ORGANIZED FOR "THE INCREASE AND DIFFUSION OF GEOGRAPHIC KNOWLEDGE"

To carry out the purposes for which it was founded sixty-four years ago, the National Geographic Society publishes the National Geographic Magazine monthly. All receipts are invested in The Magazine itself or expended directly to promote geographic knowledge.

Articles and photographs are desired. For material The Magazine uses, generous remuneration is made.

In addition to the editorial and photographic surveys constantly being made, The Society has sponsored more than 100 scientific expeditions, some of which required years of field work to achieve their objectives.

The Society's notable expeditions have pushed back the historic horizons of the southwestern United States to a period nearly eight centuries before Columbus crossed the Atlantic. By dating the ruins of the vast communal dwellings in that region, The Society's researches solved secrets that had puzzled historians for three hundred years.

In Mexico The Society and the Smithsonian Institution, January 16, 1939, discovered the oldest work of man in the Americas for which we have a date. This slab of stone is engraved in Mayan characters with a date which means November 4, 291 B. C. (Spinden Correlation). It antedates by 200 years anything heretofore dated in America, and reveals a great center of early American culture, previously unknown.

On November 11, 1935, in a flight sponsored jointly by the National Geographic Society and the U. S. Army Air Corps, the world's largest balloon, *Explorer II*, ascended to the world altitude record of 72,395 feet. Capt. Albert W. Stevens and Capt. Orvil A. Anderson took aloft in the gondola nearly a ton of scientific instruments, and obtained results of extraordinary value.

A notable undertaking in the history of astronomy was launched in 1949 by The Society in cooperation with the Palomar Observatory of the California Institute of Technology. This project will require four years to photomap the vast reaches of space, and will provide the first sky atlas for observatories all over the world.

In 1948 The Society sent out seven expeditions to study the eclipse of the sun along a 5,320-mile arc from Burma to the Aleutians. The fruitful results helped link geodetic surveys of North America and Asia.

The Society granted $25,000, and in addition $75,000 was contributed by individual members, to help preserve for the American people the finest of the giant sequoia trees in the Giant Forest of Sequoia National Park of California.

One of the world's largest icefields and glacial systems outside the polar regions was discovered in Alaska and Yukon by Bradford Washburn while exploring for The Society and the Harvard Institute of Exploration, 1938.

NATIONAL GEOGRAPHIC MAGAZINE

Cumulative Index

Volume I

1899–1946

Gilbert Grosvenor,
Editor

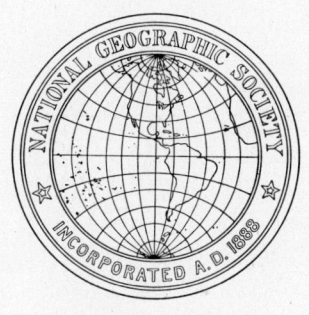

NATIONAL GEOGRAPHIC SOCIETY

WASHINGTON 6, D.C., U.S.A.

NATIONAL GEOGRAPHIC MAGAZINE
CUMULATIVE INDEX
Volume I

January, 1899–December, 1946

Volume II of this index covers issues beginning January, 1947.

The National Geographic Society publishes semi-annually for each volume (six issues) of The Magazine a detailed, comprehensive index which is mailed, upon their request, to members who bind their copies as works of reference.

A

AAFTTC (Army Air Forces Technical Training Command). *See* Army Air Forces Training Command.

Abaiang (Atoll), Gilbert Islands:

Gilbert Islands in the Wake of Battle. By W. Robert Moore. Vol. LXXXVII, pp. 129-162, 11 ills. in black and white, 19 ills. in color, 1 two-thirds-page map, Feb., 1945.

Round About Grim Tarawa. 19 ills. in color from natural-color photographs by W. Robert Moore. Vol. LXXXVII, pp. 137-160, Feb., 1945.

Abbot, C. G.:

Do Volcanic Explosions Affect Our Climate? By C. G. Abbot. Vol. XXIV, pp. 181-198, 9 ills., 1 diagram, Feb., 1913.

Hunting an Observatory: A Successful Search for a Dry Mountain on Which to Establish the National Geographic Society's Solar Radiation Station. By C. G. Abbot. Vol. L, pp. 503-518, 13 ills., 1 quarter-page map, Oct., 1926.

Measuring the Sun's Heat and Forecasting the Weather: The National Geographic Society to Maintain a Solar Station in a Remote Part of the World to Coöperate with Smithsonian Institution Stations in California and Chile. By C. G. Abbot. Vol. XLIX, pp. 111-126, 15 ills., 1 chart, Jan., 1926.

Abbot, John M.:

Buried City of Ceylon. By John M. Abbot. Vol. XVII, pp. 613-622, 8 ills., Nov., 1906.

Abdul Aziz al Saud (King of Saudi Arabia). *See* Al Saud.

Abemama (Atoll), Gilbert Islands:

Gilbert Islands in the Wake of Battle. By W. Robert Moore. Vol. LXXXVII, pp. 129-162, 11 ills. in black and white, 19 ills. in color, 1 two-thirds-page map, Feb., 1945.

Aboard a Blimp Hunting U-boats: A Day above the Atlantic Reveals Navy Talk and Navy Ways, Creeping Convoys, and Torpedoed Wrecks. By Mason Sutherland, Vol. LXXXIV, pp. 79-96, 18 ills., July, 1943.

Aborigines:

Australia's Stone Age Men. 8 ills. in color from natural-color photographs by Charles P. Mountford. Vol. LXXXIX, pp. 105-112, Jan., 1946.

Earth's Most Primitive People: A Journey with the Aborigines of Central Australia. By Charles P. Mountford. Vol. LXXXIX, pp. 89-112, 10 ills. in black and color, 8 ills. in color, 1 half-page map, Jan., 1946.

Abruzzi, Duke of the:

Duke of the Abruzzi in the Himalayas. Vol. XXI, pp. 245-249, Mar., 1910.

Honors to Peary (Presentation of Hubbard Medal). Vol. XVIII, pp. 49-60, 1 ill., Jan., 1907.

ABSD (Advanced Base Sectional Dock). *See* Docks, Floating Dry.

Abydos, Egypt:

Excavations at Abydos. Vol. XIV, pp. 358-359, Sept., 1903.

Reconstructing Egypt's History. By Wallace N. Stearns. Vol. XXIV, pp. 1021-1042, 21 ills., Sept., 1913.

Resurrection of Ancient Egypt. By James Baikie. Vol. XXIV, pp. 957-1020, 46 ills., 1 page map, Sept., 1913.

Sacred Ibis Cemetery and Jackal Catacombs at Abydos. By Camden M. Cobern. Vol. XXIV, pp. 1042-1056, 10 ills., Sept., 1913.

Abyssinia. *See* Ethiopia.

Abyssinia, the Country and People. By Oscar T. Crosby. Vol. XII, pp. 89-102, Mar., 1901.

Aces Among Aces (Aviators). By Laurence La Tourette Driggs. Vol. XXXIII, pp. 568-580, 9 ills., June, 1918.

Aces of Aviation (Gulls). 16 ills. from photographs by A. H. Hall. Vol. XLVII, pp. 665-672, June, 1925.

Aces of the Air. By Capt. Jacques De Sieyes. Vol. XXXIII, pp. 5-9, 2 ills., Jan., 1918.

Acorn, a Possibly Neglected Source of Food. By C. Hart Merriam. Vol. XXXIV, pp. 129-137, 8 ills., Aug., 1918.

Across French and Spanish Morocco. By Harriet Chalmers Adams. Vol. XLVII, pp. 327-356, 19 ills. in black and white, 16 ills. in color, 1 half-page map, Mar., 1925.

Across Madagascar by Boat, Auto, Railroad, and Filanzama. By Charles F. Swingle. Vol. LVI, pp. 179-211, 42 ills., 1 half-page and 1 three-quarters-page maps, Aug., 1929.

Across the Equator with the American Navy. By Herbert Corey. Vol. XXXIX, pp. 571-624, 53 ills., June, 1921.

Across the Midi in a Canoe: Two Americans Paddle Along the Canals of Southern France from the Atlantic to the Mediterranean. By Melville Chater. Vol. LII, pp. 127-167, 49 ills., 1 half-page map, Aug., 1927.

Across Tibet from India to China. By Lt. Col. Ilia Tolstoy, AUS. Vol. XC, pp. 169-222, 41 ills., 1 half-page map, Aug., 1946.

Across Widest Africa (Ethiopia, French Somaliland, and Nuer Country). By A. Henry Savage Landor. Vol. XIX, pp. 694-737, 38 ills., 1 half-page map, Oct., 1908.

Action Photographs of the Balloon's Perfect Landing. 8 ills. in black and white, special photographs I-VIII. Vol. LXIX, Jan., 1936.

Adak (island), Aleutian Islands.
Navy Artist Paints the Aleutians. By Mason Sutherland. Paintings by Lt. William F. Draper. Vol. LXXXIV, pp. 157-176, 4 ills. in black and white, 16 ills. in color, Aug., 1943.

Adalia, Turkey:
Historic Islands and Shores of the Ægean Sea. By Ernest Lloyd Harris. Vol. XXVIII, pp. 231-262, 29 ills., 1 half-page map, Sept., 1915.

Adam, Tassilo:
Java, Queen of the East Indies. 3 ills. in color from autochromes by Tassilo Adam. Vol. LVI, pp. 334-359, Sept., 1929.

Adams, Clifton:
Arizona: Adventures in Arizona Color Photography. 14 ills. in color from autochromes by Clifton Adams. Vol. LV, pp. 28-37, Jan., 1929.

California: Sunshine Land of Fruits, Flowers, Movies, and Sport. 41 ills. in color from natural-color photographs by Clifton Adams and Fred Payne Clatworthy. Vol. LXVI, pp. 545-592, Nov., 1934.

Chicago, Titan of the Middle West. 12 ills. in color from direct color photographs by Clifton Adams. Vol. LIX, pp. 584-593, May, 1931.

England: Cradles of English History. 14 ills. in color from natural-color photographs by Clifton Adams. Vol. LIX, pp. 268-277, Mar., 1931.

England: From Stratford to the North Sea. 16 ills. in color from autochromes by Clifton Adams. Vol. LV, pp. 616-625, May, 1929.

England: Lakeland, Home of England's Nature Poets. 15 ills. in color from autochromes by Clifton Adams. Vol. LV, pp. 592-601, May, 1929.

England: Nooks and Bays of Storied England. 11 ills. in color from natural-color photographs by Clifton Adams. Vol. LXI, pp. 182-191, Feb., 1932.

Adams, Clifton—*Continued*
Florida: High Lights in the Sunshine State. 38 ills. in color from autochromes by Clifton Adams. Vol. LVII, pp. 26-83, Jan., 1930.

Gettysburg: Most Famous Battle Field in America. 9 ills. in color from natural-color photographs by Clifton Adams and Orren R. Louden. Vol. LX, pp. 66-75, July, 1931.

Haiti: Gay Colors in the Land of Black Majesty. 13 ills. in color from natural-color photographs by Clifton Adams. Vol. LXVI, pp. 445-452, Oct., 1934.

Illinois: Rambles Through the Prairie State. 15 ills. in color from direct color photographs by Clifton Adams. Vol. LIX, pp. 544-553, May, 1931.

Ireland: Hills and Dales of Erin. 11 ills. in color from autochromes by Clifton Adams. Vol. LI, pp. 316-333, Mar., 1927.

London: Highlights of London Town. 15 ills. in color from autochromes by Clifton Adams. Vol. LV, pp. 568-577, May, 1929.

Massachusetts: Coasting Through the Bay State. 12 ills. in color from natural-color photographs by Clifton Adams. Vol. LX, pp. 286-295, Sept., 1931.

Mexico: In the Land of the Montezumas. 16 ills. in color from photographs by Clifton Adams. Vol. XLIII, pp. 265-280, Mar., 1923.

Minnesota: State of Sky-Blue Water and Verdure. 11 ills. in color from natural-color photographs by Clifton Adams and Edwin L. Wisherd. Vol. LXVII, pp. 289-296, Mar., 1935.

Mount Vernon: Home of the First Farmer of America. 18 ills. in color from autochromes by Clifton Adams. Vol. LIII, pp. 604-621, May, 1928.

New England's Wonderland of Mountain, Lake, and Seascape. 14 ills. in color from natural-color photographs by Clifton Adams. Vol. LX, pp. 262-271, Sept., 1931.

New York (City): Tempo and Color of a Great City. 42 ills. in color from natural-color photographs by Clifton Adams and Edwin L. Wisherd. Vol. LVIII, pp. 538-579, Nov., 1930.

New York (State): Color Highlights of the Empire State. 30 ills. in color from natural-color photographs by Clifton Adams. Vol. LXIV, pp. 529-576, Nov., 1933.

Philadelphia: Colorful Corners of the City of Homes. 13 ills. in color from natural-color photographs by Clifton Adams and Edwin L. Wisherd. Vol. LXII, pp. 674-683, Dec., 1932.

Rhode Island: Sauntering Through the Land of Roger Williams. 14 ills. in color from natural-color photographs by Clifton Adams. Vol. LX, pp. 310-319, Sept., 1931.

Sardinia: Sardinian Smiles. 16 ills. in color from photographs by Clifton Adams. Vol. XLIII, pp. 31-46, Jan., 1923.

Vermont: Green Mountain State. 6 ills. in color from autochromes by Clifton Adams. Vol. LI, pp. 316-333, Mar., 1927.

Adams, Clifton—*Continued*

Virginia : Scenes and Shrines of the Cavalier Country. 3 ills. in color from natural-color photographs by Clifton Adams. Vol. LV, pp. 424-433, Apr., 1929.

Washington (State) : Sunset Hues in the Pacific Northwest. 8 ills. in color from natural-color photographs by Clifton Adams. Vol. LXIII, pp. 154-163, Feb., 1933.

Washington (State) : Where the Last of the West Was Won. 4 ills. in color from natural-color photographs by Clifton Adams. Vol. LXIII, pp. 178-187, Feb., 1933.

Washington, D. C. : Our Colorful City of Magnificent Distances. 17 ills. in color from natural-color photographs by Clifton Adams. Vol. LX, pp. 530-611, Nov., 1931.

Washington, D. C. : Secrets of Washington's Lure. 15 ills. in color from natural-color photographs ; 2 ills. by Clifton Adams. Vol. LVII, pp. 376-385, Mar., 1930.

Washington, D. C. : Unique Gifts of Washington to the Nation. 2 ills. in color from natural-color photographs by Clifton Adams. Vol. LV, pp. 472-481, Apr., 1929.

Adams, Cyrus C. :

United States—Land and Waters. By Cyrus C. Adams. Vol. XIV, pp. 170-185, 8 ills., 1 half-page map, May, 1903.

Adams, Harriet Chalmers :

Across French and Spanish Morocco. By Harriet Chalmers Adams. Vol. XLVII, pp. 327-356, 19 ills. in black and white, 16 ills. in color, 1 half-page map, Mar., 1925.

Adventurous Sons of Cádiz (Spain). By Harriet Chalmers Adams. Vol. XLVI, pp. 153-204, 37 ills. in black and white, 26 ills. in color, Aug., 1924.

Along the Old Inca Highway (Peru). By Harriet Chalmers Adams. Vol. XIX, pp. 231-250, 21 ills., Apr., 1908.

Altitudinal Journey Through Portugal : Rugged Scenic Beauty, Colorful Costumes, and Ancient Castles Abound in Tiny Nation That Once Ruled a Vast Empire. By Harriet Chalmers Adams. Vol. LII, pp. 567-610, 44 ills. in black and white, 17 ills. in color, 1 two-thirds-page map, Nov., 1927.

Barcelona, Pride of the Catalans. By Harriet Chalmers Adams. Vol. LV, pp. 373-402, 32 ills., Mar., 1929.

Cirenaica, Eastern Wing of Italian Libia. By Harriet Chalmers Adams. Vol. LVII, pp. 689-726, 35 ills. in black and white, 13 ills. in color, 1 two-thirds-page map, June, 1930.

Cuzco, America's Ancient Mecca. By Harriet Chalmers Adams. Vol. XIX, pp. 669-689, 19 ills., Oct., 1908.

East Indians in the New World (Trinidad). By Harriet Chalmers Adams. Vol. XVIII, pp. 485-491, 6 ills., July, 1907.

European Outpost : The Azores. By Harriet Chalmers Adams. Vol. LXVII, pp. 35-66, 25 ills. in black and white, 13 ills. in color, 1 half-page map, Jan., 1935.

Adams, Harriet Chalmers—*Continued*

First Transandine Railroad from Buenos Aires to Valparaiso. By Harriet Chalmers Adams. Vol. XXI, pp. 397-417, 14 ills., 1 quarter-page map, May, 1910.

Grand Canyon Bridge. By Harriet Chalmers Adams. Vol. XXXIX, pp. 645-650, 6 ills., June, 1921.

In French Lorraine : That Part of France Where the First American Soldiers Have Fallen. By Harriet Chalmers Adams. Vol. XXXII, pp. 499-518, 16 ills., Nov.-Dec., 1917.

Kaleidoscopic La Paz : The City of the Clouds. By Harriet Chalmers Adams. Vol. XX, pp. 119-141, 23 ills., Feb., 1909.

Longitudinal Journey Through Chile. By Harriet Chalmers Adams. Vol. XLII, pp. 219-273, 60 ills., 1 half-page map, Sept., 1922.

Madeira the Florescent. By Harriet Chalmers Adams. Vol. LXVI, pp. 81-106, 19 ills. in black and white, 13 ills. in color, 1 half-page map, July, 1934.

Madrid Out-of-Doors. By Harriet Chalmers Adams. Vol. LX, pp. 225-256, 35 ills., Aug., 1931.

Picturesque Paramaribo (Surinam). By Harriet Chalmers Adams. Vol. XVIII, pp. 365-373, 7 ills., June, 1907.

Rio de Janeiro, in the Land of Lure. By Harriet Chalmers Adams. Vol. XXXVIII, pp. 165-210, 39 ills., 1 half-page map, Sept., 1920.

River-Encircled Paraguay. By Harriet Chalmers Adams. Vol. LXIII, pp. 385-416, 35 ills., 1 third-page map, Apr., 1933.

Some Wonderful Sights in the Andean Highlands : The Oldest City in America. Sailing on the Lake of the Clouds : The Yosemite of Peru. By Harriet Chalmers Adams. Vol. XIX, pp. 597-618, 19 ills., 1 half-page map, Sept., 1908.

Volcano-Girded Salvador : A Prosperous Central American State with the Densest Rural Population in the Western World. By Harriet Chalmers Adams. Vol. XLI, pp. 189-200, 10 ills., Feb., 1922.

Adams, M. P. Greenwood :

Australia's Wild Wonderland. By M. P. Greenwood Adams. Vol. XLV, pp. 329-356, 36 ills., 1 half-page map, Mar., 1924.

Adams (Schooner) :

Capturing Giant Turtles in the Caribbean. By David D. Duncan. Vol. LXXXIV, pp. 177-190, 13 ills., 1 quarter-page map, Aug., 1943.

Adam's Second Eden (Ceylon). By Eliza R. Scidmore. Vol. XXIII, pp. 105-173, 60 ills., Feb., 1912.

Addis Ababa, Ethiopia :

Coronation Days in Addis Ababa. By W. Robert Moore. Vol. LIX, pp. 738-746, 8 ills., June, 1931.

Present-Day Scenes in the World's Oldest Empire. 27 ills. in color from natural-color photographs by W. Robert Moore. Vol. LIX, pp. 690-723, June, 1931.

Address by Commander Robert E. Peary, U. S. N., on the Assembling of the Congress in Washington, September 8, 1904. Vol. XV, pp. 387-392, Oct., 1904.

Address of the President of the Board of Managers, June 1, 1900. By Alexander Graham Bell. Vol. XI, pp. 401-408, Oct., 1900.

Adelaide, Australia :
Capital Cities of Australia. By W. Robert Moore. Vol. LXVIII, pp. 667-722, 32 ills. in black and white, 24 ills. in color, 1 two-page map, Dec., 1935.

Lonely Australia : The Unique Continent. By Herbert E. Gregory. Vol. XXX, pp. 473-568, 68 ills., 1 two-page and 4 half-page maps, Dec., 1916.

Adelaide University: Expeditions :
Earth's Most Primitive People : A Journey with the Aborigines of Central Australia. By Charles P. Mountford. Vol. LXXXIX, pp. 89-119, 10 ills. in black and white, 6 ills. in color, 1 half-page map, Jan., 1946.

Adélie Penguins:
Antarctica's Most Interesting Citizen : The Comical Penguin Is Both Romantic and Bellicose. By Worth E. Shoults. Vol. LXI, pp. 251-260, 8 ills., Feb., 1932.

Aden, Arabia :
"Flower of Paradise" : The Part Which Khat Plays in the Life of the Yemen Arab. By Charles Moser. Vol. XXXII, pp. 173-186, 10 ills., 1 page map, Aug., 1917.

Rock of Aden : The Volcanic Mountain Fortress, on the Sea Route from Suez to India, Assumes New Importance. By H. G. C. Swayne. Vol. LXVIII, pp. 723-742, 24 ills., 1 half-page map, Dec., 1935.

Adirondack Mountains, New York :
Adirondack Idyls. 10 ills. in color from natural-color photographs by Harrison Howell Walker. Vol. LXXIII, pp. 729-736, June, 1938.

New York State's Air-Conditioned Roof. By Frederick G. Vosburgh. Vol. LXXIII, pp. 715-748, 23 ills. in black and white, 10 ills. in color, 1 three-quarters-page map, June, 1938.

Adolphus Frederick, Duke of Mecklenburg:
Land of Giants and Pygmies (Ruanda). By Duke Adolphus Frederick of Mecklenburg. Vol. XXIII, pp. 367-388, 16 ills., 1 page map, Apr., 1912.

Advanced Base Sectional Dock. *See* Docks, Floating Dry.

Advances in Geographic Knowledge During the Nineteenth Century. By Maj. Gen. A. W. Greely. Vol. XII, pp. 143-152, 2 half-page maps, Apr., 1901.

Adventure (Ship) :
Columbus of the Pacific : Captain James Cook, Foremost British Navigator, Expanded the Great Sea to Correct Proportions and Won for Albion an Insular Empire by Peaceful Exploration and Scientific Study. By J. R. Hildebrand. Vol. LI, pp. 85-132, 45 ills., 1 page and 1 three-quarters-page maps, Jan., 1927.

Adventures Among the "Lost Tribes of Islam" in Eastern Darfur : A Personal Narrative of Exploring, Mapping, and Setting up a Government in the Anglo-Egyptian Sudan Borderland. By Maj. Edward Keith-Roach. Vol. XLV, pp. 41-73, 32 ills., 1 three-quarters-page map, Jan., 1924.

Adventures in Arizona Color Photography. 14 ills. in color from autochromes by Clifton Adams. Vol. LV, pp. 28-37, Jan., 1929.

Adventures in Color on Mexico's West Coast. 13 ills. in color from natural-color photographs by Fred Payne Clatworthy. Vol. LVIII, pp. 60-69, July, 1930.

Adventures With a Camera in Many Lands. By Maynard Owen Williams. Vol. XL, pp. 87-112, 24 ills., July, 1921.

Adventures with Birds of Prey. By Frank and John Craighead. Vol. LXXII, pp. 109-134, 25 ills., July, 1937.

Adventuring Down the West Coast of Mexico. By Herbert Corey. Vol. XLII, pp. 449-503, 44 ills., 1 half-page map, Nov., 1922.

Adventurous Sons of Cádiz (Spain). By Harriet Chalmers Adams. Vol. XLVI, pp. 153-204, 37 ills. in black and white, 26 ills. in color, Aug., 1924.

Aegean Regions:
Asia Minor in the Time of the Seven Wise Men. By Mary Mills Patrick. Vol. XXXVII, pp. 47-67, 19 ills., Jan., 1920.

Greece—the Birthplace of Science and Free Speech : Explorations on the Mainland and in Crete and the Aegean Isles Reveal Ancient Life Similar to That of the Present. By Richard Stillwell. Paintings by H. M. Herget. Vol. LXXXV, pp. 273-353, 13 ills. in black and white, 32 ills. in color, 1 two-page map, Mar., 1944.

Historic Islands and Shores of the Ægean Sea. By Ernest Lloyd Harris. Vol. XXVIII, pp. 231-262, 29 ills., 1 half-page map, Sept., 1915.

Isles of Greece. By Lt. Richard Stillwell, USNR. Vol. LXXXV, pp. 593-622, 11 ills. in black and white, 20 ills. in color, 1 page map, May, 1944.

Modern Odyssey in Classic Lands : Troy's Treasures, Athens' Parthenon, and Rome's First "Broad Way" Influence Today's Banks, Costumes, Jewelry, and Railroad Timetables. By Maynard Owen Williams. Vol. LXXVII, pp. 291-337, 27 ills. in black and white, 22 ills. in color, Mar., 1940.

Rhodes, and Italy's Aegean Islands. By Dorothy Hosmer. Vol. LXXIX, pp. 449-480, 32 ills., 1 map, Apr., 1941.

Santorin and Mýkonos, Ægean Gems. 8 ills. in color from natural-color photographs ; 7 ills. by B. Anthony Stewart. Vol. LXXVII, pp. 339-346, Mar., 1940.

Seeing 3,000 Years of History in Four Hours : A Panorama of Ancient, Medieval, and Modern Events Against a Background of Mythology Unfolds During an Airplane Journey from Constantinople to Athens. By Maynard Owen Williams. Vol. LIV, pp. 719-739, 24 ills., 1 two-thirds-page map, Dec., 1928.
See also Greece.

Aerial Color Photography Becomes a War Weapon. By H. H. Arnold. Vol. LXXVII, pp. 757-766, 8 ills. in color, June, 1940.

Aërial Conquest of Everest: Flying Over the World's Highest Mountain Realizes the Objective of Many Heroic Explorers. By Lieut. Col. L. V. S. Blacker. Vol. LXIV, pp. 127-162, 35 ills., 1 page map, Aug., 1933.

Aerial Invasion of Burma. By Gen. H. H. Arnold. Vol. LXXXVI, pp. 129-148, 20 ills., Aug., 1944.

Aërial Locomotion: With a Few Notes of Progress in the Constructon of an Aërodrome. By Alexander Graham Bell. Vol. XVIII, pp. 1-34, 33 ills., Jan., 1907.

Aerography:

New Frontier in the Sky. By F. Barrows Colton. Vol. XC, pp. 379-408, 28 ills., 1 diagram, Sept., 1946.

Aeronautics:

Aboard a Blimp Hunting U-boats! A Day above the Atlantic Reveals Navy Talk and Navy Ways, Creeping Convoys, and Torpedoed Wrecks. By Mason Sutherland. Vol. LXXXIV, pp. 79-96, 18 ills., July, 1943.

Aces Among Aces. By Laurence La Tourette Driggs. Vol. XXXIII, pp. 568-580, 9 ills., June, 1918.

Aces of the Air. By Capt. Jacques De Sieyes. Vol. XXXIII, pp. 5-9, 2 ills., Jan., 1918.

Admiral Byrd Received New Honor from The Society. Vol. LVIII, pp. 228-238, 4 ills., Aug., 1930.

Aërial Conquest of Everest: Flying Over the World's Highest Mountain Realizes the Objective of Many Heroic Explorers. By Lieut. Col. L. V. S. Blacker. Vol. LXIV, pp. 127-162, 35 ills., 1 page map, Aug., 1933.

Aerial Invasion of Burma. By Gen. H. H. Arnold. Vol. LXXXVI, pp. 129-148, 20 ills., Aug., 1944.

Aërial Locomotion. By Alexander Graham Bell. Vol. XVIII, pp. 1-34, 33 ills., Jan., 1907.

Air Adventures in Peru: Cruising Among Andean Peaks, Pilots and Cameramen Discover Wondrous Works of an Ancient People. By Robert Shippee. Vol. LXIII, pp. 81-120, 40 ills., 1 three-quarters-page map, Jan., 1933.

Air Conquest: From the Early Days of Giant Kites and Birdlike Gliders, the National Geographic Society Has Aided and Encouraged the Growth of Aviation. Vol. LII, pp. 233-242, 13 ills., Aug., 1927.

Air Power for Peace. By Gen. H. H. Arnold. Vol. LXXXIX, pp. 137-193, 35 ills. in black and white, 28 ills. in color, special map supplement, Feb., 1946.

America From the Air: No Such Series of Airplane Views Has Ever Before Been Printed (Photographs by Lt. Albert W. Stevens). Vol. XLVI, pp. 85-92, 8 ills., July, 1924.

America in the Air: The Future of Airplane and Airship, Economically and as Factors in National Defense. By Brig. Gen. William Mitchell. Vol. XXXIX, pp. 339-352, 8 ills., 1 three-quarters-page map, Mar., 1921.

Aeronautics—*Continued*

American Bombers Attacking from Australia. By Howell Walker. Vol. LXXXIII, pp. 49-70. 19 ills., 1 map (two-page spread), Jan., 1943.

American Wings Soar Around the World: Epic Story of the Air Transport Command of the U. S. Army Is a Saga of Yankee Daring and Doing. By Donald H. Agnew and William A. Kinney. Vol. LXXXIV, pp. 57-78, 22 ills., July, 1943.

America's Part in the Allies' Mastery of the Air. By Maj. Joseph Tulasne. Vol. XXXIII, pp. 1-5, 2 ills., Jan., 1918.

Antarctica by Sea, Land and Air. 16 ills. in gravure from photographs by the Byrd Antarctic Expedition. Vol. LVIII, pp. 158-207, Aug., 1930.

Arctic as an Air Route of the Future. By Vilhjalmur Stefansson. Vol. XLII, pp. 205-218, 8 ills., 1 page map, Aug., 1922.

Aviation in Commerce and Defense. By F. Barrows Colton. Vol. LXXVIII, pp. 685-726, 39 ills., Dec., 1940.

Ballooning in the Stratosphere: Two Balloon Ascents to Ten-Mile Altitudes Presage New Mode of Aërial Travel. By Auguste Piccard. Vol. LXIII, pp. 353-384, 34 ills., Mar., 1933.

Building America's Air Army. By Hiram Bingham. Vol. XXXIII, pp. 48-86, 43 ills., Jan., 1918.

By Seaplane to Six Continents: Cruising 60,000 Miles, Italian Argonauts of the Air See World Geography Unroll, and Break New Sky Trails Over Vast Brazilian Jungles. By Comdr. Francesco de Pinedo. Vol. LIV, pp. 247-301, 60 ills., 1 two-page map, Sept., 1928.

Canada from the Air: Flights Aggregating 10,000 Miles Reveal the Marvelous Scenic Beauties and Amazing Natural Resources of the Dominion. By J. A. Wilson. Vol. L, pp. 389-466, 76 ills., 1 page map, Oct., 1926.

Charm of Cape Breton Island: The Most Picturesque Portion of Canada's Maritime Provinces —A Land Rich in Historic Associations, Natural Resources, and Geographic Appeal. By Catherine Dunlop Mackenzie. Vol. XXXVIII, pp. 34-60, 22 ills., 1 three-quarters-page map, July, 1920.

Commander Byrd Receives the Hubbard Gold Medal: The First Explorer to Reach the North Pole by Air Receives Coveted Honor at Brilliant National Geographic Society Reception. Vol. L, pp. 377-388, 5 ills., 1 chart, Sept., 1926.

Conquest of Antarctica by Air. By Rear Adm. Richard Evelyn Byrd. Vol. LVIII, pp. 127-227, 71 ills. in black and white, 16 ills. in gravure, 1 page map, Aug., 1930.

Cruise on an Escort Carrier. By Melville Bell Grosvenor. Vol. LXXXIV, pp. 513-546, 14 ills. in black and white, 20 ills. in color, Nov., 1943.

Dr. Bell's Man-Lifting Kite. By Gilbert H. Grosvenor. Vol. XIX, pp. 35-52, 27 ills., Jan., 1908.

Aeronautics—*Continued*

8th Air Force in England. 10 ills. in color from natural-color photographs. Vol. LXXXVII, pp. 297-304, Mar., 1945.

Exploring the Earth's Stratosphere: The Holder of the American Altitude Record Describes His Experiences in Reaching the "Ceiling" of His Plane at an Elevation of Nearly Eight Miles. By Lieut. John A. Macready. Vol. L, pp. 755-776, 18 ills., Dec., 1926.

Exploring the Stratosphere. By Capt. Albert W. Stevens. Vol. LXVI, pp. 397-434, 43 ills., 1 two-thirds-page chart, Oct., 1934.

Exploring the Valley of the Amazon in a Hydroplane: Twelve Thousand Miles of Flying Over the World's Greatest River and Greatest Forest to Chart the Unknown Parima River from the Sky. By Capt. Albert W. Stevens. Vol. XLIX, pp. 353-420, 86 ills., 1 page map, Apr., 1926.

Fighting Insects with Airplanes: An Account of the Successful Use of the Flying-Machine in Dusting Tall Trees Infested with Leaf-Eating Caterpillars. By C. R. Neillie and J. S. Houser. Vol. XLI, pp. 333-338, 6 ills., Mar., 1922.

First Airship Flight Around the World: Dr. Hugo Eckener Tells of an Epochal Geographic Achievement upon the Occasion of the Bestowal of the National Geographic Society's Special Gold Medal. Vol. LVII, pp. 653-688, 37 ills., June, 1930.

First Alaskan Air Expedition. By Capt. St. Clair Streett. Vol. XLI, pp. 490-522, 37 ills., 1 page map, May, 1922.

First Flight to the North Pole. By Lieut. Comdr. Richard Evelyn Byrd. Vol. L, pp. 357-376, 14 ills., Sept., 1926.

First Natural-Color Photograph Taken in the Stratosphere. 1 ill. in color by Maj. Albert W. Stevens. Vol. LXXI, p. 340, Mar., 1937.

Flights from Arctic to Equator: Conquering the Alps, the Ice Peaks of Spitsbergen, of Persia, and Africa's Mountains of the Moon. By Walter Mittelholzer. Vol. LXI, pp. 445-498, 53 ills., 1 three-quarters-page map, Apr., 1932.

Flying. By Gilbert Grosvenor. Vol. LXIII, pp. 585-630, 33 ills. in black and white, 17 ills. in duotone, May, 1933.

Flying Around the North Atlantic. By Anne Morrow Lindbergh; Foreword by Charles A. Lindbergh. Vol. LXVI, pp. 259-337, 82 ills., 1 two-page and 1 two-thirds-page maps, Sept., 1934.

Flying in France. By Capt. André de Berroeta. Vol. XXXIII, pp. 9-26, 12 ills., Jan., 1918.

Flying Over Egypt, Sinai, and Palestine—Looking Down Upon the Holy Land During an Air Journey of Two and a Half Hours from Cairo to Jerusalem. By Brig. Gen. P. R. C. Groves and Maj. J. R. McCrindle. Vol. L, pp. 313-355, 26 ills., 1 half-page map, Sept., 1926.

Flying Our Wounded Veterans Home. By Catherine Bell Palmer. Vol. LXXXVIII, pp. 363-384, 17 ills., Sept., 1945.

Aeronautics—*Continued*

Flying Over the Arctic. By Lieut. Comdr. Richard E. Byrd. Vol. XLVIII, pp. 519-532, 10 ills., Nov., 1925.

Flying the "Hump" of the Andes. By Capt. Albert W. Stevens. Vol. LIX, pp. 595-636, 36 ills., 1 third-page map, May, 1931.

Flying the Pacific. By William Burke Miller. Vol. LXX, pp. 665-707, 39 ills., Dec., 1936.

Flying the World: In a Homemade Airplane the Author and Her Husband Enjoy 16,000 Miles of Adventurous Flight Across Europe, Asia, and America. By Gladys M. Day. Vol. LXI, pp. 655-690, 41 ills., 1 half-page map, June, 1932.

Flying the World's Longest Air-Mail Route: From Montevideo, Uruguay, Over the Andes, Up the Pacific Coast, Across Central America and the Caribbean to Miami, Florida, in 67 Thrilling Flying Hours. By Junius B. Wood. Vol. LVII, pp. 261-325, 65 ills., 1 half-page map, Mar., 1930.

Four Thousand Hours Over China. By Capt. Hans Koester. Vol. LXXIII, pp. 571-598, 25 ills., 1 two-thirds-page map, May, 1938.

From Africa to the Alps. 8 ills. in color from natural-color photographs. Vol. LXXXIX, pp. 161-168, Feb., 1946.

From London to Australia by Aëroplane: A Personal Narrative of the First Aërial Voyage Half Around the World. By Sir Ross Smith. Vol. XXXIX, pp. 229-339, 76 ills. in black and white, 8 ills. in color, 1 page map, Mar., 1921.

Future of the Airplane. By Rear Adm. Robert E. Peary. Vol. XXXIII, pp. 107-113, 4 ills., Jan., 1918.

Gentlemen Adventurers of the Air: Many Regions of Canada's Vast Wilderness, Long Hidden Even from Fur Trappers, Are Now Revealed by Exploring Airmen. By J. A. Wilson. Vol. LVI, pp. 597-642, 55 ills., 1 page map, Nov., 1929.

Germany's Air Program. Vol. XXXIII, p. 114, Jan., 1918.

Gliders—Silent Weapons of the Sky. By William H. Nicholas. Vol. LXXXVI, pp. 149-160, 8 ills., Aug., 1944.

Helium, the New Balloon Gas. By G. Sherburne Rogers. Vol. XXXV, pp. 441-456, 11 ills., May, 1919.

How Latin America Looks from the Air: U. S. Army Airplanes Hurdle the High Andes, Brave Brazil Jungles, and Follow Smoking Volcanoes to Map New Sky Paths Around South America. By Maj. Herbert A. Dargue. Vol. LII, pp. 451-502, 52 ills., 1 page map, Oct., 1927.

How the United States Grew. By McFall Kerbey. Vol. LXIII, pp. 631-649, 17 ills., 1 page map, May, 1933.

In Honor of the Army and Aviation (National Geographic Society Banquet). Vol. XXII, pp. 267-284, 1 ill., Mar., 1911.

Aeronautics—*Continued*

Into Primeval Papua by Seaplane : Seeking Disease-Resisting Sugar Cane, Scientists Find Neolithic Man in Unmapped Nooks of Sorcery and Cannibalism. By E. W. Brandes. Vol. LVI, pp. 253-332, 98 ills., 1 three-quarters-page map, Sept., 1929.

Italy's Eagles of Combat and Defense : Heroic Achievements of Aviators Above the Adriatic, the Apennines and the Alps. By Gen. P. Tozzi. Vol. XXXIII, pp. 38-47, 8 ills., Jan., 1918.

Life-Story of an American Airman in France : Extracts from the Letters of Stuart Walcott, Who, Between July and December, 1917, Learned to Fly in French Schools of Aviation, Won Fame at the Front, and Fell Near Saint Souplet. Vol. XXXIII, pp. 86-106, 9 ills., Jan., 1918.

Looking Down on Europe : The Thrills and Advantages of Sight-Seeing by Airplane, as Demonstrated on a 6,500-Mile Tour Over Commercial Aviation Routes. By Lieut. J. Parker Van Zandt. Vol. XLVII, pp. 261-326, 67 ills., 1 half-page map, Mar., 1925.

Looking Down on Europe Again : Crisscrossing Air Tracks Reveal Nature's Scenic Masterpieces and Man's Swift-changing Boundaries and Structures. By J. Parker Van Zandt. Vol. LXXV, pp. 791-822, 31 ills., 1 page map, June, 1939.

MacMillan Arctic Expedition Returns : U. S. Navy Planes Make First Series of Overland Flights in the Arctic and National Geographic Society Staff Obtains Valuable Data and Specimens for Scientific Study. By Donald B. MacMillan. Vol. XLVIII, pp. 477-518, 42 ills., Nov., 1925.

Maneuvers of Military Planes Disclose Majestic Aërial Views. 17 ills. in duotone from U. S. Army and Navy official photographs. Vol. LXIII, pp. 598-615, May, 1933.

Man's Amazing Progress in Conquering the Air. By J. R. Hildebrand. Vol. XLVI, pp. 93-122, 28 ills., 1 diagram, July, 1924.

Man's Farthest Aloft : Rising to 13.71 Miles, the National Geographic Society-U. S. Army Stratosphere Expedition Gathers Scientific Data at Record Altitude. By Capt. Albert W. Stevens. Action Photographs of the Balloon's Perfect Landing included. Vol. LXIX, pp. 59-94, 39 ills., 1 quarter-page map, Jan., 1936.

Mapping the Antarctic from the Air : The Aërial Camera Earns Its Place as the Eyes and Memory of the Explorer. By Capt. Ashley C. McKinley. Vol. LXII, pp. 471-485, 13 ills., special map supplement, Oct., 1932.

Men-Birds Soar on Boiling Air. By Frederick G. Vosburgh. Vol. LXXIV, pp. 123-140, 15 ills., July, 1938.

My Flight Across Antarctica. By Lincoln Ellsworth. Vol. LXX, pp. 1-35, 37 ills., 1 page map, July, 1936.

My Flight from Hawaii. By Amelia Earhart. Vol. LXVII, pp. 593-609, 4 ills. in black and white, 8 ills. in duotone, May, 1935.

Aeronautics—*Continued*

My Four Antarctic Expeditions : Explorations of 1933-39 Have Stricken Vast Areas from the Realm of the Unknown. By Lincoln Ellsworth. Vol. LXXVI, pp. 129-138, 9 ills., 1 page map, July, 1939.

National Geographic Society-U. S. Army Air Corps Stratosphere Flight of 1935 in Balloon *Explorer II* (Contributed Technical Papers, Stratosphere Series, No. 2). Vol. LXXI, p. 340, Mar., 1937 ; p. 802, June, 1937.

Navigating the *Norge* (Airship) from Rome to the North Pole and Beyond : The Designer and Pilot of the First Dirigible to Fly Over the Top of the World Describes a Thrilling Voyage of More Than 8,000 Miles. By Gen. Umberto Nobile. Vol. LII, pp. 177-215, 36 ills., 1 page map, Aug., 1927.

Navy Wings over the Pacific. 12 ills. in color from natural-color photographs. Vol. LXXXVI, pp. 241-248, Aug., 1944.

New Frontier in the Sky. By F. Barrows Colton. Vol. XC, pp. 379-408, 28 ills., 1 diagram, Sept., 1946.

New Queen of the Seas (Aircraft Carrier). By Melville Bell Grosvenor. Vol. LXXXII, pp. 1-30, 27 ills., 1 drawing, 1 two-page map, July, 1942.

Non-Stop Flight Across America. By Lieut. John A Macready. Photographs by Lieut. Albert W. Stevens. Vol. XLVI, pp. 1-83, 68 ills., 1 page and 1 half-page maps, July, 1924.

On the Trail of the Air Mail : A Narrative of the Experiences of the Flying Couriers Who Relay the Mail Across America at a Speed of More Than 2,000 Miles a Day. By Lieut. J. Parker Van Zandt. Vol. XLIX, pp. 1-61, 67 ills., 1 two-thirds-page map, Jan., 1926.

On the Wings of the Wind : In Motorless Planes, Pilots Ride in Flying-Fox Fashion, Cruising on Upward Air Streams and Lifted by the Suction of Moving Clouds. By Howard Siepen. Vol. LV, pp. 751-780, 40 ills., June, 1929.

Our Conquest of the Pacific : The Narrative of the 7,400-Mile Flight from San Francisco to Brisbane in Three Ocean Hops. By Squadron-Leader Charles E. Kingsford-Smith and Flight-Lieut. Charles T. P. Ulm. Vol. LIV, pp. 371-402, 27 ills., 1 two-thirds-page map, Oct., 1928.

Our Global Strong Arm. 10 ills. in color from U. S. Army Air Forces official photographs. Vol. LXXXIX, pp. 145-152, Feb., 1946.

Our Search for the Lost Aviators : An Arctic Area Larger Than Montana First Explored in Hunt for Missing Russians. By Sir Hubert Wilkins. Vol. LXXIV, pp. 141-172, 29 ills., 1 two-page map, Aug., 1938.

Our Transatlantic Flight. By Comdr. Richard Evelyn Byrd. Vol. LII, pp. 347-368, 17 ills., 1 half-page map, Sept., 1927.

Over the Roof of Our Continent (Mount McKinley). By Bradford Washburn. Vol. LXXIV, pp. 78-98, 17 ills. in duotone, 1 half-page map, July, 1938.

Painting History in the Pacific. 19 ills. in color from paintings by Lt. William F. Draper. Vol. LXXXVI, pp. 409-424, Oct., 1944.

Aeronautics—*Continued*

Photographing the Eclipse of 1932 from the Air: From Five Miles Above the Earth's Surface, the National Geographic Society-Army Air Corps Survey Obtains Successful Photographs of the Moon's Shadow. By Capt. Albert W. Stevens. Vol. LXII, pp. 581-596, 18 ills., Nov., 1932.

Pocket Carriers Fight the Submarines. 20 ills. in color from U. S. Navy official photographs. Vol. LXXXIV, pp. 521-544, Nov., 1943.

Polar Airship. By Walter Wellman. Vol. XVII, pp. 208-228, 5 diagrams, Apr., 1906.

President Coolidge Bestows Lindbergh Award: The National Geographic Society's Hubbard Medal Is Presented to Aviator Before the Most Notable Gathering in the History of Washington. Vol. LIII, pp. 132-140, 4 ills., Jan., 1928.

Remarkable Photograph of Lilienthal's Gliding Machine. By R. W. Wood. Vol. XIX, p. 596, 1 ill., Aug., 1908.

Report of the Second Stratosphere Expedition. Vol. LXVIII, pp. 535-536, Oct., 1935.

Return to Florence. By 1st Lt. Benjamin C. McCartney. Vol. LXXXVII, pp. 257-296, 18 ills. in black and white, 18 ills. in color, Mar., 1945.

Seeing America from the *Shenandoah*: An Account of the Record-Making 9,000-Mile Flight from the Atlantic to the Pacific Coast and Return in the Navy's American-built, American-manned Airship. By Junius B. Wood. Vol. XLVII, pp. 1-47, 39 ills., 1 page map, 1 diagram, Jan., 1925.

Seeing America with Lindbergh: The Record of a Tour of More Than 20,000 Miles ·by Airplane Through Forty-eight States on Schedule Time. By Lieut. Donald E. Keyhoe. Vol. LIII, pp. 1-46, 46 ills., 1 page map, Jan., 1928.

Seeing the World from the Air. By Sir Alan J. Cobham. Vol. LIII, pp. 349-384, 37 ills., 1 three-quarters-page map, Mar., 1928.

Seeing 3,000 Years of History in Four Hours: A Panorama of Ancient, Medieval, and Modern Events Against a Background of Mythology Unfolds During an Airplane Journey from Constantinople to Athens. By Maynard Owen Williams. Vol. LIV, pp. 719-739, 24 ills., 1 two-thirds-page map, Dec., 1928.

Skypaths Through Latin America: Flying From Our Nation's Capital Southward Over Jungles, Remote Islands, and Great Cities on an Aërial Survey of the East Coast of South America. By Frederick Simpich. Vol. LIX, pp. 1-79, 77 ills., 1 page map, Jan., 1931.

Society Announces New Flight into the Stratosphere. By Gilbert Grosvenor. Vol. LXVII, pp. 265-272, 2 ills. in black and white, 1 sketch map, Feb., 1935.

Society Awards Hubbard Medal to Anne Morrow Lindbergh. Vol. LXV, pp. 791-794, 4 ills., June, 1934.

Society's Special Medal Awarded to Amelia Earhart: First Woman to Receive Geographic Distinction at Brilliant Ceremony in the National Capital. Vol. LXII, pp. 358-367, 7 ills., Sept., 1932.

Aeronautics—*Continued*

Studies Planned for New Stratosphere Flight with Helium. Vol. LXVII, pp. 795-800, 5 ills., June, 1935.

Take-off for Japan. 22 ills. in color from U. S. Navy official photographs. Vol. LXXXVIII, pp. 193-208, Aug., 1945.

Tales of the British Air Service. By Maj. William A. Bishop. Vol. XXXIII, pp. 27-37, 12 ills., Jan., 1918.

Tetrahedral Kite. Vol. XIV, p. 294, 1 ill., July, 1903.

Tetrahedral Principle in Kite Structure. By Alexander Graham Bell. Vol. XIV, pp. 219-251, 89 ills., 15 diagrams, June, 1903.

They Sustain the Wings (Ground Crews). By Frederick Simpich. Vol. LXXXIV, pp. 333-354, 19 ills., Sept., 1943.

To Bogotá and Back by Air: The Narrative of a 9,500-Mile Flight from Washington, Over Thirteen Latin American Countries and Return, in the Single-Seater Airplane *Spirit of St. Louis*. By Col. Charles A. Lindbergh. Vol. LIII, pp. 529-601, 98 ills., 1 two-thirds-page map, May, 1928.

To Seek the Unknown in the Arctic: United States Navy Flyers to Aid MacMillan Expedition Under the Auspices of the National Geographic Society in Exploring Vast Area. Vol. XLVII, pp. 673-675, 1 ill., 1 half-page map, June, 1925.

Unexplored Philippines from the Air: Map-Making over Jungle Lands Never Before Seen by White Men. By Lieut. George W. Goddard. Vol. LVIII, pp. 311-343, 38 ills., 1 quarter-page map, Sept., 1930.

Walter Wellman's Expedition to the North Pole. Vol. XVII, pp. 205-207, 1 chart, Apr., 1906.

World's Largest Free Balloon to Explore Stratosphere. Vol. LXVI, pp. 107-110, 2 ills., July, 1934.

Your Navy as Peace Insurance. By Fleet Admiral Chester W. Nimitz. Vol. LXXXIX, pp. 681-736, 32 ills. in black and white, 26 ills. in color, June, 1946.

Your New World of Tomorrow. By F. Barrows Colton. Vol. LXXXVIII, pp. 385-410, 25 ills., Oct., 1945.

Your Society Sponsors an Expedition to Explore the Stratosphere. Vol. LXV, pp. 528-530, 1 ill., Apr., 1934.

Afghanistan:

Afghan Borderland. By Ellsworth Huntington. Part I: The Russian Frontier. Vol. XX, pp. 788-799, 14 ills., Sept., 1909. Part II: The Persian Frontier. Vol. XX, pp. 866-876, 12 ills., Oct., 1909.

Afghanistan Makes Haste Slowly. By Maynard Owen Williams. Vol. LXIV, pp. 731-769, 33 ills. in black and white, 12 ills. in color, 1 two-thirds-page map, Dec., 1933.

Back to Afghanistan. By Maynard Owen Williams. Vol. XC, pp. 517-544, 27 ills., 1 page map, Oct., 1946.

Afghanistan—*Continued*

Bright Pages from an Asiatic Travel Log. 4 ills. in color from natural-color photographs by Maynard Owen Williams. Vol. LXII, pp. 544-553, Nov., 1932.

Citroën Trans-Asiatic Expedition Reaches Kashmir: Scientific Party Led by Georges-Marie Haardt Successfully Crosses Syria, Iraq, Persia, and Afghanistan to Arrive at the Pamir. By Maynard Owen Williams. Vol. LX, pp. 387-443, 62 ills., 1 page map, Oct., 1931.

Every-Day Life in Afghanistan. By Frederick Simpich and "Haji Mirza Hussein." Vol. XXXIX, pp. 85-110, 26 ills., 1 three-quarters-page map, Jan., 1921.

Kingdom of Many Tribes. 12 ills. in color from natural-color photographs by Maynard Owen Williams. Vol. LXIV, pp. 745-752, Dec., 1933.

Afield with the Spiders: Web Hunting in the Marshlands and Woodlands and Along the Lanes. By Henry E. Ewing. Vol. LXIV, pp. 163-194, 26 ills. in black and white, 64 ills. in color, Aug., 1933.

Africa:

Across Widest Africa. By A. Henry Savage Landor. Vol. XIX, pp. 694-737, 38 ills., 1 half-page map, Oct., 1908.

Africa, the Largest Game Preserve in the World. By John B. Torbert. Vol. XI, pp. 445-448, 1 page map, Nov., 1900.

Africa First of 1943 Global Warfare Maps. By William H. Nicholas. Text accompanying special map supplement in colors. Vol. LXXXIII, pp. 261-276, 13 ills., Feb., 1943.

Africa on Parade. 14 ills. in color from natural-color photographs by Lawrence Thaw. Vol. LXXIV, pp. 343-350, Sept., 1938.

African Scenes from the Equator to the Cape. Vol. XLII, pp. 431-446, 16 ills., Oct., 1922.

Amid the Snow Peaks of the Equator: A Naturalist's Explorations Around Ruwenzori, with an Excursion to the Congo State, and an Account of the Terrible Scourge of Sleeping Sickness. By A. F. R. Wollaston. Vol. XX, pp. 256-277, 11 ills., Mar., 1909.

Cairo to Cape Town, Overland: an Adventurous Journey of 135 Days, Made by an American Man and His Wife, Through the Length of the African Continent. By Felix Shay. Vol. XLVII, pp. 123-260, 118 ills., 1 half-page map, Feb., 1925.

Camera Adventures in the African Wilds. Photographs by A. Radclyffe Dugmore (Book Review). Vol. XXI, pp. 385-396, 11 ills., May, 1910.

Elephant Hunting in Equatorial Africa with Rifle and Camera. By Carl E. Akeley. Vol. XXIII, pp. 779-810, 30 ills., Aug., 1912.

Explorations in Central East Africa. Vol. XII, pp. 42-43, Jan., 1901.

Flags of Europe, Asia and Africa. By Byron McCandless and Gilbert Grosvenor. Vol. XXXII, pp. 372-385, 100 ills. in color, Oct., 1917.

Africa—*Continued*

Flights from Arctic to Equator: Conquering the Alps, the Ice Peaks of Spitsbergen, of Persia, and Africa's Mountains of the Moon. By Walter Mittelholzer. Vol. LXI, pp. 445-498, 53 ills., 1 three-quarters-page map, Apr., 1932.

Here and There in Northern Africa. By Frank Edward Johnson. Vol. XXV, pp. 1-132, 113 ills., Jan., 1914.

In Civilized French Africa. By James F. J. Archibald. Vol. XX, pp. 302-311, 14 ills., Mar., 1909.

In the Valley of the Niger. Vol. XIX, p. 164, Mar., 1908.

Magnetic Survey of Africa. By Dr. L. A. Bauer. Vol. XX, pp. 291-297, 6 ills., Mar., 1909.

Methods of Exploration in Africa. By Maj. A. St. H. Gibbons. Vol. XV, pp. 408-410, Oct., 1904.

Mr. Roosevelt's "African Game Trails." Vol. XXI, pp. 953-962, 9 ills., Nov., 1910.

National Geographic Society's New Map of Africa. By Gilbert Grosvenor. Text accompanying special supplement in colors. Vol. LXVII, pp. 731-752, 20 ills. in duotone, June, 1935.

Nature's Most Amazing Mammal: Elephants, Unique Among Animals, Have Many Human Qualities When Wild That Make Them Foremost Citizens of Zoo and Circus. By Edmund Heller. Vol. LXV, pp. 729-759, 37 ills., June, 1934.

Pathfinder of the East: Setting Sail to Find "Christians and Spices," Vasco da Gama Met Amazing Adventures, Founded an Empire, and Changed the History of Western Europe. By J. R. Hildebrand. Vol. LII, pp. 503-550, 43 ills., 1 two-thirds-page map, Nov., 1927.

Peoples and Places of Northern Africa. Vol. XLII, pp. 363-378, 16 ills., Oct., 1922.

Recent French Explorations in Africa. By Charles Rabot. Vol. XIII, pp. 119-132, 20 ills., Apr., 1902.

Recent Geographic Advances, Especially in Africa. By Maj. Gen. A. W. Greely. Vol. XXII, pp. 383-398, 5 ills., 5 page maps, Apr., 1911.

Sailing Forbidden Coasts. By Ida Treat. Vol. LX, pp. 357-386, 31 ills., 1 quarter-page map, Sept., 1931.

Scenes of Sunny Africa. 20 ills. in duotone. Vol. LXVII, pp. 735-750, June, 1935.

Seeing the World from the Air. By Sir Alan J. Cobham. Vol. LIII, pp. 349-384, 37 ills., 1 three-quarters-page map, Mar., 1928.

Society's New Map of Africa. Text accompanying special map supplement in colors. Vol. XLII, pp. 447-448, Oct., 1922.

Three-Wheeling Through Africa: Two Adventurers Cross the So-called Dark Continent North of Lake Chad on Motorcycles with Side Cars. By James C. Wilson. Vol. LXV, pp. 37-92, 64 ills., 1 two-page map, Jan., 1934.

Africa—*Continued*

Through the Deserts and Jungles of Africa by Motor: Caterpillar Cars Make 15,000-Mile Trip from Algeria to Madagascar in Nine Months. By Georges-Marie Haardt. Vol. XLIX, pp. 651-720, 95 ills., 1 two-thirds-page map, June, 1926.

Through the Heart of Africa. Vol. XI, pp. 408-411, Oct., 1900.

Trans-Africa Safari: A Motor Caravan Rolls Across Sahara and Jungle Through Realms of Dusky Potentates and the Land of Big-Lipped Women. By Lawrence Copley Thaw and Margaret Stout Thaw. Vol. LXXIV, pp. 327-364, 29 ills. in black and white, 14 ills. in color, 1 two-thirds-page map, Sept., 1938.

Transporting a Navy Through the Jungles of Africa in War Time. By Frank J. Magee. Vol. XLII, pp. 331-362, 31 ills., Oct., 1922.

Where Exploration Is Needed (Africa). Vol. XI, p. 163, Apr., 1900.

Wings Over Nature's Zoo in Africa. 20 ills. in duotone from photographs by Reginald A. Bourlay. Vol. LXXVI, pp. 527-542, Oct., 1939.

See also Algeria; Anglo-Egyptian Sudan; Angola; Belgian Congo; Cameroons; Egypt; Eritrea; Ethiopia; French West Africa; Gold Coast; Kenya Colony; Liberia; Libia; Morocco; Mozambique; Nigeria; South-West Africa; Southern Rhodesia; Tanganyika Territory; Tunisia; Uganda; Union of South Africa.

African Rainbow. 10 ills. in color from natural-color photographs by W. Robert Moore. Vol. LXXXVI, pp. 289-296, Sept., 1944.

African Scenes from the Equator to the Cape. Vol. XLII, pp. 431-446, 16 ills., Oct., 1922.

Agave. *See* Henequen.

Ageless Luster of Greece and Rhodes. 16 ills. in duotone by Arnold Genthe. Vol. LXXIII, pp. 477-492, Apr., 1938.

Ageton, (Lt.) Arthur A.:
Annapolis, Cradle of the Navy. By Lieut. Arthur A. Ageton. Vol. LXIX, pp. 789-800, 13 ills. in color, June, 1936.

Agnew, Donald H.:
American Wings Soar Around the World: Epic Story of the Air Transport Command of the U. S. Army Is a Saga of Yankee Daring and Doing. By Donald H. Agnew and William A. Kinney. Vol. LXXXIV, pp. 57-78, 22 ills., July, 1943.

Agra, India:
Through the Heart of Hindustan: A Teeming Highway Extending for Fifteen Hundred Miles, from the Khyber Pass to Calcutta. By Maynard Owen Williams. Vol. XL, pp. 433-467, 29 ills., Nov., 1921.

Agricultural and Botanical Explorers:
Aleutians: Riddle of the Aleutians: A Botanist Explores the Origin of Plants on Ever-misty Islands Now Enshrouded in the Fog of War. By Isobel Wylie Hutchison. Vol. LXXXII, pp. 769-792, 24 ills., Dec., 1942.

Asia: Hunter of Plants. By David Fairchild. Vol. XXXVI, pp. 57-77, 18 ills., July, 1919.

Canary Islands: Hunting for Plants in the Canary Islands. By David Fairchild. Vol. LVII, pp. 607-652, 37 ills. in black and white, 39 ills. in color, 1 third-page map, May, 1930.

Caribbean Regions: Hunting Useful Plants in the Caribbean. By David Fairchild. Vol. LXVI, pp. 705-737, 39 ills., Dec., 1934.

China: Experiences of a Lone Geographer: An American Agricultural Explorer Makes His Way Through Brigand-Infested Central China en Route to the Amne Machin Range, Tibet. By Joseph F. Rock. Vol. XLVIII, pp. 331-347, 16 ills., 1 quarter-page map, Sept., 1925.

China: Exploring a Grass Wonderland of Wild West China. By Ray G. Johnson. Vol. LXXXV, pp. 713-742, 24 ills., 1 half-page map, June, 1944.

China: Peacetime Plant Hunting About Peiping. By P. H. and J. H. Dorsett. Vol. LXXII, pp. 509-534, 21 ills., 1 two-thirds-page map, Oct., 1937.

China: Road to Wang Ye Fu: An Account of the Work of the National Geographic Society's Central-China Expedition in the Mongol Kingdom of Ala Shan. By Frederick R. Wulsin. Vol. XLIX, pp. 197-234, 44 ills., 1 third-page map, Feb., 1926.

China: Through the Great River Trenches of Asia: National Geographic Society Explorer Follows the Yangtze, Mekong, and Salwin Through Mighty Gorges, Some of Whose Canyon Walls Tower to a Height of More Than Two Miles. By Joseph F. Rock. Vol. L, pp. 133-186, 47 ills., 1 half-page map, Aug., 1926.

Colombia: Round About Bogotá: A Hunt for New Fruits and Plants Among the Mountain Forests of Colombia's Unique Capital. By Wilson Popenoe. Vol. XLIX, pp. 127-160, 34 ills., 1 third-page map, Feb., 1926.

Ecuador: Quinine Hunters in Ecuador. By Froelich Rainey. Vol. LXXXIX, pp. 341-363, 21 ills., 1 half-page map, Mar., 1946.

Ethiopia: Caravan Journey Through Abyssinia: From Addis Ababa Through Lalibela, the Strange Jerusalem of Ethiopia, in Search of New Grains for American Farms. By Harry V. Harlan. Vol. XLVII, pp. 613-663, 46 ills., 1 half-page map, June, 1925.

New Guinea: Into Primeval Papua by Seaplane: Seeking Disease-Resisting Sugar Cane, Scientists Find Neolithic Man in Unmapped Nooks of Sorcery and Cannibalism. By E. W. Brandes. Vol. LVI, pp. 253-332, 98 ills., 1 three-quarters-page map, Sept., 1929.

Our Plant Immigrants. By David Fairchild. Vol. XVII, pp. 179-201, 29 ills., Apr., 1906.

Agricultural and Botanical Explorers—*Continued*

U. S. S. R.: Roaming Russia's Caucasus: Rugged Mountains and Hardy Fighters Guard the Soviet Union's Caucasian Treasury of Manganese and Oil. By Rolf Singer. Vol. LXXXII, pp. 91-121, 33 ills., July, 1942.

Agricultural Capacity of Alaska: What Population Can the Territory Support? By C. C. Georgeson. Vol. XX, pp. 676-679, July, 1909.

Agricultural Possibilities in Tropical Mexico. By Dr. Pehr Olsson-Seffer. Vol. XXI, pp. 1021-1040, 18 ills., Dec., 1910.

Agriculture:

Alaska: Agricultural Capacity of Alaska: What Population Can the Territory Support? By C. C. Georgeson. Vol. XX, pp. 676-679, July, 1909.

Alaska: Agriculture in Alaska. By Henry Gannett. Vol. XIII, p. 112, Mar., 1902.

Alaska: Gardening in Northern Alaska. By Middleton Smith. Vol. XIV, pp. 355-357, Sept., 1903.

Argentina: Life on the Argentine Pampa. By Frederick Simpich. Vol. LXIV, pp. 449-491, 41 ills. in black and white, 8 ills. in color, Oct., 1933.

Ascension Island: Greens Grow for GI's on Soilless Ascension. By W. Robert Moore. Vol. LXXXVIII, pp. 219-230, 12 ills., Aug., 1945.

Australia: Beyond Australia's Cities. By W. Robert Moore. Vol. LXX, pp. 709-747, 27 ills. in black and white, 12 ills. in color, Dec., 1936.

Bulgaria, Farm Land Without a Farmhouse: A Nation of Villagers Faces the Challenge of Modern Machinery and Urban Life. By Maynard Owen Williams. Vol. LXII, pp. 185-218, 19 ills. in black and white, 27 ills. in color, 1 half-page map, Aug., 1932.

California: Man Without the Hoe. Vol. XXI, pp. 967-969, 2 ills., Nov., 1910.

California: More Water for California's Great Central Valley. By Frederick Simpich. Vol. XC, pp. 645-664, 16 ills., 1 page map, Nov., 1946.

California: Seed Farms in California. By A. J. Wells. Vol. XXIII, pp. 515-530, 14 ills., May, 1912.

China: Farmers Since the Days of Noah: China's Remarkable System of Agriculture Has Kept Alive the Densest Population in the World. By Adam Warwick. Vol. LI, pp. 469-500, 37 ills., Apr., 1927.

China: Geography of China: The Influence of Physical Environment on the History and Character of the Chinese People. By Frank Johnson Goodnow. Vol. LI, pp. 651-664, 11 ills., June, 1927.

China: How Half the World Works. By Alice Tisdale Hobart and Mary A. Nourse. Vol. LXI, pp. 509-524, 22 ills., Apr., 1932.

China: Hunter of Plants. By David Fairchild. Vol. XXXVI, pp. 57-77, 18 ills., July, 1919.

Agriculture—*Continued*

China Fights Erosion with U. S. Aid. By Walter C. Lowdermilk. Vol. LXXXVII, pp. 641-680, 10 ills. in black and white, 26 ills. in color, June, 1945.

Denmark and the Danes. By Maurice Francis Egan. Vol. XLII, pp. 115-164, 38 ills., 1 three-quarters-page map, Aug., 1922.

Egypt: Land of Egypt: A Narrow Green Strip of Fertility Stretching for a Thousand Miles Through Walls of Desert. By Alfred Pearce Dennis. Vol. XLIX, pp. 271-298, 28 ills., 1 half-page map, Mar., 1926.

England: Britain Fights in the Fields. By Francis A. Flood. Vol. LXXVI, pp. 31-65, 17 ills. in black and white, 21 ills. in color, July, 1944.

Georgia: Marching Through Georgia Sixty Years After: Multifold Industries and Diversified Agriculture Are Restoring the Prosperity of America's Largest State East of the Mississippi. By Ralph A. Graves. Vol. L, pp. 259-311, 47 ills., Sept., 1926.

How the World Is Fed. By William Joseph Showalter. Vol. XXIX, pp. 1-110, 101 ills., Jan., 1916.

Japan: Agriculture in Japan. By Consul General Bellows. Vol. XV, pp. 323-326, Aug., 1904.

Mexico: Agricultural Possibilities in Tropical Mexico. By Dr. Pehr Olsson-Seffer. Vol. XXI, pp. 1021-1040, 18 ills., Dec., 1910.

Mexico: Mexican Hacienda. By J. E. Kirkwood. Vol. XXV, pp. 563-584, 18 ills., May, 1914.

Mexico: Notes on Southern Mexico. By G. N. Collins and C. B. Doyle. Vol. XXII, pp. 301-320, 16 ills., 1 page map, Mar., 1911.

Mexico: Unearthing America's Ancient History: Investigation Suggests That the Maya May Have Designed the First Astronomical Observatory in the New World in Order to Cultivate Corn. By Sylvanus Griswold Morley. Vol. LX, pp. 99-126, 28 ills., July, 1931.

Mount Vernon: Home of the First Farmer of America. By Worth E. Shoults. Vol. LIII, pp. 603-628, 6 ills. in black and white, 26 ills. in color, May, 1928.

New Jersey Now! By E. John Long. Vol. LXIII, pp. 519-583, 49 ills. in black and white, 24 ills. in color, 1 page and 1 two-thirds-page maps, May, 1933.

New Plant Immigrants. By David Fairchild. Vol. XXII, pp. 879-907, 34 ills., Oct., 1911.

New York: Black Acres: A Thrilling Sketch in the Vast Volume of Who's Who Among the Peoples That Make America. By Dorothea D. and Fred Everett. Vol. LXXX, pp. 631-652, 13 ills. in black and white, 12 ills. in color, Nov., 1941.

New York: Fruitful Shores of the Finger Lakes. By Harrison Howell Walker. Vol. LXXIX, pp. 559-594, 15 ills. in black and white, 22 ills. in color, 1 two-thirds-page map, May, 1941.

Agriculture—*Continued*

North Carolina : Motor-Coaching Through North Carolina. By Melville Chater. Vol. XLIX, pp. 475-523, 43 ills., 1 third-page map, May, 1926.

Oregon Finds New Riches. By Leo A. Borah. Vol. XC, pp. 681-728, 15 ills. in black and white, 28 ills. in color, 1 two-page map, Dec., 1946.

Palestine : Village Life in the Holy Land. By John D. Whiting. Vol. XXV, pp. 249-314, 27 ills. in black and white, 22 ills. in color, Mar., 1914.

Palestine Today. By Francis Chase, Jr. Vol. XC, pp. 501-516, 16 ills., Oct., 1946.

Panama : Farming on the Isthmus of Panama. By Dillwyn M. Hazlett. Vol. XVII, pp. 229-234, 15 ills., Apr., 1906.

Peru : Staircase Farms of the Ancients : Astounding Farming Skill of Ancient Peruvians Who Were Probably the Most Industrious and Highly Organized People in History. By O. F. Cook. Vol. XXIX, pp. 474-534, 48 ills., May, 1916.

Philippine Islands : Economic Conditions of the Philippines. By Max L. Tornow. Vol. X, pp. 33-64, 10 ills., Feb., 1899.

Texas Delta of an American Nile : Orchards and Gardens Replace Thorny Jungle in the Southmost Tip of the Lone Star State. By McFall Kerbey. Vol. LXXV, pp. 51-96, 27 ills. in black and white, 24 ills. in color, 1 page map, Jan., 1939.

United States : America Fights on the Farms. 21 ills. in color from natural-color photographs. Vol. LXXXVI, pp. 33-48, July, 1944.

United States : Big Things of the West. By Charles F. Holder. Vol. XIV, pp. 279-282, 2 ills., July, 1903.

United States : Boys' and Girls' Agricultural Clubs. Vol. XXII, pp. 639-641, 4 ills., July, 1911.

United States : Discovery of Cancer in Plants. Vol. XXIV, pp. 53-70, 12 ills., Jan., 1913.

United States : Farmers Keep Them Eating. By Frederick Simpich. Vol. LXXXIII, pp. 435-458, 22 ills., Apr., 1943.

United States : Farmers of the United States. Vol. XVI, pp. 39-46, Jan., 1905.

United States : Forming New Fashions in Food : The Bearing of Taste on One of Our Great Food Economies, the Dried Vegetable, Which Is Developing into a Big War Industry. By David Fairchild. Vol. XXXIII, pp. 356-368, 11 ills., Apr., 1918.

United States : Helping the Farmers. Vol. XV, pp. 82-85, 1 ill., Feb., 1905.

United States : Helping the Farmers. Vol. XVIII, pp. 746-749, Nov., 1907.

United States : Helping to Solve the Allies' Food Problem : America Calls for a Million Young Soldiers of the Commissary to Volunteer for Service in 1918. By Ralph A. Graves. Vol. XXXIII, pp. 170-194, 23 ills., Feb., 1918.

United States : Inoculating the Ground. Vol. XV, pp. 225-228, 2 ills., May, 1904.

Agriculture—*Continued*

United States : Its Soils and Their Products. By H. W. Wiley. Vol. XIV, pp. 263-279, 11 ills., July, 1903.

United States : Modern Alchemist (Work of the Department of Agriculture). By James Wilson. Vol. XVIII, pp. 778-795, 6 ills., Dec., 1907.

United States : Our Greatest Plant Food (Phosphorus). By Guy Elliott Mitchell. Vol. XXI, pp. 783-791, 7 ills., Sept., 1910.

United States : Our Plant Immigrants. By David Fairchild. Vol. XVII, pp. 179-201, 29 ills., Apr., 1906.

United States : Pests and Parasites. By Charles Lester Marlatt. Vol. XXII, pp. 321-346, 29 ills., 2 three-quarters-page maps, Apr., 1911.

United States : Protecting the United States from Plant Pests. By Charles Lester Marlatt. Vol. XL, pp. 205-218, 16 ills., Aug., 1921.

United States : Soldiers of the Soil : Our Food Crops Must Be Greatly Increased. By David F. Houston. Vol. XXXI, pp. 273-280, 4 ills., Mar., 1917.

United States : Southwest : Its Splendid Natural Resources, Agricultural Wealth, and Scenic Beauty. By N. H. Darton. Vol. XXI, pp. 631-665, 21 ills., 1 page map, Aug., 1910.

United States : Spirit of the West : The Wonderful Agricultural Development Since the Dawn of Irrigation. By C. J. Blanchard. Vol. XXI, pp. 333-360, 15 ills., Apr., 1910.

United States : War, Patriotism, and the Food Supply. By Frederick V. Coville. Vol. XXXI, pp. 254-256, Mar., 1917.

United States : What the United States Government Does to Promote Agriculture. Vol. XIV, pp. 35-39, Jan., 1903.

See also individual products and industries.

Agualulcos (Indians) :
Isthmus of Tehuantepec : The Bridge of the World's Commerce. By Helen Olsson-Seffer. Vol. XXI, pp. 991-1002, 6 ills., Dec., 1910.

Aikman, Lonnelle Davison:
Bizarre Battleground—the Lonely Aleutians. By Lonnelle Davison. Vol. LXXXII, pp. 316-317, 1 ill., Sept., 1942.

Platinum in the World's Work. By Lonnelle Davison. Vol. LXXII, pp. 345-360, 17 ills., Sept., 1937.

Ailinglapalap (Atoll), Marshall Islands :
Marshallese Are Happy Again. 20 ills. in color from natural-color photographs by W. Robert Moore. Vol. LXXXVIII, pp. 337-360, Sept., 1945.

Our New Military Wards, the Marshalls. By W. Robert Moore. Vol. LXXXVIII, pp. 325-360, 14 ills. in black and white, 20 ills. in color, 1 half-page map, Sept., 1945.

Air Adventures in Peru : Cruising Among Andean Peaks, Pilots and Cameramen Discover Wondrous Works of an Ancient People. By Robert Shippee. Vol. LXIII, pp. 81-120, 40 ills., 1 three-quarters-page map, Jan., 1933.

Air Bases:
Air Power for Peace. By Gen. H. H. Arnold. Vol. LXXXIX, pp. 137-193, 35 ills. in black and white, 28 ills. in color, special map supplement, Feb., 1946.

Americans Stand Guard in Greenland. By Andrew H. Brown. Vol. XC, pp. 457-500, 23 ills. in black and white, 19 ills. in color, 1 page map, Oct., 1946.

China's Hand-built Air Bases. 9 ills. from photographs. Vol. LXXXVIII, pp. 231-236, Aug., 1945.

Servicing Arctic Airbases. By Robert A. Bartlett. Vol. LXXXIX, pp. 602-616, 3 ills. in black and white, 10 ills. in color, 1 half-page map, May, 1946.
See also Airfields.

Air Carrier Contract Personnel:
Heroes of Wartime Science and Mercy. By Elizabeth W. King. Vol. LXXXIV, pp. 715-740, 11 ills. in black and white, 334 ills. in color, Dec., 1943.

Air Commando Force. *See* U. S. First Air Commando Force.

Air Conquest: From the Early Days of Giant Kites and Birdlike Gliders, the National Geographic Society Has Aided and Encouraged the Growth of Aviation. Vol. LII, pp. 233-242, 13 ills., Aug., 1927.

Air Cruising Through New Brazil: A National Geographic Reporter Spots Vast Resources Which the Republic's War Declaration Adds to Strength of United Nations. By Henry Albert Phillips. Vol. LXXXII, pp. 503-536, 32 ills., Oct., 1942.

Air Evacuation of Wounded:
Flying Our Wounded Veterans Home. By Catherine Bell Palmer. Vol. LXXXVIII, pp. 363-384, 17 ills., Sept., 1945.

Air Force. *See* U. S. Army Air Forces.

Air Mail:
Flying the "Hump" of the Andes. By Capt. Albert W. Stevens. Vol. LIX, pp. 595-636, 36 ills., 1 third-page map, May, 1931.

Flying the World's Longest Air-Mail Route: From Montevideo, Uruguay, Over the Andes, Up the Pacific Coast, Across Central America and the Caribbean to Miami, Florida, in 67 Thrilling Flying Hours. By Junius B. Wood. Vol. LVII, pp. 261-325, 65 ills., 1 half-page map, Mar., 1930.

On the Trail of the Air Mail: A Narrative of the Experiences of the Flying Couriers Who Relay the Mail Across America at a Speed of More than 2,000 Miles a Day. By Lieut. J. Parker Van Zandt. Vol. XLIX, pp. 1-61, 67 ills., 1 two-thirds-page map, Jan., 1926.

Air Power for Peace. By Gen. H. H. Arnold. Vol. LXXXIX, pp. 137-193, 35 ills. in black and white, 28 ills. in color, special map supplement, Feb., 1946.

Air Raids:
Air Power for Peace. By Gen. H. H. Arnold. Vol. LXXXIX, pp. 137-193, 35 ills. in black and white, 28 ills. in color, special map supplement, Feb., 1946.

A City That Refused to Die (Plymouth, England). By Harvey Klemmer. Vol. LXXXIX, pp. 211-236, 13 ills. in black and white, 9 ills. in color, 1 half-page map, Feb., 1946.

Everyday Life in Wartime England. By Harvey Klemmer. Vol. LXXIX, pp. 497-534, 48 ills., Apr., 1941.

Front-line Town of Britain's Siege (Dover). By Harvey Klemmer. Vol. LXXXV, pp. 105-128, 21 ills., Jan., 1944.

Malta Invicta. By Bartimeus (A Captain in the Royal Navy). Vol. LXXXIII, pp. 375-400, 27 ills., 1 half-page map, Mar., 1943.

Return to Florence. By 1st Lt. Benjamin C. McCartney. Vol. LXXXVII, pp. 257-296, 18 ills. in black and white, 18 ills. in color, Mar., 1945.
See also Bombs, Flying.

Air Transport Command, U. S. Army Air Forces:
American Wings Soar Around the World: Epic Story of the Air Transport Command of the U. S. Army Is a Saga of Yankee Daring and Doing. By Donald H. Agnew and William A. Kinney. Vol. LXXXIV, pp. 57-78, 22 ills., July, 1943.

Flying Our Wounded Veterans Home. By Catherine Bell Palmer. Vol. LXXXVIII, pp. 363-384, 17 ills., Sept., 1945.
See also Air Carrier Contract Personnel.

Aircraft Carriers:
Navy Wings over the Pacific. 12 ills. in color from natural-color photographs. Vol. LXXXVI, pp. 241-248, Aug., 1944.

New Queen of the Seas. By Melville Bell Grosvenor. Vol. LXXXII, pp. 1-30, 27 ills., 1 drawing, 1 two-page map, July, 1942.

Painting History in the Pacific. 19 ills. in color from paintings by Lt. William F. Draper. Vol. LXXXVI, pp. 409-424, Oct., 1944.

Saga of the Carrier *Princeton.* By Capt. William H. Buracker, USN. Vol. LXXXVIII, pp. 189-218, 8 ills. in black and white, 22 ills. in color, 1 map (two-page spread), Aug., 1945.

Ships That Won the Greatest Naval War. 26 ills. in color from U. S. Navy official photographs. Vol. LXXXIX, pp. 697-736, June, 1946.

Take-off for Japan. 22 ills. in color from U. S. Navy official photographs. Vol. LXXXVIII, pp. 193-208, Aug., 1945.

Victory's Portrait in the Marianas. By Lt. William Franklin Draper, USNR. With 17 ills. in color from paintings by the author. Vol. LXXXVIII, pp. 599-616, Nov., 1945.

Your Navy as Peace Insurance. By Fleet Admiral Chester W. Nimitz. Vol. LXXXIX, pp. 681-736, 32 ills. in black and white, 26 ills. in color, June, 1946.
See also Escort Carriers.

Aircraft Industry:
American Industries Geared for War. By Thornton Oakley. With 16 ills. in color from paintings by the author. Vol. LXXXII, pp. 716-734, 1 ill. in black and white, Dec., 1942.

Michigan Fights. By Harvey Klemmer. Vol. LXXXVI, pp. 677-715, 20 ills. in black and white, 19 ills. in color, 1 page-and-a-half map, Dec., 1944.

Miracle of War Production: For Victory the United States Transforms Its Complex Industry into the Biggest Factory and Mightiest Arsenal the World Has Ever Known. By Albert W. Atwood. Paintings by Thornton Oakley. Vol. LXXXII, pp. 693-715, 17 ills. in black and white, 16 ills. in color, Dec., 1942

Women at Work. By La Verne Bradley. Vol. LXXXVI, pp. 193-220, 23 ills., Aug., 1944.

Aircraft Insignia, Spirit of Youth. By Gerard Hubbard. Vol. LXXXIII, pp. 710-722, 3 ills. in black and white, 337 ills. in color, June, 1943.

Airfields:
Ascension Island, an Engineering Victory. By Lt. Col. Frederick J. Clarke. Vol. LXXXV, pp. 623-640, 21 ills., May, 1944.

See also Air Bases.

Airplane Carriers. *See* Aircraft Carriers; Escort Carriers.

Airplanes. *See* Aeronautics; Aircraft Industry; Bombers; Seaplanes.

Airplanes Come to the Isles of Spice: Once Magnet of World Explorers, the Moluccas Again Stand at Crossroads of History in the Netherlands Indies. By Maynard Owen Williams. Vol. LXXIX, pp. 535-558, 26 ills., 1 page map, May, 1941.

Airships. *See* Blimps; *Shenandoah.*

Aisawa (Dance):
Two Great Moorish Religious Dances (Tangier, Morocco). By George Edmund Holt. Vol. XXII, pp. 776-785, 6 ills., Aug., 1911.

Ak Bulak, U. S. S. R.:
Observing an Eclipse in Asiatic Russia. By Irvine C. Gardner. Vol. LXXI, pp. 179-197, 19 ills. in black and white, 1 ill. in color, Feb., 1937.

Akeley, Carl E.:
Elephant Hunting in Equatorial Africa with Rifle and Camera. By Carl E. Akeley. Vol. XXIII, pp. 779-810, 30 ills., Aug., 1912.

Al Saud, Abdul Aziz (King of Saudi Arabia):
Guest in Saudi Arabia. By Maynard Owen Williams. Vol. LXXXVIII, pp. 463-487, 24 ills., 1 two-thirds-page map, Oct., 1945.

Ala Shan (Mongol Kingdom):
Road to Wang Ye Fu: An Account of the Work of the National Geographic Society's Central-China Expedition in the Mongol Kingdom of Ala Shan. By Frederick R. Wulsin. Vol. XLIX, pp. 197-234, 44 ills., 1 third-page map, Feb., 1926.

Alabama:
Smoke Over Alabama. By Frederick Simpich. Vol. LX, pp. 703-758, 43 ills. in black and white, 26 ills. in color, 1 page map, Dec., 1931.

Where the New South Challenges the Old. 26 ills. in color from natural-color photographs by Edwin L. Wisherd. Vol. LX, pp. 716-749, Dec., 1931.

Alamogordo, New Mexico:
White Sands of Alamogordo: A Dry Ocean of Granular Gypsum Billows Under Desert Winds in a New National Playground. By Carl P. Russell. Vol. LXVIII, pp. 250-264, 12 ills., Aug., 1935.

Åland (Islands), Finland:
Flashes from Finland. 19 ills. from photographs. Vol. LXXVII, pp. 239-254, Feb., 1940.

Where the Sailing Ship Survives. By A. J. Villiers. Vol. LXVII, pp. 101-128, 31 ills., 1 half-page map, Jan., 1935.

Alaouite (Region), Syria:
New Alphabet of the Ancients Is Unearthed: An Inconspicuous Mound in Northern Syria Yields Archeological Treasures of Far-Reaching Significance. By F. A. Schaeffer. Vol. LVIII, pp. 477-516, 47 ills., 1 quarter-page map, Oct., 1930.

Secrets from Syrian Hills: Explorations Reveal World's Earliest Known Alphabet, Deciphered from Schoolboy Slates and Dictionaries of 3,000 Years Ago. By Claude F. A. Schaeffer. Vol. LXIV, pp. 97-126, 40 ills., 1 third-page map, July, 1933.

Alaska:
Agricultural Capacity of Alaska: What Population Can the Territory Support? By C. C. Georgeson. Vol. XX, pp. 676-679, July, 1909.

Agriculture in Alaska. By Henry Gannett. Vol. XIII, p. 112, Mar., 1902.

Alaska—Our Northwestern Outpost. 16 ills. in color from natural-color photographs by Ernest H. Gruening, Amos Burg, and Froelich Rainey. Vol. LXXXII, pp. 297-308, Sept., 1942.

Alaskan Boundary. By John W. Foster. Vol. X, pp. 425-456, 10 page maps, Nov., 1899.

Alaskan Boundary Decision. Vol. XIV, p. 423, Nov., 1903.

Alaskan Boundary Dispute. Vol. XIV, p. 79, Feb., 1903.

Alaskan Boundary Tribunal. By John W. Foster. Vol. XV, pp. 1-12, 1 half-page map, special map supplement, Jan., 1904.

Alaskan Brown Bear. By Wilfred H. Osgood. Vol. XX, pp. 332-333, Apr., 1909.

Alaskan Highway an Engineering Epic: Mosquitoes, Mud, and Muskeg Minor Obstacles of 1,671-mile Race to Throw the Alcan Life Line Through Thick Forests and Uninhabited Wilderness. By Froelich Rainey. Vol. LXXXIII, pp. 143-168, 21 ills., 3 maps, Feb., 1943.

Alaska—*Continued*

Alaska's New Railway. Vol. XXVIII, pp. 567-589, 20 ills., Dec., 1915.

Anglo-American Polar Expedition. Vol. XVIII, p. 796, Dec., 1907.

Awe-Inspiring Spectacle of the Valley of Ten Thousand Smokes, Discovered and Explored by National Geographic Society Expeditions. Vol. XXXIII, supplement, Feb., 1918.

Big Game of Alaska. By Wilfred H. Osgood. Vol. XX, pp. 624-636, 10 ills., July, 1909.

"Breaking Up" of the Yukon. By Capt. George S. Gibbs. Vol. XVII, pp. 268-272, 6 ills., May, 1906.

Brooks Alaskan Expedition. Vol. XIII, p. 389, Oct., 1902.

Building the Alaskan Telegraph System. By Capt. William Mitchell. Vol. XV, pp. 357-361, Sept., 1904.

Camel of the Frozen Desert (Reindeer). By Carl J. Lomen. Vol. XXXVI, pp. 538-556, 19 ills., Dec., 1919.

Cape Nome Gold District. By F. C. Schrader. Vol. XI, pp. 15-23, 3 ills., 1 page map, Jan., 1900.

Charting a Coast-Line of 26,000 Miles. Vol. XX, pp. 608-609, July, 1909.

Coal Fields of Alaska. Vol. XXI, pp. 82-87, 6 ills., Jan., 1910.

Coal Resources of Alaska. Vol. XIII, pp. 172-174, May, 1902.

Conquest of Mount Crillon. By Bradford Washburn. Vol. LXVII, pp. 361-400, 40 ills., 2 half-page maps, Mar., 1935.

Copper River Delta. By E. D. Preston. Vol. XI, pp. 29-31, Jan., 1900.

Decision of the Alaskan Boundary Tribunal. Vol. XV, pp. 12-14, Jan., 1904.

Discovering Alaska's Oldest Arctic Town (Ipiutak) : A Scientist Finds Ivory-eyed Skeletons of a Mysterious People and Joins Modern Eskimos in the Dangerous Spring Whale Hunt. By Froelich G. Rainey. Vol. LXXXII, pp. 319-336, 15 ills., Sept., 1942.

Economic Evolution of Alaska. By Maj. Gen. A. W. Greely. Vol. XX, pp. 585-593, 4 ills., July, 1909.

Evidences of Recent Volcanic Action in Southeast Alaska. Vol. XVII, pp. 173 and 176, Mar., 1906.

Explorations in Alaska. Vol. X, pp. 269-271, July, 1899.

Exploring Frozen Fragments of American History : On the Trail of Early Eskimo Colonists Who Made a 55-Mile Crossing from the Old World to the New. By Henry B. Collins, Jr. Vol. LXXV, pp. 633-656, 24 ills., 1 two-thirds-page map, May, 1939.

First Alaskan Air Expedition. By Capt. St. Clair Streett. Vol. XLI, pp. 499-552, 37 ills., 1 page map, May, 1922.

Game Country Without Rival in America : The Proposed Mount McKinley National Park. By Stephen R. Capps. Vol. XXXI, pp. 69-84, 14 ills., 1 half-page map, Jan., 1917.

Alaska—*Continued*

Gardening in Northern Alaska. By Middleton Smith. Vol. XIV, pp. 355-357, Sept., 1903.

General Geography of Alaska. By Henry Gannett. Vol. XII, pp. 180-196, 9 ills., May, 1901.

Geography of Alaska. By Alfred H. Brooks. Vol. XV, pp. 213-219, special map supplement in colors, May, 1904.

Glaciers of Alaska. By Grove Karl Gilbert. Vol. XV, pp. 449-450, Nov., 1904.

Greely's "Handbook of Alaska." By Gilbert H. Grosvenor. Vol. XX, pp. 491-492, May, 1909.

Growing Camp in the Tanana Gold Fields, Alaska. By Sidney Paige. Vol. XVI, pp. 104-111, 4 ills., Mar., 1905.

Harriman Alaska Expedition. By Henry Gannett. Vol. X, pp. 507-512, 1 chart, 1 page map, Dec., 1899.

Harriman Alaska Expedition in Coöperation with the Washington Academy of Sciences. By Gilbert H. Grosvenor. Vol. X, pp. 225-227, June, 1899.

How Much Is Known of Alaska? By Alfred H. Brooks. Vol. XVII, pp. 112-114, Feb., 1906.

Hunting the Great Brown Bear of Alaska. By George Mixter, 2nd. Vol. XX, pp. 313-332, 35 ills., Apr., 1909.

Jack in the Box : An Account of the Strange Performances of the Most Wonderful Island in the World (Bogoslof Volcano). By Capt. F. M. Munger. Vol. XX, pp. 194-199, 8 ills., Feb., 1909.

Ketchikan. Vol. XVI, p. 508, 1 ill., Nov., 1905.

Kodiak not Kadiak. Vol. XII, pp. 397-398, Nov., 1901.

Lake Clark, a Little Known Alaskan Lake. By Wilfred H. Osgood. Vol. XV, pp. 326-331, 2 ills., 1 half-page map, Aug., 1904.

Magnetic Observations in Alaska. By Daniel L. Hazard. Vol. XX, pp. 675-676, 1 page map, July, 1909.

Making the Fur Seal Abundant. By Hugh M. Smith. Vol. XXII, pp. 1139-1165, 18 ills., 1 half-page map, Dec., 1911.

Mapping the Home of the Great Brown Bear : Adventures of the National Geographic Society's Pavlof Volcano Expedition to Alaska. By Dr. Thomas A. Jaggar. Vol. LV, pp. 109-134, 30 ills., 1 three-quarters-page map, Jan., 1929.

Marking the Alaskan Boundary. Vol. XIX, pp. 176-189, 16 ills., Mar., 1908.

Marking the Alaskan Boundary. By Thomas Riggs, Jr. Vol. XX, pp. 593-607, 17 ills., July, 1909.

Mind's Eye Map of America. By Franklin K. Lane. Vol. XXXVII, pp. 479-518, 25 ills. in black and white, 8 ills. in color, June, 1920.

Monarchs of Alaska (Mountains). By R. H. Sargent. Vol. XX, pp. 610-623, 9 ills., July, 1909.

Alaska—*Continued*

Mountains on Unimak Island. By Ferdinand Westdahl. Vol. XIV, pp. 90-99, 4 ills., 1 page and 1 half-page maps, Mar., 1903.

Muir Glacier. By C. L. Andrews. Vol. XIV, pp. 441-445, 2 ills., 1 quarter-page map, Dec., 1903.

Nakwasina Goes North: A Man, a Woman, and a Pup Cruise from Tacoma to Juneau in a 17-foot Canoe. By Jack Calvin. Vol. LXIV, pp. 1-42, 24 ills., 1 page map, July, 1933.

National Geographic Society Alaskan Expedition. Vol. XX, pp. 581-584, June, 1909.

National Geographic Society Researches in Alaska. By Lawrence Martin. Vol. XXII, pp. 537-561, 17 ills., 1 page and 4 half-page maps, June, 1911.

National Geographic Society's Alaskan Expedition. Vol. XXI, p. 370, Apr., 1910.

National Geographic Society's Alaskan Expedition of 1909. By Ralph S. Tarr and Lawrence Martin. Vol. XXI, pp. 1-54, 42 ills., 12 maps, Jan., 1910.

Nation's Undeveloped Resources. By Franklin K. Lane. Vol. XXV, pp. 183-225, 32 ills., Feb., 1914.

Nome Gold Fields. Vol. XIX, pp. 384-385, May, 1908.

Northern Crusoe's Island: Life on a Fox Farm Off the Coast of Alaska, Far from Contact with the World Eleven Months a Year. By Margery Pritchard Parker. Vol. XLIV, pp. 313-326, 15 ills., 1 eighth-page map, Sept., 1923.

Note on the Activity of Shishaldin Volcano. By Homer P. Ritter. Vol. XVI, p. 249, May, 1905.

Opening of the Alaskan Territory. By Harrington Emerson. Vol. XIV, pp. 99-106, 5 ills., Mar., 1903.

Origin of the Name "Cape Nome." Vol. XII, p. 398, Nov., 1901.

Our Air Frontier in Alaska. By Major General H. H. Arnold. Vol. LXXVIII, pp. 487-504, 15 ills., 1 page map, Oct., 1940.

Our Greatest National Monument: The National Geographic Society Completes Its Explorations in the Valley of Ten Thousand Smokes. By Robert F. Griggs. Vol. XL, pp. 219-292, 73 ills. in black and white, 16 ills. in color, 1 page and 1 three-quarters-page maps, Sept., 1921.

Over the Roof of Our Continent. By Bradford Washburn. Vol. LXXIV, pp. 78-98, 17 ills. in duotone, 1 half-page map, July, 1938.

Photography in Glacial Alaska. By O. D. von Engeln. Vol. XXI, pp. 54-62, 4 ills., Jan., 1910.

Plan for Climbing Mt. McKinley. By Alfred H. Brooks and D. L. Reaburn. Vol. XIV, pp. 30-35, 1 page map, Jan., 1903.

Possibilities of Alaska. By C. C. Georgeson. Vol. XIII, pp. 81-85, Mar., 1902.

Proposed Surveys in Alaska in 1902. By Alfred H. Brooks. Vol. XIII, pp. 133-135, Apr., 1902.

Alaska—*Continued*

Railway Routes in Alaska. By Alfred H. Brooks. Vol. XVIII, pp. 164-190, 9 ills., 7 page and 1 half-page maps, 2 diagrams, Mar., 1907.

Recent Eruption of Katmai Volcano in Alaska. By George C. Martin. Vol. XXIV, pp. 131-181, 45 ills., 1 page map, 1 diagram, Feb., 1913.

Recession of the Glaciers of Glacier Bay, Alaska. By Fremont Morse. Vol. XIX, pp. 76-78, 1 page map, Jan., 1908.

Reindeer in Alaska. By Gilbert H. Grosvenor. Vol. XIV, pp. 126-149, 17 ills., 1 half-page map, Apr., 1903.

Returns from Alaska. Vol. XVI, p. 513, 1 page map, Nov., 1905.

Shishaldin (Mountain) as a Field for Exploration. By Joseph Stanley-Brown. Vol. X, pp. 281-288, 3 ills., 1 quarter-page map, Aug., 1899.

Some Notes on the Fox Island Passes, Alaska. By I. I. Gilbert. Vol. XVI, pp. 427-429, Sept., 1905.

Stikine River in 1898. By Eliza R. Scidmore. Vol. X, pp. 1-15, 4 ills., Jan., 1899.

Strategic Alaska Looks Ahead: Our Vast Territory, Now Being More Closely Linked to Us by Road and Rail, Embodies the American Epic of Freedom, Adventure, and the Pioneer Spirit. By Ernest H. Gruening. Vol. LXXXII, pp. 281-315, 18 ills. in black and white, 16 ills. in color, 1 two-page map, Sept., 1942.

Surveying the 141st Meridian (Boundary Line Between Canada and Alaska). By Thomas Riggs, Jr. Vol. XXIII, pp. 685-713, 46 ills., 1 page map, July, 1912.

Ten Thousand Smokes Now a National Monument: The President of the United States Sets Aside for the American People the Extraordinary Valley Discovered and Explored by the National Geographic Society. Vol. XXXV, pp. 359-366, 5 ills., Apr., 1919.

To-day on "The Yukon Trail of 1898." By Amos Burg. Vol. LVIII, pp. 85-126, 52 ills., 1 two-thirds-page map, July, 1930.

Transportation Methods in Alaska. By Capt. George S. Gibbs. Vol. XVII, pp. 69-82, 19 ills., Feb., 1906.

Valley of Ten Thousand Smokes: An Account of the Discovery and Exploration of the Most Wonderful Volcanic Region in the World. By Robert F. Griggs. Vol. XXXIII, pp. 115-169, 46 ills., panorama, 1 half-page map, Feb., 1918.

Valley of Ten Thousand Smokes: National Geographic Society Explorations in the Katmai District of Alaska. By Robert F. Griggs. Vol. XXXI, pp. 12-68, 51 ills., 1 half-page map, Jan., 1917.

Volcanoes of Alaska. Report by Capt. K. W. Perry. Vol. XXIII, pp. 824-832, 11 ills., Aug., 1912.

White Sheep, Giant Moose, and Smaller Game of the Kenai Peninsula, Alaska. By George Shiras, 3d. Vol. XXIII, pp. 423-494, 59 ills., 1 two-page map, May, 1912.

Alaska—*Continued*

World Inside a Mountain : Aniakchak, the New Volcanic Wonderland of the Alaska Peninsula, Is Explored. By Bernard R. Hubbard. Vol. LX, pp. 319-345, 34 ills., 1 half-page map, Sept., 1931.

World's Highest Altitudes and First Ascents. By Charles E. Fay. Vol. XX, pp. 493-530, 25 ills., June, 1909.

Wrangell Mountains, Alaska. By Walter C. Mendenhall. Vol. XIV, pp. 395-407, 3 ills., panorama, Nov., 1903.

Wrangell Mountains. Panorama taken by W. C. Mendenhall from the ridge east of the Dadina River. Vol. XIV, supplement, Nov., 1903.

See also Aleutian Islands ; Kodiak (Island) ; McKinley, Mount.

Alaska Military Highway:
Alaskan Highway an Engineering Epic : Mosquitoes, Mud, and Muskeg Minor Obstacles of 1,671-mile Race to Throw the Alcan Life Line Through Thick Forests and Uninhabited Wilderness. By Froelich Rainey. Vol. LXXXIII, pp. 143-168, 21 ills., 3 maps, Feb., 1943.

Alaskan Boundary. By John W. Foster. Vol. X, pp. 425-456, 10 page maps, Nov., 1899.

Alaskan Boundary Decision. Vol. XIV, p. 423, Nov., 1903.

Alaskan Boundary Dispute. Vol. XIV, p. 79, Feb., 1903.

Alaskan Boundary Tribunal. By John W. Foster. Vol. XV, pp. 1-12, 1 half-page map, special map supplement, Jan., 1904.

Alaskan Brown Bear. By Wilfred H. Osgood. Vol. XX, pp. 332-333, Apr., 1909.

Alaskan Brown Bear : The Largest Carnivorous Animal Extant. Vol. XXX, colored supplement, Nov., 1916.

Alaskan-Canadian Military Highway. *See* Alaska Military Highway.

Alaskan Highway an Engineering Epic : Mosquitoes, Mud, and Muskeg Minor Obstacles of 1,671-mile Race to Throw the Alcan Life Line Through Thick Forests and Uninhabited Wilderness. By Froelich Rainey. Vol. LXXXIII, pp. 143-168, 21 ills., 3 maps, Feb., 1943.

Alaska's New Railway. Vol. XXVIII, pp. 567-589, 20 ills., Dec., 1915.

Albania:
Albanians. By Theron J. Damon. Vol. XXIII, pp. 1090-1103, 14 ills., Nov., 1912.

Changing Map in the Balkans. By Frederick Moore. Vol. XXIV, pp. 199-226, 27 ills., 1 page map, Feb., 1913.

Europe's Newest Kingdom : After Centuries of Struggle, Albania at Last Enjoys an Era of Peace and Stability. By Melville Chater. Vol. LIX, pp. 131-191, 37 ills. in black and white, 25 ills. in color, 1 half-page map, Feb., 1931.

Albania—*Continued*

Men of the Eagle in Their Mountain Eyrie. 39 ills. in color from natural-color photographs by Luigi Pellerano. Vol. LIX, pp. 142-191, Feb., 1931.

Races of Europe. By Edwin A. Grosvenor. Vol. XXXIV, pp. 441-534, 62 ills., 2 page maps, special map supplement in colors, Dec., 1918.

Recent Observations in Albania. By Brig. Gen. George P. Scriven. Vol. XXXIV, pp. 90-114, 21 ills., 1 half-page map, Aug., 1918.

Young Turk. By Rear Adm. Colby M. Chester. Vol. XXII, pp. 42-89, 39 ills., Jan., 1912.

Albanians. By Theron J. Damon. Vol. XXIII, pp. 1090-1103, 14 ills., Nov., 1912.

Albatrosses (Birds) :
Bird City (Laysan Island, Hawaii). Vol. XV, pp. 494-498, 6 ills., Dec., 1904.

Birds of the High Seas : Albatrosses and Petrels ; Gannets, Man-o'-war-birds, and Tropic-birds. By Robert Cushman Murphy. Paintings by Maj. Allan Brooks. Vol. LXXIV, pp. 226-251, 7 ills. in black and white, 36 portraits in color, Aug., 1938.

South Georgia, an Outpost of the Antarctic. By Robert Cushman Murphy. Vol. XLI, pp. 409-444, 41 ills., 2 half-page maps, Apr., 1922.

Wings Over the Bounding Main. 36 portraits in color from paintings by Maj. Allan Brooks. Vol. LXXIV, pp. 237-251, Aug., 1938.

Albee, Ruth:
Family Afoot in Yukon Wilds : Two Young Children and Their Parents Live Off the Country in the Northwest Canada Wilderness Now To Be Traversed by the Alaska Highway. By William Hamilton Albee, with Ruth Albee. Vol. LXXXI, pp. 589-616, 18 ills. in black and white, 14 ills. in color, May, 1942.

Albee, William Hamilton:
Family Afoot in Yukon Wilds : Two Young Children and Their Parents Live Off the Country in the Northwest Canada Wilderness Now To Be Traversed by the Alaska Highway. By William Hamilton Albee, with Ruth Albee. Vol. LXXXI, pp. 589-616, 18 ills. in black and white, 14 ills. in color, May, 1942.

Alberta (Province), Canada :
Columbia (River) Turns on the Power. By Maynard Owen Williams. Vol. LXXIX, pp. 749-792, 25 ills. in black and white, 18 ills. in color, June, 1941.

Exploration in the Canadian Rockies. Vol. X, pp. 135-136, Apr., 1899.

Hunting Big Game of Other Days : A Boating Expedition in Search of Fossils in Alberta, Canada. By Barnum Brown. Vol. XXXV, pp. 407-429, 24 ills., 1 page map, May, 1919.

Landslides and Rock Avalanches. By Guy Elliott Mitchell. Vol. XXI, pp. 277-287, 6 ills., Apr., 1910.

Monarch of the Canadian Rockies (Mount Robson). By Charles D. Walcott. Vol. XXIV, pp. 626-639, 13 ills., panorama, May, 1913.

Alberta (Province), Canada—*Continued*

Monarch of the Canadian Rockies—Robson Peak. Vol. XXIV, panorama, May, 1913.

Mother of Rivers: An Account of a Photographic Expedition to the Great Columbia Ice Field of the Canadian Rockies. By Lewis R. Freeman. Vol. XLVII, pp. 377-446, 60 ills., 2 maps, Apr., 1925.

Peaks and Parks of Western Canada. 11 ills. from photographs; 5 ills. by W. J. Oliver. Vol. LXXX, pp. 516-526, Oct., 1941.

Peaks and Trails in the Canadian Alps. 16 ills. in duotone from photographs by Byron Harmon and Clifford White. Vol. LXV, pp. 627-642, May, 1934.

Recent Exploration in the Canadian Rockies. By Walter D. Wilcox. Part I, Vol. XIII, pp. 151-168, 12 ills., 1 page map, May, 1902. Part II, Vol. XIII, pp. 185-200, 9 ills., June, 1902.

Albrecht, Florence Craig:

Austro-Italian Mountain Frontiers. By Florence Craig Albrecht. Vol. XXVII, pp. 321-376, 60 ills., 1 page map, Apr., 1915.

Channel Ports—And Some Others. By Florence Craig Albrecht. Vol. XXVIII, pp. 1-55, 45 ills., July, 1915.

City of Jacqueline (Ter Goes, Netherlands). By Florence Craig Albrecht. Vol. XXVII, pp. 29-56, 31 ills., Jan., 1915.

Frontier Cities of Italy. By Florence Craig Albrecht. Vol. XXVII, pp. 533-586, 45 ills., June, 1915.

London. By Florence Craig Albrecht. Vol. XXVIII, pp. 263-294, 28 ills., Sept., 1915.

Splendor of Rome. By Florence Craig Albrecht. Vol. XLI, pp. 593-626, 28 ills., June, 1922.

Town of Many Gables (Münster, Germany). By Florence Craig Albrecht. Vol. XXVII, pp. 107-140, 28 ills., Feb., 1915.

"Alcan" Highway. *See* Alaska Military Highway.

Alden, Carroll Storrs:

Megaspelæon, the Oldest Monastery in Greece. By Carroll Storrs Alden. Vol. XXIV, pp. 310-323, 11 ills., Mar., 1913.

Alderney (Island), Channel Islands:

Channel Islands. By Edith Carey. Vol. XXXVIII, pp. 143-164, 24 ills., 1 quarter-page map, Aug., 1920.

Aleppo, Syria:

From Jerusalem to Aleppo. By John D. Whiting. Vol. XXIV, pp. 71-113, 30 ills., 1 half-page map, Jan., 1913.

Impressions of Asiatic Turkey. By Steven van Rensselaer Trowbridge. Vol. XXVI, pp. 598-609, 6 ills., Dec., 1914.

Syria and Lebanon Taste Freedom. By Maynard Owen Williams. With 21 ills. in color from natural-color photographs by the author. Vol. XC, pp. 729-763, 16 ills. in black and white, Dec., 1946.

Alert Anatolia. 13 ills. in black and white from photographs. Vol. LXXXV, pp. 481-492, Apr., 1944.

Aleutian Islands, Alaska:

Bizarre Battleground—the Lonely Aleutians. By Lonnelle Davison. Vol. LXXXII, pp. 316-317, 1 ill., Sept., 1942.

Jack in the Box: An Account of the Strange Performances of the Most Wonderful Island in the World (Bogoslof Volcano). By Capt. F. M. Munger. Vol. XX, pp. 194-199, 8 ills., Feb., 1909.

Navy Artist Paints the Aleutians. By Mason Sutherland. Paintings by Lt. William F. Draper. Vol. LXXXIV, pp. 157-176, 4 ills. in black and white, 16 ills. in color, Aug., 1943.

Riddle of the Aleutians: A Botanist Explores the Origin of Plants on Ever-misty Islands Now Enshrouded in the Fog of War. By Isobel Wylie Hutchison. Vol. LXXXII, pp. 769-792, 24 ills., Dec., 1942.

See also Unimak.

Aleuts (People):

Indians of Our North Pacific Coast. By Matthew W. Stirling. Paintings by W. Langdon Kihn. Vol. LXXXVII, pp. 25-52, 3 ills. in black and white, 16 ills. in color, Jan., 1945.

Algeria:

American Eclipse Expedition. By Rear Adm. Colby M. Chester. Vol. XVII, pp. 589-612, 23 ills., 1 color plate, Nov., 1906.

Americans on the Barbary Coast. By Willard Price. Vol. LXXXIV, pp. 1-31, 13 ills. in black and white, 10 ills. in color, 1 map (two-page spread), July, 1943.

Biskra, the Ziban Queen. By Mrs. George C. Bosson, Jr. Vol. XIX, pp. 563-593, 29 ills., 1 eighth-page map, Aug., 1908.

Conquest of the Sahara by the Automobile. Vol. XLV, pp. 87-93, 9 ills., 1 three-quarters-page map, Jan., 1924.

Country of the Ant Men. By Thomas H. Kearney. Vol. XXII, pp. 367-382, 11 ills., 1 half-page map, Apr., 1911.

Date Gardens of the Jerid. By Thomas H. Kearney. Vol. XXI, pp. 543-567, 20 ills., July, 1910.

Eastward from Gibraltar: Overland Route Across North Africa to Tunisia and Libia. By Cyrus French Wicker. Vol. LXXXIII, pp. 115-142, 28 ills., Jan., 1943.

Here and There in Northern Africa. By Frank Edward Johnson. Vol. XXV, pp. 1-132, 113 ills., Jan., 1914.

In Civilized French Africa. By James F. J. Archibald. Vol. XX, pp. 302-311, 14 ills., Mar., 1909.

On the Fringe of the Great Desert. 32 ills. in color from autochromes by Gervais Courtellemont. Vol. LIII, pp. 206-223, Feb., 1928.

Trans-Africa Safari: A Motor Caravan Rolls Across Sahara and Jungle Through Realms of Dusky Potentates and the Land of Big-Lipped Women. By Lawrence Copley Thaw and Margaret Stout Thaw. Vol. LXXIV, pp. 327-364, 29 ills. in black and white, 14 ills. in color, 1 two-thirds-page map, Sept., 1938.

See also Algiers.

Algiers, Algeria :

Eastward from Gibraltar : Overland Route Across North Africa to Tunisia and Libia. By Cyrus French Wicker. Vol. LXXXIII, pp. 115-142, 28 ills., Jan., 1943.

On the Fringe of the Great Desert. 32 ills. in color from autochromes by Gervais Courtellemont. Vol. LIII, pp. 206-223, Feb., 1928.

White City of Algiers. By Lieut. Col. Gordon Casserly. Vol. LIII, pp. 206-232, 9 ills. in black and white, 32 ills. in color, Feb., 1928.

Algonquian Indians:

America's First Settlers, the Indians. By Matthew W. Stirling. Vol. LXXII, pp. 535-596, 34 ills. in black and white, 24 ills. in color, Nov., 1937.

Algué, (Father) José:

Manila Observatory. By Father José Algué. Vol. XI, pp. 427-438, 2 ills., Nov., 1900.

Ali Goes to the Clinic. By Herndon and Mary Hudson. Vol. XC, pp. 764-766, 2 ills., Dec., 1946.

Alice (Yacht) :

Southward Ho! in the "Alice." By Henry Howard. Vol. LXXIII, pp. 265-312, 38 ills. in black and white, 13 ills. in color, 2 maps, Mar., 1938.

Alikuluf Indians:

Indian Tribes of Southern Patagonia, Tierra del Fuego, and the Adjoining Islands. By J. B. Hatcher. Vol. XII, pp. 12-22, 4 ills., Jan., 1901.

Inside Cape Horn. By Amos Burg. Vol. LXXII, pp. 743-783, 29 ills. in black and white, 10 ills. in color, 1 two-page map, Dec., 1937.

Alkmaar, Netherlands :

North Holland Cheese Market. By Hugh M. Smith. Vol. XXI, pp. 1051-1066, 17 ills., Dec., 1910.

Allagash Country, Maine :

In the Allagash Country. By Kenneth Fuller Lee. Vol. LV, pp. 505-520, 19 ills., Apr., 1929.

Allahabad, India :

Through the Heart of Hindustan : A Teeming Highway Extending for Fifteen Hundred Miles, from the Khyber Pass to Calcutta. By Maynard Owen Williams. Vol. XL, pp. 433-467, 29 ills., Nov., 1921.

Alleman, Irvin E.:

Seals of Our Nation, States, and Territories. 84 ills. in color from paintings by Carlotta Gonzales Lahey, Irvin E. Alleman, and Theodora Price. Vol. XC, pp. 17-32, July, 1946.

Allen, Arthur A.:

Ambassadors of Good Will (Birds) : Annual Messengers from Our Neighbor Republics to the South Bring Cheer and Add Interest to the Out-of-Doors. By Arthur A. Allen. Vol. LXXXI, pp. 786-796, 13 ills. in color, June, 1942.

Allen, Arthur A.—*Continued*

Bag of Bird Portraits. 24 ills. in color from natural-color photographs ; 23 ills. by Arthur A. Allen. Vol. LXXXV, pp. 697-712, June, 1944.

Birds of Timberline and Tundra. By Arthur A. Allen. With 24 ills. in color from natural-color photographs by the author. Vol. XC, pp. 313-339, 8 ills. in black and white, Sept., 1946.

Birds on the Home Front. By Arthur A. Allen. Vol. LXXXIV, pp. 32-56, 7 ills. in black and white, 30 ills. in color, July, 1943.

Blackbirds and Orioles. By Arthur A. Allen. Paintings by Maj. Allan Brooks. Vol. LXVI, pp. 111-130, 48 portraits in color, July, 1934.

Color Close-ups of Familiar Birds. 14 ills. in color from natural-color photographs by Arthur A. Allen. Vol. LXXV, pp. 779-786, June, 1939.

Hunting with a Microphone the Voices of Vanishing Birds. By Arthur A. Allen. Vol. LXXI, pp. 697-723, 32 ills., June, 1937.

Shore Birds, Cranes, and Rails : Willets, Plovers, Stilts, Phalaropes, Sandpipers, and Their Relatives Deserve Protection. By Arthur A. Allen. Paintings by Maj. Allan Brooks. Vol. LXXII, pp. 183-222, 4 ills. in black and white, 101 portraits in color, Aug., 1937.

Sights and Sounds of the Winged World : Study of Birds to Make National Geographic Color Photographs Yields Rich Scientific Knowledge of Their Habits and Behavior. By Arthur A. Allen. Vol. LXXXVII, pp. 721-744, 1 ill. in black and white, 2 drawings, 26 ills. in color, June, 1945.

Stalking Birds With a Color Camera : An Expert in Avian Habits Persuades His Subjects to Sit Where He Wants Them, Even in His Hat. By Arthur A. Allen. Vol. LXXV, pp. 777-789, 3 ills. in black and white, 14 ills. in color, June, 1939.

Tanagers and Finches : Their Flashes of Color and Lilting Songs Gladden the Hearts of American Bird Lovers East and West. By Arthur A. Allen. Paintings by Maj. Allan Brooks. Vol. LXVII, pp. 505-532, 6 ills. in black and white, 55 portraits in color, Apr., 1935.

Touring for Birds with Microphone and Color Cameras. By Arthur A. Allen. Vol. LXXXV, pp. 689-712, 3 ills. in black and white, 24 ills. in color, June, 1944.

Allenby, Edmund Henry Hynman:

Old Jewel in the Proper Setting : An Eye-Witness' Account of the Reconquest of the Holy Land by Twentieth Century Crusaders. By Charles W. Whitehair. Vol. XXXIV, pp. 325-344, 17 ills., Oct., 1918.

Allied Military Government:

Americans Help Liberated Europe Live Again. By Lt. Col. Frederick Simpich, Jr. Vol. LXXXVII, pp. 747-768, 17 ills., June, 1945.

Europe's Looted Art. By John Walker. Vol. LXXXIX, pp. 39-52, 11 ills., Jan., 1946.

See also American Military Government.

Almada, Lisbon, Portugal :
Lisbon, the City of the Friendly Bay. By Clifford Albion Tinker. Vol. XLII, pp. 504-552, 30 ills. in black and white, 16 ills. in color, 1 quarter-page map, Nov., 1922.

Almasy, Paul:
Madagascar : Mystery Island : Japan's Push into the Indian Ocean Swings the Searchlight of World Attention to This Huge French Sentinel off the African Coast. By Paul Almasy. Vol. LXXXI, pp. 797-830, 37 ills., 3 maps, June, 1942.

Along London's Coronation Route. By Maynard Owen Williams. Vol. LXXI, pp. 609-632, 22 ills., 1 half-page map, May, 1937.

Along Our Side of the Mexican Border. By Frederick Simpich. Vol. XXXVIII, pp. 61-80, 9 ills., 1 quarter-page map, July, 1920.

Along the Banks of the Colorful Nile. 23 ills. in color from autochromes lumière by Gervais Courtellemont. Vol. L, pp. 322-339, Sept., 1926.

Along the Nile, Through Egypt and the Sudan. By Frederick Simpich. Vol. XLII, pp. 379-410, 29 ills., Oct., 1922.

Along the Old Inca Highway. By Harriet Chalmers Adams. Vol. XIX, pp. 231-250, 21 ills., Apr., 1908.

Along the Old Mandarin Road of Indo-China. By W. Robert Moore. Vol. LX, pp. 157-199, 32 ills. in black and white, 28 ills. in color, 1 quarter-page map, Aug., 1931.

Along the Old Silk Routes : A Motor Caravan with Air-conditioned Trailer Retraces Ancient Roads from Paris across Europe and Half of Asia to Delhi. By Lawrence Copley Thaw and Margaret S. Thaw. Vol. LXXVIII, pp. 453-486, 33 ills., 1 map, Oct., 1940.

Along the Old Spanish Road in Mexico : Life Among the People of Nayarit and Jalisco, Two of the Richest States of the Southern Republic. By Herbert Corey. Vol. XLIII, pp. 225-281, 36 ills. in black and white, 16 ills. in color, 1 half-page map, Mar., 1923.

Along the Way of the Magi. 14 ills. in color from autochromes by American Colony Photographers. Vol. LVI, pp. 708-717, Dec., 1929.

Alpacas:
Camels of the Clouds. By W. H. Hodge. Vol. LXXXIX, pp. 641-656, 15 ills., 1 half-page map, May, 1946.

Alphabets:
New Alphabet of the Ancients Is Unearthed : An Inconspicuous Mound in Northern Syria Yields Archeological Treasures of Far-Reaching Significance. By F. A. Schaeffer. Vol. LVIII, pp. 477-516, 47 ills., 1 quarter-page map, Oct., 1930.

Secrets from Syrian Hills : Explorations Reveal World's Earliest Known Alphabet, Deciphered from Schoolboy Slates and Dictionaries of 3,000 Years Ago. By Claude F. A. Schaeffer. Vol. LXIV, pp. 97-126, 40 ills., 1 third-page map, July, 1933.

Alphabets—*Continued*
Turkey Goes to School. By Maynard Owen Williams. Vol. LV, pp. 95-108, 17 ills., Jan., 1929.

Alpine Peaks and Pastures of South Island (New Zealand). 11 ills. in color from natural-color photographs by W. Robert Moore. Vol. LXIX, pp. 205-212, Feb., 1936.

Alpine Villagers of Austria. 15 ills. in color from autochromes by Hans Hildenbrand and Wilhelm Tobien. Vol. LVI, pp. 668-677, Dec., 1929.

Alps:
Alpine Villagers of Austria. 15 ills. in color from autochromes by Hans Hildenbrand and Wilhelm Tobien. Vol. LVI, pp. 668-677, Dec., 1929.

Ascent of Mont Blanc. By Walter Woodburn Hyde. Vol. XXIV, pp. 861-942, 69 ills., Aug., 1913.

Austro-Italian Mountain Frontiers. By Florence Craig Albrecht. Vol. XXVII, pp. 321-376, 60 ills., 1 page map, Apr., 1915.

Beauty of the Bavarian Alps. By Col. Fitzhugh Lee Minnigerode. Vol. XLIX, pp. 632-649, 16 ills. in color, June, 1926.

Flights from Arctic to Equator : Conquering the Alps, the Ice Peaks of Spitsbergen, of Persia, and Africa's Mountains of the Moon. By Walter Mittelholzer. Vol. LXI, pp. 445-498, 53 ills., 1 three-quarters-page map, Apr., 1932.

In Valais. By Louise Murray. Vol. XXII, pp. 249-256, 6 ills., Mar., 1910.

Letters from the Italian Front. By Marchesa Louise de Rosales to Ethel Mather Bagg. Vol. XXXII, pp. 46-67, 22 ills., July, 1917.

Majesty of the Matterhorn. Vol. XXIII, supplement, May, 1912.

Manless Alpine Climbing : The First Woman to Scale the Grépon, the Matterhorn, and Other Famous Peaks Without Masculine Support Relates Her Adventures. By Miriam O'Brien Underhill. Vol. LXVI, pp. 131-170, 30 ills. in black and white, 12 ills. in color, Aug., 1934.

Over the Alps to Brenner Pass. 15 ills. from photographs, 1 two-page map. Vol. LXXXIV, pp. 701-714, Dec., 1943.

Scenes in Switzerland. 13 ills. from photographs. Vol. XXI, pp. 257-268, Mar., 1910.

Skiing in Switzerland's Realm of Winter Sports. 10 ills. in duotone from photographs by Jean Gaberell, E. Gyger, and A. Klopfenstein. Vol. LXIII, pp. 344-353, Mar., 1933.

Swiss Cherish Their Ancient Liberties. 21 ills. from photographs. Vol. LXXIX, pp. 481-496, Apr., 1941.

This Was Austria. 18 ills. from photographs. Vol. LXXXVIII, pp. 71-86, July, 1945.

Woman's Climbs in the High Alps. By Dora Keen. Vol. XXII, pp. 642-675, 26 ills., July, 1911.

World's Highest Altitudes and First Ascents. By Charles E. Fay. Vol. XX, pp. 493-530, 25 ills., June, 1909.

Al Qosh (Monastery), Iraq :
Mountain Tribes of Iran and Iraq. By Harold Lamb. Vol. LXXXIX, pp. 385-408, 15 ills., 1 two-page map, Mar., 1946.

Alsace (Region), France :
In French Lorraine : That Part of France Where the First American Soldiers Have Fallen. By Harriet Chalmers Adams. Vol. XXXII, pp. 499-518, 16 ills., Nov.-Dec., 1917.

In Smiling Alsace, Where France Has Resumed Sway. Vol. LII, pp. 168-176, 11 ills. in color, Aug., 1927.

Altai Mountains, Outer Mongolia-Sinkiang :
Western Siberia and the Altai Mountains : With Some Speculations on the Future of Siberia. By James Bryce. Vol. XXXIX, pp. 469-507, 39 ills., May, 1921.

Altair (Ship) :
Sailing Forbidden Coasts. By Ida Treat. Vol. LX, pp. 357-386, 31 ills., 1 quarter-page map, Sept., 1931.

Altitudes :
Highest Point in Each State. Vol. XX, pp. 338-541, 2 ills., June, 1909.

World's Highest Altitudes and First Ascents. By Charles E. Fay. Vol. XX, pp. 493-530, 25 ills., June, 1909.

Altitudinal Journey Through Portugal : Rugged Scenic Beauty, Colorful Costumes, and Ancient Castles Abound in Tiny Nation That Once Ruled a Vast Empire. By Harriet Chalmers Adams. Vol. LII, pp. 567-610, 44 ills. in black and white, 17 ills. in color, 1 two-thirds-page map, Nov., 1927.

Amami O Shima (Island), Ryukyu Retto :
Peacetime Rambles in the Ryukyus. By William Leonard Schwartz. Vol. LXXXVII, pp. 543-561, 12 ills., 1 two-thirds-page and 1 half-page maps, May, 1945.

Amazon River :
Amazon, Father of Waters : The Earth's Mightiest River Drains a Basin of More Than 2,700,-000 Square Miles, from Which Came Originally the World's Finest Rubber. By W. L. Schurz. Vol. XLIX, pp. 445-463, 15 ills., Apr., 1926.

Exploring the Valley of the Amazon in a Hydroplane : Twelve Thousand Miles of Flying Over the World's Greatest River and Greatest Forest to Chart the Unknown Parima River from the Sky. By Capt. Albert W. Stevens. Vol. XLIX, pp. 353-420, 86 ills., 1 page map, Apr., 1926.

Fishing and Hunting Tales from Brazil. By Dewey Austin Cobb. Vol. XX, pp. 917-920, Oct., 1909.

Journey by Jungle Rivers to the Home of the Cock-of-the-Rock : Naturalists Enter the Amazon, Voyage Through the Heart of Tropical South America, and Emerge at the Mouth of the Orinoco. By Ernest G. Holt. Vol. LXIV, pp. 585-630, 49 ills., 1 two-thirds-page map, Nov., 1933.

New Peruvian Route to the Plain of the Amazon. By Solon I. Bailey. Vol. XVII, pp. 432-448, 12 ills., Aug., 1906.

Ambassadors of Good Will (Birds) : Annual Messengers from Our Neighbor Republics to the South Bring Cheer and Add Interest to the Out-of-Doors. By Arthur A. Allen. Vol. LXXXI, pp. 786-796, 13 ills. in color, June, 1942.

Ambergris :
Islands of Bermuda : A British Colony with a Unique Record in Popular Government. By William Howard Taft. Vol. XLI, pp. 1-26, 15 ills., 1 three-quarters-page map, Jan., 1922.

Amchitka (Island), Aleutian Islands :
Navy Artist Paints the Aleutians. By Mason Sutherland. Paintings by Lt. William F. Draper. Vol. LXXXIV, pp. 157-176, 4 ills. in black and white, 16 ills. in color, Aug., 1943.

America (Airplane) :
Our Transatlantic Flight. By Comdr. Richard Evelyn Byrd. Vol. LII, pp. 347-368, 17 ills., 1 half-page map, Sept., 1927.

America Fights on the Farms. 21 ills. in color from natural-color photographs. Vol. LXXXVI, pp. 33-48, July, 1944.

America from the Air : No Such Series of Airplane Views Has Ever Before Been Printed. Photographs by Lieut. Albert W. Stevens. Vol. XLVI, pp. 85-92, 8 ills., July, 1924.

America in the Air : The Future of Airplane and Airship, Economically and as Factors in National Defense. By Brig. Gen. William Mitchell. Vol. XXXIX, pp. 339-352, 8 ills., 1 three-quarters-page map, Mar., 1921.

America on the Move. 26 illustrations from photographs by J. Baylor Roberts, B. Anthony Stewart, and others. Vol. XC, pp. 357-378, Sept., 1946.

American Airmen in the Azores. 10 ills. in color from natural-color photographs. Vol. LXXXIX, pp. 177-184, Feb., 1946.

American Alma Maters in the Near East. By Maynard Owen Williams. Vol. LXXXVIII, pp. 237-256, 16 ills., Aug., 1945.

American Association for the Advancement of Science. By Gilbert H. Grosvenor. Vol. X, pp. 355-359, Sept., 1899.

American Berries of Hill, Dale, and Wayside. Vol. XXXV, pp. 168-184, 1 ill. in black and white, 28 ills. in color, Feb., 1919.

American Birds of Prey—A Review of Their Value. Vol. XXXVIII, pp. 460-467, 6 ills., Dec., 1920.

American Bombers Attacking from Australia. By Howell Walker. Vol. LXXXIII, pp. 49-70, 19 ills., 1 map (two-page spread), Jan., 1943.

American College for Girls, Turkey. *See* İstanbul Woman's College.

American Colony Photographers : Jerusalem : Along the Way of the Magi. 14 ills. in color from autochromes by American Colony Photographers. Vol. LVI, pp. 708-717, Dec., 1929.

American Colony Photographers: Jerusalem—
Continued

Palestine. 21 ills. in color from photographs by the American Colony Photographers, Jerusalem. Vol. XXV, pp. 265-313, Mar., 1914.

American Decorations and Insignia of Honor and Service. By Col. Robert E. Wyllie. Vol. XXXVI, pp. 502-526, 6 ills. in black and white, 119 ills. in color, Dec., 1919.

American Deserts. Vol. XV, pp. 152-163, 7 ills., 1 half-page map, Apr., 1904.

American Development of the Philippines. Vol. XIV, pp. 197-203, 4 ills., May, 1903.

American Discoverers of the Antarctic Continent. By Maj. Gen. A. W. Greely. Vol. XXIII, pp. 298-312, 7 ills., 1 page map, Mar., 1912.

American Discoveries in Egypt. Vol. XVIII, pp. 801-806, 8 ills., Dec., 1907.

American Eclipse Expedition. By Rear Adm. Colby M. Chester. Vol. XVII, pp. 589-612, 23 ills., 1 color plate, Nov., 1906.

American Fable (Conservation of Natural Resources). By Gifford Pinchot. Vol. XIX, pp. 345-350, May, 1908.

American Fighters Visit Bible Lands. By Maynard Owen Williams. With 23 ills. in color from natural-color photographs by the author. Vol. LXXXIX, pp. 311-340, 10 ills. in black and white, Mar., 1946.

American Floating Exposition. Vol. XII, pp. 204-205, May, 1901.

American Forestry Association:
Summer Meeting of the American Forestry Association. Vol. XIII, pp. 352-358, Sept., 1902.

American Game Birds. By Henry Wetherbee Henshaw. Vol. XXVIII, pp. 105-158, 4 ills. in black and white, 72 ills. in color, Aug., 1915.

American Gibraltar: Notes on the Danish West Indies. Vol. XXX, pp. 89-96, 4 ills., 1 page map, July, 1916.

American Girl Cycles Across Romania : Two-wheel Pilgrim Pedals the Land of Castles and Gypsies, Where Roman Empire Traces Mingle With Remnants of Oriental Migration. By Dorothy Hosmer. Vol. LXXIV, pp. 557-588, 31 ills., 1 page map, Nov., 1938.

American Goods in China. Vol. XVII, pp. 173-175, 4 ills., Mar., 1906.

American Industries Geared for War. By Thornton Oakley. With 16 ills. in color from paintings by the author. Vol. LXXXII, pp. 716-734, 1 ill. in black and white, Dec., 1942.

American Military Government:
Sunset in the East (Japan). By Blair A. Walliser. Vol. LXXXIX, pp. 797-812, 17 ills., June, 1946.

American Museum of Natural History: Expeditions :

Fighting Giants of the Humboldt. By David D. Duncan. Vol. LXXIX, pp. 373-400, 28 ills., 1 half-page map, Mar., 1941.

On the Bottom of a South Sea Pearl Lagoon. By Roy Waldo Miner. Vol. LXXIV, pp. 365-390, 17 ills. in black and white, 8 ills. in color, Sept., 1938.

Unknown New Guinea : Circumnavigating the World in a Flying Boat, American Scientists Discover a Valley of 60,000 People Never Before Seen by White Men. By Richard Archbold. Vol. LXXIX, pp. 315-344, 28 ills., 1 two-thirds-page map, Mar., 1941.

American National Red Cross:
American Red Cross in Italy. By Mabel Boardman. Vol. XX, pp. 396-397, Apr., 1909.

America's Duty. By Newton D. Baker. Vol. XXXI, pp. 453-457, 4 ills., May, 1917.

Bind the Wounds of France. By Herbert C. Hoover. Vol. XXXI, pp. 439-444, 5 ills., May, 1917.

Great Mississippi Flood of 1927 : Since White Man's Discovery This Mighty River Has Served Him Well, Yet It Has Brought Widespread Devastation Along Its Lower Reaches. By Frederick Simpich. Vol. LII, pp. 243-289, 53 ills., 1 half-page map, Sept., 1927.

Healer of Humanity's Wounds. Vol. XXXIV, pp. 308-324, 16 ills., Oct., 1918.

Heroes of Wartime Science and Mercy. By Elizabeth W. King. Vol. LXXXIV, pp. 715-740, 11 ills. in black and white, 334 ills. in color, Dec., 1943.

Honors to the American Navy (National Geographic Society Banquet). Vol. XX, pp. 77-95, Jan., 1909.

Keep Our Red Cross. By Woodrow Wilson. Vol. XXXI, p. 422, May, 1917.

National Geographic Society (Speech by Mabel Boardman). Vol. XXIII, pp. 272-298, 5 ills., Mar., 1912.

Our Armies of Mercy. By Henry P. Davison. Vol. XXXI, pp. 423-427, 3 ills., May, 1917.

Poisoned World. By William Howard Taft. Vol. XXXI, pp. 459-467, 7 ills., May, 1917.

Red Cross Girl Overseas. By Margaret Cotter. Vol. LXXXVI, pp. 745-768, 22 ills., Dec., 1944.

Red Cross Spirit. By Eliot Wadsworth. Vol. XXXI, pp. 467-474, 8 ills., May, 1917.

Stand by the Soldier. By Gen. John J. Pershing. Vol. XXXI, pp. 457-459, 1 ill., May, 1917.

Symbol of Service to Mankind. By Stockton Axson. Vol. XXXIII, pp. 375-390, 11 ills., Apr., 1918.

American Pathfinders in the Pacific. By William H. Nicholas. Vol. LXXXIX, pp. 617-640, 17 ills., 1 two-page map, May, 1946.

American People Must Become Ship-Minded. By Edward N. Hurley. Vol. XXXIV, pp. 201-211. 7 ills., Sept., 1918.

American Potash for America. By Guy Elliott Mitchell. Vol. XXII, pp. 398-405, 4 ills., Apr., 1911.

American Progress in Cuba. Vol. XIII, p. 76, Feb., 1902.

American Progress in Habana. Vol. XIII, pp. 97-108, 10 ills., Mar., 1902.

American Scene. 29 ills. from winning photographs in the Sixth Annual Newspaper National Snapshot Awards, with explanatory note. Vol. LXXIX, pp. 220-246, Feb., 1941.

American Soldier in Reykjavík. By Corporal Luther M. Chovan. Vol. LXXXVIII, pp. 536-568, 6 ills. in black and white, 34 ills. in color, Nov., 1945.

American Transportation Vital to Victory. By Thornton Oakley. With 16 ills. in color from paintings by the author. Vol. LXXXIV, pp. 671-688, Dec., 1943.

American University at Cairo, Egypt:
American Alma Maters in the Near East. By Maynard Owen Williams. Vol. LXXXVIII, pp. 237-256, 16 ills., Aug., 1945.

American University of Beirut, Lebanon:
American Alma Maters in the Near East. By Maynard Owen Williams. Vol. LXXXVIII, pp. 237-256, 16 ills., Aug., 1945.

American Virgins (Virgin Islands): After Dark Days, These Adopted Daughters of the United States Are Finding a New Place in the Caribbean Sun. By DuBose Heyward and Daisy Reck. Vol. LXXVIII, pp. 273-308, 15 ills. in black and white, 23 ills. in color, 1 two-thirds-page map, Sept., 1940.

American Wild Flowers. 29 ills. in color from paintings by Mary E. Eaton. Vol. XXVII, pp. 483-517, May, 1915.

American Wings Soar Around the World: Epic Story of the Air Transport Command of the U. S. Army Is a Saga of Yankee Daring and Doing. By Donald H. Agnew and William A. Kinney. Vol. LXXXIV, pp. 57-78, 22 ills., July, 1943.

Americana. 11 ills. from winning photographs in the Seventh Annual Newspaper National Snapshot Awards. Vol. LXXXI, pp. 657-666, May, 1942.

Americanization:
New York—The Metropolis of Mankind. By William Joseph Showalter. Vol. XXXIV, pp. 1-49, 39 ills., July, 1918.
What Is It to Be an American? By Franklin K. Lane. Vol. XXXIII, pp. 348-354, 4 ills., 1 diagram, Apr., 1918.

Americans Help Liberated Europe Live Again. By Lt. Col. Frederick Simpich, Jr. Vol. LXXXVII, pp. 747-768, 17 ills., June, 1945.

Americans in the Caribbean. By Luis Marden. Vol. LXXXI, pp. 723-758, 16 ills. in black and white, 22 ills. in color, 1 half-page map, June, 1942.

Americans on the Barbary Coast (Africa). By Willard Price. Vol. LXXXIV, pp. 1-31, 13 ills. in black and white, 10 ills. in color, 1 map (two-page spread), July, 1943.

Americans Stand Guard in Greenland. By Andrew H. Brown. Vol. XC, pp. 457-500, 23 ills. in black and white, 19 ills. in color, 1 page map, Oct., 1946.

America's Amazing Railway Traffic. By William Joseph Showalter. Vol. XLIII, pp. 353-404, 46 ills., 1 third-page map, Apr., 1923.

America's Debt to the Hen. By Harry R. Lewis. Vol. LI, pp. 453-467, 15 ills., Apr., 1927.

America's Duty. By Newton D. Baker. Vol. XXXI, pp. 453-457, 4 ills., May, 1917.

America's First Settlers, the Indians. By Matthew W. Stirling. Vol. LXXII, pp. 535-596, 34 ills. in black and white, 24 ills. in color, Nov., 1937.

America's Most Valuable Fishes. By Hugh M. Smith. Vol. XXIII, pp. 494-514, 17 ills., May, 1912.

America's New Crescent of Defense (Air and Naval Bases). 8 ills. from photographs, 1 page map. Vol. LXXVIII, pp. 621-628, Nov., 1940.

America's New Soldier Cities: The Geographical and Historical Environment of the National Army Cantonments and National Guard Camps. By William Joseph Showalter. Vol. XXXII, pp. 438-476, 18 ills., 1 page map in colors, Nov.-Dec., 1917.

America's Part in the Allies' Mastery of the Air. By Maj. Joseph Tulasne. Vol. XXXIII, pp. 1-5, 2 ills., Jan., 1918.

America's South Sea Soldiers (American Samoa). By Lorena MacIntyre Quinn. Vol. XXXVI, pp. 267-274, 8 ills., Sept., 1919.

America's Surpassing Fisheries: Their Present Condition and Future Prospects, and How the Federal Government Fosters Them. By Hugh M. Smith. Vol. XXIX, pp. 546-583, 35 ills., June, 1916.

Amernath (Cave), India:
Pilgrimage to Amernath, Himalayan Shrine of the Hindu Faith. By Louise Ahl Jessop. Vol. XL, pp. 512-542, 29 ills., Nov., 1921.

AMG. *See* Allied Military Government.

Amid the Snow Peaks of the Equator: A Naturalist's Explorations Around Ruwenzori, with an Excursion to the Congo State, and an Account of the Terrible Scourge of Sleeping Sickness. By A. F. R. Wollaston. Vol. XX, pp. 256-277, 11 ills., Mar., 1909.

Amid the Snows of Switzerland. Vol. XLI, pp. 277-292, 16 ills., Mar., 1922.

Amidst the Templed Hills of Greece. 13 ills. in color from natural-color photographs by Maynard Owen Williams. Vol. LVIII, pp. 664-673, Dec., 1930.

Amiens, France :
Beauties of France. By Arthur Stanley Riggs. Vol. XXVIII, pp. 391-491, 73 ills. in black and white, 16 ills. in color, 1 half-page map, Nov., 1915.

Amne Machin Shan (Mountains), China :
Experiences of a Lone Geographer : An American Agricultural Explorer Makes His Way Through Brigand-Infested Central China en Route to the Amne Machin Range, Tibet. By Joseph F. Rock. Vol. XLVIII, pp. 331-347, 16 ills., 1 quarter-page map, Sept., 1925.

Seeking the Mountains of Mystery : An Expedition on the China-Tibet Frontier to the Unexplored Amnyi Machen Range, One of Whose Peaks Rivals Everest. By Joseph F. Rock. Vol. LVII, pp. 131-185, 54 ills., 1 two-page map, Feb., 1930.

Among the Bethlehem Shepherds : A Visit to the Valley Which David Probably Recalled When He Wrote the Twenty-Third Psalm. By John D. Whiting. Vol. L, pp. 729-753, 19 ills., Dec., 1926.

Among the Big Knot Lois of Hainan : Wild Tribesmen With Topknots Roam the Little-known Interior of This Big and Strategically Important Island in the China Sea. By Leonard Clark. Vol. LXXIV, pp. 391-418, 28 ills., 1 two-thirds-page map, Sept., 1938.

Among the Big Trees of California. By John R. White. Vol. LXVI, pp. 219-232, 14 ills., Aug., 1934.

Among the Cannibals of Belgian Kongo (Taken from the Notes of E. Torday). Vol. XXI, pp. 968-971, 4 ills., Nov., 1910.

Among the "Craters of the Moon" : An Account of the First Expeditions Through the Remarkable Volcanic Lava Beds of Southern Idaho. By R. W. Limbert. Vol. XLV, pp. 303-328, 23 ills., 1 two-thirds-page map, Mar., 1924.

Among the Great Himalayan Glaciers. Vol. XIII, pp. 405-406, Nov., 1902.

Among the Highlands of the Equator Republic (Ecuador). 12 ills. in color from autochromes by Jacob Gayer. Vol. LV, pp. 68-77, Jan., 1929.

Among the Hill Tribes of Burma—An Ethnological Thicket. By Sir George Scott. Vol. XLII, pp. 293-321, 22 ills., Mar., 1922.

Among the Hill Tribes of Sumatra. By W. Robert Moore. Vol. LVII, pp. 187-227, 31 ills. in black and white, 25 ills. in color, 1 half-page map, Feb., 1930.

Among the Mahogany Forests of Cuba. By Walter D. Wilcox. Vol. XIX, pp. 485-498, 6 ills., 1 page map, July, 1908.

Among the Peaks and Parks of the Rockies (Colorado). 12 ills. in color from natural-color photographs by Fred Payne Clatworthy and H. L. Standley. Vol. LXII, pp. 38-47, July, 1932.

Among the People of Cathay (China). 16 full-page ills. in duotone. Vol. LI, pp. 701-716, June, 1927.

Among the Plains and Hill People of Siam. 14 ills. in color from natural-color photographs by Amos Burg, Gervais Courtellemont, and W. Robert Moore. Vol. LXV, pp. 563-570, May, 1934.

Among the Snows and Flowers of Peru. 25 ills. in color from natural-color photographs by Jacob Gayer. Vol. LVII, pp. 732-765, June, 1930.

Among the Zapotecs of Mexico : A Visit to the Indians of Oaxaca, Home State of the Republic's Great Liberator, Juárez, and Its Most Famous Ruler, Diaz. By Herbert Corey. Vol. LI, pp. 501-553, 59 ills., 1 two-thirds-page map, May, 1927.

Amphibious Force, U. S. Navy :
Landing Craft for Invasion. By Melville Bell Grosvenor. Vol. LXXXVI, pp. 1-30, 26 ills., July, 1944.

Amphibious Training Base, Solomons Island, Maryland :
Landing Craft for Invasion. By Melville Bell Grosvenor. Vol. LXXXVI, pp. 1-30, 26 ills., July, 1944.

Amritsar, India :
Through the Heart of Hindustan : A Teeming Highway Extending for Fifteen Hundred Miles, from the Khyber Pass to Calcutta. By Maynard Owen Williams. Vol. XL, pp. 433-467, 29 ills., Nov., 1921.

Amsterdam, Netherlands :
Behind Netherlands Sea Ramparts : Dikes and Pumps Keep Ocean and Rivers at Bay While a Busy People Carries on Peacetime Work. By McFall Kerbey. Vol. LXXVII, pp. 255-290, 26 ills. in black and white, 11 ills. in duotone, 1 two-thirds-page map, Feb., 1940.

Glimpses of Holland. By William Wisner Chapin. Vol. XXVII, pp. 1-29, 26 ills., Jan., 1915.

Holland Rises from War and Water. By Thomas R. Henry. Vol. LXXXIX, pp. 237-260, 18 ills., 1 seven-eighths-page map, Feb., 1946.

Amu Darya (Oxus River), U. S. S. R. :
Surveying Through Khoresm : A Journey into Parts of Asiatic Russia Which Have Been Closed to Western Travelers Since the World War. By Lyman D. Wilbur. Vol. LXI, pp. 753-780, 31 ills., 1 two-thirds-page map, June, 1932.

Amundsen, Roald:
Amundsen's Attainment of the South Pole. Vol. XXIII, pp. 205-208, 1 ill., 1 page map, Feb., 1912.

Election of Roald Amundsen as Honorary Member of The Society. Vol. XVIII, p. 51, Jan., 1907.

Honors for Amundsen (Presentation of Hubbard Medal). Vol. XIX, pp. 55-76, 13 ills., Jan., 1908.

Honors to Amundsen and Peary (Presentation of Special Gold Medal). Vol. XXIV, pp. 113-130, 5 ills., Jan., 1913.

Amundsen, Roald—*Continued*

Modern Viking. Vol. XVII, pp. 38-40, 1 page map, Jan., 1906.

Norwegian Expedition to the Magnetic North Pole by Roald Amundsen. Vol. XIV, pp. 293-294, July, 1903.

Anatolia:

Alert Anatolia. 13 ills. from photographs. Vol. LXXXV, pp. 481-492, Apr., 1944.

East of Constantinople : Glimpses of Village Life in Anatolia, the Battleground of East and West, Where the Turks Reorganized Their Forces After the World War. By Melville Chater. Vol. XLIII, pp. 509-534, 27 ills., 1 three-quarters-page map, May, 1923.

Turkey, Where Earthquakes Followed Timur's Trail. 15 ills. from photographs by Maynard Owen Williams. Vol. LXXVII, pp. 395-406, Mar., 1940.

Turkish Republic Comes of Age. By Maynard Owen Williams. Vol. LXXXVII, pp. 581-616, 4 ills. in black and white, 29 ills. in color, 1 map (two-page spread), May, 1945.

See also Asia Minor ; Turkey.

Ancestor of the British Navy : England's Oldest Known War Vessel Is Unearthed, Laden with Remarkable Treasures of an Anglo-Saxon Ruler. By C. W. Phillips. Vol. LXXIX, pp. 247-268, 22 ills. in black and white, 4 drawings, Feb., 1941.

Ancient Capital (Boghaz Keui, Turkey). By Isabel F. Dodd. Vol. XXI, pp. 111-124, 11 ills., Feb., 1910.

Ancient Carthage in the Light of Modern Excavation. By Count Byron Khun de Prorok. Vol. XLV, pp. 391-423, 27 ills. in black and white, 16 ills. in color, 1 half-page map, Apr., 1924.

Ancient Iceland, New Pawn of War. 21 ills. from photographs, 1 page map. Vol. LXXX, pp. 75-90, July, 1941.

Ancient Rome Brought to Life. By Rhys Carpenter. Paintings by H. M. Herget. Vol. XC, pp. 567-633, 2 ills. in black and white, 32 ills. in color, 1 half-page map, Nov., 1946.

Ancient Temples and Modern Guns in Thailand. 10 ills. from photographs ; 6 ills. by Maynard Owen Williams. Vol. LXXX, pp. 653-660, Nov., 1941.

Andalusia (Region), Spain :

In Andalusia, Home of Song and Sunshine. 14 ills. in color from autochromes by Gervais Courtellemont. Vol. LV, pp. 300-309, Mar., 1929.

Anderson, George E.:

Wonderful Canals of China. By George E. Anderson. Vol. XVI, pp. 68-69, Feb., 1905.

Anderson, (Maj. Gen.) Orvil A.:

Exploring the Stratosphere. By Capt. Albert W. Stevens. Vol. LXVI, pp. 397-434, 43 ills., 1 two-thirds-page chart, Oct., 1934.

Hubbard Medals Awarded to Stratosphere Explorers : Presentation by General Pershing. Vol. LXIX, pp. 713-714, May, 1936.

Anderson, (Maj. Gen.) Orvil A.—*Continued*

Man's Farthest Aloft : Rising to 13.71 Miles, the National Geographic Society-U. S. Army Stratosphere Expedition Gathers Scientific Data at Record Altitude. By Capt. Albert W. Stevens. Vol. LXIX, pp. 59-94, 39 ills., 1 quarter-page map, Jan., 1936.

Andes Mountains:

Air Adventures in Peru : Cruising Among Andean Peaks, Pilots and Cameramen Discover Wondrous Works of an Ancient People. By Robert Shippee. Vol. LXIII, pp. 81-120, 40 ills., 1 three-quarters-page map, Jan., 1933.

Among the Snows and Flowers of Peru. 8 ills. in color from natural-color photographs by Jacob Gayer. Vol. LVII, pp. 732-765, June, 1930.

Bolivia—Tin Roof of the Andes. By Henry Albert Phillips. Vol. LXXXIII, pp. 309-332, 5 ills. in black and white, 20 ills. in color, Mar., 1943.

Chile's Land of Fire and Water : Smoking Volcanoes and Ice-hooded Peaks Stand Sentinel Over Limpid Lakes in the Far Southern Andes. By W. Robert Moore. Vol. LXXX, pp. 91-110, 9 ills. in black and white, 10 ills. in color, 1 page map, July, 1941.

First Transandine Railroad from Buenos Aires to Valparaiso. By Harriet Chalmers Adams. Vol. XXI, pp. 397-417, 14 ills., 1 quarter-page map, May, 1910.

Flying the "Hump" of the Andes. By Capt. Albert W. Stevens. Vol. LIX, pp. 595-636, 36 ills., 1 third-page map, May, 1931.

Flying the World's Longest Air Mail Route : From Montevideo, Uruguay, Over the Andes, Up the Pacific Coast, Across Central America and the Caribbean to Miami, Florida, in 67 Thrilling Flying Hours. By Junius B. Wood. Vol. LVII, pp. 261-325, 65 ills., 1 half-page map, Mar., 1930.

Forgotten Valley of Peru : Conquered by Incas, Scourged by Famine, Plagues, and Earthquakes, Colca Valley Shelters the Last Fragment of an Ancient Andean Tribe. By Robert Shippee. Vol. LXV, pp. 111-132, 22 ills., 1 two-thirds-page map, Jan., 1934.

Heart of Aymará Land : A Visit to Tiahuanacu, Perhaps the Oldest City of the New World, Lost Beneath the Drifting Sand of Centuries in the Bolivian Highlands. By Stewart E. McMillin. Vol. LI, pp. 213-256, 23 ills. in black and white, 18 ills. in color, 1 half-page map, Feb., 1927.

High Lights in the Peruvian and Bolivian Andes. 18 ills. in color from autochromes by W. Robert Moore. Vol. LI, pp. 218-235, Feb., 1927.

How Latin America Looks from the Air : U. S. Army Airplanes Hurdle the High Andes, Grave Brazil Jungles, and Follow Smoking Volcanoes to Map New Sky Paths Around South America. By Maj. Herbert A. Dargue. Vol. LII, pp. 451-502, 52 ills., 1 page map, Oct., 1927.

Longitudinal Journey Through Chile. By Harriet Chalmers Adams. Vol. XLII, pp. 219-273, 60 ills., 1 half-page map, Sept., 1922.

Andes Mountains—*Continued*

Lure of Lima, City of the Kings. By William Joseph Showalter. Vol. LVII, pp. 727-784, 41 ills., June, 1930.

New Peruvian Route to the Plain of the Amazon. By Solon I. Bailey. Vol. XVII, pp. 432-448, 12 ills., Aug., 1906.

Over the Andes to Bogotá. Vol. XL, pp. 353-373, 19 ills., Oct., 1921.

Some Wonderful Sights in the Andean Highlands : The Oldest City in America. Sailing on the Lake of the Clouds : The Yosemite of Peru. By Harriet Chalmers Adams. Vol. XIX, pp. 597-618, 19 ills., 1 half-page map, Sept., 1908.

Volcanoes of Ecuador, Guideposts in Crossing South America. By G. M. Dyott. Vol. LV, pp. 49-93, 42 ills. in black and white, 12 ills. in color, 1 half-page map, Jan., 1929.

World's Highest Altitudes and First Ascents. By Charles E. Fay. Vol. XX, pp. 493-530, 25 ills., June, 1909.

World's Highest International Telephone Cable. Vol. LVIII, pp. 722-731, 8 ills., Dec., 1930.

Andorra:

Andorra—Mountain Museum of Feudal Europe. By Lawrence A. Fernsworth. Vol. LXIV, pp. 493-512, 21 ills., 1 third-page map, Oct., 1933.

Unique Republic, Where Smuggling Is an Industry. By Herbert Corey. Vol. XXXIII, pp. 279-299, 16 ills., 1 half-page map, Mar., 1918.

Andorra la Vella, Andorra :

Andorra—Mountain Museum of Feudal Europe. By Lawrence A. Fernsworth. Vol. LXIV, pp. 493-512, 21 ills., 1 third-page map, Oct., 1933.

Andreanof Islands, Aleutians. *See* Adak (Island).

Andrews, C. L.:

Muir Glacier (Alaska). By C. L. Andrews. Vol. XIV, pp. 441-445, 2 ills., 1 quarter-page map, Dec., 1903.

Andrews, Roy Chapman:

Explorations in the Gobi Desert. By Roy Chapman Andrews. Vol. LXIII, pp. 653-716, 50 ills. in black and white, 20 ills. in color, 1 half-page map, June, 1933.

Exploring Unknown Corners of the "Hermit Kingdom" (Chosen). By Roy Chapman Andrews. Vol. XXXVI, pp. 24-48, 30 ills., 1 page map, July, 1919.

Shore-Whaling : A World Industry. By Roy Chapman Andrews. Vol. XXII, pp. 411-442, 34 ills., May, 1911.

Andros (Island), West Indies :

Coral Castle Builders of Tropic Seas. By Roy Waldo Miner. Vol. LXV, pp. 703-728, 15 ills. in black and white, 8 ills. in color, 1 two-thirds-page and 1 third-page maps, June, 1934.

Angaur (Island), Palau Islands, Carolines :

South from Saipan. By W. Robert Moore. Vol. LXXXVII, pp. 441-474, 11 ills. in black and white, 17 ills. in color, 1 half-page map, Apr., 1945.

Angers, France :

Beauties of France. By Arthur Stanley Riggs. Vol. XXVIII, pp. 391-491, 73 ills. in black and white, 16 ills. in color, 1 half-page map, Nov., 1915.

Angkor, Cambodia :

Enigma of Cambodia. 6 ills. in color from autochromes by Gervais Courtellemont. Vol. LIV, pp. 306-323, Sept., 1928.

Forgotten Ruins of Indo-China. By Jacob E. Conner. Vol. XXIII, pp. 209-272, 63 ills., 1 page and 1 three-quarters-page maps, Mar., 1912.

Four Faces of Siva : The Mystery of Angkor. By Robert J. Casey. Vol. LIV, pp. 303-332, 13 ills. in black and white, 6 ills. in color, 1 third-page map, Sept., 1928.

Angler (Fish) :

Fishes That Carry Lanterns. Vol. XXI, pp. 453-456, 5 ills., May, 1910.

Purple Veil : A Romance of the Sea. Vol. XVI, pp. 337-341, 9 ills., July, 1905.

Anglo-American Polar Expedition. By E. de K. Leffingwell. Vol. XVIII, p. 796, Dec., 1907.

Anglo-Egyptian Sudan:

Adventures Among the "Lost Tribes of Islam" in Eastern Darfur : A Personal Narrative of Exploring, Mapping, and Setting Up a Government in the Anglo-Egyptian Sudan Borderland. By Maj. Edward Keith-Roach. Vol. XLV, pp. 41-73, 32 ills., 1 three-quarters-page map, Jan., 1924.

Along the Nile, Through Egypt and the Sudan. By Frederick Simpich. Vol. XLII, pp. 379-410, 29 ills., Oct., 1922.

Crossing the Untraversed Libyan Desert : The Record of a 2,200-Mile Journey of Exploration Which Resulted in the Discovery of Two Oases of Strategic Importance on the Southwestern Frontier of Egypt. By A. M. Hassanein. Vol. XLVI, pp. 233-277, 46 ills., 1 half-page map, Sept., 1924.

New British Empire of the Sudan. By Herbert L. Bridgman. Vol. XVII, pp. 241-267, 32 ills., 1 quarter-page map, May, 1906.

Two Fighting Tribes of the Sudan. By Merian C. Cooper. Photographs by Ernest B. Schoedsack. Vol. LVI, pp. 465-486, 27 ills., 1 two-thirds-page map, Oct., 1929.

Unbeliever Joins the Hadj : On the Age-Old Pilgrimage to Mecca, Babies Are Born, Elders Die, and Families May Halt a Year to Earn Funds in Distant Lands. By Owen Tweedy. Vol. LXV, pp. 761-789, 30 ills., 1 page map, June, 1934.

Anglo-Japanese Alliance:

Purpose of the Anglo-Japanese Alliance. By Eki Hioki. Vol. XVI, pp. 333-337, July, 1905.

Anglo-Venezuelan Boundary Dispute. By Marcus Baker. Vol. XI, pp. 129-144, 2 ills., 1 page map, Apr., 1900.

Angmagssalik, Greenland :
Desolate Greenland, Now an American Outpost. 17 ills. from photographs ; 12 ills. by Willie Knutsen ; 4 ills. by F. Vogel. Vol. LXXX, pp. 393-406, Sept., 1941.

Angola:
Angola, the Last Foothold of Slavery. Vol. XXI, pp. 625-630, 6 ills., July, 1910.

Angra do Heroismo, Terceira (Island), Azores : American Airmen in the Azores. 10 ills. in color from natural-color photographs. Vol. LXXXIX, pp. 177-184, Feb., 1946.

Aniakchak Crater, Alaska :
World Inside a Mountain : Aniakchak, the New Volcanic Wonderland of the Alaska Peninsula, Is Explored. By Bernard R. Hubbard. Vol. LX, pp. 319-345, 34 ills., 1 half-page map, Sept., 1931.

Animal Wealth of the United States. By Francis E. Warren. Vol. XVII, pp. 511-524, 6 ills., 2 diagrams, Sept., 1906.

Animals. *See* Mammals.

Animals Were Allies, Too. 16 ills. from photographs. Vol. LXXXIX, pp. 75-88, Jan., 1946.

Ankara, Turkey :
Alert Anatolia. 13 ills. from photographs. Vol. LXXXV, pp. 481-492, Apr., 1944.

Star and Crescent on Parade. 29 ills. in color from natural-color photographs by Maynard Owen Williams. Vol. LXXXVII, pp. 585-616, May, 1945.

Transformation of Turkey : New Hats and New Alphabet are the Surface Symbols of the Swiftest National Changes in Modern Times. By Douglas Chandler. Vol. LXXV, pp. 1-50, 27 ills. in black and white, 23 ills. in color, 1 map, Jan., 1939.

Turkish Republic Comes of Age. By Maynard Owen Williams. Vol. LXXXVII, pp. 581-616, 4 ills. in black and white, 29 ills. in color, 1 map (two-page spread), May, 1945.

Annam (State), French Indo-China :
Along the Old Mandarin Road of Indo-China. By W. Robert Moore. Vol. LX, pp. 157-199, 32 ills. in black and white, 28 ills. in color, 1 quarter-page map, Aug., 1931.

Under the French Tricolor in Indo-China. 28 ills. in color from natural-color photographs by W. Robert Moore. Vol. LX, pp. 166-199, Aug., 1931.

Annapolis, Maryland :
Annapolis, Cradle of the Navy. By Lt. Arthur A. Ageton. Vol. LXIX, pp. 789-800, 13 ills. in color, June, 1936.

June Week at Annapolis, Cradle of the Navy. 13 ills. in color from natural-color photographs. Vol. LXIX, pp. 791-798, June, 1936.

Old Line State Cyclorama. 22 ills. in color from natural-color photographs by W. Robert Moore, B. Anthony Stewart, and others. Vol. LXXIX, pp. 409-432, Apr., 1941.

Anopheles Mosquitoes:
Life Story of the Mosquito. By Graham Fairchild. With 10 ills. in color from paintings. Vol. LXXXV, pp. 180-195, 5 ills. in black and white, 1 drawing, Feb., 1944.

Saboteur Mosquitoes. By Harry H. Stage. Vol. LXXXV, pp. 165-179, 12 ills., Feb., 1944.

Ant Men (Tribespeople) :
Country of the Ant Men (Algeria). By Thomas H. Kearney. Vol. XXII, pp. 367-382, 11 ills., 1 half-page map, Apr., 1911.

Antarctic Regions:
Admiral Byrd Receives New Honor from The Society. Vol. LVIII, pp. 228-238, 4 ills., Aug., 1930.

American Claims in the Antarctic. Vol. XIV, pp. 77-78, Feb., 1903.

American Discoverers of the Antarctic Continent. By Maj. Gen. A. W. Greely. Vol. XXIII, pp. 298-312, 7 ills., 1 page map, Mar., 1912.

American South Polar Expedition. Vol. XIX, pp. 885-888, Dec., 1908.

Amundsen's Attainment of the South Pole (Roald Amundsen Awarded the Hubbard Medal by the National Geographic Society). Vol. XXIII, pp. 205-208, 1 ill., 1 page map, Feb., 1912.

Antarctic Climate. Vol. X, pp. 520-521, Dec., 1899.

Antarctic Continent. Vol. XV, pp. 185-186, Apr., 1904.

Antarctica by Sea, Land and Air. 16 ills. in gravure from photographs by the Byrd Antarctic Expedition. Vol. LVIII, pp. 158-207, Aug., 1930.

Antarctica's Most Interesting Citizen : The Comical Penguin Is Both Romantic and Bellicose. By Worth E. Shoults. Vol. LXI, pp. 251-260, 8 ills., Feb., 1932.

Belgian Antarctic Expedition. Vol. X, pp. 229-230, June, 1899.

British Antarctic Expedition. Vol. XII, pp. 339-345, Sept., 1901.

British Antarctic Expedition under Captain Robert F. Scott. Vol. XLV, pp. 255-270, 16 ills., Mar., 1924.

British South Polar Expedition. Vol. XIV, pp. 210-212, May, 1903.

Conquest of Antarctica by Air. By Rear Adm. Richard Evelyn Byrd. Vol. LVIII, pp. 127-227, 71 ills. in black and white, 16 ills. in gravure, 1 page map, Aug., 1930.

Expeditions in the Arctic and Antarctic. Vol. XIII, pp. 179-180, May, 1902.

Exploring the Ice Age in Antarctica. By Richard Evelyn Byrd. Vol. LXVIII, pp. 399-474, 1 page and 1 two-page maps, Oct., 1935.

Geography. By Sir W. J. L. Wharton. Vol. XVI, pp. 493-495, Nov., 1905.

German South Polar Expedition. Vol. XII, p. 311, Aug., 1901.

German South Polar Expedition. Vol. XIV, pp. 296-297, July, 1903.

German South Polar Expedition. By Dr. Georg Kollm. Vol. XII, pp. 377-379, Oct., 1901.

Antarctic Regions—*Continued*

Great Ice Barrier. By Henry Gannett. Vol. XXI, pp. 173-174, 1 Ill., Feb., 1910.

Heart of the Antarctic. By Ernest H. Shackleton. Vol. XX, pp. 972-1007, 27 ills., 1 half-page map, Nov., 1909.

Honors to the American Navy (Banquet). Vol. XX, pp. 77-95, Jan., 1909.

Ice-Wrapped Continent. By Gilbert H. Grosvenor. Vol. XVIII, pp. 95-117, 20 ills., 1 half-page map, Feb., 1907.

Life in the Antarctic. Vol. XLII, pp. 655-662, 16 ills., Dec., 1922.

Lure of the Land of Ice. Vol. XLV, pp. 255-270, 16 ills., Mar., 1924.

Mapping the Antarctic from the Air : The Aërial Camera Earns Its Place as the Eyes and Memory of the Explorer. By Capt. Ashley C. McKinley. Special map supplement in colors. Vol. LXII, pp. 471-485, 13 ills., Oct., 1932.

Motor Sledges in the Antarctic. Vol. XVIII, pp. 214-215, Mar., 1907.

My Flight Across Antarctica. By Lincoln Ellsworth. Vol. LXX, pp. 1-35, 37 ills., 1 page map, July, 1936.

My Four Antarctic Expeditions : Explorations of 1933-39 Have Stricken Vast Areas from the Realm of the Unknown. By Lincoln Ellsworth. Vol. LXXVI, pp. 129-138, 9 ills., 1 page map, July, 1939.

National Geographic Society Honors Byrd Antarctic Expedition. Vol. LXVIII, pp. 107-114, 6 ills., July, 1935.

Plans for Reaching the South Pole. By Gilbert H. Grosvenor. Vol. X, pp. 316-319, special map supplement, Aug., 1899.

Race for the South Pole (Presentation of Hubbard Medal to Shackleton). Vol. XXI, pp. 185-186, Mar., 1910.

Sailing the Seven Seas in the Interest of Science : Adventures Through 157,000 Miles of Storm and Calm, from Arctic to Antarctic and Around the World, in the Non-Magnetic Yacht *Carnegie*. By J. P. Ault. Vol. XLII, pp. 631-690, 47 ills., 1 chart, Dec., 1922.

Scottish Antarctic Expedition. Vol. XIV, p. 162, Apr., 1903.

Shackleton's Farthest South. Vol. XX, pp. 398-402, 1 half-page map, Apr., 1909.

Society's Map of the Antarctic. Text accompanying special supplement in colors. Vol. LXII, pp. 485-486, 1 ill., Oct., 1932.

Society's Special Medal Is Awarded to Dr. Thomas C. Poulter : Admiral Byrd's Second-in-Command and Senior Scientist Is Accorded High Geographic Honor. Vol. LXXII, pp. 105-108, 2 ills., July, 1937.

Some Recent Statements About the Antarctic. Vol. XV, p. 266, June, 1904.

South Georgia, an Outpost of the Antarctic. By Robert Cushman Murphy. Vol. XLI, pp. 409-444, 41 ills., 2 half-page maps, Apr., 1922.

South Polar Expedition (Proposed by Peary for Consideration of National Geographic Society). Vol. XXI, pp. 167-170, 1 page map, Feb., 1910.

Antarctic Regions—*Continued*

South Polar Explorations. Vol. XII, p. 47, Jan., 1901.

South Polar Explorations. Vol. XXII, pp. 406-409, 4 ills., 1 page map, Apr., 1911.

Swedish South Polar Expedition. Vol. XII, p. 406, Nov., 1901.

Swedish South Polar Expedition. Vol. XIV, p. 296, July, 1903.

Termination Land. By Edwin Swift Balch. Vol. XV, pp. 220-221, May, 1904.

Wilkes' and D'Urville's Discoveries in Wilkes Land. By Rear Adm. John Elliott Pillsbury. Vol. XXI, pp. 171-173, Feb., 1910.

Work in the Antarctics. Vol. XII, pp. 203-204, May, 1901.

Work in the Arctic and Antarctic. Vol. XI, pp. 164-165, Apr., 1900.

Work in the Far South. Vol. XIV, p. 109, 1 half-page chart, Mar., 1903.

Antarctica By Sea, Land and Air. 16 ills. in gravure from photographs by the Byrd Antarctic Expedition. Vol. LVIII, pp. 158-207, Aug., 1930.

Antarctica's Most Interesting Citizen : The Comical Penguin Is Both Romantic and Bellicose. By Worth E. Shoults. Vol. LXI, pp. 251-260, 8 ills., Feb., 1932.

Antelope, American. *See* Pronghorns.

Anthony, A. W.:
Cruise Among Desert Islands (Baja California). By A. W. Anthony and G. Dallas Hanna. Vol. XLIV, pp. 71-99, 32 ills., 1 quarter-page map, July, 1923.

Anthony, H. E.:
Over Trail and Through Jungle in Ecuador : Indian Head-Hunters of the Interior, an Interesting Study in the South American Republic. By H. E. Anthony. Vol. XL, pp. 327-352, 28 ills., Oct., 1921.

Anthropology:
America's First Settlers, the Indians. By Matthew W. Stirling. Vol. LXXII, pp. 535-596, 34 ills. in black and white, 24 ills. in color, Nov., 1937.

Australia's Stone Age Men. 8 ills. in color from natural-color photographs by Charles P. Mountford. Vol. LXXXIX, pp. 105-112, Jan., 1946.

Aztecs Under the War God's Reign. 10 ills. in color from paintings by H. M. Herget. Vol LXXI, pp. 735-742, June, 1937.

Battle-Line of Languages in Western Europe : A Problem in Human Geography More Perplexing Than That of International Boundaries. By A. L. Guerard. Vol. XLIII, pp. 145-180, 36 ills., Feb., 1923.

Bedouin Life in Bible Lands : The Nomads of the "Houses of Hair" Offer Unstinted Hospitality to an American. By John D. Whiting. Vol. LXXI, pp. 59-83, 27 ills., 1 third-page map, Jan., 1937.

Anthropology—*Continued*

Burma : Where India and China Meet : In the Massive Mountains of Southeast Asia, Swarming Road Builders Wage the "War of the Highways" for Free China and Her Allies. By John LeRoy Christian. Vol. LXXXIV, pp. 489-512, 18 ills., 1 page map, Oct., 1943.
Contains text references and illustrations of the following peoples : Chins, Kachins, Karens, Kaws, Padaungs, Shans.

Cradle of Civilization : Historic Lands Along the Euphrates and Tigris Rivers Where Briton Is Fighting Turk. By James Baikie. Vol. XXIX, pp. 127-162, 25 ills., Feb., 1916.

Discovering Alaska's Oldest Arctic Town (Ipiutak) : A Scientist Finds Ivory-eyed Skeletons of a Mysterious People and Joins Modern Eskimos in the Dangerous Spring Whale Hunt. By Froelich G. Rainey. Vol. LXXXII, pp. 319-336, 15 ills., Sept., 1942.

Dusky Tribesmen of French West Africa. 26 ills. in color from natural-color photographs by Enzo de Chetelat. Vol. LXXIX, pp. 639-662, May, 1941.

Earth's Most Primitive People : A Journey with the Aborigines of Central Australia. By Charles P. Mountford. Vol. LXXXIX, pp. 89-112, 10 ills. in black and white, 8 ills. in color, 1 half-page map, Jan., 1946.

Faces and Fashions of Asia's Changeless Tribes. 26 ills. in color from paintings and drawings by Alexandre Iacovleff. Vol. LXIX, pp. 21-36, Jan., 1936.

Few Thoughts Concerning Eugenics. By Alexander Graham Bell. Vol. XIX, pp. 119-123, Feb., 1908.

How Old Is Man ? By Theodore Roosevelt. Vol. XXIX, pp. 111-127, 12 ills., 1 page and 2 half-page maps, Feb., 1916.

I Lived on Formosa. By Joseph W. Ballantine. Vol. LXXXVII, pp. 1-24, 19 ills., 1 page and 1 half-page maps, Jan., 1945.
Contains information on the seven aboriginal tribes and pictures of the Paiwan and Taiyal tribesmen.

In the Empire of the Aztecs : Mexico City Is Rich in Relics of a People Who Practiced Human Sacrifice, Yet Loved Flowers, Education, and Art. By Frank H. H. Roberts, Jr. Vol. LXXI, pp. 725-750, 14 ills. in black and white, 10 ills. in color, June, 1937.

Indian Tribes of Pueblo Land. By Matthew W. Stirling. Vol. LXXVIII, pp. 549-596, 16 ills. in black and white, 25 ills. in color, Nov., 1940.

Indians of Our Western Plains. By Matthew W. Stirling. Paintings by W. Langdon Kihn. Vol. LXXXVI, pp. 73-108, 14 ills. in black and white, 16 ills. in color, July, 1944.

Mountain Tribes of Iran and Iraq. By Harold Lamb. Vol. LXXXIX, pp. 385-408, 15 ills., 1 two-page map, Mar., 1946.

National Growth and National Character. By W J McGee. Vol. X, pp. 185-206, June, 1899.

New Guinea's Mountain and Swampland Dwellers. By Col. Ray T. Elsmore. Vol. LXXXVIII, pp. 671-694, 15 ills. in black and white, 7 ills. in color, 1 half-page map, Dec., 1945.

Anthropology—*Continued*

Nigeria : From the Bight of Benin to Africa's Desert Sands. By Helen Trybulowski Gilles. Vol. LXXXV, pp. 537-568, 17 ills. in black and white, 10 ills. in color, 1 half-page map, May, 1944.
Contains information on the following peoples : Bororoje ; Egbas ; Fulani ; Hausa ; Ibo ; Ijebas ; Yorubas.

Origin of Stefansson's Blond Eskimo. By Maj. Gen. A. W. Greely. Vol. XXIII, pp. 1224-1238, 10 ills., 1 page map, Dec., 1912.

Our Immigration Laws from the Viewpoint of National Eugenics. By Robert De C. Ward. Vol. XXIII, pp. 38-41, Jan., 1912.

Parade of Life Through the Ages : Records in Rocks Reveal a Strange Procession of Prehistoric Creatures, from Jellyfish to Dinosaurs, Giant Sloths, Saber-toothed Tigers, and Primitive Man. By Charles R. Knight. With 24 ills. in color from paintings by the author. Vol. LXXXI, pp. 141-184, 13 ills. in black and white, Feb., 1942.

Races of Europe. By Edwin A. Grosvenor. Vol. XXXIV, pp. 441-534, 62 ills., 2 page maps, special map supplement in colors, Dec., 1918.

Red Men of the Southwest. 25 ills. in color from paintings by W. Langdon Kihn. Vol. LXXVIII, pp. 557-596, Nov., 1940.

Sex, Nativity, and Color of the People of the United States. By Gilbert H. Grosvenor. Vol. XII, pp. 381-389, 17 charts, Nov., 1901.

Shan Tribes Make Burma's Hills Flash With Color. 15 ills. in color from natural-color photographs by W. Robert Moore. Vol. LX, pp. 454-463, Oct., 1931.
Contains information on the following tribes : Kang, Kaw, Khun, Lahu Na, Lahu Shi, Shan, Wa.

Strange Tribes in the Shan States of Burma. 15 ills. in color from natural-color photographs by W. Robert Moore. Vol. LVIII, pp. 246-255, Aug., 1930.
Contains information on the following tribes : Kang, Kaw, Khun, Lahu Na, Lahu Shi, Shan.

Supposed Birthplace of Civilizations. Vol. XVI, pp. 499-504, 6 ills., Nov., 1905.

Unknown New Guinea : Circumnavigating the World in a Flying Boat, American Scientists Discover a Valley of 60,000 People Never Before Seen by White Men. By Richard Archbold. Vol. LXXIX, pp. 315-344, 28 ills., 1 two-thirds-page map, Mar., 1941.

War Finds Its Way to Gilbert Islands : United States Forces Dislodge Japanese from Enchanted Atolls Which Loom Now as Stepping Stones along South Sea Route from Australia to Hawaii. By Sir Arthur Grimble. Vol. LXXXIII, pp. 71-92, 19 ills., 1 half-page map, Jan., 1943.

When Red Men Ruled Our Forests. 24 ills. in color from paintings by W. Langdon Kihn. Vol. LXXII, pp. 551-590, Nov., 1937.

Anthropology—*Continued*

Who Shall Inherit Long Life? On the Existence of a Natural Process at Work Among Beings Tending to Improve the Vigor and Vitality of Succeeding Generations. By Alexander Graham Bell. Vol. XXXV, pp. 505-514, 13 ills., June, 1919.

With the Nomads of Central Asia : A Summer's Sojourn in the Tekes Valley, Plateau Paradise of Mongol and Turkic Tribes. By Edward Murray. Vol. LXIX, pp. 1-57, 43 ills. in black and white, 26 ills. in color, 1 half-page map, Jan., 1936.

Woman's Experiences among Stone Age Solomon Islanders : Primitive Life Remains Unchanged in Tropical Jungleland Where United States Forces Now Are Fighting. By Eleanor Schirmer Oliver. Vol. LXXXII, pp. 813-836, 26 ills., 1 half-page map, Dec., 1942.

Work of the Bureau of American Ethnology. By W J McGee. Vol. XII, pp. 367-372, Oct., 1901.

Yap Meets the Yanks. By David D. Duncan, USMC. With 11 ills. in color from natural-color photographs by the author. Vol. LXXXIX, pp. 364-372, Mar., 1946.

See also Arabs ; Archeology ; Cliff Dwellers ; Dyaks ; Eskimos ; Indians of Central America ; Indians of Mexico ; Indians of North America ; Indians of South America ; Lapps ; Mongols ; Moros ; Tibetans ; Troglodytes and Christian "Troglodytes."

Anticosti Island, Canada :
Anticosti Island, Nugget of the North. By Eugene E. Wilson. Vol. LXXXI, pp. 121-140, 19 ills., 1 two-thirds-page map, Jan., 1942.

Antigua, Guatemala :
Guatemala, the Country of the Future. By Edine Frances Tisdel. Vol. XXI, pp. 596-624, 33 ills., 1 three-quarters-page map, July, 1910.

To Market in Guatemala. By Luis Marden. With 19 ills. in color from natural-color photographs by Giles Greville Healey and Charles S. Pineo. Vol. LXXXVIII, pp. 87-104, July, 1945.

Antigua (Island), West Indies :
Americans in the Caribbean. By Luis Marden. Vol. LXXXI, pp. 723-758, 16 ills. in black and white, 22 ills. in color, 1 half-page map, June, 1942.

British West Indian Interlude. By Anne Rainey Langley. Vol. LXXIX, pp. 1-46, 23 ills. in black and white, 21 ills. in color, 2 page maps, Jan., 1941.

War Echoes in the West Indies. 22 ills. in color from natural-color photographs by Luis Marden. Vol. LXXXI, pp. 731-754, June, 1942.

West Indies Links in a Defense Chain. 21 ills. in color from natural-color photographs ; 20 ills. by Edwin L. Wisherd. Vol. LXXIX, pp. 9-32, Jan., 1941.

Antilles, Greater. *See* Cuba ; Dominican Republic ; Haiti ; Jamaica ; Puerto Rico.

Antilles, Lesser. *See* Antigua ; Aruba ; Bonaire ; Curaçao ; Dominica ; Guadeloupe ; Martinique ; Saba ; St. Kitts ; St. Lucia ; St. Vincent ; Trinidad ; Virgin Islands.

Antioch the Glorious. By William H. Hall. Vol. XXXVIII, pp. 81-103, 20 ills., 1 half-page map, Aug., 1920.

Antiquities:
The Greek Way. By Edith Hamilton. Vol. LXXXV, pp. 257-271, 12 ills., Mar., 1944.

The Roman Way. By Edith Hamilton. Vol. XC, pp. 545-565, 14 ills., 1 two-page map, Nov., 1946.

See also Archeology *and* names of ancient cities and countries.

Antlered Majesties of Many Lands (Deer). 23 ills. in color from paintings by Walter A. Weber. Vol. LXXVI, pp. 479-510, Oct., 1939.

Antofagasta, Chile :
Longitudinal Journey Through Chile. By Harriet Chalmers Adams. Vol. XLII, pp. 219-273, 60 ills., 1 half-page map, Sept., 1922.

Ants (Insects) :
Color Glows in the Guianas, French and Dutch. By Nicol Smith. Vol. LXXXIII, pp. 459-480, 8 ills. in black and white, 13 ills. in color, 1 two-thirds-page map, Apr., 1943.
Contains information on the Atta Ant.

Living Casks of Honey. By Jennie E. Harris. Vol. LXVI, pp. 193-199, 4 ills., Aug., 1934.

Lonely Australia : The Unique Continent. By Herbert E. Gregory. Vol. XXX, pp. 473-568, 68 ills., 1 two-page and 4 half-page maps, Dec., 1916.

Monsters of Our Back Yard. By David Fairchild. Vol. XXIV, pp. 575-626, 38 ills., May, 1913.

Notes About Ants and Their Resemblance to Man. By William Morton Wheeler. Vol. XXIII, pp. 731-766, 32 ills., 2 diagrams, Aug., 1912.

Red Ant Versus the Boll Weevil. Vol. XV, pp. 262-264, June, 1904.

Stalking Ants, Savage and Civilized : A Naturalist Braves Bites and Stings in Many Lands to Learn the Story of an Insect Whose Ways Often Parallel Those of Man. By W. M. Mann. Vol. LXVI, pp. 171-192, 7 ills. in black and white, 18 ills. in color, Aug., 1934.

Work and War in the World of Ants. 18 ills. in color from paintings by Hashime Murayama. Vol. LXVI, pp. 179-186, Aug., 1934.

Anuradhpura, Ceylon :
Adam's Second Eden. By Eliza R. Scidmore. Vol. XXIII, pp. 105-173, 60 ills., Feb., 1912.

Buried City of Ceylon. By John M. Abbot. Vol. XVII, pp. 613-622, 8 ills., Nov., 1906.

Anzacs:
Facing War's Challenge "Down Under." 20 ills. in color from natural-color photographs by Howell Walker. Vol. LXXXI, pp. 425-456, Apr., 1942.

Anzacs—*Continued*

Making of an Anzac. By Howell Walker. Vol. LXXXI, pp. 409-456, 31 ills. in black and white, 20 ills. in color, 1 two-page map, Apr., 1942.

Apache Indians:

Along Our Side of the Mexican Border. By Frederick Simpich. Vol. XXXVIII, pp. 61-80, 9 ills., 1 quarter-page map, July, 1920.

Indian Tribes of Pueblo Land. By Matthew W. Stirling. Vol. LXXVIII, pp. 549-596, 16 ills. in black and white, 25 ills. in color, Nov., 1940.

North American Indian. Vol. XIX, pp. 448-454, 5 ills., June, 1908.

Apes:

Manlike Apes of Jungle and Mountain. 10 ills. in color from paintings by Elie Cheverlange. Vol. LXXVIII, pp. 221-228, Aug., 1940.

Man's Closest Counterparts: Heavyweight of Monkeydom Is the "Old Man" Gorilla, by Far the Largest of the Four Great Apes. By William M. Mann. Vol. LXXVIII, pp. 213-236, 10 ills. in black and white, 10 ills. in color, Aug., 1940.

Aphids:

An Insect Community Lives in Flower Heads. By James G. Needham. Vol. XC, pp. 340-356, 5 ills. in black and white, 11 ills. in color, Sept., 1946.

Aphrodisias (Ancient City):

Buried Cities of Asia Minor. By Ernest L. Harris. Vol. XX, pp. 1-18, 10 ills., Jan., 1909.

Apia, Samoa:

Sailing the Seven Seas in the Interest of Science: Adventures Through 157,000 Miles of Storm and Calm, from Arctic to Antarctic and Around the World, in the Non-Magnetic Yacht *Carnegie*. By J. P. Ault. Vol. XLII, pp. 631-690, 47 ills., 1 chart, Dec., 1922.

Appeal to Members of the National Geographic Society (Food Conservation). Vol. XXXIII, pp. 347-348, 2 ills., Apr., 1918.

Apperception in Geography. By M. E. Kelton. Vol. XI, pp. 192-199, May, 1900.

Approach to Peiping. By Maj. John W. Thomason, Jr. Vol. LXIX, pp. 275-308, 24 ills., 1 page map, Feb., 1936.

Approaching Washington by Tidewater Potomac. By Paul Wilstach. Vol. LVII, pp. 372-392, 7 ills., Mar., 1930.

'Aqaba, Trans-Jordan:

On the Trail of King Solomon's Mines: The Bible, in Addition to Its Spiritual Values, Continues to Prove a Rich Geography and Guide to Exploration of the Holy Land. By Nelson Glueck. Vol. LXXXV, pp. 233-256, 20 ills., 1 page map, Feb., 1944.

Aquariums:

Bright Flashes from Pacific Corals (Fishes). 24 ills. in color from natural-color photographs by Walter H. Chute. Vol. LXXIX, pp. 349-372, Mar., 1941.

Aquariums—*Continued*

Net Results from Oceania: Collecting Aquarium Specimens in Tropical Pacific Waters. By Walter H. Chute. Vol. LXXIX, pp. 347-372, 8 ills. in black and white, 24 ills. in color, Mar., 1941.

Rainbow Denizens of the Aquarium. 16 ills. in color from natural-color photographs by Edwin L. Wisherd. Vol. LXV, pp. 97-104, Jan., 1934.

Treasure-House of the Gulf Stream: The Completion and Opening of the New Aquarium and Biological Laboratory at Miami, Florida. By John Oliver La Gorce. Vol. XXXIX, pp. 53-68, 5 ills. in black and white, 16 ills. in color, Jan., 1921.

Tropical Fish Immigrants Reveal New Nature Wonders. By Walter H. Chute. Vol. LXV, pp. 93-110, 8 ills. in black and white, 16 ills. in color, Jan., 1934.

Aqueducts:

Carrying Water Through a Desert. By Burt A. Heinly. Vol. XXI, pp. 568-596, 19 ills., 1 half-page map, July, 1910.

New York—The Metropolis of Mankind. By William Joseph Showalter. Vol. XXXIV, pp. 1-49, 39 ills., July, 1918.

Staircase Farms of the Ancients: Astounding Farming Skill of Ancient Peruvians Who Were Probably the Most Industrious and Highly Organized People in History. By O. F. Cook. Vol. XXIX, pp. 474-534, 48 ills., May, 1916.

Arabia (Peninsula):

Arabia, the Desert of the Sea. By Archibald Forder. Vol. XX, pp. 1039-1062, 20 ills., 1 page map, Dec., 1909.

Damascus and Mecca Railway. Vol. XII, p. 408, Nov., 1901.

"Flower of Paradise": The Part Which Khat Plays in the Life of the Yemen Arab. By Charles Moser. Vol. XXXII, pp. 173-186, 10 ills., 1 page map, Aug., 1917.

Into Burning Hadhramaut: The Arab Land of Frankincense and Myrrh, Ever a Lodestone of Western Exploration. By D. van der Meulen. Vol. LXII, pp. 387-429, 44 ills., 1 two-thirds-page map, Oct., 1932.

Mecca the Mystic: A New Kingdom Within Arabia (Hejaz). By S. M. Zwemer. Vol. XXXII, pp. 157-172, 13 ills., Aug., 1917.

Notes on Oman. By S. M. Zwemer. Vol. XXII, pp. 89-98, 8 ills., 1 half-page map, Jan., 1911.

One Thousand Miles of Railway Built for Pilgrims and Not for Dividends (Damascus to Mecca). By Col. F. R. Maunsell. Vol. XX, pp. 156-172, 13 ills., 1 three-quarters-page map, Feb., 1909.

Rise of the New Arab Nation. By Frederick Simpich. Vol. XXXVI, pp. 369-393, 17 ills., 1 page map, Nov., 1919.

Travels in Arabia and Along the Persian Gulf. By David G. Fairchild. Vol. XV, pp. 139-151, 20 ills., Apr., 1904.

Arabia (Peninsula)—*Continued*

Unbeliever Joins the Hadj: On the Age-Old Pilgrimage to Mecca, Babies Are Born, Elders Die, and Families May Halt a Year to Earn Funds in Distant Lands. By Owen Tweedy. Vol. LXV, pp. 761-789, 30 ills., 1 page map, June, 1934.

Visit to Three Arab Kingdoms: Transjordania, Iraq and the Hedjaz Present Many Problems to European Powers. By Junius B. Wood. Vol. XLIII, pp. 535-568, 30 ills., 1 three-quarters-page map, May, 1923.

See also Aden; Mecca; Saudi Arabia.

Arabs:

Ali Goes to the Clinic. By Herndon and Mary Hudson. Vol. XC, pp. 764-766, 2 ills., Dec., 1946.

Along the Nile, Through Egypt and the Sudan. By Frederick Simpich. Vol. XLII, pp. 379-410, 29 ills., Oct., 1922.

Among the Bethlehem Shepherds: A Visit to the Valley Which David Probably Recalled When He Wrote the Twenty-third Psalm. By John D. Whiting. Vol. L, pp. 729-753, 19 ills., Dec., 1926.

Archeology, the Mirror of the Ages: Our Debt to the Humble Delvers in the Ruins at Carchemish and at Ur. By C. Leonard Woolley. Vol. LIV, pp. 207-226, 19 ills., Aug., 1928.

Bedouin Life in Bible Lands: The Nomads of the "Houses of Hair" Offer Unstinted Hospitality to an American. By John D. Whiting. Vol. LXXI, pp. 59-83, 27 ills., 1 third-page map, Jan., 1937.

Cirenaica, Eastern Wing of Italian Libia. By Harriet Chalmers Adams. Vol. LVII, pp. 689-726, 35 ills. in black and white, 13 ills. in color, 1 two-thirds-page map, June, 1930.

Cirenaica, On the Edge of the Saharan Sands. 9 ills. in color from natural-color photographs by Luigi Pellerano. Vol. LVII, pp. 692-701, June, 1930.

Forty Years Among the Arabs. By John Van Ess. Vol. LXXXII, pp. 385-420, 27 ills., 1 two-page map, Sept., 1942.

Guest in Saudi Arabia. By Maynard Owen Williams. Vol. LXXXVIII, pp. 463-487, 24 ills., 1 two-thirds-page map, Oct., 1945.

Here and There in Northern Africa. By Frank Edward Johnson. Vol. XXV, pp. 1-132, 113 ills., Jan., 1914.

Mole Men: An Account of the Troglodytes of Southern Tunisia. By Frank Edward Johnson. Vol. XXII, pp. 787-846, 60 ills., Sept., 1911.

New Light on Ancient Ur: Excavations at the Site of the City of Abraham Reveal Geographical Evidence of the Biblical Story of the Flood. By M. E. L. Mallowan. Vol. LVII, pp. 95-130, 44 ills., 1 three-quarters-page map. Jan., 1930.

On the Fringe of the Great Desert (Algeria). 32 ills. in color from autochromes by Gervais Courtellemont. Vol. LIII, pp. 206-223, Feb., 1928.

Arabs—*Continued*

On the Trail of King Solomon's Mines: The Bible, in Addition to Its Spiritual Values, Continues to Prove a Rich Geography and Guide to Exploration of the Holy Land. By Nelson Glueck. Vol. LXXXV, pp. 233-256, 20 ills., 1 page map, Feb., 1944.

Palestine Today. By Francis Chase, Jr. Vol. XC, pp. 501-516, 16 ills., Oct., 1946.

Pearl Fishing in the Red Sea. By Henri de Monfreid. Vol. LXXII, pp. 597-626, 24 ills., 1 two-thirds-page map, Nov., 1937.

Pilgrims' Progress to Mecca. 22 ills. in duotone; 18 ills. by Oscar Marcus. Vol. LXXII, pp. 627-642, Nov., 1937.

Where Adam and Eve Lived. By Frederick and Margaret Simpich. Vol. XXVI, pp. 546-588, 35 ills., Dec., 1914.

White City of Algiers. By Lieut. Col. Gordon Casserly. Vol. LIII, pp. 206-232, 9 ills. in black and white, 3 ills. in color, Feb., 1928.

See also Arabia.

Aran Islands, Eire:

Timeless Arans: The Workaday World Lies Beyond the Horizon of Three Rocky Islets Off the Irish Coast. By Robert Cushman Murphy. Vol. LIX, pp. 747-775, 35 ills., 1 quarter-page map, June, 1931.

Araucanian Indians:

Chile's Land of Fire and Water: Smoking Volcanoes and Ice-hooded Peaks Stand Sentinel Over Limpid Lakes in the Far Southern Andes. By W. Robert Moore. Vol. LXXX, pp. 91-110, 9 ills. in black and white, 10 ills. in color, 1 page map, July, 1941.

Longitudinal Journey Through Chile. By Harriet Chalmers Adams. Vol. XLII, pp. 219-273, 60 ills., 1 half-page map, Sept., 1922.

Arbitration Treaties. By William Howard Taft. Vol. XXII, pp. 1165-1172, Dec., 1911.

Arbutus (Flower):

American Wild Flowers. 29 ills. in color from paintings by Mary E. Eaton. Vol. XXVII, pp. 483-517, May, 1915.

Cultivation of the Mayflower. By Frederick V. Coville. Vol. XXVII, pp. 518-519, 1 ill., May, 1915.

Arch-Isolationists, the San Blas Indians: Coconuts Serve as Cash on Islands Off the Panama Coast Where Tribesmen Cling to Their Ancient Ways and Discourage Visitors. By Corinne B. Feeney. Vol. LXXIX, pp. 193-220, 15 ills. in black and white, 12 ills. in color, 1 sixth-page map, Feb., 1941.

Archæology in the Air. By Eliza R. Scidmore. Vol. XVIII, pp. 150-163, 11 ills., Mar., 1907.

Archangel, U. S. S. R.:

Murman Coast: Arctic Gateway for American and Allied Expeditionary Forces in Northern European Russia. Vol. XXXV, pp. 331-348, 30 ills., 1 half-page map, Apr., 1919.

Archbold, Richard:

Unknown New Guinea : Circumnavigating the World in a Flying Boat, American Scientists Discover a Valley of 60,000 People Never Before Seen by White Men. By Richard Archbold. Vol. LXXIX, pp. 315-344, 28 ills., 1 two-thirds-page map, Mar., 1941.

Archeology:

Adam's Second Eden (Ceylon). By Eliza R. Scidmore. Vol. XXIII, pp. 105-173, 60 ills., Feb., 1912.

Air Adventures in Peru : Cruising Among Andean Peaks, Pilots and Cameramen Discover Wondrous Works of an Ancient People. By Robert Shippee. Vol. LXIII, pp. 81-120, 40 ills., 1 three-quarters-page map, Jan., 1933.

American Discoveries in Egypt. Vol. XVIII, pp. 801-806, 8 ills., Dec., 1907.

Ancestor of the British Navy : England's Oldest Known War Vessel Is Unearthed, Laden with Remarkable Treasures of an Anglo-Saxon Ruler. By C. W. Phillips. Vol. LXXIX, pp. 247-268, 22 ills. in black and white, 4 drawings, Feb., 1941.

Ancient Capital (Boghaz Keui, Turkey). By Isabel F. Dodd. Vol. XXI, pp. 111-124, 11 ills., Feb., 1910.

Ancient Carthage in the Light of Modern Excavation. By Count Byron Khun de Prorok. Vol. XLV, pp. 391-423, 27 ills. in black and white, 16 ills. in color, 1 half-page map, Apr., 1924.

Ancient Rome Brought to Life. By Rhys Carpenter. Paintings by H. M. Herget. Vol. XC, pp. 567-633, 2 ills. in black and white, 32 ills. in color, 1 half-page map, Nov., 1946.

Archæology in the Air. By Eliza R. Scidmore. Vol. XVIII, pp. 150-163, 11 ills., Mar., 1907.

Archeology, the Mirror of the Ages : Our Debt to the Humble Delvers in the Ruins of Carchemish and at Ur. By C. Leonard Woolley. Vol. LIV, pp. 207-226, 19 ills., Aug., 1928.

At the Tomb of Tutankhamen : An Account of the Opening of the Royal Egyptian Sepulcher Which Contained the Most Remarkable Funeral Treasures Unearthed in Historic Times. By Maynard Owen Williams. Vol. XLIII, pp. 461-508, 53 ills., 1 half-page map, May, 1923.

Aztecs Under the War God's Reign. 10 ills. in color from paintings by H. M. Herget. Vol. LXXI, pp. 735-742, June, 1937.

Buried Cities of Asia Minor. By Ernest L. Harris. Vol. XX, pp. 1-18, 10 ills., Jan., 1909.

Buried City of Ceylon. By John M. Abbott. Vol. XVII, pp. 613-622, 8 ills., Nov., 1906.

Channel Islands. By Edith Carey. Vol. XXXVIII, pp. 143-164, 24 ills., 1 quarter-page map, Aug., 1920.

Chichen Itzá, an Ancient American Mecca : Recent Excavations in Yucatan Are Bringing to Light the Temples, Palaces, and Pyramids of America's Most Holy Native City. By Sylvanus Griswold Morley. Vol. XLVII, pp. 63-95, 34 ills., 1 half-page map, 1 diagram, Jan., 1925.

Archeology—*Continued*

China's Treasures. By Frederick McCormick. Vol. XXIII, pp. 996-1040, 50 ills., Oct., 1912.

Cone-Dwellers of Asia Minor : A Primitive People Who Live in Nature-Made Apartment Houses, Fashioned by Volcanic Violence and Trickling Streams. By J. R. Sitlington Sterrett. Vol. XXXV, pp. 281-331, 52 ills., 1 half-page map, Apr., 1919.

Cradle of Civilization : The Historic Lands Along the Euphrates and Tigris Rivers Where Briton Is Fighting Turk. By James Baikie. Vol. XXIX, pp. 127-162, 25 ills., Feb., 1916.

Crete, Where Sea-Kings Reigned. By Agnes N. Stillwell. Vol. LXXXIV, pp. 547-568, 20 ills., 1 page map, Nov., 1943.

Daily Life in Ancient Egypt (Part I). Daily Life in Ancient Egypt : *The Later Period* (Part II). By William C. Hayes. Paintings by H. M. Herget. Vol. LXXX, pp. 419-515, 34 ills. in black and white, 32 ills. in color, 1 two-thirds-page map, Oct., 1941.

Discovering Alaska's Oldest Arctic Town (Ipiutak) : A Scientist Finds Ivory-eyed Skeletons of a Mysterious People and Joins Modern Eskimos in the Dangerous Spring Whale Hunt. By Froelich G. Rainey. Vol. LXXXII, pp. 319-336, 15 ills., Sept., 1942.

Discovering the New World's Oldest Dated Work of Man : A Maya Monument Inscribed 291 B. C. is Unearthed Near a Huge Stone Head by a Geographic-Smithsonian Expedition in Mexico. By Matthew W. Stirling. Vol. LXXVI, pp. 183-218, 40 ills., 1 half-page map, Aug., 1939.

Discovering the Oldest Statues in the World : A Daring Explorer Swims Through a Subterranean River of the Pyrenees and Finds Rock Carvings Made 20,000 Years Ago. By Norbert Casteret. Vol. XLVI, pp. 123-152, 24 ills., 1 half and 1 quarter-page maps, Aug., 1924.

Enigma of Cambodia. 6 ills. in color from autochromes by Gervais Courtellemont. Vol. LIV, pp. 306-323, Sept., 1928.

Everyday Life in Pueblo Bonito : As Disclosed By the National Geographic Society's Archeologic Explorations in the Chaco Canyon National Monument, New Mexico. By Neil M. Judd. Vol. XLVIII, pp. 227-262, 37 ills., 1 two-thirds-page map, Sept., 1925.

Excavations at Abydos. By W. M. Flinders Petrie. Vol. XIV, pp. 358-359, Sept., 1903.

Excavations at Nippur (Iraq). Vol. XI, p. 392, Oct., 1900.

Excavations at Quirigua, Guatemala. By Sylvanus Griswold Morley. Vol. XXIV, pp. 339-361, 24 ills., 1 diagram, Mar., 1913.

Excavations of M. de Morgan at Susa. Vol. XII, p. 315, Aug., 1901.

Expedition Unearths Buried Masterpieces of Carved Jade (Cerro de las Mesas, Mexico). By Matthew W. Stirling. Vol. LXXX, pp. 277-302, 14 ills. in black and white, 20 ills. in color, 1 two-thirds-page map, Sept., 1941.

Explorations in Crete. By Edith H. Hall. Vol. XX, pp. 778-787, 15 ills., Sept., 1909.

Archeology—*Continued*

Exploration in Peru. Vol. XXIII, pp. 416-422, 7 ills., 1 half-page map, Apr., 1912.

Explorations in the Gobi Desert. By Roy Chapman Andrews. Vol. LXIII, pp. 653-716, 50 ills. in black and white, 20 ills. in color, 1 half-page map, June, 1933.

Exploring Frozen Fragments of American History: On the Trail of Early Eskimo Colonists Who Made a 55-Mile Crossing from the Old World to the New. By Henry B. Collins, Jr. Vol. LXXV, pp. 633-656, 24 ills., 1 two-thirds-page map, May, 1939.

Exploring in the Canyon of Death (Arizona): Remains of a People Who Dwelt in Our Southwest at Least 4,000 Years Ago Are Revealed. By Earl H. Morris. Vol. XLVIII, pp. 263-300, 24 ills. in black and white, 22 ills. in color, Sept., 1925.

Exploring the Secrets of Persepolis. By Charles Breasted. Vol. LXIV, pp. 381-420, 48 ills., 1 half-page map, 1 plan, Oct., 1933.

Finding Jewels of Jade in a Mexican Swamp (La Venta). By Matthew W. and Marion Stirling. Vol. LXXXII, pp. 635-661, 15 ills. in black and white, 12 ills. in color, 1 two-thirds-page map, Nov., 1942.

Foremost Intellectual Achievement of Ancient America: The Hieroglyphic Inscriptions on the Monuments in the Ruined Cities of Mexico, Guatemala, and Honduras Are Yielding the Secrets of the Maya Civilization. By Sylvanus Griswold Morley. Vol. XLI, pp. 109-130, 27 ills., 17 diagrams, special map supplement, Feb., 1922.

Forgotten Ruins of Indo-China. By Jacob E. Conner. Vol. XXIII, pp. 209-272, 63 ills., 1 page and 1 three-quarters-page maps, Mar., 1912.

Four Faces of Siva: The Mystery of Angkor (Cambodia). By Robert J. Casey. Vol. LIV, pp. 303-332, 13 ills. in black and white, 27 ills. in color, 1 third-page map, Sept., 1928.

From Jerusalem to Aleppo. By John D. Whiting. Vol. XXIV, pp. 71-113, 30 ills., 1 half-page map, Jan., 1913.

Further Explorations in the Land of the Incas: The Peruvian Expedition of 1915 of the National Geographic Society and Yale University. By Hiram Bingham. Vol. XXIX, pp. 431-473, 29 ills., 1 page and 1 half-page maps, panorama, May, 1916.

Geography of the Jordan. By Nelson Glueck. Vol. LXXXVI, pp. 719-744, 23 ills., 1 page map, Dec., 1944.

Great Stone Faces of Eastern Island. 11 ills. from photographs. Vol. LXXXV, pp. 225-232, Feb., 1944.

Great Stone Faces of the Mexican Jungle: Five Colossal Heads and Numerous Other Monuments of Vanished Americans Are Excavated by the Latest National Geographic-Smithsonian Expedition. By Matthew W. Stirling. Vol. LXXVIII, pp. 309-334, 26 ills., 1 map, Sept., 1940.

Archeology—*Continued*

Greatest Achievement of Ancient Man in America, the Fortress of Sacsahuaman, Peru. Vol. XXIX, panorama, May, 1916.

Greece—the Birthplace of Science and Free Speech: Explorations on the Mainland and in Crete and the Aegean Isles Reveal Ancient Life Similar to That of the Present. By Richard Stillwell. Paintings by H. M. Herget. Vol. LXXXV, pp. 273-353, 13 ills. in black and white, 32 ills. in color, 1 two-page map, Mar., 1944.

Greece of Today. By George Higgins Moses. Vol. XXVIII, pp. 295-329, 27 ills., Oct., 1915.

Greek Bronzes. Vol. XXIII, p. 104, Jan., 1912.

Greek Bronzes of Tunisia. By Frank Edward Johnson. Vol. XXIII, pp. 89-103, 11 ills., Jan., 1912.

Guatemala, the Country of the Future. By Edine Frances Tisdel. Vol. XXI, pp. 596-624, 33 ills., 1 three-quarters-page map, July, 1910.

Heart of Aymará Land: A Visit to Tiahuanacu, Perhaps the Oldest City of the New World, Lost Beneath the Drifting Sands of Centuries in the Bolivian Highlands. By Stewart E. McMillin. Vol. LI, pp. 213-256, 23 ills. in black and white, 18 ills. in color, 1 half-page map, Feb., 1927.

Hewers of Stone (Mitla, Mexico). By Jeremiah Zimmerman. Vol. XXI, pp. 1002-1020, 11 ills., Dec., 1910.

Home of a Forgotten Race: Mysterious Chichen Itzá, in Yucatan, Mexico. By Edward H. Thompson. Vol. XXV, pp. 585-648, 59 ills., June, 1914.

Homer's Troy Today. By Jacob E. Conner. Vol. XXVII, pp. 520-532, 11 ills., 1 half-page map, May, 1915.

In the Empire of the Aztecs: Mexico City Is Rich in Relics of a People Who Practiced Human Sacrifice, Yet Loved Flowers, Education, and Art. By Frank H. H. Roberts, Jr. Vol. LXXI, pp. 725-750, 14 ills. in black and white, 10 ills. in color, June, 1937.

In the Wonderland of Peru. By Hiram Bingham. Vol. XXIV, pp. 387-574, 250 ills., 1 three-quarters-page map, 3 diagrams, Apr., 1913.

Indian Village of Baum (Ohio). By H. C. Brown. Vol. XII, pp. 272-274, July, 1901.

Interesting Visit to the Ancient Pyramids of San Juan Teotihuacan. By A. C. Galloway. Vol. XXI, pp. 1041-1050, 8 ills., 1 page map, Dec., 1910.

La Venta's Green Stone Tigers (Mexico). By Matthew W. Stirling. Vol. LXXXIV, pp. 321-332, 4 ills. in black and white, 6 ills. in color, 1 two-thirds-page map, Sept., 1943.

Life, Culture, and History of the Egyptians. 32 ills. in color from paintings by H. M. Herget. Vol. LXXX, pp. 436-514, Oct., 1941.

Little-Known Sardinia. By Helen Dunstan Wright. Vol. XXX, pp. 97-120, 23 ills. 1 page map, Aug., 1916.

Archeology—_Continued_

Luster of Ancient Mexico (Aztecs). By William H. Prescott. Vol. XXX, pp. 1-32, 22 ills., July, 1916.

Malta: The Halting Place of Nations: First Account of Remarkable Prehistoric Tombs and Temples Recently Unearthed on the Island. By William Arthur Griffiths. Vol. XXXVII, pp. 445-478, 35 ills., 1 third-page map, May, 1920.

Mexico's Deep South Yields New Treasure (Tabasco and Chiapas). 12 ills. in color from natural-color photographs by Richard H. Stewart. Vol. LXXXII, pp. 649-656, Nov., 1942.

Modern Odyssey in Classic Lands: Troy's Treasures, Athens' Parthenon, and Rome's First "Broad Way" Influence Today's Banks, Costumes, Jewelry, and Railroad Timetables. By Maynard Owen Williams. Vol. LXXVII, pp. 291-337, 27 ills. in black and white, 22 ills. in color, Mar., 1940.

Mole Men: An Account of the Troglodytes of Southern Tunisia. By Frank Edward Johnson. Vol. XXII, pp. 787-846, 60 ills., Sept., 1911.

Monte Albán (Mexico), Richest Archeological Find in America: A Tomb in Oaxaca, Mexico, Yields Treasures Which Reveal the Splendid Culture of the Mixtecs. By Dr. Alfonso Caso. Vol. LXII, pp. 487-512, 28 ills., Oct., 1932.

Mysterious Prehistoric Monuments of Brittany (France). By Charles Buxton Going. Vol. XLIV, pp. 53-69, 16 ills., July, 1923.

Mysterious Temples of the Jungle: The Prehistoric Ruins of Guatemala. By W. F. Sands. Vol. XXIV, pp. 324-338, 10 ills., Mar., 1913.

Mystery of Easter Island. By Mrs. Scoresby Routledge. Vol. XL, pp. 628-646, 13 ills., 1 page map, Dec., 1921.

New Alphabet of the Ancients Is Unearthed: An Inconspicuous Mound in Northern Syria Yields Archeological Treasures of Far-Reaching Significance. By F. A. Schaeffer. Vol. LVIII, pp. 477-516, 47 ills., 1 quarter-page map, Oct., 1930.

New Light on Ancient Ur: Excavations at the Site of the City of Abraham Reveal Geographical Evidence of the Biblical Story of the Flood. By M. E. L. Mallowan. Vol. LVII, pp. 95-130, 44 ills., 1 three-quarters-page map, Jan., 1930.

New National Geographic Society Expedition: Ruins of Chaco Canyon, New Mexico, Nature-Made Treasure-Chest of Aboriginal American History, to be Excavated and Studied; Work Begins This Month. Vol. XXXIX, pp. 637-643, 7 ills., June, 1921.

On the Trail of King Solomon's Mines: The Bible, in Addition to Its Spiritual Values, Continues to Prove a Rich Geography and Guide to Exploration of the Holy Land. By Nelson Glueck. Vol. LXXXV, pp. 233-256, 20 ills., 1 page map, Feb., 1944.

Archeology—_Continued_

Petra, Ancient Caravan Stronghold: Mysterious Temples and Tombs, Carved in Glowing Cliffs of Eroded Sandstone, Are Remnants of a City David Longed to Storm. By John D. Whiting. Vol. LXVII, pp. 129-165, 15 ills. in black and white, 21 ills. in color, 1 half-page and 1 quarter-page maps, Feb., 1935.

Portraits of Ancient Mayas, a Peace-Loving People. 10 ills. in color from paintings by H. M. Herget. Vol. LXVIII, pp. 553-560, Nov., 1935.

Prehistoric Ruin of Tsankawi (New Mexico). By George L. Beam. Vol. XX, pp. 807-822, 12 ills., Sept., 1909.

Preserving Ancient America's Finest Sculptures (Guatemala). By J. Alden Mason. Vol. LXVII, pp. 537-570, 24 ills. in black and white, 10 ills. in color, Nov., 1935.

Pueblo Bonito, the Ancient: The National Geographic Society's Third Expedition to the Southwest Seeks to Read in the Rings of Trees the Secret of the Age of Ruins. By Neil M. Judd. Vol. XLIV, pp. 99-108, 9 ills., 1 diagram, July, 1923.

Pueblo Bonito Expedition of the National Geographic Society. By Neil M. Judd. Vol. XLI, pp. 323-331, 10 ills., 1 diagram, Mar., 1922.

Pushing Back History's Horizon: How the Pick and Shovel Are Revealing Civilizations That Were Ancient When Israel Was Young. By Albert T. Clay. Vol. XXIX, pp. 162-216, 47 ills., 1 page map, Feb., 1916.

Recent Discoveries in Egypt. Vol. XII, pp. 396-397, Nov., 1901.

Reconstructing Egypt's History. By Wallace N. Stearns. Vol. XXIV, pp. 1021-1042, 21 ills., Sept., 1913.

Resurrection of Ancient Egypt. By James Baikie. Vol. XXIV, pp. 957-1020, 46 ills., 1 page map, Sept., 1913.

Rock City of Petra. By Franklin E. Hoskins. Vol. XVIII, pp. 283-291, 5 ills., May, 1907.

Rose-Red City of Rock (Petra, Trans-Jordan). 21 ills. in color from natural-color photographs by G. E. Matson. Vol. LXVII, pp. 145-160, Feb., 1935.

Ruined Cities of Asia Minor. By Ernest L. Harris. Vol. XIX, pp. 741-760, 11 ills., Nov., 1908.

Ruins at Selinus (Sicily). By Marion Crawford. Vol. XX, p. 117, Jan., 1909.

Ruins of Cuicuilco May Revolutionize Our History of Ancient America: Lofty Mound Sealed and Preserved by Great Lava Flow for Perhaps Seventy Centuries Is Now Being Excavated in Mexico. By Byron Cummings. Vol. XLIV, pp. 203-220, 21 ills., 1 third-page map, Aug., 1923.

Sacred Ibis Cemetery and Jackal Catacombs at Abydos. By Camden M. Cobern. Vol. XXIV, pp. 1042-1056, 10 ills., Sept., 1913.

Sea-Kings of Crete. By James Baikie. Vol. XXIII, pp. 1-25, 13 ills., Jan., 1912.

Archeology—*Continued*

Secret of the Southwest Solved by Talkative Tree Rings: Horizons of American History Are Carried Back to A. D. 700 and a Calendar for 1,200 Years Established by National Geographic Society Expeditions. By Andrew Ellicott Douglass. Vol. LVI, pp. 737-770, 33 ills., 1 two-thirds-page map, Dec., 1929.

Secrets from Syrian Hills: Explorations Reveal World's Earliest Known Alphabet, Deciphered from Schoolboy Slates and Dictionaries of 3,000 Years Ago. By Claude F. A. Schaeffer. Vol. LXIV, pp. 97-126, 40 ills., 1 third-page map, July, 1933.

Sicily: Island of Vivid Beauty and Crumbling Glory. 22 ills. in color from autochromes lumière by Luigi Pellerano. Vol. LII, pp. 432-449, Oct., 1927.

Sigiriya, "A Fortress in the Sky". By Wilson K. Norton. Vol. XC, pp. 665-680, 14 ills., 1 two-thirds-page map, Nov., 1946.

Some Ruined Cities of Asia Minor. By Ernest L. Harris. Vol. XIX, pp. 833-858, 19 ills., Dec., 1908.

Staircase Farms of the Ancients: Astounding Farming Skill of Ancient Peruvians Who Were Probably the Most Industrious and Highly Organized People in History. By O. F. Cook. Vol. XXIX, pp. 474-534, 48 ills., May, 1916.

Stone Idols of the Andes Reveal a Vanished People: Remarkable Relics of One of the Oldest Aboriginal Cultures of America are Unearthed in Colombia's San Agustín Region. By Hermann von Walde Waldegg. Vol. LXXVII, pp. 627-647, 22 ills., 1 map, May, 1940.

Storied Islands of the South Sea. 20 ills. in color from natural-color photographs by Irving Johnson, Malcolm Evans, and others. Vol. LXXXI, pp. 9-40, Jan., 1942.

Story of Machu Picchu: The Peruvian Expeditions of the National Geographic Society and Yale University. By Hiram Bingham. Vol. XXVII, pp. 171-217, 35 ills., Feb., 1915.

Supposed Birthplace of Civilizations. Vol. XVI, pp. 499-504, 6 ills., Nov., 1905.

Today in the Feathered Serpent's City (Chichen Itzá). 25 ills. in color from natural-color photographs by Luis Marden. Vol. LXX, pp. 599-614, Nov., 1936.

Treasure-trove of Old Mexican Jade (Cerro de las Mesas). 20 ills. in color from natural-color photographs by Richard H Stewart. Vol. LXXX, pp. 293-316, Sept., 1941.

Unearthing America's Ancient History: Investigation Suggests That the Maya May Have Designed the First Astronomical Observatory in the New World in Order to Cultivate Corn. By Sylvanus Griswold Morley. Vol. LX, pp. 99-126, 28 ills., July, 1931.

Where Early Christians Lived in Cones of Rock: A Journey to Cappadocia in Turkey Where Strange Volcanic Pinnacles Are Honeycombed With Hermit Cells and Monasteries. By John D. Whiting. Vol. LXXVI, pp. 763-802, 20 ills. in black and white, 20 ills. in color, 1 half-page map, Dec., 1939.

Archeology—*Continued*

Yucatán, Home of the Gifted Maya: Two Thousand Years of History Reach Back to Early American Temple Builders, Corn Cultivators, and Pioneers in Mathematics. By Sylvanus Griswold Morley. Vol. LXX, pp. 591-644, 28 ills. in black and white, 35 ills. in color, 1 two-thirds-page map, Nov., 1936.

See also Antiquities.

Archibald, James F. J.:

In Civilized French Africa. By James F. J. Archibald. Vol. XX, pp. 302-311, 14 ills., Mar., 1909.

Architecture:

Cathedrals of England: An Artist's Pilgrimage to These Majestic Monuments of Man's Genius and Faith. By Norman Wilkinson. Vol. LXXVI, pp. 741-762, 3 ills. in black and white, 16 ills. in gravure from dry-point engravings by the author, Dec., 1939.

Cathedrals of the Old and New World. By J. Bernard Walker. Vol. XLII, pp. 61-114, 50 ills., July, 1922.

Charleston: Where Mellow Past and Present Meet. By DuBose Heyward. Vol. LXXV, pp. 273-312, 20 ills. in black and white, 24 ills. in color, 1 page map, Mar., 1939.

Color and Customs of Sweden's Château Country. 13 ills. in color from natural-color photographs by Gustav Heurlin. Vol. LXVI, pp. 33-40, July, 1934.

Country-House Life in Sweden: In Castle and Cottage the Landed Gentry Gallantly Keep the Old Traditions. By Amelie Posse-Brázdová. Vol. LXVI, pp. 1-64, 51 ills. in black and white, 13 ills. in color, 1 page map, July, 1934.

Culture Still Lights Our Wartime Capital. 9 ills. in color from natural-color photographs by B. Anthony Stewart. Vol. LXXXI, pp. 337-344, Mar., 1942.

Nation's Capital by Night. By Volkmar Wentzel. With 16 illustrations in duotone from photographs by the author. Vol. LXXVII, pp. 514-530, Apr., 1940.

Nepal: A Little-Known Kingdom. By John Claude White. Vol. XXXVIII, pp. 245-283, 32 ills., 1 half-page map, Oct., 1920.

Our Nation's Capital on Parade. 16 ills. in color from natural-color photographs by B. Anthony Stewart, Walter M. Edwards, and others Vol. LXXXIV, pp. 265-288, Sept., 1943.

Peking, the City of the Unexpected. By James Arthur Muller. Vol. XXXVIII, pp. 335-355, 18 ills., Nov., 1920.

Restoration of Colonial Williamsburg. By W. A. R. Goodwin. Vol. LXXI, pp. 402-443, 21 ills. in black and white, 25 ills. in color, Apr., 1937.

Sculptured Gates to English Learning (Cambridge University). 19 ills. in color from natural-color photographs by B. Anthony Stewart. Vol. LXXXIX, pp. 417-440, Apr., 1946.

Architecture—*Continued*

Smallest State in the World: Vatican City on Its 108 Acres Is a Complete Sovereignty Internationally Recognized. By W. Coleman Nevils. Vol. LXXV, pp. 377-412, 37 ills., 1 two-page map, Mar., 1939.

Virginia's Colonial Heritage (Williamsburg). 25 ills. in color from natural-color photographs. Vol. LXXI, pp. 417-440, Apr., 1937.

Wartime Washington. By William H. Nicholas. Vol. LXXXIV, pp. 257-290, 12 ills. in black and white, 16 ills. in color, Sept., 1943.

Washington, Home City and Show Place: To Residents and Visitors the Nation's Capital Presents Varied Sides as the City Steadily Grows in Beauty and Stature. By Leo A. Borah. Vol. LXXI, pp. 663-695, 11 ills. in black and white, 20 ills. in color, June, 1937.

Washington—Storehouse of Knowledge. By Albert W. Atwood. Vol. LXXXI, pp. 325-359, 20 ills. in black and white, 9 ills. in color, Mar., 1942.

Washington of Tradition Builds for the Future. 20 ills. in color from natural-color photographs. Vol. LXXI, pp. 671-694, June, 1937.

Wonders of the New Washington: Efficient Modern Structures Rise in the Biggest Government Building Program Since the Capital City Was Founded in a Wilderness. By Frederick G. Vosburgh. Vol. LXVII, pp. 457-488, 20 ills. in black and white, 13 ills. in color, Apr., 1935.

See also Archeology; Castles; Cathedrals and Churches; Houses and Homes; Mosques; Palaces; Temples; Tombs.

Arctic Birds:

Birds of Timberline and Tundra. By Arthur A. Allen. With 24 ills. in color from natural-color photographs by the author. Vol. XC, pp. 313-339, 8 ills. in black and white, Sept., 1946.

Arctic Regions:

Anglo-American Polar Expedition. By E. de K. Leffingwell. Vol. XVIII, p. 796, Dec., 1907.

Arctic as an Air Route of the Future. By Vilhjalmur Stefansson. Vol. XLII, pp. 205-218, 8 ills., 1 page map, Aug., 1922.

Arctic Expeditions Commanded by Americans. Vol. XVIII, pp. 458-468, 10 ills., July, 1907.

Baldwin-Ziegler Arctic Expedition. Vol. XIII, pp. 358-359, Sept., 1902.

Bowdoin (Ship) in North Greenland: Arctic Explorers Place Tablet to Commemorate Sacrifices of the Lady Franklin Bay Expedition. By Donald B. MacMillan. Vol. XLVII, pp. 677-722, 49 ills., June, 1925.

Coast Guard Patrol in Greenland. 9 ills. in color from natural-color photographs by Lieut. Thomas S. La Farge. Vol. LXXXIII, pp. 565-572, May, 1943.

Commander Byrd at the North Pole. Reproduction in color of the painting by N. C. Wyeth, National Geographic Society, Washington, D. C. Vol. LIII, supplement, May, 1928.

Commander Byrd Receives the Hubbard Gold Medal: The First Explorer to Reach the North Pole by Air Receives Coveted Honor at Brilliant National Geographic Society Reception. Vol. L, pp. 377-388, 5 ills., 1 chart, Sept., 1926.

Arctic Regions—*Continued*

Desolate Greenland, Now an American Outpost. 17 ills. from photographs; 12 ills. by Willie Knutsen; 4 ills. by F. Vogel. Vol. LXXX, pp. 393-406, Sept., 1941.

Discovering Alaska's Oldest Arctic Town: A Scientist Finds Ivory-eyed Skeletons of a Mysterious People and Joins Modern Eskimos in the Dangerous Spring Whale Hunt. By Froelich G. Rainey. Vol. LXXXII, pp. 319-336, 15 ills., Sept., 1942.

Discovery of the North Pole. Vol. XXI, pp. 63-82, Jan., 1910.

Discovery of the Pole (First Reports by Dr. F. A. Cook and Robert E. Peary). Vol. XX, pp. 892-896, 11 ills., 1 page map, Oct., 1909.

Drifting Across the Pole. Vol. XVII, pp. 40-42, 1 ill., Jan., 1906.

European Tributes to Peary. Vol. XXI, pp. 536-540, 4 ills., June, 1910.

Europe's Northern Nomads. 12 ills. in color from natural-color photographs by Jack Kuhne. Vol. LXXVI, pp. 657-664, Nov., 1939.

Farthest North (Peary). Vol. XVII, pp. 638-644, 9 ills., Nov., 1906.

Fighting the Polar Ice. Vol. XVIII, pp. 72-77, 7 ills., Jan., 1907.

First Flight to the North Pole. By Lieut. Comdr. Richard Evelyn Byrd. Vol. L, pp. 357-376, 14 ills., Sept., 1926.

First Natural-Color Photographs from the Arctic. 22 ills. in color from natural-color photographs by Jacob Gayer and Maynard Owen Williams. Vol. XLIX, pp. 300-317, Mar., 1926.

Flights from Arctic to Equator: Conquering the Alps, the Ice Peaks of Spitsbergen, of Persia, and Africa's Mountains of the Moon. By Walter Mittelholzer. Vol. LXI, pp. 445-498, 53 ills., 1 three-quarters-page map, Apr., 1932.

Flying Over the Arctic. By Lieut. Comdr. Richard E. Byrd. Vol. XLVIII, pp. 519-532, 10 ills., Nov., 1925.

Greenland—U. S. Base in the Arctic. 5 ills. in color from natural-color photographs by James K. Penfield. Vol. LXXXII, pp. 373-376, Sept., 1942.

Greenland from 1898 to Now: "Captain Bob," Who Went North with Peary, Tells of 42 Years of Exploration in the Orphan Island of New Aerial and Naval Interest. By Robert A. Bartlett. Vol. LXXVIII, pp. 111-140, 25 ills., 1 two-page map, July, 1940.

Greenland Turns to America. By James K. Penfield. Vol. LXXXII, pp. 369-383, 7 ills. in black and white, 5 ills. in color, 1 two-page map, Sept., 1942.

Honors for Amundsen. Vol. XIX, pp. 55-76, 13 ills., Jan., 1908.

Honors to the American Navy. Vol. XX, pp. 77-95, Jan., 1909.

Lure of the Frozen Desert. Vol. XXIII, panorama, Dec., 1912.

Arctic Regions—*Continued*

MacMillan Arctic Expedition Returns: U. S. Navy Planes Make First Series of Overhead Flights in the Arctic and National Geographic Society Staff Obtains Valuable Data and Specimens for Scientific Study. By Donald B. MacMillan. Vol. XLVIII, pp. 477-518, 42 ills., Nov., 1925.

MacMillan Arctic Expedition Sails. Vol. XLVIII, pp. 225-226, 3 ills., Aug., 1925.

MacMillan in the Field. Vol. XLVIII, pp. 473-476, 3 ills., Oct., 1925.

Map of the North Polar Regions. Text accompanying special map supplement. Vol. XVIII, pp. 454-455, July, 1907.

Meteorological Observations of the Second Wellman Expedition. By Evelyn B. Baldwin. Vol. X, pp. 512-516, Dec., 1899.

Midnight Sun in the Klondike. By Alice Rollins Crane. Vol. XII, pp. 66-67, 1 ill., Feb., 1901.

Mission of the *Diana* (Peary Arctic Club). Vol. X, p. 273, July, 1899.

Mr. Ziegler and the National Geographic Society. Vol. XIV, pp. 251-254, June, 1903.

Modern Viking (Amundsen). Vol. XVII, pp. 38-40, 1 page map, Jan., 1906.

Nansen's "Farthest North" Eclipsed. Vol. XI, pp. 411-413, Oct., 1900.

National Geographic Society (Records of North Pole Discovery). Vol. XXI, p. 276, Mar., 1910.

Naturalist with MacMillan in the Arctic. By Walter N. Koelz. Vol. XLIX, pp. 299-318, 22 ills. in color, Mar., 1926.

Navigating the *Norge* (Airship) from Rome to the North Pole and Beyond: The Designer and Pilot of the First Dirigible to Fly Over the Top of the World Describes a Thrilling Voyage of More Than 8,000 Miles. By Gen. Umberto Nobile. Vol. LII, pp. 177-215, 36 ills., 1 page map, Aug., 1927.

Nearest the Pole (Rear Adm. Robert E. Peary's Address to The Society). Vol. XVIII, pp. 446-450, July, 1907.

No Man's Land—Spitzbergen. Vol. XVIII, pp. 455-458, July, 1907.

Nomads of Arctic Lapland: Mysterious Little People of a Land of the Midnight Sun Live Off the Country Above the Arctic Circle. By Clyde Fisher. Vol. LXXVI, pp. 641-676, 28 ills. in black and white, 12 ills. in color, 1 page map, Nov., 1939.

North Pole (Peary). Vol. XX, pp. 921-922, Nov., 1909.

North Pole (Resolutions of The Society Acknowledging Peary's Discovery). Vol. XX, pp. 1008-1009, Nov., 1909.

Norwegian Expedition to the Magnetic North Pole by Roald Amundsen. Vol. XIV, pp. 293-294, July, 1903.

Origin of Stefansson's Blond Eskimo. By Maj. Gen. A. W. Greely. Vol. XXIII, pp. 1224-1238, 10 ills., 1 page map, Dec., 1912.

Arctic Regions—*Continued*

Our Search for the Lost Aviators: An Arctic Area Larger Than Montana First Explored in Hunt for Missing Russians. By Sir Hubert Wilkins. Vol. LXXIV, pp. 141-172, 29 ills., 1 two-page map, Aug., 1938.

Peary and the North Pole. Vol. XIV, pp. 379-381, Oct., 1903.

Peary as a Leader: Incidents from the Life of the Discoverer of the North Pole Told by One of His Lieutenants on the Expedition Which Reached the Goal. By Donald B. MacMillan. Vol. XXXVII, pp. 293-317, 20 ills., 1 page map, Apr., 1920.

Peary on the North Pole. Vol. XIV, pp. 28-29, 1 page map, Jan., 1903.

Peary's Explorations in the Far North. By Gilbert Grosvenor. Vol. XXXVII, pp. 318-322, 3 ills., Apr., 1920.

Peary's Polar Expedition. Vol. XIX, p. 447, June, 1908.

Peary's Twenty Years' Service in the Arctics. Vol. XVIII, pp. 451-454, July, 1907.

Peary's Work and Prospects. By H. L. Bridgman. Vol. X, pp. 414-415, Oct., 1899.

Peary's Work in 1900 and 1901. Vol. XII, pp. 357-361, 2 ills., Oct., 1901.

Peary's Work in 1901-1902. By Gilbert H. Grosvenor. Vol. XIII, pp. 384-386, Oct., 1902.

Polar Airship. By Walter Wellman. Vol. XVII, pp. 208-228, 4 diagrams, Apr., 1906.

Polar Photography. By Anthony Fiala. Vol. XVIII, pp. 140-142, Feb., 1907.

Return of Wellman. By J. Howard Gore. Vol. X, pp. 348-351, 2 ills., Sept., 1899.

Russian Expedition to Spitzbergen. Vol. XII, p. 404, Nov., 1901.

Sailing the Seven Seas in the Interest of Science: Adventures Through 157,000 Miles of Storm and Calm, from Arctic to Antarctic and Around the World, in the Non-Magnetic Yacht *Carnegie*. By J. P. Ault. Vol. XLII, pp. 631-690, 47 ills., 1 chart, Dec., 1922.

Scientific Aspects of the MacMillan Arctic Expedition. Vol. XLVIII, pp. 349-354, 5 ills., Sept., 1925.

Servicing Arctic Airbases. By Robert A. Bartlett. Vol. LXXXIX, pp. 602-616, 3 ills. in black and white, 10 ills. in color, 1 half-page map, May, 1946.

Seventy-five Days in the Arctics. By Max Fleischman. Vol. XVIII, pp. 439-446, 5 ills., July, 1907.

Some Indications of Land in the Vicinity of the North Pole. By R. A. Harris. Vol. XV, pp. 255-261, 1 page map, June, 1904.

Sverdrup's Work in the Arctics. Vol. XII, pp. 460-461, 1 page map, Dec., 1902.

Ten Years of the Peary Arctic Club. By Herbert L. Bridgman. Vol. XIX, pp. 661-668, 3 ills., Sept., 1908.

Through Franz Josef Land. Vol. X, p. 362, Sept., 1899.

Arctic Regions—*Continued*

To Seek the Unknown in the Arctic: United States Navy Fliers to Aid MacMillan Expedition Under the Auspices of the National Geographic Society in Exploring Vast Area. Vol. XLVII, pp. 673-675, 1 ill., 1 half-page map, June, 1925.

Value of Arctic Exploration. By Comdr. Robert E. Peary. Vol. XIV, pp. 429-436, Dec., 1903.

Voyage of the *Morrissey*. 10 ills. in color from natural-color photographs by Daniel S. Turner and Sherman A. Wengerd. Vol. LXXXIX, pp. 609-616, May, 1946.

Walter Wellman's Expedition to the North Pole. Vol. XVII, pp. 205-207, 1 chart, Apr., 1906.

Wellman Polar Expedition. Vol. X, pp. 361-362, Sept., 1899.

Wellman Polar Expedition. Vol. XVII, p. 712, Dec., 1906.

Wellman Polar Expedition. By J. Howard Gore. Vol. X, pp. 267-268, July, 1899.

Wellman Polar Expedition. By Walter Wellman. Vol. X, pp. 481-505, 10 ills., 1 half-page map, 1 diagram, Dec., 1899.

With an Exile in Arctic Siberia: The Narrative of a Russian Who Was Compelled to Turn Polar Explorer for Two Years. By Vladimir M. Zenzinov. Vol. XLVI, pp. 695-718, 30 ills., 1 half-page map, Dec., 1924.

Women's Winter on Spitsbergen. By Martha Phillips Gilson. Vol. LIV, pp. 227-246, 20 ills., 1 three-quarters-page map, Aug., 1928.

Work in the Arctic and Antarctic. Vol. XI, pp. 164-165, Apr., 1900.

Ziegler Polar Expedition. Vol. XIV, pp. 414-417, 5 ills., Nov., 1903.

Ziegler Polar Expedition. Vol. XV, pp. 427-428, Oct., 1904.

Ziegler Polar Expedition. Vol. XVI, pp. 439-440, Sept., 1905.

Area of the Philippines. Vol. X, pp. 182-183, May, 1899.

Arecuna Indians:

Kaieteur and Roraima: The Great Falls and the Great Mountain of the Guianas. By Henry Edward Crampton. Vol. XXXVIII, pp. 227-244, 12 ills., 1 half-page map, Sept., 1920.

Through Brazil to the Summit of Mount Roraima. By G. H. H. Tate. Vol. LVIII, pp. 585-605, 24 ills., 1 half-page map, Nov., 1930.

Argaeus, Mount, Turkey:

Cone-Dwellers of Asia Minor: A Primitive People Who Live in Nature-Made Apartment Houses, Fashioned by Volcanic Violence and Trickling Streams. By J. R. Sitlington Sterrett. Vol. XXXV, pp. 281-331, 52 ills., 1 half-page map, Apr., 1919.

Argentina:

Argentina-Chile Boundary Award. Vol. XIV, pp. 115-116, Mar., 1903.

Argentine-Chile Boundary. Vol. XIII, p. 117, Mar., 1902.

Argentine-Chile Boundary Dispute. Vol. XIII, pp. 27-28, Jan., 1902.

Argentina—*Continued*

Awakening of Argentina and Chile: Progress in the Lands That Lie Below Capricorn. By Bailey Willis. Vol. XXX, pp. 121-142, 14 ills., Aug., 1916.

Buenos Aires and Its River of Silver: A Journey Up the Paraná and Paraguay to the Chaco Cattle Country. By William R. Barbour. Vol. XL, pp. 393-432, 38 ills., Oct., 1921.

Buenos Aires to Washington by Horse: A Solitary Journey of Two and a Half Years, Through Eleven American Republics, Covers 9,600 Miles of Mountain and Plain, Desert and Jungle. By A. F. Tschiffely. Vol. LV, pp. 135-196, 75 ills., 1 page map, Feb., 1929.

Chile-Argentina Boundary Dispute. Vol. XIII, p. 220, June, 1902.

Falls of Iguazu. By Marie Robinson Wright. Vol. XVII, pp. 456-460, 4 ills., Aug., 1906.

Fertile Pampas of Argentine. Vol. XVII, pp. 453-456, Aug., 1906.

First Transandine Railroad from Buenos Aires to Valparaiso. By Harriet Chalmers Adams. Vol. XXI, pp. 397-417, 41 ills., 1 quarter-page map, May, 1910.

Flying the World's Longest Air-Mail Route: From Montevideo, Uruguay, Over the Andes, Up the Pacific Coast, Across Central America and the Caribbean to Miami, Florida, in 67 Thrilling Flying Hours. By Junius B. Wood. Vol. LVII, pp. 261-325, 65 ills., 1 half-page map, Mar., 1930.

Indian Tribes of Southern Patagonia, Tierra del Fuego, and the Adjoining Islands. By J. B. Hatcher. Vol. XII, pp. 12-22, 4 ills., Jan., 1901.

Life on the Argentine Pampa. By Frederick Simpich. Vol. LXIV, pp. 449-491, 41 ills. in black and white, 8 ills. in color, Oct., 1933.

Pioneer Gaucho Days. 8 ills. in color from paintings by Cesáreo Bernaldo de Quirós. Vol. LXIV, pp. 453-460, Oct., 1933.

Some Geographic Features of Southern Patagonia, With a Discussion of Their Origin. By J. B. Hatcher. Vol. XI, pp. 41-55, 4 ills., Feb., 1900.

World's Great Waterfalls: Visits to Mighty Niagara, Wonderful Victoria, and Picturesque Iguazu. By Theodore W. Noyes. Vol. L, pp. 29-59, 29 ills., July, 1926.

See also Buenos Aires.

Argosy of Geography (Sailing Ship). Vol. XXXIX, supplement, Jan., 1921.

Arica, Chile-Peru:

Some Personal Experiences with Earthquakes. By Rear Adm. L. G. Billings. Vol. XXVII, pp. 57-71, 7 ills., Jan., 1915.

Ariza, John Francis:

Dismal Swamp in Legend and History: George Washington Owned Large Tracts in Region Which He Described as a "Glorious Paradise." By John Francis Ariza. Vol. LXII, pp. 121-130, 11 ills., July, 1932.

Arizona:

Adventures in Arizona Color Photography. 14 ills. in color from autochromes by Clifton Adams. Vol. LV, pp. 28-37, Jan., 1929.

Along Our Side of the Mexican Border. By Frederick Simpich. Vol. XXXVIII, pp. 61-80, 9 ills., 1 quarter-page map, July, 1920.

Arizona and New Mexico. By B. S. Rodey. Vol. XVII, pp. 100-102, 2 ills., Feb., 1906.

Arizona Comes of Age. By Frederick Simpich. Vol. LV, pp. 1-47, 40 ills. in black and white, 14 ills. in color, 1 two-thirds-page map, Jan., 1929.

Arizona Sands, Home of the Cactus King. 11 ills. from photographs. Vol. LXXI, pp. 521-528, Apr., 1937.

Call of the West. By C. J. Blanchard. Vol. XX, pp. 403-437, 20 ills., 1 three-quarters-page map, May, 1909.

Camp Fires on Desert and Lava (Book Review). Vol. XXI, pp. 715-718, 3 ills., Aug., 1910.

Encircling Navajo Mountain (Utah) with a Pack-Train: An Expedition to a Hitherto Untraversed Region of Our Southwest Discovers a New Route To Rainbow Natural Bridge. By Charles L. Bernheimer. Vol. XLIII, pp. 197-224, 33 ills., 1 half-page map, Feb., 1923.

Experiences in the Grand Canyon. By Ellsworth and Emery Kolb. Vol. XXVI, pp. 99-184, 70 ills., 1 page map, Aug., 1914.

Exploring in the Canyon of Death: Remains of a People Who Dwelt in Our Southwest at Least 4,000 Years Ago Are Revealed. By Earl H. Morris. Vol. XLVIII, pp. 263-300, 24 ills. in black and white, 22 ills. in color, Sept., 1925.

Flaming Cliffs of Monument Valley. By Lt. Jack Breed, USNR. With 9 ills. in color from natural-color photographs by the author and Warren T. Mithoff. Vol. LXXXVIII, pp. 452-461, Oct., 1945.

Grand Canyon Bridge. By Harriet Chalmers Adams. Vol. XXXIX, pp. 645-650, 6 ills., June, 1921.

Highest Dam in the World (Roosevelt Dam). Vol. XVI, pp. 440-441, Sept., 1905.

Home-Making by the Government: An Account of the Eleven Immense Irrigating Projects to be Opened in 1908. By C. J. Blanchard. Vol. XIX, pp. 250-287, 23 ills., Apr., 1908.

Man Without the Hoe. Vol. XXI, pp. 967-969, 2 ills., Dec., 1910.

Mysterious Tomb of a Giant Meteorite (Meteor Crater, Arizona). By William D. Boutwell. Vol. LIII, pp. 721-730, 10 ills., June, 1928.

Notes on the Deserts of the United States and Mexico (Extracted from a publication of Dr. Daniel T. MacDougal). Vol. XXI, pp. 691-714, 16 ills., Aug., 1910.

Old Yuma Trail. By W J McGee. Part I, Vol. XII, pp. 103-107, Mar., 1901. Part II, Vol. XII, pp. 129-143, 7 ills., 1 page map, Apr., 1901.

Ostrich Farming in the United States. Vol. XVII, pp. 569-574, 6 ills., Oct., 1906.

Arizona—Continued

Saguaro, Cactus Camel of Arizona. By Forrest Shreve. Vol. LXXXVIII, pp. 695-704, 9 ills. in color, Dec., 1945.

Saguaro, King of the Arizona Desert. 9 ills. in color from natural-color photographs by Esther Henderson, Jack Breed, and Max Kegley. Vol. LXXXVIII, pp. 697-704, Dec., 1945.

Saguaro Forest. By H. L. Shantz. Vol. LXXI, pp. 515-532, 18 ills., Apr., 1937.

Scenes from America's Southwest. Vol. XXXIX, pp. 651-664, 14 ills., June, 1921.

Secret of the Southwest Solved by Talkative Tree Rings: Horizons of American History Are Carried Back to A. D. 700 and a Calendar for 1,200 Years Established by National Geographic Society Expeditions. By Andrew Ellicott Douglass. Vol. LVI, pp. 737-770, 33 ills., 1 two-thirds-page map, Dec., 1929.

Seeing Our Spanish Southwest. By Frederick Simpich. Vol. LXXVII, pp. 711-756, 25 ills. in black and white, 17 ills. in duotone, special map supplement, June, 1940.

Snake Dance. By Marion L. Oliver. Vol. XXII, pp. 107-137, 31 ills., Feb., 1911.

Southwest: Its Splendid Natural Resources, Agricultural Wealth, and Scenic Beauty. By N. H. Darton. Vol. XXI, pp. 631-665, 21 ills., 1 page map, Aug., 1910.

Surveying the Grand Canyon of the Colorado: An account of the 1923 Boating Expedition of the United States Geological Survey. By Lewis R. Freeman. Vol. XLV, pp. 471-548, 62 ills., 1 three-quarters-page map, May, 1924.

Arkansas:

Arkansas Rolls Up Its Sleeves. By Frederick Simpich. Vol. XC, pp. 273-312, 16 ills. in black and white, 23 ills. in color, 1 map (two-page spread), Sept., 1946.

Arkansas Traveler of 1946. 23 ills. in color from natural-color photographs by Willard R. Culver. Vol. XC, pp. 289-312, Sept., 1946.

Great Mississippi Flood of 1927: Since White Man's Discovery This Mighty River Has Served Him Well, Yet It Has Brought Widespread Devastation Along Its Lower Reaches. By Frederick Simpich. Vol. LII, pp. 243-289, 53 ills., 1 half-page map, Sept., 1927.

Land of a Million Smiles (Ozarks). By Frederick Simpich. Vol. LXXXIII, pp. 589-623, 14 ills. in black and white, 20 ills. in color, 1 two-thirds-page map, May, 1943.

Work and Play in the Ozarks. 20 ills. in color from natural-color photographs by B. Anthony Stewart and J. Baylor Roberts. Vol. LXXXIII, pp. 597-620, May, 1943.

Arles, France:

Camargue, the Cowboy Country of Southern France. By Dr. André Vialles. Vol. XLII, pp. 1-34, 33 ills., 1 half-page map, July, 1922.

Arlington County, Virginia:

Wartime Washington. By William H. Nicholas. Vol. LXXXIV, pp. 257-290, 12 ills. in black and white, 16 ills. in color, Sept., 1943.

Arlington National Cemetery, Virginia:
Fame's Eternal Camping Ground: Beautiful Arlington, Burial Place of America's Illustrious Dead. By Enoch A. Chase. Vol. LIV, pp. 621-638, 19 ills., Nov., 1928.

Armed Forces, U. S. *See* U. S. Armed Forces.

Armenia and Armenians:
Armenia and the Armenians. By Hester Donaldson Jenkins. Vol. XXVIII, pp. 329-360, 27 ills., 1 half-page map, Oct., 1915.

Between Massacres in Van. By Maynard Owen Williams. Vol. XXXVI, pp. 181-184, 3 ills., Aug., 1919.

Cone-Dwellers of Asia Minor: A Primitive People Who Live in Nature-Made Apartment Houses, Fashioned by Volcanic Violence and Trickling Streams. By J. R. Sitlington Sterrett. Vol. XXXV, pp. 281-331, 52 ills., 1 half-page map, Apr., 1919.

East of Constantinople: Glimpses of Village Life in Anatolia, the Battleground of East and West, Where the Turks Reorganized Their Forces After the World War. By Melville Chater. Vol. XLIII, pp. 509-534, 27 ills., 1 three-quarters-page map, May, 1923.

Fringe of Verdure Around Asia Minor. By Ellsworth Huntington. Vol. XXI, pp. 761-775, 15 ills., Sept., 1910.

Land of the Stalking Death: A Journey Through Starving Armenia on an American Relief Train. By Melville Chater. Vol. XXXVI, pp. 393-420, 23 ills., Nov., 1919.

Mountaineers of the Euphrates. By Ellsworth Huntington. Vol. XX, pp. 142-156, 13 ills., Feb., 1909.

Old Post-Road from Tiflis to Erivan. By Esther Lancraft Hovey. Vol. XII, pp. 300-309, 9 ills., Aug., 1901.

Races of Europe. By Edwin A. Grosvenor. Vol. XXXIV, pp. 441-534, 62 ills., 2 page maps, special map supplement in colors, Dec., 1918.

Under the Heel of the Turk: A Land with a Glorious Past, a Present of Abused Opportunities, and a Future of Golden Possibilities. By William H. Hall. Vol. XXXIV, pp. 50-69, 14 ills., July, 1918.

Armies:
The Citizen Army of Holland. By Hendrik Willem Van Loon. Vol. XXIX, pp. 609-622, 9 ills., June, 1916.

The Citizen Army of Switzerland. Vol. XXVIII, pp. 502-510, 7 ills., Nov., 1915.

Fiji Patrol on Bougainville. By David D. Duncan. Vol. LXXXVII, pp. 87-104, 9 ills. in black and white, 11 ills. in color, Jan., 1945.

India Mosaic. By Peter Muir and Frances Muir. Vol. LXXXIX, pp. 443-470, 5 ills. in black and white, 22 ills. in color, 1 half-page map, Apr., 1946.
See also U. S. Army.

Armistice Day and the American Battle Fields. By J. J. Jusserand. Vol. LVI, pp. 509-554, 32 ills. in black and white, 23 ills. in color, Nov., 1929.

Armorica (Region), France. *See* Brittany.

Army Air Forces. *See* U. S. Army Air Forces.

Army Air Forces Technical Training Command. *See* Army Air Forces Training Command.

Army Air Forces Training Command:
They Sustain the Wings (Ground Crews). By Frederick Simpich. Vol. LXXXIV, pp. 333-354, 19 ills., Sept., 1943.

Army Dogs. *See* War Dogs.

Army Engineer Explores Nicaragua: Mapping a Route for a New Canal Through the Largest of Central American Republics. By Lieut. Col. Dan I. Sultan. Vol. LXI, pp. 593-627, 39 ills., 1 two-thirds-page map, May, 1932.

Army Map Service. *See* U. S. Army Map Service.

Army Transportation Corps. *See* U. S. Army Transportation Corps.

Arnautköy, Turkey:
American Alma Maters in the Near East. By Maynard Owen Williams. Vol. LXXXVIII, pp. 237-256, 16 ills., Aug., 1945.

Arnold, Frederic K.:
Islands Adrift: St. Pierre and Miquelon: In a Key Position on the North Atlantic Air Route, France's Oldest Colony Rides Out Another Storm. By Frederic K. Arnold. Vol. LXXX, pp. 743-768, 23 ills., 1 fifth-page map, Dec., 1941.

Arnold, (Gen.) H. H.:
Aerial Color Photography Becomes a War Weapon. By H. H. Arnold. Vol. LXXVII, pp. 757-766, 8 ills. in color, June, 1940.

Aerial Invasion of Burma. By Gen. H. H. Arnold. Vol. LXXXVI, pp. 129-148, 20 ills., Aug., 1944.

Air Power for Peace. By Gen. H. H. Arnold. Vol. LXXXIX, pp. 137-193, 35 ills. in black and white, 28 ills. in color, special map supplement, Feb., 1946.

Our Air Frontier in Alaska. By Major General H. H. Arnold. Vol. LXXVIII, pp. 487-504, 15 ills., 1 page map, Oct., 1940.

Arnold Arboretum:
Kingdom of Flowers: An Account of the Wealth of Trees and Shrubs of China and of What the Arnold Arboretum, with China's Help, is Doing to Enrich America. By Ernest H. Wilson. Vol. XXII, pp. 1003-1035, 24 ills., Nov., 1911.

Around the Clock with Your Soldier Boy. By Frederich Simpich. Vol. LXXX, pp. 1-36, 42 ills., July, 1941.

Around-the-World American Exposition. By O. P. Austin. Vol. XII, pp. 49-53, 1 page chart, Feb., 1901.

Around the World for Animals. By William M. and Lucile Q. Mann. Vol. LXXIII, pp. 665-714, 33 ills. in black and white, 23 ills. in color, 1 page map, June, 1938.

Around the World in the *Islander* (Ship) : A Narrative of the Adventures of a Solitary Voyager on His Four-Year Cruise in a Thirty-Four-Foot Sailing Craft. By Capt. Harry Pidgeon. Vol. LIII, pp. 141-205, 75 ills., 1 two-page map, Feb., 1928.

Around the World with the Salvation Army. By Evangeline Booth. Vol. XXXVII, pp. 346-368, 23 ills., Apr., 1920.

Art Supplements. *See* Pictorial Enlargements and Panoramas.

Artesian Water Predictions. Vol. XXI, pp. 361-363, 1 ill., Apr., 1910.

Artist Adventures on the Island of Bali. By Franklin Price Knott. Vol. LIII, pp. 326-347, 20 ills. in color, Mar., 1928.

Arts:
Europe's Looted Art. By John Walker. **Vol.** LXXXIX, pp. 39-52, 11 ills., Jan., 1946.

Manchuria : Mukden, the Manchu Home, and Its Great Art Museum. By Eliza R. Scidmore. Vol. XXI, pp. 289-320, 30 ills., Apr., 1910.

Persia : Exploring the Secrets of Persepolis. By Charles Breasted. Vol. LXIV, pp. 381-420, 48 ills., 1 half-page map, 1 plan, Oct., 1933.

Vatican : Smallest State in the World : Vatican City on Its 108 Acres Is a Complete Sovereignty Internationally Recognized. By W. Coleman Nevils. Vol. LXXV, pp. 377-412, 37 ills., 1 two-page map, Mar., 1939.

See also Archeology ; Architecture ; Paintings ; Sculpture.

Artvin, Turkey :
On the Turks' Russian Frontier : Everyday Life in the Fastnesses between the Black Sea and Ararat, Borderland of Oil and Minerals that Hitler Covets. By Edward Stevenson Murray. Vol. LXXX, pp. 367-392, 21 ills., 1 half-page map, Sept., 1941.

Aruba (Island), West Indies :
Curaçao and Aruba, Oil Isles of the Caribbean. 10 ills. in color from natural-color photographs by Philip Hanson Hiss and Robert Yarnall Richie. Vol. LXXXIII, pp. 175-182, Feb., 1943.

Curaçao and Aruba on Guard. By W. Robert Moore. Vol. LXXXIII, pp. 169-192, 12 ills. in black and white, 10 ills. in color, 4 maps, Feb., 1943.

As London Toils and Spins. By Frederick Simpich. Vol. LXXI, pp. 1-57, 38 ills. in black and white, 23 ills. in color, Jan., 1937.

As São Paulo Grows : Half the World's Coffee Beans Flavor the Life and Speed the Growth of an Inland Brazil City. By W. Robert Moore. Vol. LXXV, pp. 657-688, 33 ills., 1 two-thirds-page map, May, 1939.

As Seen from a Dutch Window. By James Howard Gore. Vol. XIX, pp. 619-634, 3 ills., Sept., 1908.

"As the Tuan Had Said." By George M. Hanson. Vol. LXIV, pp. 631-644, 19 ills., Nov., 1933.

As 2,000 Ships Are Born. By Frederick Simpich. Vol. LXXXI, pp. 551-588, 34 ills., May, 1942.

Ascension Island, Atlantic Ocean :
Ascension Island, an Engineering Victory. By Lt. Col. Frederick J. Clarke. Vol. LXXXV, pp. 623-640, 21 ills., May, 1944.

Greens Grow for GI's on Soilless Ascension. By W. Robert Moore. Vol. LXXXVIII, pp. 219-230, 12 ills., Aug., 1945.

Ascent of Mont Blanc. By Walter Woodburn Hyde. Vol. XXIV, pp. 861-942, 69 ills., Aug., 1913.

Ashanti (Division), Gold Coast :
Revolt of the Ashantis. Vol. XI, p. 244, 1 third-page map, June, 1900.

Ashley River Gardens, South Carolina :
Ashley River and Its Gardens. By E. T. H. Shaffer. Vol. XLIX, pp. 525-550, 6 ills. in black and white, 7 ills. in color, May, 1926.

Exploring the Atlantic Seaboard With a Color Camera. 7 ills. in color from autochromes by Jacob Gayer. Vol. XLIX, pp. 532-549, May, 1926.

Ashokan Reservoir, New York :
New York—The Metropolis of Mankind. By William Joseph Showalter. Vol. XXXIV, pp. 1-49, 39 ills., July, 1918.

Asia:
Adventures with a Camera in Many Lands. By Maynard Owen Williams. Vol. XL, pp. 87-112, 24 ills., July, 1921.

Along the Old Silk Routes : A Motor Caravan with Air-conditioned Trailer Retraces Ancient Roads from Paris across Europe and Half of Asia to Delhi. By Lawrence Copley Thaw and Margaret S. Thaw. Vol. LXXVIII, pp. 453-486, 33 ills., 1 map, Oct., 1940.

Asia : The Cradle of Humanity. By W J McGee. Vol. XII, pp. 281-290, Aug., 1901.

Bright Pages from an Asiatic Travel Log. 12 ills. in color from natural-color photographs by Maynard Owen Williams. Vol. LXII, pp. 544-553, Nov., 1932.

By Coolie and Caravan Across Central Asia : Narrative of a 7,900-Mile Journey of Exploration and Research Over "the Roof of the World," from the Indian Ocean to the Yellow Sea. By William J. Morden. Vol. LII, pp. 369-431, 73 ills., 1 page map, Oct., 1927.

Citroën Trans-Asiatic Expedition Reaches Kashmir : Scientific Party Led by Georges-Marie Haardt Successfully Crosses Syria, Iraq, Persia, and Afghanistan to Arrive at the Pamir. By Maynard Owen Williams. Vol. LX, pp. 387-443, 62 ills., 1 page map, Oct., 1931.

Commercial Prize of the Orient. By O. P. Austin. Vol. XVI, pp. 399-423, 10 ills., 1 page map, 10 charts, Sept., 1905.

Desert Road to Turkestan : Twentieth Century Travel Through Innermost Asia, Along Caravan Trails Over Which Oriental Commerce Was Borne from China to the Medieval Western World. By Owen Lattimore. Vol. LV, pp. 661-702, 45 ills., 1 two-thirds-page map, June, 1929.

Asia—*Continued*

Faces and Fashions of Asia's Changeless Tribes. 26 ills. in color from paintings and drawings by Alexandre Iacovleff. Vol. LXIX, pp. 21-36, Jan., 1936.

First Over the Roof of the World by Motor : The Trans-Asiatic Expedition Sets New Records for Wheeled Transport in Scaling Passes of the Himalayas. By Maynard Owen Williams. Vol. LXI, pp. 321-363, 45 ills., 2 half-page maps, Mar., 1932.

Flags of Europe, Asia, and Africa. By Byron McCandless and Gilbert Grosvenor. Vol. XXXII, pp. 372-385, 100 ills. in color, Oct., 1917.

From England to India by Automobile : An 8,527-Mile Trip Through Ten Countries, from London to Quetta, Requires Five and a Half Months. By Maj. F. A. C. Forbes-Leith. Vol. XLVIII, pp. 191-223, 33 ills., 1 third-page map, Aug., 1925.

From London to Australia by Aëroplane : A Personal Narrative of the First Aërial Voyage Half Around the World. By Sir Ross Smith. Vol. XXXIX, pp. 229-339, 76 ills. in black and white, 8 ills. in color, 1 page map, Mar., 1921.

From the Mediterranean to the Yellow Sea by Motor : The Citroën-Haardt Expedition Successfully Completes Its Dramatic Journey. By Maynard Owen Williams. Vol. LXII, pp. 513-580, 45 ills. in black and white, 25 ills. in color, 2 half-page maps, Nov., 1932.

Geographical Pivot of History (Steppes of Central Asia). By H. J. Mackinder. Vol. XV, pp. 331-335, Aug., 1904.

Glimpses of Asia. Vol. XXXIX, pp. 553-568, 16 ills., May, 1921.

Land of Genghis Khan in Its True Colors. 13 ills. in color from natural-color photographs by Maynard Owen Williams. Vol. LXII, pp. 568-577, Nov., 1932.

Link Relations of Southwestern Asia. By Talcott Williams. Part I, Vol. XII, pp. 249-265, 2 page and 9 half-page maps, July, 1901. Part II, Vol. XII, pp. 291-299, 1 half-page map, Aug., 1901.

New Map of Asia. Text accompanying special map supplement in colors. Vol. XXXIX, pp. 552-570, 17 ills., May, 1921.

New Map Shows Asia's Role in Global Warfare. Text accompanying special map supplement in colors. Vol. LXXXII, pp. 767-768, Dec., 1942.

New Road to Asia. By Owen Lattimore. Vol. LXXXVI, pp. 641-676, 15 ills. in black and white, 26 ills. in color, Dec., 1944.

On the World's Highest Plateaus : Through an Asiatic No Man's Land to the Desert of Ancient Cathay. By Hellmut de Terra. Vol. LIX, pp. 319-367, 39 ills. in black and white, 32 ills. in color, 1 two-thirds-page map, Mar., 1931.

Place Names in Eastern Asia. Vol. XV, p. 136, Mar., 1904.

Race Prejudice in the Far East. By Melville E. Stone. Vol. XXI, pp. 973-985, 6 ills., Dec., 1910.

Asia—*Continued*

Seeing the World from the Air. By Sir Alan J. Cobham. Vol. LIII, pp. 349-384, 37 ills., 1 three-quarters-page map, Mar., 1928.

Society's New Map of Asia. Text accompanying special map supplement in colors. Vol. LXIV, pp. 770-772, 1 ill., Dec., 1933.

Society's New Map of Southeast Asia. Text accompanying special map supplement in colors. Vol. LXXXVI, pp. 449-450, 1 ill., Oct., 1944.

Sven Hedin's Explorations in Central Asia. Vol. XII, pp. 393-395, Nov., 1901.

Trans-Asiatic Expedition Starts. By Georges-Marie Haardt. Vol. LIX, pp. 776-782, 6 ills., June, 1931.

With the Nomads of Central Asia : A Summer's Sojourn in the Tekes Valley, Plateau Paradise of Mongol and Turkic Tribes. By Edward Murray. Vol. LXIX, pp. 1-57, 43 ills. in black and white, 26 ills. in color, 1 half-page map, Jan., 1936.

World's Greatest Overland Explorer : How Marco Polo Penetrated Farthest Asia, "Discovered" Many Lands Unknown to Europe, and Added Numerous Minerals, Animals, Birds, and Plants to Man's Knowledge. By J. R. Hildebrand. Vol. LIV, pp. 505-568, 53 ills., 1 two-page map, Nov., 1928.

See also names of individual countries.

Asia Minor:

Asia Minor in the Time of the Seven Wise Men. By Mary Mills Patrick. Vol. XXXVII, pp. 47-67, 19 ills., Jan., 1920.

Buried Cities of Asia Minor. By Ernest Lloyd Harris. Vol. XX, pp. 1-18, 10 ills., Jan., 1909.

Cone-Dwellers of Asia Minor : A Primitive People Who Live in Nature-Made Apartment Houses, Fashioned by Volcanic Violence and Trickling Streams. By J. R. Sitlington Sterrett. Vol. XXXV, pp. 281-331, 52 ills., 1 half-page map, Apr., 1919.

Crossing Asia Minor, the Country of the New Turkish Republic. By Maj. Robert Whitney Imbrie. Vol. XLVI, pp. 445-472, 31 ills., 1 quarter-page map, Oct., 1924.

Fringe of Verdure Around Asia Minor. By Ellsworth Huntington. Vol. XXI, pp. 761-775, 15 ills., Sept., 1910.

Peculiar Caves of Asia Minor. By Elizabeth H. Brewer. Vol. XXII, pp. 870-875, 5 ills., Sept., 1911.

Ruined Cities of Asia Minor. By Ernest Lloyd Harris. Vol. XIX, pp. 741-760, 11 ills., Nov., 1908.

Scenes in Asia Minor. Vol. XX, pp. 174-193, 34 ills., 1 three-quarters-page map, Feb., 1909.

Sketch of the Geographical History of Asia Minor. By Sir William Ramsay. Vol. XLII, pp. 553-570, 12 ills., Nov., 1922.

Some Ruined Cities of Asia Minor. By Ernest Lloyd Harris. Vol. XIX, pp. 833-858, 19 ills., Dec., 1908.

See also Anatolia ; Turkey.

Asquith, Herbert Henry:
Tribute to America. By Herbert Henry Asquith. Vol. XXXI, pp. 294-296, 2 ills., Apr. 1917.

Assam (Province), India :
Stilwell Road—Land Route to China. By Nelson Grant Tayman. Vol. LXXXVII, pp. 681-698, 18 ills., June, 1945.

Assisi, Italy :
Inehaustible Italy. By Arthur Stanley Riggs. Vol. XXX, pp. 273-368, 76 ills., 1 page map, Oct., 1916.

Assumed Inconstancy in the Level of Lake Nicaragua : A Question of Permanency of the Nicaragua Canal. By C. Willard Hayes. Vol. XI, pp. 156-161, Apr., 1900.

Assyria (Ancient Empire) :
Cradle of Civilization : The Historic Lands Along the Euphrates and Tigris Rivers Where Briton Is Fighting Turk. By James Baikie. Vol. XXIX, pp. 127-162, 25 ills., Feb., 1916.
Pushing Back History's Horizon : How the Pick and Shovel Are Revealing Civilizations That Were Ancient When Israel Was Young. By Albert T. Clay. Vol. XXIX, pp. 162-216, 47 ills., 1 page map, Feb., 1916.

Astronomy:
American Eclipse Expedition. By Rear Adm. Colby M. Chester. Vol. XVII, pp. 589-612, 23 ills., 1 color plate, Nov., 1906.
Eclipse Adventures on a Desert Isle (Canton). By Capt. J. F. Hellweg. Vol. LXXII, pp. 377-394, 14 ills., 1 two-thirds-page map, Sept., 1937.
Exploring the Glories of the Firmament. By William Joseph Showalter. Vol. XXXVI, pp. 153-181, 17 ills., 3 charts, 1 diagram, Aug., 1919.
Girdling the Globe. Vol. XV, p. 236, May, 1904.
Heavens Above : On Land, Sea, and in the Air the Stars Serve Modern Man as Map, Compass, and Clock. By Donald H. Menzel. With 12 charts, designed by the author, showing star positions for each month, and 13 drawings of the constellations by Carlotta Gonzales Lahey. Vol. LXXXIV, pp. 97-128, 1 map (two-page spread), July, 1943.
How to Use the Star Charts. Text accompanying 12 star charts designed by Donald H. Menzel. Vol. LXXXIV, pp. 116-128, July, 1943.
Interviewing the Stars : How Twentieth Century Astronomers are Inducing the Heavens to Reveal Their Secrets. By William Joseph Showalter. Vol. XLVII, pp. 97-122, 18 ills., 2 charts, 1 diagram, Jan., 1925.
Magic Mountain (Mount Wilson, California). By J. N. Patterson. Vol. XIX, pp. 457-468, 9 ills., July, 1908.
Manila Observatory. By Father José Algué. Vol. XI, pp. 427-438, 2 ills., Nov., 1900.
National Geographic Society's Eclipse Expedition to Norfolk, Virginia. By Marcus Baker. Vol. XI, p. 320, Aug., 1900.
Natural-color photograph of an eclipse. 1 ill. in color by Irvine C. Gardner. Vol. LXXI, p. 178, Feb., 1937.

Astronomy—*Continued*
Nature's Most Dramatic Spectacle (Eclipse). By S. A. Mitchell. Vol. LXXII, pp. 361-376, 16 ills., 1 half-page map, Sept., 1937.
News of the Universe : Mars Swings Nearer the Earth, Sunspots Wane, and a Giant New Telescopic Eye Soon Will Peer Into Unexplored Depths of Space. By F. Barrows Colton. Vol. LXXVI, pp. 1-32, 23 ills. in black and white, 10 ills. in color, July, 1939.
Observing a Total Eclipse of the Sun : Dimming Solar Light for a Few Seconds Entails Years of Work for Science and Attracts Throngs to "Nature's Most Magnificent Spectacle." By Paul A. McNally. Vol. LXII, pp. 597-605, 6 ills., Nov., 1932.
Observing an Eclipse in Asiatic Russia. By Irvine C. Gardner. Vol. LXXI, pp. 179-197, 19 ills. in black and white, 1 ill. in color, Feb., 1937.
Photographing the Eclipse of 1932 from the Air : From Five Miles Above the Earth's Surface, the National Geographic Society-Army Air Corps Survey Obtains Successful Photographs of the Moon's Shadow. By Capt. Albert W. Stevens. Vol. LXII, pp. 581-596, 18 ills., Nov., 1932.
Scientific Work of the National Geographic Society's Eclipse Expedition to Norfolk, Virginia. By Simon Newcomb. Vol. XI, pp. 321-324, Aug., 1900.
Solar System's Eternal Show. 10 ills. in color from paintings by Charles Bittinger. Vol. LXXVI, pp. 17-24, July, 1939.
Special Telegraphic Time Signal from the Naval Observatory. Vol. XV, pp. 411-415, Oct., 1904.
To Observe Solar Eclipse. Vol. XVI, p. 88, Feb., 1905.
Total Eclipse of the Sun, May 28, 1900. By Frank H. Bigelow. Vol. XI, pp. 33-34, Jan., 1900.
Unfurling Old Glory on Canton Island. 11 ills. in color ; 1 painting and 1 kodachrome photograph of the eclipse. Vol. LXXIII, pp. 753-760, June, 1938.
See also Solar Radiation.

Asunción, Paraguay :
Color Cruising in Paraguay. 11 ills. in color from natural-color photographs by Fenno Jacobs. Vol. LXXXIV, pp. 465-472, Oct., 1943.
River-Encircled Paraguay. By Harriet Chalmers Adams. Vol. LXIII, pp. 385-416, 35 ills., 1 third-page map, Apr., 1933.
Through Paraguay and Southern Matto Grosso. By Sir Christopher H. Gibson. Vol. LXXXIV. pp. 459-488, 20 ills. in black and white, 11 ills. in color, 1 two-thirds-page map, Oct., 1943.

At Ease in the South Seas. By Maj. Frederick Simpich, Jr. Vol. LXXXV, pp. 79-104, 32 ills., Jan., 1944.

At Home on the Oceans : Whales and Sharks Make Exciting Neighbors for a Professor's Wife. Turned Able Seaman, On a Three-year Voyage Around the World. By Edith Bauer Strout. Vol. LXXVI, pp. 33-86, 54 ills., 1 map, July, 1939.

At the Tomb of Tutankhamen : An Account of the Opening of the Royal Egyptian Sepulcher Which Contained the Most Remarkable Funeral Treasures Unearthed in Historic Times. By Maynard Owen Williams. Vol. XLIII, pp. 461-508, 53 ills., 1 half-page map, May, 1923.

Atatürk, Mustapha Kemal:
Turkish Republic Comes of Age. By Maynard Owen Williams. Vol. LXXXVII, pp. 581-616, 4 ills. in black and white, 29 ills. in color, 1 map (two-page spread), May, 1945.

Athens, Greece :
Classic Greece Merges Into 1941 News. 19 ills. from photographs ; 15 ills. by B. Anthony Stewart ; 3 ills. by Maynard Owen Williams. Vol. LXXIX, pp. 93-108, Jan., 1941.

"Glory That Was Greece." By Alexander Wilbourne Weddell. Vol. XLII, pp. 571-630, 51 ills., 1 three-quarters-page map, Dec., 1922.

Greece of Today. By George Higgins Moses. Vol. XXVIII, pp. 295-329, 27 ills., Oct., 1915.

Modern Odyssey in Classic Lands : Troy's Treasures, Athens' Parthenon, and Rome's First "Broad Way" Influence Today's Banks, Costumes, Jewelry, and Railroad Timetables. By Maynard Owen Williams. Vol. LXXII, pp. 291-337, 27 ills. in black and white, 22 ills. in color, Mar., 1940.

New Greece, the Centenarian, Forges Ahead. By Maynard Owen Williams. Vol. LVIII, pp. 649-721, 51 ills. in black and white, 40 ills. in color, 1 three-quarters-page map, Dec., 1930.

Whirlpool of the Balkans. By George Higgins Moses. Vol. XXXIX, pp. 179-197, 15 ills., Feb., 1921.

Athos, Mount, Greece :
Hoary Monasteries of Mount Athos. By H. G. Dwight. Vol. XXX, pp. 249-272, 24 ills., 1 half-page map, Sept., 1916.

Atitlan, Lake, Guatemala :
Guatemala, the Country of the Future. By Edine Frances Tisdel. Vol. XXI, pp. 596-624, 33 ills., 1 three-quarters-page map, July, 1910.

Atkeson, Ray:
"Where Rolls the Oregon." 28 ills. in color from natural-color photographs by Ray Atkeson. Vol. XC, pp. 689-728, Dec., 1946.

Atkins, Paul M.:
French West Africa in Wartime. By Paul M. Atkins. Vol. LXXXI, pp. 371-408, 37 ills., 2 maps, Mar., 1942.

Atkinson, Agnes Akin:
Befriending Nature's Children : An Experiment With Some of California's Wild Folk. By Agnes Akin Atkinson. Vol. LXI, pp. 199-215, 26 ills., Feb., 1932.

Atkinson, Agnes Akin—*Continued*
Where Birds and Little Animals Find Haven (Eaton Canyon Bird and Game Sanctuary). By Agnes Akin Atkinson. Vol. LXX, pp. 232-241, 14 ills., Aug., 1936.

Atkinson, Edward:
Some Lessons in Geography. By Edward Atkinson. Vol. XVI, pp. 193-198, Apr., 1905.

Atlantic City, New Jersey :
New Jersey Now ! By E. John Long. Vol. LXIII, pp. 519-583, 49 ills. in black and white, 24 ills. in color, 1 page and 1 two-thirds-page maps, May, 1933.

Atlantic Ocean:
Battle-Ground of Nature : The Atlantic Seaboard. By John Oliver La Gorce. Vol. XXXIII, pp. 511-546, 23 ills., 4 half-page maps, June, 1918.

Flying Around the North Atlantic. By Anne Morrow Lindbergh ; Foreword by Charles A. Lindbergh. Vol. LXVI, pp. 259-337, 82 ills., 1 two-page and 1 two-thirds-page maps, Sept., 1934.

New Map of the Atlantic Ocean : Foremost Sea of Commerce Becomes World's Battleground and Its Peaceful Islands Rise to Strategic Importance. By Leo A. Borah and Wellman Chamberlin. Text accompanying special map supplement in colors. Vol. LXXX, pp. 407-418, 9 ills., Sept., 1941.

Our Global Ocean—Last and Vast Frontier. By F. Barrows Colton. Vol. LXXXVII, pp. 105-128, 19 ills., 1 drawing, Jan., 1945.

Our Transatlantic Flight. By Comdr. Richard Evelyn Byrd. Vol. LII, pp. 347-368, 17 ills., 1 half-page map, Sept., 1927.

Sindbads of Science : Narrative of a Windjammer's Specimen-Collecting Voyage to the Sargasso Sea, to Senegambian Africa and Among Islands of High Adventure in the South Atlantic. By George Finlay Simmons. Vol. LII, pp. 1-75, 89 ills., 1 two-thirds-page map, July, 1927.

Standing Iceberg Guard in the North Atlantic : International Patrol Safeguards the Lives of Thousands of Travelers and Protects Transatlantic Liners from a "Titanic" Fate. By Lieut. Comdr. F. A. Zeusler. Vol. L, pp. 1-28, 29 ills., 1 half-page map, July, 1926.

World That Rims the Narrowing Atlantic : Latest Ten-color Map Supplement Shows Four Continents and New Transatlantic Air Routes Which Make This Ocean Only One Day Wide. By James M. Darley. Text accompanying special map supplement in colors. Vol. LXXVI, pp. 139-142, 1 ill., July, 1939.

Atlas Mountains, Morocco :
Beyond the Grand Atlas : Where the French Tricolor Flies Beside the Flag of the Sultan of Morocco. By V. C. Scott O'Connor. Vol. LXI, pp. 261-319, 52 ills. in black and white, 12 ills. in color, 1 two-thirds-page map, Mar., 1932.

Atlases. *See* Map Articles *and* Index to Maps. p. 594.

Atomic Bomb and Atomic Power:
Air Power for Peace. By Gen. H. H. Arnold. Vol. LXXXIX, pp. 137-193, 35 ills. in black and white, 28 ills. in color, special map supplement, Feb., 1946.

Farewell to Bikini. By Carl Markwith. Vol. XC, pp. 97-116, 16 ills., July, 1946.

Your New World of Tomorrow. By F. Barrows Colton. Vol. LXXXVIII, pp. 385-410, 25 ills., Oct., 1945.

Atrevida Glacier, Alaska:
National Geographic Society's Alaskan Expedition of 1909. By Ralph S. Tarr and Lawrence Martin. Vol. XXI, pp. 1-54, 42 ills., 12 maps, Jan., 1910.

Atta Ants:
Color Glows in the Guianas, French and Dutch. By Nichol Smith. Vol. LXXXIII, pp. 459-480, 8 ills. in black and white, 13 ills. in color, 1 two-thirds-page map, Apr., 1943.

Attar of Roses:
Bulgaria's Valley of Roses. 13 ills. in color from natural-color photographs by Wilhelm Tobien and Georg Paskoff. Vol. LXII, pp. 186-195, Aug., 1932.

Atwood, Albert W.:
Coal: Prodigious Worker for Man. By Albert W. Atwood. Vol. LXXXV, pp. 569-592, 19 ills., 1 drawing, May, 1944.

Healing Arts in Global War: As Weapons Grow Deadlier, Scientific Medicine Pits Its Ever-rising Skill Against Them. By Albert W Atwood. Vol. LXXXIV, pp. 599-618, 17 ills., Nov., 1943.

Long River of New England: In War and Peace, from Mountain Wilderness to the Sea, Flows the Connecticut River, Through a Valley Abounding in History, Scenery, Inventive Genius, and Industry. By Albert W. Atwood. Vol. LXXXIII, pp. 401-434, 12 ills. in black and white, 24 ills. in color, 1 two-thirds-page map, Apr., 1943.

Miracle of War Production: For Victory the United States Transforms Its Complex Industry into the Biggest Factory and Mightiest Arsenal the World Has Ever Known. By Albert W. Atwood. Paintings by Thornton Oakley. Vol. LXXXII, pp. 693-715, 17 ills. in black and white, 16 ills. in color, Dec., 1942.

Northeast of Boston. By Albert W. Atwood. Vol. LXXXVIII, pp. 257-292, 12 ills. in black and white, 17 ills. in color, special map supplement, Sept., 1945.

Potomac, River of Destiny. By Albert W. Atwood. Vol. LXXXVIII, pp. 33-70, 15 ills. in black and white, 18 ills. in color, 1 map (two-page spread), July, 1945.

Revealing Earth's Mightiest Ocean (Pacific). By Albert W. Atwood. Vol. LXXXI, pp. 291-306, 10 ills., special map supplement, Sept., 1943.

Tidewater Virginia, Where History Lives. By Albert W. Atwood. Vol. LXXXI, pp. 617-656, 18 ills. in black and white, 20 ills. in color, 1 page map, May, 1942.

Atwood, Albert W.—*Continued*
Washington—Storehouse of Knowledge. By Albert W. Atwood. Vol. LXXXI, pp. 325-359, 20 ills. in black and white, 9 ills. in color, Mar., 1942.

Atwood, Wallace W., Jr.:
Crater Lake and Yosemite Through the Ages. By Wallace W. Atwood, Jr. Paintings by Eugene Kingman. Vol. LXXI, pp. 327-343, 7 ills. in black and white, 13 ills. in color, Mar., 1937.

August First in Gruyères (Switzerland). By Melville Bell Grosvenor. Vol. LXX, pp. 137-168, 12 ills. in black and white, 23 ills. in color, Aug., 1936.

Augusta Natural Bridge, Utah:
Colossal Natural Bridges of Utah. Vol. XV, pp. 367-369, 2 ills., Sept., 1904.

Augustus—Emperor and Architect: Two Thousand Years Ago Was Born the Physically Frail But Spiritually Great Roman Who Became the Master of His World. By W. Coleman Nevils. Vol. LXXIV, pp. 535-556, 17 ills., 1 half-page map, Oct., 1938.

Auklets (Birds):
Birds of the Northern Seas. By Alexander Wetmore. Paintings by Maj. Allan Brooks. Vol. LXIX, pp. 95-122, 12 ills. in black and white, 34 portraits in color, Jan., 1936.

Auks (Birds):
Auks and Their Northland Neighbors. 34 portraits in color from paintings by Maj. Allan Brooks. Vol. LXIX, pp. 101-116, Jan., 1936.

Birds of the Northern Seas. By Alexander Wetmore. Paintings by Maj. Allan Brooks. Vol. LXIX, pp. 95-122, 12 ills. in black and white, 34 portraits in color, Jan., 1936.

Ault, J. P.:
Sailing the Seven Seas in the Interest of Science: Adventures Through 157,000 Miles of Storm and Calm, from Arctic to Antarctic and Around the World, in the Non-Magnetic Yacht *Carnegie.* By J. P. Ault. Vol. XLII, pp. 631-690, 47 ills., 1 chart, Dec., 1922.

Auroras:
Mystery of Auroras: National Geographic Society and Cornell University Study Spectacular Displays in the Heavens. Vol. LXXV, pp. 689-690, May, 1939.

See also National Geographic Society: Research.

Austin, O. P.:
Around-the-World American Exposition. By O. P. Austin. Vol. XII, pp. 49-53, 1 page chart, Feb., 1901.

Colonial Systems of the World. By O. P. Austin. Vol. X, pp. 21-26, Jan., 1899.

Commerce of Mexico and the United States. By O. P. Austin. Vol. XIII, pp. 25-26, Jan., 1902.

Commercial Development of Japan. By O. P. Austin. Vol. X, pp. 329-337, Sept., 1899.

Austin, O. P.—*Continued*

Commercial Importance of Samoa. By O. P. Austin. Vol. X, pp. 218-220, June, 1899.

Commercial Prize of the Orient. By O. P. Austin. Vol. XVI, pp. 399-423, 10 ills., 1 page map, 10 charts, Sept., 1905.

National Geographic Society (O. P. Austin Elected Secretary). Vol. XIV, p. 425, Nov., 1903.

Our New Possessions and the Interest They Are Exciting. By O. P. Austin. Vol. XI, pp. 32-33, Jan., 1900.

Probable Effect of the Panama Canal on the Commercial Geography of the World. By O. P. Austin. Vol. XXV, pp. 245-248, Feb., 1914.

Problems of the Pacific—The Commerce of the Great Ocean. By O. P. Austin. Vol. XIII, pp. 303-318, 7 maps, Aug., 1902.

Progress of the National Geographic Society (Report of O. P. Austin). Vol. XXIV, pp. 251-256, 1 ill., Feb., 1913.

Queer Methods of Travel in Curious Corners of the World. By O. P. Austin. Vol. XVIII, pp. 687-715, 29 ills., Nov., 1907.

Remarkable Growth of Europe During Forty Years of Peace. By O. P. Austin. Vol. XXVI, pp. 272-274, Sept., 1914.

United States : Her Industries. By O. P. Austin. Vol. XIV, pp. 301-320, 24 diagrams, Aug., 1903.

Australia :

American Bombers Attacking from Australia. By Howell Walker. Vol. LXXXIII, pp. 49-70, 19 ills., 1 map (two-page spread), Jan., 1943.

At Ease in the South Seas. By Maj. Frederick Simpich, Jr. Vol. LXXXV, pp. 79-104, 32 ills., Jan., 1944.

Australia's Future. By Walter J. Ballard. Vol. XVI, pp. 570-571, Dec., 1905.

Australia's Stone Age Men. 8 ills. in color from natural-color photographs by Charles P. Mountford. Vol. LXXXIX, pp. 105-112, Jan., 1946.

Australia's Wild Wonderland. By M. P. Greenwood Adams. Vol. XLV, pp. 329-356, 36 ills., 1 half-page map, Mar., 1924.

Beyond Australia's Cities. By W. Robert Moore. Vol. LXX, pp. 709-747, 27 ills. in black and white, 12 ills. in color, Dec., 1936.

British Commonwealth of Nations : "Organized Freedom" Around the World. By Eric Underwood. Vol. LXXXIII, pp. 485-524, 31 ills., Apr., 1943.

Capital Cities of Australia. By W. Robert Moore. Vol. LXVIII, pp. 667-722, 32 ills. in black and white, 24 ills. in color, 1 two-page map, Dec., 1935.

Completion of the Cable Between Canada and Australia. Vol. XIII, p. 410, Nov., 1902.

Earth's Most Primitive People : A Journey with the Aborigines of Central Australia. By Charles P. Mountford. Vol. LXXXIX, pp. 89-112, 10 ills. in black and white, 8 ills. in color, 1 half-page map, Jan., 1946.

Australia—*Continued*

Facing War's Challenge "Down Under." 20 ills. in color from natural-color photographs by Howell Walker. Vol. LXXXI, pp. 425-456, Apr., 1942.

Fairy Wrens of Australia : The Little Long-tailed "Blue Birds of Happiness" Rank High Among the Island Continent's Remarkable Birds. By Neville W. Cayley. With 8 ills. in color from paintings by the author. Vol. LXXXVIII, pp. 488-498, 1 ill. in black and white, Oct., 1945.

Flashes of Color in the Fifth Continent. 24 ills. in color from natural-color photographs by W. Robert Moore. Vol. LXVIII, pp. 681-704, Dec., 1935.

From London to Australia by Aëroplane : A Personal Narrative of the First Aërial Voyage Half Around the World. By Sir Ross Smith. Vol. XXXIX, pp. 229-339, 76 ills. in black and white, 8 ills. in color, 1 page map, Mar., 1921.

Great Barrier Reef and Its Isles : The Wonder and Mystery of Australia's World-Famous Geographical Feature. By Charles Barrett. Vol. LVIII, pp. 355-384, 38 ills., 1 half-page map, Sept., 1930.

Great Britain's Bread Upon the Waters : Canada and Her Other Daughters. By William Howard Taft. Vol. XXIX, pp. 217-272, 56 ills., Mar., 1916.

Koala, or Australian Teddy Bear. By F. Lewis. Vol. LX, pp. 346-355, 13 ills., Sept., 1931.

Lonely Australia : The Unique Continent. By Herbert E. Gregory. Vol. XXX, pp. 473-568, 68 ills., 1 two-page and 4 half-page maps, Dec., 1916.

Making of an Anzac. By Howell Walker. Vol. LXXXI, pp. 409-456, 31 ills. in black and white, 20 ills. in color, 1 two-page map, Apr., 1942.

Sailing the Seven Seas in the Interest of Science : Adventures Through 157,000 Miles of Storm and Calm, from Arctic to Antarctic and Around the World, in the Non-Magnetic Yacht *Carnegie*. By J. P. Ault. Vol. XLII, pp. 631-690, 47 ills., 1 chart, Dec., 1922.

Seeing the World from the Air. By Sir Alan J. Cobham. Vol. LIII, pp. 349-384, 37 ills., 1 three-quarters-page map, Mar., 1928.

Shark-Fishing—An Australian Industry. By Norman Ellison. Vol. LXII, pp. 369-386, 22 ills., Sept., 1932.

Sunny Corners of Kangaroo Land. 12 ills. in color from natural-color photographs by W. Robert Moore. Vol. LXX, pp. 713-720, Dec., 1936.

Tallest Tree that Grows (Eucalyptus). By Edgerton R. Young. Vol. XX, pp. 664-667, 3 ills., July, 1909.

What the Fighting Yanks See. By Wanda Burnett. Vol. LXXXVI, pp. 451-476, 27 ills., Oct., 1944.

Australia—*Continued*

Where Nature Runs Riot: On Australia's Great Barrier Reef Marine Animals Grow to Unusual Size, Develop Strange Weapons of Attack and Defense, and Acquire Brilliant Colors. By T. C. Roughley. Vol. LXXVII, pp. 823-850, 18 ills. in black and white, 15 ills. in color, 1 page map, June, 1940.

See also Darwin ; Sydney.

Australia's Future. By Walter J. Ballard. Vol. XVI, pp. 570-571, Dec., 1905.

Australia's Patchwork Creature, the Platypus: Man Succeeds in Making Friends with This Duck-billed, Fur-coated Paradox which Lays Eggs and Suckles Its Young. By Charles H. Holmes. Vol. LXXVI, pp. 273-282, 13 ills., Aug., 1939.

Australia's Stone Age Men. 8 ills. in color from natural-color photographs by Charles P. Mountford. Vol. LXXXIX, pp. 105-112, Jan., 1946.

Australia's Wild Wonderland. By M. P. Greenwood Adams. Vol. XLV, pp. 329-356, 36 ills., 1 half-page map, Mar., 1924.

Austria:

Alpine Villagers of Austria. 13 ills. in color from autochromes by Hans Hildenbrand and Wilhelm Tobien. Vol. LVI, pp. 668-677, Dec., 1929.

Austrian Album. 13 ills. in color from natural-color photographs by Hans Hildenbrand and Wilhelm Tobien. Vol. LXXI, pp. 457-464, Apr., 1937.

Austrian August—and September. By W. Robert Moore. Vol. LXXIII, pp. 493-524, 11 ills. in black and white, 19 ills. in color, Apr., 1938.

Austrian Kodachromes from a Candid Camera. 19 ills. in color from natural-color photographs by W. Robert Moore. Vol. LXXIII, pp. 501-524, Apr., 1938.

Austro-Italian Mountain Frontiers. By Florence Craig Albrecht. Vol. XXVII, pp. 321-376, 60 ills., 1 page map, Apr., 1915.

Danube, Highway of Races: From the Black Forest to the Black Sea, Europe's Most Important River Has Borne the Traffic of Centuries. By Melville Chater. Vol. LVI, pp. 643-697, 54 ills., Dec., 1929.

Entering the Front Doors of Medieval Towns: The Adventures of an American Woman and Her Daughter in a Folding Boat on Eight Rivers of Germany and Austria. By Cornelia Stratton Parker. Vol. LXI, pp. 365-394, 23 ills., 1 two-thirds-page map, Mar., 1932.

Flags of Austria-Hungary, Bulgaria, Germany, and Turkey. By Byron McCandless and Gilbert Grosvenor. Vol. XXXII, pp. 386-388, 38 ills. in color, Oct., 1917.

Land of Contrast: Austria-Hungary. By D. W. and A. S. Iddings. Vol. XXIII, pp. 1188-1218, 34 ills., Dec., 1912.

Merry Maskers of Imst. 14 ills. from photographs by Frances C. Fuerst. Vol. LXX, pp. 201-208, Aug., 1936.

Austria—*Continued*

New Map of Europe: Showing the Boundaries Established by the Peace Conference at Paris and by Subsequent Decisions of the Supreme Council of the Allied and Associated Powers. By Ralph A. Graves. Text accompanying special map supplement in colors. Vol. XXXIX, pp. 157-177, 18 ills., Feb., 1921.

Salzkammergut, a Playground of Austria. By Florence Polk Holding. Vol. LXXI, pp. 445-484, 34 ills. in black and white, 13 ills. in color, 1 third-page map, Apr., 1937.

Styria, a Favored Vacation Land of Central Europe. By Melville Bell Grosvenor. Vol. LXII, pp. 430-439, 14 ills. in color, Oct., 1932.

Summering in Styria, Austria's Rural Playground. 14 ills. in color from natural-color photographs by Hans Hildenbrand. Vol. LXII, pp. 430-439, Oct., 1932.

This Was Austria. 18 ills. from photographs. Vol. LXXXVIII, pp. 71-86, July, 1945.

Tyrol, the Happy Mountain Land. 11 ills. in color from natural-color photographs by Hans Hildenbrand. Vol. LXI, pp. 370-379, Mar., 1932.

See also Vienna.

Austrian Album. 13 ills. in color from natural-color photographs by Hans Hildenbrand and Wilhelm Tobien. Vol. LXXI, pp. 457-464, Apr., 1937.

Austrian August—and September. By W. Robert Moore. Vol. LXXIII, pp. 493-524, 11 ills. in black and white, 19 ills. in color, Apr., 1938.

Austrian Kodachromes from a Candid Camera. 19 ills. in color from natural-color photographs by W. Robert Moore. Vol. LXXIII, pp. 501-524, Apr., 1938.

Austria-Hungary. *See* Austria ; Hungary.

Austro-Hungarian Floating Exposition. Vol. XII, p. 164, Apr., 1901.

Austro-Italian Mountain Frontiers. By Florence Craig Albrecht. Vol. XXVII, pp. 321-376, 60 ills., 1 page map, Apr., 1915.

Automobile Industry: An American Art That Has Revolutionized Methods in Manufacturing and Transformed Transportation. By William Joseph Showalter. Vol. XLIV, pp. 337-414, 76 ills., Oct., 1923.

Auvergne, France:

Beauties of France. By Arthur Stanley Riggs. Vol. XXVIII, pp. 391-491, 73 ills. in black and white, 16 ills. in color, 1 half-page map, Nov., 1915.

Avalanches:

Landslides and Rock Avalanches. By Guy Elliott Mitchell. Vol. XXI, pp. 277-287, 6 ills., Apr., 1910.

Avengers (Torpedo Bombers):

Cruise on an Escort Carrier. By Melville Bell Grosvenor. Vol. LXXXIV, pp. 513-546, 14 ills. in black and white, 20 ills. in color, Nov., 1943.

Avengers (Torpedo Bombers)—*Continued*
Take-off for Japan. 22 ills. in color from natural-color photographs. Vol. LXXXVIII, pp. 193-208, Aug., 1945.

Aviation. *See* Aeronautics.

Aviation Cadets, U. S. Navy:
Pocket Carriers Fight the Submarines. 20 ills. in color from U. S. Navy official photographs. Vol. LXXXIV, pp. 521-544, Nov., 1943.

Aviation in Commerce and Defense. By F. Barrows Colton. Vol. LXXVIII, pp. 685-726, 39 ills., Dec., 1940.

Aviation Medicine:
Flying Our Wounded Veterans Home. By Catherine Bell Palmer. Vol. LXXXVIII, pp. 363-384, 17 ills., Sept., 1945.

Healing Arts in Global War: As Weapons Grow Deadlier, Scientific Medicine Pits Its Ever-rising Skill Against Them. By Albert W. Atwood. Vol. LXXXIV, pp. 599-618, 17 ills., Nov., 1943.

New Frontier in the Sky. By F. Barrows Colton. Vol. XC, pp. 379-408, 28 ills., 1 diagram, Sept., 1946.

Aviators. *See* Aeronautics.

Avocet (Ship):
Eclipse Adventures on a Desert Isle (Canton). By Capt. J. F. Hellweg. Vol. LXXII, pp. 377-394, 14 ills., 1 two-thirds-page map, Sept., 1937.

Avon River, England:
Through the Heart of England in a Canadian Canoe. By R. J. Evans. Vol. XLI, pp. 473-497, 26 ills., 1 half-page map, May, 1922.

Awakened Continent to the South of Us. By Elihu Root. Vol. XVIII, pp. 61-72, Jan., 1907.

Awakening of Argentina and Chile: Progress in the Lands That Lie Below Capricorn. By Bailey Willis. Vol. XXX, pp. 121-142, 14 ills., Aug., 1916.

Awe-Inspiring Spectacle of the Valley of Ten Thousand Smokes, Discovered and Explored by National Geographic Society Expeditions. Vol. XXXIII, supplement, Feb., 1918.

Axson, Stockton:
Symbol of Service to Mankind (American National Red Cross). By Stockton Axson. Vol. XXXIII, pp. 375-390, 11 ills., Apr., 1918.

Ayers Rock, Australia:
Earth's Most Primitive People: A Journey with the Aborigines of Central Australia. By Charles P. Mountford. Vol. LXXXIX, pp. 89-112, 10 ills. in black and white, 8 ills. in color, 1 half-page map, Jan., 1946.

Aymará Indians:
Heart of Aymará Land: A Visit to Tiahuanacu, Perhaps the Oldest City of the New World, Lost Beneath the Drifting Sand of Centuries in the Bolivian Highlands. By Stewart E. McMillin. Vol. LI, pp. 213-256, 23 ills. in black and white, 18 ills. in color, 1 half-page map, Feb., 1927.

Aymará Land, Bolivia:
Heart of Aymará Land: A Visit to Tiahuanacu, Perhaps the Oldest City of the New World, Lost Beneath the Drifting Sand of Centuries in the Bolivian Highlands. By Stewart E. McMillin. Vol. LI, pp. 213-256, 23 ills. in black and white, 18 ills. in color, 1 half-page map, Feb., 1927.

Azerbaijan:
British Take Baku. Vol. XXXIV, pp. 163-164, 1 ill., Aug., 1918.

Russia's Orphan Races: Picturesque Peoples Who Cluster on the Southeastern Borderland of the Vast Slav Dominions. By Maynard Owen Williams. Vol. XXXIV, pp. 245-278, 26 ills., 1 page map, Oct., 1918.

Azon Bombs:
Air Power for Peace. By Gen. H. H. Arnold. Vol. LXXXIX, pp. 137-193, 35 ills. in black and white, 28 ills. in color, special map supplement, Feb., 1946.

Azores (Islands), Atlantic Ocean:
American Airmen in the Azores. 10 ills. in color from natural-color photographs. Vol. LXXXIX, pp. 177-184, Feb., 1946.

Azores: Picturesque and Historic Half-Way House of American Transatlantic Aviators. By Arminius T. Haeberle. Vol. XXXV, pp. 514-545, 26 ills., 1 page map, June, 1919.

Azores, Communications Hub of the Atlantic. 13 ills. in color from natural-color photographs by Wilhelm Tobien. Vol. LXVII, pp. 41-48, Jan., 1935.

European Outpost: The Azores. By Harriet Chalmers Adams. Vol. LXVII, pp. 35-66, 25 ills. in black and white, 13 ills. in color, 1 half-page map, Jan., 1935.

New Map of the Atlantic Ocean: Foremost Sea of Commerce Becomes World's Battleground and Its Peaceful Islands Rise to Strategic Importance. By Leo A. Borah and Wellman Chamberlin. Text accompanying special map supplement in colors. Vol. LXXX, pp. 407-418, 9 ills., Sept., 1941.

Aztecs:
Adventuring Down the West Coast of Mexico. By Herbert Corey. Vol. XLII, pp. 449-503, 44 ills., 1 half-page map, Nov., 1922.

Aztecs Under the War God's Reign. 10 ills. in color from paintings by H. M. Herget. Vol. LXXI, pp. 735-742, June, 1937.

Foremost Intellectual Achievement of Ancient America: The Hieroglyphic Inscriptions on the Monuments in the Ruined Cities of Mexico, Guatemala, and Honduras Are Yielding the Secrets of the Maya Civilization. By Sylvanus Griswold Morley. Vol. XLI, pp. 109-130, 27 ills., 17 diagrams, special map supplement in colors, Feb., 1922.

In the Empire of the Aztecs: Mexico City Is Rich in Relics of a People Who Practiced Human Sacrifice, Yet Loved Flowers, Education, and Art. By Frank H. H. Roberts, Jr. Vol. LXXI, pp. 725-750, 14 ills. in black and white, 10 ills. in color, June, 1937.

Aztecs—*Continued*

Interesting Visit to the Ancient Pyramids of San Juan Teotihuacan. By A. C. Galloway. Vol. XXI, pp. 1041-1050, 8 ills., 1 page map, Dec., 1910.

Isthmus of Tehuantepec: The Bridge of the World's Commerce. By Helen Olsson-Seffer. Vol. XXI, pp. 991-1002, 6 ills., Dec., 1910.

Luster of Ancient Mexico. By William H. Prescott. Vol. XXX, pp. 1-32, 22 ills., July, 1916.

Venice of Mexico. By Walter Hough. Vol. XXX, pp. 69-88, 18 ills., July, 1916.

B

B-17's. *See* Flying Fortresses.

B-24's. *See* Liberators.

B-26's. *See* Marauders.

Baalbek, Lebanon:

From Jerusalem to Aleppo. By John D. Whiting. Vol. XXIV, pp. 71-113, 30 ills., 1 half-page map, Jan., 1913.

"Babes in the Woods" (Bears). Vol. XXXII, supplement, Aug., 1917.

Babylonia:

Cradle of Civilization: The Historic Lands Along the Euphrates and Tigris Rivers Where Briton Is Fighting Turk. By James Baikie. Vol. XXIX, pp. 127-162, 25 ills., Feb., 1916.

Excavations at Nippur. Vol. XI, p. 392, Oct., 1900.

Most Historic Lands on Earth. Vol. XXVI, pp. 614-615, 1 page map, Dec., 1914.

New Light on Ancient Ur: Excavations at the Site of the City of Abraham Reveal Geographical Evidence of the Biblical Story of the Flood. By M. E. L. Mallowan. Vol. LXXI, pp. 95-130, 44 ills., 1 three-quarters-page map, Jan., 1930.

Pushing Back History's Horizon: How the Pick and Shovel Are Revealing Civilizations That Were Ancient When Israel Was Young. By Albert T. Clay. Vol. XXIX, pp. 162-216, 47 ills., 1 page map, Feb., 1916.

Where Adam and Eve Lived. By Frederick and Margaret Simpich. Vol. XXVI, pp. 546-588, 35 ills., Dec., 1914.

Back to Afghanistan. By Maynard Owen Williams. Vol. XC, pp. 517-544, 27 ills., 1 page map, Oct., 1946.

Bad Godesberg, Germany. *See* Godesberg.

Bad Lands of South Dakota. By N. H. Darton. Vol. X, pp. 339-343, 4 ills., Sept., 1899.

Baddeck, Nova Scotia:

Charm of Cape Breton Island: The Most Picturesque Portion of Canada's Maritime Provinces—A Land Rich in Historic Associations, Natural Resources, and Geographic Appeal. By Catherine Dunlop MacKenzie. Vol. XXXVIII, pp. 34-60, 22 ills., 1 three-quarters-page map, July, 1920.

Baddeck, Nova Scotia—*Continued*

Salty Nova Scotia: In Friendly New Scotland Gaelic Songs Still Answer the Skirling Bagpipes. By Andrew H. Brown. Vol. LXXVII, pp. 575-624, 30 ills. in black and white, 21 ills. in color, 1 two-page map, May, 1940.

Baden (State), Germany:

Wandering Through the Black Forest. 13 ills. in color from autochromes by Hans Hildenbrand. Vol. LIV, pp. 658-667, Dec., 1928.

Badges, Military and Naval:

Decorations, Medals, Service Ribbons, Badges, and Women's Insignia. Vol. LXXXIV, pp. 414-444, 6 ills. in black and white, 376 ills. in color, Oct., 1943.

Baffin Island, Canada:

Servicing Arctic Airbases. By Robert A. Bartlett. Vol. LXXXIX, pp. 602-616, 3 ills. in black and white, 10 ills. in color, 1 half-page map, May, 1946.

Voyage of the *Morrissey*. 10 ills. in color from natural-color photographs by Daniel S. Turner and Sherman A. Wengerd. Vol. LXXXIX, pp. 609-616, May, 1946.

Baffinland (Island), Canada:

Dr. Bell's Survey in Baffinland. By W J McGee. Vol. XIII, p. 113, Mar., 1902.

Bag of Bird Portraits. 24 ills. in color from natural-color photographs; 23 ills. by Arthur A. Allen. Vol. LXXXV, pp. 697-712, June, 1944.

Bagg, Ethel Mather:

Letters from the Italian Front. By Marchesa Louise de Rosales to Ethel Mather Bagg. Vol. XXXII, pp. 46-67, 22 ills., July, 1917.

Baghdad, Iraq:

Travels in Arabia and Along the Persian Gulf. By David G. Fairchild. Vol. XV, pp. 139-151, 20 ills., Apr., 1904.

Where Adam and Eve Lived. By Frederick and Margaret Simpich. Vol. XXVI, pp. 546-588, 35 ills., Dec., 1914.

Bahama Islands, West Indies:

Bahama Holiday. By Frederick Simpich. Vol. LXIX, pp. 219-245, 29 ills., 1 half-page map, Feb., 1936.

Coral Castle Builders of Tropic Seas. By Roy Waldo Miner. Vol. LXV, pp. 703-728, 15 ills. in black and white, 8 ills. in color, 1 two-thirds-page and 1 third-page maps, June, 1934.

Devil-Fishing in the Gulf Stream. By John Oliver La Gorce. Vol. XXXV, pp. 476-488, 7 ills., June, 1919.

Bahia, Brazil. *See* Salvador.

Bahrein Islands, Persian Gulf:

Bahrein: Port of Pearls and Petroleum. By Maynard Owen Williams. Vol. LXXXIX, pp. 195-210, 6 ills. in black and white, 11 ills. in color, 1 half-page map, Feb., 1946.

Oil Comes to Bahrein, Port of Pearls. 11 ills. in color from natural-color photographs by Maynard Owen Williams. Vol. LXXXIX, pp. 201-208, Feb., 1946.

Bahrein Islands, Persian Gulf—*Continued*
Rise of the New Arab Nation. By Frederick Simpich. Vol. XXXVI, pp. 369-393, 17 ills., 1 page map, Nov., 1919.

Baikal, Lake, U. S. S. R.:
Western Siberia and the Altai Mountains : With Some Speculations on the Future of Siberia. By James Bryce. Vol. XXXIX, pp. 469-507, 39 ills., May, 1921.

Baikie, James:
Cradle of Civilization : The Historic Lands Along the Euphrates and Tigris Rivers Where Briton Is Fighting Turk. By James Baikie. Vol. XXIX, pp. 127-162, 25 ills., Feb., 1916.

Resurrection of Ancient Egypt. By James Baikie. Vol. XXIV, pp. 957-1020, 46 ills., 1 page map, Sept., 1913.

Sea-Kings of Crete. By James Baikie. Vol. XXIII, pp. 1-25, 13 ills., Jan., 1912.

Bailey, Alfred M.:
Birds and Beasts of Mexico's Desert Islands. 12 ills. in color from natural-color photographs ; 8 ills. by Ed N. Harrison ; 4 ills. by Alfred M. Bailey and Robert J. Niedrach. Vol. LXXX, pp. 353-360, Sept., 1941.

Cruise of the *Kinkajou:* Among Desert Islands of Mexico Voyagers Find Outdoor Laboratories for the Naturalist and Ideal Fishing Grounds for the Sportsman. By Alfred M. Bailey. Vol. LXXX, pp. 339-366, 13 ills. in black and white, 12 ills. in color, 1 page map, Sept., 1941.

High Country of Colorado. By Alfred M. Bailey. With 23 ills. in color from natural-color photographs by the author, Robert J. Niedrach, and F. G. Brandenburg. Vol. XC, pp. 43-72, 9 ills. in black and white, July, 1946.

Nature and Man in Ethiopia. By Wilfred H. Osgood. Vol. LIV, pp. 121-176, 64 ills., 1 two-thirds-page map, Aug., 1928.
Contains photographs by the author and Alfred M. Bailey, a member of the Abyssinian Expedition of 1926-1927.

Bailey, Solon I.:
New Peruvian Route to the Plain of the Amazon. By Solon I. Bailey. Vol. XVII, pp. 432-448, 12 ills., Aug., 1906.

Bailey, Truman:
Samoa—South Sea Outpost of the U. S. Navy. 20 ills. from photographs by Truman Bailey. Vol. LXXIX, pp. 615-630, May, 1941.

Bailey, Vernon:
Bats of the Carlsbad Cavern. By Vernon Bailey. Vol. XLVIII, pp. 321-330, 11 ills., Sept., 1925.

Bainbridge, Oliver:
Chinese Jews. By Oliver Bainbridge. Vol. XVIII, pp. 621-632, 7 ills., Oct., 1907.

Baja California (Lower California), Mexico :
Adventuring Down the West Coast of Mexico. By Herbert Corey. Vol. XLII, pp. 449-503, 44 ills., 1 half-page map, Nov., 1922.

Baja California (Lower California), Mexico—*Continued*
Baja California Wakes Up. By Frederick Simpich. Vol. LXXXII, pp. 253-275, 19 ills., 1 page map, Aug., 1942.

Cruise Among Desert Islands. By G. Dallas Hanna and A. W. Anthony. Vol. XLIV, pp. 71-99, 32 ills., 1 quarter-page map, July, 1923.

Cruise of the *Kinkajou:* Among Desert Islands of Mexico Voyagers Find Outdoor Laboratories for the Naturalist and Ideal Fishing Grounds for the Sportsman. By Alfred M. Bailey. Vol. LXXX, pp. 339-366, 13 ills. in black and white, 12 ills. in color, 1 page map, Sept., 1941.

Land of Drought and Desert—Lower California : Two Thousand Miles on Horseback Through the Most Extraordinary Cacti Forests in the World. By E. W. Nelson. Vol. XXII, pp. 443-474, 25 ills., 1 page and 1 half-page maps, May, 1911.

Mexican Land of Canaan : Marvelous Riches of the Wonderful West Coast of Our Neighbor Republic. By Frederick Simpich. Vol. XXXVI, pp. 307-330, 16 ills., 1 page map, Oct., 1919.

Baker, Marcus:
Anglo-Venezuelan Boundary Dispute. By Marcus Baker. Vol. XI, pp. 129-144, 2 ills., 1 page map, Apr., 1900.

Lost Boundary of Texas. By Marcus Baker. Vol. XII, pp. 430-432, Dec., 1901.

Marcus Baker (Memorial Address by William H. Dall). Vol. XV, pp. 40-43, 1 ill., Jan. 1904.

National Geographic Society's Eclipse Expedition to Norfolk, Virginia. By Marcus Baker. Vol. XI, p. 320, Aug., 1900.

Sarichef's Atlas, 1826. By Marcus Baker. Vol. XIII, pp. 86-92, Mar., 1902.

Baker, Newton D.:
America's Duty. By Newton D. Baker. Vol. XXXI, pp. 453-457, 4 ills., May, 1917.

Baker, Roy W.:
Balearics, Island Sisters of the Mediterranean. By Roy W. Baker. Vol. LIV, pp. 177-206, 11 ills. in black and white, 29 ills. in color, 1 quarter-page map, Aug., 1928.

Bakhtiari (Tribespeople) :
Mountain Tribes of Iran and Iraq. By Harold Lamb. Vol. LXXXIX, pp. 385-408, 15 ills., 1 two-page map, Mar., 1946.

Bakluzan Dere (Tribespeople) :
Cone-Dwellers of Asia Minor : A Primitive People Who Live in Nature-Made Apartment Houses, Fashioned by Volcanic Violence and Trickling Streams. By J. R. Sitlington Sterrett. Vol. XXXV, pp. 281-331, 52 ills., 1 half-page map, Apr., 1919.

Baku, U. S. S. R.:
British Take Baku. Vol. XXXIV, pp. 163-164, 1 ill., Aug., 1918.

Russia's Orphan Races : Picturesque Peoples Who Cluster on the Southeastern Borderland of the Vast Slav Dominions. By Maynard Owen Williams. Vol. XXXIV, pp. 245-278, 26 ills., 1 page map, Oct., 1918.

Balaton, Lake, Hungary:
Hungary, a Kingdom Without a King: A Tour from Central Europe's Largest Lake to the Fertile Plains of the Danube and the Tisza. By Elizabeth P. Jacobi. Vol. LXI, pp. 691-728, 22 ills. in black and white, 27 ills. in color, 1 half-page map, June, 1932.

Balch, Edwin Swift:
Highest Camps and Climbs. By Edwin Swift Balch. Vol. XVII, p. 713, Dec., 1906.

Termination Land (Antarctica). By Edwin Swift Balch. Vol. XV, pp. 220-221, May, 1940.

Baldwin, Evelyn B.:
Baldwin-Ziegler Arctic Expedition. Vol. XIII, pp. 358-359, Sept., 1902.

Meteorological Observations of the Second Wellman Expedition. By Evelyn B. Baldwin. Vol. X, pp. 512-516, Dec., 1899.

Balearic Islands, Spain:
Balearics, Island Sisters of the Mediterranean. By Roy W. Baker. Vol. LIV, pp. 177-206, 11 ills. in black and white, 29 ills. in color, 1 quarter-page map, Aug., 1928.

Keeping House in Majorca. By Phoebe Binney Harnden. Vol. XLV, pp. 425-440, 18 ills., 1 quarter-page map, Apr., 1924.

Spain's Enchanted Isles. 29 ills. in color from autochromes by Gervais Courtellemont. Vol. LIV, pp. 182-199, Aug., 1928.

Balfour, Arthur J.:
Oldest Free Assemblies: Address of Right Hon. Arthur J. Balfour in the United States House of Representatives, May 5, 1917. Vol. XXXI, pp. 368-371, Apr., 1917.

Bali (Island), Netherlands Indies:
Artist Adventures on the Island of Bali. By Franklin Price Knott. Vol. LIII, pp. 326-347, 20 ills. in color, Mar., 1928.

Bali, Gem of the Netherlands Indies. 11 ills. in color from natural-color photographs; 10 ills. by Maynard Owen Williams. Vol. LXXV, pp. 329-336, Mar., 1939.

Bali and Points East: Crowded, Happy Isles of the Flores Sea Blend Rice Terraces, Dance Festivals, and Amazing Music in Their Pattern of Living. By Maynard Owen Williams. Vol. LXXV, pp. 313-352, 33 ills. in black and white, 11 ills. in color, 1 two-thirds-page map, Mar., 1939.

Ways and Byways of an Island Paradise. 9 ills. from photographs. Vol. LXXV, pp. 345-352, Mar., 1939.

Balim (River), Netherlands New Guinea:
"Shangri-la" in Panorama. 7 ills. in color from natural-color photographs by Ray T. Elsmore. Vol. LXXXVIII, pp. 681-688, Dec., 1945.

Balkan Peninsula:
Changing Map in the Balkans. By Frederick Moore. Vol. XXIV, pp. 199-226, 27 ills., 1 page map, Feb., 1913.

Balkan Peninsula—*Continued*
Danube, Highway of Races: From the Black Forest to the Black Sea, Europe's Most Important River Has Borne the Traffic of Centuries. By Melville Chater. Vol. LVI, pp. 643-697, 54 ills., Dec., 1929.

Great Turk and His Lost Provinces. By William E. Curtis. Vol. XIV, pp. 45-61, 7 ills., Feb., 1903.

Map of Europe Including the New Balkan States. Text accompanying special map supplement in colors. Vol. XXVI, pp. 191-192, Aug., 1914.

New Map of Europe: Showing the Boundaries Established by the Peace Conference at Paris and by Subsequent Decisions of the Supreme Council of the Allied and Associated Powers. By Ralph A. Graves. Text accompanying special map supplement in colors. Vol. XXXIX, pp. 157-177, 18 ills., Feb., 1921.

Races of Europe. By Edwin A. Grosvenor. Vol. XXXIV, pp. 441-534, 62 ills., 2 page maps, special map supplement, Dec., 1918.

Two Possible Solutions for the Eastern Problem. By James Bryce. Vol. XXIII, pp. 1149-1157, 5 ills., 1 page map, Nov., 1912.

Whirlpool of the Balkans. By George Higgins Moses. Vol. XXXIX, pp. 179-197, 15 ills., Feb., 1921.

See also Albania; Bulgaria; Greece; Turkey; Yugoslavia.

Ball, (Capt.) Albert:
Tales of the British Air Service. By Maj. William A. Bishop. Vol. XXXIII, pp. 27-37, 12 ills., Jan., 1918.

Ball, J. H.:
Surf-Boarders Capture California. 8 ills. from photographs by J. H. Ball. Vol. LXXXVI, pp. 355-362, Sept., 1944.

Ball, (Sir) Robert:
Eruption of Krakatoa. By Sir Robert Ball. Vol. XIII, pp. 200-204, June, 1902.

Ballantine, Joseph W.:
I Lived on Formosa. By Joseph W. Ballantine. Vol. LXXXVII, pp. 1-24, 19 ills., 1 page and 1 half-page maps, Jan., 1945.

Ballard, Walter J.:
Australia's Future. By Walter J. Ballard. Vol. XVI, pp. 570-571, Dec., 1905.

European Populations. By Walter J. Ballard. Vol. XVI, p. 432, Sept. 1905.

Population of Japan. By Walter J. Ballard. Vol. XVI, p. 482, Oct., 1905.

Ballestas (Islands), Peru:
Peru's Wealth-Producing Birds: Vast Riches in the Guano Deposits of Cormorants, Pelicans, and Petrels Which Nest on Her Barren, Rainless Coast. By R. E. Coker. Vol. XXXVII, pp. 537-566, 28 ills., June, 1920.

Ballooning in the Stratosphere: Two Balloon Ascents to Ten-Mile Altitudes Presage New Mode of Aërial Travel. By Auguste Piccard. Vol. LXIII, pp. 353-384, 34 ills., Mar., 1933.

Balloons. *See* Aeronautics.

Balmat, Jacques:
Ascent of Mont Blanc. By Walter Woodburn Hyde. Vol. XXIV, pp. 861-942, 69 ills., Aug., 1913.

Balogh, Rudolf:
Rural Hungarian Rhapsody. 20 ills. in color from natural-color photographs by Rudolf Balogh and Hans Hildenbrand. Vol. LXXIII, pp. 17-48, Jan., 1938.

Yugoslavia : Where Oriental Hues Splash Europe. 34 ills. in color from natural-color photographs by Konstantin J. Kostich and Rudolf Balogh. Vol. LXXV, pp. 699-738, June, 1939.

Balsas, Río, Mexico :
Down Mexico's Río Balsas. By John W. Webber. With 9 ills. in color from natural-color photographs by the author, Kenneth Segerstrom, and Jack Breed. Vol. XC, pp. 253-272, 5 ills. in black and white, 1 half-page map, Aug., 1946.

Baltic Region, Europe :
Estonia : At Russia's Baltic Gate : War Often Has Ravaged This Little Nation Whose Identity Was Long Submerged in the Vast Sea of Russian Peoples. By Baroness Irina Ungern-Sternberg. Vol. LXXVI, pp. 803-834, 33 ills., 1 half-page map, Dec., 1939.

Flying Around the Baltic. By Douglas Chandler. Vol. LXXIII, pp. 767-806, 31 ills. in black and white, 13 ills. in duotone, 1 half-page map, June, 1938.
See also names of individual countries and cities.

Baltimore, Maryland :
Colossal Work in Baltimore. By Calvin W. Hendrick. Vol. XX, pp. 365-373, 6 ills., Apr., 1909.

Maryland Presents—— By W. Robert Moore. Vol. LXXIX, pp. 401-448, 17 ills. in black and white, 32 ills. in color, 1 map (two-page spread), Apr., 1941.

Maytime in the Heart of Maryland (Sherwood Gardens). 10 ills. in color from natural-color photographs by B. Anthony Stewart and Charles Martin. Vol. LXXIX, pp. 441-448, Apr., 1941.

Old Line State Cyclorama. 22 ills. in color from natural-color photographs by W. Robert Moore, B. Anthony Stewart, and others. Vol. LXXIX, pp. 409-432, Apr., 1941.

Baluchistan (Province), India :
Adventures With a Camera in Many Lands. By Maynard Owen Williams. Vol. XL, pp. 87-112, 24 ills., July, 1921.

Bambalas (Tribespeople) :
Curious and Characteristic Customs of Central African Tribes (Belgian Congo). By E. Torday. Vol. XXXVI, pp. 342-368, 35 ills., Oct., 1919.

Bamboos (Plants) :
Lessons from Japan. Vol. XV, pp. 221-225, 3 ills., May, 1904.

New Plant Immigrants. By David Fairchild. Vol. XXII, pp. 879-907, 34 ills., Oct., 1911.

Bamian (Region), Afghanistan :
Back to Afghanistan. By Maynard Owen Williams. Vol. XC, pp. 517-544, 27 ills., 1 page map, Oct., 1946.

Bampton, England :
England's Wild Moorland Ponies. 10 ills. from photographs. Vol. LXXXIX, pp. 129-136, Jan., 1946.

Bananas (Fruit) :
Costa Rica, Land of the Banana. By Paul B. Popenoe. Vol. XLI, pp. 201-220, 17 ills., Feb., 1922.

How the World Is Fed. By William Joseph Showalter. Vol. XXIX, pp. 1-110, 101 ills., Jan., 1916.

Land of the Painted Oxcarts (Costa Rica). By Luis Marden. With 31 ills. in color from natural-color photographs by the author. Vol. XC, pp. 409-456, 30 ills. in black and white, 1 half-page map, Oct., 1946.

Where Our Bananas Come From (Costa Rica). By Edwin R. Fraser. Vol. XXIII, pp. 713-730, 14 ills., July, 1912.

Bandai-San (Mountain), Japan :
Do Volcanic Explosions Affect Our Climate? By C. G. Abbot. Vol. XXIV, pp. 181-198, 9 ills., 1 diagram, Feb., 1913.

Bangkok, Siam :
Ancient Temples and Modern Guns in Thailand. 10 ills. from photographs ; 6 ills. by Maynard Owen Williams. Vol. LXXX, pp. 653-660, Nov., 1941.

Coronation of His Majesty King Maha-Vajira-vudh of Siam. By Col. Lea Febiger. Vol. XXIII, pp. 389-416, 25 ills., Apr., 1912.

Hunting the Chaulmoogra Tree. By Joseph F. Rock. Vol. XLI, pp. 243-276, 39 ills., 1 page map, Mar., 1922.

"Land of the Free" in Asia : Siam Has Blended New With Old in Her Progressive March to Modern Statehood in the Family of Nations. By W. Robert Moore. Vol. LXV, pp. 531-576, 28 ills. in black and white, 26 ills. in color, 1 two-thirds-page map, May, 1934.

Temples and Ceremonies of Kaleidoscopic Bangkok. 12 ills. in color from natural-color photographs by Amos Burg, Gervais Courtellemont, and W. Robert Moore. Vol. LXV, pp. 547-554, May, 1934.

Banishing the Devil of Disease Among the Nashi : Weird Ceremonies Performed by an Aboriginal Tribe in the Heart of Yünnan Province, China. By Joseph F. Rock. Vol. XLVI, pp. 473-499, 26 ills., 1 half-page map, Nov., 1924.

Banninga, John J.:
Indian Census of 1911. By John J. Banninga. Vol. XXII, pp. 633-638, 4 ills., July, 1911.

Marriage of the Gods (Religious Festival). By John J. Banninga. Vol. XXIV, pp. 1314-1330, 16 ills., Dec., 1913.

Banquets. *See* National Geographic Society : Banquets.

Barbados (Island), West Indies:

British West Indian Interlude. By Anne Rainey Langley. Vol. LXXIX, pp. 1-46, 23 ills. in black and white, 21 ills. in color, 2 page maps, Jan., 1941.

West Indies Links in a Defense Chain. 21 ills. in color from natural-color photographs; 20 ills. by Edwin L. Wisherd. Vol. LXXIX, pp. 9-32, Jan., 1941.

Barbour, Thomas:

Further Notes on Dutch New Guinea. By Thomas Barbour. Vol. XIX, pp. 527-545, 19 ills., Aug., 1908.

Notes on a Zoölogical Collecting Trip to Dutch New Guinea. By Thomas Barbour. Vol. XIX, pp. 469-484, 12 ills., 2 page maps, July, 1908.

Notes on Burma. By Thomas Barbour. Vol. XX, pp. 841-866, 34 ills., Oct., 1909.

Barbour, William R.:

Buenos Aires and Its River of Silver: A Journey Up the Paraná and Paraguay to the Chaco Cattle Country. By William R. Barbour. Vol. XL, pp. 393-432, 38 ills., Oct., 1921.

Barcelona, Spain:

Barcelona, Pride of the Catalans. By Harriet Chalmers Adams. Vol. LV, pp. 373-402, 32 ills., Mar., 1929.

See also Montserrat (Shrine).

Bare Feet and Burros of Haiti. By Oliver P. Newman. Vol. LXXXVI, pp. 307-328, 10 ills. in black and white, 10 ills. in color, 1 half-page map, Sept., 1944.

Barnes, A. H.:

Beauty Spots in the United States. 4 ills. in color from photographs by A. H. Barnes. Vol. XXIX, pp. 406-409, Apr., 1916.

Great White Monarch of the Pacific Northwest (Mount Rainier). By A. H. Barnes. Vol. XXIII, pp. 593-626, 31 ills., 1 half-page map, June, 1912.

Barra, Francisco Leon de la:

In Honor of the Army and Aviation (Speech by Senor de la Barra). Vol. XXII, pp. 267-284, Mar., 1911.

Barrage of the Nile. By Day Allen Willey. Vol. XXI, pp. 175-184, 14 ills., Feb., 1910.

Barrett, Charles:

Great Barrier Reef and Its Isles: The Wonder and Mystery of Australia's World-Famous Geographical Feature. By Charles Barrett. Vol. LVIII, pp. 355-384, 38 ills., 1 half-page map, Sept., 1930.

Barrett, John:

China: Her History and Development. By John Barrett. Vol. XII, pp. 209-218, June, 1901.

China: Her History and Development. By John Barrett. Vol. XII, pp. 266-272, July, 1901.

Discovery of the North Pole (Speech by John Barrett). Vol. XXI, pp. 63-82, Jan., 1910.

Latin America and Colombia. By John Barrett. Vol. XVII, pp. 692-709, 10 ills., Dec., 1906.

Barrett, John—*Continued*

Philippine Islands and Their Environment. By John Barrett. Vol. XI, pp. 1-14, Jan., 1900.

Barrett, O. W.:

Impressions and Scenes of Mozambique. By O. W. Barrett. Vol. XXI, pp. 807-830, 31 ills., Oct., 1910.

Barro Colorado Island, Panama Canal Zone:

Who Treads Our Trails? A Camera Trapper Describes His Experiences on an Island in the Canal Zone, a Natural-History Laboratory in the American Tropics. By Frank M. Chapman. Vol. LII, pp. 331-345, 18 ills., 1 half-page map, Sept., 1927.

Barrows, David P.:

Colorado Desert. By David P. Barrows. Vol. XI, pp. 336-351, 4 ills., 1 page map, Sept., 1900.

Bartimeus (pseudonym):

Malta Invicta. By Bartimeus (A Captain in the Royal Navy). Vol. LXXXIII, pp. 375-400, 27 ills., 1 half-page map, Mar., 1943.

Bartlett, Charles H.:

Untoured Burma. By Charles H. Bartlett. Vol. XXIV, pp. 835-853, 17 ills., July, 1913.

Bartlett, (Capt.) Robert A.:

Discovery of the North Pole (Presentation of Hubbard Gold Medal to Captain Bartlett). Vol. XXI, pp. 63-82, Jan., 1910.

Greenland from 1898 to Now: "Captain Bob," Who Went North with Peary, Tells of 42 Years of Exploration in the Orphan Island of New Aerial and Naval Interest. By Robert A. Bartlett. Vol. LXXVIII, pp. 111-140, 25 ills., 1 two-page map, July, 1940.

Resolution Awarding Medal to Captain Bartlett. Vol. XX, p. 1009, Nov., 1909.

Sealing Saga of Newfoundland. By Capt. Robert A. Bartlett. Vol. LVI, pp. 91-130, 44 ills., July, 1929.

Servicing Arctic Airbases. By Robert A. Bartlett. Vol. LXXXIX, pp. 602-616, 3 ills. in black and white, 10 ills. in color, 1 half-page map, May, 1946.

Barton, Otis:

Half Mile Down: Strange Creatures, Beautiful and Grotesque as Figments of Fancy, Reveal Themselves at Windows of the Bathysphere. By William Beebe. Vol. LXVI, pp. 661-704, 28 ills. in black and white, 16 ills. in color, 1 third-page map, Dec., 1934.

Basques (People):

Land of the Basques: Home of a Thrifty, Picturesque People, Who Take Pride in the Sobriquet, "The Yankees of Spain." By Harry A. McBride. Vol. XLI, pp. 63-87, 25 ills., 1 three-quarters-page map, Jan., 1922.

Races of Europe. By Edwin A. Grosvenor. Vol. XXXIV, pp. 441-534, 62 ills., 2 page maps, special map supplement in colors, Dec., 1918.

Basra, Iraq:

From London to Australia by Aëroplane: A Personal Narrative of the First Aërial Voyage Half Around the World. By Sir Ross Smith. Vol. XXXIX, pp. 229-339, 76 ills. in black and white, 8 ills. in color, 1 page map, Mar., 1921.

Bassaris (Tribespeople):

Dusky Tribesmen of French West Africa. 26 ills. in color from natural-color photographs by Enzo de Chetelat. Vol. LXXIX, pp. 639-662, May, 1941.

Batak Highlands, Sumatra:

By Motor Through the East Coast and Batak Highlands of Sumatra. By Melvin A. Hall. Vol. XXXVII, pp. 68-102, 27 ills., Jan., 1920.

Batavia, Java:

Java Assignment. By Dee Bredin. Vol. LXXXI, pp. 89-119, 32 ills., 1 two-thirds-page map, Jan., 1942.

Traveler's Notes on Java. By Henry G. Bryant. Vol. XXI, pp. 91-111, 17 ills., Feb., 1910.

Batchelder, A. G.:

Immediate Necessity for Military Highways. By A. G. Batchelder. Vol. XXXII, pp. 477-499, 22 ills., Nov.-Dec., 1917.

Bathing and Burning Ghats at Benares. By Eliza R. Scidmore. Vol. XVIII, pp. 118-128, 7 ills., Feb., 1907.

Bathymetrical Survey of the Fresh-Water Lakes of England. Vol. XII, p. 408, Nov., 1901.

Bathysphere:

Half Mile Down: Strange Creatures, Beautiful and Grotesque as Figments of Fancy, Reveal Themselves at Windows of the Bathysphere. By William Beebe. Vol. LXVI, pp. 661-704, 28 ills. in black and white, 16 ills. in color, 1 third-page map, Dec., 1934.

Round Trip to Davy Jones's Locker: Peering into Mysteries a Quarter Mile Down in the Open Sea, by Means of the Bathysphere. By William Beebe. Vol. LIX, pp. 653-678, 14 ills. in black and white, 8 ills. in color, 1 quarter-page map, June, 1931.

Bats:

Bats of the Carlsbad Cavern (New Mexico). By Vernon Bailey. Vol. XLVIII, pp. 321-330, 11 ills., Sept., 1925.

Mexican Land of Canaan: Marvelous Riches of the Wonderful West Coast of Our Neighbor Republic. By Frederick Simpich. Vol. XXXVI, pp. 307-330, 16 ills., 1 page map, Oct., 1919.

Mystery Mammals of the Twilight. By Donald R. Griffin. Vol. XC, pp. 117-134, 19 ills., July, 1946.

Nature's Transformation at Panama: The Remarkable Changes in Faunal and Physical Conditions in the Gatun Lake Region. By George Shiras, 3d. Vol. XXVIII, pp. 159-194, 33 ills., 2 page maps, Aug., 1915.

Battle Glacier, Canada:

Some Tramps Across the Glaciers and Snowfields of British Columbia. By Howard Palmer. Vol. XXI, pp. 457-487, 25 ills., June, 1910.

Battle-Gound of Nature: The Atlantic Seaboard. By John Oliver La Gorce. Vol. XXXIII, pp. 511-546, 23 ills., 4 half-page maps, June, 1918.

Battle-Line of Languages in Western Europe: A Problem in Human Geography More Perplexing Than That of International Boundaries. By A. L. Guerard. Vol. XLIII, pp. 145-180, 36 ills., Feb., 1923.

Battlefields:

Armistice Day and the American Battle Fields. By J. J. Jusserand. Vol. LVI, pp. 509-554, 32 ills. in black and white, 23 ills. in color, Nov., 1929.

Battle Fields of France Eleven Years After. 23 ills. in color from autochromes by Gervais Courtellemont. Vol. LVI, pp. 522-539, Nov., 1929.

Most Famous Battle Field in America (Gettysburg). 14 ills. in color from natural-color photographs by Clifton Adams and Orren R. Louden. Vol. LX, pp. 66-75, July, 1931.

Our National War Memorials in Europe. By Gen. John J. Pershing. Vol. LXV, pp. 1-36, 24 ills. in black and white, 11 ills. in color, 1 half-page map, Jan., 1934.

"Time Will Not Dim the Glory of Their Deeds." 11 ills. in color from natural-color photographs by W. Robert Moore. Vol. LXV, pp. 17-24, Jan., 1934.

Battleships:

Battleship *Missouri* Comes of Age. 11 ills. in color from U. S. Navy official photographs. Vol. LXXXVII, pp. 353-360, Mar., 1945.

Ships That Won the Greatest Naval War. 26 ills. in color from U. S. Navy official photographs. Vol. LXXXIX, pp. 697-736, June, 1946.

Victory's Portrait in the Marianas. By Lt. William Franklin Draper, USNR. With 17 ills. in color from paintings by the author. Vol. LXXXVIII, pp. 599-616, Nov., 1945.

Your Navy as Peace Insurance. By Fleet Admiral Chester W. Nimitz. Vol. LXXXIX, pp. 681-736, 32 ills. in black and white, 26 ills. in color, June, 1946.

Battling with the Panama Slides. By William Joseph Showalter. Vol. XXV, pp. 133-153, 15 ills., Feb., 1914.

Bauer, (Dr.) L. A.:

Magnetic Survey of Africa. By Dr. L. A. Bauer. Vol. XX, pp. 291-297, 6 ills., Mar., 1909.

Magnetic Survey of the Pacific Ocean. By Dr. L. A. Bauer. Vol. XVII, p. 237, Apr., 1906.

Magnetic Survey of the United States. By Dr. L. A. Bauer. Vol. XIII, pp. 92-95, 1 half-page map, Mar., 1902.

Bauer, (Dr.) L. A.—*Continued*

Magnetic Work of the Coast and Geodetic Survey. By Dr. L. A. Bauer. Vol. X, pp. 288-289, Aug., 1899.

Most Curious Craft Afloat : The Compass in Navigation and the Work of the Non-Magnetic Yacht *Carnegie*. By Dr. L. A. Bauer. Vol. XXI, pp. 223-245, 31 ills., Mar., 1910.

San Francisco Earthquake of April 18, 1906, as Recorded by the Coast and Geodetic Survey Magnetic Observatories. By Dr. L. A. Bauer and J. E. Burbank. Vol. XVII, pp. 298-300, May, 1906.

Work in the Pacific Ocean of the Magnetic Survey Yacht *Galilee*. By Dr. L. A. Bauer. Vol. XVIII, pp. 601-611, 15 ills., Sept., 1907.

Bauer, Siegbert:

Behind the Scenes in the Home of the Passion Play (Oberammergau, Germany). 11 ills. in color from natural-color photographs ; 4 ills. by Siegbert Bauer. Vol. LXVIII, pp. 753-760, Dec., 1935.

Baum, Ohio :

Indian Village of Baum. By H. C. Brown. Vol. XII, pp. 272-274, July, 1901.

Bavaria (Region), Germany :

Beauty of the Bavarian Alps. By Col. Fitzhugh Lee Minnigerode. Vol. XLIX, pp. 632-649, 16 ills. in color, June, 1926.

From Chalet to Palace in Bavaria. 14 ills. in color from autochromes by Hans Hildenbrand. Vol. LIV, pp. 602-601, Dec., 1928.

Races of Europe. By Edwin A. Grosvenor. Vol. XXXIV, pp. 441-534, 62 ills., 2 page maps, special map supplement, Dec., 1918.

See also Dinkelsbühl ; Nördlingen ; Oberammergau ; Rothenburg.

Bayeux Tapestry:

Beauties of France. By Arthur Stanley Riggs. Vol. XXVIII, pp. 391-491, 73 ills. in black and white, 16 ills. in color, 1 half-page map, Nov., 1915.

Baynes, Ernest Harold:

Mankind's Best Friend (Dog) : Companion of His Solitude, Advance Guard in the Hunt and Ally of the Trenches. By Ernest Harold Baynes. Vol. XXXV, pp. 185-201, 11 ills., Mar., 1919.

Our Common Dogs. By Ernest Harold Baynes and Louis Agassiz Fuertes. Vol. XXXV, pp. 201-253, 73 ills. in color, Mar., 1919.

Bazaars:

Peiping's Happy New Year : Lunar Celebration Attracts Throngs to Temple Fairs, Motley Bazaars, and Age-old Festivities. By George Kin Leung. Vol. LXX, pp. 749-792, 31 ills. in black and white, 16 ills. in color, Dec., 1936.

BB (Boat) :

Experimental boat of Dr. Alexander Graham Bell, driven by aërial propellers. Vol. XVIII, ill. 671, Oct., 1907.

Beaches and Bathers of the Jersey Shore. 11 ills. in color from natural-color photographs by Edwin L. Wisherd. Vol. LXIII, pp. 534-543, May, 1933.

Beacons of the Sea. By George R. Putnam. Vol. XXIV, pp. 1-53, 65 ills., 1 three-quarters-page map, 2 diagrams, Jan., 1913.

Beaconsfield, England : Toy Town :

Bekonscot, England's Toy-Size Town. By Andrew H. Brown and B. Anthony Stewart. Vol. LXXI, pp. 649-661, 2 ills. in black and white, 15 ills. in color, May, 1937.

Tableaux in an English Lilliput. 15 ills. in color from natural-color photographs by B. Anthony Stewart. Vol. LXXI, pp. 653-660, May, 1937.

Beam, George L.:

Prehistoric Ruin of Tsankawi (New Mexico). By George L. Beam. Vol. XX, pp. 807-822, 12 ills., Sept., 1909.

Bearing of Physiography Upon Suess' Theories. By William M. Davis. Vol. XV, p. 430, Oct., 1904.

Bears:

Alaskan Brown Bear. By Wilfred H. Osgood. Vol. XX, pp. 332-333, Apr., 1909.

Alaskan Brown Bear : The Largest Carnivorous Animal Extant. Vol. XXX, colored supplement, Nov., 1916.

"Babes in the Woods." Vol. XXXII, supplement, Aug., 1917.

Bear Hunt. Vol. XIX, p. 222, Mar., 1908.

Bear Hunt in Montana. By Arthur Alvord Stiles. Vol. XIX, pp. 149-154, 5 ills., Feb., 1908.

Big Game of Alaska. By Wilfred H. Osgood. Vol. XX, pp. 624-636, 10 ills., July, 1909.

Hunting Bears on Horseback. By Alan D. Wilson. Vol. XIX, pp. 350-356, 4 ills., May, 1908.

Hunting the Great Brown Bear of Alaska. By George Mixter, 2d. Vol. XX, pp. 313-332, 35 ills., Apr., 1909.

Hunting the Grizzly in British Columbia. By Joseph Wendle. Vol. XVIII, pp. 612-615, 3 ills., Sept., 1907.

Larger North American Mammals. By Edward W. Nelson. Vol. XXX, pp. 385-472, 24 ills. in black and white, 50 ills. in color, Nov., 1916.

Lords of the Rockies : Photographing Big Game Animals in Their Primeval Surroundings; from Arizona to Canada, Brings Adventure to Two Wilderness Wanderers. By Wendell and Lucie Chapman. Vol. LXXVI, pp. 87-128, 14 ills. in black and white, 28 ills. in color, July, 1939.

Once in a Lifetime : Black Bears Rarely Have Quadruplets, But Goofy Did—and the Camera Caught Her Nursing Her Remarkable Family. By Paul B. Kinney. Vol. LXXX, pp. 249-258, 11 ills., Aug., 1941.

Beaumont, Arthur:

Painting the Army on Maneuvers. By Arthur Beaumont. Text accompanying 16 colored illustrations from paintings by the author. Vol. LXXXII, pp. 601-602, Nov., 1942.

Ships of Our Navy. 8 ills. in color from paintings by Arthur Beaumont. Vol. LXXX, pp. 329-336, Sept., 1941.

U. S. Army (Painting the Army on Maneuvers). 16 ills. in color from paintings by Arthur Beaumont. Vol. LXXXII, pp. 577-600, Nov., 1942.

Beauties of France. By Arthur Stanley Riggs. Vol. XXVIII, pp. 391-491. 73 ills. in black and white, 16 ills. in color, 1 half-page map, Nov., 1915.

Beauties of the Severn Valley. By Frank Wakeman. Vol. LXIII, pp. 417-452, 24 ills. in black and white, 15 ills. in color, 1 three-quarters-page map, Apr., 1933.

Beautiful Belgium, Restored by Peace. 16 ills. in color from autochromes by Paul G. Guillumette and A. Buyssens. Vol. LVI, pp. 554-563, Nov., 1929.

Beautiful Ecuador. By Joseph Lee. Vol. XVIII, pp. 80-91. 9 ills.. Feb.. 1907.

Beauty, History, and Romance Enrich the Château Country (France). 10 ills. in color from autochromes by Gervais Courtellemont. Vol. LVIII, pp. 466-475, Oct., 1930.

Beauty of the Bavarian Alps. By Col. Fitzhugh Lee Minnigerode. Vol. XLIX, pp. 632-649, 16 ills. in color, June, 1926.

Beavers:

Mickey the Beaver: Animal Engineer Performs for the Camera as a Star in the Activities of His Species. By James MacGillivray. Vol. LIV, pp. 741-756, 23 ills., Dec., 1928.

Wild Animals That Took Their Own Pictures by Day and by Night. By George Shiras, 3d. Vol. XXIV, pp. 763-834, 68 ills., 1 page map, July, 1913.

Wild Life of Lake Superior, Past and Present: The Habits of Deer, Moose, Wolves, Beavers, Muskrats, Trout, and Feathered Wood-Folk Studied with Camera and Flashlight. By George Shiras. 3d. Vol. XL. pp. 113-204, 77 ills., 1 half-page map, Aug., 1921.

Beck, Charles W., Jr.:

Rothenburg, the City Time Forgot. By Charles W. Beck, Jr. Vol. XLIX, pp. 184-194, 8 ills. in color, Feb., 1926.

Beck, Francis:

California Trapdoor Spider Performs Engineering Marvels. By Lee Passmore. Vol. LXIV, pp. 195-211, 23 ills., Aug., 1933.

Beck, Rollo H.:

South Sea Islands: Iridescent Isles of the South Seas. 12 ills. in color from photographs by Rollo H. Beck. Vol. XLVIII, pp. 403-418, Oct., 1925.

Bedouins (Tribespeople):

Ali Goes to the Clinic. By Herndon and Mary Hudson. Vol. XC, pp. 764-766, 2 ills., Dec., 1946.

Among the Bethlehem Shepherds: A Visit to the Valley Which David Probably Recalled When He Wrote the Twenty-Third Psalm. By John D. Whiting. Vol. L, pp. 729-753, 19 ills., Dec., 1926.

Bedouin Life in Bible Lands: The Nomads of the "Houses of Hair" Offer Unstinted Hospitality to an American. By John D. Whiting. Vol. LXXI, pp. 59-83, 27 ills., 1 third-page map, Jan., 1937.

Cirenaica, Eastern Wing of Italian Libia. By Harriet Chalmers Adams. Vol. LVII, pp. 689-726, 35 ills. in black and white, 13 ills. in color, 1 two-thirds-page map, June, 1930.

Forty Years Among the Arabs. By John Van Ess. Vol. LXXXII, pp. 385-420, 27 ills., 1 two-page map, Sept., 1942.

On the Trail of King Solomon's Mines: The Bible, in Addition to Its Spiritual Values, Continues to Prove a Rich Geography and Guide to Exploration of the Holy Land. By Nelson Glueck. Vol. LXXXV, pp. 233-256, 20 ills., 1 page map, Feb., 1944.

Where Adam and Eve Lived. By Frederick and Margaret Simpich. Vol. XXVI, pp. 546-588, 35 ills., Dec., 1914.

Beebe, William:

Depths of the Sea: Strange Life Forms a Mile Below the Surface. By William Beebe. Vol. LXI, pp. 65-88, 15 ills. in black and white, 8 ills. in color, 1 half-page map, Jan., 1932.

Half Mile Down: Strange Creatures, Beautiful and Grotesque as Figments of Fancy, Reveal Themselves at Windows of the Bathysphere. By William Beebe. Vol. LXVI, pp. 661-704, 28 ills. in black and white, 16 ills. in color, 1 third-page map, Dec., 1934.

Round Trip to Davy Jones's Locker: Peering into Mysteries a Quarter Mile Down in the Open Sea, by Means of the Bathysphere. By William Beebe. Vol. LIX, pp. 653-678, 14 ills. in black and white, 8 ills. in color, 1 quarter-page map, June, 1931.

Society Takes Part in Three Geographic Expeditions. Vol. LXV, pp. 625-626, May, 1934.

Wonderer Under Sea. By William Beebe. Vol. LXII, pp. 741-758, 13 ills. in black and white, 8 ills. in color, Dec., 1932.

Beech, (Dr.) Joseph:

Eden of the Flowery Republic (Szechwan Province, China). By Dr. Joseph Beech. Vol. XXXVIII, pp. 355-390, 18 ills. in black and white, 16 ills. in color, Nov., 1920.

Beechey Island, Arctic Region:

Location of the Sir John Franklin Monument. By James White. Vol. XIX, p. 596, Aug., 1908.

Beehive Homes:

Stone Beehive Homes of Italian Peasants. 12 ills. in color from autochromes by Luigi Pellerano and L. U. C. E. Vol. LVII, pp. 234-243, Feb., 1930.

Stone Beehive Homes of the Italian Heel: In Trulli-Land the Native Builds His Dwelling and Makes His Field Arable in the Same Operation. By Paul Wilstach. Vol. LVII, pp. 229-260, 25 ills. in black and white, 12 ills. in color, 1 quarter-page map, Feb., 1930.

Bees (Insects) :

In Field and Hive with the Busy Honeybee. 16 ills. in color from paintings by Hashime Murayama. Vol. LXVII, pp. 417-424, Apr., 1935.

Man's Winged Ally, the Busy Honeybee: Modern Research Adds a New Chapter to Usefulness of the Insect Which Has Symbolized Industry Since Early Bible Times. By James I. Hambleton. Vol. LXVII, pp. 401-428, 18 ills. in black and white, 10 ills. in color, Apr., 1935.

Monsters of Our Back Yards. By David Fairchild. Vol. XXIV, pp. 575-626, 38 ills., May, 1913.

Our Friends, the Bees. By A. I. Root and E. R. Root. Vol. XXII, pp. 675-694, 21 ills., July, 1911.

Beetles:

Explorers of a New Kind: Successful Introduction of Beetles and Parasites to Check Ravages of the Gipsy-Moth and Brown-Tail Moth. By L. O. Howard. Vol. XXVI, pp. 37-07, 11 ills. in black and white, 5 ills. in color, July, 1914.

Monsters of Our Back Yards. By David Fairchild. Vol. XXIV, pp. 575-626, 38 ills., May, 1913.

Protecting the United States from Plant Pests. By Charles Lester Marlatt. Vol. XL, pp. 205-218, 16 ills., Aug., 1921.

Befriending Nature's Children: An Experiment With Some of California's Wild Folk. By Agnes Akin Atkinson. Vol. LXI, pp. 199-215, 26 ills., Feb., 1932.

Begram, Afghanistan :

Back to Afghanistan. By Maynard Owen Williams. Vol. XC, pp. 517-544, 27 ills., 1 page map, Oct., 1946.

Behind Netherlands Sea Ramparts: Dikes and Pumps Keep Ocean and Rivers at Bay While a Busy People Carries on Peacetime Work. By McFall Kerbey. Vol. LXXVII, pp. 255-290, 26 ills. in black and white, 11 ills. in duotone, 1 two-thirds-page map, Feb., 1940.

Behind New Delhi's News (India). 13 ills. in color from natural-color photographs by Maynard Owen Williams. Vol. LXXXII, pp. 477-484, Oct., 1942.

Behind the Lines in Italy. By Corporal Macon Reed, Jr. Vol. LXXXVI, pp. 109-128, 20 ills., July, 1944.

Behind the Mask of Modern Japan. By Willard Price. Vol. LXXXVIII, pp. 513-535, 14 ills., Nov., 1945.

Behind the News in Singapore. By Frederick Simpich. Vol. LXXVIII, pp. 83-110, 26 ills., 1 map, July, 1940.

Behind the Scenes in the Home of the Passion Play (Oberammergau, Germany). 11 ills. in color from natural-color photographs. Vol. LXVIII, pp. 753-760, Dec., 1935.

Beirut, Lebanon :

American Alma Maters in the Near East. By Maynard Owen Williams. Vol. LXXXVIII, pp. 237-256, 16 ills., Aug., 1945.

Syria : The Land Link of History's Chain. By Maynard Owen Williams. Vol. XXXVI, pp. 437-462, 20 ills., 1 quarter-page map, Nov., 1919.

Syria and Lebanon Taste Freedom. By Maynard Owen Williams. With 21 ills. in color from natural-color photographs by the author. Vol. XC, pp. 729-763, 16 ills. in black and white, Dec., 1946.

Bekonscot (Toy Town), Beaconsfield, England : Bekonscot, England's Toy-Size Town. By Andrew H. Brown and B. Anthony Stewart. Vol. LXXI, pp. 649-661, 2 ills. in black and white, 15 ills. in colors, May, 1937.

Tableaux in an English Lilliput. 15 ills. in color from natural-color photographs by B. Anthony Stewart. Vol. LXXI, pp. 653-660, May, 1937.

Belaunsaran, Isabel:

Cuernavaca, the Sun Child of the Sierras (Mexico). By Russell Hastings Millward. Vol. XXII, pp. 291-301, 9 ills., Mar., 1911.

Beled el Jerid (Region), Tunisia :

Date Gardens of the Jerid. By Thomas H. Kearney. Vol. XXI, pp. 543-567, 20 ills., July, 1910.

Belém, Brazil :

Air Cruising Through New Brazil: A National Geographic Reporter Spots Vast Resources Which the Republic's War Declaration Adds to Strength of United Nations. By Henry Albert Phillips. Vol. LXXXII, pp. 503-536, 32 ills., Oct., 1942.

Belgian Antarctic Expedition. Vol. X, pp. 229-230, June, 1899.

Belgian Congo:

Amid the Snow Peaks of the Equator: A Naturalist's Explorations Around Ruwenzori, with an Excursion to the Congo State, and an Account of the Terrible Scourge of Sleeping Sickness. By A. F. R. Wollaston. Vol. XX, pp. 256-277, 11 ills., Mar., 1909.

Among the Cannibals of Belgian Kongo (Taken From the Notes of E. Torday). Vol. XXI, pp. 968-971, 4 ills., Nov., 1910.

Curious and Characteristic Customs of Central African Tribes. By E. Torday. Vol. XXXVI, pp. 342-368, 35 ills., Oct., 1919.

Belgian Congo—_Continued_

Journey Through the Eastern Portion of the Congo State. By Maj. P. H. G. Powell-Cotton. Vol. XIX, pp. 155-163, 9 ills., Mar., 1908.

Keeping House on the Congo. By Ruth Q. Mc-Bride. Vol. LXXII, pp. 643-670, 29 ills., Nov., 1937.

Land of Giants and Pygmies (Ruanda). By Duke Adolphus Frederick of Mecklenburg. Vol. XXIII, pp. 367-388, 16 ills., 1 page map, Apr., 1912.

Lloyd's Journey Across the Great Pygmy Forest. Vol. X, pp. 26-30, Jan., 1899.

Recent Geographic Advances, Especially in Africa. By Maj. Gen. A. W. Greely. Vol. XXII, pp. 383-398, 5 ills., 5 page maps, Apr., 1911.

Some Peculiar Features of Central African Geography. By Samuel P. Verner. Vol. XV, p. 448, Nov., 1904.

Trans-Africa Safari: A Motor Caravan Rolls Across Sahara and Jungle Through Realms of Dusky Potentates and the Land of Big-Lipped Women. By Lawrence Copley Thaw and Margaret Stout Thaw. Vol. LXXIV, pp. 327-364, 29 ills. in black and white, 14 ills. in color, 1 two-thirds-page map, Sept., 1938.

Transporting a Navy Through the Jungles of Africa in War Time. By Frank J. Magee, Vol. XLII, pp. 331-362, 31 ills., Oct., 1922.

Truth About the Congo. Vol. XVIII, pp. 807-813, 6 ills., Dec., 1907.

We Keep House on an Active Volcano: After Flying to Study a Spectacular Eruption in Belgian Congo, a Geologist Settles Down on a Newborn Craterless Vent for Eight Months' Study. By Dr. Jean Verhoogen. Vol. LXXVI, pp. 511-550, 28 ills., 1 two-thirds-page map, Oct., 1939.

Where Exploration Is Needed (Africa). Vol. XI, p. 163, Apr., 1900.

Belgian Portraits. 20 ills. in color from natural-color photographs by B. Anthony Stewart. Vol. LXXIII, pp. 413-444, Apr., 1938.

Belgium:

Beautiful Belgium, Restored by Peace. 16 ills. in color from autochromes by Paul G. Guillumette and A. Buyssens. Vol. LVI, pp. 554-563, Nov., 1929.

Belgian Portraits. 20 ills. in color from natural-color photographs by B. Anthony Stewart. Vol. LXXIII, pp. 413-444, Apr., 1938.

Belgium—Europe in Miniature. By Douglas Chandler. Vol. LXXIII, pp. 397-450, 34 ills. in black and white, 20 ills. in color, Apr. 1938.

Belgium: The Innocent Bystander. By William Joseph Showalter. Vol. XXVI, pp. 223-264, 35 ills., Sept., 1914.

Belgium's Plight. By John H. Gade. Vol. XXXI, pp. 433-439, 3 ills., May, 1917.

Low Countries Await Liberation. 10 ills. from photographs. Vol. LXXXVI, pp. 221-228, Aug., 1944.

Belgium—_Continued_

New Map of Europe: Showing the Boundaries Established by the Peace Conference at Paris and by Subsequent Decisions of the Supreme Council of Allied and Associated Powers. By Ralph A. Graves. Text acompanying special map supplement in colors. Vol. XXXIX, pp. 157-177, 18 ills., Feb., 1921.

Races of Europe. By Edwin A. Grosvenor. Vol. XXXIV, pp. 441-534, 62 ills., 2 page maps, special map supplement in colors, Dec., 1918.

Singing Towers of Holland and Belgium. By William Gorham Rice. Vol. XLVII, pp. 357-376, 22 ills., Mar., 1925.

Through the Back Doors of Belgium: Artist and Author Paddle for Three Weeks Along 200 Miles of Low-Countries Canals in a Canadian Canoe. By Melville Chater. Vol. XLVII, pp. 499-540, 39 ills., 1 half-page map, May, 1925.

Belgium's Plight. By John H. Gade. Vol. XXXI, pp. 433-439, 3 ills., May, 1917.

Belknap, (Capt.) Reginald R.:
North Sea Mine Barrage. By Capt. Reginald R. Belknap. Vol. XXXV, pp. 85-110, 23 ills., 1 diagram, 1 page map, Feb. 1919.

Bell, Alexander Graham:

Address of the President to the Board of Managers, June 1, 1900 (Early History of The Society). By Alexander Graham Bell. Vol. XI, pp. 401-408, Oct., 1900.

Aërial Locomotion: With a Few Notes of Progress in the Construction of an Aërodrome. By Alexander Graham Bell. Vol. XVIII, pp. 1-34, 33 ills., Jan., 1907.

Air Conquest: From the Early Days of Giant Kites and Birdlike Gliders, the National Geographic Society Has Aided and Encouraged the Growth of Aviation. Vol. LII, pp. 233-242, 13 ills., Aug., 1927.

Alexander Graham Bell (Announcement of the Death of Alexander Graham Bell). Vol. XLII, p. 302, portrait, Sept., 1922.

The "BB," experimental boat of Dr. Alexander Graham Bell, driven by aërial propellers. Vol. XVIII, ill. 671, Oct., 1907.

Charm of Cape Breton Island: The Most Picturesque Portion of Canada's Maritime Provinces—A Land Rich in Historic Associations, Natural Resources, and Geographic Appeal (Dr. Bell's Laboratories and Home). By Catherine Dunlop Mackenzie. Vol. XXXVIII, pp. 34-60, 22 ills., 1 three-quarters-page map, July, 1920.

Daughter of, marries Gilbert Grosvenor. Vol. XXIII, p. 274, Mar., 1912.

Discovery and Invention. By Alexander Graham Bell. Vol. XXV, pp. 649-655, June, 1914.

Dr. Bell's Man-Lifting Kite. By Gilbert H. Grosvenor. Vol. XIX, pp. 35-52, 27 ills., Jan., 1908.

Dr. Bell's Tetrahedral Tower. By Gilbert H. Grosvenor. Vol. XVIII, pp. 671-675, 7 ills., Oct., 1907.

Bell, Alexander Graham—*Continued*

Employs Gilbert Grosvenor, Apr. 1, 1899, for the National Geographic Society. Vol. XXIII, p. 274, Mar., 1912.

Few Thoughts Concerning Eugenics. By Alexander Graham Bell. Vol. XIX, pp. 119-123, Feb., 1908.

Future of the Airplane (Dr. Bell's Support of Aviation). By Rear Adm. Robert E. Peary. Vol. XXXIII, pp. 107-113, 4 ills., Jan., 1918.

Honors to Peary (Address by Alexander Graham Bell). Vol. XVIII, pp. 49-60, 1 ill., Jan., 1907.

National Geographic Society (Address by Alexander Graham Bell Concerning Early History of The Society). Vol. XXIII, pp. 272-298, 5 ills., Mar., 1912.

National Geographic Society (Resignation of Alexander Graham Bell as President of The Society). Vol. XIV, pp. 254-255, June, 1903.

Our Heterogeneous System of Weights and Measures. By Alexander Graham Bell. Vol. XVII, pp. 158-170, Mar., 1906.

Prehistoric Telephone Days. By Alexander Graham Bell. Vol. XLI, pp. 223-241, 17 ills., Mar., 1922.

President of The Society. Vol. X, p. 222, June, 1899.

Prizes for the Inventor: Some of the Problems Awaiting Solution. By Alexander Graham Bell. Vol. XXXI, pp. 131-146, 7 ills., Feb. 1917.

Tetrahedral Kite. Vol. XIV, p. 294, 1 ill., July, 1903.

Tetrahedral Principle in Kite Structure. By Alexander Graham Bell. Vol. XIV, pp. 219-251, 89 ills., 15 diagrams, June, 1903.

Voice Voyages by the National Geographic Society: A Tribute to the Geographical Achievements of the Telephone (Address by Alexander Graham Bell). Vol. XXIX, pp. 296-326, 15 ills., 1 chart, Mar., 1916.

Who Shall Inherit Long Life? On the Existence of a National Process at Work Among Human Beings Tending to Improve the Vigor and Vitality of Succeeding Generations. By Alexander Graham Bell. Vol. XXXV, pp. 505-514, 13 ills., June, 1919.

See also Largelamb, H. A. (pseudonym).

Bell, Alexander Melville:

Prehistoric Telephone Days. By Alexander Graham Bell. Vol. XLI, pp. 223-241, 17 ills., Mar., 1922.

Bell, Carl S.:

Bolivia—Tin Roof of the Andes. 20 ills. in color from natural-color photographs by Carl S. Bell and Fenno Jacobs. Vol. LXXXIII, pp. 311-326, Mar., 1943.

Bell, Robert J.:

Dr. Bell's Survey in Baffinland. By W J McGee. Vol. XIII, p. 113, Mar., 1902.

Bell Towers:

Singing Towers of Holland and Belgium. By William Gorham Rice. Vol. XLVII, pp. 357-376, 22 ills., Mar., 1925.

Bellows (Consul General):

Agriculture in Japan. By Consul General Bellows. Vol. XV, pp. 323-326, Aug., 1904.

Belo Horizonte, Brazil:

Air Cruising Through New Brazil: A National Geographic Reporter Spots Vast Resources Which the Republic's War Declaration Adds to Strength of United Nations. By Henry Albert Phillips. Vol. LXXXII, pp. 503-536, 32 ills., Oct., 1942.

Bright Facets of Brazil. 18 ills. in color from natural-color photographs by W. Robert Moore. Vol. LXXXV, pp. 49-72, Jan., 1944.

Benares, India:

Bathing and Burning Ghats at Benares. By Eliza R. Scidmore. Vol. XVIII, pp. 118-128, 7 ills., Feb., 1907.

Through the Heart of Hindustan: A Teeming Highway Extending for Fifteen Hundred Miles, from the Khyber Pass to Calcutta. By Maynard Owen Williams. Vol. XL, pp. 433-467, 29 ills., Nov., 1921.

Beneath Colombia's Azure Skies. 18 ills. in color from natural-color photographs; 17 ills. by Luis Marden. Vol. LXXVIII, pp. 513-536, Oct., 1940.

Bengasi, Libia:

Red Cross Girl Overseas. By Margaret Cotter. Vol. LXXXVI, pp. 745-768, 22 ills., Dec., 1944.

Benguet—The Garden of the Philippines. Vol. XIV, pp. 203-210, 6 ills., May, 1903.

Bennett, Floyd:

Commander Byrd Receives the Hubbard Gold Medal: The First Explorer to Reach the North Pole by Air Receives Coveted Honor at Brilliant National Geographic Society Reception (Also Presentation of Hubbard Gold Medal to Floyd Bennett). Vol. L, pp. 377-388, 5 ills., 1 chart, Sept., 1926.

Bentley, Wilson A.:

Magic Beauty of Snow and Dew. By Wilson A. Bentley. Vol. XLII, pp. 103-112, 9 ills., Jan., 1923.

Snow Crystals. 31 ills. from photographs by Wilson A. Bentley. Vol. XV, pp. 30-37, Jan., 1904.

Bequests. *See* National Geographic Society: Bequests.

Berbers (Tribespeople):

Morocco, the "Land of the Extreme West" and the Story of My Captivity. By Ion Perdicaris. Vol. XVII, pp. 117-157, 24 ills., Mar., 1906.

Berchtesgaden, Germany:

This Was Austria. 18 ills. from photographs. Vol. LXXXVIII, pp. 71-86, July, 1945.

Bergen, Norway :

White War in Norway. By Thomas R. Henry. Vol. LXXXVIII, pp. 617-640, 23 ills., 1 three-quarters-page map, Nov., 1945.

Berlin, Germany :

Changing Berlin. By Douglas Chandler. Vol. LXXI, pp. 131-177, 30 ills. in black and white, 24 ills. in color, Feb., 1937.

Life and Luster of Berlin. 24 ills. in color from natural-color photographs by Wilhelm Tobien and Hans Hildenbrand. Vol. LXXI, pp. 147-177, Feb., 1937.

Renascent Germany. By Lincoln Eyre. Vol. LIV, pp. 639-717, 59 ills. in black and white, 39 ills. in color, Dec., 1928.

Bermuda Islands, Atlantic Ocean :

Americans in the Caribbean. By Luis Marden. Vol. LXXXI, pp. 723-758, 16 ills. in black and white, 22 ills. in color, 1 half-page map, June, 1942.

Depths of the Sea : Strange Life Forms a Mile Below the Surface. By William Beebe. Vol. LXI, pp. 65-88, 15 ills. in black and white, 8 ills. in color, 1 half-page map, Jan., 1932.

Half Mile Down : Strange Creatures, Beautiful and Grotesque as Figments of Fancy, Reveal Themselves at Windows of the Bathysphere. By William Beebe. Vol. LXVI, pp. 661-704, 28 ills. in black and white, 16 ills. in color, 1 third-page map, Dec., 1934.

Happy Landing in Bermuda. By E. John Long. Vol. LXXV, pp. 213-238, 14 ills. in black and white, 12 ills. in color, Feb., 1939.

Islands of Bermuda : A British Colony with a Unique Record in Popular Government. By William Howard Taft. Vol. XLI, pp. 1-26, 15 ills., 1 three-quarters-page map, Jan., 1922.

Mid-Ocean Color Log. 12 ills. in color from natural-color photographs ; 9 ills. by E. John Long. Vol. LXXV, pp. 221-228, Feb., 1939.

Round Trip to Davy Jones's Locker : Peering into Mysteries a Quarter Mile Down in the Open Sea, by Means of the Bathysphere. By William Beebe. Vol. LIX, pp. 653-678, 14 ills. in black and white, 8 ills. in color, 1 quarter-page map, June, 1931.

Bernheimer, Charles L.:

Encircling Navajo Mountain (Utah) with a Pack-Train : An Expedition to a Hitherto Untraversed Region of Our Southwest Discovers a New Route to Rainbow Natural Bridge. By Charles L. Bernheimer. Vol. XLIII, pp. 197-224, 33 ills., 1 half-page map, Feb., 1923.

Bernstorff, Johann Heinrich, Count von:

Honors to Colonel Goethals : The Presentation by President Woodrow Wilson, of the National Geographic Society Special Gold Medal, and Addresses by Secretary of State Bryan, the French Ambassador, the German Ambassador, and Congressman James R. Mann. Vol. XXV, pp. 677-690, 6 ills., June, 1914.

In Honor of the Army and Aviation (Address by Count von Bernstorff). Vol. XXII, pp. 267-284, 1 ill., Mar., 1911.

Berries:

American Berries of Hill, Dale, and Wayside. Vol. XXXV, pp. 168-184, 1 ill. in black and white, 28 ills. in color, Feb., 1919.

Contains descriptions and illustrations of the following species : American Bittersweet, American Cranberry, American Holly, American Mountain Ash, Bayberry, Black Alder, Black Gum, Blue Cohosh, Blueleaf Greenbriar, Bunchberry, Chokeberries, Coral Berry, Early Highbush Blueberry, Highbush Blueberry, Highbush Cranberry, Longspine Thorn, Mapleleaf Arrowwood, Roundleaf Greenbriar, Shadbush, Silky Cornel, Smooth Sumac, Snowberry, Spicebush, Sweet Cherry, Sweet Elder, Wild Black Cherry, Wintergreen.

Taming the Wild Blueberry. By Frederick V. Coville. Vol. XXII, pp. 137-147, 5 ills., Feb., 1911.

Wild Blueberry Tamed : The New Industry of the Pine Barrens of New Jersey. By Frederick V. Coville. Vol. XXIX, pp. 535-546, 10 ills., June, 1916.

Berroeta, (Capt.) André de:

Flying in France. By Capt. André de Berroeta. Vol. XXXIII, pp. 9-26, 12 ills., Jan., 1918.

Beryl:

India's Treasures Helped the Allies. By John Fischer. Vol. LXXXIX, pp. 501-522, 18 ills., Apr., 1946.

Beside the Bosporus, Divider of Continents. 11 ills. in color from natural-color photographs by Maynard Owen Williams. Vol. LVI, pp. 492-501, Oct., 1929.

Bessarabia (Division), Romania :

Roumania and Its Rubicon. By John Oliver La Gorce. Vol. XXX, pp. 185-202, 11 ills., Sept., 1916.

Bethell, Union Noble:

Voice Voyages by the National Geographic Society : A Tribute to the Geographic Achievements of the Telephone (Address by Union Noble Bethell). Vol. XXIX, pp. 296-326, 5 ills., 1 chart, Mar., 1916.

Bethlehem and the Christmas Story. By John D. Whiting. Vol. LVI, pp. 699-735, 27 ills. in black and white, 14 ills. in color, Dec., 1929.

Betio Island, Tarawa, Gilbert Islands :

Gilbert Islands in the Wake of Battle. By W. Robert Moore. Vol. LXXXVII, pp. 129-162, 11 ills. in black and white, 19 ills. in color, 1 two-thirds-page map, Feb., 1945.

Between Massacres in Van (Turkey). By Maynard Owen Williams. Vol. XXXVI, pp. 181-184, 3 ills., Aug., 1919.

Between the Heather and the North Sea : Bold English Headlands Once Sheltered Sea Robbers, Later Were Ports of Wooden Ships, Centers of the Jet and Alum Trades, To-day Are Havens of Adventurous Fishing Fleets. By Leo Walmsley. Vol. LXIII, pp. 197-232, 41 ills., Feb., 1933.

Beukema, (Lt. Col.) Herman:

West Point and the Gray-Clad Corps. By Lieut. Col. Herman Beukema. Vol. LXIX, pp. 777-788, 10 ills. in color, June, 1936.

Bevan, Bernard:

Travels with a Donkey in Mexico: Three Adventurers Trudge from Oaxaca to Acapulco, 400 Miles, Through Back Country, Their Equipment Carried by Burros. By Bernard Bevan. Vol. LXVI, pp. 757-788, 36 ills., 1 page map, Dec., 1934.

Beyond Australia's Cities. By W. Robert Moore. Vol. LXX, pp. 709-747, 27 ills. in black and white, 12 ills. in color, Dec., 1936.

Beyond the Clay Hills: An Account of the National Geographic Society's Reconnaissance of a Previously Unexplored Section in Utah. By Neil M. Judd. Vol. XLV, pp. 275-302, 28 ills., 1 half-page map, Mar., 1924.

Beyond the Grand Atlas: Where the French Tricolor Flies Beside the Flag of the Sultan of Morocco. By V. C. Scott O'Connor. Vol. LXI, pp. 261-319, 52 ills. in black and white, 12 ills. in color, 1 two-thirds-page map, Mar., 1932.

Beyrouth, Lebanon. *See* Beirut.

Bhatgaon, Nepal:

Nepal: A Little-Known Kingdom. By John Claude White. Vol. XXXVIII, pp. 245-283, 32 ills., 1 half-page map, Oct., 1920.

Bhutan:

Castles in the Air: Experiences and Journeys in Unknown Bhutan. By John Claude White. Vol. XXV, pp. 365-455, 74 ills., 1 page map, Apr., 1914.

Bible Lands:

American Alma Maters in the Near East. By Maynard Owen Williams. Vol. LXXXVIII, pp. 237-256, 16 ills., Aug., 1945.

American Fighters Visit Bible Lands. By Maynard Owen Williams. With 23 ills. in color from natural-color photographs by the author. Vol. LXXXIX, pp. 311-340, 10 ills. in black and white, Mar., 1946.

Bombs over Bible Lands. By Frederick Simpich and W. Robert Moore. Vol. LXXX, pp. 141-180, 34 ills., 1 two-page map, Aug., 1941.

Change Comes to Bible Lands. By Frederick Simpich. Vol. LXXIV, pp. 695-750, 40 ills. in black and white, 25 ills. in color, special map supplement, Dec., 1938.

Geography of the Jordan. By Nelson Glueck. Vol. LXXXVI, pp. 719-744, 23 ills., 1 page map, Dec., 1944.

In the Land of Moses and Abraham. 25 ills. in color from natural-color photographs by W. Robert Moore. Vol. LXXIV, pp. 711-742, Dec., 1938.

On the Trail of King Solomon's Mines: The Bible, in Addition to Its Spiritual Values, Continues to Prove a Rich Geography and Guide to Exploration of the Holy Land. By Nelson Glueck. Vol. LXXXV, pp. 233-256, 20 ills., 1 page map, Feb., 1944.

Bible Lands—*Continued*

Society's Map of Bible Lands. By Gilbert Grosvenor. Text accompanying special map supplement in colors. Vol. LXXIV, pp. 751-754, 3 ills., Dec., 1938.

The Society's New Map of Bible Lands. Text accompanying special map supplement in colors. Vol. XC, pp. 815-816, Dec., 1946.

See also Arabia; Egypt; Iraq; Lebanon; Levant States; Palestine; Syria; Trans-Jordan; Turkey.

Bicycle Trips:

American Girl Cycles Across Romania: Two-wheel Pilgrim Pedals the Land of Castles and Gypsies, Where Roman Empire Traces Mingle With Remnants of Oriental Migration. By Dorothy Hosmer. Vol. LXXIV, pp. 557-588, 31 ills., 1 page map, Nov., 1938.

On Danish By-Lanes: An American Cycles Through the Quaint City of Lace, the Curiosity Town Where Time Stands Still, and Even Finds a Frontier in the Farming Kingdom. By Willis Lindquist. Vol. LXXVII, pp. 1-34, 21 ills. in black and white, 10 ills. in color, 1 three-quarters-page map, Jan., 1940.

Pedaling Through Poland: An American Girl Free-wheels Alone from Kraków, and Its Medieval Byways, Toward Ukraine's Restive Borderland. By Dorothy Hosmer. Vol. LXXV, pp. 739-775, 38 ills., 2 maps, June, 1939.

Bidens Pilosa. See Shepherd's Needles.

Big Game of Alaska. By Wilfred H. Osgood. Vol. XX, pp. 624-636, 10 ills., July, 1909.

Big Oklahoma. By Bird S. McGuire. Vol. XVII, pp. 103-105, 1 ill., Feb., 1906.

Big Things of the West. By Charles F. Holder. Vol. XIV, pp. 279-282, 2 ills., July, 1903.

Big Trees:

Among the Big Trees of California. By John R. White. Vol. LXVI, pp. 219-232, 14 ills., Aug., 1934.

National Geographic Society Completes Its Gifts of Big Trees. Vol. XL, pp. 85-86, July, 1921.

Oldest Living Thing ("General Sherman Tree"). Vol. XXIX, supplement, Apr., 1916.

Our Big Trees Saved. Vol. XXXI, pp. 1-11, 10 ills., Jan., 1917.

Our National Parks. By L. F. Schmeckebier. Vol. XXIII, pp. 531-579, 41 ills., 1 page map, June, 1912.

Bigelow, Frank H.:

International Cloud Work of the Weather Bureau. By Frank H. Bigelow. Vol. X, pp. 351-354, Sept., 1899.

Scientific Work of Mount Weather Meteorological Research Observatory. By Frank H. Bigelow. Vol. XV, pp. 442-445, Nov., 1904.

Studies on the Rate of Evaporation at Reno, Nevada, and in the Salton Sink. By Frank H. Bigelow. Vol. XIX, pp. 19-28, 5 ills., Jan., 1908.

Bigelow, Frank H.—*Continued*

Total Eclipse of the Sun, May 28, 1900. By Frank H. Bigelow. Vol. XI, pp. 33-34, Jan., 1900.

Bighorn Mountains, Wyoming:

Bighorn Mountains. By N. H. Darton. Vol. XVIII, pp. 355-364, 7 ills., 1 page map, June, 1907.

Bighorns (Sheep) :

Lords of the Rockies : Photographing Big Game Animals in Their Primeval Surroundings, from Arizona to Canada, Brings Adventure to Two Wilderness Wanderers. By Wendell and Lucie Chapman. Vol. LXXVI, pp. 87-128, 14 ills. in black and white, 28 ills. in color, July, 1939.

Stalking Big Game with Color Camera. 28 ills. in color from natural-color photographs by Wendell Chapman. Vol. LXXVI, pp. 89-128, July, 1939.

Bikini (Atoll), Marshall Islands:

American Pathfinders in the Pacific. By William H. Nicholas. Vol. LXXXIX, pp. 617-640, 17 ills., 1 two-page map, May, 1946.

Farewell to Bikini. By Carl Markwith. Vol. XC, pp. 97-116, 16 ills., July, 1946.

Bilbao, Spain :

Land of the Basques : Home of a Thrifty, Picturesque People, Who Take Pride in the Sobriquet, "The Yankees of Spain." By Harry A. McBride. Vol. XLI, pp. 63-87, 25 ills., 1 three-quarters-page map, Jan., 1922.

Billings, (Rear Adm.) L. G.:

Some Personal Experiences with Earthquakes. By Rear Adm. L. G. Billings. Vol. XXVII, pp. 57-71, 7 ills., Jan., 1915.

Billions of Barrels of Oil Locked Up in Rocks. By Guy Elliott Mitchell. Vol. XXXIII, pp. 195-205, 10 ills., Feb., 1918.

Bind the Wounds of France. By Herbert C. Hoover. Vol. XXXI, pp. 439-444, 5 ills., May, 1917.

Bingham, Hiram:

Building America's Air Army. By Hiram Bingham. Vol. XXXIII, pp. 48-86, 43 ills., Jan., 1918.

Explorations in Peru. Vol. XXIII, pp. 416-422, 7 ills., 1 half-page map, Apr., 1912.

Further Explorations in the Land of the Incas : The Peruvian Expedition of 1915 of the National Geographic Society and Yale University. By Hiram Bingham. Vol. XXIX, pp. 431-473, 29 ills., 1 page and 1 half-page maps, panorama, May, 1916.

Honors to Amundsen and Peary (Speech by Hiram Bingham). Vol. XXIV, pp. 113-130, 5 ills., Jan., 1913.

In the Wonderland of Peru. By Hiram Bingham. Vol. XXIV, pp. 387-574, 250 ills., 3 diagrams, 1 three-quarters-page map, Apr., 1913.

Bingham, Hiram—*Continued*

Story of Machu Picchu : The Peruvian Expeditions of the National Geographic Society and Yale University. By Hiram Bingham. Vol. XXVII, pp. 171-217, 35 ills., Feb., 1915.

Bira, Celebes (Island) :

Seafarers of South Celebes. By G. E. P. Collins. Vol. LXXXVII, pp. 53-78, 25 ills., 1 two-thirds-page map, Jan., 1945.

Bird, F. L.:

Modern Persia and Its Capital : And an Account of an Ascent of Mount Demavend, the Persian Olympus. By F. L. Bird. Vol. XXXIX, pp. 353-400, 47 ills., Apr., 1921.

Bird Banding, the Telltale of Migratory Flight : A Modern Method of Learning the Flight-Ways and Habits of Birds. By W. W. Nelson. Vol. LIII, pp. 91-131, 49 ills., 1 third-page map, Jan., 1928.

Bird Beauties of the Tanager and Finch Families. 55 portraits in color from paintings by Maj. Allan Brooks. Vol. LXVII, pp. 513-528, Apr., 1935.

Bird City (Laysan Island, Hawaii). Vol. XV, pp. 494-498, 6 ills., Dec., 1904.

Bird Life Among Lava Rock and Coral Sand : The Chronicle of a Scientific Expedition in Little-Known Islands of Hawaii. By Alexander Wetmore. Vol. XLVIII, pp. 77-108, 36 ills., 1 half-page map, July, 1925.

Birds:

Adventures with Birds of Prey. By Frank and John Craighead. Vol. LXXII, pp. 109-134, 25 ills., July, 1937.

Ambassadors of Good Will : Annual Messengers from Our Neighbor Republics to the South Bring Cheer and Add Interest to the Out-of-Doors. By Arthur A. Allen. Vol. LXXXI, pp. 786-796, 13 ills. in color, June, 1942.
Contains descriptions and colored illustrations of the following : Belted Kingfisher, Bobolink, Cardinal, Prothonotary Warbler, Red-eyed Vireo, Red-headed Woodpecker, Redwing, Tree Swallow, Wood Thrush, Yellow-billed Cuckoo, Yellow-breasted Chat.

American Birds of Prey—A Review of Their Value. Vol. XXXVIII, pp. 460-467, 6 ills., Dec., 1920.

American Game Birds. By Henry Wetherbee Henshaw. Vol. XXVIII, pp. 105-158, 4 ills. in black and white, 72 ills. in color, Aug., 1915.
Contains descriptions and illustrations of the following : Cranes, Ducks, Geese, Grouse, Pheasants, Pigeons, Plovers, Quails, Rails, Sandpipers, Snipes, Stilts, Swans.

Amid the Snow Peaks of the Equator : A Naturalist's Explorations Around Ruwenzori with an Excursion to the Congo State, and an Account of the Terrible Scourge of Sleeping Sickness. By A. F. R. Wollaston. Vol. XX, pp. 256-277, 11 ills., Mar., 1909.

Birds—*Continued*

Around the World for Animals. By William M. and Lucile Q. Mann. Vol. LXXIII, pp. 665-714, 33 ills. in black and white, 23 ills. in color, 1 page map, June, 1938.

Auks and Their Northland Neighbors. 34 portraits in color from paintings by Maj. Allan Brooks. Vol. LXIX, pp. 101-116, Jan., 1936.
Contains illustrations of the following: Auklets, Auks, Dovekies, Guillemots, Murrelets, Murres, Puffins.

Bag of Bird Portraits. 24 ills. in color from natural-color photographs; 23 ills. by Arthur A. Allen. Vol. LXXXV, pp. 697-712, June, 1944.
Contains colored illustrations of the following: Burrowing Owl, California Blue Grosbeak, California Clapper Rail, California Woodpecker, Clark's Nutcracker, Coppery-tailed Trogon, Eastern Brown Pelican, Eastern Song Sparrow, Florida Ground Dove, Gambel's Quail, Hoyt's Horned Lark, Mourning Dove, Nighthawk, Purple Gallinule, Red-eyed Towhee, Reddish Egret, Sandhill Crane, Saw-whet Owl, Scissor-tailed Flycatcher, Sennett's Oriole, Snow Bunting, Snowy Egret, Western Gull, Western Horned Owl, Yellow Warbler.

Befriending Nature's Children: An Experiment With Some of California's Wild Folk. By Agnes Akin Atkinson. Vol. LXI, pp. 199-215, 26 ills., Feb., 1932.

Bird Banding, the Telltale of Migratory Flight: A Modern Method of Learning the Flight-Ways and Habits of Birds. By E. W. Nelson. Vol. LIII, pp. 91-131, 49 ills., 1 third-page map, Jan., 1928.

Bird Beauties of the Tanager and Finch Families. 55 portraits in color from paintings by Maj. Allan Brooks. Vol. LXVII, pp. 513-528, Apr., 1935.

Bird City (Laysan Island, Hawaii). Vol. XV, pp. 494-498, 6 ills., Dec., 1904.

Bird Life Among Lava Rock and Coral Sand: The Chronicle of a Scientific Expedition to Little-Known Islands of Hawaii. By Alexander Wetmore. Vol. XLVIII, pp. 77-108, 36 ills., 1 half-page map, July, 1925.

Birds and Beasts of Mexico's Desert Islands. 12 ills. in color from natural-color photographs; 8 ills. by Ed N. Harrison; 4 ills. by Alfred M. Bailey and Robert J. Niedrach. Vol. LXXX, pp. 353-360, Sept., 1941.

Birds in Glossy Black and Vivid Color. 48 portraits in color from paintings by Maj. Allan Brooks. Vol. LXVI, pp. 113-128, July, 1934.
Contains illustrations of the following: Blackbirds, Bobolinks, Cowbirds, Grackles, Meadowlarks, Orioles, Shrikes, Vireos, Waxwings.

Birds May Bring You More Happiness Than the Wealth of the Indies. By Frank M. Chapman. Vol. XXIV, pp. 699-714, 15 ills., June, 1913.

Birds of Lake and Lagoon, Marsh and Seacoast. 24 portraits in color from paintings by Maj. Allan Brooks. Vol. LXV, pp. 313-328, Mar., 1934.

Birds—*Continued*

Contains illustrations of the following: Cormorants, Grebes, Loons, Pelicans.

Birds of the High Seas: Albatrosses and Petrels; Gannets, Man-o'-war-birds, and Tropic-birds. By Robert Cushman Murphy. Paintings by Maj. Allan Brooks. Vol. LXXIV, pp. 226-251, 7 ills. in black and white, 36 portraits in color, Aug., 1938.

Birds of the Northern Seas. By Alexander Wetmore. Paintings by Maj. Allan Brooks. Vol. LXIX, pp. 95-122, 12 ills. in black and white, 34 portraits in color, Jan., 1936.
Contains descriptions and illustrations of the following: Auklets, Auks, Dovekies, Guillemots, Murrelets, Murres, Puffins.

Birds of Timberline and Tundra. By Arthur A. Allen. With 24 ills. in color from natural-color photographs by the author. Vol. XC, pp. 313-339, 8 ills. in black and white, Sept., 1946.
Contains descriptions and illustrations of the following: Arctic Loons, Arctic Terns, Black-pole Warblers, Bonaparte's Gulls, Dowitchers, Golden Plovers, Harris's Sparrows, Herring Gulls, Horned Grebes, Hoyt's Horned Larks, Hudsonian Curlews, Lapland Longspurs, Least Sandpipers, Lesser Yellowlegs, Northern Phalaropes, Northern Shrikes, Parasitic Jaeger, Pintail Ducks, Pipits, Red-backed Sandpipers, Semipalmated Plovers, Semipalmated Sandpipers, Snow Buntings, Starlings, Stilt Sandpipers, Tree Sparrows, White-crowned Sparrows, Wild Geese, Willow Ptarmigans, Yellow Warblers.

Birds of Town and Country. By Henry Wetherbee Henshaw. Vol. XXV, pp. 494-531, 2 ills. in black and white, 64 ills. in color, May, 1914.
Contains descriptions and illustrations of the following: Blackbirds, Eagles, Finches, Flycatchers, Gulls, Hawks, Herons, Hummingbirds, Jays, Kingfishers, Orioles, Owls, Sparrows, Starlings, Swallows, Swifts, Tanagers, Terns, Thrushes, Titmice, Vireos, Vultures, Waxwings, Whippoorwills, Wood Warblers, Woodpeckers.

Birds on the Home Front. By Arthur A. Allen. Vol. LXXXIV, pp. 32-56, 7 ills. in black and white, 30 ills. in color, July, 1943.
Contains descriptions and illustrations of the following: Canada Geese, Catbirds, Chickadees, Chuck-will's-widow, Cowbirds, Flickers, Flycatchers, Gallinules, Grebes, Grouse, Hummingbirds, Meadowlarks, Orioles, Owls, Peregrines, Plovers, Ptarmigans, Puffins, Rails, Redstarts, Shrikes, Skimmers, Swallows, Vireos, Warblers, Waxwings.

Birds That Cruise the Coast and Inland Waters. By T. Gilbert Pearson. Paintings by Maj. Allan Brooks. Vol. LXV, pp. 299-328, 15 ills. in black and white, 24 portraits in color, Mar., 1934.
Contains descriptions and illustrations of the following: Cormorants, Darters, Grebes, Loons, Pelicans.

Blackbirds and Orioles. By Arthur A. Allen. Paintings by Maj. Allan Brooks. Vol. LXVI, pp. 111-130, 48 portraits in color, July, 1934.

Birds—*Continued*

Blithe Birds of Dooryard, Bush, and Brake. 37 portraits in color from paintings by Maj. Allan Brooks. Vol. LXV, pp. 579-594, May, 1934.
Contains illustrations of the following: Chickadees, Kinglets, Nuthatches, Titmice, Wrens.

Bright-hued Pets of Cage and Aviary. 51 portraits in color from paintings by Maj. Allan Brooks. Vol. LXXIV, pp. 783-790, Dec., 1938.

Camps and Cruises of an Ornithologist. By George Shiras, 3d. Vol. XX, pp. 438-463, 30 ills., May, 1909.

Canaries and Other Cage-Bird Friends. By Alexander Wetmore. Vol. LXXIV, pp. 775-806, 19 ills. in black and white, 51 portraits in color, Dec., 1938.

Color Close-ups of Familiar Birds. 14 ills. in color from natural-color photographs by Arthur A. Allen. Vol. LXXV, pp. 779-786, June, 1939.
Contains illustrations of the following: American Bittern, Blue Jay, Cedar Waxwing, Chipping Sparrow, Eastern Bluebird, Eastern Meadowlark, Goldfinch, Least Bittern, Purple Finch, Redwing, Robin, Scarlet Tanager, Wood Thrush.

Crows, Magpies, and Jays: Unusual Intelligence Has Earned a Unique Position for These Birds. By T. Gilbert Pearson. Paintings by Maj. Allan Brooks. Vol. LXIII, pp. 51-79, 16 ills. in black and white, 17 ills. in color, Jan., 1933.

Cruise of the *Kinkajou*: Among Desert Islands of Mexico Voyagers Find Outdoor Laboratories for the Naturalist and Ideal Fishing Grounds for the Sportsman. By Alfred M. Bailey. Vol. LXXX, pp. 339-366, 13 ills. in black and white, 12 ills. in color, 1 page map, Sept., 1941.
Contains information on the following: Auklets, Belding's Plovers, Black Oystercatchers, Black Turnstones, Black-vented Shearwaters, Blue-footed Boobies, Brewster's Boobies, Brown Towhees, Cactus Wrens, Cape Gilded Flickers, Caracaras, Cardinals, Cardon Woodpeckers, Cormorants, Frazar's Oystercatchers, Gnat-catchers, Heermann's Gulls, Horned Larks, Hudsonian Curlews, Lark Buntings, Man-o'-war-birds, Mockingbirds, Noddy Terns, Ospreys, Pelicans, Petrels, Ravens, Red-billed Tropic-birds, Red-footed Boobies, Red Phalaropes, Rock Wrens, San Lucas Quail, San Lucas Sparrows, San Lucas Woodpeckers, Sooty Terns, Thrashers, Townsend's Shearwaters, Verdins, Vultures, Wandering Tattlers, White-winged Doves, Willets, Wyman's Gulls, Yellow-legged Gulls.

Eagle, King of Birds and His Kin. By Alexander Wetmore. Paintings by Maj. Allan Brooks. Vol. LXIV, pp. 43-95, 23 ills. in black and white, 28 ills. in color, July, 1933.

Eagles, Hawks, and Vultures. 28 ills. in color from paintings by Maj. Allan Brooks. Vol. LXIV, pp. 65-94, July, 1933.

Birds—*Continued*

Encouraging Birds Around the Home. By Frederick H. Kennard. Vol. XXV, pp. 315-344, 36 ills., Mar., 1914.

Far-Flying Wild Fowl and Their Foes. By Maj. Allan Brooks. Vol. LXVI, pp. 487-528, 6 ills. in black and white, 93 portraits in color, Oct., 1934.
Contains descriptions and illustrations of the following: Ducks, Geese, Swans.

Feathered Foragers of Swamp and Shore. 101 portraits in color from paintings by Maj. Allan Brooks. Vol. LXXII, pp. 191-222, Aug., 1937.

Fifty Common Birds of Farm and Orchard. By Henry Wetherbee Henshaw. Vol. XXIV, pp. 669-697, 50 ills. in color, June, 1913.
Contains descriptions and illustrations of the following: Blackbirds, Creepers, Crows, Cuckoos, Doves, Flycatchers, Grouse, Gulls, Hawks, Jays, Kinglets, Larks, Nighthawks, Nuthatches, Orioles, Owls, Plovers, Quail, Shrikes, Sparrows, Swallows, Terns, Thrashers, Thrushes, Titmice, Wood Warblers, Woodpeckers, Wrens.

Flycatchers and Other Friends in Feathers. 36 portraits in color from paintings by Maj. Allan Brooks. Vol. LXIX, pp. 807-822, June, 1936.
Contains illustrations of the following: Anis, Cuckoos, Flycatchers, Kingbirds, Kingfishers, Parrots.

Further Explorations in the Land of the Incas: The Peruvian Expedition of 1915 of the National Geographic Society and Yale University. By Hiram Bingham. Vol. XXIX, pp. 431-473, 29 ills., 1 page and 1 half-page maps, panorama, May, 1916.

Game Birds of Prairie, Forest, and Tundra. By Alexander Wetmore. Vol. LXX, pp. 461-500, 5 ills. in black and white, 60 portraits in color, Oct., 1936.
Contains descriptions and illustrations of the following: Doves, Grouse, Pigeons, Ptarmigans, Quails.

Geographic Achievement (Reprint of Bird Bulletin). Vol. XXIV, pp. 667-668, June, 1913.

Guillemot Eggs. Vol. XIV, pp. 386-388, 1 ill., Oct., 1903.

High Country of Colorado. By Alfred M. Bailey. With 23 ills. in color from natural-color photographs by the author, Robert J. Niedrach, and F. G. Brandenburg. Vol. XC, pp. 43-72, 9 ills. in black and white, July, 1946.
Contains text references and illustrations of the following: Bluebirds, Flickers, Golden Eagles, Goshawks, Grosbeaks, Hawks, Hummingbirds, Juncos, Owls, Pine Grosbeaks, Ptarmigans, Robins, Sage Grouse, Sap-suckers, Sparrows, Vireos, Warblers, Woodpeckers.

Humming Birds, Swifts and Goatsuckers. 36 ills. in color from paintings by Maj. Allan Brooks. Vol. LXII, pp. 75-88, July, 1932.

Hunted Birds of Field and Wild. 60 portraits in color from paintings by Maj. Allan Brooks. Vol. LXX, pp. 469-500, Oct., 1936.
Contains illustrations of the following: Doves, Grouse, Pigeons, Ptarmigans, Quails.

Birds—*Continued*

Hunting Birds With a Camera: A Record of Twenty Years of Adventure in Obtaining Photographs of Feathered Wild Life in America. By William L. Finley. Vol. XLIV, pp. 161-201, 37 ills., Aug., 1923.

Hunting with a Microphone the Voices of Vanishing Birds. By Arthur A. Allen. Vol. LXXI, pp. 697-723, 32 ills., June, 1937.

Hunting with the Lens. By Howard H. Cleaves. Vol. XXVI, pp. 1-35, 47 ills., July, 1914.

Ibises, Herons, and Flamingos. 24 ills. in color from paintings by Maj. Allan Brooks. Vol. LXII, pp. 454-469, Oct., 1932.

Journey by Jungle Rivers to the Home of the Cock-of-the-Rock: Naturalists Enter the Amazon, Voyage Through the Heart of Tropical South America, and Emerge at the Mouth of the Orinoco. By Ernest G. Holt. Vol. LXIV, pp. 585-630, 4 ills., 1 two-thirds-page map, Nov., 1933.

Large Wading Birds: Long Legs and Remarkable Beaks, as Well as Size, Form and Color, Distinguish the Herons, Ibises, and Flamingos. By T. Gilbert Pearson. Paintings by Maj. Allan Brooks. Vol. LXII, pp. 441-469, 13 ills. in black and white, 24 ills. in color, Oct., 1932.

Life with an Indian Prince: As Guests of a Maharaja's Brother, Two Young American Naturalists Study Age-old Methods of Hunting with Trained Falcons and Cheetahs and Savor the Pomp of Royal India. By John and Frank Craighead. Vol. LXXXI, pp. 235-272, 38 ills., 1 sixth-page map, Feb., 1942.

Lonely Australia: The Unique Continent. By Herbert E. Gregory. Vol. XXX, pp. 473-568, 68 ills., 1 two-page and 4 half-page maps, Dec., 1916.

Masters of Flight. Vol. XXXVI, pp. 49-56, 8 ills., July, 1919.

National Geographic Society's New "Book of Birds." Vol. LXXI, p. 723, June, 1937. Vol. LXXII, p. 183, Aug., 1937. Vol. LXXIV, p. 226, Aug., 1938; p. 775, Dec., 1938. Vol. LXXVII, p. 121, Jan., 1940.

Naturalist with MacMillan in the Arctic. By Walter N. Koelz. Vol. XLIX, pp. 299-318, 22 ills. in color, Mar., 1926.

Naturalist's Journey Around Vera Cruz and Tampico. By Frank M. Chapman. Vol. XXV, pp. 532-562, 31 ills., May, 1914.

One Season's Game Bag with the Camera. By George Shiras, 3d. Vol. XIX, pp. 387-446, 70 ills., June, 1908.

Our Greatest Travelers: Birds That Fly from Pole to Pole and Shun the Darkness: Birds That Make 2,500 Miles in a Single Flight. By Wells W. Cooke. Vol. XXII, pp. 346-365, 4 page and 8 half-page maps, Apr., 1911.

Our Policemen of the Air. Vol. XXIV, p. 698, June, 1913.

Birds—*Continued*

Parrots, Kingfishers, and Flycatchers: Strange Trogons and Curious Cuckoos are Pictured with these Other Birds of Color, Dash, and Courage. By Alexander Wetmore. Paintings by Maj. Allan Brooks. Vol. LXIX, pp. 801-828, 9 ills. in black and white, 36 portraits in color, June, 1936.

Peru's Wealth-Producing Birds: Vast Riches in the Guano Deposits of Cormorants, Pelicans, and Petrels Which Nest on Her Barren, Rainless Coast. By R. E. Coker. Vol. XXXVII, pp. 537-566, 28 ills., June, 1920.

Photographing Wild Game with Flashlight and Camera. By George Shiras, 3d. Vol. XVII, pp. 366-423, 70 ills., July, 1906.

Policemen of the Air. By Henry Wetherbee Henshaw. Vol. XIX, pp. 79-118, 38 ills., Feb., 1908.

Romance of Science in Polynesia: An Account of Five Years of Cruising Among the South Sea Islands. By Robert Cushman Murphy. Vol. XLVIII, pp. 355-426, 66 ills. in black and white, 16 ills. in color, 3 half-page maps, Oct., 1925.

Seeking the Smallest Feathered Creatures: Humming Birds, Peculiar to the New World, Are Found from Canada and Alaska to the Strait of Magellan. Swifts and Goatsuckers, Their Nearest Relatives. By Alexander Wetmore. Paintings by Maj. Allan Brooks. Vol. LXII, pp. 65-89, 9 ills. in black and white, 36 ills. in color, July, 1932.

Shore Birds, Cranes, and Rails: Willets, Plovers, Stilts, Phalaropes, Sandpipers, and Their Relatives Deserve Protection. By Arthur A. Allen. Paintings by Maj. Allan Brooks. Vol. LXXII, pp. 183-222, 4 ills. in black and white, 101 portraits in color, Aug., 1937.

Sights and Sounds of the Winged World: Study of Birds to Make National Geographic Color Photographs Yields Rich Scientific Knowledge of Their Habits and Behavior. By Arthur A. Allen. Vol. LXXXVII, pp. 721-744, 1 ill. in black and white, 2 drawings, 26 ills. in color, June, 1945.

Contains colored illustrations of the following: Albino Rose-breasted Grosbeak, Baltimore Oriole, Bank Swallow, Black-billed Cuckoo, Black-capped Chickadee, Bronzed Grackle, Chestnut-sided Warbler, Crested Flycatcher, Downy Woodpecker, Forster's Tern, Hairy Woodpecker, Kingbird, Long-billed Marsh Wren, Marsh Hawk, Orchard Oriole, Pectoral Sandpiper, Pileated Woodpecker, Prairie Chicken, Redpoll, Rose-breasted Grosbeak, Rough-winged Swallow, Sharp-tailed Grouse, Wilson's Phalarope, Woodcock, Yellow-throat.

Sindbads of Science: Narrative of a Windjammer's Specimen-Collecting Voyage to the Sargasso Sea, to Senegambian Africa and Among Islands of High Adventure in the South Atlantic. By George Finlay Simmons. Vol. LII, pp. 1-75, 89 ills., 1 two-thirds-page map, July, 1927.

Birds—*Continued*

Some Songsters and Flyers of Wide Repute. 42 portraits in color from paintings by Maj. Allan Brooks. Vol. LXIX, pp. 529-544, Apr., 1936.

Contains illustrations of the following: Swallows, Thrashers, Thrushes.

South Florida's Amazing Everglades: Encircled by Populous Places Is a Seldom-visited Area of Rare Birds, Prairies, Cowboys, and Teaming Wild Life of Big Cypress Swamp. By John O'Reilly. Vol. LXXVII, pp. 115-142, 26 ills., 1 page map, Jan., 1940.

Contains the following: Burrowing Owl, Everglade Kite, Florida Cormorant, Florida Crane, Great White Heron, Limpkin, Pelican, Roseate Spoonbill, Snowy Egret, White Ibis.

South Georgia, an Outpost of the Antarctic. By Robert Cushman Murphy. Vol. XLI, pp. 409-444, 41 ills., 2 half-page maps, Apr., 1922.

Sparrows, Towhees, and Longspurs. 43 paintings in color from life by Maj. Allan Brooks and Walter A. Weber. Vol. LXXV, pp. 361-375, Mar., 1939.

Sparrows, Towhees, and Longspurs: These Happy Little Singers Make Merry in Field, Forest, and Desert Throughout North America. By T. Gilbert Pearson. Vol. LXXV, pp. 353-376, 5 ills. in black and white, 43 ills. in color, Mar., 1939.

Stalking Birds With a Color Camera: An Expert in Avian Habits Persuades His Subjects to Sit Where He Wants Them, Even in His Hat. By Arthur A. Allen. Vol. LXXV, pp. 777-789, 3 ills. in black and white, 14 ills. in color, June, 1939.

Tanagers and Finches: Their Flashes of Color and Lilting Songs Gladden the Hearts of American Bird Lovers East and West. By Arthur A. Allen. Paintings by Maj. Allan Brooks. Vol. LXVII, pp. 505-532, 6 ills. in black and white, 55 portraits in color, Apr., 1935.

Thrushes, Thrashers, and Swallows: Robins and Bluebirds are Familiar Members of a Famous Musical Family Which Includes the Hermit Thrush and European Nightingale. By T. Gilbert Pearson. Paintings by Maj. Allan Brooks. Vol. LXIX, pp. 523-546, 6 ills. in black and white, 42 paintings from life, Apr., 1936.

Touring for Birds with Microphone and Color Cameras. By Arthur A. Allen. Vol. LXXXV, pp. 689-712, 3 ills. in black and white, 24 ills. in color, June, 1944.

Contains descriptions and illustrations of the birds of Arizona, Texas, and California and a discussion of the "Life Zone Theory" which treats of the distribution of bird fauna in relation to temperature.

Unique Island of Mount Desert. By George B. Door, Ernest Howe Forbush, and M. L. Fernald. Vol. XXVI, pp. 75-89, 7 ills., July, 1914.

Viking Life in the Storm-Cursed Faeroes. By Leo Hansen. Vol. LVIII, pp. 607-648, 49 ills., 1 half-page map, Nov., 1930.

We Live Alone, and Like It—On an Island (Skokholm). By R. M. Lockley. Vol. LXXIV, pp. 252-278, 27 ills., Aug., 1938.

Birds—*Continued*

Contains descriptions and illustrations of the following: Auks, Cormorants, Gannets, Gulls, Petrels, Puffins, Shearwaters.

What the Fighting Yanks See. By Wanda Burnett. Vol. LXXXVI, pp. 451-476, 27 ills., Oct., 1944.

Contains information on the following: Birds of Paradise, Cassowaries, Frogmouths, Grebes, Hornbills, Laughing Jack, Laughing Jackass, Lories, Love Terns, Parakeets, Parrots, Pink Cockatoos, White Cockatoos.

Where Birds and Little Animals Find Haven (Eaton Canyon Bird and Game Sanctuary). By Agnes Akin Atkinson. Vol. LXX, pp. 232-241, 14 ills., Aug., 1936.

Where Roosevelt Will Hunt (Africa). By Sir Harry Johnston. Vol. XX, pp. 207-256, 43 ills., special map supplement in colors, Mar., 1909.

White Sheep, Giant Moose, and Smaller Game of the Kenai Peninsula, Alaska. By George Shiras, 3d. Vol. XXIII, pp. 423-494, 59 ills., 1 page and 1 two-page maps, May, 1912.

Wild Geese, Ducks, and Swans. 93 portraits in color from paintings by Maj. Allan Brooks. Vol. LXVI, pp. 493-524, Oct., 1934.

Wild Life of Lake Superior, Past and Present: The Habits of Deer, Moose, Wolves, Beavers, Muskrats, Trout, and Feathered Wood-Folk Studied with Camera and Flashlight. By George Shiras, 3d. Vol. XL, pp. 113-204, 77 ills., special supplement, 1 half-page map, Aug., 1921.

Wild Life of the Atlantic and Gulf Coasts: A Field Naturalist's Photographic Record of Nearly Half a Century of Fruitful Exploration. By George Shiras, 3d. Vol. XLII, pp. 261-309, 62 ills., Sept., 1932.

Wildlife of Tabasco and Veracruz (Mexico). By Walter A. Weber. With 19 ills. in color from paintings by the author. Vol. LXXXVII, pp. 187-216, 7 ills. in black and white, 1 two-thirds-page map, Feb., 1945.

Contains colored illustrations of the following: Ant Tanager, Araçari Toucan, Black-bellied Tree Duck, Black-headed Trogon, Black Vulture, Blue Tanager, Crested Curassow, Crimson-collared Tanager, Finfoot, Forest Sparrow, Jacamar, King Vulture, Laughing Falcon, Least Kingfisher, Lesson's Oriole, Massena Trogon, Mexican Ant Thrush, Mexican Black Hawk, Mexican Jaçana, Mexican Motmot, Muscovy Duck, Oropendola, Plush Tanager, Quail Dove, Redstart, Ringed Kingfisher, Royal Flycatcher, Squirrel Cuckoo, Sulphur-breasted Toucan, Tiger Bittern, Veracruz Ivory-billed Woodpecker, White Snake Hawk, White-throated Bat Falcon, Yellow-headed Amazon, Yellow-tailed Oriole, Yellow-thighed Manakin.

Winged Denizens of Woodland, Stream, and Marsh. By Alexander Wetmore. Paintings by Maj. Allan Brooks. Vol. LXV, pp. 577-596, 37 portraits in color, May, 1934.

Contains descriptions and illustrations of the following: Chickadees, Creepers, Dippers, Gnatcatchers, Kinglets, Nuthatches, Titmice, Wren-tits, Wrens.

Birds—*Continued*

Wings Over the Bounding Main (Ocean Birds). 36 portaits in color from paintings by Maj. Allan Brooks. Vol. LXXIV, pp. 237-251, Aug., 1938.

See also Cormorants; Crows; Ducks; Eagles; Falcons; Flamingos; Geese; Gulls; Hawks; Ibises; Ostriches; Owls; Pelicans; Penguins; Petrels; Pigeons; Poultry; Quetzals; Sparrows; Terns; Warblers; Woodpeckers; Wrens.

Bird's-Eye View of the Panama Canal. Vol. XXIII, colored supplement, Feb., 1912.

Birkinbine, John:

Our Neighbor, Mexico. By John Birkinbine. Vol. XXII, pp. 475-508, 26 ills., special map supplement in colors, May, 1911.

Bishop, (Maj.) William A.:

Tales of the British Air Service. By Maj. William A. Bishop. Vol. XXXIII, pp. 27-37, 12 ills., Jan., 1918.

Biskra, the Ziban Queen. By Mrs. George C. Bosson, Jr. Vol. XIX, pp. 563-593, 29 ills., 1 eighth-page map, Aug., 1908.

Bison:

Lords of the Rockies : Photographing Big Game Animals in Their Primeval Surroundings, from Arizona to Canada, Brings Adventure to Two Wilderness Wanderers. By Wendell and Lucie Chapman. Vol. LXXVI, pp. 87-128, 14 ills. in black and white, 28 ills. in color, July, 1939.

Stalking Big Game with Color Camera. 28 ills. in color from natural-color photographs by Wendell Chapman. Vol. LXXVI, pp. 89-128, July, 1939.

Bit of Elizabethan England in America : Fisher Folk of the Islands off North Carolina Conserved the Speech and Customs of Sir Walter Raleigh's Colonists. By Blanch Nettleton Epler. Vol. LXIV, pp. 695-730, 43 ills., 1 three-quarters-page map, Dec., 1933.

Bitterns (Birds) :

Large Wading Birds : Long Legs and Remarkable Beaks, as Well as Size, Form, and Color, Distinguish the Herons, Ibises, and Flamingos. By T. Gilbert Pearson ; Paintings by Maj. Allan Brooks. Vol. LXII, pp. 441-469, 1 ill. in black and white, 3 ills. in color, Oct., 1932.

Bittinger, Charles:

Solar System's Eternal Show. 10 ills. in color from paintings by Charles Bittinger. Vol. LXXVI, pp. 17-24, July, 1939.

Unfurling Old Glory on Canton Island. 11 ills. in color ; 1 painting of the eclipse by Charles Bittinger. Vol. LXXIII, pp. 753-760, June, 1938.

Bizarre Battleground—the Lonely Aleutians. By Lonnelle Davison. Vol. LXXXII, pp. 316-317, 1 ill., Sept., 1942.

Bizerte, Tunisia :

Eastward from Gibraltar : Overland Route Across North Africa to Tunisia and Libia. By Cyrus French Wicker. Vol. LXXXIII, pp. 115-142, 28 ills., Jan., 1943.

Black Acres (Mucklands of New York) : A Thrilling Sketch in the Vast Volume of Who's Who Among the Peoples That Make America. By Dorothea D. and Fred Everett. Vol. LXXX, pp. 631-652, 13 ills. in black and white, 12 ills. in color, Nov., 1941.

Black Bears:

Once in a Lifetime : Black Bears Rarely Have Quadruplets, But Goofy Did—and the Camera Caught Her Nursing Her Remarkable Family. By Paul B. Kinney. Vol. LXXX, pp. 249-258, 11 ills., Aug., 1941.

Black Death (Epidemic) :

Fearful Famines of the Past : History Will Repeat Itself Unless the American People Conserve Their Resources. By Ralph A. Graves Vol. XXXII, pp. 68-90, 11 ills., July, 1917.

Black Forest, Germany :

Freiburg—Gateway to the Black Forest. By Alicia O'Reardon Overbeck. Vol. LXIV, pp. 213-252, 40 ills. in black and white, 11 ills. in color, Aug., 1933.

Peasant Life in the Black Forest. By Karl Frederick Geiser. Vol. XIX, pp. 635-649, 12 ills., Sept., 1908.

Wandering Through the Black Forest. 13 ills. in color from autochromes by Hans Hildenbrand. Vol. LIV, pp. 658-667, Dec., 1928.

Black-Headed Gulls in London. By A. H. Hall. Vol. XLII, pp. 664-672, 16 ills., June, 1925.

Black Hills (South Dakota), Once Hunting Grounds of the Red Men. Vol. LII, pp. 305-329, 18 ills., Sept., 1927.

Black Republic—Liberia. By Sir Harry Johnston and Ernest Lyon. Vol. XVIII, pp. 334-343, 9 ills., May, 1907.

Black Sea:

Gates to the Black Sea : The Dardanelles, the Bosphorus, and the Sea of Marmora. By Harry Griswold Dwight. Vol. XXVII, pp. 435-459, 27 ills., May, 1915.

Blackbirds:

Blackbirds and Orioles. By Arthur A. Allen. Paintings by Maj. Allan Brooks. Vol. LXVI, pp. 111-130, 12 portraits in color, July, 1934.

Blacker, (Lt. Col.) L. V. S.:

Aërial Conquest of Everest : Flying Over the World's Highest Mountain Realizes the Objective of Many Heroic Explorers. By Lt. Col. L. V. S. Blacker. Vol. LXIV, pp. 127-162, 35 ills., 1 page map, Aug., 1933.

Blackman, Leopold G.:

Pacific: The Most-Explored and Least-Known Region of the Globe. By Leopold G. Blackman. Vol. XIX, pp. 546-563, 11 ills., 1 three-quarters-page map, Aug., 1908.

Blake, Thomas Edward:

Waves and Thrills at Waikiki (Honolulu). 8 ills. in duotone by Thomas Edward Blake. Vol. LXVII, pp. 597-604, May, 1935.

Blanc, Mont, France:

Ascent of Mont Blanc. By Walter Woodburn Hyde. Vol. XXIV, pp. 861-942, 69 ills., Aug., 1913.

Woman's Climbs in the High Alps. By Dora Keen. Vol. XXII, pp. 642-675, 26 ills., July, 1911.

Blanchard, C. J.:

Call of the West. By C. J. Blanchard. Vol. XX, pp. 403-437, 20 ills., three-quarters-page map, May, 1909.

Home-Making by the Government: An Account of the Eleven Immense Irrigating Projects to be Opened in 1908. By C. J. Blanchard. Vol. XIX, pp. 250-287, 23 ills., Apr., 1908.

Millions for Moisture: An Account of the Work of the United States Reclamation Service. By C. J. Blanchard. Vol. XVIII, pp. 217-243, 22 ills., Apr., 1907.

Spirit of the West (United States): The Wonderful Agricultural Development Since the Dawn of Irrigation. By C. J. Blanchard. Vol. XXI, pp. 333-360, 15 ills., Apr., 1910.

Winning the West. By C. J. Blanchard. Vol. XVII, pp. 82-99, 10 ills., 1 page map, Feb., 1906.

Blanchard, Frieda Cobb:

Tuatara: "Living Fossils" Walk on Well-Nigh Inaccessible Rocky Islands off the Coast of New Zealand. By Frieda Cobb Blanchard. Vol. LXVII, pp. 649-662, 14 ills., 1 half-page map, May, 1935.

Blayney, Thomas Lindsey:

Journey in Morocco: "The Land of the Moors." By Thomas Lindsey Blayney. Vol. XXII, pp. 750-776, 24 ills., 1 page map, Aug., 1911.

Blimps:

Aboard a Blimp Hunting U-boats: A Day above the Atlantic Reveals Navy Talk and Navy Ways, Creeping Convoys, and Torpedoed Wrecks. By Mason Sutherland. Vol. LXXXIV, pp. 79-96, 18 ills., July, 1943.

Bliss, Howard S.:

Sunshine in Turkey. By Howard S. Bliss. Vol. XX, pp. 66-76, 1 ill., Jan., 1909.

Blithe Birds of Dooryard, Bush, and Brake. 37 portraits in color from paintings by Maj. Allan Brooks. Vol. LXV, pp. 579-594, May, 1934.

Bloch, Sara:

Sheep Dog Trials in Llangollen: Trained Collies Perform Marvels of Herding in the Cambrian Stakes, Open to the World. By Sara Bloch. Vol. LXXVII, pp. 559-574, 17 ills., Apr. 1940.

"Blood, Toil, Tears, and Sweat": An American Tells the Story of Britain's War Effort, Summed up in Prime Minister Churchill's Unflinching Words. By Harvey Klemmer. Vol. LXXXII, pp. 141-166, 19 ills., Aug., 1942.

Bloodworms:

The Worm Turns. By Samuel Sandrof. Vol. LXXXIX, pp. 775-786, 14 ills., June, 1946.

Blossom (Ship):

Sindbads of Science: Narrative of a Windjammer's Specimen-Collecting Voyage to the Sargasso Sea, to Senegambian Africa and Among Islands of High Adventure in the South Atlantic. By George Finlay Simmons. Vol. LII, pp. 1-75, 89 ills., 1 two-thirds-page map, July, 1927.

Blount, (Col.) Henry F.:

Resolution in Memory of Col. Henry F. Blount. Vol. XXXIII, p. 371, Apr., 1918.

Blue, Rupert:

Conserving the Nation's Man-Power: Disease Weakens Armies, Cripples Industry, Reduces Production. How the Government Is Sanitating the Civil Zones Around Cantonment Areas. A Nation-Wide Campaign for Health. By Rupert Blue. Vol. XXXII, pp. 254-278, 17 ills., Sept., 1917.

Blue Crab. Vol. XVII, p. 46, Jan., 1906.

Blue Seas and Brilliant Costumes Along the Brittany Coast. 29 ills. in color from autochromes by Gervais Courtellemont. Vol. LVI, pp. 142-175, Aug., 1929.

Blueberries:

Taming the Wild Blueberry. By Frederick V. Coville. Vol. XXII, pp. 137-147, 5 ills., Feb., 1911.

Wild Blueberry Tamed: The New Industry of the Pine Barrens of New Jersey. By Frederick V. Coville. Vol. XXIX, pp. 535-546, 10 ills., June, 1916.

Board of Managers. *See* National Geographic Society: Board of Managers.

Board of Trustees. *See* National Geographic Society: Board of Trustees.

Boardman, Mabel:

American Red Cross in Italy. By Mabel Boardman. Vol. XX, pp. 396-397, Apr., 1909.

Honors to the American Navy (Address by Mabel Boardman). Vol. XX, pp. 77-95, Jan., 1909.

National Geographic Society (Address by Mabel Boardman). Vol. XXIII, pp. 273-298, 5 ills., Mar., 1912.

Boats:

The "BB," experimental boat of Dr. Alexander Graham Bell, driven by aërial propellers. Vol. XVIII, ill. 671, Oct., 1907.

China's Teeming Life on the Rivers and Sea. 18 ills. in duotone from photographs by Paul De Gaston and W. Robert Moore. Vol. LXVI, pp. 625-640, Nov., 1934.

Cosmopolitan Shanghai, Key Seaport of China. By W. Robert Moore. Vol. LXII, pp. 311-335, 19 ills., Sept., 1932.

Glass-Bottom Boat. By Charles Frederick Holder. Vol. XX, pp. 761-778, 17 ills., Sept., 1909.

Ho for the Soochow Ho. By Mabel Craft Deering. Vol. LI, pp. 623-649, 32 ills., 1 three-quarters-page map, June, 1927.

House-Boat Days in the Vale of Kashmir. By Florence H. Morden. Vol. LVI, pp. 437-463, 22 ills. in black and white, 30 ills. in color, Oct., 1929.

Landing Craft for Invasion. By Melville Bell Grosvenor. Vol. LXXXVI, pp. 1-30, 26 ills., July, 1944.

Life Afloat in China: Tens of Thousands of Chinese in Congested Ports Spend Their Entire Existence on Boats. By Robert F. Fitch. Vol. LI, pp. 665-686, 28 ills., June, 1927.

Macao, "Land of Sweet Sadness": The Oldest European Settlement in the Far East, Long the Only Haven for Distressed Mariners in the China Sea. By Edgar Allen Forbes. Vol. LXII, pp. 807 357, 13 ills. in black and white, 11 ills. in color, Sept., 1932.

Miniatures of Macao (China). 11 ills. in color from natural-color photographs by W. Robert Moore. Vol. LXII, pp. 340-349, Sept., 1932.

Ore-Boat Unloaders. By W. M. Gregory. Vol. XVIII, pp. 343-345, 1 ill., May, 1907.

Pirate-Fighters of the South China Sea. By Robert Cardwell. Vol. LXXXIX, pp. 787-796, 11 ills., June, 1946.

Ships, from Dugouts to Dreadnoughts. By Capt. Dudley W. Knox. Vol. LXXIII, pp. 57-98, 27 ills. in black and white, 16 ills. in gravure, Jan., 1938.

Speediest Boat. Vol. XXII, pp. 875-878, 2 ills., Sept., 1911.

Surveying the Grand Canyon of the Colorado: An Account of the 1923 Boating Expedition of the United States Geological Survey. By Lewis R. Freeman. Vol. XLV, pp. 471-548, 62 ills., 1 three-quarters-page map, May, 1924.

Transporting a Navy Through the Jungles of Africa in War Time. By Frank J. Magee. Vol. XLII, pp. 331-362, 31 ills., Oct., 1922.

Tuna Harvest of the Sea: A Little-known Epic of the Ocean Is the Story of Southern California's Far-ranging Tuna Fleet. By John Degelman. Vol. LXXVIII, pp. 393-408, 17 ills., Sept., 1940.

See also Canoes and Canoe Trips; Ships and Shipping; Voyages.

Bodine, Margaret L.:

Holidays with Humming Birds. By Margaret L. Bodine. Vol. LIII, pp. 731-742, 15 ills., June, 1928.

Boghaz Keui, Turkey:

Ancient Capital. By Isabel F. Dodd. Vol. XXI, pp. 111-124, 11 ills., Feb., 1910.

Bogoslof (Volcanic Island), Aleutian Islands:

Jack in the Box: An Account of the Strange Performances of the Most Wonderful Island in the World. By Capt. F. M. Munger. Vol. XX, pp. 194-199, 8 ills., Feb., 1909.

Riddle of the Aleutians: A Botanist Explores the Origin of Plants on Ever-misty Islands Now Enshrouded in the Fog of War. By Isobel Wylie Hutchison. Vol. LXXXII, pp. 769-792, 24 ills., Dec., 1942.

Bogotá, Colombia:

Beneath Colombia's Azure Skies. 18 ills. in color from natural-color photographs; 17 ills. by Luis Marden. Vol. LXXVIII, pp. 513-536, Oct., 1940.

Hail Colombia! By Luis Marden. Vol. LXXVIII, pp. 505-536, 10 ills. in black and white, 18 ills. in color, 1 third-page map, Oct., 1940.

Over the Andes to Bogotá. By Frank M. Chapman. Vol. XL, pp. 353-373, 18 ills., Oct., 1921.

Round About Bogotá: A Hunt for New Fruits and Plants Among the Mountain Forests of Colombia's Unique Capital. By Wilson Popenoe. Vol. XLIX, pp. 127-160, 34 ills., 1 third-page map, Feb., 1926.

Bohemia and the Czechs. By Aleš Hrdlička. Vol. XXXI, pp. 163-187, 18 ills., Feb., 1917.

Bolivia:

Bolivia—A Country Without a Debt. By Ignacio Calderon. Vol. XVIII, pp. 573-586, 4 ills., Sept., 1907.

Bolivia, Land of Fiestas. By Alicia O'Reardon Overbeck. Vol. LXVI, pp. 645-660, 16 ills., 1 half-page map, Nov., 1934.

Bolivia—Tin Roof of the Andes. By Henry Albert Phillips. Vol. LXXXIII, pp. 309-332, 5 ills. in black and white, 20 ills. in color, Mar., 1943.

Buenos Aires to Washington by Horse: A Solitary Journey of Two and a Half Years, Through Eleven American Republics, Covers 9,600 Miles of Mountain and Plain, Desert and Jungle. By A. F. Tschiffely. Vol. LV, pp. 135-196, 75 ills., 1 page map, Feb., 1929.

From Panama to Patagonia. By Charles M. Pepper. Vol. XVII, pp. 449-452, 1 ill., Aug., 1906.

Heart of Aymará Land: A Visit to Tiahuanacu, Perhaps the Oldest City of the New World, Lost Beneath the Drifting Sand of Centuries in the Bolivian Highlands. By Stewart E. McMillin. Vol. LI, pp. 213-256, 23 ills. in black and white, 18 ills. in color, 1 half-page map, Feb., 1927.

Bolivia—*Continued*

High Lights in the Peruvian and Bolivian Andes. 18 ills. in color from autochromes by W. Robert Moore. Vol. LI, pp. 218-235, Feb., 1927.

Road to Bolivia. By William E. Curtis. Vol. XI, pp. 208-224, 7 ills., June, 1900.

Road to Bolivia. By William E. Curtis. Vol. XI, pp. 264-280, 6 ills., July, 1900.

Some Wonderful Sights in the Andean Highlands : The Oldest City in America. Sailing on the Lake of the Clouds : The Yosemite of Peru. By Harriet Chalmers Adams. Vol. XIX, pp. 597-618, 19 ills., 1 half-page map, Sept., 1908.

Tin, the Cinderella Metal. By Alicia O'Reardon Overbeck. Vol. LXXVIII, pp. 659-684, 24 ills., Nov., 1940.

What the Latin American Republics Think of the Pan-American Conferences. Vol. XVII, pp. 474-479, Aug., 1906.

See also La Paz.

Boll Weevil (Insect) :

Red Ant Versus the Boll Weevil. Vol. XV, pp. 262-264, June, 1904.

Bombay, India :

Parsees and the Towers of Silence at Bombay, India. By William Thomas Fee. Vol. XVI, pp. 529-554, 16 ills., Dec., 1905.

Bombers:

Air Power for Peace. By Gen. H. H. Arnold. Vol. LXXXIX, pp. 137-193, 35 ills. in black and white, 28 ills. in color, special map supplement, Feb., 1946.

American Bombers Attacking from Australia. By Howell Walker. Vol. LXXXIII, pp. 49-70, 19 ills., 1 map (two-page spread), Jan., 1943.

Cruise on an Escort Carrier. By Melville Bell Grosvenor. Vol. LXXXIV, pp. 513-546, 14 ills. in black and white, 20 ills. in color, Nov., 1943.

8th Air Force in England. 10 ills. in color from U. S. Army Air Forces official photographs. Vol. LXXXVII, pp. 297-304, Mar., 1945.

From Africa to the Alps. 8 ills. in color from U. S. Army Air Forces official photographs. Vol. LXXXIX, pp. 161-168, Feb., 1946.

Navy Wings over the Pacific. 12 ills. in color from U. S. Navy official photographs. Vol. LXXXVI, pp. 241-248, Aug., 1944.

New Queen of the Seas. By Melville Bell Grosvenor. Vol. LXXXII, pp. 1-30, 27 ills., 1 drawing, 1 two-page map, July, 1942.

Our Global Strong Arm. 10 ills. in color from U. S. Army Air Forces official photographs. Vol. LXXXIX, pp. 145-152, Feb., 1946.

Painting History in the Pacific. 19 ills. in color from paintings by Lt. William F. Draper, USNR. Vol. LXXXVI, pp. 409-424, Oct., 1944.

Pocket Carriers Fight the Submarines. 20 ills. in color from U. S. Navy official photographs. Vol. LXXXIV, pp. 521-544, Nov., 1943.

Bombers—*Continued*

Return to Florence. By 1st Lt. Benjamin C. McCartney. Vol. LXXXVII, pp. 257-296, 18 ills. in black and white, 18 ills. in color, Mar., 1945.

Saga of the Carrier *Princeton*. By Capt. William H. Buracker, USN. Vol. LXXXVIII, pp. 189-218, 8 ills. in black and white, 22 ills. in color, 1 map (two-page spread), Aug., 1945.

Take-off for Japan. 22 ills. in color from U. S. Navy official photographs. Vol. LXXXVIII, pp. 193-208, Aug., 1945.

Bombs, Flying :

Air Power for Peace. By Gen. H. H. Arnold. Vol. LXXXIX, pp. 137-193, 35 ills. in black and white, 28 ills. in color, special map supplement, Feb., 1946.

London Wins the Battle. By Marquis W. Childs. Vol. LXXXVIII, pp. 129-152, 21 ills., Aug., 1945.

Bombs over Bible Lands. By Frederick Simpich and W. Robert Moore. Vol. LXXX, pp. 141-180, 34 ills., 1 two-page map, Aug., 1941.

Bonaire (Island), West Indies :

Curaçao and Aruba on Guard. By W. Robert Moore. Vol. LXXXIII, pp. 169-192, 12 ills. in black and white, 10 ills. in color, 4 maps, Feb., 1943.

Bonaparte, Charles J.:

Honors to Peary (Address by Charles J. Bonaparte). Vol. XVIII, pp. 49-60, 1 ill., Jan., 1907.

Bonds Between the Americas. By Frederick Simpich. Vol. LXXII, pp. 785-808, 22 ills. Dec., 1937.

Bonin Islands, Pacific Ocean. *See* Ogasawara Shoto.

Bonivard, François de:

Millennial City : The Romance of Geneva, Capital of the League of Nations. By Ralph A. Graves. Vol. XXXV, pp. 457-476, 11 ills., June, 1919.

Bonn, Germany :

War's Wake in the Rhineland. By Thomas R. Henry. Vol. LXXXVIII, pp. 1-32, 29 ills., 1 third-page map, July, 1945.

Bonnie Scotland, Postwar Style. By Isobel Wylie Hutchison. Vol. LXXXIX, pp. 545-601, 14 ills. in black and white, 38 ills. in color, 1 two-page map, May, 1946.

Book of Monsters (Insects). By David and Marian Fairchild. Vol. XXVI, pp. 89-98, 7 ills., July, 1914.

Booth, Evangeline:

Around the World with the Salvation Army. By Evangeline Booth. Vol. XXXVII, pp. 346-368, 23 ills., Apr., 1920.

Borah, Leo A.:

Connecticut, Prodigy of Ingenuity: Factories Play a Symphony of Industry Amid Colonial Scenes in the State of Steady Habits. By Leo A. Borah. Vol. LXXIV, pp. 279-326, 25 ills. in black and white, 25 ills. in color, 1 two-page map, Sept., 1938.

Diamond Delaware, Colonial Still: Tradition Rules the "Three Lower Counties" Over Which William Penn and Lord Baltimore Went to Law. By Leo A. Borah. Vol. LXVIII, pp. 367-398, 25 ills. in black and white, 15 ills. in color, 1 page map, Sept., 1935.

Home Folk around Historic Cumberland Gap. By Leo A. Borah. Vol. LXXXIV, pp. 741-768, 25 ills., 1 quarter-page map, Dec., 1943.

Iowa, Abiding Place of Plenty: The State Where the Tall Corn Grows Provides the Nation with a Tenth of Its Food Supply. By Leo A. Borah. Vol. LXXVI, pp. 143-182, 15 ills. in black and white, 20 ills. in color, 1 two-page map, Aug., 1939.

Kentucky, Boone's Great Meadow: The Bluegrass State Celebrates Its Sesquicentennial As It Helps the Nation Gird for War. By Leo A. Borah. Vol. LXXXII, pp. 57-89, 13 ills. in black and white, 21 ills. in color, 1 map (two-page spread), July, 1942.

Nebraska, the Cornhusker State. By Leo A. Borah. Vol. LXXXVII, pp. 513-542, 6 ills. in black and white, 23 ills. in color, 1 map (two-page spread), May, 1945.

New Map of the Atlantic Ocean: Foremost Sea of Commerce Becomes World's Battleground and Its Peaceful Islands Rise to Strategic Importance. By Leo A. Borah and Wellman Chamberlin. Text accompanying special map supplement in colors. Vol. LXXX, pp. 407-418, 9 ills., Sept., 1941.

Oregon Finds New Riches. By Leo A. Borah. Vol. XC, pp. 681-728, 15 ills. in black and white, 28 ills. in color, 1 two-page map, Dec., 1946.

Patriotic Pilgrimage to Eastern National Parks: History and Beauty Live Along Paved Roads, Once Indian Trails, Through Virginia, North Carolina, Tennessee, Kentucky, and West Virginia. By Leo A. Borah. Vol. LXV, pp. 663-702, 18 ills. in black and white, 28 ills. in color, 1 two-page map, June, 1934.

Some Odd Pages from the Annals of the Tulip: A "Made" Flower of Unknown Origin Took Medieval Europe by Storm and Caused a Financial Panic in the Netherlands. By Leo A. Borah. Vol. LXIV, pp. 321-343, 13 ills. in black and white, 10 ills. in color, Sept., 1933.

Utah, Carved by Winds and Waters: The Beehive State, Settled Only 89 Years Ago, Stands a Monument to the Courage of Its Founders. By Leo A. Borah. Vol. LXIX, pp. 577-623, 20 ills. in black and white, 22 ills. in color, 1 two-page map, May, 1936.

Washington, the Evergreen State: The Amazing Commonwealth of the Pacific Northwest Which Has Emerged from the Wilderness in a Span of Fifty Years. By Leo A. Borah. Vol. LXIII, pp. 131-196, 50 ills. in black and white, 26 ills. in color, 1 two-page map, Feb., 1933.

Borah, Leo A.—*Continued*

Washington, Home City and Show Place: To Residents and Visitors the Nation's Capital Presents Varied Sides as the City Steadily Grows in Beauty and Stature. By Leo A. Borah. Vol. LXXI, pp. 663-695, 11 ills. in black and white, 20 ills. in color, June, 1937.

Borchgrevink, (Comdr.) C. E.:

National Geographic Society Expedition in the West Indies. Vol. XIII, pp. 209-213, 2 half-page maps, June, 1902.

National Geographic Society Expedition to Martinique and St. Vincent. Vol. XIII, pp. 183-184, 2 ills., June, 1902.

Borneo:

Colonial Government in Borneo. By James M. Hubbard. Vol. XI, pp. 359-363, Sept., 1900.

Keeping House in Borneo. By Virginia Hamilton. Vol. LXXXVIII, pp. 293-324, 28 ills., 1 page map, Sept., 1945.

Notes on the Sea Dyaks of Borneo. By Edwin H. Gomes. Vol. XXII, pp. 695-723, 26 ills., Aug., 1911.

Sarawak: The Land of the White Rajahs. By Harrison W. Smith. Vol. XXXV, pp. 110-167, 58 ills., 1 half-page map, Feb., 1919.

Bornholm (Island), Denmark:

Bornholm—Denmark in a Nutshell. By Mason Sutherland. Vol. LXXXVII, pp. 239-256, 20 ills., 1 half-page map, Feb., 1945.

"Bornholmers" (Herring):

Bornholm—Denmark in a Nutshell. By Mason Sutherland. Vol. LXXXVII, pp. 239-256, 20 ills., 1 half-page map, Feb., 1945.

Bosnia:

East of the Adriatic: Notes on Dalmatia, Montenegro, Bosnia, and Herzegovina. By Kenneth McKenzie. Vol. XXIII, pp. 1159-1187, 37 ills., 1 page map, Dec., 1912.

Great Turk and His Lost Provinces. By William Eleroy Curtis. Vol. XIV, pp. 45-61, 7 ills., Feb., 1903.

Where East Meets West: A Visit to Picturesque Dalmatia, Montenegro, and Bosnia. By Marian Cruger Coffin. Vol. XIX, pp. 309-344, 26 ills., 1 half-page map, May, 1908.

Bosporus (Strait):

Beside the Bosporus, Divider of Continents. 11 ills. in color from natural-color photographs by Maynard Owen Williams. Vol. LVI, pp. 492-501, Oct., 1929.

Constantinople and Sancta Sophia. By Edwin A. Grosvenor. Vol. XXVII, pp. 459-482, 21 ills., May, 1915.

Gates to the Black Sea: The Dardanelles, the Bosphorus, and the Sea of Marmora. By Harry Griswold Dwight. Vol. XXVII, pp. 435-459, 27 ills., May, 1915.

Seeing 3,000 Years of History in Four Hours: A Panorama of Ancient, Medieval, and Modern Events Against a Background of Mythology Unfolds During an Airplane Journey from Constantinople to Athens. By Maynard Owen Williams. Vol. LIV, pp. 719-739, 24 ills., 1 two-thirds-page map, Dec., 1928.

Bosporus (Strait)—*Continued*

Summer Holidays on the Bosporus. By Maynard Owen Williams. Vol. LVI, pp. 487-508, 13 ills. in black and white, 11 ills. in color, 1 half-page map, Oct., 1929.

Bosque, Fernando del:

Expedition into Texas of Fernando del Bosque, Standard-Bearer of the King, Don Carlos II, in the Year 1675. Translated from an Old, Unpublished Spanish Manuscript. By Betty B. Brewster. Vol. XIV, pp. 339-348, Sept., 1903.

Bosshard, W.:

Life on the Steppes and Oases of Chinese Turkestan. 32 ills. in color from natural-color photographs by W. Bosshard. Vol. LIX, pp. 332-357, Mar., 1931.

Bosson, (Mrs.) George C., Jr.:

Biskra, the Ziban Queen. By Mrs. George C. Bosson, Jr. Vol. XIX, pp. 563-593, 29 ills., 1 eighth-page map, Aug., 1908.

Notes on Normandy. By Mrs. George C. Bosson, Jr. Vol. XXI, pp. 775-782, 5 ills., Sept., 1910.

Sicily, the Battle-Field of Nations and of Nature. By Mrs. George C. Bosson, Jr. Vol. XX, pp. 96-118, 25 ills., 1 page map, Jan., 1909.

Bostelmann, Else:

Carnivores of a Lightless World (Fishes). 8 ills. in color from paintings by Else Bostelmann. Vol. LXVI, pp. 693-700, Dec., 1934.

Exploring Neptune's Hidden World of Vivid Color. 8 ills. in color from paintings by E. Bostelmann. Vol. LXII, pp. 747-754, Dec., 1932.

Fantastic Sea Life from Abyssal Depths. 8 ills. in color from paintings by E. Bostelmann. Vol. LXI, pp. 71-78, Jan., 1932.

Flashes From Ocean Deeps. 16 ills. in color from paintings by Else Bostelmann, Helen D. Tee-Van, and E. J. Geske. Vol. LXVI, pp. 677-700, Dec., 1934.

Luminous Life in the Depths of the Sea. 8 ills. in color from paintings by E. Bostelmann. Vol. LIX, pp. 667-674, June, 1931.

Monster and Midget Squid and Octopuses. 8 ills. in color from paintings by Else Bostelmann. Vol. LXVIII, pp. 193-200, Aug., 1935.

Multi-Hued Marvels of a Coral Reef. 8 ills. in color from paintings by Else Bostelmann. Vol. LXV, pp. 719-726, June, 1934.

Sea Floor Aquarelles from Tongareva. 8 ills. in color from paintings by Else Bostelmann. Vol. LXXIV, pp. 383-390, Sept., 1938.

Strange Creatures of Sunny Seas (Mollusks, Crustaceans, etc.). 8 ills. in color from paintings by Else Bostelmann. Vol. LXXI, pp. 211-218, Feb., 1937.

Undersea Gardens of the North Atlantic Coast. 8 ills. in color from paintings by Else Bostelmann. Vol. LXX, pp. 217-224, Aug., 1936.

Whales, Porpoises, and Dolphins. 31 ills. in color from paintings by Else Bostelmann. Vol. LXXVII, pp. 41-80, Jan., 1940.

Boston, Massachusetts:

Boston Through Midwest Eyes. By Frederick Simpich. Vol. LXX, pp. 37-82, 24 ills. in black and white, 31 ills. in color, July, 1936.

Hub City, Cradle of American Liberty. 31 ills. in color from natural-color photographs by B. Anthony Stewart and Luis Marden. Vol. LXX, pp. 49-72, July, 1936.

Bosworth, Abbie L.:

Life in a Norway Valley: An American Girl Is Welcomed Into the Homemaking and Haying of Happy Hallingdal. By Abbie L. Bosworth. Vol. LXVII, pp. 627-648, 21 ills., 1 half-page map, May, 1935.

Botany. *See* Agricultural and Botanical Explorers; Flowers; Plants; Trees.

Botflies (Insects):

Life Story of the Mosquito. By Graham Fairchild. With 10 ills. in color from paintings. Vol. LXXXV, pp. 180-195, 5 ills. in black and white, 1 drawing, Feb., 1944.

Bougainville (Island), Solomon Islands:

Fiji Patrol on Bougainville. By David D. Duncan. Vol. LXXXVII, pp. 87-104, 9 ills. in black and white, 11 ills. in color, Jan., 1945.

Jungle War: Bougainville and New Caledonia. 17 ills. in color from paintings by Lieut. William F. Draper. Vol. LXXXV, pp. 417-432, Apr., 1944.

Woman's Experiences among Stone Age Solomon Islanders: Primitive Life Remains Unchanged in Tropical Jungleland Where United States Forces Now Are Fighting. By Eleanor Schirmer Oliver. Vol. LXXXII, pp. 813-836, 26 ills., 1 half-page map, Dec., 1942.

Boulton, Laura C.:

Timbuktu and Beyond: Desert City of Romantic Savor and Salt Emerges into World Life Again as Trading Post of France's Vast African Empire. By Laura C. Boulton. Vol. LXXIX, pp. 631-670, 18 ills. in black and white, 26 ills. in color, 1 map (two-page spread), May, 1941.

Boundaries:

Alaskan Boundary. By John W. Foster. Vol. X, pp. 425-456, 10 page maps, special map supplement, Nov., 1899.

Alaskan Boundary Decision. Vol. XIV, p. 423, Nov., 1903.

Alaskan Boundary Dispute. Vol. XIV, p. 79, Feb., 1903.

Alaskan Boundary Tribunal. By John W. Foster. Vol. XV, pp. 1-12, 1 half-page map, special map supplement, Jan., 1904.

Along Our Side of the Mexican Border. By Frederick Simpich. Vol. XXXVIII, pp. 61-80, 9 ills., 1 quarter-page map, July, 1920.

Anglo-Venezuelan Boundary Dispute. By Marcus Baker. Vol. XI, pp. 129-144, 2 ills., 1 page map, Apr., 1900.

Boundaries—*Continued*

Argentina-Chile Boundary Award. Vol. XIV, pp. 115-116, Mar., 1903.

Argentine-Chile Boundary. Vol. XIII, p. 117, Mar., 1902.

Argentine-Chile Boundary Dispute. Vol. XIII, pp. 27-28, Jan., 1902.

Battle-Line of Languages in Western Europe: A Problem in Human Geography More Perplexing Than That of International Boundaries. By A. L. Guerard. Vol. XLIII, pp. 145-180, 36 ills., Feb., 1923.

Boundaries of Territorial Acquisitions. Vol. XII, pp. 373-377, 1 page chart, Oct., 1901.

Brazil-French Guiana Boundary Decision. Vol. XII, p. 83, Feb., 1901.

California and Nevada Boundary. Vol. X, pp. 416-417, Oct., 1899.

Canadian Boundary. By John W. Foster. Vol. XIV, pp. 85-89, Mar., 1903.

Charting a Coast-Line of 20,000 Miles (Alaska). Vol. XX, pp. 608-609, July, 1909.

Chile-Argentina Boundary Dispute. Vol. XIII, p. 220, June, 1902.

Decision of the Alaskan Boundary Tribunal. Vol. XV, pp. 12-14, Jan., 1904.

Geographic's New Map of Germany and Its Approaches: With a Review of The Society's Maps of Europe. By Gilbert Grosvenor. Text accompanying special map supplement in colors. Vol. LXXXVI, pp. 66-72, 1 ill., July, 1944.
  Contains information on the boundary changes in Europe (1912-1940).

How the United States Grew. By McFall Kerbey. Vol. LXIII, pp. 631-649, 17 ills., 1 page map, May, 1933.

Idaho and Montana Boundary Line. By Richard U. Goode. Vol. XI, pp. 23-29, 1 ill., Jan., 1900.

Location of the Boundary Between Nicaragua and Costa Rica. By Arthur P. Davis. Vol. XII, pp. 22-28, 1 ill., 1 half-page map, Jan., 1901.

Lost Boundary of Texas. By Marcus Baker. Vol. XII, pp. 430-432, Dec., 1901.

Marking the Alaskan Boundary. Vol. XIX, pp. 176-189, 16 ills., Mar., 1908.

Marking the Alaskan Boundary. By Thomas Riggs, Jr. Vol XX, pp. 593-607, 17 ills., July, 1909.

New Map of Europe: Showing the Boundaries Established by the Peace Conference at Paris and by Subsequent Decisions of the Supreme Council of the Allied and Associated Powers. By Ralph A. Graves. Text accompanying special map supplement in colors. Vol. XXXIX, pp. 157-177, 18 ills., Feb., 1921.

Original Boundary Stones of the District of Columbia. By Ernest A. Shuster, Jr. Vol. XX, pp. 356-359, 6 ills., 1 half-page map, Apr., 1909.

Surveying the 141st Meridian (Boundary Line Between Canada and Alaska). By Thomas Riggs, Jr. Vol. XXIII, pp. 685-713, 46 ills., 1 page map, July, 1912.

Boundaries—*Continued*

Wandering Islands in the Rio Grande. By Mrs. Albert S. Burleson. Vol. XXIV, pp. 381-386, 2 ills., 1 three-quarters-page map, Mar., 1913.

Boundary Changes in Europe from 1912 to 1940. *See* Review of The Society's Maps of Europe.

Bourchier, James D.:

Rise of Bulgaria. By James D. Bourchier. Vol. XXIII, pp. 1104-1118, 13 ills., Nov., 1912.

Bourges, France:

Beauties of France. By Arthur Stanley Riggs. Vol. XXVIII, pp. 391-491, 73 ills. in black and white, 16 ills. in color, 1 half-page map, Nov., 1915.

Bourlay, Reginald A.:

Wings Over Nature's Zoo in Africa. 20 ills. in duotone from photographs by Reginald A. Bourlay. Vol. LXXVI, pp. 527-542, Oct., 1939.

Boutwell, William Dow:

Mysterious Tomb of a Giant Meteorite (Meteor Crater, Arizona). By William D. Boutwell. Vol. LIII, pp. 721-730, 10 ills., June, 1928.

Old World Charm in Modern Quebec. 9 ills. in color from natural-color photographs by William Dow Boutwell. Vol. LVII, pp. 506-515, Apr., 1930.

Quebec, Capital of French Canada. By William Dow Boutwell. Vol. LVII, pp. 515-522, 6 ills. in black and white, 12 ills. in color, Apr., 1930.

Bouvet Island, Antarctic Region:

Definite Location of Bouvet Island. By O. H. Tittmann. Vol. X, pp. 413-414, Oct., 1899.

Bovey, Wilfrid:

Gaspé Peninsula Wonderland. By Wilfrid Bovey. Vol. LXVIII, pp. 209-230, 13 ills. in black and white, 15 ills. in color, 1 half-page map, Aug., 1935.

Bowdoin (Ship) in North Greenland: Arctic Explorers Place Tablet to Commemorate Sacrifices of the Lady Franklin Bay Expedition. By Donald B. MacMillan. Vol. XLVII, pp. 677-722, 49 ills., June, 1925.

Bowers, George M.:

Planting Fishes in the Ocean. By George M. Bowers. Vol. XVIII, pp. 715-723, 5 ills., Nov., 1907.

Boxer Uprising: China:

Causes that Led Up to the Siege of Peking. By W. A. P. Martin. Vol. XII, pp. 53-63, 1 ill., Feb., 1901.

Chinese "Boxers." By Llewellyn James Davies. Vol. XI, pp. 281-287, July, 1900.

Shifting Scenes on the Stage of New China. Vol. XXXVIII, pp. 422-428, 4 ills., Nov., 1920.

Boy Scouts:

Star and Crescent on Parade. 29 ills. in color from natural-color photographs, by Maynard Owen Williams. Vol. LXXXVII, pp. 585-616, May, 1945.

Youth Explores Its World. By Frederick Simpich. Vol. LXV, pp. 643-662, 21 ills., May, 1934.

Boyden, Amanda:

Changing Shanghai. By Amanda Boyden. Vol. LXXII, pp. 485-508, 21 ills., 1 two-thirds-page and 1 quarter-page maps, Oct., 1937.

Boyhood of (Sir Walter) Raleigh. Reproduction in color of the painting by Sir John Millais, Tate Gallery, London. Vol. XLIX, text, p. 596; supplement, May, 1926.

Boys' and Girls' Agricultural Clubs. Vol. XXII, pp. 639-641, 4 ills., July, 1911.

Bracq, Jean C.:

Colonial Expansion of France. By Jean C. Bracq. Vol. XI, pp. 225-238, 1 page map, June, 1900.

Bradley, La Verne:

San Francisco : Gibraltar of the West Coast. By La Verne Bradley. Vol. LXXXIII, pp. 279-308, 28 ills., Mar., 1943.

Women at Work. By La Verne Bradley. Vol. LXXXVI, pp. 193-220, 23 ills., Aug., 1944.

Women in Uniform. By La Verne Bradley. Vol. LXXXIV, pp. 445-458, 10 ills., Oct., 1943.

Bradley, Walter W.:

Some Mexican Transportation Scenes. By Walter W. Bradley. Vol. XXI, pp. 985-991, 10 ills., Dec., 1910.

Braemar, Scotland :

Clans in Kilt and Plaidie Gather at Braemar. 11 ills. in color from natural-color photographs by Maynard Owen Williams. Vol. LXVIII, pp. 153-160, Aug., 1935.

Brahmaputra (River), India-Tibet :

The Tsangpo. By James Mascarene Hubbard. Vol. XII, pp. 32-35, Jan., 1901.

Brandes, E. W.:

Into Primeval Papua by Seaplane : Seeking Disease-Resisting Sugar Cane, Scientists Find Neolithic Man in Unmapped Nooks of Sorcery and Cannibalism. By E. W. Brandes. Vol. LVI, pp. 253-332, 98 ills., 1 three-quarters-page map, Sept., 1929.

Branner, J. C.:

Recent Ascent of Itambé (Brazil). By J. C. Branner. Vol. X, p. 183, May, 1899.

Brazil:

Air Cruising Through New Brazil : A National Geographic Reporter Spots Vast Resources Which the Republic's War Declaration Adds to Strength of United Nations. By Henry Albert Phillips. Vol. LXXXII, pp. 503-536, 32 ills., Oct., 1942.

Brazil—*Continued*

Amazon, Father of Waters : The Earth's Mightiest River Drains a Basin of More Than 2,700,-000 Square Miles, from Which Came Originally the World's Finest Rubber. By W. L. Schurz. Vol. XLIX, pp. 445-463, 15 ills., Apr., 1926.

Brazil and Peru. Vol. XVII, pp. 203-204, Apr., 1906.

Brazil-French Guiana Boundary Decision. Vol. XII, p. 83, Feb., 1901.

Brazil's Potent Weapons. By W. Robert Moore. Vol. LXXXV, pp. 41-78, 16 ills. in black and white, 18 ills. in color, 1 two-page map, Jan., 1944.

Bright Facets of Brazil. 18 ills. in color from natural-color photographs by W. Robert Moore. Vol. LXXXV, pp. 49-72, Jan., 1944.

By Seaplane to Six Continents : Cruising 60,000 Miles, Italian Argonauts of the Air See World Geography Unroll, and Break New Sky Trails Over Vast Brazilian Jungles. By Comdr. Francesco de Pinedo. Vol. LIV, pp. 247-301, 60 ills., 1 two-page map, Sept., 1928.

Cowboys and Caymans of Marajó. 12 ills. in color from natural-color photographs by Desmond Holdridge. Vol. LXXIV, pp. 645-652, Nov., 1938.

Exploring the Valley of the Amazon in a Hydroplane : Twelve Thousand Miles of Flying Over the World's Greatest River and Greatest Forest to Chart the Unknown Parima River from the Sky. By Capt. Albert W. Stevens. Vol. XLIX, pp. 353-420, 86 ills., 1 page map, Apr., 1926.

Falls of Iguazu. By Marie Robinson Wright. Vol. XVII, pp. 456-460, 4 ills., Aug., 1906.

Fishing and Hunting Tales from Brazil. By Dewey Austin Cobb. Vol. XX, pp. 917-920, Oct., 1909.

Gigantic Brazil and Its Glittering Capital. By Frederick Simpich. Vol. LVIII, pp. 733-778, 54 ills., 1 page map, Dec., 1930.

How Latin America Looks from the Air : U. S. Army Airplanes Hurdle the High Andes, Brave Brazil Jungles, and Follow Smoking Volcanoes to Map New Sky Paths Around South America. By Maj. Herbert A. Dargue. Vol. LII, pp. 451-502, 52 ills., 1 page map, Oct., 1927.

In Humboldt's Wake : Narrative of a National Geographic Society Expedition Up the Orinoco and Through the Strange Casiquiare Canal to Amazonian Waters. By Ernest G. Holt. Vol. LX, pp. 621-644, 27 ills., 1 two-thirds-page map, Nov., 1931.

Journey by Jungle Rivers to the Home of the Cock-of-the-Rock : Naturalists Enter the Amazon, Voyage Through the Heart of Tropical South America, and Emerge at the Mouth of the Orinoco. By Ernest G. Holt. Vol. LXIV, pp. 585-630, 49 ills., 1 two-thirds-page map, Nov., 1933.

Recent Ascent of Itambé. By J. C. Branner. Vol. X, p. 183, May, 1899.

Brazil—*Continued*

Skypaths Through Latin America : Flying From Our Nation's Capital Southward Over Jungles, Remote Islands, and Great Cities on an Aërial Survey of the East Coast of South America. By Frederick Simpich. Vol. LIX, pp. 1-79, 77 ills., 1 page map, Jan., 1931.

South America Fifty Years Hence. By Charles M. Pepper. Vol. XVII, pp. 427-432, special map supplement in colors, Aug., 1906.

Through Brazil to the Summit of Mount Roraima. By G. H. H. Tate. Vol. LVIII, pp. 585-605, 24 ills., 1 half-page map, Nov., 1930.

Through Paraguay and Southern Matto Grosso. By Sir Christopher H. Gibson. Vol. LXXXIV, pp. 459-488, 20 ills. in black and white, 11 ills. in color, 1 two-thirds-page map, Oct., 1943.

Visit to the Brazilian Coffee Country. By Robert De C. Ward. Vol. XXII, pp. 908-931, 19 ills., 1 half-page map, Oct., 1911.

Wonder Island of the Amazon Delta : On Marajó Cowboys Ride Oxen, Tree-dwelling Animals Throng Dense Forests, While Strange Fishes and Birds Help Make a Zoologist's Paradise. By Hugh B. Cott. Vol. LXXIV, pp. 635-670, 30 ills. in black and white, 12 ills. in color, 1 half-page map, Nov., 1938.

World's Great Waterfalls : Visits to Mighty Niagara, Wonderful Victoria, and Picturesque Iguazu. By Theodore W. Noyes. Vol. L, pp. 29-59, 29 ills., July, 1926.

See also Rio de Janeiro ; Santos ; São Paulo.

Brazil's Potent Weapons. By W Robert Moore, Vol. LXXXV, pp. 41-78, 16 ills. in black and white, 18 ills. in color, 1 two-page map, Jan., 1944.

Bread Making:

Bread Making in Many Lands. Vol. XIX, pp. 165-179, 15 ills., Mar., 1908.

How the World Is Fed. By William Joseph Showalter. Vol. XXIX, pp. 1-110, 101 ills., Jan., 1916.

"Breaking Up" of the Yukon. By Capt. George S. Gibbs. Vol. XVII, pp. 268-272, 6 ills., May, 1906.

Breasted, Charles:

Exploring the Secrets of Persepolis. By Charles Breasted. Vol. LXIV, pp. 381-420, 48 ills., 1 half-page map, 1 plan, Oct., 1933.

Bredin, Dee:

Java Assignment. By Dee Bredin. Vol. LXXXI, pp. 89-119, 32 ills., 1 two-thirds-page map, Jan., 1942.

Breed, Austin A.:

Spain and Morocco. 6 ills. in color from photographs by Austin A. Breed. Vol. XXXI, pp. 257-270, Mar., 1917.

Breed, (Lt.) Jack:

Flaming Cliffs of Monument Valley. By Lt. Jack Breed, USNR. With 9 ills. in color from natural-color photographs by the author and Warren T. Mithoff. Vol. LXXXVIII, pp. 452-461, Oct., 1945.

Brewer, Elizabeth H.:

Peculiar Caves of Asia Minor. By Elizabeth H. Brewer. Vol. XXII, pp. 870 875, 5 ills., Sept., 1911.

Brewster, Betty B.:

Expedition into Texas of Fernando del Bosque, Standard-Bearer of the King, Don Carlos II. in the Year 1675. Translated from an Old, Unpublished Spanish Manuscript. By Betty B. Brewster. Vol. XIV, pp. 339-348, Sept., 1903.

Bridges:

Bridges, from Grapevine to Steel. By Frederick Simpich. Vol. LXIX, pp. 391-406, 13 ills., Mar., 1936.

California's Coastal Redwood Realm : Along a Belt of Tall Trees a Giant Bridge Speeds the Winning of Our Westernmost Frontier. By J. R. Hildebrand. Vol. LXXV, pp. 133-184, 31 ills. in black and white, 17 ills. in color, 1 page-and-a-half map, Feb., 1939.

Bridges, Natural :

Colossal Natural Bridges of Utah. Vol. XV, pp. 367-369, 2 ills., Sept., 1904.

Encircling Navajo Mountain (Utah) with a Pack-Train : An Expedition to a Hitherto Untraversed Region of Our Southwest Discovers a New Route to Rainbow Natural Bridge. By Charles L. Bernheimer. Vol. XLIII, pp. 197-224, 33 ills., 1 half-page map, Feb., 1923.

Great Natural Bridges of Utah. Vol. XVIII, pp. 199-204, 3 ills., Mar., 1907.

Great Natural Bridges of Utah. By Byron Cummings. Vol. XXI, pp. 157-167, 7 ills., Feb., 1910.

Great Rainbow Natural Bridge of Southern Utah. By Joseph E. Pogue. Vol. XXII, pp. 1048-1056, 6 ills., Nov., 1911.

Bridgman, Herbert L.:

New British Empire of the Sudan. By Herbert L. Bridgman. Vol. XVII, pp. 241-267, 32 ills., 1 quarter-page map, May, 1906.

Peary's Work and Prospects. Vol. X, pp. 414-415, Oct., 1899.

Ten Years of the Peary Arctic Club. By Herbert L. Bridgman. Vol. XIX, pp. 661-668, 3 ills., Sept., 1908.

Brigham, Albert Perry:

Introduction to Physical Geography. By Albert Perry Brigham and Grove Karl Gilbert. Vol. XIV, pp. 21-26, 6 ills., Jan., 1903.

Bright Angel Trail, Arizona :

Experiences in the Grand Canyon. By Ellsworth and Emery Kolb. Vol. XXVI, pp. 99-184 70 ills., 1 page map, Aug., 1914.

Bright Bits in Poland's Mountainous South. 16 ills. in color from natural-color photographs by Hans Hildenbrand. Vol. LXVII, pp. 353-360, Mar., 1935.

Bright Corners of Time-Mellowed Germany. 11 ills. in color from natural-color photographs by Hans Hildenbrand and Wilhelm Tobien. Vol. LXIV, pp. 222-231, Aug., 1933.

Bright Facets of Brazil. 18 ills. in color from natural-color photographs by W. Robert Moore. Vol. LXXXV, pp. 49-72, Jan., 1944.

Bright Facets of Italy's Grandeur. 9 ills. in color from natural-color photographs; 8 ills. by B. Anthony Stewart. Vol. LXXVII, pp. 355-362, Mar., 1940.

Bright Flashes from Pacific Corals (Fishes). 24 ills. in color from natural-color photographs by Walter H. Chute. Vol. LXXIX, pp. 349-372, Mar., 1941.

Bright-hued Pets of Cage and Aviary. 51 portraits in color from paintings by Maj. Allan Brooks. Vol. LXXIV, pp. 783-790, Dec., 1938.

Bright Pages from an Asiatic Travel Log. 12 ills. in color from natural-color photographs by Maynard Owen Williams. Vol. LXII, pp. 544-553, Nov., 1932.

Bright Patterns of Long Island Life. 18 ills. in color from natural-color photographs; 14 ills. by Willard R. Culver. Vol. LXXV, pp. 429-460, Apr., 1939.

Bringing the World to Our Foreign-Language Soldiers: How a Military Training Camp Is Solving a Seemingly Unsurmountable Problem by Using The Geographic. By Christina Krysto. Vol. XXXIV, pp. 81-90, 4 ills., Aug., 1918.

Briquets (Fuel):

Ideal Fuel: The American Coal Briquetting Industry. By Guy Elliott Mitchell. Vol. XXI, pp. 1067-1074, 4 ills., Dec., 1910.

Brisbane, Australia:

Capital Cities of Australia. By W. Robert Moore. Vol. LXVIII, pp. 667-722, 32 ills. in black and white, 24 ills. in color, 1 two-page map, Dec., 1935.

Britain Fights in the Fields. By Francis A. Flood. Vol. LXXXVI, pp. 31-65, 17 ills. in black and white, 21 ills. in color, July, 1944.

Britain Just Before the Storm: A Canadian Canoe Threads Old English Waterways Athrob with the Midlands' Industrial Life. By Amos Burg. Vol. LXXVIII, pp. 185-212, 14 ills. in black and white, 9 ills. in color, 1 two-thirds-page map, Aug., 1940.

British Antarctic Expedition. Vol. XII, pp. 339-345, Sept., 1901.

British Antarctic Expedition under Captain Robert F. Scott. Vol. XLV, pp. 255-270, 16 ills., Mar., 1924.

British Association for the Advancement of Science:

Geography at the British Association. Vol. XI, pp. 475-478, Dec., 1900.

British Colonial Scenes. Vol. XXIX, pp. 233-248, 16 ills., Mar., 1916.

British Columbia (Province), Canada:

Alaskan Highway an Engineering Epic: Mosquitoes, Mud, and Muskeg Minor Obstacles of 1,671-mile Race to Throw the Alcan Life Line Through Thick Forests and Uninhabited Wilderness. By Froelich Rainey. Vol. LXXXIII, pp. 143-168, 21 ills., 3 maps, Feb., 1943.

Columbia (River) Turns on the Power. By Maynard Owen Williams. Vol. LXXIX, pp. 749-792, 25 ills. in black and white, 18 ills. in color, June, 1941.

Exploration in the Canadian Rockies. Vol. X, pp. 135-136, Apr., 1899.

Factors Which Modify the Climate of Victoria, British Columbia. By Arthur W. McCurdy. Vol. XVIII, pp. 345-348, 2 quarter-page maps, May, 1907.

Forests of Canada. Vol. XIV, pp. 106-108, Mar., 1903.

Geologist's Paradise (Canadian Rockies). By Charles D. Walcott. Vol. XXII, pp. 509-536, 28 ills., panorama, June, 1911.

Hunting the Grizzly in British Columbia. By Joseph Wendle. Vol. XVIII, pp. 612-615, 3 ills., Sept., 1907.

Life on a Yukon Trail. By Alfred Pearce Dennis. Part I, Vol. X, pp. 377-391, 8 ills., 1 page map, Oct., 1899. Part II, Vol. X, pp. 457-466, 7 ills., Nov., 1899.

Monarch of the Canadian Rockies (Mount Robson). By Charles D. Walcott. Vol. XXIV, pp. 626-639, 13 ills., panorama, May, 1913.

Monarch of the Canadian Rockies—Robson Peak. Vol. XXIV, panorama, May, 1913.

Nakwasina Goes North: A Man, a Woman, and a Pup Cruise from Tacoma to Juneau in a 17-Foot Canoe. By Jack Calvin. Vol. LXIV, pp. 1-42, 24 ills., 1 page map, July, 1933.

On the Trail of a Horse Thief (Columbia River). By Herbert W. Gleason. Vol. XXXV, pp. 349-358, 6 ills., Apr., 1919.

Peaks and Parks of Western Canada. 11 ills. from photographs; 5 ills. by W. J. Oliver. Vol. LXXX, pp. 516-526, Oct., 1941.

Peaks and Trails in the Canadian Alps. 16 ills. in duotone from photographs by Byron Harmon and Clifford White. Vol. LXV, pp. 627-642, May, 1934.

Recent Exploration in the Canadian Rockies. By Walter D. Wilcox. Part I, Vol. XIII, pp. 151-168, 12 ills., 1 page map, May, 1902. Part II, Vol. XIII, pp. 185-200, 9 ills., June, 1902.

Some Tramps Across the Glaciers and Snowfields of British Columbia. By Howard Palmer. Vol. XXI, pp. 457-487, 25 ills., June, 1910.

Stikine River in 1898. By Eliza R. Scidmore. Vol. X, pp. 1-15, 4 ills., Jan., 1899.

Tweedsmuir Park: The Diary of a Pilgrimage. By The Lady Tweedsmuir of Elsfield. Vol. LXXIII, pp. 451-476, 22 ills., 1 half-page and 1 third-page maps, Apr., 1938.

British Columbia (Province), Canada—*Continued*

Vast Timber Belts of Canada. Vol. XVII, pp. 509-511, Sept., 1906.

Wartime in the Pacific Northwest. By Frederick Simpich. Vol. LXXXII, pp. 421-464, 25 ills. in black and white, 23 ills. in color, 1 half-page map, Oct., 1942.

British Commonwealth of Nations:

British Commonwealth of Nations: "Organized Freedom" Around the World. By Eric Underwood. Vol. LXXXIII, pp. 485-524, 31 ills., Apr., 1943.

United States and the British Empire. By Leonard David Gammans. Vol. LXXXVII, pp. 562-564, May, 1945.

Yanks at Westminster. By Capt. Leonard David Gammans. Vol. XC, pp. 223-252, 6 ills. in black and white, 19 ills. in color, Aug., 1946.

See also Great Britain; Northern Ireland; *and* names of colonies and dominions.

British East Africa:

Amid the Snow Peaks of the Equator: A Naturalist's Exploration Around Ruwenzori, with an Excursion to the Congo State, and an Account of the Terrible Scourge of Sleeping Sickness. By A. F. R. Wollaston. Vol. XX, pp. 256-277, 11 ills., Mar., 1909.

British Commonwealth of Nations: "Organized Freedom" Around the World. By Eric Underwood. Vol. LXXXIII, pp. 485-524, 31 ills., Apr., 1943.

Elephant Hunting in Equatorial Africa with Rifle and Camera. By Carl E. Akeley. Vol. XXIII, pp. 779-810, 30 ills., Aug., 1912.

Great African Lake (Victoria). By Sir Henry M. Stanley. Vol. XIII, pp. 169-172, 1 half-page map, May, 1902.

Uganda, "Land of Something New": Equatorial African Area Reveals Snow-Crowned Peaks, Crater Lakes, Jungle-Story Beasts, Human Giants, and Forest Pygmies. By Jay Marston. Vol. LXXI, pp. 109-130, 22 ills., 1 two-thirds-page map, Jan., 1937.

When a Drought Blights Africa: Hippos and Elephants Are Driven Insane by Suffering, in the Lorian Swamp, Kenya Colony. By Capt. A. T. Curle. Vol. LV, pp. 521-528, 9 ills., Apr., 1929.

Where Roosevelt Will Hunt. By Sir Harry Johnston. Vol. XX, pp. 207-256, 43 ills., special map supplement, Mar., 1909.

Wild Man and Wild Beast in Africa. By Theodore Roosevelt. Vol. XXII, pp. 1-33, 41 ills., 1 page map, Jan., 1911.

Zanzibar. By Mrs. Harris R. Childs. Vol. XXIII, pp. 810-824, 11 ills., Aug., 1912.

British Empire. *See* British Commonwealth of Nations.

British Guiana:

Anglo-Venezuelan Boundary Dispute. By Marcus Baker. Vol. XI, pp. 129-144, 2 ills., 1 page map, Apr., 1900.

British Guiana—*Continued*

Impression of the Guiana Wilderness. By Angelo Heilprin. Vol. XVIII, pp. 373-381, 6 ills., June, 1907.

Kaieteur and Roraima: The Great Falls and the Great Mountain of the Guianas. By Henry Edward Crampton. Vol. XXXVIII, pp. 227-244, 12 ills., 1 half-page map, Sept., 1920.

New World to Explore: In the Tree-Roof of the British Guiana Forest Flourishes Much Hitherto-Unknown Life. By Maj. R. W. G. Hingston. Vol. LXII, pp. 617-642, 35 ills., Nov., 1932.

Notes from a Naturalist's Experiences in British Guiana. By C. H. Eigenmann. Vol. XXII, pp. 859-870, 8 ills., Sept., 1911.

World's Greatest Waterfall: The Kaieteur Fall, in British Guiana. By Leonard Kennedy. Vol. XXII, pp. 846-859, 6 ills., 1 page map, Sept., 1911.

British Honduras:

Notes on Central America. Vol. XVIII, pp. 272-278, 1 ill., 1 half-page map, Apr., 1907.

British Isles:

Modern Pilgrim's Map of the British Isles. By Andrew H. Brown. Text accompanying special map supplement in colors. Vol. LXXI, pp. 795-802, 3 ills., June, 1937.

See also Channel Islands; Great Britain; Man, Isle of; Scilly Isles; Skokholm; Wight, Isle of.

British Malaya:

British Commonwealth of Nations: "Organized Freedom" Around the World. By Eric Underwood. Vol. LXXXIII, pp. 485-524, 31 ills., Apr., 1943.

See also Singapore.

British New Guinea. *See* Papua.

British Pacific Cable. Vol. XII, p. 78, Feb., 1901.

British South Africa. *See* Union of South Africa.

British South Africa and the Transvaal. By F. F. Hilder. Vol. XI, pp. 81-96, 7 ills., Mar., 1900.

British South Polar Expedition. Vol. XIV, pp. 210-212, May, 1903.

British Take Baku. Vol. XXXIV, pp. 163-164, 1 ill., Aug., 1918.

British West Africa:

British Commonwealth of Nations: "Organized Freedom" Around the World. By Eric Underwood. Vol. LXXXIII, pp. 485-524, 31 ills., Apr., 1943.

Notes on the Ekoi. By P. A. Talbot. Vol. XXIII, pp. 32-38, 8 ills., Jan., 1912.

Three-Wheeling Through Africa: Two Adventurers Cross the So-called Dark Continent North of Lake Chad on Motorcycles with Side Cars. By James C. Wilson. Vol. LXV, pp. 37-92, 64 ills., 1 two-page map, Jan., 1934.

See also Gold Coast; Nigeria.

British West Indian Interlude. By Anne Rainey Langley. Vol. LXXIX, pp. 1-46, 23 ills. in black and white, 21 ills. in color, 2 page maps, Jan., 1941.

British West Indies:

Americans in the Caribbean. By Luis Marden. Vol. LXXXI, pp. 723-758, 16 ills. in black and white, 22 ills. in color, 1 half-page map, June, 1942.

British Commonwealth of Nations: "Organized Freedom" Around the World. By Eric Underwood. Vol. LXXXIII, pp. 485-524, 31 ills., Apr., 1943.

British West Indian Interlude. By Anne Rainey Langley. Vol. LXXIX, pp. 1-46, 23 ills. in black and white, 21 ills. in color, 2 page maps, Jan., 1941.

War Echoes in the West Indies. 22 ills. in color from natural-color photographs by Luis Marden. Vol. LXXXI, pp. 731-754. June, 1942.

West Indies Links in a Defense Chain. 21 ills. in color from natural-color photographs; 20 ills. by Edwin L. Wisherd. Vol. LXXIX, pp. 9-32, Jan., 1941.

See also Bahama Islands; Cayman Islands; Jamaica; St. Vincent; Trinidad.

British Yukon Telegraph. Vol. XII, p. 164, Apr., 1901.

Brittany (Region), France:

Beauties of France. By Arthur Stanley Riggs. Vol. XXVIII, pp. 391-491, 73 ills. in black and white, 16 ills. in color, 1 half-page map, Nov., 1915.

Brittany: The Land of the Sardine. By Hugh M. Smith. Vol. XX, pp. 541-573, 23 ills., June, 1909.

Coasts of Normandy and Brittany. By W. Robert Moore. Vol. LXXXIV, pp. 205-232, 5 ills. in black and white, 21 ills. in color, 1 two-page map, Aug., 1943.

France of Today. By Maj. Gen. A. W. Greely. Vol. XXVI, pp. 193-222, 27 ills., Sept., 1914.

Mysterious Prehistoric Monuments of Brittany. By Charles Buxton Going. Vol. XLIV, pp. 53-69, 16 ills., July, 1923.

Normandy and Brittany in Brighter Days. 21 ills. in color from natural-color photographs by W. Robert Moore, Peter Upton Muir, and others. Vol. LXXXIV, pp. 209-232, Aug., 1943.

Rural Scenes in Brittany. Vol. XLIV, pp. 11-26, 16 ills., July, 1923.

Saint Malo, Ancient City of Corsairs: An Old Brittany Seaport Whose Past Bristles with Cannons and Cutlasses. By Junius B. Wood. Vol. LVI, pp. 131-177, 28 ills. in black and white, 29 ills. in color, 1 two-thirds-page map, Aug., 1929.

Scenes from France. Vol. XL, pp. 29-44, 16 ills., July, 1921.

Brittany (Region), France—*Continued*

Through the Back Doors of France: A Seven Weeks' Voyage in a Canadian Canoe from St. Malo, Through Brittany and the Château Country, to Paris. By Melville Chater. Vol. XLIV, pp. 1-51, 55 ills., 1 half-page map, July, 1923.

Where Bretons Wrest a Living from the Sea. 23 ills. from photographs by F. W. Goro. Vol. LXXI, pp. 751-766, June, 1937.

Broad, Philip:

Within the Halls of Cambridge (University). By Philip Broad. Vol. LXX, pp. 333-349, 7 ills. in black and white, 12 ills. in color, Sept., 1936.

Broadbill. *See* Swordfish.

Brookfield, Charles M.:

Cannon on Florida Reefs Solve Mystery of Sunken Ship. By Charles M. Brookfield. Vol. LXXX, pp. 807-824, 20 ills., 1 map (on pen and ink drawing), Dec., 1941.

Brooklyn, New York:

Spin Your Globe to Long Island: Only Six States Have More People than the Insular Empire that Ranges from a World's Fair Through Potato Patches, Princely Estates, and Historic Shrines. By Frederick Simpich. Vol. LXXV, pp. 413-460, 25 ills. in black and white, 18 ills. in color, Apr., 1939.

Brooks, Alfred H.:

Brooks Alaskan Expedition. Vol. XIII, p. 389, Oct., 1902.

Geography of Alaska. By Alfred H. Brooks. Vol. XV, pp. 213-219, special map supplement, May, 1904.

How Much Is Known of Alaska. By Alfred H. Brooks. Vol. XVII, pp. 112-114, 1 ill., 1 third-page map, Feb., 1906.

Ice Cliffs on White River, Yukon Territory. By Alfred H. Brooks and C. Willard Hayes. Vol. XI, pp. 199-201, May, 1900.

Plan for Climbing Mount McKinley. By Alfred H. Brooks and D. L. Reaburn. Vol. XIV, pp. 30-35, 1 page map, Jan., 1903.

Proposed Surveys in Alaska in 1902. By Alfred H. Brooks. Vol. XIII, pp. 133-135, Apr., 1902.

Railway Routes in Alaska. By Alfred H. Brooks. Vol. XVIII, pp. 164-190, 9 ills., 7 page and 1 half-page maps, 2 diagrams, Mar., 1907.

Brooks, (Maj.) Allan:

Auks and Their Northland Neighbors. 34 portraits in color from paintings by Maj. Allan Brooks. Vol. LXIX, pp. 101-116, Jan., 1936. Contains illustrations of the following: Auklets, Auks, Dovekies, Guillemots, Murrelets, Murres, Puffins.

Bird Beauties of the Tanager and Finch Families. 55 portraits in color from paintings by Maj. Allan Brooks. Vol. LXVII, pp. 513-528, Apr., 1935.

Brooks, (Maj.) Allan—*Continued*

Birds in Glossy Black and Vivid Color. 48 portraits in color from paintings by Maj. Allan Brooks. Vol. LXVI, pp. 113-128, July, 1934.
Contains illustrations of the following: Blackbirds, Bobolinks, Cowbirds, Grackles, Meadowlarks, Orioles, Shrikes, Vireos, Waxwings.

Birds of Lake and Lagoon, Marsh and Seacoast. 24 portraits in color from paintings by Maj. Allan Brooks. Vol. LXV, pp. 313-328, Mar., 1934.
Contains illustrations of the following: Cormorants, Grebes, Loons, Pelicans.

Blithe Birds of Dooryard, Bush, and Brake. 37 portraits in color from paintings by Maj. Allan Brooks. Vol. LXV, pp. 579-594, May, 1934.
Contains illustrations of the following: Chickadees, Kinglets, Nuthatches, Titmice, Wrens.

Bright hued Pets of Cage and Aviary. 51 portraits in color from paintings by Maj. Allan Brooks. Vol. LXXIV, pp. 738-790, Dec., 1938.

Crows, Magpies, and Jays. 17 ills. in color from paintings by Maj. Allan Brooks. Vol. LXIII, pp. 64-79, Jan., 1933.

Eagles, Hawks, and Vultures. 28 ills. in color from paintings by Maj. Allan Brooks. Vol. LXIV, pp. 65-94, July, 1933.

Far-Flying Wild Fowl and Their Foes. By Maj. Allan Brooks. Vol. LXVI, pp. 487-528, 6 ills. in black and white, 93 portraits in color, Oct., 1934.
Contains descriptions and illustrations of the following: Ducks, Geese, Swans.

Feathered Foragers of Swamp and Shore. 101 portraits in color from paintings by Maj. Allan Brooks. Vol. LXXII, pp. 191-222, Aug., 1937.

Flycatchers and Other Friends in Feathers. 36 portraits in color from paintings by Maj. Allan Brooks. Vol. LXIX, pp. 807-822, June, 1936.
Contains illustrations of the following: Anis, Cuckoos, Flycatchers, Kingbirds, Kingfishers, Parrots.

Humming Birds, Swifts, and Goatsuckers. 36 ills. in color from paintings by Maj. Allan Brooks. Vol. LXII, pp. 75-88, July, 1932.

Hunted Birds of Field and Wild. 60 portraits in color from paintings by Maj. Allan Brooks. Vol. LXX, pp. 469-500, Oct., 1936.
Contains illustrations of the following: Doves, Grouse, Pigeons, Ptarmigans, Quails.

Ibises, Herons, and Flamingos. 24 ills. in color from paintings by Maj. Allan Brooks. Vol. LXII, pp. 454-469, Oct., 1932.

North American Woodpeckers. 25 ills. in color from paintings by Maj. Allan Brooks. Vol. LXIII, pp. 465-478, Apr., 1933.

Silent-Winged Owls of North America. 21 portraits in color from paintings by Maj. Allan Brooks. Vol. LXVII, pp. 225-240, Feb., 1935.

Some Songsters and Flyers of Wide Repute. 42 portraits in color from paintings by Maj. Allan Brooks. Vol. LXIX, pp. 529-544, Apr., 1936.
Contains illustrations of the following: Swallows, Thrushes, Thrashers.

Brooks, (Maj.) Allan—*Continued*

Sparrows, Towhees, and Longspurs. 43 paintings in color from life by Maj Allan Brooks and Walter A. Weber. Vol. LXXV, pp. 361-375, Mar., 1939.

Wild Geese, Ducks, and Swans. 93 portraits in color from paintings by Maj. Allan Brooks. Vol. LXVI, pp. 493-524, Oct., 1934.

Wings Over the Bounding Main (Ocean Birds). 36 portraits in color from paintings by Maj. Allan Brooks. Vol. LXXIV, pp. 237-251, Aug., 1938.

Brooks, Sydney:

What Great Britain Is Doing (War Preparations). By Sydney Brooks. Vol. XXXI, pp. 193-210, 7 ills., Mar., 1917.

Broughton, (Lady) Vera:

Modern Dragon Hunt on Komodo: An English Yachting Party Traps and Photographs the Huge and Carnivorous Dragon Lizard of the Lesser Sundas. By Lady Broughton. Vol. LXX, pp. 321-331, 12 ills. in duotone, Sept., 1936.

Brown, Andrew H.:

Americans Stand Guard in Greenland. By Andrew H. Brown. Vol. XC, pp. 457-500, 23 ills. in black and white, 19 ills. in color, 1 page map, Oct., 1946.

Bekonscot, England's Toy-Size Town. By Andrew H. Brown and B. Anthony Stewart. Vol. LXXI, pp. 649-661, 2 ills. in black and white, 15 ills. in color, May, 1937.

Modern Pilgrim's Map of the British Isles. By Andrew H. Brown. Text accompanying special map supplement in colors. Vol. LXXI, pp. 795-802, 3 ills., June, 1937.

Salty Nova Scotia: In Friendly New Scotland Gaelic Songs Still Answer the Skirling Bagpipes. By Andrew H. Brown. Vol. LXXVII, pp. 575-624, 30 ills. in black and white, 21 ills. in color, 1 two-page map, May, 1940.

Brown, Barnum:

Hunting Big Game of Other Days: A Boating Expedition in Search of Fossils in Alberta, Canada. By Barnum Brown. Vol. XXXV, pp. 407-429, 24 ills., 1 page map, May, 1919.

Brown, G. M. L.:

Three Old Ports on the Spanish Main. By G. M. L. Brown. Vol. XVII, pp. 622-638, 12 ills., Nov., 1906.

Brown, H. C.:

Indian Village of Baum (Ohio). By H. C. Brown. Vol. XII, pp. 272-274, July, 1901.

Brown, Josephine A.:

6,000 Miles over the Roads of Free China. By Josephine A. Brown. Vol. LXXXV, pp. 355-384, 30 ills., 1 two-thirds-page map, Mar., 1944.

Brown, Robert Marshall:

Simple Method of Proving That the Earth Is Round. By Robert Marshall Brown. Vol. XVIII, pp. 771-774, 5 diagrams, Dec., 1907.

Brownsville, Texas:

Texas Delta of an American Nile: Orchards and Gardens Replace Thorny Jungle in the Southmost Tip of the Lone Star State. By McFall Kerbey. Vol. LXXV, pp. 51-96, 27 ills. in black and white, 24 ills. in color, 1 page map, Jan., 1939.

Brukkaros, Mount, Africa:

Hunting an Observatory: A Successful Search for a Dry Mountain on Which to Establish the National Geographic Society's Solar Radiation Station. By C. G. Abbot. Vol. L, pp. 503-518, 13 ills., 1 quarter-page map, Oct., 1926.

Keeping House for the "Shepherds of the Sun." By Mrs. William H. Hoover. Vol. LVII, pp. 483-506, 17 ills., 1 third-page map, Apr., 1930.

Brussels, Belgium:

Belgium—Europe in Miniature. By Douglas Chandler. Vol. LXXIII, pp. 397-450, 34 ills. in black and white, 20 ills. in color, Apr., 1938.

Bryan, William Jennings:

Honors to Colonel Goethals: The Presentation, by President Woodrow Wilson, of the National Geographic Society Special Gold Medal, and Addresses by Secretary of State Bryan, the French Ambassador, the German Ambassador, and Congressman James R. Mann. Vol. XXV, pp. 677-690, 6 ills., June, 1914.

Bryant, Henry G.:

Traveler's Notes on Java. By Henry G. Bryant. Vol. XXI, pp. 91-111, 17 ills., Feb., 1910.

Bryce, James:

Discovery of the North Pole (Address by James Bryce). Vol. XXI, pp. 63-82, Jan., 1910.

Honors for Amundsen (Address by James Bryce). Vol. XIX, pp. 55-76, 13 ills., Jan. 1908.

Honors to Amundsen and Peary (Address by James Bryce). Vol. XXIV, pp. 113-130, 5 ills., Jan., 1913.

Impressions of Palestine. By James Bryce. Vol. XXVII, pp. 293-317, 18 ills., 1 page map, Mar., 1915.

In Honor of the Army and Aviation (Address by James Bryce). Vol. XXII, pp. 267-284, 1 ill., Mar., 1911.

National Geographic Society (Announcing the Election of James Bryce, British Ambassador, as an Honorary Member of The Society). Vol. XXIII, pp. 272-298, 5 ills., Mar., 1912.

Nation's Capital. By James Bryce. Vol. XXIV, pp. 717-750, 26 ills., June, 1913.

Scenery of North America. By James Bryce, Vol. XLI, pp. 339-389, 45 ills., Apr., 1922.

Two Possible Solutions for the Eastern Problem. By James Bryce. Vol. XXIII, pp. 1149-1157, 5 ills., 1 page map, Nov., 1912.

Bryce, James—*Continued*

Western Siberia and the Altai Mountains: With Some Speculations on the Future of Siberia. By James Bryce. Vol. XXXIX, pp. 469-507, 39 ills., May, 1921.

Bryce Canyon National Park, Utah:

Bursts of Color in Sculptured Utah. 22 ills. in color from natural-color photographs. Vol. LXIX, pp. 593-616, May, 1936.

Photographing the Marvels of the West in Colors. By Fred Payne Clatworthy. Vol. LIII, pp. 694-719, 8 ills. in color, June, 1928.

Bubonic Plague:

Conquest of Bubonic Plague in the Philippines. Vol. XIV, pp. 185-195, 7 ills., May, 1903.

History and Geographic Distribution of Bubonic Plague. By George M. Sternberg. Vol. XI, pp. 97-113, Mar., 1900.

Buchan, Susan Charlotte (Lady Tweedsmuir):

Tweedsmuir Park: The Diary of a Pilgrimage. By The Lady Tweedsmuir of Elsfield. Vol. LXXIII, pp. 451-476, 22 ills., I half-page and 1 third-page maps, Apr., 1938.

Bucharest, Romania:

Roumania, the Pivotal State. By James Howard Gore. Vol. XXVIII, pp. 360-390, 32 ills., Oct., 1915.

Roumania and Its Rubicon. By John Oliver La Gorce. Vol. XXX, pp. 185-202, 11 ills., Sept., 1916.

Budapest, Hungary:

Budapest, Twin City of the Danube. By J. R. Hildebrand. Vol. LXI, pp. 729-742, 3 ills. in black and white, 10 ills. in duotone, June, 1932.

Land of Shepherd Kings. By C. Townley-Fullam. Vol. XXVI, pp. 311-393, 92 ills., 1 page map, Oct., 1914.

Saint Stephens Fête in Budapest. By De Witt Clinton Falls. Vol. XVIII, pp. 548-558, 9 ills., Aug., 1907.

Tale of Three Cities. By Thomas R. Henry. Vol. LXXXVIII, pp. 641-669, 23 ills., Dec., 1945.

Buddhism:

Adam's Second Eden (Ceylon). By Eliza R. Scidmore. Vol. XXIII, pp. 105-173, 60 ills., Feb., 1912.

Buddhist Calm Survives Along China's Great Wall. 10 ills. in color; 4 paintings by Mary Augusta Mullikin and Anna M. Hotchkis and 6 natural-color photographs. Vol. LXXIII, pp. 321-328, Mar., 1938.

China's Great Wall of Sculpture: Man-hewn Caves and Countless Images Form a Colossal Art Wonder of Early Buddhism. By Mary Augusta Mullikin. Vol. LXXIII, pp. 313-348, 23 ills. in black and white, 10 ills. in color, 1 third-page map, Mar., 1938.

Koyasan, the Japanese Valhalla. By Eliza R. Scidmore. Vol. XVIII, pp. 650-670, 14 ills., Oct., 1907.

Buddhism—*Continued*

Puto, the Enchanted Island. By Robert F. Fitch. Vol. LXXXIX, pp. 373-384, 11 ills., 1 third-page map, Mar., 1946.

See also Lamaism.

Buddhist Calm Survives Along China's Great Wall. 10 ills. in color; 4 paintings by Mary Augusta Mullikin and Anna M. Hotchkis and 6 natural-color photographs. Vol. LXXIII, pp. 321-328, Mar., 1938.

Buenos Aires, Argentina :

Buenos Aires : Queen of the River of Silver. By Maynard Owen Williams. Vol. LXXVI, pp. 561-600, 22 ills. in black and white, 24 ills. in color, 1 half-page map, Nov., 1939.

Buenos Aires—Metropolis of the Pampas. 24 ills. in color from natural-color photographs by Luis Marden and Maynard Owen Williams. Vol. LXXVI, pp. 577-600, Nov., 1939.

Buenos Aires and Its River of Silver : A Journey Up the Paraná and Paraguay to the Chaco Cattle Country. By William R. Barbour. Vol. XL, pp. 393-432, 38 ills., Oct., 1921.

Buenos Aires to Washington by Horse : A Solitary Journey of Two and a Half Years, Through Eleven American Republics, Covers 9,600 Miles of Mountain and Plain, Desert and Jungle. By A. F. Tschiffely. Vol. LV, pp. 135-196, 75 ills., 1 page map, Feb., 1929.

Fertile Pampas of Argentine. Vol. XVII, pp. 453-456, Aug., 1906.

First Transandine Railroad from Buenos Aires to Valparaiso. By Harriet Chalmers Adams. Vol. XXI, pp. 397-417, 14 ills., 1 quarter-page map, May, 1910.

Buffalo, American. *See* Bison.

Building America's Air Army. By Hiram Bingham. Vol. XXXIII, pp. 48-86, 43 ills., Jan., 1918.

Building the Alaskan Telegraph System. By Brig. Gen. William Mitchell. Vol. XV, pp. 357-361, Sept., 1904.

Buildings. *See* Architecture ; National Geographic Society : Buildings.

Bukhara, U. S. S. R. :

Land of Lambskins : An Expedition to Bukhara, Russian Central Asia, to Study the Karakul Sheep Industry. By Robert K. Nabours. Vol. XXXVI, pp. 77-88, 15 ills., July, 1919.

Russia's Orphan Races : Picturesque Peoples Who Cluster on the Southeastern Borderland of the Vast Slav Dominions. By Maynard Owen Williams. Vol. XXXIV, pp. 245-278, 26 ills., 1 page map, Oct., 1918.

Bulawayo, Southern Rhodesia :

Rhodesia, Hobby and Hope of Cecil Rhodes. By W. Robert Moore. Vol. LXXXVI, pp. 281-306, 13 ills. in black and white, 10 ills. in color, 1 half-page map, Sept., 1944.

Bulgaria:

Bulgaria, Farm Land Without a Farmhouse : A Nation of Villagers Faces the Challenge of Modern Machinery and Urban Life. By Maynard Owen Williams. Vol. LXII, pp. 185-218, 19 ills. in black and white, 27 ills. in color, 1 half-page map, Aug., 1932.

Bulgaria, the Peasant State. Vol. XIX, pp. 760-773, 14 ills., Nov., 1908.

Bulgaria and Its Women. By Hester Donaldson Jenkins. Vol. XXVII, pp. 377-400, 22 ills., Apr., 1915.

Bulgaria's Valley of Roses. 13 ills. in color from natural-color photographs by Wilhelm Tobien and Georg Paskoff. Vol. LXII, pp. 186-195, Aug., 1932.

Changing Map in the Balkans. By Frederick Moore. Vol. XXIV, pp. 199-226, 27 ills., 1 page map, Feb., 1913.

Flags of Austria-Hungary, Bulgaria, Germany, and Turkey. By Byron McCandless and Gilbert Grosvenor. Vol. XXXII, pp. 386-388, 38 ills. in color, Oct., 1917.

Great Turk and His Lost Provinces. By W. E. Curtis. Vol. XIV, pp. 45-61, 7 ills., Feb., 1903.

In the Shadow of Bulgarian Monasteries. 14 ills. in color from natural-color photographs by Wilhelm Tobien and Georg Paskoff. Vol. LXII, pp. 202-211, Aug., 1932.

Races of Europe. By Edwin A. Grosvenor. Vol. XXXIV, pp. 441-534, 62 ills., 2 page maps, special map supplement in colors, Dec., 1918.

Rise of Bulgaria. By James D. Bourchier. Vol. XXIII, pp. 1104-1118, 13 ills., Nov., 1912.

Whirlpool of the Balkans. By George Higgins Moses. Vol. XXXIX, pp. 179-197, 15 ills., Feb., 1921.

See also Tirnova.

Bulgaria's Valley of Roses. 13 ills. in color from natural-color photographs by Wilhelm Tobien and Georg Paskoff. Vol. LXII, pp. 186-195, Aug., 1932.

Bulhak, Jan:

Wilno, Stepchild of the Polish Frontier. 13 ills. in duotone ; 8 ills. by Jan Bulhak. Vol. LXXIII, pp. 777-784, June, 1938.

Bull-Fighting:

Camargue, the Cowboy Country of Southern France. By Dr. André Vialles. Vol. XLII, pp. 1-34, 33 ills., 1 half-page map, July, 1922.

Bumstead, Albert H.:

Appointed Chief Cartographer, National Geographic Society. Vol. LXIX, p. 130, Jan., 1936.

First Flight to the North Pole. By Lieut. Comdr. Richard Evelyn Byrd. Vol. L, pp. 357-376, 14 ills., Sept., 1926.

Buracker, (Capt.) William H.:

Saga of the Carrier *Princeton*. By Capt. William H. Buracker, USN. Vol. LXXXVIII, pp. 189-218, 8 ills. in black and white, 22 ills. in color, 1 map (two-page spread), Aug., 1945.

Burbank, J. E.:

San Francisco Earthquake of April 18, 1906, as Recorded by the Coast and Geodetic Survey Magnetic Observatories. By Dr. L. A. Bauer and J. E. Burbank. Vol. XVII, pp. 298-300, May, 1906.

Burdekin, H. B.:

Shadowy London by Night. 8 ills. by H. B. Burdekin. Vol. LXVIII, pp. 177-184, Aug., 1935.

Burden, W. Douglas:

Stalking the Dragon Lizard on the Island of Komodo. By W. Douglas Burden. Vol. LII, pp. 216-232, 21 ills., Aug., 1927.

Burden France Has Borne. By Granville Fortescue. Vol. XXXI, pp. 322-344, 19 ills., Apr., 1917.

Burdsall, Richard L.:

Climbing Mighty Minya Konka : Americans First Scaled Mountain That Now Is Landmark of China's New Skyway. By Richard L. Burdsall and Terris Moore. Vol. LXXXIII, pp. 625-650, 23 ills., 1 page map, May, 1943.

Burg, Amos:

Alaska—Our Northwestern Outpost. 16 ills. in color from natural-color photographs by Ernest H. Gruening, Amos Burg, and Froelich Rainey. Vol. LXXXII, pp. 297-308, Sept., 1942.

Britain Just Before the Storm : A Canadian Canoe Threads Old English Waterways Athrob with the Midlands' Industrial Life. By Amos Burg. Vol. LXXVIII, pp. 185-212, 14 ills. in black and white, 9 ills. in color, 1 two-thirds-page map, Aug., 1940.

Canals and Pageants of Peacetime England. 9 ills. in color from natural-color photographs ; 6 ills. by Amos Burg. Vol. LXXVIII, pp. 197-204, Aug., 1940.

Color Glimpses of the Changing South Seas. 14 ills. in color from natural-color photographs by Amos Burg. Vol. LXV, pp. 281-288, Mar., 1934.

Inside Cape Horn. By Amos Burg. Vol. LXXII, pp. 743-783, 29 ills. in black and white, 10 ills. in color, 1 two-page map, Dec., 1937.

Land of the Horn, America's Tiptoe. 10 ills. in color from natural-color photographs by Amos Burg. Vol. LXXII, pp. 751-758, Dec., 1937.

Native Son's Rambles in Oregon. By Amos Burg. Vol. LXV, pp. 173-234, 39 ills. in black and white, 24 ills. in color, 1 two-page map, Feb., 1934.

On Mackenzie's Trail to the Polar Sea. By Amos Burg. Vol. LX, pp. 127-156, 32 ills., 1 page map, Aug., 1931.

Scenes and Round-Ups of the Beaver State (Oregon). 24 ills. in color from natural-color photographs by Amos Burg. Vol. LXV, pp. 181-212, Feb., 1934.

To-day on "The Yukon Trail of 1898." By Amos Burg. Vol. LVIII, pp. 85-126, 52 ills., 1 two-thirds-page map, July, 1930.

Burial Mounds:

Indians of the Southeastern United States. By Matthew W. Stirling. Paintings by W. Langdon Kihn. Vol. LXXXIX, pp. 53-74, 8 ills. in black and white, 8 ills. in color, Jan., 1946.

Burial Ship:

Ancestor of the British Navy : England's Oldest Known War Vessel Is Unearthed, Laden with Remarkable Treasures of an Anglo-Saxon Ruler. By C. W. Phillips. Vol. LXXIX, pp. 247-268, 22 ills. in black and white, 4 drawings, Feb., 1941.

Buried Cities of Asia Minor. By Ernest L. Harris. Vol. XX, pp. 1-18, 10 ills., Jan., 1909.

Buried City of Ceylon. By John M. Abbot. Vol. XVII, pp. 613-622, 8 ills., Nov., 1906.

Burke, Eric Keast:

Modern Life in the Cradle of Civilization (Iraq). 16 ills. in color from photographs by Eric Keast Burke. Vol. XLI, pp. 391-406, Apr., 1922.

Burke, Walter:

Hurdle Racing in Canoes : A Thrilling and Spectacular Sport Among the Maoris of New Zealand. By Walter Burke. Vol. XXXVII, pp. 440-444, 6 ills., May, 1920.

Burleson, (Mrs.) Albert S.:

Wandering Islands of the Rio Grande. By Mrs. Albert S. Burleson. Vol. XXIV, pp. 381-386, 2 ills., 1 three-quarters-page map, Mar., 1913.

Burma:

Aerial Invasion of Burma. By Gen. H. H. Arnold. Vol. LXXXVI, pp. 129-148, 20 ills., Aug., 1944.

Among the Hill Tribes of Burma—An Ethnological Thicket. By Sir George Scott. Vol. XLI, pp. 293-321, 22 ills., Mar., 1922.

British Commonwealth of Nations : "Organized Freedom" Around the World. By Eric Underwood. Vol. LXXXIII, pp. 485-524, 31 ills., Apr., 1943.

Burma : Where India and China Meet : In the Massive Mountains of Southeast Asia, Swarming Road Builders Wage the "War of the Highway" for Free China and Her Allies. By John LeRoy Christian. Vol. LXXXIV, pp. 489-512, 18 ills., 1 page map, Oct., 1943.

Burma Road, Back Door to China : Like the Great Wall of Ancient Times, This Mighty Mountain Highway Has Been Built by Myriad Chinese to Help Defend Their Homeland. By Frank Outram and G. E. Fane. Vol. LXXVIII, pp. 629-658, 26 ills., 1 two-thirds-page map, Nov., 1940.

Five Thousand Temples of Pagān : Burma's Sacred City Is a Place of Enchantment in the Midst of Ruins. By William H. Roberts. Vol. LX, pp. 445-454, 9 ills., Oct., 1931.

Hunting the Chaulmoogra Tree. By Joseph F. Rock. Vol. XLI, pp. 243-276, 39 ills., 1 page map, Mar., 1922.

Notes on Burma. By Thomas Barbour. Vol. XX, pp. 841-866, 34 ills., Oct., 1909.

Burma—*Continued*

Shan Tribes Make Burma's Hills Flash with Color. 15 ills. in color from natural-color photographs by W. Robert Moore. Vol. LX, pp. 454-463, Oct., 1931.

Stilwell Road—Land Route to China. By Nelson Grant Tayman. Vol. LXXXVII, pp. 681-698, 18 ills., June, 1945.

Strange Tribes in the Shan States of Burma. 15 ills. in color from natural-color photographs by W. Robert Moore. Vol. LVIII, pp. 247-254, Aug., 1930.

The Society's New Map of India and Burma. Text accompanying special map supplement in colors. Vol. LXXXIX, p. 544, Apr., 1946.

Untoured Burma. By Charles H. Bartlett. Vol. XXIV, pp. 835-853, 17 ills., July, 1913.

Working Teak in the Burma Forests: The Sagacious Elephant is Man's Ablest Ally in the Logging Industry of the Far East. By A. W. Smith. Vol. LVIII, pp. 239-256, 5 ills. in black and white, 15 ills. in color, Aug., 1930.

Yank Meets Native. By Wanda Burnett. Vol. LXXXVIII, pp. 105-128, 24 ills., July, 1945.

Burma Road:

Burma: Where India and China Meet: In the Massive Mountains of Southeast Asia, Swarming Road Builders Wage the "War of the Highways" for Free China and Her Allies. By John LeRoy Christian. Vol. LXXXIV, pp. 489-512, 18 ills., 1 page map, Oct., 1943.

China Opens Her Wild West: In the Mountaingirt Heart of a Continent a New China Has Been Created During the Years of War. By Owen Lattimore. Vol. LXXXII, pp. 337-367, 21 ills. in black and white, 11 ills. in color, 1 map (two-page spread), Sept., 1942.

Stilwell Road—Land Route to China. By Nelson Grant Tayman. Vol. LXXXVII, pp. 681-698, 18 ills., June, 1945.

Burnett, Wanda:

Cape Cod People and Places. By Wanda Burnett. Vol. LXXXIX, pp. 737-774, 17 ills. in black and white, 24 ills. in color, 1 half-page map, June, 1946.

What the Fighting Yanks See. By Wanda Burnett. Vol. LXXXVI, pp. 451-476, 27 ills., Oct., 1944.

Yank Meets Native. By Wanda Burnett. Vol. LXXXVIII, pp. 105-128, 24 ills., July, 1945.

Burning the Roads. Vol. XVII, pp. 538-586, 4 ills., Oct., 1906.

Burpee, Lawrence J.:

Canada's Awakening North. By Lawrence J. Burpee. Vol. LXIX, pp. 749-767, 18 ills., June, 1936.

New Brunswick Down by the Sea. By Lawrence J. Burpee. Vol. LXXIX, pp. 595-614, 14 ills., 1 page map, May, 1941.

Burr, Franklin L.:

Burr Prize awarded to Capt. Albert W. Stevens. Vol. LXV, p. 626, May, 1934.

Burr, Mary C.:

Fund bequeathed to The Society by Mary C. Burr. Vol. LXV, p. 626, May, 1934.

Burr, William H.:

Republic of Panama. By William H. Burr. Vol. XV, pp. 57-73, 7 ills., Feb., 1904.

Burrall, Jessie L.:

Sight-Seeing in School: Taking Twenty Million Children on a Picture Tour of the World. By Jessie L. Burrall. Vol. XXXV, pp. 489-503, 14 ills., June, 1919.

Burritt, Charles H.:

Mining Bureau of the Philippine Islands. By Charles H. Burritt. Vol. XIV, pp. 418-419, Nov., 1903.

Burroughs, G. H. G.:

Perahera Processions of Ceylon. By G. H. G. Burroughs. Vol. LXII, pp. 90-100, 1 ill. in black and white, 8 ills. in duotone, July, 1932.

Bursts of Color in Sculptured Utah. 22 ills. in color from natural-color photographs. Vol. LXIX, pp. 593-616, May, 1936.

Burton, Theodore:

Honors for Amundsen (Address by Theodore Burton). Vol. XIX, pp. 55-76, 13 ills., Jan., 1908.

Buryat-Mongol Autonomous Soviet Socialist Republic, R. S. F. S. R. :

New Road to Asia. By Owen Lattimore. Vol. LXXXVI, pp. 641-676, 15 ills. in black and white, 26 ills. in color, Dec., 1944.

Buryats (People) :

New Road to Asia. By Owen Lattimore. Vol. LXXXVI, pp. 641-676, 15 ills. in black and white, 26 ills. in color, Dec., 1944.

Sunny Siberia. 26 ills. in color from natural-color photographs by Owen Lattimore. Vol. LXXXVI, pp. 649-672, Dec., 1944.

Busy Corner—the Cape of Good Hope: Ships Bound for Faraway Battlegrounds Stream Past Capetown, "Tavern of the Seas," and Other Ports of Virile South Africa. By W. Robert Moore. Vol. LXXXII, pp. 197-223, 11 ills. in black and white, 11 ills. in color, 1 two-thirds-page map, Aug., 1942.

Butter Exports from Siberia. Vol. XIII, p. 34, Jan., 1902.

Butter Festival:

Demon Dancers and Butter Gods of Choni. 16 ills. in color from photographs by Joseph F. Rock. Vol. LIV, pp. 584-601, Nov., 1928.

Life Among the Lamas of Choni: Describing the Mystery Plays and Butter Festival in the Monastery of an Almost Unknown Tibetan Principality in Kansu Province, China. By Joseph F. Rock. Vol. LIV, pp. 569-619, 34 ills. in black and white, 16 ills. in color, 1 half-page map, Nov., 1928.

Butterflies:

Butterflies—Try and Get Them. By Laurence Ilsley Hewes. Vol. LXIX, pp. 667-678, 15 ills. in black and white, 9 ills. in color, May, 1936.

Butterfly Travelers: Some Varieties Migrate Thousands of Miles. By C. B. Williams. Vol. LXXI, pp. 568-585, 1 ill. in black and white, 8 ills. in color, May, 1937.

Monsters of Our Back Yards. By David Fairchild. Vol. XXIV, pp. 575-626, 38 ills., May, 1913.

Nomads Among the Butterflies. 8 ills. in color; 3 paintings by Hashime Murayama and 5 natural-color photographs by Willard R. Culver. Vol. LXXI, pp. 569-584, May, 1937.

Strange Habits of Familiar Moths and Butterflies. By William Joseph Showalter. Vol. LII, pp. 77-126, 28 ills. in black and white, 169 ills. in color, July, 1927.

Contains descriptions and illustrations of species of the following families: Danaidae, Hesperiidae, Lycaenidae, Nymphalidae, Papilionidae, Pieridae, Satyridae.

Where Our Moths and Butterflies Roam. Vol. LII, pp. 105-126, July, 1927.

Who's Who Among the Butterflies. By Austin H. Clark. Vol. LXIX, pp. 679-692, 15 ills. in black and white, 9 ills. in color, May, 1936.

Winged Jewels from Many Lands. 9 ills. in color; 3 paintings by Hashime Murayama and 6 natural-color photographs by Willard R. Culver. Vol. LXIX, pp. 673-688, May, 1936.

Butterfly Travelers: Some Varieties Migrate Thousands of Miles. By C. B. Williams. Vol. LXXI, pp. 568-585, 1 ill. in black and white, 8 ills. in color, May, 1937.

Buxton, B. H.:

Corner of Old Württemberg (Germany). By B. H. Buxton. Vol. XXII, pp. 931-947, 17 ills., 1 half-page map, Oct., 1911.

Buyssens, A.:

Beautiful Belgium, Restored by Peace. 5 ills. in color from autochromes by A. Buyssens. Vol. LVI, pp. 554-563, Nov., 1929.

Tulip Time in the Netherlands. 10 ills. in color from natural-color photographs by Wilhelm Tobien and A. Buyssens. Vol. LXIV, pp. 325-332, Sept., 1933.

BW-1. *See* Narsarssuak, Greenland.

By Car and Steamer Around Our Inland Seas. By Maynard Owen Williams. Vol. LXV, pp. 451-491, 29 ills. in black and white, 8 ills. in duotone, 1 two-page map, Apr., 1934.

By Coolie and Caravan Across Central Asia: Narrative of a 7,900-Mile Journey of Exploration and Research Over "the Roof of the World," from the Indian Ocean to the Yellow Sea. By William J. Morden. Vol. LII, pp. 369-431, 73 ills., 1 page map, Oct., 1927.

By Felucca Down the Nile: Giant Dams Rule Egypt's Lifeline River, Yet Village Life Goes On As It Did in the Time of the Pharaohs. By Willard Price. Vol. LXXVII, pp. 435-476, 21 ills. in black and white, 22 ills. in color, 1 two-page map, Apr., 1940.

By-Laws. *See* National Geographic Society: By-Laws.

By Motor Through the East Coast and Batak Highlands of Sumatra. By Melville A. Hall. Vol. XXXVII, pp. 68-102, 27 ills., Jan., 1920.

By Motor Trail Across French Indo-China. By Maynard Owen Williams. Vol. LXVIII, pp. 487-534, 31 ills. in black and white, 27 ills. in color, 1 page map, Oct., 1935.

By Sail Across Europe. By Merlin Minshall. Vol. LXXI, pp. 533-567, 38 ills., 1 two-thirds-page map, May, 1937.

By Seaplane to Six Continents: Cruising 60,000 Miles, Italian Argonauts of the Air See World Geography Unroll, and Break New Sky Trails Over Vast Brazilian Jungles. By Comdr. Francesco de Pinedo. Vol. LIV, pp. 247-301, 60 ills., 1 two-page map, Sept., 1928.

Byagha (Castle), Bhutan:

Castles in the Air—Experiences and Journeys in Unknown Bhutan. By John Claude White. Vol. XXV, pp. 365-455, 74 ills., 1 page map, Apr., 1914.

Byrd, (Rear Adm.) Richard Evelyn:

Admiral Byrd Receives New Honor from The Society (Presentation of Special Gold Medal). Vol. LVIII, pp. 228-238, 4 ills., Aug., 1930.

Air Conquest: From the Early Days of Giant Kites and Birdlike Gliders, the National Geographic Society Has Aided and Encouraged the Growth of Aviation. Vol. LII, pp. 233-242, 13 ills., Aug., 1927.

Antarctica by Sea, Land and Air. 16 ills. in gravure from photographs by the Byrd Antarctic Expedition. Vol. LVIII, pp. 158-207, Aug., 1930.

Commander Byrd at the North Pole. Reproduction in color of the painting by N. C. Wyeth, National Geographic Society, Washington, D. C. Vol. LIII, supplement, May, 1928.

Commander Byrd Receives the Hubbard Gold Medal: The First Explorer to Reach the North Pole by Air Receives Coveted Honor at Brilliant National Geographic Society Reception (Address by Comdr. Byrd). Vol. L, pp. 377-388, 5 ills., 1 chart, Sept., 1926.

Conquest of Antarctica by Air. By Rear Adm. Richard Evelyn Byrd. Vol. LVIII, pp. 127-227, 71 ills. in black and white, 16 ills. in gravure, 1 page map, Aug., 1930.

Exploring the Ice Age in Antarctica. By Richard Evelyn Byrd. Vol. LXVIII, pp. 399-474, 72 ills., 1 page and 1 two-page maps, Oct., 1935.

First Flight to the North Pole. By Lieut. Comdr. Richard Evelyn Byrd. Vol. L, pp. 357-376, 14 ills., Sept., 1926.

Byrd, (Rear Adm.) Richard Evelyn—*Continued*

Flying Over the Arctic. By Lieut. Comdr. Richard E. Byrd. Vol. XLVIII, pp. 519-532, 10 ills., Nov., 1925.

National Geographic Society Honors Byrd Antarctic Expedition. Vol. LXVIII, pp. 107-114, 6 ills., July, 1935.

Our Transatlantic Flight. By Comdr. Richard Evelyn Byrd. Vol. LII, pp. 347-368, 17 ills., 1 half-page map, Sept., 1927.

Society Takes Part in Three Geographic Expeditions. Vol. LXV, pp. 625-626, May, 1934.

Byrd Antarctic Expeditions:

Admiral Byrd Receives New Honor from The Society. Vol. LVIII, pp. 228-238, 4 ills., Aug., 1930.

Antarctica by Sea, Land and Air. 16 ills. in gravure from photographs by the Byrd Antarctic Expedition. Vol. LVIII, pp. 158-207, Aug., 1930.

Conquest of Antarctica by Air. By Rear Adm. Richard Evelyn Byrd. Vol. LVIII, pp. 127-227, 71 ills. in black and white, 16 ills. in gravure, 1 page map, Aug., 1930.

Exploring the Ice Age in Antarctica. By Richard Evelyn Byrd. Vol. LXVIII, pp. 399-474, 72 ills., 1 page and 1 two-page maps, Oct., 1935.

Mapping the Antarctic from the Air: The Aërial Camera Earns Its Place as the Eyes and Memory of the Explorer. By Capt. Ashley C. McKinley. Special map supplement in colors. Vol. LXII, pp. 471-485, 13 ills., Oct., 1932.

Society Takes Part in Three Geographic Expeditions. Vol. LXV, pp. 625-626, May, 1934.

Society's Special Medal Is Awarded to Dr. Thomas C. Poulter: Admiral Byrd's Second-in-Command and Senior Scientist Is Accorded High Geographic Honor. Vol. LXXII, pp. 105-108, 2 ills., July, 1937.

Byrne, Donn:

Ireland: The Rock Whence I Was Hewn. By Donn Byrne. Vol. LI, pp. 257-326, 68 ills. in black and white, 11 ills. in color, 1 page map, Mar., 1927.

Byroads and Backwoods of Manchuria: Where Violent Contrasts of Modernism and Unaltered Ancient Tradition Clash. By Owen Lattimore. Vol. LXI, pp. 101-130, 27 ills., 1 three-quarters-page map, Jan., 1932.

Byzantium:

Constantinople Today. By Solita Solano. Vol. XLI, pp. 647-680, 40 ills., 1 three-quarters-page map, June, 1922.

C

Cables:

British Pacific Cable. Vol. XII, p. 78, Feb., 1901.

Completion of the Cable Between Canada and Australia. Vol. XIII, p. 410, Nov., 1902.

Cables—*Continued*

German Submarine Cable System. Vol. XII, p. 163, Apr., 1901.

Girdling the Globe. Vol. XV, p. 236, May, 1904.

Influence of Submarine Cables Upon Military and Naval Supremacy. By Capt. George O. Squier. Vol. XII, pp. 1-12, Jan., 1901.

New French Ocean Cables. Vol. XII, pp. 315-316, Aug., 1901.

United States Government Telegraph and Cable Lines. Vol. XV, pp. 490-494, 3 page maps, Dec., 1904.

World's Highest International Telephone Cable. Vol. LVIII, pp. 722-731, 8 ills., Dec., 1930.

Cacao Industry:

São Tomé, the Chocolate Island. By William Leon Smyser. Vol. LXXXIX, pp. 657-680, 23 ills., 1 third-page map, May, 1946.

Cacti:

Arizona Sands, Home of the Cactus King. 11 ills. from photographs. Vol. LXXI, pp. 521-528, Apr., 1937.

Canyons and Cacti of the American Southwest. 22 ills. in color from natural-color photographs by Edwin L. Wisherd, Jacob Gayer and Charles Martin. Vol. XLVIII, pp. 275-290, Sept., 1925.

Fantastic Plants of Our Western Deserts. 8 ills. by Frank M. Campbell. Vol. XLV, pp. 33-40, Jan., 1924.

Land of Drought and Desert—Lower California: Two Thousand Miles on Horseback Through the Most Extraordinary Cacti Forests in the World. By Edward W. Nelson. Vol. XXII, pp. 443-474, 25 ills., 1 page and 1 half-page maps, May, 1911.

Notes on the Deserts of the United States and Mexico (Extracted from a publication of Dr. Daniel T. MacDougal). Vol. XXI, pp. 691-714, 16 ills., Aug., 1910.

Utilizing the Desert. Vol. XVI, pp. 242-244, 3 ills., May, 1905.

See also Saguaro.

Cadets. *See* Aviation Cadets.

Cádiz, Spain:

Adventurous Sons of Cádiz. By Harriet Chalmers Adams. Vol. XLVI, pp. 153-204, 37 ills. in black and white, 26 ills. in color, Aug., 1924.

Caesar's City Today (Rome). 21 ills. in color from natural-color photographs by Bernard F. Rogers, Jr., and Luigi Pellerano. Vol. LXXI, pp. 285-316, Mar., 1937.

Caetani, Gelasio:

Redemption of the Pontine Marshes: By Draining the Malarial Wastes Around Rome, Italy Has Created a Promised Land. By Gelasio Caetani. Vol. LXVI, pp. 201-217, 9 ills. in black and white, 12 ills. in color, 1 two-thirds-page map, Aug., 1934.

Caetani, Gelasio—*Continued*

Story and the Legends of the Pontine Marshes: After Many Centuries of Fruitless Effort, Italy Is to Inaugurate a Gigantic Enterprise to Drain the Fertile Region Southeast of Rome. By Gelasio Caetani. Vol. XLV, pp. 357-390, 34 ills., Apr., 1924.

Cahalane, Victor H.:

Deer of the World: As Workers, Pets, and Graceful "Living Statuary" in Parks and Estates, These Versatile Creatures Have Endeared Themselves to Mankind. By Victor H. Cahalane. Vol. LXXVI, pp. 463-510, 20 ills. in black and white, 23 ills. in color, Oct., 1939.

King of Cats and His Court (Leopards, Lions, and Tigers). By Victor H. Cahalane. Paintings by Walter A. Weber. Vol. LXXXIII, pp. 217-259, 9 ills. in black and white, 20 ills. in color, Feb., 1943.

Cahuilla, Lake, California:

Lake Cahuilla: The Ancient Lake of the Colorado Desert. Vol. XVIII, p. 830, Dec., 1907.

Cairo, Egypt:

American Alma Maters in the Near East. By Maynard Owen Williams. Vol. LXXXVIII, pp. 237-256, 16 ills., Aug., 1945.

American Fighters Visit Bible Lands. By Maynard Owen Williams. With 23 ills. in color from natural-color photographs by the author. Vol. LXXXIX, pp. 311-340, 10 ills. in black and white, Mar., 1946.

Cairo to Cape Town, Overland: An Adventurous Journey of 135 Days, Made by an American Man and His Wife, Through the Length of the African Continent. By Felix Shay. Vol. XLVII, pp. 123-260, 118 ills., 1 half-page map, Feb., 1925.

Red Cross Girl Overseas. By Margaret Cotter. Vol. LXXXVI, pp. 745-768, 22 ills., Dec., 1944.

Calabria (Department), Italy:

Country Where Going to America Is an Industry (Sicily). By Arthur H. Warner. Vol. XX, pp. 1063-1102, 41 ills., Dec., 1909.

Daily Life in Calabria. Vol. XLIII, pp. 181-196, 16 ills., Feb., 1923.

Calculations of Population in June, 1900. By Henry Farquhar. Vol. X, pp. 406-413, Oct., 1899.

Calcutta, India:

Through the Heart of Hindustan: A Teeming Highway Extending for Fifteen Hundred Miles, from the Khyber Pass to Calcutta. By Maynard Owen Williams. Vol. XL, pp. 433-467, 29 ills., Nov., 1921.

Calderon, Alfredo Alvarez:

Peru—Its Resources, Development, and Future. By Alfredo Alvarez Calderon. Vol. XV, pp. 311-323, Aug., 1904.

Calderon, Ignacio:

Bolivia—A Country Without a Debt. By Ignacio Calderon. Vol. XVIII, pp. 573-586, 4 ills., Sept., 1907.

What the Latin American Republics Think of the Pan-American Conferences. Address by Ignacio Calderon. Vol. XVII, pp. 474-479, Aug., 1906.

Cali, Colombia:

Over the Andes to Bogotá. By Frank M. Chapman. Vol. XL, pp. 353-373, 19 ills., Oct., 1921.

Calicut, India:

Pathfinder of the East: Setting Sail to Find "Christians and Spices," Vasco da Gama Met Amazing Adventures, Founded an Empire, and Changed the History of Western Europe. By J. R. Hildebrand. Vol. LII, pp. 503-550, 43 ills., 1 two-thirds-page map, Nov., 1927.

Vasco da Gama at the Court of the Zamorin of Calicut. Reproduction in color of the painting by José Velloso Salgado, Sociedade de Geographia de Lisboa. Vol. LII, supplement, Nov., 1927.

California:

Among the Big Trees of California. By John R. White. Vol. LXVI, pp. 219-232, 14 ills., Aug., 1934.

Befriending Nature's Children: An Experiment With Some of California's Wild Folk. By Agnes Akin Atkinson. Vol. LXI, pp. 199-215, 26 ills., Feb., 1932.

Bringing the World to Our Foreign-Language Soldiers: How a Military Training Camp Is Solving a Seemingly Unsurmountable Problem by Using The Geographic. By Christina Krysto. Vol. XXXIV, pp. 81-90, 4 ills., Aug., 1918.

California—85 Years After the Gold Rush. 23 ills. in color from natural-color photographs by B. Anthony Stewart. Vol. LXIX, pp. 325-356, Mar., 1936.

California, Our Lady of Flowers. By Chapin Hall. Vol. LV, pp. 703-750, 20 ills. in black and white, 30 ills. in color, June, 1929.

California and Nevada Boundary. By C. H. Sinclair. Vol. X, pp. 416-417, Oct., 1899.

California Earthquake. Vol. XVII, pp. 325-343, 27 ills., June, 1906.

California Says It with Wild Flowers. By Francis Woodworth. With 9 ills. in color from natural-color photographs by B. Anthony Stewart. Vol. LXXXI, pp. 492-501, Apr., 1942.

California's Coastal Redwood Realm: Along a Belt of Tall Trees a Giant Bridge Speeds the Winning of Our Westernmost Frontier. By J. R. Hildebrand. Vol. LXXV, pp. 133-184, 31 ills. in black and white, 17 ills. in color, 1 page-and-a-half map, Feb., 1939.

Carrying Water Through a Desert: The Story of the Los Angeles Aqueduct. By Burt A. Heinly. Vol. XXI, pp. 568-596, 19 ills., 1 half-page map, July, 1910.

California—*Continued*

Colorado Desert. By David P. Barrows. Vol. XI, pp. 337-351, 4 ills., 1 page map, Sept., 1900.

Colorado Desert. By W. C. Mendenhall. Vol. XX, pp. 681-701, 16 ills., Aug., 1909.

Crater Lake and Yosemite Through the Ages. By Wallace W. Atwood, Jr. Paintings by Eugene Kingman. Vol. LXXI, pp. 327-343, 7 ills. in black and white, 13 ills. in color, Mar., 1937.

Deserts of Nevada and the Death Valley. By Robert H. Chapman. Vol. XVII, pp. 482-497, 9 ills., 1 chart, Sept., 1906.

Ever Changing California, Land of Startling Contrasts. 30 ills. in color from autochromes by Charles Martin. Vol. LV, pp. 704-745, June, 1929.

Forestry in California. Vol. XVI, pp. 480-481, Oct., 1905.

Glass-Bottom Boat. By Charles Frederick Holder. Vol. XX, pp. 761-778, 17 ills., Sept., 1909.

Golden Gate, and Redwood Evergreens. 17 ills. in color from natural-color photographs by B. Anthony Stewart. Vol. LXXV, pp. 149-160, Feb., 1939.

Lake Cahuilla : The Ancient Lake of the Colorado Desert. Vol. XVIII, p. 830, Dec., 1907.

Land of the Best. By Gilbert H. Grosvenor. Vol. XXIX, pp. 327-430, 71 ills. in black and white, 33 ills. in color, panorama, Apr., 1916.

Lowest Point in the United States (Death Valley, California). Vol. XVIII, pp. 824-825, Dec., 1907.

Magic Mountain (Mount Wilson). By J. N. Patterson. Vol. XIX, pp. 457-468, 9 ills., July, 1908.

Man Without the Hoe. Vol. XXI, pp. 967-969, 2 ills., Dec., 1910.

Mind's-Eye Map of America. By Franklin K. Lane. Vol. XXXVII, pp. 479-518, 25 ills. in black and white, 8 ills. in color, June, 1920.

More Water for California's Great Central Valley. By Frederick Simpich. Vol. XC, pp. 645-664, 16 ills., 1 page map, Nov., 1946.

National Geographic Society Completes Its Gifts of Big Trees. Vol. XL, pp. 85-86, July, 1921.

New Inland Sea (Salton Sea). By Arthur P. Davis. Vol. XVIII, pp. 36-49, 8 ills., 1 page map, Jan., 1906.

Northern California at Work. By Frederick Simpich. Vol. LXIX, pp. 309-389, 36 ills. in black and white, 41 ills. in color, 1 two-page and 1 third-page maps, Mar., 1936.

Oil Fields of Texas and California. Vol. XII, pp. 276-278, July, 1901.

Origin of Yosemite Valley. By Henry Gannett. Vol. XII, pp. 86-87, Feb., 1901.

Ostrich Farming in the United States. Vol. XVII, pp. 569-574, 6 ills., Oct., 1906.

Our Big Trees Saved. Vol. XXXI, pp. 1-11, 10 ills., Jan., 1917.

California—*Continued*

Our National Parks. By L. F. Schmeckebier. Vol. XXIII, pp. 531-579, 11 ills., 1 page map, June, 1912.

Reclamation of Arid Land in California. Vol. XIV, pp. 78-79, Feb., 1903.

Redwood Forest of the Pacific Coast. By Henry Gannett. Vol. X, pp. 145-159, 6 ills., 1 page map, May, 1899.

Remarkable Salt Deposit (Salton Sea). By Charles F. Holder. Vol. XII, pp. 390-392, 2 ills., Nov., 1901.

Salton Sea and the Rainfall of the Southwest. By Alfred J. Henry. Vol. XVIII, pp. 244-248, Apr., 1907.

Saving the Redwoods. By Madison Grant. Vol. XXXVII, pp. 519-536, 10 ills., June, 1920.

Seed Farms in California. By A. J. Wells. Vol. XXIII, pp. 515-530, 14 ills., May, 1912.

Seeing Our Spanish Southwest. By Frederick Simpich. Vol. LXXVII, pp. 711-756, 25 ills. in black and white, 17 ills. in duotone, special map supplement, June, 1940.

Southern California at Work. By Frederick Simpich. Vol. LXVI, pp. 529-600, 39 ills. in black and white, 41 ills. in color, 1 two-page map, Nov., 1934.

Southwest : Its Splendid Natural Resources, Agricultural Wealth, and Scenic Beauty. By N. H. Darton. Vol. XXI, pp. 631-665, 21 ills., 1 page map, Aug., 1910.

Studies on the Rate of Evaporation at Reno, Nevada, and in the Salton Sink. Vol. XIX, pp. 19-28, 5 ills,, Jan., 1908.

Sunshine Land of Fruits, Flowers, Movies, and Sport. 41 ills. in color from natural-color photographs by Clifton Adams and Fred Payne Clatworthy. Vol. LXVI, pp. 545-592, Nov., 1934.

Surf-Boarders Capture California. 8 ills. from photographs by J. H. Ball. Vol. LXXXVI, pp. 355-362, Sept., 1944.

Topographic Work of the United States Geological Survey in 1902. Vol. XIII, pp. 326-328, Aug., 1902.

Where Birds and Little Animals Find Haven (Eaton Canyon Bird and Game Sanctuary). By Agnes Akin Atkinson. Vol. LXX, pp. 232-241, 14 ills., Aug., 1936.

Where Spring Paints a State with Wild Flowers. 18 ills. in color from natural-color photographs by B. Anthony Stewart. Vol. LXIX, pp. 365-380, Mar., 1936.

Wild Ducks as Winter Guests in a City Park. By Joseph Dixon. Vol. XXXVI, pp. 331-343, 11 ills., Oct., 1919.

Wonderland of California. By Herman Whitaker. Vol. XXVIII, pp. 56-104, 45 ills., July, 1915.

See also Colorado Desert : San Diego ; San Francisco ; Santa Catalina (Island).

California, Lower. *See* Baja California.

California Trapdoor Spider Performs Engineering Marvels. By Lee Passmore. Vol. LXIV, pp. 195-211, 23 ills., Aug., 1933.

California's Coastal Redwood Realm: Along a Belt of Tall Trees a Giant Bridge Speeds the Winning of Our Westernmost Frontier. By J. R. Hildebrand. Vol. LXXV, pp. 133-184, 31 ills. in black and white, 17 ills. in color, 1 page-and-a-half map, Feb., 1939.

Call of the West. By C. J. Blanchard. Vol. XX, pp. 403-437, 20 ills., 1 half-page map, May, 1909.

Call to the Colors. Vol. XXXI, pp. 345-361, 17 ills., Apr., 1917.

Calvin, Jack:

Nakwasina Goes North: A Man, a Woman, and a Pup Cruise from Tacoma to Juneau in a 17-Foot Canoe. By Jack Calvin. Vol. LXIV, pp. 1-42, 24 ills., 1 page map, July, 1933.

Calvin, John:

Millennial City: The Romance of Geneva, the Capital of the League of Nations. By Ralph A. Graves. Vol. XXXV, pp. 457-476, 11 ills., June, 1919.

Calvo, Joaquin Bernardo:

What the Latin American Republics Think of the Pan-American Conferences. Address by Joaquin Bernardo Calvo. Vol. XVII, pp. 474-479, Aug., 1906.

Camargue, The Cowboy Country of Southern France. By Dr. André Vialles. Vol. XLII, pp. 1-34, 33 ills., 1 half-page map, July, 1922.

Cambodia (Protectorate), French Indo-China:

Along the Old Mandarin Road of Indo-China. By W. Robert Moore. Vol. LX, pp. 157-199, 32 ills. in black and white, 28 ills. in color, 1 quarter-page map, Aug., 1931.

Enigma of Cambodia. 27 ills. in color from autochromes by Gervais Courtellemont. Vol. LIV, pp. 306-323, Sept., 1928.

Forgotten Ruins of Indo-China. By Jacob E. Conner. Vol. XXIII, pp. 209-272, 63 ills., 1 page and 1 three-quarters-page maps, Mar., 1912.

Four Faces of Siva: The Mystery of Angkor. By Robert J. Casey. Vol. LIV, pp. 303-332, 13 ills. in black and white, 27 ills. in color, 1 third-page map, Sept., 1928.

Under the French Tricolor in Indo-China. 28 ills. in color from natural-color photographs by W. Robert Moore. Vol. LX, pp. 166-199, Aug., 1931.

Cambrian Stakes (Sheep Dog Trials):

Sheep Dog Trials in Llangollen: Trained Collies Perform Marvels of Herding in the Cambrian Stakes, Open to the World. By Sara Bloch. Vol. LXXVII, pp. 559-574, 17 ills., Apr., 1940.

Cambridge, England:

Sculptured Gates to English Learning (Cambridge University). 19 ills. in color from natural-color photographs by B. Anthony Stewart. Vol. LXXXIX, pp. 417-440, Apr., 1946.

Cambridge, England—*Continued*

A Texan Teaches American History at Cambridge University. By J. Frank Dobie. Vol. LXXXIX, pp. 409-441, 9 ills. in black and white, 19 ills. in color, Apr., 1946.

Where the Winding Cam Mirrors Cambridge (University) Spires. 12 ills. in color from natural-color photographs by Bernard Wakeman and Walter M. Edwards. Vol. LXX, pp. 339-346, Sept., 1936.

Within the Halls of Cambridge (University). By Philip Broad. Vol. LXX, pp. 333-349, 7 ills. in black and white, 12 ills. in color, Sept., 1936.

Camel, Man's Humpy, Grumpy Servant. 11 ills. in duotone. Vol. LXXXII, pp. 393-400, Sept., 1942.

Camel of the Frozen Desert (Reindeer). By Carl J. Lomen. Vol. XXXVI, pp. 538-556, 19 ills., Dec., 1919.

Camels:

Camel, Man's Humpy, Grumpy Servant. 11 ills. in duotone. Vol. LXXXII, pp. 393-400, Sept., 1942.

Here and There in Northern Africa. By Frank Edward Johnson. Vol. XXV, pp. 1-132, 113 ills., Jan., 1914.

Road to Wang Ye Fu: An Account of the Work of the National Geographic Society's Central-China Expedition in the Mongol Kingdom of Ala Shan. By Frederick R. Wulsin. Vol. XLIX, pp. 197-234, 44 ills., 1 third-page map, Feb., 1926.

Camels of the Clouds (Lamoids). By W. H. Hodge. Vol. LXXXIX, pp. 641-656, 15 ills., 1 half-page map, May, 1946.

Camera Adventures in the African Wilds. By A. Radclyffe Dugmore. Vol. XXI, pp. 385-396, 11 ills., May, 1910.

Camera Cruising in the Philippines. 12 ills. in color from natural-color photographs by J. Baylor Roberts, Fenno Jacobs, and others. Vol. LXXXVI, pp. 545-552, Nov., 1944.

Camera Pastels in French Canada. 25 ills. in color from natural-color photographs by Harrison Howell Walker. Vol. LXXV, pp. 601-624, May, 1939.

Cameroons (Cameroun):

Africa on Parade. 14 ills. in color from natural-color photographs by Lawrence Thaw. Vol. LXXIV, pp. 343-350, Sept., 1938.

Mandate of Cameroun: A Vast African Territory Ruled by Petty Sultans Under French Sway. By John W. Vandercook. Vol. LIX, pp. 225-260, 49 ills., 1 two-thirds-page map, Feb., 1931.

Trans-Africa Safari: A Motor Caravan Rolls Across Sahara and Jungle Through Realms of Dusky Potentates and the Land of Big-Lipped Women. By Lawrence Copley Thaw and Margaret Stout Thaw. Vol. LXXIV, pp. 327-364, 29 ills. in black and white, 14 ills. in color, 1 two-thirds-page map, Sept., 1938.

Cameroons Mountain, Cameroons:

Timbuktu and Beyond: Desert City of Romantic Savor and Salt Emerges into World Life Again as Trading Post of France's Vast African Empire. By Laura C. Boulton. Vol. LXXIX, pp. 631-670, 18 ills. in black and white, 26 ills. in color, 1 map (two-page spread), May, 1941.

Camp Fires on Desert and Lava. Vol. XXI, pp. 715-718, 3 ills., Aug., 1910.

Campbell, Alfred S.:

Guernsey, the Friendly Island. By Alfred S. Campbell. Vol. LXXIII, pp. 361-396, 28 ills. in black and white, 11 ills. in color, Mar., 1938.

Campbell, Frank M.:

Fantastic Plants of Our Western Deserts. 8 ills. by Frank M. Campbell. Vol. XLV, pp. 33-40, Jan., 1924.

Campbell, Marius R.:

How Long Will the Coal Reserves of the United States Last? By Marius R. Campbell. Vol. XVIII, pp. 129-138, 1 half-page map, 5 diagrams, Feb., 1907.

Camphor:

Formosa the Beautiful. By Alice Ballantine Kirjassoff. Vol. XXXVII, pp. 246-292, 60 ills., 1 half-page map, Mar., 1920.

Camps and Cruises of an Ornithologist. By George Shiras, 3d. Vol. XX, pp. 438-463, 30 ills., May, 1909.

Canada:

Alaskan Highway an Engineering Epic: Mosquitoes, Mud, and Muskeg Minor Obstacles of 1,671-mile Race to Throw the Alcan Life Line Through Thick Forests and Uninhabited Wilderness. By Froelich Rainey. Vol. LXXXIII, pp. 143-168, 21 ills., 3 maps, Feb., 1943.

British Commonwealth of Nations: "Organized Freedom" Around the World. By Eric Underwood. Vol. LXXXIII, pp. 485-524, 31 ills., Apr., 1943.

Canada from the Air: Flights Aggregating 10,000 Miles Reveal the Marvelous Scenic Beauties and Amazing Natural Resources of the Dominion. By J. A. Wilson. Vol. L, pp. 389-466, 76 ills., 1 page map, Oct., 1926.

Canada's Awakening North. By Lawrence J. Burpee. Vol. LXIX, pp. 749-767, 18 ills., June, 1936.

Canada's War Effort: A Canadian Pictures the Swift and Sweeping Transformation from a Peaceful Dominion to a Nation Geared for War. By Bruce Hutchison. Vol. LXXX, pp. 553-590, 40 ills., Nov., 1941.

Canadian Boundary. By John W. Foster. Vol. XIV, pp. 85-89, Mar., 1903.

Canadian Immigration. Vol. XVII, p. 356, June, 1906.

Columbia (River) Turns on the Power. By Maynard Owen Williams. Vol. LXXIX, pp. 749-792, 25 ills. in black and white, 18 ills. in color, June, 1941.

Canada—*Continued*

Completion of the Cable Between Canada and Australia. Vol. XIII, p. 410, Nov., 1902.

Conquest of Mount Logan: North America's Second Highest Peak Yields to the Intrepid Attack of Canadian Climbers. By H. F. Lambart. Vol. XLIX, pp. 597-631, 40 ills., June, 1926.

Decision of the Alaskan Boundary Tribunal Under the Treaty of January 24, 1903, Between the United States and Great Britain. Vol. XV, pp. 12-14, Jan., 1904.

Exploring Yukon's Glacial Stronghold. By Bradford Washburn. Vol. LXIX, pp. 715-747, 28 ills., 1 two-page map, June, 1936.

First Alaskan Air Expedition. By Capt. St. Clair Streett. Vol. XLI, pp. 499-552, 37 ills., 1 page map, May, 1922.

Forests of Canada. Vol. XIV, pp. 106-108, Mar., 1903.

Forests of Canada. By Sir Wilfrid Laurier. Vol. XVII, pp. 504-509, Sept., 1906.

Gentlemen Adventurers of the Air: Many Regions of Canada's Vast Wilderness, Long Hidden Even from Fur Trappers, Are Now Revealed by Exploring Airmen. By J. A. Wilson. Vol. LVI, pp. 597-642, 55 ills., 1 page map, Nov., 1929.

Great Britain's Bread Upon the Waters: Canada and Her Other Daughters. By William Howard Taft. Vol. XXIX, pp. 217-272, 56 ills., Mar., 1916.

How Canada Went to the Front. By T. B. Macaulay. Vol. XXXIV, pp. 297-307, 6 ills., Oct., 1918.

New Trans-Canada Railway. Vol. XIV, pp. 214-215, 1 quarter-page map, May, 1903.

On Mackenzie's Trail to the Polar Sea. By Amos Burg. Vol. LX, pp. 127-156, 32 ills., 1 page map, Aug., 1931.

On the Trail of a Horse Thief (Columbia River). By Herbert W. Gleason. Vol. XXXV, pp. 349-358, 6 ills., Apr., 1919.

Peaks and Parks of Western Canada. 11 ills. from photographs; 5 ills. by W. J. Oliver. Vol. LXXX, pp. 516-526, Oct., 1941.

Place Names in Canada. Vol. X, pp. 519-520, Dec., 1899.

Possibilities of the Hudson Bay Country. Vol. XVIII, pp. 209-213, 3 ills., Mar., 1907.

Society Maps Northwestern United States and Neighboring Canadian Provinces. Text accompanying special map supplement in colors. Vol. LXXIX, pp. 805-806, June, 1941.

Society's New Map of Canada. Text accompanying special map supplement in colors. Vol. LXIX, pp. 769-776, 10 ills., June, 1936.

Sources of the Saskatchewan. By Walter D. Wilcox. Vol. X, pp. 113-134, 5 ills., 1 chart, Apr., 1899.

Surveying the 141st Meridian (Boundary Line Between Canada and Alaska). By Thomas Riggs, Jr. Vol. XXIII, pp. 685-713, 46 ills., 1 page map, July, 1912.

To-day on "The Yukon Trail of 1898." By Amos Burg. Vol. LVIII, pp. 85-126, 52 ills., 1 two-thirds-page map, July, 1930.

Canada—*Continued*

Vast Timber Belts of Canada. Vol. XVII, pp. 509-511, Sept., 1906.

See also Alberta; Anticosti Island; Baffin Island; British Columbia; Churchill; New Brunswick; Nova Scotia; Ontario; Quebec; Toronto; Yukon Territory.

Canada's Awakening North. By Lawrence J. Burpee. Vol. LXIX, pp. 749-767, 18 ills., June, 1936.

Canada's War Effort: A Canadian Pictures the Swift and Sweeping Transformation from a Peaceful Dominion to a Nation Geared for War. By Bruce Hutchison. Vol. LXXX, pp. 553-590, 40 ills., Nov., 1941.

Canadian Boundary. By John W. Foster. Vol. XIV, pp. 85-89, Mar., 1903.

Canadian Immigration. Vol. XVII, p. 356, June, 1906.

Canadian Rocky Mountains:

Exploration in the Canadian Rockies. Vol. X, pp. 135-136, Apr., 1899.

Geologist's Paradise. By Charles D. Walcott. Vol. XXII, pp. 509-536, 28 ills., panorama, June, 1911.

Monarch of the Canadian Rockies (Mount Robson). By Charles D. Walcott. Vol. XXIV, pp. 626-639, 13 ills., panorama, May, 1913.

Monarch of the Canadian Rockies—Robson Peak. Vol. XXIV, panorama, May, 1913.

Mother of Rivers: An Account of a Photographic Expedition to the Great Columbia Ice Field of the Canadian Rockies. By Lewis R. Freeman. Vol. XLVII, pp. 377-446, 60 ills., 2 maps, Apr., 1925.

Our Mountain Panorama. Vol. XXII, supplement, June, 1911.

Peaks and Parks of Western Canada. 11 ills. from photographs; 5 ills. by W. J. Oliver. Vol. LXXX, pp. 516-526, Oct., 1941.

Peaks and Trails in the Canadian Alps. 16 ills. in duotone from photographs by Byron Harmon and Clifford White. Vol. LXV, pp. 627-642, May, 1934.

Recent Exploration in the Canadian Rockies. By Walter D. Wilcox. Part I, Vol. XIII, pp. 151-168, 12 ills., 1 page map, May, 1902. Part II, Vol. XIII, pp. 185-200, 9 ills., June, 1902.

Some Tramps Across the Glaciers and Snowfields of British Columbia. By Howard Palmer. Vol. XXI, pp. 457-487, 25 ills., June, 1910.

World's Highest Altitudes and First Ascents. By Charles E. Fay. Vol. XX, pp. 493-530, 25 ills., June, 1909.

Canal from the Atlantic to the Mediterranean. Vol. XI, pp. 122-123, Mar., 1900.

Canal Zone, Panama:

Who Treads Our Trails? A Camera Trapper Describes His Experiences on an Island in the Canal Zone, a Natural-History Laboratory in the American Tropics. By Frank M. Chapman. Vol. LII, pp. 331-345, 18 ills., 1 half-page map, Sept., 1927.

See also Panama Canal.

Canals:

Across the Midi in a Canoe: Two Americans Paddle Along the Canals of Southern France from the Atlantic to the Mediterranean. By Melville Chater. Vol. LII, pp. 127-167, 49 ills., 1 half-page map, Aug., 1927.

Army Engineer Explores Nicaragua: Mapping a Route for a New Canal Through the Largest of Central American Republics. By Lieut. Col. Dan I. Sultan. Vol. LXI, pp. 593-627, 39 ills., 1 two-thirds-page map, May, 1932.

Britain Just Before the Storm: A Canadian Canoe Threads Old English Waterways Athrob with the Midlands' Industrial Life. By Amos Burg. Vol. LXXVIII, pp. 185-212, 14 ills. in black and white, 9 ills. in color, 1 two-thirds page map, Aug., 1940.

By Sail Across Europe. By Merlin Minshall. Vol. LXXI, pp. 533-567, 38 ills., 1 two-thirds-page map, May, 1937.

Canal from the Atlantic to the Mediterranean. Vol. XI, pp. 122-123, Mar., 1900.

Canals and Pageants of Peacetime England. 9 ills. in color from natural-color photographs; 6 ills. by Amos Burg. Vol. LXXVIII, pp. 197-204, Aug., 1940.

Cape Cod Canal. By Commodore J. W. Miller. Vol. XXVI, pp. 185-190, 3 ills., 1 half-page map, Aug., 1914.

Deep-Water Route from Chicago to the Gulf. Vol. XVIII, pp. 676-685, 3 ills., 1 page map, Oct., 1907.

Glimpses of Holland. By William Wisner Chapin. Vol. XXVII, pp. 1-29, 26 ills., Jan., 1915.

Grand Canal Panorama (China). By Willard Price. Vol. LXXI, pp. 487-514, 31 ills., 1 half-page map, Apr., 1937.

Great Canals of the World. Vol. XVI, pp. 475-479, Oct., 1905.

Ho for the Soochow Ho. By Mabel Craft Deering. Vol. LI, pp. 623-640, 32 ills., 1 three-quarters-page map, June, 1927.

Industrial Titan of America: Pennsylvania, Once the Keystone of the Original Thirteen, Now the Keystone of Forty-eight Sovereign States. By John Oliver La Gorce. Vol. XXXV, pp. 367-406, 33 ills., 1 page map, May, 1919.

Isthmian Canal Commission. Vol. XI, pp. 160-161, Apr., 1900.

Latest Route Proposed for the Isthmian Canal—Mandingo Route. Vol. XIII, pp. 64-70, 1 page chart, Feb., 1902.

Life Afloat in China: Tens of Thousands of Chinese in Congested Ports Spend Their Entire Existence on Boats. By Robert F. Fitch. Vol. LI, pp. 665-686, 28 ills., June, 1927.

Canals—*Continued*

New Erie Canal. Vol. XVI, pp. 568-570, 1 page map, Dec., 1905.

Nicaragua and the Isthmian Routes. By A. P. Davis. Vol. X, pp. 247-266, 8 ills., 2 diagrams, July, 1899.

Shantung—China's Holy Land. By Charles K. Edmunds. Vol. XXXVI, pp. 231-252, 21 ills., 1 half-page map, Sept., 1919.

Surveying Through Khoresm: A Journey into Parts of Asiatic Russia Which Have Been Closed to Western Travelers Since the World War. By Lyman D. Wilbur. Vol. XLI, pp. 753-780, 31 ills., 1 two-thirds-page map, June, 1932.

Through the Back Doors of Belgium: Artist and Author Paddle for Three Weeks Along 200 Miles of Low-Countries Canals in a Canadian Canoe. By Melville Chater. Vol. XLVII, pp. 499-540, 39 ills., 1 half-page map, May, 1925.

Through the Back Doors of France: A Seven Weeks' Voyage in a Canadian Canoe, from St. Malo, Through Brittany and the Château Country, to Paris. By Melville Chater. Vol. XLIV, pp. 1-51, 55 ills., 1 half-page map, July, 1923.

Through the Heart of England in a Canadian Canoe. By R. J. Evans. Vol. XLI, pp. 473-497, 26 ills., 1 half-page map, May, 1922.

Wonderful Canals of China. By George E. Anderson. Vol. XVI, pp. 68-69, Feb., 1905.

Wonderful Canals of China. By F. H. King. Vol. XXIII, pp 931-958, 35 ills., 5 half-page maps, Oct., 1912.

See also Chesapeake and Ohio Canal; Nicaragua Canal; Panama Canal; Suez Canal.

Canaries:

Bright-hued Pets of Cage and Aviary. 51 portraits in color from paintings by Maj. Allan Brooks. Vol. LXXIV, pp. 783-790, Dec., 1938.

Canaries and Other Cage-Bird Friends. By Alexander Wetmore. Vol. LXXIV, pp. 775-806, 19 ills. in black and white, 51 portraits in color, Dec., 1938.

Canary Islands, Atlantic Ocean:

Elysium for the Beauty-Seeking Traveler. 14 ills. in color from natural-color photographs by Wilhelm Tobien. Vol. LVII, pp. 630-639, May, 1930.

Hunting for Plants in the Canary Islands. By David Fairchild. Vol. LVII, pp. 607-652, 37 ills. in black and white, 39 ills. in color, 1 third-page map, May, 1930.

In the Canary Islands, Where Streets Are Carpeted with Flowers. 13 ills. in color from natural-color photographs by Wilhelm Tobien. Vol. LVII, pp. 614-623, May, 1930.

New Map of the Atlantic Ocean: Foremost Sea of Commerce Becomes World's Battleground and Its Peaceful Islands Rise to Strategic Importance. By Leo A. Borah and Wellman Chamberlin. Text accompanying special map supplements in colors. Vol. LXXX, pp. 407-418, 9 ills., Sept., 1941.

Canary Islands, Atlantic Ocean—*Continued*

Scenes in the Fortunate Isles. 12 ills. in color from natural-color photographs by Wilhelm Tobien. Vol. LVII, pp. 598-607, May, 1930.

Canberra, Australia:

Capital Cities of Australia. By W. Robert Moore. Vol. LXVIII, pp. 667-722, 32 ills. in black and white, 24 ills. in color, 1 two-page map, Dec., 1935.

Cancer:

Discovery of Cancer in Plants. Vol. XXIV, pp. 53-70, 12 ills., Jan., 1913.

Candee, Helen Churchill:

Life's Pattern on the Italian Riviera. By Helen Churchill Candee. Vol. LXVII, pp. 67-100, 25 ills. in black and white, 12 ills. in color, 1 two-thirds-page map, Jan., 1935.

Normandy—Choice of the Vikings. By Helen Churchill Candee. Vol. LXIX, pp. 625-665, 25 ills. in black and white, 22 ills. in duotone, 1 two-thirds-page map, May, 1936.

Summering in an English Cottage: Quiet and Loveliness Invite Contemplation in the Extra "Room," the Garden of the Thatched House. By Helen Churchill Candee. Vol. LXVII, pp. 429-456, 32 ills., Apr., 1935.

Candia, Crete (Island):

Crete, Where Sea-Kings Reigned. By Agnes N. Stillwell. Vol. LXXXIV, pp. 547-568, 20 ills., 1 page map, Nov., 1943.

Canek (Mayan Hero):

Home of a Forgotten Race: Mysterious Chichen Itzá in Yucatan, Mexico. By Edward H. Thompson. Vol. XXV, pp. 585-648, 59 ills., June, 1914.

Cannibals:

Among the Cannibals of Belgian Kongo (Taken from Notes of E. Torday). Vol. XXI, pp. 968-971, 4 ills., Nov., 1910.

Curious and Characteristic Customs of Central African Tribes (Belgian Congo). By E. Torday. Vol. XXXVI, pp. 342-368, 35 ills., Oct., 1919.

Luster of Ancient Mexico (Aztecs). By William H. Prescott. Vol. XXX, pp. 1-31, 22 ills., July, 1916.

Vanishing People of the South Seas: The Tragic Fate of the Marquesan Cannibals, Noted for Their Warlike Courage and Physical Beauty. By John W. Church. Vol. XXXVI, pp. 275-306, 22 ills., 1 half-page map, Oct., 1919.

Canning:

Forming New Fashions in Food: The Bearing of Taste on One of Our Great Food Economies, the Dried Vegetable, Which Is Developing into a Big War Industry. By David Fairchild. Vol. XXXIII, pp. 356-368, 11 ills., Apr., 1918.

How the World Is Fed. By William Joseph Showalter. Vol. XXIX, pp. 1-110, 101 ills., Jan., 1916.

Cannon, Joseph:

Discovery of the North Pole (Speech by Joseph Cannon). Vol. XXI, pp. 63-82, Jan., 1910.

Cannon:

Cannon on Florida Reefs Solve Mystery of Sunken Ship. By Charles M. Brookfield. Vol. LXXX, pp. 807-824, 20 ills., 1 map (on pen and ink drawing), Dec., 1941.

Pirate-Fighters of the South China Sea. By Robert Cardwell. Vol. LXXXIX, pp. 787-796, 11 ills., June, 1946.

Canoeing Down the River Jordan : Voyagers in Rubber Boats Find the Bible Stream Little Tamed Today as It Plunges to the Dead Sea Over the Earth's Lowest River Bed. By John D. Whiting. Vol. LXXVIII, pp. 781-808, 19 ills., 1 page map, Dec., 1940.

Canoes and Canoe Trips:

Across the Midi in a Canoe : Two Americans Paddle Along the Canals of Southern France from the Atlantic to the Mediterranean. By Melville Chater. Vol. LII, pp. 127-167, 49 ills., 1 half-page map, Aug., 1927.

Britain Just Before the Storm : A Canadian Canoe Threads Old English Waterways Athrob with the Midlands' Industrial Life. By Amos Burg. Vol. LXXVIII, pp. 185-212, 14 ills. in black and white, 9 ills. in color, 1 two-thirds-page map, Aug., 1940.

Canoeing Down the River Jordan : Voyagers in Rubber Boats Find the Bible Stream Little Tamed Today as It Plunges to the Dead Sea Over the Earth's Lowest River Bed. By John D. Whiting. Vol. LXXVIII, pp. 781-808, 19 ills., Dec., 1940.

Entering the Front Doors of Medieval Towns : The Adventures of an American Woman and Her Daughter in a Folding Boat on Eight Rivers of Germany and Austria. By Cornelia Stratton Parker. Vol. LXI, pp. 365-394, 23 ills., 1 two-thirds-page map, Mar., 1932.

Hurdle Racing in Canoes : A Thrilling and Spectacular Sport Among the Maoris of New Zealand. By Walter Burke. Vol. XXXVII, pp. 440-444, 6 ills., May, 1920.

Nakwasina Goes North : A Man, a Woman, and a Pup Cruise from Tacoma to Juneau in a 17-Foot Canoe. By Jack Calvin. Vol. LXIV, pp. 1-42, 24 ills., 1 page map, July, 1933.

On Mackenzie's Trail to the Polar Sea. By Amos Burg. Vol. LX, pp. 127-156, 32 ills., 1 page map, Aug., 1931.

Through the Back Doors of Belgium. Artist and Author Paddle for Three Weeks Along 200 Miles of Low-Countries Canals in a Canadian Canoe. By Melville Chater. Vol. XLVII, pp. 499-540, 39 ills., 1 half-page map, May, 1925.

Through the Back Doors of France : A Seven Weeks' Voyage in a Canadian Canoe from St. Malo, Through Brittany and the Château Country, to Paris. By Melville Chater. Vol. XLIV, pp. 1-51, 55 ills., 1 half-page map, July, 1923.

Through the Heart of England in a Canadian Canoe. By R. J. Evans. Vol. XLI, pp. 473-497, 26 ills., 1 half-page map, May, 1922.

Canoes and Canoe Trips—*Continued*

To-day on "The Yukon Trail of 1898." By Amos Burg. Vol. LVIII, pp. 85-126, 52 ills., 1 two-thirds-page map, July, 1930.

Canova, Enrique C.:

Cuba—The Isle of Romance. By Enrique C. Canova. Vol. LXIV, pp. 345-380, 34 ills., 1 page map, Sept., 1933.

West Virginia : Treasure Chest of Industry. By Enrique C. Canova. Vol. LXXVIII, pp. 141-184, 19 ills. in black and white, 21 ills. in color, 1 two-page map, Aug., 1940.

Cantigny, France :

National Geographic Society's Memorial to American Troops : Fountain and Water Supply System Presented to Historic French Town of Cantigny, Where Our Overseas Soldiers Won Their First Victory in the World War. Vol. XLIV, pp. 675-678, 4 ills., Dec., 1923.

Canton, China :

Changing Canton. 20 ills. from photographs by Siukee Mack, Alfred T. Palmer, and Kinchue Wong. Vol. LXXII, pp. 711-726, Dec., 1937.

Canton Island, Phoenix Islands :

American Pathfinders in the Pacific. By William H. Nicholas. Vol. LXXXIX, pp. 617-640, 17 ills., 1 two-page map, May, 1946.

Crusoes of Canton Island : Life on a Tiny Pacific Atoll That Has Flashed Into World Importance. By Irvine C. Gardner. Vol. LXXIII, pp. 749-766, 7 ills. in black and white, 11 ills. in color, June, 1938.

Eclipse Adventures on a Desert Isle. By Capt. J. F. Hellweg. Vol. LXXII, pp. 377-394, 14 ills., 1 two-thirds-page map, Sept., 1937.

Nature's Most Dramatic Spectacle (Eclipse). By S. A. Mitchell. Vol. LXXII, pp. 361-376, 16 ills., 1 half-page map, Sept., 1937.

Unfurling Old Glory on Canton Island. 11 ills. in color ; 1 painting by Charles Bittinger and 10 natural-color photographs. Vol. LXXIII, pp. 753-760, June, 1938.

Canyon of Death, Arizona :

Exploring in the Canyon of Death : Remains of a People Who Dwelt in Our Southwest at Least 4,000 Years Ago Are Revealed. By Earl H. Morris. Vol. XLVIII, pp. 263-300, 24 ills. in black and white, 22 ills. in color, Sept., 1925.

Canyons and Cacti of the American Southwest. 22 ills. in color from natural-color photographs by Edwin L. Wisherd, Jacob Gayer, and Charles Martin. Vol. XLVIII, pp. 275-290, Sept., 1925.

Cape Breton Island, Nova Scotia :

Charm of Cape Breton Island : The Most Picturesque Portion of Canada's Maritime Provinces—A Land Rich in Historic Associations, Natural Resources, and Geographic Appeal. By Catherine Dunlop Mackenzie. Vol. XXXVIII, pp. 34-60, 22 ills., 1 three-quarters-page map, July, 1920.

Cape Breton Island, Nova Scotia—*Continued*

Salty Nova Scotia: In Friendly New Scotland Gaelic Songs Still Answer the Skirling Bagpipes. By Andrew H. Brown. Vol. LXXVII, pp. 575-624, 30 ills. in black and white, 21 ills. in color, 1 two-page map, May, 1940.

Tartan Tints New Scotland. 21 ills. in color from natural-color photographs; 12 ills. by John Mills, Jr.; 7 ills. by W. R. MacAskill. Vol. LXXVII, pp. 591-622, May, 1940.

Cape Cod, Massachusetts:

Cape Cod Canal. By Commodore J. W. Miller. Vol. XXVI, pp. 185-190, 3 ills., 1 half-page map, Aug., 1914.

Cape Cod People and Places. By Wanda Burnett. Vol. LXXXIX, pp. 737-774, 17 ills. in black and white, 24 ills. in color, 1 half-page map, June, 1946.

Collarin' Cape Cod: Experiences on Board a U. S. Navy Destroyer in a Wild Winter Storm. By Lieut. H. R. Thurber. Vol. XLVIII, pp. 427-472, 46 ills., Oct., 1925.

Cape Horn, Chile:

Cape Horn Grain-Ship Race: The Gallant *Parma* Leads the Vanishing Fleet of Square-Riggers Through Raging Gales and Irksome Calms 16,000 Miles, from Australia to England. By A. J. Villiers. Vol. LXIII, pp. 1-39, 38 ills., Jan., 1933.

Inside Cape Horn. By Amos Burg. Vol. LXXII, pp. 743-783, 29 ills. in black and white, 10 ills. in color, 1 two-page map, Dec., 1937.

Land of the Horn, America's Tiptoe. 10 ills. in color from natural-color photographs by Amos Burg. Vol. LXXII, pp. 751-758, Dec., 1937.

Cape Nome, Alaska:

Cape Nome Gold District (Alaska). By F. C. Schrader. Vol. XI, pp. 15-23, 3 ills., 1 page map, Jan., 1900.

Origin of the Name "Cape Nome." Vol. XII, p. 398, Nov., 1901.

Cape of Good Hope Province, Union of South Africa:

Busy Corner—the Cape of Good Hope: Ships Bound for Faraway Battlegrounds Stream Past Capetown, "Tavern of the Seas," and Other Ports of Virile South Africa. By W. Robert Moore. Vol. LXXXII, pp. 197-223, 11 ills. in black and white, 11 ills. in color, 1 two-thirds-page map, Aug., 1942.

Cape of Good Hope: The Floral Province. By Melville Chater. Vol. LIX, pp. 391-430, 29 ills., Apr., 1931.

Color at Africa's Southern Tip. 11 ills. in color from natural-color photographs by W. Robert Moore. Vol. LXXXII, pp. 213-220, Aug., 1942.

See also Capetown.

Cape-to-Cairo Railway:

Transporting a Navy Through the Jungles of Africa in War Time. By Frank J. Magee. Vol. XLII, pp. 331-362, 31 ills., Oct., 1922.

Cape-to-Cairo Telegraph. Vol. XII, pp. 162-163, Apr., 1901.

Cape-to-Cairo Telegraph. Vol. XIII, pp. 76-77, Feb., 1902.

Cape Verde Islands, Atlantic Ocean:

New Map of the Atlantic Ocean: Foremost Sea of Commerce Becomes World's Battleground and Its Peaceful Islands Rise to Strategic Importance. By Leo A. Borah and Wellman Chamberlin. Text accompanying special map supplement in colors. Vol. LXXX, pp. 407-418, 9 ills., Sept., 1941.

Sindbads of Science: Narrative of a Windjammer's Specimen-Collecting Voyage to the Sargasso Sea, to Senegambian Africa and Among Islands of High Adventure in the South Atlantic. By George Finlay Simmons. Vol. LII, pp. 1-75, 89 ills., 1 two-thirds-page map, July, 1927.

Capetown, Union of South Africa:

Busy Corner—the Cape of Good Hope: Ships Bound for Faraway Battlegrounds Stream Past Capetown, "Tavern of the Seas," and Other Ports of Virile South Africa. By W. Robert Moore. Vol. LXXXII, pp. 197-223, 11 ills. in black and white, 11 ills. in color, 1 two-thirds-page map, Aug., 1942.

Cairo to Cape Town, Overland: An Adventurous Journey of 135 Days, Made by an American Man and His Wife, Through the Length of the African Continent. By Felix Shay. Vol. LXVII, pp. 123-260, 118 ills., 1 half-page map, Feb., 1925.

Sailing the Seven Seas in the Interest of Science: Adventures Through 157,000 Miles of Storm and Calm, from Arctic to Antarctic and Around the World, in the Non-Magnetic Yacht *Carnegie*. By J. P. Ault. Vol. XLII, pp. 631-690, 47 ills., 1 chart, Dec., 1922.

Under the South African Union. By Melville Chater. Vol. LIX, pp. 391-512, 97 ills. in black and white, 38 ills. in color, 1 two-page map, Apr., 1931.

Capital and Chief Seaport of Chile (Santiago and Valparaíso). By W. Robert Moore. Vol. LXXXVI, pp. 477-500, 15 ills. in black and white, 8 ills. in color, 1 third-page map, Oct., 1944.

Capital and Country of Old Cathay. 16 ills. in duotone. Vol. LXIII, pp. 748-765, June, 1933.

Capital Cities of Australia. By W. Robert Moore. Vol. LXVIII, pp. 667-722, 32 ills. in black and white, 24 ills. in color, 1 two-page map, Dec., 1935.

Capitol (United States), Wonder Building of the World. By Gilbert Grosvenor. Vol. XLIII, pp. 603-638, 17 ills., June, 1923.

Cappadocia:

Cone-Dwellers of Asia Minor: A Primitive People Who Live in Nature-Made Apartment Houses, Fashioned by Volcanic Violence and Trickling Streams. By J. R. Sitlington Sterrett. Vol. XXXV, pp. 281-331, 52 ills., 1 half-page map, Apr., 1919.

Multicolored Cones of Cappadocia. 20 ills. in color from natural-color photographs by Eric Matson. Vol. LXXVI, pp. 769-800, Dec., 1939.

Cappadocia—*Continued*

Peculiar Caves of Asia Minor. By Elizabeth H. Brewer. Vol. XXII, pp. 870-875, 5 ills., Sept., 1911.

Star and Crescent on Parade. 29 ills. in color from natural-color photographs by Maynard Owen Williams. Vol. LXXXVII, pp. 585-616, May, 1945.

Turkish Republic Comes of Age. By Maynard Owen Williams. Vol. LXXXVII, pp. 581-616, 4 ills. in black and white, 29 ills. in color, 1 map (two-page spread), May, 1945.

Where Early Christians Lived in Cones of Rock: A Journey to Cappadocia in Turkey Where Strange Volcanic Pinnacles Are Honeycombed with Hermit Cells and Monasteries. By John D. Whiting. Vol. LXXVI, pp. 763-802, 20 ills. in black and white, 20 ills. in color, 1 half-page map, Dec., 1939.

Capps, Stephen R.:

Game Country Without Rival in America: The Proposed Mount McKinley National Park. By Stephen R. Capps. Vol. XXXI, pp. 69-84, 14 ills., 1 half-page map, Jan., 1917.

Capri (Island), Italy:

Capri, the Island Retreat of Roman Emperors. 12 ills. from photographs by Morgan Heiskell. Vol. XLI, pp. 627-638, June, 1922.

Inexhaustible Italy. By Arthur Stanley Riggs. Vol. XXX, pp. 273-368, 76 ills., 1 page map, Oct., 1916.

Isle of Capri: An Imperial Residence and Probable Wireless Station of Ancient Rome. By John A. Kingman. Vol. XXXVI, pp. 213-231, 17 ills., Sept., 1919.

Capturing Giant Turtles in the Caribbean. By David D. Duncan. Vol. LXXXIV, pp. 177-190, 13 ills., 1 quarter-page map, Aug., 1943.

Caracas, Venezuela:

Caracas, Cradle of the Liberator: The Spirit of Simón Bolívar, South American George Washington, Lives On in the City of His Birth. By Luis Marden. Vol. LXXVII, pp. 477-513, 18 ills. in black and white, 19 ills. in color, Apr., 1940.

I Kept House in a Jungle: The Spell of Primeval Tropics in Venezuela, Riotous With Strange Plants, Animals, and Snakes, Enthralls a Young American Woman. By Anne Rainey Langley. Vol. LXXV, pp. 97-132, 28 ills., 1 third-page map, Jan., 1939.

Modern Venezuelan Vignettes. 9 ills. from photographs. Vol. LXXV, pp. 113-120, Jan., 1939.

Venezuela's Capital—City of Contrasts. 19 ills. in color from natural-color photographs by Luis Marden. Vol. LXXVII, pp. 483-506, Apr., 1940.

Caravan Journey Through Abyssinia: From Addis Ababa Through Lalibela, the Strange Jerusalem of Ethiopia, in Search of New Grains for American Farms. By Harry V. Harlan. Vol. XLVII, pp. 613-663, 46 ills., 1 half-page map, June, 1925.

Caravels of Columbus. Reproduction in color of the painting by N. C. Wyeth, National Geographic Society, Washington, D. C. Vol. LIV, text, p. 55; supplement, July, 1928.

Carchemish (Ancient City):

Archeology, the Mirror of the Ages: Our Debt to the Humble Delvers in the Ruins at Carchemish and at Ur. By C. Leonard Woolley. Vol. LIV, pp. 207-226, 19 ills., Aug., 1928.

Cardwell, Robert:

Pirate-Fighters of the South China Sea. By Robert Cardwell. Vol. LXXXIX, pp. 787-796, 11 ills., June, 1946.

Carey, Edith:

Channel Islands. By Edith Carey. Vol. XXXVIII, pp. 143-164, 24 ills., 1 quarter-page map, Aug., 1920.

Caribbean Regions:

Americans in the Caribbean. By Luis Marden. Vol. LXXXI, pp. 723-758, 16 ills. in black and white, 22 ills. in color, 1 half-page map, June, 1942.

Capturing Giant Turtles in the Caribbean. By David D. Duncan. Vol. LXXXIV, pp. 177-190, 13 ills., 1 quarter-page map, Aug., 1943.

Haunts of the Caribbean Corsairs: The West Indies a Geographic Background for the Most Adventurous Episodes in the History of the Western Hemisphere. By Nell Ray Clarke. Vol. XLI, pp. 147-187, 27 ills., Feb., 1922.

Heart of a Hemisphere: Of Vital Importance Is the Area Portrayed in The Society's New Map of Mexico, Central America, and the West Indies. Text accompanying special map supplement in colors. Vol. LXXVI, pp. 739-740, 1 ill., Dec., 1939.

Hunting Useful Plants in the Caribbean. By David Fairchild. Vol. LXVI, pp. 705-737, 39 ills., Dec., 1934.

Our Map of the Countries of the Caribbean. Text accompanying special map supplement in colors. Vol. XLI, pp. 221-222, Feb., 1922.

Society's New Caribbean Map: Mexico, Central America, and the West Indies—Gateway of Discovery. Text accompanying special map supplement in colors. Vol. LXVI, pp. 738-740, 1 ill., Dec., 1934.

See also West Indies *and* names of individual countries and islands.

Caribou (Animals):

Big Game of Alaska. By Wilfred H. Osgood. Vol. XX, pp. 624-636, 10 ills., July, 1909.

Game Country Without Rival in America: The Proposed Mount McKinley National Park. By Stephen R. Capps. Vol. XXXI, pp. 69-84, 14 ills., 1 half-page map, Jan., 1917.

Carillons:

Singing Towers of Holland and Belgium. By William Gorham Rice. Vol. XLVII, pp. 357-376, 22 ills., Mar., 1925.

Carioca Carnival (Rio de Janeiro). 34 ills. in color from natural-color photographs by W. Robert Moore. Vol. LXXVI, pp. 291-322, Sept., 1939.

Carlsbad Caverns, New Mexico:

Bats of the Carlsbad Cavern. By Vernon Bailey. Vol. XLVIII, pp. 321-330, 11 ills., Sept., 1925.

New Discoveries in Carlsbad Cavern: Vast Subterranean Chambers with Spectacular Decorations are Explored, Surveyed, and Photographed. By Willis T. Lee. Vol. XLVIII, pp. 301-319, 19 ills., 1 three-quarters-page map, Sept., 1925.

Visit to Carlsbad Cavern: Recent Explorations of a Limestone Cave in the Guadalupe Mountains of New Mexico Reveal a Natural Wonder of the First Magnitude. By Willis T. Lee. Vol. XLV, pp. 1-40, 42 ills., Jan., 1924.

Carnegie, Andrew:

Discovery of the North Pole (Speech by Andrew Carnegie). Vol. XXI, pp. 63-82, Jan., 1910.

Carnegie Institution of Washington:

Carnegie Institution. Vol. XIX, p. 124, Feb., 1908.

Geologists in China. Vol. XVIII, pp. 640-644, Oct., 1907.

Most Curious Craft Afloat: The Compass in Navigation and the Work of the Non-Magnetic Yacht *Carnegie*. By Dr. L. A. Bauer. Vol. XXI, pp. 223-245, 31 ills., Mar., 1910.

Recent Magnetic Work by the Carnegie Institution of Washington. Vol. XVII, p. 648, Nov., 1906.

Sailing the Seven Seas in the Interest of Science: Adventures Through 157,000 Miles of Storm and Calm, from Arctic to Antarctic and Around the World, in the Non-Magnetic Yacht *Carnegie*. By J. P. Ault. Vol. XLII, pp. 631-690, 47 ills., 1 chart, Dec., 1922.

Carnivals:

Carioca Carnival (Rio de Janeiro). 34 ills. in color from natural-color photographs by W. Robert Moore. Vol. LXXVI, pp. 291-322, Sept., 1939.

Carnival Days on the Riviera. By Maynard Owen Williams. Vol. L, pp. 467-501, 21 ills., Oct., 1926.

Rio Panorama: Breath-taking Is This Fantastic City amid Peaks, Palms, and Sea, and in Carnival Time It Moves to the Rhythm of Music. By W. Robert Moore. Vol. LXXVI, pp. 283-324, 12 ills. in black and white, 34 ills. in color, Sept., 1939.

Carnivores of a Lightless World (Fishes). 8 ills. in color from paintings by Else Bostelmann. Vol. LXVI, pp. 693-700, Dec., 1934.

Caroline Islands, Pacific Ocean:

American Pathfinders in the Pacific. By William H. Nicholas. Vol. LXXXIX, pp. 617-640, 17 ills., 1 two-page map, May, 1946.

Caroline Islands. Vol. X, p. 227, June, 1899.

Caroline Islands, Pacific Ocean—*Continued*

Hidden Key to the Pacific: Piercing the Web of Secrecy Which Long Has Veiled Japanese Bases in the Mandated Islands. By Willard Price. Vol. LXXXI, pp. 759-785, 28 ills., 1 map (two-page spread), June, 1942.

South from Saipan. By W. Robert Moore. Vol. LXXXVII, pp. 441-474, 11 ills. in black and white, 17 ills. in color, 1 half-page map, Apr., 1945.

Yap and Other Pacific Islands under Japanese Mandate. By Junius B. Wood. Vol. XL, pp. 591-627, 34 ills., 1 two-thirds-page map, Dec., 1921.

See also Palau Islands; Yap.

Carpenter, Frank G.:

Awarded Jane M. Smith Life Membership. Vol. XXXVII, p. 342, Apr., 1920.

Carpenter, Rhys:

Ancient Rome Brought to Life. By Rhys Carpenter. Paintings by H. M. Herget. Vol. XC, pp. 567-633, 2 ills. in black and white, 32 ills. in color, 1 half-page map, Nov., 1946.

Carriers, Airplane. *See* Aircraft Carriers; Escort Carriers.

Carrying the Color Camera Through Unmapped China. 24 ills. in color from natural-color photographs by Joseph F. Rock. Vol. LVIII, pp. 402-435, Oct., 1930.

Carrying Water Through a Desert. The Story of the Los Angeles Aqueduct. By Burt A. Heinly. Vol. XXI, pp. 568-596, 19 ills., 1 half-page map, July, 1910.

Carson City, Nevada:

Nevada, Desert Treasure House. By W. Robert Moore. Vol. LXXXIX, pp. 1-38, 16 ills. in black and white, 20 ills. in color, 1 four-fifths-page map, Jan., 1946.

Cartago, Costa Rica:

Costa Rica—Vulcan's Smithy. By Henry Pittier. Vol. XXI, pp. 494-525, 30 ills., 2 half-page maps, June, 1910.

Carter, (Maj. Gen.) William Harding:

Story of the Horse: The Development of Man's Companion in War Camp, on Farm, in the Marts of Trade, and in the Field of Sports. By Maj. Gen. William Harding Carter. Vol. XLIV, pp. 455-566, 62 ills. in black and white, 24 ills. in color, Nov., 1923.

Carthage (Ancient City):

Ancient Carthage in the Light of Modern Excavation. By Count Byron Khun de Prorok. Vol. XLV, pp. 391-423, 27 ills. in black and white, 16 ills. in color, 1 half-page map, Apr., 1924.

Cartography. *See* Map Making.

Carts. *See* Oxcarts.

Carty, John J.:

Voice Voyages by the National Geographic Society: A Tribute to the Geographical Achievements of the Telephone (Address by John J. Carty). Vol. XXIX, pp. 296-326, 15 ills., 1 chart, Mar., 1916.

Carving, Wood. *See* Totem Poles.

Carvings, Stone. *See* Archeology; Sculpture; Stone Faces (Monuments).

Casablanca, Morocco:

Casablanca Smiles. 10 ills. in color from natural-color photographs by Herbert P. MacNeal. Vol. LXXXIV, pp. 17-24, July, 1943.

Eastward from Gibraltar: Overland Route Across North Africa to Tunisia and Libia. By Cyrus French Wicker. Vol. LXXXIII, pp. 115-142, 28 ills., Jan., 1943.

Casasus, Joaquin D.:

What the Latin American Republics Think of the Pan-American Conferences. Address by Joaquin D. Casasus. Vol. XVII, pp. 474-479, Aug., 1906.

Cascade Mountains, Oregon:

Scenes Among the High Cascades in Central Oregon. By Ira A. Williams. Vol. XXIII, pp. 578-592, 11 ills., June, 1912.

Casey, Robert J.:

Four Faces of Siva: The Mystery of Angkor (Cambodia). By Robert J. Casey. Vol. LIV, pp. 303-332, 13 ills. in black and white, 6 ills. in color, 1 third-page map, Sept., 1928.

Caso, Alfonso:

Monte Albán, Richest Archeological Find in America: A Tomb in Oaxaca, Mexico, Yields Treasures Which Reveal the Splendid Culture of the Mixtecs. By Alfonso Caso. Vol. LXII, pp. 487-512, 28 ills., Oct., 1932.

Cassava (Plant):

Dumboy, the National Dish of Liberia. By G. N. Collins. Vol. XXII, pp. 84-88, 5 ills., Jan., 1911.

Casserly, (Lt. Col.) Gordon:

Fez, Heart of Morocco: Africa's "Imperial City" Retains Its Teeming Streets, Cluttered Shops, Glamorous Moorish Homes and Mosques, Amid the Peace of French Rule. By Gordon Casserly. Vol. LXVII, pp. 663-694, 13 ills. in black and white, 27 ills. in color, June, 1935.

Tripolitania (Africa), Where Rome Resumes Sway: The Ancient Trans-Mediterranean Empire, on the Fringe of the Libyan Desert, Becomes a Promising Modern Italian Colony. By Col. Gordon Casserly. Vol. XLVIII, pp. 131-161, 27 ills. in black and white, 9 ills. in color, 1 two-thirds-page map, Aug., 1925.

White City of Algiers. By Lieut. Col. Gordon Casserly. Vol. LIII, pp. 206-232, 9 ills. in black and white, 32 ills. in color, Feb., 1928.

Castaways:

They Survived at Sea. By Lt. Comdr. Samuel F. Harby. Vol. LXXXVII, pp. 617-640, 22 ills., May, 1945.

Castelrosso (Island), Aegean Sea:

Rhodes, and Italy's Aegean Islands. By Dorothy Hosmer. Vol. LXXIX, pp. 449-480, 32 ills., 1 map, Apr., 1941.

Casteret, Norbert:

Discovering the Oldest Statues in the World: A Daring Explorer Swims Through a Subterranean River of the Pyrenees and Finds Rock Carvings Made 20,000 Years Ago. By Norbert Casteret. Vol. XLVI, pp. 123-152, 24 ills., 1 half and 1 quarter-page maps, Aug., 1924.

Castle, William R.:

Hawaii, Then and Now: Boyhood Recollections and Recent Observations by An American Whose Grandfather Came to the Islands 102 Years Ago. By William R. Castle. Vol. LXXIV, pp. 419-462, 30 ills. in black and white, 10 ills. in color, 1 page-and-a-half map, Oct., 1938.

Tokyo To-day. By William R. Castle, Jr. Vol. LXI, pp. 131-162, 33 ills., Feb., 1932.

Castles:

Beyond the Grand Atlas: Where the French Tricolor Flies Beside the Flag of the Sultan of Morocco. By V. C. Scott O'Connor. Vol. LXI, pp. 261-319, 52 ills. in black and white, 12 ills. in color, 1 two-thirds-page map, Mar., 1932.

Castles, Shrines, and Parks of Japanese Pilgrimage. 10 ills. in color from natural-color photographs by W. Robert Moore. Vol. LXIX, pp. 457-464, Apr., 1936.

Castles in the Air: Experiences and Journeys in Unknown Bhutan. By John Claude White. Vol. XXV, pp. 365-455, 74 ills., 1 page map, Apr., 1914.

Color and Customs of Sweden's Château Country. 13 ills. in color from natural-color photographs by Gustav Heurlin. Vol. LXVI, pp. 33-40, July, 1934.

Country-House Life in Sweden: In Castle and Cottage the Landed Gentry Gallantly Keep the Old Traditions. By Amelie Posse-Brázdová. Vol. LXVI, pp. 1-64, 51 ills. in black and white, 13 ills. in color, 1 page map, July, 1934.

Crusader Castles of the Near East. By William H. Hall. Vol. LIX, pp. 369-390, 19 ills., 1 third-page map, Mar., 1931.

Danube, Highway of Races: From the Black Forest to the Black Sea, Europe's Most Important River Has Borne the Traffic of Centuries. By Melville Chater. Vol. LVI, pp. 643-697, 54 ills., Dec., 1929.

How Warwick Was Photographed in Color. By Maynard Owen Williams. Vol. LXX, pp. 83-93, 13 ills. in color, July, 1936.

Hunting Castles in Italy. By Melville Chater. Vol. LXVIII, pp. 329-366, 25 ills. in black and white, 13 ills. in color, 1 page and 1 quarter-page maps, Sept., 1935.

Castles—*Continued*

Palaces and Peasants in Rome's Old Colony (Romania). 14 ills. in color from natural-color photographs by Wilhelm Tobien. Vol. LXV, pp. 439-446, Apr., 1934.

Road of the Crusaders : A Historian Follows the Steps of Richard the Lion Heart and Other Knights of the Cross Over the "Via Dei." By Harold Lamb. Vol. LXIV, pp. 645-693, 46 ills. in black and white, 13 ills. in color, 1 page map, Dec., 1933.

Transylvania and Its Seven Castles : A Motor Circuit Through Rumania's New Province of Racial Complexity and Architectural Charm. By J. Theodore Marriner. Vol. XLIX, pp. 319-352, 35 ills., 1 half-page map, Mar., 1926.

War's Wake in the Rhineland. By Thomas R. Henry. Vol. LXXXVIII, pp. 1-32, 29 ills., 1 third-page map, July, 1945.

Warwick Castle, Stage for Old England's Pageantry. 13 ills. in color from natural-color photographs by Maynard Owen Williams. Vol. LXX, pp. 85-92, July, 1936.

See also Châteaux ; Palaces.

Castles and Progress in Portugal. By W. Robert Moore. Vol. LXXIII, pp. 133-188, 36 ills. in black and white, 24 ills. in color, 1 half-page map, Feb., 1938.

Catalina Island, California. *See* Santa Catalina.

Catalpa (Tree) :

Hardy Catalpa. Vol. XIV, pp. 348-353, 4 ills., Sept., 1903.

Catdom's Royalty Photographed in Color. 25 ills. in color from natural-color photographs by Willard R. Culver. Vol. LXXIV, pp. 597-628, Nov., 1938.

Caterpillars :

An Insect Community Lives in Flower Heads. By James G. Needham. Vol. XC, pp. 340-356, 5 ills. in black and white, 11 ills. in color, Sept., 1946.

Fighting Insects with Airplanes : An Account of the Successful Use of the Flying-Machine in Dusting Tall Trees Infected with Leaf-Eating Caterpillars. By C. R. Neillie and J. S. Houser. Vol. XLI, pp. 333-338, 6 ills., Mar., 1922.

Strange Habits of Familiar Moths and Butterflies. By William Joseph Showalter. Vol. LII, pp. 77-126, 28 ills. in black and white, 169 ills. in color, July, 1927.

Cathedrals and Churches :

Beauties of France. By Arthur Stanley Riggs. Vol. XXVIII, pp. 391-491, 73 ills. in black and white, 16 ills. in color, 1 half-page map, Nov., 1915.

Cathedrals of England : An Artist's Pilgrimage to These Majestic Monuments of Man's Genius and Faith. By Norman Wilkinson. Vol. LXXVI, pp. 741-762, 3 ills. in black and white, 16 ills. in gravure from dry-point engravings by the author, Dec., 1939.

Cathedrals and Churches—*Continued*

Cathedrals of the Old and New World. By J. Bernard Walker. Vol. XLII, pp. 61-114, 50 ills., July, 1922.

Clock Turns Back in Yugoslavia : The Fortified Monastery of Mountain-girt Dečani Survives Its Six Hundredth Birthday. By Ethel Chamberlain Porter. Vol. LXXXV, pp. 493-512, 20 ills., 1 page map, Apr., 1944.

Constantinople and Sancta Sophia. By Edwin A. Grosvenor. Vol. XXVII, pp. 459-482, 21 ills., May, 1915.

Constantinople Today. By Solita Solano. Vol. XLI, pp. 647-680, 40 ills., 1 three-quarters-page map, June, 1922.

Glimpses of the Russian Empire. By William Wisner Chapin. Vol. XXIII, pp. 1043-1078, 51 ills. in color, 1 three-quarters-page map, Nov., 1912.

Inexhaustible Italy. By Arthur Stanley Riggs. Vol. XXX, pp. 273-368, 76 ills., 1 page map, Oct., 1916.

Splendor of Rome. By Florence Craig Albrecht. Vol. XLI, pp. 593-626, 28 ills., June, 1922.

Venice. By Karl Stieler. Vol. XXVII, pp. 587-630, 42 ills., 1 page and 1 quarter-page maps, June, 1915.

See also Chapels ; St. Magnus' Cathedral.

Cats :

Catdom's Royalty Photographed in Color. 25 ills. in color from natural-color photographs by Willard R. Culver. Vol. LXXIV, pp. 597-628, Nov., 1938.

Panther of the Hearth : Lithe Grace and Independence of Spirit Contribute to the Appeal of Cats, "The Only Domestic Animal Man Has Never Conquered." By Frederick B. Eddy. Vol. LXXIV, pp. 589-634, 22 ills. in black and white, 25 ills. in color, Nov., 1938.

Cats, Wild :

King of Cats and His Court. By Victor H. Cahalane. Paintings by Walter A. Weber. Vol. LXXXIII, pp. 217-259, 9 ills. in black and white, 20 ills. in color, Feb., 1943.
    Contains descriptions and colored illustrations of the following : African Wildcat, Bengal Tiger, Bobcat, Cheetah, Clouded Leopard, European Wildcat, Golden Cat, Jaguar, Jaguarundi, Leopard, Lion, Lynx, Marbled Cat, Ocelot, Pallas's Cat, Puma, Serval, Siberian Tiger, Snow Leopard, Tabby, Tiger Cat.

Catskill Aqueduct, New York :

New York—The Metropolis of Mankind. By William Joseph Showalter. Vol. XXXIV, pp. 1-49, 39 ills., July, 1918.

Cattle and Cattle Raising :

Beyond Australia's Cities. By W. Robert Moore. Vol. LXX, pp. 709-747, 27 ills. in black and white, 12 ills. in color, Dec., 1936.

Exploring a Grass Wonderland of Wild West China. By Ray G. Johnson. Vol. LXXXV, pp. 713-742, 24 ills., 1 half-page map, June, 1944.

Cattle and Cattle Raising—*Continued*

Grass Makes Wyoming Fat. By Frederick Simpich. Vol. LXXXVIII, pp. 153-188, 13 ills. in black and white, 19 ills. in color, 1 two-page map, Aug., 1945.

Life on the Argentine Pampa. By Frederick Simpich. Vol. LXIV, pp. 449-491, 41 ills. in black and white, 8 ills. in color, Oct., 1933.

Lonely Australia : The Unique Continent. By Herbert E. Gregory. Vol. XXX, pp. 473-568, 68 ills., 1 two-page and 4 half-page maps, Dec., 1916.

Nebraska, The Cornhusker State. By Leo A. Borah. Vol. LXXXVII, pp. 513-542, 6 ills. in black and white, 23 ills. in color, 1 map (two-page spread), May, 1945.

Taurine World : Cattle and Their Place in the Human Scheme—Wild Types and Modern Breeds in Many Lands. By Alvin Howard Sanders. Vol. XLVIII, pp. 591-710, 76 ills. in black and white, 20 ills. in color, Dec., 1925.
Contains descriptions and illustrations of the following breeds : Aberdeen-Angus, Banteng, Brahman, Brown Swiss, Devon, Dutch Belted, Gaur, Guernsey, Hereford, Holstein-Friesian, Indian Buffalo, Jersey, Nivernais-Charolais, Red Africander, Red Polls, Shorthorn, Texas Longhorn, West Highlander, Wild White, Yak.

Through Paraguay and Southern Matto Grosso. By Sir Christopher H. Gibson. Vol. LXXXIV, pp. 459-488, 20 ills. in black and white, 11 ills. in color, 1 two-thirds-page map, Oct., 1943.

Welcome to Wyoming. 19 ills. in color from natural-color photographs ; 18 ills. by B. Anthony Stewart. Vol. LXXXVIII, pp. 161-184, Aug., 1945.

Wonder Island of the Amazon Delta : On Marajó Cowboys Ride Oxen, Tree-dwelling Animals Throng Dense Forests, While Strange Fishes and Birds Help Make a Zoologist's Paradise. By Hugh B. Cott. Vol. LXXIV, pp. 635-670, 30 ills. in black and white, 12 ills. in color, 1 half-page map, Nov., 1938.

Cauca (River), Colombia :

Over the Andes to Bogotá. By Frank M. Chapman. Vol. XL, pp. 353-373, 19 ills., Oct., 1921.

Caucasus (Mountains), U. S. S. R. :

Island in the Sea of History : The Highlands of Daghestan. By George Kennan. Vol. XXIV, pp. 1086-1140, 49 ills., 1 page map, Oct., 1913.

Roaming Russia's Caucasus : Rugged Mountains and Hardy Fighters Guard the Soviet Union's Caucasian Treasury of Manganese and Oil. By Rolf Singer. Vol. LXXXII, pp. 91-121, 33 ills., July, 1942.

World's Highest Altitudes and First Ascents. By Charles E. Fay. Vol. XX, pp. 493-530, 25 ills., June, 1909.

Cause of Earthquakes. By Robert F. Griggs. Vol. XLIV, pp. 443-451, 5 ills., 1 page map, Oct., 1923.

Cause of the Earth's Heat. Vol. XVI, pp. 124-125, 1 ill., Mar., 1905.

Causes That Led Up to the Siege of Pekin. By W. A. P. Martin. Vol. XII, pp. 53-63, 1 ill., Feb., 1901.

Cave Dwellers. *See* Cliff Dwellers ; Troglodytes and Christian "Troglodytes."

Cave Temples, China :

Buddhist Calm Survives Along China's Great Wall. 10 ills. in color ; 4 paintings by Mary Augusta Mullikin and Anna M. Hotchkis and 6 natural-color photographs. Vol. LXXIII, pp. 321-328, Mar., 1938.

China's Great Wall of Sculpture : Man-hewn Caves and Countless Images Form a Colossal Art Wonder of Early Buddhism. By Mary Augusta Mullikin. Vol. LXXIII, pp. 313-348, 23 ills. in black and white, 10 ills. in color, 1 third-page map, Mar., 1938.

Caves:

Discovering the Oldest Statues in the World : A Daring Explorer Swims Through a Subterranean River of the Pyrenees and Finds Rock Carvings Made 20,000 Years Ago. By Norbert Casteret. Vol. XLVI, pp. 123-152, 24 ills., 1 half and 1 quarter-page maps, Aug., 1924.

Ice Caves and Frozen Wells. By W J McGee. Vol. XII, pp. 433-434, Dec., 1901.

Impressions of Palestine. By James Bryce. Vol. XXVII, pp. 293-317, 18 ills., 1 page map, Mar., 1915.

See also Carlsbad Caverns ; Luray Caverns.

Caviar Fishermen of Romania : From Vâlcov, "Little Venice" of the Danube Delta, Bearded Russian Exiles Go Down to the Sea. By Dorothy Hosmer. Vol. LXXVII, pp. 407-434, 29 ills., 1 third-page map, Mar., 1940.

Cayenne, French Guiana :

Color Glows in the Guianas, French and Dutch. By Nicol Smith. Vol. LXXXIII, pp. 459-480, 8 ills. in black and white, 13 ills. in color, 1 two-thirds-page map, Apr., 1943.

Cayley, Neville W.:

Fairy Wrens of Australia : The Little Long-tailed "Blue Birds of Happiness" Rank High Among the Island Continent's Remarkable Birds. By Neville W. Cayley. With 8 ills. in color from paintings by the author. Vol. LXXXVIII, pp. 488-498, 1 ill. in black and white, Oct., 1945.

Pastel Wrens from "Down Under." 8 ills. in color from paintings by N. W. Cayley. Vol. LXXXVIII, pp. 489-496, Oct., 1945.

Cayman Islands, West Indies :

Capturing Giant Turtles in the Caribbean. By David D. Duncan. Vol. LXXXIV, pp. 177-190, 13 ills., 1 quarter-page map, Aug., 1943.

Caymans (Alligators) :

Cowboys and Caymans of Marajó (Brazil). 12 ills. in color from natural-color photographs by Desmond Holdridge. Vol. LXXIV, pp. 645-652, Nov., 1938.

Caymans (Alligators)—*Continued*

Wonder Island of the Amazon Delta : On Marajó Cowboys Ride Oxen, Tree-dwelling Animals Throng Dense Forests, While Strange Fishes and Birds Help Make a Zoologist's Paradise. By Hugh B. Cott. Vol. LXXIV, pp. 635-670, 30 ills. in black and white, 12 ills. in color, 1 half-page map, Nov., 1938.

Cedars of Lebanon:

From Jerusalem to Aleppo. By John D. Whiting. Vol. XXIV, pp. 71-113, 30 ills., 1 half-page map, Jan., 1913.

Syria and Lebanon Taste Freedom. By Maynard Owen Williams. With 21 ills. in color from natural-color photographs by the author. Vol. XC, pp. 729-763, 16 ills. in black and white, Dec., 1946.

Cedros (Island), Mexico :

Cruise Among Desert Islands. By G. Dallas Hanna and A. W. Anthony. Vol. XLIV, pp. 71-99, 32 ills., 1 quarter-page map, July, 1923.

Celebes (Island), Netherlands Indies :

Celebes : New Man's Land of the Indies. By Maynard Owen Williams. Vol. LXXVIII, pp. 51-82, 33 ills., 1 page map, July, 1940.

Life and Death in Toradjaland. 22 ills. from photographs ; 11 ills. by Maynard Owen Williams : 8 ills. by Helene Fischer. Vol. LXXVIII, pp. 65-80, July, 1940.

Seafarers of South Celebes. By G. E. P. Collins. Vol. LXXXVII, pp. 53-78, 25 ills., 1 two-thirds-page map, Jan., 1945.

Celebrating Christmas on the Meuse. By Capt. Clifton Lisle. Vol. XXXVI, pp. 527-537, 5 ills., Dec., 1919.

Cemeteries:

Armistice Day and the American Battle Fields. By J. J. Jusserand. Vol. LVI, pp. 509-554, 32 ills. in black and white, 23 ills. in color, Nov., 1929.

Fame's Eternal Camping Ground : Beautiful Arlington (Virginia), Burial Place of America's Illustrious Dead. By Enoch A. Chase. Vol. LIV, pp. 621-638, 19 ills., Nov., 1928.

"Glory That Was Greece." By Alexander Wilbourne Weddell. Vol. XLII, pp. 571-630, 51 ills., 1 three-quarters-page map, Dec., 1922.

Our National War Memorials in Europe. By Gen. John J. Pershing. Vol. LXV, pp. 1-36, 24 ills. in black and white, 11 ills. in color, 1 half-page map, Jan., 1934.

"Time Will Not Dim the Glory of Their Deeds." 11 ills. in color from natural-color photographs by W. Robert Moore. Vol. LXV, pp. 17-24, Jan., 1934.

Census of 1900 (United States). By Dr. F. H. Wines. Vol. XI, pp. 34-36, Jan., 1900.

Central America:

Buenos Aires to Washington by Horse : A Solitary Journey of Two and a Half Years, Through Eleven American Republics, Covers 9,600 Miles of Mountain and Plain, Desert and Jungle. By A. F. Tschiffely. Vol. LV, pp. 135-196, 75 ills., 1 page map, Feb., 1929.

Central America—*Continued*

Countries of the Caribbean. By William Joseph Showalter. Vol. XXIV, pp. 227-250, 23 ills., Feb., 1913.

Heart of a Hemisphere : Of Vital Importance is the Area Portrayed in The Society's New Map of Mexico, Central America, and the West Indies. Text accompanying special map supplement in colors. Vol. LXXVI, pp. 739-740, 1 ill., Dec., 1939.

How Latin America Looks from the Air : U. S. Army Airplanes Hurdle the High Andes, Brave Brazil Jungles, and Follow Smoking Volcanoes to Map New Sky Paths Around South America. By Maj. Herbert A. Dargue. Vol. LII, pp. 451-502, 52 ills., 1 page map, Oct., 1927.

Notes on Central America. Vol. XVIII, pp. 272-278, 1 ill., 1 half-page map, Apr., 1907.

Our Map of the Countries of the Caribbean. Text accompanying special map supplement in colors. Vol. XLI, pp. 221-222, Feb., 1922.

Rubber Plantations in Mexico and Central America. Vol. XIV, pp. 409-414, 7 ills., Nov., 1903.

Shattered Capitals of Central America. By Herbert J. Spinden. Vol. XXXVI, pp. 185-212, 32 ills., 1 page map, Sept., 1919.

Society's New Caribbean Map : Mexico, Central America, and the West Indies—Gateway of Discovery. Text accompanying special map supplement in colors. Vol. LXVI, pp. 738-740, 1 ill., Dec., 1934.

To Bogotá and Back by Air : The Narrative of a 9,500-Mile Flight from Washington, Over Thirteen Latin-American Countries and Return, in the Single-Seater Airplane *Spirit of St. Louis*. By Col. Charles A. Lindbergh. Vol. LIII, pp. 529-601, 98 ills., 1 two-thirds-page map, May, 1928.

See also Costa Rica ; El Salvador ; Guatemala ; Honduras ; Nicaragua ; Panama.

Central Asiatic Expedition:

Explorations in the Gobi Desert. By Roy Chapman Andrews. Vol. LXIII, pp. 653-716, 50 ills. in black and white, 20 ills. in color, 1 half-page map, June, 1933.

Nomad Life and Fossil Treasures of Mongolia. 20 ills. in color from photographs by J. B. Shackelford. Vol. LXIII, pp. 669-701, June, 1933.

Central Great Plains (United States). Vol. XVI, pp. 389-397, Aug., 1905.

Central Valley, California :

More Water for California's Great Central Valley. By Frederick Simpich. Vol. XC, pp. 645-664, 16 ills., 1 page map, Nov., 1946.

Cephalopoda:

Marauders of the Sea. By Roy Waldo Miner. Vol. LXVIII, pp. 185-207, 12 ills. in black and white, 8 ills. in color, Aug., 1935.

Monster and Midget Squid and Octopuses. 8 ills. in color from paintings by Else Bostelmann. Vol. LXVIII, pp. 193-200, Aug., 1935.

See also Squid.

Cerameicus (Cemetery), Athens:

"Glory That Was Greece." By Alexander Wilbourne Weddell. Vol. XLII, pp. 571-630, 51 ills., 1 three-quarters-page map, Dec., 1922.

Ceramics:

World's Ancient Porcelain Center (Kingtehchen, China). By Frank B. Lenz. Vol. XXXVIII, pp. 391-406, 17 ills., Nov., 1920.

Cerro de las Mesas, Mexico:

Expedition Unearths Buried Masterpieces of Carved Jade. By Matthew W. Stirling. Vol. LXXX, pp. 277-302, 14 ills. in black and white, 20 ills. in color, 1 two-thirds-page map, Sept., 1941.

Jungle Housekeeping for a Geographic Expedition. By Marion Stirling. Vol. LXXX, pp. 303-327, 15 ills., Sept., 1941.

Treasure-trove of Old Mexican Jade. 20 ills. in color from natural-color photographs by Richard H. Stewart. Vol. LXXX, pp. 293-316, Sept., 1941.

Certain Citizens of the Warm Sea. By Louis L. Mowbray. Vol. XLI, pp. 27-62, 18 ills. in black and white, 16 ills. in color, Jan., 1922.

Cetaceans. *See* Dolphins; Porpoises; Whales.

Cetinje, Yugoslavia:

East of the Adriatic: Notes on Dalmatia, Montenegro, Bosnia, and Herzegovina. By Kenneth McKenzie. Vol. XXIII, pp. 1159-1187, 37 ills., 1 page map, Dec., 1912.

Greece and Montenegro. By George Higgins Moses. Vol. XXIV, pp. 281-310, 24 ills., Mar., 1913.

Whirlpool of the Balkans. By George Higgins Moses. Vol. XXXIX, pp. 179-197, 15 ills., Feb., 1921.

Ceylon (Island), Indian Ocean:

Adam's Second Eden. By Eliza R. Scidmore. Vol. XXIII, pp. 105-173, 60 ills., Feb., 1912.

Archæology in the Air. By Eliza R. Scidmore. Vol. XVIII, pp. 150-163, 11 ills., Mar., 1907.

British Commonwealth of Nations: "Organized Freedom" Around the World. By Eric Underwood. Vol. LXXXIII, pp. 485-524, 31 ills., Apr., 1943.

Buried City of Ceylon. By John M. Abbot. Vol. XVII, pp. 613-622, 8 ills., Nov., 1906.

Fishing for Pearls in the Indian Ocean. By Bella Sidney Woolf. Vol. XLIX, pp. 161-183, 24 ills., Feb., 1926.

India and Ceylon. 8 ills. in color from autochromes by Helen Messinger Murdoch. Vol. XXXIX, pp. 281-288, Mar., 1921.

Pearl Fisheries of Ceylon. By Hugh M. Smith. Vol. XXIII, pp. 173-194, 13 ills., 1 quarter-page map, Feb., 1912.

Perahera Processions of Ceylon. By G. H. G. Burroughs. Vol. LXII, pp. 90-100, 1 ill. in black and white, 8 ills. in duotone, July, 1932.

Ceylon (Island), Indian Ocean—*Continued*

Sailing the Seven Seas in the Interest of Science: Adventures Through 157,000 Miles of Storm and Calm, from Arctic to Antarctic and Around the World, in the Non-Magnetic Yacht *Carnegie.* By J. P. Ault. Vol. XLII, pp. 631-690, 47 ills., 1 chart, Dec., 1922.

Sigiriya, "A Fortress in the Sky." By Wilson K. Norton. Vol. XC, pp. 665-680, 14 ills., 1 two-thirds-page map, Nov., 1946.

CG-4A's (Cargo Gliders):

Gliders—Silent Weapons of the Sky. By William H. Nicholas. Vol. LXXXVI, pp. 149-160, 8 ills., Aug., 1944.

Chaco (Region), South America:

Buenos Aires and Its River of Silver: A Journey Up the Paraná and Paraguay to the Chaco Cattle Country. By William R. Barbour. Vol. XL, pp. 393-432, 38 ills., Oct., 1921.

Through Paraguay and Southern Matto Grosso. By Sir Christopher H. Gibson. Vol. LXXXIV, pp. 459-488, 20 ills. in black and white, 11 ills. in color, 1 two-thirds-page map, Oct., 1943.

Chaco Boreal (Region), Paraguay:

Through Paraguay and Southern Matto Grosso. By Sir Christopher H. Gibson. Vol. LXXXIV, pp. 459-488, 20 ills. in black and white, 11 ills. in color, 1 two-thirds-page map, Oct., 1943.

Chaco Canyon, New Mexico:

Everyday Life in Pueblo Bonito: As Disclosed by the National Geographic Society's Archeologic Explorations in the Chaco Canyon National Monument, New Mexico. By Neil M. Judd. Vol. XLVIII, pp. 227-262, 37 ills., 1 two-thirds-page map, Sept., 1925.

New National Geographic Society Expedition: Ruins of Chaco Canyon, New Mexico, Nature-Made Treasure-Chest of Aboriginal American History, To Be Excavated and Studied; Work Begins This Month. Vol. XXXIX, pp. 637-643, 7 ills., June, 1921.

Pueblo Bonito, the Ancient: The National Geographic Society's Third Expedition to the Southwest Seeks to Read in the Rings of Trees the Secret of the Age of Ruins. By Neil M. Judd. Vol. XLIV, pp. 99-108, 9 ills., 1 diagram, July, 1923.

Pueblo Bonito Expedition of the National Geographic Society. By Neil M. Judd. Vol. XLI, pp. 323-331, 10 ills., 1 diagram, Mar., 1922.

Chad Territory:

Recent Geographic Advances, Especially in Africa. By Maj. Gen. A. W. Greely. Vol. XXII, pp. 383-398, 5 ills., 5 page maps, Apr., 1911.

Three-Wheeling Through Africa: Two Adventurers Cross the So-Called Dark Continent North of Lake Chad on Motorcycles with Side Cars. By James C. Wilson. Vol. LXV, pp. 37-92, 64 ills., 1 two-page map, Jan., 1934.

Chaman, India :

Back to Afghanistan. By Maynard Owen Williams. Vol. XC, pp. 517-544, 27 ills., 1 page map, Oct., 1946.

Chamberlin, Rollin T.:

Populous and Beautiful Szechuan : A Visit to the Restless Province of China, in which the Present Revolution Began. By Rollin T. Chamberlin. Vol. XXII, pp. 1094-1119, 26 ills., 1 half-page map, Dec., 1911.

Chamberlin, Wellman:

New Map of the Atlantic Ocean : Foremost Sea of Commerce Becomes World's Battleground and Its Peaceful Islands Rise to Strategic Importance. By Leo A. Borah and Wellman Chamberlin. Text accompanying special map supplement in colors. Vol. LXXX, pp. 407-418, 9 ills., Sept., 1941.

Chamonix, France :

Ascent of Mont Blanc. By Walter Woodburn Hyde. Vol. XXIV, pp. 861-942, 69 ills., Aug., 1913.

Chamorros (Tribespeople) :

South from Saipan. By W. Robert Moore. Vol. LXXXVII, pp. 441-447, 11 ills. in black and white, 17 ills. in color, 1 half-page map, Apr., 1945.

Champ, W. S.:

Annual Dinner of the National Geographic Society (Speech by W. S. Champ). Vol. XVII, pp. 22-37, Jan., 1908.

Report Concerning Ziegler Polar Expedition. By W. S. Champ. Vol. XV, pp. 427-428, Oct., 1904.

Champéry, Switzerland :

In Valais. By Louise Murray. Vol. XXI, pp. 249-256, 6 ills., Mar., 1910.

Chandler, Douglas:

Belgium—Europe in Miniature. By Douglas Chandler. Vol. LXXIII, pp. 397-450, 34 ills. in black and white, 20 ills. in color, Apr., 1938.

Changing Berlin. By Douglas Chandler. Vol. LXXI, pp. 131-177, 30 ills. in black and white, 24 ills. in color, Feb., 1937.

Flying Around the Baltic. By Douglas Chandler. Vol. LXXIII, pp. 767-806, 31 ills. in black and white, 13 ills. in duotone, 1 half-page map, June, 1938.

Kaleidoscopic Land of Europe's Youngest King : Yugoslavia Holds a Mosaic of Slavs and the City Where Pistol Shots Touched Off the World War. By Douglas Chandler. Vol. LXXV, pp. 691-738, 18 ills. in black and white, 34 ills. in color, 2 maps, June, 1939.

Transformation of Turkey : New Hats and New Alphabet Are the Surface Symbols of the Swiftest National Changes in Modern Times. By Douglas Chandler. Vol. LXXV, pp. 1-50, 27 ills. in black and white, 23 ills. in color, 1 map, Jan., 1939.

Chandler, J. S.:

Madura Temples. By J. S. Chandler. Vol. XIX, pp. 218-222, 4 ills., Mar., 1908.

Change Comes to Bible Lands. By Frederick Simpich. Vol. LXXIV, pp. 695-750, 40 ills. in black and white, 25 ills. in color, special map supplement, Dec., 1938.

Changing Berlin. By Douglas Chandler. Vol. LXXI, pp. 131-177, 30 ills. in black and white, 24 ills. in color, Feb., 1937.

Changing Canton. 20 ills. from photographs by Siukee Mack, Alfred T. Palmer, and Kinchue Wong. Vol. LXXII, pp. 711-726, Dec., 1937.

Changing Map in the Balkans. By Frederick Moore. Vol. XXIV, pp. 199-226, 27 ills., 1 page map, Feb., 1913.

Changing Palestine. By Maj. Edward Keith-Roach. Vol. LXV, pp. 493-527, 43 ills., 1 half-page map, Apr., 1934.

Changing Shanghai. By Amanda Boyden. Vol. LXXII, pp. 485-508, 21 ills., 1 two-thirds-page and 1 quarter-page maps, Oct., 1937.

Channel Indians. *See* Alikuluf Indians ; Yahgans.

Channel Islands:

Channel Islands. By Edith Carey. Vol. XXXVIII, pp. 143-164, 24 ills., 1 fourth-page map, Aug., 1920.

Feudal Isle of Sark : Where Sixteenth Century Laws Are Still Observed. By Sibyl Hathaway (La Dame de Serk). Vol. LXII, pp. 101-119, 21 ills., 1 half-page map, July, 1932.

See also Guernsey.

Channel Ports—And Some Others (England). By Florence Craig Albrecht. Vol. XXVIII, pp. 1-55, 45 ills., July, 1915.

Chantier (Ship) :

First Flight to the North Pole. By Lieut. Comdr. Richard Evelyn Byrd. Vol. L, pp. 357-376, 14 ills., Sept., 1926.

Chapels:

Our National War Memorials in Europe. By Gen. John J. Pershing. Vol. LXV, pp. 1-36, 24 ills. in black and white, 11 ills. in color, 1 half-page map, Jan., 1934.

"Time Will Not Dim the Glory of Their Deeds." 11 ills. in color from natural-color photographs by W. Robert Moore. Vol. LXV, pp. 17-24, Jan., 1934.

See also Cathedrals and Churches.

Chapin, William Wisner:

Empire of Romance—India. 5 ills. in color from photographs by William Wisner Chapin. Vol. XL, pp. 483-494, Nov., 1921.

Glimpses of Holland. By William Wisner Chapin. Vol. XXVII, pp. 1-29, 26 ills., Jan., 1915.

Glimpses of Japan. By William Wisner Chapin. Vol. XXII, pp. 965-1002, 10 ills. in black and white, 34 ills. in color, Nov., 1911.

Glimpses of Korea and China. By William Wisner Chapin. Vol. XXI, pp. 895-934, 11 ills. in black and white, 39 ills. in color, Nov., 1910.

Chapin, William Wisner—*Continued*

Glimpses of the Russian Empire. By William Wisner Chapin. Vol. XXIII, pp. 1043-1078, 51 ills. in color, 1 three-quarters-page map, Nov., 1912.

Japan. 34 ills. in color from photographs by William Wisner Chapin. Vol. XXII, pp. 973-996, Nov., 1911.

Korea and China. 39 ills. in color from photographs by William Wisner Chapin. Vol. XXI, pp. 903-926, Nov., 1910.

Russian Empire. 51 ills. in color from photographs by William Wisner Chapin. Vol. XXIII, pp. 1047-1070, Nov., 1912.

Chapman, Frank M.:

Birds May Bring You More Happiness Than the Wealth of the Indies. By Frank M. Chapman. Vol. XXIV, pp. 699-714, 15 ills., June, 1913.

Naturalist's Journey Around Vera Cruz and Tampico. By Frank M. Chapman. Vol. XXV, pp. 532-562, 31 ills., May, 1914.

Over the Andes to Bogotá. By Frank M. Chapman. Vol. XL, pp. 353-373, 19 ills., Oct., 1921.

Who Treads Our Trails? A Camera Trapper Describes His Experiences on an Island in the Canal Zone, a Natural-History Laboratory in the American Tropics. By Frank M. Chapman. Vol. LII, pp. 331-345, 18 ills., 1 half-page map, Sept., 1927.

Chapman, Lucie:

Lords of the Rockies: Photographing Big Game Animals in Their Primeval Surroundings, from Arizona to Canada, Brings Adventure to Two Wilderness Wanderers. By Wendell and Lucie Chapman. Vol. LXXVI, pp. 87-128, 14 ills. in black and white, 28 ills. in color, July, 1939.

With Wild Animals in the Rockies. By Lucie and Wendell Chapman. Vol. LXVIII, pp. 231-249, 26 ills. in duotone, Aug., 1935.

Chapman, Robert H.:

Deserts of Nevada and the Death Valley. By Robert H. Chapman. Vol. XVII, pp. 482-497, 9 ills., 1 chart, Sept., 1906.

Drowned Empire (Swamp Drainage). By Robert H. Chapman. Vol. XIX, pp. 190-199, 10 ills., Mar., 1908.

Our Northern Rockies. By Robert H. Chapman. Vol. XIII, pp. 361-372, 10 ills., Oct., 1902.

Chapman, Wendell:

Lords of the Rockies: Photographing Big Game Animals in Their Primeval Surroundings, from Arizona to Canada, Brings Adventure to Two Wilderness Wanderers. By Wendell and Lucie Chapman. Vol. LXXVI, pp. 87-128, 14 ills. in black and white, 28 ills. in color, July, 1939.

Stalking Big Game with Color Camera. 28 ills. in color from natural-color photographs by Wendell Chapman. Vol. LXXVI, pp. 89-128, July, 1939.

Chapman, Wendell—*Continued*

With Wild Animals in the Rockies. By Lucie and Wendell Chapman. Vol. LXVIII, pp. 231-249, 26 ills. in duotone, Aug., 1935.

Chapter from Japanese History. By Eki Hioki. Vol. XVI, pp. 220-228, May, 1905.

Char-à-Bancs in Cornwall. By Herbert Corey. Vol. XLVI, pp. 653-694, 44 ills., 1 half-page map, Dec., 1924.

Character of Our Immigration, Past and Present. By Z. F. McSweeny. Vol. XVI, pp. 1-15, 1 chart, Jan., 1905.

Characteristics of the Japanese People. By Baron Kentaro Kaneko. Vol. XVI, pp. 93-100, Mar., 1905.

Charcot, Jean:

Election of Jean Charcot as Honorary Member of The Society. Vol. XXIV, pp. 122, 124-125, Jan., 1913.

Charleston, South Carolina:

Charleston: A Colonial Rhapsody. 24 ills. in color from natural-color photographs by B. Anthony Stewart. Vol. LXXV, pp. 289-312, Mar., 1939.

Charleston: Where Mellow Past and Present Meet. By DuBose Heyward. Vol. LXXV, pp. 273-312, 20 ills. in black and white, 24 ills. in color, 1 page map, Mar., 1939.

Heroes' Return. By William H. Nicholas. Vol. LXXXVII, pp. 333-352, 19 ills., Mar., 1945.

Charm and Color Distinguish Norman Byways. 13 ills. in color from natural-color photographs by Gervais Courtellemont. Vol. LXI, pp. 90-99, Jan., 1932.

Charm of Cape Breton Island: The Most Picturesque Portion of Canada's Maritime Provinces—A Land Rich in Historic Associations, Natural Resources, and Geographic Appeal. By Catherine Dunlop Mackenzie. Vol. XXXVIII, pp. 34-60, 22 ills., 1 three-quarters-page map, July, 1920.

Charm Spots Along England's Harassed Coast. 16 ills. in duotone from photographs. Vol. LXXVIII, pp. 237-252, Aug., 1940.

Charting a Coast-Line of 26,000 Miles (Alaska). Vol. XX, pp. 608-609, July, 1909.

Charting a World at War. By William H. Nicholas. Vol. LXXXVI, pp. 617-640, 23 ills., 1 drawing, Nov., 1944.

Charts, Star. *See* Star Charts.

Chase, Enoch A.:

Fame's Eternal Camping Ground: Beautiful Arlington (Virginia), Burial Place of America's Illustrious Dead. By Enoch A. Chase. Vol. LIV, pp. 621-638, 19 ills., Nov., 1928.

Chase, Francis, Jr.:

Palestine Today. By Francis Chase, Jr. Vol. XC, pp. 501-516, 16 ills., Oct., 1946.

Châteaux:

Anticosti Island, Nugget of the North. By Eugene E. Wilson. Vol. LXXXI, pp. 121 140, 19 ills., 1 two-thirds-page map, Jan., 1942.

Beauty, History, and Romance Enrich the Château Country (France). 10 ills. in color from autochromes by Gervais Courtellemont. Vol. LVIII, pp. 466-475, Oct., 1930.

Château Land—France's Pageant on the Loire. Vol. LVIII, pp. 466-475, 10 ills. in color, Oct., 1930.

Color and Customs of Sweden's Château Country. 13 ills. in color from natural-color photographs by Gustav Heurlin. Vol. LXVI, pp. 33-40, July, 1934.

Country-House Life in Sweden: In Castle and Cottage the Landed Gentry Keep the Old Traditions. By Amelie Posse-Brázdová. Vol. LXVI, pp. 1-64, 51 ills. in black and white, 13 ills. in color, 1 page map, July, 1934.

Through the Back Doors of France: A Seven Weeks' Voyage in a Canadian Canoe from St. Malo, Through Brittany and the Château Country, to Paris. By Melville Chater. Vol. XLIV, pp. 1-51, 55 ills., 1 half-page map, July, 1923.

See also Castles.

Chater, Melville:

Across the Midi in a Canoe: Two Americans Paddle Along the Canals of Southern France from the Atlantic to the Mediterranean. By Melville Chater. Vol. LII, pp. 127-167, 49 ills., 1 half-page map, Aug., 1927.

Dalmatian Days: Coasting Along Debatable Shores Where Latin and Slav Meet. By Melville Chater. Vol. LIII, pp. 47-90, 26 ills. in black and white, 17 ills. in color, 1 two-thirds-page map, Jan., 1928.

Danube, Highway of Races: From the Black Forest to the Black Sea, Europe's Most Important River Has Borne the Traffic of Centuries. By Melville Chater. Vol. LVI, pp. 643-697, 54 ills., Dec., 1929.

East of Constantinople: Glimpses of Village Life in Anatolia, the Battleground of East and West, Where the Turks Reorganized Their Forces After the World War. By Melville Chater. Vol. XLIII, pp. 509-534, 27 ills., 1 three-quarters-page map, May, 1923.

Europe's Newest Kingdom: After Centuries of Struggle, Albania at Last Enjoys an Era of Peace and Stability. By Melville Chater. Vol. LIX, pp. 131-191, 37 ills. in black and white, 25 ills. in color, 1 half-page map, Feb., 1931.

Faces and Flowers Below the Tropics (Union of South Africa). 14 ills. in color from natural-color photographs by Melville Chater. Vol. LIX, pp. 452-461, Apr., 1931.

History's Greatest Trek: Tragedy Stalks Through the Near East as Greece and Turkey Exchange Two Million of Their People. By Melville Chater. Vol. XLVIII, pp. 533-590, 52 ills. in black and white, 32 ills. in color, Nov., 1925.

Chater, Melville—*Continued*

Hunting Castles in Italy. By Melville Chater. Vol. LXVIII, pp. 329-366, 25 ills. in black and white, 13 ills. in color, 1 page and 1 quarter-page maps, Sept., 1935.

Jugoslavia—Ten Years After. By Melville Chater. Vol. LVIII, pp. 257-309, 44 ills. in black and white, 25 ills. in color, 1 three-quarters-page map, Sept., 1930.

Kizilbash Clans of Kurdistan. By Melville Chater. Vol. LIV, pp. 485-504, 22 ills., Oct., 1928.

Land of the Stalking Death: A Journey Through Starving Armenia on an American Relief Train. By Melville Chater. Vol. XXXVI, pp. 393-420, 23 ills., Nov., 1919.

Michigan, Mistress of the Lakes. By Melville Chater. Vol. LIII, pp. 269-325, 65 ills., 1 page and 1 three-quarters-page maps, Mar., 1928.

Motor-Coaching Through North Carolina. By Melville Chater. Vol. XLIX, pp. 475-523, 43 ills., 1 third-page map, May, 1926.

Ohio, The Gateway State. By Melville Chater. Vol. LXI, pp. 525-591, 58 ills. in black and white, 13 ills. in color, 1 three-quarters-page map, May, 1932.

Rediscovering the Rhine: A Trip by Barge from the Sea to the Headwaters of Europe's Storied Stream. By Melville Chater. Vol. XLVIII, pp. 1-43, 44 ills., July, 1925.

Rhodesia, the Pioneer Colony: In the Land of Sheba's Gold and Rhodes' Diamonds Emerge Model Towns and Modern Mines. By Melville Chater. Vol. LXVII, pp. 753 782, 31 ills, June, 1935.

Scenes on High Veld and Low (Union of South Africa). 13 ills. in color from natural-color photographs by Melville Chater. Vol. LIX, pp. 492-501, Apr., 1931.

Skirting the Shores of Sunrise: Seeking and Finding "The Levant" in a Journey by Steamer, Motor-Car, and Train from Constantinople to Port Said. By Melville Chater. Vol. L, pp. 649-728, 60 ills. in black and white, 34 ills. in color, 1 two-thirds-page map, Dec., 1926.

Through the Back Doors of Belgium: Artist and Author Paddle for Three Weeks Along 200 Miles of Low-Countries Canals in a Canadian Canoe. By Melville Chater. Vol. XLVII, pp. 499-540, 39 ills., 1 half-page map, May, 1925.

Through the Back Doors of France: A Seven Weeks' Voyage in a Canadian Canoe, from St. Malo, Through Brittany and the Château Country, to Paris. By Melville Chater. Vol. XLIV, pp. 1-51, 55 ills., 1 half-page map, July, 1923.

Trekking South Africa with a Color Camera. 11 ills. in color from natural-color photographs by Melville Chater. Vol. LIX, pp. 412-421, Apr., 1931.

Under the South African Union. By Melville Chater. Vol. LIX, pp. 391-512, 97 ills. in black and white, 38 ills. in color, 1 two-page map, Apr., 1931.

Chater, Melville—*Continued*

Contents : Cape of Good Hope : The Floral Province.—Orange Free State : The Prairie Province.—Natal : The Garden Province.—The Transvaal : The Treasure-House Province.

Zigzagging Across Sicily. By Melville Chater. Vol. XLVI, pp. 303-352, 44 ills., 1 half-page map, Sept., 1924.

Chatham, Massachusetts :

Cape Cod People and Places. By Wanda Burnett. Vol. LXXXIX, pp. 737-774, 17 ills. in black and white, 24 ills. in color, 1 half-page map, June, 1946.

Chaulmoogra Oil:

Hunting the Chaulmoogra Tree. By Joseph F. Rock. Vol. XLI, pp. 243-276, 39 ills., 1 page map, Mar., 1922.

Cheese:

Glimpses of Holland. By William Wisner Chapin. Vol. XXVII, pp. 1-29, 26 ills., Jan., 1915.

North Holland Cheese Market. By Hugh M. Smith. Vol. XXI, pp. 1051-1066, 17 ills., Dec., 1910.

Chekiang (Province), China :

China's Wonderland—Yen Tang Shan. 8 ills. in color from camera paintings by Herbert Clarence White, Deng Bao-ling, and Hwang Yao-tso. Vol. LXXII, pp. 687-694, Dec., 1937.

Chelan National Forest, Washington :

Forest Lookout. By Ella E. Clark. With 9 ills. in color from natural-color photographs by the author. Vol. XC, pp. 73-96, 8 ills. in black and white, July, 1946.

Chemical Discussion of Analyses of Volcanic Ejecta from Martinique and St. Vincent. By W. F. Hillebrand. Vol. XIII, pp. 296-299, July, 1902.

Chemistry:

Chemists Make a New World : Creating Hitherto Unknown Raw Materials, Science Now Disrupts Old Trade Routes and Revamps the World Map of Industry. By Frederick Simpich. Vol. LXXVI, pp. 601-640, 22 ills. in black and white, 26 ills. in color, Nov., 1939.

From Nature's Hidden Building Blocks (Synthetic Products). 26 ills. in color from natural-color photographs by Willard R. Culver. Vol. LXXVI, pp. 609-640, Nov., 1939.

Chemists Make a New World : Creating Hitherto Unknown Raw Materials, Science Now Disrupts Old Trade Routes and Revamps the World Map of Industry. By Frederick Simpich. Vol. LXXVI, pp. 601-640, 22 ills. in black and white, 26 ills. in color, Nov., 1939.

Chengtu, China :

Eden of the Flowery Republic. By Joseph Beech. Vol. XXXVIII, pp. 355-390, 18 ills. in black and white, 16 ills. in color, Nov., 1920.

Chengtu, China—*Continued*

Populous and Beautiful Szechuan : A Visit to the Restless Province of China, in Which the Present Revolution Began. By Rollin T. Chamberlin. Vol. XXII, pp. 1094-1119, 26 ills., 1 half-page map, Dec., 1911.

Chesapeake and Ohio Canal:

Potomac, River of Destiny. By Albert W. Atwood. Vol. LXXXVIII, pp. 33-70, 15 ills. in black and white, 18 ills. in color, 1 map (two-page spread), July, 1945.

Chesapeake Bay:

Tides of Chesapeake Bay. By E. D. Preston. Vol. X, pp. 391-392, Oct., 1899.

Chesapeake Bay Region:

Chesapeake Odyssey : An 18-foot Sailboat Follows the Course of Captain John Smith around This Spacious Bay of History, Commerce, Sea Food, and Nautical Lore. By John Maloney. Vol. LXXVI, pp. 357-392, 32 ills., 1 page map, Sept., 1939.

Chess (Game) :

Ströbeck (Germany), Home of Chess : A Medieval Village in the Harz Mountains of Germany Teaches the Royal Game in Its Public School. By Harriet Geithmann. Vol. LIX, pp. 637-652, 8 ills. in black and white, 14 ills. in color, May, 1931.

Chester, (Rear Adm.) Colby M.:

American Eclipse Expedition. By Rear Adm. Colby M. Chester. Vol. XVII, pp. 589-612, 23 ills., 1 color plate, Nov., 1906.

Discovery of North Pole (Speech by Rear Adm. Colby M. Chester). Vol. XXI, pp. 63-82, Jan., 1910.

Haiti : A Degenerating Island. By Rear Adm. Colby M. Chester. Vol. XIX, pp. 200-217, 5 ills., 1 quarter-page map, Mar., 1908.

Panama Canal. By Rear Adm. Colby M. Chester. Vol. XVI, pp. 445-467, 8 ills., Oct., 1905.

Some Early Geographers of the United States. By Rear Adm. Colby M. Chester. Vol. XV, pp. 392-404, Oct., 1904.

Young Turk. By Rear Adm. Colby M. Chester. Vol. XXIII, pp. 42-89, 39 ills., Jan., 1912.

Chetelat, Eleanor de:

My Domestic Life in French Guinea : An American Woman Accompanies Her Husband, a French Geologist, on His Explorations in a Little-Known Region. By Eleanor de Chételat. Vol. LXVII, pp. 695-730, 48 ills., 1 half-page map, June, 1935.

Chetelat, Enzo de:

Dusky Tribesmen of French West Africa. 26 ills. in color from natural-color photographs by Enzo de Chetelat. Vol. LXXIX, pp. 639-662, May, 1941.

South Sea Isle of Mineral Mountains (New Caledonia). 12 ills. in color from natural-color photographs by Enzo de Chetelat. Vol. LXXXII, pp. 33-40, July, 1942.

Chetelat, Enzo de—*Continued*

War Awakened New Caledonia: Swift Changes Take Place on the South Pacific Island of Mineral Wealth Defended by Free French and American Troops. By Enzo de Chetelat. Vol. LXXXII, pp. 31-55, 14 ills. in black and white, 12 ills. in color, 1 two-thirds-page map, July, 1942.

Chetwode, Penelope:

Nepal, the Sequestered Kingdom. By Penelope Chetwode. Vol. LXVII, pp. 319-352, 27 ills. in black and white, 15 ills. in color, 1 half-page map, Mar., 1935.

Cheverlange, Elie:

Manlike Apes of Jungle and Mountain. 10 ills. in color from paintings by Elie Cheverlange. Vol. LXXVIII, pp. 221-228, Aug., 1940.

Who's Who in the Monkey World. 40 portraits in color from paintings by Elie Cheverlange. Vol. LXXIII, pp. 625-642, May, 1938.

Cheyenne, Wyoming:

Grass Makes Wyoming Fat. By Frederick Simpich. Vol. LXXXVIII, pp. 153-188, 13 ills. in black and white, 19 ills. in color, 1 two-page map, Aug., 1945.

Chiapas (State), Mexico:

Finding Jewels of Jade in a Mexican Swamp. By Matthew W. and Marion Stirling. Vol. LXXXII, pp. 635-661, 15 ills. in black and white, 12 ills. in color, 1 two-thirds-page map, Nov., 1942.

Chicago, Illinois:

Chicago, Titan of the Middle West. 12 ills. in color from direct color photographs by Clifton Adams. Vol. LIX, pp. 584-593, May, 1931.

Chicago Today and Tomorrow: A City Whose Industries Have Changed the Food Status of the World and Transformed the Economic Situation of a Billion People. By William Joseph Showalter. Vol. XXXV, pp. 1-42, 28 ills., 1 page map, Jan., 1919.

Deep-Water Route from Chicago to the Gulf. Vol. XVIII, pp. 676-685, 3 ills., 1 page map, Oct., 1907.

Great Canals of the World. Vol. XVI, pp. 475-479, Oct., 1905.

Illinois, Crossroads of the Continent. By Junius B. Wood. Vol. LIX, pp. 523-594, 51 ills. in black and white, 12 ills. in color, special map supplement, May, 1931.

Chichen Itzá, Mexico:

Chichen Itzá, an Ancient American Mecca: Recent Excavations in Yucatan Are Bringing to Light the Temples, Palaces, and Pyramids of America's Most Holy Native City. By Sylvanus Griswold Morley. Vol. XLVII, pp. 63-95, 34 ills., 1 half-page map, 1 diagram, Jan., 1925.

Home of a Forgotten Race—Mysterious Chichen Itzá, in Yucatan, Mexico. By Edward H. Thompson. Vol. XXV, pp. 585-648, 59 ills., June, 1914.

Chichen Itzá, Mexico—*Continued*

Life and Death in Ancient Maya Land. 10 ills. in color from paintings by H. M. Herget. Vol. LXX, pp. 623-630, Nov., 1936.

Today in the Feathered Serpent's City. 25 ills. in color from natural-color photographs by Luis Marden. Vol. LXX, pp. 599-614, Nov., 1936.

Unearthing America's Ancient History: Investigation Suggests That the Maya May Have Designed the First Astronomical Observatory in the New World in Order to Cultivate Corn. By Sylvanus Griswold Morley. Vol. LX, pp. 99-126, 28 ills., July, 1931.

Chichi Jima (Peel Island), Ogasawara Shoto:

Springboards to Tokyo. By Willard Price. Vol. LXXXVI, pp. 385-407, 16 ills., Oct., 1944.

Chiengmai, Siam:

Hunting the Chaulmoogra Tree. By Joseph F. Rock. Vol. XLI, pp. 243-276, 39 ills., 1 page map, Mar., 1922.

Childhood Scenes in Many Lands. Vol. XXXI, pp. 147-162, 16 ills., Feb., 1917.

Children of the World. Vol. XIX, pp. 126-140, 15 ills., Feb., 1908.

Childs, (Mrs.) Harris R. (Eleanor Stuart):

Zanzibar. By Mrs. Harris R. Childs. Vol. XXIII, pp. 810-824, 11 ills., Aug., 1912.

Childs, Marquis W.:

London Wins the Battle. By Marquis W. Childs. Vol. LXXXVIII, pp. 129-152, 21 ills., Aug., 1945.

Chile:

Argentina-Chile Boundary Award. Vol. XIV, pp. 115-116, Mar., 1903.

Argentine-Chile Boundary. Vol. XIII, p. 117, Mar., 1902.

Argentine-Chile Boundary Dispute. Vol. XIII, pp. 27-28, Jan., 1902.

Awakening of Argentina and Chile: Progress in the Lands That Lie Below Capricorn. By Bailey Willis. Vol. XXX, pp. 121-142, 14 ills., Aug., 1916.

Capital and Chief Seaport of Chile (Santiago and Valparaíso). By W. Robert Moore. Vol. LXXXVI, pp. 477-500, 15 ills. in black and white, 8 ills. in color, 1 third-page map, Oct., 1944.

Chile-Argentina Boundary Dispute. Vol. XIII, p. 220, June, 1902.

Chile's Disputes with Peru and Bolivia. Vol. XII, pp. 401-402, Nov., 1901.

Chile's Land of Fire and Water: Smoking Volcanoes and Ice-hooded Peaks Stand Sentinel Over Limpid Lakes in the Far Southern Andes. By W. Robert Moore. Vol. LXXX, pp. 91-110, 9 ills. in black and white, 10 ills. in color, 1 page map, July, 1941.

First Transandine Railroad from Buenos Aires to Valparaiso. By Harriet Chalmers Adams. Vol. XXI, pp. 397-417, 14 ills., 1 quarter-page map, May, 1910.

Chile—*Continued*

Flying the "Hump" of the Andes. By Capt. Albert W. Stevens. Vol. LIX, pp. 595-636, 36 ills., 1 third-page map, May, 1931.

Flying the World's Longest Air-Mail Route: From Montevideo, Uruguay, Over the Andes, Up the Pacific Coast, Across Central America and the Caribbean to Miami, Florida, in 67 Thrilling Flying Hours. By Junius B. Wood. Vol. LVII, pp. 261-325, 65 ills., 1 half-page map, Mar., 1930.

From Panama to Patagonia. By Charles M. Pepper. Vol. XVII, pp. 449-452, 1 ill., Aug., 1906.

Indian Tribes of Southern Patagonia, Tierra del Fuego, and the Adjoining Islands. By J. B. Hatcher. Vol. XII, pp. 12-22, 4 ills., Jan., 1901.

Inside Cape Horn. By Amos Burg. Vol. LXXII, pp. 743-783, 29 ills. in black and white, 10 ills. in color, 1 two-page map, Dec., 1937.

Land of the Horn, America's Tiptoe. 10 ills. in color from natural-color photographs by Amos Burg. Vol. LXXII, pp. 751-758, Dec., 1937.

Longitudinal Journey Through Chile. By Harriet Chalmers Adams. Vol. XLII, pp. 219-273, 60 ills., 1 half-page map, Sept., 1922.

On a Chilean Hacienda. 8 ills. in color from natural-color photographs by E. P. Haddon. Vol. LXXXVI, pp. 489-496, Oct., 1944.

Scenes of Beauty in Copper Land. 25 ills. in color from autochromes by Jacob Gayer. Vol. LV, pp. 198-215, Feb., 1929.

Some Geographic Features of Southern Patagonia, With a Discussion of Their Origin. By J. B. Hatcher. Vol. XI, pp. 41-55, 4 ills., Feb., 1900.

Some Personal Experiences with Earthquakes (Arica). By Rear Adm. L. G. Billings. Vol. XXVII, pp. 57-71, 7 ills., Jan., 1915.

Sunshine Over the Chilean Lakes. 10 ills. in color from natural-color photographs by W. Robert Moore and John Swope. Vol. LXXX, pp. 97-104, July, 1941.

Twin Stars of Chile: Valparaiso, the Gateway, and Santiago, the Capital—Key Cities with a Progressive Present and a Romantic Past. By William Joseph Showalter. Vol. LV, pp. 197-247, 35 ills. in black and white, 25 ills. in color, Feb., 1929.

See also Easter Island; Juan Fernández Island.

Chile's Disputes with Peru and Bolivia. Vol. XII, pp. 401-402, Nov., 1901.

Chile's Land of Fire and Water: Smoking Volcanoes and Ice-hooded Peaks Stand Sentinel Over Limpid Lakes in the Far Southern Andes. By W. Robert Moore. Vol. LXXX, pp. 91-110, 9 ills. in black and white, 10 ills. in color, 1 page map, July, 1941.

Chilkat Tlingit (Indian Tribe):

Indians of Our North Pacific Coast. By Matthew W. Sterling. Paintings by W. Langdon Kihn. Vol. LXXXVII, pp. 25-52, 3 ills. in black and white, 16 ills. in color, Jan., 1945.

Chimpanzees:

Manlike Apes of Jungle and Mountain. 10 ills. in color from paintings by Elie Cheverlange. Vol. LXXVIII, pp. 221-228, Aug., 1940.

Man's Closest Counterparts: Heavyweight of Monkeydom Is the "Old Man" Gorilla, by Far the Largest of the Four Great Apes. By William M. Mann. Vol. LXXVIII, pp. 213-236, 10 ills. in black and white, 10 ills. in color, Aug., 1940.

Chimú Civilization:

Air Adventures in Peru: Cruising Among Andean Peaks, Pilots and Cameramen Discover Wondrous Works of an Ancient People. By Robert Shippee. Vol. LXIII, pp. 81-120, 40 ills., 1 three-quarters-page map, Jan., 1933.

China:

American Goods in China. Vol. XVII, pp. 173-175, 4 ills., Mar., 1906.

Among the People of Cathay. 16 ills. in duotone. Vol. LI, pp. 701-716, June, 1927.

Banishing the Devil of Disease Among the Nashi: Weird Ceremonies Performed by an Aboriginal Tribe in the Heart of Yünnan Province, China. By Joseph F. Rock. Vol. XLVI, pp. 473-499, 26 ills., 1 half-page map, Nov., 1924.

Buddhist Calm Survives Along China's Great Wall. 10 ills. in color; 4 paintings by Mary Augusta Mullikin and Anna M. Hotchkis and 6 natural-color photographs. Vol. LXXIII, pp. 321-328, Mar., 1938.

Burma Road, Back Door to China: Like the Great Wall of Ancient Times, This Mighty Mountain Highway Has Been Built by Myriad Chinese to Help Defend Their Homeland. By Frank Outram and G. E. Fane. Vol. LXXVIII, pp. 629-658, 26 ills., 1 two-thirds-page map, Nov., 1940.

Capital and Country of Old Cathay. 16 ills. in duotone. Vol. LXIII, pp. 748-765, June, 1933.

Carrying the Color Camera Through Unmapped China. 24 ills. in color from natural-color photographs by Joseph F. Rock. Vol. LVIII, pp. 402-435, Oct., 1930.

Causes that Led Up to the Siege of Pekin. By W. A. P. Martin. Vol. XII, pp. 53-63, 1 ill., Feb., 1901.

China. By John W. Foster. Vol. XV, pp. 463-478, 2 page maps, Dec., 1904.

China: Her History and Development. By John Barrett. Vol. XII, pp. 209-218, June, 1901.

China: Her History and Development. By John Barrett. Vol. XII, pp. 266-272, July, 1901.

China and Her People: Some Reflections on Their Manners and Customs, Habits and Lives. By Comdr. Harrie Webster. Vol. XI, pp. 309-319, 3 ills., Aug., 1900.

China and the United States. By Sir Chentung Liang-Cheng. Vol. XVI, pp. 554-557, Dec., 1905.

China Fights Erosion with U. S. Aid. By Walter C. Lowdermilk. Vol. LXXXVII, pp. 641-680, 10 ills. in black and white, 26 ills. in color, June, 1945.

China—*Continued*

China Opens Her Wild West (Yünnan): In the Mountain-girt Heart of a Continent a New China Has Been Created During the Years of War. By Owen Lattimore. Vol. LXXXII, pp. 337-367, 21 ills. in black and white, 11 ills. in color, 1 map (two-page spread), Sept., 1942.

China's Great Wall of Sculpture: Man-hewn Caves and Countless Images Form a Colossal Art Wonder of Early Buddhism. By Mary Augusta Mullikin. Vol. LXXIII, pp. 313-348, 23 ills. in black and white, 10 ills. in color, 1 third-page map, Mar., 1938.

China's Hand-built Air Bases. 9 ills. from photographs. Vol. LXXXVIII, pp. 231-236, Aug., 1945.

China's Teeming Life on the Rivers and Sea. 18 ills. in duotone from photographs by Paul De Gaston and W. Robert Moore. Vol. LXVI, pp. 625-640, Nov., 1934.

China's Treasures. By Frederick McCormick. Vol. XXIII, pp. 996-1040, 50 ills., Oct., 1912.

China's Wonderland—Yen Tang Shan (Chekiang Province). 8 ills. in colors from camera paintings by Herbert Clarence White, Deng Bao-ling, and Hwang Yao-tso. Vol. LXXII, pp. 687-694, Dec., 1937.

Chinese "Boxers." By Llewellyn James Davies. Vol. XI, pp. 281-287, July, 1900.

Chinese Jews. By Oliver Bainbridge. Vol. XVIII, pp. 621-632, 7 ills., Oct., 1907.

Chinese Paradox. By Harvey Maitland Watts. Vol. XI, pp. 352-358, 2 ills., Sept., 1900.

Chinese Pigeon Whistles. Vol. XXIV, pp. 715-716, 1 ill., June, 1913.

Climbing Mighty Minya Konka: Americans First Scaled Mountain That Now Is Landmark of China's New Skyway. By Richard L. Burdsall and Terris Moore. Vol. LXXXIII, pp. 625-650, 23 ills., 1 page map, May, 1943.

Coastal Cities of China. By W. Robert Moore. Vol. LXVI, pp. 601-643, 12 ills. in black and white, 18 ills. in duotone, 14 ills. in color, 1 page map, Nov., 1934.

Cotton and the Chinese Boycott. From an address by President Roosevelt to the citizens of Atlanta, October 20, 1905. Vol. XVI, pp. 516-517, Nov., 1905.

Curious and Characteristic Customs of China. By Kenneth F. Junor. Vol. XXI, pp. 791-806, 7 ills., Sept., 1910.

Demon Dancers and Butter Gods of Choni. 16 ills. in color from photographs by Joseph F. Rock. Vol. LIV, pp. 584-601, Nov., 1928.

Descendants of Confucious (Industries in Shantung). By Maynard Owen Williams. Vol. XXXVI, pp. 253-265, 16 ills., Sept., 1919.

Desert Road to Turkestan: Twentieth Century Travel Through Innermost Asia, Along Caravan Trails Over Which Oriental Commerce Was Once Borne from China to the Medieval Western World. By Owen Lattimore. Vol. LV, pp. 661-702, 45 ills., 1 two-thirds-page map, June, 1929.

China—*Continued*

Eden of the Flowery Republic. By Joseph Beech. Vol. XXXVIII, pp. 355-390, 18 ills. in black and white, 16 ills. in color, Nov., 1920.

Experiences of a Lone Geographer: An American Agricultural Explorer Makes His Way Through Brigand-Infested Central China en Route to the Amne Machin Range, Tibet. By Joseph F. Rock. Vol. XLVIII, pp. 331-347, 16 ills., 1 quarter-page map, Sept., 1925.

Exploring a Grass Wonderland of Wild West China. By Ray G. Johnson. Vol. LXXXV, pp. 713-742, 24 ills., 1 half-page map, June, 1944.

Farmers Since the Days of Noah: China's Remarkable System of Agriculture Has Kept Alive the Densest Population in the World. By Adam Warwick. Vol. LI, pp. 469-500, 37 ills., Apr., 1927.

Fearful Famines of the Past: History Will Repeat Itself Unless the American People Conserve Their Resources. By Ralph A. Graves. Vol. XXXII, pp. 68-90, 11 ills., July, 1917.

Foreigners and Foreign Firms in China. Vol. XI, p. 330, Aug., 1900.

Four Thousand Hours Over China. By Capt. Hans Koester. Vol. LXXIII, pp. 571-598, 25 ills., 1 two-thirds-page map, May, 1938.

From the Mediterranean to the Yellow Sea by Motor: The Citroën-Haardt Expedition Successfully Completes Its Dramatic Journey. By Maynard Owen Williams. Vol. LXII, pp. 513-580, 45 ills. in black and white, 25 ills. in color, 2 half-page maps, Nov., 1932.

Geography of China: The Influence of Physical Environment on the History and Character of the Chinese People. By Frank Johnson Goodnow. Vol. LI, pp. 651-664, 11 ills., June, 1927.

Geologists in China. Vol. XVIII, pp. 640-644, Oct., 1907.

Glimpses of Korea and China. By William W. Chapin. Vol. XXI, pp. 895-934, 11 ills. in black and white, 39 ills. in color, Nov., 1910.

Glories of the Minya Konka: Magnificent Snow Peaks of the China-Tibetan Border Are Photographed at Close Range by a National Geographic Society Expedition. By Joseph F. Rock. Vol. LVIII, pp. 385-437, 35 ills. in black and white, 24 ills. in color, 1 three-quarters-page map, Oct., 1930.

Grand Canal Panorama. By Willard Price. Vol. LXXI, pp. 487-514, 31 ills., 1 half-page map, Apr., 1937.

Great Wall of China. By James H. Wilson. Vol. XI, pp. 372-374, 1 ill., Sept., 1900.

Great Wall of China Near Nankow Pass. Vol. XLIII, panorama, Feb., 1923.

Hairnet Industry in North China. By H. W. Robinson. Vol. XLIV, pp. 327-336, 10 ills., Sept., 1923.

Ho for the Soochow Ho. By Mabel Craft Deering. Vol. LI, pp. 623-649, 32 ills., 1 three-quarters-page map, June, 1927.

China—*Continued*

How Half the World Works. By Alice Tisdale Hobart and Mary A. Nourse. Vol. LXI, pp. 509-524, 22 ills., Apr., 1932.

Hunan—The Closed Province of China. By William Barclay Parsons. Vol. XI, pp. 393-400, 1 ill., 1 half-page map, Oct., 1900.

Hunter of Plants. By David Fairchild. Vol. XXXVI, pp. 57-77, 18 ills., July, 1919.

Jade. By S. E. Easter. Vol. XIV, pp. 9-17, 2 half-page maps, Jan., 1903.

Japan, America, and the Orient. By Eki Hioki. Vol. XVII, pp. 498-504, Sept., 1906.

Japan and China—Some Comparisons. By Comdr. Harrie Webster. Vol. XII, pp. 69-77, 2 ills., Feb., 1901.

Kingdom of Flowers : An Account of the Wealth of Trees and Shrubs of China and of What the Arnold Arboretum, with China's Help, Is Doing to Enrich America. By Ernest H. Wilson. Vol. XXII, pp. 1003-1035, 24 ills., Nov., 1911.

Konka Risumgongba, Holy Mountain of the Outlaws. By Joseph F. Rock. Vol. LX, pp. 1-65, 36 ills. in black and white, 43 ills. in color, 1 three-quarters-page map, July, 1931.

Lama's Motor-Car. By Ethan C. Le Munyon. Vol. XXIV, pp. 640-670, 34 ills., May, 1913.

Land of Genghis Khan in Its True Colors. 6 ills. in color from natural-color photographs by Maynard Owen Williams. Vol. LXII, pp. 568-577, Nov., 1932.

Land of the Crossbow (Yünnan Province). By George Forrest. Vol. XXI, pp. 132-156, 15 ills., 1 page map, Feb., 1910.

Land of the Yellow Lama : National Geographic Society Explorer Visits the Strange Kingdom of Muli, Beyond the Likiang Snow Range of Yünnan Province, China. By Joseph F. Rock. Vol. XLVII, pp. 447-491, 39 ills., 1 half-page map, Apr., 1925.

Landscaped Kwangsi, China's Province of Pictorial Art. By G. Weidman Groff and T. C. Lau. Vol. LXXII, pp. 671-710, 33 ills., 1 half-page map, Dec., 1937.

Lessons from China. Vol. XX, pp. 18-29, 8 ills., Jan., 1909.

Life Afloat in China : Tens of Thousands of Chinese in Congested Ports Spend Their Entire Existence on Boats. By Robert F. Fitch. Vol. LI, pp. 665-686, 28 ills., June, 1927.

Life Along the Central China Coast. 14 ills. in color from natural-color photographs by W. Robert Moore. Vol. LXII, pp. 316-325, Sept., 1932.

Life Among the Lamas of Choni : Describing the Mystery Plays and Butter Festival in the Monastery of an Almost Unknown Tibetan Principality in Kansu Province, China. By Joseph F. Rock. Vol. LIV, pp. 569-619, 34 ills. in black and white, 16 ills. in color, 1 half-page map, Nov., 1928.

"Man in the Street" in China. By Guy Magee, Jr. Vol. XXXVIII, pp. 406-421, 15 ills., Nov., 1920.

China—*Continued*

Map-Changing Medicine. By William Joseph Showalter. Vol. XLII, pp. 303-330, 26 ills., Sept., 1922.

Mrs. Bishop's "The Yangtze Valley and Beyond." By Eliza R. Scidmore. Vol. XI, pp. 366-368, Sept., 1900.

National Geographic Society's Yünnan Province Expedition. By Gilbert Grosvenor. Vol. XLVII, pp. 493-498, 5 ills., Apr., 1925.

New China and the Printed Page. By Paul Hutchinson. Vol. LI, pp. 687-722, 37 ills., June, 1927.

Peacetime Plant Hunting About Peiping. By P. H. and J. H. Dorsett. Vol. LXXII, pp. 509-534, 21 ills., 1 two-thirds-page map, Oct., 1937.

Pirate-Fighters of the South China Sea. By Robert Cardwell. Vol. LXXXIX, pp. 787-796, 11 ills., June, 1946.

Populous and Beautiful Szechuan : A Visit to the Restless Province of China, in Which the Present Revolution Began. By Rollin T. Chamberlin. Vol. XXII, pp. 1094-1119, 26 ills., 1 half-page map, Dec., 1911.

Present Conditions in China. By John W. Foster. Vol. XVII, pp. 651-672, 709-711, Dec., 1906.

Present Conditions in China. By Frederick McCormick. Vol. XXII, pp. 1120-1138, 12 ills., Dec., 1911.

Problems in China. By James M. Hubbard. Vol. XI, pp. 297-308, 3 ills., special map supplement, Aug., 1900.

Race Prejudice in the Far East. By Melville E. Stone. Vol. XXI, pp. 973-985, 6 ills., Dec., 1910.

Raft Life on the Hwang Ho. By W. Robert Moore. Vol. LXI, pp. 743-752, 14 ills., June, 1932.

Road to Wang Ye Fu : An Account of the Work of the National Geographic Society's Central-China Expedition in the Mongol Kingdom of Ala Shan. By Frederick R. Wulsin. Vol. XLIX, pp. 197-234, 44 ills., 1 third-page map, Feb., 1926.

Salt for China's Daily Rice. 11 ills. from photographs. Vol. LXXXVI, pp. 329-336, Sept., 1944.

Scenes in the Celestial Republic. 16 ills. in duotone. Vol. XLIX, pp. 217-232, Feb., 1926.

Seeking the Mountains of Mystery : An Expedition on the China-Tibet Frontier to the Unexplored Amnyi Machen Range, One of Whose Peaks Rivals Everest. By Joseph F. Rock. Vol. LVII, pp. 131-185, 54 ills., 1 two-page map, Feb., 1930.

Shantung—China's Holy Land. By Charles K. Edmunds. Vol. XXXVI, pp. 231-252, 21 ills., 1 half-page map, Sept., 1919.

Shifting Scenes on the Stage of New China. Vol. XXXVIII, pp. 422-428, 4 ills., Nov., 1920.

Singan—The Present Capital of the Chinese Empire. By James Mascarene Hubbard. Vol. XII, pp. 63-66, 1 ill., Feb., 1901.

China—*Continued*

6,000 Miles over the Roads of Free China. By Josephine A. Brown. Vol. LXXXV, pp. 355-384, 30 ills., 1 two-thirds-page map, Mar., 1944.

Society's New Map of China. By James M. Darley. Text accompanying special map supplement in colors. Vol. LXXXVII, pp. 745-746, June, 1945.

South of the Clouds—Yünnan. 11 ills. in color from natural-color photographs by Owen Lattimore and Frank Outram. Vol. LXXXII, pp. 349-356, Sept., 1942.

Stilwell Road—Land Route to China. By Nelson Grant Tayman. Vol. LXXXVII, pp. 681-698, 18 ills., June, 1945.

Taming "Flood Dragons" Along China's Hwang Ho (River). By Oliver J. Todd. Vol. LXXXI, pp. 205-234, 26 ills., 1 half-page map, Feb., 1942.

Thousand Miles Along the Great Wall of China: The Mightiest Barrier Ever Built by Man Has Stood Guard Over the Land of Chin for Twenty Centuries. By Adam Warwick. Vol. XLIII, pp. 113-143, 27 ills., panorama, 1 page and 1 half-page maps, Feb., 1923.

Through the Great River Trenches of Asia: National Geographic Society Explorer Follows the Yangtze, Mekong, and Salwin Through Mighty Gorges, Some of Whose Canyon Walls Tower to a Height of More Than Two Miles. By Joseph F. Rock. Vol. L, pp. 133-186, 47 ills., 1 half-page map, Aug., 1926.

Today on the China Coast. By John B. Powell. Vol. LXXXVII, pp. 217-238, 17 ills., 1 page map, Feb., 1945.

Tsung-Li-Yamen (Foreign Office). By Eliza R. Scidmore. Vol. XI, pp. 291-292, 1 diagram, 1 two-thirds-page map, July, 1900.

Western Progress in China. Vol. XII, pp. 434-436, Dec., 1901.

"Where the Mountains Walked": An Account of the Recent Earthquake in Kansu Province, China, Which Destroyed 100,000 Lives. By Upton Close and Elsie McCormick. Vol. XLI, pp. 445-464, 23 ills., 1 three-quarters-page map, May, 1922.

With the Devil Dancers of China and Tibet. 43 ills. in color from natural-color photographs by Joseph F. Rock. Vol. LX, pp. 18-59, July, 1931.

Wonderful Canals of China. By George E. Anderson. Vol. XVI, pp. 68-69, Feb., 1905.

Wonderful Canals of China. By F. H. King. Vol. XXIII, pp. 931-958, 35 ills., 5 half-page maps, Oct., 1912.

World's Ancient Porcelain Center (Kingtehchen). By Frank B. Lenz. Vol. XXXVIII, pp. 391-406, 17 ills., Nov., 1920.

World's Greatest Overland Explorer: How Marco Polo Penetrated Farthest Asia, "Discovered" Many Lands Unknown to Europe, and Added Numerous Minerals, Animals, Birds, and Plants to Man's Knowledge. By J. R. Hildebrand. Vol. LIV, pp. 505-568, 53 ills., 1 two-page map, Nov., 1928.

China—*Continued*

See also Canton ; Hainan (Island) ; Hong Kong ; Kunming ; Macau ; Manchuria (Manchukuo) ; Mongolia ; Nanking ; Peiping ; Puto Shan (Island) ; Shanghai ; Sinkiang ; Tibet ; Tsinghai ; Yünnan.

China's Great Wall of Sculpture: Man-hewn Caves and Countless Images Form a Colossal Art Wonder of Early Buddhism. By Mary Augusta Mullikin. Vol. LXXIII, pp. 313-348, 23 ills. in black and white, 10 ills. in color, 1 third-page map, Mar., 1938.

China's Hand-built Air Bases. 9 ills. from photographs. Vol. LXXXVIII, pp. 231-236, Aug., 1945.

China's Teeming Life on the Rivers and Sea. 18 ills. in duotone from photographs by Paul De Gaston and W. Robert Moore. Vol. LXVI, pp. 625-640, Nov., 1934.

China's Treasures. By Frederick McCormick. Vol. XXIII, pp. 996-1040, 50 ills., Oct., 1912.

China's Wonderland—Yen Tang Shan (Chekiang Province). 8 ills. in color from camera paintings by Herbert Clarence White, Deng Baoling, and Hwang Yao-tso. Vol. LXXII, pp. 687-694, Dec., 1937.

Chincha Islands, Peru :

Peru's Wealth-Producing Birds: Vast Riches in the Guano Deposits of Cormorants, Pelicans, and Petrels Which Nest on Her Barren, Rainless Coast. By R. E. Coker. Vol. XXXVII, pp. 537-566, 28 ills., June, 1920.

Chinese (People) :

China and Her People : Some Reflections on Their Manners and Customs, Habits and Lives. By Comdr. Harrie Webster. Vol. XI, pp. 309-319, 3 ills., Aug., 1900.

Geography of China : The Influence of Physical Environment on the History and Character of the Chinese People. By Frank Johnson Goodnow. Vol. LI, pp. 651-664, 11 ills., June, 1927.

I Lived on Formosa. By Joseph W. Ballantine. Vol. LXXXVII, pp. 1-24, 19 ills., 1 page and 1 half-page maps, Jan., 1945.

Chinese "Boxers." By Llewellyn James Davies. Vol. XI, pp. 281-287, July, 1900.

Chinese Jews. By Oliver Bainbridge. Vol. XVIII, pp. 621-632, 7 ills., Oct., 1907.

Chinese Labor for Mexico. Vol. XVI, pp. 481-482, Oct., 1905.

Chinese Paradox. By Harvey Maitland Watts. Vol. XI, pp. 354-358, 2 ills., Sept., 1900.

Chinese Pigeon Whistles. Vol. XXIV, pp. 715-716, 1 ill., June, 1913.

Chinese Turkistan. *See* Sinkiang.

Chinghai (Province), China:

Seeking the Mountains of Mystery: An Expedition on the China-Tibet Frontier to the Unexplored Amnyi Machen Range, One of Whose Peaks Rivals Everest. By Joseph F. Rock. Vol. LVII, pp. 131-185, 54 ills., 1 two-page map, Feb., 1930.

Chingtehchen. See Kingtehchen.

Chinini, Tunisia:

Mole Men: An Account of the Troglodytes of Southern Tunisia. By Frank Edward Johnson. Vol. XXII, pp. 787-846, 60 ills., Sept., 1911.

Chios (Island), Greece:

Historic Islands and Shores of the Ægean Sea. By Ernest Lloyd Harris. Vol. XXVIII, pp. 231-262, 29 ills., 1 half-page map, Sept., 1915.

Chipmunks:

Into the Land of the Chipmunk. By Ruth Alexander Nichols. Vol. LX, pp. 77-98, 28 ills., July, 1931.

Chippewa (Indian Tribe):

America's First Settlers, the Indians. By Matthew W. Stirling. Vol. LXXII, pp. 535-596, 34 ills. in black and white, 24 ills. in color, Nov., 1937.

When Red Men Ruled Our Forests. 24 ills. in color from paintings by W. Langdon Kihn. Vol. LXXII, pp. 551-590, Nov., 1937.

Chippewa Forest Reservation, Minnesota:

Summer Meeting of the American Forestry Association. Vol. XIII, pp. 352-358, Sept., 1902.

Chita, U. S. S. R.:

Far Eastern Republic. By Junius B. Wood. Vol. XLI, pp. 565-592, 29 ills., 1 three-quarters-page map, June, 1922.

"Chocolate Island." See São Tomé.

Chocos (Indians):

Land That Links the Americas (Panama). 22 ills. in color from natural-color photographs by Luis Marden. Vol. LXXX, pp. 601-624, Nov., 1941.

Little-Known Parts of Panama. By Henry Pittier. Vol. XXIII, pp. 627-662, 35 ills., 1 page map, July, 1912.

Cholera:

Changing Map in the Balkans. By Frederick Moore. Vol. XXIV, pp. 199-226, 27 ills., 1 page map, Feb., 1913.

Choni, China:

Demon Dancers and Butter Gods of Choni. 16 ills. in color from photographs by Joseph F. Rock. Vol. LIV, pp. 584-601, Nov., 1928.

Life Among the Lamas of Choni: Describing the Mystery Plays and Butter Festival in the Monastery of an Almost Unknown Tibetan Principality in Kansu Province, China. By Joseph F. Rock. Vol. LIV, pp. 569-619, 34 ills. in black and white, 16 ills. in color, 1 half-page map, Nov., 1928.

Choqquequirau, Peru:

In the Wonderland of Peru. By Hiram Bingham. Vol. XXIV, pp. 387-574, 250 ills., 3 diagrams, 1 three-quarters-page map, Apr., 1913.

Chosen. See Korea.

Chovan, (Cpl.) Luther M.:

American Soldier in Reykjavík. By Corporal Luther M. Chovan. Vol. LXXXVIII, pp. 536-568, 6 ills. in black and white, 34 ills. in color, Nov., 1945.

Iceland Defrosted. 34 ills. in color from natural color photographs by Luther M. Chovan. Vol. LXXXVIII, pp. 537-568, Nov., 1945.

Christ of the Andes, Argentina-Chile:

First Transandine Railroad from Buenos Aires to Valparaiso. By Harriet Chalmers Adams. Vol. XXI, pp. 397-417, 41 ills., 1 quarter-page map, May, 1910.

Christian, John LeRoy:

Burma: Where India and China Meet: In the Massive Mountains of Southeast Asia, Swarming Road Builders Wage the "War of the Highways" for Free China and Her Allies. By John LeRoy Christian. Vol. LXXXIV, pp. 489-512, 18 ills., 1 page map, Oct., 1943.

Christmas:

Bethlehem and the Christmas Story. By John D. Whiting. Vol. LVI, pp. 699-735, 27 ills. in black and white, 14 ills. in color, Dec., 1929.

Celebrating Christmas on the Meuse. By Capt. Clifton Lisle. Vol. XXXVI, pp. 527-537, 5 ills., Dec., 1919.

Christmas Island, Indian Ocean:

At Home on the Oceans: Whales and Sharks Make Exciting Neighbors for a Professor's Wife Turned Able Seaman, On a Three-year Voyage Around the World. By Edith Bauer Strout. Vol. LXXVI, pp. 33-86, 54 ills., 1 map, July, 1939.

Christophe's Citadel, Haiti:

Little-Known Marvel of the Western Hemisphere: Christophe's Citadel, a Monument to the Tyranny and Genius of Haiti's King of Slaves. By Maj. G. H. Osterhout, Jr. Vol. XXXVIII, pp. 468-482, 13 ills., Dec., 1920.

Chromatic Highlights of Korea. 13 ills. in color from natural-color photographs by W. Robert Moore. Vol. LXIV, pp. 429-436, Oct., 1933.

Chronometer and Time Service of the U. S. Naval Observatory and the Present Status of Standard Time. By Lieut. Comdr. Edward Everett Hayden. Vol. XV, pp. 430-431, Oct., 1904.

Chuan, Shoaching H.:

Most Extraordinary City in the World: Notes on Lhasa—The Mecca of the Buddhist Faith. By Shoaching H. Chuan. Vol. XXIII, pp. 959-995, 60 ills., Oct., 1912.

Chugach Mountains, Alaska:

National Geographic Society's Alaskan Expedition of 1909. By Ralph S. Tarr and Lawrence Martin. Vol. XXI, pp. 1-54, 42 ills., 4 page and 7 half-page maps, Jan., 1910.

Chunchos (Indians):

New Peruvian Route to the Plain of the Amazon. By Solon I. Bailey. Vol. XVII, pp. 432-448, 12 ills., Aug., 1906.

Chungking, China:

Eden of the Flowery Republic. By Joseph Beech. Vol. XXXVIII, pp. 355-390, 18 ills. in black and white, 16 ills. in color, Nov., 1920.

Church, D. B.:

Valley of Ten Thousand Smokes: An Account of the Discovery and Exploration of the Most Wonderful Volcanic Region in the World. By Robert F. Griggs. Vol. XXXIII, pp. 115-169, 16 ills., 1 half page map, panorama, Feb., 1918.

Church, John W.:

Vanishing People of the South Seas: The Tragic Fate of the Marquesan Cannibals. Noted for Their Warlike Courage and Physical Beauty. By John W, Church. Vol. XXXVI, pp. 275-306, 22 ills., 2 half-page maps, Oct., 1919.

Churches. *See* Cathedrals and Churches; Chapels.

Churchill, Canada:

Birds of Timberline and Tundra. By Arthur A. Allen. With 24 ills. in color from natural-color photographs by the author. Vol. XC, pp. 313-339, 8 ills. in black and white, Sept., 1946.

Chute, Walter H.:

Bright Flashes from Pacific Corals (Fishes). 24 ills. in color from natural-color photographs by Walter H. Chute. Vol. LXXIX, pp. 349-372, Mar., 1941.

Net Results from Oceania: Collecting Aquarium Specimens in Tropical Pacific Waters. By Walter H. Chute. Vol. LXXIX, pp. 347-372, 8 ills. in black and white, 24 ills. in color, Mar., 1941.

Tropical Fish Immigrants Reveal New Nature Wonders. By Walter H. Chute. Vol. LXV, pp. 93-110, 8 ills. in black and white, 16 ills. in color, Jan., 1934.

Cinchona:

Quinine Hunters in Ecuador. By Froelich Rainey. Vol. LXXXIX, pp. 341-363, 21 ills., 1 half-page map, Mar., 1946.

Cincinnati, Ohio:

Ohio, The Gateway State. By Melville Chater. Vol. LXI, pp. 525-591, 58 ills. in black and white, 13 ills. in color, 1 three-quarters-page map, May, 1932.

Cintra, Portugal:

Woods and Gardens of Portugal. By Martin Humé. Vol. XXI, pp. 883-894, 8 ills., Oct., 1910.

Circuses:

Color Camera Explores the Country That Moves by Night. 29 ills. in color from natural-color photographs by Richard H. Stewart, W. Robert Moore, Orren R. Louden, and Jacob Gayer. Vol, LX, pp. 478-511, Oct., 1931.

Land of Sawdust and Spangles—A World in Miniature. By Francis Beverly Kelley. Vol. LX, pp. 463-516, 35 ills. in black and white, 29 ills. in color, Oct., 1931.

Cirenaica (District), Libia:

Cirenaica, Eastern Wing of Italian Libia. By Harriet Chalmers Adams. Vol. LVII, pp. 689-726, 35 ills. in black and white, 13 ills. in color, 1 two-thirds-page map, June, 1930.

Cirenaica, On the Edge of the Saharan Sands. 13 ills. in color from natural-color photographs by Luigi Pellerano. Vol. LVII, pp. 692-701, June, 1930.

Crossing the Untraversed Libyan Desert: The Record of a 2,200-Mile Journey of Exploration Which Resulted in the Discovery of Two Oases of Strategic Importance on the Southwestern Frontier of Egypt. By A. M. Hassanein. Vol. XLVI, pp. 233-277, 46 ills., 1 half-page map, Sept., 1924.

Tripoli: A Land of Little Promise. By Adolph L. Vischer. Vol. XXII, pp. 1035-1047, 6 ills., 1 half-page map, Nov., 1911.

Cities That Gold and Diamonds Built: Transvaal Treasures Have Created Bustling Johannesburg and Fostered Pretoria, Administrative Capital of the South African Union. By W. Robert Moore. Vol. LXXXII, pp. 735-766, 20 ills. in black and white, 9 ills. in color, 1 two-thirds-page map, Dec., 1942.

Citizen Army of Holland. By Henrik Willem Van Loon. Vol. XXIX, pp. 609-622, 9 ills., June, 1916.

Citizen Army of Switzerland. Vol. XXVIII, pp. 502-510, 7 ills., Nov., 1915.

Citroën-Haardt Trans-Asiatic Expedition:

Citroën Trans-Asiatic Expedition Reaches Kashmir: Scientific Party Led by Georges-Marie Haardt Successfully Crosses Syria, Iraq, Persia, and Afghanistan to Arrive at the Pamir. By Maynard Owen Williams. Vol. LX, pp. 387-443, 62 ills., 1 page map, Oct., 1931.

First Over the Roof of the World by Motor: The Trans-Asiatic Expedition Sets New Records for Wheeled Transport in Scaling Passes of the Himalayas. By Maynard Owen Williams. Vol. LXI, pp. 321-363, 45 ills., 2 half-page maps, Mar., 1932.

From the Mediterranean to the Yellow Sea by Motor: The Citroën-Haardt Expedition Successfully Completes Its Dramatic Journey. By Maynard Owen Williams. Vol. LXII, pp. 513-580, 45 ills. in black and white, 25 ills. in color, 2 half-page maps, Nov., 1932.

Trans-Asiatic Expedition Starts. By Georges-Marie Haardt. Vol. LIX, pp. 776-782, 6 ills., June, 1931.

City Learns to Smile Again (Nancy, France). By Maj. Frederick G. Vosburgh. Vol. LXXXVII, pp. 361-384, 23 ills., 1 two-thirds-page map, Mar., 1945.

City of Jacqueline (Ter Goes, Netherlands). By Florence Craig Albrecht. Vol. XXVII, pp. 29-56, 31 ills., Jan., 1915.

City of Realized Dreams (San Francisco). By Franklin K. Lane. Vol. XXVII, pp. 169-171, Feb., 1915.

City That Refused to Die (Plymouth, England). By Harvey Klemmer. Vol. LXXXIX, pp. 211-236, 13 ills. in black and white, 9 ills. in color, 1 half-page map, Feb., 1946.

Civil Air Patrol:

Heroes of Wartime Science and Mercy. By Elizabeth W. King. Vol. LXXXIV, pp. 715-740, 11 ills. in black and white, 334 ills. in color, Dec., 1943.

Civil War (United States) :

Fame's Eternal Camping Ground: Beautiful Arlington (Virginia), Burial Place of America's Illustrious Dead. By Enoch A. Chase. Vol. LIV, pp. 621-638, 19 ills., Nov., 1928.

Most Famous Battle Field in America (Gettysburg). 14 ills. in color from natural-color photographs by Clifton Adams and Orren R. Louden. Vol. LX, pp. 66-75, July, 1931.

Clans in Kilt and Plaidie Gather at Braemar (Scotland). 11 ills. in color from natural-color photographs by Maynard Owen Williams. Vol. LXVIII, pp. 153-160, Aug., 1935.

Clark, Austin H.:

Potent Personalities—Wasps and Hornets: Though Often Painfully Stung, Mankind Profits Immeasurably from the Pest-Killing Activities of These Fiery Little Flyers. By Austin H. Clark. Vol. LXXII, pp. 47-72, 18 ills. in black and white, 12 ills. in color, July, 1937.

Who's Who Among the Butterflies. By Austin H. Clark. Vol. LXIX, pp. 679-692, 15 ills. in black and white, 9 ills. in color, May, 1936.

Clark, Charles Upson:

Romantic Spain. By Charles Upson Clark. Vol. XXI, pp. 187-215, 40 ills., 1 half-page map, Mar., 1910.

Clark, D. Worth:

Idaho Made the Desert Bloom. By D. Worth Clark. Vol. LXXXV, pp. 641-688, 21 ills. in black and white, 20 ills. in color, 1 page map, June, 1944.

Clark, Ella E.:

Forest Lookout. By Ella E. Clark. With 9 ills. in color from natural-color photographs by the author. Vol. XC, pp. 73-96, 8 ills. in black and white, July, 1946.

Clark, Hubert Lyman:

Paradise of the Tasman (Lord Howe Island) : A Pacific Island Provides the Palms Which Decorate Hotels, Churches, Steamships, and Homes. By Hubert Lyman Clark. Vol. LXVIII, pp. 115-136, 24 ills., 1 half-page map, July, 1935.

Clark, James L.:

Morden-Clark Asiatic Expedition : By Coolie and Caravan Across Central Asia : Narrative of a 7,900-Mile Journey of Exploration and Research Over "the Roof of the World," from the Indian Ocean to the Yellow Sea. By William J. Morden. Vol. LII, pp. 369-431, 73 ills., 1 page map, Oct., 1927.

Clark, Joe:

Home Folk around Historic Cumberland Gap. By Leo A. Borah. Vol. LXXXIV, pp. 741-768, 25 ills., 1 quarter-page map, Dec., 1943.

Clark, Leonard:

Among the Big Knot Lois of Hainan : Wild Tribesmen With Topknots Roam the Little-known Interior of This Big and Strategically Important Island in the China Sea. By Leonard Clark. Vol. LXXIV, pp. 391-418, 28 ills., 1 two-thirds-page map, Sept., 1938.

Clark, Lake, Alaska :

Lake Clark, a Little-Known Alaskan Lake. By Wilfred H. Osgood. Vol. XV, pp. 326-331, 2 ills., 1 half-page map, Aug., 1904.

Clarke, (Lt. Col.) Frederick J.:

Ascension Island, an Engineering Victory. By Lt. Col. Frederick J. Clarke. Vol. LXXXV, pp. 623-640, 21 ills., May, 1944.

Clarke, Nell Ray:

Haunts of the Caribbean Corsairs : The West Indies a Geographic Background for the Most Adventurous Episodes in the History of the Western Hemisphere. By Nell Ray Clarke. Vol. XLI, pp. 147-187, 27 ills., Feb., 1922.

Classic Greece Merges Into 1941 News. 19 ills. from photographs ; 15 ills. by B. Anthony Stewart ; 3 ills. by Maynard Owen Williams. Vol. LXXIX, pp. 93-108, Jan., 1941.

Classic Lands:

Ancient Rome Brought to Life. By Rhys Carpenter. Paintings by H. M. Herget. Vol. XC, pp. 567-633, 2 ills. in black and white, 32 ills. in color, 1 half-page map, Nov., 1946.

Classic Greece Merges Into 1941 News. 19 ills. from photographs ; 15 ills. by B. Anthony Stewart ; 3 ills. by Maynard Owen Williams. Vol. LXXIX, pp. 93-108, Jan., 1941.

Greece—the Birthplace of Science and Free Speech : Explorations on the Mainland and in Crete and the Aegean Isles Reveal Ancient Life Similar to That of the Present. By Richard Stillwell. Paintings by H. M. Herget. Vol. LXXXV, pp. 273-353, 13 ills. in black and white, 32 ills. in color, 1 two-page map, Mar., 1944.

Classic Lands—*Continued*

Italy, From Roman Ruins to Radio: History of Ancient Bridge Building and Road Making Repeats Itself in Modern Public Works and Engineering Projects. By John Patric. Vol. LXXVII, pp. 347-394, 27 ills. in black and white, 9 ills. in color, Mar., 1940.

Italy's Monuments Tell Rome's Magnificence. 8 ills. from photographs; 7 ills. by B. Anthony Stewart. Vol. LXXVII, pp. 371-378, Mar., 1940.

Map Links Classic World with 1940. Text accompanying special map supplement in colors. Vol. LXXVII, p. 338, Mar., 1940.

Modern Odyssey in Classic Lands: Troy's Treasures, Athens' Parthenon, and Rome's First "Broad Way" Influence Today's Banks, Costumes, Jewelry, and Railroad Timetables. By Maynard Owen Williams. Vol. LXXVII, pp. 291-337, 27 ills. in black and white, 22 ills. in color, Mar., 1940.

Ruins at Selinus (Sicily). By Marion Crawford. Vol. XIX, p. 117, Jun., 1909.

See also Athens; Carthage; Greece; Rome; Troy.

Clatworthy, Fred Payne:

California: Sunshine Land of Fruits, Flowers, Movies and Sport. 14 ills. in color from natural-color photographs by Fred Payne Clatworthy. Vol. LXVI, pp. 585-592, Nov., 1934.

Colorado: Among the Peaks and Parks of the Rockies. 11 ills. in color from natural-color photographs by Fred Payne Clatworthy. Vol. LXII, pp. 38-47, July, 1932.

Mexico: Adventures in Color on Mexico's West Coast. 13 ills. in color from natural-color photographs by Fred Payne Clatworthy. Vol. LVIII, pp. 60-69, July, 1930.

United States: Photographing the Marvels of the West in Colors. By Fred Payne Clatworthy. Vol. LIII, pp. 694-719, 30 ills. in color, June, 1928.

United States: Scenic Glories of Western United States. 8 ills. in color from autochromes by Fred Payne Clatworthy. Vol. LVI, pp. 223-230, Aug., 1929.

United States: Western Views in the Land of the Best. 16 ills. in color from autochromes by Fred Payne Clatworthy. Vol. XLIII, pp. 404-421, Apr., 1923.

Clay, Albert T.:

Pushing Back History's Horizon: How the Pick and Shovel Are Revealing Civilizations That Were Ancient When Israel Was Young. By Albert T. Clay. Vol. XXIX, pp. 162-216, 47 ills., 1 page map, Feb., 1916.

Clay Hills, Utah:

Beyond the Clay Hills: An Account of the National Geographic Society's Reconnaissance of a Previously Unexplored Section of Utah. By Neil M. Judd. Vol. XLV, pp. 275-302, 28 ills., 1 half-page map, Mar., 1924.

Cleaves, Howard H.:

Hunting with the Lens (Birds). By Howard H. Cleaves, Vol. XXVI, pp, 1-35, 47 ills., July, 1914.

Clements, Edith S.:

Floral Garlands of Prairie, Plain, and Woodland. 125 flower paintings in color by Edith S. Clements. Vol. LXXVI, pp. 224-270, Aug., 1939.

Flower Pageant of the Midwest: From March to November Nature Embroiders an Ever-changing Pattern of Living Color. By Edith S. and Frederic E. Clements. Vol. LXXVI, pp. 219-271, 1 ill. in black and white, 125 flower paintings in color, Aug., 1939.

Wild Flowers of the West (United States). By Edith S. Clements. Vol. LI, pp. 566-622, 207 ills. in color, May, 1927.

Clements, Frederic E.:

Family Tree of the Flowers. By Frederic E. Clements and William Joseph Showalter. Vol. LI, pp. 555-563, 1 ill. in black and white, 1 ill. in color, May, 1927.

Flower Pageant of the Midwest: From March to November Nature Embroiders an Ever-changing Pattern of Living Color. By Edith S. and Frederic E. Clements. Vol. LXXVI, pp. 219-271, 1 ill. in black and white, 125 flower paintings in color, Aug., 1939.

Cleveland, Ohio:

Ohio, The Gateway State. By Melville Chater. Vol. LXI, pp. 525-591, 58 ills. in black and white, 13 ills. in color, 1 three-quarters-page map, May, 1932.

Cliff Dwellers:

Isle of Frankincense (Socotra, Arabian Sea). By Charles K. Moser. Vol. XXXIII, pp. 266-278, 11 ills., Mar., 1918.

Prehistoric Ruin of Tsankawi (New Mexico). By George L. Beam. Vol. XX, pp. 807-822, 12 ills., Sept., 1909.

Climate:

Antarctic Climate. Vol. X, pp. 520-521, Dec., 1899.

Deforestation and Climate. Vol. XVI, pp. 397-398, Aug., 1905.

Do Volcanic Explosions Affect Our Climate? By C. G. Abbot. Vol. XXIV, pp. 181-198, 9 ills., 1 diagram, Feb., 1913.

Factors Which Modify the Climate of Victoria, British Columbia. By Arthur W. McCurdy. Vol. XVIII, pp. 345-348, 2 quarter-page maps, May, 1907.

Further Explorations in the Land of the Incas: The Peruvian Expedition of 1915 of the National Geographic Society and Yale University. By Hiram Bingham. Vol. XXIX, pp. 431-473, 29 ills., 1 page and 1 half-page maps, panorama, May, 1916.

Geography. By Sir W. J. L. Wharton. Vol. XVI, pp. 483-498, Nov., 1905.

Is Climatic Aridity Impending on the Pacific Slope? The Testimony of the Forest. By J. B. Leiberg. Vol. X, pp. 160-181, May, 1899.

Southwest (United States): Its Splendid Natural Resources, Agricultural Wealth, and Scenic Beauty. By N. H. Darton. Vol. XXI, pp. 631-665, 21 ills., 1 page map, Aug., 1910.

Climate—*Continued*

Weather Fights and Works for Man. By F. Barrows Colton. Vol. LXXXIV, pp. 641-670, 22 ills. in black and white, 3 drawings, Dec., 1943.

See also Meteorology.

Climatic Laboratories, U. S. Army:

Fit to Fight Anywhere. By Frederick Simpich. Vol. LXXXIV, pp. 233-256, 26 ills., Aug., 1943.

Climbing Mighty Minya Konka: Americans First Scaled Mountain That Now Is Landmark of China's New Skyway. By Richard L. Burdsall and Terris Moore. Vol. LXXXIII, pp. 625-650, 23 ills., 1 page map, May, 1943.

Clinic, Hospital: Deir ez Zor, Syria:

Ali Goes to the Clinic. By Herndon and Mary Hudson. Vol. XC, pp. 764-766, 2 ills., Dec., 1946.

Clipper Ships (Seaplanes):

Flying the Pacific. By William Burke Miller. Vol. LXX, pp. 665-707, 39 ills., Dec., 1936.

Clock Turns Back in Yugoslavia: The Fortified Monastery of Mountain-girt Dečani Survives Its Six Hundredth Birthday. By Ethel Chamberlain Porter. Vol. LXXXV, pp. 493-512, 20 ills., 1 page map, Apr., 1944.

Close, Upton:

"Where the Mountains Walked": An Account of the Recent Earthquake in Kansu Province, China, Which Destroyed 100,000 Lives. By Upton Close and Elsie McCormick. Vol. XLI, pp. 445-464, 23 ills., 1 three-quarters-page map, May, 1922.

Close-Ups of a People Without a Country (Saar). 23 ills. in duotone. Vol. LXVII, pp. 249-264, Feb., 1935.

Clothing and Equipment Tests, U. S. Army:

Fit to Fight Anywhere. By Frederick Simpich. Vol. LXXXIV, pp. 233-256, 26 ills., Aug., 1943.

Clouds:

Forecasting the Weather. By Alfred J. Henry. Vol. XV, pp. 285-292, 6 ills., 1 chart, July, 1904.

International Cloud Work of the Weather Bureau. By Frank H. Bigelow. Vol. X, pp. 351-354, Sept., 1899.

Our Heralds of Storm and Flood (U. S. Weather Bureau). By Gilbert H. Grosvenor. Vol. XVIII, pp. 586-601, 15 ills., 1 chart, Sept., 1907.

Toilers of the Sky: Tenuous Clouds Perform the Mighty Task of Shaping the Earth and Sustaining Terrestrial Life. By McFall Kerbey. Vol. XLVIII, pp. 163-189, 33 ills., Aug., 1925.

Warfare on Our Eastern Coast. By John Oliver La Gorce. Vol. XXVIII, pp. 195-230, 29 ills., 2 charts, Sept., 1915.

Clouds—*Continued*

Weather Fights and Works for Man. By F. Barrows Colton. Vol. LXXXIV, pp. 641-670, 22 ills. in black and white, 3 drawings, Dec., 1943.

Clovelly, England:

Channel Ports—And Some Others. By Florence Craig Albrecht. Vol. XXVIII, pp. 1-55, 45 ills., July, 1915.

Cnossus, Crete (Island):

Crete, Where Sea-Kings Reigned. By Agnes N. Stillwell. Vol. LXXXIV, pp. 547-568, 20 ills., 1 page map, Nov., 1943.

Coal and Coal Mining:

Charm of Cape Breton Island: The Most Picturesque Portion of Canada's Maritime Provinces—A Land Rich in Historic Associations, Natural Resources, and Geographic Appeal. By Catherine Dunlop Mackenzie. Vol. XXXVIII, pp. 34-60, 22 ills., 1 three quarters-page map, July, 1920.

Coal: Prodigious Worker for Man. By Albert W. Atwood. Vol. LXXXV, pp. 569-592, 19 ills., 1 drawing, May, 1944.

Coal—Ally of American Industry. By William Joseph Showalter. Vol. XXXIV, pp. 407-434, 23 ills., Nov., 1918.

Coal Fields of Alaska. Vol. XXI, pp. 83-87, 6 ills., Jan., 1910.

Coal Resources of Alaska. Vol. XIII, pp. 172-174, May, 1902.

Course of the Retail Coal Trade. By Dr. David T. Day. Vol. XIII, pp. 394-398, Nov., 1902.

Efforts to Obtain Energy from Coal. Vol. XVIII, pp. 138-140, Feb., 1907.

How Long Will the Coal Reserves of the United States Last? By Marius R. Campbell. Vol. XVIII, pp. 129-138, 1 half-page map, 5 diagrams, Feb., 1907.

Ideal Fuel (Briquets). By Guy Elliott Mitchell. Vol. XXI, pp. 1066-1074, 4 ills., Dec., 1910.

Nation's Undeveloped Resources (Alaska). By Franklin K. Lane. Vol. XXV, pp. 183-225, 32 ills., Feb., 1914.

New Source of Power (Lignite). By Guy Elliott Mitchell. Vol. XXI, pp. 935-944, 7 ills., Nov., 1910.

Our Coal Lands. By Guy Elliott Mitchell. Vol. XXI, pp. 446-451, 5 ills., May, 1910.

Story of the Ruhr. By Frederick Simpich. Vol. XLI, pp. 553-564, 11 ills., 1 third-page map, May, 1922.

Coast and Geodetic Survey: Its Present Work. By E. D. Preston. Vol. X, pp. 268-269, July, 1899.

Coast Guard Patrol in Greenland. 9 ills. in color from natural-color photographs by Lieut. Thomas S. La Farge. Vol. LXXXIII, pp. 565-572, May, 1943.

Coastal Cities of China. By W. Robert Moore. Vol. LXVI, pp. 601-643, 12 ills. in black and white, 18 ills. in duotone, 14 ills. in color, 1 page map, Nov., 1934.

Coral Fishes:

Bright Flashes from Pacific Corals. 24 ills. in color from natural-color photographs by Walter H. Chute. Vol. LXXIX, pp. 349-372, Mar., 1941.

Net Results from Oceania : Collecting Aquarium Specimens in Tropical Pacific Waters. By Walter H. Chute. Vol. LXXIX, pp. 347-372, 8 ills. in black and white, 24 ills. in color, Mar., 1941.

Corey, Carol:

Day with Our Boys in the Geographic Wards. By Carol Corey. Vol. XXXIV, pp. 69-80, 8 ills., July, 1918.

From the Trenches to Versailles. By Carol Corey. Vol. XXXII, pp. 535-550, 12 ills., Nov.-Dec., 1917.

Plain Tales from the Trenches : As Told Over the Tea Table in Blighty—A Soldier's "Home" in Paris. By Carol Corey. Vol. XXXIII, pp. 300-312, 7 ills., Mar., 1918.

Corey, Herbert:

Across the Equator with the American Navy. By Herbert Corey. Vol. XXXIX, pp. 571-624, 53 ills., June, 1921.

Adventuring Down the West Coast of Mexico. By Herbert Corey. Vol. XLII, pp. 449-503, 44 ills., 1 half-page map, Nov., 1922.

Along the Old Spanish Road in Mexico : Life Among the People of Nayarit and Jalisco, Two of the Richest States of the Southern Republic. By Herbert Corey. Vol. XLIII, pp. 225-281, 36 ills. in black and white, 16 ills. in color, 1 half-page map, Mar., 1923.

Among the Zapotecs of Mexico : A Visit to the Indians of Oaxaca, Home State of the Republic's Great Liberator, Juárez, and Its Most Famous Ruler, Diaz. By Herbert Corey. Vol. LI, pp. 501-553, 59 ills., 1 two-thirds-page map, May, 1927.

Char-à-Bancs in Cornwall. By Herbert Corey. Vol. XLVI, pp. 653-694, 44 ills., 1 half-page map, Dec., 1924.

Cooties and Courage. By Herbert Corey. Vol. XXXIII, pp. 495-509, 10 ills., June, 1918.

Down Devon Lanes. By Herbert Corey. Vol. LV, pp. 529-568, 45 ills., 1 two-thirds-page map, May, 1929.

Green Mountain State (Vermont). By Herbert Corey. Vol. LI, pp. 333-369, 40 ills. in black and white, 6 ills. in color, 1 page map, Mar., 1927.

Isthmus of Tehuantepec (Mexico). By Herbert Corey. Vol. XLV, pp. 549-579, 25 ills., May, 1924.

London from a Bus Top. By Herbert Corey. Vol. XLIX, pp. 551-596, 44 ills., May, 1926.

On the Monastir Road. By Herbert Corey. Vol. XXXI, pp. 383-412, 31 ills., May, 1917.

Shopping Abroad for Our Armies in France. By Herbert Corey. Vol. XXXIII, pp. 206-218, 6 ills., Feb., 1918.

Corey, Herbert—*Continued*

Unique Republic, Where Smuggling Is an Industry (Andorra). By Herbert Corey. Vol. XXXIII, pp. 279-299, 16 ills., 1 half-page map, Mar., 1918.

Corinth Canal, Greece :

Great Canals of the World. Vol. XVI, pp. 475-479, Oct., 1905.

Cork. Vol. XIX, pp. 690-693, 3 ills., Oct., 1908.

Cormorants (Birds) :

Birds of Lake and Lagoon, Marsh and Seacoast. 7 portraits in color from paintings by Maj. Allan Brooks. Vol. LXV, pp. 313-328, Mar., 1934.

Birds That Cruise the Coast and Inland Waters. By T. Gilbert Pearson ; Paintings by Maj. Allan Brooks. Vol. LXV, pp. 299-328, 5 ills. in black and white, 7 portraits in color, Mar., 1934.

Fisheries of Japan. By Hugh M. Smith. Vol. XVI, pp. 201-220, 13 ills., May, 1905.

Most Valuable Bird in the World. By Robert Cushman Murphy. Vol. XLVI, pp. 279-302, 25 ills., 1 half-page map, Sept., 1924.

Peru's Wealth-Producing Birds : Vast Riches in the Guano Deposits of Cormorants, Pelicans, and Petrels Which Nest on Her Barren, Rainless Coast. Vol. XXXVII, pp. 537-566, 28 ills., June, 1920.

White Sheep, Giant Moose and Smaller Game of the Kenai Peninsula, Alaska. By George Shiras, 3d. Vol. XXIII, pp. 423-494, 59 ills., 1 two-page map, May, 1912.

Corn:

How the World Is Fed. By William Joseph Showalter. Vol. XXIX, pp. 1-110, 101 ills., Jan., 1916.

Staircase Farms of the Ancients : Astounding Farming Skill of Ancient Peruvians Who Were Probably the Most Industrious and Highly Organized People in History. By O. F. Cook. Vol. XXIX, pp. 474-534, 48 ills., May, 1916.

Corn and Color in the Hawkeye State (Iowa). 20 ills. in color from natural-color photographs ; 19 ills. by J. Baylor Roberts. Vol. LXXVI, pp. 151-174, Aug., 1939.

Cornell University: Research :

Aurora Borealis research under the auspices of the National Geographic Society and Cornell University. Vol. LXXIX, p. 580, May, 1941. Vol. LXXXVI, p. 640, Nov., 1944. Vol. XC, p. 387, Sept., 1946.

Mystery of Auroras : National Geographic Society and Cornell University Study Spectacular Displays in the Heavens. Vol. LXXV, pp. 689-690, May, 1939.

Corner of Old Württemberg (Germany). By B. H. Buxton. Vol. XXII, pp. 931-947, 17 ills., 1 half-page map, Oct., 1911.

Cornhusker State Highlights (Nebraska). 23 ills. in color from natural-color photographs by B. Anthony Stewart. Vol. LXXXVII, pp. 521-536, May, 1945.

Cornwall, England :

Channel Ports—And Some Others. By Florence Craig Albrecht. Vol. XXVIII, pp. 1-55, 45 ills., July, 1915.

Char-à-Bancs in Cornwall. By Herbert Corey. Vol. XLVI, pp. 653-694, 44 ills., 1 half-page map, Dec., 1924.

Corona, Solar :

Natural-color photograph of an eclipse. 1 ill. in color by Irvine C. Gardner. Vol. LXXI, p. 178, Feb., 1937.

Nature's Most Dramatic Spectacle. By S. A. Mitchell. Vol. LXXII, pp. 361-376, 16 ills., 1 half-page map, Sept., 1937.

Observing an Eclipse in Asiatic Russia. By Irvine C. Gardner. Vol. LXXI, pp. 179-197, 19 ills. in black and white, 1 ill. in color, Feb., 1937.

Unfurling Old Glory on Canton Island. 11 ills. in color ; 1 painting and 1 kodachrome photograph of the eclipse. Vol. LXXIII, pp. 753-760, June, 1938.

Coronations:

Along London's Coronation Route. By Maynard Owen Williams. Vol. LXXI, pp. 609-632, 22 ills., 1 half-page map, May, 1937.

Coronation Days in Addis Ababa. By W. Robert Moore. Vol. LIX, pp. 738-746, 8 ills., June, 1931.

Coronation of His Majesty King Maha-Vajira-vudh of Siam. By Col. Lea Febiger. Vol. XXIII, pp. 389-416, 25 ills., Apr., 1912.

Present-Day Scenes in the World's Oldest Empire. 27 ills. in color from natural-color photographs by W. Robert Moore. Vol. LIX, pp. 690-723, June, 1931.

Corpus Christi Celebration:

In the Canary Islands, Where Streets Are Carpeted With Flowers. 13 ills. in color from natural-color photographs by Wilhelm Tobien. Vol. LVII, pp. 614-623, May, 1930.

Correct Display of the Stars and Stripes. By Gilbert Grosvenor and Byron McCandless. Vol. XXXII, pp. 404-413, 8 ills., Oct., 1917.

Corsica (Island), Mediterranean Sea :

Coasts of Corsica : Impressions of a Winter's Stay in the Island Birthplace of Napoleon. By Maynard Owen Williams. Vol. XLIV, pp. 221-312, 88 ills., special supplement, 1 page and 1 quarter-page maps, Sept., 1923.

Peasant Home in Corsica. Vol. XLIV, supplement, Sept., 1923.

Cortés, Hernando:

On the Cortés Trail. By Luis Marden. Vol. LXXVIII, pp. 335-375, 17 ills. in black and white, 22 ills. in color, 1 map, Sept., 1940.

Cos (Island), Aegean Sea :

Rhodes, and Italy's Aegean Islands. By Dorothy Hosmer. Vol. LXXIX, pp. 449-480, 32 ills., 1 map, Apr., 1941.

Cosmic Rays:

Ballooning in the Stratosphere : Two Balloon Ascents to Ten-Mile Altitudes Presage New Mode of Aërial Travel. By Auguste Piccard. Vol. LXIII, pp. 353-384, 34 ills., Mar., 1933.

New Frontier in the Sky. By F. Barrows Colton. Vol. XC, pp. 379-408, 28 ills., 1 diagram, Sept., 1946.

Series of flights under auspices of National Geographic Society, U. S. Army Air Forces, and Bartol Research Foundation of the Franklin Institute. Vol. XC, p. 387 ; ill. 388, Sept., 1946.

Cosmopolitan Shanghai, Key Seaport of China. By W. Robert Moore. Vol. LXII, pp. 311-335, 19 ills., Sept., 1932.

Costa, Guido:

Island of Sardinia and Its People : Traces of Many Civilizations to be Found in the Speech, Customs, and Costumes of This Picturesque Land. By Guido Costa. Vol. XLIII. pp. 1-75, 63 ills. in black and white, 16 ills. in color, 1 three-quarters and 1 quarter-page maps, Jan., 1923.

Costa Rica:

Costa Rica, Land of the Banana. By Paul B. Popenoe. Vol. XLI, pp. 201-220, 17 ills., Feb., 1922.

Costa Rica—Vulcan's Smithy. By Henry Pittier. Vol. XXI, pp. 494-525, 30 ills., 2 half-page maps, June, 1910.

Countries of the Caribbean. By William Joseph Showalter. Vol. XXIV, pp. 227-250, 23 ills., Feb., 1913.

Land of the Painted Oxcarts. By Luis Marden. With 31 ills. in color from natural-color photographs by the author. Vol. XC, pp. 409-456, 30 ills., in black and white, 1 half-page map, Oct., 1946.

Location of the Boundary Between Nicaragua and Costa Rica. By Arthur P. Davis. Vol. XII, pp. 22-28, 1 ill., 1 half-page map, Jan., 1901.

Methods of Obtaining Salt in Costa Rica. Vol. XIX, pp. 28-34, 7 ills., 1 diagram, Jan., 1908.

Notes on Central America. Vol. XVIII, pp. 272-278, 1 ill., 1 half-page map, Apr., 1907.

Shattered Capitals of Central America. By Herbert J. Spinden. Vol. XXXVI, pp. 185-212, 32 ills., 1 page map, Sept., 1919.

Where Our Bananas Come From. By Edwin R. Fraser. Vol. XXIII, pp. 713-730, 14 ills., July, 1912.

Costume Pageants in the French Pyrenees. 24 ills. in color from natural-color photographs by W. Robert Moore. Vol. LXXII, pp. 435-450, Oct., 1937.

Costumes:

Carioca Carnival. 34 ills. in color from natural-color photographs by W. Robert Moore. Vol. LXXVI, pp. 291-322, Sept., 1939.

Rainbow Costumes of Poland's Peasants. 11 ills. in color from natural-color photographs by Hans Hildenbrand and Maynard Owen Williams. Vol. LXIII, pp. 328-337, Mar., 1933.

Snowy Peaks and Old Costumes of Switzerland. 12 ills. in color from natural-color photographs by Hans Hildenbrand. Vol. LXVI, pp. 147-154, Aug., 1934.

Types and Costumes of Old Sweden. 30 ills. in color from autochromes lumière by Gustav Heurlin, G. W. Cronquist, Wilhelm Tobien, and Charles Martin. Vol. LIV, pp. 424-441, Oct., 1928.

See also material on individual countries.

Cotidal Lines for the World. By R. A. Harris. Vol. XVII, pp. 303-309, 2 page and 1 half-page maps, special map supplement, June, 1906.

Cott, Hugh B.:

Wonder Island of the Amazon Delta : On Marajó Cowboys Ride Oxen, Tree-dwelling Animals Throng Dense Forests, While Strange Fishes and Birds Help Make a Zoologist's Paradise. By Hugh B. Cott. Vol. LXXIV, pp. 635-670, 30 ills. in black and white, 12 ills. in color, 1 half-page map, Nov., 1938.

Cotter, Margaret:

Red Cross Girl Overseas. By Margaret Cotter. Vol. LXXXVI, pp. 745-768, 22 ills., Dec., 1944.

Cotton and Cotton Industry:

Cotton : Foremost Fiber of the World. By J. R. Hildebrand. Vol. LXXIX, pp. 137-192, 31 ills. in black and white, 34 ills. in color, Feb., 1941.

Cotton and the Chinese Boycott. From an address by President Roosevelt to the citizens of Atlanta, October 20, 1905. Vol. XVI, pp. 516-517, Nov., 1905.

Cotton for England. Vol. XV, p. 39, Jan., 1904.

Farmers of the United States. Vol. XVI, pp. 39-46, Jan., 1905.

Golden Fleece of Dixie. 34 ills. in color from natural-color photographs by Willard R. Culver. Vol. LXXIX, pp. 153-192, Feb., 1941.

Massachusetts—Beehive of Business. By William Joseph Showalter. Vol. XXXVII, pp. 203-245, 41 ills., Mar., 1920.

Modern Alchemist (Work of Department of Agriculture). By James Wilson. Vol. XVIII, pp. 778-795, 6 ills., Dec., 1907.

Our Plant Immigrants. By David Fairchild. Vol. XVII, pp. 179-201, 29 ills., Apr., 1906.

Paper From Cotton Stalks. Vol. XVII, p. 425, July, 1906.

Countries of the Caribbean. By William Joseph Showalter. Vol. XXIV, pp. 227-250, 23 ills., Feb., 1913.

Country-House Life in Sweden : In Castle and Cottage the Landed Gentry Gallantly Keep the Old Traditions. By Amelie Posse-Brázdová. Vol. LXVI, pp. 1-64, 51 ills. in black and white, 13 ills. in color, 1 page map, July, 1934.

Country Life in Norway : The Beneficent Gulf Stream Enables One-third of the People in a Far-north, Mountainous Land to Prosper on Farms. By Axel H. Oxholm. Vol. LXXV, pp. 493-528, 17 ills. in black and white, 20 ills. in color, 1 two-thirds-page map, Apr., 1939.

Country of the Ant Men (Sahara). By Thomas H. Kearney. Vol. XXII, pp. 367-382, 11 ills., 1 half-page map, Apr., 1911.

Country Where Going to America Is an Industry (Sicily). By Arthur H. Warner. Vol. XX, pp. 1063-1102, 41 ills., Dec., 1909.

Course of the Retail Coal Trade. By Dr. David T. Day. Vol. XIII, pp. 394-398, Nov., 1902.

Courtellemont, Gervais:

Africa : Camera's Color Records of North Africa. 16 ills. in color from autochromes lumière by Gervais Courtellemont. Vol. XLVII, pp. 333-340, Mar., 1925.

Algeria : On the Fringe of the Great Desert. 32 ills. in color from autochromes by Gervais Courtellemont. Vol. LIII, pp. 206-223, Feb., 1928.

Asia : Sun-Painted Scenes in the Near East. 32 ills. in color from autochromes lumière by Gervais Courtellemont. Vol. XLVIII, pp. 541-556, Nov., 1925.

Balearics : Spain's Enchanted Isles. 29 ills. in color from autochromes by Gervais Courtellemont. Vol. LIV, pp. 182-199, Aug., 1928.

Brittany : Blue Seas and Brilliant Costumes Along the Brittany Coast. 29 ills. in color from autochromes by Gervais Courtellemont. Vol. LVI, pp. 142-175, Aug., 1929.

Cambodia : Enigma of Cambodia. 27 ills. in color from autochromes by Gervais Courtellemont. Vol. LIV, pp. 306-323, Sept., 1928.

Egypt : Along the Banks of the Colorful Nile. 23 ills. in color from autochromes lumière by Gervais Courtellemont. Vol. L, pp. 322-339, Sept., 1926.

France : Battle Fields of France Eleven Years After. 23 ills. in color from autochromes by Gervais Courtellemont. Vol. LVI, pp. 522-539, Nov., 1929.

France : Beauty, History, and Romance Enrich the Château Country. 10 ills. in color from autochromes by Gervais Courtellemont. Vol. LVIII, pp. 466-475, Oct., 1930.

France : Charm and Color Distinguish Norman Byways. 13 ills. in color from natural-color photographs by Gervais Courtellemont. Vol. LXI, pp. 90-99, Jan., 1932.

France : Fifteenth-Century Vignettes of Compiègne. 15 ills. in color from natural-color photographs by Gervais Courtellemont. Vol. LXII, pp. 608-617, Nov., 1932.

Courtellemont, Gervais—Continued

France : Flashes of Color Throughout France. 28 ills. in color from autochromes by Gervais Courtellemont. Vol. XLVI, pp. 529-544, Nov., 1924.

France : In Smiling Alsace, Where France Has Resumed Sway. 11 ills. in color from autochromes lumière by Gervais Courtellemont. Vol. LII, pp. 168-177, Aug., 1927.

France : Versailles the Magnificent. 14 ills. in color from autochromes lumière by Gervais Courtellemont. Vol. XLVII, pp. 53-60, Jan., 1925.

Holy Land : In the Birthplace of Christianity. 7 ills. in color from autochromes lumière by Gervais Courtellemont. Vol. L, pp. 696-721, Dec., 1926.

India : Streets and Palaces of Colorful India. 34 ills. in color from autochromes lumière by Gervais Courtellemont. Vol. L, pp. 60-85, July, 1926.

Morocco : In the Land of Cruel Desert and Majestic Mountain. 10 ills. in color from natural-color photographs by Gervais Courtellemont. Vol. LXI, pp. 306-315, Mar., 1932.

Portugal : Rainbow Portraits of Portugal. 17 ills. in color from autochromes lumière by Gervais Courtellemont. Vol. LII, pp. 550-567, Nov., 1927.

Spain : Color Camera Records Scenes in Eastern Spain. 13 ills. in color from autochromes by Gervais Courtellemont. Vol. LV, pp. 364-373, Mar., 1929.

Spain : Color Contrasts in Northern Spain. 14 ills. in color from natural-color photographs by Gervais Courtellemont. Vol. LIX, pp. 112-121, Jan., 1931.

Spain : Glories Past and Present of Northern Spain. 13 ills. in color from autochromes by Gervais Courtellemont. Vol. LV, pp. 340-349, Mar., 1929.

Spain : In Andalusia, Home of Song and Sunshine. 14 ills. in color from autochromes by Gervais Courtellemont. Vol. LV, pp. 300-309, Mar., 1929.

Spain : Moorish Spain. 26 ills. in color from autochromes by Gervais Courtellemont. Vol. XLVI, pp. 163-178, Aug., 1924.

Tunisia, Where Sand and Desert Meet. 16 ills. in color from autochromes by Gervais Courtellemont. Vol. XLV, pp. 415-423, Apr., 1924.

Coville, Frederick V.:

Cultivation of the Mayflower. By Frederick V. Coville. Vol. XXVII, pp. 518-519, 1 ill., May, 1915.

National Geographic Society (Memorial Tribute to Frederick V. Coville). Vol. LXXI, p. 662, 1 ill., May, 1937.

Quills of a Porcupine. By Frederick V. Coville. Vol. XXIII, pp. 25-31, 5 ills., Jan., 1912.

Taming the Wild Blueberry. By Frederick V. Coville. Vol. XXII, pp. 137-147, 5 ills., Feb., 1911.

Coville, Frederick V.—Continued

War, Patriotism, and the Food Supply. By Frederick V. Coville. Vol. XXXI, pp. 254-256, Mar., 1917.

Wild Blueberry Tamed : The New Industry of the Pine Barrens of New Jersey. By Frederick V. Coville. Vol. XXIX, pp. 535-546, 10 ills., June, 1916.

Coville, Lilian Grosvenor:

Here in Manchuria : Many Thousand Lives Were Lost and More Than Half the Crops Destroyed by the Floods of 1932. By Lilian Grosvenor Coville. Vol. LXIII, pp. 233-256, 26 ills., Feb., 1933.

Cowboys:

Cowboys and Caymans of Marajó (Brazil). 12 ills. in color from natural-color photographs by Desmond Holdridge. Vol. LXXIV, pp. 645-652, Nov., 1938.

Grass Makes Wyoming Fat. By Frederick Simpich. Vol. LXXXVIII, pp. 153-188, 13 ills. in black and white, 19 ills. in color, 1 two-page map, Aug., 1945.

On a Chilean Hacienda. 8 ills. in color from natural-color photographs by E. P. Haddon. Vol. LXXXVI, pp. 489-496, Oct., 1944.

Welcome to Wyoming. 19 ills. in color from natural-color photographs ; 18 ills. by B. Anthony Stewart. Vol. LXXXVIII, pp. 161-184, Aug., 1945.

"Where Rolls the Oregon." 28 ills. in color from natural-color photographs by Ray Atkeson. Vol. XC, pp. 689-728, Dec., 1946.

Wonder Island of the Amazon Delta : On Marajó Cowboys Ride Oxen, Tree-dwelling Animals Throng Dense Forests, While Strange Fishes and Birds Help Make a Zoologist's Paradise. By Hugh B. Cott. Vol. LXXIV, pp. 635-670, 30 ills. in black and white, 12 ills. in color, 1 half-page map, Nov., 1938.

Cowes, Isle of Wight :

England's Sun Trap Isle of Wight. By J. R. Hildebrand. Vol. LXVII, pp. 1-33, 22 ills. in black and white, 14 ills. in color, 1 half-page map, Jan., 1935.

Crabs:

Blue Crab. Vol. XVII, p. 46, Jan., 1906.

Crabs and Crablike Curiosities of the Sea. By William Crowder. Vol. LIV, pp. 57-72, 10 ills. in black and white, 8 ills. in color, July, 1928. Contains descriptions and illustrations of the following species : Blue, Fiddler, Hermit, Horseshoe, Rock, Spider, Swimming.

Strange Sights in Far-Away Papua. By A. E. Pratt. Vol. XVIII, pp. 559-572, 7 ills., Sept., 1907.

Cradle of Civilization : Historic Lands Along the Euphrates and Tigris Rivers Where Briton Is Fighting Turk. By James Baikie. Vol. XXIX, pp. 127-162, 25 ills., Feb., 1916.

Cradles of English History. 15 ills. in color from natural-color photographs by Clifton Adams and Bernard Wakeman. Vol. LIX, pp. 268-277, Mar., 1931.

Craige, (Capt.) John Houston:

Haitian Vignettes. By Capt. John Houston Craige. Vol. LXVI, pp. 435-485, 40 ills. in black and white, 13 ills. in color, 1 quarter-page map, Oct., 1934.

Craighead, Frank:

Adventures with Birds of Prey. By Frank and John Craighead. Vol. LXXII, pp. 109-134, 25 ills., July, 1937.

In Quest of the Golden Eagle: Over Lonely Mountain and Prairie Soars This Rare and Lordly Bird, But Three Youths from the East Catch Up With Him at Last. By John and Frank Craighead. Vol. LXXVII, pp. 693-710, 17 ills., May, 1940.

Life with an Indian Prince: As Guests of a Maharaja's Brother, Two Young American Naturalists Study Age-old Methods of Hunting with Trained Falcons and Cheetahs and Savor the Pomp of Royal India. By John and Frank Craighead. Vol. LXXXI, pp. 235-272, 38 ills., 1 sixth-page map, Feb., 1942.

Craighead, John:

Adventures with Birds of Prey. By Frank and John Craighead. Vol. LXXII, pp. 109-134, 25 ills., July, 1937.

In Quest of the Golden Eagle: Over Lonely Mountain and Prairie Soars This Rare and Lordly Bird, But Three Youths from the East Catch Up With Him at Last. By John and Frank Craighead. Vol. LXXVII, pp. 693-710, 17 ills., May, 1940.

Life with an Indian Prince: As Guests of a Maharaja's Brother, Two Young American Naturalists Study Age-old Methods of Hunting with Trained Falcons and Cheetahs and Savor the Pomp of Royal India. By John and Frank Craighead. Vol. LXXXI, pp. 235-272, 38 ills., 1 sixth-page map, Feb., 1942.

Crampton, Henry Edward:

Kaieteur and Roraima: The Great Falls and the Great Mountain of the Guianas. By Henry Edward Crampton. Vol. XXXVIII, pp. 227-244, 12 ills., 1 half-page map, Sept., 1920.

Crane, Alice Rollins:

Midnight Sun in the Klondike. By Alice Rollins Crane. Vol. XII, pp. 66-67, 1 ill., Feb., 1901.

Northern Lights. By Alice Rollins Crane. Vol. XII, pp. 68-69, 1 ill., Feb., 1901.

Cranes:

Feathered Foragers of Swamp and Shore. 101 portraits in color from paintings by Maj. Allan Brooks. Vol. LXXII, pp. 191-222, Aug., 1937.

Cranes—*Continued*

Shore Birds, Cranes, and Rails: Willets, Plovers, Stilts, Phalaropes, Sandpipers, and Their Relatives Deserve Protection. By Arthur A. Allen. Paintings by Maj. Allan Brooks. Vol. LXXII, pp. 183-222, 4 ills. in black and white, 101 portraits in color, Aug., 1937.

Crater Lake, Oregon:

"Where Rolls the Oregon." 28 ills. in color from natural-color photographs by Ray Atkeson. Vol. XC, pp. 689-728, Dec., 1946.

Crater Lake National Park, Oregon:

Crater Lake, Oregon. Vol. XIII, p. 221, June, 1902.

Crater Lake and Yosemite Through the Ages. By Wallace W. Atwood, Jr. Paintings by Eugene Kingman. Vol. LXXI, pp. 327-343, 7 ills. in black and white, 13 ills. in color, Mar., 1937.

Our National Parks. By L. F. Schmeckebier. Vol. XXIII, pp. 531-579, 41 ills., 1 page map, June, 1912.

Craters of the Moon National Monument, Idaho:

Among the "Craters of the Moon": An Account of the First Expeditions Through the Remarkable Volcanic Lava Beds of Southern Idaho. By R. W. Limbert. Vol. XLV, pp. 303-328, 23 ills., 1 two-thirds-page map, Mar., 1924.

Crawfish:

Certain Citizens of the Warm Sea. By Louis L. Mowbray. Vol. XLI, pp. 27-62, 18 ills. in black and white, 16 ills. in color, Jan., 1922.

Crawford, Marion:

Ruins at Selinus (Sicily). By Marion Crawford. Vol. XX, p. 117, Jan., 1909.

Crawfurd, Oswald:

Greatness of Little Portugal. By Oswald Crawfurd. Vol. XXI, pp. 867-883, 12 ills., Oct., 1910.

Creeks (Indians):

Indians of the Southeastern United States. By Matthew W. Stirling. Paintings by W. Langdon Kihn. Vol. LXXXIX, pp. 53-74, 8 ills. in black and white, 8 ills. in color, Jan., 1946.

Cresson, W. P.:

Persia: The Awakening East. By W. P. Cresson. Vol. XIX, pp. 356-384, 21 ills., 1 quarter-page map, May, 1908.

Crete (Island), Greece:

Classic Greece Merges Into 1941 News. 19 ills. from photographs; 15 ills. by B. Anthony Stewart; 3 ills. by Maynard Owen Williams. Vol. LXXIX, pp. 93-108, Jan., 1941.

Crete, Where Sea-Kings Reigned. By Agnes N. Stillwell. Vol. LXXXIV, pp. 547-568, 20 ills., 1 page map, Nov., 1943.

Crete (Island), Greece—*Continued*

Cruising to Crete: Four French Girls Set Sail in a Breton Yawl for the Island of the Legendary Minotaur. By Marthe Oulié and Mariel Jean-Brunhes. Vol. LV, pp. 249-272, 15 ills. in black and white, 14 ills. in color, 1 page map, Feb., 1929.

Explorations in Crete. By Edith H. Hall. Vol. XX, pp. 778-787, 15 ills., Sept., 1909.

Greece—the Birthplace of Science and Free Speech: Explorations on the Mainland and in Crete and the Aegean Isles Reveal Ancient Life Similar to That of the Present. By Richard Stillwell. Paintings by H. M. Herget. Vol. LXXXV, pp. 273-353, 13 ills. in black and white, 32 ills. in color, 1 two-page map, Mar., 1944.

Sea-Kings of Crete. By James Baikie. Vol. XXIII, pp. 1-25, 13 ills., Jan., 1912.

Where Ancient Sea Kings Held Sway. 14 ills. in color from autochromes by Maynard Owen Williams. Vol. LV, pp. 254-263, Feb., 1929.

Crimea Reborn. By Eddy Gilmore. Vol. LXXXVII, pp. 487-512, 23 ills., 1 half-page map, Apr., 1945.

Crimean Autonomous Soviet Socialist Republic, R. S. F. S. R.:

Crimea Reborn. By Eddy Gilmore. Vol. LXXXVII, pp. 487-512, 23 ills., 1 half-page map, Apr., 1945.

Critchell, Laurence Sanford:

Crossroads of the Caribbean (Trinidad). By Laurence Sanford Critchell. Vol. LXXII, pp. 319-344, 18 ills. in black and white, 14 ills. in color, 1 half-page map, Sept., 1937.

Croatia:

In Quaint, Curious Croatia. By Felix J. Koch. Vol. XIX, pp. 809-832, 37 ills., Dec., 1908.

Cronquist, G. W.:

Types and Costumes of Old Sweden. 2 ills. in color from autochromes lumière by G. W. Cronquist. Vol. LIV, pp. 424-441, Oct., 1928.

Crosby, Oscar T.:

Abyssinia, the Country and People. By Oscar T. Crosby. Vol. XII, pp. 89-102, Mar., 1901.

Crosby Expedition to Tibet. Vol. XV, pp. 228-231, 3 ills., May, 1904.

Crossing Asia Minor, the Country of the New Turkish Republic. By Maj. Robert Whitney Imbrie. Vol. XLVI, pp. 445-472, 31 ills., 1 quarter-page map, Oct., 1924.

Crossing the Untraversed Libyan Desert: The Record of a 2,200-Mile Journey of Exploration Which Resulted in the Discovery of Two Oases of Strategic Importance on the Southwestern Frontier of Egypt. By A. M. Hassanein. Vol. XLVI, pp. 233-277, 46 ills., 1 half-page map, Sept., 1924.

Crossroads of the Caribbean (Trinidad). By Laurence Sanford Critchell. Vol. LXXII, pp. 319-344, 18 ills. in black and white, 14 ills. in color, 1 half-page map, Sept., 1937.

Crow, Bird Citizen of Every Land: A Feathered Rogue Who Has Many Fascinating Traits and Many Admirable Qualities Despite His Marauding Propensities. By E. R. Kalmbach. Vol. XXXVII, pp. 322-337, 10 ills., Apr., 1920.

Crow Indians:

Friendly Crows in Festive Panoply. 13 ills. in color from natural-color photographs by Edwin L. Wisherd. Vol. LII, pp. 314-323, Sept., 1927.

Crowder, William:

Crabs and Crablike Curiosities of the Sea. By William Crowder. Vol. LIV, pp. 57-72, 10 ills. in black and white, 8 ills. in color, July, 1928.

Jellyfishes—Living Draperies of Color. 8 ills. in color from paintings by William Crowder. Vol. L, pp. 193-200, Aug., 1926.

Life of the Moon-Jelly. By William Crowder. Vol. L, pp. 187-202, 6 ills. in black and white, 1 ill. in color, Aug., 1926.

Living Jewels of the Sea (Plankton). By William Crowder. Vol. LII, pp. 290-304, 8 ills. in black and white, 8 ills. in color, Sept., 1927.

Marvels of Mycetozoa: Exploration of a Long Island Swamp Reveals Some of the Secrets of the Slime Molds, Dwelling on the Borderland Between the Plant and Animal Kingdoms. By William Crowder. Vol. XLIX, pp. 421-443, 5 ills. in black and white, 16 ills. in color, Apr., 1926.

Crows (Birds):

Crow, Bird Citizen of Every Land: A Feathered Rogue Who Has Many Fascinating Traits and Many Admirable Qualities Despite His Marauding Propensities. By E. R. Kalmbach. Vol. XXXVII, pp. 322-337, 10 ills., Apr., 1920.

Crows, Magpies, and Jays: Unusual Intelligence Has Earned a Unique Position for These Birds. By T. Gilbert Pearson. Paintings by Maj. Allan Brooks. Vol. LXIII, pp. 51-79, 4 ills. in black and white, 2 ills. in color, Jan., 1933.

Cruise Among Desert Islands (Baja California). By G. Dallas Hanna and A. W. Anthony. Vol. XLIV, pp. 71-99, 32 ills., 1 quarter-page map, July, 1923.

Cruise of the *Kinkajou:* Among Desert Islands of Mexico Voyagers Find Outdoor Laboratories for the Naturalist and Ideal Fishing Grounds for the Sportsman. By Alfred M. Bailey. Vol. LXXX, pp. 339-366, 13 ills. in black and white, 12 ills. in color, 1 page map, Sept., 1941.

Cruise on an Escort Carrier. By Melville Bell Grosvenor. Vol. LXXXIV, pp. 513-546, 14 ills. in black and white, 20 ills. in color, Nov., 1943.

Cruising to Crete : Four French Girls Set Sail in a Breton Yawl for the Island of the Legendary Minotaur. By Marthe Oulié and Mariel Jean-Brunhes. Vol. LV, pp. 249-272, 15 ills. in black and white, 14 ills. in color, 1 page map, Feb., 1929.

Crusader Castles of the Near East. By William H. Hall. Vol. LIX, pp. 369-390, 19 ills., 1 third-page map, Mar., 1931.

Crusaders:

Crusader Castles of the Near East. By William H. Hall. Vol. LIX, pp. 369-390, 19 ills., 1 third-page map, Mar., 1931.

Road of the Crusaders : A Historian Follows the Steps of Richard the Lion Heart and Other Knights of the Cross Over the "Via Dei." By Harold Lamb. Vol. LXIV, pp. 645-693, 46 ills. in black and white, 13 ills. in color, 1 page map, Dec., 1933.

Souvenirs of Knighthood in Rhodes. 13 ills. in color from natural-color photographs by Luigi Pellerano. Vol. LXIV, pp. 665-672, Dec., 1933.

Crusoe, Robinson:

Voyage to the Island Home of Robinson Crusoe (Juan Fernández). By Waldo L. Schmitt. Vol. LIV, pp. 353-370, 24 ills., Sept., 1928.

Crusoes of Canton Island : Life on a Tiny Pacific Atoll That Has Flashed Into World Importance. By Irvine C. Gardner. Vol. LXXIII, pp. 749-766, 7 ills. in black and white, 11 ills. in color, June, 1938.

Crustaceans:

America's Surpassing Fisheries : Their Present Condition and Future Prospects and How the Federal Government Fosters Them. By Hugh M. Smith. Vol. XXIX, pp. 546-583, 35 ills., June, 1916.

Certain Citizens of the Warm Sea. By Louis L. Mowbray. Vol. XLI, pp. 27-62, 18 ills. in black and white, 16 ills. in color, Jan., 1922.

Denizens of Our Warm Atlantic Waters. By Roy Waldo Miner. Vol. LXXI, pp. 199-219, 10 ills. in black and white, 8 ills. in color, Feb., 1937.

Fantastic Dwellers in a Coral Fairyland (Great Barrier Reef). 15 ills. in color from natural-color photographs by T. C. Roughley. Vol. LXXVII, pp. 831-838, June, 1940.

Gleaming Fishes of Pacific Coastal Waters. 31 portraits in color from paintings by Hashime Murayama. Vol. LXXIV, pp. 467-498, Oct., 1938.

Living Jewels of the Sea. By William Crowder. Vol. LII, pp. 290-304, 8 ills. in black and white, 8 ills. in color, Sept., 1927.

Sea Creatures of Our Atlantic Shores. By Roy Waldo Miner. Vol. LXX, pp. 209-231, 8 ills. in black and white, 8 ills. in color, 1 chart, Aug., 1936.

Strange Creatures of Sunny Seas. 8 ills. in color from paintings by Else Bostelmann. Vol. LXXI, pp. 211-218, Feb., 1937.

Crustaceans—*Continued*

Treasures of the Pacific : Marine Fishes and Fisheries Yield Vast Wealth from Alaska to Baja California. By Leonard P. Schultz. Vol. LXXIV, pp. 463-498, 10 ills. in black and white, 31 portraits in color, Oct., 1938.

Undersea Gardens of the North Atlantic Coast. 8 ills. in color from paintings by Else Bostelmann. Vol. LXX, pp. 217-224, Aug., 1936.

See also Crabs ; Lobsters ; Shrimp.

Cuba:

Across the Equator with the American Navy. By Herbert Corey. Vol. XXXIX, pp. 571-624, 53 ills., June, 1921.

American Progress in Cuba. Vol. XIII, p. 76, Feb., 1902.

Among the Mahogany Forests of Cuba. By Walter D. Wilcox. Vol. XIX, pp. 485-498, 6 ills., 1 page map, July, 1908.

Conditions in Cuba as Revealed by the Census. By Henry Gannett. Vol. XX, pp. 200-202, Feb., 1909.

Cuba—The Isle of Romance. By Enrique C. Canova. Vol. LXIV, pp. 345-380, 34 ills., 1 page map, Sept., 1933.

Cuba—The Pearl of the Antilles. Vol. XVII, pp. 535-568, 24 ills., special map supplement, Oct., 1906.

Cuba—The Sugar Mill of the Antilles. By William Joseph Showalter. Vol. XXXVIII, pp. 1-33, 24 ills., 1 page map, July, 1920.

Cuba and Porto Rico. Vol. XII, p. 80, Feb., 1901.

Cuban Census. Vol. XI, p. 205, 5 diagrams, May, 1900.

Cuban Railways. By Albert G. Robinson. Vol. XIII, pp. 108-110, Mar., 1902.

Development of Cuba. Vol. XIV, pp. 112-113, 1 half-page map, Mar., 1903.

Influence of Submarine Cables upon Military and Naval Supremacy. By Capt. George O. Squier. Vol. XII, pp. 1-12, Jan., 1901.

Isle of Pines. Vol. XVII, pp. 105-108, 2 ills., Feb., 1906.

Our New Possessions and the Interest They Are Exciting. By O. P. Austin. Vol. XI, pp. 32-33, Jan., 1900.

Some Recent Instances of National Altruism : The Efforts of the United States to Aid the Peoples of Cuba, Porto Rico, and the Philippines. By William H. Taft. Vol. XVIII, pp. 429-438, July, 1907.

To Bogotá and Back by Air : The Narrative of a 9,500-Mile Flight from Washington, Over Thirteen Latin-American Countries and Return, in the Single-Seater Airplane, *Spirit of St. Louis.* By Col. Charles A. Lindbergh. Vol. LIII, pp. 529-601, 98 ills., 1 two-thirds-page map, May, 1928.

Yellow Fever in Cuba. Vol. XII, p. 440, Dec., 1901.

See also Havana.

Cuban Census. Vol. XI, p. 205, 5 diagrams, May, 1900.

Cuban Railways. By Albert G. Robinson. Vol. XIII, pp. 108-110, Mar., 1902.

Cuckoos (Birds) :

Parrots, Kingfishers, and Flycatchers : Strange Trogons and Curious Cuckoos Are Pictured with These Other Birds of Color, Dash, and Courage. By Alexander Wetmore. Paintings by Maj. Allan Brooks. Vol. LXIX, pp. 801-828, 9 ills., in black and white, 36 portraits in color, June, 1936.

Cuernavaca, the Sun Child of the Sierras. By Russell Hastings Millward. Vol. XXII, pp. 291-301, 9 ills., Mar., 1911.

Cuicuilco, Mexico :

Ruins of Cuicuilco May Revolutionize Our History of Ancient America : Lofty Mound Sealed and Preserved by Great Lava Flow for Perhaps Seventy Centuries Is Now Being Excavated in Mexico. By Byron Cummings. Vol. XLIV, pp. 203-220, 21 ills., 1 third-page map, Aug., 1923.

Culiacan, Mexico :

Adventuring Down the West Coast of Mexico. By Herbert Corey. Vol. XLII, pp. 449-503, 44 ills., 1 half-page map, Nov., 1922.

Cultivation of Marine and Fresh Water Animals in Japan. By K. Mitsukuri. Vol. XVII, pp. 524-531, 5 ills., Sept., 1906.

Cultivation of the Mayflower. By Frederick V. Coville. Vol. XXVII, pp. 518-519, 1 ill., May, 1915.

Culture Still Lights Our Wartime Capital (Washington, D. C.). 9 ills. in color from natural-color photographs by B. Anthony Stewart. Vol. LXXXI, pp. 337-344, Mar., 1942.

Culver, Willard R.:

Arkansas Traveler of 1946. 23 ills. in color from natural-color photographs by Willard R. Culver. Vol. XC, pp. 289-312, Sept., 1946.

Butterflies : Nomads Among the Butterflies. 8 ills. in color ; 3 paintings by Hashime Murayama and 5 natural-color photographs by Willard R. Culver. Vol. LXXI, pp. 569-584, May, 1937.

Butterflies : Winged Jewels from Many Lands. 9 ills. in color ; 3 paintings by Hashime Murayama and 6 natural-color photographs by Willard R. Culver. Vol. LXIX, pp. 673-688, May, 1936.

Catdom's Royalty Photographed in Color. 25 ills. in color from natural-color photographs by Willard R. Culver. Vol. LXXIV, pp. 597-628, Nov., 1938.

Chemistry : From Nature's Hidden Building Blocks. 26 ills. in color from natural-color photographs by Willard R. Culver. Vol. LXXVI, pp. 609-640, Nov., 1939.

Connecticut : Old and New Blend in Yankeeland. 25 ills. in color from natural-color photographs ; 7 ills. by Willard R. Culver. Vol. LXXIV, pp. 295-326, Sept., 1938.

Culver, Willard R.—*Continued*

Cotton : Golden Fleece of Dixie. 34 ills. in color from natural-color photographs by Willard R. Culver. Vol. LXXIX, pp. 153-192, Feb., 1941.

Dogs in Toyland. 16 ills. in color from natural-color photographs by Willard R. Culver. Vol. LXXXV, pp. 473-480, Apr., 1944.

Food : Flavor and Savor of American Foods. 25 ills. in color from natural-color photographs by J. Baylor Roberts, Willard R. Culver, and others. Vol. LXXXI, pp. 289-320, Mar., 1942.

Glass : From Sand to Seer and Servant of Man. 22 ills. in color from natural-color photographs by Willard R. Culver. Vol. LXXXIII, pp. 17-48, Jan., 1943.

Indiana : Hoosier Haunts and Holidays. 27 ills. in color from natural-color photographs by Willard R. Culver. Vol. LXX, pp. 283-314, Sept., 1936.

Insects : A Community of Dwarfs. 11 Illustrations in color from natural-color photographs by Willard R. Culver. Vol. XC, pp. 345-352, Sept., 1946.

New York : Bright Patterns of Long Island Life. 18 ills. in color from natural-color photographs ; 14 ills. by Willard R. Culver. Vol. LXXV, pp. 429-460, Apr., 1939.

Potomac : George Washington's Historic River. 18 ills. in color from natural-color photographs by Willard R. Culver and Robert F. Sisson. Vol. LXXXVIII, pp. 41-64, July, 1945.

Rubber : From Trees to Tires and Toys. 26 ills. in color from natural-color photographs by Willard R. Culver and J. Baylor Roberts. Vol. LXXVII, pp. 159-190, Feb., 1940.

Virginia, Maryland, and Delaware : Tri-State Medley. 10 ills. in color from natural-color photographs by Willard R. Culver. Vol. LXXIV, pp. 33-40, July, 1938.

Virginia's Colonial Heritage (Williamsburg). 25 ills. in color from natural-color photographs ; 4 ills. by Willard R. Culver. Vol. LXXI, pp. 417-440, Apr., 1937.

Washington of Tradition Builds for the Future. 20 ills. in color from natural-color photographs ; 3 ills. by Willard R. Culver. Vol. LXXI, pp. 671-694, June, 1937.

Cumana, Venezuela :

Three Old Ports on the Spanish Main. By G. M. L. Brown. Vol. XVII, pp. 622-638, 12 ills., Nov., 1906.

Cumberland, Maryland :

Potomac, River of Destiny. By Albert W. Atwood. Vol. LXXXVIII, pp. 33-70, 15 ills. in black and white, 18 ills. in color, 1 map (two-page spread), July, 1945.

Cumberland Gap (Region), United States :

Home Folk around Historic Cumberland Gap. By Leo A. Borah. Vol. LXXXIV, pp. 741-768, 25 ills., 1 quarter-page map, Dec., 1943.

Cummings, Byron:

Great Natural Bridges of Utah. By Byron Cummings. Vol. XXI, pp. 157-167, 7 ills., Feb., 1910.

Ruins of Cuicuilco May Revolutionize Our History of Ancient America : Lofty Mound Sealed and Preserved by Great Lava Flow for Perhaps Seventy Centuries Is Now Being Excavated in Mexico. By Byron Cummings. Vol. XLIV, pp. 203-220, 21 ills., 1 third-page map, Aug., 1923.

Cuna Indians. *See* San Blas Indians.

Curaçao (Island), West Indies :

Curaçao and Aruba, Oil Isles of the Caribbean. 10 ills. in color from natural-color photographs by Philip Hanson Hiss and Robert Yarnall Richie. Vol. LXXXIII, pp. 175-182, Feb., 1943.

Curaçao and Aruba on Guard. By W. Robert Moore. Vol. LXXXIII, pp. 169-192, 12 ills. in black and white, 10 ills in color, 4 maps, Feb., 1943.

Curari (Poison). *See* Urari.

Curious and Characteristic Customs of Central African Tribes (Belgian Congo). By E. Torday. Vol. XXXVI, pp. 342-368, 35 ills., Oct., 1919.

Curious and Characteristic Customs of China. By Kenneth F. Junor. Vol. XXI, pp. 791-806, 7 ills., Sept., 1910.

Curious Scenes in Out of the Way Places. Vol. XXIV, pp. 751-762, 12 ills. from photographs, June, 1913.

Curityba, Brazil :

Air Cruising Through New Brazil : A National Geographic Reporter Spots Vast Resources Which the Republic's War Declaration Adds to Strength of United Nations. By Henry Albert Phillips. Vol. LXXXII, pp. 503-536, 32 ills., Oct., 1942.

Curle, (Capt.) A. T.:

When a Drought Blights Africa : Hippos and Elephants Are Driven Insane by Suffering, in the Lorian Swamp, Kenya Colony. By Capt. A. T. Curle. Vol. LV, pp. 521-528, 9 ills., Apr., 1929.

Curtis, Asahel:

National Parks. 3 ills. in color from photographs by Asahel Curtis. Vol. XXXVII, pp. 513-517, June, 1920.

Washington (State) : Sunset Hues in the Pacific Northwest. 5 ills. in color from natural-color photographs by Asahel Curtis. Vol. LXIII, pp. 154-163, Feb., 1933.

Washington (State) : Where the Last of the West Was Won. 8 ills. in color from natural-color photographs by Asahel Curtis. Vol. LXIII, pp. 178-187, Feb., 1933.

Curtis, William Eleroy:

Great Turk and His Lost Provinces. By William Eleroy Curtis. Vol. XIV, pp. 45-61, 7 ills., Feb., 1903.

Curtis, William Eleroy—*Continued*

Honors to the American Navy (Address by William Eleroy Curtis). Vol. XX, pp. 77-95, Jan., 1909.

Revolution in Russia. By William Eleroy Curtis. Vol. XVIII, pp. 302-316, May, 1907.

Road to Bolivia. By William Eleroy Curtis. Vol. XI, pp. 208-224, 7 ills., June, 1900.

Road to Bolivia. By William Eleroy Curtis. Vol. XI, pp. 264-280, 6 ills., July, 1900.

Curvature of the Earth : Photograph Showing the Division Between the Troposphere and Stratosphere and also the Actual Curvature of the Earth. Special supplement from aërial photograph by Capt. Albert W. Stevens. Vol. LXIX, supplement, May, 1936.

Curzon, Marquess, of Kedleston:

In the Diamond Mountains : Adventures Among the Buddhist Monasteries of Eastern Korea. By Marquess Curzon of Kedleston. Vol. XLVI, pp. 353-374, 21 ills., 1 quarter-page map, Oct., 1924.

Curzon, (Lady) Mary Irene. *See* Ravensdale, The Baroness.

Cushing, Frank Hamilton:

Biography of Frank Hamilton Cushing. Vol. XI, p. 206, May, 1900.

Customs:

China and Her People : Some Reflections on Their Manners and Customs, Habits and Lives. By Comdr. Harrie Webster. Vol. XI, pp. 309-319, 3 ills., Aug., 1900.

Curious and Characteristic Customs of Central African Tribes (Belgian Congo). By E. Torday. Vol. XXXVI, pp. 342-368, 35 ills., Oct., 1919.

Curious and Characteristic Customs of China. By Kenneth F. Junor. Vol. XXI, pp. 791-806, 7 ills., Sept., 1910.

Yank Meets Native. By Wanda Burnett. Vol. LXXXVIII, pp. 105-128, 24 ills., July, 1945.

See also Coronations ; Dances ; Festivals ; Marriage Customs ; Religious Ceremonies *and* material on individual countries.

Cutler, A. W.:

Announcement of the Death of A. W. Cutler. Vol. XLII, p. 34, July, 1922.

Portugal, the Land of Henry the Navigator. 16 ills. in color from photographs by A. W. Cutler. Vol. XLII, pp. 517-532, Nov., 1922.

Cutting, C. Suydam:

Sky-high in Lama Land. 12 ills. from photographs by C. Suydam Cutting. Vol. XC, pp. 185-196, Aug., 1946.

Cuzco, Peru :

Among the Snows and Flowers of Peru. 7 ills. in color from natural-color photographs by Jacob Gayer. Vol. LVII, pp. 732-765, June, 1930.

Cuzco, America's Ancient Mecca. By Harriet Chalmers Adams. Vol. XIX, pp. 669-689, 19 ills., Oct., 1908.

Cuzco, Peru—*Continued*

Further Explorations in the Land of the Incas: Peruvian Expedition of 1915 of the National Geographic Society and Yale University. By Hiram Bingham. Vol. XXIX, pp. 431-473, 29 ills., 1 page and 1 half-page maps, panorama, May, 1916.

In the Wonderland of Peru. By Hiram Bingham. Vol. XXIV, pp. 387-574, 250 ills., 3 diagrams, 1 three-quarters-page map, Apr., 1913.

Incas: Empire Builders of the Andes. By Philip Ainsworth Means. Vol. LXXIII, pp. 225-264, 26 ills. in black and white, 10 ills. in color, Feb., 1938.

Story of Machu Picchu: The Peruvian Expedition of the National Geographic Society and Yale University. By Hiram Bingham. Vol. XXVII, pp. 171-217, 35 ills., Feb., 1915.

CVE's. *See* Escort Carriers.

Cyclades (Islands), Greece:

Isles of Greece. By Lt. Richard Stillwell, USNR. Vol. LXXXV, pp. 593-622, 11 ills. in black and white, 20 ills. in color, 1 page map, May, 1944.

Modern Odyssey in Classic Lands: Troy's Treasures, Athens' Parthenon, and Rome's First "Broad Way" Influence Today's Banks, Costumes, Jewelry, and Railroad Timetables. By Maynard Owen Williams. Vol. LXXVII, pp. 291-337, 27 ills. in black and white, 22 ills. in color, Mar., 1940.

Santorin and Mýkonos, Aegean Gems. 8 ills. in color from natural-color photographs; 7 ills. by B. Anthony Stewart. Vol. LXXVII, pp. 339-346, Mar., 1940.

Cygnet (Kite):

Dr. Bell's Man-Lifting Kite. By Gilbert H. Grosvenor. Vol. XIX, pp. 35-52, 27 ills., Jan., 1908.

Cyprus (Island), Mediterranean Sea:

American Fighters Visit Bible Lands. By Maynard Owen Williams. With 23 ills. in color from natural-color photographs by the author. Vol. LXXIX, pp. 311-340, 10 ills. in black and white, Mar., 1946.

Unspoiled Cyprus: The Traditional Island Birthplace of Venus Is One of the Least Sophisticated of Mediterranean Lands. By Maynard Owen Williams. Vol. LIV, pp. 1-55, 55 ills. in black and white, 10 ills. in color, 1 half-page map, July, 1928.

Czechoslovakia:

Bohemia and the Czechs. By Aleš Hrdlička. Vol. XXXI, pp. 163-187, 18 ills., Feb., 1917.

Costumes of Czechoslovakia. 19 ills. in color from natural-color photographs by Hans Hildenbrand. Vol. LI, pp. 724-741, June, 1927.

Czechoslovakia, Key-Land to Central Europe. By Maynard Owen Williams. Vol. XXXIX, pp. 111-156, 45 ills., 1 quarter-page map, Feb., 1921.

Czechoslovakia—*Continued*

Czechoslovakian Cyclorama. 30 ills. in color from natural-color photographs by W. Robert Moore. Vol. LXXIV, pp. 181-220, Aug., 1938.

Czechoslovaks, Yankees of Europe. By John Patric. Vol. LXXIV, pp. 173-225, 23 ills. in black and white, 30 ills. in color, 1 map, Aug., 1938.

Danube, Highway of Races: From the Black Forest to the Black Sea, Europe's Most Important River Has Borne the Traffic of Centuries. By Melville Chater. Vol. LVI, pp. 643-697, 54 ills., Dec., 1929.

Hospitality of the Czechs. By Worth E. Shoults. Vol. LI, pp. 723-742, 19 ills. in color, June, 1927.

Land of Contrast: Austria-Hungary. By D. W. and A. S. Iddings. Vol. XXIII, pp. 1188-1218, 34 ills., Dec., 1912.

New Map of Europe: Showing the Boundaries Established by the Peace Conference at Paris and by Subsequent Decisions of the Supreme Council of the Allied and Associated Powers. By Ralph A. Graves. Text accompanying special map supplement. Vol. XXXIX, pp. 157-177, 18 ills., Feb., 1921.

Races of Europe. By Edwin A. Grosvenor. Vol. XXXIV, pp. 441-534, 62 ills., 2 page maps, Dec., 1918.

When Czechoslovakia Puts a Falcon Feather in Its Cap. By Maynard Owen Williams. Vol. LXIII, pp. 40-49, 13 ills. in color, Jan., 1933.

See also Prague.

Czechoslovakian Cyclorama. 30 ills. in color from natural-color photographs by W. Robert Moore. Vol. LXXIV, pp. 181-220, Aug., 1938.

Czechoslovaks, Yankees of Europe. By John Patric. Vol. LXXIV, pp. 173-225, 23 ills. in black and white, 30 ills. in color, 1 map, Aug., 1938.

D

Daghestan Autonomous Soviet Socialist Republic, R. S. F. S. R.:

An Island in the Sea of History: The Highlands of Daghestan. By George Kennan. Vol. XXIV, pp. 1086-1140, 49 ills., 1 page map, Oct., 1913.

Roaming Russia's Caucasus: Rugged Mountains and Hardy Fighters Guard the Soviet Union's Caucasian Treasury of Manganese and Oil. By Rolf Singer. Vol. LXXXII, pp. 91-121, 33 ills., July, 1942.

Daily Life in Ancient Egypt (Part I). Daily Life in Ancient Egypt: *The Later Period* (Part II). By William C. Hayes. Paintings by H. M. Herget. Vol. LXXX, pp. 419-515, 34 ills. in black and white, 32 ills. in color, 1 two-thirds-page map, Oct., 1941.

Daily Life in Calabria (Italy). Vol. XLIII, pp. 181-196, 16 ills., Feb., 1923.

Dairen (Dalny), Manchuria:

Building of Dalny. Vol. XIV, p. 360, Sept., 1903.

Japan Faces Russia in Manchuria. By Willard Price. Vol. LXXXII, pp. 603-634, 30 ills., 1 page map, Nov., 1942.

Mukden, the Manchu Home, and Its Great Art Museum. By Eliza R. Scidmore. Vol. XXI, pp. 289-320, 30 ills., Apr., 1910.

Daitotei, Formosa:

Formosa the Beautiful. By Alice Ballantine Kirjassoff. Vol. XXXVII, pp. 246-292, 60 ills., 1 half-page map, Mar., 1920.

Dakar, Sénégal:

French West Africa in Wartime. By Paul M. Atkins. Vol. LXXXI, pp. 371-408, 37 ills., 2 maps, Mar., 1942.

Timbuktu and Beyond: Desert City of Romantic Savor and Salt Emerges into World Life Again as Trading Post of France's Vast African Empire. By Laura C. Boulton. Vol. LXXIX, pp. 631-670, 18 ills. in black and white, 26 ills. in color, 1 map (two-page spread), May, 1941.

Dalai Lama:

Across Tibet from India to China. By Lt. Col. Ilia Tolstoy, AUS. Vol. XC, pp. 169-222, 41 ills., 1 half-page map, Aug., 1946.

Sky-high in Lama Land. 12 ills. from photographs by C. Suydam Cutting. Vol. XC, pp. 185-196, Aug., 1946.

Dalarne, Sweden:

In Beautiful Delecarlia. By Lillian Gore. Vol. XX, pp. 464-477, 13 ills., May, 1909.

Dall, William H.:

How Long a Whale May Carry a Harpoon. By William H. Dall. Vol. X, pp. 136-137, Apr., 1899.

Marcus Baker (Address by William H. Dall). Vol. XV, pp. 40-43, 1 ill., Jan., 1904.

Dalmatia:

Dalmatian Days: Coasting Along Debatable Shores Where Latin and Slav Meet. By Melville Chater. Vol. LIII, pp. 47-90, 26 ills. in black and white, 17 ills. in color, 1 two-thirds-page map, Jan., 1928.

East of the Adriatic: Notes on Dalmatia, Montenegro, Bosnia, and Herzegovina. By Kenneth McKenzie. Vol. XXIII, pp. 1159-1187, 37 ills., 1 page map, Dec., 1912.

Where East Meets West: A Visit to Picturesque Dalmatia, Montenegro, and Bosnia. By Marian Cruger Coffin. Vol. XIX, pp. 309-344, 26 ills., 1 half-page map, May, 1908.

Dalmatian Days: Coasting Along Debatable Shores Where Latin and Slav Meet. By Melville Chater. Vol. LIII, pp. 47-90, 26 ills. in black and white, 17 ills. in color, 1 two-thirds-page map, Jan., 1928.

Dalny, Manchuria. *See* Dairen.

Damascus, Syria:

Damascus, the Pearl of the Desert. By Archibald Forder. Vol. XXII, pp. 62-82, 19 ills., 1 three-quarters-page map, Jan., 1911.

Syria and Lebanon Taste Freedom. By Maynard Owen Williams. With 21 ills. in color from natural-color photographs by the author. Vol. XC, pp. 729-763, 16 ills. in black and white, Dec., 1946.

Damascus and Mecca Railway:

Damascus and Mecca Railway. Vol. XII, p. 408, Nov., 1901.

One Thousand Miles of Railway Built for Pilgrims and Not for Dividends. By Col. F. R. Maunsell. Vol. XX, pp. 156-172, 13 ills., 1 three-quarters-page map, Feb., 1909.

Damon, Theron J.:

Albanians. By Theron J. Damon. Vol. XXIII, pp. 1090-1103, 14 ills., Nov., 1912.

Dampier, William:

Revealing Earth's Mightiest Ocean (Pacific). By Albert W. Atwood. Vol. LXXXIV, pp. 291-306, 10 ills., special map supplement, Sept., 1943.

Dams:

By Felucca Down the Nile: Giant Dams Rule Egypt's Lifeline River, Yet Village Life Goes On As It Did in the Time of the Pharaohs. By Willard Price. Vol. LXXVII, pp. 435-476, 21 ills. in black and white, 22 ills. in color, 1 two-page map, Apr., 1940.

Columbia (River) Turns on the Power. By Maynard Owen Williams. Vol. LXXIX, pp. 749-792, 25 ills. in black and white, 18 ills. in color, June, 1941.

Highest Dam in the World (Roosevelt Dam). Vol. XVI, pp. 440-441, Sept., 1905.

Marble Dams of Rajputana. By Eleanor Maddock. Vol. XL, pp. 468-499, 13 ills. in black and white, 16 ills. in color, Nov., 1921.

More Water for California's Great Central Valley. By Frederick Simpich. Vol. XC, pp. 645-664, 16 ills., 1 page map, Nov., 1946.

Panama Canal. By Lieut. Col. William L. Sibert. Vol. XXV, pp. 153-183, 24 ills., Feb., 1914.

Taming the Outlaw Missouri River. By Frederick Simpich. Vol. LXXXVIII, pp. 569-598, 25 ills., 1 two-page map, Nov., 1945.

Danakil (Tribespeople):

Sailing Forbidden Coasts. By Ida Treat. Vol. LX, pp. 357-386, 31 ills., 1 quarter-page map, Sept., 1931.

Dances:

Artist Adventures on the Island of Bali. 9 ills. in color from autochromes by Franklin Price Knott. Vol. LIII, pp. 328-345, Mar., 1928.

Bali, Gem of the Netherlands Indies. 11 ills. in color from natural-color photographs; 10 ills. by Maynard Owen Williams. Vol. LXXV, pp. 329-336, Mar., 1939.

Dances—*Continued*

Bali and Points East: Crowded, Happy Isles of the Flores Sea Blend Rice Terraces, Dance Festivals, and Amazing Music in Their Pattern of Living. By Maynard Owen Williams. Vol. LXXV, pp. 313-352, 33 ills. in black and white, 11 ills. in color, 1 two-thirds-page map, Mar., 1939.

Costume Pageants in the French Pyrenees. 24 ills. in color from natural-color photographs by W. Robert Moore. Vol. LXXII, pp. 435-450, Oct., 1937.

Demon Dancers and Butter Gods of Choni. 16 ills. in color from photographs by Joseph F. Rock. Vol. LIV, pp. 584-601, Nov., 1928.

Enigma of Cambodia. 27 ills. in color from autochromes by Gervais Courtellemont. Vol. LIV, pp. 306-323, Sept., 1928.

Field Sports Among the Wild Men of Northern Luzon. By Dean C. Worcester. Vol. XXII, pp. 215-267, 17 ills., 1 half-page map, Mar., 1911.

Four Faces of Siva: The Mystery of Angkor. By Robert J. Casey. Vol. LIV, pp. 303-332, 13 ills. in black and white, 27 ills. in color, 1 third-page map, Sept., 1928.

"Glory That Was Greece." By Alexander Wilbourne Weddell. Vol. XLII, pp. 571-630, 51 ills., 1 three-quarters-page map, Dec., 1922.

Head-Hunters of Northern Luzon. By Dean C. Worcester. Vol. XXIII, pp. 833-930, 102 ills., 1 page map, Sept., 1912.

Here and There in Northern Africa. By Frank Edward Johnson. Vol. XXV, pp. 1-132, 113 ills., Jan., 1914.

Impressions and Scenes in Mozambique. By O. W. Barrett. Vol. XXI, pp. 807-830, 31 ills., Oct., 1910.

Island in the Sea of History (Daghestan). By George Kennan. Vol. XXIV, pp. 1086-1140, 49 ills., 1 page map, Oct., 1913.

Java, Queen of the East Indies. 10 ills. in color from autochromes by W. Robert Moore and Tassilo Adam. Vol. LVI, pp. 334-359, Sept., 1929.

Land of the Basques: Home of a Thrifty, Picturesque People, Who Take Pride in the Sobriquet, "The Yankees of Spain." By Harry A. McBride. Vol. XLI, pp. 63-87, 25 ills., 1 three-quarters-page map, Jan., 1922.

Life Among the Lamas of Choni: Describing the Mystery Plays and Butter Festival in the Monastery of an Almost Unknown Tibetan Principality in Kansu Province, China. By Joseph F. Rock. Vol. LIV, pp. 569-619, 34 ills. in black and white, 16 ills. in color, 1 half-page map, Nov., 1928.

Mexican Indian Flying Pole Dance. By Helga Larsen. Vol. LXXI, pp. 387-400, 13 ills., Mar., 1937.

Perahera Processions of Ceylon. By G. H. G. Burroughs. Vol. LXII, pp. 90-100, 1 ill. in black and white, 8 ills. in duotone, July, 1932.

Roumania and Its Rubicon. By John Oliver La Gorce. Vol. XXX, pp. 185-202, 11 ills., Sept., 1916.

Dances—*Continued*

Samoa—South Sea Outpost of the U. S. Navy. 20 ills. from photographs by Truman Bailey. Vol. LXXIX, pp. 615-630, May, 1941.

Snake Dance (Hopi Indians). By Marion Oliver. Vol. XXII, pp. 107-137, 31 ills., Feb., 1911.

Two Great Moorish Religious Dances. By George Edmund Holt. Vol. XXII, pp. 776-785, 6 ills., Aug., 1911.

Vanishing People of the South Seas: The Tragic Fate of the Marquesan Cannibals, Noted for Their Warlike Courage and Physical Beauty. By John W. Church. Vol. XXXVI, pp. 275-306, 22 ills., 1 half-page map, Oct., 1919.

Daniels, Josephus:

Gem of the Ocean: Our American Navy. By Josephus Daniels. Vol. XXXIII, pp. 313-335, 35 ills., Apr., 1918.

Voice Voyages by the National Geographic Society: A Tribute to the Geographic Achievements of the Telephone (Address by Josephus Daniels). Vol. XXIX, pp. 296-326, 5 ills., 1 chart, Mar., 1916.

Danish West Indies. *See* Virgin Islands.

Danish West Indies. Vol. XIII, pp. 72-73, Feb., 1902.

Danube (River), Europe:

Budapest, Twin City of the Danube. By J. R. Hildebrand. Vol. LXI, pp. 729-742, 3 ills. in black and white, 10 ills. in duotone, June, 1932.

Danube, Highway of Races: From the Black Forest to the Black Sea, Europe's Most Important River Has Borne the Traffic of Centuries. By Melville Chater. Vol. LVI, pp. 643-697, 54 ills., Dec., 1929.

Danube Delta, Romania:

Caviar Fishermen of Romania: From Vâlcov, "Little Venice" of the Danube Delta, Bearded Russian Exiles Go Down to the Sea. By Dorothy Hosmer. Vol. LXXVII, pp. 407-434, 29 ills., 1 third-page map, Mar., 1940.

Danzig:

Flying Around the Baltic. By Douglas Chandler. Vol. LXXIII, pp. 767-806, 31 ills. in black and white, 13 ills. in duotone, 1 half-page map, June, 1938.

Historic Danzig: Last of the City-States. By William and Alicelia Franklin. Vol. LXXVI, pp. 677-696, 26 ills., Nov., 1939.

War Clouds Over Danzig and Poland's Port. 8 ills. from photographs. Vol. LXXVI, pp. 551-558, Oct., 1939.

Dardanelles:

Gates to the Black Sea: The Dardanelles, the Bosphorus, and the Sea of Marmora. By Harry Griswold Dwight. Vol. XXVII, pp. 435-459, 27 ills., May, 1915.

Darfur (Province), Anglo-Egyptian Sudan:

Adventures Among the "Lost Tribes of Islam" In Eastern Darfur: A Personal Narrative of Exploring, Mapping, and Setting Up a Government in the Anglo-Egyptian Sudan Borderland. By Maj. Edward Keith-Roach. Vol. XLV, pp. 41-73, 32 ills., 1 three-quarters-page map, Jan., 1924.

Dargue, (Maj.) Herbert A.:

How Latin America Looks from the Air: U. S. Army Airplanes Hurdle the High Andes, Brave Brazil Jungles, and Follow Smoking Volcanoes to Map New Sky Paths Around South America. By Maj. Herbert A. Dargue. Vol. LII, pp. 451-502, 52 ills., 1 page map, Oct., 1927.

Darley, James M.:

Society Maps Northwestern United States and Neighboring Canadian Provinces. Text accompanying special map supplement in colors. Vol. LXXIX, pp. 805-806, June, 1941.

Society's New Map of China. By James M. Darley. Text accompanying special map supplement in colors. Vol. LXXXVII, pp. 745-746, June, 1945.

World That Rims the Narrowing Atlantic: Latest Ten-color Map Supplement Shows Four Continents and New Transatlantic Air Routes Which Make This Ocean Only One Day Wide. By James M. Darley. Text accompanying special map supplement in colors. Vol. LXXVI, pp. 139-142, 1 ill., July, 1939.

Dartmouth Outing Club:

Skiing Over the New Hampshire Hills. By Fred H. Harris. Vol. XXXVII, pp. 133-164, 35 ills., Feb., 1920.

Darton, N. H.:

Bad Lands of South Dakota. By N. H. Darton. Vol. X, pp. 339-343, 4 ills., Sept., 1899.

Bighorn Mountains. By N. H. Darton. Vol. XVIII, pp. 355-364, 7 ills., 1 page map, June, 1907.

Mexico—The Treasure House of the World. By N. H. Darton. Vol. XVIII, pp. 492-519, 23 ills., Aug., 1907.

Our Pacific Northwest. By N. H. Darton. Vol. XX, pp. 645-663, 12 ills., 2 half-page maps, July, 1909.

Southwest (United States): Its Splendid Natural Resources, Agricultural Wealth, and Scenic Beauty. By N. H. Darton. Vol. XXI, pp. 631-665, 21 ills., 1 page map, Aug., 1910.

Texas, Our Largest State. By N. H. Darton. Vol. XXIV, pp. 1330-1360, 22 ills., 2 half-page maps, Dec., 1913.

Darwin, Australia:

Life in Dauntless Darwin: A National Geographic Staff Writer Gives a Vivid Description of the Australian Town That Guards the Continent's Northern Door. By Howell Walker. Vol. LXXXII, pp. 123-138, 17 ills., 1 sixth-page map, July, 1942.

Dasara Ceremonies:

India at Work and Play. 22 ills. in color from natural-color photographs by Peter Upton Muir, Maynard Owen Williams, and Frances Muir. Vol. LXXXIX, pp. 449-464, Apr., 1946.

Indian Mosaic. By Peter Muir and Frances Muir. Vol. LXXXIX, pp. 443-470, 5 ills. in black and white, 22 ills. in color, 1 half-page map, Apr., 1946.

Dasheen (Vegetable):

In Honor of the Army and Aviation. Vol. XXII, pp. 267-284, 5 ills., Mar., 1911.

Date Gardens of the Jerid. By Thomas H. Kearney. Vol. XXI, pp. 543-567, 20 ills., July, 1910.

Date Palms:

Date Gardens of the Jerid. By Thomas H. Kearney. Vol. XXI, pp. 543-567, 20 ills., July, 1910.

Here and There in Northern Africa. By Frank Edward Johnson. Vol. XXV, pp. 1-132, 113 ills., Jan., 1914.

National Geographic Society (Announcing the election of James Bryce, British Ambassador, as an Honorary Member of The Society). Vol. XXIII, pp. 272-298, 5 ills., Mar., 1912.

New Plant Immigrants. By David Fairchild. Vol. XXII, pp. 879-907, 34 ills., Oct., 1911.

Our Plant Immigrants. By David Fairchild. Vol. XVII, pp. 179-210, 29 ills., Apr., 1906.

Davao, Philippine Islands:

Mindanao, on the Road to Tokyo. By Frederick Simpich. Vol. LXXXVI, pp. 539-574, 26 ills. in black and white, 12 ills. in color, 1 two-page map, Nov., 1944.

Davidson, George:

Origin of the Name "Cape Nome." By George Davidson. Vol. XII, p. 398, Nov., 1901.

Davies, Llewellyn James:

Chinese "Boxers." By Llewellyn James Davies. Vol. XI, pp. 281-287, July, 1900.

Davis, Arthur P.:

Four Prominent Geographers. Vol. XVIII, pp. 425-428, 4 ills., June, 1907.

Location of the Boundary Between Nicaragua and Costa Rica. By Arthur P. Davis. Vol. XII, pp. 22-28, 1 ill., 1 half-page map, Jan., 1901.

New Inland Sea (Salton Sea). By Arthur P. Davis. Vol. XVIII, pp. 36-49, 8 ills., 1 page map, Jan., 1907.

Nicaragua and the Isthmian Routes. By Arthur P. Davis. Vol. X, pp. 247-266, 8 ills., 2 diagrams, July, 1899.

Water Supply for the Nicaragua Canal. By Arthur P. Davis. Vol. XI, pp. 363-365, Sept., 1900.

Davis, (Lt. Comdr.) Noel:

Removal of the North Sea Mine Barrage. By Lieut. Comdr. Noel Davis. Vol. XXXVII, pp. 103-133, 28 ills., 2 half-page maps, Feb., 1920.

Davis, W. M.:

Bearing of Physiography Upon Seuss' Theories. By W. M. Davis. Vol. XV, p. 430, Oct., 1904.

Practical Exercises in Geography. By W. M. Davis. Vol. XI, pp. 62-78, Feb., 1900.

Rational Element in Geography. By W. M. Davis. Vol. X, pp. 466-473, 2 diagrams, Nov., 1899.

Davison, Henry P.:

Our Armies of Mercy (American National Red Cross). By Henry P. Davison. Vol. XXXI, pp. 423-427, 3 ills., May, 1917.

Davison, Lonnelle. *See* Aikman, Lonnelle Davison.

Dawson, George M.:

George M. Dawson (Biography). Vol. XII, p. 197, 1 ill., May, 1901.

Day, Charles Healy and **Gladys M.:**

Flying the World: In a Homemade Airplane the Author and Her Husband Enjoy 16,000 Miles of Adventurous Flight Across Europe, Asia, and America. By Gladys M. Day. Vol. LXI, pp. 655-690, 41 ills., 1 half-page map, June, 1932.

Day, (Dr.) David T.:

Course of the Retail Coal Trade. By Dr. David T. Day. Vol. XIII, pp. 394-398, Nov., 1902.

Day with Our Boys in the Geographic Wards. By Carol Corey. Vol. XXXIV, pp. 69-80, 8 ills., July, 1918.

Dayaks (Tribespeople). *See* Dyaks.

Dealings of the United States with the Nations of the World. Vol. XV, pp. 186-187, Apr., 1904.

Dearborn, N.:

Pest of English Sparrows. By N. Dearborn. Vol. XXI, pp. 948-952, 4 ills., Nov., 1910.

Death Valley, California:

Deserts of Nevada and the Death Valley. By Robert H. Chapman. Vol. XVII, pp. 482-497, 9 ills., 1 chart, Sept., 1906.

Lowest Point in the United States. Vol. XVIII, pp. 824-825, Dec., 1907.

Dečani Monastery, Yugoslavia:

Clock Turns Back in Yugoslavia: The Fortified Monastery of Mountain-girt Dečani Survives Its Six Hundredth Birthday. By Ethel Chamberlain Porter. Vol. LXXXV, pp. 493-512, 20 ills., 1 page map, Apr., 1944.

Decapods. *See* Crabs; Lobster; Shrimp.

De Chetelat, Enzo. *See* Chetelat, Enzo de.

Decision of the Alaskan Boundary Tribunal. Vol. XV, pp. 12-14, Jan., 1904.

Decorations, Military and Naval:

Decorations, Medals, Service Ribbons, Badges, and Women's Insignia. Vol. LXXXIV, pp. 414-444, 6 ills. in black and white, 376 ills. in color, Oct., 1943.

Heraldry of Heroism. By Arthur E. Du Bois. Vol. LXXXIV, pp. 409-413, 2 ills., 1 third-page map, Oct., 1943.

Insignia and Decorations of the United States Armed Forces. By Gilbert Grosvenor. Vol. LXXXVII, pp. 185-186, Feb., 1945.

Deep-Sea Exploring Expedition of the Steamer *Albatross.* By Hugh M. Smith. Vol. X, pp. 291-296, 2 ills., 1 diagram, Aug., 1899.

Deep-Water Route from Chicago to the Gulf. Vol. XVIII, pp. 676-685, 3 ills., 1 page map, Oct., 1907.

Deer:

Antlered Majesties of Many Lands. 23 ills. in color from paintings by Walter A. Weber. Vol. LXXVI, pp. 479-510, Oct., 1939.

Deer Farming in the United States. Vol. XXI, pp. 269-276, 2 ills., Mar., 1910.

Deer of the World: As Workers, Pets, and Graceful "Living Statuary" in Parks and Estates, These Versatile Creatures Have Endeared Themselves to Mankind. By Victor H. Cahalane. Vol. LXXVI, pp. 463-510, 20 ills. in black and white, 23 ills. in color, Oct., 1939.

Doe and Twin Fawns. Flashlight photograph by George Shiras, 3d. Vol. XXIV, supplement, July, 1913. Vol. LXXVI, ill. 475, Oct., 1939.

Hark! Vol. XL, special supplement, Aug., 1921.

Larger North American Mammals. By E. W. Nelson. Vol. XXX, pp. 385-472, 24 ills. in black and white, 50 ills. in color, special supplement in color, 1 page and 1 half-page maps, Nov., 1916.

Wild Animals That Took Their Own Pictures by Day and by Night. By George Shiras, 3d. Vol. XXIV, pp. 763-834, 68 ills., 1 page map, July, 1913.

Wild Life of Lake Superior, Past and Present: The Habits of Deer, Moose, Wolves, Beavers, Muskrats, Trout, and Feathered Wood-Folk Studied with Camera and Flashlight. By George Shiras, 3d. Vol. XL, pp. 113-204, 77 ills., special supplement, 1 half-page map, Aug., 1921.

See also Mule Deer.

Deering, Mabel Craft:

Chosen—Land of Morning Calm. By Mabel Craft Deering. Vol. LXIV, pp. 421-448, 20 ills. in black and white, 13 ills. in color, 1 two-thirds-page map, Oct., 1933.

Ho for the Soochow Ho. By Mabel Craft Deering. Vol. LI, pp. 623-649, 32 ills., 1 three-quarters-page map, June, 1927.

Defense Bases. *See* Air Bases; U. S. Defense Bases.

Definite Location of Bouvet Island. By O. H. Tittmann. Vol. X, pp. 413-414, Oct., 1899.

De Forest, J. H.:

Why Nik-ko Is Beautiful. By J. H. De Forest. Vol. XIX, pp. 300-308, 8 ills., Apr., 1908.

Deforestation and Climate. Vol. XVI, pp. 397-398, Aug., 1905.

De Gaston, Paul:

China's Teeming Life on the Rivers and Sea. 16 ills. in duotone from photographs by Paul De Gaston. Vol. LXVI, pp. 625-640, Nov., 1934.

Degelman, John:

Tuna Harvest of the Sea: A Little-known Epic of the Ocean Is the Story of Southern California's Far-ranging Tuna Fleet. By John Degelman. Vol. LXXVIII, pp. 393-408, 17 ills., Sept., 1940.

Dehodencq, Alfred:

Fate Directs the Faltering Footsteps of Columbus. Reproduction in color of the painting by Alfred Dehodencq, Paris. Vol. LIV, supplement, Sept., 1928.

Deir-el-Bahari, Egypt:

Reconstructing Egypt's History. By Wallace N. Stearns. Vol. XXIV, pp. 1021-1042, 21 ills., Sept., 1913.

Resurrection of Ancient Egypt. By James Baikie. Vol. XXIV, pp. 957-1020, 46 ills., 1 page map, Sept., 1913.

Deir ez Zor, Syria:

Ali Goes to the Clinic. By Herndon and Mary Hudson. Vol. XC, pp. 764-766, 2 ills., Dec., 1946.

Delaware:

Diamond Delaware, Colonial Still: Tradition Rules the "Three Lower Counties" Over Which William Penn and Lord Baltimore Went to Law. By Leo A. Borah. Vol. LXVIII, pp. 367-398, 25 ills. in black and white, 15 ills. in color, 1 page map, Sept., 1935.

First in Statehood, Delaware Retains Its Graciousness. 15 ills. in color from natural-color photographs by B. Anthony Stewart. Vol. LXVIII, pp. 377-384, Sept., 1935.

Delectable Shrimp: Once a Culinary Stepchild, Today a Gulf Coast Industry. By Harlan Major. Vol. LXXXVI, pp. 501-512, 11 ills., 1 two-thirds-page map, Oct., 1944.

Delhi, India:

Behind New Delhi's News. 13 ills. in color from natural-color photographs by Maynard Owen Williams. Vol. LXXXII, pp. 477-484, Oct., 1942.

India at Work and Play. 22 ills. in color from natural-color photographs by Peter Upton Muir, Maynard Owen Williams, and Frances Muir. Vol. LXXXIX, pp. 449-464, Apr., 1946.

Delhi, India—*Continued*

India Mosaic. By Peter Muir and Frances Muir. Vol. LXXXIX, pp. 443-470, 5 ills. in black and white, 22 ills. in color, 1 half-page map, Apr., 1946.

New Delhi Goes Full Time. By Maynard Owen Williams. Vol. LXXXII, pp. 465-494, 17 ills. in black and white, 13 ills. in color, 1 page map, Oct., 1942.

Temples of India. 54 ills. from photographs by W. M. Zumbro. Vol. XX, pp. 922-971, Nov., 1909.

Through the Heart of Hindustan: A Teeming Highway Extending for Fifteen Hundred Miles, from the Khyber Pass to Calcutta. By Maynard Owen Williams. Vol. XL, pp. 433-467, 29 ills., Nov., 1921.

Deli, Sumatra:

By Motor Through the East Coast and Batak Highlands of Sumatra. By Melvin A. Hall. Vol. XXXVII, pp. 68-102, 27 ills., Jan., 1920.

Delos (Island), Aegean Sea:

Isles of Greece. By Lt. Richard Stillwell, USNR. Vol. LXXXV, pp. 593-622, 11 ills. in black and white, 20 ills. in color, 1 page map, May, 1944.

Delphi, Greece:

"Glory That Was Greece." By Alexander Wilbourne Weddell. Vol. XLII, pp. 571-630, 51 ills., 1 three-quarters-page map, Dec., 1922.

Delphic Festival (1930):

Festival Days on the Slopes of Mount Parnassus (Greece). 14 ills. in color from natural-color photographs by Maynard Owen Williams. Vol. LVIII, pp. 712-721, Dec., 1930.

Demavend, Mount, Iran:

Modern Persia and Its Capital: And an Account of an Ascent of Mount Demavend, the Persian Olympus. By F. L. Bird. Vol. XXXIX, pp. 353-400, 47 ills., Apr., 1921.

Democracy's Royal Palace (Westminster). 19 ills. in color from natural-color photographs by B. Anthony Stewart. Vol. XC, pp. 233-248, Aug., 1946.

Demolishing Germany's North Sea Ramparts. By Stuart E. Jones. Vol. XC, pp. 635-644, 1 ill. in black and white, 10 ills. in color, Nov., 1946.

Demon Dancers:

Demon Dancers and Butter Gods of Choni. 16 ills. in color from photographs by Joseph F. Rock. Vol. LIV, pp. 584-601, Nov., 1928.

With the Devil Dancers of China and Tibet. 43 ills. in color from natural-color photographs by Joseph F. Rock. Vol. LX, pp. 18-59, July, 1931.

Demon-Possessed Tibetans and Their Incredible Feats. 12 ills. in color from natural-color photographs. Vol. LXVIII, pp. 479-486, Oct., 1935.

Denby, Edwin:

Memorial to Peary: The National Geographic Society Dedicates Monument in Arlington National Cemetery to Discoverer of the North Pole (Address by Edwin Denby). Vol. XLI, pp. 639-646, 4 ills., June, 1922.

Deng Bao-ling:

China's Wonderland—Yen Tang Shan (Chekiang Province). 8 ills. in color from camera paintings by Herbert Clarence White, Deng Bao-ling, and Hwang Yao-tso. Vol. LXXII, pp. 687-694, Dec., 1937.

Denizens of Our Warm Atlantic Waters (Mollusks, Crustaceans, etc.). By Roy Waldo Miner. Vol. LXXI, pp. 199-219, 10 ills. in black and white, 8 ills. in color, Feb., 1937.

Denmark:

Denmark, Land of Farms and Fisheries. 14 ills. in color from natural-color photographs by Gustav Heurlin. Vol. LXI, pp. 222-231, Feb., 1932.

Denmark—Land of Tranquility. 10 ills. in color from natural-color photographs. Vol. LXXVII, pp. 17-24, Jan., 1940.

Denmark and the Danes. By Maurice Francis Egan. Vol. XLII, pp. 115-164, 38 ills., 1 three-quarters-page map, Aug., 1922.

On Danish By-Lanes: An American Cycles Through the Quaint City of Lace, the Curiosity Town Where Time Stands Still, and Even Finds a Frontier in the Farming Kingdom. By Willis Lindquist. Vol. LXXVII, pp. 1-34, 21 ills. in black and white, 10 ills. in color, 1 three-quarters-page map, Jan., 1940.

Royal Copenhagen, Capital of a Farming Kingdom: A Fifth of Denmark's Thrifty Population Resides in a Metropolis Famous for Its Porcelains, Its Silver, and Its Lace. By J. R. Hildebrand. Vol. LXI, pp. 217-250, 26 ills. in black and white, 14 ills. in color, Feb., 1932.

See also Bornholm (Island).

Dennis, Alfred Pearce:

Land of Egypt: A Narrow Green Strip of Fertility Stretching for a Thousand Miles Through Walls of Desert. By Alfred Pearce Dennis. Vol. XLIX, pp. 271-298, 28 ills., 1 half-page map, Mar., 1926.

Life on a Yukon Trail. By Alfred Pearce Dennis. Part I, Vol. X, pp. 377-391, 8 ills., 1 page map, Oct., 1899. Part II, Vol. X, pp. 457-466, 7 ills., Nov., 1899.

Norway, a Land of Stern Reality: Where Descendants of the Sea Kings of Old Triumphed Over Nature and Wrought a Nation of Arts and Crafts. By Alfred Pearce Dennis. Vol. LVIII, pp. 1-44, 31 ills. in black and white, 27 ills. in color, July, 1930.

Dent du Requin (Mountain), France:

Woman's Climbs in the High Alps. By Dora Keen. Vol. XXII, pp. 642-675, 26 ills., July, 1911.

Denver, Colorado:

Colorado, a Barrier That Became a Goal: Where Water Has Transformed Dry Plains Into Verdant Farms, and Highways Have Opened up Mineral and Scenic Wealth. By McFall Kerbey. Vol. LXII, pp. 1-63, 56 ills. in black and white, 12 ills. in color, 1 page map, July, 1932.

Depths of the Sea: Strange Life Forms a Mile Below the Surface. By William Beebe. Vol. LXI, pp. 65-88, 15 ills. in black and white, 8 ills. in color, 1 half-page map, Jan., 1932.

Descendants of Confucius (Industries in Shantung). By Maynard Owen Williams. Vol. XXXVI, pp. 253-265, 16 ills., Sept., 1919.

Desert Road to Turkestan: Twentieth Century Travel Through Innermost Asia, Along Caravan Trails Over Which Oriental Commerce Was Once Borne from China to the Medieval Western World. By Owen Lattimore. Vol. LV, pp. 661-702, 45 ills., 1 two-thirds-page map, June, 1929.

Deserts:

Africa: Cirenaica, Eastern Wing of Italian Libia. By Harriet Chalmers Adams. Vol. LVII, pp. 689-726, 35 ills. in black and white, 13 ills. in color, 1 two-thirds-page map, June, 1930.

Africa: Conquest of the Sahara by the Automobile. Vol. XLV, pp. 87-93, 9 ills., 1 three-quarters-page map, Jan., 1924.

Africa: Country of the Ant Men (Algeria). By Thomas H. Kearney. Vol. XXII, pp. 367-382, 11 ills., 1 half-page map, Apr., 1911.

Africa: Crossing the Untraversed Libyan Desert: The Record of a 2,200-Mile Journey of Exploration Which Resulted in the Discovery of Two Oases of Strategic Importance on the Southwestern Frontier of Egypt. By A. M. Hassanein. Vol. XLVI, pp. 233-277, 46 ills., 1 half-page map, Sept., 1924.

Africa: French Conquest of the Sahara. By Charles Rabot. Vol. XVI, pp. 76-80, 1 ill., Feb., 1905.

Africa: Here and There in Northern Africa (Sahara). By Frank Edward Johnson. Vol. XXV, pp. 1-132, 113 ills., Jan., 1914.

Africa: Hour of Prayer: In the Sahara Desert. Vol. XXII, supplement, Apr., 1911.

Africa: Mysteries of the Desert (Sahara). By Hanns Vischer. Vol. XXII, pp. 1056-1059, Nov., 1911.

Africa: On the Fringe of the Great Desert (Algeria). 32 ills. in color from autochromes by Gervais Courtellemont. Vol. LIII, pp. 206-223, Feb., 1928.

Africa: Three-Wheeling Through Africa: Two Adventurers Cross the So-Called Dark Continent North of Lake Chad on Motorcycles with Side Cars. By James C. Wilson. Vol. LXV, pp. 37-92, 64 ills., 1 two-page map, Jan., 1934.

Deserts—*Continued*

Africa : Through the Deserts and Jungles of Africa by Motor : Caterpillar Cars Make 15,000-Mile Trip from Algeria to Madagascar in Nine Months. By Georges-Marie Haardt. Vol. XLIX, pp. 651-720, 95 ills., 1 two-thirds-page map, June, 1926.

Africa : Timbuktu in the Sands of the Sahara. By Capt. Cecil D. Priest. Vol. XLV, pp. 73-85, 16 ills., Jan., 1924.

Africa : Time's Footprints in Tunisian Sands. By Maynard Owen Williams. Vol. LXXI, pp. 345-386, 43 ills., 1 page and 1 half-page maps, Mar., 1937.

Arabia : Guest in Saudi Arabia. By Maynard Owen Williams. Vol. LXXXVIII, pp. 463-487, 24 ills., 1 two-thirds-page map, Oct., 1945.

Arabia, the Desert of the Sea. By Archibald Forder. Vol. XX, pp. 1039-1062, 20 ills., 1 page map, Dec., 1909.

Asia : Life in the Great Desert of Central Asia. By Ellsworth Huntington. Vol. XX, pp. 749-760, 12 ills., Aug., 1909.

Australia : Lonely Australia : The Unique Continent. By Herbert E. Gregory. Vol. XXX, pp. 473-568, 68 ills., 1 two-page and 4 half-page maps, Dec., 1916.

Mexico : Camp Fires on Desert and Lava. Vol. XXI, pp. 715-718, 3 ills., Aug., 1910.

Mexico : Land of Drought and Desert—Lower California ; Two Thousand Miles on Horseback Through the Most Extraordinary Cacti Forests in the World. By E. W. Nelson. Vol. XXII, pp. 443-474, 25 ills., special supplement in color, 1 page and 1 half-page maps, May, 1911.

Mongolia : Desert Road to Turkestan : Twentieth Century Travel Through Innermost Asia, Along Caravan Trails Over Which Oriental Commerce Was Once Borne from China to the Medieval Western World. By Owen Lattimore. Vol. LV, pp. 661-702, 45 ills., 1 two-thirds-page map, June, 1929.

Mongolia : Lama's Motor-Car : A Trip Across the Gobi Desert by Motor-Car. By Ethan C. Le Munyon. Vol. XXIV, pp. 640-670, 34 ills., May, 1913.

United States : American Deserts. Vol. XV, pp. 152-163, 7 ills., 1 half-page map, Apr., 1904.

United States : Arizona Sands, Home of the Cactus King. 11 ills. from photographs. Vol. LXXI, pp. 521-528, Apr., 1937.

United States : Canyon and Cacti of the American Southwest. 22 ills. in color from natural-color photographs by Jacob Gayer, Charles Martin, and Edwin L. Wisherd. Vol. XLVIII, pp. 275-290, Sept., 1925.

United States : Carrying Water Through a Desert : The Story of the Los Angeles Aqueduct. By Burt A. Heinly. Vol. XXI, pp. 568-596, 19 ills., 1 half-page map, July, 1910.

United States : Colorado Desert. By W. C. Mendenhall. Vol. XX, pp. 681-701, 16 ills., Aug., 1909.

Deserts—*Continued*

United States : Deserts of Nevada and the Death Valley. By Robert H. Chapman. Vol. XVII, pp. 482-497, 9 ills., 1 chart, Sept., 1906.

United States : Fantastic Plants of Our Western Deserts. 8 ills. by Frank M. Campbell. Vol. XLV, pp. 33-40, Jan., 1924.

United States : Is Climatic Aridity Impending on the Pacific Slope ? The Testimony of the Forest. By J. B. Leiberg. Vol. X, pp. 160-181, May, 1899.

United States : Notes on the Deserts of the United States and Mexico (Extracted from a Publication of Dr. Daniel T. MacDougal). Vol. XXI, pp. 691-714, 16 ills., Aug., 1910.

United States : Saguaro, Cactus Camel of Arizona. By Forrest Shreve. Vol. LXXXVIII, pp. 695-704, 9 ills. in color, Dec., 1945.

United States : Saguaro, King of the Arizona Desert. 9 ills. in color from natural-color photographs by Esther Henderson, Jack Breed, and Max Kegley. Vol. LXXXVIII, pp. 697-704, Dec., 1945.

United States : Saguaro Forest (Arizona). By H. L. Shantz. Vol. LXXI, pp. 515-532, 18 ills., Apr., 1937.

United States : Scenery of North America. By James Bryce. Vol. XLI, pp. 339-389, 45 ills., Apr., 1922.

United States : Southwest : Its Splendid Natural Resources, Agricultural Wealth and Scenic Beauty. By N. H. Darton. Vol. XXI, pp. 631-665, 21 ills., 1 page map, Aug., 1910.

See also Reclamation of Land.

De Sieyes, (Capt.) Jacques:

Aces of the Air. By Capt. Jacques De Sieyes. Vol. XXXIII, pp. 5-9, 2 ills., Jan., 1918.

Desolate Greenland, Now an American Outpost. 17 ills. from photographs ; 12 ills. by Willie Knutsen ; 4 ills. by F. Vogel. Vol. LXXX, pp. 393-406, Sept., 1941.

Destruction of Pompeii as Interpreted by the Volcanic Eruptions of Martinique. By Angelo Heilprin. Vol. XV, p. 431, Oct., 1904.

Detroit, Michigan :

Michigan Fights. By Harvey Klemmer. Vol. LXXXVI, pp. 677-715, 20 ills. in black and white, 19 ills. in color, 1 page-and-a-half map, Dec., 1944.

Devastated Poland. By Frederic C. Walcott. Vol. XXXI, pp. 445-452, 7 ills., May, 1917.

Development of Nevada. Vol. XV, p. 166, Apr., 1904.

Devil-Fishing in the Gulf Stream. By John Oliver La Gorce. Vol. XXXV, pp. 476-488, 7 ills., June, 1919.

Deville Névé (Glacier), British Columbia :

Some Tramps Across the Glaciers and Snowfields of British Columbia. By Howard Palmer. Vol. XXI, pp. 457-487, 25 ills., June, 1910.

Devon (County), England:

Down Devon Lanes. By Herbert Corey. Vol. LV, pp. 529-568, 45 ills., 1 two-thirds-page map, May, 1929.

See also Bampton; Clovelly.

Dew:

Magic Beauty of Snow and Dew. By Wilson A. Bentley. Vol. XLIII, pp. 103-112, 9 ills., Jan., 1923.

Dewey, (Adm.) George:

Election of Admiral Dewey as Honorary Member of The Society. Vol. XVIII, p. 51, Jan., 1907.

Diamond Delaware, Colonial Still: Tradition Rules the "Three Lower Counties" Over Which William Penn and Lord Baltimore Went to Law. By Leo A. Borah. Vol. LXVIII, pp. 367-398, 25 ills. in black and white, 15 ills. in color, 1 page map, Sept., 1935.

Diamond Mines:

Diamond Mines of South Africa. By Gardiner F. Williams. Vol. XVII, pp. 344-356, 11 ills., June, 1906.

Under the South African Union. By Melville Chater. Vol. LIX, pp. 391-512, 97 ills. in black and white, 38 ills. in color, 1 two-page map, Apr., 1931.

Diamond Mountains, Korea:

In the Diamond Mountains: Adventures Among the Buddhist Monasteries of Eastern Korea. By Marquess Curzon of Kedleston. Vol. XLVI, pp. 353-374, 21 ills., 1 quarter-page map, Oct., 1924.

Diana (Ship):

Mission of the *Diana* (Peary Arctic Club). Vol. X, p. 273, July, 1899.

Peary's Explorations in 1898-1899. Vol. X, pp. 415-416, Oct., 1899.

Diary of a Voyage from San Francisco to Tahiti and Return, 1901. By S. P. Langley. Vol. XII, pp. 412-429, 10 ills., 1 page and 1 half-page maps, Dec., 1901.

Dieppe, France:

Rehearsal at Dieppe. By W. Robert Moore. Vol. LXXXII, pp. 495-502, 6 ills., Oct., 1942.

Dikes:

Dikes of Holland. By Gerard H. Matthes. Vol. XII, pp. 219-234, 3 ills., 7 charts, June, 1901.

Mending Dikes in the Netherlands. 20 ills. from photographs by Lawrence Earl. Vol. XC, pp. 791-806, Dec., 1946.

Diller, J. S.:

Volcanic Rocks of Martinique and St. Vincent: Collected by Robert T. Hill and Israel C. Russell. By J. S. Diller. Vol. XIII, pp. 285-296, July, 1902.

Dillon, Raymond A.:

War Finds Its Way to Gilbert Islands: United States Forces Dislodge Japanese from Enchanted Atolls Which Loom Now as Stepping Stones along South Sea Route from Australia to Hawaii. By Sir Arthur Grimble. Photographs by Dr. Raymond A. Dillon. Vol. LXXXIII, pp. 71-92, 19 ills., 1 half-page map, Jan., 1943.

Dinkas (Tribespeople):

Across Widest Africa. By. A. Henry Savage Landor. Vol. XIX, pp. 694-737, 38 ills., 1 half-page map, Oct. 1908.

Dinkelsbühl (Germany), Romantic Vision From the Past. Vol. LX, pp. 689-702, 4 ills. in black and white, 12 ills. in color, Dec., 1931.

Dinosaurs:

Hunting Big Game of Other Days: A Boating Expedition in Search of Fossils in Alberta, Canada. By Barnum Brown. Vol. XXXV, pp. 407-429, 24 ills., 1 page map, May, 1919.

Parade of Life Through the Ages: Records in Rocks Reveal a Strange Procession of Prehistoric Creatures, from Jellyfish to Dinosaurs, Giant Sloths, Saber-toothed Tigers, and Primitive Man. By Charles R. Knight. With 24 ills. in color from paintings by the author. Vol. LXXXI, pp. 141-184, 13 ills. in black and white, Feb., 1942.

Contains descriptions and colored illustrations of the following: Ceratosaurus, Diplodocus, Parasaurolophus, Protoceratops, Stegosaurus, Styracosaurus, *Tyrannosaurus rex*.

Dipo, the Little Desert "Kangaroo." By Walter E. Ketcham. Vol. LXXVIII, pp. 537-548, 14 ills., Oct., 1940.

Directory of Officers and Counsellors of Geographic Societies of the United States. Vol. XIV, pp. 392-394, Oct., 1903.

Discoverers:

American Pathfinders in the Pacific. By William H. Nicholas. Vol. LXXXIX, pp. 617-640, 17 ills., 1 two-page map, May, 1946.

Columbus, Christopher: Fate Directs the Faltering Footsteps of Columbus. Reproduction in color of the painting by Alfred Dehodencq, Paris. Vol. LIV, supplement, Sept., 1928.

Cook, (Capt.) James: Columbus of the Pacific: Captain James Cook, Foremost British Navigator, Expanded the Great Sea to Correct Proportions and Won for Albion an Insular Empire by Peaceful Exploration and Scientific Study. By J. R. Hildebrand. Vol. LI, pp. 85-132, 45 ills., 1 page and 1 three-quarters-page maps, Jan., 1927.

The Discoverer. Reproduction in color of the painting by N. C. Wyeth, National Geographic Society, Washington, D. C. Vol. LIII, text, p. 347; supplement, Mar., 1928.

Discoverers—*Continued*

Gama, Vasco da : Pathfinder of the East : Setting Sail to Find "Christians and Spices," Vasco da Gama Met Amazing Adventures, Founded an Empire, and Changed the History of Western Europe. By J. R. Hildebrand. Vol. LII, pp. 503-550, 43 ills., 1 two-thirds-page map, Nov., 1927.

Gama, Vasco da : Vasco da Gama at the Court of the Zamorin of Calicut. Reproductions in color of the painting by José Velloso Salgado, Sociedade de Geographia de Lisboa. Vol. LII, supplement, Nov., 1927.

Henry Hudson, Magnificent Failure : Just 330 Years Ago He and His Mutinous Crew Found Manhattan Covered With "Goodly Oakes" and Fought Indians in New York Harbor. By Frederick G. Vosburgh. Vol. LXXV, pp. 461-490, 21 ills., Apr., 1939.

Magellan, Ferdinand : Greatest Voyage in the Annals of the Sea. By J. R. Hildebrand. Vol. LXII, pp. 699-739, 35 ills., 2 half-page maps, Dec., 1932.

Revealing Earth's Mightiest Ocean (Pacific). By Albert W. Atwood. Vol. LXXXIV, pp. 291-306, 10 ills., special map supplement, Sept., 1943.

See also Agricultural and Botanical Explorers ; Antarctic Regions ; Arctic Regions ; Geography ; National Geographic Society : Expeditions ; *and* Voyages.

Discovering Alaska's Oldest Arctic Town (Ipiutak) : A Scientist Finds Ivory-eyed Skeletons of a Mysterious People and Joins Modern Eskimos in the Dangerous Spring Whale Hunt. By Froelich G. Rainey. Vol. LXXXII, pp. 319-336, 15 ills., Sept., 1942.

Discovering the New World's Oldest Dated Work of Man : A Maya Monument Inscribed 291 B. C. is Unearthed Near a Huge Stone Head by a Geographic-Smithsonian Expedition in Mexico. By Matthew W. Stirling. Vol. LXXVI, pp. 183-218, 40 ills., 1 half-page map, Aug., 1939.

Discovering the Oldest Statues in the World : A Daring Explorer Swims Through a Subterranean River of the Pyrenees and Finds Rock Carvings Made 20,000 Years Ago. By Norbert Casteret. Vol. XLVI, pp. 123-152. 24 ills., 1 half and 1 quarter-page maps, Aug., 1924.

Discovery (Ship) :

Heart of the Antarctic. By Ernest H. Shackleton. Vol. XX, pp. 972-1007, 27 ills., 1 half-page map, Nov., 1909.

Discovery and Invention. By Alexander Graham Bell. Vol. XXV, pp. 649-655, June, 1914.

Discovery of Cancer in Plants. Vol. XXIV, pp. 53-70, 12 ills., Jan., 1913.

Discovery of the North Pole. Vol. XXI, pp. 63-82, Jan., 1910.

Discovery of the Pole (First Reports by Peary and Cook). Vol. XX, pp. 892-896, 11 ills., 1 page map, Oct., 1909.

Diseases :

Ali Goes to the Clinic. By Herndon and Mary Hudson. Vol. XC, pp. 764-766, 2 ills., Dec., 1946.

Amid the Snow Peaks of the Equator : A Naturalist's Explorations Around Ruwenzori, with an Excursion to the Congo State, and an Account of the Terrible Scourge of Sleeping Sickness. By A. F. R. Wollaston. Vol. XX, pp. 256-277, 11 ills., Mar., 1909.

Changing Map of the Balkans. By Frederick Moore. Vol. XXIV, pp. 199-226, 27 ills., 1 page map, Feb., 1913.

Conquest of Bubonic Plague in the Philippines. Vol. XIV, pp. 185-195, 7 ills., May, 1903.

Discovery of Cancer in Plants. Vol. XXIV, pp. 53-70, 12 ills., Jan., 1913.

Diseases of the Philippines. Vol. XI, pp. 123-124, Mar., 1900.

Economic Loss to the People of the United States Through Insects That Carry Disease. By L. O. Howard. Vol. XX, pp. 735-749. Aug., 1909.

Fearful Famines of the Past : History Will Repeat Itself Unless the American People Conserve Their Resources. By Ralph A. Graves. Vol. XXXII, pp. 68-90, 11 ills., July, 1917.

History and Geographic Distribution of Bubonic Plague. By George M. Sternberg. Vol. XI, pp. 97-113, Mar., 1900.

Life Story of the Mosquito. By Graham Fairchild. With 10 ills. in color from paintings. Vol. LXXXV, pp. 180-195, 5 ills. in black and white, 1 drawing, Feb., 1944.

Map-Changing Medicine. By William Joseph Showalter. Vol. XLII, pp. 303-330, 26 ills., Sept., 1922.

Our Army Versus a Bacillus. Vol. XXIV, pp. 1146-1152, 5 ills., 1 diagram, Oct., 1913.

Redeeming the Tropics. By William Joseph Showalter. Vol. XXV, pp. 344-364, 13 ills., Mar., 1914.

Saboteur Mosquitoes. By Harry H. Stage. Vol. LXXXV, pp. 165-179, 12 ills., Feb., 1944.

Tracking the Columbian Ground-Squirrel to Its Burrow : Loss of Millions to Crops and Danger of the Spread of Spotted Fever Necessitated Study of Peculiar Rodent of Western North America. By William T. Shaw. Vol. XLVII, pp. 587-596, 13 ills., May, 1925.

See also Sanitation.

Dismal Swamp in Legend and History : George Washington Owned Large Tracts in Region Which He Described as a "Glorious Paradise." By John Francis Ariza. Vol. LXII, pp. 121-130, 11 ills., July, 1932.

District of Columbia. *See* Washington, D. C.

Ditmars, Raymond L. :

Reptiles of All Lands. By Raymond L. Ditmars. Vol. XXII, pp. 601-633, 32 ills., July 1911.

Diving, Ocean :

On the Bottom of a South Sea Pearl Lagoon. By Roy Waldo Miner. Vol. LXXIV, pp. 365-390, 17 ills. in black and white, 8 ills. in color, Sept., 1938.

Round Trip to Davy Jones's Locker : Peering into Mysteries a Quarter Mile Down in the Open Sea, by Means of the Bathysphere. By William Beebe. Vol. LIX, pp. 653-678, 14 ills. in black and white, 8 ills. in color, 1 quarter-page map, June, 1931.

Sea Floor Aquarelles from Tongareva. 8 ills. in color from paintings by Else Bostelmann. Vol. LXXIV, pp. 383-390, Sept., 1938.

Wonderer Under Sea. By William Beebe. Vol. LXII, pp. 741-758, 13 ills. in black and white, 8 ills. in color, Dec., 1932.

Dixon, Joseph:

Wild Ducks as Winter Guests in a City Park. By Joseph Dixon. Vol. XXXVI, pp. 331-342, 11 ills., Oct., 1919.

Djakarta, Java. *See* Batavia.

Do Volcanic Explosions Affect Our Climate? By C. G. Abbot. Vol. XXIV, pp. 181-198, 9 ills., 1 diagram, Feb., 1913.

Do Your Bit for America : A Proclamation by President Wilson to the American People. By Woodrow Wilson. Vol. XXXI, pp. 287-293, 2 ills., Apr., 1917.

Dobie, J. Frank:

A Texan Teaches American History at Cambridge University. By J. Frank Dobie. Vol. LXXXIX, pp. 409-441, 9 ills. in black and white, 19 ills. in color, Apr., 1946.

Docks, Floating Dry :

Your Navy as Peace Insurance. By Fleet Admiral Chester W. Nimitz. Vol. LXXXIX, pp. 681-736, 32 ills. in black and white, 26 ills. in color, June, 1946.

Dr. Bell's Man-Lifting Kite. By Gilbert H. Grosvenor. Vol. XIX, pp. 35-52, 27 ills., Jan., 1908.

Dr. Bell's Tetrahedral Tower. By Gilbert H. Grosvenor. Vol. XVIII, pp. 671-675, 7 ills., Oct., 1907.

Dodd, Isabel F.:

Ancient Capital (Boghaz Keui, Turkey). By Isabel F. Dodd. Vol. XXI, pp. 111-124, 11 ills., Feb., 1910.

Dodecanese Islands, Aegean Sea :

Historic Islands and Shores of the Aegean Sea. By Ernest L. Harris. Vol. XXVIII, pp. 231-262, 29 ills., 1 half-page map, Sept., 1915.

Rhodes, and Italy's Aegean Islands. By Dorothy Hosmer. Vol. LXXIX, pp. 449-480, 32 ills., 1 map, Apr., 1941.

See also Rhodes (Island).

Dodge, Richard E.:

Teaching of Physical Geography in Elementary Schools. By Richard E. Dodge. Vol. XI, pp. 470-475, Dec., 1900.

Doe and Twin Fawns. Vol. XXIV, special supplement, July, 1913. Vol. LXXVI, ill. 475, Oct., 1939.

Dogs:

Animals Were Allies, Too. 16 ills. from photographs. Vol. LXXXIX, pp. 75-88, Jan., 1946.

Dogs in Toyland. 16 ills. in color from natural-color photographs by Willard R. Culver. Vol. LXXXV, pp. 473-480, Apr., 1944.

Dogs of Duty and Devotion. By Frederick G. Vosburgh. Vol. LXXX, pp. 769-774, 3 ills., Dec., 1941.

Field Dogs in Action. By Freeman Lloyd. Paintings by Edward Herbert Miner. Vol. LXXI, pp. 85-108, 8 ills. in black and white, 36 portraits in color, Jan., 1937.

Contains descriptions and illustrations of the following breeds : Chesapeake Bay Retriever, Clumber Spaniel, Cocker Spaniel, Curly-coated Retriever, Dachshund, English Setter, English Springer Spaniel, Field Spaniel, Flat-coated Retriever, German Short-haired Pointer, Golden Retriever, Gordon Setter, Irish Red Setter, Irish Water Spaniel, Labrador Retriever, Pointer, Sussex Spaniel, Wire-haired Pointing Griffon.

Gallant Little Sportsmen of the Terrier Tribe. 33 portraits in color from paintings by Edward Herbert Miner. Vol. LXIX, pp. 253-268, Feb., 1936.

Hark to the Hounds. By Freeman Lloyd. Paintings by Edward Herbert Miner. Vol. LXXII, pp. 453-484, 18 ills. in black and white, 31 portraits in color, Oct., 1937.

Contains descriptions and illustrations of the following breeds : Afghan Hound, American Foxhound, Basset Hound, Beagle, Bloodhound, Borzoi, or Russian Wolfhound, Deerhound, English Foxhound, Greyhound, Harrier, Irish Wolfhound, Otterhound, Rampur Hound, Saluki, Welsh Foxhound, Whippet.

Hunters All : A Roll Call of the Hounds. 31 portraits in color from paintings by Edward Herbert Miner. Vol. LXXII, pp. 467-482, Oct., 1937.

Lure of the Frozen Desert (Polar Regions). Vol. XXIII, panorama, Dec., 1912.

Mankind's Best Friend : Companion of His Solitude, Advance Guard in the Hunt, and Ally of the Trenches. By Ernest Harold Baynes. Vol. XXXV, pp. 185-201, 11 ills., Mar., 1919.

Man's Hunting Partner, the Field Dog. 36 portraits in color from paintings by Edward Herbert Miner. Vol. LXXI, pp. 89-104, Jan., 1937.

Man's Oldest Ally, the Dog : Since Cave-Dweller Days This Faithful Friend Has Shared the Work, Exploration, and Sport of Humankind. By Freeman Lloyd. Paintings by Edward Herbert Miner. Vol. LXIX, pp. 247-274, 13 ills. in black and white, 33 portraits in color, Feb., 1936.

Dogs—*Continued*

Contains descriptions and illustrations of the following breeds: Airedale Terrier, Bedlington Terrier, Bull Terrier, Cairn Terrier, Dandie Dinmont Terrier, Irish Terrier, Kerry Blue Terrier, Lakeland Terrier, Manchester Terrier, Miniature Schnauzer, Scottish Terrier, Sealyham Terrier, Skye Terrier, Smooth Fox Terrier, Standard Schnauzer, Welsh Terrier, West Highland White Terrier, and Wirehaired Fox Terrier.

Non-sporting Dogs. By Freeman Lloyd. Paintings by Walter A. Weber. Vol. LXXXIV, pp. 569-588, 9 ills. in black and white, 8 ills. in color from paintings from life, Nov., 1943.

Contains descriptions and colored illustrations of the following breeds: Boston Terrier, Chow, Dalmatian, English Bulldog, French Bulldog, Keeshond, Poodle, Schipperke.

Other Working Dogs and the Wild Species. By Stanley P. Young. Paintings by Walter A. Weber. Vol. LXXXVI, pp. 363-384, 12 ills. in black and white, 9 ills. in color, Sept., 1944.

Our Common Dogs. By Louis Agassiz Fuertes and Ernest Harold Baynes. Vol. XXXV, pp. 201-253, 73 ills. in color, Mar., 1919.

Contains descriptions and illustrations of the following breeds: Basset, Beagle, Belgian Shepherd, Bloodhound, Brussels Griffon, Bulldogs, Chihuahua, Chow, Collies, Dachshund, Dalmatian, English Sheep-Dog, Eskimo, Foxhound, German Police, Great Dane, Greyhound, Irish Wolfhound, Mastiff, Mexican Hairless, Newfoundland, Norwegian Elkhound, Otterhound, Pekingese, Persian Gazellehound, Pointer, Pomeranian, Poodles, Pug, Pyrenean Sheep-Dog, Retrievers, Russian Wolfhound, St. Bernard, Samoyed, Schipperke, Scottish Deerhound, Setters, Spaniels, Spitz, Terriers, Whippet.

Sagacity and Courage of Dogs: Instances of the Remarkable Intelligence and Unselfish Devotion of Man's Best Friend Among Dumb Animals. Vol. XXXV, pp. 253-275, 14 ills., Mar., 1919.

Sheep Dog Trials in Llangollen: Trained Collies Perform Marvels of Herding in the Cambrian Stakes, Open to the World. By Sara Bloch. Vol. LXXVII, pp. 559-574, 17 ills., Apr., 1940.

Sheep-Killers—The Pariahs of Dogkind. Vol. XXXV, pp. 275-280, 3 ills., Mar., 1919.

Toy Dogs, Pets of Kings and Commoners. By Freeman Lloyd. Vol. LXXXV, pp. 459-480, 8 ills. in black and white, 16 ills. in color, Apr., 1944.

Wild Dogs and Working Dogs. 9 ills. in color from paintings by Walter A. Weber. Vol. LXXXVI, pp. 369-376, Sept., 1944.

Working Dogs of the World. By Freeman Lloyd. Paintings by Edward Herbert Miner. Vol. LXXX, pp. 776-806, 12 ills. in black and white, 20 ills. in color, Dec., 1941.

Dogs—*Continued*

Contains descriptions and colored illustrations of the following breeds: Alaskan Malemute, Australian Kelpie, Belgian Sheep Dog, Bouvier de Flandres, Boxer, Briard, Bull Mastiff, Collie, Doberman Pinscher, Eskimo, German Shepherd, Giant Schnauzer, Great Dane, Great Pyrenees, Kuvasz, Mastiff, Newfoundland, Norwegian Elkhound, Old English Sheep Dog, Rottweiler, St. Bernard, Samoyede, Shetland Sheep Dog, Siberian Husky, Welsh Corgi.

Your Dog Joins Up. By Frederick Simpich. Vol. LXXXIII, pp. 93-113, 25 ills., Jan., 1943.

Dolan, (Capt.) Brooke, 2d:

Across Tibet from India to China. By Lt. Col. Ilia Tolstoy, AUS. Vol. XC, pp. 169-222, 41 ills., 1 half-page map, Aug., 1946.

Dolomites (Mountains), Italy:

Land of Contrast: Austria-Hungary. By D. W. and A. S. Iddings. Vol. XXIII, pp. 1188-1218, 34 ills., Dec., 1912.

Dolphins (Mammals):

Whales, Giants of the Sea: Wonder Mammals, Biggest Creatures of All Time, Show Tender Affection for Young, But Can Maim or Swallow Human Hunters. By Remington Kellogg. Vol. LXXVII, pp. 35-90, 25 ills. in black and white, 31 ills. in color, Jan., 1940.

Whales, Porpoises, and Dolphins. 31 ills. in color from paintings by Else Bostelmann. Vol. LXXVII, pp. 41-80, Jan., 1940.

Domestic Fowls of Field, Park, and Farmyard. 16 ills. in color from paintings by Hashime Murayama. Vol. LVII, pp. 329-360, Mar., 1930.

Dominica (Island), West Indies:

British West Indian Interlude. By Anne Rainey Langley. Vol. LXXIX, pp. 1-46, 23 ills. in black and white, 21 ills. in color, 2 page maps, Jan., 1941.

Report by Robert T. Hill on Volcanic Disturbances in the West Indies. Vol. XIII, pp. 223-267, 13 ills., 2 half and 1 quarter-page maps, July, 1902.

West Indies Links in a Defense Chain. 21 ills. in color from natural-color photographs; 20 ills. by Edwin L. Wisherd. Vol. LXXIX, pp. 9-32, Jan., 1941.

Dominican Republic:

Arbitration Treaties. By William Howard Taft. Vol. XXII, pp. 1165-1172, Dec., 1911.

Dominican Republic, Land of Plenty. 11 ills. in color from natural-color photographs by B. Anthony Stewart. Vol. LXXXV, pp. 209-216, Feb., 1944.

Haiti: A Degenerating Island. By Rear Adm. Colby M. Chester. Vol. XIX, pp. 200-217, 5 ills., 1 quarter-page map, Mar., 1908.

Haiti, the Home of Twin Republics. By Sir Harry Johnston. Vol. XXXVIII, pp. 483-496, 11 ills., 1 third-page map, Dec., 1920.

Dominican Republic—*Continued*

Hispaniola Rediscovered. By Jacob Gayer. Vol. LIX, pp. 80-112, 12 ills. in black and white, 28 ills. in color, Jan., 1931.

Land Columbus Loved. By Oliver P. Newman. Vol. LXXXV, pp. 197-224, 15 ills. in black and white, 11 ills. in color, 1 two-thirds-page map, Feb., 1944.

Scenic Resources of the Dominican Republic. By Jacob Gayer. Vol. LIX, pp. 80-105, Jan., 1931.

Wards of the United States : Notes on What Our Country Is Doing for Santo Domingo, Nicaragua, and Haiti. Vol. XXX, pp. 143-177, 36 ills., Aug., 1916.

Dorjun (Ship) :

Inside Cape Horn. By Amos Burg. Vol. LXXII, pp. 743-783, 29 ills. in black and white, 10 ills. in color, 1 two-page map, Dec., 1937.

Dorr, George B.:

Unique Island of Mount Desert. By George B. Dorr, M. L. Fernald, and Ernest Howe Forbush. Vol. XXVI, pp. 75-89, 7 ills., July, 1914.

Dorsett, J. H.:

Mount Vernon : Home of the First Farmer of America. 3 ills. in color from autochromes by J. H. Dorsett. Vol. LIII, pp. 604-621, May, 1928.

Peacetime Plant Hunting About Peiping. By P. H. and J. H. Dorsett. Vol. LXXII, pp. 509-534, 21 ills., 1 two-thirds-page map, Oct., 1937.

Dorsett, P. H.:

Peacetime Plant Hunting About Peiping. By P. H. and J. H. Dorsett. Vol. LXXII, pp. 509-534, 21 ills., 1 two-thirds-page map, Oct., 1937.

Doubtful Island of the Pacific. By James D. Hague. Vol. XV, pp. 478-489, 1 ill., 2 page maps, Dec., 1904.

Douglass, Andrew Ellicott:

Secret of the Southwest Solved by Talkative Tree Rings : Horizons of American History Are Carried Back to A. D. 700 and a Calendar for 1,200 Years Established by National Geographic Society Expeditions. By Andrew Ellicott Douglass. Vol. LVI, pp. 737-770, 33 ills., 1 two-thirds-page map, Dec., 1929.

Douirat, Tunisia :

Mole Men : An Account of the Troglodytes of Southern Tunisia. By Frank Edward Johnson. Vol. XXII, pp. 787-846, 60 ills., Sept., 1911.

Dovekies (Birds) :

Birds of the Northern Seas. By Alexander Wetmore. Paintings by Maj. Allan Brooks. Vol. LXIX, pp. 95-122, 12 ills. in black and white, 34 portraits in color, Jan., 1936.

Dover, England :

Front-line Town of Britain's Siege. By Harvey Klemmer. Vol. LXXXV, pp. 105-128, 21 ills., Jan., 1944.

Doves:

Game Birds of Prairie, Forest, and Tundra. By Alexander Wetmore. Vol. LXX, pp. 461-500, 5 ills. in black and white, 60 portraits in color, Oct., 1936.

Down Devon Lanes. By Herbert Corey. Vol. LV, pp. 529-568, 45 ills., 1 two-thirds-page map, May, 1929.

Down Idaho's River of No Return (Salmon River). By Philip J. Shenon and John C. Reed. Vol. LXX, pp. 95-136, 43 ills., 1 page and 1 two-thirds-page maps, July, 1936.

Down Mexico's Río Balsas. By John W. Webber. With 9 ills. in color from natural-color photographs by the author, Kenneth Segerstrom, and Jack Breed. Vol. XC, pp. 253-272, 5 ills. in black and white, 1 half-page map, Aug., 1946.

Down the Rio Grande : Tracing this Strange, Turbulent Stream on Its Long Course from Colorado to the Gulf of Mexico. By Frederick Simpich. Vol. LXXVI, pp. 415-462, 28 ills. in black and white, 24 ills. in color, 6 maps, Oct., 1939.

Doyle, C. B.:

Notes on Southern Mexico (Agricultural Products). By C. B. Doyle and G. N. Collins. Vol. XXII, pp. 301-320, 16 ills., 1 half-page map, Mar., 1911.

Dragon Lizards:

Modern Dragon Hunt on Komodo : An English Yachting Party Traps and Photographs the Huge and Carnivorous Dragon Lizard of the Lesser Sundas. By Lady Broughton. Vol. LXX, pp. 321-331, 12 ills. in duotone, Sept., 1936.

Stalking the Dragon Lizard on the Island of Komodo. By W. Douglas Burden. Vol. LII, pp. 216-232, 21 ills., Aug., 1927.

Drainage. *See* Reclamation of Land.

Drainage of Wet Lands. Vol. XVII, pp. 713-714, Dec., 1906.

Draper, (Lt.) William F.:

Jungle War : Bougainville and New Caledonia. 17 ills. in color from paintings by Lieut. William F. Draper. Vol. LXXXV, pp. 417-432, Apr., 1944.

Navy Artist Paints the Aleutians. 16 ills. in color from paintings by Lt. William F. Draper. Vol. LXXXIV, pp. 161-176, Aug., 1943.

Painting History in the Pacific. 19 ills. in color from paintings by Lt. William F. Draper. Vol. LXXXVI, pp. 409-424, Oct., 1944.

Victory's Portrait in the Marianas. By Lt. William Franklin Draper, USNR. With 17 ills. in color from paintings by the author. Vol. LXXXVIII, pp. 599-616, Nov., 1945.

Dream Ship : The Story of a Voyage of Adventure More Than Half Around the World in a 47-Foot Lifeboat. By Ralph Stock. Vol. XXXIX, pp. 1-52, 43 ills., 1 page map, Jan., 1921.

Drift of Floating Bottles in the Pacific Ocean. By James Page. Vol. XII, pp. 337-339, Sept., 1901.

Drifting Across the Pole. Vol. XVII, pp. 40-42, 1 ill., Jan., 1906.

Driggs, Laurence La Tourette:

Aces Among Aces. By Laurence La Tourette Driggs. Vol. XXXIII, pp. 568-580, 9 ills., June, 1918.

Drowned Empire (Swamp Drainage). By Robert H. Chapman. Vol. XIX, pp. 190-199, 10 ills., Mar., 1908.

Druses (People) :

Syria and Lebanon Taste Freedom. By Maynard Owen Williams. With 21 ills. in color from natural-color photographs by the author. Vol. XC, pp. 729-763, 16 ills. in black and white, Dec., 1946.

Dry Tortugas Islands, Gulf of Mexico :

First Autochromes from the Ocean Bottom! Marine Life in Its Natural Habitat Along the Florida Keys Is Successfully Photographed in Colors.. Vol. LI, pp. 56-60, 8 ills. in color, Jan., 1927.

Life on a Coral Reef : The Fertility and Mystery of the Sea Studied Beneath the Waters Surrounding Dry Tortugas. By W. H. Longley. Vol. LI, pp. 61-83, 22 ills. in black and white, 8 ills. in color, Jan., 1927.

Du Bois, Arthur E.:

Heraldry of Heroism. By Arthur E. Du Bois. Vol. LXXXIV, pp. 409-413, 2 ills., 1 third-page map, Oct., 1943.

Traditions and Glamour of Insignia. By Arthur E. Du Bois. Vol. LXXXIII, pp. 652-655, 3 ills., June, 1943.

Du Chaillu, Paul:

Paul Du Chaillu (Biography). Vol. XIV, pp. 282-285, July, 1903.

Ducks:

American Game Birds. By Henry Wetherbee Henshaw. Vol. XXVIII, pp. 105-158, 4 ills. in black and white, 72 ills. in color, Aug., 1915.

Domestic Fowls of Field, Park, and Farmyard. 6 ills. in color from paintings by Hashime Murayama. Vol. LVII, pp. 328-361, Mar., 1930.

Far-Flying Wild Fowl and Their Foes. By Maj. Allan Brooks. Vol. LXVI, pp. 487-528, 6 ills. in black and white, 74 portraits in color, Oct., 1934.

Fowls of Forest and Stream Tamed by Man. By Morley A. Jull. Vol. LVII, pp. 327-371, 27 ills. in black and white, 16 ills. in color, Mar., 1930.

Contains descriptions and illustrations of the following species : Aylesbury, Black East India, Blue Swedish, Buff, Cayuga, Crested White, Gray Call, Khaki Campbell, Muscovy, Pekin, Rouen, Runner.

Saving the Ducks and Geese. By Wells W. Cooke. Vol. XXIV, pp. 361-380, 7 ills., 7 half-page maps, Feb., 1913.

Ducks—*Continued*

Wild Ducks as Winter Guests in a City Park. By Joseph Dixon. Vol. XXXVI, pp. 331-342, 11 ills., Oct., 1919.

Wild Geese, Ducks, and Swans. 74 portraits in color from paintings by Maj. Allan Brooks. Vol. LXVI, pp. 493-524, Oct., 1934.

Wild Life of the Atlantic and Gulf Coasts : A Field Naturalist's Photographic Record of Nearly Half a Century of Fruitful Exploration. By George Shiras, 3d. Vol. LXII, pp. 261-309, 62 ills., Sept., 1932.

Dug-Gye Jong (Fort), Bhutan :

Castles in the Air—Experiences and Journeys in Unknown Bhutan. By John Claude White. Vol. XXV, pp. 365-455, 75 ills., 1 page map, Apr., 1914.

Dugmore, A. Radclyffe:

Camera Adventures in the African Wilds. By A. Radclyffe Dugmore. Vol. XXI, pp. 385-396, 11 ills., May, 1910.

Duke of the Abruzzi in the Himalayas. Vol. XXI, pp. 245-249, Mar., 1910.

Dumboy, the National Dish of Liberia. By G. N. Collins. Vol. XXII, pp. 84-88, 5 ills., Jan., 1911.

Dumont D'Urville, Jules Sebastien César:

Wilkes' and D'Urville's Discoveries in Wilkes Land. By Rear Adm. John Elliott Pillsbury. Vol. XXI, pp. 171-173, Feb., 1910.

Dunant, Henri:

Symbol of Service to Mankind. By Stockton Axson. Vol. XXXIII, pp. 375-390, 11 ills., Apr., 1918.

Duncan, David D.:

Capturing Giant Turtles in the Caribbean. By David D. Duncan. Vol. LXXXIV, pp. 177-190, 13 ills., 1 quarter-page map, Aug., 1943.

Coffee Is King in El Salvador. 27 ills. in color from natural-color photographs by Luis Marden and David D. Duncan. Vol. LXXXVI, pp. 585-616, Nov., 1944.

Fighting Giants of the Humboldt (Fish and Squid). By David D. Duncan. Vol. LXXIX, pp. 373-400, 28 ills., 1 half-page map, Mar., 1941.

Fiji Patrol on Bougainville. By David D. Duncan. Vol. LXXXVII, pp. 87-104, 9 ills. in black and white, 11 ills. in color, Jan., 1945.

Okinawa, Threshold to Japan. By Lt. David D. Duncan, USMC. With 22 ills. in color from natural-color photographs by the author and others. Vol. LXXXVIII, pp. 411-428, Oct., 1945.

Yap Meets the Yanks. By David D. Duncan, USMC. With 11 ills. in color from natural-color photographs by the author. Vol. LXXXIX, pp. 364-372, Mar., 1946.

Dundee, Scotland :

Low Road, High Road, Around Dundee. By Maurice P. Dunlap. Vol. LXIX, pp. 547-576, 35 ills., 1 half-page map, Apr., 1936.

Dunlap, Maurice Pratt:

Low Road, High Road, Around Dundee (Scotland). By Maurice P. Dunlap. Vol. LXIX, pp. 547-576, 35 ills., 1 half-page map, Apr., 1936.

Outwitting the Water Demons of Kashmir. By Maurice Pratt Dunlap. Vol. XL, pp. 499-511, 9 ills., Nov., 1921.

Du Puy, William Atherton:

Geography of Money. By William Atherton Du Puy. Vol. LII, pp. 745-768, 31 ills., Dec., 1927.

Durban, Natal:

Under the South African Union. By Melville Chater. Vol. LIX, pp. 391-512, 97 ills. in black and white, 38 ills. in color, 1 two-page map, Apr., 1931.

Durbars:

Castles in the Air—Experiences and Journeys in Unknown Bhutan. By John Claude White. Vol. XXV, pp. 365-455, 74 ills., 1 page map, Apr., 1914.

In the Realms of the Maharajas. By Lawrence Copley Thaw and Margaret S. Thaw. Vol. LXXVIII, pp. 727-780, 14 ills. in black and white, 40 ills. in color, 1 page map, Dec., 1940.

Princely India, Resplendent with Jewels and Gold. 40 ills. in color from natural-color photographs by Lawrence Copley Thaw. Vol. LXXVIII, pp. 733-780, Dec., 1940.

Dusky Tribesmen of French West Africa. 26 ills. in color from natural-color photographs by Enzo de Chetelat. Vol. LXXIX, pp. 639-662, May, 1941.

Dutch East Indies. *See* Netherlands East Indies.

Dutch Guiana. *See* Surinam.

Dutch New Guinea. *See* Netherlands New Guinea.

Dwellings. *See* Châteaux; Cliff Dwellers; Cone Dwellings; Estates; Houses and Homes; Housing; Huts.

Dwight, Harry Griswold:

Gates to the Black Sea: The Dardanelles, the Bosphorus, and the Sea of Marmora. By Harry Griswold Dwight. Vol. XXVII, pp. 435-459, 27 ills., May, 1915.

Hoary Monasteries of Mount Athos (Greece). By Harry Griswold Dwight. Vol. XXX, pp. 249-272, 24 ills., 1 half-page map, Sept., 1916.

Life in Constantinople. By Harry Griswold Dwight. Vol. XXVI, pp. 521-545, 25 ills., Dec., 1914.

Saloniki. By Harry Griswold Dwight. Vol. XXX, pp. 203-232, 28 ills., Sept., 1916.

Dyaks (Tribespeople):

Keeping House in Borneo. By Virginia Hamilton. Vol. LXXXVIII, pp. 293-324, 28 ills., 1 page map, Sept., 1945.

Notes on the Sea Dyaks of Borneo. By Edwin H. Gomes. Vol. XXII, pp. 695-723, 26 ills., Aug., 1911.

Dyaks (Tribespeople)—*Continued*

Sarawak: The Land of the White Rajahs. By Harrison W. Smith. Vol. XXXV, pp. 110-167, 58 ills., 1 half-page map, Feb., 1919.

Dyar, (Dr.) Harrison G.:

Where Our Moths and Butterflies Roam. Vol. LII, pp. 105-126, July, 1927.

Dyott, G. M.:

Volcanoes of Ecuador, Guideposts in Crossing South America. By G. M. Dyott. Vol. LV, pp. 49-93, 42 ills. in black and white, 12 ills. in color, 1 half-page map, Jan., 1929.

E

Eagle, King of Birds, and His Kin. By Alexander Wetmore. Paintings by Maj. Allan Brooks. Vol. LXIV, pp. 43-95, 23 ills. in black and white, 28 ills. in color, July, 1933.

Eagle in Action: An Intimate Study of the Eyrie Life of America's National Bird. By Francis H. Herrick. Vol. LV, pp. 635-660, 20 ills., May, 1929.

Eagles.

Eagle, King of Birds, and His Kin. By Alexander Wetmore. Paintings by Maj. Allan Brooks. Vol. LXIV, pp. 43-95, 23 ills. in black and white, 28 ills. in color, July, 1933.

Eagle in Action: An Intimate Study of the Eyrie Life of America's National Bird. By Francis H. Herrick. Vol. LV, pp. 635-660, 20 ills., May, 1929.

Eagles, Hawks, and Vultures. 28 ills. in color from paintings by Maj. Allan Brooks. Vol. LXIV, pp. 65-94, July, 1933.

In Quest of the Golden Eagle: Over Lonely Mountain and Prairie Soars This Rare and Lordly Bird, But Three Youths from the East Catch Up With Him at Last. By John and Frank Craighead. Vol. LXXVII, pp. 693-710, 17 ills., May, 1940.

Earhart, Amelia:

My Flight from Hawaii. By Amelia Earhart. Vol. LXVII, pp. 593-609, 4 ills. in black and white, 8 ills. in duotone, May, 1935.

Society's Special Medal Awarded to Amelia Earhart: First Woman to Receive Geographic Distinction at Brilliant Ceremony in the National Capital (Address by Amelia Earhart). Vol. LXII, pp. 358-367, 7 ills., Sept., 1932.

Earl, Lawrence:

Mending Dikes in the Netherlands. 20 ills. from photographs by Lawrence Earl. Vol. XC, pp. 791-806, Dec., 1946.

Earthquakes:

Antioch the Glorious. By William H. Hall. Vol. XXXVIII, pp. 81-103, 20 ills., 1 half-page map, Aug., 1920.

Cause of Earthquakes. By Robert F. Griggs. Vol. XLIV, pp. 443-451, 5 ills., 1 page map, Oct., 1923.

Earthquakes—*Continued*

Charting a World at War. By William H. Nicholas. Vol. LXXXVI, pp. 617-640, 23 ills., 1 drawing, Nov., 1944.

Costa Rica—Vulcan's Smithy. By Henry Pittier. Vol. XXI, pp. 494-525, 30 ills., 2 half-page maps, June, 1910.

Echoes of the San Francisco Earthquake. By Robert E. C. Stearns. Vol. XVIII, pp. 351-353, 1 ill., May, 1907.

Eighth International Geographic Congress, September, 1904. Vol. XV, pp. 415-418, Oct., 1904.

Geography of Japan : With Special Reference to Its Influence on the Character of the Japanese People. By Walter Weston. Vol. XL, pp. 45-84, 23 ills. in black and white, 16 ills. in color, July, 1921.

How the Earth Telegraphed Its Tokyo Quake to Washington. By Rev. Francis A. Tondorf. Vol. XLIV, pp. 453-454, 1 ill., Oct., 1923.

Probable Cause of the San Francisco Earthquake. By Frederick Leslie Ransome. Vol. XVII, pp. 280-296, 9 ills., May, 1906.

Record of the Great Earthquake Written in Washington by the Seismograph of the United States Weather Bureau. By C. F. Marvin. Vol. XVII, pp. 296-298, May, 1906.

Reelfoot—An Earthquake Lake (Tennessee). By Wilbur A. Nelson. Vol. XLV, pp. 95-114, 20 ills., Jan., 1924.

Sakurajima, Japan's Greatest Volcanic Eruption : A Convulsion of Nature Whose Ravages Were Minimized by Scientific Knowledge, Compared with the Terrors and Destruction of the Recent Tokyo Earthquake. By Dr. Thomas Augustus Jaggar. Vol. XLV, pp. 441-470, 32 ills., 1 half-page map, Apr., 1924.

San Francisco Earthquake. Vol. XVII, pp. 325-343, 26 ills., June, 1906.

San Francisco Earthquake of April 18, 1906, as Recorded by the Coast and Geodetic Survey Magnetic Observatories. By Dr. L. A. Bauer and J. E. Burbank. Vol. XVII, pp. 298-300, May, 1906.

Shattered Capitals of Central America. By Herbert J. Spinden. Vol. XXXVI, pp. 185-212, 32 ills., 1 page map, Sept., 1919.

Some Personal Experiences with Earthquakes (Chile-Peru). By Rear Adm. L. G. Billings. Vol. XXVII, pp. 57-71, 7 ills., Jan., 1915.

Turkey, Where Earthquakes Followed Timur's Trail (Text references only). 15 ills. from photographs by Maynard Owen Williams. Vol. LXXVII, pp. 395-406, Mar., 1940.

"Where the Mountains Walked" : an Account of the Recent Earthquake in Kansu Province, China, Which Destroyed 100,000 Lives. By Upton Close and Elsie McCormick. Vol. XLI, pp. 445-464, 23 ills., 1 three-quarters-page map, May, 1922.

World's Most Cruel Earthquake (Messina). By Charles W. Wright. Vol. XX, pp. 373-396, 22 ills., 1 page and 1 three-quarters-page maps, Apr., 1909.

Earth's Most Primitive People : A Journey with the Aborigines of Central Australia. By Charles P. Mountford. Vol. LXXXIX, pp. 89-112, 10 ills. in black and white, 8 ills. in color, 1 half-page map, Jan., 1946.

East, Ben:

Winter Sky Roads to Isle Royal (Michigan). By Ben East. Vol. LX, pp. 759-774, 18 ills., 1 half-page map, Dec., 1931.

East Indians:

East Indians in the New World (Trinidad). By Harriet Chalmers Adams. Vol. XVIII, pp. 485-491, 6 ills., July, 1907.

India at Work and Play. 22 ills. in color from natural-color photographs by Peter Upton Muir, Maynard Owen Williams, and Frances Muir. Vol. LXXXIX, pp. 449-464, Apr., 1946.

India Mosaic. By Peter Muir and Frances Muir. Vol. LXXXIX, pp. 443-470, 5 ills. in black and white, 22 ills. in color, 1 half-page map, Apr., 1946.

East Indies. *See* Netherlands East Indies.

East of Constantinople : Glimpses of Village Life in Anatolia, the Battleground of East and West, Where the Turks Reorganized Their Forces After the World War. By Melville Chater. Vol. XLIII, pp. 509-534, 27 ills., 1 three-quarters-page map, May, 1923.

East of Suez to the Mount of the Decalogue : Following the Trail Over Which Moses Led the Israelites from the Slave-Pens of Egypt to Sinai. By Maynard Owen Williams. Vol. LII, pp. 709-743, 32 ills., 1 three-quarters-page map, Dec., 1927.

East of the Adriatic : Notes on Dalmatia, Montenegro, Bosnia, and Herzegovina. By Kenneth McKenzie. Vol. XXIII, pp. 1159-1187, 37 ills., 1 page map, Dec., 1912.

East Prussia:

Flying Around the Baltic. By Douglas Chandler. Vol. LXXIII, pp. 767-806, 31 ills. in black and white, 13 ills. in duotone, 1 half-page map, June, 1938.

Easter, S. E.:

Jade. By S. E. Easter. Vol. XIV, pp. 9-17, 2 half-page maps, Jan., 1903.

Easter Island, Pacific Ocean :

Great Stone Faces of Easter Island. 11 ills. from photographs. Vol. LXXXV, pp. 225-232, Feb., 1944.

Mystery of Easter Island. By Mrs. Scoresby Routledge. Vol. XL, pp. 628-646, 13 ills., 1 page map, Dec., 1921.

Romance of Science in Polynesia : An Account of Five Years of Cruising Among the South Sea Islands. By Robert Cushman Murphy. Vol. XLVIII, pp. 355-426, 66 ills. in black and white, 16 ills. in color, 3 half-page maps, Oct., 1925.

Easter Island, Pacific Ocean—*Continued*

Sailing the Seven Seas in the Interest of Science : Adventures Through 157,000 Miles of Storm and Calm, from Arctic to Antarctic and Around the World, in the Non-Magnetic Yacht *Carnegie.* By J. P. Ault. Vol. XLII, pp. 631-690, 47 ills., 1 chart, Dec., 1922.

Storied Islands of the South Sea. 20 ills. in color from natural-color photographs by Irving Johnson, Malcolm Evans, and others. Vol. LXXXI, pp. 9-40, Jan., 1942.

Westward Bound in the *Yankee.* By Irving and Electa Johnson. Vol. LXXXI, pp. 1-44, 25 ills. in black and white, 20 ills. in color, 1 three-quarters-page map, Jan., 1942.

Eastern Hemisphere:

Map of Discovery. Reproduction in color of the painting by N. C. Wyeth, National Geographic Society, Washington, D. C. Vol. LIV, text, p. 568 ; supplement, Nov., 1928.

Eastern Woodland Indians:

America's first Settlers, the Indians. By Matthew W. Stirling. Vol. LXXII, pp. 535-596, 34 ills. in black and white, 24 ills. in color, Nov., 1937.

When Red Men Ruled Our Forests. 24 ills. in color from paintings by W. Langdon Kihn. Vol. LXXII, pp. 551-590, Nov., 1937.

Eastward from Gibraltar : Overland Route Across North Africa to Tunisia and Libia. By Cyrus French Wicker. Vol. LXXXIII, pp. 115-142, 28 ills., Jan., 1943.

Eaton, Mary E.:

Berries (American). 29 ills. in color from paintings by Mary E. Eaton. Vol. XXXV, pp. 173-180, Feb., 1919.

Flowers. 47 ills. in color from paintings by Mary E. Eaton. Vol. XLV, pp. 613-628, June, 1924.

Flowers (American Wild Flowers). 29 ills. in color from paintings by Mary E. Eaton. Vol. XXVII, pp. 483-506, May, 1915.

Flowers (Common American Wild Flowers). 17 ills. in color from paintings by Mary E. Eaton. Vol. XXIX, pp. 591-606, June, 1916.

Flowers (State Flowers). 30 ills. in color from paintings by Mary E. Eaton. Vol. XXXI, pp. 501-516, June, 1917.

Midsummer Wild Flowers. 38 ills. in color from paintings by Mary E. Eaton. Vol. XLII, pp. 37-52, July, 1922.

Pages From the Floral Life of America. 55 ills. in color from paintings by Mary E. Eaton. Vol. XLVIII, pp. 47-70, July, 1925.

Eaton Canyon Bird and Game Sanctuary, California :

Where Birds and Little Animals Find Haven. By Agnes Akin Atkinson. Vol. LXX, pp. 232-241, 14 ills., Aug., 1936.

Eberlein, Harold Donaldson:

Some Forgotten Corners of London : Many Places of Beauty and Historic Interest Repay the Search of the Inquiring Visitor. By Harold Donaldson Eberlein. Vol. LXI, pp. 163-198, 25 ills., Feb., 1932.

Visits to the Old Inns of England : Historic Homes of Hospitality for the Wayfarer Dot the Length and Breadth of the Kingdom. By Harold Donaldson Eberlein. Vol. LIX, pp. 261-285, 17 ills. in black and white, 15 ills. in color, Mar., 1931.

Echagüe, J. Ortiz:

Flashing Fashions of Old Spain. 26 ills. in duotone by J. Ortiz Echagüe. Vol. LXIX, pp. 413-428, Mar., 1936.

Echoes from Yugoslavia. 16 ills. from photographs. Vol. LXXIX, pp. 793-804, June, 1941.

Echoes of the San Francisco Earthquake. By Robert E. C. Stearns. Vol. XVIII, pp. 351-353, 1 ill., May, 1907.

Echoes of Whaling Days (Nantucket). 8 ills. in color from natural-color photographs by B. Anthony Stewart. Vol. LXXXV, pp. 449-456, Apr., 1944.

Eckener, Hugo:

First Airship Flight Around the World : Dr. Hugo Eckener Tells of an Epochal Geographic Achievement upon the Occasion of the Bestowal of the National Geographic Society's Special Gold Medal. Vol. LVII, pp. 653-688, 37 ills., June, 1930.

Eclipses:

American Eclipse Expedition. By Rear Adm. Colby M. Chester. Vol. XVII, pp. 589-612, 23 ills., 1 color plate, Nov., 1906.

Eclipse Adventures on a Desert Isle (Canton). By Capt. J. F. Hellweg. Vol. LXXII, pp. 377-394, 14 ills., 1 two-thirds-page map, Sept., 1937.

National Geographic Society's Eclipse Expedition to Norfolk, Virginia. By Marcus Baker. Vol. XI, p. 320, Aug., 1900.

Natural-color photograph of an eclipse. 1 ill. in color by Irvine C. Gardner. Vol. LXXI, p. 178, Feb., 1937.

Nature's Most Dramatic Spectacle. By S. A. Mitchell. Vol. LXXII, pp. 361-376, 16 ills., 1 half-page map, Sept., 1937.

Observing a Total Eclipse of the Sun : Dimming Solar Light for a Few Seconds Entails Years of Work for Science and Attracts Throngs to "Nature's Most Magnificent Spectacle." By Paul A. McNally. Vol. LXII, pp. 597-605, 6 ills., Nov., 1932.

Observing an Eclipse in Asiatic Russia. By Irvine C. Gardner. Vol. LXXI, pp. 179-197, 19 ills. in black and white, 1 ill. in color, Feb., 1937.

Eclipses—*Continued*

Photographing the Eclipse of 1932 from the Air : From Five Miles Above the Earth's Surface, the National Geographic Society–Army Air Corps Survey Obtains Successful Photographs of the Moon's Shadow. By Capt. Albert W. Stevens. Vol. LXII, pp. 581-596, 18 ills., Nov., 1932.

Scientific Work of the National Geographic Society's Eclipse Expedition to Norfolk, Virginia. By Simon Newcomb. Vol. XI, pp. 321-324, Aug., 1900.

To Observe Solar Eclipse. Vol. XVI, p. 88, Feb., 1905.

Total Eclipse of the Sun, May 28, 1900. By F. H. Bigelow. Vol. XI, pp. 33-34, Jan., 1900.

Unfurling Old Glory on Canton Island. 11 ills. in color ; 1 painting and 1 kodachrome photograph of the eclipse. Vol. LXXIII, pp. 753-760, June, 1938.

Economic Condition of the Philippines. By Max L. Tornow. Vol. X, pp. 33-64, 10 ills., Feb., 1899.

Economic Evolution of Alaska. By Maj. Gen. A. W. Greely. Vol. XX, pp. 585-593, 4 ills., July, 1909.

Economic Loss to the People of the United States Through Insects That Carry Disease. By L. O. Howard. Vol. XX, pp. 735-749, Aug., 1909.

Ecuador:

Among the Highlands of the Equator Republic. 12 ills. in color from autochromes by Jacob Gayer. Vol. LV, pp. 68-77, Jan., 1929.

Beautiful Ecuador. By Joseph Lee. Vol. XVIII, pp. 80-91, 9 ills., Feb., 1907.

From Sea to Clouds in Ecuador. By W. Robert Moore. Vol. LXXX, pp. 717-740, 11 ills. in black and white, 9 ills. in color, Dec., 1941.

Mrs. Robinson Crusoe in Ecuador. By Mrs. Richard C. Gill. Vol. LXV, pp. 133-172, 43 ills. in black and white, 1 half-page map, Feb., 1934.

Over Trail and Through Jungle in Ecuador : Indian Head-Hunters of the Interior, an Interesting Study in the South American Republic. By H. E. Anthony. Vol. XL, pp. 327-352, 28 ills., Oct., 1921.

Quinine Hunters in Ecuador. By Froelich Rainey. Vol. LXXXIX, pp. 341-363, 21 ills., 1 half-page map, Mar., 1946.

Road to Bolivia. By William E. Curtis. Vol. XI, pp. 208-224, 7 ills., June, 1900.

Volcanoes of Ecuador, Guideposts in Crossing South America. By G. M. Dyott. Vol. LV, pp. 49-93, 42 ills. in black and white, 12 ills. in color, 1 half-page map, Jan., 1929.

Where Snow Peaks Temper the Tropics. 9 ills. in color from natural-color photographs by W. Robert Moore. Vol. LXXX, pp. 727-734, Dec., 1941.

Edam Cheese:

North Holland Cheese Market. By Hugh M. Smith. Vol. XXI, pp. 1051-1066, 17 ills., Dec., 1910.

Eddy, Frederick B.:

Panther of the Hearth : Lithe Grace and Independence of Spirit Contribute to the Appeal of Cats, "The Only Domestic Animal Man Has Never Conquered." By Frederick B. Eddy. Vol. LXXIV, pp. 589-634, 22 ills. in black and white, 25 ills. in color, Nov., 1938.

Eden, Garden of :

Cradle of Civilization : The Historic Lands Along the Euphrates and Tigris Rivers Where Briton Is Fighting Turk. By James Baikie. Vol. XXIX, pp. 127-162, 25 ills., Feb., 1916.

Where Adam and Eve Lived (Baghdad). By Frederick and Margaret Simpich. Vol. XXVI, pp. 546-588, 35 ills., Dec., 1914.

Eden of the Flowery Republic (Szechuan). By Joseph Beech. Vol. XXXVIII, pp. 355-390, 18 ills. in black and white, 16 ills. in color, Nov., 1920.

Edgerton, (Prof.) Harold E.:

Mystery Mammals of the Twilight (Bats). By Donald R. Griffin. Vol. XC, pp. 117-134, 19 ills., July, 1946.

Edinburgh, Scotland :

Bonnie Scotland, Postwar Style. By Isobel Wylie Hutchison. Vol. LXXXIX, pp. 545-601, 14 ills. in black and white, 38 ills. in color, 1 two-page map, May, 1946.

Edinburgh, Athens of the North : Romantic History of Cramped Medieval City Vies With Austere Beauty of Newer Wide Streets and Stately Squares. By J. R. Hildebrand. Vol. LXII, pp. 219-246, 19 ills. in black and white, 8 ills. in duotone, Aug., 1932.

Heather Paints the Highlands. 38 ills. in color from natural-color photographs by B. Anthony Stewart. Vol. LXXXIX, pp. 561-600, May, 1946.

Scotland in Wartime. By Isobel Wylie Hutchison. Vol. LXXXIII, pp. 723-743, 19 ills., June, 1943.

Vagabonding in England : A Young American Works His Way Around the British Isles and Sees Sights from an Unusual Point of View. By John McWilliams. Vol. LXV, pp. 357-398, 39 ills., 1 three-quarters-page map, Mar., 1934.

Editorial Department. *See* National Geographic Society : Editorial Department.

Edmunds, Charles K.:

Shantung—China's Holy Land. By Charles K. Edmunds. Vol. XXXVI, pp. 231-252, 21 ills., 1 half-page map, Sept., 1919.

Edom. *See* Trans-Jordan.

Educating the Filipinos. Vol. XVI, pp. 46-49, Jan., 1905.

Education:

Bringing the World to Our Foreign-Language Soldiers: How a Military Training Camp Is Solving a Seemingly Unsurmountable Problem by Using The Geographic. By Christina Krysto. Vol. XXXIV, pp. 81-90, 4 ills., Aug., 1918.

Denmark and the Danes. By Maurice Francis Egan. Vol. XLII, pp. 115-164, 38 ills., 1 three-quarters-page map, Aug., 1922.

Educating the Filipinos. Vol. XVI, pp. 46-49, Jan., 1905.

New York—The Metropolis of Mankind. By William Joseph Showalter. Vol. XXXIV, pp. 1-49, 39 ills., July, 1918.

Present Conditions in China. By John W. Foster. Vol. XVII, pp. 651-672, pp. 709-711, Dec., 1906.

Sight-Seeing in School: Taking Twenty Million Children on a Picture Tour of the World. By Jessie L. Burrall. Vol. XXXV, pp. 489-503, 14 ills., June, 1919.

Teaching of Physical Geography in the Elementary Schools. By Richard E. Dodge. Vol. XI, pp. 470-475, Dec., 1900.

Edwards, (Col.) Clarence R.:

Governing the Philippine Islands. By Col. Clarence R. Edwards. Vol. XV, pp. 273-284, 5 ills., July, 1904.

Work of the Bureau of Insular Affairs. By Col. Clarence R. Edwards. Vol. XV, pp. 239-255, 8 ills., June, 1904.

Edwards, Walter M.:

Our Nation's Capital on Parade. 16 ills. in color from natural-color photographs by B. Anthony Stewart, Walter M. Edwards, and others. Vol. LXXXIV, pp. 265-288, Sept., 1943.

Where the Winding Cam Mirrors Cambridge (University) Spires. 12 ills. in color from natural-color photographs by Bernard Wakeman and Walter M. Edwards. Vol. LXX, pp. 339-346, Sept., 1936.

Eels:

Mysterious Life of the Common Eel. By Hugh M. Smith. Vol. XXIV, pp. 1140-1146, 3 ills., Oct., 1913.

Efate (Island), New Hebrides:

Palms and Planes in the New Hebrides. By Maj. Robert D. Heinl, Jr. Vol. LXXXVI, pp. 229-256, 17 ills. in black and white, 12 ills. in color, 1 four-fifths-page map, Aug., 1944.

Effie M. Morrissey (Schooner):

Servicing Arctic Airbases. By Robert A. Bartlett. Vol. LXXXIX, pp. 602-616, 3 ills. in black and white, 10 ills. in color, 1 half-page map, May, 1946.

Voyage of the *Morrissey*. 10 ills. in color from natural-color photographs by Daniel S. Turner and Sherman A. Wengerd. Vol. LXXXIX, pp. 609-616, May, 1946.

Efforts to Obtain Greater Energy from Coal. Vol. XVIII, pp. 138-140, Feb., 1907.

Egan, Maurice Francis:

Denmark and the Danes. By Maurice Francis Egan. Vol. XLII, pp. 115-164, 38 ills., 1 three-quarters-page map, Aug., 1922.

Norway and the Norwegians. By Maurice Francis Egan. Vol. XLV, pp. 647-696, 45 ills., June, 1924.

Egrets (Birds):

Ibises, Herons, and Flamingos. 4 ills. in color from paintings by Maj. Allan Brooks. Vol. LXII, pp. 454-469, Oct., 1932.

Large Wading Birds: Long Legs and Remarkable Beaks, as Well as Size, Form, and Color, Distinguish the Herons, Ibises, and Flamingos. By T. Gilbert Pearson. Paintings by Maj. Allan Brooks. Vol. LXII, pp. 441-469, 2 ills. in black and white, 4 ills. in color, Oct., 1932.

Egypt:

Along the Banks of the Colorful Nile. 23 ills. in color from autochromes lumière by Gervais Courtellemont. Vol. L, pp. 322-339, Sept., 1926.

Along the Nile, Through Egypt and the Sudan. By Frederick Simpich. Vol. XLII, pp. 379-410, 29 ills., Oct., 1922.

American Alma Maters in the Near East. By Maynard Owen Williams. Vol. LXXXVIII, pp. 237-256, 16 ills., Aug., 1945.

American Discoveries in Egypt. Vol. XVIII, pp. 801-806, 8 ills., Dec., 1907.

American Fighters Visit Bible Lands. By Maynard Owen Williams. With 23 ills. in color from natural-color photographs by the author. Vol. LXXXIX, pp. 311-340, 10 ills. in black and white, Mar., 1946.

At the Tomb of Tutankhamen: An Account of the Opening of the Royal Egyptian Sepulcher Which Contained the Most Remarkable Funeral Treasures Unearthed in Historic Times. By Maynard Owen Williams. Vol. XLIII, pp. 461-508, 53 ills., 1 half-page map, May, 1923.

Barrage of the Nile. By Day Allen Willey. Vol. XXI, pp. 175-184, 14 ills., Feb., 1910.

British Commonwealth of Nations: "Organized Freedom" Around the World. By Eric Underwood. Vol. LXXXIII, pp. 485-524, 31 ills., Apr., 1943.

By Felucca Down the Nile: Giant Dams Rule Egypt's Lifeline River, Yet Village Life Goes On As It Did in the Time of the Pharaohs. By Willard Price. Vol. LXXVII, pp. 435-476, 21 ills. in black and white, 22 ills. in color, 1 two-page map, Apr., 1940.

Cairo to Cape Town, Overland: An Adventurous Journey of 135 Days, Made by an American Man and His Wife, Through the Length of the African Continent. By Felix Shay. Vol. XLVII, pp. 123-260, 118 ills., 1 half-page map, Feb., 1925.

Change Comes to Bible Lands. By Frederick Simpich. Vol. LXXIV, pp. 695-750, 40 ills. in black and white, 25 ills. in color, special map supplement, Dec., 1938.

Egypt—*Continued*

Crossing the Untraversed Libyan Desert: The Record of a 2,200-Mile Journey of Exploration Which Resulted in the Discovery of Two Oases of Strategic Importance on the Southwestern Frontier of Egypt. By A. M. Hassanein. Vol. XLVI, pp. 233-277, 46 ills., 1 half-page map, Sept., 1924.

Daily Life in Ancient Egypt (Part I). Daily Life in Ancient Egypt: *The Later Period* (Part II). By William C. Hayes. Paintings by H. M. Herget. Vol. LXXX, pp. 419-515, 34 ills. in black and white, 32 ills. in color, 1 two-thirds-page map, Oct., 1941.

   Contents: Life in Lower Egypt Before the Dawn of History.—A King of Upper Egypt Conquers the Delta and Unites the Two Kingdoms.—King Djoser and the Wise I-em-hotep Usher in the Old Kingdom.—The Builder of the Great Pyramid Receives a Visit from His Mother.—The Egyptian Farmer—Winter Sowing in the Pyramid Age.—Supplies of Food for a Resident of the City of the Dead—an Old Kingdom Mastabeh Field Near Memphis.—Netting Wildfowl in the Marshes.—The Egyptian Scribe and His Equipment.—A "Dwarf of the Divine Dances from the Land of the Spirits" as a Gift to the Boy King of Egypt.—An Ancient Egyptian Brewery.—An XIth Dynasty Carpenter's Shop.—The Formal Gardens and Informal Children of Ancient Egypt.—The Egyptian Stonemason and His Craft—Construction Work on a XIIth Dynasty Pyramid Site.—An Ancient Egyptian River Fort on the Sudān Frontier.—An Egyptian Nomarch Entertains a Bedawīn Sheikh.—A King's Daughter and Her Personal Possessions.—The Founders of the New Kingdom.—The Family of King Thut-mosĕ I.—A Sea Voyage to a Remote Land.—Amun-Rĕ', "King of the Gods," Pays His Yearly Visit to Queen Hatshepsūt's Temple in Western Thebes.—Egyptian Chariots at Armageddon.—The Vintage of 1400 B. C.—A Family Outing in the Papyrus Pools.—At Home with the Average Egyptian and His Wife.—The Aten Shines, King Akh-en-Aten Dreams, and the XVIIIth Dynasty Draws to a Close.—A Wealthy Theban Is Buried in His Tomb in the Western Cliffs.—User-hēt Entertains.—Preparation of a Painted Tomb-chapel—The Egyptian Artist and His Methods.—Ramesses "the Great."—The Manufacture and Use of Brick in Ancient Egypt.—The Largest Temple Ever Erected by Man—2,000 Years Building.—The Assyrians (and Others) Come Down Like a Wolf on the Fold.

East of Suez to the Mount of the Decalogue: Following the Trail Over Which Moses Led the Israelites from the Slave-Pens of Egypt to Sinai. By Maynard Owen Williams. Vol. LII, pp. 709-743, 32 ills., 1 three-quarters-page map, Dec., 1927.

Excavations at Abydos. By W. M. Flinders Petrie. Vol. XIV, pp. 358-359, Sept., 1903.

Fearful Famines of the Past: History Will Repeat Itself Unless the American People Conserve Their Resources. By Ralph A. Graves. Vol. XXXII, pp. 68-90, 11 ills., July, 1917.

Egypt—*Continued*

Flying Over Egypt, Sinai, and Palestine: Looking Down Upon the Holy Land During an Air Journey of Two and a Half Hours from Cairo to Jerusalem. By Brig. Gen. P. R. C. Groves and Maj. J. R. McCrindle. Vol. L, pp. 313-355, 26 ills., 1 half-page map, Sept., 1926.

Land of Egypt: A Narrow Green Strip of Fertility Stretching for a Thousand Miles Through Walls of Desert. By Alfred Pearce Dennis. Vol. XLIX, pp. 271-298, 28 ills., 1 half-page map, Mar., 1926.

Life, Culture, and History of the Egyptians. 32 ills. in color from paintings by H. M. Herget. Vol. LXXX, pp. 436-514, Oct., 1941.

Old-New Battle Grounds of Egypt and Libia. By W. Robert Moore. Vol. LXXVIII, pp. 809-820, 8 ills., 1 third-page map, Dec., 1940.

Recent Discoveries in Egypt. Vol. XII, pp. 396-397, Nov., 1901.

Reconstructing Egypt's History. By Wallace N. Stearns. Vol. XXIV, pp. 1021-1042, 21 ills., Sept., 1913.

Red Cross Girl Overseas. By Margaret Cotter. Vol. LXXXVI, pp. 745-768, 22 ills., Dec., 1944.

Resurrection of Ancient Egypt. By James Baikie. Vol. XXIV, pp. 957-1020, 46 ills., 1 page map, Sept., 1913.

Route Over Which Moses Led the Children of Israel Out of Egypt. By Franklin E. Hoskins. Vol. XX, pp. 1011-1038, 24 ills., 1 page map, Dec., 1909.

Sacred Ibis Cemetery and Jackal Catacombs at Abydos. By Camden M. Cobern. Vol. XXIV, pp. 1042-1056, 10 ills., Sept., 1913.

Suez Canal: Short Cut to Empires. By Maynard Owen Williams. Vol. LXVIII, pp. 611-632, 19 ills., 1 half-page map, Nov., 1935.

Sunrise and Sunset from Mount Sinai. By Sartell Prentice, Jr., Vol. XXIII, pp. 1242-1282, 34 ills., 1 page map, Dec., 1912.

Under Egypt's Golden Sun. 22 ills. in color from natural-color photographs by B. Anthony Stewart. Vol. LXXVII, pp. 451-466, Apr., 1940.

War Meets Peace in Egypt. By Grant Parr and G. E. Janssen. Vol. LXXXI, pp. 503-526, 25 ills., 1 page map, Apr., 1942.

Eigenmann, C. H.:

Notes from a Naturalist's Experiences in British Guiana. By C. H. Eigenmann. Vol. XXII, pp. 859-870, 8 ills., Sept., 1911.

8th Air Force in England. 10 ills. in color from U. S. Army Air Forces official photographs. Vol. LXXXVII, pp. 297-304, Mar., 1945.

Eighth International Geographic Congress. *See* International Geographic Congress.

Eigner, Julius:

Rise and Fall of Nanking. By Julius Eigner. Vol. LXXIII, pp. 189-224, 37 ills., Feb., 1938.

Eire:

British Commonwealth of Nations: "Organized Freedom" Around the World. By Eric Underwood. Vol. LXXXIII, pp. 485-524, 31 ills., Apr., 1943.

Old Ireland, Mother of New Erie: By Whatever Name, 'Tis the Same Fair Land With the Grass Growing Green on the Hills of Her and the Peat Smoke Hanging Low. By Harrison Howell Walker. Vol. LXXVII, pp. 649-691, 19 ills. in black and white, 18 ills. in color, 1 page map, May, 1940.

When Irish Skies Are Smiling. 18 ills. in color from natural-color photographs by Harrison Howell Walker. Vol. LXXVII, pp. 663-686, May, 1940.

Eklingi (Temple), India:

Marble Dams of Rajputana. By Eleanor Maddock. Vol. XL, pp. 468-499, 13 ills. in black and white, 16 ills. in color, Nov., 1921.

Ekoi (Tribespeople):

Notes on the Ekoi (Nigeria). By P. A. Talbot. Vol. XXIII, pp. 32-38, 8 ills., Jan., 1912.

Elburz Mountains, Iran:

Modern Persia and Its Capital: And an Account of an Ascent of Mount Demavend, the Persian Olympus. By F. L. Bird. Vol. XXXIX, pp. 353-400, 47 ills., Apr., 1921.

Electronics:

Your New World of Tomorrow. By F. Barrows Colton. Vol. LXXXVIII, pp. 385-410, 25 ills., Oct., 1945.

Elephant Hunting in Equatorial Africa with Rifle and Camera. By Carl E. Akeley. Vol. XXIII, pp. 779-810, 30 ills., Aug., 1912.

Elephant Seals:

Birds and Beasts of Mexico's Desert Islands. 12 ills. in color from natural-color photographs; 8 ills. by Ed N. Harrison; 4 ills. by Alfred M. Bailey and Robert J. Niedrach. Vol. LXXX, pp. 353-360, Sept., 1941.

Cruise of the *Kinkajou:* Among Desert Islands of Mexico Voyagers Find Outdoor Laboratories for the Naturalist and Ideal Fishing Grounds for the Sportsman. By Alfred M. Bailey. Vol. LXXX, pp. 339-366, 13 ills. in black and white, 12 ills. in color, 1 page map, Sept., 1941.

South Georgia, an Outpost of the Antarctic. By Robert Cushman Murphy. Vol. XLI, pp. 409-444, 41 ills., 2 half-page maps, Apr., 1922.

Elephants:

Color Camera Explores the Country That Moves by Night. 29 ills. in color from natural-color photographs by Richard H. Stewart, W. Robert Moore, Orren R. Louden, and Jacob Gayer. Vol. LX, pp. 478-511, Oct., 1931.

Elephant Hunting in Equatorial Africa with Rifle and Camera. By Carl E. Akeley. Vol. XXIII, pp. 779-810, 30 ills., Aug., 1912.

Greatest Hunt in the World. By Eliza R. Scidmore. Vol. XVII, pp. 673-692, 17 ills., Dec., 1906.

Elephants—*Continued*

Land of Sawdust and Spangles—A World in Miniature. By Francis Beverly Kelley. Vol. LX, pp. 463-516, 35 ills. in black and white, 29 ills. in color, Oct., 1931.

Nature's Most Amazing Mammal: Elephants, Unique Among Animals, Have Many Human Qualities When Wild That Make Them Foremost Citizens of Zoo and Circus. By Edmund Heller. Vol. LXV, pp. 729-759, 37 ills., June, 1934.

Perahera Processions of Ceylon. By G. H. G. Burroughs. Vol. LXII, pp. 90-100, 1 ill. in black and white, 8 ills. in duotone, July, 1932.

Warfare of the Jungle Folk: Campaigning Against Tigers, Elephants, and Other Wild Animals in Northern Siam. By Merian C. Cooper. Photographs by Ernest B. Schoedsack. Vol. LIII, pp. 233-268, 33 ills., Feb., 1928.

When a Drought Blights Africa: Hippos and Elephants Are Driven Insane by Suffering, in the Lorain Swamp, Kenya Colony. By Capt. A. T. Curle. Vol. LV, pp. 521-528, 9 ills., Apr., 1929.

Where Roosevelt Will Hunt. By Sir Harry Johnston. Vol. XX, pp. 207-256, 43 ills., special map supplement in colors, Mar., 1909.

Wild Man and Wild Beast in Africa. By Theodore Roosevelt. Vol. XXII, pp. 1-33, 41 ills., 1 page map, Jan., 1911.

Wings Over Nature's Zoo in Africa. 20 ills. in duotone from photographs by Reginald A. Bourlay. Vol. LXXVI, pp. 527-542, Oct., 1939.

Working Teak in the Burma Forests: The Sagacious Elephant Is Man's Ablest Ally in the Logging Industry of the Far East. By A. W. Smith. Vol. LVIII, pp. 239-256, 5 ills. in black and white, 15 ills. in color, Aug., 1930.

Eliot, Charles W.:

Need of Conserving the Beauty and Freedom of Nature in Modern Life. By Charles W. Eliot. Vol. XXVI, pp. 67-74, 4 ills., July, 1914.

Ellice Islands, Pacific Ocean:

American Pathfinders in the Pacific. By William H. Nicholas. Vol. LXXXIX, pp. 617-640, 17 ills., 1 two-page map, May, 1946.

Ellis, William T.:

Voyaging on the Volga Amid War and Revolution: War-Time Sketches on Russia's Great Waterway. By William T. Ellis. Vol. XXXIII, pp. 245-265, 16 ills., Mar., 1918.

Ellison, Norman:

Shark Fishing—An Australian Industry. By Norman Ellison. Vol. LXII, pp. 369-386, 22 ills., Sept., 1932.

Ellsworth, Lincoln:

Ellsworth Awarded the Hubbard Medal. Vol. LXX, p. 36, July, 1936.

My Flight Across Antarctica. By Lincoln Ellsworth. Vol. LXX, pp. 1-35, 37 ills., 1 page map, July, 1936.

Ellsworth, Lincoln—*Continued*

My Four Antarctic Expeditions : Explorations of 1933-39 Have Stricken Vast Areas from the Realm of the Unknown. By Lincoln Ellsworth. Vol. LXXVI, pp. 129-138, 9 ills., 1 page map, July, 1939.

El Oued (Oasis), Algeria :

Country of the Ant Men (Algeria). By Thomas H. Kearney. Vol. XXII, pp. 367-382, 11 ills., 1 half-page map, Apr., 1911.

El Paso, Texas :

Along Our Side of the Mexican Border. By Frederick Simpich. Vol. XXXVIII, pp. 61-80, 9 ills., 1 quarter-page map, July, 1920.

El Salvador:

Coffee Is King in El Salvador. By Luis Marden. Vol. LXXXVI, pp. 575-616, 22 ills. in black and white, 27 ills. in color, 1 half-page map, Nov., 1944.

Countries of the Caribbean. By William Joseph Showalter. Vol. XXIV, pp. 227-250, 23 ills., Feb., 1913.

Notes on Central America. Vol. XVIII, pp. 272-278, 1 ill., 1 half-page map, Apr., 1907.

Shattered Capitals of Central America. By Herbert J. Spinden. Vol. XXXVI, pp. 185-212, 32 ills., 1 page map, Sept., 1919.

Volcano-Girded Salvador : A Prosperous Central American State with the Densest Rural Population in the Western World. By Harriet Chalmers Adams. Vol. XLI, pp. 189-200, 10 ills., Feb., 1922.

Elsmore, (Col.) Ray T.:

New Guinea's Mountain and Swampland Dwellers. By Col. Ray T. Elsmore. Vol LXXXVIII, pp. 671-694, 15 ills. in black and white, 7 ills. in color, 1 half-page map, Dec., 1945.

"Shangri-la" in Panorama. 7 ills. in color from natural-color photographs by Ray T. Elsmore. Vol. LXXXVIII, pp. 681-688, Dec., 1945.

Elysium for the Beauty-Seeking Traveler (Canary Islands). 14 ills. in color from natural-color photographs by Wilhelm Tobien. Vol. LVII, pp. 630-639, May, 1930.

Emancipation of Mohammedan Women. By Mary Mills Patrick. Vol. XX, pp. 42-66, 19 ills., Jan., 1909.

Emerson, Harrington:

Opening of the Alaskan Territory. By Harrington Emerson. Vol. XIV, pp. 99-106, 5 ills., Mar., 1903.

Emigration from Siberia. Vol. XIII, pp. 32-33, Jan., 1902.

Emperor Worship:

Behind the Mask of Modern Japan. By Willard Price. Vol. LXXXVIII, pp. 513-535, 14 ills., Nov., 1945.

Empire of Romance—India. 16 ills. in color from photographs. Vol. XL, pp. 481-496, Nov., 1921.

Empire of the Risen Sun (Japan). By William Elliot Griffis. Vol. XLIV, pp. 415-443, 21 ills., Oct., 1923.

Empire State Onions and Pageantry (New York). 12 ills. in color from natural-color photographs by J. Baylor Roberts and Volkmar Wentzel. Vol. LXXX, pp. 641-648, Nov., 1941.

Emu Wrens:

Fairy Wrens of Australia : The Little Long-tailed "Blue Birds of Happiness" Rank High Among the Island Continent's Remarkable Birds. By Neville W. Cayley. With 8 ills. in color from paintings by the author. Vol. LXXXVIII, pp. 488-498, 1 ill. in black and white, Oct., 1945.

Pastel Wrens from "Down Under." 8 ills. in color from paintings by N. W. Cayley. Vol. LXXXVIII, pp. 489-496, Oct., 1945.

Encircling Navajo Mountain (Utah) with a Pack-Train : An Expedition to a Hitherto Untraversed Region of Our Southwest Discovers a New Route to Rainbow Natural Bridge. By Charles L. Bernheimer. Vol. XLIII, pp. 197-224, 33 ills., 1 half-page map, Feb., 1923.

Encouraging Birds Around the Home. By Frederick H. Kennard. Vol. XXV, pp. 315-344, 36 ills., Mar., 1914.

Endeavour (Ship) :

Columbus of the Pacific : Captain James Cook, Foremost British Navigator, Expanded the Great Sea to Correct Proportions and Won for Albion an Insular Empire by Peaceful Exploration and Scientific Study. By J. R. Hildebrand. Vol. LI, pp. 85-132, 45 ills., 1 page and 1 three-quarters-page maps, Jan., 1927.

Engeln, O. D. von:

Photography in Glacial Alaska. By O. D. von Engeln. Vol. XXI, pp. 54-62, 4 ills., Jan., 1910.

Engineering:

Alaskan Highway an Engineering Epic : Mosquitoes, Mud, and Muskeg Minor Obstacles of 1,671-mile Race to Throw the Alcan Life Line Through Thick Forests and Uninhabited Wilderness. By Froelich Rainey. Vol. LXXXIII, pp. 143-168, 21 ills., 3 maps, Feb., 1943.

Ascension Island, an Engineering Victory. By Lt. Col. Frederick J. Clarke. Vol. LXXXV, pp. 623-640, 21 ills., May., 1944.

Greens Grow for GI's on Soilless Ascension. By W. Robert Moore. Vol. LXXXVIII, pp. 219-230, 12 ills., Aug., 1945.

Mending Dikes in the Netherlands. 20 ills. from photographs by Lawrence Earl. Vol. XC, pp. 791-806, Dec., 1946.

Normandy's Made-in-England Harbors. Vol. LXXXVII, pp. 565-580, 16 ills., 1 quarter-page map, May, 1945.

Oil for Victory Piped under the Sea. 9 ills. from photographs. Vol. LXXXVIII, pp. 721-726, Dec., 1945.

See also Aqueducts ; Bridges ; Canals ; Dams ; Floods and Flood Control ; Highways and Roads ; Reclamation of Land.

England:

Ancestor of the British Navy: England's Oldest Known War Vessel Is Unearthed, Laden with Remarkable Treasures of an Anglo-Saxon Ruler. By C. W. Phillips. Vol. LXXIX, pp. 247-268, 22 ills. in black and white, 4 drawings, Feb., 1941.

Bathymetrical Survey of the Freshwater Lakes of England. Vol. XII, p. 408, Nov., 1901.

Beauties of the Severn Valley. By Frank Wakeman. Vol. LXIII, pp. 417-452, 24 ills. in black and white, 15 ills. in color, 1 three-quarters-page map, Apr., 1933.

Between the Heather and the North Sea: Bold English Headlands Once Sheltered Sea Robbers, Later Were Ports of Wooden Ships, Centers of the Jet and Alum Trades, To-day Are Havens of Adventurous Fishing Fleets. By Leo Walmsley. Vol. LXIII, pp. 197-232, 41 ills., Feb., 1933.

"Blood, Toil, Tears, and Sweat": An American Tells the Story of Britain's War Effort, Summed up in Prime Minister Churchill's Unflinching Words. By Harvey Klemmer. Vol. LXXXII, pp. 141-166, 19 ills., Aug., 1942.

Britain Fights in the Fields. By Francis A. Flood. Vol. LXXXVI, pp. 31-65, 17 ills. in black and white, 21 ills. in color, July, 1944.

Britain Just Before the Storm: A Canadian Canoe Threads Old English Waterways Athrob with the Midlands' Industrial Life. By Amos Burg. Vol. LXXVIII, pp. 185-212, 14 ills. in black and white, 9 ills. in color, 1 two-thirds-page map, Aug., 1940.

British Commonwealth of Nations: "Organized Freedom" Around the World. By Eric Underwood. Vol. LXXXIII, pp. 485-524, 31 ills., Apr., 1943.

British Isles. Vol. XXVIII, pp. 551-566, 16 ills., Dec., 1915.

Canals and Pageants of Peacetime England. 9 ills. in color from natural-color photographs; 6 ills. by Amos Burg. Vol. LXXVIII, pp. 197-204, Aug., 1940.

Cathedrals of England: An Artist's Pilgrimage to These Majestic Monuments of Man's Genius and Faith. By Norman Wilkinson. Vol. LXXVI, pp. 741-762, 3 ills. in black and white, 16 ills. in gravure from dry-point engravings by the author, Dec., 1939. Vol. LXXVI, text, p. 762, Dec., 1939.

Channel Ports—And Some Others. By Florence Craig Albrecht. Vol. XXVIII, pp. 1-55, 45 ills., July, 1915.

Char-à-Bancs in Cornwall. By Herbert Corey. Vol. XLVI, pp. 653-694, 44 ills., 1 half-page map, Dec., 1924.

Charm Spots Along England's Harassed Coast. 16 ills. in duotone from photographs. Vol. LXXVIII, pp. 237-252, Aug., 1940.

Cotton for England. Vol. XV, p. 39, Jan., 1904.

Cradles of English History. 15 ills. in color from natural-color photographs by Clifton Adams and Bernard Wakeman. Vol. LIX, pp. 268-277, Mar., 1931.

England—*Continued*

Democracy's Royal Palace (Westminster). 19 ills. in color from natural-color photographs by B. Anthony Stewart. Vol. XC, pp. 233-248, Aug., 1946.

Down Devon Lanes. By Herbert Corey. Vol. LV, pp. 529-568, 45 ills., 1 two-thirds-page map, May, 1929.

8th Air Force in England. 10 ills. in color from U. S. Army Air Forces official photographs. Vol. LXXXVII, pp. 297-304, Mar., 1945.

England's Island Garden of Rocks and Flowers (Isle of Wight). 14 ills. in color from natural-color photographs by W. Robert Moore. Vol. LXVII, pp. 17-24, Jan., 1935.

England's Lake District, Fountainhead of Poetry. 10 ills. in color from natural-color photographs. Vol. LXIX, pp. 513-520, Apr., 1936.

England's Sun Trap Isle of Wight. By J. R. Hildebrand. Vol. LXVII, pp, 1-33, 22 ills. in black and white, 14 ills. in color, 1 half-page map, Jan., 1935.

Europe's Endangered Fish Supply: War and the North Sea Fisheries. Vol. XXVII, pp. 141-152, 9 ills., 1 half-page map, Feb., 1915.

Everyday Life in Wartime England. By Harvey Klemmer. Vol. LXXIX, pp. 497-534, 48 ills., Apr., 1941.

From Stratford to the North Sea. 16 ills. in color from autochromes by Clifton Adams. Vol. LV, pp. 616-625, May, 1929.

Great Britain on Parade. By Maynard Owen Williams. Vol. LXVIII, pp. 137-184, 40 ills. in black and white, 11 ills. in color, Aug., 1935.

Informal Salute to the English Lakes. By Maynard Owen Williams. Vol. LXIX, pp. 511-521, 10 ills. in color, Apr., 1936.

Lakeland, Home of England's Nature Poets. 15 ills. in color from autochromes by Clifton Adams. Vol. LV, pp. 592-601, May, 1929.

Lend-Lease Is a Two-way Benefit: Innovation in Creative Statesmanship Pools Resources of United Nations, and Supplies American Forces Around the World. By Francis Flood. Vol. LXXXIII, pp. 745-761, 14 ills., June, 1943.

Modern Pilgrim's Map of the British Isles. By Andrew H. Brown. Text accompanying special map supplement in colors. Vol. LXXI, pp. 795-802, 3 ills., June, 1937.

Nooks and Bays of Storied England. 13 ills. in color from natural-color photographs by Clifton Adams and Bernard Wakeman. Vol. LXI, pp. 182-191, Feb., 1932.

Oldest Nation of Europe: Geographical Factors in the Strength of Modern England. By Roland G. Usher. Vol. XXVI, pp. 393-414, 11 ills., Oct., 1914.

One Hundred British Seaports. Vol. XXXI, pp. 84-94, 10 ills., 1 page map, Jan., 1917.

Penn Country in Sussex: Home of Pennsylvania's Founder Abounds in Quaker History and Memories of Adventurous Smugglers. By Col. P. T. Etherton. Vol. LXVIII, pp. 59-90, 32 ills., 1 page map, July, 1935.

England—*Continued*

Preservation of England's Historic and Scenic Treasures. By Eric Underwood. Vol. LXXXVII, pp. 413-440, 24 ills., 1 two-page map, Apr., 1945.

Rural Britain Carries On. By Harvey Klemmer. Vol. LXXX, pp. 527-552, 27 ills., Oct., 1941.

Summering in an English Cottage: Quiet and Loveliness Invite Contemplation in the Extra "Room," the Garden of the Thatched House. By Helen Churchill Candee. Vol. LXVII, pp. 429-456, 32 ills., Apr., 1935.

Thames, England's Gateway to the World. 10 ills. in color from natural-color photographs by B. Anthony Stewart. Vol. LXXV, pp. 253-260, Feb., 1939.

Through the English Lake District Afoot and Awheel. By Ralph A. Graves. Vol. LV, pp. 577-603, 19 ills. in black and white, 15 ills. in color, 1 quarter-page map, May, 1929.

Through the Heart of England in a Canadian Canoe. By R. J. Evans. Vol. XLI, pp. 473-497, 26 ills., 1 half-page map, May, 1922.

Time and Tide on the Thames. By Frederick Simpich. Vol. LXXV, pp. 239-272, 23 ills. in black and white, 10 ills. in color, 1 map, Feb., 1939.

Tour in the English Fenland. By Christopher Marlowe. Vol. LV, pp. 605-634, 26 ills. in black and white, 5 ills. in color, 1 half-page map, May, 1929.

Transportation in England. Vol. XVI, p. 88, Feb., 1905.

Vacation in a Fifteenth Century English Manor House. By George Alden Sanford. Vol. LIII, pp. 629-636, 8 ills., May, 1928.

Vagabonding in England: A Young American Works His Way Around the British Isles and Sees Sights from an Unusual Point of View. By John McWilliams. Vol. LXV, pp. 357-398, 39 ills., 1 three-quarters-page map, Mar., 1934.

Visits to the Old Inns of England: Historic Homes of Hospitality for the Wayfarer Dot the Length and Breadth of the Kingdom. By Harold Donaldson Eberlein. Vol. LIX, pp. 261-285, 17 ills. in black and white, 15 ills. in color, Mar., 1931.

Wayfaring down the Winding Severn. 15 ills. in color from natural-color photographs by Frank and Bernard Wakeman. Vol. LXIII, pp. 432-441, Apr., 1933.

When the Herring Fleet Comes to Great Yarmouth. By W. Robert Moore. Vol. LXVI, pp. 233-250, 19 ills., Aug., 1934.

Yanks at Westminster. By Capt. Leonard David Gammans. Vol. XC, pp. 223-252, 6 ills. in black and white, 19 ills. in color, Aug., 1946.

See also Bampton; Beaconsfield; Cambridge; Dover; Great Britain; London; Man, Isle of; Oxford; Plymouth; Scilly Islands; Southampton; Warwick; Winchester.

England's Wild Moorland Ponies. 10 ills. from photographs. Vol. LXXXIX, pp. 129-136, Jan., 1946.

English Channel:

Oil for Victory Piped under the Sea. 9 ills. from photographs. Vol. LXXXVIII, pp. 721-726, Dec., 1945.

Engravings and Etchings:

Cathedrals of England: An Artist's Pilgrimage to These Majestic Monuments of Man's Genius and Faith. By Norman Wilkinson. Vol. LXXVI, pp. 741-762, 3 ills. in black and white, 16 ills. in gravure from dry-point engravings by the author, Dec., 1939.

Ships of the Centuries. 16 ills. in gravure from original etchings by Norman Wilkinson. Vol. LXXIII, pp. 65-80; text, p. 98, Jan., 1938.

Enigma of Cambodia (French Indo-China). 27 ills. in color from autochromes by Gervais Courtellemont. Vol. LIV, pp. 306-323, Sept., 1928.

Eniwetok (Atoll), Marshall Islands:

Our New Military Wards, the Marshalls. By W. Robert Moore. Vol. LXXXVIII, pp. 325-360, 14 ills. in black and white, 20 ills. in color, 1 half-page map, Sept., 1945.

Entering the Front Doors of Medieval Towns: The Adventures of an American Woman and Her Daughter in a Folding Boat on Eight Rivers of Germany and Austria. By Cornelia Stratton Parker. Vol. LXI, pp. 365-394, 23 ills., 1 two-thirds-page map, Mar., 1932.

Entertainment. *See* Sports and Games.

Entomology. *See* Insects.

Entre Ríos (Province), Argentina:

Pioneer Gaucho Days. 8 ills. in color from paintings by Cesáreo Bernaldo de Quirós. Vol. LXIV, pp. 453-460, Oct., 1933.

Ephesus (Ancient City):

Some Ruined Cities of Asia Minor. By Ernest L. Harris. Vol. XIX, pp. 833-858, 19 ills., Dec., 1908.

Epler, Blanch Nettleton:

Bit of Elizabethan England in America: Fisher Folk of the Islands Off North Carolina Conserved the Speech and Customs of Sir Walter Raleigh's Colonists. By Blanch Nettleton Epler. Vol. LXIV, pp. 695-730, 43 ills., 1 three-quarters-page map, Dec., 1933.

Erebus, Mount, Antarctica:

Heart of the Antarctic. By Ernest H. Shackleton. Vol. XX, pp. 972-1007, 27 ills., 1 half-page map, Nov., 1909.

Erg, El (Region), Algeria:

Country of the Ant Men. By Thomas H. Kearney. Vol. XXII, pp. 367-382, 11 ills., 1 page map, Apr., 1911.

Erie, Lake:

Rainfall and the Level of Lake Erie. By E. L. Moseley. Vol. XIV, pp. 327-328, Aug., 1903.

Erie, Lake—*Continued*

Submerged Valleys in Sandusky Bay. By E. L. Moseley. Vol. XIII, pp. 398-403, 4 charts, Nov., 1902.

Testing the Currents of Lake Erie. By E. L. Moseley. Vol. XIV, pp. 41-42, Jan., 1903.

Erie, Pennsylvania :

Industrial Titan of America : Pennsylvania, Once the Keystone of the Original Thirteen, Now the Keystone of Forty-eight Sovereign States. By John Oliver La Gorce. Vol. XXXV, pp. 367-406, 33 ills., 1 page map, May, 1919.

Erie Canal, New York :

New Erie Canal. Vol. XVI, pp. 568-570, 1 page map, Dec., 1905.

Eritrea:

With the Italians in Eritrea : Torrid Colony Between the Red Sea and Ethiopia, 2,600 Miles by Sea from Rome, Is Mobilization Place of Fascist Troops and Planes. By Harald P. Lechenperg. Vol. LXVIII, pp. 265-295, 34 ills., 1 two-page map, Sept., 1935.

Erivan, U. S. S. R. :

Land of the Stalking Death : A Journey Through Starving Armenia on an American Relief Train. By Melville Chater. Vol. XXXVI, pp. 393-420, 23 ills., Nov., 1919.

Old Post-Road from Tiflis to Erivan. By Esther Lancraft Hovey. Vol. XII, pp. 300-309, 9 ills., Aug., 1901.

Ernst Thaelmann (Collective Farm), U. S. S. R. : Sunny Siberia. 26 ills. in color from natural-color photographs by Owen Lattimore. Vol. LXXXVI, pp. 649-672, Dec., 1944.

Erosion. *See* Soil Erosion.

Erratic (Geologic Formation of the United States). By O. A. Ljungstedt. Vol. XXI, pp. 525-531, 4 ills., 1 three-quarters-page map, June, 1910.

Eruption of Krakatoa. By Sir Robert Ball. Vol. XIII, pp. 200-204, June, 1902.

Eruption of Mount Vesuvius, April 7-8, 1906. By Dr. Thomas Augustus Jaggar. Vol. XVII, pp. 318-325, 6 ills., June, 1906.

Eruptions of La Soufrière, St. Vincent, in May, 1902. By Edmund Otis Hovey. Vol. XIII, pp. 444-459, 4 ills., Dec., 1902.

Erzurum, Turkey :

Turkish Republic Comes of Age. By Maynard Owen Williams. Vol. LXXXVII, pp. 581-616, 4 ills. in black and white, 29 ills. in color, 1 map (two-page spread), May, 1945.

Escort Carriers:

Cruise on an Escort Carrier. By Melville Bell Grosvenor. Vol. LXXXIV, pp. 513-546, 14 ills. in black and white, 20 ills. in color, Nov., 1943.

Pocket Carriers Fight the Submarines. 20 ills. in color from natural-color photographs. Vol. LXXXIV, pp. 521-544, Nov., 1943.

Escort Carriers—*Continued*

Ships That Won the Greatest Naval War. 26 ills. in color from U. S. Navy official photographs. Vol. LXXXIX, pp. 697-736, June, 1946.

Your Navy as Peace Insurance. By Fleet Admiral Chester W. Nimitz. Vol. LXXXIX, pp. 681-736, 32 ills. in black and white, 26 ills. in color, June, 1946.

Esdraelon (Plain), Palestine :

Impressions of Palestine. By James Bryce. Vol. XXVII, pp. 293-317, 18 ills., 1 page map, Mar., 1915.

Eskimos:

Alaska—Our Northwestern Outpost. 16 ills. in color from natural-color photographs by Ernest H. Gruening, Amos Burg, and Froelich Rainey. Vol. LXXXII, pp. 297-308, Sept., 1942.

Coast Guard Patrol in Greenland. 9 ills. in color from natural-color photographs by Lieut. Thomas S. La Farge. Vol. LXXXIII, pp. 565-572, May, 1943.

Desolate Greenland, Now an American Outpost. 17 ills. from photographs ; 12 ills. by Willie Knutsen ; 4 ills. by F. Vogel. Vol. LXXX, pp. 393-406, Sept., 1941.

Discovering Alaska's Oldest Arctic Town : A Scientist Finds Ivory-eyed Skeletons of a Mysterious People and Joins Modern Eskimos in the Dangerous Spring Whale Hunt. By Froelich G. Rainey. Vol. LXXXII, pp. 319-336, 15 ills., Sept., 1942.

Exploring Frozen Fragments of American History : On the Trail of Early Eskimo Colonists Who Made a 55-Mile Crossing from the Old World to the New. By Henry B. Collins, Jr. Vol. LXXV, pp. 633-656, 24 ills., 1 two-thirds-page map, May, 1939.

First Natural-Color Photographs from the Arctic. 22 ills. in color from natural-color photographs by Jacob Gayer and Maynard Owen Williams. Vol. XLIX, pp. 300-317, Mar., 1926.

Greenland from 1898 to Now : "Captain Bob," Who Went North with Peary, Tells of 42 Years of Exploration in the Orphan Island of New Aerial and Naval Interest. By Robert A. Bartlett. Vol. LXXVIII, pp. 111-140, 25 ills., 1 two-page map, July, 1940.

Origin of Stefansson's Blond Eskimo. By Maj. Gen. A. W. Greely. Vol. XXIII, pp. 1224-1238, 10 ills., 1 page map, Dec., 1912.

Peary as a Leader : Incidents from the Life of the Discoverer of the North Pole Told by One of His Lieutenants on the Expedition Which Reached the Goal. By Donald B. MacMillan. Vol. XXXVII, pp. 293-317, 20 ills., 1 page map, Apr., 1920.

Espíritu Santo (Island), New Hebrides :

Painting History in the Pacific. 19 ills. in color from paintings by Lt. William F. Draper. Vol. LXXXVI, pp. 409-424, Oct., 1944.

Estates:

Channel Islands: Feudal Isle of Sark: Where Sixteenth-Century Laws Are Still Observed. By Sibyl Hathaway (La Dame de Serk). Vol. LXII, pp. 101-119, 21 ills., 1 half-page map, July, 1932.

England: Preservation of England's Historic and Scenic Treasures. By Eric Underwood. Vol. LXXXVII, pp. 413-440, 24 ills., 1 two-page map, Apr., 1945.

England: Vacation in a Fifteenth Century English Manor House. By George Alden Sanford. Vol. LIII, pp. 629-636, 8 ills., May, 1928.

Mexican Hacienda. By J. E. Kirkwood. Vol. XXV, pp. 563-584, 18 ills., May, 1914.

Monticello: Jefferson's Little Mountain: Romance Enfolds Monticello, the Restored Home of the Author of the Declaration of Independence. By Paul Wilstach. Vol. LV, pp. 481-503, 12 ills. in black and white, 12 ills. in color, Apr., 1929.

Monticello, One of America's Most Historic Shrines. 12 ills. in color from natural-color photographs by Edwin L. Wisherd, Charles Martin, and Jacob Gayer. Vol. LV, pp. 488-497, Apr., 1929.

Mount Vernon: Home of the First Farmer of America. By Worth E. Shoults. Vol. LIII, pp. 603-628, 6 ills. in black and white, 26 ills. in color, May, 1928.

South Carolina: Ashley River and Its Gardens. By E. T. H. Shaffer. Vol. XLIX, pp. 525-550, 6 ills. in black and white, 7 ills. in color, May, 1926.

South Carolina: Exploring the Atlantic Seaboard With a Color Camera. 7 ills. in color from autochromes by Jacob Gayer. Vol. XLIX, pp. 532-549, May, 1926.

Sweden: Color and Customs of Sweden's Château Country. 13 ills. in color from natural-color photographs by Gustav Heurlin. Vol. LXVI, pp. 33-40, July, 1934.

Sweden: Country-House Life in Sweden: In Castle and Cottage the Landed Gentry Gallantly Keep the Old Traditions. By Amelie Posse-Brázdová. Vol. LXVI, pp. 1-64, 51 ills. in black and white, 13 ills. in color, 1 page map, July, 1934.

Virginia—A Commonwealth That Has Come Back. By William Joseph Showalter. Vol. LV, pp. 403-472, 69 ills. in black and white, 13 ills. in color, 1 page map, Apr., 1929.

Virginia: Gardens and Shrines of Old Virginia. 20 ills. in color from natural-color photographs by B. Anthony Stewart and J. Baylor Roberts. Vol. LXXXI, pp. 623-646, May, 1942.

Virginia: Tidewater Virginia, Where History Lives. By Albert W. Atwood. Vol. LXXXI, pp. 617-656, 18 ills. in black and white, 20 ills. in color, 1 page map, May, 1942.

See also Haciendas.

Estonia:

Estonia: At Russia's Baltic Gate: War Often Has Ravaged This Little Nation Whose Identity Was Long Submerged in the Vast Sea of Russian Peoples. By Baroness Irina Ungern-Sternberg. Vol. LXXVI, pp. 803-834, 33 ills., 1 half-page map, Dec., 1939.

Estonia—*Continued*

Flying Around the Baltic. By Douglas Chandler. Vol. LXXIII, pp. 767-806, 31 ills. in black and white, 13 ills. in duotone, 1 half-page map, June, 1938.

New Map of Europe: Showing the Boundaries Established by the Peace Conference at Paris and by Subsequent Decisions of the Supreme Council of Allied and Associated Powers. By Ralph A. Graves. Text accompanying special map supplement in colors. Vol. XXXIX, pp. 157-177, 18 ills., Feb., 1921.

Races of Europe. By Edwin A. Grosvenor. Vol. XXXIV, 441-534, 62 ills., special map supplement in colors, 2 page maps, Dec., 1918.

Etherton, (Col.) P. T.:

Penn Country in Sussex (England): Home of Pennsylvania's Founder Abounds in Quaker History and Memories of Adventurous Smugglers. By Col. P. T. Etherton. Vol. LXVIII, pp. 59-90, 32 ills., 1 page map, July, 1935.

Ethiopia (Abyssinia):

Abyssinia—The Country and People. By Oscar T. Crosby. Vol. XII, pp. 89-102, Mar., 1901.

Across Widest Africa. By A. Henry Savage Landor. Vol. XIX, pp. 694-737, 38 ills., 1 half-page map, Oct., 1908.

Caravan Journey Through Abyssinia: From Addis Ababa Through Lalibela, the Strange Jerusalem of Ethiopia, in Search of New Grains for American Farms. By Harry V. Harlan. Vol. XLVII, pp. 613-663, 46 ills., 1 half-page map, June, 1925.

Consul Skinner's Mission to Abyssinia. Vol. XV, pp. 164-166, 1 ill., Apr., 1904.

Coronation Days in Addis Ababa. By W. Robert Moore. Vol LIX, pp. 738-746, 8 ills., June, 1931.

Explorations in Central East Africa. Vol. XII, pp. 42-43, Jan., 1901.

Geography of Abyssinia. Vol. XII, pp. 274-276, July, 1901.

Life's Tenor in Ethiopia: Africa's Land of Early Christianity Now Yields Minerals for Modern Industry. By James Loder Park. Vol. LXVII, pp. 783-793, 8 ills., June, 1935.

Modern Ethiopia: Haile Selassie the First, Formerly Ras Tafari, Succeeds to the World's Oldest Continuously Sovereign Throne. By Addison E. Southard. Vol. LIX, pp. 679-738, 47 ills. in black and white, 27 ills. in color, 1 two-thirds-page map, June, 1931.

Nature and Man in Ethiopia. By Wilfred H. Osgood. Vol. LIV, pp. 121-176, 64 ills., 1 two-thirds-page map, Aug., 1928.

Open-Air Law Courts of Ethiopia. 18 ills. by Harald P. Lechenperg. Vol. LXVIII, pp. 633-646, Nov., 1935.

Present Day Scenes in the World's Oldest Empire. 27 ills. in color from natural-color photographs by Robert Moore. Vol. LIX, pp. 690-723, June, 1931.

Ethiopia (Abyssinia)—*Continued*

Traveling in the Highlands of Ethiopia. By Leo B. Roberts. Vol. LXVIII, pp. 297-328, 37 ills., Sept., 1935.

Ethnology. *See* Anthropology.

Etruscans:

Ancient Rome Brought to Life. By Rhys Carpenter. Paintings by H. M. Herget. Vol. XC, pp. 567-633, 2 ills. in black and white, 32 ills. in color, 1 half-page map, Nov., 1946.

Eucalyptus (Tree) :

Lonely Australia : The Unique Continent. By Herbert E. Gregory. Vol. XXX, pp. 473-568, 68 ills., 1 two-page and 4 half-page maps, Dec., 1916.

Notes on the Eucalyptus Tree from the United States Forest Service. Vol. XX, pp. 668-673, 4 ills., July, 1909.

Tallest Tree That Grows. By Edgerton R. Young. Vol. XX, pp. 664-667, 3 ills., July, 1909.

Eugenics:

Few Thoughts Concerning Eugenics. By Alexander Graham Bell. Vol. XIX, pp. 119-123, Feb., 1908.

Our Immigration Laws from the Viewpoint of National Eugenics. By Robert De C. Ward. Vol. XXIII, pp. 38-41, Jan., 1912.

Who Shall Inherit Long Life ? On the Existence of a Natural Process at Work Among Beings Tending to Improve the Vigor and Vitality of Succeeding Generations. By Alexander Graham Bell. Vol. XXXV, pp. 505-514, 13 ills., June, 1919.

Euphrates (River), Asia :

Cradle of Civilization : The Historic Lands Along The Euphrates and Tigris Rivers Where Briton Is Fighting Turk. By James Baikie. Vol. XXIX, pp. 127-162, 25 ills., Feb., 1916.

Mountaineers of the Euphrates. By Ellsworth Huntington. Vol. XX, pp. 142-156, 13 ills., Feb., 1909.

Mystic Nedjef, the Shia Mecca. By Frederick Simpich. Vol. XXVI, pp. 589-598, 4 ills., Dec., 1914.

Where Adam and Eve Lived (Baghdad). By Frederick and Margaret Simpich. Vol. XXVI, pp. 546-588, 25 ills., Dec., 1914.

Europe:

Along the Old Silk Routes : A Motor Caravan with Air-conditioned Trailer Retraces Ancient Roads from Paris across Europe and Half of Asia to Delhi. By Lawrence Copley Thaw and Margaret S. Thaw. Vol. LXXVIII, pp. 453-486, 33 ills., 1 map, Oct., 1940.

Americans Help Liberated Europe Live Again. By Lt. Col. Frederick Simpich, Jr. Vol. LXXXVII, pp. 747-768, 17 ills., June, 1945.

Europe—*Continued*

Battle Line of Languages in Western Europe : A Problem in Human Geography More Perplexing Than That of International Boundaries. By A. L. Guerard. Vol. XLIII, pp. 145-180, 36 ills., Feb., 1923.

By Sail Across Europe. By Merlin Minshall. Vol. LXXI, pp. 533-567, 38 ills., 1 two-thirds-page map, May, 1937.

European Populations. By Walter J. Ballard. Vol. XVI, p. 432, Sept., 1905.

European Scenes. Vol. XXXII, pp. 519-534, 16 ills., Nov.-Dec., 1917.

Europe's Endangered Fish Supply : War and the North Sea Fisheries. Vol. XXVII, pp. 141-152, 9 ills., 1 half-page map, Feb., 1915.

Europe's Looted Art. By John Walker. Vol. LXXXIX, pp. 39-52, 11 ills., Jan., 1946.

Flags of Europe, Asia and Africa. By Byron McCandless and Gilbert Grosvenor. Vol. XXXII, pp. 372-385, 100 ills. in color, Oct., 1917.

Flying Around the Baltic. By Douglas Chandler. Vol. LXXIII, pp. 767-806, 31 ills. in black and white, 13 ills. in duotone, 1 half-page map, June, 1938.

Flying Around the North Atlantic. By Anne Morrow Lindberg. Foreword by Charles A. Lindbergh. Vol. LXVI, pp. 259-337, 82 ills., 1 two-page and 1 two-thirds-page maps, Sept., 1934.

From Africa to the Alps. 8 ills. in color from U. S. Army Air Forces official photographs. Vol. LXXXIX, pp. 161-168, Feb., 1946.

From England to India by Automobile : An 8,527-Mile Trip Through Ten Countries, from London to Quetta, Requires Five and a Half Months. By Maj. F. A. C. Forbes-Leith. Vol. XLVIII, pp. 191-223, 33 ills., 1 third-page map, Aug., 1925.

From London to Australia by Aëroplane : A Personal Narrative of the First Aërial Voyage Half Around the World. By Sir Ross Smith. Vol. XXXIX, pp. 229-339, 76 ills. in black and white, 8 ills. in color, 1 page map, Mar., 1921.

Geographic's New Map of Europe and the Mediterranean. By Gilbert Grosvenor. Text accompanying special map supplement in colors. Vol. LXXIII, pp. 525-528, 1 ill., Apr., 1938.

Geographic's New Map of Germany and Its Approaches : With a Review of The Society's Maps of Europe. By Gilbert Grosvenor. Text accompanying special map supplement in colors. Vol. LXXXVI, pp. 66-72, 1 ill., July, 1944.

Contains information on the Boundary Changes in Europe from 1912 to 1940.

Looking Down on Europe : The Thrills and Advantages of Sight-Seeing by Airplane, as Demonstrated on a 6,500-Mile Tour Over Commercial Aviation Routes. By Lieut. J. Parker Van Zandt. Vol. XLVII, pp. 261-326, 67 ills., 1 half-page map, Mar., 1925.

Europe—*Continued*

Looking Down on Europe Again: Crisscrossing Air Tracks Reveal Nature's Scenic Masterpieces and Man's Swift-changing Boundaries and Structures. By J. Parker Van Zandt. Vol. LXXV, pp. 791-822, 31 ills., 1 page map, June, 1939.

Map of Europe, Including the New Balkan States. Text accompanying special map supplement in colors. Vol. XXVI, pp. 191-192, Aug., 1914.

National Geographic War Zone Map. Text accompanying special map supplement in colors. Vol. XXIX, p. 494, May, 1918.

New Map of Europe: Showing the Boundaries Established by the Peace Conference at Paris and by Subsequent Decisions of the Supreme Council of the Allied and Associated Powers. By Ralph A. Graves. Text accompanying special map supplement in colors. Vol. XXXIV, pp. 157-177, 18 ills., Feb., 1921.

New Map of Europe and the Near East. Text accompanying special map supplement in colors. Vol. LXXXIII, pp. 762-763, 1 ill., June, 1943.

New Map of Europe Records War Changes. Text accompanying special map supplement in colors. Vol. LXXVII, p. 625, May, 1940.

Races of Europe. By Edwin A. Grosvenor. Vol. XXXIV, pp. 441-534, 62 ills., 2 page maps, special map supplement in colors, Dec., 1918.

Remarkable Growth of Europe During 40 Years of Peace. By O. P. Austin. Vol. XXVI, pp. 272-274, Sept., 1914.

Scenes in Europe. Vol. XXVIII, pp. 551-566, 16 ills., Dec., 1915.

Scenes in Europe. Vol. XXX, pp. 233-248, 16 ills. in color, Sept., 1916.

Society's New Map of Central Europe and the Mediterranean. Text accompanying special map supplement in colors. Vol. LXXVI, pp. 559-560, Oct., 1939.

Society's New Map of Europe. Text by Gilbert Grosvenor. Vol. LVI, pp. 771-774, Dec., 1929.

Tale of Three Cities (Prague, Vienna, Budapest). By Thomas R. Henry. Vol. LXXXVIII, pp. 641-669, 23 ills., Dec., 1945.

Wayside Scenes in Europe. Vol. XXV, pp. 226-244, 19 ills., Feb., 1914.

Wayside Scenes in Europe. Vol. XXVII, pp. 401-416, 16 ills., Apr., 1915.

See also names of individual countries.

European Outpost: The Azores. By Harriet Chalmers Adams. Xol. LXVII, pp. 35-66, 25 ills. in black and white, 13 ills. in color, 1 half-page map, Jan., 1935.

European Populations. By Walter J. Ballard. Vol. XVI, p. 432, Sept., 1905.

European Tributes to Peary. Vol. XXI, pp. 536-540, 4 ills., June, 1910.

European War. *See* World War I.

Europe's Endangered Fish Supply: War and the North Sea Fisheries. Vol. XXVII, pp. 141-152, 9 ills., 1 half-page map, Feb., 1915.

Europe's Looted Art. By John Walker. Vol. LXXXIX, pp. 39-52, 11 ills., Jan., 1946.

Europe's Newest Kingdom: After Centuries of Struggle, Albania at Last Enjoys an Era of Peace and Stability. By Melville Chater. Vol. LIX, pp. 131-191, 37 ills. in black and white, 25 ills. in color, 1 half-page map, Feb., 1931.

Europe's Northern Nomads (Lapps). 12 ills. in color from natural-color photographs by Jack Kuhne. Vol. LXXVI, pp. 657-664, Nov., 1939.

Evans, Malcolm:

Storied Islands of the South Sea. 20 ills. in color from natural-color photographs; 5 ills. by Malcolm Evans. Vol. LXXXI, pp. 9-40, Jan., 1942.

Evans, R. J.:

Through the Heart of England in a Canadian Canoe. By R. J. Evans. Vol. XLI, pp. 473-497, 26 ills., 1 half-page map, May, 1922.

Evans, (Rear Adm.) Robley D.:

Honors to the American Navy (Address by Rear Adm. Robley D. Evans). Vol. XX, pp. 77-95, Jan., 1909.

Ever Changing California, Land of Startling Contrasts. 30 ills. in color from autochromes by Charles Martin. Vol. LV, pp. 704-745, June, 1929.

Everest, Mount, Nepal-Tibet:

Aërial Conquest of Everest. Flying Over the World's Highest Mountain Realizes the Objective of Many Heroic Explorers. By Lieut. Col. L. V. S. Blacker. Vol. LXIV, pp. 127-162, 35 ills., 1 page map, Aug., 1933.

Everett, Dorothea D.:

Black Acres: A Thrilling Sketch in the Vast Volume of Who's Who Among the Peoples That Make America. By Dorothea D. and Fred Everett. Vol. LXXX, pp. 631-652, 13 ills. in black and white, 12 ills. in color, Nov., 1941.

Everett, Fred:

Black Acres: A Thrilling Sketch in the Vast Volume of Who's Who Among the Peoples That Make America. By Dorothea D. and Fred Everett. Vol. LXXX, pp. 631-652, 13 ills. in black and white, 12 ills. in color, Nov., 1941.

Everglades (Region), Florida:

South Florida's Amazing Everglades: Encircled by Populous Places Is a Seldom-visited Area of Rare Birds, Prairies, Cowboys, and Teeming Wild Life of Big Cypress Swamp. By John O'Reilly. Vol. LXXVII, pp. 115-142, 26 ills., 1 page map, Jan., 1940.

Evermann, (Dr.) Barton Warren:

Bureau of Fisheries. By Dr. Barton Warren Evermann. Vol. XV, pp. 191-212, 11 ills., 3 diagrams, May, 1904.

Everyday Life in Afghanistan. By Frederick Simpich and Haji Mirza Hussein. Vol. XXXIX, pp. 85-110, 26 ills., 1 three-quarters-page map, Jan., 1921.

Everyday Life in Pueblo Bonito: As Disclosed by the National Geographic Society's Archeologic Explorations in the Chaco Canyon National Monument, New Mexico. By Neil M. Judd. Vol. XLVIII, pp. 227-262, 37 ills., 1 two-thirds-page map, Sept., 1925.

Everyday Life in Wartime England. By Harvey Klemmer. Vol. LXXIX, pp. 497-534, 48 ills., Apr., 1941.

Evidences of Recent Volcanic Action in Southeast Alaska. Vol. XVII, pp. 173 and 176, Mar., 1906.

Evolution of Russian Government. By Edwin A. Grosvenor. Vol. XVI, pp. 309-332, 16 ills., July, 1905.

Ewing, Henry E.:

Afield with the Spiders: Web Hunting in the Marshlands and Woodlands and Along the Lanes. By Henry E. Ewing. Vol. LXIV, pp. 163-194, 26 ills. in black and white, 64 ills. in color, Aug., 1933.

Excavations at Abydos. By W. M. Flinders Petrie. Vol. XIV, pp. 358-359, Sept., 1903.

Excavations at Nippur (Iraq). Vol. XI, p. 392, Oct., 1900.

Excavations at Quirigua, Guatemala. By Sylvanus Griswold Morley. Vol. XXIV, pp. 339-361, 24 ills., 1 diagram, Mar., 1913.

Excavations of M. de Morgan at Susa. Vol. XII, p. 315, Aug., 1901.

Excursions. See National Geographic Society: Excursions.

Exmoor Ponies:

England's Wild Moorland Ponies. 10 ills. from photographs. Vol. LXXXIX, pp. 129-136, Jan., 1946.

Expansion of England. By Edwin D. Mead. Vol. XI, pp. 249-263, July, 1900.

Expedition into Texas of Fernando del Bosque, Standard-Bearer of the King, Don Carlos II, in the Year 1675. Translated from an Old, Unpublished Spanish Manuscript. By Betty B. Brewster. Vol. XIV, pp. 339-348, Sept., 1903.

Expedition to Turkestan. Vol. XIV, p. 215, May, 1903.

Expedition Unearths Buried Masterpieces of Carved Jade (Cerro de las Mesas, Mexico). By Matthew W. Stirling. Vol. LXXX, pp. 277-302, 14 ills. in black and white, 20 ills. in color, 1 two-thirds-page map, Sept., 1941.

Expeditions:

By Coolie and Caravan Across Central Asia: Narrative of a 7,900-Mile Journey of Exploration and Research Over the "Roof of the World," from the Indian Ocean to the Yellow Sea (Morden-Clark Asiatic Expedition). By William J. Morden. Vol. LII, pp. 369-431, 73 ills., 1 page map, Oct., 1927.

Expeditions—*Continued*

Climbing Mighty Minya Konka: Americans First Scaled Mountain That Now is Landmark of China's New Skyway. By Richard L. Burdsall and Terris Moore. Vol. LXXXIII, pp. 625-650, 23 ills., 1 page map, May, 1943.

Crosby Expedition to Tibet. Vol. XV, pp. 228-231, 3 ills., May, 1904.

Earth's Most Primitive People: A Journey with the Aborigines of Central Australia. By Charles P. Mountford. Vol. LXXXIX, pp. 89-112, 10 ills. in black and white, 8 ills. in color, 1 half-page map, Jan., 1946.

Expeditions in the Arctic and Antarctic. Vol. XIII, pp. 179-180, May, 1902.

Fit to Fight Anywhere (Quartermaster Corps Expedition). By Frederick Simpich. Vol. LXXXIV, pp. 233-256, 26 ills., Aug., 1943.

Quinine Hunters in Ecuador. By Froelich Rainey. Vol. LXXXIX, pp. 341-363, 21 ills., 1 half-page map, Mar., 1946.

See also American Museum of Natural History; Antarctic Regions; Arctic Regions; Lady Franklin Bay Expedition; MacMillan Arctic Expeditions; Mountain Climbing; National Geographic Society: Expeditions; Shedd Aquarium; Smithsonian Institution.

Experiences in the Grand Canyon. By Ellsworth and Emery Kolb. Vol. XXVI, pp. 99-184, 70 ills., 1 page map, Aug., 1914.

Experiences of a Lone Geographer: An American Agricultural Explorer Makes His Way Through Brigand-Infested Central China en Route to the Amne Machin Range, Tibet. By Joseph F. Rock. Vol. XLVIII, pp. 331-347, 16 ills., 1 quarter-page map, Sept., 1925.

Exploration. *See* Agricultural and Botanical Explorers; Discoverers; Expeditions.

Exploration During Victoria's Reign. Vol. XII, p. 160, Apr., 1901.

Exploration in the Canadian Rockies. Vol. X, pp. 135-136, Apr., 1899.

Explorations in Alaska. Vol. X, pp. 269-271, July, 1899.

Explorations in Central East Africa. Vol. XII, pp. 42-43, Jan., 1901.

Explorations in Crete. By Edith H. Hall. Vol. XX, pp. 778-787, 15 ills., Sept., 1909.

Explorations in Peru. Vol. XXIII, pp. 416-422, 7 ills., 1 half-page map, Apr., 1912.

Explorations in the Gobi Desert. By Roy Chapman Andrews. Vol. LXIII, pp. 653-716, 50 ills. in black and white, 20 ills. in color, 1 half-page map, June, 1933.

Explorations in Tibet. Vol. XIV, pp. 353-355, Sept., 1903.

Explorer (Balloon):

Exploring the Stratosphere. By Capt. Albert W. Stevens. Vol. LXVI, pp. 397-434, 43 ills., 1 two-thirds-page chart, Oct., 1934.

Explorer II (Balloon):

First natural-color photograph taken in the stratosphere. 1 ill. in color by Maj. Albert W. Stevens. Vol. LXXI, p. 340, Mar., 1937.

National Geographic Society-U. S. Army Air Corps Stratosphere Flight of 1935 in Balloon *Explorer II* (Contributed Technical Papers, Stratosphere Series, No. 2). Vol. LXXI, p. 340, Mar., 1937; p. 802, June, 1937.

Explorers. *See* Agricultural and Botanical Explorers; Discoverers.

Explorers of a New Kind: Successful Introduction of Beetles and Parasites to Check Ravages of the Gypsy-Moth and Brown-Tail Moth. By L. O. Howard. Vol. XXVI, pp. 38-67, 11 ills. in black and white, 5 ills. in color, July, 1914.

Exploring a Grass Wonderland of Wild West China. By Ray G. Johnson. Vol. LXXXV, pp. 713-742, 24 ills., 1 half-page map, June, 1944.

Exploring Frozen Fragments of American History: On the Trail of Early Eskimo Colonists Who Made a 55-Mile Crossing from the Old World to the New. By Henry B. Collins, Jr. Vol. LXXV, pp. 633-656, 24 ills., 1 two-thirds-page map, May, 1939.

Exploring in the Canyon of Death (Arizona): Remains of a People Who Dwelt in Our Southwest at Least 4,000 Years Ago Are Revealed. By Earl H. Morris. Vol. XLVIII, pp. 263-300, 24 ills. in black and white, 22 ills. in color, Sept., 1925.

Exploring Neptune's Hidden World of Vivid Color. 8 ills. in color from paintings by E. Bostelmann. Vol. LXII, pp. 747-754, Dec., 1932.

Exploring the Atlantic Seaboard with a Color Camera. 18 ills. in color from autochromes by Charles Martin and Jacob Gayer. Vol. XLIX, pp. 532-549, May, 1926.

Exploring the Earth's Stratosphere: The Holder of the American Altitude Record Describes His Experiences in Reaching the "Ceiling" of His Plane at an Elevation of Nearly Eight Miles. By Lieut. John A. Macready. Vol. L, pp. 755-776, 18 ills., Dec., 1926.

Exploring the Glories of the Firmament. By William Joseph Showalter. Vol. XXXVI, pp. 153-181, 17 ills., 3 charts, 1 diagram, Aug., 1919.

Exploring the Ice Age in Antarctica. By Richard Evelyn Byrd. Vol. LXVIII, pp. 399-474, 72 ills., 1 page and 1 two-page maps, Oct., 1935.

Exploring the Mysteries of Plant Life. By William Joseph Showalter. Vol. XLV, pp. 581-646, 41 ills. in black and white, 47 ills. in color, June, 1924.

Exploring the Secrets of Persepolis. By Charles Breasted. Vol. LXIV, pp. 381-420, 48 ills., 1 half-page map, 1 plan, Oct., 1933.

Exploring the Stratosphere. By Capt. Albert W. Stevens. Vol. LXVI, pp. 397-434, 43 ills., 1 two-thirds-page chart, Oct., 1934.

Exploring the Valley of the Amazon in a Hydroplane: Twelve Thousand Miles of Flying Over the World's Greatest River and Greatest Forest to Chart the Unknown Parima River from the Sky. By Capt. Albert W. Stevens. Vol. XLIX, pp. 353-420, 86 ills., 1 page map, Apr., 1926.

Exploring the Wonders of the Insect World. By William Joseph Showalter. Vol. LVI, pp. 1-90, 59 ills. in black and white, 269 ills. in color, July, 1929.

Exploring Tibet. Vol. XII, pp. 403-404, Nov., 1901.

Exploring Unknown Corners of the "Hermit Kingdom." By Roy Chapman Andrews. Vol. XXXVI, pp. 24-48, 30 ills., 1 page map, July, 1919.

Exploring Yukon's Glacial Stronghold. By Bradford Washburn. Vol. LXIX, pp. 715-747, 28 ills., 1 two-page map, June, 1936.

Exports of Manufactures. Vol. XVI, pp. 434-437, Sept., 1905.

Expositions:

American Floating Exposition. Vol. XII, pp. 204-205, May, 1901.

Around-the-World American Exposition. By O. P. Austin. Vol. XII, pp. 49-53, 1 page chart, Feb., 1901.

Austro-Hungarian Floating Exposition. Vol. XII, p. 164, Apr., 1901.

City of Realized Dreams (San Francisco). By Franklin K. Lane. Vol. XXVII, pp. 169-171, Feb., 1915.

Philippine Exhibit at the Pan American Exposition. By D. O. Noble Hoffmann. Vol. XII, pp. 119-122, Mar., 1901.

Extinct Reptiles Found in Nodules. By H. A. Largelamb. Vol. XVII, pp. 170-173, 9 ills., Mar., 1906.

Eyre, Edward John:

Edward John Eyre (Biography). Vol. XIII, p. 75, Feb., 1902.

Eyre, Lincoln:

Renascent Germany. By Lincoln Eyre. Vol. LIV, pp. 639-717, 59 ills. in black and white, 39 ills. in color, Dec., 1928.

Ezion-geber, Trans-Jordan:

On the Trail of King Solomon's Mines: The Bible, in Addition to Its Spiritual Values, Continues to Prove a Rich Geography and Guide to Exploration of the Holy Land. By Nelson Glueck. Vol. LXXXV, pp. 233-256, 20 ills., 1 page map, Feb., 1944.

F

Fabulous Yellowstone: Even Stranger Than the Tales of Early Trappers is the Truth About This Steaming Wonderland. By Frederick G. Vosburgh. Vol. LXXVII, pp. 769-794, 15 ills. in black and white, 9 ills. in color, 1 two-thirds-page map, June, 1940.

Face of Japan. By W. Robert Moore. Vol. LXXXVIII, pp. 753-768, 14 ills., special map supplement, Dec., 1945.

Face of the Netherlands Indies. 20 ills. from photographs by Maynard Owen Williams and others. Vol. LXXXIX, pp. 261-276, Feb., 1946.

Faces, Stone (Monuments). *See* Stone Faces.

Faces and Fashions of Asia's Changeless Tribes. 26 ills. in color from paintings and drawings by Alexandre Iacovleff. Vol. LXIX, pp. 21-36, Jan., 1936.

Faces and Flowers Below the Tropics (Union of South Africa). 14 ills. in color from natural-color photographs by Melville Chater. Vol. LIX, pp. 452-461, Apr., 1931.

Facing War's Challenge "Down Under" (Australia and New Zealand). 20 ills. in color from natural-color photographs by Howell Walker. Vol. LXXXI, pp. 425-456, Apr., 1942.

Factors Which Modify the Climate of Victoria, British Columbia. By Arthur W. McCurdy. Vol. XVIII, pp. 345-348, 2 quarter-page maps, May, 1907.

Facts about the Philippines. By Frederick Simpich. Vol. LXXXI, pp. 185-202, 17 ills., 1 page map, Feb., 1942.

Faeroe Islands, North Atlantic Ocean:

Viking Life in the Storm-Cursed Faeroes. By Leo Hansen. Vol. LVIII, pp. 607-648, 49 ills., 1 half-page map, Nov., 1930.

Fairbanks, Charles W.:

Honors for Amundsen (Address by Charles W. Fairbanks). Vol. XIX, pp. 55-76, 13 ills., Jan., 1908.

Honors to the American Navy (Address by Charles W. Fairbanks). Vol. XX, pp. 77-95, Jan., 1909.

Fairchild, David:

Book of Monsters. By David and Marian Fairchild. Vol. XXVI, pp. 89-98, 7 ills., July, 1914.

Forming New Fashions in Food: The Bearing of Taste on One of Our Great Food Economies, the Dried Vegetable, Which Is Developing Into a Big War Industry. By David Fairchild. Vol. XXXIII, pp. 356-368, 11 ills., Apr., 1918.

Hunter of Plants. By David Fairchild. Vol. XXXVI, pp. 57-77, 18 ills., July, 1919.

Hunting for Plants in the Canary Islands. By David Fairchild. Vol. LVII, pp. 607-652, 37 ills. in black and white, 39 ills. in color, 1 third-page map, May, 1930.

Fairchild, David—*Continued*

Hunting Useful Plants in the Caribbean. By David Fairchild. Vol. LXVI, pp. 705-737, 39 ills., Dec., 1934.

Jungles of Panama. By David Fairchild. Vol. XLI, pp. 131-145, 14 ills., Feb., 1922.

Madeira, on the Way to Italy. By David Fairchild. Vol. XVIII, pp. 751-771, 18 ills., Dec., 1907.

Monsters of Our Back Yards. By David Fairchild. Vol. XXIV, pp. 575-626, 38 ills., May, 1913.

New Plant Immigrants. By David Fairchild. Vol. XXII, pp. 879-907, 34 ills., Oct., 1911.

Our Plant Immigrants. By David Fairchild. Vol. XVII, pp. 179-201, 29 ills., Apr., 1906.

Travels in Arabia and Along the Persian Gulf. By David Fairchild. Vol. XV, pp. 139-151, 20 ills., Apr., 1904.

Fairchild, Graham:

Life Story of the Mosquito. By Graham Fairchild. With 10 ills. in color from paintings. Vol. LXXXV, pp. 180-195, 5 ills. in black and white, 1 drawing, Feb., 1944.

Fairchild, Marian:

Book of Monsters. By David and Marian Fairchild. Vol. XXVI, pp. 89-98, 7 ills., July, 1914.

Fairs:

England's Wild Moorland Ponies. 10 ills. from photographs. Vol. LXXXIX, pp. 129-136, Jan., 1946.

Peiping's Happy New Year: Lunar Celebration Attracts Throngs to Temple Fairs, Motley Bazaars, and Age-Old Festivities. By George Kin Leung. Vol. LXX, pp. 749-792, 31 ills. in black and white, 16 ills. in color, Dec., 1936.

Fairy Terns of the Atolls. By Lewis Wayne Walker. Vol. XC, pp. 807-814, 9 ills., Dec., 1946.

Fairy Wrens:

Fairy Wrens of Australia: The Little Long-tailed "Blue Birds of Happiness" Rank High Among the Island Continent's Remarkable Birds. By Neville W. Cayley. With 8 ills. in color from paintings by the author. Vol. LXXXVIII, pp. 488-498, 1 ill. in black and white, Oct., 1945.

Pastel Wrens from "Down Under." 8 ills. in color from paintings by N. W. Cayley. Vol. LXXXVIII, pp. 489-496, Oct., 1945.

Falcon Island, Pacific Ocean:

Falcon, the Pacific's Newest Island. By J. Edward Hoffmeister and Harry S. Ladd. Vol. LIV, pp. 757-766, 8 ills., 1 half-page map, Dec., 1928.

Falconry:

Adventures with Birds of Prey. By Frank and John Craighead. Vol. LXXII, pp. 109-134, 25 ills., July, 1937.

Falconry—*Continued*

Eagle, King of Birds, and His Kin. By Alexander Wetmore. Paintings by Maj. Allan Brooks. Vol. LXIV, pp. 43-95, 23 ills. in black and white, 28 ills. in color, July, 1933.

Falconry, the Sport of Kings. By Louis Agassiz Fuertes. Vol. XXXVIII, pp. 429-460, 12 ills. in black and white, 12 ills. in color, Dec., 1920.

Life with an Indian Prince: As Guests of a Maharaja's Brother, Two Young American Naturalists Study Age-old Methods of Hunting with Trained Falcons and Cheetahs and Savor the Pomp of Royal India. By John and Frank Craighead. Vol. LXXXI, pp. 235-272, 38 ills., 1 sixth-page map, Feb., 1942.

Falcons:

American Birds of Prey—A Review of Their Value. Vol. XXXVIII, pp. 460-467, 6 ills., Dec., 1920.

Eagles, Hawks, and Vultures. 28 ills. in color from paintings by Maj. Allan Brooks. Vol. LXIV, pp. 64-95, July, 1933.

In Quest of the Golden Eagle: Over Lonely Mountain and Prairie Soars This Rare and Lordly Bird, But Three Youths from the East Catch Up With Him at Last. By John and Frank Craighead. Vol. LXXVII, pp. 693-710, 17 ills., May, 1940.

Life with an Indian Prince: As Guests of a Maharaja's Brother, Two Young American Naturalists Study Age-old Methods of Hunting with Trained Falcons and Cheetahs and Savor the Pomp of Royal India. By John and Frank Craighead. Vol. LXXXI, pp. 235-272, 38 ills., 1 sixth-page map, Feb., 1942.

Week-Ends with the Prairie Falcon: A Commuter Finds Recreation in Scaling Cliffs to Observe the Nest Life and Flying Habits of These Elusive Birds. By Frederick Hall Fowler. Vol. LXVII, pp. 611-626, 21 ills., May, 1935.

Falling Mountain, Alaska:

Valley of Ten Thousand Smokes: An Account of the Discovery and Exploration of the Most Wonderful Volcanic Region in the World. By Robert F. Griggs. Vol. XXXIII, pp. 115-169, 46 ills., 1 half-page map, panorama, Feb., 1918.

Falls, De Witt Clinton:

Saint Stephen's Fête in Budapest. By De Witt Clinton Falls. Vol. XVIII, pp. 548-558, 9 ills., Aug., 1907.

Falls. *See* Waterfalls.

Falls of Iguazu. By Marie Robinson Wright. Vol. XVII, pp. 456-460, 4 ills., Aug., 1906.

Faltboats:

Entering the Front Doors of Medieval Towns: The Adventures of an American Woman and Her Daughter in a Folding Boat on Eight Rivers of Germany and Austria. By Cornelia Stratton Parker. Vol. LXI, pp. 365-394, 23 ills., 1 two-thirds-page map, Mar., 1932.

Fame's Eternal Camping Ground: Beautiful Arlington (Virginia), Burial Place of America's Illustrious Dead. By Enoch A. Chase. Vol. LIV, pp. 621-638, 19 ills., Nov., 1928.

Familiar Grasses and Their Flowers. By E. J. Geske and W. J. Showalter. Vol. XXXIX, pp. 625-636, 8 ills. in color, June, 1921.

Family Afoot in Yukon Wilds: Two Young Children and Their Parents Live Off the Country in the Northwest Canada Wilderness Now To Be Traversed by the Alaska Highway. By William Hamilton Albee, with Ruth Albee. Vol. LXXXI, pp. 589-616, 18 ills. in black and white, 14 ills. in color, May, 1942.

Family Tree of the Flowers. By Frederic E. Clements and William Joseph Showalter. Vol. LI, pp. 555-563, 1 ill. in black and white, 1 ill. in color, May, 1927.

Famines:

Fearful Famines of the Past: History Will Repeat Itself Unless the American People Conserve Their Resources. By Ralph A. Graves. Vol. XXXII, pp. 68-90, 11 ills., July, 1917.

Forerunners of Famine. By Frederick C. Walcott. Vol. XXXIII, pp. 336-347, 4 ills., 4 diagrams, 1 half-page map, Apr., 1918.

Land of the Stalking Death: A Journey Through Starving Armenia on an American Relief Train. By Melville Chater. Vol. XXXVI, pp. 393-420, 23 ills., Nov., 1919.

Fane, G. E.:

Burma Road, Back Door to China: Like the Great Wall of Ancient Times, This Mighty Mountain Highway Has Been Built by Myriad Chinese to Help Defend Their Homeland. By Frank Outram and G. E. Fane. Vol. LXXVIII, pp. 629-658, 26 ills., 1 two-thirds-page map, Nov., 1940.

Fantastic Dwellers in a Coral Fairyland (Great Barrier Reef). 15 ills. in color from natural-color photographs by T. C. Roughley. Vol. LXXVII, pp. 831-838, June, 1940.

Fantastic Plants of Our Western Deserts. 8 ills. by Frank M. Campbell. Vol. XLV, pp. 33-40, Jan., 1924.

Fantastic Sea Life From Abyssal Depths. 8 ills. in color from paintings by E. Bostelmann. Vol. LXI, pp. 71-78, Jan., 1932.

Far East:

Indian Ocean Map Spans Far East News Centers. Text accompanying special map supplement in colors. Vol. LXXIX, pp. 345-346, 1 ill., Mar., 1941.

See also Borneo; British Malaya; Celebes; China; Formosa; French Indo-China; Japan; Java; Korea; Manchuria; Moluccas; New Guinea; Philippine Islands; Siam; Singapore; Sumatra; Timor.

Far Eastern Republic (U. S. S. R.). By Junius B. Wood. Vol. XLI, pp. 565-592, 29 ills., 1 three-quarters-page map, June, 1922.

Far-Flying Wild Fowl and Their Foes. By Maj. Allan Brooks. Vol. LXVI, pp. 487-528, 6 ills. in black and white, 93 portraits in color, Oct., 1934.

Farewell to Bikini. By Carl Markwith. Vol. XC, pp. 97-116, 16 ills., July, 1946.

Farmers' Friends Among the Wasps and Hornets. 12 ills. in color from paintings by Hashime Murayama. Vol. LXXII, pp. 57-64, July, 1937.

Farmers Keep Them Eating. By Frederick Simpich. Vol. LXXXIII, pp. 435-458, 22 ills., Apr., 1943.

Farmers of the United States. Vol. XVI, pp. 39-46, Jan., 1905.

Farmers Since the Days of Noah: China's Remarkable System of Agriculture Has Kept Alive the Densest Population in the World. By Adam Warwick. Vol. LI, pp. 469-500, 37 ills., Apr., 1927.

Farming. See Agriculture.

Farming on the Isthmus of Panama. By Dillwyn M. Hazlett. Vol. XVII, pp. 229-234, 5 ills., Apr., 1906.

Farms. See Ernst Thaelmann (Collective Farm); Gan Shemuel; Högakull.

Farms and Workshops of "The Garden State" (New Jersey). 13 ills. in color from natural-color photographs by Edwin L. Wisherd. Vol. LXIII, pp. 558-567, May, 1933.

Faroe Islands. See Faeroe Islands.

Farquhar, Henry:
Calculations of Population in June, 1900. By Henry Farquhar. Vol. X, pp. 406-413, Oct., 1899.

Farthest North (Peary). Vol. XVII, pp. 638-644, 9 ills., Nov., 1906.

Farthest-North Republic: Olympic Games and Arctic Flying Bring Sequestered Finland into New Focus of World Attention. By Alma Luise Olson. Vol. LXXIV, pp. 499-533, 25 ills. in black and white, 12 ills. in color, 1 page map, Oct., 1938.

Fate Directs the Faltering Footsteps of Columbus. Reproduction in color of the painting by Alfred Dehodencq, Paris. Vol. LIV, supplement, Sept., 1928.

Fatu-Hiva (Island), Marquesas Islands:
Turning Back Time in the South Seas. By Thor Heyerdahl. Vol. LXXIX, pp. 109-136, 33 ills., 2 maps, Jan., 1941.

Fay, Charles E.:
World's Highest Altitude and First Ascents. By Charles E. Fay. Vol. XX, pp. 493-530, 25 ills., June, 1909.

Fayetteville, Arkansas:
Arkansas Rolls Up Its Sleeves. By Frederick Simpich. Vol. XC, pp. 273-312, 16 ills. in black and white, 23 ills. in color, 1 map (two-page spread), Sept., 1946.

Fearful Famines of the Past: History Will Repeat Itself Unless the American People Conserve Their Resources. By Ralph A. Graves. Vol. XXXII, pp. 68-90, 11 ills., July, 1917.

Feathered Foragers of Swamp and Shore. 101 portraits in color from paintings by Maj. Allan Brooks. Vol. LXXII, pp. 191-222, Aug., 1937.

Febiger, (Col.) Lea:
Coronation of His Majesty King Maha-Vajiravudh of Siam. By Col. Lea Febiger. Vol. XXIII, pp. 389-416, 25 ills., Apr., 1912.

Federal Fish Farming; or Planting Fish by the Billion. By Hugh M. Smith. Vol. XXI, pp. 418-446, 22 ills., May, 1910.

Fee, William Thomas:
Parsees and the Towers of Silence at Bombay, India. By William Thomas Fee. Vol. XVI, pp. 529-554, 16 ills., Dec., 1905.

Feeney, Corinne B.:
Arch-Isolationist, the San Blas Indians: Coconuts Serve as Cash on Islands Off the Panama Coast Where Tribesmen Cling to Their Ancient Ways and Discourage Visitors. By Corinne B. Feeney. Vol. LXXIX, pp. 193-220, 15 ills. in black and white, 12 ills. in color, 1 sixth-page map, Feb., 1941.

Fen District, England:
Tour in the English Fenland. By Christopher Marlowe. Vol. LV, pp. 605-634, 26 ills. in black and white, 5 ills. in color, 1 half-page map, May, 1929.

Ferguson, Alfred F.:
Report of Annual Dinner of the National Geographic Society. By Albert F. Ferguson. Vol. XVII, pp. 22-23, Jan., 1906.

Fernald, M. L.:
Unique Island of Mount Desert. By George B. Dorr, M. L. Fernald, and Ernest Howe Forbush. Vol. XXVI, pp. 75-89, 7 ills., July, 1914.

Ferns:
Ferns as a Hobby. By William R. Maxon. Vol. XLVII, pp. 541-586, 29 ills. in black and white, 16 ills. in color, May, 1925.

  Contains descriptions and illustrations of the following ferns: Adder's Tongue, Bracken, Bulblet Bladder, Christmas, Climbing, Common Wood, Dwarf Spleenwort, Eastern Lady, Interrupted, Maidenhair, Marginal, Marsh, Rattlesnake, Royal, Sensitive, Walking.

Marvels of Fern Life. 16 ills. in color from paintings by E. J. Geske. Vol. XLVII, pp. 547-562, May, 1925.

Fernsworth, Lawrence A.:
Andorra—Mountain Museum of Feudal Europe. By Lawrence A. Fernsworth. Vol. LXIV, pp. 493-512, 21 ills., 1 third-page map, Oct., 1933.

Ferrara, Italy :

Inexhaustible Italy. By Arthur Stanley Riggs. Vol. XXX, pp. 273-368, 76 ills., 1 page map, Oct., 1916.

Fertile Pampas of Argentine. Vol. XVII, pp. 453-456, Aug., 1906.

Fertilizers:

American Potash for America. By Guy Elliott Mitchell. Vol. XXII, pp. 398-405, 4 ills., Apr., 1911.

Farmers Since the Days of Noah : China's Remarkable System of Agriculture Has Kept Alive the Densest Population in the World. By Adam Warwick. Vol. LI, pp. 469-500, 37 ills., Apr., 1927.

Inoculating the Ground. Vol. XV, pp. 225-228, 2 ills., May, 1904.

Most Valuable Bird in the World (Guanay). By Robert Cushman Murphy. Vol. XLVI, pp. 279-302, 25 ills., 1 half-page map, Sept., 1924.

Our Greatest Plant Food (Phosphorus). By Guy Elliott Mitchell. Vol. XXI, pp. 783-791, 7 ills., 1 diagram, Sept., 1910.

Peru's Wealth-Producing Birds : Vast Riches in the Guano Deposits of Cormorants, Pelicans, and Petrels Which Nest on Her Barren, Rainless Coast. By R. E. Coker. Vol. XXXVII, pp. 537-566, 28 ills., June, 1920.

Festivals:

August First in Gruyères. By Melville Bell Grosvenor. Vol. LXX, pp. 137-168, 12 ills. in black and white, 23 ills. in color, Aug., 1936.

Azores : Picturesque and Historic Half-Way House of American Transatlantic Aviators. By Arminius T. Haeberle. Vol. XXXV, pp. 514-545, 26 ills., 1 page map, June, 1919.

Bolivia, Land of Fiestas. By Alicia O'Reardon Overbeck. Vol. LXVI, pp. 645-660, 16 ills., 1 half-page map, Nov., 1934.

Carnival Days on the Riviera. By Maynard Owen Williams. Vol. L, pp. 467-501, 21 ills., Oct., 1926.

Clans in Kilt and Plaidie Gather at Braemar (Scotland). 11 ills. in color from natural-color photographs by Maynard Owen Williams. Vol. LXVIII, pp. 153-160, Aug., 1935.

Coronation of His Majesty King Maha-Vajira-vudh of Siam. By Col. Lea Febiger. Vol. XXIII, pp. 389-416, 25 ills., Apr., 1912.

Costume Pageants in the French Pyrenees. 24 ills. in color from natural-color photographs by W. Robert Moore. Vol. LXXII, pp. 435-450, Oct., 1937.

Czechoslovakia, Key-Land to Central Europe. By Maynard Owen Williams. Vol. XXXIX, pp. 111-156, 45 ills., 1 quarter-page map, Feb., 1921.

Demon Dancers and Butter Gods of Choni. 16 ills. in color from photographs by Joseph F. Rock. Vol. LIV, pp. 584-601, Nov., 1928.

Festivals—*Continued*

Demon-Possessed Tibetans and Their Incredible Feats. 12 ills. in color from natural-color photographs. Vol. LXVIII, pp. 479-486, Oct., 1935.

Empire State Onions and Pageantry (New York). 12 ills. in color from natural-color photographs by J. Baylor Roberts and Volkmar Wentzel. Vol. LXXX, pp. 641-648, Nov., 1941.

Festival Days on the Slopes of Mount Parnassus (Greece). 14 ills. in color from natural-color photographs by Maynard Owen Williams. Vol. LVIII, pp. 712-721, Dec., 1930.

Fifteenth - Century Vignettes of Compiègne (France). 15 ills. in color from natural-color photographs by Gervais Courtellemont. Vol. LXII, pp. 608-617, Nov., 1932.

Fire-Walking Hindus of Singapore. By L. Elizabeth Lewis. Vol. LIX, pp. 513-522, 12 ills., Apr., 1931.

Great Britain on Parade. By Maynard Owen Williams. Vol. LXVIII, pp. 137-184, 40 ills. in black and white, 11 ills. in color, Aug., 1935.

Heather Paints the Highlands (Scotland). 38 ills. in color from natural-color photographs by B. Anthony Stewart. Vol. LXXXIX, pp. 561-600, May, 1946.

India at Work and Play. 22 ills. in color from natural-color photographs by Peter Upton Muir, Maynard Owen Williams, and Frances Muir. Vol. LXXXIX, pp. 449-464, Apr., 1946.

Life Among the Lamas of Choni : Describing the Mystery Plays and Butter Festival in the Monastery of an Almost Unknown Tibetan Principality in Kansu Province, China. By Joseph F. Rock. Vol. LIV, pp. 569-619, 34 ills. in black and white, 16 ills. in color, 1 half-page map, Nov., 1928.

Maid of France Rides By : Compiègne, Where Joan of Arc Fought Her Last Battle, Celebrates Her Fifth Centenary. By Inez Buffington Ryan. Vol. LXII, pp. 607-617, 15 ills. in color, Nov., 1932.

Marriage of the Gods. By John J. Banninga. Vol. XXIV, pp. 1314-1330, 16 ills., Dec., 1913.

Medieval Pageantry in Modern Nördlingen. 12 ills. in color from autochromes by Hans Hildenbrand. Vol. LIV, pp. 706-715, Dec., 1928.

Merry Maskers of Imst (Austria). 14 ills. from photographs by Francis C. Fuerst. Vol. LXX, pp. 201-208, Aug., 1936.

Mexican Indian Flying Pole Dance. By Helga Larsen. Vol. LXXI, pp. 387-400, 13 ills., Mar., 1937.

North Carolina Colorcade. 21 ills. in color from natural-color photographs ; 19 ills. by J. Baylor Roberts. Vol. LXXX, pp. 189-220, Aug., 1941.

Peiping's Happy New Year : Lunar Celebration Attracts Throngs to Temple Fairs, Motley Bazaars, and Age-old Festivities. By George Kin Leung. Vol. LXX, pp. 749-792, 31 ills. in black and white, 16 ills. in color, Dec., 1936.

Festivals—*Continued*

Perahera Processions of Ceylon. By G. H. G. Burroughs. Vol. LXII, pp. 90-100, 1 ill. in black and white, 8 ills. in duotone, July, 1932.

Rothenburg, the City Time Forgot. By Charles W. Beck, Jr. Vol. XLIX, pp. 184-194, 8 ills. in color, Feb., 1926.

Saint Stephen's Fête in Budapest. By De Witt Clinton Falls. Vol. XVIII, pp. 548-558, 9 ills., Aug., 1907.

Siena's Palio, an Italian Inheritance from the Middle Ages. By Marie Louise Handley. Vol. L, pp. 245-258, 3 ills., Aug., 1926.

Some Aspects of Rural Japan. By Walter Weston. Vol. XLII, pp. 275-301, 12 ills. in black and white, 16 ills. in color, Sept., 1922.

Sungmas, the Living Oracles of the Tibetan Church. By Joseph F. Rock. Vol. LXVIII, pp. 475-486, 1 ill. in black and white, 12 ills. in color, Oct., 1935.

When Czechoslovakia Puts a Falcon Feather in Its Cap. By Maynard Owen Williams. Vol. LXIII, pp. 40-49, 13 ills. in color, Jan., 1933.

When Golden Praha Entertains the Majestic Sokol Festival. 13 ills. in color from natural-color photographs by Hans Hildenbrand. Vol. LXIII, pp. 40-49, Jan., 1933.

With the Devil Dancers of China and Tibet. 43 ills. in color from natural-color photographs by Joseph F. Rock. Vol. LX, pp. 18-59, July, 1931.

See also Carnivals.

Feudal Isle of Sark: Where Sixteenth-Century Laws Are Still Observed. By Sibyl Hathaway (La Dame de Serk). Vol. LXII, pp. 101-119, 21 ills., 1 half-page map, July, 1932.

Fevers. *See* Malaria; Spotted Fever; Typhoid Fever; Yellow Fever.

Few Glimpses into Russia. By Lieut. Zinovi Pechkoff. Vol. XXXII, pp. 238-253, 10 ills., Sept., 1917.

Few Thoughts Concerning Eugenics. By Alexander Graham Bell. Vol. XIX, pp. 119-123, Feb., 1908.

Fez, Morocco:

Fez, Heart of Morocco: Africa's "Imperial City" Retains Its Teeming Streets, Cluttered Shops, Glamorous Moorish Homes and Mosques, Amid the Peace of French Rule. By Gordon Casserly. Vol. LXVII, pp. 663-694, 13 ills. in black and white, 27 ills. in color, June, 1935.

Journey in Morocco: "The Land of the Moors." By Thomas Lindsey Blayney. Vol. XXII, pp. 750-776, 24 ills., 1 page map, Aug., 1911.

Fiala, Anthony:

Annual Dinner of the National Geographic Society (Speech by Anthony Fiala). Vol. XVII, pp. 22-37, Jan., 1906.

Polar Photography. By Anthony Fiala. Vol. XVIII, pp. 140-142, Feb., 1907.

Fiala, Anthony—*Continued*

Ziegler Polar Expedition (Report by Anthony Fiala). Vol. XIV, pp. 414-417, 5 ills., Nov., 1903.

Field Courses in Geology. Vol. XVI, p. 250, May, 1905.

Field Dogs:

Field Dogs in Action. By Freeman Lloyd. Paintings by Edward Herbert Miner. Vol. LXXI, pp. 85-108, 8 ills. in black and white, 36 portraits in color, Jan., 1937.

Contains descriptions and illustrations of the following breeds: Chesapeake Bay Retriever, Clumber Spaniel, Cocker Spaniel, Curly-coated Retriever, Dachshund, English Setter, English Springer Spaniel, Field Spaniel, Flat-coated Retriever, Gordon Setter, Irish Red Setter, Irish Water Spaniel, Labrador Retriever, Pointer, Sussex Spaniel, Wirehaired Pointing Griffon.

Man's Hunting Partner, the Field Dog. 36 portraits in color from paintings by Edward Herbert Miner. Vol. LXXI, pp. 89-104, Jan., 1937.

Field Sports Among the Wild Men of Northern Luzon. By Dean C. Worcester. Vol. XXII, pp. 216-267, 17 ills., 1 half-page map, Mar., 1911.

Fieldwork of the United States Geological Survey for the Season 1902. Vol. XIII, pp. 322-325, Aug., 1902.

Fifteenth – Century Vignettes of Compiègne (France). 15 ills. in color from natural-color photographs by Gervais Courtellement. Vol. LXII, pp. 608-617, Nov., 1932.

Fifty Common Birds of Farm and Orchard. By Henry Wetherbee Henshaw. Vol. XXIV, pp. 669-697, 50 ills. in color, June, 1913.

Fight Against Forest Fires. By Henry S. Graves. Vol. XXIII, pp. 662-683, 19 ills., July, 1912.

Fight at the Timber-Line. By John Oliver La Gorce. Vol. XLII, pp. 165-196, 32 ills., Aug., 1922.

Fight the Flies. Vol. XXI, pp. 383-385, May, 1910.

Fighting Giants of the Humboldt (Fish and Squid). By David D. Duncan. Vol. LXXIX, pp. 373-400, 28 ills., 1 half-page map, Mar., 1941.

Fighting Insects with Airplanes: An Account of the Successful Use of the Flying Machine in Dusting Tall Trees Infested with Leaf-Eating Caterpillars. By C. R. Neillie and J. S. Houser. Vol. XLI, pp. 333-338, 6 ills., Mar., 1922.

Fighting the Polar Ice. Vol. XVIII, pp. 72-77, 7 ills., Jan., 1907.

Fiji Islands, Pacific Ocean:

American Pathfinders in the Pacific. By William H. Nicholas. Vol. LXXXIX, pp. 617-640, 17 ills., 1 two-page map, May, 1946.

Fiji Islands, Pacific Ocean—*Continued*

British Commonwealth of Nations: "Organized Freedom" Around the World. By Eric Underwood. Vol. LXXXIII, pp. 485-524, 31 ills., Apr., 1943.

In the Savage South Seas. By Beatrice Grimshaw. Vol. XIX, pp. 1-19, 21 ills., Jan., 1908.

Net Results from Oceania: Collecting Aquarium Specimens in Tropical Pacific Waters. By Walter H. Chute. Vol. LXXIX, pp. 347-372, 8 ills. in black and white, 24 ills. in color, Mar., 1941.

Treasure Islands of Australasia: New Guinea, New Caledonia, and Fiji Trace across the South Pacific a Fertile Crescent Incredibly Rich in Minerals and Foods. By Douglas L. Oliver. Vol. LXXXI, pp. 691-722, 23 ills., 1 two-page map, June, 1942.

Fiji Patrol on Bougainville. By David D. Duncan. Vol. LXXXVII, pp. 87-104, 9 ills. in black and white, 11 ills. in color, Jan., 1945.

Fijians:

Fiji Patrol on Bougainville. By David D. Duncan. Vol. LXXXVII, pp. 87-104, 9 ills. in black and white, 11 ills. in color, Jan., 1945.

Financial and Commercial Statistics of the Principal Countries of the World. Vol. XVIII, pp. 420-423, June, 1907.

Finches (Birds):

Bird Beauties of the Tanager and Finch Families. 55 portraits in color from paintings by Maj. Allan Brooks. Vol. LXVII, pp. 513-528, Apr., 1935.

Bright-hued Pets of Cage and Aviary. 51 portraits in color from paintings by Maj. Allan Brooks. Vol. LXXIV, pp. 783-790, Dec., 1938.

Canaries and Other Cage-Bird Friends. By Alexander Wetmore. Vol. LXXIV, pp. 775-806, 19 ills. in black and white, 51 portraits in color, Dec., 1938.

Tanagers and Finches: Their Flashes of Color and Lilting Songs Gladden the Hearts of American Bird Lovers East and West. By Arthur A. Allen. Paintings by Maj. Allan Brooks. Vol. LXVII, pp. 505-532, 6 ills. in black and white, 55 portraits in color, Apr., 1935.

Finding Jewels of Jade in a Mexican Swamp (La Venta). By Matthew W. and Marion Stirling. Vol. LXXXII, pp. 635-661, 15 ills. in black and white, 12 ills. in color, 1 two-thirds-page map, Nov., 1942.

Finger Lakes Region, New York:

Fruitful Shores of the Finger Lakes. By Harrison Howell Walker. Vol. LXXIX, pp. 559-594, 15 ills. in black and white, 22 ills. in color, 1 two-thirds-page map, May, 1941.

Finland:

Farthest-North Republic: Olympic Games and Arctic Flying Bring Sequestered Finland into New Focus of World Attention. By Alma Luise Olson. Vol. LXXIV, pp. 499-533, 25 ills. in black and white, 12 ills. in color, 1 page map, Oct., 1938.

Finland—*Continued*

Finland: Land of Sky-Blue Lakes. 12 ills. in color from natural-color photographs by Konstantin J. Kostich. Vol. LXXIV, pp. 515-522, Oct., 1938.

Flashes from Finland. 19 ills. from photographs. Vol. LXXVI, pp. 239-254, Feb., 1940.

Flying Around the Baltic. By Douglas Chandler. Vol. LXXIII, pp. 767-806, 31 ills. in black and white, 13 ills. in duotone, 1 half-page map, June, 1938.

New Map of Europe: Showing the Boundaries Established by the Peace Conference at Paris and by Subsequent Decisions of the Supreme Council of the Allied and Associated Powers. By Ralph A. Graves. Text accompanying special map supplement in colors. Vol. XXXIX, pp. 157-177, 18 ills., Feb., 1921.

Notes on Finland. By Baroness Alletta Korff. Vol. XXI, pp. 493-494, June, 1910.

Races of Europe. By Edwin A. Grosvenor. Vol. XXXIV, pp. 441-534, 62 ills., 2 page maps, special map supplement in colors, Dec., 1918.

Where Women Vote. By Baroness Alletta Korff. Vol. XXI, pp. 487-493, June, 1910.

See also Åland (Islands); Helsinki.

Finley, John H.:

Red Cross Spirit Speaks (Poem). By John H. Finley. Vol. XXXI, p. 474, May, 1917.

Finley, William L.:

Hunting Birds With a Camera: A Record of Twenty Years of Adventure in Obtaining Photographs of Feathered Wild Life in America. By William L. Finley. Vol. XLIV, pp. 161-201, 37 ills., Aug., 1923.

Fire-Walking Hindus of Singapore. By L. Elizabeth Lewis. Vol. LIX, pp. 513-522, 12 ills., Apr., 1931.

First Air Commando Force, U. S.:

Aerial Invasion of Burma. By Gen. H. H. Arnold. Vol. LXXXVI, pp. 129-148, 20 ills., Aug., 1944.

First Airship Flight Around the World: Dr. Hugo Eckener Tells of an Epochal Geographic Achievement upon the Occasion of the Bestowal of the National Geographic Society's Special Gold Medal. Vol. LVII, pp. 653-688, 37 ills., June, 1930.

First Alaskan Air Expedition. By Capt. St. Clair Streett. Vol. XLI, pp. 499-552, 37 ills., 1 page map, May, 1922.

First American Census of Porto Rico. Vol. XI, p. 328, Aug., 1900.

First Autochromes from the Ocean Bottom: Marine Life in Its Natural Habitat Along the Florida Keys Is Successfully Photographed in Colors. Vol. LI, pp. 56-61, 8 ills. in color, Jan., 1927.

1st Battalion, Fiji Infantry Regiment:

Fiji Patrol on Bougainville. By David D. Duncan. Vol. LXXXVII, pp. 87-104, 9 ills. in black and white, 11 ills. in color, Jan., 1945.

First Families of Southeastern America (Indians). 8 ills. in color from paintings by W. Langdon Kihn. Vol. LXXXIX, pp. 65-72, Jan., 1946.

First Flight to the North Pole. By Lieut. Comdr. Richard Evelyn Byrd. Vol. L, pp. 357-376, 14 ills., Sept., 1926.

First in Statehood, Delaware Retains Its Graciousness. 15 ills. in color from natural-color photographs by B. Anthony Stewart. Vol. LXVIII, pp. 377-384, Sept., 1935.

First Journey Across Alaska. Vol. XV, p. 267, June, 1904.

First National Park East of Mississippi River (Mount Desert Island, Maine). Vol. XXIX, pp. 622-626, 5 ills., June, 1916.

First natural-color photograph of an eclipse ever reproduced. 1 ill. in color by Irvine C. Gardner. Vol. LXXI, p. 178, Feb., 1937.

First natural-color photograph taken in the stratosphere. 1 ill. in color by Maj. Albert W. Stevens. Vol. LXXI, p. 340, Mar., 1937.

First Natural-Color Photographs from the Arctic. 22 ills. in color from natural-color photographs by Jacob Gayer and Maynard Owen Williams. Vol. XLIX, pp. 300-317, Mar., 1926.

First Over the Roof of the World by Motor: The Trans-Asiatic Expedition Sets New Records for Wheeled Transport in Scaling Passes of the Himalayas. By Maynard Owen Williams. Vol. LXI, pp. 321-363, 45 ills., 2 half-page maps, Mar., 1932.

First Transandine Railroad from Buenos Aires to Valparaiso. By Harriet Chalmers Adams. Vol. XXI, pp. 397-417, 14 ills., 1 quarter-page map, May, 1910.

Fischer, Helene:

Life and Death in Toradjaland. 22 ills. from photographs; 8 ills. by Helene Fischer. Vol. LXXVIII, pp. 65-80, July, 1940.

Mexican Land of Lakes and Lacquers (Pátzcuaro Region). 22 ills. from photographs by Helene Fischer and Luis Marquez. Vol. LXXI, pp. 633-648, May, 1937.

Fischer, John:

India's Treasures Helped the Allies. By John Fischer. Vol. LXXXIX, pp. 501-522, 18 ills., Apr., 1946.

Fish Hawks. *See* Ospreys.

Fisher, Clyde:

Nomads of Arctic Lapland: Mysterious Little People of a Land of the Midnight Sun Live Off the Country Above the Arctic Circle. By Clyde Fisher. Vol. LXXVI, pp. 641-676, 28 ills. in black and white, 12 ills. in color, 1 page map, Nov., 1939.

Fisher, Franklin L.:

Insect Rivals of the Rainbow. Text by Franklin L. Fisher. Vol. LVI, pp. 28-90, July, 1929.

Fisher, Franklin L.—*Continued*

Palace of Versailles, Its Park and the Trianons. By Franklin L. Fisher. Vol. XLVII, pp. 49-62, 4 ills. in black and white, 14 ills. in color, Jan., 1925.

Fisher, Walter L.:

Honors to Amundsen and Peary (Speech by Walter L. Fisher). Vol. XXIV, pp. 113-130, 5 ills., Jan., 1913.

Fishes and Fisheries:

America's Most Valuable Fishes. By Hugh M. Smith. Vol. XXIII, pp. 494-514, 17 ills., May, 1912.

Contains descriptions and illustrations of the following species: Blueback Salmon, Chinook Salmon, Dog Salmon, Humpback Salmon, Silver Salmon.

America's Surpassing Fisheries: Their Present Condition and Future Prospects, and How the Federal Government Fosters Them. By Hugh M. Smith. Vol. XXIX, pp. 546-583, 35 ills., June, 1916.

Bornholm—Denmark in a Nutshell. By Mason Sutherland. Vol. LXXXVII, pp. 239-256, 20 ills., 1 half-page map, Feb., 1945.

Contains information on the "Bornholmer" (Herring).

Bright Flashes from Pacific Corals. 24 ills. in color from natural-color photographs by Walter H. Chute. Vol. LXXIX, pp. 349-372, Mar., 1941.

Contains illustrations of the following: Achilles Tang, *Balistapus aculeatus,* Banded Dascyllus, Bar Diagonal Butterflyfish, Birdfish, Black Tang, Black Triggerfish, Blackline Hawkfish, Blue Parrotfish, Bluegreen Chromide, Bluelined Wrasse, Bluespotted Niggerfish, Bluestriped Butterflyfish, Brown-spotted Grouper, *Chaetodon trifasciatus, Cheilinus bimaculatus,* Clown Goby, Clown Wrasse, Common Moray, Common Scorpion, Convict Tang, *Dascyllus albisella,* Fantail Filefish, Flying Gurnard, Gray Wrasse, Green Birdfish, Hawaiian Butterflyfish, *Hemitaurichthys zoster,* "Hinalea Hilu," "Hinalea Lolo," Lionfish, Longfin Butterflyfish, Longfin Razorfish, Longnose Butterflyfish, Moorish Idol, Moray Eel, Orangespot Tang, Orangestriped Triggerfish, Pinktail Triggerfish, Polkadot Moray, Polkadot Wrasse, "Pooú," Potter's Pomacentrid, Rectangular Triggerfish, Red Goatfish, Red Bigeye, Red Squirrelfish, Redline Wrasse, Ringed Hawkfish, Saddle Wrasse, Sailfin Tang, Sandfish, Sergeant Major, Spot Diagonal Butterflyfish, Spot Pomacentrid, Spot Wrasse, Spotted Rockfish, Spotted White Moray, Striped Apagon, Threadfish, Threestriped Coralfish, "Ulua," "Umauma Lei," Whiteline Hawkfish, Whiteline Squirrelfish, Whiteline Triggerfish, Yellow Blenny, Yellow Jack, Yellow Tang, Yelloweye Tang, Yellowspot Goatfish.

Brittany: The Land of the Sardine. By Hugh M. Smith. Vol. XX, pp. 541-573, 23 ills., June, 1909.

Bureau of Fisheries. By Barton Warren Evermann. Vol. XV, pp. 191-212, 11 ills., 3 diagrams, May, 1904.

Fishes and Fisheries—*Continued*

Carnivores of a Lightless World. 8 ills. in color from paintings by Else Bostelmann. Vol. LXVI, pp. 693-700, Dec., 1934.

Caviar Fishermen of Romania: From Vâlcov, "Little Venice" of the Danube Delta, Bearded Russian Exiles Go Down to the Sea. By Dorothy Hosmer. Vol. LXXVII, pp., 407-434, 29 ills., 1 third-page map, Mar., 1940.

Certain Citizens of the Warm Sea. By Louis L. Mowbray. Vol. XLI, pp. 27-62, 18 ills. in black and white, 16 ills. in color, Jan., 1922.
    Contains descriptions and illustrations of the following species: Amber Jack, Barracuda, Bone-Fish, Crawfish, Dolphin, Gag, Grouper, Kingfish, Margate Fish, Moon Fish, Mutton Fish, Sailfish, Spanish Mackerel, Tarpon, Yellow Jack.

Coffee Is King in El Salvador. By Luis Marden. Vol. LXXXVI, pp. 575-616, 22 ills. in black and white, 27 ills. in color, 1 half-page map, Nov., 1944.
    Contains description and illustration of the four-eyed fish, *Anableps dowei*.

"Compleat Angler" Fishes for Fossils. By Imogene Powell. Vol. LXVI, pp. 251-258, 7 ills., Aug., 1934.

Cruise of the *Kinkajou:* Among Desert Islands of Mexico Voyagers Find Outdoor Laboratories for the Naturalist and Ideal Fishing Grounds for the Sportsman (Fishing for Marlin and Wahoo). By Alfred M. Bailey. Vol. LXXX, pp. 339-366, 13 ills. in black and white, 12 ills. in color, 1 page map, Sept., 1941.

Cultivation of Marine and Fresh Water Animals in Japan. By K. Mitsukuri. Vol. XVII, pp. 524-531, 5 ills., Sept., 1906.

Depths of the Sea: Strange Life Forms a Mile Below the Surface. By William Beebe. Vol. LXI, pp. 65-88, 15 ills. in black and white, 8 ills. in color, 1 half-page map, Jan., 1932.

Devil-Fishing in the Gulf Stream. By John Oliver La Gorce. Vol. XXXV, pp. 476-488, 7 ills., June, 1919.

Dream Ship: The Story of a Voyage of Adventure More Than Half Around the World in a 47-Foot Lifeboat. By Ralph Stock. Vol. XXXIX, pp. 1-52, 43 ills., 1 page map, Jan., 1921.

Europe's Endangered Fish Supply: War and the North Sea Fisheries. Vol. XXVII, pp. 141-152, 9 ills., 1 half-page map, Feb., 1915.

Exploring Neptune's Hidden World of Vivid Color. 8 ills. in color from paintings by E. Bostelmann. Vol. LXII, pp. 747-754, Dec., 1932.

Fantastic Sea Life From Abyssal Depths. 8 ills. in color from paintings by E. Bostelmann. Vol. LXI, pp. 71-78, Jan., 1932.

Federal Fish Farming; or, Planting Fish by the Billion. By Hugh M. Smith. Vol. XXI, pp. 418-446, 22 ills., May, 1910.

Fighting Giants of the Humboldt. By David D. Duncan. Vol. LXXIX, pp. 373-400, 28 ills., 1 half-page map, Mar., 1941.

Fishes and Fisheries—*Continued*

Contains information on the following: Giant Manta Ray, Marlin, Squid, Swordfish, Whale.

First Autochromes from the Ocean Bottom: Marine Life in Its Natural Habitat Along the Florida Keys Is Successfully Photographed in Colors. Vol. LI, pp. 56-61, 8 ills. in color, Jan., 1927.

Fisheries of Japan. By Hugh M. Smith. Vol. XV, pp. 362-364, Sept., 1904.

Fisheries of Japan. By Hugh M. Smith. Vol. XVI, pp. 201-220, 13 ills., May, 1905.

Fishes and Fisheries of Our North Atlantic Seaboard. By John Oliver La Gorce. Vol. XLIV, pp. 567-634, 35 ills. in black and white, 16 ills. in color, Dec., 1923.
    Contains descriptions and illustrations of the following species: Alewife, Butter-Fish, Codfish, Cusk, Flounder, Haddock, Hake, Halibut, Herring, Lobster, Mackerel, Pollock, Salmon, Scup, Shad, Smelt, Sturgeon, Swordfish, Tautog, Tilefish, Tuna, Whiting.

Fishes That Build Nests and Take Care of Their Young. Vol. XVIII, pp. 400-412, 16 ills., June, 1907.

Fishes That Carry Lanterns. Vol. XXI, pp. 453-456, 5 ills., May, 1910.

Fishing for Pearls in the Indian Ocean. By Bella Sidney Woolf. Vol. XLIX, pp. 161-183, 24 ills., Feb., 1926.

Fishing in Pacific Coast Streams. By Leonard P. Schultz. Vol. LXXV, pp. 185-212, 10 ills. in black and white, 54 portraits in color, Feb., 1939.
    Contains descriptions and illustrations of the following species: Chinook Salmon, Chum Salmon, Cutthroat Trout, Dolly Varden Trout, Eulachon, Golden Trout, Pink Salmon, Piute Trout, Rainbow Trout, Red Salmon, Sacramento Perch, Sacramento Pike, Sacramento Sucker, Silver Salmon, Steelhead Trout, Three-Spined Stickleback, White Sturgeon, Yellowstone Trout.

Flashes From Ocean Deeps. 16 ills. in color from paintings by Else Bostelmann, Helen D. Tee-Van, and E. J. Geske. Vol. LXVI, pp. 677-700, Dec., 1934.

Fresh-Water Denizens of the Far West. 54 portraits in color from paintings by Hashime Murayama. Vol. LXXV, pp. 193-204, Feb., 1939.

Glass-Bottom Boat. By Charles Frederick Holder. Vol. XX, pp. 761-778, 17 ills., Sept., 1909.

Gleaming Fishes of Pacific Coastal Waters. 31 portraits in color from paintings by Hashime Murayama. Vol. LXXIV, pp. 467-498, Oct., 1938.

Golden Trout. Vol. XVII, p. 424, July, 1906.

Goldfish and Their Cultivation in America. By Hugh M. Smith. Vol. XLVI, pp. 375-400, 14 ills. in black and white, 8 ills. in color, Oct., 1924.

Fishes and Fisheries—*Continued*

Half Mile Down : Strange Creatures, Beautiful and Grotesque as Figments of Fancy, Reveal Themselves at Windows of the Bathysphere. By William Beebe. Vol. LXVI, pp. 661-704, 28 ills. in black and white, 16 ills. in color, 1 third-page map, Dec., 1934.

Helping the Filipino Fisheries. Vol. XVIII, pp. 795-796, Dec., 1907.

Interesting Citizens of the Gulf Stream. By Dr. John T. Nichols. Vol. XXXIX, pp. 69-84, 11 ills. in black and white, 16 ills. in color, Jan., 1921.

Contains descriptions and illustrations of the following species : Angel-Fish, Blue Striped Grunt, Buffalo Trunkfish, Butterfly Fish, Cow Pilot, Cowfish, Cuckold, Four-Eyed Fish, Green Moray, Pork Fish, Portuguese Man-of-War, Queen Trigger-Fish, Rainbow Parrot-Fish, Rock Hind, Sea Horse, Shark Sucker, Spade Fish, Squirrel Fish, Yellow Tail.

Iridescent Denizens of the Miniature Aquarium. 8 ills. in color from paintings by Hashime Murayama. Vol. LIX, pp. 291-300, Mar., 1931.

Islands Adrift : St. Pierre and Miquelon : In a Key Position on the North Atlantic Air Route, France's Oldest Colony Rides Out Another Storm. By Frederic K. Arnold. Vol. LXXX, pp. 743-768, 23 ills., 1 fifth-page map, Dec., 1941.

Jumping Salmon. Vol. XIX, p. 124, 1 ill., Feb., 1908.

King Herring : An Account of the World's Most Valuable Fish, the Industries It Supports, and the Part It Has Played in History. By Hugh M. Smith. Vol. XX, pp. 701-735, 21 ills., Aug., 1909.

Land of Lakes and Volcanoes. By Luis Marden. With 17 ills. in color from natural-color photographs by the author. Vol. LXXXVI, pp. 161-192, 11 ills. in black and white, 1 two-thirds-page map, Aug., 1944.

Life on a Coral Reef : The Fertility and Mystery of the Sea Studied Beneath the Waters Surrounding Dry Tortugas. By W. H. Longley. Vol. LI, pp. 61-83, 22 ills. in black and white, 8 ills. in color, Jan., 1927.

Contains descriptions and illustrations of the following species : Barracuda, Black Angel Fish, Gold-Browned Gnathypops, Gray Snapper, Nassau Grouper, Razor Fish, Red Parrot Fish, Squirrel Fish, Trunkfish, Yellow-Finned Grouper, Yellow Goatfish, Yellowtail.

Life on the Grand Banks : An Account of the Sailor-Fishermen Who Harvest the Shoal Waters of North America's Eastern Coasts. By Frederick William Wallace. Vol. XL, pp. 1-28, 29 ills., July, 1921.

Luminous Life in the Depths of the Sea. 8 ills. in color from paintings by E. Bostelmann. Vol. LIX, pp. 667-674, June, 1931.

The Maine American and the American Lobster. By John D. Lucas. Vol. LXXXIX, pp. 523-543, 19 ills., Apr., 1946.

Mysterious Life of the Common Eel. By Hugh M. Smith. Vol. XXIV, pp. 1140-1146, 3 ills., Oct., 1913.

Fishes and Fisheries—*Continued*

Native Oysters of the West Coast. By Robert E. C. Stearns. Vol. XIX, pp. 224-226, Mar., 1908.

Net Results from Oceania : Collecting Aquarium Specimens in Tropical Pacific Waters. By Walter H. Chute. Vol. LXXIX, pp. 347-372, 8 ills. in black and white, 24 ills. in color, Mar., 1941.

Contains information on the following : Butterflyfishes, Coralfishes, Dwarf Pterois, Giant Burrfishes, Goatfishes, Gobies, Hawkfishes, Lionfishes, Morays, Mud-Springers, Poison Puffers, Poison Toadfishes, Pomacentrids, Razorfishes, Rock Skippers, Squirrelfishes, Tangs, Triggerfishes, Wrasses.

Newfoundland, North Atlantic Rampart : From the "First Base of American Defense" Planes Fly to Britain's Aid over Stout Fishing Schooners of the Grand Banks. By George Whiteley, Jr. Vol. LXXX, pp. 111-140, 26 ills., 1 two-thirds-page map, July, 1941.

Notes from a Naturalist's Experiences in British Guiana. By C. H. Eigenmann. Vol. XXII, pp. 859-870, 8 ills., Sept., 1911.

Notes on the Sea Dyaks of Borneo. By Edwin H. Gomes. Vol. XXII, pp. 695-723, 26 ills., Aug., 1911.

On the Bottom of a South Sea Pearl Lagoon. By Roy Waldo Miner. Vol. LXXIV, pp. 365-390, 17 ills. in black and white, 8 ills. in color, Sept., 1938.

Oregon Finds New Riches. By Leo A. Borah. Vol. XC, pp. 681-728, 15 ills. in black and white, 28 ills. in color, 1 two-page map, Dec., 1946.

Our Fish Immigrants. By Hugh M. Smith. Vol. XVIII, pp. 382-400, 3 ills., June, 1907.

Our Global Ocean—Last and Vast Frontier. By F. Barrows Colton. Vol. LXXXVII, pp. 105-128, 19 ills., 1 drawing, Jan., 1945.

Our Heritage of the Fresh Waters : Biographies of the Most Widely Distributed of the Important Food and Game Fishes of the United States. By Charles Haskins Townsend. Vol. XLIV, pp. 109-159, 25 ills. in black and white, 16 ills. in color, Aug., 1923.

Contains descriptions and illustrations of the following species : Black Bass, Brook Trout, Calico Bass, Catfish, Common Eel, Drum, Eastern Pickerel, Lake Sturgeon, Lake Trout, Muskellunge, Pike, Pike-Perch, Rainbow Trout, Rock Bass, White Perch, Whitefish, Yellow Perch.

Our Smallest Possession—Guam. By William E. Safford. Vol. XVI, pp. 229-237, 5 ills., May, 1905.

Oysters : The World's Most Valuable Water Crop. By Hugh M. Smith. Vol. XXIV, pp. 257-281, 21 ills., Mar., 1913.

Pearl Fisheries of Ceylon. By Hugh M. Smith. Vol. XXIII, pp. 173-194, 13 ills., 1 quarter-page map, Feb., 1912.

Pearl Fishing in the Red Sea. By Henri de Monfreid. Vol. LXXII, pp. 597-626, 24 ills., 1 two-thirds-page map, Nov., 1937.

Fishes and Fisheries—*Continued*

Planting Fishes in the Ocean. By George M. Bowers. Vol. XVIII, pp. 715-723, 5 ills., Nov., 1907.

Purple Veil: A Romance of the Sea. Vol. XVI, pp. 337-341, 9 ills., July, 1905.

Rainbow Denizens of the Aquarium. 16 ills. in color from natural-color photographs by Edwin L. Wisherd. Vol. LXV, pp. 97-104, Jan., 1934.

Rise of the New Arab Nation. By Frederick Simpich. Vol. XXXVI, pp. 369-393, 17 ills., 1 page map, Nov., 1919.

    Contents: Pearl Fisheries.

Round Trip to Davy Jones's Locker: Peering into Mysteries a Quarter Mile Down in the Open Sea, by Means of the Bathysphere. By William Beebe. Vol. LIX, pp. 653-678, 14 ills. in black and white, 8 ills. in color, 1 quarter-page map, June, 1931.

Sailing the Seven Seas in the Interest of Science: Adventures Through 157,000 Miles of Storm and Calm, from Arctic to Antarctic and Around the World, in the Non-Magnetic Yacht *Carnegie*. By J. P. Ault. Vol. XLII, pp. 631-690, 47 ills., 1 chart, Dec., 1922.

Sea Floor Aquarelles from Tongareva. 8 ills. in color from paintings by Else Bostelmann. Vol. LXXIV, pp. 383-390, Sept., 1938.

Shark Fishing—An Australian Industry. By Norman Ellison. Vol. LXII, pp. 369-386, 22 ills., Sept., 1932.

Some Giant Fishes of the Seas. By Hugh M. Smith. Vol. XX, pp. 637-644, 6 ills., July, 1909.

    Contains descriptions and illustrations of the following species: Basking Shark, "Devil-Fish," Jew-Fish, Man-Eater Shark, Ribbon-Fish, Saw-Fish, Sleeper Shark, Sun-Fish, Tunny, Whale Shark.

Treasure-House of the Gulf Stream: The Completion and Opening of the New Aquarium and Biological Laboratory at Miami, Florida. By John Oliver La Gorce. Vol. XXXIX, pp. 53-68, 5 ills. in black and white, 16 ills. in color, Jan., 1921.

Treasures of the Pacific: Marine Fishes and Fisheries Yield Vast Wealth from Alaska to Baja California. By Leonard P. Schultz. Vol. LXXIV, pp. 463-498, 10 ills. in black and white, 31 portraits in color, Oct., 1938.

Tropical Fish Immigrants Reveal New Nature Wonders. By Walter H. Chute. Vol. LXV, pp. 93-110, 8 ills. in black and white, 16 ills. in color, Jan., 1934.

Tropical Toy Fishes: More Than 600 Varieties of Aquarium Pygmies Afford a Fascinating Field of Zoölogical Study in the Home. By Ida Mellen. Vol. LIX, pp. 287-317, 20 ills. in black and white, 8 ills. in color, Mar., 1931.

Tuna Harvest of the Sea: A Little-known Epic of the Ocean Is the Story of Southern California's Far-ranging Tuna Fleet. By John Degelman. Vol. LXXVIII, pp. 393-408, 17 ills., Sept., 1940.

Fishes and Fisheries—*Continued*

War and Ocean Geography. By Gilbert Grosvenor. Vol. XXXIV, pp. 230-242, 6 ills., 1 page map, Sept., 1918.

When the Father of Waters Goes on a Rampage: An Account of the Salvaging of Food-Fishes from the Overflowed Lands of the Mississippi River. By Hugh M. Smith. Vol. XXXVII, pp. 369-386, 18 ills., Apr., 1920.

When the Herring Fleet Comes to Great Yarmouth. By W. Robert Moore. Vol. LXVI, pp. 233-250, 19 ills., Aug., 1934.

Where Bretons Wrest a Living from the Sea. 23 ills. from photographs by F. W. Goro. Vol. LXXI, pp. 751-766, June, 1937.

Where Nature Runs Riot: On Australia's Great Barrier Reef Marine Animals Grow to Unusual Size, Develop Strange Weapons of Attack and Defense, and Acquire Brilliant Colors. By T. C. Roughley. Vol. LXXVII, pp. 823-850, 18 ills. in black and white, 15 ills. in color, 1 page map, June, 1940.

Wonderer Under Sea. By William Beebe. Vol. LXII, pp. 741-758, 13 ills. in black and white, 8 ills. in color, Dec., 1932.

Fishing and Hunting Tales from Brazil. By Dewey Austin Cobb. Vol. XX, pp. 917-920, Oct., 1909.

Fishing for Pearls in the Indian Ocean. By Bella Sidney Woolf. Vol. XLIX, pp. 161-183, 24 ills., Feb., 1926.

Fishing in Pacific Coast Streams (Salmon, Trout, etc.). By Leonard P. Schultz. Vol. LXXV, pp. 185-212, 10 ills. in black and white, 54 portraits in color, Feb., 1939.

Fissure Lake, Alaska:

Valley of Ten Thousand Smokes: An Account of the Discovery and Exploration of the Most Wonderful Volcanic Region in the World. By Robert F. Griggs. Vol. XXXIII, pp. 115-169, 46 ills., 1 half-page map, panorama, Feb., 1918.

Fit to Fight Anywhere (Army Quartermaster Tests). By Frederick Simpich. Vol. LXXXIV, pp. 233-256, 26 ills., Aug., 1943.

Fita-Fitas (Samoan Soldiers):

America's South Sea Soldiers. By Lorena MacIntyre Quinn. Vol. XXXVI, pp. 267-274, 8 ills., Sept., 1919.

Fitch, Robert F.:

China. 4 ills. in color from photographs by Robert F. Fitch. Vol. XXXVIII, pp. 377-389, Nov., 1920.

Life Afloat in China: Tens of Thousands of Chinese in Congested Ports Spend Their Entire Existence on Boats. By Robert F. Fitch. Vol. LI, pp. 665-686, 28 ills., June, 1927.

Puto, the Enchanted Island. By Robert F. Fitch. Vol. LXXXIX, pp. 373-384, 11 ills., 1 third-page map, Mar., 1946.

Five Thousand Temples of Pagän: Burma's Sacred City Is a Place of Enchantment in the Midst of Ruins. By William H. Roberts. Vol. LX, pp. 445-454, 9 ills., Oct., 1931.

Fjords and Fjells of Viking Land (Norway). 27 ills. in color from natural-color photographs by Gustav Heurlin. Vol. LVIII, pp. 12-45, July, 1930.

Flags:

Correct Display of the Stars and Stripes. By Byron McCandless and Gilbert Grosvenor. Vol. XXXII, pp. 404-413, 8 ills., Oct., 1917.

Flags Famous in American History. By Byron McCandless and Gilbert Grosvenor. Vol. XXXII, pp. 341-361, 92 ills. in color, Oct., 1917.

Flags of Austria-Hungary, Bulgaria, Germany, and Turkey. By Byron McCandless and Gilbert Grosvenor. Vol. XXXII, pp. 386-388, 38 ills. in color, Oct., 1917.

Flags of Europe, Asia, and Africa. By Byron McCandless and Gilbert Grosvenor. Vol. XXXII, pp. 372-385, 100 ills. in color, Oct., 1917.

Flags of Our Army, Navy, and Government Departments. By Byron McCandless and Gilbert Grosvenor. Vol. XXXII, pp. 305-322, 3 ills. in black and white, 300 ills. in color, Oct., 1917.

Flags of Pan-America. By Byron McCandless and Gilbert Grosvenor. Vol. XXXII, pp. 361-369, 62 ills. in color, Oct., 1917.

Flags of the British Empire. By Byron McCandless and Gilbert Grosvenor. Vol. XXXII, pp. 378-385, 158 ills. in color, Oct., 1917.

Flags of the World. By Gilbert Grosvenor and William J. Showalter. Vol. LXVI, pp. 339-396, 10 ills. in black and white, 808 ills. in color, Sept., 1934.

Heroic Flags of the Middle Ages. By Byron McCandless and Gilbert Grosvenor. Vol. XXXII, pp. 388-399, 96 ills. in color, Oct., 1917.

Makers of the Flag. By Franklin K. Lane. Vol. XXXII, p. 304, Oct., 1917.

Naval Flags of the World. By Byron McCandless and Gilbert Grosvenor. Vol. XXXII, pp. 347-369, 211 ills. in color, Oct., 1917.

Our Flag Number. By Gilbert Grosvenor. Vol. XXXII, pp. 281-284, 2 ills., Oct., 1917.

Our State Flags. By Byron McCandless and Gilbert Grosvenor. Vol. XXXII, pp. 323-341, 1 ill. in black and white, 57 ills. in color, Oct., 1917.

Pennants of Patriotism 200 Years Ago. By Byron McCandless and Gilbert Grosvenor. Vol. XXXII, pp. 399-403, 75 ills. in color, Oct., 1917.

Story of the American Flag. By Byron McCandless and Gilbert Grosvenor. Vol. XXXII, pp. 286-303, 12 ills., Oct., 1917.

Unfurling Old Glory on Canton Island. 11 ills. in color; 1 painting by Charles Bittinger and 10 natural-color photographs. Vol. LXXIII, pp. 753-760, June, 1938.

See also National Geographic Society : Flag.

Flame-Feathered Flamingos of Florida. By W. A. Watts. With 9 ills. in color from natural-color photographs by W. F. Gerecke. Vol. LXXIX, pp. 56-65, Jan., 1941.

Flaming Cliffs of Monument Valley. By Lt. Jack Breed, USNR. With 9 ills. in color from natural-color photographs by the author and Warren T. Mithoff. Vol. LXXXVIII, pp. 452-461, Oct., 1945.

Flamingos:

Camps and Cruises of an Ornithologist. By George Shiras, 3d. Vol. XX, pp. 438-463, 30 ills., May, 1909.

Flame-Feathered Flamingos of Florida. By W. A. Watts. With 9 ills. in color from natural-color photographs by W. F. Gerecke. Vol. LXXIX, pp. 56-65, Jan., 1941.

Large Wading Birds : Long Legs and Remarkable Beaks, as Well as Size, Form, and Color, Distinguish the Herons, Ibises, and Flamingos. By T. Gilbert Pearson. Paintings by Maj. Allan Brooks. Vol. LXII, pp. 441-469, 2 ills. in black and white, 1 ill. in color, Oct., 1932.

Remarkable Photographs of Flamingo Nests. Vol. XV, pp. 82-83, 1 ill., Feb., 1904.

Story of the Flamingo. Vol. XVI, p. 50, Jan., 1905.

Flandrin, M.:

Modern Life in Morocco, Western Outpost of Islam. 27 ills. in color from natural-color photographs by M. Flandrin. Vol. LXVII, pp. 679-694, June, 1935.

Flashes from Finland. 19 ills. from photographs. Vol. LXXVII, pp. 239-254, Feb., 1940.

Flashes from Ocean Deeps. 16 ills. in color from paintings by Else Bostelmann, Helen D. Tee-Van and E. J. Geske. Vol. LXVI, pp. 677-700, Dec., 1934.

Flashes of Color in the Fifth Continent (Australia). 24 ills. in color from natural-color photographs by W. Robert Moore. Vol. LXVIII, pp. 681-704, Dec., 1935.

Flashing Fashions of Old Spain. 26 ills. in duotone by J. Ortiz Echagüe. Vol. LXIX, pp. 413-428, Mar., 1936.

Flashlight Story of an Albino Porcupine and of a Cunning but Unfortunate Coon. By George Shiras, 3d. Vol. XXII, pp. 572-596, 26 ills., June, 1911.

Flashlights from the Jungle. Vol. XVIII, pp. 534-548, 11 ills., Aug., 1907.

Flavor and Savor of American Foods. 25 ills. in color from natural-color photographs by J. Baylor Roberts, Willard R. Culver, and others. Vol. LXXXI, pp. 289-320, Mar., 1942.

Flecks of Color in the Fertile Fields of Louisiana. 14 ills. in color from natural-color photographs by Edwin L. Wisherd. Vol. LVII, pp. 418-427, Apr., 1930.

Fleischman, Max:

Seventy-five Days in the Arctics. By Max Fleischman. Vol. XVIII, pp. 439-446, 5 ills., July, 1907.

Flies:

Book of Monsters. By David and Marian Fairchild. Vol. XXVI, pp. 89-98, 7 ills., July, 1914.

A Community of Dwarfs. 11 illustrations in color from natural-color photographs by Willard R. Culver. Vol. XC, pp. 345-352, Sept., 1946.

Economic Loss to the People of the United States Through Insects That Carry Disease. By L. O. Howard. Vol. XX, pp. 735-749, Aug., 1909.

Explorers of a New Kind: Successful Introduction of Beetles and Parasites to Check Ravages of the Gipsy-Moth and Brown-Tail Moth. By L. O. Howard. Vol. XXVI, pp. 38-67, 11 ills. in black and white, 5 ills. in color, July, 1914.

Fight the Flies. Vol. XXI, pp. 383-385, May, 1910.

House-Fly. By N. A. Cobb. Vol. XXI, pp. 371-380, 4 ills., May, 1910.

An Insect Community Lives in Flower Heads. By James G. Needham. Vol. XC, pp. 340-356, 5 ills. in black and white, 11 ills. in color, Sept., 1946.

    Contains descriptions and illustrations of the following: Baccha Flies, Bandwing Flies, Clearwing Flies, Spotwing Flies.

Marvels of Metamorphosis: A Scientific "G-man" Pursues Rare Trapdoor Spider Parasites for Three Years With a Spade and a Candid Camera. By George Elwood Jenks. Vol. LXXIV, pp. 807-828, 39 ills., Dec., 1938.

Notes on the Distances Flies Can Travel. By N. A. Cobb. Vol. XXI, pp. 380-383, May, 1910.

Flights from Arctic to Equator: Conquering the Alps, the Ice Peaks of Spitsbergen, of Persia, and Africa's Mountains of the Moon. By Walter Mittelholzer. Vol. LXI, pp. 445-498, 53 ills., 1 three-quarters-page map, Apr., 1932.

Floating Dry Docks. *See* Docks.

Floating Expositions. *See* Expositions.

Flood, Francis A.:

Britain Fights in the Fields. By Francis A. Flood. Vol. LXXXVI, pp. 31-65, 17 ills. in black and white, 21 ills. in color, July, 1944.

Lend-Lease Is a Two-way Benefit: Innovation in Creative Statesmanship Pools Resources of United Nations, and Supplies American Forces Around the World. By Francis Flood. Vol. LXXXIII, pp. 745-761, 14 ills., June, 1943.

Three-Wheeling Through Africa: Two Adventurers Cross the So-Called Dark Continent North of Lake Chad on Motorcycles with Side Cars. By James C. Wilson. Vol. LXV, pp. 37-92, 64 ills., 1 two-page map, Jan., 1934.

Floods and Flood Control:

Forecasting the Weather and Storms. By Willis L. Moore. Vol. XVI, pp. 255-305, 5 ills., 20 charts, June, 1905.

Floods and Flood Control—*Continued*

Great Mississippi Flood of 1927: Since White Man's Discovery This Mighty River Has Served Him Well, Yet It Has Brought Widespread Devastation Along Its Lower Reaches. By Frederick Simpich. Vol. LII, pp. 243-289, 53 ills., 1 half-page map, Sept., 1927.

Men Against the Rivers (Mississippi and Ohio Rivers). By Frederick Simpich. Vol. LXXI, pp. 767-794, 22 ills., 1 page-and-a-half and 1 quarter-page maps, June, 1937.

More Water for California's Great Central Valley. By Frederick Simpich. Vol. XC, pp. 645-664, 16 ills., 1 page map, Nov., 1946.

Our Heralds of Storm and Flood (U. S. Weather Bureau). By Gilbert H. Grosvenor. Vol. XVIII, pp. 586-601, 15 ills., 1 chart, Sept., 1907.

Taming "Flood Dragons" Along China's Hwang Ho (River). By Oliver J. Todd. Vol. LXXXI, pp. 205-234, 26 ills., 1 half-page map, Feb., 1942.

Taming the Outlaw Missouri River. By Frederick Simpich. Vol. LXXXVIII, pp. 569-598, 25 ills., 1 two-page map, Nov., 1945.

Weather Bureau. By Willis L. Moore. Vol. XII, pp. 363-369, Oct., 1901.

Weather Bureau and the Recent Floods. By H. C. Frankenfield. Vol. XIV, pp. 285-290, 2 ills., July, 1903.

When the Father of Waters Goes on a Rampage: An Account of the Salvaging of Food-Fishes from the Overflowed Lands of the Mississippi River. By Hugh M. Smith. Vol. XXXVII, pp. 369-386, 18 ills., Apr., 1920.

Flora. *See* Flowers.

Floral Carpets:

In the Canary Islands, Where Streets Are Carpeted with Flowers. 13 ills. in color from natural-color photographs by Wilhelm Tobien. Vol. LVII, pp. 614-623, May, 1930.

Floral Emblems:

Our State Flowers: Floral Emblems Chosen by the Commonwealths. By Gilbert Grosvenor. Vol. XXXI, pp. 481-517, 30 ills. in color, June, 1917.

Floral Garlands of Prairie, Plain, and Woodland. 125 flower paintings in color by Edith S. Clements. Vol. LXXVI, pp. 224-270, Aug., 1939.

Florence, Italy:

Inexhaustible Italy. By Arthur Stanley Riggs. Vol. XXX, pp. 273-368, 76 ills., 1 page map, Oct., 1916.

Northern Italy: Scenic Battleground. 18 ills. in color from natural-color photographs; 13 ills. by B. Anthony Stewart and 3 ills. by Lt. Benjamin C. McCartney. Vol. LXXXVII, pp. 265-288, Mar., 1945.

Return to Florence. By 1st Lt. Benjamin C. McCartney. Vol. LXXXVII, pp. 257-296, 18 ills. in black and white, 18 ills. in color, Mar., 1945.

Floriculture:

Garden Isles of Scilly: Geologists May Throw Stones at Legend of Lost Lyonnesse, But Natives Grow Flowers in Glass Houses for London. By W. Robert Moore. Vol. LXXIV, pp. 755-774, 9 ills. in black and white, 13 ills. in color, 1 half-page map, Dec., 1938.

Scillies: Isles of Wrecks and Golden Daffodils. 13 ills. in color from natural-color photographs by B. Anthony Stewart, Maynard Owen Williams, and W. Robert Moore. Vol. LXXIV, pp. 759-766, Dec., 1938.

Florida:

Certain Citizens of the Warm Sea. By Louis L. Mowbray. Vol. XLI, pp. 27-62, 18 ills. in black and white, 16 ills. in color, Jan., 1922.

Devil-Fishing in the Gulf Stream. By John Oliver La Gorce. Vol. XXXV, pp. 476-488, 7 ills., June, 1919.

Flame-Feathered Flamingos of Florida. By W. A. Watts. With 9 ills. in color from natural-color photographs by W. F. Gerecke. Vol. LXXIX, pp. 56-65, Jan., 1941.

Florida—The Fountain of Youth. By John Oliver La Gorce. Vol. LVII, pp. 1-93, 73 ills. in black and white, 41 ills. in color, special map supplement in colors, Jan., 1930.

Growth of Florida. Vol. XVII, p. 424, July, 1906.

Gulf Coast Towns Get into the Fight. 19 ills. in color from natural-color photographs; 17 ills. by J. Baylor Roberts. Vol. LXXXV, pp. 17-40, Jan., 1944.

High Lights in the Sunshine State. 41 ills. in color from autochromes by Clifton Adams and Charles Edward Hagle. Vol. LVII, pp. 26-83, Jan., 1930.

How We Use the Gulf of Mexico. By Frederick Simpich. Vol. LXXXV, pp. 1-40, 20 ills. in black and white, 19 ills. in color, 1 two-page map, Jan., 1944.

Interesting Citizens of the Gulf Stream. By Dr. John T. Nichols. Vol. XXXIX, pp. 69-84, 11 ills. in black and white, 16 ills. in color, Jan., 1921.

South Florida's Amazing Everglades: Encircled by Populous Places Is a Seldom-visited Area of Rare Birds, Prairies, Cowboys, and Teeming Wild Life of Big Cypress Swamp. By John O'Reilly. Vol. LXXVII, pp. 115-142, 26 ills., 1 page map, Jan., 1940.

Treasure-House of the Gulf Stream: The Completion and Opening of the New Aquarium and Biological Laboratory at Miami, Florida. By John Oliver La Gorce. Vol. XXXIX, pp. 53-68, 5 ills. in black and white, 16 ills. in color, Jan., 1921.

Wild Life of the Atlantic and Gulf Coasts: A Field Naturalist's Photographic Record of Nearly Half a Century of Fruitful Exploration. By George Shiras, 3d. Vol. LXII, pp. 261-309, 62 ills., Sept., 1932.

See also Florida Keys; Key West.

Florida Keys:

Cannon on Florida Reefs Solve Mystery of Sunken Ship. By Charles M. Brookfield. Vol. LXXX, pp. 807-824, 20 ills., 1 map (on pen and ink drawing), Dec., 1941.

First Autochromes from the Ocean Bottom: Marine Life in Its Natural Habitat Along the Florida Keys Is Successfully Photographed in Colors. Vol. LI, pp. 56-60, 8 ills. in color, Jan., 1927.

Florida Keys. By John Gifford. Vol. XVII, pp. 5-16, 13 ills., 1 half-page map, Jan., 1906.

Life on a Coral Reef: The Fertility and Mystery of the Sea Studied Beneath the Waters Surrounding Dry Tortugas. By W. H. Longley. Vol. LI, pp. 61-83, 22 ills. in black and white, 8 ills. in color, Jan., 1927.

See also Key West.

Flow Onward, Connecticut (River)! 24 ills. in color from natural-color photographs; 22 ills. by B. Anthony Stewart. Vol. LXXXIII, pp. 409-432, Apr., 1943.

"Flower of Paradise": The Part Which Khat Plays in the Life of the Yemen Arab. By Charles Moser. Vol. XXXII, pp. 173-186, 10 ills., 1 page map, Aug., 1917.

Flower Pageant of the Midwest: From March to November Nature Embroiders an Ever-changing Pattern of Living Color. By Edith S. and Frederic E. Clements. Vol. LXXVI, pp. 219-271, 1 ill. in black and white, 125 flower paintings in color, Aug., 1939.

Flowers:

American Berries of Hill, Dale, and Wayside. Vol. XXXV, pp. 168-184, 1 ill. in black and white, 28 ills. in color, Feb., 1919.

American Wild Flowers. Vol. XXVII, pp. 483-517, 29 ills. in color, May, 1915.

Contains descriptions and illustrations of the following species: American Holly, Bindweed, Bittersweet, Black Haw, Black-Eyed Susan, Blue Flag, Bluebell, Blue-Eyed Grass, Broad - Leaved Arrow - Head, Bulb - Bearing Loosestrife, Buttercup, Canada Lily, Cardinal Flower, Day Flower, Evening Primrose, Jewel Weed, Moth Mullen, Partridge Berry, Purple Flowering Raspberry, Purple Loosestrife, Showy Lady's-Slipper, Star Grass, Trailing Arbutus, Turk's Cap Lily, Virginia Strawberry, Wild Columbine, Wild Geranium, Wild Pink, Witch Hazel.

Ashley River and Its Gardens (South Carolina). By E. T. H. Shaffer. Vol. XLIX, pp. 525-550, 6 ills. in black and white, 7 ills. in color, May, 1926.

California, Our Lady of Flowers. By Chapin Hall. Vol. LV, pp. 703-750, 20 ills. in black and white, 30 ills. in color, June, 1929.

California Says It with Wild Flowers. By Francis Woodworth. With 9 ills. in color from natural-color photographs by B. Anthony Stewart. Vol. LXXXI, pp. 492-501, Apr., 1942.

Flowers—*Continued*

Contains descriptions and colored illustrations of the following: Babyblue-eyes, Blazingstar, Blueblossom, Collinsia, Coreopsis, Dandelion, Eveningprimrose, Farewell-to-spring, Flannel Bush, Ithuriel's Spear, Lupine, Monkeyflower, Mustard, Owlclover, Poppy, *Rosa californica*, Toyon, Yellowdaisy, Tidytip.

Canyons and Cacti of the American Southwest. 22 ills. in color from natural-color photographs by Edwin L. Wisherd, Jacob Gayer, and Charles Martin. Vol. XLVIII, pp. 274-290, 22 ills., Sept., 1925.

Common American Wild Flowers. Vol. XXIX, pp. 584-609, 17 ills. in color, June, 1916.

Contains descriptions and illustrations of the following species: Chicory, Common Mullen, Butter-and-Eggs, Butterfly-Weed, Button Bush, Fireweed, Forget-Me-Not, Fringed Gentian, Jack-in-the-Pulpit, New England Aster, Poison Ivy, Spotted Boneset, Steeple Bush, Swamp Rose-Mallow, Virginia Creeper, Wild Yellow Plum, Yarrow.

A Community of Dwarfs. 11 ills. in color from natural-color photographs by Willard R. Culver. Vol. XC, pp. 345-352, Sept., 1946.

Contains illustrations of the insects that live in flower heads.

Cultivation of the Mayflower. By Frederick V. Coville. Vol. XXVII, pp. 518-519, 1 ill., May, 1915.

Exploring the Mysteries of Plant Life. By William Joseph Showalter. Vol. XLV, pp. 581-610, 11 ills. in black and white, 47 ills. in color, June, 1924.

Contains descriptions and illustrations of the following species: Alfalfa, Amsonia, Arethusa, Bindweed, Blackberry-Lily, Checkerbloom, Cobaea Pentstemon, Coneflower, Creeping Polemonium, Daylily, Goldmoss, Grays Lily, Ground-Ivy, Honeysuckle, Meadow-Parsnip, Phlox, Pitcherplant, Poppy-Mallow, Rhododendron, Rose Pogonia, St. Johnswort, Shootingstar, Snow-on-the-Mountain, Spatterdock, Springbeauty, Wildbergamot, Woodbetony, Woodsorrel, Yellow Ladyslipper.

Familiar Grasses and Their Flowers. By E. J. Geske and W. J. Showalter. Vol. XXXIX, pp. 625-636, 8 ills. in color, June, 1921.

Family Tree of the Flowers. By Frederic E. Clements and William Joseph Showalter. Vol. LI, pp. 555-563, 1 ill. in black and white, 1 ill. in color, May, 1927.

Floral Garlands of Prairie, Plain, and Woodland. 125 flower paintings in color by Edith S. Clements. Vol. LXXVI, pp. 224-270, Aug., 1939.

Flower Pageant of the Midwest: From March to November Nature Embroiders an Ever-changing Pattern of Living Color. By Edith S. and Frederic E. Clements. Vol. LXXVI, pp. 219-271, 1 ill. in black and white, 125 flower paintings in color, Aug., 1939.

Contains descriptions and illustrations of the following families: Acanthus, Amaryllis, Aster, Bluebell, Borage, Buckwheat, Buttercup, Cactus, Caper, Dogbane, Evening Primrose, Evening Star, Gentian, Geranium, Heath, Iris,

Flowers—*Continued*

Lily, Mallow, Meadow Beauty, Mint, Morning-Glory, Mustard, Orchid, Oxalis, Pea, Phlox, Pink, Poppy, Potato, Primrose, Purslane, Snapdragon, Spiderwort, Spurge, Touch-Me-Not, Verbena, Violet, Witch Hazel.

Garden Isles of Scilly: Geologists May Throw Stones at Legend of Lost Lyonnesse, But Natives Grow Flowers in Glass Houses for London. By W. Robert Moore. Vol. LXXIV, pp. 755-774, 9 ills. in black and white, 13 ills. in color, 1 half-page map, Dec., 1938.

Great White Monarch of the Pacific Northwest (Mount Rainier). By A. H. Barnes. Vol. XXIII, pp. 593-626, 31 ills., 1 half-page map, June, 1912.

High Country of Colorado. By Alfred M. Bailey. With 23 ills. in color from natural-color photographs by the author, Robert J. Niedrach, and F. G. Brandenburg. Vol. XC, pp. 43-72, 9 ills. in black and white, July, 1946.

Contains text references and illustrations of the following: Arnica, Asters, Bistort, Columbine, Golden Avens, Geranium, Indian Paintbrush, King's Crown, Marigolds, Mountain Sunflower, Parsley, Shooting Stars, Snow Lily, Wild Onion, Wild Rose, Wood Lilies.

An Insect Community Lives in Flower Heads. By James G. Needham. Vol. XC, pp. 340-356, 5 ills. in black and white, 11 ills. in color, Sept., 1946.

Kingdom of Flowers: An Account of the Wealth of Trees and Shrubs of China and of What the Arnold Arboretum, with China's Help, Is Doing to Enrich America. By Ernest H. Wilson. Vol. XXII, pp. 1003-1035, 24 ills., Nov., 1911.

Midsummer Wild Flowers. Vol. XLII, pp. 35-59, 16 ills. in color, July, 1922.

Contains descriptions and illustrations of the following varieties: American Waterlily, Aster, Beach Pea, Blue Vervain, Bluebell, Broom, Closed Gentian, Corn Cockle, Corydalis, Dodder, Early Goldenrod, English Plaintain, False-Foxglove, Field Mustard, Gayfeather, Golden St. John's-Wort, Groundcherry, Hairy Pentstemon, Hyssop Skullcap, Milkweed, Milkwort, Mistflower, Pickerelweed, Pokeweed, Pricklepoppy, Purple Avens, Purple Wildbergamot, Rosemallow, Sheep Laurel, Sheep Sorrel, Silver Aster, Spiderwort, Sweetshrub, Tansy, Teasel, Turtlehead, Venus Looking-Glass, Yellow Fringed Orchid.

Our State Flowers: Floral Emblems Chosen by the Commonwealths. By Gilbert Grosvenor. Vol. XXXI, pp. 481-517, 30 ills. in color, June, 1917.

Contains descriptions and illustrations of the following families: Apple, Bitter Root, Cactus, Carnation, Colorado Columbine, Daisy, Golden Poppy, Goldenrod, Indian Paintbrush, Magnolia, Mistletoe, Moccasin Flower, Mountain Laurel, Orange, Oregon Grape, Pasque Flower, Peach, Pine, Red Clover, Rhododendron, Rose, Sagebrush, Sahuaro, Sego Lily, Sunflower, Syringa, Texas Bluebonnet, Trumpet Vine, Violet.

Flowers—*Continued*

Pages from the Floral Life of America. Vol. XLVIII, pp. 44-75, 55 ills. in color, July, 1925.

Contains descriptions and illustrations of the following families: Acanthus, Amaranth, Amaryllis, Apple, Arum, Aster, Bicknell, Bladderwort, Borage, Broom-Rape, Buckthorn, Buckwheat, Bunchflower, Caper, Chicory, Diapensia, Dogwood, Evening-Primrose, Figwort, Four-O'Clock, Fumitory, Gentian, Ginseng, Gooseberry, Goosefoot, Gourd, Heath, Horsetail, Lily-of-the-Valley, Logania, Madder, Magnolia, Meadowbeauty, Milkwort, Milkweed, Mimosa, Nettle, Olive, Parsley, Passionflower, Pea, Plantain, Pondweed, Ragweed, Rush, Saxifrage, Senna, Sundew, Waterlily.

Photographing the Marvels of the West in Colors. 6 ills. in color from natural-color photographs by Fred Payne Clatworthy. Vol. LIII, pp. 694-719, June, 1928.

Riddle of the Aleutians: A Botanist Explores the Origin of Plants on Ever-misty Islands Now Enshrouded in the Fog of War. By Isobel Wylie Hutchison. Vol. LXXXII, pp. 769-792, 24 ills., Dec., 1942.

Scillies: Isles of Wrecks and Golden Daffodils. 13 ills. in color from natural-color photographs by B. Anthony Stewart, Maynard Owen Williams, and W. Robert Moore. Vol. LXXIV, pp. 759-766, Dec., 1938.

Some Odd Pages from the Annals of the Tulip: A "Made" Flower of Unknown Origin Took Medieval Europe by Storm and Caused a Financial Panic in the Netherlands. By Leo A. Borah. Vol. LXIV, pp. 321-343, 13 ills. in black and white, 10 ills. in color, Sept., 1933.

Spring's Gay Bouquets Deck the Nation's Capital. 10 ills. in color from natural-color photographs by Harrison Howell Walker. Vol. LXXIV, pp. 17-24, July, 1938.

Sunshine Land of Fruits, Flowers, Movies, and Sport. 41 ills. in color from natural-color photographs by Clifton Adams and Fred Payne Clatworthy. Vol. LXVI, pp. 545-592, Nov., 1934.

Tulip Time in the Netherlands. 10 ills. in color from natural-color photographs by Wilhelm Tobien and A. Buyssens. Vol. LXIV, pp. 325-332, Sept., 1933.

Under the South African Union. By Melville Chater. Vol. LIX, pp. 391-512, 97 ills. in black and white, 38 ills. in color, 1 two-page map, Apr., 1931.

Where Spring Paints a State with Wild Fowers (California). 18 ills. in color from natural-color photographs by B. Anthony Stewart. Vol. LXIX, pp. 365-380, Mar., 1936.

Wild Flowers of the West (United States). By Edith S. Clements. Vol. LI, pp. 566-622, 207 ills. in color, May, 1927.

Contains descriptions and illustrations of the following families: Aster, Bellflower, Borage, Broom-Rape, Buckthorn, Buckwheat, Cactus, Caper, Chicory, Crowfoot, Dogbane, Evening-Primrose, Evening-Star, Figwort, Flax, Four-O'Clock, Fumitory, Gentian, Ger-

Flowers—*Continued*

anium, Gooseberry, Heath, Honeysuckle, Indianpipe, Iris, Leadwort, Lily, Lobelia, Mallow, Mesembryanthemum, Milkweed, Milkwort, Mint, Morning-Glory, Mustard, Orchid, Orpine, Parsley, Pea, Phlox, Pink, Poppy, Potato, Primrose, Purslane, Rockrose, Rose, St. Johnswort, Saxifrage, Violet, Waterleaf, Wintergreen, Woodsorrel.

See also Gardens; Orchids.

Flycatchers (Birds):

Birds on the Home Front. By Arthur A. Allen. Vol. LXXXIV, pp. 32-56, 7 ills. in black and white, 30 ills. in color, July, 1943.

Flycatchers and Other Friends in Feathers. 36 portraits in color from paintings by Maj. Allan Brooks. Vol. LXIX, pp. 807-822, June, 1936.

Parrots, Kingfishers, and Flycatchers: Strange Trogons and Curious Cuckoos are Pictured with these Other Birds of Color, Dash, and Courage. By Alexander Wetmore. Paintings by Maj. Allan Brooks. Vol. LXIX, pp. 801-828, 9 ills. in black and white, 36 portraits in color, June, 1936.

Flying. By Gilbert Grosvenor. Vol. LXIII, pp. 585-630, 33 ills. in black and white, 17 ills. in duotone, May, 1933.

Flying Around the Baltic. By Douglas Chandler. Vol. LXXIII, pp. 767-806, 31 ills. in black and white, 13 ills. in duotone, 1 half-page map, June, 1938.

Flying Around the North Atlantic. By Anne Morrow Lindbergh; Foreword by Charles A. Lindbergh. Vol. LXVI, pp. 259-337, 82 ills., 1 two-page and 1 two-thirds-page maps, Sept., 1934.

Flying Fortresses:

American Bombers Attacking from Australia. By Howell Walker. Vol. LXXXIII, pp. 49-70, 19 ills., 1 map (two-page spread), Jan., 1943.

8th Air Force in England. 10 ills. in color from U. S. Army Air Forces official photographs. Vol. LXXXVII, pp. 297-304, Mar., 1945.

Flying in France. By Capt. André de Berroeta. Vol. XXXIII, pp. 9-26, 12 ills., Jan., 1918.

Flying Our Wounded Veterans Home. By Catherine Bell Palmer. Vol. LXXXVIII, pp. 363-384, 17 ills., Sept., 1945.

Flying Over Egypt, Sinai, and Palestine: Looking Down Upon the Holy Land During an Air Journey of Two and a Half Hours from Cairo to Jerusalem. By Brig. Gen. P. R. C. Groves and Maj. J. R. McCrindle. Vol. L, pp. 313-355, 26 ills., 1 half-page map, Sept., 1926.

Flying Over the Arctic. By Lieut. Comdr. Richard E. Byrd. Vol. XLVIII, pp. 519-532, 10 ills., Nov., 1925.

Flying Pole Dance:

Mexican Indian Flying Pole Dance. By Helga Larsen. Vol. LXXI, pp. 387-400, 13 ills., Mar., 1937.

Flying the "Hump" of the Andes. By Capt. Albert W. Stevens. Vol. LIX, pp. 595-636, 36 ills., 1 third-page map, May, 1931.

Flying the Pacific. By William Burke Miller. Vol. LXX, pp. 665-707, 39 ills., Dec., 1936.

Flying the World: In a Homemade Airplane the Author and Her Husband Enjoy 16,000 Miles of Adventurous Flight Across Europe, Asia, and America. By Gladys M. Day. Vol. LXI, pp. 655-690, 41 ills., 1 half-page map, June, 1932.

Flying the World's Longest Air Mail Route: From Montevideo, Uruguay, Over the Andes, Up the Pacific Coast, Across Central America and the Caribbean to Miami, Florida, in 67 Thrilling Flying Hours. By Junius B. Wood. Vol. LVII, pp. 261-325, 65 ills., 1 half-page map, Mar., 1930.

Foehn (Wind):

Americans Stand Guard in Greenland. By Andrew H. Brown. Vol. XC, pp. 457-500, 23 ills. in black and white, 19 ills. in color, 1 page map, Oct., 1946.

Folkner, Roland P.:

Conditions in Liberia. By Roland P. Folkner, George Sale, and Emmett J. Scott. Vol. XXI, pp. 729-741, 9 ills., Sept., 1910.

Folliard, Edward T.:

Martinique, Caribbean Question Mark. By Edward T. Folliard. Vol. LXXIX, pp. 47-55, 9 ills., Jan., 1941.

Fonck, René:

Aces Among Aces. By Laurence La Tourette Driggs. Vol. XXXIII, pp. 568-580, 9 ills., June, 1918.

Food:

Acorn, a Possibly Neglected Source of Food. By C. Hart Merriam. Vol. XXXIV, pp. 129-137, 8 ills., Aug., 1918.

America Fights on the Farms. 21 ills. in color from natural-color photographs. Vol. LXXXVI, pp. 33-48, July, 1944.

America's Debt to the Hen. By Harry R. Lewis. Vol. LI, pp. 453-467, 15 ills., Apr., 1927.

Appeal to Members of the National Geographic Society (Food Conservation). Vol. XXXIII, pp. 347-348, 2 ills., Apr., 1918.

Britain Fights in the Fields. By Francis A. Flood. Vol. LXXXVI, pp. 31-65, 17 ills. in black and white, 21 ills. in color, July, 1944.

Deer Farming in the United States. Vol. XXI, pp. 269-276, 2 ills., Mar., 1910.

Delectable Shrimp: Once A Culinary Stepchild, Today A Gulf Coast Industry. By Harlan Major. Vol. LXXXVI, pp. 501-512, 11 ills., 1 two-thirds-page map, Oct., 1944.

Dumboy, the National Dish of Liberia. By G. N. Collins. Vol. XXII, pp. 84-88, 5 ills., Jan., 1911.

Food—*Continued*

Farmers Keep Them Eating. By Frederick Simpich. Vol. LXXXIII, pp. 435-458, 22 ills., Apr., 1943.

Farmers Since the Days of Noah: China's Remarkable System of Agriculture Has Kept Alive the Densest Population in the World. By Adam Warwick. Vol. LI, pp. 469-500, 37 ills., Apr., 1927.

Fearful Famines of the Past: History Will Repeat Itself Unless the American People Conserve Their Resources. By Ralph A. Graves. Vol. XXXII, pp. 68-90, 11 ills., July, 1917.

Flavor and Savor of American Foods. 25 ills. in color from natural-color photographs by J. Baylor Roberts, Willard R. Culver, and others. Vol. LXXXI, pp. 289-320, Mar., 1942.

Food Armies of Liberty. By Herbert Hoover. Vol. XXXII, pp. 187-196, 6 ills., Sept., 1917.

Food for Our Allies in 1919. By Herbert Hoover. Vol. XXXIV, pp. 242-244, Sept., 1918.

Forerunners of Famine. By Frederic C. Walcott. Vol. XXXIII, pp. 336-347, 4 ills., 4 diagrams, 1 half-page map, Apr., 1918.

Forming New Fashions in Food: The Bearing of Taste on One of Our Great Food Economies, the Dried Vegetable, Which Is Developing Into a Big War Industry. By David Fairchild. Vol. XXXIII, pp. 356-368, 11 ills., Apr., 1918.

Greens Grow for GI's on Soilless Ascension. By W. Robert Moore. Vol. LXXXVIII, pp. 219-230, 12 ills., Aug., 1945.

Helping to Solve the Allies' Food Problem: America Calls for a Million Young Soldiers of the Commissary to Volunteer for Service in 1918. By Ralph A. Graves. Vol. XXXIII, pp. 170-194, 23 ills., Feb., 1918.

How the World Is Fed. By William Joseph Showalter. Vol. XXIX, pp. 1-110, 101 ills., Jan., 1916.

Jungle Housekeeping for a Geographic Expedition (Cerro de las Mesas, Mexico). By Marion Stirling. Vol. LXXX, pp. 303-327, 15 ills., Sept., 1941.

Lend-Lease Is a Two-way Benefit: Innovation in Creative Statesmanship Pools Resources of United Nations, and Supplies American Forces Around the World. By Francis Flood. Vol. LXXXIII, pp. 745-761, 14 ills., June, 1943.

Nuts and Their Uses as Foods. Vol. XVIII, p. 800, Dec., 1907.

Peacetime Plant Hunting About Peiping. By P. H. and J. H. Dorsett. Vol. LXXII, pp. 509-534, 21 ills., 1 two-thirds-page map, Oct., 1937.

Reviving a Lost Art. Vol. XXXI, pp. 475-481, 9 ills., June, 1917.

Revolution in Eating: Machine Food Age—Born of Roads, Research, and Refrigeration—Makes the United States the Best-fed Nation in History. By J. R. Hildebrand. Vol. LXXXI, pp. 273-324, 33 ills. in black and white, 25 ills. in color, Mar., 1942.

Food—*Continued*

Round About Bogotá: A Hunt for New Fruits and Plants Among the Mountain Forests of Colombia's Unique Capital. By Wilson Popenoe. Vol. XLIX, pp. 127-160, 34 ills., 1 third-page map, Feb., 1926.

War, Patriotism, and the Food Supply. By Frederick V. Coville. Vol. XXXI, pp. 254-256, Mar., 1917.

Weapon of Food. By Herbert Hoover. Vol. XXXII, pp. 197-24?, 15 ills., Sept., 1917.

Wokas, a Primitive Indian Food. Vol. XV, pp. 182-185, 3 ills., Apr., 1904.

Your New World of Tomorrow. By F. Barrows Colton. Vol. LXXXVIII, pp. 385-410, 25 ills., Oct., 1945.

See also Agriculture; Fishes and Fisheries; Fruits; Vegetables.

Foote, John:

Geography of Medicines: War's Effect Upon the World's Sources of Supply. By John Foote. Vol. XXXII, pp. 213-238, 25 ills., Sept., 1917.

Medicine Fakes and Fakers of All Ages: Strange Stories of Nostrums and Kingly Quacks in Every Era and Clime. By John Foote. Vol. XXXV, pp. 67-84, 14 ills., Jan., 1919.

Foran, W. Robert:

Tristan da Cunha, Isles of Contentment: On Lonely Sea Spots of Pirate Lore and Shipwrecks Seven Families Live Happily Far from War Rumors and World Changes. By W. Robert Foran. Vol. LXXIV, pp. 671-694, 23 ills., 1 half-page map, Nov., 1938.

Forbes, Edgar Allen:

Macao (China), "Land of Sweet Sadness": The Oldest European Settlement in the Far East, Long the Only Haven for Distressed Mariners in the China Sea. By Edgar Allen Forbes. Vol. LXII, pp. 337-357, 13 ills. in black and white, 11 ills. in color, Sept., 1932.

Notes on the Only American Colony in the World (Liberia). By Edgar Allen Forbes. Vol. XXI, pp. 719-729, 14 ills., Sept., 1910.

Forbes-Leith, (Maj.) F. A. C.:

From England to India by Automobile: An 8,527-Mile Trip Through Ten Countries, from London to Quetta, Requires Five and a Half Months. By Maj. F. A. C. Forbes-Leith. Vol. XLVIII, pp. 191-223, 33 ills., 1 third-page map, Aug., 1925.

Forbush, Ernest Howe:

Unique Island of Mount Desert. By George B. Dorr, M. L. Fernald, and Ernest Howe Forbush. Vol. XXVI, pp. 75-89, 7 ills., July, 1914.

Ford, Richard:

Seville, More Spanish Than Spain: The City of the Ibero-American Exposition, Which Opens This Spring, Presents a Tapestry of Many Ages and of Nations Old and New. By Richard Ford. Vol. LV, pp. 273-310, 35 ills. in black and white, 2 ills. in color, Mar., 1929.

Forder, Archibald:

Arabia, the Desert of the Sea. By Archibald Forder. Vol. XX, pp. 1039-1062, 20 ills., Dec., 1909.

Damascus, the Pearl of the Desert. By Archibald Forder. Vol. XXII, pp. 62-82, 19 ills., 1 three-quarters-page map, Jan., 1911.

Forecasting the Weather. By Alfred J. Henry. Vol. XV, pp. 285-292, 6 ills., 1 chart, July, 1904.

Forecasting the Weather and Storms. By Willis L. Moore. Vol. XVI, pp. 255-305, 5 ills., 20 charts, June, 1905.

Foreign-Born of the United States. Vol. XXVI, pp. 265-271, 14 diagrams, Sept., 1914.

Foreign Commerce of the United States in 1903. Vol. XIV, pp. 359-360, Sept., 1903.

Foreigners and Foreign Firms in China. Vol. XI, p. 330, Aug., 1900.

Foremost Intellectual Achievement of Ancient America: The Hieroglyphic Inscriptions on the Monuments in the Ruined Cities of Mexico, Guatemala, and Honduras Are Yielding the Secrets of the Maya Civilization. By Sylvanus Griswold Morley. Vol. XLI, pp. 109-130, 27 ills., 17 diagrams, special map supplement in colors, Feb., 1922.

Forerunners of Famine. By Frederic C. Walcott. Vol. XXXIII, pp. 336-347, 4 ills., 4 diagrams, 1 half-page map, Apr., 1918.

Forest Fires in the Adirondacks in 1903. By H. M. Sutter. Vol. XV, p. 224, May, 1904.

Forest Lookout. By Ella E. Clark. With 9 ills. in color from natural-color photographs by the author. Vol. XC, pp. 73-96, 8 ills. in black and white, July, 1946.

Forest Reserves of the United States. By Gifford Pinchot. Vol. XI, pp. 369-372, 1 three-quarters-page map, Sept., 1900.

Forests and Forestry:

Amazon, the Father of Waters: The Earth's Mightiest River Drains a Basin of More Than 2,700,000 Square Miles, from Which Came Originally the World's Finest Rubber. By W. L. Schurz. Vol. XLIX, pp. 445-463, 15 ills., Apr., 1926.

Among the Big Trees of California. By John R. White. Vol. LXVI, pp. 219-232, 14 ills., Aug., 1934.

Among the Mahogany Forests of Cuba. By Walter D. Wilcox. Vol. XIX, pp. 485-498, 6 ills., 1 page map, July, 1908.

By Seaplane to Six Continents: Cruising 60,000 Miles, Italian Argonauts of the Air See World Geography Unroll, and Break New Sky Trails Over Vast Brazilian Jungles. By Comdr. Francesco de Pinedo. Vol. LIV, pp. 247-301, 60 ills., 1 two-page map, Sept., 1928.

Forests and Forestry—*Continued*

California's Coastal Redwood Realm: Along a Belt of Tall Trees a Giant Bridge Speeds the Winning of Our Westernmost Frontier. By J. R. Hildebrand. Vol. LXXV, pp. 133-184, 31 ills. in black and white, 17 ills. in color, 1 page-and-a-half map, Feb., 1939.

Comparison of Our Unprotected with Our Protected Forests. Vol. XIX, pp. 739-740, Oct., 1908.

Deforestation and Climate. Vol. XVI, pp. 397-398, Aug., 1905.

Exploring the Valley of the Amazon in a Hydroplane: Twelve Thousand Miles of Flying Over the World's Greatest River and Greatest Forest to Chart the Unknown Parima River from the Sky. By Capt. Albert W. Stevens. Vol. XLIX, pp. 353-420, 86 ills., 1 page map, Apr., 1926.

Exploring Unknown Corners of the "Hermit Kingdom" (Korea). By Roy Chapman Andrews. Vol. XXXVI, pp. 24-48, 80 ills., 1 page map, July, 1919.

Fight Against Forest Fires. By Henry S. Graves. Vol. XXIII, pp. 662-683, 19 ills., July, 1912.

Fight at the Timber-Line. By John Oliver La Gorce. Vol. XLII, pp. 165-196, 32 ills., Aug., 1922.

Forest Fires in the Adirondacks in 1903. By H. M. Suter. Vol. XV, p. 224, May, 1904.

Forest Lookout. By Ella E. Clark. With 9 ills. in color from natural-color photographs by the author. Vol. XC, pp. 73-96, 8 ills. in black and white, July, 1946.

Forest Reserves of the United States. By Gifford Pinchot. Vol. XI, pp. 369-372, 1 three-quarters-page map, Sept., 1900.

Forestry at Home and Abroad. By Gifford Pinchot. Vol. XVI, pp. 375-388, 8 ills., Aug., 1905.

Forestry in California. Vol. XVI, pp. 480-481, Oct., 1905.

Forests of Canada. Vol. XIV, pp. 106-108, Mar., 1903.

Forests of Canada. By Sir Wilfrid Laurier. Vol. XVII, pp. 504-509, Sept., 1906.

Forests Vital to Our Welfare (From an Address by President Roosevelt at Raleigh, North Carolina, October 19, 1905). Vol. XVI, pp. 515-516, Nov., 1905.

Government Assistance in Handling Forest Lands. Vol. XV, pp. 450-452, Nov., 1904.

Impression of the Guiana Wilderness. By Angelo Heilprin. Vol. XVIII, pp. 373-381, 6 ills., June, 1907.

Impressions of Asiatic Turkey. By Stephen van Rensselaer Trowbridge. Vol. XXVI, pp. 598-609, 6 ills., Dec., 1914.

Influence of Forestry upon the Lumber Industry of the United States. By Overton W. Price. Vol. XIV, pp. 381-386, 2 ills., Oct., 1903.

Forests and Forestry—*Continued*

Is Climatic Aridity Impending on the Pacific Slope? The Testimony of the Forest. By J. B. Leiberg. Vol. X, pp. 160-181, May, 1899.

Jungles of Panama. By David Fairchild. Vol. XLI, pp. 131-145, 14 ills., Feb., 1922.

Lessons from China (Forest Destruction). Vol. XX, pp. 18-29, 8 ills., Jan., 1909.

New World to Explore: the Tree-Roof of the British Guiana Forest Flourishes Much Hitherto-Unknown Life. By Maj. R. W. G. Hingston. Vol. LXII, pp. 617-642, 35 ills., Nov., 1932.

Notes on the Eucalyptus Tree from the United States Forest Service. Vol. XX, pp. 668-673, 4 ills., July, 1909.

Notes on the Forest Service. Vol. XVIII, pp. 142-145, 3 ills., Feb., 1907.

Our Big Trees Saved. Vol. XXXI, pp. 1-11, 10 ills., Jan., 1917.

Protecting Our Forests from Fire. By James Wilson. Vol. XXII, pp. 98-100, 5 ills., Jan., 1911.

Redwood Forest of the Pacific Coast. By Henry Gannett. Vol. X, pp. 145-159, 6 ills., 1 page map, May, 1899.

Relation of Forests and Forest Fires. By Gifford Pinchot. Vol. X, pp. 393-403, 7 ills., Oct., 1899.

Saving the Forests. By Herbert A. Smith. Vol. XVIII, pp. 519-534, 7 ills., Aug., 1907.

Summer Meeting of the American Forestry Association. Vol. XIII, pp. 352-358, Sept., 1902.

Tallest Tree That Grows (Eucalyptus). By Edgerton R. Young. Vol. XX, pp. 664-667, 3 ills., July, 1909.

Timberlines. Vol. XIV, pp. 80-81, Feb., 1903.

Timberlines. By Israel C. Russell. Vol. XV, pp. 47-49, Jan., 1904.

Two Great Undertakings (Work of U. S. Bureau of Reclamation and U. S. Forest Service). Vol. XVII, pp. 645-647, Nov., 1906.

Value of the United States Forest Service. Vol. XX, pp. 29-41, 14 ills., Jan., 1909.

Vast Timber Belts of Canada. Vol. XVII, pp. 509-511, Sept., 1906.

When Our Country Is Fifty Years Older. By Raphael Zon. Vol. XX, pp. 573-580, 2 ills., 1 diagram, June, 1909.

Working Teak in the Burma Forests: The Sagacious Elephant Is Man's Ablest Ally in the Logging Industry of the Far East. By A. W. Smith. Vol. LVIII, pp. 239-256, 5 ills. in black and white, 15 ills. in color, Aug., 1930.

See also Trees.

Forgotten Ruins of Indo-China. By Jacob E. Conner. Vol. XXIII, pp. 209-272, 63 ills., 1 page and 1 three-quarters-page maps, Mar., 1912.

Forgotten Valley of Peru : Conquered by Incas, Scourged by Famine, Plagues, and Earthquakes, Colca Valley Shelters the Last Fragment of an Ancient Andean Tribe. By Robert Shippee. Vol. LXV, pp. 111-132, 22 ills., 1 two-thirds-page map, Jan., 1934.

Forming New Fashions in Food : The Bearing of Taste on One of Our Great Food Economies, the Dried Vegetable, Which Is Developing Into a Big War Industry. By David Fairchild. Vol. XXXIII, pp. 356-368, 11 ills., Apr., 1918.

Formosa (Island), China Sea :

Formosa the Beautiful. By Alice Ballantine Kirjassoff. Vol. XXXVII, pp. 246-292, 60 ills., 1 half-page map, Mar., 1920.

I Lived on Formosa. By Joseph W. Ballantine. Vol. LXXXVII, pp. 1-24, 19 ills., 1 page and 1 half-page maps, Jan., 1945.

Forrest, George:

Land of the Crossbow (Yünnan Province, China). By George Forrest. Vol. XXI, pp. 132-156, 15 ills., 1 page map, Feb., 1910.

Fort Peck Dam, Montana :

Taming the Outlaw Missouri River. By Frederick Simpich. Vol. LXXXVIII, pp. 569-598, 25 ills., 1 two-page map, Nov., 1945.

Fort Wrangell, Alaska :

Stikine River in 1898. By Eliza R. Scidmore. Vol. X, pp. 1-15, 4 ills., Jan., 1899.

Fortescue, Granville:

Burden France Has Borne. By Granville Fortescue. Vol. XXXI, pp. 322-344, 19 ills., Apr., 1917.

Training the New Armies of Liberty : Camp Lee, Virginia's Home for the National Army. By Granville Fortescue. Vol. XXXII, pp. 421-437, 8 ills., 1 page map in colors, Nov.-Dec., 1917.

Forts:

Greatest Achievement of Ancient Man in America, the Fortress of Sacsahuaman (Peru). Vol. XXIX, panorama, May, 1916.

Little-Known Marvel of the Western Hemisphere : Christophe's Citadel, a Monument to the Tyranny and Genius of Haiti's King of Slaves. By Maj. G. H. Osterhout, Jr. Vol. XXXVIII, pp. 468-482, 13 ills., Dec., 1920.

Sigiriya, "A Fortress in the Sky." By Wilson K. Norton. Vol. XC, pp. 665-680, 14 ills., 1 two-thirds-page map, Nov., 1946.

Forty Years Among the Arabs. By John Van Ess. Vol. LXXXII, pp. 385-420, 27 ills., 1 two-page map, Sept., 1942.

Foshag, (Dr.) William F.:

Paricutín, the Cornfield That Grew a Volcano (Mexico). By James A. Green. Vol. LXXXV, pp. 129-164, 16 ills. in black and white, 21 ills. in color, 1 third-page map, Feb., 1944.

Fossils. *See* Paleontology.

Foster, John W.:

Alaskan Boundary. By John W. Foster. Vol. X, pp. 425-456, 10 page maps, Nov., 1899.

Alaskan Boundary Tribunal. By John W. Foster. Vol. XV, pp. 1-12, special map supplement, 1 half-page map, Jan., 1904.

Canadian Boundary. By John W. Foster. Vol. XIV, pp. 85-89, Mar., 1903.

China. By John W. Foster. Vol. XV, pp. 463-478, 2 page maps, Dec., 1904.

Latin American Constitutions and Revolutions. By John W. Foster. Vol. XII, pp. 169-175, May, 1901.

New Mexico. By John W. Foster. Vol. XIII, pp. 1-24, 11 ills., 2 page maps, Jan., 1902.

Present Conditions in China. By John W. Foster. Vol. XVII, pp. 651-672, 709-711, Dec., 1906.

Foum Tatahouine, Tunisia :

Mole Men : An Account of the Troglodytes of Southern Tunisia. By Frank Edward Johnson. Vol. XXII, pp. 787-846, 60 ills., Sept., 1911.

Four Faces of Siva : The Mystery of Angkor (Cambodia). By Robert J. Cassey. Vol. LIV, pp. 303-332, 13 ills. in black and white, 6 ills. in color, 1 third-page map, Sept., 1928.

Four Prominent Geographers. Vol. XVIII, pp. 425-428, 4 ills., June, 1907.

Contains biographies and portraits of the following : Arthur P. Davis, Frederick Haynes Newell, George Otis Smith, and Charles D. Walcott.

Four Thousand Hours Over China. By Capt. Hans Koester. Vol. LXXIII, pp. 571-598, 25 ills., 1 two-thirds-page map, May, 1938.

Fowl. *See* Poultry.

Fowl of the Old and New World. 29 ills. in color from paintings by Hashime Murayama. Vol. LI, pp. 421-436, Apr., 1927.

Fowler, Frederick Hall:

Week-Ends with the Prairie Falcon : A Commuter Finds Recreation in Scaling Cliffs to Observe the Nest Life and Flying Habits of These Elusive Birds. By Frederick Hall Fowler. Vol. LXVII, pp. 611-626, 21 ills., May, 1935.

Fowliang, China. *See* Kingtehchen.

Fowls of Forest and Stream Tamed by Man. By Morley A. Jull. Vol. LVII, pp. 327-371, 27 ills. in black and white, 16 ills. in color, Mar., 1930.

Contains descriptions and illustrations of the following fowls : Ducks, Geese, Guinea Fowl, Peafowl, Swans, Turkeys.

Fox Farming:

Northern Crusoe's Island : Life on a Fox Farm Off the Coast of Alaska, Far from Contact with the World Eleven Months a Year. By Margery Pritchard Parker. Vol. XLIV, pp. 313-326, 15 ills., 1 eighth-page map, Sept., 1923.

The Policemen of the Air (Birds). By Henry Wetherbee Henshaw. Vol. XIX, pp. 79-118, 38 ills., Feb., 1908.

Contains information on fox farming.

Fox Island Passes, Alaska :

Some Notes on the Fox Island Passes, Alaska. By J. J. Gilbert. Vol. XVI, pp. 427-429, Sept., 1905.

France:

Aces Among Aces (Aviators). By Laurence La Tourette Driggs. Vol. XXXIII, pp. 568-580, 9 ills., June, 1918.

Aces of the Air. By Capt. Jacques De Sieyes. Vol. XXXIII, pp. 5-9, 2 ills., Jan., 1918.

Across the Midi in a Canoe : Two Americans Paddle Along the Canals of Southern France from the Atlantic to the Mediterranean. By Melville Chater. Vol. LII, pp. 127-167, 49 ills., 1 half-page map, Aug., 1927.

Americans Help Liberated Europe Live Again. By Lt. Col. Frederick Simpich, Jr. Vol. LXXXVII, pp. 747-768, 17 ills., June, 1945.

Armistice Day and the American Battle Fields. By J. J. Jusserand. Vol. LVI, pp. 509-554, 32 ills. in black and white, 20 ills. in color, Nov., 1929.

Ascent of Mont Blanc. By Walter Woodburn Hyde. Vol. XXIV, pp. 861-942, 69 ills., Aug., 1913.

Battle Fields of France Eleven Years After. 23 ills. in color from autochromes by Gervais Courtellemont. Vol. LVI, pp. 522-539, Nov., 1929.

Beauties of France. By Arthur Stanley Riggs. Vol. XXVIII, pp. 391-491, 73 ills. in black and white, 16 ills. in color, 1 half-page map, Nov., 1915.

Beauty, History, and Romance Enrich the Château Country. 10 ills. in color from autochromes by Gervais Courtellemont. Vol. LVIII, pp. 466-475, Oct., 1930.

Bind the Wounds of France. By Herbert C. Hoover. Vol. XXXI, pp. 439-444, 5 ills., May, 1917.

Blue Seas and Brilliant Costumes Along the Brittany Coast. 29 ills. in color from autochromes by Gervais Courtellemont. Vol. LVI, pp. 142-175, Aug., 1929.

Brittany : The Land of the Sardine. By Hugh M. Smith. Vol. XX, pp. 541-573, 23 ills., June, 1909.

Burden France Has Borne. By Granville Fortescue. Vol. XXXI, pp. 322-344, 19 ills., Apr., 1917.

Camargue, the Cowboy Country of Southern France. By Dr. André Vialles. Vol. XLII, pp. 1-34, 33 ills., 1 half-page map, July, 1922.

France—*Continued*

Canal from the Atlantic to the Mediterranean. Vol. XI, pp. 122-123, Mar., 1900.

Carnival Days on the Riviera. By Maynard Owen Williams. Vol. L, pp. 467-501, 21 ills., Oct., 1926.

Celebrating Christmas on the Meuse. By Capt. Clifton Lisle. Vol. XXXVI, pp. 527-537, 5 ills., Dec., 1919.

Charm and Color Distinguish Norman Byways. 13 ills. in color from natural-color photographs by Gervais Courtellemont. Vol. LXI, pp. 90-99, Jan., 1932.

Château Land—France's Pageant on the Loire. Vol. LVIII, pp. 466-475, 10 ills. in color, Oct., 1930.

A City Learns to Smile Again (Nancy). By Maj. Frederick G. Vosburgh. Vol. LXXXVII, pp. 361-384, 23 ills., 1 two-thirds-page map, Mar., 1945.

Coasts of Normandy and Brittany. By W. Robert Moore. Vol. LXXXIV, pp. 205-232, 5 ills. in black and white, 21 ills. in color, 1 two page map, Aug., 1943.

Colonial Expansion of France. By Jean C. Bracq. Vol. XI, pp. 225-238, 1 page map, June, 1900.

Cooties and Courage. By Herbert Corey. Vol. XXXIII, pp. 495-509, 10 ills., June, 1918.

Costume Pageants in the French Pyrenees. 24 ills. in color from natural-color photographs by W. Robert Moore. Vol. LXXII, pp. 435-450, Oct., 1937.

Day with Our Boys in the Geographic Wards. By Carol Corey. Vol. XXXIV, pp. 69-80, 8 ills., July, 1918.

Discovering the Oldest Statues in the World : A Daring Explorer Swims Through a Subterranean River of the Pyrenees and Finds Rock Carvings Made 20,000 Years Ago. By Norbert Casteret. Vol. XLVI, pp. 123-152, 24 ills., 1 half and 1 quarter-page maps, Aug., 1924.

Fearful Famines of the Past : History Will Repeat Itself Unless the American People Conserve Their Resources. By Ralph A. Graves. Vol. XXXII, pp. 68-90, 11 ills., July, 1917.

Flashes of Color Throughout France. 28 ills. in color from autochromes by Gervais Courtellemont. Vol. XLVI, pp. 529-544, Nov., 1924.

Flying in France. By Capt. André de Berroeta. Vol. XXXIII, pp. 9-26, 12 ills., Jan., 1918.

France Farms as War Wages : An American Explores the Rich Rural Region of the Historic Paris Basin. By Harrison Howell Walker. Vol. LXXVII, pp. 201-238, 16 ills. in black and white, 18 ills. in color, 1 map, Feb., 1940.

France of Sunshine and Flowers. 21 ills. in color from autochromes lumière by Maynard Owen Williams, Gervais Courtellemont, and Hans Hildenbrand. Vol. L, pp. 481-496, Oct., 1926.

France of Today. By Maj. Gen. A. W. Greely. Vol. XXVI, pp. 193-222, 27 ills., Sept., 1914.

France—*Continued*

From the Trenches to Versailles. By Carol Corey. Vol. XXXII, pp. 535-550, 12 ills., Nov.-Dec., 1917.

In French Lorraine : That Part of France Where the First American Soldiers Have Fallen. By Harriet Chalmers Adams. Vol. XXXII, pp. 499-518, 16 ills., Nov.-Dec., 1917.

In Smiling Alsace, Where France Has Resumed Sway. Vol. LII, pp. 168-176, 11 ills. in color, Aug., 1927.

Italy, France, Switzerland. Vol. XXVIII, pp. 439-454, 16 ills. in color, Nov., 1915.

Land of William the Conqueror : Where Northmen Came to Build Castles and Cathedrals. By Inez Buffington Ryan. Vol. LXI, pp. 89-99, 13 ills. in color, Jan., 1932.

Life Story of an American Airman in France : Extracts from the Letters of Stuart Walcott, Who, Between July and December, 1917, Learned to Fly in French Schools of Aviation, Won Fame at the Front, and Fell Near Saint Souplet. Vol. XXXIII, pp. 86-106, 9 ills., Jan., 1918.

Manless Alpine Climbing : The First Woman to Scale the Grépon, the Matterhorn, and Other Famous Peaks Without Masculine Support Relates Her Adventures. By Miriam O'Brien Underhill. Vol. LXVI, pp. 131-170, 30 ills. in black and white, 12 ills. in color, Aug., 1934.

Mont St. Michel, a Medieval Masterpiece. 22 ills. in duotone. Vol. LXIX, pp. 633-648, May, 1936.

Mysterious Prehistoric Monuments of Brittany. By Charles Buxton Going. Vol. XLIV, pp. 53-69, 16 ills., July, 1923.

National Geographic Society's Memorial to American Troops : Fountain and Water Supply System Presented to Historic French Town of Cantigny, Where Our Overseas Soldiers Won Their First Victory in the World War. Vol. XLIV, pp. 675-678, 4 ills., Dec., 1923.

Normandy—Choice of the Vikings. By Helen Churchill Candee. Vol. LXIX, pp. 625-665, 25 ills. in black and white, 22 ills. in duotone, 1 two-thirds-page map, May, 1936.

Normandy and Brittany in Brighter Days. 21 ills. in color from natural-color photographs by W. Robert Moore, Peter Upton Muir, and others. Vol. LXXXIV, pp. 209-232, Aug., 1943.

Normandy's Made-in-England Harbors. Vol. LXXXVII, pp. 565-580, 16 ills., 1 quarter-page map, May, 1945.

Notes on Normandy. By Mrs. George C. Bosson, Jr. Vol. XXI, pp. 775-782, 5 ills., Sept., 1910.

Our First Alliance. By J. J. Jusserand. Vol. XXXI, pp. 518-548, 8 ills., June, 1917.

Our Friends, the French : An Appraisal of the Traits and Temperament of the Citizens of Our Sister Republic. By Carl Holliday. Vol. XXXIV, pp. 345-377, 29 ills., Nov., 1918.

France—*Continued*

Our Heritage of Liberty : An Address Before the United States Senate by M. Viviani, President of the French Commission to the United States, May 1, 1917. Vol. XXXI, pp. 365-367, 1 ill., Apr., 1917.

Our National War Memorials in Europe. By Gen. John J. Pershing. Vol. LXV, pp. 1-36, 24 ills. in black and white, 11 ills. in color, 1 half-page map, Jan., 1934.

Our Second Alliance. By J. J. Jusserand. Vol. XXXI, pp. 565-566, 1 ill., June, 1917.

Our Transatlantic Flight. By Comdr. Richard Evelyn Byrd. Vol. LII, pp. 347-368, 17 ills., 1 half-page map, Sept., 1927.

Outspeaking of a Great Democracy : The Proceedings of the Chamber of Deputies of France on Friday, April 6, 1917, as Reported in the "Journal Officiel de La République Française." Vol. XXXI, pp. 362-365, 1 ill., Apr., 1917.

Plain Tales from the Trenches : As Told Over the Tea Table in Blighty—A Soldier's "Home" in Paris. By Carol Corey. Vol. XXXIII, pp. 300-312, 7 ills., Mar., 1918.

Price of Liberty, Equality, Fraternity. Vol. XXXIV, p. 377, Nov., 1918.

Races of Europe. By Edwin A. Grosvenor. Vol. XXXIV, pp. 441-534, 62 ills., special map supplement in colors, 2 page maps, Dec., 1918.

Republics—The Ladder to Liberty. By David Jayne Hill. Vol. XXXI, pp. 240-254, 5 ills., 2 page maps, Mar., 1917.

Scenes from France. Vol. XL, pp. 29-44, 16 ills., July, 1921.

Shopping Abroad for Our Armies in France. By Herbert Corey. Vol. XXXIII, pp. 206-218, 6 ills., Feb., 1918.

Skyline Drive in the Pyrenees. By W. Robert Moore. Vol. LXXII, pp. 434-452, 24 ills. in color, Oct., 1937.

Some French Pastorals. 18 ills. in color from natural-color photographs by Harrison Howell Walker. Vol. LXXVII, pp. 207-230, Feb., 1940.

Through the Back Doors of France : A Seven Weeks' Voyage in a Canadian Canoe from St. Malo, Through Brittany and the Château Country, to Paris. By Melville Chater. Vol. XLIV, pp. 1-51, 55 ills., 1 half-page map, July, 1923.

Ties That Bind : Our Natural Sympathy with English Traditions, the French Republic, and the Russian Outburst for Liberty. By John Sharp Williams. Vol. XXXI, pp. 281-286, 4 ills., Mar., 1917.

"Time Will Not Dim the Glory of Their Deeds" (World War Memorials). 11 ills. in color from natural-color photographs by W. Robert Moore. Vol. LXV, pp. 17-24, Jan., 1934.

Where Bretons Wrest a Living from the Sea. 23 ills. from photographs by F. W. Goro. Vol. LXXI, pp. 751-766, June, 1937.

France—*Continued*

World's Debt to France. Vol. XXVIII, pp. 491-501, 7 ills., Nov., 1915.

See also Compiègne ; Corsica (Island) ; Dieppe ; Marseille ; Paris ; St. Malo ; Versailles.

Frank, Alberta (Province), Canada :

Landslides and Rock Avalanches. By Guy Elliott Mitchell. Vol. XXI, pp. 277-287, 6 ills., Apr., 1910.

Frankenfield, H. C.:

Kite Work of the Weather Bureau. By H. C. Frankenfield. Vol. XI, pp. 55-62, Feb., 1900.

Weather Bureau and the Recent Floods. By H. C. Frankenfield. Vol. XIV, pp. 285-290, 2 ills., July, 1903.

Frankincense:

Isle of Frankincense (Socotra, Arabian Sea). By Charles K. Moser. Vol. XXXIII, pp. 266-278, 11 ills., Mar., 1918.

Franklin, Alicelia:

Historic Danzig : Last of the City-States. By William and Alicelia Franklin. Vol. LXXVI, pp. 677-696, 26 ills., Nov., 1939.

Franklin, Benjamin:

Historic City of Brotherly Love : Philadelphia, Born of Penn and Strengthened by Franklin, a Metropolis of Industries, Homes and Parks. By John Oliver La Gorce. Vol. LXII, pp. 643-697, 49 ills. in black and white, 13 ills. in color, Dec., 1932.

Franklin, (Sir) John:

Location of the Sir John Franklin Monument. By James White. Vol. XIX, p. 596, Aug., 1908.

Franklin, William:

Historic Danzig : Last of the City-States. By William and Alicelia Franklin. Vol. LXXVI, pp. 677-696, 26 ills., Nov., 1939.

Franklin Institute:

Series of flights under auspices of National Geographic Society, U. S. Army Air Forces, and Bartol Research Foundation of the Franklin Institute, to study cosmic rays. Vol. XC, p. 387 ; ill. 388, Sept., 1946.

Franz Josef Land, Arctic Region :

Through Franz Josef Land. Vol. X, p. 362, Sept., 1899.

Wellman Polar Expedition. By Walter Wellman. Vol. X, pp. 481-505, 10 ills., 1 half-page map, 1 diagram, Dec., 1899.

Fraser, Edwin R.:

Where Our Bananas Come From (Costa Rica). By Edwin R. Fraser. Vol. XXIII, pp. 713-730, 14 ills., July, 1912.

Freeman, Lewis R.:

Mother of Rivers : An Account of a Photographic Expedition to the Great Columbia Ice Field of the Canadian Rockies. By Lewis R. Freeman. Vol. XLVII, pp. 377-446, 60 ills., 1 three-quarters and 1 quarter-page maps, Apr., 1925.

Freeman, Lewis R.—*Continued*

Surveying the Grand Canyon of the Colorado : An Account of the 1923 Boating Expedition of the United States Geological Survey. By Lewis R. Freeman. Vol. XLV, pp. 471-548, 62 ills., 1 three-quarters-page map, May, 1924.

Trailing History Down the Big Muddy : In the Homeward Wake of Lewis and Clark, a Folding Steel Skiff Bears Its Lone Pilot on a 2,000-Mile Cruise on the Yellowstone-Missouri. By Lewis R. Freeman. Vol. LIV, pp. 73-120, 51 ills., 1 half-page map, July, 1928.

Freiburg (Germany)—Gateway to the Black Forest. By Alicia O'Reardon Overbeck. Vol. LXIV, pp. 213-252, 40 ills. in black and white, 11 ills. in color, Aug., 1933.

Freighters of Fortune on our Great Lakes. 8 ills. in duotone from photographs by Maynard Owen Williams. Vol. LXV, pp. 463-470, Apr., 1934.

French and Indian War:

Travels of George Washington : Dramatic Episodes in His Career as the First Geographer of the United States. By William Joseph Showalter. Vol. LXI, pp. 1-63, 50 ills., 5 maps, special supplement in colors, Jan., 1932.

French Conquest of the Sahara. By Charles Rabot. Vol. XVI, pp. 76-80, 1 ill., Feb., 1905.

French Equatorial Africa:

Three-Wheeling Through Africa : Two Adventurers Cross the So-called Dark Continent North of Lake Chad on Motorcycles with Side Cars. By James C. Wilson. Vol. LXV, pp. 37-92, 64 ills., 1 two-page map, Jan., 1934.

French Guiana:

Brazil-French Guiana Boundary Decision. Vol. XII, p. 83, Feb., 1901.

Color Glows in the Guianas, French and Dutch. By Nicol Smith. Vol. LXXXIII, pp. 459-480, 8 ills. in black and white, 13 ills. in color, 1 two-thirds-page map, Apr., 1943.

French Guinea:

Dusky Tribesmen of French West Africa. 26 ills. in color from natural-color photographs by Enzo de Chetelat. Vol. LXXIX, pp. 639-662, May, 1941.

My Domestic Life in French Guinea : An American Woman Accompanies Her Husband, a French Geologist, on His Explorations in a Little-Known Region. By Eleanor de Chételat. Vol. LXVII, pp. 695-730, 48 ills., 1 half-page map, June, 1935.

French Indo-China:

Along the Old Mandarin Road of Indo-China. By W. Robert Moore. Vol. LX, pp. 157-199, 32 ills. in black and white, 28 ills. in color, 1 quarter-page map, Aug., 1931.

By Motor Trail Across French Indo-China. By Maynard Owen Williams. Vol. LXVIII, pp. 487-534, 31 ills. in black and white, 27 ills. in color, 1 page map, Oct., 1935.

Enigma of Cambodia. 27 ills. in color from autochromes by Gervais Courtellemont. Vol. LIV, pp. 306-323, Sept., 1928.

French Indo-China—*Continued*

Forgotten Ruins of Indo-China. By Jacob E. Conner. Vol. XXIII, pp. 209-272, 63 ills., 1 page and 1 three-quarters-page maps, Mar., 1912.

Four Faces of Siva: The Mystery of Angkor. By Robert J. Casey. Vol. LIV, pp. 303-332, 13 ills. in black and white, 27 ills. in color, 1 third-page map, Sept., 1928.

Glimpses of Asia. Vol. XXXIX, pp. 553-568, 16 ills., May, 1921.

Tricolor Rules the Rainbow in French Indo-China. 27 ills. in color from natural-color photographs by Maynard Owen Williams. Vol. LXVIII, pp. 495-518, Oct., 1935.

Under the French Tricolor in Indo-China. 28 ills. in color from natural-color photographs by W. Robert Moore. Vol. LX, pp. 166-199, Aug., 1931.

French Morocco. *See* Morocco.

French North Africa:

Americans on the Barbary Coast. By Willard Price. Vol. LXXXIV, pp. 1-31, 13 ills. in black and white, 10 ills. in color, 1 map (two-page spread), July, 1943.

Casablanca Smiles. 10 ills. in color from natural-color photographs by Herbert P. MacNeal. Vol. LXXXIV, pp. 17-24, July, 1943.

Eastward from Gibraltar: Overland Route Across North Africa to Tunisia and Libia. By Cyrus French Wicker. Vol. LXXXIII, pp. 115-142, 28 ills., Jan., 1943.

In Civilized French Africa. By James F. J. Archibald. Vol. XX, pp. 302-311, 14 ills., Mar., 1909.

Yank Meets Native. By Wanda Burnett. Vol. LXXXVIII, pp. 105-128, 24 ills., July, 1945.

See also Algeria; Morocco; Tunisia.

French Somaliland:

Across Widest Africa. By A. Henry Savage Landor. Vol. XIX, pp. 694-737, 38 ills., 1 half-page map, Oct., 1908.

Sailing Forbidden Coasts. By Ida Treat. Vol. LX, pp. 357-386, 31 ills., 1 quarter-page map, Sept., 1931.

French Sudan:

Timbuktu, in the Sands of the Sahara. By Capt. Cecil D. Priest. Vol. XLV, pp. 73-85, 16 ills., Jan., 1924.

Timbuktu and Beyond: Desert City of Romantic Savor and Salt Emerges into World Life Again as Trading Post of France's Vast African Empire. By Laura C. Boulton. Vol. LXXIX, pp. 631-670, 18 ills. in black and white, 26 ills. in color, 1 map (two-page spread), May, 1941.

French West Africa:

Dusky Tribesmen of French West Africa. 26 ills. in color from natural-color photographs by Enzo de Chetelat. Vol. LXXIX, pp. 639-662, May, 1941.

French West Africa—*Continued*

French Conquest of the Sahara. By Charles Rabot. Vol. XVI, pp. 76-80, 1 ill., Feb., 1905.

French West Africa in Wartime. By Paul M. Atkins. Vol. LXXXI, pp. 371-408, 37 ills., 2 maps, Mar., 1942.

My Domestic Life in French Guinea: An American Woman Accompanies Her Husband, a French Geologist, on His Explorations in a Little-Known Region. By Eleanor de Chételat. Vol. LXVII, pp. 695-730, 48 ills., 1 half-page map, June, 1935.

Recent French Explorations in Africa. By Charles Rabot. Vol. XIII, pp. 119-132, 20 ills., Apr., 1902.

Sindbads of Science: Narrative of a Windjammer's Specimen-Collecting Voyage to the Sargasso Sea, to Senegambian Africa and Among Islands of High Adventure in the South Atlantic. By George Finlay Simmons. Vol. LII, pp. 1-75, 89 ills., 1 two-thirds-page map, July, 1927.

Three-Wheeling Through Africa: Two Adventurers Cross the So-called Dark Continent North of Lake Chad on Motorcycles with Side Cars. By James C. Wilson. Vol. LXV, pp. 37-92, 64 ills., 1 two-page map, Jan., 1934.

Timbuktu, in the Sands of the Sahara. By Capt. Cecil D. Priest. Vol. XLV, pp. 73-85, 16 ills., Jan., 1924.

Timbuktu and Beyond: Desert City of Romantic Savor and Salt Emerges into World Life Again as Trading Post of France's Vast African Empire. By Laura C. Boulton. Vol. LXXIX, pp. 631-670, 18 ills. in black and white, 26 ills. in color, 1 map (two-page spread), May, 1941.

French West Indies. *See* Guadeloupe; Martinique.

Frescoes:

Multicolored Cones of Cappadocia. 20 ills. in color from natural-color photographs by Eric Matson. Vol. LXXVI, pp. 769-800, Dec., 1939.

Fresh-water Denizens of the Far West (Salmon, Trout, etc.). 54 portraits in color from paintings by Hashime Murayama. Vol. LXXV, pp. 193-204, Feb., 1939.

Friant Dam, California:

More Water for California's Great Central Valley. By Frederick Simpich. Vol. XC, pp. 645-664, 16 ills., 1 page map, Nov., 1946.

Friendly Bay, Portugal:

Lisbon, the City of the Friendly Bay. By Clifford Albion Tinker. Vol. XLII, pp. 504-552, 30 ills. in black and white, 16 ills. in color, 1 quarter-page map, Nov., 1922.

Friendly Crows (Indians) in Festive Panoply. 13 ills. in color from natural-color photographs by Edwin L. Wisherd. Vol. LII, pp. 314-323, Sept., 1927.

Friendly Islands. *See* Tonga Islands.

Friendly Journeys in Japan : A Young American Finds a Ready Welcome in the Homes of the Japanese During Leisurely Travels Through the Islands. By John Patric. Vol. LXIX, pp. 441-480, 28 ills. in black and white, 10 ills. in color, 1 two-thirds-page map, Apr., 1936.

Friends of Our Forests. By Henry Wetherbee Henshaw. Vol. XXXI, pp. 297-321, 1 ill. in black and white, 32 ills. in color, Apr., 1917.

Fringe of Verdure Around Asia Minor. By Ellsworth Huntington. Vol. XXI, pp. 761-775, 15 ills., Sept., 1910.

Frisian Islands. *See* North Frisian Islands.

Frog That Eats Bats and Snakes : In Captivity, This Big Jungle Amphibian Exhibits an Extraordinary Appetite. By Kenneth W. Vinton. Vol. LXXIII, pp. 657-664, 11 ills., May, 1938.

Frogs:

Frog That Eats Bats and Snakes : In Captivity, This Big Jungle Amphibian Exhibits an Extraordinary Appetite. By Kenneth W. Vinton. Vol. LXXIII, pp. 657-664, 11 ills., May, 1938.

Iridescent Beauty of Frogs and Toads. 14 ills. in color from paintings by Hashime Murayama. Vol. LXI, pp. 635-642, May, 1932.

Our Friend the Frog. By Doris M. Cochran. Vol. LXI, pp. 629-654, 16 ills. in black and white, 14 ills. in color, May, 1932.

From Africa to the Alps. 8 ills. in color from U. S. Army Air Forces official photographs. Vol. LXXXIX, pp. 161-168, Feb., 1946.

From Chalet to Palace in Bavaria (Germany). 14 ills. in color from autochromes by Hans Hildenbrand. Vol. LIV, pp. 682-691, Dec., 1928.

From England to India by Automobile : An 8,527-mile Trip Through Ten Countries, from London to Quetta, Requires Five and a Half Months. By Maj. F. A. C. Forbes-Leith. Vol. XLVIII, pp. 191-223, 33 ills., 1 third-page map, Aug., 1925.

From Granada to Gibraltar—A Tour of Southern Spain. By Harry A. McBride. Vol. XLVI, pp. 205-232, 23 ills., Aug., 1924.

From Jerusalem to Aleppo. By John D. Whiting. Vol. XXIV, pp. 71-113, 30 ills., 1 half-page map, Jan., 1913.

From London to Australia by Aëroplane : A Personal Narrative of the First Aërial Voyage Half Around the World. By Sir Ross Smith. Vol. XXXIX, pp. 229-339, 76 ills. in black and white, 8 ills. in color, 1 page map, Mar., 1921.

From Nature's Hidden Building Blocks (Synthetic Chemical Products). 26 ills. in color from natural-color photographs by Willard R. Culver. Vol. LXXVI, pp. 609-640, Nov., 1939.

From Notch to Notch in the White Mountains : Soaring Heights of New Hampshire Attract Multitudes to America's Oldest Mountain Recreation Area. By Leonard Cornell Roy. Vol. LXXII, pp. 73-104, 30 ills., special map supplement, July, 1937.

From Panama to Patagonia. By Charles M. Pepper. Vol. XVII, pp. 449-452, 1 ill., Aug., 1906.

From Sand to Seer and Servant of Man (Glassmaking). 22 ills. in color from natural-color photographs by Willard R. Culver. Vol. LXXXIII, pp. 17-48, Jan., 1943.

From Sea to Clouds in Ecuador. By W. Robert Moore. Vol. LXXX, pp. 717-740, 11 ills. in black and white, 9 ills. in color, Dec., 1941.

From Stratford to the North Sea (England). 16 ills. in color from autochromes by Clifton Adams. Vol. LV, pp. 616-625, May, 1929.

From the Halls of Montezuma (Mexico). 21 ills. in color from natural-color photographs by Richard H. Stewart and others. Vol. LXXXV, pp. 137-164, Feb., 1944.

From the Mediterranean to the Yellow Sea by Motor : The Citroën-Haardt Expedition Successfully Completes Its Dramatic Journey. By Maynard Owen Williams. Vol. LXII, pp. 513-580, 45 ills. in black and white, 25 ills. in color, 2 half-page maps, Nov., 1932.

From the Plains of Madras to the Snows of Kashmir. Vol. XLVI, pp. 561-576, 16 ills., Nov., 1924.

From the Trenches to Versailles. By Carol Corey. Vol. XXXII, pp. 535-550, 12 ills., Nov.-Dec., 1917.

From the War-Path to the Plow. By Franklin K. Lane. Vol. XXVII, pp. 72-87, 12 ills., Jan., 1915.

Front-line Town of Britain's Siege (Dover). By Harvey Klemmer. Vol. LXXXV, pp. 105-128, 21 ills., Jan., 1944.

Frontier Cities of Italy. By Florence Craig Albrecht. Vol. XXVII, pp. 533-586, 45 ills., June, 1915.

Frost:

Magic Beauty of Snow and Dew. By Wilson A. Bentley. Vol. XLIII, pp. 103-112, 9 ills., Jan., 1923.

Frozen Foods:

Your New World of Tomorrow. By F. Barrows Colton. Vol. LXXXVIII, pp. 385-410, 25 ills., Oct., 1945.

Fruitful Shores of the Finger Lakes (New York). By Harrison Howell Walker. Vol. LXXIX, pp. 559-594, 15 ills. in black and white, 22 ills. in color, 1 two-thirds-page map, May, 1941.

Fruits:

Agricultural Possibilities in Tropical Mexico. By Dr. Pehr Olsson-Seffer. Vol. XXI, pp. 1021-1040, 18 ills., Dec., 1910.

American Berries of Hill, Dale, and Wayside. Vol. XXXV, pp. 168-184, 1 ill. in black and white, 28 ills. in color, Feb., 1919.

Costa Rica, Land of the Banana. By Paul B. Popenoe. Vol. XLI, pp. 201-220, 17 ills., Feb., 1922.

Fruits—*Continued*

Date Gardens of the Jerid (Northern Africa). By Thomas H. Kearney. Vol. XXI, pp. 543-567, 20 ills., July, 1910.

Flavor and Savor of American Foods. 25 ills. in color from natural-color photographs by J. Baylor Roberts, Willard R. Culver, and others. Vol. LXXXI, pp. 289-320, Mar., 1942.

Fruitful Shores of the Finger Lakes (New York). By Harrison Howell Walker. Vol. LXXIX, pp. 559-594, 15 ills. in black and white, 22 ills. in color, 1 two-thirds-page map, May, 1941.

Introduction of the Mango. Vol. XIV, pp. 320-327, 5 ills., Aug., 1903.

More Water for California's Great Central Valley. By Frederick Simpich. Vol. XC, pp. 645-664, 16 ills., 1 page map, Nov., 1946.

New Plant Immigrants. By David Fairchild. Vol. XXII, pp. 879-907, 34 ills., Oct., 1911.

Peacetime Plant Hunting About Peiping. By P. H. and J. H. Dorsett. Vol. LXXII, pp. 509-534, 21 ills., 1 two-thirds-page map, Oct., 1937.

Reviving a Lost Art (Drying Fruits and Vegetables). Vol. XXXI, pp. 475-481, 9 ills., June, 1917.

Rio Grande Cornucopia Under a Winter Sun. 24 ills. in color from natural-color photographs by B. Anthony Stewart. Vol. LXXV, pp. 65-96, Jan., 1939.

Round About Bogotá: A Hunt for New Fruits and Plants Among the Mountain Forests of Colombia's Unique Capital. By Wilson Popenoe. Vol. XLIX, pp. 127-160, 34 ills., 1 third-page map, Feb., 1926.

Taming the Wild Blueberry. By Frederick V. Coville. Vol. XXII, pp. 137-147, 5 ills., Feb., 1911.

Texas Delta of an American Nile: Orchards and Gardens Replace Thorny Jungle in the Southmost Tip of the Lone Star State. By McFall Kerbey. Vol. LXXV, pp. 51-96, 27 ills. in black and white, 24 ills. in color, 1 page map, Jan., 1939.

United States: Its Soils and Their Products. By H. W. Wiley. Vol. XIV, pp. 263-279, 11 ills., July, 1903.

Where Our Bananas Come From (Costa Rica). By Edwin R. Fraser. Vol. XXIII, pp. 713-730, 14 ills., July, 1912.

Wild Blueberry Tamed: The New Industry of the Pine Barrens of New Jersey. By Frederick V. Coville. Vol. XXIX, pp. 535-546, 10 ills., June, 1916.

Fuel:

Conversion of Old Newspapers and Candle Ends into Fuel. Vol. XXXI, pp. 568-570, 3 ills., June, 1917.

Ideal Fuel: The American Coal Briquetting Industry. By Guy Elliott Mitchell. Vol. XXI, pp. 1066-1074, 4 ills., Dec., 1910.

See also Coal and Coal Mining.

Fuerst, Francis C.:

Merry Maskers of Imst (Austria). 14 ills. from photographs by Francis C. Fuerst. Vol. LXX, pp. 201-208, Aug., 1936.

Fuertes, Louis Agassiz:

Birds (American Game Birds). 72 ills. in color from paintings by Louis Agassiz Fuertes. Vol. XXVIII, pp. 109-144, Aug., 1915.

Birds (Common Birds of Farm and Orchard). 50 ills. in color from paintings by Louis Agassiz Fuertes. Vol. XXIV, pp. 673-697, June, 1913.

Birds (Common Birds of Town and Country). 64 ills. in color from paintings by Louis Agassiz Fuertes. Vol. XXV, pp. 499-530, May, 1914.

Birds (Warblers). 32 ills. in color from paintings by Louis Agassiz Fuertes. Vol. XXXI, pp. 305-320, Apr., 1917.

Dogs. 73 ills. in color from paintings by Louis Agassiz Fuertes. Vol. XXXV, pp. 202-263, Mar., 1919.

Dogs: Our Common Dogs. By Louis Agassiz Fuertes and Ernest Harold Baynes. Vol. XXXV, pp. 201-253, 73 ills. in color, Mar., 1919.

Falconry, the Sport of Kings. By Louis Agassiz Fuertes. Vol. XXXVIII, pp. 429-460, 12 ills. in black and white, 12 ills. in color, Dec., 1920.

Falcons. 12 ills. in color from paintings by Louis Agassiz Fuertes. Vol. XXXVIII, pp. 441-456, Dec., 1920.

Mammals: Larger Mammals of North America. 49 ills. in color from paintings by Louis Agassiz Fuertes. Vol. XXX, pp. 409-471, Nov., 1916.

Mammals: Smaller Mammals of North America. 59 ills. in color from paintings by Louis Agassiz Fuertes. Vol. XXXIII, pp. 404-465, May, 1918.

Fuji (Peak), Japan:

Geography of Japan: With Special Reference to Its Influence on the Character of the Japanese People. By Walter Weston. Vol. XL, pp. 45-84, 23 ills. in black and white, 16 ills. in color, July, 1921.

Fulah (Tribespeople):

Dusky Tribesmen of French West Africa. 26 ills. in color from natural-color photographs by Enzo de Chetelat. Vol. LXXIX, pp. 639-662, May, 1941.

Fumaroles:

Valley of Ten Thousand Smokes: An Account of the Discovery and Exploration of the Most Wonderful Volcanic Region in the World. By Robert F. Griggs. Vol. XXXIII, pp. 115-169, 46 ills., panorama, 1 half-page map, Feb., 1918.

Funchal, Madeira (Island) :

Madeira the Florescent. By Harriet Chalmers Adams. Vol. LXVI, pp. 81-106, 19 ills. in black and white, 13 ills. in color, 1 half-page map, July, 1934.

Fundy, Bay of, Canada :

Tides in the Bay of Fundy. Vol. XVI, pp. 71-76, 4 ills., Feb., 1905.

Fungi:

Common Mushrooms of the United States. By Louis C. C. Krieger. Vol. XXXVII, pp. 387-439, 37 ills. in black and white, 16 ills. in color, May, 1920.

Fur Farming. *See* Fox Farming.

Further Explorations in the Land of the Incas : The Peruvian Expedition of 1915 of the National Geographic Society and Yale University. By Hiram Bingham. Vol. XXIX, pp. 431-473, 29 ills., 1 page and 1 half-page maps, panorama, May, 1916.

Further Notes on Dutch New Guinea. By Thomas Barbour. Vol. XIX, pp. 527-545, 19 ills., Aug., 1908.

Future of the Airplane. By Rear Adm. Robert E. Peary. Vol. XXXIII, pp. 107-113, 4 ills., Jan., 1918.

Fuzzy-Wuzzies (Tribespeople) :

Two Fighting Tribes of the Sudan. By Merian C. Cooper. Photographs by Ernest B. Schoedsack. Vol. LVI, pp. 465-486, 27 ills., 1 two-thirds-page map, Oct., 1929.

G

Gaberell, Jean:

Skiing in Switzerland's Realm of Winter Sports. 6 ills. in duotone from photographs by Jean Gaberell. Vol. LXIII, pp. 344-353, Mar., 1933.

Gabes, Tunisia :

Mole Men : An Account of the Troglodytes of Southern Tunisia. By Frank Edward Johnson. Vol. XXII, pp. 787-846, 60 ills., Sept., 1911.

Gade, John H.:

Belgium's Plight. By John H. Gade. Vol. XXXI, pp. 433-439, 3 ills., May, 1917.

Gadsden Purchase:

Boundaries of Territorial Acquisitions. Vol. XII, pp. 373-377, 1 page chart, Oct., 1901.

Galápagos Islands, Pacific Ocean :

At Home on the Oceans : Whales and Sharks Make Exciting Neighbors for a Professor's Wife, Turned Able Seaman, On a Three-year Voyage Around the World. By Edith Bauer Strout. Vol. LXXVI, pp. 33-86, 54 ills., 1 map, July, 1939.

Dream Ship : The Story of a Voyage of Adventure More Than Half Around the World in a 47-Foot Lifeboat. By Ralph Stock. Vol. XXXIX, pp. 1-52, 43 ills., 1 page map, Jan., 1921.

Galápagos Islands, Pacific Ocean—*Continued*

Westward Bound in the *Yankee.* By Irving and Electa Johnson. Vol. LXXXI, pp. 1-44, 25 ills. in black and white, 20 ills. in color, 1 three-quarters-page map, Jan., 1942.

Galicia:

Partitioned Poland. By William Joseph Showalter. Vol. XXVII, pp. 88-106, 12 ills., Jan., 1915.

Galilee, Sea of, Palestine :

Geography of the Jordan. By Nelson Glueck. Vol. LXXXVI, pp. 719-744, 23 ills., 1 page map, Dec., 1944.

Impressions of Palestine. By James Bryce. Vol. XXVII, pp. 293-317, 18 ills., 1 page map, Mar., 1915.

Galilee (Ship) :

Work in the Pacific Ocean of the Magnetic Survey Yacht *Galilee.* By Dr. L. A. Bauer. Vol. XVIII, pp. 601-611, 15 ills., Sept., 1907.

Gall Midges. *See* Midges.

Gallant Little Sportsmen of the Terrier Tribe. 33 portraits in color from paintings by Edward Herbert Miner. Vol. LXIX, pp. 253-268, Feb., 1936.

Galloway, A. C.:

Interesting Visit to the Ancient Pyramids of San Juan Teotihuacan. By A. C. Galloway. Vol. XXI, pp. 1041-1050, 8 ills., 1 page map, Dec., 1910.

Galveston, Texas :

How We Use the Gulf of Mexico. By Frederick Simpich. Vol. LXXXV, pp. 1-40, 20 ills. in black and white, 19 ills. in color, 1 two-page map, Jan., 1944.

Lessons of Galveston. By W J McGee. Vol. XI, pp. 377-383, Oct., 1900.

Texas, Our Largest State. By N. H. Darton. Vol. XXIV, pp. 1330-1360, 22 ills., 2 half-page maps, Dec., 1913.

Gama, Vasco da:

Pathfinder of the East : Setting Sail to Find "Christians and Spices," Vasco da Gama Met Amazing Adventures, Founded an Empire, and Changed the History of Western Europe. By J. R. Hildebrand. Vol. LII, pp. 503-550, 43 ills., 1 two-thirds-page map, Nov., 1927.

Vasco da Gama at the Court of the Zamorin of Calicut. Reproduction in color of the painting by José Velloso Salgado, Sociedade de Geographia de Lisboa. Vol. LII, supplement, Nov., 1927.

Game. *See* Mammals.

Game and Fur-Bearing Animals and Their Influence on the Indians of the Northwest. By Townsend W. Thorndike. Vol. XV, p. 431, Oct., 1904.

Game Birds:

American Game Birds. By Henry Wetherbee Henshaw. Vol. XXVIII, pp. 105-158, 4 ills. in black and white, 72 ills. in color, Aug., 1915.

Game Birds—*Continued*

Contains descriptions and illustrations of the following : Cranes, Ducks, Geese, Grouse, Pheasants, Pigeons, Plovers, Quails, Rails, Sandpipers, Snipes, Stilts, Swans.

Birds on the Home Front. By Arthur A. Allen. Vol. LXXXIV, pp. 32-56, 7 ills. in black and white, 30 ills. in color, July, 1943.

Far-Flying Wild Fowl and Their Foes. By Maj. Allan Brooks. Vol. LXVI, pp. 487-528, 6 ills. in black and white, 93 portraits in color, Oct., 1934.

Contains descriptions and illustrations of the following : Ducks, Geese, Swans.

Game Birds of Prairie, Forest and Tundra. By Alexander Wetmore. Vol. LXX, pp. 461-500, 5 ills. in black and white, 60 portraits in color, Oct., 1936.

Hunted Birds of Field and Wild. 60 portraits in color from paintings by Maj. Allan Brooks. Vol. LXX, pp. 469-500, Oct., 1936.

Contains illustrations of the following : Doves, Grouse, Pigeons, Ptarmigans, Quails.

Wild Geese, Ducks, and Swans. 93 portraits in color from paintings by Maj. Allan Brooks. Vol. LXVI, pp. 493-524, Oct., 1934.

Game Country Without Rival in America : The Proposed Mount McKinley National Park. By Stephen R. Capps. Vol. XXXI, pp. 69-84, 14 ills., 1 half-page map, Jan., 1917.

Game Fowl (Game Cocks) :

Races of Domestic Fowl. By Morley A. Jull. Vol. LI, pp. 379-452, 67 ills. in black and white, 29 ills. in color, Apr., 1927.

Sarawak : The Land of the White Rajahs. By Harrison W. Smith. Vol. XXXV, pp. 110-167, 58 ills., 1 half-page map, Feb., 1919.

Game Preserves:

Africa, the Largest Game Preserve in the World. By John B. Torbert. Vol. XI, pp. 445-448, 1 page map, Nov., 1900.

Game Country Without Rival in America : The Proposed Mount McKinley National Park. By Stephen R. Capps. Vol. XXXI, pp. 69-84, 14 ills., 1 half-page map, Jan., 1917.

Where Birds and Little Animals Find Haven (Eaton Canyon Bird and Game Sanctuary). By Agnes Akin Atkinson. Vol. LXX, pp. 232-241, 14 ills., Aug., 1936.

Games. *See* Sports and Games.

Gammans, Leonard David:

United States and the British Empire. By Leonard David Gammans. Vol. LXXXVII, pp. 562-564, May, 1945.

Yanks at Westminster. By Capt. Leonard David Gammans. Vol. XC, pp. 223-252, 6 ills. in black and white, and 19 ills. in color, Aug., 1946.

Gan Shemuel, Palestine :

Palestine Today. By Francis Chase, Jr. **Vol.** XC, pp. 501-516, 16 ills., Oct., 1946.

Gannets:

Birds of the High Seas : Albatrosses and Petrels ; Gannets, Man-o'-war-birds, and Tropic-birds. By Robert Cushman Murphy. Paintings by Maj. Allan Brooks. Vol. LXXIV, pp. 226-251, 7 ills. in black and white, 36 portraits in color, Aug., 1938.

Wings Over the Bounding Main. 36 portraits in color from paintings by Maj. Allan Brooks. Vol. LXXIV, pp. 237-251, Aug., 1938.

Gannett, Henry:

Agriculture in Alaska. By Henry Gannett. Vol. XIII, p. 112, Mar., 1902.

Chairman of Research Committee. Vol. XX, p. 486, May, 1909.

Committee Appointed to Consider Claims of Peary and Cook. Vol. XX, pp. 921-922, Nov., 1909.

Conditions in Cuba as Revealed by the Census. By Henry Gannett. Vol. XX, pp. 200-202, Feb., 1909.

Conservation League of America. By Henry Gannett. Vol. XIX, pp. 737-739, Oct., 1908.

Death Notice. Vol. XXVI, p. 520, Nov., 1914.

Elected Member of the Geographical Society of Paris. Vol. XVIII, p. 428, June, 1907.

General Geography of Alaska. By Henry Gannett. Vol. XII, pp. 180-196, 9 ills., May, 1901.

Great Ice Barrier (Antarctica). By Henry Gannett. Vol. XXI, pp. 173-174, 1 ill., Feb., 1910.

Harriman Alaska Expedition. By Henry Gannett. Vol. X, pp. 507-512, 1 chart, 1 page map, Dec., 1899.

Henry Gannett (Biography). Vol. XXVI, pp. 609-613, 1 ill., Dec., 1914.

Honors to Amundsen and Peary (Speech by Henry Gannett). Vol. XXIV, pp. 113-130, 5 ills., Jan., 1913.

In Honor of the Army and Aviation (Speech by Henry Gannett). Vol. XXII, pp. 267-284, 1 ill., Mar., 1911.

Judge of Prize Essay Contest. Vol. X, p. 32, Jan., 1899.

National Geographic Society (Announcing the Election of Henry Gannett as Vice-President of The Society). Vol. XVI, p. 87, Feb., 1905.

National Geographic Society (Announcing the Election of Henry Gannett as President of The Society). Vol. XXI, pp. 88-90, Jan., 1910.

National Geographic Society (Speech by Henry Gannett). Vol. XXIII, pp. 273-298, 5 ills., Mar., 1912.

Notes (Election as Honorary Member of the Geographical Society of Paris). Vol. XVIII, p. 428, June, 1907.

Origin of the Yosemite Valley. By Henry Gannett. Vol. XII, pp. 86-87, Feb., 1901.

Philippine Islands and Their People. By Henry Gannett. Vol. XV, pp. 91-112, 13 ills., Mar., 1904.

Population of the United States. By Henry Gannett. Vol. XXII, pp. 34-48, 9 diagrams, 3 half-page maps, Jan., 1911.

Gannett, Henry—*Continued*

Recent Population Figures. By Henry Gannett. Vol. XXII, pp. 785-786, Aug., 1911.

Redwood Forest of the Pacific Coast. By Henry Gannett. Vol. X, pp. 145-159, 6 ills., 1 page map, May, 1899.

Gardening in Northern Alaska. By Middleton Smith. Vol. XIV, pp. 355-357, Sept., 1903.

Gardens:

Bulgaria : Tirnova, the City of Hanging Gardens. By Felix J. Koch. Vol. XVIII, pp. 632-640, 7 ills., Oct., 1907.

England : Bekonscot, England's Toy-Size Town. By Andrew H. Brown and B. Anthony Stewart. Vol. LXXI, pp. 649-661, 2 ills. in black and white, 15 ills. in color, May, 1937.

England : Summering in an English Cottage : Quiet and Loveliness Invite Contemplation in the Extra "Room," the Garden of the Thatched House. By Helen Churchill Candee. Vol. LXVII, pp. 429-456, 32 ills., Apr., 1935.

England : Tableaux in an English Lilliput (Bekonscot). 15 ills. in color from natural-color photographs by B. Anthony Stewart. Vol. LXXI, pp. 653-660, May, 1937.

England : Vacation in a Fifteenth Century English Manor House. By George Alden Sanford. Vol. LIII, pp. 629-636, 8 ills., May, 1928.

England's Island Garden of Rocks and Flowers (Isle of Wight). 14 ills. in color from natural-color photographs by W. Robert Moore. Vol. LXVII, pp. 17-24, Jan., 1935.

France : Palace of Versailles : Its Park and the Trianons. By Franklin L. Fisher. Vol. XLVII, pp. 49-62, 4 ills. in black and white, 14 ills. in color, Jan., 1925.

Maryland : Maytime in the Heart of Maryland (Sherwood Gardens). 10 ills. in color from natural-color photographs by B. Anthony Stewart and Charles Martin. Vol. LXXIX, pp. 441-448, Apr., 1941.

Mount Vernon : Home of the First Farmer of America. By Worth E. Shoults. Vol. LIII, pp. 603-628, 6 ills. in black and white, 26 ills. in color, May, 1928.

Portugal : Woods and Gardens of Portugal. By Martin Hume. Vol. XXI, pp. 883-894, 8 ills., Oct., 1910.

Scilly Isles : Garden Isles of Scilly : Geologists May Throw Stones at Legend of Lost Lyonnesse, But Natives Grow Flowers in Glass Houses for London. By W. Robert Moore. Vol. LXXIV, pp. 755-774, 9 ills. in black and white, 13 ills. in color, 1 half-page map, Dec., 1938.

South Carolina : Ashley River and Its Gardens. By E. T. H. Shaffer. Vol. XLIX, pp. 525-550, 6 ills. in black and white, 7 ills. in color, May, 1926.

South Carolina : Charleston : A Colonial Rhapsody. 24 ills. in color from natural-color photographs by B. Anthony Stewart. Vol. LXXV, pp. 289-312, Mar., 1939.

South Carolina : Charleston : Where Mellow Past and Present Meet. By DuBose Heyward. Vol. LXXV, pp. 273-312, 20 ills. in black and white, 24 ills. in color, 1 page map, Mar., 1939.

Gardens—*Continued*

South Carolina : Exploring the Atlantic Seaboard with a Color Camera. 7 ills. in color from autochromes by Jacob Gayer. Vol. XLIX, pp. 532-549, May, 1926.

Virginia : Gardens and Shrines of Old Virginia. 20 ills. in color from natural-color photographs by B. Anthony Stewart and J. Baylor Roberts. Vol. LXXXI, pp. 623-646, May, 1942.

Gardens of the West. Vol. XVI, pp. 118-123, 7 ills., Mar., 1905.

Gardner, Irvine C.:

Crusoes of Canton Island : Life on a Tiny Pacific Atoll That Has Flashed Into World Importance. By Irvine C. Gardner. Vol. LXXIII, pp. 749-766, 7 ills. in black and white, 11 ills. in color, June, 1938.

Natural-color photograph of 1936 eclipse. 1 ill. in color by Irvine C. Gardner. Vol. LXXI, p. 178, Feb., 1937.

Natural-color photograph of 1937 eclipse. 1 ill. in color by Irvine C. Gardner. Vol. LXXIII, p. 756, June, 1938.

Observing an Eclipse in Asiatic Russia. By Irvine C. Gardner. Vol. LXXI, pp. 179-197, 19 ills. in black and white, 1 ill. in color, Feb., 1937.

Garriott, E. B.:

West Indian Hurricane of August 7-14, 1899. By E. B. Garriott. Vol. X, pp. 343-348, 1 diagram, Sept., 1899.

West Indian Hurricane of September 1-12, 1900. By E. B. Garriott. Vol. XI, pp. 384-392, 4 charts, Oct., 1900.

West Indian Hurricane of September 10-11, 1898. By E. B. Garriott. Vol. X, pp. 17-20, Jan., 1899.

Garrison, C. L.:

Geography for Teachers. By C. L. Garrison. Vol. X, pp. 223-225, June, 1899.

Gases:

Helium, the New Balloon Gas. By G. Sherburne Rogers. Vol. XXXV, pp. 441-456, 11 ills., May, 1919.

Natural-Gas, Oil, and Coal Supply of the United States. Vol. XV, p. 186, Apr., 1904.

Valley of Ten Thousand Smokes: An Account of the Discovery and Exploration of the Most Wonderful Volcanic Region in the World. By Robert F. Griggs. Vol. XXXIII, pp. 115-169, 46 ills., 1 half-page map, panorama, Feb., 1918.

Gasoline:

Oil for Victory Piped under the Sea. 9 ills. from photographs. Vol. LXXXVIII, pp. 721-726, Dec., 1945.

Gaspé Peninsula, Canada :

Gaspé Peninsula Wonderland. By Wilfrid Bovey. Vol. LXVIII, pp. 209-230, 13 ills. in black and white, 15 ills. in color, 1 half-page map, Aug., 1935.

Gaspé Peninsula, Canada—*Continued*

Remnants of Royal France in Canada. 15 ills. in color from natural-color photographs by B. Anthony Stewart. Vol. LXVIII, pp. 217-224, Aug., 1935.

Gates and Gateways:

Sculptured Gates to English Learning (Cambridge University). 19 ills. in color from natural-color photographs by B. Anthony Stewart. Vol. LXXXIX, pp. 417-440, Apr., 1946.

Gates to the Black Sea : The Dardanelles, the Bosphorus, and the Sea of Marmora. By Harry Griswold Dwight. Vol. XXVII, pp. 435-459, 27 ills., May, 1915.

Gatun Lake, Panama :

Nature's Transformation at Panama : Remarkable Changes in Faunal and Physical Conditions in the Gatun Lake Region. By George Shiras, 3d. Vol. XXVIII, pp. 159-194, 33 ills., 2 page maps, Aug., 1915.

Gatun Locks and Dam, Panama :

Panama Canal. By Lieut. Col. William L. Sibert. Vol. XXV, pp. 153-183, 24 ills., Feb., 1914.

Gauchos (Plainsmen) :

Life on the Argentine Pampa. By Frederick Simpich. Vol. LXIV, pp. 449-491, 41 ills. in black and white, 8 ills. in color, Oct., 1933.

Pioneer Gaucho Days. 8 ills. in color from paintings by Cesáreo Bernaldo de Quirós. Vol. LXIV, pp. 453-460, Oct., 1933.

Gay Colors in the Land of Black Majesty (Haiti). 13 ills. in color from natural-color photographs by Clifton Adams. Vol. LXVI, pp. 445-452, Oct., 1934.

Gayer, Jacob:

Arctic Regions : First Natural-Color Photographs from the Arctic. 19 ills. in color from natural-color photographs by Jacob Gayer. Vol. XLIX, pp. 300-317, Mar., 1926.

Chile : Scenes of Beauty in Copper Land. 25 ills. in color from autochromes by Jacob Gayer. Vol. LV, pp. 198-215, Feb., 1929.

Dominican Republic : Hispaniola Rediscovered. By Jacob Gayer. Vol. LIX, pp. 80-112, 12 ills. in black and white, 28 ills. in color, Jan., 1931.

Dominican Republic : Scenic Resources of the Dominican Republic. 28 ills. in color from natural-color photographs by Jacob Gayer. Vol. LIX, pp. 81-104, Jan., 1931.

Ecuador : Among the Highlands of the Equator Republic. 12 ills. in color from autochromes by Jacob Gayer. Vol. LV, pp. 68-77, Jan., 1929.

Guatemala : In the Land of the Quetzal. 20 ills. in color from autochromes lumière by Jacob Gayer. Vol. L, pp. 610-627, Nov., 1926.

Jamaica : Color Palette of the Caribbean. 11 ills. in color from autochromes lumière by Jacob Gayer. Vol. LI, pp. 44-56, Jan., 1927.

Gayer, Jacob—*Continued*

Ohio : Where the Winning of the West Began. 13 ills. in color from natural-color photographs by Jacob Gayer. Vol. LXI, pp. 562-571, May, 1932.

Peru : Among the Snows and Flowers of Peru. 25 ills. in color from natural-color photographs by Jacob Gayer. Vol. LVII, pp. 732-765, June, 1930.

United States : Canyons and Cacti of the American Southwest. 14 ills. in color from natural-color photographs by Jacob Gayer. Vol. XLVIII, pp. 283-290, Sept., 1925.

United States : Exploring the Atlantic Seaboard with a Color Camera. 8 ills. in color from autochromes by Jacob Gayer. Vol. XLIX, pp. 532-549, May, 1926.

Washington, D. C. : Our Colorful City of Magnificent Distances. 4 ills. in color from natural-color photographs by Jacob Gayer. Vol. LX, pp. 530-611, Nov., 1931.

Washington, D. C. : Springtime Wreathes a Garland for the Nation's Capital. 13 ills. in color from natural-color photographs ; 3 ills. by Jacob Gayer. Vol. LXVII, pp. 473-480, Apr., 1935.

Gazetteers:

Dictionary of Universal Geography. Vol. XVII, p. 114, Feb., 1906.

Gazetteers of the States. Vol. XV, pp. 369-370, Sept., 1904.

Gdynia, Poland :

War Clouds Over Danzig and Poland's Port. 8 ills. from photographs. Vol. LXXVI, pp. 551-558, Oct., 1939.

Geese:

American Game Birds. By Henry Wetherbee Henshaw. Vol. XXVIII, pp. 105-158, 4 ills. in black and white, 72 ills. in color, Aug., 1915.

Domestic Fowls of Field, Park, and Farmyard. 3 ills. in color from paintings by Hashime Murayama. Vol. LVII, pp. 328-361, Mar., 1930.

Far-Flying Wild Fowl and Their Foes. By Maj. Allan Brooks. Vol. LXVI, pp. 487-528, 6 ills. in black and white, 16 portraits in color, Oct., 1934.

Fowls of Forest and Stream Tamed by Man. By Morley A. Jull. Vol. LVII, pp. 327-371, 27 ills. in black and white, 16 ills. in color, Mar., 1930.

Contains descriptions and illustrations of the following species : Canadian, Chinese, Egyptian, Embden, Gray African, Sebastopol, Toulouse.

Saving the Ducks and Geese. By Wells W. Cooke. Vol. XXIV, pp. 361-380, 7 ills., 7 half-page maps, Feb., 1913.

Wild Geese, Ducks, and Swans. 16 portraits in color from paintings by Maj. Allan Brooks. Vol. LXVI, pp. 493-524, Oct., 1934.

Geikie Glacier, British Columbia :

Some Tramps Across the Glaciers and Snowfields of British Columbia. By Howard Palmer. Vol. XXI, pp. 457-487, 25 ills., June, 1910.

Geiser, Karl Frederick:

Peasant Life in the Black Forest. By Karl Frederick Geiser. Vol. XIX, pp. 635-649, 12 ills., Sept., 1908.

Geithmann, Harriet:

Ströbeck, Home of Chess : A Medieval Village in the Harz Mountains of Germany Teaches the Royal Game in Its Public School. By Harriet Geithmann. Vol. LIX, pp. 637-652, 8 ills. in black and white, 14 ills. in color, May, 1931.

Gem of the Ocean : Our American Navy. By Josephus Daniels. Vol. XXXIII, pp. 313-335, 35 ills., Apr., 1918.

Gems:

Diamond Mines of South Africa. By Gardiner F. Williams. Vol. XVII, pp. 344-356, 11 ills., June, 1906.

Fishing for Pearls in the Indian Ocean. By Bella Sidney Woolf. Vol. XLIX, pp. 161-183, 24 ills., Feb., 1926.

Pearl Fisheries of Ceylon. By Hugh M. Smith. Vol. XXIII, pp. 173-194, 13 ills., 1 fourth-page map, Feb., 1912.

Precious Stones. Vol. XIV, pp. 451-458, 4 ills., Dec., 1903.

See also Jade.

Gems of the Italian Lakes. By Arthur Ellis Mayer. Vol. XXIV, pp. 943-956, 13 ills., Aug., 1913.

General Geography of Alaska. By Henry Gannett. Vol. XII, pp. 180-196, 9 ills., May, 1901.

General Grant National Park, California :

Our National Parks. By L. F. Schmeckebier. Vol. XXIII, pp. 531-579, 41 ills., 1 page map, June, 1912.

"General Sherman Tree,"** Sequoia National Park, California :

Oldest Living Thing. Vol. XXIX, supplement, Apr., 1916.

Genesis of the Williamsburg Restoration. By John D. Rockefeller, Jr. Vol. LXXI, p. 401, Apr., 1937.

Geneva, Lake, Switzerland–France :

Lake Geneva : Cradle of Conferences. By F. Barrows Colton. Vol. LXXII, pp. 727-742, 12 ills., 1 third-page map, Dec., 1937.

Geneva, Switzerland :

Millennial City : The Romance of Geneva, the Capital of the League of Nations. By Ralph A. Graves. Vol. XXXV, pp. 457-476, 11 ills., June, 1919.

Genoa, Italy :

Frontier Cities of Italy. By Florence Craig Albrecht. Vol. XXVII, pp. 533-586, 45 ills., June, 1915.

Genoa, Italy—*Continued*

Genoa, Where Columbus Learned to Love the Sea. By McFall Kerbey. Vol. LIV, pp. 333-352, 20 ills., Sept., 1928.

Inexhaustible Italy. By Arthur Stanley Riggs. Vol. XXX, pp. 273-368, 76 ills., 1 page map, Oct., 1916.

Genthe, Arnold:

Ageless Luster of Greece and Rhodes. 16 ills. in duotone by Arnold Genthe. Vol. LXXIII, pp. 477-492, Apr., 1938.

Genthe, Martha Krug:

German Geographers and German Geography. By Martha Krug Genthe. Vol. XII, pp. 324-337, Sept., 1901.

Gentle Folk Settle Stern Saguenay : On French Canada's Frontier Homespun Colonists Keep the Customs of Old Norman Settlers. By Harrison Howell Walker. Vol. LXXV, pp. 595-632, 15 ills. in black and white, 25 ills. in color, 1 map, May, 1939.

Gentlemen Adventurers of the Air : Many Regions of Canada's Vast Wilderness, Long Hidden Even from Fur Trappers, Are Now Revealed by Exploring Airmen. By J. A. Wilson. Vol. LVI, pp. 597-642, 55 ills., 1 page map, Nov., 1929.

Geodesy:

Charting a World at War. By William H. Nicholas. Vol. LXXXVI, pp. 617-640, 23 ills., 1 drawing, Nov., 1944.

Recent Contributions to Our Knowledge of the Earth's Shape and Size, by the United States Coast and Geodetic Survey. By C. A. Schott. Vol. XII, pp. 36-41, 1 ill., 1 chart, Jan., 1901.

Simple Method of Proving That the Earth Is Round. By Robert Marshall Brown. Vol. XVIII, pp. 771-774, 5 diagrams, Dec., 1907.

Geographic Achievement. Vol. XXIV, pp. 667-668, June, 1913.

Geographic Congress. *See* International Geographic Congress.

Geographic Facts from Report of the Taft Philippine Commission. Vol. XII, pp. 114-119, Mar., 1901.

Geographic Names:

Geographic Names in the United States and the Stories They Tell. By R. H. Whitbeck. Vol. XVI, pp. 100-104, Mar., 1905.

Geographic Nomenclature. By E. W. Hilgard. Vol. XI, pp. 36-37, Jan., 1900.

Kodiak Not Kadiak. Vol. XII, pp. 397-398, Nov., 1901.

Origin of American State Names. By Frederick W. Lawrence. Vol. XXXVIII, pp. 104-143, 34 ills., Aug., 1920.

Origin of the Name "Cape Nome." Vol. XII, p. 398, Nov., 1901.

Place Names in Canada. Vol. X, pp. 519-520, Dec., 1899.

Geographic Names—*Continued*

Place Names in Eastern Asia. Vol. XV, p. 136, Mar., 1904.

Place Names of the United States. Vol. XIII, pp. 403-405, Nov., 1902.

Porto Rico or Puerto Rico? By Robert T. Hill. Vol. X, pp. 516-571, Dec., 1899.

Puerto Rico, not Porto Rico. Vol. XI, pp. 37-38, Jan., 1900.

See also U. S. Geographic Board.

Geographic Societies:

Directory of Officers and Councilors of Geographic Societies of the United States. Vol. XIV, pp. 392-394, Oct., 1903.

See also National Geographic Society.

Geographical Congress at Berlin. Vol. X, p. 296, Aug., 1899.

Geographical Distribution of Insanity in the United States. By William A. White. Vol. XIV, pp. 361-378, 6 charts, Oct., 1903.

Geographical Exploration : Its Moral and Material Results. By Maj. Gen. A. W. Greely. Vol. XVII, pp. 1-5, Jan., 1906.

Geographical Pivot of History (Steppes of Central Asia). By H. J. Mackinder. Vol. XV, pp. 331-335, Aug., 1904.

Geographic's New Map of Europe and the Mediterranean. By Gilbert Grosvenor. Text accompanying special map supplement in colors. Vol. LXXIII, pp. 525-528, 1 ill., Apr., 1938.

Geographic's New Map of Germany and Its Approaches : With a Review of The Society's Maps of Europe. By Gilbert Grosvenor. Text accompanying special map supplement in colors. Vol. LXXXVI, pp. 66-72, 1 ill., July, 1944.

Geography:

Advances in Geographic Knowledge During the Nineteenth Century. By Maj. Gen. A. W. Greely. Vol. XII, pp. 143-152, 2 half-page maps, Apr., 1901.

Apperception in Geography. By M. E. Kelton. Vol. XI, pp. 192-199, May, 1900.

Bearing of Physiography Upon Suess' Theories. By William M. Davis. Vol. XV, p. 430, Oct., 1904.

Geographical Exploration : Its Moral and Material Results. By Maj. Gen. A. W. Greely. Vol. XVII, pp. 1-5, Jan., 1906.

Geography. By Sir W. J. L. Wharton. Vol. XVI, pp. 483-498, Nov., 1905.

Geography and Culture. Vol. XVI, pp. 70-71, Feb., 1905.

Geography and Some Explorers. By Joseph Conrad. Vol. XLV, pp. 239-274, 29 ills., Mar., 1924.

Geography at the British Association. Vol. XI, pp. 475-478, Dec., 1900.

Geography for Teachers. By C. L. Garrison. Vol. X, pp. 223-225, June, 1899.

Geography in the University of Chicago. Vol. XIV, pp. 163-164, Apr., 1903.

Geography—*Continued*

Geography of Abyssinia. Vol. XII, pp. 274-276, July, 1901.

Geography of Alaska. By Alfred H. Brooks. Vol. XV, pp. 213-219, special map supplement, May, 1904.

Geography of China : The Influence of Physical Environment on the History and Character of the Chinese People. By Frank Johnson Goodnow. Vol. LI, pp. 651-664, 11 ills., June, 1927.

Geography of Japan : With Special Reference to Its Influence on the Character of the Japanese People. By Walter Weston. Vol. XL, pp. 45-84, 23 ills. in black and white, 16 ills. in color, July, 1921.

Geography of Our Foreign Trade. By Frederick Simpich. Vol. XLI, pp. 89-108, 25 ills., Jan., 1922.

German Geographers and German Geography. By Martha Krug Genthe. Vol. XII, pp. 324-337, Sept., 1901.

Imagination and Geography. Vol. XVIII, p. 825, Dec., 1907.

International Flat Globe and Geographical History. Vol. XVIII, pp. 281-282, April, 1907.

Introduction to Physical Geography. By Grove Karl Gilbert and Albert Perry Brigham. Vol. XIV, pp. 21-26, 6 ills., Jan., 1903.

Practical Exercises in Geography. By W. M. Davis. Vol. XI, pp. 62-78, Feb., 1900.

Probable Effect of the Panama Canal on the Commercial Geography of the World. By O. P. Austin. Vol. XXV, pp. 245-248, Feb., 1914.

Rational Element in Geography. By W. M. Davis. Vol. X, pp. 466-473, 2 diagrams, Nov., 1899.

Recent Geographic Advances, Especially in Africa. By Maj. Gen. A. W. Greely. Vol. XXII, pp. 383-398, 5 ills., 5 page maps, Apr., 1911.

Sight-Seeing in School : Taking Twenty Million Children on a Picture Tour of the World. By Jessie L. Burrall. Vol. XXXV, pp. 489-503, 14 ills., June, 1919.

Some Early Geographers of the United States. By Rear Adm. Colby M. Chester. Vol. XV, pp. 392-404, Oct., 1904.

Some Lessons in Geography. By Edward Atkinson. Vol. XVI, pp. 193-198, Apr., 1905.

Teaching of Geography. By Ralph S. Tarr. Vol. XIII, pp. 55-64, Feb., 1902.

Teaching of Physical Geography in Elementary Schools. By Richard E. Dodge. Vol. XI, pp. 470-475, Dec., 1900.

See also Discoverers ; Expeditions ; National Geographic Society : Expeditions ; Oceanography.

Geography of a Hurricane : A Doughnut-shaped Storm Turned Back Time in New England to Candlelight Days, but Revealed Anew Yankee Courage and Ingenuity. By F. Barrows Colton. Vol. LXXV, pp. 529-552, 20 ills., 1 page map, Apr., 1939.

Geography of Games : How the Sports of Nations Form a Gazetteer of the Habits and Histories of Their Peoples. By J. R. Hildebrand. Vol. XXXVI, pp. 89-144, 61 ills., Aug., 1919.

Geography of Medicines : War's Effect upon the World's Sources of Supply. By John Foote. Vol. XXXII, pp. 213-238, 26 ills., Sept., 1917.

Geography of Money. By William Atherton Du Puy. Vol. LII, pp. 745-768, 31 ills., Dec., 1927.

Geography of the Jordan. By Nelson Glueck. Vol. LXXXVI, pp. 719-744, 23 ills., 1 page map, Dec., 1944.

Geologic Folios in Schools. Vol. XVI, pp. 244-247, May, 1905.

Geologists in China. Vol. XVIII, pp. 640-644, Oct., 1907.

Geologist's Paradise (Canadian Rockies). By Charles D. Walcott. Vol. XXII, pp. 509-536, 28 ills., panorama, June, 1911.

Geology:

Cause of the Earth's Heat. Vol. XVI, pp. 124-125, 1 ill., Mar., 1905.

Central Great Plains (United States). Vol. XVI, pp. 389-397, Aug., 1905.

Crater Lake and Yosemite Through the Ages. By Wallace W. Atwood, Jr. Paintings by Eugene Kingman. Vol. LXXI, pp. 327-343, 7 ills. in black and white, 13 ills. in color, Mar., 1937.

Erratic. By O. A. Ljungstedt. Vol. XXI, pp. 525-531, 4 ills., 1 three-quarters-page map, June, 1910.

Field Courses in Geology. Vol. XVI, p. 250, May, 1905.

Geologist's Paradise (Canadian Rockies). By Charles D. Walcott. Vol. XXII, pp. 509-536, 28 ills., panorama, June, 1911.

Landslides and Rock Avalanches. By Guy Elliott Mitchell. Vol. XXI, pp. 277-287, 6 ills., Apr., 1910.

Limiting Width of Meander Belts. By Mark S. W. Jefferson. Vol. XIII, pp. 373-384, 6 charts, Oct., 1902.

Multicolored Cones of Cappadocia. 20 ills. in color from natural-color photographs by Eric Matson. Vol. LXXVI, pp. 769-800, Dec., 1939.

Porto Rico. By Robert T. Hill. Vol. X, pp. 93-112, 13 ills., Mar., 1899.

Report by Robert T. Hill on the Volcanic Disturbances in the West Indies. Vol. XIII, pp. 223-267, 13 ills., 2 half and 1 quarter-page maps, July, 1902.

Volcanic Rocks of Martinique and St. Vincent : Collected by Robert T. Hill and Israel C. Russell. By J. S. Diller. Vol. XIII, pp. 285-296, July, 1902.

Geology—*Continued*

We Keep House on an Active Volcano : After Flying to Study a Spectacular Eruption in Belgian Congo, a Geologist Settles Down on a Newborn Craterless Vent for Eight Months' Study. By Dr. Jean Verhoogen. Vol. LXXVI, pp. 511-550, 28 ills., 1 two-thirds-page map, Oct., 1939.

Where Early Christians Lived in Cones of Rock : A Journey to Cappadocia in Turkey Where Strange Volcanic Pinnacles Are Honeycombed With Hermit Cells and Monasteries. By John D. Whiting. Vol. LXXVI, pp. 763-802, 20 ills. in black and white. 20 ills. in color, 1 half-page map, Dec., 1939.

See also Earthquakes ; Geysers ; Glaciers ; U. S. Geological Survey ; Volcanoes.

Geomagnetism:

Charting a World at War. By William H. Nicholas. Vol. LXXXVI, pp. 617-640, 23 ills., 1 drawing, Nov., 1944.

Magnetic Disturbances Caused by the Explosion of Mont Pelée. Vol. XIII, pp. 208-209, June, 1902.

Magnetic Observations in Alaska. By Daniel L. Hazard. Vol. XX, pp. 675-676, July, 1909.

Magnetic Survey of Africa. By Dr. L. A. Bauer. Vol. XX, pp. 291-297, 6 ills., Mar., 1909.

Magnetic Survey of the Pacific. Vol. XIX, pp. 447-448, June, 1908.

Magnetic Survey of the Pacific Ocean. By Dr. L. A. Bauer. Vol. XVII, p. 237, Apr., 1906.

Magnetic Survey of the United States. By Dr. L. A. Bauer. Vol. XIII, pp. 92-95, 1 half-page map, Mar., 1902.

Magnetic Work of the Coast and Geodetic Survey. By Dr. L. A. Bauer. Vol. X, pp. 288-289, Aug., 1899.

Most Curious Craft Afloat : The Compass in Navigation and the Work of the Non-Magnetic Yacht *Carnegie*. By Dr. L. A. Bauer. Vol. XXI, pp. 223-245, 31 ills., Mar., 1910.

Our Guardians on the Deep. By William Joseph Showalter. Vol. XXV, pp. 655-677, 15 ills., 1 chart, June, 1914.

Recent Magnetic Work by the Carnegie Institution of Washington. Vol. XVII, p. 648, Nov., 1906.

Sailing the Seven Seas in the Interest of Science : Adventures Through 157,000 Miles of Storm and Calm, from Arctic to Antarctic and Around the World, in the Non-Magnetic Yacht *Carnegie*. By J. P. Ault. Vol. XLII, pp. 631-690, 47 ills., 1 chart, Dec., 1922.

Work in the Pacific Ocean of the Magnetic Survey Yacht *Galilee*. By Dr. L. A. Bauer. Vol. XVIII, pp. 601-611, 15 ills., Sept., 1907.

George Washington's Historic River (Potomac). 18 ills. in color from natural-color photographs by Willard R. Culver and Robert F. Sisson. Vol. LXXXVIII, pp. 41-64, July, 1945.

Georgeson, C. C.:

Agriculture Capacity of Alaska: What Population Can the Territory Support? By C. C. Georgeson. Vol. XX, pp. 676-679, July, 1909.

Possibilities of Alaska. By C. C. Georgeson. Vol. XIII, pp. 81-85, Mar., 1902.

Georgetown, Washington, D. C.:

Potomac, River of Destiny. By Albert W. Atwood. Vol. LXXXVIII, pp. 33-70, 15 ills. in black and white, 18 ills. in color, 1 map (two-page spread), July, 1945.

Georgia:

Golden Isles of Guale. By W. Robert Moore. Vol. LXV, pp. 235-264, 35 ills., 1 three-quarters-page map, Feb., 1934.

Marching Through Georgia Sixty Years After: Multifold Industries and Diversified Agriculture Are Restoring the Prosperity of America's Largest State East of the Mississippi. By Ralph A. Graves. Vol. L, pp. 259-311, 47 ills., Sept., 1926.

Okefinokee Wilderness: Exploring the Mystery Land of the Suwannee River Reveals Natural Wonders and Fascinating Folklore. By Francis Harper. Vol. LXV, pp. 597-624, 35 ills., 1 two-thirds-page map, May, 1934.

Georgian Soviet Socialist Republic, U. S. S. R.:

Land of the Stalking Death: A Journey Through Starving Armenia on an American Relief Train. By Melville Chater. Vol. XXXVI, pp. 393-420, 23 ills., Nov., 1919.

Roaming Russia's Caucasus: Rugged Mountains and Hardy Fighters Guard the Soviet Union's Caucasian Treasury of Manganese and Oil. By Rolf Singer. Vol. LXXXII, pp. 91-121, 33 ills., July, 1942.

Russia's Orphan Races: Picturesque Peoples Who Cluster on the Southeastern Borderland of the Vast Slav Dominions. By Maynard Owen Williams. Vol. XXXIV, pp. 254-278, 26 ills., 1 page map, Oct., 1918.

Gerbéviller, France:

In French Lorraine: That Part of France Where the First American Soldiers Have Fallen. By Harriet Chalmers Adams. Vol. XXXII, pp. 499-518, 16 ills., Nov.-Dec., 1917.

Gerecke, W. F.:

Flamingos (Flame-Feathered Flamingos of Florida). 9 ills. in color from natural-color photographs by W. F. Gerecke. Vol. LXXIX, pp. 57-64, Jan., 1941.

Gerizim (Mountain), Palestine:

Last Israelitish Blood Sacrifice: How the Vanishing Samaritans Celebrate the Passover on Sacred Mount Gerizim. By John D. Whiting. Vol. XXXVII, pp. 1-46, 40 ills., 1 half-page map, Jan., 1920.

German Geographers and German Geography. By Martha Krug Genthe. Vol. XII, pp. 324-337, Sept., 1901.

German Nation. Vol. XXVI, pp. 275-310, 28 ills., Sept., 1914.

German Route to India. By Gilbert H. Grosvenor. Vol. XI, pp. 202-204, 1 page map, May, 1900.

German South Polar Expedition. Vol. XII, p. 311, Aug., 1901.

German South Polar Expedition. By Dr. Georg Kollm. Vol. XII, pp. 377-379, Oct., 1901.

German Submarine Cable System. Vol. XII, p. 163, Apr., 1901.

Germany:

Aces Among Aces (Aviators). By Laurence La Tourette Driggs. Vol. XXXIII, pp. 568-580, 9 ills., June, 1918.

Americans Help Liberated Europe Live Again. By Lt. Col. Frederick Simpich, Jr. Vol. LXXXVII, pp. 747-768, 17 ills., June, 1945.

Beauty of the Bavarian Alps. By Col. Fitzhugh Lee Minnigerode. Vol. XLIX, pp. 632-649, 16 ills. in color, June, 1926.

Bright Corners of Time-Mellowed Germany. 11 ills. in color from natural-color photographs by Hans Hildenbrand and Wilhelm Tobien. Vol. LXIV, pp. 222-231, Aug., 1933.

Close-Ups of a People Without a Country. 23 ills. in duotone. Vol. LXVII, pp. 249-264, Feb., 1935.

Cologne, Key City of the Rhineland. By Francis Woodworth. Vol. LXIX, pp. 829-848, 18 ills., 1 half-page map, June, 1936.

Corner of Old Württemberg. By B. H. Buxton. Vol. XXII, pp. 931-947, 17 ills., 1 half-page map, Oct., 1911.

Danube, Highway of Races: From the Black Forest to the Black Sea, Europe's Most Important River Has Borne the Traffic of Centuries. By Melville Chater. Vol. LVI, pp. 643-697, 54 ills., Dec., 1929.

Entering the Front Doors of Medieval Towns: The Adventures of an American Woman and Her Daughter in a Folding Boat on Eight Rivers of Germany and Austria. By Cornelia Stratton Parker. Vol. LXI, pp. 365-394, 23 ills., 1 two-thirds-page map, Mar., 1932.

Flags of Austria-Hungary, Bulgaria, Germany, and Turkey. By Byron McCandless and Gilbert Grosvenor. Vol. XXXII, pp. 386-388, 38 ills. in color, Oct., 1917.

From Chalet to Palace in Bavaria. 14 ills. in color from autochromes by Hans Hildenbrand. Vol. LIV, pp. 682-691, Dec., 1928.

Geographic's New Map of Germany and Its Approaches: With a Review of The Society's Maps of Europe. By Gilbert Grosvenor. Text accompanying special map supplement in colors. Vol. LXXXVI, pp. 66-72, 1 ill., July, 1944.

German Nation. Vol. XXVI, pp. 275-310, 28 ills., Sept., 1914.

German Submarine Cable System. Vol. XII, p. 163, Apr., 1901.

Germany's Air Program. Vol. XXXIII, p. 114, Jan., 1918.

Germany's Dream of World Domination. Vol. XXXIII, pp. 559-567, 3 ills., June, 1918.

Germany—*Continued*

Great Canals of the World. Vol. XVI, pp. 475-479, Oct., 1905.

Grimm's Fairyland in Northwestern Germany. 14 ills. in color from natural-color photographs by Hans Hildenbrand and Wilhelm Tobien. Vol. LIX, pp. 640-649, May, 1931.

Industrial Training of the German People. Vol. XVI, pp. 111-114, Mar., 1905.

Map of the New Germany. Vol. XXXV, pp. 545-546, 1 page map, June, 1919.

New Map of Europe: Showing the Boundaries Established by the Peace Conference at Paris and by Subsequent Decisions of the Supreme Council of the Allied and Associated Powers. By Ralph A. Graves. Text accompanying special map supplement in colors. Vol. XXXIX, pp. 157-177, 18 ills., Feb., 1921.

Peasant Life in the Black Forest. By Karl Frederick Geiser. Vol. XIX, pp. 635-649, 12 ills., Sept., 1908.

Prussianism. By Robert Lansing. Vol. XXXIII, pp. 546-557, 5 ills., June, 1918.

Races of Europe. By Edwin A. Grosvenor. Vol. XXXIV, pp. 441-534, 62 ills., special map supplement in colors, 2 page maps, Dec., 1918.

Rediscovering the Rhine: A Trip by Barge from the Sea to the Headwaters of Europe's Storied Stream. By Melville Chater. Vol. XLVIII, pp. 1-43, 44 ills., July, 1925.

Renascent Germany. By Lincoln Eyre. Vol. LIV, pp. 639-717, 59 ills. in black and white, 39 ills. in color, Dec., 1928.

Story of the Ruhr. By Frederick Simpich. Vol. XLI, pp. 553-564, 11 ills., 1 third-page map, May, 1922.

Town of Many Gables (Münster). By Florence Craig Albrecht. Vol. XXVII, pp. 107-140, 28 ills., Feb., 1915.

Wandering Through the Black Forest. 13 ills. in color from autochromes by Hans Hildenbrand. Vol. LIV, pp. 658-667, Dec., 1928.

War's Wake in the Rhineland. By Thomas R. Henry. Vol. LXXXVIII, pp. 1-32, 29 ills., 1 third-page map, July, 1945.

Wends of the Spreewald. By Frederick Simpich. Vol. XLIII, pp. 327-336, 12 ills., Mar., 1923.

What Is the Saar? By Frederick Simpich. Vol. LXVII, pp. 241-264, 5 ills. in black and white, 23 ills. in duotone, 1 half-page and 1 third-page maps, Feb., 1935.

See also Berlin; Dinkelsbühl; East Prussia; Freiburg; Hamburg; Helgoland (Island); Nördlingen; Oberammergau; R o t h e n b u r g ; Ströbeck.

Germany's Air Program. Vol. XXXIII, p. 114, Jan., 1918.

Germany's Dream of World Domination. Vol. XXXIII, pp. 559-567, 3 ills., June, 1918.

Geske, E. J.:

Beauties of Our Common Grasses. 8 ills. in color from paintings by E. J. Geske. Vol. XXXIX, pp. 627-634, June, 1921.

Familiar Grasses and Their Flowers. By E. J. Geske and W. J. Showalter. Vol. XXXIX, pp. 625-636, 8 ills. in color, June, 1921.

Marvels of Fern Life. 16 ills. in color from paintings by E. J. Geske. Vol. XLVII, pp. 547-562, May, 1925.

Gettysburg, Pennsylvania:

Most Famous Battle Field in America. 14 ills. in color from natural-color photographs by Clifton Adams and Orren R. Louden. Vol. LX, pp. 66-75, July, 1931.

Geysers:

Costa Rica—Vulcan's Smithy. By Henry Pittier. Vol. XXI, pp. 494-525, 30 ills., 2 half-page maps, June, 1910.

Fabulous Yellowstone: Even Stranger Than the Tales of Early Trappers is the Truth About This Steaming Wonderland. By Frederick G. Vosburgh. Vol. LXXVII, pp. 769-794, 15 ills. in black and white, 9 ills. in color, 1 two-thirds-page map, June, 1940.

Waimangu and the Hot-Spring Country of New Zealand: The World's Greatest Geyser Is One of Many Natural Wonders in a Land of Inferno and Vernal Paradise. By Joseph C. Grew. Vol. XLVIII, pp. 109-130, 19 ills., 1 third-page map, Aug., 1925.

Where Hot Pools Seethe and Geysers Spout (Yellowstone). 9 ills. in color from natural-color photographs by Edwin L. Wisherd. Vol. LXXVII, pp. 775-782, June, 1940.

Ghazni, Afghanistan:

Back to Afghanistan. By Maynard Owen Williams. Vol. XC, pp. 517-544, 27 ills., 1 page map, Oct., 1946.

Gibbons, (Maj.) A. St. H.:

Methods of Exploration in Africa. By Maj. A. St. H. Gibbons. Vol. XV, pp. 408-410, Oct., 1904.

Gibbons:

Manlike Apes of Jungle and Mountain. 10 ills. in color from paintings by Elie Cheverlange. Vol. LXXVIII, pp. 221-228, Aug., 1940.

Man's Closest Counterparts: Heavyweight of Monkeydom Is the "Old Man" Gorilla, by Far the Largest of the Four Great Apes. By William M. Mann. Vol. LXXVIII, pp. 213-236, 10 ills. in black and white, 10 ills. in color, Aug., 1940.

Gibbs, (Capt.) George S.:

"Breaking Up" of the Yukon. By Capt. George S. Gibbs. Vol. XVII, pp. 268-272, 6 ills., May, 1906.

Transportation Methods in Alaska. Vol. XVII, pp. 69-82, 19 ills., Feb., 1906.

Gibraltar:

American Eclipse Expedition. By Rear Adm. Colby M. Chester. Vol. XVII, pp. 589-612, 23 ills., 1 color plate, Nov., 1906.

Gibraltar—*Continued*

From Granada to Gibraltar—A Tour of Southern Spain. By Harry A. McBride. Vol. XLVI, pp. 205-232, 23 ills., Aug., 1924.

Rock of Gibraltar: Key to the Mediterranean. 17 ills. from photographs. Vol. LXXVIII, pp. 376-391, Sept., 1940.

Gibson, (Sir) Christopher H.:

Through Paraguay and Southern Matto Grosso. By Sir Christopher H. Gibson. Vol. LXXXIV, pp. 459-488, 20 ills. in black and white, 11 ills. in color, 1 two-thirds-page map, Oct., 1943.

Gifford, John:

Florida Keys. By John Gifford. Vol. XVII, pp. 5-16, 13 ills., 1 half-page map, Jan., 1906.

Gigantic Brazil and Its Glittering Capital. By Frederick Simpich. Vol. LVIII, pp. 733-778, 54 ills., 1 page map, Dec., 1930.

Gilbert, Grove Karl:

Discovery of the North Pole (Presentation of Hubbard Gold Medal). Vol. XXI, pp. 63-82, Jan., 1910.

Election of Grove Karl Gilbert as Vice-President of The Society. Vol. XV, p. 176, Apr., 1904.

Glaciers of Alaska. By Grove Karl Gilbert. Vol. XV, pp. 449-450, Nov., 1904.

Grove Karl Gilbert (Biography). Vol. XI, p. 289, 1 ill., July, 1900.

Introduction to Physical Geography. By Albert Perry Brigham and Grove Karl Gilbert. Vol. XIV, pp. 21-26, 6 ills., Jan., 1903.

Mr. Ziegler and the National Geographic Society. Vol. XIV, pp. 251-254, June, 1903.

Speech of welcome to Eighth International Geographic Congress. Vol. XV, p. 419, Oct., 1904.

Gilbert, J. J.:

Some Notes on the Fox Island Passes, Alaska. By J. J. Gilbert. Vol. XVI, pp. 427-429, Sept., 1905.

Gilbert Islands, Pacific Ocean:

American Pathfinders in the Pacific. By William H. Nicholas. Vol. LXXXIX, pp. 617-640, 17 ills., 1 two-page map, May, 1946.

Gilbert Islands in the Wake of Battle. By W. Robert Moore. Vol. LXXXVII, pp. 129-162, 11 ills. in black and white, 19 ills. in color, 1 two-thirds-page map, Feb., 1945.

Round About Grim Tarawa. 19 ills. in color from natural-color photographs by W. Robert Moore. Vol. LXXXVII, pp. 137-160, Feb., 1945.

War Finds Its Way to Gilbert Islands: United States Forces Dislodge Japanese from Enchanted Atolls Which Loom Now as Stepping Stones along South Sea Route from Australia to Hawaii. By Sir Arthur Grimble. Vol. LXXXIII, pp. 71-92, 19 ills., 1 half-page map, Jan., 1943.

Gilded Domes Against an Azure Sky (Iran). 13 ills. in color from natural-color photographs by Stephen H. Nyman. Vol. LXXVI, pp. 339-346, Sept., 1939.

Gill, Richard C.:

Mrs. Robinson Crusoe in Ecuador. By Mrs. Richard C. Gill. Vol. LXV, pp. 133-172, 43 ills. in black and white, 1 half-page map, Feb., 1934.

Gill, (Mrs.) Richard C.:

Mrs. Robinson Crusoe in Ecuador. By Mrs. Richard C. Gill. Vol. LXV, pp. 133-172, 43 ills. in black and white, 1 half-page map, Feb., 1934.

Gilles, Helen Trybulowski:

Nigeria: From the Bight of Benin to Africa's Desert Sands. By Helen Trybulowski Gilles. Vol. LXXXV, pp. 537-568, 17 ills. in black and white, 10 ills. in color, 1 half-page map, May, 1944.

Gilman, Daniel C.:

Late Daniel C. Gilman (Biography). Vol. XIX, p. 883, 1 ill., Dec., 1908.

Gilmore, Eddy:

Crimea Reborn. By Eddy Gilmore. Vol. LXXXVII, pp. 487-512, 23 ills., 1 half-page map, Apr., 1945.

I Learn About the Russians. By Eddy Gilmore. Vol. LXXXIV, pp. 619-640, 21 ills., Nov., 1943.

Liberated Ukraine. By Eddy Gilmore. Vol. LXXXV, pp. 513-536, 22 ills., 1 page map, May, 1944.

Gilson, Martha Phillips:

Woman's Winter on Spitsbergen. By Martha Phillips Gilson. Vol. LIV, pp. 227-246, 20 ills., 1 three-quarters-page map, Aug., 1928.

Gipson, Henry Clay:

Peru on Parade. 20 ills. in color from natural-color photographs by Henry Clay Gipson and Jack Kuhne. Vol. LXXXII, pp. 173-196, Aug., 1942.

Giraffes:

Where Roosevelt Will Hunt (Africa). By Sir Harry Johnston. Vol. XX, pp. 207-256, 43 ills., special map supplement in colors, Mar., 1909.

Girdling the Globe. Vol. XV, p. 236, May, 1904.

Girl Scouts:

Star and Crescent on Parade (Turkey). 29 ills. in color from natural-color photographs by Maynard Owen Williams. Vol. LXXXVII, pp. 585-616, May, 1945.

Glacier Bay, Alaska:

Recession of the Glaciers of Glacier Bay, Alaska. By Fremont Morse. Vol. XIX, pp. 76-78, 1 page map, Jan., 1908.

Glacier National Park, Montana:

New National Park. By Guy Elliott Mitchell. Vol. XXI, pp. 215-223, 6 ills., Mar., 1910.

Our National Parks. By L. F. Schmeckebier. Vol. XXIII, pp. 531-579, 41 ills., 1 page map, June, 1912.

Glaciers:

Among the Great Himalayan Glaciers. Vol. XIII, pp. 405-406, Nov., 1902.

Ascent of Mont Blanc. By Walter Woodburn Hyde. Vol. XXIV, pp. 861-942, 69 ills., Aug., 1913.

Conquest of Mount Logan : North America's Second Highest Peak Yields to the Intrepid Attack of Canadian Climbers. By H. F. Lambart. Vol. XLIX, pp. 597-631, 40 ills., June, 1926.

Crater Lake and Yosemite Through the Ages. By Wallace W. Atwood, Jr. Paintings by Eugene Kingman. Vol. LXXI, pp. 327-343, 7 ills. in black and white, 13 ills. in color, Mar., 1937.

Form of Glacier Terminals. Vol. XXII, p. 786, Aug., 1911.

Glaciers of Alaska. By Grove Karl Gilbert. Vol. XV, pp. 449-450, Nov., 1904.

Great White Monarch of the Pacific Northwest (Mount Rainier). By A. H. Barnes. Vol. XXIII, pp. 595-626, 31 ills., 1 half-page map, June, 1912.

Is Our Noblest Volcano Awakening to New Life : A Description of the Glaciers and Evidences of Volcanic Activity of Mount Hood. By A. H. Sylvester. Vol. XIX, pp. 515-525, 5 ills., 1 page map, July, 1908.

Monarch of the Canadian Rockies. By Charles D. Walcott. Vol. XXIV, pp. 626-639, 13 ills., panorama, May, 1913.

Muir Glacier. By C. L. Andrews. Vol. XIV, pp. 441-445, 2 ills., 1 third-page map, Dec., 1903.

National Geographic Society Researches in Alaska. By Lawrence Martin. Vol. XXII, pp. 537-561, 17 ills., 1 page and 4 half-page maps, June, 1911.

National Geographic Society's Alaskan Expedition of 1909. By Ralph S. Tarr and Lawrence Martin. Vol. XXI, pp. 1-54, 42 ills., 4 page and 7 half-page maps, Jan., 1910.

Note on Glacier Discovery. By W. H. Jackson. Vol. XVII, p. 587, Oct., 1906.

Photography in Glacial Alaska. By O. D. von Engeln. Vol. XXI, pp. 54-62, 4 ills., Jan., 1910.

Recession of the Glaciers of Glacier Bay, Alaska. By Fremont Morse. Vol. XIX, pp. 76-78, 1 page map, Jan., 1908.

Scenes Among the High Cascades in Central Oregon. By Ira A. Williams. Vol. XXIII, pp. 578-592, 11 ills., June, 1912.

Some Tramps Across the Glaciers and Snowfields of British Columbia. By Howard Palmer. Vol. XXI, pp. 457-487, 25 ills., June, 1910.

Stikine River in 1898 (British Columbia). By Eliza R. Scidmore. Vol. X, pp. 1-15, 4 ills., Jan., 1899.

Wonderland of Glaciers and Snow (Mount Rainier National Park). By Milnor Roberts. Vol. XX, pp. 530-537, 8 ills., June, 1909.

Glamour of Historic Havana. 9 ills. in black and white from photographs by F. S. Lincoln. Vol. LXIV, pp. 357-364, Sept., 1933.

Glamour of Mexico—Old and New. 15 ills. in color from natural-color photographs by L. Pérez Parra. Vol. LXV, pp. 345-352, Mar., 1934.

Glasgow, Scotland :

Bonnie Scotland, Postwar Style. By Isobel Wylie Hutchison. Vol. LXXXIX, pp. 545-601, 14 ills. in black and white, 38 ills. in color, 1 two-page map, May, 1946.

Glass and Glassmaking:

From Sand to Seer and Servant of Man. 22 ills. in color from natural-color photographs by Willard R. Culver. Vol. LXXXIII, pp. 17-48, Jan., 1943.

Glass "Goes to Town." By J. R. Hildebrand. Vol. LXXXIII, pp. 1-48, 28 ills. in black and white, 22 ills. in color, Jan., 1943.

Industrial Titan of America : Pennsylvania, Once the Keystone of the Original Thirteen, Now the Keystone of Forty-eight Sovereign States. By John Oliver La Gorce. Vol. XXXV, pp. 367-406, 33 ills., 1 page map, May, 1919.

Glass-Bottom Boat. By Charles Frederick Holder. Vol. XX, pp. 761-778, 17 ills., Sept., 1909.

Glassey, Frank P. S.:

Helsingfors (Finland)—A Contrast in Light and Shade. By Frank P. S. Glassey. Vol. XLVII, pp. 597-612, 20 ills., May, 1925.

Gleaming Fishes of Pacific Coastal Waters. 31 portraits in color from paintings by Hashime Murayama. Vol. LXXIV, pp. 467-498, Oct., 1938.

Gleason, Herbert W.:

On the Trail of a Horse Thief (British Columbia). By Herbert W. Gleason. Vol. XXXV, pp. 349-358, 6 ills., Apr., 1919.

Winter Rambles in Thoreau's Country. By Herbert W. Gleason. Vol. XXXVII, pp. 165-180, 15 ills., Feb., 1920.

Glen Canyon, Utah :

Experiences in the Grand Canyon. By Ellsworth and Emery Kolb. Vol. XXVI, pp. 99-184, 70 ills., 1 page map, Aug., 1914.

Glenfinnan, Scotland :

Heather Paints the Highlands. 38 ills. in color from natural-color photographs by B. Anthony Stewart. Vol. LXXXIX, pp. 561-600, May, 1946.

Glenora, British Columbia :

Stikine River in 1898. By Eliza R. Scidmore. Vol. X, pp. 1-15, 4 ills., Jan., 1899.

Glide Bombs:

Air Power for Peace. By Gen. H. H. Arnold. Vol. LXXXIX, pp. 137-193, 35 ills. in black and white, 28 ills. in color, special map supplement, Feb., 1946.

Gliders:

Aerial Invasion of Burma. By Gen. H. H. Arnold. Vol. LXXXVI, pp. 129-148, 20 ills., Aug., 1944.

Gliders—*Continued*

Air Conquest: From the Early Days of Giant Kites and Birdlike Gliders, the National Geographic Society Has Aided and Encouraged the Growth of Aviation. Vol. LII, pp. 233-242, 13 ills., Aug., 1927.

Gliders—Silent Weapons of the Sky. By William H. Nicholas. Vol. LXXXVI, pp. 149-160, 8 ills., Aug., 1944.

Men-Birds Soar on Boiling Air. By Frederick G. Vosburgh. Vol. LXXIV, pp. 123-140, 15 ills., July, 1938.

On the Wings of the Wind: In Motorless Planes, Pilots Ride in Flying-Fox Fashion, Cruising on Upward Air Streams and Lifted by the Suction of Moving Clouds. By Howard Siepen. Vol. LV, pp. 751-780, 40 ills., June, 1929.

Remarkable Photograph of Lilienthal's Gliding Machine. By R. W. Wood. Vol. XIX, p. 596, 1 ill., Aug., 1908.

Glimpses East and West in America. Vol. XLV, pp. 531-546, 16 ills., May, 1924.

Glimpses of Asia. Vol. XXXIX, pp. 553-568, 16 ills., May, 1921.

Glimpses of Holland. By William Wisner Chapin. Vol. XXVII, pp. 1-29, 26 ills., Jan., 1915.

Glimpses of Japan. By William Wisner Chapin. Vol. XXII, pp. 965-1002, 10 ills. in black and white, 34 ills. in color, Nov., 1911.

Glimpses of Korea and China. By William Wisner Chapin. Vol. XXI, pp. 895-934, 11 ills. in black and white, 39 ills. in color, Nov., 1910.

Glimpses of Siberia, the Russian "Wild East." By Cody Marsh. Vol. XXXVIII, pp. 512-536, 26 ills., Dec., 1920.

Glimpses of the Russian Empire. By William Wisner Chapin. Vol. XXIII, pp. 1043-1078, 51 ills. in color, 1 three-quarters-page map, Nov., 1912.

Glories of the Minya Konka: Magnificent Snow Peaks of the China-Tibetan Border Are Photographed at Close Range by a National Geographic Society Expedition. By Joseph F. Rock. Vol. LVIII, pp. 385-437, 35 ills. in black and white, 24 ills. in color, 1 three-quarters-page map, Oct., 1930.

Glories Past and Present of Northern Spain. 13 ills. in color from autochromes by Gervais Courtellemont. Vol. LV, pp. 340-349, Mar., 1929.

"Glory That Was Greece." By Alexander Wilbourne Weddell. Vol. XLII, pp. 571-603, 51 ills., 1 three-quarters-page map, Dec., 1922.

"Glory That Was Greece." 32 ills. in color from paintings by H. M. Herget. Vol. LXXXV, pp. 290-352, Mar., 1944.

Glory That Was Imperial Peking. By W. Robert Moore. Vol. LXIII, pp. 745-780, 18 ills. in black and white, 16 ills. in duotone, June, 1933.

Gloucester, Massachusetts:

Northeast of Boston. By Albert W. Atwood. Vol. LXXXVIII, pp. 257-292, 12 ills. in black and white, 17 ills. in color, special map supplement, Sept., 1945.

Where New England Meets the Sea. 17 ills. in color from natural-color photographs by B. Anthony Stewart. Vol. LXXXVIII, pp. 265-288, Sept., 1945.

Glueck, Nelson:

Geography of the Jordan. Vol. LXXXVI, pp. 719-744, 23 ills., 1 page map, Dec., 1944.

On the Trail of King Solomon's Mines: The Bible, in Addition to Its Spiritual Values, Continues to Prove a Rich Geography and Guide to Exploration of the Holy Land. By Nelson Glueck. Vol. LXXXV, pp. 233-256, 20 ills., 1 page map, Feb., 1944.

Gnatcatchers (Birds):

Winged Denizens of Woodland, Stream, and Marsh. By Alexander Wetmore. Paintings by Maj. Allan Brooks. Vol. LXV, pp. 577-596, 4 portraits in color, May, 1934.

Goats:

Milch Goat. Vol. XVI, p. 237, 1 ill., May, 1905.

Goatsuckers (Birds):

Humming Birds, Swifts and Goatsuckers. 6 ills. in color from paintings by Maj. Allan Brooks. Vol. LXII, pp. 75-88, July, 1932.

Seeking the Smallest Feathered Creatures: Humming Birds, Peculiar to the New World, Are Found from Canada and Alaska to the Strait of Magellan. Swifts and Goatsuckers, Their Nearest Relatives. By Alexander Wetmore. Paintings by Maj. Allan Brooks. Vol. LXII, pp. 65-89, 1 ill. in black and white, 6 ills. in color, July, 1932.

Gobi (Desert), Outer Mongolia–China:

Desert Road to Turkestan: Twentieth Century Travel Through Innermost Asia, Along Caravan Trails Over Which Oriental Commerce Was Once Borne from China to the Medieval Western World. By Owen Lattimore. Vol. LV, pp. 661-702, 45 ills., 1 two-thirds-page map, June, 1929.

Explorations in the Gobi Desert. By Roy Chapman Andrews. Vol. LXIII, pp. 653-716, 50 ills. in black and white, 20 ills. in color, 1 half-page map, June, 1933.

Lama's Motor-Car. By Ethan C. Le Munyon. Vol. XXIV, pp. 640-670, 34 ills., May, 1913.

Nomad Life and Fossil Treasures of Mongolia. 20 ills. in color from photographs by J. B. Shackelford. Vol. LXIII, pp. 669-701, June, 1933.

Goddard, (Maj.) George W.:

Aerial Color Photography Becomes a War Weapon. By H. H. Arnold. Vol. LXXVII, pp. 757-766, 8 ills. in color from natural-color photographs by Major George W. Goddard, June, 1940.

Goddard, (Maj.) George W.—*Continued*

Unexplored Philippines from the Air : Map-Making over Jungle Lands Never Before Seen by White Men. By Lieut. George W. Goddard. Vol. LVIII, pp. 311-343, 38 ills., 1 quarter-page map, Sept., 1930.

Godesberg, Bad, Germany :

War's Wake in the Rhineland. By Thomas R. Henry. Vol. LXXXVIII, pp. 1-32, 29 ills., 1 third-page map, July, 1945.

Godthaab, Greenland :

Greenland—U. S. Base in the Arctic. 5 ills. in color from natural-color photographs by James K. Penfield. Vol. LXXXII, pp. 373-376, Sept., 1942.

Greenland Turns to America. By James K. Penfield. Vol. LXXXII, pp. 369-383, 7 ills. in black and white, 5 ills. in color, 1 two-page map, Sept., 1942.

Goes, Netherlands :

City of Jacqueline. By Florence Craig Albrecht. Vol. XXVII, pp. 29-56, 31 ills., Jan., 1915.

Goethals, (Col.) George W.:

Honors to Colonel Goethals : The Presentation, by President Woodrow Wilson, of the National Geographic Society Special Gold Medal, and Addresses by Secretary of State Bryan, the French Ambassador, the German Ambassador, and Congressman James R. Mann. Vol. XXV, pp. 677-690, 6 ills., June, 1914.

Panama Canal. By Lieut. Col. George W. Goethals. Vol. XX, pp. 334-355, 7 ills., 1 half-page map, 1 diagram, Apr., 1909.

Panama Canal. By Col. George W. Goethals. Vol. XXII, pp. 148-211, 49 ills., 2 half-page maps, 1 diagram, Feb., 1911.

Going, Charles Buxton :

Mysterious Prehistoric Monuments of Brittany (France). By Charles Buxton Going. Vol. XLIV, pp. 53-69, 16 ills., July, 1923.

Goja (Ship) :

Modern Viking. Vol. XVII, pp. 38-40, 1 ill., 1 page map, Jan., 1906.

Gold and Gold Mining:

Beyond Australia's Cities. By W. Robert Moore. Vol. LXX, pp. 709-747, 27 ills. in black and white, 12 ills. in color, Dec., 1936.

Cape Nome Gold District (Alaska). By F. C. Schrader. Vol. XI, pp. 15-23, 3 ills., 1 page map, Jan., 1900.

Cities That Gold and Diamonds Built : Transvaal Treasures Have Created Bustling Johannesburg and Fostered Pretoria, Administrative Capital of the South African Union. By W. Robert Moore. Vol. LXXXII, pp. 735-766, 20 ills. in black and white, 9 ills. in color, 1 two-thirds-page map, Dec., 1942.

Colorado, a Barrier That Became a Goal : Where Water Has Transformed Dry Plains Into Verdant Farms, and Highways Have Opened up Mineral and Scenic Wealth. By McFall Kerbey. Vol. LXII, pp. 1-63, 56 ills. in black and white, 12 ills. in color, 1 page map, July, 1932.

Gold and Gold Mining—*Continued*

Gold in the Philippines. By F. F. Hilder. Vol. XI, pp. 465-470, Dec., 1900.

Growing Camp in the Tanana Gold Fields. By Sidney Paige. Vol. XVI, pp. 104-111, 4 ills., Mar., 1905.

Lonely Australia : The Unique Continent. By Herbert E. Gregory. Vol. XXX, pp. 473-568, 68 ills., 1 two-page and 4 half-page maps, Dec., 1916.

Men and Gold. By Frederick Simpich. Vol. LXIII, pp. 481-518, 33 ills. in black and white, 11 ills. in duotone, Apr., 1933.

Nome Gold Fields. Vol. XIX, pp. 384-385, May, 1908.

Quest of Gold and the Goldsmith's Art. 11 ills. in duotone. Vol. LXIII, pp. 488-497, Apr., 1933.

Under the South African Union. By Melville Chater. Vol. LIX, pp. 391-512, 97 ills. in black and white, 38 ills. in color, 1 two-page map, Apr., 1931.

World's Production of Gold (From an Address to the American Banker's Convention, by F. A. Vanderlip, October 11, 1905). Vol. XVI, pp. 571-572, Dec., 1905.

Gold Coast, Africa :

Revolt of the Ashantis. Vol. XI, p. 244, 1 third-page map, June, 1900.

Golden Eagles:

In Quest of the Golden Eagle : Over Lonely Mountain and Prairie Soars This Rare and Lordly Bird, But Three Youths from the East Catch Up With Him at Last. By John and Frank Craighead. Vol. LXXVII, pp. 693-710, 17 ills., May, 1940.

Golden Fleece of Dixie (Cotton). 34 ills. in color from natural-color photographs by Willard R. Culver. Vol. LXXIX, pp. 153-192, Feb., 1941.

Golden Gate, and Redwood Evergreens (California). 17 ills. in color from natural-color photographs by B. Anthony Stewart. Vol. LXXV, pp. 149-160, Feb., 1939.

Golden Isles of Guale (Sea Islands, Georgia). By W. Robert Moore. Vol. LXV, pp. 235-264, 35 ills., 1 three-quarters-page map, Feb., 1934.

Golden Trout. Vol. XVII, p. 424, July, 1906.

Goldfish:

Fisheries of Japan. By Hugh M. Smith. Vol. XVI, pp. 201-220, 13 ills., May, 1905.

Goldfish and Their Cultivation in America. By Hugh M. Smith. Vol. XLVI, pp. 375-400, 14 ills. in black and white, 8 ills. in color, Oct., 1924.

Gomes, Edwin H.:

Notes on the Sea Dyaks of Borneo. By Edwin H. Gomes. Vol. XXII, pp. 695-723, 26 ills., Aug., 1911.

Good Hope, Cape of, South Africa:

Busy Corner—the Cape of Good Hope: Ships Bound for Faraway Battlegrounds Stream Past Capetown, "Tavern of the Seas," and Other Ports of Virile South Africa. By W. Robert Moore. Vol. LXXXII, pp. 197-223, 11 ills. in black and white, 11 ills. in color, 1 two-thirds-page map, Aug., 1942.

Cape of Good Hope: The Floral Province. By Melville Chater. Vol. LIX, pp. 391-430, 29 ills., Apr., 1931.

Color at Africa's Southern Tip. 11 ills. in color from natural-color photographs by W. Robert Moore. Vol. LXXXII, pp. 213-220, Aug., 1942.

Goode, Richard U.:

Idaho and Montana Boundary Line. By Richard U. Goode. Vol. XI, pp. 23-29, 1 ill., Jan., 1900.

Richard Urquhart Goode (Biography). Vol. XIV, pp. 424-425, 1 ill., Nov., 1903.

Gooding, Paul:

Tahiti: A Playground of Nature. By Paul Gooding. Vol. XXXVIII, pp. 301-326, 16 ills., 1 half-page map, Oct., 1920.

Goodnow, Frank Johnson:

Geography of China: The Influence of Physical Environment on the History and Character of the Chinese People. By Frank Johnson Goodnow. Vol. LI, pp. 651-664, 11 ills., June, 1927.

Goodwin, W. A. R.:

Restoration of Colonial Williamsburg. By W. A. R. Goodwin. Vol. LXXI, pp. 402-443, 21 ills. in black and white, 25 ills. in color, Apr., 1937.

Goose Fish:

Purple Veil: A Romance of the Sea. Vol. XIV, pp. 337-341, 9 ills., July, 1905.

Gophers:

Into the Land of the Chipmunk. By Ruth Alexander Nichols. Vol. LX, pp. 77-98, 28 ills., July, 1931.

Gore, James Howard:

As Seen from a Dutch Window. By James Howard Gore. Vol. XIX, pp. 619-634, 3 ills., Sept., 1908.

Discovery of the North Pole (Speech by James Howard Gore). Vol. XXI, pp. 63-82, Jan., 1910.

Holland's War With the Sea. By James Howard Gore. Vol. XLIII, pp. 283-325, 39 ills., 1 third-page map, Mar., 1923.

Return of Wellman. By J. Howard Gore. Vol. X, pp. 348-351, 2 ills., Sept., 1899.

Roumania, the Pivotal State. By James Howard Gore. Vol. XXVIII, pp. 360-390, 32 ills., Oct., 1915.

Wellman Polar Expedition (Arctic). By J. Howard Gore. Vol. X, pp. 267-268, July, 1899.

Gore, Lillian:

In Beautiful Delecarlia (Sweden). By Lillian Gore. Vol. XX, pp. 464-477, 13 ills., May, 1909.

Gorgonians (Coral):

First Autochromes from the Ocean Bottom. 8 ills. in color from autochromes by W. H. Longley and Charles Martin. Vol. LI, pp. 56-61, Jan., 1927.

Life on a Coral Reef: The Fertility and Mystery of the Sea Studied Beneath the Waters Surrounding Dry Tortugas. By W. H. Longley. Vol. LI, pp. 61-83, 22 ills. in black and white, 8 ills. in color, Jan., 1927.

Gorillas:

Manlike Apes of Jungle and Mountain. 10 ills. in color from paintings by Elie Cheverlange. Vol. LXXVIII, pp. 221-228, Aug., 1940.

Man's Closest Counterparts: Heavyweight of Monkeydom Is the "Old Man" Gorilla, by Far the Largest of the Four Great Apes. By William M. Mann. Vol. LXXVIII, pp. 213-236, 10 ills. in black and white, 10 ills. in color, Aug., 1940.

Gorki (Nizhni Novgorod), R. S. F. S. R.:

Voyaging on the Volga Amid War and Revolution: War-Time Sketches on Russia's Great Waterway. By William T. Ellis. Vol. XXXIII, pp. 245-265, 16 ills., Mar., 1918.

Gorman, Martin W.:

Ice Cliffs on White River, Yukon Territory. By Martin W. Gorman. Vol. XI, pp. 113-117, Mar., 1900.

Goro, F. W.:

Where Bretons Wrest a Living from the Sea. 23 ills. from photographs by F. W. Goro. Vol. LXXI, pp. 751-766, June, 1937.

Goulder, Harvey:

Honors for Amundsen (Address by Harvey Goulder). Vol. XIX, pp. 55-76, 13 ills., Jan., 1908.

Governing the Philippine Islands. By Col. Clarence R. Edwards. Vol. XV, pp. 273-284, 5 ills., July, 1904.

Government:

Colonial Government in Borneo. By James M. Hubbard. Vol. XI, pp. 359-363, Sept., 1900.

Colonial Systems of the World. By O. P. Austin. Vol. X, pp. 21-26, Jan., 1899.

Democracy's Royal Palace (Westminster). 19 ills. in color from natural-color photographs by B. Anthony Stewart. Vol. XC, pp. 233-248, Aug., 1946.

Oldest Free Assemblies: Address of Right Hon. Arthur J. Balfour, in the United States House of Representatives, May 5, 1917. Vol. XXXI, pp. 368-371, Apr., 1917.

United States and the British Empire. By Leonard David Gammans. Vol. LXXXVII, pp. 562-564, May, 1945.

Government—*Continued*

Yanks at Westminster. By Capt. Leonard David Gammans. Vol. XC, pp. 223-252, 6 ills. in black and white, 19 ills. in color, Aug., 1946.
See also Allied Military Government.

Government Assistance in Handling Forest Lands. Vol. XV, pp. 450-452, Nov., 1904.

Grace Harwar (Ship) :

Rounding the Horn in a Windjammer. By A. J. Villiers. Vol. LIX, pp. 191-224, 36 ills., 1 two-thirds-page map, Feb., 1931.

Graf Zeppelin (Airship) :

First Airship Flight Around the World: Dr. Hugo Eckener Tells of an Epochal Geographic Achievement upon the Occasion of the Bestowal of the National Geographic Society's Special Gold Medal. Vol. LVII, pp. 653-688, 37 ills., June, 1930.

Graham Land, Antarctica :

American Discoverers of the Antarctic Continent. By Maj. Gen. A. W. Greely. Vol. XXIII, pp. 298-312, 7 ills., 1 page map, Mar., 1912.

Granada, Spain :

From Granada to Gibraltar—A Tour of Southern Spain. By Harry A. McBride. Vol. XLVI, pp. 205-232, 23 ills., Aug., 1924.

Grand Banks, Newfoundland :

Life on the Grand Banks : An Account of the Sailor-Fishermen Who Harvest the Shoal Waters of North America's Eastern Coasts. By Frederick William Wallace. Vol. XL, pp. 1-28, 29 ills., July, 1921.

Grand Canal, China :

Grand Canal Panorama (China). By Willard Price. Vol. LXXI, pp. 487-514, 31 ills., 1 half-page map, Apr., 1937.
Shantung—China's Holy Land. By Charles K. Edmunds. Vol. XXXVI, pp. 231-252, 21 ills., 1 half-page map, Sept., 1919.

Grand Canyon, Arizona :

Experiences in the Grand Canyon. By Ellsworth and Emery Kolb. Vol. XXVI, pp. 99-184, 70 ills., 1 page map, Aug., 1914.
Grand Canyon Bridge. By Harriet Chalmers Adams. Vol. XXXIX, pp. 645-650, 6 ills., June, 1921.
Photographing the Marvels of the West in Colors. By Fred Payne Clatworthy. Vol. LIII, pp. 694-719, 5 ills. in color, June, 1928.
Scenery of North America. By James Bryce. Vol. XLI, pp. 339-389, 45 ills., Apr., 1922.
Scenic Glories of Western United States. 8 ills. in color from autochromes by Fred Payne Clatworthy. Vol. LVI, pp. 223-230, Aug., 1929.
Southwest: Its Splendid Natural Resources, Agricultural Wealth, and Scenic Beauty. By N. H. Darton. Vol. XXI, pp. 631-665, 21 ills., 1 page map, Aug., 1910.

Grand Canyon, Arizona—*Continued*

Surveying the Grand Canyon of the Colorado : An Account of the 1923 Boating Expedition of the United States Geological Survey. By Lewis R. Freeman. Vol. XLV, pp. 471-548, 62 ills., 1 three-quarters-page map, May, 1924.

Grand Coulee Dam, Washington :

Columbia (River) Turns on the Power. By Maynard Owen Williams. Vol. LXXIX, pp. 749-792, 25 ills. in black and white, 18 ills. in color, June, 1941.

Grand Duchy of Luxemburg : A Miniature Democratic State of Many Charms Against a Feudal Background. By Maynard Owen Williams. Vol. XLVI, pp. 501-528, 28 ills., 1 quarter-page map, Nov., 1924.

Grand Union Canal, England :

Britain Just Before the Storm : A Canadian Canoe Threads Old English Waterways Athrob with the Midlands' Industrial Life. By Amos Burg. Vol. LXXVIII, pp. 185-212, 14 ills. in black and white, 9 ills. in color, 1 two-thirds-page map, Aug., 1940.

Grand Valley, Netherlands New Guinea :

New Guinea's Mountain and Swampland Dwellers. By Col. Ray T. Elsmore. Vol. LXXXVIII, pp. 671-694, 15 ills. in black and white, 7 ills. in color, 1 half-page map, Dec., 1945.
"Shangri-la" in Panorama. 7 ills. in color from natural-color photographs by Ray T. Elsmore. Vol. LXXXVIII, pp. 681-688, Dec., 1945.

Grande Baie, Canada :

Camera Pastels in French Canada. 25 ills. in color from natural-color photographs by Harrison Howell Walker. Vol. LXXV, pp. 601-624, May, 1939.
Gentle Folk Settle Stern Saguenay : On French Canada's Frontier Homespun Colonists Keep the Customs of Old Norman Settlers. By Harrison Howell Walker. Vol. LXXV, pp. 595-632, 15 ills. in black and white, 25 ills. in color, 1 map, May, 1939.

Grandest and Most Mighty Terrestrial Phenomenon : The Gulf Stream. By Rear Adm. John Elliott Pillsbury. Vol. XXIII, pp. 767-778, 1 ill., 2 diagrams, 2 page and 1 half-page maps, Aug., 1912.

Granite City of the North : Austere Stockholm, Sweden's Prosperous Capital, Presents a Smiling Aspect in Summer. By Ralph A. Graves. Vol. LIV, pp. 403-424, 23 ills. in black and white, 6 ills. in color, Oct., 1928.

Grant, G. A.:

Western National Parks Invite America Out of Doors. 12 ills. in duotone from photographs by G. A. Grant. Vol. LXVI, pp. 65-80, July, 1934.

Grant, Madison:

Saving the Redwoods. By Madison Grant. Vol. XXXVII, pp. 519-536, 10 ills., June, 1920.

Grape Culture:

Fruitful Shores of the Finger Lakes (New York). By Harrison Howell Walker. Vol. LXXIX, pp. 559-594, 15 ills. in black and white, 22 ills. in color, 1 two-thirds-page map, May, 1941.

Grape-Growing Industry in the United States. Vol. XIV, pp. 445-451, 5 ills., Dec., 1903.

Grass Makes Wyoming Fat. By Frederick Simpich. Vol. LXXXVIII, pp. 153-188, 13 ills. in black and white, 19 ills. in color, 1 two-page map, Aug., 1945.

"Grass Never Grows Where the Turkish Hoof Has Trod." By Edwin Pears. Vol. XXIII, pp. 1132-1148, 19 ills., Nov., 1912.

Grasse, (Adm.) François Joseph Paul de:

Our First Alliance. By J. J. Jusserand. Vol. XXXI, pp. 518-548, 8 ills., June, 1917.

Grasses:

American Wild Flowers. Vol. XXVII, pp. 483-517, 29 ills. in color, May, 1915.

Exploring a Grass Wonderland of Wild West China. By Ray G. Johnson. Vol. LXXXV, pp. 713-742, 24 ills., 1 half-page map, June, 1944.

Familiar Grasses and Their Flowers. By E. J. Geske and W. J. Showalter. Vol. XXXIX, pp. 625-636, 8 ills. in color, June, 1921.

Contains descriptions and illustrations of the following species: Barnyard Grass, Kentucky Bluegrass, Orchard Grass, Purple-Top, Redtop, Rye-Grass, Timothy, Yellow Foxtail.

Graves, Henry S.:

Fight Against Forest Fires. By Henry S. Graves. Vol. XXIII, pp. 662-683, 19 ills., July, 1912.

Graves, Ralph A.:

Fearful Famines of the Past: History Will Repeat Itself Unless the American People Conserve Their Resources. By Ralph A. Graves. Vol. XXXII, pp. 68-90, 11 ills., July, 1917.

Granite City of the North: Austere Stockholm, Sweden's Prosperous Capital, Presents a Smiling Aspect in Summer. By Ralph A. Graves. Vol. LIV, pp. 403-424, 23 ills. in black and white, 6 ills. in color, Oct., 1928.

Helping to Solve the Allies' Food Problem: America Calls for a Million Young Soldiers of the Commissary to Volunteer for Service in 1918. By Ralph A. Graves. Vol. XXXIII, pp. 170-194, 23 ills., Feb., 1918.

Human Emotion Recorded by Photography. Vol. XXXVIII, pp. 284-300, 16 ills., Oct., 1920.

Louisiana, Land of Perpetual Romance. By Ralph A. Graves. Vol. LVII, pp. 393-482, 84 ills. in black and white, 29 ills. in color, special map supplement in colors, Apr., 1930.

Marching Through Georgia Sixty Years After: Multifold Industries and Diversified Agriculture Are Restoring the Prosperity of America's Largest State East of the Mississippi. By Ralph A. Graves. Vol. L, pp. 259-311, 47 ills., Sept., 1926.

Graves, Ralph A.—*Continued*

Memorial Tribute of the Board of Trustees and Officers of the National Geographic Society to Ralph A. Graves, Late Senior Assistant Editor of the National Geographic Magazine. Vol. LXII, p. 606, 1 ill., Nov., 1932.

Millennial City: The Romance of Geneva, Capital of the League of Nations. By Ralph A. Graves. Vol. XXXV, pp. 457-476, 13 ills., June, 1919.

New Map of Europe: Showing the Boundaries Established by the Peace Conference at Paris and by Subsequent Decisions of the Supreme Council of the Allied and Associated Powers. By Ralph A. Graves. Text accompanying special map supplement in colors. Vol. XXXIX, pp. 157-177, 18 ills., Feb., 1921.

Ships for the Seven Seas: The Story of America's Maritime Needs. Her Capabilities and Her Achievements. By Ralph A. Graves. Vol. XXXIV, pp. 165-200, 24 ills., Sept., 1918.

Short Visit to Wales: Historic Associations and Scenic Beauties Contend for Interest in the Little Land Behind the Hills. By Ralph A. Graves. Vol. XLIV, pp. 635-675, 37 ills., 1 half-page map, Dec., 1923.

Through the English Lake District Afoot and Awheel. By Ralph A. Graves. Vol. LV, pp. 577-603, 19 ills. in black and white, 15 ills. in color, 1 quarter-page map, May, 1929.

Gravosa, Yugoslavia:

East of the Adriatic: Notes on Dalmatia, Montenegro, Bosnia, and Herzegovina. By Kenneth McKenzie. Vol. XXIII, pp. 1159-1187, 37 ills., 1 page map, Dec., 1912.

Great African Lake (Victoria). By Sir Henry M. Stanley. Vol. XIII, pp. 169-172, 1 half-page map, May, 1902.

Great American Desert, Utah:

Nation's Undeveloped Resources. By Franklin K. Lane. Vol. XXV, pp. 183-225, 32 ills., Feb., 1914.

Great Barrier Reef, Australia:

Fantastic Dwellers in a Coral Fairyland. 15 ills. in color from natural-color photographs by T. C. Roughley. Vol. LXXVII, pp. 831-838, June, 1940.

Great Barrier Reef and Its Isles: The Wonder and Mystery of Australia's World-Famous Geographical Feature. By Charles Barrett. Vol. LVIII, pp. 355-384, 38 ills., 1 half-page map, Sept., 1930.

Where Nature Runs Riot: On Australia's Great Barrier Reef Marine Animals Grow to Unusual Size, Develop Strange Weapons of Attack and Defense, and Acquire Brilliant Colors. By T. C. Roughley. Vol. LXXVII, pp. 823-850, 18 ills. in black and white, 15 ills. in color, 1 page map, June, 1940.

Great Britain:

Britain Fights in the Fields. By Francis A. Flood. Vol. LXXXVI, pp. 31-65, 17 ills. in black and white, 21 ills. in color, July, 1944.

Great Britain—*Continued*

British Commonwealth of Nations: "Organized Freedom" Around the World. By Eric Underwood. Vol. LXXXIII, pp. 485-524, 31 ills., Apr., 1943.

British Isles. Vol. XXVIII, pp. 551-566, 16 ills., Dec., 1915.

Democracy's Royal Palace (Westminster). 19 ills. in color from natural-color photographs by B. Anthony Stewart. Vol. XC, pp. 233-248, Aug., 1946.

Expansion of England. By Edwin D. Mead. Vol. XI, pp. 249-263, July, 1900.

Fearful Famines of the Past: History Will Repeat Itself Unless the American People Conserve Their Resources. By Ralph A. Graves. Vol. XXXII, pp. 68-90, 11 ills., July, 1917.
Contents: Famines in England.

Flags of the British Empire. By Byron McCandless and Gilbert Grosvenor. Vol. XXXII, pp. 378-385, 158 ills. in color, Oct., 1917.

Great Britain in the Yangtze Valley. Vol. XII, p. 163, Apr., 1901.

Great Britain on Parade. By Maynard Owen Williams. Vol. LXVIII, pp. 137-184, 40 ills. in black and white, 11 ills. in color, Aug., 1935.

Great Britain's Bread Upon the Waters: Canada and Her Other Daughters. By William Howard Taft. Vol. XXIX, pp. 217-272, 56 ills., Mar., 1916.

Lend-Lease Is a Two-way Benefit: Innovation in Creative Statesmanship Pools Resources of United Nations, and Supplies American Forces Around the World. By Francis Flood. Vol. LXXXIII, pp. 745-761, 14 ills., June, 1943.

Oldest Free Assemblies: Address of Right Hon. Arthur J. Balfour, in the United States House of Representatives, May 5, 1917. Vol. XXXI, pp. 368-371, Apr., 1917.

One Hundred British Seaports. Vol. XXXI, pp. 84-94, 10 ills., 1 page map, Jan., 1917.

Races of Europe. By Edwin A. Grosvenor. Vol. XXXIV, pp. 441-534, 62 ills., 2 page maps, Dec., 1918.

Shipbuilding in the United Kingdom in 1898. Vol. X, pp. 138-139, Apr., 1899.

Some Significant Facts Concerning the Foreign Trade of Great Britain. Vol. XI, p. 480, Dec., 1900.

Tales of the British Air Service. By Maj. William A. Bishop. Vol. XXXIII, pp. 27-37, 12 ills., Jan., 1918.

Ties that Bind: Our Natural Sympathy with English Traditions, the French Republic, and the Russian Outburst for Liberty. By John Sharp Williams. Vol. XXXI, pp. 281-286, 4 ills., Mar., 1917.

What Great Britain Is Doing (War Preparations). By Sydney Brooks. Vol. XXXI, pp. 193-210, 7 ills., Mar., 1917.

What the War Has Done for Britain. By Judson C. Welliver. Vol. XXXIV, pp. 278-297, 13 ills., Oct., 1918.

Great Britain—*Continued*

Yanks at Westminster. By Capt. Leonard David Gammans. Vol. XC, pp. 223-252, 6 ills. in black and white, 19 ills. in color, Aug., 1946.
See also England; Scotland; Wales.

Great Britain's Bread Upon the Waters: Canada and Her Other Daughters. By William Howard Taft. Vol. XXIX, pp. 217-272, 56 ills., Mar., 1916.

Great Canals of the World. Vol. XVI, pp. 475-479, Oct., 1905.

Great Falls, Potomac River:

Great Falls of the Potomac. By Gilbert Grosvenor. Vol. LIII, pp. 385-400, 19 ills., Mar., 1928.

Potomac, River of Destiny. By Albert W. Atwood. Vol. LXXXVIII, pp. 33-70, 15 ills. in black and white. 18 ills. in color, 1 map (two-page spread), July, 1945.

Great Ice Barrier, Antarctica:

Geography. By Sir W. J. L. Wharton. Vol. XVI, pp. 483-498, Nov., 1905.

Great Ice Barrier. By Henry Gannett. Vol. XXI, pp. 173-174, 1 ill., Feb., 1910.

Ice-Wrapped Continent. By Gilbert H. Grosvenor. Vol. XVIII, pp. 95-117, 20 ills., 1 half-page map, Feb., 1907.

Great Lakes, United States-Canada:

By Car and Steamer Around Our Inland Seas. By Maynard Owen Williams. Vol. LXV, pp. 451-491, 29 ills. in black and white, 8 ills. in duotone, 1 two-page map, Apr., 1934.

Freighters of Fortune on Our Great Lakes. 8 ills. in duotone from photographs by Maynard Owen Williams. Vol. LXV, pp. 463-470, Apr., 1934.

Great Lakes and Great Industries. 19 ills. in color from natural-color photographs by B. Anthony Stewart, Alfred T. Palmer, and Willard R. Culver. Vol. LXXXVI, pp. 689-712, Dec., 1944.

Honors for Amundsen (Banquet). Vol. XIX, pp. 55-76, 13 ills., Jan., 1908.

Rainfall and the Level of Lake Erie. By E. L. Moseley. Vol. XIV, pp. 327-328, Aug., 1903.

Submerged Valleys in Sandusky Bay. By E. L. Moseley. Vol. XIII, pp. 398-403, 4 charts, Nov., 1902.

Testing the Currents of Lake Erie. By E. L. Moseley. Vol. XIV, pp. 41-42, Jan., 1903.

Variations in Lake Levels and Atmospheric Precipitation. By Alfred J. Henry. Vol. X, pp. 403-406, 1 diagram, Oct., 1899.

Great Mississippi Flood of 1927: Since White Man's Discovery This Mighty River Has Served Him Well, Yet It Has Brought Widespread Devastation Along Its Lower Reaches. By Frederick Simpich. Vol. LII, pp. 243-289, 53 ills., 1 half-page-map, Sept., 1927.

Great Natural Bridges of Utah. Vol. XVIII, pp. 199-204, 3 ills., Mar., 1907.

Great Natural Bridges of Utah. By Byron Cummings. Vol. XXI, pp. 157-167, 7 ills., Feb., 1910.

Great Rainbow Natural Bridge of Southern Utah. By Joseph E. Pogue. Vol. XXII, pp. 1048-1056, 6 ills., Nov., 1911.

Great Smoky Mountains:

Rambling Around the Roof of Eastern America. By Leonard C. Roy. Vol. LXX, pp. 243-266, 25 ills., 1 page map, Aug., 1936.

Great Stone Faces of Easter Island. 11 ills. from photographs. Vol. LXXXV, pp. 225-232, Feb., 1944.

Great Stone Faces of the Mexican Jungle : Five Colossal Heads and Numerous Other Monuments of Vanished Americans Are Excavated by the Latest National Geographic-Smithsonian Expedition. By Matthew W. Stirling. Vol. LXXVIII, pp. 309-334, 26 ills., 1 map, Sept., 1940.

Great Turk and His Lost Provinces. By William E. Curtis. Vol. XIV, pp. 45-61, 7 ills., Feb., 1903.

Great Wall of China:

China's Treasures. By Frederick McCormick. Vol. XXIII, pp. 996-1040, 50 ills., Oct., 1912.

Great Wall of China. By James H. Wilson. Vol. XI, pp. 372-374, 1 ill., Sept., 1900.

Great Wall of China Near Nankow Pass. Vol. XLIII, panorama, Feb., 1923.

Peking, the City of the Unexpected. By James Arthur Muller. Vol. XXXVIII, pp. 335-355, 18 ills., Nov., 1920.

Thousand Miles Along the Great Wall of China : The Mightiest Barrier Ever Built by Man Has Stood Guard Over the Land of Chin for Twenty Centuries. By Adam Warwick. Vol. XLIII, pp. 113-143, 27 ills., panorama, 1 page and 1 half-page maps, Feb., 1923.

Great White Monarch of the Pacific Northwest (Mount Rainier). By A. H. Barnes. Vol. XXIII, pp. 593-626, 31 ills., 1 half-page map, June, 1912.

Great Yarmouth, England :

When the Herring Fleet Comes to Great Yarmouth. By W. Robert Moore. Vol. LXVI, pp. 233-250, 19 ills., Aug., 1934.

Greater Antilles. *See* Cuba ; Dominican Republic ; Haiti ; Jamaica ; Puerto Rico.

Greater New York . . . Metropolis of Mankind. Special supplement from aërial photograph by Capt. Albert W. Stevens. Vol. LXIV, supplement, Nov., 1933.

Greater Sunda Islands. *See* Borneo ; Celebes ; Java ; Sumatra.

Greatest Achievement of Ancient Man in America, the Fortress of Sacsahuaman, Peru. Vol. XXIX, panorama, May, 1916.

Greatest Hunt in the World (Elephant Hunting). By Eliza R. Scidmore. Vol. XVII, pp. 673-692, 17 ills., Dec., 1906.

Greatest Volcanoes of Mexico. By A. Melgareio. Vol. XXI, pp. 741-760, 22 ills., Sept., 1910.

Greatest Voyage in the Annals of the Sea. By J. R. Hildebrand. Vol. LXII, pp. 699-739, 35 ills., 2 half-page maps, Dec., 1932.

Greatness of Little Portugal. By Oswald Crawfurd. Vol. XXI, pp. 867-883, 12 ills., Oct., 1910.

Grebes (Birds) :

Birds of Lake and Lagoon, Marsh and Seacoast. 9 portraits in color from paintings by Maj. Allan Brooks. Vol. LXV, pp. 313-328, Mar., 1934.

Birds That Cruise the Coast and Inland Waters. By T. Gilbert Pearson. Paintings by Maj. Allan Brooks. Vol. LXV, pp. 299-328, 2 ills. in black and white, 9 portraits in color, Mar., 1934.

Greece:

Ageless Luster of Greece and Rhodes. 16 ills. in duotone by Arnold Genthe. Vol. LXXIII, pp. 477-492, Apr., 1938.

Amidst the Templed Hills of Greece. 13 ills. in color from natural-color photographs by Maynard Owen Williams. Vol. LVIII, pp. 664-673, Dec., 1930.

Changing Map in the Balkans. By Frederick Moore. Vol. XXIV, pp. 199-226, 27 ills., 1 page map, Feb., 1913.

Classic Greece Merges Into 1941 News. 19 ills. from photographs ; 15 ills. by B. Anthony Stewart ; 3 ills. by Maynard Owen Williams. Vol. LXXIX, pp. 93-108, Jan., 1941.

Festival Days on the Slopes of Mount Parnassus. 14 ills. in color from natural-color photographs by Maynard Owen Williams. Vol. LVIII, pp. 712-721, Dec., 1930.

"Glory That Was Greece." By Alexander Wilbourne Weddell. Vol. XLII, pp. 571-630, 51 ills., 1 three-quarters-page map, Dec., 1922.

"Glory That Was Greece." 32 ills. in color from paintings by H. M. Herget. Vol. LXXXV, pp. 290-352, Mar., 1944.

"Grass Never Grows Where the Turkish Hoof Has Trod." By Edwin Pears. Vol. XXIII, pp. 1132-1148, 19 ills., Nov., 1912.

Great Turk and His Lost Provinces. By William E. Curtis. Vol. XIV, pp. 45-61, 7 ills., Feb., 1903.

Greece and Montenegro. By George Higgins Moses. Vol. XXIV, pp. 281-310, 24 ills., Mar., 1913.

Greece of Today. By George Higgins Moses. Vol. XXVIII, pp. 295-329, 27 ills., Oct., 1915.

Greece—the Birthplace of Science and Free Speech : Explorations on the Mainland and in Crete and the Aegean Isles Reveal Ancient Life Similar to That of the Present. By Richard Stillwell. Paintings by H. M. Herget.

Greece—*Continued*

Vol. LXXXV, pp. 273-353, 13 ills. in black and white, 32 ills. in color, 1 two-page map, Mar., 1944.

Contents: Boy and Girl Grappling Bulls at Cnossus: Crete.—Travelers at a Mycenaean Palace.—A Fountain House of 2,500 Years Ago.—Chariot Race at Olympia.—Athena's Gift to Greece Was the Precious Olive.—Fishermen in the Gulf of Corinth.—Hauling a Ship over the Isthmus.—The Famous Oracle at Delphi.—Young Spartans Were Tough.—Leonidas' Immortal Sacrifice at Thermopylae.—The Persians Storm the Acropolis.—Xerxes Watching the Battle of Salamis, 480 B. C.—To Greeks We Owe Our Love of Athletics.—An Athenian School.—Weaving and Spinning.—Herodotus—Geographer and Historian.—Pericles and Pheidias in the Parthenon.—The Panathenaic Procession Brings a New Robe to Athena.—Setting a Capital on the Erechtheum.—An Athenian Wedding Party.—Socrates Enjoys a Banquet. Greek Women Used Mascara and Beauty Lotions.—Voting in the Market Place at Athens.—Potter Making Clay Figurines.—Hippocrates, Father of Medicine.—Phryne Poses for Praxiteles.—The Countryside Is Smiling; "Therefore, Ye Soft Pipes, Play on."—Alexander Calls on Diogenes the Cynic.—Alexander Defeats Darius the Persian at Issus, 333 B. C.—In Such a Theater Orestes and Electra Played Their Tragic Roles.—A Key to the Classic Sea Was the Port of Delos.—Archimedes Discovered the Law of Specific Gravity.

The Greek Way. By Edith Hamilton. Vol. LXXXV, pp. 257-271, 12 ills., Mar., 1944.

History's Greatest Trek: Tragedy Stalks Through the Near East as Greece and Turkey Exchange Two Million of Their People. By Melville Chater. Vol. XLVIII, pp. 533-590, 52 ills. in black and white, 32 ills. in color, Nov., 1925.

Hoary Monasteries of Mount Athos. By H. G. Dwight. Vol. XXX, pp. 249-272, 24 ills., 1 half-page map, Sept., 1916.

Megaspelæon, the Oldest Monastery in Greece. By Carroll Storrs Alden. Vol. XXIV, pp. 310-323, 11 ills., Mar., 1913.

Modern Odyssey in Classic Lands: Troy's Treasures, Athens' Parthenon, and Rome's First "Broad Way" Influence Today's Banks, Costumes, Jewelry, and Railroad Timetables. By Maynard Owen Williams. Vol. LXXVII, pp. 291-337, 27 ills. in black and white, 22 ills. in color, Mar., 1940.

New Greece, the Centenarian, Forges Ahead. By Maynard Owen Williams. Vol. LVIII, pp. 649-721, 51 ills. in black and white, 40 ills. in color, 1 three-quarters-page map, Dec., 1930.

New Map of Europe: Showing the Boundaries Established by the Peace Conference at Paris and by Subsequent Decisions of the Supreme Council of the Allied and Associated Powers. By Ralph A. Graves. Text accompanying special map supplement in colors. Vol. XXXIX, pp. 157-177, 18 ills., Feb., 1921.

Greece—*Continued*

Races of Europe. By Edwin A. Grosvenor. Vol. XXXIV, pp. 441-534, 62 ills., 2 page maps, special map supplement in colors, Dec., 1918.

Saloniki. By H. G. Dwight. Vol. XXX, pp. 203-232, 28 ills., Sept., 1916.

Scenes Along the Byways of Hellas. 13 ills. in color from natural-color photographs by Maynard Owen Williams. Vol. LVIII, pp. 688-697. Dec., 1930.

Seeing 3,000 Years of History in Four Hours: A Panorama of Ancient, Medieval, and Modern Events Against a Background of Mythology Unfolds During an Airplane Journey from Constantinople to Athens. By Maynard Owen Williams. Vol. LIV, pp. 719-739, 24 ills., 1 two-thirds-page map, Dec., 1928.

Today's Evidence of Grecian Glory. 22 ills. in color from natural-color photographs by B. Anthony Stewart. Vol. LXXVII, pp. 307-322, Mar., 1940.

Whirlpool of the Balkans. By George Higgins Moses. Vol. XXXIX, pp. 179-197, 15 ills., Feb., 1921.

With the Monks at Meteora: Monasteries of Thessaly. By Elizabeth Perkins. Vol. XX, pp. 799-807, 5 ills., Sept., 1909.

See also Crete (Island); Cyclades (Islands); Dodecanese Islands.

Greek Bronzes. Text regarding requests for photographs. Vol. XXIII, p. 104, Jan., 1912.

Greek Bronzes of Tunisia. By Frank Edward Johnson. Vol. XXIII, pp. 89-103, 11 ills., Jan., 1912.

Greek Drama:

Festival Days on the Slopes of Mount Parnassus. 6 ills. in color from natural-color photographs by Maynard Owen Williams. Vol. LVIII, pp. 712-721, Dec., 1930.

Greek Way. By Edith Hamilton. Vol. LXXXV, pp. 257-271, 12 ills., Mar., 1944.

Greeks, Ancient:

Greece—the Birthplace of Science and Free Speech: Explorations on the Mainland and in Crete and the Aegean Isles Reveal Ancient Life Similar to That of the Present. By Richard Stillwell. Paintings by H. M. Herget. Vol. LXXXV, pp. 273-353, 13 ills. in black and white, 32 ills. in color, 1 two-page map, Mar., 1944.

The Greek Way. By Edith Hamilton. Vol. LXXXV, pp. 257-271, 12 ills., Mar., 1944.

Greely, (Maj. Gen.) A. W.:

Advances in Geographic Knowledge During the Nineteenth Century. By Maj. Gen. A. W. Greely. Vol. XII, pp. 143-152, 2 half-page maps, Apr., 1901.

American Discoverers of the Antarctic Continent. By Maj. Gen. A. W. Greely. Vol. XXIII, pp. 298-312, 7 ills., 1 page map, Mar., 1912.

Greely, (Maj. Gen.) A. W.—*Continued*

Bowdoin (Ship) in North Greenland : Arctic Explorers Place Tablet to Commemorate Sacrifices of the Lady Franklin Bay Expedition. By Donald B. MacMillan. Vol. XLVII, pp. 677-722, 49 ills., June, 1925.

Economic Evolution of Alaska. By Maj. Gen. A. W. Greely. Vol. XX, pp. 585-593, 4 ills., July, 1909.

Farthest North Reached by General Greely. Vol. XVIII, p. 50, Jan., 1907.

France of Today. By Maj. Gen. A. W. Greely. Vol. XXVI, pp. 193-222, 27 ills., Sept., 1914.

Geographical Exploration : Its Moral and Material Results. By Maj. Gen. A. W. Greely. Vol. XVII, pp. 1-5, Jan., 1906.

Greely's "Handbook of Alaska." By Gilbert H. Grosvenor. Vol. XX, pp. 491-492, May, 1909.

Honors to the American Navy (Address by Maj. Gen. A. W. Greely). Vol. XX, pp. 77-95, Jan., 1909.

Hurricanes on the Coast of Texas. By Maj. Gen. A. W. Greely. Vol. XI, pp. 442-445, Nov., 1900.

In Honor of the Army and Aviation (Address by Maj. Gen. A. W. Greely). Vol. XXII, pp. 267-284, Mar., 1911.

Land of Promise (Siberia). By Maj. Gen. A. W. Greely. Vol. XXIII, pp. 1078-1090, 7 ills., Nov., 1912.

National Geographic Society in War Time. By Maj. Gen. A. W. Greely. Vol. XXXIII, pp. 369-375, 5 ills., Apr., 1918.

National Geographic Society Notes (Election of Gen. Greely as Chairman of the Committee on Eighth International Geographic Congress). Vol. XIII, pp. 218-219, 1 ill., June, 1902.

National Geographic Society's Notable Year (Address by Maj. Gen. A. W. Greely). Vol. XXXVII, pp. 338-345, 2 ills., Apr., 1920.

Origin of Stefansson's Blond Eskimo. By Maj. Gen. A. W. Greely. Vol. XXIII, pp. 1224-1238, 10 ills., 1 page map, Dec., 1912.

Recent Geographic Advances, Especially in Africa. By Maj. Gen. A. W. Greely. Vol. XXII, pp. 383-398, 5 ills., 5 page maps, Apr., 1911.

Russia in Recent Literature. By Maj. Gen. A. W. Greely. Vol. XVI, pp. 564-568, Dec., 1905.

Greely, (Brig. Gen.) John N.:

Iran in Wartime : Through Fabulous Persia, Hub of the Middle East, Americans, Britons, and Iranians Keep Sinews of War Moving to the Embattled Soviet Union. By John N. Greely. Vol. LXXXIV, pp. 129-156, 26 ills., 1 page map, Aug., 1943.

Greely's "Handbook of Alaska." By Gilbert H. Grosvenor. Vol. XX, pp. 491-492, May, 1909.

Green, James A.:

Paricutín, the Cornfield That Grew a Volcano (Mexico). By James A. Green. Vol. LXXXV, pp. 129-164, 16 ills. in black and white, 21 ills. in color, 1 third-page map, Feb., 1944.

Green, (Dr.) Thomas E.:

Making of a Japanese Newspaper. By Dr. Thomas E. Green. Vol. XXXVIII, pp. 327-334, 5 ills., Oct., 1920.

Green Gruyère, Home of a Swiss Cheese. 23 ills. in color from natural-color photographs by Bernard F. Rogers, Jr. Vol. LXX, pp. 145-168, Aug., 1936.

Green Mountain State (Vermont). By Herbert Corey. Vol. LI, pp. 333-369, 40 ills. in black and white, 6 ills. in color, 1 page map, Mar., 1927.

Green River, Utah-Wyoming :

Experiences in the Grand Canyon. By Ellsworth and Emory Kolb. Vol. XXVI, pp. 99-184, 70 ills., 1 page map, Aug., 1914.

Greenland:

Americans Stand Guard in Greenland. By Andrew H. Brown. Vol. XC, pp. 457-500, 23 ills. in black and white, 19 ills. in color, 1 page map, Oct., 1946.

Bowdoin (Ship) in North Greenland : Arctic Explorers Place Tablet to Commemorate Sacrifices of the Lady Franklin Bay Expedition. By Donald B. MacMillan. Vol. XLVII, pp. 677-722, 49 ills., June, 1925.

Coast Guard Patrol in Greenland. 9 ills. in color from natural-color photographs by Lieut. Thomas S. La Farge. Vol. LXXXIII, pp. 565-572, May, 1943.

Desolate Greenland, Now an American Outpost. 17 ills. from photographs ; 12 ills. by Willie Knutsen ; 4 ills. by F. Vogel. Vol. LXXX, pp. 393-406, Sept., 1941.

First Natural-Color Photographs from the Arctic. 22 ills. in color from natural-color photographs by Jacob Gayer and Maynard Owen Williams. Vol. XLIX, pp. 300-317, Mar., 1926.

Flying Around the North Atlantic. By Anne Morrow Lindbergh. Foreword by Charles A. Lindbergh. Vol. LXVI, pp. 259-337, 82 ills., 1 two-page and 1 two-thirds-page maps, Sept., 1934.

Flying Over the Arctic. By Lieut. Comdr. Richard E. Byrd. Vol. XLVIII, pp. 519-532, 10 ills., Nov., 1925.

Greenland—U. S. Base in the Arctic. 5 ills. in color from natural-color photographs by James K. Penfield. Vol. LXXXII, pp. 373-376, Sept., 1942.

Greenland from 1898 to Now : "Captain Bob," Who Went North with Peary, Tells of 42 Years of Exploration in the Orphan Island of New Aerial and Naval Interest. By Robert A. Bartlett. Vol. LXXVIII, pp. 111-140, 25 ills., 1 two-page map, July, 1940.

Greenland Turns to America. By James K. Penfield. Vol. LXXXII, pp. 369-383, 7 ills. in black and white, 5 ills. in color, 1 two-page map, Sept., 1942.

Hunting Trip to Northern Greenland. By Fullerton Merrill. Vol. XI, pp. 118-122, Mar., 1900.

Greenland—*Continued*

MacMillan Arctic Expedition Returns: U. S. Navy Planes Make First Series of Overhead Flights in the Arctic and National Geographic Society Staff Obtains Valuable Data and Specimens for Scientific Study. By Donald B. MacMillan. Vol. XLVIII, pp. 477-518, 42 ills., Nov., 1925.

Naturalist with MacMillan in the Arctic. By Walter N. Koelz. Vol. XLIX, pp. 299-318, 22 ills. in color, Mar., 1926.

Origin of Stefansson's Blond Eskimo. By Maj. Gen. A. W. Greely. Vol. XXIII, pp. 1224-1238, 10 ills., 1 page map, Dec., 1912.

Scenes from Greenland. Vol. XX, pp. 877-891, 15 ills., Oct., 1909.

Servicing Arctic Airbases. By Robert A. Bartlett. Vol. LXXXIX, pp. 602-616, 3 ills. in black and white, 10 ills. in color, 1 half-page map, May, 1946.

Uncle Sam's Icebox Outposts. 19 ills. in color from natural-color photographs by John E. Schneider and Robert B. Sykes, Jr. Vol. XC, pp. 473-496, Oct., 1946.

Greens Grow for GI's on Soilless Ascension. By W. Robert Moore. Vol. LXXXVIII, pp. 219-230, 12 ills., Aug., 1945.

Gregory, Herbert E.:

Lonely Australia: The Unique Continent. By Herbert E. Gregory. Vol. XXX, pp. 473-568, 68 ills., 1 two-page and 4 half-page maps, Dec., 1916.

Gregory, W. M.:

Ore-Boat Unloaders. By W. M. Gregory. Vol. XVIII, pp. 343-345, 1 ill., May, 1907.

Grenada (Island), West Indies:

British West Indian Interlude. By Anne Rainey Langley. Vol. LXXIX, pp. 1-46, 23 ills. in black and white, 21 ills. in color, 2 page maps, Jan., 1941.

Grenfell, (Sir) Wilfred T.:

Land of Eternal Warring (Labrador). By Sir Wilfred T. Grenfell. Vol. XXI, pp. 665-690, 24 ills., Aug., 1910.

Grew, Joseph C.:

Japan and the Pacific. By Joseph C. Grew. Vol. LXXXV, pp. 385-414, 29 ills., 17 island maps (two pages), Apr., 1944.

Waimangu and the Hot-Spring Country of New Zealand: The World's Greatest Geyser Is One of Many Natural Wonders in a Land of Inferno and Vernal Paradise. By Joseph C. Grew. Vol. XLVIII, pp. 109-130, 19 ills., 1 third-page map, Aug., 1925.

Griffin, Donald R.:

Mystery Mammals of the Twilight (Bats). By Donald R. Griffin. Vol. XC, pp. 117-134, 19 ills., July, 1946.

Griffis, William Elliot:

Empire of the Risen Sun (Japan). By William Elliot Griffis. Vol XLIV, pp. 415-443, 21 ills., Oct., 1923.

Griffis, William Elliot—*Continued*

Japan, Child of the World's Old Age: An Empire of Mountainous Islands, Whose Alert People Constantly Conquer Harsh Forces of Land, Sea, and Sky. By William Elliot Griffis. Vol. LXIII, pp. 257-301, 37 ills. in black and white, 12 ills. in color, Mar., 1933.

Griffiths, William Arthur:

Malta: The Halting Place of Nations: First Account of Remarkable Prehistoric Tombs and Temples Recently Unearthed on the Island. By William Arthur Griffiths. Vol. XXXVII, pp. 445-478, 35 ills., 1 third-page map, May, 1920.

Griggs, Robert F.:

Awarded Jane M. Smith Life Membership. Vol. XXXVII, p. 342, Apr., 1920.

Cause of Earthquakes. By Robert F. Griggs. Vol. XLIV, pp. 443-451, 5 ills., 1 page map, Oct., 1923.

Our Greatest National Monument: The National Geographic Society Completes Its Explorations in the Valley of Ten Thousand Smokes. By Robert F. Griggs. Vol XL, pp. 219-292, 73 ills. in black and white, 16 ills. in color, 1 page and 1 three-quarters-page maps, Sept., 1921.

Valley of Ten Thousand Smokes: An Account of the Discovery and Exploration of the Most Wonderful Volcanic Region in the World. By Robert F. Griggs. Vol. XXXIII, pp. 115-169, 46 ills., 1 half-page map, panorama, Feb., 1918.

Valley of Ten Thousand Smokes: National Geographic Society Explorations in the Katmai District of Alaska. By Robert F. Griggs. Vol. XXXI, pp. 12-68, 51 ills., 1 half-page map, Jan., 1917.

Grimble, (Sir) Arthur:

War Finds Its Way to Gilbert Islands: United States Forces Dislodge Japanese from Enchanted Atolls Which Loom Now as Stepping Stones along South Sea Route from Australia to Hawaii. By Sir Arthur Grimble. Vol. LXXXIII, pp. 71-92, 19 ills., 1 half-page map, Jan., 1943.

Grimes, S. A.:

Birds on the Home Front. 30 ills. in color from natural-color photographs by Arthur A. Allen, S. A. Grimes, and others. Vol. LXXXIV, pp. 33-56, July, 1943.

Grimm's Fairyland in Northwestern Germany. 14 ills. in color from natural-color photographs by Hans Hildenbrand and Wilhelm Tobien. Vol. LIX, pp. 640-649, May, 1931.

Grimsby, England:

Europe's Endangered Fish Supply: War and the North Sea Fisheries. Vol. XXVII, pp. 141-152, 9 ills., 1 half-page map, Feb., 1915.

Grimshaw, Beatrice:

In the Savage South Seas. By Beatrice Grimshaw. Vol. XIX, pp. 1-19, 21 ills., Jan., 1908.

Grini (Concentration Camp), Norway:

White War in Norway. By Thomas R. Henry. Vol. LXXXVIII, pp. 617-640, 23 ills., 1 three-quarters-page map, Nov., 1945.

Grinnell, Alton G.:

Our Army Versus a Bacillus. By Alton G. Grinnell. Vol. XXIV, pp. 1146-1152, 5 ills., 1 diagram, Oct., 1913.

Griscom, Lloyd C.:

Annual Dinner of the National Geographic Society (Speech by Lloyd C. Griscom). Vol. XVII, pp. 22-37, Jan., 1906.

Groff, G. Weidman:

Landscaped Kwangsi, China's Province of Pictorial Art. By G. Weidman Groff and T. C. Lau. Vol. LXXII, pp. 671-710, 33 ills., 1 half-page map, Dec., 1937.

Grosvenor, Edwin A.:

Constantinople and Sancta Sophia. By Edwin A. Grosvenor. Vol. XXVII, pp. 459-482, 21 ills., May, 1915.

Evolution of Russian Government. By Edwin A. Grosvenor. Vol. XVI, pp. 309-332, 16 ills., July, 1905.

Growth of Russia. By Edwin A. Grosvenor. Vol. XI, pp. 169-185, 2 page and 3 half-page maps, May, 1900.

Races of Europe: The Graphic Epitome of a Never-Ceasing Human Drama. The Aspirations, Failures, Achievements, and Conflicts of the Polyglot People of the Most Densely Populated Continent. By Edwin A. Grosvenor. Vol. XXXIV, pp. 441-534, 62 ills., 2 page maps, special map supplement, Dec., 1918.

Siberia. By Edwin A. Grosvenor. Vol. XII, pp. 317-324, Sept., 1901.

Grosvenor, Gilbert:

Admiral Byrd Receives New Honor from The Society (Address by Gilbert Grosvenor). Vol. LVIII, pp. 228-238, 4 ills., Aug., 1930.

Air Conquest: From the Early Days of Giant Kites and Birdlike Gliders, the National Geographic Society Has Aided and Encouraged the Growth of Aviation (History of The Society). Vol. LII, pp. 233-242, 13 ills., Aug., 1927.

Alaska's New Railway. Vol. XXXVIII, pp. 567-589, 20 ills., Dec., 1915.

Alexander Graham Bell's appreciation of. Vol. XXIII, p. 274, Mar., 1912.

America from the Air: No Such Series of Airplane Views Has Ever Before Been Printed. Vol. XLVI, pp. 85-92, 8 ills., July, 1924.

American Association for the Advancement of Science. By Gilbert H. Grosvenor. Vol. X, pp. 355-359, Sept., 1899.

American Development of the Philippines. Vol. XIV, pp. 197-203, 4 ills., May, 1903.

American Progress in Habana. Vol. XIII, pp. 97-108, 10 ills., Mar., 1902.

Amundsen's Attainment of the South Pole. Vol. XXIII, pp. 205-208, 1 ill., 1 page map, Feb., 1912.

Grosvenor, Gilbert—*Continued*

Annual Dinner of the National Geographic Society (Early History of The Society). Vol. XVII, pp. 22-37, Jan., 1906.

Appeal to Members of the National Geographic Society (Food Conservation). Vol. XXXII, pp. 347-348, 2 ills., Apr., 1918.

Appointment of Gilbert H. Grosvenor as Editor, April 1, 1899. Vol. XXIII, p. 274, Mar., 1912.

Belgian Antarctic Expedition. Vol. X, pp. 229-230, June, 1899.

Benguet—The Garden of the Philippines. Vol. XIV, pp. 203-210, 6 ills., May, 1903.

Bird City (Laysan Island, Hawaii). Vol. XV, pp. 494-498, 6 ills., Dec., 1904.

Black Hills (South Dakota), Once Hunting Grounds of the Red Men. Vol. LII, pp. 305-329, 18 ills., Sept., 1927.

Boys' and Girls' Agricultural Clubs. Vol. XXII, pp. 639-641, 4 ills., July, 1911.

British Antarctic Expedition. Vol. XII, pp. 339-345, Sept., 1901.

Bulgaria, the Peasant State. Vol. XIX, pp. 760-773, 14 ills., Nov., 1908.

Capitol (United States), Wonder Building of the World. By Gilbert Grosvenor. Vol. XLIII, pp. 603-638, 17 ills., June, 1923.

Chairman, committee of arrangements, for banquet honoring Peary. Vol. XVIII, p. 58, Jan., 1907.

Charting a Coast-Line of 26,000 Miles (Alaska). Vol. XX, pp. 608-609, July, 1909.

Château Land—France's Pageant on the Loire. Vol. LVIII, pp. 466-475, 10 ills. in color, Oct., 1930.

Citizen Army of Switzerland. Vol. XXVIII, pp. 502-510, 7 ills., Nov., 1915.

Colossal Natural Bridges of Utah. Vol. XV, pp. 367-369, 2 ills., Sept., 1904.

Commander Byrd Receives the Hubbard Gold Medal: The First Explorer to Reach the North Pole by Air Receives Coveted Honor at Brilliant National Geographic Society Reception (Address by Gilbert Grosvenor). Vol. L, pp. 377-388, 5 ills., 1 chart, Sept., 1926.

Commander Peary's New Vessel. Vol. XVI, p. 192, Apr., 1905.

Comments on the Notable Features of the First Census Report of the Philippine Islands. Vol. XVI, pp. 191-192, Apr., 1905.

Conquest of Bubonic Plague in the Philippines. Vol. XIV, pp. 185-195, 7 ills., May, 1903.

Conquest of the Sahara by the Automobile. Vol. XLV, pp. 87-93, 9 ills., 1 three-quarters-page map, Jan., 1924.

Correct Display of the Stars and Stripes. By Gilbert Grosvenor and B. McCandless. Vol. XXXII, pp. 404-413, 8 ills., Oct., 1917.

Cousin of President William Howard Taft. Vol. XVII, p. 25, Jan., 1906.

Discovery of Cancer in Plants. Vol. XXIV, pp. 53-70, 12 ills., Jan., 1913.

Discovery of the North Pole. Vol. XXI, pp. 63-82, Jan., 1910.

Grosvenor, Gilbert—*Continued*

Dr. Bell's Man-Lifting Kite. By Gilbert H. Grosvenor. Vol. XIX, pp. 35-52, 27 ills., Jan., 1908.

Dr. Bell's Tetrahedral Tower. By Gilbert H. Grosvenor. Vol. XVIII, pp. 671-675, 7 ills., Oct., 1907.

Drifting Across the Pole. Vol. XVII, pp. 40-42, 1 ill., Jan., 1906.

Du Chaillu, Paul. *See* Paul Du Chaillu.

Editor of Report of Proceedings of Eighth International Geographic Congress. Vol. XVI, p. 199, Apr., 1905.

Editorial Policy. *See* National Geographic Society : Editorial Department.

Educating the Filipinos. Vol. XVI, pp. 46-49, Jan., 1905.

Election of Gilbert Grosvenor as President of The Society. Vol. XXXVII, p. 345, Apr., 1920.

European Tributes to Peary. Vol. XXI, pp. 536-540, 4 ills., June, 1910.

Europe's Endangered Fish Supply : The War and the North Sea Fisheries. Vol. XXVII, pp. 141-152, 9 ills., 1 half-page map, Feb., 1915.

Explorations in Alaska. Vol. X, pp. 269-271, July, 1899.

Explorations in Central East Africa. Vol. XII, pp. 42-43, Jan., 1901.

Explorations in Peru. Vol. XXIII, pp. 416-422, 7 ills., 1 half-page map, Apr., 1912.

Explorations in Tibet. Vol. XIV, pp. 353-355, Sept., 1903.

Farthest North (Report from Adm. Peary). Vol. XVII, pp. 638-644, 9 ills., Nov., 1906.

First Airship Flight Around the World : Dr. Hugo Eckener Tells of an Epochal Geographic Achievement upon the Occasion of the Bestowal of the National Geographic Society's Special Gold Medal (Presentation Address by Gilbert Grosvenor). Vol. LVII, pp. 653-688, 37 ills., June, 1930.

Fishes That Build Nests and Take Care of Their Young. Vol. XVIII, pp. 400-412, 16 ills., June, 1907.

Fishes That Carry Lanterns. Vol. XXI, pp. 453-456, 5 ills., May, 1910.

Flags Famous in American History. By Gilbert Grosvenor and Byron McCandless. Vol. XXXII, pp. 341-361, 92 ills. in color, Oct., 1917.

Flags of Austria-Hungary, Bulgaria, Germany, and Turkey. By Gilbert Grosvenor and Byron McCandless. Vol. XXXII, pp. 386-388, 38 ills. in color, Oct., 1917.

Flags of Europe, Asia, and Africa. By Gilbert Grosvenor and Byron McCandless. Vol. XXXII, pp. 372-385, 100 ills. in color, Oct., 1917.

Flags of Our Army, Navy, and Government Departments. By Gilbert Grosvenor and Byron McCandless. Vol. XXXII, pp. 305-322, 3 ills. in black and white, 300 ills. in color, Oct., 1917.

Grosvenor, Gilbert—*Continued*

Flags of Pan-America. By Gilbert Grosvenor and Byron McCandless. Vol. XXXII, pp. 361-369, 62 ills. in color, Oct., 1917.

Flags of the British Empire. By Gilbert Grosvenor and Byron McCandless. Vol. XXXII, pp. 378-385, 158 ills. in color, Oct., 1917.

Flags of the World. By Gilbert Grosvenor and William J. Showalter. Vol. LXVI, pp. 339-396, 10 ills. in black and white, 808 ills. in color, Sept., 1934.

Flying. By Gilbert Grosvenor. Vol. LXIII, pp. 585-630, 33 ills. in black and white, 17 ills. in duotone, May, 1933.

Foreign-Born of the United States. Vol. XXVI, pp. 265-271, 14 diagrams, Sept., 1914.

Four Prominent Geographers. Vol. XVIII, pp. 425-428, 4 ills., June, 1907.

Geographic Achievement. Vol. XXIV, pp. 667-668, June, 1913.

Geographic Facts from Report of the Taft Philippine Commission. Vol. XII, pp. 114-119, Mar., 1901.

German Nation. Vol. XXVI, pp. 275-310, 28 ills., Sept., 1914.

German Route to India. By Gilbert H. Grosvenor. Vol. XI, pp. 202-204, 1 page map, May, 1900.

German South Polar Expedition. Vol. XII, p. 311, Aug., 1901.

Germany's Air Program. Vol. XXXIII, p. 114, Jan., 1918.

Germany's Dream of World Domination. Vol. XXXIII, pp. 559-567, 3 ills., 1 page map, June, 1918.

Gilbert Grosvenor Trail, Antarctica. Vol. LVIII, pp. 184, 193, 198 ; air view 218, Aug., 1930.

Great Falls of the Potomac. By Gilbert Grosvenor. Vol. LIII, pp. 385-400, 19 ills., Mar., 1928.

Great Natural Bridges of Utah. Vol. XVIII, pp. 199-204, 3 ills., Mar., 1907.

Greek Bronzes. Text regarding requests for photographs. Vol. XXIII, p. 104, Jan., 1912.

Greely's "Handbook of Alaska." By Gilbert H. Grosvenor. Vol. XX, pp. 491-492, May, 1909.

Haiti and Its Regeneration by the United States. Vol. XXXVIII, pp. 497-511, 10 ills., Dec., 1920.

Harriman Alaska Expedition in Coöperation with the Washington Academy of Sciences. By Gilbert H. Grosvenor. Vol. X, pp. 225-227, June, 1899.

Hawaiian Islands : America's Strongest Outpost of Defense—The Volcanic and Floral Wonderland of the World. By Gilbert Grosvenor. Vol. XLV, pp. 115-238, 106 ills. in black and white, 21 ills. in color, 1 page and 5 half-page maps, 1 diagram, Feb., 1924.

Healer of Humanity's Wounds. Vol. XXXIV, pp. 308-324, 16 ills., Oct., 1918.

Henry Gannett (Tribute to Late President of The Society). Vol. XXVI, pp. 609-613, 1 ill., Dec., 1914.

Grosvenor, Gilbert—*Continued*

Heroic Flags of the Middle Ages. By Gilbert Grosvenor and Byron McCandless. Vol. XXXII, pp. 388-399, 96 ills. in color, Oct., 1917.

History of National Geographic Society. *See* National Geographic Society : History.

Home, Summer. *See* Grosvenor, Gilbert : Photographs by : Beinn Bhreagh.

Home, Wild Acres, Maryland. Vol. LI, ill. 202, Feb., 1927. Vol. LVII, ill. 592, May, 1930.

Honors for Amundsen (Presentation of Hubbard Medal). Vol. XIX, pp. 55-76, 13 ills., Jan., 1908.

Honors to Amundsen and Peary (Presentation of Special Gold Medal to Amundsen). Vol. XXIV, pp. 113-130, 5 ills., Jan., 1913.

Honors to Colonel Goethals : The Presentation by President Woodrow Wilson of the National Geographic Society Special Gold Medal, and Addresses by Secretary of State Bryan, the French Ambassador, the German Ambassador, and Congressman James R. Mann (Address by Gilbert H. Grosvenor.) Vol. XXV, pp. 677-690, 6 ills., June, 1914.

Honors to Peary (Presentation of Hubbard Medal). Vol. XVIII, pp. 49-60, 1 ill., Jan., 1907.

Honors to the American Navy (Banquet). Vol. XX, pp. 77-95, Jan., 1909.

Hospital Heroes Convict the Cootie. Vol. XXXIII, p. 510, June, 1918.

How the World Is Shod. Vol. XIX, pp. 649-660, Sept., 1908.

Hubbard Medals Awarded to Stratosphere Explorers : Presentation by General Pershing (Address by Gilbert Grosvenor.) Vol. LXIX, p. 713, May, 1936.

Ice-Wrapped Continent. By Gilbert H. Grosvenor. Vol. XVIII, pp. 95-117, 20 ills., 1 half-page map, Feb., 1907.

Improvements in the City of Manila. Vol. XIV, pp. 195-197, 1 ill., May, 1903.

In Honor of the Army and Aviation (Banquet). Vol. XXII, pp. 267-284, 1 ill., Mar., 1911.

Inoculating the Ground. Vol. XV, pp. 225-228, 2 ills., May, 1904.

Insignia and Decorations of the United States Armed Forces. By Gilbert Grosvenor. Vol. LXXXVII, pp. 185-186, Feb., 1945.

Insignia of the Uniformed Forces of the United States. By Gilbert Grosvenor and Byron McCandless. Vol. XXXII, pp. 413-419, 318 ills., Oct., 1917.

Insignia of the United States Armed Forces. By Gilbert Grosvenor. With 991 illustrations in color. Vol. LXXXIII, p. 651, June, 1943.

Introducing Reindeer into Labrador. Vol. XVIII, p. 686, Oct., 1907.

Italian Race. By Gilbert Grosvenor. Vol. XXXIII, p. 47, Jan., 1918.

John Wesley Powell. By Gilbert H. Grosvenor. Vol. XIII, pp. 392-394, 1 ill., Nov., 1902.

Lake Grosvenor, Alaska, named for Gilbert Grosvenor. Vol. XL, pp. 222, 287 ; ill. 284, 288, Sept., 1921. Vol. L, ill. 89, July, 1926.

Grosvenor, Gilbert—*Continued*

Land of the Best (United States). By Gilbert H. Grosvenor. Vol. XXIX, pp. 327-430, 71 ills. in black and white, 33 ills. in color, panorama, Apr., 1916.

Lessons from Japan. Vol. XV, pp. 221-225, 3 ills., May, 1904.

Lloyd's Journey Across the Great Pygmy Forest (Belgian Congo). Vol. X, pp. 26-30, Jan., 1899.

MacMillan Arctic Expedition Sails. Vol. XLVIII, pp. 225-226, 3 ills., Aug., 1925.

MacMillan in the Field. Vol. XLVIII, pp. 473-476, 3 ills., Oct., 1925.

Marking the Alaskan Boundary. Vol. XIX, pp. 176-189, 16 ills., Mar., 1908.

Married Elsie May Bell. Vol. XXIII, p. 274. Mar., 1912. Vol. LXIX, p. 148, Jan., 1936.

Maryland Pilgrimage : Visits to Hallowed Shrines Recall the Major Rôle Played by This Prosperous State in the Development of Popular Government in America. By Gilbert Grosvenor. Vol. LI, pp. 133-212, 88 ills., special map supplement, Feb., 1927.

Memorial to Peary : The National Geographic Society Dedicates Monument in Arlington National Cemetery to Discoverer of the North Pole (Address by Gilbert Grosvenor). Vol. XLI, pp. 639-645, 4 ills., June, 1922.

Mission of the *Diana*. Vol. X, p. 273, July, 1899.

Mr. Coolidge Becomes a Member of The Society's Board of Trustees. Vol. LV, p. 750, June, 1929.

Mr. Roosevelt's "African Game Trails." Vol. XXI, pp. 953-962, 9 ills., Nov., 1910.

Mr. Ziegler and the National Geographic Society. Vol. XIV, pp. 251-254, June, 1903.

Modern Viking (Amundsen). Vol. XVII, pp. 38-40, 1 page map, Jan., 1906.

Most Historic Lands on Earth. Vol. XXVI, pp. 614-615, 1 page map, Dec., 1914.

Mount Grosvenor, China. Vol. LVIII, p. 415, color plates VII, X, Oct., 1930.

Muir Glacier. Vol. XIV, pp. 441-445, 2 ills., 1 fourth-page map, Dec., 1903.

Murman Coast : Arctic Gateway for American and Allied Expeditionary Forces in Northern European Russia. Vol. XXXV, pp. 331-348, 30 ills., 1 half-page map, Apr., 1919.

Mystery of Auroras : National Geographic Society and Cornell University Study Spectacular Displays in the Heavens. Vol. LXXV, pp. 689-690, May, 1939.

Nansen received by Dr. Grosvenor. Vol. LVIII, ill. 22, July, 1930.

Nansen's "Farthest North" Eclipsed. Vol. XI, pp. 411-413, Oct., 1900.

National Geographic Society (Discovery of the North Pole). Vol. XXI, p. 276, Mar., 1910.

National Geographic Society (Dr. Grosvenor's Work as Editor of The Magazine). Vol. XXIII, pp. 273-298, 5 ills., Mar., 1912.

National Geographic Society (Early History of The Society). Vol. XXIII, pp. 272-298, 5 ills., Mar., 1912.

Grosvenor, Gilbert—*Continued*

National Geographic Society (Expeditions). Vol. XXXIII, p. 170, Feb., 1918.

National Geographic Society (Jane M. Smith Bequest). Vol. XXIII, p. 104, Jan., 1912.

National Geographic Society (Proceedings). By Gilbert Grosvenor. Vol. X, pp. 474-475, Nov., 1899.

National Geographic Society (Proceedings). Vol. XXVII, p. 218, Feb., 1915.

National Geographic Society (Roosevelt's African Expedition). Vol. XXI, pp. 365-370, 5 ills., Apr., 1910.

National Geographic Society Alaska Expedition. Vol. XX, pp. 581-584, June, 1909.

National Geographic Society and Geographic Work. Vol. XX, pp. 485-487, May, 1909.

National Geographic Society and Its Magazine. By Gilbert Grosvenor. Vol. LXIX, pp. 123-164, 24 ills., Jan., 1936.

National Geographic Society and Its New Building. Vol. XXV, pp. 161-170, 11 ills., Apr., 1914.

National Geographic Society Completes Its Gifts of Big Trees. Vol. XL, pp. 85-86, July, 1921.

National Geographic Society Expedition to Martinique and St. Vincent. Vol. XIII, pp. 183-184, 2 ills., June, 1902.

National Geographic Society Expeditions in New Mexico. By Gilbert Grosvenor. Vol. LVI, p. 737, Dec., 1929.

National Geographic Society's Alaskan Expedition. Vol. XXI, p. 370, Apr., 1910.

National Geographic Society's Expedition in the West Indies. Vol. XIII, pp. 209-213, 2 half-page maps, June, 1902.

National Geographic Society's Memorial to American Troops: Fountain and Water Supply System Presented to Historic French Town of Cantigny, Where Our Overseas Soldiers Won Their First Victory in the World War. Vol. XLIV, pp. 675-678, 4 ills., Dec., 1923.

National Geographic Society's Notable Year (Announcement of the Election of Dr. Grosvenor as President of The Society). Vol. XXXVII, pp. 338-345, 2 ills., Apr., 1920.

National Geographic Society's Yünnan Province Expedition. By Gilbert Grosvenor. Vol. XLVII, pp. 493-498, 5 ills., Apr., 1925.

Naval Flags of the World. By Gilbert Grosvenor and Byron McCandless. Vol. XXXII, pp. 347-369, 211 ills. in color, Oct., 1917.

New Cone of Mont Pelée. Vol. XIV, pp. 422-423, 2 ills., Nov., 1903.

New English Province of Northern Nigeria. Vol. XV, pp. 433-442, 9 ills., Nov., 1904.

New National Geographic Society Expedition (Chaco Canyon). Vol. XXXIX, pp. 637-643, 7 ills., June, 1921.

Next International Geographical Congress to be Held in Washington. By Gilbert H. Grosvenor. Vol. XII, pp. 351-357, 4 ills., Oct., 1901.

Nicaragua, Largest of Central American Republics. Vol. LI, pp. 370-378, 15 ills., Mar., 1927.

Nicaragua Canal. Vol. XII, pp. 28-32, 2 ills., 1 half-page map, Jan., 1901.

Grosvenor, Gilbert—*Continued*

No Man's Land—Spitzbergen. Vol. XVIII, pp. 455-458, July, 1907.

North Pole (Appointment of Committee to Consider Claims of Peary and Cook). Vol. XX, pp. 921-922, Nov., 1909.

North Pole (Resolutions of The Society Acknowledging Peary's Discovery). Vol. XX, pp. 1008-1009, Nov., 1909.

Notes on Macedonia. Vol. XIX, pp. 790-802, 15 ills., 1 page map, Nov., 1908.

Notes on Panama and Colombia. Vol. XIV, pp. 458-466, 12 ills., Dec., 1903.

Notes on Turbulent Nicaragua. Vol. XX, pp. 1102-1116, 13 ills., 1 page map, Dec., 1909.

Office of the Editor. Vol. XXV, ill. 460, Apr., 1914.

One Hundred British Seaports. Vol. XXXI, pp. 84-94, 10 ills., 1 page map, Jan., 1917.

Our Big Trees Saved. Vol. XXXI, pp. 1-11, 10 ills., Jan., 1917.

Our Colored Pictures. Vol. XXI, pp. 965-967, Nov., 1910.

Our Desert Panorama. Text accompanying special supplement. Vol. XXII, pp. 409-410, 1 ill., Apr., 1911.

Our Flag Number. By Gilbert Grosvenor. Vol. XXXII, pp. 281-284, 2 ills., Oct., 1917.

Our Foreign-Born Citizens. Vol. XXXI, pp. 95-130, 36 ills., 1 page map, 8 diagrams, Feb., 1917.

Our Heralds of Storm and Flood (U. S. Weather Bureau). By Gilbert H. Grosvenor. Vol. XVIII, pp. 586-601, 15 ills., 1 chart, Sept., 1907.

Our Immigration During 1904. Vol. XVI, pp. 15-27, 6 ills., 2 charts, Jan., 1905.

Our Mountain Panorama (Canadian Rockies). Vol. XXII, p. 521, 1 ill., June, 1911.

Our Policemen of the Air (Birds). Vol. XXIV, p. 698, June, 1913.

Our State Flags. By Gilbert Grosvenor and Byron McCandless. Vol. XXXII, pp. 323-341, 1 ill. in black and white, 57 ills. in color, Oct., 1917.

Our State Flowers: Floral Emblems Chosen by the Commonwealths. By Gilbert Grosvenor. Vol. XXXI, pp. 481-517, 30 ills. in color, June, 1917.

Paul Du Chaillu (Dr. Grosvenor's First Guest). Vol. XIV, pp. 282-285, 1 ill., July, 1903.

Peary on the North Pole. Vol. XIV, pp. 28-29, 1 page map, Jan., 1903.

Peary to Try Again. Vol. XVIII, p. 281, Apr., 1907.

Peary's Explorations in the Far North. By Gilbert Grosvenor. Vol. XXXVII, pp. 318-322, 3 ills., Apr., 1920.

Peary's Polar Expedition. Vol. XIX, p. 447, June, 1908.

Peary's Work in 1900 and 1901. Vol. XII, pp. 357-361, 2 ills., Oct., 1901.

Peary's Work in 1901-1902. By Gilbert H. Grosvenor. Vol. XIII, pp. 384-386, Oct., 1902.

Grosvenor, Gilbert—*Continued*

Pennants of Patriotism 200 Years Ago. By Gilbert Grosvenor and Byron McCandless. Vol. XXXII, pp. 399-403, 75 ills. in color, Oct., 1917.

Plans for Reaching the South Pole. By Gilbert H. Grosvenor. Vol. X, pp. 316-319, Aug., 1899.

Practical Patriotism (National Geographic Society's War Work). Vol. XXXII, pp. 279-280, Sept., 1917.

President Calvin Coolidge is introduced by Dr. Grosvenor to Members of The Society on the occasion of the presentation of the Hubbard Gold Medals to Commander Richard E. Byrd and Floyd Bennett. Vol. L, p. 377, Sept., 1926.

President Coolidge Bestows Lindbergh Award: The National Geographic Society's Hubbard Medal Is Presented to Aviator Before the Most Notable Gathering in the History of Washington (Address by Gilbert Grosvenor). Vol. LIII, pp. 132-140, 4 ills., Jan., 1928.

President Herbert Hoover is introduced by Dr. Grosvenor to Members of The Society on the occasion of the presentation of The Society's Special Gold Medal to Amelia Earhart. Vol. LXII, pp. 358, 359, 362, Sept., 1932.

President Herbert Hoover is introduced by Dr. Grosvenor to Members of The Society on the occasion of the presentation of The Society's Special Gold Medal to Adm. Richard E. Byrd. Vol. LVIII, pp. 229, 231, Aug., 1930.

Price of Liberty, Equality, Fraternity. Vol. XXXIV, p. 377, Nov., 1918.

Progress of the National Geographic Society (Report by Gilbert H. Grosvenor). Vol. XXIV, pp. 251-256, 1 ill., Feb., 1913.

Progress on the Panama Canal. By Gilbert H. Grosvenor. Vol. XVI, pp. 467-475, 1 half-page map, Oct., 1905.

Prosperous Porto Rico. Vol. XVII, p. 712, Dec., 1906.

Race for the South Pole (Presentation of Hubbard Medal to Shackleton). Vol. XXI, pp. 185-186, Mar., 1910.

The "Races of Europe" Number. Vol. XXXIV, p. 440, Nov., 1918.

Railways, Rivers, and Strategic Towns in Manchuria. Vol. XI, pp. 326-327, Aug., 1900.

Reindeer in Alaska. By Gilbert H. Grosvenor. Vol. XIV, pp. 126-149, 17 ills., 1 half-page map, Apr., 1903.

Report of the Director and Editor of the National Geographic Society for the Year 1914. By Gilbert H. Grosvenor. Vol. XXVII, pp. 318-320, Mar., 1915.

Report of the Second Stratosphere Expedition. Vol. LXVIII, pp. 535-536, Oct., 1935.

Revelation of the Filipinos. By Gilbert H. Grosvenor. Vol. XVI, pp. 139-192, 130 ills., Apr., 1905.

Sagacity and Courage of Dogs: Instances of the Remarkable Intelligence and Unselfish Devotion of Man's Best Friend Among Dumb Animals. Vol. XXXV, pp. 253-275, 14 ills., Mar., 1919.

Grosvenor, Gilbert—*Continued*

Scientific Aspects of the MacMillan Arctic Expedition. Vol. XLVIII, pp. 349-354, 5 ills., Sept., 1925.

Servia and Montenegro. Vol. XIX, pp. 774-789, 24 ills., Nov., 1908.

Sex, Nativity, and Color of the People of the United States. By Gilbert H. Grosvenor. Vol. XII, pp. 381-389, 17 charts, Nov., 1901.

Shackleton's Farthest South. Vol. XX, pp. 398-402, 1 half-page map, Apr., 1909.

Sheep-Killers—The Pariahs of Dogkind. Vol. XXXV, pp. 275-280, 3 ills., Mar., 1919.

Snow Crystals. Vol. XV, pp. 30-37, 31 ills., Jan., 1904.

Society Announces New Flight into the Stratosphere. By Gilbert Grosvenor. Vol. LXVII, pp. 265-272, 2 ills. in black and white, 1 sketch map, Feb., 1935.

Society Awards Hubbard Medal to Anne Morrow Lindbergh (Address by Gilbert Grosvenor). Vol. LXV, pp. 791-794, 4 ills., June, 1934.

Society Takes Part in Three Geographic Expeditions. Vol. LXV, pp. 625-626, May, 1934.

Society's New "Book of Birds." Edited by Gilbert Grosvenor and Alexander Wetmore. Vol. LXXI, p. 723, June, 1937. Vol. LXXII, p. 183, Aug., 1937. Vol. LXXIV, p. 226, Aug., 1938; p. 775, Dec., 1938. Vol. LXXVII, p. 121, Jan., 1940.

Society's Special Medal Awarded to Amelia Earhart: First Woman to Receive Geographic Distinction at Brilliant Ceremony in the National Capital (Address by Gilbert Grosvenor). Vol. LXII, pp. 358-367, 7 ills., Sept., 1932.

Society's Special Medal Is Awarded to Dr. Thomas C. Poulter: Admiral Byrd's Second-in-Command and Senior Scientist Is Accorded High Geographic Honor (Presentation Is Made by Gilbert Grosvenor). Vol. LXXII, pp. 105-108, 2 ills., July, 1937.

Some Facts About Japan. Vol. XV, pp. 446-448, Nov., 1904.

Some of Our Immigrants. Vol. XVIII, pp. 317-334, 21 ills., May, 1907.

Son-in-law of Alexander Graham Bell. Vol. XXIII, p. 274, Mar., 1912.

South Polar Expedition (Proposed by Peary for Consideration of National Geographic Society). Vol. XXI, pp. 167-170, 1 page map, Feb., 1910.

South Polar Explorations. Vol. XXII, pp. 406-409, 4 ills., 1 page map, Apr., 1911.

Speediest Boat. Vol. XXII, pp. 875-878, 2 ills., Sept., 1911.

Spirit of The Geographic. Vol. XXXIV, pp. 434-440, 4 ills., Nov., 1918.

Story of the American Flag. By Gilbert Grosvenor and Byron McCandless. Vol. XXXII, pp. 286-303, 12 ills., Oct., 1917.

Streets and Palaces of Colorful India. Vol. L, pp. 60-85, 34 ills. in color, July, 1926.

Studies Planned for New Stratosphere Flight with Helium. Vol. LXVII, pp. 795-800, 5 ills., June, 1935.

Grosvenor, Gilbert—*Continued*

Suggested Field for Exploration (Volcanic Disturbances in Mexico, Central America, and the West Indies). Vol. XIV, pp. 290-291, July, 1903.

Supposed Birthplace of Civilizations. Vol. XVI, pp. 499-504, 6 ills., Nov., 1905.

Tailed People of Nigeria. Vol. XXIII, pp. 1239-1242, 3 ills., Dec., 1912.

Ten Thousand Smokes Now a National Monument. Vol. XXXV, pp. 359-366, 5 ills., Apr., 1919.

To Seek the Unknown in the Arctic: United States Navy Fliers to Aid MacMillan Expedition Under the Auspices of the National Geographic Society in Exploring Vast Area. Vol. XLVII, pp. 673-675, 1 ill., 1 half-page map, June, 1925.

Tribute by Admiral Byrd. Vol. LXXII, p. 106, July, 1937.

United States Government Telegraph and Cable Lines. Vol. XV, pp. 490-494, 3 page maps, Dec., 1904.

The U. S. Signal Corps. By Gilbert H. Grosvenor. Vol. XIV, pp. 467-468, Dec., 1903.

Value of the United States Forest Service. Vol. XX, pp. 29-41, 14 ills., Jan., 1909.

Voice Voyages by the National Geographic Society: A Tribute to the Geographical Achievements of the Telephone. Vol. XXIX, pp. 296-326, 15 ills., 1 chart, Mar., 1916.

Volcanoes. By Gilbert H. Grosvenor. Vol. XIII, pp. 204-208, 1 page map, June, 1902.

War and Ocean Geography. By Gilbert Grosvenor. Vol. XXXIV, pp. 230-242, 6 ills., 1 page map, Sept., 1918.

War Work of The Society directed by Gilbert Grosvenor. Vol. XXXIII, p. 375, Apr., 1918.

Wards of the United States. Vol. XXX, pp. 143-177, 36 ills., Aug., 1916.

Washington Through the Years: On Rolling Wooded Hills and Colonial Tobacco Fields, Where George Washington Dreamed Our Nation's Great Capital, His Gorgeous Vision Comes True. By Gilbert Grosvenor. Vol. LX, pp. 517-619, 67 ills. in black and white, 49 ills. in color, 1 page map, Nov., 1931.

What the United States Geological Survey Has Done in Twenty-five Years. Vol. XV, pp. 365-366, 2 ills., Sept., 1905.

What the United States Government Does to Promote Agriculture. Vol. XIV, pp. 35-39, Jan., 1903.

Where Our Moths and Butterflies Roam. Vol. LII, pp. 105-126, July, 1927.

Where the Sard Holds Sway. Vol. XLIX, pp. 464-474, 1 ill. in black and white, 9 ills. in color, Apr., 1926.

Women and Children of the East. Vol. XVIII, pp. 248-271, 28 ills., Apr., 1907.

Wonderland of Science. Vol. XXVII, pp. 153-169, 15 ills., Feb., 1915.

Work in the Arctic and Antarctic. Vol. XI, pp. 164-165, Apr., 1900.

World's Debt to France. Vol. XXVIII, pp. 491-501, 7 ills., Nov., 1915.

Grosvenor, Gilbert—*Continued*

World's Highest International Telephone Cable. Vol. LVIII, pp. 722-731, 8 ills., Dec., 1930.

World's Largest Free Balloon to Explore Stratosphere. Vol. LXVI, pp. 107-110, 2 ills., July, 1934.

Young Russia: The Land of Unlimited Possibilities. By Gilbert H. Grosvenor. Vol. XXVI, pp. 421-520, 85 ills. in black and white, 17 ills. in color, Nov., 1914.

Your Society Aids War Effort. Vol. LXXXIII, pp. 277-278, 1 ill., Feb., 1943.

Your Society Sponsors an Expedition to Explore the Stratosphere. Vol. LXV, pp. 528-530, 1 ill., Apr., 1934.

Ziegler Polar Expedition. Vol. XIV, pp. 414-417, 5 ills., Nov., 1903.

Addresses by Gilbert Grosvenor:

Byrd, Adm. Richard E., awarded The Society's Special Gold Medal. Vol. LVIII, pp. 229, 231, Aug., 1930.

Byrd, Adm. Richard E., honored at reception Vol. LXVIII, pp. 107-108, July, 1935.

Byrd, Commander Richard E., awarded the Hubbard Gold Medal. Vol. L, pp. 377, 383, Sept., 1926.

Earhart, Amelia, awarded The Society's Special Gold Medal. Vol. LXII, pp. 359, 362, Sept., 1932.

Eckener, Dr. Hugo, awarded The Society's Special Gold Medal. Vol. LVII, pp. 653, 655, 681, 688, June, 1930.

Ellsworth, Lincoln, awarded the Hubbard Medal. Vol. LXX, p. 36, July, 1936.

Goethals, Col. George W., awarded The Society's Special Gold Medal. Vol. XXV, pp. 679-680, June, 1914.

Lindbergh, Anne Morrow, awarded the Hubbard Medal. Vol. LXV, pp. 791-792, June, 1934.

Lindbergh, Charles A., awarded the Hubbard Medal. Vol. LIII, pp. 134, 137, Jan., 1928.

Peary, Robert E., Memorial unveiled in Arlington National Cemetery. Vol. XLI, pp. 641, 643, June, 1922.

Poulter, Dr. Thomas C., awarded The Society's Special Gold Medal. Vol. LXXII, p. 105, July, 1937.

Speech on opening of The Society's fifty-fifth annual series of lectures in Constitution Hall, Nov. 20, 1942. Vol. LXXXIII, pp. 277-278, Feb., 1943.

Stevens, Capt. Albert W., and Anderson, Capt. Orvil A., awarded Hubbard Medals. Vol. LXIX, p. 713, May, 1936.

Map Articles:

Geographic's New Map of Europe and the Mediterranean. By Gilbert Grosvenor. Text accompanying special map supplement in colors. Vol. LXXIII, pp. 525-528, 1 ill., Apr., 1938.

Geographic's New Map of Germany and Its Approaches: With a Review of The Society's Maps of Europe. By Gilbert Grosvenor. Text accompanying special map supplement in colors. Vol. LXXXVI, pp. 66-72, 1 ill., July, 1944.

Grosvenor, Gilbert—*Continued*

Map Articles—*Continued*

Heart of a Hemisphere : Of Vital Importance is the Area Portrayed in The Society's New Map of Mexico, Central America, and the West Indies. Text accompanying special map supplement in colors. Vol. LXXVI, pp. 739-740, 1 ill., Dec., 1939.

Indian Ocean Map Spans Far East News Centers. Text accompanying special map supplement in colors. Vol. LXXIX, pp. 345-346, 1 ill., Mar., 1941.

The Latest Map of Mexico. Text accompanying special map supplement in colors. Vol. XXX, p. 88, July, 1916.

Manchuria and Korea. Text accompanying special map supplement. Vol. XV, pp. 128-129, 2 half-page maps, Mar., 1904.

Map Links Classic World with 1940. Text accompanying special map supplement in colors. Vol. LXXVII, p. 338, Mar., 1940.

Map of Europe, Including the New Balkan States. Text accompanying special map supplement in colors. Vol. XXVI, pp. 191-192, Aug., 1914.

Map of Mediterranean Regions. Text accompanying special map supplement in colors. Vol. XXIII, p. 104, Jan., 1912.

Map of the New Germany. Vol. XXXV, pp. 545-546, 1 page map, June, 1919.

Map of the North Polar Regions. Text accompanying special map supplement in colors. Vol. XVIII, pp. 454-455, July, 1907.

Map of the Northern and Southern Hemispheres. Text accompanying special map supplement in colors. Vol. LXXXIII, pp. 481-483, Apr., 1943.

Map of the Philippines. Text accompanying special map supplement. Vol. XIII, p. 31, Jan., 1902.

Maps for Victory : National Geographic Society's Charts Used in War on Land, Sea, and in the Air. By Gilbert Grosvenor. Text accompanying special map supplement in colors. Vol. LXXXI, pp. 667-690, 28 ills., May, 1942.

National Geographic Map of Japan, Regions of Asia, and the Pacific. Text accompanying special map supplement in colors. Vol. LXXXV, pp. 415-416, Apr., 1944.

National Geographic Society's Map of Northeastern United States. Text accompanying special map supplement in colors. Vol. LXXXVIII, pp. 361-362, Sept., 1945.

National Geographic Society's New Map of Africa. By Gilbert Grosvenor. Text accompanying special map supplement in colors. Vol. LXVII, pp. 731-752, 20 ills. in duotone, June, 1935.

National Geographic Society's New Map of the World. Text accompanying special map supplement in colors. Vol. LXVIII, pp. 796-798, Dec., 1935.

National Geographic War-Zone Map. Text accompanying special map supplement in colors. Vol. XXXIII, p. 494, May, 1918.

New Map of Asia. Text accompanying special map supplement in colors. Vol. XXXIX, pp. 552-570, 17 ills., May, 1921.

Grosvenor, Gilbert—*Continued*

Map Articles—*Continued*

New Map of Europe : Showing the Boundaries Established by the Peace Conference at Paris and by Subsequent Decisions of the Supreme Council of the Allied and Associated Powers. By Ralph A. Graves. Text accompanying special map supplement in colors. Vol. XXXIX, pp. 157-177, 18 ills., Feb., 1921.

New Map of Europe Records War Changes. Text accompanying special map supplement in colors. Vol. LXXVII, p. 625, May, 1940.

New Map Shows Asia's Role in Global Warfare. Text accompanying special map supplement in colors. Vol. LXXXII, pp. 767-768, Dec., 1942.

New Map Shows Immense Pacific Battleground. Text accompanying special map supplement in colors. Vol. LXXXI, pp. 203-204, Feb., 1942.

New National Geographic Society Map Charts South America's Wartime Importance. Text accompanying special map supplement in colors. Vol. LXXXII, pp. 537-540, 2 ills., Oct., 1942.

New World Map Gives Backdrop for Headlines. Text accompanying special map supplement in colors. Vol. LXXX, pp. 741-742, 1 ill., Dec., 1941.

North Polar Map. Compiled by Gilbert Grosvenor. Vol. XX, p. 915, Oct., 1909.

Our Map of North America. Text accompanying special map supplement in colors. Vol. XLV, p. 580, May, 1924.

Our Map of the Countries of the Caribbean. Text accompanying special map supplement in colors. Vol. XLI, pp. 221-222, Feb., 1922.

Our Map of the Pacific. Text accompanying special map supplement in colors. Vol. XL, pp. 647-648, 1 half-page map, Dec., 1921.

Our Map of the Races of Europe. Text accompanying special map supplement in colors. Vol. XXXIV, pp. 535-536, Dec., 1918.

Our Map of the United States. Text accompanying special map supplement in colors. Vol. XLIII, p. 460, Apr., 1923.

Postwar Portrait of the United States. Text accompanying special map supplement in colors. Vol. XC, pp. 135-136, July, 1946.

Society's Map of Bible Lands. By Gilbert Grosvenor. Text accompanying special map supplement in colors. Vol. LXXIV, pp. 751-754, 3 ills., Dec., 1938.

Society's Map of South America. By Gilbert Grosvenor. Text accompanying special map supplement in colors. Vol. LXXII, pp. 809-810, Dec., 1937.

Society's Map of the Antarctic. Text accompanying special map supplement in colors. Vol. LXII, pp. 485-486, 1 ill., Oct., 1932.

Society's Map of the Reaches of New York City. Text accompanying special map supplement in colors. Vol. LXXV, pp. 491-492, April, 1939.

Society's New Caribbean Map : Mexico, Central America, and the West Indies—Gateway of Discovery. Text accompanying special map supplement in colors. Vol. LXVI, pp. 738-740, 1 ill., Dec., 1934.

Grosvenor, Gilbert—*Continued*

Map Articles—*Continued*

Society's New Map of Africa. Text accompanying special map supplement in colors. Vol. XLII, pp. 447-448, Oct., 1922.

Society's New Map of Asia. Text accompanying special map supplement in colors. Vol. LXIV, pp. 770-772, 1 ill., Dec., 1933.

Society's New Map of Bible Lands. Text accompanying special map supplement in colors. Vol. XC, pp. 815-816, Dec., 1946.

Society's New Map of Central Europe and the Mediterranean. Text accompanying special map supplement in colors. Vol. LXXVI, pp. 559-560, Oct., 1939.

Society's New Map of Europe. By Gilbert Grosvenor. Text accompanying special map supplement in colors. Vol. LVI, pp. 771-774, Dec., 1929.

Society's New Map of India and Burma. Text accompanying special map supplement in colors. Vol. LXXXIX, p. 544, Apr., 1946.

Society's New Map of South America. Text accompanying special map supplement in colors. Vol. XL, pp. 374-392, 17 ills., Oct., 1921.

Society's New Map of Southeast Asia. Text accompanying special map supplement in colors. Vol. LXXXVI, pp. 449, 450, 1 ill., Oct., 1944.

Society's New Map of Soviet Russia. Text accompanying special map supplement in colors. Vol. LXXXVI, pp. 716-718, Dec., 1944.

Society's New Map of the Pacific. By Gilbert Grosvenor. Text accompanying special map supplement in colors. Vol. LXX, pp. 793-796, Dec., 1936.

Society's New Map of the United States. Text accompanying special map supplement in colors. Vol. LXIII, pp. 650-652, 1 ill., May, 1933.

Society's New Map of the World. Text accompanying special map supplement in colors. Vol. XLII, pp. 690-691, Dec., 1922.

Southwest Trails from Horse to Motor. Text accompanying special map supplement in colors. Vol. LXXVII, p. 767, June, 1940.

The Story of the Map. Text accompanying special map supplement in colors. Vol. LXII, pp. 759-774, 11 ills., Dec., 1932.

The Travels of George Washington : Dramatic Episodes in His Career as the First Geographer of the United States. By William Joseph Showalter. Text accompanying special map supplement in colors. Vol. LXI, pp. 1-63, 50 ills., 4 maps, Jan., 1932.

Western Front Map Embraces Three Continents. Text accompanying special map supplement in colors. Vol. LXXXII, pp. 139-140, July, 1942.

Map Supplements edited by Gilbert Grosvenor :

Africa (Prepared from Latest Geographical Data by Gilbert H. Grosvenor, Editor). Vol. XX, special supplement in colors, 15½ x 20 inches, Mar., 1909.

Grosvenor, Gilbert—*Continued*

Map Supplements—*Continued*

Africa. Vol. XLII, special supplement in colors, 27 x 30 inches, Oct., 1922.

Africa, with Inset showing Airways and Relief. Vol. LXVII, special supplement in colors, 29 x 31½ inches, June, 1935.

Africa, with Insets of the Cape Verde Islands, Relief Map, and a Table of Airline Distances in Statute Miles. Vol. LXXXIII, special supplement in colors, 29¼ x 31½ inches, Feb., 1943.

Alaska. Vol. XV, special supplement in colors, 36 x 42 inches, May, 1904.

Alaska. Vol. XXV, special supplement in colors, 15¼ x 20 inches, Feb., 1914.

Alaskan Boundary Decision. Vol. XV, special supplement, 12 x 12½ inches, Jan., 1904.

Antarctic Regions, with Inset Maps showing Antarctic Archipelago, King Edward VII Land and Part of Marie Byrd Land, and Byrd's South Pole Flight. Vol. LXII, special supplement in colors, 19½ x 26½ inches, Oct., 1932.

Arctic Regions. Vol. XLVIII, special supplement in colors, 19¼ x 18 inches, Nov., 1925.

Asia and Adjacent Areas, with Table of Airline Distances in Statute Miles. Vol. LXXXII, special supplement in colors, 40 x 26½ inches, Dec., 1942.

Asia and Adjacent Regions. Vol. LXIV, special supplement in colors, 30¾ x 38 inches, Dec., 1933.

Asia and Adjoining Europe with a Portion of Africa. Vol. XXXIX, special supplement in colors, 28 x 36 inches, May, 1921.

Atlantic Ocean, with Inset of Isthmus of Panama. Vol. LXXVI, special supplement in colors, 25 x 31 inches, July, 1939.

Atlantic Ocean, with Inset of Isthmus of Panama and a Table of Airline Distances in Statute Miles. Vol. LXXX, special supplement in colors, 31¼ x 25 inches, Sept., 1941.

Balkan States and Central Europe. Vol. XXVI, special supplement in colors, 17 x 22½ inches, Aug., 1914.

Bible Lands and the Cradle of Western Civilization, with Insets showing Jerusalem, the Holy Land, Economic Development, Route of the Exodus, St. Paul's Travels, Crusades, and Empire of Alexander the Great. Vol. LXXIV, special supplement in colors, 25 x 35 inches, Dec., 1938.

Bible Lands and the Cradle of Western Civilization, with Insets showing the Holy Land Today, Holy Land in Biblical Times, Jerusalem, Traditional Route of the Exodus, St. Paul's Travels, and the Seven Churches, and the Crusades. Vol. XC, special supplement in colors, 32 x 22 inches, Dec., 1946.

Bird's-Eye View of the Panama Canal (Picture of a Relief Map). Vol. XXIII, special supplement in colors, 9 x 18 inches, Feb., 1912.

Grosvenor, Gilbert—*Continued*

Map Supplements—*Continued*

Canada, with Insets showing Natural Regions, Precipitation and Temperature, Main Natural Resources, Routes of Explorers and Time Zones. Vol. LXIX, special supplement in colors, 27 x 40 inches, June, 1936.

Central Europe and the Mediterranean. Vol. LXXVI, special supplement in colors, 36½ x 26½ inches, Oct., 1939.

Chart of the World on Mercator's Projection. Vol. XVI, special supplement in colors, 25 x 45 inches, Feb., 1905.

Chart Shewing Part of the Coast of N. W. America (Vancouver's Chart No. I). Vol. X, special supplement, 15½ x 18 inches, Nov., 1899.

Chart Shewing Part of the Coast of N. W. America (Vancouver's Chart No. II). Vol. X, special supplement, 15½ x 18 inches, Nov., 1899.

China. Vol. LXXXVII, special supplement in colors, 37 x 26½ inches, June, 1945.

China and Its Territories. Vol. XXIII, special supplement in colors, 17 x 23 inches, Oct., 1912.

Classical Lands of the Mediterranean. Vol. LXXVII, special supplement in colors, 35¼ x 26 inches, Mar., 1940.

Cotidal Lines for the World; or, Lines of Simultaneous High Water at Each Hour and Half Hour of Greenwich Lunar Time. Vol. XVII, special supplement, 8 x 14 inches, June, 1906.

Countries Bordering the Mediterranean Sea. Vol. XXIII, special supplement in colors, 9 x 18 inches, Jan., 1912.

Countries of the Caribbean, Including Mexico, Central America, the West Indies and the Panama Canal, with Detailed Insets of the Panama Canal and the Canal Zone, Porto Rico and the Virgin Islands, and Guantanamo Bay, Cuba. Vol. XLI, special supplement in colors, 25 x 44 inches, Feb., 1922.

Cuba. Vol. XVII, special supplement in colors, 12 x 24 inches, Oct., 1906.

Europe, Shewing Countries as Established by the Peace Conference at Paris. Vol. XXXIX, special supplement in colors, 30 x 33 inches, Feb., 1921.

Europe and Adjoining Portions of Africa and Asia. Vol. XXVIII, special supplement in colors, 28 x 32 inches, July, 1915.

Europe and the Mediterranean. Vol. LXXIII, special supplement in colors, 34 x 39 inches, Apr., 1938.

Europe and the Near East. Vol. LVI, special supplement in colors, 34¼ x 39¼ inches, Dec., 1929.

Europe and the Near East, as of April 1, 1940. Vol. LXXVII, special supplement in colors, 39 x 34 inches, May, 1940.

Grosvenor, Gilbert—*Continued*

Map Supplements—*Continued*

Europe and the Near East, with Inset Map of the Middle East, and a Table of Distances between the Principal Ports via Shortest Navigable Routes. Vol. LXXXIII, special supplement in colors, 39 x 34 inches, June, 1943.

Florida, with Insets of the following Areas: Miami-Palm Beach, Pensacola, Jacksonville-St. Augustine, St. Petersburg-Sarasota-Tampa. Vol. LVII, special supplement in colors, 12½ x 13¼ inches, Jan., 1930.

Germany and Its Approaches, with International Boundaries as of September 1, 1939, the day Germany invaded Poland and Boundaries as of January 1, 1938, before Germany seized Austria and Czechoslovakia. Vol. LXXXVI, special supplement in colors, 33½ x 26½ inches, July, 1944.

Greater New York . . . Metropolis of Mankind. Special supplement from aërial photograph by Capt. Albert W. Stevens. Vol. LXIV, Nov., 1933.

Historic and Scenic Reaches of the Nation's Capital. Vol. LXXIV, special supplement in colors, 26½ x 31¼ inches, July, 1938.

Illinois, with Inset of Chicago. Vol. LIX, special supplement in colors, 12½ x 19 inches, May, 1931.

India and Burma, with Insets of Bombay and Calcutta Areas. Verso of Map: Political Subdivisions and The Political Geography of India. Vol. LXXXIX, special supplement in colors, 30 x 25 inches, Apr., 1946.

Indian Ocean, including Australia, New Zealand and Malaysia. Vol. LXXIX, special supplement in colors, 25½ x 32¾ inches, Mar., 1941.

Japan and Adjacent Regions of Asia and the Pacific Ocean, with Insets of Industrial Centers of Japan and the Marshall Islands. Vol. LXXXV, special supplement in colors, 26½ x 34½ inches, Apr., 1944.

Japan and Korea, with Insets of Kuril Islands, Pescadores, Karafuto, Ryukyu Islands, Okinawa, Formosa, Tokyo Area, and a Location Map of Japan in the Western Pacific. Vol. LXXXVIII, special supplement in colors, 37 x 26½ inches, Dec., 1945.

Location of the Panama Canal. Vol. XVI, special supplement in colors, 24 x 33 inches, Oct., 1905.

Louisiana, with Inset of New Orleans. Vol. LVII, special supplement in colors, 13 x 13¼ inches, Apr., 1930.

Mall, Washington, D. C. Vol. XXVII, special supplement in colors, Mar., 1915.

Grosvenor, Gilbert—*Continued*

Map Supplements—*Continued*

Map of Central America, Cuba, Porto Rico, and the Islands of the Caribbean Sea, with Inset of the Panama Canal and Canal Zone. Vol. XXIV, special supplement in colors, 12½ x 19 inches, Feb., 1913.

Map of Discovery (Eastern Hemisphere). Reproduction in color of the painting by N. C. Wyeth, National Geographic Society, Washington, D. C. Vol. LIV, text, p. 568 ; supplement, Nov., 1928.

Map of Discovery (Western Hemisphere). Reproduction in color of the painting by N. C. Wyeth, National Geographic Society, Washington, D. C. Vol. LV, text, p. 93 ; supplement, Jan., 1929.

Map of Northwestern United States and Neighboring Canadian Provinces. Vol. LXXIX, special supplement in colors, 24½ by 36 inches, June, 1941.

Map of the Region Adjacent to the Nicaragua Canal Route. Vol. X, special supplement, 7½ x 10½ inches, July, 1899.

Map of the Seat of War in Africa, Prepared in the War Department, Adjutant General's Office, Military Information Division, with an Inset of South Africa. Vol. X, special supplement, 33 x 45 inches, Dec., 1899.

Map of the World (in Eastern and Western Hemispheres), with Insets showing Land and Water Hemispheres, Density of Population, Time Zones, and World Mapping. Vol. LXXX, special supplement in colors, 41 x 22 inches, Dec., 1941.

Maryland, Delaware, and District of Columbia. Vol. LI, special supplement in colors, 12 x 18 inches, Feb., 1927.

Mexico. Vol. XXII, special supplement in colors, 17 x 24½ inches, May, 1911.

Mexico. Vol. XXV, special supplement in colors, 17 x 24½ inches, May, 1914.

Mexico. Vol. XXX, special supplement in colors, 20 x 29 inches, July, 1916.

Mexico, Central America, and the West Indies. Vol. LXVI, special supplement in colors, 23 x 40 inches, Dec., 1934.

Mexico, Central America, and the West Indies. Vol. LXXVI, special supplement in colors, 24 x 41 inches, Dec., 1939.

Modern Pilgrim's Map of the British Isles. Vol. LXXI, special supplement in colors, 29 x 35 inches, June, 1937.

North America. Vol. XLV, special supplement in colors, 27 x 37 inches, May, 1924.

North America, with Inset of the Aleutian Islands. Vol. LXXXI, special supplement in colors, 26½ x 33 inches, May, 1942.

North Carolina, South Carolina, Georgia, and Eastern Tennessee. Vol. L, special supplement in colors, 14¾ x 19 inches, Sept., 1926.

Grosvenor, Gilbert—*Continued*

Map Supplements—*Continued*

North Polar Regions. Vol. XVIII, special supplement in colors, 17½ x 17½ inches, July, 1907.

Northeastern China. Vol. XI, p. 336, special supplement, 18½ x 35½ inches, Sept., 1900.

Northeastern United States, with Inset of Southeastern New England. Vol. LXXXVIII, special supplement in colors, 41 x 26½ inches, Sept., 1945.

Northern and Southern Hemispheres, with Insets of Time Zones, World Terrain, and Tables of Airline Distances in Four Hemispheres. Vol. LXXXIII, special supplement in colors, 41 x 22 inches, Apr., 1943.

Northern Hemisphere, with Tables showing Airline Distances in the Pacific, the Atlantic, the Arctic, and the Americas. Vol. LXXXIX, special supplement in colors, 21¾ x 21 inches, Feb., 1946.

Pacific Ocean, with Inset Maps of Important Islands and Groups. Vol. LXX, special supplement in colors, 31 x 38 inches, Dec., 1936 ; revised in 1942.

Pacific Ocean and the Bay of Bengal, with Inset Maps of Important Islands, and Table of Airline Distances in Statute Miles. Vol. LXXXIV, special supplement in colors, 36½ x 26½ inches, Sept., 1943.

Philippine Islands. Vol. XVI, special supplement in colors, 23 x 36 inches, Aug., 1905.

Philippine Islands as the Geographical Center of the Far East. Vol. XI, special supplement, 7½ x 10¾ inches, Jan., 1900.

Philippines. Vol. XIII, special supplement in two sheets, Jan., 1902.

Philippines, with Insets of Manila, Lingayen Gulf, and a Location Map of the Philippines. Vol. LXXXVII, special supplement in colors, 17½ x 26 inches, Mar., 1945.

Pilot Chart of the North Atlantic Ocean for February, 1903. Vol. XIV, special supplement, 32 x 21¾ inches, Feb., 1903.

Races of Europe and Adjoining Portions of Asia and Africa. Vol. XXXIV, special supplement in colors, 19¾ x 31 inches, Dec., 1918.

Reaches of New York City. Vol. LXXV, special supplement in colors, 26½ x 29 inches, Apr., 1939.

Seat of War in Manchuria (Beginning Just North of Mukden, and Covering the Country North to Harbin and East to Vladivostok). Vol. XVI, special supplement in colors, 18 x 44 inches, June, 1905.

South America. Vol. XVII, special supplement in colors, 8 x 11 inches, Aug., 1906.

South America. Vol. XL, special supplement in colors, 26 x 36 inches, Oct., 1921.

Grosvenor, Gilbert—*Continued*

Map Supplements—*Continued*

South America, with Inset Maps of Airways and Relief, Chief Natural Resources, Precipitation and Temperature, and the Galápagos Islands. Edited by Gilbert Grosvenor. Vol. LXXII, special supplement in colors, 26¾ x 37½ inches, Dec., 1937.

South America, with Insets of the Galápagos Islands, Chief Natural Resources, Precipitation and Temperature, Airways and Relief, and a Table of Airline Distances and Flying Times in Hours. Vol. LXXII, special supplement in colors, 26½ x 37¼ inches, Oct., 1942.

South Polar Regions—Showing Routes of the Proposed Antarctic Expeditions. Vol. X, special supplement, 8 x 8 inches, Aug., 1899.

Southeast Asia and Pacific Islands from the Indies and the Philippines to the Solomons, with 22 Inset Maps of Important Cities and Islands. Vol. LXXXVI, special supplement in colors, 41 x 26½ inches, Oct., 1944.

Southwestern United States. Vol. LXXVII, special supplement in colors, 35 x 26 inches, June, 1940.

Sovereignty and Mandate Boundary Lines in 1921 of the Islands of the Pacific. Vol. XL, special supplement in colors, 19 x 25 inches, Dec., 1921.

Theater of Military Operations in Luzon, 1899. Vol. X, special supplement, 23½ x 38 inches, June, 1899.

Theater of War in Europe, Africa, and Western Asia, with Table of Airline Distances in Statute Miles. Vol. LXXXII, special supplement in colors, 26½ x 31 inches, July, 1942.

Theater of War in the Pacific Ocean, with Table of Airline Distances in Statute Miles. Vol. LXXXI, special supplement in colors, 20½ x 26½ inches, Feb., 1942.

Travels of George Washington. Vol. LXI, special supplement in colors, 20 x 29 inches, Jan., 1932.

The Ultimate Washington (Plan Laid Out by the Commission of 1901 for the National Capital). Vol. XXVII, special supplement in colors, Mar., 1915.

Union of Soviet Socialist Republics, with International Boundaries according to Russian Treaties and Claims as of October 1, 1944. Boundaries of January 1, 1938, are shown in red. Vol. LXXXVI, special supplement in colors, 40 x 25 inches, Dec., 1944.

United States, with Insets of Important Cities. Vol. XLIII, special supplement in colors, 26½ x 36¼ inches, Apr., 1923.

United States, with Insets showing Army Corps Areas and Population of the States (1940). Vol. LXXVIII, special supplement in colors, 41 x 26½ inches, Dec., 1940.

Grosvenor, Gilbert—*Continued*

Map Supplements—*Continued*

United States and Adjoining Portions of Canada and Mexico. Vol. LXIII, special supplement in colors, 26 x 40 inches, May, 1933.

The United States of America, with Insets of United Nations Area and East of Maine. Vol. XC, special supplement in colors, 26½ x 41 inches, July, 1946.

War Map of Manchuria and Korea. Vol. XV, special supplement, 36 x 42 inches, Mar., 1904.

Western Theatre of War, with Inset of France and Belgium. Vol. XXXIII, special supplement, 26 x 31 inches, May, 1918.

White Mountains of New Hampshire. Vol. LXXII, special supplement in colors, 17 x 20 inches, July, 1937.

World. Vol. XLII, special supplement in colors, 27½ x 40 inches, Dec., 1922.

World, with Insets showing Arctic and Antarctic Regions, Natural Vegetation and Ocean Currents, and Density of Population and Prevailing Winds. Vol. LXII, special supplement in colors, 26 x 38½ inches, Dec., 1932.

World (in Eastern and Western Hemispheres), with Insets showing Land and Water Hemispheres, and Time Zones. Vol. LXVIII, special supplement in colors, 23 x 44 inches, Dec., 1935.

World Map, with Insets of Arctic and Antarctic Regions, Territories Occupied by Belligerents in First and Second World Wars, and Table of Geographical Equivalents and Abbreviations. Vol. LXXXIV, special supplement in colors, 41 x 26½ inches, Dec., 1943.

Photographs by Gilbert Grosvenor:

Algeciras, Spain, Docks at. Vol. LV, p. 318, Mar., 1929.

Alhambra, Spain, Hall of the Ambassadors. Vol. LV, p. 327, Mar., 1929.

Alligator, King, St. Augustine, Florida. Vol. XXII, p. 612, July, 1911.

Alligators, Big, St. Augustine, Florida. Vol. XXII, p. 611, July, 1911.

Alligators, Young, St. Augustine, Florida. Vol. XXII, p. 610, July, 1911.

Amitabha, Yun Kang Caves, China. Vol. LXXIII, p. 342, Mar., 1938.

Ape-Ape and Ferns on Slopes of Haleakala, Hawaii. Vol. XLV, p. 171, Feb., 1924.

Ape-Ape Foliage, Puohokamoa Gulch, Island of Maui. Vol. XLV, p. 156, Feb., 1924.

Ape-Ape Plants, Hawaii. Vol. LXXIV, p. 422, Oct., 1938.

Artificial Lakes, Arizona. Vol. LV, p. 40, Jan., 1929.

Aspy Bay, Cape Breton, Nova Scotia. Vol. XXXVIII, p. 57 (upper), July, 1920.

Baddeck, Cape Breton, Nova Scotia. Vol. XXXVIII, p. 36 (lower), July, 1920.

Grosvenor, Gilbert—*Continued*

Photographs by—*Continued*

Baddeck Harbor, Nova Scotia. Vol. LIII, p. 508, Apr., 1928.

Baltic Sea, Bathing at Bornholm, Denmark. Vol. XLII, p. 158, Aug., 1922.

Barn Dance, Chéticamp, Nova Scotia. Vol. LXXVII, p. 611, May, 1940.

Bartlett, (Capt.) Sam. Vol. XVII, p. 643, Nov., 1906.

Bazaar, Jewish, Russia. Vol. XXVI, p. 460, Nov., 1914.

Bazaar, Moscow, Russia. Vol. XXVI, p. 462, Nov., 1914.

Beggar, Nizhni-Novgorod, Russia. Vol. XXXIII, p. 250, Mar., 1918.

Beinn Bhreagh, Baddeck, Nova Scotia, Summer Home of Alexander Graham Bell. Vol. XLI, p. 238, Mar., 1922.

Bell, Alexander Graham and Alexander Melville. Vol. XLI, p. 233, Mar., 1922.

Bell, Alexander Graham and Mrs. Alexander Graham, at Baddeck, Nova Scotia. Vol. XXXVIII, p. 41 (lower), July, 1920.

Bell, Alexander Graham and Mrs. Alexander Graham, with Daughters and Grandchildren, at Baddeck, Nova Scotia. Vol. XLI, p. 236, Mar., 1922.

Bell, Alexander Graham, and Three Grandchildren, Cape Breton, Nova Scotia. Vol. XXXVIII, p. 59, July, 1920.

Bell, Alexander Graham, Hauling Down Kite, Cape Breton Island, Nova Scotia. Vol. LXXVII, p. 612, May, 1940.

Bells, Cart of, Nizhni-Novgorod, Russia. Vol. XXVI, p. 424 (lower), Nov., 1914.

Blood-Letting by Marrakech Surgeons, Morocco. Vol. LXI, p. 289, Mar., 1932.

Boat, Submerged Hydroplane Type, Dr. Bell's "HD-4," Cape Breton, Nova Scotia. Vol. XXXVIII, pp. 47-49, July, 1920.

Boats, Driven by Aërial Propellers, "B B." Vol. XVIII, p. 671, Oct., 1907.

Bou Jeloud, Gate of, Morocco. Vol. LXI, p. 265, Mar., 1932.

Bouleceet Harbor, Cape Breton, Nova Scotia. Vol. XXXVIII, p. 54 (lower), July, 1920.

Boys, Nizhni-Novgorod, Russia. Vol. XXVI, p. 492 (left), Nov., 1914.

Bras d'Or Lake from Beinn Bhreagh, Nova Scotia. Vol. L, p. 426, Oct., 1926.

Bras d'Or Lakes, Nova Scotia. Vol. XXIX, p. 226, Mar., 1916.

Bras d'Or Lakes, Nova Scotia. Vol. XXXVIII, p. 36 (upper), July, 1920.

Bridegroom, Nizhni-Novgorod, Russia. Vol. XXVI, p. 478 (right), Nov., 1914.

Bridgman, Herbert L. Vol. XVII, p. 643, Nov., 1906.

Bullock Team, San José, Costa Rica. Vol. LIII, p. 563 (lower), May, 1928.

Cab Driver, Nizhni-Novgorod, Russia. Vol. XXXIII, p. 251, Mar., 1918.

Cacti, Giant Saguaro. Vol. LXXI, pp. 522, 527 (left), Apr., 1937.

Grosvenor, Gilbert—*Continued*

Photographs by—*Continued*

Cactus, Barrel (or Bisnaga). Vol. LXXI, p. 524 (lower), Apr., 1937.

Cactus, Giant Saguaro. Vol. LV, p. 10, Jan., 1929.

Cannon, Captured from Napoleon, Moscow, Russia. Vol. XXVI, pp. 450-451, Nov., 1914.

Canyon Lake, Arizona. Vol. LV, p. 19, Jan., 1929.

Cape North, Cape Breton, Nova Scotia. Vol. XXXVIII, p. 57 (lower), July, 1920.

Cart, Nizhni-Novgorod, Russia. Vol. XXVI, p. 480 (upper and lower), Nov., 1914.

Carved Robes of Buddha, Yun Kang Caves. Vol. LXXIII, p. 346, Mar., 1938.

Cathedral of Our Saviour, Moscow, Russia. Vol. XXVI, pp. 441, 469, Nov., 1914.

Children, American. Vol. XXXI, p. 158, Feb., 1917.

Children, Andalusian, Spain. Vol. LV, p. 320, Mar., 1929.

Children, Moscow, Russia. Vol. XXVI, p. 447, Nov., 1914.

Children of New Mexico. Vol. LXXIII, p. 557, May, 1938.

Circassians, Moscow, Russia. Vol. XXVI, p. 487, Nov., 1914.

Clock of Bou Inania, Fez, Morocco. Vol. LXVII, p. 670, June, 1935.

Coachman, Moscow, Russia. Vol. XXVI, p. 464 (left), Nov., 1914.

Codfish, Cape Breton, Nova Scotia. Vol. XXXVIII, p. 56 (lower), July, 1920.

Colorful Wonders of the Hawaiian Islands. 3 ills. in color from photographs by Gilbert Grosvenor. Vol. XLV, pp. 198-203, Feb., 1924.

Crenelated Wall, Nanking. Vol. LXXIII, p. 207, Feb., 1938.

Cross Manor, Oldest House in Maryland. Vol. LI, p. 138, Feb., 1927.

Cypress Trees, Garden of Palacio de Generalife, near Alhambra, Spain. Vol. LV, pp. 328, 329, Mar., 1929.

Dr. and Mrs. Gilbert Grosvenor Photographed Before Entrance to Shih Chia Fo Temple. Vol. LXXIII, p. 319, Mar., 1938.

Edinburgh Royal High School, Scotland. Vol. XLI, p. 231, Mar., 1922.

El Hassan, Chief of Zaian Tribe, Morocco. Vol. LXI, p. 270, Mar., 1932.

Elsie's Harbor, Bras d'Or Lakes, Cape Breton, Nova Scotia. Vol. XXXVIII, p. 54 (upper), July, 1920.

Escorial, Church-Palace near Madrid, Spain. Vol. LX, p. 251, Aug., 1931.

Fair, Nizhni-Novgorod, Russia. Vol. XXXI, p. 237, Mar., 1917.

Fence of Old Ties, Between Cordova and Toledo, Spain. Vol. LV, p. 353, Mar., 1929.

Fern, Bird's Nest, Hawaii. Vol. XLV, p. 126, Feb., 1924.

Grosvenor, Gilbert—*Continued*

Photographs by—*Continued*

Finland, Coast of, near Helsingfors. Vol. XXXII, p. 28, July, 1917.

Fish Catch, Bahamas, Fish Bitten in Half Before Landed. Vol. LXIX, p. 239, Feb., 1936.

Flame Tree, Honolulu, Hawaii. Vol. XLV, plate XIII, p. 203, Feb., 1924.

Fortress, "on the Fringe of the Grand Atlas," Morocco. Vol. LXI, p. 286, Mar., 1932.

Fortune-Teller with Pet, Nizhni-Novgorod, Russia. Vol. XXVI, p. 497, Nov., 1914.

Funeral, Moscow, Russia. Vol. XXVI, p. 454, Nov., 1914.

General Sherman Tree, Sequoia National Park, California. Vol. XXIX, p. 414, Apr., 1916. Vol. LXIX, p. 140, Jan., 1936.

Girl, Moscow, Russia, with Glimpse of the University. Vol. XXVI, p. 492 (right), Nov., 1914.

Glacier National Park, Montana. Vol. XXXVII, p. 484, June, 1920.

Göta Canal, Sweden. Vol. LIV, p. 454, Oct., 1928.

Grace Harwar, Full Rigged at Sea. Vol. LIX, p. 218, Feb., 1931.

Grace Harwar, Overhauled by a Liner. Vol. LIX, p. 219, Feb., 1931.

Great Wall, China. Vol. LXXII, p. 525, Oct., 1937.

Greek Theater, Epidaurus. Vol. LXXXV, p. 275, Mar., 1944.

Grosvenor, Mrs. Gilbert, at Tai Shan (Mountain), China. Vol. LXXXVII, pp. 703, 704, 708, 716, 717, June, 1945.

Gypsies, Moscow, Russia. Vol. XXVI, p. 491, Nov., 1914.

Haleakala, World's Greatest Extinct Crater, Hawaii. Vol. XLV, plate VIII, Feb., 1924.

Haleakala Crater, Hawaii, Floor and Two Dead Cones. Vol. XLV, plate IX, Feb., 1924.

Haleakala Crater, Hawaii, Small Corner of. Vol. XLV, p. 147, Feb., 1924.

Helsingfors Harbor, Finland. Vol. XXVI, p. 510, Nov., 1914.

Hong Kong Junks. Vol. LXXIII, p. 91, Jan., 1938.

Houghton, Michigan, Wharf Scene. Vol. XXIX, p. 360, Apr., 1916.

Iberian Chapel, Moscow, Russia. Vol. XXVI, p. 467, Nov., 1914.

Interior View of Wu Ta Tung, Yun Kang Caves. Vol. LXXIII, p. 330, Mar., 1938.

Karouiine Mosque, Fez, Morocco. Vol. LXVII, p. 668, June, 1935.

Khenifra, Morocco. Vol. LXI, p. 269, Mar., 1932.

Khenifra, Morocco, Castle at. Vol. LXI, p. 268, Mar., 1932.

Kite, Hauled Down at Cape Breton, Nova Scotia. Vol. XXXVIII, p. 45, July, 1920.

Kite, Man-Lifting, Over Bras d'Or Lakes, Nova Scotia. Vol. XXXVIII, p. 44, July, 1920.

Grosvenor, Gilbert—*Continued*

Photographs by—*Continued*

Kite, Used in Early Aviation. Vol. XXXVIII, p. 38, July, 1920. Vol. LII, p. 235, Aug., 1927.

Kites, Tetrahedral, of Alexander Graham Bell. Vol. XVIII, p. 24, Jan., 1907.

Koa Tree, Hawaii National Park. Vol. XLV, p. 144, Feb., 1924.

Kremlin, Moscow, Russia. Vol. L, p. 520, Nov., 1926.

Kremlin, Moscow, Russia, Battlements. Vol. XXVI, p. 430, Nov., 1914.

Kremlin, Moscow, Russia, Bells. Vol. XXVI, pp. 438, 439, Nov., 1914.

Kremlin, Moscow, Russia, Boys Visiting. Vol. XXVI, p. 488, Nov., 1914.

Kremlin, Moscow, Russia, Guards. Vol. XXVI, p. 444 (right), Nov., 1914.

Kremlin, Moscow, Russia, Inside Redeemer Gate. Vol. XXVI, p. 434, Nov., 1914.

Kremlin, Moscow, Russia, Redeemer Gate. Vol. XXVI, pp. 432, 433, Nov., 1914.

Kremlin, Moscow, Russia, Russian Mothers Visit. Vol. XXVI, p. 446, Nov., 1914.

Kremlin, Moscow, Russia, with Cathedral of Our Savior and Redeemer Gate. Vol. XXVI, p. 468, Nov., 1914.

Lahaina Roadstead, Island of Maui. Vol. XLV, p. 165, Feb., 1924.

Lava River Bed where Flow Passed from Halemaumau, Hawaii. Vol. XLV, p. 236, Feb., 1924.

Loa, Lava on Slopes of, Hawaii. Vol. XLV, p. 188, Feb., 1924.

Lotus-Bossed Doorway, Yun Kang Caves, China. Vol. LXXIII, p. 334, Mar., 1938.

McAskill, Angus, Boot and Waistcoat of Cape Breton's Giant. Vol. XXXVIII, p. 55, July, 1920.

Málaga to Granada Road, Spain. Vol. LV, p. 315, Mar., 1929.

Market of Bab Mahrouk, Fez, Morocco, Muffled Figures Dicker for Wool. Vol. LXVII, p. 664, June, 1935.

Mauna Loa, Hawaii, Dead Cones on. Vol. XLV, p. 208, Feb., 1924.

Mauna Loa, Hawaii, Resthouse on. Vol. XLV, p. 182, Feb., 1924.

Mauna Loa, Hawaii, Slopes of. Vol. XLV, p. 209, Feb., 1924.

Medals of Service, Russian Errand Boy's. Vol. XXVI, p. 425, Nov., 1914.

Milkmaid, Stockholm, Sweden. Vol. XXIX, p. 46, Jan., 1916.

Monastery of Miracles, Moscow, Russia. Vol. XXVI, p. 440, Nov., 1914.

Morrison Family, Nine Sons of, St. Ann's, Cape Breton, Nova Scotia. Vol. XXXV, p. 506, June, 1919.

Morrison Family, Parents and Nine Sons of, Baddeck, Nova Scotia. Vol. XXIX, p. 220, Mar., 1916.

Morro Castle, Havana, Cuba. Vol. LII, p. 497, Oct., 1927.

Grosvenor, Gilbert—*Continued*

Photographs by—*Continued*

Morro Castle, Havana, Cuba. Vol. LVII, p. 582, May, 1930.

Moujik, Nizhni-Novgorod, Russia. Vol. XXVI, p. 479 (left), Nov., 1914.

Nuevitas, Cuba, Seaplane Docks. Vol. LXIII, p. 630, May, 1933.

Nun, Moscow, Russia. Vol. XXVI, p. 457 (right), Nov., 1914.

Olympic Forest, Washington. Vol. XXIX, p. 421, Apr., 1916.

Pagoda, Canton, China. Vol. LXXII, p. 724, Dec., 1937.

Panoehoe Region, Hawaii. Vol. XLV, p. 210, Feb., 1924.

Peary, (Rear Adm.) Robert E. Vol. XVII, p. 639, Nov., 1906.

Peasant, Nizhni-Novgorod, Russia. Vol. XXVI, p. 478 (left), Nov., 1914.

Peasant Woman, Nizhni-Novgorod, Russia. Vol. XXVI, p. 479 (middle), Nov., 1914.

Peasant Woman and Child, Nizhni-Novgorod, Russia. Vol. XXVI, p. 479 (right), Nov., 1914.

Peddler of Pictures, Russia. Vol. XXVI, p. 457 (left), Nov., 1914.

Peking Carts. Vol. LXXIII, p. 314, Mar., 1938.

Picnic, Game Played at, Chéticamp, Nova Scotia. Vol. LXXVII, p. 605, May, 1940.

Pigeons, Amherst College, Massachusetts. Vol. XLIX, p. 97, Jan., 1926.

Pigeons, Feeding in Red Square, Moscow, Russia. Vol. XXVI, p. 452, Nov., 1914.

Policeman, Nizhni-Novgorod, Russia. Vol. XXXIII, p. 254, Mar., 1918.

Policeman, Petrograd, Russia. Vol. XXVI, p. 426, Nov., 1914.

Port Royal, Jamaica. Vol. LI, p. 3, Jan., 1927.

Porter, in front of St. Isaac's Cathedral, Petrograd, Russia. Vol. XXVI, p. 509, Nov., 1914.

Priest and Wife, Moscow, Russia. Vol. XXVI, p. 444 (left), Nov., 1914.

Priest and Wife and Two Children, Russia. Vol. XXVI, p. 463, Nov., 1914.

Priests, Russia. Vol. XXVI, p. 465, Nov., 1914.

Prisoner, Nizhni-Novgorod, Russia. Vol. XXVI, p. 476 (lower), Nov., 1914.

Puna, Hawaii, Beach. Vol. XLV, p. 148 (upper), Feb., 1924.

Puna, Hawaii, Lava Rock Hurled above the Cliff. Vol. XLV, p. 148 (lower), Feb., 1924.

Railway Station, Nizhni-Novgorod, Russia. Vol. XXVI, p. 474, Nov., 1914.

Restored Figure in Yun Kang Caves. Vol. LXXIII, p. 335, Mar., 1938.

Resurrection Church, Petrograd, Russia. Vol. XXVI, p. 499, Nov., 1914.

Grosvenor, Gilbert—*Continued*

Photographs by—*Continued*

Russia. 10 ills. in color from photographs by Gilbert H. Grosvenor. Vol. XXVI, pp. 487-499, Nov., 1914.

Russian, Young, Moscow, Russia. Vol. XXVI, p. 464 (right), Nov., 1914.

Russian Group. Vol. XXVI, p. 490, Nov., 1914.

Russian Group in Street. Vol. XXXI, p. 235 (right), Mar., 1917.

Russian Making Sign of the Cross. Vol. XXVI, p. 443, Nov., 1914.

Russian Schoolboys, Moscow. Vol. XXXII, p. 30, July, 1917.

Saba, West Indies, Volcanic Cone. Vol. LIII, p. 583, May, 1928.

St. Anns, Bay of, Cape Breton, Nova Scotia. Vol. XXXVIII, p. 52, July, 1920.

St. Basil's Cathedral, Moscow, Russia. Vol. XXVI, p. 493, Nov., 1914.

St. Isaac's Golden Dome, Petrograd, Russia. Vol. XXVI, p. 485, Nov., 1914.

St. Kitts, West Indies. Vol. LIII, p. 582, May, 1928.

St. Nicholas Lutheran Church, Helsingfors, Finland. Vol. XXVI, p. 511, Nov., 1914.

Saloon, Vodka, Nizhni-Novgorod, Russia. Vol. XXVI, p. 481, Nov., 1914.

San Pedro de Macoris, Dominican Republic, Refueling Clipper Ship. Vol. LXIII, p. 629, May, 1933.

São Paulo, Brazil, Market Place. Vol. LVIII, p. 770, Dec., 1930.

Schoolboys, Costa Rica. Vol. LIII, p. 563 (upper), May, 1928.

Schoolboys, Russia. Vol. XXVI, p. 459, Nov., 1914.

Schoolboys and Priest, Moscow, Russia. Vol. XXVI, p. 448, Nov., 1914.

Schoolmaster and Boys, Moscow, Russia. Vol. XXXI, p. 235 (left), Mar., 1917.

Sequoia National Park, California. Vol. XXXI, p. 8, Jan., 1917.

Sheep, Twin Bearing, Cape Breton, Nova Scotia. Vol. XXXVIII, p. 41 (upper), July, 1920.

Shops, Selling Icons, Moscow, Russia. Vol. XXVI, p. 461, Nov., 1914.

Shrine, Nizhni-Novgorod, Russia. Vol. XXVI, p. 477, Nov., 1914.

Shrine in a Bazaar, Petrograd, Russia. Vol. XXXII, p. 45, July, 1917.

Shrines, Moscow, Russia. Vol. XXVI, pp. 427, 458, 466, Nov., 1914.

Soldiers, Petrograd, Russia. Vol. XXVI, p. 505, Nov., 1914.

South Ingonish Harbor, Cape Breton, Nova Scotia. Vol. XXXVIII, p. 58, July, 1920.

Statue, Peter the Great, Petrograd, Russia. Vol. XXVI, p. 504, Nov., 1914.

Statue, A Trial, in front of University, Nizhni-Novgorod, Russia. Vol. XXVI, p. 424 (upper), Nov., 1914.

Stork's Nest, Morocco. Vol. LXI, p. 301, Mar., 1932.

Grosvenor, Gilbert—*Continued*

Photographs by—*Continued*

Stratobowl, South Dakota, Photographer's Perch. Vol. LXIX, p. 696, May, 1936.

Straw Carried by Donkeys, Spain. Vol. LV, p. 333, Mar., 1929.

Street Scene, Moscow, Russia. Vol. XXXI, p. 225, Mar., 1917.

Sun Yat-Sen Memorial, Nanking. Vol. LXXIII, p. 195, Feb., 1938.

Tai Shan (Mountain), China, Chair Bearers. Vol. LXXXVII, pp. 702, 706, 708, 710, June, 1945.

Tai Shan (Mountain), China, Dragon's Throat Stairs. Vol. LXXXVII, p. 711, June, 1945.

Tai Shan (Mountain), China, Great Stone Road. Vol. LXXXVII, p. 704, June, 1945.

Tai Shan (Mountain), China, Halfway House. Vol. LXXXVII, p. 707, June, 1945.

Tai Shan (Mountain), China, Inscriptions. Vol. LXXXVII, p. 712, June, 1945.

Tai Shan (Mountain), China, Jade Emperor's Summit. Vol. LXXXVII, p. 717, June, 1945.

Tai Shan (Mountain), China, Pilgrim Way. Vol. LXXXVII, pp. 702, 706, 707, 708, 710, 711, June, 1945.

Tai Shan (Mountain), China, South Heavenly Gate. Vol. LXXXVII, p. 709, June, 1945.

Tai Shan (Mountain), China, Tablet Without Inscription. Vol. LXXXVII, p. 716, June, 1945.

Tai Shan (Mountain), China, Temple of the Jade Emperor. Vol. LXXXVII, pp. 714, 716, June, 1945.

Tai Shan (Mountain), China, Temple of the Mother of the Great Bear. Vol. LXXXVII, p. 703, June, 1945.

Tai Shan (Mountain), China, Tower of Ten Thousand Fairies. Vol. LXXXVII, p. 702, June, 1945.

Tatar Merchant, Nizhni-Novgorod Fair, Russia. Vol. XXVI, p. 475, Nov., 1914.

Temple of Heaven, Peiping, China. Vol. LXXII, p. 511, Oct., 1937.

Tent, Chief El Hassan's, Morocco. Vol. LXI, p. 271, Mar., 1932.

Theater, Great Imperial, Moscow, Russia. Vol. L, p. 581, Nov., 1926.

Tower, Beinn Bhreagh, Baddeck, Nova Scotia. Vol. XXXVIII, p. 43, July, 1920.

Trout Pool, near Cheticamp, Cape Breton, Nova Scotia. Vol. XXXVIII, p. 56 (upper), July, 1920.

Tuna Fish, Cape Breton, Nova Scotia. Vol. XLIV, p. 592, Dec., 1923.

United States Marines, Peiping, China. Vol. LXXII, p. 518, Oct., 1937.

Volcanoes, Costa Rica. Vol. LIII, p. 562, May, 1928.

Volga River, Russia, Boat on. Vol. XXVI, p. 476 (upper), Nov., 1914.

Volga River at Nizhni-Novgorod, Russia. Vol. XXVI, p. 472, Nov., 1914.

Grosvenor, Gilbert—*Continued*

Photographs by—*Continued*

Water Front, Nizhni-Novgorod, Russia. Vol. XXVI, p. 473, Nov., 1914.

White Sands, Alamogordo, New Mexico. Vol. LXVIII, pp. 252-256, Aug., 1935.

Wild Acres, Maryland. Vol. LI, p. 202, Feb., 1927.

Workmen, Moscow, Russia. Vol. XXVI, pp. 455, 489, Nov., 1914.

Wu Chou Shan Caves, China. Vol. LXXIII, p. 317, Mar., 1938.

Záhara, Tower and Battlements, Spain. Vol. LV, p. 322, Mar., 1929.

Photographs of Gilbert Grosvenor. Vol. XXV, p. 460, Apr., 1914. Vol. XLI, p. 240, Mar., 1922; p. 640, June, 1922. Vol. XLVIII, p. 224, Aug., 1925; p. 476, Oct., 1925. Vol. L, p. 380, Sept., 1926. Vol. LIII, p. 135, Jan., 1928. Vol. LVII, pp. 583, 592, May, 1930. Vol. LVIII, p. 22, July, 1930; pp. 230-233, Aug., 1930. Vol. LXII, p. 366, Sept., 1932. Vol. LXV, pp. 790, 792, June, 1934. Vol. LXVII, p. 137, Feb., 1935. Vol. LXVIII, pp. 112, 114, July, 1935. Vol. LXIX, pp. 126, 129, 132, 133, 134, 137, 139, 159, Jan., 1936; p. 712, May, 1936. Vol. LXXII, p. 107, July, 1937. Vol. LXXIII, p. 319, Mar., 1938. Vol. LXXXVII, p. 717, June, 1945. Vol. LXXXIX, p. 141, Feb., 1946.

Grosvenor, Melville Bell:

August First in Gruyères (Switzerland). By Melville Bell Grosvenor. Vol. LXX, pp. 137-168, 12 ills. in black and white, 23 ills. in color, Aug., 1936.

Color Camera's First Aërial Success. By Melville Bell Grosvenor. Vol. LVIII, pp. 344-353, 9 ills. in color, Sept., 1930.

Cruise on an Escort Carrier. By Melville Bell Grosvenor. Vol. LXXXIV, pp. 513-546, 14 ills. in black and white, 20 ills. in color, Nov., 1943.

Landing Craft for Invasion. By Melville Bell Grosvenor. Vol. LXXXVI, pp. 1-30, 26 ills., July, 1944.

New Queen of the Seas (Aircraft Carrier). By Melville Bell Grosvenor. Vol. LXXXII, pp. 1-30, 27 ills., 1 drawing, 1 two-page map, July, 1942.

Poland, Land of the White Eagle. By Melville Bell Grosvenor. Vol. LXI, pp. 435-445, 12 ills. in color, Apr., 1932.

Styria (Austria), a Favored Vacation Land of Central Europe. By Melville Bell Grosvenor. Vol. LXII, pp. 430-439, 14 ills. in color, Oct., 1932.

Ground Crews, U. S. Army Air Forces:

They Sustain the Wings. By Frederick Simpich. Vol. LXXXIV, pp. 333-354, 19 ills., Sept., 1943.

Grouse (Bird) :

Game Birds of Prairie, Forest, and Tundra. By Alexander Wetmore. Vol. LXX, pp. 461-500, 5 ills. in black and white, 60 portraits in color, Oct., 1936.

Hunted Birds of Field and Wild. 60 portraits in color from paintings by Maj. Allan Brooks. Vol. LXX, pp. 469-500, Oct., 1936.

Wild Life of Lake Superior, Past and Present : The Habits of Deer, Moose, Wolves, Beavers, Muskrats, Trout, and Feathered Wood-Folk Studied with Camera and Flashlight. By George Shiras, 3d. Vol. XL, pp. 113-204, 77 ills., supplement, 1 half-page map, Aug., 1921.

See also Sage Grouse.

Groves, (Brig. Gen.) P. R. C.:

Flying Over Egypt, Sinai, and Palestine : Looking Down Upon the Holy Land During an Air Journey of Two and a Half Hours from Cairo to Jerusalem. By Brig. Gen. P. R. C. Groves and Maj. J. R. McCindle. Vol. I, pp. 313-355, 26 ills., 1 half-page map, Sept., 1926.

Growing Camp in the Tanana Gold Fields, Alaska. By Sidney Paige. Vol. XVI, pp. 104-111, 4 ills., Mar., 1905.

Growth of Florida. Vol. XVII, p. 424, July, 1906.

Growth of Maritime Commerce. Vol. X, pp. 30-31, Jan., 1899.

Growth of Russia. By Edwin A. Grosvenor. Vol. XI, pp. 169-185, 2 page and 3 half-page maps, May, 1900.

Gruening, Ernest H.:

Alaska—Our Northwestern Outpost. 16 ills. in color from natural-color photographs by Ernest H. Gruening, Amos Burg, and Froelich Rainey. Vol. LXXXII, pp. 297-308, Sept., 1942.

Strategic Alaska Looks Ahead : Our Vast Territory, Now Being More Closely Linked to Us by Road and Rail, Embodies the American Epic of Freedom, Adventure, and the Pioneer Spirit. By Ernest H. Gruening. Vol. LXXXII, pp. 281-315, 18 ills. in black and white, 16 ills. in color, 1 two-page map, Sept., 1942.

Gruntvig, (Bishop) Nikolai Frederik Severin: Denmark and the Danes. By Maurice Francis Egan. Vol. XLII, pp. 115-164, 38 ills., three-quarters-page map, Aug., 1922.

Gruyères, Switzerland :

August First in Gruyères. By Melville Bell Grosvenor. Vol. LXX, pp. 137-168, 12 ills. in black and white, 23 ills. in color, Aug., 1936.

Green Gruyère, Home of a Swiss Cheese. 23 ills. in color from natural-color photographs by Bernard F. Rogers, Jr. Vol. LXX, pp. 145-168, Aug., 1936.

Guadalajara, Mexico :

Vignettes of Guadalajara. By Frederick Simpich. Vol. LXV, pp. 329-356, 20 ills. in black and white, 15 ills. in color, 1 third-page map. Mar., 1934.

Guadalcanal (Island), Solomon Islands :

At Ease in the South Seas. By Maj. Frederick Simpich, Jr. Vol. LXXXV, pp. 79-104, 32 ills., Jan., 1944.

What the Fighting Yanks See. By Wanda Burnett. Vol. LXXXVI, pp. 451-476, 27 ills., Oct., 1944.

Guadalupe (Island), Mexico :

Cruise Among the Desert Islands. By G. Dallas Hanna and A. W. Anthony. Vol. XLIV, pp. 71-99, 32 ills., 1 quarter-page map, July, 1923.

Guadalupe Mountains, New Mexico–Texas :

Visit to Carlsbad Cavern : Recent Explorations of a Limestone Cave in the Guadalupe Mountains of New Mexico Reveal a Natural Wonder of the First Magnitude. By Willis T. Lee. Vol. XLV, pp. 1-40, 42 ills., Jan., 1924.

Guadeloupe (Island), West Indies :

Colorful Paths in Martinique and Guadeloupe. 13 ills. in color from natural-color photographs by Edwin L. Wisherd. Vol. LXXIII, pp. 281-288, Mar., 1938.

Report by Robert T. Hill on Volcanic Disturbances in the West Indies. Vol. XIII, pp. 223-267, 13 ills., 2 half-page and 1 quarter-page maps, July, 1902.

Guale. *See* Sea Islands, Georgia.

Guam (Island), Marianas Islands :

Guam—Perch of the China Clippers. By Margaret M. Higgins. Vol. LXXIV, pp. 99-122, 23 ills., 1 third-page map, July, 1938.

Our Smallest Possession—Guam. By William E. Safford. Vol. XVI, pp. 229-237, 5 ills., May, 1905.

Springboards to Tokyo. By Willard Price. Vol. LXXXVI, pp. 385-407, 16 ills., Oct., 1944.

Victory's Portrait in the Marianas. By Lt. William Franklin Draper, USNR. With 17 ills. in color from paintings by the author. Vol. LXXXVIII, pp. 599-616, Nov., 1945.

Guanacos:

Camels of the Clouds. By W. H. Hodge. Vol. LXXXIX, pp. 641-656, 15 ills., 1 half-page map, May, 1946.

Guanajuato, Mexico :

Treasure Chest of Mercurial Mexico (Silver Mines). By Frank H. Probert. Vol. XXX, pp. 33-68, 33 ills., July, 1916.

Guanayes (Birds) :

Most Valuable Bird in the World. By Robert Cushman Murphy. Vol. XLVI, pp. 279-302, 25 ills., 1 half-page map, Sept., 1924.

Guano (Fertilizer) :

Most Valuable Bird in the World (Guanay). By Robert Cushman Murphy. Vol. XLVI, pp. 279-302, 25 ills., 1 half-page map, Sept., 1924.

Guano (Fertilizer)—*Continued*

Peru's Wealth-Producing Birds: Vast Riches in the Guano Deposits of Cormorants, Pelicans, and Petrels Which Nest on Her Barren, Rainless Coast. By R. E. Coker. Vol. XXXVII, pp. 537-566, 28 ills., June, 1920.

Guantanamo Bay, Cuba:

Across the Equator With the American Navy. By Herbert Corey. Vol. XXXIX, pp. 571-624, 53 ills., June, 1921.

Guarequi (Plant):

Notes on the Deserts of the United States and Mexico (Extracted from a Publication by Dr. Daniel T. MacDougal). Vol. XXI, pp. 691-714, 16 ills., Aug., 1910.

Guatemala:

Buenos Aires to Washington by Horse: A Solitary Journey of Two and a Half Years, Through Eleven American Republics, Covers 9,600 Miles of Mountain and Plain, Desert and Jungle. By A. F. Tschiffely. Vol. LV, pp. 135-196, 75 ills., 1 page map, Feb., 1929.

Countries of the Caribbean. By William Joseph Showalter. Vol. XXIV, pp. 227-250, 23 ills., Feb., 1913.

Excavations at Quirigua, Guatemala. By Sylvanus Griswold Morley. Vol. XXIV, pp. 339-361, 24 ills., 1 diagram, Mar., 1913.

Foremost Intellectual Achievement of Ancient America: The Hieroglyphic Inscriptions on the Monuments in the Ruined Cities of Mexico, Guatemala, and Honduras Are Yielding the Secrets of the Maya Civilization. By Sylvanus Griswold Morley. Vol. XLI, pp. 109-130, 27 ills., 17 diagrams, special map supplement, Feb., 1922.

Guatemala: Land of Volcanoes and Progress: Cradle of Ancient Mayan Civilization, Redolent with Its Later Spanish and Indian Ways, Now Reaping Prosperity from Bananas and Coffee. By Thomas F. Lee. Vol. L, pp. 599-648, 32 ills. in black and white, 20 ills. in color, 1 page map, Nov., 1926.

Guatemala, the Country of the Future. By Edine Frances Tisdel. Vol. XXI, pp. 596-624, 33 ills., 1 three-quarters-page map, July, 1910.

Guatemala Interlude: In the Land of the Quetzal a Modern Capital Contrasts With Primitive Indian Villages and the "Pompeii of America." By E. John Long. Vol. LXX, pp. 429-460, 22 ills. in black and white, 13 ills. in color, 1 page map, Oct., 1936.

In the Land of the Quetzal. 20 ills. in color from autochromes lumière by Jacob Gayer. Vol. L, pp. 610-627, Nov., 1926.

Mysterious Temples of the Jungle: The Prehistoric Ruins of Guatemala. By W. F. Sands. Vol. XXIV, pp. 324-338, 10 ills., Mar., 1913.

Notes on Central America. Vol. XVIII, pp. 272-278, 1 ill., 1 half-page map, Apr., 1907.

Preserving Ancient America's Finest Sculptures. By J. Alden Mason. Vol. LXVIII, pp. 537-570, 24 ills. in black and white, 10 ills. in color, Nov., 1935.

Guatemala—*Continued*

Shattered Capitals of Central America. By Herbert J. Spinden. Vol. XXXVI, pp. 185-212, 32 ills., 1 page map, Sept., 1919.

To Market in Guatemala. By Luis Marden. With 19 ills. in color from natural-color photographs by Giles Greville Healey and Charles S. Pineo. Vol. LXXXVIII, pp. 87-104, July, 1945.

Unearthing America's Ancient History: Investigation Suggests That the Maya May Have Designed the First Astronomical Observatory in the New World in Order to Cultivate Corn. By Sylvanus Griswold Morley. Vol. LX, pp. 99-126, 28 ills., July, 1931.

Where Man's Garb Rivals the Quetzal. 13 ills. in color from natural-color photographs by Luis Marden. Vol. LXX, pp. 437-444, Oct., 1936.

Guayaquil, Ecuador:

Beautiful Ecuador. By Joseph Lee. Vol. XVIII, pp. 80-91, 9 ills., Feb., 1907.

From Sea to Clouds in Ecuador. By W. Robert Moore. Vol. LXXX, pp. 717-740, 11 ills. in black and white, 9 ills. in color, Dec., 1941.

Over Trail and Through Jungle in Ecuador: Indian Head-Hunters of the Interior, an Interesting Study in the South American Republic. By H. E. Anthony. Vol. XL, pp. 327-352, 28 ills., Oct., 1921.

Guaymas, Mexico:

Adventuring Down the West Coast of Mexico. By Herbert Corey. Vol. XLII, pp. 449-503, 44 ills., 1 half-page map, Nov., 1922.

Guaymi Indians:

Little-Known Parts of Panama. By Henry Pittier. Vol. XXIII, pp. 627-662, 35 ills., 1 page map, July, 1912.

Guelma, Algeria:

American Eclipse Expedition. By Rear Adm. Colby M. Chester. Vol. XVII, pp. 589-612, 23 ills., 1 color plate, Nov., 1906.

Guérande (Peninsula), France:

Where Bretons Wrest a Living from the Sea. 23 ills. from photographs by F. W. Goro. Vol. LXXI, pp. 751-766, June, 1937.

Guerard, A. L.:

Battle-Line of Languages in Western Europe: A Problem in Human Geography More Perplexing Than That of International Boundaries. By A. L. Guerard. Vol. XLIII, pp. 145-180, 36 ills., Feb., 1923.

Guermessa, Tunisia:

Here and There in Northern Africa. By Frank Edward Johnson. Vol. XXV, pp. 1-132, 113 ills., Jan., 1914.

Guernsey (Island), Channel Islands:

Channel Islands. By Edith Carey. Vol. XXXVIII, pp. 143-164, 24 ills., 1 quarter-page map, Aug., 1920.

Guernsey (Island), Channel Islands—*Continued*

Contented Guernsey. 11 ills. in color from natural-color photographs by B. Anthony Stewart. Vol. LXXIII, pp. 377-384, Mar., 1938.

Guernsey, the Friendly Island. By Alfred S. Campbell. Vol. LXXIII, pp. 361-396, 28 ills. in black and white, 11 ills. in color, Mar., 1938.

Guerrero (State), Mexico:

Down Mexico's Río Balsas. By John W. Webber. With 9 ills. in color from natural-color photographs by the author, Kenneth Segerstrom, and Jack Breed. Vol. XC, pp. 253-272, 5 ills. in black and white, 1 half-page map, Aug., 1946.

Guest in Saudi Arabia. By Maynard Owen Williams. Vol. LXXXVIII, pp. 463-487, 24 ills., 1 two-thirds-page map, Oct., 1945.

Guiana, British. *See* British Guiana.

Guiana, Dutch. *See* Surinam.

Guiana, French. *See* French Guiana.

Guilford (Suburb), Baltimore. *See* Sherwood Gardens.

Guillemot Eggs. Vol. XIV, pp. 386-388, 1 ill., Oct., 1903.

Guillemots (Birds):

Birds of the Northern Seas. By Alexander Wetmore. Paintings by Maj. Allan Brooks. Vol. LXIX, pp. 95-122, 12 ills. in black and white, 34 portraits in color, Jan., 1936.

Guillemot Eggs. Vol. XIV, pp. 386-388, 1 ill., Oct., 1903.

Guillumette, Paul G.:

Belgium: Beautiful Belgium, Restored by Peace. 11 ills. in color from autochromes by Paul G. Guillumette. Vol. LVI, pp. 554-563, Nov., 1929.

Guinea, French. *See* French Guinea.

Guinea Fowl:

Fowls of Forest and Stream Tamed by Man. By Morley A. Jull. Vol. LVII, pp. 327-371, 27 ills. in black and white, 16 ills. in color, Mar., 1930.

Gulf Coast, United States:

Delectable Shrimp: Once a Culinary Stepchild, Today a Gulf Coast Industry. By Harlan Major. Vol. LXXXVI, pp. 501-512, 11 ills., 1 two-thirds-page map, Oct., 1944.

Gulf Coast Towns Get into the Fight. 19 ills. in color from natural-color photographs; 17 ills. by J. Baylor Roberts. Vol. LXXXV, pp. 17-40, Jan., 1944.

How We Use the Gulf of Mexico. By Frederick Simpich. Vol. LXXXV, pp. 1-40, 20 ills. in black and white, 19 ills. in color, 1 two-page map, Jan., 1944.

Gulf Stream:

Certain Citizens of the Warm Sea. By Louis L. Mowbray. Vol. XLI, pp. 27-62, 18 ills. in black and white, 16 ills. in color, Jan., 1922.

Devil-Fishing in the Gulf Stream. By John Oliver La Gorce. Vol. XXXV, pp. 476-488, 7 ills., June, 1919.

Grandest and Most Mighty Terrestrial Phenomenon: The Gulf Stream. By Rear Adm. John Elliott Pillsbury. Vol. XXIII, pp. 767-778, 1 ill., 2 diagrams, 2 page and 1 half-page maps, Aug., 1912.

Interesting Citizens of the Gulf Stream. By Dr. John T. Nichols. Vol. XXXIX, pp. 69-84, 11 ills. in black and white, 16 ills. in color, Jan., 1921.

Ocean Currents. By James Page. Vol. XIII, pp. 135-142, Apr., 1902.

Treasure-House of the Gulf Stream: The Completion and Opening of the New Aquarium and Biological Laboratory at Miami, Florida. By John Oliver La Gorce. Vol. XXXIX, pp. 53-68, 5 ills. in black and white, 16 ills. in color, Jan., 1921.

Gull-billed Terns:

Pelican Profiles. By Lewis Wayne Walker. Vol. LXXXIV, pp. 589-598, 5 ills. in black and white, 8 ills. in color, Nov., 1943.

Contains information on the Gull-billed Tern of the Salton Sea Area, California.

Gulls (Birds):

Black-Headed Gulls in London. By A. H. Hall. Vol. XLVII, pp. 604-672, 16 ills., June, 1925.

White Sheep, Giant Moose, and Smaller Game of the Kenai Peninsula, Alaska. By George Shiras, 3d. Vol. XXIII, pp. 423-494, 59 ills., 1 page and 1 two-page maps, May, 1912.

Guns. *See* Cannon; Weapons.

Gurkha (Hindu Caste):

Nepal: A Little-Known Kingdom. By John Claude White. Vol. XXXVIII, pp. 245-283, 32 ills., 1 half-page map, Oct., 1920.

Guynemer, Georges:

Aces of the Air. By Capt. Jacques De Sieyes. Vol. XXXIII, pp. 5-9, 2 ills., Jan., 1918.

Gyangtse, Tibet:

Across Tibet from India to China. By Lt. Col. Ilia Tolstoy, AUS. Vol. XC, pp. 169-222, 41 ills., 1 half-page map, Aug., 1946.

Gygis alba. *See* Fairy Terns.

Gypsies:

American Girl Cycles Across Romania: Two-wheel Pilgrim Pedals the Land of Castles and Gypsies, Where Roman Empire Traces Mingle With Remnants of Oriental Migration. By Dorothy Hosmer. Vol. LXXIV, pp. 557-588, 31 ills., 1 page map, Nov., 1938.

Camargue, the Cowboy Country of Southern France. By Dr. André Vialles. Vol. XLII, pp. 1-34, 33 ills., 1 half-page map, July, 1922.

Gypsies—*Continued*

Hungary : A Land of Shepherd Kings. By C. Townley-Fullam. Vol. XXVI, pp. 311-393, 92 ills., 1 page map, Oct., 1914.

Races of Europe. By Edwin A. Grosvenor. Vol. XXXIV, pp. 441-534, 62 ills., 2 page maps, special map supplement, Dec., 1918.

Gypsum:

White Sands of Alamogordo (New Mexico) : A Dry Ocean of Granular Gypsum Billows Under Desert Winds in a New National Playground. By Carl P. Russell. Vol. LXVIII, pp. 250-264, 12 ills., Aug., 1935.

Gypsy-Moth:

Explorers of a New Kind : Successful Introduction of Beetles and Parasites to Check Ravages of the Gipsy-Moth and Brown-Tail Moth. By L. O. Howard. Vol. XXVI, pp. 38-67, 11 ills. in black and white, 5 ills. in color, July, 1914.

The Gypsy Moth. Vol. XVII, pp. 460-464, 5 ills., Aug., 1906.

Pests and Parasites : Why We Need a National Law to Prevent the Importation of Insect-Infested and Diseased Plants. By Charles Lester Marlatt. Vol. XXII, pp. 321-346, 29 ills., 2 three-quarters-page maps, Apr., 1911.

Gyroscope (Toy):

Primitive Gyroscope in Liberia. By G. N. Collins. Vol. XXI, pp. 531-535, 3 ills., June, 1910.

H

Haakon VII (Norwegian King):

White War in Norway. By Thomas R. Henry. Vol. LXXXVIII, pp. 617-640, 23 ills., 1 three-quarters-page map, Nov., 1945.

Haardt, Georges-Marie:

Citroën Trans-Asiatic Expedition Reaches Kashmir : Scientific Party Led by Georges-Marie Haardt Successfully Crosses Syria, Iraq, Persia, and Afghanistan to Arrive at the Pamir. By Maynard Owen Williams. Vol. LX, pp. 387-443, 62 ills., 1 page map, Oct., 1931.

First Over the Roof of the World by Motor : The Trans-Asiatic Expedition Sets New Records for Wheeled Transport in Scaling Passes of the Himalayas. By Maynard Owen Williams. Vol. LXI, pp. 321-363, 45 ills., 2 half-page maps, Mar., 1932.

From the Mediterranean to the Yellow Sea by Motor : The Citroën-Haardt Expedition Successfully Completes Its Dramatic Journey. By Maynard Owen Williams. Vol. LXII, pp. 513-580, 45 ills. in black and white, 25 ills. in color, 2 half-page maps, Nov., 1932.

Through the Deserts and Jungles of Africa by Motor : Caterpillar Cars Make 15,000-Mile Trip from Algeria to Madagascar in Nine Months. By Georges-Marie Haardt. Vol. XLIX, pp. 651-720, 95 ills., 1 two-thirds-page map, June, 1926.

Trans-Asiatic Expedition Starts. By Georges-Marie Haardt. Vol. LIX, pp. 776-782, 6 ills., June, 1931.

Habana, Cuba. *See* Havana.

Haciendas:

Mexican Hacienda. By J. E. Kirkwood. Vol. XXV, pp. 563-584, 18 ills., May, 1914.

Mrs. Robinson Crusoe in Ecuador. By Mrs. Richard C. Gill. Vol. LXV, pp. 133-172, 43 ills. in black and white, 1 half-page map, Feb., 1934.

On a Chilean Hacienda. 8 ills. in color from natural-color photographs by E. P. Haddon. Vol. LXXXVI, pp. 489-496, Oct., 1944.

Haddon, E. P.:

On a Chilean Hacienda. 8 ills. in color from natural-color photographs by E. P. Haddon. Vol. LXXXVI, pp. 489-496, Oct., 1944.

Hadhramaut:

Into Burning Hadhramaut : The Arab Land of Frankincense and Myrrh, Ever a Lodestone of Western Exploration. By D. van der Meulen. Vol. LXII, pp. 387-429, 44 ills., 1 two-thirds-page map, Oct., 1932.

Hadj (Mohammedan Pilgrimage):

Unbeliever Joins the Hadj : On the Age-Old Pilgrimage to Mecca, Babies Are Born, Elders Die, and Families May Halt a Year to Earn Funds in Distant Lands. By Owen Tweedy. Vol. LXV, pp. 761-789, 30 ills., 1 page map, June, 1934.

Haeberle, Arminius T.:

Azores : Picturesque and Historic Half-Way House of American Transatlantic Aviators. By Arminius T. Haeberle. Vol. XXXV, pp. 514-545, 26 ills., 1 page map, June, 1919.

Hagelbarger, Paul R.:

Valley of Ten Thousand Smokes : An Account of the Discovery and Exploration of the Most Wonderful Volcanic Region in the World. By Robert F. Griggs. Vol. XXXIII, pp. 115-169, 46 ills., 1 half-page map, panorama, Feb., 1918.

Hagerstown, Maryland :

Potomac, River of Destiny. By Albert W. Atwood. Vol. LXXXVIII, pp. 33-70, 15 ills. in black and white, 18 ills. in color, 1 map (two-page spread), July, 1945.

Hague, James D.:

Doubtful Island of the Pacific. By James D. Hague. Vol. XV, pp. 478-489, 1 ill., 2 page maps, Dec., 1904.

Recent Report from the "Doubtful Island Region." By James D. Hague. Vol. XVIII, pp. 205-208, 2 page maps, Mar., 1907.

Hague, The, Netherlands :

Glimpses of Holland. By William Wisner Chapin. Vol. XXVII, pp. 1-29, 26 ills., Jan., 1915.

Holland Rises from War and Water. By Thomas R. Henry. Vol. LXXXIX, pp. 237-260, 18 ills., 1 seven-eighths-page map, Feb., 1946.

Haha Jima (Island), Ogasawara Shoto :

Springboards to Tokyo. By Willard Price. Vol. LXXXVI, pp. 385-407, 16 ills., Oct., 1944.

Haida (Indian Tribe) :

Indians of Our North Pacific Coast. By Matthew W. Stirling. Paintings by W. Langdon Kihn. Vol. LXXXVII, pp. 25-52, 3 ills. in black and white, 16 ills. in color, Jan., 1945.

Totem-pole Builders. 16 ills. in color from paintings by W. Langdon Kihn. Vol. LXXXVII, pp. 33-48, Jan., 1945.

Haifa, Palestine :

Palestine Today. By Francis Chase, Jr. Vol. XC, pp. 501-516, 16 ills., Oct., 1946.

Syria : The Land Link of History's Chain. By Maynard Owen Williams. Vol. XXXVI, pp. 437-462, 20 ills., 1 quarter-page map, Nov., 1919.

Hail Colombia ! By Luis Marden. Vol. LXXVIII, pp. 505-536, 10 ills. in black and white, 18 ills. in color, 1 third-page map, Oct., 1940.

Hailstorms:

Prevention of Hailstorms by the Use of Cannon. Vol. XI, pp. 239-241, June, 1900.

Hainan (Island), China :

Among the Big Knot Lois of Hainan : Wild Tribesmen With Topknots Roam the Little-known Interior of This Big and Strategically Important Island in the China Sea. By Leonard Clark. Vol. LXXIV, pp. 391-418, 28 ills., 1 two-thirds-page map, Sept., 1938.

Hairnet Industry in North China. By H. W. Robinson. Vol. XLIV, pp. 327-336, 10 ills., Sept., 1923.

Haiti:

Bare Feet and Burros of Haiti. By Oliver P. Newman. Vol. LXXXVI, pp. 307-328, 10 ills. in black and white, 10 ills. in color, 1 half-page map, Sept., 1944.

Gay Colors in the Land of Black Majesty. 13 ills. in color from natural-color photographs by Clifton Adams. Vol. LXVI, pp. 445-452, Oct., 1934.

Haiti : A Degenerating Island. By Rear Adm. Colby M. Chester. Vol. XIX, pp. 200-217, 5 ills., 1 quarter-page map, Mar., 1908.

Haiti, the Home of Twin Republics. By Sir Harry Johnston. Vol. XXXVIII, pp. 483-496, 11 ills., 1 third-page map, Dec., 1920.

Haiti and Its Regeneration by the United States. Vol. XXXVIII, pp. 497-511, 10 ills., Dec., 1920.

Haiti Goes to Market. 10 ills. in color from natural-color photographs by B. Anthony Stewart. Vol. LXXXVI, pp. 313-320, Sept., 1944.

Haitian Vignettes. By Capt. John Houston Craige. Vol. LXVI, pp. 435-485, 40 ills. in black and white, 13 ills. in color, 1 quarter-page map, Oct., 1934.

Haiti—*Continued*

Little-Known Marvel of the Western Hemisphere : Christophe's Citadel, a Monument to the Tyranny and Genius of Haiti's King of Slaves. By Maj. G. H. Osterhout, Jr. Vol. XXXVIII, pp. 468-482, 13 ills., Dec., 1920.

Wards of the United States : Notes on What Our Country Is Doing for Santo Domingo, Nicaragua, and Haiti. Vol. XXX, pp. 143-177, 36 ills., Aug., 1916.

Haitian Vignettes. By Capt. John Houston Craige. Vol. LXVI, pp. 435-485, 40 ills. in black and white, 13 ills. in color, 1 quarter-page map, Oct., 1934.

Hal Saflieni (Temple), Malta :

Malta : The Halting Place of Nations : First Account of Remarkable Prehistoric Tombs and Temples Recently Unearthed on the Island. By William Arthur Griffiths. Vol. XXXVII, pp. 445-478, 35 ills., 1 third-page map, May, 1920.

Hale, Edward E.:

Philip Nolan and the *Levant*. By Edward E. Hale. Vol. XVI, pp. 114-116, Mar., 1905.

Half Mile Down : Strange Creatures, Beautiful and Grotesque as Figments of Fancy, Reveal Themselves at Windows of the Bathysphere. By William Beebe. Vol. LXVI, pp. 661-704, 28 ills. in black and white, 16 ills. in color, 1 third-page map, Dec., 1934.

Halifax, Lord (Edward Frederick Lindley Wood) :

India—Yesterday, Today, and Tomorrow. By Lord Halifax. Vol. LXXXIV, pp. 385-408, 20 ills., 1 two-page map, Oct., 1943.

Hall, A. H.:

Aces of Aviation (Gulls). 16 ills. from photographs by A. H. Hall. Vol. XLVII, pp. 665-672, June, 1925.

Black-Headed Gulls in London. By A. H. Hall. Vol. XLVII, pp. 664-672, 16 ills., June, 1925.

Hall, Chapin:

California, Our Lady of Flowers. By Chapin Hall. Vol. LV, pp. 703-750, 20 ills. in black and white, 30 ills. in color, June, 1929.

Hall, Edith H.:

Explorations in Crete. By Edith H. Hall. Vol. XX, pp. 778-787, 15 ills., Sept., 1909.

Hall, Josef W. *See* Close, Upton.

Hall, Melvin A.:

By Motor Through the East Coast and Batak Highlands of Sumatra. By Melvin A. Hall. Vol. XXXVII, pp. 68-102, 27 ills., Jan., 1920.

Hall, William H.:

Antioch the Glorious. By William H. Hall. Vol. XXXVIII, pp. 81-103, 20 ills., 1 half-page map, Aug., 1920.

Crusader Castles of the Near East. By William H. Hall. Vol. LIX, pp. 369-390, 19 ills., 1 third-page map, Mar., 1931.

Hall, William H.—*Continued*

Under the Heel of the Turk: A Land with a Glorious Past, A Present of Abused Opportunities, and a Future of Golden Possibilities. By William H. Hall. Vol. XXXIV, pp. 50-69, 14 ills., July, 1918.

Hallingdal Valley, Norway:

Life in a Norway Valley: An American Girl Is Welcomed Into the Homemaking and Haying of Happy Hallingdal. By Abbie L. Bosworth. Vol. LXVII, pp. 627-648, 21 ills., 1 half-page map, May, 1935.

Hama, Syria:

From Jerusalem to Aleppo. By John D. Whiting. Vol. XXIV, pp. 71-113, 30 ills., 1 half-page map, Jan., 1913.

Hamada el Homra (Desert), Libia:

Mysteries of the Desert. By Hanns Vischer. Vol. XXII, pp. 1056-1059, Nov., 1911.

Hamadsha (Dance):

Two Great Moorish Religious Dances. By George Edmund Holt. Vol. XXII, pp. 776-785, 6 ills., Aug., 1911.

Hambleton, James I.:

Man's Winged Ally, the Busy Honeybee: Modern Research Adds a New Chapter to Usefulness of the Insect Which Has Symbolized Industry Since Early Bible Times. By James I. Hambleton. Vol. LXVII, pp. 401-428, 18 ills. in black and white, 16 ills. in color, Apr., 1935.

Hamburg, Germany:

Hamburg Speaks with Steam Sirens. By Frederick Simpich. Vol. LXIII, pp. 717-744, 32 ills., June, 1933.

Hamilton, Edith:

The Greek Way. By Edith Hamilton. Vol. LXXXV, pp. 257-271, 12 ills., Mar., 1944.

The Roman Way. By Edith Hamilton. Vol. XC, pp. 545-565, 14 ills., 1 two-page map, Nov., 1946.

Hamilton, Virginia:

Keeping House in Borneo. By Virginia Hamilton. Vol. LXXXVIII, pp. 293-324, 28 ills., 1 page map, Sept., 1945.

Hammerfest, Norway:

Sailing the Seven Seas in the Interest of Science: Adventures Through 157,000 Miles of Storm and Calm, from Arctic to Antarctic and Around the World, in the Non-Magnetic Yacht *Carnegie.* By J. P. Ault. Vol. XLII, pp. 631-690, 47 ills., 1 chart, Dec., 1922.

Hammond, (Mrs.) John Hays:

National Geographic Society (Speech by Mrs. John Hays Hammond). Vol. XXIII, pp. 273-298, 5 ills., Mar., 1912.

Hammurabi, Code of:

Pushing Back History's Horizon: How the Pick and Shovel Are Revealing Civilizations That Were Ancient When Israel Was Young. By Albert T. Clay. Vol. XXXIX, pp. 162-216, 47 ills., 1 page map, Feb., 1916.

Handley, Marie Louise:

Siena's Palio, an Italian Inheritance from the Middle Ages. By Marie Louise Handley. Vol. L, pp. 245-258, 3 ills., Aug., 1926.

Hangchow, China:

Ho for the Soochow Ho. By Mabel Craft Deering. Vol. LI, pp. 623-649, 32 ills., 1 three-quarters-page map, June, 1927.

Hanna, G. Dallas:

Cruise Among Desert Islands (Baja California). By A. W. Anthony and G. Dallas Hanna. Vol. XLIV, pp. 71-99, 32 ills., 1 quarter-page map, July, 1923.

Hansen, Leo:

Viking Life in the Storm-Cursed Faeroes. By Leo Hansen. Vol. LVIII, pp. 607-648, 49 ills., 1 half-page map, Nov., 1930.

Hanson, Earl:

Island of the Sagas (Iceland). By Earl Hanson. Vol. LIII, pp. 499-511, 22 ills., Apr., 1928.

Hanson, Elisha:

Man's Feathered Friends of Longest Standing: Peoples of Every Clime and Age Have Lavished Care and Affection Upon Lovely Pigeons. By Elisha Hanson. Vol. XLIX, pp. 63-110, 35 ills. in black and white, 12 ills. in color, Jan., 1926.

Hanson, George M.:

"As the Tuan Had Said." By George M. Hanson. Vol. LXIV, pp. 631-644, 19 ills., Nov., 1933.

Happy Landing in Bermuda. By E. John Long. Vol. LXXV, pp. 213-238, 14 ills. in black and white, 12 ills. in color, Feb., 1939.

Harbin, Manchuria:

Here in Manchuria: Many Thousand Lives Were Lost and More Than Half the Crops Destroyed by the Floods of 1932. By Lilian Grosvenor Coville. Vol. LXIII, pp. 233-256, 26 ills., Feb., 1933.

Japan Faces Russia in Manchuria. By Willard Price. Vol. LXXXII, pp. 603-634, 30 ills., 1 page map, Nov., 1942.

Land of Promise. By Maj. Gen. A. W. Greely. Vol. XXIII, pp. 1078-1090, 7 ills., Nov., 1912.

Russian Development of Manchuria. By Henry B. Miller. Vol. XV, pp. 113-127, 11 ills., 1 half-page map, Mar., 1904.

Harbors and Ports:

Between the Heather and the North Sea: Bold English Headlands Once Sheltered Sea Robbers, Later Were Ports of Wooden Ships, Centers of the Jet and Alum Trades, To-day Are Havens of Adventurous Fishing Fleets. By Leo Walmsley. Vol. LXIII, pp. 197-232, 41 ills., Feb., 1933.

Capital and Chief Seaport of Chile. By W. Robert Moore. Vol. LXXXVI, pp. 477-500, 15 ills. in black and white, 8 ills. in color, 1 third-page map, Oct., 1944.

Harbors and Ports—*Continued*

Channel Ports—And Some Others. By Florence Craig Albrecht. Vol. XXVIII, pp. 1-55, 45 ills., July, 1915.

Charm Spots Along England's Harassed Coast. 16 ills. in duotone from photographs. Vol. LXXVIII, pp. 237-252, Aug., 1940.

Cosmopolitan Shanghai, Key Seaport of China. By W. Robert Moore. Vol. LXII, pp. 311-335, 19 ills., Sept., 1932.

Heroes' Return (Charleston, S. C.). By William H. Nicholas. Vol. LXXVII, pp. 333-352, 19 ills., Mar., 1945.

Jobos Harbor (Puerto Rico). Vol. X, p. 206, June, 1899.

Marseille, Battle Port of Centuries. By a Staff Correspondent. Vol. LXXXVI, pp. 425-448, 24 ills., 1 three-quarters-page map, Oct., 1944.

Normandy's Made-in-England Harbors. Vol. LXXXVII, pp. 565-580, 16 ills., 1 quarter-page map, May, 1945.

One Hundred British Seaports. Vol. XXXI, pp. 84-94, 10 ills., 1 page map, Jan., 1917.

Three Old Ports on the Spanish Main. By G. M. L. Brown. Vol. XVII, pp. 622-638, 12 ills., Nov., 1906.

Today on the China Coast. By John B. Powell. Vol. LXXXVII, pp. 217-238, 17 ills., 1 page map, Feb., 1945.

When the Herring Fleet Comes to Great Yarmouth. By W. Robert Moore. Vol. LXVI, pp. 233-250, 19 ills., Aug., 1934.

Harby, (Lt. Comdr.) Samuel F.:

They Survived at Sea. By Lt. Comdr. Samuel F. Harby. Vol. LXXXVII, pp. 617-640, 22 ills., May, 1945.

Harding, Warren G.:

President Harding present at unveiling of the Peary Memorial in Arlington National Cemetery, Apr. 6, 1922. Vol. XLI, p. 639 ; ill. 640, 642, June, 1922.

Hardy Catalpa. Vol. XIV, pp. 348-353, 4 ills., Sept., 1903.

Hargrave, Laurence:

Tetrahedral Principle in Kite Structure. By Alexander Graham Bell. Vol. XIV, pp. 219-251, 89 ills., 15 diagrams, June, 1903.

Hark! (Deer). Vol. XL, supplement, Aug., 1921.

Hark to the Hounds. By Freeman Lloyd. Paintings by Edward Herbert Miner. Vol. LXXII, pp. 453-484, 18 ills. in black and white, 31 portraits in color, Oct., 1937.

Harlan, Harry V.:

Caravan Journey Through Abyssinia : From Addis Ababa Through Lalibela, the Strange Jerusalem of Ethiopia, in Search of New Grains for American Farms. By Harry V. Harlan. Vol. XLVII, pp. 613-663, 46 ills., 1 half-page map, June, 1925.

Harmon, Byron:

Peaks and Trails in the Canadian Alps. 13 ills. in duotone from photographs by Byron Harmon. Vol. LXV, pp. 627-642, May, 1934.

Harnden, Phoebe Binney:

Keeping House in Majorca. By Phoebe Binney Harnden. Vol. XLV, pp. 425-440, 18 ills., 1 quarter-page map, Apr., 1924.

Harper, Francis:

Okefinokee Wilderness : Exploring the Mystery Land of the Suwannee River Reveals Natural Wonders and Fascinating Folklore. By Francis Harper. Vol. LXV, pp. 597-624, 35 ills., 1 two-thirds-page map, May, 1934.

Harpers Ferry, West Virginia :

George Washington's Historic River (Potomac). 18 ills. in color from natural-color photographs by Willard R. Culver and Robert F. Sisson. Vol. LXXXVIII, pp. 41-64, July, 1945.

Potomac, River of Destiny. By Albert W. Atwood. Vol. LXXXVIII, pp. 33-70, 15 ills. in black and white, 18 ills. in color, 1 map (two-page spread), July, 1945.

Harput, Turkey :

Mountaineers of the Euphrates. By Ellsworth Huntington. Vol. XX, pp. 142-156, 13 ills., Feb., 1909.

Harriman, Pennsylvania :

Ships for the Seven Seas : The Story of America's Maritime Needs, Her Capabilities and Her Achievements. By Ralph A. Graves. Vol. XXXIV, pp. 165-200, 24 ills., Sept., 1918.

Harriman Alaska Expedition. By Henry Gannett. Vol. X, pp. 507-512, 1 chart, 1 page map, Dec., 1899.

Harriman Alaska Expedition in Coöperation with the Washington Academy of Sciences. By Gilbert H. Grosvenor. Vol. X, pp. 225-227, June, 1899.

Harris, Ernest Lloyd:

Buried Cities of Asia Minor. By Ernest Lloyd Harris. Vol. XX, pp. 1-18, 10 ills., Jan., 1909.

Historic Islands and Shores of the Ægean Sea. By Ernest Lloyd Harris. Vol. XXVIII, pp. 231-262, 29 ills., 1 half-page map, Sept., 1915.

Ruined Cities of Asia Minor. By Ernest Lloyd Harris. Vol. XIX, pp. 741-760, 11 ills., Nov., 1908.

Some Ruined Cities of Asia Minor. By Ernest Lloyd Harris. Vol. XIX, pp. 833-858, 19 ills., Dec., 1908.

Harris, Fred H.:

Skiing Over the New Hampshire Hills. By Fred H. Harris. Vol. XXXVII, pp. 133-164, 37 ills., Feb., 1920.

Harris, Jennie E.:

Living Casks of Honey (Ants). By Jennie E. Harris. Vol. LXVI, pp. 193-199, 4 ills., Aug., 1934.

Harris, R. A.:

Cotidal Lines for the World. By R. A. Harris. Vol. XVII, pp. 303-309, special map supplement, 2 page and 1 half-page maps, June, 1906.

Some Indications of Land in the Vicinity of the North Pole. By R. A. Harris. Vol. XV, pp. 255-261, 1 page map, June, 1904.

Harrison, Ed N.:

Birds and Beasts of Mexico's Desert Islands. 12 ills. in color from natural-color photographs by Ed N. Harrison, Alfred M. Bailey, and Robert J. Niedrach. Vol. LXXX, pp. 353-360, Sept., 1941.

Hart, Albert Bushnell:

Judge of Prize Essay Contest. Vol. X, p. 32, Jan., 1899.

Hartford, Connecticut:

Connecticut, Prodigy of Ingenuity: Factories Play a Symphony of Industry Amid Colonial Scenes in the State of Steady Habits. By Leo A. Borah. Vol. LXXIV, pp. 279-326, 25 ills. in black and white, 25 ills. in color, 1 two-page map, Sept., 1938.

Harvard University: Biological Laboratories:

Mystery Mammals of the Twilight (Bats). By Donald R. Griffin. Vol. XC, pp. 117-134, 19 ills., July, 1946.

Hasanoğlan, Turkey: Village Institutes:

Turkish Republic Comes of Age. By Maynard Owen Williams. Vol. LXXXVII, pp. 581-616, 4 ills. in black and white, 29 ills. in color, 1 map (two-page spread), May, 1945.

Hassanein, A. M.:

Crossing the Untraversed Libyan Desert: The Record of a 2,200-Mile Journey of Exploration Which Resulted in the Discovery of Two Oases of Strategic Importance on the Southwestern Frontier of Egypt. By A. M. Hassanein. Vol. XLVI, pp. 233-277, 46 ills., 1 half-page map, Sept., 1924.

Hatay:

In the Land of Moses and Abraham. 25 ills. in color from natural-color photographs by W. Robert Moore. Vol. LXXIV, pp. 711-742, Dec., 1938.

Hatcher, J. B.:

Indian Tribes of Southern Patagonia, Tierra del Fuego, and the Adjoining Islands. By J. B. Hatcher. Vol. XII, pp. 12-22, 4 ills., Jan., 1901.

Some Geographic Features of Southern Patagonia, With a Discussion of Their Origin. By J. B. Hatcher. Vol. XI, pp. 41-55, 4 ills., Feb., 1900.

Hathaway, Sibyl (La Dame de Serk):

Feudal Isle of Sark: Where Sixteenth-Century Laws Are Still Observed. By Sibyl Hathaway (La Dame de Serk). Vol. LXII, pp. 101-119, 21 ills., 1 half-page map, July, 1932.

Hatteras Island, North Carolina:

Bit of Elizabethan England in America: Fisher Folk of the Islands Off North Carolina Conserved the Speech and Customs of Sir Walter Raleigh's Colonists. By Blanch Nettleton Epler. Vol. LXIV, pp. 695-730, 43 ills., 1 three-quarters-page map, Dec., 1933.

Where the Wind Does the Work. By Collier Cobb. Vol. XVII, pp. 310-317, 9 ills., 1 page map, June, 1906.

Hatteria (Reptile). *See* Tuatara.

Haunts of the Caribbean Corsairs: The West Indies, a Geographic Background for the Most Adventurous Episodes in the History of the Western Hemisphere. By Nell Ray Clarke. Vol. XLI, pp. 147-187, 27 ills., Feb., 1922.

Havana (Habana), Cuba:

American Progress in Habana. Vol. XIII, pp. 97-108, 10 ills., Mar., 1902.

Cuba—The Isle of Romance. By Enrique C. Canova. Vol. LXIV, pp. 345-380, 34 ills., 1 page map, Sept., 1933.

Cuba—The Sugar Mill of the Antilles. By William Joseph Showalter. Vol. XXXVIII, pp. 1-33, 24 ills., 1 page map, July, 1920.

Glamour of Historic Havana. 9 ills. in black and white from photographs by F. S. Lincoln. Vol. LXIV, pp. 357-364, Sept., 1933.

Havasupai Indians:

Experiences in the Grand Canyon. By Ellsworth and Emery Kolb. Vol. XXVI, pp. 99-184, 70 ills., 1 page map, Aug., 1914.

Indian Tribes of Pueblo Land. By Matthew W. Stirling. Vol. LXXVIII, pp. 549-596, 16 ills. in black and white, 25 ills. in color, Nov., 1940.

Hawaii, Territory of:

American Pathfinders in the Pacific. By William H. Nicholas. Vol. LXXXIX, pp. 617-640, 17 ills., 1 two-page map, May, 1946.

Bird City. Vol. XV, pp. 494-498, 6 ills., Dec., 1904.

Bird Life Among Lava Rock and Coral Sand: The Chronicle of a Scientific Expedition to Little-Known Islands of Hawaii. By Alexander Wetmore. Vol. XLVIII, pp. 77-108, 36 ills., 1 half-page map, July, 1925.

Hawaii, Then and Now: Boyhood Recollections and Recent Observations by an American Whose Grandfather Came to the Islands 102 Years Ago. By William R. Castle. Vol. LXXIV, pp. 419-462, 30 ills. in black and white, 10 ills. in color, 1 page-and-a-half map, Oct., 1938.

Hawaii for Homes. By H. P. Wood. Vol. XIX, pp. 298-299, Apr., 1908.

Hawaiian Islands: America's Strongest Outpost of Defense—The Volcanic and Floral Wonderland of the World. By Gilbert Grosvenor. Vol. XLV, pp. 115-238, 106 ills. in black and white, 21 ills. in color, 1 page, 4 half-page, and 1 quarter-page maps, 1 diagram, Feb., 1924.

Hawaii, Territory of—_Continued_

Key to the Pacific. By George C. Perkins. Vol. XIX, pp. 295-298, 1 half-page map, Apr., 1908.

Leis from Aloha Land. 10 ills. in color from natural-color photographs; 8 ills. by Richard H. Stewart. Vol. LXXIV, pp. 435-442, Oct., 1938.

Life on the Hawaii "Front" : All-out Defense and Belt Tightening of Pacific Outpost Foreshadow the Things to Come on Mainland. By Lieut. Frederick Simpich, Jr. Vol. LXXXII, pp. 541-560, 19 ills., 1 half-page map, Oct., 1942.

My Flight from Hawaii. By Amelia Earhart. Vol. LXVII, pp. 593-609, 4 ills. in black and white, 8 ills. in duotone, May, 1935.

Net Results from Oceania : Collecting Aquarium Specimens in Tropical Pacific Waters. By Walter H. Chute. Vol. LXXIX, pp. 347-372, 8 ills. in black and white, 24 ills. in color, Mar., 1941.

Waves and Thrills at Waikiki. 8 ills. in duotone by Thomas Edward Blake. Vol. LXVII, pp. 597-604, May, 1935.

Hawaiian Islands : America's Strongest Outpost of Defense—The Volcanic and Floral Wonderland of the World. By Gilbert Grosvenor. Vol. XLV, pp. 115-238, 106 ills. in black and white, 21 ills. in color, 1 page, 4 half-page, and 1 quarter-page maps, 1 diagram, Feb., 1924.

Hawke (Ship) :

By Sail Across Europe. By Merlin Minshall. Vol. LXXI, pp. 533-567, 38 ills., 1 two-thirds-page map, May, 1937.

Hawks:

Adventures with Birds of Prey. By Frank and John Craighead. Vol. LXXII, pp. 109-134, 25 ills., July, 1937.

American Birds of Prey—A Review of Their Value. Vol. XXXVIII, pp. 460-467, 6 ills., Dec., 1920.

Eagle, King of Birds, and His Kin. By Alexander Wetmore. Paintings by Maj. Allan Brooks. Vol. LXIV, pp. 43-95, 23 ills. in black and white, 28 ills. in color, July, 1933.

Eagles, Hawks, and Vultures. 28 ills. in color from paintings by Maj. Allan Brooks. Vol. LXIV, pp. 65-94, July, 1933.

Falconry, the Sport of Kings. By Louis Agassiz Fuertes. Vol. XXXVIII, pp. 429-460, 12 ills. in black and white, 12 ills. in color, Dec., 1920.

Hunting with the Lens. By Howard H. Cleaves. Vol. XXVI, pp. 1-35, 47 ills., July, 1914.

In Quest of the Golden Eagle : Over Lonely Mountain and Prairie Soars This Rare and Lordly Bird, But Three Youths from the East Catch Up With Him at Last. By John and Frank Craighead. Vol. LXXVII, pp. 693-710, 17 ills., May, 1940.

Hawks—_Continued_

Life with an Indian Prince : As Guests of a Maharaja's Brother, Two Young American Naturalists Study Age-old Methods of Hunting with Trained Falcons and Cheetahs and Savor the Pomp of Royal India. By John and Frank Craighead. Vol. LXXXI, pp. 235-272, 38 ills., 1 sixth-page map, Feb., 1942.

Photographing the Nest Life of the Osprey. By Capt. C. W. R. Knight. Vol. LXII, pp. 247-260, 25 ills., Aug., 1932.

Hayden, (Lt. Comdr.) Edward Everett:

Chronometer and Time Service of the U. S. Naval Observatory and the Present Status of Standard Time. By Lieut. Comdr. Edward Everett Hayden. Vol. XV, pp. 430-431, Oct., 1904.

Hayes, C. Willard:

Assumed Inconstancy in the Level of Lake Nicaragua : A Question of Permanency of the Nicaragua Canal. By C. Willard Hayes. Vol. XI, pp. 156-161, Apr., 1900.

Ice Cliffs on White River, Yukon Territory. By Alfred H. Brooks and C. Willard Hayes. Vol. XI, pp. 199-201, May, 1900.

Physiography of the Nicaragua Canal Route. By C. Willard Hayes. Vol. X, pp. 233-246, special map supplement, 2 page and 1 half-page maps, July, 1899.

Hayes, William C.:

Daily Life in Ancient Egypt (Part I). Daily Life in Ancient Egypt: _The Later Period_ (Part II). By William C. Hayes. Paintings by H. M. Herget. Vol. LXXX, pp. 419-515, 34 ills. in black and white, 32 ills. in color, 1 two-thirds-page map, Oct., 1941.

Hazard, Daniel L.:

Magnetic Observations in Alaska. By Daniel L. Hazard. Vol. XX, pp. 675-676, 1 page map, July, 1909.

Hazen, Henry Allen:

Henry Allen Hazen (Biography). Vol. XI, pp. 78-79, Feb., 1900.

Hazlett, Dillwyn M.:

Farming on the Isthmus of Panama. By Dillwyn M. Hazlett. Vol. XVII, pp. 229-234, 5 ills., Apr., 1906.

Head-Hunters:

Field Sports Among the Wild Men of Northern Luzon. By Dean C. Worcester. Vol. XXII, pp. 215-267, 17 ills., 1 half-page map, Mar., 1911.

Formosa the Beautiful. By Alice Ballantine Kirjassoff. Vol. XXXVII, pp. 246-292, 60 ills., 1 half-page map, Mar., 1920.

Head-Hunters of Northern Luzon. By Dean C. Worcester. Vol. XXIII, pp. 833-930, 102 ills., 1 page map, Sept., 1912.

I Lived on Formosa. By Joseph W. Ballantine. Vol. LXXXVII, pp. 1-24, 19 ills., 1 page and 1 half-page maps, Jan., 1945.

Head-Hunters—*Continued*

Into Primeval Papua by Seaplane : Seeking Disease-Resisting Sugar Cane, Scientists Find Neolithic Man in Unmapped Nooks of Sorcery and Cannibalism. By E. W. Brandes. Vol. LVI, pp. 253-332, 98 ills., 1 three-quarters-page map, Sept., 1929.

New Guinea's Mountain and Swampland Dwellers. By Col. Ray T. Elsmore. Vol. LXXXVIII, pp. 671-694, 15 ills. in black and white, 7 ills. in color, 1 half-page map, Dec., 1945.

Over Trail and Through Jungle in Ecuador : Indian Head-Hunters of the Interior, an Interesting Study in the South American Republic. By H. E. Anthony. Vol. XL, pp. 327-352, 28 ills., Oct., 1921.

Healer of Humanity's Wounds (American Red Cross). Vol. XXXIV, pp. 308-324, 16 ills., Oct., 1918.

Healey, Giles Greville:

To Market in Guatemala. 19 ills. in color from natural-color photographs by Giles Greville Healey and Charles S. Pineo. Vol. LXXXVIII, pp. 89-104, July, 1945.

Healing Arts in Global War : As Weapons Grow Deadlier, Scientific Medicine Pits Its Ever-rising Skill Against Them. By Albert W. Atwood. Vol. LXXXIV, pp. 599-618, 17 ills., Nov., 1943.

Health and Morale of America's Citizen Army : Personal Observations of Conditions in Our Soldier Cities by a Former Commander-in-Chief of the United States Army and Navy. By William Howard Taft. Vol. XXXIII, pp. 219-245, 22 ills., Mar., 1918.

Hearn, Lafcadio:

Lafcadio Hearn on the Island and People of Martinique. Vol. XIII, pp. 214-216, June, 1902.

Heart of a Hemisphere : Of Vital Importance is the Area Portrayed in The Society's New Map of Mexico, Central America, and the West Indies. Text accompanying special map supplement in colors. Vol. LXXVI, pp. 739-740, 1 ill., Dec., 1939.

Heart of Aymará Land : A Visit to Tiahuanacu, Perhaps the Oldest City of the New World, Lost Beneath the Drifting Sand of Centuries in the Bolivian Highlands. By Stewart E. McMillin. Vol. LI, pp. 213-256, 23 ills. in black and white, 18 ills. in color, 1 half-page map, Feb., 1927.

Heart of the Antarctic. By Ernest H. Shackleton. Vol. XX, pp. 972-1007, 27 ills., 1 half-page map, Nov., 1909.

Heather Paints the Highlands (Scotland). 38 ills. in color from natural-color photographs by B. Anthony Stewart. Vol. LXXXIX, pp. 561-600, May, 1946.

Heavens Above : On Land, Sea, and in the Air the Stars Serve Modern Man as Map, Compass, and Clock. By Donald H. Menzel. With 12 charts, designed by the author, showing star positions for each month, and 13 drawings of the constellations by Carlotta Gonzales Lahey. Vol. LXXXIV, pp. 97-128, 1 map (two-page spread), July, 1943.

Hedin, (Dr.) Sven:

Dr. Sven Hedin (Biography). Vol. XIV, pp. 26-29, Jan., 1903.

Sven Hedin in Tibet. Vol. XIII, pp. 96-97, Mar., 1902.

Sven Hedin's Explorations in Central Asia. Vol. XII, pp. 393-395, Nov., 1901.

Heilprin, Angelo:

Destruction of Pompeii as Interpreted by the Volcanic Eruptions of Martinique. By Angelo Heilprin. Vol. XV, p. 431, Oct., 1904.

Impression of the Guiana Wilderness. By Angelo Heilprin. Vol. XVIII, pp. 373-381, 6 ills., June, 1907.

National Geographic Society Expedition in the West Indies. Vol. XIII, pp. 209-213, 2 half-page maps, June, 1902.

Shattered Obelisk of Mont Pelée. By Angelo Heilprin. Vol. XVII, pp. 465-474, 5 ills., Aug., 1906.

Heinicke, Alfred:

Persia. 4 ills. in color from photographs by Alfred Heinicke. Vol. XXXIX, pp. 401-416, Apr., 1921.

Heinl, (Maj.) Robert D., Jr.:

Palms and Planes in the New Hebrides. By Maj. Robert D. Heinl, Jr. Vol. LXXXVI, pp. 229-256, 17 ills. in black and white, 12 ills. in color, 1 four-fifths-page map, Aug., 1944.

Heinly, Burt A.:

Carrying Water Through a Desert : The Story of the Los Angeles Aqueduct. By Burt A. Heinly. Vol. XXI, pp. 568-596, 19 ills., 1 half-page map, July, 1910.

Heiskell, Morgan:

Capri, the Island Retreat of Roman Emperors. 12 ills. from photographs by Morgan Heiskell. Vol. XLI, pp. 627-638, June, 1922.

Hejaz (Arab Kingdom) :

Visit to Three Arab Kingdoms : Transjordania, Iraq, and the Hedjaz Present Many Problems to European Powers. By Junius B. Wood. Vol. XLIII, pp. 535-568, 30 ills., 1 three-quarters-page map, May, 1923.

Helgoland (Island), Germany :

Demolishing Germany's North Sea Ramparts. By Stuart E. Jones. Vol. XC, pp. 635-644, 1 ill. in black and white, 10 ills. in color, Nov., 1946.

Helium:

Helium, the New Balloon Gas. By G. Sherburne Rogers. Vol. XXXV, pp. 441-456, 11 ills., May, 1919.

Helium—*Continued*

Modern Transmutation of the Elements. By Sir William Ramsay. Vol. XVII, pp. 201-203, Apr., 1906.

Studies Planned for New Stratosphere Flight with Helium. Vol. LXVII, pp. 795-800, 5 ills., June, 1935.

Hell, Norway:

White War in Norway. By Thomas R. Henry. Vol. LXXXVIII, pp. 617-640, 23 ills., 1 three-quarters-page map, Nov., 1945.

Hellcats (Airplanes):

Take-off for Japan. 22 ills. in color from natural-color photographs. Vol. LXXXVIII, pp. 193-208, Aug., 1945.

Heller, Edmund:

Nature's Most Amazing Mammal: Elephants, Unique Among Animals, Have Many Human Qualities When Wild That Make Them Foremost Citizens of Zoo and Circus. By Edmund Heller. Vol. LXV, pp. 729-759, 37 ills., June, 1934.

Hellweg, (Capt.) J. F.:

Eclipse Adventures on a Desert Isle (Canton). By Capt. J. F. Hellweg. Vol. LXXII, pp. 377-394, 14 ills., 1 two-thirds-page map, Sept., 1937.

Helping Navigation. Vol. XI, pp. 162-163, Apr., 1900.

Helping the Farmers. Vol. XV, pp. 82-85, 1 ill., Feb., 1905.

Helping the Farmers. Vol. XVIII, pp. 746-749, Nov., 1907.

Helping the Filipino Fisheries. Vol. XVIII, pp. 795-796, Dec., 1907.

Helping to Solve Our Allies' Food Problem: America Calls for a Million Young Soldiers of the Commissary to Volunteer for Service in 1918. By Ralph A. Graves. Vol. XXXIII, pp. 170-194, 23 ills., Feb., 1918.

Helsingfors, Finland. *See* Helsinki.

Helsinki, Finland:

Farthest-North Republic: Olympic Games and Arctic Flying Bring Sequestered Finland into New Focus of World Attention. By Alma Luise Olson. Vol. LXXIV, pp. 499-533, 25 ills. in black and white, 12 ills. in color, 1 page map, Oct., 1938.

Finland: Land of Sky-Blue Lakes. 12 ills. in color from natural-color photographs by Konstantin J. Kostich. Vol. LXXIV, pp. 515-522, Oct., 1938.

Flashes from Finland. 19 ills. from photographs. Vol. LXXVII, pp. 239-254, Feb., 1940.

Flying Around the Baltic. By Douglas Chandler. Vol. LXXIII, pp. 767-806, 31 ills. in black and white, 13 ills. in duotone, 1 half-page map, June, 1938.

Helsingfors—A Contrast in Light and Shade. By Frank P. S. Glassey. Vol. XLVII, pp. 597-612, 20 ills., May, 1925.

Hemisphere Map Articles:

Map of the Northern and Southern Hemispheres. Text accompanying special map supplement in colors. Vol. LXXXIII, pp. 481-483, Apr., 1943.

New World Map Gives Backdrop for Headlines (Eastern and Western Hemispheres). Text accompanying special map supplement in colors. Vol. LXXX, pp. 741-742, 1 ill., Dec., 1941.

Henderson, Esther:

Saguaro, King of the Arizona Desert. 9 ills. in color from natural-color photographs by Esther Henderson, Jack Breed, and Max Kegley. Vol. LXXXVIII, pp. 697-704, Dec., 1945.

Hendrick, Calvin W.:

Colossal Work in Baltimore. By Calvin W. Hendrick. Vol. XX, pp. 365-373, 6 ills., Apr., 1909.

Henequen—The Yucatan Fiber. By E. H. Thompson. Vol. XIV, pp. 150-158, 6 ills., Apr., 1903.

Henry, Alfred J.:

Forecasting the Weather. By Alfred J. Henry. Vol. XV, pp. 285-292, 6 ills., 1 chart, July, 1904.

Report by Alfred J. Henry. Vol. XIII, p. 80, Feb., 1902.

Resignation of Alfred J. Henry as Secretary of The Society. Vol. XIV, p. 425, Nov., 1903.

Salton Sea and the Rainfall of the Southwest. By Alfred J. Henry. Vol. XVIII, pp. 244-248, Apr., 1907.

Storm of February 25-28, 1902. By Alfred J. Henry. Vol. XIII, pp. 110-112, 1 chart, Mar., 1902.

Variations in Lake Levels and Atmospheric Precipitation. By Alfred J. Henry. Vol. X, pp. 403-406, 1 diagram, Oct., 1899.

Henry, Thomas R.:

Holland Rises from War and Water. By Thomas R. Henry. Vol. LXXXIX, pp. 237-260, 18 ills., 1 seven-eighths-page map, Feb., 1946.

Tale of Three Cities. By Thomas R. Henry. Vol. LXXXVIII, pp. 641-669, 23 ills., Dec., 1945.

War's Wake in the Rhineland. By Thomas R. Henry. Vol. LXXXVIII, pp. 1-32, 29 ills., 1 third-page map, July, 1945.

White War in Norway. By Thomas R. Henry. Vol. LXXXVIII, pp. 617-640, 23 ills., 1 three-quarters-page map, Nov., 1945.

Henry Hudson, Magnificent Failure: Just 330 Years Ago He and His Mutinous Crew Found Manhattan Covered With "Goodly Oakes" and Fought Indians in New York Harbor. By Frederick G. Vosburgh. Vol. LXXV, pp. 461-490, 21 ills., Apr., 1939.

Henshaw, Henry Wetherbee:

American Game Birds. By Henry Wetherbee Henshaw. Vol. XXVIII, pp. 105-158, 4 ills. in black and white, 72 ills. in color, Aug., 1915.

Henshaw, Henry Wetherbee—*Continued*

Birds of Town and Country. By Henry Wetherbee Henshaw. Vol. XXV, pp. 494-531, 2 ills. in black and white, 64 ills. in color, May, 1914.

Fifty Common Birds of Farm and Orchard. By Henry Wetherbee Henshaw. Vol. XXIV, pp. 669-697, 50 ills. in color, June, 1913.

Friends of Our Forests. By Henry Wetherbee Henshaw. Vol. XXXI, pp. 297-321, 1 ill. in black and white, 32 ills. in color, Apr., 1917.

Policemen of the Air. By Henry Wetherbee Henshaw. Vol. XIX, pp. 79-118, 38 ills., Feb., 1908.

Hērákleion, Crete (Island). *See* Candia.

Heraldry of Heroism (Decorations and Medals). By Arthur E. Du Bois. Vol. LXXXIV, pp. 409-413, 2 ills., 1 third-page map, Oct., 1943.

Herbert, Charles W.:

Island Treasures of the Caribbean. 23 ills. in color from natural-color photographs by Edwin L. Wisherd and C. W. Herbert. Vol. LXXVIII, pp. 281-304, Sept., 1940.

Saba, Crater Treasure of the Indies. By Charles W. Herbert. Vol. LXXVIII, pp. 597-620, 14 ills. in black and white, 12 ills. in color, 1 map (inset), Nov., 1940.

Up and Down on Saba (Island). 12 ills. in color from natural-color photographs by Charles W. Herbert. Vol. LXXVIII, pp. 605-612, Nov., 1940.

Here and There in Northern Africa. By Frank Edward Johnson. Vol. XXV, pp. 1-132, 113 ills., Jan., 1914.

Here in Manchuria: Many Thousand Lives Were Lost and More Than Half the Crops Destroyed by the Floods of 1932. By Lilian Grosvenor Coville. Vol. LXIII, pp. 233-256, 26 ills., Feb., 1933.

Herget, H. M.:

Aztecs Under the War God's Reign. 10 ills. in color from paintings by H. M. Herget. Vol. LXXI, pp. 735-742, June, 1937.

Egyptians: Life, Culture, and History of the Egyptians. 32 ills. in color from paintings by H. M. Herget. Vol. LXXX, pp. 436-514, Oct., 1941.

Greeks: "Glory That Was Greece." 32 ills. in color from paintings by H. M. Herget. Vol. LXXXV, pp. 290-352, Mar., 1944.

Incas: In the Realm of the Sons of the Sun. 10 ills. in color from paintings by H. M. Herget. Vol. LXXIII, pp. 229-236, Feb., 1938.

Mayas: Life and Death in Ancient Maya Land. 10 ills. in color from paintings by H. M. Herget. Vol. LXX, pp. 623-630, Nov., 1936.

Mayas: Portraits of Ancient Mayas, a Peace-Loving People. 10 ills. in color from paintings by H. M. Herget. Vol. LXVIII, pp. 553-560, Nov., 1935.

Herget, H. M.—*Continued*

Romans: Ancient Rome Brought to Life. 32 ills. in color from paintings by H. M. Herget. Vol. XC, pp. 570-633, Nov., 1946.

Herki (Tribespeople):

Mountain Tribes of Iran and Iraq. By Harold Lamb. Vol. LXXXIX, pp. 385-408, 15 ills., 1 two-page map, Mar., 1946.

Herm (Island), Channel Islands:

Channel Islands. By Edith Carey. Vol. XXXVIII, pp. 143-164, 24 ills., 1 quarter-page map, Aug., 1920.

Heroes of Wartime Science and Mercy. By Elizabeth W. King. Vol. LXXXIV, pp. 715-740, 11 ills. in black and white, 334 ills. in color, Dec., 1943.

Heroes' Return. By William H. Nicholas. Vol. LXXXVII, pp. 333-352, 19 ills., Mar., 1945.

Heroic Flags of the Middle Ages. By Gilbert Grosvenor and Byron McCandless. Vol. XXXII, pp. 388-399, 96 ills. in color, Oct., 1917.

Herons:

Ibises, Herons, and Flamingos. 11 ills. in color from paintings by Maj. Allan Brooks. Vol. LXII, pp. 454-469, Oct., 1932.

Large Wading Birds: Long Legs and Remarkable Beaks, as Well as Size, Form and Color, Distinguish the Herons, Ibises, and Flamingos. By T. Gilbert Pearson. Paintings by Maj. Allan Brooks. Vol. LXII, pp. 441-469, 7 ills. in black and white, 11 ills. in color, Oct., 1932.

Herrick, Francis H.:

Eagle in Action: An Intimate Study of the Eyrie Life of America's National Bird. By Francis H. Herrick. Vol. LV, pp. 635-660, 20 ills., May, 1929.

Herring:

Bornholm—Denmark in a Nutshell. By Mason Sutherland. Vol. LXXXVII, pp. 239-256, 20 ills., 1 half-page map, Feb., 1945.

Fishes and Fisheries of Our North Atlantic Seaboard. By John Oliver La Gorce. Vol. XLIV, pp. 567-634, 35 ills. in black and white, 16 ills. in color, Dec., 1923.

King Herring: An Account of the World's Most Valuable Fish, the Industries It Supports, and the Part It Has Played in History. By Hugh M. Smith. Vol. XX, pp. 701-735, 21 ills., Aug., 1909.

When the Herring Fleet Comes to Great Yarmouth. By W. Robert Moore. Vol. LXVI, pp. 233-250, 19 ills., Aug., 1934.

Hersey, (Maj.) Henry E.:

Member of Wellman Polar Expedition. Vol. XVII, p. 205, Apr., 1906. Vol. XVII, p. 712, Dec., 1906.

Herzegovina:

East of the Adriatic: Notes on Dalmatia, Montenegro, Bosnia, and Herzegovina. By Kenneth McKenzie. Vol. XXIII, pp. 1159-1187, 37 ills., 1 page map, Dec., 1912.

Where East Meets West: A Visit to Picturesque Dalmatia, Montenegro, and Bosnia. By Marian Cruger Coffin. Vol. XIX, pp. 309-344, 26 ills., 1 half-page map, May, 1908.

Herzfeld, (Dr.) Ernst Emil:

Exploring the Secrets of Persepolis. By Charles Breasted. Vol. LXIV, pp. 381-420, 48 ills., 1 half-page map, 1 plan, Oct., 1933.

Heurlin, Gustav:

Denmark, Land of Farms and Fisheries. 14 ills. in color from natural-color photographs by Gustav Heurlin. Vol. LXI, pp. 222-231, Feb., 1932.

Norway: Fjords and Fjells of Viking Land. 27 ills. in color from natural-color photographs by Gustav Heurlin. Vol. LVIII, pp. 12-45, July, 1930.

Sweden: Color and Customs of Sweden's Chateau Country. 13 ills. in color from natural-color photographs by Gustav Heurlin. Vol. LXVI, pp. 33-40, July, 1934.

Sweden: Types and Costumes of Old Sweden. 23 ills. in color from autochromes lumière by Gustav Heurlin. Vol. LIV, pp. 424-441, Oct., 1928.

Hewers of Stone (Mitla, Mexico). By Jeremiah Zimmerman. Vol. XXI, pp. 1002-1020, 11 ills., Dec., 1910.

Hewes, Laurence Ilsley:

Butterflies—Try and Get Them. By Laurence Ilsley Hewes. Vol. LXIX, pp. 667-678, 15 ills. in black and white, 9 ills. in color, May, 1936.

Heyerdahl, Thor:

Turning Back Time in the South Seas (Fatu-Hiva Island). By Thor Heyerdahl. Vol. LXXIX, pp. 109-136, 33 ills., 2 maps, Jan., 1941.

Heyward, DuBose:

American Virgins: After Dark Days, These Adopted Daughters of the United States Are Finding a New Place in the Caribbean Sun. By DuBose Heyward and Daisy Reck. Vol. LXXVIII, pp. 273-308, 15 ills. in black and white, 23 ills. in color, 1 two-thirds-page map, Sept., 1940.

Charleston: Where Mellow Past and Present Meet. By DuBose Heyward. Vol. LXXV, pp. 273-312, 20 ills. in black and white, 24 ills. in color, 1 page map, Mar., 1939.

Hialeah Park, Florida:

Flame-Feathered Flamingos of Florida. By W. A. Watts. With 9 ills. in color from natural-color photographs by W. F. Gerecke. Vol. LXXIX, pp. 56-65, Jan., 1941.

Hidden Glacier, Alaska:

National Geographic Society's Alaska Expedition of 1909. By Ralph S. Tarr and Lawrence Martin. Vol. XXI, pp. 1-54, 42 ills., 4 page and 7 half-page maps, Jan., 1910.

Hidden Key to the Pacific: Piercing the Web of Secrecy Which Long Has Veiled Japanese Bases in the Mandated Islands. By Willard Price. Vol. LXXXI, pp. 759-785, 28 ills., 1 map (two-page spread), June, 1942.

Hidden Perils of the Deep. By G. R. Putnam. Vol. XX, pp. 822-837, 19 diagrams, 3 charts, Sept., 1909.

Hidden Valley, Netherlands New Guinea. *See* Grand Valley.

Hierapolis (Ancient City):

Ruined Cities of Asia Minor. By Ernest L. Harris. Vol. XIX, pp. 741-760, 11 ills., Nov., 1908.

Higgins, Margaret M.:

Guam—Perch of the China Clippers. By Margaret M. Higgins. Vol. LXXIV, pp. 99-122, 23 ills., 1 third-page map, July, 1938.

High Country of Colorado. By Alfred M. Bailey. With 23 ills. in color from natural-color photographs by the author, Robert J. Niedrach, and F. G. Brandenburg. Vol. XC, pp. 43-72, 9 ills. in black and white, July, 1946.

High Lights in the Peruvian and Bolivian Andes. 18 ills. in color from autochromes by W. Robert Moore. Vol. LI, pp. 218-235, Feb., 1927.

High Lights in the Sunshine State (Florida). 41 ills. in color from autochromes by Clifton Adams and Charles Edward Hagle. Vol. LVII, pp. 26-83, Jan., 1930.

High Road and Low Through the Mountain State (West Virginia). 21 ills. in color from natural-color photographs by B. Anthony Stewart and Volkmar Wentzel. Vol. LXXVIII, pp. 157-180, Aug., 1940.

Highest Camp in the World. Vol. XVII, pp. 647-648, Nov., 1906.

Highest Camps and Climbs. By Edwin Swift Balch. Vol. XVII, p. 713, Dec., 1906.

Highest Dam in the World (Roosevelt Dam). Vol. XVI, pp. 440-441, Sept., 1905.

Highest Point in Each State. Vol. XX, pp. 539-541, 2 ills., June, 1909.

Highlights of London Town. 15 ills. in color from autochromes by Clifton Adams. Vol. LV, pp. 568-577, May, 1929.

Highlights of the Volunteer State: Men and Industry in Tennessee Range from Pioneer Stages to Modern Machine Age. By Leonard Cornell Roy. Vol. LXXV, pp. 553-594, 20 ills. in black and white, 22 ills. in color, 1 map, May, 1939.

Highways and Roads:

Alaskan Highway an Engineering Epic: Mosquitoes, Mud, and Muskeg Minor Obstacles of 1,671-mile Race to Throw the Alcan Life Line Through Thick Forests and Uninhabited Wilderness. By Froelich Rainey. Vol. LXXXIII, pp. 143-168, 21 ills., 3 maps, Feb., 1943.

Burma: Where India and China Meet: In the Massive Mountains of Southeast Asia, Swarming Road Builders Wage the "War of the Highways" for Free China and Her Allies. By John LeRoy Christian. Vol. LXXXIV, pp. 489-512, 18 ills., 1 page map, Oct., 1943.

Burma Road: China Opens Her Wild West: In the Mountain-girt Heart of a Continent a New China Has Been Created During the Years of War. By Owen Lattimore. Vol. LXXXII, pp. 337-367, 21 ills. in black and white, 11 ills. in color, 1 map (two-page spread), Sept., 1942.

Burma Road, Back Door to China: Like the Great Wall of Ancient Times, This Mighty Mountain Highway Has Been Built by Myriad Chinese to Help Defend Their Homeland. By Frank Outram and G. E. Fane. Vol. LXXVIII, pp. 629-658, 26 ills., 1 two-thirds-page map, Nov., 1940.

Burning the Roads. Vol. XVII, pp. 583-586, 4 ills., Oct., 1906.

Immediate Necessity for Military Highways. By A. G. Batchelder. Vol. XXXII, pp. 477-499, 22 ills., Nov.-Dec., 1917.

Land of the Free in Africa. By Harry A. McBride. Vol. XLII, pp. 411-430, 22 ills., Oct., 1922.

Old Post-Road from Tiflis to Erivan. By Esther Lancraft Hovey. Vol. XII, pp. 300-309, 9 ills., Aug., 1901.

6,000 Miles over the Roads of Free China. By Josephine A. Brown. Vol. LXXXV, pp. 355-384, 30 ills., 1 two-thirds-page map, Mar., 1944.

Stilwell Road—Land Route to China. By Nelson Grant Tayman. Vol. LXXXVII, pp. 681-698, 18 ills., June, 1945.

U. S. Roads in War and Peace. By Frederick Simpich. Vol. LXXX, pp. 687-716, 27 ills., Dec., 1941.

Hildebrand, J. R.:

Budapest, Twin City of the Danube. By J. R. Hildebrand. Vol. LXI, pp. 729-742, 3 ills. in black and white, 10 ills. in duotone, June, 1932.

California's Coastal Redwood Realm: Along a Belt of Tall Trees a Giant Bridge Speeds the Winning of Our Westernmost Frontier. By J. R. Hildebrand. Vol. LXXV, pp. 133-184, 31 ills. in black and white, 17 ills. in color, 1 page-and-a-half map, Feb., 1939.

Columbus of the Pacific: Captain James Cook, Foremost British Navigator, Expanded the Great Sea to Correct Proportions and Won for Albion an Insular Empire by Peaceful Exploration and Scientific Study. By J. R. Hildebrand. Vol. LI, pp. 85-132, 45 ills., 1 page and 1 three-quarters-page maps, Jan., 1927.

Hildebrand, J. R.—*Continued*

Cotton: Foremost Fiber of the World. By J. R. Hildebrand. Vol. LXXIX, pp. 137-192, 31 ills. in black and white, 34 ills. in color, Feb., 1941.

Edinburgh, Athens of the North: Romantic History of Cramped Medieval City Vies With Austere Beauty of Newer Wide Streets and Stately Squares. By J. R. Hildebrand. Vol. LXII, pp. 219-246, 19 ills. in black and white, 8 ills. in duotone, Aug., 1932.

England's Sun Trap Isle of Wight. By J. R. Hildebrand. Vol. LXVII, pp. 1-33, 22 ills. in black and white, 14 ills. in color, 1 half-page map, Jan., 1935.

Geography of Games: How the Sports of Nations Form a Gazetteer of the Habits and Histories of Their People. By J. R. Hildebrand. Vol. XXXVI, pp. 89-144, 61 ills., Aug., 1919.

Glass "Goes to Town." By J. R. Hildebrand. Vol. LXXXIII, pp. 1-48, 28 ills. in black and white, 22 ills. in color, Jan., 1943.

Greatest Voyage in the Annals of the Sea. By J. R. Hildebrand. Vol. LXII, pp. 699-739, 35 ills., 2 half-page maps, Dec., 1932.

Machines Come to Mississippi. By J. R. Hildebrand. Vol. LXXII, pp. 263-318, 34 ills. in black and white, 26 ills. in color, 1 two-page map, Sept., 1937.

Man's Amazing Progress in Conquering the Air. By J. R. Hildebrand. Vol. XLVI, pp. 93-122, 28 ills., 1 diagram, July, 1924.

Our Most Versatile Vegetable Product: Rubber Drops from Millions of Tropical Trees Are Transformed by Genii Chemists into Myriad Articles, from Tires to Teething Rings. By J. R. Hildebrand. Vol. LXXVII, pp. 143-200, 51 ills. in black and white, 26 ills. in color, Feb., 1940.

Pathfinder of the East: Setting Sail to Find "Christians and Spices," Vasco da Gama Met Amazing Adventures, Founded an Empire, and Changed the History of Western Europe. By J. R. Hildebrand. Vol. LII, pp. 503-550, 43 ills., 1 two-thirds-page map, Nov., 1927.

Revolution in Eating: Machine Food Age—Born of Roads, Research, and Refrigeration—Makes the United States the Best-fed Nation in History. By J. R. Hildebrand. Vol. LXXXI, pp. 273-324, 33 ills. in black and white, 25 ills. in color, Mar., 1942.

Royal Copenhagen, Capital of a Farming Kingdom: A Fifth of Denmark's Thrifty Population Resides in a Metropolis Famous for Its Porcelains, Its Silver, and Its Lace. By J. R. Hildebrand. Vol. LXI, pp. 217-250, 26 ills. in black and white, 14 ills. in color, Feb., 1932.

Sources of Washington's Charm (District of Columbia). By J. R. Hildebrand. Vol. XLIII, pp. 639-680, 46 ills., June, 1923.

Trains of Today—and Tomorrow. By J. R. Hildebrand. Vol. LXX, pp. 535-589, 51 ills., Nov., 1936.

Hildebrand, J. R.—*Continued*

World's Greatest Overland Explorer: How Marco Polo Penetrated Farthest Asia, "Discovered" Many Lands Unknown to Europe, and Added Numerous Minerals, Animals, Birds, and Plants to Man's Knowledge. By J. R. Hildebrand. Vol. LIV, pp. 505-568, 53 ills., 1 two-page map, Nov., 1928.

Hildenbrand, Hans:

Austria: Alpine Villagers of Austria. 14 ills. in color from autochromes by Hans Hildenbrand. Vol. LVI, pp. 668-677, Dec., 1929.

Austria: Summering in Styria, Austria's Rural Playground. 14 ills. in color from natural-color photographs by Hans Hildenbrand. Vol. LXII, pp. 430-439, Oct., 1932.

Austria: Tyrol, the Happy Mountain Land. 11 ills. in color from natural-color photographs by Hans Hildenbrand. Vol. LXI, pp. 370-379, May, 1932.

Austrian Album. 13 ills. in color from natural-color photographs by Hans Hildenbrand and Wilhelm Tobien. Vol. LXXI, pp. 457-464, Apr., 1937.

Czechoslovakia: Costumes of Czechoslovakia. 19 ills. in color from natural-color photographs by Hans Hildenbrand. Vol. LI, pp. 724-741, June, 1927.

Czechoslovakia: When Golden Praha Entertains the Majestic Sokol Festival. 13 ills. in color from natural-color photographs by Hans Hildenbrand. Vol. LXIII, pp. 40-49, Jan., 1933.

France of Sunshine and Flowers. 3 ills. in color from autochromes lumière by Hans Hildenbrand. Vol. L, pp. 481-496, Oct., 1926.

Germany: Beauty of the Bavarian Alps. 16 ills. in color from autochromes lumière by Hans Hildenbrand. Vol. XLIX, pp. 632-649, June, 1926.

Germany: Bright Corners of Time-Mellowed Germany. 9 ills. in color from natural-color photographs by Hans Hildenbrand. Vol. LXIV, pp. 222-231, Aug., 1933.

Germany: Dinkelsbühl, Romantic Vision From the Past. 12 ills. in color from natural-color photographs by Hans Hildenbrand. Vol. LX, pp. 692-701, Dec., 1931.

Germany: From Chalet to Palace in Bavaria. 14 ills. in color from autochromes by Hans Hildenbrand. Vol. LIV, pp. 682-691, Dec., 1928.

Germany: Grimm's Fairyland in Northwestern Germany. 9 ills. in color from natural-color photographs by Hans Hildenbrand. Vol. LIX, pp. 640-649, May, 1931.

Germany: Life and Luster of Berlin. 24 ills. in color from natural-color photographs by Wilhelm Tobien and Hans Hildenbrand. Vol. LXXI, pp. 147-177, Feb., 1937.

Germany: Medieval Pageantry in Modern Nördlingen. 12 ills. in color from autochromes by Hans Hildenbrand. Vol. LIV, pp. 706-715, Dec., 1928.

Hildenbrand, Hans—*Continued*

Germany: Rothenburg, the City Time Forgot. 8 ills. from natural-color photographs by Hans Hildenbrand. Vol. XLIX, pp. 184-193, Feb., 1926.

Germany: Wandering Through the Black Forest. 13 ills. in color from autochromes by Hans Hildenbrand. Vol. LIV, pp. 658-667, Dec., 1928.

Holy Land: In the Birthplace of Christianity. 10 ills. in color from autochromes lumière by Hans Hildenbrand. Vol. L, pp. 696-721, Dec., 1926.

Hungary: Rainbow Hues from Hungary. 26 ills. in color from natural-color photographs by Hans Hildenbrand. Vol. LXI, pp. 696-729, June, 1932.

Hungary: Rural Hungarian Rhapsody. 20 ills. in color from natural-color photographs by Rudolf Balogh and Hans Hildenbrand. Vol. LXXIII, pp. 17-48, Jan., 1938.

Italy: Colorful Patinas of Northern Italy. 13 ills. in color from natural-color photographs; 9 ills. by Hans Hildenbrand. Vol. LXVIII, pp. 337-344, Sept. 1935.

Italy: Man and Nature Paint Italian Scenes in Prodigal Colors. 33 ills. in color from autochromes by Hans Hildenbrand. Vol. LIII, pp. 442-467, Apr., 1928.

Italy: Neopolitan Blues and Imperial Purple of Roman Italy. 8 ills. in color from natural-color photographs by Hans Hildenbrand. Vol. LXVI, pp. 203-210, Aug., 1934.

Italy: Under Radiant Italian Skies. 8 ills. in color from autochromes by Hans Hildenbrand. Vol. L, pp. 248-257, Aug., 1926.

Italy: Where the Blue Begins on the Italian Coast. 12 ills. in color from natural-color photographs by Hans Hildenbrand. Vol. LXVII, pp. 81-88, Jan., 1935.

Poland: Bright Bits in Poland's Mountainous South. 16 ills. in color from natural-color photographs by Hans Hildenbrand. Vol. LXVII, pp. 353-360, Mar., 1935.

Poland: In the Land of the White Eagle. 12 ills. in color from natural-color photographs by Hans Hildenbrand. Vol. LXI, pp. 437-444, Apr., 1932.

Poland: Rainbow Costumes of Poland's Peasants. 10 ills. in color from natural-color photographs by Hans Hildenbrand. Vol. LXIII, pp. 328-337, Mar., 1933.

Switzerland: Snowy Peaks and Old Costumes of Switzerland. 12 ills. in color from natural-color photographs by Hans Hildenbrand. Vol. LXVI, pp. 147-154, Aug., 1934.

Yugoslavia: Color Brightens Rustic Life in Jugoslavia. 23 ills. in color from natural-color photographs by Hans Hildenbrand. Vol. LVIII, pp. 272-305, Sept., 1930.

Yugoslavia: Medieval Glory Haunts the Eastern Adriatic. 17 ills. in color from autochromes by Hans Hildenbrand. Vol. LIII, pp. 64-81, Jan., 1928.

Hilder, Frank Frederick:

British South Africa and the Transvaal. By F. F. Hilder. Vol. XI, pp. 81-96, 7 ills., Mar., 1900.

Frank Frederick Hilder (Biography). Vol. XII, pp. 84-86, Feb., 1901.

Gold in the Philippines. By F. F. Hilder. Vol. XI, pp. 465-470, Dec., 1900.

Hilgard, E. W.:

Geographic Nomenclature. By E. W. Hilgard. Vol. XI, pp. 36-37, Jan., 1900.

Hill, David Jayne:

Original Territory of the United States. By David Jayne Hill. Vol. X, pp. 73-92, Mar., 1899.

Republics—The Ladder to Liberty. By David Jayne Hill. Vol. XXXI, pp. 240-254, 5 ills., 2 page maps, Mar., 1917.

Hill, Ebenezer J.:

Trip Through Siberia. By Ebenezer J. Hill. Vol. XIII, pp. 37-54, 17 ills., 1 quarter-page map, Feb., 1902.

Hill, Robert T.:

National Geographic Society Expedition in the West Indies. Vol. XIII, pp. 209-213, 2 half-page maps, June, 1902.

National Geographic Society Expedition to Martinique and St. Vincent. Vol. XIII, pp. 183-184, 2 ills., June, 1902.

Porto Rico. By Robert T. Hill. Vol. X, pp. 93-112, 13 ills., Mar., 1899.

Porto Rico or Puerto Rico? By Robert T. Hill. Vol. X, pp. 516-517, Dec., 1899.

Report by Robert T. Hill on the Volcanic Disturbances in the West Indies. Vol. XIII, pp. 223-267, 13 ills., 2 half and 1 quarter-page maps, July, 1902.

Volcanic Rocks of Martinique and St. Vincent: Collected by Robert T. Hill and Israel C. Russell. By J. S. Diller. Vol. XIII, pp. 285-296, July, 1902.

Hillebrand, W. F.:

Chemical Discussion of Analyses of Volcanic Ejecta from Martinique and St. Vincent. By W. F. Hillebrand. Vol. XIII, pp. 296-299, July, 1902.

Hills and Dales of Erin. 11 ills. in color from autochromes by Clifton Adams. Vol. LI, pp. 316-333, Mar., 1927.

Himalayas (Mountains), India-Tibet:

Aërial Conquest of Everest: Flying Over the World's Highest Mountain Realizes the Objective of Many Heroic Explorers. By Lieut. Col. L. V. S. Blacker. Vol. LXIV, pp. 127-162, 35 ills., 1 page map, Aug., 1933.

Among the Great Himalayan Glaciers. Vol. XIII, pp. 405-406, Nov., 1902.

Castles in the Air: Experiences and Journeys In Unknown Bhutan. By John Claude White. Vol. XXV, pp. 365-455, 74 ills., 1 page map, Apr., 1914.

Himalayas (Mountains), India-Tibet—*Continued*

Duke of the Abruzzi in the Himalayas. Vol. XXI, pp. 245-249, Mar., 1910.

First Over the Roof of the World by Motor: The Trans-Asiatic Expedition Sets New Records for Wheeled Transport in Scaling Passes of the Himalayas. By Maynard Owen Williams. Vol. LXI, pp. 321-363, 45 ills., 2 half-page maps, Mar., 1932.

Highest Camp in the World. Vol. XVII, pp. 647-648, Nov., 1906.

Nepal: A Little-Known Kingdom. By John Claude White. Vol. XXXVIII, pp. 245-283, 32 ills., 1 half-page map, Oct., 1920.

Pilgrimage to Amernath, Himalayan Shrine of the Hindu Faith. By Louise Ahl Jessop. Vol. XL, pp. 512-542, 29 ills., Nov., 1921.

Record Ascents in the Himalayas. Vol. XIV, pp. 420-421, Nov., 1903.

World's Highest Altitudes and First Ascents. By Charles E. Fay. Vol. XX, pp. 493-530, 25 ills., June, 1909.

Hindus and Hinduism:

Bathing and Burning Ghats at Benares. By Eliza R. Scidmore. Vol. XVIII, pp. 118-128, 7 ills., Feb., 1907.

Fire-Walking Hindus of Singapore. By L. Elizabeth Lewis. Vol. LIX, pp. 513-522, 12 ills., Apr., 1931.

India—Yesterday, Today, and Tomorrow. By Lord Halifax. Vol. LXXXIV, pp. 385-408, 20 ills., 1 two-page map, Oct., 1943.

India Mosaic. By Peter Muir and Frances Muir. Vol. LXXXIX, pp. 443-470, 5 ills. in black and white, 22 ills. in color, 1 half-page map, Apr., 1946.

Marriage of the Gods (Festival at Madura, India). By John J. Banninga. Vol. XXIV, pp. 1314-1330, 16 ills., Dec., 1913.

Religious Penances and Punishments Self-Inflicted by the Holy Men of India. By W. M. Zumbro. Vol. XXIV, pp. 1257-1314, 69 ills., Dec., 1913.

Yank Meets Native. By Wanda Burnett. Vol. LXXXVIII, pp. 105-128, 24 ills., July, 1945.

Hindustan (Region), India:

Through the Heart of Hindustan: A Teeming Highway Extending for Fifteen Hundred Miles, from the Khyber Pass to Calcutta. By Maynard Owen Williams. Vol. XL, pp. 443-467, 29 ills., Nov., 1921.

Hine, James S.:

Valley of Ten Thousand Smokes: An Account of the Discovery and Exploration of the Most Wonderful Volcanic Region in the World. By Robert F. Griggs. Vol. XXXIII, pp. 115-169, 46 ills., 1 half-page map, panorama, Feb., 1918.

Hingston, (Maj.) R. W. G.:

New World to Explore: In the Tree-Roof of the British Guiana Forest Flourishes Much Hitherto-Unknown Life. By Maj. R. W. G. Hingston. Vol. LXII, pp. 617-642, 35 ills., Nov., 1932.

Hioki, Eki:

Chapter from Japanese History. By Eki Hioki. Vol. XVI, pp. 220-228, May, 1905.

Japan, America, and the Orient. By Eki Hioki. Vol. XVII, pp. 498-504, Sept., 1906.

Purpose of the Anglo-Japanese Alliance. By Eki Hioki. Vol. XVI, pp. 333-337, July, 1905.

Hippopotamuses:

When a Drought Blights Africa: Hippos and Elephants Are Driven Insane by Suffering, in the Lorian Swamp, Kenya Colony. By Capt. A. T. Curle. Vol. LV, pp. 521-528, 9 ills., Apr., 1929.

Hirohito (Japanese Emperor):

Behind the Mask of Modern Japan. By Willard Price. Vol. LXXXVIII, pp. 513-535, 14 ills., Nov., 1945.

Hispaniola (Island), West Indies. *See* Dominican Republic; Haiti.

Hispaniola Rediscovered (Dominican Republic). By Jacob Gayer. Vol. LIX, pp. 80-112, 12 ills. in black and white, 28 ills. in color, Jan., 1931.

Hiss, Philip Hanson:

Curaçao and Aruba, Oil Isles of the Caribbean. 10 ills. in color from natural-color photographs by Philip Hanson Hiss and Robert Yarnall Richie. Vol. LXXXIII, pp. 175-182, Feb., 1943.

Surinam Subjects of Queen Wilhelmina 13 ills. in color from natural-color photographs by Philip Hanson Hiss. Vol. LXXXIII, pp. 465-472, Apr., 1943.

Historic City of Brotherly Love: Philadelphia, Born of Penn and Strengthened by Franklin, a Metropolis of Industries, Homes and Parks. By John Oliver La Gorce. Vol. LXII, pp. 643-697, 49 ills. in black and white, 13 ills. in color, Dec., 1932.

Historic Danzig: Last of the City-States. By William and Alicelia Franklin. Vol. LXXVI, pp. 677-696, 26 ills., Nov., 1939.

Historic Islands and Shores of the Ægean Sea. By Ernest Lloyd Harris. Vol. XXVIII, pp. 231-262, 29 ills., 1 half-page map, Sept., 1915.

History and Geographic Distribution of Bubonic Plague. By George M. Sternberg. Vol. XI, pp. 97-113, Mar., 1900.

History's Greatest Trek: Tragedy Stalks Through the Near East as Greece and Turkey Exchange Two Million of Their People. By Melville Chater. Vol. XLVIII, pp. 533-590, 52 ills. in black and white, 32 ills. in color, Nov., 1925.

Hitchcock, A. S.:

Controlling Sand Dunes in the United States and Europe. By A. S. Hitchcock. Vol. XV, pp. 43-47, 4 ills., Jan., 1904.

Hittites (People):

Ancient Capital (Boghaz Keui, Turkey). By Isabel F. Dodd. Vol. XXI, pp. 111-124, 11 ills., Feb., 1910.

Hittites (People)—*Continued*

Sketch of the Geographical History of Asia Minor. By Sir William Ramsay. Vol. XLII, pp. 553-570, 12 ills., Nov., 1922.

Syria: The Land Link of History's Chain. By Maynard Owen Williams. Vol. XXXVI, pp. 437-462, 20 ills., 1 quarter-page map, Nov., 1919.

Ho for the Soochow Ho (China). By Mabel Craft Deering. Vol. LI, pp. 623-649, 32 ills., 1 three-quarters-page map, June, 1927.

Hoary Monasteries of Mount Athos (Greece). By H. G. Dwight. Vol. XXX, pp. 249-272, 24 ills., 1 half-page map, Sept., 1916.

Hobart, Alice Tisdale:

How Half the World Works. By Alice Tisdale Hobart and Mary A. Nourse. Vol. LXI, pp. 509-524, 22 ills., Apr., 1932.

Hobart, Tasmania:

Capital Cities of Australia. By W. Robert Moore. Vol. LXVIII, pp. 667-722, 32 ills. in black and white, 24 ills. in color, 1 two-page map, Dec., 1935.

Hodge, W. H.:

Camels of the Clouds (Lamoids). By W. H. Hodge. Vol. LXXXIX, pp. 641-656, 15 ills., 1 half-page map, May, 1946.

Hoffmann, D. O. Noble:

Philippine Exhibit at the Pan-American Exposition. By D. O. Noble Hoffmann. Vol. XII, pp. 119-122, Mar., 1901.

Hoffmeister, J. Edward:

Falcon, the Pacific's Newest Island. By J. Edward Hoffmeister and Harry S. Ladd. Vol. LIV, pp. 757-766, 8 ills., 1 half-page map, Dec., 1928.

Hog Island, Pennsylvania:

Ships for the Seven Seas: The Story of America's Maritime Needs, Her Capabilities and Her Achievements. By Ralph A. Graves. Vol. XXXIV, pp. 165-200, 24 ills., Sept., 1918.

Högakull (Farm), Sweden:

Life's Flavor on a Swedish Farm: From the Rocky Hills of Småland Thousands of Sturdy Citizens Have Emigrated to the United States. By Willis Lindquist. Vol. LXXVI, pp. 393-414, 23 ills., 1 quarter-page map, Sept., 1939.

Hogbin, H. Ian:

Coconuts and Coral Islands (Ontong Java). By H. Ian Hogbin. Vol. LXV, pp. 256-298, 24 ills. in black and white, 14 ills. in color, 1 half-page map, Mar., 1934.

Holder, Charles Frederick:

Big Things of the West. By Charles F. Holder. Vol. XIV, pp. 279-282, 2 ills., July, 1903.

Glass-Bottom Boat. By Charles Frederick Holder. Vol. XX, pp. 761-778, 17 ills., Sept., 1909.

Remarkable Salt Deposit. By Charles F. Holder. Vol. XII, pp. 390-392, 2 ills., Nov., 1901.

Holding, Florence Polk:

Salzkammergut, a Playground of Austria. By Florence Polk Holding. Vol. LXXI, pp. 445-485, 34 ills. in black and white, 13 ills. in color, 1 third-page map, Apr., 1937.

Holdridge, Desmond:

Cowboys and Caymans of Marajó (Brazil). 12 ills. in color from natural-color photographs by Desmond Holdridge. Vol. LXXIV, pp. 645-652, Nov., 1938.

Holidays Among the Hill Towns of Umbria and Tuscany. By Paul Wilstach. Vol. LIII, pp. 401-442, 40 ills., 1 page map, Apr., 1928.

Holidays with Humming Birds. By Margaret L. Bodine. Vol. LIII, pp. 731-742, 15 ills., June, 1928.

Holland. *See* Netherlands.

Holliday, Carl:

Our Friends, the French: An Appraisal of the Traits and Temperament of the Citizens of Our Sister Republic. By Carl Holliday. Vol. XXXIV, pp. 345-377, 29 ills., Nov., 1918.

Holmes, Charles H.:

Australia's Patchwork Creature, the Platypus: Man Succeeds in Making Friends with This Duck-billed, Fur-coated Paradox which Lays Eggs and Suckles Its Young. By Charles H. Holmes. Vol. LXXVI, pp. 273-282, 13 ills., Aug., 1939.

Holmes, Henrietta Allen:

Spell of Romania: An American Woman's Narrative of Her Wanderings Among Colorful People and Long-Hidden Shrines. By Henrietta Allen Holmes. Vol. LXV, pp. 399-450, 37 ills. in black and white, 29 ills. in color, 1 half-page map, Apr., 1934.

Holmes, William H.:

Awarded Jane M. Smith Life Membership. Vol. XXXVII, p. 342, Apr., 1920.

Holt, Ernest G.:

In Humboldt's Wake: Narrative of a National Geographic Society Expedition Up the Orinoco and Through the Strange Casiquiare Canal to Amazonian Waters. By Ernest G. Holt. Vol. LX, pp. 621-644, 27 ills., 1 two-thirds-page map, Nov., 1931.

Journey by Jungle Rivers to the Home of the Cock-of-the-Rock: Naturalists Enter the Amazon, Voyage Through the Heart of Tropical South America, and Emerge at the Mouth of the Orinoco. By Ernest G. Holt. Vol. LXIV, pp. 585-630, 49 ills., 1 two-thirds-page map, Nov., 1933.

Holt, George Edmund:

Two Great Moorish Religious Dances. By George Edmund Holt. Vol. XXII, pp. 776-785, 6 ills., Aug., 1911.

Holy Land. *See* Palestine.

Home Folk around Historic Cumberland Gap. By Leo A. Borah. Vol. LXXXIV, pp. 741-768, 25 ills., 1 quarter-page map, Dec., 1943.

Home Life and Industry in the Netherlands. 11 ills. in duotone from photographs. Vol. LXXVII, pp. 271-278, Feb., 1940.

Home-Making by the Government: An Account of the Eleven Immense Irrigating Projects to be Opened in 1908. By C. J. Blanchard. Vol. XIX, pp. 250-287, 23 ills., Apr., 1908.

Home of a Forgotten Race: Mysterious Chichen Itzá in Yucatan, Mexico. By Edward H. Thompson. Vol. XXV, pp. 585-648, 59 ills., June, 1914.

Home of the First Farmer of America (Mount Vernon). By Worth E. Shoults. Vol. LIII, pp. 603-628, 6 ills. in black and white, 26 ills. in color, May, 1928.

Home of the National Geographic. Vol. XVI, p. 342, July, 1905.

Homer's Troy Today. By Jacob E. Conner. Vol. XXVII, pp. 520-532, 11 ills., 1 half-page map, May, 1915.

Homra, Hamada el (Desert), Libia:

Mysteries of the Desert. By Hanns Vischer. Vol. XXII, pp. 1056-1059, Nov., 1911.

Honduran Highlights. With 11 ills. in color from natural-color photographs by H. C. Lanks. Vol. LXXXI, pp. 360-369, Mar., 1942.

Honduras:

Countries of the Caribbean. By William Joseph Showalter. Vol. XXIV, pp. 227-250, 23 ills., Feb., 1913.

Foremost Intellectual Achievement of Ancient America: The Hieroglyphic Inscriptions on the Monuments in the Ruined Cities of Mexico, Guatemala, and Honduras are Yielding the Secrets of the Maya Civilization. By Sylvanus Griswold Morley. Vol. XLI, pp. 109-130, 27 ills., 17 diagrams, special map supplement in colors, Feb., 1922.

Honduran Highlights. With 11 ills. in color from natural-color photographs by H. C. Lanks. Vol. LXXXI, pp. 360-369, Mar., 1942.

Little Journey in Honduras. By F. J. Youngblood. Vol. XXX, pp. 177-184, 6 ills., Aug., 1916.

Notes on Central America. Vol. XVIII, pp. 272-278, 1 ill., 1 half-page map, Apr., 1907.

Honduras, British. *See* British Honduras.

Honey Ants:

Living Casks of Honey. By Jennie E. Harris. Vol. LXVI, pp. 193-199, 4 ills., Aug., 1934.

Honeybees:

In Field and Hive with the Busy Honeybee. 16 ills. in color from paintings by Hashime Murayama. Vol. LXVII, pp. 417-424, Apr., 1935.

Man's Winged Ally, the Busy Honeybee: Modern Research Adds a New Chapter to Usefulness of the Insect Which Has Symbolized Industry Since Early Bible Times. By James I. Hambleton. Vol. LXVII, pp. 401-428, 18 ills. in black and white, 16 ills. in color, Apr., 1935.

Hong Kong, China :

Hong Kong—Britain's Far-flung Outpost in China. 16 ills. from photographs. Vol. LXXIII, pp. 349-360, Mar., 1938.

1940 Paradox in Hong Kong. By Frederick Simpich. Vol. LXXVII, pp. 531-558, 24 ills., 3 maps, Apr., 1940.

Today on the China Coast. By John B. Powell. Vol. LXXXVII, pp. 217-238, 17 ills., 1 page map, Feb., 1945.

Honolulu, Hawaii :

Hawaii, Then and Now : Boyhood Recollections and Recent Observations by an American Whose Grandfather Came to the Islands 102 Years Ago. By William R. Castle. Vol. LXXIV, pp. 419-462, 30 ills. in black and white, 10 ills. in color, 1 page-and-a-half map, Oct., 1938.

Life on the Hawaii "Front" : All-out Defense and Belt Tightening of Pacific Outpost Foreshadow the Things to Come on Mainland. By Lieut. Frederick Simpich, Jr. Vol. LXXXII, pp. 541-560, 19 ills., 1 half-page map, Oct., 1942.

Waves and Thrills at Waikiki. 8 ills. in duotone by Thomas Edward Blake. Vol. LXVII, pp. 597-604, May, 1935.

Honorary Members. *See* National Geographic Society : Honorary Members.

Honors for Amundsen. Vol. XIX, pp. 55-76, 13 ills., Jan., 1908.

Honors to Amundsen and Peary (National Geographic Society Banquet). Vol. XXIV, pp. 113-130, 5 ills., Jan., 1913.

Honors to Colonel Goethals : The Presentation, by President Woodrow Wilson, of the National Geographic Society Special Gold Medal, and Addresses by Secretary of State Bryan, the French Ambassador, the German Ambassador, and Congressman James R. Mann. Vol. XXV, pp. 677-690, 6 ills., June, 1914.

Honors to Peary (Presentation of Hubbard Medal). Vol. XVIII, pp. 49-60, 1 ill., Jan., 1907.

Honors to the American Navy. Vol. XX, pp. 77-95, Jan., 1909.

Hood, Mount, Oregon :

Is Our Noblest Volcano Awakening to New Life : A Description of the Glaciers and Evidences of Volcanic Activity of Mount Hood. By A. H. Sylvester. Vol. XIX, pp. 515-525, 5 ills., 1 page map, July, 1908.

Oregon Finds New Riches. By Leo A. Borah. Vol. XC, pp. 681-728, 15 ills. in black and white, 28 ills. in color, 1 two-page map, Dec., 1946.

Hookworm (Disease) :

Map-Changing Medicine. By William Joseph Showalter. Vol. XLII, pp. 303-330, 26 ills., Sept., 1922.

Redeeming the Tropics. By William Joseph Showalter, Vol. XXV, pp. 344-364, 13 ills., Mar., 1914,

Hoosier Haunts and Holidays (Indiana). 27 ills. in color from natural-color photographs by Willard R. Culver. Vol. LXX, pp. 283-314, Sept., 1936.

Hoover, Herbert :

Admiral Byrd Receives New Honor from The Society (Address by Herbert Hoover). Vol. LVIII, pp. 228-238, 4 ills., Aug., 1930.

Bind the Wounds of France. By Herbert C. Hoover. Vol. XXXI, pp. 439-444, 5 ills., May, 1917.

Food Armies of Liberty. By Herbert Hoover. Vol. XXXII, pp. 187-196, Sept., 1917.

Food for Our Allies in 1919. By Herbert Hoover. Vol. XXXIV, pp. 242-244, Sept., 1918.

Great Mississippi Flood of 1927 : Since White Man's Discovery This Mighty River Has Served Him Well, Yet It Has Brought Widespread Devastation Along Its Lower Reaches. By Frederick Simpich. Vol. LII, pp. 243-289, 53 ills., 1 half-page map, Sept., 1927.

Society's Special Medal Awarded to Amelia Earhart : First Woman to Receive Geographic Distinction (Address by Herbert Hoover). Vol. LXII, pp. 358-367, 7 ills., Sept., 1932.

Weapon of Food. By Herbert Hoover. Vol. XXXII, pp. 197-212, 15 ills., Sept., 1917.

Hoover, (Mrs.) Herbert :

Member of National Geographic Society since 1902. Vol. LVIII, p. 231, Aug., 1930. Vol. LXII, p. 362, Sept., 1932.

Hoover, (Mrs.) William H. :

Keeping House for the "Shepherds of the Sun.' By Mrs. William H. Hoover. Vol. LVII, pp 483-506, 17 ills., 1 map, Apr., 1930.

Hopeh (Province), China :

Grand Canal Panorama. By Willard Price. Vol. LXXI, pp. 487-514, 31 ills., 1 half-page map, Apr., 1937.

Peacetime Plant Hunting About Peiping. By P. H. and J. H. Dorsett. Vol. LXXII, pp. 509-534, 21 ills., 1 two-thirds-page map, Oct., 1937.

Hopi Indians :

Everyday Life in Pueblo Bonito : As Disclosed by the National Geographic Society's Archeologic Explorations in the Chaco Canyon National Monument, New Mexico. By Neil M Judd. Vol. XLVIII, pp. 227-262, 37 ills., 1 two-thirds-page map, Sept., 1925.

Exploring in the Canyon of Death : Remains of a People Who Dwelt in Our Southwest at Least 4,000 Years Ago Are Revealed. By Earl H. Morris. Vol. XLVIII, pp. 263-300, 24 ills. in black and white, 22 ills. in color, Sept., 1925.

Indian Tribes of Pueblo Land. By Matthew W. Stirling. Vol. LXXVIII, pp. 549-596, 16 ills. in black and white, 25 ills. in color, Nov., 1940.

Land of the Best. By Gilbert H. Grosvenor. Vol. XXIX, pp. 327-430, 71 ills. in black and white, 33 ills. in color, panorama, Apr., 1916.

Hopi Indians—*Continued*

North American Indians. Vol. XVIII, pp. 469-484, 14 ills., July, 1907.

Photographing the Marvels of the West in Colors. By Fred Payne Clatworthy. Vol. LIII, pp. 694-719, 30 ills. in color, June, 1928.

Red Men of the Southwest. 25 ills. in color from paintings by W. Langdon Kihn. Vol. LXXVIII, pp. 557-596, Nov., 1940.

Scenes from America's Southwest. Vol. XXXIX, pp. 651-664, 14 ills., June, 1921.

Secret of the Southwest Solved by Talkative Tree Rings: Horizons of American History Are Carried Back to A. D. 700 and a Calendar for 1,200 Years Established by National Geographic Society Expeditions. By Andrew Ellicott Douglass. Vol. LVI, pp. 737-770, 33 ills., 1 two-thirds-page map, Dec., 1929.

Snake Dance. By Marion L. Oliver. Vol. XXII, pp. 107-137, 31 ills., Feb. 1911.

Horace—Classic Poet of the Countryside. By W. Coleman Nevils. Vol. LXVIII pp. 771-795, 22 ills., 1 page map, Dec., 1935.

Horgan, James C.:

Bequest to The Society by James C. Horgan. Vol. XXXVII, p. 338, 2 ills., Apr., 1920.

Horn, Cape, Chile:

Cape Horn Grain-Ship Race: The Gallant *Parma* Leads the Vanishing Fleet of Square-Riggers Through Raging Gales and Irksome Calms 16,000 Miles, from Australia to England. By A. J. Villiers. Vol. LXIII, pp. 1-39, 38 ills., Jan., 1933.

Inside Cape Horn. By Amos Burg. Vol. LXXII, pp. 743-783, 29 ills. in black and white, 10 ills. in color, 1 two-page map, Dec., 1937.

Land of the Horn, America's Tiptoe. 10 ills. in color from natural-color photographs by Amos Burg. Vol. LXXII, pp. 751-758, Dec., 1937.

Rounding the Horn in a Windjammer. By A. J. Villiers. Vol. LIX, pp. 191-224, 36 ills., 1 two-thirds-page map, Feb., 1931.

Hornets:

Farmers' Friends Among the Wasps and Hornets. 12 ills. in color from paintings by Hashime Murayama. Vol. LXXII, pp. 57-64, July, 1937.

Potent Personalities—Wasps and Hornets: Though Often Painfully Stung, Mankind Profits Immeasurably from the Pest-Killing Activities of These Fiery Little Flyers. By Austin H. Clark. Vol. LXXII, pp. 47-72, 18 ills. in black and white, 12 ills. in color, July, 1937.

Horse Racing:

Kentucky, Boone's Great Meadow: The Bluegrass State Celebrates Its Sesquicentennial As It Helps the Nation Gird for War. By Leo A. Borah. Vol. LXXXII, pp. 57-89, 13 ills. in black and white, 21 ills. in color, 1 map (two-page spread), July, 1942.

People of the Wilderness: The Mongols, Once the Terror of All Christendom, Now a Primitive, Harmless Nomad Race. By Adam Warwick. Vol. XXXIX, pp. 507-551, 59 ills., May, 1921.

Horse Racing—*Continued*

Siena's Palio, an Italian Inheritance from the Middle Ages. By Marie Louise Handley. Vol. L, pp. 245-258, 3 ills., Aug., 1926.

Story of the Horse: The Development of Man's Companion in War Camp, on Farm, in the Marts of Trade, and in the Field of Sports. By Maj. Gen. William Harding Carter. Vol. XLIV, pp. 455-566, 62 ills. in black and white, 24 ills. in color, Nov., 1923.

Horse Thief Creek, British Columbia:

On the Trail of a Horse Thief. By Herbert W. Gleason. Vol. XXXV, pp. 349-358, 6 ills., Apr., 1919.

Horseback Journey:

Buenos Aires to Washington by Horse: A Solitary Journey of Two and a Half Years, Through Eleven American Republics, Covers 9,600 Miles of Mountain and Plain, Desert and Jungle. By A. F. Tschiffely. Vol. LV, pp. 135-196, 75 ills., 1 page map, Feb., 1929.

Horses:

Horses of the World. 24 ills. in color from paintings by Edward Herbert Miner. Vol. XLIV, pp. 479-526, Nov., 1923.

Kentucky, Boone's Great Meadow: The Bluegrass State Celebrates Its Sesquicentennial As It Helps the Nation Gird for War. By Leo A. Borah. Vol. LXXXII, pp. 57-89, 13 ills. in black and white, 21 ills. in color, 1 map (two-page spread), July, 1942.

People of the Wilderness: The Mongols, Once the Terror of All Christendom, Now a Primitive, Harmless Nomad Race. By Adam Warwick. Vol. XXXIX, pp. 507-551, 59 ills., May, 1921.

Siena's Palio, an Italian Inheritance from the Middle Ages. By Marie Louise Handley. Vol. L, pp. 245-258, 3 ills., Aug., 1926.

Story of the Horse: The Development of Man's Companion in War Camp, on Farm, in the Marts of Trade, and in the Field of Sports. By Maj. Gen. William Harding Carter. Vol. XLIV, pp. 455-566, 62 ills. in black and white, 24 ills. in color, Nov., 1923.

See also Ponies.

Horticulture. *See* Floriculture; Fruits; Gardens; Plants.

Hoskins, Franklin E.:

Rock City of Petra. By Franklin E. Hoskins. Vol. XVIII, pp. 283-291, 5 ills., May, 1907.

Route Over Which Moses Led the Children of Israel Out of Egypt. By Franklin E. Hoskins. Vol. XX, pp. 1011-1038, 24 ills., Dec., 1909.

Hosmer, Dorothy:

American Girl Cycles Across Romania: Two-wheel Pilgrim Pedals the Land of Castles and Gypsies, Where Roman Empire Traces Mingle With Remnants of Oriental Migration. By Dorothy Hosmer. Vol. LXXIV, pp. 557-588, 31 ills., 1 page map, Nov., 1938.

Hosmer, Dorothy—*Continued*

Caviar Fishermen of Romania: From Vâlcov, "Little Venice" of the Danube Delta, Bearded Russian Exiles Go Down to the Sea. By Dorothy Hosmer. Vol. LXXVII, pp. 407-434, 29 ills., 1 third-page map, Mar., 1940.

Pedaling Through Poland: An American Girl Free-wheels Alone from Kraków, and Its Medieval Byways, Toward Ukraine's Restive Borderland. By Dorothy Hosmer. Vol. LXXV, pp. 739-775, 38 ills., 2 maps, June, 1939.

Rhodes, and Italy's Aegean Islands. By Dorothy Hosmer. Vol. LXXIX, pp. 449-480, 32 ills., 1 map, Apr., 1941.

Hospital, American: Deir ez Zor, Syria:

Ali Goes to the Clinic. By Herndon and Mary Hudson. Vol. XC, pp. 764-766, 2 ills., Dec., 1946.

Hospital Heroes Convict the Cootie. Vol. XXXIII, p. 510, June, 1918.

Hospital Ships:

Heroes' Return. By William H. Nicholas. Vol. LXXXVII, pp. 333-352, 19 ills., Mar., 1945.

Hospitality of the Czechs. By Worth E. Shoults. Vol. LI, pp. 723-742, 19 ills. in color, June, 1927.

Hot Springs:

Fabulous Yellowstone: Even Stranger Than the Tales of Early Trappers is the Truth About This Steaming Wonderland. By Frederick G. Vosburgh. Vol. LXXVII, pp. 769-794, 15 ills. in black and white, 9 ills. in color, 1 two-thirds-page map, June, 1940.

Our National Parks. By L. F. Schmeckebier. Vol. XXIII, pp. 531-579, 41 ills., 1 page map, June, 1912.

Waimangu and the Hot-Spring Country of New Zealand: The World's Greatest Geyser Is One of Many Natural Wonders in a Land of Inferno and Vernal Paradise. By Joseph C. Grew. Vol. XLVIII, pp. 109-130, 19 ills., 1 third-page map, Aug., 1925.

Where Hot Pools Seethe and Geysers Spout. 9 ills. in color from natural-color photographs by Edwin L. Wisherd. Vol. LXXVII, pp. 775-782, June, 1940.

Why Nik-ko is Beautiful. By J. H. De Forest. Vol. XIX, pp. 300-308, 8 ills., Apr., 1908.

Hot Springs, Arkansas:

Arkansas Rolls Up Its Sleeves. By Frederick Simpich. Vol. XC, pp. 273-312, 16 ills. in black and white, 23 ills. in color, 1 map (two-page spread), Sept., 1946.

Hotchkis, Anna M.:

Buddhist Calm Survives Along China's Great Wall. 10 ills. in color; 4 paintings by Mary Augusta Mullikin and Anna M. Hotchkis and 6 natural-color photographs. Vol. LXXIII, pp. 321-328, Mar., 1938.

Hough, Walter:

Venice of Mexico (Aztec Lake Country). By Walter Hough. Vol. XXX, pp. 69-88, 18 ills., July, 1916.

Houma, Louisiana:

Delectable Shrimp: Once a Culinary Stepchild, Today a Gulf Coast Industry. By Harlan Major. Vol. LXXXVI, pp. 501-512, 11 ills., 1 two-thirds-page map, Oct., 1944.

Hounds:

Hark to the Hounds. By Freeman Lloyd. Paintings by Edward Herbert Miner. Vol. LXXII, pp. 453-484, 18 ills. in black and white, 31 portraits in color, Oct., 1937.

Contains descriptions and illustrations of the following breeds: Afghan Hound, American Foxhound, Basset Hound, Beagle, Bloodhound, Borzoi, or Russian Wolfhound, Deerhound, English Foxhound, Greyhound, Harrier, Irish Wolfhound, Otterhound, Rampur Hound, Saluki, Welsh Foxhound, Whippet.

Hunters All: A Roll Call of the Hounds. 31 portraits in color from paintings by Edward Herbert Miner. Vol. LXXII, pp. 467-482, Oct., 1937.

Hour of Prayer. In the Sahara Desert. Vol. XXII, supplement, Apr., 1911.

House-Fly. By N. A. Cobb. Vol. XXI, pp. 371-380, 4 ills., May, 1910.

Houseboats:

China: Ho for the Soochow Ho. By Mabel Craft Deering. Vol. LI, pp. 623-649, 32 ills., 1 three-quarters-page map, June, 1927.

China: Life Afloat in China: Tens of Thousands of Chinese in Congested Ports Spend Their Entire Existence on Boats. By Robert F. Fitch. Vol. LI, pp. 665-686, 28 ills., June, 1927.

Kashmir: House-Boat Days in the Vale of Kashmir. By Florence H. Morden. Vol. LVI, pp. 437-463, 22 ills. in black and white, 30 ills. in color, Oct., 1929.

Houser, J. S.:

Fighting Insects with Airplanes: An Account of the Successful Use of the Flying-Machine in Dusting Tall Trees Infested with Leaf-Eating Caterpillars. By J. S. Houser and C. R. Neillie. Vol. XLI, pp. 333-338, 6 ills., Mar., 1922.

Houses and Homes:

Alabama: Smoke Over Alabama. By Frederick Simpich. Vol. LX, pp. 703-758, 43 ills. in black and white, 26 ills. in color, 1 page map, Dec., 1931.

Cape Cod People and Places. By Wanda Burnett. Vol. LXXXIX, pp. 737-774, 17 ills. in black and white, 24 ills. in color, 1 half-page map, June, 1946.

Delaware: Diamond Delaware, Colonial Still: Tradition Rules the "Three Lower Counties" Over Which William Penn and Lord Baltimore Went to Law. By Leo A. Borah. Vol. LXVIII, pp. 367-398, 25 ills. in black and white, 15 ills. in color, 1 page map, Sept., 1935.

England: Preservation of England's Historic and Scenic Treasures. By Eric Underwood. Vol. LXXXVII, pp. 413-440, 24 ills., 1 two-page map, Apr., 1945.

Houses and Homes—*Continued*

England: Summering in an English Cottage: Quiet and Loveliness Invite Contemplation in the Extra "Room," the Garden of the Thatched House. By Helen Churchill Candee. Vol. LXVII, pp. 429-456, 32 ills., Apr., 1935.

England: Vacation in a Fifteenth Century English Manor House. By George Alden Sanford. Vol. LIII, pp. 629-636, 8 ills., May, 1928.

England's Island Garden of Rocks and Flowers (Isle of Wight). 14 ills. in color from natural-color photographs by W. Robert Moore. Vol. LXVII, pp. 17-24, Jan., 1935.

Georgia: Marching Through Georgia Sixty Years After: Multifold Industries and Diversified Agriculture Are Restoring the Prosperity of America's Largest State East of the Mississippi. By Ralph A. Graves. Vol. L, pp. 259-311, 47 ills., Sept., 1926.

Indiana Journey. By Frederick Simpich. Vol. LXX, pp. 267-320, 32 ills. in black and white, 27 ills. in color, 1 two-page map, Sept., 1936.

Italy: Stone Beehive Homes of Italian Peasants. 4 ills. in color from autochromes by Luigi Pellerano. Vol. LVII, pp. 234-243, Feb., 1930.

Italy: Stone Beehive Homes of the Italian Heel: In Trulli-Land the Native Builds His Dwelling and Makes His Field Arable in the Same Operation. By Paul Wilstach. Vol. LVII, pp. 229-260, 25 ills. in black and white, 12 ills. in color, 1 quarter-page map, Feb., 1930.

Louisiana, Land of Perpetual Romance. By Ralph A. Graves. Vol. LVII, pp. 393-482, 84 ills. in black and white, 29 ills. in color, special map supplement, Apr., 1930.

Maryland Pilgrimage: Visits to Hallowed Shrines Recall the Major Rôle Played by This Prosperous State in the Development of Popular Government in America. By Gilbert Grosvenor. Vol. LI, pp. 133-212, 88 ills., special map supplement, Feb., 1927.

Massachusetts: Northeast of Boston. By Albert W. Atwood. Vol. LXXXVIII, pp. 257-292, 12 ills. in black and white, 17 ills. in color, special map supplement, Sept., 1945.

Mississippi: Machines Come to Mississippi. By J. R. Hildebrand. Vol. LXXII, pp. 263-318, 34 ills. in black and white, 26 ills. in color, 1 two-page map, Sept., 1937.

Ohio: The Gateway State. By Melville Chater. Vol. LXI, pp. 525-591, 58 ills. in black and white, 13 ills. in color, 1 three-quarters-page map, May, 1932.

Pennsylvania: Penn's Land of Modern Miracles. By John Oliver La Gorce. Vol. LXVIII, pp. 1-58, 28 ills. in black and white, 39 ills. in color, 1 two-page map, July, 1935.

Sark: Feudal Isle of Sark: Where Sixteenth-Century Laws Are Still Observed. By Sibyl Hathaway (La Dame de Serk). Vol. LXII, pp. 101-119, 21 ills., 1 half-page map, July, 1932.

South Carolina: Ashley River and Its Gardens. By E. T. H. Shaffer. Vol. XLIX, pp. 525-550, 6 ills. in black and white, 7 ills. in color, May, 1926.

Houses and Homes—*Continued*

Sweden: Color and Customs of Sweden's Château Country. 13 ills. in color from natural-color photographs by Gustav Heurlin. Vol. LXVI, pp. 33-40, July, 1934.

Sweden: Country-House Life in Sweden: In Castle and Cottage the Landed Gentry Gallantly Keep the Old Traditions. By Amelie Posse-Brázdová. Vol. LXVI, pp. 1-64, 51 ills. in black and white, 13 ills. in color, 1 page map, July, 1934.

Tennessee: Highlights of the Volunteer State: Men and Industry in Tennessee Range from Pioneer Stages to Modern Machine Age. By Leonard Cornell Roy. Vol. LXXV, pp. 553-594, 20 ills. in black and white, 22 ills. in color, 1 map, May, 1939.

United States: Exploring the Atlantic Seaboard with a Color Camera. 11 ills. in color from autochromes by Charles Martin and Jacob Gayer. Vol. XLIX, pp. 532-549, May, 1926.

United States: Some Human Habitations. By Collier Cobb. Vol. XIX, pp. 509-515, 5 ills., July, 1908.

Virginia: Fame's Eternal Camping Ground: Beautiful Arlington, Burial Place of America's Illustrious Dead. By Enoch A. Chase. Vol. LIV, pp. 621-638, 19 ills., Nov., 1928.

Virginia: Gardens and Shrines of Old Virginia. 20 ills. in color from natural-color photographs by B. Anthony Stewart and J. Baylor Roberts. Vol. LXXXI, pp. 623-646, May, 1942.

Virginia: Home of the First Farmer of America (Mount Vernon). By Worth E. Shoults. Vol. LIII, pp. 603-628, 6 ills. in black and white, 26 ills. in color, May, 1928.

Virginia: Jefferson's Little Mountain: Romance Enfolds Monticello, the Restored Home of the Author of the Declaration of Independence. By Paul Wilstach. Vol. LV, pp. 481-503, 12 ills. in black and white, 12 ills. in color, Apr., 1929.

Virginia: Monticello, One of America's Most Historic Shrines. 12 ills. in color from natural-color photographs by Edwin L. Wisherd, Charles Martin, and Jacob Gayer. Vol. LV, pp. 488-497, Apr., 1929.

Virginia: Tidewater Virginia, Where History Lives. By Albert W. Atwood. Vol. LXXXI, pp. 617-656, 18 ills. in black and white, 20 ills. in color, 1 page map, May, 1942.

Virginia—A Commonwealth That Has Come Back. By William Joseph Showalter. Vol. LV, pp. 403-472, 69 ills. in black and white, 13 ills. in color, 1 page map, Apr., 1929.

See also Castles; Châteaux; Cone Dwellings; Housing; Palaces.

Houses of Parliament. *See* Parliament.

Housing, U. S. Government:

Wartime Washington. By William H. Nicholas. Vol. LXXXIV, pp. 257-290, 12 ills. in black and white, 16 ills. in color, Sept., 1943.

Houston, David F.:

Soldiers of the Soil: Our Food Crops Must Be Greatly Increased. By David F. Houston. Vol. XXXI, pp. 273-280, 4 ills., Mar., 1917.

Houston-Mount Everest Flight:

Aërial Conquest of Everest: Flying over the World's Highest Mountain Realizes the Objective of Many Heroic Explorers. By Lieut. Col. L. V. S. Blacker. Vol. LXIV, pp. 127-162, 35 ills., 1 page map, Aug., 1933.

Hovey, Edmund Otis:

Eruptions of La Soufrière, St. Vincent, in May, 1902. By Edmund Otis Hovey. Vol. XIII, pp. 444-459, 4 ills., Dec., 1902.

Hovey, Esther Lancraft:

Old Post-Road from Tiflis to Erivan. By Esther Lancraft Hovey. Vol. XII, pp. 300-309, 9 ills., Aug., 1901.

Hovey, H. C.:

Skeleton in Luray Cave. By H. C. Hovey. Vol. XVII, pp. 425-426, July, 1906.

How Canada Went to the Front. By T. B. Macaulay. Vol. XXXIV, pp. 297-307, 6 ills., Oct., 1918.

How Half the World Works. By Alice Tisdale Hobart and Mary A. Nourse. Vol. LXI, pp. 509-524, 22 ills., Apr., 1932.

How Latin America Looks from the Air: U. S. Army Airplanes Hurdle the High Andes, Brave Brazil Jungles, and Follow Smoking Volcanoes to Map New Sky Paths Around South America. By Maj. Herbert A. Dargue. Vol. LII, pp. 451-502, 52 ills., 1 page map, Oct., 1927.

How Long a Whale May Carry a Harpoon. By William H. Dall. Vol. X, pp. 136-137, Apr., 1899.

How Long Will the Coal Reserves of the United States Last? By Marius R. Campbell. Vol. XVIII, pp. 129-138, 5 diagrams, 1 half-page map, Feb., 1907.

How Much is Known of Alaska. By Alfred H. Brooks. Vol. XVII, pp. 112-114, Feb., 1906.

How Old Is Man? By Theodore Roosevelt. Vol. XXIX, pp. 111-127, 12 ills., 1 page and 2 half-page maps, Feb., 1916.

How the Earth Telegraphed Its Tokyo Quake to Washington. By Rev. Francis A. Tondorf. Vol. XLIV, pp. 453-454, 1 ill., Oct., 1923.

How the United States Grew. By McFall Kerbey. Vol. LXIII, pp. 631-649, 17 ills., 1 page map, May, 1933.

How the World Is Fed. By William Joseph Showalter. Vol. XXIX, pp. 1-110, 101 ills., Jan., 1916.

How the World Is Shod. Vol. XIX, pp. 649-660, 12 ills., Sept., 1908.

How to Use the Star Charts. Text accompanying 12 star charts designed by Donald H. Menzel. Vol. LXXXIV, pp. 116-128, July, 1943.

How Warwick (Castle) Was Photographed in Color. By Maynard Owen Williams. Vol. LXX, pp. 83-93, 13 ills. in color, July, 1936.

How We Fight with Photographs. By F. Barrows Colton. Vol. LXXXVI, pp. 257-280, 22 ills., Sept., 1944.

How We Use the Gulf of Mexico. By Frederick Simpich. Vol. LXXXV, pp. 1-40, 20 ills. in black and white, 19 ills. in color, 1 two-page map, Jan., 1944.

Howard, Henry:

Southward Ho! in the "Alice." By Henry Howard. Vol. LXXIII. pp. 265-312. 38 ills. in black and white, 13 ills. in color, 2 maps, Mar., 1938.

Howard, L. O.:

Economic Loss to the People of the United States Through Insects That Carry Disease. By L. O. Howard. Vol. XX, pp. 735-749, Aug., 1909.

Explorers of a New Kind: Successful Introduction of Beetles and Parasites to Check Ravages of the Gipsy-Moth and Brown-Tail-Moth. Vol. XXVI, pp. 38-67, 11 ills. in black and white, 5 ills. in color, July, 1914.

Hrdlička, Aleš:

Bohemia and the Czechs. By Aleš Hrdlička. Vol. XXXI, pp. 163-187, 18 ills., Feb., 1917.

Huave Indians:

Isthmus of Tehuantepec: The Bridge of the World's Commerce. By Helen Olsson-Seffer, Vol. XXI, pp. 991-1002, 6 ills., Dec., 1910.

Hub City (Boston), Cradle of American Liberty. 31 ills. in color from natural-color photographs by B. Anthony Stewart and Luis Marden. Vol. LXX, pp. 49-72, July, 1936.

Hubbard, Bernard R.:

Society Takes Part in Three Geographic Expeditions. Vol. LXV, pp. 625-626, May, 1934.

World Inside a Mountain: Aniakchak, the New Volcanic Wonderland of the Alaska Peninsula, Is Explored. By Bernard R. Hubbard. Vol. LX, pp. 319-345, 34 ills., 1 half-page map, Sept., 1931.

Hubbard, Gardiner Greene:

Dedication of Hubbard Memorial Hall, National Geographic Society, and Hubbard Memorial Window, Church of the Covenant, Washington, D. C. Vol. XIII, pp. 174-175, May, 1902.

Hubbard Glacier, Alaska, named for Gardiner Greene Hubbard. Vol. XLIX, p. 599, June, 1926.

Memorial Building. Vol. XI, pp. 406-407, Oct., 1900.

President of The Society. Vol. X, p. 222, June, 1899.

Toast to the Memory of Gardiner Greene Hubbard. Vol. XVII, p. 24, Jan., 1906.

Hubbard, (Mrs.) Gardiner Greene:

Tribute of Respect to the Memory of Mrs. Gardiner Greene Hubbard, Adopted by the Board of Managers of the National Geographic Society at a Special Meeting held at Hubbard Memorial Hall, October 23, 1909. Vol. XX, p. 1008, Nov., 1909.

Hubbard, Gerard:

Aircraft Insignia, Spirit of Youth. By Gerard Hubbard. Vol. LXXXIII, pp. 710-722, 3 ills. in black and white, 337 ills. in color, June, 1943.

Hubbard, James Mascarene:

Colonial Government in Borneo. By James M. Hubbard. Vol. XI, pp. 359-363, Sept., 1900.

Problems in China. By James M. Hubbard. Vol. XI, pp. 297-308, 3 ills., special map supplement, Aug., 1900.

Singan—The Present Capital of the Chinese Empire. By James Mascarene Hubbard. Vol. XII, pp. 63-66, 1 ill., Feb., 1901.

The Tsangpo. By James Mascarene Hubbard. Vol. XII, pp. 32-35, Jan., 1901.

Hubbard, (Gen.) Thomas H.:

Discovery of the North Pole (Speech by Gen. Thomas H. Hubbard). Vol. XXI, pp. 63-82, Jan., 1910.

Hubbard Glacier, Alaska :

National Geographic Society's Alaskan Expedition of 1909. By Ralph S. Tarr and Lawrence Martin. Vol. XXI, pp. 1-54, 42 ills., 4 page and 7 half-page maps, Jan., 1910.

Hubbard Medal:

Air Conquest : From the Early Days of Giant Kites and Birdlike Gliders, the National Geographic Society Has Aided and Encouraged the Growth of Aviation. Vol. LII, pp. 233-242, 13 ills., Aug., 1927.

"Captain Bob" Bartlett awarded the Hubbard Medal. Vol. LXXXIX, p. 609, May, 1946.

Commander Byrd Receives the Hubbard Gold Medal : The First Explorer to Reach the North Pole by Air Receives Coveted Honor at Brilliant National Geographic Society Reception. Vol. L, pp. 377-388, 5 ills., 1 chart, Sept., 1926.

Discovery of the North Pole (Awarded to Robert Bartlett and Grove Karl Gilbert). Vol. XXI, pp. 63-82, Jan., 1910.

Ellsworth Awarded the Hubbard Medal. Vol. LXX, p. 36, July, 1936.

Honors for Amundsen (Presentation of Hubbard Gold Medal by Charles W. Fairbanks). Vol. XIX, pp. 55-76, 13 ills., Jan., 1908.

Honors to Peary (Presentation of Hubbard Gold Medal by President Roosevelt). Vol. XVIII, pp. 49-60, 1 ill., Jan., 1907.

Hubbard Medals Awarded to Stratosphere Explorers : Presentation by General Pershing. Vol. LXIX, pp. 713-714, May, 1936.

National Geographic Society's Notable Year (Awarded to Stefansson). Vol. XXXVII, pp. 338-345, 2 ills., Apr., 1920.

Hubbard Medal—*Continued*

President Coolidge Bestows Lindbergh Award : The National Geographic Society's Hubbard Medal Is Presented to Aviator Before the Most Notable Gathering in the History of Washington. Vol. LIII, pp. 132-140, 4 ills., Jan., 1928.

President Harry S. Truman presents Hubbard Medal to Gen. H. H. Arnold. Vol. LXXXIX, ill. 141, Feb., 1946.

Race for the South Pole (Presentation of Hubbard Gold Medal to Shackleton by President Taft). Vol. XXI, pp. 185-186, Mar., 1910.

Society Awards Hubbard Medal to Anne Morrow Lindbergh. Vol. LXV, pp. 791-794, 4 ills., June, 1934.

Hubbard Memorial Hall:

Home of the National Geographic Society. Vol. XVI, p. 342, July, 1905.

Hubbard Memorial Building (Laying of Cornerstone). Vol. XIII, pp. 174-176, May, 1902.

National Geographic Society and Its New Building. Vol. XXV, pp. 454-470, 11 ills., Apr., 1914.

New Home of the National Geographic Society. Vol. XV, pp. 176-181, 5 ills., Apr., 1904.

Opening of Building. Vol. XIV, p. 217, May, 1903.

Plans for Memorial Building. Vol. XI, pp. 406-407, Oct., 1900.

Hudson, Henry:

Henry Hudson, Magnificent Failure : Just 330 Years Ago He and His Mutinous Crew Found Manhattan Covered With "Goodly Oakes" and Fought Indians in New York Harbor. By Frederick G. Vosburgh. Vol. LXXV, pp. 461-490, 21 ills., Apr., 1939.

Hudson, Herndon and **Mary:**

Ali Goes to the Clinic. By Herndon and Mary Hudson. Vol. XC, pp. 764-766, 2 ills., Dec., 1946.

Hudsonian Birds:

Birds of Timberline and Tundra. By Arthur A. Allen. With 24 ills. in color from natural-color photographs by the author. Vol. XC, pp. 313-339, 8 ills. in black and white, Sept., 1946.

Human Emotions Recorded by Photography. By Ralph A. Graves. Vol. XXXVIII, pp. 284-300, 16 ills., Oct., 1920.

Humboldt Current, Pacific Ocean :

Fighting Giants of the Humboldt (Fish and Squid). By David D. Duncan. Vol. LXXIX, pp. 373-400, 28 ills., 1 half-page map, Mar., 1941.

Hume, Martin:

Woods and Gardens of Portugal. By Martin Hume. Vol. XXI, pp. 883-894, 8 ills., Oct. 1910.

Hummingbirds:

Holidays with Humming Birds. By Margaret L. Bodine. Vol. LIII, pp. 731-742, 15 ills., June, 1928.

Hummingbirds—*Continued*

Humming Birds, Swifts and Goatsuckers. 24 ills. in color from paintings by Maj. Allan Brooks. Vol. LXII, pp. 75-88, July, 1932.

Seeking the Smallest Feathered Creatures: Humming Birds, Peculiar to the New World, Are Found from Canada and Alaska to the Strait of Magellan. Swifts and Goatsuckers, Their Nearest Relatives. By Alexander Wetmore. Paintings by Maj. Allan Brooks. Vol. LXII, pp. 65-89, 6 ills. in black and white, 25 ills. in color, July, 1932.

Hunan—The Closed Province of China. By William Barclay Parsons. Vol. XI, pp. 393-400, 1 ill., 1 half-page map, Oct., 1900.

Hungary:

Danube, Highway of Races: From the Black Forest to the Black Sea, Europe's Most Important River Has Borne the Traffic of Centuries. By Melville Chater. Vol. LVI, pp. 643-697, 54 ills., Dec., 1929.

Flags of Austria-Hungary, Bulgaria, Germany, and Turkey. By Gilbert Grosvenor and Byron McCandless. Vol. XXXII, pp. 386-388, 38 ills. in color, Oct., 1917.

Hungary: A Land of Shepherd Kings. By C. Townley-Fullam. Vol. XXVI, pp. 311-393, 92 ills., 1 page map, Oct., 1914.

Hungary, a Kingdom Without a King: A Tour from Central Europe's Largest Lake to the Fertile Plains of the Danube and the Tisza. By Elizabeth P. Jacobi. Vol. LXI, pp. 691-728, 22 ills. in black and white, 27 ills. in color, 1 half-page map, June, 1932.

Land of Contrast: Austria-Hungary. By D. W. and A. S. Iddings. Vol. XXIII, pp. 1188-1218, 34 ills., Dec., 1912.

Magyar Mirth and Melancholy. By John Patric. Vol. LXXIII, pp. 1-55, 33 ills. in black and white, 20 ills. in color, 1 half-page map, Jan., 1938.

Rainbow Hues from Hungary. 27 ills. in color from natural-color photographs by Hans Hildenbrand. Vol. LXI, pp. 696-729, June, 1932.

Rural Hungarian Rhapsody. 20 ills. in color from natural-color photographs by Rudolf Balogh and Hans Hildenbrand. Vol. LXXIII, pp. 17-48, Jan., 1938.

Sunday in Mezőkövesd. By Margery Rae. Vol. LXVII, pp. 489-504, 22 ills., Apr., 1935.

See also Budapest.

Hunted Birds of Field and Wild. 60 portraits in color from paintings by Maj. Allan Brooks. Vol. LXX, pp. 469-500, Oct., 1936.

Hunter of Plants. By David Fairchild. Vol. XXXVI, pp. 57-77, 18 ills., July, 1919.

Hunters All: A Roll Call of the Hounds. 31 portraits in color from paintings by Edward Herbert Miner. Vol. LXXII, pp. 467-482, Oct., 1937.

Hunting an Observatory: A Successful Search for a Dry Mountain on Which to Establish the National Geographic Society's Solar Radiation Station. By C. G. Abbot. Vol. L, pp. 503-518, 13 ills., 1 quarter-page map, Oct., 1926.

Hunting Bears on Horseback (Wyoming). By Alan D. Wilson. Vol. XIX, pp. 350-356, 4 ills., May, 1908.

Hunting Big Game in Portuguese East Africa. By R. C. F. Maugham. Vol. XVIII, pp. 723-730, 7 ills., Nov., 1907.

Hunting Big Game of Other Days: A Boating Expedition in Search of Fossils in Alberta, Canada. By Barnum Brown. Vol. XXXV, pp. 407-429, 24 ills., 1 page map, May, 1919.

Hunting Birds With a Camera: A Record of Twenty Years of Adventure in Obtaining Photographs of Feathered Wild Life in America. By William L. Finley. Vol. XLIV, pp. 161-201, 37 ills., Aug., 1923.

Hunting Castles in Italy. By Melville Chater. Vol. LXVIII, pp. 329-366, 25 ills. in black and white, 13 ills. in color, 1 page and 1 quarter-page maps, Sept., 1935.

Hunting for Plants in the Canary Islands. By David Fairchild. Vol. LVII, pp. 607-652, 37 ills. in black and white, 39 ills. in color, 1 third-page map, May, 1930.

Hunting the Chaulmoogra Tree. By Joseph F. Rock. Vol. XLI, pp. 243-276, 39 ills., 1 page map, Mar., 1922.

Hunting the Great Brown Bear of Alaska. By George Mixter, 2d. Vol. XX, pp. 313-332, 35 ills., Apr., 1909.

Hunting the Grizzly in British Columbia. By Joseph Wendle. Vol. XVIII, pp. 612-615, 3 ills., Sept., 1907.

Hunting the Walrus. Vol. XXII, pp. 285-290, 10 ills., Mar., 1911.

Hunting Trip to Northern Greenland. By Fullerton Merrill. Vol. XI, pp. 118-122, Mar., 1900.

Hunting Useful Plants in the Caribbean. By David Fairchild. Vol. LXVI, pp. 705-737, 39 ills., Dec., 1934.

Hunting with a Microphone the Voices of Vanishing Birds. By Arthur A. Allen. Vol. LXXI, pp. 697-723, 32 ills., June, 1937.

Hunting with the Lens (Birds). By Howard H. Cleaves. Vol. XXVI, pp. 1-35, 47 ills., July, 1914.

Huntington, Ellsworth:

Afghan Borderland, Part I: The Russian Frontier. By Ellsworth Huntington. Vol. XX, pp. 788-799, 14 ills., Sept., 1909.

Afghan Borderland, Part II: The Persian Frontier. By Ellsworth Huntington. Vol. XX, pp. 866-876, 12 ills., Oct., 1909.

Huntington, Ellsworth—*Continued*

Fringe of Verdure Around Asia Minor. By Ellsworth Huntington. Vol. XXI, pp. 761-775, 15 ills., Sept., 1910.

Life in the Great Desert of Central Asia. By Ellsworth Huntington. Vol. XX, pp. 749-760, 12 ills., Aug., 1909.

Lost Wealth of the Kings of Midas. By Ellsworth Huntington. Vol. XXI, pp. 831-846, 15 ills., Oct., 1910.

Medieval Tales of the Lop Basin in Central Asia. By Ellsworth Huntington. Vol. XIX, pp. 288-295, 9 ills., Apr., 1908.

Mountaineers of the Euphrates. By Ellsworth Huntington. Vol. XX, pp. 142-156, 13 ills., Feb., 1909.

Huntley, Montana :

Call of the West. By C. J. Blanchard. Vol. XX, pp. 403-437, 20 ills., 1 half-page map, May, 1909.

Hunza (State), India :

First Over the Roof of the World by Motor. By Maynard Owen Williams. Vol. LXI, pp. 321-363, 45 ills., 2 half-page maps, Mar., 1932.

Hurdle Racing in Canoes : A Thrilling and Spectacular Sport Among the Maoris of New Zealand. By Walter Burke. Vol. XXXVII, pp. 440-444, 6 ills., May, 1920.

Hurley, Edward N.:

American People Must Become Ship-Minded. By Edward N. Hurley. Vol. XXXIV, pp. 201-211, 7 ills., Sept., 1918.

Hurley, (Capt.) Frank:

Pictorial Jaunt Through Papua. 22 ills. from photographs by Capt. Frank Hurley. Vol. LI, pp. 109-124, Jan., 1927.

Hürlimann, Martin:

Remote Nepal, Land of Mystery. 15 ills. in color from natural-color photographs by Martin Hürlimann. Vol. LXVII, pp. 329-336, Mar., 1935.

Huron (Indian Tribe) :

America's First Settlers, the Indians. By Matthew W. Stirling. Vol. LXXII, pp. 535-596, 34 ills. in black and white, 24 ills. in color, Nov. 1937.

When Red Men Ruled Our Forests. 24 ills. in color from paintings by W. Langdon Kihn. Vol. LXXII, pp. 551-590, Nov., 1937.

Hurricanes:

Cape Cod People and Places. By Wanda Burnett. Vol. LXXXIX, pp. 737-774, 17 ills. in black and white, 24 ills. in color, 1 half-page map, June, 1946.

Charting a World at War. By William H. Nicholas. Vol. LXXXVI, pp. 617-640, 23 ills., 1 drawing, Nov., 1944.

Forecasting the Weather and Storms. By Willis L. Moore. Vol. XVI, pp. 255-306, 5 ills., 20 charts, June, 1905.

Hurricanes—*Continued*

Geography of a Hurricane : A Doughnut-shaped Storm Turned Back Time in New England to Candlelight Days, but Revealed Anew Yankee Courage and Ingenuity. By F. Barrows Colton. Vol. LXXV, pp. 529-552, 20 ills., 1 page map, Apr., 1939.

Hurricanes on the Coast of Texas. By Maj. Gen. A. W. Greely. Vol. XI, pp. 442-445, Nov., 1900.

Islands of Bermuda : A British Colony with a Unique Record in Popular Government. By William Howard Taft. Vol. XLI, pp. 1-26, 15 ills., 1 three-quarters-page map, Jan., 1922.

Lessons of Galveston. By W J McGee. Vol. XI, pp. 377-383, Oct., 1900.

West Indian Hurricane of August 7-14, 1899. By E. B. Garriott. Vol. X, pp. 343-348, 1 diagram, Sept., 1899.

West Indian Hurricane of September 1-12, 1900. By E. B. Garriott. Vol. XI, pp. 384-392, Oct., 1900.

West Indian Hurricane of September 10-11, 1898. By E. B. Garriott. Vol. X, pp. 17-20, Jan., 1899.

Hussein, Haji Mirza (Col. Oscar von Niedermeyer):

Every-Day Life in Afghanistan. By Haji Mirza Hussein and Frederick Simpich. Vol. XXXIX, pp. 85-110, 26 ills., 1 three-quarters-page map, Jan., 1921.

Hutchinson, Paul:

New China and the Printed Page. By Paul Hutchinson. Vol. LI, pp. 687-722, 37 ills., June, 1927.

Hutchison, Bruce,

Canada's War Effort: A Canadian Pictures the Swift and Sweeping Transformation from a Peaceful Dominion to a Nation Geared for War. By Bruce Hutchison. Vol. LXXX, pp. 553-590, 40 ills., Nov., 1941.

Hutchison, George W.:

Memorial Tribute to George W. Hutchison. Vol. LXXXVII, p. 720, 1 ill., June, 1945.

See also National Geographic Society : Secretary.

Hutchison, Isobel Wylie:

Bonnie Scotland, Postwar Style. By Isobel Wylie Hutchison. Vol. LXXXIX, pp. 545-601, 14 ills. in black and white, 38 ills. in color, 1 two-page map, May, 1946.

Riddle of the Aleutians : A Botanist Explores the Origin of Plants on Ever-misty Islands Now Enshrouded in the Fog of War. By Isobel Wylie Hutchison. Vol. LXXXII, pp. 769-792, 24 ills., Dec., 1942.

Scotland in Wartime. By Isobel Wylie Hutchison. Vol. LXXXIII, pp. 723-743, 19 ills., June, 1943.

Wales in Wartime. By Isobel Wylie Hutchison. Vol. LXXXV, pp. 751-768, 16 ills., 1 page map, June, 1944.

Walking Tour Across Iceland. By Isobel Wylie Hutchison. Vol. LIII, pp. 467-497, 36 ills., 1 half-page map, Apr., 1928.

Huts:

Some Human Habitations. By Collier Cobb. Vol. XIX, pp. 509-515, 5 ills., July, 1908.

Hwang Ho (Yellow River), China :

Raft Life on the Hwang Ho. By W. Robert Moore. Vol. LXI, pp. 743-752, 14 ills., June, 1932.

Shantung—China's Holy Land. By Charles K. Edmunds. Vol. XXXVI, pp. 231-252, 21 ills., 1 half-page map, Sept., 1919.

Taming "Flood Dragons" Along China's Hwang Ho. By Oliver J. Todd. Vol. LXXXI, pp. 205-234, 26 ills., 1 half-page map, Feb., 1942.

Hwang Yao-tso:

China's Wonderland—Yen Tang Shan (Chekiang Province). 8 ills. in color from camera paintings by Herbert Clarence White, Deng Baoling, and Hwang Yao-tso. Vol. LXXII, pp. 687-694, Dec., 1937.

Hyannis, Massachusetts :

Cape Cod People and Places. By Wanda Burnett. Vol. LXXXIX, pp. 737-774, 17 ills. in black and white, 24 ills. in color, 1 half-page map, June, 1946.

Hyde, John:

National Geographic Society (Early History of The Society). By John Hyde. Vol. X, pp. 220-223, June, 1899.

Hyde, Walter Woodburn:

Ascent of Mont Blanc. By Walter Woodburn Hyde. Vol. XXIV, pp. 861-942, 69 ills., Aug., 1913.

Hydrographic Work of the U. S. Geological Survey. Vol. XI, pp. 324-325, 1 ill., Aug., 1900.

Hydrography:

Battle-Ground of Nature : The Atlantic Seaboard. By John Oliver La Gorce. Vol. XXXIII, pp. 511-546, 23 ills., 4 half-page maps, June, 1918.

Charting a World at War. By William H. Nicholas. Vol. LXXXVI, pp. 617-640, 23 ills., 1 drawing, Nov., 1944.

Helping Navigation. Vol. XI, pp. 162-163, Apr., 1900.

Hidden Perils of the Deep. By G. R. Putnam. Vol. XX, pp. 822-837, 19 diagrams, 3 charts, Sept., 1909.

Hydrographic Work of the U. S. Geological Survey. Vol. XI, pp. 324-325, 1 ill., Aug., 1900.

Marine Hydrographic Surveys of the Coasts of the World. By George W. Littlehales. Vol. XVI, pp. 63-67, 1 page map, Feb., 1905.

Our Guardians on the Deep. By William Joseph Showalter. Vol. XXV, pp. 655-677, 15 ills., 1 chart, June, 1914.

Servicing Arctic Airbases. By Robert A. Bartlett. Vol. LXXXIX, pp. 602-616, 3 ills. in black and white, 10 ills. in color, 1 half-page map, May, 1946.

Warfare on Our Eastern Coast. By John Oliver La Gorce. Vol. XXVIII, pp. 195-230, 29 ills., 2 charts, Sept., 1915.

Hydrography—*Continued*

Work of the United States Hydrographic Office. By Comdr. W. H. H. Southerland. Vol. XIV, pp. 61-75, Feb., 1903.

Hydroplanes. *See* Seaplanes.

Hydroponics:

Greens Grow for GI's on Soilless Ascension. By W. Robert Moore. Vol. LXXXVIII, pp. 219-230, 12 ills., Aug., 1945.

I

I Kept House in a Jungle : The Spell of Primeval Tropics in Venezuela, Riotous With Strange Plants, Animals, and Snakes, Enthralls a Young American Woman. By Anne Rainey Langley. Vol. LXXV, pp. 97-132, 28 ills., 1 third-page map, Jan., 1939.

I Learn About the Russians. By Eddy Gilmore. Vol. LXXXIV, pp. 010-010, 21 ills., Nov., 1943.

I Lived on Formosa. By Joseph W. Ballantine. Vol. LXXXVII, pp. 1-24, 19 ills., 1 page and 1 half-page maps, Jan., 1945.

Iacovleff, Alexandre:

Faces and Fashions of Asia's Changeless Tribes. 26 ills. in color from paintings and drawings by Alexandre Iacovleff. Vol. LXIX, pp. 21-36, Jan., 1936.

Ibises (Birds) :

Ibises, Herons, and Flamingos. 4 ills. in color from paintings by Maj. Allan Brooks. Vol. LXII, pp. 454-469, Oct., 1932.

Large Wading Birds : Long Legs and Remarkable Beaks, as Well as Size, Form, and Color, Distinguish the Herons, Ibises, and Flamingos. By T. Gilbert Pearson. Paintings by Maj. Allan Brooks. Vol. LXII, pp. 441-469, 1 ill. in black and white, 4 ills. in color, Oct., 1932.

Sacred Ibis Cemetery and Jackal Catacombs at Abydos. By Camden M. Cobern. Vol. XXIV, pp. 1042-1056, 10 ills., Sept., 1913.

Ibn Saud (King of Saudi Arabia). *See* Al Saud.

Ibu, Bougainville Island :

Fiji Patrol on Bougainville. By David D. Duncan. Vol. LXXXVII, pp. 87-104, 9 ills. in black and white, 11 ills. in color, Jan., 1945.

Ice Caves and Frozen Wells. By W J McGee. Vol. XII, pp. 433-434, Dec., 1901.

Ice Cliffs on White River, Yukon Territory. By Martin W. Gorman. Vol. XI, pp. 113-117, Mar., 1900.

Ice Cliffs on White River, Yukon Territory. By C. Willard Hayes and Alfred H. Brooks. Vol. XI, pp. 199-201, May, 1900.

Ice Patrol. *See* International Ice Patrol.

Ice-Wrapped Continent (Antarctica). By Gilbert H. Grosvenor. Vol. XVIII, pp. 95-117, 20 ills., 1 half-page map, Feb., 1907.

Icebergs:

Coast Guard Patrol in Greenland. 9 ills. in color from natural-color photographs by Lieut. Thomas S. La Farge. Vol. LXXXIII, pp. 565-572, May, 1943.

Sailing the Seven Seas in the Interest of Science: Adventures Through 157,000 Miles of Storm and Calm, from Arctic to Antarctic and Around the World, in the Non-Magnetic Yacht *Carnegie*. By J. P. Ault. Vol. XLII, pp. 631-690, 47 ills., 1 chart, Dec., 1922.

Standing Iceberg Guard in the North Atlantic: International Patrol Safeguards the Lives of Thousands of Travelers and Protects Transatlantic Liners from a "Titanic" Fate. By Lieut. Comdr. F. A. Zeusler. Vol. L, pp. 1-28, 29 ills., 1 half-page map, July, 1926.

Iceland:

American Soldier in Reykjavík. By Corporal Luther M. Chovan. Vol. LXXXVIII, pp. 536-568, 6 ills. in black and white, 34 ills. in color, Nov., 1945.

Ancient Iceland, New Pawn of War. 21 ills. from photographs, 1 page map. Vol. LXXX, pp. 75-90, July, 1941.

Iceland Defrosted. 34 ills. in color from natural-color photographs by Luther M. Chovan. Vol. LXXXVIII, pp. 537-568, Nov., 1945.

Island of the Sagas. By Earl Hanson. Vol. LIII, pp. 499-511, 22 ills., Apr., 1928.

Land of Fire. By Jon Stefansson. Vol. XVIII, pp. 741-744, Nov., 1907.

Proposed Meteorological Station in Iceland. Vol. X, p. 228, June, 1899.

Sailing the Seven Seas in the Interest of Science: Adventures Through 157,000 Miles of Storm and Calm, from Arctic to Antarctic and Around the World, in the Non-Magnetic Yacht *Carnegie*. By J. P. Ault. Vol. XLII, pp. 631-690, 47 ills., 1 chart, Dec., 1922.

Visit to Lonely Iceland. By Perley H. Noyes. Vol. XVIII, pp. 731-741, 12 ills., Nov., 1907.

Walking Tour Across Iceland. By Isobel Wylie Hutchison. Vol. LIII, pp. 467-497, 36 ills., 1 half-page map, Apr., 1928.

Id Festival:

India at Work and Play. 22 ills. in color from natural-color photographs by Peter Upton Muir, Maynard Owen Williams, and Frances Muir. Vol. LXXXIX, pp. 449-464, Apr., 1946.

Idaho:

Among the "Craters of the Moon": An Account of the First Expeditions Through the Remarkable Volcanic Lava Beds of Southern Idaho. By R. W. Limbert. Vol. XLV, pp. 303-328, 23 ills., 1 two-thirds-page map, Mar., 1924.

Down Idaho's River of No Return (Salmon River). By Philip J. Shenon and John C. Reed. Vol. LXX, pp. 95-136, 43 ills., 1 page and 1 two-thirds-page maps, July, 1936.

Idaho and Montana Boundary Line. By Richard U. Goode. Vol. XI, pp. 23-29, 1 ill., Jan., 1900.

Idaho—*Continued*

Idaho Made the Desert Bloom. By D. Worth Clark. Vol. LXXXV, pp. 641-688, 21 ills. in black and white, 20 ills. in color, 1 page map, June, 1944.

Mind's-Eye Map of America. By Franklin K. Lane. Vol. XXXVII, pp. 479-518, 25 ills. in black and white, 8 ills. in color, June, 1920.

Prosperous Idaho (An Interview with Governor Gooding, of Idaho, Published in the New York *Sun*, December, 1905). Vol. XVII, pp. 16-22, Jan., 1906.

Iddings, A. S. and D. W.:

Land of Contrast: Austria-Hungary. By A. S. and D. W. Iddings. Vol. XXIII, pp. 1188-1218, 34 ills., Dec., 1912.

Ideal Fuel: The American Coal Briquetting Industry. By Guy Elliott Mitchell. Vol. XXI, pp. 1066-1074, 4 ills., Dec., 1910.

Ifitamin, North-East New Guinea:

New Guinea's Mountain and Swampland Dwellers. By Col. Ray T. Elsmore. Vol. LXXXVIII, pp. 671-694, 15 ills. in black and white, 7 ills. in color, 1 half-page map, Dec., 1945.

Igdrasil (Boat):

At Home on the Oceans: Whales and Sharks Make Exciting Neighbors for a Professor's Wife, Turned Able Seaman, On a Three-year Voyage Around the World. By Edith Bauer Strout. Vol. LXXVI, pp. 33-86, 54 ills., 1 map, July, 1939.

Iguazu Falls, Argentina-Brazil:

Falls of Iguazu. By Marie Robinson Wright. Vol. XVII, pp. 456-460, 4 ills., Aug., 1906.

World's Great Waterfalls: Visits to Mighty Niagara, Wonderful Victoria, and Picturesque Iguazu. By Theodore W. Noyes. Vol. L, pp. 29-59, 29 ills., July, 1926.

Illinois:

Illinois, Crossroads of the Continent. By Junius B. Wood. Vol. LIX, pp. 523-594, 51 ills. in black and white, 27 ills. in color, special map supplement in colors, May, 1931.

Rambles Through the Prairie State. 15 ills. in color from direct color photographs by Clifton Adams. Vol. LIX, pp. 544-553, May, 1931.

See also Chicago.

Imagination and Geography. Vol. XVIII, p. 825, Dec., 1907.

Imbrie, (Maj.) Robert Whitney:

Crossing Asia Minor, the Country of the New Turkish Republic. By Maj. Robert Whitney Imbrie. Vol. XLVI, pp. 445-472, 31 ills., 1 quarter-page map, Oct., 1924.

Immediate Necessity for Military Highways. By A. G. Batchelder. Vol. XXXII, pp. 477-499, 22 ills., Nov.-Dec., 1917.

Immigration:

Canadian Immigration. Vol. XVII, p. 356, June, 1906.

Character of Our Immigration, Past and Present. By Z. F. McSweeny. Vol. XVI, pp. 1-15, 1 chart, Jan., 1905.

Foreign-Born of the United States. Vol. XXVI, pp. 265-271, 14 diagrams, Sept., 1914.

Immigration and Naturalization. Vol. XVI, pp. 51-52, Jan., 1905.

Immigration to the Southern States. Vol. XVI, pp. 517-519, Nov., 1905.

New York—The Metropolis of Mankind. By William Joseph Showalter. Vol. XXXIV, pp. 1-49, 39 ills., July, 1918.

Our Foreign-Born Citizens. Vol. XXXI, pp. 95-130, 36 ills., 1 page map, 8 diagrams, Feb., 1917.

Our Immigration During 1904. Vol. XVI, pp. 15-27, 6 ills., 2 charts, Jan., 1905.

Our Immigration In 1905. Vol. XVI, pp. 434-435, Sept., 1905.

Our Immigration Laws from the Viewpoint of National Eugenics. By Robert De C. Ward. Vol. XXIII, pp. 38-41, Jan., 1912.

Sex, Nativity, and Color of the People of the United States. By Gilbert H. Grosvenor. Vol. XII, pp. 381-389, 17 charts, Nov., 1901.

Some of Our Immigrants. Vol. XVIII, pp. 317-334, 21 ills., May, 1907.

South American Immigration. Vol. XIII, p. 587, Oct., 1906.

Imperial Rome Reborn. By John Patric. Vol. LXXI, pp. 269-325, 34 ills. in black and white, 21 ills. in color, Mar., 1937.

Imphal, India :

Manipur—Where Japan Struck at India. 11 ills. from photographs, 1 page map. Vol. LXXXV, pp. 743-750, June, 1944.

Important New Guide for Shipping : Navassa Light, on a Barren Island in the West Indies, Is the First Signal for the Panama Canal. By George R. Putnam. Vol. XXXIV, pp. 401-406, 3 ills., 1 half-page map, Nov., 1918.

Impression of the Guiana Wilderness. By Angelo Heilprin. Vol. XVIII, pp. 373-381, 6 ills., June, 1907.

Impressions and Scenes of Mozambique. By O. W. Barrett. Vol. XXI, pp. 807-830, 31 ills., Oct., 1910.

Impressions of Asiatic Turkey. By Stephen van Rensselaer Trowbridge. Vol. XXVI, pp. 598-609, 6 ills., Dec., 1914.

Impressions of Palestine. By James Bryce. Vol. XXVII, pp. 293-317, 18 ills., 1 page map, Mar., 1915.

Improvements in the City of Manila. Vol. XIV, pp. 195-197, 1 ill., May, 1903.

Improvements in the Republic of Panama. Vol. XVI, pp. 441-442, Sept., 1905.

Imst, Austria :

Merry Maskers of Imst. 14 ills. from photographs by Francis C. Fuerst. Vol. LXX pp. 201-208, Aug., 1936.

In Andalusia, Home of Song and Sunshine. 14 ills. in color from autochromes by Gervais Courtellemont. Vol. LV, pp. 300-309, Mar., 1929.

In Beautiful Delecarlia (Sweden). By Lillian Gore. Vol. XX, pp. 464-477, 13 ills., May, 1909.

In Civilized French Africa. By James F. J. Archibald. Vol. XX, pp. 302-311, 14 ills., Mar., 1909.

In Field and Hive with the Busy Honeybee. 16 ills. in color from paintings by Hashime Murayama. Vol. LXVII, pp. 417-424, Apr., 1935.

In French Lorraine : That Part of France Where the First American Soldiers Have Fallen. By Harriet Chalmers Adams. Vol. XXXII, pp. 499-518, 16 ills., Nov.-Dec., 1917.

In Honor of the Army and Aviation (National Geographic Society Banquet). Vol. XXII, pp. 267-284, 1 ill., Mar., 1911.

In Humboldt's Wake : Narrative of a National Geographic Society Expedition Up the Orinoco and Through the Strange Casiquiare Canal to Amazonian Waters. By Ernest G. Holt. Vol. LX, pp. 621-644, 27 ills., 1 two-thirds-page map, Nov., 1931.

In Montezuma's Painted Land. 22 ills. in color from natural-color photographs ; 21 ills. by Luis Marden. Vol. LXXVIII, pp. 345-368, Sept., 1940.

In Quaint, Curious Croatia. By Felix J. Koch. Vol. XIX, pp. 809-832, 37 ills., Dec., 1908.

In Quest of the Golden Eagle : Over Lonely Mountain and Prairie Soars This Rare and Lordly Bird, But Three Youths from the East Catch Up With Him at Last. By John and Frank Craighead. Vol. LXXVII, pp. 693-710, 17 ills., May, 1940.

In Smiling Alsace, Where France Has Resumed Sway. 11 ills. in color from autochromes lumière by Gervais Courtellemont. Vol. LII, pp. 168-177, Aug., 1927.

In the Allagash Country (Maine). By Kenneth Fuller Lee. Vol. LV, pp. 505-520, 19 ills., Apr., 1929.

In the Birthplace of Christianity. 34 ills. in color from autochromes lumière by Hans Hildenbrand, Maynard Owen Williams, and Gervais Courtellemont. Vol. L, pp. 696-721, Dec., 1926.

In the Canary Islands, Where Streets Are Carpeted with Flowers. 13 ills. in color from natural-color photographs by Wilhelm Tobien. Vol. LVII, pp. 614-623, May, 1930.

In the Diamond Mountains: Adventures Among the Buddhist Monasteries of Eastern Korea. By Marquess Curzon of Kedleston. Vol. XLVI, pp. 353-374, 21 ills., 1 quarter-page map, Oct., 1924.

In the Empire of the Aztecs: Mexico City Is Rich in Relics of a People Who Practiced Human Sacrifice, Yet Loved Flowers, Education, and Art. By Frank H. H. Roberts, Jr. Vol. LXXI. pp. 725-750, 14 ills. in black and white, 10 ills. in color, June, 1937.

In the Land of Cruel Desert and Majestic Mountain (Morocco). 12 ills. in color from natural-color photographs by Gervais Courtellemont and M. Flandrin. Vol. LXI, pp. 306-315, Mar., 1932.

In the Land of Kublai Khan (Mongolia). Vol. XLI, pp. 465-472, 16 ills. in color, May, 1922.

In the Land of Moses and Abraham. 25 ills. in color from natural-color photographs by W. Robert Moore. Vol. LXXIV, pp. 711-742, Dec., 1938.

In the Land of the Montezumas. 16 ills. in color from photographs by Clifton Adams. Vol. XLIII, pp. 265-280, Mar., 1923.

In the Land of the Quetzal (Guatemala). 20 ills. in color from autochromes lumière by Jacob Gayer. Vol. L, pp. 610-627, Nov., 1926.

In the Land of the White Eagle (Poland). 12 ills. in color from natural-color photographs by Hans Hildenbrand. Vol. LXI, pp. 437-444, Apr., 1932.

In the Land of Windmills and Wooden Shoes. 16 ills. from photographs by Donald McLeish. Vol. XLIII, pp. 297-312, Mar., 1923.

In the Pennsylvania Dutch Country. By Elmer C. Stauffer. Vol. LXXX, pp. 37-74, 20 ills. in black and white, 22 ills. in color, 1 map (pen and ink drawing), July, 1941.

In the Realm of the Sons of the Sun (Incas). 10 ills. in color from paintings by H. M. Herget. Vol. LXXIII, pp. 229-236, Feb., 1938.

In the Realms of the Maharajas. By Lawrence Copley Thaw and Margaret S. Thaw. Vol. LXXVIII, pp. 727-780, 14 ills. in black and white, 40 ills. in color, 1 page map, Dec. 1940.

In the Savage South Seas. By Beatrice Grimshaw. Vol. XIX pp. 1-19, 21 ills., Jan., 1908.

In the Shadow of Bulgarian Monasteries. 14 ills. in color from natural-color photographs by Wilhelm Tobien and Georg Paskoff. Vol. LXII, pp. 202-211, Aug., 1932.

In the Wonderland of Peru. By Hiram Bingham. Vol. XXIV, pp. 387-574, 250 ills., 3 diagrams, 1 three-quarters-page map, Apr., 1913.

In Valais (Switzerland). By Louise Murray. Vol. XXI, pp. 249-256, 6 ills., Mar., 1910.

Incas (Indians):

Air Adventures in Peru: Cruising Among Andean Peaks, Pilots and Cameramen Discover Wondrous Works of an Ancient People. By Robert Shippee. Vol. LXIII, pp. 81-120, 40 ills., 1 three-quarters-page map, Jan., 1933.

Along the Old Inca Highway. By Harriet Chalmers Adams. Vol. XIX, pp. 231-250, 21 ills., Apr., 1908.

Cuzco, America's Ancient Mecca. By Harriet Chalmers Adams. Vol. XIX, pp. 669-689, 19 ills., Oct., 1908.

Explorations in Peru. Vol. XXIII, pp. 416-422. 7 ills., 1 half-page map, Apr., 1912.

Further Explorations in the Land of the Incas: The Peruvian Expedition of 1915 of the National Geographic Society and Yale University. By Hiram Bingham. Vol. XXIX, pp. 431-473, 29 ills., 1 page and 1 half-page maps, panorama, May, 1916.

Heart of Aymará Land: A Visit to Tiahuanacu, Perhaps the Oldest City of the New World, Lost Beneath the Drifting Sand of Centuries in the Bolivian Highlands. By Stewart E. McMillin. Vol. LI, pp. 213-256, 23 ills. in black and white, 18 ills. in color, 1 half-page map, Feb., 1927.

Honors to Amundsen and Peary (Banquet). Vol. XXIV, pp. 113-130, 5 ills., Jan., 1913.
 Contents: Address by Hiram Bingham on the Peruvian Expedition.

In the Realm of the Sons of the Sun. 10 ills. in color from paintings by H. M. Herget. Vol. LXXIII, pp. 229-236, Feb., 1938.

In the Wonderland of Peru. By Hiram Bingham. Vol. XXIV, pp. 387-574, 250 ills., 3 diagrams, 1 three-quarters-page map, Apr., 1913.

Incas: Empire Builders of the Andes. By Philip Ainsworth Means. Vol. LXXIII, pp. 225-264, 26 ills. in black and white, 10 ills. in color, Feb., 1938.

Pith of Peru: A Journey from Talara to Machu Picchu, with Memorable Stopovers. By Henry Albert Phillips. Vol. LXXXII, pp. 167-196, 6 ills. in black and white, 20 ills. in color, 1 page map, Aug., 1942.

Ruins of an Ancient Inca Capital, Machu Picchu. Vol. XXIV, panorama, Apr., 1913.

Some Wonderful Sights in the Andean Highlands: The Oldest City in America. Sailing on the Lake of the Clouds: The Yosemite of Peru. By Harriet Chalmers Adams. Vol. XIX, pp. 579-618, 19 ills., 1 half-page map, Sept., 1908.

Staircase Farms of the Ancients: Astounding Farming Skill of Ancient Peruvians, Who Were Probably the Most Industrious and Highly Organized People in History. By O. F. Cook. Vol. XXIX, pp. 474-534, 48 ills., May, 1916.

Story of Machu Picchu: The Peruvian Expeditions of the National Geographic Society and Yale University. By Hiram Bingham. Vol. XXVII, pp. 171-217, 50 ills., Feb., 1915.

Independence-class Light Carrier. *See Princeton.*

India:

Across Tibet from India to China. By Lt. Col. Ilia Tolstoy, AUS. Vol. XC, pp. 169-222, 41 ills., 1 half-page map, Aug., 1946.

Aërial Conquest of Everest: Flying Over the World's Highest Mountain Realizes the Objective of Many Heroic Explorers. By Lieut. Col. L. V. S. Blacker. Vol. LXIV, pp. 127-162, 35 ills., 1 page map, Aug., 1933.

Among the Great Himalayan Glaciers. Vol. XIII, pp. 405-406, Nov., 1902.

British Commonwealth of Nations: "Organized Freedom" Around the World. By Eric Underwood. Vol. LXXXIII, pp. 485-524, 31 ills., Apr., 1943.

Empire of Romance—India. 16 ills. in color from photographs. Vol. XL, pp. 481-496, Nov., 1921.

Fearful Famines of the Past: History Will Repeat Itself Unless the American People Conserve Their Resources. By Ralph A. Graves. Vol. XXXII, pp. 68-90, 11 ills., July, 1917.

First Over the Roof of the World by Motor: The Trans-Asiatic Expedition Sets New Records for Wheeled Transport in Scaling Passes of the Himalayas. By Maynard Owen Williams. Vol. LXI, pp. 321-363, 45 ills., 2 half-page maps, Mar., 1932.

Flying the World: In a Homemade Airplane the Author and Her Husband Enjoy 16,000 Miles of Adventurous Flight Across Europe, Asia, and America. By Gladys M. Day. Vol. LXI, pp. 655-690, 41 ills., 1 half-page map, June, 1932.

In the Realms of the Maharajas. By Lawrence Copley Thaw and Margaret S. Thaw. Vol. LXXVIII, pp. 727-780, 14 ills. in black and white, 40 ills. in color, 1 page map, Dec., 1940.

India—Yesterday, Today, and Tomorrow. By Lord Halifax. Vol. LXXXIV, pp. 385-408, 20 ills., 1 two-page map, Oct., 1943.

India and Ceylon. 8 ills. in color from autochromes by Helen Messinger Murdoch. Vol. XXXIX, pp. 281-288, Mar., 1921.

India at Work and Play. 22 ills. in color from natural-color photographs by Peter Upton Muir, Maynard Owen Williams, and Frances Muir. Vol. LXXXIX, pp. 449-464, Apr., 1946.

India Mosaic. By Peter Muir and Frances Muir. Vol. LXXXIX, pp. 443-470, 5 ills. in black and white, 22 ills. in color, 1 half-page map, Apr., 1946.

Indian Census of 1911. By John J. Banninga. Vol. XXII, pp. 633-638, 4 ills., July, 1911.

India's Treasures Helped the Allies. By John Fischer. Vol. LXXXIX, pp. 501-522, 18 ills., Apr., 1946.

Life with an Indian Prince: As Guests of a Maharaja's Brother, Two Young American Naturalists Study Age-old Methods of Hunting with Trained Falcons and Cheetahs and Savor the Pomp of Royal India. By John and Frank Craighead. Vol. LXXXI, pp. 235-272, 38 ills., 1 sixth-page map, Feb., 1942.

India—*Continued*

Manipur—Where Japan Struck at India. 11 ills. from photographs, 1 page map. Vol. LXXXV, pp. 743-750, June, 1944.

Marble Dams of Rajputana. By Eleanor Maddock. Vol. XL, pp. 468-499, 13 ills. in black and white, 16 ills. in color, Nov., 1921.

Marriage of the Gods (Religious Festival at Madura, India). By John J. Banninga. Vol. XXIV, pp. 1314-1330, 16 ills., Dec., 1913.

Nature's Most Amazing Mammal: Elephants, Unique Among Animals, Have Many Human Qualities When Wild That Make Them Foremost Citizens of Zoo and Circus. By Edmund Heller. Vol. LXV, pp. 729-759, 37 ills., June, 1934.

Old Mines and Mills in India. Vol. XX, pp. 489-490, 2 ills., May, 1909.

On the World's Highest Plateaus: Through an Asiatic No Man's Land to the Desert of Ancient Cathay. By Hellmut de Terra. Vol. LIX, pp. 319-367, 60 ills. in black and white, 32 ills. in color, 1 two-thirds-page map, Mar., 1931.

Oriental Pageantry of Northern India. 30 ills. in color from natural-color photographs by Franklin Price Knott. Vol. LVI, pp. 428-461, Oct., 1929.

Parsees and the Towers of Silence at Bombay, India. By William Thomas Fee. Vol. XVI, pp. 529-554, 16 ills., Dec., 1905.

Pathfinder of the East: Setting Sail to Find "Christians and Spices," Vasco da Gama Met Amazing Adventures, Founded an Empire, and Changed the History of Western Europe. By J. R. Hildebrand. Vol. LII, pp. 503-550, 43 ills., 1 two-thirds-page map, Nov., 1927.

Pilgrimage to Amernath, Himalayan Shrine of the Hindu Faith. By Louise Ahl Jessop. Vol. XL, pp. 512-542, 29 ills., Nov., 1921.

Princely India, Resplendent with Jewels and Gold. 40 ills. in color from natural-color photographs by Lawrence Copley Thaw. Vol. LXXVIII, pp. 733-780, Dec., 1940.

Race Prejudice in the Far East. By Melville E. Stone. Vol. XXI, pp. 973-985, 6 ills., Dec., 1910.

Religious Penances and Punishments Self-Inflicted by the Holy Men of India. By W. M. Zumbro. Vol. XXIV, pp. 1257-1314, 69 ills., Dec., 1913.

The Society's New Map of India and Burma. Text accompanying special map supplement in colors. Vol. LXXXIX, p. 544, Apr., 1946.

South of Khyber Pass. By Maynard Owen Williams. Vol. LXXXIX, pp. 471-500, 31 ills., Apr., 1946.

Stilwell Road—Land Route to China. By Nelson Grant Tayman. Vol. LXXXVII, pp. 681-698, 18 ills., June, 1945.

Streets and Palaces of Colorful India. 34 ills. in color from autochromes lumière by Gervais Courtellemont. Vol. L, pp. 60-85, July, 1926.

India—*Continued*

Temples of India. 54 ills. from photographs by W. M. Zumbro. Vol. XX, pp. 922-971, Nov., 1909.

Through the Heart of Hindustan: A Teeming Highway Extending for Fifteen Hundred Miles, from the Khyber Pass to Calcutta. By Maynard Owen Williams. Vol. XL, pp. 433-467, 29 ills., Nov., 1921.

Tiger-Hunting in India. By Brig. Gen. William Mitchell. Vol. XLVI, pp. 545-598, 46 ills., 1 quarter-page map, Nov., 1924.

United States and the British Empire. By Leonard David Gammans. Vol. LXXXVII, pp. 562-564, May, 1945.

Vasco da Gama at the Court of the Zamorin of Calicut. Reproduction in color of the painting by José Velloso Salgado, Sociedade de Geographia de Lisboa. Vol. LII, supplement, Nov., 1927.

Yank Meets Native. By Wanda Burnett. Vol. LXXXVIII, pp. 105-128, 24 ills., July, 1945

See also Benares; Delhi; Kashmir; Madura; New Delhi.

Indian Census of 1911. By John J. Banninga. Vol. XXII, pp. 633-638, 4 ills., July, 1911.

Indian Haven—Off the San Blas Coast (Mulatas Archipelago). 12 ills. in color from natural-color photographs by Lieut. Dayton Seiler. Vol. LXXIX, pp. 209-216, Feb., 1941.

Indian Ocean:

Fishing for Pearls in the Indian Ocean. By Bella Sidney Woolf. Vol. XLIX, pp. 161-183, 24 ills., Feb., 1926.

Indian Ocean Map Spans Far East News Centers. Text accompanying special map supplement in colors. Vol. LXXIX, pp. 345-346, 1 ill., Mar., 1941.

Indian Tribes of Pueblo Land. By Matthew W. Stirling. Vol. LXXVIII, pp. 549-596, 16 ills. in black and white, 25 ills. in color, Nov., 1940.

Indian Tribes of Southern Patagonia, Tierra del Fuego, and the Adjoining Islands. By J. B. Hatcher. Vol. XII, pp. 12-22, 4 ills., Jan., 1901.

Indian Village of Baum (Ohio). By H. C. Brown. Vol. XII, pp. 272-274, July, 1901.

Indiana:

Hoosier Haunts and Holidays. 27 ills. in color from natural-color photographs by Willard R. Culver. Vol. LXX, pp. 283-314, Sept., 1936.

Indiana Journey. By Frederick Simpich. Vol. LXX, pp. 267-320, 32 ills. in black and white, 27 ills. in color, 1 two-page map, Sept., 1936.

Indiana's Unrivaled Sand-Dunes—A National Park Opportunity. By Orpheus Moyer Schantz. Vol. XXXV, pp. 430-441, 18 ills., May, 1919.

Indians, East. *See* East Indians.

Indians of Central America:

Arch-Isolationists, the San Blas Indians: Coconuts Serve as Cash on Islands Off the Panama Coast Where Tribesmen Cling to Their Ancient Ways and Discourage Visitors. By Corinne B. Feeney. Vol. LXXIX, pp. 193-220, 15 ills. in black and white, 12 ills. in color, 1 sixth-page map, Feb., 1941.

Guatemala Interlude: In the Land of the Quetzal a Modern Capital Contrasts With Primitive Indian Villages and the "Pompeii of America." By E. John Long. Vol. LXX, pp. 429-460, 22 ills. in black and white, 13 ills. in color, 1 page map, Oct., 1936.
   Contains information on the Cakchiquels. Quichés, Sololás, and Tzutuhiles.

Indian Haven—Off the San Blas Coast (Mulatas Archipelago). 12 ills. in color from natural-color photographs by Lieut. Dayton Seiler. Vol. LXXIX, pp. 209-216, Feb., 1941.

Land That Links the Americas (Panama). 22 ills. in color from natural-color photographs by Luis Marden. Vol. LXXX, pp. 601-624, Nov., 1941.
   Contains illustrations of the Choco and San Blas Indians.

Little-Known Parts of Panama. By Henry Pittier. Vol. XXIII, pp. 627-662, 35 ills., 1 page map, July, 1912.
   Contains descriptions and illustrations of the Chocoes, Guaymies, and San Blas Indians.

To Market in Guatemala. By Luis Marden. With 19 ills. in color from natural-color photographs by Giles Greville Healey and Charles S. Pineo. Vol. LXXXVIII, pp. 87-104, July, 1945.

Where Man's Garb Rivals the Quetzal (Guatemala). 13 ills. in color from natural-color photographs by Luis Marden. Vol. LXX, pp. 437-444, Oct., 1936.
   Contains illustrations of Indians of the following types: Santo Tomás, Sololá, Todos Santos, and Tzutuhile.

See also Mayas; Quichés.

Indians of Mexico:

Adventuring Down the West Coast of Mexico. By Herbert Corey. Vol. XLII, pp. 449-503, 44 ills., 1 half-page map, Nov., 1922.
   Contains information on the Aztecs and Seri Indians.

Discovering the New World's Oldest Dated Work of Man: A Maya Monument Inscribed 291 B. C. is Unearthed Near a Huge Stone Head by a Geographic-Smithsonian Expedition in Mexico. By Matthew W. Stirling. Vol. LXXVI, pp. 183-218, 40 ills., 1 half-page map, Aug., 1939.

Expedition Unearths Buried Masterpieces of Carved Jade (Cerro de las Mesas). By Matthew W. Stirling. Vol. LXXX, pp. 277-302, 14 ills. in black and white, 20 ills. in color, 1 two-thirds-page map, Sept., 1941.

Finding Jewels of Jade in a Mexican Swamp. By Matthew W. and Marion Stirling. Vol. LXXXII, pp. 635-661, 15 ills. in black and white, 12 ills. in color, 1 two-thirds-page map, Nov., 1942.

Indians of Mexico—*Continued*

Contains text references and illustrations of the Zoque Indians, Zotzil Indians, and the Maya ruins at Palenque.

Great Stone Faces of the Mexican Jungle: Five Colossal Heads and Numerous Other Monuments of Vanished Americans Are Excavated by the Latest National Geographic-Smithsonian Expedition. By Matthew W. Stirling. Vol. LXXVIII, pp. 309-334, 26 ills., 1 map, Sept., 1940.

Isthmus of Tehuantepec: The Bridge of the World's Commerce. By Helen Olsson-Seffer. Vol. XXI, pp. 991-1002, 6 ills., Dec., 1910.
Contains descriptions of the following types: Agualulcos, Aztecs, Huaves, Mijes, Zapotecs, and Zoques.

La Venta's Green Stone Tigers. By Matthew W. Stirling. Vol. LXXXIV, pp. 321-332, 4 ills. in black and white, 6 ills. in color, 1 two-thirds-page map, Sept., 1943.

Parícutin the Cornfield That Grew a Volcano. By James A. Green. Vol. LXXXV, pp. 129-164, 16 ills. in black and white, 21 ills. in color, 1 third-page map, Feb., 1944.
Contains text references and illustrations of the Tarascan Indians.

See also Aztecs; Mayas; Mixtec Indians; Otomi Indians; Seri Indians; Tarascan Indians; Toltecs; Yaqui Indians; Zapotec Indians.

Indians of North America:

Acorn, a Possibly Neglected Source of Food. By C. Hart Merriam. Vol. XXXIV, pp. 129-137, 8 ills., Aug., 1918.
Contains descriptions and illustrations of the Indians of California.

Along Our Side of the Mexican Border. By Frederick Simpich. Vol. XXXVIII, pp. 61-80, 9 ills., 1 quarter-page map, July, 1920.
Contains information on the following types: Apache, Coahuila, Cocopah, Pima, and Yuma.

America's First Settlers, the Indians. By Matthew W. Stirling. Vol. LXXII, pp. 535-596, 34 ills. in black and white, 24 ills. in color, Nov., 1937.
Contains information on the following types: Algonquian, Assiniboin, Cayuga, Chippewa, Delaware, Huron, Iroquois, Malecite, Menominee, Mohawk, Mohican, Natchez, Nez Percé, Oneida, Onondago, Passamaquoddy, Penobscot, Seneca, Shawnee, Shoshoni, Tuscarora, Wampanoag.

Everyday Life in Pueblo Bonito: As Disclosed by the National Geographic Society's Archeologic Explorations in the Chaco Canyon National Monument, New Mexico. By Neil M. Judd. Vol. XLVIII, pp. 227-262, 37 ills., 1 two-thirds-page map, Sept., 1925.

Exploring in the Canyon of Death: Remains of a People Who Dwelt in Our Southwest at Least 4,000 Years Ago Are Revealed. By Earl H. Morris. Vol. XLVIII, pp. 263-300, 24 ills. in black and white, 22 ills. in color, Sept., 1925.

First Families of Southeastern America. 8 ills. in color from paintings by W. Langdon Kihn. Vol. LXXXIX, pp. 65-72, Jan., 1946.

Indians of North America—*Continued*

Contains illustrations of the following types: Burial Mound Builders, Choctaws, Natchez, Seminole, Taensa, Temple Mound Builders.

From the War-Path to the Plow. By Franklin K. Lane. Vol. XXVII, pp. 72-87, 12 ills., Jan., 1915.
Contains information on the following types: Apache, Blackfeet, Cherokee, Crow, and Osage.

Game and Fur-Bearing Animals and Their Influence on the Indians of the Northwest. By Townsend W. Thorndike. Vol. XV, p. 431, Oct., 1904.

Grass Makes Wyoming Fat. By Frederick Simpich. Vol. LXXXVIII, pp. 153-188, 13 ills. in black and white, 19 ills. in color, 1 two-page map, Aug., 1945.

Indian Tribes of Pueblo Land. By Matthew W. Stirling. Vol. LXXVIII, pp. 549-596, 16 ills. in black and white, 25 ills. in color, Nov., 1940.
Contains information on the following types: Apaches, Basket Makers, Cliff Dwellers, Cocopas, Comanches, Havasupais, Hochokams, Hopis, Kiowas, Mojaves, Navajos, Paiutes, Papagos, Pimas, Utes, Yavapais, Yumas, Zunis.

Indian Village of Baum (Ohio). By H. C. Brown. Vol. XII, pp. 272-274, July, 1901.

Indians of Our North Pacific Coast. By Matthew W. Stirling. Paintings by W. Langdon Kihn. Vol. LXXXVII, pp. 25-52, 3 ills. in black and white, 16 ills. in color, Jan., 1945.
Contains information and illustrations of the following tribes: Bellacoola, Haida, Kwakiutl, Niska, Nootka, Pomo, Tlingit, Tsimshian.

Indians of Our Western Plains. By Matthew W. Stirling. Paintings by W. Langdon Kihn. Vol. LXXXVI, pp. 73-108, 14 ills. in black and white, 16 ills. in color, July, 1944.
Contains information and illustrations of the following tribes: Arapaho, Arikara, Bannock, Blackfeet, Caddo, Cheyenne, Chippewa, Comanche, Crow, Dakota, Hidatsa, Iowa, Kansas, Kiowa, Mandan, Missouri, Osage, Pawnee, Quapaw, Shoshoni, Sioux, Ute, Waco, Wichita.

Indians of the Southeastern United States. By Matthew W. Stirling. Paintings by W. Langdon Kihn. Vol. LXXXIX, pp. 53-74, 8 ills. in black and white, 8 ills. in color, Jan., 1946.
Contains information on the following: Attacapan, Biloxi, Burial Mound Period, Caddoan, Calusa, Catawba, Cheraw, Cherokee, Chickasaw, Chitmachan, Choctaw, Creek, Hitchiti, Muskhogean, Natchez, Pamunkey, Powhatan Confederacy, Seminole, Shawnee, Temple Mound Period, Timucuan, Tunican, Yuchi.

Land of the Best. By Gilbert H. Grosvenor. Vol. XXIX, pp. 327-430, 71 ills. in black and white, 33 ills. in color, panorama, Apr., 1916.
Contains illustrations of the following types: Acoma, Blackfeet, Hopi, Pueblo.

Indians of North America—*Continued*

Nature Paints New Mexico. 25 ills. in color from natural-color photographs by Richard H. Stewart. Vol. LXXIII, pp. 537-568, May, 1938.

    Contains illustrations of the following types: Isleta, Navajo, San Ildefonso, Santa Clara, and Taos.

New Mexico Melodrama. By Frederick Simpich. Vol. LXXIII, pp. 529-569, 19 ills. in black and white, 25 ills. in color, 1 two-page map, May, 1938.

The North American Indian. Vol. XIX, pp. 448-454, 5 ills., June, 1908.

    Contains information and illustrations of the following tribes: Apache, Havasupai, Maricopa, Mohave, Navajo, Papago, Pima, Walapai, Yuma.

North American Indians. Vol. XVIII, pp. 469-484, 14 ills., July, 1907.

    Contains illustrations of the following types: Acoma, Apache, Crow, Hopi, Mohave, Navajo, San Ildefonso, Zuñi.

Origin of American State Names. By Frederick W. Lawrence. Vol. XXXVIII, pp. 104-143, 34 ills., Aug., 1920.

Photographing the Marvels of the West in Colors. By Fred Payne Clatworthy. Vol. LIII, pp. 694-719, 4 ills. in color, June, 1928.

    Contains colored illustrations of the Hopis and Sioux, and text references to the Utes, Cheyennes, and Arapahoes.

Red Men of the Southwest. 25 ills. in color from paintings by W. Landon Kihn. Vol. LXXVIII, pp. 557-596, Nov., 1940.

    Contains illustrations of the following types: Acoma, Apache, Cliff Dwellers, Havasupai, Hohokam, Hopi, Laguna, Navajo, Pima, San Ildefonso, Tewa, Yaqui, Yuma, Zuni.

Scenes from America's Southwest. 14 ills. from photographs by Frederick I. Monsen and Charles Martin. Vol. XXXIX, pp. 651-664, June, 1921.

    Contains illustrations of the Hopi and Laguna Indians, and the following ruins and localities: Canyon De Chelly, Canyon Del Muerto, Mesa Verde, Painted Desert, Pueblo Bonito, Tyuonyi, Walpi.

Secret of the Southwest Solved by Talkative Tree Rings: Horizons of American History Are Carried Back to A. D. 700 and a Calendar for 1,200 Years Established by National Geographic Society Expeditions. By Andrew Ellicott Douglass. Vol. LVI, pp. 737-770, 33 ills., 1 two-thirds-page map, Dec., 1929.

Taming the Outlaw Missouri River. By Frederick Simpich. Vol. LXXXVIII, pp. 569-598, 25 ills., 1 two-page map, Nov., 1945.

Totem-pole Builders. 16 ills. in color from paintings by W. Langdon Kihn. Vol. LXXXVII, pp. 33-48, Jan., 1945.

    Contains illustrations of the following tribes: Bellacoola, Haida, Niska, Nootka, Pomo, Tlingit, Tsimshian.

Indians of North America—*Continued*

Travels of George Washington: Dramatic Episodes in His Career as the First Geographer of the United States. By William Joseph Showalter. Vol. LXI, pp. 1-63, 50 ills., 5 maps, special supplement in colors, Jan., 1932.

    Contains information on Washington's dealings with the Half-King.

Welcome to Wyoming. 19 ills. in color from natural-color photographs; 18 ills. by B. Anthony Stewart. Vol. LXXXVIII, pp. 161-184, Aug., 1945.

    Contains illustrations of the Shoshoni.

When Red Men Ruled Our Forests. 24 ills. in color from paintings by W. Langdon Kihn. Vol. LXXII, pp. 551-590, Nov., 1937.

    Contains illustrations of the following types: Chippewa, Huron, Iroquois, Massachusetts, Menominee, Mohawk, Penobscot, Pequot, Sauk and Fox, Seneca, Shawnee.

See also Crow Indians; Havasupai Indians; Hopi Indians; Klamath Indians; Navajos; Ojibways; Papago Indians; Seminole Indians; Sioux Indians; Tahltan Indians.

Indians of South America:

Bolivia—Tin Roof of the Andes. By Henry Albert Phillips. Vol. LXXXIII, pp. 309-332, 5 ills. in black and white, 20 ills. in color, Mar., 1943.

Camels of the Clouds (Lamoids). By W. H. Hodge. Vol. LXXXIX, pp. 641-656, 15 ills., 1 half-page map, May, 1946.

    Contains information on the Quichua and Aymará Indians.

Chile's Land of Fire and Water: Smoking Volcanoes and Ice-hooded Peaks Stand Sentinel Over Limpid Lakes in the Far Southern Andes. By W. Robert Moore. Vol. LXXX, pp. 91-110, 9 ills. in black and white, 10 ills. in color, 1 page map, July, 1941.

    Contains text references and illustrations of the Araucanian Indians.

Further Explorations in the Land of the Incas: The Peruvian Expedition of 1915 of the National Geographic Society and Yale University. By Hiram Bingham. Vol. XXIX, pp. 431-473, 29 ills., 1 page and 1 half-page maps, panorama, May, 1916.

    Contains information on the Incas and the present-day Indians of the Lowlands and Highlands.

High Lights in the Peruvian and Bolivian Andes. 12 ills. in color from autochromes by W. Robert Moore. Vol. LI, pp. 218-235, Feb., 1927.

In the Wonderland of Peru. By Hiram Bingham. Vol. XXIV, pp. 387-574, 250 ills., 3 diagrams, 1 three-quarters-page map, Apr., 1913.

    Contains descriptions and illustrations of the Highland Indians of Southern Peru.

Indian Tribes of Southern Patagonia, Tierra del Fuego, and the Adjoining Islands. By J. B. Hatcher. Vol. XII, pp. 12-22, 4 ills., Jan., 1901.

    Contains descriptions and illustrations of the following: Alaculoffs (Alikulufs), Onas, Tehuelches, and Yahgans.

Indians of South America—*Continued*

Inside Cape Horn. By Amos Burg. Vol. LXXII, pp. 743-783, 29 ills. in black and white, 10 ills. in color, 1 two-page map, Dec., 1937.

Contains information on the following: Alikulufs, Onas, and Yahgans.

Longitudinal Journey Through Chile. By Harriet Chalmers Adams. Vol. XLII, pp. 219-273, 60 ills., 1 half-page map, Sept., 1922.

Contains descriptions and illustrations of the following: Alacaluf (Alikuluf) Indians, Araucanian Indians, Ona Indians, and Yahgan Indians.

Peru on Parade. 20 ills. in color from natural-color photographs by Henry Clay Gipson and Jack Kuhne. Vol. LXXII, pp. 173-196, Aug., 1942.

Pith of Peru: A Journey from Talara to Machu Picchu, with Memorable Stopovers. By Henry Albert Phillips. Vol. LXXXII, pp. 167-196, 6 ills. in black and white, 20 ills. in color, 1 page map, Aug., 1942.

Quinine Hunters in Ecuador. By Froelich Rainey. Vol. LXXXIX, pp. 341-363, 21 ills., 1 one-half-page map, Mar., 1946.

Stone Idols of the Andes Reveal a Vanished People: Remarkable Relics of One of the Oldest Aboriginal Cultures of America are Unearthed in Colombia's San Agustín Region. By Hermann von Walde-Waldegg. Vol. LXXVII, pp. 627-647, 22 ills., 1 map, May, 1940.

Where Snow Peaks Temper the Tropics (Ecuador). 9 ills. in color from natural-color photographs by W. Robert Moore. Vol. LXXX, pp. 727-701, Dec., 1941.

See also Arecuna Indians; Aymará Indians; Chunchos; Incas; Jivaro Indians; Quichua Indians.

India's Treasures Helped the Allies. By John Fischer. Vol. LXXXIX, pp. 501-522, 18 ills., Apr., 1946.

Indispensable Sheep. Vol. LIII, pp. 512-528, 20 ills., Apr., 1928.

Indochina. *See* French Indo-China.

Indonesia. *See* Netherlands East Indies.

Industrial Titan of America: Pennsylvania, Once the Keystone of the Original Thirteen, Now the Keystone of Forty-eight Sovereign States. By John Oliver La Gorce. Vol. XXXV, pp. 367-406, 33 ills., 1 page map, May, 1919.

Industrial Training of the German People. Vol. XVI, pp. 111-114, Mar., 1905.

Industries:

Automobile Industry: An American Art That Has Revolutionized Methods in Manufacturing and Transformed Transportation. By William Joseph Showalter. Vol. XLIV, pp. 337-414, 76 ills., Oct., 1923.

Blueberry Culture: Wild Blueberry Tamed: The New Industry of the Pine Barrens of New Jersey. By Frederick V. Coville. Vol. XXIX, pp. 535-546, 10 ills., June, 1916.

Cacao: São Tomé, the Chocolate Island. By William Leon Smyser. Vol. LXXXIX, pp. 657-680, 23 ills., 1 third-page map, May, 1946.

Industries—*Continued*

Cinchona: Quinine Hunters in Ecuador. By Froelich Rainey. Vol. LXXXIX, pp. 341-363. 21 ills., 1 half-page map, Mar., 1946.

Coal: Ideal Fuel: The American Coal Briquetting Industry. By Guy Elliott Mitchell. Vol. XXI. pp. 1066-1074, 4 ills., Dec., 1910.

Coal: Prodigious Worker for Man. By Albert W. Atwood. Vol. LXXXV, pp. 569-592, 19 ills., 1 drawing, May, 1944.

Coal—Ally of American Industry. By William Joseph Showalter. Vol. XXXIV, pp. 407-434, 23 ills., Nov., 1918.

Coffee Is King in El Salvador. By Luis Marden. Vol. LXXXVI, pp. 575-616, 22 ills. in black and white, 27 ills. in color, 1 half-page map, Nov., 1944.

Cork. Vol. XIX, pp. 690-693, 3 ills., Oct., 1908.

Cotton: Foremost Fiber of the World. By J. R. Hildebrand. Vol. LXXIX, pp. 137-192, 31 ills. in black and white 34 ills. in color, Feb., 1941.

Cotton: Golden Fleece of Dixie. 34 ills. in color from natural-color photographs by Willard R. Culver. Vol. LXXIX, pp. 153-192, Feb., 1941.

Floriculture: Garden Isles of Scilly: Geologists May Throw Stones at Legend of Lost Lyonnesse, but Natives Grow Flowers in Glass Houses for London. By W. Robert Moore. Vol. LXXIV, pp. 755-774, 9 ills. in black and white, 13 ills. in color, 1 half-page map, Dec., 1938.

Floriculture: Scillies: Isles of Wrecks and Golden Daffodils. 13 ills. in color from natural-color photographs by B. Anthony Stewart, Maynard Owen Williams, and W. Robert Moore. Vol. LXXIV, pp. 759-766, Dec., 1938.

Fruits and Vegetables: Rio Grande Cornucopia Under a Winter Sun. 24 ills. in color from natural-color photographs by B. Anthony Stewart. Vol. LXXV, pp. 65-96, Jan., 1939.

Fruits and Vegetables: Texas Delta of an American Nile: Orchards and Gardens Replace Thorny Jungle in the Southmost Tip of the Lone Star State. By McFall Kerbey. Vol. LXXV, pp. 51-96, 27 ills. in black and white, 24 ills. in color, 1 page map, Jan., 1939.

Glass: From Sand to Seer and Servant of Man. 22 ills. in color from natural-color photographs by Willard R. Culver. Vol. LXXXIII, pp. 17-48, Jan., 1943.

Glass "Goes to Town." By J. R. Hildebrand. Vol. LXXXIII, pp. 1-48, 28 ills. in black and white, 22 ills. in color, Jan., 1943.

Grape-Growing Industry in the United States. Vol. XIV, pp. 445-451, 5 ills., Dec., 1903.

Hairnet Industry in North China. By H. W. Robinson. Vol. XLIV, pp. 327-336, 10 ills., Sept., 1923.

Lobster Fishing: The Maine American and the American Lobster. By John D. Lucas. Vol. LXXXIX, pp. 523-543, 19 ills., Apr., 1946.

Industries—*Continued*

Lumber : Influence of Forestry upon the Lumber Industry of the United States. By Overton W. Price. Vol. XIV, pp. 381-386, 2 ills., Oct., 1903.

Lumber : Lumber Business of the Government. Vol. XVII, pp. 531-533, Sept., 1906.

Lumber : Lumbering in Manchuria. By Henry B. Miller. Vol. XV, pp. 130-132, 2 ills., Mar., 1904.

Lumber : Redwood Forest of the Pacific Coast. By Henry Gannett. Vol. X, pp. 145-159, 6 ills., 1 page map, May, 1899.

Lumber : Working Teak in the Burma Forests : The Sagacious Elephant Is Man's Ablest Ally in the Logging Industry of the Far East. By A. W. Smith. Vol. LVIII, pp. 239-256, 5 ills. in black and white, 15 ills. in color, Aug., 1930.

Metal Sinews of Strength : This Is a War of Many Metals, for We Live in an Age of Alloys. By Frederick G. Vosburgh. Vol. LXXXI, pp. 457-491, 35 ills., Apr., 1942.

Nitrate : Longitudinal Journey Through Chile. By Harriet Chalmers Adams. Vol. XLII, pp. 219-273, 60 ills., 1 half-page map, Sept., 1922.

Paper : Lessons from Japan. Vol. XV, pp. 221-225, 3 ills., May, 1904.

Paper : Paper from Cotton Stalks. Vol. XVII, p. 425, July, 1906.

Pearl : Fishing for Pearls in the Indian Ocean. By Bella Sidney Woolf. Vol. XLIX, pp. 161-183, 24 ills., Feb., 1926.

Petroleum : Curaçao and Aruba, Oil Isles of the Caribbean. 10 ills. in color from natural-color photographs by Philip Hanson Hiss and Robert Yarnall Richie. Vol. LXXXIII, pp. 175-182, Feb., 1943.

Petroleum : Curaçao and Aruba on Guard. By W. Robert Moore. Vol. LXXXIII, pp. 169-192, 12 ills. in black and white, 10 ills. in color, 4 maps, Feb., 1943.

Petroleum : So Oklahoma Grew Up. By Frederick Simpich. Vol. LXXIX, pp. 269-314, 30 ills. in black and white, 19 ills. in color, 1 page map, Mar., 1941.

Petroleum : Today's World Turns on Oil. By Frederick Simpich. Vol. LXXIX, pp. 703-748, 22 ills., in black and white, 2 drawings, 21 ills. in color, June, 1941.

Platinum in the World's Work. By Lonnelle Davison. Vol. LXXII, pp. 345-360, 17 ills., Sept., 1937.

Porcelain : World's Ancient Porcelain Center (Kingtehchen). By Frank B. Lenz. Vol. XXXVIII, pp. 391-406, 17 ills., Nov., 1920.

Poultry : America's Debt to the Hen. By Harry R. Lewis. Vol. LI, pp. 453-467, 15 ills., Apr., 1927.

Poultry : Races of Domestic Fowl. By Morley A. Jull. Vol. LI, pp. 379-452, 67 ills. in black and white, 29 ills. in color, Apr., 1927.

Rose Oil : Bulgaria's Valley of Roses. 13 ills. in color from natural-color photographs by Wilhelm Tobien and Georg Paskoff. Vol. LXII, pp. 186-195, Aug., 1932.

Industries—*Continued*

Rubber : From Trees to Tires and Toys. 26 ills. in color from natural-color photographs by Willard R. Culver and J. Baylor Roberts. Vol. LXXVII, pp. 159-190, Feb., 1940.

Rubber : Our Most Versatile Vegetable Product : Rubber Drops from Millions of Tropical Trees Are Transformed by Genii Chemists into Myriad Articles, from Tires to Teething Rings. By J. R. Hildebrand. Vol. LXXVII, pp. 143-200, 51 ills. in black and white, 26 ills. in color. Feb., 1940.

Rubber : Singapore, Crossroads of the East : The World's Greatest Mart for Rubber and Tin Was in Recent Times a Pirate-Haunted, Tiger-Infested Jungle Isle. By Frederick Simpich. Vol. XLIX, pp. 235-269, 32 ills., 1 half-page map, Mar., 1926.

Sale for China's Daily Rice. 11 ills. from photographs. Vol. LXXXVI, pp. 329-336, Sept., 1944.

Sheep : Indispensable Sheep. Vol. LIII, pp. 512-528, 20 ills., Apr., 1928.

Sheep : Land of Lambskins : An Expedition to Bokhara, Russian Central Asia, to Study the Karakul Sheep Industry. By Robert K. Nabours. Vol. XXXVI, pp. 77-88, 15 ills., July, 1919.

Shipbuilding : As 2,000 Ships Are Born. By Frederick Simpich. Vol. LXXXI, pp. 551-588, 34 ills., May, 1942.

Shipbuilding : Our Industrial Victory. By Charles M. Schwab. Vol. XXXIV, pp. 212-229, 17 ills., Sept., 1918.

Shore-Whaling : A World Industry. By Roy Chapman Andrews. Vol. XXII, pp. 411-442, 34 ills., May, 1911.

Shrimp : Delectable Shrimp : Once a Culinary Stepchild, Today a Gulf Coast Industry. By Harlan Major. Vol. LXXXVI, pp. 501-512, 11 ills., 1 two-thirds-page-map, Oct., 1944.

Silk : How Half the World Works. By Alice Tisdale Hobart and Mary A. Nourse. Vol. LXI, pp. 509-524, 22 ills., Apr., 1932.

Steel : Industry's Greatest Asset—Steel. By William Joseph Showalter. Vol. XXXII, pp. 121-156, 34 ills., Aug., 1917.

Steel : "Magnetic City" (Magnitogorsk), Core of Valiant Russia's Industrial Might. By John Scott. Vol. LXXXIII, pp. 525-556, 27 ills., 1 two-page map, May, 1943,

Sugar : Agricultural Possibilities in Tropical Mexico. By Dr. Pehr Olsson-Seffer. Vol. XXI, pp. 1021-1040, 18 ills., Dec., 1910.

Sugar : Cuba—The Sugar Mill of the Antilles. By William Joseph Showalter. Vol. XXVIII, pp. 1-33, 24 ills., 1 page map, July, 1920.

Sugar : How the World Is Fed. By William Joseph Showalter. Vol. XXIX, pp. 1-110, 101 ills., Jan., 1916.

Synthetic Products : Chemists Make a New World : Creating Hitherto Unknown Raw Materials, Science Now Disrupts Old Trade Routes and Revamps the World Map of Industry. By Frederick Simpich. Vol. LXXVI, pp. 601-640. 22 ills. in black and white, 26 ills. in color Nov., 1939.

Industries—*Continued*

Synthetic Products: From Nature's Hidden Building Blocks. 26 ills. in color from natural-color photographs by Willard R. Culver. Vol. LXXVI, pp. 609-640, Nov., 1939.

Tin, the Cinderella Metal. By Alicia O'Reardon Overbeck. Vol. LXXVIII, pp. 659-684, 24 ills., Nov., 1940.

War Industries: American Industries Geared for War. By Thornton Oakley. With 16 ills. in color from paintings by the author. Vol. LXXXII, pp. 716-734, 1 ill., Dec., 1942.

War Industries: Brazil's Potent Weapons. By W. Robert Moore. Vol. LXXXV, pp. 41-78, 16 ills. in black and white, 18 ills. in color, 1 two-page map, Jan., 1944.

War Industries: Bright Facets of Brazil. 18 ills. in color from natural-color photographs by W. Robert Moore. Vol. LXXXV, pp. 49-72, Jan., 1944.

War Industries: Great Lakes and Great Industries. 19 ills. in color from natural-color photographs by B. Anthony Stewart, Alfred T. Palmer, and Willard R. Culver. Vol. LXXXVI, pp. 689-712, Dec., 1944.

War Industries: India's Treasures Helped the Allies. By John Fischer. Vol. LXXXIX, pp. 501-522, 18 ills., Apr., 1946.

War Industries: Michigan Fights. By Harvey Klemmer. Vol. LXXXVI, pp. 677-715, 20 ills. in black and white, 19 ills. in color, 1 page-and-a-half map, Dec., 1944.

War Industries: Miracle of War Production: For Victory the United States Transforms Its Complex Industry into the Biggest Factory and Mightiest Arsenal the World Has Ever Known. By Albert W. Atwood. Paintings by Thornton Oakley. Vol. LXXXII, pp. 693-715, 17 ills. in black and white, 16 ills. in color, Dec., 1942.

War Industries: Women at Work. By La Verne Bradley. Vol. LXXXVI, pp. 193-220, 23 ills., Aug., 1944.

War Industries: Yield of Texas. By Frederick Simpich. Vol. LXXXVII, pp. 163-184, 15 ills., 1 two-page map, Feb., 1945.

Worm Digging (Fishing Bait): The Worm Turns. By Samuel Sandrof. Vol. LXXXIX, pp. 775-786, 14 ills., June, 1946.

See also Agriculture; Bananas; Cattle and Cattle Raising; Codfish and Codfish Industry; Coffee; Meat Industry and Trade; Mines and Mining; Motion Picture Industry; Paper Industry; Rug Industry; Shark Fishing; Sheep and Sheep Raising; Shoes and Shoe Industry; Silk Industry; Tobacco Industry; Transportation; Turtling; *and* country and state articles describing local industries.

Industry's Greatest Asset—Steel. By William Joseph Showalter. Vol. XXXII, pp. 121-156, 34 ills., Aug., 1917.

Inexhaustible Italy. By Arthur Stanley Riggs. Vol. XXX, pp. 273-368, 76 ills., 1 page map, Oct., 1916.

Infantrymen—The Fighters of War. By Brig. Gen. W. H. Wilbur. Vol. LXXXVI, pp. 513-538, 22 ills., Nov., 1944.

Influence of Forestry upon the Lumber Industry of the United States. By Overton W. Price. Vol. XIV, pp. 381-386, 2 ills., Oct., 1903.

Influence of Geographical Conditions on Military Operations in South Africa. By Maj. W. A. Simpson. Vol. XI, pp. 186-192, 1 half-page map, May, 1900.

Influence of Submarine Cables upon Military and Naval Supremacy. By Capt. George O. Squier. Vol. XII, pp. 1-12, Jan., 1901.

Informal Salute to the English Lakes. By Maynard Owen Williams. Vol. LXIX, pp. 511-521, 10 ills. in color, Apr., 1936.

Inner Mongolia. *See* Mongolia.

Inns:

England: Cradles of English History. 6 ills. in color from natural-color photographs by Clifton Adams. Vol. LIX, pp. 268-277, Mar., 1931.

England: Visits to the Old Inns of England: Historic Homes of Hospitality for the Wayfarer Dot the Length and Breadth of the Kingdom. By Harold Donaldson Eberlein. Vol. LIX, pp. 261-285, 17 ills. in black and white, 15 ills. in color, Mar., 1931.

Inoculating the Ground. Vol. XV, pp. 225-228, 2 ills., May, 1904.

Insanity:

Geographical Distribution of Insanity in the United States. By William A. White. Vol. XIV, pp. 361-378, 6 charts, Oct., 1903.

Insect Community Lives in Flower Heads. By James G. Needham. Vol. XC, pp. 340-356, 5 ills. in black and white, 11 ills. in color, Sept., 1946.

Insects:

Amid the Snow Peaks of the Equator: A Naturalist's Explorations Around Ruwenzori, With an Excursion to the Congo State, and an Account of the Terrible Scourge of Sleeping Sickness. By A. F. R. Wollaston. Vol. XX, pp. 256-277, 11 ills., Mar., 1909.

Book of Monsters. By David and Marian Fairchild. Vol. XXVI, pp. 89-98, 7 ills., July, 1914.

A Community of Dwarfs. 11 illustrations in color from natural-color photographs by Willard R. Culver. Vol. XC, pp. 345-352, Sept., 1946.

Cooties and Courage. By Herbert Corey. Vol. XXXIII, pp. 495-509, 10 ills., June, 1918.

Economic Loss to the People of the United States Through Insects That Carry Disease. By L. O. Howard. Vol. XX, pp. 735-749, Aug., 1909.

Explorers of a New Kind: Successful Introduction of Beetles and Parasites to Check Ravages of the Gipsy-Moth and Brown-Tail Moth. By L. O. Howard. Vol. XXVI, pp. 38-67, 11 ills. in black and white, 5 ills. in color, July, 1914.

Insects—*Continued*

Exploring the Wonders of the Insect World. By William Joseph Showalter. Vol. LVI, pp. 1-90, 59 ills. in black and white, 269 ills. in color, July, 1929.

Fighting Insects with Airplanes : An Account of the Successful Use of the Flying-Machine in Dusting Tall Trees Infested with Leaf-Eating Caterpillars. By C. R. Neillie and J. S. Houser. Vol. XLI, pp. 333-338, 6 ills., Mar., 1922.

Hospital Heroes Convict the Cootie. Vol. XXXIII, p. 510, June, 1918.

An Insect Community Lives in Flower Heads. By James G. Needham. Vol. XC, pp. 340-356, 5 ills. in black and white, 11 ills. in color, Sept., 1946.
    Contains descriptions and illustrations of the following : Ants, Aphids, Baccha Flies, Bandwing Flies, Clearwing Flies, Mealy Bugs, Midges, Moths, Spotwing Flies.

Insect Rivals of the Rainbow. 269 ills. in color from natural-color photographs by Edwin L. Wisherd and paintings by Hashime Murayama. Vol. LVI, pp. 28-85, July, 1929.

Jungles of Panama. By David Fairchild. Vol. XLI, pp. 131-145, 14 ills., Feb., 1922.

Marvels of Metamorphosis : A Scientific "G-man" Pursues Rare Trapdoor Spider Parasites for Three Years With a Spade and a Candid Camera. By George Elwood Jenks. Vol. LXXIV, pp. 807-828, 39 ills., Dec., 1938.

Monsters of Our Back Yards. By David Fairchild. Vol. XXIV, pp. 575-626, 38 ills., May, 1913.
    Contains descriptions and illustrations of various species of the following insects : Ant, Bee, Bee-Fly, Butterfly, Cicada, Cockroach, Cricket, Dragon Fly, Grasshopper, Ground-Beetle, Hornet, Horsefly, June Beetle, June-Bug, Katydid, Long-Horned Beetle, Mosquito, Spider, Squash-Bug.

Our Insect Fifth Column : Alien Enemies Take Steady Toll of Food, Trees, and Treasure by Boring from Within. By Frederick G. Vosburgh. Paintings by Hashime Murayama. Vol. LXXX, pp. 225-248, 14 ills. in black and white, 10 ills. in color, Aug., 1941.

Pests and Parasites : Why We Need a National Law to Prevent the Importation of Insect-Infested and Diseased Plants. By Charles Lester Marlatt. Vol. XXII, pp. 321-346, 29 ills., 2 three-quarters-page maps, Apr., 1911.

Protecting the United States from Plant Pests. By Charles Lester Marlatt. Vol. XL, pp. 205-218, 16 ills., Aug., 1921.

Red Ant Versus the Boll Weevil. Vol. XV, pp. 262-264, June, 1904.

Rogues' Gallery of Imported Pests. 10 ills. in color from paintings by Hashime Murayama. Vol. LXXX, pp. 237-244, Aug., 1941.
    Contains colored illustrations of the following : Boll Weevil, *Centeter cinerea,* Digger Wasp, European Cabbage Butterfly, European Corn Borer, Gladiolus Thrips, Gypsy Moth, Japanese Beetle, Mexican Bean Beetle, Sweet Potato Weevil, White-fringed Beetle.

Insects—*Continued*

See also Ants ; Bees ; Butterflies ; Flies ; Hornets ; Locusts ; Mosquitoes ; Moths ; Wasps.

Inside Cape Horn. By Amos Burg. Vol. LXXII, pp. 743-783, 29 ills. in black and white, 10 ills. in color, 1 two-page map, Dec., 1937.

Insignia:

Aircraft Insignia, Spirit of Youth. By Gerard Hubbard. Vol. LXXXIII, pp. 710-722, 3 ills. in black and white, 337 ills. in color, June, 1943.

American Decorations and Insignia of Honor and Service. By Col. Robert E. Wyllie. Vol. XXXVI, pp. 502-526, 6 ills. in black and white, 119 ills. in color, Dec., 1919.

Decorations, Medals, Service Ribbons, Badges, and Women's Insignia. Vol. LXXXIV, pp. 414-444, 6 ills. in black and white, 376 ills. in color, Oct., 1943.

Heroes of Wartime Science and Mercy. By Elizabeth W. King. Vol. LXXXIV, pp. 715-740, 11 ills. in black and white, 334 ills. in color, Dec., 1943.
    Contains descriptions and illustrations of insignia of the following organizations : Air Carrier Contract Personnel, American Red Cross, Civil Air Patrol, U. S. Army Transportation Corps Vessels, U. S. Coast and Geodetic Survey, U. S. Maritime Service, U. S. Public Health Service.

Insignia and Decorations of the United States Armed Forces. By Gilbert Grosvenor. Vol. LXXXVII, pp. 185-186, Feb., 1945.

Insignia of the Uniformed Forces of the United States. By Byron McCandless and Gilbert Grosvenor. Vol. XXXII, pp. 413-419, 318 ills., Oct., 1917.

Insignia of the United States Armed Forces. By Gilbert Grosvenor. With 991 illustrations in color. Vol. LXXXIII, p. 651, June, 1943.

Romance of Military Insignia : How the United States Government Recognizes Deeds of Heroism and Devotion to Duty. By Col. Robert E. Wyllie. Vol. XXXVI, pp. 463-501, 27 ills., Dec., 1919.

Traditions and Glamour of Insignia. By Arthur E. Du Bois. Vol. LXXXIII, pp. 652-655, 3 ills., June, 1943.

United States Military Insignia. Vol. LXXXIII, pp. 656-693, 7 ills. in black and white, 12 drawings, 311 ills. in color, June, 1943.

United States Navy, Marine Corps, and Coast Guard Insignia. Vol. LXXXIII, pp. 694-709, 5 ills. in black and white, 343 ills. in color, June, 1943.

See also Seals.

Interesting Citizens of the Gulf Stream. By Dr. John T. Nichols. Vol. XXXIX, pp. 69-84, 11 ills. in black and white, 16 ills. in color, Jan., 1921.

Interesting Visit to the Ancient Pyramids of San Juan Teotihuacan. By A. C. Galloway. Vol. XXI, pp. 1041-1050, 8 ills., 1 page map, Dec., 1910.

International Arbitration and Its Possibilities. Vol. XI, p. 162, Apr., 1900.

International Cloud Work of the Weather Bureau. By Frank H. Bigelow. Vol. X, pp. 351-354, Sept., 1899.

International Flat Globe and Geographical History. Vol. XVIII, pp. 281-282, Apr., 1907.

International Geographic Congress:

Address by Commander Robert E. Peary, U. S. N., on the Assembling of the Congress in Washington, September 8, 1904. Vol. XV, pp. 387-392, Oct., 1904.

Chairman of Committee on Eighth Congress. Vol. XIII, p. 219, June, 1902. Vol. XIV, pp. 254-255, June, 1903.

Delegates to Ninth Congress. Vol. XIX, pp. 385-386, May, 1908.

Eighth International Geographic Congress. Vol. XIV, pp. 388, 390, Oct., 1903.

Eighth International Geographic Congress. Vol. XV, pp. 419-426, 2 ills., Oct., 1904.

Eighth International Geographic Congress, Washington, 1904. Vol. XV, pp. 74-77, Feb., 1904.

Eighth International Geographic Congress, Washington, 1904. Vol. XV, pp. 297-310, July, 1904.

General Program of Eighth International Geographic Congress. Vol. XV, pp. 373-386, Sept., 1904.

Geographical Congress at Berlin. Vol. X, p. 296, Aug., 1899. Vol. X, p. 480, Nov., 1899.

International Geographic Congress. Vol. XIV, p. 292, July, 1903.

Next International Geographical Congress to Be Held in Washington. By Gilbert H. Grosvenor. Vol. XII, pp. 351-357, 4 ills., Oct., 1901.

Ninth International Geographic Congress, Geneva, Switzerland, 1908. Vol. XVIII, p. 491, July, 1907.

Publication of Proceedings of Eighth Congress. Vol. XVI, pp. 198-199, Apr., 1905.

Resolutions Adopted by the Eighth International Geographic Congress, September, 1904. Vol. XV, pp. 415-418, Oct., 1904.

Special Telegraphic Time Signal from the Naval Observatory. Vol. XV, pp. 411-415, Oct., 1904.

International Ice Patrol:

Coast Guard Patrol in Greenland. 9 ills. in color from natural-color photographs by Lieut. Thomas S. La Farge. Vol. LXXXIII, pp. 565-572, May, 1943.

Standing Iceberg Guard in the North Atlantic: International Patrol Safeguards the Lives of Thousands of Travelers and Protects Transatlantic Liners from a "Titanic" Fate. By Lieut. Comdr. F. A. Zeusler. Vol. L, pp. 1-28, 29 ills., 1 half-page map, July, 1926.

International Millionth Map of the World. By Bailey Willis. Vol. XXI, pp. 125-132, 1 diagram, Feb., 1910.

Interoceanic Canal. By Emory R. Johnson. Vol. X, pp. 311-316, Aug., 1899.

Interviewing the Stars: How Twentieth Century Astronomers Are Inducing the Heavens to Reveal Their Secrets. By William Joseph Showalter. Vol. XLVII, pp. 97-122, 18 ills., 2 charts, 1 diagram, Jan., 1925.

Into Burning Hadhramaut (Arabia): The Arab Land of Frankincense and Myrrh, Ever a Lodestone of Western Exploration. By D. van der Meulen. Vol. LXII, pp. 387-429, 44 ills., 1 two-thirds-page map, Oct., 1932.

Into Primeval Papua by Seaplane: Seeking Disease-Resisting Sugar Cane, Scientists Find Neolithic Man in Unmapped Nooks of Sorcery and Cannibalism. By E. W. Brandes. Vol. LVI, pp. 253-332, 98 ills., 1 three-quarters-page map, Sept., 1929.

Into the Land of the Chipmunk. By Ruth Alexander Nichols. Vol. LX, pp. 77-98, 28 ills., July, 1931.

Introducing Reindeer into Labrador. Vol. XVIII, p. 686, Oct., 1907.

Introduction of the Mango. Vol. XIV, pp. 320-327, 5 ills., Aug., 1903.

Introduction to Physical Geography. By Grove Karl Gilbert and Albert Perry Brigham. Vol. XIV, pp. 21-26, 6 ills., Jan., 1903.

Inventors and Inventions:

Long River of New England: In War and Peace, from Mountain Wilderness to the Sea, Flows the Connecticut River Through a Valley Abounding in History, Scenery, Inventive Genius, and Industry. By Albert W. Atwood. Vol. LXXXIII, pp. 401-434, 12 ills. in black and white, 24 ills. in color, 1 two-thirds-page map, Apr., 1943.

Iowa:

Corn and Color in the Hawkeye State. 20 ills. in color from natural-color photographs; 19 ills. by J. Baylor Roberts. Vol. LXXVI, pp. 151-174, Aug., 1939.

Iowa, Abiding Place of Plenty: The State Where the Tall Corn Grows Provides the Nation with a Tenth of Its Food Supply. By Leo A. Borah. Vol. LXXVI, pp. 143-182, 15 ills. in black and white, 20 ills. in color, 1 two-page map, Aug., 1939.

Iowa-class Battleship. *See Missouri.*

Ipiutak, Alaska:

Discovering Alaska's Oldest Arctic Town: A Scientist Finds Ivory-eyed Skeletons of a Mysterious People and Joins Modern Eskimos in the Dangerous Spring Whale Hunt. By Froelich G. Rainey. Vol. LXXXII, pp. 319-336, 15 ills., Sept., 1942.

Iran (Persia):

Afghan Borderland. By Ellsworth Huntington. Part I: The Russian Frontier. Vol. XX, pp. 788-799, 14 ills., Sept., 1909. Part II: The Persian Frontier. Vol. XX, pp. 866-876, 12 ills., Oct., 1909.

Iran (Persia)—*Continued*

Citroën Trans-Asiatic Expedition Reaches Kashmir : Scientific Party Led by Georges-Marie Haardt Successfully Crosses Syria, Iraq, Persia, and Afghanistan to Arrive at the Pamir. By Maynard Owen Williams. Vol. LX, pp. 387-443, 62 ills., 1 page map, Oct., 1931.

Excavations of M. de Morgan at Susa. Vol. XII, p. 315, Aug., 1901.

Exploring the Secrets of Persepolis. By Charles Breasted. Vol. LXIV, pp. 381-420, 48 ills., 1 half-page map, 1 plan, Oct., 1933.

Flights from Arctic to Equator : Conquering the Alps, the Ice Peaks of Spitsbergen, of Persia, and Africa's Mountains of the Moon. By Walter Mittelholzer. Vol. LXI, pp. 445-498, 53 ills., 1 three-quarters-page map, Apr., 1932.

From England to India by Automobile : An 8,527-Mile Trip Through Ten Countries, from London to Quetta, Requires Five and a Half Months. By Maj. F. A. C. Forbes-Leith. Vol. XLVIII, pp. 191-223, 33 ills., 1 third-page map, Aug., 1925.

German Route to India. By Gilbert H. Grosvenor. Vol. XI, pp. 202-204, 1 page map, May, 1900.

Gilded Domes Against an Azure Sky. 13 ills. in color from natural-color photographs by Stephen H. Nyman. Vol. LXXVI, pp. 339-346, Sept., 1939.

Iran in Wartime : Through Fabulous Persia, Hub of the Middle East, Americans, Britons, and Iranians Keep Sinews of War Moving to the Embattled Soviet Union. By John N. Greely. Vol. LXXXIV, pp. 129-156, 26 ills., 1 page map, Aug., 1943.

Modern Persia and Its Capital : And an Account of an Ascent of Mount Demavend, the Persian Olympus. By F. L. Bird. Vol. XXXIX, pp. 353-400, 47 ills., Apr., 1921.

Mountain Tribes of Iran and Iraq. By Harold Lamb. Vol. LXXXIX, pp. 385-408, 15 ills., 1 two-page map, Mar., 1946.

Mountaineers of the Euphrates. By Ellsworth Huntington. Vol. XX, pp. 142-156, 13 ills., Feb., 1909.

Old and New in Persia : In This Ancient Land Now Called Iran a Modern Sugar Factory Rears Its Head Near the Palace of Darius the Great. By The Baroness Ravensdale. Vol. LXXVI, pp. 325-355, 20 ills. in black and white, 13 ills. in color, 1 two-thirds-page map, Sept., 1939.

Persia : The Awakening East. By W. P. Cresson. Vol. XIX, pp. 356-384, 21 ills., 1 fourth-page map, May, 1908.

Persia—Past and Present. Vol. XVIII, pp. 91-95, 6 ills., Feb., 1907.

Persian Caravan Sketches : The Land of the Lion and the Sun as Seen on a Summer Caravan Trip. By Harold F. Weston. Vol. XXXIX, pp. 417-468, 46 ills. in black and white, 16 ills. in color, 1 three-quarters-page map, Apr., 1921.

Talk About Persia and Its Women. By Ella C. Sykes. Vol. XXI, pp. 847-866, 22 ills., Oct., 1910.

Iran (Persia)—*Continued*

Travels in Arabia and Along the Persian Gulf. By David G. Fairchild. Vol. XV, pp. 139-151, 20 ills., Apr., 1904.

Iraq:

Archeology, the Mirror of the Ages : Our Debt to the Humble Delvers in the Ruins at Carchemish and at Ur. By C. Leonard Woolley. Vol. LIV, pp. 207-226, 19 ills., Aug., 1928.

Bombs over Bible Lands. By Frederick Simpich and W. Robert Moore. Vol. LXXX, pp. 141-180, 34 ills., 1 two-page map, Aug., 1941.

Change Comes to Bible Lands. By Frederick Simpich. Vol. LXXIV, pp. 695-750, 40 ills. in black and white, 25 ills. in color, special map supplement, Dec., 1938.

Cradle of Civilization : The Historic Lands Along the Euphrates and Tigris Rivers Where Briton Is Fighting Turk. By James Baikie. Vol. XXIX, pp. 127-162, 25 ills., Feb., 1916.

Excavations at Nippur. Vol. XI, p. 392, Oct., 1900.

Forty Years Among the Arabs. By John Van Ess. Vol. LXXXII, pp. 385-420, 27 ills., 1 two-page map, Sept., 1942.

From England to India by Automobile : An 8,527-Mile Trip Through Ten Countries, from London to Quetta, Requires Five and a Half Months. By Maj. F. A. C. Forbes-Leith. Vol. XLVIII, pp. 191-223, 33 ills., 1 third-page map, Aug., 1925.

Modern Life in the Cradle of Civilization. Vol. XLI, pp. 390-407, 16 ills. in color, Apr., 1922.

Most Historic Lands on Earth. Vol. XXVI, pp. 614-615, 1 page map, Dec., 1914.

Mountain Tribes of Iran and Iraq. By Harold Lamb. Vol. LXXXIX, pp. 385-408, 15 ills., 1 two-page map, Mar., 1946.

Mountaineers of the Euphrates. By Ellsworth Huntington. Vol. XX, pp. 142-156, 13 ills., Feb., 1909.

Mystic Nedjef, the Shia Mecca. By Frederick Simpich. Vol. XXVI, pp. 589-598, 4 ills., Dec., 1914.

New Light on Ancient Ur : Excavations at the Site of the City of Abraham Reveal Geographical Evidence of the Biblical Story of the Flood. By M. E. L. Mallowan. Vol. LVII, pp. 95-130, 44 ills., 1 three-quarters-page map, Jan., 1930.

Pushing Back History's Horizon : How the Pick and Shovel Are Revealing Civilizations That Were Ancient When Israel Was Young. By Albert T. Clay. Vol. XXIX, pp. 162-216, 47 ills., 1 page map, Feb., 1916.

Travels in Arabia and Along the Persian Gulf. By David G. Fairchild. Vol. XV, pp. 139-151, 20 ills., Apr., 1904.

Under the Heel of the Turk : A Land with a Glorious Past, a Present of Abused Opportunities, and a Future of Golden Possibilities. By William H. Hall. Vol. XXXIV, pp. 50-69, 14 ills., July, 1918.

Iraq—*Continued*

Visit to Three Arab Kingdoms: Transjordania, Iraq, and the Hedjaz Present Many Problems to European Powers. By Junius B. Wood. Vol. XLIII, pp. 535-568, 30 ills., 1 three-quarters-page map, May, 1923.

Where Adam and Eve Lived. By Frederick and Margaret Simpich. Vol. XXVI, pp. 546-588, 35 ills., Dec., 1914.

Ireland:

British Isles. Vol. XXVIII, pp. 551-566, 16 ills., Dec., 1915.

Fearful Famines of the Past: History Will Repeat Itself Unless the American People Conserve Their Resources. By Ralph A. Graves. Vol. XXXII, pp. 68-90, 11 ills., July, 1917.

Hills and Dales of Erin. 11 ills. in color from autochromes by Clifton Adams. Vol. LI, pp. 316-333, Mar., 1927.

Ireland: The Rock Whence I Was Hewn. By Donn Byrne. Vol. LI, pp. 257-326, 68 ills. in black and white, 11 ills. in color, 1 page map, Mar., 1927.

Mist and Sunshine of Ulster. By Bernard F. Rogers, Jr. Vol. LXVIII, pp. 571-610, 23 ills. in black and white, 21 ills. in color, 1 three-quarters-page map, Nov., 1935.

Old Ireland, Mother of New Eire: By Whatever Name, 'Tis the Same Fair Land With the Grass Growing Green on the Hills of Her and the Peat Smoke Hanging Low. By Harrison Howell Walker. Vol. LXXVII, pp. 649-691, 19 ills. in black and white, 18 ills. in color, 1 page map, May, 1940.

Rambles Through Ulster, Northern Tip of the Shamrock Isle. 21 ills. in color from natural-color photographs by Bernard F. Rogers, Jr. Vol. LXVIII, pp. 577-600, Nov., 1935.

When Irish Skies Are Smiling. 18 ills. in color from natural-color photographs by Harrison Howell Walker. Vol. LXXVII, pp. 663-686, May, 1940.

See also Aran Islands; Eire; Northern Ireland.

Iridescent Beauty of Frogs and Toads. 14 ills. in color from paintings by Hashime Murayama. Vol. LXI, pp. 635-642, May, 1932.

Iridescent Denizens of the Miniature Aquarium. 8 ills. in color from paintings by Hashime Murayama. Vol. LIX, pp. 291-300, Mar., 1931.

Iridescent Isles of the South Seas. 16 ills. in color; 12 natural-color photographs; 4 paintings by Hashime Murayama. Vol. XLVIII, pp. 403-418, Oct., 1925.

Iroquois Indians:

America's First Settlers, the Indians. By Matthew W. Stirling. Vol. LXXII, pp. 535-596, 34 ills. in black and white, 24 ills. in color, Nov., 1937.

When Red Men Ruled Our Forests. 24 ills. in color from paintings by W. Langdon Kihn. Vol. LXXII, pp. 551-590, Nov., 1937.

Irrawaddy (River), Burma:

Untoured Burma. By Charles H. Bartlett. Vol. XXIV, pp. 835-853, 17 ills., July, 1913.

Irrigation:

Call of the West. By C. J. Blanchard. Vol. XX, pp. 403-437, 20 ills., 1 half-page map, May, 1909.

China Fights Erosion with U. S. Aid. By Walter C. Lowdermilk. Vol. LXXXVII, pp. 641-680, 10 ills. in black and white, 26 ills. in color, June, 1945.

Farmers Since the Days of Noah: China's Remarkable System of Agriculture Has Kept Alive the Densest Population in the World. By Adam Warwick. Vol. LI, pp. 469-500, 37 ills., Apr., 1927.

Home-Making by the Government: An Account of the Eleven Immense Irrigating Projects to be Opened in 1908. By C. J. Blanchard. Vol. XIX, pp. 250-287, 23 ills., Apr., 1908.

More Water for California's Great Central Valley. By Frederick Simpich. Vol. XC, pp. 645-664, 16 ills., 1 page map, Nov., 1946.

Spirit of the West: The Wonderful Agricultural Development Since the Dawn of Irrigation. By C. J. Blanchard. Vol. XXI, pp. 332-360, 15 ills., Apr., 1910.

Is Climatic Aridity Impending on the Pacific Slope? The Testimony of the Forest. By J. B. Leiberg. Vol. X, pp. 160-181, May, 1899.

Is Our Noblest Volcano Awakening to New Life: A Description of the Glaciers and Evidences of Volcanic Activity of Mount Hood. By A. H. Sylvester. Vol. XIX, pp. 515-525, 5 ills., 1 page map, July, 1908.

Isabela Island, Mexico:

Cruise of the *Kinkajou:* Among Desert Islands of Mexico Voyagers Find Outdoor Laboratories for the Naturalist and Ideal Fishing Grounds for the Sportsman. By Alfred M. Bailey. Vol. LXXX, pp. 339-366, 13 ills. in black and white, 12 ills. in color, 1 page map, Sept., 1941.

Isfahan, Iran:

Iran in Wartime: Through Fabulous Persia, Hub of the Middle East, Americans, Britons, and Iranians Keep Sinews of War Moving to the Embattled Soviet Union. By John N. Greely. Vol. LXXXIV, pp. 129-156, 26 ills., 1 page map, Aug., 1943.

Persian Caravan Sketches: The Land of the Lion and the Sun as Seen on a Summer Caravan Trip. By Harold F. Weston. Vol. XXXIX, pp. 417-468, 46 ills. in black and white, 16 ills. in color, 1 three-quarters-page map, Apr., 1921.

Islam. *See* Mohammedans and Mohammedanism.

Islamabad, India:

Pilgrimage to Amernath, Himalayan Shrine of the Hindu Faith. By Louise Ahl Jessop. Vol. XL, pp. 512-542, 29 ills., Nov., 1921.

Island in the Sea of History: The Highlands of Daghestan. By George Kennan. Vol. XXIV, pp. 1086-1140, 49 ills., 1 page map, Oct., 1913.

Island of Nias, at the Edge of the World. By Mabel Cook Cole. Vol. LX, pp. 201-224, 26 ills., 1 quarter-page map, Aug., 1931.

Island of Sardinia and Its People: Traces of Many Civilizations to Be Found in the Speech, Customs, and Costumes of This Picturesque Land. By Guido Costa. Vol. XLIII, pp. 1-75, 63 ills. in black and white, 16 ills. in color, 1 three-quarters and 1 quarter-page maps, Jan., 1923.

Island of the Sagas (Iceland). By Earl Hanson. Vol. LIII, pp. 499-511, 22 ills., Apr., 1928.

Island Treasures of the Caribbean (Virgin Islands). 23 ills. in color from natural-color photographs by Edwin L. Wisherd and C. W. Herbert. Vol. LXXVIII, pp. 281-304, Sept., 1940.

Islander (Ship):
Around the World in the *Islander:* A Narrative of the Adventures of a Solitary Voyager on His Four-Year Cruise in a Thirty-Four-Foot Sailing Craft. By Capt. Harry Pidgeon. Vol. LIII, pp. 141-205, 75 ills., 1 two-page map, Feb., 1928.

Islands. *See* Pacific Islands *and* names of individual islands and group of islands.

Islands Adrift: St. Pierre and Miquelon: In a Key Position on the North Atlantic Air Route, France's Oldest Colony Rides Out Another Storm. By Frederick K. Arnold. Vol. LXXX, pp. 743-768, 23 ills., 1 fifth-page map, Dec., 1941.

Islands of the Pacific. By J. P. Thomson. Vol. XL, pp. 543-558, 15 ills., special map supplement, Dec., 1921.

Isle of Capri: An Imperial Residence and Probable Wireless Station of Ancient Rome. By John A. Kingman. Vol. XXXVI, pp. 213-231, 17 ills., Sept., 1919.

Isle of Frankincense (Socotra, Arabian Sea). By Charles K. Moser. Vol. XXXIII, pp. 266-278, 11 ills., Mar., 1918.

Isle of Man. *See* Man, Isle of.

Isle of Pines. Vol. XVII, pp. 105-108, 2 ills., Feb., 1906.

Isle of Wight. *See* Wight, Isle of.

Isle Royale, Michigan:
Winter Sky Roads to Isle Royal. By Ben East. Vol. LX, pp. 759-774, 18 ills., 1 half-page map, Dec., 1931.

Isles, Bay of, South Georgia:
South Georgia, an Outpost of the Antarctic. By Robert Cushman Murphy. Vol. XLI, pp. 409-444, 41 ills., 2 half-page maps, Apr., 1922.

Isles of Greece. By Lt. Richard Stillwell, USNR. Vol. LXXXV, pp. 593-622, 11 ills. in black and white, 20 ills. in color, 1 page map, May, 1944.

Isles of Spice. *See* Moluccas.

Isola Bella (Island), Italy:
Gems of the Italian Lakes. By Arthur Ellis Mayer. Vol. XXIV, pp. 943-956, 13 ills., Aug., 1913.

Ispahan, Iran. *See* Isfahan.

Israel. *See* Palestine.

Istanbul, Turkey:
Alert Anatolia. 13 ills. from photographs. Vol. LXXXV, pp. 481-492, Apr., 1944.

Constantinople and Sancta Sophia. By Edwin A. Grosvenor. Vol. XXVII, pp. 459-482, 21 ills., May, 1915.

Constantinople Today. By Solita Solano. Vol. XLI, pp. 647-680, 40 ills., 1 three-quarters-page map, June, 1922.

Life in Constantinople. By Harry Griswold Dwight. Vol. XXVI, pp. 521-545, 25 ills., Dec., 1914.

Old Pattern and New in Turkey. 23 ills. in color from natural-color photographs by Bernard F. Rogers, Jr. Vol. LXXV, pp. 17-48, Jan., 1939.

Star and Crescent on Parade. 29 ills. in color from natural-color photographs by Maynard Owen Williams. Vol. LXXXVII, pp. 585-616, May, 1945.

Transformation of Turkey: New Hats and New Alphabet are the Surface Symbols of the Swiftest National Changes in Modern Times. By Douglas Chandler. Vol. LXXV, pp. 1-50, 27 ills. in black and white, 23 ills. in color, 1 map, Jan., 1939.

Turkish Republic Comes of Age. By Maynard Owen Williams. Vol. LXXXVII, pp. 581-616, 4 ills. in black and white, 29 ills. in color, 1 map (two-page spread), May, 1945.

Istanbul Amerikan Koleji, Turkey:
American Alma Maters in the Near East. By Maynard Owen Williams. Vol. LXXXVIII, pp. 237-256, 16 ills., Aug., 1945.

Istanbul Woman's College, Arnautköy, Turkey:
American Alma Maters in the Near East. By Maynard Owen Williams. Vol. LXXXVIII, pp. 237-256, 16 ills., Aug., 1945.

Isthmian Canal Commission. Vol. XI, pp. 160-161, Apr., 1900.

Isthmian Canal Problem. By W J McGee. Vol. X, pp. 363-364, Sept., 1899.

Isthmus of Tehuantepec (Mexico). By Herbert Corey. Vol. XLV, pp. 549-579, 25 ills., May, 1924.

Isthmus of Tehuantepec (Mexico): The Bridge of the World's Commerce. By Helen Olsson-Seffer. Vol. XXI, pp. 991-1002, 6 ills., Dec., 1910.

Italian Islands of the Aegean. *See* Dodecanese Islands.

Italian Race. By Gilbert Grosvenor. Vol. XXXIII, p. 47, Jan., 1918.

Italy:

Aces Among Aces (Aviators). By Laurence La Tourette Driggs. Vol. XXXIII, pp. 568-580, 9 ills., June, 1918.

American Red Cross in Italy. By Mabel Boardman. Vol. XX, pp. 396-397, Apr., 1909.

Ascent of Mont Blanc. By Walter Woodburn Hyde. Vol. XXIV, pp. 861-942, 69 ills., Aug., 1913.

Austro-Italian Mountain Frontiers. By Florence Craig Albrecht. Vol. XXVII, pp. 321-376, 60 ills., 1 page map, Apr., 1915.

Behind the Lines in Italy. By Corporal Macon Reed, Jr. Vol. LXXXVI, pp. 109-128, 20 ills., July, 1944.

Bright Facets of Italy's Grandeur. 9 ills. in color from natural-color photographs; 8 ills. by B. Anthony Stewart. Vol. LXXVII, pp. 355-362, Mar., 1940.

Colorful Patinas of Northern Italy. 13 ills. in color from natural-color photographs. Vol. LXVIII, pp. 337-344, Sept., 1935.

Daily Life in Calabria. Vol. XLIII, pp. 181-196, 16 ills., Feb., 1923.

Eruption of Mount Vesuvius, April 7-8, 1906. By Dr. Thomas Augustus Jaggar. Vol. XVII, pp. 318-325, 6 ills., June, 1906.

From Africa to the Alps. 8 ills. in color from U. S. Army Air Forces official photographs. Vol. LXXXIX, pp. 161-168, Feb., 1946.

From England to India by Automobile: An 8,527-Mile Trip Through Ten Countries, from London to Quetta, Requires Five and a Half Months. By Maj. F. A. C. Forbes-Leith. Vol. XLVIII, pp. 191-223, 33 ills., 1 third-page map, Aug., 1925.

Frontier Cities of Italy. By Florence Craig Albrecht. Vol. XXVII, pp. 533-586, 45 ills., June, 1915.

Gems of the Italian Lakes. By Arthur Ellis Mayer. Vol. XXIV, pp. 943-956, 13 ills., Aug., 1913.

Holidays Among the Hill Towns of Umbria and Tuscany. By Paul Wilstach. Vol. LIII, pp. 401-442, 40 ills., 1 page map, Apr., 1928.

Horace—Classic Poet of the Countryside. By W. Coleman Nevils. Vol. LXVIII, pp. 771-795, 22 ills., 1 page map, Dec., 1935.

Hunting Castles in Italy. By Melville Chater. Vol. LXVIII, pp. 329-366, 25 ills. in black and white, 13 ills. in color, 1 page and 1 quarter-page maps, Sept., 1935.

Inexhaustible Italy. By Arthur Stanley Riggs. Vol. XXX, pp. 273-368, 76 ills., 1 page map, Oct., 1916.

Italian, French, and Swiss Scenes. 16 ills. in color from natural-color photographs by Donald McLeish and Arthur Stanley Riggs. Vol. XXVIII, pp. 439-454, Nov., 1915.

Italian Race. By Gilbert Grosvenor. Vol. XXXIII, p. 47, Jan., 1918.

Italy, France, Switzerland. Vol. XXVIII, pp. 439-454, 16 ills. in color, Nov., 1915.

Italy—Continued

Italy, From Roman Ruins to Radio: History of Ancient Bridge Building and Road Making Repeats Itself in Modern Public Works and Engineering Projects. By John Patric. Vol. LXXVII, pp. 347-394, 27 ills. in black and white, 9 ills. in color, Mar., 1940.

Italy, Land of History and Romance. Vol. XLV, pp. 375-390, 16 ills., Apr., 1924.

Italy's Eagles of Combat and Defense: Heroic Achievements of Aviators Above the Adriatic, the Apennines, and the Alps. By Gen. P. Tozzi. Vol. XXXIII, pp. 38-47, 8 ills., Jan., 1918.

Italy's Monuments Tell Rome's Magnificence. 8 ills. from photographs; 7 ills. by B. Anthony Stewart. Vol. LXXVII, pp. 371-378, Mar., 1940.

Letters from the Italian Front. By Marchesa Louise de Rosales to Ethel Mather Bagg. Vol. XXXII, pp. 46-67, 22 ills., July, 1917.

Life's Pattern on the Italian Riviera. By Helen Churchill Candee. Vol. LXVII, pp. 67-100, 25 ills. in black and white, 12 ills. in color, 1 two-thirds-page map, Jan., 1935.

Majesty of the Matterhorn. Vol. XXIII, supplement, May, 1912.

Man and Nature Paint Italian Scenes in Prodigal Colors. 33 ills. in color from autochromes by Hans Hildenbrand. Vol. LIII, pp. 119-167, Apr., 1928.

Mount Vesuvius. Vol. XVII, pp. 272-279, 7 ills., May, 1906.

Neapolitan Blues and Imperial Purple of Roman Italy. 12 ills. in color from natural-color photographs by Hans Hildenbrand, Luigi Pellerano, and Gervais Courtellemont. Vol. LXVI, pp. 203-210, Aug., 1934.

New Map of Europe: Showing the Boundaries Established by the Peace Conference at Paris and by Subsequent Decisions of the Supreme Council of the Allied and Associated Powers. By Ralph A. Graves. Text accompanying special map supplement in colors. Vol. XXXIX, pp. 157-177, 18 ills., Feb., 1921.

Northern Italy: Scenic Battleground. 18 ills. in color from natural-color photographs; 13 ills. by B. Anthony Stewart and 3 ills. by Lt. Benjamin C. McCartney. Vol. LXXXVII, pp. 265-288, Mar., 1945.

Over the Alps to Brenner Pass. 15 ills. from photographs, 1 two-page map. Vol. LXXXIV, pp. 701-714, Dec., 1943.

Perennial Geographer: After 2,000 Years Vergil Is Still the Most Widely Read of Latin Poets —First to Popularize the Geography of the Roman Empire. By W. Coleman Nevils. Vol. LVIII, pp. 439-465, 29 ills., Oct., 1930.

Races of Europe. By Edwin A. Grosvenor. Vol. XXXIV, pp. 441-534, 62 ills., 2 page maps, special map supplement in colors, Dec., 1918.

Italy—*Continued*

Redemption of the Pontine Marshes : By Drain-ing the Malarial Wastes Around Rome, Italy Has Created a Promised Land. By Gelasio Caetani. Vol. LXVI, pp. 201-217, 9 ills. in black and white, 12 ills. in color, 1 two-thirds-page map, Aug., 1934.

Scenes in Italy. Vol. XXI, pp. 321-332, 12 ills., Apr., 1910.

Sojourning in the Italy of Today. By Mrs. Kenneth Roberts. Vol. LXX, pp. 351-396, 46 ills., 1 two-thirds-page map, Sept., 1936.

Stone Beehive Homes of Italian Peasants. 12 ills. in color from autochromes by Luigi Pel-lerano and L.U.C.E. Vol. LVII, pp. 234-243, Feb., 1930.

Stone Beehive Homes of the Italian Heel : In Trulli-Land the Native Builds His Dwelling and Makes His Field Arable in the Same Operation. By Paul Wilstach. Vol. LVII, pp. 229-260, 25 ills. in black and white, 12 ills. in color, 1 quarter-page map, Feb., 1930.

Story and the Legends of the Pontine Marshes : After Many Centuries of Fruitless Effort, Italy Is to Inaugurate a Gigantic Enterprise to Drain the Fertile Region Southeast of Rome. By Gelasio Caetani. Vol. XLV, pp. 357-390, 34 ills., 1 half-page map, Apr., 1924.

Under Radiant Italian Skies. 8 ills. in color from autochromes by Hans Hildenbrand. Vol. L, pp. 248-257, Aug., 1926.

Where the Blue Begins on the Italian Coast. 12 ills. in color from natural-color photographs by Hans Hildenbrand. Vol. LXVII, pp. 81-88, Jan., 1935.

See also Capri (Island) ; Florence ; Genoa ; Rome ; Sardinia (Island) ; Sicily (Island) ; Siena ; Vatican City ; Venice.

Italy's Eagles of Combat and Defense : Heroic Achievements of Aviators Above the Adriatic, the Apennines, and the Alps. By Gen. P. Tozzi. Vol. XXXIII, pp. 38-47, 8 ills., Jan., 1918.

Itambé (Peak), Brazil :

Recent Ascent of Itambé. By J. C. Branner. Vol. X, p. 183, May, 1899.

Ithera (Oasis), Arabia :

Arabia, the Desert of the Sea. By Archibald Forder. Vol. XX, pp. 1039-1062, 20 ills., 1 page map, Dec., 1909.

Ivan IV, The Terrible :

Young Russia : The Land of Unlimited Possibili-ties. By Gilbert H. Grosvenor. Vol. XXVI, pp. 421-520, 85 ills. in black and white, 17 ills. in color, Nov., 1914.

Izalco Volcano, El Salvador :

Coffee Is King in El Salvador. By Luis Marden. Vol. LXXXVI, pp. 575-616, 22 ills. in black and white, 27 ills. in color, 1 half-page map, Nov., 1944.

İzmir (Smyrna), Turkey :

History's Greatest Trek : Tragedy Stalks Through the Near East as Greece and Turkey Exchange Two Million of Their People. By Melville Chater. Vol. XLVIII, pp. 533-590, 52 ills. in black and white, 32 ills. in color, Nov., 1925.

Some Ruined Cities of Asia Minor. By Ernest L. Harris. Vol. XIX, pp. 833-858, 19 ills., Dec., 1908.

Turkish Republic Comes of Age. By Maynard Owen Williams. Vol. LXXXVII, pp. 581-616. 4 ills. in black and white, 29 ills. in color, 1 map (two-page spread), May, 1945.

J

Jack in the Box : An Account of the Strange Per-formances of the Most Wonderful Island in the World (Bogoslof Volcano, Alaska). By Capt. F. M. Munger. Vol. XX, pp. 194-199, 8 ills., Feb., 1909.

Jackals :

Sacred Ibis Cemetery and Jackal Catacombs at Abydos. By Camden M. Cobern. Vol. XXIV, pp. 1042-1056, 10 ills., Sept., 1913.

Jackson, W. H. :

Note on Glacier Discovery. By W. H. Jackson. Vol. XVII, p. 587, Oct., 1906.

Jackson, Mississippi :

Machines Come to Mississippi. By J. R. Hilde-brand. Vol. LXXII, pp. 263-318, 34 ills. in black and white, 26 ills. in color, 1 two-page map, Sept., 1937.

Magnolia State Mosaic. 26 ills. in color from natural-color photographs by J. Baylor Rob-erts. Vol. LXXII, pp. 279-310, Sept., 1937.

Jacobi, Elizabeth P. :

Hungary, a Kingdom Without a King : A Tour from Central Europe's Largest Lake to the Fertile Plains of the Danube and the Tisza. By Elizabeth P. Jacobi. Vol. LXI, pp. 691-728. 22 ills. in black and white, 27 ills. in color, 1 half-page map, June, 1932.

Jacobins (Pigeons) :

Man's Feathered Friends of Longest Standing : Peoples of Every Clime and Age Have Lavished Care and Affection Upon Lovely Pigeons. By Elisha Hanson. Vol. XLIX, pp. 63-110, 35 ills. in black and white, 12 ills. in color, Jan., 1926.

Jacobs, Fenno :

Bolivia—Tin Roof of the Andes. 20 ills. in color from natural-color photographs by Carl S. Bell and Fenno Jacobs. Vol. LXXXIII, pp. 311-326, Mar., 1943.

Paraguay : Color Cruising in Paraguay. 11 ills. in color from natural-color photographs by Fenno Jacobs. Vol. LXXXIV, pp. 465-472, Oct., 1943.

Jacobs, Fenno—*Continued*

Philippines : Camera Cruising in the Philippines. 12 ills. in color from natural-color photographs by J. Baylor Roberts, Fenno Jacobs, and others. Vol. LXXXVI, pp. 545-552, Nov., 1944.

Jacqueline (Countess of Holland) :

City of Jacqueline (Goes, Netherlands). By Florence Craig Albrecht. Vol. XXVII, pp. 29-56, 31 ills., Jan., 1915.

Jade:

Expedition Unearths Buried Masterpieces of Carved Jade (Cerro de las Mesas, Mexico). By Matthew W. Stirling. Vol. LXXX, pp. 277-302, 14 ills. in black and white, 20 ills. in color, 1 two-thirds-page map, Sept., 1941.

Finding Jewels of Jade in a Mexican Swamp (La Venta). By Matthew W. and Marion Stirling. Vol. LXXXII, pp. 635-661, 15 ills. in black and white, 12 ills. in color, 1 two-thirds-page map, Nov., 1942.

Jade. By S. E. Easter. Vol. XIV, pp. 9-17, 2 half-page maps, Jan., 1903.

La Venta's Green Stone Tigers. By Matthew W. Stirling. Vol. LXXXIV, pp. 321-332, 4 ills. in black and white, 6 ills. in color, 1 two-thirds-page map, Sept., 1943.

Mexico's Deep South Yields New Treasure (La Venta). 12 ills. in color from natural-color photographs by Richard H. Stewart. Vol. LXXXII, pp. 640-656, Nov., 1942.

Treasure-trove of Old Mexican Jade (Cerro de las Mesas). 20 ills. in color from natural-color photographs by Richard H. Stewart. Vol. LXXX, pp. 293-316, Sept., 1941.

Jaggar, (Dr.) Thomas Augustus:

Eruption of Mount Vesuvius, April 7-8, 1906. By Dr. Thomas Augustus Jaggar. Vol. XVII, pp. 318-325, 6 ills., June, 1906.

Living on a Volcano: An Unspoiled Patch of Polynesia Is Niuafoō, Nicknamed "Tin Can Island" by Stamp Collectors. By Thomas A. Jaggar. Vol. LXVIII, pp. 91-106, 17 ills., 1 half-page map, July, 1935.

Mapping the Home of the Great Brown Bear: Adventures of the National Geographic Society's Pavlof Volcano Expedition to Alaska. By Dr. Thomas Augustus Jaggar. Vol. LV, pp. 109-134, 30 ills., 1 three-quarters-page map, Jan., 1929.

Sakurajima, Japan's Greatest Volcanic Eruption : A Convulsion of Nature Whose Ravages Were Minimized by Scientific Knowledge, Compared with the Terrors and Destruction of the Recent Tokyo Earthquake. By Dr. Thomas Augustus Jaggar. Vol. XLV, pp. 441-470, 32 ills., 1 half-page map, Apr., 1924.

Jaipur, India :

Oriental Pageantry of Northern India. 8 ills. in color from natural-color photographs by Franklin Price Knott. Vol. LVI, pp. 428-461, Oct., 1929.

Jalisco (State), Mexico :

Along the Old Spanish Road in Mexico : Life Among the People of Nayarit and Jalisco, Two of the Richest States of the Southern Republic. By Herbert Corey. Vol. XLIII, pp. 225-281, 36 ills. in black and white, 16 ills. in color, 1 half-page map, Mar., 1923.

See also Guadalajara.

Jamaica:

Color Palette of the Caribbean. 11 ills. in color from autochromes lumière by Jacob Gayer. Vol. LI, pp. 45-56, Jan., 1927.

Jamaica, the Isle of Many Rivers. By John Oliver La Gorce. Vol. LI, pp. 1-55, 38 ills. in black and white, 11 ills. in color, 1 page map, Jan., 1927.

See also Cayman Islands.

Jammu and Kashmir. *See* Kashmir.

Janssen, G. E.:

War Meets Peace in Egypt. By Grant Parr and G. E. Janssen. Vol. LXXXI, pp. 503-526, 25 ills., 1 page map, Apr., 1942.

Janssen Observatory, Mont Blanc :

Ascent of Mont Blanc. By Walter Woodburn Hyde. Vol. XXIV, pp. 861-942, 69 ills., Aug., 1913.

Jap Rule in the Hermit Nation (Korea). By Willard Price. Vol. LXXXVIII, pp. 429-451, 19 ills., 1 page map, Oct., 1945.

Japan:

Agriculture in Japan. By Consul General Bellows. Vol. XV, pp. 323-326, Aug., 1904.

Behind the Mask of Modern Japan. By Willard Price. Vol. LXXXVIII, pp. 513-535, 14 ills., Nov., 1945.

Castles, Shrines, and Parks of Japanese Pilgrimage. 10 ills. in color from natural-color photographs by W. Robert Moore. Vol. LXIX, pp. 457-464, Apr., 1936.

Chapter from Japanese History. By Eki Hioki. Vol. XVI, pp. 220-228, May, 1905.

Characteristics of the Japanese People. By Baron Kentaro Kaneko. Vol. XVI, pp. 93-100, Mar., 1905.

Commercial Development of Japan. By O. P. Austin. Vol. X, pp. 329-337, Sept., 1899.

Cultivation of Marine and Fresh Water Animals in Japan. By K. Mitsukuri. Vol. XVII, pp. 524-531, 5 ills., Sept., 1906.

Empire of the Risen Sun. By William Elliot Griffis. Vol. XLIV, pp. 415-443, 21 ills., Oct., 1923.

Face of Japan. By W. Robert Moore. Vol. LXXXVIII, pp. 753-768, 14 ills., special map supplement, Dec., 1945.

Fisheries of Japan. By Hugh M. Smith. Vol. XV, pp. 362-364, Sept., 1904.

Fisheries of Japan. By Hugh M. Smith. Vol. XVI, pp. 201-220, 13 ills., May, 1905.

Japan—*Continued*

Friendly Journeys in Japan: A Young American Finds a Ready Welcome in the Homes of the Japanese During Leisurely Travels Through the Islands. By John Patric. Vol. LXIX, pp. 441-480, 28 ills. in black and white, 10 ills. in color, 1 two-thirds-page map, Apr., 1936.

Geography of Japan: With Special Reference to Its Influence on the Character of the Japanese People. By Walter Weston. Vol. XL, pp. 45-84, 23 ills. in black and white, 16 ills. in color, July, 1921.

Glimpses of Japan. By William W. Chapin. Vol. XXII, pp. 965-1002, 10 ills. in black and white, 34 ills. in color, Nov., 1911.

How the Earth Telegraphed Its Tokyo Quake to Washington. By Rev. Francis A. Tondorf. Vol. XLIV, pp. 453-454, 1 ill., Oct., 1923.

Japan. Vol. XXVI, pp. 415-420, 6 ills., Oct., 1914.

Japan, America, and the Orient. By Eki Hioki. Vol. XVII, pp. 498-504, Sept., 1906.

Japan, Child of the World's Old Age: An Empire of Mountainous Islands, Whose Alert People Constantly Conquer Harsh Forces of Land, Sea, and Sky. By William Elliot Griffis. Vol. LXIII, pp. 257-301, 37 ills. in black and white, 12 ills. in color, Mar., 1933.

Japan and China—Some Comparisons. By Comdr. Harrie Webster. Vol. XII, pp. 69-77, 2 ills., Feb., 1901.

Japan and the Pacific. By Joseph C. Grew. Vol. LXXXV, pp. 385-414, 29 ills., 17 island maps (two pages), Apr., 1944.

Japan and the United States. Vol. XVI, pp. 432-434, 1 ill., Sept., 1905.

Japan Faces Russia in Manchuria. By Willard Price. Vol. LXXXII, pp. 603-634, 30 ills., 1 page map, Nov., 1942.

Koyasan, the Japanese Valhalla. By Eliza R. Scidmore. Vol. XVIII, pp. 650-670, 14 ills., Oct., 1907.

Lessons from Japan. Vol. XV, pp. 221-225, 3 ills., May, 1904.

Life and Color Under the Rising Sun. 12 ills. in color from natural-color photographs by W. Robert Moore and Kiyoshi Sakamoto. Vol. LXIII, pp. 288-297, Mar., 1933.

Making of a Japanese Newspaper. By Dr. Thomas E. Green. Vol. XXXVIII, pp. 327-334, 5 ills., Oct., 1920.

Motor Trails in Japan. By W. Robert Moore. Vol. LXIII, pp. 303-318, 17 ills., Mar., 1933.

National Geographic Map of Japan, Regions of Asia, and the Pacific. Text accompanying special map supplement in colors. Vol. LXXXV, pp. 415-416, Apr., 1944.

Observations on the Russo-Japanese War in Japan and Manchuria. By Dr. Louis Livingston Seaman. Vol. XVI, pp. 80-82, Feb., 1905.

Population of Japan. By Walter J. Ballard. Vol. XVI, p. 482, Oct., 1905.

Purpose of the Anglo-Japanese Alliance. By Eki Hioki. Vol. XVI, pp. 333-337, July, 1905.

Japan—*Continued*

Race Prejudice in the Far East. By Melville E. Stone. Vol. XXI, pp. 973-985, 6 ills., Dec., 1910.

Sakurajima, Japan's Greatest Volcanic Eruption: A Convulsion of Nature Whose Ravages Were Minimized by Scientific Knowledge, Compared with the Terrors and Destruction of the Recent Tokyo Earthquake. By Dr. Thomas Augustus Jaggar. Vol. XLV, pp. 441-470, 32 ills., 1 half-page map, Apr., 1924.

Some Aspects of Rural Japan. By Walter Weston. Vol. XLII, pp. 275-301, 12 ills. in black and white, 16 ills. in color, Sept., 1922.

Some Facts About Japan. Vol. XV, pp. 446-448, Nov., 1904.

Some Impressions of 150,000 Miles of Travel. By William Howard Taft. Vol. LVII, pp. 523-598, 80 ills., May, 1930.

Sunset in the East (Japan). By Blair A. Walliser. Vol. LXXXIX, pp. 797-812, 17 ills., June, 1946.

Tokyo To-day. By William R. Castle, Jr. Vol. LXI, pp. 131-162, 33 ills., Feb., 1932.

Torii Gate. Vol. XXII, color plate, page 982, Nov., 1911.

Tradition Lingers in Modern Japan. 11 ills. in color from natural-color photographs by W. Robert Moore. Vol. LXXIII, pp. 117-124, Jan., 1938.

Unknown Japan: A Portrait of the People Who Make Up One of the Two Most Fanatical Nations in the World. By Willard Price. Vol. LXXXII, pp. 225-252, 30 ills., Aug., 1942.

Why Nik-ko Is Beautiful. By J. H. De Forest. Vol. XIX, pp. 300-308, 8 ills., Apr., 1908.

Women's Work in Japan. By Mary A. Nourse. Vol. LXXIII, pp. 99-132, 32 ills. in black and white, 11 ills. in color, Jan., 1938.

Young Japan. By Eliza R. Scidmore. Vol. XXVI, pp. 36-64, 11 ills. in color, July, 1914.

See also Kazan Retto; Ogasawara Shoto; Okinawa; Ryukyu Retto; *and* the following mandates and occupied territories: Caroline Islands; Formosa; Korea; Manchuria (Manchukuo); Marianas Islands; Marshall Islands; Palau Islands.

Japanese (People):

Characteristics of the Japanese People. By Baron Kentaro Kaneko. Vol. XVI, pp. 93-100, Mar. 1905.

Geography of Japan: With Special Reference to Its Influence on the Character of the Japanese People. By Walter Weston. Vol. XL, pp. 45-84, 23 ills. in black and white, 16 ills. in color, July, 1921.

Unknown Japan: A Portrait of the People Who Make Up One of the Two Most Fanatical Nations in the World. By Willard Price. Vol. LXXXII, pp. 225-252, 30 ills., Aug., 1942.

Jauf, Saudi Arabia:

Arabia, the Desert of the Sea. By Archibald Forder. Vol. XX, pp. 1039-1062, 20 ills., 1 page map, Dec. 1909.

Java:

The Face of the Netherlands Indies. 20 ills. from photographs by Maynard Owen Williams and others. Vol. LXXXIX, pp. 261-276, Feb., 1946.

Java, Queen of the East Indies. 29 ills. in color from autochromes by W. Robert Moore and Tassilo Adam. Vol. LVI, pp. 334-359, Sept., 1929.

Java Assignment. By Dee Bredin. Vol. LXXXI, pp. 89-119, 32 ills., 1 two-thirds-page map, Jan., 1942.

Through Java in Pursuit of Color. By W. Robert Moore. Vol. LVI, pp. 333-362, 9 ills. in black and white, 29 ills. in color, 1 third-page map, Sept., 1929.

Traveler's Notes on Java. By Henry G. Bryant. Vol. XXI, pp. 91-111, 17 ills., Feb., 1910.

Jays:

Crows, Magpies, and Jays: Unusual Intelligence Has Earned a Unique Position for These Birds. By T. Gilbert Pearson. Paintings by Maj. Allan Brooks. Vol. LXIII, pp. 51-79, 16 ills. in black and white, 17 ills. in color, Jan., 1933.

White Sheep, Giant Moose, and Smaller Game of the Kenai Peninsula, Alaska. By George Shiras, 3d. Vol. XXIII, pp. 423-494, 59 ills., 1 page and 1 two-page maps, May, 1912.

Jean-Brunhes, Mariel:

Cruising to Crete: Four French Girls Set Sail in a Breton Yawl for the Island of the Legendary Minotaur. By Marthe Oulié and Mariel Jean-Brunhes. Vol. LV, pp. 249-272, 15 ills. in black and white, 14 ills. in color, 1 page map, Feb., 1929.

Jefferson, Mark S. W.:

Limiting Width of Meander Belts. By Mark S. W. Jefferson. Vol. XIII, pp. 373-385, 6 charts, Oct., 1902.

Jefferson, Thomas:

Jefferson's Little Mountain: Romance Enfolds Monticello, the Restored Home of the Author of the Declaration of Independence. By Paul Wilstach. Vol. LV, pp. 481-503, 12 ills. in black and white, 12 ills. in color, Apr., 1929.

Jefferson's Little Mountain: Romance Enfolds Monticello, the Restored Home of the Author of the Declaration of Independence. By Paul Wilstach. Vol. LV, pp. 481-503, 12 ills. in black and white, 12 ills. in color, Apr., 1929.

Jellyfishes:

Jellyfishes—Living Draperies of Color. 8 ills. in color from paintings by William Crowder. Vol. L, pp. 193-200, Aug., 1926.
Contains descriptions and illustrations of the following species: Aurelia Aurita, Beroe Cucumis, Cunoctantha Octonaria, Cyanea Capillata, Dactylometra Quinquecirra, Eutima Variabilis, Gionionemus Murbachii, Linerges Mercurius, Mnemiopsis Leidyi, Pelagia Cyanella, Pleurobrachia Rhododactyla, Sarsia Mirabilis, Stomolophus Meleagris, Zygodactyla Groenlandica.

Jellyfishes—*Continued*

Life of the Moon-Jelly. By William Crowder. Vol. L, pp. 187-202, 6 ills. in black and white, 1 ill. in color, Aug., 1926.

Jenkins, Hester Donaldson:

Armenia and the Armenians. By Hester Donaldson Jenkins. Vol. XXVIII, pp. 329-360, 27 ills., 1 half-page map, Oct., 1915.

Bulgaria and Its Women. By Hester Donaldson Jenkins. Vol. XXVII, pp. 377-400, 22 ills., Apr., 1915.

Jenks, George Elwood:

Marvels of Metamorphosis: A Scientific "G-man" Pursues Rare Trapdoor Spider Parasites for Three Years With a Spade and a Candid Camera. By George Elwood Jenks. Vol. LXXIV, pp. 807-828, 39 ills., Dec., 1938.

Jericho, Palestine:

Geography of the Jordan. By Nelson Glueck. Vol. LXXXVI, pp. 719-744, 23 ills., 1 page map, Dec., 1944.

Jerid (Region), Algeria-Tunisia:

Date Gardens of the Jerid. By Thomas H. Kearney. Vol. XXI, pp. 543-567, 20 ills., July, 1910.

Jersey (Island), Channel Islands:

Channel Islands. By Edith Carey. Vol. XXXVIII, pp. 143-164, 24 ills., 1 quarter-page map, Aug., 1920.

Jerusalem, Holy Land:

American Fighters Visit Bible Lands. By Maynard Owen Williams. With 23 ills. in color from natural-color photographs by the author. Vol. LXXXIX, pp. 311-340, 10 ills. in black and white, Mar., 1946.

Changing Palestine. By Maj. Edward Keith-Roach. Vol. LXV, pp. 493-527, 43 ills., 1 half-page map, Apr., 1934.

Color Records from the Changing Life of the Holy City. By Maynard Owen Williams. Vol. LII, pp. 682-707, 27 ills. in color, Dec., 1927.

Crusader Castles of the Near East. By William H. Hall. Vol. LIX, pp. 369-390, 19 ills., 1 third-page map, Mar., 1931.

In the Birthplace of Christianity. 8 ills. in color from autochromes lumière by Hans Hildenbrand and Gervais Courtellemont. Vol. L, pp. 696-721, Dec., 1926.

Jerusalem's Locust Plague: Being a Description of the Recent Locust Influx into Palestine, and Comparing Same with Ancient Locust Invasions as Narrated in the Old World's History Book, the Bible. By John D. Whiting. Vol. XXVIII, pp. 511-550, 25 ills., 1 page map, Dec., 1915.

Old Jewel in the Proper Setting: An Eye-Witness' Account of the Reconquest of the Holy Land by Twentieth Century Crusaders. By Charles W. Whitehair. Vol. XXXIV, pp. 325-344, 17 ills., Oct., 1918.

Jerusalem, Holy Land—*Continued*

Pageant of Jerusalem : The Capital of the Land of Three Great Faiths Is Still the Holy City for Christian, Moslem, and Jew. By Maj. Edward Keith-Roach. Vol. LII, pp. 635-681, 57 ills., Dec., 1927.

Palestine Today. By Francis Chase, Jr. Vol. XC, pp. 501-516, 16 ills., Oct., 1946.

Village Life in the Holy Land. By John D. Whiting. Vol. XXV, pp. 249-314, 27 ills. in black and white, 22 ills. in color, Mar., 1914.

Jerusalem's Locust Plague : Being a Description of the Recent Locust Influx into Palestine, and Comparing Same with the Ancient Locust Invasions as Narrated in the Old World's History Book, the Bible. By John D. Whiting. Vol. XXVIII, pp. 511-550, 25 ills., 1 page map, Dec., 1915.

Jessop, Louise Ahl:

Pilgrimage to Amernath, Himalayan Shrine of the Hindu Faith. By Louise Ahl Jessop. Vol. XL, pp. 512-542, 29 ills., Nov., 1921.

Jesup, Morris K.:

Election of Morris K. Jesup as Honorary Member of The Society. Vol. XVIII, p. 51, Jan., 1907.

Jet Propulsion:

Air Power for Peace. By Gen. H. H. Arnold. Vol. LXXXIX, pp. 137-193, 35 ills. in black and white, 28 ills. in color, special map supplement, Feb., 1946.

New Frontier in the Sky. By F. Barrows Colton. Vol. XC, pp. 379-408, 28 ills., 1 diagram, Sept., 1946.

Your New World of Tomorrow. By F. Barrows Colton. Vol. LXXXVIII, pp. 385-410, 25 ills., Oct., 1945.

Jewels:

Princely India, Resplendent with Jewels and Gold. 40 ills. in color from natural-color photographs by Lawrence Copley Thaw. Vol. LXXVIII, pp. 733-780, Dec., 1940.

Jews:

American Fighters Visit Bible Lands. By Maynard Owen Williams. With 23 ills. in color from natural-color photographs by the author. Vol. LXXXIX, pp. 311-340, 10 ills. in black and white, Mar., 1946.

Chinese Jews. By Oliver Bainbridge. Vol. XVIII, pp. 621-632, 7 ills., Oct., 1907.

Palestine Today. By Francis Chase, Jr. Vol. XC, pp. 501-516, 16 ills., Oct., 1946.

Pedaling Through Poland : An American Girl Free-wheels Alone from Kraków, and Its Medieval Byways, Toward Ukraine's Restive Borderland. By Dorothy Hosmer. Vol. LXXV, pp. 739-775, 38 ills., 2 maps, June, 1939.

Progressive World Struggle of the Jews for Civil Equality. By William Howard Taft. Vol. XXXVI, pp. 1-23, 14 ills., July, 1919.

Races of Europe. By Edwin A. Grosvenor. Vol. XXXIV, pp. 441-534, 62 ills., 2 page maps, special map supplement, Dec., 1918.

Jhelum (River), India :

Pilgrimage to Amernath, Himalayan Shrine of the Hindu Faith. By Louise Ahl Jessop. Vol. XL, pp. 512-542, 29 ills., Nov., 1921.

Jidda, Saudi Arabia :

Guest in Saudi Arabia. By Maynard Owen Williams. Vol. LXXXVIII, pp. 463-487, 24 ills., 1 two-thirds-page map, Oct., 1945.

Mecca the Mystic : A New Kingdom Within Arabia. By S. M. Zwemer. Vol. XXXII, pp. 157-172, 13 ills., Aug., 1917.

Rise of the New Arab Nation. By Frederick Simpich. Vol. XXXVI, pp. 369-393, 17 ills., 1 page map, Nov., 1919.

Unbeliever Joins the Hadj : On the Age-Old Pilgrimage to Mecca, Babies Are Born, Elders Die, and Families May Halt a Year to Earn Funds in Distant Lands. By Owen Tweedy. Vol. LXV, pp. 761-789, 30 ills., 1 page map, June, 1934.

Jivaro Indians:

Over Trail and Through Jungle in Ecuador : Indian Head-Hunters of the Interior, an Interesting Study in the South American Republic. By H. E. Anthony. Vol. XL, pp. 327-352, 28 ills., Oct., 1921.

Joan of Arc:

Fifteenth-Century Vignettes of Compiègne (France). 15 ills. in color from natural-color photographs by Gervais Courtellemont. Vol. LXII, pp. 608-617, Nov., 1932.

Maid of France Rides By : Compiègne, Where Joan of Arc Fought Her Last Battle, Celebrates Her Fifth Centenary. By Inez Buffington Ryan. Vol. LXII, pp. 607-617, 15 ills. in color, Nov., 1932.

Jobos Harbor (Puerto Rico). Vol. X, p. 206, June, 1899.

Johannesburg, Transvaal :

Cities That Gold and Diamonds Built : Transvaal Treasures Have Created Bustling Johannesburg and Fostered Pretoria, Administrative Capital of the South African Union. By W. Robert Moore. Vol. LXXXII, pp. 735-766, 20 ills. in black and white, 9 ills. in color, 1 two-thirds-page map, Dec., 1942.

Under the South African Union. By Melville Chater. Vol. LIX, pp. 391-512, 97 ills. in black and white, 38 ills. in color, 1 two-page map, Apr., 1931.

John G. Shedd Aquarium, Chicago. *See* Shedd Aquarium.

Johns Hopkins University, Baltimore, Maryland :

Maryland Pilgrimage : Visits to Hallowed Shrines Recall the Major Rôle Played by This Prosperous State in the Development of Popular Government in America. By Gilbert Grosvenor. Vol. LI, pp. 133-212, 88 ills., 1 map, Feb., 1927.

Johnson, Electa:

Westward Bound in the *Yankee.* By Irving and Electa Johnson. Vol. LXXXI, pp. 1-44, 25 ills. in black and white, 20 ills. in color, 1 three-quarters-page map, Jan., 1942.

Johnson, Emory R.:

Interoceanic Canal. By Emory R. Johnson. Vol. X, pp. 311-316, Aug., 1899.

Johnson, Frank Edward:

Greek Bronzes of Tunisia. By Frank Edward Johnson. Vol. XXIII, pp. 89-103, 11 ills., Jan., 1912.

Here and There in Northern Africa. By Frank Edward Johnson. Vol. XXV, pp. 1-132, 113 ills., Jan., 1914.

Mole Men: An Account of the Troglodytes of Southern Tunisia. By Frank Edward Johnson. Vol. XXII, pp. 787-846, 60 ills., Sept., 1911.

Sacred City of the Sands (Kairouan, Tunisia). By Frank Edward Johnson. Vol. XXII, pp. 1061-1093, 25 ills., 1 half-page map, Dec., 1911.

Tunis of Today. By Frank Edward Johnson. Vol. XXII, pp. 723-749, 24 ills., Aug., 1911.

Johnson, Irving:

Storied Islands of the South Sea. 20 ills. in color from natural-color photographs; 13 ills. by Irving Johnson. Vol. LXXXI, pp. 9-40, Jan., 1942.

Westward Bound in the *Yankee.* By Irving and Electa Johnson. Vol. LXXXI, pp. 1-44, 25 ills. in black and white, 20 ills. in color, 1 three-quarters-page map, Jan., 1942.

Johnson, Ray G.:

Exploring a Grass Wonderland of Wild West China. By Ray G. Johnson. Vol. LXXXV, pp. 713-742, 24 ills., 1 half-page map, June, 1944.

Johnston, (Sir) Harry:

Black Republic—Liberia. By Sir Harry Johnston and Ernest Lyon. Vol. XVIII, pp. 334-343, 9 ills., May, 1907.

Haiti, the Home of Twin Republics. By Sir Harry Johnston. Vol. XXXVIII, pp. 483-496, 11 ills., 1 third-page map, Dec., 1920.

Where Roosevelt Will Hunt (Africa). By Sir Harry Johnston. Vol. XX, pp. 207-256, 43 ills., special map supplement, Mar., 1909.

Jonas, Lucien:

Three Drawings of the World War. 3 ills. from drawings by Lucien Jonas. Vol. XXXIII, pp. 355-357, Apr., 1918.

Jones, Frank I.:

Katmai. 16 ills. from natural-color photographs by Frank I. Jones. Vol. XL, pp. 271-278, Sept., 1921.

Jones, Stuart E.:

Demolishing Germany's North Sea Ramparts. By Stuart E. Jones. Vol. XC, pp. 635-644, 1 ill. in black and white, 10 ills. in color, Nov., 1946.

Jordan. *See* Trans-Jordan.

Jordan (River), Palestine:

Canoeing Down the River Jordan: Voyagers in Rubber Boats Find the Bible Stream Little Tamed Today as It Plunges to the Dead Sea Over the Earth's Lowest River Bed. By John D. Whiting. Vol. LXXVIII, pp. 781-808, 19 ills., 1 page map, Dec., 1940.

Geography of the Jordan. By Nelson Glueck. Vol. LXXXVI, pp. 719-744, 23 ills., 1 page map, Dec., 1944.

Joseph Conrad (Ship):

North About. By Alan J. Villiers. Vol. LXXI, pp. 221-250, 24 ills., Feb., 1937.

Josephine Ford (Airplane):

First Flight to the North Pole. By Lieut. Comdr. Richard Evelyn Byrd. Vol. L, pp. 357-376, 14 ills., Sept., 1926.

Journalism:

China: New China and the Printed Page. By Paul Hutchinson. Vol. LI, pp. 687-722, 37 ills., June, 1927.

Japan: Making of a Japanese Newspaper. By Dr. Thomas E. Green. Vol. XXXVIII, pp. 327-334, 5 ills., Oct., 1920.

Journey by Jungle Rivers to the Home of the Cock-of-the-Rock: Naturalists Enter the Amazon, Voyage Through the Heart of Tropical South America, and Emerge at the Mouth of the Orinoco. By Ernest G. Holt. Vol. LXIV, pp. 585-630, 49 ills., 1 two-thirds-page map, Nov., 1933.

Journey in Morocco: "The Land of the Moors." By Thomas Lindsey Blayney. Vol. XXII, pp. 750-776, 24 ills., 1 page map, Aug., 1911.

Journey Through the Eastern Portion of the Congo State. By Maj. P. H. G. Powell-Cotton. Vol. XIX, pp. 155-163, 9 ills., Mar., 1908.

Juan Fernández Island, Pacific Ocean:

Voyage to the Island Home of Robinson Crusoe. By Waldo L. Schmitt. Vol. LIV, pp. 353-370, 24 ills., Sept., 1928.

Juárez, Benito:

Among the Zapotecs of Mexico: A Visit to the Indians of Oaxaca, Home State of the Republic's Great Liberator, Juárez, and Its Most Famous Ruler, Diaz. By Herbert Corey. Vol. LI, pp. 501-553, 59 ills., 1 two-thirds-page map, May, 1927.

Judd, Neil M.:

Beyond the Clay Hills: An Account of the National Geographic Society's Reconnaissance of a Previously Unexplored Section in Utah. By Neil M. Judd. Vol. XLV, pp. 275-302, 28 ills., 1 half-page map, Mar., 1924.

Everyday Life in Pueblo Bonito: As Disclosed by the National Geographic Society's Archeologic Explorations in the Chaco Canyon National Monument, New Mexico. By Neil M. Judd. Vol. XLVIII, pp. 227-262, 37 ills., 1 two-thirds-page map, Sept., 1925.

Judd, Neil M.—*Continued*

Pueblo Bonito, the Ancient: The National Geographic Society's Third Expedition to the Southwest Seeks to Read in the Rings of Trees the Secret of the Age of Ruins. By Neil M. Judd. Vol. XLIV, pp. 99-108, 9 ills., 1 diagram, July, 1923.

Pueblo Bonito Expedition of the National Geographic Society. By Neil M. Judd. Vol. XLI, pp. 323-331, 10 ills., 1 diagram, Mar., 1922.

Jugoslavia. *See* Yugoslavia.

Jugoslavia—Ten Years After. By Melville Chater. Vol. LVIII, pp. 257-309, 44 ills. in black and white, 25 ills. in color, 1 three-quarters-page map, Sept., 1930.

Jull, Morley A.:

Fowls of Forest and Stream Tamed by Man. By Morley A. Jull. Vol. LVII, pp. 327-371, 27 ills. in black and white, 15 ills. in color, Mar., 1930.

Races of Domestic Fowl. By Morley A. Jull. Vol. LI, pp. 379-452, 67 ills. in black and white, 29 ills., in color, Apr., 1927.

Jumping Salmon. Vol. XIX, p. 124, 1 ill., Feb., 1908.

June Week at Annapolis, Cradle of the Navy. 13 ills. in color from natural-color photographs. Vol. LXIX, pp. 791-798, June, 1936.

Jungle Housekeeping for a Geographic Expedition. By Marion Stirling. Vol. LXXX, pp. 303-327, 15 ills., Sept., 1941.

Jungle War: Bougainville and New Caledonia. 17 ills. in color from paintings by Lieut. William F. Draper. Vol. LXXXV, pp. 417-432, Apr., 1944.

Jungles:

Africa: Through the Deserts and Jungles of Africa by Motor: Caterpillar Cars Make 15,000-Mile Trip from Algeria to Madagascar in Nine Months. By Georges-Marie Haardt. Vol. XLIX, pp. 651-720, 95 ills., 1 two-thirds-page map, June, 1926.

Brazil: By Seaplane to Six Continents: Cruising 60,000 Miles, Italian Argonauts of the Air See World Geography Unroll, and Break New Sky Trails Over Vast Brazilian Jungles. By Comdr. Francesco de Pinedo. Vol. LIV, pp. 247-301, 60 ills., 1 two-page map, Sept., 1928.

Brazil: Exploring the Valley of the Amazon in a Hydroplane: Twelve Thousand Miles of Flying Over the World's Greatest River and Greatest Forest to Chart the Unknown Parima River from the Sky. By Capt. Albert W. Stevens. Vol. XLIX, pp. 353-420, 86 ills., 1 page map, Apr., 1926.

British Guiana: New World to Explore: In the Tree-Roof of the British Guiana Forest Flourishes Much Hitherto-Unknown Life. By Maj. R. W. G. Hingston. Vol. LXII, pp. 617-642, 35 ills., Nov., 1932.

Jungles—*Continued*

Burma: Working Teak in the Burma Forests: The Sagacious Elephant Is Man's Ablest Ally in the Logging Industry of the Far East. By A. W. Smith. Vol. LVIII, pp. 239-256, 5 ills. in color, Aug., 1930.

Ecuador: Mrs. Robinson Crusoe in Ecuador. By Mrs. Richard C. Gill. Vol. LXV, pp. 133-172, 43 ills., 1 half-page map, Feb., 1934.

Guatemala: Mysterious Temples of the Jungle: The Prehistoric Ruins of Guatemala. By W. F. Sands. Vol. XXIV, pp. 324-338, 10 ills., Mar., 1913.

Panama: Jungles of Panama. By David Fairchild. Vol. XLI, pp. 131-145, 14 ills., Feb., 1922.

Siam: Warfare of the Jungle Folk: Campaigning Against Tigers, Elephants, and Other Wild Animals in Northern Siam. By Merian C. Cooper. Photographs by Ernest B. Schoedsack. Vol. LIII, pp. 233-268, 33 ills., Feb., 1928.

Tanganyika: Flashlights from the Jungle. Vol. XVIII, pp. 534-548, 11 ills., Aug., 1907.

Venezuela: I Kept House in a Jungle: The Spell of Primeval Tropics in Venezuela, Riotous With Strange Plants, Animals, and Snakes, Enthralls a Young American Woman. By Anne Rainey Langley. Vol. LXXV, pp. 97-132, 28 ills., 1 third-page map, Jan., 1939.

Junks (Boats):

Cosmopolitan Shanghai, Key Seaport of China. By W. Robert Moore. Vol. LXII, pp. 311-335, 19 ills., Sept., 1932.

Life Afloat in China: Tens of Thousands of Chinese in Congested Ports Spend Their Entire Existence on Boats. By Robert F. Fitch. Vol. LI, pp. 665-686, 28 ills., June, 1927.

Macao, "Land of Sweet Sadness": The Oldest European Settlement in the Far East, Long the Only Haven for Distressed Mariners in the China Sea. By Edgar Allen Forbes. Vol. LXII, pp. 337-357, 13 ills. in black and white, 11 ills. in color, Sept., 1932.

Pirate-Fighters of the South China Sea. By Robert Cardwell. Vol. LXXXIX, pp. 787-796, 11 ills., June, 1946.

Junor, (Dr.) Kenneth F.:

Curious and Characteristic Customs of China. By Kenneth F. Junor. Vol. XXI, pp. 791-806, 7 ills., Sept., 1910.

Jusserand, J. J.:

Armistice Day and the American Battlefields. By J. J. Jusserand. Vol. LVI, pp. 509-554, 32 ills. in black and white, 23 ills. in color, Nov., 1929.

Discovery of the North Pole (Address by J. J. Jusserand). Vol. XXI, pp. 63-80, Jan., 1910.

Honors for Amundsen (Address by J. J. Jusserand). Vol. XIX, pp. 55-76, 13 ills., Jan., 1908.

Honors to Amundsen and Peary (Address by J. J. Jusserand). Vol. XXIV, pp. 113-130, 5 ills., Jan., 1913.

Jusserand, J. J.—*Continued*

Honors to Colonel Goethals : The Presentation, by President Woodrow Wilson, of the National Geographic Society Special Gold Medal, and Addresses by Secretary of State Bryan, the French Ambassador, the German Ambassador, and Congressman James R. Mann (Election of J. J. Jusserand as Honorary Member of The Society). Vol. XXV, pp. 677-690, 6 ills., June, 1914.

Our First Alliance. By J. J. Jusserand. Vol. XXXI, pp. 518-548, 8 ills., June, 1917.

Our Second Alliance. By J. J. Jusserand. Vol. XXXI, pp. 565-566, 1 ill., June, 1917.

Jute:

India's Treasures Helped the Allies. By John Fischer. Vol. LXXXIX, pp. 501-522, 18 ills., Apr., 1946.

Jyekundo (Yushu), China :

Across Tibet from India to China. By Lt. Col. Ilia Tolstoy, AUS. Vol. XC, pp. 169-222, 41 ills., 1 half-page map, Aug., 1946.

K

Kabul, Afghanistan :

Back to Afghanistan. By Maynard Owen Williams. Vol. XC, pp. 517-544, 27 ills., 1 page map, Oct., 1946.

Kaf, Arabia :

Arabia, the Desert of the Sea. By Archibald Forder. Vol. XX, pp. 1039-1062, 20 ills., 1 page map, Dec., 1909.

Kafirs (Tribespeople) :

Impressions and Scenes of Mozambique. By O. W. Barrett. Vol. XXI, pp. 807-830, 31 ills., Oct., 1910.

Kahn, (Mirza) Ali Kuli:

National Geographic Society (Speech by Mirza Ali Kuli Kahn). Vol. XXIII, pp. 273-298, 5 ills., Mar., 1912.

Kaieteur Falls, British Guiana :

Kaieteur and Roraima : The Great Falls and the Great Mountain of the Guianas. By Henry Edward Crampton. Vol. XXXVIII, pp. 227-244, 12 ills., 1 half-page map, Sept., 1920.

World's Greatest Waterfall : The Kaieteur Fall, in British Guiana. By Leonard Kennedy. Vol. XXII, pp. 846-859, 6 ills., 1 page map, Sept., 1911.

Kaijo (Songdo), Korea :

Chosen—Land of Morning Calm. By Mabel Craft Deering. Vol. LXIV, pp. 421-448, 20 ills. in black and white, 13 ills. in color, 1 two-thirds-page map, Oct., 1933.

Kairouan, Tunisia :

Eastward from Gibraltar : Overland Route Across North Africa to Tunisia and Libia. By Cyrus French Wicker. Vol. LXXXIII, pp. 115-142, 28 ills., Jan., 1943.

Kairouan, Tunisia—*Continued*

Sacred City of the Sands. By Frank Edward Johnston. Vol. XXII, pp. 1061-1093, 25 ills., 1 half-page map, Dec., 1911.

Kaiser Wilhelm Canal, Germany :

Great Canals of the World. Vol. XVI, pp. 475-479, Oct., 1905.

Kaleidoscopic Land of Europe's Youngest King : Yugoslavia Holds a Mosaic of Slavs and the City Where Pistol Shots Touched Off the World War. By Douglas Chandler. Vol. LXXV, pp. 691-738, 18 ills. in black and white, 34 ills. in color, 2 maps, June, 1939.

Kaleidoscopic La Paz : The City of the Clouds. By Harriet Chalmers Adams. Vol. XX, pp. 119-141, 23 ills., Feb., 1909.

Kalmbach, E. R.:

Crow, Bird Citizen of Every Land : A Feathered Rogue Who Has Many Fascinating Traits and Many Admirable Qualities Despite His Marauding Propensities. By E. R. Kalmbach. Vol. XXXVII, pp. 322-337, 10 ills., Apr., 1920.

Kalmucks (Tribespeople) :

With the Nomads of Central Asia : A Summer's Sojourn in the Tekes Valley, Plateau Paradise of Mongol and Turkic Tribes. By Edward Murray. Vol. LXIX, pp. 1-57, 43 ills. in black and white, 26 ills. in color, 1 half-page map, Jan., 1936.

Kampanzan, Formosa (Island) :

Formosa the Beautiful. By Alice Ballantine Kirjassoff. Vol. XXXVII, pp. 246-292, 60 ills., 1 half-page map, Mar., 1920.

Kandahar, Afghanistan :

Back to Afghanistan. By Maynard Owen Williams. Vol. XC, pp. 517-544, 27 ills., 1 page map, Oct., 1946.

Kandy, Ceylon :

Adam's Second Eden. By Eliza R. Scidmore. Vol. XXIII, pp. 105-173, 60 ills., Feb., 1912.

Perahera Processions of Ceylon. By G. H. G. Burroughs. Vol. LXII, pp. 90-100, 1 ill. in black and white, 8 ills. in duotone, July, 1932.

Kaneko, (Baron) Kentaro:

Characteristics of the Japanese People. By Baron Kentaro Kaneko. Vol. XVI, pp. 93-100, Mar., 1905.

Kangaroo Rat:

Dipo, the Little Desert "Kangaroo." By Walter E. Ketcham. Vol. LXXVIII, pp. 537-548, Oct., 1940.

Kano, Nigeria :

Kano, Mud-made City. 10 ills. in color from natural-color photographs by George W. Scott and K. S. Twitchell. Vol. LXXXV, pp. 545-552, May, 1944.

Nigeria : From the Bight of Benin to Africa's Desert Sands. By Helen Trybulowski Gilles. Vol. LXXXV, pp. 537-568, 17 ills. in black and white, 10 ills. in color, 1 half-page map, May, 1944.

Kansas:

Speaking of Kansas. By Frederick Simpich. Vol. LXXII, pp. 135-182, 37 ills. in black and white, 12 ills. in color, 1 two-page map, Aug., 1937.

Views and Hues of the Sunflower State. 12 ills. in color from natural-color photographs by Richard H. Stewart. Vol. LXXII, pp. 151-158, Aug., 1937.

Kansas City, Missouri:

Taming the Outlaw Missouri River. By Frederick Simpich. Vol. LXXXVIII, pp. 569-598, 25 ills., 1 two-page map, Nov., 1945.

These Missourians. By Frederick Simpich. Vol. LXXXIX, pp. 277-310, 12 ills. in black and white, 22 ills. in color, 1 map (two-page spread), Mar., 1946.

Kansu (Province), China:

China Fights Erosion with U. S. Aid. By Walter C. Lowdermilk. Vol. LXXXVII, pp. 641-680, 10 ills. in black and white, 26 ills. in color, June, 1945.

"Where the Mountains Walked": An Account of the Recent Earthquake in Kansu Province, China, Which Destroyed 100,000 Lives. By Upton Close and Elsie McCormick. Vol. XLI, pp. 445-464, 23 ills., 1 three-quarters-page map, May, 1922.

See also Choni.

Karaganda, U. S. S. R.:

New Road to Asia. By Owen Lattimore. Vol. LXXXVI, pp. 641-676, 15 ills. in black and white, 26 ills. in color, Dec., 1944.

Karakul Sheep:

Land of the Lambskins: An Expedition to Bokhara, Russian Central Asia, to Study the Karakul Sheep Industry. By Robert K. Nabours. Vol. XXXVI, pp. 77-88, 15 ills., July, 1919.

Karbala (Kerbela), Iraq:

Mystic Nedjef, the Shia Mecca. By Frederick Simpich. Vol. XXVI, pp. 589-598, 4 ills., Dec., 1914.

Karens (Tribespeople):

Among the Hill Tribes of Burma—An Ethnological Thicket. By Sir George Scott. Vol. XLII, pp. 293-321, 22 ills., Mar., 1922.

Burma: Where India and China Meet: In the Massive Mountains of Southeast Asia, Swarming Road Builders Wage the "War of the Highways" for Free China and Her Allies. By John LeRoy Christian. Vol. LXXXIV, pp. 489-512, 18 ills., 1 page map, Oct., 1943.

Notes on Burma. By Thomas Barbour. Vol. XX, pp. 841-866, 34 ills., Oct., 1909.

Karnak, Egypt:

Resurrection of Ancient Egypt. By James Baikie. Vol. XXIV, pp. 957-1020, 46 ills., 1 page map, Sept., 1913.

Kärnten (Austrian Province):

Entering the Front Doors of Medieval Towns: The Adventures of an American Woman and Her Daughter in a Folding Boat on Eight Rivers of Germany and Austria. By Cornelia Stratton Parker. Vol. LXI, pp. 365-394, 23 ills., 1 two-thirds-page map, Mar., 1932.

Karyés, Greece:

Hoary Monasteries of Mount Athos. By H. G. Dwight. Vol. XXX, pp. 249-272, 24 ills., 1 half-page map, Sept., 1916.

Kashgais (Tribespeople):

Mountain Tribes of Iran and Iraq. By Harold Lamb. Vol. LXXXIX, pp. 385-408, 15 ills., 1 two-page map, Mar., 1946.

Kashmir:

First Over the Roof of the World by Motor: The Trans-Asiatic Expedition Sets New Records for Wheeled Transport in Scaling Passes of the Himalayas. By Maynard Owen Williams. Vol. LXI, pp. 321-363, 45 ills., 2 half-page maps, Mar., 1932.

House-Boat Days in the Vale of Kashmir. By Florence H. Morden. Vol. LVI, pp. 437-463, 22 ills. in black and white, 10 ills. in color, Oct., 1929.

On the World's Highest Plateaus: Through an Asiatic No Man's Land to the Desert of Ancient Cathay. By Hellmut de Terra. Vol. LIX, pp. 319-367, 39 ills. in black and white, 32 ills. in color, 1 two-thirds-page map, Mar., 1931.

Oriental Pageantry of Northern India. 10 ills. in color from natural-color photographs by Franklin Price Knott. Vol. LVI, pp. 428-461, Oct., 1929.

Outwitting the Water Demons of Kashmir. By Maurice Pratt Dunlap. Vol. XL, pp. 499-511, 9 ills., Nov., 1921.

Pilgrimage to Amernath, Himalayan Shrine of the Hindu Faith. By Louise Ahl Jessop. Vol. XL, pp. 512-542, 29 ills., Nov., 1921.

Katmai, Mount, Alaska:

Our Greatest National Monument: The National Geographic Society Completes Its Explorations in the Valley of Ten Thousand Smokes. By Robert F. Griggs. Vol. XL, pp. 219-292, 73 ills. in black and white, 16 ills. in color, 2 page and 1 three-quarters-page maps, Sept., 1921.

Recent Eruption of Katmai Volcano in Alaska. By George C. Martin. Vol. XXIV, pp. 131-181, 45 ills., 1 page map, 1 diagram, Feb., 1913.

Ten Thousand Smokes Now a National Monument: The President of the United States Sets Aside for the American People the Extraordinary Valley Discovered and Explored by the National Geographic Society. Vol. XXXV, pp. 359-366, 5 ills., Apr., 1919.

Valley of Ten Thousand Smokes: An Account of the Discovery and Exploration of the Most Wonderful Volcanic Region in the World. By Robert F. Griggs. Vol. XXXIII, pp. 115-169, 46 ills., 1 half-page map, panorama, Feb., 1918.

Katmai, Mount, Alaska—*Continued*

Valley of Ten Thousand Smokes: National Geographic Society's Explorations in the Katmai District of Alaska. By Robert F. Griggs. Vol. XXXI, pp. 12-68, 51 ills., 1 half-page map, Jan., 1917.

Volcanoes of Alaska. Report by Capt. K. W. Perry. Vol. XXIII, pp. 824-832, 11 ills., Aug., 1912.

Kaws (Tribespeople):

Burma: Where India and China Meet: In the Massive Mountains of Southeast Asia, Swarming Road Builders Wage the "War of the Highways" for Free China and Her Allies. By John LeRoy Christian. Vol. LXXXIV, pp. 489-512, 18 ills., 1 page map, Oct., 1943.

Shan Tribes Make Burma's Hills Flash With Color. 15 ills. in color from natural-color photographs by W. Robert Moore. Vol. LX, pp. 454-463, Oct., 1931.

Strange Tribes in the Shan States of Burma. 15 ills. in color from natural-color photographs by W. Robert Moore. Vol. LVIII, pp. 246-255, Aug., 1930.

Kayans (Tribespeople):

Sarawak: The Land of the White Rajahs. By Harrison W. Smith. Vol. XXXV, pp. 110-167, 28 ills., 1 half-page map, Feb., 1919.

Kazakh Soviet Socialist Republic, U. S. S. R.:

New Road to Asia. By Owen Lattimore. Vol. LXXXVI, pp. 641-676, 15 ills. in black and white, 26 ills. in color, Dec., 1944.

See also Ak Bulak.

Kazakhs:

New Road to Asia. By Owen Lattimore. Vol. LXXXVI, pp. 641-676, 15 ills. in black and white, 26 ills. in color, Dec., 1944.

Sunny Siberia. 26 ills. in color from natural-color photographs by Owen Lattimore. Vol. LXXXVI, pp. 649-672, Dec., 1944.

Kazan Retto (Volcano Islands), Pacific Ocean:

Springboards to Tokyo. By Willard Price. Vol. LXXXVI, pp. 385-407, 16 ills., Oct., 1944.

Kboo, a Liberian Game. By G. N. Collins. Vol. XXI, pp. 944-948, 3 ills., Nov., 1910.

Kearney, Thomas H.:

Country of the Ant Men. By Thomas H. Kearney. Vol. XXII, pp. 367-382, 11 ills., 1 half-page map, Apr., 1911.

Date Gardens of the Jerid. By Thomas H. Kearney. Vol. XXI, pp. 543-567, 20 ills., July, 1910.

Kearny, Camp, California:

Bringing the World to Our Foreign-Language Soldiers: How a Military Training Camp Is Solving a Seemingly Unsurmountable Problem by Using The Geographic. By Christina Krysto. Vol. XXXIV, pp. 81-90, 4 ills., Aug., 1918.

Kebon Djahe, Sumatra:

By Motor Through the East Coast and Batak Highlands of Sumatra. By Melvin A. Hall. Vol. XXXVII, pp. 68-102, 27 ills., Jan., 1920.

Keen, Dora:

Woman's Climbs in the High Alps. By Dora Keen. Vol. XXII, pp. 642-675, 26 ills., July, 1911.

Keeping House for the "Shepherds of the Sun." By Mrs. William H. Hoover. Vol. LVII, pp. 483-506, 17 ills., 1 third-page map, Apr., 1930.

Keeping House in Borneo. By Virginia Hamilton. Vol. LXXXVIII, pp. 293-324, 28 ills., 1 page map, Sept., 1945.

Keeping House in Majorca. By Phoebe Binney Harnden. Vol. XLV, pp. 425-440, 18 ills., 1 quarter-page map, April, 1924.

Keeping House on the Congo. By Ruth Q. McBride. Vol. LXXII, pp. 643-670, 29 ills., Nov., 1937.

Keijo, Korea. *See* Seoul.

Keith-Roach, (Maj.) Edward:

Adventures Among the "Lost Tribes of Islam" in Eastern Darfur: A Personal Narrative of Exploring, Mapping, and Setting Up a Government in the Anglo-Egyptian Sudan Borderland. By Major Edward Keith-Roach. Vol. XLV, pp. 41-73, 32 ills., 1 three-quarters-page map, Jan., 1924.

Changing Palestine. By Maj. Edward Keith-Roach. Vol. LXV, pp. 493-527, 43 ills., 1 half-page map, Apr., 1934.

Pageant of Jerusalem: The Capital of the Land of Three Great Faiths Is Still the Holy City for Christian, Moslem, and Jew. By Maj. Edward Keith-Roach. Vol. LII, pp. 635-681, 57 ills., Dec., 1927.

Kèkawngdu (Tribespeople):

Among the Hill Tribes of Burma—An Ethnological Thicket. By Sir George Scott. Vol. XLII, pp. 293-321, 22 ills., Mar., 1922.

Kelley, Francis Beverly:

Land of Sawdust and Spangles—A World in Miniature. By Francis Beverly Kelley. Vol. LX, pp. 463-516, 35 ills. in black and white, 29 ills. in color, Oct., 1931.

Kellogg, Remington:

Whales, Giants of the Sea: Wonder Mammals, Biggest Creatures of All Times, Show Tender Affection for Young, But Can Maim or Swallow Human Hunters. By Remington Kellogg. Vol. LXXVII, pp. 35-90, 25 ills. in black and white, 31 ills. in color, Jan., 1940.

Kelton, M. E.:

Apperception in Geography. By M. E. Kelton. Vol. XI, pp. 192-199, May, 1900.

Kemal Atatürk. *See* Mustapha Kemal.

Kenai Peninsula, Alaska:

White Sheep, Giant Moose, and Smaller Game of the Kenai Peninsula, Alaska. By George Shiras, 3d. Vol. XXIII, pp. 423-494, 59 ills., 1 page and 1 two-page maps, May, 1912.

Kennan, George:

Island in the Sea of History : The Highlands of Daghestan. By George Kennan. Vol. XXIV, pp. 1086-1140, 49 ills., 1 page map, Oct., 1913.

Kennard, Frederick H.:

Encouraging Birds Around the Home. By Frederick H. Kennard. Vol. XXV, pp. 315-344, 36 ills., Mar., 1914.

Kennedy, Leonard:

World's Greatest Waterfall : The Kaieteur Fall, in British Guiana. By Leonard Kennedy. Vol. XXII, pp 846-859, 6 ills., 1 page map, Sept., 1911.

Kent (County), England :

Britain Fights in the Fields. By Francis A. Flood. Vol. LXXXVI, pp. 31-65, 17 ills. in black and white, 21 ills. in color, July, 1944.

Charm Spots Along England's Harassed Coast. 16 ills. in duotone from photographs. Vol. LXXVIII, pp. 237-252, Aug., 1940.

See also Dover.

Kentucky:

Home Folk around Historic Cumberland Gap. By Leo A. Borah. Vol. LXXXIV, pp. 741-768, 25 ills., 1 quarter-page map, Dec., 1943.

Kentucky, Boone's Great Meadow : The Bluegrass State Celebrates Its Sesquicentennial As It Helps the Nation Gird for War. By Leo A. Borah. Vol. LXXXII, pp. 57-89, 13 ills. in black and white, 21 ills. in color, 1 map (two-page spread), July, 1942.

Modern Scenes in the Land of Lincoln's Birth. 15 ills. in color from natural-color photographs by Edwin L. Wisherd. Vol. LXV, pp. 695-702, June, 1934.

Patriotic Pilgrimage to Eastern National Parks : History and Beauty Live Along Paved Roads, Once Indian Trails, Through Virginia, North Carolina, Tennessee, Kentucky, and West Virginia. By Leo A. Borah. Vol. LXV, pp. 663-702, 18 ills. in black and white, 28 ills. in color, 1 two-page map, June, 1934.

Sun Shines Bright in Kentucky. 21 ills. in color from natural-color photographs by B. Anthony Stewart, Volkmar Wentzel, and Ray Scott. Vol. LXXXII, pp. 65-88, July, 1942.

Kenya Colony, Africa :

When a Drought Blights Africa : Hippos and Elephants Are Driven Insane by Suffering, in the Lorian Swamp, Kenya Colony. By Capt. A. T. Curle. Vol. LV, pp. 521-528, 9 ills., Apr., 1929.

Where Roosevelt Will Hunt. By Sir Harry Johnston. Vol. XX, pp. 207-256, 43 ills., special map supplement in colors, Mar., 1909.

Kepner, (Maj. Gen.) William E.:

Exploring the Stratosphere. By Capt. Albert W. Stevens. Vol. LXVI, pp. 397-434, 43 ills., 1 two-thirds-page chart, Oct., 1934.

Kerbela, Iraq. *See* Karbala.

Kerbey, McFall:

Behind Netherlands Sea Ramparts : Dikes and Pumps Keep Ocean and Rivers at Bay While a Busy People Carries on Peacetime Work. By McFall Kerbey. Vol. LXXVII, pp. 255-290, 26 ills. in black and white, 11 ills. in duotone, 1 two-thirds-page map, Feb., 1940.

Colorado, a Barrier That Became a Goal : Where Water Has Transformed Dry Plains Into Verdant Farms and Highways Have Opened up Mineral and Scenic Wealth. By McFall Kerbey. Vol. LXII, pp. 1-63, 56 ills. in black and white, 12 ills. in color, 1 page map, July, 1932.

Genoa, Where Columbus Learned to Love the Sea. By McFall Kerbey. Vol. LIV, pp. 333-352, 20 ills., Sept., 1928.

How the United States Grew. By McFall Kerbey. Vol. LXIII, pp. 631-649, 17 ills., 1 page map, May, 1933.

Texas Delta of an American Nile : Orchards and Gardens Replace Thorny Jungle in the Southmost Tip of the Lone Star State. By McFall Kerbey. Vol. LXXV, pp. 51-96, 27 ills. in black and white, 24 ills. in color, 1 page map, Jan., 1939.

Toilers of the Sky : Tenuous Clouds Perform the Mighty Task of Shaping the Earth and Sustaining Terrestrial Life. By McFall Kerbey. Vol. XLVIII, pp. 163-189, 33 ills., Aug., 1925.

Kerensky, Alexander:

Russia from Within : Her War of Yesterday, Today, and Tomorrow. By Stanley Washburn. Vol. XXXII, pp. 91-120, 30 ills., Aug., 1917.

Russia's Man of the Hour : Alexander Kerensky's First Speeches and Proclamations. Vol. XXXII, pp. 24-45, 17 ills., July, 1917.

Ketcham, Walter E.:

Dipo, the Little Desert "Kangaroo." By Walter E. Ketcham. Vol. LXXVIII, pp. 537-548, 14 ills., Oct., 1940.

Ketchikan, Alaska :

Ketchikan. Vol. XVI, p. 508, 1 ill., Nov., 1905.

Key to the Pacific (Territory of Hawaii). By George C. Perkins. Vol. XIX, pp. 295-298, 1 half-page map, Apr., 1908.

Key West, Florida :

Capturing Giant Turtles in the Caribbean. By David D. Duncan. Vol. LXXXIV, pp. 177-190, 13 ills., 1 quarter-page map, Aug., 1943.

Keyhoe, (Lt.) Donald E.:

Seeing America With Lindbergh : The Record of a Tour of More Than 20,000 Miles by Airplane Through Forty-eight States on Schedule Time. By Lieut. Donald E. Keyhoe. Vol. LIII, pp. 1-46, 46 ills., 1 page map, Jan., 1928.

Kharkov, U. S. S. R. :

Liberated Ukraine. By Eddy Gilmore. Vol. LXXXV, pp. 513-536, 22 ills., 1 page map, May, 1944.

Kharkov, U.S.S.R.—*Continued*

Ukraine, Past and Present. By Nevin O. Winter. Vol. XXXIV, pp. 114-128, 14 ills., Aug., 1918.

Khat (Flower) :

"Flower of Paradise" : The Part Which Khat Plays in the Life of the Yemen Arab. By Charles Moser. Vol. XXXII, pp. 173-186, 10 ills., 1 page map, Aug., 1917.

Khatmandu, Nepal :

Nepal : A Little-Known Kingdom. By John Claude White. Vol. XXXVIII, pp. 245-283, 32 ills., 1 half-page map, Oct., 1920.

Khoresm:

Surveying Through Khoresm : A Journey into Parts of Asiatic Russia Which Have Been Closed to Western Travelers Since the World War. By Lyman D. Wilbur. Vol. LXI, pp. 753-780, 31 ills., 1 two-thirds-page map, June, 1932.

Khun (Tribespeople) :

Strange Tribes in the Shan States of Burma. 15 ills. in color from natural-color photographs by W. Robert Moore. Vol. LVIII, pp. 246-255, Aug., 1930.

Khun de Prorok, Count Byron. *See* Prorok, (Count) Byron Khun de.

Khyber Pass, India :

Through the Heart of Hindustan : A Teeming Highway Extending for Fifteen Hundred Miles, from the Khyber Pass to Calcutta. By Maynard Owen Williams. Vol. XL, pp. 433-467, 29 ills., Nov., 1921.

Kiangsi (Province), China :

World's Ancient Porcelain Center. By Frank B. Lenz. Vol. XXXVIII, pp. 391-406, 17 ills., Nov., 1920.

Kienlung (Emperor of China) :

Mukden, the Manchu Home and Its Great Art Museum. By Eliza R. Scidmore. Vol. XXI, pp. 289-320, 30 ills., Apr., 1910.

Kiev, U. S. S. R.:

Liberated Ukraine. By Eddy Gilmore. Vol. LXXXV, pp. 513-536, 22 ills., 1 page map, May, 1944.

Ukraine, Past and Present. By Nevin O. Winter. Vol. XXXIV, pp. 114-128, 14 ills., Aug., 1918.

Kihn, W. Langdon:

First Families of Southeastern America (Indians). 8 ills. in color from paintings by W. Langdon Kihn. Vol. LXXXIX, pp. 65-72, Jan., 1946.

Indians of Our Western Plains. 16 ills. in color from paintings by W. Langdon Kihn. Vol. LXXXVI, pp. 81-96, July, 1944.

Palette from Spain. By W. Langdon Kihn. Vol. LXIX, pp. 407-440, 16 ills. in black and white, 26 ills. in duotone, 1 half-page map, Mar., 1936.

Kihn, W. Langdon—*Continued*

Red Men of the Southwest. 25 ills. in color from paintings by W. Langdon Kihn. Vol. LXXVIII, pp. 557-596, Nov., 1940.

Totem-pole Builders. 16 ills. in color from paintings by W. Langdon Kihn. Vol. LXXXVII, pp. 33-48, Jan., 1945.

When Red Men Ruled Our Forests. 24 ills. in color from paintings by W. Langdon Kihn. Vol. LXXII, pp. 551-590, Nov., 1937.

Killdeer (Bird) :

Hunting with the Lens. By Howard H. Cleaves. Vol. XXVI, pp. 1-35, 47 ills., July, 1914.

Kinaling, Sumatra :

By Motor Through the East Coast and Batak Highlands of Sumatra. By Melvin A. Hall. Vol. XXXVII, pp. 68-102, 27 ills., Jan., 1920.

King, Elizabeth W.:

Heroes of Wartime Science and Mercy. By Elizabeth W. King. Vol. LXXXIV, pp. 715-740, 11 ills. in black and white, 334 ills. in color, Dec., 1943.

Seals of Our Nation, States, and Territories. By Elizabeth W. King. Paintings by Carlotta Gonzales Lahey, Irvin E. Alleman, and Theodora Price. Vol. XC, pp. 1-42, 14 ills. in black and white, 84 ills. in color, July, 1946.

King, F. H.:

Awarded Grant Squires Prize. Vol. XXIV, p. 115, Jan., 1913.

Wonderful Canals of China. By F. H. King. Vol. XXIII, pp. 931-958, 35 ills., 5 half-page maps, Oct., 1912.

King Herring : An Account of the World's Most Valuable Fish, the Industries It Supports, and the Part It Has Played in History. By Hugh M. Smith. Vol. XX, pp. 701-735, 21 ills., Aug., 1909.

King of Cats and His Court (Leopards, Lions, and Tigers). By Victor H. Cahalane. Paintings by Walter A. Weber. Vol. LXXXIII, pp. 217-259, 9 ills. in black and white, 20 ills. in color, Feb., 1943.

Kingdom of Flowers : An Account of the Wealth of Trees and Shrubs of China and of What the Arnold Arboretum, with China's Help, Is Doing to Enrich America. By Ernest H. Wilson. Vol. XXII, pp. 1003-1035, 24 ills., Nov., 1911.

Kingdom of Many Tribes (Afghanistan). 12 ills. in color from natural-color photographs by Maynard Owen Williams. Vol. LXIV, pp. 745-752, Dec., 1933.

Kingdom of Servia. By William Joseph Showalter. Vol. XXVII, pp. 417-432, 12 ills., 1 page map, Apr., 1915.

Kingfishers (Birds) :

Flycatchers and Other Friends in Feathers. 36 portraits in color from paintings by Maj. Allan Brooks. Vol. LXIX, pp. 807-822, June, 1936.

Kingfishers (Birds)—*Continued*

Parrots, Kingfishers, and Flycatchers: Strange Trogons and Curious Cuckoos are Pictured with these Other Birds of Color, Dash, and Courage. By Alexander Wetmore. Paintings by Maj. Allan Brooks. Vol. LXIX, pp. 801-828, 9 ills. in black and white, 36 portraits in color, June, 1936.

Kinglets (Birds):

Winged Denizens of Woodland, Stream, and Marsh. By Alexander Wetmore. Paintings by Maj. Allan Brooks. Vol. LXV, pp. 577-596, 4 portraits in color, May, 1934.

Kingman, Eugene:

Crater Lake and Yosemite Through the Ages. 13 ills. in color from paintings by Eugene Kingman. Vol. LXXI, pp. 333-339, Mar., 1937.

Kingman, John A.:

Isle of Capri: An Imperial Residence and Probable Wireless Station of Ancient Rome. By John A. Kingman. Vol. XXXVI, pp. 213-231, 17 ills., Sept., 1919.

Kingsford-Smith, Charles E.:

Our Conquest of the Pacific: The Narrative of the 7,400-Mile Flight from San Francisco to Brisbane in Three Ocean Hops. By Squadron-Leader Charles E. Kingsford-Smith and Flight-Lieut. Charles T. P. Ulm. Vol. LIV, pp. 371-402, 27 ills., 1 two-thirds-page map, Oct., 1928.

Kingston, Jamaica:

Jamaica, the Isle of Many Rivers. By John Oliver La Gorce. Vol. LI, pp. 1-55, 38 ills. in black and white, 11 ills. in color, 1 page map, Jan., 1927.

Kingtehchen, China:

World's Ancient Porcelain Center. By Frank B. Lenz. Vol. XXXVIII, pp. 391-406, 17 ills., Nov., 1920.

Kinkajou (Yacht):

Cruise of the *Kinkajou:* Among Desert Islands of Mexico Voyagers Find Outdoor Laboratories for the Naturalist and Ideal Fishing Grounds for the Sportsman. By Alfred M. Bailey. Vol. LXXX, pp. 339-366, 13 ills. in black and white, 12 ills. in color, 1 page map, Sept., 1941.

Kinney, Paul B.:

Once in a Lifetime: Black Bears Rarely Have Quadruplets, But Goofy Did—and the Camera Caught Her Nursing Her Remarkable Family. By Paul B. Kinney. Vol. LXXX, pp. 249-258, 11 ills., Aug., 1941.

Kinney, William A.:

American Wings Soar Around the World: Epic Story of the Air Transport Command of the U. S. Army Is a Saga of Yankee Daring and Doing. By Donald H. Agnew and William A. Kinney. Vol. LXXXIV, pp. 57-78, 22 ills., July, 1943.

Kirchhoff, C.:

United States—Her Mineral Resources. By C. Kirchhoff. Vol. XIV, pp. 331-339, Sept., 1903.

Kirghiz (Tribespeople):

First Over the Roof of the World by Motor: The Trans-Asiatic Expedition Sets New Records for Wheeled Transport in Scaling Passes of the Himalayas. By Maynard Owen Williams. Vol. LXI, pp. 321-363, 45 ills., 2 half-page maps, Mar., 1932.

With the Nomads of Central Asia: A Summer's Sojourn in the Tekes Valley, Plateau Paradise of Mongol and Turkic Tribes. By Edward Murray. Vol. LXIX, pp. 1-57, 43 ills. in black and white, 26 ills. in color, 1 half-page map, Jan., 1936.

Kirjassoff, Alice Ballantine:

Formosa the Beautiful. By Alice Ballantine Kirjassoff. Vol. XXXVII, pp. 246-292, 60 ills., 1 half-page map, Mar., 1920.

Kirkwood, J. E.:

Mexican Hacienda. By J. E. Kirkwood. Vol. XXV, pp. 563-584, 18 ills., May, 1914.

Kite Work of the Weather Bureau. By H. C. Frankenfield. Vol. XI, pp. 55-62, Feb., 1900.

Kites:

Aërial Locomotion: With a Few Notes of Progress in the Construction of an Aërodrome. By Alexander Graham Bell. Vol. XVIII, pp. 1-34, 36 ills., Jan., 1907.

Air Conquest: From the Early Days of Giant Kites and Birdlike Gliders, the National Geographic Society Has Aided and Encouraged the Growth of Aviation. Vol. LII, pp. 233-242, 13 ills., Aug., 1927.

Dr. Bell's Man-Lifting Kite. By Gilbert H. Grosvenor. Vol. XIX, pp. 35-52, 27 ills., Jan., 1908.

Kite Work of the Weather Bureau. By H. C. Frankenfield. Vol. XI, pp. 55-62, Feb., 1900.

The Tetrahedral Kite. Vol. XIV, p. 294, 1 ill., July, 1903.

The Tetrahedral Principle in Kite Structure. By Alexander Graham Bell. Vol. XIV, pp. 219-251, 79 ills., 15 diagrams, June, 1903.

Kites (Birds):

Eagle, King of Birds, and His Kin. By Alexander Wetmore. Paintings by Maj. Allan Brooks. Vol. LXIV, pp. 43-95, 2 ills. in black and white, 6 ills. in color, July, 1933.

Eagles, Hawks, and Vultures. 6 ills. in color from paintings by Maj. Allan Brooks. Vol. LXIV, pp. 64-95, July, 1933.

Kizilbash Clans of Kurdistan. By Melville Chater. Vol. LIV, pp. 485-504, 22 ills., Oct., 1928.

Klamath Indians:

Wokas, a Primitive Indian Food. Vol. XV, pp. 182-185, 3 ills., Apr., 1904.

Klemmer, Harvey:

"Blood, Toil, Tears, and Sweat": An American Tells the Story of Britain's War Effort, Summed up in Prime Minister Churchill's Unflinching Words. By Harvey Klemmer. Vol. LXXXII, pp. 141-166, 19 ills., Aug., 1942.

Klemmer, Harvey—*Continued*

A City That Refused to Die (Plymouth, England). By Harvey Klemmer. Vol. LXXXIX, pp. 211-236, 13 ills. in black and white, 9 ills. in color, 1 half-page map, Feb., 1946.

Convoys to Victory. By Harvey Klemmer. Vol. LXXXIII, pp. 193-216, 24 ills., Feb., 1943.

Everyday Life in Wartime England. By Harvey Klemmer. Vol. LXXIX, pp. 497-534, 48 ills., Apr., 1941.

Front-line Town of Britain's Siege (Dover). By Harvey Klemmer. Vol. LXXXV, pp. 105-128, 21 ills., Jan., 1944.

Lend-Lease and the Russian Victory. By Harvey Klemmer. Vol. LXXXVIII, pp. 499-512, 6 ills., Oct., 1945.

Lisbon—Gateway to Warring Europe. By Harvey Klemmer. Vol. LXXX, pp. 259-276, 18 ills., Aug., 1941.

Michigan Fights. By Harvey Klemmer. Vol. LXXXVI, pp. 677-715, 20 ills. in black and white, 19 ills. in color, 1 page-and-a-half map, Dec., 1944.

Rural Britain Carries On. By Harvey Klemmer. Vol. LXXX, pp. 527-552, 27 ills., Oct., 1941.

Knight, (Capt.) C. W. R.:

Photographing the Nest Life of the Osprey. By Capt. C. W. R. Knight. Vol. LXII, pp. 247-260, 25 ills., Aug., 1932.

Knight, Charles R.:

Parade of Life Through the Ages; Records in Rocks Reveal a Strange Procession of Prehistoric Creatures, from Jellyfish to Dinosaurs, Giant Sloths, Saber-toothed Tigers, and Primitive Man. By Charles R. Knight. With 24 ills. in color from paintings by the author. Vol. LXXXI, pp. 141-184, 13 ills. in black and white, Feb., 1942.

Knight, Wilbur C.:

Wyoming Fossil Fields Expedition of July, 1899. By Wilbur C. Knight. Vol. XI, pp. 449-465, 8 ills., Dec., 1900.

Knossos, Crete (Island). *See* Cnossus.

Knott, Franklin Price:

Bali: Artist Adventures on the Island of Bali. By Franklin Price Knott. Vol. LIII, pp. 326-347, 20 ills. in color, Mar., 1928.

India: Oriental Pageantry of Northern India. 30 ills. in color from natural-color photographs by Franklin Price Knott. Vol. LVI, pp. 428-461, Oct., 1929.

North Africa. 16 ills. in color from autochromes by Franklin Price Knott. Vol. XXX, pp. 233-248, Sept., 1916.

United States: Beauty Spots in the United States. 23 ills. in color from autochromes by Franklin Price Knott. Vol. XXIX, pp. 379-405, Apr., 1916.

Knox, (Capt.) Dudley W.:

Ships, from Dugouts to Dreadnoughts. By Capt. Dudley W. Knox. Vol. LXXIII, pp. 57-98, 27 ills. in black and white, 16 ills. in gravure, Jan., 1938.

Knutsen, Willie:

Desolate Greenland, Now an American Outpost. 17 ills. from photographs; 12 ills. by Willie Knutsen; 4 ills. by F. Vogel. Vol. LXXX, pp. 393-406, Sept., 1941.

Koala, or Australian Teddy Bear. By F. Lewis. Vol. LX, pp. 346-355, 13 ills., Sept., 1931.

Koch, Felix J.:

In Quaint, Curious Croatia. By Felix J. Koch. Vol. XIX, pp. 809-832, 37 ills., Dec., 1908.

Tirnova, the City of Hanging Gardens. By Felix J. Koch. Vol. XVIII, pp. 632-640, 7 ills., Oct., 1907.

Kodiak (Island), Alaska:

Kodiak not Kadiak. Vol. XII, pp. 397-398, Nov., 1901.

Navy Artist Paints the Aleutians. By Mason Sutherland. Paintings by Lt. William F. Draper. Vol. LXXXIV, pp. 157-176, 4 ills. in black and white, 16 ills. in color, Aug., 1943.

Recent Eruption of Katmai Volcano in Alaska. By George C. Martin. Vol. XXIV, pp. 131-181, 45 ills., 1 diagram, 1 page map, Feb., 1913.

Valley of Ten Thousand Smokes: National Geographic Society Explorations in the Katmai District of Alaska. By Robert F. Griggs. Vol. XXXI, pp. 12-68, 51 ills., 1 half-page map, Jan., 1917.

Volcanoes of Alaska (Eruption of Mt. Katmai in June, 1912). Vol. XXIII, pp. 824-832, 11 ills., Aug., 1912.

Koelz, Walter N.:

Naturalist with MacMillan in the Arctic. By Walter N. Koelz. Vol. XLIX, pp. 299-318, 22 ills. in color, Mar., 1926.

Koester, (Capt.) Hans:

Four Thousand Hours Over China. By Capt. Hans Koester. Vol. LXXIII, pp. 571-598, 25 ills., 1 two-thirds-page map, May, 1938.

Kolb, Ellsworth:

Experiences in the Grand Canyon. By Ellsworth and Emery Kolb. Vol. XXVI, pp. 99-184, 70 ills., 1 page map, Aug., 1914.

Kolb, Emery:

Experiences in the Grand Canyon. By Ellsworth and Emery Kolb. Vol. XXVI, pp. 99-184, 70 ills., 1 page map, Aug., 1914.

Kold, Kristen:

Denmark and the Danes. By Maurice Francis Egan. Vol. XLII, pp. 115-164, 38 ills., 1 three-quarters-page map, Aug., 1922.

Kollm, (Dr.) Georg:

German South Polar Expedition. By Dr. Georg Kollm. Vol. XII, pp. 377-379, Oct., 1901.

Komensky, Jan Amos:

Bohemia and the Czechs. By Aleš Hrdlička. Vol. XXXI, pp. 163-187, 18 ills., Feb., 1917.

Komodo (Island), Netherlands Indies:

Modern Dragon Hunt on Komodo: An English Yachting Party Traps and Photographs the Huge and Carnivorous Dragon Lizard of the Lesser Sundas. By Lady Broughton. Vol. LXX, pp. 321-331, 12 ills. in duotone, Sept., 1936.

Stalking the Dragon Lizard on the Island of Komodo. By W. Douglas Burden. Vol. LII, pp. 216-232, 21 ills., Aug., 1927.

Komsomolsk, U. S. S. R.:

New Road to Asia. By Owen Lattimore. Vol. LXXXVI, pp. 641-676, 15 ills. in black and white, 26 ills. in color, Dec., 1944.

Konka Risumgongba, Holy Mountain of the Outlaws. By Joseph F. Rock. Vol. LX, pp. 1-65, 36 ills. in black and white, 43 ills. in color, 1 three-quarters-page map, July, 1931.

Korea:

Chosen—Land of Morning Calm. By Mabel Craft Deering. Vol. LXIV, pp. 421-448, 20 ills. in black and white, 13 ills. in color, 1 two-thirds-page map, Oct., 1933.

Chromatic Highlights of Korea. 13 ills. in color from natural-color photographs by W. Robert Moore. Vol. LXIV, pp. 429-436, Oct., 1933.

Exploring the Unknown Corners of the "Hermit Kingdom." By Roy Chapman Andrews. Vol. XXXVI, pp. 24-48, 30 ills., 1 page map, July, 1919.

Glimpses of Korea and China. By William W. Chapin. Vol. XXI, pp. 895-934, 11 ills. in black and white, 39 ills. in color, Nov., 1910.

Hunter of Plants. By David Fairchild. Vol. XXXVI, pp. 57-77, 18 ills., July, 1919.

In the Diamond Mountains: Adventures Among the Buddhist Monasteries of Eastern Korea. By Marquess Curzon of Kedleston. Vol. XLVI, pp. 353-374, 21 ills., 1 quarter-page map, Oct., 1924.

Jap Rule in the Hermit Nation. By Willard Price. Vol. LXXXVIII, pp. 429-451, 19 ills., 1 page map, Oct., 1945.

Korea. Vol. XIX, pp. 872-877, 10 ills., Dec., 1908.

Korea—The Hermit Nation. By Comdr. Harrie Webster. Vol. XI, pp. 145-155, 7 ills., Apr., 1900.

Manchuria and Korea. Vol. XV, pp. 128-129, special map supplement, 2 half-page maps, Mar., 1904.

Notes and Scenes from Korea. Vol. XIX, pp. 498-508, 14 ills., July, 1908.

Passing of Korea. Vol. XVII, pp. 575-580, 5 ills., Oct., 1906.

Some Facts About Korea. Vol. XV, p. 79, Feb., 1904.

Korff, (Baroness) Alletta:

Notes on Finland. By Baroness Alletta Korff. Vol. XXI, pp. 493-494, June, 1910.

Where Women Vote (Finland). By Baroness Alletta Korff. Vol. XXI, pp. 487-493, June, 1910.

Kostich, Konstantin J.:

Finland: Land of Sky-Blue Lakes. 12 ills. in color from natural-color photographs by Konstantin J. Kostich. Vol. LXXIV, pp. 515-522, Oct., 1938.

Yugoslavia: Where Oriental Hues Splash Europe. 34 ills. in color from natural-color photographs by Konstantin J. Kostich and Rudolph Balogh. Vol. LXXV, pp. 699-738, June, 1939.

Koyasan, the Japanese Valhalla. By Eliza R. Scidmore. Vol. XVIII, pp. 650-670, 14 ills., Oct., 1907.

Kpwesis (Tribespeople):

Land of the Free in Africa. By Harry A. McBride. Vol. XLII, pp. 411-430, 22 ills., Oct., 1922.

Krakatau (Island), Netherlands Indies:

Do Volcanic Explosions Affect Our Climate? By C. G. Abbot. Vol. XXIV, pp. 181-198, 9 ills., 1 diagram, Feb., 1913.

Eruption of Krakatoa. By Sir Robert Ball. Vol. XIII, pp. 200-204, June, 1902.

Kraków, Poland:

Pedaling Through Poland: An American Girl Free-wheels Alone from Kraków, and Its Medieval Byways, Toward Ukraine's Restive Borderland. By Dorothy Hosmer. Vol. LXXV, pp. 739-775, 38 ills., 2 maps, June, 1939.

Poland, Land of the White Eagle. By Melville Bell Grosvenor. With 12 illustrations in color from natural-color photographs by Hans Hildenbrand. Vol. LXI, pp. 435-445, 12 ills. in color, Apr., 1932.

Kreider, Herman H.:

Looking in on the Everyday Life of New Turkey. 7 ills. in color from natural-color photographs by Herman H. Kreider. Vol. LXI, pp. 500-509, Apr., 1932.

Kremlin, Moscow:

Rebirth of Religion in Russia: The Church Reorganized While Bolshevik Cannon Spread Destruction in the Nation's Holy of Holies. By Thomas Whittemore. Vol. XXXIV, pp. 378-401, 16 ills., Nov., 1918.

Russia of the Hour: Giant Battle Ground for Theories of Economy, Society, and Politics, as Observed by an Unbiased Correspondent. By Junius B. Wood. Vol. L, pp. 519-598, 81 ills., Nov., 1926.

Krieger, Louis C. C.:

Common Mushrooms of the United States. By Louis C. C. Krieger. Vol. XXXVII, pp. 387-439, 37 ills. in black and white, 16 ills. in color, May, 1920.

Mushrooms. 16 ills. in color from paintings by Louis C. C. Krieger. Vol. XXXVII, pp. 423-438, May, 1920.

Kruisinga, J. C. M.:

New Country Awaits Discovery: The Draining of the Zuider Zee Makes Room for the Excess Population of the Netherlands. By J. C. M. Kruisinga. Vol. LXIV, pp. 293-320, 20 ills. in black and white, 13 ills. in color, 1 three-quarters and 1 half-page maps, Sept., 1933.

Krung Thep, Thailand. *See* Bangkok.

Krus (Tribespeople) :

Land of the Free in Africa. By Harry A. Mc-
Bride. Vol. XLII, pp. 411-430, 22 ills., Oct.,
1922.

Krysto, Christina:

Bringing the World to Our Foreign-Language
Soldiers : How a Military Training Camp Is
Solving a Seemingly Unsurmountable Problem
by Using The Geographic. By Christina
Krysto. Vol. XXXIV, pp. 81-90, 4 ills., Aug.,
1918.

Kublai Khan:

World's Greatest Overland Explorer : How Marco
Polo Penetrated Farthest Asia, "Discovered"
Many Lands Unknown to Europe, and Added
Numerous Minerals, Animals, Birds, and Plants
to Man's Knowledge. By J. R. Hildebrand.
Vol. LIV, pp. 505-568, 53 ills., 1 two-page map,
Nov., 1928.

Kuhne, Jack:

Europe's Northern Nomads. 12 ills. in color
from natural-color photographs by Jack Kuhne.
Vol. LXXVI, pp. 657-664, Nov., 1939.

Norwegian Fjords and Folkways. 20 ills. in
color from natural-color photographs ; 19 ills.
by Jack Kuhne. Vol. LXXV, pp. 501-524,
Apr., 1939.

Peru on Parade. 20 ills. in color from natural-
color photographs by Henry Clay Gipson and
Jack Kuhne. Vol. LXXXII, pp. 173-196, Aug.,
1942.

Kuibyshev, U. S. S. R. :

Mother Volga Defends Her Own. By Maynard
Owen Williams. Vol. LXXXII, pp. 793-811, 21
ills., Dec., 1942.

Kulusuk, Greenland :

Uncle Sam's Icebox Outposts. 19 ills. in color
from natural-color photographs by John E.
Schneider and Robert B. Sykes, Jr. Vol. XC,
pp. 473-496, Oct., 1946.

Kunming, China :

Kunming, Southwestern Gateway to China. By
Joseph E. Passantino. With 18 ills. in color
from natural-color photographs by the author.
Vol. XC, pp. 137-168, 12 ills. in black and
white, Aug., 1946.

Kurds (People) :

Kizilbash Clans of Kurdistan. By Melville Chater.
Vol. LIV, pp. 485-504, 22 ills., Oct., 1928.

Mountain Tribes of Iran and Iraq. By Harold
Lamb. Vol. LXXXIX, pp. 385-408, 15 ills., 1
two-page map, Mar., 1946.

Mountaineers of the Euphrates. By Ellsworth
Huntington. Vol. XX, pp. 142-156, 13 ills.,
Feb., 1909.

Persian Caravan Sketches : The Land of the Lion
and the Sun as Seen on a Summer Caravan
Trip. By Harold F. Weston. Vol. XXXIX,
pp. 417-468, 46 ills. in black and white, 16 ills.
in color, 1 page map, Apr., 1921.

Kusaie (Island), Caroline Islands :

Hidden Key to the Pacific : Piercing the Web of
Secrecy Which Long Has Veiled Japanese
Bases in the Mandated Islands. By Willard
Price. Vol. LXXXI, pp. 759-785, 28 ills., 1
map (two-page spread), June, 1942.

Kuzzililar, Turkey :

Fringe of Verdure Around Asia Minor. By Ellsworth Huntington. Vol. XXI, pp. 761-775, 15
ills., Sept., 1910.

Kwajalein (Atoll), Marshall Islands :

Marshallese Are Happy Again. 20 ills. in color
from natural-color photographs by W. Robert
Moore. Vol. LXXXVIII, pp. 337-360, Sept.,
1945.

Our New Military Wards, the Marshalls. By W.
Robert Moore. Vol. LXXXVIII, pp. 325-360,
14 ills. in black and white, 20 ills. in color,
1 half-page map, Sept., 1945.

Kwakiutl (Indian Tribe) :

Indians of Our North Pacific Coast. By Matthew
W. Stirling. Paintings by W. Langdon Kihn.
Vol. LXXXVII, pp. 25-52, 3 ills. in black and
white, 16 ills. in color, Jan., 1945.

Kwangsi (Province), China :

Landscaped Kwangsi, China's Province of Pictorial Art. By G. Weidman Groff and T. C.
Lau. Vol. LXXII, pp. 671-710, 33 ills., 1 half-
page map, Dec., 1937.

Kyoto, Japan :

Glimpses of Japan. By William W. Chapin. Vol.
XXII, pp. 965-1002, 10 ills. in black and white,
34 ills. in color, Nov., 1911.

L

Laboratories. *See* Climatic Laboratories.

Labrador:

Introducing Reindeer in Labrador. Vol. XVIII,
p. 686, Oct., 1907.

Labrador Expedition. Vol. XV, p. 185, Apr.,
1904.

Land of Eternal Warring. By Sir Wilfred T.
Grenfell. Vol. XXI, pp. 665-690, 24 ills., Aug.,
1910.

MacMillan Arctic Expedition Returns : U. S.
Navy Planes Make First Series of Overhead
Flights in the Arctic and National Geographic
Society Staff Obtains Valuable Data and Speci-
mens for Scientific Study. By Donald B. Mac-
Millan. Vol. XLVIII, pp. 477-518, 42 ills.,
Nov., 1925.

Origin of "Labrador." Vol. XVII, pp. 587-588,
Oct., 1906.

Ladd, Harry S.:

Falcon, the Pacific's Newest Island. By J. Edward Hoffmeister and Harry S. Ladd. Vol.
LIV, pp. 757-766, 8 ills., 1 half-page map, Dec.,
1928.

Ladrones Islands, Pacific Ocean. *See* Marianas
Islands.

Lady Franklin Bay Expedition:

Bowdoin (Ship) in North Greenland: Arctic Explorers Place Tablet to Commemorate Sacrifices of the Lady Franklin Bay Expedition. By Donald B. MacMillan. Vol. XLVII, pp. 677-722, 49 ills., June, 1925.

La Farge, (Lt.) Thomas S.:

Coast Guard Patrol in Greenland. 9 ills. in color from natural-color photographs by Lieut. Thomas S. La Farge. Vol. LXXXIII, pp. 565-572, May, 1943.

Lafayette, Marquis de:

Our First Alliance. By J. J. Jusserand. **Vol.** XXXI, pp. 518-548, 8 ills., June, 1917.

Lafayette Escadrille:

Armistice Day and the American Battle Fields. By J. J. Jusserand. Vol. LVI, pp. 509-554, 32 ills. in black and white, 23 ills. in color, Nov., 1929.

Life Story of an American Airman in France: Extracts from the Letters of Stuart Walcott, Who, Between July and December, 1917, Learned to Fly in French Schools of Aviation, Won Fame at the Front, and Fell Near Saint Souplet. Vol. XXXIII, pp. 86-106, 9 ills., Jan., 1918.

Lafayette National Park, Maine:

Unique Island of Mount Desert. By George B. Dorr, Ernest Howe Forbush, and M. L. Fernald. Vol. XXVI, pp. 75-89, 7 ills., July, 1914.

Lafcadio Hearn on the Island and People of Martinique. Vol. XIII, pp. 214-216, June, 1902.

La Gorce, John Oliver:

The Argosy of Geography (Sailing Ship). Photograph by John Oliver La Gorce. Vol. XXXIX, supplement, Jan., 1921.

Battle-Ground of Nature: The Atlantic Seaboard. By John Oliver La Gorce. Vol. XXXIII, pp. 511-546, 23 ills., 4 maps, June, 1918.

Devil-Fishing in the Gulf Stream. By John Oliver La Gorce. Vol. XXXV, pp. 476-488, 7 ills., June, 1919.

Employed by National Geographic Society. Vol. LXIX, p. 152, Jan., 1936.

Expedition to the Bahamas led by Dr. La Gorce. Vol. LXII, p. 452, Oct., 1932.

Fight at the Timber-Line. By John Oliver La Gorce. Vol. XLII, pp. 165-196, 32 ills., Aug., 1922.

Fishes and Fisheries of Our North Atlantic Seaboard. By John Oliver La Gorce. Vol. XLIV, pp. 567-634, 35 ills. in black and white, 16 ills. in color, Dec., 1923.

Florida—The Fountain of Youth. By John Oliver La Gorce. Vol. LVII, pp. 1-93, 73 ills. in black and white, 41 ills. in color, special map supplement, Jan., 1930.

Historic City of Brotherly Love: Philadelphia, Born of Penn and Strengthened by Franklin, a Metropolis of Industries, Homes and Parks. By John Oliver La Gorce. Vol. LXII, pp. 643-697, 49 ills. in black and white, 13 ills. in color, Dec., 1932.

La Gorce, John Oliver—*Continued*

Industrial Titan of America: Pennsylvania, Once the Keystone of the Original Thirteen, Now the Keystone of Forty-eight Sovereign States. By John Oliver La Gorce. Vol. XXXV, pp. 367-406, 33 ills., 1 page map, May, 1919.

Jamaica, the Isle of Many Rivers. By John Oliver La Gorce. Vol. LI, pp. 1-55, 38 ills. in black and white, 11 ills. in color, 1 page map, Jan., 1927.

Meteorological Station, Antarctica, named for Dr. La Gorce. Vol. LVIII, p. 184; ill. 193, Aug., 1930.

Mount La Gorce, Alaska, named for Dr. La Gorce. Vol. XL, pp. 222, 287, Sept., 1921.

National Geographic Society's Notable Year (Announcement of the Election of Dr. La Gorce as Vice-President of The Society). Vol. XXXVII, pp. 338-345, 2 ills., Apr., 1920.

Penn's Land of Modern Miracles (Pennsylvania). By John Oliver La Gorce. Vol. LXVIII, pp. 1-58, 28 ills. in black and white, 39 ills. in color, 1 two-page map, July, 1935.

Pirate Rivers and Their Prizes: The Warfare of Waterways Has Sometimes Changed the Geography of Our Continents. By John Oliver La Gorce. Vol. L, pp. 87-132, 48 ills., 1 half-page map, July, 1926.

Porto Rico, the Gate of Riches: Amazing Prosperity Has Been the Lot of Ponce de León's Isle Under American Administration. By John Oliver La Gorce. Vol. XLVI, pp. 599-651, 46 ills. in black and white, 12 ills. in color, 1 half-page map, Dec., 1924.

Roumania and Its Rubicon. By John Oliver La Gorce. Vol. XXX, pp. 185-202, 11 ills., Sept., 1916.

Treasure-House of the Gulf Stream: The Completion and Opening of the New Aquarium and Biological Laboratory at Miami, Florida. By John Oliver La Gorce. Vol. XXXIX, pp. 53-68, 5 ills. in black and white, 16 ills. in color, Jan., 1921.

Warfare on Our Eastern Coast. By John Oliver La Gorce. Vol. XXVIII, pp. 195-230, 29 ills., 2 charts, Sept., 1915.

Lagos, Nigeria:

Nigeria: From the Bight of Benin to Africa's Desert Sands. By Helen Trybulowski Gilles. Vol. LXXXV, pp. 537-568, 17 ills. in black and white, 10 ills. in color, 1 half-page map, May, 1944.

Lahey, Carlotta Gonzales:

Heavens Above: On Land, Sea, and in the Air the Stars Serve Modern Man as Map, Compass, and Clock. By Donald H. Menzel. With 12 charts, designed by the author, showing star positions for each month, and 13 drawings of the constellations by Carlotta Gonzales Lahey. Vol. LXXXIV, pp. 97-128, 1 map (two-page spread), July, 1943.

Seals of Our Nation, States, and Territories. 84 ills. in color from paintings by Carlotta Gonzales Lahey, Irvin E. Alleman, and Theodora Price. Vol. XC, pp. 17-32, July, 1946.

Lahore, India :

Through the Heart of Hindustan : A Teeming Highway Extending for Fifteen Hundred Miles, from the Khyber Pass to Calcutta. By Maynard Owen Williams. Vol. XL, pp. 433-467, 29 ills., Nov., 1921.

Lake Cahuilla : The Ancient Lake of the Colorado Desert. Vol. XVIII, p. 830, Dec., 1907.

Lake Clark, a Little-Known Alaskan Lake. By Wilfred H. Osgood. Vol. XV, pp. 326-331, 2 ills., 1 half-page map, Aug., 1904.

Lake District, Chile :

Chile's Land of Fire and Water : Smoking Volcanoes and Ice-hooded Peaks Stand Sentinel Over Limpid Lakes in the Far Southern Andes. By W. Robert Moore. Vol. LXXX, pp. 91-110, 9 ills. in black and white, 10 ills. in color, 1 page map, July, 1941.

Lake District, England :

England's Lake District, Fountainhead of Poetry. 10 ills. in color from natural-color photographs. Vol. LXIX, pp. 513-520, Apr., 1936.

Informal Salute to the English Lakes. By Maynard Owen Williams. Vol. LXIX, pp. 511-521, 10 ills. in color, Apr., 1936.

Lakeland, Home of England's Nature Poets. 15 ills. in color from autochromes by Clifton Adams. Vol. LV, pp. 592-601, May, 1929.

Through the English Lake District Afoot and Awheel. By Ralph A. Graves. Vol. LV, pp. 577-603, 19 ills. in black and white, 15 ills. in color, 1 quarter-page map, May, 1929.

Lake Geneva : Cradle of Conferences. By F. Barrows Colton. Vol. LXXII, pp. 727-742, 12 ills., 1 third-page map, Dec., 1937.

Lakehurst, New Jersey : U. S. Naval Air Station :

Aboard a Blimp Hunting U-boats : A Day above the Atlantic Reveals Navy Talk and Navy Ways, Creeping Convoys, and Torpedoed Wrecks. By Mason Sutherland. Vol. LXXXIV, pp. 79-96, 18 ills., July, 1943.

Lakeland, Home of England's Nature Poets. 15 ills. in color from autochromes by Clifton Adams. Vol. LV, pp. 592-601, May, 1929.

Lakes:

Bathymetrical Survey of the Fresh-Water Lakes of England. Vol. XII, p. 408, Nov., 1901.

Gems of the Italian Lakes. By Arthur Ellis Mayer. Vol. XXIV, pp. 943-956, 13 ills., Aug., 1913.
Contains text references and illustrations of Como, Lugano, and Maggiore.

Land of Lakes and Volcanoes (Nicaragua). By Luis Marden. With 17 ills. in color from natural-color photographs by the author. Vol. LXXXVI, pp. 161-192, 11 ills. in black and white, 1 two-thirds-page map, Aug., 1944.

Variations in Lake Levels and Atmospheric Precipitation. By Alfred J. Henry. Vol. X, pp. 403-406, 1 diagram, Oct., 1899.

Lakes—Continued

See also Atitlan ; Baikal ; Balaton ; Cahuilla ; Clark ; Como ; Crater Lake ; Erie ; Finger Lakes Region ; Fissure Lake ; Gatun Lake ; Geneva ; Great Lakes ; Lake District, Chile ; Lake District, England ; Lugano ; Maggiore ; Merritt ; Naivasha ; Raj Samand ; Superior ; Titicaca ; Toba ; Victoria Lake ; Windermere ; Xochimilco.

Lalibela, Ethiopia :

Caravan Journey Through Abyssinia : From Addis Ababa Through Lalibela, the Strange Jerusalem of Ethiopia, in Search of New Grains for American Farms. By Harry V. Harlan. Vol. XLVII, pp. 613-663, 46 ills., 1 half-page map, June, 1925.

Lamaism:

Across Tibet from India to China. By Lt. Col. Ilia Tolstoy, AUS. Vol. XC, pp. 169-222, 41 ills., 1 half-page map, Aug., 1946.

Castles in the Air—Experiences and Journeys in Unknown Bhutan. By John Claude White. Vol. XXV, pp. 365-455, 74 ills., 1 page map, Apr., 1914.

Demon Dancers and Butter Gods of Choni. 16 ills. in color from photographs by Joseph F. Rock. Vol. LIV, pp. 584-601, Nov., 1928.

Demon-Possessed Tibetans and Their Incredible Feats. 12 ills. in color from natural-color photographs. Vol. LXVIII, pp. 479-486, Oct., 1935.

Konka Risumgongba, Holy Mountain of the Outlaws. By Joseph F. Rock. Vol. LX, pp. 1-65, 36 ills. in black and white, 43 ills. in color, 1 three-quarters-page map, July, 1931.

Lama's Motor-Car. By Ethan C. Le Munyon. Vol. XXIV, pp. 640-670, 34 ills., May, 1913.

Land of the Yellow Lama : National Geographic Society Explorer Visits the Strange Kingdom of Muli, Beyond the Likiang Snow Range of Yünnan Province, China. By Joseph F. Rock. Vol. XLVII, pp. 447-491, 39 ills., 1 half-page map, Apr., 1925.

Life Among the Lamas of Choni : Describing the Mystery Plays and Butter Festival in the Monastery of an Almost Unknown Tibetan Principality in Kansu Province, China. By Joseph F. Rock. Vol. LIV, pp. 569-619, 34 ills. in black and white, 16 ills. in color, 1 half-page map, Nov., 1928.

Most Extraordinary City in the World : Notes on Lhasa—The Mecca of the Buddhist Faith. By Shaoching H. Chuan. Vol. XXIII, pp. 959-995, 60 ills., Oct., 1912.

Seeking the Mountains of Mystery : An Expedition on the China-Tibet Frontier to the Unexplored Amnyi Machen Range, One of Whose Peaks Rivals Everest. By Joseph F. Rock. Vol. LVII, pp. 131-185, 54 ills., 1 two-page map, Feb., 1930.

Sky-high in Lama Land. 12 ills. from photographs by C. Suydam Cutting. Vol. XC, pp. 185-196, Aug., 1946.

Sungmas, the Living Oracles of the Tibetan Church. By Joseph F. Rock. Vol. LXVIII, pp. 475-486, 1 ill. in black and white, 12 ills. in color, Oct., 1935.

Lamaism—*Continued*

With the Devil Dancers of China and Tibet. 43 ills. in color from natural-color photographs by Joseph F. Rock. Vol. LX, pp. 18-59, July, 1931.

World's Strangest Capital (Lhasa, Tibet). By John Claude White. Vol. XXIX, pp. 273-295, 19 ills., panorama, Mar., 1916.

See also Lhasa.

Lama's Motor-Car. By Ethan C. Le Munyon. Vol. XXIV, pp. 640-670, 34 ills., May, 1913.

Lamb, Harold:

Mountain Tribes of Iran and Iraq. By Harold Lamb. Vol. LXXXIX, pp. 385-408, 15 ills., 1 two-page map, Mar., 1946.

Road of the Crusaders: A Historian Follows the Steps of Richard the Lion Heart and Other Knights of the Cross Over the "Via Dei." By Harold Lamb. Vol. LXIV, pp. 645-693, 46 ills. in black and white, 13 ills. in color, 1 page map, Dec., 1933.

Lambart, H. F.:

Conquest of Mount Logan: North America's Second Highest Peak Yields to the Intrepid Attack of Canadian Climbers. By H. F. Lambart. Vol. XLIX, pp. 597-631, 40 ills., June, 1926.

Lamoids:

Camels of the Clouds. By W. H. Hodge. Vol. LXXXIX, pp. 641-656, 15 ills., 1 half-page map, May, 1946.

Lancaster (County), Pennsylvania:

Pennsylvania Dutch—In a Land of Milk and Honey. 10 ills. in color from natural-color photographs by J. Baylor Roberts. Vol. LXXIV, pp. 49-56, July, 1938.

Land Columbus Loved (Dominican Republic). By Oliver P. Newman. Vol. LXXXV, pp. 197-224, 15 ills. in black and white, 11 ills. in color, 1 two-thirds-page map, Feb., 1944.

Land of a Million Smiles (Ozarks). By Frederick Simpich. Vol. LXXIII, pp. 589-623, 14 ills. in black and white, 20 ills. in color, 1 two-thirds-page map, May, 1943.

Land of Contrast: Austria-Hungary. By D. W. and A. S. Iddings. Vol. XXIII, pp. 1188-1218, 34 ills., Dec., 1912.

Land of Drought and Desert—Lower California: Two Thousand Miles on Horseback Through the Most Extraordinary Cacti Forests in the World. By E. W. Nelson. Vol. XXII, pp. 443-474, 25 ills., 1 page and 1 half-page maps, May, 1911.

Land of Egypt: A Narrow Green Strip of Fertility Stretching for a Thousand Miles Through Walls of Desert. By Alfred Pearce Dennis. Vol. XLIX, pp. 271-298, 28 ills., 1 half-page map, Mar., 1926.

Land of Eternal Warring (Labrador). By Sir Wilfred T. Grenfell. Vol. XXI, pp. 665-690, 24 ills., Aug., 1910.

Land of Fire (Iceland). By Jon Stefansson. Vol. XVIII, pp. 741-744, Nov., 1907.

Land of Genghis Khan in Its True Colors. 18 ills. in color from natural-color photographs by Maynard Owen Williams. Vol. LXII, pp. 568-577, Nov., 1932.

Land of Giants and Pygmies (Ruanda). By Duke Adolphus Frederick of Mecklenburg. Vol. XXIII, pp. 367-388, 16 ills., 1 page map, Apr., 1912.

Land of Lakes and Volcanoes (Nicaragua). By Luis Marden. With 17 ills. in color from natural-color photographs by the author. Vol. LXXXVI, pp. 161-192, 11 ills. in black and white, 1 two-thirds-page map, Aug., 1944.

Land of Lambskins: An Expedition to Bokhara, Russian Central Asia to Study the Karakul Sheep Industry. By Robert K. Nabours. Vol. XXXVI, pp. 77-88, 15 ills., July, 1919.

Land of Promise (Siberia). By Maj. Gen. A. W. Greely. Vol. XXIII, pp. 1078-1090, 7 ills., Nov., 1912.

Land of Sagebrush and Silver (Nevada). 20 ills. in color from natural-color photographs by W. Robert Moore. Vol. LXXXIX, pp. 9-32, Jan., 1946.

Land of Sawdust and Spangles—A World in Miniature. By Francis Beverly Kelley. Vol. LX, pp. 463-516, 35 ills. in black and white, 29 ills. in color, Oct., 1931.

Land of the Basques: Home of a Thrifty, Picturesque People, Who Take Pride in the Sobriquet, "The Yankees of Spain." By Harry A. McBride. Vol. XLI, pp. 63-87, 25 ills., 1 three-quarters-page map, Jan., 1922.

Land of the Best (United States). By Gilbert H. Grosvenor. Vol. XXIX, pp. 327-430, 71 ills. in black and white, 33 ills. in color, panorama, Apr., 1916.

Land of the Crossbow (Yünnan Province, China). By George Forrest. Vol. XXI, pp. 132-156, 15 ills., 1 page map, Feb., 1910.

Land of the Free in Africa. By Harry A. McBride. Vol. XLII, pp. 411-430, 22 ills., Oct., 1922.

"Land of the Free" in Asia: Siam Has Blended New With Old in Her Progressive March to Modern Statehood in the Family of Nations. By W. Robert Moore. Vol. LXV, pp. 531-576, 28 ills. in black and white, 26 ills. in color, 1 two-thirds-page map, May, 1934.

Land of the Horn, America's Tiptoe. 10 ills. in color from natural-color photographs by Amos Burg. Vol. LXXII, pp. 751-758, Dec., 1937.

Land of the Painted Oxcarts (Costa Rica). By Luis Marden. With 31 ills. in color from natural-color photographs by the author. Vol XC, pp. 409-456. 30 ills. in black and white, 1 half-page map, Oct., 1946.

Land of the Stalking Death : A Journey Through Starving Armenia on an American Relief Train. By Melville Chater. Vol. XXXVI, pp. 393-420, 23 ills., Nov., 1919.

Land of the Yellow Lama : National Geographic Society Explorer Visits the Strange Kingdom of Muli, Beyond the Likiang Snow Range of Yünnan Province, China. By Joseph F. Rock. Vol. XLVII, pp. 447-491, 39 ills., 1 half-page map, Apr., 1925.

Land of William the Conqueror (Normandy) : Where Northmen Came to Build Castles and Cathedrals. By Inez Buffington Ryan. Vol. LXI, pp. 89-99, 13 ills. in color, Jan., 1932.

Land That Links the Americas (Panama). 22 ills. in color from natural-color photographs by Luis Marden. Vol. LXXX, pp. 601-624, Nov., 1941.

Landing Craft for Invasion. By Melville Bell Grosvenor. Vol. LXXXVI, pp. 1-30, 26 ills., July, 1944.

Landor, A. Henry Savage:

Across Widest Africa. By A. Henry Savage Landor. Vol. XIX, pp. 694-737, 38 ills., 1 half-page map, Oct., 1908.

Landscape Architecture:

Need of Conserving the Beauty and Freedom of Nature in Modern Life. By Charles W. Eliot. Vol. XXVI, pp. 67-74, 4 ills., July, 1914.

Landscaped Kwangsi, China's Province of Pictorial Art. By G. Weidman Groff and T. C. Lau. Vol. LXXII, pp. 671-710, 33 ills., 1 half-page map, Dec., 1937.

Landslides:

Landslides and Rock Avalanches. By Guy Elliott Mitchell. Vol. XXI, pp. 277-287, 6 ills., Apr., 1910.

"Where the Mountains Walked" : An Account of the Recent Earthquake in Kansu Province, China, Which Destroyed 100,000 Lives. By Upton Close and Elsie McCormick. Vol. XLI, pp. 445-464, 23 ills., 1 three-quarters-page map, May, 1922.

Lane, Franklin K.:

City of Realized Dreams (San Francisco). By Franklin K. Lane. Vol. XXVII, pp. 169-171, Feb., 1915.

From the War-Path to the Plow. By Franklin K. Lane. Vol. XXVII, pp. 72-87, 12 ills., Jan., 1915.

Makers of the Flag. By Franklin K. Lane. Vol. XXXII, p. 304, Oct., 1917.

Mind's-Eye Map of America. By Franklin K. Lane. Vol. XXXVII, pp. 479-518, 25 ills. in black and white, 8 ills. in color, June, 1920.

Nation's Pride (United States). By Franklin K. Lane. Vol. XXVIII, pp. 589-606, 6 ills., Dec., 1915.

Nation's Undeveloped Resources (United States). By Franklin K. Lane. Vol. XXV, pp. 183-225, 32 ills., Feb., 1914.

Lane, Franklin K.—Continued

Voice Voyages by the National Geographic Society : A Tribute to the Geographical Achievements of the Telephone (Address by Franklin K. Lane). Vol. XXIX, pp. 296-326, 15 ills., 1 chart, Mar., 1916.

What Is It to be an American ? By Franklin K. Lane. Vol. XXXIII, pp. 348-354, 4 ills., 1 diagram, Apr., 1918.

Lang, Anton, Jr.:

Where Bible Characters Live Again : Everyday Life in Oberammergau, World Famous for Its Passion Play, Reaches a Climax at Christmas. By Anton Lang, Jr. Vol. LXVIII, pp. 743-769, 19 ills. in black and white, 11 ills. in color, 1 third-page map, Dec., 1935.

Langlade Island (Petite Miquelon). See Miquelon.

Langley, Anne Rainey:

British West Indian Interlude. By Anne Rainey Langley. Vol. LXXIX, pp. 1-46, 23 ills. in black and white, 21 ills. in color, 2 page maps, Jan., 1941.

I Kept House in a Jungle : The Spell of Primeval Tropics in Venezuela, Riotous With Strange Plants, Animals, and Snakes, Enthralls a Young American Woman. By Anne Rainey Langley. Vol. LXXV, pp. 97-132, 28 ills., 1 third-page map, Jan., 1939.

Langley, S. P.:

Aërial Locomotion. By Alexander Graham Bell. Vol. XVIII, pp. 1-34, 33 ills., Jan., 1907.

Biography of S. P. Langley. Vol XVII, p, 170, Mar., 1906.

Diary of a Voyage from San Francisco to Tahiti and Return, 1901. By S. P. Langley. Vol. XII, pp. 413-429, 10 ills., 1 page and 1 half-page maps, Dec., 1901.

Languages:

Battle-Line of Languages in Western Europe : A Problem in Human Geography More Perplexing Than That of International Boundaries. By A. L. Guerard. Vol. XLIII, pp. 145-180, 36 ills., Feb., 1923.

New Alphabet of the Ancients Is Unearthed : An Inconspicuous Mound in Northern Syria Yields Archeological Treasures of Far-Reaching Significance. By F. A. Schaeffer. Vol. LVIII, pp. 477-516, 47 ills., 1 quarter-page map, Oct., 1930.

New China and the Printed Page. By Paul Hutchinson. Vol. LI, pp. 687-722, 37 ills., June, 1927.

Secrets from Syrian Hills : Explorations Reveal World's Earliest Known Alphabet, Deciphered from Schoolboy Slates and Dictionaries of 3,000 Years Ago. By Claude F. A. Schaeffer. Vol. LXIV, pp. 97-126, 40 ills., 1 third-page map, July, 1933.

Turkey Goes to School. By Maynard Owen Williams. Vol. LV, pp. 95-108, 17 ills., Jan., 1929.

World's Words. By William H. Nicholas. Vol. LXXXIV, pp. 689-700, 8 ills., 1 two-page map. Dec., 1943.

Lanks, H. C.:

Honduran Highlights. 11 ills. in color from natural-color photographs by H. C. Lanks. Vol. LXXXI, pp. 361-368, Mar., 1942.

Lansing, Robert:

Prussianism. By Robert Lansing. Vol. XXXIII, pp. 546-557, 5 ills., June, 1918.

Laodicea (Ancient City):

Ruined Cities of Asia Minor. By Ernest L. Harris. Vol. XIX, pp. 741-760, 11 ills., Nov., 1908.

La Paz, Bolivia:

Bolivia—Tin Roof of the Andes. By Henry Albert Phillips. Vol. LXXXIII, pp. 309-332, 5 ills. in black and white, 20 ills. in color, Mar., 1943.

Kaleidoscopic La Paz: The City of the Clouds. By Harriet Chalmers Adams. Vol. XX, pp. 119-141, 23 ills., Feb., 1909.

La Paz, Mexico:

Adventuring Down the West Coast of Mexico. By Herbert Corey. Vol. XLII, pp. 449-503, 44 ills., 1 half-page map, Nov., 1922.

Lapland:

Europe's Northern Nomads. 12 ills. in color from natural-color photographs by Jack Kuhne. Vol. LXXVI, pp. 657-664, Nov., 1939.

Nomads of Arctic Lapland: Mysterious Little People of a Land of the Midnight Sun Live Off the Country Above the Arctic Circle. By Clyde Fisher. Vol. LXXVI, pp. 641-676, 28 ills. in black and white, 12 ills. in color, 1 page map, Nov., 1939.

Lapps:

Europe's Northern Nomads. 12 ills. in color from natural-color photographs by Jack Kuhne. Vol. LXXVI, pp. 657-664, Nov., 1939.

Nomads of Arctic Lapland: Mysterious Little People of a Land of the Midnight Sun Live Off the Country Above the Arctic Circle. By Clyde Fisher. Vol. LXXVI, pp. 641-676, 28 ills. in black and white, 12 ills. in color, 1 page map, Nov., 1939.

Large Wading Birds: Long Legs and Remarkable Beaks, as Well as Size, Form, and Color, Distinguish the Herons, Ibises, and Flamingos. By T. Gilbert Pearson. Paintings by Maj. Allan Brooks. Vol. LXII, pp. 441-469, 13 ills. in black and white, 24 ills. in color, Oct., 1932.

Largelamb, H. A. (pseudonym):

Extinct Reptiles Found in Nodules. By H. A. Largelamb. Vol. XVII, pp. 170-173, 9 ills., Mar., 1906.

Notes on the Remarkable Habits of Certain Turtles and Lizards. By H. A. Largelamb. Vol. XVIII, pp. 413-419, 12 ills., June, 1907.

Purple Veil: A Romance of the Sea. Vol. XVI, pp. 337-341, 9 ills., July, 1905.

See also Bell, Alexander Graham.

Larger North American Mammals. By E. W. Nelson. Vol. XXX, pp. 385-472, 24 ills. in black and white, 49 ills. in color, supplement in color, Nov., 1916.

Larsen, Helga:

Mexican Indian Flying Pole Dance. By Helga Larsen. Vol. LXXI, pp. 387-400, 13 ills., Mar., 1937.

Last Israelitish Blood Sacrifice: How the Vanishing Samaritans Celebrate the Passover on Sacred Mount Gerizim. By John D. Whiting. Vol. XXXVII, pp. 1-46, 40 ills., 1 half-page map, Jan., 1920.

Latakia:

Antioch the Glorious. By William H. Hall. Vol. XXXVIII, pp. 81-103, 20 ills., 1 half-page map, Aug., 1920.

Crusader Castles of the Near East. By William H. Hall. Vol. LIX, pp. 369-390, 19 ills., 1 third-page map, Mar., 1931.

New Alphabet of the Ancients Is Unearthed: An Inconspicuous Mound in Northern Syria Yields Archeological Treasures of Far-Reaching Significance. By F. A. Schaeffer. Vol. LVIII, pp. 477-516, 47 ills., 1 quarter-page map, Oct., 1930.

Road of the Crusaders: A Historian Follows the Steps of Richard the Lion Heart and Other Knights of the Cross Over the "Via Dei." By Harold Lamb. Vol. LXIV, pp. 645-693, 46 ills. in black and white, 13 ills. in color, 1 page map, Dec., 1933.

Secrets from Syrian Hills: Explorations Reveal World's Earliest Known Alphabet, Deciphered from Schoolboy Slates and Dictionaries of 3,000 Years Ago. By Claude F. A. Schaeffer. Vol. LXIV, pp. 97-126, 40 ills., 1 third-page map, July, 1933.

Latest Map of Mexico. Text accompanying special map supplement in colors. Vol. XXX, p. 88, July, 1916.

Latest Route Proposed for the Isthmian Canal—Mandingo Route. Vol. XIII, pp. 64-70, 1 page chart, Feb., 1902.

Latin America:

Buenos Aires to Washington by Horse: A Solitary Journey of Two and a Half Years, Through Eleven American Republics, Covers 9,600 Miles of Mountain and Plain, Desert and Jungle. By A. F. Tschiffely. Vol. LV, pp. 135-196, 75 ills., 1 page map, Feb., 1929.

Flags of Pan-America. By Byron McCandless and Gilbert Grosvenor. Vol. XXXII, pp. 361-369, 62 ills. in color, Oct., 1917.

Flying the World's Longest Air-Mail Route: From Montevideo, Uruguay, Over the Andes. Up the Pacific Coast, Across Central America and the Caribbean to Miami, Florida, in 67 Thrilling Flying Hours. By Junius B. Wood. Vol. LVII, pp. 261-325, 65 ills., 1 half-page map, Mar., 1930.

Latin America—*Continued*

How Latin America Looks from the Air: U. S. Army Airplanes Hurdle the High Andes, Brave Brazil Jungles, and Follow Smoking Volcanoes to Map New Sky Paths Around South America. By Maj. Herbert A. Dargue. Vol. LII, pp. 451-502, 42 ills., 1 page map, Oct., 1927.

Latin America and Columbia. By John Barrett. Vol. XVII, pp. 692-709, 10 ills., Dec., 1906.

Latin American Constitutions and Revolutions. By John W. Foster. Vol. XII, pp. 169-175, May, 1901.

Peace of Latin America. Vol. XVI, pp. 479-480, Oct., 1905.

Skypaths Through Latin America: Flying From Our Nation's Capital Southward Over Jungles, Remote Islands, and Great Cities on an Aërial Survey of the East Coast of South America. By Frederick Simpich. Vol. LIX, pp. 1-79, 77 ills., 1 page map, Jan., 1931.

To Bogotá and Back by Air: The Narrative of a 9,500-Mile Flight from Washington, Over Thirteen Latin-American Countries and Return, in the Single-Seater Airplane *Spirit of St. Louis*. By Col. Charles A. Lindbergh. Vol. LIII, pp. 529-601, 98 ills., 1 two-thirds-page map, May, 1928.

What the Latin American Republics Think of the Pan American Conferences. Vol. XVII, pp. 474-479, Aug., 1906.

See also names of individual countries.

Latin American Constitutions and Revolutions. By John W. Foster. Vol. XII, pp. 169-175, May, 1901.

Lattimore, Owen:

Byroads and Backwoods of Manchuria: Where Violent Contrasts of Modernism and Unaltered Ancient Tradition Clash. By Owen Lattimore. Vol. LXI, pp. 101-130, 27 ills., 1 three-quarters-page map, Jan., 1932.

China Opens Her Wild West (Yünnan): In the Mountain-girt Heart of a Continent a New China Has Been Created During the Years of War. By Owen Lattimore. Vol. LXXXII, pp. 337-367, 21 ills. in black and white, 11 ills. in color, 1 map (two-page spread), Sept., 1942.

Desert Road to Turkestan: Twentieth Century Travel Through Innermost Asia, Along Caravan Trails Over Which Oriental Commerce Was Once Borne from China to the Medieval Western World. By Owen Lattimore. Vol. LV, pp. 661-702, 45 ills., 1 two-thirds-page map, June, 1929.

New Road to Asia. By Owen Lattimore. Vol. LXXXVI, pp. 641-676, 15 ills. in black and white, 26 ills. in color, Dec., 1944.

South of the Clouds—Yünnan. 11 ills. in color from natural-color photographs by Owen Lattimore and Frank Outram. Vol. LXXXII, pp. 349-356, Sept., 1942.

Sunny Siberia. 26 ills. in color from natural-color photographs by Owen Lattimore. Vol. LXXXVI, pp. 649-672, Dec., 1944.

Latvia:

Flying Around the Baltic. By Douglas Chandler. Vol. LXXIII, pp. 767-806, 31 ills. in black and white, 13 ills. in duotone, 1 half-page map, June, 1938.

Latvia, Home of the Letts: One of the Baltic Republics Which Is Successfully Working Its Way to Stability. By Maynard Owen Williams. Vol. XLVI, pp. 401-443, 48 ills., 1 half-page map, Oct., 1924.

Races of Europe. By Edwin A. Grosvenor. Vol. XXXIV, pp. 441-534, 62 ills., 2 page maps, special map supplement, Dec., 1918.

Lau, T. C.:

Landscaped Kwangsi, China's Province of Pictorial Art. By G. Weidman Groff and T. C. Lau. Vol. LXXII, pp. 671-710, 33 ills., 1 half-page map, Dec., 1937.

Laurier, (Sir) Wilfrid:

Forests of Canada. By Sir Wilfrid Laurier. Vol. XVII, pp. 504-509, Sept., 1906.

Laurinburg-Maxton Army Air Base, North Carolina:

Gliders—Silent Weapons of the Sky. By William H. Nicholas. Vol. LXXXVI, pp. 149-160, 8 ills., Aug., 1944.

La Venta, Mexico:

Finding Jewels of Jade in a Mexican Swamp. By Matthew W. and Marion Stirling. Vol. LXXXII, pp. 635-661, 15 ills. in black and white, 12 ills. in color, 1 two-thirds-page map, Nov., 1942.

Great Stone Faces of the Mexican Jungle; Five Colossal Heads and Numerous Other Monuments of Vanished Americans Are Excavated by the Latest National Geographic-Smithsonian Expedition. By Matthew W. Stirling. Vol. LXXVIII, pp. 309-334, 26 ills., 1 map, Sept., 1940.

La Venta's Green Stone Tigers. By Matthew W. Stirling. Vol. LXXXIV, pp. 321-332, 4 ills. in black and white, 6 ills. in color, 1 two-thirds-page map, Sept., 1943.

Mexico's Deep South Yields New Treasure. 12 ills. in color from natural-color photographs by Richard H. Stewart. Vol. LXXXII, pp. 649-656, Nov., 1942.

Wildlife of Tabasco and Veracruz. By Walter A. Weber. With 19 ills. in color from paintings by the author. Vol. LXXXVII, pp. 187-216, 7 ills. in black and white, 1 two-thirds-page map, Feb., 1945.

La Venta's Green Stone Tigers. By Matthew W. Stirling. Vol. LXXXIV, pp. 321-332, 4 ills. in black and white, 6 ills. in color, 1 two-thirds-page map, Sept., 1943.

Law Courts:

Open-Air Law Courts of Ethiopia. 18 ills. by Harald P. Lechenperg. Vol. LXVIII, pp. 633-646, Nov., 1935.

Lawrence, Frederick W.:

Origin of American State Names. By Frederick W. Lawrence. Vol. XXXVIII, pp. 104-143, 34 ills., Aug., 1920.

Laysan (Island), Hawaii:

Bird City. Vol. XV, pp. 494-498, 6 ills., Dec., 1904.

Bird Life Among Lava Rock and Coral Sand: The Chronicle of a Scientific Expedition to Little-Known Islands of Hawaii. By Alexander Wetmore. Vol. XLVIII, pp. 77-108, 36 ills., 1 half-page map, July, 1925.

LCIs (Landing Craft, Infantry):

Landing Craft for Invasion. By Melville Bell Grosvenor. Vol. LXXXVI, pp. 1-30, 26 ills., July, 1944.

LCTs (Landing Craft, Tank):

Landing Craft for Invasion. By Melville Bell Grosvenor. Vol. LXXXVI, pp. 1-30, 26 ills., July, 1944.

Leach's Petrel: His Nursery on Little Duck Island. By Arnold Wood. Vol. XX, pp. 360-365, 7 ills., Apr., 1909.

Leaf-cutting Ants. *See* Atta Ants.

League of Nations:

League of Nations, What It Means and Why It Must Be. By William Howard Taft. Vol. XXXV, pp. 43-66, 15 ills., Jan., 1919.

Millennial City: The Romance of Geneva, the Capital of the League of Nations. By Ralph A. Graves. Vol. XXXV, pp. 457-476, 11 ills., June, 1919.

Lebanon:

American Alma Maters in the Near East. By Maynard Owen Williams. Vol. LXXXVIII, pp. 237-256, 16 ills., Aug., 1945.

Crusader Castles of the Near East. By William H. Hall. Vol. LIX, pp. 369-390, 19 ills., 1 third-page map, Mar., 1931.

From Jerusalem to Aleppo. By John D. Whiting. Vol. XXIV, pp. 71-113, 30 ills., 1 half-page map, Jan., 1913.

In the Land of Moses and Abraham. 25 ills. in color from natural-color photographs by W. Robert Moore. Vol. LXXIV, pp. 711-742, Dec., 1938.

Road of the Crusaders: A Historian Follows the Steps of Richard the Lion Heart and Other Knights of the Cross Over the "Via Dei." By Harold Lamb. Vol. LXIV, pp. 645-693, 46 ills. in black and white, 13 ills. in color, 1 page map, Dec., 1933.

Skirting the Shores of Sunrise: Seeking and Finding "The Levant" in a Journey by Steamer, Motor-Car, and Train from Constantinople to Port Said. By Melville Chater. Vol. L, pp. 649-728, 60 ills. in black and white, 34 ills. in color, 1 two-thirds-page map, Dec., 1926.

Syria and Lebanon Taste Freedom. By Maynard Owen Williams. With 21 ills. in color from natural-color photographs by the author. Vol. XC, pp. 729-763, 16 ills. in black and white, Dec., 1946.

Lechenperg, Harald P.:

Open-Air Law Courts of Ethiopia. 18 ills. by Harald P. Lechenperg. Vol. LXVIII, pp. 633-646, Nov., 1935.

Lechenperg, Harald P.—*Continued*

With the Italians in Eritrea: Torrid Colony Between the Red Sea and Ethiopia, 2,600 Miles by Sea from Rome, Is Mobilization Place of Fascist Troops and Planes. By Harald P. Lechenperg. Vol. LXVIII, pp. 265-295, 34 ills., 1 two-page map, Sept., 1935.

Le Conte, Joseph:

Joseph Le Conte (Biography). Vol. XII, pp. 309-311, 1 ill., Aug., 1901.

Joseph Le Conte (Biography). Vol. XLII, p. 302, Sept., 1922.

Ledo–Burma Road. *See* Stilwell Road.

Ledo Road:

Stilwell Road—Land Route to China. By Nelson Grant Tayman. Vol. LXXXVII, pp. 681-698, 18 ills., June, 1945.

Lee, Joseph:

Beautiful Ecuador. By Joseph Lee. Vol. XVIII, pp. 80-91, 9 ills., Feb., 1907.

Lee, Kenneth Fuller:

In the Allagash Country (Maine). By Kenneth Fuller Lee. Vol. LV, pp. 505-520, 19 ills., Apr., 1929.

Lee, Thomas F.:

Guatemala: Land of Volcanoes and Progress: Cradle of Ancient Mayan Civilization Redolent With Its Later Spanish and Indian Ways, Now Reaping Prosperity from Bananas and Coffee. By Thomas F. Lee. Vol. L, pp. 599-648, 32 ills. in black and white, 20 ills. in color, 1 page map, Nov., 1926.

Lee, Willis T.:

New Discoveries in Carlsbad Cavern (New Mexico): Vast Subterranean Chambers with Spectacular Decorations Are Explored, Surveyed, and Photographed. By Willis T. Lee. Vol. XLVIII, pp. 301-319, 19 ills., 1 three-quarters-page map, Sept., 1925.

Visit to Carlsbad Cavern: Recent Explorations of a Limestone Cave in the Guadalupe Mountains of New Mexico Reveal a Natural Wonder of the First Magnitude. By Willis T. Lee. Vol. XLV, pp. 1-40, 42 ills., Jan., 1924.

Lee, Camp, Virginia:

Training the New Armies of Liberty: Camp Lee, Virginia's Home for the National Army. By Granville Fortescue. Vol. XXXII, pp. 421-437, 8 ills., 1 page map in colors, Nov.-Dec., 1917.

Leeward Islands, Hawaii:

Bird Life Among Lava Rock and Coral Sand: The Chronicle of a Scientific Expedition to Little-Known Islands of Hawaii. By Alexander Wetmore. Vol. XLVIII, pp. 77-108, 36 ills., 1 half-page map, July, 1925.

Leeward Islands, West Indies:

British West Indian Interlude. By Anne Rainey Langley. Vol. LXXIX, pp. 1-46, 23 ills. in black and white, 21 ills. in color, 2 page maps, Jan., 1941.

Leeward Islands, West Indies—*Continued*

See also Antigua ; Dominica ; Guadeloupe ; Martinique ; Saba ; St. Kitts ; Virgin Islands.

Leffingwell, E. de K.:

Anglo-American Polar Expedition. By E. de K. Leffingwell. Vol. XVIII, p. 796, Dec., 1907.

Legends:

War's Wake in the Rhineland. By Thomas R. Henry. Vol. LXXXVIII, pp. 1-32, 29 ills., 1 third-page map, July, 1945.

Leiberg, J. B.:

Is Climatic Aridity Impending on the Pacific Slope? The Testimony of the Forest. By J. B. Leiberg. Vol. X, pp. 160-181, May, 1899.

Leis from Aloha Land (Hawaii). 10 ills. in color from natural-color photographs ; 8 ills. by Richard H. Stewart. Vol. LXXIV, pp. 435-442, Oct., 1938.

Le Munyon, Ethan C.:

Lama's Motor-Car. By Ethan C. Le Munyon. Vol. XXIV, pp. 640-670, 34 ills., May, 1913.

Lend-Lease:

Iran in Wartime: Through Fabulous Persia, Hub of the Middle East, Americans, Britons, and Iranians Keep Sinews of War Moving to the Embattled Soviet Union. By John N. Greely. Vol. LXXXIV, pp. 129-156, 26 ills., 1 page map, Aug., 1943.

Lend-Lease and the Russian Victory. By Harvey Klemmer. Vol. LXXXVIII, pp. 499-512, 6 ills., Oct., 1945.

Lend-Lease Is a Two-way Benefit: Innovation in Creative Statesmanship Pools Resources of United Nations, and Supplies American Forces Around the World. By Francis Flood. Vol. LXXXIII, pp. 745-761, 14 ills., June, 1943.

Leningrad, R. S. F. S. R.:

Glimpses of the Russian Empire. By William Wisner Chapin. Vol. XXIII, pp. 1043-1078, 51 ills. in color, 1 three-quarters-page map, Nov., 1912.

Young Russia: The Land of Unlimited Possibilities. By Gilbert H. Grosvenor. Vol. XXVI, pp. 421-520, 85 ills. in black and white, 17 ills. in color, Nov., 1914.

Lenz, Frank B.:

World's Ancient Porcelain Center (Kingtehchen). By Frank B. Lenz. Vol. XXXVIII, pp. 391-406, 17 ills., Nov., 1920.

Leopards:

King of Cats and His Court. By Victor H. Cahalane. Paintings by Walter A. Weber. Vol. LXXXIII, pp. 217-259, 9 ills. in black and white, 20 ills. in color, Feb., 1943.

Leprosy:

Hunting the Chaulmoogra Tree. By Joseph F. Rock. Vol. XLI, pp. 243-276, 39 ills., 1 page map, Mar., 1922.

Lesbos (Island). *See* Mytilene.

Lesser Antilles. *See* Antigua ; Aruba ; Bonaire ; Curaçao ; Dominica ; Guadeloupe ; Martinique ; Saba ; St. Kitts ; St. Lucia ; St. Vincent ; Trinidad ; Virgin Islands.

Lesser Sunda Islands. *See* Bali ; Timor.

Lessons from China (Forestry). Vol. XX, pp. 18-29, 8 ills., Jan., 1909.

Lessons from Japan. Vol. XV, pp. 221-225, 3 ills., May, 1904.

Lessons of Galveston. By W J McGee. Vol. XI, pp. 377-383, Oct., 1900.

Letters from the Italian Front. By Marchesa Louise de Rosales to Ethel Mather Bagg. Vol. XXXII, pp. 46-67, 22 ills., July, 1917.

Leuaniua (Island), Solomon Islands:

Coconuts and Coral Islands. By H. Ian Hogbin. Vol. LXV, pp. 265-298, 24 ills. in black and white, 14 ills. in color, 1 half-page map, Mar., 1934.

Leung, George Kin:

Peiping's Happy New Year: Lunar Celebration Attracts Throngs to Temple Fairs, Motley Bazaars, and Age-old Festivities. By George Kin Leung. Vol. LXX, pp. 749-792, 31 ills. in black and white, 16 ills. in color, Dec., 1936.

Levant (Ship):

Philip Nolan and the *Levant*. By Edward E. Hale. Vol. XVI, pp. 114-116, Mar., 1905.

Levant States:

Change Comes to Bible Lands. By Frederick Simpich. Vol. LXXIV, pp. 695-750, 40 ills. in black and white, 25 ills. in color, special map supplement, Dec., 1938.

Crusader Castles of the Near East. By William H. Hall. Vol. LIX, pp. 369-390, 19 ills., 1 third-page map, Mar., 1931.

Damascus, the Pearl of the Desert. By Archibald Forder. Vol. XXII, pp. 62-82, 19 ills., 1 three-quarters-page map, Jan., 1911.

Damascus and Mecca Railway. Vol. XII, p. 408, Nov., 1901.

From Jerusalem to Aleppo. By John D. Whiting. Vol. XXIV, pp. 71-113, 30 ills., 1 half-page map, Jan., 1913.

Impressions of Asiatic Turkey. By Stephen van Rensselaer Trowbridge. Vol. XXVI, pp. 598-609, 6 ills., Dec., 1914.

In the Land of Moses and Abraham. 25 ills. in color from natural-color photographs by W. Robert Moore. Vol. LXXIV, pp. 711-742, Dec., 1938.

New Alphabet of the Ancients Is Unearthed: An Inconspicuous Mound in Northern Syria Yields Archeological Treasures of Far-Reaching Significance. By F. A. Schaeffer. Vol. LVIII, pp. 477-516, 47 ills., 1 quarter-page map, Oct., 1930.

Levant States—*Continued*

One Thousand Miles of Railway Built for Pilgrims and Not for Dividends. By Col. F. R. Maunsell. Vol. XX, pp. 156-172, 13 ills., 1 three-quarters-page map, Feb., 1909.

Road of the Crusaders: A Historian Follows the Steps of Richard the Lion Heart and Other Knights of the Cross Over the "Via Dei." By Harold Lamb. Vol. LXIV, pp. 645-693, 46 ills. in black and white, 13 ills. in color, 1 page map, Dec., 1933.

Scenes in Asia Minor. Vol. XX, pp. 174-193, 34 ills., 1 three-quarters-page map, Feb., 1909.

Secrets from Syrian Hills: Explorations Reveal World's Earliest Known Alphabet, Deciphered from Schoolboy Slates and Dictionaries of 3,000 Years Ago. By Claude F. A. Schaeffer. Vol. LXIV, pp. 97-126, 40 ills., 1 third-page map, July, 1933.

Skirting the Shores of Sunrise: Seeking and Finding "The Levant" in a Journey by Steamer, Motor-Car, and Train from Constantinople to Port Said. By Melville Chater. Vol. L, pp. 649-728, 60 ills. in black and white, 24 ills. in color, 1 two-thirds-page map, Dec., 1926.

Under the Heel of the Turk: A Land with a Glorious Past, a Present of Abused Opportunities and a Future of Golden Possibilities. By William H. Hall. Vol. XXXIV, pp. 50-69, 14 ills., July, 1918.

Levees:

Great Mississippi Flood of 1927: Since White Man's Discovery This Mighty River Has Served Him Well, Yet It Has Brought Widespread Devastation Along Its Lower Reaches. By Frederick Simpich. Vol. LII, pp. 243-289, 53 ills., 1 half-page map, Sept., 1927.

Lewis, F.:

Koala, or Australian Teddy Bear. By F. Lewis. Vol. LX, pp. 346-355, 13 ills., Sept., 1931.

Lewis, Harry R.:

America's Debt to the Hen. By Harry R. Lewis. Vol. LI, pp. 453-467, 15 ills., Apr., 1927.

Lewis, L. Elizabeth:

Fire-Walking Hindus of Singapore. By L. Elizabeth Lewis. Vol. LIX, pp. 513-522, 12 ills., Apr., 1931.

Lewis and Clark Expedition Route:

Trailing History Down the Big Muddy: In the Homeward Wake of Lewis and Clark, a Folding Steel Skiff Bears Its Lone Pilot on a 2,000-Mile Cruise on the Yellowstone-Missouri. By Lewis R. Freeman. Vol. LIV, pp. 73-120, 51 ills., 1 half-page map, July, 1928.

Lhasa, Tibet:

Across Tibet from India to China. By Lt. Col. Ilia Tolstoy, AUS. Vol. XC, pp. 169-222, 41 ills., 1 half-page map, Aug., 1946.

Explorations in Tibet. Vol. XIV, pp. 353-355, Sept., 1903.

Lhasa—The Mecca of the Buddhist Faith. Vol. XXIX, panorama, Mar., 1916.

Lhasa, Tibet—*Continued*

Most Extraordinary City in the World: Notes on Lhasa—The Mecca of the Buddhist Faith. By Shaoching H. Chuan. Vol. XXIII, pp. 959-995, 60 ills., Oct., 1912.

Notes on Tibet. Vol. XV, pp. 292-294, 1 ill., July, 1904.

Sky-high in Lama Land. 12 ills. from photographs by C. Suydam Cutting. Vol. XC, pp. 185-196, Aug., 1946.

Views of Lhasa. Vol. XVI, pp. 27-38, 11 ills., Jan., 1905.

World's Strangest Capital. By John Claude White. Vol. XXIX, pp. 273-295, 19 ills., panorama, Mar., 1916.

Liang-Cheng, (Sir) Chentung:

China and the United States. By Sir Chentung Liang-Cheng. Vol. XVI, pp. 554-557, Dec., 1905.

Liberated Ukraine. By Eddy Gilmore. Vol. LXXXV, pp. 513-536, 22 ills., 1 page map, May, 1944.

Liberators (Bombers):

8th Air Force in England. 10 ills. in color from U. S. Army Air Forces official photographs. Vol. LXXXVII, pp. 297-304, Mar., 1945.

Liberia:

Black Republic—Liberia. By Sir Harry Johnston and Ernest Lyon. Vol. XVIII, pp. 334-343, 9 ills., May, 1907.

Conditions in Liberia. By Roland P. Folkner, George Sale, and Emmett J. Scott. Vol. XXI, pp. 729-741, 9 ills., Sept., 1910.

Dumboy, the National Dish of Liberia. By G. N. Collins. Vol. XXII, pp. 84-88, 5 ills., Jan., 1911.

Kboo, a Liberian Game. By G. N. Collins. Vol. XXI, pp. 944-948, 3 ills., Nov., 1910.

Land of the Free in Africa. By Harry A. McBride. Vol. XLII, pp. 411-430, 22 ills., Oct., 1922.

Notes on the Only American Colony in the World. By Edgar Allen Forbes. Vol. XXI, pp. 719-729, 14 ills., Sept., 1910.

Primitive Gyroscope in Liberia. By G. N. Collins. Vol. XXI, pp. 531-535, 3 ills., June, 1910.

Liberia, Costa Rica:

Land of the Painted Oxcarts. By Luis Marden. With 31 ills. in color from natural-color photographs by the author. Vol. XC, pp. 409-456, 30 ills. in black and white, 1 half-page map, Oct., 1946.

Libia:

Cirenaica, Eastern Wing of Italian Libia. By Harriet Chalmers Adams. Vol. LVII, pp. 689-726, 35 ills. in black and white, 13 ills. in color, 1 two-thirds-page map, June, 1930.

Cirenaica, on the Edge of the Saharan Sands. 13 ills. in color from natural-color photographs by Luigi Pellerano. Vol. LVII, pp. 692-701, June, 1930.

Libia—*Continued*

Crossing the Untraversed Libyan Desert: The Record of a 2,200-Mile Journey of Exploration Which Resulted in the Discovery of Two Oases of Strategic Importance on the Southwestern Frontier of Egypt. By A. M. Hassanein. Vol. XLVI, pp. 233-277, 46 ills., 1 half-page map, Sept., 1924.

Here and There in Northern Africa. By Frank Edward Johnson. Vol. XXV, pp. 1-132, 113 ills., Jan., 1914.

Mysteries of the Desert. By Hanns Vischer. Vol. XXII, pp. 1056-1059, Nov., 1911.

Old-New Battle Grounds of Egypt and Libia. By W. Robert Moore. Vol. LXXVIII, pp. 809-820, 8 ills., 1 third-page map, Dec., 1940.

Tripoli: A Land of Little Promise. By Adolf L. Vischer. Vol. XXII, pp. 1035-1047, 6 ills., 1 half-page map, Nov., 1911.

Tripolitania, Where Rome Resumes Sway: The Ancient Trans-Mediterranean Empire, on the Fringe of the Libyan Desert, Becomes a Promising Modern Italian Colony. By Col. Gordon Casserly. Vol. XLVIII, pp. 131-161, 27 ills. in black and white, 9 ills. in color, 1 two-thirds-page map, Aug., 1925.

See also Bengasi; Tripoli.

Libian Desert, Africa:

Crossing the Untraversed Libyan Desert: The Record of a 2,200-Mile Journey of Exploration Which Resulted in the Discovery of Two Oases of Strategic Importance on the Southwestern Frontier of Egypt. By A. M. Hassanein. Vol. XLVI, pp. 233-277, 46 ills., 1 half-page map, Sept., 1924.

Library. *See* National Geographic Society: Library.

Liechtenstein:

Round About Liechtenstein: A Tiny Principality Which the Visitor May Encompass in a Single View Affords Adventurous Climbs Among Steep Pastures and Quaint Villages. By Maynard Owen Williams. Vol. LII, pp. 611-634, 18 ills., 1 half-page map, Nov., 1927.

Life, Culture, and History of the Egyptians. 32 ills. in color from paintings by H. M. Herget. Vol. LXXX, pp. 436-514, Oct., 1941.

Life Afloat in China: Tens of Thousands of Chinese in Congested Ports Spend Their Entire Existence on Boats. By Robert F. Fitch. Vol. LI, pp. 665-686, 28 ills., June, 1927.

Life Along the Central China Coast. 14 ills. in color from natural-color photographs by W. Robert Moore. Vol. LXII, pp. 316-325, Sept., 1932.

Life Among the Lamas of Choni: Describing the Mystery Plays and Butter Festival in the Monastery of an Almost Unknown Tibetan Principality in Kansu Province, China. By Joseph F. Rock. Vol. LIV, pp. 569-619, 34 ills. in black and white, 16 ills. in color, 1 half-page map, Nov., 1928.

Life Among the People of Eastern Tibet. By Dr. A. L. Shelton. Vol. XL, pp. 293-326, 35 ills., 1 half-page map, Sept., 1921.

Life and Color Under the Rising Sun (Japan). 12 ills. in color from natural-color photographs by W. Robert Moore and Kiyoshi Sakamoto. Vol. LXIII, pp. 288-297, Mar., 1933.

Life and Death in Ancient Maya Land (Yucatán). 10 ills. in color from paintings by H. M. Herget. Vol. LXX, pp. 623-630, Nov., 1936.

Life and Luster of Berlin. 24 ills. in color from natural-color photographs by Wilhelm Tobien and Hans Hildenbrand. Vol. LXXI, pp. 147-177, Feb., 1937.

Life Grows Grim in Singapore. By H. Gordon Minnigerode. Vol. LXXX, pp. 661-686, 17 ills. in black and white, 9 ills. in color, 1 half-page map, Nov., 1941.

Life in a Norway Valley: An American Girl Is Welcomed Into the Homemaking and Haying of Happy Hallingdal. By Abbie L. Bosworth. Vol. LXVII, pp. 627-648, 21 ills., 1 half-page map, May, 1935.

Life in Constantinople. By H. G. Dwight. Vol. XXVI, pp. 521-545, 25 ills., Dec., 1914.

Life in Dauntless Darwin: A National Geographic Staff Writer Gives a Vivid Description of the Australian Town That Guards the Continent's Northern Door. By Howell Walker. Vol. LXXXII, pp. 123-138, 17 ills., 1 sixth-page map, July, 1942.

Life in Our Fighting Fleet (U. S. Navy). By F. Barrows Colton. Vol. LXXIX, pp, 671-702, 30 ills., June, 1941.

Life in the Great Desert of Central Asia. By Ellsworth Huntington. Vol. XX, pp. 749-760, 12 ills., Aug., 1909.

Life Members. *See* National Geographic Society: Life Members.

Life of the Moon-Jelly. By William Crowder. Vol. L, pp. 187-202, 6 ills. in black and white, 1 ill. in color, Aug., 1926.

Life on a Coral Reef: The Fertility and Mystery of the Sea Studied Beneath the Waters Surrounding Dry Tortugas. By W. H. Longley. Vol. LI, pp. 61-83, 22 ills. in black and white, 8 ills. in color, Jan., 1927.

Life on a Yukon Trail. By Alfred Pearce Dennis. Part I, Vol. X, pp. 377-391, 8 ills., 1 page map, Oct., 1899. Part II, Vol. X, pp. 457-466, 7 ills., Nov., 1899.

Life on the Argentine Pampa. By Frederick Simpich. Vol. LXIV, pp. 449-491, 41 ills. in black and white, 8 ills. in color, Oct., 1933.

Life on the Grand Banks: An Account of the Sailor-Fishermen Who Harvest the Shoal Waters of North America's Eastern Coasts. By Frederick William Wallace. Vol. XL, pp. 1-28, 29 ills., July, 1921.

Life on the Hawaii "Front": All-out Defense and Belt Tightening of Pacific Outpost Foreshadow the Things to Come on Mainland. By Lieut. Frederick Simpich, Jr. Vol. LXXXII, pp. 541-560, 19 ills., 1 half-page map, Oct., 1942.

Life on the Steppes and Oases of Chinese Turkestan. 32 ills. in color from natural-color photographs by W. Bosshard. Vol. LIX, pp. 332-357, Mar., 1931.

Life Story of an American Airman in France : Extracts from the Letters of Stuart Walcott, Who, Between July and December, 1917, Learned to Fly in French Schools of Aviation, Won Fame at the Front, and Fell Near Saint Souplet. Vol. XXXIII, pp. 86-106, 9 ills., Jan., 1918.

Life Story of the Mosquito. By Graham Fairchild. With 10 ills. in color from paintings. Vol. LXXXV, pp. 180-195, 5 ills. in black and white, 1 drawing, Feb., 1944.

Life with an Indian Prince : As Guests of a Maharaja's Brother, Two Young American Naturalists Study Age-old Methods of Hunting with Trained Falcons and Cheetahs and Savor the Pomp of Royal India. By John and Frank Craighead. Vol. LXXXI, pp. 235-272, 38 ills., 1 sixth-page map, Feb., 1942.

Life with Our Fighting Coast Guard. By F. Barrows Colton. Vol. LXXXIII, pp. 557-588, 22 ills. in black and white, 9 ills. in color, May, 1943.

Life's Color in Wisconsin. 27 ills. in color from natural-color photographs ; 23 ills. by B. Anthony Stewart. Vol. LXXII, pp. 17-40, July, 1937.

Life's Flavor on a Swedish Farm : From the Rocky Hills of Småland Thousands of Sturdy Citizens Have Emigrated to the United States. By Willis Lindquist. Vol. LXXVI, pp. 393-414, 23 ills., 1 quarter-page map, Sept., 1939.

Life's Pattern on the Italian Riviera. By Helen Churchill Candee. Vol. LXVII, pp. 67-100, 25 ills. in black and white, 12 ills. in color, 1 two-thirds-page map, Jan., 1935.

Life's Tenor in Ethiopia : Africa's Land of Early Christianity Now Yields Minerals for Modern Industry. By James Loder Park. Vol. LXVII, pp. 783-793, 8 ills., June, 1935.

Lighthouses:

Battle-Ground of Nature : The Atlantic Seaboard. By John Oliver La Gorce. Vol. XXXIII, pp. 511-546, 23 ills., 4 half-page maps, June, 1918.

Beacons of the Sea. By George R. Putnam. Vol. XXIV, pp. 1-53, 65 ills., 2 diagrams, 1 three-quarters-page map, Jan., 1913.

Important New Guide for Shipping : Navassa Light, on a Barren Island in the West Indies, Is the First Signal for the Panama Canal. By George R. Putnam. Vol. XXXIV, pp. 401-406, 3 ills., 1 half-page map, Nov., 1918.

Isle of Capri : An Imperial Residence and Probable Wireless Station of Ancient Rome. By John A. Kingman. Vol. XXXVI, pp. 213-231, 17 ills., Sept., 1919.

New Safeguards for Ships in Fog and Storm. By George R. Putnam. Vol. LXX, pp. 169-200, 28 ills., 2 charts, Aug., 1936.

Lighthouses—*Continued*

Warfare on Our Eastern Coast. By John Oliver La Gorce. Vol. XXVIII, pp. 195-230, 29 ills., 2 charts, Sept., 1915.

Lightships:

New Safeguards for Ships in Fog and Storm. By George R. Putnam. Vol. LXX, pp. 169-200, 28 ills., 2 charts, Aug., 1936.

Lilienthal, Otto:

Aërial Locomotion. By Alexander Graham Bell. Vol. XVIII, pp. 1-34, 33 ills., Jan., 1907.

Remarkable Photographs of Lilienthal's Gliding Machine. By R. W. Wood. Vol. XIX, p. 596, 1 ill., Aug., 1908.

Lima, Peru :

Lure of Lima, City of the Kings. By William Joseph Showalter. Vol. LVII, pp. 727-784, 41 ills., June, 1930.

Limbert, R. W.:

Among the "Craters of the Moon" : An Account of the First Expeditions Through the Remarkable Volcanic Lava Beds of Southern Idaho. By R. W. Limbert. Vol. XLV, pp. 303-328, 23 ills., 1 two-thirds-page map, Mar., 1924.

Limited Water Supply of the Arid Region. By Frederick H. Newell. Vol. XI, pp. 438-442, Nov.. 1900.

Limiting Width of Meander Belts. By Mark S. W. Jefferson. Vol. XIII, pp. 373-384, 6 charts, Oct., 1902.

Limón, Costa Rica :

Land of the Painted Oxcarts. By Luis Marden. With 31 ills. in color from natural-color photographs by the author. Vol. XC, pp. 409-456, 30 ills. in black and white, 1 half-page map, Oct., 1946.

Lincoln, F. S.:

Glamour of Historic Havana. 9 ills. in black and white from photographs by F. S. Lincoln. Vol. LXIV, pp. 357-364, Sept., 1933.

Lincoln, Nebraska :

Cornhusker State Highlights. 23 ills. in color from natural-color photographs by B. Anthony Stewart. Vol. LXXXVII, pp. 521-536, May. 1945.

Nebraska, the Cornhusker State. By Leo A. Borah. Vol. LXXXVII, pp. 513-542, 6 ills. in black and white, 23 ills. in color, 1 map (two-page spread), May, 1945.

Lincoln Memorial, Washington, D. C. :

Lincoln Memorial. By William Howard Taft. Vol. XLIII, pp. 597-602, 5 ills., June, 1923.

Views of the Lincoln Memorial in Washington. Vol. XLII, pp. 197-204, 8 ills., Aug., 1922.

Lindbergh, Anne Morrow:

Flying Around the North Atlantic. By Anne Morrow Lindbergh. Foreword by Charles A. Lindbergh. Vol. LXVI, pp. 259-337, 82 ills.. 1 two-page and 1 two-thirds-page maps, Sept.. 1934.

Lindbergh, Anne Morrow—*Continued*

Society Awards Hubbard Medal to Anne Morrow Lindbergh. Vol. LXV, pp. 791-794, 4 ills., June, 1934.

Lindbergh, (Col.) Charles A.:

Air Conquests: From the Early Days of Giant Kites and Birdlike Gliders, the National Geographic Society Has Aided and Encouraged the Growth of Aviation. Vol. LII, pp. 233-242, 13 ills., Aug., 1927.

Flying Around the North Atlantic. By Anne Morrow Lindbergh; Foreword by Charles A. Lindbergh. Vol. LXVI, pp. 259-337, 82 ills., 1 two-page and 1 two-thirds-page maps, Sept., 1934.

President Coolidge Bestows Lindbergh Award: The National Geographic Society's Hubbard Medal Is Presented to Aviator Before the Most Notable Gathering in the History of Washington (Address by Colonel Lindbergh). Vol. LIII, pp. 127-140, 4 ills. Jan., 1928.

Seeing America with Lindbergh: The Record of a Tour of More Than 20,000 Miles by Airplane Through Forty-eight States on Schedule Time. By Lieut. Donald E. Keyhoe. Vol. LIII, pp. 1-46, 46 ills., 1 page map, Jan., 1928.

To Bogotá and Back by Air: The Narrative of a 9,500-Mile Flight from Washington, Over Thirteen Latin-American Countries and Return, in the Single-Seater Airplane *Spirit of St. Louis.* By Col. Charles A. Lindbergh. Vol. LIII, pp. 529-601, 98 ills., 1 two-thirds-page map, May, 1928.

Lindquist, Willis:

Life's Flavor on a Swedish Farm: From the Rocky Hills of Småland Thousands of Sturdy Citizens Have Emigrated to the United States. By Willis Lindquist. Vol. LXXVI, pp. 393-414, 23 ills., 1 quarter-page map, Sept., 1939.

On Danish By-Lanes: An American Cycles Through the Quaint City of Lace, the Curiosity Town Where Time Stands Still, and Even Finds a Frontier in the Farming Kingdom. By Willis Lindquist. Vol. LXXVII, pp. 1-34, 21 ills. in black and white, 10 ills. in color, 1 three-quarters-page map, Jan., 1940.

Lindsay Island, Antarctic Region:

Sailing the Seven Seas in the Interest of Science: Adventures Through 157,000 Miles of Storm and Calm, from Arctic to Antarctic and Around the World, in the Non-Magnetic Yacht *Carnegie.* By J. P. Ault. Vol. XLII, pp. 631-690, 47 ills., 1 chart, Dec., 1922.

Lingnan University, Canton, China: Expedition:

Landscaped Kwangsi, China's Province of Pictorial Art. By G. Weidman Groff and T. C. Lau. Vol. LXXII, pp. 671-710, 33 ills., 1 half-page map, Dec., 1937.

Link Relations of Southwestern Asia. By Talcott Williams. Part I, Vol. XII, pp. 249-265, 2 page and 8 half-page maps, July, 1901. Part II, Vol. XII, pp. 291-299, 1 half-page map, Aug., 1901.

Lions:

King of Cats and His Court. By Victor H. Cahalane. Paintings by Walter A. Weber. Vol. LXXXIII, pp. 217-259, 9 ills. in black and white, 20 ills. in color, Feb., 1943.

Wild Man and Wild Beast in Africa. By Theodore Roosevelt. Vol. XXII, pp. 1-33, 41 ills., 1 page map, Jan., 1911.

Lipovan Fishermen:

Caviar Fishermen of Romania: From Vâlcov, "Little Venice" of the Danube Delta, Bearded Russian Exiles Go Down to the Sea. By Dorothy Hosmer. Vol. LXXVII, pp. 407-434, 29 ills., 1 third-page map, Mar., 1940.

Lisbon, Portugal:

Castles and Progress in Portugal. By W. Robert Moore. Vol. LXXIII, pp. 133-188, 36 ills. in black and white, 24 ills. in color, 1 half-page map, Feb., 1938.

Lisbon—Gateway to Warring Europe. By Harvey Klemmer. Vol. LXXX, pp. 259-276, 18 ills., Aug., 1941.

Lisbon, the City of the Friendly Bay. By Clifford Albion Tinker. Vol. XLII, pp. 504-552, 30 ills. in black and white, 16 ills. in color, 1 quarter-page map, Nov., 1922.

Woods and Gardens of Portugal. By Martin Hume. Vol. XXI, pp. 883-894, 8 ills., Oct., 1910.

Lisle, (Capt.) Clifton:

Celebrating Christmas on the Meuse. By Capt. Clifton Lisle. Vol. XXXVI, pp. 527-537, 5 ills., Dec., 1919.

Lithuania:

Flying Around the Baltic. By Douglas Chandler. Vol. LXXIII, pp. 767-806, 31 ills. in black and white, 13 ills. in duotone, 1 half-page map, June, 1938.

Little America, Antarctica:

Antarctica by Sea, Land and Air. 16 ills. in gravure from photographs by the Byrd Antarctic Expedition. Vol. LVIII, pp. 158-207, Aug., 1930.

Conquest of Antarctica by Air. By Rear Adm. Richard Evelyn Byrd. Vol. LVIII, pp. 127-227, 71 ills. in black and white, 16 ills. in gravure, 1 page map, Aug., 1930.

Mapping the Antarctic from the Air: The Aërial Camera Earns Its Place as the Eyes and Memory of the Explorer. By Capt. Ashley C. McKinley. Vol. LXII, pp. 471-485, 13 ills., special map supplement, Oct., 1932.

Little Duck Island, Maine:

Leach's Petrel: His Nursery on Little Duck Island. By Arnold Wood. Vol. XX, pp. 360-365, 7 ills., Apr., 1909.

"Little Gray Lady." *See* Nantucket (Island).

Little Journey in Honduras. By F. J. Youngblood. Vol. XXX, pp. 177-184, 6 ills., Aug., 1916.

Little-Known Marvel of the Western Hemisphere: Christophe's Citadel, a Monument to the Tyranny and Genius of Haiti's King of Slaves. By Maj. G. H. Osterhout, Jr. Vol. XXXVIII, pp. 468-482, 13 ills., Dec., 1920.

Little-Known Parts of Panama. By Henry Pittier. Vol. XXIII, pp. 627-662, 35 ills., 1 page map, July, 1912.

Little-Known Sardinia. By Helen Dunstan Wright. Vol. XXX, pp. 97-120, 23 ills., 1 page map, Aug., 1916.

Little Norway (Training Center), Toronto, Canada:

Norway, an Active Ally. By Wilhelm Morgenstierne. Vol. LXXXIII, pp. 333-357, 24 ills., 1 two-thirds-page map, Mar., 1943.

Little Rock, Arkansas:

Arkansas Rolls Up Its Sleeves. By Frederick Simpich. Vol. XC, pp. 273-312, 16 ills. in black and white, 23 ills. in color, 1 map (two-page spread), Sept., 1946.

Arkansas Traveler of 1946. 23 ills. in color from natural-color photographs by Willard R. Culver. Vol. XC, pp. 289-312, Sept., 1946.

Littlehales, George W.:

Marine Hydrographic Surveys of the Coasts of the World. By George W. Littlehales. Vol. XVI, pp. 63-67, 1 page map, Feb., 1905.

Livestock:

America Fights on the Farms. 21 ills. in color from natural-color photographs. Vol. LXXXVI, pp. 33-48, July, 1944.

Britain Fights in the Fields. By Francis A. Flood. Vol. LXXXVI, pp. 31-65, 17 ills. in black and white, 21 ills. in color, July, 1944.

Cornhusker State Highlights (Nebraska). 23 ills. in color from natural-color photographs by B. Anthony Stewart. Vol. LXXXVII, pp. 521-536, May, 1945.

Exploring a Grass Wonderland of Wild West China. By Ray G. Johnson. Vol. LXXXV, pp. 713-742, 24 ills., 1 half-page map, June, 1944.

Grass Makes Wyoming Fat. By Frederick Simpich. Vol. LXXXVIII, pp. 153-188, 13 ills. in black and white, 19 ills. in color, 1 two-page map, Aug., 1945.

Idaho Made the Desert Bloom. By D. Worth Clark. Vol. LXXXV, pp. 641-688, 21 ills. in black and white, 20 ills. in color, 1 page map, June, 1944.

Nebraska, the Cornhusker State. By Leo A. Borah. Vol. LXXXVII, pp. 513-542, 6 ills. in black and white, 23 ills. in color, 1 map (two-page spread), May, 1945.

See also Cattle and Cattle Raising; Goats; Sheep and Sheep Raising.

Living Casks of Honey (Ants). By Jennie E. Harris. Vol. LXVI, pp. 193-199, 4 ills., Aug., 1934.

Living Jewels of the Sea (Plankton). By William Crowder. Vol. LII, pp. 290-304, 8 ills. in black and white, 8 ills. in color, Sept., 1927.

Living on a Volcano: An Unspoiled Patch of Polynesia Is Niuafoō, Nicknamed "Tin Can Island" by Stamp Collectors. By Thomas A. Jaggar. Vol. LXVIII, pp. 91-106, 17 ills., 1 half-page map, July, 1935.

Lizards:

Lonely Australia: The Unique Continent. By Herbert E. Gregory. Vol. XXX, pp. 473-568, 68 ills., 1 two-page and 4 half-page maps, Dec., 1916.
Contains descriptions of the following species: Monitor, Skink, Slow-worm.

Modern Dragon Hunt on Komodo: An English Yachting Party Traps and Photographs the Huge and Carnivorous Dragon Lizard of the Lesser Sundas. By Lady Broughton. Vol. LXX, pp. 321-331, 12 ills. in duotone, Sept., 1936.

Notes on the Remarkable Habits of Certain Turtles and Lizards. By H. A. Largelamb. Vol. XVIII, pp. 413-419, 12 ills., June, 1907.
Contains descriptions and illustrations of the following species: Glass "Snake," Mexican Horned Lizard, Pacific Horned Lizard, Plated Lizard, Regal Horned Lizard, Two-Footed Worm Lizard.

Reptiles of All Lands. By Raymond L. Ditmars. Vol. XXII, pp. 601-633, 32 ills., July, 1911.
Contains descriptions and illustrations of the following species: Black Tegu, Flying Dragon, Gecko, Gila Monster, Horned Lizard, Iguana, Malayan Kabara-Goya, Monitor, Spiny Lizard.

Stalking the Dragon Lizard on the Island of Komodo. By W. Douglas Burden. Vol. LII, pp. 216-232, 21 ills., Aug., 1927.

Ljungstedt, O. A.:

Erratic (Geologic Formation of the United States). By O. A. Ljungstedt. Vol. XXI, pp. 525-531, 4 ills., 1 three-quarters-page map, June, 1910.

Llamas:

Camels of the Clouds. By W. H. Hodge. Vol. LXXXIX, pp. 641-656, 15 ills., 1 half-page map, May, 1946.

Llangollen, Wales:

Sheep Dog Trials in Llangollen: Trained Collies Perform Marvels of Herding in the Cambrian Stakes, Open to the World. By Sara Bloch. Vol. LXXVII, pp. 559-574, 17 ills., Apr., 1940.

Lloyd, Freeman:

Field Dogs in Action. By Freeman Lloyd. Paintings by Edward Herbert Miner. Vol. LXXI, pp. 85-108, 8 ills. in black and white, 36 portraits in color, Jan., 1937.

Hark to the Hounds. By Freeman Lloyd. Paintings by Edward Herbert Miner. Vol. LXXII, pp. 453-484, 18 ills. in black and white, 31 portraits in color, Oct., 1937.

Lloyd, Freeman—Continued

Man's Oldest Ally, the Dog : Since Cave-Dweller Days This Faithful Friend Has Shared the Work, Exploration, and Sport of Humankind. By Freeman Lloyd. Paintings by Edward Herbert Miner. Vol. LXIX, pp. 247-274, 13 ills. in black and white, 33 portraits in color, Feb., 1936.

Non-sporting Dogs. By Freeman Lloyd. Paintings by Walter A. Weber. Vol. LXXXIV, pp. 569-588, 9 ills. in black and white, 8 ills. in color from paintings from life, Nov., 1943.

Toy Dogs, Pets of Kings and Commoners. By Freeman Lloyd. Vol. LXXXV, pp. 459-480, 8 ills. in black and white, 16 ills. in color, Apr., 1944.

Working Dogs of the World. By Freeman Lloyd. Paintings by Edward Herbert Miner. Vol. LXXX, pp. 776-806, 12 ills. in black and white, 20 ills. in color, Dec., 1941.

Lloyd, Henry Demarest:

Problems of the Pacific—New Zealand. By Henry Demarest Lloyd. Vol. XIII, pp. 342-352, Sept., 1902.

Lloyd's Journey Across the Great Pygmy Forest (Belgian Congo). Vol. X, pp. 26-30, Jan., 1899.

Loanda, Angola :

Angola, the Last Foothold of Slavery. Vol. XXI, pp. 625-630, 6 ills., July, 1910.

Lobos Islands, Peru :

Peru's Wealth-Producing Birds : Vast Riches in the Guano Deposits of Cormorants, Pelicans, and Petrels Which Nest on Her Barren, Rainless Coast. By R. E. Coker. Vol. XXXVII, pp. 537-566, 28 ills., June, 1920.

Lobsters:

The Maine American and the American Lobster. By John D. Lucas. Vol. LXXXIX, pp. 523-543, 19 ills., Apr., 1946.

Location of the Boundary Between Nicaragua and Costa Rica. By Arthur P. Davis. Vol. XII, pp. 22-28, 1 ill., 1 half-page map, Jan., 1901.

Lockley, R. M.:

We Live Alone, and Like It—On an Island (Skokholm). By R. M. Lockley. Vol. LXXIV, pp. 252-278, 27 ills., Aug., 1938.

Locusts:

Here and There in Northern Africa. By Frank Edward Johnson. Vol. XXV, pp. 1-132, 113 ills., Jan., 1914.

Jerusalem's Locust Plague : Being a Description of the Recent Locust Influx Into Palestine, and Comparing Same with the Ancient Locust Invasions as Narrated in the Old World's History Book, the Bible. By John D. Whiting. Vol. XXVIII, pp. 511-550, 25 ills., 1 page map, Dec., 1915.

Life in the Great Desert of Central Asia. By Ellsworth Huntington. Vol. XX, pp. 749-760, 12 ills., Aug., 1909.

Lodore Canyon, Colorado :

Experiences in the Grand Canyon. By Ellsworth and Emery Kolb. Vol. XXVI, pp. 99-184, 70 ills., 1 page map, Aug., 1914.

Logan, Mount, Canada :

Conquest of Mount Logan : North America's Second Highest Peak Yields to the Intrepid Attack of Canadian Climbers. By H. F. Lambart. Vol. XLIX, pp. 597-631, 40 ills., June, 1926.

Loire (River), France :

Beauty, History, and Romance Enrich the Château Country. 10 ills. in color from autochromes by Gervais Courtellemont. Vol. LVIII, pp. 466-475, Oct., 1930.

Château Land—France's Pageant on the Loire. Vol. LVIII, pp. 466-475, 10 ills. in color, Oct., 1930.

Lois (Tribespeople) .

Among the Big Knot Lois of Hainan : Wild Tribesmen With Topknots Roam the Little-known Interior of This Big and Strategically Important Island in the China Sea. By Leonard Clark. Vol. LXXIV, pp. 391-418, 28 ills., 1 two-thirds-page map, Sept., 1938.

Loja, Ecuador :

Over Trail and Through Jungle in Ecuador : Indian Head-Hunters of the Interior, an Interesting Study in the South American Republic. By H. E. Anthony. Vol. XL, pp. 327-352, 28 ills., Oct., 1921.

Lombardy (Department), Italy :

Inexhaustible Italy. By Arthur Stanley Riggs. Vol. XXX, pp. 273-368, 76 ills., 1 page map, Oct., 1916.

Lomen, Carl J.:

Camel of the Frozen Desert (Reindeer). By Carl J. Lomen. Vol. XXXVI, pp. 538-556, 19 ills., Dec., 1919.

London, England :

Along London's Coronation Route. By Maynard Owen Williams. Vol. LXXI, pp. 609-632, 22 ills., 1 half-page map, May, 1937.

As London Toils and Spins. By Frederick Simpich. Vol. LXXI, pp. 1-57, 38 ills. in black and white, 23 ills. in color, Jan., 1937.

Black-Headed Gulls in London. By A. H. Hall. Vol. XLVII, pp. 664-672, 16 ills., June, 1925.

Democracy's Royal Palace. 19 ills. in color from natural-color photographs by B. Anthony Stewart. Vol. XC, pp. 233-248, Aug., 1946.

Everyday Life in Wartime England. By Harvey Klemmer. Vol. LXXIX, pp. 497-534, 48 ills., Apr., 1941.

Highlights of London Town. 15 ills. in color from autochromes by Clifton Adams. Vol. LV, pp. 568-577, May, 1929.

London. By Florence Craig Albrecht. Vol. XXVIII, pp. 263-294, 28 ills., Sept., 1915.

London, England—*Continued*

London from a Bus Top. By Herbert Corey. Vol. XLIX, pp. 551-596, 44 ills., May, 1926.

London Wins the Battle. By Marquis W. Childs. Vol. LXXXVIII, pp. 129-152, 21 ills., Aug., 1945.

Pomp and Pulse of Modern London. 23 ills. in color from natural-color photographs by B. Anthony Stewart. Vol. LXXI, pp. 17-48, Jan., 1937.

Shadowy London by Night. 8 ills. by H. B. Burdekin. Vol. LXVIII, pp. 177-184, Aug., 1935.

Some Forgotten Corners of London : Many Places of Beauty and Historic Interest Repay the Search of the Inquiring Visitor. By Harold Donaldson Eberlein. Vol. LXI, pp. 163-198, 25 ills., Feb., 1932.

Vagabonding in England : A Young American Works His Way Around the British Isles and Sees Sights from an Unusual Point of View. By John McWilliams. Vol. LXV, pp. 357-398, 39 ills., 1 three-quarters-page map, Mar., 1934.

When GI Joes Took London. By Maj. Frederick Simpich, Jr. Vol. LXXXVI, pp. 337-354, 18 ills., Sept., 1944.

Yanks at Westminster. By Capt. Leonard David Gammans. Vol. XC, pp. 223-252, 6 ills. in black and white, 19 ills. in color, Aug., 1946.

Lonely Australia : The Unique Continent. By Herbert E. Gregory. Vol. XXX, pp. 473-568, 68 ills., 1 two-page and 4 half-page maps, Dec., 1916.

Long, E. John:

Guatemala Interlude : In the Land of the Quetzal a Modern Capital Contrasts With Primitive Indian Villages and the "Pompeii of America." By E. John Long. Vol. LXX, pp. 429-460, 22 ills. in black and white, 13 ills. in color, 1 page map, Oct., 1936.

Happy Landing in Bermuda. By E. John Long. Vol. LXXV, pp. 213-238, 14 ills. in black and white, 12 ills. in color, Feb., 1939.

Mid-Ocean Color Log (Bermuda). 12 ills. in color from natural-color photographs ; 9 ills. by E. John Long. Vol. LXXV, pp. 221-228, Feb., 1939.

Montserrat, Spain's Mountain Shrine. By E. John Long. Vol. LXIII, pp. 121-130, 10 ills., Jan., 1933.

New Jersey Now ! By E. John Long. Vol. LXIII, pp. 519-583, 49 ills. in black and white, 24 ills. in color, 1 page and 1 two-thirds-page maps, May, 1933.

Oxford, Mother of Anglo-Saxon Learning. By E. John Long. Vol. LVI, pp. 563-596, 31 ills., Nov., 1929.

Puerto Rico : Watchdog of the Caribbean : Venerable Domain Under American Flag Has New Role as West Indian Stronghold and Sentinel of the Panama Canal. By E. John Long. Vol. LXXVI, pp. 697-738, 24 ills. in black and white, 23 ills. in color, Dec., 1939.

Long Island, New York :

Bright Patterns of Long Island Life. 18 ills. in color from natural-color photographs ; 14 ills. by Willard R. Culver. Vol. LXXV, pp. 429-460, Apr., 1939.

Marvels of Mycetozoa : Exploration of a Long Island Swamp Reveals Some of the Secrets of the Slime Molds, Dwelling on the Borderland Between the Plant and Animal Kingdoms. By William Crowder. Vol. XLIX, pp. 421-443, 5 ills. in black and white, 16 ills. in color, Apr., 1926.

Spin Your Globe to Long Island : Only Six States Have More People than the Insular Empire that Ranges from a World's Fair Through Potato Patches, Princely Estates, and Historic Shrines. By Frederick Simpich. Vol. LXXV, pp. 413-460, 25 ills. in black and white, 18 ills. in color, Apr., 1939.

Long Palei (Village), Sarawak :

Sarawak : The Land of the White Rajahs. By Harrison W. Smith. Vol. XXXV, pp. 110-167, 58 ills., 1 half-page map, Feb., 1919.

Long River of New England : In War and Peace, from Mountain Wilderness to the Sea, Flows the Connecticut River, Through a Valley Abounding in History, Scenery, Inventive Genius, and Industry. By Albert W. Atwood. Vol. LXXXIII, pp. 401-434, 12 ills. in black and white, 24 ills. in color, 1 two-thirds-page map, Apr., 1943.

Longevity:

Who Shall Inherit Long Life ? On the Existence of a Natural Process at Work Among Human Beings Tending to Improve the Vigor and Vitality of Succeeding Generations. By Alexander Graham Bell. Vol. XXXV, pp. 505-514, 13 ills., June, 1919.

Longitudinal Journey Through Chile. By Harriet Chalmers Adams. Vol. XLII, pp. 219-273, 60 ills., 1 half-page map, Sept., 1922.

Longley, W. H.:

First Autochromes from the Ocean Bottom : Marine Life in Its Natural Habitat Along the Florida Keys Is Successfully Photographed in Colors. Vol. LI, pp. 56-61, 8 ills. in color, Jan., 1927.

Life on a Coral Reef : The Fertility and Mystery of the Sea Studied Beneath the Waters Surrounding Dry Tortugas. By W. H. Longley. Vol. LI, pp. 61-83, 22 ills. in black and white, 8 ills. in color, Jan., 1927.

Looking Down on Europe : The Thrills and Advantages of Sight-Seeing by Airplane, as Demonstrated on a 6,500-Mile Tour Over Commercial Aviation Routes. By Lieut. J. Parker Van Zandt. Vol. XLVII, pp. 261-326, 67 ills., 1 half-page map, Mar., 1925.

Looking Down on Europe Again : Crisscrossing Air Tracks Reveal Nature's Scenic Masterpieces and Man's Swift-changing Boundaries and Structures. By J. Parker Van Zandt. Vol. LXXV, pp. 791-822, 31 ills., 1 page map, June, 1939.

Looking in on the Everyday Life of New Turkey. 12 ills. in color from natural-color photographs by Herman H. Kreider, Maynard Owen Williams, and Gervais Courtellemont. Vol. LXI, pp. 499-509, Apr., 1932.

Loons (Birds) :

Birds of Lake and Lagoon, Marsh and Seacoast. 6 portraits in color from paintings by Maj. Allan Brooks. Vol. LXV, pp. 313-328, Mar., 1934.

Birds of Timberline and Tundra. By Arthur A. Allen. With 24 ills. in color from natural-color photographs by the author. Vol. XC, pp. 313-339, 8 ills. in black and white, Sept., 1946.

Birds That Cruise the Coast and Inland Waters. By T. Gilbert Pearson. Paintings by Maj. Allan Brooks. Vol. LXV, pp. 299-328, 1 ill. in black and white, 6 portraits in color, Mar., 1934.

Lop Basin, Sinkiang :

Medieval Tales of the Lop Basin in Central Asia. By Ellsworth Huntington. Vol. XIX, pp. 288-295, 9 ills., Apr., 1908.

Lord Howe (Island), New South Wales :

Paradise of the Tasman : A Pacific Island Provides the Palms Which Decorate Hotels, Churches, Steamships, and Homes. By Hubert Lyman Clark. Vol. LXVIII, pp. 115-136, 24 ills., 1 half-page map, July, 1935.

Lord Howe Islands. *See* Ontong Java.

Lords of the Rockies : Photographing Big Game Animals in Their Primeval Surroundings, from Arizona to Canada, Brings Adventure to Two Wilderness Wanderers. By Wendell and Lucie Chapman. Vol. LXXVI, pp. 87-128, 14 ills. in black and white, 28 ills. in color, July, 1939.

Lorian Swamp, Kenya Colony :

When a Drought Blights Africa : Hippos and Elephants Are Driven Insane by Suffering, in the Lorian Swamp, Kenya Colony. By Capt. A. T. Curle. Vol. LV, pp. 521-528, 9 ills., Apr., 1929.

Lorraine (Region), France :

A City Learns to Smile Again (Nancy, France). By Maj. Frederick G. Vosburgh. Vol. LXXXVII, pp. 361-384, 23 ills., 1 two-thirds-page map, Mar., 1945.

In French Lorraine : That Part of France Where the First American Soldiers Have Fallen. By Harriet Chalmers Adams. Vol. XXXII, pp. 499-518, 16 ills., Nov.-Dec., 1917.

Los Angeles, California :

Carrying Water Through a Desert : The Story of the Los Angeles Aqueduct. By Burt A. Heinly. Vol. XXI, pp. 568-596, 19 ills., 1 half-page map, July, 1910.

Southern California at Work. By Frederick Simpich. Vol. LXVI, pp. 529-600, 39 ills. in black and white, 41 ills. in color, 1 two-page map, Nov., 1934.

Loss of Life by Lightning. Vol. XIII, p. 115, Mar., 1902.

Loss of Property From Lightning. Vol. XII, p. 82, Feb., 1901.

Lost Boundary of Texas. By Marcus Baker. Vol. XII, pp. 430-432, Dec., 1901.

Lost Wealth of the Kings of Midas. By Ellsworth Huntington. Vol. XXI, pp. 831-846, 15 ills., Oct., 1910.

Louden, Orren R.:

Circus : Color Camera Explores the Country That Moves by Night. 5 ills. in color from natural-color photographs by Orren R. Louden. Vol. LX, pp. 478-511, Oct., 1931.

Gettysburg : Most Famous Battle Field in America. 5 ills. in color from natural-color photographs by Orren R. Louden. Vol. LX, pp. 66-75, July, 1931.

Washington, D. C.: Our Colorful City of Magnificent Distances. 7 ills. in color from natural-color photographs by Orren R. Louden. Vol. LX, pp. 530-611, Nov., 1931.

Washington, D. C. : Secrets of Washington's Lure. 7 ills. in color from natural-color photographs by Orren R. Louden. Vol. LVII, pp. 376-385, Mar., 1930.

Washington, D. C. : Springtime Wreathes a Garland for the Nation's Capital. 13 ills. in color from natural-color photographs ; 3 ills. by Orren R. Louden. Vol. LXVII, pp. 473-480, Apr., 1935.

Louisiana:

Color Camera Records of New Orleans. 15 ills. in color from natural-color photographs by Edwin L. Wisherd. Vol. LVII, pp. 458-467, Apr., 1930.

Delectable Shrimp : Once a Culinary Stepchild, Today a Gulf Coast Industry. By Harlan Major. Vol. LXXXVI, pp. 501-512, 11 ills., 1 two-thirds-page map, Oct., 1944.

Flecks of Color in the Fertile Fields of Louisiana. 14 ills. in color from natural-color photographs by Edwin L. Wisherd. Vol. LVII, pp. 418-427, Apr., 1930.

Great Mississippi Flood of 1927 : Since White Man's Discovery This Mighty River Has Served Him Well, Yet It Has Brought Widespread Devastation Along Its Lower Reaches. By Frederick Simpich. Vol. LII, pp. 243-289, 53 ills., 1 half-page map, Sept., 1927.

How We Use the Gulf of Mexico. By Frederick Simpich. Vol. LXXXV, pp. 1-40, 20 ills. in black and white, 19 ills. in color, 1 two-page map, Jan., 1944.

Louisiana, Land of Perpetual Romance. By Ralph A. Graves. Vol. LVII, pp. 393-482, 84 ills. in black and white, 29 ills. in color, special map supplement in colors, Apr., 1930.

Louisiana Purchase:

Boundaries of Territorial Acquisitions. Vol. XII, pp. 373-377, 1 page chart, Oct., 1901.

Love Terns (Birds). *See* Fairy Terns.

Low Countries Await Liberation (Belgium and Netherlands). 10 ills. from photographs. Vol. LXXXVI, pp. 221-228, Aug., 1944.

Low Road, High Road, Around Dundee (Scotland). By Maurice P. Dunlap. Vol. LXIX, pp. 547-576, 35 ills., 1 half-page map, Apr., 1936.

Lowdermilk, Walter C.:
China Fights Erosion with U. S. Aid. By Walter C. Lowdermilk. Vol. LXXXVII, pp. 641-680, 10 ills. in black and white, 26 ills. in color, June, 1945.

Lower California. *See* Baja California.

Lowest Point in the United States (Death Valley, California). Vol. XVIII, pp. 824-825, Dec., 1907.

LSTs (Landing Ship, Tank) :
Landing Craft for Invasion. By Melville Bell Grosvenor. Vol. LXXXVI, pp. 1-30, 26 ills., July, 1944.

Lualaba (River), Belgian Congo :
Transporting a Navy Through the Jungles of Africa in War Time. By Frank J. Magee. Vol. XLII, pp. 331-362, 31 ills., Oct., 1922.

Lucas, John D.:
The Maine American and the American Lobster. By John D. Lucas. Vol. LXXXIX, pp. 523-543, 19 ills., Apr., 1946.

Lucia Glacier, Alaska :
National Geographic Society's Alaskan Expedition of 1909. By Ralph S. Tarr and Lawrence Martin. Vol. XXI, pp. 1-54, 42 ills., 4 page and 7 half-page maps, Jan., 1910.

Lugano, Lake, Italy :
Frontier Cities of Italy. By Florence Craig Albrecht. Vol. XXVII, pp. 533-586, 45 ills., June, 1915.

Gems of the Italian Lakes. By Arthur Ellis Mayer. Vol. XXIV, pp. 943-956, 13 ills., Aug., 1913.

Luke, (Sir) Harry:
Maltese Islands : Cicero's Land of "Honey and Roses," and Stronghold of the Knights, Again Is Focus of Naval Strategy. By Sir Harry Luke. Vol. LXVIII, pp. 647-666, 20 ills., 1 half-page and 1 third-page maps, Nov., 1935.

Lumber Business of the Government. Vol. XVII, pp. 531-533, Sept., 1906.

Lumbering:
Influence of Forestry upon the Lumber Industry of the United States. By Overton W. Price. Vol. XIV, pp. 381-386, 2 ills., Oct., 1903.

Lumber Business of the Government. Vol. XVII, pp. 531-533, Sept., 1906.

Lumbering in Manchuria. By Henry B. Miller. Vol. XV, pp. 130-132, 2 ills., Mar., 1904.

Redwood Forest of the Pacific Coast. By Henry Gannett. Vol. X, pp. 145-159, 6 ills., 1 page map, May, 1899.

Working Teak in the Burma Forests : The Sagacious Elephant Is Man's Ablest Ally in the Logging Industry of the Far East. By A. W. Smith. Vol. LVIII, pp. 239-256, 5 ills. in black and white, 15 ills. in color, Aug., 1930.

Luminous Life in the Depths of the Sea. 8 ills. in color from paintings by E. Bostelmann. Vol. LIX, pp. 667-674, June, 1931.

Lunéville, France :
In French Lorraine : That Part of France Where the First American Soldiers Have Fallen. By Harriet Chalmers Adams. Vol. XXXII, pp. 499-518, 16 ills., Nov.-Dec., 1917.

Luray Caverns, Virginia :
Luray Caverns. Vol. XVII, pp. 358-362, 3 ills., June, 1906.

Skeleton in Luray Cave. By H. C. Hovey. Vol. XVII, pp. 425-426, July, 1906.

Lure of Lima, City of the Kings. By William Joseph Showalter. Vol. LVII, pp. 727-784, 41 ills., June, 1930.

Lure of the Frozen Desert (Polar Regions). Vol. XXII, panorama, Dec., 1912.

Lure of the Land of Ice (Antarctic Regions). Vol. XLV, pp. 255-270, 16 ills., Mar., 1924.

Lurs (Tribespeople) :
Mountain Tribes of Iran and Iraq. By Harold Lamb. Vol. LXXXIX, pp. 385-408, 15 ills., 1 two-page map, Mar., 1946.

Luster of Ancient Mexico (Aztecs). By William H. Prescott. Vol. XXX, pp. 1-32, 22 ills., July, 1916.

Luxembourg (Grand Duchy) :
Grand Duchy of Luxemburg: A Miniature Democratic State of Many Charms Against a Feudal Background. By Maynard Owen Williams. Vol. XLVI, pp. 501-528, 28 ills., 1 quarter-page map, Nov., 1924.

Luxor, Egypt :
Resurrection of Ancient Egypt. By James Baikie. Vol. XXIV, pp. 957-1020, 46 ills., 1 page map, Sept., 1913.

Luzon (Island), Philippine Islands :
Camera Cruising in the Philippines. 12 ills. in color from natural-color photographs by J. Baylor Roberts, Fenno Jacobs, and others. Vol. LXXXVI, pp. 545-552, Nov., 1944.

Field Sports Among the Wild Men of Northern Luzon. By Dean C. Worcester. Vol. XXII, pp. 215-267, 17 ills., 1 half-page map, Mar., 1911.

Head-Hunters of Northern Luzon. By Dean C. Worcester. Vol. XXIII, pp. 833-930, 102 ills., 1 page map, Sept., 1912.

Non-Christian Peoples of the Philippine Islands. By Dean C. Worcester. Vol. XXIV, pp. 1157-1256, 41 ills. in black and white, 48 ills. in color, Nov., 1913.

Taal Volcano and Its Recent Destructive Eruption. By Dean C. Worcester. Vol. XXIII, pp. 313-368, 40 ills., 4 half-page maps, 1 diagram. Apr., 1912.

What Luzon Means to Uncle Sam. By Frederick Simpich. Vol. LXXXVII, pp. 305-332, 25 ills., special map supplement, Mar., 1945.

Lyon, Ernest:

Black Republic—Liberia. By Sir Harry Johnston and Ernest Lyon. Vol. XVIII, pp. 334-343, 9 ills., May, 1907.

Lyttelton, New Zealand:

Sailing the Seven Seas in the Interest of Science: Adventures Through 157,000 Miles of Storm and Calm, from Arctic to Antarctic and Around the World in the Non-Magnetic Yacht *Carnegie*. By J. P. Ault. Vol. XLII, pp. 631-690, 47 ills., 1 chart, Dec., 1922.

M

Macao, China. *See* Macau.

MacAskill, W. R.:

Tartan Tints New Scotland (Nova Scotia). 21 ills. in color from natural-color photographs by John Mills, Jr., W. R. MacAskill, and others. Vol. LXXVII, pp. 591-622, May, 1940.

Macau, China:

Macao, "Land of Sweet Sadness": The Oldest European Settlement in the Far East, Long the Only Haven for Distressed Mariners in the China Sea. By Edgar Allen Forbes. Vol. LXII, pp. 337-357, 13 ills. in black and white, 11 ills. in color, Sept., 1932.

Miniatures of Macao. 11 ills. in color from natural-color photographs by W. Robert Moore. Vol. LXII, pp. 340-349, Sept., 1932.

Macaulay, (Hon.) T. B.:

How Canada Went to the Front. By T. B. Macaulay. Vol. XXXIV, pp. 297-307, 6 ills., Oct., 1918.

McBride, Harry A.:

From Granada to Gibraltar—A Tour of Southern Spain. By Harry A. McBride. Vol. XLVI, pp. 205-232, 23 ills., Aug., 1924.

Land of the Basques: Home of a Thrifty, Picturesque People, Who Take Pride in the Sobriquet, "The Yankees of Spain." By Harry A. McBride. Vol. XLI, pp. 63-87, 25 ills., 1 three-quarters-page map, Jan., 1922.

Land of the Free in Africa. By Harry A. McBride. Vol. XLII, pp. 411-430, 22 ills., Oct., 1922.

On the Bypaths of Spain. By Harry A. McBride. Vol. LV, pp. 311-364, 50 ills. in black and white, 13 ills. in color, 1 two-thirds-page map, Mar., 1929.

Pursuing Spanish Bypaths Northwest of Madrid. By Harry A. McBride. Vol. LIX, pp. 121-130, 6 ills. in black and white, 12 ills. in color, 1 two-thirds-page map, Jan., 1931.

McBride, Ruth Q.:

Keeping House on the Congo. By Ruth Q. McBride. Vol. LXXII, pp. 643-670, 29 ills., Nov., 1937.

Old Masters in a New National Gallery. By Ruth Q. McBride. Vol. LXXVIII, pp. 1-50, 11 ills. in black and white, 32 color reproductions of masterpieces, July, 1940.

McBride, Ruth Q.—*Continued*

Turbulent Spain. By Ruth Q. McBride. Vol LXX, pp. 397-427, 25 ills., 1 two-page map, Oct., 1936.

McCandless, Byron:

Correct Display of the Stars and Stripes. By Gilbert Grosvenor and Byron McCandless. Vol. XXXII, pp. 404-413, 8 ills., Oct., 1917.

Flags Famous in American History. By Gilbert Grosvenor and Byron McCandless. Vol. XXXII, pp. 341-361, 92 ills. in color, Oct., 1917.

Flags of Austria-Hungary, Bulgaria, Germany, and Turkey. By Gilbert Grosvenor and Byron McCandless. Vol. XXXII, pp. 386-388, 38 ills. in color, Oct., 1917.

Flags of Europe, Asia, and Africa. By Gilbert Grosvenor and Byron McCandless. Vol. XXXII, pp. 372-385, 100 ills. in color, Oct., 1917.

Flags of Our Army, Navy, and Government Departments. By Gilbert Grosvenor and Byron McCandless. Vol. XXXII, pp. 305-322, 3 ills. in black and white, 300 ills. in color, Oct., 1917.

Flags of Pan-America. By Gilbert Grosvenor and Byron McCandless. Vol. XXXII, pp. 361-369, 62 ills. in color, Oct., 1917.

Flags of the British Empire. By Gilbert Grosvenor and Byron McCandless. Vol. XXXII, pp. 378-385, 158 ills. in color, Oct., 1917.

Heroic Flags of the Middle Ages. By Gilbert Grosvenor and Byron McCandless. Vol. XXXII, pp. 388-399, 96 ills. in color, Oct., 1917.

Insignia of the Uniformed Forces of the United States. By Gilbert Grosvenor and Byron McCandless. Vol. XXXII, pp. 413-419, 318 ills., Oct., 1917.

Naval Flags of the World. By Gilbert Grosvenor and Byron McCandless. Vol. XXXII, pp. 347-369, 211 ills. in color, Oct., 1917.

Our State Flags. By Gilbert Grosvenor and Byron McCandless. Vol. XXXII, pp. 323-341, 1 ill. in black and white, 57 ills. in color, Oct., 1917.

Pennants of Patriotism 200 Years Ago. By Gilbert Grosvenor and Byron McCandless. Vol. XXXII, pp. 399-403, 75 ills. in color, Oct., 1917.

Story of the American Flag. By Gilbert Grosvenor and Byron McCandless. Vol. XXXII, pp. 286-303, 12 ills., Oct., 1917.

McCartney, (Lt.) Benjamin C.:

Northern Italy: Scenic Battleground. 18 ills. in color from natural-color photographs; 13 ills. by B. Anthony Stewart and 3 ills. by Lt. Benjamin C. McCartney. Vol. LXXXVII, pp. 265-288, Mar., 1945.

Return to Florence. By 1st Lt. Benjamin C. McCartney. Vol. LXXXVII, pp. 257-296, 18 ills. in black and white, 18 ills. in color, Mar., 1945.

McClure, Henry Herbert:

Shortening Time Across the Continent. By Henry Herbert McClure. Vol. XIII, pp. 319-321, Aug., 1902.

McCormick, Elsie:

"Where the Mountains Walked": An Account of the Recent Earthquake in Kansu Province, China, Which Destroyed 100,000 Lives. By Upton Close and Elsie McCormick. Vol. XLI, pp. 445-464, 23 ills., 1 three-quarters-page map, May, 1922.

McCormick, Frederick:

China's Treasures. By Frederick McCormick. Vol. XXIII, pp. 996-1040, 50 ills., Oct., 1912.

Present Conditions in China. By Frederick McCormick. Vol. XXII, pp. 1120-1138, 12 ills., Dec., 1911.

MacCracken, William P.:

President Coolidge Bestows Lindbergh Award: The National Geographic Society's Hubbard Medal Is Presented to Aviator Before the Most Notable Gathering in the History of Washington (Address by Secretary MacCracken). Vol. LIII, pp. 132-140, 4 ills., Jan., 1928.

McCrindle, (Maj.) J. R.:

Flying Over Egypt, Sinai, and Palestine: Looking Down Upon the Holy Land During an Air Journey of Two and a Half Hours from Cairo to Jerusalem. By Brig. Gen. P. R. C. Groves and Maj. J. R. McCrindle. Vol. L, pp. 313-355, 26 ills., 1 half-page map, Sept., 1926.

McCudden, James Byford:

Aces Among Aces. By Laurence La Tourette Driggs. Vol. XXXIII, pp. 568-580, 9 ills., June, 1918.

McCurdy, Arthur W.:

Factors Which Modify the Climate of Victoria, British Columbia. By Arthur W. McCurdy. Vol. XVIII, pp. 345-348, 2 quarter-page maps, May, 1907.

MacDougal, (Dr.) Daniel T.:

More Changes of the Colorado River. By D. T. MacDougal. Vol. XIX, pp. 52-54, 1 page map, Jan., 1908.

Notes on the Deserts of the United States and Mexico (Extracted from a Publication of Dr. Daniel T. MacDougal). Vol. XXI, pp. 691-714, 16 ills., Aug., 1910.

Macedonia:

"Grass Never Grows Where the Turkish Hoof Has Trod." By Edwin Pears. Vol. XXIII, pp. 1132-1148, 19 ills., Nov., 1912.

Great Turk and His Lost Provinces. By William E. Curtis. Vol. XIV, pp. 45-61, 7 ills., Feb., 1903.

Hoary Monasteries of Mount Athos. By H. G. Dwight. Vol. XXX, pp. 249-272, 24 ills., 1 half-page map, Sept., 1916.

New Greece, the Centenarian, Forges Ahead. By Maynard Owen Williams. Vol. LXIII, pp. 649-721, 51 ills. in black and white, 40 ills. in color, 1 three-quarters-page map, Dec., 1930.

Notes on Macedonia. Vol. XIX, pp. 790-802, 15 ills., 1 page map, Nov., 1908.

On the Monastir Road. By Herbert Corey. Vol. XXXI, pp. 383-412, 31 ills., May, 1917.

Macedonia—_Continued_

Races and Religions of Macedonia. By Luigi Villari. Vol. XXIII, pp. 1118-1132, 14 ills., Nov., 1912.

Saloniki. By H. G. Dwight. Vol. XXX, pp. 203-232, 28 ills., Sept., 1916.

Whirlpool of the Balkans. By George Higgins Moses. Vol. XXXIX, pp. 179-197, 15 ills., Feb., 1921.

McGee, Anita Newcomb:

Judge of Prize Essay Contest. Vol. X, p. 32, Jan., 1899.

McGee, W J:

Asia: The Cradle of Humanity. By W J McGee. Vol. XII, pp. 281-290, Aug., 1901.

Chairman of Committee on Eighth International Geographic Congress. Vol. XIV, pp. 254-255, June, 1903.

Dr. Bell's Survey in Baffinland. By W J McGee. Vol. XIII, p. 113, Mar., 1902.

Ice Caves and Frozen Wells. By W J McGee. Vol. XII, pp. 433-434, Dec., 1901.

Isthmian Canal Problem. By W J McGee. Vol. X, pp. 363-364, Sept., 1899.

Lessons of Galveston. By W J McGee. Vol. XI, pp. 377-383, Oct., 1900.

National Growth and National Character. By W J McGee. Vol. X, pp. 185-206, June, 1899.

New Home of the National Geographic Society (Election of W J McGee as President of The Society). Vol. XV, pp. 176-181, 5 ills., Apr., 1904.

Old Yuma Trail. By W J McGee. Part I. Vol. XII, pp. 103-107, Mar., 1901. Part II, Vol. XII, pp. 129-143, 7 ills., 1 page map, Apr., 1901.

Problems of the Pacific—The Great Ocean in World Growth. By W J McGee. Vol. XIII, pp. 333-342, Sept., 1902.

Work of the Bureau of American Ethnology. By W J McGee. Vol. XII, pp. 369-372, Oct., 1901.

MacGillivray, James:

Mickey the Beaver: An Animal Engineer Performs for the Camera as a Star in the Activities of His Species. By James MacGillivray. Vol. LIV, pp. 741-756, 23 ills., Dec., 1928.

McGregor Mountain, Washington:

Forest Lookout. By Ella E. Clark. With 9 ills. in color from natural-color photographs by the author. Vol. XC, pp. 73-96, 8 ills. in black and white, July, 1946.

McGuire, Bird S.:

Big Oklahoma. By Bird S. McGuire. Vol. XVII, pp. 103-105, 1 ill., Feb., 1906.

Machines Come to Mississippi. By J. R. Hildebrand. Vol. LXXII, pp. 263-318, 34 ills. in black and white, 26 ills. in color, 1 two-page map, Sept., 1937.

Machu Picchu, Peru:

Further Explorations in the Land of the Incas: The Peruvian Expedition of 1915 of the National Geographic Society and Yale University. By Hiram Bingham. Vol. XXIX, pp. 431-473, 29 ills., 1 page and 1 half-page maps, panorama, May, 1916.

Honors to Amundsen and Peary (National Geographic Society Banquet). Vol. XXIV, pp. 113-130, 5 ills., Jan., 1913.

In the Wonderland of Peru. By Hiram Bingham. Vol. XXIV, pp. 387-574, 250 ills., 1 three-quarters-page map, 3 diagrams, Apr., 1913.

Pith of Peru: A Journey from Talara to Machu Picchu, with Memorable Stopovers. By Henry Albert Phillips. Vol. LXXXII, pp. 167-196, 6 ills. in black and white, 20 ills. in color, 1 page map, Aug., 1942.

Ruins of an Ancient Inca Capital. Vol. XXIV, panorama, Apr., 1913.

Story of Machu Picchu: The Peruvian Expedition of the National Geographic Society and Yale University. By Hiram Bingham. Vol. XXVII, pp. 171-217, 35 ills., Feb., 1915.

Mack, Siukee:

Changing Canton (China). 20 ills. from photographs by Siukee Mack, Alfred T. Palmer, and Kinchue Wong. Vol. LXXII, pp. 711-726, Dec., 1937.

MacKenzie, Catherine Dunlop:

Charm of Cape Breton Island: The Most Picturesque Portion of Canada's Maritime Provinces—A Land Rich in Historic Associations, Natural Resources, and Geographic Appeal. By Catherine Dunlop MacKenzie. Vol. XXXVIII, pp. 34-60, 22 ills., 1 three-quarters-page map, July, 1920.

McKenzie, Kenneth:

East of the Adriatic: Notes on Dalmatia, Montenegro, Bosnia, and Herzegovina. By Kenneth McKenzie. Vol. XXIII, pp. 1159-1187, 37 ills., 1 page map, Dec., 1912.

Mackenzie (River), Canada:

On Mackenzie's Trail to the Polar Sea. By Amos Burg. Vol. LX, pp. 127-156, 32 ills., 1 page map, Aug., 1931.

Mackinder, H. J.:

Geographical Pivot of History (Steppes of Central Asia). By H. J. Mackinder. Vol. XV, pp. 331-335, Aug., 1904.

McKinley, (Capt.) Ashley C.:

Mapping the Antarctic from the Air: The Aërial Camera Earns Its Place as the Eyes and Memory of the Explorer. By Capt. Ashley C. McKinley. Vol. LXII, pp. 471-485, 13 ills., special map supplement, Oct., 1932.

McKinley, William:

Proceedings of the National Geographic Society, Session 1898-'99 (Election of President McKinley to Honorary Membership in The Society). Vol. X, pp. 143-144, Apr., 1899.

McKinley, Mount, Alaska:

Fit to Fight Anywhere (Quartermaster Corps Expedition). By Frederick Simpich. Vol. LXXXIV, pp. 233-256, 26 ills., Aug., 1943.

Game Country Without Rival in America: The Proposed Mount McKinley National Park. By Stephen R. Capps. Vol. XXXI, pp. 69-84, 14 ills., 1 half-page map, Jan., 1917.

Monarchs of Alaska. By R. H. Sargent. Vol. XX, pp. 610-623, 9 ills., July, 1909.

Mount McKinley. By Robert Muldrow. Vol. XII, pp. 312-313, 1 half-page map, Aug., 1901.

Over the Roof of Our Continent. By Bradford Washburn. Vol. LXXIV, pp. 78-98, 17 ills. in duotone, 1 half-page map, July, 1938.

Plan for Climbing Mt. McKinley. By Alfred H. Brooks and D. L. Reaburn. Vol. XIV, pp. 30-35, 1 page map, Jan., 1903.

McKnew, Thomas W.:

McKnew, Thomas W.: Impressing the Society's Seal on Membership Certificate. Vol. XC, ill. 39, July, 1946.

McLeish, Donald:

In the Land of Windmills and Wooden Shoes. 16 ills. from photographs by Donald McLeish. Vol. XLIII, pp. 297-312, Mar., 1923.

Italy, France, Switzerland. 10 ills. in color from photographs by Donald McLeish. Vol. XXVIII, pp. 439-450, Nov., 1915.

Vacation in Holland. 8 ills. in color from photographs by Donald McLeish. Vol. LVI, pp. 366-375, Sept., 1929.

McMaster, John Bach:

Judge of Prize Essay Contest. Vol. X, p. 32, Jan., 1899.

MacMillan, Donald B.:

Bowdoin (Ship) in North Greenland: Arctic Explorers Place Tablet to Commemorate Sacrifices of the Lady Franklin Bay Expedition. Vol. XLVII, pp. 677-722, 49 ills., June, 1925.

MacMillan Arctic Expedition Returns: U. S. Navy Planes Make First Series of Overland Flights in the Arctic and National Geographic Society Staff Obtains Valuable Data and Specimens for Scientific Study. By Donald B. MacMillan. Vol. XLVIII, pp. 477-518, 42 ills., Nov., 1925.

Peary as a Leader: Incidents from the Life of the Discoverer of the North Pole Told by One of His Lieutenants on the Expedition Which Reached the Goal. Vol. XXXVII, pp. 293-317, 20 ills., 1 page map, Apr., 1920.

MacMillan Arctic Expeditions:

Bowdoin (Ship) in North Greenland: Arctic Explorers Place Tablet to Commemorate Sacrifices of the Lady Franklin Bay Expedition. Vol. XLVII, pp. 677-722, 49 ills., June, 1925.

First Natural-Color Photographs from the Arctic. 22 ills. in color from natural-color photographs by Maynard Owen Williams and Jacob Gayer. Vol. XLIX, pp. 300-317, Mar., 1926.

MacMillan Arctic Expeditions—*Continued*

Flying Over the Arctic. By Lieut. Comdr. Richard E. Byrd. Vol. XLVIII, pp. 519-532, 10 ills., Nov., 1925.

MacMillan Arctic Expedition Returns : U. S. Navy Planes Make First Series of Overland Flights in the Arctic and National Geographic Society Staff Obtains Valuable Data and Specimens for Scientific Study. By Donald B. MacMillan. Vol. XLVIII, pp. 477-518, 42 ills., Nov., 1925.

MacMillan Arctic Expedition Sails. Vol. XLVIII, pp. 225-226, 3 ills., Aug., 1925.

MacMillan in the Field. Vol. XLVIII, pp. 473-476, 3 ills., Oct., 1925.

Naturalist with MacMillan in the Arctic. By Walter N. Koelz. Vol. XLIX, pp. 299-318, 22 ills. in color, Mar., 1926.

Scientific Aspects of the MacMillan Arctic Expedition. Vol. XLVIII, pp. 349-354, 5 ills., Sept., 1925.

To Seek the Unknown in the Arctic : United States Navy Flyers to Aid MacMillan Expedition Under the Auspices of the National Geographic Society in Exploring Vast Area. Vol. XLVII, pp. 673-675, 1 ill., 1 half-page map, June, 1925.

McMillin, Stewart E.:

Heart of Aymará Land : A Visit to Tiahuanacu, Perhaps the Oldest City of the New World, Lost Beneath the Drifting Sand of Centuries in the Bolivian Highlands. By Stewart E. McMillin. Vol. LI, pp. 213-256, 23 ills. in black and white, 18 ills. in color, 1 half-page map, Feb., 1927.

McNally, Paul A.:

Observing a Total Eclipse of the Sun : Dimming Solar Light for a Few Seconds Entails Years of Work for Science and Attracts Throngs to "Nature's Most Magnificent Spectacle." By Paul A. McNally. Vol. LXII, pp. 597-605, 6 ills., Nov., 1932.

MacNeal, Herbert P.:

Casablanca Smiles. 10 ills. in color from natural-color photographs by Herbert P. MacNeal. Vol. LXXXIV, pp. 17-24, July, 1943.

Macready, (Lt.) John A.:

Exploring the Earth's Stratosphere : The Holder of the American Altitude Record Describes His Experiences in Reaching the "Ceiling" of His Plane at an Elevation of Nearly Eight Miles. By Lieut. John A. Macready. Vol. L, pp. 755-776, 18 ills., Dec., 1926.

Non-Stop Flight Across America. By Lieut. John A. Macready. Photographs by Lieut. Albert W. Stevens. Vol. XLVI, pp. 1-83, 68 ills., 1 page and 1 half-page maps, July, 1924.

McSweeny, Z. F.:

Character of Our Immigration, Past and Present. By Z. F. McSweeny. Vol. XVI, pp. 1-15, 1 chart, Jan., 1905.

McWilliams, John:

Vagabonding in England : A Young American Works His Way Around the British Isles and Sees Sights from an Unusual Point of View. By John McWilliams. Vol. LXV, pp. 357-398, 39 ills., 1 three-quarters-page map, Mar., 1934.

Madagascar:

Across Madagascar by Boat, Auto, Railroad, and Filanzana. By Charles F. Swingle. Vol. LVI, pp. 179-211, 42 ills., 1 half-page and 1 three-quarters-page maps, Aug., 1929.

Madagascar : Mystery Island : Japan's Push into the Indian Ocean Swings the Searchlight of World Attention to This Huge French Sentinel off the African Coast. By Paul Almasy. Vol. LXXXI, pp. 797-830, 37 ills., 3 maps, June, 1942.

Ma'dan (Tribespeople) :

Forty Years Among the Arabs. By John Van Ess. Vol. LXXXII, pp. 385-420, 27 ills., 1 two-page map, Sept., 1942.

Maddock, Eleanor:

Marble Dams of Rajputana. By Eleanor Maddock. Vol. XL, pp. 468-499, 13 ills. in black and white, 16 ills. in color, Nov., 1921.

Madeira (Island), Atlantic Ocean :

Madeira, on the Way to Italy. By David Fairchild. Vol. XVIII, pp. 751-771, 18 ills., Dec., 1907.

Madeira the Florescent. By Harriet Chalmers Adams. Vol. LXVI, pp. 81-106, 19 ills. in black and white, 13 ills. in color, 1 half-page map, July, 1934.

Mirrors of Madeira, Rock Garden of the Atlantic. 13 ills. in color from natural-color photographs by Wilhelm Tobien. Vol. LXVI, pp. 89-96, July, 1934.

Madrid, Spain :

Madrid Out-of-Doors. By Harriet Chalmers Adams. Vol. LX, pp. 225-256, 35 ills., Aug., 1931.

We Escape from Madrid. By Gretchen Schwinn. Vol. LXXI, pp. 251-268, 15 ills., Feb., 1937.

Madura, India :

Madura Temples. By J. S. Chandler. Vol. XIX, pp. 218-222, 4 ills., Mar., 1908.

Marriage of the Gods (Religious Festival). By John J. Banninga. Vol. XXIV, pp. 1314-1330, 16 ills., Dec., 1913.

Temples of India. 54 ills. from photographs by W. M. Zumbro. Vol. XX, pp. 922-971, Nov., 1909.

Magdalena (River), Colombia :

Over the Andes to Bogotá. By Frank M. Chapman. Vol. XL, pp. 353-373, 19 ills., Oct., 1921.

Magdalena Bay, Mexico:

Land of Drought and Desert—Lower California: Two Thousand Miles on Horseback Through the Most Extraordinary Cacti Forests in the World. By E. W. Nelson. Vol. XXII, pp. 443-474, 25 ills., 1 page and 1 half-page maps, May, 1911.

Magee, Frank J.:

Transporting a Navy Through the Jungles of Africa in War Time. By Frank J. Magee. Vol. XLII, pp. 331-362, 31 ills., Oct., 1922.

Magee, Guy, Jr.:

"Man in the Street" in China. By Guy Magee, Jr. Vol. XXXVIII, pp. 406-421, 15 ills., Nov., 1920.

Mageik, Mount, Alaska:

Valley of Ten Thousand Smokes: An Account of the Discovery and Exploration of the Most Wonderful Volcanic Region in the World. By Robert F. Griggs. Vol. XXXIII, pp. 115-169, 46 ills., 1 half-page map, panorama, Feb., 1918.

Valley of Ten Thousand Smokes: National Geographic Society Explorations in the Katmai District of Alaska. By Robert F. Griggs. Vol. XXXI, pp. 12-68, 51 ills., 1 half-page map, Jan., 1917.

Magellan, Ferdinand:

Greatest Voyage in the Annals of the Sea. By J. R. Hildebrand. Vol. LXII, pp. 699-739, 35 ills., 2 half-page maps, Dec., 1932.

Maggiore, Lake, Italy:

Frontier Cities of Italy. By Florence Craig Albrecht. Vol. XXVII, pp. 533-586, 45 ills., June, 1915.

Gems of the Italian Lakes. By Arthur Ellis Mayer. Vol. XXIV, pp. 943-956, 13 ills., Aug., 1913.

Magic Beauty of Snow and Dew. By Wilson A. Bentley. Vol. XLIII, pp. 103-112, 9 ills., Jan., 1923.

Magic Mountain (Mount Wilson, California). By J. N. Patterson. Vol. XIX, pp. 457-468, 9 ills., July, 1908.

Magnesia (Ancient City):

Buried Cities of Asia Minor. By Ernest L. Harris. Vol. XX, pp. 1-18, 10 ills., Jan., 1909.

Some Ruined Cities of Asia Minor. By Ernest L. Harris. Vol. XIX, pp. 833-858, 19 ills., Dec., 1908.

"Magnetic City" (Magnitogorsk), Core of Valiant Russia's Industrial Might. By John Scott. Vol. LXXXIII, pp. 525-556, 27 ills., 1 two-page map, May, 1943.

Magnetic Disturbance Caused by the Explosion of Mont Pelée. Vol. XIII, pp. 208-209, June, 1902.

Magnetic Observations in Alaska. By Daniel L. Hazard. Vol. XX, pp. 675-676, 1 page map, July, 1909.

Magnetic Survey of Africa. By Dr. L. A. Bauer. Vol. XX, pp. 291-297, 6 ills., Mar., 1909.

Magnetic Survey of the Pacific. Vol. XIX, pp. 447-448, June, 1908.

Magnetic Survey of the Pacific Ocean. By Dr. L. A. Bauer. Vol. XVII, p. 237, Apr., 1906.

Magnetic Survey of the United States. By Dr. L. A. Bauer. Vol. XIII, pp. 92-95, 1 half-page map, Mar., 1902.

Magnetic Work of the Coast and Geodetic Survey. By Dr. L. A. Bauer. Vol. X, pp. 288-289, Aug., 1899.

Magnetism, Terrestrial. *See* Geomagnetism.

Magnitogorsk, R. S. F. S. R.:

"Magnetic City," Core of Valiant Russia's Industrial Might. By John Scott. Vol. LXXXIII, pp. 525-556, 27 ills., 1 two-page map, May, 1943.

Magnitude of the New World Metropolis (New York City). 8 ills. in gravure. Vol. LVIII, pp. 522-531, Nov., 1930.

Magnolia Gardens, South Carolina:

Ashley River and Its Gardens. By E. T. H. Shaffer. Vol. XLIX, pp. 525-550, 6 ills. in black and white, 7 ills. in color, May, 1926.

Magnolia State Mosaic (Mississippi). 26 ills. in color from natural-color photographs by J. Baylor Roberts. Vol. LXXII, pp. 279-310, Sept., 1937.

Magpies (Birds):

Crows, Magpies, and Jays: Unusual Intelligence Has Earned a Unique Position for These Birds. By T. Gilbert Pearson. Paintings by Maj. Allan Brooks. Vol. LXIII, pp. 51-79, 2 ills. in color, Jan., 1933.

Magyar Mirth and Melancholy. By John Patric. Vol. LXXIII, pp. 1-55, 33 ills. in black and white, 20 ills. in color, 1 half-page map, Jan., 1938.

Magyars (People):

Hungary: A Land of Shepherd Kings. By C. Townley-Fullam. Vol. XXVI, pp. 311-393, 92 ills., 1 page map, Oct., 1914.

Land of Contrast: Austria-Hungary. By D. W. and A. S. Iddings. Vol. XXIII, pp. 1188-1218, 34 ills., Dec., 1912.

Magyar Mirth and Melancholy. By John Patric. Vol. LXXIII, pp. 1-55, 33 ills. in black and white, 20 ills. in color, 1 half-page map, Jan., 1938.

Races of Europe. By Edwin A. Grosvenor. Vol. XXXIV, pp. 441-534, 62 ills., 2 page maps, special map supplement in colors, Dec., 1918.

Rural Hungarian Rhapsody. 20 ills. in color from natural-color photographs by Rudolf Balogh and Hans Hildenbrand. Vol. LXXIII, pp. 17-48, Jan., 1938.

Maha-Vajiravudh (King of Siam):

Coronation of His Majesty King Maha-Vajiravudh of Siam. By Col. Lea Febiger. Vol. XXIII, pp. 389-416, 25 ills., Apr., 1912.

Mahdia, Tunisia:

Greek Bronzes of Tunisia. By Frank Edward Johnson. Vol. XXIII, pp. 89-103, 11 ills., Jan., 1912.

Mahoganies (Trees):

Among the Mahogany Forests of Cuba. By Walter D. Wilcox. Vol. XIX, pp. 485-498, 6 ills., 1 page map, July, 1908.

Maid of France Rides By: Compiègne, Where Joan of Arc Fought Her Last Battle, Celebrates Her Fifth Centenary. By Inez Buffington Ryan. Vol. LXII, pp. 607-617, 15 ills. in color, Nov., 1932.

Maine:

First National Park East of Mississippi River (Mount Desert Island). Vol. XXIX, pp. 622-626, 5 ills., June, 1916.

In the Allagash Country. By Kenneth Fuller Lee. Vol. LV, pp. 505-520, 19 ills., Apr., 1929.

Leach's Petrel: His Nursery on Little Duck Island. By Arnold Wood. Vol. XX, pp. 360-365, 7 ills., Apr., 1909.

Maine, the Outpost State: Some Forgotten Incidents in the Life of an Old and Stout-Hearted Commonwealth. By George Otis Smith. Vol. LXVII, pp. 533-592, 35 ills. in black and white, 39 ills. in color, 1 two-page map, May, 1935.

The Maine American and the American Lobster. By John D. Lucas. Vol. LXXXIX, pp. 523-543, 19 ills., Apr., 1946.

Northeast of Boston. By Albert W. Atwood. Vol. LXXXVIII, pp. 257-292, 12 ills. in black and white, 17 ills. in color, special map supplement, Sept., 1945.

Pine-Scented, Harbor-Dented Maine. 39 ills. in color from natural-color photographs by B. Anthony Stewart and Robert F. Maxcy. Vol. LXVII, pp. 549-588, May, 1935.

Unique Island of Mount Desert. By George B. Dorr, Ernest Howe Forbush, and M. L. Fernald. Vol. XXVI, pp. 75-89, 7 ills., July, 1914.

Where New England Meets the Sea. 17 ills. in color from natural-color photographs by B. Anthony Stewart. Vol. LXXXVIII, pp. 265-288, Sept., 1945.

The Worm Turns. By Samuel Sandrof. Vol. LXXXIX, pp. 775-786, 14 ills., June, 1946. Contains information on the worm-digging industry.

Majesty of the Matterhorn. Vol. XXIII, supplement, May, 1912.

Major, Harlan:

Delectable Shrimp: Once a Culinary Stepchild, Today a Gulf Coast Industry. By Harlan Major. Vol. LXXXVI, pp. 501-512, 11 ills., 1 two-thirds-page map, Oct., 1944.

Majorca (Island), Balearic Islands:

Keeping House in Majorca. By Phoebe Binney Harnden. Vol. XLV, pp. 425-440, 18 ills., 1 quarter-page map, Apr., 1924.

Majuro (Atoll), Marshall Islands:

Marshallese Are Happy Again. 20 ills. in color from natural-color photographs by W. Robert Moore. Vol. LXXXVIII, pp. 337-360, Sept., 1945.

Our New Military Wards, the Marshalls. By W. Robert Moore. Vol. LXXXVIII, pp. 325-360, 14 ills. in black and white, 20 ills. in color, 1 half-page map, Sept., 1945.

Makers of the Flag. By Franklin K. Lane. Vol. XXXII, p. 304, Oct., 1917.

Makin (Atoll), Gilbert Islands:

Gilbert Islands in the Wake of Battle. By W. Robert Moore. Vol. LXXXVII, pp. 129-162. 11 ills. in black and white, 19 ills. in color, 1 two-thirds-page map, Feb., 1945.

Round About Grim Tarawa. 19 ills. in color from natural-color photographs by W. Robert Moore. Vol. LXXXVII, pp. 137-160, Feb., 1945.

Making of a Japanese Newspaper. By Dr. Thomas E. Green. Vol. XXXVIII, pp. 327-334, 5 ills., Oct., 1920.

Making of an Anzac. By Howell Walker. Vol. LXXXI, pp. 409-456, 31 ills. in black and white, 20 ills. in color, 1 two-page map, Apr., 1942.

Making of Military Maps. By William H. Nicholas. Vol. LXXXIII, pp. 765-778, 17 ills., June, 1943.

Making the Fur Seal Abundant. By Hugh M. Smith. Vol. XXII, pp. 1139-1165, 18 ills., 1 half-page map, Dec., 1911.

Malaria:

Economic Loss to the People of the United States Through Insects That Carry Disease. By L. O. Howard. Vol. XX, pp. 735-749, Aug., 1909.

Life Story of the Mosquito. By Graham Fairchild. With 10 ills. in color from paintings. Vol. LXXXV, pp. 180-195, 5 ills. in black and white, 1 drawing, Feb., 1944.

Map-Changing Medicine. By William Joseph Showalter. Vol. XLII, pp. 303-330, 26 ills., Sept., 1922.

Redeeming the Tropics. By William Joseph Showalter. Vol. XXV, pp. 344-354, 13 ills., Mar., 1914.

Saboteur Mosquitoes. By Harry H. Stage. Vol. LXXXV, pp. 165-179, 12 ills., Feb., 1944.

Malaspina Glacier, Alaska:

National Geographic Society's Alaskan Expedition of 1909. By Ralph S. Tarr and Lawrence Martin. Vol. XXI, pp. 1-54, 42 ills., 4 page and 7 half-page maps, Jan., 1910.

Malay Archipelago. *See* Borneo; Celebes; Java; Moluccas; New Guinea; Philippine Islands; Timor.

Malay Peninsula. *See* British Malaya; Siam; Singapore.

Malcolm, Ian:

Needs Abroad. By Ian Malcolm. Vol. XXXI, pp. 427-433, 5 ills., May, 1917.

Mall, Washington, D. C. Vol. XXVII, colored panorama, Mar., 1915.

Mallowan, M. E. L.:

New Light on Ancient Ur: Excavations at the Site of the City of Abraham Reveal Geographical Evidence of the Biblical Story of the Flood. By M. E. L. Mallowan. Vol. LVII, pp. 95-130, 44 ills., 1 three-quarters-page map, Jan., 1930.

Maloney, John:

Chesapeake Odyssey: An 18-foot Sailboat Follows the Course of Captain John Smith around This Spacious Bay of History, Commerce, Sea Food, and Nautical Lore. By John Maloney. Vol. LXXVI, pp. 357-392, 32 ills., 1 page map, Sept., 1939.

Malta (Island), Mediterranean Sea:

Malta: The Halting Place of Nations: First Account of Remarkable Prehistoric Tombs and Temples Recently Unearthed on the Island. By William Arthur Griffiths. Vol. XXXVII, pp. 445-478, 35 ills., 1 third-page map, May, 1920.

Malta Invicta. By Bartimeus (A Captain in the Royal Navy). Vol. LXXXIII, pp. 375-400, 27 ills., 1 half-page map, Mar., 1943.

Maltese Islands: Cicero's Land of "Honey and Roses," and Stronghold of the Knights, Again Is Focus of Naval Strategy. By Sir Harry Luke. Vol. LXVIII, pp. 647-666, 20 ills., 1 half-page and 1 third-page maps, Nov., 1935.

Races of Europe. By Edwin A. Grosvenor. Vol. XXXIV, pp. 441-534, 62 ills., 2 page maps, special map supplement, Dec., 1918.

Wanderers Awheel in Malta: British Stronghold Has Been a Steppingstone of Conquest Since Phoenicians Cruised the Mediterranean and St. Paul Was Shipwrecked There. By Richard Walter. Vol. LXXVIII, pp. 253-272, 17 ills., 2 maps, Aug., 1940.

Maltese Islands: Cicero's Land of "Honey and Roses," and Stronghold of the Knights, Again Is Focus of Naval Strategy. By Sir Harry Luke. Vol. LXVIII, pp. 647-666, 20 ills., 1 half-page and 1 third-page maps, Nov., 1935.

Mammals:

Animal Wealth of the United States. By Francis E. Warren. Vol. XVII, pp. 511-524, 6 ills., 2 diagrams, Sept., 1906.

Animals Were Allies, Too. 16 ills. from photographs. Vol. LXXXIX, pp. 75-88, Jan., 1946.

Contains illustrations of the following: Camels, Carabaos, Cattle, Dogs, Donkeys, Elephants, Horses, Monkeys, Mules, Oxen.

Around the World for Animals. By William M. and Lucile Q. Mann. Vol. LXXIII, pp. 665-714, 33 ills. in black and white, 23 ills. in color, 1 page map, June, 1938.

Befriending Nature's Children: An Experiment With Some of California's Wild Folk. By Agnes Akin Atkinson. Vol. LXI, pp. 199-215, 26 ills., Feb., 1932.

Big Game of Alaska. By Wilfred H. Osgood. Vol. XX, pp. 624-636, 10 ills., July, 1909.

Mammals—*Continued*

Camera Adventures in the African Wilds. By A. Radclyffe Dugmore. Vol. XXI, pp. 385-396, 11 ills., May, 1910.

Color Camera Explores the Country That Moves by Night. 29 ills. in color from natural-color photographs by Richard H. Stewart, W. Robert Moore, Orren R. Louden, and Jacob Gayer. Vol. LX, pp. 478-511, Oct., 1931.

Flashlight Story of An Albino Porcupine and of a Cunning but Unfortunate Coon. By George Shiras, 3d. Vol. XXII, pp. 572-596, 26 ills., June, 1911.

Flashlights from the Jungle. Vol. XVIII, pp. 534-548, 11 ills., Aug., 1907.

Game and Fur-Bearing Animals and Their Influence on the Indians of the Northwest. By Townsend W. Thorndike. Vol. XV, p. 431, Oct., 1904.

Game Country Without Rival in America: The Proposed Mount McKinley National Park. By Stephen R. Capps. Vol. XXXI, pp. 69-84, 14 ills., 1 half-page map, Jan., 1917.

Hunting Big Game in Portuguese East Africa. By R. C. F. Maugham. Vol. XVIII, pp. 723-730, 7 ills., Nov., 1907.

Land of Eternal Warring (Labrador). By Sir Wilfred T. Grenfell. Vol. XXI, pp. 665-690, 24 ills., Aug., 1910.

Land of Sawdust and Spangles—A World in Miniature. By Francis Beverly Kelley. Vol. LX, pp. 463-516, 35 ills. in black and white, 29 ills. in color, Oct., 1931.

Larger North American Mammals. By E. W. Nelson. Vol. XXX, pp. 385-472, 24 ills. in black and white, 49 ills. in color, special supplement in color, Nov., 1916.

Contains descriptions and illustrations of various species of the following mammals: Antelope, Badger, Bear, Beaver, Buffalo, Caribou, Coyote, Deer, Elk, Eyra, Fisher, Fox, Goat, Jaguar, Lion, Lynx, Manati, Moose, Musk-Ox, Ocelot, Opossum, Otter, Peccary, Raccoon, Seal, Sheep, Walrus, Whale, Wolf, Wolverine.

Lords of the Rockies: Photographing Big Game Animals in Their Primeval Surroundings, from Arizona to Canada, Brings Adventure to Two Wilderness Wanderers. By Wendell and Lucie Chapman. Vol. LXXVI, pp. 87-128, 14 ills. in black and white, 28 ills. in color, July, 1939.

Mr. Roosevelt's "African Game Trails." Vol. XXI, pp. 953-962, 9 ills., Nov., 1910.

Naturalist's Journey Around Vera Cruz and Tampico. By Frank M. Chapman. Vol. XXV, pp. 533-561, 30 ills., May, 1914.

Nature's Transformation at Panama: The Remarkable Changes in Faunal and Physical Conditions in the Gatun Lake Region. By George Shiras, 3d. Vol. XXVIII, pp. 159-194, 33 ills., 2 page maps, Aug., 1915.

One Season's Game-Bag with the Camera. By George Shiras, 3d. Vol. XIX, pp. 387-446, 70 ills., June, 1908.

Mammals—*Continued*

Photographing Wild Game with Flashlight and Camera. By George Shiras, 3d. Vol. XVII, pp. 366-423, 70 ills., July, 1906.

Policemen of the Air. By Henry Wetherbee Henshaw. Vol. XIX, pp. 79-118, 38 ills., Feb., 1908.

Contents : Many of the Small Mammals Become Pests.—Wolves Cause Millions of Dollars of Loss Yearly.—Fox Farming.—Life and Crop Zones.—Game Protection and Kindred Subjects.—Big-Game Refuges.

Quills of a Porcupine. By Frederick V. Coville. Vol. XXIII, pp. 25-31, 5 ills., Jan., 1912.

Smaller Mammals of North America. By E. W. Nelson. Vol. XXXIII, pp. 391-493, 29 ills. in black and white, 59 ills. in color, May, 1918.

Contains descriptions and illustrations of various species of the following mammals : Armadillo, Bat, Beaver, Cat, Chipmunk, Ferret, Gopher, Hare, Lemming, Marmot, Marten, Mink, Mole, Mouse, Muskrat, Porcupine, Prairie-Dog, Rabbit, Rat, Shrew, Skunk, Squirrel, Weasel, Woodrat.

Stalking Big Game with Color Camera. 28 ills. in color from natural-color photographs by Wendell Chapman. Vol. LXXVI, pp. 89-128, July, 1939.

Tiger-Hunting in India. By Brig. Gen. William Mitchell. Vol. XLVI, pp. 545-598, 46 ills., 1 quarter-page map, Nov., 1924.

Warfare of the Jungle Folk: Campaigning Against Tigers, Elephants, and Other Wild Animals in Northern Siam. By Merian C. Cooper. Photographs by Ernest B. Schoedsack. Vol. LIII, pp. 233-268, 33 ills., Feb., 1928.

What the Fighting Yanks See. By Wanda Burnett. Vol. LXXXVI, pp. 451-476, 27 ills., Oct., 1944.

When a Drought Blights Africa: Hippos and Elephants Are Driven Insane by Suffering, in the Lorian Swamp, Kenya Colony. By Capt. A. T. Curle. Vol. LV, pp. 521-528, 9 ills., Apr., 1929.

Where Birds and Little Animals Find Haven (Eaton Canyon Bird and Game Sanctuary). By Agnes Akin Atkinson. Vol. LXX, pp. 232-241, 14 ills., Aug., 1936.

Where Roosevelt Will Hunt (Africa). By Sir Harry Johnston. Vol. XX, pp. 207-256, 43 ills., special map supplement in colors, Mar., 1909.

White Sheep, Giant Moose, and Smaller Game of the Kenai Peninsula, Alaska. By George Shiras, 3d. Vol. XXIII, pp. 423-494, 59 ills., 1 page and 1 two-page maps, May, 1912.

Who Treads Our Trails? A Camera Trapper Describes His Experiences on an Island in the Canal Zone, a Natural-History Laboratory in the American Tropics. By Frank M. Chapman. Vol. LII, pp. 331-345, 18 ills., 1 half-page map, Sept., 1927.

Wild Animals That Took Their Own Pictures by Day and by Night. By George Shiras, 3d. Vol. XXIV, pp. 763-834, 68 ills., 1 page map, July, 1913.

Mammals—*Continued*

Wild Life of Lake Superior, Past and Present : The Habits of Deer, Moose, Wolves, Beavers, Muskrats, Trout, and Feathered Wood-Folk Studied with Camera and Flashlight. By George Shiras, 3d. Vol. XL, pp. 113-204, 77 ills., special supplement, 1 half-page map, Aug., 1921.

Wild Life of the Atlantic and Gulf Coasts: A Field Naturalist's Photographic Record of Nearly Half a Century of Fruitful Exploration. By George Shiras, 3d. Vol. LXII, pp. 261-309, 62 ills., Sept., 1932.

Wild Man and Wild Beast in Africa. By Theodore Roosevelt. Vol. XXII, pp. 1-33, 41 ills., 1 page map, Jan., 1911.

Wings Over Nature's Zoo in Africa. 20 ills. in duotone from photographs by Reginald A. Bourlay. Vol. LXXVI, pp. 527-542, Oct., 1939.

With Wild Animals in the Rockies. By Lucie and Wendell Chapman. Vol. LXVIII, pp. 231-249, 26 ills. in duotone, Aug., 1935.

Wonder Island of the Amazon Delta : On Marajó Cowboys Ride Oxen, Tree-dwelling Animals Throng Dense Forests, While Strange Fishes and Birds Help Make a Zoologist's Paradise. By Hugh B. Cott. Vol. LXXIV, pp. 635-670, 30 ills. in black and white, 12 ills. in color, 1 half-page map, Nov., 1938.

See also Apes ; Bats ; Bears ; Camels ; Cats ; Cattle and Cattle Raising ; Deer ; Dogs ; Dolphins ; Elephant Seals ; Elephants ; Goats ; Horses ; Jackals ; Lamoids ; Monkeys ; Paleontology ; Platypus ; Porcupines ; Porpoises ; Reindeer ; Rodents ; Seals ; Sheep and Sheep Raising ; Walruses ; Whales ; Wild Cats ; Wolves.

Mammoth :

Strange and Remarkable Beast. Vol. XVIII, p. 620, 1 ill., Sept., 1907.

Man, Isle of, England :

Isle of Man. By Capt. F. H. Mellor. Vol. LXXI, pp. 587-608, 13 ills. in black and white, 12 ills. in color, 1 third-page map, May, 1937.

Sunny Corners in a Friendly Isle. 12 ills. in color from natural-color photographs by B. Anthony Stewart. Vol. LXXI, pp. 601-608, May, 1937.

Man and Nature Paint Italian Scenes in Prodigal Colors. 33 ills. in color from autochromes by Hans Hildenbrand. Vol. LIII, pp. 442-467, Apr., 1928.

"Man in the Street" in China. By Guy Magee, Jr. Vol. XXXVIII, pp. 406-421, 15 ills., Nov., 1920.

Man-O'-War-Birds :

Birds of the High Seas : Albatrosses and Petrels ; Gannets, Man-o'-war-birds, and Tropic-birds. By Robert Cushman Murphy. Paintings by Maj. Allan Brooks. Vol. LXXIV, pp. 226-251, 7 ills. in black and white, 36 portraits in color, Aug., 1938.

Man Without the Hoe. Vol. XXI, pp. 967-969, 2 ills., Nov., 1910.

Managua, Nicaragua :

Land of Lakes and Volcanoes. By Luis Marden. With 17 ills. in color from natural-color photographs by the author. Vol. LXXXVI, pp. 161-192, 11 ills. in black and white, 1 two-thirds-page map, Aug., 1944.

Manama, Bahrein Islands :

Bahrein : Port of Pearls and Petroleum. By Maynard Owen Williams. Vol. LXXXIX, pp. 195-210, 6 ills. in black and white, 11 ills. in color, 1 half-page map, Feb., 1946.

Oil Comes to Bahrein, Port of Pearls. 11 ills. in color from natural-color photographs by Maynard Owen Williams. Vol. LXXXIX, pp. 201-208, Feb., 1946.

Manáos, Brazil :

Air Cruising Through New Brazil : A National Geographic Reporter Spots Vast Resources Which the Republic's War Declaration Adds to Strength of United Nations. By Henry Albert Phillips. Vol. LXXXII, pp. 503-536, 32 ills., Oct., 1942.

Manchester Ship Canal, England :

Great Canals of the World. Vol. XVI, pp. 475-479, Oct., 1905.

Manchukuo. *See* Manchuria.

Manchuria :

Building of Dalny (Dairen). Vol. XIV, p. 360, Sept., 1903.

Byroads and Backwoods of Manchuria : Where Violent Contrasts of Modernism and Unaltered Ancient Tradition Clash. By Owen Lattimore. Vol. LXI, pp. 101-130, 27 ills., 1 three-quarters-page map, Jan., 1932.

Here in Manchuria : Many Thousand Lives Were Lost and More than Half the Crops Destroyed by the Floods of 1932. By Lilian Grosvenor Coville. Vol. LXIII, pp. 233-256, 26 ills., Feb., 1933.

Japan Faces Russia in Manchuria. By Willard Price. Vol. LXXXII, pp. 603-634, 30 ills., 1 page map, Nov., 1942.

Land of Promise. By Maj. Gen. A. W. Greely. Vol. XXIII, pp. 1078-1090, 7 ills., Nov., 1912.

Lumbering in Manchuria. By Henry B. Miller. Vol. XV, pp. 130-132, 2 ills., Mar., 1904.

Manchuria, Promised Land of Asia : Invaded by Railways and Millions of Settlers, This Vast Region Now Recalls Early Boom Days in the American West. By Frederick Simpich. Vol. LVI, pp. 379-428, 58 ills., 1 two-thirds-page map, Oct., 1929.

Manchuria and Korea. Text accompanying special map supplement. Vol. XV, pp. 128-129, 2 half-page maps, Mar., 1904.

Mukden, the Manchu Home, and Its Great Art Museum. By Eliza R. Scidmore. Vol. XXI, pp. 289-320, 30 ills., Apr., 1910.

Notes on Manchuria. By Henry B. Miller. Vol. XV, pp. 261-262, June, 1904.

Observations on the Russo-Japanese War in Japan and Manchuria. By Louis Livingston Seaman. Vol. XVI, pp. 80-82, Feb., 1905.

Manchuria—*Continued*

Railways, Rivers, and Strategic Towns in Manchuria. Vol. XI, pp. 326-327, Aug., 1900.

Russian Development of Manchuria. By Henry B. Miller. Vol. XV, pp. 113-127, 11 ills., 1 half-page map, Mar., 1904.

Mandalay, Burma :

Notes on Burma. By Thomas Barbour. Vol. XX, pp. 841-866, 34 ills., Oct., 1909.

Mandarin Road, French Indo-China :

Along the Old Mandarin Road of Indo-China. By W. Robert Moore. Vol. LX, pp. 157-199, 32 ills. in black and white, 28 ills. in color, 1 quarter-page map, Aug., 1931.

Under the French Tricolor in Indo-China. 28 ills. in color from natural-color photographs by W. Robert Moore. Vol. LX, pp. 166-199, Aug., 1931.

Mandate of Cameroun : A Vast African Territory Ruled by Petty Sultans Under French Sway. By John W. Vandercook. Vol. LIX, pp. 225-260, 49 ills., 1 two-thirds-page map, Feb., 1931.

Maneuvers of Military Planes Disclose Majestic Aërial Views. 17 ills. in duotone from U. S. Army and Navy official photographs. Vol. LXIII, pp. 598-615, May, 1933.

Manganese :

India's Treasures Helped the Allies. By John Fischer. Vol. LXXXIX, pp. 501-522, 18 ills., Apr., 1946.

Mangbettu (Tribespeople) :

Trans-Africa Safari : A Motor Caravan Rolls Across Sahara and Jungle Through Realms of Dusky Potentates and the Land of Big-Lipped Women. By Lawrence Copley Thaw and Margaret Stout Thaw. Vol. LXXIV, pp. 327-364, 29 ills. in black and white, 14 ills. in color, 1 two-thirds-page map, Sept., 1938.

Mangoes (Trees) :

Introduction of the Mango. Vol. XIV, pp. 320-327, 5 ills., Aug., 1903.

New Plant Immigrants. By David Fairchild. Vol. XXII, pp. 879-907, 34 ills., Oct., 1911.

Manihiki Island, Pacific Ocean :

Sailing the Seven Seas in the Interest of Science : Adventures Through 157,000 Miles of Storm and Calm, from Arctic to Antarctic and Around the World, in the Non-Magnetic Yacht *Carnegie*. By J. P. Ault. Vol. XLII, pp. 631-690, 47 ills., 1 chart, Dec., 1922.

Manila, Luzon, Philippine Islands :

Economic Condition of the Philippines. By Max L. Tornow. Vol. X, pp. 33-64, 10 ills., Feb., 1899.

Facts about the Philippines. By Frederick Simpich. Vol. LXXXI, pp. 185-202, 17 ills., 1 page map, Feb., 1942.

Improvements in the City of Manila. Vol. XIV, pp. 195-197, 1 ill., May, 1903.

Manila, Luzon, Philippine Islands—*Continued*

Manila and the Philippines. By Maj. A. Falkner von Sonnenburg. Vol. X, pp. 65-72, Feb., 1899.

Manila Observatory. By Father José Algué. Vol. XI, pp. 427-438, 2 ills., Nov., 1900.

Return to Manila. By Frederick Simpich. Vol. LXXVIII, pp. 409-451, 21 ills. in black and white, 21 ills. in color, 1 half-page map, Oct., 1940.

Smiling, Happy Philippines. 21 ills. in color from natural-color photographs; 19 ills. by J. Baylor Roberts. Vol. LXXVIII, pp. 425-448, Oct., 1940.

What Luzon Means to Uncle Sam. By Frederick Simpich. Vol. LXXXVII, pp. 305-332, 25 ills., special map supplement, Mar., 1945.

Manipur (State), India:

Manipur—Where Japan Struck at India. 11 ills. from photographs, 1 page map. Vol. LXXXV, pp. 743-750, June, 1944.

Manitoba (Province), Canada. *See* Churchill.

Mankind's Best Friend (Dog): Companion of His Solitude, Advance Guard in the Hunt, and Ally of the Trenches. By Ernest Harold Baynes. Vol. XXXV, pp. 185-201, 11 ills., Mar., 1919.

Manless Alpine Climbing: The First Woman to Scale the Grépon, the Matterhorn, and Other Famous Peaks Without Masculine Support Relates Her Adventures. By Miriam O'Brien Underhill. Vol. LXVI, pp. 131-170, 30 ills. in black and white, 12 ills. in color, Aug., 1934.

Manlike Apes of Jungle and Mountain. 10 ills. in color from paintings by Elie Cheverlange. Vol. LXXVIII, pp. 221-228, Aug., 1940.

Mann, James R.:

Honors to Colonel Goethals: The Presentation, by President Woodrow Wilson, of the National Geographic Society Special Gold Medal, and Addresses by Secretary of State Bryan, the French Ambassador, the German Ambassador, and Congressman James R. Mann. Vol. XXV, pp. 677-690, 6 ills., June, 1914.

Mann, Lucile Q.:

Around the World for Animals. By William M. and Lucile Q. Mann. Vol. LXXIII, pp. 665-714, 33 ills. in black and white, 23 ills. in color, 1 page map, June, 1938.

Mann, William M.:

Around the World for Animals. By William M. and Lucile Q. Mann. Vol. LXXIII, pp. 665-714, 33 ills. in black and white, 23 ills. in color, 1 page map, June, 1938.

Man's Closest Counterparts: Heavyweight of Monkeydom Is the "Old Man" Gorilla, by Far the Largest of the Four Great Apes. By William M. Mann. Vol. LXXVIII, pp. 213-236, 10 ills. in black and white, 10 ills. in color, Aug., 1940.

Monkey Folk. By William M. Mann. Vol. LXXIII, pp. 615-655, 24 ills. in black and white, 40 portraits in color, May, 1938.

Mann, William M.—*Continued*

Stalking Ants, Savage and Civilized: A Naturalist Braves Bites and Stings in Many Lands to Learn the Story of an Insect Whose Ways Often Parallel Those of Man. By W. M. Mann. Vol. LXVI, pp. 171-192, 7 ills. in black and white, 18 ills. in color, Aug., 1934.

Man's Amazing Progress in Conquering the Air. By J. R. Hildebrand. Vol. XLVI, pp. 93-122, 28 ills., 1 diagram, July, 1924.

Man's Closest Counterparts: Heavyweight of Monkeydom Is the "Old Man" Gorilla, by Far the Largest of the Four Great Apes. By William M. Mann. Vol. LXXVIII, pp. 213-236, 10 ills. in black and white, 10 ills. in color, Aug., 1940.

Man's Farthest Aloft: Rising to 13.71 Miles, the National Geographic Society-U. S. Army Stratosphere Expedition Gathers Scientific Data at Record Altitude. By Capt. Albert W. Stevens. Action Photographs of the Balloon's Perfect Landing included. Vol. LXIX, pp. 59-94, 39 ills., 1 quarter-page map, Jan., 1936.

Man's Feathered Friends of Longest Standing: Peoples of Every Clime and Age Have Lavished Care and Affection Upon Lovely Pigeons. By Elisha Hanson. Vol. XLIX, pp. 63-110, 35 ills. in black and white, 12 ills. in color, Jan., 1926.

Man's Hunting Partner, the Field Dog. 36 portraits in color from paintings by Edward Herbert Miner. Vol. LXXI, pp. 89-104, Jan., 1937.

Man's Oldest Ally, the Dog: Since Cave-Dweller Days This Faithful Friend Has Shared the Work, Exploration, and Sport of Humankind. By Freeman Lloyd. Paintings by Edward Herbert Miner. Vol. LXIX, pp. 247-274, 13 ills. in black and white, 33 portraits in color, Feb., 1936.

Man's Winged Ally, the Busy Honeybee: Modern Research Adds a New Chapter to Usefulness of the Insect Which Has Symbolized Industry Since Early Bible Times. By James I. Hambleton. Vol. LXVII, pp. 401-428, 18 ills. in black and white, 16 ills. in color, Apr., 1935.

Maoris (Tribespeople):

Hurdle Racing in Canoes: A Thrilling and Spectacular Sport Among the Maoris of New Zealand. By Walter Burke. Vol. XXXVII, pp. 440-444, 6 ills., May, 1920.

Maoris of New Zealand. Vol. XVIII, pp. 191-199, 8 ills., Mar., 1907.

Map (Island), Caroline Islands:

Mysterious Micronesia: Yap, Map, and Other Islands Under Japanese Mandate are Museums of Primitive Man. By Willard Price. Vol. LXIX, pp. 481-510, 37 ills., 1 half-page map, Apr., 1936.

Map Articles—*Continued*

Western Front Map Embraces Three Continents (Europe, Africa, Asia). Text accompanying special map supplement in colors. Vol. LXXXII, pp. 139-140, July, 1942.

World That Rims the Narrowing Atlantic: Latest Ten-color Map Supplement Shows Four Continents and New Transatlantic Air Routes Which Make This Ocean Only One Day Wide. By James M. Darley. Text accompanying special map supplement in colors. Vol. LXXVI, pp. 139-142, 1 ill., July, 1939.

Your Society Aids War Effort. Vol. LXXXIII, pp. 277-278, 1 ill., Feb., 1943.

Map-Changing Medicine. By William Joseph Showalter. Vol. XLII, pp. 303-330, 26 ills., Sept., 1922.

Map Links Classic World with 1940. Text accompanying special map supplement in colors. Vol. LXXVII, p. 338, Mar., 1940.

Map Making:

Charting a World at War. By William H. Nicholas. Vol. LXXXVI, pp. 617-640, 23 ills., 1 drawing, Nov., 1944.

Making of Military Maps. By William H. Nicholas. Vol. LXXXIII, pp. 765-778, 17 ills., June, 1943.

Maps for Victory: National Geographic Society's Charts Used in War on Land, Sea, and in the Air. By Gilbert Grosvenor. Vol. LXXXI, pp. 667-690, 28 ills., May, 1942.

Story of the Map. Text accompanying special map supplement in colors. Vol. LXII, pp. 759-774, 11 ills., Dec., 1932.

Unexplored Philippines from the Air: Map Making over Jungle Lands Never Before Seen by White Men. By Lieut. George W. Goddard. Vol. LVIII, pp. 311-343, 38 ills., 1 quarter-page map, Sept., 1930.

Map of the Northern and Southern Hemispheres. Text accompanying special map supplement in colors. Vol. LXXXIII, pp. 481-483, Apr., 1943.

Mapping the Antarctic from the Air: The Aërial Camera Earns Its Place as the Eyes and Memory of the Explorer. By Capt. Ashley C. McKinley. Vol. LXII, pp. 471-485, 13 ills., special map supplement in colors, Oct., 1932.

Mapping the Home of the Great Brown Bear: Adventures of the National Geographic Society's Pavlof Volcano Expedition to Alaska. By Dr. Thomas A. Jaggar. Vol. LV, pp. 109-134, 30 ills., 1 three-quarters-page map, Jan., 1929.

Maps. *See* Index to Maps, p. 594.

Maps, Sky. *See* Star Charts.

Maps for Victory: National Geographic Society's Charts Used in War on Land, Sea, and in the Air. By Gilbert Grosvenor. Text accompanying special map supplement in colors. Vol. LXXXI, pp. 667-690, 28 ills., May, 1942.

Maps of Discovery:

Eastern Hemisphere. Reproduction in color of the painting by N. C. Wyeth, National Geographic Society, Washington, D. C. Vol. LIV, text, p. 568; supplement, Nov., 1928.

Western Hemisphere. Reproduction in color of the painting by N. C. Wyeth, National Geographic Society, Washington, D. C. Vol. LV, text, p. 93; supplement Jan., 1929.

Mapuches (Indians). *See* Araucanian Indians.

Marajó Island, Brazil:

Cowboys and Caymans of Marajó. 12 ills. in color from natural-color photographs by Desmond Holdridge. Vol. LXXIV, pp. 645-652, Nov., 1938.

Wonder Island of the Amazon Delta: On Marajó Cowboys Ride Oxen, Tree-dwelling Animals Throng Dense Forests, While Strange Fishes and Birds Help Make a Zoologist's Paradise. By Hugh B. Cott. Vol. LXXIV, pp. 635-670, 30 ills. in black and white, 12 ills. in color, 1 half-page map, Nov., 1938.

Marakei (Atoll), Gilbert Islands:

Gilbert Islands in the Wake of Battle. By W. Robert Moore. Vol. LXXXVII, pp. 129-162, 11 ills. in black and white, 19 ills. in color, 1 two-thirds-page map, Feb., 1945.

Round About Grim Tarawa. 19 ills. in color from natural-color photographs by W. Robert Moore. Vol. LXXXVII, pp. 137-160, Feb., 1945.

Marathon (Plain), Greece:

"Glory That Was Greece." By Alexander Wilbourne Weddell. Vol. XLII, pp. 571-630, 51 ills., 1 three-quarters-page map, Dec., 1922.

Marauders (Bombers):

Return to Florence. By 1st Lt. Benjamin C. McCartney. Vol. LXXXVII, pp. 257-296, 18 ills. in black and white, 18 ills. in color, Mar., 1945.

Marauders of the Sea (Squid and Octopuses). By Roy Waldo Miner. Vol. LXVIII, pp. 185-207, 12 ills. in black and white, 8 ills. in color, Aug., 1935.

Marble Canyon, Arizona:

Experiences in the Grand Canyon. By Ellsworth and Emory Kolb. Vol. XXVI, pp. 99-184, 70 ills., 1 page map, Aug., 1914.

Marble Dams of Rajputana. By Eleanor Maddock. Vol. XL, pp. 468-499, 13 ills. in black and white, 16 ills. in color, Nov., 1921.

Marblehead, Massachusetts:

Northeast of Boston. By Albert W. Atwood. Vol. LXXXVIII, pp. 257-292, 12 ills. in black and white, 17 ills. in color, special map supplement, Sept., 1945.

Marching Through Georgia Sixty Years After: Multifold Industries and Diversified Agriculture Are Restoring the Prosperity of America's Largest State East of the Mississippi. By Ralph A. Graves. Vol. L, pp. 259-311, 47 ills., Sept., 1926.

Marcus, Oscar:

Pilgrims' Progress to Mecca.   22 ills. in duotone; 18 ills. by Oscar Marcus.   Vol. LXXII, pp. 627-642, Nov., 1937.

Marden, Luis:

Americans in the Caribbean. By Luis Marden. Vol. LXXXI, pp. 723-758, 16 ills. in black and white, 22 ills. in color, 1 half-page map, June, 1942.

Beneath Colombia's Azure Skies. 18 ills. in color from natural-color photographs; 17 ills. by Luis Marden. Vol. LXXVIII, pp. 513-536, Oct., 1940.

Buenos Aires—Metropolis of the Pampas. 24 ills. in color from natural-color photographs by Luis Marden and Maynard Owen Williams. Vol. LXXVI, pp. 577-600, Nov., 1939.

Caracas, Cradle of the Liberator: The Spirit of Simón Bolívar, South American George Washington, Lives On in the City of His Birth. By Luis Marden. Vol. LXXVII, pp. 477-513, 18 ills. in black and white, 19 ills. in color, Apr., 1940.

Coffee Is King in El Salvador. By Luis Marden. With 27 ills. in color from natural-color photographs by the author and David D. Duncan. Vol. LXXXVI, pp. 575-616, 22 ills. in black and white, 1 half-page map, Nov., 1944.

Hail Colombia! By Luis Marden. Vol. LXXVIII, pp. 505-536, 10 ills. in black and white, 18 ills. in color, 1 third-page map, Oct., 1940.

Hub City (Boston), Cradle of American Liberty. 31 ills. in color from natural-color photographs; 26 ills. by Luis Marden. Vol. LXX, pp. 49-72, July, 1936.

In Montezuma's Painted Land (Mexico). 22 ills. in color from natural-color photographs; 21 ills. by Luis Marden. Vol. LXXVIII, pp. 345-368, Sept., 1940.

Land of Lakes and Volcanoes (Nicaragua). By Luis Marden. With 17 ills. in color from natural-color photographs by the author. Vol. LXXXVI, pp. 161-192, 11 ills. in black and white, 1 two-thirds-page map, Aug., 1944.

Land of the Painted Oxcarts (Costa Rica). By Luis Marden. With 31 ills. in color from natural-color photographs by the author. Vol. XC, pp. 409-456, 30 ills. in black and white, 1 half-page map, Oct., 1946.

Land That Links the Americas (Panama). 22 ills. in color from natural-color photographs by Luis Marden. Vol. LXXX, pp. 601-624, Nov., 1941.

Old and New Blend in Yankeeland (Connecticut). 25 ills. in color from natural-color photographs; 10 ills. by Luis Marden. Vol. LXXIV, pp. 295-326, Sept., 1938.

Marden, Luis—_Continued_

On the Cortés Trail (Mexico). By Luis Marden. Vol. LXXVIII, pp. 335-375, 17 ills. in black and white, 22 ills. in color, 1 map, Sept., 1940.

Panama, Bridge of the World. By Luis Marden. Vol. LXXX, pp. 591-630, 23 ills. in black and white, 22 ills. in color, 1 half-page map, Nov., 1941.

Riatas and Romance on the Rio Grande. 24 ills. in color from natural-color photographs; 23 ills. by Luis Marden. Vol. LXXVI, pp. 431-462, Oct., 1939.

To Market in Guatemala. By Luis Marden. With 19 ills. in color from natural-color photographs by Giles Greville Healey and Charles S. Pineo. Vol. LXXXVIII, pp. 87-104, July, 1945.

Today in the Feathered Serpent's City (Chichen Itzá). 25 ills. in color from natural-color photographs by Luis Marden. Vol. LXX, pp. 599-614, Nov., 1936.

Venezuela's Capital—City of Contrasts. 19 ills. in color from natural-color photographs by Luis Marden. Vol. LXXVII, pp. 483-506, Apr., 1940.

Virginia's Colonial Heritage (Williamsburg). 25 ills. in color from natural-color photographs; 8 ills. by Luis Marden. Vol. LXXI, pp. 417-440, Apr., 1937.

War Echoes in the West Indies. 22 ills. in color from natural-color photographs by Luis Marden. Vol. LXXXI, pp. 731-754, June, 1942.

Where Man's Garb Rivals the Quetzal (Guatemala). 13 ills. in color from natural-color photographs by Luis Marden. Vol. LXX, pp. 437-444, Oct., 1936.

Marianas Islands, Pacific Ocean:

American Pathfinders in the Pacific. By William H. Nicholas. Vol. LXXXIX, pp. 617-640, 17 ills., 1 two-page map, May, 1946.

Hidden Key to the Pacific: Piercing the Web of Secrecy Which Long Has Veiled Japanese Bases in the Mandated Islands. By Willard Price. Vol. LXXXI, pp. 759-785, 28 ills., 1 map (two-page spread), June, 1942.

South from Saipan. By W. Robert Moore. Vol. LXXXVII, pp. 441-474, 11 ills. in black and white, 17 ills. in color, 1 half-page map, Apr., 1945.

Springboards to Tokyo. By Willard Price. Vol. LXXXVI, pp. 385-407, 16 ills., Oct., 1944.

Victory's Portrait in the Marianas. By Lt. William Franklin Draper, USNR. With 17 ills. in color from paintings by the author. Vol. LXXXVIII, pp. 599-616, Nov., 1945.

See also Guam.

Marine Biology:

America's Most Valuable Fishes. By Hugh M. Smith. Vol. XXIII, pp. 494-514, 17 ills., May, 1912.

Carnivores of a Lightless World. 8 ills. in color from paintings by Else Bostelmann. Vol. LXVI, pp. 693-700, Dec., 1934.

Marine Biology—*Continued*

Certain Citizens of the Warm Sea. By Louis L. Mowbray. Vol. XLI, pp. 27-62, 18 ills. in black and white, 16 ills. in color, Jan., 1922.

Coral Castle Builders of Tropic Seas. By Roy Waldo Miner. Vol. LXV, pp. 703-728, 15 ills. in black and white, 8 ills. in color, 1 two-thirds-page and 1 third-page maps, June, 1934.

Crabs and Crablike Curiosities of the Sea. By William Crowder. Vol. LIV, pp. 57-72, 10 ills. in black and white, 8 ills. in color, July, 1928.

Cultivation of Marine and Fresh Water Animals in Japan. By K. Mitsukuri. Vol. XVII, pp. 524-531, 5 ills., Sept., 1906.

Deep-Sea Exploring Expedition of the Steamer *Albatross*. By Hugh M. Smith. Vol. X, pp. 291-296, 2 ills., 1 diagram, Aug., 1899.

Denizens of Our Warm Atlantic Waters. By Roy Waldo Miner. Vol. LXXI, pp. 199-219, 10 ills. in black and white, 8 ills. in color, Feb., 1937.

Depths of the Sea: Strange Life Forms a Mile Below the Surface. By William Beebe. Vol. LXI, pp. 65-88, 15 ills. in black and white, 8 ills. in color, 1 half-page map, Jan., 1932.

Exploring Neptune's Hidden World of Vivid Color. 8 ills. in color from paintings by E. Bostelmann. Vol. LXII, pp. 747-754, Dec., 1932.

Fantastic Dwellers in a Coral Fairyland (Great Barrier Reef). 15 ills. in color from natural-color photographs by T. C. Roughley. Vol. LXXVII, pp. 831-838, June, 1940.

Fantastic Sea Life from Abyssal Depths. 8 ills. in color from paintings by E. Bostelmann. Vol. LXI, pp. 71-78, Jan., 1932.

First Autochromes from the Ocean Bottom: Marine Life in Its Natural Habitat Along the Florida Keys Is Successfully Photographed in Colors. Vol. LI, pp. 56-61, 8 ills. in color, Jan., 1927.

Fishes and Fisheries of Our North Atlantic Seaboard. By John Oliver La Gorce. Vol. XLIV, pp. 567-634, 35 ills. in black and white, 16 ills. in color, Dec., 1923.

Fishes That Build Nests and Take Care of Their Young. Vol. XVIII, pp. 400-412, 16 ills., June, 1907.

Fishes That Carry Lanterns. Vol. XXI, pp. 453-456, 5 ills., May, 1910.

Fishing in Pacific Coast Streams. By Leonard P. Schultz. Vol. LXXV, pp. 185-212, 10 ills. in black and white, 54 portraits in color, Feb., 1939.

Flashes From Ocean Deeps. 14 ills. in color from paintings by Else Bostelmann. Vol. LXVI, pp. 677-700, Dec., 1934.

Fresh-Water Denizens of the Far West. 54 portraits in color from paintings by Hashime Murayama. Vol. LXXV, pp. 193-204, Feb., 1939.

Glass-Bottom Boat. By Charles Frederick Holder. Vol. XX, pp. 761-778, 17 ills., Sept., 1909.

Marine Biology—*Continued*

Gleaming Fishes of Pacific Coastal Waters. 31 portraits in color from paintings by Hashime Murayama. Vol. LXXIV, pp. 467-498, Oct., 1938.

Great Barrier Reef and Its Isles: The Wonder and Mystery of Australia's World-Famous Geographical Feature. By Charles Barrett. Vol. LVIII, pp. 355-384, 38 ills., 1 two-thirds-page map, Sept., 1930.

Half Mile Down: Strange Creatures, Beautiful and Grotesque as Figments of Fancy, Reveal Themselves at Windows of the Bathysphere. By William Beebe. Vol. LXVI, pp. 661-704, 28 ills. in black and white, 16 ills. in color, 1 third-page map, Dec., 1934.

Interesting Citizens of the Gulf Stream. By Dr. John T. Nichols. Vol. XXXIX, pp. 69-84, 11 ills. in black and white, 16 ills. in color, Jan., 1921.

Jellyfishes—Living Draperies of Color. 8 ills. in color from paintings by William Crowder. Vol. L, pp. 193-200, Aug., 1926.

King Herring: An Account of the World's Most Valuable Fish, the Industries It Supports, and the Part It Has Played in History. By Hugh M. Smith. Vol. XX, pp. 701-735, 21 ills., Aug., 1909.

Life of the Moon-Jelly. By William Crowder. Vol. L, pp. 187-202, 6 ills. in black and white, 1 ill. in color, Aug., 1926.

Life on a Coral Reef: The Fertility and Mystery of the Sea Studied Beneath the Waters Surrounding Dry Tortugas. By W. H. Longley. Vol. LI, pp. 61-83, 22 ills. in black and white, 8 ills. in color, Jan., 1927.

Living Jewels of the Sea (Plankton). By William Crowder. Vol. LII, pp. 290-304, 8 ills. in black and white, 8 ills. in color, Sept., 1927.

Luminous Life in the Depths of the Sea. 8 ills. in color from paintings by E. Bostelmann. Vol. LIX, pp. 667-674, June, 1931.

Multi-Hued Marvels of a Coral Reef. 8 ills. in color from paintings by Else Bostelmann. Vol. LXV, pp. 719-726, June, 1934.

Mysterious Life of the Common Eel. By Hugh M. Smith. Vol. XXIV, pp. 1140-1146, 3 ills., Oct., 1913.

Native Oysters of the West Coast. By Robert E. C. Stearns. Vol. XIX, pp. 224-226, Mar., 1908.

Notes from a Naturalist's Experiences in British Guiana. By C. H. Eigenmann. Vol. XXII, pp. 859-870, 8 ills., Sept., 1911.

On the Bottom of a South Sea Pearl Lagoon. By Roy Waldo Miner. Vol. LXXIV, pp. 365-390, 17 ills. in black and white, 8 ills. in color, Sept., 1938.

Oysters: The World's Most Valuable Water Crop. By Hugh M. Smith. Vol. XXIV, pp. 257-281, 21 ills., Mar., 1913.

Planting Fishes in the Ocean. By George M. Bowers. Vol. XVIII, pp. 715-723, 5 ills., Nov., 1907.

Purple Veil: A Romance of the Sea. Vol. XVI, pp. 337-341, 9 ills., July, 1905.

Marine Biology—*Continued*

Rainbow Denizens of the Aquarium (Tropical Fish). 16 ills. in color from natural-color photographs by Edwin L. Wisherd. Vol. LXV, pp. 97-104, Jan., 1934.

Round Trip to Davy Jones's Locker : Peering into Mysteries a Quarter Mile Down in the Open Sea, by Means of the Bathysphere. By William Beebe. Vol. LIX, pp. 653-678, 14 ills. in black and white, 8 ills. in color, 1 quarter-page map, June, 1931.

Sea Creatures of Our Atlantic Shores. By Roy Waldo Miner. Vol. LXX, pp. 209-231, 8 ills. in black and white, 8 ills. in color, 1 chart, Aug., 1936.

Sea Floor Aquarelles from Tongareva. 8 ills. in color from paintings by Else Bostelmann. Vol. LXXIV, pp. 383-390, Sept., 1938.

Some Giant Fishes of the Seas. By Hugh M. Smith. Vol. XX, pp. 637-644, 6 ills., July, 1909.

Strange Creatures of Sunny Seas. 8 ills. in color from paintings by Else Bostelmann. Vol. LXXI, pp. 211-218, Feb., 1937.

Treasure-House of the Gulf Stream : The Completion and Opening of the New Aquarium and Biological Laboratory at Miami, Florida. By John Oliver La Gorce. Vol. XXXIX, pp. 53 68, 5 ills. in black and white, 16 ills. in color, Jan., 1921.

Treasures of the Pacific : Marine Fishes and Fisheries Yield Vast Wealth from Alaska to Baja California. By Leonard P. Schultz. Vol. LXXIV, pp. 463-498, 10 ills. in black and white, 31 portraits in color, Oct., 1938.

Tropical Fish Immigrants Reveal New Nature Wonders. By Walter H. Chute. Vol. LXV, pp. 93-110, 8 ills. in black and white, 16 ills. in color, Jan., 1934.

Tropical Toy Fishes : More Than 600 Varieties of Aquarium Pygmies Afford a Fascinating Field of Zoölogical Study in the Home. By Ida Mellen. Vol. LIX, pp. 287-317, 20 ills. in black and white, 8 ills. in color, Mar., 1931.

Undersea Gardens of the North Atlantic Coast. 8 ills. in color from paintings by Else Bostelmann. Vol. LXX, pp. 217-224, Aug., 1936.

Where Nature Runs Riot : On Australia's Great Barrier Reef Marine Animals Grow to Unusual Size, Develop Strange Weapons of Attack and Defense, and Acquire Brilliant Colors. By T. C. Roughley. Vol. LXXVII, pp. 823-850, 18 ills. in black and white, 15 ills. in color, 1 page map, June, 1940.

Wonderer Under Sea. By William Beebe. Vol. LXII, pp. 741-758, 13 ills. in black and white, 8 ills. in color, Dec., 1932.

Marine Hydrographic Surveys of the Coasts of the World. By George W. Littlehales. Vol. XVI, pp. 63-67, 1 page map, Feb., 1905.

Marine Worms:

The Worm Turns. By Samuel Sandrof. Vol. LXXXIX, pp. 775-786, 14 ills., June, 1946.

Marines, U. S. *See* U. S. Marine Corps.

Marken (Island), Netherlands :

Glimpses of Holland. By William W. Chapin. Vol. XXVII, pp. 1-29, 26 ills., Jan., 1915.

Markets:

Down Mexico's Río Balsas. 9 ills. in color from natural-color photographs by John W. Webber, Kenneth Segerstrom, and Jack Breed. Vol. XC, pp. 257-264, Aug., 1946.

Haiti Goes to Market. 10 ills. in color from natural-color photographs by B. Anthony Stewart. Vol. LXXXVI, pp. 313-320, Sept., 1944.

Kano (Nigeria), Mud-Made City. 10 ills. in color from natural-color photographs by George W. Scott and K. S. Twitchell. Vol. LXXXV, pp. 545-552, May, 1944.

Manipur—Where Japan Struck at India. 11 ills. from photographs, 1 page map. Vol. LXXXV, pp. 743-750, June, 1944.

North Holland Cheese Market. By Hugh M. Smith. Vol. XXI, pp. 1051-1066, 17 ills., Dec., 1910.

Oil Comes to Bahrein, Port of Pearls. 11 ills. in color from natural-color photographs by Maynard Owen Williams. Vol. LXXXIX, pp. 201-208, Feb., 1946.

Syria and Lebanon Taste Freedom. By Maynard Owen Williams. With 21 ills. in color from natural-color photographs by the author. Vol. XC, pp. 729-763, 16 ills. in black and white, Dec., 1946.

To Market in Guatemala. By Luis Marden. With 19 ills. in color from natural-color photographs by Giles Greville Healey and Charles S. Pineo. Vol. LXXXVIII, pp. 87-104, July, 1945.

Marking the Alaskan Boundary. Vol. XIX, pp. 176-189, 16 ills., Mar., 1908.

Marking the Alaskan Boundary. By Thomas Riggs, Jr. Vol. XX, pp. 593-607, 17 ills., July, 1909.

Markwith, Carl:

Farewell to Bikini. By Carl Markwith. Vol. XC, pp. 97-116, 16 ills., July, 1946.

Marlatt, Charles Lester:

Pests and Parasites : Why We Need a National Law to Prevent the Importation of Insect-Infested and Diseased Plants. By Charles Lester Marlatt. Vol. XXII, pp. 321-346, 29 ills., 2 three-quarters-page maps, Apr., 1911.

Protecting the United States from Plant Pests. By Charles Lester Marlatt. Vol. XL, pp. 205-218, 16 ills., Aug., 1921.

Marlin (Fish) :

Fighting Giants of the Humboldt. By David D. Duncan. Vol. LXXIX, pp. 373-400, 28 ills., 1 half-page map, Mar., 1941.

Marlowe, Christopher:

Tour in the English Fenland. By Christopher Marlowe. Vol. LV, pp. 605-634, 26 ills. in black and white, 5 ills. in color, 1 half-page map, May, 1929.

Marmora, Sea of :

Gates to the Black Sea : The Dardanelles, the Bosphorus, and the Sea of Marmora. By H. G. Dwight. Vol. XXVII, pp. 435-459, 27 ills., May, 1915.

Marqueen Islands. *See* Tauu Islands.

Marquesas Islands, Pacific Ocean :

At Home on the Oceans : Whales and Sharks Make Exciting Neighbors for a Professor's Wife, Turned Able Seaman, On a Three-year Voyage Around the World. By Edith Bauer Strout. Vol. LXXVI, pp. 33-86, 54 ills., 1 map, July, 1939.

Diary of a Voyage from San Francisco to Tahiti and Return, 1901. By S. P. Langley. Vol. XII, pp. 413-429, 10 ills., 1 page and 1 half-page maps, Dec., 1901.

Dream Ship : The Story of a Voyage of Adventure More Than Half Around the World in a 47-Foot Lifeboat. By Ralph Stock. Vol. XXXIX, pp. 1-52, 43 ills., 1 page map, Jan., 1921.

Romance of Science in Polynesia : An Account of Five Years of Cruising Among the South Sea Islands. By Robert Cushman Murphy. Vol. XLVIII, pp. 355-426, 66 ills. in black and white, 16 ills. in color, 3 half-page maps, Oct., 1925.

Vanishing People of the South Seas : The Tragic Fate of the Marquesan Cannibals, Noted for Their Warlike Courage and Physical Beauty. By John W. Church. Vol. XXXVI, pp. 275-306, 22 ills., 1 half page map, Oct., 1919.

See also Fatu-Hiva (Island).

Marquez, Luis:

Mexican Land of Lakes and Lacquers (Pátzcuaro Region). 22 ills. from photographs by Helene Fischer and Luis Marquez. Vol. LXXI, pp. 633-648, May, 1937.

Marrak Point, Greenland :

Uncle Sam's Icebox Outposts. 19 ills. in color from natural-color photographs by John E. Schneider and Robert B. Sykes, Jr. Vol. XC, pp. 473-496, Oct., 1946.

Marrakech, Morocco :

Americans on the Barbary Coast. By Willard Price. Vol. LXXXIV, pp. 1-31, 13 ills. in black and white, 10 ills. in color, 1 map (two-page spread), July, 1943.

Marriage Customs:

Among the Hill Tribes of Burma—An Ethnological Thicket. By Sir George Scott. Vol. XLII, pp. 293-321, 22 ills., Mar., 1922.

Beauties of France. By Arthur Stanley Riggs. Vol. XXVIII, pp. 391-491, 73 ills. in black and white, 16 ills. in color, 1 half-page map, Nov., 1915.

"Flower of Paradise" : The Part Which Khat Plays in the Life of the Yemen Arab. By Charles Moser. Vol. XXXII, pp. 173-186, 10 ills., 1 page map, Aug., 1917.

Marriage Customs—*Continued*

In the Realms of the Maharajas. By Lawrence Copley Thaw and Margaret S. Thaw. Vol. LXXVIII, pp. 727-780, 14 ills. in black and white, 40 ills. in color, 1 page map, Dec., 1940.

Journey in Morocco : "The Land of the Moors." By Thomas Lindsey Blayney. Vol. XXII, pp. 750-776, 24 ills., 1 page map, Aug., 1911.

Princely India, Resplendent with Jewels and Gold. 40 ills. in color from natural-color photographs by Lawrence Copley Thaw. Vol. LXXVIII, pp. 733-780, Dec., 1940.

Pushing Back History's Horizon : How the Pick and Shovel Are Revealing Civilizations That Were Ancient When Israel Was Young. By Albert T. Clay. Vol. XXIX, pp. 162-216, 47 ills., 1 page map, Feb., 1916.

Roumania and Its Rubicon. By John Oliver La Gorce. Vol. XXX, pp. 185-202, 11 ills., Sept., 1916.

Vanishing People of the South Seas : The Tragic Fate of the Marquesan Cannibals, Noted for Their Warlike Courage and Physical Beauty. By John W. Church. Vol. XXXVI, pp. 275-306, 22 ills., 1 half-page map, Oct., 1919.

Village Life in the Holy Land. By John D. Whiting. Vol. XXV, pp. 249-314, 27 ills. in black and white, 22 ills. in color, Mar., 1914.

Marriage of the Gods (Religious Festival, Madura, India). By John J. Banninga. Vol. XXIV, pp. 1314-1330, 16 ills., Dec., 1913.

Marriner, J. Theodore:

Transylvania and Its Seven Castles : A Motor Circuit Through Rumania's New Province of Racial Complexity and Architectural Charm. By J. Theodore Marriner. Vol. XLIX, pp. 319-352, 35 ills., 1 half-page map, Mar., 1926.

Marseille (France), Battle Port of Centuries. By a Staff Correspondent. Vol. LXXXVI, pp. 425-448, 24 ills., 1 three-quarters-page map, Oct., 1944.

Marsh, Cody:

Glimpses of Siberia, the Russian "Wild East." By Cody Marsh. Vol. XXXVIII, pp. 512-536, 26 ills., Dec., 1920.

Marsh, O. C.:

O. C. Marsh (Biography). Vol. X, pp. 181-182, May, 1899.

Marshall Islands, Pacific Ocean :

American Pathfinders in the Pacific. By William H. Nicholas. Vol. LXXXIX, pp. 617-640, 17 ills., 1 two-page map, May, 1946.

Farewell to Bikini. By Carl Markwith. Vol. XC, pp. 97-116, 16 ills., July, 1946.

Hidden Key to the Pacific : Piercing the Web of Secrecy Which Long Has Veiled Japanese Bases in the Mandated Islands. By Willard Price. Vol. LXXXI, pp. 759-785, 28 ills., 1 map (two-page spread), June, 1942.

Marshall Islands, Pacific Ocean—*Continued*

Marshallese Are Happy Again. 20 ills. in color from natural-color photographs by W. Robert Moore. Vol. LXXXVIII, pp. 337-360, Sept., 1945.

Our New Military Wards, the Marshalls. By W. Robert Moore. Vol. LXXXVIII, pp. 325-360, 14 ills. in black and white, 20 ills. in color, 1 half-page map, Sept., 1945.

Yap and Other Pacific Islands Under Japanese Mandate. By Junius B. Wood. Vol. XL, pp. 591-627, 34 ills., 1 two-thirds-page map, Dec., 1921.

Marshallese Are Happy Again. 20 ills. in color from natural-color photographs by W. Robert Moore. Vol. LXXXVIII, pp. 337-360, Sept., 1945.

Marston, Jay:

Uganda, "Land of Something New": Equatorial African Area Reveals Snow-Crowned Peaks, Crater Lakes, Jungle-Story Beasts, Human Giants, and Forest Pygmies. By Jay Marston. Vol. LXXI, pp. 109-130, 22 ills., 1 two-thirds-page map, Jan., 1937.

Marsupials:

Koala, or Australian Teddy Bear. By F. Lewis. Vol. LX, pp. 346-355, 13 ills., Sept., 1931.

What the Fighting Yanks See. By Wanda Burnett. Vol. LXXXVI, pp. 451-476, 27 ills., Oct., 1944.

Martin, Charles:

California: Ever Changing California, Land of Startling Contrasts. 30 ills. in color from autochromes by Charles Martin. Vol. LV, pp. 704-745, June, 1929.

Fish: First Autochromes from the Ocean Bottom: Marine Life in Its Natural Habitat Along the Florida Keys Is Successfully Photographed in Colors. Vol. LI, pp. 56-61, 8 ills. in color, Jan., 1927.

Monticello, One of America's Most Historic Shrines. 3 ills. in color from natural-color photographs by Charles Martin. Vol. LV, pp. 488-497, Apr., 1929.

Philippines. 48 ills. in color from photographs by Dean C. Worcester and Charles Martin. Vol. XXIV, pp. 1161-1192, Nov., 1913.

Puerto Rico: Colorful Porto Rico. 12 ills. from natural-color photographs by Charles Martin. Vol. XLVI, pp. 631-642, Dec., 1924.

Sungmas (Oracles): Demon-Possessed Tibetans and Their Incredible Feats. 12 ills. in color from natural-color photographs; 3 ills. by Charles Martin. Vol. LXVIII, pp. 479-486, Oct., 1935.

United States: Exploring the Atlantic Seaboard with a Color Camera. 10 ills. in color from autochromes by Charles Martin. Vol. XLIX, pp. 532-549, May, 1926.

Virginia: Scenes and Shrines of the Cavalier Country. 7 ills. in color from natural-color photographs by Charles Martin. Vol. LV, pp. 424-433, Apr., 1929.

Martin, Charles—*Continued*

Washington, D. C.: Our Colorful City of Magnificent Distances. 10 ills. in color from natural-color photographs by Charles Martin. Vol. LX, pp. 530-611, Nov., 1931.

Washington, D. C.: Secrets of Washington's Lure. 3 ills. in color from natural-color photographs by Charles Martin. Vol. LVII, pp. 376-385, Mar., 1930.

Washington, D. C.: Unique Gifts of Washington to the Nation. 5 ills. in color from natural-color photographs by Charles Martin. Vol. LV, pp. 472-481, Apr., 1929.

Washington, D. C.: Winter Lights and Shadows in the Nation's Capital. 21 ills. in duotone; 3 ills. by Charles Martin. Vol. LXVII, pp. 201-216, Feb., 1935.

Washington (D. C.), the Pride of the Nation. 16 ills. in color from autochromes by Charles Martin. Vol. XLIII, pp. 617-632, June, 1923.

Martin, George C.:

Recent Eruption of Katmai Volcano in Alaska. By George C. Martin. Vol. XXIV, pp. 131-181, 45 ills., 1 page map, 1 diagram, Feb., 1913.

Martin, Lawrence:

National Geographic Society's Alaskan Expedition of 1909. By Ralph S. Tarr and Lawrence Martin. Vol. XXI, pp. 1-54, 42 ills., 12 maps, Jan., 1910.

National Geographic Society's Researches in Alaska. By Lawrence Martin. Vol. XXII, pp. 537-561, 17 ills., 1 page and 4 half-page maps, June, 1911.

Martin, (Dr.) W. A. P.:

Causes That Led Up to the Siege of Pekin. By Dr. W. A. P. Martin. Vol. XII, pp. 53-63, 1 ill., Feb., 1901.

Martin, Mount, Alaska:

Our Greatest National Monument: The National Geographic Society Completes Its Explorations in the Valley of Ten Thousand Smokes. By Robert F. Griggs. Vol. XL, pp. 219-292, 73 ills. in black and white, 16 ills. in color, 1 page and 1 three-quarters-page maps, Sept., 1921.

Valley of Ten Thousand Smokes: The National Geographic Society Explorations in the Katmai District of Alaska. By Robert F. Griggs. Vol. XXXI, pp. 12-68, 51 ills., 1 half-page map, Jan., 1917.

Martinique (Island), West Indies:

Chemical Discussion of Analyses of Volcanic Ejecta from Martinique and St. Vincent. By W. F. Hillebrand. Vol. XIII, pp. 296-299, July, 1902.

Colorful Paths in Martinique and Guadeloupe. 13 ills. in color from natural-color photographs by Edwin L. Wisherd. Vol. LXXIII, pp. 281-288, Mar., 1938.

Destruction of Pompeii as Interpreted by the Volcanic Eruptions of Martinique. By Angelo Heilprin. Vol. XV, p. 431, Oct., 1904.

Martinique (Island), West Indies—*Continued*

Lafcadio Hearn on the Island and People of Martinique. Vol. XIII, pp. 214-216, June, 1902.

Magnetic Disturbance Caused by the Explosion of Mont Pelée. Vol. XIII, pp. 208-209, June, 1902.

Martinique, Caribbean Question Mark. By Edward T. Folliard. Vol. LXXIX, pp. 47-55, 9 ills., Jan., 1941.

National Geographic Society Expedition to Martinique and St. Vincent. Vol. XIII, pp. 183-184, 2 ills., June, 1902.

National Geographic Society's Expedition in the West Indies. Vol. XIII, pp. 209-213, 2 half-page maps, June, 1902.

New Cone of Mont Pelée. Vol. XIV, pp. 422-423, 2 ills., Nov., 1903.

Recent Volcanic Eruptions in the West Indies. By Israel C. Russell. Vol. XIII, pp. 267-285, 7 ills., July, 1902.

Report by Robert T. Hill on the Volcanic Disturbances in the West Indies. Vol. XIII, pp. 223-267, 13 ills., 2 page and 1 quarter-page maps, July, 1902.

Reports of Vessels as to the Range of Volcanic Dust. By James Page. Vol. XIII, pp. 299-301, July, 1902.

Shattered Obelisk of Mount Pelée. By Angelo Heilprin. Vol. XVII, pp. 465-474, 5 ills., Aug., 1906.

Southward Ho! in the "Alice." By Henry Howard. Vol. LXXIII, pp. 265-312, 38 ills. in black and white, 13 ills. in color, 2 maps, Mar., 1938.

Volcanic Eruptions on Martinique and St. Vincent. By Israel C. Russell. Vol. XIII, pp. 415-436, 10 ills., Dec., 1902.

Volcanic Rocks of Martinique and St. Vincent: Collected by Robert T. Hill and Israel C. Russell. By J. S. Diller. Vol. XIII, pp. 285-296, July, 1902.

Martinsburg, West Virginia :

Potomac, River of Destiny. By Albert W. Atwood. Vol. LXXXVIII, pp. 33-70, 15 ills. in black and white, 18 ills. in color, 1 map (two-page spread), July, 1945.

Marvelous Prosperity of the South. Vol. XVIII, p. 685, Oct., 1905.

Marvels of Fern Life. 16 ills. in color from paintings by E. J. Geske. Vol. XLVII, pp. 547-562, May, 1925.

Marvels of Metamorphosis : A Scientific "G-man" Pursues Rare Trapdoor Spider Parasites for Three Years With a Spade and a Candid Camera. By George Elwood Jenks. Vol. LXXIV, pp. 807-828, 39 ills., Dec., 1938.

Marvels of Mycetozoa : Exploration of a Long Island Swamp Reveals Some of the Secrets of the Slime Molds, Dwelling on the Borderland Between the Plant and Animal Kingdoms. By William Crowder. Vol. XLIX, pp. 421-443, 5 ills. in black and white, 16 ills. in color, Apr., 1926.

Marvin, C. F.:

Record of the Great Earthquake Written in Washington by the Seismograph of the United States Weather Bureau. By C. F. Marvin. Vol. XVII, pp. 296-298, May, 1906.

Maryland:

Approaching Washington by Tidewater Potomac. By Paul Wilstach. Vol. LVII, pp. 372-392, 7 ills., Mar., 1930.

Chesapeake Odyssey : An 18-foot Sailboat Follows the Course of Captain John Smith around This Spacious Bay of History, Commerce, Sea Food, and Nautical Lore. By John Maloney. Vol. LXXVI, pp. 357-392, 32 ills., 1 page map, Sept., 1939.

Colossal Work in Baltimore. By Calvin W. Hendrick. Vol. XX, pp. 365-373, 6 ills., Apr., 1909.

George Washington's Historic River (Potomac). 18 ills. in color from natural-color photographs by Willard R. Culver and Robert F. Sisson. Vol. LXXXVIII, pp. 41-64, July, 1945.

Maryland Pilgrimage : Visits to Hallowed Shrines Recall the Major Rôle Played by This Prosperous State in the Development of Popular Government in America. By Gilbert Grosvenor. Vol. LI, pp. 133-212, 88 ills., special map supplement, Feb., 1927.

Maryland Presents— By W. Robert Moore. Vol. LXXIX, pp. 401-448, 17 ills. in black and white, 32 ills. in color, 1 map (two-page spread), Apr., 1941.

Maytime in the Heart of Maryland. 10 ills. in color from natural-color photographs by B. Anthony Stewart and Charles Martin. Vol. LXXIX, pp. 441-448, Apr., 1941.

Old Line State Cyclorama. 22 ills. in color from natural-color photographs by W. Robert Moore, B. Anthony Stewart, and others. Vol. LXXIX, pp. 409-432, Apr., 1941.

Potomac, River of Destiny. By Albert W. Atwood. Vol. LXXXVIII, pp. 33-70, 15 ills. in black and white, 18 ills. in color, 1 map (two-page spread), July, 1945.

Roads from Washington. By John Patric. Vol. LXXIV, pp. 1-48, 27 ills. in black and white, 30 ills. in color, special map supplement, July, 1938.

Society's Map of Historic and Scenic Reaches of the Nation's Capital. Text accompanying special map supplement in colors. Vol. LXXIV, pp. 57-58, July, 1938.

Travels of George Washington : Dramatic Episodes in His Career as the First Geographer of the United States. By William Joseph Showalter. Vol. LXI, pp. 1-63, 50 ills., 5 maps, special map supplement, Jan., 1932.

Tri-State Medley. 10 ills. in color from natural-color photographs by Willard R. Culver. Vol. LXXIV, pp. 33-40, July, 1938.

Wartime Washington. By William H. Nicholas. Vol. LXXXIV, pp. 257-290, 12 ills. in black and white, 16 ills. in color, Sept., 1943.

See also Annapolis ; Solomons Island.

Masai (Tribespeople) :

Where Roosevelt Will Hunt. By Sir Harry Johnston. Vol. XX, pp. 207-256, 43 ills., special map supplement, Mar., 1909.

Wild Man and Wild Beast in Africa. By Theodore Roosevelt. Vol. XXII, pp. 1-33, 41 ills., 1 page map, Jan., 1911.

Masks:

Merry Maskers of Imst (Austria). 14 ills. from photographs by Francis C. Fuerst. Vol. LXX, pp. 201-208, Aug., 1936.

Mason, J. Alden:

Preserving Ancient America's Finest Sculptures (Guatemala). By J. Alden Mason. Vol. LXVIII, pp. 537-570, 24 ills. in black and white, 10 ills. in color, Nov., 1935.

Massachusetts:

Cape Cod Canal. By Commodore J. W. Miller. Vol. XXVI, pp. 185-190, 3 ills., 1 half-page map, Aug., 1914.

Cape Cod People and Places. By Wanda Burnett. Vol. LXXXIX, pp. 737-774, 17 ills. in black and white, 24 ills. in color, 1 half-page map, June, 1946.

Coasting Through the Bay State. 12 ills. in color from natural-color photographs by Clifton Adams. Vol. LX, pp. 286-295, Sept., 1931.

Collarin' Cape Cod : Experiences on Board a U. S. Navy Destroyer in a Wild Winter Storm. By Lieut. H. R. Thurber. Vol. XLVIII, pp. 427-472, 46 ills., Oct., 1925.

Flow Onward Connecticut (River) ! 24 ills. in color from natural-color photographs ; 22 ills. by B. Anthony Stewart. Vol. LXXXIII, pp. 409-432, Apr., 1943.

Long River of New England : In War and Peace, from Mountain Wilderness to the Sea, Flows the Connecticut River, Through a Valley Abounding in History, Scenery, Inventive Genius, and Industry. By Albert W. Atwood. Vol. LXXXIII, pp. 401-434, 12 ills. in black and white, 24 ills. in color, 1 two-thirds-page map, Apr., 1943.

Massachusetts—Beehive of Business. By William Joseph Showalter. Vol. XXXVII, pp. 203-245, 41 ills., Mar., 1920.

Massachusetts and Its Position In the Life of the Nation. By Calvin Coolidge. Vol. XLIII, pp. 337-352, 9 ills., Apr., 1923.

Northeast of Boston. By Albert W. Atwood. Vol. LXXXVIII, pp. 257-292, 12 ills. in black and white, 17 ills. in color, special map supplement, Sept., 1945.

Sauntering Through the Land of Roger Williams. 5 ills. in color from natural-color photographs by Clifton Adams. Vol. LX, pp. 310-319, Sept., 1931.

Where New England Meets the Sea. 17 ills. in color from natural-color photographs by B. Anthony Stewart. Vol. LXXXVIII, pp. 265-288, Sept., 1945.

Winter Rambles in Thoreau's Country. By Herbert W. Gleason. Vol. XXXVII, pp. 165-180, 15 ills., Feb., 1920.

See also Boston ; Nantucket (Island).

Massachusetts Indians:

America's First Settlers, the Indians. By Matthew W. Stirling. Vol. LXXII, pp. 535-596, 34 ills. in black and white, 24 ills. in color, Nov., 1937.

When Red Men Ruled Our Forests. 24 ills. in color from paintings by W. Langdon Kihn. Vol. LXXII, pp. 551-590, Nov., 1937.

Masters of Flight (Birds). Vol. XXXVI, pp. 49-56, 8 ills., July, 1919.

Mather, Stephen T.:

Awarded Jane M. Smith Life Membership. Vol. XXXVII, p. 342, Apr., 1920.

Matmata, Tunisia :

Mole Men : An Account of the Troglodytes of Southern Tunisia. By Frank Edward Johnson. Vol. XXII, pp. 787-846, 60 ills., Sept., 1911.

Matsang (River), Tibet :

The Tsangpo. By James Mascarene Hubbard. Vol. XII, pp. 32-35, Jan., 1901.

Matson, G. E.:

Multicolored Cones of Cappadocia. 20 ills. in color from natural-color photographs by Eric Matson. Vol. LXXVI, pp. 769-800, Dec., 1939.

Rose-Red City of Rock (Petra, Trans-Jordan). 21 ills. in color from natural-color photographs by G. E. Matson. Vol. LXVII, pp. 145-160, Feb., 1935.

Matterhorn (Mountain), Alps :

Majesty of the Matterhorn. Vol. XXIII, supplement, May, 1912.

Woman's Climbs in the High Alps. By Dora Keen. Vol. XXII, pp. 642-675, 26 ills., July, 1911.

Matthes, Gerard H.:

Dikes of Holland. By Gerard H. Matthes. Vol. XII, pp. 219-234, 3 ills., 7 charts, June, 1901.

Matto Grosso (State), Brazil :

Through Paraguay and Southern Matto Grosso. By Sir Christopher H. Gibson. Vol. LXXXIV, pp. 459-488, 20 ills. in black and white, 11 ills. in color, 1 two-thirds-page map, Oct., 1943.

Maugham, R. C. F.:

Hunting Big Game in Portuguese East Africa. By R. C. F. Maugham. Vol. XVIII, pp. 723-730, 7 ills., Nov., 1907.

Maunsell, (Col.) F. R.:

One Thousand Miles of Railway Built for Pilgrims and Not for Dividends (Damascus to Mecca). By Col. F. R. Maunsell. Vol. XX, pp. 156-172, 13 ills., 1 three-quarters-page map, Feb., 1909.

Maury, Matthew Fontaine:

Gem of the Ocean : Our American Navy. By Josephus Daniels. Vol. XXXIII, pp. 313-335 35 ills., Apr., 1918.

Maxcy, Robert F.:

Pine-Scented, Harbor-Dented Maine. 39 ills. in color from natural-color photographs by B. Anthony Stewart and Robert F. Maxcy. Vol. LXVII, pp. 549-588, May, 1935.

Maxon, William R.:

Ferns as a Hobby. By William R. Maxon. Vol. XLVII, pp. 541-586, 29 ills. in black and white, 16 ills. in color, May, 1925.

Mayas (Indians) :

Chichen Itzá, an Ancient American Mecca : Recent Excavations in Yucatan Are Bringing to Light the Temples, Palaces, and Pyramids of America's Most Holy Native City. By Sylvanus Griswold Morley. Vol. XLVII, pp. 63-95, 34 ills., 1 half-page map, 1 diagram, Jan., 1925.

Discovering the New World's Oldest Dated Work of Man : A Maya Monument Inscribed 291 B. C. is Unearthed Near a Huge Stone Head by a Geographic-Smithsonian Expedition in Mexico. By Matthew W. Stirling. Vol. LXXVI, pp. 183-218, 40 ills., 1 half-page map, Aug., 1939.

Excavations at Quirigua, Guatemala. By Sylvanus Griswold Morley. Vol. XXIV, pp. 339-361, 24 ills., 1 diagram, Mar., 1913.

Finding Jewels of Jade in a Mexican Swamp (Palenque Ruins). By Matthew W. and Marion Stirling. Vol. LXXXII, pp. 635-661, 15 ills. in black and white, 12 ills. in color, 1 two-thirds-page map, Nov., 1942.

Foremost Intellectual Achievement of Ancient America : The Hieroglyphic Inscriptions on the Monuments in the Ruined Cities of Mexico, Guatemala, and Honduras Are Yielding the Secrets of the Maya Civilization. By Sylvanus Griswold Morley. Vol. XLI, pp. 109-130, 27 ills., 17 diagrams, special map supplement in colors, Feb., 1922.

Home of a Forgotten Race : Mysterious Chichen Itzá in Yucatan, Mexico. By Edward H. Thompson. Vol. XXV, pp. 585-648, 59 ills., June, 1914.

Life and Death in Ancient Maya Land. 10 ills. in color from paintings by H. M. Herget. Vol. LXX, pp. 623-630, Nov., 1936.

Mexico's Deep South Yields New Treasure (Palenque Ruins). 12 ills. in color from natural-color photographs by Richard H. Stewart. Vol. LXXXII, pp. 649-656, Nov., 1942.

Mysterious Temples of the Jungle : The Prehistoric Ruins of Guatemala. By W. F. Sands. Vol. XXIV, pp. 324-338, 10 ills., Mar., 1913.

Portraits of Ancient Mayas, a Peace-Loving People. 10 ills. in color from paintings by H. M. Herget. Vol. LXVIII, pp. 553-560, Nov., 1935.

Preserving Ancient America's Finest Sculptures (Guatemala). By J. Alden Mason. Vol. LXVIII, pp. 537-570, 24 ills. in black and white, 10 ills. in color, Nov., 1935.

To Market in Guatemala. By Luis Marden. With 19 ills. in color from natural-color photographs by Giles Greville Healey and Charles S. Pineo. Vol. LXXXVIII, pp. 87-104, July, 1945.

Mayas (Indians)—*Continued*

Today in the Feathered Serpent's City (Chichen Itzá). 25 ills. in color from natural-color photographs by Luis Marden. Vol. LXX, pp. 599-614, Nov., 1936.

Unearthing America's Ancient History : Investigation Suggests That the Maya May Have Designed the First Astronomical Observatory in the New World in Order to Cultivate Corn. By Sylvanus Griswold Morley. Vol. LX, pp. 99-126, 28 ills., July, 1931.

Yucatán, Home of the Gifted Maya : Two Thousand Years of History Reach Back to Early American Temple Builders, Corn Cultivators, and Pioneers in Mathematics. By Sylvanus Griswold Morley. Vol. LXX, pp. 591-644, 28 ills. in black and white, 35 ills. in color, 1 two-thirds-page map, Nov., 1936.

Mayer, Alfred Goldsborough:

Our Neglected Southern Coast. By Alfred Goldsborough Mayer. Vol. XIX, pp. 859-871, 10 ills., Dec., 1908.

Mayer, Arthur Ellis:

Gems of the Italian Lakes. By Arthur Ellis Mayer. Vol. XXIV, pp. 943-956, 13 ills., Aug., 1913.

Mayflower. *See* Arbutus.

Maynard, Clarence F.:

Valley of Ten Thousand Smokes : An Account of the Discovery and Exploration of the Most Wonderful Volcanic Region in the World. By Robert F. Griggs. Vol. XXXIII, pp. 115-169, 46 ills., 1 half-page map, panorama, Feb., 1918.

Maytime in the Heart of Maryland (Sherwood Gardens). 10 ills. in color from natural-color photographs by B. Anthony Stewart and Charles Martin. Vol. LXXIX, pp. 441-448, Apr., 1941.

Mazatlan, Mexico :

Adventuring Down the West Coast of Mexico. By Herbert Corey. Vol. XLII, pp. 449-503, 44 ills., 1 half-page map, Nov., 1922.

M'chopis (Tribespeople) :

Impressions and Scenes in Mozambique. By O. W. Barrett. Vol. XXI, pp. 807-830, 31 ills., Oct., 1910.

Mead, Edwin D.:

Expansion of England. By Edwin D. Mead. Vol. XI, pp. 249-263, July, 1900.

Mealy Bugs:

An Insect Community Lives in Flower Heads. By James G. Needham. Vol. XC, pp. 340-356, 5 ills. in black and white, 11 ills. in color, Sept., 1946.

Means, Philip Ainsworth:

Incas : Empire Builders of the Andes. By Philip Ainsworth Means. Vol. LXXIII, pp. 225-264, 26 ills. in black and white, 10 ills. in color, Feb., 1938.

Measuring the Sun's Heat and Forecasting the Weather: The National Geographic Society to Maintain a Solar Station in a Remote Part of the World to Coöperate with Smithsonian Institution Stations in California and Chile. By C. G. Abbot. Vol. XLIX, pp. 111-126, 15 ills., 1 chart, Jan., 1926.

Meat Industry and Trade:

Farmers Keep Them Eating. By Frederick Simpich. Vol. LXXXIII, pp. 435-458, 22 ills., Apr., 1943.

Flavor and Savor of American Foods. 25 ills. in color from natural-color photographs by J. Baylor Roberts, Willard R. Culver, and others. Vol. LXXXI, pp. 289-320, Mar., 1942.

Nebraska, the Cornhusker State. By Leo A. Borah. Vol. LXXXVII, pp. 513-542, 6 ills. in black and white, 23 ills. in color, 1 map (two-page spread), May, 1945.

Revolution in Eating: Machine Food Age—Born of Roads, Research, and Refrigeration—Makes the United States the Best-fed Nation in History. By J. R. Hildebrand. Vol. LXXXI, pp. 273-324, 33 ills. in black and white, 25 ills. in color, Mar., 1942.

Mecca, Saudi Arabia:

Damascus and Mecca Railway. Vol. XII, p. 408, Nov., 1901.

Mecca the Mystic: A New Kingdom Within Arabia (Hejaz). By S. M. Zwemer. Vol. XXXII, pp. 157-172, 13 ills., Aug., 1917.

One Thousand Miles of Railway Built for Pilgrims and Not for Dividends (Damascus to Mecca). By Col. F. R. Maunsell. Vol. XX, pp. 156-172, 13 ills., 1 three-quarters-page map, Feb., 1909.

Pilgrims' Progress to Mecca. 22 ills. in duotone; 18 ills. by Oscar Marcus. Vol. LXXII, pp. 627-642, Nov., 1937.

Mechanics, Airplane:

They Sustain the Wings. By Frederick Simpich. Vol. LXXXIV, pp. 333-354, 19 ills., Sept., 1943.

Medals:

American Decorations and Insignia of Honor and Service. By Col. Robert E. Wyllie. Vol. XXXVI, pp. 502-526, 6 ills. in black and white, 119 ills. in color, Dec., 1919.

Decorations, Medals, Service Ribbons, Badges, and Women's Insignia. Vol. LXXXIV, pp. 414-444, 6 ills. in black and white, 376 ills. in color, Oct 1943.

Heraldry of Heroism. By Arthur E. Du Bois. Vol. LXXXIV, pp. 409-413, 2 ills., 1 third-page map, Oct., 1943.

Romance of Military Insignia: How the United States Government Recognizes Deeds of Heroism and Devotion to Duty. By Col. Robert E. Wyllie. Vol. XXXVI, pp. 463-501, 27 ills., Dec., 1919.

See also National Geographic Society: Medals.

Medan, Sumatra:

By Motor Through the East Coast and Batak Highlands of Sumatra. By Melvin A. Hall. Vol. XXXVII, pp. 68-102, 27 ills., Jan., 1920.

Médenine, Tunisia:

Mole Men: An Account of the Troglodytes of Southern Tunisia. By Frank Edward Johnson. Vol. XXII, pp. 787-846, 60 ills., Sept., 1911.

Medicine and Health:

Ali Goes to the Clinic. By Herndon and Mary Hudson. Vol. XC, pp. 764-766, 2 ills., Dec., 1946.

Flying Our Wounded Veterans Home. By Catherine Bell Palmer. Vol. LXXXVIII, pp. 363-384, 17 ills., Sept., 1945.

Geography of Medicines: War's Effect upon the World's Sources of Supply. By John Foote. Vol. XXXII, pp. 213-238, 25 ills., Sept., 1917.

Healing Arts in Global War: As Weapons Grow Deadlier, Scientific Medicine Pits Its Ever-rising Skill Against Them. By Albert W. Atwood. Vol. LXXXIV, pp. 599-618, 17 ills., Nov., 1943.

Life Story of the Mosquito. By Graham Fairchild. With 10 ills. in color from paintings. Vol. LXXXV, pp. 180-195, 5 ills. in black and white, 1 drawing, Feb., 1944.

Map-Changing Medicine. By William Joseph Showalter. Vol. XLII, pp. 303-330, 26 ills., Sept., 1922.

Medicine Fakes and Fakers of All Ages: Strange Stories of Nostrums and Kingly Quacks in Every Era and Clime. By John Foote. Vol. XXXV, pp. 67-84, 14 ills., Jan., 1919.

New Frontier in the Sky. By F. Barrows Colton. Vol. XC, pp. 379-408, 28 ills., 1 diagram, Sept., 1946.

1940 Paradox in Hong Kong. By Frederick Simpich. Vol. LXXVII, pp. 531-558, 24 ills., 3 maps, Apr., 1940.

Redeeming the Tropics. By William Joseph Showalter. Vol. XXV, pp. 344-364, 13 ills., Mar., 1914.

Saboteur Mosquitoes. By Harry H. Stage. Vol. LXXXV, pp. 165-179, 12 ills., Feb., 1944.

Your New World of Tomorrow. By F. Barrows Colton. Vol. LXXXVIII, pp. 385-410, 25 ills., Oct. 1945.

See also Diseases; Sanitation.

Medieval Glory Haunts the Eastern Adriatic. 17 ills. in color from autochromes by Hans Hildenbrand. Vol. LIII, pp. 64-81, Jan., 1928.

Medieval Pageantry in Modern Nördlingen (Germany). 12 ills. in color from autochromes by Hans Hildenbrand. Vol. LIV, pp. 706-715, Dec., 1928.

Medieval Tales of the Lop Basin in Central Asia. By Ellsworth Huntington. Vol. XIX, pp. 288-295, 9 ills., Apr., 1908.'

Mediterranean Regions:

From Africa to the Alps. 8 ills. in color from U. S. Army Air Forces official photographs. Vol. LXXXIX, pp. 161-168, Feb., 1946.

Geographic's New Map of Europe and the Mediterranean. By Gilbert Grosvenor. Text accompanying special map supplement in colors. Vol. LXXIII, pp. 525-528, 1 ill., Apr., 1938.

Mediterranean Checkerboard. By Frederick Simpich. Vol. LXXXI, pp. 527-550, 20 ills., 1 map (two-page spread), Apr., 1942

Mediterranean Regions. Text accompanying special map supplement in colors. Vol. XXIII, p. 104, Jan., 1912.

Society's New Map of Central Europe and the Mediterranean. Text accompanying special map supplement in colors. Vol. LXXVI, pp. 559-560, Oct., 1939.

See also Balearic Islands; Corsica; Crete; Cyprus; Malta; Sardinia; Sicily; *and* names of individual countries.

Meetings. *See* National Geographic Society: Meetings.

Megaspelæon, the Oldest Monastery in Greece. By Carroll Storrs Alden. Vol. XXIV, pp. 310-323, 11 ills., Mar., 1913.

Mekong (River), China:

Through the Great River Trenches of Asia: National Geographic Society Explorer Follows the Yangtze, Mekong, and Salwin Through Mighty Gorges, Some of Whose Canyon Walls Tower to a Height of More Than Two Miles. By Joseph F. Rock. Vol. L, pp. 133-186, 47 ills., 1 half-page map, Aug., 1926.

Melanesia:

In the Savage South Seas. By Beatrice Grimshaw. Vol. XIX, pp. 1-19, 21 ills., Jan., 1908.

Islands of the Pacific. By J. P. Thomson. Vol. XL, pp. 543-558, 15 ills., special map supplement, Dec., 1921.

North About. By Alan J. Villiers. Vol. LXXI, pp. 221-250, 24 ills., Feb., 1937.

Treasure Islands of Australasia: New Guinea, New Caledonia, and Fiji Trace across the South Pacific a Fertile Crescent Incredibly Rich in Minerals and Foods. By Douglas L. Oliver. Vol. LXXXI, pp. 691-722, 23 ills., 1 two-page map, June, 1942.

See also Bougainville; Fiji Islands; Munda; New Caledonia; New Guinea; New Hebrides; Solomon Islands.

Melbourne, Australia:

Capital Cities of Australia. By W. Robert Moore. Vol. LXVIII, pp. 667-722, 32 ills. in black and white, 24 ills. in color, 1 two-page map, Dec., 1935.

Lonely Australia: The Unique Continent. By Herbert E. Gregory. Vol. XXX, pp. 473-568, 68 ills., 1 two-page and 4 half-page maps, Dec., 1916.

Melgareio, A.:

Greatest Volcanoes of Mexico. By A. Melgareio. Vol. XXI, pp. 741-760, 22 ills., Sept., 1910.

Mellen, Ida:

Tropical Toy Fishes: More Than 600 Varieties of Aquarium Pygmies Afford a Fascinating Field of Zoölogical Study in the Home. By Ida Mellen. Vol. LIX, pp. 287-317, 20 ills. in black and white, 8 ills. in color, Mar., 1931.

Mellor, (Capt.) F. H.:

Isle of Man. By Capt. F. H. Mellor. Vol. LXXI, pp. 587-608, 13 ills. in black and white, 12 ills. in color, 1 third-page map, May, 1937.

Memorials:

Our National War Memorials in Europe. By Gen. John J. Pershing. Vol. LXV, pp. 1-36, 24 ills. in black and white, 11 ills. in color, 1 half-page map, Jan., 1934.

"Time Will Not Dim the Glory of Their Deeds." 11 ills. in color from natural-color photographs by W. Robert Moore. Vol. LXV, pp. 17-24, Jan., 1934.

See also Cemeteries; National Geographic Society: Memorials.

Men Against the Rivers (Mississippi and Ohio Rivers). By Frederick Simpich. Vol. LXXI, pp. 767-794, 22 ills., 1 page-and-a-half and 1 quarter-page maps, June, 1937.

Men and Gold. By Frederick Simpich. Vol. LXIII, pp. 481-518, 33 ills. in black and white, 11 ills. in duotone, Apr., 1933.

Men-Birds Soar on Boiling Air (Sailplanes). By Frederick G. Vosburgh. Vol. LXXIV, pp. 123-140, 15 ills., July, 1938.

Men of the Eagle in Their Mountain Eyrie (Albania). 39 ills. in color from natural-color photographs by Luigi Pellerano. Vol. LIX, pp. 142-191, Feb., 1931.

Mendaña, Alvaro de:

Revealing Earth's Mightiest Ocean (Pacific). By Albert W. Atwood. Vol. LXXXIV, pp. 291-306, 10 ills., special map supplement, Sept., 1943.

Mendenhall, Walter C.:

Colorado Desert. By W. C. Mendenhall. Vol. XX, pp. 681-701, 16 ills., Aug., 1909.

Wrangell Mountains, Alaska. By Walter C. Mendenhall. Vol. XIV, pp. 395-407, 3 ills., panorama, Nov., 1903.

Wrangell Mountains (Alaska). Panorama taken by W. C. Mendenhall from the ridge east of the Dadina River. Vol. XIV, supplement, Nov., 1903.

Mending Dikes in the Netherlands. 20 ills. from photographs by Lawrence Earl. Vol. XC, pp. 791-806, Dec., 1946.

Mengo, Uganda:

Where Roosevelt Will Hunt. By Sir Harry Johnston. Vol. XX, pp. 207-256, 43 ills., special map supplement in colors, Mar., 1909.

Menominee (Indian Tribe) :

America's First Settlers, the Indians. By Matthew W. Stirling. Vol. LXXII, pp. 535-596, 34 ills. in black and white, 24 ills. in color, Nov., 1937.

When Red Men Ruled Our Forests. 24 ills. in color from paintings by W. Langdon Kihn. Vol. LXXII, pp. 551-590, Nov., 1937.

Menzel, Donald H.:

Heavens Above : On Land, Sea, and in the Air the Stars Serve Modern Man as Map, Compass, and Clock. By Donald H. Menzel. With 12 charts, designed by the author, showing star positions for each month, and 13 drawings of the constellations by Carlotta Gonzales Lahey. Vol. LXXXIV, pp. 97-128, 1 map (two-page spread), July, 1943.

How to Use the Star Charts. Text accompanying 12 star charts designed by Donald H. Menzel. Vol. LXXXIV, pp. 116-128, July, 1943.

Merriam, C. Hart:

Acorn, a Possibly Neglected Source of Food. By C. Hart Merriam. Vol. XXXIV, pp. 129-137, 8 ills., Aug., 1918.

Merrill, Fullerton:

Hunting Trip to Northern Greenland. By Fullerton Merrill. Vol. XI, pp. 118-122, Mar., 1900.

Merritt, Lake, Oakland, California :

Wild Ducks as Winter Guests in a City Park. By Joseph Dixon. Vol. XXXVI, pp. 331-342, 11 ills., Oct., 1919.

Merry Maskers of Imst (Austria). 14 ills. from photographs by Francis C. Fuerst. Vol. LXX, pp. 201-208, Aug., 1936.

Mesa Verde National Park, Colorado :

Our National Parks. By L. F. Schmeckebier. Vol. XXIII, pp. 531-579, 41 ills., 1 page map, June, 1912.

Meshed, Iran :

Gilded Domes Against an Azure Sky. 13 ills. in color from natural-color photographs by Stephen H. Nyman. Vol. LXXVI, pp. 339-346, Sept., 1939.

Mesopotamia. *See* Iraq.

Messerias (Tribespeople) :

Two Fighting Tribes of the Sudan. By Merian C. Cooper. Photographs by Ernest B. Schoedsack. Vol. LVI, pp. 465-486, 27 ills., 1 two-thirds-page map, Oct., 1929.

Messina, Sicily :

World's Most Cruel Earthquake. By Charles W. Wright. Vol. XX, pp. 373-396, 22 ills., 1 page and 1 three-quarters-page maps, Apr., 1909.

Metal Sinews of Strength : This Is a War of Many Metals, for We Live in an Age of Alloys. By Frederick G. Vosburgh. Vol. LXXXI, pp. 457-491, 35 ills., Apr., 1942.

Metals:

Metal Sinews of Strength : This Is a War of Many Metals, for We Live in an Age of Alloys. By Frederick G. Vosburgh. Vol. LXXXI, pp. 457-491, 35 ills., Apr., 1942.

See also Gold and Gold Mining ; Platinum ; Radium ; Silver and Silver Mining ; Tin.

Metamorphosis:

Marvels of Metamorphosis : A Scientific "G-man" Pursues Rare Trapdoor Spider Parasites for Three Years With a Spade and a Candid Camera. By George Elwood Jenks. Vol. LXXIV, pp. 807-828, 39 ills., Dec., 1938.

Meteorites:

Mysterious Tomb of a Giant Meteorite (Meteor Crater, Arizona). By William D. Boutwell. Vol. LIII, pp. 721-730, 10 ills., June, 1928.

Meteorological Observations of the Second Wellman Expedition. By Evelyn B. Baldwin. Vol. X, pp. 512-516, Dec., 1899.

Meteorology:

Americans Stand Guard in Greenland. By Andrew H. Brown. Vol. XC, pp. 457-500, 23 ills. in black and white, 19 ills. in color, 1 page map, Oct., 1946.

Forecasting the Weather. By Alfred J. Henry. Vol. XV, pp. 285-292, 6 ills., 1 chart, July, 1904.

Forecasting the Weather and Storms. By Willis L. Moore. Vol. XVI. pp. 255-306, 5 ills., 20 charts, June, 1905.

Hurricanes on the Coast of Texas. By Maj. Gen. A. W. Greely. Vol. XI, pp. 442-445, Nov., 1900.

Ice Caves and Frozen Wells. By W J McGee. Vol. XIII, pp. 433-434, Dec., 1901.

International Cloud Work of the Weather Bureau. By Frank H. Bigelow. Vol. X, pp. 351-354, Sept., 1899.

Kite Work of the Weather Bureau. By H. C. Frankenfield. Vol. XI, pp. 55-62, Feb., 1900.

Loss of Life by Lightning. Vol. XIII, p. 115, Mar., 1902.

Loss of Property From Lightning. Vol. XII, p. 82, Feb., 1901.

Magic Beauty of Snow and Dew. By Wilson A. Bentley. Vol. XLIII, pp. 103-112, 9 ills., Jan., 1923.

Manila Observatory. By Father José Algué. Vol. XI, pp. 427-438, 2 ills., Nov., 1900.

Measuring the Sun's Heat and Forecasting the Weather : The National Geographic Society to Maintain a Solar Station in a Remote Part of the World to Coöperate with Smithsonian Institution Stations in California and Chile. By C. G. Abbot. Vol. XLIX, pp. 111-126, 15 ills., 1 chart, Jan., 1926.

Men-Birds Soar on Boiling Air. By Frederick G. Vosburgh. Vol. LXXIV, pp. 123-140, 15 ills., July, 1938.

Meteorological Observations of the Second Wellman Expedition. By Evelyn B. Baldwin. Vol. X, pp. 512-516, Dec., 1899.

Meteorology—*Continued*

Meteorology in the Philippines. Vol. X, pp. 271-272, July, 1899.

Mystery of Auroras : National Geographic Society and Cornell University Study Spectacular Displays in the Heavens. Vol. LXXV, pp. 689-690, May, 1939.

New Frontier in the Sky. By F. Barrows Colton. Vol. XC, pp. 379-408, 28 ills., 1 diagram, Sept., 1946.

Our Heralds of Storm and Flood. By Gilbert H. Grosvenor. Vol. XVIII, pp. 586-601, 15 ills., 1 chart, Sept., 1907.

Philippine Weather Service. Vol. XV, pp. 77-78, Feb., 1904.

Prevention of Hailstorms by the Use of Cannon. Vol. XI, pp. 239-241, June, 1900.

Project for the Exploration of the Atmosphere Over the Tropical Oceans. By A. Lawrence Rotch. Vol. XV, p. 430, Oct., 1904.

Proposed Meteorological Station in Iceland. Vol. X, p. 228, June, 1899.

Salton Sea and the Rainfall of the Southwest. By Alfred J. Henry. Vol. XVIII, pp. 244-248, Apr., 1907.

Scientific Work of Mount Weather Meteorological Observatory. By Frank H. Bigelow. Vol. XV, pp. 442-445, Nov., 1904.

Snow Crystals. By Wilson A. Bentley. Vol. XV, pp. 30-37, 31 ills., Jan., 1904.

Storm of February 25-28, 1902. By Alfred J. Henry. Vol. XIII, pp. 110-112, 1 chart, Mar., 1902.

Studies on the Rate of Evaporation at Reno, Nevada, and in the Salton Sink. By Frank H. Bigelow. Vol. XIX, pp. 20-28, 5 ills., Jan., 1908.

Toilers of the Sky : Tenuous Clouds Perform the Mighty Task of Shaping the Earth and Sustaining Terrestrial Life. By McFall Kerbey. Vol. XLVIII, pp. 163-189, 33 ills., Aug., 1925.

United States Weather Bureau. Vol. XIII, pp. 71-72, Feb., 1902.

United States Weather Bureau. By James Wilson. Vol. XV, pp. 37-39, Jan., 1904.

United States Weather Bureau at the Paris Exposition. Vol. XII, pp. 81-82. Feb., 1901.

Variations in Lake Levels and Atmospheric Precipitation. By Alfred J. Henry. Vol. X, pp. 403-406, 1 diagram, Oct., 1899.

Weather Bureau. By Willis L. Moore. Vol. XII, pp. 363-369, Oct., 1901.

Weather Bureau and the Recent Floods. By H. C. Frankenfield. Vol. XIV, pp. 285-290, 2 ills., July, 1903.

Weather Fights and Works for Man. By F. Barrows Colton. Vol. LXXXIV, pp. 641-670, 22 ills. in black and white, 3 drawings, Dec., 1943.

West Indian Hurricane of August 7-14, 1899. By E. B. Garriott. Vol. X, pp. 343-348, 1 diagram, Sept., 1899.

West Indian Hurricane of September 1-12, 1900. By E. B. Garriott. Vol. XI, pp. 384-392, Oct., 1900.

Meteorology—*Continued*

West Indian Hurricane of September 10-11, 1898. By E. B. Garriott. Vol. X, pp. 17-20, Jan., 1899.

See also Climate ; Hurricanes ; Winds.

Methods of Exploration in Africa. By Maj. A. St. H. Gibbons. Vol. XV, pp. 408-410, Oct., 1904.

Methods of Obtaining Salt in Costa Rica. Vol. XIX, pp. 28-34, 7 ills., 1 diagram, Jan., 1908.

Meulen, D. van der. *See* Van der Meulen, D.

Mewar (State), India. *See* Udaipur.

Mexican Hacienda. By J. E. Kirkwood. Vol. XXV, pp. 563-584, 18 ills., May, 1914.

Mexican Indian Flying Pole Dance. By Helga Larsen. Vol. LXXI, pp. 387-400, 13 ills., Mar., 1937.

Mexican Land of Canaan : Marvelous Riches of the Wonderful West Coast of Our Neighbor Republic. By Frederick Simpich. Vol. XXXVI, pp. 307-330, 16 ills., 1 page map, Oct., 1919.

Mexican Land of Lakes and Lacquers (Pátzcuaro Region). 22 ills. from photographs by Helene Fischer and Luis Marquez. Vol. LXXI, pp. 633-648, May, 1937.

Mexico:

Adventures in Color on Mexico's West Coast. 13 ills. in color from natural-color photographs by Fred Payne Clatworthy. Vol. LVIII, pp. 60-69, July, 1930.

Adventuring Down the West Coast of Mexico. By Herbert Corey. Vol. XLII, pp. 449-503, 44 ills., 1 half-page map, Nov., 1922.

Agricultural Possibilities in Tropical Mexico. By Dr. Pehr Olsson-Seffer. Vol. XXI, pp. 1021-1040, 18 ills., Dec., 1910.

Along Our Side of the Mexican Border. By Frederick Simpich. Vol. XXXVIII, pp. 61-80, 9 ills., 1 quarter-page map, July, 1920.

Along the Old Spanish Road in Mexico : Life Among the People of Nayarit and Jalisco, Two of the Richest States of the Southern Republic. By Herbert Corey. Vol. XLIII, pp. 225-281, 36 ills. in black and white, 16 ills. in color, 1 half-page map, Mar., 1923.

Among the Zapotecs of Mexico : A Visit to the Indians of Oaxaca, Home State of the Republic's Great Liberator, Juárez, and Its Most Famous Ruler, Diaz. By Herbert Corey. Vol. LI, pp. 501-553, 59 ills., 1 two-thirds-page map, May, 1927.

Baja California Wakes Up. By Frederick Simpich. Vol. LXXXII, pp. 253-275, 19 ills., 1 page map, Aug., 1942.

Boundaries of Territorial Acquisitions. Vol. XII, pp. 373-377, 1 page chart, Oct., 1901.

Buenos Aires to Washington by Horse : A Solitary Journey of Two and a Half Years, Through Eleven American Republics, Covers 9,600 Miles of Mountain and Plain, Desert and Jungle. By A. F. Tschiffely. Vol. LV, pp. 135-196, 75 ills., 1 page map, Feb., 1929.

Mexico—*Continued*

Camp Fires on Desert and Lava (Book Review). Vol. XXI, pp. 715-718, 3 ills., Aug., 1910.

Chichen Itzá, an Ancient American Mecca: Recent Excavations in Yucatan Are Bringing to Light the Temples, Palaces, and Pyramids of America's Most Holy Native City. By Sylvanus Griswold Morley. Vol. XLVII, pp. 63-95, 34 ills., 1 half-page map, 1 diagram, Jan., 1925.

Chinese Labor for Mexico. Vol. XVI, pp. 481-482, Oct., 1905.

Colorado Desert. By W. C. Mendenhall. Vol. XX, pp. 681-701, 16 ills., Aug., 1909.

Commerce of Mexico and the United States. By O. P. Austin. Vol. XIII, pp. 25-26, Jan., 1902.

Cruise Among Desert Islands (Baja California). By A. W. Anthony and G. Dallas Hanna. Vol. XLIV, pp. 71-99, 32 ills., 1 quarter-page map, July, 1923.

Cruise of the *Kinkajou*: Among Desert Islands of Mexico Voyagers Find Outdoor Laboratories for the Naturalist and Ideal Fishing Grounds for the Sportsman. By Alfred M. Bailey. Vol. LXXX, pp. 339-366, 13 ills. in back and white, 12 ills. in color, 1 page map, Sept., 1941.

Cuernavaca, the Sun Child of the Sierras. By Russell Hastings Millward. Vol. XXII, pp. 291-301, 9 ills., Mar., 1911.

Discovering the New World's Oldest Dated Work of Man: A Maya Monument Inscribed 291 B. C. is Unearthed Near a Huge Stone Head by a Geographic-Smithsonian Expedition in Mexico. By Matthew W. Stirling. Vol. LXXVI pp. 183-218, 40 ills., 1 half-page map, Aug., 1939.

Down Mexico's Río Balsas. By John W. Webber. With 9 ills. in color from natural-color photographs by the author, Kenneth Segerstrom, and Jack Breed. Vol. XC, pp. 253-272, 5 ills. in black and white, 1 half-page map, Aug., 1946.

Down the Rio Grande: Tracing this Strange, Turbulent Stream on Its Long Course from Colorado to the Gulf of Mexico. By Frederick Simpich. Vol. LXXVI, pp. 415-462, 28 ills. in black and white, 24 ills. in color, 6 maps, Oct., 1939.

Expedition into Texas of Fernando del Bosque, Standard-Bearer of the King, Don Carlos II, in the Year 1675. Translated from an Old, Unpublished Spanish Manuscript. By Betty B. Brewster. Vol. XIV, pp. 339-348, Sept., 1903.

Expedition Unearths Buried Masterpieces of Carved Jade (Cerro de las Mesas). By Matthew W. Stirling. Vol. LXXX, pp. 277-302, 14 ills. in black and white, 20 ills. in color, 1 two-thirds-page map, Sept., 1941.

Finding Jewels of Jade in a Mexican Swamp (La Venta). By Matthew W. and Marion Stirling. Vol. LXXXII, pp. 635-661, 15 ills. in black and white, 12 ills. in color, 1 two-thirds-page map, Nov., 1942.

Mexico—*Continued*

Foremost Intellectual Achievement of Ancient America: The Hieroglyphic Inscriptions on the Monuments in the Ruined Cities of Mexico, Guatemala, and Honduras Are Yielding the Secrets of the Maya Civilization. By Sylvanus Griswold Morley. Vol. XLI, pp. 109-130, 27 ills., 17 diagrams, special map supplement, Feb., 1922.

From the Halls of Montezuma. 21 ills. in color from natural-color photographs by Richard H. Stewart and others. Vol. LXXXV, pp. 137-164, Feb., 1944.

Glamour of Mexico—Old and New. 15 ills. in color from natural-color photographs by L. Pérez Parra. Vol. LXV, pp. 345-352, Mar., 1934.

Great Stone Faces of the Mexican Jungle: Five Colossal Heads and Numerous Other Monuments of Vanished Americans Are Excavated by the Latest National Geographic-Smithsonian Expedition. By Matthew W. Stirling. Vol. LXXVIII, pp. 309-334, 26 ills., 1 map, Sept., 1940.

Greatest Volcanoes of Mexico. By A. Melgareio. Vol. XXI, pp. 741-760, 22 ills., Sept., 1910.

Heart of a Hemisphere: Of Vital Importance is the Area Portrayed in The Society's New Map of Mexico, Central America, and the West Indies. Text accompanying special map supplement in colors. Vol. LXXVI, pp. 739-740, 1 ill., Dec., 1939.

Henequen—The Yucatan Fiber. By E. H. Thompson. Vol. XIV, pp. 150-158, 6 ills., Apr., 1903.

Hewers of Stone. By Jeremiah Zimmerman. Vol. XXI, pp. 1002-1020, 11 ills., Dec., 1910.

Home of a Forgotten Race: Mysterious Chichen Itzá in Yucatan, Mexico. By Edward H. Thompson. Vol. XXV, pp. 585-648, 59 ills., June, 1914.

In Montezuma's Painted Land. 22 ills. in color from natural-color photographs; 21 ills. by Luis Marden. Vol. LXXVIII, pp. 345-368, Sept, 1940.

Interesting Visit to the Ancient Pyramids of San Juan Teotihuacan. By A. C. Galloway. Vol. XXI, pp. 1041-1050, 8 ills., 1 page map, Dec., 1910.

Isthmus of Tehuantepec. By Herbert Corey. Vol. XLV, pp. 549-579, 25 ills., May, 1924.

Isthmus of Tehuantepec: The Bridge of the World's Commerce. By Helen Olsson-Seffer. Vol. XXI, pp. 991-1002, 6 ills., Dec., 1910.

Jungle Housekeeping for a Geographic Expedition (Cerro de las Mesas). By Marion Stirling. Vol. LXXX, pp. 303-327, 15 ills., Sept., 1941.

Land of Drought and Desert—Lower California: Two Thousand Miles on Horseback Through the Most Extraordinary Cacti Forests in the World. By E. W. Nelson. Vol. XXII, pp. 443-474, 25 ills., 1 page and 1 half-page maps, May, 1911.

Latest Map of Mexico. Text accompanying special map supplement in colors. Vol. XXX, p. 88, July, 1916.

Mexico—*Continued*

La Venta's Green Stone Tigers. By Matthew W. Stirling. Vol. LXXXIV, pp. 321-332, 4 ills. in black and white, 6 ills. in color, 1 two-thirds-page map, Sept., 1943.

Life and Death in Ancient Maya Land. 10 ills. in color from paintings by H. M. Herget. Vol. LXX, pp. 623-630, Nov., 1936.

Luster of Ancient Mexico (Aztecs). By William H. Prescott. Vol. XXX, pp. 1-32, 22 ills., July, 1916.

Mexican Hacienda. By J. E. Kirkwood. Vol. XXV, pp. 563-584, 18 ills., May, 1914.

Mexican Indian Flying Pole Dance. By Helga Larsen. Vol. LXXI, pp. 387-400, 13 ills., Mar., 1937.

Mexican Land of Canaan: Marvelous Riches of the Wonderful West Coast of Our Neighbor Republic. By Frederick Simpich. Vol. XXXVI, pp. 307-330, 16 ills., 1 page map, Oct., 1919.

Mexican Land of Lakes and Lacquers (Pátzcuaro Region). 22 ills. from photographs by Helene Fischer and Luis Marquez. Vol. LXXI, pp. 633-648, May, 1937.

Mexico—The Treasure House of the World. By N. H. Darton. Vol. XVIII, pp. 492-519, 23 ills., Aug., 1907.

Mexico and Mexicans. By William Joseph Showalter. Vol. XXV, pp. 471-493, 17 ills., special map supplement, May, 1914.

Mexico of Today. By Don Juan N. Navarro. Part I, Vol. XII, pp. 152-157, Apr., 1901. Part II, Vol. XII, pp. 176-179, May, 1901. Part III, Vol. XII, pp. 235-238, June, 1901.

Mexico's Deep South Yields New Treasure (Tabasco and Chiapas). 12 ills. in color from natural-color photographs by Richard H. Stewart. Vol. LXXXII, pp. 649-656, Nov., 1942.

Modern Progress and Age-Old Glamour in Mexico. Vol. LXVI, pp. 741-756, 22 ills. in duotone, Dec., 1934.

Monte Albán, Richest Archeological Find in America: A Tomb in Oaxaca, Mexico, Yields Treasures Which Reveal the Splendid Culture of the Mixtecs. By Dr. Alfonso Caso. Vol. LXII, pp. 487-512, 28 ills., Oct., 1932.

More Changes in the Colorado River. By D. T. MacDougal. Vol. XIX, pp. 52-54, 1 page map, Jan., 1908.

Naturalist's Journey Around Vera Cruz and Tampico. By Frank M. Chapman. Vol. XXV, pp. 532-562, 31 ills., May, 1914.

New Mexico. By John W. Foster. Vol. XIII, pp. 1-24, 11 ills., 2 page maps, Jan., 1902.

Notes on Southern Mexico (Agricultural Products). By G. N. Collins and C. B. Doyle. Vol. XXII, pp. 301-320, 16 ills., 1 half-page map, Mar., 1911.

Notes on the Deserts of the United States and Mexico (Extracted from a Publication of Dr. Daniel T. MacDougal). Vol. XXI, pp. 691-714, 16 ills., Aug., 1910.

Oil Treasure of Mexico. By Russell Hastings Millward. Vol. XIX, pp. 803-805, 1 ill., Nov., 1908.

Mexico—*Continued*

Old Yuma Trail. By W J McGee. Part I, Vol. XII, pp. 103-107, Mar., 1901. Part II, Vol. XII, pp. 129-143, 7 ills., 1 page map, Apr., 1901.

On the Cortés Trail. By Luis Marden. Vol. LXXVIII, pp. 335-375, 17 ills. in black and white, 22 ills. in color, 1 map, Sept., 1940.

Our Map of the Countries of the Caribbean. Text accompanying special map supplement in colors. Vol. XLI, pp. 221-222, Feb., 1922.

Our Neighbor, Mexico. By John Birkinbine. Vol. XXII, pp. 475-508, 26 ills., special map supplement, May, 1911.

Paricutín, the Cornfield That Grew a Volcano. By James A. Green. Vol. LXXXV, pp. 129-164, 16 ills. in black and white, 21 ills. in color, 1 third-page map, Feb., 1944.

Riatas and Romance on the Rio Grande. 24 ills. in color from natural-color photographs; 23 ills. by Luis Marden. Vol. LXXVI, pp. 431-462, Oct., 1939.

Rubber Plantations in Mexico and Central America. Vol. XIV, pp. 409-414, 7 ills., Nov., 1903.

Ruins of Cuicuilco May Revolutionize Our History of Ancient America: Lofty Mound Sealed and Preserved by Great Lava Flow for Perhaps Seventy Centuries Is Now Being Excavated in Mexico. By Byron Cummings. Vol. XLIV, pp. 203-220, 21 ills., 1 third-page map, Aug., 1923.

Society's New Caribbean Map: Mexico, Central America, and the West Indies—Gateway of Discovery. Text accompanying special map supplement in colors. Vol. LXVI, pp. 738-740, 1 ill., Dec., 1934.

Some Mexican Transportation Scenes. By Walter W. Bradley. Vol. XXI, pp. 985-991, 10 ills., Dec., 1910.

To Bogotá and Back by Air: The Narrative of a 9,500-Mile Flight from Washington, Over Thirteen Latin-American Countries and Return, in the Single-Seater Airplane *Spirit of St. Louis.* By Col. Charles A. Lindbergh. Vol. LIII, pp. 529-601, 98 ills., 1 two-thirds-page map, May, 1928.

Today in the Feathered Serpent's City (Chichen Itzá). 25 ills. in color from natural-color photographs by Luis Marden. Vol. LXX, pp. 599-614, Nov., 1936.

Travels with a Donkey in Mexico: Three Adventurers Trudge from Oaxaca to Acapulco, 400 Miles, Through Back Country, Their Equipment Carried by Burros. By Bernard Bevan. Vol. LXVI, pp. 757-788, 36 ills., 1 page map, Dec., 1934.

Treasure Chest of Mercurial Mexico (Silver Mines in Guanajuato). By Frank H. Probert. Vol. XXX, pp. 33-68, 33 ills., July, 1916.

Treasure-trove of Old Mexican Jade (Cerro de las Mesas). 20 ills. in color from natural-color photographs by Richard H. Stewart. Vol. LXXX, pp. 293-316, Sept., 1941.

Mexico—*Continued*

Unearthing America's Ancient History : Investigation Suggests That the Maya May Have Designed the First Astronomical Observatory in the New World in Order to Cultivate Corn. By Sylvanus Griswold Morley. Vol. LX, pp. 99-126, 28 ills., July, 1931.

Venice of Mexico (Aztec Lake Country). By Walter Hough. Vol. XXX, pp. 69-88, 18 ills., July, 1916.

Vignettes of Guadalajara. By Frederick Simpich. Vol. LXV, pp. 329-356, 20 ills. in black and white, 15 ills. in color, 1 third-page map, Mar., 1934.'

Wandering Islands in the Rio Grande. By Mrs. Albert S. Burleson. Vol. XXIV, pp. 381-386, 2 ills., 1 three-quarters-page map, Mar., 1913.'

Wildlife of Tabasco and Veracruz. By Walter A. Weber. With 19 ills. in color from paintings by the author. Vol. LXXXVII, pp. 187-216, 7 ills. in black and white, 1 two-thirds-page map, Feb., 1945.

Winter Expedition in Southwestern Mexico. By E. W. Nelson. Vol. XV, pp. 341-356, 14 ills., Sept., 1904.

Yucatán, Home of the Gifted Maya : Two Thousand Years of History Reach Back to Early American Temple Builders, Corn Cultivators, and Pioneers in Mathematics. By Sylvanus Griswold Morley. Vol. LXX, pp. 591-644, 28 ills. in black and white, 35 ills. in color, 1 two-thirds-page map, Nov., 1936.

See also Mexico, D. F.

Mexico, D. F. (Mexico City) :

From the Halls of Montezuma. 21 ills. in color from natural-color photographs by Richard H. Stewart and others. Vol. LXXXV, pp. 137-164, Feb., 1944.

In the Empire of the Aztecs : Mexico City Is Rich in Relics of a People Who Practiced Human Sacrifice, Yet Loved Flowers, Education, and Art. By Frank H. H. Roberts, Jr. Vol. LXXI, pp. 725-750, 14 ills. in black and white, 10 ills. in color, June, 1937.

Mexico and Mexicans. By William Joseph Showalter. Vol. XXV, pp. 471-493, 17 ills., special map supplement, May, 1914.

Modern Progress and Age-Old Glamour in Mexico. Vol. LXVI, pp. 741-756, 22 ills. in duotone, Dec., 1934.

North America's Oldest Metropolis : Through 600 Melodramatic Years, Mexico City Has Grown in Splendor and Achievement. By Frederick Simpich. Vol. LVIII, pp. 45-84, 34 ills., July, 1930.

Mexico, Gulf of :

Delectable Shrimp : Once a Culinary Stepchild, Today a Gulf Coast Industry. By Harlan Major. Vol. LXXXVI, pp. 501-512, 11 ills., 1 two-thirds-page map, Oct., 1944.

Gulf Coast Towns Get into the Fight. 19 ills. in color from natural-color photographs ; 17 ills. by J. Baylor Roberts. Vol. LXXXV, pp. 17-40, Jan., 1944.

Mexico, Gulf of—*Continued*

How We Use the Gulf of Mexico. By Frederick Simpich. Vol. LXXXV, pp. 1-40, 20 ills. in black and white, 19 ills. in color, 1 two-page map, Jan., 1944.

Mexico's Deep South Yields New Treasure (Tabasco and Chiapas). 12 ills. in color from natural-color photographs by Richard H. Stewart. Vol. LXXXII, pp. 649-656, Nov., 1942.

Meyer, Frank N.:

Hunter of Plants. By David Fairchild. Vol. XXXVI, pp. 57-77, 18 ills., July, 1919.

Mezőkövesd, Hungary :

Sunday in Mezőkövesd. By Margery Rae. Vol. LXVII, pp. 489-504, 22 ills., Apr. 1935.

Miami, Florida. *See* Hialeah Park ; Miami Aquarium.

Miami Aquarium, Miami, Florida :

Treasure-House of the Gulf Stream : The Completion and Opening of the New Aquarium and Biological Laboratory at Miami, Florida. By John Oliver La Gorce. Vol. XXXIX, pp. 53-68, 5 ills. in black and white, 16 ills. in color, Jan., 1921.

Mica (Sheet Mica) :

India's Treasures Helped the Allies. By John Fischer. Vol. LXXXIX, pp. 501-522, 18 ills., Apr., 1946.

Mice:

Plague of Mice. **Vol. XX, pp. 478-485, 7** ills., May, 1909.

Michigan:

By Car and Steamer Around Our Inland Seas. By Maynard Owen Williams. Vol. LXV, pp. 451-491, 29 ills. in black and white, 8 ills. in duotone, 1 two-page map, Apr., 1934.

Great Lakes and Great Industries. 19 ills. in color from natural-color photographs by B. Anthony Stewart, Alfred T. Palmer, and Willard R. Culver. Vol. LXXXVI, pp. 689-712, Dec., 1944.

Michigan, Mistress of the Lakes. By Melville Chater. Vol. LIII, pp. 269-325, 65 ills., 1 page and 1 three-quarters-page maps, Mar., 1928.

Michigan Fights. By Harvey Klemmer. Vol. LXXXVI, pp. 677-715, 20 ills. in black and white, 19 ills. in color, 1 page-and-a-half map, Dec., 1944.

Summer Meeting of the American Forestry Association. Vol. XIII, pp. 352-358, Sept., 1902.

Winter Sky Roads to Isle Royal. By Ben East. Vol. LX, pp. 759-774, 18 ills., 1 half-page map, Dec., 1931.

Michoacán (State), Mexico :

Down Mexico's Río Balsas. By John W. Webber. With 9 ills. in color from natural-color photographs by the author, Kenneth Segerstrom, and Jack Breed. Vol. XC, pp. 253-272, 5 ills. in black and white, 1 half-page map, Aug., 1946.

Mexican Land of Lakes and Lacquers (Pátzcuaro Region). 22 ills. from photographs by Helene Fischer and Luis Marquez. Vol. LXXI, pp. 633-648, May, 1937.

Michoacán (State), Mexico—*Continued*

Paricutín, the Cornfield That Grew a Volcano. By James A. Green. Vol. LXXXV, pp. 129-164, 16 ills. in black and white, 21 ills. in color, 1 third-page map, Feb., 1944.

Mickey the Beaver: An Animal Engineer Performs for the Camera as a Star in the Activities of His Species. By James MacGillivray. Vol. LIV, pp. 741-756, 23 ills., Dec., 1928.

Micronesia:

Hidden Key to the Pacific: Piercing the Web of Secrecy Which Long Has Veiled Japanese Bases in the Mandated Islands. By Willard Price. Vol. LXXXI, pp. 759-785, 28 ills., 1 map (two-page spread), June, 1942.

Mysterious Micronesia: Yap, Map, and Other Islands Under Japanese Mandate are Museums of Primitive Man. By Willard Price. Vol. LXIX, pp. 481-510, 37 ills., 1 half-page map, Apr., 1936.

Nauru, the Richest Island in the South Seas. By Rosamond Dodson Rhone. Vol. XL, pp. 559-589, 24 ills., Dec., 1921.

Yap and Other Pacific Islands Under Japanese Mandate. By Junius B. Wood. Vol. XL, pp. 591-627, 34 ills., 1 two-thirds-page map, Dec., 1921.

See also Caroline Islands; Gilbert Islands; Guam; Marianas Islands; Marshall Islands; Palau Islands.

Middleton Island, Alaska:

A Northern Crusoe's Island: Life on a Fox Farm Off the Coast of Alaska, Far from Contact with the World Eleven Months a Year. By Margery Pritchard Parker. Vol. XLIV, pp. 313-326, 15 ills., 1 eighth-page map, Sept., 1923.

Middleton Place Gardens, South Carolina:

Ashley River and Its Gardens. By E. T. H. Shaffer. Vol. XLIX, pp. 525-550, 6 ills. in black and white, 7 ills. in color, May, 1926.

Midges:

An Insect Community Lives in Flower Heads. By James G. Needham. Vol. XC, pp. 340-356, 5 ills. in black and white, 11 ills. in color, Sept., 1946.

Midi (Region), France:

Across the Midi in a Canoe: Two Americans Paddle Along the Canals of Southern France from the Atlantic to the Mediterranean. By Melville Chater. Vol. LII, pp. 127-167, 49 ills., 1 half-page map, Aug., 1927.

Midnight Sun in the Klondike. By Alice Rollins Crane. Vol. XII, pp. 66-67, 1 ill., Feb., 1901.

Mid-ocean Color Log (Bermuda Islands). 12 ills. in color from natural-color photographs; 9 ills. by E. John Long. Vol. LXXV, pp. 221-228, Feb., 1939.

Midsummer Wild Flowers. Vol. XLII, pp. 35-59, 16 ills. in color, July, 1922.

Midway (Islands), Pacific Ocean:

American Pathfinders in the Pacific. By William H. Nicholas. Vol. LXXXIX, pp. 617-640, 17 ills., 1 two-page map, May, 1946.

Mijes (Indians):

Isthmus of Tehuantepec: The Bridge of the World's Commerce. By Helen Olsson-Seffer. Vol. XXI, pp. 991-1002, 6 ills., Dec., 1910.

Milan, Italy:

Frontier Cities of Italy. By Florence Craig Albrecht. Vol. XXVII, pp. 533-586, 45 ills., June, 1915.

Milch Goat. Vol. XVI, p. 237, 1 ill., May, 1905.

Miletus (Ancient City):

Some Ruined Cities of Asia Minor. By Ernest L. Harris. Vol. XIX, pp. 833-858, 19 ills., Dec., 1908.

Military Government and Occupation. *See* Allied Military Government.

Military Maps:

Making of Military Maps. By William H. Nicholas. Vol. LXXXIII, pp. 765-778, 17 ills., June, 1943.

Millais, (Sir) John:

Boyhood of (Sir Walter) Raleigh. Reproduction in color of the painting by Sir John Millais, Tate Gallery, London. Vol. XLIX, text, p. 506; supplement, May, 1926.

Millennial City: The Romance of Geneva, Capital of the League of Nations. By Ralph A. Graves. Vol. XXXV, pp. 457-476, 13 ills., June, 1919.

Miller, Henry B.:

Lumbering in Manchuria. By Henry B. Miller. Vol. XV, pp. 130-132, 2 ills., Mar., 1904.

Notes on Manchuria. By Henry B. Miller. Vol. XV, pp. 261-262, June, 1904.

Russian Development of Manchuria. By Henry B. Miller. Vol. XV, pp. 113-127, 11 ills., 1 half-page map, Mar., 1904.

Miller, (Commodore) J. W.:

Cape Cod Canal. By Commodore J. W. Miller. Vol. XXVI, pp. 185-190, 3 ills., 1 half-page map, Aug., 1914.

Miller, William Alexander:

Copyright of a Map or Chart. By William Alexander Miller. Vol. XIII, pp. 437-443, Dec., 1902.

Miller, William Burke:

Flying the Pacific. By William Burke Miller. Vol. LXX, pp. 665-707, 39 ills., Dec., 1936.

Millions for Moisture: An Account of the Work of the United States Reclamation Service. By C. J. Blanchard. Vol. XVIII, pp. 217-243, 22 ills., Apr., 1907.

Mills, John, Jr.:

Tartan Tints New Scotland (Nova Scotia). 21 ills. in color from natural-color photographs by John Mills, Jr., W. R. MacAskill and others. Vol. LXXXVII, pp. 591-622, May, 1940.

Millward, Russell Hastings:

Cuernavaca, the Sun Child of the Sierras (Mexico). By Russell Hastings Millward. Vol. XXII, pp. 291-301, 9 ills., Mar., 1911.

Natal : The Garden Colony. By Russell Hastings Millward. Vol. XX, pp. 278-291, 16 ills., Mar., 1909.

Oil Treasure of Mexico. By Russell Hastings Millward. Vol. XIX, pp. 803-805, 1 ill., Nov., 1908.

Minas Gerais (State), Brazil :

Brazil's Potent Weapons. By W. Robert Moore. Vol. LXXXV, pp. 41-78, 16 ills. in black and white, 18 ills. in color, 1 two-page map, Jan., 1944.

Bright Facets of Brazil. 18 ills. in color from natural-color photographs by W. Robert Moore. Vol. LXXXV, pp. 49-72, Jan., 1944.

Mindanao (Island), Philippine Islands :

Camera Cruising in the Philippines. 12 ills. in color from natural-color photographs by J. Baylor Roberts, Fenno Jacobs, and others. Vol. LXXXVI, pp. 545-552, Nov., 1944.

Mindanao, on the Road to Tokyo. By Frederick Simpich. Vol. LXXXVI, pp. 539-574, 26 ills. in black and white, 12 ills. in color, 1 two-page map, Nov., 1944.

Mind's-Eye Map of America. By Franklin K. Lane. Vol. XXXVII, pp. 479-518, 25 ills. in black and white, 8 ills. in color, June, 1920.

Miner, Edward Herbert:

Announcement of Death of. Vol. LXXX, p. 769, Dec., 1941.

Cattle of the World. 20 ills. in color from paintings by Edward Herbert Miner. Vol. XLVIII, pp. 639-678, Dec., 1925.

Dogs : Gallant Little Sportsmen of the Terrier Tribe. 33 portraits in color from paintings by Edward Herbert Miner. Vol. LXIX, pp. 253-268, Feb., 1936.

Dogs : Hunters All : A Roll Call of the Hounds. 31 portraits in color from paintings by Edward Herbert Miner. Vol. LXXII, pp. 467-482, Oct., 1937.

Dogs : Man's Hunting Partner, the Field Dog. 36 portraits in color from paintings by Edward Herbert Miner. Vol. LXXI, pp. 89-104, Jan., 1937.

Dogs (Working Dogs of the World). 20 ills. in color from paintings by Edward Herbert Miner. Vol. LXXX, pp. 775-806, Dec., 1941.

Horses of the World. 24 ills. in color from paintings by Edward Herbert Miner. Vol. XLIV, pp. 479-526, Nov., 1923.

Painting the Terrier Series (Acknowledgments). By Edward Herbert Miner. Vol. LXIX, pp. 273-274, Feb., 1936.

Miner, Roy Waldo:

Coral Castle Builders of Tropic Seas. By Roy Waldo Miner. Vol. LXV, pp. 703-728, 15 ills. in black and white, 8 ills. in color, 1 two-thirds-page and 1 third-page maps, June, 1934.

Denizens of Our Warm Atlantic Waters (Mollusks, Crustaceans, etc.). By Roy Waldo Miner. Vol. LXXI, pp. 199-219, 10 ills. in black and white, 8 ills. in color, Feb., 1937.

Marauders of the Sea. By Roy Waldo Miner. Vol. LXVIII, pp. 185-207, 12 ills. in black and white, 8 ills. in color, Aug., 1935.

On the Bottom of a South Sea Pearl Lagoon. By Roy Waldo Miner. Vol. LXXIV, pp. 365-390, 17 ills. in black and white, 8 ills. in color, Sept., 1938.

Sea Creatures of Our Atlantic Shores (Mollusks, Crustaceans, etc.) By Roy Waldo Miner. Vol. LXX, pp. 209-231, 8 ills. in black and white, 8 ills. in color, 1 chart, Aug., 1936.

Minerals:

Brazil's Potent Weapons. By W. Robert Moore. Vol. LXXXV, pp. 41-78, 16 ills. in black and white, 18 ills. in color, 1 two-page map, Jan., 1944.

Bright Facets of Brazil. 18 ills. in color from natural-color photographs by W. Robert Moore. Vol. LXXXV, pp. 49-72, Jan., 1944.

India's Treasures Helped the Allies. By John Fischer. Vol. LXXXIX, pp. 501-522, 18 ills., Apr., 1946.

See also Metals ; Mines and Mining.

Mines, Submarine :

North Sea Mine Barrage. By Capt. Reginald R. Belknap. Vol. XXXV, pp. 85-110, 23 ills., 1 page map, 1 diagram, Feb., 1919.

Removal of the North Sea Mine Barrage. By Lieut. Comdr. Noel Davis. Vol. XXXVII, pp. 103-133, 28 ills., 2 half-page maps, Feb., 1920.

Mines and Mining:

Beyond Australia's Cities. By W. Robert Moore. Vol. LXX, pp. 709-747, 27 ills. in black and white, 12 ills. in color, Dec., 1936.

Bolivia—Tin Roof of the Andes. By Henry Albert Phillips. Vol. LXXXIII, pp. 309-332, 5 ills. in black and white, 20 ills. in color, Mar., 1943.

Brazil's Potent Weapons. By W. Robert Moore. Vol. LXXXV, pp. 41-78, 16 ills. in black and white, 18 ills. in color, 1 two-page map, Jan., 1944.

Bright Facets of Brazil. 18 ills. in color from natural-color photographs by W. Robert Moore. Vol. LXXXV, pp. 49-72, Jan., 1944.

Burma : Where India and China Meet : In the Massive Mountains of Southeast Asia, Swarming Road Builders Wage the "War of the Highways" for Free China and Her Allies. By John LeRoy Christian. Vol. LXXXIV, pp. 489-512, 18 ills., 1 page map, Oct., 1943.

Mines and Mining—*Continued*

Cities That Gold and Diamonds Built : Transvaal Treasures Have Created Bustling Johannesburg and Fostered Pretoria, Administrative Capital of the South African Union. By W. Robert Moore. Vol. LXXXII, pp. 735-766, 20 ills. in black and white, 9 ills. in color, 1 two-thirds-page map, Dec., 1942.

Coal : Prodigious Worker for Man. By Albert W. Atwood. Vol. LXXXV, pp. 569-592, 19 ills., 1 drawing, May, 1944.

Coal—Ally of American Industry. By William Joseph Showalter. Vol. XXXIV, pp. 407-434, 23 ills., Nov., 1918.

Coal Fields of Alaska. Vol. XXI, pp. 83-87, 6 ills., Jan., 1910.

Colorado, a Barrier That Became a Goal : Where Water Has Transformed Dry Plains Into Verdant Farms, and Highways Have Opened up Mineral and Scenic Wealth. By McFall Kerbey. Vol. LXII, pp. 1-63, 56 ills. in black and white, 12 ills. in color, 1 page map, July, 1932.

Diamond Mines of South Africa. By Gardiner F. Williams. Vol. XVII, pp. 344-356, 11 ills., June, 1906.

India's Treasures Helped the Allies. By John Fischer. Vol. LXXXIX, pp. 501-522, 18 ills., Apr., 1946.

Industry's Greatest Asset—Steel. By William Joseph Showalter. Vol. XXXII, pp. 121-156, 34 ills., Aug., 1917.

Lonely Australia : The Unique Continent. By Herbert E. Gregory. Vol. XXX, pp 473-568, 68 ills., 1 two-page and 4 half-page maps, Dec., 1916.

Men and Gold. By Frederick Simpich. Vol. LXIII, pp. 481-518, 33 ills. in black and white, 11 ills. in duotone, Apr., 1933.

Mexican Hacienda. By J. E. Kirkwood. Vol. XXV, pp. 563-584, 18 ills., May, 1914.

Mexico—The Treasure House of the World. By N. H. Darton. Vol. XVIII, pp. 492-519, 23 ills., Aug., 1907.

Mining Bureau of the Philippine Islands. By Charles H. Burritt. Vol. XIV, pp. 418-419, Nov., 1903.

Nevada, Desert Treasure House. By W. Robert Moore. Vol. LXXXIX, pp. 1-38, 16 ills. in black and white, 20 ills. in color, 1 four-fifths-page map, Jan., 1946.

Old Mines and Mills in India. Vol. XX, pp. 489-490, 2 ills., May, 1909.

Ore-Boat Unloaders. By W. M. Gregory. Vol. XVIII, pp. 343-345, 1 ill., May, 1907.

Pieces of Silver. By Frederick Simpich. Vol. LXIV, pp. 253-292, 49 ills., Sept., 1933.

Platinum in the World's Work. By Lonnelle Davison. Vol. LXXII, pp. 345-360, 17 ills., Sept., 1937.

Precious Stones. Vol. XIV, pp. 451-458, 4 ills., Dec., 1903.

Quest of Gold and the Goldsmith's Art. 11 ills. in duotone. Vol. LXIII, pp. 488-497, Apr., 1933.

Mines and Mining—*Continued*

Rhodesia, Hobby and Hope of Cecil Rhodes. By W. Robert Moore. Vol. LXXXVI, pp. 281-306, 13 ills. in black and white, 10 ills. in color, 1 half-page map, Sept., 1944.

Story of the Ruhr. By Frederick Simpich. Vol. XLI, pp. 553-564, 11 ills., 1 third-page map, May, 1922.

Tin, the Cinderella Metal. By Alicia O'Reardon Overbeck. Vol. LXXVIII, pp. 659-684, 24 ills., Nov., 1940.

Treasure Chest of Mercurial Mexico. By Frank H. Probert. Vol. XXX, pp. 33-68, 33 ills., July, 1916.

Under the South African Union. By Melville Chater. Vol. LIX, pp. 391-512, 97 ills. in black and white, 38 ills. in color, 1 two-page map, Apr., 1931.

United States—Her Mineral Resources. By C. Kirchhoff. Vol. XIV, pp. 331-339, Sept., 1903.

War Awakened New Caledonia : Swift Changes on the South Pacific Island of Mineral Wealth Defended by Free French and American Troops. By Enzo de Chetelat. Vol. LXXXII, pp. 31-55, 14 ills. in black and white, 12 ills. in color, 1 two-thirds-page map, July, 1942.

Miniatures of Macao (China). 11 ills. in color from natural-color photographs by W. Robert Moore. Vol. LXII, pp. 340-349, Sept., 1932.

Minneapolis, Minnesota : Northwestern Aeronautical Corporation :

Gliders—Silent Weapons of the Sky. By William H Nicholas. Vol. LXXXVI, pp. 149-160, 8 ills., Aug., 1944.

Minnesota:

Minnesota, Mother of Lakes and Rivers. By Glanville Smith. Vol. LXVII, pp. 273-318, 42 ills. in black and white, 11 ills. in color, 1 two-page map, Mar., 1935.

State of Sky-Blue Water and Verdure. 11 ills. in color from natural-color photographs by Clifton Adams and Edwin L. Wisherd. Vol. LXVII, pp. 289-296, Mar., 1935.

Wild Life of Lake Superior, Past and Present : The Habits of Deer, Moose, Wolves, Beavers, Muskrats, Trout, and Feathered Wood-Folk Studied with Camera and Flashlight. By George Shiras, 3d. Vol. XL, pp. 113-204, 77 ills, supplement, 1 half-page map, Aug., 1921.

See also Minneapolis.

Minnigerode, (Col.) Fitzhugh Lee:

Beauty of the Bavarian Alps. By Col. Fitzhugh Lee Minnigerode. Vol. XLIX, pp. 632-649, 16 ills. in color, June, 1926.

Minnigerode, H. Gordon:

Life Grows Grim in Singapore. By H. Gordon Minnigerode. Vol. LXXX, pp. 661-686, 17 ills. in black and white, 9 ills. in color, 1 half-page map, Nov., 1941.

Minshall, Merlin:

By Sail Across Europe. By Merlin Minshall Vol. LXXI, pp. 533-567, 38 ills., 1 two-thirds-page map, May, 1937.

Minya Konka (Mountains), China:

Carrying the Color Camera Through Unmapped China. 24 ills. in color from natural-color photographs by Joseph F. Rock. Vol. LVIII, pp. 402-435, Oct., 1930.

Climbing Mighty Minya Konka: Americans First Scaled Mountain That Now Is Landmark of China's New Skyway. By Richard L. Burdsall and Terris Moore. Vol. LXXXIII, pp. 625-650, 23 ills., 1 page map, May, 1943.

Glories of the Minya Konka: Magnificent Snow Peaks of the China-Tibetan Border Are Photographed at Close Range by a National Geographic Society Expedition. By Joseph F. Rock. Vol. LVIII, pp. 385-437, 35 ills. in black and white, 24 ills. in color, 1 three-quarters-page map, Oct., 1930.

Miquelon (Island), Atlantic Ocean:

Islands Adrift: St. Pierre and Miquelon: In a Key Position on the North Atlantic Air Route, France's Oldest Colony Rides Out Another Storm. Vol. LXXX, pp. 743-768, 23 ills., 1 fifth-page map, Dec., 1941.

Miracle of Talking by Telephone. By F. Barrows Colton. Vol. LXXII, pp. 395-433, 41 ills., Oct., 1937.

Miracle of War Production: For Victory the United States Transforms Its Complex Industry into the Biggest Factory and Mightiest Arsenal the World Has Ever Known. By Albert W. Atwood. Paintings by Thornton Oakley. Vol. LXXXII, pp. 693-715, 17 ills. in black and white, 16 ills. in color, Dec., 1942.

Miram Shah, India:

South of Khyber Pass. By Maynard Owen Williams. Vol. LXXXIX, pp. 471-500, 31 ills., Apr., 1946.

Mirrors of Madeira, Rock Garden of the Atlantic. 13 ills. in color from natural-color photographs by Wilhelm Tobien. Vol. LXVI, pp. 89-96, July, 1934.'

Mission of the *Diana* (Peary Arctic Club). Vol. X, p. 273, July, 1899.

Mississippi:

Burning the Roads. Vol. XVII, pp. 583-586, 4 ills., Oct., 1906.

Machines Come to Mississippi. By J. R. Hildebrand. Vol. LXXII, pp. 263-318, 34 ills. in black and white, 26 ills. in color, 1 two-page map, Sept., 1937.

Magnolia State Mosaic. 26 ills. in color from natural-color photographs by J. Baylor Roberts. Vol. LXXII, pp. 279-310, Sept., 1937.

Mississippi (River), United States:

Deep-Water Route from Chicago to the Gulf. Vol. XVIII, pp. 676-685, 3 ills., 1 page map, Oct., 1907.'

Great Mississippi Flood of 1927: Since White Man's Discovery This Mighty River Has Served Him Well, Yet It Has Brought Widespread Devastation Along Its Lower Reaches. By Frederick Simpich. Vol. LII, pp. 243-289, 53 ills., 1 half-page map, Sept., 1927.

Mississippi (River), United States—*Continued*

Honors for Amundsen (National Geographic Society Banquet). Vol. XIX, pp. 55-76, 13 ills., Jan., 1908.

Louisiana, Land of Perpetual Romance. By Ralph A. Graves. Vol. LVII, pp. 393-482, 84 ills. in black and white, 29 ills. in color, special map supplement in colors, Apr., 1930.

Men Against the Rivers. By Frederick Simpich. Vol. LXXI, pp. 767-794, 22 ills., 1 page-and-a-half and 1 quarter-page maps, June, 1937.

When the Father of Waters Goes on a Rampage: An Account of the Salvaging of Food-Fishes from the Overflowed Lands of the Mississippi River. By Hugh M. Smith. Vol. XXXVII, pp. 369-386, 18 ills., Apr., 1920.'

Missouri:

Land of a Million Smiles (Ozarks). By Frederick Simpich. Vol. LXXXIII, pp. 589-623, 14 ills. in black and white, 20 ills. in color, 1 two-thirds-page map, May, 1943.

Missouri, Mother of the West. By Frederick Simpich. Vol. XLIII, pp. 421-460, 35 ills., Apr., 1923.

Missouri Mirrors of 1946. 22 ills. in color from natural-color photographs by Richard H. Stewart. Vol. LXXXIX, pp. 285-308, Mar., 1946.

Taming the Outlaw Missouri River. By Frederick Simpich. Vol. LXXXVIII, pp. 569-598, 25 ills., 1 two-page map, Nov., 1945.

These Missourians. By Frederick Simpich. Vol. LXXXIX, pp. 277-310, 12 ills. in black and white, 22 ills. in color, 1 map (two-page spread), Mar., 1946.

Work and Play in the Ozarks. 20 ills. in color from natural-color photographs by B. Anthony Stewart and J. Baylor Roberts. Vol. LXXXIII, pp. 597-620, May, 1943.

Missouri (River), United States:

Taming the Outlaw Missouri River. By Frederick Simpich. Vol. LXXXVIII, pp. 569-598, 25 ills., 1 two-page map, Nov., 1945.

Trailing History Down the Big Muddy: In the Homeward Wake of Lewis and Clark, a Folding Steel Skiff Bears Its Lone Pilot on a 2,000-Mile Cruise on the Yellowstone-Missouri. By Lewis R. Freeman. Vol. LIV, pp. 73-120, 51 ills., 1 half-page map, July, 1928.

Missouri River Basin:

Taming the Outlaw Missouri River. By Frederick Simpich. Vol. LXXXVIII, pp. 569-598, 25 ills., 1 two-page map, Nov., 1945.

Missouri (Battleship):

Battleship *Missouri* Comes of Age. 11 ills. in color from natural-color photographs. Vol. LXXXVII, pp. 353-360, Mar., 1945.

Mist and Sunshine of Ulster (Northern Ireland). By Bernard F. Rogers, Jr. Vol. LXVIII, pp. 571-610, 23 ills. in black and white, 21 ills. in color, 1 three-quarters-page map, Nov., 1935.

Mr. Roosevelt's "African Game Trails." Vol. XXI, pp. 953-962, 9 ills., Nov., 1910.

Mr. Ziegler and the National Geographic Society. Vol. XIV, pp. 251-254, June, 1903.

Mistletoe. Vol. XXI, p. 965, 3 ills., Nov., 1910.

Mistral, Frédéric:

Camargue, the Cowboy Country of Southern France. By Dr. André Vialles. Vol. XLII, pp. 1-34, 33 ills., 1 half-page map, July, 1922.

Mrs. Bishop's "The Yangtze Valley and Beyond." By Eliza R. Scidmore. Vol. XI, pp. 366-368, Sept., 1900.

Mrs. Robinson Crusoe in Ecuador. By Mrs. Richard C. Gill. Vol. LXV, pp. 133-172, 43 ills. in black and white, 1 half-page map, Feb., 1934.

Mitchell, Guy Elliott:

American Potash for America. By Guy Elliott Mitchell. Vol. XXII, pp. 398-405, 4 ills., Apr., 1911.

Billions of Barrels of Oil Locked Up in Rocks. By Guy Elliott Mitchell. Vol. XXXIII, pp. 195-205, 10 ills., Feb., 1918.

Ideal Fuel: The American Coal Briquetting Industry. By Guy Elliott Mitchell. Vol. XXI, pp. 1066-1074, 4 ills., Dec., 1910.

Landslides and Rock Avalanches. By Guy Elliott Mitchell. Vol. XXI, pp. 277-287, 6 ills., Apr., 1910.

New National Park (Glacier National Park). By Guy Elliott Mitchell. Vol. XXI, pp. 215-223, 6 ills., Mar., 1910.

New Source of Power (Lignite). By Guy Elliott Mitchell. Vol. XXI, pp. 935-944, 7 ills., Nov., 1910.

Our Coal Lands. By Guy Elliott Mitchell. Vol. XXI, pp. 446-451, 5 ills., May, 1910.

Our Greatest Plant Food (Phosphorus). By Guy Elliott Mitchell. Vol. XXI, pp. 783-791, 7 ills., 1 diagram, Sept., 1910.

Mitchell, S. A.:

Nature's Most Dramatic Spectacle (Eclipse). By S. A. Mitchell. Vol. LXXII, pp. 361-376, 16 ills., 1 half-page map, Sept., 1937.

Mitchell, (Brig. Gen.) William:

America in the Air: The Future of Airplane and Airship, Economically and as Factors in National Defense. By Brig. Gen. William Mitchell. Vol. XXXIX, pp. 339-352, 8 ills., 1 three-quarters-page map, Mar., 1921.

Building the Alaskan Telegraph System. By Brig. Gen. William Mitchell. Vol. XV, pp. 357-361, Sept., 1904.

Tiger-Hunting in India. By Brig. Gen. William Mitchell. Vol. XLVI, pp. 545-598, 46 ills., 1 quarter-page map, Nov., 1924.

Mitla, Mexico:

Hewers of Stone. By Jeremiah Zimmerman. Vol. XXI, pp. 1002-1020, 11 ills., Dec., 1910.

Mitsukuri, K.:

Cultivation of Marine and Fresh Water Animals in Japan. By K. Mitsukuri. Vol. XVII, pp. 524-531, 5 ills., Sept., 1906.

Mittelholzer, Walter:

Flights from Arctic to Equator: Conquering the Alps, the Ice Peaks of Spitsbergen, of Persia, and Africa's Mountains of the Moon. By Walter Mittelholzer. Vol. LXI, pp. 445-498. 53 ills., 1 three-quarters-page map, Apr., 1932.

Mixtec Indians:

Monte Albán, Richest Archeological Find in America: A Tomb in Oaxaca, Mexico, Yields Treasures Which Reveal the Splendid Culture of the Mixtecs. By Dr. Alfonso Caso. Vol. LXII, pp. 487-512, 28 ills., Oct., 1932.

Mixter, George:

Hunting the Great Brown Bear of Alaska. By George Mixter. Vol. XX, pp. 313-332, 35 ills., Apr., 1909.

Modern Alchemist (U. S. Department of Agriculture). By James Wilson. Vol. XVIII, pp. 778-795, 6 ills., Dec., 1907.

Modern Dragon Hunt on Komodo: An English Yachting Party Traps and Photographs the Huge and Carnivorous Dragon Lizard of the Lesser Sundas. By Lady Broughton. Vol. LXX, pp. 321-331, 12 ills. in duotone, Sept., 1936.

Modern Ethiopia: Haile Selassie the First, Formerly Ras Tafari, Succeeds to the World's Oldest Continuously Sovereign Throne. By Addison E. Southard. Vol. LIX, pp. 679-738, 47 ills. in black and white, 27 ills. in color, 1 two-thirds-page map, June, 1931.

Modern Life in Morocco, Western Outpost of Islam. 27 ills. in color from natural-color photographs by M. Flandrin. Vol. LXVII, pp. 679-694, June, 1935.

Modern Life in the Cradle of Civilization (Iraq). Vol. XLI, pp. 390-407, 16 ills. in color, Apr., 1922.

Modern Odyssey in Classic Lands: Troy's Treasures, Athens' Parthenon, and Rome's First "Broad Way" Influence Today's Banks, Costumes, Jewelry, and Railroad Timetables. By Maynard Owen Williams. Vol. LXXVII, pp. 291-337, 27 ills. in black and white, 22 ills. in color, Mar., 1940.

Modern Persia and Its Capital: And an Account of an Ascent of Mount Demavend, the Persian Olympus. By F. L. Bird. Vol. XXXIX, pp. 353-400, 47 ills., Apr., 1921.

Modern Pilgrim's Map of the British Isles. By Andrew H. Brown. Text acompanying special map supplement in colors. Vol. LXXII, pp. 795-802, 3 ills., June, 1937.

Modern Progress and Age-Old Glamour in Mexico. Vol. LXVI, pp. 741-756, 22 ills. in duotone, Dec., 1934.

Modern Saga of the Seas: The Narrative of a 17,000-Mile Cruise on a 40-Foot Sloop by the Author, His Wife, and a Baby, Born on the Voyage. By Erling Tambs. Vol. LX, pp. 645-688, 49 ills., 1 half-page map, Dec., 1931.

Modern Scenes in the Land of Lincoln's Birth (Kentucky). 15 ills. in color from natural-color photographs by Edwin L. Wisherd. Vol. LXV, pp. 695-702, June, 1934.

Modern Transmutation of the Elements. By Sir William Ramsay. Vol. XVII, pp. 201-203, Jan., 1906.

Modern Venezuelan Vignettes. 9 ills. from photographs. Vol. LXXV, pp. 113-120, Jan., 1939.

Modern Viking (Amundsen). Vol. XVII, pp. 38-40, 1 page map, Jan., 1906.

Mohammedans and Mohammedanism:

Color Records from the Changing Life of the Holy City (Jerusalem). By Maynard Owen Williams. Vol. LII, pp. 682-707, 27 ills. in color, Dec., 1927.

Emancipation of Mohammedan Women. By Mary Mills Patrick. Vol. XX, pp. 42-66, 19 ills., Jan., 1909.

India—Yesterday, Today, and Tomorrow. By Lord Halifax. Vol. LXXXIV, pp. 385-408, 20 ills., 1 two-page map, Oct., 1943.

India at Work and Play. 22 ills. in color from natural-color photographs by Peter Upton Muir, Maynard Owen Williams, and Frances Muir. Vol. LXXXIX, pp. 449-464, Apr., 1946.

India Mosaic. By Peter Muir and Frances Muir. Vol. LXXXIX, pp. 443-470, 5 ills. in black and white, 22 ills. in color, 1 half-page map, Apr., 1946.

Mecca the Mystic: A New Kingdom Within Arabia (Hejaz). By S. M. Zwemer. Vol. XXXII, pp. 157-172, 13 ills., Aug., 1917.

Mystic Nedjef, the Shia Mecca. By Frederick Simpich. Vol. XXVI, pp. 589-598, 4 ills., Dec., 1914.

Pageant of Jerusalem: The Capital of the Land of Three Great Faiths Is Still the Holy City for Christian, Moslem, and Jew. By Maj. Edward Keith-Roach. Vol. LII, pp. 635-681, 57 ills., Dec., 1927.

Pilgrims' Progress to Mecca. 22 ills. in duotone; 18 ills. by Oscar Marcus. Vol. LXXII, pp. 627-642, Nov., 1937.

Races and Religions of Macedonia. By Luigi Villari. Vol. XXIII, pp. 1118-1132, 14 ills., Nov., 1912.

Sacred City of the Sands (Kairouan, Tunisia). By Frank Edward Johnson. Vol. XXII, pp. 1061-1093, 25 ills., 1 half-page map, Dec., 1911.

Unbeliever Joins the Hadj: On the Age-Old Pilgrimage to Mecca, Babies Are Born, Elders Die, and Families May Halt a Year to Earn Funds in Distant Lands. By Owen Tweedy. Vol. LXV, pp. 761-789, 30 ills., 1 page map, June, 1934.

See also Moros.

Mohave Desert, California:

Carrying Water Through a Desert: The Story of the Los Angeles Aqueduct. By Burt A. Heinly. Vol. XXI, pp. 568-596, 19 ills., 1 half-page map, July, 1910.

Mohawk (Indian Tribe):

America's First Settlers, the Indians. By Matthew W. Stirling. Vol. LXXII, pp. 535-596, 34 ills. in black and white, 24 ills. in color, Nov., 1937.

When Red Men Ruled Our Forests. 24 ills. in color from paintings by W. Langdon Kihn. Vol. LXXII, pp. 551-590, Nov., 1937.

Mole Men: An Account of the Troglodytes of Southern Tunisia. By Frank Edward Johnson. Vol. XXII, pp. 787-846, 60 ills., Sept., 1911.

Mollusks:

America's Surpassing Fisheries: Their Present Condition and Future Prospects, and How the Federal Government Fosters Them. By Hugh M. Smith. Vol. XXIX, pp. 546-583, 35 ills., June, 1916.

Cultivation of Marine and Fresh Water Animals in Japan. By K. Mitsukuri. Vol. XVII, pp. 524-531, Sept., 1906.

Denizens of Our Warm Atlantic Waters. By Roy Waldo Miner. Vol. LXXI, pp. 199-219, 10 ills. in black and white, 8 ills. in color, Feb., 1937.

Dream Ship: The Story of a Voyage of Adventure More Than Half Around the World in a 47-Foot Lifeboat. By Ralph Stock. Vol. XXXIX, pp. 1-52, 43 ills., 1 page map, Jan., 1921.

Fantastic Dwellers in a Coral Fairyland (Great Barrier Reef). 15 ills. in color from natural-color photographs by T. C. Roughley. Vol. LXXVII, pp. 831-838, June, 1940.

Marauders of the Sea. By Roy Waldo Miner. Vol. LXVIII, pp. 185-207, 12 ills. in black and white, 8 ills. in color, Aug., 1935.

Monster and Midget Squid and Octopuses. 8 ills. in color from paintings by Else Bostelmann. Vol. LXVIII, pp. 193-200, Aug., 1935.

Native Oysters of the West Coast. By Robert E. C. Stearns. Vol. XIX, pp. 224-226, Mar., 1908.

Pearl Fisheries of Ceylon. By Hugh M. Smith. Vol. XXIII, pp. 173-194, 13 ills., 1 quarter-page map, Feb., 1912.

Rise of the New Arab Nation. By Frederick Simpich. Vol. XXXVI, pp. 369-393, 17 ills., 1 page map, Nov., 1919.

Sea Creatures of Our Atlantic Shores. By Roy Waldo Miner. Vol. LXX, pp. 209-231, 8 ills. in black and white, 8 ills. in color, 1 chart, Aug., 1936.

Strange Creatures of Sunny Seas. 8 ills. in color from paintings by Else Bostelmann. Vol. LXXI, pp. 211-218, Feb., 1937.

Undersea Gardens of the North Atlantic Coast. 8 ills. in color from paintings by Else Bostelmann. Vol. LXX, pp. 217-224, Aug., 1936.

Mollusks—*Continued*

World's Most Valuable Water Crop. By Hugh M. Smith. Vol. XXIV, pp. 257-281, 21 ills., Mar., 1913.

Moluccas (Islands), Netherlands Indies:

Airplanes Come to the Isles of Spice: Once Magnet of World Explorers, the Moluccas Again Stand at Crossroads of History in the Netherlands Indies. By Maynard Owen Williams. Vol. LXXIX, pp. 535-558, 26 ills., 1 page map, May, 1941.

Mombasa, Kenya Colony:

Where Roosevelt Will Hunt. By Sir Harry Johnston. Vol. XX, pp. 207-256, 43 ills., special map supplement in colors, Mar., 1909.

Monarch of the Canadian Rockies (Mount Robson). By Charles D. Walcott. Vol. XXIV, pp. 626-639, 13 ills., panorama, May, 1913.

Monarch of the Canadian Rockies—Robson Peak. Vol. XXIV, panorama, May, 1913.

Monarchs of Alaska (Mountains). By R. H. Sargent. Vol. XX, pp. 610-623, 9 ills., July, 1909.

Monasteries:

Across Tibet from India to China. By Lt. Col. Ilia Tolstoy, AUS. Vol. XC, pp. 169-222, 41 ills., 1 half-page map, Aug., 1946.

Castles in the Air: Experiences and Journeys in Unknown Bhutan. By John Claude White. Vol. XXV, pp. 365-455, 74 ills., 1 page map, Apr., 1914.

Clock Turns Back in Yugoslavia: The Fortified Monastery of Mountain-girt Dečani Survives Its Six Hundredth Birthday. By Ethel Chamberlain Porter. Vol. LXXXV, pp. 493-512, 20 ills., 1 page map, Apr., 1944.

Frontier Cities of Italy. By Florence Craig Albrecht. Vol. XXVII, pp. 533-586, 45 ills., June, 1915.

Hoary Monasteries of Mount Athos (Greece). By H. G. Dwight. Vol. XXX, pp. 249-272, 24 ills., 1 half-page map, Sept., 1916.

In the Diamond Mountains: Adventures Among the Buddhist Monasteries of Eastern Korea. By Marquess Curzon of Kedleston. Vol. XLVI, pp. 353-374, 21 ills., 1 quarter-page map, Oct., 1924.

In the Shadow of Bulgarian Monasteries. 14 ills. in color from natural-color photographs by Wilhelm Tobien and Georg Paskoff. Vol. LXII, pp. 202-211, Aug., 1932.

Land of the Yellow Lama: National Geographic Society Explorer Visits the Strange Kingdom of Muli, Beyond the Likiang Snow Range of Yünnan Province, China. By Joseph F. Rock. Vol. XLVII, pp. 447-491, 39 ills., 1 half-page map, Apr., 1925.

Megaspelæon, the Oldest Monastery in Greece. By Carroll Storrs Alden. Vol. XXIV, pp. 310-323, 11 ills., Mar., 1913.

Montserrat, Spain's Mountain Shrine. By E. John Long. Vol. LXIII, pp. 121-130, 10 ills., Jan., 1933.

Monasteries—*Continued*

Most Extraordinary City in the World: Notes on Lhasa—The Mecca of the Buddhist Faith. By Shaoching H. Chuan. Vol. XXIII, pp. 959-995, 60 ills., Oct., 1912.

Multicolored Cones of Cappadocia. 20 ills. in color from natural-color photographs by Eric Matson. Vol. LXXVI, pp. 760-800, Dec., 1939.

Puto, the Enchanted Island. By Robert F. Fitch. Vol. LXXXIX, pp. 373-384, 11 ills., 1 third-page map, Mar., 1946.

Route Over Which Moses Led the Children of Israel Out of Egypt. By Franklin E. Hoskins. Vol. XX, pp. 1011-1038, 24 ills., 1 page map. Dec., 1909.

Sunrise and Sunset from Mount Sinai. By Sartell Prentice, Jr. Vol. XXIII, pp. 1242-1282, 34 ills., 1 page map, Dec., 1912.

Where Early Christians Lived in Cones of Rock: A Journey to Cappadocia in Turkey Where Strange Volcanic Pinnacles Are Honeycombed With Hermit Cells and Monasteries. By John D. Whiting. Vol. LXXVI, pp. 763-802, 20 ills. in black and white, 20 ills. in color, 1 half-page map, Dec., 1939.

Whirlpool of the Balkans. By George Higgins Moses. Vol. XXXIX, pp. 179-197, 15 ills., Feb., 1921.

With the Monks at Meteora: The Monasteries of Thessaly. By Elizabeth Perkins. Vol. XX, pp. 799-807, 5 ills., Sept., 1909.

World's Strangest Capital (Lhasa, Tibet). By John Claude White. Vol. XXIX, pp. 273-295, 19 ills., panorama, Mar., 1916.

See also Al Qosh.

Monastir, Yugoslavia:

On the Monastir Road. By Herbert Corey. Vol. XXXI, pp. 383-412, 31 ills., May, 1917.

Money:

Geography of Money. By William Atherton Du Puy. Vol. LII, pp. 745-768, 31 ills., Dec., 1927.

Pieces of Silver. By Frederick Simpich. Vol. LXIV, pp. 253-292, 49 ills., Sept., 1933.

Monfreid, Henri de:

Pearl Fishing in the Red Sea. By Henri de Monfreid. Vol. LXXII, pp. 597-626, 24 ills., 1 two-thirds-page map, Nov., 1937.

Mongolia:

By Coolie and Caravan Across Central Asia: Narrative of a 7,900-Mile Journey of Exploration and Research Over "the Roof of the World," from the Indian Ocean to the Yellow Sea. By William J. Morden. Vol. LII, pp. 369-431, 73 ills., 1 page map, Oct., 1927.

Desert Road to Turkestan: Twentieth Century Travel Through Innermost Asia, Along Caravan Trails Over Which Oriental Commerce Was Once Borne from China to the Medieval Western World. By Owen Lattimore. Vol. LV, pp. 661-702, 45 ills., 1 two-thirds-page map, June, 1929.

Mongolia—*Continued*

Explorations in the Gobi Desert. By Roy Chapman Andrews. Vol. LXIII, pp. 653-716, 50 ills. in black and white, 20 ills. in color, 1 half-page map, June, 1933.

In the Land of Kublai Khan. 16 ills. in color from autochromes by M. Stephane Passet. Vol. XLI, pp. 465-472, May, 1922.

Lama's Motor-Car. By Ethan C. Le Munyon. Vol. XXIV, pp. 640-670, 34 ills., May, 1913.

Land of Genghis Khan in Its True Colors. 6 ills. in color from natural-color photographs by Maynard Owen Williams. Vol. LXII, pp. 568-577, Nov., 1932.

Nomad Life and Fossil Treasures of Mongolia. 20 ills. in color from photographs by J. B. Shackelford. Vol. LXIII, pp. 669-701, June, 1933.

People of the Wilderness: The Mongols, Once the Terror of All Christendom, Now a Primitive, Harmless, Nomad Race. By Adam Warwick. Vol. XXXIX, pp. 507-551, 59 ills., May, 1921.

Road to Wang Ye Fu: An Account of the Work of the National Geographic Society's Central-China Expedition in the Mongol Kingdom of Ala Shan. By Frederick R. Wulsin. Vol. XLIX, pp. 197-234, 44 ills., 1 third-page map, Feb., 1926.

Thousand Miles Along the Great Wall of China: The Mightiest Barrier Ever Built by Man Has Stood Guard Over the Land of Chin for Twenty Centuries. By Adam Warwick. Vol. XLIII, pp. 113-143, 27 ills., panorama, 1 page and 1 half-page maps, Feb., 1923.

World's Greatest Overland Explorer: How Marco Polo Penetrated Farthest Asia, "Discovered" Many Lands Unknown to Europe, and Added Numerous Minerals, Animals, Birds, and Plants to Man's Knowledge. By J. R. Hildebrand. Vol. LIV, pp. 505-568, 53 ills., 1 two-page map, Nov., 1928.

Mongols:

Japan Faces Russia in Manchuria. By Willard Price. Vol. LXXXII, pp. 603-634, 30 ills., 1 page map, Nov., 1942.

New Road to Asia. By Owen Lattimore. Vol. LXXXVI, pp. 641-676, 15 ills. in black and white, 26 ills. in color, Dec., 1944.

Nomad Life and Fossil Treasures of Mongolia. 20 ills. in color from photographs by J. B. Shackelford. Vol. LXIII, pp. 669-700, June, 1933.

People of the Wilderness: The Mongols, Once the Terror of All Christendom, Now a Primitive, Harmless, Nomad Race. By Adam Warwick. Vol. XXXIX, pp. 507-551, 59 ills., May, 1921.

Sunny Siberia. 26 ills. in color from natural-color photographs by Owen Lattimore. Vol. LXXXVI, pp. 649-672, Dec., 1944.

With the Nomads of Central Asia: A Summer's Sojourn in the Tekes Valley, Plateau Paradise of Mongol and Turkic Tribes. By Edward Murray. Vol. LXIX, pp. 1-57, 43 ills. in black and white, 26 ills. in color, 1 half-page map, Jan., 1936.

Monkeys:

Monkey Folk. By William M. Mann. Vol. LXXIII, pp. 615-655, 24 ills. in black and white, 40 portraits in color, May, 1938.

Who's Who in the Monkey World. 40 portraits in color from paintings by Elie Cheverlange. Vol. LXXIII, pp. 625-648, May, 1938.

See also Apes.

Monrovia, Liberia:

Land of the Free in Africa. By Harry A. McBride. Vol. XLII, pp. 411-430, 22 ills., Oct., 1922.

Notes on the Only American Colony in the World. By Edgar Allen Forbes. Vol. XXI, pp. 719-729, 14 ills., Sept., 1910.

Monster and Midget Squid and Octopuses. 8 ills. in color from paintings by Else Bostelmann. Vol. LXVIII, pp. 193-200, Aug., 1935.

Monsters of Our Back Yards. By David Fairchild. Vol. XXIV, pp. 575-626, 38 ills., May, 1913.

Mont St. Michel (France), a Medieval Masterpiece. 22 ills. in duotone. Vol. LXIX, pp. 633-648, May, 1936.

Montana:

Bear Hunt in Montana. By Arthur Alvord Stiles. Vol. XIX, pp. 149-154, 5 ills., Feb., 1908.

Call of the West. By C. J. Blanchard. Vol. XX, pp. 403-437, 20 ills., 1 half-page map, May, 1909.

Friendly Crows (Indians) in Festive Panoply. 13 ills. in color from natural-color photographs by Edwin L. Wisherd. Vol. LII, pp. 314-323, Sept., 1927.

Idaho and Montana Boundary Line. By Richard U. Goode. Vol. XI, pp. 23-29, 1 ill., Jan., 1900.

New National Park (Glacier National Park). By Guy Elliott Mitchell. Vol. XXI, pp. 215-223, 6 ills., Mar., 1910.

Our National Parks. By L. F. Schmeckebier. Vol. XXIII, pp. 531-579, 41 ills., 1 page map, June, 1912.

Our Northern Rockies. By R. H. Chapman. Vol. XIII, pp. 361-372, 10 ills., Oct., 1902.

Taming the Outlaw Missouri River. By Frederick Simpich. Vol. LXXXVIII, pp. 569-598, 25 ills., 1 two-page map, Nov., 1945.

Monte Albán, Richest Archeological Find in America: A Tomb in Oaxaca, Mexico, Yields Treasures Which Reveal the Splendid Culture of the Mixtecs. By Dr. Alfonso Caso. Vol. LXII, pp. 487-512, 28 ills., Oct., 1932.

Montenegro:

East of the Adriatic: Notes on Dalmatia, Montenegro, Bosnia, and Herzegovina. By Kenneth McKenzie. Vol. XXIII, pp. 1159-1187, 37 ills., 1 page map, Dec., 1912.

Greece and Montenegro. By George Higgins Moses. Vol. XXIV, pp. 281-310, 24 ills., Mar., 1913.

Montenegro—*Continued*

New Map of Europe : Showing the Boundaries Established by the Peace Conference at Paris and by Subsequent Decisions of the Supreme Council of the Allied and Associated Powers. By Ralph A. Graves. Text accompanying special map supplement in colors. Vol. XXXIX, pp. 157-177, 18 ills., Feb., 1921.

Races of Europe. By Edwin A. Grosvenor. Vol. XXXIV, pp. 441-534, 62 ills., 2 page maps, special map supplement in colors, Dec., 1918.

Servia and Montenegro. Vol. XIX, pp. 774-789, 24 ills., Nov., 1908.

Where East Meets West : A Visit to Picturesque Dalmatia, Montenegro, and Bosnia. By Marian Cruger Coffin. Vol. XIX, pp. 309-344, 26 ills., 1 half-page map, May, 1908.

Whirlpool of the Balkans. By George Higgins Moses. Vol. XXXIX, pp. 179-197, 15 ills., Feb., 1921.

Montespan Grotto, France :

Discovering the Oldest Statues in the World : A Daring Explorer Swims Through a Subterranean River of the Pyrenees and Finds Rock Carvings Made 20,000 Years Ago. By Norbert Casteret. Vol. XLVI, pp. 123-152, 24 ills., 1 half-page and 1 quarter-page maps, Aug., 1924.

Monticello, Virginia :

Jefferson's Little Mountain : Romance Enfolds Monticello, the Restored Home of the Author of the Declaration of Independence. By Paul Wilstach. Vol. LV, pp. 481-503, 12 ills. in black and white, 12 ills. in color, Apr., 1929.

Monticello, One of America's Most Historic Shrines. 12 ills. in color from natural-color photographs by Edwin L. Wisherd, Charles Martin, and Jacob Gayer. Vol. LV, pp. 488-497, Apr., 1929.

Montserrat, Spain's Mountain Shrine. By E. John Long. Vol. LXIII, pp. 121-130, 10 ills., Jan., 1933.

Monument Valley, Utah-Arizona :

Flaming Cliffs of Monument Valley. By Lt. Jack Breed, USNR. With 9 ills. in color from natural-color photographs by the author and Warren T. Mithoff. Vol. LXXXVIII, pp. 452-461, Oct., 1945.

Monuments. *See* Memorials.

Monuments, Archeological. *See* Archeology.

Monuments, Fine Arts, and Archives Branch, Military Government :

Europe's Looted Art. By John Walker. Vol. LXXXIX, pp. 39-52, 11 ills., Jan., 1946.

Moon Jellyfish :

Life of the Moon-Jelly. By William Crowder. Vol. L, pp. 187-202, 6 ills. in black and white, 8 ills. in color, Aug., 1926.

Moore, Charles :

Transformation of Washington (D. C.) : A Glance at the History and Along the Vista of the Future of the Nation's Capital. By Charles Moore. Vol. XLIII, pp. 569-595, 16 ills., 2 page maps, June, 1923.

Moore, Frederick :

Changing Map in the Balkans. By Frederick Moore. Vol. XXIV, pp. 199-226, 27 ills., 1 page map, Feb., 1913.

Rumania and Her Ambitions. By Frederick Moore. Vol. XXIV, pp. 1057-1085, 34 ills., Oct., 1913.

Moore, J. Hampton :

Honors for Amundsen (Address by J. Hampton Moore). Vol. XIX, pp. 55-76, 13 ills., Jan., 1908.

National Geographic Society (Pamphlet by J. Hampton Moore on Discovery of North Pole). Vol. XXI, p. 276, Mar., 1910.

Moore, Terris.

Climbing Mighty Minya Konka : Americans First Scaled Mountain That Now Is Landmark of China's New Skyway. By Richard L. Burdsall and Terris Moore. Vol. LXXXIII, pp. 625-650, 23 ills., 1 page map, May, 1943.

Moore, W. Robert :

African Rainbow. 10 ills. in color from natural-color photographs by W. Robert Moore. Vol. LXXXVI, pp. 289-296, Sept., 1944.

Along the Old Mandarin Road of Indo-China. By W. Robert Moore. Vol. LX, pp. 157-199, 32 ills. in black and white, 28 ills. in color. 1 quarter-page map, Aug., 1931.

Alpine Peaks and Pastures of South Island (New Zealand). 11 ills. in color from natural-color photographs by W. Robert Moore. Vol. LXIX, pp. 205-212, Feb., 1936.

Among the Hill Tribes of Sumatra. By W. Robert Moore. Vol. LVII, pp. 187-227, 31 ills. in black and white, 25 ills. in color, 1 half-page map, Feb., 1930.

Among the Plains and Hill People of Siam. 12 ills. in color from natural-color photographs by W. Robert Moore. Vol. LXV, pp. 563-570, May, 1934.

As São Paulo Grows : Half the World's Coffee Beans Flavor the Life and Speed the Growth of an Inland Brazil City. By W. Robert Moore. Vol. LXXV, pp. 657-688, 33 ills., 1 two-thirds-page map, May, 1939.

Austrian August—and September. By W. Robert Moore. Vol. LXXIII, pp. 493-524, 11 ills. in black and white, 19 ills. in color, Apr., 1938.

Austrian Kodachromes from a Candid Camera. 19 ills. in color from natural-color photographs by W. Robert Moore. Vol. LXXIII, pp. 501-524, Apr., 1938.

Beyond Australia's Cities. By W. Robert Moore. Vol. LXX, pp. 709-747, 27 ills. in black and white, 12 ills. in color, Dec., 1936.

Bombs over Bible Lands. By Frederick Simpich and W. Robert Moore. Vol. LXXX, pp. 141-180, 34 ills., 1 two-page map, Aug., 1941.

Moore, W. Robert—*Continued*

Brazil's Potent Weapons. By W. Robert Moore. Vol. LXXXV, pp. 41-78, 16 ills. in black and white, 18 ills. in color, 1 two-page map, Jan., 1944.

Bright Facets of Brazil. 18 ills. in color from natural-color photographs by W. Robert Moore. Vol. LXXXV, pp. 49-72, Jan., 1944.

Buddhist Calm Survives Along China's Great Wall. 10 ills. in color ; 3 ills. from natural-color photographs by W. Robert Moore. Vol. LXXIII, pp. 321-328, Mar., 1938.

Busy Corner—the Cape of Good Hope : Ships Bound for Faraway Battlegrounds Stream Past Capetown, "Tavern of the Seas," and Other Ports of Virile South Africa. By W. Robert Moore. Vol. LXXXII, pp. 197-223, 11 ills. in black and white, 11 ills. in color, 1 two-thirds-page map, Aug., 1942.

Capital and Chief Seaport of Chile. By W. Robert Moore. Vol. LXXXVI, pp. 477-500, 15 ills. in black and white, 8 ills. in color, 1 third-page map, Oct., 1944.

Capital Cities of Australia. By W. Robert Moore. Vol. LXVIII, pp. 667-722, 32 ills. in black and white, 24 ills. in color, 1 two-page map, Dec., 1935.

Carioca Carnival (Rio de Janeiro). 34 ills. in color from natural-color photographs by W. Robert Moore. Vol. LXXVI, pp. 291-322, Sept., 1939.

Castles, Shrines, and Parks of Japanese Pilgrimage. 10 ills. in color from natural-color photographs by W. Robert Moore. Vol. LXIX, pp. 457-464, Apr., 1936.

Castles and Progress in Portugal. By W. Robert Moore. Vol. LXXIII, pp. 133-188, 36 ills. in black and white, 24 ills. in color, 1 half-page map, Feb., 1938.

Chile's Land of Fire and Water : Smoking Volcanoes and Ice-hooded Peaks Stand Sentinel Over Limpid Lakes in the Far Southern Andes. By W. Robert Moore. Vol. LXXX, pp. 91-110, 9 ills. in black and white, 10 ills. in color, 1 page map, July, 1941.

Chromatic Highlights of Korea. 13 ills. in color from natural-color photographs by W. Robert Moore. Vol. LXIV, pp. 429-436, Oct., 1933.

Cities That Gold and Diamonds Built : Transvaal Treasures Have Created Bustling Johannesburg and Fostered Pretoria, Administrative Capital of the South African Union. By W. Robert Moore. Vol. LXXXII, pp. 735-766, 20 ills. in black and white, 9 ills. in color, 1 two-thirds-page map, Dec., 1942.

Coastal Cities of China. By W. Robert Moore. Vol. LXVI, pp. 601-643, 12 ills. in black and white, 18 ills. in duotone, 14 ills. in color, 1 page map, Nov., 1934.

Coasts of Normandy and Brittany. By W. Robert Moore. Vol. LXXXIV, pp. 205-232, 5 ills. in black and white, 21 ills. in color, 1 two-page map, Aug., 1943.

Moore, W. Robert—*Continued*

Color at Africa's Southern Tip. 11 ills. in color from natural-color photographs by W. Robert Moore. Vol. LXXXII, pp. 213-220, Aug., 1942.

Color Camera Explores the Country That Moves by Night. 8 ills. in color from natural-color photographs by W. Robert Moore. Vol. LX, pp. 478-511, Oct., 1931.

Color Close-ups of Europe's Corner Land (Portugal). 24 ills. in color from natural-color photographs by W. Robert Moore. Vol. LXXIII, pp. 149-180, Feb., 1938.

Coronation Days in Addis Ababa (Ethiopia). By W. Robert Moore. Vol. LIX, pp. 738-746, 8 ills., June, 1931.

Cosmopolitan Shanghai, Key Seaport of China. By W. Robert Moore. Vol. LXII, pp. 311-335, 19 ills., Sept., 1932.

Costume Pageants in the French Pyrenees. 24 ills. in color from natural-color photographs by W. Robert Moore. Vol. LXXII, pp. 435-450, Oct., 1937.

Curaçao and Aruba on Guard. By W. Robert Moore. Vol. LXXXIII, pp. 169-192, 12 ills. in black and white, 10 ills. in color, 4 maps, Feb., 1943.

Czechoslovakian Cyclorama. 30 ills. in color from natural-color photographs by W. Robert Moore. Vol. LXXIV, pp. 181-220, Aug., 1938.

England's Island Garden of Rocks and Flowers (Isle of Wight). 14 ills. in color from natural-color photographs by W. Robert Moore. Vol. LXVII, pp. 17-24, Jan., 1935.

Face of Japan. By W. Robert Moore. Vol. LXXXVIII, pp. 753-768, 14 ills., special map supplement, Dec., 1945.

Flashes of Color in the Fifth Continent (Australia). 24 ills. in color from natural-color photographs by W. Robert Moore. Vol. LXVIII, pp. 681-704, Dec., 1935.

From Sea to Clouds in Ecuador. By W. Robert Moore. Vol. LXXX, pp. 717-740, 11 ills. in black and white, 9 ills. in color, Dec., 1941.

Garden Isles of Scilly : Geologists May Throw Stones at Legend of Lost Lyonnesse, But Natives Grow Flowers in Glass Houses for London. By W. Robert Moore. Vol. LXXIV, pp. 755-774, 9 ills. in black and white, 13 ills. in color, 1 half-page map, Dec., 1938.

Gilbert Islands in the Wake of Battle. By W. Robert Moore. Vol. LXXXVII, pp. 129-162, 11 ills. in black and white, 19 ills. in color, 1 two-thirds-page map, Feb., 1945.

Glory That Was Imperial Peking. By W. Robert Moore. Vol. LXIII, pp. 745-780, 18 ills. in black and white, 16 ills. in duotone, June, 1933.

Golden Isles of Guale (Sea Islands, Georgia). By W. Robert Moore. Vol. LXV, pp. 235-264, 35 ills., 1 three-quarters-page map, Feb., 1934.

Greens Grow for GI's on Soilless Ascension. By W. Robert Moore. Vol. LXXXVIII, pp. 219-230, 12 ills., Aug., 1945.

Moore, W. Robert—*Continued*

High Lights in the Peruvian and Bolivian Andes. 18 ills. in color from autochromes by W. Robert Moore. Vol. LI, pp. 218-235, Feb., 1927.

In the Land of Moses and Abraham. 25 ills. in color from natural-color photographs by W. Robert Moore. Vol. LXXIV, pp. 711-742, Dec., 1938.

Java, Queen of the East Indies. 26 ills. in color from autochromes by W. Robert Moore. Vol. LVI, pp. 334-359, Sept., 1929.

Land of Sagebrush and Silver (Nevada). 20 ills. in color from natural-color photographs by W. Robert Moore. Vol. LXXXIX, pp. 9-32, Jan., 1946.

"Land of the Free" in Asia : Siam Has Blended New With Old in Her Progressive March to Modern Statehood in the Family of Nations. By W. Robert Moore. Vol. LXV, pp. 531-576, 28 ills. in black and white, 26 ills. in color, 1 two-thirds-page map, May, 1934.

Life Along the Central China Coast. 14 ills. in color from natural-color photographs by W. Robert Moore. Vol. LXII, pp. 316-325, Sept., 1932.

Life and Color Under the Rising Sun. 9 ills. in color from natural-color photographs by W. Robert Moore and Kiyoshi Sakamoto. Vol. LXIII, pp. 288-297, Mar., 1933.

Marshallese Are Happy Again. 20 ills. in color from natural-color photographs by W. Robert Moore. Vol. LXXXVIII, pp. 337-360, Sept., 1945.

Maryland Presents— By W. Robert Moore. Vol. LXXIX, pp. 401-448, 17 ills. in black and white, 32 ills. in color, 1 map (two-page spread), Apr., 1941.

Miniatures of Macao (China). 11 ills. in color from natural-color photographs by W. Robert Moore. Vol. LXII, pp. 340-349, Sept., 1932.

Motor Trails in Japan. By W. Robert Moore. Vol. LXIII, pp. 303-318, 17 ills., Mar., 1933.

Nevada, Desert Treasure House. By W. Robert Moore. Vol. LXXXIX, pp. 1-38, 16 ills. in black and white, 20 ills. in color, 1 four-fifths-page map, Jan., 1946.

New Zealand "Down Under." By W. Robert Moore. Vol. LXIX, pp. 165-218, 31 ills. in black and white, 23 ills. in color, 1 two-page map, Feb., 1936.

Normandy and Brittany in Brighter Days. 21 ills. in color from natural-color photographs by W. Robert Moore, Peter Upton Muir, and others. Vol. LXXXIV, pp. 209-232, Aug., 1943.

North Island of New Zealand : A Vulcan's Playground. 12 ills. in color from natural-color photographs by W. Robert Moore. Vol. LXIX, pp. 181-188, Feb., 1936.

Old Line State Cyclorama (Maryland). 22 ills. in color from natural-color photographs ; 17 ills. by W. Robert Moore. Vol. LXXIX, pp. 409-432, Apr., 1941.

Moore, W. Robert— *Continued*

Old-New Battle Grounds of Egypt and Libia. By W. Robert Moore. Vol. LXXVIII, pp. 809-820, 8 ills., 1 third-page map, Dec., 1940.

Our New Military Wards, the Marshalls. By W. Robert Moore. Vol. LXXXVIII, pp. 325-360, 14 ills. in black and white, 20 ills. in color, 1 half-page map, Sept., 1945.

Peiping, City of Dust and Color. 13 ills. in color from natural-color photographs by W. Robert Moore. Vol. LXVI, pp. 609-619, Nov., 1934.

Present Day Scenes in the World's Oldest Empire (Ethiopia). 27 ills. in color from natural-color photographs by W. Robert Moore. Vol. LIX, pp. 690-723, June, 1931.

Raft Life on the Hwang Ho. By W. Robert Moore. Vol. LXI, pp. 743-752, 14 ills., June, 1932.

Rehearsal at Dieppe (France). By W. Robert Moore. Vol. LXXXII, pp. 495-502, 6 ills., Oct., 1942.

Rhodesia, Hobby and Hope of Cecil Rhodes. By W. Robert Moore. Vol. LXXXVI, pp. 281-306, 13 ills. in black and white, 10 ills. in color, 1 half-page map, Sept., 1944.

Rio Panorama : Breath-taking Is This Fantastic City amid Peaks, Palms, and Sea, and in Carnival Time It Moves to the Rhythm of Music. By W. Robert Moore. Vol. LXXVI, pp. 283-324, 12 ills. in black and white, 34 ills. in color, Sept., 1939.

Round About Grim Tarawa. 19 ills. in color from natural-color photographs by W. Robert Moore. Vol. LXXXVII, pp. 137-160, Feb., 1945.

Saipan and Tinian, Take-offs to Tokyo. 17 ills. in color from natural-color photographs ; 15 ills. by W. Robert Moore. Vol. LXXXVII, pp. 453-468, Apr., 1945.

Shan Tribes Make Burma's Hills Flash With Color. 15 ills. in color from natural-color photographs by W. Robert Moore. Vol. LX, pp. 454-463, Oct., 1931.

Skyline Drive in the Pyrenees. By W. Robert Moore. Vol. LXXII, pp. 434-452, 24 ills. in color, Oct., 1937.

South from Saipan. By W. Robert Moore. Vol. LXXXVII, pp. 441-474, 11 ills. in black and white, 17 ills. in color, 1 half-page map, Apr., 1945.

Strange Tribes in the Shan States of Burma. 15 ills. in color from natural-color photographs by W. Robert Moore. Vol. LVIII, pp. 246-255, Aug., 1930.

Sumatra, a Ribbon of Color on the Equator. 25 ills. in color from autochromes by W. Robert Moore. Vol. LVII, pp. 194-219, Feb., 1930.

Sunny Corners of Kangaroo Land (Australia). 12 ills. in color from natural-color photographs by W. Robert Moore. Vol. LXX, pp. 713-720, Dec., 1936.

Sunny South Africa. 9 ills. in color from natural-color photographs by W. Robert Moore. Vol. LXXXII, pp. 749-756, Dec., 1942.

Moore, W. Robert—*Continued*

Sunshine Over the Chilean Lakes. 10 ills. in color from natural-color photographs by W. Robert Moore and John Swope. Vol. LXXX, pp. 97-104, July, 1941.

Temples and Ceremonies of Kaleidoscopic Bangkok. 9 ills. in color from natural-color photographs by W. Robert Moore. Vol. LXV, pp. 547-554, May, 1934.

Through Java in Pursuit of Color. By W. Robert Moore. Vol. LVI, pp. 333-362, 9 ills. in black and white, 29 ills. in color, 1 third-page map, Sept., 1929.

"Time Will Not Dim the Glory of Their Deeds" (World War Memorials). 11 ills. in color from natural-color photographs by W. Robert Moore. Vol. LXV, pp. 17-24, Jan., 1934.

Tradition Lingers in Modern Japan. 11 ills. in color from natural-color photographs by W. Robert Moore. Vol. LXXIII, pp. 117-124, Jan., 1938.

Under the French Tricolor in Indo-China. 28 ills. in color from natural-color photographs by W. Robert Moore. Vol. LX, pp. 166-199, Aug., 1931.

When the Herring Fleet Comes to Great Yarmouth. By W. Robert Moore. Vol. LXVI, pp. 233-250, 19 ills., Aug., 1934.

Where Snow Peaks Temper the Tropics (Ecuador). 9 ills. in color from natural-color photographs by W. Robert Moore. Vol. LXXX, pp. 727-734, Dec., 1941.

Moore, Willis L.:

Annual Dinner of the National Geographic Society (Speeches by Willis L. Moore). Vol. XVII, pp. 22-37, Jan., 1906.

Discovery of the North Pole (Speeches by Willis L. Moore). Vol. XXI, pp. 63-82, Jan., 1910.

Forecasting the Weather and Storms. By Willis L. Moore. Vol. XVI, pp. 255-305, 5 ills., 20 charts, June, 1905.

Honors for Amundsen (Speeches by Willis L. Moore). Vol. XIX, pp. 55-76, 13 ills., Jan., 1908.

Honors to Peary (Speeches by Willis L. Moore). Vol. XVIII, pp. 49-60, 1 ill., Jan., 1907.

Honors to the American Navy (Speeches by Willis L. Moore). Vol. XX, pp. 77-95, Jan., 1909.

National Geographic Society (Announcement of the Election of Willis L. Moore as President of The Society). Vol. XVI, p. 87, Feb., 1905.

Weather Bureau. By Willis L. Moore. Vol. XII, pp. 363-369, Oct., 1901.

Moorish Spain. 26 ills. in color from autochromes lumière by Gervais Courtellemont. Vol. XLVI, pp. 163-178, Aug., 1924.

Moose:

Big Game of Alaska. By Wilfred H. Osgood. Vol. XX, pp. 624-636, 10 ills., July, 1909.

Moose—*Continued*

Deer of the World : As Workers, Pets, and Graceful "Living Statuary" in Parks and Estates. These Versatile Creatures Have Endeared Themselves to Mankind. By Victor H. Cahalane. Vol. LXXVI, pp. 463-510, 20 ills. in black and white, 23 ills. in color, Oct., 1939.

Lords of the Rockies : Photographing Big Game Animals in Their Primeval Surroundings, from Arizona to Canada, Brings Adventure to Two Wilderness Wanderers. By Wendell and Lucie Chapman. Vol. LXXVI, pp. 87-128, 14 ills. in black and white, 28 ills. in color, July, 1939.

One Season's Game-Bag with the Camera. By George Shiras, 3d. Vol. XIX, pp. 387-446, 70 ills., June, 1908.

Stalking Big Game with Color Camera. 28 ills. in color from natural-color photographs by Wendell Chapman. Vol. LXXVI, pp. 89-128, July, 1939.

White Sheep, Giant Moose, and Smaller Game of the Kenai Peninsula, Alaska. By George Shiras, 3d. Vol. XXIII, pp. 423-494, 59 ills., 1 two-page map, May, 1912.

Wild Animals That Took Their Own Pictures by Day and by Night. By George Shiras, 3d. Vol. XXIV, pp. 763-834, 68 ills., 1 page map, July, 1913.

Wild Life of Lake Superior, Past and Present : The Habits of Deer, Wolves, Beavers, Muskrats, Trout, and Feathered Wood-Folk Studied with Camera and Flashlight. By George Shiras, 3d. Vol. XL, pp. 113-204, 77 ills., supplement, 1 half-page map, Aug., 1921.

Morden, Florence H.:

House-Boat Days in the Vale of Kashmir. By Florence H. Morden. Vol. LVI, pp. 437-463, 22 ills. in black and white, 30 ills. in color, Oct., 1929.

Morden, William J.:

By Coolie and Caravan Across Central Asia : Narrative of a 7,900-Mile Journey of Exploration and Research Over "the Roof of the World," from the Indian Ocean to the Yellow Sea. By William J. Morden. Vol. LII, pp. 369-431, 73 ills., 1 page map, Oct., 1927.

More Changes of the Colorado River. By D. T. MacDougal. Vol. XIX, pp. 52-54, 1 page map, Jan., 1908.

More Water for California's Great Central Valley. By Frederick Simpich. Vol. XC, pp. 645-664, 16 ills., 1 page map, Nov., 1946.

Morgan, Edwin V.:

Samoan Islands. By Edwin V. Morgan. Vol. XI, pp. 417-426, Nov., 1900.

Morgan, (Sir) Henry:

Haunts of the Caribbean Corsairs : The West Indies a Geographic Background for the Most Adventurous Episodes in the History of the Western Hemisphere. By Nell Ray Clarke. Vol. XLI, pp. 147-187, 27 ills., Feb., 1922.

Morgan, M. de:

Excavations of M. de Morgan at Susa. **Vol.** XII, p. 315, Aug., 1901.

Morgenstierne, Wilhelm:

Norway, an Active Ally. By Wilhelm Morgenstierne. Vol. LXXXIII, pp. 333-357, 24 ills., 1 two-thirds-page map, Mar., 1943.

Morley, Sylvanus Griswold:

Chichen Itzá, an Ancient American Mecca : Recent Excavations in Yucatan Are Bringing to Light the Temples, Palaces, and Pyramids of America's Most Holy Native City. By Sylvanus Griswold Morley. Vol. XLVII, pp. 63-95, 34 ills., 1 half-page map, 1 diagram, Jan., 1925.

Excavations at Quirigua, Guatemala. By Sylvanus Griswold Morley. Vol. XXIV, pp. 339-361, 24 ills., 1 diagram, Mar., 1913.

Foremost Intellectual Achievement of Ancient America : The Hieroglyphic Inscriptions on the Monuments in the Ruined Cities of Mexico, Guatemala, and Honduras Are Yielding the Secrets of the Maya Civilization. By Sylvanus Griswold Morley. Vol. XLI, pp. 109-130, 27 ills., 17 diagrams, special map supplement in colors, Feb., 1922.

Unearthing America's Ancient History : Investigation Suggests That the Maya May Have Designed the First Astronomical Observatory in the New World in Order to Cultivate Corn. By Sylvanus Griswold Morley. Vol. LX, pp. 99-126, 28 ills., July, 1931.

Yucatán, Home of the Gifted Maya : Two Thousand Years of History Reach Back to Early American Temple Builders, Corn Cultivators, and Pioneers in Mathematics. By Sylvanus Griswold Morley. Vol. LXX, pp. 591-644, 28 ills. in black and white, 35 ills. in color, 1 two-thirds-page map, Nov., 1936.

Morocco:

Across French and Spanish Morocco. By Harriet Chalmers Adams. Vol. XLVII, pp. 327-356, 19 ills. in black and white, 16 ills. in color, 1 half-page map, Mar., 1925.

Americans on the Barbary Coast. By Willard Price. Vol. LXXXIV, pp. 1-31, 13 ills. in black and white, 10 ills. in color, 1 map (two-page spread), July, 1943.

Beyond the Grand Atlas : Where the French Tricolor Flies Beside the Flag of the Sultan of Morocco. By V. C. Scott O'Connor. Vol. LXI, pp. 261-319, 52 ills. in black and white, 12 ills. in color, 1 two-thirds-page map, Mar., 1932.

Eastward from Gibraltar : Overland Route Across North Africa to Tunisia and Libia. By Cyrus French Wicker. Vol. LXXXIII, pp. 115-142, 28 ills., Jan., 1943.

Fez, Heart of Morocco : Africa's "Imperial City" Retains Its Teeming Streets, Cluttered Shops, Glamorous Moorish Homes and Mosques, Amid the Peace of French Rule. By Gordon Casserly. Vol. LXVII, pp. 663-694, 13 ills. in black and white, 27 ills. in color, June, 1935.

Morocco—_Continued_

In the Land of Cruel Desert and Majestic Mountain. 12 ills. in color from natural-color photographs by Gervais Courtellemont and M. Flandrin. Vol. LXI, pp. 306-315, Mar., 1932.

Journey in Morocco : "The Land of the Moors." By Thomas Lindsey Blayney. Vol. XXII, pp. 750-776, 24 ills., 1 page map, Aug., 1911.

Modern Life in Morocco, Western Outpost of Islam. 27 ills. in color from natural-color photographs by M. Flandrin. Vol. LXVII, pp. 679-694, June, 1935.

Morocco, the "Land of the Extreme West," and the Story of My Captivity. By Ion Perdicaris. Vol. XVII, pp. 117-157, 24 ills., Mar., 1906.

Notes on Morocco. Vol. XVII, p. 157, Mar., 1906.

People of Morocco. Vol. XVII, p. 108, 1 ill., Feb., 1906.

Scenes from North Africa. Vol. XVIII, pp. 615-619, 4 ills., Sept., 1907.

Two Great Moorish Religious Dances. By George Edmund Holt. Vol. XXII, pp. 776-785, 6 ills., Aug., 1911.

See also Casablanca.

Moros (People) :

Mindanao, on the Road to Tokyo. By Frederick Simpich. Vol. LXXXVI, pp. 539-574, 26 ills. in black and white, 12 ills. in color, 1 two-page map, Nov., 1944.

Morris, Earl H.:

Exploring in the Canyon of Death (Arizona) : Remains of a People Who Dwelt in Our Southwest at Least 4,000 Years Ago Are Revealed. By Earl H. Morris. Vol. XLVIII, pp. 263-300, 24 ills. in black and white, 22 ills. in color, Sept., 1925.

Morrissey (Schooner). _See Effie M. Morrissey._

Morristown, New Jersey : Seeing Eye School :

Dogs of Duty and Devotion. By Frederick G. Vosburgh. Vol. LXXX, pp. 769-774, 3 ills., Dec., 1941.

Morse, Fremont:

Recession of the Glaciers of Glacier Bay, Alaska. By Fremont Morse. Vol. XIX, pp. 76-78, 1 page map, Jan., 1908.

Moscow, U. S. S. R. :

Glimpses of the Russian Empire. By William Wisner Chapin. Vol. XXIII, pp. 1043-1078, 51 ills. in color, 1 three-quarters-page map, Nov., 1912.

I Learn About the Russians. By Eddy Gilmore. Vol. LXXXIV, pp. 619-640, 21 ills., Nov., 1943.

Rebirth of Religion in Russia : The Church Reorganized While Bolshevik Cannon Spread Destruction in the Nation's Holy of Holies. By Thomas Whittemore. Vol. XXXIV, pp. 378-401, 16 ills., Nov., 1918.

Moscow, U. S. S. R.—*Continued*

Russia of the Hour: Giant Battle Ground for Theories of Economy, Society, and Politics, as Observed by an Unbiased Correspondent. By Junius B. Wood. Vol. L, pp. 519-598, 81 ills., Nov., 1926.

Young Russia: Land of Unlimited Possibilities. By Gilbert H. Grosvenor. Vol. XXVI, pp. 421-520, 85 ills. in black and white, 17 ills. in color, Nov., 1914.

Moseley, E. L.:

Rainfall and the Level of Lake Erie. By E. L. Moseley. Vol. XIV, pp. 327-328, Aug., 1903.

Submerged Valleys in Sandusky Bay (Ohio). By E. L. Moseley. Vol. XIII, pp. 398-403, 4 charts, Nov., 1902.

Testing the Currents of Lake Erie. By E. L. Moseley. Vol. XIV, pp. 41-42, Jan., 1903.

Moser, Charles K.:

"Flower of Paradise": The Part Which Khat Plays in the Life of the Yemen Arab. By Charles K. Moser. Vol. XXXII, pp. 173-186, 10 ills., 1 page map, Aug., 1917.

Isle of Frankincense (Socotra, Arabian Sea). By Charles K. Moser. Vol. XXXIII, pp. 266-278, 11 ills., Mar., 1918.

Moses, George Higgins:

Greece and Montenegro. By George Higgins Moses. Vol. XXIV, pp. 281-310, 24 ills., Mar., 1913.

Greece of Today. By George Higgins Moses. Vol. XXVIII, pp. 295-329, 27 ills., Oct., 1915.

New Hampshire, the Granite State. By George Higgins Moses. Vol. LX, pp. 257-310, 47 ills. in black and white, 5 ills. in color, 1 page map, Sept., 1931.

Whirlpool of the Balkans. By George Higgins Moses. Vol. XXXIX, pp. 179-197, 15 ills., Feb., 1921.

Moslems. *See* Mohammedans and Mohammedanism; Moros.

Mosques:

Gilded Domes Against an Azure Sky. 13 ills. in color from natural-color photographs by Stephen H. Nyman. Vol. LXXVI, pp. 339-346, Sept., 1939.

See also Sancta Sophia.

Mosquito Cays, Caribbean Sea:

Capturing Giant Turtles in the Caribbean. By David D. Duncan. Vol. LXXXIV, pp. 177-190, 13 ills., 1 quarter-page map, Aug., 1943.

Mosquitoes:

Life Story of the Mosquito. By Graham Fairchild. With 10 ills. in color from paintings. Vol. LXXXV, pp. 180-195, 5 ills. in black and white, 1 drawing, Feb., 1944.

Saboteur Mosquitoes. By Harry H. Stage. Vol. LXXXV, pp. 165-179, 12 ills., Feb., 1944.

Most Curious Craft Afloat, the Compass in Navigation and the Work of the Non-Magnetic Yacht *Carnegie*. By Dr. L. A. Bauer. Vol. XXI, pp. 223-245, 31 ills., Mar., 1910.

Most Extraordinary City in the World: Notes on Lhasa—The Mecca of the Buddhist Faith. By Shaoching H. Chuan. Vol. XXIII, pp. 959-995, 60 ills., Oct., 1912.

Most Famous Battle Field in America (Gettysburg). 14 ills. in color from natural-color photographs by Clifton Adams and Orren R. Louden. Vol. LX, pp. 66-75, July, 1931.

Most Historic Lands on Earth. Vol. XXVI, pp. 614-615, 1 page map, Dec., 1914.

Most Valuable Bird in the World (Guanay). By Robert Cushman Murphy. Vol. XLVI, pp. 279-302, 25 ills., 1 half-page map, Sept., 1924.

Mother of Rivers: An Account of a Photographic Expedition to the Great Columbia Ice Field of the Canadian Rockies. By Lewis R. Freeman. Vol. XLVII, pp. 377-446, 60 ills., 1 three-quarters-page and 1 quarter-page maps, Apr., 1925.

Mother Volga Defends Her Own (U. S. S. R.). By Maynard Owen Williams. Vol. LXXXII, pp. 793-811, 21 ills., Dec., 1942.

Mothers of Many Lands. Vol. XXXI, pp. 549-564, 16 ills., June, 1917.

Moths:

An Insect Community Lives in Flower Heads. By James G. Needham. Vol. XC, pp. 340-356, 5 ills. in black and white, 11 ills. in color, Sept., 1946.

Explorers of a New Kind: Successful Introduction of Beetles and Parasites to Check Ravages of the Gipsy-Moth and Brown-Tail Moth. By L. O. Howard. Vol. XXVI, pp. 38-67, 11 ills. in black and white, 5 ills. in color, July, 1914.

Exploring the Wonders of the Insect World. By William Joseph Showalter. Vol. LVI, pp. 1-90, 59 ills. in black and white, 269 ills. in color, July, 1929.

Gypsy Moth. Vol. XVII, pp. 460-464, 5 ills., Aug., 1906.

Insect Rivals of the Rainbow. 269 ills. in color from natural-color photographs by Edwin L. Wisherd and paintings by Hashime Murayama. Vol. LVI, pp. 28-85, July, 1929.

Pests and Parasites: Why We Need a National Law to Prevent the Importation of Insect-Infected and Diseased Plants. By Charles Lester Marlatt. Vol. XXII, pp. 321-346, 29 ills., 2 three-quarters-page maps, Apr., 1911.

Strange Habits of Familiar Moths and Butterflies. By William Joseph Showalter. Vol. LII, pp. 77-126, 28 ills. in black and white, 169 ills. in color, July, 1927.

Contains descriptions and illustrations of species of the following families: Arctiidæ, Ceratocampidæ, Noctuidæ, Saturniidæ, Sphingidæ.

Where Our Moths and Butterflies Roam. Vol. LII, pp. 105-126, July, 1927.

Motion Picture Industry:

Southern California at Work. By Frederick Simpich. Vol. LXVI, pp. 529-600, 39 ills. in black and white, 41 ills. in color, 1 two-page map, Nov., 1934.

Motor-Coaching Through North Carolina. By Melville Chater. Vol. XLIX, pp. 475-523, 43 ills., 1 third-page map, May, 1926.

Motor Trails in Japan. By W. Robert Moore. Vol. LXIII, pp. 303-318, 17 ills., Mar., 1933.

Mound Builders:

Indian Village of Baum (Ohio). By H. C. Brown. Vol. XII, pp. 272-274, July, 1901.

Indians of the Southeastern United States. By Matthew W. Stirling. Paintings by W. Langdon Kihn. Vol. LXXXIX, pp. 53-74, 8 ills. in black and white, 8 ills. in color, Jan., 1946.

Mount Desert Island, Maine:

First National Park East of the Mississippi River. Vol. XXIX, pp. 622-626, 5 ills., June, 1916.

Need of Conserving the Beauty and Freedom of Nature in Modern Life. By Charles W. Eliot. Vol. XXVI, pp. 67-74, 4 ills., July, 1914.

Northeast of Boston. By Albert W. Atwood. Vol. LXXXVIII, pp. 257-292, 12 ills. in black and white, 17 ills. in color, special map supplement, Sept., 1945.

Unique Island of Mount Desert. By George B. Dorr, Ernest Howe Forbush, and M. L. Fernald. Vol. XXVI, pp. 75-89, 7 ills., July, 1914.

Mount McKinley. By Robert Muldrow. Vol. XII, pp. 312-313, 1 half-page map, Aug., 1901.

Mount McKinley National Park, Alaska:

Game Country Without Rival in America: The Proposed Mount McKinley National Park. By Stephen R. Capps. Vol. XXXI, pp. 69-84, 14 ills., 1 half-page map, Jan., 1917.

Mount Rainier National Park, Washington:

Great White Monarch of the Pacific Northwest. By A. H. Barnes. Vol. XXIII, pp. 593-626, 31 ills., 1 half-page map, June, 1912.

Our National Parks. By L. F. Schmeckebier. Vol. XXIII, pp. 531-579, 41 ills., 1 page map, June, 1912.

Wonderland of Glaciers and Snow. By Milnor Roberts. Vol. XX, pp. 530-537, 8 ills., June, 1909.

Mount Vernon, Virginia:

Home of the First Farmer of America. By Worth E. Shoults. Vol. LIII, pp. 603-628, 6 ills. in black and white, 26 ills. in color, May, 1928.

Mount Weather Meteorological Observatory, Virginia:

Scientific Work of Mount Weather Meteorological Observatory. By Frank H. Bigelow. Vol. XV, pp. 442-445, Nov., 1904.

Mountain Climbing:

Amid the Snow Peaks of the Equator: A Naturalist's Explorations Around Ruwenzori, with an Excursion to the Congo State, and an Account of the Terrible Scourge of Sleeping Sickness. By A. F. R. Wollaston. Vol. XX, pp. 256-277, 11 ills., Mar., 1909.

Ascent of Mont Blanc. By Walter Woodburn Hyde. Vol. XXIV, pp. 861-942, 69 ills., Aug., 1913.

Climbing Mighty Minya Konka: Americans First Scaled Mountain That Now Is Landmark of China's New Skyway. By Richard L. Burdsall and Terris Moore. Vol. LXXXIII, pp. 625-650, 23 ills., 1 page map, May, 1943.

Conquest of Mount Crillon (Alaska). By Bradford Washburn. Vol. LXVII, pp. 361-400, 40 ills., 2 half-page maps, Mar., 1935.

Conquest of Mount Logan: North America's Second Highest Peak Yields to the Intrepid Attack of Canadian Climbers. By H. F. Lambart. Vol. XLIX, pp. 597-631, 40 ills., June, 1926.

Duke of the Abruzzi in the Himalayas. Vol. XXI, pp. 245-249, Mar., 1910.

Glories of the Minya Konka: Magnificent Snow Peaks of the China-Tibetan Border Are Photographed at Close Range by a National Geographic Society Expedition. By Joseph F. Rock. Vol. LVIII, pp. 385-437, 35 ills. in black and white, 24 ills. in color, 1 three-quarters-page map, Oct., 1930.

Highest Camp in the World. Vol. XVII, pp. 647-648, Nov., 1906.

Highest Camps and Climbs. By Edwin Swift Balch. Vol. XVII, p. 713, Dec., 1906.

Konka Risumgongba, Holy Mountain of the Outlaws. By Joseph F. Rock. Vol. LX, pp. 1-65, 36 ills. in black and white, 43 ills. in color, 1 three-quarters-page map, July, 1931.

Manless Alpine Climbing: The First Woman to Scale the Grépon, the Matterhorn, and Other Famous Peaks Without Masculine Support Relates Her Adventures. By Miriam O'Brien Underhill. Vol. LXVI, pp. 131-170, 30 ills. in black and white, 12 ills. in color, Aug., 1934.

Modern Persia and Its Capital: And an Account of an Ascent of Mount Demavend, the Persian Olympus. By F. L. Bird. Vol. XXXIX, pp. 353-400, 47 ills., Apr., 1921.

Monarch of the Canadian Rockies (Mount Robson). By Charles D. Walcott. Vol. XXIV, pp. 626-639, 13 ills., panorama, May, 1913.

Plan for Climbing Mount McKinley. By Alfred H. Brooks and D. L. Reaburn. Vol. XIX, pp. 30-35, 1 page map, Jan., 1903.

Recent Ascent of Itambé. By J. C. Branner. Vol. X, p. 183, May, 1899.

Record Ascent in the Himalayas. Vol. XIV, pp. 420-421, Nov., 1903.

Seeking the Mountains of Mystery: An Expedition on the China-Tibet Frontier to the Unexplored Amnyi Machen Range, One of Whose Peaks Rivals Everest. By Joseph F. Rock. Vol. LVII, pp. 131-185, 54 ills., 1 two-page map, Feb., 1930.

Mountain Climbing—*Continued*

Through Brazil to the Summit of Mount Roraima. By G. H. H. Tate. Vol. LVIII, pp. 585-605, 24 ills., 1 half-page map, Nov., 1930.

Volcanoes of Ecuador, Guideposts in Crossing South America. By G. M. Dyott. Vol. LV, pp. 49-93, 42 ills. in black and white, 12 ills. in color, 1 half-page map, Jan., 1929.

Woman's Climbs in the High Alps. By Dora Keen. Vol. XXII, pp. 642-675, 26 ills., July, 1911.

World's Highest Altitudes and First Ascents. By Charles E. Fay. Vol. XX, pp. 493-530, 25 ills., June, 1909.

Mountain Sheep:

Lords of the Rockies : Photographing Big Game Animals in Their Primeval Surroundings, from Arizona to Canada, Brings Adventure to Two Wilderness Wanderers. By Wendell and Lucie Chapman. Vol. LXXVI, pp. 87-128, 14 ills. in black and white, 28 ills. in color, July, 1939.

Stalking Big Game with Color Camera. 28 ills. in color from natural-color photographs by Wendell Chapman. Vol. LXXVI, pp. 89-128, July, 1939.

Mountain Tribes of Iran and Iraq. By Harold Lamb. Vol. LXXXIX, pp. 385-408, 15 ills., 1 two-page map, Mar., 1946.

Mountaineers: Tennessee-Kentucky :

Home Folk around Historic Cumberland Gap. By Leo A. Borah. Vol. LXXXIV, pp. 741-768, 25 ills., 1 quarter-page map, Dec., 1943.

Mountaineers of the Euphrates. By Ellsworth Huntington. Vol. XX, pp. 142-156, 13 ills., Feb., 1909.

Mountains. *See* Adirondack Mountains ; Alps ; Altai Mountains ; Amne Machin Shan ; Andes ; Argaeus, Mount ; Athos, Mount ; Atlas Mountains ; Bandai-San ; Bighorn Mountains ; Blanc, Mont ; Brukkaros, Mount ; Cameroons Mountain ; Canadian Rocky Mountains ; Caucasus ; Chugach Mountains ; Demavend, Mount ; Dent du Requin ; Diamond Mountains ; Dolomites ; Elburz Mountains ; Erebus, Mount ; Everest, Mount ; Falling Mountain ; Gerizim ; Great Smoky Mountains ; Guadalupe Mountains ; Himalayas ; Hood, Mount ; Itambé ; Izalco Volcano ; Katmai ; Konka Risumgongba ; Logan, Mount ; McKinley, Mount ; Martin, Mount ; Matterhorn ; Minya Konka ; Muli, Mount ; Navajo Mountain ; Novarupta ; Nyamlagira ; Orizaba ; Parnassus ; Pavlof Volcano ; Pelée, Mont ; Perry Peak ; Poás ; Popocatepetl ; Pyrenees ; Rainier, Mount ; Robson, Mount ; Rocky Mountains ; Roraima ; Rosa, Monte ; Ruwenzori ; St. Elias ; Sakurajima ; San Juan Mountains ; San Salvador Volcano ; Selkirk Mountains ; Shishaldin ; Soufrière ; Tai Shan ; Vesuvius ; Volcanoes ; Weisshorn ; White Mountains ; Wilson, Mount ; Wrangell Mountains.

Mountains of the Moon. *See* Ruwenzori.

Mountains on Unimak Island, Alaska. By Ferdinand Westdahl. Vol. XIV, pp. 90-99, 4 ills., 1 page and 1 half-page maps, Mar., 1903.

Mountford, Charles P.:

Australia's Stone Age Men. 8 ills. in color from natural-color photographs by Charles P. Mountford. Vol. LXXXIX, pp. 105-112, Jan., 1946.

Earth's Most Primitive People : A Journey with the Aborigines of Central Australia. By Charles P. Mountford. Vol. LXXXIX, pp. 89-112, 10 ills. in black and white, 8 ills. in color, 1 half-page map, Jan., 1946.

Mowbray, Louis L.:

Certain Citizens of the Warm Sea. By Louis L. Mowbray. Vol. XLI, pp. 27-62, 18 ills. in black and white, 16 ills. in color, Jan., 1922.

Mozambique:

Hunting Big Game in Portugese East Africa. By R. C. F. Maugham. Vol. XVIII, pp. 723-730, 7 ills., Nov., 1907.

Impressions and Scenes in Mozambique. By O. W. Barrett. Vol. XXI, pp. 807-830, 31 ills., Oct., 1910.

Wings Over Nature's Zoo in Africa. 20 ills. in duotone from photographs by Reginald A. Bourlay. Vol. LXXVI, pp. 527-542, Oct., 1939.

Mtzkhet, U. S. S. R.:

Russia's Orphan Races : Picturesque Peoples Who Cluster on the Southeastern Borderland of the Vast Slav Dominions. By Maynard Owen Williams. Vol. XXXIV, pp. 245-278, 26 ills., 1 page map, Oct., 1918.

Mughs (Tribespeople) :

India's Treasures Helped the Allies. By John Fischer. Vol. LXXXIX, pp. 501-522, 18 ills., Apr., 1946.

Muharrage (Town and Island), Bahrein Islands :

Bahrein : Port of Pearls and Petroleum. By Maynard Owen Williams. Vol. LXXXIX, pp. 195-210, 6 ills. in black and white, 11 ills. in color, 1 half-page map, Feb., 1946.

Muir, Frances:

India at Work and Play. 22 ills. in color from natural-color photographs by Peter Upton Muir, Maynard Owen Williams, and Frances Muir. Vol. LXXXIX, pp. 449-464, Apr., 1946.

India Mosaic. By Peter Muir and Frances Muir. Vol. LXXXIX, pp. 443-470, 5 ills. in black and white, 22 ills. in color, 1 half-page map, Apr., 1946.

Muir, Peter Upton:

India at Work and Play. 22 ills. in color from natural-color photographs by Peter Upton Muir, Maynard Owen Williams, and Frances Muir. Vol. LXXXIX, pp. 449-464, Apr., 1946.

India Mosaic. By Peter Muir and Frances Muir. Vol. LXXXIX, pp. 443-470, 5 ills. in black and white, 22 ills. in color, 1 half-page map, Apr., 1946.

Muir, Peter Upton—*Continued*

Normandy and Brittany in Brighter Days. 21 ills. in color from natural-color photographs by W. Robert Moore, Peter Upton Muir, and others. Vol. LXXXIV, pp. 209-232, Aug., 1943.

Muir Glacier, Alaska :

Muir Glacier. By C. L. Andrews. Vol. XIV, pp. 441-445, 2 ills., 1 quarter-page map, Dec., 1903.

Mukden, Manchuria :

Japan Faces Russia in Manchuria. By Willard Price. Vol. LXXXII, pp. 603-634, 30 ills., 1 page map, Nov., 1942.

Mukden, the Manchu Home, and Its Great Art Museum. By Eliza R. Scidmore. Vol. XXI, pp. 289-320, 30 ills., Apr., 1910.

Mula Mulai (Ship) :

Seafarers of South Celebes. By G. E. P. Collins. Vol. LXXXVII, pp. 57-78, 25 ills., 1 two-thirds-page map, Jan., 1945.

Mulatas Archipelago, Panama :

Arch-Isolationists, the San Blas Indians : Coconuts Serve as Cash on Islands Off the Panama Coast Where Tribesmen Cling to Their Ancient Ways and Discourage Visitors. By Corinne B. Feeney. Vol. LXXIX, pp. 193-220, 15 ills. in black and white, 12 ills. in color, 1 sixth-page map, Feb., 1941.

Indian Haven—Off the San Blas Coast. 12 ills. in color from natural-color photographs by Lieut. Dayton Seiler. Vol. LXXIX, pp. 209-216, Feb., 1941.

Mulberry (Artificial Harbor), Normandy Coast :

Normandy's Made-in-England Harbors. Vol. LXXXVII, pp. 565-580, 16 ills., 1 quarter-page map, May, 1945.

Muldrow, Robert:

Mount McKinley. By Robert Muldrow. Vol. XII, pp. 312-313, 1 half-page map, Aug., 1901.

Mule Deer:

High Country of Colorado. By Alfred M. Bailey. With 23 ills. in color from natural-color photographs by the author, Robert J. Niedrach, and F. G. Brandenburg. Vol. XC, pp. 43-72, 9 ills. in black and white, July, 1946.

Muli (Lama Kingdom) :

Land of the Yellow Lama : National Geographic Society Explorer Visits the Strange Kingdom of Muli, Beyond the Likiang Snow Range of Yünnan Province, China. By Joseph F. Rock. Vol. XLVII, pp. 447-491, 39 ills., 1 half-page map, Apr., 1925.

Muli, Mount, Borneo :

Sarawak : The Land of the White Rajahs. By Harrison W. Smith. Vol. XXXV, pp. 110-167, 58 ills., 1 half-page map, Feb., 1919.

Muller, James Arthur:

Peking, the City of the Unexpected. By James Arthur Muller. Vol. XXXVIII, pp. 335-355, 18 ills., Nov., 1920.

Mullikin, Mary Augusta:

Buddhist Calm Survives Along China's Great Wall. 10 ills. in color ; 4 paintings by Mary Augusta Mullikin and Anna M. Hotchkis and 6 natural-color photographs. Vol. LXXIII, pp. 321-328, Mar., 1938.

China's Great Wall of Sculpture : Man-hewn Caves and Countless Images Form a Colossal Art Wonder of Early Buddhism. By Mary Augusta Mullikin. Vol. LXXIII, pp. 313-348, 23 ills. in black and white, 10 ills. in color, 1 third-page map, Mar., 1938.

Tai Shan, Sacred Mountain of the East. By Mary Augusta Mullikin. Vol. LXXXVII, pp. 699-719, 18 ills., 1 page map, June, 1945.

Multicolored Cones of Cappadocia. 20 ills. in color from natural-color photographs by Eric Matson. Vol. LXXVI, pp. 769-800, Dec., 1939.

Multi-Hued Marvels of a Coral Reef. 8 ills. in color from paintings by Else Bostelmann. Vol. LXV, pp. 719-726, June, 1934.

Munda, New Georgia (Island), Solomon Islands :

Painting History in the Pacific. 19 ills. in color from paintings by Lt. William F. Draper. Vol. LXXXVI, pp. 409-424, Oct., 1944.

Munger, (Capt.) F. M.:

Jack in the Box : An Account of the Strange Performances of the Most Wonderful Island in the World (Bogoslof Volcano, Alaska). By Capt. F. M. Munger. Vol. XX, pp. 194-199, 8 ills., Feb., 1909.

Münster, Germany :

Town of Many Gables. By Florence Craig Albrecht. Vol. XXVII, pp. 107-140, 28 ills., Feb., 1915.

Murayama, Hashime:

Ants : Work and War in the World of Ants. 18 ills. in color from paintings by Hashime Murayama. Vol. LXVI, pp. 179-186, Aug., 1934.

Bees : In Field and Hive with the Busy Honeybee. 16 ills. in color from paintings by Hashime Murayama. Vol. LXVII, pp. 417-424, Apr., 1935.

Birds. 4 ills. in color from paintings by Hashime Murayama. Vol. XLVIII, pp. 412-415, Oct., 1925.

Birds : Iridescent Isles of the South Seas. 16 ills. in color ; 4 paintings by Hashime Murayama. Vol. XLVIII, pp. 403-418, Oct., 1925.

Birds : Pigeons of Resplendent Plumage. 12 ills. in color from paintings by Hashime Murayama. Vol. XLIX, pp. 65-76, Jan., 1926.

Butterflies : Nomads Among the Butterflies. 8 ills. in color ; 3 paintings by Hashime Murayama and 5 natural-color photographs by Willard R. Culver. Vol. LXXI, pp. 569-584, May, 1937.

Butterflies : Winged Jewels from Many Lands. 9 ills. in color ; 3 paintings by Hashime Murayama and 6 natural-color photographs by Willard R. Culver. Vol. LXIX, pp. 673-688, May, 1936.

Murayama, Hashime—*Continued*

Fish. 16 ills. in color from paintings by Hashime Murayama. Vol. XXXIX, pp. 61-68, Jan., 1921.

Fish. 16 ills. in color from paintings by Hashime Murayama. Vol. XLI, pp. 37-52, Jan., 1922.

Fish : Fresh-Water Denizens of the Far West. 54 portraits in color from paintings by Hashime Murayama. Vol. LXXV, pp. 193-204, Feb., 1939.

Fish : Fresh-Water Fishes of the United States. 16 ills. in color from paintings by Hashime Murayama. Vol. XLIV, pp. 133-148, Aug., 1923.

Fish : Gleaming Fishes of Pacific Coastal Waters. 31 portraits in color from paintings by Hashime Murayama. Vol. LXXIV, pp. 467-498, Oct., 1938.

Fish : Goldfish and Their Cultivation. 8 ills. in color from paintings by Hashime Murayama. Vol. XLVI, pp. 385-392, Oct., 1924.

Fish : Iridescent Denizens of the Miniature Aquarium. 8 ills. in color from paintings by Hashime Murayama. Vol. LIX, pp. 291-300, Mar., 1931.

Fish : North Atlantic Fishes. 16 ills. in color from paintings by Hashime Murayama. Vol. XLIV, pp. 613-628, Dec., 1923.

Fowl : Domestic Fowls of Field, Park, and Farmyard. 16 ills. in color from paintings by Hashime Murayama. Vol. LVII, pp. 329-360, Mar., 1930.

Fowl of the Old and New World. 29 ills. in color from paintings by Hashime Murayama. Vol. LI, pp. 421-436, Apr., 1927.

Frogs and Toads : Iridescent Beauty of Frogs and Toads. 14 ills. in color from paintings by Hashime Murayama. Vol. LXI, pp. 635-642, May, 1932.

Insects : Exploring the Wonders of the Insect World. By William Joseph Showalter. 1 ill. in black and white, 3 ills. in color from paintings by Hashime Murayama. Vol. LVI, pp. 1-90, July, 1929.

Insects : Rogues' Gallery of Imported Pests. 10 ills. in color from paintings by Hashime Murayama. Vol. LXXX, pp. 237-244, Aug., 1941.

Spiders : Nature's Ingenious Spinners. 64 ills. in color from paintings by Hashime Murayama. Vol. LXIV, pp. 167-174, Aug., 1933.

Wasps and Hornets : Farmers' Friends Among the Wasps and Hornets. 12 ills. in color from paintings by Hashime Murayama. Vol. LXXII, pp. 57-64, July, 1937.

Murdoch, Helen Messinger:

India and Ceylon. 8 ills. in color from autochromes by Helen Messinger Murdoch. Vol. XXXIX, pp. 281-288, Mar., 1921.

Murdoch, L. H.:

Why Great Salt Lake Has Fallen. By L. H. Murdoch. Vol. XIV, pp. 75-77, Feb., 1903.

Murman Coast : Arctic Gateway for American and Allied Expeditionary Forces in Northern European Russia. Vol. XXXV, pp. 331-348, 30 ills., 1 half-page map, Apr., 1919.

Murphy, Robert Cushman:

Birds of the High Seas : Albatrosses and Petrels ; Gannets, Man-o'-war-birds, and Tropic-birds. By Robert Cushman Murphy. Paintings by Maj. Allan Brooks. Vol. LXXIV, pp. 226-251, 7 ills. in black and white, 36 portraits in color, Aug., 1938.

Most Valuable Bird in the World (Guanay). By Robert Cushman Murphy. Vol. XLVI, pp. 279-302, 25 ills., 1 half-page map, Sept., 1924.

Romance of Science in Polynesia : An Account of Five Years of Cruising Among the South Sea Islands. By Robert Cushman Murphy. Vol. XLVIII, pp. 355-426, 66 ills. in black and white, 16 ills. in color, 3 half-page maps, Oct., 1925.

South Georgia, an Outpost of the Antarctic. By Robert Cushman Murphy. Vol. XLI, pp. 409-444, 41 ills., 2 half-page maps, Apr., 1922.

Timeless Arans : The Workaday World Lies Beyond the Horizon of Three Rocky Islets Off the Irish Coast. By Robert Cushman Murphy. Vol. LIX, pp. 747-775, 35 ills., 1 quarter-page map, June, 1931.

Murray, Edward Stevenson:

On the Turks' Russian Frontier : Everyday Life in the Fastnesses between the Black Sea and Ararat, Borderland of Oil and Minerals that Hitler Covets. By Edward Stevenson Murray. Vol. LXXX, pp. 367-392, 21 ills., 1 half-page map, Sept., 1941.

With the Nomads of Central Asia : A Summer's Sojourn in the Tekes Valley, Plateau Paradise of Mongol and Turkic Tribes. By Edward Murray. Vol. LXIX, pp. 1-57, 43 ills. in black and white, 26 ills. in color, 1 half-page map, Jan., 1936.

Murray, (Sir) John:

Sir John Murray (Biography). Vol. XII, pp. 238-240, 1 ill., June, 1901.

Murray, Louise:

In Valais (Switzerland). By Louise Murray. Vol. XXI, pp. 249-256, 6 ills., Mar., 1910.

Murrelets (Birds) :

Birds of the Northern Seas. By Alexander Wetmore. Paintings by Maj. Allan Brooks. Vol. LXIX, pp. 95-122, 12 ills. in black and white, 34 portraits in color, Jan., 1936.

Murres (Birds) :

Birds of the Northern Seas. By Alexander Wetmore. Paintings by Maj. Allan Brooks. Vol. LXIX, pp. 95-122, 12 ills. in black and white, 34 portraits in color, Jan., 1936.

Murzuch, Libia :

Mysteries of the Desert. By Hanns Vischer. Vol. XXII, pp. 1056-1059, Nov., 1911.

Musan, Korea :

Exploring Unknown Corners of the "Hermit Kingdom." By Roy Chapman Andrews. Vol. XXXVI, pp. 24-48, 30 ills., 1 page map, July, 1919.

Mushrooms:

Common Mushrooms of the United States. By Louis C. C. Krieger. Vol. XXXVII, pp. 387-439, 37 ills. in black and white, 16 ills. in color, May, 1920.

Muskrats:

Wild Animals That Took Their Own Pictures by Day and by Night. By George Shiras, 3d. Vol. XXIV, pp. 763-834, 68 ills., 1 page map, July, 1913.

Wild Life of Lake Superior, Past and Present : The Habits of Deer, Moose, Wolves, Beavers, Muskrats, Trout, and Feathered Wood-Folk Studied with Camera and Flashlight. By George Shiras, 3d. Vol. XL, pp. 113-204, 77 ills., supplement, 1 half-page map, Aug., 1921.

Mustapha Kemal (President of Turkey) :

Turkish Republic Comes of Age. By Maynard Owen Williams. Vol. LXXXVII, pp. 581-616, 4 ills. in black and white, 29 ills. in color, 1 map (two-page spread), May, 1945.

My Domestic Life in French Guinea : An American Woman Accompanies Her Husband, a French Geologist, on His Explorations in a Little-Known Region. By Eleanor de Chételat. Vol. LXVII, pp. 695-730, 48 ills., 1 half-page map, June, 1935.

My Flight Across Antarctica. By Lincoln Ellsworth. Vol. LXX, pp. 1-35, 37 ills., 1 page map, July, 1936.

My Flight from Hawaii. By Amelia Earhart. Vol. LXVII, pp. 593-609, 4 ills. in black and white, 8 ills. in duotone, May, 1935.

My Four Antarctic Expeditions : Explorations of 1933-39 Have Stricken Vast Areas from the Realm of the Unknown. By Lincoln Ellsworth. Vol. LXXVI, pp. 129-138, 9 ills., 1 page map, July, 1939.

Mycetozoa:

Marvels of Mycetozoa : Exploration of a Long Island Swamp Reveals Some of the Secrets of the Slime Molds, Dwelling on the Borderland Between the Plant and Animal Kingdoms. By William Crowder. Vol. XLIX, pp. 421-443, 5 ills. in black and white, 16 ills. in color, Apr., 1926.

Contains descriptions and illustrations of the following species : Arcyria Denudata, Arcyria Ferruginea, Badhamia Papaveracea, Comatricha Pulchella, Diachea Leucopoda, Dictydium Cancellatum, Diderma Testaceum, Fuligo Septica, Globuliferum, Lamproderma Arcyrionema, Lamproderma Violaceum, Leocarpus Fragilis, Physarum Lateritium, Physarum Viride, Stemonitis Splendens, Trichia Persimilis.

Mýkonos (Island), Aegean Sea :

Isles of Greece. By Lt. Richard Stillwell, USNR. Vol. LXXXV, pp. 593-622, 11 ills. in black and white, 20 ills. in color, 1 page map, May, 1944.

Santorin and Mýkonos, Aegean Gems. 8 ills. in color from natural-color photographs ; 7 ills. by B. Anthony Stewart. Vol. LXXVII, pp. 339-346, Mar., 1940.

Mysore, India :

India at Work and Play. 22 ills. in color from natural-color photographs by Peter Upton Muir, Maynard Owen Williams, and Frances Muir. Vol. LXXXIX, pp. 449-464, Apr., 1946.

India Mosaic. By Peter Muir and Frances Muir. Vol. LXXXIX, pp. 443-470, 5 ills. in black and white, 22 ills. in color, 1 half-page map, Apr., 1946.

Mysteries of the Desert (Sahara). By Hanns Vischer. Vol. XXII, pp. 1056-1059, Nov., 1911.

Mysterious Life of the Common Eel. By Hugh M. Smith. Vol. XXIV, pp. 1140-1146, 3 ills., Oct., 1913.

Mysterious Micronesia : Yap, Map, and Other Islands Under Japanese Mandate are Museums of Primitive Man. By Willard Price. Vol. LXIX, pp. 481-510, 37 ills., 1 half-page map, Apr., 1936.

Mysterious Prehistoric Monuments of Brittany (France). By Charles Buxton Going. Vol. XLIV, pp. 53-69, 16 ills., July, 1923.

Mysterious Temples of the Jungle : The Prehistoric Ruins of Guatemala. By W. F. Sands. Vol. XXIV, pp. 324-338, 10 ills., Mar., 1913.

Mysterious Tomb of a Giant Meteorite (Meteor Crater, Arizona). By William D. Boutwell. Vol. LIII, pp. 721-730, 10 ills., June, 1928.

Mystery Mammals of the Twilight (Bats). By Donald R. Griffin. Vol. XC, pp. 117-134, 19 ills., July, 1946.

Mystery of Auroras : National Geographic Society and Cornell University Study Spectacular Displays in the Heavens. Vol. LXXV, pp. 689-690, May, 1939.

Mystery of Easter Island. By Mrs. Scoresby Routledge. Vol. XL, pp. 628-646, 13 ills., 1 page map, Dec., 1921.

Mystic Nedjef, the Shia Mecca. By Frederick Simpich. Vol. XXVI, pp. 589-598, 4 ills., Dec., 1914.

Mytilene (Island), Greece :

Some Ruined Cities of Asia Minor. By Ernest L. Harris. Vol. XIX, pp. 833-858, 19 ills., Dec., 1908.

N

Nablus (Shechem), Palestine :

Last Israelitish Blood Sacrifice : How the Vanishing Samaritans Celebrate the Passover on Sacred Mount Gerizim. By John D. Whiting. Vol. XXXVII, pp. 1-46, 40 ills., 1 half-page map, Jan., 1920.

Nabours, Robert K.:

Land of Lambskins : An Expedition to Bokhara, Russian Central Asia, to Study the Karakul Sheep Industry. By Robert K. Nabours. Vol. XXXVI, pp. 77-88, 15 ills., July, 1919.

Nabuco, Joaquim:

What the Latin American Republics Think of the Pan-American Conferences (Address by the Brazilian Ambassador). Vol. XVII, pp. 474-479, Aug., 1906.

Nagas (Tribespeople) :

Women of All Nations. Vol. XXII, pp. 49-61, 12 ills., Jan., 1911.

Naha, Okinawa (Island), Ryukyu Retto :

Peacetime Rambles in the Ryukyus. By William Leonard Schwartz. Vol. LXXXVII, pp. 543-561, 12 ills., 1 two-thirds-page and 1 half-page maps, May, 1945.

Naivasha (Lake), Kenya Colony :

Where Roosevelt Will Hunt. By Sir Harry Johnston. Vol. XX, pp. 207-256, 43 ills., special map supplement, Mar., 1909.

Najaf, An, Iraq :

Mystic Nedjef, the Shia Mecca. By Frederick Simpich. Vol. XXVI, pp. 589-598, 4 ills., Dec., 1914.

Nakwasina Goes North : A Man, a Woman, and a Pup Cruise from Tacoma to Juneau in a 17-foot Canoe. By Jack Calvin. Vol. LXIV, pp. 1-42, 24 ills., 1 page map, July, 1933.

Nancy, France :

A City Learns to Smile Again. By Maj. Frederick G. Vosburgh. Vol. LXXXVII, pp. 361-384, 23 ills., 1 two-thirds-page map, Mar., 1945.

In French Lorraine : That Part of France Where the First American Soldiers Have Fallen. By Harriet Chalmers Adams. Vol. XXXII, pp. 499-518, 16 ills., Nov.-Dec., 1917.

Nanking, China :

Rise and Fall of Nanking. By Julius Eigner. Vol. LXXIII, pp. 189-224, 37 ills., Feb., 1938.

Nansen's "Farthest North" Eclipsed. Vol. XI, pp. 411-413, Oct., 1900.

Nantucket (Island), Massachusetts :

Echoes of Whaling Days. 8 ills. in color from natural-color photographs by B. Anthony Stewart. Vol. LXXXV, pp. 449-456, Apr., 1944.

Nantucket—Little Gray Lady. By William H. Nicholas. Vol. LXXXV, pp. 433-458, 14 ills. in black and white, 8 ills. in color, 1 half-page map, Apr., 1944.

Naples, Italy :

Inexhaustible Italy. By Arthur Stanley Riggs. Vol. XXX, pp. 273-368, 76 ills., 1 page map, Oct., 1916.

Napoleon I:

Coasts of Corsica : Impressions of a Winter's Stay in the Island Birthplace of Napoleon. By Maynard Owen Williams. Vol. XLIV, pp. 221-312, 88 ills., special supplement, 1 page and 1 quarter-page maps, Sept., 1923.

Narsak, Greenland :

Americans Stand Guard in Greenland. By Andrew H. Brown. Vol. XC, pp. 457-500, 23 ills. in black and white, 19 ills. in color, 1 page map, Oct., 1946.

Narsarssuak, Greenland :

Americans Stand Guard in Greenland. By Andrew H. Brown. Vol. XC, pp. 457-500, 23 ills. in black and white, 19 ills. in color, 1 page map, Oct., 1946.

Nashi (Tribespeople) :

Banishing the Devil of Disease Among the Nashi : Weird Ceremonies Performed by an Aboriginal Tribe in the Heart of Yünnan Province, China. By Joseph F. Rock. Vol. XLVI, pp. 473-499, 26 ills., 1 half-page map, Nov., 1924.

Natal (Province), Union of South Africa :

Natal : The Garden Colony. By Russell Hastings Millward. Vol. XX, pp. 278-291, 16 ills., Mar., 1909.

Natal : The Garden Province. By Melville Chater. Vol. LIX, pp. 447-478, 29 ills., Apr., 1931.

Natchez Indians:

Indians of the Southeastern United States. By Matthew W. Stirling. Paintings by W. Langdon Kihn. Vol. LXXXIX, pp. 53-74, 8 ills. in black and white, 8 ills. in color, Jan., 1946.

National Forests:

Forest Lookout. By Ella E. Clark. With 9 ills. in color from natural-color photographs by the author. Vol. XC, pp. 73-96, 8 ills. in black and white, July, 1946.

National Gallery of Art, Washington, D. C. :

Old Masters in a New National Gallery. By Ruth Q. McBride. Vol. LXXVIII, pp. 1-50, 11 ills. in black and white, 32 color reproductions of masterpieces, July, 1940.

National Geographic Magazine:

Associate Editor. *See* National Geographic Society : Vice-President.

Bringing the World to Our Foreign-Language Soldiers : How a Military Training Camp Is Solving a Seemingly Unsurmountable Problem by Using The Geographic. By Christina Krysto. Vol. XXXIV, pp. 81-90, 4 ills., Aug., 1918.

Censorship of The Magazine. Vol. LXXXIV, p. 280, Sept., 1943.

National Geographic Magazine—*Continued*

Clay added to coating of paper gives greater luster to photographs. Vol. LXXIV, p. 753, Dec., 1938.

Comments on The Magazine. Vol. XXV, pp. 465, 468-469, Apr., 1913.

Correspondence Department opened. Vol. XVII, p. 37, Jan., 1906.

Early years of The Magazine. Vol. X, pp. 221-222, June, 1899.

Editor. *See* Grosvenor, Gilbert.

First extensive article in America on gliders published in the National Geographic Magazine. Vol. LXXIV, p. 123, July, 1938.

Gliders, German, First report of, appeared in The Magazine in 1929. Vol. LXXXVI, p. 150, Aug., 1944.

History of The Magazine (Speech by Alexander Graham Bell). Vol. XXIII, pp. 273-274, Mar., 1912.

Increase in circulation of The Magazine. Vol. XXIII, p. 208, Feb., 1912 ; p. 274, Mar., 1912. Vol. XXIV, pp. 252-253, Feb., 1913. Vol. XXV, p. 680, June, 1914. Vol. XXXVII, p. 343, Apr., 1920.

Letter from President Woodrow Wilson to Dr. Grosvenor (Congratulations on the Flag Number). Vol. XXXII, p. 549, Nov.-Dec., 1917.

Map Supplements. *See* National Geographic Society: Map Supplement Articles, Map Supplements (Text and Illustrations) ; *and* Index to Maps, p. 594.

National Geographic Magazine, the first to publish a complete set of full-color pictures of the better-known whales, dolphins, and porpoises. Vol. LXXVII, p. 35, Jan., 1940.

National Geographic Magazine and the U. S. Board on Geographic Names. Vol. X, pp. 517-519, Dec., 1899.

National Geographic Society and Its Magazine. By Gilbert Grosvenor. Vol. LXIX, pp. 123-164, 24 ills., Jan., 1936.
Binding of 125
Early issues........125, 135, 149, 150, 161
Flag numbers 160
Geographical distribution of copies..161, 163–164
Ink 123
Map supplements 130, 155
Nature library 160
Photographs and paintings.128–129, 143, 150, 153–154, 155, 157, 158 ; ill. 142
Policy and guiding principles.......123, 149
State articles 160
Subject matter 125, 128–129, 130, 143, 153–154, 155, 160–161, 162
Value and service rendered....123, 128, 161–162

Number of copies per month. Vol. LXXXI, pp. 474, 484, Apr., 1942.

Paper manufactured for The Magazine. Vol. XXXVII, pp. 234-245, 9 ills., Mar., 1920.

Photographs. *See* National Geographic Society: Paintings ; Photography.

Policy of The Magazine. Vol. XX, p. 486, May, 1909.

National Geographic Magazine—*Continued*

Printing The Magazine. Vol. LXXXI, p. 484 ; ill. 474, Apr., 1942.

Publication of first aerial color photographs. Vol. LXXVII, p. 757, June, 1940.

Publication of *Revista Geográfica Americana* inspired by National Geographic Magazine. Vol. LXXVI, p. 573, Nov., 1939.

Report by Gilbert H. Grosvenor for the Year 1912. Vol. XXIV, pp. 251-255, Feb., 1913.

Report of the Director and Editor of the National Geographic Society for the Year 1914 (Policy of The Magazine). By Gilbert H. Grosvenor. Vol. XXVII, pp. 318-320, Mar., 1915.

Various uses of The Geographic's map supplements. Vol. LXXIII, p. 525, Apr., 1938.

See also National Geographic Society : Editorial Department.

National Geographic Map of Japan, Regions of Asia, and the Pacific. Text accompanying special map supplement in colors. Vol. LXXXV, pp. 415-416, Apr., 1944.

National Geographic Society:

Aeronautics:

Admiral Byrd Receives New Honor from The Society (Presentation by President Hoover of Special Gold Medal). Vol. LVIII, pp. 228–238, 4 ills., Aug., 1930.
Achievements of Byrd Antarctic Expedition 231–232
Bumstead sun-compass praised by Byrd.. 233
Byrd Antarctic Expedition aided by The Society 232

Aëronautics promoted by The Society. Vol. XLVI, p. 122, July, 1924.

Air Conquest : From the Early Days of Giant Kites and Birdlike Gliders, the National Geographic Society Has Aided and Encouraged the Growth of Aviation. Vol. LII, pp. 233-242, 13 ills., Aug., 1927.
Aërial photography sponsored by The Society 240
Articles on aviation published in The Magazine 233–234, 240–242
Banquet celebrating progress in aviation.. 233
Bell, Alexander Graham : Kite experiments of ....233 ; ill. 235, 236
Bumstead sun-compass, Byrd's use of 238 ; ill. 242
Expeditions aided by The Society....234, 238 ; ill. 239
Hubbard Gold Medal awarded Lindbergh 241-242 ; ill. 234
Hubbard Gold Medals awarded Comdr. Byrd and Floyd Bennett......238 ; ill. 239
Peary's prophecy regarding aviation..... 234

First Airship Flight Around the World : Dr. Hugo Eckener Tells of an Epochal Geographic Achievement upon the Occasion of the Bestowal of the National Geographic Society's Special Gold Medal. Vol. LVII, pp. 653–688, 37 ills., June, 1930.
Four aviators awarded Society's medals.. 655
Presentation of medal to Dr. Eckener by Dr. Grosvenor...................653–655
Service of aviation to geography........ 655

National Geographic Society—*Continued*

Aeronautics—*Continued*

In Honor of the Army and Aviation. Vol.
XXII, pp. 267–284, 1 ill., Mar., 1911.
Appreciation of S. P. Langley........ 279
Aviation in Germany......270–271; ill. 271
Importance of aviation in warfare....278–280
Wright, Wilbur: Address by........279–281
President Coolidge Bestows Lindbergh
Award: The National Geographic Society's
Hubbard Medal Is Presented to Aviator
Before the Most Notable Gathering in the
History of Washington. Vol. LIII, pp.
132–140, 4 ills., Jan., 1928.
Aviation aided by The Society.......... 135
Aviators at ceremony................. 132
Contributions of U. S. to aviation...... 138
Lindbergh's achievements 134–135
Motion picture of aviation history....139–140
Society Awards Hubbard Medal to Anne Mor-
row Lindbergh. Vol. LXV, pp. 791-794,
4 ills., June, 1934.
Aërial photography sponsored by The So-
ciety 794
Aviation sponsored by The Society...... 791
Tribute to Mrs. Lindbergh by Dr. Grosve-
nor 791–792
Society's Special Medal Awarded to Amelia
Earhart: First Woman to Receive Geo-
graphic Distinction at Brilliant Ceremony
in the National Capital. Vol. LXII, pp.
358–367, 7 ills., Sept., 1932.
Aviation sponsored by The Society...... 362
Earhart, Amelia: Account of Transat-
lantic flight....358, 363–367; ill. 359, 360
Tribute to Miss Earhart by Dr. Grosvenor 359
Tribute to Miss Earhart by President
Hoover 362–363
See also Aeronautics, p. 5; Expeditions:
Stratosphere.

Air-raid wardens, Demonstration given for.
Vol. LXXXI, ill. 460, Apr., 1942.

Air travel by The Society's Staff. Vol.
LXIII, pp. 587, 628, May, 1933.

Annex. *See* Buildings.

Aquariums. Vol. LXV, ill. 107, Jan., 1934.

Banquets:

Announcement of Annual Banquet. Vol.
XVII, p. 714, Dec., 1906.
Guests 714
Announcement of Annual Banquet. Vol.
XIX, p. 805, Nov., 1908; p. 888, Dec.,
1908.
Announcement of Annual Banquet, Decem-
ber 20, 1905. Vol. XVI, p. 570, Dec., 1905.
Guests 570
Annual Banquet, January 26, 1912. Vol.
XXIII, pp. 272–298, 5 ills., Mar., 1912.
American Red Cross................288–290
Announcement of election of James Bryce
as Honorary Member.......272, 275–276
Bell, Alexander Graham: Speeches by
272–276, 280, 282, 284,
287, 290, 292, 293
Boardman, Mabel: Speech by.......288–290
Bryce, James: Speech by..........276–280
Date-growing experiments in America.... 293
Expeditions of The Society........... 275

National Geographic Society—*Continued*

Banquets—*Continued*

Gannett, Henry: Speech by........... 272
Geography of food................... 283
Growth of The Society.............272–274
Guests 272, 293–298
Hammond, (Mrs.) John Hays: Speech by
292–293
Importance of trigonometrical surveys
284, 287
Kahn, (Mirza) Ali Kuli: Speech by..281–282
Message from President Taft.......... 282
Nitobe, (Dr.) Inazu: Speech by.....290–292
Progress of The Magazine under its Edi-
tor, Gilbert H. Grosvenor............ 274
Tittmann, O. H.: Speech by.......284, 287
Wiley, (Dr.) Harvey W.: Speech by..282–284
Annual Banquet of the National Geographic
Society. Vol. XVII, pp. 22–37, Jan., 1906.
Achievements of the American press....29–32
Champ, W. S.: Speech by............35–36
Committee for banquet............... 37
Definition of geography.............. 24
Fiala, Anthony: Speech by...........32–34
Greely, (Brig. Gen.) A. W.: Speech by... 36
Griscom, Floyd C.: Speech by.........27–29
Guests 22–23, 36–37
History of The Society..............23–24
Newspaper account of dinner.........22–23
Scott, Charles F.: Speech by.........29–32
Taft, William H.: Speech by.........25–26
Taft, (Mr. and Mrs.) William H.: Guests
of honor 22
Toast in memory of Gardiner Greene Hub-
bard 24
Toast to the President and the Flag....25–26
Toastmaster (Willis L. Moore)...23–25,
26–27, 29, 32, 34–35
Wellman, Walter: Speech by.......... 36
Ziegler Polar Expedition.............32–36
Discovery of the North Pole (Presentation
of Special Gold Medal to Peary by Willis
L. Moore, and Hubbard Gold Medal to
Bartlett by James Bryce). Vol. XXI, pp.
63–82, Jan., 1910.
Abruzzi, Duke of the: Message from.... 64
Barrett, John: Speech by............. 79
Bartlett, (Capt.) Robert A.: Acceptance
speech by 77–78
Bryce, James: Presentation speech by..75–77
Cannon, Joseph: Speech by..........66–67
Carnegie, Andrew: Speech by.........68–69
Chester, (Rear Adm.) Colby M.: Speech
by 69–73
Guests 63, 79–82
History of Peary's explorations........69–73
Hubbard, (Gen.) Thomas H.: Speech by
78–79
Hubbard Gold Medal awarded to Grove
Karl Gilbert 63, 75
Hubbard Gold Medal presented to Capt.
Robert A. Bartlett by James Bryce
63, 75–77
Jusserand, J. J.: Speech by..........64–66
Medals received by Peary............. 73
Moore, Willis L.: Presentation speech by
73–74
Peary, Robert E.: Acceptance speech by
74–75
Peary Arctic Club...................78–79

National Geographic Society—*Continued*
Banquets—*Continued*

Planches, Baron Mayor des : Speech by ... 64
Purpose and organization of The Society
  67–68
Roosevelt, Theodore : Message from..... 63
Special Gold Medal presented to Peary
  by Willis L. Moore.............63, 74–75
Toastmaster (Willis L. Moore)......63,
  66–69, 73–75, 78–79

Honors for Amundsen (Presentation of Hub-
bard Gold Medal by Charles W. Fair-
banks). Vol. XIX, pp. 55–76, 13 ills.,
Jan., 1908.
Amundsen, Roald : Speech by.......... 57
Bryce, James : Speech by.............62–64
Burton, Theodore : Speech by.........66–68
Fairbanks, Charles W.: Presentation
  speech by 55–57
Forestry in America.................64–65
Goulder, Harvey : Speech by..........69–72
Great Lakes 69–72
Guests 55, 57, 74–76
Importance of geography.............62–64
Jusserand, J. J.: Speech by..........57–61
McGee, W J : Speech by.............. 69
Mississippi River 66–68
Moore, J. Hampton : Speech by........72–74
Norse explorations 58
Rivers of the Atlantic coast.........72–74
Toastmaster (Willis L. Moore)....55, 57,
  61–62, 64, 68–69, 72

Honors to Amundsen and Peary (Presenta-
tion of Special Gold Medal to Amundsen
by Peary). Vol. XXIV, pp. 113–130,
Jan., 1913.
Amundsen, Roald : Speech of acceptance
  129–130
Award of Grant Squires Prize to F. H.
  King 115
Bingham, Hiram : Account of Peruvian
  Expedition 116–117
Bryce, James : Speech and farewell..117–119
Buildings of The Society............ill. 126
Election of Jean Charcot as Honorary
  Member 122, 124–125
Fields of exploration...............118–119
Finances 115
Fisher, Walter L.: Speech on Alaska and
  Hawaii 125, 127
Gannett, Henry : Speech by........... 115
Guests 113
Jusserand, J. J.: Speech by..........122–125
Membership 113, 115
Need of instruction in geography....121–122
Photograph of distinguished guests and
  officers of The Society.............. 114
Polar exploration 127–130
Presentation of Special Gold Medal to
  Amundsen by Peary.....129 ; ill. 120, 128
Redfield, William C.: Speech by.....121–122
Toastmaster (Robert E. Peary).....115,
  117, 119, 122, 125, 127–129, 130

Honors to Colonel Goethals : The Presentation, by President Woodrow Wilson, of
the National Geographic Society Special
Gold Medal. Vol. XXV, pp. 677-690, 6
ills., June, 1914.
Announcement of the election of J. J. Jusserand as Honorary Member......679, 688

National Geographic Society—*Continued*
Banquets—*Continued*

Bernstorff, Johann Heinrich, Count von :
  Speech by 684
Goethals, (Col.) George W.: Acceptance
  speech by 683–684
Grosvenor, Gilbert : Address by..... 679–680
Guests 677
Jusserand, J. J.: Speech by........688, 690
Magazine circulation 679
Mann, James R.: Speech by........... 687
Membership statistics 679
Panama Canal..........679, 680, 683, 687
Toastmaster (William Jennings Bryan)
  679, 680, 684, 687, 688, 690
Wilson, Woodrow : Presentation speech by
  679, 680, 683

Honors to Peary (Presentation of Hubbard
Gold Medal by President Roosevelt). Vol.
XVIII, pp. 49–60, 1 ill., Jan., 1907.
Abruzzi, Duke of the : Tribute to......50–51
Achievements of members.............. 50
Bell, Alexander Graham : Speech by....53–54
Bonaparte, Charles J : Speech by......51–52
Committee for banquet................ 58
Cook, Frederick A.: Speech by........54–56
Expeditions by Frederick A. Cook.....54–56
Guests 49, 58–60
History of The Society............... 49
Honorary Members 51
Peary, Robert E.: Speeches by.....50, 57–58
Planches, Baron Mayor des : Speech by.. 50
Roosevelt, Theodore : Presentation speech
  by 56–57
Toastmaster (Willis L. Moore)...49–50,
  51, 53, 56
U. S. Navy........................51–53

Honors to the American Navy. Vol. XX, pp.
77–95, Jan., 1909.
Achievements of The Society.......... 77
Boardman, Mabel : Speech by.........84–86
Curtis, William Eleroy : Speech by....82–84
Evans, (Rear Adm.) Robley D.: Speech by
  91–93
Exploration and research promoted by the
  Navy 79–80, 90
Fairbanks, Charles W.: Speech by......77–78
Geographic research 89–90
Greely, (Maj. Gen.) A. W.: Speech by..89–90
Guests 93–95
Newberry, Truman H.: Speech by.....79–81
Theme of speeches................... 77
Toastmaster (Willis L. Moore)...77–78,
  82, 84, 86, 89, 91
Weeks, John M.: Speech by..........86–89
Work of the Red Cross..............84–86

In Honor of the Army and Aviation. Vol.
XXII, pp. 267–284, 1 ill., Mar., 1911.
Announcement of the election of President
  Taft as Honorary Member.......267, 276
Appreciation of S. P. Langley.......... 279
Aviation in Germany.............270–271
Barra, Francisco Leon de la : Speech by
  272–273
Bernstorff, Johann Heinrich, Count von :
  Speech by 270–271
Bryce, James : Speech by..........275–276
Commercial routes of the world.....272–273
Committee for banquet................ 281
Fields of exploration..............275–276

National Geographic Society—*Continued*
Banquets—*Continued*

Greely, (Maj. Gen.) A. W.: Speech by 278–279
Guests 267, 281–284
Introduction of dasheen (vegetable).267;
    ill. 268, 269
Taft, William Howard: Speech by....276–277
Toastmaster (Gen. John M. Wilson)..268,
    270–272, 275–279
Wood, (Maj. Gen.) Leonard: Speech by.. 278
Work of The Society................. 267
Wright, Wilbur: Speech by.........279–281
Voice Voyages by the National Geographic
    Society: A Tribute to the Geographical
    Achievements of the Telephone. Vol.
    XXIX, 15 ills., 1 chart, Mar., 1916.
Bell, Alexander Graham: Speech by..315–316
Bell, Alexander Graham: Telephone in-
    vented by..296, 297, 306, 310, 316–318, 320
Bethell, Union Noble: Speech by....319–322
Carty, John J.: Speech by............. 316
Carty, John J.: Telephone demonstration
    by 297–302
Daniels, Josephus: Speech by........322–326
Geographical census of telephones....320–321
Geographical importance of telephone.310, 312
Guests ....296–297; ill. 298
History of the telephone and telegraph
    306–310, 315–318, 324
Long distance telephone demonstration
    297–302; map, p. 297; ill. 301
Setting telephone poles.............ill. 307
Speakers' table ....ill. 298
Telephone Building, Buffalo, New York
    ill. 308
Telephone Building, El Paso, Texas..ill. 303
Telephone cables ....ill. 311
Toastmaster (Franklin K. Lane)....305–306
U. S. Navy wireless system.......324, 326
Vail, Theodore N.: Speech by.......306–315
Wireless telephone demonstration....302–305

Bequests:

Fund bequeathed by Mary C. Burr. Vol.
    LXV, p. 626, May, 1934.
James C. Horgan Bequest. Vol. XXXVII,
    p. 338, Apr., 1920.
Jane M. Smith Bequest for Life Member-
    ships. Vol. XXIII, p. 104, Jan., 1912.
    Vol. XXXVII, pp. 342-343, Apr., 1920.
Recent Bequests by Members of the National
    Geographic Society. Vol. XLIX, p. 474,
    Apr., 1926.
    Designated use of funds............... 474
    Nealley, George True: Fund given by.... 474
    White, Abbie M.: Fund given by........ 474

Board of Managers:

Amendment of By-laws. Vol. XVI, p. 53,
    Jan., 1905.
Announcement of the Deaths of Brig. Gen.
    John M. Wilson, Rear Adm. John E. Pills-
    bury, and Rear Adm. Robert E. Peary.
    Vol. XXXVII, p. 345, Apr., 1920.
Appreciation of Marcus Baker. Vol. XV, pp.
    40-43, 1 ill., Jan., 1904.
Claims of Peary and Cook referred to Com-
    mittee on Research. Vol. XX, pp. 921-
    922, Nov., 1909.
Election of Israel C. Russell. Vol. XIII, pp.
    218-219, 1 ill., June, 1902.

National Geographic Society—*Continued*
Board of Managers—*Continued*

Election of John Oliver La Gorce. Vol.
    XXXVII, p. 345, Apr., 1920.
Election of Members. Vol. XVI, p. 87, Feb.,
    1905. Vol. XXI, p. 88, Jan., 1910.
    Vol. XXII, p. 211, Feb., 1911.
Election of O. H. Tittmann as President,
    and John E. Pillsbury as Vice-President
    of The Society. Vol. XXVII, p. 218, Feb.,
    1915.
National Geographic Society in War Time.
    By Maj. Gen. A. W. Greely. Vol. XXXIII,
    pp. 269-275, 5 ills., Apr., 1918.
    Committee to present Honorary Member-
        ship to President Wilson............ 369
    Election of Woodrow Wilson as Honorary
        Member 369
    Resolution in memory of Col. Henry F.
        Blount 371
    William Howard Taft elected to the Board
        of Managers....................... 371
North Pole. Vol. XX, pp. 1008-1009, Nov.,
    1909.
    Committee appointed to consider claims
        of Cook............................1009
    Report of committee on claims of Cook
        and Peary..........................1008
    Resolution acknowledging Peary's discov-
        ery 1008
    Resolution awarding medals to Peary and
        Bartlett 1008–1009
Photograph of Board of Managers. Vol.
    XXIV, p. 114, Jan., 1913. Vol. LXIX,
    p. 126, Jan., 1936.
Research Fund established. Vol. XX, p. 486,
    May, 1909.
Resolution authorizing purchase of Big
    Trees. Vol. XXXI, p. 5, Jan., 1917.
Resolution concerning Wellman Polar Ex-
    pedition. Vol. XVII, p. 205, Apr., 1906.
Resolution in Memory of Henry Gannett.
    Vol. XXVI, pp. 609–613, Dec., 1914.
Resolution subscribing to Peary Expedition
    of 1907-1908. Vol. XVIII, p. 281, Apr.,
    1907.
Resolution withdrawing Subscription to
    South Polar Expedition of Peary Arctic
    Club. Vol. XXI, p. 365, Apr., 1910.
Resolutions concerning Medals. Vol. XX, p.
    487, May, 1909.
Tribute of Respect to the Memory of Mrs.
    Gardiner Greene Hubbard. Vol. XX, p.
    1008, Nov., 1909.
See also Board of Trustees; History.

Board of Trustees:

Colbert, Rear Adm. L. O. Vol. LXXXIV,
    ill. 458, Oct., 1943. Vol. LXXXVI, p.
    640; ill. 618, Nov., 1944.
Coolidge, Calvin: Election of. Vol. LV, p.
    750, June, 1929.
Gannett, Henry: Naming of Electric Peak,
    Yellowstone National Park. Vol. LXXVII,
    p. 794, June, 1940.
Greely, Maj. Gen. Adolphus W. Vol.
    LXXXIV, p. 133, Aug., 1943.

National Geographic Society—*Continued*

Board of Trustees—*Continued*

Kettering, Charles F.   Vol. LXXXVI, ill. 703, Dec., 1944.

Members of Board.   Vol. LXI, p. 403, Apr., 1932.   Vol. LXV, pp. 792-793, June, 1934.

Merriam, Dr. C. Hart.   Vol. LXXXV, p. 694, June, 1944.

National Geographic Society (Memorial Tribute to Frederick V. Coville).   Vol. LXXI, p. 662, 1 ill., May, 1937.

Peary, Robert E.: Election of.   Vol. XLI, p. 643, June, 1922.

Pershing, (Gen.) John J.: Photograph of.   Vol. LXXI, p. 517, Apr., 1937.

Photograph of Members of Board of Trustees, June, 1929.   Vol. LVII, p. 592, May, 1930.

Photograph of the Board of Trustees, December 14, 1921.   Vol. XLI, p. 240, Mar., 1922.   Vol. LXIX, p. 133, Jan., 1936.

Photograph of Trustees and Officers of The Society in 1930.   Vol. LXIX, p. 159, Jan., 1936.

Presentation of Hubbard Medal by President Truman to Gen. H. H. Arnold.   Vol. LXXXIX, ill. 141, Feb., 1946.

Proposed Amendment to By-laws regarding Trustees.   Vol. XXXVII, p. 292, Mar., 1920.

Redwood Groves, California, named for Franklin K. Lane and Stephen T. Mather.   Vol. LXIX, p. 343, Mar., 1936.

Taft, William Howard.   Vol. LXXIV, p. 312, Sept., 1938.

Taft, William Howard: Birthplace of.   Vol. LXI, ill. 591, May, 1932.

Taft, William Howard: Funeral of.   Vol. LVII, ill. 597, May, 1930.

U. S. Coast and Geodetic Survey Directors, Members of the Board of Trustees.   Vol. LXXXVI, p. 640; ill. 618, Nov., 1944.

Wetmore, Dr. Alexander.   Vol. LXXXVI, p. 161, Aug., 1944.

See also Board of Managers; History.

Buildings:

Air-conditioning plant.   Vol. LXIII, p. 574, May, 1933.

Annex.   Vol. LXIX, ill. 125, Jan., 1936.

Aquariums.   Vol. LXV, ill. 107, Jan., 1934.

Building stone used in New Office Building.   Vol. LXVII, p. 486, Apr., 1935.

Cafeteria.   Vol. LXXXII, p. 209, Aug., 1942.

Explorers' Hall.   Vol. LXV, pp. 791, 794, June, 1934.   Vol. LXXXI, color plate II, p. 338, Mar., 1942; p. 657, May, 1942.

Façade of Executive and Editorial Offices illuminated.   Vol. LXVII, duotone plate XVI, p. 216, Feb., 1935.

National Geographic Society—*Continued*
Buildings—*Continued*

Foyer of The Society's Headquarters.   Vol. LXIX, ill. 157, Jan., 1936.   Vol. XC, ill. 11, July, 1946.

Funeral Cortège of William Howard Taft passes The Society's Headquarters.   Vol. LVII, ill. 597, May, 1930.

Home of the National Geographic Society.   Vol. XVI, p. 342, July, 1905.
    Deed of trust for Hubbard Memorial Hall 342
    Resolution of thanks to donors of building 342

Hubbard Memorial Building.   Vol. XIII, pp. 174–176, May, 1902.
    Contents of cornerstone............174–176
    Dedication to Gardiner Greene Hubbard.. 175
    Laying of cornerstone.............174–175

Hubbard Memorial Hall.   Vol. XVII, p. 24, Jan., 1906.

Lobby.   *See* Foyer.

Location of Headquarters and Annex.   Vol. XLI, air view, p. 522, May, 1922.   Vol. XLII, air view, p. 390, April, 1923; p. 659, air view, p. 586, June, 1923.   Vol. LXXIV, p. 189, Aug., 1938.   Vol. LXXXI, air view, p. 356, Mar., 1942.

Map Department.   Vol. LXIII, ill. 651, June, 1933.   Vol. LXXXI, ill. 333, Mar., 1942; ill. 675, 680, May, 1942.

Mural, "The Discoverer," in Hubbard Memorial Hall.   Vol. LXXIV, p. 77, July, 1938.

National Geographic Society and Its New Building.   Vol. XXV, pp. 454–470, 11 ills., Apr., 1914.
    Architecture and plan................ 459
    Correspondence 465
    Editorial rooms ....459; ill. 460, 461
    Exterior ....ill. 454
    General office ....ill. 456
    Hubbard Memorial Hall....457; ill. 454, 464
    Index department..................ill. 463
    Library 459
    Mail room........................ill. 462

New Building of The Society.   Vol. LX, ill. 544, Nov., 1931.   Vol. LXV, ill. 794, June, 1934.   Vol. LXVI, ill. 434, Oct., 1934.

New Home of the National Geographic Society.   Vol. XV, pp. 176–181, Apr., 1904.
    Entrance hall.....................ill. 178
    Exterior ....ill. 177
    Fireplace ....ill. 180
    Library and meeting hall.......ill. 179, 181
    Opening 176

Office of Gilbert Grosvenor.   Vol. XXV, ill. 460, Apr., 1914.

Office of John Oliver La Gorce.   Vol. XXV, ill. 461, Apr., 1914.   Vol. LXIX, ill. 156, Jan., 1936.

Opening of Hubbard Memorial Hall.   Vol. XIV, p. 217, May, 1903.

Photographic Laboratory.   Vol. LXIV, ill. 277, Sept., 1933.   Vol. LXVII, p. 486, Apr., 1935.   Vol. LXXI, p. 670, June, 1937.

National Geographic Society—*Continued*
Buildings—*Continued*

Photographic Library. Vol. LXXXIV, p. 289; ill. 274, Sept., 1943.

Photographs of Hubbard Memorial Hall and new Office Building. Vol. XXIV, p. 126, Jan., 1913. Vol. XLIII, pp. 669, 670, June, 1923. Vol. LIII, p. 133, Jan., 1928. Vol. LXVII, duotone plate XVI, p. 216, Feb., 1935. Vol. LXIX, p. 124, Jan., 1936.

Plans for Hubbard Memorial Hall. Vol. XI, pp. 406–407, Oct., 1900.

Plans for New Building. Vol. XXIV, pp. 251–252, Feb., 1913.

Seal, Bronze, in lobby floor. Vol. LXIX, ill. 157, Jan., 1936. Vol. XC, ill. 11, July, 1946.

By-Laws:

Adoption of By-laws. Vol. XII, p. 208, May, 1901.

Amendment concerning Board of Managers. Vol. XVI, p. 53, Jan., 1905.

Copy of By-laws. Vol. XVI, pp. 137–138, Mar., 1905.

Copy of By-laws adopted May 16, 1902. Vol. XIV, pp. 123–124, Mar., 1903.

Creation of a Class of Fellows. Vol. XIII, p. 220, June, 1902.

Notice of proposed Amendments. Vol. XIII, p. 182, May, 1902.

Proposed change in By-laws. Vol. XVIII, pp. 826–829, Dec., 1907.

Proposed change regarding Membership. Vol. XI, p. 404, Oct., 1900.

Proposed changes in By-laws. Vol. XXXVII, p. 292, Mar., 1920.
  Amendments 292
  Board of Trustees.................... 292
  Dues 292

Proposed changes in By-laws, especially regarding Membership. Vol. XII, pp. 167–168, Apr., 1901.

Cartographic Department. *See* Buildings: Map Department.

Committees:

Advisory Committee for Stratosphere Flight. Vol. LXVI, pp. 109-110, July, 1934; pp. 398, 411, Oct., 1934.

Appointment of Committee to nominate President. Vol. XIV, p. 254, June, 1903.

Chairman of Committee on Eighth International Geographic Congress. Vol. XIII, p. 219, June, 1902. Vol. XIV, p. 254, June, 1903.

Committee appointed to consider claims of Cook. Vol. XX, p. 1009, Nov., 1909.

Committee appointed to consider claims of Peary and Cook. Vol. XX, pp. 921–922, 1008, Nov., 1909.

Committee appointed to examine records of Byrd Arctic Expedition. Vol. L, pp. 377, 385–388, Sept., 1926.
  Members of committee................ 384
  Reports approving records.....377, 384-388

National Geographic Society—*Continued*
Committees—*Continued*

Committee to present Honorary Membership to President Wilson. Vol. XXXIII, p. 369, Apr., 1918.

Committees for 1906. Vol. XVII, p. 240, Apr., 1906.

Committees of 1907. Vol. XVIII, p. 216, Mar., 1907.

Editorial Committee. Vol. X, p. 222, June, 1899.

Prize Committee. Vol. X, p. 32, Jan., 1899.

Research Committee. Vol. XVII, p. 205, Apr., 1906. Vol. XX, p. 486, May, 1909; pp. 921–922, Nov., 1909.

Standing Committees appointed by Alexander Graham Bell. Vol. XIII, p. 118, Mar., 1902; p. 150, Apr., 1902.

Cruise sponsored by the National Geographic Society and Woods Hole Oceanographic Institution. Vol. LXXXVII, p. 106, Jan., 1945.

Editorial Department:

Announcement of the Death of Ralph A. Graves, Senior Assistant Editor. Vol. LXII, p. 606, Nov., 1932.

Assistant Editor appointed. Vol. X, p. 222, June, 1899.

Borah, Leo. Vol. LXXXV, p. 677, June, 1944.

Editorial Committee. Vol. X, p. 222, June, 1899.

Grosvenor, Gilbert H.: Address by. Vol. XXV, pp. 679-680, June, 1914.

Grosvenor, Gilbert H.: Alexander Graham Bell's appreciation of. Vol. XXIII, p. 274, Mar., 1912.

Grosvenor, Gilbert H.: Appointed Editor in 1899. Vol. XXIII, p. 274, Mar., 1912.

Grosvenor, Gilbert H.: President Taft's appreciation of. Vol. XXII, p. 276, Mar., 1911.

Grosvenor, Gilbert H.: Private Office of Editor. Vol. XXV, ill. 460, Apr., 1914.

La Gorce, John Oliver: Private Office of Associate Editor. Vol. XXV, ill. 461, Apr., 1914. Vol. LXIX, ill. 156, Jan., 1936.

Nygaard, Arnvid, Chief Translator. Vol. LXXXIV, ill. 695, Dec., 1943.

Policy of The Magazine. Vol. XX, p. 486, May, 1909.

Report of the Director and Editor of the National Geographic Society for the Year 1914. By Gilbert H. Grosvenor. Vol. XVII, pp. 318–320, Mar., 1915.
  Dr. Grosvenor's first years as Editor..318–319
  Growth of The Society since 1899....319, 320
  Magazine policy adopted by Dr. Grosvenor 319

Report of the Editor for 1912. Vol. XXIV, pp. 251-255, Feb., 1913.
  Advertising policy.................... 253
  Appreciation in Boston Herald.....253, 255

National Geographic Society—*Continued*
Editorial Department—*Continued*

Educational purpose.................. 253
Increase in circulation.............252-253

See also President, Vice President

Engravings and Etchings:

Cathedrals of England. 16 ills. in gravure from dry-point engravings by Norman Wilkinson. Vol. LXXVI, pp. 745-760; text, p. 762, Dec., 1939.

Ships of the Centuries. 16 ills. in gravure from original etchings by Norman Wilkinson. Vol. LXXIII, pp. 65-80; text, p. 98, Jan., 1938.

Excursions:

Annual Excursion to Annapolis, Maryland. Vol. XIV, p. 217, May, 1903.

Annual Excursion to Brandywine, Delaware. Vol. XII, p. 208, May, 1901.

Annual Excursion to Gettysburg, Pennsylvania. Vol. XIII, p. 150, Apr., 1902.

Annual Excursion to Luray Caverns, Virginia. Vol. XVII, p. 302, May, 1906; pp. 358-359, 3 ills., June, 1906.

National Geographic Society Eclipse Expedition to Norfolk, Virginia. Vol. XI, p. 320, Aug., 1900.

Scientific Work of the National Geographic Society's Eclipse Expedition to Norfolk, Virginia. By Simon Newcomb. Vol. XI, pp. 321-324, Aug., 1900.

Expeditions:

Africa: Hunting an Observatory: A Successful Search for a Dry Mountain on Which to Establish the National Geographic Society's Solar Radiation Station. By C. G. Abbot. Vol. L, pp. 503-518, 13 ills., 1 quarter-page map, Oct., 1926.

Africa: Keeping House for the "Shepherds of the Sun." By Mrs. William H. Hoover. Vol. LVII, pp. 483-506, 17 ills., 1 third-page map, Apr., 1930.

Africa: Measuring the Sun's Heat and Forecasting the Weather: The National Geographic Society to Maintain a Solar Station in a Remote Part of the World to Coöperate with Smithsonian Institution Stations in California and Chile. By C. G. Abbot. Vol. XLIX, pp. 111–126, 15 ills., 1 chart, Jan., 1926.

Africa: National Geographic Society (Reports and Cables concerning Roosevelt's African Expedition). Vol. XXI, pp. 365-370, 5 ills., Apr., 1910.

Africa: Under the South African Union. By Melville Chater. Vol. LIX, pp. 391-512, 97 ills. in black and white, 38 ills. in color, 1 two-page map, Apr., 1931.

National Geographic Society—*Continued*
Expeditions—*Continued*

Air Conquest: From the Early Days of Giant Kites and Birdlike Gliders, the National Geographic Society Has Aided and Encouraged the Growth of Aviation (History of The Society). Vol. LII, pp. 233-242, 13 ills., Aug., 1927.

Alaska: Appropriation for, and Personnel of, 1919 Katmai Expedition. Vol. XXXV, p. 366, Apr., 1919.

Alaska: Appropriation for Fifth Expedition to the Valley of Ten Thousand Smokes. Vol. XXXIII, p. 372, Apr., 1918.

Alaska: Contributors to Alaskan Expedition of 1909. Vol. XXI, p. 88, Jan., 1910.

Alaska: Exploring Frozen Fragments of American History: On the Trail of Early Eskimo Colonists Who Made a 55-Mile Crossing from the Old World to the New. By Henry B. Collins, Jr. Vol. LXXV, pp. 633-650, 21 ills., 1 two-thirds-page map, May, 1939.

Alaska: Father Hubbard's Alaskan Explorations. Vol. LXV, pp. 625-626, May, 1934.

Alaska: Mapping the Home of the Great Brown Bear: Adventures of the National Geographic Society's Pavlof Volcano Expedition to Alaska. By Dr. Thomas Augustus Jaggar. Vol. LV, pp. 109-134, 30 ills., 1 three-quarters-page map, Jan., 1929.

Alaska: Mount Katmai Region (1915-1916). Vol. LXXXIV, p. 157, Aug., 1943.

Alaska: National Geographic Society Alaska Expedition. Vol. XX, pp. 581-584, June, 1909.

Alaska: National Geographic Society-Harvard University Alaska Expedition (1938). Vol. LXXXI, p. 675, May, 1942.

Alaska: National Geographic Society-Harvard University Mount McKinley Flight Expedition (1936). Vol. LXXXII, p. 310, Sept., 1942.

Alaska: National Geographic Society Researches in Alaska. By Lawrence Martin. Vol. XXII, pp. 537-561, 17 ills., 1 page and 4 half-page maps, June, 1911.

Alaska: National Geographic Society's Alaskan Expedition. Vol. XXI, p. 370, Apr., 1910.

Alaska: National Geographic Society's Alaskan Expedition of 1909. By Ralph S. Tarr and Lawrence Martin. Vol. XXI, pp. 1-54, 42 ills., 12 maps, Jan., 1910.

Alaska: Our Greatest National Monument: The National Geographic Society Completes Its Explorations in the Valley of Ten Thousand Smokes. By Robert F. Griggs. Vol. XL, pp. 219-292, 73 ills. in black and white, 16 ills. in color, 1 page and 1 three-quarters-page maps, Sept., 1921.

National Geographic Society—*Continued*
Expeditions—*Continued*

Alaska : Over the Roof of Our Continent (Mount McKinley). By Bradford Washburn. Vol. LXXIV, pp. 78-98, 17 ills. in duotone, 1 half-page map, July, 1938.

Alaska : Photography in Glacial Alaska. By O. D. von Engeln. Vol. XXI, pp. 54-62, 4 ills., Jan., 1910.

Alaska : Recent Eruption of Katmai Volcano in Alaska. By George C. Martin. Vol. XXIV, pp. 131-181, 45 ills., 1 page map, 1 diagram, Feb., 1913.

Alaska : Report of Sixth Katmai Expedition. Vol. XXXVII, p. 338, Apr., 1920.

Alaska : Ten Thousand Smokes Now a National Monument : The President of the United States Sets Aside for the American People the Extraordinary Valley Discovered and Explored by the National Geographic Society. Vol. XXXV, pp. 359-366, 5 ills., Apr., 1919.

Alaska : Valley of Ten Thousand Smokes : An Account of the Discovery and Exploration of the Most Wonderful Volcanic Region in the World. By Robert F. Griggs. Vol. XXXIII, pp. 115-169, 46 ills., 1 half-page map, panorama, Feb., 1918.

Alaska : Valley of Ten Thousand Smokes : National Geographic Society Explorations in the Katmai District of Alaska. By Robert F. Griggs. Vol. XXXI, pp. 12-68, 51 ills., 1 half-page map, Jan., 1917.

Alaska : Volcanoes of Alaska (Report by Capt. K. W. Perry). Vol. XXIII, pp. 824-832, 11 ills., Aug., 1912.

Antarctic Regions : Conquest of Antarctica by Air. By Rear Adm. Richard Evelyn Byrd. Vol. LVIII, pp. 127-227, 71 ills. in black and white, 16 ills. in gravure, 1 page map, Aug., 1930.

Antarctic Regions : Exploring the Ice Age in Antarctica. By Richard Evelyn Byrd. Vol. LXVIII, pp. 399-474, 72 ills., 1 page and 1 two-page maps, Oct., 1935.

Antarctic Regions : Mapping the Antarctic from the Air : The Aërial Camera Earns Its Place as the Eyes and Memory of the Explorer. By Capt. Ashley C. McKinley. Vol. LXII, pp. 471-485, 13 ills., special map supplement, Oct., 1932.

Antarctic Regions : Second Byrd Antarctic Expedition. Vol. LXV, p. 626, May, 1934.

Antarctic Regions : Society's Special Medal Is Awarded to Dr. Thomas C. Poulter : Admiral Byrd's Second-in-Command and Senior Scientist Is Accorded High Geographic Honor. Vol. LXXII, pp. 105-108, 2 ills., July, 1937.

Antarctic Regions : South Polar Expedition (Proposed by Peary for Consideration of National Geographic Society). Vol. XXI, pp. 167-170, 1 page map, Feb., 1910.

National Geographic Society—*Continued*
Expeditions—*Continued*

Arctic Regions : *Bowdoin* (Ship) in North Greenland : Arctic Explorers Place Tablet to Commemorate Sacrifices of the Lady Franklin Bay Expedition. By Donald B. MacMillan. Vol. XLVII, pp. 677-722, 49 ills., June, 1925.

Arctic Regions : Farthest North (Peary Expedition). Vol. XVII, pp. 638-644, 9 ills., Nov., 1906.

Arctic Regions : Fighting the Polar Ice (Ziegler Polar Expedition). Vol. XVIII, pp. 72-78, 7 ills., Jan., 1907.

Arctic Regions : First Natural-Color Photographs from the Arctic. 22 ills. in color from natural-color photographs by Jacob Gayer and Maynard Owen Williams. Vol. XLIX, pp. 300-317, Mar., 1926.

Arctic Regions : Flying Over the Arctic. By Lieut. Comdr. Richard E. Byrd. Vol. XLVIII, pp. 519-532, 10 ills., Nov., 1925.

Arctic Regions : MacMillan Arctic Expedition Returns : U. S. Navy Planes Make First Series of Overland Flights in the Arctic and National Geographic Society Staff Obtains Valuable Data and Specimens for Scientific Study. By Donald B. MacMillan. Vol. XLVIII, pp. 477-518, 42 ills., Nov., 1925.

Arctic Regions : MacMillan Arctic Expedition Sails. Vol. XLVIII, pp. 225-226, 3 ills., Aug., 1925.

Arctic Regions : MacMillan in the Field. Vol. XLVIII, pp. 473-476, 3 ills., Oct., 1925.

Arctic Regions : Meteorological Observations of the Second Wellman Expedition. By Evelyn B. Baldwin. Vol. X, pp. 512-516, Dec., 1899.

Arctic Regions : Mr. Ziegler and the National Geographic Society. Vol. XIV, pp. 251-254, June, 1903.

Arctic Regions : Naturalist with MacMillan in the Arctic. By Walter N. Koelz. Vol. XLIX, pp. 299-318, 22 ills. in color, Mar., 1926.

Arctic Regions : Nearest the Pole (Address by Robert E. Peary to The Society). Vol. XVIII, pp. 446-450, July, 1907.

Arctic Regions : Peary to Try Again. Vol. XVIII, p. 281, Apr., 1907.

Arctic Regions : Peary's Polar Expedition. Vol. XIX, p. 447, June, 1908.

Arctic Regions : Polar Airship (Wellman Expedition). By Walter Wellman. Vol. XVII, pp. 208-228, 4 diagrams, Apr., 1906.

Arctic Regions : Polar Photography (Ziegler Polar Expedition). By Anthony Fiala. Vol. XVIII, pp. 140-142, Feb., 1907.

Arctic Regions : Report of Ziegler Polar Expedition by Anthony Fiala. Vol. XVII, pp. 32-34, Jan., 1906.

Arctic Regions : Return of Wellman. By J. Howard Gore. Vol. X, pp. 348-351, 2 ills., Sept., 1899.

National Geographic Society—*Continued*
Expeditions—*Continued*

Arctic Regions : Scientific Aspects of the Mac-Millan Arctic Expedition. Vol. XLVIII, pp. 349-354, 5 ills., Sept., 1925.

Arctic Regions : To Seek the Unknown in the Arctic : United States Navy Flyers to Aid MacMillan Expedition Under the Auspices of the National Geographic Society in Exploring Vast Area. Vol. XLVII, pp. 673-675, 1 ill., 1 half-page map, June, 1925.

Arctic Regions : Walter Wellman's Expedition to the North Pole. Vol. XVII, pp. 205-207, 1 chart, Apr., 1906.

Arctic Regions : Wellman Expedition. Vol. LIV, p. 242, Aug., 1928.

Arctic Regions : Wellman Polar Expedition. Vol. X, pp. 361-362, Sept., 1899.

Arctic Regions : Wellman Polar Expedition. Vol. X, pp. 481-505, 10 ills., 1 half-page map, 1 diagram, Dec., 1899.

Arctic Regions : Wellman Polar Expedition. Vol. XVII, p. 712, Dec., 1906.

Arctic Regions : Wellman Polar Expedition. By J. Howard Gore. Vol. X, pp. 267-268, July, 1899.

Arctic Regions : Ziegler Polar Expedition. Vol. XIV, pp. 414-417, 5 ills., Nov., 1903.

Arctic Regions : Ziegler Polar Expedition. Vol. XV, pp. 427-428, Oct., 1904.

Arctic Regions : Ziegler Polar Expedition. Vol. XVI, p. 198, Apr., 1905.

Arctic Regions : Ziegler Polar Expedition. Vol. XVI, p. 355, July, 1905.

Arctic Regions : Ziegler Polar Expedition. Vol. XVI, pp. 439-440, Sept., 1905.

Arctic Regions : Ziegler Polar Expedition. Speeches by Anthony Fiala and W. S. Champ. Vol. XVII, pp. 32-36, Jan., 1906.

Arizona : Exploring in the Canyon of Death : Remains of a People Who Dwelt in Our Southwest at Least 4,000 Years Ago Are Revealed. By Earl H. Morris. Vol. XLVIII, pp. 263-300, 24 ills. in black and white, 22 ills. in color, Sept., 1925.

Arizona : Photographic Party in Cañon del Muerto. Vol. XLVIII, p. 265, Sept., 1925.

Arizona : Secret of the Southwest Solved by Talkative Tree Rings : Horizons of American History Are Carried Back to A. D. 700 and a Calendar for 1,200 Years Established by National Geographic Society Expeditions. By Andrew Ellicott Douglass. Vol. LVI, pp. 737-770, 33 ills., 1 two-thirds-page map, Dec., 1929.

Asia : Citroën-Haardt Trans-Asiatic and Thaw Expeditions. Vol. LXXX, p. 157, Aug., 1941.

Asia : Citroën Trans-Asiatic Expedition Reaches Kashmir : Scientific Party Led by Georges-Marie Haardt Successfully Crosses Syria, Iraq, Persia, and Afghanistan to Arrive at the Pamir. By Maynard Owen Williams. Vol. LX, pp. 387-443, 62 ills., 1 page map, Oct., 1931.

National Geographic Society—*Continued*
Expeditions—*Continued*

Asia : First Over the Roof of the World by Motor : The Trans-Asiatic Expedition Sets New Records for Wheeled Transport in Scaling Passes of the Himalayas. By Maynard Owen Williams. Vol. LXI, pp. 321-363, 45 ills., 2 half-page maps, Mar., 1932.

Asia : From the Mediterranean to the Yellow Sea by Motor : The Citroën-Haardt Expedition Successfully Completes Its Dramatic Journey. By Maynard Owen Williams. Vol. LXII, pp. 513-580, 45 ills. in black and white, 25 ills. in color, 2 half-page maps, Nov., 1932.

Asia : Trans-Asiatic Expedition Starts. By Georges-Marie Haardt. Vol. LIX, pp. 776-782, 6 ills., June, 1931.

Bahamas : Flamingos studied by The Society's Expedition. Vol. LXII, p. 452, Oct., 1932.

Canada : Exploring Yukon's Glacial Stronghold. By Bradford Washburn. Vol. LXIX, pp. 715-747, 28 ills., 1 two-page map, June, 1936.

Canada : National Geographic Society-U. S. Geological Survey Expedition. Vol. XLIX, p. 597 ; ill. 598, 599, June, 1926.

Canada : National Geographic Society Yukon Expedition (1935). Vol. LXXIV, p. 79, July, 1938.

Cape Horn : Inside Cape Horn. By Amos Burg. Vol. LXXII, pp. 743-783, 29 ills. in black and white, 10 ills. in color, 1 two-page map, Dec., 1937.

China : Banishing the Devil of Disease Among the Nashi : Weird Ceremonies Performed by an Aboriginal Tribe in the Heart of Yünnan Province, China. By Joseph F. Rock. Vol. XLVI, pp. 473-499, 26 ills., 1 half-page map, Nov., 1924.

China : Carrying the Color Camera Through Unmapped China. 24 ills. in color from natural-color photographs by Joseph F. Rock. Vol. LVIII, pp. 402-435, Oct., 1930.

China : Expeditions of Joseph F. Rock. Vol. LXIV, p. 279, Sept., 1933.

China : Glories of the Minya Konka : Magnificent Snow Peaks of the China-Tibetan Border Are Photographed at Close Range by a National Geographic Society Expedition. By Joseph F. Rock. Vol. LVIII, pp. 385-437, 35 ills. in black and white, 24 ills. in color, 1 three-quarters-page map, Oct., 1930.

China : Konka Risumgongba, Holy Mountain of the Outlaws. By Joseph F. Rock. Vol. LX, pp. 1-65, 36 ills. in black and white, 43 ills. in color, 1 three-quarters-page map, July, 1931.

China : Land of the Yellow Lama : National Geographic Society Explorer Visits the Strange Kingdom of Muli, Beyond the Likiang Snow Range of Yünnan Province, China. By Joseph F. Rock. Vol. XLVII, pp. 447-491, 39 ills., 1 half-page map, Apr., 1925.

National Geographic Society—*Continued*
Expeditions—*Continued*

China : Landscaped Kwangsi, China's Province of Pictorial Art. By G. Weidman Groff and T. C. Lau. Vol. LXXII, pp. 671-710, 33 ills., 1 half-page map, Dec., 1937.

China : National Geographic Society Expeditions led by Dr. Joseph F. Rock. Vol. LXXXI, p. 331, Mar., 1942.

China : National Geographic Society's Yünnan Province Expedition. By Gilbert Grosvenor. Vol. XLVII, pp. 493-498, 5 ills., Apr., 1925.

China : Road to Wang Ye Fu : An Account of the Work of the National Geographic Society's Central-China Expedition in the Mongol Kingdom of Ala Shan. By Frederick R. Wulsin. Vol. XLIX, pp. 197-234, 44 ills., 1 third-page map, Feb., 1926.

China : Seeking the Mountains of Mystery : An Expedition on the China-Tibet Frontier to the Unexplored Amnyi Machen Range, One of Whose Peaks Rivals Everest. By Joseph F. Rock. Vol. LVII, pp. 131-185, 54 ills., 1 two-page map, Feb., 1930.

China : Through the Great River Trenches of Asia : National Geographic Society Explorer Follows the Yangtze, Mekong, and Salwin Through Mighty Gorges, Some of Whose Canyon Walls Tower to a Height of More Than Two Miles. By Joseph F. Rock. Vol. L, pp. 133-186, 47 ills., 1 half-page map, Aug., 1926.

Cosmic Rays : Series of flights under auspices of National Geographic Society, U. S. Army Air Forces, and Bartol Research Foundation of the Franklin Institute. Vol. XC, p. 387 ; ill. 388, Sept., 1946.

Deep-Sea : Half Mile Down : Strange Creatures, Beautiful as Figments of Fancy, Reveal Themselves at Windows of the Bathysphere. By William Beebe. Vol. LXVI, pp. 661-704, 28 ills. in black and white, 16 ills. in color, 1 third-page map, Dec., 1934.

Deep-Sea : National Geographic Society-William Beebe Expedition. Vol. LXV, p. 625, May, 1934.

Deep-Sea Diving Record of National Geographic Society-William Beebe Expedition. Vol. LXXII, p. 419, Oct., 1937. Vol. LXXVI, p. 140, July, 1939.

East Indies : Around the World for Animals. By William M. and Lucile Q. Mann. Vol. LXXIII, pp. 665-714, 33 ills. in black and white, 23 ills. in color, 1 page map, June, 1938.

East Indies : National Geographic Society-Smithsonian Institution Expedition to the Netherlands Indies. Vol. LXXI, p. 668, June, 1937. Vol. LXXIII, pp. 647, 650, 651, May, 1938. Vol. LXXXI, p. 326, Mar., 1942.

Eclipse : Camera of National Geographic Society-Bureau of Standards Eclipse Expedition of 1936. Vol. LXXII, ill. 374, Sept., 1937.

National Geographic Society—*Continued*
Expeditions—*Continued*

Eclipse : National Geographic Society-National Bureau of Standards Expedition (1940). Vol. LXXIX, p. 163, Feb., 1941.

Eclipse : National Geographic Society-U. S. Navy Eclipse Expedition (1937). Vol. LXXIII, p. 749 ; ill. 764, June, 1938. Vol. LXXX, p. 741, Dec., 1941.

Eclipse : National Geographic Society's Eclipse Expedition to Norfolk, Virginia. By Marcus Baker. Vol. XI, p. 320, Aug., 1900.

Eclipse : Natural-color photograph of (1936) eclipse. 1 ill. in color by Irvine C. Gardner. Vol. LXXI, p. 178, Feb., 1937.

Eclipse : Nature's Most Dramatic Spectacle. By S. A. Mitchell. Vol. LXXII, pp. 361-376, 16 ills., 1 half-page map, Sept., 1937.

Eclipse : Observing an Eclipse in Asiatic Russia. By Irvine C. Gardner. Vol. LXXI, pp. 179-197, 19 ills. in black and white, 1 ill. in color, Feb., 1937.

Eclipse : Photographing the Eclipse of 1932 from the Air : From Five Miles Above the Earth's Surface, the National Geographic Society-Army Air Corps Survey Obtains Successful Photographs of the Moon's Shadow. By Capt. Albert W. Stevens. Vol. LXII, pp. 581-596, 18 ills., Nov., 1932.

Eclipse : Scientific Work of the National Geographic Society's Eclipse Expedition to Norfolk, Virginia. By Simon Newcomb. Vol. XI, pp. 321-324, Aug., 1900.

Eclipse : Unfurling Old Glory on Canton Island. 11 ills. in color ; 1 painting and 1 kodachrome photograph of the eclipse. Vol. LXXIII, pp. 753-760, June, 1938.

Eclipse Adventures on a Desert Isle (Canton). By Capt. J. F. Hellweg. Vol. LXXII, pp. 377-394, 14 ills., 1 two-thirds-page map, Sept., 1937.

Expeditions of 1912. Vol. XXIV, p. 251, Feb., 1913.

Idaho : Down Idaho's River of No Return (Salmon River). By Philip J. Shenon and John C. Reed. Vol. LXX, pp. 95-136, 43 ills., 1 page and 1 two-thirds-page maps, July, 1936.

Latin America : Flamingos photographed from air. Vol. LXII, ill. 453, Oct., 1932.

Latin America : Skypaths Through Latin America : Flying From Our Nation's Capital Southward Over Jungles, Remote Islands, and Great Cities on an Aërial Survey of the East Coast of South America. By Frederick Simpich. Vol. LIX, pp. 1-79, 77 ills., 1 page map, Jan., 1931.

Mexico : Cruise Among Desert Islands. By G. Dallas Hanna and A. W. Anthony. Vol. XLIV, pp. 71-99, 32 ills., 1 quarter-page map, July, 1923.

National Geographic Society—*Continued*
Expeditions—*Continued*

Mexico : Discovering the New World's Oldest Dated Work of Man : A Maya Monument Inscribed 291 B. C. is Unearthed Near a Huge Stone Head by a Geographic-Smithsonian Expedition in Mexico. By Matthew W. Stirling. Vol. LXXVI, pp. 183-218, 40 ills., 1 half-page-map, Aug., 1939.

Mexico : Excavations at Cuicuilco. Vol. LX, p. 107, July, 1931.

Mexico : Expedition Unearths Buried Masterpieces of Carved Jade (Cerro de las Mesas). By Matthew W. Stirling. Vol. LXXX, pp. 277-302, 14 ills. in black and white, 20 ills. in color, 1 two-thirds-page map, Sept., 1941.

Mexico : Great Stone Faces of the Mexican Jungle : Five Colossal Heads and Numerous Other Monuments of Vanished Americans Are Excavated by the Latest National Geographic-Smithsonian Expedition. By Matthew W. Stirling Vol LXXVIII, pp. 309-334, 26 ills., 1 map, Sept., 1940.

Mexico : Jungle Housekeeping for a Geographic Expedition (Cerro de las Mesas). By Marion Stirling. Vol. LXXX, pp. 303-327, 15 ills., Sept., 1941.

Mexico : La Venta's Green Stone Tigers. By Matthew W. Stirling. Vol. LXXXIV, pp. 321-332, 4 ills. in black and white, 6 ills. in color, 1 two-thirds-page map, Sept., 1943.

Mexico : National Geographic Society-Smithsonian Institution Archeological Expedition to Cerro de las Mesas, Veracruz (1941). Vol. LXXXII, pp. 635, 642, 649, Nov., 1942. Vol. LXXXIV, p. 323, Sept., 1943.

Mexico : National Geographic Society-Smithsonian Institution Archeological Expedition to La Venta, Tabasco (1940). Vol. LXXXII, pp. 635, 642, Nov., 1942.

Mexico : National Geographic Society-Smithsonian Institution Archeological Expedition to La Venta, Tabasco (1942). Vol. LXXXIV, pp. 321, 323, Sept., 1943.

Mexico : National Geographic Society-Smithsonian Institution Archeological Expedition to La Venta, Tabasco (1943). Vol. LXXXVII, pp. 187, 193 ; ill. 190, Feb., 1945.

Mexico : National Geographic Society-Smithsonian Institution Expedition to Mexico (1936). Vol. LXXXIV, pp. 699-700, Dec., 1943.

Mexico : National Geographic Society-Smithsonian Institution Expedition to Veracruz (1938-1939). Vol. LXXXI, p. 338, Mar., 1942.

Mexico : Ruins of Cuicuilco May Revolutionize Our History of Ancient America : Lofty Mound Sealed and Preserved by Great Lava Flow for Perhaps Seventy Centuries Is Now Being Excavated in Mexico. By Byron Cummings. Vol. XLIV, pp. 203-220, 21 ills., 1 third-page map, Aug., 1923.

National Geographic Society—*Continued*
Expeditions—*Continued*

Mexico : Treasure-trove of Old Mexican Jade (Cerro de las Mesas). 20 ills. in color from natural-color photographs by Richard H. Stewart. Vol. LXXX, pp. 293-316, Sept., 1941.

Mexico : Wildlife of Tabasco and Veracruz. By Walter A. Weber. With 19 ills. in color from paintings by the author. Vol. LXXXVII, pp. 187-216, 7 ills. in black and white, 1 two-thirds-page map, Feb., 1945.

New Mexico : Carlsbad Caverns. Vol. LXXIII, pp. 530, 560, May, 1938. Vol. LXXVII, pp. 718, 724, June, 1940.

New Mexico : Everyday Life in Pueblo Bonito : As Disclosed by the National Geographic Society's Archeologic Explorations in the Chaco Canyon National Monument, New Mexico. By Neil M. Judd. Vol. XLVIII, pp. 227-262, 37 ills., 1 two-thirds-page map, Sept., 1925.

New Mexico : New Discoveries in Carlsbad Cavern : Vast Subterranean Chambers with Spectacular Decorations Are Explored, Surveyed, and Photographed. By Willis T. Lee. Vol. XLVIII, pp. 301-319, 19 ills., 1 three-quarters-page map, Sept., 1925.

New Mexico : New National Geographic Society Expedition : Ruins of Chaco Canyon, New Mexico, Nature-Made Treasure-Chest of Aboriginal American History, to Be Excavated and Studied ; Work Begins This Month. Vol. XXXIX, pp. 637-643, 7 ills., June, 1921.

New Mexico : Pueblo Bonito. Vol. LXXIII, pp. 547, 551, May, 1938. Vol. LXXVII, p. 767, June, 1940.

New Mexico : Pueblo Bonito, the Ancient : The National Geographic Society's Third Expedition to the Southwest Seeks to Read in the Rings of Trees the Secret of the Age of Ruins. By Neil M. Judd. Vol. XLIV, pp. 99-108, 9 ills., 1 diagram, July, 1923.

New Mexico : Pueblo Bonito Expedition of the National Geographic Society. By Neil M. Judd. Vol. XLI, pp. 323-331, 10 ills., 1 diagram, Mar., 1922.

New Mexico : Secret of the Southwest Solved by Talkative Tree Rings : Horizons of American History Are Carried Back to A. D. 700 and a Calendar for 1,200 Years Established by National Geographic Society Expeditions. By Andrew Ellicott Douglass. Vol. LVI, pp. 737–770, 33 ills., 1 two-page map, Dec., 1929.

Peru : Explorations in Peru. Vol. XXIII, pp. 416-422, 7 ills., 1 half-page map, Apr., 1912.

Peru : Further Explorations in the Land of the Incas : The Peruvian Expedition of 1915 of the National Geographic Society and Yale University. By Hiram Bingham. Vol. XXIX, pp. 431-473, 29 ills., 1 page and 1 half-page maps, panorama, May, 1916.

National Geographic Society—*Continued*
Expeditions—*Continued*

Peru : Honors to Amundsen and Peary (Address by Hiram Bingham). Vol. XXIV, pp. 116–117, Jan., 1913.

Peru : In the Wonderland of Peru. By Hiram Bingham. Vol. XXIV, pp. 387-574, 250 ills., 1 three-quarters-page map, 3 diagrams, Apr., 1913.

Peru : National Geographic Society-Yale University Peruvian Expeditions. Vol. LXXIII, pp. 244, 256, 258, Feb., 1938. Vol. LXXXII, pp. 187, 192, Aug., 1942.

Peru : Staircase Farms of the Ancients : Astounding Farming Skill of Ancient Peruvians Who Were Probably the Most Industrious and Highly Organized People in History. By O. F. Cook. Vol. XXIX, pp. 474-534, 48 ills., May, 1916.

Peru : Story of Machu Picchu : The Peruvian Expedition of the National Geographic Society and Yale University. By Hiram Bingham. Vol. XXVII, pp. 171-217, 35 ills., Feb., 1915.

Salmon River : National Geographic Society-United States Geological Survey Expedition. Vol. LXXXV, p. 643, June, 1944.

Sicily : Announcement of Messina Expedition. Vol. XX, p. 118, 1 map, Jan., 1909.

Sicily : Messina earthquake (1909). Vol. LXXXIV, p. 314, Sept., 1943.

Sicily : World's Most Cruel Earthquake. By Charles W. Wright. Vol. XX, pp. 373-396, 22 ills., 1 page and 1 three-quarters-page maps, Apr., 1909.

South Dakota : National Geographic Society-South Dakota School of Mines Paleontological Expedition to the Badlands of South Dakota (1940). Vol. LXXXI, p. 161, Feb., 1942.

Stratosphere : Capt. Albert W. Stevens (now Lt. Col., ret.) and Capt. Orvil A. Anderson (now Brig. Gen.) photographed with Sioux Indians in front of gondola. Vol. LXXXVI, ill. 106, July, 1944.

Stratosphere : Exploring the Stratosphere. By Capt. Albert W. Stevens. Vol. LXVI, pp. 397-434, 43 ills., 1 two-thirds-page chart, Oct., 1934.

Stratosphere : First natural-color photograph taken in the stratosphere. 1 ill. in color by Maj. Albert W. Stevens. Vol. LXXI, p. 340, Mar., 1937.

Stratosphere : Helium used by National Geographic Society-U. S. Army Air Corps Expedition, 1935, to inflate *Explorer II.* Vol. LXXII, p. 363, Sept., 1937.

Stratosphere : Infrared sensitive plates used in photographing curvature of the earth from record altitude of 72,395 feet. Vol. LXXXVI, p. 265, Sept., 1944.

National Geographic Society—*Continued*
Expeditions—*Continued*

Stratosphere : Man's Farthest Aloft : Rising to 13.71 Miles, the National Geographic Society-U. S. Army Stratosphere Expedition Gathers Scientific Data at Record Altitude. By Capt. Albert W. Stevens. Action Photographs of the Balloon's Perfect Landing included. Vol. LXIX, pp. 59-94, 39 ills., 1 quarter-page map, Jan., 1936.

Stratosphere : National Geographic Society-U. S. Army Air Corps Flight insured by Lloyd's. Vol. LXXI, p. 34, Jan., 1937.

Stratosphere : National Geographic Society-U. S. Army Air Corps Stratosphere Flight of 1935 in Balloon *Explorer II* (Contributed Technical Papers, Stratosphere Series, No. 2). Vol. LXXI, p. 340, Mar., 1937 ; p. 802, June, 1937.

Stratosphere : National Geographic Society-U. S. Army Air Corps Stratosphere Flights. Vol. LXXXII, p. 444, Oct., 1942. Vol. XC, p. 379, Sept., 1946.

Stratosphere : Report of the Second Stratosphere Expedition. Vol. LXVIII, pp. 535-536, Oct., 1935.

Stratosphere : Scientific Results of the World-Record Stratosphere Flight. By Capt. Albert W. Stevens. Vol. LXIX, pp. 693-712, 15 ills., May, 1936.

Stratosphere : Society Announces New Flight into the Stratosphere. By Gilbert Grosvenor. Vol. LXVII, pp. 265-272, 2 ills. in black and white, 1 sketch map, Feb., 1935.

Stratosphere : Spectograph carried on National Geographic Society-U. S. Army Air Corps Expedition, 1935. Vol. LXXII, p. 372, Sept., 1937.

Stratosphere : Studies Planned for New Stratosphere Flight with Helium. Vol. LXVII, pp. 795-800, 5 ills., June, 1935.

Stratosphere : World's Largest Free Balloon to Explore Stratosphere. Vol. LXVI, pp. 107-110, 2 ills., July, 1934.

Stratosphere : Your Society Sponsors an Expedition to Explore the Stratosphere. Vol. LXV, pp. 528-530, 1 ill., Apr., 1934.

Utah : Beyond the Clay Hills : An Account of the National Geographic Society's Reconnaissance of a Previously Unexplored Section in Utah. By Neil M. Judd. Vol. XLV, pp. 275-302, 28 ills., 1 half-page map, Mar., 1924.

Utah : Expedition to Moki Canyon (1923). Vol. LXXIX, p. 143, Feb., 1941.

Venezuela-Brazil : In Humboldt's Wake : Narrative of a National Geographic Society Expedition Up the Orinoco and Through the Strange Casiquiare Canal to Amazonian Waters. By Ernest G. Holt. Vol. LX, pp. 621-644, 27 ills., 1 two-thirds-page map, Nov., 1931.

National Geographic Society—*Continued*
Expeditions—*Continued*

Venezuela-Brazil: Journey by Jungle Rivers to the Home of the Cock-of-the-Rock: Naturalists Enter the Amazon, Voyage Through the Heart of Tropical South America, and Emerge at the Mouth of the Orinoco. By Ernest G. Holt. Vol. LXIV, pp. 585-630, 49 ills., 1 two-thirds-page map, Nov., 1933.

West Indies: Martinique Island (1902). Vol. LXXIII, p. 292, Mar., 1938. Vol. LXXIX, p. 48, Jan., 1941.

West Indies: Members of The Society on Expedition to Martinique and St. Vincent. Vol. XIII, p. 219, June, 1902.

West Indies: National Geographic Society Expedition in the West Indies. Vol. XIII, pp. 209-213, 2 half-page maps, June, 1902.

West Indies: National Geographic Society Expedition to Martinique and St. Vincent. Vol. XIII, pp. 183-184, 2 ills., June, 1902.

West Indies: Recent Volcanic Eruptions in the West Indies. By Israel C. Russell. Vol. XIII, pp. 267-285, 7 ills., July, 1902.

West Indies: Report by Robert T. Hill on the Volcanic Disturbances in the West Indies. Vol. XIII, pp. 223-267, 13 ills., 2 page and 1 half-page maps, July, 1902.

West Indies: Volcanic Eruptions on Martinique and St. Vincent. By Israel C. Russell. Vol. XIII, pp. 415-436, 10 ills., Dec., 1902.

West Indies: Volcanic Rocks of Martinique and St. Vincent: Collected by Robert T. Hill and Israel C. Russell. By J. S. Diller. Vol. XIII, pp. 285-296, July, 1902.

See also Stratosphere Balloon; History.

Fellows:

Alexander Graham Bell's proposal regarding Fellows. Vol. X, pp. 404-405, Oct., 1900.

Change in By-laws instituting a Class of Fellows. Vol. XIII, p. 220, June, 1902.

Notice of Proposed Amendment to the By-Laws of the National Geographic Society. Vol. XIII, p. 182, May, 1902.

Finances:

Finances. Vol. XI, p. 405, Oct., 1900. Vol. XVII, pp. 23-24, Jan., 1906. Vol. XXIII, pp. 273, 275, Mar., 1912. Vol. XXIV, p. 115, Jan., 1913; p. 252, Feb., 1913. Vol. XXVII, pp. 318, 320, Mar., 1915.

Research Fund established. Vol. XX, p. 486, May, 1909.

Treasurer's Reports. Vol. XIII, p. 80, Feb., 1902. Vol. XXI, pp. 89-90, Jan., 1910. Vol. XXII, p. 214, Feb., 1911. Vol. XXIV, p. 256, Feb., 1913.

See also Bequests; Prizes.

Flag:

Bathysphere cable. Vol. LXIX, ill. 153, Jan., 1936.

National Geographic Society—*Continued*
Flag—*Continued*

Canton Island: National Geographic Society-U. S. Navy Eclipse Expedition (1937). Vol. LXXII, p. 388; ill. 385, Sept., 1937. Vol. LXXIII, ill. 764; color plates I, p. 753; II, p. 754; VI, p. 758, June, 1938.

Dundee Island, Antarctic: Ellsworth Antarctic Expedition. Vol. LXXXIV, ill. 301, Sept., 1943.

Hubbard Gold Medal presentation to Anne Morrow Lindbergh. Vol. LXIX, ill. 137, Jan., 1936.

Katmai mast on Naknek Lake, Alaska. Vol. XL, ill. 238, Sept., 1921.

National Geographic Society Flag. Vol. LXVI, p. 364; color plate, p. 367, Sept., 1934.

Silverash (Ship). Vol. LXXIII, ill. 700, June, 1938.

Special Gold Medal presentation to Dr. Thomas C. Poulter. Vol. LXXII, ill. 107, July, 1937.

Stratocamp, South Dakota. Vol. LXVI, ill. 404, Oct., 1934.

Stratosphere balloon rigging. Vol. LXIX, ill. 70, Jan., 1936.

Sumatra: National Geographic Society-Smithsonian Institution East Indies Expedition. Vol. LXXIII, color plates VIII, p. 688; XIII, p. 709, June, 1938.

Travel-stained flag, to be taken on aërial survey to Latin America. Vol. LIX, ill. 2, Jan., 1931.

Valley of Ten Thousand Smokes. Vol. XL, ill. 238, Sept., 1921.

World travels made by The Society's Flag. Vol. LVII, p. 655, June, 1930.

Yukon flight of Bradford Washburn. Vol. LXIX, ill. 717, June, 1936.

Founders:

Greely, Maj. Gen. Adolphus W. Vol. LXXXIV, p. 133, Aug., 1943.

History:

Achievements of The Society. Vol. XXXIII, p. 170, Feb., 1918.

Address by Alexander Graham Bell on history of National Geographic Magazine, Jan. 26, 1912. Vol. XXIII, pp. 272-276, Mar., 1912.

Address of the President to the Board of Managers, June 1, 1900. By Alexander Graham Bell. Vol. XI, pp. 401-408, 1 chart, Oct., 1900.

Annual Dinner of the National Geographic Society. Vol. XVII, pp. 22-37, Jan., 1906.
    Finances...........................23–24
    Founders............................ 23
    Hubbard Memorial Hall 24
    Membership 23

National Geographic Society. By John Hyde. Vol. X, pp. 220-223, June, 1899.
    Assistant Editor appointed............ 222
    Editorial Committee 222

National Geographic Society—*Continued*
History—*Continued*

Influence of The Society............... 222
Magazine 221–222
Members..........................221, 223
Object................................ 221
Presidents 222

National Geographic Society and Its Magazine. By Gilbert Grosvenor. Vol. LXIX,
pp. 123-164, 24 ills., Jan., 1936.
Aid rendered scientific exploration and
research......123, 124–125, 140, 141,
143, 150, 154
Banquets....................150; ill. 127
Board of Managers....135, 138, 139, 144,
148, 152, 155; ill. 126, 129
Board of Trustees.....129, 131, 152, 153,
154, 155, 162; ill. 129, 133, 138, 159
Buildings........131, 148, 152, 155; ill.
124, 125, 126, 133, 156, 157
Certificate presented Gilbert Grosvenor.. 155
Committees..........136, 139, 144, 152, 154
Cumulative Index.........123, 125, 161, 162
Employees 125, 131, 162
Expeditions......124–125, 126, 141, 147;
ill. 143, 146, 151, 153, 158
Flag...................124; ill. 137, 153
History and organization...131, 134–135,
136–137, 138, 144–145, 148, 150, 152,
154, 155, 162
Library ....128; ill. 124
Luncheon in honor of Col. Theodore
Roosevelt.........................ill. 129
Medals and medal presentations....127,
149, 154, 161; ill. 127, 134, 136, 137,
138, 139
Membership......123–124, 125, 130, 134,
135, 145, 148, 152, 155, 161, 163–164
Officers and staff members..128, 131, 134,
138, 139, 148, 152, 154, 155,
162; ill. 126, 156, 157, 159
Offices...........................ill. 156
Photographic achievements.128–129, 143,
150, 153–154, 155, 157, 158; ill. 142
Purpose and policies of The Society..123,
134–135, 145, 148, 162
Seal of The Society.................ill. 157
Unveiling of Peary Memorial........ill. 132
National Geographic Society and Its New
Building. Vol. XXV, pp. 454-470, 11 ills.,
Apr., 1914.
Expeditions 459, 465
Geographical distribution of membership
468–470
Growth of The Society............455, 457
Photograph of officers and members..... 458

National Geographic Society's Notable Year.
Vol. XXXVII, pp. 338-345, 2 ills., Apr.,
1920.
Announcement of the deaths of Brig. Gen.
John M. Wilson, Rear Adm. John E.
Pillsbury, and Rear Adm. Robert E.
Peary 345
Award of Eight Jane M. Smith life mem-
berships......................342–343
Election of Gilbert Grosvenor as President 345
Election of John Oliver La Gorce as Vice-
President 345
Geographic News Bulletins and School
Service 343

National Geographic Society—*Continued*
History—*Continued*

Greely, (Maj. Gen.) A. W.: Presentation
of medal to Stefansson by........339–342
Hubbard Gold Medal awarded to Stefans-
son............................338–342
James C. Horgan Bequest............. 338
Magazine circulation.................. 343
Peary, (Rear Adm.) Robert E.: Last pub-
lic appearance of................... 339
Photograph of Peary, Stefansson, and
Greely............................ 318
Previous recipients of Jane M. Smith life
memberships...................... 342
Purpose of The Society............... 345
Sixth Katmai Expedition............. 338

Report of the Director and Editor of the
National Geographic Society for the
Year 1914. By Gilbert H. Grosvenor. Vol.
XVII, pp. 318-320, Mar., 1915.
Appropriations for research............ 320
Assets............................318–320
Bell, Alexander Graham: Funds contrib-
uted by 318
Early history of The Society.......... 319
Growth of The Society since 1907....... 320
Lecturers 320
Magazine policy adopted by Dr. Grosvenor 319
Membership 318

Report of the Editor for 1912. Vol. XXIV,
pp. 251-255, Feb., 1913.
Expeditions 251
Funds 251–252
Growth of The Magazine.............. 252
Growth of The Society............... 252
Membership 255

Speech by Alexander Graham Bell at An-
nual Banquet, January, 1912. Vol.
XXIII, pp. 272-275, Mar., 1912.
Buildings 273
Change in membership policy........... 273
Committee on Research............... 275
Expeditions......................... 275
Fellows 274
Finances.......................273, 275
Founding........................... 273
Gilbert H. Grosvenor elected Editor of
Magazine in 1899................... 274
Magazine policy and growth........273–274

Speech by James Howard Gore at Annual
Banquet, January, 1910. Vol. XXI, pp.
67-68, Jan., 1910.
Membership........................ 67
Organization 67–68
Purpose............................ 67

See also Banquets; Board of Managers;
Board of Trustees; Buildings; By-Laws;
Meetings; Members and Membership; Re-
ceptions.

Honorary Members:

Amundsen, Roald. Vol. XIX, p. 57, Jan.,
1908.
Bryce, James: Election of. Vol. XXIII, pp.
272, 275–276, Mar., 1912.
Charcot, Jean: Election of. Vol. XXIV, p.
122, Jan., 1913.

National Geographic Society—*Continued*
Honorary Members—*Continued*

Election of Adm. George Dewey, Roald Amundsen, and Morris K. Jesup. Vol. XVIII, p. 51, Jan., 1907.

Jesup, Morris K.: Photograph of. Vol. XVIII, p. 460, July, 1907.

Jusserand, J. J.: Election of. Vol. XXV, pp. 679, 688, June, 1914.

List of Honorary Members. Vol. XVIII, p. 51, Jan., 1907. Vol. XXII, p. 214, Feb., 1911.

McKinley, William: Election of. Vol. X, p. 143, Apr., 1899.

Peary, Robert E.: Election of. Vol. XLI, p. 643, June, 1922.

Taft, William H.: Election of. Vol. XXII, p. 214, Feb., 1911; pp. 267, 276, Mar., 1911.

Truman, Harry S., Honorary Life Member. Vol. LXXXIX, p. 141, Feb., 1946.

Wilson, Woodrow: Election of. Vol. XXXIII, p. 369, Apr., 1918.

Insignia Publications. *See* Publications.

International Geographic Congress:

Address by Comdr. Peary at Eighth Congress. Vol. XV, pp. 387-392, Oct., 1904.

Chairman of Committee on Eighth Congress. Vol. XIII, p. 219, June, 1902. Vol. XIV, pp. 254-255, June, 1903.

Delegates to Ninth Congress. Vol. XIX, pp. 385-386, May, 1908.

Delegates to Seventh Congress. Vol. X, p. 296, Aug., 1899; p. 480, Nov., 1899.

Eighth International Geographic Congress. Vol. XIV, pp. 388, 390, Oct., 1903.
Committee on arrangements........... 390
Plans 388, 390

Eighth International Geographic Congress. Vol. XV, pp. 74-77, Feb., 1904.
American societies coöperating......... 74
Discussion subjects 75-76
Membership 75
Officers and committees..............76-77
Publications......................... 75
Sessions and excursions.............. 74

Eighth International Geographic Congress. Vol. XV, pp. 297-310, July, 1904.
American societies coöperating........ 297
Headquarters........................ 298
Lectures and papers................306-310
Meetings 297-298
Membership 301-302
Officers and committees............304-305
Program 299-301
Publications......................... 303
Registration 298
Subjects for discussion............302-303
Transportation...................... 301

Eighth International Geographic Congress. Vol. XV, pp. 419-426, 2 ills., Oct., 1904.
Entertainment...........420, 423, 424-425
Gilbert, Grove Karl: Speech by........ 419
Meetings and papers..............420, 424

National Geographic Society—*Continued*
International Geographic Congress
—*Continued*

Photographs of members..........421, 422
Telegram sent to President Roosevelt.... 420
Walcott, Charles D.: Speech by........ 419

International Geographic Congress. Vol. XIV, p. 292, July, 1903.
Appointment of committees........... 292
Plans for eighth Congress.............. 292

Next International Geographical Congress to be Held in Washington. By Gilbert H. Grosvenor. Vol. XII, pp. 351-357, 4 ills., Oct., 1901.
Delegates to seventh Congress.......... 352
Delegates to sixth Congress............ 352
Invitation for eighth Congress extended by The Society....................352-353
Plans for entertainment of Congress..356-357

Ninth International Geographic Congress, Geneva, Switzerland, 1908. Vol. XVIII, p. 491, July, 1907.

Program of Eighth International Geographic Congress. Vol. XV, pp. 373-386, Sept., 1904.
Map of Washington, D. C.............. 375
Officers and committees............384-386
Washington sessions................. 383

Publication of Proceedings of Eighth International Geographic Congress. Vol. XVI, pp. 198-199, Apr., 1905.
Editors 199
Resolutions......................... 199

Resolutions Adopted by the Eighth International Geographic Congress. Vol. XV, pp. 415-418, Oct., 1904.

Library:

Fund bequeathed to The Society by George T. Nealley to be used in purchasing books for the Library. Vol. XLIX, p. 474, Apr., 1926.

Library. Vol. XXIV, p. 252, Feb., 1913; p. 459, Apr., 1913. Vol. LXV, ill. 794, June, 1934. Vol. LXXXIX, p. 331, Mar., 1946.

Life Members:

Award of Eight Jane M. Smith Life Memberships. Vol. XXXVII, pp. 342-343, Apr., 1920.
List and account of recipients.......342-343
Previous recipients.................. 342
Reasons for awards................342-343

Jane M. Smith Bequest for Life Memberships. Vol. XXIII, p. 104, Jan., 1912.

Life Members. Vol. XXII, p. 211, Feb., 1910. Vol. XXIV, p. 255, Feb., 1913.

See also Honorary Members.

Map Department. *See* Buildings.

Map Rack presented to President Truman. Vol. LXXXIX, p. 290, Mar., 1946.

Map Supplement Articles:

Africa First of 1943 Global Warfare Maps. By William H. Nicholas. Text accompanying special map supplement in colors. Vol. LXXXIII, pp. 261-276, 13 ills., Feb., 1943.

National Geographic Society—*Continued*
Map Supplement Articles—*Continued*

Western Front Map Embraces Three Continents (Europe, Africa, Asia). Text accompanying special map supplement in colors. Vol. LXXXII, pp. 139-140, July, 1942.

World That Rims the Narrowing Atlantic: Latest Ten-color Map Supplement Shows Four Continents and New Transatlantic Air Routes Which Make This Ocean Only One Day Wide. By James M. Darley. Text accompanying special map supplement in colors. Vol. LXXVI, pp. 139-142, 1 ill., July, 1939.

Your Society Aids War Effort. Vol. LXXXIII, pp. 277-278, 1 ill., Feb., 1943.

Map Supplements (Text and Illustrations):

Date of issue printed on each Geographic map. Vol. LXXXVI, p. 69, July, 1944.

Key to foreign names for physical features. Vol. LXXXVI, p. 68, July, 1944.

Map supplement of Canada used by Sir Hubert Wilkins in air navigation. Vol. LXXIV, p. 142, Aug., 1938.

Master drawing, Tacking highway routes over. Vol. LXXIX, ill. 436, Apr., 1942.

Number, Total, of maps printed since December, 1941. Vol. LXXXVI, p. 450, Oct., 1944.

Number of maps printed annually. Vol. LXXIX, p. 419, Apr., 1941.

Number of supplements for 1941. Vol. LXXXI, p. 333, Mar., 1942.

Printed by A. Hoen and Company, Inc. Vol. LXXIX, pp. 419, 436, Apr., 1941. Vol. LXXXI, ill. 679, May, 1942.

"Rediscovering America" series of decorated charts on sections of the United States. Vol. LXXIX, p. 805, June, 1941.

Series of charts on sections of the United States. Vol. LXXXVIII, p. 362, Sept., 1945.

Various uses of The Society's map supplements by Army and Navy, Government Departments, embassies, clubs, offices, etc. Vol. LXXXI, p. 333, Mar., 1942; pp. 671-673, 674; ill. 668-674, 682-684, 686-690, May, 1942; p. 691, June, 1942. Vol. LXXXII, ill. 670, 671, Nov., 1942. Vol. LXXXIII, p. 265; ill. 278, Feb., 1943. Vol. LXXXV, p. 83; ill. 93, Jan., 1944; p. 415, Apr., 1944. Vol. LXXXVI, pp. 66-67, 71, 72; ill. 69, July, 1944; p. 263; ill. 279, Sept., 1944; p. 450; ill. 450, Oct., 1944. Vol. LXXXVIII, ill. 7, July, 1945; pp. 709, 753, Dec., 1945.

Wartime map series. Vol. LXXXI, p. 203, Feb., 1942. Vol. LXXXII, p. 139, July, 1942; pp. 767, 768, Dec., 1942. Vol. LXXXV, pp. 415, 416, Apr., 1944. Vol. LXXXVI, pp. 449, 450, Oct., 1944; p. 716, Dec., 1944. Vol. LXXXVII, p. 745, June, 1945.

Maps. *See* Index to Maps, p. 594.

National Geographic Society—*Continued*

Medals:

Admiral Byrd Receives New Honor from The Society (Presentation by President Hoover of Special Gold Medal). Vol. LVIII, pp. 228-238, 4 ills., Aug., 1930.
Basis of award 232
Photograph of medal 235
Presentation by President Hoover . . 231–232 ; ill. 233
Two of The Society's Medals awarded Byrd 229

Air Conquest: From the Early Days of Giant Kites and Birdlike Gliders the National Geographic Society Has Aided and Encouraged the Growth of Aviation (Hubbard Gold Medal Awarded Lindbergh). Vol. LII, pp. 233-242, 13 ills., Aug., 1927.
Basis of award 241, 242
Byrd, (Comdr.) Richard E.: Lindbergh notified by 241
Inscription .... ill. 234
Letter from Gilbert Grosvenor announcing award 242
Photograph of medal 234
Previous recipients 242

"Captain Bob" Bartlett awarded the Hubbard Medal. Vol. LXXXIX, p. 609, May, 1946.

Commander Byrd Receives the Hubbard Gold Medal: The First Explorer to Reach the North Pole by Air Receives Coveted Honor at Brilliant National Geographic Society Reception (Also Presentation of Hubbard Gold Medal to Floyd Bennett). Vol. L, pp. 377-388, 5 ills., 1 chart, Sept., 1926.
Acceptance of medal by Comdr. Byrd . 379–383
Basis of awards 378–379
Bennett, Floyd: Hubbard Gold Medal presented to 377–379
Comparison of Peary's and Byrd's achievements 377–378
Photographs of medals 382, 385
Presentation of medals by President Coolidge .... 377–379 ; ill. 380
Previous recipients 377

Discovery of the North Pole. Vol. XXI, pp. 63-82, Jan., 1910.
Basis of awards 63,   75
Hubbard Gold Medal awarded to Grove Karl Gilbert 63,   75
Hubbard Gold Medal presented to Capt. Robert A. Bartlett by James Bryce 63, 75–77
Inscriptions 63
Special Gold Medal presented to Peary by Willis L. Moore 63, 73–74
Telegrams of congratulations 63,   64

Ellsworth Awarded the Hubbard Medal. Vol. LXX, p. 36, July, 1936.
Acceptance speech 36
Grosvenor, Gilbert: Exploits of Lincoln Ellsworth related by 36
Presentation speech by President Franklin D. Roosevelt 36

National Geographic Society—*Continued*
Medals—*Continued*

First Airship Flight Around the World: Dr. Hugo Eckener Tells of an Epochal Geographic Achievement upon the Occasion of the Bestowal of the National Geographic Society's Special Gold Medal. Vol. LVII, pp. 653-688, 37 ills., June, 1930.
  Acceptance speech by Dr. Eckener....655–681
  Basis of award........................ 653
  Inscription 655
  Presentation by Gilbert Grosvenor...653–655
  Previous recipients 655
  Telegram of congratulations from Byrd.. 688

Honors for Amundsen (Presentation of Hubbard Gold Medal by Charles W. Fairbanks). Vol. XIX, pp. 55-76, 13 ills., Jan., 1908.
  Basis of award........................ 56
  Presentation 56–57

Honors to Amundsen and Peary (Special Gold Medal Presented to Amundsen by Peary). Vol. XXIV, pp. 113-130, Jan., 1913.
  Amundsen's acceptance speech.......129–130
  Photograph of medal................... 128
  Photograph of presentation ceremony.... 120
  Presentation by Peary................. 129

Honors to Colonel Goethals: The Presentation, by President Woodrow Wilson, of the National Geographic Society Special Gold Medal, and Addresses by Secretary of State Bryan, the French Ambassador, the German Ambassador, and Congressman James R. Mann. Vol. XXV, pp. 677-690, 6 ills., June, 1914.
  Acceptance speech 683–684
  Basis of award..............679, 680, 683
  Inscription 679
  Presentation speech 679, 680, 683
  Previous recipients 679

Honors to Peary (Presentation of Hubbard Gold Medal by President Roosevelt). Vol. XVIII, pp. 49-60, 1 ill., Jan., 1907.
  Basis of award........................ 56
  Design and inscription.........49; ill. 48
  Presentation 57

Hubbard Medals Awarded to Stratosphere Explorers: Presentation by General Pershing. Vol. LXIX, pp. 713-714, May, 1936.
  Address by Gilbert Grosvenor.......... 713
  Presentation ....713–714; ill. 712

National Geographic Society's Notable Year (Award of Hubbard Gold Medal to Stefansson). Vol. XXXVII, pp. 338-345, 2 ills., Apr., 1920.
  Achievements of Stefansson........339–342
  Basis of award........................ 340
  Peary, (Rear Adm.) Robert E.: Tribute to Stefansson by 339
  Photograph of Peary, Stefansson, and Greely 318
  Presentation of medal by Maj. Gen. A. W. Greely 339–342
  Tribute to Stefansson by members of Greely International Polar Expedition. 342

National Geographic Society—*Continued*
Medals—*Continued*

President Coolidge Bestows Lindbergh Award: The National Geographic Society's Hubbard Medal Is Presented to Aviator Before the Most Notable Gathering in the History of Washington. Vol. LIII, pp. 132-140, 4 ills., Jan., 1928.
  Acceptance by Lindbergh...........135, 137
  Inscription 139
  Presentation by President Coolidge..134–135; ill. 139

President Truman presents Hubbard Medal to Gen. H. H. Arnold, Nov. 16, 1945. Vol. LXXXIX, ill. 141, Feb., 1946.

Race for the South Pole (Presentation of Hubbard Gold Medal to Sir Ernest H. Shackleton). Vol. XXI, pp. 185-186, Mar., 1910.
  Acceptance speech by Shackleton........ 186
  Basis of award........................ 185
  Distinguished audience 185
  Presentation speech by President Taft... 186

Resolution Awarding Medals to Peary and Bartlett. Vol. XX, pp. 1008-1009, Nov., 1909.

Resolutions Concerning Medals (The National Geographic Society and Geographic Work). Vol. XX, pp. 486-487, May, 1909.
  Basis of awards....................... 487
  Endowment of awards................... 487
  Purpose of medals..................... 486
  Recommendations for awards............ 487
  Society medals 487
  Special medals 487
  Squires, Grant: Endowment by......... 487

Society Awards Hubbard Medal to Anne Morrow Lindbergh. Vol. LXV, pp. 791-794, 4 ills., June, 1934.
  Acceptance by Mrs. Lindbergh.......... 792
  Basis of award........................ 791
  Bumstead, Albert H.: Medal designed by. 793
  Design and inscription........791, 792, 793
  Messages of congratulation............ 793
  Photograph of......................... 793
  Presentation by Dr. Grosvenor..791–792; ill. 792
  Previous recipients................791, 792
  Projection used for map design on medal 793

Society's Special Medal Awarded to Amelia Earhart: First Woman to Receive Geographic Distinction at Brilliant Ceremony in the National Capital. Vol. LXII, pp. 358-367, 7 ills., Sept., 1932.
  Acceptance by Miss Earhart.......363, 367
  Inscription 359
  Photograph of medal................... 366
  Presentation by President Hoover....358, 362–363; ill. 366
  Presidents of the U. S. who have presented The Society's medals.......... 362
  Previous recipients................359, 362

Society's Special Medal Is Awarded to Dr. Thomas C. Poulter: Admiral Byrd's Second-in-Command and Senior Scientist Is Accorded High Geographic Honor. Vol. LXXII, pp. 105-108, 2 ills., July, 1937.
  Acceptance by Dr. Poulter.........105–106
  Basis of award........................ 105

National Geographic Society—*Continued*
  Medals—*Continued*

Byrd, (Rear Adm.) R. E.: Tribute to Dr.
  Poulter by 106–108
Photograph of medal................. 107
Presentation by Dr. Grosvenor..105; ill. 107

Special Gold Medal presented to Peary. Vol.
  XXI, ill. 540, June, 1910.

Meetings:

Annual Meeting, January 10, 1902. Vol.
  XIII, p. 80, Feb., 1902.
  Report of Secretary concerning member-
    ship 80
  Treasurer's report................... 80

Annual Meeting, January 13, 1905. Vol.
  XVI, p. 87, Feb., 1905.
  Board of Managers: Election of members. 87
  Henry Gannett elected Vice-President.... 87
  Secretary's report................... 87
  Willis L. Moore elected President....... 87

Annual Meeting, January 14, 1910. Vol.
  XXI, pp. 88-90, Jan., 1910.
  Board of Managers: Election of members. 88
  Election of officers................... 88
  Secretary's report...................88–89
  Treasurer's report...................89–90

Annual Meeting, January 13, 1911. Vol.
  XXII, pp. 211, 214, Feb., 1911.
  Board of Managers: Election of members 211
  Election of officers................... 211
  Membership 211, 214
  President Taft elected Honorary Member. 214
  Secretary's report................211, 214
  Treasurer's report................... 214

Meeting of Board of Managers. Vol. XIV,
  pp. 254-255, June, 1903.
  Appointment of Chairman of Committee
    on Eighth International Geographic
    Congress 254–255
  Appointment of Presidential Nominating
    Committee 254
  Resignation of Alexander Graham Bell as
    President 254

Meeting of Board of Managers. Vol. XVII,
  p. 205, Apr., 1906.
  Maj. Henry E. Hersey appointed repre-
    sentative of The Society on Wellman
    Expedition 205
  Resolution concerning Wellman Polar Ex-
    pedition 205

Meeting of Board of Managers. Vol. XVIII,
  p. 281, Apr., 1907.
  Resolution subscribing to Peary Expedi-
    tion of 1907-1908................... 281

Meeting of Board of Managers (The National
  Geographic Society and Geographic
  Work). Vol. XX, pp. 486-487, May, 1909.
  Research fund established............. 486
  Resolutions concerning medals......... 487

Meeting of Board of Managers. Vol. XX,
  pp. 921-922, Nov., 1909.
  Claims of Peary and Cook referred to
    Committee on Research............. 921

Meeting of Board of Managers. Vol. XX,
  pp. 1008-1009, Nov., 1909.
  Report of committee on claims of Cook
    and Peary........................1008

National Geographic Society—*Continued*
  Meetings—*Continued*

Resolution appointing committee to con-
  sider claims of Cook................1009
Resolution awarding medals to Peary and
  Bartlett 1008–1009
Tribute in memory of Mrs. Gardiner
  Greene Hubbard...................1008

Meeting of Board of Managers. Vol. XXI,
  p. 365, Apr., 1910.
  Resolution withdrawing subscription to
    South Polar Expedition............. 365

Meeting of Board of Managers. Vol. XXVI,
  pp. 609-610, Dec., 1914.
  Tribute to Henry Gannett..........609–610

Meeting of Board of Managers. Vol. XXVII,
  p. 218, Feb., 1915.
  John E. Pillsbury elected Vice-President. 218
  O. H. Tittmann elected President....... 218

Notice of Annual Meeting, January 13, 1905.
  Vol. XVI, p. 53, Jan., 1905.

Proceedings of the National Geographic Society, Session 1898-1899. Vol. X, pp.
  143-144, Apr., 1899.
  Election of new members............. 144
  President McKinley elected Honorary
    Member 143

Proceedings of the National Geographic Society, Session 1898-1899. Vol. X, pp.
  327-328, Aug., 1899.
  Annual reception..................... 328

See also Board of Managers; Board of
  Trustees.

Members and Membership:

Achievements of Members. Vol. XVIII, p.
  50, Jan., 1907.

Africa, Members in. Vol. LXVII, pp. 731-
  732, June, 1935.

Argentina and Iceland, Membership in. Vol.
  LXXI, pp. 30-31, Jan., 1937.

Ascension Island—2 Members. Vol. LXXXV,
  p. 635, May, 1944.

Bahrein Island—26 Members. Vol.
  LXXXIX, p. 209, Feb., 1946.

Belgian Merchant, a Member for fifteen
  years. Vol. LXXIII, p. 446, Apr., 1938.

Buenos Aires—1,527 Members. Vol. LXXVI,
  p. 585, Nov., 1939.

Canada. Vol. LXIX, p. 769, June, 1936.

Certificate of newly elected Member. Vol.
  XC, ill. 39, July, 1946.

Change in Membership Policy. Vol. XI, p.
  289, July, 1900; pp. 403-404, Oct., 1900.
  Vol. XXIII, p. 273, Mar., 1912.

Chart of Membership, 1888-1900. Vol. XI,
  p. 402, Oct., 1900.

Dues. Vol. XI, p. 406, Oct., 1900. Vol.
  XXXVII, p. 292, Mar., 1920. Vol.
  XXXVIII, p. 80, July, 1920.

Election of New Members. Vol. X, p. 144,
  Apr., 1899. Vol. XC, p. 39, July, 1946.

National Geographic Society—*Continued*
Members and Membership—*Continued*

El Salvador—7 Members of Álvarez family. Vol. LXXXVI, p. 577, Nov., 1944.

Europe, Members in. Vol. LVI, p. 771, Dec., 1929.

Geographical distribution of. Vol. XXI, pp. 88-89, Jan., 1910. Vol. XXII, pp. 211, 214, Feb., 1911. Vol. XXIV, p. 255, Feb., 1913. Vol. XXV, pp. 468-470, Apr., 1914; p. 679, June, 1914. Vol. LIII, p. 137, Jan., 1928; pp. 173, 192, Feb., 1928. Vol. LXIX, pp. 163-164, Jan., 1936. Vol. LXXVIII, p. 61, July, 1940.

Iceland and Argentina, Membership in. Vol. LXXI, pp. 30-31, Jan., 1937.

Idaho : Uncle Dave ("Cougar Dave" Lewis). Vol. LXXXV, p. 679, June, 1944.

Increase in Membership. Vol. XI, p. 289, July, 1900; p. 403, Oct., 1900. Vol. XXI, p. 88, Jan., 1910. Vol. XXII, p. 211, Feb., 1911. Vol. XXIII, pp. 272-273, Mar., 1912. Vol. XXIV, pp. 252, 255, Feb., 1913. Vol. XXVII, p. 318, Mar., 1915.

Intellectual calibre of Members. Vol. XVII, p. 23, Jan., 1906.

King Fuad I a Member. Vol. LXV, p. 658, May, 1934.

Lord Howe Island, Membership in. Vol. LXVIII, pp. 126, 136, July, 1935.

Louis Tungwenuk, Westernmost Member on the American Continent. Vol. LXXV, pp. 650-651; ill. 646, May, 1939.

Malacca, Members from. Vol. LV, color plate XIV, p. 478, Apr., 1929.

Martinique Member. Vol. LXXIII, ill. 297, Mar., 1938.

Mauritius Island — 55 Members. Vol. LXXVI, p. 73, July, 1939.

Members using Geographic map in following text of Roosevelt's address. Vol. LXXXI, p. 667; ill. 669, May, 1942.

Mrs. Herbert Hoover, a Member. Vol. LVIII, p. 231, Aug., 1930. Vol. LXII, p. 362, Sept., 1932.

Nicaragua : Chinese merchant of Bluefields. Vol. LXXXVI, pp. 177-178, Aug., 1944.

Notice of Proposed Amendments to the By-Laws of the National Geographic Society. Vol. XIII, p. 182, May, 1902.

Number of Members. Vol. X, p. 221, June, 1899. Vol. XIII, p. 80, Feb., 1902. Vol. XIV, p. 217, May, 1903. Vol. XVI, p. 87, Feb., 1905; p. 241, May, 1905. Vol. XVII, p. 23, Jan., 1906. Vol. XXI, p. 67, Jan., 1910. Vol. XXII, p. 267, Mar., 1911. Vol. XXIV, p. 113, Jan., 1913. Vol. XXV, p. 679, June, 1914. Vol. L, p. 377, Sept., 1926. Vol. LXXIII, p. 525, Apr., 1938. Vol. LXXVII, p. 625, May, 1940; p. 767, June, 1940. Vol. LXXVIII, p. 61, July, 1940. Vol. LXXIX, p. 345, Mar., 1941. Vol. LXXX, p. 741, Dec., 1941. Vol. LXXXI, p. 203, Feb., 1942;

National Geographic Society—*Continued*
Members and Membership—*Continued*

p. 333, Mar., 1942; p. 667, May, 1942. Vol. LXXXII, p. 139, July, 1942; p. 276, Aug., 1942; p. 537, Oct., 1942; p. 767, Dec., 1942. Vol. LXXXIII, p. 261, Feb., 1943. Vol. LXXXV, p. 415, Apr., 1944. Vol. LXXXVI, p. 60, July, 1944; p. 710, Dec., 1944. Vol. LXXXVII, p. 745, June, 1945. Vol. LXXXVIII, p. 361, Sept., 1945. Vol. XC, pp. 34, 39, 135, July, 1946; p. 815, Dec., 1946.

Ohio, Conneaut, Members in. Vol. LXV, p. 458, Apr., 1934.

Peary, Robert E., a Charter Member. Vol. XLI, p. 641, June, 1922.

Proposed change in By-laws. Vol. XII, p. 167, Apr., 1901.

Scotland. Vol. LXXXIX, p. 550, May, 1946.

South American Members—Farthest South. Vol. LXXII, p. 750; ill. 761, Dec., 1937.

Tibetan Member. Vol. XC, p. 198; ill. 179, Aug., 1946.

See also Honorary Members ; Life Members.

Memorials:

Bowdoin (Ship) in North Greenland : Arctic Explorers Place Tablet to Commemorate Sacrifices of the Lady Franklin Bay Expedition. By Donald B. MacMillan. Vol. XLVII, pp. 677-722, 49 ills., June, 1925.
Christmas message from Greely to MacMillan 684
History of Lady Franklin Bay Expedition 677-679
Photographs of memorial........... 700, 706
Site of memorial..................... 688
Unveiling ceremony............... 688, 700

Memorial Fountain, Cantigny, France. Vol. LVI, ill. 548, Nov., 1929. Vol. LXV, ill. 34, Jan., 1934.

Memorial to Peary : The National Geographic Society Dedicates Monument in Arlington National Cemetery to Discoverer of the North Pole. Vol. XLI, pp. 639-646, 4 ills., June, 1922.
Design 646
Inscriptions 645-646
Photographs 644, 646
Unveiling ....639 ; ill. 640, 644

Memorial to Peary, Unveiling of. Vol. LVII, ill. 583, May, 1930. Vol. LXIX, ill. 132, Jan., 1936.

Memorial to Robert E. Peary, Photograph of. Vol. LIV, ill. 632, Nov., 1928.

Monument to Rear Adm. Charles Wilkes. Vol. LIV, ill. 633, Nov., 1928.

National Geographic Society's Memorial to American Troops : Fountain and Water Supply System Presented to Historic French Town of Cantigny, Where Our Overseas Soldiers Won Their First Victory in the World War. Vol. XLIV, pp. 675-678, 4 ills., Dec., 1923.
American Legion Color Guard........ill. 676

National Geographic Society—*Continued*
Memorials—*Continued*

Dedication of.......................... 675

Fund for memorial.................... 676

Gore, James Howard: Presentation address by 675–676

Museum:

Exhibit case.   Vol. LX, color plate XVII, p. 578, Nov., 1931.

Hebrew Shekel presented to. Vol. LXIV, ill. 259, Sept., 1933.

Varied exhibitions.   Vol. LXXI, p. 670, June, 1937.

Yünnan Expedition exhibit.   Vol. LXVII, color plate VII, p. 479, Apr., 1935. Vol. LXVIII, color plates III, p. 481; VII, p. 485, Oct., 1935.

Musical Composition:

"National Geographic Society March," composed and dedicated by Captain Thomas F. Darcy, leader of the United States Army Band, Washington. Vol. LXIX, p. 122, Jan., 1936.

News Bulletin Service:

Current Newspaper Maps, a special feature of the News Bulletin Service. Vol. LXXX, p. 741, Dec., 1941.

North Pole Discovery:

Discovery of the North Pole. Vol. XXI, pp. 63-82, Jan., 1910.
  Account of Peary's explorations........69–73
  Hubbard Gold Medal presented to Capt. Robert A. Bartlett..............63, 75–77
  Special Gold Medal presented to Peary 63, 74–75

Discovery of the Pole. Vol. XX, pp. 892-915, 11 ills., 1 page map, Oct., 1909.
  Cook, Frederick A.: Report by.....892–896
  Peary, Robert E.: Report by........896–915

Memorial to Peary: The National Geographic Society Dedicates Monument in Arlington National Cemetery to Discoverer of the North Pole. Vol. XLI, pp. 639-646, 4 ills., June, 1922.
  Denby, Edwin: Speech by...643-645; ill. 642
  Grosvenor, Gilbert: Address by......641–643
  Members and guests present....639, 641;
                                   ill. 640, 642
  Peary a charter member of The Society.. 641
  Peary's career.....................643–645
  Peary's first address to The Society..... 641
  Peary's last public appearance, last article, and last photograph were for The Society 641
  Recognition of Peary by The Society.... 643
  Roosevelt, (Col.) Theodore: Speech by... 645
  Stafford, (Mrs.) Edward: Monument unveiled by.................639; ill. 644

North Pole. Vol. XX, pp. 921-922, Nov., 1909.
  Committee appointed to consider claims of Peary and Cook.................921–922

North Pole. Vol. XX, pp. 1008-1009, Nov., 1909.

National Geographic Society—*Continued*
North Pole Discovery—*Continued*

Committee appointed to consider claims of Cook 1009

Medals awarded Peary and Bartlett
                              1008–1009

Recognition of Peary's discovery........1008

"Peary's Discovery of the North Pole" (Pamphlet by J. Hampton Moore), presented to Members of The Society. Vol. XXI, p. 276, Mar., 1910.

See also Expeditions: Arctic Regions.

Notary Public. Vol. XC, ill. 7, July, 1946.

Officers:

Photograph of Officers and Board of Managers in 1913. Vol. XXIV, p. 114, Jan., 1913. Vol. LXIX, p. 126, Jan., 1936.

Photograph of Officers and Trustees in 1930. Vol. LXIX, p. 159, Jan., 1936.

Presentation of Hubbard Medal by President Truman to Gen. H. H. Arnold. Vol. LXXXIX, ill. 141, Feb., 1946.

See also President; Secretary; Treasurer; Vice-President.

Offices. *See* Buildings.

Paintings:

Aleutians: Navy Artist Paints the Aleutians. 16 ills. in color from paintings by Lt. William F. Draper. Vol. LXXXIV, pp. 161-176, Aug., 1943.

Ants: Work and War in the World of Ants. 18 ills. in color from paintings by Hashime Murayama. Vol. LXVI, pp. 179-186, Aug., 1934.

Bees: In Field and Hive With the Busy Honeybee. 16 ills. in color from paintings by Hashime Murayama. Vol. LXVII, pp. 417-424, Apr., 1935.

Berries (American Berries of Hill, Dale, and Wayside). 29 ills. in color from paintings by Mary E. Eaton. Vol. XXXV, pp. 173-180, Feb., 1919.

Bird Beauties of the Tanager and Finch Families. 55 portraits in color from paintings by Maj. Allan Brooks. Vol. LXVII, pp. 513-528, Apr., 1935.

Birds (American Game Birds). 72 ills. in color from paintings by Louis Agassiz Fuertes. Vol. XXVIII, pp. 109-144, Aug., 1915.

Birds (Common Birds of Farm and Orchard). 50 ills. in color from paintings by Louis Agassiz Fuertes. Vol. XXIV, pp. 673-697, June, 1913.

Birds (Warblers of North America). 32 ills. in color from paintings by Louis Agassiz Fuertes. Vol. XXXI, pp. 305-320, April, 1917.

Birds: Auks and Their Northland Neighbors. 34 portraits in color from paintings by Maj. Allan Brooks. Vol. LXIX, pp. 101-116, Jan., 1936.

National Geographic Society—*Continued*

Paintings—*Continued*

Birds: Blithe Birds of Dooryard, Bush, and Brake. 37 portraits in color from paintings by Maj. Allan Brooks. Vol. LXV, pp. 579-594, May, 1934.

Birds: Bright-hued Pets of Cage and Aviary. 51 portraits in color from paintings by Maj. Allan Brooks. Vol. LXXIV, pp. 783-790, Dec., 1938.

Birds: Crows, Magpies, and Jays. 17 ills. in color from paintings by Maj. Allan Brooks. Vol. LXIII, pp. 65-78, Jan., 1933.

Birds: Eagles, Hawks, and Vultures. 48 ills. in color from paintings by Maj. Allan Brooks. Vol. LXIV, pp. 65-94, July, 1933.

Birds: Falconry, the Sport of Kings. 12 ills. in color from paintings by Louis Agassiz Fuertes. Vol. XXXVIII, pp. 441-456, Dec., 1920.

Birds: Feathered Foragers of Swamp and Shore. 101 portraits in color from paintings by Maj. Allan Brooks. Vol. LXXII, pp. 191-222, Aug., 1937.

Birds: Flycatchers and Other Friends in Feathers. 36 portraits in color from paintings by Maj. Allan Brooks. Vol. LXIX, pp. 807-822, June, 1936.

Birds: Humming Birds, Swifts and Goatsuckers. 36 ills. in color from paintings by Maj. Allan Brooks. Vol. LXII, pp. 75-88, July, 1932.

Birds: Hunted Birds of Field and Wild. 60 portraits in color from paintings by Maj. Allan Brooks. Vol. LXX, pp. 469-500, Oct., 1936.

Birds: Ibises, Herons, and Flamingos. 24 ills. in color from paintings by Maj. Allan Brooks. Vol. LXII, pp. 455-468, Oct., 1932.

Birds: Iridescent Isles of the South Seas. 16 ills. in color; 4 paintings by Hashime Murayama. Vol. XLVIII, pp. 403-418, Oct., 1925.

Birds: North American Woodpeckers. 25 ills. in color from paintings by Maj. Allan Brooks. Vol. LXIII, pp. 465-478, Apr., 1933.

Birds: Pastel Wrens from "Down Under." 8 ills. in color from paintings by N. W. Cayley. Vol. LXXXVIII, pp. 489-496, Oct., 1945.

Birds: Pigeons of Resplendent Plumage. 12 ills. in color from paintings by Hashime Murayama. Vol. XLIX, pp. 65-76, Jan., 1926.

Birds: Silent-Winged Owls of North America. 21 portraits in color from paintings by Maj. Allan Brooks. Vol. LXVII, pp. 225-240, Feb., 1935.

Birds: Some Songsters and Flyers of Wide Repute (Thrushes, Thrashers, and Swallows). 42 portraits in color from paintings by Maj. Allan Brooks. Vol. LXIX, pp. 529-544, Apr., 1936.

National Geographic Society—*Continued*

Paintings—*Continued*

Birds: Sparrows, Towhees, and Longspurs: These Happy Little Singers Make Merry in Field, Forest, and Desert Throughout North America. 43 portraits in color from paintings by Maj. Allan Brooks and Walter A. Weber. Vol. LXXV, pp. 361-373, Mar., 1939.

Birds: Wild Geese, Ducks, and Swans. 93 portraits in color from paintings by Maj. Allan Brooks. Vol. LXVI, pp. 493-524, Oct., 1934.

Birds: Wings Over the Bounding Main (Ocean Birds). 36 portraits in color from paintings by Maj. Allan Brooks. Vol. LXXIV, pp. 237-251, Aug., 1938.

Birds in Glossy Black and Vivid Color. 48 portraits in color from paintings by Maj. Allan Brooks. Vol. LXVI, pp. 113-128, July, 1934.

Birds of Lake and Lagoon, Marsh and Seacoast. 24 portraits in color from paintings by Maj. Allan Brooks. Vol. LXV, pp. 313-328, Mar., 1934.

Birds of Town and Country. 64 ills. in color from paintings by Louis Agassiz Fuertes. Vol. XXV, pp. 499-530, May, 1914.

Butterflies: Nomads Among the Butterflies. 8 ills. in color; 3 paintings by Hashime Murayama. Vol. LXXI, pp. 569-584, May, 1937.

Butterflies: Winged Jewels From Many Lands. 9 ills. in color; 3 paintings by Hashime Murayama. Vol. LXIX, pp. 673-688, May, 1936.

Cattle of the World. 20 ills. in color from paintings by Edward Herbert Miner. Vol. XLVIII, pp. 639-678, Dec., 1925.

Cephalopods: Monster and Midget Squid and Octopuses. 8 ills. in color from paintings by Else Bostelmann. Vol. LXVIII, pp. 193-200, Aug., 1935.

China: Buddhist Calm Survives Along China's Great Wall. 10 ills. in color; 4 paintings by Mary Augusta Mullikin and Anna M. Hotchkis. Vol. LXXIII, pp. 321-328, Mar., 1938.

China's Wonderland—Yen Tang Shan (Chekiang Province). 8 ills. in color from camera paintings by Herbert Clarence White, Deng Bao-ling, and Hwang Yao-tso. Vol. LXXII, pp. 687-694, Dec., 1937.

Coral: Multi-Hued Marvels of a Coral Reef. 8 ills. in color from paintings by Else Bostelmann. Vol. LXV, pp. 719-726, June, 1934.

Crabs and Crablike Curiosities of the Sea. 8 ills. in color from paintings by William Crowder. Vol. LIV, pp. 63-70, July, 1928.

Crater Lake and Yosemite Through the Ages. 13 ills. in color from paintings by Eugene Kingman. Vol. LXXI, pp. 333-339, Mar., 1937.

National Geographic Society—*Continued*
Paintings—*Continued*

Crustaceans and Mollusks: Strange Creatures of Sunny Seas. 8 ills. in color from paintings by Else Bostelmann. Vol. LXXI, pp. 211-218, Feb., 1937.

Deer: Antlered Majesties of Many Lands. 23 ills. in color from paintings by Walter A. Weber. Vol. LXXVI, pp. 479-510, Oct., 1939.

Dogs (Our Common Dogs). 73 ills. in color from paintings by Louis Agassiz Fuertes. Vol. XXXV, pp. 202-263, May, 1919.

Dogs (Working Dogs of the World). 20 ills. in color from paintings by Edward Herbert Miner. Vol. LXXX, pp. 775-806, Dec., 1941.

Dogs: Gallant Little Sportsmen of the Terrier Tribe. 33 portraits in color from paintings by Edward Herbert Miner. Vol. LXIX, pp. 253-268, Feb., 1936.

Dogs: Hunters All: A Roll Call of the Hounds. 31 portraits in color from paintings by Edward Herbert Miner. Vol. LXXII, pp. 467-482, Oct., 1937.

Dogs: Man's Hunting Partner, the Field Dog. 36 portraits in color from paintings by Edward Herbert Miner. Vol. LXXI, pp. 89-104, Jan., 1937.

Dogs: Non-sporting Dogs. 8 ills. in color from paintings from life by Walter A. Weber. Vol. LXXXIV, pp. 577-584, Nov., 1943.

Dogs: Wild Dogs and Working Dogs. 9 ills. in color from paintings by Walter A. Weber. Vol. LXXXVI, pp. 369-376, Sept., 1944.

Egypt: Life, Culture, and History of the Egyptians. 32 ills. in color from paintings by H. M. Herget. Vol. LXXX, pp. 436-514, Oct., 1941.

Faces and Fashions of Asia's Changeless Tribes. 26 ills. in color from paintings and drawings by Alexandre Iacovleff. Vol. LXIX, pp. 21-36, Jan., 1936.

Ferns: Marvels of Fern Life. 16 ills. in color from paintings by E. J. Geske. Vol. XLVII, pp. 547-562, May, 1925.

Fishes (Certain Citizens of the Warm Sea). 16 ills. in color from paintings by Hashime Murayama. Vol. XLI, pp. 37-52, Jan., 1922.

Fishes (Goldfish and Their Cultivation in America). 8 ills. in color from paintings by Hashime Murayama. Vol. XLVI, pp. 385-392, Oct., 1924.

Fishes (Treasure-House of the Gulf Stream). 16 ills. in color from paintings by Hashime Murayama. Vol. XXXIX, pp. 61-68, Jan., 1921.

Fishes: Flashes From Ocean Deeps. 16 ills. in color from paintings by Else Bostelmann, Helen D. Tee-Van, and E. J. Geske. Vol. LXVI, pp. 677-700, Dec., 1934.

National Geographic Society—*Continued*
Paintings—*Continued*

Fishes: Fresh-Water Denizens of the Far West (Salmon, Trout, etc.). 54 portraits in color from paintings by Hashime Murayama. Vol. LXXV, pp. 193-204, Feb., 1939.

Fishes: Fresh-Water Fishes of the United States. 16 ills. in color from paintings by Hashime Murayama. Vol. XLIV, pp. 133-148, Aug., 1923.

Fishes: Gleaming Fishes of Pacific Coastal Waters. 31 portraits in color from paintings by Hashime Murayama. Vol. LXXIV, pp. 467-498, Oct., 1938.

Fishes: Iridescent Denizens of the Miniature Aquarium. 8 ills. in color from paintings by Hashime Murayama. Vol. LIX, pp. 293-300, Mar., 1931.

Fishes: Luminous Life in the Depths of the Sea. 8 ills. in color from paintings by E. Bostelmann. Vol. LIX, pp. 667-674, June, 1931.

Fishes of Our North Atlantic Seaboard. 16 ills. in color from paintings by Hashime Murayama. Vol. XLIV, pp. 613-628, Dec., 1923.

Flowers (American Wild Flowers). 29 ills. in color from paintings by Mary E. Eaton. Vol. XXVII, pp. 483-506, May, 1915.

Flowers (Common American Wild Flowers). 17 ills. in color from paintings by Mary E. Eaton. Vol. XXIX, pp. 591-606, June, 1916.

Flowers (Exploring the Mysteries of Plant Life). 47 ills. in color from paintings by Mary E. Eaton. Vol. XLV, pp. 613-628, June, 1924.

Flowers (Midsummer Wild Flowers). 38 ills. in color from paintings by Mary E. Eaton. Vol. XLII, pp. 37-52, July, 1922.

Flowers (Our State Flowers). 30 ills. in color from paintings by Mary E. Eaton. Vol. XXXI, pp. 501-516, June, 1917.

Flowers (Pages From the Floral Life of America). 55 ills. in color from paintings by Mary E. Eaton. Vol. XLVIII, pp. 47-70, July, 1925.

Flowers: Floral Garlands of Prairie, Plain, and Woodland. 125 flower paintings in color by Edith S. Clements. Vol. LXXVI, pp. 224-270, Aug.. 1939.

Flowers: Wild Flowers of the West. 207 ills. in color from paintings by Edith S. Clements. Vol. LI, pp. 557-620, May, 1927.

Fowl: Domestic Fowls of Field, Park, and Farmyard. 16 ills. in color from paintings by Hashime Murayama. Vol. LVII, pp. 329-360, Mar., 1930.

Fowl of the Old and New World. 29 ills. in color from paintings by Hashime Murayama. Vol. LI, pp. 421-436, Apr., 1927.

National Geographic Society—*Continued*

Paintings—*Continued*

Frogs: Iridescent Beauty of Frogs and Toads. 14 ills. in color from paintings by Hashime Murayama. Vol. LXI, pp. 635-642, May, 1932.

Gauchos: Pioneer Gaucho Days. 8 ills. in color from paintings by Cesáreo Bernaldo de Quirós. Vol. LXIV, pp. 453-460, Oct., 1933.

Grasses: Beauties of Our Common Grasses. 8 ills. in color from paintings by E. J. Geske. Vol. XXXIX, pp. 627-634, June, 1921.

Greece: "Glory That Was Greece." 32 ills. in color from paintings by H. M. Herget. Vol. LXXXV, pp. 290-352, Mar., 1944.

Horses of the World. 24 ills. in color from paintings by Edward Herbert Miner. Vol. XLIV, pp. 479-526, Nov., 1923.

Indians: Aztecs Under the War God's Reign. 10 ills. in color from paintings by H. M. Herget. Vol. LXXI, pp. 735-742, June, 1937.

Indians: First Families of Southeastern America. 8 ills. in color from paintings by W. Langdon Kihn. Vol. LXXXIX, pp. 65-72, Jan., 1946.

Indians: In the Realm of the Sons of the Sun (Incas). 10 ills. in color from paintings by H. M. Herget. Vol. LXXIII, pp. 229-236, Feb., 1938.

Indians: Life and Death in Ancient Maya Land (Yucatán). 10 ills. in color from paintings by H. M. Herget. Vol. LXX, pp. 623-630, Nov., 1936.

Indians: Portraits of Ancient Mayas, a Peace-Loving People. 10 ills. in color from paintings by H. M. Herget. Vol. LXVIII, pp. 553-560, Nov., 1935.

Indians: Red Men of the Southwest. 25 ills. in color from paintings by W. Langdon Kihn. Vol. LXXVIII, pp. 557-596, Nov., 1940.

Indians: Totem-pole Builders. 16 ills. in color from paintings by W. Langdon Kihn. Vol. LXXXVII, pp. 33-48, Jan., 1945.

Indians: When Red Men Ruled Our Forests. 24 ills. in color from paintings by W. Langdon Kihn. Vol. LXXII, pp. 551-590, Nov., 1937.

Indians of Our Western Plains. 16 ills. in color from paintings by W. Langdon Kihn. Vol. LXXXVI, pp. 81-96, July, 1944.

Insect Rivals of the Rainbow. 24 ills. in color; 3 paintings by Hashime Murayama. Vol. LVI, pp. 29-84, July, 1929.

Insects: Rogues' Gallery of Imported Pests. 10 ills. in color from paintings by Hashime Murayama. Vol. LXXX, pp. 237-244, Aug., 1941.

National Geographic Society—*Continued*

Paintings—*Continued*

Jellyfishes—Living Draperies of Color. 8 ills. in color from paintings by William Crowder. Vol. L, pp. 193-200, Aug., 1926.

Jungle War: Bougainville and New Caledonia. 17 ills. in color from paintings by Lieut. William F. Draper. Vol. LXXXV, pp. 417-432, Apr., 1944.

Leopards, Lions, and Tigers (King of Cats and His Court). 20 ills. in color from paintings by Walter A. Weber. Vol. LXXXIII, pp. 223-254, Feb., 1943.

Mammals (Larger North American Mammals). 49 ills. in color from paintings by Louis Agassiz Fuertes. Vol. XXX, pp. 409-471, Nov., 1916.

Mammals (Smaller Mammals of North America). 59 ills. in color from paintings by Louis Agassiz Fuertes. Vol. XXXIII, pp. 404-465, May, 1918.

Marianas: Victory's Portrait in the Marianas. 17 ills. in color from paintings by Lt. William F. Draper, USNR. Vol. LXXXVIII, pp. 601-616, Nov., 1945.

Marine Biology: Exploring Neptune's Hidden World of Vivid Color. 8 ills. in color from paintings by E. Bostelmann. Vol. LXII, pp. 747-754, Dec., 1932.

Marine Biology: Fantastic Sea Life From Abyssal Depths. 8 ills. in color from paintings by E. Bostelmann. Vol. LXI, pp. 71-78, Jan., 1932.

Marine Biology: Sea Floor Aquarelles from Tongareva. 8 ills. in color from paintings by Else Bostelmann. Vol. LXXIV, pp. 383-390, Sept., 1938.

Marine Biology: Undersea Gardens of the North Atlantic Coast. 8 ills. in color from paintings by Else Bostelmann. Vol. LXX, pp. 217-224, Aug., 1936.

Monkeys: Manlike Apes of Jungle and Mountain. 10 ills. in color from paintings by Elie Cheverlange. Vol. LXXVIII, pp. 221-228, Aug., 1940.

Monkeys: Who's Who in the Monkey World. 40 portraits in color from paintings by Elie Cheverlange. Vol. LXXIII, pp. 625-648, May, 1938.

Mosquitoes: Life Story of the Mosquito. 10 ills. in color from paintings. Vol. LXXXV, pp. 181-188, Feb., 1944.

Mushrooms (Common Mushrooms of the United States). 16 ills. in color from paintings by Louis C. C. Krieger. Vol. XXXVII, pp. 423-438, May, 1920.

Mycetozoa: Marvels of Mycetozoa. 16 ills. in color from paintings by William Crowder. Vol. XLIX, pp. 425-440, Apr., 1926.

Pacific War: Painting History in the Pacific. 19 ills. in color from paintings by Lt. William F. Draper. Vol. LXXXVI, pp. 409-424, Oct., 1944.

National Geographic Society—*Continued*

Paintings—*Continued*

Paleontology : Parade of Life Through the Ages. 24 ills. in color from paintings by Charles R. Knight. Vol. LXXXI, pp. 149-180, Feb., 1942.

Plankton : Living Jewels of the Sea. 8 ills. in color from paintings by William Crowder. Vol. LII, pp. 291-298, Sept., 1927.

Rome : Ancient Rome Brought to Life. 32 ills. in color from paintings by H. M. Herget. Vol. XC, pp. 570-633, Nov., 1946.

Science Works for Mankind. 16 ills. in color from paintings by Thornton Oakley. Vol. LXXXVIII, pp. 737-752, Dec., 1945.

Seals of Our Nation, States, and Territories. 84 ills. in color from paintings by Carlotta Gonzales Lahey, Irvin E. Alleman, and Theodora Price. Vol. XC, pp. 17-32, July, 1946.

Ships of Our Navy. 8 ills. in color from paintings by Arthur Beaumont. Vol. LXXX, pp. 329-336, Sept., 1941.

Solar System's Eternal Show. 10 ills. in color from paintings by Charles Bittinger. Vol. LXXVI, pp. 17-24, July, 1939.

Spiders : Nature's Ingenious Spinners. 64 ills. in color from paintings by Hashime Murayama. Vol. LXIV, pp. 167-174, Aug., 1933.

Transportation (American Transportation Vital to Victory). 16 ills. in color from paintings by Thornton Oakley. Vol. LXXXIV, pp. 673-688, Dec., 1943.

U. S. Army (Painting the Army on Maneuvers). 16 ills. in color from paintings by Arthur Beaumont. Vol. LXXXII, pp. 577-600, Nov., 1942.

War Industries (American Industries Geared for War). 16 ills. in color from paintings by Thornton Oakley. Vol. LXXXII, pp. 717-732, Dec., 1942.

Wasps and Hornets : Farmers' Friends Among the Wasps and Hornets. 12 ills. in color from paintings by Hashime Murayama. Vol. LXXII, pp. 57-64, July, 1937.

Whales, Porpoises, and Dolphins. 31 ills. in color from paintings by Else Bostelmann. Vol. LXXVII, pp. 41-80, Jan., 1940.

Wildlife of Tabasco and Veracruz (Mexico). 19 ills. in color from paintings by Walter A. Weber. Vol. LXXXVII, pp. 193-208, Feb., 1945.

Paintings (Text) :

American Industries Geared for War. By Thornton Oakley. Text accompanying 16 colored illustrations from paintings by the author. Vol. LXXXII, pp. 716-734, 1 ill. in black and white, Dec., 1942.

National Geographic Society—*Continued*

Paintings (Text)—*Continued*

American Transportation Vital to Victory. By Thornton Oakley. Text accompanying 16 colored illustrations from paintings by the author. Vol. LXXXIV, pp. 671-672, Dec., 1943.

Navy Artist Paints the Aleutians. By Mason Sutherland. Text accompanying 16 colored illustrations from paintings by Lt. William F. Draper. Vol. LXXXIV, pp. 157-160, 4 ills. in black and white, Aug., 1943.

Painting History in the Pacific. Text accompanying 19 colored illustrations from paintings by Lt. William F. Draper. Vol. LXXXVI, p. 408, Oct., 1944.

Painting the Army on Maneuvers. By Arthur Beaumont. Text accompanying 16 colored illustrations from paintings by the author. Vol. LXXXII, pp. 601-602, Nov., 1942.

Painting the Field Dog Series (Acknowledgments). Vol. LXXI, p. 108, Jan., 1937.

Painting the Hound Series (Acknowledgments). Vol. LXXII, p. 484, Oct., 1937.

Paintings by Alexandre Iacovleff owned by The Society. Vol. LXIX, color plates IV, page 24 ; V, page 25, Jan., 1936.

Photographic Exhibits, Newspaper :

American Scene. 29 ills. from winning photographs in the Sixth Annual Newspaper National Snapshot Awards (1940), with explanatory note. Vol. LXXIX, pp. 220-246, Feb., 1941.

Americana. 11 ills. from winning photographs in the Seventh Annual Newspaper National Snapshot Awards (1941). Vol. LXXXI, pp. 657-666, May, 1942.

Photographic Laboratory. *See* Buildings.

Photographic Library. *See* Buildings.

Preservation of wild life encouraged by The Society. Vol. LXII, p. 263, Sept., 1932.

President :

Bell, Alexander Graham. Vol. X, p. 222, June, 1899.

Bell, Alexander Graham : Announcement of the Death of. Vol. XLII, p. 302, portrait, Sept., 1922.

Bell, Alexander Graham : Photograph of. Vol. XII, p. 353, Oct., 1901.

Bell, Alexander Graham : Photograph of. Inaugurates Telephone Service, New York to Chicago. Vol. LXXII, p. 397, Oct., 1937.

Bell, Alexander Graham : Resignation of. Vol. XIV, p. 254, June, 1903.

Gannett, Henry : Biography of. Vol. XXVI, pp. 609-613, 1 ill., Dec., 1914.

National Geographic Society—*Continued*
President—*Continued*

Gannett, Henry: Chief Geographer, U. S. Geological Survey, and President of The Society from 1910 to 1914. Vol. XC, p. 95, July, 1946.

Gannett, Henry: Death of. Vol. XXVI, p. 520, Nov., 1914.

Gannett, Henry: Election of. Vol. XXI, p. 88, Jan., 1910.

Gannett, Henry: Speeches by. Vol. XXII, p. 267, Mar., 1911. Vol. XXIII, p. 272, Mar., 1912. Vol. XXIV, p. 115, Jan., 1913.

Gilbert, Grove Karl: Career of. Vol. XI, p. 289, 1 ill., July, 1900.

Gilbert, Grove Karl: Eighth International Geographic Congress welcomed by. Vol. XV, p. 419, Oct., 1904.

Grosvenor, Gilbert: Address and introductions upon the occasion of the presentation of Hubbard Gold Medal to Charles A. Lindbergh. Vol. LIII, pp. 132, 134, 137, Jan., 1928.

Grosvenor, Gilbert: Address and introductions upon the occasion of the presentation of Hubbard Gold Medal to Commander Byrd. Vol. L, pp. 377, 383, Sept., 1926.

Grosvenor, Gilbert: Address given at the reception to Admiral Byrd. Vol. LXVIII, pp. 107-108, July, 1935.

Grosvenor, Gilbert: Address upon opening of The Society's fifty-fifth annual series of lectures in Constitution Hall, November 20, 1942. Vol. LXXXIII, pp. 277-278, Feb., 1943.

Grosvenor, Gilbert: Address upon the occasion of the presentation of Hubbard Gold Medal to Anne Morrow Lindbergh. Vol. LXV, pp. 791-792, June, 1934.

Grosvenor, Gilbert: Address upon the occasion of the presentation of Hubbard Gold Medal to Lincoln Ellsworth. Vol. LXX, p. 36, July, 1936.

Grosvenor, Gilbert: Address upon the occasion of the presentation of Hubbard Gold Medals to Captain Albert W. Stevens and Captain Orvil A. Anderson. Vol. LXIX, pp. 713-714, May, 1936.

Grosvenor, Gilbert: Address upon the occasion of the presentation of Special Gold Medal to Admiral Byrd. Vol. LVIII, pp. 229-231, Aug., 1930.

Grosvenor, Gilbert: Address upon the occasion of the presentation of Special Gold Medal to Amelia Earhart. Vol. LXII, pp. 359, 362, Sept., 1932.

Grosvenor, Gilbert: Address upon the occasion of the presentation of Special Gold Medal to Dr. Thomas C. Poulter. Vol. LXXII, p. 105, July, 1937.

Grosvenor, Gilbert: Address upon the occasion of the presentation of Special Gold Medal to Eckener. Vol. LVII, pp. 653-655, 681, 688, June, 1930.

National Geographic Society—*Continued*
President—*Continued*

Grosvenor, Gilbert: Address upon the occasion of the unveiling of the Peary memorial. Vol. XLI, pp. 641, 643, June, 1922.

Grosvenor, Gilbert: Air travel by. Vol. LXIII, p. 628, May, 1933.

Grosvenor, Gilbert: Alexander Graham Bell pays tribute to. Vol. LXIX, p. 148, Jan., 1936.

Grosvenor, Gilbert: Boyhood, spent in Turkey. Vol. LXXXVIII, pp. 237, 238, Aug., 1945.

Grosvenor, Gilbert: Byrd's North Pole flight aided by. Vol. L, p. 381, Sept., 1926.

Grosvenor, Gilbert: Cornerstone Document signed by. Vol. LXIX, p. 152, Jan., 1936.

Grosvenor, Gilbert: Election of. Vol. XXXVII, p. 345, Apr., 1920.

Grosvenor, Gilbert: Engaged as Editor, April 1, 1899. Vol. XXIII, p. 274, Mar., 1912.

Grosvenor, Gilbert: Gilbert Grosvenor Trail, Antarctica. Vol. LXIII, pp. 184, 193, 198; air view 218, Aug., 1930.

Grosvenor, Gilbert: Home of. Vol. LI, ill. 202, Feb., 1927. Vol. LVII, ill. 592, May, 1930.

Grosvenor, Gilbert: Lake, Alaskan, named for. Vol. XL, pp. 222, 287; ill. 284, 288, Sept., 1921. Vol. L, ill. 89, July, 1926.

Grosvenor, Gilbert: Letter announcing award of Hubbard Medal to Lindbergh. Vol. LII, p. 242, Aug., 1927.

Grosvenor, Gilbert: MacMillan Arctic Expedition. Vol. XLVIII, p. 226; ill. 224, Aug., 1925; ill. 476, Oct., 1925.

Grosvenor, Gilbert: Mount Grosvenor, China. Vol. LVIII, p. 415; color plates VII, p. 402; X, p. 428, Oct., 1930.

Grosvenor, Gilbert: Nansen received by. Vol. LVIII, ill. 22, July, 1930.

Grosvenor, Gilbert: Photographs of. Vol. XLI, p. 240, Mar., 1922; p. 640, June, 1922. Vol. XLVIII, p. 224, Aug., 1925; p. 476, Oct., 1925. Vol. L, p. 380, Sept., 1926. Vol. LIII, p. 135, Jan., 1928. Vol. LVII, pp. 583, 592, May, 1930. Vol. LVIII, p. 22, July, 1930; pp. 230, 233, Aug., 1930. Vol. LXII, p. 366, Sept., 1932. Vol. LXV, pp. 790, 792, June, 1934. Vol. LXVII, p. 137, Feb., 1935. Vol. LXVIII, pp. 112, 114, July, 1935. Vol. LXIX, pp. 126, 129, 132, 133, 134, 137, 139, 159, Jan., 1936; p. 712, May, 1936. Vol. LXXII, p. 107, July, 1937. Vol. LXXIII, p. 319, Mar., 1938. Vol. LXXVII, p. 717, June, 1945.

Grosvenor, Gilbert: Presentation of Hubbard Medal by President Truman to Gen. H. H. Arnold. Vol. LXXXIX, ill. 141, Feb., 1946.

Hubbard, Gardiner Greene. Vol. X, p. 222, June, 1899. Vol. XVII, pp. 23, 24, Jan., 1906.

National Geographic Society—*Continued*
President—*Continued*

Hubbard, Gardiner Greene : Alaskan Glacier named for. Vol. XLIX, p. 599, June, 1926.

Hubbard, Gardiner Greene : Dedication of Hubbard Memorial Hall. Vol. XIII, pp. 174-176, May, 1902.

Hubbard, Gardiner Greene : Seal of The Society designed under his supervision. Vol. XC, p. 34, July, 1946.

Hubbard, Gardiner Greene : Tribute to Mrs. Hubbard. Vol. XX, p. 1008, Nov., 1909.

McGee, W J : Election of. Vol. XV, p. 176, Apr., 1904.

Moore, Willis L. : Election of. Vol. XVI, p. 87, Feb., 1905.

Moore, Willis L. : Photograph of. Vol. XVIII, p. 587, Sept., 1907.

Moore, Willis L. : Special Gold Medal presented to Peary by. Vol. XXI, pp. 73-74, Jan., 1910.

Moore, Willis L. : Speeches by. Vol. XVII, pp. 23-27, 29, 32, 34-35, Jan., 1906. Vol. XVIII, pp. 49-51, 53, 56, Jan., 1907. Vol. XIX, pp. 55, 57, 61-62, 64, 68-69, 72, Jan., 1908. Vol. XX, pp. 77, 78, 82, 84, 86, 89, 91, Jan., 1909. Vol. XXI, pp. 63, 67-69, 73-74, 78-79, Jan., 1910.

Pillsbury, (Rear Adm.) John E. : Death of. Vol. XXXVII, p. 345, Apr., 1920.

Pillsbury, (Rear Adm.) John E. : Photograph of. Vol. XXXVII, p. 341, Apr., 1920.

Tittmann, O. H. : Election of. Vol. XXVII, p. 218, Feb., 1915.

See also Grosvenor, Gilbert *and* names of former presidents.

Presidents of the United States Address National Geographic Society:

Coolidge, Calvin : Presentation of Hubbard Gold Medals to Commander Byrd and Floyd Bennett. Vol. L, pp. 377-379 ; ill. 380, Sept., 1926. Vol. LII, ill. 239, Aug., 1927.

Coolidge, Calvin : Presentation of Hubbard Medal to Charles Lindbergh. Vol. LIII, pp. 134-135 ; ill. 139, Jan., 1928.

Hoover, Herbert : Presentation of Society's Special Medal to Amelia Earhart. Vol. LXII, pp. 358, 362-363 ; ill. 366, Sept., 1932.

Hoover, Herbert : Presentation of Special Gold Medal to Admiral Byrd. Vol. LVIII, pp. 231-232 ; ill. 233, Aug., 1930.

Presidents of the United States who have presented The Society's medals. Vol. LXII, p. 362, Sept., 1932.

Roosevelt, Theodore : Address, "Wild Man and Wild Beast in Africa," delivered before The Society, Nov. 18, 1910. Vol. XXII, pp. 1-33, Jan., 1911. Vol. LXII, p. 358, Sept., 1932.

Roosevelt, Theodore : Presentation of Hubbard Gold Medal to Robert Peary. Vol. XVIII, pp. 56-57, Jan., 1907. Vol. XXXVII, pp. 293, 322, Apr., 1920. Vol. LXII, p. 362, Sept., 1932.

National Geographic Society—*Continued*
Presidents of the United States Address National Geographic Society—*Continued*

Taft, William Howard : Address at Annual Dinner of The Society. Vol. XVII, pp. 22-37, Jan., 1906.

Taft, William Howard : Address upon Election as Honorary Member of The Society. Vol. XXII, pp. 267-284, 1 ill., Mar., 1911.

Taft, William Howard : Presentation of Hubbard Gold Medal to Sir Ernest H. Shackleton. Vol. XXI, p. 186, Mar., 1910.

Wilson, Woodrow : Presentation of Special Gold Medal to Colonel Goethals. Vol. XXV, pp. 679, 680, 683, June, 1914.

See also, for articles and additional information, Coolidge, Calvin ; Harding, Warren G. ; Hoover, Herbert ; McKinley, William ; Roosevelt, Franklin D. ; Roosevelt, Theodore ; Taft, William Howard ; Truman, Harry S. ; Wilson, Woodrow ; *and* National Geographic Society : Banquets.

Press Reports:

Article on The Society in Boston *Herald*, November 23, 1907. Vol. XVIII, p. 825, Dec., 1907.

Prizes:

Essay Contest on Norse Discoveries in America. Vol. X, pp. 31-32, Jan., 1899.
Chairman of Prize Committee 32
Judges of contest 32
Rules of contest 31-32

Essay Contest on Norse Discoveries in America. Vol. XI, p. 246, June, 1900.
Award of prizes 246

Franklin L. Burr Prize awarded to Capt. Albert W. Stevens. Vol. LXV, p. 626, May, 1934.

Grant Squires Prize awarded to F. H. King. Vol. XXIV, p. 115, Jan., 1913.

Property:

Purchase of lot adjoining Hubbard Memorial Hall. Vol. XX, p. 487, May, 1909.

Publications:

Book of Fishes. Vol. LXXXI, p. 730, June, 1942.

Book of Flags. Vol. LXXIX, p. 162, Feb., 1941.

Complete Reprints of Insignia Available. Vol. LXXXIV, p. 740, Dec., 1943.

Hunting Wild Life with Camera and Flashlight. By George Shiras, 3d. Vol. LXXVI, p. 87, July, 1939. Vol. LXXIX, p. 612, May, 1941. Vol. LXXXIII, p. 248, Feb., 1943.

Insignia and Decorations of the United States Armed Forces. Vol. LXXXVII, p. 185, Feb., 1945.

Insignia and Decorations of the United States Armed Forces. By Gilbert Grosvenor. Vol. LXXXVII, pp. 185-186, Feb., 1945.

National Geographic Society-U. S. Army Air Corps Stratosphere Flight of 1935 in Balloon *Explorer II* (Contributed Technical Papers, Stratosphere Series, No. 2). Vol. LXXI, p. 340, Mar., 1937 ; p. 802, June, 1937.

National Geographic Society—*Continued*
Publications—*Continued*

National Geographic Society's New "Book
of Birds." Vol. LXXI, p. 723, June,
1937. Vol. LXXII, p. 183, Aug., 1937.
Vol. LXXIV, p. 226, Aug., 1938; p. 775,
Dec., 1938. Vol. LXXVII, p. 121, Jan.,
1940.

Reprints Available for Mosquito, Classic
Greece, and Insignia Articles. Vol.
LXXXV, p. 536, May, 1944.

Reprints of Insignia. Vol. LXXXIV, color
plate XVI, p. 288, Sept., 1943; p. 488,
Oct., 1943; p. 740, Dec., 1943. Vol.
LXXXV, p. 536, May, 1944.

Revised Edition of Insignia, December 1,
1944. Vol. LXXXVII, p. 185, Feb., 1945.

Valley of Ten Thousand Smokes. Vol.
LXXXIV, p. 157, Aug., 1943. Vol.
LXXXV, p. 154, Feb., 1944.

See also National Geographic Magazine.

Receptions:

Admiral Byrd Receives New Honor from The
Society. Vol. LVIII, pp. 228-238, 4 ills.,
Aug., 1930.
 Article for The Magazine prepared by
  Byrd ....228 ; ill. 229
 Audience and distinguished guests...228,
  234–238
 Byrd (Rear Adm.), Richard E.: Address
  by 228, 232–233
 Byrd, (Rear Adm.) Richard E.: Gratitude
  for Society's aid................... 232
 Decorations 228
 Grosvenor, Gilbert: Introduction of Pres-
  ident Hoover 229–231
 Guests on platform................... 228
 Luncheon in honor of Byrd and his party
  232–233
 Members of Byrd Expedition guests of The
  Society ....232, 238 ; ill. 230
 Mrs. Hoover long a member of The Society 231
 Motion pictures of Byrd Expedition.... 232
 Presentation of Special Gold Medal by
  President Hoover.........231-232 ; ill. 233
 Reception by President Hoover at White
  House...........................ill. 230
 Travels of President Hoover............ 231

Annual Reception, March 22, 1899. Vol. X,
p. 328, Aug., 1899.

Annual Reception, April 12, 1901. Vol. XII,
p. 167, Apr., 1901 ; p. 208, May, 1901.

Commander Byrd Receives the Hubbard Gold
Medal : The First Explorer to Reach the
North Pole by Air Receives Coveted Honor
at Brilliant National Geographic Society
Reception (Also Presentation of Hub-
bard Gold Medal to Floyd Bennett). Vol.
L, pp. 377-388, 5 ills., 1 chart, Sept., 1926.
 Byrd, (Comdr.) Richard E.: Acceptance
  speech by 379–383
 Chart of route of flight.............. 386
 Committee appointed to examine Byrd's
  records 377, 384–385
 Coolidge, Calvin : Presentation speech by
  377–379
 Difficulties of Byrd's achievement....... 384

National Geographic Society—*Continued*
Receptions—*Continued*

 Finances and equipment of Byrd Arctic
  Expedition 382
 Grosvenor, Gilbert : Byrd Arctic Expedi-
  tion aided by..................... 381
 Grosvenor, Gilbert : Speeches by....377, 383
 Importance of aviation in Arctic explora-
  tion 382–383
 Instruments used by Byrd Arctic Expedi-
  tion ....ill. 378, 379
 Introduction of President Coolidge by Dr.
  Grosvenor......................... 377
 MacMillan Expedition aided by The So-
  ciety..........................379, 381
 Members and guests present............ 377
 Personnel of Byrd Arctic Expedition.... 381
 Presentation ceremony.............ill. 380
 Record of flight...................385–388
 Reports of committee approving Byrd's
  records...................377, 384–388
 Tribute to Bumstead sun-compass...381 ;
  ill. 378
 Wilbur, Curtis D.: Speech by.......383–384

First Airship Flight Around the World : Dr.
Hugo Eckener Tells of an Epochal Geo-
graphic Achievement upon the Occasion of
the Bestowal of the National Geographic
Society's Special Gold Medal. Vol. LVII,
pp. 653–688, 37 ills., June, 1930.
 Byrd, (Rear Adm.) Richard E.: Telegram
  of congratulations from.............. 688
 Eckener, (Dr.) Hugo: Acceptance speech
  by 655–681
 Grosvenor, Gilbert : Presentation speech
  653–655
 Members of audience.................. 653
 Tribute to Dr. Eckener............653, 655
 World travels of The Society's flag...... 655

National Geographic Society Honors Byrd
Antarctic Expedition. Vol. LXVIII, pp.
107-114, 6 ills., July, 1935.
 Byrd, (Rear Adm.) Richard E.: Address
  by.................107, 108–109 ; ill. 111
 Grosvenor, Gilbert : Address by.....107–108
 Grosvenor, Gilbert : Scroll presented by
  107, 108 ; ill. 112, 114
 Tribute to men of the Expedition....... 109

President Coolidge Bestows Lindbergh
Award : The National Geographic So-
ciety's Hubbard Medal Is Presented to
Aviator Before the Most Notable Gather-
ing in the History of Washington. Vol.
LIII, pp. 132-140, 4 ills., Jan., 1928.
 Contributions of U. S. to aviation...... 138
 Coolidge, Calvin : Presentation speech by
  132, 134–135 ; ill. 135
 Geographical distribution of The Society's
  members 137
 Grosvenor, Gilbert : Speech presenting
  President Coolidge..............132, 134
 Grosvenor, Gilbert : Speech presenting Sec-
  retary MacCracken.................. 137
 Guests of honor on platform.....132 ; ill. 135
 Lindbergh introduced by President Cool-
  idge 133–134
 Lindbergh's speech of acceptance....135, 137
 MacCracken, William P.: Speech by..137–139
 Members and guests present....132, 140 ;
  ill. 135

National Geographic Society—*Continued*
Receptions—*Continued*

Motion picture of history of aviation.139–140
Presentation ceremony........132–133,
                                    134–135 ; ill. 139
Radio broadcast of ceremony.......... 139
Ticket lines ....ill. 133

Society Awards Hubbard Medal to Anne
   Morrow Lindbergh. Vol. LXV, pp. 791-
   794, 4 ills., June, 1934.
   Grosvenor, Gilbert : Presentation speech
      by 791–792
   Guests 791, 792–793
   Lindbergh, Anne Morrow : Acceptance
      speech by 792
   Photographs of Officers and Mrs. Lind-
      bergh 790

Society's Special Medal Awarded to Amelia
   Earhart : First Woman to Receive Geo-
   graphic Distinction at Brilliant Ceremony
   in the National Capital. Vol. LXII, pp.
   358-367, 7 ills., Sept., 1932.
   Arrival of Miss Earhart............ill. 364
   Audience 358–359
   Decorations 358
   Earhart, Amelia : Account of transat-
      lantic flight....358, 363–367 ; ill. 359, 360
   First accounts of explorers contained in
      The Magazine..................... 358
   Grosvenor, Gilbert : Address introducing
      President Hoover 359, 362
   Guests on platform 358–359
   Hoover, Herbert : Presentation by...358,
                                        362–363
   Luncheon in honor of Miss Earhart..... 358
   Reception of Miss Earhart by President
      Hoover at the White House........ill. 366
   Tribute to Mrs. Hoover............... 362

Reprints. *See* Publications.

Research:

Appropriations for research. **Vol. XXVII,**
   p. 320, Mar., 1915.

Aurora Borealis : Mystery of Auroras : National Geographic Society and Cornell University Study Spectacular Displays in the
   Heavens. Vol. LXXV, pp. 689-690, May,
   1939.

Aurora Borealis : Research under the auspices of the National Geographic Society
   and Cornell University. Vol. LXXIX, p.
   580, May, 1941. Vol. LXXXVI, p. 640,
   Nov., 1944. Vol. XC, p. 387, Sept., 1946.

Cosmic Rays : Series of flights under auspices
   of National Geographic Society, U. S.
   Army Air Forces, and Bartol Research
   Foundation. Vol. XC, p. 387 ; ill. 388,
   Sept., 1946.

Promotion of research by The Society. Vol.
   XX, pp. 486-487, May, 1909.

Solar Radiation : Hunting an Observatory :
   A Successful Search for a Dry Mountain
   on Which to Establish the National Geographic Society's Solar Radiation Station.
   By C. G. Abbot. Vol. L, pp. 503-518, 13
   ills., 1 quarter-page map, Oct., 1926.

National Geographic Society—*Continued*
Research—*Continued*

Solar Radiation : Measuring the Sun's Heat
   and Forecasting the Weather : The Na-
   tional Geographic Society to Maintain a
   Solar Station in a Remote Part of the
   World to Coöperate with Smithsonian
   Institution Stations in California and
   Chile. By C. G. Abbot. Vol. XLIX, pp.
   111-126, 15 ills., 1 chart, Jan., 1926.

Solar Radiation : National Geographic Society-Smithsonian Institution solar radiation station, Mount Brukkaros, South
   West Africa. Vol. LVII, p. 483, Apr.,
   1930.

See also Expeditions.

Rhododendrons:

Rhododendron seeds presented to Golden
   Gate Park, San Francisco, by The Society.
   Vol. LV, p. 729, June, 1929. Vol. LXI,
   p. 428, Apr., 1932.

Rhododendrons presented to Kew Gardens,
   London, by The Society. Vol. LV, color
   plate IV, p. 572, May, 1929. Vol. LXVIII,
   pp. 143, 147 ; ill. 146, Aug., 1935.

School Service Department:

Geographic News Bulletins. Vol. XXXVII,
   p. 343, Apr., 1920.

Schoolroom Aids Provided by the National
   Geographic Society. Vol. LXXX, p. 366,
   Sept., 1941 ; p. 824, Dec., 1941.

Sight-seeing in School : Taking Twenty Mil-
   lion Children on a Picture Tour of the
   World. By Jessie L. Burrall. Vol. XXXV,
   pp. 489-503, 14 ills., June, 1919.
   Educational value of The Society's photo-
      graphs 499
   Pictorial Geography series.............503
   Separate picture sets for schools........ 501
   Use of The Magazine in schools......497, 499

Seal:

Authorization and design of The Society's
   Seal. Vol. XC, p. 34 ; color plate, p. 28,
   July, 1946.

Bronze Seal of The Society, set in lobby
   floor. Vol. LXIX, ill. 157, Jan., 1936. Vol.
   XC, ill. 11, July, 1946.

Secretary impressing The Society's Seal on
   Membership Certificate. Vol. XC, ill. 39,
   July, 1946.

Society's Seal on marker erected by Eclipse
   Expedition on Canton Island. Vol. LXXII,
   ill. 376, Sept., 1937.

Secretary:

Austin, O. P. : Election of. Vol. XIV, p.
   425, Nov., 1903.

Austin, O. P. : Report by. Vol. XVI, p. 87,
   Feb., 1905.

Austin, O. P. : Report by. Vol. XXI, pp.
   88-89, Jan., 1910.

Austin, O. P. : Report by. Vol. XXII, pp.
   211, 214, Feb., 1911.

National Geographic Society—*Continued*

Secretary—*Continued*

Austin, O. P.: Report by. Vol. XXIV, p. 255, Feb., 1913.

Henry, A. J.: Report by. Vol. XIII, p. 80, Feb., 1902.

Henry, A. J.: Resignation of. Vol. XIV, p. 425, Nov., 1903.

Hutchison, George W.: Memorial Tribute to George W. Hutchison. Vol. LXXXVII, p. 720, 1 ill., June, 1945.

Hutchison, George W.: Photographs of. Vol. LXV, p. 790, June, 1934. Vol. LXXIX, color plate, p. 432, Apr., 1941.

McGee, W J: Speech by. Vol. XIX, p. 69, Jan., 1908.

McKnew, Thomas W.: Impressing The Society's Seal on Membership Certificate. Vol. XC, ill. 39, July, 1946.

McKnew, Thomas W.: Presentation of Hubbard Medal by President Truman to Gen. H. H. Arnold. Vol. LXXXIX, ill. 141, Feb., 1946.

Newell, Frederick Haynes: Resignation of. Vol. X, p. 474, Nov., 1899.

Stanley-Brown, Joseph: Election of. **Vol. X,** p. 475, Nov., 1899.

See also names of secretaries.

Sequoia National Park:

National Geographic Society Completes Its Gifts of Big Trees. Vol. XL, pp. 85-86, July, 1921.

Amount of funds subscribed..........85–86

Area of purchase......................85 86

Contributors to fund.................. 85

Fall, Albert B.: Letter acknowledging gift 86

Our Big Trees Saved. Vol. XXXI, pp. 1-11, 10 ills., Jan., 1917.

Letter from Gilbert H. Grosvenor to Secretary Lane announcing gift..........5, 7

Letter from Secretary Lane acknowledging gift 7

Resolution of Board of Managers appropriating purchase fund............. 5

Tablet commemorating The Society to be placed on one of the trees........... 7

Photograph of Sequoia National Park. Vol. LXIV, duotone plate V, p. 21, July, 1933.

Society's gift of Big Trees. Vol. LXVI, p. 231, Aug., 1934.

Tablet commemorating Society's gift. Vol. LV, ill. 719, 733, June, 1929. Vol. LXVI, ill. 225, Aug., 1934.

Staff Members. *See* Editorial Department.

Stratosphere Balloon:

Explorer II. Vol. LXXIX, p. 168, Feb., 1941. Vol. LXXXI, p. 471, Apr., 1942.

See also National Geographic Society: Expeditions: Stratosphere.

Supplements. *See* Index to Maps, p. 594; Pictorial Enlargements and Panoramas.

National Geographic Society—*Continued*

Translators. Vol. LXXXIV, p. 698; ill. 695, Dec., 1943.

Treasurer:

Edson, John Joy: Photograph of. Vol. LXV, p. 790, June, 1934.

Edson, John Joy: Report by. Vol. XIII, p. 80, Feb., 1902.

Edson, John Joy: Report by. Vol. XXI, pp. 89-90, Jan., 1910.

Edson, John Joy: Report by. Vol. XXII, p. 214, Feb., 1911.

Edson, John Joy: Report by. Vol. XXIV, p. 256, Feb., 1913.

Fleming, Robert V.: Presentation of Hubbard Medal by President Truman to Gen. H. H. Arnold. Vol. LXXXIX, ill. 141, Feb., 1946.

Vice-President:

Gannett, Henry: Chairman of committee appointed to consider claims of Cook and Peary. Vol. XX, pp. 921-922, Nov., 1909.

Gannett, Henry: Chairman of Research Committee. Vol. XX, p. 486, May, 1909.

Gannett, Henry: Elected Member of Geographical Society of Paris. Vol. XVIII, p. 428, June, 1907.

Gannett, Henry: Election of. Vol. XVI, p. 87, Feb., 1905.

Gilbert, Grove Karl: Election of. Vol. XV, p. 176, Apr., 1904.

La Gorce, John Oliver: Election of. Vol. XXXVI, p. 345, Apr., 1920.

La Gorce, John Oliver: Expedition to the Bahamas. Vol. LXII, p. 452, Oct., 1932.

La Gorce, John Oliver: Meteorological station, Antarctica, named for. Vol. LVIII, p. 184; ill. 193, Aug., 1930.

La Gorce, John Oliver: Mountain, Alaskan, named for. Vol. XL, pp. 222, 287, Sept., 1921.

La Gorce, John Oliver: Photographs of. Vol. XLVIII, p. 352, Sept., 1925. Vol. LVIII, p. 230, Aug., 1930. Vol. LIX, p. 2, Jan., 1931. Vol. LX, p. 391, Oct., 1931. Vol. LXII, p. 366, Sept., 1932. Vol. LXV, p. 790, June, 1934. Vol. LXIX, pp. 126, 133, 134, 156, 159, Jan., 1936. Vol. LXXXIV, p. 336, Sept., 1943.

La Gorce, John Oliver: Presentation of Hubbard Medal by President Truman to Gen. H. H. Arnold. Vol. LXXXIX, ill. 141, Feb., 1946.

McGee, W J: Photograph of. Vol. XII, p. 354, Oct., 1901.

Pillsbury, John E.: Election of. Vol. XXVII, p. 218, Feb., 1915.

Tittmann, O. H.: Election of. Vol. XXI, p. 88, Jan., 1910.

National Geographic Society—*Continued*
Vice-President—*Continued*

Tittmann, O. H.: Speech by. Vol. XXIII, pp. 284, 287, Mar., 1912.

See also names of vice-presidents.

War Work (World Wars I and II) :

Appeal to Members of the National Geographic Society. Vol. XXXIII, pp. 347, 348, Apr., 1918.

Army, Navy, Government Departments, and private organizations use The Society's maps, photographs, and publications. Vol. LXXXI, p. 333, Mar., 1942. Vol. LXXXII, p. 767, Dec., 1942. Vol. LXXXIII, p. 265, Feb., 1943 ; p. 482, Apr., 1943 ; pp. 763, 766 ; ill. 763, June, 1943. Vol. LXXXIV, pp. 288, 289 ; ill. 274, Sept., 1943. Vol. LXXXV, p. 83 ; ill. 93, Jan., 1944 ; p. 415, Apr., 1944. Vol. LXXXVI, pp. 66-67, 71, 72 ; ill. 69, July, 1944 ; p. 263 ; ill. 279, Sept., 1944 ; p. 450 ; ill. 450, Oct., 1944. Vol. LXXXVIII, ill. 7, July, 1945 ; pp. 709, 753, Dec., 1945.

Blood donors. Vol. LXXXIV, ill. 610, Nov., 1943.

Day With Our Boys in the Geographic Wards. By Carol Corey. Vol. XXXIV, pp. 69-80, 8 ills., July, 1918.

National Geographic Society in War Time. By Maj. Gen. A. W. Greely. Vol. XXXIII, pp. 369-375, 5 ills., Apr., 1918.
    Liberty Loan investment............372–373
    National Geographic wards........373, 375
    President Wilson's suggestions regarding The Society's war work.............. 369
    Society's war work directed by Gilbert Grosvenor 375
    U. S. Military Hospitals. ill. 370, 371 372, 373
    War Savings Stamp club.............. 373

Practical Patriotism. Vol. XXXII, pp. 279-280, Sept., 1917.
    American Red Cross campaign aided by.. 279
    Food conservation advertised by........ 280
    Liberty Loan campaigns aided by....279, 280
    National Geographic Society Ward...... 280
    Patriotic flag number of The Magazine 279, 280
    Red Cross work by members of staff.... 279
    Services of addressing department donated 279
    Subscriptions donated to Army and Navy. 280

Spirit of The Geographic. Vol. XXXIV, pp. 434-440, 4 ills., Nov., 1918.
    Contributions received 434-435, 437
    Geographic wards 434-435, 437, 440
    Message from a soldier in a Geographic ward 440

Your Society Aids War Effort. Vol. LXXXIII, pp. 277-278, 1 ill., Feb., 1943.

National Geographic Society and Geographic Work. Vol. XX, pp. 485-487, May, 1909.

National Geographic Society's Map of Northeastern United States. Text accompanying special map supplement in colors. Vol. LXXXVIII, pp. 361-362, Sept., 1945.

National Geographic Society's Notable Year. Vol. XXXVII, pp. 338-345, 2 ills., Apr., 1920.

National Growth and National Character. By W J McGee. Vol. X, pp. 185-206, June, 1899.

National Monuments:

Arizona Sands, Home of the Cactus King. 11 ills. from photographs. Vol. LXXI, pp. 521-528, Apr., 1937.

Bursts of Color in Sculptured Utah. 22 ills. in color from natural-color photographs. Vol. LXIX, pp. 593-616, May, 1936.

Colossal Natural Bridges of Utah. Vol. XV, pp. 367-369, 2 ills., Sept., 1904.

Crater Lake and Yosemite Through the Ages. By Wallace W. Atwood, Jr. Paintings by Eugene Kingman. Vol. LXXI, pp. 327-343, 7 ills. in black and white, 13 ills. in color, Mar., 1937.

Everyday Life in Pueblo Bonito : As Disclosed by the National Geographic Society's Archeologic Explorations in the Chaco Canyon National Monument, New Mexico. By Neil M. Judd. Vol. XLVIII, pp. 227-262, 37 ills., 1 two-thirds-page map, Sept., 1925.

Great Natural Bridges of Utah. Vol. XVIII, pp. 199-204, 3 ills., Mar., 1907.

Great Natural Bridges of Utah. By Byron Cummings. Vol. XXI, pp. 157-167, 7 ills., Feb., 1910.

Great Rainbow Natural Bridge of Southern Utah. By Joseph E. Pogue. Vol. XXII, pp. 1048-1056, 6 ills., Nov., 1911.

New National Geographic Society Expedition : Ruins of Chaco Canyon, New Mexico, Nature-Made Treasure-Chest of Aboriginal American History, to be Excavated and Studied ; Work Begins This Month. Vol. XXXIX, pp. 637-643, 7 ills., June, 1921.

Our Greatest National Monument : The National Geographic Society Completes Its Explorations In the Valley of Ten Thousand Smokes. By Robert F. Griggs. Vol. XL, pp. 219-292, 73 ills. in black and white, 16 ills. in color, 1 page and 1 three-quarters-page maps, Sept., 1921.

Our National Parks. By L. F. Schmeckebier. Vol. XXIII, pp. 531-579, 41 ills., 1 page map, June, 1912.

Photographing the Marvels of the West in Colors. By Fred Payne Clatworthy. Vol. LIII, pp. 694-719, 30 ills. in color, June, 1928.

Pueblo Bonito Expedition of the National Geographic Society. By Neil M. Judd. Vol. XLI, pp. 323-331, 10 ills., 1 diagram, Mar., 1922.

Recent Eruption of Katmai Volcano in Alaska. By George C. Martin. Vol. XXIV, pp. 131-181, 45 ills., 1 page map, 1 diagram, Feb., 1913.

Saguaro Forest (Arizona). By H. L. Shantz. Vol. LXXI, pp. 515-532, 18 ills., Apr., 1937.

Scenery of North America. By James Bryce. Vol. XLI, pp. 339-389, 45 ills., Apr., 1922.

National Monuments—*Continued*

Ten Thousand Smokes Now a National Monument: The President of the United States Sets Aside for the American People the Extraordinary Valley Discovered and Explored by the National Geographic Society. Vol. XXXV, pp. 359-366, 5 ills., Apr., 1919.

Valley of Ten Thousand Smokes: An Account of the Discovery and Exploration of the Most Wonderful Volcanic Region in the World. By Robert F. Griggs. Vol. XXXIII, pp. 115-169, 46 ills., 1 half-page map, panorama, Feb., 1918.

Valley of Ten Thousand Smokes: National Geographic Society's Explorations in the Katmai District of Alaska. By Robert F. Griggs. Vol. XXXI, pp. 12-68, 51 ills., 1 half-page map, Jan., 1917.

Volcanoes of Alaska (Eruption of Mt. Katmai in June, 1912). Vol. XXIII, pp. 824-832, 11 ills., Aug., 1912.

Wheeler National Monument. Vol. XX, pp. 837-840, 4 ills., Sept., 1909.

White Sands of Alamogordo (New Mexico): A Dry Ocean of Granular Gypsum Billows Under Desert Winds in a New National Playground. By Carl P. Russell. Vol. LXVIII, pp. 250-264, 12 ills., Aug., 1935.

National Parks:

Among the Big Trees of California. By John R. White. Vol. LXVI, pp. 219-232, 14 ills., Aug., 1934.

Bats of Carlsbad Cavern (New Mexico). By Vernon Bailey. Vol. XLVIII, pp. 321-330, 11 ills., Sept., 1925.

Bursts of Color in Sculptured Utah. 22 ills. in color from natural-color photographs. Vol. LXIX, pp. 593-616, May, 1936.

Fabulous Yellowstone: Even Stranger Than the Tales of Early Trappers is the Truth About This Steaming Wonderland. By Frederick G. Vosburgh. Vol. LXXVII, pp. 769-794, 15 ills. in black and white, 9 ills. in color, 1 two-thirds-page map, June, 1940.

First National Park East of Mississippi River (Mount Desert Island). Vol. XXIX, pp. 622-626, 5 ills., June, 1916.

Game Country Without Rival in America: The Proposed Mount McKinley National Park. By Stephen R. Capps. Vol. XXXI, pp. 69-84, 14 ills., 1 half-page map, Jan., 1917.

Grand Canyon Bridge. By Harriet Chalmers Adams. Vol. XXXIX, pp. 645-650, 8 ills., June, 1921.

Indiana's Unrivaled Sand-Dunes—A National Park Opportunity. By Orpheus Moyer Schantz. Vol. XXXV, pp. 430-441, 18 ills., May, 1919.

Land of the Best. By Gilbert H. Grosvenor. Vol. XXIX, pp. 327-430, 71 ills. in black and white, 33 ills. in color, panorama, Apr., 1916.

Mind's-Eye Map of America. By Franklin K. Lane. Vol. XXXVII, pp. 479-518, 25 ills. in black and white, 8 ills. in color, June, 1920.

National Parks—*Continued*

National Geographic Society Completes Its Gifts of Big Trees. Vol. XL, pp. 85-86, July, 1921.

Nature's Scenic Marvels of the West. 17 ills. in duotone. Vol. LXIV, pp. 16-33, July, 1933.

New Discoveries in Carlsbad Cavern (New Mexico); Vast Subterranean Chambers with Spectacular Decorations Are Explored, Surveyed, and Photographed. By Willis T. Lee. Vol. XLVIII, pp. 301-319, 19 ills., 1 three-quarters-page map, Sept., 1925.

New National Park (Glacier National Park). By Guy Elliott Mitchell. Vol. XXI, pp. 215-223, 6 ills., Mar., 1910.

Our Big Trees Saved. Vol. XXXI, pp. 1-11, 10 ills., Jan., 1917.

Our National Parks. By L. F. Schmeckebier. Vol. XXIII, pp. 531-579, 41 ills., 1 page map, June, 1912.

Patriotic Pilgrimage to Eastern National Parks: History and Beauty Live Along Paved Roads, Once Indian Trails, Through Virginia, North Carolina, Tennessee, Kentucky, and West Virginia. By Leo A. Borah. Vol. LXV, pp. 669-702, 18 ills. in black and white, 28 ills. in color, 1 two-page map, June, 1934.

Peaks and Parks of Western Canada. 11 ills. from photographs; 5 ills. by W. J. Oliver. Vol. LXXX, pp. 516-526, Oct., 1941.

Photographing the Marvels of the West in Colors. By Fred Payne Clatworthy. Vol. LIII, pp. 694-719, 30 ills. in color, June, 1928.

Rambling Around the Roof of Eastern America (Great Smoky Mountains). By Leonard C. Roy. Vol. LXX, pp. 243-266, 25 ills., 1 page map, Aug., 1936.

Restoration of Colonial Williamsburg. By W. A. R. Goodwin. Vol. LXXI, pp. 402-443, 21 ills. in black and white, 25 ills. in color, Apr., 1937.

Scenery of North America. By James Bryce. Vol. XLI, pp. 339-389, 45 ills., Apr., 1922.

Scenic Glories of Western United States. 5 ills. in color from autochromes by Fred Payne Clatworthy. Vol. LVI, pp. 222-231, Aug., 1929.

Unique Island of Mount Desert. By George B. Dorr, Ernest Howe Forbush, and M. L. Fernald. Vol. XXVI, pp. 75-89, 7 ills., July, 1914.

United States: Western Views in the Land of the Best. 16 ills. in color from autochromes by Fred Payne Clatworthy. Vol. XLIII, pp. 405-420, Apr., 1923.

Virginia's Colonial Heritage. 25 ills. in color from natural-color photographs. Vol. LXXI, pp. 417-440, Apr., 1937.

Western National Parks Invite America Out of Doors. 17 ills. in duotone from photographs by G. A. Grant, W. M. Rush, Merl La Voy, and J. S. Dixon. Vol. LXVI, pp. 65-80, July, 1934.

Where Hot Pools Seethe and Geysers Spout (Yellowstone). 9 ills. in color from natural-color photographs by Edwin L. Wisherd. Vol. LXXVII, pp. 775-782, June, 1940.

National Parks—*Continued*

Wonderland of California. By Herman Whitaker. Vol. XXVIII, pp. 56-104, 45 ills., July, 1915.

Wonderland of Glaciers and Snow (Mt. Rainier National Park). By Milnor Roberts. Vol. XX, pp. 530-537, 8 ills., June, 1909.

National Trust for Places of Historic Interest or Natural Beauty:

Preservation of England's Historic and Scenic Treasures. By Eric Underwood. Vol. LXXXVII, pp. 413-440, 24 ills., 1 two-page map, Apr., 1945.

Nation's Capital (Washington, D. C.). By James Bryce. Vol. XXIV, pp. 717-750, 26 ills., June, 1913.

Nation's Capital by Night (Washington, D. C.). By Volkmar Wentzel. With 16 illustrations in duotone from photographs by the author. Vol. LXXVII, pp. 514-530, Apr., 1940.

Nation's Pride (Natural Resources). By Franklin K. Lane. Vol. XXVIII, pp. 589-606, 6 ills., Dec., 1915.

Nation's Undeveloped Resources. By Franklin K. Lane. Vol. XXV, pp. 183-225, 32 ills., Feb., 1914.

Native Oysters of the West Coast. By Robert E. C. Stearns. Vol. XIX, pp. 224-226, Mar., 1908.

Native Son's Rambles in Oregon. By Amos Burg. Vol. LXV, pp. 173-234, 39 ills. in black and white, 24 ills. in color, 1 two-page map, Feb., 1934.

Natural Bridges:

Colossal Natural Bridges of Utah. Vol. XV, pp. 367-369, 2 ills., Sept., 1904.

Encircling Navajo Mountain with a Pack-Train: An Expedition to a Hitherto Untraversed Region of Our Southwest Discovers a New Route to Rainbow Natural Bridge. By Charles L. Bernheimer. Vol. XLIII, pp. 197-224, 33 ills., 1 half-page map, Feb., 1923.

Great Natural Bridges of Utah. Vol. XVIII, pp. 199-204, 3 ills., Mar., 1907.

Great Natural Bridges of Utah. By Byron Cummings. Vol. XXI, pp. 157-167, 7 ills., Feb., 1910.

Great Rainbow Natural Bridge of Southern Utah. By Joseph E. Pogue. Vol. XXII, pp. 1048-1056, 6 ills., Nov., 1911.

Natural-color photograph of an eclipse. 1 ill. in color by Irvine C. Gardner. Vol. LXXI, p. 178, Feb., 1937.

Natural-Gas, Oil and Coal Supply of the United States. Vol. XV, p. 186, Apr., 1904.

Natural History:

What the Fighting Yanks See. By Wanda Burnett. Vol. LXXXVI, pp. 451-476, 27 ills., Oct., 1944.

Natural History—*Continued*

Wildlife of Tabasco and Veracruz (Mexico). By Walter A. Weber. With 19 ills. in color from paintings by the author. Vol. LXXXVII, pp. 187-216, 7 ills. in black and white, 1 two-thirds-page map, Feb., 1945.

See also Birds; Crustaceans; Fishes and Fisheries; Insects; Mammals; Marine Biology; Mollusks; Paleontology; Plants; Reptiles; Wildlife.

Naturalist with MacMillan in the Arctic. By Walter N. Koelz. Vol. XLIX, pp. 299-318, 22 ills. in color, Mar., 1926.

Naturalist's Journey Around Vera Cruz and Tampico. By Frank M. Chapman. Vol. XXV, pp. 532-562, 31 ills., May, 1914.

Nature and Man in Ethiopia. By Wilfred H. Osgood. Vol. LIV, pp. 121-176, 64 ills., 1 two-thirds-page map, Aug., 1928.

Nature Paints New Mexico. 25 ills. in color from natural-color photographs by Richard H. Stewart. Vol. LXXIII, pp. 537-568, May, 1938.

Nature's Ingenious Spinners (Spiders). 64 ills. in color from paintings by Hashime Murayama. Vol. LXIV, pp. 167-174, Aug., 1933.

Nature's Most Amazing Mammal: Elephants, Unique Among Animals, Have Many Human Qualities When Wild That Make Them Foremost Citizens of Zoo and Circus. By Edmund Heller. Vol. LXV, pp. 729-759, 37 ills., June, 1934.

Nature's Most Dramatic Spectacle (Eclipse). By S. A. Mitchell. Vol. LXXII, pp. 361-376, 16 ills., 1 half-page map, Sept., 1937.

Nature's Scenic Marvels of the West. 17 ills. in duotone. Vol. LXIV, pp. 16-33, July, 1933.

Nature's Transformation at Panama: Remarkable Changes in Faunal and Physical Conditions in the Gatun Lake Region. By George Shiras, 3d. Vol. XXVIII, pp. 159-194, 33 ills., 2 page maps, Aug., 1915.

Nauru, the Richest Island in the South Seas. By Rosamond Dodson Rhone. Vol. XL, pp. 559-589, 24 ills., Dec., 1921.

Navajo Indian Reservation, Utah-Arizona:

Flaming Cliffs of Monument Valley. By Lt. Jack Breed, USNR. With 9 ills. in color from natural-color photographs by the author and Warren T. Mithoff. Vol. LXXXVIII, pp. 452-461, Oct., 1945.

Navajo Mountain, Utah:

Encircling Navajo Mountain with a Pack-Train: An Expedition to a Hitherto Untraversed Region of Our Southwest Discovers a New Route to Rainbow Natural Bridge. By Charles L. Bernheimer. Vol. XLIII, pp. 197-224, 33 ills., 1 half-page map, Feb., 1923.

Navajos (Indians) :

Flaming Cliffs of Monument Valley. By Lt. Jack Breed, USNR. With 9 ills. in color from natural-color photographs by the author and Warren T. Mithoff. Vol. LXXXVIII, pp. 452-461, Oct., 1945.

Indian Tribes of Pueblo Land. By Matthew W. Stirling. Vol. LXXVIII, pp. 549-596, 16 ills. in black and white, 25 ills. in color, Nov., 1940.

New Mexico Melodrama. By Frederick Simpich. Vol. LXXIII, pp. 529-569, 19 ills. in black and white, 25 ills. in color, 1 two-page map, May, 1938.

Red Men of the Southwest. 25 ills. in color from paintings by W. Langdon Kihn. Vol. LXXVIII, pp. 557-596, Nov., 1940.

Naval Air Transport Service:

Flying Our Wounded Veterans Home. By Catherine Bell Palmer. Vol. LXXXVIII, pp. 363-384, 17 ills., Sept., 1945.

Naval Flags of the World. By Byron McCandless and Gilbert Grosvenor. Vol. XXXII, pp. 347-369, 311 ills. in color, Oct., 1917.

Navarro, Don Juan N.:

Mexico of Today. By Don Juan N. Navarro. Part I, Vol. XII, pp. 152-157, Apr., 1901. Part II, Vol. XII, pp. 176-179, May, 1901. Part III, Vol. XII, pp. 235-238, June, 1901.

Navassa Island, West Indies:

Important New Guide to Shipping: Navassa Light, on a Barren Island in the West Indies, Is the First Signal for the Panama Canal. By George R. Putnam. Vol. XXXIV, pp. 401-406, 3 ills., 1 half-page map, Nov., 1918.

Navigating the *Norge* (Airship) from Rome to the North Pole and Beyond: The Designer and Pilot of the First Dirigible to Fly Over the Top of the World Describes a Thrilling Voyage of More Than 8,000 Miles. By Gen. Umberto Nobile. Vol. LII, pp. 177-215, 36 ills., 1 page map, Aug., 1927.

Navigation:

Heavens Above: On Land, Sea, and in the Air the Stars Serve Modern Man as Map, Compass, and Clock. By Donald H. Menzel. With 12 charts, designed by the author, showing star positions for each month, and 13 drawings of the constellations by Carlotta Gonzales Lahey. Vol. LXXXIV, pp. 97-128, 1 map (two-page spread), July, 1943.

Revealing Earth's Mightiest Ocean (Pacific). By Albert W. Atwood. Vol. LXXXIV, pp. 291-306, 10 ills., special map supplement, Sept., 1943.

Navigators. *See* Discoverers; Raleigh, (Sir) Walter.

Navy Artist Paints the Aleutians. By Mason Sutherland. Paintings by Lt. William F. Draper. Vol. LXXXIV, pp. 157-176, 4 ills. in black and white, 16 ills. in color, Aug., 1943.

Navy Wings over the Pacific. 12 ills. in color from U. S. Navy official photographs. Vol. LXXXVI, pp. 241-248, Aug., 1944.

Nayarit (State), Mexico :

Along the Old Spanish Road in Mexico: Life Among the People of Nayarit and Jalisco, Two of the Richest States of the Southern Republic. By Herbert Corey. Vol. XLIII, pp. 225-281, 36 ills. in black and white, 16 ills. in color, 1 half-page map, Mar., 1923.

Nealley, George True:

Recent Bequests by Members of the National Geographic Society. Vol. XLIX, p. 474, Apr., 1926.

Neapolitan Blues and Imperial Purple of Roman Italy. 12 ills. in color from natural-color photographs by Hans Hildenbrand, Luigi Pellerano, and Gervais Courtellemont. Vol. LXVI, pp. 203-210, Aug., 1934.

Near East:

American Alma Maters in the Near East. By Maynard Owen Williams. Vol. LXXXVIII, pp. 237-256, 16 ills., Aug., 1945.

New Map of Europe and the Near East. Text accompanying special map supplement in colors. Vol. LXXXIII, pp. 762-763, 1 ill., June, 1943.

See also Egypt; Iraq; Lebanon; Palestine; Syria; Trans-Jordan; Turkey.

Nearest the Pole (Rear Adm. Robert E. Peary's Address to The Society). Vol. XVIII, pp. 446-450, July, 1907.

Nebaj, Guatemala :

To Market in Guatemala. By Luis Marden. With 19 ills. in color from natural-color photographs by Giles Greville Healey and Charles S. Pineo. Vol. LXXXVIII, pp. 87-104, July, 1945.

Nebraska:

Cornhusker State Highlights. 23 ills. in color from natural-color photographs by B. Anthony Stewart. Vol. LXXXVII, pp. 521-536, May, 1945.

Nebraska, the Cornhusker State. By Leo A. Borah. Vol. LXXXVII, pp. 513-542, 6 ills. in black and white, 23 ills. in color, 1 map (two-page spread), May, 1945.

Taming the Outlaw Missouri River. By Frederick Simpich. Vol. LXXXVIII, pp. 569-598, 25 ills., 1 two-page map, Nov., 1945.

Nedjef. *See* Najaf.

Need of Conserving the Beauty and Freedom of Nature in Modern Life. By Charles W. Eliot. Vol. XXVI, pp. 67-74, 4 ills., July, 1914.

Needham, James G.:

An Insect Community Lives in Flower Heads. By James G. Needham. Vol. XC, pp. 340-356, 5 ills. in black and white, 11 ills. in color, Sept., 1946.

Needs Abroad. By Ian Malcolm. Vol. XXXI, pp. 427-433, 5 ills., May, 1917.

Neillie, C. R.:

Fighting Insects With Airplanes: An Account of the Successful Use of the Flying-Machine in Dusting Tall Trees Infested With Leaf-Eating Caterpillars. By C. R. Neillie and J. S. Houser. Vol. XLI, pp. 333-338, 6 ills., Mar., 1922.

Nejd. *See* Saudi Arabia.

Nelson, E. W.:

Awarded Jane M. Smith Life Membership. Vol. XXXVII, p. 342, Apr., 1920.

Bird Banding, the Telltale of Migratory Flight: A Modern Method of Learning the Flight-Ways and Habits of Birds. By E. W. Nelson. Vol. LIII, pp. 91-131, 49 ills., 1 third-page map, Jan., 1928.

Land of Drought and Desert—Lower California: Two Thousand Miles on Horseback Through the Most Extraordinary Cacti Forests in the World. By E. W. Nelson. Vol. XXII, pp. 443-474, 25 ills., 1 page and 1 half-page maps, May, 1911.

Larger North American Mammals. By E. W. Nelson. Vol. XXX, pp. 385-472, 24 ills. in black and white, 50 ills. in color, special supplement in color, Nov., 1916.

Rat Pest: The Labor of 200,000 Men in the United States Required to Support Rats, Man's Most Destructive and Dangerous Enemy. By E. W. Nelson. Vol. XXXII, pp. 1-23, 21 ills., July, 1917.

Smaller Mammals of North America. By E. W. Nelson. Vol. XXXIII, pp. 391-493, 29 ills. in black and white, 59 ills. in color, May, 1918.

Winter Expedition in Southwestern Mexico. By E. W. Nelson. Vol. XV, pp. 341-356, 14 ills., Sept., 1904.

Nelson, Wilbur A.:

Reelfoot—An Earthquake Lake (Tennessee). By Wilbur A. Nelson. Vol. XLV, pp. 95-114, 20 ills., Jan., 1924.

Nepal:

Aërial Conquest of Everest: Flying Over the World's Highest Mountain Realizes the Objective of Many Heroic Explorers. By Lieut. Col. L. V. S. Blacker. Vol. LXIV, pp. 127-162, 35 ills., 1 page map, Aug., 1933.

Nepal: A Little-Known Kingdom. By John Claude White. Vol. XXXVIII, pp. 245-283, 32 ills., 1 half-page map, Oct., 1920.

Nepal, the Sequestered Kingdom. By Penelope Chetwode. Vol. LXVII, pp. 319-352, 27 ills. in black and white, 15 ills. in color, 1 half-page map, Mar., 1935.

Remote Nepal, Land of Mystery. 15 ills. in color from natural-color photographs by Martin Hürlimann. Vol. LXVII, pp. 329-336, Mar., 1935.

Nervion River, Spain:

Land of the Basques: Home of a Thrifty, Picturesque People, Who Take Pride in the Sobriquet, "The Yankees of Spain." By Harry A. McBride. Vol. XLI, pp. 63-87, 25 ills., 1 three-quarters-page map, Jan., 1922.

Net Results from Oceania: Collecting Aquarium Specimens in Tropical Pacific Waters. By Walter H. Chute. Vol. LXXIX, pp. 347-372, 8 ills. in black and white, 24 ills. in color, Mar., 1941.

Netherlands:

As Seen from a Dutch Window. By James Howard Gore. Vol. XIX, pp. 619-634, 3 ills., Sept., 1908.

Behind Netherlands Sea Ramparts: Dikes and Pumps Keep Ocean and Rivers at Bay While a Busy People Carries on Peacetime Work. By McFall Kerbey. Vol. LXXVII, pp. 255-290, 26 ills. in black and white, 11 ills. in duotone, 1 two-thirds-page map, Feb., 1940.

Citizen Army of Holland. By Hendrik Willem Van Loon. Vol. XXIX, pp. 609-622, 9 ills., June, 1916.

City of Jacqueline (Goes, Netherlands). By Florence Craig Albrecht. Vol. XXVII, pp. 29-56, 31 ills., Jan., 1915.

Dikes of Holland. By Gerard H. Matthes. Vol. XII, pp. 219-234, 7 charts, 3 ills., June, 1901.

Glimpses of Holland. By William Wisner Chapin. Vol. XXVII, pp. 1-29, 26 ills., Jan., 1915.

Holland Rises from War and Water. By Thomas R. Henry. Vol. LXXXIX, pp. 237-260, 18 ills., 1 seven-eighths-page map, Feb., 1946.

Holland's War With the Sea. By James Howard Gore. Vol. XLIII, pp. 283-325, 39 ills., 1 third-page map, Mar., 1923.

Home Life and Industry in the Netherlands. 11 ills. in duotone from photographs. Vol. LXXVII, pp. 271-278, Feb., 1940.

In the Land of Windmills and Wooden Shoes. 16 ills. from photographs by Donald McLeish. Vol. XLIII, pp. 297-312, Mar., 1923.

Low Countries Await Liberation. 10 ills. from photographs. Vol. LXXXVI, pp. 221-228, Aug., 1944.

Mending Dikes in the Netherlands. 20 ills. from photographs by Lawrence Earl. Vol. XC, pp. 791-806, Dec., 1946.

New Country Awaits Discovery: The Draining of the Zuider Zee Makes Room for the Excess Population of the Netherlands. By J. C. M. Kruisinga. Vol. LXIV, pp. 293-320, 20 ills. in black and white, 13 ills. in color, 1 three-quarters and 1 half-page maps, Sept., 1933.

Nooks and Bays Around the Zuider Zee. 13 ills. in color from natural color photographs by Wilhelm Tobien, Gervais Courtellemont, and Franklin Price Knott. Vol. LXIV, pp. 301-308, Sept., 1933.

North Holland Cheese Market. By Hugh M. Smith. Vol. XXI, pp. 1051-1066, 17 ills., Dec., 1910.

Races of Europe. By Edwin A. Grosvenor. Vol. XXXIV, pp. 441-534, 62 ills., 2 page maps, special map supplement, Dec., 1918.

Rediscovering the Rhine: A Trip by Barge from the Sea to the Headwaters of Europe's Storied Stream. By Melville Chater. Vol. XLVIII, pp. 1-43, 44 ills., July, 1925.

Singing Towers of Holland and Belgium. By William Gorham Rice. Vol. XLVII, pp. 357-376, 22 ills., Mar., 1925.

Netherlands—*Continued*

Some Odd Pages from the Annals of the Tulip: A "Made" Flower of Unknown Origin Took Medieval Europe by Storm and Caused a Financial Panic in the Netherlands. By Leo A. Borah. Vol. LXIV, pp. 321-343, 13 ills. in black and white, 10 ills. in color, Sept., 1933.

Tulip Time in the Netherlands. 10 ills. in color from natural-color photographs by Wilhelm Tobien and A. Buyssens. Vol. LXIV, pp. 325-332, Sept., 1933.

Vacation in Holland. By George Alden Sanford. Vol. LVI, pp. 363-378, 6 ills. in black and white, 8 ills. in color, 1 two-thirds-page map, Sept., 1929.

Netherlands East Indies:

Around the World for Animals. By William M. and Lucile Q. Mann. Vol. LXXIII, pp. 665-714, 33 ills. in black and white, 23 ills. in color, 1 page map, June, 1938.

The Face of the Netherlands Indies. 20 ills. from photographs by Maynard Owen Williams and others. Vol. LXXXIX, pp. 261-276, Feb., 1946.

From London to Australia by Aëroplane: A Personal Narrative of the First Aërial Voyage Half Around the World. By Sir Ross Smith. Vol. XXXIX, pp. 229-339, 76 ills., in black and white, 8 ills. in color, 1 page map, Mar., 1921.

Greatest Voyage in the Annals of the Sea. By J. R. Hildebrand. Vol. LXII, pp. 699-739, 35 ills., 2 half-page maps, Dec., 1932.

Netherlands Indies: Patchwork of Peoples. 23 ills. in color from natural-color photographs by Maynard Owen Williams. Vol. LXXIII, pp. 681-712, June, 1938.

See also Bali; Borneo; Celebes; Java; Komodo; Krakatau; Moluccas; New Guinea; Nias; Sumatra; Timor.

Netherlands New Guinea:

Further Notes on Dutch New Guinea. By Thomas Barbour. Vol. XIX, pp. 527-545, 19 ills., Aug., 1908.

New Guinea's Mountain and Swampland Dwellers. By Col. Ray T. Elsmore. Vol. LXXXVIII, pp. 671-694, 15 ills. in black and white, 7 ills. in color, 1 half-page map, Dec., 1945.

Notes on a Zoölogical Collecting Trip to Dutch New Guinea. By Thomas Barbour. Vol. XIX, pp. 469-484, 12 ills., 2 half-page maps, July, 1908.

"Shangri-la" in Panorama. 7 ills. in color from natural-color photographs by Ray T. Elsmore. Vol. LXXXVIII, pp. 681-688, Dec., 1945.

Netherlands West Indies. *See* Aruba; Bonaire; Curaçao; Saba.

Nevada:

California and Nevada Boundary. By C. H. Sinclair. Vol. X, pp. 416-417, Oct., 1899.

Deserts of Nevada and the Death Valley. By Robert H. Chapman. Vol. XVII, pp. 482-497, 9 ills., 1 chart, Sept., 1906.

Nevada—*Continued*

Development of Nevada. Vol. XV, p. 166, Apr., 1904.

Land of Sagebrush and Silver. 20 ills. in color from natural-color photographs by W. Robert Moore. Vol. LXXXIX, pp. 9-32, Jan., 1946.

Nevada, Desert Treasure House. By W. Robert Moore. Vol. LXXXIX, pp. 1-38, 16 ills. in black and white, 20 ills. in color, 1 four-fifths-page map, Jan., 1946.

Plague of Mice. Vol. XX, pp. 478-485, 7 ills., May, 1909.

Studies on the Rate of Evaporation at Reno, Nevada, and in the Salton Sink. By Frank H. Bigelow. Vol. XIX, pp. 20-28, 5 ills., Jan., 1908.

Sulphur Mine in Nevada. Vol. XV, p. 498, Dec., 1904.

Nevils, W. Coleman:

Augustus—Emperor and Architect: Two Thousand Years Ago Was Born the Physically Frail But Spiritually Great Roman Who Became the Master of His World. By W. Coleman Nevils. Vol. LXXIV, pp. 535-556, 17 ills., 1 half-page map, Oct., 1938.

Horace—Classic Poet of the Countryside. By W. Coleman Nevils. Vol. LXVIII, pp. 771-795, 22 ills., 1 page map, Dec., 1935.

Perennial Geographer: After 2,000 Years Vergil Is Still the Most Widely Read of Latin Poets—First to Popularize the Geography of the Roman Empire. By W. Coleman Nevils. Vol. LVIII, pp. 439-465, 29 ills., Oct., 1930.

Smallest State in the World: Vatican City on Its 108 Acres Is a Complete Sovereignty Internationally Recognized. By W. Coleman Nevils. Vol. LXXV, pp. 377-412, 37 ills., 1 two-page map, Mar., 1939.

New Alphabet of the Ancients Is Unearthed: An Inconspicuous Mound in Northern Syria Yields Archeological Treasures of Far-Reaching Significance. By F. A. Schaeffer. Vol. LVIII, pp. 477-516, 47 ills., 1 quarter-page map, Oct., 1930.

New Britain (Island), Bismarck Archipelago:

Islands of the Pacific. By J. P. Thomson. Vol. XL, pp. 543-558, 15 ills., special map supplement, Dec., 1921.

New British Empire of the Sudan. By Herbert L. Bridgman. Vol. XVII, pp. 241-267, 32 ills., 1 quarter-page map, May, 1906.

New Brunswick (Province), Canada:

New Brunswick Down by the Sea. By Lawrence J. Burpee. Vol. LXXIX, pp. 595-614, 14 ills., 1 page map, May, 1941.

New Caledonia (Island), Pacific Ocean:

At Ease in the South Seas. By Maj. Frederick Simpich, Jr. Vol. LXXXV, pp. 79-104, 32 ills., Jan., 1944.

Jungle War: Bougainville and New Caledonia. 17 ills. in color from paintings by Lieut. William F. Draper. Vol. LXXXV, pp. 417-432, Apr., 1944.

New Caledonia (Island), Pacific Ocean—*Continued*

South Sea Isle of Mineral Mountains. 12 ills. in color from natural-color photographs by Enzo de Chetelat. Vol. LXXXII, pp. 33-40, July, 1942.

Treasure Islands of Australasia: New Guinea, New Caledonia, and Fiji Trace across the South Pacific a Fertile Crescent Incredibly Rich in Minerals and Foods. By Douglas L. Oliver. Vol. LXXXI, pp. 691-722, 23 ills., 1 two-page map, June, 1942.

War Awakened New Caledonia: Swift Changes Take Place on the South Pacific Island of Mineral Wealth Defended by Free French and American Troops. By Enzo de Chetelat. Vol. LXXXII, pp. 31-55, 14 ills. in black and white, 12 ills. in color, 1 two-thirds-page map, July, 1942.

Yank Meets Native. By Wanda Burnett. Vol. LXXXVIII, pp. 105-128, 24 ills., July, 1945.

New China and the Printed Page. By Paul Hutchinson. Vol. LI, pp. 687-722, 37 ills., June, 1927.

New Cone of Mont Pelée. Vol. XIV, pp. 422-423, 2 ills., Nov., 1903.

New Country Awaits Discovery: The Draining of the Zuider Zee Makes Room for the Excess Population of the Netherlands. By J. C. M. Kruisinga. Vol. LXIV, pp. 293-320, 20 ills. in black and white, 13 ills. in color, 1 three-quarters and 1 half-page maps, Sept., 1933.

New Delhi, India:

Behind New Delhi's News. 13 ills. in color from natural-color photographs by Maynard Owen Williams. Vol. LXXXII, pp. 477-484, Oct., 1942.

New Delhi Goes Full Time. By Maynard Owen Williams. Vol. LXXXII, pp. 465-494, 17 ills. in black and white, 13 ills. in color, 1 page map, Oct., 1942.

New Discoveries in Carlsbad Cavern (New Mexico): Vast Subterranean Chambers with Spectacular Decorations Are Explored, Surveyed, and Photographed. By Willis T. Lee. Vol. XLVIII, pp. 301-319, 19 ills., 1 three-quarters-page map, Sept., 1925.

New England, United States:

Cape Cod People and Places. By Wanda Burnett. Vol. LXXXIX, pp. 737-774, 17 ills. in black and white, 24 ills. in color, 1 half-page map, June, 1946.

Flow Onward, Connecticut (River)! 24 ills. in color from natural-color photographs; 22 ills. by B. Anthony Stewart. Vol. LXXXIII, pp. 409-432, Apr., 1943.

From Notch to Notch in the White Mountains: Soaring Heights of New Hampshire Attract Multitudes to America's Oldest Mountain Recreation Area. By Leonard Cornell Roy. Vol. LXXII, pp. 73-104, 30 ills., special map supplement, July, 1937.

New England, United States—*Continued*

Geography of a Hurricane: A Doughnut-shaped Storm Turned Back Time in New England to Candlelight Days, but Revealed Anew Yankee Courage and Ingenuity. By F. Barrows Colton. Vol. LXXV, pp. 529-552, 20 ills., 1 page map, Apr., 1939.

Long River of New England: In War and Peace, from Mountain Wilderness to the Sea, Flows the Connecticut River, Through a Valley Abounding in History, Scenery, Inventive Genius, and Industry. By Albert W. Atwood. Vol. LXXXIII, pp. 401-434, 12 ills. in black and white, 24 ills. in color, 1 two-thirds-page map, Apr., 1943.

New England Ski Trails: Snow and Ice Sports Transform Whittier's Winters of Snowbound Seclusion Into Seasons of Outdoor Recreation. By Daniel Rochford. Vol. LXX, pp. 645-664, 11 ills. in black and white, 13 ills. in color, Nov., 1936.

New England's Wonderland of Mountain, Lake, and Seascape. 14 ills. in color from natural-color photographs by Clifton Adams. Vol. LX, pp. 262-271, Sept., 1931.

Northeast of Boston. By Albert W. Atwood. Vol. LXXXVIII, pp. 257-292, 12 ills. in black and white, 17 ills. in color, special map supplement, Sept., 1945.

Sport and Color Amid New England Snows. 13 ills. in color from natural-color photographs by B. Anthony Stewart. Vol. LXX, pp. 647-654, Nov., 1936.

Where New England Meets the Sea. 17 ills. in color from natural-color photographs by B. Anthony Stewart. Vol. LXXXVIII, pp. 265-288, Sept., 1945.

See also Connecticut; Maine; Massachusetts; New Hampshire; Rhode Island; Vermont.

New England's Wonderland of Mountain, Lake, and Seascape. 14 ills. in color from natural-color photographs by Clifton Adams. Vol. LX, pp. 262-271, Sept., 1931.

New English Province of Northern Nigeria. Vol. XV, pp. 433-442, 9 ills., Nov., 1904.

New Erie Canal. Vol. XVI, pp. 568-570, 1 page map, Dec., 1905.

New French Ocean Cables. Vol. XII, pp. 315-316, Aug., 1901.

New Frontier in the Sky. By F. Barrows Colton. Vol. XC, pp. 379-408, 28 ills., 1 diagram, Sept., 1946.

New Georgia (Island), Solomon Islands. *See* Munda.

New Greece, the Centenarian, Forges Ahead. By Maynard Owen Williams. Vol. LVIII, pp. 649-721, 51 ills. in black and white, 40 ills. in color, 1 three-quarters-page map, Dec., 1930.

New Guinea:

Further Notes on Dutch New Guinea. By Thomas Barbour. Vol. XIX, pp. 527-545, 19 ills., Aug., 1908.

New Guinea—*Continued*

Into Primeval Papua by Seaplane : Seeking Disease-Resisting Sugar Cane, Scientists Find Neolithic Man in Unmapped Nooks of Sorcery and Cannibalism. By E. W. Brandes. Vol. LVI, pp. 253-332, 98 ills., 1 three-quarters-page map, Sept., 1929.

Islands of the Pacific. By J. P. Thomson. Vol. XL, pp. 543-558, 15 ills., special map supplement, Dec., 1921.

New Guinea's Mountain and Swampland Dwellers. By Col. Ray T. Elsmore. Vol. LXXXVIII, pp. 671-694, 15 ills. in black and white, 7 ills. in color, 1 half-page map, Dec., 1945.

Notes on a Zoölogical Collecting Trip to Dutch New Guinea. By Thomas Barbour. Vol. XIX, pp. 469-484, 12 ills., 2 half-page maps, July, 1908.

Pictorial Jaunt Through Papua. 22 ills. from photographs by Capt. Frank Hurley. Vol. LI, pp. 109-124, Jan., 1927.

"Shangri-la" in Panorama. 7 ills. in color from natural-color photographs by Ray T. Elsmore. Vol. LXXXVIII, pp. 681-688, Dec., 1945.

Strange Sights in Far-Away Papua. B. A. E. Pratt. Vol. XVIII, pp. 559-572, 7 ills., Sept., 1907.

Treasure Islands of Australasia : New Guinea, New Caledonia, and Fiji Trace across the South Pacific a Fertile Crescent Incredibly Rich in Minerals and Foods. By Douglas L. Oliver. Vol. LXXXI, pp. 691-722, 23 ills., 1 two-page map, June, 1942.

Unknown New Guinea : Circumnavigating the World in a Flying Boat, American Scientists Discover a Valley of 60,000 People Never Before Seen by White Men. By Richard Archbold. Vol. LXXIX, pp. 315-344, 28 ills., 1 two-thirds-page map, Mar., 1941.

What the Fighting Yanks See. By Wanda Burnett. Vol. LXXXVI, pp. 451-476, 27 ills., Oct., 1944.

Yank Meets Native. By Wanda Burnett. Vol. LXXXVIII, pp. 105-128, 24 ills., July, 1945.

New Guinea's Mountain and Swampland Dwellers. By Col. Ray T. Elsmore. Vol. LXXXVIII, pp. 671-694, 15 ills. in black and white, 7 ills. in color, 1 half-page map, Dec., 1945.

New Hampshire :

Flow Onward, Connecticut (River) ! 24 ills. in color from natural-color photographs ; 22 ills. by B. Anthony Stewart. Vol. LXXXIII, pp. 409-432, Apr., 1943.

Long River of New England : In War and Peace, from Mountain Wilderness to the Sea, Flows the Connecticut River, Through a Valley Abounding in History, Scenery, Inventive Genius, and Industry. By Albert W. Atwood. Vol. LXXXIII, pp. 401-434, 12 ills. in black and white, 24 ills. in color, 1 two-thirds-page map, Apr., 1943.

New England's Wonderland of Mountain, Lake, and Seascape. 5 ills. in color from natural-color photographs by Clifton Adams. Vol. LX, pp. 262-271, Sept., 1931.

New Hampshire—*Continued*

New Hampshire, the Granite State. By George Higgins Moses. Vol. LX, pp. 257-310, 47 ills. in black and white, 5 ills. in color, 1 page map, Sept., 1931.

Skiing Over the New Hampshire Hills. By Fred H. Harris. Vol. XXXVII, pp. 133-164, 37 ills., Feb., 1920.

See also Portsmouth.

New Hebrides (Islands), Pacific Ocean :

In the Savage South Seas. By Beatrice Grimshaw. Vol. XIX, pp. 1-19, 21 ills., Jan., 1908.

Palms and Planes in the New Hebrides. By Maj. Robert D. Heinl, Jr. Vol. LXXXVI, pp. 229-256, 17 ills. in black and white, 12 ills. in color, 1 four-fifths-page map, Aug., 1944.

See also Espíritu Santo.

New Home of the National Geographic Society. Vol. XV, pp. 176-181, 5 ills., Apr., 1904.

New Inland Sea (Salton Sea). By Arthur P. Davis. Vol. XVIII, pp. 36-49, 8 ills., 1 page map, Jan., 1906.

New Jersey :

Beaches and Bathers of the Jersey Shore. 11 ills. in color from natural-color photographs by Edwin L. Wisherd. Vol. LXIII, pp. 534-543, May, 1933.

Farms and Workshops of "The Garden State." 13 ills. in color from natural-color photographs by Edwin L. Wisherd. Vol. LXIII, pp. 558-567, May, 1933.

New Jersey Now ! By E. John Long. Vol. LXIII, pp. 519-583, 49 ills. in black and white, 24 ills. in color, 1 page and 1 two-thirds-page maps, May, 1933.

Wild Blueberry Tamed : The New Industry of the Pine Barrens of New Jersey. By Frederick V. Coville. Vol. XXIX, pp. 535-546, 10 ills., June, 1916.

See also Lakehurst ; Morristown.

New Light on Ancient Ur : Excavations at the Site of the City of Abraham Reveal Geographical Evidence of the Biblical Story of the Flood. By M. E. L. Mallowan. Vol. LVII, pp. 95-130, 44 ills., 1 three-quarters-page map, Jan., 1930.

New Map of Asia. Text accompanying special map supplement in colors. Vol. XXXIX, pp. 552-570, 17 ills., May, 1921.

New Map of Europe : Showing the Boundaries Established by the Peace Conference at Paris and by Subsequent Decisions of the Supreme Council of the Allied and Associated Powers. By Ralph A. Graves. Text accompanying special map supplement in colors. Vol. XXXIX, pp. 157-177, 18 ills., Feb., 1921.

New Map of Europe and the Near East. Text accompanying special map supplement in colors. Vol. LXXXIII, pp. 762-763, 1 ill., June, 1943.

New Map of Europe Records War Changes. Text accompanying special map supplement in colors. Vol. LXXVII, p. 625, May, 1940.

New Map of the Atlantic Ocean: Foremost Sea of Commerce Becomes World's Battleground and Its Peaceful Islands Rise to Strategic Importance. By Leo A. Borah and Wellman Chamberlin. Text accompanying special map supplement in colors. Vol. LXXX, pp. 407-418, 9 ills., Sept., 1941.

New Map Reveals the Progress and Wonders of Our Country. Text accompanying special map supplement in colors. Vol. LXIII, pp. 650-652, 1 ill., May, 1933.

New Map Shows Asia's Role in Global Warfare. Text accompanying special map supplement in colors. Vol. LXXXII, pp. 767-768, Dec., 1942.

New Map Shows Immense Pacific Battleground. Text accompanying special map supplement in colors. Vol. LXXXI, pp. 203-204, Feb., 1942.

New Mexico:

Arizona and New Mexico. By B. S. Rodey. Vol. XVII, pp. 100-102, 2 ills., Feb., 1906.

Bats of the Carlsbad Cavern. By Vernon Bailey. Vol. XLVIII, pp. 321-330, 11 ills., Sept., 1925.

Call of the West. By C. J. Blanchard. Vol. XX, pp. 403-437, 20 ills., 1 half-page map, May, 1909.

Canyons and Cacti of the American Southwest. 22 ills. in color from natural-color photographs by Edwin L. Wisherd, Jacob Gayer, and Charles Martin. Vol. XLVIII, pp. 275-290, Sept., 1925.

Down the Rio Grande: Tracing this Strange, Turbulent Stream on Its Long Course from Colorado to the Gulf of Mexico. By Frederick Simpich. Vol. LXXVI, pp. 415-462, 28 ills. in black and white, 24 ills. in color, 6 maps, Oct., 1939.

Everyday Life in Pueblo Bonito: As Disclosed by the National Geographic Society's Archeologic Explorations in the Chaco Canyon National Monument, New Mexico. By Neil M. Judd. Vol. XLVIII, pp. 227-262, 37 ills., 1 two-thirds-page map, Sept., 1925.

Nature Paints New Mexico. 25 ills. in color from natural-color photographs by Richard H. Stewart. Vol. LXXIII, pp. 537-568, May, 1938.

New Discoveries in Carlsbad Cavern: Vast Subterranean Chambers with Spectacular Decorations Are Explored, Surveyed, and Photographed. By Willis T. Lee. Vol. XLVIII, pp. 301-319, 19 ills., 1 three-quarters-page map, Sept., 1925.

New Mexico Melodrama. By Frederick Simpich. Vol. LXXIII, pp. 529-569, 19 ills. in black and white, 25 ills. in color, 1 two-page map, May, 1938.

New Mexico—Continued

New National Geographic Society Expedition: Ruins of Chaco Canyon, New Mexico, Nature-Made Treasure-Chest of Aboriginal American History, to be Excavated and Studied; Work Begins This Month. Vol. XXXIX, pp. 637-643, 7 ills., June, 1921.

Notes on the Deserts of the United States and Mexico (Extracted from a Publication of Dr. Daniel T. MacDougal). Vol. XXI, pp. 691-714, 16 ills., Aug., 1910.

Prehistoric Ruin of Tsankawi. By George L. Beam. Vol. XX, pp. 807-822, 12 ills., Sept., 1909.

Pueblo Bonito, the Ancient: The National Geographic Society's Third Expedition to the Southwest Seeks to Read in the Rings of Trees the Secret of the Age of Ruins. By Neil M. Judd. Vol. XLIV, pp. 99-108, 9 ills., 1 diagram, July, 1923.

Pueblo Bonito Expedition of the National Geographic Society. By Neil M. Judd. Vol. XLI, pp. 323-331, 10 ills., 1 diagram, Mar., 1922.

Scenes from America's Southwest. Vol. XXXIX, pp. 651-664, 14 ills., June, 1921.

Secret of the Southwest Solved by Talkative Tree Rings: Horizons of American History Are Carried Back to A. D. 700 and a Calendar for 1,200 Years Established by National Geographic Society Expeditions. By Andrew Ellicott Douglass. Vol. LVI, pp. 737-770, 33 ills., 1 two-thirds-page map, Dec., 1929.

Seeing Our Spanish Southwest. By Frederick Simpich. Vol. LXXVII, pp. 711-756, 25 ills. in black and white, 17 ills. in duotone, special map supplement, June, 1940.

Southwest: Its Splendid Natural Resources, Agricultural Wealth, and Scenic Beauty. By N. H. Darton. Vol. XXI, pp. 631-665, 21 ills., 1 page map, Aug., 1910.

Visit to Carlsbad Cavern: Recent Explorations of a Limestone Cave in the Guadalupe Mountains of New Mexico Reveal a Natural Wonder of the First Magnitude. By Willis T. Lee. Vol. XLV, pp. 1-40, 42 ills., Jan., 1924.

White Sands of Alamogordo: A Dry Ocean of Granular Gypsum Billows Under Desert Winds in a New National Playground. By Carl P. Russell. Vol. LXVIII, pp. 250-264, 12 ills., Aug., 1935.

New National Geographic Society Expedition: Ruins of Chaco Canyon, New Mexico, Nature-Made Treasure-Chest of Aboriginal American History, to be Excavated and Studied; Work Begins This Month. Vol. XXXIX, pp. 637-643, 7 ills., June, 1921.

New National Geographic Society Map Charts South America's Wartime Importance. Text accompanying special map supplement in colors. Vol. LXXXII, pp. 537-540, 2 ills., Oct., 1942.

New National Park (Glacier National Park). By Guy Elliott Mitchell. Vol. XXI, pp. 215-223, 6 ills., Mar., 1910.

New Orleans, Louisiana :

Color Camera Records of New Orleans. 15 ills. in color from natural-color photographs by Edwin L. Wisherd. Vol. LVII, pp. 458-467, Apr., 1930.

Louisiana, Land of Perpetual Romance. By Ralph A. Graves. Vol. LVII, pp. 393-482, 84 ills. in black and white, 29 ills. in color, special map supplement in color, Apr., 1930.

New Peruvian Route to the Plain of the Amazon. By Solon I. Bailey. Vol. XVII, pp. 432-448, 12 ills., Aug., 1906.

New Plant Immigrants. By David Fairchild. Vol. XXII, pp. 879-907, 34 ills., Oct., 1911.

New Queen of the Seas (Aircraft Carrier). By Melville Bell Grosvenor. Vol. LXXXII, pp. 1-30, 27 ills., 1 drawing, 1 two-page map, July, 1942.

New Road to Asia (U. S. S. R.). By Owen Lattimore. Vol. LXXXVI, pp. 641-676, 15 ills. in black and white, 26 ills. in color, Dec., 1944.

New Safeguards for Ships in Fog and Storm. By George R. Putnam. Vol. LXX, pp. 169-200, 28 ills., 2 charts, Aug., 1936.

New Source of Power : Billions of Tons of Lignite, Previously Thought Too Poor Coal for Commercial Use, Are Made Easily Available. By Guy Elliott Mitchell. Vol. XXI, pp. 935-944, 7 ills., Nov., 1910.

New South Wales (State), Australia :

Shark Fishing—An Australian Industry. By Norman Ellison. Vol. LXII, pp. 369-386, 22 ills., Sept., 1932.

See also Lord Howe (Island).

New Trans-Canada Railway. Vol. XIV, pp. 214-215, 1 quarter-page map, May, 1903.

New World Map Gives Backdrop for Headlines. Text accompanying special map supplement in colors. Vol. LXXX, pp. 741-742, 1 ill., Dec., 1941.

New World to Explore : In the Tree-Roof of the British Guiana Forest Flourishes Much Hitherto-Unknown Life. By Maj. R. W. G. Hingston. Vol. LXII, pp. 617-642, 35 ills., Nov., 1932.

New Year Celebrations:

Peiping's Happy New Year : Lunar Celebration Attracts Throngs to Temple Fairs, Motley Bazaars, and Age-old Festivities. By George Kin Leung. Vol. LXX, pp. 749-792, 31 ills. in black and white, 16 ills. in color, Dec., 1936.

New York (City) :

Greater New York . . . Metropolis of Mankind. Special supplement from aërial photograph by Capt. Albert W. Stevens. Vol. LXIV, supplement, Nov., 1933.

New York (City)—*Continued*

Magnitude of the New World Metropolis. 8 ills. in gravure. Vol. LVIII, pp. 522-531, Nov., 1930.

New York—The Metropolis of Mankind. By William Joseph Showalter. Vol. XXXIV, pp. 1-49, 39 ills., July, 1918.

Society's Map of the Reaches of New York City. Text accompanying special map supplement in colors. Vol. LXXV, pp. 491-492, Apr., 1939.

Tempo and Color of a Great City. 42 ills. in color from natural-color photographs by Clifton Adams and Edwin L. Wisherd. Vol. LVIII, pp. 538-579, Nov., 1930.

This Giant That Is New York. By Frederick Simpich. Vol. LVIII, pp. 517-583, 26 ills. in black and white. 8 ills. in gravure, 42 ills. in color, Nov., 1930.

New York (State) :

Adirondack Idyls. 10 ills. in color from natural-color photographs by Harrison Howell Walker. Vol. LXXIII, pp. 729-736, June, 1938.

Black Acres : A Thrilling Sketch in the Vast Volume of Who's Who Among the Peoples That Make America. By Dorothea D. and Fred Everett. Vol. LXXX, pp. 631-652, 13 ills. in black and white, 12 ills. in color, Nov., 1941.

Color Highlights of the Empire State. 35 ills. in color from natural-color photographs by Clifton Adams, James A. G. Davey, and Edwin L. Wisherd. Vol. LXIV, pp. 529-576, Nov., 1933.

Commercial Importance of the State of New York. Vol. XV, p. 429, Oct., 1904.

Empire State Onions and Pageantry. 12 ills. in color from natural-color photographs by J. Baylor Roberts and Volkmar Wentzel. Vol. LXXX, pp. 641-648, Nov., 1941.

Fruitful Shores of the Finger Lakes. By Harrison Howell Walker. Vol. LXXIX, pp. 559-594, 15 ills. in black and white, 22 ills. in color, 1 two-thirds page map, May, 1941.

New Erie Canal. Vol. XVI, pp. 568-570, 1 page map, Dec., 1905.

New York—An Empire Within a Republic. By William Joseph Showalter. Vol. LXIV, pp. 513-584, 47 ills. in black and white, 35 ills. in color, 1 two-page map, Nov., 1933.

New York State's Air-Conditioned Roof (Adirondacks). By Frederick G. Vosburgh. Vol. LXXIII, pp. 715-748, 23 ills. in black and white, 10 ills. in color, 1 three-quarters-page map, June, 1938.

Niagara at the Battle Front. By William Joseph Showalter. Vol. XXXI, pp. 413-422, 6 ills., May, 1917.

Spin Your Globe to Long Island : Only Six States Have More People than the Insular Empire that Ranges from a World's Fair Through Potato Patches, Princely Estates, and Historic Shrines. By Frederick Simpich. Vol. LXXV, pp. 413-460, 25 ills. in black and white, 18 ills. in color, Apr., 1939.

See also New York (City) ; West Point.

New Zealand:

Alpine Peaks and Pastures of South Island. 11 ills. in color from natural-color photographs by W. Robert Moore. Vol. LXIX, pp. 205-212, Feb., 1936.

At Home on the Oceans: Whales and Sharks Make Exciting Neighbors for a Professor's Wife, Turned Able Seaman, On a Three-Year Voyage Around the World. By Edith Bauer Strout. Vol. LXXVI, pp. 33-86, 54 ills., 1 map, July, 1939.

British Commonwealth of Nations: "Organized Freedom" Around the World. By Eric Underwood. Vol. LXXXIII, pp. 485-524, 31 ills., Apr., 1943.

Facing War's Challenge "Down Under." 20 ills. in color from natural-color photographs by Howell Walker. Vol. LXXXI, pp. 425-456, Apr., 1942.

Great Britain's Bread Upon the Waters: Canada and Her Other Daughters. By William Howard Taft. Vol. XXIX, pp. 217-272, 56 ills., Mar., 1916.

Hurdle Racing in Canoes: A Thrilling and Spectacular Sport Among the Maoris of New Zealand. By Walter Burke. Vol. XXXVII, pp. 440-444, 6 ills., May, 1920.

Making of an Anzac. By Howell Walker. Vol. LXXXI, pp. 409-456, 31 ills. in black and white, 20 ills. in color, 1 two-page map, Apr., 1942.

Maoris of New Zealand. Vol. XVIII, pp. 191-199, 8 ills., Mar., 1907.

New Zealand "Down Under." By W. Robert Moore. Vol. LXIX, pp. 165-218, 31 ills. in black and white, 23 ills. in color, 1 two-page map, Feb., 1936.

North Island of New Zealand: A Vulcan's Playground. 12 ills. in color from natural-color photographs by W. Robert Moore. Vol. LXIX, pp. 181-188, Feb., 1936.

Problems of the Pacific—New Zealand. By Henry Demarest Lloyd. Vol. XIII, pp. 342-352, Sept., 1902.

Tuatara: "Living Fossils" Walk on Well-Nigh Inaccessible Rocky Islands off the Coast of New Zealand. By Frieda Cobb Blanchard. Vol. LXVII, pp. 649-662, 14 ills., 1 half-page map, May, 1935.

Waimangu and the Hot-spring Country of New Zealand: The World's Greatest Geyser Is One of Many Natural Wonders in a Land of Inferno and Vernal Paradise. By Joseph C. Grew. Vol. XLVIII, pp. 109-130, 19 ills., 1 third-page map, Aug., 1925.

World's Highest Altitudes and First Ascents. By Charles E. Fay. Vol. XX, pp. 493-530, 25 ills., June, 1909.

Newberry, Truman H.:

Honors to the American Navy (Address by T. H. Newberry). Vol. XX, pp. 77-95, Jan., 1909.

Newburyport, Massachusetts:

Northeast of Boston. By Albert W. Atwood. Vol. LXXXVIII, pp. 257-292, 12 ills. in black and white, 17 ills. in color, special map supplement, Sept., 1945.

Newcomb, Simon:

Scientific Work of the National Geographic Society's Eclipse Expedition to Norfolk, Virginia. By Simon Newcomb. Vol. XI, pp. 321-324, Aug., 1900.

Newell, Frederick H.:

Four Prominent Geographers. Vol. XVIII, pp. 425-428, 4 ills., June, 1907.

Limited Water Supply of the Arid Region. By Frederick H. Newell. Vol. XI, pp. 438-442, Nov., 1900.

National Geographic Society (Resignation of Frederick H. Newell as Secretary of The Society). By Gilbert H. Grosvenor. Vol. X, pp. 474-475, Nov., 1899.

Reclamation of the West. By F. H. Newell. Vol. XV, pp. 15-30, 6 ills., 7 half-page maps, Jan., 1904.

Newfoundland:

King Herring: An Account of the World's Most Valuable Fish, the Industries It Supports, and the Part It Has Played in History. By Hugh M. Smith. Vol. XX, pp. 701-735, 21 ills., Aug., 1909.

Life on the Grand Banks: An Account of the Sailor-Fishermen Who Harvest the Shoal Waters of North America's Eastern Coasts. By Frederick William Wallace. Vol. XL, pp. 1-28, 29 ills., July, 1921.

Newfoundland, North Atlantic Rampart: From the "First Base of American Defense" Planes Fly to Britain's Aid over Stout Fishing Schooners of the Grand Banks. By George Whiteley, Jr. Vol. LXXX, pp. 111-140, 26 ills., 1 two-thirds-page map, July, 1941.

Sealing Saga of Newfoundland. By Capt. Robert A. Bartlett. Vol. LVI, pp. 91-130, 44 ills., July, 1929.

Newman, Oliver P.:

Bare Feet and Burros of Haiti. By Oliver P. Newman. Vol. LXXXVI, pp. 307-328, 10 ills. in black and white, 10 ills. in color, 1 half-page map, Sept., 1944.

Land Columbus Loved (Dominican Republic). By Oliver P. Newman. Vol. LXXXV, pp. 197-224, 15 ills. in black and white, 11 ills. in color, 1 two-thirds-page map, Feb., 1944.

News of the Universe: Mars Swings Nearer the Earth, Sunspots Wane, and a Giant New Telescopic Eye Soon Will Peer Into Unexplored Depths of Space. By F. Barrows Colton. Vol. LXXVI, pp. 1-32, 23 ills. in black and white, 10 ills. in color, July, 1939.

Newspapers:

American Scene. 29 ills. from winning photographs in the Sixth Annual Newspaper National Snapshot Awards, with explanatory note. Vol. LXXIX, pp. 220-246, Feb., 1941.

Americana. 11 ills. from winning photographs in the Seventh Annual Newspaper National Snapshot Awards. Vol. LXXXI, pp. 657-666, May, 1942.

Newspapers—*Continued*

Making of a Japanese Newspaper. By Dr. Thomas E. Green. Vol. XXXVIII, pp. 327-334, 5 ills., Oct., 1920.

New China and the Printed Page. By Paul Hutchinson. Vol. LI, pp. 687-722, 37 ills., June, 1927.

Next International Geographical Congress to be Held in Washington. By Gilbert H. Grosvenor. Vol. XII, pp. 351-357, 4 ills., Oct., 1901.

Niagara Falls:

Niagara at the Battle Front. By William Joseph Showalter. Vol. XXXI, pp. 413-422, 6 ills., May, 1917.

World's Great Waterfalls: Visits to Mighty Niagara, Wonderful Victoria, and Picturesque Iguazu. By Theodore W. Noyes. Vol. L, pp. 29-59, 29 ills., July, 1926.

Niagaras of Five Continents. Vol. XXXVIII, pp. 211-226, 16 ills., Sept., 1920.

Nias (Island), Netherlands Indies:

Island of Nias, at the Edge of the World. By Mable Cook Cole. Vol. LX, pp. 201-224, 26 ills., 1 quarter-page map, Aug., 1931.

Nicaragua:

Army Engineer Explores Nicaragua: Mapping a Route for a New Canal Through the Largest of Central American Republics. By Lieut. Col. Dan I. Sultan. Vol. LXI, pp. 593-627, 39 ills., 1 two-thirds-page map, May, 1932.

Countries of the Caribbean. By William Joseph Showalter. Vol. XXIV, pp. 227-250, 23 ills., Feb., 1913.

Flying the World's Longest Air-Mail Route: From Montevideo, Uruguay, Over the Andes, Up the Pacific Coast, Across Central America and the Caribbean to Miami, Florida, in 67 Thrilling Flying Hours. By Junius B. Wood. Vol. LVII, pp. 261-325, 65 ills., 1 half-page map, Mar., 1930.

Land of Lakes and Volcanoes. By Luis Marden. With 17 ills. in color from natural-color photographs by the author. Vol. LXXXVI, pp. 161-192, 11 ills. in black and white, 1 two-thirds-page map, Aug., 1944.

Location of the Boundary Between Nicaragua and Costa Rica. By Arthur P. Davis. Vol. XII, pp. 22-28, 1 ill., 1 half-page map, Jan., 1901.

Nicaragua, Largest of Central American Republics. Vol. LI, pp. 370-378, 15 ills., Mar. 1927.

Nicaragua and the Isthmian Routes. By Arthur P. Davis. Vol. X, pp. 247-266, 8 ills., 2 diagrams, July, 1899.

Notes on Central America. Vol. XVIII, pp. 272-278, 1 ill., 1 half-page map, Apr., 1907.

Notes on Turbulent Nicaragua. Vol. XX, pp. 1102-1116, 13 ills., 1 page map, Dec., 1909.

Shattered Capitals of Central America. By Herbert J. Spinden. Vol. XXXVI, pp. 185-212, 32 ills., 1 page map, Sept., 1919.

Nicaragua—*Continued*

Wards of the United States: Notes on What Our Country Is Doing for Santo Domingo, Nicaragua, and Haiti. Vol. XXX, pp. 143-177, 36 ills., Aug., 1916.

See also Nicaragua Canal.

Nicaragua Canal:

Army Engineer Explores Nicaragua: Mapping a Route for a New Canal Through the Largest of Central American Republics. By Lieut. Col. Dan I. Sultan. Vol. LXI, pp. 593-627, 39 ills., 1 two-thirds-page map, May, 1932.

Assumed Inconstancy in the Level of Lake Nicaragua: A Question of Permanency of the Nicaragua Canal. By C. Willard Hayes. Vol. XI, pp. 156-161, Apr., 1900.

Completed Report of the Isthmian Canal Commission. Vol. XII, p. 441, Dec., 1901.

Isthmian Canal Problem. By W J McGee. Vol. X, pp. 363-364, Sept., 1899.

Nicaragua and the Isthmian Routes. By Arthur P. Davis. Vol. X, pp. 247-266, 8 ills., 2 diagrams, July, 1899.

Nicaragua Canal. Vol. XII, pp. 28-32, 2 ills., 1 half-page map, Jan., 1901.

Physiography of the Nicaragua Canal Route. By C. Willard Hayes. Vol. X, pp. 233-246, 2 page and 1 half-page maps, special map supplement, July, 1899.

Proposed American Interoceanic Canal in Its Commercial Aspects. By Joseph Nimmo, Jr. Vol. X, pp. 297-310, Aug., 1899.

Water Supply for the Nicaragua Canal. By Arthur P. Davis. Vol. XI, pp. 363-365, Sept., 1900.

Nice, France:

Carnival Days on the Riviera. By Maynard Owen Williams. Vol. L, pp. 467-501, 21 ills., Oct., 1926.

Nicholas, William H.:

Africa First of 1943 Global Warfare Maps. By William H. Nicholas. Text accompanying special map supplement in colors. Vol. LXXXIII, pp. 261-276, 13 ills., Feb., 1943.

American Pathfinders in the Pacific. By William H. Nicholas. Vol. LXXXIX, pp. 617-640, 17 ills., 1 two-page map, May, 1946.

Charting a World at War. By William H. Nicholas. Vol. LXXXVI, pp. 617-640, 23 ills., 1 drawing, Nov., 1944.

Gliders—Silent Weapons of the Sky. By William H. Nicholas. Vol. LXXXVI, pp. 149-160, 8 ills., Aug., 1944.

Heroes' Return. By William H. Nicholas. Vol. LXXXVII, pp. 333-352, 19 ills., Mar., 1945.

Making of Military Maps. By William H. Nicholas. Vol. LXXXIII, pp. 765-778, 17 ills., June, 1943.

Nantucket—Little Gray Lady. By William H. Nicholas. Vol. LXXXV, pp. 433-458, 14 ills. in black and white, 8 ills. in color, 1 half-page map, Apr., 1944.

Nicholas, William H.—*Continued*

Wartime Washington. By William H. Nicholas. Vol. LXXXIV, pp. 257-290, 12 ills. in black and white, 16 ills. in color, Sept., 1943.

World's Words. By William H. Nicholas. Vol. LXXXIV, pp. 689-700, 8 ills., 1 two-page map, Dec., 1943.

Nichols, (Dr.) John T.:

Interesting Citizens of the Gulf Stream. By Dr. John T. Nichols. Vol. XXXIX, pp. 69-84, 11 ills. in black and white, 16 ills. in color, Jan., 1921.

Nichols, Ruth Alexander:

Into the Land of the Chipmunk. By Ruth Alexander Nichols. Vol. LX, pp. 77-98, 28 ills., July, 1931.

Niedermeyer, (Col.) Oscar von (Haji Mirza Hussein):

Every-Day Life in Afghanistan. By Haji Mirza Hussein and Frederick Simpich. Vol. XXXIX, pp. 85-110, 26 ills., 1 three-quarters-page map, Jan., 1921.

Niedrach, Robert J.:

Birds and Beasts of Mexico's Desert Islands. 12 ills. in color from natural-color photographs; 8 ills. by Ed N. Harrison; 4 ills. by Alfred M. Bailey and Robert J. Niedrach. Vol. LXXX, pp. 353-360, Sept., 1941.

High Country of Colorado. 23 ills. in color from natural-color photographs by Alfred M. Bailey, Robert J. Niedrach, and F. G. Brandenburg. Vol. XC, pp. 49-64, July, 1946.

Niger Colony:

Three-Wheeling Through Africa : Two Adventurers Cross the So-called Dark Continent North of Lake Chad on Motorcycles with Side Cars. By James C. Wilson. Vol. LXV, pp. 37-92, 64 ills., 1 two-page map, Jan., 1934.

Niger River Valley:

In the Valley of the Niger (Africa). Vol. XIX, p. 164, Mar., 1908.

Nigeria:

British Commonwealth of Nations : "Organized Freedom" Around the World. By Eric Underwood. Vol. LXXXIII, pp. 485-524, 31 ills., Apr., 1943.

Kano, Mud-Made City. 10 ills. in color from natural-color photographs by George W. Scott and K. S. Twitchell. Vol. LXXXV, pp. 545-552, May, 1944.

New English Province of Northern Nigeria. Vol. XV, pp. 433-442, 9 ills., Nov., 1904.

Nigeria : From the Bight of Benin to Africa's Desert Sands. By Helen Trybulowski Gilles. Vol. LXXXV, pp. 537-568, 17 ills. in black and white, 10 ills. in color, 1 half-page map, May, 1944.

Notes on the Ekoi. By P. A. Talbot. Vol. XXIII, pp. 32-38, 8 ills., Jan., 1912.

Tailed People of Nigeria. Vol. XXIII, pp. 1239-1242, 3 ills., Dec., 1912.

Nigeria—*Continued*

Three-Wheeling Through Africa : Two Adventurers Cross the So-called Dark Continent North of Lake Chad on Motorcycles with Side Cars. By James C. Wilson. Vol. LXV, pp. 37-92, 64 ills., 1 two-page map, Jan., 1934.

Timbuktu and Beyond : Desert City of Romantic Savor and Salt Emerges into World Life Again as Trading Post of France's Vast African Empire. By Laura C. Boulton. Vol. LXXIX, pp. 631-670, 18 ills. in black and white, 26 ills. in color, 1 map (two-page spread), May, 1941.

Trans-Africa Safari : A Motor Caravan Rolls Across Sahara and Jungle Through Realms of Dusky Potentates and the Land of Big-Lipped Women. By Lawrence Copley Thaw and Margaret Stout Thaw. Vol. LXXIV, pp. 327-364, 29 ills. in black and white, 14 ills. in color, 1 two-thirds-page map, Sept., 1938.

Nightingale, Florence:

Symbol of Service to Mankind. By Stockton Axson. Vol. XXXIII, pp. 375-390, 11 ills., Apr., 1918.

Nikko, Japan :

Glimpses of Japan. By William W. Chapin. Vol. XXII, pp. 965-1002, 10 ills. in black and white, 34 ills. in color, Nov., 1911.

Why Nik-ko is Beautiful. By J. H. De Forest. Vol. XIX, pp. 300-308, 8 ills., Apr., 1908.

Nile (River), Egypt :

Along the Nile, Through Egypt and the Sudan. By Frederick Simpich. Vol. XLII, pp. 379-410, 29 ills., Oct., 1922.

Barrage of the Nile. By Day Allen Willey. Vol. XXI, pp. 175-184, 14 ills., Feb., 1910.

By Felucca Down the Nile : Giant Dams Rule Egypt's Lifeline River, Yet Village Life Goes On As It Did in the Time of the Pharaohs. By Willard Price. Vol. LXXVII, pp. 435-476, 21 ills. in black and white, 22 ills. in color, 1 two-page map, Apr., 1940.

Land of Egypt : A Narrow Green Strip of Fertility Stretching for a Thousand Miles Through Walls of Desert. By Alfred Pearce Dennis. Vol. XLIX, pp. 271-298, 28 ills., 1 half-page map, Mar., 1926.

Nilson, Elizabeth W.:

Rural Sweden Through American Eyes : A Visitor in Peacetime Finds Warmth, Welcome, and Strange Folkways On a Century-old Farm. By Elizabeth W. Nilson. Vol. LXXVII, pp. 795-822, 8 ills. in black and white, 22 ills. in color, June, 1940.

Nimitz, (Adm.) Chester W.:

Your Navy as Peace Insurance. By Fleet Admiral Chester W. Nimitz. Vol. LXXXIX, pp. 681-736, 32 ills. in black and white, 26 ills. in color, June, 1946.

Nimmo, Joseph, Jr.:

Proposed American Interoceanic Canal in Its Commercial Aspects. By Joseph Nimmo, Jr. Vol. X, pp. 297-310, Aug., 1899.

1940 Paradox in Hong Kong. By Frederick Simpich. Vol. LXXVII, pp. 531-558, 24 ills., 3 maps, Apr., 1940.

Nippur, Iraq :

Excavations at Nippur. Vol. XI, p. 392, Oct., 1900.

Nitobe, (Dr.) Inazu:

National Geographic Society (Speech by Dr. Inazu Nitobe). Vol. XXIII, pp. 273-298, 5 ills., Mar., 1912.

Nitrate Industry:

Longitudinal Journey Through Chile. By Harriet Chalmers Adams. Vol. XLII, pp. 219-273, 61 ills., 1 half-page map, Sept., 1922.

Niuafoō (Island), Tonga Islands :

Living on a Volcano : An Unspoiled Patch of Polynesia Is Niuafoō, Nicknamed "Tin Can Island" by Stamp Collectors. By Thomas A. Jaggar. Vol. LXVIII, pp. 91-106, 17 ills., 1 half-page map, July, 1935.

Nizhni Novgorod. *See* Gorki.

No Man's Land—Spitzbergen. Vol. XVIII, pp. 455-458, July, 1907.

Nobile, (Gen.) Umberto:

Navigating the *Norge* (Airship) from Rome to the North Pole and Beyond : The Designer and Pilot of the First Dirigible to Fly Over the Top of the World Describes a Thrilling Voyage of More Than 8,000 Miles. By Gen. Umberto Nobile. Vol. LII, pp. 177-215, 36 ills., 1 page map, Aug., 1927.

Nomad Life and Fossil Treasures of Mongolia. 20 ills. in color from photographs by J. B. Shackelford. Vol. LXIII, pp. 669-701, June, 1933.

Nomads:

Mountain Tribes of Iran and Iraq. By Harold Lamb. Vol. LXXXIX, pp. 385-408, 15 ills., 1 two-page map, Mar., 1946.

New Road to Asia. By Owen Lattimore. Vol. LXXXVI, pp. 641-676, 15 ills. in black and white, 26 ills. in color, Dec., 1944.

Sunny Siberia. 26 ills. in color from natural-color photographs by Owen Lattimore. Vol. LXXXVI, pp. 649-672, Dec., 1944.

See also Bedouins ; Lapps.

Nomads Among the Butterflies. 8 ills. in color ; 3 paintings by Hashime Murayama and 5 natural-color photographs by Willard R. Culver. Vol. LXXI, pp. 569-584, May, 1937.

Nomads of Arctic Lapland : Mysterious Little People of a Land of the Midnight Sun Live Off the Country Above the Arctic Circle. By Clyde Fisher. Vol. LXXVI, pp. 641-676, 28 ills. in black and white, 12 ills. in color, 1 page map, Nov., 1939.

Nome, Alaska :

Cape Nome Gold District. By F. C. Schrader. Vol. XI, pp. 15-23, 3 ills., 1 page map, Jan., 1900.

Nome Gold Fields. Vol. XIX, pp. 384-385, May, 1908.

Nome, Cape, Alaska :

Cape Nome Gold District. By F. C. Schrader. Vol. XI, pp. 15-23, 3 ills., 1 page map, Jan., 1900.

Origin of the Name "Cape Nome." Vol. XII, p. 398, Nov., 1901.

Non-Christian Peoples of the Philippine Islands. By Dean C. Worcester. Vol. XXIV, pp. 1157-1256, 41 ills. in black and white, 48 ills. in color, Nov., 1913.

Non-sporting Dogs. By Freeman Lloyd. Paintings by Walter A. Weber. Vol. LXXXIV, pp. 569-588, 9 ills. in black and white, 8 ills. in color from paintings from life, Nov., 1943.

Contains descriptions and illustrations of the following breeds : Boston Terrier, Chow, Dalmatian, English Bulldog, French Bulldog, Keeshond, Poodle, Schipperke.

Non-Stop Flight Across America. By Lieut. John A. Macready. Photographs by Albert W. Stevens. Vol. XLVI, pp. 1 89, 68 ills., 1 page and 1 half-page maps, July, 1924.

Nonsatong, Korea :

Exploring Unknown Corners of the "Hermit Kingdom." By Roy Chapman Andrews. Vol. XXXVI, pp. 24-48, 30 ills., 1 page map, July, 1919.

Nonsuch Island, Bermuda :

Depths of the Sea : Strange Life Forms a Mile Below the Surface. By William Beebe. Vol. LXI, pp. 65-88, 15 ills. in black and white, 8 ills. in color, 1 half-page map, Jan., 1932.

Round Trip to Davy Jones's Locker : Peering into Mysteries a Quarter Mile Down in the Open Sea, by Means of the Bathysphere. By William Beebe. Vol. LIX, pp. 653-678, 14 ills. in black and white, 8 ills. in color, 1 quarter-page map, June, 1931.

Nooks and Bays Around the Zuider Zee. 13 ills. in color from natural-color photographs by Wilhelm Tobien, Gervais Courtellemont, and Franklin Price Knott. Vol. LXIV, pp. 301-308, Sept., 1933.

Nooks and Bays of Storied England. 13 ills. in color from natural-color photographs by Clifton Adams and Bernard Wakeman. Vol. LXI, pp. 182-191, Feb., 1932.

Nootka (Indian Tribe) :

Indians of Our North Pacific Coast. By Matthew W. Stirling. Paintings by W. Langdon Kihn. Vol. LXXXVII, pp. 25-52, 3 ills. in black and white, 16 ills. in color, Jan., 1945.

Nördlingen, Germany :

Medieval Pageantry in Modern Nördlingen. 12 ills. in color from autochromes by Hans Hildenbrand. Vol. LIV, pp. 706-715, Dec., 1928.

Norge (Airship):

Navigating the *Norge* from Rome to the North Pole and Beyond: The Designer and Pilot of the First Dirigible to Fly Over the Top of the World Describes a Thrilling Voyage of More Than 8,000 Miles. By Gen. Umberto Nobile. Vol. LII, pp. 177-215, 36 ills., 1 page map, Aug., 1927.

Normandy (Region), France:

Beauties of France. By Arthur Stanley Riggs. Vol. XXVIII, pp. 391-491, 73 ills. in black and white, 16 ills. in color, 1 half-page map, Nov., 1915.

Charm and Color Distinguish Norman Byways. 13 ills. in color from natural-color photographs by Gervais Courtellement. Vol. LXI, pp. 90-99, Jan., 1932.

Coasts of Normandy and Brittany. By W. Robert Moore. Vol. LXXXIV, pp. 205-232, 5 ills. in black and white, 21 ills. in color, 1 two-page map, Aug., 1943.

France Farms as War Wages: An American Explores the Rich Rural Region of the Historic Paris Basin. By Harrison Howell Walker. Vol. LXXVII, pp. 201-238, 16 ills. in black and white, 18 ills. in color, 1 map, Feb., 1940.

Land of William the Conqueror: Where Northmen Came to Build Castles and Cathedrals. By Inez Buffington Ryan. Vol. LXI, pp. 89-99, 13 ills. in color, Jan., 1932.

Mont St. Michel, a Medieval Masterpiece. 22 ills. in duotone. Vol. LXIX, pp. 633-648, May, 1936.

Normandy—Choice of the Vikings. By Helen Churchill Candee. Vol. LXIX, pp. 625-665, 25 ills. in black and white, 22 ills. in duotone, 1 two-thirds-page map, May, 1936.

Normandy and Brittany in Brighter Days. 21 ills. in color from natural-color photographs by W. Robert Moore, Peter Upton Muir, and others. Vol. LXXXIV, pp. 209-232, Aug., 1943.

Normandy's Made-in-England Harbors. Vol. LXXXVII, pp. 565-580, 16 ills., 1 quarter-page map, May, 1945.

Notes on Normandy. By Mrs. George C. Bosson, Jr. Vol. XXI, pp. 775-782, 5 ills., Sept., 1910.

Some French Pastorals. 18 ills. in color from natural-color photographs by Harrison Howell Walker. Vol. LXXVII, pp. 207-230, Feb., 1940.

Normandy's Made-in-England Harbors. Vol. LXXXVII, pp. 565-580, 16 ills., 1 quarter-page map, May, 1945.

North About (Sailing Ship, *Joseph Conrad*). By Alan J. Villiers. Vol. LXXI, pp. 221-250, 24 ills., Feb., 1937.

North America:

Maps for Victory: National Geographic Society's Charts Used in War on Land, Sea, and in the Air. By Gilbert Grosvenor. Text accompanying special map supplement in colors. Vol. LXXXI, pp. 667-690, 28 ills., May, 1942.

North America—*Continued*

Our Map of North America. Text accompanying special map supplement in colors. Vol. XLV, p. 580, May, 1924.

See also names of individual countries.

North American Indian. Vol. XIX, pp. 448-454, 5 ills., June, 1908.

North American Indians. Vol. XVIII, pp. 469-484, 14 ills., July, 1907.

North American Woodpeckers. 25 ills. in color from paintings by Maj. Allan Brooks. Vol. LXIII, pp. 465-478, Apr., 1933.

North America's Oldest Metropolis: Through 600 Melodramatic Years, Mexico City Has Grown in Splendor and Achievement. By Frederick Simpich. Vol. LVIII, pp. 45-84, 34 ills., July, 1930.

North Carolina:

Bit of Elizabethan England in America: Fisher Folk of the Islands Off North Carolina Conserved the Speech and Customs of Sir Walter Raleigh's Colonists. By Blanch Nettleton Epler. Vol. LXIV, pp. 695-730, 43 ills., 1 three-quarters-page map, Dec., 1933.

Dismal Swamp in Legend and History: George Washington Owned Large Tracts in Region Which He Described as a "Glorious Paradise." By John Frances Ariza. Vol. LXII, pp. 121-130, 11 ills., July, 1932.

Gliders—Silent Weapons of the Sky (Laurinburg-Maxton Army Air Base). By William H. Nicholas. Vol. LXXXVI, pp. 149-160, 8 ills., Aug., 1944.

Motor-Coaching Through North Carolina. By Melville Chater. Vol. XLIX, pp. 475-523, 43 ills., 1 third-page map, May, 1926.

North Carolina Colorcade. 21 ills. in color from natural-color photographs; 19 ills. by J. Baylor Roberts. Vol. LXXX, pp. 189-220, Aug., 1941.

Patriotic Pilgrimage to Eastern National Parks: History and Beauty Live Along Paved Roads, Once Indian Trails, Through Virginia, North Carolina, Tennessee, Kentucky, and West Virginia. By Leo A. Borah. Vol. LXV, pp. 663-702, 18 ills. in black and white, 28 ills. in color, 1 two-page map, June, 1934.

Rambling Around the Roof of Eastern America (Great Smoky Mountains). By Leonard C. Roy. Vol. LXX, pp. 243-266, 25 ills., 1 page map, Aug., 1936.

Some Human Habitations. By Collier Cobb. Vol. XIX, pp. 509-515, 5 ills., July, 1908.

Tarheelia on Parade: Versatile and Vibrant, North Carolina in a Generation Has Climbed New Economic Heights. By Leonard C. Roy. Vol. LXXX, pp. 181-224, 24 ills. in black and white, 21 ills. in color, 1 map (two-page spread), Aug., 1941.

Where the Wind Does the Work (Cape Hatteras). By Collier Cobb. Vol. XVII, pp. 310-317, 9 ills., 1 page map, June, 1906.

North Carolina—*Continued*

Wild Gardens of the Southern Appalachians. 13 ills. in color from natural-color photographs by Edwin L. Wisherd, Laurence V. Jolliffe, and Clifton Adams. Vol. XLV, pp. 679-686, June, 1934.

North Dakota:

New Source of Power: Billions of Tons of Lignite, Previously Thought Too Poor Coal for Commercial Use, Are Made Easily Available. By Guy Elliott Mitchell. Vol. XXI, pp. 935-944, 7 ills., Nov., 1910.

Taming the Outlaw Missouri River. By Frederick Simpich. Vol. LXXXVIII, pp. 569-598, 25 ills., 1 two-page map, Nov., 1945.

North Frisian Islands, Germany:

Demolishing Germany's North Sea Ramparts. By Stuart E. Jones. Vol. XC, pp. 635-644, 1 ill. in black and white, 10 ills. in color, Nov., 1946.

North Holland Cheese Market. By Hugh M. Smith.

Vol. XXI, pp. 1051-1066, 17 ills., Dec., 1910.

North Island of New Zealand: A Vulcan's Play-

ground. 12 ills. in color from natural-color photographs by W. Robert Moore. Vol. LXIX, pp. 181-188, Feb., 1936.

North Pole:

Commander Byrd at the North Pole. Reproduction in color of the painting by N. C. Wyeth, National Geographic Society, Washington, D. C. Vol. LIII, supplement, May, 1928.

Commander Byrd Receives the Hubbard Gold Medal: The First Explorer to Reach the North Pole by Air Receives Coveted Honor at Brilliant National Geographic Society Reception. Vol. L, pp. 377-388, 5 ills., 1 chart, Sept., 1926.

Discovery of the North Pole (National Geographic Society Banquet). Vol. XXI, pp. 63-82, Jan., 1910.

Discovery of the Pole (First Reports by Peary and Cook). Vol. XX, pp. 892-896, 11 ills., 1 page map, Oct., 1909.

European Tributes to Peary. Vol. XXI, pp. 536-540, 4 ills., June, 1910.

Farthest North. Vol. XVII, pp. 638-644, 9 ills., Nov., 1906.

First Flight to the North Pole. By Lieut. Comdr. Richard Evelyn Byrd. Vol. L, pp. 357-376, 14 ills., Sept., 1926.

Honors to Peary (Presentation of Hubbard Gold Medal). Vol. XVIII, pp. 49-60, 1 ill., Jan., 1907.

Contains Commander Peary's reasons, methods, and desires to reach the Pole. This medal presented for arctic exploration farthest north, 87° 6', Dec. 15, 1906.

Memorial to Peary: The National Geographic Society Dedicates Monument in Arlington National Cemetery to Discoverer of the North Pole. Vol. XLI, pp. 639-646, 4 ills., June, 1922.

North Pole—*Continued*

National Geographic Society (Records of North Pole Discovery). Vol. XXI, p. 276, Mar., 1910.

Navigating the *Norge* (Airship) from Rome to the North Pole and Beyond: The Designer and Pilot of the First Dirigible to Fly Over the Top of the World Describes a Thrilling Voyage of More than 8,000 Miles. By Gen. Umberto Nobile. Vol. LII, pp. 177-215, 36 ills., 1 page map, Aug., 1927.

Nearest the Pole (Address by Robert E. Peary to The Society). Vol. XVIII, pp. 446-450, special map supplement, July, 1907.

North Pole (Appointment of a Committee by The Society to Consider Claims of Peary and Cook). Vol. XX, pp. 921-922, Nov., 1909.

North Pole (Resolutions of The Society Acknowledging Peary's Discovery). Vol. XX, pp. 1008-1009, Nov., 1909.

Peary and the North Pole. Vol. XIV, pp. 379-381, Oct., 1903.

Peary as a Leader: Incidents from the Life of the Discoverer of the North Pole Told by One of His Lieutenants on the Expedition Which Reached the Goal. By Donald B. MacMillan. Vol. XXXVII, pp. 293-317, 20 ills., 1 page map, Apr., 1920.

Peary on the North Pole. Vol. XIV, pp. 28-29, 1 page map, Jan., 1903.

Peary to Try Again. Vol. XVIII, p. 281, Apr., 1907.

Peary's Explorations in the Far North. By Gilbert Grosvenor. Vol. XXXVII, pp. 318-322, 3 ills., Apr., 1920.

Peary's Polar Expedition. Vol. XIX, p. 447, June, 1908.

Peary's Twenty Years' Service in the Arctics. Vol. XVIII, pp. 451-454, July, 1907.

Some Indications of Land in the Vicinity of the North Pole. By R. A. Harris. Vol. XV, pp. 255-261, 1 page map, June, 1904.

Value of Arctic Exploration. By Comdr. Robert E. Peary. Vol. XIV, pp. 429-436, Dec., 1903.

See also Arctic Regions.

North Sea:

Demolishing Germany's North Sea Ramparts (Helgoland). By Stuart E. Jones. Vol. XC, pp. 635-644, 1 ill. in black and white, 10 ills. in color, Nov., 1946.

Europe's Endangered Fish Supply: The War and the North Sea Fisheries. Vol. XXVII, pp. 141-152, 9 ills., 1 half-page map, Feb., 1915.

North Sea Mine Barrage. By Capt. Reginald R. Belknap. Vol. XXXV, pp. 85-110, 23 ills., 1 page map, 1 diagram, Feb., 1919.

Removal of the North Sea Mine Barrage. By Lieut. Comdr. Noel Davis. Vol. XXXVII, pp. 103-133, 28 ills., 2 half-page maps, Feb., 1920.

Northeast of Boston. By Albert W. Atwood. Vol.

LXXXVIII, pp. 257-292, 12 ills. in black and white, 17 ills. in color, special map supplement, Sept., 1945.

Northeastern Woodland Indians. *See* Eastern Woodland Indians.

Northern California at Work. By Frederick Simpich. Vol. LXIX, pp. 309-389, 36 ills. in black and white, 41 ills. in color, 1 two-page and 1 third-page maps, Mar., 1936.

Northern Crusoe's Island: Life on a Fox Farm Off the Coast of Alaska, Far from Contact with the World Eleven Months a Year. By Margery Pritchard Parker. Vol. XLIV, pp. 313-326, 15 ills., 1 eighth-page map, Sept., 1923.

Northern Hemisphere:

Map of the Northern and Southern Hemispheres. Text accompanying special map supplement in colors. Vol. LXXXIII, pp. 481-483, Apr., 1943.

Northern Ireland:

British Commonwealth of Nations: "Organized Freedom" Around the World. By Eric Underwood. Vol. LXXXIII, pp. 485-524, 31 ills., Apr., 1943.

Mist and Sunshine of Ulster. By Bernard F. Rogers, Jr. Vol. LXVIII, pp. 571-610, 23 ills. in black and white, 21 ills. in color, 1 three-quarters-page map, Nov., 1935.

Rambles Through Ulster, Northern Tip of the Shamrock Isle. 21 ills. in color from natural-color photographs by Bernard F. Rogers, Jr. Vol. LXVIII, pp. 577-600, Nov., 1935.

Yanks in Northern Ireland. 15 ills. from photographs. Vol. LXXXIV, pp. 191-204, Aug., 1943.

Northern Italy: Scenic Battleground. 18 ills. in color from natural-color photographs; 13 ills. by B. Anthony Stewart and 3 ills. by Lt. Benjamin C. McCartney. Vol. LXXXVII, pp. 265-288, Mar., 1945.

Northern Lights. By Alice Rollins Crane. Vol. XII, pp. 68-69, 1 ill., Feb., 1901.

Northwest Coast Indians:

Indians of Our North Pacific Coast. By Matthew W. Stirling. Paintings by W. Langdon Kihn. Vol. LXXXVII, pp. 25-52, 3 ills. in black and white, 16 ills. in color, Jan., 1945.

Totem-pole Builders. 16 ills. in color from paintings by W. Langdon Kihn. Vol. LXXXVII, pp. 33-48, Jan., 1945.

North-West Frontier Province, India:

South of Khyber Pass. By Maynard Owen Williams. Vol. LXXXIX, pp. 471-500, 31 ills., Apr., 1946.

Northwest Passage:

Honors for Amundsen (Banquet). Vol. XIX, pp. 55-76, 13 ills., Jan., 1908.

Modern Viking (Amundsen). Vol. XVII, pp. 38-40, 1 page map, Jan., 1906.

Northwest Territories, Canada:

Canada's Awakening North. By Lawrence J. Burpee. Vol. LXIX, pp. 749-767, 18 ills., June, 1936.

Northwestern Aeronautical Corporation, Minneapolis, Minnesota:

Gliders—Silent Weapons of the Sky. By William H. Nicholas. Vol. LXXXVI, pp. 149-160, 8 ills., Aug., 1944.

Norton, Wilson K.:

Sigiriya, "A Fortress in the Sky." By Wilson K. Norton. Vol. XC, pp. 665-680, 14 ills., 1 two-thirds-page map, Nov., 1946.

Norway:

Comparison of Norway and Sweden. Vol. XVI, pp. 429-431, Sept., 1905.

Country Life in Norway: The Beneficent Gulf Stream Enables One-Third of the People in a Far-north, Mountainous Land to Prosper on Farms. By Axel H. Oxholm. Vol. LXXV, pp. 493-528, 17 ills. in black and white, 20 ills. in color, 1 two-thirds-page map, Apr., 1939.

Europe's Northern Nomads (Lapps). 12 ills. in color from natural-color photographs by Jack Kuhne. Vol. LXXVI, pp. 657-664, Nov., 1939.

Fjords and Fjells of Viking Land. 27 ills. in color from natural-color photographs by Gustav Heurlin. Vol. LVIII, pp. 12-45, July, 1930.

King Herring: An Account of the World's Most Valuable Fish, the Industries It Supports, and the Part It Has Played in History. By Hugh M. Smith. Vol. XX, pp. 701-735, 21 ills., Aug., 1909.

Life in a Norway Valley: An American Girl Is Welcomed Into the Homemaking and Haying of Happy Hallingdal. By Abbie L. Bosworth. Vol. LXVII, pp. 627-648, 21 ills., 1 half-page map, May, 1935.

Norway, A Land of Stern Reality: Where Descendants of the Sea Kings of Old Triumphed Over Nature and Wrought a Nation of Arts and Crafts. By Alfred Pearce Dennis. Vol. LVIII, pp. 1-44, 31 ills. in black and white, 27 ills. in color, July, 1930.

Norway, an Active Ally. By Wilhelm Morgenstierne. Vol. LXXXIII, pp. 333-357, 24 ills., 1 two-thirds-page map, Mar., 1943.

Norway and the Norwegians. By Maurice Francis Egan. Vol. XLV, pp. 647-696, 45 ills., June, 1924.

Norwegian Fjords and Folkways. 20 ills. in color from natural-color photographs; 19 ills. by Jack Kuhne. Vol. LXXV, pp. 501-524, Apr., 1939.

Notable Norwegian Publication. By Charles Rabot. Vol. XV, pp. 370-371, Sept., 1904.

Sailing the Seven Seas in the Interest of Science: Adventures Through 157,000 Miles of Storm and Calm, from Arctic to Antarctic and Around the World, in the Non-Magnetic Yacht *Carnegie*. By J. P. Ault. Vol. XLII, pp. 631-690, 47 ills., 1 chart, Dec., 1922.

White War in Norway. By Thomas R. Henry. Vol. LXXXVIII, pp. 617-640, 23 ills., 1 three-quarters-page map, Nov., 1945.

Norwegian Expedition to the Magnetic North Pole by Roald Amundsen. Vol. XIV, pp. 293-294, July, 1903.

Norwegian Fjords and Folkways. 20 ills. in color from natural-color photographs; 19 ills. by Jack Kuhne. Vol. LXXV, pp. 501-524, Apr., 1939.

Norwegian Seamen and Ships:

Convoys to Victory. By Harvey Klemmer. Vol. LXXXIII, pp. 193-216, 24 ills., Feb., 1943.

Notes About Ants and Their Resemblance to Man. By William Morton Wheeler. Vol. XXIII, pp. 731-766, 32 ills., 2 diagrams, Aug., 1912.

Notes and Scenes from Korea. Vol. XIX, pp. 498-508, 14 ills., July, 1908.

Notes from a Naturalist's Experiences in British Guiana. By C. H. Eigenmann. Vol. XXII, pp. 859-870, 8 ills., Sept., 1911.

Notes on a Zoölogical Collecting Trip to Dutch New Guinea. By Thomas Barbour. Vol. XIX, pp. 469-484, 12 ills., 2 half-page maps, July, 1908.

Notes on Burma. By Thomas Barbour. Vol. XX, pp. 841-866, 34 ills., Oct., 1909.

Notes on Central America. Vol. XVIII, pp. 272-278, 1 ill., 1 half-page map, Apr., 1907.

Notes on Finland. By Baroness Alletta Korff. Vol. XXI, pp. 493-494, June, 1910.

Notes on Macedonia. Vol. XIX, pp. 790-802, 15 ills., 1 page map, Nov., 1908.

Notes on Manchuria. By Henry B. Miller. Vol. XV, pp. 261-262, June, 1904.

Notes on Morocco. Vol. XVII, p. 157, Mar., 1906.

Notes on Normandy. By Mrs. George C. Bosson, Jr. Vol. XXI, pp. 775-782, 5 ills., Sept., 1910.

Notes on Oman. By S. M. Zwemer. Vol. XXII, pp. 89-98, 8 ills., 1 half-page map, Jan., 1911.

Notes on Panama and Colombia. Vol. XIV, pp. 458-466, 12 ills., Dec., 1903.

Notes on Rumania. Vol. XXIII, pp. 1218-1225, 8 ills., Dec., 1912.

Notes on Southern Mexico (Agricultural Products). By G. N. Collins and C. B. Doyle. Vol. XXII, pp. 301-320, 16 ills., 1 half-page map, Mar., 1911.

Notes on Tahiti. By H. W. Smith. Vol. XXII, pp. 947-963, 17 ills., Oct., 1911.

Notes on the Deserts of the United States and Mexico (Extracted from a Publication of Dr. Daniel T. MacDougal). Vol. XXI, pp. 691-714, 16 ills., Aug., 1910.

Notes on the Distances Flies Can Travel. By N. A. Cobb. Vol. XXI, pp. 380-383, May, 1910.

Notes on the Ekoi (Nigeria). By P. A. Talbot. Vol. XXIII, pp. 32-38, 8 ills., Jan., 1912.

Notes on the Eucalyptus Tree from the United States Forest Service. Vol. XX, pp. 668-673, 4 ills., July, 1909.

Notes on the Forest Service. Vol. XVIII, pp. 142-145, 3 ills., Feb., 1907.

Notes on the Only American Colony in the World (Liberia). By Edgar Allen Forbes. Vol. XXI, pp. 719-729, 14 ills., Sept., 1910.

Notes on the Panama Canal. By Theodore P. Shonts. Vol. XVII, pp. 362-363, June, 1906.

Notes on the Remarkable Habits of Certain Turtles and Lizards. By H. A. Largelamb. Vol. XVIII, pp. 413-419, 12 ills., June, 1907.

Notes on the Sea Dyaks of Borneo. By Edwin H. Gomes. Vol. XXII, pp. 695-723, 26 ills., Aug., 1911.

Notes on Tibet. Vol. XV, pp. 292-294, 1 ill., July, 1904.

Notes on Troy. Vol. XXVII, pp. 531-532, 1 half-page map, Apr., 1915.

Notes on Turbulent Nicaragua. Vol. XX, pp. 1102-1116, 13 ills., 1 page map, Dec., 1909.

Nourse, Mary A.:

How Half the World Works. By Alice Tisdale Hobart and Mary A. Nourse. Vol. LXI, pp. 509-524, 22 ills., Apr., 1932.

Women's Work in Japan. By Mary A. Nourse. Vol. LXXIII, pp. 99-132, 32 ills. in black and white, 11 ills. in color, Jan., 1938.

Nova Scotia (Province), Canada:

Charm of Cape Breton Island: The Most Picturesque Portion of Canada's Maritime Provinces—A Land Rich in Historic Associations, Natural Resources, and Geographic Appeal. By Catherine Dunlop Mackenzie. Vol. XXXVIII, pp. 34-60, 22 ills., 1 three-quarters-page map, July, 1920.

Salty Nova Scotia: In Friendly New Scotland Gaelic Songs Still Answer the Skirling Bagpipes. By Andrew H. Brown. Vol. LXXVII, pp. 575-624, 30 ills. in black and white, 21 ills. in color, 1 two-page map, May, 1940.

Tartan Tints New Scotland. 21 ills. in color from natural-color photographs by John Mills, Jr., W. R. MacAskill, and others. Vol. LXXVII, pp. 591-622, May, 1940.

Tides in the Bay of Fundy. Vol. XVI, pp. 71-76, 4 ills., Feb., 1905.

Novarupta (Volcano), Alaska:

Valley of Ten Thousand Smokes: An Account of the Discovery and Exploration of the Most Wonderful Volcanic Region in the World. By Robert F. Griggs. Vol. XXXIII, pp. 115-169, 46 ills., 1 half-page map, panorama, Feb., 1918.

Noyes, Perley H.:

Visit to Lonely Iceland. By Perley H. Noyes. Vol. XVIII, pp. 731-741, 12 ills., Nov., 1907.

Noyes, Theodore W.:

World's Great Waterfalls: Visits to Mighty Niagara, Wonderful Victoria, and Picturesque Iguazu. By Theodore W. Noyes. Vol. L, pp. 29-59, 29 ills., July, 1926.

Nubas (Tribespeople) :

Two Fighting Tribes of the Sudan. By Merian C. Cooper. Photographs by Ernest B. Schoedsack. Vol. LVI, pp. 465-486, 27 ills., 1 two-thirds-page map, Oct., 1929.

Nuers (Tribespeople) :

Across Widest Africa. By A. Henry Savage Landor. Vol. XIX, pp. 694-737, 38 ills., 1 half-page map, Oct., 1908.

Nunivak (Island), Bering Sea :

Alaska—Our Northwestern Outpost. 16 ills. in color from natural-color photographs by Ernest H. Gruening, Amos Burg, and Froelich Rainey. Vol. LXXXII, pp. 297-308, Sept., 1942.

Nursing:

Flying Our Wounded Veterans Home. By Catherine Bell Palmer. Vol. LXXXVIII, pp. 363-384, 17 ills., Sept., 1945.

Heroes' Return. By William H. Nicholas. Vol. LXXXVII, pp. 333-352, 19 ills., Mar., 1945.

Nuthatches (Birds) :

Winged Denizens of Woodland, Stream, and Marsh. By Alexander Wetmore. Paintings by Maj. Allan Brooks. Vol. LXV, pp. 577-596, 5 portraits in color, May, 1934.

Nuts and Their Uses as Foods. Vol. XVIII, p. 800, Dec., 1907.

Nyamlagira (Volcano), Belgian Congo :

We Keep House on an Active Volcano : After Flying to Study a Spectacular Eruption in Belgian Congo, a Geologist Settles Down on a Newborn Craterless Vent for Eight Months' Study. By Dr. Jean Verhoogen. Vol. LXXVI, pp. 511-550, 28 ills., 1 two-thirds-page map, Oct., 1939.

Nyman, Stephen H.:

Gilded Domes Against an Azure Sky (Iran). 13 ills. in color from natural-color photographs by Stephen H. Nyman. Vol. LXXVI, pp. 339-346, Sept., 1939.

O

Oakland, California :

Wild Ducks as Winter Guests in a City Park. By Joseph Dixon. Vol. XXXVI, pp. 331-342, 11 ills., Oct., 1919.

Oakley, Thornton:

Industries : American Industries Geared for War. By Thornton Oakley. With 16 ills. in color from paintings by the author. Vol. LXXXII, pp. 716-734, 1 ill. in black and white, Dec., 1942.

Science Works for Mankind. 16 ills. in color from paintings by Thornton Oakley. Vol. LXXXVIII, pp. 737-752, Dec., 1945.

Transportation : American Transportation Vital to Victory. By Thornton Oakley. With 16 ills. in color from paintings by the author. Vol. LXXXIV, pp. 671-688, Dec., 1943.

Oaxaca (State), Mexico :

Among the Zapotecs of Mexico : A Visit to the Indians of Oaxaca, Home State of the Republic's Great Liberator, Juárez, and Its Most Famous Ruler, Diaz. By Herbert Corey. Vol. LI, pp. 501-553, 59 ills., 1 two-thirds-page map, May, 1927.

Hewers of Stone. By Jeremiah Zimmerman. Vol. XXI, pp. 1002-1020, 11 ills., Dec., 1910.

Monte Albán, Richest Archeological Find in America : A Tomb in Oaxaca, Mexico, Yields Treasures Which Reveal the Splendid Culture of the Mixtecs. By Dr. Alfonso Caso. Vol. LXII, pp. 487-512, 28 ills., Oct., 1932.

Oberammergau, Germany :

Behind the Scenes in the Home of the Passion Play. 11 ills. in color from natural-color photographs. Vol. LXVIII, pp. 753-760, Dec., 1935.

Where Bible Characters Live Again : Everyday Life in Oberammergau, World Famous for Its Passion Play, Reaches a Climax at Christmas. By Anton Lang, Jr. Vol. LXVIII, pp. 743-769, 19 ills. in black and white, 11 ills. in color, 1 third-page map, Dec., 1935.

Observations on the Russo-Japanese War in Japan and Manchuria. By Louis Livingston Seaman. Vol. XVI, pp. 80-82, Feb., 1905.

Observing a Total Eclipse of the Sun : Dimming Solar Light for a Few Seconds Entails Years of Work for Science and Attracts Throngs to "Nature's Most Magnificent Spectacle." By Paul A. McNally. Vol. LXII, pp. 597-605, 6 ills., Nov., 1932.

Observing an Eclipse in Asiatic Russia. By Irvine C. Gardner. Vol. LXXI, pp. 179-197, 19 ills. in black and white, 1 ill. in color, Feb., 1937.

Oceania. *See* Pacific Islands.

Oceanography:

Charting a World at War. By William H. Nicholas. Vol. LXXXVI, pp. 617-640, 23 ills., 1 drawing, Nov., 1944.

Cotidal Lines for the World. By R. A. Harris. Vol. XVII, pp. 303-309, 2 page and 1 half-page maps, special map supplement, June, 1906.

Drift of Floating Bottles in the Pacific Ocean. By James Page. Vol. XII, pp. 337-339, Sept., 1901.

Grandest and Most Mighty Terrestrial Phenomenon : The Gulf Stream. By Rear Adm. John Elliott Pillsbury. Vol. XXIII, pp. 767-778, 1 ill., 2 page and 1 half-page maps, 2 diagrams, Aug., 1912.

Ocean Currents. By James Page. Vol. XIII, pp. 135-142, Apr., 1902.

Our Global Ocean—Last and Vast Frontier. By F. Barrows Colton. Vol. LXXXVII, pp. 105-128, 19 ills., 1 drawing, Jan., 1945.

Our Guardians on the Deep. By William Joseph Showalter. Vol. XXV, pp. 655-677, 15 ills., 1 chart, June, 1914.

Oceanography—*Continued*

Tides in the Bay of Fundy. Vol. XVI, pp. 71-76, 4 ills., Feb., 1905.

Tides of Chesapeake Bay. By E. D. Preston. Vol. X, pp. 391-392, Oct., 1899.

War and Ocean Geography. By Gilbert Grosvenor. Vol. XXXIV, pp. 200-212, 0 ills., 1 page map, Sept., 1918.

See also Hydrography.

O'Connor, V. C. Scott:

Beyond the Grand Atlas: Where the French Tricolor Flies Beside the Flag of the Sultan of Morocco. By V. C. Scott O'Connor. Vol. LXI, pp. 261-319, 52 ills. in black and white, 12 ills. in color, 1 two-thirds-page map, Mar., 1932.

Old France in Modern Canada. By V. C. Scott O'Connor. Vol. LXVII, pp. 167-200, 36 ills., 1 page map, Feb., 1935.

Octopuses:

Marauders of the Sea. By Roy Waldo Miner. Vol. LXVIII, pp. 185-207, 12 ills. in black and white, 8 ills. in color, Aug., 1935.

Monster and Midget Squid and Octopuses. 8 ills. in color from paintings by Else Bostelmann. Vol. LXVIII, pp. 193-200, Aug., 1935.

Odessa, U. S. S. R.:

Ukraine, Past and Present. By Nevin O. Winter. Vol. XXXIV, pp. 114-128, 14 ills., Aug., 1918.

Ogasawara Shoto (Bonin Islands), Pacific Ocean:

American Pathfinders in the Pacific. By William H. Nicholas. Vol. LXXXIX, pp. 617-640, 17 ills., 1 two-page map, May, 1946.

Hidden Key to the Pacific: Piercing the Web of Secrecy Which Long Has Veiled Japanese Bases in the Mandated Islands. By Willard Price. Vol. LXXXI, pp. 759-785, 28 ills., 1 map (two-page spread), June, 1942.

Springboards to Tokyo. By Willard Price. Vol. LXXXVI, pp. 385-407, 16 ills., Oct., 1944.

Ohio:

Indian Village of Baum. By H. C. Brown. Vol. XII, pp. 272-274, July, 1901.

Ohio, The Gateway State. By Melville Chater. Vol. LXI, pp. 525-591, 58 ills. in black and white, 13 ills. in color, 1 three-quarters-page map, May, 1932.

Submerged Valleys in Sandusky Bay. By E. L. Moseley. Vol. XIII, pp. 398-403, 4 charts, Nov., 1902.

Where the Winning of the West Began. 13 ills. in color from natural-color photographs by Jacob Gayer. Vol. LXI, pp. 562-571, May, 1932.

See also Wright Field.

Ohio (River), United States:

Men Against the Rivers. By Frederick Simpich. Vol. LXXI, pp. 767-794, 22 ills., 1 page-and-a-half and 1 quarter-page maps, June, 1937.

Ohio (River), United States—*Continued*

Ohio, The Gateway State. By Melville Chater. Vol. LXI, pp. 525-591, 58 ills. in black and white, 13 ills. in color, 1 three-quarters-page map, May, 1932.

Travels of George Washington: Dramatic Episodes in His Career as the First Geographer of the United States. By William Joseph Showalter. Vol. LXI, pp. 1-63, 50 ills., 5 maps, special supplement in colors, Jan., 1932.

Oil. *See* Petroleum.

Oil Comes to Bahrein, Port of Pearls. 11 ills. in color from natural-color photographs by Maynard Owen Williams. Vol. LXXXIX, pp. 201-208, Feb., 1946.

Oil Fields of Texas and California. Vol. XII, pp. 276-278, July, 1901.

Oil for Victory Piped under the Sea. 9 ills. from photographs. Vol. LXXXVIII, pp. 721-726, Dec., 1945.

Oil Treasure of Mexico. By Russell Hastings Millward. Vol. XIX, pp. 803-805, 1 ill., Nov., 1908.

Ojibways (Indians):

Wild Life of Lake Superior, Past and Present: The Habits of Deer, Moose, Wolves, Beavers, Muskrats, Trout, and Feathered Wood-Folk Studied with Camera and Flashlight. By George Shiras, 3d. Vol. XL, pp. 113-204, 77 ills., 1 half-page map, Aug., 1921.

Okefinokee (Swamp), Georgia-Florida:

Okefinokee Wilderness: Exploring the Mystery Land of the Suwannee River Reveals Natural Wonders and Fascinating Folklore. By Francis Harper. Vol. LXV, pp. 597-624, 35 ills., 1 two-thirds-page map, May, 1934.

Okinawa (Island), Ryukyu Retto:

American Pathfinders in the Pacific. By William H. Nicholas. Vol. LXXXIX, pp. 617-640, 17 ills., 1 two-page map, May, 1946.

Okinawa, Threshold to Japan. By Lt. David D. Duncan, USMC. With 22 ills. in color from natural-color photographs by the author and others. Vol. LXXXVIII, pp. 411-428, Oct., 1945.

Peacetime Rambles in the Ryukyus. By William Leonard Schwartz. Vol. LXXXVII, pp. 543-561, 12 ills., 1 two-thirds-page and 1 half-page maps, May, 1945.

Oklahoma:

Big Oklahoma. By Bird S. McGuire. Vol. XVII, pp. 103-105, 1 ills., Feb., 1906.

So Oklahoma Grew Up. By Frederick Simpich. Vol. LXXIX, pp. 269-314, 30 ills. in black and white, 19 ills. in color, 1 page map, Mar., 1941.

Sunshine over Oklahoma. 19 ills. in color from natural-color photographs by B. Anthony Stewart. Vol. LXXIX, pp. 277-308, Mar., 1941.

Oklahoma City, Oklahoma:

So Oklahoma Grew Up. By Frederick Simpich. Vol. LXXIX, pp. 269-314, 30 ills. in black and white, 19 ills. in color, 1 page map, Mar., 1941.

Olcott, Charles S.:

Orkneys and Shetlands—A Mysterious Group of Islands. By Charles S. Olcott. Vol. XXXIX, pp. 197-228, 33 ills., Feb., 1921.

Old and New Blend in Yankeeland (Connecticut). 25 ills. in color from natural-color photographs. Vol. LXXIV, pp. 295-326, Sept., 1938.

Old and New in Persia: In This Ancient Land Now Called Iran a Modern Sugar Factory Rears Its Head Near the Palace of Darius the Great. By The Baroness Ravensdale. Vol. LXXVI, pp. 325-355, 20 ills. in black and white, 13 ills. in color, 1 two-thirds-page map, Sept., 1939.

Old France in Modern Canada. By V. C. Scott O'Connor. Vol. LXVII, pp. 167-200, 36 ills., 1 page map, Feb., 1935.

Old Ireland, Mother of New Eire: By Whatever Name, 'Tis the Same Fair Land With the Grass Growing Green on the Hills of Her and the Peat Smoke Hanging Low. By Harrison Howell Walker. Vol. LXXVII, pp. 649-691, 19 ills. in black and white, 18 ills. in color, 1 page map, May, 1940.

Old Jewel in the Proper Setting: An Eyewitness' Account of the Reconquest of the Holy Land by Twentieth Century Crusaders. By Charles W. Whitehair. Vol. XXXIV, pp. 325-344, 17 ills., Oct., 1918.

Old Line State Cyclorama (Maryland). 22 ills. in color from natural-color photographs by W. Robert Moore, B. Anthony Stewart, and others. Vol. LXXIX, pp. 409-432, Apr., 1941.

Old Masters in a New National Gallery. By Ruth Q. McBride. Vol. LXXVIII, pp. 1-50, 11 ills. in black and white, 32 color reproductions of masterpieces, July, 1940.

Old Mines and Mills in India. Vol. XX, pp. 489-490, 2 ills., May, 1909.

Old-New Battle Grounds of Egypt and Libia. By W. Robert Moore. Vol. LXXVIII, pp. 809-820, 8 ills., 1 third-page map, Dec., 1940.

Old Pattern and New in Turkey. 23 ills. in color from natural-color photographs by Bernard F. Rogers, Jr. Vol. LXXV, pp. 17-48, Jan., 1939.

Old Post-Road from Tiflis to Erivan. By Esther Lancraft Hovey. Vol. XII, pp. 300-309, 9 ills., Aug., 1901.

Old World Charm in Modern Quebec. 12 ills. in color from natural-color photographs by William D. Boutwell, Jacob Gayer, Edwin L. Wisherd, and Clifton Adams. Vol. LVII, pp. 506-515, Apr., 1930.

Old Yuma Trail. By W J McGee. Part I, Vol. XII, pp. 103-107, Mar., 1901. Part II, Vol. XII, pp. 129-143, 7 ills., 1 page map, Apr., 1901.

Oldest Free Assemblies: Address of Right Hon. Arthur J. Balfour, in the United States House of Representatives, May 5, 1917. Vol. XXXI, pp. 368-371, Apr., 1917.

Oldest Living Thing ("General Sherman Tree"). Vol. XXIX, supplement, Apr., 1916.

Oldest Nation of Europe: Geographical Factors in the Strength of Modern England. By Roland G. Usher. Vol. XXVI, pp. 393-414, 11 ills., Oct., 1914.

Oliver, Douglas L.:

Treasure Islands of Australasia: New Guinea, New Caledonia, and Fiji Trace across the South Pacific a Fertile Crescent Incredibly Rich in Minerals and Foods. By Douglas L. Oliver. Vol. LXXXI, pp. 691-722, 23 ills., 1 two-page map, June, 1942.

Oliver, Eleanor Schirmer:

Woman's Experiences among Stone Age Solomon Islanders: Primitive Life Remains Unchanged in Tropical Jungleland Where United States Forces Now Are Fighting. By Eleanor Schirmer Oliver. Vol. LXXXII, pp. 813-836, 26 ills., 1 half-page map, Dec., 1942.

Oliver, Marion L.:

Snake Dance (Hopi Indians). By Marion L. Oliver. Vol. XXII, pp. 107-137, 31 ills., Feb., 1911.

Oliver, W. J.:

Peaks and Parks of Western Canada. 11 ills. from photographs; 5 ills. by W. J. Oliver. Vol. LXXX, pp. 516-526, Oct., 1941.

Olmec Civilization:

Great Stone Faces of the Mexican Jungle: Five Colossal Heads and Numerous Other Monuments of Vanished Americans Are Excavated by the Latest National Geographic-Smithsonian Expedition. By Matthew W. Stirling. Vol. LXXVIII, pp. 309-334, 26 ills., 1 map, Sept., 1940.

See also La Venta, Mexico.

Olson, Alma Luise:

Farthest-North Republic: Olympic Games and Arctic Flying Bring Sequestered Finland into New Focus of World Attention. By Alma Luise Olson. Vol. LXXIV, pp. 499-533, 25 ills. in black and white, 12 ills. in color, 1 page map, Oct., 1938.

Sweden, Land of White Birch and White Coal. By Alma Luise Olson. Vol. LIV, pp. 441-484, 51 ills. in black and white, 29 ills. in color, Oct., 1928.

Olsson-Seffer, Helen:

Isthmus of Tehuantepec (Mexico): The Bridge of the World's Commerce. By Helen Olsson-Seffer. Vol. XXI, pp. 991-1002, 6 ills., Dec., 1910.

Olsson-Seffer, (Dr.) Pehr:

Agricultural Possibilities in Tropical Mexico. By Dr. Pehr Olsson-Seffer. Vol. XXI, pp. 1021-1040, 18 ills., Dec., 1910.

Omaha, Nebraska:

Cornhusker State Highlights. 23 ills. in color from natural-color photographs by D. Anthony Stewart. Vol. LXXXVII, pp. 521-536, May, 1945.

Nebraska, the Cornhusker State. By Leo A. Borah. Vol. LXXXVII, pp. 513-542, 6 ills. in black and white, 23 ills. in color, 1 map (two-page spread), May, 1945.

Omaha Beach (Artificial Harbor), Normandy Coast, France:

Normandy's Made-in-England Harbors. Vol. LXXXVII, pp. 565-580, 16 ills., 1 quarter-page map, May, 1945.

Oman (Sultanate), Arabia:

Notes on Oman. By S. M. Zwemer. Vol. XXII, pp. 89-98, 8 ills., 1 half-page map, Jan., 1911.

Omsk, R. S. F. S. R.:

Land of Promise (Siberia). By Maj. Gen. A. W. Greely. Vol. XXIII, pp. 1078-1090, 7 ills., Nov., 1912.

On a Chilean Hacienda. 8 ills. in color from natural-color photographs by E. P. Haddon. Vol. LXXXVI, pp. 489-496, Oct., 1944.

On Danish By-Lanes: An American Cycles Through the Quaint City of Lace, the Curiosity Town Where Time Stands Still, and Even Finds a Frontier in the Farming Kingdom. By Willis Lindquist. Vol. LXXVII, pp. 1-34, 21 ills. in black and white, 10 ills. in color, 1 three-quarters-page map, Jan., 1940.

On Goes Wisconsin: Strength and Vigor Mark This Midwestern State, With Its Woods and Lakes and Its Blend of Sturdy Nationalities. By Glanville Smith. Vol. LXXII, pp. 1-46, 25 ills. in black and white, 27 ills. in color, 1 two-page map, July, 1937.

On Mackenzie's Trail to the Polar Sea. By Amos Burg. Vol. LX, pp. 127-156, 32 ills., 1 page map, Aug., 1931.

On the Bottom of a South Sea Pearl Lagoon. By Roy Waldo Miner. Vol. LXXIV, pp. 365-390, 17 ills. in black and white, 8 ills. in color, Sept., 1938.

On the Bypaths of Spain. By Harry A. McBride. Vol. LV, pp. 311-364, 50 ills. in black and white, 13 ills. in color, 1 two-thirds-page map, Mar., 1929.

On the Cortés Trail. By Luis Marden. Vol. LXXVIII, pp. 335-375, 17 ills. in black and white, 22 ills. in color, 1 map, Sept., 1940.

On the Fringe of the Great Desert (Algeria). 32 ills. in color from autochromes by Gervais Courtellemont. Vol. LIII, pp. 206-223, Feb., 1928.

On the Monastir Road. By Herbert Corey. Vol. XXXI, pp. 383-412, 31 ills., May, 1917.

On the Shores of the Caribbean. Vol. XLI, pp. 157-172, 16 ills., Feb., 1922.

On the Trail of a Horse Thief (British Columbia). By Herbert W. Gleason. Vol. XXXV, pp. 349-350, 6 ills., Apr., 1919.

On the Trail of King Solomon's Mines: The Bible, in Addition to Its Spiritual Values, Continues to Prove a Rich Geography and Guide to Exploration of the Holy Land. By Nelson Glueck. Vol. LXXXV, pp. 233-256, 20 ills., 1 page map, Feb., 1944.

On the Trail of the Air Mail: A Narrative of the Experiences of the Flying Couriers Who Relay the Mail Across America at a Speed of More Than 2,000 Miles a Day. By Lieut. J. Parker Van Zandt. Vol. XLIX, pp. 1-61, 67 ills., 1 two-thirds-page map, Jan., 1926.

On the Turks' Russian Frontier: Everyday Life In the Fastnesses between the Black Sea and Ararat, Borderland of Oil and Minerals that Hitler Covets. By Edward Stevenson Murray. Vol. LXXX, pp. 367-392, 21 ills., 1 half-page map, Sept., 1941.

On the Wings of the Wind: In Motorless Planes, Pilots Ride in Flying-Fox Fashion, Cruising on Upward Air Streams and Lifted by the Suction of Moving Clouds. By Howard Siepen. Vol. LV, pp. 751-780, 40 ills., June, 1929.

On the World's Highest Plateaus: Through an Asiatic No Man's Land to the Desert of Ancient Cathay. By Hellmut de Terra. Vol LIX, pp. 319-367, 39 ills. in black and white, 32 ills. in color, 1 two-thirds-page map, Mar., 1931.

Ona Indians:

Indian Tribes of Southern Patagonia, Tierra del Fuego, and the Adjoining Islands. By J. B. Hatcher. Vol. XII, pp. 12-22, 4 ills., Jan., 1901.

Once in a Lifetime: Black Bears Rarely Have Quadruplets, But Goofy Did—and the Camera Caught Her Nursing Her Remarkable Family. By Paul B. Kinney. Vol. LXXX, pp. 249-258, 11 ills., Aug., 1941.

One Hundred British Seaports. Vol. XXXI, pp. 84-94, 10 ills., 1 page map, Jan., 1917.

One Season's Game-Bag with the Camera. By George Shiras, 3d. Vol. XIX, pp. 387-446, 70 ills., June, 1908.

One Thousand Miles of Railway Built for Pilgrims and Not for Dividends (Damascus to Mecca). By Col. F. R. Maunsell. Vol. XX, pp. 156-172, 13 ills., 1 three-quarters-page map, Feb., 1909.

Onions and Onion Growing:

Black Acres (Mucklands of New York): A Thrilling Sketch in the Vast Volume of Who's Who Among the Peoples That Make America. By Dorothea D. and Fred Everett. Vol. LXXX, pp. 631-652, 13 ills. in black and white, 12 ills. in color, Nov., 1941.

Ontario (Province), Canada:

Ontario, Next Door: Alert, Energetic, and Resourceful, Its British Pluck and Skill in Arts and Trades Gain for This Province a High Place Under the Union Jack. By Frederick Simpich. Vol. LXII, pp. 131-183, 54 ills., 1 three-quarters-page map, Aug., 1932.

Ontong Java (Islands), Solomon Islands:

Coconuts and Coral Islands. By H. Ian Hogbin. Vol. LXV, pp. 265-298, 24 ills. in black and white, 14 ills. in color, 1 half-page map, Mar., 1934.

Open-Air Law Courts of Ethiopia. 18 ills. by Harald P. Lechenperg. Vol. LXVIII, pp. 633-646, Nov., 1935.

Opening of the Alaskan Territory. By Harrington Emerson. Vol. XIV, pp. 99-106, 5 ills., Mar., 1903.

Operation Crossroads (Atomic Bomb Tests):

Farewell to Bikini. By Carl Markwith. Vol. XC, pp. 97-116, 16 ills., July, 1946.

Operation Pluto: World War II:

Oil for Victory Piped under the Sea. 9 ills. from photographs. Vol. LXXXVIII, pp. 721-726, Dec., 1945.

Oraibi, Arizona:

Snake Dance (Hopi Indians). By Marion L. Oliver. Vol. XXII, pp. 107-137, 31 ills., Feb., 1911.

Oran, Algeria:

Eastward from Gibraltar: Overland Route Across North Africa to Tunisia and Libia. By Cyrus French Wicker. Vol. LXXXIII, pp. 115-142, 28 ills., Jan., 1943.

Orange County, New York:

Black Acres: A Thrilling Sketch in the Vast Volume of Who's Who Among the Peoples That Make America. By Dorothea D. and Fred Everett. Vol. LXXX, pp. 631-652, 13 ills. in black and white, 12 ills. in color, Nov., 1941.

Orange Free State, Union of South Africa:

Orange Free State: The Prairie Province. By Melville Chater. Vol. LIX, pp. 431-444, 11 ills., Apr., 1931.

Orangutans:

Manlike Apes of Jungle and Mountain. 10 ills. in color from paintings by Elie Cheverlange. Vol. LXXVIII, pp. 221-228, Aug., 1940.

Man's Closest Counterparts: Heavyweight of Monkeydom Is the "Old Man" Gorilla, by Far the Largest of the Four Great Apes. By William M. Mann. Vol. LXXVIII, pp. 213-236, 10 ills. in black and white, 10 ills. in color, Aug., 1940.

Orchids:

Land of the Painted Oxcarts (Costa Rica). By Luis Marden. With 31 ills. in color from natural-color photographs by the author. Vol. XC, pp. 409-456, 30 ills. in black and white, 1 half-page map, Oct., 1946.

Ore-Boat Unloaders. By W. M. Gregory. Vol. XVIII, pp. 343-345, 1 ill., May, 1907.

Oregon:

Columbia (River) Turns on the Power. By Maynard Owen Williams. Vol. LXXIX, pp. 749-792, 25 ills. in black and white, 18 ills. in color, June, 1941.

Crater Lake, Oregon. Vol. XIII, p. 221, June, 1902.

Crater Lake and Yosemite Through the Ages. By Wallace W. Atwood, Jr. Paintings by Eugene Kingman. Vol. LXXI, pp. 327-343, 7 ills. in black and white, 13 ills. in color, Mar., 1937.

Is Our Noblest Volcano Awakening to New Life: A Description of the Glaciers and Evidences of Volcanic Activity of Mount Hood. By A. H. Sylvester. Vol. XIX, pp. 515-525, 5 ills., 1 page map, July, 1908.

Native Son's Rambles in Oregon. By Amos Burg. Vol. LXV, pp. 173-234, 39 ills. in black and white, 24 ills. in color, 1 two-page map, Feb., 1934.

Oregon Finds New Riches. By Leo A. Borah. Vol. XC, pp. 681-728, 15 ills. in black and white, 28 ills. in color, 1 two-page map, Dec., 1946.

Our Pacific Northwest. By N. H. Darton. Vol. XX, pp. 645-663, 12 ills., 2 half-page maps, July, 1909.

Scenes Among the High Cascades in Central Oregon. By Ira A. Williams. Vol. XXIII, pp. 578-592, 11 ills., June, 1912.

Scenes and Round-Ups of the Beaver State. 24 ills. in color from natural-color photographs by Amos Burg. Vol. LXV, pp. 181-212, Feb., 1934.

Topographic Work of the United States Geological Survey in 1902. Vol. XIII, pp. 326-328, Aug., 1902.

Wartime in the Pacific Northwest. By Frederick Simpich. Vol. LXXXII, pp. 421-464, 25 ills. in black and white, 23 ills. in color, 1 half-page map, Oct., 1942.

Where Fog and Sun Paint the Pacific. 23 ills. in color from natural-color photographs by J. Baylor Roberts. Vol. LXXXII, pp. 437-460, Oct., 1942.

"Where Rolls the Oregon." 28 ills. in color from natural-color photographs by Ray Atkeson. Vol. XC, pp. 689-728, Dec., 1946.

Oregon Territory:

Boundaries of Territorial Acquisitions. Vol. XII, pp. 373-377, 1 page chart, Oct., 1901.

Oregon Trail:

Grass Makes Wyoming Fat. By Frederick Simpich. Vol. LXXXVIII, pp. 158-188, 13 ills. in black and white, 19 ills. in color, 1 two-page map, Aug., 1945.

Idaho Made the Desert Bloom. By D. Worth Clark. Vol. LXXXV, pp. 641-688, 21 ills. in black and white, 20 ills. in color, 1 page map, June, 1944.

Oregon Trail—*Continued*

Nebraska, the Cornhusker State. By Leo A. Borah. Vol. LXXXVII, pp. 513-542, 6 ills. in black and white, 23 ills. in color, 1 map (two-page spread), May, 1945.

O'Reilly, John:

South Florida's Amazing Everglades: Encircled by Populous Places Is a Seldom-visited Area of Rare Birds, Prairies, Cowboys, and Teeming Wild Life of Big Cypress Swamp. By John O'Reilly. Vol. LXXVII, pp. 115-142, 26 ills., 1 page map, Jan., 1940.

Oriental Pageantry of Northern India. 30 ills. in color from natural-color photographs by Franklin Price Knott. Vol. LVI, pp. 428-461, Oct., 1929.

Origin of American State Names. By Frederick W. Lawrence. Vol. XXXVIII, pp. 104-143, 34 ills., Aug., 1920.

Origin of "Labrador." Vol. XVII, pp. 587-588, Oct., 1906.

Origin of Stefansson's Blond Eskimo. By Maj. Gen. A. W. Greely. Vol. XXIII, pp. 1224-1238, 10 ills., 1 page map, Dec., 1912.

Origin of the Name "Cape Nome." Vol. XII, p. 398, Nov., 1901.

Origin of the Yosemite Valley. By Henry Gannett. Vol. XII, pp. 86-87, Feb., 1901.

Original Boundary Stones of the District of Columbia. By Ernest A. Shuster, Jr. Vol. XX, pp. 356-359, 6 ills., 1 half-page map., Apr., 1909.

Original Territory of the United States. By David J. Hill. Vol. X, pp. 73-92, Mar., 1899.

Orinoco (River), Venezuela :

In Humboldt's Wake: Narrative of a National Geographic Society Expedition Up the Orinoco and Through the Strange Casiquiare Canal to Amazonian Waters. By Ernest G. Holt. Vol. LX, pp. 621-644, 27 ills., 1 two-thirds-page map, Nov., 1931.

Orioles:

Blackbirds and Orioles. By Arthur A. Allen. Paintings by Maj. Allan Brooks. Vol. LXVI, pp. 111-130, 12 portraits in color, July, 1934.

Orizaba (Volcano), Mexico :

Greatest Volcanoes of Mexico. By A. Melgareio. Vol. XXI, pp. 741-760, 22 ills., Sept., 1910.

Naturalist's Journey Around Vera Cruz and Tampico. By Frank M. Chapman. Vol. XXV, pp. 532-562, 31 ills., May, 1914.

Orkneys and Shetlands—A Mysterious Group of Islands. By Charles S. Olcott. Vol. XXXIX, pp. 197-228, 33 ills., Feb., 1921.

Osgood, Wilfred H.:

Alaskan Brown Bear. By Wilfred H. Osgood. Vol. XX, pp. 332-333, Apr., 1909.

Big Game of Alaska. By Wilfred H. Osgood. Vol. XX, pp. 624-636, 10 ills., July, 1909.

Osgood, Wilfred H.—*Continued*

Lake Clark, a Little-Known Alaskan Lake. By Wilfred H. Osgood. Vol. XV, pp. 326-331, 2 ills., 1 half-page map, Aug., 1904.

Nature and Man in Ethiopia. By Wilfred H. Osgood. Vol. LIV, pp. 121-176, 64 ills., 1 two-thirds-page map, Aug., 1928.

Oslo, Norway :

White War in Norway. By Thomas R. Henry. Vol. LXXXVIII, pp. 617-640, 23 ills., 1 three-quarters-page map, Nov., 1945.

Ospreys:

Cruise of the *Kinkajou* : Among Desert Islands of Mexico Voyagers Find Outdoor Laboratories for the Naturalist and Ideal Fishing Grounds for the Sportsman. By Alfred M. Bailey. Vol. LXXX, pp. 339-366, 13 ills. in black and white, 12 ills. in color, 1 page map, Sept., 1941.

The Eagle, King of Birds, and His Kin. By Alexander Wetmore. Paintings by Maj. Allan Brooks. Vol. LXIV, pp. 43-95, 23 ills. in black and white, 28 ills. in color, July, 1933.

Photographing the Nest Life of the Osprey. By Capt. C. W. R. Knight. Vol. LXII, pp. 247-260, 25 ills., Aug., 1932.

Osterhout, (Maj.) G. H., Jr.:

Little-Known Marvel of the Western Hemisphere : Christophe's Citadel, a Monument to the Tyranny and Genius of Haiti's King of Slaves. By Maj. G. H. Osterhout, Jr. Vol. XXXVIII, pp. 468-482, 13 ills., Dec., 1920.

Ostrich Farming in the United States. Vol. XVII, pp. 569-574, 6 ills., Oct., 1906.

Ostriches:

Ostrich Farming in the United States. Vol. XVII, pp. 569-574, 6 ills., Oct., 1906.

Other Working Dogs and the Wild Species. By Stanley P. Young. Paintings by Walter A. Weber. Vol. LXXXVI, pp. 363-384, 12 ills. in black and white, 9 ills. in color, Sept., 1944.

Otomi Indians:

Mexican Indian Flying Pole Dance. By Helga Larsen. Vol. LXXI, pp. 387-400, 13 ills., Mar., 1937.

Ottawa, Canada :

Ontario, Next Door : Alert, Energetic, and Resourceful, Its British Pluck and Skill in Arts and Trades Gain for This Province a High Place Under the Union Jack. By Frederick Simpich. Vol. LXII, pp. 131-183, 54 ills., 1 three-quarters-page map, Aug., 1932.

Oued Souf (Region), Algeria :

Country of the Ant Men. By Thomas H. Kearney. Vol. XXII, pp. 367-382, 11 ills., 1 half-page map, Apr., 1911.

Oulié, Marthe:

Cruising to Crete : Four French Girls Set Sail in a Breton Yawl for the Island of the Legendary Minotaur. By Marthe Oulié and Mariel Jean-Brunhes. Vol. LV, pp. 249-272, 15 ills. in black and white, 14 ills. in color, 1 page map, Feb., 1929.

Our Air Frontier in Alaska. By Major General H. H. Arnold. Vol. LXXVIII, pp. 487-504, 15 ills., 1 page map, Oct., 1940.

Our Armies of Mercy (Red Cross). By Henry P. Davison. Vol. XXXI, pp. 423-427, 3 ills., May, 1917.

Our Army Versus a Bacillus. By Alton G. Grinnell. Vol. XXIV, pp. 1146-1152, 5 ills., 1 diagram, Oct., 1913.

Our Big Trees Saved. Vol. XXXI, pp. 1-11, 10 ills., Jan., 1917.

Our Coal Lands. By Guy Elliott Mitchell. Vol. XXI, pp. 446-451, 5 ills., May, 1910.

Our Colored Pictures. Vol. XXI, pp. 965-967, Nov., 1910.

Our Colorful City of Magnificent Distances (Washington, D. C.). 49 ills. in color from natural-color photographs by Staff Photographers and Capt. A. W. Stevens. Vol. LX, pp. 530-611, Nov., 1931.

Our Common Dogs. By Louis Agassiz Fuertes and Ernest Harold Baynes. Vol. XXXV, pp. 201-253, 73 ills. in color, Mar., 1919.

Our Conquest of the Pacific: The Narrative of the 7,400-Mile Flight from San Francisco to Brisbane in Three Ocean Hops. By Squadron-Leader Charles E. Kingsford-Smith and Flight-Lieut. Charles T. P. Ulm. Vol. LIV, pp. 371-402, 27 ills., 1 two-thirds-page map, Oct., 1928.

Our First Alliance. By J. J. Jusserand. Vol. XXXI, pp. 518-548, 8 ills., June, 1917.

Our Fish Immigrants. By Hugh M. Smith. Vol. XVIII, pp. 382-400, 3 ills., June, 1907.

Our Flag Number. By Gilbert Grosvenor. Vol. XXXII, pp. 281-284, 2 ills., Oct., 1917.

Our Foreign-Born Citizens. Vol. XXXI, pp. 95-130, 36 ills., 1 page map, 8 diagrams, Feb., 1917.

Our Friend the Frog. By Doris M. Cochran. Vol. LXI, pp. 629-654, 16 ills. in black and white, 14 ills. in color, May, 1932.

Our Friends, the Bees. By A. I. and E. R. Root. Vol. XXII, pp. 675-694, 21 ills., July, 1911.

Our Friends, the French: An Appraisal of the Traits and Temperament of the Citizens of Our Sister Republic. By Carl Holliday. Vol. XXXIV, pp. 345-377, 29 ills., Nov., 1918.

Our Global Ocean—Last and Vast Frontier. By F. Barrows Colton. Vol. LXXXVII, pp. 105-128, 19 ills., 1 drawing, Jan., 1945.

Our Global Strong Arm (Air Power). 10 ills. in color from natural-color photographs. Vol. LXXXIX, pp. 145-152, Feb., 1946.

Our Greatest National Monument: The National Geographic Society Completes Its Explorations in the Valley of Ten Thousand Smokes. By Robert F. Griggs. Vol. XL, pp. 219-292, 73 ills. in black and white, 16 ills. in color, 2 page and 1 three-quarters-page maps, Sept., 1921.

Our Greatest Plant Food (Phosphorus). By Guy Elliott Mitchell. Vol. XXI, pp. 783-791, 7 ills., 1 diagram, Sept., 1910.

Our Greatest Travelers: Birds That Fly from Pole to Pole and Shun the Darkness: Birds That Make 2,500 Miles in a Single Flight. By Wells W. Cooke. Vol. XXII, pp. 346-365, 4 page and 8 half-page maps, Apr., 1911.

Our Guardians on the Deep. By William Joseph Showalter. Vol. XXV, pp. 655-677, 15 ills., 1 chart, June, 1914.

Our Heralds of Storm and Flood. By Gilbert H. Grosvenor. Vol. XVIII, pp. 586-601, 15 ills., 1 chart, Sept., 1907.

Our Heritage of Liberty: An Address Before the United States Senate by M. Viviani, President of the French Commission to the United States, May 1, 1917. Vol. XXXI, pp. 365-367, 1 ill., Apr., 1917.

Our Heritage of the Fresh Waters: Biographies of the Most Widely Distributed of the Important Food and Game Fishes of the United States. By Charles Haskins Townsend. Vol. XLIV, pp. 109-159, 25 ills. in black and white, 16 ills. in color, Aug., 1923.

Our Heterogeneous System of Weights and Measures. By Alexander Graham Bell. Vol. XVII, pp. 158-169, Mar., 1906.

Our Immigration During 1904. Vol. XVI, pp. 15-27, 6 ills., 2 charts, Jan., 1905.

Our Immigration in 1905. Vol. XVI, pp. 434-435, Sept., 1905.

Our Immigration Laws from the Viewpoint of National Eugenics. By Robert De C. Ward. Vol. XXIII, pp. 38-41, Jan., 1912.

Our Industrial Victory. By Charles M. Schwab. Vol. XXXIV, pp. 212-229, 17 ills., Sept., 1918.

Our Insect Fifth Column: Alien Enemies Take Steady Toll of Food, Trees, and Treasure by Boring from Within. By Frederick G. Vosburgh. Paintings by Hashime Murayama. Vol. LXXX, pp. 225-248, 14 ills. in black and white, 10 ills. in color, Aug., 1941.

Our Littlest Ally (San Marino). By Alice Rohe. Vol. XXXIV, pp. 139-163, 17 ills., Aug., 1918.

Our Map of North America. Text accompanying special map supplement in colors. Vol. XLV, p. 580, May, 1924.

Our Map of the Countries of the Caribbean. Text accompanying special map supplement in colors. Vol. XLI, pp. 221-222, Feb., 1922.

Our Map of the Pacific. Text accompanying special map supplement in colors. Vol. XL, pp. 647-648, 1 ill., Dec., 1921.

Our Map of the Races of Europe. Text accompanying special map supplement in colors. Vol. XXXIV, pp. 535-536, Dec., 1918.

Our Map of the United States. Text accompanying special map supplement in colors. Vol. XLIII, p. 460, Apr., 1923.

Our Most Versatile Vegetable Product: Rubber Drops from Millions of Tropical Trees Are Transformed by Genii Chemists into Myriad Articles, from Tires to Teething Rings. By J. R. Hildebrand. Vol. LXXVII, pp. 143-200, 51 ills. in black and white, 26 ills. in color, Feb., 1940.

Our Mountain Panorama (Canadian Rockies). Vol. XXII, panorama, June, 1911.

Our National Parks. By L. F. Schmeckebier. Vol. XXIII, pp. 531-579, 41 ills., 1 page map, June, 1912.

Our National War Memorials in Europe. By Gen. John J. Pershing. Vol. LXV, pp. 1-36, 24 ills. in black and white, 11 ills. in color, 1 half-page map, Jan., 1934.

Our Nation's Capital (Washington, D. C.) on Parade. 16 ills. in color from natural-color photographs by B. Anthony Stewart, Walter M. Edwards, and others. Vol. LXXXIV, pp. 265-288, Sept., 1943.

Our Neglected Southern Coast. By Alfred Goldsborough Mayer. Vol. XIX, pp. 859-871, 10 ills., Dec., 1908.

Our Neighbor, Mexico. By John Birkinbine. Vol. XXII, pp. 475-508, 26 ills., special map supplement in colors, May, 1911.

Our New Military Wards, the Marshalls. By W. Robert Moore. Vol. LXXXVIII, pp. 325-360, 14 ills. in black and white, 20 ills. in color, 1 half-page map, Sept., 1945.

Our New Possessions and the Interest They Are Exciting. By O. P. Austin. Vol. XI, pp. 32-33, Jan., 1900.

Our Northern Rockies. By R. H. Chapman. Vol. XIII, pp. 361-372, 10 ills., Oct., 1902.

Our Pacific Northwest. By N. H. Darton. Vol. XX, pp. 645-663, 12 ills., 2 half-page maps, July, 1909.

Our Plant Immigrants. By David Fairchild. Vol. XVII, pp. 179-201, 29 ills., Apr., 1906.

Our Policemen of the Air (Birds). Vol. XXIV, p. 698, June, 1913.

Our Present Population. Vol. XV, p. 232, May, 1904.

Our Search for the Lost Aviators: An Arctic Area Larger than Montana First Explored in Hunt for Missing Russians. By Sir Hubert Wilkins. Vol. LXXIV, pp. 141-172, 29 ills., 1 two-page map, Aug., 1938.

Our Second Alliance. By J. J. Jusserand. Vol. XXXI, pp. 565-566, 1 ill., June, 1917.

Our Smallest Possession—Guam. By William E. Safford. Vol. XVI, pp. 229-237, 5 ills., May, 1905.

Our State Flags. By Gilbert Grosvenor and Byron McCandless. Vol. XXXII, pp. 323-341, 1 ill in black and white, 57 ills. in color, Oct., 1917.

Our State Flowers: Floral Emblems Chosen by the Commonwealths. By Gilbert Grosvenor. Vol. XXXI, pp. 481-517, 30 ills. in color, June, 1917.

Our Transatlantic Flight. By Comdr. Richard Evelyn Byrd. Vol. LII, pp. 347-368, 17 ills., 1 half-page map, Sept., 1927.

Out in San Francisco: Fed on Gold Dust and Fattened by Sea Trade, a Pioneer Village Becomes a Busy World Port. By Frederick Simpich. Vol. LXI, pp. 395-434, 38 ills., Apr., 1932.

Outram, Frank:

Burma Road, Back Door to China: Like the Great Wall of Ancient Times, This Mighty Mountain Highway Has Been Built by Myriad Chinese to Help Defend Their Homeland. By Frank Outram and G. E. Fane. Vol. LXXVIII, pp. 629-658, 26 ills., 1 two-thirds-page map, Nov., 1940.

Outspeaking of a Great Democracy: The Proceedings of the Chamber of Deputies of France on Friday, April 6, 1917, as Reported in the "Journal Officiel de La République Française." Vol. XXXI, pp. 362-365, 1 ill., Apr., 1917.

Outwitting the Water Demons of Kashmir. By Maurice Pratt Dunlap. Vol. XL, pp. 499-511, 9 ills., Nov., 1921.

Over the Alps to Brenner Pass. 15 ills. from photographs, 1 two-page map. Vol. LXXXIV, pp. 701-714, Dec., 1943.

Over the Andes to Bogotá. By Frank M. Chapman. Vol. XL, pp. 353-373, 19 ills., Oct., 1921.

Over the Roof of Our Continent (Mount McKinley). By Bradford Washburn. Vol. LXXIV, pp. 78-98, 17 ills. in duotone, 1 half-page map, July, 1938.

Over Trail and Through Jungle in Ecuador: Indian Head-Hunters of the Interior, an Interesting Study in the South American Republic. By H. E. Anthony. Vol. XL, pp. 327-352, 28 ills., Oct., 1921.

Overbeck, Alicia O'Reardon:

Bolivia, Land of Fiestas. By Alicia O'Reardon Overbeck. Vol. LXVI, pp. 645-660, 16 ills., 1 half-page map, Nov., 1934.

Freiburg (Germany)—Gateway to the Black Forest. By Alicia O'Reardon Overbeck. Vol. LXIV, pp. 213-252, 40 ills. in black and white, 11 ills. in color, Aug., 1933.

Tin, the Cinderella Metal. By Alicia O'Reardon Overbeck. Vol. LXXVIII, pp. 659-684, 24 ills., Nov., 1940.

Ovis Poli (Sheep):

By Coolie and Caravan Across Central Asia: Narrative of a 7,900-Mile Journey of Exploration and Research Over "the Roof of the World," from the Indian Ocean to the Yellow Sea. By William J. Morden. Vol. LII, pp. 369-431, 73 ills., 1 page map, Oct., 1927.

Owls:

American Birds of Prey—A Review of Their Value. Vol. XXXVIII, pp. 460-467, 6 ills., Dec., 1920.

In Quest of the Golden Eagle: Over Lonely Mountain and Prairie Soars This Rare and Lordly Bird, But Three Youths from the East Catch Up With Him at Last. By John and Frank Craighead. Vol. LXXVII, pp. 693-710, 17 ills., May, 1940.

Photoflashing Western Owls. By Lewis W. Walker. Vol. LXXXVII, pp. 475-486, 6 ills. in black and white, 7 ills. in color, Apr., 1945.
Contains descriptions and illustrations of the following: Elf Owl, Great Horned Owl, Long-eared Owl, Screech Owl.

Shadowy Birds of the Night. By Alexander Wetmore. Vol. LXVII, pp. 217-240, 5 ills. in black and white, 21 portraits in color, Feb., 1935.

Silent-Winged Owls of North America. 21 portraits in color from paintings by Maj. Allan Brooks. Vol. LXVII, pp. 225-240, Feb., 1935.

Oxcarts:

Land of the Painted Oxcarts (Costa Rica). By Luis Marden. With 31 ills. in color from natural-color photographs by the author. Vol. XC, pp. 409-456, 30 ills. in black and white, 1 half-page map, Oct., 1946.

Oxford, England:

Oxford (University), Mother of Anglo-Saxon Learning. By E. John Long. Vol. LVI, pp. 563-596, 31 ills., Nov., 1929.

Through the Heart of England in a Canadian Canoe. By R. J. Evans. Vol. XLI, pp. 473-497, 26 ills., 1 half-page map, May, 1922.

Oxholm, Axel H.:

Country Life in Norway: The Beneficent Gulf Stream Enables One-third of the People in a Far-north, Mountainous Land to Prosper on Farms. By Axel H. Oxholm. Vol. LXXV, pp. 493-528, 17 ills. in black and white, 20 ills. in color, 1 two-thirds-page map, Apr., 1939.

Oxus (River), Afghanistan-U. S. S. R. *See* Amu Darya.

Oysters:

America's Surpassing Fisheries: Their Present Condition and Future Prospects, and How the Federal Government Fosters Them. By Hugh M. Smith. Vol. XXIX, pp. 546-583, 35 ills., June, 1916.

Cultivation of Marine and Fresh Water Animals in Japan. By K. Mitsukuri. Vol. XVII, pp. 524-531, 5 ills., Sept., 1906.

Oysters—*Continued*

Dream Ship: The Story of a Voyage of Adventure More Than Half Around the World in a 47-Foot Lifeboat. By Ralph Stock. Vol. XXXIX, pp. 1-52, 43 ills., 1 page map, Jan., 1921.

Maryland Pilgrimage: Visits to Hallowed Shrines Recall the Major Rôle Played by This Prosperous State in the Development of Popular Government in America. By Gilbert Grosvenor. Vol. LI, pp. 133-212, 88 ills., special map supplement, Feb., 1927.

Native Oysters of the West Coast. By Robert E. C. Stearns. Vol. XIX, pp. 224-226, Mar., 1908.

Pearl Fisheries of Ceylon. By Hugh M. Smith. Vol. XXIII, pp. 173-194, 13 ills., 1 quarter-page map, Jan., 1912.

Rise of the New Arab Nation. By Frederick Simpich. Vol. XXXVI, pp. 369-393, 17 ills., 1 page map, Nov., 1919.

World's Most Valuable Water Crop. By Hugh M. Smith. Vol. XXIV, pp. 257-281, 21 ills., Mar., 1913.

Ozarks (Plateau), United States:

Arkansas Rolls Up Its Sleeves. By Frederick Simpich. Vol. XC, pp. 273-312, 16 ills. in black and white, 23 ills. in color, 1 map (two-page spread), Sept., 1946.

Land of a Million Smiles. By Frederick Simpich. Vol. LXXXIII, pp. 589-623, 14 ills. in black and white, 20 ills. in color, 1 two-thirds-page map, May, 1943.

Work and Play in the Ozarks. 20 ills. in color from natural-color photographs by B. Anthony Stewart and J. Baylor Roberts. Vol. LXXXIII, pp. 597-620, May, 1943.

P

Pacific Islands:

American Pathfinders in the Pacific. By William H. Nicholas. Vol. LXXXIX, pp. 617-640, 17 ills., 1 two-page map, May, 1946.

Around the World in the *Islander* (Ship): A Narrative of the Adventures of a Solitary Voyager on his Four-Year Cruise in a Thirty-Four-Foot Sailing Craft. By Capt. Harry Pidgeon. Vol. LIII, pp. 141-205, 75 ills., 1 two-page map, Feb., 1928.

At Ease in the South Seas. By Maj. Frederick Simpich, Jr. Vol. LXXXV, pp. 79-104, 32 ills., Jan., 1944.

At Home on the Oceans: Whales and Sharks Make Exciting Neighbors for a Professor's Wife, Turned Able Seaman, On a Three-year Voyage Around the World. By Edith Bauer Strout. Vol. LXXVI, pp. 33-86, 54 ills., 1 map, July, 1939.

Color Glimpses of the Changing South Seas. 14 ills. in color from natural-color photographs by Amos Burg. Vol. LXV, pp. 281-288, Mar., 1934.

Diary of a Voyage from San Francisco to Tahiti and Return, 1901. By S. P. Langley. Vol. XII, pp. 413-429, 10 ills., 1 page and 1 half-page maps, Dec., 1901.

Pacific Islands—*Continued*

Dream Ship : The Story of a Voyage of Adventure More Than Half Around the World in a 47-Foot Lifeboat. By Ralph Stock. Vol. XXXIX, pp. 1-52, 43 ills., 1 page map, Jan., 1921.

Fairy Terns of the Atolls. By Lewis Wayne Walker. Vol. XC, pp. 807-814, 9 ills., Dec., 1946.

Greatest Voyage in the Annals of the Sea. By J. R. Hildebrand. Vol. LXII, pp. 699-739, 35 ills., 2 half-page maps, Dec., 1932.

Hidden Key to the Pacific : Piercing the Web of Secrecy Which Long Has Veiled Japanese Bases in the Mandated Islands. By Willard Price. Vol. LXXXI, pp. 759-785, 28 ills., 1 map (two-page spread), June, 1942.

In the Savage South Seas. By Beatrice Grimshaw. Vol. XIX, pp. 1-19, 21 ills., Jan., 1908.

Iridescent Isles of the South Seas. 16 ills. in color from photographs ; 12 ills. by Rollo H. Beck. Vol. XLVIII, pp. 403-418, Oct., 1925.

Islands of the Pacific. By J. P. Thomson. Vol. XL, pp. 543-558, 15 ills., special map supplement, Dec., 1921.

Jungle War : Bougainville and New Caledonia. 17 ills. in color from paintings by Lieut. William F. Draper. Vol. LXXXV, pp. 417-432, Apr., 1944.

Living on a Volcano : An Unspoiled Patch of Polynesia Is Niuafoō, Nicknamed "Tin Can Island" by Stamp Collectors. By Thomas A. Jaggar. Vol. LXVIII, pp. 91-106, 17 ills., 1 half-page map, July, 1935.

Modern Saga of the Seas : The Narrative of a 17,000-Mile Cruise on a 40-Foot Sloop by the Author, His Wife, and a Baby, Born on the Voyage. By Erling Tambs. Vol. LX, pp. 645-688, 49 ills., 1 half-page map, Dec., 1931.

Mysterious Micronesia : Yap, Map, and Other Islands Under Japanese Mandate are Museums of Primitive Man. By Willard Price. Vol. LXIX, pp. 481-510, 37 ills., 1 half-page map, Apr., 1936.

New Map Shows Immense Pacific Battleground. Text accompanying special map supplement in colors. Vol. LXXXI, pp. 203-204, Feb., 1942.

North About. By Alan J. Villiers. Vol. LXXI, pp. 221-250, 24 ills., Feb., 1937.
　　Contains information on the following islands : Balabac, Philippines ; Balimbing, Philippines ; Barahun, Solomons ; Bongao, Philippines ; Florida, Solomons ; Guadalcanal, Solomons ; Kawio, Pacific Ocean ; Kiriwina, Trobriand Islands ; Lusancay Islands, Pacific Ocean ; Mambahenauhan, Sulu Sea ; Nissan, Solomons ; Santa Ana, Solomons ; Santa Catalina, Solomons ; Tawitawi, Philippines.

Our New Possessions and the Interest They Are Exciting. By O. P. Austin. Vol. XI, pp. 32-33, Jan., 1900.

Painting History in the Pacific. 19 ills. in color from paintings by Lt. William F. Draper. Vol. LXXXVI, pp. 409-424, Oct., 1944.

Pacific Islands—*Continued*

Pilgrim Sails the Seven Seas : A Schooner Yacht Out of Boston Drops in at Desert Isles and South Sea Edens in a Leisurely Two-Year Voyage. By Harold Peters. Vol. LXXII, pp. 223-262, 36 ills., Aug., 1937.

Revealing Earth's Mightiest Ocean. By Albert W. Atwood. Vol. LXXXIV, pp. 291-306, 10 ills., special map supplement, Sept., 1943.

Romance of Science in Polynesia : An Account of Five Years of Cruising Among the South Sea Islands. By Robert Cushman Murphy. Vol. XLVIII, pp. 355-426, 66 ills. in black and white, 16 ills. in color, 3 half-page maps, Oct., 1925.

Society's New Map of Southeast Asia. Text accompanying special map supplement in colors. Vol. LXXXVI, pp. 449-450, 1 ill., Oct., 1944.

South from Saipan. By W. Robert Moore. Vol. LXXXVII, pp. 441-474, 11 ills. in black and white, 17 ills. in color, 1 half-page map, Apr., 1945.

Springboards to Tokyo. By Willard Price. Vol. LXXXVI, pp. 385-407, 16 ills., Oct., 1944.

Storied Islands of the South Sea. 20 ills. in color from natural-color photographs by Irving Johnson, Malcolm Evans, and others. Vol. LXXXI, pp. 9-40, Jan., 1942.
　　Contains illustrations of Easter Island, Galápagos Islands, Pitcairn, Samoa, Santa Cruz, and Solomon Islands.

Treasure Islands of Australasia : New Guinea, New Caledonia, and Fiji Trace across the South Pacific a Fertile Crescent Incredibly Rich in Minerals and Foods. By Douglas L. Oliver. Vol. LXXXI, pp. 691-722, 23 ills., 1 two-page map, June, 1942.

Westward Bound in the *Yankee*. By Irving and Electa Johnson. Vol. LXXXI, pp. 1-44, 25 ills. in black and white, 20 ills. in color, 1 three-quarters-page map, Jan., 1942.
　　Contains information and illustrations of Easter Island, Galápagos Islands, Pitcairn, Samoa, Santa Cruz, and Solomon Islands.

What the Fighting Yanks See. By Wanda Burnett. Vol. LXXXVI, pp. 451-476, 27 ills., Oct., 1944.

Yap and Other Pacific Islands Under Japanese Mandate. By Junius B. Wood. Vol. XL, pp. 591-627, 34 ills., 1 two-thirds-page map, Dec., 1921.

See also Aleutian Islands ; Canton Island ; Caroline Islands ; Easter Island ; Falcon Island ; Fatu-Hiva (Island) ; Fiji Islands ; Gilbert Islands ; Guam ; Hawaii ; Marianas Islands ; Marquesas Islands ; Marshall Islands ; Nauru ; New Caledonia ; New Guinea ; New Hebrides ; Niuafoō ; Okinawa ; Philippine Islands ; Ryukyu Retto ; Samoa ; Society Islands ; Solomon Islands ; Tongareva ; Wake.

Pacific Northwest, United States :

Columbia (River) Turns on the Power. By Maynard Owen Williams. Vol. LXXIX, pp. 749-792, 25 ills. in black and white, 18 ills. in color, June, 1941.

Pacific Northwest, United States—*Continued*

Great White Monarch of the Pacific Northwest (Mount Rainier). By A. H. Barnes. Vol. XXIII, pp. 593-626, 31 ills., 1 half-page map, June, 1912.

Our Pacific Northwest. By N. H. Darton. Vol. XX, pp. 645-663, 12 ills., 2 half-page maps, July, 1909.

Society Maps Northwestern United States and Neighboring Canadian Provinces. Text accompanying special map supplement in colors. Vol. LXXIX, pp. 805-806, June, 1941.

Wartime in the Pacific Northwest. By Frederick Simpich. Vol. LXXXII, pp. 421-464, 25 ills. in black and white, 23 ills. in color, 1 half-page map, Oct., 1942.

Where Fog and Sun Paint the Pacific. 23 ills. in color from natural-color photographs by J. Baylor Roberts. Vol. LXXXII, pp. 437-460, Oct., 1942.

See also Oregon ; Washington.

Pacific Ocean:

Columbus of the Pacific : Captain James Cook, Foremost British Navigator, Expanded the Great Sea to Correct Proportions and Won for Albion an Insular Empire by Peaceful Exploration and Scientific Study. By J. R. Hildebrand. Vol. LI, pp. 85-132, 45 ills., 1 page and 1 three-quarters-page maps, Jan., 1927.

Deep-Sea Exploring Expedition of the Steamer *Albatross.* By Hugh M. Smith. Vol. X, pp. 291-296, 2 ills., 1 diagram, Aug., 1899.

Doubtful Island in the Pacific. By James D. Hague. Vol. XV, pp. 478-489, 1 ill., 2 page maps, Dec., 1904.

Flying the Pacific. By William Burke Miller. Vol. LXX, pp. 665-707, 39 ills., Dec., 1936.

Islands of the Pacific. By J. P. Thomson. Vol. XL, pp. 543-558, 15 ills., special map supplement in colors, Dec., 1921.

Magnetic Survey of the Pacific. Vol. XIX, pp. 447-448, June, 1908.

Magnetic Survey of the Pacific Ocean. By Dr. L. A. Bauer. Vol. XVII, p. 237, Apr., 1906.

New Map Shows Immense Pacific Battleground. Text accompanying special map supplement in colors. Vol. LXXXI, pp. 203-204, Feb., 1942.

Our Global Ocean—Last and Vast Frontier. By F. Barrows Colton. Vol. LXXXVII, pp. 105-128, 19 ills., 1 drawing, Jan., 1945.

Our Map of the Pacific. Text accompanying special map supplement in colors. Vol. XL, pp. 647-648, 1 ill., Dec., 1921.

Pacific : The Most Explored and Least-Known Region of the Globe. By Leopold G. Blackman. Vol. XIX, pp. 546-563, 11 ills., 1 three-quarters-page map, Aug., 1908.

Problems of the Pacific—The Commerce of the Great Ocean. By O. P. Austin. Vol. XIII, pp. 303-318, 7 page and 1 half-page maps, Aug., 1902.

Problems of the Pacific—The Great Ocean in World Growth. By W J McGee. Vol. XIII, pp. 333-342, Sept., 1902.

Pacific Ocean—*Continued*

Recent Report from the "Doubtful Island Region." By James D. Hague. Vol. XVIII, pp. 205-208, 2 page maps, Mar., 1907.

Revealing Earth's Mightiest Ocean. By Albert W. Atwood. Vol. LXXXIV, pp. 291-306, 10 ills., special map supplement, Sept., 1943.

Romance of Science in Polynesia : An Account of Five Years of Cruising Among the South Sea Islands. By Robert Cushman Murphy. Vol. XLVIII, pp. 355-426, 66 ills. in black and white, 16 ills. in color, 3 half-page maps, Oct., 1925.

Sailing the Seven Seas in the Interest of Science : Adventures Through 157,000 Miles of Storm and Calm, from Arctic to Antarctic and Around the World, in the Non-Magnetic Yacht *Carnegie.* By J. P. Ault. Vol. XLII, pp. 631-690, 47 ills., 1 chart, Dec., 1922.

Search for the Lost Island of the Pacific. Vol. XV, pp. 425-426, Oct., 1904.

Society's New Map of the Pacific. By Gilbert Grosvenor. Text accompanying special map supplement in colors. Vol. LXX, pp. 793-796, Dec., 1936.

Work in the Pacific Ocean of the Magnetic Survey Yacht *Galilee.* By Dr. L. A. Bauer. Vol. XVIII, pp. 601-611, 15 ills., Sept., 1907.

See also Pacific Islands.

Padaungs (Tribespeople) :

Among the Hill Tribes of Burma—An Ethnological Thicket. By Sir George Scott. Vol. XLII, pp. 293-321, 22 ills., Mar., 1922.

Burma : Where India and China Meet : In the Massive Mountains of Southeast Asia, Swarming Road Builders Wage the "War of the Highways" for Free China and Her Allies. By John LeRoy Christian. Vol. LXXXIV, pp. 489-512, 18 ills., 1 page map, Oct., 1943.

Pagan, Burma :

Five Thousand Temples of Pagān : Burma's Sacred City Is a Place of Enchantment in the Midst of Ruins. By William H. Roberts. Vol. LX, pp. 445-454, 9 ills., Oct., 1931.

Untoured Burma. By Charles H. Bartlett. Vol. XXIV, pp. 835-853, 17 ills., July, 1913.

Page, James:

Drift of Floating Bottles in the Pacific Ocean. By James Page. Vol. XII, pp. 337-339, Sept., 1901.

Ocean Currents. By James Page. Vol. XIII, pp. 135-142, Apr., 1902.

Reports of Vessels as to the Range of Volcanic Dust. By James Page. Vol. XIII, pp. 299-301, July, 1902.

Sailing Ship and the Panama Canal. By James Page. Vol. XV, pp. 167-176, 2 charts, Apr., 1904.

Pageant of Jerusalem : The Capital of the Land of Three Great Faiths Is Still the Holy City for Christian, Moslem, and Jew. By Maj. Edward Keith-Roach. Vol. LII, pp. 635-681, 57 ills., Dec., 1927.

Pages from the Floral Life of America. Vol. XLVIII, pp. 44-75, 55 ills. in color, July, 1925.

Pago-Pago, Samoa :

America's South Sea Soldiers. By Lorena Mac-Intýre Quinn. Vol. XXVI, pp. 267-274, 8 ills., Sept., 1919.

Sailing the Seven Seas in the Interest of Science : Adventures Through 157,000 Miles of Storm and Calm, from Arctic to Antarctic and Around the World, in the Non-Magnetic Yacht *Carnegie.* By J. P. Ault. Vol. XLII, pp. 631-690, 47 ills., 1 chart, Dec., 1922.

Samoa—South Sea Outpost of the U. S. Navy. 20 ills. from photographs by Truman Bailey. Vol. LXXIX, pp. 615-630, May, 1941.

Pahuatlán, Mexico :

Mexican Indian Flying Pole Dance. By Helga Larsen. Vol. LXXI, pp. 387-400, 13 ills., Mar., 1937.

Paige, Sidney:

Growing Camp in the Tanana Gold Fields, Alaska. By Sidney Paige. Vol. XVI, pp. 104-111, 4 ills., Mar., 1905.

Painting History in the Pacific. 19 ills. in color from paintings by Lt. William F. Draper. Vol. LXXXVI, pp. 409-424, Oct., 1944.

Painting the Army on Maneuvers. By Arthur Beaumont. With 16 ills. in color from paintings by the author. Vol. LXXXII, pp. 601-602, Nov., 1942.

Paintings:

Democracy's Royal Palace (Westminster). 19 ills. in color from natural-color photographs by B. Anthony Stewart. Vol. XC, pp. 233-248, Aug., 1946.

Europe's Looted Art. By John Walker. Vol. LXXXIX, 11 ills., Jan., 1946.

Faces and Fashions of Asia's Changeless Tribes. 26 ills. in color from paintings and drawings by Alexandre Iacovleff. Vol. LXIX, pp. 21-36, Jan., 1936.

How Warwick (Castle) Was Photographed in Color. By Maynard Owen Williams. Vol. LXX, pp. 83-93, 13 ills. in color, July, 1936.

Old Masters in a New National Gallery. By Ruth Q. McBride. Vol. LXXVIII, pp. 1-50, 11 ills. in black and white, 32 color reproductions of masterpieces, July, 1940.

Contents : Mellon and Kress Collections.

Pioneer Gaucho Days. 8 ills. in color from paintings by Cesáreo Bernaldo de Quirós. Vol. LXIV, pp. 453-460, Oct., 1933.

See also National Geographic Society : Paintings.

Palaces:

India : Streets and Palaces of Colorful India. Vol. L, pp. 60-85, 34 ills. in color, July, 1926.

Mexico : Chichen Itzá, an Ancient American Mecca : Recent Excavations in Yucatan Are Bringing to Light the Temples, Palaces, and Pyramids of America's Most Holy Native City. By Sylvanus Griswold Morley. Vol. XLVII, pp. 63-95, 34 ills., 1 half-page map, 1 diagram, Jan., 1925.

Palaces *Continued*

Persia : Exploring the Secrets of Persepolis. By Charles Breasted. Vol. LXIV, pp. 381-420, 48 ills., 1 half page map, 1 plan, Oct., 1933.

Romania : Palaces and Peasants in Rome's Old Colony. 14 ills. in color from natural-color photographs by Wilhelm Tobien. Vol. LXV, pp. 439-446, Apr., 1934.

See also Castles ; Châteaux ; Potala ; Versailles ; Westminster, Palace of.

Palaris (Ships) :

Seafarers of South Celebes. By G. E. P. Collins. Vol. LXXXVII, pp. 53-78, 25 ills., 1 two-thirds-page map, Jan., 1945.

Palau Islands, Caroline Islands :

Hidden Key to the Pacific : Piercing the Web of Secrecy Which Long Has Veiled Japanese Bases in the Mandated Islands. By Willard Price. Vol. LXXXI, pp. 759-785, 28 ills., 1 map (two-page spread), June, 1942.

Painting History in the Pacific. 19 ills. in color from paintings by Lt. William F. Draper. Vol. LXXXVI, pp. 409-424, Oct., 1944.

South from Saipan. By W. Robert Moore. Vol. LXXXVII, pp. 441-474, 11 ills. in black and white, 17 ills. in color, 1 half-page map, Apr., 1945.

Yap and Other Pacific Islands Under Japanese Mandate. By Junius B. Wood. Vol. XL, pp. 591-627, 34 ills., 1 two-thirds-page map, Dec., 1921.

Palenque Ruins, Mexico :

Finding Jewels of Jade in a Mexican Swamp. By Matthew W. and Marion Stirling. Vol. LXXXII, pp. 635-661, 15 ills. in black and white, 12 ills. in color, 1 two-thirds-page map, Nov., 1942.

Mexico's Deep South Yields New Treasure. 12 ills. in color from natural-color photographs by Richard H. Stewart. Vol. LXXXII, pp. 649-656, Nov., 1942.

Paleontology:

Birds May Bring You More Happiness Than the Wealth of the Indies. By Frank M. Chapman. Vol. XXIV, pp. 699-714, 15 ills., June, 1913.

"Compleat Angler" Fishes for Fossils. By Imogene Powell. Vol. LXVI, pp. 251-258, 7 ills., Aug., 1934.

Explorations in the Gobi Desert. By Roy Chapman Andrews. Vol. LXIII, pp. 653-716, 50 ills. in black and white, 20 ills. in color, 1 half-page map, June, 1933.

Extinct Reptiles Found in Nodules. By H. A. Largelamb. Vol. XVII, pp. 170-173, 9 ills., Mar., 1906.

How Old Is Man? By Theodore Roosevelt. Vol. XXIX, pp. 111-127, 12 ills., 1 page and 2 half-page maps, Feb., 1916.

Hunting Big Game of Other Days : A Boating Expedition in Search of Fossils in Alberta, Canada. By Barnum Brown. Vol. XXXV, pp. 407-429, 24 ills., 1 page map, May, 1919.

Paleontology—*Continued*

Larger North American Mammals. By E. W. Nelson. Vol. XXX, pp. 385-472, 24 ills. in black and white, 50 ills. in color, special supplement in color, Nov., 1916.

Our Coal Lands. By Guy Elliott Mitchell. Vol. XXI, pp. 446-451, 5 ills., May, 1910.

Parade of Life Through the Ages: Records in Rocks Reveal a Strange Procession of Prehistoric Creatures, from Jellyfish to Dinosaurs, Giant Sloths, Saber-toothed Tigers, and Primitive Man. By Charles R. Knight. With 24 ills. in color from paintings by the author. Vol. LXXXI, pp. 141-184, 13 ills. in black and white, Feb., 1942.

Contains descriptions and colored illustrations of the following: American Mastodon, Archaeopteryx, Arsinoitherium, Ceratosaurus, Cladoselache, Cro-Magnon Man, Dimetrodon, Dinichthys, Diplodocus, Eohippus, Eryops, Eurypterid, Glyptodon, Hyaenodon, Lake Dwellers, Macrauchenia, Megaceros, Megatherium, Moa, Mosasaurus, Naosaurus, Neanderthal Man, Parasaurolophus, Protoceratops, Pteranodon, Pterodactyl, Saber-toothed Tiger, Stegosaurus, Styracosaurus, Titanotherium, Toxodon, *Tyrannosaurus rex*, Uintatherium, Woolly Mammoth.

Reptiles of All Lands. By Raymond L. Ditmars. Vol. XXII, pp. 601-633, 32 ills., July, 1911.

Contains illustrations of the following: Brontosaurus, Diplodocus, Stegosaurus.

Strange and Remarkable Beast (Mammoth). Vol. XVIII, p. 620, 1 ill., Sept., 1907.

Wyoming Fossil Fields Expedition of July, 1899. By Wilbur C. Knight. Vol. XI, pp. 449-465, 8 ills., Dec., 1900.

Palermo, Sicily:

Sicily, the Battlefield of Nations and of Nature. By Mrs. George C. Bosson, Jr. Vol. XX, pp. 96-118, 25 ills., 1 page map, Jan., 1909.

Sicily Again in the Path of War. By Maynard Owen Williams. Vol. LXXXIV, pp. 307-320, 7 ills., 1 map (two-page spread), Sept., 1943.

Palestine:

Along the Way of the Magi. 14 ills. in color from autochromes by American Colony Photographers. Vol. LVI, pp. 708-717, Dec., 1929.

American Fighters Visit Bible Lands. By Maynard Owen Williams. With 23 ills. in color from natural-color photographs by the author. Vol. LXXXIX, pp. 311-340, 10 ills. in black and white, Mar., 1946.

Among the Bethlehem Shepherds: A Visit to the Valley Which David Probably Recalled When He Wrote the Twenty-third Psalm. By John D. Whiting. Vol. L, pp. 729-753, 19 ills., Dec., 1926.

Bethlehem and the Christmas Story. By John D. Whiting. Vol. LVI, pp. 699-735, 27 ills. in black and white, 14 ills. in color, Dec., 1929.

Bombs over Bible Lands. By Frederick Simpich and W. Robert Moore. Vol. LXXX, pp. 141-180, 34 ills., 1 two-page map, Aug., 1941.

Palestine—*Continued*

Canoeing Down the River Jordan: Voyagers in Rubber Boats Find the Bible Stream Little Tamed Today as It Plunges to the Dead Sea Over the Earth's Lowest River Bed. By John D. Whiting. Vol. LXXVIII, pp. 781-808, 19 ills., 1 page map, Dec., 1940.

Change Comes to Bible Lands. By Frederick Simpich. Vol. LXXIV, pp. 695-750, 40 ills. in black and white, 25 ills. in color, special map supplement, Dec., 1938.

Changing Palestine. By Maj. Edward Keith-Roach. Vol. LXV, pp. 493-527, 43 ills., 1 half-page map, Apr., 1934.

Crusader Castles of the Near East. By William H. Hall. Vol. LIX, pp. 369-390, 19 ills., 1 third-page map, Mar., 1931.

Flying Over Egypt, Sinai, and Palestine: Looking Down Upon the Holy Land During an Air Journey of Two and a Half Hours from Cairo to Jerusalem. By Brig. Gen. P. R. C. Groves and Maj. J. R. McCrindle. Vol. L, pp. 313-355, 26 ills., 1 half-page map, Sept., 1926.

Geography of the Jordan. By Nelson Glueck. Vol. LXXXVI, pp. 719-744, 23 ills., 1 page map, Dec., 1944.

Impressions of Palestine. By James Bryce. Vol. XXVII, pp. 293-317, 18 ills., 1 page map, Mar., 1915.

In the Birthplace of Christianity. 34 ills. in color from autochromes lumière by Hans Hildenbrand, Maynard Owen Williams, and Gervais Courtellemont. Vol. L, pp. 696-721, Dec., 1926.

In the Land of Moses and Abraham. 25 ills. in color from natural-color photographs by W. Robert Moore. Vol. LXXIV, pp. 711-742, Dec., 1938.

Jerusalem's Locust Plague: Being a Description of the Recent Locust Influx into Palestine, and Comparing Same with the Ancient Locust Invasions as Narrated in the Old World's History Book, the Bible. By John D. Whiting. Vol. XXVIII, pp. 511-550, 25 ills., 1 page map, Dec., 1915.

Last Israelitish Blood Sacrifice: How the Vanishing Samaritans Celebrate the Passover on Sacred Mount Gerizim. By John D. Whiting. Vol. XXXVII, pp. 1-46, 40 ills., 1 half-page map, Jan., 1920.

Old Jewel in the Proper Setting: An Eye-witness' Account of the Reconquest of the Holy Land by Twentieth Century Crusaders. By Charles W. Whitehair. Vol. XXXIV, pp. 325-344, 17 ills., Oct., 1918.

On the Trail of King Solomon's Mines: The Bible, in Addition to Its Spiritual Values, Continues to Prove a Rich Geography and Guide to Exploration of the Holy Land. By Nelson Glueck. Vol. LXXXV, pp. 233-256, 20 ills., 1 page map, Feb., 1944.

Palestine. 21 ills. in color from photographs by the American Colony Photographers. Vol. XXV, pp. 265-313, Mar., 1914.

Palestine Today. By Francis Chase, Jr. Vol. XC, pp. 501-516, 16 ills., Oct., 1946.

Palestine—*Continued*

Road of the Crusaders: A Historian Follows the Steps of Richard the Lion Heart and Other Knights of the Cross Over the "Via Dei." By Harold Lamb. Vol. LXIV, pp. 645-693, 46 ills. in black and white, 13 ills. in color, 1 page map, Dec., 1933.

Skirting the Shores of Sunrise: Seeking and Finding "The Levant" in a Journey by Steamer, Motor-Car, and Train from Constantinople to Port Said. By Melville Chater. Vol. L, pp. 649-728, 60 ills. in black and white, 34 ills. in color, 1 two-thirds-page map, Dec., 1926.

Village Life in the Holy Land. By John D. Whiting. Vol. XXV, pp. 249-314, 27 ills. in black and white, 22 ills. in color, Mar., 1914.

See also Jerusalem.

Palette from Spain. By W. Langdon Kihn. Vol. LXIX, pp. 407-440, 16 ills. in black and white, 26 ills. in duotone, 1 half-page map, Mar., 1936.

Palio (Horse Race):

Siena's Palio, an Italian Inheritance from the Middle Ages. By Marie Louise Handley. Vol. L, pp. 245-258, 3 ills., Aug., 1926.

Palmer, Alfred T.:

China: Changing Canton. 20 ills. from photographs by Siukee Mack, Alfred T. Palmer, and Kinchue Wong. Vol. LXXII, pp. 711-726, 20 ills., Dec., 1937.

Great Lakes and Great Industries. 19 ills. in color from natural-color photographs by Alfred T. Palmer, B. Anthony Stewart, and Willard R. Culver. Vol. LXXXVI, pp. 689-712, Dec., 1944.

Palmer, Catherine Bell:

Flying Our Wounded Veterans Home. By Catherine Bell Palmer. Vol. LXXXVIII, pp. 363-384, 17 ills., Sept., 1945.

Palmer, Howard:

Some Tramps Across the Glaciers and Snowfields of British Columbia. By Howard Palmer. Vol. XXI, pp. 457-487, 25 ills., June, 1910.

Palmerston Island, Pacific Ocean:

Dream Ship: The Story of a Voyage of Adventure More Than Half Around the World in a 47-Foot Lifeboat. By Ralph Stock. Vol. XXXIX, pp. 1-52, 43 ills., 1 page map, Jan., 1921.

Palms (Trees):

The Palms. Vol. XXII, supplement, Dec., 1911.

Paradise of the Tasman (Lord Howe Island): A Pacific Island Provides the Palms Which Decorate Hotels, Churches, Steamships, and Homes. By Hubert Lyman Clark. Vol. LXVIII, pp. 115-136, 24 ills., 1 half-page map, July, 1935.

See also Date Palms.

Palms and Planes in the New Hebrides. By Maj Robert D. Heinl, Jr. Vol. LXXXVI, pp. 229-256, 17 ills. in black and white, 12 ills. in color, 1 four-fifths-page map, Aug., 1944.

Pan American Airways:

Flight Expedition: Over the Roof of Our Continent (Mount McKinley). By Bradford Washburn. Vol. LXXIV, pp. 78-98, 17 ills. in duotone, 1 half-page map, July, 1938.

Flying the Pacific. By William Burke Miller. Vol. LXX, pp. 665-707, 39 ills., Dec., 1936.

Pan American Conferences:

What the Latin American Republics Think of the Pan American Conferences. Vol. XVII, pp. 474-479, Aug., 1906.

Pan American Good Will Flyers:

How Latin America Looks from the Air: U. S. Army Airplanes Hurdle the High Andes, Brave Brazil Jungles, and Follow Smoking Volcanoes to Map New Sky Paths Around South America. By Maj. Herbert A. Dargue. Vol. LII, pp. 451-502, 52 ills., 1 page map, Oct., 1927.

Pan-American Railway. Vol. XV, pp. 232-233, May, 1904.

Panama:

Farming on the Isthmus of Panama. By Dillwyn M. Hazlett. Vol. XVII, pp. 229-234, 5 ills., Apr., 1906.

Improvements in the Republic of Panama. Vol. XVI, pp. 441-442, Sept., 1905.

Jungles of Panama. By David Fairchild. Vol. XLI, pp. 131-145, 14 ills., Feb., 1922.

Land That Links the Americas. 22 ills. in color from natural-color photographs by Luis Marden. Vol. LXXX, pp. 601-624, Nov., 1941.

Latest Route Proposed for the Isthmian Canal— Mandingo Route. Vol. XIII, pp. 64-70, 1 page chart, Feb., 1902.

Little-Known Parts of Panama. By Henry Pittier. Vol. XXIII, pp. 627-662, 35 ills., 1 page map, July, 1912.

Nature's Transformation at Panama: The Remarkable Changes in Faunal and Physical Conditions in the Gatun Lake Region. By George Shiras, 3d. Vol. XXVIII, pp. 159-194, 33 ills., 2 page maps, Aug., 1915.

Notes on Panama and Colombia. Vol. XIV, pp. 458-466, 12 ills., Dec., 1903.

Panama, Bridge of the World. By Luis Marden. Vol. LXXX, pp. 591-630, 23 ills. in black and white, 22 ills. in color, 1 half-page map, Nov., 1941.

Redeeming the Tropics. By William Joseph Showalter. Vol. XXV, pp. 344-364, 13 ills., Mar., 1914.

Republic of Panama. By William H. Burr. Vol. XV, pp. 57-73, 7 ills., Feb., 1904.

Panama—*Continued*

Who Treads Our Trails? A Camera Trapper Describes His Experiences on an Island in the Canal Zone, a Natural-History Laboratory in the American Tropics. By Frank M. Chapman. Vol. LII, pp. 331-345, 18 ills., 1 half-page map, Sept., 1927.

See also Mulatas Archipelago.

Panama Canal:

Battling with the Panama Slides. By William Joseph Showalter. Vol. XXV, pp. 133-153, 15 ills., Feb., 1914.

Bird's-Eye View of the Panama Canal. Vol. XXIII, special supplement in color, Feb., 1912.

Completed Report of the Isthmian Canal Commission. Vol. XII, p. 441, Dec., 1901.

Dream Ship: The Story of a Voyage of Adventure More Than Half Around the World in a 47-Foot Lifeboat. By Ralph Stock. Vol. XXXIX, pp. 1-52, 43 ills., 1 page map, Jan., 1921.

Honors to Colonel Goethals: The Presentation by President Woodrow Wilson of the National Geographic Society Special Gold Medal. Vol. XXV, pp. 677-690, 6 ills., June, 1914.

Interoceanic Canal. By Emory R. Johnson. Vol. X, pp. 311-316, Aug., 1899.

Nicaragua and the Isthmian Routes. By Arthur P. Davis. Vol. X, pp. 247-266, 8 ills., 2 diagrams, July, 1899.

Notes on the Panama Canal. By Theodore P. Shonts. Vol. XVII, pp. 362-363, June, 1906.

Panama, Bridge of the World. By Luis Marden. Vol. LXXX, pp. 591-630, 23 ills. in black and white, 22 ills. in color, 1 half-page map, Nov., 1941.

Panama Canal. By Rear Adm. Colby M. Chester. Vol. XVI, pp. 445-467, 8 ills., Oct., 1905.

Panama Canal. By Lieut. Col. George W. Goethals. Vol. XX, pp. 334-355, 7 ills., 1 half-page map, 1 diagram, Apr., 1909.

Panama Canal. By Col. George W. Goethals. Vol. XXII, pp. 148-211, 49 ills., 2 half-page maps, 1 diagram, Feb., 1911.

Panama Canal. By Theodore P. Shonts. Vol. XVII, pp. 55-68, 5 ills., Feb., 1906.

Panama Canal. By William Joseph Showalter. Vol. XXIII, pp. 195-205, special map supplement in colors, Feb., 1912.

Panama Canal. By Lt. Col. William L. Sibert. Vol. XXV, pp. 153-183, 24 ills., Feb., 1914.

Probable Effect of the Panama Canal on the Commercial Geography of the World. By O. P. Austin. Vol. XXV, pp. 245-248, Feb., 1914.

Progress on the Panama Canal. By Gilbert H. Grosvenor. Vol. XVI, pp. 467-475, 1 half-page map, Oct., 1905.

Proposed American Interoceanic Canal in Its Commercial Aspects. By Joseph Nimmo, Jr. Vol. X, pp. 297-310, Aug., 1899.

Republic of Panama. By William H. Burr. Vol. XV, pp. 57-73, 7 ills., Feb., 1904.

Panama Canal—*Continued*

What Has Been Accomplished by the United States Toward Building the Panama Canal. By Theodore P. Shonts. Vol. XVI, pp. 558-564, Dec., 1905.

Work on the Isthmus. Vol. XVII, pp. 586-587, Oct., 1906.

Panama-Pacific International Exposition:

City of Realized Dreams (San Francisco). By Franklin K. Lane. Vol. XXVII, pp. 169-171, Feb., 1915.

Panoramas. *See* Pictorial Enlargements and Panoramas.

Panther of the Hearth: Lithe Grace and Independence of Spirit Contribute to the Appeal of Cats, "The Only Domestic Animal Man Has Never Conquered." By Frederick B. Eddy. Vol. LXXIV, pp. 589-634, 22 ills. in black and white, 25 ills. in color, Nov., 1938.

Papago Indians:

Old Yuma Trail. By W J McGee. Vol. XII, pp. 103-107, Mar., 1901.

Old Yuma Trail. By W J McGee. Vol. XII, pp. 129-143, 7 ills., 1 page map, Apr., 1901.

Papeete, Tahiti:

Notes on Tahiti. By Harrison W. Smith. Vol. XXII, pp. 947-963, 17 ills., Oct., 1911.

Tahiti: A Playground of Nature. By Paul Gooding. Vol. XXXVIII, pp. 301-326, 16 ills., 1 half-page map, Oct., 1920.

Paper Industry:

Lessons from Japan. Vol. XV, pp. 221-225, 3 ills., May, 1904.

Massachusetts—Beehive of Business. By William Joseph Showalter. Vol. XXXVII, pp. 203-245, 41 ills., Mar., 1920.

Paper From Cotton Stalks. Vol. XVII, p. 425, July, 1906.

Papua (Territory), New Guinea:

Further Notes on Dutch New Guinea. By Thomas Barbour. Vol. XIX, pp. 527-545, 19 ills., Aug., 1908.

Into Primeval Papua by Seaplane: Seeking Disease-Resisting Sugar Cane, Scientists Find Neolithic Man in Unmapped Nooks of Sorcery and Cannibalism. By E. W. Brandes. Vol. LVI, pp. 253-332, 98 ills., 1 three-quarters-page map, Sept., 1929.

Notes on a Zoölogical Collecting Trip to Dutch New Guinea. By Thomas Barbour. Vol. XIX, pp. 469-484, 12 ills., 2 half-page maps, July, 1908.

Pictorial Jaunt Through Papua. 22 ills. from photographs by Capt. Frank Hurley. Vol. LI, pp. 109-124, Jan., 1927.

Strange Sights in Far-Away Papua. By A. E. Pratt. Vol. XVIII, pp. 559-572, 7 ills., Sept., 1907.

Parade of Life Through the Ages: Records in Rocks Reveal a Strange Procession of Prehistoric Creatures, from Jellyfish to Dinosaurs, Giant Sloths, Saber-toothed Tigers, and Primitive Man. By Charles R. Knight. With 24 ills. in color from paintings by the author. Vol. LXXXI, pp. 141-184, 13 ills. in black and white, Feb., 1942.

Paradise of the Tasman (Lord Howe Island): A Pacific Island Provides the Palms Which Decorate Hotels, Churches, Steamships, and Homes. By Hubert Lyman Clark. Vol. LXVIII, pp. 115-136, 24 ills., 1 half-page map, July, 1935.

Paraguay:

Buenos Aires and Its River of Silver: A Journey Up the Paraná and Paraguay to the Chaco Cattle Country. By William R. Barbour. Vol. XL, pp. 393-432, 38 ills., Oct., 1921.

Color Cruising in Paraguay. 11 ills. in color from natural-color photographs by Fenno Jacobs. Vol. LXXXIV, pp. 465-472, Oct., 1943.

Falls of Iguazu. By Marie Robinson Wright. Vol. XVII, pp. 456-460, 4 ills., Aug., 1906.

River-Encircled Paraguay. By Harriet Chalmers Adams. Vol. LXIII, pp. 385-416, 35 ills., 1 third-page map, Apr., 1933.

Through Paraguay and Southern Matto Grosso. By Sir Christopher H. Gibson. Vol. LXXXIV, pp. 459-488, 20 ills. in black and white, 11 ills. in color, 1 two-thirds-page map, Oct., 1943.

Paraguay (River), Argentina-Paraguay:

Buenos Aires and Its River of Silver: A Journey Up the Paraná and Paraguay to the Chaco Cattle Country. By William R. Barbour. Vol. XL, pp. 393-432, 38 ills., Oct., 1921.

Through Paraguay and Southern Matto Grosso. By Sir Christopher H. Gibson. Vol. LXXXIV, pp. 459-488, 20 ills. in black and white, 11 ills. in color, 1 two-thirds-page map, Oct., 1943.

Paramaribo, Surinam:

Color Glows in the Guianas, French and Dutch. By Nicol Smith. Vol. LXXXIII, pp. 459-480, 8 ills. in black and white, 13 ills. in color, 1 two-thirds-page map, Apr., 1943.

Picturesque Paramaribo. By Harriet Chalmers Adams. Vol. XVIII, pp. 365-373, 7 ills., June, 1907.

Surinam Subjects of Queen Wilhelmina. 13 ills. in color from natural-color photographs by Philip Hanson Hiss. Vol. LXXXIII, pp. 465-472, Apr., 1943.

Paraná (River), South America:

Buenos Aires and Its River of Silver: A Journey Up the Paraná and Paraguay to the Chaco Cattle Country. By William R. Barbour. Vol. XL, pp. 393-432, 38 ills., Oct., 1921.

Through Paraguay and Southern Matto Grosso. By Sir Christopher H. Gibson. Vol. LXXXIV, pp. 459-488, 20 ills. in black and white, 11 ills. in color, 1 two-thirds-page map, Oct., 1943.

Paricutin, the Cornfield That Grew a Volcano (Mexico). By James A. Green. Vol. LXXXV, pp. 129-164, 16 ills. in black and white, 21 ills. in color, 1 third-page map, Feb., 1944.

Parima (River), Brazil:

Exploring the Valley of the Amazon in a Hydroplane: Twelve Thousand Miles of Flying Over the World's Greatest River and Greatest Forest to Chart the Unknown Parima River from the Sky. By Capt. Albert W. Stevens. Vol. XLIX, pp. 353-420, 86 ills., 1 page map, Apr., 1926.

Paris, France:

Paris Delivered. 10 ills. from photographs. Vol. LXXXVII, pp. 79-86, Jan., 1945.

Paris Freed. By Maj. Frederick Simpich, Jr. Vol. LXXXVII, pp. 385-412, 14 ills. in black and white, 12 ills. in color, Apr., 1945.

Paris in Spring. By Maynard Owen Williams. Vol. LXX, pp. 501-534, 30 ills., Oct. 1936.

Paris Lives Again. By M. O. Williams. Vol. XC, pp. 767-790, 24 ills. Dec. 1946.

Seeing Paris on a 48-Hour Pass. 12 ills. in color from U. S. Army official photographs. Vol. LXXXVII, pp. 401-412, Apr., 1945.

Paris Basin (Region), France:

France Farms as War Wages: An American Explores the Rich Rural Region of the Historic Paris Basin. By Harrison Howell Walker. Vol. LXXVII, pp. 201-238, 16 ills. in black and white, 18 ills. in color, 1 map, Feb., 1940.

Some French Pastorals. 18 ills. in color from natural-color photographs by Harrison Howell Walker. Vol. LXXVII, pp. 207-230, Feb., 1940.

Park, James Loder:

Life's Tenor in Ethiopia: Africa's Land of Early Christianity Now Yields Minerals for Modern Industry. By James Loder Park. Vol. LXVII, pp. 783-793, 8 ills., June, 1935.

Parker, Cornelia Stratton:

Entering the Front Doors of Medieval Towns: The Adventures of an American Woman and Her Daughter in a Folding Boat on Eight Rivers of Germany and Austria. By Cornelia Stratton Parker. Vol. LXI, pp. 365-394, 23 ills., 1 two-thirds-page map, Mar., 1932.

Parker, Margery Pritchard:

Northern Crusoe's Island: Life on a Fox Farm Off the Coast of Alaska, Far from Contact with the World Eleven Months a Year. By Margery Pritchard Parker. Vol. XLIV, pp. 313-326, 15 ills., 1 eighth-page map, Sept., 1923.

Parks. *See* National Parks.

Parliament (British):

Democracy's Royal Palace. 19 ills. in color from natural-color photographs by B. Anthony Stewart. Vol. XC, pp. 233-248, Aug., 1946.

Parliament (British)—*Continued*

Oldest Free Assemblies : Address of Right Hon. Arthur J. Balfour, in the United States House of Representatives, May 5, 1917. Vol. XXXI, pp. 368-371, Apr., 1917.

Yanks at Westminster. By Capt. Leonard David Gammans. Vol. XC, pp. 223-252, 6 ills. in black and white, 19 ills. in color, Aug., 1946.

Parma (Ship) :

Cape Horn Grain-Ship Race : The Gallant *Parma* Leads the Vanishing Fleet of Square-Riggers Through Raging Gales and Irksome Calms 16,000 Miles from Australia to England. By A. J. Villiers. Vol. LXIII, pp. 1-39, 38 ills., Jan., 1933.

Parnassus, Mount, Greece :

Festival Days on the Slopes of Mount Parnassus. 14 ills. in color from natural-color photographs by Maynard Owen Williams. Vol. LVIII, pp. 712-721, Dec., 1930.

Paro Jong (Fort), Bhutan :

Castles in the Air—Experiences and Journeys in Unknown Bhutan. By John Claude White. Vol. XXV, pp. 365-455, 74 ills., 1 page map, Apr., 1914.

Paro-Ta-Tshang (Monastery), Bhutan :

Castles in the Air—Experiences and Journeys in Unknown Bhutan. By John Claude White. Vol. XXV, pp. 365-455, 74 ills., 1 page map, Apr., 1914.

Parr, Grant:

War Meets Peace in Egypt. By Grant Parr and G. E. Janssen. Vol. LXXXI, pp. 503-526, 25 ills., 1 page map, Apr., 1942.

Parra, L. Pérez:

Glamour of Mexico—Old and New. 15 ills. in color from natural-color photographs by L. Pérez Parra. Vol. LXV, pp. 345-352, Mar., 1934.

Parrots:

Flycatchers and Other Friends in Feathers. 36 portraits in color from paintings by Maj. Allan Brooks. Vol. LXIX, pp. 807-822, June, 1936.

Parrots, Kingfishers, and Flycatchers : Strange Trogons and Curious Cuckoos are Pictured with these Other Birds of Color, Dash, and Courage. By Alexander Wetmore. Paintings by Maj. Allan Brooks. Vol. LXIX, pp. 801-828, 9 ills. in black and white, 36 portraits in color, June, 1936.

Parsees and the Towers of Silence at Bombay, India. By William Thomas Fee. Vol. XVI, pp. 529-554, 15 ills., Dec., 1905.

Parsons, William Barclay:

Hunan—The Closed Province of China. By William Barclay Parsons. Vol. XI, pp. 393-400, 1 half-page map, 1 ill., Oct., 1900.

Partitioned Poland. By William Joseph Showalter. Vol. XXVII, pp. 88-106, 12 ills., Jan., 1915.

Pashpati, Nepal :

Nepal : A Little-Known Kingdom. By John Claude White. Vol. XXXVIII, pp. 245-283, 32 ills., 1 half-page map, Oct., 1920.

Passantino, Joseph E.:

Kunming, Southwestern Gateway to China. By Joseph E. Passantino. With 18 ills. in color from natural-color photographs by the author. Vol. XC, pp. 137-168, 12 ills. in black and white, Aug., 1946.

Passet, M. Stephane:

Mongolia : In the Land of Kublai Khan. 16 ills. in color from autochromes by M. Stephane Passet. Vol. XLI, pp. 465-472, May, 1922.

Passing of Korea. Vol. XVII, pp. 575-580, 5 ills., Oct., 1906.

Passion Play: Oberammergau, Germany :

Behind the Scenes in the Home of the Passion Play. 11 ills. in color from natural-color photographs. Vol. LXVIII, pp. 753-760, Dec., 1935.

Where Bible Characters Live Again : Everyday Life in Oberammergau, World Famous for Its Passion Play, Reaches a Climax at Christmas. By Anton Lang, Jr. Vol. LXVIII, pp. 743-769, 19 ills. in black and white, 11 ills. in color, 1 third-page map, Dec., 1935.

Passmore, Lee:

California Trapdoor Spider Performs Engineering Marvels. By Lee Passmore. Vol. LXIV, pp. 195-211, 23 ills., Aug., 1933.

Passover:

Last Israelitish Blood Sacrifice : How the Vanishing Samaritans Celebrate the Passover on Sacred Mount Gerizim. By John D. Whiting. Vol. XXXVII, pp. 1-46, 40 ills., 1 half-page map, Jan., 1920.

Pastel Wrens from "Down Under." 8 ills. in color from paintings by N. W. Cayley. Vol. LXXXVIII, pp. 489-496, Oct., 1945.

Patagonia (Region), South America :

Indian Tribes of Southern Patagonia, Tierra del Fuego, and the Adjoining Islands. By J. B. Hatcher. Vol. XII, pp. 12-22, 4 ills., Jan., 1901.

Some Geographic Features of Southern Patagonia, With a Discussion of Their Origin. By J. B. Hatcher. Vol. XI, pp. 41-55, 4 ills., Feb., 1900.

Patan, Nepal :

Nepal : A Little-Known Kingdom. By John Claude White. Vol. XXXVIII, pp. 245-283, 32 ills., 1 half-page map, Oct., 1920.

Pathans (Tribespeople) :

South of Khyber Pass (India). By Maynard Owen Williams. Vol. LXXXIX, pp. 471-500, 31 ills., Apr., 1946.

Pathfinder of the East : Setting Sail to Find "Christians and Spices," Vasco da Gama Met Amazing Adventures, Founded an Empire, and Changed the History of Western Europe. By J. R. Hildebrand. Vol. LII, pp. 503-550, 43 ills., 1 two-thirds-page map, Nov., 1927.

Patmos (Island), Aegean Sea:

Rhodes, and Italy's Aegean Islands. By Dorothy Hosmer. Vol. LXXIX, pp. 449-480, 32 ills., 1 map, Apr., 1911.

Patric, John:

Czechoslovakia, Yankees of Europe. By John Patric. Vol. LXXIV, pp. 173-225, 23 ills. in black and white, 30 ills. in color, 1 map, Aug., 1938.

Friendly Journeys in Japan: A Young American Finds a Ready Welcome in the Homes of the Japanese During Leisurely Travels Through the Islands. By John Patric. Vol. LXIX, pp. 441-480, 28 ills. in black and white, 10 ills. in color, 1 two-thirds-page map, Apr., 1936.

Imperial Rome Reborn. By John Patric. Vol. LXXI, pp. 269-325, 34 ills. in black and white, 21 ills. in color, Mar., 1937.

Italy, From Roman Ruins to Radio: History of Ancient Bridge Building and Road Making Repeats Itself in Modern Public Works and Engineering Projects. By John Patric. Vol. LXXVII, pp. 347-394, 27 ills. in black and white, 9 ills. in color, Mar., 1940.

Magyar Mirth and Melancholy. By John Patric. Vol. LXXIII, pp. 1-55, 33 ills. in black and white, 20 ills. in color, 1 half-page map, Jan., 1938.

Roads from Washington (D. C.). By John Patric. Vol. LXXIV, pp. 1-48, 27 ills. in black and white, 30 ills. in color, special map supplement, July, 1938.

Patrick, Mary Mills:

Asia Minor in the Time of the Seven Wise Men. By Mary Mills Patrick. Vol. XXXVII, pp. 47-67, 19 ills., Jan., 1920.

Emancipation of Mohammedan Women. By Mary Mills Patrick. Vol. XX, pp. 42-66, 19 ills., Jan., 1909.

Patriotic Pilgrimage to Eastern National Parks: History and Beauty Live Along Paved Roads, Once Indian Trails, Through Virginia, North Carolina, Tennessee, Kentucky, and West Virginia. By Leo A. Borah. Vol. LXV, pp. 663-702, 18 ills. in black and white, 28 ills. in color, 1 two-page map, June, 1934.

Patterson, J. N.:

Magic Mountain (Mount Wilson, California). By J. N. Patterson. Vol. XIX, pp. 457-468, 9 ills., July, 1908.

Pátzcuaro Region, Mexico:

Mexican Land of Lakes and Lacquers. 22 ills. from photographs by Helene Fischer and Luis Marquez. Vol. LXXI, pp. 633-648, May, 1937.

Paul Du Chaillu (Biography). Vol. XIV, pp. 282-285, July, 1903.

Pavia, Italy:

Frontier Cities of Italy. By Florence Craig Albrecht. Vol. XXVII, pp. 533-586, 45 ills., June, 1915.

Pavlof Volcano, Alaska:

Mapping the Home of the Great Brown Bear: Adventures of the National Geographic Society's Pavlof Volcano Expedition to Alaska. By Dr. Thomas Augustus Jaggar. Vol. LV, pp. 109-134, 30 ills., 1 three-quarters-page map, Jan., 1929.

Peace Conference: Paris, France:

Paris Lives Again. By M. O. Williams. Vol. XC, pp. 767-790, 24 ills., Dec., 1946.

Peace of Latin America. Vol. XVI, pp. 479-480, Oct., 1905.

Peacetime Plant Hunting About Peiping. By P. H. and J. H. Dorsett. Vol. LXXII, pp. 509-534, 21 ills., 1 two-thirds-page map, Oct., 1937.

Peacetime Rambles in the Ryukyus. By William Leonard Schwartz. Vol. LXXXVII, pp. 543-561, 12 ills., 1 two-thirds-page and 1 half-page maps, May, 1945.

Peafowl:

Fowls of Forest and Stream Tamed by Man. By Morley A. Jull. Vol. LVII, pp. 327-371, 27 ills. in black and white, 16 ills. in color, Mar., 1930.

Peaks and Parks of Western Canada. 11 ills. from photographs; 5 ills. by W. J. Oliver. Vol. LXXX, pp. 516-526, Oct., 1941.

Peaks and Trails in the Canadian Alps. 16 ills. in duotone from photographs by Byron Harmon and Clifford White. Vol. LXV, pp. 627-642, May, 1934.

Pearl Fisheries:

Bahrein: Port of Pearls and Petroleum. By Maynard Owen Williams. Vol. LXXXIX, pp. 195-210, 6 ills. in black and white, 11 ills. in color, 1 half-page map, Feb., 1946.

Cultivation of Marine and Fresh Water Animals in Japan. By K. Mitsukuri. Vol. XVII, pp. 524-531, 5 ills., Sept., 1906.

Dream Ship: The Story of a Voyage of Adventure More Than Half Around the World in a 47-foot Lifeboat. By Ralph Stock. Vol. XXXIX, pp. 1-52, 43 ills., 1 page map, Jan., 1921.

Fishing for Pearls in the Indian Ocean. By Bella Sidney Woolf. Vol. XLIX, pp. 161-183, 24 ills., Feb., 1926.

On the Bottom of a South Sea Pearl Lagoon. By Roy Waldo Miner. Vol. LXXIV, pp. 365-390, 17 ills. in black and white, 8 ills. in color, Sept., 1938.

Pearl and Turtle Farms in Japan. Vol. XV, p. 427, Oct., 1904.

Pearl Fisheries of Ceylon. By Hugh M. Smith. Vol. XXIII, pp. 173-194, 13 ills., 1 quarter-page map, Feb., 1912.

Rise of the New Arab Nation. By Frederick Simpich. Vol. XXXVI, pp. 369-393, 17 ills., 1 page map, Nov., 1919.

Pearl Fishing in the Red Sea. By Henri de Monfreid. Vol. LXXII, pp. 597-626, 24 ills., 1 two-thirds-page map, Nov., 1937.

Pears, Edwin:

"Grass Never Grows Where the Turkish Hoof Has Trod." By Edwin Pears. Vol. XXIII, pp. 1132-1148, 19 ills., Nov., 1912.

Pearson, T. Gilbert:

Birds That Cruise the Coast and Inland Waters. By T. Gilbert Pearson. Paintings by Maj. Allan Brooks. Vol. LXV, pp. 299-328, 15 ills. in black and white, 24 portraits in color, Mar., 1934.

Crows, Magpies, and Jays: Unusual Intelligence Has Earned a Unique Position for These Birds. By T. Gilbert Pearson. Paintings by Maj. Allan Brooks. Vol. LXIII, pp. 51-79, 16 ills. in black and white, 17 ills. in color, Jan., 1933.

Large Wading Birds: Long Legs and Remarkable Beaks, as Well as Size, Form, and Color, Distinguish the Herons, Ibises, and Flamingos. By T. Gilbert Pearson. Paintings by Maj. Allan Brooks. Vol. LXII, pp. 441-469, 13 ills. in black and white, 24 ills. in color, Oct., 1932.

Sparrows, Towhees, and Longspurs: These Happy Little Singers Make Merry in Field, Forest, and Desert Throughout North America. By T. Gilbert Pearson. Vol. LXXV, pp. 353-376, 5 ills. in black and white, 43 ills. in color, Mar., 1939.

Thrushes, Thrashers, and Swallows: Robins and Bluebirds are Familiar Members of a Famous Musical Family Which Includes the Hermit Thrush and European Nightingale. By T. Gilbert Pearson. Paintings by Maj. Allan Brooks. Vol. LXIX, pp. 523-546, 6 ills. in black and white, 42 paintings from life, Apr., 1936.

Woodpeckers, Friends of Our Forests. By T. Gilbert Pearson. Paintings by Maj. Allan Brooks. Vol. LXIII, pp. 453-479, 12 ills. in black and white, 25 ills. in color, Apr., 1933.

Peary, Robert E.:

Account of Peary's Explorations. By Rear Adm. Colby M. Chester. Vol. XXI, pp. 69-73, Jan., 1910.

Address by Commander Robert E. Peary, U. S. N., on the Assembling of the Congress in Washington, September 8, 1904. Vol. XV, pp. 387-392, Oct., 1904.

Commander Peary's New Vessel. Vol. XVI, p. 192, Apr., 1905.

Discovery of the North Pole (Presentation of Special Gold Medal). Vol. XXI, pp. 63-82, Jan., 1910.

Discovery of the Pole: First Report by Commander Robert E. Peary, September 6, 1909. Vol. XX, pp. 893-916, 11 ills., 1 page map, Oct., 1909.

European Tributes to Peary. Vol. XXI, pp. 536-540, 4 ills., June, 1910.

Farthest North. Vol. XVII, pp. 638-644, 9 ills., Nov., 1906.

Future of the Airplane. By Rear Adm. Robert E. Peary. Vol. XXXIII, pp. 107-113, 4 ills., Jan., 1918.

Peary, Robert E.—_Continued_

Honors to Amundsen and Peary (Speeches by Robert E. Peary). Vol. XXIV, pp. 113-130, 5 ills., Jan., 1913.

Honors to Peary (Presentation of Hubbard Medal by President Roosevelt). Vol. XVIII, pp. 49-60, 1 ill., Jan., 1907.

Memorial to Peary: The National Geographic Society Dedicates Monument in Arlington National Cemetery to Discoverer of the North Pole. Vol. XLI, pp. 639-646, 4 ills., June, 1922.

National Geographic Society (Records of North Pole Discovery). Vol. XXI, p. 276, Mar., 1910.

National Geographic Society's Notable Year (Address by Rear Adm. Robert E. Peary). Vol. XXXVII, pp. 338-345, 2 ills., Apr., 1920.

Nearest the Pole (Rear Adm. Robert E. Peary's Address to The Society). Vol. XVIII, pp. 446-450, special map supplement, July, 1907.

North Pole (Appointment of a Committee by The Society to Consider Claims of Peary and Cook). Vol. XX, pp. 921-922, Nov., 1909.

North Pole (Resolutions of The Society Acknowledging Peary's Discovery). Vol. XX, pp. 1008-1009, Nov., 1909.

Peary and the North Pole. Vol. XIV, pp. 379-381, Oct., 1903.

Peary as a Leader: Incidents from the Life of the Discoverer of the North Pole Told by One of His Lieutenants on the Expedition Which Reached the Goal. By Donald B. MacMillan. Vol. XXXVII, pp. 293-317, 20 ills., 1 page map, Apr., 1920.

Peary on the North Pole. Vol. XIV, pp. 28-29, 1 page map, Jan., 1903.

Peary to Try Again. Vol. XVIII, p. 281, Apr., 1907.

Peary's Explorations in 1898-1899. Vol. X, pp. 415-416, Oct., 1899.

Peary's Explorations in the Far North. By Gilbert Grosvenor. Vol. XXXVII, pp. 318-322, 3 ills., Apr., 1920.

Peary's Polar Expedition. Vol. XIX, p. 447, June, 1908.

Peary's Twenty Years' Service in the Arctics. Vol. XVIII, pp. 451-454, July, 1907.

Peary's Work and Prospects. Vol. X, pp. 414-415, Oct., 1899.

Peary's Work in 1900 and 1901. Vol. XII, pp. 357-361, 2 ills., Oct., 1901.

Peary's Work in 1901-1902. By Gilbert H. Grosvenor. Vol. XIII, pp. 384-386, Oct., 1902.

South Polar Expedition (Proposed by Peary for Consideration of National Geographic Society). Vol. XXI, pp. 167-170, 1 page map, Feb., 1910.

Value of Arctic Exploration. By Rear Adm. Robert E. Peary. Vol. XIV, pp. 429-436, Dec., 1903.

Peary Arctic Club:

Letter of appreciation to Comdr. Robert E. Peary, signed by Theodore Roosevelt. Vol. XIV, p. 330, Aug., 1903.

Mission of the *Diana*. Vol. X, p. 273, July, 1899.

Peary Arctic Club. Vol. XIII, p. 146, Apr., 1902.

Ten Years of the Peary Arctic Club. By Herbert L. Bridgman. Vol. XIX, pp. 661-668, 3 ills., Sept., 1908.

Peasant Home in Corsica. Vol. XLIV, supplement, Sept., 1923.

Peasant Life in the Black Forest. By Karl Frederick Geiser. Vol. XIX, pp. 635-649, 12 ills., Sept., 1908.

Pechkoff, (Lt.) Zinovi:

Few Glimpses into Russia. By Lieut. Zinovi Pechkoff. Vol. XXXII, pp. 238-253, 10 ills., Sept., 1917.

Peculiar Caves of Asia Minor. By Elizabeth H. Brewer. Vol. XXII, pp. 870-875, 5 ills., Sept., 1911.

Pedaling Through Poland: An American Girl Free-wheels Alone from Kraków, and Its Medieval Byways, Toward Ukraine's Restive Borderland. By Dorothy Hosmer. Vol. LXXV, pp. 739-775, 38 ills., 2 maps, June, 1939.

Peel Island, Bonin Islands. *See* Chichi Jima.

Peiping (Peking), China:

Approach to Peiping. By Maj. John W. Thomason, Jr. Vol. LXIX, pp. 275-308, 24 ills., 1 page map, Feb., 1936.

Capital and Country of Old Cathay. 16 ills. in duotone. Vol. LXIII, pp. 748-765, June, 1933.

Causes That Led Up to the Siege of Pekin. By W. A. P. Martin. Vol. XII, pp. 53-63, 1 ill., Feb., 1901.

Glimpses of Korea and China. By William W. Chapin. Vol. XXI, pp. 895-934, 11 ills. in black and white, 39 ills. in color, Nov., 1910.

Glory That Was Imperial Peking. By W. Robert Moore. Vol. LXIII, pp. 745-780, 18 ills. in black and white, 16 ills. in duotone, June, 1933.

Map-Changing Medicine. By William Joseph Showalter. Vol. XLII, pp. 303-330, 26 ills., Sept., 1922.

Peacetime Plant Hunting About Peiping. By P. H. and J. H. Dorsett. Vol. LXXII, pp. 509-534, 21 ills., 1 two-thirds-page map, Oct., 1937.

Peiping, City of Dust and Color. 14 ills. in color from natural-color photographs by W. Robert Moore and Owen Lattimore. Vol. LXVI, pp. 609-619, Nov., 1934.

Peiping Panorama in Vivid Pigments. 16 ills. in color from camera paintings by H. C. and J. H. White, Deng Bao-ling, and Hwang Yao-tso. Vol. LXX, pp. 753-784, Dec., 1936.

Peiping (Peking), China—*Continued*

Peiping's Happy New Year: Lunar Celebration Attracts Throngs to Temple Fairs, Motley Bazaars, and Age-old Festivities. By George Kin Leung. Vol. LXX, pp. 749-792, 31 ills. in black and white, 16 ills. in color, Dec., 1936.

Peking, the City of the Unexpected. By James Arthur Muller. Vol. XXXVIII, pp. 005-055, 18 ills., Nov., 1920.

Peiping's Happy New Year: Lunar Celebration Attracts Throngs to Temple Fairs, Motley Bazaars, and Age-old Festivities. By George Kin Leung. Vol. LXX, pp. 749-792, 31 ills. in black and white, 16 ills. in color, Dec., 1936.

Peking, China. *See* Peiping.

Peking, the City of the Unexpected. By James Arthur Muller. Vol. XXXVIII, pp. 335-355, 18 ills., Nov., 1920.

Pelée, Mont (Volcano), Martinique:

Magnetic Disturbance Caused by the Explosion of Mont Pelée. Vol. XIII, pp. 208-209, June, 1902.

National Geographic Society's Expedition in the West Indies. Vol. XIII, pp. 209-213, 2 half-page maps, June, 1902.

New Cone of Mont Pelée. Vol. XIV, pp. 422-423, 2 ills., Nov., 1903.

Recent Volcanic Eruptions in the West Indies. By Israel C. Russell. Vol. XIII, pp. 267-285, 7 ills., July, 1902.

Report by Robert T. Hill on the Volcanic Disturbances in the West Indies. Vol. XIII, pp. 223-267, 13 ills., 2 page and 1 half-page maps, July, 1902.

Shattered Obelisk of Mont Pelée. By Angelo Heilprin. Vol. XVII, pp. 465-474, 5 ills., Aug., 1906.

Volcanic Eruptions on Martinique and St. Vincent. By Israel C. Russell. Vol. XIII, pp. 415-436, 10 ills., Dec., 1902.

Peleliu (Island), Palau Islands, Carolines:

South from Saipan. By W. Robert Moore. Vol. LXXXVII, pp. 441-414, 11 ills. in black and white, 17 ills. in color, 1 half-page map, Apr., 1945.

Pelican Profiles. By Lewis Wayne Walker. Vol. LXXXIV, pp. 589-598, 5 ills. in black and white, 8 ills. in color, Nov., 1943.

Pelicans (Birds):

Birds of Lake and Lagoon, Marsh and Seacoast. 24 portraits in color from paintings by Maj. Allan Brooks. Vol. LXV, pp. 313-328, Mar., 1934.

Birds That Cruise the Coast and Inland Waters. By T. Gilbert Pearson. Paintings by Maj. Allan Brooks. Vol. LXV, pp. 299-328, 7 ills. in black and white, 2 portraits in color, Mar., 1934.

Pelican Profiles. By Lewis Wayne Walker. Vol. LXXXIV, pp. 589-598, 5 ills. in black and white, 8 ills. in color, Nov., 1943.

Pelicans (Birds)—*Continued*

Peru's Wealth-Producing Birds : Vast Riches in the Guano Deposits of Cormorants, Pelicans, and Petrels Which Nest on Her Barren, Rainless Coast. By R. E. Coker. Vol. XXXVII, pp. 537-566, 28 ills., June, 1920.

Pellerano, Luigi:

Albania : Men of the Eagle in Their Mountain Eyrie. 39 ills. in color from natural-color photographs by Luigi Pellerano. Vol. LIX, pp. 142-191, Feb., 1931.

Cirenaica, On the Edge of the Saharan Sands. 13 ills. in color from natural-color photographs by Luigi Pellerano. Vol. LVII, pp. 692-701, June, 1930.

Italy : Caesar's City Today (Rome). 21 ills. in color from natural-color photographs by Bernard F. Rogers, Jr., and Luigi Pellerano. Vol. LXXI, pp. 285-316, Mar., 1937.

Italy : Stone Beehive Homes of Italian Peasants. 5 ills. in color from autochromes by Luigi Pellerano. Vol. LVII, pp. 234-243, Feb., 1930.

Libia : Under Italian Libia's Burning Sun. 9 ills. in color from autochromes lumière by Luigi Pellerano. Vol. XLVIII, pp. 141-148, Aug., 1925.

Rhodes : Souvenirs of Knighthood in Rhodes. 13 ills. in color from natural-color photographs by Luigi Pellerano. Vol. LXIV, pp. 665-672, Dec., 1933.

Sardinia : Where the Sard Holds Sway. 9 ills. in color from autochromes by Luigi Pellerano. Vol. XLIX, pp. 464-474, Apr., 1926.

Sicily : Island of Vivid Beauty and Crumbling Glory. 22 ills. in color from autochromes lumière by Luigi Pellerano. Vol. LII, pp. 432-449, Oct., 1927.

Penck, Albrecht:

Plan of a Map of the World. By Albrecht Penck. Vol. XV, pp. 405-408, Oct., 1904.

Pendleton, Oregon :

"Where Rolls the Oregon." 28 ills. in color from natural-color photographs by Ray Atkeson. Vol. XC, pp. 689-728, Dec., 1946.

Penfield, James K.:

Greenland—U. S. Base in the Arctic. 5 ills. in color from natural-color photographs by James K. Penfield. Vol. LXXXII, pp. 373-376, Sept., 1942.

Greenland Turns to America. By James K. Penfield. Vol. LXXXII, pp. 369-383, 7 ills. in black and white, 5 ills. in color, 1 two-page map, Sept., 1942.

Penguins (Birds) :

Antarctica's Most Interesting Citizen : The Comical Penguin Is Both Romantic and Bellicose. By Worth E. Shoults. Vol. LXI, pp. 251-260, 8 ills., Feb., 1932.

South Georgia, an Outpost of the Antarctic. By Robert Cushman Murphy. Vol. XLI, pp. 409-444, 41 ills., 2 half-page maps, Apr., 1922.

Penn, William:

Historic City of Brotherly Love : Philadelphia, Born of Penn and Strengthened by Franklin, a Metropolis of Industries, Homes, and Parks. By John Oliver La Gorce. Vol. LXII, pp. 643-697, 49 ills. in black and white, 13 ills. in color, Dec., 1932.

Penn Country in Sussex (England) : Home of Pennsylvania's Founder Abounds in Quaker History and Memories of Adventurous Smugglers. By Col. P. T. Etherton. Vol. LXVIII, pp. 59-90, 32 ills., 1 page map, July, 1935.

Pennants of Patriotism 200 Years Ago. By Gilbert Grosvenor and Byron McCandless. Vol. XXXII, pp. 399-403, 75 ills. in color, Oct., 1917.

Penn's Land of Modern Miracles (Pennsylvania). By John Oliver La Gorce. Vol. LXVIII, pp. 1-58, 28 ills. in black and white, 39 ills. in color, 1 two-page map, July, 1935.

Pennsylvania:

In the Pennsylvania Dutch Country. By Elmer C. Stauffer. Vol. LXXX, pp. 37-74, 20 ills. in black and white, 22 ills. in color, 1 map (pen and ink drawing), July, 1941.

Industrial Titan of America : Pennsylvania, Once the Keystone of the Original Thirteen, Now the Keystone of Forty-eight Sovereign States. By John Oliver La Gorce. Vol. XXXV, pp. 367-406, 33 ills., 1 page map, May, 1919.

Penn's Land of Modern Miracles. By John Oliver La Gorce. Vol. LXVIII, pp. 1-58, 28 ills. in black and white, 39 ills. in color, 1 two-page map, July, 1935.

Pennsylvania Dutch—In a Land of Milk and Honey. 10 ills. in color from natural-color photographs by J. Baylor Roberts. Vol. LXXIV, pp. 49-56, July, 1938.

Pennsylvania's Land of Plenty. 22 ills. in color from natural-color photographs by Harrison Howell Walker. Vol. LXXX, pp. 41-64, July, 1941.

Roads from Washington. By John Patric. Vol. LXXIV, pp. 1-48, 27 ills. in black and white, 30 ills. in color, special map supplement, July, 1938.

Today in the Land of Penn and Franklin. 39 ills. in color from natural-color photographs by Edwin L. Wisherd. Vol. LXVIII, pp. 13-52, July, 1935.

Travels of George Washington : Dramatic Episodes in His Career as the First Geographer of the United States. By William Joseph Showalter. Vol. LXI, pp. 1-63, 50 ills., 5 maps, special map supplement, Jan., 1932.

See also Gettysburg ; Philadelphia.

Pennsylvania Dutch (People) :

In the Pennsylvania Dutch Country. By Elmer C. Stauffer. Vol. LXXX, pp. 37-74, 20 ills. in black and white, 22 ills. in color, 1 map (pen and ink drawing), July, 1941.

Pennsylvania Dutch (People)—*Continued*

Pennsylvania's Land of Plenty. 22 ills. in color from natural-color photographs by Harrison Howell Walker. Vol. LXXX, pp. 41-64, July, 1941.

Pennsylvania's Land of Plenty. 22 ills. in color from natural color photographs by Harrison Howell Walker. Vol. LXXX, pp. 41-64, July, 1941.

Penobscot (Indian Tribe):

America's First Settlers, the Indians. By Matthew W. Stirling. Vol. LXXII, pp. 535-596, 34 ills. in black and white, 24 ills. in color, Nov., 1937.

When Red Men Ruled Our Forests. 24 ills. in color from paintings by W. Langdon Kihn. Vol. LXXII, pp. 551-590, Nov., 1937.

Penrhyn Island, Pacific Ocean. *See* Tongareva.

Penrose, (Dr.) C. B.:

Bear Hunt. Vol. XIX, p. 222, Mar., 1908.

Bear Hunt in Montana. By Arthur Alvord Stiles. Vol. XIX, pp. 149-154, 5 ills., Feb., 1908.

People of Morocco. Vol. XVII, p. 108, 1 ill., Feb., 1906.

People of the Wilderness: The Mongols, Once the Terror of All Christendom, Now a Primitive, Harmless, Nomad Race. By Adam Warwick. Vol. XXXIX, pp. 507-551, 59 ills., May, 1921.

Peoples and Places of Northern Africa. Vol. XLII, pp. 363-378, 16 ills., Oct., 1922.

People's Fight Against Slavery. By Hon. Henry A. Wallace. Reprint of address delivered at a dinner of the Free World Association, May 8, 1942. Vol. LXXXII, pp. 276-280, 1 ill., Aug., 1942.

Pepper, Charles M.:

From Panama to Patagonia. By Charles M. Pepper. Vol. XVII, pp. 449-452, 1 ill., Aug., 1906.

South America Fifty Years Hence. By Charles M. Pepper. Vol. XVII, pp. 428-432, special map supplement, Aug., 1906.

Pequot (Indian Tribe):

America's First Settlers, the Indians. By Matthew W. Stirling. Vol. LXXII, pp. 535-596, 34 ills. in black and white, 24 ills. in color, Nov., 1937.

When Red Men Ruled Our Forests. 24 ills. in color from paintings by W. Langdon Kihn. Vol. LXXII, pp. 551-590, Nov., 1937.

Perahera Processions of Ceylon. By G. H. G. Burroughs. Vol. LXII, pp. 90-100, 1 ill. in black and white, 8 ills. in duotone, July, 1932.

Perdicaris, Ion:

Morocco, the "Land of the Extreme West," and the Story of My Captivity. By Ion Perdicaris. Vol. XVII, pp. 117-157, 24 ills., Mar., 1906.

Perennial Geographer: After 2,000 Years Vergil Is Still the Most Widely Read of Latin Poets—First to Popularize the Geography of the Roman Empire. By W. Coleman Nevils. Vol. LVIII, pp. 439-465, 29 ills., Oct., 1930.

Pergamus (Ancient City):

Buried Cities of Asia Minor. By Ernest L. Harris. Vol. XX, pp. 1-18, 10 ills., Jan., 1909.

Perigueux, France:

Beauties of France. By Arthur Stanley Riggs. Vol. XXVIII, pp. 391-491, 73 ills. in black and white, 16 ills. in color, 1 half-page map, Nov., 1915.

Perkins, Elizabeth:

With the Monks at Meteora: The Monasteries of Thessaly. By Elizabeth Perkins. Vol. XX, pp. 799-807, 5 ills., Sept., 1909.

Perkins, George C.:

Key to the Pacific (Territory of Hawaii). By George C. Perkins. Vol. XIX, pp. 295-298, 1 half-page map, Apr., 1908.

Pernambuco, Brazil. *See* Recife.

Perry, (Capt.) K. W.:

Volcanoes of Alaska. Report by Capt. K. W. Perry. Vol. XXIII, pp. 824-832, 11 ills., Aug., 1912.

Perry, (Commodore) Matthew Calbraith:

Chapter from Japanese History. By Eki Hioki. Vol. XVI, pp. 220-228, May, 1905.

Gem of the Ocean: Our American Navy. By Josephus Daniels. Vol. XXXIII, pp. 313-335, 35 ills., Apr., 1918.

Some Early Geographers of the United States. By Rear Adm. Colby M. Chester. Vol. XV, pp. 392-404, Oct., 1904.

Perry Peak (Volcano), Alaska:

Jack in the Box: An Account of the Strange Performances of the Most Wonderful Island in the World. By Capt. F. M. Munger. Vol. XX, pp. 194-199, 8 ills., Feb., 1909.

Persepolis, Iran:

Exploring the Secrets of Persepolis. By Charles Breasted. Vol. LXIV, pp. 381-420, 48 ills., 1 half-page map, 1 plan, Oct., 1933.

Pershing, (Gen.) John J.:

Hubbard Medals Awarded to Stratosphere Explorers: Presentation by General Pershing. Vol. LXIX, pp. 713-714, May, 1936.

Our National War Memorials in Europe. By Gen. John J. Pershing. Vol. LXV, pp. 1-36, 24 ills. in black and white, 11 ills. in color, 1 half-page map, Jan., 1934.

Shopping Abroad for Our Armies in France. By Herbert Corey. Vol. XXXIII, pp. 206-218, 6 ills., Feb., 1918.

Stand by the Soldier. By Gen. John J. Pershing. Vol. XXXI, pp. 457-459, 1 ill., May, 1917.

Persia. *See* Iran.

Persia: The Awakening East. By W. P. Cresson. Vol. XIX, pp. 356-384, 21 ills., 1 quarter-page map, May, 1908.

Persia—Past and Present. Vol. XVIII, pp. 91-95, 6 ills., Feb., 1907.

Persian Caravan Sketches : The Land of the Lion and the Sun as Seen on a Summer Caravan Trip. By Harold F. Weston. Vol. XXXIX, pp. 417-468, 46 ills. in black and white, 16 ills. in color, 1 three-quarters-page map, Apr., 1921.

Persian Cats:

Catdom's Royalty Photographed in Color. 25 ills. in color from natural-color photographs by Willard R. Culver. Vol. LXXIV, pp. 597-628, Nov., 1938.

Panther of the Hearth : Lithe Grace and Independence of Spirit Contribute to the Appeal of Cats. "The Only Domestic Animal Man Has Never Conquered." By Frederick B. Eddy. Vol. LXXIV, pp. 589-634, 22 ills. in black and white, 25 ills. in color, Nov., 1938.

Perth, Australia :

Capital Cities of Australia. By W. Robert Moore. Vol. LXVIII, pp. 667-722, 32 ills. in black and white, 24 ills. in color, 1 two-page map, Dec., 1935.

Peru:

Air Adventures in Peru : Cruising Among Andean Peaks, Pilots and Cameramen Discover Wondrous Works of an Ancient People. By Robert Shippee. Vol. LXIII, pp. 81-120, 40 ills., 1 three-quarters-page map, Jan., 1933.

Along the Old Inca Highway. By Harriet Chalmers Adams. Vol. XIX, pp. 231-250, 21 ills., Apr., 1908.

Among the Snows and Flowers of Peru. 25 ills. in color from natural-color photographs by Jacob Gayer. Vol. LVII, pp. 732-765, June, 1930.

Brazil and Peru. Vol. XVII, pp. 203-204, Apr., 1906.

Buenos Aires to Washington by Horse : A Solitary Journey of Two and a Half Years, Through Eleven American Republics, Covers 9,600 Miles of Mountain and Plain, Desert and Jungle. By A. F. Tschiffely. Vol. LV, pp. 135-196, 75 ills., 1 page map, Feb., 1929.

Camels of the Clouds (Lamoids). By W. H. Hodge. Vol. LXXXIX, pp. 641-656, 15 ills., 1 half-page map, May, 1946.

Chile's Disputes With Peru and Bolivia. Vol. XII, pp. 401-402, Nov., 1901.

Cuzco, America's Ancient Mecca. By Harriet Chalmers Adams. Vol. XIX, pp. 669-689, 19 ills., Oct., 1908.

Explorations in Peru. Vol. XXIII, pp. 416-422, 7 ills., 1 half-page map, Apr., 1912.

Flying the World's Longest Air-Mail Route : From Montevideo, Uruguay, Over the Andes, Up the Pacific Coast, Across Central America and the Caribbean to Miami, Florida, in 67 Thrilling Flying Hours. By Junius B. Wood. Vol. LVII, pp. 261-325, 65 ills., 1 half-page map, Mar., 1930.

Peru—*Continued*

Forgotten Valley of Peru : Conquered by Incas, Scourged by Famine, Plagues and Earthquakes, Colca Valley Shelters the Last Fragment of an Ancient Andean Tribe. By Robert Shippee. Vol. LXV, pp. 111-132, 22 ills., 1 two-thirds-page map, Jan., 1934.

From Panama to Patagonia. By Charles M. Pepper. Vol. XVII, pp. 449-452, 1 ill., Aug., 1906.

Further Explorations in the Land of the Incas : The Peruvian Expedition of 1915 of the National Geographic Society and Yale University. By Hiram Bingham. Vol. XXIX, pp. 431-473, 29 ills., 1 page and 1 half-page maps, panorama, May, 1916.

Greatest Achievement of Ancient Man in America, the Fortress of Sacsahuaman, Peru. Vol. XXIX, supplement, May, 1916.

High Lights in the Peruvian and Bolivian Andes. 18 ills. in color from autochromes by W. Robert Moore. Vol. LI, pp. 218-235, Feb., 1927.

Honors to Amundsen and Peary (Banquet). Vol. XXIV, pp. 113-130, 5 ills., Jan., 1913.

How Latin America Looks from the Air : U. S. Army Airplanes Hurdle the High Andes, Brave Brazil Jungles, and Follow Smoking Volcanoes to Map New Sky Paths Around South America. By Maj. Herbert A. Dargue. Vol. LII, pp. 451-502, 52 ills., 1 page map, Oct., 1927.

In the Wonderland of Peru. By Hiram Bingham. Vol. XXIV, pp. 387-574, 250 ills., 1 three-quarters-page map, 3 diagrams, Apr., 1913.

Incas : Empire Builders of the Andes. By Philip Ainsworth Means. Vol. LXXIII, pp. 225-264, 26 ills. in black and white, 10 ills. in color, Feb., 1938.

Lure of Lima, City of the Kings. By William Joseph Showalter. Vol. LVII, pp. 727-784, 41 ills., June, 1930.

Most Valuable Bird in the World (Guanay). By Robert Cushman Murphy. Vol. XLVI, pp. 279-302, 25 ills., 1 half-page map, Sept., 1924.

New Peruvian Route to the Plain of the Amazon. By Solon I. Bailey. Vol. XVII, pp. 432-448, 12 ills., Aug., 1906.

Peru—Its Resources, Development, and Future. By Alfredo Alvarez Calderon. Vol. XV, pp. 311-323, Aug., 1904.

Peru on Parade. 20 ills. in color from natural-color photographs by Henry Clay Gipson and Jack Kuhne. Vol. LXXXII, pp. 173-196, Aug., 1942.

Peru's Wealth-Producing Birds : Vast Riches in the Guano Deposits of Cormorants, Pelicans, and Petrels Which Nest on Her Barren, Rainless Coast. By R. E. Coker. Vol. XXXVII, pp. 537-566, 28 ills., June, 1920.

Pith of Peru : A Journey from Talara to Machu Picchu, with Memorable Stopovers. By Henry Albert Phillips. Vol. LXXXII, pp. 167-196, 6 ills. in black and white, 20 ills. in color, 1 page map, Aug., 1942.

Peru—*Continued*

Road to Bolivia. By William E. Curtis. Part I, Vol. XI, pp. 208-224, 7 ills., June, 1900. Part II, Vol. XI, pp. 264-280, 6 ills., July, 1900.

Ruins of an Ancient Inca Capital, Machu Picchu. Vol. XXIV, panorama, Apr., 1913.

Some Personal Experiences with Earthquakes (Arica). By Rear Adm. L. G. Billings. Vol. XXVII, pp. 57-71, 7 ills., Jan., 1915.

Some Wonderful Sights in the Andean Highlands: The Oldest City in America. Sailing on the Lake of the Clouds: The Yosemite of Peru. By Harriet Chalmers Adams. Vol. XIX, pp. 597-618, 19 ills., 1 half-page map, Sept., 1908.

Staircase Farms of the Ancients: Astounding Farming Skill of Ancient Peruvians Who Were Probably the Most Industrious and Highly Organized People in History. By O. F. Cook. Vol. XXIX, pp. 474-534, 48 ills., May, 1916.

Story of Machu Picchu: The Peruvian Expeditions of the National Geographic Society and Yale University. By Hiram Bingham. Vol. XXVII, pp. 171-217, 35 ills., Feb., 1915.

Perugia, Italy :

Inexhaustible Italy. By Arthur Stanley Riggs. Vol. XXX, pp. 273-368, 76 ills., 1 page map, Oct., 1916.

Peru's Wealth-Producing Birds: Vast Riches in the Guano Deposits of Cormorants, Pelicans, and Petrels Which Nest on Her Barren, Rainless Coast. By R. E. Coker. Vol. XXXVII, pp. 537-566, 28 ills., June, 1920.

Peshawar, India :

South of Khyber Pass. By Maynard Owen Williams. Vol. LXXXIX, pp. 471-500, 31 ills., Apr., 1946.

Through the Heart of Hindustan : A Teeming Highway Extending for Fifteen Hundred Miles, from the Khyber Pass to Calcutta. By Maynard Owen Williams. Vol. XL, pp. 433-467, 29 ills., Nov., 1921.

Pest of English Sparrows. By N. Dearborn. Vol. XXI, pp. 948-952, 4 ills., Nov., 1910.

Pests and Parasites: Why We Need a National Law to Prevent the Importation of Insect-Infested and Diseased Plants. By Charles Lester Marlatt. Vol. XXII, pp. 321-346, 29 ills., 2 three-quarters-page maps, Apr., 1911.

Peter I, The Great :

Young Russia : The Land of Unlimited Possibilities. By Gilbert H. Grosvenor. Vol. XXVI, pp. 421-520, 85 ills. in black and white, 17 ills. in color, Nov., 1914.

Peters, Harold:

"Pilgrim" Sails the Seven Seas : A Schooner Yacht Out of Boston Drops in at Desert Isles and South Sea Edens in a Leisurely Two-Year Voyage. By Harold Peters. Vol. LXXII, pp. 223-262, 36 ills., Aug., 1937.

Peters, William J.:

Mr. Ziegler and the National Geographic Society. Vol. XIV, pp. 251-254, June, 1903.

Petra, Trans-Jordan :

Arabia, the Desert of the Sea. By Archibald Forder. Vol. XX, pp. 1039-1062, 20 ills., 1 page map, Dec., 1909.

Petra, Ancient Caravan Stronghold : Mysterious Temples and Tombs, Carved in Glowing Cliffs of Eroded Sandstone, Are Remnants of a City David Longed to Storm. By John D. Whiting. Vol. LXVII, pp. 129-165, 15 ills. in black and white, 21 ills. in color, 1 half-page and 1 quarter-page maps, Feb., 1935.

Rock City of Petra. By Franklin E. Hoskins. Vol. XVIII, pp. 283-291, 5 ills., May, 1907.

Rose-Red City of Rock. 21 ills. in color from natural-color photographs by G. E. Matson. Vol. LXVII, pp. 145-160, Feb., 1935.

Petrels (Birds) :

Birds of the High Seas : Albatrosses and Petrels ; Gannets, Man-o'-war-birds, and Tropic-birds. By Robert Cushman Murphy. Paintings by Maj. Allan Brooks. Vol. LXXIV, pp. 226-251, 7 ills. in black and white, 36 portraits in color, Aug., 1938.

Leach's Petrel : His Nursery on Little Duck Island. By Arnold Wood. Vol. XX, pp. 360-365, 7 ills., Apr., 1909.

Peru's Wealth-Producing Birds : Vast Riches in the Guano Deposits of Cormorants, Pelicans, and Petrels Which Nest on Her Barren, Rainless Coast. By R. E. Coker. Vol. XXXVII, pp. 537-566, 28 ills., June, 1920.

Wings Over the Bounding Main. 36 portraits in color from paintings by Maj. Allan Brooks. Vol. LXXIV, pp. 237-251, Aug., 1938.

Petrie, W. M. Flinders:

Excavations at Abydos. By W. M. Flinders Petrie. Vol. XIV, pp. 358-359, Sept., 1903.

Petrograd. *See* Leningrad.

Petroleum:

Bahrein : Port of Pearls and Petroleum. By Maynard Owen Williams. Vol. LXXXIX, pp. 195-210, 6 ills. in black and white, 11 ills. in color, 1 half-page map, Feb., 1946.

Billions of Barrels of Oil Locked up in Rocks. By Guy Elliott Mitchell. Vol. XXXIII, pp. 195-205, 10 ills., Feb., 1918.

Bombs over Bible Lands. By Frederick Simpich and W. Robert Moore. Vol. LXXX, pp. 141-180, 34 ills., 1 two-page map, Aug., 1941.

Curaçao and Aruba, Oil Isles of the Caribbean. 10 ills. in color from natural-color photographs by Philip Hanson Hiss and Robert Yarnall Richie. Vol. LXXXIII, pp. 175-182, Feb., 1943.

Curaçao and Aruba on Guard. By W. Robert Moore. Vol. LXXXIII, pp. 169-192, 12 ills. in black and white, 10 ills. in color, 4 maps, Feb., 1943.

Guest in Saudi Arabia. By Maynard Owen Williams. Vol. LXXXVIII, pp. 463-487, 24 ills., 1 two-thirds-page map, Oct., 1945.

Petroleum—*Continued*

Nation's Undeveloped Resources. By Franklin K. Lane. Vol. XXV, pp. 183-225, 32 ills., Feb., 1914.

Natural-Gas, Oil and Coal Supply of the United States. Vol. XV, p. 186, Apr., 1904.

Oil Fields of Texas and California. Vol. XII, pp. 276-278, July, 1901.

Oil for Victory Piped under the Sea. 9 ills. from photographs. Vol. LXXXVIII, pp. 721-726, Dec., 1945.

Oil Treasure of Mexico. By Russell Hastings Millward. Vol. XIX, pp. 803-805, 1 ill., Nov., 1908.

Petroleum Serves—From Lamps to Wheels. 21 ills. in color from natural-color photographs; 20 ills. by B. Anthony Stewart. Vol. LXXIX, pp. 707-738, June, 1941.

So Oklahoma Grew Up. By Frederick Simpich. Vol. LXXIX, pp. 269-314, 30 ills. in black and white, 19 ills. in color, 1 page map, Mar., 1941.

Today's World Turns on Oil. By Frederick Simpich. Vol. LXXIX, pp. 703-748, 22 ills. in black and white, 2 drawings, 21 ills. in color, June, 1941.

Where the World Gets Its Oil: But Where Will Our Children Get It When American Wells Cease to Flow? By George Otis Smith. Vol. XXXVII, pp. 181-202, 21 ills., 1 page and 2 half-page maps, Feb., 1920.

Pfingstl, W.:

Behind the Scenes in the Home of the Passion Play (Oberammergau, Germany). 11 ills. in color from natural-color photographs; 4 ills. by W. Pfingstl. Vol. LXVIII, pp. 753-760, Dec., 1935.

Philadelphia (Ancient City):

Buried Cities of Asia Minor. By Ernest L. Harris. Vol. XX, pp. 1-18, 10 ills., Jan., 1909.

Philadelphia, Pennsylvania:

Colorful Corners of the City of Homes. 13 ills. in color from natural-color photographs by Clifton Adams and Edwin L. Wisherd. Vol. LXII, pp. 674-683, Dec., 1932.

Historic City of Brotherly Love: Philadelphia, Born of Penn and Strengthened by Franklin, a Metropolis of Industries, Homes and Parks. By John Oliver La Gorce. Vol. LXII, pp. 643-697, 49 ills. in black and white, 13 ills. in color, Dec., 1932.

Philae (Island), Egypt:

Resurrection of Ancient Egypt. By James Baikie. Vol. XXIV, pp. 957-1020, 46 ills., 1 page map, Sept., 1913.

Philip Nolan and the *Levant*. By Edward E. Hale. Vol. XVI, pp. 114-116, Mar., 1905.

Philippine Clipper (Seaplane):

Flying the Pacific. By William Burke Miller. Vol. LXX, pp. 665-707, 39 ills., Dec., 1936.

Philippine Islands (Republic of the Philippines):

American Development of the Philippines. Vol. XIV, pp. 197-203, 4 ills., May, 1903.

Area of the Philippines. Vol. X, pp. 182-183, May, 1899.

"As the Tuan Had Said." By George M. Hanson. Vol. LXIV, pp. 631-644, 19 ills., Nov., 1933.

Benguet—The Garden of the Philippines. Vol. XIV, pp. 203-210, 6 ills., May, 1903.

Camera Cruising in the Philippines. 12 ills. in color from natural-color photographs by J. Baylor Roberts, Fenno Jacobs, and others. Vol. LXXXVI, pp. 545-552, Nov., 1944.

Conquest of Bubonic Plague in the Philippines. Vol. XIV, pp. 185-195, 7 ills., May, 1903.

Diseases of the Philippines. Vol. XI, pp. 123-124, Mar., 1900.

Economic Condition of the Philippines. By Max L. Tornow. Vol. X, pp. 33-64, 10 ills., Feb., 1899.

Educating the Filipinos. Vol. XVI, pp. 46-49, Jan., 1905.

Facts about the Philippines. By Frederick Simpich. Vol. LXXXI, pp. 185-202, 17 ills., 1 page map, Feb., 1942.

Field Sports Among the Wild Men of Northern Luzon. By Dean C. Worcester. Vol. XXII, pp. 215-267, 17 ills., 1 half-page map, Mar., 1911.

Geographic Facts from Report of the Taft Philippine Commission. Vol. XII, pp. 114-119, Mar., 1901.

Gold in the Philippines. By F. F. Hilder. Vol. XI, pp. 465-470, Dec., 1900.

Governing the Philippine Islands. By Col. Clarence R. Edwards. Vol. XV, pp. 273-284, 5 ills., July, 1904.

Head-Hunters of Northern Luzon. By Dean C. Worcester. Vol. XXIII, pp. 833-930, 102 ills., 1 page map, Sept., 1912.

Helping the Filipino Fisheries. Vol. XVIII, pp. 795-796, Dec., 1907.

Meteorology in the Philippines. Vol. X, pp. 271-272, July, 1899.

Mindanao, on the Road to Tokyo. By Frederick Simpich. Vol. LXXXVI, pp. 539-574, 26 ills. in black and white, 12 ills. in color, 1 two-page map, Nov., 1944.

Mining Bureau of the Philippine Islands. By Charles H. Burritt. Vol. XIV, pp. 418-419, Nov., 1903.

Non-Christian Peoples of the Philippine Islands. By Dean C. Worcester. Vol. XXIV, pp. 1157-1256, 41 ills. in black and white, 48 ills. in color, Nov., 1913.

Our Own Possessions and the Interest They Are Exciting. By O. P. Austin. Vol. XI, pp. 32-33, Jan., 1900.

Philippine Exhibit at Pan American Exposition. By D. O. Noble Hoffmann. Vol. XII, pp. 119-122, Mar., 1901.

Philippine Islands and Their Environment. By John Barrett. Vol. XI, pp. 1-14, special map supplement, 1 two-page map, Jan., 1900.

Philippine Islands (Republic of the Philippines)
—*Continued*

Philippine Islands and Their People. By Henry Gannett. Vol. XV, pp. 91-112, 13 ills., Mar., 1904.

Philippine Weather Service. Vol. XV, pp. 77-78, Feb., 1904.

Philippines. By William Howard Taft. Vol. XVI, pp. 361-375, 3 ills., special map supplement, Aug., 1905.

Progress in the Philippines. Vol. XVI, pp. 116-118, Mar., 1905.

Progress in the Philippines. Vol. XVI, pp. 513-514, 2 ills., Nov., 1905.

Return to Manila. By Frederick Simpich. Vol. LXXVIII, pp. 409-451, 21 ills. in black and white, 21 ills. in color, 1 half-page map, Oct., 1940.

Revelation of the Filipinos. Vol. XVI, pp. 139-192, 130 ills., Apr., 1905.

Smiling, Happy Philippines. 21 ills. in color from natural-color photographs; 19 ills. by J. Baylor Roberts. Vol. LXXVIII, pp. 425-448, Oct., 1940.

Some Impressions of 150,000 Miles of Travel. By William Howard Taft. Vol. LVII, pp. 523-598, 80 ills., May, 1930.

Some Recent Instances of National Altruism. By William Howard Taft. Vol. XVIII, pp. 429-438, July, 1907.

Surveying the Philippine Islands. By George H. Putnam. Vol. XIV, pp. 437-441, 4 ills., Dec., 1903.

Taal Volcano and Its Recent Destructive Eruption. By Dean C. Worcester. Vol. XXIII, pp. 313-368, 40 ills., 4 half-page maps, 1 diagram, Apr., 1912.

Ten Years in the Philippines. By William Howard Taft. Vol. XIX, pp. 141-148, Feb., 1908.

Unexplored Philippines from the Air: Map-Making Over Jungle Lands Never Before Seen by White Men. By Lieut. George W. Goddard. Vol. LVIII, pp. 311-343, 38 ills., 1 quarter-page map, Sept., 1930.

What Luzon Means to Uncle Sam. By Frederick Simpich. Vol. LXXXVII, pp. 305-332, 25 ills., special map supplement, Mar., 1945.

Work of the Bureau of Insular Affairs. By Col. Clarence R. Edwards. Vol. XV, pp. 239-255, 8 ills., June, 1904.

See also Manila.

Phillips, C. W.:

Ancestor of the British Navy: England's Oldest Known War Vessel Is Unearthed, Laden with Remarkable Treasures of an Anglo-Saxon Ruler. By C. W. Phillips. Vol. LXXIX, pp. 247-268, 22 ills. in black and white, 4 drawings, Feb., 1941.

Phillips, Henry Albert:

Air Cruising Through New Brazil: A National Geographic Reporter Spots Vast Resources Which the Republic's War Declaration Adds to Strength of United Nations. By Henry Albert Phillips. Vol. LXXXII, pp. 503-536, 32 ills., Oct., 1942.

Phillips, Henry Albert—*Continued*

Bolivia—Tin Roof of the Andes. By Henry Albert Phillips. Vol. LXXXIII, pp. 309-332, 5 ills. in black and white, 20 ills. in color, Mar., 1943.

Pith of Peru: A Journey from Talara to Machu Picchu, with Memorable Stopovers. By Henry Albert Phillips. Vol. LXXXII, pp. 167-196, 6 ills. in black and white, 20 ills. in color, 1 page map, Aug., 1942.

Phoenix Islands, Pacific Ocean.

American Pathfinders in the Pacific. By William H. Nicholas. Vol. LXXXIX, pp. 617-640, 17 ills., 1 two-page map, May, 1946.

See also Canton Island.

Phosphates:

Nauru: Richest Island in the South Seas. By Rosamond Dodson Rhone. Vol. XL, pp. 559-589, 24 ills., Dec., 1921.

Our Greatest Plant Food. By Guy Elliott Mitchell. Vol. XXI, pp. 783-791, 7 ills., 1 diagram, Sept., 1910.

Photoflashing Western Owls. By Lewis W. Walker. Vol. LXXXVII, pp. 475-486, 6 ills. in black and white, 7 ills. in color, Apr., 1945.

Photographing the Eclipse of 1932 from the Air: From Five Miles Above the Earth's Surface, the National Geographic Society-Army Air Corps Survey Obtains Successful Photographs of the Moon's Shadow. By Capt. Albert W. Stevens. Vol. LXII, pp. 581-596, 18 ills., Nov., 1932.

Photographing the Marvels of the West in Colors. By Fred Payne Clatworthy. Vol. LIII, pp. 694-719, 30 ills. in color, June, 1928.

Photographing the Nest Life of the Osprey. By Capt. C. W. R. Knight. Vol. LXII, pp. 247-260, 25 ills., Aug., 1932.

Photographing Wild Game with Flashlight and Camera. By George Shiras, 3d. Vol. XVII, pp. 366-423, 70 ills., July, 1906.

Photography:

Adventures with Birds of Prey. By Frank and John Craighead. Vol. LXXII, pp. 109-134, 25 ills., July, 1937.

American Scene. 29 ills. from winning photographs in the Sixth Annual Newspaper National Snapshot Awards, with explanatory note. Vol. LXXIX, pp. 220-246, Feb., 1941.

Americana. 11 ills. from winning photographs in the Seventh Annual Newspaper National Snapshot Awards. Vol. LXXXI, pp. 657-666, May, 1942.

First natural-color photograph of an eclipse ever reproduced. 1 ill. in color by Irvine C. Gardner. Vol. LXXI, p. 178, Feb., 1937.

How Warwick (Castle) Was Photographed in Color. By Maynard Owen Williams. Vol. LXX, pp. 83-93, 13 ills. in color, July, 1936.

Photography—*Continued*

How We Fight with Photographs. By F. Barrows Colton. Vol. LXXXVI, pp. 257-280, 22 ills., Sept., 1944.

In Quest of the Golden Eagle: Over Lonely Mountain and Prairie Soars This Rare and Lordly Bird, But Three Youths from the East Catch Up With Him at Last. By John and Frank Craighead. Vol. LXXVII, pp. 693-710, 17 ills., May, 1940.

Lords of the Rockies: Photographing Big Game Animals in Their Primeval Surroundings, from Arizona to Canada, Brings Adventure to Two Wilderness Wanderers. By Wendell and Lucie Chapman. Vol. LXXVI, pp. 87-128, 14 ills. in black and white, 28 ills. in color, July, 1939.

Mystery Mammals of the Twilight (Bats). By Donald R. Griffin. Vol. XC, pp. 117-134, 19 ills., July, 1946.

Contains photographs taken by the high-speed camera developed by Prof. Harold E. Edgerton.

Nation's Capital by Night. By Volkmar Wentzel. With 16 illustrations in duotone from photographs by the author. Vol. LXXVII, pp. 514-530, Apr., 1940.

Natural-color photograph of the 1937 eclipse. 1 ill. in color by Irvine C. Gardner. Vol. LXXIII, p. 756, June, 1938.

Nature's Most Dramatic Spectacle (Eclipse). By S. A. Mitchell. Vol. LXXII, pp. 361-376, 16 ills., 1 half-page map, Sept., 1937.

Net Results from Oceania: Collecting Aquarium Specimens in Tropical Pacific Waters. By Walter H. Chute. Vol. LXXIX, pp. 347-372, 8 ills. in black and white, 24 ills. in color, Mar., 1941.

Observing an Eclipse in Asiatic Russia. By Irvine C. Gardner. Vol. LXXI, pp. 179-197, 19 ills. in black and white, 1 ill. in color, Feb., 1937.

On the Bottom of a South Sea Pearl Lagoon. By Roy Waldo Miner. Vol. LXXIV, pp. 365-390, 17 ills. in black and white, 8 ills. in color, Sept., 1938.

Photographing the Marvels of the West in Colors. By Fred Payne Clatworthy. Vol. LIII, pp. 694-719, 30 ills. in color, June, 1928.

Photography in Glacial Alaska. By O. D. von Engeln. Vol. XXI, pp. 54-62, 4 ills., Jan., 1910.

Polar Photography. By Anthony Fiala. Vol. XVIII, pp. 140-142, Feb., 1907.

Stalking Birds With a Color Camera: An Expert in Avian Habits Persuades His Subjects to Sit Where He Wants Them, Even in His Hat. By Arthur A. Allen. Vol. LXXV, pp. 777-789, 3 ills. in black and white, 14 ills. in color, June, 1939.

Photography, Aerial:

Aerial Color Photography Becomes a War Weapon. By H. H. Arnold. Vol. LXXVII, pp. 757-766, 8 ills. in color, June, 1940.

Photography, Aerial—*Continued*

Aërial Conquest of Everest: Flying Over the World's Highest Mountain Realizes the Objective of Many Heroic Explorers. By Lieut. Col. L. V. S. Blacker. Vol. LXIV, pp. 127-162, 35 ills., 1 page map, Aug., 1933.

Air Adventures in Peru: Cruising Among Andean Peaks, Pilots and Cameramen Discover Wondrous Works of an Ancient People. By Robert Shippee. Vol. LXIII, pp. 81-120, 40 ills., 1 three-quarters-page map, Jan., 1933.

America from the Air: No Such Series of Airplane Views Has Ever Before Been Printed. 8 ills. from photographs by Capt. Albert W. Stevens. Vol. XLVI, pp. 85-92, July, 1924.

By Seaplane to Six Continents: Cruising 60,000 Miles, Italian Argonauts of the Air See World Geography Unroll, and Break New Sky Trails Over Vast Brazilian Jungles. By Comdr. Francesco de Pinedo. Vol. LIV, pp. 247-301, 60 ills., 1 two-page map, Sept., 1928.

Canada from the Air: Flights Aggregating 10,000 Miles Reveal the Marvelous Scenic Beauties and Amazing Natural Resources of the Dominion. By J. A. Wilson. Vol. L, pp. 389-466, 76 ills., 1 page map, Oct., 1926.

Color Camera's First Aërial Success. By Melville Bell Grosvenor. Vol. LVIII, pp. 344-353, 9 ills. in color, Sept., 1930.

Conquest of Antarctica by Air. By Rear Adm. Richard Evelyn Byrd. Vol. LVIII, pp. 127-227, 71 ills. in black and white, 16 ills. in gravure, 1 page map, Aug., 1930.

Curvature of the Earth: Photograph Showing the Division Between the Troposphere and Stratosphere and also the Actual Curvature of the Earth. Special supplement from aërial photograph by Capt. Albert W. Stevens. Vol. LXIX, supplement, May, 1936.

Exploring the Stratosphere. By Capt. Albert W. Stevens. Vol. LXVI, pp. 397-434, 43 ills., 1 two-thirds-page chart, Oct., 1934.

Exploring the Valley of the Amazon in a Hydroplane: Twelve Thousand Miles of Flying Over the World's Greatest River and Greatest Forest to Chart the Unknown Parima River from the Sky. By Capt. Albert W. Stevens. Vol. XLIX, pp. 353-420, 86 ills., 1 page map, Apr., 1926.

First Airship Flight Around the World: Dr. Hugo Eckener Tells of an Epochal Geographic Achievement upon the Occasion of the Bestowal of the National Geographic Society's Special Gold Medal. Vol. LVII, pp. 653-688, 37 ills., June, 1930.

First Alaskan Air Expedition. By Capt. St. Clair Streett. Vol. XLI, pp. 499-552, 37 ills., 1 page map, May, 1922.

First natural-color photograph taken in the stratosphere. 1 ill. in color by Maj. Albert W. Stevens. Vol. LXXI, p. 340, Mar., 1937.

Photography, Aerial—*Continued*

Flying Around the North Atlantic. By Anne Morrow Lindbergh. Foreword by Charles A. Lindbergh. Vol. LXVI, pp. 259-337, 82 ills., 1 two-page and 1 two-thirds-page maps, Sept., 1934.

Flying Over Egypt, Sinai, and Palestine—Looking Down Upon the Holy Land During an Air Journey of Two and a Half Hours from Cairo to Jerusalem. By Brig. Gen. P. R. C. Groves and Maj. J. R. McCrindle. Vol. L, pp. 313-355, 26 ills., 1 half-page map, Sept., 1926.

Flying the "Hump" of the Andes. By Capt. Albert W. Stevens. Vol. LIX, pp. 595-636, 36 ills., 1 third-page map, May, 1931.

Flying the World's Longest Air-Mail Route: From Montevideo, Uruguay, Over the Andes, Up the Pacific Coast, Across Central America and the Caribbean to Miami, Florida, in 67 Thrilling Flying Hours. By Junius B. Wood. Vol. LVII, pp. 261-325, 65 ills., 1 half-page map, Mar., 1930.

From London to Australia by Aëroplane: A Personal Narrative of the First Aërial Voyage Half Around the World. By Sir Ross Smith. Vol. XXXIX, pp. 229-339, 76 ills. in black and white, 8 ills. in color, 1 page map, Mar., 1921.

Greater New York . . . Metropolis of Mankind. Special supplement from aërial photograph by Capt. Albert W. Stevens. Vol. LXIV, supplement, Nov., 1933.

How Latin America Looks from the Air: U. S. Army Airplanes Hurdle the High Andes, Brave Brazil Jungles, and Follow Smoking Volcanoes to Map New Sky Paths Around South America. By Maj. Herbert A. Dargue. Vol. LII, pp. 451-502, 52 ills., 1 page map, Oct., 1927.

Looking Down on Europe: The Thrills and Advantages of Sight-Seeing by Airplane, as Demonstrated on a 6,500-Mile Tour Over Commercial Aviation Routes. By Lieut. J. Parker Van Zandt. Vol. XLVII, pp. 261-326, 67 ills., 1 half-page map, Mar., 1925.

Mapping the Antarctic from the Air: The Aërial Camera Earns Its Place as the Eyes and Memory of the Explorer. By Capt. Ashley C. McKinley. Vol. LXII, pp. 471-485, 13 ills., special map supplement in colors, Oct., 1932.

Non-Stop Flight Across America. By Lieut. John A. Macready. Photographs by Lieut. Albert W. Stevens. Vol. XLVI, pp. 1-83, 68 ills., 1 page and 1 half-page maps, July, 1924.

On the Trail of the Air Mail: A Narrative of the Experiences of the Flying Couriers Who Relay the Mail Across America at a Speed of More Than 2,000 Miles a Day. By Lieut. J. Parker Van Zandt. Vol. XLIX, pp. 1-61, 67 ills., 1 two-thirds-page map, Jan., 1926.

Over the Roof of Our Continent (Mount McKinley). By Bradford Washburn. Vol. LXXIV, pp. 78-98, 17 ills. in duotone, 1 half-page map, July, 1938.

Photography, Aerial—*Continued*

Photographing the Eclipse of 1932 from the Air: From Five Miles Above the Earth's Surface, the National Geographic Society–Army Air Corps Survey Obtains Successful Photographs of the Moon's Shadow. By Capt. Albert W. Stevens. Vol. LXII, pp. 581-596, 18 ills., Nov., 1932.

Seeing America from the *Shenandoah*: An Account of the Record-Making 9,000-Mile Flight from the Atlantic to the Pacific Coast and Return in the Navy's American-built, American-manned Airship. By Junius B. Wood. Vol. XLVII, pp. 1-47, 39 ills., 1 page map, 1 diagram, Jan., 1925.

Seeing America with Lindbergh: The Record of a Tour of More than 20,000 Miles by Airplane Through Forty-eight States on Schedule Time. By Lieut. Donald E. Keyhoe. Vol. LIII, pp. 1-46, 46 ills., 1 page map, Jan., 1928.

Seeing the World from the Air. By Sir Alan J. Cobham. Vol. LIII, pp. 349-384, 37 ills., 1 three-quarters-page map, Mar., 1928.

Seeing 3,000 Years of History in Four Hours: A Panorama of Ancient, Medieval, and Modern Events Against a Background of Mythology Unfolds During an Airplane Journey from Constantinople to Athens. By Maynard Owen Williams. Vol. LIV, pp. 719-739, 24 ills., 1 two-thirds-page map, Dec., 1928.

Skypaths Through Latin America: Flying From Our Nation's Capital Southward Over Jungles, Remote Islands, and Great Cities on an Aërial Survey of the East Coast of South America. By Frederick Simpich. Vol. LIX, pp. 1-79, 77 ills., 1 page map, Jan., 1931.

To Bogotá and Back by Air: The Narrative of a 9,500-Mile Flight from Washington, Over Thirteen Latin-American Countries and Return, in the Single-Seater Airplane *Spirit of St. Louis*. By Col. Charles A. Lindbergh. Vol. LIII, pp. 529-601, 98 ills., 1 two-thirds-page map, May, 1928.

Unexplored Philippines from the Air: Map-Making over Jungle Lands Never Before Seen by White Men. By Lieut. George W. Goddard. Vol. LVIII, pp. 311-343, 38 ills., 1 quarter-page map, Sept., 1930.

Wings Over Nature's Zoo in Africa. 20 ills. in duotone from photographs by Reginald A. Bourlay. Vol. LXXVI, pp. 527-542, Oct., 1939.

Photography, Flashlight:

Doe and Twin Fawns. Flashlight photograph by George Shiras, 3d. Vol. XXIV, supplement, July, 1913. Vol. LXXVI, ill. 475, Oct., 1939.

Flashlight Story of an Albino Porcupine and of a Cunning but Unfortunate Coon. By George Shiras, 3d. Vol. XXII, pp. 572-596, 26 ills., June, 1911.

Flashlights from the Jungle. Vol. XVIII, pp. 534-548, 11 ills., Aug., 1907.

Hark! (Deer). Vol. XL, supplement, Aug., 1921.

Photographing Wild Game with Flashlight and Camera. By George Shiras, 3d. Vol. XVII, pp. 366-423, 70 ills., July, 1906.

Photography, Flashlight—*Continued*

Wild Animals That Took Their Own Pictures by Day and by Night. By George Shiras, 3d. Vol. XXIV, pp. 763-834, 68 ills., 1 page map, July, 1913.

Wild Life of Lake Superior, Past and Present: The Habits of Deer, Moose, Wolves, Beavers, Muskrats, Trout, and Feathered Wood-Folk Studied with Camera and Flashlight. By George Shiras, 3d. Vol. XL, pp. 113-204, 77 ills., 1 half-page map, supplement, Aug., 1921.

Photography, High-speed Flash:

Mystery Mammals of the Twilight (Bats). By Donald R. Griffin. Vol. XC, pp. 117-134, 19 ills., July, 1946.
  Contents: Photographs taken by the high-speed camera developed by Prof. Harold E. Edgerton.

Phrygia (Ancient Region):

Lost Wealth of the Kings of Midas. By Ellsworth Huntington. Vol. XXI, pp. 831-846, 15 ills., Oct., 1910.

Phyle (Fortress), Greece:

"Glory That Was Greece." By Alexander Wilbourne Weddell. Vol. XLII, pp. 571-603, 51 ills., 1 three-quarters-page map, Dec., 1922.

Physalia (Yacht):

Our Neglected Southern Coast. By Alfred Goldsborough Mayer. Vol. XIX, pp. 859-871, 10 ills., Dec., 1908.

Physiography of the Nicaragua Canal Route. By C. Willard Hayes. Vol. X, pp. 233-246, special map supplement, 2 page and 1 half-page maps, July, 1899.

Piccard, Auguste:

Ballooning in the Stratosphere: Two Balloon Ascents to Ten-Mile Altitudes Presage New Mode of Aërial Travel. By Auguste Piccard. Vol. LXIII, pp. 353-384, 34 ills., Mar., 1933.

Pictorial Enlargements and Panoramas:

Alaskan Brown Bear: The Largest Carnivorous Animal Extant. Vol. XXX, colored supplement, Nov., 1916.

The Argosy of Geography (Sailing Ship). Vol. XXXIX, supplement, Jan., 1921.

Awe-Inspiring Spectacle of the Valley of Ten Thousand Smokes, Discovered and Explored by National Geographic Society Expeditions. Vol. XXXIII, panorama, Feb., 1918.

"Babes in the Woods" (Bears). Vol. XXXII, supplement, Aug., 1917.

Bird's-Eye View of the Panama Canal. Vol. XXIII, colored panorama, Feb., 1912.

Boyhood of (Sir Walter) Raleigh. Reproduction in color of the painting by Sir John Millais, Tate Gallery, London. Vol. XLIX, text, p. 596; supplement, May, 1926.

Pictorial Enlargements and Panoramas—*Continued*

Caravels of Columbus. Reproduction in color of the painting by N. C. Wyeth, National Geographic Society, Washington, D. C. Vol. LIV, text, p. 55; supplement, July, 1928.

Cathedrals of England. 16 ills. in gravure from dry-point engravings by Norman Wilkinson. Vol. LXXVI, pp. 745-760; text, p. 762, Dec., 1939.

Commander Byrd at the North Pole. Reproduction in color of the painting by N. C. Wyeth, National Geographic Society, Washington, D. C. Vol. LIII, supplement, May, 1928.

Curvature of the Earth: Photograph Showing the Division Between the Troposphere and Stratosphere and also the Actual Curvature of the Earth. Special supplement from aërial photograph by Capt. Albert W. Stevens. Vol. LXIX, supplement, May, 1936.

The Discoverer. Reproduction in color of the painting by N. C. Wyeth, National Geographic Society, Washington, D. C. Vol. LIII, text, p. 347; supplement, Mar., 1928.

Doe and Twin Fawns. Flashlight photograph by George Shiras, 3d. Vol. XXIV, supplement, July, 1913. Vol. LXXVI, ill. 475, Oct., 1939.

Fate Directs the Faltering Footsteps of Columbus. Reproduction in color of the painting by Alfred Dehodencq, Paris. Vol. LIV, supplement, Sept., 1928.

Great Wall of China Near Nankow Pass. Vol. XLIII, panorama, Feb., 1923.

Greater New York . . . Metropolis of Mankind. Special supplement from aërial photograph by Capt. Albert W. Stevens. Vol. LXIV, supplement, Nov., 1933.

Greatest Achievement of Ancient Man in America, the Fortress Sacsahuaman, Peru. Vol. XXIX, panorama, May, 1916.

Hark! (Deer). Vol. XL, supplement, Aug., 1921.

Hour of Prayer: In the Sahara Desert. Vol. XXII, supplement, Apr., 1911.

Lhasa—The Mecca of the Buddhist Faith. Vol. XXIX, panorama, Mar., 1916.

Lure of the Frozen Desert (Polar Regions). Vol. XXII, panorama, Dec., 1912.

Majesty of the Matterhorn. Vol. XXIII, supplement, May, 1912.

Mall, Washington, D. C. Vol. XXVII, colored panorama, Mar., 1915.

Map of Discovery (Eastern Hemisphere). Reproduction in color of the painting by N. C. Wyeth, National Geographic Society, Washington, D. C. Vol. LIV, text, p. 568; supplement, Nov., 1928.

Pictorial Enlargements and Panoramas—*Continued*

Map of Discovery (Western Hemisphere). Reproduction in color of the painting by N. C. Wyeth, National Geographic Society, Washington, D. C. Vol. LV, text, p. 93 ; supplement, Jan., 1929.

Monarch of the Canadian Rockies—Robson Peak. Vol. XXIV, panorama, May, 1913.

Oldest Living Thing ("General Sherman Tree"). Vol. XXIX, supplement, Apr., 1916.

Our Mountain Panorama (Canadian Rockies). Vol. XXII, panorama, June, 1911.

The Palms (Trees). Vol. XXII, supplement, Dec., 1911.

Peasant Home in Corsica. Vol. XLIV, supplement, Sept., 1923.

Ruins of an Ancient Inca Capital, Machu Picchu. Vol. XXIV, panorama, Apr., 1913.

Rumanian Peasant Girl. Vol. XXIV, p. 1084, Oct., 1913.

Ships of the Centuries. 16 ills. in gravure from etchings by Norman Wilkinson. Vol. LXXIII, pp. 65-80 ; text, p. 98, Jan., 1938.

Torii Gate, Japan. Vol. XXII, color plate, p. 982, Nov., 1911.

Ultimate Washington (Plan Laid Out by the Commission of 1901 for the National Capital), Vol. XXVII, colored panorama, Mar., 1915.

Vasco da Gama at the Court of the Zamorin of Calicut. Reproduction in color of the painting by José Velloso Salgado, Sociedade de Geographia de Lisboa. Vol. LII, supplement, Nov., 1927.

Wrangell Mountains (Alaska). Panorama taken by W. C. Mendenhall from the ridge east of the Dadina River. Vol. XIV, supplement, Nov., 1903.

Pictorial Jaunt Through Papua. 22 ills. from photographs by Capt. Frank Hurley. Vol. LI, pp. 109-124, Jan., 1927.

Picturesque Paramaribo. By Harriet Chalmers Adams. Vol. XVIII, pp. 365-373, 7 ills., June, 1907.

Pidgeon, (Capt.) Harry:

Around the World in the *Islander* (Ship) : A Narrative of the Adventures of a Solitary Voyager on his Four-Year Cruise in a Thirty-Four-Foot Sailing Craft. By Capt. Harry Pidgeon. Vol. LIII, pp. 141-205, 75 ills., 1 two-page map, Feb., 1928.

Pieces of Silver. By Frederick Simpich. Vol. LXIV, pp. 253-292, 49 ills., Sept., 1933.

Pigeons:

American Game Birds. By Henry Wetherbee Henshaw. Vol. XXVIII, pp. 105-158, 4 ills. in black and white, 72 ills. in color, Aug., 1915.

Chinese Pigeon Whistles. Vol. XXIV, pp. 715-716, 1 ill., June, 1913.

Game Birds of Prairie, Forest, and Tundra. By Alexander Wetmore. Vol. LXX, pp. 461-500, 5 ills. in black and white, 60 portraits in color, Oct., 1936.

Hunted Birds of Field and Wild. 60 portraits in color from paintings by Maj. Allan Brooks. Vol. LXX, pp. 469-500, Oct., 1936.

Man's Feathered Friends of Longest Standing : Peoples of Every Clime and Age Have Lavished Care and Affection Upon Lovely Pigeons. By Elisha Hanson. Vol. XLIX, pp. 63-110, 35 ills. in black and white, 12 ills. in color, Jan., 1926.

Pigeons of Resplendent Plumage. 12 ills. in color from paintings by Hashime Murayama. Vol. XLIX, pp. 65-76, Jan., 1926.

Contains descriptions and illustrations of the following species : Barb, Carneau, Carrier, Dragoon, Fantail, Helmet, Homer, Jacobin, King, Magpie, Mondaine, Nun, Oriental Frill, Park, Pouter, Swallow, Tumbler, Victoria Crowned.

Wild Life of Lake Superior, Past and Present : The Habits of Deer, Moose, Wolves, Beavers, Muskrats, Trout, and Feathered Wood-Folk Studied with Camera and Flashlight. By George Shiras, 3d. Vol. XL, pp. 113-204, 77 ills., supplement, 1 half-page map, Aug., 1921.

Pilgrim Sails the Seven Seas : A Schooner Yacht Out of Boston Drops in at Desert Isles and South Sea Edens in a Leisurely Two-Year Voyage. By Harold Peters. Vol. LXXII, pp. 223-262, 36 ills., Aug., 1937.

Pilgrimage to Amernath, Himalayan Shrine of the Hindu Faith. By Louise Ahl Jessop. Vol. XL, pp. 512-542, 29 ills., Nov., 1921.

Pilgrims and Pilgrimages:

Pilgrimage to Amernath, Himalayan Shrine of the Hindu Faith. By Louise Ahl Jessop. Vol. XL, pp. 512-542, 29 ills., Nov., 1921.

Pilgrims' Progress to Mecca. 22 ills. in duotone ; 18 ills. by Oscar Marcus. Vol. LXXII, pp. 627-642, Nov., 1937.

Puto, the Enchanted Island. By Robert F. Fitch. Vol. LXXXIX, pp. 373-384, 11 ills., 1 third-page map, Mar., 1946.

Tai Shan, Sacred Mountain of the East. By Mary Augusta Mullikin. Vol. LXXXVII, pp. 699-719, 18 ills., 1 page map, June, 1945.

Unbeliever Joins the Hadj : On the Age-Old Pilgrimage to Mecca, Babies Are Born, Elders Die, and Families May Halt a Year to Earn Funds in Distant Lands. By Owen Tweedy. Vol. LXV, pp. 761-789, 30 ills., 1 page map, June, 1934.

Pilgrims Still Stop at Plymouth (England). By Maynard Owen Williams. Vol. LXXIV, pp. 59-77, 19 ills., July, 1938.

Pillsbury, (Rear Adm.) John Elliott:

Election of Adm. Pillsbury as Vice-President of The Society. Vol. XVII, p. 218, Feb., 1915.

Grandest and Most Mighty Terrestrial Phenomenon : The Gulf Stream. By Rear Adm. John Elliott Pillsbury. Vol. XXIII, pp. 767-778, 1 ill., 2 diagrams, 2 page and 1 half-page maps, Aug., 1912.

National Geographic Society's Notable Year (Announcement of Admiral Pillsbury's Death). Vol. XXXVII, pp. 338-345, 2 ills., Apr., 1920.

Wilkes' and D'Urville's Discoveries in Wilkes Land. By Rear Adm. John Elliott Pillsbury. Vol. XXI, pp. 171-173, Feb., 1910.

Pinchot, Gifford:

American Fable (Conservation of Resources). By Gifford Pinchot. Vol. XIX, pp. 345-350, May, 1908.

Forest Reserves of the United States. By Gifford Pinchot. Vol. XI, pp. 369-372, 1 three-quarters-page map, Sept., 1900.

Forestry at Home and Abroad. By Gifford Pinchot. Vol. XVI, pp. 375-388, 8 ills., Aug., 1905.

Relation of Forests and Forest Fires. By Gifford Pinchot. Vol. X, pp. 393-403, 7 ills., Oct., 1899.

Pine-Scented, Harbor-Dented Maine. 39 ills. in color from natural-color photographs by B. Anthony Stewart and Robert F. Maxcy. Vol. LXVII, pp. 549-588, May, 1935.

Pinedo, (Comdr.) Francesco de:

By Seaplane to Six Continents : Cruising 60,000 Miles, Italian Argonauts of the Air See World Geography Unroll and Break New Sky Trails Over Vast Brazilian Jungles. By Comdr. Francesco de Pinedo. Vol. LIV, pp. 247-301, 60 ills., 1 two-page map, Sept., 1928.

Pineo, Charles S.:

To Market in Guatemala. 19 ills. in color from natural-color photographs by Giles Greville Healey and Charles S. Pineo. Vol. LXXXVIII, pp. 89-104, July, 1945.

Pines, Isle of, Cuba :

Isle of Pines. Vol. XVII, pp. 105-108, 2 ills., Feb., 1906.

Pioneer Gaucho Days. 8 ills. in color from paintings by Cesáreo Bernaldo de Quirós. Vol. LXIV, pp. 453-460, Oct., 1933.

Pipelines:

Oil for Victory Piped under the Sea. 9 ills. from photographs. Vol. LXXXVIII, pp. 721-726, Dec., 1945.

Pirate-Fighters of the South China Sea. By Robert Cardwell. Vol. LXXXIX, pp. 787-796, 11 ills., June, 1946.

Pirate Rivers and Their Prizes : The Warfare of Waterways Has Sometimes Changed the Geography of Our Continents. By John Oliver La Gorce. Vol. L, pp. 87-132, 48 ills., 1 half-page map, July, 1926.

Pirates:

Haunts of the Caribbean Corsairs : The West Indies a Geographic Background for the Most Adventurous Episodes in the History of the Western Hemisphere. By Nell Ray Clarke. Vol. XLI, pp. 147-187, 27 ills., Feb., 1922.

Pirate-Fighters of the South China Sea. By Robert Cardwell. Vol. LXXXIX, pp. 787-796, 11 ills., June, 1946.

Pisa, Italy :

From London to Australia by Aëroplane : A Personal Narrative of the First Aërial Voyage Half Around the World. By Sir Ross Smith. Vol. XXXIX, pp. 229-339, 76 ills. in black and white, 8 ills. in color, 1 page map., Mar., 1921.

Inexhaustible Italy. By Arthur Stanley Riggs. Vol. XXX, pp. 273-368, 76 ills., 1 page map, Oct., 1916.

Pitcairn Island, Pacific Ocean :

Westward Bound in the *Yankee.* By Irving and Electa Johnson. Vol. LXXXI, pp. 1-44, 25 ills. in black and white, 20 ills. in color, 1 three-quarters-page map, Jan., 1942.

Pith of Peru : A Journey from Talara to Machu Picchu, with Memorable Stopovers. By Henry Albert Phillips. Vol. LXXXII, pp. 167-196, 6 ills. in black and white, 20 ills. in color, 1 page map, Aug., 1942.

Pittier, Henry:

Costa Rica—Vulcan's Smithy. By Henry Pittier. Vol. XXI, pp. 494-525, 30 ills., 2 half-page maps, June, 1910.

Little-Known Parts of Panama. By Henry Pittier. Vol. XXIII, pp. 627-662, 35 ills., 1 page map, July, 1912.

Place Names in Canada. Vol. X, pp. 519-520, Dec., 1899.

Place Names in Eastern Asia. Vol. XV, p. 136, Mar., 1904.

Place Names of the United States. Vol. XIII, pp. 403-405, Nov., 1902.

Plague of Mice. Vol. XX, pp. 478-485, 7 ills., May, 1909.

Plain Tales from the Trenches : As Told Over the Tea Table in Blighty—A Soldier's "Home" in Paris. By Carol Corey. Vol. XXXIII, pp. 300-312, 7 ills., Mar., 1918.

Plains Indians: United States :

Indians of Our Western Plains. By Matthew W. Stirling. Paintings by W. Langdon Kihn. Vol. LXXXVI, pp. 73-108, 14 ills. in black and white, 16 ills. in color, July, 1944.

Plan for Climbing Mount McKinley. By Alfred H. Brooks and D. L. Reaburn. Vol. XIV, pp. 30-35, 1 page map, Jan., 1903.

Plan of a Map of the World. By Albrecht Penck. Vol. XV, pp. 405-408, Oct. 1904.

Planches, Baron Mayor des:

Discovery of the North Pole (Address by Baron Mayor des Planches). Vol. XXI, pp. 63-82, Jan., 1910.

Honors to Peary (Address by Baron Mayor des Planches). Vol. XVIII, pp. 49-60, 1 ill., Jan., 1907.

Plankton:

Living Jewels of the Sea. By William Crowder. Vol. LII, pp. 290-304, 8 ills. in black and white, 8 ills. in color, Sept., 1927.

Contains descriptions and illustrations of animal and plant forms, especially species of the following: Crustaceans, Dinoflagellates, Foraminifers, Radiolarians, Diatoms.

Plans for Reaching the South Pole. By Gilbert H. Grosvenor. Vol. X, pp. 316-319, Aug., 1899.

Planting Fishes in the Ocean. By George M. Bowers. Vol. XVIII, pp. 715-723, 5 ills., Nov., 1907.

Plants:

American Deserts. Vol. XV, pp. 152-163, 7 ills., 1 half-page map, Apr., 1904.

Big Things of the West. By Charles F. Holder. Vol. XIV, pp. 279-282, 2 ills., July, 1903.

Canyons and Cacti of the American Southwest. 22 ills. in color from natural-color photographs by Edwin L. Wisherd, Jacob Gayer, and Charles Martin. Vol. XLVIII, pp. 275-290, Sept., 1925.

Common Mushrooms of the United States. By Louis C. C. Krieger. Vol. XXXVII, pp. 387-439, 37 ills. in black and white, 16 ills. in color, May, 1920.

A Community of Dwarfs. 11 ills. in color from natural-color photographs by Willard R. Culver. Vol. XC, pp. 345-352, Sept., 1946.

Contains information on the insects that live in the plant, shepherd's needles.

Discovery of Cancer in Plants. Vol. XXIV, pp. 53-70, 12 ills., Jan., 1913.

Exploring a Grass Wonderland of Wild West China. By Ray G. Johnson. Vol. LXXXV, pp. 713-742, 24 ills., 1 half-page map, June, 1944.

Exploring the Mysteries of Plant Life. By William Joseph Showalter. Vol. XLV, pp. 581-646, 41 ills. in black and white, 47 ills. in color, June, 1924.

Contains descriptions and illustrations of the following species: Alfalfa, Amsonia, Arethusa, Barberry, Bindweed, Bittersweet, Blackberry-Lily, Bladdernut, Bur-Reed, Burnet, Carrionflower, Cattail, Checkerbloom, Cobaea Pentstemon, Coneflower, Creeping Polemonium, Curly Dock, Daylily, Garlic, Goldmoss, Grays Lily, Ground-Ivy, Honeysuckle, Lizardtail, Meadow-Parsnip, Moonseed, Phlox, Pitcherplant, Poppy-Mallow, Pussy Willow, Rhododendron, Rose Pogonia, St. Johnswort, Shootingstar, Snow-on-the-Mountain, Spatterdock, Springbeauty, Sumac, Swallow-Wort, Sweetflag, Sweet Gale, Wildbergamot, Wildginger, Withe-Rod, Woodbetony, Woodsorrel, Yellow Ladyslipper.

Plants—Continued

Familiar Grasses and Their Flowers. By E. J. Geske and W. J. Showalter. Vol. XXXIX, pp. 625-636, 8 ills. in color, June, 1921.

Fantastic Plants of Our Western Deserts. 8 ills. by Frank M. Campbell. Vol. XLV, pp. 33-40, Jan., 1924.

Ferns as a Hobby. By William R. Maxon. Vol. XLVII, pp. 541-586, 29 ills. in black and white, 16 ills. in color, May, 1925.

Goldfish and Their Cultivation in America. By Hugh M. Smith. Vol. XLVI, pp. 375-400, 14 ills. in black and white, 8 ills. in color, Oct., 1924.

Contains text references and colored illustrations of the following ornamental plants grown in aquaria: Fanwort, Spatterdock, Water Seedbox, Waterweed.

Henequen—The Yucatan Fiber. By E. H. Thompson. Vol. XIV, pp. 150-158, 6 ills., Apr., 1903.

Hunter of Plants. By David Fairchild. Vol. XXXVI, pp. 57-77, 19 ills., July, 1919.

Hunting for Plants in the Canary Islands. By David Fairchild. Vol. LVII, pp. 607-652, 37 ills. in black and white, 39 ills. in color, 1 third-page map, May, 1930.

Hunting Useful Plants in the Caribbean. By David Fairchild. Vol. LXVI, pp. 705-737, 39 ills., Dec., 1934.

An Insect Community Lives in Flower Heads (Shepherd's Needles). By James G. Needham. Vol. XC, pp. 340-356, 5 ills. in black and white, 11 ills. in color, Sept., 1946.

Kingdom of Flowers: An Account of the Wealth of Trees and Shrubs of China and of What the Arnold Arboretum, with China's Help, Is Doing to Enrich America. By Ernest H. Wilson. Vol. XXII, pp. 1003-1035, 24 ills., Nov., 1911.

Mistletoe. Vol. XXI, p. 965, Nov., 1910.

New Plant Immigrants. By David Fairchild. Vol. XXII, pp. 879-907, 34 ills., Oct., 1911.

Our Plant Immigrants. By David Fairchild. Vol. XVII, pp. 179-201, 29 ills., Apr., 1906.

Peacetime Plant Hunting About Peiping. By P. H. and J. H. Dorsett. Vol. LXXII, pp. 509-534, 21 ills., 1 two-thirds-page map, Oct., 1937.

Pests and Parasites: Why We Need a National Law to Prevent the Importation of Insect-Infested and Diseased Plants. By Charles Lester Marlatt. Vol. XXII, pp. 321-346, 29 ills., 2 three-quarters-page maps, Apr., 1911.

Protecting the United States from Plant Pests. By Charles Lester Marlatt. Vol. XL, pp. 205-218, 16 ills., Aug., 1921.

Riddle of the Aleutians: A Botanist Explores the Origin of Plants on Ever-misty Islands Now Enshrouded in the Fog of War. By Isobel Wylie Hutchison. Vol. LXXXII, pp. 769-792, 24 ills., Dec., 1942.

Round About Bogotá: A Hunt for New Fruits and Plants Among the Mountain Forests of Colombia's Unique Capital. By Wilson Popenoe. Vol. XLIX, pp. 127-160, 34 ills., 1 quarter-page map, Feb., 1926.

Plants—*Continuea*

See also Agricultural and Botanical Explorers; Agriculture; Cacti; Flowers; Fruits; Gardens; Seaweeds; Shrubs; Trees.

Plastics:

Chemists Make a New World: Creating Hitherto Unknown Raw Materials, Science Now Disrupts Old Trade Routes and Revamps the World Map of Industry. By Frederick Simpich. Vol. LXXVI, pp. 601-640, 22 ills. in black and white, 26 ills. in color, Nov., 1939.

From Nature's Hidden Building Blocks. 26 ills. in color from natural-color photographs by Willard R. Culver. Vol. LXXVI, pp. 609-640, Nov., 1939.

Platinum:

Platinum in the World's Work. By Lonnelle Davison. Vol. LXXII, pp. 345-360, 17 ills., Sept., 1937.

Platypus:

Australia's Patchwork Creature, the Platypus: Man Succeeds in Making Friends with This Duck-billed, Fur-coated Paradox which Lays Eggs and Suckles Its Young. By Charles H. Holmes. Vol. LXXVI, pp. 273-282, 13 ills., Aug., 1939.

Plovers (Birds):

Birds of Timberline and Tundra. By Arthur A. Allen. With 24 ills. in color from natural-color photographs by the author. Vol. XC, pp. 313-339, 8 ills. in black and white, Sept., 1946.

Feathered Foragers of Swamp and Shore. 101 portraits in color from paintings by Maj. Allan Brooks. Vol. LXXII, pp. 191-222, Aug., 1937.

Our Greatest Travelers: Birds That Fly from Pole to Pole and Shun the Darkness: Birds That Make 2,500 Miles in a Single Flight. By Wells W. Cooke. Vol. XXII, pp. 346-366, 1 ill., 12 page and half-page maps, Apr., 1911.

Shore Birds, Cranes, and Rails: Willets, Plovers, Stilts, Phalaropes, Sandpipers, and Their Relatives Deserve Protection. By Arthur A. Allen. Paintings by Maj. Allan Brooks. Vol. LXXII, pp. 183-222, 4 ills. in black and white, 101 portraits in color, Aug., 1937.

Pluto, Operation, World War II. *See* Operation Pluto.

Plymouth, England:

Channel Ports—And Some Others. By Florence Craig Albrecht. Vol. XXVIII, pp. 1-55, 45 ills., July, 1915.

A City That Refused to Die. By Harvey Klemmer. Vol. LXXXIX, pp. 211-236, 13 ills. in black and white, 9 ills. in color, 1 half-page map, Feb., 1946.

Pilgrims Still Stop at Plymouth. By Maynard Owen Williams. Vol. LXXIV, pp. 59-77, 19 ills., July, 1938.

Poás (Mountain), Costa Rica:

Costa Rica—Vulcan's Smithy. By Henry Pittier. Vol. XXI, pp. 494-525, 30 ills., 2 half-page maps, June, 1910.

Pocket Carriers Fight the Submarines. 20 ills. in color from U. S. Navy official photographs. Vol. LXXXIV, pp. 521-544, Nov., 1943.

Pogue, Joseph E.:

Great Rainbow Natural Bridge of Southern Utah. By Joseph E. Pogue. Vol. XXII, pp. 1048-1056, 6 ills., Nov. 1911.

Poisoned World. By William Howard Taft. Vol. XXXI, pp. 459-467, 7 ills., May, 1917.

Poitou (French Province):

Beauties of France. By Arthur Stanley Riggs. Vol. XXVIII, pp. 391-491, 73 ills. in black and white, 16 ills. in color, 1 half-page map, Nov., 1915.

Poland:

Bright Bits in Poland's Mountainous South. 16 ills. in color from natural-color photographs by Hans Hildenbrand. Vol. LXVII, pp. 353-360, Mar., 1935.

Devastated Poland. By Frederic C. Walcott. Vol. XXXI, pp. 445-452, 7 ills., May, 1917.

New Map of Europe: Showing the Boundaries Established by the Peace Conference at Paris and by Subsequent Decisions of the Supreme Council of the Allied and Associated Powers. By Ralph A. Graves. Text accompanying special map supplement in colors. Vol. XXXIX, pp. 157-177, 18 ills., Feb., 1921.

Partitioned Poland. By William Joseph Showalter. Vol. XXVII, pp. 88-106, 12 ills., Jan., 1915.

Pedaling Through Poland: An American Girl Free-wheels Alone from Kraków, and Its Medieval Byways, Toward Ukraine's Restive Borderland. By Dorothy Hosmer. Vol. LXXV, pp. 739-775, 38 ills., 2 maps, June, 1939.

Poland, Land of the White Eagle. By Melville Bell Grosvenor. With 12 ills. in color from natural-color photographs by Hans Hildenbrand. Vol. LXI, pp. 435-445, 12 ills. in color, Apr., 1932.

Poland of the Present. By Maynard Owen Williams. Vol. LXIII, pp. 319-344, 19 ills. in black and white, 11 ills. in color, Mar., 1933.

Races of Europe. By Edwin A. Grosvenor. Vol. XXXIV, pp. 441-534, 62 ills., 2 page maps, special map supplement, Dec., 1918.

Rainbow Costumes of Poland's Peasants. 11 ills. in color from natural-color photographs by Hans Hildenbrand and Maynard Owen Williams. Vol. LXIII, pp. 328-337, Mar., 1933.

Struggling Poland: A Journey in Search of the Picturesque Through the Most Populous of the New States of Europe. By Maynard Owen Williams. Vol. L, pp. 203-244, 48 ills., 1 two-thirds-page map, Aug., 1926.

Poland—*Continued*

Wilno, Stepchild of the Polish Frontier. 13 ills. in duotone. Vol. LXXIII, pp. 777-784, June, 1938.

See also Gdynia.

Polar Airship. By Walter Wellman. Vol. XVII, pp. 208-228, 4 diagrams, Apr., 1906.

Polar Expeditions. *See* Antarctic Regions; Arctic Regions; *and* National Geographic Society: Expeditions: Antarctic, Arctic.

Polar Photography. By Anthony Fiala. Vol. XVIII, pp. 140-142, Feb., 1907.

Polar Regions. *See* Antarctic Regions; Arctic Regions.

Poles (People):

Black Acres: A Thrilling Sketch in the Vast Volume of Who's Who Among the Peoples That Make America. By Dorothea D. and Fred Everett. Vol. LXXX, pp. 631-652, 13 ills. in black and white, 12 ills in color. Nov., 1941.

Empire State Onions and Pageantry (New York). 12 ills. in color from natural-color photographs by J. Baylor Roberts and Volkmar Wentzel. Vol. LXXX, pp. 641-648, Nov., 1941.

Policemen of the Air (Birds). By Henry Wetherbee Henshaw. Vol. XIX, pp. 79-118, 38 ills., Feb., 1908.

Polo, Marco:

World's Greatest Overland Explorer: How Marco Polo Penetrated Farthest Asia, "Discovered" Many Lands Unknown to Europe, and Added Numerous Minerals, Animals, Birds, and Plants to Man's Knowledge. By J. R. Hildebrand. Vol. LIV, pp. 505-568, 53 ills., 1 two-page map, Nov., 1928.

Polperro, England:

Channel Ports—And Some Others. By Florence Craig Albrecht. Vol. XXVIII, pp. 1-55, 45 ills., July, 1915.

Polynesia:

Around the World in the "Islander" (Ship): A Narrative of the Adventures of a Solitary Voyager on His Four-Year Cruise in a Thirty-Four-Foot Sailing Craft. By Capt. Harry Pidgeon. Vol. LIII, pp. 141-205, 75 ills., 1 two-page map, Feb., 1928.

At Home on the Oceans: Whales and Sharks Make Exciting Neighbors for a Professor's Wife, Turned Able Seaman, On a Three-year Voyage Around the World. By Edith Bauer Strout. Vol. LXXVI, pp. 33-86, 54 ills., 1 map, July, 1939.

Color Glimpses of the Changing South Seas. 14 ills. in color from natural-color photographs by Amos Burg. Vol. LXV, pp. 281-288, Mar., 1934.

Diary of a Voyage from San Francisco to Tahiti and Return, 1901. By S. P. Langley. Vol. XII, pp. 413-429, 10 ills., 1 page and 1 half-page maps, Dec., 1901.

Polynesia—*Continued*

Dream Ship: The Story of a Voyage of Adventure More Than Half Around the World in a 47-Foot Lifeboat. By Ralph Stock. Vol. XXXIX, pp. 1-52, 43 ills., 1 page map, Jan., 1921.

Greatest Voyage in the Annals of the Sea. By J. R. Hildebrand. Vol. LXII, pp. 699-739, 35 ills., 2 half-page maps, Dec., 1932.

Iridescent Isles of the South Seas. 16 ills. in color from photographs; 12 ills. by Rollo H. Beck. Vol. XLVIII, pp. 403-418, Oct., 1925.

Islands of the Pacific. By J. P. Thomson. Vol. XL, pp. 543-558, 15 ills., special map supplement, Dec., 1921.

Living on a Volcano: An Unspoiled Patch of Polynesia Is Niuafoō, Nicknamed "Tin Can Island" by Stamp Collectors. By Thomas A. Jaggar. Vol. LXVIII, pp. 91-106, 17 ills., 1 half-page map, July, 1935.

Modern Saga of the Seas: The Narrative of a 17,000-Mile Cruise on a 40-Foot Sloop by the Author, His Wife, and a Baby, Born on the Voyage. By Erling Tambs. Vol. LX, pp. 645-688, 49 ills., 1 half-page map, Dec., 1931.

Pilgrim Sails the Seven Seas: A Schooner Yacht Out of Boston Drops in at Desert Isles and South Sea Edens in a Leisurely Two-Year Voyage. By Harold Peters. Vol. LXXII, pp. 223-262, 36 ills., Aug., 1937.

Romance of Science in Polynesia: An Account of Five Years of Cruising Among the South Sea Islands. By Robert Cushman Murphy. Vol. XLVIII, pp. 355-426, 66 ills. in black and white, 16 ills. in color, 3 half-page maps, Oct., 1925.

See also Canton Island; Easter Island; Falcon Island; Fatu-Hiva; Hawaii; Marquesas Islands; Pitcairn Island; Samoa Islands; Society Islands; Tongareva.

Polyps (Marine Animals):

Coral Castle Builders of Tropic Seas. By Roy Waldo Miner. Vol. LXV, pp. 703-728, 15 ills. in black and white, 8 ills. in color, 1 two-thirds-page and 1 third-page maps, June, 1934.

Multi-Hued Marvels of a Coral Reef. 8 ills. in color from paintings by Else Bostelmann. Vol. LXV, pp. 719-726, June, 1934.

Pomp and Pulse of Modern London. 23 ills. in color from natural-color photographs by B. Anthony Stewart. Vol. LXXI, pp. 17-48, Jan., 1937.

Pompeii, Italy:

Destruction of Pompeii as Interpreted by the Volcanic Eruptions of Martinique. By Angelo Heilprin. Vol. XV, p. 431, Oct., 1904.

Ponape (Island), Caroline Islands:

Hidden Key to the Pacific: Piercing the Web of Secrecy Which Long Has Veiled Japanese Bases in the Mandated Islands. By Willard Price. Vol. LXXXI, pp. 759-785, 28 ills., 1 map (two-page spread), June, 1942.

Yap and Other Pacific Islands Under Japanese Mandate. By Junius B. Wood. Vol. XL, pp. 591-627, 34 ills., 1 two-thirds-page map, Dec., 1921.

Ponies:

England's Wild Moorland Ponies. 10 ills. from photographs. Vol. LXXXIX, pp. 129-136, Jan., 1946.

Ponta Delgada, Azores:

Azores: Picturesque and Historic Half-Way House of American Transatlantic Aviators. By Arminius T. Haeberle. Vol. XXXV, pp. 514-545, 26 ills., 1 page map, June, 1919.

Pontine Marshes, Italy:

Redemption of the Pontine Marshes: By Draining the Malarial Wastes Around Rome, Italy Has Created a Promised Land. By Gelasio Caetani. Vol. LXVI, pp. 201-217, 9 ills. in black and white, 12 ills. in color, 1 two-thirds-page map, Aug., 1934.

Story and the Legends of the Pontine Marshes: After Many Centuries of Fruitless Effort, Italy Is to Inaugurate a Gigantic Enterprise to Drain the Fertile Region Southeast of Rome. By Gelasio Caetani. Vol. XLV, pp. 357-390, 34 ills., Apr., 1924.

Popenoe, Paul B.:

Costa Rica, Land of the Banana. By Paul B. Popenoe. Vol. XLI, pp. 201-220, 17 ills., Feb., 1922.

Popenoe, Wilson:

Round About Bogotá: A Hunt for New Fruits and Plants Among the Mountain Forests of Colombia's Unique Capital. By Wilson Popenoe. Vol. XLIX, pp. 127-160, 34 ills., 1 third-page map, Feb., 1926.

Popocatepetl (Mountain), Mexico:

Greatest Volcanoes of Mexico. By A. Melgareio. Vol. XXI, pp. 741-760, 22 ills., Sept., 1910.

Population:

Calculations of Population in June, 1900. By Henry Farquhar. Vol. X, pp. 406-413, Oct., 1899.

European Populations. By Walter J. Ballard. Vol. XVI, p. 432, Sept., 1905.

Indian Census of 1911. By John J. Banninga. Vol. XXII, pp. 633-638, 4 ills., July, 1911.

Population of Japan. By Walter J. Ballard. Vol. XVI, p. 482, Oct., 1905.

Population of the United States. By Henry Gannett. Vol. XXII, pp. 34-48, 3 half-page maps, 9 diagrams, Jan., 1911.

Proportion of Children in the United States. Vol. XVI, pp. 504-508, 2 charts, Nov., 1905.

Recent Population Figures. By Henry Gannett. Vol. XXII, pp. 785-786, Aug., 1911.

Remarkable Growth of Europe During 40 Years of Peace. By O. P. Austin. Vol. XXVI, pp. 272-274, Sept., 1914.

Urban Population of United States. Vol. XII, pp. 345-346, Sept., 1901.

White Population of the Chief British Colonies. Vol. XIV, p. 360, Sept., 1903.

Populous and Beautiful Szechuan: A Visit to the Restless Province of China in which the Present Revolution Began. By Rollin T. Chamberlin. Vol. XXII, pp. 1094-1119, 26 ills., 1 half-page map, Dec., 1911.

Porcelain:

World's Ancient Porcelain Center (Kingtehchen). By Frank B. Lenz. Vol. XXXVIII, pp. 391-406, 17 ills., Nov., 1920.

Porcupines:

Flashlight Story of an Albino Porcupine and of a Cunning but Unfortunate Coon. By George Shiras, 3d. Vol. XXII, pp. 572-596, 26 ills., June, 1911.

Quills of a Porcupine. By Frederick V. Coville. Vol. XXIII, pp. 25-31, 5 ills., Jan., 1912.

Smaller Mammals of North America. By E. W. Nelson. Vol. XXXIII, pp. 391-493, 29 ills. in black and white, 59 ills. in color, May, 1918.

Wild Animals That Took Their Own Pictures by Day and by Night. By George Shiras, 3d. Vol. XXIV, pp. 763-834, 68 ills., 1 page map, July, 1913.

Porpoises:

Whales, Giants of the Sea: Wonder Mammals, Biggest Creatures of All Time, Show Tender Affection for Young, But Can Maim or Swallow Human Hunters. By Remington Kellogg. Vol. LXXVII, pp. 35-90, 25 ills. in black and white, 31 ills. in color, Jan., 1940.

Whales, Porpoises, and Dolphins. 31 ills. in color from paintings by Else Bostelmann. Vol. LXXVII, pp. 41-80, Jan., 1940.

Port-au-Prince, Haiti:

Bare Feet and Burros of Haiti. By Oliver P. Newman. Vol. LXXXVI, pp. 307-328, 10 ills. in black and white, 10 ills. in color, 1 half-page map, Sept., 1944.

Haiti, the Home of Twin Republics. By Sir Harry Johnston. Vol. XXXVIII, pp. 483-496, 11 ills., 1 third-page map, Dec., 1920.

Haitian Vignettes. By John Houston Craige. Vol. LXVI, pp. 435-485, 40 ills. in black and white, 13 ills. in color, 1 quarter-page map, Oct., 1934.

Port-of-Spain, Trinidad:

Crossroads of the Caribbean. By Laurence Sanford Critchell. Vol. LXXII, pp. 319-344, 18 ills. in black and white, 14 ills. in color, 1 half-page map, Sept., 1937.

Tropic Color in Trinidad. 14 ills. in color from natural-color photographs by Edwin L. Wisherd. Vol. LXXII, pp. 327-334, Sept., 1937.

Porter, Ethel Chamberlain:

Clock Turns Back in Yugoslavia: Fortified Monastery of Mountain-girt Dečani Survives Its Six Hundredth Birthday. By Ethel Chamberlain Porter. Vol. LXXXV, pp. 493-512, 20 ills., 1 page map, Apr., 1944.

Porter, Russell W.:

Member of Ziegler Polar Expedition. Vol. XVII, p. 35, Jan., 1906.

Portland, Oregon:

Oregon Finds New Riches. By Leo A. Borah. Vol. XC, pp. 681-728, 15 ills. in black and white, 28 ills. in color, 1 two-page map, Dec., 1946.

Porto Alegre, Brazil:

Air Cruising Through New Brazil: A National Geographic Reporter Spots Vast Resources Which the Republic's War Declaration Adds to Strength of United Nations. By Henry Albert Phillips. Vol. LXXXII, pp. 503-536, 32 ills., Oct., 1942.

Porto Rico. See Puerto Rico.

Porto Rico. By Robert T. Hill. Vol. X, pp. 93-112, 13 ills., Mar., 1899.

Porto Rico, the Gate of Riches: Amazing Prosperity Has Been the Lot of Ponce de León's Isle Under American Administration. By John Oliver La Gorce. Vol. XLVI, pp. 599-651, 46 ills. in black and white, 12 ills. in color, 1 half-page map, Dec., 1924.

Porto Rico or Puerto Rico? By Robert T. Hill. Vol. X, pp. 516-517, Dec., 1899.

Portraits of Ancient Mayas, a Peace-Loving People. 10 ills. in color from paintings by H. M. Herget. Vol. LXVIII, pp. 553-560, Nov., 1935.

Ports. See Harbors and Ports.

Portsmouth, New Hampshire:

Northeast of Boston. By Albert W. Atwood. Vol. LXXXVIII, pp. 257-292, 12 ills. in black and white, 17 ills. in color, special map supplement, Sept., 1945.

Portugal:

Altitudinal Journey Through Portugal: Rugged Scenic Beauty, Colorful Costumes, and Ancient Castles Abound in Tiny Nation That Once Ruled a Vast Empire. By Harriet Chalmers Adams. Vol. LII, pp. 567-610, 44 ills. in black and white, 17 ills. in color, 1 two-thirds-page map, Nov., 1927.

Castles and Progress in Portugal. By W. Robert Moore. Vol. LXXIII, pp. 133-188, 36 ills. in black and white, 24 ills. in color, 1 half-page map, Feb., 1938.

Color Close-ups of Europe's Corner Land. 24 ills. in color from natural-color photographs by W. Robert Moore. Vol. LXXIII, pp. 149-180, Feb., 1938.

Greatness of Little Portugal. By Oswald Crawfurd. Vol. XXI, pp. 867-883, 12 ills., Oct., 1910.

Pathfinder of the East: Setting Sail to Find "Christians and Spices," Vasco da Gama Met Amazing Adventures, Founded an Empire, and Changed the History of Western Europe. By J. R. Hildebrand. Vol. LII, pp. 503-550, 43 ills., 1 two-thirds-page map, Nov., 1927.

Portugal, the Land of Henry the Navigator. 16 ills. in color from photographs by A. W. Cutler. Vol. XLII, pp. 517-532, Nov., 1922.

Races of Europe. By Edwin A. Grosvenor. Vol. XXXIV, pp. 441-534, 62 ills., 2 page maps, special map supplement, Dec., 1918.

Rainbow Portraits of Portugal. 17 ills. in color from autochromes lumière by Gervais Courtellemont. Vol. LII, pp. 550-567, Nov., 1927.

Portugal—Continued

Woods and Gardens of Portugal. By Martin Hume. Vol. XXI, pp. 883-894, 8 ills., Oct., 1910.

See also Azores (Islands); Lisbon; Madeira (Islands); São Tomé (Island).

Portuguese East Africa. See Mozambique.

Portuguese Timor:

Timor a Key to the Indies. By Stuart St. Clair. Vol. LXXXIV, pp. 355-384, 33 ills., 1 third-page map, Sept., 1943.

Portuguese West Africa. See Angola.

Posse-Brázdová, Amelie:

Country-House Life in Sweden: In Castle and Cottage the Landed Gentry Gallantly Keep the Old Traditions. By Amelie Posse-Brázdová. Vol. LXVI, pp. 1-64, 51 ills. in black and white, 13 ills. in color, 1 page map, July, 1934.

Possibilities of Alaska. By C. C. Georgeson. Vol. XIII, pp. 81-85, Mar., 1902.

Possibilities of the Hudson Bay Country. Vol. XVIII, pp. 209-213, 3 ills., Mar., 1907.

Postwar Portrait of the United States. Text accompanying special map supplement in colors. Vol. XC, pp. 135-136, July, 1946.

Potala (Monastery), Tibet:

Sky-high in Lama Land. 12 ills. from photographs by C. Suydam Cutting. Vol. XC, pp. 185-196, Aug., 1946.

World's Strangest Capital (Lhasa, Tibet). By John Claude White. Vol. XXIX, pp. 273-395, 19 ills., panorama, Mar., 1916.

Potash:

American Potash for America. By Guy Elliott Mitchell. Vol. XXII, pp. 398-405, 4 ills., Apr., 1911.

Potent Personalities—Wasps and Hornets: Though Often Painfully Stung, Mankind Profits Immeasurably from the Pest-Killing Activities of These Fiery Little Flyers. By Austin H. Clark. Vol. LXXII, pp. 47-72, 18 ills. in black and white, 12 ills. in color, July, 1937.

Potomac (River), United States:

Approaching Washington by Tidewater Potomac. By Paul Wilstach. Vol. LVII, pp. 372-392, 7 ills., Mar., 1930.

George Washington's Historic River. 18 ills. in color from natural-color photographs by Willard R. Culver and Robert F. Sisson. Vol. LXXXVIII, pp. 41-64, July, 1945.

Great Falls of the Potomac. By Gilbert Grosvenor. Vol. LIII, pp. 385-400, 19 ills., Mar., 1928.

Potomac, River of Destiny. By Albert W. Atwood. Vol. LXXXVIII, pp. 33-70, 15 ills. in black and white, 18 ills. in color, 1 map (two-page spread), July, 1945.

Potosí, Bolivia:

Bolivia—Tin Roof of the Andes. By Henry Albert Phillips. Vol. LXXXIII, pp. 309-332, 5 ills. in black and white, 20 ills. in color, Mar., 1943.

Pottery:

World's Ancient Porcelain Center (Kingteh-chen). By Frank B. Lenz. Vol. XXXVIII, pp. 391-406, 17 ills., Nov., 1920.

Poulter, (Dr.) Thomas C.:

Society's Special Medal Is Awarded to Dr. Thomas C. Poulter: Admiral Byrd's Second-in-Command and Senior Scientist Is Accorded High Geographic Honor. Vol. LXXII, pp. 105-108, 2 ills., July, 1937.

Poultry:

America's Debt to the Hen. By Harry R. Lewis. Vol. LI, pp. 453-467, 15 ills., Apr., 1927.

Domestic Fowls of Field, Park, and Farmyard. 16 ills. in color from paintings by Hashime Murayama. Vol. LVII, pp. 329-360, Mar., 1930.

Fowl of the Old and New World. 29 ills. in color from paintings by Hashime Murayama. Vol. LI, pp. 421-436, Apr., 1927.

Fowls of Forest and Stream Tamed by Man. By Morley A. Jull. Vol. LVII, pp. 327-371, 27 ills. in black and white, 16 ills. in color, Mar., 1930.
　　Contains descriptions and illustrations of the following: Ducks, Geese, Guinea Fowl, Pea-fowl, Swans, Turkeys.

Races of Domestic Fowl. By Morley A. Jull. Vol. LI, pp. 379-452, 67 ills. in black and white, 29 ills. in color, Apr., 1927.
　　Contains descriptions and illustrations of the following species: Ancona, Andalusian, Araucana, Bantam, Brahma, Campine, Cochin, Cornish, Dominique, Frizzle, Hamburg, Houdan, Jersey Black Giant, Langshan, Leghorn, Minorca, Plymouth Rock, Polish, Red Jungle Fowl, Rhode Island Red, Silkie, Sussex, Wyandotte, Yokohama.

Powell, Imogene:

"Compleat Angler" Fishes for Fossils. By Imogene Powell. Vol. LXVI, pp. 251-258, 7 ills., Aug., 1934.

Powell, John B.:

Today on the China Coast. By John B. Powell. Vol. LXXXVII, pp. 217-238, 17 ills., 1 page map, Feb., 1945.

Powell, John Wesley:

John Wesley Powell (Biography). By Gilbert H. Grosvenor. Vol. XIII, pp. 392-395, 1 ill., Nov., 1902.

Powell, W. B.:

Chairman of National Geographic Society Prize Committee. Vol. X, p. 32, Jan., 1899.

Powell-Cotton, (Maj.) P. H. G.:

Journey Through the Eastern Portion of the Congo State. By Maj. P. H. G. Powell-Cotton. Vol. XIX, pp. 155-163, 9 ills., Mar., 1908.

Powhatan Confederacy:

Indians of the Southeastern United States. By Matthew W. Stirling. Paintings by W. Langdon Kihn. Vol. LXXXIX, pp. 53-74, 8 ills. in black and white, 8 ills. in color, Jan., 1946.

Practical Exercises in Geography. By W. M. Davis. Vol. XI, pp. 62-78, Feb., 1900.

Practical Patriotism (National Geographic Society's War Work). Vol. XXXII, pp. 279-280, Sept., 1917.

Prague (Praha), Czechoslovakia:

Czechoslovakia, the Key-Land to Central Europe. By Maynard Owen Williams. Vol. XXXIX, pp. 111-156, 45 ills., 1 quarter-page map, Feb., 1921.

Czechoslovaks, Yankees of Europe. By John Patric. Vol. LXXIV, pp. 173-225, 23 ills. in black and white, 30 ills. in color, 1 map, Aug., 1938.

A Tale of Three Cities. By Thomas R. Henry. Vol. LXXXVIII, pp. 641-669, 23 ills., Dec., 1945.

When Czechoslovakia Puts a Falcon Feather in Its Cap. By Maynard Owen Williams. Vol. LXIII, pp. 40-49, 13 ills. in color, Jan., 1933.

When Golden Praha Entertains the Majestic Sokol Festival. 13 ills. in color from natural-color photographs by Hans Hildenbrand. Vol. LXIII, pp. 40-49, Jan., 1933.

Praha, Czechoslovakia. *See* Prague.

Prairie Falcons:

In Quest of the Golden Eagle: Over Lonely Mountain and Prairie Soars This Rare and Lordly Bird, But Three Youths from the East Catch Up With Him at Last. By John and Frank Craighead. Vol. LXXVII, pp. 693-710, 17 ills., May, 1940.

Week-Ends With the Prairie Falcon: A Commuter Finds Recreation in Scaling Cliffs to Observe the Nest Life and Flying Habits of These Elusive Birds. By Frederick Hall Fowler. Vol. LXVII, pp. 611-626, 21 ills., May, 1935.

Pratt, A. E.:

Strange Sights in Far-Away Papua. By A. E. Pratt. Vol. XVIII, pp. 559-572, 7 ills., Sept., 1907.

Praus (Ships):

Seafarers of South Celebes. By G. E. P. Collins. Vol. LXXXVII, pp. 53-78, 25 ills., 1 two-thirds-page map, Jan., 1945.

Precious Stones. Vol. XIV, pp. 451-458, 4 ills., Dec., 1903.

Prehistoric Animals. *See* Paleontology.

Prehistoric Ruin of Tsankawi (New Mexico). By George L. Beam. Vol. XX, pp. 807-822, 12 ills., Sept., 1909.

Prehistoric Telephone Days. By Alexander Graham Bell. Vol. XLI, pp. 223-241, 17 ills., Mar., 1922.

Prentice, Sartell, Jr.:

Sunrise and Sunset from Mount Sinai. By Sartell Prentice, Jr. Vol. XXIII, pp. 1242-1282, 34 ills., 1 page map, Dec., 1912.

Prescott, William H.:

Luster of Ancient Mexico (Aztecs). By William H. Prescott. Vol. XXX, pp. 1-32, 22 ills., July, 1916.

Present Conditions in China. By John W. Foster. Vol XVII, pp. 651-672, 709-711, Dec., 1906.

Present Conditions in China. By Frederick McCormick. Vol. XXII, pp. 1120-1138, 12 ills., Dec., 1911.

Present Day Scenes in the World's Oldest Empire (Ethiopia). 27 ills. in color from natural-color photographs by W. Robert Moore. Vol. LIX, pp. 690-723, June, 1931.

Preservation of England's Historic and Scenic Treasures. By Eric Underwood. Vol. LXXXVII, pp. 413-440, 24 ills., 1 two-page map, Apr., 1945.

Preserving Ancient America's Finest Sculptures (Guatemala). By J. Alden Mason. Vol. LXVIII. pp. 537-570. 24 ills. in black and white, 10 ills. in color, Nov., 1935.

Preston, E. D.:

Coast and Geodetic Survey: Its Present Work. By E. D. Preston. Vol. X, pp. 268-269, July, 1899.

Copper River Delta. By E. D. Preston. Vol. XI, pp. 29-31, Jan., 1900.

Tides of Chesapeake Bay. By E. D. Preston. Vol. X, pp. 391-392, Oct., 1899.

Pretoria, Transvaal, Union of South Africa :

Cities That Gold and Diamonds Built : Transvaal Treasures Have Created Bustling Johannesburg and Fostered Pretoria, Administrative Capital of the South African Union. By W. Robert Moore. Vol. LXXXII, pp. 735-766, 20 ills. in black and white, 9 ills. in color, 1 two-thirds-page map, Dec., 1942.

Under the South African Union. By Melville Chater. Vol. LIX, pp. 391-512, 97 ills. in black and white, 38 ills. in color, 1 two-page map, Apr., 1931.

Prevention of Hailstorms by the Use of Cannon. Vol. XI, pp. 239-241, June, 1900.

Pribilof Islands, Alaska :

Making the Fur Seal Abundant. By Hugh M. Smith. Vol. XXII, pp. 1139-1165, 18 ills., 1 half-page map, Dec., 1911.

Price, Overton W.:

Influence of Forestry upon the Lumber Industry of the United States. By Overton W. Price. Vol. XIV, pp. 381-386, 2 ills., Oct., 1903.

Price, Theodora:

Seals of Our Nation, States, and Territories. 84 ills. in color from paintings by Carlotta Gonzales Lahey, Irvin E. Alleman, and Theodora Price. Vol. XC, pp. 17-32, July, 1946.

Price, Willard:

Americans on the Barbary Coast. By Willard Price. Vol. LXXXIV, pp. 1-31, 13 ills. in black and white, 10 ills. in color, 1 map (two-page spread), July, 1943.

Behind the Mask of Modern Japan. By Willard Price. Vol. LXXXVIII, pp. 513-535, 14 ills., Nov., 1945.

By Felucca Down the Nile : Giant Dams Rule Egypt's Lifeline River, Yet Village Life Goes On As It Did in the Time of the Pharaohs. By Willard Price. Vol. LXXVII, pp. 435-476, 21 ills. in black and white, 22 ills. in color, 1 two-page map, Apr., 1940.

Grand Canal Panorama (China). By Willard Price. Vol. LXXI, pp. 487-514, 31 ills., 1 half-page map, Apr., 1937.

Hidden Key to the Pacific : Piercing the Web of Secrecy Which Long Has Veiled Japanese Bases in the Mandated Islands. By Willard Price. Vol. LXXXI, pp. 759-785, 28 ills., 1 map (two-page spread), June, 1942.

Jap Rule in the Hermit Nation (Korea). By Willard Price. Vol. LXXXVIII, pp. 429-451, 19 ills., 1 page map, Oct., 1945.

Japan Faces Russia in Manchuria. By Willard Price. Vol. LXXXII, pp. 603-634, 30 ills., 1 page map, Nov., 1942.

Mysterious Micronesia : Yap, Map, and Other Islands Under Japanese Mandate are Museums of Primitive Man. By Willard Price. Vol. LXIX, pp. 481-510, 37 ills., 1 half-page map, Apr., 1936.

Springboards to Tokyo. By Willard Price. Vol. LXXXVI, pp. 385-407, 16 ills., Oct., 1944.

Unknown Japan : A Portrait of the People Who Make Up One of the Two Most Fanatical Nations in the World. By Willard Price. Vol. LXXXII, pp. 225-252, 30 ills., Aug., 1942.

Price of Free World Victory (Title of address delivered by the Honorable Henry A. Wallace at a dinner of the Free World Association, May 8, 1942). *See* People's Fight Against Slavery.

Price of Liberty, Equality, Fraternity. Vol. XXXIV, p. 377, Nov., 1918.

Priene, Turkey :

Some Ruined Cities of Asia Minor. By Ernest L. Harris. Vol. XIX, pp. 833-858, 19 ills., Dec., 1908.

Priest, (Capt.) Cecil D.:

Timbuktu, in the Sands of the Sahara. By Capt. Cecil D. Priest. Vol. XLV, pp. 73-85, 16 ills., Jan., 1924.

Primitive Gyroscope in Liberia. By G. N. Collins. Vol. XXI, pp. 531-535, 3 ills., June, 1910.

Princely India, Resplendent with Jewels and Gold. 40 ills. in color from natural-color photographs by Lawrence Copley Thaw. Vol. LXXVIII, pp. 733-780, Dec., 1940.

Princeton (Carrier) :

Saga of the Carrier *Princeton*. By Capt. William H. Buracker, USN. Vol. LXXXVIII, pp. 189-218, 8 ills. in black and white, 22 ills. in color, 1 map (two-page spread), Aug., 1945.

Pritchett, Henry S.:

Judge of Prize Essay Contest. Vol. X, p. 32, Jan., 1899.

Prizes. *See* National Geographic Society : Prizes.

Prizes for the Inventor : Some of the Problems Awaiting Solution. By Alexander Graham Bell. Vol. XXXI, pp. 131-146, 7 ills., Feb., 1917.

Probable Cause of the San Francisco Earthquake. By Frederick Leslie Ransome. Vol. XVII, pp. 280-296, 9 ills., 2 page maps, May, 1906.

Probable Effect of the Panama Canal on the Commercial Geography of the World. By O. P. Austin. Vol. XXV, pp. 245-248, Feb., 1914.

Probert, Frank H.:

Treasure Chest of Mercurial Mexico (Silver Mines in Guanajuato). By Frank H. Probert. Vol. XXX, pp. 33-68, 33 ills., July, 1916.

Problems in China. By James M. Hubbard. Vol. XI, pp. 297-308, 3 ills., special map supplement, Aug., 1900.

Problems of the Pacific—New Zealand. By Henry Demarest Lloyd. Vol. XIII, pp. 342-352, Sept., 1902.

Problems of the Pacific—The Commerce of the Great Ocean. By O. P. Austin. Vol. XIII, pp. 303-318, 7 page and 1 half-page maps, Aug., 1902.

Problems of the Pacific—The Great Ocean in World Growth. By W J McGee. Vol. XIII, pp. 333-342, Sept., 1902.

Proboscis Worm. *See* Bloodworms.

Production of Whalebone. Vol. XIX, pp. 883-885, 2 ills., Dec., 1908.

Progress in Surveying the United States. By O. H. Tittmann. Vol. XVII, pp. 110-112, 1 ill., Feb., 1906.

Progress in the Philippines. Vol. XVI, pp. 116-118, Mar., 1905.

Progress in the Philippines. Vol. XVI, pp. 513-514, 2 ills., Nov., 1905.

Progress of the National Geographic Society. Vol. XXIV, pp. 251-256, 1 ill., Feb., 1913.

Progress on the Panama Canal. By Gilbert H. Grosvenor. Vol. XVI, pp. 467-475, 1 half-page map, Oct., 1905.

Progressive World Struggle of the Jews for Civil Equality. By William Howard Taft. Vol. XXXVI, pp. 1-23, 14 ills., July, 1919.

Project for the Exploration of the Atmosphere Over the Tropical Oceans. By A. Lawrence Rotch. Vol. XV, p. 430, Oct., 1904.

Pronghorns:

Stalking Big Game with Color Camera. 28 ills. in color from natural-color photographs by Wendell Chapman. Vol. LXXVI, pp. 89-128, July, 1939.

Proportion of Children in the United States. Vol. XVI, pp. 504-508, 2 charts, Nov., 1905.

Proposed American Interoceanic Canal in Its Commercial Aspects. By Joseph Nimmo, Jr. Vol. X, pp. 297-310, Aug., 1899.

Proposed Meteorological Station in Iceland. Vol. X, p. 228, June, 1899.

Proposed Surveys in Alaska in 1902. By Alfred H. Brooks. Vol. XIII, pp. 133-135, Apr., 1902.

Prorok, (Count) Byron Khun de:

Ancient Carthage in the Light of Modern Excavation. By Count Byron Khun de Prorok. Vol. XLV, pp. 391-423, 27 ills. in black and white, 16 ills. in color, 1 half-page map, Apr., 1924.

Prosperous Idaho (An Interview with Governor Gooding, of Idaho, Published in the New York *Sun*, Dec., 1905). Vol. XVII, pp. 16-22, Jan., 1906.

Prosperous Porto Rico. Vol. XVII, p. 712, Dec., 1906.

Protecting Our Forests from Fire. By James Wilson. Vol. XXII, pp. 98-106, 5 ills., Jan., 1911.

Protecting the United States from Plant Pests. By Charles Lester Marlatt. Vol. XL, pp. 205-218, 16 ills., Aug., 1921.

Provence (French Province) :

Camargue, the Cowboy Country of Southern France. By Dr. André Vialles. Vol. XLII, pp. 1-34, 33 ills., 1 half-page map, July, 1922.

Provincetown, Massachusetts :

Cape Cod People and Places. By Wanda Burnett. Vol. LXXXIX, pp. 737-774, 17 ills. in black and white, 24 ills. in color, 1 half-page map, June, 1946.

Prussianism. By Robert Lansing. Vol. XXXIII, pp. 546-557, 5 ills., June, 1918.

Psalms. *See* Twenty-third Psalm.

Ptarmigans (Birds) :

Birds of Timberline and Tundra. By Arthur A. Allen. With 24 ills. in color from natural-color photographs by the author. Vol. XC, pp. 313-339, 8 ills. in black and white, Sept., 1946.

Game Birds of Prairie, Forest, and Tundra. By Alexander Wetmore. Vol. LXX, pp. 461-500, 5 ills. in black and white, 60 portraits in color, Oct., 1936.

White Sheep, Giant Moose, and Smaller Game of the Kenai Peninsula, Alaska. By George Shiras, 3d. Vol. XXIII, pp. 423-494, 59 ills., 1 page and 1 two-page maps, May, 1912.

Puebla (State), Mexico :

Mexican Indian Flying Pole Dance. By Helga Larsen. Vol. LXXI, pp. 387-400, 13 ills., Mar., 1937.

Pueblo Bonito, New Mexico :

Everyday Life in Pueblo Bonito : As Disclosed by the National Geographic Society's Archeologic Explorations in the Chaco Canyon National Monument, New Mexico. By Neil M. Judd. Vol. XLVIII, pp. 227-262, 37 ills., 1 two-thirds-page map, Sept., 1925.

New National Geographic Society Expedition ; Ruins of Chaco Canyon, New Mexico, Nature-Made Treasure-Chest of Aboriginal American History, to be Excavated and Studied ; Work Begins This Month. Vol. XXXIX, pp. 637-643, 7 ills., June, 1921.

Pueblo Bonito, the Ancient : The National Geographic Society's Third Expedition to the Southwest Seeks to Read in the Rings of Trees the Secret of the Age of Ruins. By Neil M. Judd. Vol. XLIV, pp. 99-108, 9 ills., 1 diagram, July, 1923.

Pueblo Bonito Expedition of the National Geographic Society. By Neil M. Judd. Vol. XLI, pp. 323-331, 10 ills., 1 diagram, Mar., 1922.

See also Tree Rings.

Pueblo Indians :

Everyday Life in Pueblo Bonito : As Disclosed by the National Geographic Society's Archeologic Explorations in the Chaco Canyon National Monument, New Mexico. By Neil M. Judd. Vol. XLVIII, pp. 227-262, 37 ills., 1 two-thirds-page map, Sept., 1925.

Indian Tribes of Pueblo Land. By Matthew W. Stirling. Vol. LXXVIII, pp. 549-596, 16 ills. in black and white, 25 ills. in color, Nov., 1940.

Nature Paints New Mexico. 25 ills. in color from natural-color photographs by Richard H. Stewart. Vol. LXXIII, pp. 537-568, May, 1938.

New Mexico Melodrama. By Frederick Simpich. Vol. LXXIII, pp. 529-569, 19 ills. in black and white, 25 ills. in color, 1 two-page map, May, 1938.

Red Men of the Southwest. 25 ills. in color from paintings by W. Langdon Kihn. Vol. LXXVIII, pp. 557-596, Nov., 1940.

Scenes from America's Southwest. Vol. XXXIX, pp. 651-664, 14 ills., June, 1921.

See also Hopi Indians.

Pueblo Viejo (Ruins), Mexico :

La Venta's Green Stone Tigers. By Matthew W. Stirling. Vol. LXXXIV, pp. 321-332, 4 ills. in black and white, 6 ills. in color, 1 two-thirds-page map, Sept., 1943.

Puerto Rico :

Countries of the Caribbean. By William Joseph Showalter. Vol. XXIV, pp. 227-250, 23 ills., Feb., 1913.

First American Census of Porto Rico. Vol. XI, p. 328, Aug., 1900.

Geographic Nomenclature. By E. W. Hilgard. Vol. XI, pp. 36-37, Jan., 1900.

Jobos Harbor. Vol. X, p. 206, June, 1899.

Our New Possessions and the Interest They Are Exciting. By O. P. Austin. Vol. XI, pp. 32-33, Jan., 1900.

Puerto Rico—Continued

Porto Rico. By Robert T. Hill. Vol. X, pp. 93-112, 13 ills., Mar., 1899.

Porto Rico, the Gate of Riches : Amazing Prosperity Has Been the Lot of Ponce de León's Isle Under American Administration. By John Oliver La Gorce. Vol. XLVI, pp. 599-651, 46 ills. in black and white, 12 ills. in color, 1 half-page map, Dec., 1924.

Porto Rico or Puerto Rico ? By Robert T. Hill. Vol. X, pp. 516-571, Dec., 1899.

Proceedings of the National Geographic Society (Report of Lecture on Puerto Rico by Hon. William F. Willoughby). Vol. XIII, pp. 466-470, Dec., 1902.

Prosperous Porto Rico. Vol. XVII, p. 712, Dec., 1906.

Puerto Rico : Watchdog of the Caribbean : Venerable Domain Under American Flag Has New Role as West Indian Stronghold and Sentinel of the Panama Canal. By E. John Long. Vol. LXXVI, pp. 697-738, 24 ills. in black and white, 23 ills. in color, Dec., 1939.

Puerto Rico, not Porto Rico. Vol. XI, pp. 37-38, Jan., 1900.

Puerto Rico Polychromes. 23 ills. in color from natural-color photographs by Edwin L. Wisherd. Vol. LXXVI, pp. 713-736, Dec., 1939.

Rediscovery of Puerto Rico. Vol. X, pp. 359-360, Sept., 1899.

Some Recent Instances of National Altruism : The Efforts of the United States to Aid the Peoples of Cuba, Porto Rico, and the Philippines. By William Howard Taft. Vol. XVIII, pp. 429-438, July, 1907.

U. S. Signal Corps in Porto Rico. Vol. XI, pp. 242-243, 1 page map, June, 1900.

Puffins (Birds) :

Birds of the Northern Seas. By Alexander Wetmore. Paintings by Maj. Allan Brooks. Vol. LXIX, pp. 95-122, 12 ills. in black and white, 34 portraits in color, Jan., 1936.

Puget Sound, Washington :

Our Pacific Northwest. By N. H. Darton. Vol. XX, pp. 645-663, 12 ills., 2 half-page maps, July, 1909.

Punta Arenas, Chile :

Longitudinal Journey Through Chile. By Harriet Chalmers Adams. Vol. XLII, pp. 219-273, 60 ills., 1 half-page map, Sept., 1922.

Purple Veil : A Romance of the Sea. Vol. XVI, pp. 337-341, 9 ills., July, 1905.

Purpose of the Anglo-Japanese Alliance. By Eki Hioki. Vol. XVI, pp. 333-337, July, 1905.

Pursuing Spanish Bypaths Northwest of Madrid. By Harry A. McBride. Vol. LIX, pp. 121-130, 6 ills. in black and white, 12 ills. in color, 1 two-thirds-page map, Jan., 1931.

Pushing Back History's Horizon : How the Pick and Shovel Are Revealing Civilizations That Were Ancient When Israel Was Young. By Albert T. Clay. Vol. XXIX, pp. 162-216, 47 ills., 1 page map, Feb., 1916.

Putnam, Amelia Earhart. *See* Earhart, Amelia.

Putnam, George R.:

Beacons of the Sea. By George R. Putnam. Vol. XXIV, pp. 1-53, 65 ills., 2 diagrams, 1 three-quarters-page map, Jan., 1913.

Hidden Perils of the Deep. By George R. Putnam. Vol. XX, pp. 822-837, 3 charts, 19 diagrams, Sept., 1909.

Important New Guide for Shipping: Navassa Light, on a Barren Island in the West Indies, Is the First Signal for the Panama Canal. By George R. Putnam. Vol. XXXIV, pp. 401-406, 3 ills., 1 half-page map, Nov., 1918.

New Safeguards for Ships in Fog and Storm. By George R. Putnam. Vol. LXX, pp. 169-200, 28 ills., 2 charts, Aug., 1936.

Surveying the Philippine Islands. By George R. Putnam. Vol. XIV, pp. 437-441, 4 ills., Dec., 1903.

Puto Shan (Island), East China Sea:

Puto, the Enchanted Island. By Robert F. Fitch. Vol. LXXXIX, pp. 373-384, 11 ills., 1 third-page map, Mar., 1946.

Pygmies (Tribespeople):

Journey Through the Eastern Portion of the Congo State. By Maj. P. H. G. Powell-Cotton. Vol. XIX, pp. 155-163, 9 ills., Mar., 1908.

Lloyd's Journey Across the Great Pygmy Forest (Belgian Congo). Vol. X, pp. 26-30, Jan., 1899.

Pyramids:

Chichen Itzá, an Ancient American Mecca: Recent Excavations in Yucatan Are Bringing to Light the Temples, Palaces, and Pyramids of America's Most Holy Native City. By Sylvanus Griswold Morley. Vol. XLVII, pp. 63-95, 34 ills., 1 half-page map, 1 diagram, Jan., 1925.

Interesting Visit to the Ancient Pyramids of San Juan Teotihuacan. By A. C. Galloway. Vol. XXI, pp. 1041-1050, 8 ills., 1 page map, Dec., 1910.

Resurrection of Ancient Egypt. By James Baikie. Vol. XXIV, pp. 957-1020, 46 ills., 1 page map, Sept., 1913.

Pyrenees (Mountains), France-Spain:

Andorra—Mountain Museum of Feudal Europe. By Lawrence A. Fernsworth. Vol. LXIV, pp. 493-512, 21 ills., 1 third-page map, Oct., 1933.

Costume Pageants in the French Pyrenees. 24 ills. in color from natural-color photographs by W. Robert Moore. Vol. LXXII, pp. 435-450, Oct., 1937.

Discovering the Oldest Statues in the World: A Daring Explorer Swims Through a Subterranean River of the Pyrenees and Finds Rock Carvings Made 20,000 Years Ago. By Norbert Casteret. Vol. XLVI, pp. 123-152, 24 ills., 1 half-page and 1 quarter-page maps, Aug., 1924.

Skyline Drive in the Pyrenees (France). By W. Robert Moore. Vol. LXXII, pp. 434-452, 24 ills. in color, Oct., 1937.

Q

QM, the Fighting Storekeeper. By Frederick Simpich. Paintings by Arthur Beaumont. Vol. LXXXII, pp. 561-600, 22 ills. in black and white, 16 ills. in color, Nov., 1942.

Quails (Birds):

Game Birds of Prairie, Forest, and Tundra. By Alexander Wetmore. Paintings by Maj. Allan Brooks. Vol. LXX, pp. 461-500, 5 ills. in black and white, 60 ills. in color, Oct., 1936.

Hunted Birds of Field and Wild. 60 portraits in color from paintings by Maj. Allan Brooks. Vol. LXX, pp. 469-500, Oct., 1936.

Quartermaster Corps, U. S. Army. *See* U. S. Army Quartermaster Corps.

Quebec (City), Canada:

Old France in Modern Canada. By V. C. Scott O'Connor. Vol. LXVII, pp. 167-200, 36 ills., 1 page map, Feb., 1935.

Old World Charm in Modern Quebec. 12 ills. in color from natural-color photographs by William D. Boutwell, Jacob Gayer, Edwin L. Wisherd, and Clifton Adams. Vol. LVII, pp. 506-515, Apr., 1930.

Quebec, Capital of French Canada. By William Dow Boutwell. Vol. LVII, pp. 515-522, 6 ills. in black and white, 12 ills. in color, Apr., 1930.

Quebec (Province), Canada:

Camera Pastels in French Canada. 25 ills. in color from natural-color photographs by Harrison Howell Walker. Vol. LXXV, pp. 601-624, May, 1939.

Gaspé Peninsula Wonderland. By Wilfrid Bovey. Vol. LXVIII, pp. 209-230, 13 ills. in black and white, 15 ills. in color, 1 half-page map, Aug., 1935.

Gentle Folk Settle Stern Saguenay: On French Canada's Frontier Homespun Colonists Keep the Customs of Old Norman Settlers. By Harrison Howell Walker. Vol. LXXV, pp. 595-632, 15 ills. in black and white, 25 ills. in color, 1 map, May, 1939.

Old France in Modern Canada. By V. C. Scott O'Connor. Vol. LXVII, pp. 167-200, 36 ills., 1 page map, Feb., 1935.
Contents: St. Lawrence and Saguenay Regions.

Old World Charm in Modern Quebec. 12 ills. in color from natural-color photographs by William D. Boutwell, Jacob Gayer, Edwin L. Wisherd, and Clifton Adams. Vol. LVII, pp. 506-515, Apr., 1930.

Quebec, Capital of French Canada. By William Dow Boutwell. Vol. LVII, pp. 515-522, 6 ills. in black and white, 12 ills. in color, Apr., 1930.

Remnants of Royal France in Canada. 15 ills. in color from natural-color photographs by B. Anthony Stewart. Vol. LXVIII, pp. 217-224, Aug., 1935.

Servicing Arctic Airbases. By Robert A. Bartlett. Vol. LXXXIX, pp. 602-616, 3 ills. in black and white, 10 ills. in color, 1 half-page map, May, 1946.

See also Anticosti Island.

Queensland (State), Australia. *See* Great Barrier Reef.

Queer Methods of Travel in Curious Corners of the World. By O. P. Austin. Vol. XVIII, pp. 687-715, 29 ills., Nov., 1907.

Quest of Gold and the Goldsmith's Art. 11 ills. in duotone. Vol. LXIII, pp. 488-497, Apr., 1933.

Quetzals:

Land of the Painted Oxcarts (Costa Rica). By Luis Marden. With 31 ills. in color from natural-color photographs by the author. Vol. XC, pp. 409-456, 30 ills. in black and white, 1 half-page map, Oct., 1946.

Quichés (Indians):

Guatemala: Land of Volcanoes and Progress: Cradle of Ancient Mayan Civilization, Redolent With Its Later Spanish and Indian Ways, Now Reaping Prosperity from Bananas and Coffee. By Thomas F. Lee. Vol. L, pp. 599-648, 32 ills. in black and white, 20 ills. in color, 1 page map, Nov., 1926.

Guatemala Interlude: In the Land of the Quetzal a Modern Capital Contrasts With Primitive Indian Villages and the "Pompeii of America." By E. John Long. Vol. LXX, pp. 429-460, 22 ills. in black and white, 13 ills. in color, 1 page map, Oct., 1936.

In the Land of the Quetzal. 20 ills. in color from autochromes lumière by Jacob Gayer. Vol. L, pp. 610-627, Nov., 1926.

Quichua Indians:

Along the Old Inca Highway. By Harriet Chalmers Adams. Vol. XIX, pp. 231-250, 21 ills., Apr., 1908.

Cuzco, America's Ancient Mecca. By Harriet Chalmers Adams. Vol. XIX, pp. 669-689, 19 ills., Oct., 1908.

Over Trail and Through Jungle in Ecuador: Indian Head-Hunters of the Interior, an Interesting Study in the South American Republic. By H. E. Anthony. Vol. XL, pp. 327-352, 28 ills., Oct., 1921.

Quills of a Porcupine. By Frederick V. Coville. Vol. XXIII, pp. 25-31, 5 ills., Jan., 1912.

Quinine Hunters in Ecuador. By Froelich Rainey. Vol. LXXXIX, pp. 341-363, 21 ills., 1 half-page map, Mar., 1946.

Quinn, Lorena MacIntyre:

America's South Sea Soldiers (American Samoa). By Lorena MacIntyre Quinn. Vol. XXXVI, pp. 267-274, 8 ills., Sept., 1919.

Quirigua, Guatemala:

Excavations at Quirigua, Guatemala. By Sylvanus Griswold Morley. Vol. XXIV, pp. 339-361, 24 ills., 1 diagram, Mar., 1913.

Mysterious Temples of the Jungle: The Prehistoric Ruins of Guatemala. By W. F. Sands. Vol. XXIV, pp. 324-338, 10 ills., Mar., 1913.

Quirós, Cesáreo Bernaldo de:

Pioneer Gaucho Days. 8 ills. in color from paintings by Cesáreo Bernaldo de Quirós. Vol. LXIV, pp. 453-460, Oct., 1933.

Quirós, Pedro Fernández de:

Revealing Earth's Mightiest Ocean (Pacific). By Albert W. Atwood. Vol. LXXXIV, pp. 291-306, 10 ills., special map supplement, Sept., 1943.

Quito, Ecuador:

From Sea to Clouds in Ecuador. By W. Robert Moore. Vol. LXXX, pp. 717-740, 11 ills. in black and white, 9 ills. in color, Dec., 1941.

Over Trail and Through Jungle in Ecuador: Indian Head-Hunters of the Interior, an Interesting Study in the South American Republic. By H. E. Anthony. Vol. XL, pp. 327-352, 28 ills., Oct., 1921.

R

Rabat, Morocco:

Eastward from Gibraltar: Overland Route Across North Africa to Tunisia and Libia. By Cyrus French Wicker. Vol. LXXXIII, pp. 115-142, 28 ills., Jan., 1943.

Rabbits:

Lonely Australia: The Unique Continent. By Herbert E. Gregory. Vol. XXX, pp. 473-568, 68 ills., 1 two-page and 4 half-page maps, Dec., 1916.

Wild Animals That Took Their Own Pictures by Day and by Night. By George Shiras, 3d. Vol. XXIV, pp. 763-834, 68 ills., 1 page map, July, 1913.

Rabot, Charles:

French Conquest of the Sahara. By Charles Rabot. Vol. XVI, pp. 76-80, 1 ill., Feb., 1905.

Notable Norwegian Publication. By Charles Rabot. Vol. XV, pp. 370-371, Sept., 1904.

Recent French Explorations in Africa. By Charles Rabot. Vol. XIII, pp. 119-132, 20 ills., Apr., 1902.

Raccoons:

Flashlight Story of an Albino Porcupine and of a Cunning but Unfortunate Coon. By George Shiras, 3d. Vol. XXII, pp. 572-596, 26 ills., June, 1911.

Race for the South Pole (Presentation of Hubbard Medal to Shackleton). Vol. XXI, pp. 185-186, Mar., 1910.

Race Prejudice in the Far East. By Melville E. Stone. Vol. XXI, pp. 973-985, 6 ills., Dec., 1910.

Races of Domestic Fowl. By Morley A. Jull. Vol. LI, pp. 379-452, 67 ills. in black and white, 29 ills. in color, Apr., 1927.

Races of Europe: The Graphic Epitome of a Never-Ceasing Human Drama. The Aspirations, Failures, Achievements, and Conflicts of the Polyglot People of the Most Densely Populated Continent. By Edwin A. Grosvenor. Vol. XXXIV, pp. 441-534, 62 ills., 2 page maps, special map supplement, Dec., 1918.

Radar:

Air Power for Peace. By Gen. H. H. Arnold. Vol. LXXXIX, pp. 137-193, 35 ills. in black and white, 28 ills. in color, special map supplement, Feb., 1946.

New Frontier in the Sky. By F. Barrows Colton. Vol. XC, pp. 379-408, 28 ills., 1 diagram, Sept., 1946.

Your New World of Tomorrow. By F. Barrows Colton. Vol. LXXXVIII, pp. 385-410, 25 ills., Oct., 1945.

Radio:

Air Power for Peace. By Gen. H. H. Arnold. Vol. LXXXIX, pp. 137-193, 35 ills. in black and white, 28 ills. in color, special map supplement, Feb., 1946.

Miracle of Talking by Telephone. By F. Barrows Colton. Vol. LXXII, pp. 395-433, 41 ills., Oct., 1937.

New Frontier in the Sky. By F. Barrows Colton. Vol. XC, pp. 379-408, 28 ills., 1 diagram, Sept., 1946.

New Safeguards for Ships in Fog and Storm. By George R. Putnam. Vol. LXX, pp. 169-200, 28 ills., 2 charts, Aug., 1936.

Voice Voyages by the National Geographic Society: A Tribute to the Geographic Achievements of the Telephone. Vol. XXIX, pp. 296-326, 15 ills., 1 chart, Mar., 1916

Winged Words—New Weapon of War. By F. Barrows Colton. Vol. LXXXII, pp. 663-692, 29 ills., 2 two-thirds-page maps, Nov., 1942.

Your New World of Tomorrow. By F. Barrows Colton. Vol. LXXXVIII, pp. 385-410, 25 ills., Oct., 1945.

Radio Stations:

Americans Stand Guard in Greenland. By Andrew H. Brown. Vol. XC, pp. 457-500, 23 ills. in black and white, 19 ills. in color, 1 page map, Oct., 1946.

Radium:

Cause of the Earth's Heat. Vol. XVI, pp. 124-125, 1 ill., Mar., 1905.

Helium, the New Balloon Gas. By G. Sherburne Rogers. Vol. XXXV, pp. 441-456, 11 ills., May, 1919.

Prizes for the Inventor: Some of the Problems Awaiting Solution. By Alexander Graham Bell. Vol. XXXI, pp. 131-146, 7 ills., Feb., 1917.

Rae, Margery:

Sunday in Mezőkövesd, Hungary. By Margery Rae. Vol. LXVII, pp. 489-504, 22 ills., Apr., 1935.

Raft Life on the Hwang Ho. By W. Robert Moore. Vol. LXI, pp. 743-752, 14 ills., June, 1932.

Railroads:

Alaska's New Railway. Vol. XXVIII, pp. 567-589, 20 ills., Dec., 1915.

America's Amazing Railway Traffic. By William Joseph Showalter. Vol. XLIII, pp. 353-404, 46 ills., 1 third-page map, Apr., 1923.

Railroads—*Continued*

Commercial Valuation of Railway Operating Property in the United States. Vol. XVI, pp. 438-439, Sept., 1905.

Cuban Railways. By Albert G. Robinson. Vol. XIII, pp. 108-110, Mar., 1902.

First Transandine Railroad from Buenos Aires to Valparaiso. By Harriet Chalmers Adams. Vol. XXI, pp. 397-417, 14 ills., 1 quarter-page map, May, 1910.

Manchuria, Promised Land of Asia: Invaded by Railways and Millions of Settlers, This Vast Region Now Recalls Early Boom Days in the American West. By Frederick Simpich. Vol. LVI, pp. 379-428, 58 ills., 1 two-thirds-page map, Oct., 1929.

Maryland Pilgrimage: Visits to Hallowed Shrines Recall the Major Rôle Played by This Prosperous State in the Development of Popular Government in America. By Gilbert Grosvenor. Vol. LI, pp. 133-212, 88 ills., special map supplement, Feb., 1927.

One Thousand Miles of Railway Built for Pilgrims and Not for Dividends (Damascus to Mecca). By Col. F. R. Maunsell. Vol. XX, pp. 156-172, 13 ills., 1 three-quarters-page map, Feb. 1909.

Pan-American Railway. Vol. XV, pp. 232-233, May, 1904.

Railroads and Canals. Vol. X, p. 420, Oct., 1899.

Railway Construction and Improvements. Vol. XI, p. 163, Apr., 1900.

Railway Routes in Alaska. By Alfred H. Brooks. Vol. XVIII, pp. 164-190, 9 ills., 7 page and 1 half-page maps, 2 diagrams, Mar., 1907.

Railways, Rivers, and Strategic Towns in Manchuria. Vol. XI, pp. 326-327, Aug., 1900.

Russian Railways. Vol. XI, p. 243, June, 1900.

Shortening Time Across the Continent. By Henry Herbert McClure. Vol. XIII, pp. 319-321, Aug., 1902.

Trains of Today—and Tomorrow. By J. R. Hildebrand. Vol. LXX, pp. 535-589, 51 ills., Nov., 1936.

Winning the War of Supply. By F. Barrows Colton. Vol. LXXXVIII, pp. 705-736, 23 ills., Dec., 1945.

Rails (Birds):

Feathered Foragers of Swamp and Shore. 101 portraits in color from paintings by Maj. Allan Brooks. Vol. LXXII, pp. 191-222, Aug., 1937.

Shore Birds, Cranes, and Rails: Willets, Plovers, Stilts, Phalaropes, Sandpipers, and Their Relatives Deserve Protection. By Arthur A. Allen. Paintings by Maj. Allan Brooks. Vol. LXXII, pp. 183-222, 4 ills. in black and white, 101 portraits in color, Aug., 1937.

Railway Construction and Improvements. Vol. XI, p. 163, Apr., 1900.

Railway Routes in Alaska. By Alfred H. Brooks. Vol. XVIII, pp. 164-190, 9 ills., 7 page and 1 half-page maps, 2 diagrams, Mar., 1907.

Railways, Rivers, and Strategic Towns in Manchuria. Vol. XI, pp. 326-327, Aug., 1900.

Rainbow Costumes of Poland's Peasants. 11 ills. in color from natural-color photographs by Hans Hildenbrand and Maynard Owen Williams. Vol. LXIII, pp. 328-337, Mar., 1933.

Rainbow Denizens of the Aquarium. 16 ills. in color from natural-color photographs by Edwin L. Wisherd. Vol. LXV, pp. 97-104, Jan., 1934.

Rainbow Hues from Hungary. 27 ills. in color from natural-color photographs by Hans Hildenbrand. Vol. LXI, pp. 696-729, June, 1932.

Rainbow Natural Bridge, Utah :

Encircling Navajo Mountain with a Pack-Train: An Expedition to a Hitherto Untraversed Region of Our Southwest Discovers a New Route to Rainbow Natural Bridge. By Charles L. Bernheimer. Vol. XLIII, pp. 197-224, 33 ills., 1 half-page map, Feb., 1923.

Great Rainbow Natural Bridge of Southern Utah. By Joseph E. Pogue. Vol. XXII, pp. 1048-1056, 6 ills., Nov., 1911.

Rainbow Portraits of Portugal. 17 ills. in color from autochromes lumière by Gervais Courtellemont. Vol. LII, pp. 550-567, Nov., 1927.

Rainey, Froelich G.:

Alaskan Highway an Engineering Epic: Mosquitoes, Mud, and Muskeg Minor Obstacles of 1,671-mile Race to Throw the Alcan Life Line Through Thick Forests and Uninhabited Wilderness. By Froelich Rainey. Vol. LXXXIII, pp. 143-168, 21 ills., 3 maps, Feb., 1943.

Discovering Alaska's Oldest Arctic Town: A Scientist Finds Ivory-eyed Skeletons of a Mysterious People and Joins Modern Eskimos in the Dangerous Spring Whale Hunt. By Froelich G. Rainey. Vol. LXXXII, pp. 319-336, 15 ills., Sept., 1942.

Quinine Hunters in Ecuador. By Froelich Rainey. Vol. LXXXIX, pp. 341-363, 21 ills., 1 half-page map, Mar., 1946.

Rainfall and the Level of Lake Erie. By E. L. Moseley. Vol. XIV, pp. 327-328, Aug., 1903.

Rainier, Mount, Washington :

Great White Monarch of the Pacific Northwest. By A. H. Barnes. Vol. XXIII, pp. 593-626, 31 ills., 1 half-page map, June, 1912.

Our National Parks. By L. F. Schmeckebier. Vol. XXIII, pp. 531-579, 41 ills., 1 page map, June, 1912.

Wonderland of Glaciers and Snow. By Milnor Roberts. Vol. XX, pp. 530-537, 8 ills., June, 1909.

Raj Samand (Lake), India :

Marble Dams of Rajputana. By Eleanor Maddock. Vol. XL, pp. 468-499, 13 ills. in black and white, 16 ills. in color, Nov., 1921.

Rajputana (States), India :

Marble Dams of Rajputana. By Eleanor Maddock. Vol. XL, pp. 468-499, 13 ills. in black and white, 16 ills. in color, Nov., 1921.

Raleigh, (Sir) Walter:

Boyhood of Raleigh. Reproduction in color of the painting by Sir John Millais. Tate Gallery, London. Vol. XLIX, text, p. 596 ; supplement, May, 1926.

Ralik Chain, Marshalls. *See* Bikini ; Rongerik.

Rambles Through the Prairie State (Illinois). 15 ills. in color from direct color photographs by Clifton Adams. Vol. LIX, pp. 544-553, May, 1931.

Rambles Through Ulster, Northern Tip of the Shamrock Isle. 21 ills. in color from natural-color photographs by Bernard F. Rogers, Jr. Vol. LXVIII, pp. 577-600, Nov., 1935.

Rambling Around the Roof of Eastern America (Great Smoky Mountains). By Leonard C. Roy. Vol. LXX, pp. 243-266, 25 ills., 1 page map, Aug., 1936.

Ramsay, (Sir) William:

Modern Transmutation of the Elements. By Sir William Ramsay. Vol. XVII, pp. 201-203, Apr., 1906.

Sketch of the Geographical History of Asia Minor. By Sir William Ramsay. Vol. XLII, pp. 553-570, 12 ills., Nov., 1922.

Ranches:

On a Chilean Hacienda. 8 ills. in color from natural-color photographs by E. P. Haddon. Vol. LXXXVI, pp. 489-496, Oct., 1944.

Rand District, South Africa. *See* Witwatersrand.

Rangoon, Burma :

Notes on Burma. By Thomas Barbour. Vol. XX, pp. 841-866, 34 ills., Oct., 1909.

Ransome, Frederick Leslie:

Probable Cause of the San Francisco Earthquake. By Frederick Leslie Ransome. Vol. XVII, pp. 280-296, 9 ills., 2 page maps, May, 1906.

Rapa Nui (Island), Pacific Ocean. *See* Easter Island.

Ras at Tannura (Cape), Saudi Arabia. *See* Tannura, Ras at.

Ras Shamra, Latakia :

New Alphabet of the Ancients Is Unearthed: An Inconspicuous Mound in Northern Syria Yields Archeological Treasures of Far-Reaching Significance. By F. A. Schaeffer. Vol. LVIII, pp. 477-516, 47 ills., 1 quarter-page map, Oct., 1930.

Secrets from Syrian Hills: Explorations Reveal World's Earliest Known Alphabet, Deciphered from Schoolboy Slates and Dictionaries of 3,000 Years Ago. By Claude F. A. Schaeffer. Vol. LXIV, pp. 97-126, 40 ills., 1 third-page map, July, 1933.

Rat Pest : The Labor of 200,000 Men in the United States Required to Support Rats, Man's Most Destructive and Dangerous Enemy. By E. W. Nelson. Vol. XXXII, pp. 1-23, 21 ills., July, 1917.

Rational Element in Geography. By W. M. Davis. Vol. X, pp. 466-473, 2 diagrams, Nov., 1899.

Rats:

Rat Pest: The Labor of 200,000 Men in the United States Required to Support Rats, Man's Most Destructive and Dangerous Enemy. By E. W. Nelson. Vol. XXXII, pp. 1-23, 21 ills., July, 1917.

Ravens (Birds) :

Crows, Magpies, and Jays : Unusual Intelligence Has Earned a Unique Position for These Birds. By T. Gilbert Pearson. Paintings by Maj. Allan Brooks. Vol. LXIII, pp. 51-79, 16 ills. in black and white, 17 ills. in color, Jan., 1933.

Ravensdale, The Baroness:

Old and New in Persia : In This Ancient Land Now Called Iran a Modern Sugar Factory Rears Its Head Near the Palace of Darius the Great. By The Baroness Ravensdale. Vol. LXXVI, pp. 325-355, 20 ills. in black and white, 13 ills. in color, 1 two-thirds-page map, Sept., 1939.

Reaburn, D. L.:

Plan for Climbing Mt. McKinley. By Alfred H. Brooks and D. L. Reaburn. Vol. XIV, pp. 30-35, 1 page map, Jan., 1903.

Rebirth of Religion in Russia : The Church Reorganized While Bolshevik Cannon Spread Destruction in the Nation's Holy of Holies. By Thomas Whittemore. Vol. XXXIV, pp. 378-401, 16 ills., Nov. 1918.

Recent Ascent of Itambé (Brazil). By J. C. Branner. Vol. X, p. 183, May, 1899.

Recent Bequests by Members of the National Geographic Society. Vol. XLIX, p. 474, Apr., 1926.

Recent Contributions to Our Knowledge of the Earth's Shape and Size, by the United States Coast and Geodetic Survey. By C. A. Schott. Vol. XII, pp. 36-41, 1 ill., 1 chart, Jan., 1901.

Recent Discoveries in Egypt. Vol. XII, pp. 396-397, Nov., 1901.

Recent Eruption of Katmai Volcano in Alaska. By George C. Martin. Vol. XXIV, pp. 131-181, 45 ills., 1 diagram, 1 page map, Feb., 1913.

Recent Exploration in the Canadian Rockies. By Walter D. Wilcox. Part I, Vol. XIII, pp. 151-168, 12 ills., 1 page map, May, 1902. Part II, Vol. XIII, pp. 185-200, 9 ills., June, 1902.

Recent French Explorations in Africa. By Charles Rabot. Vol. XIII, pp. 119-132, 20 ills., Apr., 1902.

Recent Geographic Advances, Especially in Africa. By Maj. Gen. A. W. Greely. Vol. XXII, pp. 383-398, 5 ills., 5 page maps, Apr., 1911.

Recent Magnetic Work by the Carnegie Institution of Washington. Vol. XVII, p. 648, Nov., 1906.

Recent Observations in Albania. By Brig. Gen. George P. Scriven. Vol. XXXIV, pp. 90-114, 21 ills., 1 half-page map, Aug., 1918.

Recent Population Figures. By Henry Gannett. Vol. XXII, pp. 785-786, Aug., 1911.

Recent Report from the "Doubtful Island Region." By James D. Hague. Vol. XVIII, pp. 205-208, 2 page maps, Mar., 1907.

Recent Volcanic Eruptions in the West Indies. By Israel C. Russell. Vol. XIII, pp. 267-285, 7 ills., July, 1902.

Receptions. *See* National Geographic Society : Receptions.

Recession of the Glaciers of Glacier Bay, Alaska. By Fremont Morse. Vol. XIX, pp. 76-78, 1 page map, Jan., 1908.

Recife (Pernambuco), Brazil :

Air Cruising Through New Brazil : A National Geographic Reporter Spots Vast Resources Which the Republic's War Declaration Adds to Strength of United Nations. By Henry Albert Phillips. Vol. LXXXII, pp. 503-536, 32 ills., Oct., 1942.

Reck, Daisy:

American Virgins : After Dark Days, These Adopted Daughters of the United States Are Finding a New Place in the Caribbean Sun. By DuBose Heyward and Daisy Reck. Vol. LXXVIII, pp. 273-308, 15 ills. in black and white, 23 ills. in color, 1 two-thirds-page map, Sept., 1940.

Reclaiming the Swamp Lands of the United States. By Herbert M. Wilson. Vol. XVIII, pp. 292-301, 2 ills., 1 half-page map, 1 diagram, May, 1907.

Reclamation of Land:

Call of the West. By C. J. Blanchard. Vol. XX, pp. 403-437, 20 ills., 1 half-page map, May, 1909.

China Fights Erosion with U. S. Aid. By Walter C. Lowdermilk. Vol. LXXXVII, pp. 641-680, 10 ills. in black and white, 26 ills. in color, June, 1945.

Dikes of Holland. By Gerard H. Matthes. Vol. XII, pp. 219-234, 3 ills., 7 charts, June, 1901.

Drainage of Wet Lands. Vol. XVII, pp. 713-714, Dec., 1906.

Drowned Empire. By Robert H. Chapman. Vol. XIX, pp. 190-199, 10 ills., Mar., 1908.

Farmers Since the Days of Noah : China's Remarkable System of Agriculture Has Kept Alive the Densest Population in the World. By Adam Warwick. Vol. LI, pp. 469-500, 37 ills., Apr., 1927.

Holland's War With the Sea. By James Howard Gore. Vol. XLIII, pp. 283-325, 39 ills., 1 third-page map, Mar., 1923.

Home-Making by the Government: An Account of the Eleven Immense Irrigating Projects to be Opened in 1908. By C. J. Blanchard. Vol. XIX, pp. 250-287, 23 ills., Apr., 1908.

Reclamation of Land—*Continued*

Land of Egypt : A Narrow Green Strip of Fertility Stretching for a Thousand Miles Through Walls of Desert. By Alfred Pearce Dennis. Vol. XLIX, pp. 271-298, 28 ills., 1 half-page map, Mar., 1926.

Limited Water Supply of the Arid Region. By Frederick H. Newell. Vol. XI, pp. 438-442, Nov., 1900.

Mending Dikes in the Netherlands. 20 ills. from photographs by Lawrence Earl. Vol. XC, pp. 791-806, Dec., 1946.

Millions for Moisture : An Account of the Work of the United States Reclamation Service. By C. J. Blanchard. Vol. XVIII, pp. 217-243, 22 ills., Apr., 1907.

More Water for California's Great Central Valley. By Frederick Simpich. Vol. XC, pp. 645-664, 16 ills., 1 page map, Nov., 1946.

Nation's Undeveloped Resources. By Franklin K. Lane. Vol. XXV, pp. 183-225, 32 ills., Feb., 1914.

New Country Awaits Discovery : The Draining of the Zuider Zee Makes Room for the Excess Population of the Netherlands. By J. C. M. Kruisinga. Vol. LXIV, pp. 293-320, 20 ills. in black and white, 13 ills. in color, 1 three-quarters and 1 half-page maps, Sept., 1933.

New Mexico (Drainage of the Valley of Mexico). By John W. Foster. Vol. XIII, pp. 1-24, 11 ills., 2 page maps, Jan., 1902.

Reclaiming the Swamp Lands of the United States. By Herbert M. Wilson. Vol. XVIII, pp. 292-301, 2 ills., 1 half-page map, 1 diagram, May, 1907.

Reclamation in Wyoming and Colorado. Vol. XIV, p. 166, Apr., 1903.

Reclamation of the West. By F. H. Newell. Vol. XV, pp. 15-30, 6 ills., 7 half-page maps, Jan., 1904.

Redemption of the Pontine Marshes : By Draining the Malarial Wastes Around Rome, Italy Has Created a Promised Land. By Gelasio Caetani. Vol. LXVI, pp. 201-217, 9 ills. in black and white, 12 ills. in color, 1 two-thirds-page map, Aug., 1934.

Spirit of the West : The Wonderful Agricultural Development Since the Dawn of Irrigation. By C. J. Blanchard. Vol. XXI, pp. 332-360, 15 ills., Apr., 1910.

Staircase Farms of the Ancients : Astounding Farming Skill of Ancient Peruvians Who Were Probably the Most Industrious and Highly Organized People in History. By O. F. Cook. Vol. XXIX, pp. 474-534, 48 ills., May, 1916.

Story and the Legends of the Pontine Marshes : After Many Centuries of Fruitless Effort, Italy Is to Inaugurate a Gigantic Enterprise to Drain the Fertile Region Southeast of Rome. By Gelasio Caetani. Vol. XLV, pp. 357-390, 34 ills., Apr., 1924.

Surveying Through Khoresm : A Journey into Parts of Asiatic Russia Which Have Been Closed to Western Travelers Since the World War. By Lyman D. Wilbur. Vol. LXI, pp. 753-780, 31 ills., 1 two-thirds-page map, June, 1932.

Reclamation of Land—*Continued*

Taming the Outlaw Missouri River. By Frederick Simpich. Vol. LXXXVIII, pp. 569-598, 25 ills., 1 two-page map, Nov., 1945.

Two Great Undertakings (Work of U. S. Bureau of Reclamation and U. S. Forest Service). Vol. XVII, pp. 645-647, Nov., 1906.

Winning the West. By C. J. Blanchard. Vol. XVII, pp. 82-99, 10 ills., 1 page map, Feb., 1906.

Reconstructing Egypt's History. By Wallace N. Stearns. Vol. XXIV, pp. 1021-1042, 21 ills., Sept., 1913.

Record Ascents in the Himalayas. Vol. XIV, pp. 420-421, Nov., 1903.

Record of the Great Earthquake Written in Washington by the Seismograph of the United States Weather Bureau. By C. F. Marvin. Vol. XVII, pp. 296-298, May, 1906.

Red Ant Versus the Boll Weevil. Vol. XV, pp. 262-264, June, 1904.

Red Cross :

Needs Abroad. By Ian Malcolm. Vol. XXXI, pp. 427-433, 5 ills., May, 1917.

The Red Cross Spirit Speaks (Poem). By John H. Finley. Vol. XXXI, p. 474, May, 1917.

Symbol of Service to Mankind. By Stockton Axson. Vol. XXXIII, pp. 375-390, 11 ills., Apr., 1918.

See also American National Red Cross.

Red Cross Girl Overseas. By Margaret Cotter. Vol. LXXXVI, pp. 745-768, 22 ills., Dec. 1944.

Red Men of the Southwest (Pueblo Indians). 25 ills. in color from paintings by W. Langdon Kihn. Vol. LXXVIII, pp. 557-596, Nov., 1940.

Red Sea :

Pearl Fishing in the Red Sea. By Henri de Monfreid. Vol. LXXII, pp. 597-626, 24 ills., 1 two-thirds-page map, Nov., 1937.

Redeeming the Tropics. By William Joseph Showalter. Vol. XXV, pp. 344-364, 13 ills., Mar., 1914.

Redemption of the Pontine Marshes : By Draining the Malarial Wastes Around Rome, Italy Has Created a Promised Land. By Gelasio Caetani. Vol. LXVI, pp. 201-217, 9 ills. in black and white, 12 ills. in color, 1 two-thirds-page map, Aug., 1934.

Redfield, William C. :

Honors to Amundsen and Peary (Speech by William C. Redfield). Vol. XXIV, pp. 113-130, 5 ills., Jan., 1913.

Rediscovering the Rhine : A Trip by Barge from the Sea to the Headwaters of Europe's Storied Stream. By Melville Chater. Vol. XLVIII, pp. 1-43, 44 ills., July, 1925.

Rediscovery of Puerto Rico. Vol. X, pp. 359-360, Sept., 1899.

Redwood Forest of the Pacific Coast. By Henry Gannett. Vol. X, pp. 145-159, 6 ills., 1 page map, May, 1899.

Redwoods (Trees):

California's Coastal Redwood Realm: Along a Belt of Tall Trees a Giant Bridge Speeds the Winning of Our Westernmost Frontier. By J. R. Hildebrand. Vol. LXXV, pp. 133-184, 31 ills. in black and white, 17 ills. in color, 1 page-and-a-half map, Feb., 1939.

Golden Gate, and Redwood Evergreens. 17 ills. in color from natural-color photographs by B. Anthony Stewart. Vol. LXXV, pp. 149-160, Feb., 1939.

Redwood Forest of the Pacific Coast. By Henry Gannett. Vol. X, pp. 145-159, 6 ills., 1 page map, May, 1899.

Saving the Redwoods. By Madison Grant. Vol. XXXVII, pp. 519-536, 10 ills., June, 1920.

Reed, John C.:

Down Idaho's River of No Return (Salmon River). By Philip J. Shenon and John C. Reed. Vol. LXX, pp. 95-136, 43 ills., 1 page and 1 two-thirds-page maps, July, 1936.

Reed, (Cpl.) Macon, Jr.:

Behind the Lines in Italy. By Corporal Macon Reed, Jr. Vol. LXXXVI, pp. 109-128, 20 ills., July, 1944.

Reelfoot—An Earthquake Lake (Tennessee). By Wilbur A. Nelson. Vol. XLV, pp. 95-114, 20 ills., Jan., 1924.

Rehabilitation:

Americans Help Liberated Europe Live Again. By Lt. Col. Frederick Simpich, Jr. Vol. LXXXVII, pp. 747-768, 17 ills., June, 1945.

Rehearsal at Dieppe (France). By W. Robert Moore. Vol. LXXXII, pp. 495-502, 6 ills., Oct., 1942.

Reï Bouba, Cameroons:

Africa on Parade. 14 ills. in color from natural-color photographs by Lawrence Thaw. Vol. LXXIV, pp. 343-350, Sept., 1938.

Trans-Africa Safari: A Motor Caravan Rolls Across Sahara and Jungle Through Realms of Dusky Potentates and the Land of Big-Lipped Women. By Lawrence Copley Thaw and Margaret Stout Thaw. Vol. LXXIV, pp. 327-364, 29 ills. in black and white, 14 ills. in color, 1 two-thirds-page map, Sept., 1938.

Reindeer:

Camel of the Frozen Desert. By Carl J. Lomen. Vol. XXXVI, pp. 538-556, 19 ills., Dec., 1919.

Introducing Reindeer Into Labrador. Vol. XVIII, p. 686, Oct., 1907.

Reindeer in Alaska. By Gilbert H. Grosvenor. Vol. XIV, pp. 126-149, 17 ills., 1 half-page map, Apr., 1903.

Relation of Forests and Forest Fires. By Gifford Pinchot. Vol. X, pp. 393-403, 7 ills., Oct., 1899.

Religions:

Behind the Mask of Modern Japan. By Willard Price. Vol. LXXXVIII, pp. 513-535, 14 ills., Nov., 1945.
Contains information on Buddhism, Shinto, and Emperor Worship.

See also Buddhism; Confucianism; Hindus and Hinduism; Lamaism; Mohammedans and Mohammedanism; Zoroastrianism.

Religious Ceremonies:

Banishing the Devil of Disease Among the Nashi: Weird Ceremonies Performed by an Aboriginal Tribe in the Heart of Yünnan Province, China. By Joseph F. Rock. Vol. XLVI, pp. 473-499, 26 ills., 1 half-page map, Nov., 1924.

Demon Dancers and Butter Gods of Choni. 16 ills. in color from photographs by Joseph F. Rock. Vol. LIV, pp. 584-601, Nov., 1928.

Demon-Possessed Tibetans and Their Incredible Feats. 12 ills. in color from natural-color photographs. Vol. LXVIII, pp. 479-486, Oct., 1935.

Fire-Walking Hindus of Singapore. By L. Elizabeth Lewis. Vol. LIX, pp. 513-522, 12 ills., Apr., 1931.

In the Canary Islands, Where Streets are Carpeted with Flowers. 13 ills. in color from natural-color photographs by Wilhelm Tobien. Vol. LVII, pp. 614-623, May, 1930.

India at Work and Play. 22 ills. in color from natural-color photographs by Peter Upton Muir, Maynard Owen Williams, and Frances Muir. Vol. LXXXIX, pp. 449-464, Apr., 1946.

India Mosaic. By Peter Muir and Frances Muir. Vol. LXXXIX, pp. 443-470, 5 ills. in black and white, 22 ills. in color, 1 half-page map, Apr., 1946.

Last Israelitish Blood Sacrifice: How the Vanishing Samaritans Celebrate the Passover on Sacred Mount Gerizim. By John D. Whiting. Vol. XXXVII, pp. 1-46, 40 ills., 1 half-page map, Jan., 1920.

Life Among the Lamas of Choni: Describing the Mystery Plays and Butter Festival in the Monastery of an Almost Unknown Tibetan Principality in Kansu Province, China. By Joseph F. Rock. Vol. LIV, pp. 569-619, 34 ills. in black and white, 16 ills. in color, 1 half-page map, Nov., 1928.

Marriage of the Gods. By John J. Banninga. Vol. XXIV, pp. 1314-1330, 16 ills., Dec., 1913.

Pageant of Jerusalem: The Capital of the Land of Three Great Faiths Is Still the Holy City for Christian, Moslem, and Jew. By Maj. Edward Keith-Roach. Vol. LII, pp. 635-681, 57 ills., Dec., 1927.

Perahera Processions of Ceylon. By G. H. G. Burroughs. Vol. LXII, pp. 90-100, 1 ill. in black and white, 8 ills. in duotone, July, 1932.

Sacred City of the Sands (Kairouan, Tunisia). By Frank Edward Johnson. Vol. XXII, pp. 1061-1093, 25 ills., 1 half-page map, Dec., 1911.

Religious Ceremonies—*Continued*

Snake Dance (Hopi Indians). By Marion L. Oliver. Vol. XXII, pp. 107-137, 31 ills., Feb., 1911.

Sungmas, the Living Oracles of the Tibetan Church. By Joseph F. Rock. Vol. LXVIII, pp. 475-486, 1 ill. in black and white, 12 ills. in color, Oct., 1935.

Syria: The Land Link of History's Chain. By Maynard Owen Williams. Vol. XXXVI, pp. 437-462, 20 ills., 1 quarter-page map, Nov., 1919.

Two Great Moorish Religious Dances (Tangier, Morocco). By George Edmund Holt. Vol. XXII, pp. 776-785, 6 ills., Aug., 1911.

Religious Penances and Punishments Self-Inflicted by the Holy Men of India. By W. M. Zumbro. Vol. XXIV, pp. 1257-1314, 69 ills., Dec., 1913.

Remagen, Germany:

War's Wake in the Rhineland. By Thomas R. Henry. Vol. LXXXVIII, pp. 1-32, 29 ills., 1 third-page map, July, 1945.

Remarkable Growth of Europe During 40 Years of Peace. By O. P. Austin. Vol. XXIV, pp. 272-274, Sept., 1914.

Remarkable Salt Deposit. By Charles F. Holder. Vol. XII, pp. 390-392, 2 ills., Nov., 1901.

Remnants of Royal France in Canada. 15 ills. in color from natural-color photographs by B. Anthony Stewart. Vol. LXVIII, pp. 217-224, Aug., 1935.

Remote Nepal, Land of Mystery. 15 ills. in color from natural-color photographs by Martin Hürlimann. Vol. LXVII, pp. 329-336, Mar., 1935.

Removal of the North Sea Mine Barrage. By Lieut. Comdr. Noel Davis. Vol. XXXVII, pp. 103-133, 28 ills., 2 half-page maps, Feb., 1920.

Renascent Germany. By Lincoln Eyre. Vol. LIV, pp. 639-717, 59 ills. in black and white, 39 ills. in color, Dec., 1928.

Reno, Nevada:

Nevada, Desert Treasure House. By W. Robert Moore. Vol. LXXXIX, pp. 1-38, 16 ills. in black and white, 20 ills. in color, 1 four-fifths-page map, Jan., 1946.

Studies on the Rate of Evaporation at Reno, Nevada, and in the Salton Sink. By Frank H. Bigelow. Vol. XIX, pp. 20-28, 5 ills., Jan., 1908.

Report by Robert T. Hill on the Volcanic Disturbances in the West Indies. Vol. XIII, pp. 223-267, 13 ills., 2 page and 1 half-page maps, July, 1902.

Report of the Director and Editor of the National Geographic Society for the Year 1914. By Gilbert H. Grosvenor. Vol. XXVII, pp. 318-320, Mar., 1915.

Report of the Eruption of the Soufrière of St. Vincent, 1812. Vol. XIV, pp. 158-161, Apr., 1903.

Report of the Second Stratosphere Expedition. Vol. LXVIII, pp. 535-536, Oct., 1935.

Reports of Vessels as to the Range of Volcanic Dust (Martinique). By James Page. Vol. XIII, pp. 299-301, July, 1902.

Reptiles:

Certain Citizens of the Warm Sea. By Louis L. Mowbray. Vol. XLI, pp. 27-62, 18 ills. in black and white, 16 ills. in color, Jan., 1922.

Cultivation of Marine and Fresh Water Animals in Japan. By K. Mitsukuri. Vol. XVII, pp. 524-531, 5 ills., Sept., 1906.

Extinct Reptiles Found in Nodules. By H. A. Largelamb. Vol. XVII, pp. 170-173, 9 ills., Mar., 1906.

Contains information on Inostransevia and Pariasaurus.

Hunting Big Game of Other Days: A Boating Expedition in Search of Fossils in Alberta, Canada. By Barnum Brown. Vol. XXXV, pp. 407-429, 24 ills., 1 page map, May, 1919.

Lonely Australia: The Unique Continent. By Herbert E. Gregory. Vol. XXX, pp. 473-568, 68 ills., 1 two-page and 4 half-page maps, Dec., 1916.

Modern Dragon Hunt on Komodo: An English Yachting Party Traps and Photographs the Huge and Carnivorous Dragon Lizard of the Lesser Sundas. By Lady Broughton. Vol. LXX, pp. 321-331, 12 ills. in duotone, Sept., 1936.

Notes on the Remarkable Habits of Certain Turtles and Lizards. By H. A. Largelamb. Vol. XVIII, pp. 413-419, 12 ills., June, 1907.

Parade of Life Through the Ages: Records in Rocks Reveal a Strange Procession of Prehistoric Creatures, from Jellyfish to Dinosaurs, Giant Sloths, Saber-toothed Tigers, and Primitive Man. By Charles R. Knight. With 24 ills. in color from paintings by the author. Vol. LXXXI, pp. 141-184, 13 ills. in black and white, Feb., 1942.

Contains descriptions and colored illustrations of the following: Ceratosaurus, Dimetrodon, Diplodocus, Mosasaurus, Naosaurus, Parasaurolophus, Protoceratops, Pteranodon, Pterodactyl, Stegosaurus, Styracosaurus, *Tyrannosaurus rex.*

Reptiles of All Lands. By Raymond L. Ditmars. Vol. XXII, pp. 601-633, 32 ills., July, 1911.

Contents: Crocodiles and Alligators.—The Tortoises and Turtles.—The Lizards.—Snakes. —The Vipers.

Stalking the Dragon Lizard on the Island of Komodo. By W. Douglas Burden. Vol. LII, pp. 216-232, 21 ills., Aug., 1927.

Tuatara: "Living Fossils" Walk on Well-Nigh Inaccessible Rocky Islands off the Coast of New Zealand. By Frieda Cobb Blanchard. Vol. LXVII, pp. 649-662, 14 ills., 1 half-page map, May, 1935.

Reptiles—*Continued*

Wonder Island of the Amazon Delta : On Marajó Cowboys Ride Oxen, Tree-dwelling Animals Throng Dense Forests, While Strange Fishes and Birds Help Make a Zoologist's Paradise. By Hugh B. Cott. Vol. LXXIV, pp. 635-670, 30 ills. in black and white, 12 ills. in color, 1 half-page map, Nov., 1938.

See also Turtles.

Republic of Panama. By William H. Burr. Vol. XV, pp. 57-73, 7 ills., Feb., 1904.

Republics—The Ladder to Liberty. By David Jayne Hill. Vol. XXXI, pp. 240-254, 5 ills., 2 page maps, Mar., 1917.

Rescue Work:

They Survived at Sea. By Lt. Comdr. Samuel F. Harby. Vol. LXXXVII, pp. 617-640, 22 ills., May, 1945.

Resolution (Ship) :

Columbus of the Pacific : Captain James Cook, Foremost British Navigator, Expanded the Great Sea to Correct Proportions and Won for Albion an Insular Empire by Peaceful Exploration and Scientific Study. By J. R. Hildebrand. Vol. LI, pp. 85-132, 45 ills., 1 page and 1 three-quarters-page maps, Jan., 1927.

Restoration of Colonial Williamsburg. By W. A. R. Goodwin. Vol. LXXI, pp. 402-443, 21 ills. in black and white, 25 ills. in color, Apr., 1937.

Resurrection of Ancient Egypt. By James Baikie. Vol. XXIV, pp. 957-1020, 46 ills., 1 page map, Sept., 1913.

Return of Wellman. By J. Howard Gore. Vol. X, pp. 348-351, 2 ills., Sept., 1899.

Return to Florence (Italy). By 1st Lt. Benjamin C. McCartney. Vol. LXXXVII, pp. 257-296, 18 ills. in black and white, 18 ills. in color, Mar., 1945.

Return to Manila. By Frederick Simpich. Vol. LXXVIII, pp. 409-451, 21 ills. in black and white, 21 ills. in color, 1 half-page map, Oct., 1940.

Returns from Alaska. Vol. XVI, pp. 512-513, 1 page map, Nov., 1905.

Revealing Earth's Mightiest Ocean (Pacific). By Albert W. Atwood. Vol. LXXXIV, pp. 291-306, 10 ills., special map supplement, Sept., 1943.

Revelation of the Filipinos. Vol. XVI, pp. 139-192, 130 ills., April, 1905.

Review of The Society's Maps of Europe:

Geographic's New Map of Germany and Its Approaches : With a Review of The Society's Maps of Europe. By Gilbert Grosvenor. Text accompanying special map supplement in colors. Vol. LXXXVI, pp. 66-72, 1 ill., July, 1944.

Reviving a Lost Art (Drying Fruits and Vegetables). Vol. XXXI, pp. 475-481, 9 ills., June, 1917.

Revolt of the Ashantis (Gold Coast). Vol. XI, p. 244, 1 third-page map, June, 1900.

Revolution in Eating : Machine Food Age—Born of Roads, Research, and Refrigeration—Makes the United States the Best-fed Nation in History. By J. R. Hildebrand. Vol. LXXXI, pp. 273-324, 33 ills. in black and white, 25 ills. in color, Mar., 1942.

Revolution in Russia. By William Eleroy Curtis. Vol. XVIII, pp. 302-316, May, 1907.

Reykjavík, Iceland :

American Soldier in Reykjavík. By Corporal Luther M. Chovan. Vol. LXXXVIII, pp. 536-568, 6 ills. in black and white, 34 ills. in color, Nov., 1945.

Iceland Defrosted. 34 ills. in color from natural-color photographs by Luther M. Chovan. Vol. LXXXVIII, pp. 537-568, Nov., 1945.

Rhine (River), Germany :

Cologne, Key City of the Rhineland. By Francis Woodworth. Vol. LXIX, pp. 829-848, 18 ills., 1 half-page map, June, 1936.

Rediscovering the Rhine : A Trip by Barge from the Sea to the Headwaters of Europe's Storied Stream. By Melville Chater. Vol. XLVIII, pp. 1-43, 44 ills., July, 1925.

Story of the Ruhr. By Frederick Simpich. Vol. XLI, pp. 553-564, 11 ills., 1 third-page map, May, 1922.

War's Wake in the Rhineland. By Thomas R. Henry. Vol. LXXXVIII, pp. 1-32, 29 ills., 1 third-page map, July, 1945.

Rhineland (Region), Germany :

War's Wake in the Rhineland. By Thomas R. Henry. Vol. LXXXVIII, pp. 1-32, 29 ills., 1 third-page map, July, 1945.

Rhode Island:

Sauntering Through the Land of Roger Williams. 8 ills. in color from natural-color photographs by Clifton Adams. Vol. LX, pp. 310-319, Sept., 1931.

Rhodes, Cecil:

Rhodesia, Hobby and Hope of Cecil Rhodes. By W. Robert Moore. Vol. LXXXVI, pp. 281-306, 13 ills. in black and white, 10 ills. in color, 1 half-page map, Sept., 1944.

Rhodes (Island), Aegean Sea :

Ageless Luster of Greece and Rhodes. 16 ills. in duotone by Arnold Genthe. Vol. LXXIII, pp. 477-492, Apr., 1938.

Historic Islands and Shores of the Ægean Sea. By Ernest L. Harris. Vol. XXVIII, pp. 231-262, 29 ills., 1 half-page map, Sept., 1915.

Rhodes, and Italy's Aegean Islands. By Dorothy Hosmer. Vol. LXXIX, pp. 449-480, 32 ills., 1 map, Apr., 1941.

Souvenirs of Knighthood in Rhodes. 13 ills. in color from natural-color photographs by Luigi Pellerano. Vol. LXIV, pp. 665-672, Dec., 1933.

Rhodesia:

African Rainbow. 10 ills. in color from natural-color photographs by W. Robert Moore. Vol. LXXXVI, pp. 289-296, Sept., 1944.

Rhodesia, Hobby and Hope of Cecil Rhodes. By W. Robert Moore. Vol. LXXXVI, pp. 281-306, 13 ills. in black and white, 10 ills. in color, 1 half-page map, Sept., 1944.

Rhodesia, the Pioneer Colony: In the Land of Sheba's Gold and Rhodes' Diamonds Emerge Model Towns and Modern Mines. By Melville Chater. Vol. LXVII, pp. 753-782, 31 ills., June, 1935.

Wonders of the Mosi-oa-Tunga: The Falls of the Zambesi. By Louis Livingston Seaman. Vol. XXII, pp. 561-571, 6 ills., June, 1911.

World's Great Waterfalls: Visits to Mighty Niagara, Wonderful Victoria, and Picturesque Iguazu. By Theodore W. Noyes. Vol. L, pp. 29-59, 29 ills., July, 1926.

Rhododendrons, Black:

Through the Great River Trenches of Asia: National Geographic Society Explorer Follows the Yangtze, Mekong, and Salwin Through Mighty Gorges, Some of Whose Canyon Walls Tower to a Height of More Than Two Miles. By Joseph F. Rock. Vol. L, pp. 133-186, 47 ills., 1 half-page map, Aug., 1926.

Rhone, Rosamond Dodson:

Nauru, the Richest Island in the South Seas. By Rosamond Dodson Rhone. Vol. XL, pp. 559-589, 24 ills., Dec., 1921.

Riatas and Romance on the Rio Grande. 24 ills. in color from natural-color photographs; 23 ills. by Luis Marden. Vol. LXXVI, pp. 431-462, Oct., 1939.

Rice, William Gorham:

Singing Towers of Holland and Belgium. By William Gorham Rice. Vol. XLVII, pp. 357-376, 22 ills., Mar., 1925.

Rice:

How Half the World Works. By Alice Tisdale Hobart and Mary A. Nourse. Vol. LXI, pp. 509-524, 22 ills., Apr., 1932.

Some Aspects of Rural Japan. By Walter Weston. Vol. XLII, pp. 275-301, 12 ills. in black and white, 16 ills. in color, Sept., 1922.

Richmond, Virginia:

Virginia—A Commonwealth That Has Come Back. By William Joseph Showalter. Vol. LV, pp. 403-472, 5 ills. in black and white, 1 ill. in color, Apr., 1929.

Richthofen, Manfred von:

Aces Among Aces. By Laurence La Tourette Driggs. Vol. XXXIII, pp. 569-580, 9 ills., June, 1918.

Riddle of the Aleutians: A Botanist Explores the Origin of Plants on Ever-misty Islands Now Enshrouded in the Fog of War. By Isobel Wylie Hutchison. Vol. LXXXII, pp. 769-792, 24 ills., Dec., 1942.

Rift Valley, Kenya Colony:

Where Roosevelt Will Hunt. By Sir Harry Johnston. Vol. XX, pp. 207-256, 43 ills., special map supplement, Mar., 1909.

Riga, Latvia:

Flying Around the Baltic. By Douglas Chandler. Vol. LXXIII, pp. 767-806, 51 ills. in black and white, 13 ills. in duotone, 1 half-page map, June, 1938.

Riggs, Arthur Stanley:

Beauties of France. By Arthur Stanley Riggs. Vol. XXVIII, pp. 391-491, 73 ills. in black and white, 16 ills. in color, 1 half-page map, Nov., 1915.

Inexhaustible Italy. By Arthur Stanley Riggs. Vol. XXX, pp. 273-368, 76 ills., 1 page map, Oct., 1916.

Riggs, Thomas, Jr.:

Marking the Alaskan Boundary. By Thomas Riggs, Jr. Vol. XX, pp. 593-607, 17 ills., July, 1909.

Surveying the 141st Meridian (Boundary Line Between Canada and Alaska). By Thomas Riggs, Jr. Vol. XXIII, pp. 685-713, 46 ills., 1 page map, July, 1912.

Rio de Janeiro, Brazil:

Air Cruising Through New Brazil: A National Geographic Reporter Spots Vast Resources Which the Republic's War Declaration Adds to Strength of United Nations. By Henry Albert Phillips. Vol. LXXXII, pp. 503-536, 32 ills., Oct., 1942.

Brazil's Potent Weapons. By W. Robert Moore. Vol. LXXXV, pp. 41-78, 16 ills. in black and white, 18 ills. in color, 1 two-page map, Jan., 1944.

Carioca Carnival. 34 ills. in color from natural-color photographs by W. Robert Moore. Vol. LXXVI, pp. 291-322, Sept., 1939.

Gigantic Brazil and Its Glittering Capital. By Frederick Simpich. Vol. LVIII, pp. 733-778, 54 ills., 1 page map, Dec., 1930.

Rio de Janeiro, in the Land of Lure. By Harriet Chalmers Adams. Vol. XXXVIII, pp. 165-210, 39 ills., 1 half-page map, Sept., 1920.

Rio Panorama: Breath-taking Is This Fantastic City amid Peaks, Palms, and Sea, and in Carnival Time It Moves to the Rhythm of Music. By W. Robert Moore. Vol. LXXVI, pp. 283-324, 12 ills. in black and white, 34 ills. in color, Sept., 1939.

Rio Grande (River), United States-Mexico:

Down the Rio Grande: Tracing this Strange Turbulent Stream on Its Long Course from Colorado to the Gulf of Mexico. By Frederick Simpich. Vol. LXXVI, pp. 415-462, 28 ills. in black and white, 24 ills. in color, 6 maps, Oct., 1939.

Riatas and Romance on the Rio Grande. 24 ills. in color from natural-color photographs; 23 ills. by Luis Marden. Vol. LXXVI, pp. 431-462, Oct., 1939.

Wandering Islands in the Rio Grande. By Mrs. Albert S. Burleson. Vol. XXIV, pp. 381-386, 2 ills., 1 three-quarters-page map, Mar., 1913.

Rio Grande Cornucopia Under a Winter Sun (Texas). 24 ills. in color from natural-color photographs by B. Anthony Stewart. Vol. LXXV, pp. 65-96, Jan., 1939.

Rise and Fall of Nanking. By Julius Eigner. Vol. LXXIII, pp. 189-224, 37 ills., Feb., 1938.

Rise of Bulgaria. By James D. Bourchier. Vol. XXIII, pp. 1104-1118, 13 ills., Nov., 1912.

Rise of the New Arab Nation. By Frederick Simpich. Vol. XXXVI, pp. 369-393, 17 ills., 1 page map, Nov., 1919.

Ritter, Homer P.:

Note on the Activity of Shishaldin Volcano. By Homer P. Ritter. Vol. XVI, p. 249, May, 1905.

River-Encircled Paraguay. By Harriet Chalmers Adams. Vol. LXIII, pp. 385-416, 35 ills., 1 third-page map, Apr., 1933.

Rivers:

Amazon, Father of Waters: The Earth's Mightiest River Drains a Basin of More Than 2,700,-000 Square Miles, from Which Came Originally the World's Finest Rubber. By W. L. Schurz. Vol. XLIX, pp. 445-463, 15 ills., Apr., 1926.

Barrage of the Nile. By Day Allen Willey. Vol. XXI, pp. 175-184, 14 ills., Feb., 1910.

"Breaking Up" of the Yukon. By Capt. George S. Gibbs. Vol. XVII, pp. 268-272, 6 ills., May, 1906.

By Sail Across Europe. By Merlin Minshall. Vol. LXXI, pp. 533-567, 38 ills., 1 two-thirds-page map, May, 1937.

China Fights Erosion with U. S. Aid. By Walter C. Lowdermilk. Vol. LXXXVII, pp. 641-680, 10 ills. in black and white, 26 ills. in color, June, 1945.

Columbia Turns on the Power. By Maynard Owen Williams. Vol. LXXIX, pp. 749-792, 25 ills. in black and white, 18 ills. in color, June, 1941.

Deep-Water Route from Chicago to the Gulf. Vol. XVIII, pp. 676-685, 3 ills., 1 page map, Oct., 1907.

Down Mexico's Río Balsas. By John W. Webber. With 9 ills. in color from natural-color photographs by the author, Kenneth Segerstrom, and Jack Breed. Vol. XC, pp. 253-272, 5 ills. in black and white, 1 half-page map, Aug., 1946.

Geography of the Jordan. By Nelson Glueck. Vol. LXXXVI, pp. 719-744, 23 ills., 1 page map, Dec., 1944.

George Washington's Historic River (Potomac). 18 ills. in color from natural-color photographs by Willard R. Culver and Robert F. Sisson. Vol. LXXXVIII, pp. 41-64, July, 1945.

Great Falls of the Potomac. By Gilbert Grosvenor. Vol. LIII, pp. 385-400, 19 ills., Mar., 1928.

Rivers—*Continued*

Great Mississippi Flood of 1927: Since White Man's Discovery This Mighty River Has Served Him Well, Yet It Has Brought Widespread Devastation Along Its Lower Reaches. By Frederick Simpich. Vol. LII, pp. 243-289, 53 ills., 1 half-page map, Sept., 1927.

Ice Cliffs on White River, Yukon Territory. By Martin W. Gorman. Vol. XI, pp. 113-117, Mar., 1900.

Limiting Width of Meander Belts. By Mark S. W. Jefferson. Vol. XIII, pp. 373-384, 6 charts, Oct., 1902.

Long River of New England: In War and Peace, from Mountain Wilderness to the Sea, Flows the Connecticut River, Through a Valley Abounding in History, Scenery, Inventive Genius, and Industry. By Albert W. Atwood. Vol. LXXXIII, pp. 401-434, 24 ills. in black and white, 24 ills. in color, 1 two-thirds-page map, Apr., 1943.

Men Against the Rivers (Mississippi and Ohio Rivers). By Frederick Simpich. Vol. LXXI, pp. 767-794, 22 ills., 1 page-and-a-half and 1 quarter-page maps, June, 1937.

More Changes of the Colorado River. By D. T. MacDougal. Vol. XIX, pp. 52-54, 1 page map, Jan., 1908.

Mother Volga Defends Her Own. By Maynard Owen Williams. Vol. LXXXII, pp. 793-811, 21 ills., Dec., 1942.

Pirate Rivers and Their Prizes: The Warfare of Waterways Has Sometimes Changed the Geography of Our Continents. By John Oliver La Gorce. Vol. L, pp. 87-132, 48 ills., 1 half-page map, July, 1926.

Potomac, River of Destiny. By Albert W. Atwood. Vol. LXXXVIII, pp. 33-70, 15 ills. in black and white, 18 ills. in color, 1 map (two-page spread), July, 1945.

Stikine River in 1898. By Eliza R. Scidmore. Vol. X, pp. 1-15, 4 ills., Jan., 1899.

Taming "Flood Dragons" Along China's Hwang Ho (Yellow River). By Oliver J. Todd. Vol. LXXXI, pp. 205-234, 26 ills., 1 half-page map, Feb., 1942.

Taming the Outlaw Missouri River. By Frederick Simpich. Vol. LXXXVIII, pp. 569-598, 25 ills., 1 two-page map, Nov., 1945.

Through Paraguay and Southern Matto Grosso (Paraguay and Paraná Rivers). By Sir Christopher H. Gibson. Vol. LXXXIV, pp. 459-488, 20 ills. in black and white, 11 ills. in color, 1 two-thirds-page map, Oct., 1943.

The Tsangpo (Brahmaputra River). By James Mascarene Hubbard. Vol. XII, pp. 32-35, Jan., 1901.

War's Wake in the Rhineland. By Thomas R. Henry. Vol. LXXXVIII, pp. 1-32, 29 ills., 1 third-page map, July, 1945.

When the Father of Waters Goes on a Rampage: An Account of the Salvaging of Food-Fishes from the Overflowed Lands of the Mississippi River. By Hugh M. Smith. Vol. XXXVII, pp. 369-386, 18 ills., Apr., 1920.

Rivers—*Continued*

See also the following names of rivers: Amazon; Amu Darya; Avon; Balim; Brahmaputra; Cauca; Colorado; Columbia; Congo; Danube; Euphrates; Green; Hwang Ho; Irrawaddy; Jhelum; Jordan; Loire; Mackenzie; Magdalena; Matsang; Mekong; Mississippi; Missouri; Nervion, Nile, Ohio, Orinoco, Paraguay; Paraná; Parima; Potomac; Rhine; Rio Grande; Sacramento; Salmon; Salween; San Joaquin; San Juan; Saskatchewan; Seine; Stikine; Suwannee; Tejo; Thames; Tigris; Tumen; Volga; Yangtze; Yellowstone; Yukon; Zambesi.

Riviera (Region), France-Italy:

Carnival Days on the Riviera. By Maynard Owen Williams. Vol. L, pp. 467-501, 21 ills., Oct., 1926.

France of Sunshine and Flowers. 21 ills. in color from autochromes lumière by Maynard Owen Williams, Gervais Courtellemont, and Hans Hildenbrand. Vol. L, pp. 481-496, Oct., 1926.

Life's Pattern on the Italian Riviera. By Helen Churchill Candee. Vol. LXVII, pp. 67-100, 25 ills. in black and white, 12 ills. in color, 1 two-thirds-page map, Jan., 1935.

Where the Blue Begins on the Italian Coast. 12 ills. in color from natural-color photographs by Hans Hildenbrand. Vol. LXVII, pp. 81-88, Jan., 1935.

Riyadh, Saudi Arabia:

Guest in Saudi Arabia. By Maynard Owen Williams. Vol. LXXXVIII, pp. 163-187, 21 ills., 1 two-thirds-page map, Oct., 1945.

Road of the Crusaders: A Historian Follows the Steps of Richard the Lion Heart and Other Knights of the Cross Over the "Via Dei." By Harold Lamb. Vol. LXIV, pp. 645-693, 46 ills. in black and white, 13 ills. in color, 1 page map, Dec., 1933.

Road to Bolivia. By William E. Curtis. Part I, Vol. XI, pp. 208-224, 7 ills., June, 1900. Part II, Vol. XI, pp. 264-280, 6 ills., July, 1900.

Road to Wang Ye Fu: An Account of the Work of the National Geographic Society's Central-China Expedition in the Mongol Kingdom of Ala Shan. By Frederick R. Wulsin. Vol. XLIX, pp. 197-234, 44 ills., 1 third-page map, Feb., 1926.

Roads. *See* Highways and Roads.

Roads from Washington (D. C.). By John Patric. Vol. LXXIV, pp. 1-48, 27 ills. in black and white, 30 ills. in color, special map supplement, July, 1938.

Roaming Russia's Caucasus: Rugged Mountains and Hardy Fighters Guard the Soviet Union's Caucasian Treasury of Manganese and Oil. By Rolf Singer. Vol. LXXXII, pp. 91-121, 33 ills., July, 1942.

Roanoke Island, North Carolina:

Bit of Elizabethan England in America: Fisher Folk of the Islands Off North Carolina Conserved the Speech and Customs of Sir Walter Raleigh's Colonists. By Blanch Nettleton Epler. Vol. LXIV, pp. 695-730, 43 ills., 1 three-quarters-page map, Dec., 1933.

Robert College, Rumeli Hissar, Turkey:

American Alma Maters in the Near East. By Maynard Owen Williams. Vol. LXXXVIII, pp. 237-256, 16 ills., Aug., 1945.

Roberts, Frank H. H., Jr.:

In the Empire of the Aztecs: Mexico City Is Rich in Relics of a People Who Practiced Human Sacrifice, Yet Loved Flowers, Education, and Art. By Frank H. H. Roberts, Jr. Vol. LXXI, pp. 725-750, 14 ills. in black and white, 10 ills. in color, June, 1937.

Roberts, J. Baylor:

America on the Move. 26 illustrations from photographs by J. Baylor Roberts, B. Anthony Stewart, and others. Vol. XC, pp. 357-378, Sept., 1946.

Food: Flavor and Savor of American Foods. 25 ills. in color from natural-color photographs by J. Baylor Roberts, Willard R. Culver, and others. Vol. LXXXI, pp. 289-320, Mar., 1942.

Gulf Coast Towns Get into the Fight. 19 ills. in color from natural-color photographs; 17 ills. by J. Baylor Roberts. Vol. LXXXV, pp. 17-40, Jan., 1944.

Iowa: Corn and Color in the Hawkeye State. 20 ills. in color from natural-color photographs; 19 ills. by J. Baylor Roberts. Vol. LXXVI, pp. 151-174, Aug., 1939.

Mississippi: Magnolia State Mosaic. 26 ills. in color from natural-color photographs by J. Baylor Roberts. Vol. LXXII, pp. 279-310, Sept., 1937.

New York: Empire State Onions and Pageantry. 12 ills. in color from natural-color photographs by J. Baylor Roberts and Volkmar Wentzel. Vol. LXXX, pp. 641-648, Nov., 1941.

North Carolina Colorcade. 21 ills. in color from natural-color photographs; 19 ills. by J. Baylor Roberts. Vol. LXXX, pp. 189-220, Aug., 1941.

Ozarks (Plateau): Work and Play in the Ozarks. 20 ills. in color from natural-color photographs by B. Anthony Stewart and J. Baylor Roberts. Vol. LXXXIII, pp. 597-620, May, 1943.

Pacific Northwest: Where Fog and Sun Paint the Pacific. 23 ills. in color from natural-color photographs by J. Baylor Roberts. Vol. LXXXII, pp. 437-460, Oct., 1942.

Pennsylvania Dutch—In a Land of Milk and Honey. 10 ills. in color from natural-color photographs by J. Baylor Roberts. Vol. LXXIV, pp. 49-56, July, 1938.

Philippines: Camera Cruising in the Philippines. 12 ills. in color from natural-color photographs by J. Baylor Roberts, Fenno Jacobs, and others. Vol. LXXXVI, pp. 545-552, Nov., 1944.

Roberts, J. Baylor—*Continued*

Philippines : Smiling, Happy Philippines. 21 ills. in color from natural-color photographs ; 19 ills. by J. Baylor Roberts. Vol. LXXVIII, pp. 425-448, Oct., 1940.

Rubber : From Trees to Tires and Toys. 26 ills. in color from natural-color photographs by Willard R. Culver and J. Baylor Roberts. Vol. LXXVII, pp. 159-190, Feb., 1940.

Singapore—Britain's Outpost of Empire. 9 ills. in color from natural-color photographs by J. Baylor Roberts. Vol. LXXX, pp. 665-672, Nov., 1941.

Tennessee Tableaux. 22 ills. in color from natural-color photographs ; 19 ills. by J. Baylor Roberts. Vol. LXXV, pp. 569-592, May, 1939.

Washington of Tradition Builds for the Future. 20 ills. in color from natural-color photographs ; 13 ills. by J. Baylor Roberts. Vol. LXXI, pp. 671-694, June, 1937.

Roberts, (Mrs.) Kenneth:

Sojourning in the Italy of Today. By Mrs. Kenneth Roberts. Vol. LXX, pp. 351-396, 46 ills., 1 two-thirds-page map, Sept., 1936.

Roberts, Leo B.:

Traveling in the Highlands of Ethiopia. By Leo B. Roberts. Vol. LXVIII, pp. 297-328, 37 ills., Sept., 1935.

Roberts, Milnor:

Wonderland of Glaciers and Snow. By Milnor Roberts. Vol. XX, pp. 530-537, 8 ills., June, 1909.

Roberts, William H.:

Five Thousand Temples of Pagān : Burma's Sacred City Is a Place of Enchantment in the Midst of Ruins. By William H. Roberts. Vol. LX, pp. 445-454, 9 ills., Oct., 1931.

Robin Hood's Bay, England :

Between the Heather and the North Sea : Bold English Headlands Once Sheltered Sea Robbers, Later Were Ports of Wooden Ships, Centers of the Jet and Alum Trades, To-day Are Havens of Adventurous Fishing Fleets. By Leo Walmsley. Vol. LXIII, pp. 197-232, 41 ills., Feb., 1933.

Robinson, Albert G.:

Cuban Railways. By Albert G. Robinson. Vol. XIII, pp. 108-110, Mar., 1902.

Robinson, H. W.:

Hairnet Industry in North China. By H. W. Robinson. Vol. XLIV, pp. 327-336, 10 ills., Sept., 1923.

Robot Airplanes:

Air Power for Peace. By Gen. H. H. Arnold. Vol. LXXXIX, pp. 137-193, 35 ills. in black and white, 28 ills. in color, special map supplement, Feb., 1946.

Robot Bombs:

Air Power for Peace. By Gen. H. H. Arnold. Vol. LXXXIX, pp. 137-193, 35 ills. in black and white, 28 ills. in color, special map supplement, Feb., 1946.

London Wins the Battle. By Marquis W. Childs. Vol. LXXXVIII, pp. 129-152, 21 ills., Aug., 1945.

Robson, Mount, British Columbia :

Monarch of the Canadian Rockies. By Charles D. Walcott. Vol. XXIV, pp. 626-639, 13 ills., panorama, May, 1913.

Monarch of the Canadian Rockies—Robson Peak. Vol. XXIV, panorama, May, 1913.

Rochambeau, Jean B. D. de Vimeur, Comte de:

Our First Alliance. By J. J. Jusserand. Vol. XXXI, pp. 518-548, 8 ills., June, 1917.

Rochford, Daniel:

New England Ski Trails : Snow and Ice Sports Transform Whittier's Winters of Snowbound Seclusion Into Seasons of Outdoor Recreation. By Daniel Rochford. Vol. LXX, pp. 645-664, 11 ills. in black and white, 13 ills. in color, Nov., 1936.

Rock, Joseph F.:

Banishing the Devil of Disease Among the Nashi : Weird Ceremonies Performed by an Aboriginal Tribe in the Heart of Yünnan Province, China. By Joseph F. Rock. Vol. XLVI, pp. 473-499, 26 ills., 1 half-page map, Nov., 1924.

Carrying the Color Camera Through Unmapped China. 24 ills. in color from natural-color photographs by Joseph F. Rock. Vol. LVIII, pp. 402-435, Oct., 1930.

Demon Dancers and Butter Gods of Choni. 16 ills. in color from photographs by Joseph F. Rock. Vol. LIV, pp. 584-601, Nov., 1928.

Demon-Possessed Tibetans and Their Incredible Feats. 12 ills. in color from natural-color photographs ; 8 ills. by Joseph F. Rock. Vol. LXVIII, pp. 479-486, Oct., 1935.

Experiences of a Lone Geographer : An American Agricultural Explorer Makes His Way Through Brigand-infested Central China en Route to the Amne Machin Range, Tibet. By Joseph F. Rock. Vol. XLVIII, pp. 331-347, 16 ills., 1 quarter-page map, Sept., 1925.

Glories of the Minya Konka : Magnificent Snow Peaks of the China-Tibetan Border Are Photographed at Close Range by a National Geographic Society Expedition. By Joseph F. Rock. Vol. LVIII, pp. 385-437, 35 ills. in black and white, 24 ills. in color, 1 three-quarters-page map, Oct., 1930.

Hunting the Chaulmoogra Tree. By Joseph F. Rock. Vol. XLI, pp. 243-276, 39 ills., 1 page map, Mar., 1922.

Konka Risumgongba, Holy Mountain of the Outlaws. By Joseph F. Rock. Vol. LX, pp. 1-65, 36 ills. in black and white, 43 ills. in color. 1 three-quarters-page map, July, 1931.

Rock, Joseph F.—*Continued*

Land of the Yellow Lama : National Geographic Society Explorer Visits the Strange Kingdom of Muli, Beyond the Likiang Snow Range of Yünnan Province, China. By Joseph F. Rock. Vol. XLVII, pp. 447-491, 39 ills., 1 half-page map, Apr., 1925.

Life Among the Lamas of Choni : Describing the Mystery Plays and Butter Festival in the Monastery of an Almost Unknown Tibetan Principality in Kansu Province, China. By Joseph F. Rock. Vol. LIV, pp. 569-619, 34 ills. in black and white, 16 ills. in color, 1 half-page map, Nov., 1928.

Seeking the Mountains of Mystery : An Expedition on the China-Tibet Frontier to the Unexplored Amnyi Machen Range, One of Whose Peaks Rivals Everest. By Joseph F. Rock. Vol. LVII, pp. 131-185, 54 ills., 1 two-page map, Feb., 1930.

Sungmas, the Living Oracles of the Tibetan Church. By Joseph F. Rock. Vol. LXVIII, pp. 475-486, 1 ill. in black and white, 12 ills. in color, Oct., 1935.

Through the Great River Trenches of Asia : National Geographic Society Explorer Follows the Yangtze, Mekong, and Salwin Through Mighty Gorges, Some of Whose Canyon Walls Tower to a Height of More Than Two Miles. By Joseph F. Rock. Vol. L, pp. 133-186, 47 ills., 1 half-page map, Aug., 1926.

With the Devil Dancers of China and Tibet. 43 ills. in color from natural-color photographs by Joseph F. Rock. Vol. LX, pp. 18-59, July, 1931.

Rock City of Petra. By Franklin E. Hoskins. Vol. XVIII, pp. 283-291, 5 ills., May, 1907.

Rock of Aden : The Volcanic Mountain Fortress, on the Sea Route from Suez to India, Assumes New Importance. By H. G. C. Swayne. Vol. LXVIII, pp. 723-742, 24 ills., 1 half-page map, Dec., 1935.

Rock of Gibraltar : Key to the Mediterranean. 17 ills. from photographs. Vol. LXXVIII, pp. 376-391, Sept., 1940.

Rockefeller, John D., Jr.:

Genesis of the Williamsburg Restoration. By John D. Rockefeller, Jr. Vol. LXXI, p. 401, Apr., 1937.

Rocket Bombs:

London Wins the Battle. By Marquis W. Childs. Vol. LXXXVIII, pp. 129-152, 21 ills., Aug., 1945.

Rockets:

Air Power for Peace. By Gen. H. H. Arnold. Vol. LXXXIX, pp. 137-193, 35 ills. in black and white, 28 ills. in color, special map supplement, Feb., 1946.

New Frontier in the Sky. By F. Barrows Colton. Vol. XC, pp. 379-408, 28 ills., 1 diagram, Sept., 1946.

Rocky Mountain National Park, Colorado :

Photographing the Marvels of the West in Colors. By Fred Payne Clatworthy. Vol. LIII, pp. 694-719, 30 ills. in color, June, 1928.

Rocky Mountain Sheep:

High Country of Colorado. By Alfred M. Bailey. With 23 ills. in color from natural-color photographs by the author, Robert J. Niedrach, and F. G. Brandenburg. Vol. XC, pp. 43-72, 9 ills. in black and white, July, 1946.

Rocky Mountains, Canada-United States :

Among the Peaks and Parks of the Rockies. 12 ills. in color from natural-color photographs by Fred Payne Clatworthy and H. L. Standley. Vol. LXII, pp. 38-47, July, 1932.

Bighorn Mountains. By N. H. Darton. Vol. XVIII, pp. 355-364, 7 ills., 1 page map, June, 1907.

Colorado, a Barrier That Became a Goal : Where Water Has Transformed Dry Plains Into Verdant Farms, and Highways Have Opened up Mineral and Scenic Wealth. By McFall Kerbey. Vol. LXII, pp. 1 63, 56 ills. in black and white, 12 ills. in color, 1 page map, July, 1932.

Exploration in the Canadian Rockies. Vol. X, pp. 135-136, Apr., 1899.

Geologist's Paradise. By Charles D. Walcott. Vol. XXII, pp. 509-536, 28 ills., panorama, June, 1911.

Lords of the Rockies : Photographing Big Game Animals in Their Primeval Surroundings, from Arizona to Canada, Brings Adventure to Two Wilderness Wanderers. By Wendell and Lucie Chapman. Vol. LXXVI, pp. 87-128, 14 ills. in black and white, 28 ills. in color, July, 1939.

Monarch of the Canadian Rockies (Mount Robson). By Charles D. Walcott. Vol. XXIV, pp. 626-639, 13 ills., panorama, May, 1913.

Monarch of the Canadian Rockies—Robson Peak. Vol. XXIV, panorama, May, 1913.

Mother of Rivers : An Account of a Photographic Expedition to the Great Columbia Ice Field of the Canadian Rockies. By Lewis R. Freeman. Vol. XLVII, pp. 377-446, 60 ills., 1 three-quarters and 1 quarter-page maps, Apr., 1925.

Our Mountain Panorama. Vol. XXII, supplement, June, 1911.

Our Northern Rockies. By R. H. Chapman. Vol. XIII, pp. 361-372, 10 ills., Oct., 1902.

Peaks and Parks of Western Canada. 11 ills. from photographs ; 5 ills. by W. J. Oliver. Vol. LXXX, pp. 516-526, Oct., 1941.

Peaks and Trails in the Canadian Alps. 16 ills. in duotone from photographs by Byron Harmon and Clifford White. Vol. LXV, pp. 627-642, May, 1934.

Photographing the Marvels of the West in Colors. By Fred Payne Clatworthy. Vol. LIII, pp. 694-719, 30 ills. in color, June, 1928.

Recent Exploration in the Canadian Rockies. By Walter D. Wilcox. Part I, Vol. XIII, pp. 151-168, 12 ills., 1 page map, May, 1902. Part II, Vol. XIII, pp. 185-200, 9 ills., June, 1902.

Rocky Mountains, Canada-United States—*Continued*

Some Tramps Across the Glaciers and Snowfields of British Columbia. By Howard Palmer. Vol. XXI, pp. 457-487, 25 ills., June, 1910.

With Wild Animals in the Rockies. By Lucie and Wendell Chapman. Vol. LXVIII, pp. 231-249, 26 ills. in duotone, Aug., 1935.

World's Highest Altitudes and First Ascents. By Charles E. Fay. Vol. XX, pp. 493-530, 25 ills., June, 1909.

Rodents:

Dipo, the Little Desert "Kangaroo." By Walter E. Ketcham. Vol. LXXVIII, pp. 537-548, 14 ills., Oct., 1940.

Into the Land of the Chipmunk. By Ruth Alexander Nichols. Vol. LX, pp. 77-98, 28 ills., July, 1931.

Mickey the Beaver: An Animal Engineer Performs for the Camera as a Star in the Activities of His Species. By James MacGillivray. Vol. LIV, pp. 741-756, 23 ills., Dec., 1928.

Plague of Mice. Vol. XX, pp. 478-485, 7 ills., May, 1909.

Rat Pest: The Labor of 200,000 Men in the United States Required to Support Rats, Man's Most Destructive and Dangerous Enemy. By E. W. Nelson. Vol. XXXII, pp. 1-23, 21 ills., July, 1917.

Tracking the Columbian Ground-Squirrel to Its Burrow: Loss of Millions to Crops and Danger of the Spread of Spotted Fever Necessitated Study of Peculiar Rodent of Western North America. By William T. Shaw. Vol. XLVII, pp. 587-596, 13 ills., May, 1925.

Rodey, B. S.:

Arizona and New Mexico. By B. S. Rodey. Vol. XVII, pp. 100-102, 2 ills., Feb., 1906.

Rogers, Bernard F., Jr.:

Ireland: Mist and Sunshine of Ulster. By Bernard F. Rogers, Jr. Vol. LXVIII, pp. 571-610, 23 ills. in black and white, 21 ills. in color, 1 three-quarters-page map, Nov., 1935.

Ireland: Rambles Through Ulster, Northern Tip of the Shamrock Isle. 21 ills. in color from natural-color photographs by Bernard F. Rogers, Jr. Vol. LXVIII, pp. 577-600, Nov., 1935.

Italy: Caesar's City Today (Rome). 21 ills. in color from natural-color photographs by Bernard F. Rogers, Jr., and Luigi Pellerano. Vol. LXXI, pp. 285-316, Mar., 1937.

Switzerland: Green Gruyère, Home of a Swiss Cheese. 23 ills. in color from natural-color photographs by Bernard F. Rogers, Jr. Vol. LXX, pp. 145-168, Aug., 1936.

Turkey: Old Pattern and New in Turkey. 23 ills. in color from natural-color photographs by Bernard F. Rogers, Jr. Vol. LXXV, pp. 17-48, Jan., 1939.

Rogers, G. Sherburne:

Helium: The New Balloon Gas. By G. Sherburne Rogers. Vol. XXXV, pp. 441-456, 11 ills., May, 1919.

Rogues' Gallery of Imported Pests (Insects). 10 ills. in color from paintings by Hashime Murayama. Vol. LXXX, pp. 237-244, Aug., 1941.

Rohe, Alice:

Our Littlest Ally (San Marino). By Alice Rohe. Vol. XXXIV, pp. 139-163, 17 ills., Aug., 1918.

Roman Way. By Edith Hamilton. Vol. XC, pp. 545-565, 14 ills., 1 two-page map, Nov., 1946.

Romance of Discovery Series:

Caravels of Columbus. Reproduction in color of the painting by N. C. Wyeth, National Geographic Society, Washington, D. C. Vol. LIV, text, p. 55; supplement, July, 1928.

Commander Byrd at the North Pole. Reproduction in color of the painting by N. C. Wyeth, National Geographic Society, Washington, D. C. Vol. LIII, supplement, May, 1928.

The Discoverer. Reproduction in color of the painting by N. C. Wyeth, National Geographic Society, Washington, D. C. Vol. LIII, text, p. 347; supplement, Mar., 1928.

Map of Discovery (Eastern Hemisphere). Reproduction in color of the painting by N. C. Wyeth, National Geographic Society, Washington, D. C. Vol. LIV, text, p. 568; supplement, Nov., 1928.

Map of Discovery (Western Hemisphere). Reproduction in color of the painting by N. C. Wyeth, National Geographic Society, Washington, D. C. Vol. LV, text, p. 93; supplement, Jan., 1929.

Romance of Military Insignia: How the United States Government Recognizes Deeds of Heroism and Devotion to Duty. By Robert E. Wyllie. Vol. XXXVI, pp. 463-501, 27 ills., Dec., 1919.

Romance of Science in Polynesia: An Account of Five Years of Cruising Among the South Sea Islands. By Robert Cushman Murphy. Vol. XLVIII, pp. 355-426, 66 ills. in black and white, 16 ills. in color, 3 half-page maps, Oct., 1925.

Romania (Rumania):

American Girl Cycles Across Romania: Two-wheel Pilgrim Pedals the Land of Castles and Gypsies, Where Roman Empire Traces Mingle With Remnants of Oriental Migration. By Dorothy Hosmer. Vol. LXXIV, pp. 557-588, 31 ills., 1 page map, Nov., 1938.

Caviar Fishermen of Romania: From Vâlcov, "Little Venice" of the Danube Delta, Bearded Russian Exiles Go Down to the Sea. By Dorothy Hosmer. Vol. LXXVII, pp. 407-434, 29 ills., 1 third-page map, Mar., 1940.

Changing Map in the Balkans. By Frederick Moore. Vol. XXIV, pp. 199-226, 27 ills., 1 page map, Feb., 1913.

Romania (Rumania)—*Continued*

New Map of Europe : Showing the Boundaries Established by the Peace Conference at Paris and by Subsequent Decisions of the Supreme Council of the Allied and Associated Powers. By Ralph A. Graves. Text accompanying special map supplement in colors. Vol. XXXIX, pp. 157-177, 10 ills., Feb., 1921.

Notes on Rumania. Vol. XXIII, pp. 1218-1225, 8 ills., Dec., 1912.

Palaces and Peasants in Rome's Old Colony. 14 ills. in color from natural-color photographs by Wilhelm Tobien. Vol. LXV, pp. 439-446, Apr., 1934.

Races of Europe. By Edwin A. Grosvenor. Vol. XXXIV, pp. 441-534, 62 ills., 2 page maps, special map supplement, Dec., 1918.

Romania, Land of Color and Contrast. 15 ills. in color from natural-color photographs by Wilhelm Tobien. Vol. LXV, pp. 415-422, Apr., 1934.

Roumania, the Pivotal State. By James Howard Gore. Vol. XXVIII, pp. 360-390, 39 ills., Oct., 1915.

Roumania and Its Rubicon. By John Oliver La Gorce. Vol. XXX, pp. 185-202, 11 ills., Sept., 1916.

Rumania and Her Ambitions. By Frederick Moore. Vol. XXIV, pp. 1057-1085, 34 ills., Oct., 1913.

Rumanian Peasant Girl. Vol. XXIV, p. 1084, Oct., 1913.

Spell of Romania : An American Woman's Narrative of Her Wanderings Among Colorful People and Long Hidden Shrines. By Henrietta Allen Holmes. Vol. LXV, pp. 399-450, 37 ills. in black and white, 29 ills. in color, 1 half-page map, Apr., 1934.

Transylvania and Its Seven Castles : A Motor Circuit Through Rumania's New Province of Racial Complexity and Architectural Charm. By J. Theodore Marriner. Vol. XLIX, pp. 319-352, 35 ills., 1 half-page map, Mar., 1926.

Whirlpool of the Balkans. By George Higgins Moses. Vol. XXXIX, pp. 179-197, 15 ills., Feb., 1921.

Romans, Ancient :

Ancient Rome Brought to Life. By Rhys Carpenter. Paintings by H. M. Herget. Vol. XC, pp. 567-633, 2 ills. in black and white, 32 ills. in color, 1 half-page map, Nov., 1946.

The Roman Way. By Edith Hamilton. Vol. XC, pp. 545-565, 14 ills., 1 two-page map, Nov., 1946.

Romantic Spain. By Charles Upson Clark. Vol. XXI, pp. 187-215, 40 ills., 1 half-page map, Mar., 1910.

Rome, Italy :

Ancient Rome Brought to Life. By Rhys Carpenter. Paintings by H. M. Herget. Vol. XC, pp. 567-633, 2 ills. in black and white, 32 ills. in color, 1 half-page map, Nov., 1946.

Rome, Italy—*Continued*

Contents : Before Rome Was Founded.—Etruscan Funeral.—Etruscan Festival.—Bridge over the Tiber.—Market and Wharf at a Roman Port.—At the Slave Market.—The Roman Army Crosses Alcántara in Spain.—Siege of a Walled City.—Triumphal Procession.—Unconditional Surrender.—An Embassy to Caligula.—An Empress Makes Ready.—In the Gardens of Lucullus.—A Distinguished Dinner Party.—Horace's Villa in the Sabine Hills.—Interior of a Rich Man's House.—Vegetable Market.—Tunisian Farm.—Street Scene in Pompeii.—In a Pompeian Tavern.—Seaside Villas.—Roman Baths : Tepidarium.—Furnaces Beneath the Baths.—Worship of Isis.—Rehearsal for the Mysteries.—Sacrifice of the "Suovetaurilia."—In a Court of Law.—The Library in Timgad.—At the Theater.—Sea Battle in the Arena.—Diocletian's Palace at Spalato.—Dusk on the Street of Tombs.

Augustus—Emperor and Architect : Two Thousand Years Ago Was Born the Physically Frail But Spiritually Great Roman Who Became the Master of His World. By W. Coleman Nevils. Vol. LXXIV, pp. 535-556, 17 ills., 1 half-page map, Oct., 1938.

Caesar's City Today. 21 ills. in color from natural-color photographs by Bernard F. Rogers, Jr., and Luigi Pellerano. Vol. LXXI, pp. 285-316, Mar., 1937.

Fearful Famines of the Past : History Will Repeat Itself Unless the American People Conserve Their Resources. By Ralph A. Graves. Vol. XXXII, pp. 68-90, 11 ills., July, 1917.

Imperial Rome Reborn. By John Patric. Vol. LXXI, pp. 269-325, 34 ills. in black and white, 21 ills. in color, Mar., 1937.

Inexhaustible Italy. By Arthur Stanley Riggs. Vol. XXX, pp. 273-368, 76 ills., 1 page map, Oct., 1916.

Isle of Capri : An Imperial Residence and Probable Wireless Station of Ancient Rome. By John A. Kingman. Vol. XXXVI, pp. 213-231, 17 ills., Sept., 1919.

Italy's Monuments Tell Rome's Magnificence. 8 ills. from photographs ; 7 ills. by B. Anthony Stewart. Vol. LXXVII, pp. 371-378, Mar., 1940.

Perennial Geographer : After 2,000 Years Vergil Is Still Most Widely Read of Latin Poets—First to Popularize the Geography of the Roman Empire. By W. Coleman Nevils. Vol. LVIII, pp. 439-465, 29 ills., Oct., 1930.

The Roman Way. By Edith Hamilton. Vol. XC, pp. 545-565, 14 ills., 1 two-page map, Nov., 1946.

Splendor of Rome. By Florence Craig Albrecht. Vol. XLI, pp. 593-626, 28 ills., June, 1922.

See also Vatican City.

Rongerik (Atoll), Marshall Islands :

Farewell to Bikini. By Carl Markwith. Vol. XC, pp. 97-116, 16 ills., July, 1946.

Roosevelt, Franklin D.:

Ellsworth Awarded the Hubbard Medal (Presentation by Franklin D. Roosevelt). Vol. LXX, p. 36, July, 1936.

Roosevelt, Theodore:

Cotton and the Chinese Boycott (From an Address by President Roosevelt). Vol. XVI, pp. 516-517, Nov., 1905.

Forests Vital to Our Welfare (From an Address by President Roosevelt). Vol. XVI, pp. 515-516, Nov., 1905.

Honors to Peary (Address by President Roosevelt). Vol. XVIII, pp. 49-60, 1 ill., Jan., 1907.

How Old Is Man? By Theodore Roosevelt. Vol. XXIX, pp. 111-127, 12 ills., 1 page and 2 half-page maps, Feb., 1916.

Mr. Roosevelt's "African Game Trails." Vol. XXI, pp. 953-962, 9 ills., Nov., 1910.

National Geographic Society (Report and Cables Concerning African Expedition by Theodore Roosevelt). Vol. XXI, pp. 365-370, 5 ills., Apr., 1910.

Roosevelt African Trophies. Vol. XXII, pp. 103-106, 4 ills., Jan., 1911.

Where Roosevelt Will Hunt. By Sir Harry Johnston. Vol. XX, pp. 207-256, 43 ills., special map supplement, Mar., 1909.

Wild Man and Wild Beast in Africa. By Theodore Roosevelt. Vol. XXII, pp. 1-33, 41 ills., 1 page map, Jan., 1911.

Roosevelt (Ship):

Commander Peary's New Vessel. Vol. XVI, p. 192, Apr., 1905.

Roosevelt Dam, Arizona:

Highest Dam in the World. Vol. XVI, pp. 440-441, Sept., 1905.

Home-Making by the Government: An Account of the Eleven Immense Irrigating Projects to be Opened in 1908. By C. J. Blanchard. Vol. XIX, pp. 250-287, 23 ills., Apr., 1908.

Spirit of the West: The Wonderful Agricultural Development Since the Dawn of Irrigation. By C. J. Blanchard. Vol. XXI, pp. 333-360, 15 ills., Apr., 1910.

Root, A. I.:

Our Friends, the Bees. By A. I. and E. R. Root. Vol. XXII, pp. 675-694, 21 ills., July, 1911.

Root, E. R.:

Our Friends, the Bees. By A. I. and E. R. Root. Vol. XXII, pp. 675-694, 21 ills., July, 1911.

Root, Elihu:

Awakened Continent to the South of Us. By Elihu Root. Vol. XVIII, pp. 61-72, Jan., 1907.

Roraima (Mountain), British Guiana:

Kaieteur and Roraima: The Great Falls and the Great Mountain of the Guianas. By Henry Edward Crampton. Vol. XXXVIII, pp. 227-244, 12 ills., 1 half-page map, Sept., 1920.

Roraima (Mountain), British Guiana—Continued

Through Brazil to the Summit of Mount Roraima. By G. H. H. Tate. Vol. LVIII, pp. 585-605, 24 ills., 1 half-page map, Nov., 1930.

Rosa, Monte (Mountain), Alps:

Woman's Climbs in the High Alps. By Dora Keen. Vol. XXII, pp. 642-675, 26 ills., July, 1911.

Rosales, (Marchesa) Louise de:

Letters from the Italian Front. By Marchesa Louise de Rosales to Ethel Mather Bagg. Vol. XXXII, pp. 46-67, 22 ills., July, 1917.

Rose Oil Industry:

Bulgaria's Valley of Roses. 13 ills. in color from natural-color photographs by Wilhelm Tobien and Georg Paskoff. Vol. LXII, pp. 186-195, Aug., 1932.

Rose-Red City of Rock (Petra, Trans-Jordan). 21 ills. in color from natural-color photographs by G. E. Matson. Vol. LXVII, pp. 145-160, Feb., 1935.

Rotch, A. Lawrence:

Project for the Exploration of the Atmosphere Over the Tropical Oceans. By A. Lawrence Rotch. Vol. XV, p. 430, Oct., 1904.

Rothenburg, Germany:

Rothenburg, the City Time Forgot. By Charles W. Beck, Jr. Vol. XLIX, pp. 184-194, 8 ills. in color, Feb., 1926.

Rotterdam, Netherlands:

Holland Rises from War and Water. By Thomas R. Henry. Vol. LXXXIX, pp. 237-260, 18 ills., 1 seven-eighths-page map, Feb., 1946.

Rouen, France:

Beauties of France. By Arthur Stanley Riggs. Vol. XXVIII, pp. 391-491, 73 ills. in black and white, 16 ills. in color, 1 half-page map, Nov., 1915.

Coasts of Normandy and Brittany. By W. Robert Moore. Vol. LXXXIV, pp. 205-232, 5 ills. in black and white, 21 ills. in color, 1 two-page map, Aug., 1943.

Normandy and Brittany in Brighter Days. 21 ills. in color from natural-color photographs by W. Robert Moore, Peter Upton Muir, and others. Vol. LXXXIV, pp. 209-232, Aug., 1943.

Roughley, T. C.:

Fantastic Dwellers in a Coral Fairyland (Great Barrier Reef). 15 ills. in color from natural-color photographs by T. C. Roughley. Vol. LXXVII, pp. 831-838, June, 1940.

Where Nature Runs Riot: On Australia's Great Barrier Reef Marine Animals Grow to Unusual Size, Develop Strange Weapons of Attack and Defense, and Acquire Brilliant Colors. By T. C. Roughley. Vol. LXXVII, pp. 823-850, 18 ills. in black and white, 15 ills. in color, 1 page map, June, 1940.

Roumania. *See* Romania.

Roumania, the Pivotal State. By James Howard Gore. Vol. XXVIII, pp. 360-390, 32 ills., Oct., 1915.

Roumania and Its Rubicon. By John Oliver La Gorce. Vol. XXX, pp. 185-202, 11 ills., Sept., 1916.

Round About Bogotá: A Hunt for New Fruits and Plants Among the Mountain Forests of Colombia's Unique Capital. By Wilson Popenoe. Vol. XLIX, pp. 127-160, 34 ills., 1 third-page map, Feb., 1926.

Round About Grim Tarawa. 19 ills. in color from natural-color photographs by W. Robert Moore. Vol. LXXXVII, pp. 137-160, Feb., 1945.

Round About Liechtenstein: A Tiny Principality Which the Visitor May Encompass in a Single View Affords Adventurous Climbs Among Steep Pastures and Quaint Villages. By Maynard Owen Williams. Vol. LII, pp. 611-634, 18 ills., 1 half-page map, Nov., 1927.

Round Trip to Davy Jones's Locker: Peering into Mysteries a Quarter Mile Down in the Open Sea, by Means of the Bathysphere. By William Beebe. Vol. LIX, pp. 653-678, 14 ills. in black and white, 8 ills. in color, 1 quarter-page map, June, 1931.

Rounding the Horn in a Windjammer. By A. J. Villiers. Vol. LIX, pp. 191-224, 36 ills., 1 two-thirds-page map, Feb., 1931.

Route Over Which Moses Led the Children of Israel Out of Egypt. By Franklin E. Hoskins. Vol. XX, pp. 1011-1038, 24 ills., 1 page map, Dec., 1909.

Routledge, (Mrs.) Scoresby:

Mystery of Easter Island. By Mrs. Scoresby Routledge. Vol. XL, pp. 628-646, 13 ills., 1 page map, Dec., 1921.

Roy, Leonard C.:

From Notch to Notch in the White Mountains: Soaring Heights of New Hampshire Attract Multitudes to America's Oldest Mountain Recreation Area. By Leonard Cornell Roy. Vol. LXXII, pp. 73-104, 30 ills., special map supplement, July, 1937.

Highlights of the Volunteer State: Men and Industry in Tennessee Range from Pioneer Stages to Modern Machine Age. By Leonard Cornell Roy. Vol. LXXV, pp. 553-594, 20 ills. in black and white, 22 ills. in color, 1 map, May, 1939.

Rambling Around the Roof of Eastern America (Great Smoky Mountains). By Leonard C. Roy. Vol. LXX, pp. 243-266, 25 ills., 1 page map, Aug., 1936.

Tarheelia on Parade: Versatile and Vibrant, North Carolina in a Generation Has Climbed New Economic Heights. By Leonard C. Roy. Vol. LXXX, pp. 181-224, 24 ills. in black and white, 21 ills. in color, 1 map (two-page spread), Aug., 1941.

Royal Copenhagen, Capital of a Farming Kingdom: A Fifth of Denmark's Thrifty Population Resides in a Metropolis Famous for Its Porcelains, Its Silver, and Its Lace. By J. R. Hildebrand. Vol. LXI, pp. 217-250, 26 ills. in black and white, 14 ills. in color, Feb., 1932.

Royale, Isle, Michigan;

Winter Sky Roads to Isle Royal. By Ben East. Vol. LX, pp. 759-774, 18 ills., 1 half-page map, Dec., 1931.

Ruanda (Region), Belgian Congo:

Land of Giants and Pygmies. By Duke Adolphus Frederick of Mecklenburg. Vol. XXIII, pp. 367-388, 16 ills., 1 page map, Apr., 1912.

Rubber:

Amazon, Father of Waters: The Earth's Mightiest River Drains a Basin of More than 2,700,-000 Square Miles, from Which Came Originally the World's Finest Rubber. By W. L. Schurz. Vol. XLIX, pp. 445-463, 15 ills., Apr., 1926.

Our Most Versatile Vegetable Product: Rubber Drops from Millions of Tropical Trees Are Transformed by Genii Chemists into Myriad Articles, from Tires to Teething Rings. By J. R. Hildebrand. Vol. LXXVII, pp. 143-200, 51 ills. in black and white, 26 ills. in color, Feb., 1940.

Rubber: From Trees to Tires and Toys. 26 ills. in color from natural-color photographs by Willard R. Culver and J. Baylor Roberts. Vol. LXXVII, pp. 159-190, Feb., 1940.

Rubber Plantations in Mexico and Central America. Vol. XIV, pp. 409-414, 7 ills., Nov., 1903.

Singapore, Crossroads of the East: The World's Greatest Mart for Rubber and Tin Was in Recent Times a Pirate-Haunted, Tiger-Infested Jungle Isle. By Frederick Simpich. Vol. XLIX, pp. 235-269, 32 ills., 1 half-page map, Mar., 1926.

Rug Industry:

Russia's Orphan Races: Picturesque Peoples Who Cluster on the Southeastern Borderland of the Vast Slav Dominions. By Maynard Owen Williams. Vol. XXXIV, pp. 245-278, 26 ills., 1 page map, Oct., 1918.

Ruhr (District), Germany:

Story of the Ruhr. By Frederick Simpich. Vol. XLI, pp. 553-564, 11 ills., 1 third-page map, May, 1922.

Ruined Cities of Asia Minor. By Ernest L. Harris. Vol. XIX, pp. 741-760, 11 ills., Nov., 1908.

Ruins. *See* Archeology.

Ruins at Selinus (Sicily). By Marion Crawford. Vol. XX, p. 117, Jan., 1909.

Ruins of an Ancient Inca Capital, Machu Picchu. Vol. XXIV, panorama, Apr., 1913.

Ruins of Cuicuilco May Revolutionize Our History of Ancient America: Lofty Mound Sealed and Preserved by Great Lava Flow for Perhaps Seventy Centuries Is Now Being Excavated in Mexico. By Byron Cummings. Vol. XLIV, pp. 203-220, 21 ills., 1 third-page map, Aug., 1923.

Rumania. *See* Romania.

Rumania and Her Ambitions. By Frederick Moore. Vol. XXIV, pp. 1057-1085, 34 ills., Oct., 1913.

Rumanian Peasant Girl. Vol. XXIV, p. 1084, Oct., 1913.

Rumeli Hissar, Turkey:

American Alma Maters in the Near East. By Maynard Owen Williams. Vol. LXXXVIII, pp. 237-256, 16 ills., Aug., 1945.

Rural Britain Carries On. By Harvey Klemmer. Vol. LXXX, pp. 527-552, 27 ills., Oct., 1941.

Rural Hungarian Rhapsody. 20 ills. in color from natural-color photographs by Rudolf Balogh and Hans Hildenbrand. Vol. LXXIII, pp. 17-48, Jan., 1938.

Rural Sweden Through American Eyes: A Visitor in Peacetime Finds Warmth, Welcome, and Strange Folkways On a Century-old Farm. By Elizabeth W. Nilson. Vol. LXXVII, pp. 795-822, 8 ills. in black and white, 22 ills. in color, June, 1940.

Russell, Carl P.:

White Sands of Alamogordo (New Mexico): A Dry Ocean of Granular Gypsum Billows Under Desert Winds in a New National Playground. By Carl P. Russell. Vol. LXVIII, pp. 250-264, 12 ills., Aug., 1935.

Russell, Israel C.:

National Geographic Society Expedition in the West Indies. Vol. XIII, pp. 209-213, 2 half-page maps, June, 1902.

National Geographic Society Expedition to Martinique and St. Vincent. Vol. XIII, pp. 183-184, 2 ills., June, 1902.

National Geographic Society Notes (Election of Dr. Russell to Board of Managers). Vol. XIII, pp. 218-219, 1 ill., June, 1902.

Recent Volcanic Eruptions in the West Indies. By Israel C. Russell. Vol. XIII, pp. 267-285, 7 ills., July, 1902.

Timberlines. By Israel C. Russell. Vol. XV, pp. 47-49, Jan., 1904.

Volcanic Eruptions on Martinique and St. Vincent. By Israel C. Russell. Vol. XIII, pp. 415-436, 10 ills., Dec., 1902.

Volcanic Rocks of Martinique and St. Vincent: Collected by Robert T. Hill and Israel C. Russell. By J. S. Diller. Vol. XIII, pp. 285-296, July, 1902.

Russia. *See* Union of Soviet Socialist Republics.

Russia. By Charles Emory Smith. Vol. XVI, pp. 55-63, Feb., 1905.

Russia from Within: Her War of Yesterday, To-day, and Tomorrow. By Stanley Washburn. Vol. XXXII, pp. 91-120, 30 ills., Aug., 1917.

Russia in Recent Literature. By Maj. Gen. A. W. Greely. Vol. XVI, pp. 564-568, Dec., 1905.

Russia of the Hour: Giant Battle Ground for Theories of Economy, Society, and Politics, as Observed by an Unbiased Correspondent. By Junius B. Wood. Vol. L, pp. 519-598, 81 ills., Nov., 1926.

Russian Development of Manchuria. By Henry B. Miller. Vol. XV, pp. 113-127, 11 ills., 1 half-page map, Mar., 1904.

Russian Expedition to Spitzbergen. Vol. XII, p. 404, Nov., 1901.

Russian Situation and Its Significance to America. By Stanley Washburn. Vol. XXXI, pp. 371-382, 8 ills., Apr., 1917.

Russian Soviet Federated Socialist Republic, U. S. S. R.:

I Learn About the Russians. By Eddy Gilmore. Vol. LXXXIV, pp. 619-640, 21 ills., Nov., 1943.

Mother Volga Defends Her Own. By Maynard Owen Williams. Vol. LXXXII, p. 793-811, 21 ills., Dec., 1942.

New Road to Asia. By Owen Lattimore. Vol. LXXXVI, pp. 641-676, 15 ills. in black and white, 26 ills. in color, Dec., 1944.

Roaming Russia's Caucasus: Rugged Mountains and Hardy Fighters Guard the Soviet Union's Caucasian Treasury of Manganese and Oil. By Rolf Singer. Vol. LXXXII, pp. 91-121, 33 ills., July, 1942.

Society's New Map of Soviet Russia. Text accompanying special map supplement in colors. Vol. LXXXVI, pp. 716-718, Dec., 1944.

See also Crimean Autonomous Soviet Socialist Republic; Dagestan Autonomous Soviet Socialist Republic; Magnitogorsk.

Russian Turkistan. *See* Soviet Central Asia.

Russians:

I Learn About the Russians. By Eddy Gilmore. Vol. LXXXIV, pp. 619-640, 21 ills., Nov., 1943.

"Magnetic City" (Magnitogorsk), Core of Valiant Russia's Industrial Might. By John Scott. Vol. LXXXIII, pp. 525-556, 27 ills., 1 two-page map, May, 1943.

New Road to Asia. By Owen Lattimore. Vol. LXXXVI, pp. 641-676, 15 ills. in black and white, 26 ills. in color, Dec., 1944.

Roaming Russia's Caucasus: Rugged Mountains and Hardy Fighters Guard the Soviet Union's Caucasian Treasury of Manganese and Oil. By Rolf Singer. Vol. LXXXII, pp. 91-121, 33 ills., July, 1942.

Russia's Democrats. By Montgomery Schuyler. Vol. XXXI, pp. 210-240, 25 ills., Mar., 1917.

Russia's Man of the Hour: Alexander Kerensky's First Speeches and Proclamations. Vol. XXXII, pp. 24-25, 17 ills., July, 1917.

Russia's Orphan Races: Picturesque Peoples Who Cluster on the Southeastern Borderland of the Vast Slav Dominions. By Maynard Owen Williams. Vol. XXXIV, pp. 245-278, 26 ills., 1 page map, Oct., 1918.

Russia's Wheat Surplus. Vol. XVII, pp. 580-583, Oct., 1906.

Ruwenzori (Mountains), Central Africa:
Amid the Snow Peaks of the Equator: A Naturalist's Explorations Around Ruwenzori, with an Excursion to the Congo State, and an Account of the Terrible Scourge of Sleeping Sickness. By A. F. R. Wollaston. Vol. XX, pp. 256-277, 11 ills., Mar., 1909.

Flights from Arctic to Equator: Conquering the Alps, the Ice Peaks of Spitsbergen, of Persia, and Africa's Mountains of the Moon. By Walter Mittelholzer. Vol. LXI, pp. 445-498, 53 ills., 1 three-quarters-page map, Apr., 1932.

World's Highest Altitudes and First Ascents. By Charles E. Fay. Vol. XX, pp. 493-530, 25 ills., June, 1909.

Ryan, Inez Buffington:
Land of William the Conqueror (Normandy): Where Northmen Came to Build Castles and Cathedrals. By Inez Buffington Ryan. Vol. LXI, pp. 89-99, 13 ills. in color, Jan., 1932.

Maid of France Rides By: Compiègne, Where Joan of Arc Fought Her Last Battle, Celebrates Her Fifth Centenary. By Inez Buffington Ryan. Vol. LXII, pp. 607-617, 15 ills. in color, Nov., 1932.

Ryukyu Retto (Nansei Islands), Japan:
Peacetime Rambles in the Ryukyus. By William Leonard Schwartz. Vol. LXXXVII, pp. 543-561, 12 ills., 1 two-thirds-page and 1 half-page maps, May, 1945.
See also Okinawa.

S

Saar (Region), Germany:
Close-Ups of a People Without a Country. 23 ills. in duotone. Vol. LXVII, pp. 249-264, Feb., 1935.

What Is the Saar? By Frederick Simpich. Vol. LXVII, pp. 241-264, 5 ills. in black and white, 23 ills. in duotone, 1 half-page and 1 third-page maps, Feb., 1935.

Saba (Island), Leeward Islands:
Saba, Crater Treasure of the Indies. By Charles W. Herbert. Vol. LXXVIII, pp. 597-620, 14 ills. in black and white, 12 ills. in color, 1 map (inset), Nov., 1940.

Up and Down on Saba. 12 ills. in color from natural-color photographs by Charles W. Herbert. Vol. LXXVIII, pp. 605-612, Nov., 1940.

Saboteur Mosquitoes. By Harry H. Stage. Vol. LXXXV, pp. 165-179, 12 ills., Feb., 1944.

Sacramento (River), California:
More Water for California's Great Central Valley. By Frederick Simpich. Vol. XC, pp. 645-664, 16 ills., 1 page map, Nov., 1946.

Sacred City of the Sands (Kairouan, Tunisia). By Frank Edward Johnson. Vol. XXII, pp. 1061-1093, 25 ills., 1 half-page map, Dec., 1911.

Sacred Ibis Cemetery and Jackal Catacombs at Abydos. By Camden M. Cobern. Vol. XXIV, pp. 1042-1056, 10 ills., Sept., 1913.

Sacsahuaman (Fortress), Peru:
Greatest Achievement of Ancient Man in America, the Fortress of Sacsahuaman. Vol. XXIX, supplement, May, 1916.

Safford, William E.:
Our Smallest Possession—Guam. By William E. Safford. Vol. XVI, pp. 229-237, 5 ills., May, 1905.

Saga of the Carrier *Princeton*. By Capt. William H. Buracker, USN. Vol. LXXXVIII, pp. 189-218, 8 ills. in black and white, 22 ills. in color, 1 map (two-page spread), Aug., 1945.

Sagacity and Courage of Dogs: Instances of the Remarkable Intelligence and Unselfish Devotion of Man's Best Friend Among Dumb Animals. Vol. XXXV, pp. 253-275, 14 ills., Mar., 1919.

Sage Grouse:
High Country of Colorado. By Alfred M. Bailey. With 23 ills. in color from natural-color photographs by the author, Robert J. Niedrach, and F. G. Brandenburg. Vol. XC, pp. 43-72, 9 ills. in black and white, July, 1946.

Saguaro:
Arizona Sands, Home of the Cactus King. 11 ills. from photographs. Vol. LXXI, pp. 521-528, Apr., 1937.

Saguaro, Cactus Camel of Arizona. By Forrest Shreve. Vol. LXXXVIII, pp. 695-704, 9 ills. in color, Dec., 1945.

Saguaro, King of the Arizona Desert. 9 ills. in color from natural-color photographs by Esther Henderson, Jack Breed, and Max Kegley. Vol. LXXXVIII, pp. 697-704, Dec., 1945.

Saguaro Forest (Arizona). By H. L. Shantz. Vol. LXXI, pp. 515-532, 18 ills., Apr., 1937.

Saguaro National Monument, Arizona:
Arizona Sands, Home of the Cactus King. 11 ills. from photographs. Vol. LXXI, pp. 521-528, Apr., 1937.

Saguaro Forest. By H. L. Shantz. Vol. LXXI, pp. 515-532, 18 ills., Apr., 1937.

Saguenay River Region, Canada. *See* Quebec (Province).

Sahara:
Conquest of the Sahara by the Automobile. Vol. XLV, pp. 87-93, 9 ills., 1 three-quarters-page map, Jan., 1924.

Country of the Ant Men. By Thomas H. Kearney. Vol. XXII, pp. 367-382, 11 ills., 1 half-page map, Apr., 1911.

Date Gardens of the Jerid. By Thomas H. Kearney. Vol. XXI, pp. 543-567, 20 ills., July, 1910.

Sahara—*Continued*

French Conquest of the Sahara. By Charles Rabot. Vol. XVI, pp. 76-80, 1 ill., Feb., 1905.

Here and There in Northern Africa. By Frank Edward Johnson. Vol. XXV, pp. 1-132, 113 ills., Jan., 1914.

Hour of Prayer: In the Sahara Desert. Vol. XXII, supplement, Apr., 1911.

Mysteries of the Desert. By Hanns Vischer. Vol. XXII, pp. 1056-1059, Nov., 1911.

Our Desert Panorama. Text accompanying special supplement. Vol. XXII, pp. 409-410, 1 ill., Apr., 1911.

Three-Wheeling Through Africa: Two Adventurers Cross the So-called Dark Continent North of Lake Chad on Motorcycles with Side Cars. By James C. Wilson. Vol. LXV, pp. 37-92, 64 ills., 1 two-page map, Jan., 1934.

Trans-Africa Safari: A Motor Caravan Rolls Across Sahara and Jungle Through Realms of Dusky Potentates and the Land of Big-Lipped Women. By Lawrence Copley Thaw and Margaret Stout Thaw. Vol. LXXIV, pp. 327-364, 29 ills. in black and white, 14 ills. in color, 1 two-thirds-page map, Sept., 1938.

Sahuaro (Cactus). *See* Saguaro.

Sailing Forbidden Coasts (Africa). By Ida Treat. Vol. LX, pp. 357-386, 31 ills., 1 quarter-page map, Sept., 1931.

Sailing Ship and the Panama Canal. By James Page. Vol. XV, pp. 167-176, 2 charts, Apr., 1904.

Sailing the Seven Seas in the Interest of Science: Adventures Through 157,000 Miles of Storm and Calm, from Arctic to Antarctic and Around the World, in the Non-Magnetic Yacht *Carnegie*. By J. P. Ault. Vol. XLII, pp. 631-690, 47 ills., 1 chart, Dec., 1922.

Sailors, U. S. *See* U. S. Navy.

Sailplanes:

Men-Birds Soar on Boiling Air. By Frederick G. Vosburgh. Vol. LXXIV, pp. 123-140, 15 ills., July, 1938.

St. Andrews, Scotland:

Bonnie Scotland, Postwar Style. By Isobel Wylie Hutchison. Vol. LXXXIX, pp. 545-601, 14 ills. in black and white, 38 ills. in color, 1 two-page map, May, 1946.

St. Catherine Monastery, Egypt:

Route Over Which Moses Led the Children of Israel Out of Egypt. By Franklin E. Hoskins. Vol. XX, pp. 1011-1038, 24 ills., 1 page map, Dec., 1909.

St. Clair, Stuart:

Timor a Key to the Indies. By Stuart St. Clair. Vol. LXXXIV, pp. 355-384, 33 ills., 1 third-page map, Sept., 1943.

St. Croix (Island), Virgin Islands:

American Gibraltar: Notes on the Danish West Indies. Vol. XXX, pp. 89-96, 4 ills., 1 page map, July, 1916.

American Virgins: After Dark Days, These Adopted Daughters of the United States Are Finding a New Place in the Caribbean Sun. By DuBose Heyward and Daisy Reck. Vol. LXXVIII, pp. 273-308, 15 ills. in black and white, 23 ills. in color, 1 two-thirds-page map, Sept., 1940.

Island Treasures of the Caribbean. 23 ills. in color from natural-color photographs by Edwin L. Wisherd and C. W. Herbert. Vol. LXXVIII, pp. 281-304, Sept., 1940.

St. Elias (Mountain), Alaska-Yukon:

Conquest of Mount Logan: North America's Second Highest Peak Yields to the Intrepid Attack of Canadian Climbers. By H. F. Lambart. Vol. XLIX, pp. 597-631, 40 ills., June, 1926.

Monarchs of Alaska. By R. H. Sargent. Vol. XX, pp. 610-623, 9 ills., July, 1909.

National Geographic Society's Alaskan Expedition of 1909. By Ralph S. Tarr and Lawrence Martin. Vol. XXI, pp. 1-54, 42 ills., 4 page and 7 half-page maps, Jan., 1910.

St. Helena (Island), Atlantic Ocean:

Sailing the Seven Seas in the Interest of Science: Adventures Through 157,000 Miles of Storm and Calm, from Arctic to Antarctic and Around the World, in the Non-Magnetic Yacht *Carnegie*. By J. P. Ault. Vol. XLII, pp. 631-690, 47 ills., 1 chart, Dec., 1922.

St. Ives, England:

Channel Ports—And Some Others. By Florence Craig Albrecht. Vol. XXVIII, pp. 1-55, 45 ills., July, 1915.

Saint John, New Brunswick:

New Brunswick Down by the Sea. By Lawrence J. Burpee. Vol. LXXIX, pp. 595-614, 14 ills., 1 page map, May, 1941.

St. John (Island), Virgin Islands:

American Gibraltar: Notes on the Danish West Indies. Vol. XXX, pp. 89-96, 4 ills., 1 page map, July, 1916.

American Virgins: After Dark Days, These Adopted Daughters of the United States Are Finding a New Place in the Caribbean Sun. By DuBose Heyward and Daisy Reck. Vol. LXXVIII, pp. 273-308, 15 ills. in black and white, 23 ills. in color, 1 two-thirds-page map, Sept., 1940.

Island Treasures of the Caribbean. 23 ills. in color from natural-color photographs by Edwin L. Wisherd and C. W. Herbert. Vol. LXXVIII, pp. 281-304, Sept., 1940.

St. John's, Newfoundland:

Newfoundland, North Atlantic Rampart: From the "First Base of American Defense" Planes Fly to Britain's Aid over Stout Fishing Schooners of the Grand Banks. By George Whiteley, Jr. Vol. LXXX, pp. 111-140, 26 ills., 1 two-thirds-page map, July, 1941.

St. Kitts (Island), West Indies:

British West Indian Interlude. By Anne Rainey Langley. Vol. LXXIX, pp. 1-46, 23 ills. in black and white, 21 ills. in color, 2 page maps, Jan., 1941.

West Indies Links in a Defense Chain. 21 ills. in color from natural-color photographs; 20 ills. by Edwin L. Wisherd. Vol. LXXIX, pp. 9-32, Jan., 1941.

St. Lawrence (River), New York-Canada. *See* Quebec (Province).

St. Louis, Missouri:

Missouri Mirrors of 1946. 22 ills. in color from natural-color photographs by Richard H. Stewart. Vol. LXXXIX, pp. 285-308, Mar., 1946.

These Missourians. By Frederick Simpich. Vol. LXXXIX, pp. 277-310, 12 ills. in black and white, 22 ills. in color, 1 map (two-page spread), Mar., 1946.

St. Lucia (Island), West Indies:

Americans in the Caribbean. By Luis Marden. Vol. LXXXI, pp. 723-758, 16 ills. in black and white, 22 ills. in color, 1 half-page map, June, 1942.

British West Indian Interlude. By Anne Rainey Langley. Vol. LXXIX, pp. 1-46, 23 ills. in black and white, 21 ills. in color, 2 page maps, Jan., 1941.

War Echoes in the West Indies. 22 ills. in color from natural-color photographs by Luis Marden. Vol. LXXXI, pp. 731-754, June, 1942.

West Indies Links in a Defense Chain. 21 ills. in color from natural-color photographs; 20 ills. by Edwin L. Wisherd. Vol. LXXIX, pp. 9-32, Jan., 1941.

St. Magnus' Cathedral, Orkney Islands:

Orkneys and Shetlands—A Mysterious Group of Islands. By Charles S. Olcott. Vol. XXXIX, pp. 197-228, 33 ills., Feb., 1921.

St. Malo, France:

St. Malo, Ancient City of Corsairs: An Old Brittany Seaport Whose Past Bristles with Cannons and Cutlasses. By Junius B. Wood. Vol. LVI, pp. 131-177, 28 ills. in black and white, 29 ills. in color, 1 two-thirds-page map, Aug., 1929.

St. Mark's Cathedral, Venice:

Venice. By Karl Stieler. Vol. XXVII, pp. 587-630, 42 ills., 1 page and 1 quarter-page maps, June, 1915.

St. Michael's (Island), Azores:

Azores: Picturesque and Historic Half-Way House of American Transatlantic Aviators. By Arminius T. Haeberle. Vol. XXXV, pp. 514-545, 26 ills., 1 page map, June, 1919.

St. Peter's Cathedral, Rome:

Inexhaustible Italy. By Arthur Stanley Riggs. Vol. XXX, pp. 273-368, 76 ills., 1 page map, Oct., 1916.

Splendor of Rome. By Florence Claig Albrecht. Vol. XLI, pp. 593-626, 28 ills., June, 1922.

St. Pierre, Martinique:

Lafcadio Hearn on the Island and People of Martinique. Vol. XIII, pp. 214-216, June, 1902.

Recent Volcanic Eruptions in the West Indies. By Israel C. Russell. Vol. XIII, pp. 267-285, 7 ills., July, 1902.

St. Pierre and **Miquelon** (Islands), Atlantic Ocean:

Islands Adrift: St. Pierre and Miquelon: In a Key Position on the North Atlantic Air Route, France's Oldest Colony Rides Out Another Storm. By Frederic K. Arnold. Vol. LXXX, pp. 743-768, 23 ills., 1 fifth-page map, Dec., 1941.

St. Simon (Island), Georgia:

Golden Isles of Guale. By W. Robert Moore. Vol. LXV, pp. 235-264, 35 ills., 1 three-quarters-page map, Feb., 1934.

Saint Stephen's Fête in Budapest. By De Witt Clinton Falls. Vol. XVIII, pp. 548-558, 9 ills., Aug., 1907.

St. Thomas (Island), Virgin Islands:

American Gibraltar: Notes on the Danish West Indies. Vol. XXX, pp. 89-96, 4 ills., 1 page map, July, 1916.

American Virgins: After Dark Days, These Adopted Daughters of the United States Are Finding a New Place in the Caribbean Sun. By DuBose Heyward and Daisy Reck. Vol. LXXVIII, pp. 273-308, 15 ills. in black and white, 23 ills. in color, 1 two-thirds-page map, Sept., 1940.

Haunts of the Caribbean Corsairs: The West Indies a Geographic Background for the Most Adventurous Episodes in the History of the Western Hemisphere. By Nell Ray Clarke. Vol. XLI, pp. 147-187, 27 ills., Feb., 1922.

Island Treasures of the Caribbean. 23 ills. in color from natural-color photographs by Edwin L. Wisherd and C. W. Herbert. Vol. LXXVIII, pp. 281-304, Sept., 1940.

St. Vincent (Island), West Indies:

British West Indian Interlude. By Anne Rainey Langley. Vol. LXXIX, pp. 1-46, 23 ills. in black and white, 21 ills. in color, 2 page maps, Jan., 1941.

Chemical Discussion of Analyses of Volcanic Ejecta from Martinique and St. Vincent. By W. F. Hillebrand. Vol. XIII, pp. 296-299, July, 1902.

Eruptions of La Soufrière, St. Vincent, in May, 1902. By Edmund Otis Hovey. Vol. XIII, pp. 444-459, 4 ills., Dec., 1902.

National Geographic Society Expedition to Martinique and St. Vincent. Vol. XIII, pp. 183-184, 2 ills., June, 1902.

Recent Volcanic Eruptions in the West Indies. By Israel C. Russell. Vol. XIII, pp. 267-285, 7 ills., July, 1902.

Report by Robert T. Hill on Volcanic Disturbances in the West Indies. Vol. XIII, pp. 223-267, 13 ills., 2 page and 1 half-page maps, July, 1902.

St. Vincent (Island), West Indies—*Continued*

Report of the Eruption of the Soufrière of St. Vincent, 1812 (From the *Evening News* of June 30, 1812). Vol. XIV, pp. 158-161, Apr., 1903.

Reports of Vessels as to the Range of Volcanic Dust. By James Page. Vol. XIII, pp. 299-301, July, 1902.

Volcanic Eruptions on Martinique and St. Vincent. By Israel C. Russell. Vol. XIII, pp. 415-436, 10 ills., Dec., 1902.

Volcanic Rocks of Martinique and St. Vincent: Collected by Robert T. Hill and Israel C. Russell. By J. S. Diller. Vol. XIII, pp. 285-296, July, 1902.

Saipan (Island), Marianas Islands:

Hidden Key to the Pacific: Piercing the Web of Secrecy Which Long Has Veiled Japanese Bases in the Mandated Islands. By Willard Price. Vol. LXXXI, pp. 759-785, 28 ills., 1 map (two-page spread), June, 1942.

Saipan and Tinian, Take-offs to Tokyo. 17 ills. in color from natural-color photographs; 15 ills. by W. Robert Moore. Vol. LXXXVII, pp. 453-468, Apr., 1945.

South from Saipan. By W. Robert Moore. Vol. LXXXVII, pp. 441-474, 11 ills. in black and white, 17 ills. in color, 1 half-page map, 1945.

Springboards to Tokyo. By Willard Price. Vol. LXXXVI, pp. 385-407, 16 ills., Oct., 1944.

Victory's Portrait in the Marianas. By Lt. William Franklin Draper, USNR. With 17 ills. in color from paintings by the author. Vol. LXXXVIII, pp. 599-616, Nov., 1945.

Sakamoto, Kiyoshi:

Japan. 11 ills. in color from photographs by Kiyoshi Sakamoto. Vol. XL, pp. 61-76, July, 1921.

Japan: Picturesque Side of Japanese Life. 12 ills. in color from photographs by Kiyoshi Sakamoto. Vol. XLII, pp. 284-298, Sept., 1922.

Sakurajima, Japan's Greatest Volcanic Eruption: A Convulsion of Nature Whose Ravages Were Minimized by Scientific Knowledge, Compared with the Terrors and Destruction of the Recent Tokyo Earthquake. By Dr. Thomas Augustus Jaggar. Vol. XLV, pp. 441-470, 32 ills., 1 half-page map, Apr., 1924.

Sale, George:

Conditions in Liberia. By Roland P. Folkner, George Sale, and Emmett J. Scott. Vol. XXI, pp. 729-741, 9 ills., Sept., 1910.

Salé, Morocco:

Eastward from Gibraltar: Overland Route Across North Africa to Tunisia and Libia. By Cyrus French Wicker. Vol. LXXXIII, pp. 115-142, 28 ills., Jan., 1943.

Salem, Massachusetts:

Northeast of Boston. By Albert W. Atwood. Vol. LXXXVIII, pp. 257-292, 12 ills. in black and white, 17 ills. in color, special map supplement, Sept., 1945.

Salem, Massachusetts—*Continued*

Where New England Meets the Sea. 17 ills. in color from natural-color photographs by B. Anthony Stewart. Vol. LXXXVIII, pp. 265-288, Sept., 1945.

Salem, Oregon:

Oregon Finds New Riches. By Leo A. Borah. Vol. XC, pp. 681-728, 15 ills. in black and white, 28 ills. in color, 1 two-page map, Dec., 1946.

Salgado, José Velloso:

Vasco da Gama at the Court of the Zamorin of Calicut. Reproduction in color of the painting by José Velloso Salgado, Sociedade de Geographia de Lisboa. Vol. LII, supplement, Nov., 1927.

Salisbury, Southern Rhodesia:

Rhodesia, Hobby and Hope of Cecil Rhodes. By W. Robert Moore. Vol. LXXXVI, pp. 281-306, 13 ills. in black and white, 10 ills. in color, 1 half-page map, Sept., 1944.

Salmon (River), Idaho:

Down Idaho's River of No Return. By Philip J. Shenon and John C. Reed. Vol. LXX, pp. 95-136, 43 ills., 1 page and 1 two-thirds-page maps, July, 1936.

Salmon (Fish):

America's Most Valuable Fishes. By Hugh M. Smith. Vol. XXIII, pp. 494-514, 17 ills., May, 1912.

Federal Fish Farming; or, Planting Fish by the Billion. By Hugh M. Smith. Vol. XXI, pp. 418-446, 22 ills., May, 1910.

Fishing in Pacific Coast Streams. By Leonard P. Schultz. Vol. LXXV, pp. 185-212, 10 ills. in black and white, 54 portraits in color, Feb., 1939.

Fresh-Water Denizens of the Far West. 54 portraits in color from paintings by Hashime Murayama. Vol. LXXV, pp. 193-204, Feb., 1939.

Jumping Salmon. Vol. XIX, p. 124, 1 ill., Feb., 1908.

White Sheep, Giant Moose, and Smaller Game of the Kenai Peninsula, Alaska. By George Shiras, 3d. Vol. XXIII, pp. 423-494, 59 ills., 1 page and 1 two-page maps, May, 1912.

Saloniki (Greece). By H. G. Dwight. Vol. XXX, pp. 203-232, 28 ills., Sept., 1916.

Salt:

Eden of the Flowery Republic. By Joseph Beech. Vol. XXXVIII, pp. 355-390, 18 ills. in black and white, 16 ills. in color, Nov., 1920.

An Interesting Photograph (Salt Deposit, Athabasca District, Alberta). Vol. XVII, p. 237, 1 ill., Apr., 1906.

Methods of Obtaining Salt in Costa Rica. Vol. XIX, pp. 28-34, 7 ills., Jan., 1908.

Remarkable Salt Deposit. By Charles F. Holder. Vol. XII, pp. 390-392, 2 ills., Nov., 1901.

Salt for China's Daily Rice. 11 ills. from photographs. Vol. LXXXVI, pp. 329-336, Sept., 1944.

Salton Sea, California :

Colorado Desert. By W. C. Mendenhall. Vol. XX, pp. 681-701, 16 ills., Aug., 1909.

New Inland Sea. By Arthur P. Davis. Vol. XVIII, pp. 36-49, 8 ills., 1 page map, Jan., 1907.

Remarkable Salt Deposit. By Charles F. Holder. Vol. XII, pp. 390-392, 2 ills., Nov., 1901.

Salton Sea and the Rainfall of the Southwest. By Alfred J. Henry. Vol. XVIII, pp. 244-248, Apr., 1907.

Studies on the Rate of Evaporation at Reno, Nevada, and in the Salton Sink. By Frank H. Bigelow. Vol. XIX, pp. 20-28, 5 ills., Jan., 1908.

Salton Sea Bird Refuge, California :

Pelican Profiles. By Lewis Wayne Walker. Vol. LXXXIV, pp. 589-598, 5 ills. in black and white, 8 ills. in color, Nov., 1943.

Salty Nova Scotia : In Friendly New Scotland Gaelic Songs Still Answer the Skirling Bagpipes. By Andrew H. Brown. Vol. LXXVII, pp. 575-624, 30 ills. in black and white, 21 ills. in color, 1 two-page map, May, 1940.

Salvador. *See* El Salvador.

Salvador (Bahia), Brazil :

Air Cruising Through New Brazil : A National Geographic Reporter Spots Vast Resources Which the Republic's War Declaration Adds to Strength of United Nations. By Henry Albert Phillips. Vol. LXXXII, pp. 503-536, 32 ills., Oct., 1942.

Salvation Army:

Around the World with the Salvation Army. By Evangeline Booth. Vol. XXXVII, pp. 346-368, 23 ills., Apr., 1920.

Salween (River), Burma-China :

The Land of the Crossbow (Yünnan Province). By George Forrest. Vol. XXI, pp. 132-156, 15 ills., 1 page map, Feb., 1910.

Through the Great River Trenches of Asia : National Geographic Society Explorer Follows the Yangtze, Mekong, and Salwin Through Mighty Gorges, Some of Whose Canyon Walls Tower to a Height of More Than Two Miles. By Joseph F. Rock. Vol. L, pp. 133-186, 47 ills., 1 half-page map, Aug., 1926.

Salzburg (Province), Austria :

Salzkammergut, a Playground of Austria. By Florence Polk Holding. Vol. LXXI, pp. 445-485, 34 ills. in black and white, 13 ills. in color, 1 third-page map, Apr., 1937.

This Was Austria. 18 ills. from photographs. Vol. LXXXVIII, pp. 71-86, July, 1945.

Salzkammergut (Region), Austria :

Salskammergut, a Playground of Austria. By Florence Polk Holding. Vol. LXXI, pp. 445-485, 34 ills. in black and white, 13 ills. in color, 1 third-page map, Apr., 1937.

Samaritans (Sect) :

Last Israelitish Blood Sacrifice : How the Vanishing Samaritans Celebrate the Passover on Sacred Mount Gerizim. By John D. Whiting. Vol. XXXVII, pp. 1-46, 40 ills., 1 half-page map, Jan., 1920.

Samarkand, Uzbek, U. S. S. R. :

Russia's Orphan Races : Picturesque Peoples Who Cluster on the Southeastern Borderland of the Vast Slav Dominions. By Maynard Owen Williams. Vol. XXXIV, pp. 245-278, 26 ills., 1 page map, Oct., 1918.

Samoa (Islands), Pacific Ocean :

America's South Sea Soldiers. By Lorena MacIntyre Quinn. Vol. XXXVI, pp. 267-274, 8 ills., Sept., 1919.

Commercial Importance of Samoa. By O. P. Austin. Vol. X, pp. 218-220, June, 1899.

Sailing the Seven Seas in the Interest of Science : Adventures Through 157,000 Miles of Storm and Calm, from Arctic to Antarctic and Around the World in the Non-Magnetic Yacht *Carnegie.* By J. P. Ault. Vol. XLII, pp. 631-690, 47 ills., 1 chart, Dec., 1922.

Samoa : Navigators Islands. By Comdr. Harrie Webster. Vol. X, pp. 207-217, 9 ills., June, 1899.

Samoa—South Sea Outpost of the U. S. Navy. 20 ills. from photographs by Truman Bailey. Vol. LXXIX, pp. 615-630, May, 1941.

Samoan Islands. By Edwin V. Morgan. Vol. XI, pp. 417-426, Nov., 1900.

Samos (Island), Aegean Sea :

Historic Islands and Shores of the Ægean Sea. By Ernest Lloyd Harris. Vol. XXVIII, pp. 231-262, 29 ills., 1 half-page map, Sept., 1915.

San Agustín Region, Colombia :

Stone Idols of the Andes Reveal a Vanished People : Remarkable Relics of One of the Oldest Aboriginal Cultures of America are Unearthed in Colombia's San Agustín Region. By Hermann von Walde-Waldegg. Vol. LXXVII, pp. 627-647, 22 ills., 1 map, May, 1940.

San Benito Islands, Mexico :

Cruise of the *Kinkajou:* Among Desert Islands of Mexico Voyagers Find Outdoor Laboratories for the Naturalist and Ideal Fishing Grounds for the Sportsman. By Alfred M. Bailey. Vol. LXXX, pp. 339-366, 13 ills. in black and white, 12 ills. in color, 1 page map, Sept., 1941.

San Blas Indians:

Arch-Isolationists, the San Blas Indians : Coconuts Serve as Cash on Islands Off the Panama Coast Where Tribesmen Cling to Their Ancient Ways and Discourage Visitors. By Corinne B. Feeney. Vol. LXXIX, pp. 193-220, 15 ills. in black and white, 12 ills. in color, 1 sixth-page map, Feb., 1941.

Indian Haven—Off the San Blas Coast (Mulatas Archipelago). 12 ills. in color from naturalcolor photographs by Lieut. Dayton Seiler. Vol. LXXIX, pp. 209-216, Feb., 1941.

San Blas Indians—*Continued*

Land That Links the Americas (Panama). 22 ills. in color from natural-color photographs by Luis Marden. Vol. LXXX, pp. 601-624, Nov., 1941.

Little-Known Parts of Panama. By Henry Pittier. Vol. XXIII, pp. 627-662, 35 ills., 1 page map, July, 1912.

San Cristobal (Island), Galápagos Islands :

Dream Ship : The Story of a Voyage of Adventure More Than Half Around the World in a 47-Foot Lifeboat. By Ralph Stock. Vol. XXXIX, pp. 1-52, 43 ills., 1 page map, Jan., 1921.

San Diego, California :

San Diego Can't Believe It. By Frederick Simpich. Vol. LXXXI, pp. 45-80, 26 ills. in black and white, 9 ills. in color, Jan., 1942.

Sun Shines on San Diego. 9 ills. in color from natural-color photographs by B. Anthony Stewart. Vol. LXXXI, pp. 57-64, Jan., 1942.

San Francisco, California :

California Earthquake. Vol. XVII, pp. 325-343, 27 ills., June, 1906.

City of Realized Dreams. By Franklin K. Lane. Vol. XXVII, pp. 169-171, Feb., 1915.

Echoes of the San Francisco Earthquake. By Robert E. C. Stearns. Vol. XVIII, pp. 351-353, 1 ill., May, 1907.

Out in San Francisco : Fed on Gold Dust and Fattened by Sea Trade, a Pioneer Village Becomes a Busy World Port. By Frederick Simpich. Vol. LXI, pp. 395-434, 38 ills., Apr., 1932.

Probable Cause of the San Francisco Earthquake. By Frederick Leslie Ransome. Vol. XVII, pp. 280-296, 9 ills., 2 page maps, May, 1906.

Record of the Great Earthquake Written in Washington by the Seismograph of the United States Weather Bureau. By C. F. Marvin. Vol. XVII, pp. 296-298, May, 1906.

San Francisco : Gibraltar of the West Coast. By La Verne Bradley. Vol. LXXXIII, pp. 279-308, 28 ills., Mar., 1943.

San Francisco Earthquake. Vol. XVII, pp. 325-343, 26 ills., June, 1906.

San Francisco Earthquake of April 18, 1906, as Recorded by the Coast and Geodetic Survey Magnetic Observatories. By Dr. L. A. Bauer and J. E. Burbank. Vol. XVII, pp. 298-300, May, 1906.

Sea Fogs of San Francisco. Vol. XII, pp. 108-114, 5 ills., Mar., 1901.

Wonderland of California. By Herman Whitaker. Vol. XXVIII, pp. 56-104, 45 ills., July, 1915.

San Joaquin (River), California :

More Water for California's Great Central Valley. By Frederick Simpich. Vol. XC, pp. 645-664, 16 ills., 1 page map, Nov., 1946.

San José, Costa Rica :

Costa Rica, Land of the Banana. By Paul B. Popenoe. Vol. XLI, pp. 201-220, 17 ills., Feb., 1922.

Costa Rica—Vulcan's Smithy. By Henry Pittier. Vol. XXI, pp. 494-525, 30 ills., 2 half-page maps, June, 1910.

Land of the Painted Oxcarts. By Luis Marden. With 31 ills. in color from natural-color photographs by the author. Vol. XC, pp. 409-456, 30 ills. in black and white, 1 half-page map, Oct., 1946.

San Juan, Puerto Rico :

Puerto Rico : Watchdog of the Caribbean : Venerable Domain Under American Flag Has New Role as West Indian Stronghold and Sentinel of the Panama Canal. By E. John Long. Vol. LXXVI, pp. 697-738, 24 ills. in black and white, 23 ills. in color, Dec., 1939.

Puerto Rico Polychromes. 23 ills. in color from natural-color photographs by Edwin L. Wisherd. Vol. LXXVI, pp. 713-736, Dec., 1939.

San Juan (River), Utah-New Mexico :

Beyond the Clay Hills : An Account of the National Geographic Society's Reconnaissance of a Previously Unexplored Section in Utah. By Neil M. Judd. Vol. XLV, pp. 275-302, 28 ills., 1 half-page map, Mar., 1924.

San Juan de Teotihuacan, Mexico :

Interesting Visit to the Ancient Pyramids of San Juan Teotihuacan. By A. C. Galloway. Vol. XXI, pp. 1041-1050, 8 ills., 1 page map, Dec., 1910.

San Juan Mountains, Colorado-New Mexico :

Landslides and Rock Avalanches. By Guy Elliott Mitchell. Vol. XXI, pp. 277-287, 6 ills., Apr., 1910.

San Marino:

San Marino : Our Littlest Ally. By Alice Rohe. Vol. XXXIV, pp. 139-163, 17 ills., Aug., 1918.

San Salvador, El Salvador :

Coffee Is King in El Salvador. By Luis Marden. Vol. LXXXVI, pp. 575-616, 22 ills. in black and white, 27 ills. in color, 1 half-page map, Nov., 1944.

Volcano-Girded Salvador : A Prosperous Central American State with the Densest Rural Population in the Western World. By Harriet Chalmers Adams. Vol. XLI, pp. 189-200, 10 ills., Feb., 1922.

San Salvador Volcano, El Salvador :

Coffee Is King in El Salvador. By Luis Marden. Vol. LXXXVI, pp. 575-616, 22 ills. in black and white, 27 ills. in color, 1 half-page map, Nov., 1944.

San Vicente (Hacienda), Chile :

On a Chilean Hacienda. 8 ills. in color from natural-color photographs by E. P. Haddon. Vol. LXXXVI, pp. 489-496, Oct., 1944.

Sancta Sophia (Mosque), Istanbul:

Constantinople and Sancta Sophia. By Edwin A. Grosvenor. Vol. XXVII, pp. 459-482, 21 ills., May, 1915.

Constantinople Today. By Solita Solano. Vol. XLI, pp. 647-680, 40 ills., 1 three-quarters-page map, June, 1922.

Sand Dunes:

Battle Ground of Nature: The Atlantic Seaboard. By John Oliver La Gorce. Vol. XXXIII, pp. 511-546, 23 ills., 4 half-page maps, June, 1918.

Controlling Sand Dunes in the United States and Europe. By A. S. Hitchcock. Vol. XV, pp. 43-47, 4 ills., Jan., 1904.

Indiana's Unrivaled Sand-Dunes—A National Park Opportunity. By Orpheus Moyer Schantz. Vol. XXXV, pp. 430-441, 18 ills., May, 1919.

Our Neglected Southern Coast. By Alfred Goldsborough Mayer. Vol. XIX, pp. 859-871, 10 ills., Dec., 1908.

Warfare on Our Eastern Coast. By John Oliver La Gorce. Vol. XXVIII, pp. 195-230, 29 ills., 2 charts, Sept., 1915.

Where the Wind Does the Work (Cape Hatteras, North Carolina). By Collier Cobb. Vol. XVII, pp. 310-317, 9 ills., 1 page map, June, 1906.

White Sands of Alamogordo (New Mexico): A Dry Ocean of Granular Gypsum Billows Under Desert Winds in a New National Playground. By Carl P. Russell. Vol. LXVIII, pp. 250-264, 12 ills., Aug., 1935.

See also Deserts.

Sanders, Alvin Howard:

Taurine World: Cattle and Their Place in the Human Scheme—Wild Types and Modern Breeds in Many Lands. By Alvin Howard Sanders. Vol. XLVIII, pp. 591-710, 76 ills. in black and white, 20 ills. in color, Dec., 1925.

Sandpipers:

Birds of Timberline and Tundra. By Arthur A. Allen. With 24 ills. in color from natural-color photographs by the author. Vol. XC, pp. 313-339, 8 ills. in black and white, Sept., 1946.

Feathered Foragers of Swamp and Shore. 101 portraits in color from paintings by Maj. Allan Brooks. Vol. LXXII, pp. 191-222, Aug., 1937.

Shore Birds, Cranes, and Rails: Willets, Plovers, Stilts, Phalaropes, Sandpipers, and Their Relatives Deserve Protection. By Arthur A. Allen. Paintings by Maj. Allan Brooks. Vol. LXXII, pp. 183-222, 4 ills. in black and white, 101 portraits in color, Aug., 1937.

Sandrof, Samuel:

The Worm Turns. By Samuel Sandrof. Vol. LXXXIX, pp. 775-786, 14 ills., June, 1946.

Sands, W. F.:

Mysterious Temples of the Jungle: The Prehistoric Ruins of Guatemala. By W. F. Sands. Vol. XXIV, pp. 324-338, 10 ills., Mar., 1913.

Sandusky Bay, Ohio:

Submerged Valleys in Sandusky Bay. By E. L. Moseley. Vol. XIII, pp. 398-403, 4 charts, Nov., 1902.

Sandwich, Massachusetts:

Cape Cod People and Places. By Wanda Burnett. Vol. LXXXIX, pp. 737-774, 17 ills. in black and white, 24 ills. in color, 1 half-page map, June, 1946.

Sandworms:

The Worm Turns. By Samuel Sandrof. Vol. LXXXIX, pp. 775-786, 14 ills., June, 1946.

Sanford, George Alden:

Vacation in a Fifteenth Century English Manor House. By George Alden Sanford. Vol. LIII, pp. 629-636, 8 ills., May, 1928.

Vacation in Holland. By George Alden Sanford. Vol. LVI, pp. 363-378, 6 ills. in black and white, 8 ills. in color, 1 two-thirds-page map, Sept., 1929.

Sanitation:

Colossal Work in Baltimore. By Calvin W. Hendrick. Vol. XX, pp. 365-373, 6 ills., Apr., 1909.

Conserving the Nation's Man Power: Disease Weakens Armies, Cripples Industry, Reduces Production. How the Government Is Sanitating the Civil Zones Around Cantonment Areas. A Nation-Wide Campaign for Health. By Rupert Blue. Vol. XXXII, pp. 254-278, 17 ills., Sept., 1917.

Cooties and Courage. By Herbert Corey. Vol. XXXIII, pp. 495-509, 10 ills., June, 1918.

Economic Loss to the People of the United States Through Insects That Carry Disease. By L. O. Howard. Vol. XX, pp. 735-749, Aug., 1909.

New York—The Metropolis of Mankind. By William Joseph Showalter. Vol. XXXIV, pp. 1-49, 29 ills., July, 1918.

Our Army Versus a Bacillus. By Alton G. Grinnell. Vol. XXIV, pp. 1146-1152, 5 ills., 1 diagram, Oct., 1913.

Panama Canal. By Rear Adm. Colby M. Chester. Vol. XVI, pp. 445-467, 8 ills., Oct., 1905.

Redeeming the Tropics. By William Joseph Showalter. Vol. XXV, pp. 344-364, 13 ills., Mar., 1914.

Santa Catalina (Island), California:

Santa Catalina—400 Years a Lure to California Travelers. 11 ills. in color from natural-color photographs by B. Anthony Stewart. Vol. LXXXI, pp. 81-88, Jan., 1942.

Santa Fe, New Mexico:

New Mexico Melodrama. By Frederick Simpich. Vol. LXXIII, pp. 529-569, 19 ills. in black and white, 25 ills. in color, 1 two-page map, May, 1938.

Santa Fe Trail, Path to Empire. By Frederick Simpich. Vol. LVI, pp. 213-252, 35 ills. in black and white, 12 ills. in color, 1 half-page map, Aug., 1929.

Santa Maria (Seaplane) :

By Seaplane to Six Continents : Cruising 60,000 Miles, Italian Argonauts of the Air See World Geography Unroll, and Break New Sky Trails Over Vast Brazilian Jungles. By Comdr. Francesco de Pinedo. Vol. LIV, pp. 247-301, 60 ills., 1 two-page map, Sept., 1928.

Santa Tecla, El Salvador :

Coffee Is King in El Salvador. By Luis Marden. Vol. LXXXVI, pp. 575-616, 22 ills. in black and white, 27 ills. in color, 1 half-page map, Nov., 1944.

Santarem, Brazil :

Air Cruising Through New Brazil : A National Geographic Reporter Spots Vast Resources Which the Republic's War Declaration Adds to Strength of United Nations. By Henry Albert Phillips. Vol. LXXXII, pp. 503-536, 32 ills., Oct., 1942.

Santiago, Chile :

Capital and Chief Seaport of Chile. By W. Robert Moore. Vol. LXXXVI, pp. 477-500, 15 ills. in black and white, 8 ills. in color, 1 third-page map, Oct., 1944.

Twin Stars of Chile : Valparaiso, the Gateway, and Santiago, the Capital—Key Cities with a Progressive Present and a Romantic Past. By William Joseph Showalter. Vol. LV, pp. 197-247, 35 ills. in black and white, 25 ills. in color, Feb., 1929.

Santiago Atitlán, Guatemala :

To Market in Guatemala. By Luis Marden. With 19 ills. in color from natural-color photographs by Giles Greville Healey and Charles S. Pineo. Vol. LXXXVIII, pp. 87-104, July, 1945.

Santo Domingo. *See* Dominican Republic.

Santorin (Island), Aegean Sea :

Isles of Greece. By Lt. Richard Stillwell, USNR. Vol. LXXXV, pp. 593-622, 11 ills. in black and white, 20 ills. in color, 1 page map, May, 1944.

Santorin and Mýkonos, Aegean Gems. 8 ills. in color from natural-color photographs ; 7 ills. by B. Anthony Stewart. Vol. LXXVII, pp. 339-346, Mar., 1940.

Santos, Brazil :

As São Paulo Grows : Half the World's Coffee Beans Flavor the Life and Speed the Growth of an Inland Brazil City. By W. Robert Moore. Vol. LXXV, pp. 657-688, 33 ills., 1 two-thirds-page map, May, 1939.

São Paulo, Brazil :

Air Cruising Through New Brazil : A National Geographic Reporter Spots Vast Resources Which the Republic's War Declaration Adds to Strength of United Nations. By Henry Albert Phillips. Vol. LXXXII, pp. 503-536, 32 ills., Oct., 1942.

São Paulo, Brazil—*Continued*

As São Paulo Grows : Half the World's Coffee Beans Flavor the Life and Speed the Growth of an Inland Brazil City. By W. Robert Moore. Vol. LXXV, pp. 657-688, 33 ills., 1 two-thirds-page map, May, 1939.

Brazil's Potent Weapons. By W. Robert Moore. Vol. LXXXV, pp. 41-78, 16 ills. in black and white, 18 ills. in color, 1 two-page map, Jan., 1944.

Visit to the Brazilian Coffee Country. By Robert De C. Ward. Vol. XXII, pp. 908-931, 19 ills., 1 half-page map, Oct., 1911.

São Tomé (Island), Gulf of Guinea :

São Tomé, the Chocolate Island. By William Leon Smyser. Vol. LXXXIX, pp. 657-680, 23 ills., 1 third-page map, May, 1946.

Sapelo (Island), Sea Islands, Georgia :

Golden Isles of Guale. By W. Robert Moore. Vol. LXV, pp. 235-264, 35 ills., 1 three-quarters-page map, Feb., 1934.

Sarawak:

Colonial Government in Borneo. By James M. Hubbard. Vol. XI, pp. 359-363, Sept., 1900.

Keeping House in Borneo. By Virginia Hamilton. Vol. LXXXVIII, pp. 293-324, 28 ills., 1 page map, Sept., 1945.

Notes on the Sea Dyaks of Borneo. By Edwin H. Gomes. Vol. XXII, pp. 695-723, 26 ills., Aug., 1911.

Sarawak : The Land of the White Rajahs. By Harrison W. Smith. Vol. XXXV, pp. 110-167, 58 ills., 1 half-page map, Feb., 1919.

Sardines:

Brittany : The Land of the Sardine. By Hugh M. Smith. Vol. XX, pp. 541-573, 23 ills., June, 1909.

Sardinia (Island), Mediterranean Sea :

Island of Sardinia and Its People : Traces of Many Civilizations to Be Found in the Speech, Customs, and Costumes of This Picturesque Land. By Guido Costa. Vol. XLIII, pp. 1-75, 63 ills. in black and white, 16 ills. in color, 1 three-quarters and 1 quarter-page maps, Jan., 1923.

Little-Known Sardinia. By Helen Dunstan Wright. Vol. XXX, pp. 97-120, 23 ills., 1 page map, Aug., 1916.

Sardinian Smiles. 16 ills. in color from photographs by Clifton Adams. Vol. XLIII, pp. 31-46, Jan., 1923.

Where the Sard Holds Sway. Vol. XLIX, pp. 464-474, 1 ill. in black and white, 9 ills. in color, Apr., 1926.

Sardinian Smiles. 16 ills. in color from photographs by Clifton Adams. Vol. XLIII, pp. 31-46, Jan., 1923.

Sardis (Ancient City) :

Buried Cities of Asia Minor. By Ernest L. Harris. Vol. XX, pp. 1-18, 10 ills., Jan., 1909.

Sargasso Sea:

Sindbads of Science: Narrative of a Windjammer's Specimen-Collecting Voyage to the Sargasso Sea, to Senegambian Africa and Among Islands of High Adventure in the South Atlantic. By George Finlay Simmons. Vol. LII, pp. 1-75, 89 ills., 1 two-thirds-page map, July, 1927.

Sargent, R. H.:

Monarchs of Alaska. By R. H. Sargent. Vol. XX, pp. 610-623, 9 ills., July, 1909.

Sarichef's Atlas, 1826. By Marcus Baker. Vol. XIII, pp. 86-92, Mar., 1902.

Sark (Island), Channel Islands:

Channel Islands. By Edith Carey. Vol. XXXVIII, pp. 143-164, 24 ills., 1 quarter-page map, Aug., 1920.

Feudal Isle of Sark: Where Sixteenth-Century Laws Are Still Observed. By Sibyl Hathaway (La Dame de Serk). Vol. LXII, pp. 101-119, 21 ills., 1 half-page map, July, 1932.

Saskatchewan (River), Canada:

Sources of the Saskatchewan. By Walter D. Wilcox. Vol. X, pp. 113-134, 5 ills., 1 chart, Apr., 1899.

Saskatoon, Saskatchewan, Canada:

First Alaskan Air Expedition. By Capt. St. Clair Streett. Vol. XLI, pp. 499-552, 37 ills., 1 page map, May, 1922.

Al Saud, Abdul Aziz (King of Saudi Arabia):

Guest in Saudi Arabia. By Maynard Owen Williams. Vol. LXXXVIII, pp. 463-487, 24 ills., 1 two-thirds-page map, Oct., 1945.

Saudi Arabia:

Damascus and Mecca Railway. Vol. XII, p. 408, Nov., 1901.

Guest in Saudi Arabia. By Maynard Owen Williams. Vol. LXXXVIII, pp. 463-487, 24 ills., 1 two-thirds-page map, Oct., 1945.

Mecca the Mystic: A New Kingdom Within Arabia. By S. M. Zwemer. Vol. XXXII, pp. 157-172, 13 ills., Aug., 1917.

One Thousand Miles of Railway Built for Pilgrims and Not for Dividends (Damascus to Mecca). By Col. F. R. Maunsell. Vol. XX, pp. 156-172, 13 ills., 1 three-quarters-page map, Feb., 1909.

Pilgrims' Progress to Mecca. 22 ills. in duotone; 18 ills. by Oscar Marcus. Vol. LXXII, pp. 627-642, Nov., 1937.

Rise of the New Arab Nation. By Frederick Simpich. Vol. XXXVI, pp. 369-393, 17 ills., 1 page map, Nov., 1919.

Unbeliever Joins the Hadj: On the Age-Old Pilgrimage to Mecca, Babies Are Born, Elders Die, and Families May Halt a Year to Earn Funds in Distant Lands. By Owen Tweedy. Vol. LXV, pp. 761-789, 30 ills., 1 page map, June, 1934.

Visit to Three Arab Kingdoms: Transjordania, Iraq, and the Hedjaz Present Many Problems to European Powers. By Junius B. Wood. Vol. XLIII, pp. 535-568, 30 ills., 1 three-quarters-page map, May, 1923.

Sauk and Fox (Indian Tribe):

America's First Settlers, the Indians. By Matthew W. Stirling. Vol. LXXII, pp. 535-596, 34 ills. in black and white, 24 ills. in color, Nov., 1937.

When Red Men Ruled Our Forests. 24 ills. in color from paintings by W. Langdon Kihn. Vol. LXXII, pp. 551-590, Nov., 1937.

Sauntering Through the Land of Roger Williams. 14 ills. in color from natural-color photographs by Clifton Adams. Vol. LX, pp. 310-319, Sept., 1931.

Saussure, H. B. de:

Ascent of Mont Blanc. By Walter Woodburn Hyde. Vol. XXIV, pp. 861-942, 69 ills., Aug., 1913.

Saving the Ducks and Geese. By Wells W. Cooke. Vol. XXIV, pp. 361-380, 7 ills., 7 half-page maps, Feb., 1913.

Saving the Forests. By Herbert A. Smith. Vol. XVIII, pp. 519-534, 7 ills., Aug., 1907.

Saving the Redwoods. By Madison Grant. Vol. XXXVII, pp. 519-536, 10 ills., June, 1920.

Sayre, J. D.:

Valley of Ten Thousand Smokes: An Account of the Discovery and Exploration of the Most Wonderful Volcanic Region in the World. By Robert F. Griggs. Vol. XXXIII, pp. 115-169, 46 ills., 1 half-page map, panorama, Feb., 1918.

SCAT. See South Pacific Combat Air Transport.

Scenery of North America. By James Bryce. Vol. XLI, pp. 339-389, 45 ills., Apr., 1922.

Scenes Along the Byways of Hellas. 13 ills. in color from natural-color photographs by Maynard Owen Williams. Vol. LVIII, pp. 688-697, Dec., 1930.

Scenes Among the High Cascades in Central Oregon. By Ira A. Williams. Vol. XXIII, pp. 578-592, 11 ills., June, 1912.

Scenes and Round-Ups of the Beaver State (Oregon). 24 ills. in color from natural-color photographs by Amos Burg. Vol. LXV, pp. 181-212, Feb., 1934.

Scenes and Shrines of the Cavalier Country (Virginia). 13 ills. in color from natural-color photographs by Charles Martin, Edwin L. Wisherd, Jacob Gayer, and Clifton Adams. Vol. LV, pp. 424-433, Apr., 1929.

Scenes from America's Southwest. Vol. XXXIX, pp. 651-664, 14 ills., June, 1921.

Scenes from France. Vol. XL, pp. 29-44, 16 ills. July, 1921.

Scenes from Greenland. Vol. XX, pp. 877-891, 15 ills., Oct., 1909.

Scenes from North Africa. Vol. XVIII, pp. 615-619, 4 ills., Sept., 1907.

Scenes in Asia Minor. Vol. XX, pp. 174-193, 34 ills., 1 three-quarters-page map, Feb., 1909.

Scenes in Europe. Vol. XXVIII, pp. 551-566, 16 ills., Dec., 1915.

Scenes in Europe. Vol. XXX, pp. 233-248, 16 ills. in color, Sept., 1916.

Scenes in Italy. Vol. XXI, pp. 321-332, 12 ills., Apr., 1910.

Scenes in Out-of-the-Way Places. Vol. XXIV, pp. 854-860, 7 ills., July, 1913.

Scenes in Scotland. Vol. XXXII, pp. 519-534, 16 ills., Nov.-Dec., 1917.

Scenes in Switzerland. Vol. XXI, pp. 257-268, 13 ills., Mar., 1910.

Scenes in the Celestial Republic (China). 16 ills. in duotone. Vol. XLIX, pp. 217-232, Feb., 1926.

Scenes in the Fortunate Isles (Canary Islands). 12 ills. in color from natural-color photographs by Wilhelm Tobien. Vol. LVII, pp. 598-607, May, 1930.

Scenes of Beauty in Copper Land (Chile). 25 ills. in color from autochromes by Jacob Gayer. Vol. LV, pp. 198-215, Feb., 1929.

Scenes of Sunny Africa. 20 ills. in duotone. Vol. LXVII, pp. 735-750, June, 1935.

Scenes on High Veld and Low (Union of South Africa). 13 ills. in color from natural-color photographs by Melville Chater. Vol. LIX, pp. 492-501, Apr., 1931.

Scenic Glories of Western United States. 8 ills. in color from autochromes by Fred Payne Clatworthy. Vol. LVI, pp. 222-231, Aug., 1929.

Scenic Resources of the Dominican Republic. 28 ills. in color from natural-color photographs by Jacob Gayer. Vol. LIX, pp. 80-105, Jan., 1931.

Schaeffer, Claude F. A.:

New Alphabet of the Ancients Is Unearthed: An Inconspicuous Mound in Northern Syria Yields Archeological Treasures of Far-Reaching Significance. By F. A. Schaeffer. Vol. LVIII, pp. 477-516, 47 ills., 1 quarter-page map, Oct., 1930.

Secrets from Syrian Hills: Explorations Reveal World's Earliest Known Alphabet, Deciphered from Schoolboy Slates and Dictionaries of 3,000 Years Ago. By Claude F. A. Schaeffer. Vol. LXIV, pp. 97-126, 40 ills., 1 third-page map, July, 1933.

Schantz, Orpheus Moyer:

Indiana's Unrivaled Sand-Dunes—A National Park Opportunity. By Orpheus Moyer Schantz. Vol. XXXV, pp. 430-441, 18 ills., May, 1919.

Schillings, C. G.:

Flashlights from the Jungle (Extracted from a Publication by C. G. Schillings). Vol. XVIII, pp. 534-548, 11 ills., Aug., 1907.

Schleswig-Holstein (Region), Germany. *See* Helgoland.

Schmeckebier, L. F.:

Our National Parks (United States). By L. F. Schmeckebier. Vol. XXIII, pp. 531-579, 41 ills., 1 page map, June, 1912.

Schmitt, Waldo L.:

Voyage to the Island Home of Robinson Crusoe (Juan Fernández). By Waldo L. Schmitt. Vol. LIV, pp. 353-370, 24 ills., Sept., 1928.

Schneider, John E.:

Uncle Sam's Icebox Outposts. 19 ills. in color from natural-color photographs by John E. Schneider and Robert B. Sykes, Jr. Vol. XC, pp. 473-496, Oct., 1946.

Schoedsack, Ernest B.:

Two Fighting Tribes of the Sudan. By Merian C. Cooper. Photographs by Ernest B. Schoedsack. Vol. LVI, pp. 465-486, 27 ills., 1 two-thirds-page map, Oct., 1929.

Warfare of the Jungle Folk: Campaigning Against Tigers, Elephants, and Other Wild Animals in Northern Siam. By Merian C. Cooper. Photographs by Ernest B. Schoedsack. Vol. LIII, pp. 233-268, 33 ills., Feb., 1928.

Schools. *See* Training Schools; Universities and Colleges.

Schooners. *See Adams; Effie M. Morrissey; Kinkajou; Yankee.*

Schott, C. A.:

Recent Contributions to Our Knowledge of the Earth's Shape and Size, by the United States Coast and Geodetic Survey. By C. A. Schott. Vol. XII, pp. 36-41, 1 ill., 1 chart, Jan., 1901.

Schrader, F. C.:

Cape Nome Gold District (Alaska). By F. C. Schrader. Vol. XI, pp. 15-23, 3 ills., 1 page map, Jan., 1900.

Schultz, Leonard P.:

Fishing in Pacific Coast Streams. By Leonard P. Schultz. Vol. LXXV, pp. 185-212, 10 ills. in black and white, 54 portraits in color, Feb., 1939.

Treasures of the Pacific: Marine Fishes and Fisheries Yield Vast Wealth from Alaska to Baja California. By Leonard P. Schultz. Vol. LXXIV, pp. 463-498, 10 ills. in black and white, 31 portraits in color, Oct., 1938.

Schurz, W. L.:

Amazon, Father of Waters: The Earth's Mightiest River Drains a Basin of More Than 2,700,000 Square Miles, from Which Came Originally the World's Finest Rubber. By W. L. Schurz. Vol. XLIX, pp. 445-463, 15 ills., Apr., 1926.

Schuyler, Montgomery:

Russia's Democrats. By Montgomery Schuyler. Vol. XXXI, pp. 210-240, 25 ills., Mar., 1917.

Schwab, Charles M.:

Our Industrial Victory. By Charles M. Schwab. Vol. XXXIV, pp. 212-229, 17 ills., Sept., 1918.

Schwartz, William Leonard:

Peacetime Rambles in the Ryukyus. By William Leonard Schwartz. Vol. LXXXVII, pp. 543-561, 12 ills., 1 two-thirds-page and 1 half-page maps, May, 1945.

Schwinn, Gretchen:

We Escape from Madrid. By Gretchen Schwinn. Vol. LXXI, pp. 251-268, 15 ills., Feb., 1937.

Scidmore, Eliza Ruhamah:

Adam's Second Eden (Ceylon). By Eliza R. Scidmore. Vol. XXIII, pp. 105-173, 60 ills., Feb., 1912.

Archæology in the Air. By Eliza R. Scidmore. Vol. XVIII, pp. 150-163, 11 ills., Mar., 1907.

Bathing and Burning Ghats at Benares. By Eliza R. Scidmore. Vol. XVIII, pp. 118-128, 7 ills., Feb., 1907.

Greatest Hunt in the World (Elephant Hunting). By Eliza R. Scidmore. Vol. XVII, pp. 673-692, 17 ills., Dec., 1906.

Japan. 11 ills. in color from photographs by Eliza R. Scidmore. Vol. XXVI, pp. 54-64, July, 1914.

Koyasan, the Japanese Valhalla. By Eliza R. Scidmore. Vol. XVIII, pp. 650-670, 14 ills., Oct., 1907.

Mrs. Bishop's "The Yangtze Valley and Beyond." By Eliza R. Scidmore. Vol. XI, pp. 366-368, Sept., 1900.

Mukden, the Manchu Home, and Its Great Art Museum. By Eliza R. Scidmore. Vol. XXI, pp. 289-320, 30 ills., Apr., 1910.

Stikine River in 1898 (British Columbia). By Eliza R. Scidmore. Vol. X, pp. 1-15, 4 ills., Jan., 1899.

Tsung-Li-Yamen (Foreign Office, China). By Eliza R. Scidmore. Vol. XI, pp. 291-292, 1 diagram, 1 two-thirds-page map, July, 1900.

Young Japan. By Eliza R. Scidmore. Vol. XXVI, pp. 36-38, 54-64, 11 ills. in color, July, 1914.

Science:

American Association for the Advancement of Science. By Gilbert H. Grosvenor. Vol. X, pp. 355-359, Sept., 1899.

Chemists Make a New World: Creating Hitherto Unknown Raw Materials, Science Now Disrupts Old Trade Routes and Revamps the World Map of Industry. By Frederick Simpich. Vol. LXXVI, pp. 601-640, 22 ills. in black and white, 26 ills. in color, Nov., 1939.

Discovery and Invention. By Alexander Graham Bell. Vol. XXV, pp. 649-655, June, 1914.

From Nature's Hidden Building Blocks. 26 ills. in color from natural-color photographs by Willard R. Culver. Vol. LXXVI, pp. 609-640, Nov., 1939.

Prizes for the Inventor: Some of the Problems Awaiting Solution. By Alexander Graham Bell. Vol. XXXI, pp. 131-146, 7 ills., Feb., 1917.

Science—*Continued*

Science Works for Mankind. 16 ills. in color from paintings by Thornton Oakley. Vol. LXXXVIII, pp. 737-752, Dec., 1945.

See also the various branches of science.

Scientific Aspects of the MacMillan Arctic Expedition. Vol. XLVIII, pp. 545-554, 9 ills., Sept., 1925.

Scientific Results of the World-Record Stratosphere Flight. By Capt. Albert W. Stevens. Vol. LXIX, pp. 693-712, 15 ills., May, 1936.

Scientific Work of Mount Weather Meteorological Research Observatory. By Frank H. Bigelow. Vol. XV, pp. 442-445, Nov., 1904.

Scientific Work of the National Geographic Society's Eclipse Expedition to Norfolk, Virginia. By Simon Newcomb. Vol. XI, pp. 321-324, Aug., 1900.

Scillies: Isles of Wrecks and Golden Daffodils. 13 ills. in color from natural-color photographs by B. Anthony Stewart, Maynard Owen Williams, and W. Robert Moore. Vol. LXXIV, pp. 759-766, Dec., 1938.

Scilly Isles, England:

Garden Isles of Scilly: Geologists May Throw Stones at Legend of Lost Lyonnesse, But Natives Grow Flowers in Glass Houses for London. By W. Robert Moore. Vol. LXXIV, pp. 755-774, 9 ills. in black and white, 13 ills. in color, 1 half-page map, Dec., 1938.

Scillies: Isles of Wrecks and Golden Daffodils. 13 ills. in color from natural-color photographs by B. Anthony Stewart, Maynard Owen Williams, and W. Robert Moore. Vol. LXXIV, pp. 759-766, Dec., 1938.

Scotland:

Bonnie Scotland, Postwar Style. By Isobel Wylie Hutchison. Vol. LXXXIX, pp. 545-601, 14 ills. in black and white, 38 ills. in color, 1 two-page map, May, 1946.

Clans in Kilt and Plaidie Gather at Braemar. 11 ills. in color from natural-color photographs by Maynard Owen Williams. Vol. LXVIII, pp. 153-160, Aug., 1935.

Great Britain on Parade. By Maynard Owen Williams. Vol. LXVIII, pp. 137-184, 40 ills. in black and white, 11 ills. in color, Aug., 1935.

Heather Paints the Highlands. 38 ills. in color from natural-color photographs by B. Anthony Stewart. Vol. LXXXIX, pp. 561-600, May, 1946.

Low Road, High Road, Around Dundee. By Maurice P. Dunlap. Vol. LXIX, pp. 547-576, 35 ills., 1 half-page map, Apr., 1936.

Orkneys and Shetlands—A Mysterious Group of Islands. By Charles S. Olcott. Vol. XXXIX, pp. 197-228, 33 ills., Feb., 1921.

Scenes in Scotland. Vol. XXXII, pp. 519-534, 16 ills., Nov.-Dec., 1917.

Scotland—*Continued*

Scotland in Wartime. By Isobel Wylie Hutchison. Vol. LXXXIII, pp. 723-743, 19 ills., June, 1943.

See also Edinburgh.

Scott, Charles F.:

Annual Dinner of the National Geographic Society (Speech by Charles F. Scott). Vol. XVII, pp. 22-37, Jan., 1906.

Scott, Emmett J.:

Conditions in Liberia. By Roland P. Folkner, George Sale, and Emmett J. Scott. Vol. XXI, pp. 729-741, 9 ills., Sept., 1910.

Scott, (Sir) George:

Among the Hill Tribes of Burma—An Ethnological Thicket. By Sir George Scott. Vol. XLII, pp. 293-321, 22 ills., Mar., 1922.

Scott, George W.:

Kano, Mud-made City. 10 ills. in color from natural-color photographs by George W. Scott and K. S. Twitchell. Vol. LXXXV, pp. 545-552, May, 1944.

Scott, John:

"Magnetic City" (Magnitogorsk), Core of Valiant Russia's Industrial Might. By John Scott. Vol. LXXXIII, pp. 525-556, 27 ills., 1 two-page map, May, 1943.

Scott, Robert F.:

British South Polar Expedition. Vol. XIV, pp. 210-212, May, 1903.

Ice-Wrapped Continent. By Gilbert H. Grosvenor. Vol. XVIII, pp. 95-117, 20 ills., 1 half-page map, Feb., 1907.

Scouts. *See* Boy Scouts; Girl Scouts.

Scriven, (Brig. Gen.) George P.:

Recent Observations in Albania. By Brig. Gen. George P. Scriven. Vol. XXXIV, pp. 90-114, 21 ills., 1 half-page map, Aug., 1918.

Sculpture:

Buddhist Calm Survives Along China's Great Wall. 10 ills. in color; 4 paintings by Mary Augusta Mullikin and Anna M. Hotchkis and 6 natural-color photographs. Vol. LXXIII, pp. 321-328, Mar., 1938.

China's Great Wall of Sculpture: Man-hewn Caves and Countless Images Form a Colossal Art Wonder of Early Buddhism. By Mary Augusta Mullikin. Vol. LXXIII, pp. 313-348, 23 ills. in black and white, 10 ills. in color, 1 third-page map, Mar., 1938.

Discovering the New World's Oldest Dated Work of Man: A Maya Monument Inscribed 291 B. C. Is Unearthed Near a Huge Stone Head by a Geographic-Smithsonian Expedition in Mexico. By Matthew W. Stirling. Vol. LXXVI, pp. 183-218, 40 ills., 1 half-page map, Aug., 1939.

Sculpture—*Continued*

Discovering the Oldest Statues in the World: A Daring Explorer Swims Through a Subterranean River of the Pyrenees and Finds Rock Carvings Made 20,000 Years Ago. By Norbert Casteret. Vol. XLVI, pp. 123-152, 24 ills., 1 half and 1 quarter-page maps, Aug., 1924.

Exploring the Secrets of Persepolis. By Charles Breasted. Vol. LXIV, pp. 381-420, 48 ills., 1 half-page map, 1 plan, Oct., 1933.

Great Stone Faces of Easter Island. 11 ills. from photographs. Vol. LXXXV, pp. 225-232, Feb., 1944.

Great Stone Faces of the Mexican Jungle: Five Colossal Heads and Numerous Other Monuments of Vanished Americans Are Excavated by the Latest National Geographic-Smithsonian Expedition. By Matthew W. Stirling. Vol. LXXVIII, pp. 309-334, 26 ills., 1 map, Sept., 1940.

Greek Bronzes of Tunisia. By Frank Edward Johnson. Vol. XXIII, pp. 89-103, 11 ills., Jan., 1912.

Italy's Monuments Tell Rome's Magnificence. 8 ills. from photographs; 7 ills. by B. Anthony Stewart. Vol. LXXVII, pp. 371-378, Mar., 1940.

Modern Odyssey in Classic Lands: Troy's Treasures, Athens' Parthenon, and Rome's First "Broad Way" Influence Today's Banks, Costumes, Jewelry, and Railroad Timetables. By Maynard Owen Williams. Vol. LXXVII, pp. 291-337, 27 ills. in black and white, 22 ills. in color, Mar., 1940.

Mystery of Easter Island. By Mrs. Scoresby Routledge. Vol. XL, pp. 628-646, 13 ills., 1 page map, Dec., 1921.

Nation's Capital by Night. By Volkmar Wentzel. With 16 illustrations in duotone from photographs by the author. Vol. LXXVII, pp. 514-530, Apr., 1940.

Smallest State in the World: Vatican City on Its 108 Acres Is a Complete Sovereignty Internationally Recognized. By W. Coleman Nevils. Vol. LXXV, pp. 377-412, 37 ills., 1 two-page map, Mar., 1939.

Stone Idols of the Andes Reveal a Vanished People: Remarkable Relics of One of the Oldest Aboriginal Cultures of America Are Unearthed in Colombia's San Agustín Region. By Hermann von Walde-Waldegg. Vol. LXXVII, pp. 627-647, 22 ills., 1 map, May, 1940.

Storied Islands of the South Sea. 20 ills. in color from natural-color photographs by Irving Johnson, Malcolm Evans, and others. Vol. LXXXI, pp. 9-40, Jan., 1942.

Sculptured Gates to English Learning (Cambridge University). 19 ills. in color from natural-color photographs by B. Anthony Stewart. Vol. LXXXIX, pp. 417-440, Apr., 1946.

Sea Bees:

Your Navy as Peace Insurance. By Fleet Admiral Chester W. Nimitz. Vol. LXXXIX, pp. 681-736, 32 ills. in black and white, 26 ills. in color, June, 1946.

Sea Captains:

American Pathfinders in the Pacific. By William H. Nicholas. Vol. LXXXIX, pp. 617-640, 17 ills., 1 two-page map, May, 1946.

Sea Creatures of Our Atlantic Shores (Mollusks, Crustaceans, etc.). By Roy Waldo Miner. Vol. LXX, pp. 209-231, 8 ills. in black and white, 8 ills. in color, 1 chart, Aug., 1936.

Sea Elephants. *See* Elephant Seals.

Sea Floor Aquarelles from Tongareva. 8 ills. in color from paintings by Else Bostelmann. Vol. LXXIV, pp. 383-390, Sept., 1938.

Sea Fogs of San Francisco. Vol. XII, pp. 108-114, 5 ills., Mar., 1901.

Sea Islands, Georgia:

Golden Isles of Guale. By W. Robert Moore. Vol. LXV, pp. 235-264, 35 ills., 1 three-quarters-page map, Feb., 1934.

Sea-Kings of Crete. By James Baikie. Vol. XXIII, pp. 1-25, 13 ills., Jan., 1912.

Sea Rescues:

They Survived at Sea. By Lt. Comdr. Samuel F. Harby. Vol. LXXXVII, pp. 617-640, 22 ills., May, 1945.

Seafarers of South Celebes. By G. E. P. Collins. Vol. LXXXVII, pp. 53-78, 25 ills., 1 two-thirds-page map, Jan., 1945.

Sealing Saga of Newfoundland. By Capt. Robert A. Bartlett. Vol. LVI, pp. 91-130, 44 ills., July, 1929.

Seals (Mammals):

Birds and Beasts of Mexico's Desert Islands. 12 ills. in color from natural-color photographs; 8 ills. by Ed N. Harrison; 4 ills. by Alfred M. Bailey and Robert J. Niedrach. Vol. LXXX, pp. 353-360, Sept., 1941.

Cruise of the *Kinkajou:* Among Desert Islands of Mexico Voyagers Find Outdoor Laboratories for the Naturalist and Ideal Fishing Grounds for the Sportsman. By Alfred M. Bailey. Vol. LXXX, pp. 339-366, 13 ills. in black and white, 12 ills. in color, 1 page map, Sept., 1941.

Land of Eternal Warring (Labrador). By Sir Wilfred T. Grenfell. Vol. XXI, pp. 665-690, 24 ills., Aug., 1910.

Making the Fur Seal Abundant. By Hugh M. Smith. Vol. XXII, pp. 1139-1165, 18 ills., 1 half-page map, Dec., 1911.

Sealing Saga of Newfoundland. By Capt. Robert A. Bartlett. Vol. LVI, pp. 91-130, 44 ills., July, 1929.

South Georgia, an Outpost of the Antarctic. By Robert Cushman Murphy. Vol. XLI, pp. 409-444, 41 ills., 2 half-page maps, Apr., 1922.

Seals of Our Nation, States, and Territories. By Elizabeth W. King. Paintings by Carlotta Gonzales Lahey, Irvin E. Alleman, and Theodora Price. Vol. XC, pp. 1-42, 14 ills. in black and white, 84 ills. in color, July, 1946.

Contents: Seals of the States and the District of Columbia; Seals of the Territories, Island Possessions, the Canal Zone, and the Philippine Commonwealth; Great Seal of the United States and Other Federal Seals; Seals of the President and of the Government Departments.

Seaman, Louis Livingston:

Observations on the Russo-Japanese War in Japan and Manchuria. By Louis Livingston Seaman. Vol. XVI, pp. 80-82, Feb., 1905.

Wonders of the Mosi-oa-Tunga: The Falls of the Zambesi. By Louis Livingston Seaman. Vol. XXII, pp. 561-571, 6 ills., June, 1911.

Seaplanes:

By Seaplane to Six Continents: Cruising 60,000 Miles, Italian Argonauts of the Air See World Geography Unroll, and Break New Sky Trails Over Vast Brazilian Jungles. By Comdr. Francesco de Pinedo. Vol. LIV, pp. 247-301, 60 ills., 1 two-page map, Sept., 1928.

Exploring the Valley of the Amazon in a Hydroplane: Twelve Thousand Miles of Flying Over the World's Greatest River and Greatest Forest to Chart the Unknown Parima River from the Sky. By Capt. Albert W. Stevens. Vol. XLIX, pp. 353-420, 86 ills., 1 page map, Apr., 1926.

Flying. By Gilbert Grosvenor. Vol. LXIII, pp. 589-630, 33 ills. in black and white, 17 ills. in duotone, May, 1933.

Flying the Pacific. By William Burke Miller. Vol. LXX, pp. 665-707, 39 ills., Dec., 1936.

How the United States Grew. By McFall Kerbey. Vol. LXIII, pp. 631-649, 17 ills., 1 page map, May, 1933.

Into Primeval Papua by Seaplane: Seeking Disease-Resisting Sugar Cane, Scientists Find Neolithic Man in Unmapped Nooks of Sorcery and Cannibalism. By E. W. Brandes. Vol. LVI, pp. 253-332, 98 ills., 1 three-quarters-page map, Sept., 1929.

Maneuvers of Military Planes Disclose Majestic Aërial Views. 17 ills. in duotone from U. S. Army and Navy official photographs. Vol. LXIII, pp. 598-615, May, 1933.

Seeing 3,000 Years of History in Four Hours: A Panorama of Ancient, Medieval, and Modern Events Against a Background of Mythology Unfolds During an Airplane Journey from Constantinople to Athens. By Maynard Owen Williams. Vol. LIV, pp. 719-739, 24 ills., 1 two-thirds-page map, Dec., 1928.

Unknown New Guinea: Circumnavigating the World in a Flying Boat, American Scientists Discover a Valley of 60,000 People Never Before Seen by White Men. By Richard Archbold. Vol. LXXIX, pp. 315-344, 28 ills., 1 two-thirds-page map, Mar., 1941.

Seattle, Washington:

Washington, The Evergreen State: The Amazing Commonwealth of the Pacific Northwest Which Has Emerged from the Wilderness in a Span of Fifty Years. By Leo A. Borah. Vol. LXIII, pp. 131-196, 50 ills. in black and white, 26 ills. in color, 1 two-page map, Feb., 1933.

Seaweeds:

Fisheries of Japan. By Hugh M. Smith. Vol. XVI, pp. 201-220, 13 ills., May, 1905.

Seaweeds of the United States. Vol. XVI, p. 244, 2 ills., May, 1905.

Undersea Gardens of the North Atlantic Coast. 8 ills. in color from paintings by Else Bostelmann. Vol. LXX, pp. 217-224, Aug., 1936.

Second Marine Division, U. S.:

Gilbert Islands in the Wake of Battle. By W. Robert Moore. Vol. LXXXVII, pp. 129-162, 11 ills. in black and white, 19 ills. in color, 1 two-thirds-page map, Feb., 1945.

Secret of the Southwest Solved by Talkative Tree Rings: Horizons of American History Are Carried Back to A. D. 700 and a Calendar for 1,200 Years Established by National Geographic Society Expeditions. By Andrew Ellicott Douglass. Vol. LVI, pp. 737-770, 33 ills., 1 two-thirds-page map, Dec., 1929.

Secrets from Syrian Hills: Explorations Reveal World's Earliest Known Alphabet, Deciphered from Schoolboy Slates and Dictionaries of 3,000 Years Ago. By Claude F. A. Schaeffer. Vol. LXIV, pp. 97-126, 40 ills., 1 third-page map, July, 1933.

Secrets of Washington's Lure. 15 ills. in color from natural-color photographs by Staff Photographers. Vol. LVII, pp. 376-385, Mar., 1930.

Seed Farms in California. By A. J. Wells. Vol. XXIII, pp. 515-530, 14 ills., May, 1912.

Seeing America from the *Shenandoah:* An Account of the Record-Making 9,000-Mile Flight from the Atlantic to the Pacific Coast and Return in the Navy's American-built, American-manned Airship. By Junius B. Wood. Vol. XLVII, pp. 1-47, 39 ills., 1 page map, 1 diagram, Jan., 1925.

Seeing America with Lindbergh: The Record of a Tour of More than 20,000 Miles by Airplane Through Forty-eight States on Schedule Time. By Lieut. Donald E. Keyhoe. Vol. LIII, pp. 1-46, 46 ills., 1 page map, Jan., 1928.

Seeing Eye (School), Morristown, New Jersey:
Dogs of Duty and Devotion. By Frederick G. Vosburgh. Vol. LXXX, pp. 769-774, 3 ills., Dec., 1941.

Seeing Our Spanish Southwest. By Frederick Simpich. Vol. LXXVII, pp. 711-756, 25 ills. in black and white, 17 ills. in duotone, special map supplement, June, 1940.

Seeing Paris on a 48-Hour Pass. 12 ills. in color from U. S. Army official photographs. Vol. LXXXVII, pp. 401-412, Apr., 1945.

Seeing the World from the Air. By Sir Alan J. Cobham. Vol. LIII, pp. 349-384, 37 ills., 1 three-quarters-page map, Mar., 1928.

Seeing 3,000 Years of History in Four Hours: A Panorama of Ancient, Medieval, and Modern Events Against a Background of Mythology Unfolds During an Airplane Journey from Constantinople to Athens. By Maynard Owen Williams. Vol. LIV, pp. 719-739, 24 ills., 1 two-thirds-page map, Dec., 1928.

Seeking the Mountains of Mystery: An Expedition on the China-Tibet Frontier to the Unexplored Amnyi Machen Range, One of Whose Peaks Rivals Everest. By Joseph F. Rock. Vol. LVII, pp. 131-185, 54 ills., 1 two-page map, Feb., 1930.

Seeking the Smallest Feathered Creatures: Humming Birds, Peculiar to the New World, Are Found from Canada and Alaska to the Straits of Magellan. Swifts and Goatsuckers, Their Nearest Relatives. By Alexander Wetmore. Paintings by Maj. Allan Brooks. Vol. LXII, pp. 65-89, 9 ills. in black and white, 36 ills. in color, July, 1932.

Segerstrom, Kenneth:

Down Mexico's Río Balsas. 9 ills. in color from natural-color photographs by John W. Webber, Kenneth Segerstrom, and Jack Breed. Vol. XC, pp. 257-264, Aug., 1946.

Seiler, (Lt.) Dayton:

Indian Haven—Off the San Blas Coast (Mulatas Archipelago). 12 ills. in color from natural-color photographs by Lieut. Dayton Seiler. Vol. LXXIX, pp. 209-216, Feb., 1941.

Seine (River), France:

Beauties of France. By Arthur Stanley Riggs. Vol. XXVIII, pp. 391-491, 73 ills. in black and white, 16 ills. in color, 1 half-page map, Nov., 1915.

Seismology:

Charting a World at War. By William H. Nicholas. Vol. LXXXVI, pp. 617-640, 23 ills., 1 drawing, Nov., 1944.

How the Earth Telegraphed Its Tokyo Quake to Washington. By Rev. Francis A. Tondorf. Vol. XLIV, pp. 453-454, 1 ill., Oct., 1923.

Record of the Great Earthquake Written in Washington by the Seismograph of the United States Weather Bureau. By C. F. Marvin. Vol. XVII, pp. 296-298, May, 1906.

San Francisco Earthquake of April 18, 1906, as Recorded by the Coast and Geodetic Survey Magnetic Observatories. By Dr. L. A. Bauer and J. E. Burbank. Vol. XVII, pp. 298-300, May, 1906.

Selenium (Chemical Element):

Discovery and Invention. By Alexander Graham Bell. Vol. XXV, pp. 649-655, June, 1914.

Seleucus (King of Syria):
Antioch the Glorious. By William H. Hall. Vol. XXXVIII, pp. 81-103, 20 ills., 1 half-page map, Aug., 1920.

Self-Government:

United States and the British Empire. By Leonard David Gammans. Vol. LXXXVII, pp. 562-564, May, 1945.

Yanks at Westminster. By Capt. Leonard David Gammans. Vol. XC, pp. 223-252, 6 ills. in black and white, 19 ills. in color, Aug., 1946.

Selinus, Sicily:

Ruins at Selinus. By Marion Crawford. Vol. XX, p. 117, Jan., 1909.

Selkirk Mountains, British Columbia:

Some Tramps Across the Glaciers and Snowfields of British Columbia. By Howard Palmer. Vol. XXI, pp. 457-487, 25 ills., June, 1910.

Sella, Vittorio:

Africa: African Scenes from the Equator to the Cape. 16 ills. from photographs; 5 ills. by Vittorio Sella. Vol. XLII, pp. 431-446, Oct., 1922.

Africa: Amid the Snows and Swamps of Tropical Africa. 10 ills. from photographs; 7 ills. by Vittorio Sella. Vol. XLVII, pp. 163-178, Feb., 1925.

Africa: Cairo to Cape Town, Overland: An Adventurous Journey of 135 Days, Made by an American and His Wife, Through the Length of the African Continent. By Felix Shay. Vol. XLVII, pp. 123-260, 118 ills., 1 half-page map, Feb., 1925.

Contains 6 illustrations from photographs by Vittorio Sella.

Daghestan: Island in the Sea of History: The Highlands of Daghestan. By George Kennan. Vol. XXIV, pp. 1086-1140, 49 ills., 1 page map, Oct., 1913.

Contains 6 illustrations from photographs by Vittorio Sella.

Fight at the Timber-Line. By John Oliver La Gorce. Vol. XLII, pp. 165-196, 32 ills., Aug., 1922.

Contains 9 illustrations from photographs by Vittorio Sella.

Swiss Alps. 16 ills. from photographs; 11 ills. by Vittorio Sella. Vol. XXVII, pp. 187-202, Feb., 1915.

U. S. S. R.: Young Russia: The Land of Unlimited Possibilities. By Gilbert H. Grosvenor. Vol. XXVI, pp. 421-520, 85 ills. in black and white, 17 ills. in color, Nov., 1914.

Contains 4 illustrations from photographs by Vittorio Sella.

World's Highest Altitudes and First Ascents. By Charles E. Fay. Vol. XX, pp. 493-530, 25 ills., June, 1902.

Contains 9 illustrations from photographs by Vittorio Sella.

Seminole Indians:

Indians of the Southeastern United States. By Matthew W. Stirling. Paintings by W. Langdon Kihn. Vol. LXXXIX, pp. 53-74, 8 ills. in black and white, 8 ills. in color, Jan., 1946.

Seminole Indians—*Continued*

South Florida's Amazing Everglades: Encircled by Populous Places, Is a Seldom-visited Area of Rare Birds, Prairies, Cowboys, and Teeming Wild Life of Big Cypress Swamp. By John O'Reilly. Vol. LXXVII, pp. 115-142, 26 ills., 1 page map, Jan., 1940.

Seneca (Indian Tribe):

America's First Settlers, the Indians. By Matthew W. Stirling. Vol. LXXII, pp. 535-596, 34 ills. in black and white, 24 ills. in color, Nov., 1937.

When Red Men Ruled Our Forests. 24 ills. in color from paintings by W. Langdon Kihn. Vol. LXXII, pp. 551-590, Nov., 1937.

Sénégal:

French West Africa in Wartime. By Paul M. Atkins. Vol. LXXXI, pp. 371-408, 37 ills., 2 maps, Mar., 1942.

See also Dakar.

Seoul (Keijo), Korea:

Chosen—Land of Morning Calm. By Mabel Craft Deering. Vol. LXIV, pp. 421-448, 20 ills. in black and white, 13 ills. in color, 1 two-thirds-page map, Oct., 1933.

Glimpses of Korea and China. By William W. Chapin. Vol. XXI, pp. 895-934, 11 ills. in black and white, 39 ills. in color, Nov., 1910.

Jap Rule in the Hermit Nation (Korea). By Willard Price. Vol. LXXXVIII, pp. 429-451, 19 ills., 1 page map, Oct., 1945.

Sequoia National Park, California:

Among the Big Trees of California. By John R. White. Vol. LXVI, pp. 219-232, 14 ills., Aug., 1934.

Land of the Best. By Gilbert H. Grosvenor. Vol. XXIX, pp. 327-430, 71 ills. in black and white, 33 ills. in color, panorama, Apr., 1916.

National Geographic Society Completes Its Gifts of Big Trees. Vol. XL, pp. 85-86, July, 1921.

Oldest Living Thing ("General Sherman Tree"). Vol. XXIX, supplement, Apr., 1916.

Our Big Trees Saved. Vol. XXXI, pp. 1-11, 10 ills., Jan., 1917.

Our National Parks. By L. F. Schmeckebier. Vol. XXIII, pp. 531-579, 41 ills., 1 page map, June, 1912.

Sequoias (Trees):

Among the Big Trees of California. By John R. White. Vol. LXVI, pp. 219-232, 14 ills., Aug., 1934.

California's Coastal Redwood Realm: Along a Belt of Tall Trees a Giant Bridge Speeds the Winning of Our Westernmost Frontier. By J. R. Hildebrand. Vol. LXXV, pp. 133-184, 31 ills. in black and white, 17 ills. in color, 1 page-and-a-half map, Feb., 1939.

Golden Gate, and Redwood Evergreens. 17 ills. in color from natural-color photographs by B. Anthony Stewart. Vol. LXXV, pp. 149-160, Feb., 1939.

Sequoias (Trees)—*Continued*

National Geographic Society Completes Its Gifts of Big Trees. Vol. XL, pp. 85-86, July, 1921.

Oldest Living Thing ("General Sherman Tree"). Vol. XXIX, supplement, Apr., 1916.

Our Big Trees Saved. Vol. XXXI, pp. 1-11, 10 ills., Jan., 1917.

Our National Parks. By L. F. Schmeckebier. Vol. XXIII, pp. 531-579, 41 ills., 1 page map, June, 1912.

Redwood Forest of the Pacific Coast. By Henry Gannett. Vol. X, pp. 145-159, 6 ills., 1 page map, May, 1899.

Saving the Redwoods. By Madison Grant. Vol. XXXVII, pp. 519-536, 10 ills., June, 1920.

Serbia:

Changing Map in the Balkans. By Frederick Moore. Vol. XXIV, pp. 199-226, 27 ills., 1 page map, Feb., 1913.

Clock Turns Back in Yugoslavia: The Fortified Monastery of Mountain-girt Dečani Survives Its Six Hundredth Birthday. By Ethel Chamberlain Porter. Vol. LXXXV, pp. 493-512, 20 ills., 1 page map, Apr., 1944.

Great Turk and His Lost Provinces. By William E. Curtis. Vol. XIV, pp. 45-61, 7 ills., Feb., 1903.

Kingdom of Servia. By William Joseph Showalter. Vol. XXVII, pp. 417-432, 12 ills., 1 page map, Apr., 1915.

Land of Contrast: Austria-Hungary. By D. W. and A. S. Iddings. Vol. XXIII, pp. 1188-1218, 34 ills., Dec., 1912.

Races of Europe. By Edwin A. Grosvenor. Vol. XXXIV, pp. 441-534, 62 ills., 2 page maps, special map supplement, Dec., 1918.

Servia and Montenegro. Vol. XIX, pp. 774-789, 24 ills., Nov., 1908.

Seri Indians:

Adventuring Down the West Coast of Mexico. By Herbert Corey. Vol. XLII, pp. 449-503, 44 ills., 1 half-page map, Nov., 1922.

Mexican Land of Canaan: Marvelous Riches of the Wonderful West Coast of Our Neighbor Republic. By Frederick Simpich. Vol. XXXVI, pp. 307-330, 16 ills., 1 page map, Oct., 1919.

Seri Indians. Vol. XII, pp. 278-280, July, 1901.

Servia and Montenegro. Vol. XIX, pp. 774-789, 24 ills., Nov., 1908.

Service Ribbons, Military and Naval:

Decorations, Medals, Service Ribbons, Badges, and Women's Insignia. Vol. LXXXIV, pp. 414-444, 6 ills. in black and white, 376 ills. in color, Oct., 1943.

Seton, Ernest Thompson:

Smaller Mammals of North America. By E. W. Nelson. Vol. XXXIII, pp. 371-493, 29 ills. in black and white, 59 ills. in color, May, 1918.

Sevastopol, R. S. F. S. R.:

Crimea Reborn. By Eddy Gilmore. Vol. LXXXVII, pp. 487-512, 23 ills., 1 half-page map, Apr., 1945.

Seventh Annual Newspaper National Snapshot Awards:

Americana. 11 ills. from winning photographs in the Seventh Annual Newspaper National Snapshot Awards. Vol. LXXXI, pp. 657-666, May, 1942.

Seventy-Five Days in the Arctics. By Max Fleischman. Vol. XVIII, pp. 439-446, 5 ills., July, 1907.

Severn Valley, England:

Beauties of the Severn Valley. By Frank Wakeman. Vol. LXIII, pp. 417-452, 24 ills. in black and white, 15 ills. in color, 1 three-quarters-page map, Apr., 1933.

Wayfaring down the Winding Severn. 15 ills. in color from natural-color photographs by Frank and Bernard Wakeman. Vol. LXIII, pp. 432-441, Apr., 1933.

Seville, Spain:

Seville, More Spanish Than Spain: The City of the Ibero-American Exposition, Which Opens This Spring, Presents a Tapestry of Many Ages and of Nations Old and New. By Richard Ford. Vol. LV, pp. 273-310, 35 ills. in black and white, 2 ills. in color, Mar., 1929.

Sex, Nativity, and Color of the People of the United States. By Gilbert H. Grosvenor. Vol. XII, pp. 381-389, 17 charts, Nov., 1901.

Shackelford, J. B.:

Nomad Life and Fossil Treasures of Mongolia. 20 ills. in color from photographs by J. B. Shackelford. Vol. LXIII, pp. 669-701, June, 1933.

Shackleton, (Sir) Ernest H.:

Heart of the Antarctic. By Ernest H. Shackleton. Vol. XX, pp. 972-1007, 27 ills., 1 half-page map, Nov., 1909.

Race for the South Pole (Presentation of Hubbard Medal by President Taft). Vol. XXI, pp. 185-186, Mar., 1910.

Shackleton's Farthest South. Vol. XX, pp. 398-402, 1 half-page map, Apr., 1909.

South Georgia, an Outpost of the Antarctic. By Robert Cushman Murphy. Vol. XLI, pp. 409-444, 41 ills., 2 half-page maps, Apr., 1922.

Shackleton's Farthest South. Vol. XX, pp. 398-402, 1 half-page map, Apr., 1909.

Shad (Fish):

Federal Fish Farming; or, Planting Fish by the Billion. By Hugh M. Smith. Vol. XXI, pp. 418-446, 22 ills., May, 1910.

Shadowy Birds of the Night (Owls). By Alexander Wetmore. Vol. LXVII, pp. 217-240, 5 ills. in black and white, 21 portraits in color, Feb., 1935.

Shadowy London by Night. 8 ills. by H. B. Burdekin. Vol. LXVIII, pp. 177-184, Aug., 1935.

Shaffer, E. T. H.:

Ashley River and Its Gardens (South Carolina). By E. T. H. Shaffer. Vol. XLIX, pp. 525-550, 6 ills. in black and white, 7 ills. in color, May, 1926.

Shahr Kurd, Iran:

Mountain Tribes of Iran and Iraq. By Harold Lamb. Vol. LXXXIX, pp. 385-408, 15 ills., 1 two-page map, Mar., 1946.

Shan (Tribespeople):

Burma: Where India and China Meet: In the Massive Mountains of Southeast Asia, Swarming Road Builders Wage the "War of the Highways" for Free China and Her Allies. By John LeRoy Christian. Vol. LXXXIV, pp. 489-512, 18 ills., 1 page map, Oct., 1943.

Shan Tribes Make Burma's Hills Flash With Color. 15 ills. in color from natural-color photographs by W. Robert Moore. Vol. LX, pp. 454-463, Oct., 1931.

Strange Tribes in the Shan States of Burma. 15 ills. in color from natural-color photographs by W. Robert Moore. Vol. LVIII, pp. 247-254, Aug., 1930.

Shan States, Burma:

Burma: Where India and China Meet: In the Massive Mountains of Southeast Asia, Swarming Road Builders Wage the "War of the Highways" for Free China and Her Allies. By John LeRoy Christian. Vol. LXXXIV, pp. 489-512, 18 ills., 1 page map, Oct., 1943.

Shan Tribes Make Burma's Hills Flash With Color. 15 ills. in color from natural-color photographs by W. Robert Moore. Vol. LX, pp. 454-463, Oct., 1931.

Strange Tribes in the Shan States of Burma. 15 ills. in color from natural-color photographs by W. Robert Moore. Vol. LVIII, pp. 247-254, Aug., 1930.

Shanghai, China:

Changing Shanghai. By Amanda Boyden. Vol. LXXII, pp. 485-508, 21 ills., 1 two-thirds-page and 1 quarter-page maps, Oct., 1937.

Cosmopolitan Shanghai, Key Seaport of China. By W. Robert Moore. Vol. LXII, pp. 311-335, 19 ills., Sept., 1932.

Today on the China Coast. By John B. Powell. Vol. LXXXVII, pp. 217-238, 17 ills., 1 page map, Feb., 1945.

"Shangri-la," Netherlands New Guinea. *See* Grand Valley.

"Shangri-la" in Panorama (New Guinea). 7 ills. in color from natural-color photographs by Ray T. Elsmore. Vol. LXXXVIII, pp. 681-688, Dec., 1945.

Shansi (Province), China:

China's Great Wall of Sculpture: Man-hewn Caves and Countless Images Form a Colossal Art Wonder of Early Buddhism. By Mary Augusta Mullikin. Vol. LXXIII, pp. 313-348, 23 ills. in black and white, 10 ills. in color, 1 third-page map, Mar., 1938.

Shantung (Province), China:

Descendants of Confucius. By Maynard Owen Williams. Vol. XXXVI, pp. 253-265, 16 ills., Sept., 1919.

Shantung—China's Holy Land. By Charles K. Edmunds. Vol. XXVI, pp. 231-252, 21 ills., 1 half-page map, Sept., 1919.

Tai Shan, Sacred Mountain of the East. By Mary Augusta Mullikin. Vol. LXXXVII, pp. 699-719, 18 ills., 1 page map, June, 1945.

Shantz, H. L.:

Saguaro Forest (Arizona). By H. L. Shantz. Vol. LXXI, pp. 515-532, 18 ills., Apr., 1937.

Shark Fishing—An Australian Industry. By Norman Ellison. Vol. LXII, pp. 369-386, 22 ills., Sept., 1932.

Shasta Dam, California:

More Water for California's Great Central Valley. By Frederick Simpich. Vol. XC, pp. 645-664, 16 ills., 1 page map, Nov., 1946.

Shattered Capitals of Central America. By Herbert J. Spinden. Vol. XXXVI, pp. 185-212, 32 ills., 1 page map, Sept., 1919.

Shattered Obelisk of Mont Pelée. By Angelo Heilprin. Vol. XVII, pp. 465-474, 5 ills., Aug., 1906.

Shaw, William T.:

Tracking the Columbian Ground-Squirrel to Its Burrow: Loss of Millions to Crops and Danger of the Spread of Spotted Fever Necessitated Study of Peculiar Rodent of Western North America. By William T. Shaw. Vol. XLVII, pp. 587-596, 13 ills., May, 1925.

Shawnee (Indian Tribe):

America's First Settlers, the Indians. By Matthew W. Stirling. Vol. LXXII, pp. 535-596, 34 ills. in black and white, 24 ills. in color, Nov., 1937.

When Red Men Ruled Our Forests. 24 ills. in color from paintings by W. Langdon Kihn. Vol. LXXII, pp. 551-590, Nov., 1937.

Shay, Felix:

Cairo to Cape Town, Overland: An Adventurous Journey of 135 Days, Made by an American Man and His Wife, Through the Length of the African Continent. By Felix Shay. Vol. XLVII, pp. 123-260, 118 ills., 1 half-page map, Feb., 1925.

Shearwaters:

Birds of the High Seas: Albatrosses and Petrels; Gannets, Man-o'-war-birds, and Tropic-birds. By Robert Cushman Murphy. Vol. LXXIV, pp. 226-251, 7 ills. in black and white, 36 portraits in color, Aug., 1938.

Wings Over the Bounding Main. 36 portraits in color from paintings by Maj. Allan Brooks. Vol. LXXIV, pp. 237-251, Aug., 1938.

Shechem, Palestine. *See* Nablus.

Shedd Aquarium, Chicago : Expedition :

Net Results from Oceania : Collecting Aquarium Specimens in Tropical Pacific Waters. By Walter H. Chute. Vol. LXXIX, pp. 347-372, 8 ills. in black and white, 24 ills. in color, Mar., 1941.

Sheep and Sheep Raising:

Among the Bethlehem Shepherds : A Visit to the Valley Which David Probably Recalled When He Wrote the Twenty-third Psalm. By John D. Whiting. Vol. L, pp. 729-753, 19 ills., Dec., 1926.

Beyond Australia's Cities. By W. Robert Moore. Vol. LXX, pp. 709-747, 27 ills. in black and white, 12 ills. in color, Dec., 1936.

By Coolie and Caravan Across Central Asia : Narrative of a 7,900-Mile Journey of Exploration and Research Over "the Roof of the World" from the Indian Ocean to the Yellow Sea. By William J. Morden. Vol. LII, pp. 369-431, 73 ills., 1 page map, Oct., 1927.

Contains information on the Marco Polo sheep, or Ovis Poli.

Grass Makes Wyoming Fat. By Frederick Simpich. Vol. LXXXVIII, pp. 153-188, 13 ills. in black and white, 19 ills. in color, 1 two-page map, Aug., 1945.

Indispensable Sheep. Vol. LIII, pp. 512-528, 20 ills., Apr., 1928.

Land of Lambskins : An Expedition to Bokhara, Russian Central Asia, to Study the Karakul Sheep Industry. By Robert H. Nabours. Vol. XXXVI, pp. 77-88, 15 ills., July, 1919.

Lonely Australia : The Unique Continent. By Herbert E. Gregory. Vol. XXX, pp. 473-568, 68 ills., 1 two-page and 4 half-page maps, Dec., 1916.

White Sheep, Giant Moose, and Smaller Game of the Kenai Peninsula, Alaska. By George Shiras, 3d. Vol. XXIII, pp. 423-494, 59 ills., 1 page and 1 two-page maps, May, 1912.

See also Mountain Sheep.

Sheep Dogs:

Sheep Dog Trials in Llangollen : Trained Collies Perform Marvels of Herding in the Cambrian Stakes, Open to the World. By Sara Bloch. Vol. LXXVII, pp. 559-574, 17 ills., Apr., 1940.

Working Dogs of the World. By Freeman Lloyd. Paintings by Edward Herbert Miner. Vol. LXXX, pp. 776-806, 12 ills. in black and white, 20 ills. in color, Dec., 1941.

Sheep-Killers—The Pariahs of Dogkind. Vol. XXXV, pp. 275-280, 3 ills., Mar., 1919.

Shellfish. *See* Crabs ; Crustaceans ; Lobsters ; Mollusks ; Oysters ; Shrimp.

Shelton, (Dr.) A. L.:

Life Among the People of Eastern Tibet. By Dr. A. L. Shelton. Vol. XL, pp. 293-326, 35 ills., 1 half-page map, Sept., 1921.

Shenandoah (Airship) :

Seeing America from the *Shenandoah:* An Account of the Record-Making 9,000-Mile Flight from the Atlantic to the Pacific Coast and Return in the Navy's American-built, American-manned Airship. By Junius B. Wood. Vol. XLVII, pp. 1-47, 39 ills., 1 page map, 1 diagram, Jan., 1925.

Shenon, Philip J.:

Down Idaho's River of No Return (Salmon River). By Philip J. Shenon and John C. Reed. Vol. LXX, pp. 95-136, 43 ills., 1 page and 1 two-thirds-page maps, July, 1936.

Shensi (Province), China :

China Fights Erosion with U. S. Aid. By Walter C. Lowdermilk. Vol. LXXXVII, pp. 641-680, 10 ills. in black and white, 26 ills. in color, June, 1945.

See also Siking.

Shepherd's Needles (Plants) :

A Community of Dwarfs. 11 ills. in color from natural-color photographs by Willard R. Culver. Vol. XC, pp. 345-352, Sept., 1946.

An Insect Community Lives in Flower Heads. By James G. Needham. Vol. XC, pp. 340-356, 5 ills. in black and white, 11 ills. in color, Sept., 1946.

Sherwood Gardens, Maryland :

Maytime in the Heart of Maryland. 10 ills. in color from natural-color photographs by B. Anthony Stewart and Charles Martin. Vol. LXXIX, pp. 441-448, Apr., 1941.

Shetland Islands, Scotland :

Orkneys and Shetlands—A Mysterious Group of Islands. By Charles S. Olcott. Vol. XXXIX, pp. 197-228, 33 ills., Feb., 1921.

Shias (Tribespeople) :

Mystic Nedjef, the Shia Mecca. By Frederick Simpich. Vol. XXVI, pp. 589-598, 4 ills., Dec., 1914.

Shifting Scenes on the Stage of New China. Vol. XXXVIII, pp. 422-428, 4 ills., Nov., 1920.

Shigatse, Tibet :

Sky-high in Lama Land. 12 ills. from photographs by C. Suydam Cutting. Vol. XC, pp. 185-196, Aug., 1946.

Shinto:

Behind the Mask of Modern Japan. By Willard Price. Vol. LXXXVIII, pp. 513-535, 14 ills., Nov., 1945.

Ship Burial. *See* Burial Ship.

Shipbuilding:

American Industries Geared for War. By Thornton Oakley. With 16 ills. in color from paintings by the author. Vol. LXXXII, pp. 716-734, 1 ill. in black and white, Dec., 1942.

As 2,000 Ships Are Born. By Frederick Simpich. Vol. LXXXI, pp. 551-588, 34 ills., May, 1942.

Shipbuilding in the United Kingdom in 1898. Vol. X, pp. 138-139, Apr., 1899.

Shipley, L. W.:

Valley of Ten Thousand Smokes : An Account of The Discovery and Exploration of the Most Wonderful Volcanic Region in the World. By Robert F. Griggs. Vol. XXXIII, pp. 115-169, 46 ills., 1 half-page map, panorama, Feb., 1918.

Shippee, Robert:

Air Adventures in Peru : Cruising Among Andean Peaks, Pilots and Cameramen Discover Wondrous Works of an Ancient People. By Robert Shippee. Vol. LXIII, pp. 81-120, 40 ills., 1 three-quarters-page map, Jan., 1933.

Forgotten Valley of Peru : Conquered by Incas, Scourged by Famine, Plagues, and Earthquakes, Colca Valley Shelters the Last Fragment of an Ancient Andean Tribe. By Robert Shippee. Vol. LXV, pp. 111-132, 22 ills., 1 two-thirds-page map, Jan., 1934.

Ships and Shipping:

American Industries Geared for War. By Thornton Oakley. With 16 ills. in color from paintings by the author. Vol. LXXXII, pp. 716-734, 1 ill. in black and white, Dec., 1942.

American Pathfinders in the Pacific. By William H. Nicholas. Vol. LXXXIX, pp. 617-640, 17 ills., 1 two-page map, May, 1946.

American People Must Become Ship-Minded. By Edward N. Hurley. Vol. XXXIV, pp. 201-211, 7 ills., Sept., 1918.

Ancestor of the British Navy : England's Oldest Known War Vessel Is Unearthed, Laden with Remarkale Treasures of an Anglo-Saxon Ruler. By C. W. Phillips. Vol. LXXIX, pp. 247-268, 22 ills. in black and white, 4 drawings, Feb., 1941.

The Argosy of Geography (Sailing Ship). Vol. XXXIX, supplement, Jan., 1921.

As 2,000 Ships Are Born. By Frederick Simpich. Vol. LXXXI, pp. 551-588, 34 ills., May, 1942.

Battleship *Missouri* Comes of Age. 11 ills. in color from natural-color photographs. Vol. LXXXVII, pp. 353-360, Mar., 1945.

By Car and Steamer Around Our Inland Seas. By Maynard Owen Williams. Vol. LXV, pp. 451-491, 29 ills. in black and white, 8 ills. in duotone, 1 two-page map, Apr., 1934.

Cannon on Florida Reefs Solve Mystery of Sunken Ship. By Charles M. Brookfield. Vol. LXXX, pp. 807-824, 20 ills., 1 map (on pen and ink drawing), Dec., 1941.

Caravels of Columbus. Reproduction in color of the painting by N. C. Wyeth, National Geographic Society, Washington, D. C. Vol. LIV, text, p. 55 ; supplement, July, 1928.

Convoys to Victory. By Harvey Klemmer. Vol. LXXXIII, pp. 193-216, 24 ills., Feb., 1943.

Freighters of Fortune on Our Great Lakes. 8 ills. in duotone from photographs by Maynard Owen Williams. Vol. LXV, pp. 463-470, Apr., 1934.

Growth of Maritime Commerce. Vol. X, pp. 30-31, Jan., 1899.

Ships and Shipping—*Continued*

Heroes' Return. By William H. Nicholas. Vol. LXXXVII, pp. 333-352, 19 ills., Mar., 1945.

Landing Craft for Invasion. By Melville Bell Grosvenor. Vol. LXXXVI, pp. 1-30, 26 ills., July, 1944.

Life In Our Fighting Fleet. By F. Barrows Colton. Vol. LXXIX, pp. 671-702, 30 ills., June, 1941.

Life with Our Fighting Coast Guard. By F. Barrows Colton. Vol. LXXXIII, pp. 557-588, 22 ills. in black and white, 9 ills. in color, May, 1943.

Most Curious Craft Afloat : The Compass in Navigation and the Work of the Non-Magnetic Yacht *Carnegie*. By Dr. L. A. Bauer. Vol. XXI, pp. 223-245, 31 ills., Mar., 1910.

New Safeguards for Ships in Fog and Storm. By George R. Putnam. Vol. LXX, pp. 169-200, 28 ills., 2 charts, Aug., 1936.

Normandy's Made-in-England Harbors. Vol. LXXXVII, pp. 565-580, 16 ills., 1 quarter-page map, May, 1945.

North About. By Alan J. Villiers. Vol. LXXI, pp. 221-250, 24 ills., Feb., 1937.

Norway, an Active Ally. By Wilhelm Morgenstierne. Vol. LXXXIII, pp. 333-357, 24 ills., 1 two-thirds-page map, Mar., 1943.

Our Industrial Victory. By Charles M. Schwab. Vol. XXXIV, pp. 212-229, 17 ills., Sept., 1918.

Sailing Ship and the Panama Canal. By James Page. Vol. XV, pp. 167-176, 2 charts, Apr., 1904.

Seafarers of South Celebes. By G. E. P. Collins. Vol. LXXXVII, pp. 53-78, 25 ills., 1 two-thirds-page map, Jan., 1945.

Shipbuilding in the United Kingdom in 1898. Vol. X, pp. 138-139, Apr., 1899.

Ships, from Dugouts to Dreadnoughts. By Capt. Dudley W. Knox. Vol. LXXIII, pp. 57-98, 27 ills. in black and white, 16 ills. in gravure, Jan., 1938.

Ships for the Seven Seas : The Story of America's Maritime Needs, Capabilities and Her Achievements. By Ralph A. Graves. Vol. XXXIV, pp. 165-200, 24 ills., Sept., 1918.

Ships of Our Navy. 8 ills. in color from paintings by Arthur Beaumont. Vol. LXXX, pp. 329-336, Sept., 1941.

Ships of the Centuries. 16 ills. in gravure from etchings by Norman Wilkinson. Vol. LXXIII, pp. 65-80, text, p. 98, Jan., 1938.

Ships That Guard Our Ocean Ramparts. By F. Barrows Colton. Paintings by Arthur Beaumont. Vol. LXXX, pp. 328-337, 8 ills. in color, Sept., 1941.

Ships That Won the Greatest Naval War. 26 ills. in color from U. S. Navy official photographs. Vol. LXXXIX, pp. 697-736, June, 1946.

Time and Tide on the Thames. By Frederick Simpich. Vol. LXXV, pp. 239-272, 23 ills. in black and white, 10 ills. in color, 1 map, Feb., 1939.

Ships and Shipping—*Continued*

Victory's Portrait in the Marianas. By Lt. William Franklin Draper, USNR. With 17 ills. in color from paintings by the author. Vol. LXXXVIII, pp. 599-616, Nov., 1945.

Where the Sailing Ship Survives (Åland Islands). By A. J. Villiers. Vol. LXVII, pp. 101-128, 21 ills., 1 half-page map, Jan., 1935.

Your Navy as Peace Insurance. By Fleet Admiral Chester W. Nimitz. Vol. LXXXIX, pp. 681-736, 32 ills. in black and white, 26 ills. in color, June, 1946.

See also Aircraft Carriers; Boats; Escort Carriers; Junks; Lighthouses; U. S. Navy; Voyages.

Shiras, George, 3d:

Camps and Cruises of an Ornithologist. By George Shiras, 3d. Vol. XX, pp. 438-463, 30 ills., May, 1909.

Doe and Twin Fawns. Flashlight photograph by George Shiras, 3d. Vol. XXIV, supplement, July, 1913. Vol. LXXVI, ill. 475, Oct., 1939.

Flashlight Story of an Albino Porcupine and of a Cunning but Unfortunate Coon. By George Shiras, 3d. Vol. XXII, pp. 572-596, 26 ills., June, 1911.

Nature's Transformation at Panama: Remarkable Changes in Faunal and Physical Conditions in the Gatun Lake Region. By George Shiras, 3d. Vol. XXVIII, pp. 159-194, 33 ills., 2 page maps, Aug., 1915.

One Season's Game-Bag with the Camera. By George Shiras, 3d. Vol. XIX, pp. 387-446, 70 ills., June, 1908.

Photographing Wild Game with Flashlight and Camera. By George Shiras, 3d. Vol. XVII, pp. 366-423, 70 ills., July, 1906.

White Sheep, Giant Moose, and Smaller Game of the Kenai Peninsula, Alaska. By George Shiras, 3d. Vol. XXIII, pp. 423-494, 59 ills., 1 page and 1 two-page maps, May, 1912.

Wild Animals That Took Their Own Pictures by Day and by Night. By George Shiras, 3d. Vol. XXIV, pp. 763-834, 68 ills., 1 page map, July, 1913.

Wild Life of Lake Superior, Past and Present: The Habits of Deer, Moose, Wolves, Beavers, Muskrats, Trout, and Feathered Wood-Folk Studied with Camera and Flashlight. By George Shiras, 3d. Vol. XL, pp. 113-204, 77 ills., supplement, 1 half-page map, Aug., 1921.

Wild Life of the Atlantic and Gulf Coasts: A Field Naturalist's Photographic Record of Nearly Half a Century of Fruitful Exploration. By George Shiras, 3d. Vol. LXII, pp. 261-309, 62 ills., Sept., 1932.

Shishaldin (Volcano), Aleutian Islands:

Mountains on Unimak Island, Alaska. By Ferdinand Westdahl. Vol. XIV, pp. 90-99, 4 ills., 2 page and 1 half-page maps, Mar., 1903.

Note on the Activity of Shishaldin Volcano. By Homer P. Ritter. Vol. XVI, p. 249, May, 1905.

Shishaldin as a Field for Exploration. By Joseph Stanley-Brown. Vol. X, pp. 281-288, 3 ills., 1 quarter-page map, Aug., 1899.

Shoes and Shoe Industry:

Czechoslovaks, Yankees of Europe. By John Patric. Vol. LXXIV, pp. 173-225, 23 ills. in black and white, 30 ills. in color, 1 map, Aug., 1938.

How the World Is Shod. Vol. XIX, pp. 649-660, 12 ills., Sept., 1908.

Massachusetts—Beehive of Business. By William Joseph Showalter. Vol. XXXVII, pp. 203-245, 41 ills., Mar., 1920.

Shonts, Theodore P.:

Notes on the Panama Canal. By Theodore P. Shonts. Vol. XVII, pp. 362-363, June, 1906.

Panama Canal. By Theodore P. Shonts. Vol. XVII, pp. 55-68, 5 ills., Feb., 1906.

What Has Been Accomplished by the United States Toward Building the Panama Canal. By Theodore P. Shonts. Vol. XVI, pp. 558-564, Dec., 1905.

Shopping Abroad for Our Armies in France. By Herbert Corey. Vol. XXXIII, pp. 206-218, 6 ills., Feb., 1918.

Shore-Whaling: A World Industry. By Roy Chapman Andrews. Vol. XXII, pp. 411-442, 34 ills., May, 1911.

Short Visit to Wales: Historic Associations and Scenic Beauties Contend for Interest in the Little Land Behind the Hills. By Ralph A. Graves. Vol. XLIV, pp. 635-675, 37 ills., 1 half-page map, Dec., 1923.

Shortening Time Across the Continent. By Henry Herbert McClure. Vol. XIII, pp. 319-321, Aug., 1902.

Shoshone Dam, Wyoming:

Call of the West. By C. J. Blanchard. Vol. XX, pp. 403-437, 20 ills., 1 half-page map, May, 1909.

Spirit of the West: The Wonderful Agricultural Development Since the Dawn of Irrigation. By C. J. Blanchard. Vol. XXI, pp. 333-360, 15 ills., Apr., 1910.

Shoults, Worth E.:

Antarctica's Most Interesting Citizen: The Comical Penguin Is Both Romantic and Bellicose. By Worth E. Shoults. Vol. LXI, pp. 251-260, 8 ills., Feb., 1932.

Home of the First Farmer of America (Mount Vernon). By Worth E. Shoults. Vol. LIII, pp. 603-628, 6 ills. in black and white, 26 ills. in color, May, 1928.

Hospitality of the Czechs. By Worth E. Shoults. Vol. LI, pp. 723-742, 19 ills. in color, June, 1927.

Showalter, William Joseph:

America's Amazing Railway Traffic. By William Joseph Showalter. Vol. XLIII, pp. 353-404, 46 ills., 1 third-page map, Apr., 1923.

America's New Soldier Cities: The Geographical and Historical Environment of the National Army Cantonments and National Guard Camps. By William Joseph Showalter. Vol. XXXII, pp. 438-476, 18 ills., 1 page map in colors, Nov.-Dec., 1917.

Showalter, William Joseph—*Continued*

Automobile Industry: An American Art That Has Revolutionized Methods in Manufacturing and Transformed Transportation. By William Joseph Showalter. Vol. XLIV, pp. 337-414, 76 ills., Oct., 1923.

Battling with the Panama Slides. By William Joseph Showalter. Vol. XXV, pp. 133-153, 15 ills., Feb., 1914.

Belgium: The Innocent Bystander. By William Joseph Showalter. Vol. XXVI, pp. 223-264, 35 ills., Sept., 1914.

Chicago Today and Tomorrow: A City Whose Industries Have Changed the Food Status of the World and Transformed the Economic Situation of a Billion People. By William Joseph Showalter. Vol. XXXV, pp. 1-42, 28 ills., 1 page map, Jan., 1919.

Coal—Ally of American Industry. By William Joseph Showalter. Vol. XXXIV, pp. 407-434, 23 ills., Nov., 1918.

Countries of the Caribbean. By William Joseph Showalter. Vol. XXIV, pp. 227-250, 23 ills., Feb., 1913.

Cuba—The Sugar Mill of the Antilles. By William Joseph Showalter. Vol. XXXVIII, pp. 1-33, 24 ills., 1 page map, July, 1920.

Exploring the Glories of the Firmament. By William Joseph Showalter. Vol. XXXVI, pp. 153-181, 17 ills., 3 charts, 1 diagram, Aug., 1919.

Exploring the Mysteries of Plant Life. By William Joseph Showalter. Vol. XLV, pp. 581-646, 41 ills. in black and white, 47 ills. in color, June, 1924.

Exploring the Wonders of the Insect World. By William Joseph Showalter. Vol. LVI, pp. 1-90, 59 ills. in black and white, 269 ills. in color, July, 1929.

Familiar Grasses and Their Flowers. By E. J. Geske and W. J. Showalter. Vol. XXXIX, pp. 625-636, 8 ills. in color, June, 1921.

Family Tree of the Flowers. By Frederic E. Clements and William Joseph Showalter. Vol. LI, pp. 555-563, 1 ill. in black and white, 1 ill. in color, May, 1927.

Flags of the World. By Gilbert Grosvenor and William J. Showalter. Vol. LXVI, pp. 339-396, 10 ills. in black and white, 808 ills. in color, Sept., 1934.

How the World Is Fed. By William Joseph Showalter. Vol. XXIX, pp. 1-110, 101 ills., Jan., 1916.

Industry's Greatest Asset—Steel. By William Joseph Showalter. Vol. XXXII, pp. 121-156, 34 ills., Aug., 1917.

Interviewing the Stars: How Twentieth Century Astronomers Are Inducing the Heavens to Reveal Their Secrets. By William Joseph Showalter. Vol. XLVII, pp. 97-122, 18 ills., 2 charts, 1 diagram, Jan., 1925.

Kingdom of Servia. By William Joseph Showalter. Vol. XXVII, pp. 417-432, 12 ills., 1 page map, Apr., 1915.

Lure of Lima, City of the Kings. By William Joseph Showalter. Vol. LVII, pp. 727-784, 41 ills., June, 1930.

Showalter, William Joseph—*Continued*

Map-Changing Medicine. By William Joseph Showalter. Vol. XLII, pp. 303-330, 26 ills., Sept., 1922.

Massachusetts—Beehive of Business. By William Joseph Showalter. Vol. XXXVII, pp. 203-245, 41 ills., Mar., 1920.

Mexico and Mexicans. By William Joseph Showalter. Vol. XXV, pp. 471-493, 17 ills., special map supplement in colors, May, 1914.

New York—An Empire Within a Republic. By William Joseph Showalter. Vol. LXIV, pp. 513-584, 47 ills. in black and white, 35 ills. in color, 1 two-page map, Nov., 1933.

New York—The Metropolis of Mankind. By William Joseph Showalter. Vol. XXXIV, pp. 1-49, 39 ills., July, 1918.

Niagara at the Battle Front. By William Joseph Showalter. Vol. XXXI, pp. 413-422, 6 ills., May, 1917.

Our Guardians on the Deep. By William Joseph Showalter. Vol. XXV, pp. 655-677, 15 ills., 1 chart, June, 1914.

Panama Canal. By William Joseph Showalter. Vol. XXIII, pp. 195-205, special map supplement in colors, Feb., 1912.

Partitioned Poland. By William Joseph Showalter. Vol. XXVII, pp. 88-106, 12 ills., Jan., 1915.

Redeeming the Tropics. By William Joseph Showalter. Vol. XXV, pp. 344-364, 13 ills., Mar., 1914.

Strange Habits of Familiar Moths and Butterflies. By William Joseph Showalter. Vol. LII, pp. 77-126, 28 ills. in black and white, 169 ills. in color, July, 1927.

Travels of George Washington: Dramatic Episodes in His Career as the First Geographer of the United States. By William Joseph Showalter. Vol. LXI, pp. 1-63, 50 ills., 5 maps, special map supplement in colors, Jan., 1932.

Twin Stars of Chile: Valparaiso, the Gateway, and Santiago, the Capital—Key Cities with a Progressive Present and a Romantic Past. By William Joseph Showalter. Vol. LV, pp. 197-247, 35 ills. in black and white, 25 ills. in color, Feb., 1929.

Virginia—A Commonwealth That Has Come Back. By William Joseph Showalter. Vol. LV, pp. 403-472, 69 ills. in black and white, 13 ills. in color, 1 page map, Apr., 1929.

Shreve, Forrest:

Saguaro, Cactus Camel of Arizona. By Forrest Shreve. Vol. LXXXVIII, pp. 695-704, 9 ills. in color, Dec., 1945.

Shrimp:

Delectable Shrimp: Once a Culinary Stepchild, Today a Gulf Coast Industry. By Harlan Major. Vol. LXXXVI, pp. 501-512, 11 ills., 1 two-thirds-page map, Oct., 1944.

Shrines:

Behind the Mask of Modern Japan. By Willard Price. Vol. LXXXVIII, pp. 513-535, 14 ills., Nov., 1945.

Shrines—*Continued*

Castles, Shrines, and Parks of Japanese Pilgrimage. 10 ills. in color from natural-color photographs by W. Robert Moore. Vol. LXIX, pp. 457-464, Apr., 1936.

Gilded Domes Against an Azure Sky (Iran). 13 ills. in color from natural-color photographs by Stephen H. Nyman. Vol. LXXVI, pp. 339-346, Sept., 1939.

Pilgrimage to Amernath, Himalayan Shrine of the Hindu Faith. By Louise Ahl Jessop. Vol. XL, pp. 512-542, 29 ills., Nov., 1921.

Pilgrims' Progress to Mecca. 22 ills. in duotone; 18 ills. by Oscar Marcus. Vol. LXXII, pp. 627-642, Nov., 1937.

Puto, the Enchanted Island. By Robert F. Fitch. Vol. LXXXIX, pp. 373-384, 11 ills., 1 third-page map, Mar., 1946.

Tai Shan, Sacred Mountain of the East. By Mary Augusta Mullikin. Vol. LXXXVII, pp. 699-719, 18 ills., 1 page map, June, 1945.

See also Montserrat.

Shrubs:

American Berries of Hill, Dale, and Wayside. Vol. XXXV, pp. 168-184, 1 ill. in black and white, 28 ills. in color, Feb., 1919.

Kingdom of Flowers: An Account of the Wealth of Trees and Shrubs of China and of What the Arnold Arboretum, with China's Help, Is Doing to Enrich America. By Ernest H. Wilson. Vol. XXII, pp. 1003-1035, 24 ills., Nov., 1911.

See also Rhododendrons.

Shuri, Okinawa (Island), Ryukyu Retto:

Peacetime Rambles in the Ryukyus. By William Leonard Schwartz. Vol. LXXXVII, pp. 543-561, 12 ills., 1 two-thirds-page and 1 half-page maps, May, 1945.

Shush, Iran. *See* Susa.

Shuster, Ernest A., Jr.:

Original Boundary Stones of the District of Columbia. By Ernest A. Shuster, Jr. Vol. XX, pp. 356-359, 6 ills., 1 half-page map, Apr., 1909.

Siam:

Among the Plains and Hill People of Siam. 14 ills. in color from natural-color photographs by Amos Burg, Gervais Courtellemont, and W. Robert Moore. Vol. LXV, pp. 563-570, May, 1934.

Ancient Temples and Modern Guns in Thailand. 10 ills. from photographs; 6 ills. by Maynard Owen Williams. Vol. LXXX, pp. 653-660, Nov., 1941.

Coronation of His Majesty King Maha-Vaji-ravudh of Siam. By Col. Lea Febiger. Vol. XXIII, pp. 389-416, 25 ills., Apr., 1912.

Greatest Hunt in the World (Elephant Hunting). By Eliza R. Scidmore. Vol. XVII, pp. 673-692, 17 ills., Dec., 1906.

Hunting the Chaulmoogra Tree. By Joseph F. Rock. Vol. XLI, pp. 243-276, 39 ills., 1 page map, Mar., 1922.

Siam—*Continued*

"Land of the Free" in Asia: Siam Has Blended New With Old in Her Progressive March to Modern Statehood in the Family of Nations. By W. Robert Moore. Vol. LXV, pp. 531-576, 28 ills. in black and white, 26 ills. in color, 1 two-thirds-page map, May, 1934.

Temples and Ceremonies of Kaleidoscopic Bangkok. 12 ills. in color from natural-color photographs by Amos Burg, Gervais Courtellemont, and W. Robert Moore. Vol. LXV, pp. 547-554, May, 1934.

Warfare of the Jungle Folk: Campaigning Against Tigers, Elephants, and Other Wild Animals in Northern Siam. By Merian C. Cooper. Photographs by Ernest B. Schoedsack. Vol. LIII, pp. 233-268, 33 ills., Feb., 1928.

Siamese Cats:

Catdom's Royalty Photographed in Color. 25 ills. in color from natural-color photographs by Willard R. Culver. Vol. LXXIV, pp. 597-628, Nov., 1938.

Panther of the Hearth: Lithe Grace and Independence of Spirit Contribute to the Appeal of Cats, "The Only Domestic Animal Man Has Never Conquered." By Frederick B. Eddy. Vol. LXXIV, pp. 589-634, 22 ills. in black and white, 25 ills. in color, Nov., 1938.

Sian (Siking), China:

Singan—The Present Capital of the Chinese Empire. By James Mascarene Hubbard. Vol. XII, pp. 63-66, 1 ill., Feb., 1901.

Siasconset, Nantucket (Island):

Nantucket—Little Gray Lady. By William H. Nicholas. Vol. LXXXV, pp. 433-458, 14 ills. in black and white, 8 ills. in color, 1 half-page map, Apr., 1944.

Siberia:

Butter Exports from Siberia. Vol. XIII, p. 34, Jan., 1902.

Far Eastern Republic. By Junius B. Wood. Vol. XLI, pp. 565-592, 29 ills., 1 three-quarters-page map, June, 1922.

Glimpses of Siberia, the Russian "Wild East." By Cody Marsh. Vol. XXXVIII, pp. 512-536, 26 ills., Dec., 1920.

Land of Promise. By Maj. Gen. A. W. Greely. Vol. XXIII, pp. 1078-1090, 7 ills., Nov., 1912.

"Magnetic City" (Magnitogorsk), Core of Valiant Russia's Industrial Might. By John Scott. Vol. LXXXIII, pp. 525-556, 27 ills., 1 two-page map, May, 1943.

New Road to Asia. By Owen Lattimore. Vol. LXXXVI, pp. 641-676, 15 ills. in black and white, 26 ills. in color, Dec., 1944.

Siberia. By Edwin A. Grosvenor. Vol. XII, pp. 317-324, Sept., 1901.

Strange and Remarkable Beast (Mammoth). Vol. XVIII, p. 620, 1 ill., Sept., 1907.

Sunny Siberia. 26 ills. in color from natural-color photographs by Owen Lattimore. Vol. LXXXVI, pp. 649-672, Dec., 1944.

Trip Through Siberia. By Ebenezer J. Hill. Vol. XIII, pp. 37-54, 17 ills., 1 quarter-page map, Feb., 1902.

Siberia—*Continued*

Western Siberia and the Altai Mountains : With Some Speculations on the Future of Siberia. By James Bryce. Vol. XXXIX, pp. 469-507, 39 ills., May, 1921.

With an Exile in Arctic Siberia : The Narrative of a Russian Who Was Compelled to Turn Polar Explorer for Two Years. By Vladimir M. Zenzinov. Vol. XLVI, pp. 695-718, 30 ills., 1 half-page map, Dec., 1924.

Sibert, (Lt. Col.) William L.:

Panama Canal. By Lieut. Col. William L. Sibert. Vol. XXV, pp. 153-183, 24 ills., Feb., 1914.

Sicily (Island), Mediterranean Sea :

Africa First of 1943 Global Warfare Maps. By William H. Nicholas. Text accompanying special map supplement in colors. Vol. LXXXIII, pp. 261-276, 13 ills., Feb., 1943.

Country Where Going to America Is an Industry. By Arthur H. Warner. Vol. XX, pp. 1063-1102, 41 ills., Dec., 1909.

Inexhaustible Italy. By Arthur Stanley Riggs. Vol. XXX, pp. 273-368, 76 ills., 1 page map, Oct., 1916.

Ruins at Selinus. By Marion Crawford. Vol. XX, p. 117, Jan., 1909.

Sicily : Island of Vivid Beauty and Crumbling Glory. Vol. LII, pp. 432-449, 22 ills. in color, Oct., 1927.

Sicily, the Battle-Field of Nations and of Nature. By Mrs. George C. Bosson, Jr. Vol. XX, pp. 96-118, 25 ills., Jan., 1909.

Sicily Again in the Path of War. By Maynard Owen Williams. Vol. LXXXIV, pp. 307-320, 7 ills., 1 map (two-page spread), Sept., 1943.

World's Most Cruel Earthquake (Messina). By Charles W. Wright. Vol. XX, pp. 373-396, 22 ills., 1 page and 1 three-quarters-page maps, Apr., 1909.

Zigzagging Across Sicily. By Melville Chater. Vol. XLVI, pp. 303-352, 44 ills., 1 half-page map, Sept., 1924.

Siena, Italy :

Inexhaustible Italy. By Arthur Stanley Riggs. Vol. XXX, pp. 273-368, 76 ills., 1 page map, Oct., 1916.

Siena's Palio, an Italian Inheritance from the Middle Ages. By Marie Louise Handley. Vol. L, pp. 245-258, 3 ills., Aug., 1926.

Siepen, Howard:

On the Wings of the Wind : In Motorless Planes, Pilots Ride in Flying-Fox Fashion, Cruising on Upward Air Streams and Lifted by the Suction of Moving Clouds. By Howard Siepen. Vol. LV, pp. 751-780, 40 ills., June, 1929.

Sieur de Monts National Monument, Maine. *See* Mount Desert Island.

Sight-Seeing in School : Taking Twenty Million Children on a Picture Tour of the World. By Jessie L. Burrall. Vol. XXXV, pp. 489-503, 14 ills., June, 1919.

Sights and Sounds of the Winged World : Study of Birds to Make National Geographic Color Photographs Yields Rich Scientific Knowledge of Their Habits and Behavior. By Arthur A. Allen. Vol. LXXXVII, pp. 721-744, 1 ill. in black and white, 2 drawings, 26 ills. in color, June, 1945.

Sigiri (Fortress Rock), Ceylon. *See* Sigiriya.

Sigiriya (Fortress Rock), Ceylon :

Archæology in the Air. By Eliza R. Scidmore. Vol. XVIII, pp. 150-163, 11 ills., Mar., 1907.

Sigiriya, "A Fortress in the Sky." By Wilson K. Norton. Vol. XC, pp. 665-680, 14 ills., 1 two-thirds-page map, Nov., 1946.

Signal Corps, U. S. Army. *See* U. S. Army Signal Corps.

Sikang (Province), China :

Carrying the Color Camera Through Unmapped China. 24 ills. in color from natural-color photographs by Joseph F. Rock. Vol. LVIII, pp. 402-435, Oct., 1930.

Climbing Mighty Minya Konka : Americans First Scaled Mountain That Now Is Landmark of China's New Skyway. By Richard L. Burdsall and Terris Moore. Vol. LXXXIII, pp. 625-650, 23 ills., 1 page map, May, 1943.

Experiences of a Lone Geographer : An American Agricultural Explorer Makes His Way Through Brigand-infested Central China en Route to the Amne Machin Range, Tibet. By Joseph F. Rock. Vol. XLVIII, pp. 331-347, 16 ills., 1 quarter-page map, Sept., 1925.

Exploring a Grass Wonderland of Wild West China. By Ray G. Johnson. Vol. LXXXV, pp. 713-742, 24 ills., 1 half-page map, June, 1944.

Glories of the Minya Konka : Magnificent Snow Peaks of the China-Tibetan Border Are Photographed at Close Range by a National Geographic Society Expedition. By Joseph F. Rock. Vol. LVIII, pp. 385-437, 35 ills. in black and white, 24 ills. in color, 1 three-quarters-page map, Oct., 1930.

Konka Risumgongba, Holy Mountain of the Outlaws. By Joseph F. Rock. Vol. LX, pp. 1-65, 36 ills. in black and white, 43 ills. in color, 1 three-quarters-page map, July, 1931.

Land of the Yellow Lama : National Geographic Society Explorer Visits the Strange Kingdom of Muli, Beyond the Likiang Snow Range of Yünnan Province, China. By Joseph F. Rock. Vol. XLVII, pp. 447-491, 39 ills., 1 half-page map, Apr., 1925.

Populous and Beautiful Szechuan : A Visit to the Restless Province of China in which the Present Revolution Began. By Rollin T. Chamberlin. Vol. XXII, pp. 1094-1119, 26 ills., 1 half-page map, Dec., 1911.

With the Devil Dancers of China and Tibet. 43 ills. in color from natural-color photographs by Joseph F. Rock. Vol. LX, pp. 18-59, July, 1931.

Sikang Expedition:

Climbing Mighty Minya Konka : Americans First Scaled Mountain That Now Is Landmark of China's New Skyway. By Richard L. Burdsall and Terris Moore. Vol. LXXXIII, pp. 625-650, 23 ills., 1 page map, May, 1943.

Siking (Sian), China :

Singan—The Present Capital of the Chinese Empire. By James Mascarene Hubbard. Vol. XII, pp. 63-66, 1 ill., Feb., 1901.

Silent-Winged Owls of North America. 21 portraits in color from paintings by Maj. Allan Brooks. Vol. LXVII, pp. 225-240, Feb., 1935.

Silk Industry:

How Half the World Works. By Alice Tisdale Hobart and Mary A. Nourse. Vol. LXI, pp. 509-524, 22 ills., Apr., 1932.

Industrial Titan of America : Pennsylvania, Once the Keystone of the Original Thirteen, Now the Keystone of Forty-eight Sovereign States. By John Oliver La Gorce. Vol. XXXV, pp. 367-406, 33 ills., 1 page map, May, 1919.

Massachusetts—Beehive of Business. By William Joseph Showalter. Vol. XXXVII, pp. 203-245, 41 ills., Mar., 1920.

Strange Habits of Familiar Moths and Butterflies. By William Joseph Showalter. Vol. LII, pp. 77-126, 28 ills. in black and white, 169 ills. in color, July, 1927.

Silver and Silver Mining:

Pieces of Silver. By Frederick Simpich. Vol. LXIV, pp. 253-292, 49 ills., Sept., 1933.

Treasure Chest of Mercurial Mexico. By Frank H. Probert. Vol. XXX, pp. 33-68, 33 ills., July, 1916.

Silverware:

Pieces of Silver. By Frederick Simpich. Vol. LXIV, pp. 253-292, 49 ills., Sept., 1933.

Simi (Island), Aegean Sea :

Rhodes, and Italy's Aegean Islands. By Dorothy Hosmer. Vol. LXXIX, pp. 449-480, 32 ills., 1 map, Apr., 1941.

Simmons, George Finlay:

Sindbads of Science : Narrative of a Windjammer's Specimen-Collecting Voyage to the Sargasso Sea, to Senegambian Africa and Among Islands of High Adventure in the South Atlantic. By George Finlay Simmons. Vol. LII, pp. 1-75, 89 ills., 1 two-thirds-page map, July, 1927.

Simpich, Frederick:

Along Our Side of the Mexican Border. By Frederick Simpich. Vol. XXXVIII, pp. 61-80, 9 ills., 1 quarter-page map, July, 1920.

Along the Nile, Through Egypt and the Sudan. By Frederick Simpich. Vol. XLII, pp. 379-410, 29 ills., Oct., 1922.

Arizona Comes of Age. By Frederick Simpich. Vol. LV, pp. 1-47, 40 ills. in black and white, 14 ills. in color, 1 two-thirds-page map, Jan., 1929.

Simpich, Frederick—*Continued:*

Arkansas Rolls Up Its Sleeves. By Frederick Simpich. Vol. XC, pp. 273-312, 16 ills. in black and white, 23 ills. in color, 1 map (two-page spread), Sept., 1946.

Around the Clock with Your Soldier Boy. By Frederick Simpich. Vol. LXXX, pp. 1-36, 42 ills., July, 1941.

As London Toils and Spins. By Frederick Simpich. Vol. LXXI, pp. 1-57, 38 ills. in black and white, 23 ills. in color, Jan., 1937.

As 2,000 Ships Are Born. By Frederick Simpich. Vol. LXXXI, pp. 551-588, 34 ills., May, 1942.

Bahama Holiday. By Frederick Simpich. Vol. LXIX, pp. 219-245, 29 ills., 1 half-page map, Feb., 1936.

Baja California Wakes Up. By Frederick Simpich. Vol. LXXXII, pp. 253-275, 19 ills., 1 page map, Aug., 1942.

Behind the News in Singapore. By Frederick Simpich. Vol. LXXVIII, pp. 83-110, 26 ills., 1 map, July, 1940.

Bombs Over Bible Lands. By Frederick Simpich and W. Robert Moore. Vol. LXXX, pp. 141-180, 34 ills., 1 two-page map, Aug., 1941.

Bonds Between the Americas. By Frederick Simpich. Vol. LXXII, pp. 785-808, 22 ills., Dec., 1937.

Boston Through Midwest Eyes. By Frederick Simpich. Vol. LXX, pp. 37-82, 24 ills. in black and white, 31 ills. in color, July, 1936.

Bridges, from Grapevine to Steel. By Frederick Simpich. Vol. LXIX, pp. 391-406, 13 ills., Mar., 1936.

Change Comes to Bible Lands. By Frederick Simpich. Vol. LXXIV, pp. 695-750, 40 ills. in black and white, 25 ills. in color, special map supplement, Dec., 1938.

Chemists Make a New World : Creating Hitherto Unknown Raw Materials, Science Now Disrupts Old Trade Routes and Revamps the World Map of Industry. By Frederick Simpich. Vol. LXXVI, pp. 601-640, 22 ills. in black and white, 26 ills. in color, Nov., 1939.

Down the Rio Grande : Tracing this Strange, Turbulent Stream on Its Long Course from Colorado to the Gulf of Mexico. By Frederick Simpich. Vol. LXXVI, pp. 415-462, 28 ills. in black and white, 24 ills. in color, 6 maps, Oct., 1939.

Every-Day Life in Afghanistan. By Frederick Simpich and "Haji Mirza Hussein." Vol. XXXIX, pp. 85-110, 26 ills., 1 three-quarters-page map, Jan., 1921.

Facts about the Philippines. By Frederick Simpich. Vol. LXXXI, pp. 185-202, 17 ills., 1 page map, Feb., 1942.

Farmers Keep Them Eating. By Frederick Simpich. Vol. LXXXIII, pp. 435-458, 22 ills., Apr., 1943.

Fit to Fight Anywhere (Army Quartermaster Tests). By Frederick Simpich. Vol. LXXXIV, pp. 233-256, 26 ills., Aug., 1943.

Simpich, Frederick—*Continued*

Geography of Our Foreign Trade. By Frederick Simpich. Vol. XLI, pp. 89-108, 25 ills., Jan., 1922.

Gigantic Brazil and Its Glittering Capital. By Frederick Simpich. Vol. LVIII, pp. 733-778, 54 ills., 1 page map, Dec., 1930.

Grass Makes Wyoming Fat. By Frederick Simpich. Vol. LXXXVIII, pp. 153-188, 13 ills. in black and white, 19 ills. in color, 1 two-page map, Aug., 1945.

Great Mississippi Flood of 1927 : Since White Man's Discovery This Mighty River Has Served Him Well, Yet It Has Brought Widespread Devastation Along Its Lower Reaches. By Frederick Simpich. Vol. LII, pp. 243-289, 53 ills., 1 half-page map, Sept., 1927.

Hamburg Speaks with Steam Sirens. By Frederick Simpich. Vol. LXIII, pp. 717-744, 32 ills., June, 1933.

How We Use the Gulf of Mexico. By Frederick Simpich. Vol. LXXXV, pp. 1-40, 20 ills. in black and white, 19 ills. in color, 1 two-page map, Jan., 1944.

Indiana Journey. By Frederick Simpich. Vol. LXX, pp. 267-320, 32 ills. in black and white, 27 ills. in color, 1 two-page map, Sept., 1936.

Land of a Million Smiles (Ozarks). By Frederick Simpich. Vol. LXXXIII, pp. 589-623, 14 ills. in black and white, 20 ills. in color, 1 two-thirds-page map, May, 1943.

Life on the Argentine Pampa. By Frederick Simpich. Vol. LXIV, pp. 449-491, 41 ills. in black and white, 8 ills. in color, Oct., 1933.

Manchuria, Promised Land of Asia ; Invaded by Railways and Millions of Settlers, This Vast Region Now Recalls Early Boom Days in the American West. By Frederick Simpich. Vol. LVI, pp. 379-428, 58 ills., 1 two-thirds-page map, Oct., 1929.

Mediterranean Checkerboard. By Frederick Simpich. Vol. LXXXI, pp. 527-550, 20 ills., 1 map (two-page spread), Apr., 1942.

Men Against the Rivers (Mississippi and Ohio Rivers). By Frederick Simpich. Vol. LXXI, pp. 767-794, 22 ills., 1 page-and-a-half and 1 quarter-page maps, June, 1937.

Men and Gold. By Frederick Simpich. Vol. LXIII, pp. 481-518, 33 ills. in black and white, 11 ills. in duotone, Apr., 1933.

Mexican Land of Canaan : Marvelous Riches of the Wonderful West Coast of Our Neighbor Republic. By Frederick Simpich. Vol. XXXVI, pp. 307-330, 16 ills., 1 page map, Oct., 1919.

Mindanao, on the Road to Tokyo. By Frederick Simpich. Vol. LXXXVI, pp. 539-574, 26 ills. in black and white, 12 ills. in color, 1 two-page map, Nov., 1944.

Missouri, Mother of the West. By Frederick Simpich. Vol. XLIII, pp. 421-460, 35 ills., Apr., 1923.

More Water for California's Great Central Valley. By Frederick Simpich. Vol. XC, pp. 645-664, 16 ills., 1 page map, Nov., 1946.

Simpich, Frederick—*Continued*

Mystic Nedjef, the Shia Mecca. By Frederick Simpich. Vol. XXVI, pp. 589-598, 4 ills., Dec., 1914.

New Mexico Melodrama. By Frederick Simpich. Vol. LXXIII, pp. 529-569, 19 ills. in black and white, 25 ills. in color, 1 two-page map, May, 1938.

1940 Paradox in Hong Kong. By Frederick Simpich. Vol. LXXVII, pp. 531-558, 24 ills., 3 maps, Apr., 1940.

North America's Oldest Metropolis : Through 600 Melodramatic Years, Mexico City Has Grown in Splendor and Achievement. By Frederick Simpich. Vol. LVIII, pp. 45-84, 34 ills., July, 1930.

Northern California at Work. By Frederick Simpich. Vol. LXIX, pp. 309-389, 36 ills. in black and white, 41 ills. in color, 1 two-page and 1 third-page maps, Mar., 1936.

Ontario, Next Door : Alert, Energetic, and Resourceful, Its British Pluck and Skill in Arts and Trades Gain for This Province a High Place Under the Union Jack. By Frederick Simpich. Vol. LXII, pp. 131-183, 54 ills., 1 three-quarters-page map, Aug., 1932.

Out in San Francisco : Fed on Gold Dust and Fattened by Sea Trade a Pioneer Village Becomes a Busy World Port. By Frederick Simpich. Vol. LXI, pp. 395-434, 38 ills., Apr., 1932.

Pieces of Silver. By Frederick Simpich. Vol. LXIV, pp. 253-292, 49 ills., Sept., 1933.

QM, the Fighting Storekeeper. By Frederick Simpich. Paintings by Arthur Beaumont. Vol. LXXXII, pp. 561-600, 22 ills. in black and white, 16 ills. in color, Nov., 1942.

Return to Manila. By Frederick Simpich. Vol. LXXVIII, pp. 409-451, 21 ills. in black and white, 21 ills. in color, 1 half-page map, Oct., 1940.

Rise of the New Arab Nation. By Frederick Simpich. Vol. XXXVI, pp. 369-393, 17 ills., 1 page map, Nov., 1919.

San Diego Can't Believe It. By Frederick Simpich. Vol. LXXXI, pp. 45-80, 26 ills. in black and white, 9 ills. in color, Jan., 1942.

Santa Fe Trail, Path to Empire. By Frederick Simpich. Vol. LVI, pp. 213-252, 35 ills. in black and white, 12 ills. in color, 1 half-page map, Aug., 1929.

Seing Our Spanish Southwest. By Frederick Simpich. Vol. LXXVII, pp. 711-756, 25 ills. in black and white, 17 ills. in duotone, special map supplement, June, 1940.

Singapore, Crossroads of the East : The World's Greatest Mart for Rubber and Tin Was in Recent Times a Pirate-Haunted, Tiger-Infested Jungle Isle. By Frederick Simpich. Vol. XLIX, pp. 235-269, 32 ills., 1 half-page map, Mar., 1926.

Skypaths Through Latin America : Flying From Our Nation's Capital Southward Over Jungles, Remote Islands, and Great Cities on an Aërial Survey of the East Coast of South America. By Frederick Simpich. Vol. LIX, pp. 1-79, 77 ills., 1 page map, Jan., 1931.

Simpich, Frederick—*Continued*

Smoke Over Alabama. By Frederick Simpich. Vol. LX, pp. 703-758, 43 ills. in black and white, 26 ills. in color, 1 page map, Dec., 1931.

So Big Texas. By Frederick Simpich. Vol LIII, pp. 637-693, 72 ills., 1 two-page map, June, 1928.

So Oklahoma Grew Up. By Frederick Simpich. Vol. LXXIX, pp. 269-314, 30 ills. in black and white, 19 ills. in color, 1 page map, Mar., 1941.

Southern California at Work. By Frederick Simpich. Vol. LXVI, pp. 529-600, 39 ills. in black and white, 41 ills. in color, 1 two-page map, Nov., 1934.

Speaking of Kansas. By Frederick Simpich. Vol. LXXII, pp. 135-182, 37 ills. in black and white, 12 ills. in color, 1 two-page map, Aug., 1937.

Spin Your Globe to Long Island : Only Six States Have More People than the Insular Empire that Ranges from a World's Fair Through Potato Patches, Princely Estates, and Historic Shrines. By Frederick Simpich. Vol. LXXV, pp. 413-460, 25 ills. in black and white, 18 ills. in color, Apr., 1939.

Story of the Ruhr. By Frederick Simpich. Vol. XLI, pp. 553-564, 11 ills., 1 third-page map, May, 1922.

Taming the Outlaw Missouri River. By Frederick Simpich. Vol. LXXXVIII, pp. 569-598, 25 ills., 1 two-page map, Nov., 1945.

These Missourians. By Frederick Simpich. Vol. LXXXIX, pp. 277-310, 12 ills. in black and white, 22 ills. in color, 1 map (two-page spread), Mar., 1946.

They Sustain the Wings (Ground Crews). By Frederick Simpich. Vol. LXXIV, pp. 333-354, 19 ills., Sept., 1943.

This Giant That Is New York. By Frederick Simpich. Vol. LVIII, pp. 517-583, 26 ills. in black and white, 8 ills. in gravure, 42 ills. in color, Nov., 1930.

Time and Tide on the Thames. By Frederick Simpich. Vol. LXXV, pp. 239-272, 23 ills. in black and white, 10 ills. in color, 1 map, Feb., 1939.

Today's World Turns on Oil. By Frederick Simpich. Vol. LXXIX, pp. 703-748, 22 ills. in black and white, 2 drawings, 21 ills. in color, June, 1941.

U. S. Roads in War and Peace. By Frederick Simpich. Vol. LXXX, pp. 687-716, 27 ills., Dec., 1941.

Vignettes of Guadalajara (Mexico). By Frederick Simpich. Vol. LXV, pp. 329-356, 20 ills. in black and white, 15 ills. in color, 1 third-page map, Mar., 1934.

Wartime in the Pacific Northwest. By Frederick Simpich. Vol. LXXXII, pp. 421-464, 25 ills. in black and white, 23 ills. in color, 1 half-page map, Oct., 1942.

Wends of the Spreewald. By Frederick Simpich. Vol. XLIII, pp. 327-336, 12 ills., Mar., 1923.

Simpich, Frederick—*Continued*

What Is the Saar ? By Frederick Simpich. Vol. LXVII, pp. 241-264, 5 ills. in black and white. 23 ills. in duotone, 1 half-page and 1 third-page maps, Feb., 1935.

What Luzon Means to Uncle Sam. By Frederick Simpich. Vol. LXXXVII, pp. 305 332, 25 ills., special map supplement, Mar., 1945.

Where Adam and Eve Lived (Baghdad). By Frederick and Margaret Simpich. Vol. XXVI, pp. 546-588, 35 ills., Dec., 1914.

Winchester, England's Early Capital. By Frederick Simpich. Vol. LXXIX, pp. 67-92, 25 ills., 1 third-page map, Jan., 1941.

Yield of Texas. By Frederick Simpich. Vol. LXXXVII, pp. 163-184, 15 ills., 1 two-page map, Feb., 1945.

Your Dog Joins Up. By Frederick Simpich. Vol. LXXXIII, pp. 93-113, 25 ills., Jan., 1943.

Youth Explores Its World (Boy Scouts). By Frederick Simpich. Vol. LXV, pp. 643-662, 21 ills., May, 1934.

Simpich, Frederick, Jr.:

Americans Help Liberated Europe Live Again. By Lt. Col. Frederick Simpich, Jr. Vol. LXXXVII, pp. 747-768, 17 ills., June, 1945.

At Ease in the South Seas. By Maj. Frederick Simpich, Jr. Vol. LXXXV, pp. 79-104, 32 ills., Jan., 1944.

Life on the Hawaii "Front" : All-out Defense and Belt Tightening of Pacific Outpost Foreshadow the Things to Come on Mainland. By Lieut. Frederick Simpich, Jr., Vol. LXXXII, pp. 541-560, 19 ills., 1 half-page map, Oct., 1942.

Paris Freed. By Maj. Frederick Simpich, Jr. Vol. LXXXVII, pp. 385-412, 14 ills. in black and white, 12 ills. in color, Apr., 1945.

When GI Joes Took London. By Maj. Frederick Simpich, Jr. Vol. LXXXVI, pp. 337-354, 18 ills., Sept., 1944.

Simpich, Margaret:

Where Adam and Eve Lived (Baghdad). By Frederick and Margaret Simpich. Vol. XXVI, pp. 546-588, 35 ills., Dec., 1914.

Simple Method of Proving That the Earth Is Round. By Robert Marshall Brown. Vol. XVIII, pp. 771-774, 5 diagrams, Dec., 1907.

Simpson, (Maj.) W. A.:

Influence of Geographical Conditions on Military Operations in South Africa. By Maj. W. A. Simpson. Vol. XI, pp. 186-192, 1 half-page map, May, 1900.

Sinai (Peninsula), Egypt :

East of Suez to the Mount of the Decalogue : Following the Trail Over Which Moses Led the Israelites from the Slave-Pens of Egypt to Sinai. By Maynard Owen Williams. Vol. LII, pp. 709-743, 32 ills., 1 three-quarters-page map, Dec., 1927.

Sinai (Peninsula), Egypt—*Continued*

Flying Over Egypt, Sinai and Palestine: Looking Down Upon the Holy Land During an Air Journey of Two and a Half Hours from Cairo to Jerusalem. By Brig. Gen. P. R. C. Groves and Maj. J. R. McCrindle. Vol. L, pp. 313-355, 26 ills., 1 half-page map, Sept., 1926.

Route Over Which Moses Led the Children of Israel Out of Egypt. By Franklin E. Hoskins. Vol. XX, pp. 1011-1038, 24 ills., 1 page map, Dec., 1909.

Sunrise and Sunset from Mt. Sinai. By Sartell Prentice, Jr. Vol. XXIII, pp. 1242-1282, 34 ills., 1 page map, Dec., 1912.

Sinclair, C. H.:

California and Nevada Boundary. By C. H. Sinclair. Vol. X, pp. 416-417, Oct., 1899.

Sindbads of Science: Narrative of a Windjammer's Specimen-Collecting Voyage to the Sargasso Sea, to Senegambian Africa and Among Islands of High Adventure in the South Atlantic. By George Finlay Simmons. Vol. LII, pp. 1-75, 89 ills., 1 two-thirds-page map, July, 1927.

Singan—The Present Capital of the Chinese Empire. By James Mascarene Hubbard. Vol. XII, pp. 63-66, 1 ill., Feb., 1901.

Singapore, Straits Settlements:

Behind the News in Singapore. By Frederick Simpich. Vol. LXXVIII, pp. 83-110, 26 ills., 1 map, July, 1940.

Fire-Walking Hindus of Singapore. By L. Elizabeth Lewis. Vol. LIX, pp. 513-522, 12 ills., Apr., 1931.

Life Grows Grim in Singapore. By H. Gordon Minnigerode. Vol. LXXX, pp. 661-686, 17 ills. in black and white, 9 ills. in color, 1 half-page map, Nov., 1941.

Singapore—Britain's Outpost of Empire. 9 ills. in color from natural-color photographs by J. Baylor Roberts. Vol. LXXX, pp. 665-672, Nov., 1941.

Singapore: Far East Gibraltar in the Malay Jungle. 23 ills. from photographs. Vol. LXXIII, pp. 599-614, May, 1938.

Singapore, Crossroads of the East: The World's Greatest Mart for Rubber and Tin Was in Recent Times a Pirate-Haunted, Tiger-Infested Jungle Isle. By Frederick Simpich. Vol. XLIX, pp. 235-269, 32 ills., 1 half-page map, Mar., 1926.

Singer, Rolf:

Roaming Russia's Caucasus: Rugged Mountains and Hardy Fighters Guard the Soviet Union's Caucasian Treasury of Manganese and Oil. By Rolf Singer. Vol. LXXXII, pp. 91-121, 33 ills., July, 1942.

Singing Towers of Holland and Belgium. By William Gorham Rice. Vol. XLVII, pp. 357-376, 22 ills., Mar., 1925.

Sinkiang (Chinese Turkistan):

By Coolie and Caravan Across Central Asia: Narrative of a 7,900-Mile Journey of Exploration and Research Over "the Roof of the World," from the Indian Ocean to the Yellow Sea. By William J. Morden. Vol. LII, pp. 369-431, 73 ills., 1 page map, Oct., 1927.

Desert Road to Turkestan. Twentieth Century Travel Through Innermost Asia, Along Caravan Trails Over Which Oriental Commerce Was Once Borne from China to the Medieval Western World. By Owen Lattimore. Vol. LV, pp. 661-702, 45 ills., 1 two-thirds-page map, June, 1929.

First Over the Roof of the World by Motor: The Trans-Asiatic Expedition Sets New Records for Wheeled Transport in Scaling Passes of the Himalayas. By Maynard Owen Williams. Vol. LXI, pp. 321-363, 45 ills., 2 half-page maps, Mar., 1932.

From the Mediterranean to the Yellow Sea by Motor: The Citroën-Haardt Expedition Successfully Completes Its Dramatic Journey. By Maynard Owen Williams. Vol. LXII, pp. 513-580, 45 ills. in black and white, 25 ills. in color, 2 half-page maps, Nov., 1932.

Land of Genghis Khan in Its True Colors. 4 ills. in color from natural-color photographs by Maynard Owen Williams. Vol. LXII, pp. 568-577, Nov., 1932.

Life on the Steppes and Oases of Chinese Turkestan. 32 ills. in color from natural-color photographs by W. Bosshard. Vol. LIX, pp. 332-357, Mar., 1931.

Medieval Tales of the Lop Basin in Central Asia. By Ellsworth Huntington. Vol. XIX, pp. 288-295, 9 ills., Apr., 1908.

On the World's Highest Plateaus: Through an Asiatic No Man's Land to the Desert of Ancient Cathay. By Hellmut de Terra. Vol. LIX, pp. 319-367, 39 ills. in black and white, 32 ills. in color, 1 two-thirds-page map, Mar., 1931.

Sven Hedin's Explorations in Central Asia. Vol. XII, pp. 393-395, Nov., 1901.

With the Nomads of Central Asia: A Summer's Sojourn in the Tekes Valley, Plateau Paradise of Mongol and Turkic Tribes. By Edward Murray. Vol. LXIX, pp. 1-57, 43 ills. in black and white, 26 ills. in color, 1 half-page map, Jan., 1936.

Sioux Indians:

Black Hills, Once Huntings Grounds of the Red Men. Vol. LII, pp. 305-329, 18 ills., Sept., 1927.

Siracusa (Syracuse), Sicily:

Sicily, the Battlefield of Nations and of Nature. By Mrs. George C. Bosson, Jr. Vol. XX, pp. 96-118, 25 ills., 1 page map, Jan., 1909.

Sisal Hemp. *See* Henequen.

Sisson, Robert F.:

Cape Cod People and Places. 24 ills. in color from natural-color photographs; 23 ills. by Robert F. Sisson. Vol. LXXXIX, pp. 753-768, June, 1946.

Sisson, Robert F.—*Continued*

Potomac: George Washington's Historic River. 18 ills. in color from natural-color photographs by Willard R. Culver and Robert F. Sisson. Vol. LXXXVIII, pp. 41-64, July, 1945.

Sivas, Turkey:

Turkish Republic Comes of Age. By Maynard Owen Williams. Vol. LXXXVII, pp. 581-616, 4 ills. in black and white, 29 ills. in color, 1 map (two-page spread), May, 1945.

Siwai (Tribespeople):

Woman's Experiences among Stone Age Solomon Islanders: Primitive Life Remains Unchanged in Tropical Jungleland Where United States Forces Now Are Fighting. By Eleanor Schirmer Oliver. Vol. LXXXII, pp. 813-836, 26 ills., 1 half-page map, Dec., 1942.

6,000 Miles over the Roads of Free China. By Josephine A. Brown. Vol. LXXXV, pp. 355-384, 30 ills., 1 two-thirds-page map, Mar., 1944.

Sixth Annual Newspaper National Snapshot Awards:

American Scene. 29 ills. from winning photographs in the Sixth Annual Newspaper National Snapshot Awards, with explanatory note. Vol. LXXIX, pp. 220-246, Feb., 1941.

Skeleton in Luray Cave. By H. C. Hovey. Vol. XVII, pp. 425-426, July, 1906.

Sketch of the Geographical History of Asia Minor. By Sir William Ramsay. Vol. XLII, pp. 553-570, 12 ills., Nov., 1922.

Skiing (Sport):

New England Ski Trails: Snow and Ice Sports Transform Whittier's Winters of Snowbound Seclusion Into Seasons of Outdoor Recreation. By Daniel Rochford. Vol. LXX, pp. 645-664, 11 ills. in black and white, 13 ills. in color, Nov., 1936.

Skiing in Switzerland's Realm of Winter Sports. 10 ills. in duotone from photographs by Jean Gaberell, E. Gyger, and A. Klopfenstein. Vol. LXIII, pp. 344-353, Mar., 1933.

Skiing Over the New Hampshire Hills. By Fred H. Harris. Vol. XXXVII, pp. 133-164, 37 ills., Feb., 1920.

Sport and Color Amid New England Snows. 13 ills. in color from natural-color photographs by B. Anthony Stewart. Vol. LXX, pp. 647-654, Nov., 1936.

Skinner's Mission to Abyssinia. Vol. XV, pp. 164-166, 1 ill., Apr., 1904.

Skirting the Shores of Sunrise: Seeking and Finding "The Levant" in a Journey by Steamer, Motor-Car, and Train from Constantinople to Port Said. By Melville Chater. Vol. L, pp. 649-728, 60 ills. in black and white, 34 ills. in color, 1 two-thirds-page map, Dec., 1926.

Skokholm (Island), Wales:

We Live Alone, and Like It—On an Island. By R. M. Lockley. Vol. LXXIV, pp. 252-278, 27 ills., Aug., 1938.

Skuas (Birds):

South Georgia, an Outpost of the Antarctic. By Robert Cushman Murphy. Vol. XLI, pp. 409-444, 41 ills., 2 half-page maps, Apr., 1922.

Skunks:

Wild Animals That Took Their Own Pictures by Day and by Night. By George Shiras, 3d. Vol. XXIV, pp. 763-834, 68 ills., 1 page map, July, 1913.

Sky Charts. *See* Star Charts.

Sky-high in Lama Land (Tibet). 12 ills. from photographs by C. Suydam Cutting. Vol. XC, pp. 185-196, Aug., 1946.

Skyline Drive in the Pyrenees (France). By W. Robert Moore. Vol. LXXII, pp. 434-452, 24 ills. in color, Oct., 1937.

Skypaths Through Latin America: Flying From Our Nation's Capital Southward Over Jungles, Remote Islands, and Great Cities on an Aërial Survey of the East Coast of South America. By Frederick Simpich. Vol. LIX, pp. 1-79, 77 ills., 1 page map, Jan., 1931.

Skýros (Island), Aegean Sea:

Isles of Greece. By Lt. Richard Stillwell, USNR. Vol. LXXXV, pp. 593-622, 11 ills. in black and white, 20 ills. in color, 1 page map, May, 1944.

Sledge Dogs:

Dogs of Duty and Devotion. By Frederick G. Vosburgh. Vol. LXXX, pp. 769-774, 3 ills., Dec., 1941.

Working Dogs of the World. By Freeman Lloyd. Paintings by Edward Herbert Miner. Vol. LXXX, pp. 776-806, 12 ills. in black and white, 20 ills. in color, Dec., 1941.

Sleeping Sickness:

Amid the Snow Peaks of the Equator: A Naturalist's Explorations Around Ruwenzori, with an Excursion to the Congo State, and an Account of the Terrible Scourge of Sleeping Sickness. By A. F. R. Wollaston. Vol. XX, pp. 256-277, 11 ills., Mar., 1909.

Slime Molds. *See* Mycetozoa.

Småland (Region), Sweden:

Life's Flavor on a Swedish Farm: From the Rocky Hills of Småland Thousands of Sturdy Citizens Have Emigrated to the United States. By Willis Lindquist. Vol. LXXVI, pp. 393-414, 23 ills., 1 quarter-page map, Sept., 1939.

Smaller Mammals of North America. By E. W. Nelson. Vol. XXXIII, pp. 391-493, 29 ills. in black and white, 59 ills. in color, May, 1918.

Smiling, Happy Philippines. 21 ills. in color from natural-color photographs; 19 ills. by J. Baylor Roberts. Vol. LXXVIII, pp. 425-448, Oct., 1940.

Smith, A. W.:

Working Teak in the Burma Forests: The Sagacious Elephant Is Man's Ablest Ally in the Logging Industry of the Far East. By A. W. Smith. Vol. LVIII, pp. 239-256, 5 ills. in black and white, 15 ills. in color, Aug., 1930.

Smith, Charles Emory:

Russia. By Charles Emory Smith. Vol. XVI, pp. 55-63, Feb., 1905.

Smith, George Otis:

Four Prominent Geographers. Vol. XVIII, pp. 425-428, 4 ills., June, 1907.

Maine, the Outpost State: Some Forgotten Incidents in the Life of an Old and Stout-Hearted Commonwealth. By George Otis Smith. Vol. LXVII, pp. 533-592, 35 ills. in black and white, 39 ills. in color, 1 two-page map, May, 1935.

Where the World Gets Its Oil: But Where Will Our Children Get It When American Wells Cease to Flow? By George Otis Smith. Vol. XXXVII, pp. 181-202, 21 ills., 1 page and 2 half-page maps, Feb., 1920.

Smith, Glanville:

Minnesota, Mother of Lakes and Rivers. By Glanville Smith. Vol. LXVII, pp. 273-318, 42 ills. in black and white, 11 ills. in color, 1 two-page map, Mar., 1935.

On Goes Wisconsin: Strength and Vigor Mark This Midwestern State, With Its Woods and Lakes and Its Blend of Sturdy Nationalities. By Glanville Smith. Vol. LXXII, pp. 1-46, 25 ills. in black and white, 27 ills. in color, 1 two-page map, July, 1937.

Smith, Harrison W.:

Notes on Tahiti. By Harrison W. Smith. Vol. XXII, pp. 947-963, 17 ills., Oct., 1911.

Sarawak: The Land of the White Rajahs. By Harrison W. Smith. Vol. XXXV, pp. 110-167, 58 ills., 1 half-page map, Feb., 1919.

Smith, Herbert A.:

Saving the Forests. By Herbert A. Smith. Vol. XVIII, pp. 519-534, 7 ills., Aug., 1907.

Smith, Hugh M.:

America's Most Valuable Fishes. By Hugh M. Smith. Vol. XXIII, pp. 494-514, 17 ills., May, 1912.

America's Surpassing Fisheries: Their Present Condition and Future Prospects, and How the Federal Government Fosters Them. By Hugh M. Smith. Vol. XXIX, pp. 546-583, 35 ills., June, 1916.

Brittany: The Land of the Sardine. By Hugh M. Smith. Vol. XX, pp. 541-573, 23 ills., June, 1909.

Deep-Sea Exploring Expedition of the Steamer *Albatross*. By Hugh M. Smith. Vol. X, pp. 291-296, 2 ills., 1 diagram, Aug., 1899.

Federal Fish Farming: or, Planting Fish by the Billion. By Hugh M. Smith. Vol. XXI, pp. 418-446, 22 ills., May, 1910.

Fisheries of Japan. By Hugh M. Smith. Vol. XV, pp. 362-364, Sept., 1904.

Smith, Hugh M.—*Continued*

Fisheries of Japan. By Hugh M. Smith. Vol. XVI, pp. 201-220, 13 ills., May, 1905.

Goldfish and Their Cultivation in America. By Hugh M. Smith. Vol. XLVI, pp. 375-400, 14 ills. in black and white, 8 ills. in color, Oct., 1924.

King Herring: An Account of the World's Most Valuable Fish, the Industries It Supports, and the Part It Has Played in History. By Hugh M. Smith. Vol. XX, pp. 701-735, 21 ills., Aug., 1909.

Making the Fur Seal Abundant. By Hugh M. Smith. Vol. XXII, pp. 1139-1165, 18 ills., 1 half-page map, Dec., 1911.

Mysterious Life of the Common Eel. By Hugh M. Smith. Vol. XXIV, pp. 1140-1146, 3 ills., Oct., 1913.

North Holland Cheese Market. By Hugh M. Smith. Vol. XXI, pp. 1051-1066, 17 ills., Dec., 1910.

Our Fish Immigrants. By Hugh M. Smith. Vol. XVIII, pp. 382-400, 3 ills., June, 1907.

Oysters: The World's Most Valuable Water Crop. By Hugh M. Smith. Vol. XXIV, pp. 257-281, 21 ills., Mar., 1913.

Pearl Fisheries of Ceylon. By Hugh M. Smith. Vol. XXIII, pp. 173-194, 13 ills., 1 quarter-page map, Feb., 1912.

Some Giant Fishes of the Seas. By Hugh M. Smith. Vol. XX, pp. 637-644, 6 ills., July, 1909.

When the Father of Waters Goes on a Rampage: An Account of the Salvaging of Food-Fishes from the Overflowed Lands of the Mississippi River. By Hugh M. Smith. Vol. XXXVII, pp. 369-386, 18 ills., Apr., 1920.

Smith, Jane M.:

Fund for Life Memberships in The Society bequeathed by Jane M. Smith. Vol. XXIII, p. 104, Jan., 1912.

National Geographic Society's Notable Year (Award of Life Memberships Under Jane M. Smith Endowment Fund). Vol. XXXVII, pp. 338-345, 2 ills., Apr., 1920.

Smith, Middleton:

Gardening in Northern Alaska. By Middleton Smith. Vol. XIV, pp. 355-357, Sept., 1903.

Smith, Nicol:

Color Glows in the Guianas, French and Dutch. By Nicol Smith. Vol. LXXXIII, pp. 459-480, 8 ills. in black and white, 13 ills. in color, 1 two-thirds-page map, Apr., 1943.

Smith, (Sir) Ross:

From London to Australia by Aëroplane: A Personal Narrative of the First Aërial Voyage Half Around the World. By Sir Ross Smith. Vol. XXXIX, pp. 229-339, 76 ills. in black and white, 8 ills. in color, 1 page map, Mar., 1921.

Smithsonian Institution: Expeditions:

Around the World for Animals. By William M. and Lucile Q. Mann. Vol. LXXIII, pp. 665-714, 33 ills. in black and white, 23 ills. in color, 1 page map, June, 1938.

Smithsonian Institution: Expeditions—*Continued*

Discovering the New World's Oldest Dated Work of Man : A Maya Monument Inscribed 291 B. C. is Unearthed Near a Huge Stone Head by a Geographic-Smithsonian Expedition in Mexico. By Matthew W. Stirling. Vol. LXXVI, pp. 183-218, 40 ills., 1 half-page map, Aug., 1939.

Expedition Unearths Buried Masterpieces of Carved Jade. By Matthew W. Stirling. Vol. LXXX, pp. 277-302, 14 ills. in black and white, 20 ills. in color, 1 two-thirds-page map, Sept., 1941.

Exploring Frozen Fragments of American History : On the Trail of Early Eskimo Colonists Who Made a 55-Mile Crossing from the Old World to the New. By Henry B. Collins, Jr. Vol. LXXV, pp. 633-656, 24 ills., 1 two-thirds-page map, May, 1939.

Great Stone Faces of the Mexican Jungle : Five Colossal Heads and Numerous Other Monuments of Vanished Americans Are Excavated by the Latest National Geographic-Smithsonian Expedition. By Matthew W. Stirling. Vol. LXXVIII, pp. 309-334, 26 ills., 1 map, Sept., 1940.

Jungle Housekeeping for a Geographic Expedition. By Marion Stirling. Vol. LXXX, pp. 303-327, 15 ills., Sept., 1941.

La Venta's Green Stone Tigers. By Matthew W. Stirling. Vol. LXXXIV, pp. 321-332, 4 ills. in black and white, 6 ills. in color, 1 two-thirds-page map, Sept., 1943.

Measuring the Sun's Heat and Forecasting the Weather : The National Geographic Society to Maintain a Solar Station in a Remote Part of the World to Coöperate with Smithsonian Institution Stations in California and Chile. By C. G. Abbot. Vol. XLIX, pp. 111-126, 15 ills., 1 chart, Jan., 1926.

Wildlife of Tabasco and Veracruz (Mexico). By Walter A. Weber. With 19 ills. in color from paintings by the author. Vol. LXXXVII, pp. 187-216, 7 ills. in black and white, 1 two-thirds-page map, Feb., 1945.

Smoke Over Alabama. By Frederick Simpich. Vol. LX, pp. 703-758, 43 ills. in black and white, 26 ills. in color, 1 page map, Dec., 1931.

Smoky Jungle Frog:

Frog That Eats Bats and Snakes : In Captivity, This Big Jungle Amphibian Exhibits an Extraordinary Appetite. By Kenneth W. Vinton. Vol. LXXIII, pp. 657-664, 11 ills., May, 1938.

Smoky Mountains, North Carolina-Tennessee. *See* Great Smoky Mountains.

Smyrna, Turkey. *See* İzmir.

Smyser, William Leon:

São Tomé, the Chocolate Island. By William Leon Smyser. Vol. LXXXIX, pp. 657-680, 23 ills., 1 third-page map, May, 1946.

Snake Dance (Hopi Indians). By Marion L. Oliver. Vol. XXII, pp. 107-137, 31 ills., Feb., 1911.

Snakes. *See* Reptiles.

Snow:

Magic Beauty of Snow and Dew. By Wilson A. Bentley. Vol. XLIII, pp. 103-112, 9 ills., Jan., 1923.

Snow Crystals. By Wilson A. Bentley. Vol. XV, pp. 30-37, 31 ills., Jan., 1904.

Snow Scenes. Vol. XXIX, pp. 135-150, 16 ills., Jan., 1916.

Snowy Peaks and Old Costumes of Switzerland. 12 ills. in color from natural-color photographs by Hans Hildenbrand. Vol. LXVI, pp. 147-154, Aug., 1934.

So Big Texas. By Frederick Simpich. Vol. LIII, pp. 637-693, 72 ills., 1 two-page map, June, 1928.

So Oklahoma Grew Up. By Frederick Simpich. Vol. LXXIX, pp. 269-314, 30 ills. in black and white, 19 ills. in color, 1 page map, Mar., 1941.

Society Announces New Flight into the Stratosphere. By Gilbert Grosvenor. Vol. LXVII, pp. 265-272, 2 ills. in black and white, 1 sketch map, Feb., 1935.

Society Awards Hubbard Medal to Anne Morrow Lindbergh. Vol. LXV, pp. 791-794, 4 ills., June, 1934.

Society Islands, Pacific Ocean :

Diary of a Voyage from San Francisco to Tahiti and Return, 1901. By S. P. Langley. Vol. XII, pp. 413-429, 10 ills., 1 page and 1 half-page maps, Dec., 1901.

Dream Ship : The Story of a Voyage of Adventure More Than Half Around the World in a 47-Foot Lifeboat. By Ralph Stock. Vol. XXXIX, pp. 1-52, 43 ills., 1 page map, Jan., 1921.

Notes on Tahiti. By Harrison W. Smith. Vol. XXII, pp. 947-963, 17 ills., Oct., 1911.

Tahiti—A Playground of Nature. By Paul Gooding. Vol. XXXVIII, pp. 301-326, 16 ills., 1 half-page map, Oct., 1920.

Society Maps Northwestern United States and Neighboring Canadian Provinces. Text accompanying special map supplement in colors. Vol. LXXIX, pp. 805-806, June, 1941.

Society Takes Part in Three Geographic Expeditions. Vol. LXV, pp. 625-626, May, 1934.

Society's Map of Bible Lands. By Gilbert Grosvenor. Text accompanying special map supplement in colors. Vol. LXXIV, pp. 751-754, 3 ills., Dec., 1938.

Society's Map of Historic and Scenic Reaches of the Nation's Capital. Text accompanying special map supplement in colors. Vol. LXXIV, pp. 57-58, July, 1938.

Society's Map of South America. By Gilbert Grosvenor. Text accompanying special map supplement in colors. Vol. LXXII, pp. 809-810, Dec., 1937.

Society's Map of the Antarctic. Text accompanying special map supplement in colors. Vol. LXII, pp. 485-486, 1 ill., Oct., 1932.

Society's Map of the Reaches of New York City. Text accompanying special map supplement in colors. Vol. LXXV, pp. 491-492, Apr., 1939.

Society's New Caribbean Map. Mexico, Central America, and the West Indies—Gateway of Discovery. Text accompanying special map supplement in colors. Vol. LXVI, pp. 738-740, 1 ill., Dec., 1934.

Society's New Map of Africa. Text accompanying special map supplement in colors. Vol. XLII, pp. 447-448, Oct., 1922.

Society's New Map of Asia. Text accompanying special map supplement in colors. Vol. LXIV, pp. 770-772, 1 ill., Dec., 1933.

Society's New Map of Bible Lands. Text accompanying special map supplement in colors. Vol. XC, pp. 815-816, Dec., 1946.

Society's New Map of Canada. Text accompanying special map supplement in colors. Vol. LXIX, pp. 769-776, 10 ills., June, 1936.

Society's New Map of Central Europe and the Mediterranean. Text accompanying special map supplement in colors. Vol. LXXVI, pp. 559-560, Oct., 1939.

Society's New Map of China. By James M. Darley. Text accompanying special map supplement in colors. Vol. LXXXVII, pp. 745-746, June, 1945.

Society's New Map of Europe. By Gilbert Grosvenor. Text accompanying special map supplement in colors. Vol. LVI, pp. 771-774, Dec., 1929.

Society's New Map of India and Burma. Text accompanying special map supplement in colors. Vol. LXXXIX, p. 544, Apr., 1946.

Society's New Map of South America. Text accompanying special map supplement in colors. Vol. XL, pp. 374-392, 17 ills., Oct., 1921.

Society's New Map of Southeast Asia. Text accompanying special map supplement in colors. Vol. LXXXVI, pp. 449-450, 1 ill., Oct., 1944.

Society's New Map of the Pacific. By Gilbert Grosvenor. Text accompanying special map supplement in colors. Vol. LXX, pp. 793-796, Dec., 1936.

Society's New Map of the World. Text accompanying special map supplement in colors. Vol. XLII, p. 691, Dec., 1922.

Society's Special Medal Awarded to Amelia Earhart: First Woman to Receive Geographic Distinction at Brilliant Ceremony in the National Capital. Vol. LXII, pp. 358-367, 7 ills., Sept., 1932.

Society's Special Medal Is Awarded to Dr. Thomas C. Poulter: Admiral Byrd's Second-In-Command and Senior Scientist Is Accorded High Geographic Honor. Vol. LXXII, pp. 105-108, 2 ills., July, 1937.

Socotra (Island), Indian Ocean:

Isle of Frankincense. By Charles K. Moser. Vol. XXXIII, pp. 266-278, 11 ills., Mar., 1918.

Sofia, Bulgaria:

Bulgaria, Farm Land Without a Farmhouse: A Nation of Villagers Faces the Challenge of Modern Machinery and Urban Life. By Maynard Owen Williams. Vol. LXII, pp. 185-218, 19 ills. in black and white, 27 ills. in color, 1 half-page map, Aug., 1932.

Soil. *See* Agriculture.

Soil Erosion:

China Fights Erosion with U. S. Aid. By Walter C. Lowdermilk. Vol. LXXXVII, pp. 641-680, 10 ills. in black and white, 26 ills. in color, June, 1945.

Taming the Outlaw Missouri River. By Frederick Simpich. Vol. LXXXVIII, pp. 569-598, 25 ills., 1 two-page map, Nov., 1945.

Sojourning in the Italy of Today. By Mrs. Kenneth Roberts. Vol. LXX, pp. 351-396, 46 ills., 1 two-thirds-page map, Sept., 1936.

Sokol Festival:

Czechoslovakia, Key-Land to Central Europe. By Maynard Owen Williams. Vol. XXXIX, pp. 111-156, 45 ills., 1 quarter-page map, Feb., 1921.

When Czechoslovakia Puts a Falcon Feather in Its Cap. By Maynard Owen Williams. Vol. LXIII, pp. 40-49, 13 ills. in color, Jan., 1933.

When Golden Praha Entertains the Majestic Sokol Festival. 13 ills. in color from natural-color photographs by Hans Hildenbrand. Vol. LXIII, pp. 40-49, Jan., 1933.

Solano, Solita:

Constantinople Today. By Solita Solano. Vol. XLI, pp. 647-680, 40 ills., 1 three-quarters-page map, June, 1922.

Vienna—A Capital Without a Nation. By Solita Solano. Vol. XLIII, pp. 77-102, 27 ills., Jan., 1923.

Solar Radiation:

Hunting an Observatory: A Successful Search for a Dry Mountain on Which to Establish the National Geographic Society's Solar Radiation Station. By C. G. Abbot. Vol. L, pp. 503-518, 13 ills., 1 quarter-page map, Oct., 1926.

Keeping House for the "Shepherds of the Sun." By Mrs. William H. Hoover. Vol. LVII, pp. 483-506, 17 ills., 1 third-page map, Apr., 1930.

Measuring the Sun's Heat and Forecasting the Weather: The National Geographic Society to Maintain a Solar Station in a Remote Part of the World to Coöperate with Smithsonian Institution Stations in California and Chile. By C. G. Abbot. Vol. XLIX, pp. 111-126, 15 ills., 1 chart, Jan., 1926.

Solar System's Eternal Show. 10 ills. in color from paintings by Charles Bittinger. Vol. LXXVI, pp. 17-24, July, 1939.

Soldier-Crabs:

Strange Sights in Far-Away Papua. By A. E. Pratt. Vol. XVIII, pp. 559-572, 7 ills., Sept., 1907.

Soldiers:

Aerial Invasion of Burma. By Gen. H. H. Arnold. Vol. LXXXVI, pp. 129-148, 20 ills., Aug., 1944.

Contains information on the Allied troops who worked with Maj. Gen. Orde Charles Wingate.

American Fighters Visit Bible Lands. By Maynard Owen Williams. With 23 ills. in color from natural-color photographs by the author. Vol. LXXXIX, pp. 311-340, 10 ills. in black and white, Mar., 1946.

American Soldier in Reykjavík. By Corporal Luther M. Chovan. Vol. LXXXVIII, pp. 536-568, 6 ills. in black and white, 34 ills. in color, Nov., 1945.

Americans Stand Guard in Greenland. By Andrew H. Brown. Vol. XC, pp. 457-500, 23 ills. in black and white, 19 ills. in color, 1 page map, Oct., 1946.

Around the Clock with Your Soldier Boy. By Frederick Simpich. Vol. LXXX, pp. 1-36, 42 ills., July, 1941.

Fiji Patrol on Bougainville. By David D. Duncan. Vol. LXXXVII, pp. 87-104, 9 ills. in black and white, 11 ills. in color, Jan., 1945.

Flying Our Wounded Veterans Home. By Catherine Bell Palmer. Vol. LXXXVIII, pp. 363-384, 17 ills., Sept., 1945.

Heroes' Return. By William H. Nicholas. Vol. LXXXVII, pp. 333-352, 19 ills., Mar., 1945.

Iceland Defrosted. 34 ills. in color from natural-color photographs by Luther M. Chovan. Vol. LXXXVIII, pp. 537-568, Nov., 1945.

Infantrymen—The Fighters of War. By Brig. Gen. W. H. Wilbur. Vol. LXXXVI, pp. 513-538, 22 ills., Nov., 1944.

Painting the Army on Maneuvers. By Arthur Beaumont. Text accompanying 16 colored illustrations from paintings by the author. Vol. LXXXII, pp. 601-602, Nov., 1942.

Paris Delivered. 10 ills. from photographs. Vol. LXXXVII, pp. 79-86, Jan., 1945.

Paris Freed. By Maj. Frederick Simpich, Jr. Vol. LXXXVII, pp. 385-412, 14 ills. in black and white, 12 ills. in color, Apr., 1945.

Seeing Paris on a 48-Hour Pass. 12 ills. in color from U. S. Army official photographs. Vol. LXXXVII, pp. 401-412, Apr., 1945.

This Is My Own : How the United States Seems to a Citizen Soldier Back From Three Years Overseas. By Frederick G. Vosburgh. Vol. LXXXIX, pp. 113-128, 14 ills., Jan., 1946.

Soldiers—Continued

Uncle Sam's Icebox Outposts. 19 ills. in color from natural-color photographs by John E. Schneider and Robert B. Sykes, Jr. Vol. XC, pp. 473-496, Oct., 1946.

When GI Joes Took London. By Maj. Frederick Simpich, Jr. Vol. LXXXVI, pp. 337-354, 18 ills., Sept., 1944.

White War in Norway. By Thomas R. Henry. Vol. LXXXVIII, pp. 617-640, 23 ills., 1 three-quarters-page map, Nov., 1945.

Yank Meets Native. By Wanda Burnett. Vol. LXXXVIII, pp. 105-128, 24 ills., July, 1945.

Yanks in Northern Ireland. 15 ills. from photographs. Vol. LXXXIV, pp. 191-204, Aug., 1943.

See also Anzacs ; U. S. Army ; U. S. Army Air Forces ; U. S. Army Engineers ; U. S. Army Quartermaster Corps ; U. S. Army Signal Corps ; World War II.

Solomon (King of Israel) :

On the Trail of King Solomon's Mines : The Bible, in Addition to Its Spiritual Values, Continues to Prove a Rich Geography and Guide to Exploration of the Holy Land. By Nelson Glueck. Vol. LXXXV, pp. 233-256, 20 ills., 1 page map, Feb., 1944.

Solomon Islands, Pacific Ocean :

Coconuts and Coral Islands. By H. Ian Hogbin. Vol. LXV, pp. 265-298, 24 ills. in black and white, 14 ills. in color, 1 half-page map, Mar., 1934.

Islands of the Pacific. By J. P. Thomson. Vol. XL, pp. 543-558, 15 ills., special map supplement, Dec., 1921.

What the Fighting Yanks See. By Wanda Burnett. Vol. LXXXVI, pp. 451-476, 27 ills., Oct., 1944.

Woman's Experiences among Stone Age Solomon Islanders : Primitive Life Remains Unchanged in Tropical Jungleland Where United States Forces Now Are Fighting. By Eleanor Schirmer Oliver. Vol. LXXXII, pp. 813-836, 26 ills., 1 half-page map, Dec., 1942.

See also Bougainville ; Guadalcanal ; Munda.

Solomons Island, Maryland : Amphibious Training Base :

Landing Craft for Invasion. By Melville Bell Grosvenor. Vol. LXXXVI, pp. 1-30, 26 ills., July, 1944.

Soluka Creek, Alaska :

Valley of Ten Thousand Smokes : National Geographic Society Explorations in the Katmai District of Alaska. By Robert F. Griggs. Vol. XXXI, pp. 12-68, 51 ills., 1 half-page map, Jan., 1917.

Somaliland. See French Somaliland.

Some Aspects of Rural Japan. By Walter Weston. Vol. XLII, pp. 275-301, 12 ills. in black and white, 16 ills. in color, Sept., 1922.

Some Early Geographers of the United States. By Rear Adm. Colby M. Chester. Vol. XV, pp. 392-404, Oct., 1904.

Some Facts About Japan. Vol. XV, pp. 446-448, Nov., 1904.

Some Forgotten Corners of London : Many Places of Beauty and Historic Interest Repay the Search of the Inquiring Visitor. By Harold Donaldson Eberlein. Vol. LXI, pp. 163-198, 25 ills., Feb., 1932.

Some French Pastorals. 18 ills. in color from natural-color photographs by Harrison Howell Walker. Vol. LXXVII, pp. 207-230, Feb., 1940.

Some Geographic Features of Southern Patagonia, with a Discussion of Their Origin. By J. B. Hatcher. Vol. XI, pp. 41-55, 4 ills., Feb., 1900.

Some Giant Fishes of the Seas. By Hugh M. Smith. Vol. XX, pp. 637-644, 6 ills., July, 1909.

Some Human Habitations. By Collier Cobb. Vol. XIX, pp. 509-515, 5 ills., July, 1908.

Some Impressions of 150,000 Miles of Travel. By William Howard Taft. Vol. LVII, pp. 523-508, 80 ills., May, 1930.

Some Indications of Land in the Vicinity of the North Pole. By R. A. Harris. Vol. XV, pp. 255-261, 1 page map, June, 1904.

Some Lessons in Geography. By Edward Atkinson. Vol. XVI, pp. 193-198, Apr., 1905.

Some Mexican Transportation Scenes. By Walter W. Bradley. Vol. XXI, pp. 985-991, 10 ills., Dec., 1910.

Some Notes on the Fox Island Passes, Alaska. By J. J. Gilbert. Vol. XVI, pp. 427-429, Sept., 1905.

Some Notes on Venezuela. Vol. XIV, pp. 17-21, 3 ills., 1 page map, Jan., 1903.

Some Odd Pages from the Annals of the Tulip : A "Made" Flower of Unknown Origin Took Medieval Europe by Storm and Caused a Financial Panic in the Netherlands. By Leo A. Borah. Vol. LXIV, pp. 321-343, 13 ills. in black and white, 10 ills. in color, Sept., 1933.

Some of Our Immigrants. Vol. XVIII, pp. 317-334, 21 ills., May, 1907.

Some Peculiar Features of Central African Geography. By Samuel P. Verner. Vol. XV, p. 448, Nov., 1904.

Some Personal Experiences with Earthquakes (Arica, Peru). By Rear Adm. L. G. Billings. Vol. XVII, pp. 57-71, 7 ills., Jan., 1915.

Some Recent Instances of National Altruism : The Efforts of the United States to Aid the Peoples of Cuba, Porto Rico, and the Philippines. By William Howard Taft. Vol. XVIII, pp. 429-438, July, 1907.

Some Ruined Cities of Asia Minor. By Ernest L. Harris. Vol. XIX, pp. 833-858, 19 ills., Dec., 1908.

Some Songsters and Flyers of Wide Repute. 42 portraits in color from paintings by Maj. Allan Brooks. Vol. LXIX, pp. 529-544, Apr., 1936.

Some Tramps Across the Glaciers and Snowfields of British Columbia. By Howard Palmer. Vol. XXI, pp. 457-487, 25 ills., June, 1910.

Some Wonderful Sights in the Andean Highlands : The Oldest City in America. Sailing on the Lake of the Clouds : The Yosemite of Peru. By Harriet Chalmers Adams. Vol. XIX, pp. 597-618, 19 ills., 1 half-page map, Sept., 1908.

Somers, (Sir) George:

Islands of Bermuda : A British Colony With a Unique Record in Popular Government. By William Howard Taft. Vol. XLI, pp. 1-26, 15 ills., 1 three-quarters-page map, Jan., 1922.

Songdo, Korea. *See* Kaijo.

Sonnenburg, (Maj.) A. Falkner von:

Manila and the Philippines. By Maj. A. Falkner von Sonnenburg. Vol. X, pp. 65-72, Feb., 1900.

Sonora (State), Mexico :

Adventuring Down the West Coast of Mexico. By Herbert Corey. Vol. XLII, pp. 449-503, 44 ills., 1 half-page map, Nov., 1922.

Mexican Land of Canaan : Marvelous Riches of the Wonderful West Coast of Our Neighbor Republic. By Frederick Simpich. Vol. XXXVI, pp. 307-330, 16 ills., 1 page map, Oct., 1919.

Soochow Creek, China :

Ho for the Soochow Ho. By Mabel Craft Deering. Vol. LI, pp. 623-649, 32 ills., 1 three-quarters-page map, June, 1927.

Sorata, Bolivia :

Bolivia—Tin Roof of the Andes. By Henry Albert Phillips. Vol. LXXXIII, pp. 309-332, 5 ills. in black and white, 20 ills. in color, Mar., 1943.

Souf (Region), Algeria :

Country of the Ant Men. By Thomas H. Kearney. Vol. XXII, pp. 367-382, 11 ills., 1 half-page map, Apr., 1911.

Soufrière (Volcano), St. Vincent :

Eruptions of La Soufrière, St. Vincent, in May, 1902. By Edmund Otis Hovey. Vol. XIII, pp. 444-459, 4 ills., Dec., 1902.

National Geographic Society's Expedition in the West Indies. Vol. XIII, pp. 209-213, 2 half-page maps, June, 1902.

Recent Volcanic Eruptions in the West Indies. By Israel C. Russell. Vol. XIII, pp. 267-285, 7 ills., July, 1902.

Report of the Eruption of the Soufrière of St. Vincent, 1812 (From the *Evening News* of June 30, 1812). Vol. XIV, pp. 158-161, Apr., 1903.

Sources of the Saskatchewan. By Walter D. Wilcox. Vol. X, pp. 113-134, 5 ills., 1 chart, Apr., 1899.

Sources of Washington's Charm (District of Columbia). By J. R. Hildebrand. Vol. XLIII, pp. 639-680, 46 ills., June, 1923.

South Africa. *See* Union of South Africa.

South America:

Awakened Continent to the South of Us. By Elihu Root. Vol. XVIII, pp. 61-72, Jan., 1907.

Bonds Between the Americas. By Frederick Simpich. Vol. LXXII, pp. 785-808, 22 ills., Dec., 1937.

Buenos Aires and Its River of Silver: A Journey Up the Paraná and Paraguay to the Chaco Cattle Country. By William R. Barbour. Vol. XL, pp. 393-432, 38 ills., Oct., 1921.

Buenos Aires to Washington by Horse: A Solitary Journey of Two and a Half Years, Through Eleven American Republics, Covers 9,600 Miles of Mountain and Plain, Desert and Jungle. By A. F. Tschiffely. Vol. LV, pp. 135-196, 75 ills., 1 page map, Feb., 1929.

By Seaplane to Six Continents: Cruising 60,000 Miles, Italian Argonauts of the Air See World Geography Unroll, and Break New Sky Trails Over Vast Brazilian Jungles. By Comdr. Francesco de Pinedo. Vol. LIV, pp. 247-301, 60 ills., 1 two-page map, Sept., 1928.

Flags of Pan-America. By Byron McCandless and Gilbert Grosvenor. Vol. XXXII, pp. 361-369, 62 ills. in color, Oct., 1917.

Flying the "Hump" of the Andes. By Capt. Albert W. Stevens. Vol. LIX, pp. 595-636, 36 ills., 1 third-page map, May, 1931.

Flying the World's Longest Air-Mail Route: From Montevideo, Uruguay, Over the Andes, Up the Pacific Coast, Across Central America and the Caribbean to Miami, Florida, in 67 Thrilling Flying Hours. By Junius B. Wood. Vol. LVII, pp. 261-325, 65 ills., 1 half-page map, Mar., 1930.

From Panama to Patagonia. By Charles M. Pepper. Vol. XVII, pp. 449-452, 1 ill., Aug., 1906.

How Latin America Looks from the Air: U. S. Army Airplanes Hurdle the High Andes, Brave Brazil Jungles, and Follow Smoking Volcanoes to Map New Sky Paths Around South America. By Maj. Herbert A. Dargue. Vol. LII, pp. 451-502, 52 ills., 1 page map, Oct., 1927.

In Humboldt's Wake: Narrative of a National Geographic Society Expedition Up the Orinoco and Through the Strange Casiquiare Canal to Amazonian Waters. By Ernest G. Holt. Vol. LX, pp. 621-644, 27 ills., 1 two-thirds-page map, Nov., 1931.

Latin America and Colombia. By John Barrett. Vol. XVII, pp. 692-709, 10 ills., Dec., 1906.

Latin American Constitutions and Revolutions. By John W. Foster. Vol. XII, pp. 169-175, May, 1901.

New National Geographic Society Map Charts South America's Wartime Importance. Text accompanying special map supplement in colors. Vol. LXXXII, pp. 537-540, 2 ills., Oct., 1942.

South America—*Continued*

Over the Andes to Bogotá. By Frank M. Chapman. Vol. XL, pp. 353-373, 19 ills., Oct., 1921.

Peace of Latin America. Vol. XVI, pp. 479-480, Oct., 1905.

Skypaths Through Latin America: Flying From Our Nation's Capital Southward Over Jungles, Remote Islands, and Great Cities on an Aërial Survey of the East Coast of South America. By Frederick Simpich. Vol. LIX, pp. 1-79, 77 ills., 1 page map, Jan., 1931.

Society's Map of South America. By Gilbert Grosvenor. Text accompanying special map supplement in colors. Vol. LXXII, pp. 809-810, Dec., 1937.

Society's New Map of South America. Text accompanying special map supplement in colors. Vol. XL, pp. 374-392, 17 ills., Oct., 1921.

South America Fifty Years Hence. By Charles M. Pepper. Vol. XVII, pp. 427-432, special map supplement in colors, Aug., 1906.

South American Immigration. Vol. XVII, p. 587, Oct., 1906.

To Bogotá and Back by Air: The Narrative of a 9,500-Mile Flight from Washington, Over Thirteen Latin-American Countries and Return, in the Single-Seater Airplane *Spirit of St. Louis*. By Col. Charles A. Lindbergh. Vol. LIII, pp. 529-601, 98 ills., 1 two-thirds-page map, May, 1928.

What the Latin American Republics Think of the Pan American Conferences. Vol. XVII, pp. 474-479, Aug., 1906.

World's Highest International Telephone Cable. Vol. LVIII, pp. 722-731, 8 ills., Dec., 1930.

See also Argentina; Bolivia; Brazil; British Guiana; Buenos Aires; Chile; Colombia; Ecuador; French Guiana; Marajó Island; Paraguay; Peru; Rio de Janeiro; Santos; São Paulo; Surinam; Tierra del Fuego (Archipelago); Venezuela.

South American Immigration. Vol. XVII, p. 587, Oct., 1906.

South Carolina:

Ashley River and Its Gardens. By E. T. H. Shaffer. Vol. XLIX, pp. 525-550, 6 ills. in black and white, 7 ills. in color, May, 1926.

See also Charleston.

South Dakota:

Bad Lands of South Dakota. By N. H. Darton. Vol. X, pp. 339-343, 4 ills., Sept., 1899.

Black Hills, Once Hunting Grounds of the Red Men. Vol. LII, pp. 305-329, 18 ills., Sept., 1927.

Call of the West. By C. J. Blanchard. Vol. XX, pp. 403-437, 20 ills., 1 half-page map, May, 1909.

Exploring the Stratosphere. By Capt. Albert W. Stevens. Vol. LXVI, pp. 397-434, 43 ills., 1 two-thirds-page chart, Oct., 1934.

South Dakota *Continued*

Man's Farthest Aloft: Rising to 13.71 Miles, the National Geographic Society-U. S. Army Stratosphere Expedition Gathers Scientific Data at Record Altitude. By Capt. Albert W. Stevens. Action Photographs of the Balloon's Perfect Landing included. Vol. LXIX, pp. 59-94, 39 ills., 1 quarter-page map, Jan., 1936.

Taming the Outlaw Missouri River. By Frederick Simpich. Vol. LXXXVIII, pp. 569-598, 25 ills., 1 two-page map, Nov., 1945.

South Florida's Amazing Everglades: Encircled by Populous Places Is a Seldom-visited Area of Rare Birds, Prairies, Cowboys, and Teeming Wild Life of Big Cypress Swamp. By John O'Reilly. Vol. LXXVII, pp. 115-142, 26 ills., 1 page map, Jan., 1940.

South from Saipan. By W. Robert Moore. Vol. LXXXVII, pp. 441-474, 11 ills. in black and white, 17 ills. in color, 1 half-page map, Apr., 1945.

South Georgia (Island), Scotia Sea:

Sailing the Seven Seas in the Interest of Science: Adventures Through 157,000 Miles of Storm and Calm, from Arctic to Antarctic and Around the World, in the Non-Magnetic Yacht *Carnegie*. By J. P. Ault. Vol. XLII, pp. 631-690, 47 ills., 1 chart, Dec., 1922.

South Georgia, an Outpost of the Antarctic. By Robert Cushman Murphy. Vol. XLI, pp. 409-444, 41 ills., 2 half-page maps, Apr., 1922.

South Island, New Zealand:

Alpine Peaks and Pastures of South Island. 11 ills. in color from natural-color photographs by W. Robert Moore. Vol. LXIX, pp. 205-212. Feb., 1936.

South of Khyber Pass (India). By Maynard Owen Williams. Vol. LXXXIX, pp. 471-500, 31 ills., Apr., 1946.

South of the Clouds—Yünnan (China). 11 ills. in color from natural-color photographs by Owen Lattimore and Frank Outram. Vol. LXXXII, pp. 349-356, Sept., 1942.

South Pacific Combat Air Transport (SCAT):

Flying Our Wounded Veterans Home. By Catherine Bell Palmer. Vol. LXXXVIII, pp. 363-384, 17 ills., Sept., 1945.

South Pacific Islands. *See* Pacific Islands.

South Polar Expedition (Proposed by Peary for Consideration of National Geographic Society). Vol. XXI, pp. 167-170, 1 page map, Feb., 1910.

South Polar Explorations. Vol. XXII, pp. 406-409, 4 ills., 1 page map, Apr., 1911.

South Pole. *See* Antarctic Regions.

South Sea Islands. *See* Melanesia; Micronesia; Polynesia.

South Sea Isle of Mineral Mountains (New Caledonia). 12 ills. in color from natural-color photographs by Enzo de Chetelat. Vol. LXXXII, pp. 33-40, July, 1942.

South-West Africa:

Hunting an Observatory: A Successful Search for a Dry Mountain on Which to Establish the National Geographic Society's Solar Radiation Station. By C. G. Abbot. Vol. L, pp. 503-518, 13 ills., 1 quarter-page map, Oct., 1926.

Keeping House for the "Shepherds of the Sun." By Mrs. William H. Hoover. Vol. LVII, pp. 483-506, 17 ills., 1 third-page map, Apr., 1930.

Southampton—Gateway to London: The Port of Double Tides Where the "Mayflower" Moored is Rich in Sea History and Lore of Early England. By Stanley Toogood. Vol. LXXVII, pp. 91-114, 21 ills., 1 map, Jan., 1940.

Southard, Addison E.:

Modern Ethiopia. Haile Selassie the First, Formerly Ras Tafari, Succeeds to the World's Oldest Continuously Sovereign Throne. By Addison E. Southard. Vol. LIX, pp. 679-738, 47 ills. in black and white, 27 ills. in color, 1 two-thirds-page map, June, 1931.

Southeastern Indians: United States:

First Families of Southeastern America. 8 ills. in color from paintings by W. Langdon Kihn. Vol. LXXXIX, pp. 65-72, Jan., 1946.

Indians of the Southeastern United States. By Matthew W. Stirling. Paintings by W. Langdon Kihn. Vol. LXXXIX, pp. 53-74, 8 ills. in black and white, 8 ills. in color, Jan., 1946.

Southerland, (Comdr.) W. H. H.:

Work of the United States Hydrographic Office. By Comdr. W. H. H. Southerland. Vol. XIV, pp. 61-75, Feb., 1903.

Southern California at Work. By Frederick Simpich. Vol. LXVI, pp. 529-600, 39 ills. in black and white, 41 ills. in color, 1 two-page map, Nov., 1934.

Southern Hemisphere:

Map of the Northern and Southern Hemispheres. Text accompanying special map supplement in colors. Vol. LXXXIII, pp. 481-483, Apr., 1943.

Southern Rhodesia:

African Rainbow. 10 ills. in color from natural-color photographs by W. Robert Moore. Vol. LXXXVI, pp. 289-296, Sept., 1944.

Rhodesia, Hobby and Hope of Cecil Rhodes. By W. Robert Moore. Vol. LXXXVI, pp. 281-306, 13 ills. in black and white, 10 ills. in color, 1 half-page map, Sept., 1944.

Southward Ho! in the "Alice" (Atlantic and Caribbean Cruise). By Henry Howard. Vol. LXXIII, pp. 265-312, 38 ills. in black and white, 13 ills. in color, 2 maps, Mar., 1938.

Southwest Trails from Horse to Motor. Text accompanying special map supplement in colors. Vol. LXXVII, p. 767, June, 1940.

Souvenirs of Knighthood in Rhodes. 13 ills. in color from natural-color photographs by Luigi Pellerano. Vol. LXIV, pp. 665-672, Dec., 1933.

Soviet Central Asia:

Afghan Borderland. By Ellsworth Huntington. Part I: The Russian Frontier. Vol. XX, pp. 788-799, 14 ills., Sept., 1909.

Land of Lambskins: An Expedition to Bokhara, Russian Central Asia, to Study the Karakul Sheep Industry. By Robert K. Nabours. Vol. XXXVI, pp. 77-88, 15 ills., July, 1919.

Life in the Great Desert of Central Asia. By Ellsworth Huntington. Vol. XX, pp. 749-760, 12 ills., Aug., 1909.

New Road to Asia. By Owen Lattimore. Vol. LXXXVI, pp. 641-676, 15 ills. in black and white, 26 ills. in color, Dec., 1944.

Observing an Eclipse in Asiatic Russia. By Irvine C. Gardner. Vol. LXXI, pp. 179-197, 19 ills. in black and white, 1 ill. in color, Feb., 1937.

Russia's Orphan Races: Picturesque Peoples Who Cluster on the Southeastern Borderland of the Vast Slav Dominions. By Maynard Owen Williams. Vol. XXXIV, pp. 245-278, 26 ills., 1 page map, Oct., 1918.

Supposed Birthplace of Civilizations. Vol. XVI, pp. 499-504, 6 ills., Nov., 1905.

Surveying Through Khoresm: A Journey Into Parts of Asiatic Russia Which Have Been Closed to Western Travelers Since the World War. By Lyman D. Wilbur. Vol. LXI, pp. 753-780, 31 ills., 1 two-thirds-page map, June, 1932.

Where Slav and Mongol Meet. Vol. XXXVI, pp. 421-436, 16 ills. in color, Nov., 1919.

Spain:

Adventurous Sons of Cádiz. By Harriet Chalmers Adams. Vol. XLVI, pp. 153-204, 37 ills. in black and white, 26 ills. in color, Aug., 1924.

American Eclipse Expedition. By Rear Adm. Colby M. Chester. Vol. XVII, pp. 589-612, 23 ills., 1 color plate, Nov., 1906.

Color Camera Records Scenes in Eastern Spain. 13 ills. in color from autochromes by Gervais Courtellemont. Vol. LV, pp. 364-373, Mar., 1929.

Color Contrasts in Northern Spain. 14 ills. in color from natural-color photographs by Gervais Courtellemont. Vol. LIX, pp. 112-121, Jan., 1931.

Flashing Fashions of Old Spain. 26 ills. in duotone by J. Ortiz Echagüe. Vol. LXIX, pp. 413-428, Mar., 1936.

From Granada to Gibraltar—A Tour of Southern Spain. By Harry A. McBride. Vol. XLVI, pp. 205-232, 23 ills., Aug., 1924.

Glories Past and Present of Northern Spain. 13 ills. in color from autochromes by Gervais Courtellemont. Vol. LV, pp. 340-349, Mar., 1929.

Spain—*Continued*

In Andalusia, Home of Song and Sunshine. 14 ills. in color from autochromes by Gervais Courtellemont. Vol. LV, pp. 300-309, Mar., 1929.

Land of the Basques: Home of a Thrifty, Picturesque People, Who Take Pride in the Sobriquet, "The Yankees of Spain." By Harry A. McBride. Vol. XLI, pp. 63-87, 25 ills., 1 three-quarters-page map, Jan., 1922.

Montserrat, Spain's Mountain Shrine. By E. John Long. Vol. LXIII, pp. 121-130, 10 ills., Jan., 1933.

Moorish Spain. 26 ills. in color from autochromes lumière by Gervais Courtellemont. Vol. XLVI, pp. 163-178, Aug., 1924.

On the Bypaths of Spain. By Harry A. McBride. Vol. LV, pp. 311-364, 50 ills. in black and white, 13 ills. in color, 1 two-thirds-page map, Mar., 1929.

Palette from Spain. By W. Langdon Kihn. Vol. LXIX, pp. 407-440, 16 ills. in black and white, 26 ills. in duotone, 1 half-page map, Mar., 1936.

Pursuing Spanish Bypaths Northwest of Madrid. By Harry A. McBride. Vol. LIX, pp. 121-130, 6 ills. in black and white, 12 ills. in color, 1 two-thirds-page map, Jan., 1931.

Races of Europe. By Edwin A. Grosvenor. Vol. XXXIV, pp. 441-534, 62 ills., 2 page maps, special map supplement, Dec., 1918.

Rock of Gibraltar: Key to the Mediterranean. 17 ills. from photographs. Vol. LXXVIII, pp. 376-391, Sept., 1940.

Romantic Spain. By Charles Upson Clark. Vol. XXI, pp. 187-215, 40 ills., 1 half-page map, Mar., 1910.

Turbulent Spain. By Ruth Q. McBride. Vol. LXX, pp. 397-427, 25 ills., 1 two-page map, Oct., 1936.

See also Balearic Islands; Barcelona; Madrid; Seville.

Spain's Enchanted Isles (Balearic Islands). 29 ills. in color from autochromes by Gervais Courtellemont. Vol. LIV, pp. 182-199, Aug., 1928.

Spaniels:

Dogs in Toyland. 16 ills. in color from natural-color photographs by Willard R. Culver. Vol. LXXXV, pp. 473-480, Apr., 1944.

Toy Dogs, Pets of Kings and Commoners. By Freeman Lloyd. Vol. LXXXV, pp. 459-480, 8 ills. in black and white, 16 ills. in color, Apr., 1944.

Spanish American War:

Manila and the Philippines. By Maj. A. Falkner von Sonnenburg. Vol. X, pp. 65-72, Feb., 1899.

Spanish Morocco:

Across French and Spanish Morocco. By Harriet Chalmers Adams. Vol. XLVII, pp. 327-356, 19 ills. in black and white, 16 ills. in color, 1 half-page map, Mar., 1925.

Sparrows:

Birds of Timberline and Tundra. By Arthur A. Allen. With 24 ills. in color from natural-color photographs by the author. Vol. XC, pp. 313-339, 8 ills. in black and white, Sept., 1946.

Pest of English Sparrows. By N. Dearborn. Vol. XXI, pp. 948-952, 4 ills., Nov., 1910.

Sparrows, Towhees, and Longspurs. 43 paintings in color from life by Maj. Allan Brooks and Walter A. Weber. Vol. LXXV, pp. 361-375, Mar., 1939.

Sparrows, Towhees, and Longspurs: These Happy Little Singers Make Merry in Field, Forest, and Desert Throughout North America. By T. Gilbert Pearson. Vol. LXXV, pp. 353-376, 5 ills. in black and white, 43 ills. in color, Mar., 1939.

SPARS. See Women's Reserve of the U. S. Coast Guard Reserve.

Speaking of Kansas. By Frederick Simpich. Vol. LXXII, pp. 135-182, 37 ills. in black and white, 12 ills. in color, 1 two-page map, Aug., 1937.

Special Telegraphic Time Signal from the Naval Observatory. Vol. XV, pp. 411-415, Oct., 1904.

Spectroscopes:

Exploring the Glories of the Firmament. By William Joseph Showalter. Vol. XXXVI, pp. 153-181, 17 ills., 3 charts, 1 diagram, Aug., 1919.

Speediest Boat. Vol. XXII, pp. 875-878, 2 ills., Sept., 1911.

Spell of Romania: An American Woman's Narrative of Her Wanderings Among Colorful People and Long-Hidden Shrines. By Henrietta Allen Holmes. Vol. LXV, pp. 399-450, 37 ills. in black and white, 29 ills. in color, 1 half-page map, Apr., 1934.

Spices:

Airplanes Come to the Isles of Spice: Once Magnet of World Explorers, the Moluccas Again Stand at Crossroads of History in the Netherlands Indies. By Maynard Owen Williams. Vol. LXXIX, pp. 535-558, 26 ills., 1 page map, May, 1941.

Greatest Voyage in the Annals of the Sea. By J. R. Hildebrand. Vol. LXII, pp. 699-739, 35 ills., 1 page map, Dec., 1932.

How the World Is Fed. By William Joseph Showalter. Vol. XXIX, pp. 1-110, 101 ills., Jan., 1916.

Pathfinder of the East: Setting Sail to Find "Christians and Spices," Vasco da Gama Met Amazing Adventures, Founded an Empire, and Changed the History of Western Europe. By J. R. Hildebrand. Vol. LII, pp. 503-550, 43 ills., 1 two-thirds-page map, Nov., 1927.

Spider Crabs:

Crabs and Crablike Curiosities of the Sea. By William Crowder. Vol. LIV, pp. 57-72, 10 ills. in black and white, 8 ills. in color, July, 1928.

Spiders:

Afield with the Spiders: Web Hunting in the Marshlands and Woodlands and Along the Lanes. By Henry E. Ewing. Vol. LXIV, pp. 163-194, 26 ills. in black and white, 64 ills. in color, Aug., 1933.

California Trapdoor Spider Performs Engineering Marvels. By Lee Passmore. Vol. LXIV, pp. 195-211, 23 ills., Aug., 1933.

Marvels of Metamorphosis: A Scientific "G-man" Pursues Rare Trapdoor Spider Parasites for Three Years with a Spade and a Candid Camera. By George Elwood Jenks. Vol. LXXIV, pp. 807-828, 39 ills., Dec., 1938.

Nature's Ingenious Spinners. 64 ills. in color from paintings by Hashime Murayama. Vol. LXIV, pp. 167-174, Aug., 1933.

Spin Your Globe to Long Island: Only Six States Have More People than the Insular Empire that Ranges from a World's Fair Through Potato Patches, Princely Estates, and Historic Shrines. By Frederick Simpich. Vol. LXXV, pp. 413-460, 25 ills. in black and white, 18 ills. in color, Apr., 1939.

Spinden, Herbert J.:

Shattered Capitals of Central America. By Herbert J. Spinden. Vol. XXXVI, pp. 185-212, 32 ills., 1 page map, Sept., 1919.

Spirit of St. Louis (Airplane):

Seeing America with Lindbergh: The Record of a Tour of More Than 20,000 Miles by Airplane Through Forty-eight States on Schedule Time. By Lieut. Donald E. Keyhoe. Vol. LIII, pp. 1-46, 46 ills., 1 page map, Jan., 1928.

To Bogotá and Back by Air: The Narrative of a 9,500-Mile Flight from Washington, Over Thirteen Latin-American Countries and Return, in the Single-Seater Airplane Spirit of St. Louis. By Col. Charles A. Lindbergh. Vol. LIII, pp. 529-601, 98 ills., 1 two-thirds-page map, May, 1928.

Spirit of the Geographic (World War I). Vol. XXXIV, pp. 434-440, 4 ills., Nov., 1918.

Spirit of the West (United States): The Wonderful Agricultural Development Since the Dawn of Irrigation. By C. J. Blanchard. Vol. XXI, pp. 333-360, 15 ills., Apr., 1910.

Spitsbergen (Archipelago), Arctic Region:

Flights from Arctic to Equator: Conquering the Alps, the Ice Peaks of Spitsbergen, of Persia, and Africa's Mountains of the Moon. By Walter Mittelholzer. Vol. LXI, pp. 445-498, 53 ills., 1 three-quarters-page map, Apr., 1932.

No Man's Land—Spitzbergen. Vol. XVIII, pp. 455-458, July, 1907.

Russian Expedition to Spitzbergen. Vol. XII, p. 404, Nov., 1901.

Spitsbergen (Archipelago), Arctic Region—*Continued*

Woman's Winter on Spitsbergen. By Martha Phillips Gilson. Vol. LIV, pp. 227-246, 20 ills., 1 three-quarters-page map, Aug., 1928.

Splendor of Rome. By Florence Craig Albrecht. Vol. XLI, pp. 593-626, 28 ills., June, 1922.

Sponges:

Federal Fish Farming; or, Planting Fish by the Billion. By Hugh M. Smith. Vol. XXI, pp. 418-446, 22 ills., May, 1910.

Here and There in Northern Africa. By Frank Edward Johnson. Vol. XXV, pp. 1-132, 113 ills., Jan., 1914.

Spoonbills, Roseate:

Large Wading Birds: Long Legs and Remarkable Beaks, as Well as Size, Form, and Color, Distinguish the Herons, Ibises, and Flamingos. By T. Gilbert Pearson. Paintings by Maj. Allan Brooks. Vol. LXII, pp. 441-469, 1 ill. in color, Oct., 1932.

Sporades, Northern (Islands). *See* Skýros.

Sporades, Southern (Islands). *See* Dodecanese Islands.

Sports and Games:

Clans in Kilt and Plaidie Gather at Braemar (Scotland). 11 ills. in color from natural-color photographs by Maynard Owen Williams. Vol. LXVIII, pp. 153-160, Aug., 1935.

Devil-Fishing in the Gulf Stream. By John Oliver La Gorce. Vol. XXXV, pp. 476-488, 7 ills., June, 1919.

Field Sports Among the Wild Men of Northern Luzon. By Dean C. Worcester. Vol. XXII, pp. 215-267, 17 ills., 1 half-page map, Mar., 1911.

Geography of Games: How the Sports of Nations Form a Gazetteer of the Habits and Histories of Their Peoples. By J. R. Hildebrand. Vol. XXXVI, pp. 89-144, 61 ills., Aug., 1919.

Hurdle Racing in Canoes: A Thrilling and Spectacular Sport Among the Maoris of New Zealand. By Walter Burke. Vol. XXXVII, pp. 440-444, 6 ills., May, 1920.

New England Ski Trails: Snow and Ice Sports Transform Whittier's Winters of Snowbound Seclusion Into Seasons of Outdoor Recreation. By Daniel Rochford. Vol. LXX, pp. 645-664, 11 ills. in black and white, 13 ills. in color, Nov., 1936.

Sport and Color Amid New England Snows. 13 ills. in color from natural-color photographs by B. Anthony Stewart. Vol. LXX, pp. 647-654, Nov., 1936.

When Czechoslovakia Puts a Falcon Feather in Its Cap: Gymnastics. By Maynard Owen Williams. Vol. LXIII, pp. 40-49, 13 ills. in color, Jan., 1933.

See also Chess; Cock-fighting; Falconry; Horse Racing; Kboo; Skiing; Surf-board Riding; Tops.

Spotted Fever:

Tracking the Columbian Ground-Squirrel to Its Burrow: Loss of Millions to Crops and Danger of the Spread of Spotted Fever Necessitated Study of Peculiar Rodent of Western North America. By William T. Shaw. Vol. XLVII, pp. 587-596, 13 ills., May, 1925.

Spreewald (Region), Germany:

Wends of the Spreewald. By Frederick Simpich. Vol. XLIII, pp. 327-336, 12 ills., Mar., 1923.

Springboards to Tokyo. By Willard Price. Vol. LXXXVI, pp. 385-407, 16 ills., Oct., 1944.

Spring's Gay Bouquets Deck the Nation's Capital (Washington, D. C.). 10 ills. in color from natural-color photographs by Harrison Howell Walker. Vol. LXXIV, pp. 17-24, July, 1938.

Springtime Wreathes a Garland for the Nation's Capital (Washington, D. C.). 13 ills. in color from natural-color photographs. Vol. LXVII, pp. 473-480, Apr., 1935.

Squid:

Fighting Giants of the Humboldt. By David D. Duncan. Vol. LXXIX, pp. 373-400, 28 ills., 1 half-page map, Mar., 1941.

Marauders of the Sea. By Roy Waldo Miner. Vol. LXVIII, pp. 185-207, 12 ills. in black and white, 8 ills. in color, Aug., 1935.

Monster and Midget Squid and Octopuses. 8 ills. in color from paintings by Else Bostelmann. Vol. LXVIII, pp. 193-200, Aug., 1935.

Squier, (Capt.) George O.:

Influence of Submarine Cables Upon Military and Naval Supremacy. By Capt. George O. Squier. Vol. XII, pp. 1-12, Jan., 1901.

Squires, Grant:

Honors to Amundsen and Peary (Banquet). Vol. XXIV, pp. 113-130, 5 ills., Jan., 1913.

Squirrels:

Tracking the Columbian Ground-Squirrel to Its Burrow: Loss of Millions to Crops and Danger of the Spread of Spotted Fever Necessitated Study of Peculiar Rodent of Western North America. By William T. Shaw. Vol. XLVII, pp. 587-596, 13 ills., May, 1925.

Srinagar, India:

Outwitting the Water Demons of Kashmir. By Maurice Pratt Dunlap. Vol. XL, pp. 499-511, 9 ills., Nov., 1921.

Pilgrimage to Amernath, Himalayan Shrine of the Hindu Faith. By Louise Ahl Jessop. Vol. XL, pp. 512-542, 29 ills., Nov., 1921.

Stage, Harry H.:

Saboteur Mosquitoes. By Harry H. Stage. Vol. LXXXV, pp. 165-179, 12 ills., Feb., 1944.

Staircase Farms of the Ancients: Astounding Farming Skill of Ancient Peruvians, Who Were Probably the Most Industrious and Highly Organized People in History. By O. F. Cook. Vol. XXIX, pp. 474-534, 48 ills., May, 1916.

Stalking Ants, Savage and Civilized: A Naturalist Braves Bites and Stings in Many Lands to Learn the Story of an Insect Whose Ways Often Parallel Those of Man. By W. M. Mann. Vol. LXVI, pp. 171-192, 7 ills. in black and white, 18 ills. in color, Aug., 1934.

Stalking Big Game with Color Camera. 28 ills. in color from natural-color photographs by Wendell Chapman. Vol. LXXVI, pp. 89-128, July, 1939.

Stalking Birds With a Color Camera: An Expert in Avian Habits Persuades His Subjects to Sit Where He Wants Them. Even in His Hat. By Arthur A. Allen. Vol. LXXV, pp. 777-789, 3 ills. in black and white, 14 ills. in color, June, 1939.

Stalking the Dragon Lizard on the Island of Komodo. By W. Douglas Burden. Vol. LII, pp. 216-232, 21 ills., Aug., 1927.

Stand by the Soldier. By Gen. John J. Pershing. Vol. XXXI, pp. 457-459, 1 ill., May, 1917.

Standing Iceberg Guard in the North Atlantic: International Patrol Safeguards the Lives of Thousands of Travelers and Protects Transatlantic Liners from a "Titanic" Fate. By Lieut. Comdr. F. A. Zeusler. Vol. L, pp. 1-28, 29 ills., 1 half-page map, July, 1926.

Stanley, (Sir) Henry M.:

Great African Lake (Victoria). By Sir Henry M. Stanley. Vol. XIII, pp. 169-172, 1 half-page map, May, 1902.

Stanley-Brown, Joseph:

Shishaldin as a Field of Exploration (Alaska). By Joseph Stanley-Brown. Vol. X, pp. 281-288, 3 ills., 1 quarter-page map, Aug., 1899.

Star and Crescent on Parade (Turkey). 29 ills. in color from natural-color photographs by Maynard Owen Williams. Vol. LXXXVII, pp. 585-616, May, 1945.

Star Charts:

How to Use the Star Charts. Text accompanying 12 star charts designed by Donald H. Menzel. Vol. LXXXIV, pp. 116-128, July, 1943.

Stars. *See* Astronomy.

State of Sky-Blue Water and Verdure (Minnesota). 11 ills. in color from natural-color photographs by Clifton Adams and Edwin L. Wisherd. Vol. LXVII, pp. 289-296, Mar., 1935.

State Survey Articles: United States :

Alabama : Smoke Over Alabama. By Frederick Simpich. Vol. LX, pp. 703-758, 43 ills. in black and white, 26 ills. in color, 1 page map, Dec., 1931.

Arizona Comes of Age. By Frederick Simpich. Vol. LV, pp. 1-47, 40 ills. in black and white, 14 ills. in color, 1 two-thirds-page map, Jan., 1929.

Arkansas Rolls Up Its Sleeves. By Frederick Simpich. Vol. XC, pp. 273-312, 16 ills. in black and white, 23 ills. in color, 1 map (two-page spread); Sept., 1946.

California, Northern : Northern California at Work. By Frederick Simpich. Vol. LXIX, pp. 309-389, 36 ills. in black and white, 41 ills. in color, 1 two-page and 1 third-page maps, Mar., 1936.

State Survey Articles: United States—*Continued*

California, Southern : Southern California at Work. By Frederick Simpich. Vol. LXVI, pp. 529-600, 39 ills. in black and white, 41 ills. in color, 1 two-page map, Nov., 1934.

Colorado, a Barrier That Became a Goal ; Where Water Has Transformed Dry Plains Into Verdant Farms, and Highways Have Opened Up Mineral and Scenic Wealth. By McFall Kerbey. Vol. LXII, pp. 1-63, 56 ills. in black and white, 12 ills. in color, 1 page map, July, 1932.

Connecticut, Prodigy of Ingenuity : Factories Play a Symphony of Industry Amid Colonial Scenes in the State of Steady Habits. By Leo A. Borah. Vol. LXXIV, pp. 279-326, 25 ills. in black and white, 25 ills. in color, 1 two-page map, Sept., 1938.

Delaware : Diamond Delaware, Colonial Still : Tradition Rules the "Three Lower Counties" Over Which William Penn and Lord Baltimore Went to Law. By Leo A. Borah. Vol. LXVIII, pp. 307-398, 25 ills. in black and white, 15 ills. in color, 1 page map, Sept., 1935.

Florida—The Fountain of Youth. By John Oliver La Gorce. Vol. LVII, pp. 1-93, 73 ills. in black and white, 44 ills. in color, special map supplement, Jan., 1930.

Georgia : Marching Through Georgia Sixty Years After : Multifold Industries and Diversified Agriculture Are Restoring the Prosperity of America's Largest State East of the Mississippi. By Ralph A. Graves. Vol. L, pp. 259-311, 47 ills., Sept., 1926.

Idaho Made the Desert Bloom. By D. Worth Clark. Vol. LXXXV, pp. 641-688, 21 ills. in black and white, 20 ills. in color, 1 page map, June, 1944.

Illinois, Crossroads of the Continent. By Junius B. Wood. Vol. LIX, pp. 523-594, 51 ills. in black and white, 27 ills. in color, special map supplement, May, 1931.

Indiana Journey. By Frederick Simpich. Vol. LXX, pp. 267-320, 32 ills. in black and white, 27 ills. in color, 1 two-page map, Sept., 1936.

Iowa, Abiding Place of Plenty : The State Where the Tall Corn Grows Provides the Nation With a Tenth of Its Food Supply. By Leo A. Borah. Vol. LXXVI, pp. 143-182, 15 ills. in black and white, 20 ills. in color, 1 two-page map, Aug., 1939.

Kansas : Speaking of Kansas. By Frederick Simpich. Vol. LXXII, pp. 135-182, 37 ills. in black and white, 12 ills. in color, 1 two-page map, Aug., 1937.

Kentucky, Boone's Great Meadow : The Bluegrass State Celebrates Its Sesquicentennial As It Helps the Nation Gird for War. By Leo A. Borah. Vol. LXXXII, pp. 57-89, 13 ills. in black and white, 21 ills. in color, 1 map (two-page spread), July, 1942.

Louisiana, Land of Perpetual Romance. By Ralph A. Graves. Vol. LVII, pp. 393-482, 84 ills. in black and white, 29 ills. in color, special map supplement, Apr., 1930.

State Survey Articles: United States—*Continued*

Maine, the Outpost State : Some Forgotten Incidents in the Life of an Old and Stout-Hearted Commonwealth. By George Otis Smith. Vol. LXVII, pp. 533-592, 35 ills. in black and white, 39 ills. in color, 1 two-page map, May, 1935.

Maryland Pilgrimage : Visits to Hallowed Shrines Recall the Major Rôle Played by This Prosperous State in the Development of Popular Government in America. By Gilbert Grosvenor. Vol. LI, pp. 133-212, 88 ills., special map supplement, Feb., 1927.

Maryland Presents— By W. Robert Moore. Vol. LXXIX, pp. 401-448, 17 ills. in black and white, 32 ills. in color, 1 map (two-page spread), Apr., 1941.

Massachusetts—Beehive of Business. By William Joseph Showalter. Vol. XXXVII, pp. 203-245, 41 ills., Mar., 1920.

Michigan, Mistress of the Lakes. By Melville Chater. Vol. LIII, pp. 269-325, 65 ills., 1 page and 1 three-quarters-page maps, Mar., 1928.

Minnesota, Mother of Lakes and Rivers. By Glanville Smith. Vol. LXVII, pp. 273-318, 42 ills. in black and white, 11 ills. in color, 1 two-page map, Mar., 1935.

Mississippi : Machines Come to Mississippi. By J. R. Hildebrand. Vol. LXXII, pp. 263-318, 34 ills. in black and white, 26 ills. in color, 1 two-page map, Sept., 1937.

Missouri, Mother of the West. By Frederick Simpich. Vol. XLIII, pp. 421-460, 35 ills., Apr., 1923.

Missouri : These Missourians. By Frederick Simpich. Vol. LXXXIX, pp. 277-310, 12 ills. in black and white, 22 ills. in color, 1 map (two-page spread), Mar., 1946.

Nebraska, the Cornhusker State. By Leo A. Borah. Vol. LXXXVII, pp. 513-542, 6 ills. in black and white, 23 ills. in color, 1 map (two-page spread), May, 1945.

Nevada, Desert Treasure House. By W. Robert Moore. Vol. LXXXIX, pp. 1-38, 16 ills. in black and white, 20 ills. in color, 1 four-fifths-page map, Jan., 1946.

New Hampshire, the Granite State. By George Higgins Moses. Vol. LX, pp. 257-310, 47 ills. in black and white, 5 ills. in color, 1 page map, Sept., 1931.

New Jersey Now ! By E. John Long. Vol. LXIII, pp. 519-583, 49 ills. in black and white, 24 ills. in color, 1 page and 1 two-thirds-page maps, May, 1933.

New Mexico Melodrama. By Frederick Simpich. Vol. LXXIII, pp. 529-569, 19 ills. in black and white, 25 ills. in color, 1 two-page map, May, 1938.

New York—An Empire Within a Republic. By William Joseph Showalter. Vol. LXIV, pp. 513-584, 47 ills. in black and white, 35 ills. in color, 1 two-page map, Nov., 1933.

North Carolina : Motor-Coaching Through North Carolina. By Melville Chater. Vol. XLIX, pp. 475-523, 43 ills., 1 third-page map, May, 1926.

State Survey Articles: United States—*Continued*

North Carolina : Tarheelia on Parade : Versatile and Vibrant, North Carolina in a Generation Has Climbed New Economic Heights. By Leonard C. Roy. Vol. LXXX, pp. 181-224, 24 ills. in black and white, 21 ills. in color, 1 map (two-page spread), Aug., 1941.

Ohio, The Gateway State. By Melville Chater. Vol. LXI, pp. 525-591, 58 ills. in black and white, 13 ills. in color, 1 three-quarters-page map, May, 1932.

Oklahoma : So Oklahoma Grew Up. By Frederick Simpich. Vol. LXXIX, pp. 269-314, 30 ills. in black and white, 19 ills. in color, 1 page map, Mar., 1941.

Oregon : Native Son's Rambles in Oregon. By Amos Burg. Vol. LXV, pp. 173-234, 39 ills. in black and white, 24 ills. in color, 1 two-page map, Feb., 1934.

Oregon Finds New Riches. By Leo A. Borah. Vol. XC, pp. 681-728, 15 ills. in black and white, 28 ills. in color, 1 two-page map, Dec., 1946.

Pennsylvania : Industrial Titan of America : Pennsylvania, Once the Keystone of the Original Thirteen; Now the Keystone of Forty-Eight Sovereign States. By John Oliver La Gorce. Vol. XXXV, pp. 367-406, 33 ills., 1 page map, May, 1919.

Pennsylvania : Penn's Land of Modern Miracles. By John Oliver La Gorce. Vol. LXVIII, pp. 1-58, 28 ills. in black and white, 39 ills. in color, 1 two-page map, July, 1935.

Tennessee : Highlights of the Volunteer State : Men and Industry in Tennessee Range from Pioneer Stages to Modern Machine Age. By Leonard Cornell Roy. Vol. LXXV, pp. 553-594, 20 ills. in black and white, 22 ills. in color, 1 map, May, 1939.

Texas : So Big Texas. By Frederick Simpich. Vol. LIII, pp. 637-693, 72 ills., 1 two-page map, June, 1928.

Utah, Carved by Winds and Waters : The Beehive State, Settled Only 89 years Ago, Stands a Monument to the Courage of Its Founders. By Leo A. Borah. Vol. LXIX, pp. 577-623, 20 ills. in black and white, 22 ills. in color, 1 two-page map, May, 1936.

Vermont : Green Mountain State. By Herbert Corey. Vol. LI, pp. 333-369, 40 ills. in black and white, 6 ills. in color, 1 page map, Mar., 1927.

Virginia—A Commonwealth That Has Come Back. By William Joseph Showalter. Vol. LV, pp. 403-472, 69 ills. in black and white, 13 ills. in color, 1 page map, Apr., 1929.

Washington, the Evergreen State : The Amazing Commonwealth of the Pacific Northwest Which Has Emerged from the Wilderness in a Span of Fifty Years. By Leo A. Borah. Vol. LXIII, pp. 131-196, 50 ills. in black and white, 26 ills. in color, 1 two-page map, Feb., 1933.

West Virginia : Treasure Chest of Industry. By Enrique C. Canova. Vol. LXXVIII, pp. 141-184, 19 ills. in black and white, 21 ills. in color, 1 two-page map, Aug., 1940.

State Survey Articles: United States—*Continued*

Wisconsin: On Goes Wisconsin: Strength and Vigor Mark This Midwestern State, With Its Woods and Lakes and Its Blend of Sturdy Nationalities. By Glanville Smith. Vol. LXXII, pp. 1-46, 25 ills. in black and white, 27 ills. in color, 1 two-page map, July, 1937.

Wyoming: Grass Makes Wyoming Fat. By Frederick Simpich. Vol. LXXXVIII, pp. 153-188, 13 ills. in black and white, 19 ills. in color, 1 two-page map, Aug., 1945.

Statistical Atlas of the United States. Vol. XV, pp. 50-52, 2 diagrams, Jan., 1904.

Statistics:

Financial and Commercial Statistics of the Principal Countries of the World. Vol. XVIII, pp. 420-423, June, 1907.

Statistics of Cities (United States). Vol. XVI, p. 437, Sept., 1905.

Useful Facts About the Countries of the World. Vol. XVIII, pp. 424-425, June, 1907.

Statues. *See* Archeology; Sculpture; Stone Faces (Monuments).

Stauffer, Elmer C.:

In the Pennsylvania Dutch Country. By Elmer C. Stauffer. Vol. LXXX, pp. 37-74, 20 ills. in black and white, 22 ills. in color, 1 map (pen and ink drawing), July, 1941.

Stearns, Robert E. C.:

Echoes of the San Francisco Earthquake. By Robert E. C. Stearns. Vol. XVIII, pp. 351-353, 1 ill., May, 1907.

Native Oysters of the West Coast. By Robert E. C. Stearns. Vol. XIX, pp. 224-226, Mar., 1908.

Stearns, Wallace N.:

Reconstructing Egypt's History. By Wallace N. Stearns. Vol. XXIV, pp. 1021-1042, 21 ills., Sept., 1913.

Steel Industry:

India's Treasures Helped the Allies. By John Fischer. Vol. LXXXIX, pp. 501-522, 18 ills., Apr., 1946.

Industry's Greatest Asset—Steel. By William Joseph Showalter. Vol. XXXII, pp. 121-156, 34 ills., Aug., 1917.

"Magnetic City" (Magnitogorsk), Core of Valiant Russia's Industrial Might. By John Scott. Vol. LXXXIII, pp. 525-556, 27 ills., 1 two-page map, May, 1943.

Stefansson, Jon:

Land of Fire (Iceland). By Jon Stefansson. Vol. XVIII, pp. 741-744, Nov., 1907.

Stefansson, Vilhjalmur:

Arctic as an Air Route of the Future. By Vilhjalmur Stefansson. Vol. XLII, pp. 205-218, 8 ills., 1 page map, Aug., 1922.

Stefansson, Vilhjalmur—*Continued*

National Geographic Society's Notable Year (Award of Hubbard Gold Medal). Vol. XXXVII, pp. 338-345, 2 ills., Apr., 1920.

Origin of Stefansson's Blonde Eskimo. By Maj. Gen. A. W. Greely. Vol. XXIII, pp. 1224-1238, 10 ills., 1 page map, Dec., 1912.

Steiner, Albert:

Amid the Snows of Switzerland. 16 ills. in duotone by Albert Steiner. Vol. XLI, pp. 277-292, Mar., 1922.

Sternberg, George M.:

History and Geographic Distribution of Bubonic Plague. By George M. Sternberg. Vol. XI, pp. 97-113, Mar., 1900.

Sterrett, J. R. Sitlington:

Cone-Dwellers of Asia Minor: A Primitive People Who Live in Nature-Made Apartment Houses, Fashioned by Volcanic Violence and Trickling Streams. By J. R. Sitlington Sterrett. Vol. XXXV, pp. 281-331, 52 ills., 1 half-page map, Apr., 1919.

Stevens, (Lt. Col.) Albert W.:

America from the Air: No Such Series of Airplane Views Has Ever Before Been Printed. 8 ills. from photographs by Lieut. Albert W. Stevens. Vol. XLVI, pp. 85-92, July, 1924.

Curvature of the Earth: Photograph Showing the Division Between the Troposphere and Stratosphere and also the Actual Curvature of the Earth. Special supplement from aërial photographs by Capt. Albert W. Stevens. Vol. LXIX, supplement, May, 1936.

Exploring the Stratosphere. By Capt. Albert W. Stevens. Vol. LXVI, pp. 397-434, 43 ills., 1 two-thirds-page chart, Oct., 1934.

Exploring the Valley of the Amazon in a Hydroplane: Twelve Thousand Miles of Flying Over the World's Greatest River and Greatest Forest to Chart the Unknown Parima River from the Sky. By Capt. Albert W. Stevens. Vol. XLIX, pp. 353-420, 86 ills., 1 page map, Apr., 1926.

First natural-color photograph taken in the stratosphere. 1 ill. in color by Maj. Albert W. Stevens. Vol. LXXI, p. 340, Mar., 1937.

Flying the "Hump" of the Andes. By Capt. Albert W. Stevens. Vol. LIX, pp. 595-636, 36 ills., 1 third-page map, May, 1931.

Franklin L. Burr Prize awarded to Captain Stevens. Vol. LXV, p. 626, May, 1934.

Greater New York . . . Metropolis of Mankind. Special supplement from aërial photograph by Capt. Albert W. Stevens. Vol. LXIV, supplement, Nov., 1933.

Hubbard Medals Awarded to Stratosphere Explorers: Presentation by General Pershing. Vol. LXIX, pp. 713-714, May, 1936.

Stevens, (Lt. Col.) Albert W.—*Continued*

Man's Farthest Aloft: Rising to 13.71 Miles, the National Geographic Society–U. S. Army Stratosphere Expedition Gathers Scientific Data at Record Altitude. By Capt. Albert W. Stevens. Action Photographs of the Balloon's Perfect Landing included. Vol. LXIX, pp. 59-94, 39 ills., 1 quarter-page map, Jan., 1936.

National Geographic Society-U. S. Army Air Corps Stratosphere Flight of 1935 in Balloon *Explorer II* (Contributed Technical Papers, Stratosphere Series, No. 2). Vol. LXXI, p. 340, Mar., 1937; p. 802, June, 1937.

Non-Stop Flight Across America. By Lieut. John A. Macready. Photographs by Lieut. Albert W. Stevens. Vol. XLVI, pp. 1-83, 68 ills., 1 page and 1 half-page maps, July, 1924.

Our Colorful City of Magnificent Distances (Washington, D. C.). 5 ills. in color from natural-color photographs by Capt. A. W. Stevens. Vol. LX, pp. 530-611, Nov., 1931.

Photographing the Eclipse of 1932 from the Air: From Five Miles Above the Earth's Surface, the National Geographic Society–Army Air Corps Survey Obtains Successful Photographs of the Moon's Shadow. By Capt. Albert W. Stevens. Vol. LXII, pp. 581-596, 18 ills., Nov., 1932.

Scientific Results of the World-Record Stratosphere Flight. By Capt. Albert W. Stevens. Vol. LXIX, pp. 693-712, 15 ills., May, 1936.

Society Takes Part in Three Geographic Expeditions. Vol. LXV, pp. 625-626, May, 1934.

Your Society Sponsors an Expedition to Explore the Stratosphere. Vol. LXV, pp. 528-530, 1 ill., Apr., 1934.

Stewart, B. Anthony:

Aegean Islands: Isles of Greece. 20 ills. in color from natural-color photographs by Maynard Owen Williams and B. Anthony Stewart. Vol. LXXXV, pp. 601-616, May, 1944.

America on the Move. 26 ills. from photographs by J. Baylor Roberts, B. Anthony Stewart, and others. Vol. XC, pp. 357-378, Sept., 1946.

Bekonscot: Tableaux in an English Lilliput. 15 ills. in color from natural-color photographs by B. Anthony Stewart. Vol. LXXI, pp. 653-660, May, 1937.

Bekonscot, England's Toy-Size Town. By Andrew H. Brown and B. Anthony Stewart. Vol. LXXI, pp. 649-661, 2 ills. in black and white, 15 ills. in color, May, 1937.

Belgian Portraits. 20 ills. in color from natural-color photographs by B. Anthony Stewart. Vol. LXXIII, pp. 413-444, Apr., 1938.

Boston, Massachusetts: Hub City, Cradle of American Liberty. 31 ills. in color from natural-color photographs; 5 ills. by B. Anthony Stewart. Vol. LXX, pp. 49-72, July, 1936.

Stewart, B. Anthony—*Continued*

California: Golden Gate, and Redwood Evergreens. 17 ills. in color from natural-color photographs by B. Anthony Stewart. Vol. LXXV, pp. 149-160, Feb., 1939.

California: Sun Shines on San Diego. 9 ills. in color from natural-color photographs by B. Anthony Stewart. Vol. LXXXI, pp. 57-64, Jan., 1942.

California: Where Spring Paints a State with Wild Flowers. 18 ills. in color from natural-color photographs by B. Anthony Stewart. Vol. LXIX, pp. 365-380, Mar., 1936.

California—85 Years after the Gold Rush. 23 ills. in color from natural-color photographs by B. Anthony Stewart. Vol. LXIX, pp. 325-356, Mar., 1936.

California Says It with Wild Flowers. 9 ills. in color from natural-color photographs by B. Anthony Stewart. Vol. LXXXI, pp. 493-500, Apr., 1942.

Cambridge University: Sculptured Gates to English Learning. 19 ills. in color from natural-color photographs by B. Anthony Stewart. Vol. LXXXIX, pp. 417-440, Apr., 1946.

Canada: Remnants of Royal France in Canada. 15 ills. in color from natural-color photographs by B. Anthony Stewart. Vol. LXVIII, pp. 217-224, Aug., 1935.

Charleston: A Colonial Rhapsody. 24 ills. in color from natural-color photographs by B. Anthony Stewart. Vol. LXXV, pp. 289-312, Mar., 1939.

Connecticut: Old and New Blend in Yankeeland. 25 ills. in color from natural-color photographs; 4 ills. by B. Anthony Stewart. Vol. LXXIV, pp. 295-326, Sept., 1938.

Delaware: First in Statehood, Delaware Retains Its Graciousness. 15 ills. in color from natural-color photographs by B. Anthony Stewart. Vol. LXVIII, pp. 377-384, Sept., 1935.

Dominican Republic, Land of Plenty. 11 ills. in color from natural-color photographs by B. Anthony Stewart. Vol. LXXXV, pp. 209-216, Feb., 1944.

Egypt: Under Egypt's Golden Sun. 22 ills. in color from natural-color photographs by B. Anthony Stewart. Vol. LXXVII, pp. 451-466, Apr., 1940.

England: Democracy's Royal Palace (Westminster). 19 ills. in color from natural-color photographs by B. Anthony Stewart. Vol. XC, pp. 233-248, Aug., 1946.

England: Pomp and Pulse of Modern London. 23 ills. in color from natural-color photographs by B. Anthony Stewart. Vol. LXXI, pp. 17-48, Jan., 1937.

England: Thames, England's Gateway to the World. 10 ills. in color from natural-color photographs by B. Anthony Stewart. Vol. LXXV, pp. 253-260, Feb., 1939.

Great Lakes and Great Industries. 19 ills. in color from natural-color photographs by B. Anthony Stewart, Alfred T. Palmer, and Willard R. Culver. Vol. LXXXVI, pp. 689-712, Dec., 1944.

Stewart, B. Anthony—*Continued*

Greece : Classic Greece Merges Into 1941 News. 19 ills. from photographs ; 15 ills. by B. Anthony Stewart ; 3 ills. by Maynard Owen Williams. Vol. LXXIX, pp. 93-108, Jan., 1941.

Greece : Today's Evidence of Grecian Glory. 22 ills. in color from natural-color photographs by B. Anthony Stewart. Vol. LXXVII, pp. 307-322, Mar., 1940.

Guernsey : Contented Guernsey. 11 ills. in color from natural-color photographs by B. Anthony Stewart. Vol. LXXIII, pp. 377-384, Mar., 1938.

Haiti Goes to Market. 10 ills. in color from natural-color photographs by B. Anthony Stewart. Vol. LXXXVI, pp. 313-320, Sept., 1944.

Italy : Bright Facets of Italy's Grandeur. 9 ills. in color from natural-color photographs : 8 ills. by B. Anthony Stewart. Vol. LXXVII, pp. 355-362, Mar., 1940.

Italy : Northern Italy : Scenic Battleground. 18 ills. in color from natural-color photographs : 13 ills. by B. Anthony Stewart and 3 ills. by Lt. Benjamin C. McCartney. Vol. LXXXVII, pp. 265-288, Mar., 1945.

Italy's Monuments Tell Rome's Magnificence. 8 ills. from photographs ; 7 ills. by B. Anthony Stewart. Vol. LXXVII, pp. 371-378, Mar., 1940.

Kentucky : Sun Shines Bright in Kentucky. 21 ills. in color from natural-color photographs by B. Anthony Stewart, Volkmar Wentzel, and Ray Scott. Vol. LXXXII, pp. 65-88, July, 1942.

Maine : Pine-Scented Harbor-Dented Maine. 39 ills. in color from natural-color photographs by B. Anthony Stewart and Robert F. Maxey. Vol. LXVII, pp. 549-588, May, 1935.

Man, Isle of : Sunny Corners in a Friendly Isle. 12 ills. in color from natural-color photographs by B. Anthony Stewart. Vol. LXXI, pp. 601-608, May, 1937.

Maryland : Maytime in the Heart of Maryland. 10 ills. in color from natural-color photographs by B. Anthony Stewart and Charles Martin. Vol. LXXIX, pp. 441-448, Apr., 1941.

Maryland : Old Line State Cyclorama. 22 ills. in color from natural-color photographs : 3 ills., by B. Anthony Stewart. Vol. LXXIX, pp. 409-432, Apr., 1941.

Nantucket : Echoes of Whaling Days. 8 ills. in color from natural-color photographs by B. Anthony Stewart. Vol. LXXXV, pp. 449-456, Apr., 1944.

Nebraska : Cornhusker State Highlights. 23 ills. in color from natural-color photographs by B. Anthony Stewart. Vol. LXXXVII, pp. 521-536, May, 1945.

New England : Flow Onward, Connecticut (River) ! 24 ills. in color from natural-color photographs ; 22 ills. by B. Anthony Stewart. Vol. LXXXIII, pp. 409-432, Apr., 1943.

Stewart, B. Anthony—*Continued*

New England : Sport and Color Amid New England Snows. 13 ills. in color from natural-color photographs by B. Anthony Stewart. Vol. LXX, pp. 647-654, Nov., 1936.

New England : Where New England Meets the Sea. 17 ills. in color from natural-color photographs by B. Anthony Stewart. Vol. LXXXVIII, pp. 265-288, Sept., 1945.

Oklahoma : Sunshine over Oklahoma. 19 ills. in color from natural-color photographs by B. Anthony Stewart. Vol. LXXIX, pp. 277-308, Mar., 1941.

Ozarks (Plateau) : Work and Play in the Ozarks. 20 ills. in color from natural-color photographs by B. Anthony Stewart and J. Baylor Roberts. Vol. LXXXIII, pp. 597-620, May, 1943.

Petroleum Serves—From Lamps to Wheels. 21 ills. in color from natural-color photographs ; 20 ills. by B. Anthony Stewart. Vol. LXXIX, pp. 707-738, June, 1941.

Plymouth, England : A City That Refused to Die. 9 ills. in color from natural-color photographs by B. Anthony Stewart. Vol. LXXXIX, pp. 225-232, Feb., 1946.

Santa Catalina—400 Years a Lure to California Travelers. 11 ills. in color from natural-color photographs by B. Anthony Stewart. Vol. LXXXI, pp. 81-88, Jan., 1942.

Santorin and Mýkonos, Aegean Gems. 8 ills. in color from natural-color photographs ; 7 ills. by B. Anthony Stewart. Vol. LXXVII, pp. 339-346, Mar., 1940.

Scillies : Isles of Wrecks and Golden Daffodils. 13 ills. in color from natural-color photographs ; 9 ills. by B. Anthony Stewart. Vol. LXXIV, pp. 759-766, Dec., 1938.

Scotland : Heather Paints the Highlands. 38 ills. in color from natural-color photographs by B. Anthony Stewart. Vol. LXXXIX, pp. 561-600, May, 1946.

Texas : Rio Grande Cornucopia Under a Winter Sun. 24 ills. in color from natural-color photographs by B. Anthony Stewart. Vol. LXXV, pp. 65-96, Jan., 1939.

Virginia : Gardens and Shrines of Old Virginia. 20 ills. in color from natural-color photographs by B. Anthony Stewart and J. Baylor Roberts. Vol. LXXXI, pp. 623-646, May, 1942.

Washington, D. C. : Culture Still Lights Our Wartime Capital. 9 ills. in color from natural-color photographs by B. Anthony Stewart. Vol. LXXXI, pp. 337-344, Mar., 1942.

Washington, D. C. : Our Nation's Capital on Parade. 16 ills. in color from natural-color photographs by B. Anthony Stewart, Walter M. Edwards, and others. Vol. LXXXIV, pp. 265-288, Sept., 1943.

Washington, D. C. : Winter Lights and Shadows in the Nation's Capital. 21 ills. in duotone ; 6 ills. by B. Anthony Stewart. Vol. LXVII, pp. 201-216, Feb., 1935.

West Virginia : High Road and Low through the Mountain State. 21 ills. in color from natural-color photographs by B. Anthony Stewart and Volkmar Wentzel. Vol. LXXVIII, pp. 157-180, Aug., 1940.

Stewart, B. Anthony—*Continued*

Wisconsin : Life's Color in Wisconsin. 27 ills. in color from natural-color photographs ; 23 ills. by B. Anthony Stewart. Vol. LXXII, pp. 17-40, July, 1937.

Wyoming : Welcome to Wyoming. 19 ills. in color from natural-color photographs ; 18 ills. by B. Anthony Stewart. Vol. LXXXVIII, pp. 161-184, Aug., 1945.

Stewart, Richard H.:

Canton Island : Unfurling Old Glory on Canton Island. 11 ills. in color ; 7 ills. from natural-color photographs by Richard H. Stewart. Vol. LXXIII, pp. 753-760, June, 1938.

Circus : Color Camera Explores the Country That Moves by Night. 15 ills. in color from natural-color photographs by Richard H. Stewart. Vol. LX, pp. 478-511, Oct., 1931.

Hawaii : Leis from Aloha Land. 10 ills. in color from natural-color photographs ; 8 ills. by Richard H. Stewart. Vol. LXXIV, pp. 435-442, Oct., 1938.

Kansas : Views and Hues of the Sunflower State. 12 ills. in color from natural-color photographs by Richard H. Stewart. Vol. LXXII, pp. 151-158, Aug., 1937.

Mexico : From the Halls of Montezuma. 21 ills. in color from natural-color photographs by Richard H. Stewart and others. Vol. LXXXV, pp. 137-164, Feb., 1944.

Mexico : La Venta's Green Stone Tigers. 6 ills. in color from natural-color photographs by Richard H. Stewart. Vol. LXXXIV, pp. 329-332, Sept., 1943.

Mexico : Treasure-trove of Old Mexican Jade (Cerro de las Mesas). 20 ills. in color from natural-color photographs by Richard H. Stewart. Vol. LXXX, pp. 293-316, Sept., 1941.

Mexico's Deep South Yields New Treasure (Tabasco and Chiapas). 12 ills. in color from natural-color photographs by Richard H. Stewart. Vol. LXXXII, pp. 649-656, Nov., 1942.

Missouri Mirrors of 1946. 22 ills. in color from natural-color photographs by Richard H. Stewart. Vol. LXXXIX, pp. 285-308, Mar., 1946.

New Mexico : Nature Paints New Mexico. 25 ills. in color from natural-color photographs by Richard H. Stewart. Vol. LXXIII, pp. 537-568, May, 1938.

Utah : Bursts of Color in Sculptured Utah. 22 ills. in color from natural-color photographs ; 18 ills. by Richard H. Stewart. Vol. LXIX, pp. 593-616, May, 1936.

Stieler, Karl:

Venice. By Karl Stieler. Vol. XXVII, pp. 587-630, 42 ills., 1 page and 1 quarter-page maps, June, 1915.

Stikine River, Alaska-Canada :

Life on a Yukon Trail. By Alfred Pearce Dennis. Part I, Vol. X, pp. 377-391, 8 ills., 1 page map, Oct., 1899. Part II, Vol. X, pp. 457-466, 7 ills., Nov., 1899.

Stikine River, Alaska-Canada—*Continued*

Stikine River in 1898. By Eliza R. Scidmore. Vol. X, pp. 1-15, 4 ills., Jan., 1899.

Stiles, Arthur Alvord:

Bear Hunt in Montana. By Arthur Alvord Stiles. Vol. XIX, pp. 149-154, 5 ills., Feb., 1908.

Stillwell, Agnes N.:

Crete, Where Sea-Kings Reigned. By Agnes N. Stillwell. Vol. LXXXIV, pp. 547-568, 20 ills., 1 page map, Nov., 1943.

Stillwell, Richard:

Greece—the Birthplace of Science and Free Speech : Explorations on the Mainland and in Crete and the Aegean Isles Reveal Ancient Life Similar to That of the Present. By Richard Stillwell. Paintings by H. M. Herget. Vol. LXXXV, pp. 273-353, 13 ills. in black and white, 32 ills. in color, 1 two-page map, Mar., 1944.

Isles of Greece. By Lt. Richard Stillwell, USNR. Vol. LXXXV, pp. 593-622, 11 ills. in black and white, 20 ills. in color, 1 page map, May, 1944.

Stilwell Road—Land Route to China. By Nelson Grant Tayman. Vol. LXXXVII, pp. 681-698, 18 ills., June, 1945.

Stirling, Marion:

Finding Jewels of Jade in a Mexican Swamp (La Venta). By Matthew W. and Marion Stirling. Vol. LXXXII, pp. 635-661, 15 ills. in black and white, 12 ills. in color, 1 two-thirds-page map, Nov., 1942.

Jungle Housekeeping for a Geographic Expedition (Cerro de las Mesas, Mexico). By Marion Stirling. Vol. LXXX, pp. 303-327, 15 ills., Sept., 1941.

Stirling, Matthew W.:

America's First Settlers, the Indians. By Matthew W. Stirling. Vol. LXXII, pp. 535-596, 34 ills. in black and white, 24 ills. in color, Nov., 1937.

Discovering the New World's Oldest Dated Work of Man : A Maya Monument Inscribed 291 B. C. Is Unearthed Near a Huge Stone Head by a Geographic-Smithsonian Expedition in Mexico. By Matthew W. Stirling. Vol. LXXVI, pp. 183-218, 40 ills., 1 half-page map, Aug., 1939.

Expedition Unearths Buried Masterpieces of Carved Jade (Cerro de las Mesas, Mexico). By Matthew W. Stirling. Vol. LXXX, pp. 277-302, 14 ills. in black and white, 20 ills. in color, 1 two-thirds-page map, Sept., 1941.

Finding Jewels of Jade in a Mexican Swamp (La Venta). By Matthew W. and Marion Stirling. Vol. LXXXII, pp. 635-661, 15 ills. in black and white, 12 ills. in color, 1 two-thirds-page map, Nov., 1942.

Stirling, Matthew W.—*Continued*

Great Stone Faces of the Mexican Jungle: Five Colossal Heads and Numerous Other Monuments of Vanished Americans Are Excavated by the Latest National Geographic-Smithsonian Expedition. By Matthew W. Stirling. Vol. LXXVIII, pp. 309-334, 26 ills., 1 map, Sept., 1940.

Indian Tribes of Pueblo Land. By Matthew W. Stirling. Vol. LXXVIII, pp. 549-596, 16 ills. in black and white, 25 ills. in color, Nov., 1940.

Indians of Our North Pacific Coast. By Matthew W. Stirling. Paintings by W. Langdon Kihn. Vol. LXXXVII, pp. 25-52, 3 ills. in black and white, 16 ills. in color, Jan., 1945.

Indians of Our Western Plains. By Matthew W. Stirling. Paintings by W. Langdon Kihn. Vol. LXXXVI, pp. 73-108, 14 ills. in black and white, 16 ills. in color, July, 1944.

Indians of the Southeastern United States. By Matthew W. Stirling. Paintings by W. Langdon Kihn. Vol. LXXXIX, pp. 53-74, 8 ills. in black and white, 8 ills. in color, Jan., 1946.

La Venta's Green Stone Tigers. By Matthew W. Stirling. Vol. LXXXIV, pp. 321-332, 4 ills. in black and white, 6 ills. in color, 1 two-thirds-page map, Sept., 1943.

Stock, Ralph:

Dream Ship: The Story of a Voyage of Adventure More Than Half Around the World in a 47-Foot Lifeboat. By Ralph Stock. Vol. XXXIX, pp. 1-52, 43 ills., 1 page map, Jan., 1921.

Stockholm, Sweden:

Flying Around the Baltic. By Douglas Chandler. Vol. LXXIII, pp. 767-806, 31 ills. in black and white, 13 ills. in duotone, 1 half-page map, June, 1938.

Granite City of the North: Austere Stockholm, Sweden's Prosperous Capital, Presents a Smiling Aspect in Summer. By Ralph A. Graves. Vol. LIV, pp. 403-424, 23 ills. in black and white, 6 ills. in color, Oct., 1928.

Types and Costumes of Old Sweden. 30 ills. in color from autochromes lumière by Gustav Heurlin, G. W. Cronquist, Wilhelm Tobien, and Charles Martin. Vol. LIV, pp. 424-441, Oct., 1928.

Stone, Melville E.:

Race Prejudice in the Far East. By Melville E. Stone. Vol. XXI, pp. 973-985, 6 ills., Dec., 1910.

Stone Beehive Homes of Italian Peasants. 12 ills. in color from autochromes by Luigi Pellerano and L.U.C.E. Vol. LVII, pp. 234-243, Feb., 1930.

Stone Beehive Homes of the Italian Heel: In Trulli-Land the Native Builds His Dwelling and Makes His Field Arable in the Same Operation. By Paul Wilstach. Vol. LVII, pp. 229-260, 25 ills. in black and white, 12 ills. in color, 1 quarter-page map, Feb., 1930.

Stone Faces (Monuments):

Discovering the New World's Oldest Dated Work of Man: A Maya Monument Inscribed 291 B. C. Is Unearthed Near a Huge Stone Head by a Geographic-Smithsonian Expedition in Mexico. By Matthew W. Stirling. Vol. LXXVI, pp. 183-218, 40 ills., 1 half-page map, Aug., 1939.

Great Stone Faces of Easter Island. 11 ills. from photographs. Vol. LXXXV, pp. 225-232, Feb., 1944.

Great Stone Faces of the Mexican Jungle: Five Colossal Heads and Numerous Other Monuments of Vanished Americans Are Excavated by the Latest National Geographic-Smithsonian Expedition. By Matthew W. Stirling. Vol. LXXVIII, pp. 309-334, 26 ills., 1 map, Sept., 1940.

Mystery of Easter Island. By Mrs. Scoresby Routledge. Vol. XL, pp. 628-646, 13 ills., 1 page map, Dec., 1921.

Stone Idols of the Andes Reveal a Vanished People: Remarkable Relics of One of the Oldest Aboriginal Cultures of America Are Unearthed in Colombia's San Agustín Region. By Hermann von Wald-Waldegg. Vol. LXXVII, pp. 627-647, 22 ills., 1 map, May, 1940.

Storied Islands of the South Sea. 20 ills. in color from natural-color photographs by Irving Johnson, Malcolm Evans, and others. Vol. LXXXI, pp. 9-40, Jan., 1942.

Stone Idols of the Andes Reveal a Vanished People: Remarkable Relics of One of the Oldest Aboriginal Cultures of America Are Unearthed in Colombia's San Agustín Region. By Herman von Walde-Waldegg. Vol. LXXVII, pp. 627-647, 22 ills., 1 map, May, 1940.

Storied Islands of the South Sea. 20 ills. in color from natural-color photographs by Irving Johnson, Malcolm Evans, and others. Vol. LXXXI, pp. 9-40, Jan., 1942.

Contains illustrations of Easter Island, Galápagos Islands, Pitcairn, Samoa, Santa Cruz, and Solomon Islands.

Storm of February 25-28, 1902. By Alfred J. Henry. Vol. XIII, pp. 110-112, 1 chart, Mar., 1902.

Storms. *See* Meteorology.

Story and the Legends of the Pontine Marshes: After Many Centuries of Fruitless Effort, Italy Is to Inaugurate a Gigantic Enterprise to Drain the Fertile Region Southeast of Rome. By Gelasio Caetani. Vol. XLV, pp. 357-390, 34 ills., Apr., 1924.

Story of Machu Picchu: The Peruvian Expedition of the National Geographic Society and Yale University. By Hiram Bingham. Vol. XXVII, pp. 171-217, 50 ills., Feb., 1915.

Story of the American Flag. By Gilbert Grosvenor and Byron McCandless. Vol. XXXII, pp. 286-303, 12 ills., Oct., 1917.

Story of the Flamingo. Vol. XVI, p. 50, Jan., 1905.

Story of the Horse: The Development of Man's Companion in War Camp, on Farm, in the Marts of Trade, and in the Field of Sports. By Maj. Gen. William Harding Carter. Vol. XLIV, pp. 455-566, 62 ills. in black and white, 24 ills. in color, Nov., 1923.

Story of the Map. Text accompanying special map supplement in colors. Vol. LXII, pp. 759-774, 11 ills., Dec., 1932.

Story of the Ruhr. By Frederick Simpich. Vol. XLI, pp. 553-564, 11 ills., 1 third-page map, May, 1922.

Straits Settlement, Malay Peninsula. *See* Christmas Island; Cocos Islands; Singapore.

Strange and Remarkable Beast (Mammoth). Vol. XVIII, p. 620, 1 ill., Sept., 1907.

Strange Creatures of Sunny Seas (Mollusks, Crustaceans, etc.). 8 ills. in color from paintings by Else Bostelmann. Vol. LXXI, pp. 211-218, Feb., 1937.

Strange Habits of Familiar Moths and Butterflies. By William Joseph Showalter. Vol. LII, pp. 77-126, 28 ills. in black and white, 169 ills. in color, July, 1927.

Strange Sights in Far-Away Papua. By A. E. Pratt. Vol. XVIII, pp. 559-572, 7 ills., Sept., 1907.

Strange Tribes in the Shan States of Burma. 15 ills. in color from natural-color photographs by W. Robert Moore. Vol. LVIII, pp. 246-255, Aug., 1930.

Strategic Alaska Looks Ahead: Our Vast Territory, Now Being More Closely Linked to Us by Road and Rail, Embodies the American Epic of Freedom, Adventure, and the Pioneer Spirit. By Ernest H. Gruening. Vol. LXXXII, pp. 281-315, 18 ills. in black and white, 16 ills. in color, 1 two-page map, Sept., 1942.

Stratford-on-Avon, England:

Through the Heart of England in a Canadian Canoe. By R. J. Evans. Vol. XLI, pp. 473-497, 26 ills., 1 half-page map, May, 1922.

Stratosphere:

Ballooning in the Stratosphere: Two Balloon Ascents to Ten-Mile Altitudes Presage New Mode of Aërial Travel. By Auguste Piccard. Vol. LXIII, pp. 353-384, 34 ills., Mar., 1933.

Exploring the Earth's Stratosphere: The Holder of the American Altitude Record Describes His Experiences in Reaching the "Ceiling" of His Plane at an Elevation of Nearly Eight Miles. By Lieut. John A. Macready. Vol. L, pp. 755-776, 18 ills., Dec., 1926.

Exploring the Stratosphere. By Capt. Albert W. Stevens. Vol. LXVI, pp. 397-434, 43 ills., 1 two-thirds-page chart, Oct., 1934.

First natural-color photograph taken in the stratosphere. 1 ill. in color by Maj. Albert W. Stevens. Vol. LXXI, p. 340, Mar., 1937.

Stratosphere—*Continued*

Man's Farthest Aloft: Rising to 13.71 Miles, the National Geographic Society-U. S. Army Stratosphere Expedition Gathers Scientific Data at Record Altitude. By Capt. Albert W. Stevens. Action Photographs of the Balloon's Perfect Landing included. Vol. LXIX, pp. 59-94, 39 ills., 1 quarter-page map, Jan., 1936.

National Geographic Society-U. S. Army Air Corps Stratosphere Flight of 1935 in Balloon *Explorer II* (Contributed Technical Papers, Stratosphere Series, No. 2). Vol. LXXI, p. 340, Mar., 1937; p. 802, June, 1937.

Photograph Showing the Division Between the Troposphere and Stratosphere and also the Actual Curvature of the Earth. Special supplement from aërial photograph by Capt. Albert W. Stevens. Vol. LXIX, supplement, May, 1936.

Report of the Second Stratosphere Expedition. Vol. LXVIII, pp. 535-536, Oct., 1935.

Scientific Results of the World-Record Stratosphere Flight. By Capt. Albert W. Stevens. Vol. LXIX, pp. 693-712, 15 ills., May, 1936.

Society Announces New Flight into the Stratosphere. By Gilbert Grosvenor. Vol. LXVII, pp. 265-272, 2 ills. in black and white, 1 sketch map, Feb., 1935.

Studies Planned for New Stratosphere Flight with Helium. Vol. LXVII, pp. 795-800, 5 ills., June, 1935.

World's Largest Free Balloon to Explore Stratosphere. Vol. LXVI, pp. 107-110, 2 ills., July, 1934.

Your Society Sponsors an Expedition to Explore the Stratosphere. Vol. LXV, pp. 528-530, 1 ill., Apr., 1934.

Strauss, (Rear Adm.) Joseph:

Awarded Jane M. Smith Life Membership. Vol. XXXVII, p. 342, Apr., 1920.

Streets and Palaces of Colorful India. 34 ills. in color from autochromes lumière by Gervais Courtellemont. Vol. L, pp. 60-85, July, 1926.

Streett, (Capt.) St. Clair:

First Alaskan Air Expedition. By Capt. St. Clair Streett. Vol. XLI, pp. 499-552, 37 ills., 1 page map, May, 1922.

Ströbeck, Germany:

Ströbeck, Home of Chess: A Medieval Village in the Harz Mountains of Germany Teaches The Royal Game in Its Public School. By Harriet Geithmann. Vol. LIX, pp. 637-652, 8 ills. in black and white, 14 ills. in color, May, 1931.

Strout, Edith Bauer:

At Home on the Oceans: Whales and Sharks Make Exciting Neighbors for a Professor's Wife, Turned Able Seaman, On a Three-year Voyage Around the World. By Edith Bauer Strout. Vol. LXXVI, pp. 33-86, 54 ills., 1 map, July, 1939.

Struggling Poland: A Journey in Search of the Picturesque Through the Most Populous of the New States of Europe. By Maynard Owen Williams. Vol. L, pp. 203-244, 48 ills., 1 two-thirds-page map, Aug., 1926.

Stuart, Eleanor (Mrs. Harris R. Childs):

Zanzibar. By Mrs. Harris R. Childs. Vol. XXIII, pp. 810-824, 11 ills., Aug., 1912.

Studies on the Rate of Evaporation at Reno, Nevada, and in the Salton Sink. By Frank H. Bigelow. Vol. XIX, pp. 20-28, 5 ills., Jan., 1908.

Studies Planned for New Stratosphere Flight with Helium. Vol. LXVII, pp. 795-800, 5 ills., June, 1935.

Styria (Province), Austria:

Styria, a Favored Vacation Land of Central Europe. By Melville Bell Grosvenor. Vol. LXII, pp. 430-439, 14 ills. in color, Oct., 1932.

Summering in Styria, Austria's Rural Playground. 14 ills. in color from natural-color photographs by Hans Hildenbrand. Vol. LXII, pp. 430-439, Oct., 1932.

This Was Austria. 18 ills. from photographs. Vol. LXXXVIII, pp. 71-86, July, 1945.

Submarines:

Your Navy as Peace Insurance. By Fleet Admiral Chester W. Nimitz. Vol. LXXXIX, pp. 681-736, 32 ills. in black and white, 26 ills. in color, June, 1946.

Submerged Valleys in Sandusky Bay (Ohio). By E. L. Moseley. Vol. XIII, pp. 398-403, 4 charts, Nov., 1902.

Sudan (Region), Africa:

Three-Wheeling Through Africa: Two Adventurers Cross the So-called Dark Continent North of Lake Chad on Motorcycles with Side Cars. By James C. Wilson. Vol. LXV, pp. 37-92, 64 ills., 1 two-page map, Jan., 1934.

See also Anglo-Egyptian Sudan; French Sudan.

Suez Canal, Egypt:

Suez Canal: Short Cut to Empires. By Maynard Owen Williams. Vol. LXVIII, pp. 611-632, 19 ills., 1 half-page map, Nov., 1935.

Traffic on the Suez Canal. Vol. XII, p. 380, Oct., 1901.

Sugar Industry:

Agricultural Possibilities in Tropical Mexico. By Dr. Pehr Olsson-Seffer. Vol. XXI, pp. 1021-1040, 18 ills., Dec., 1910.

Cuba—The Sugar Mill of the Antilles. By William Joseph Showalter. Vol. XXXVIII, pp. 1-33, 24 ills., 1 page map, July, 1920.

How the World Is Fed. By William Joseph Showalter. Vol. XXIX, pp. 1-110, 101 ills., Jan., 1916.

Suggested Field for Exploration (Caribbean Regions). Vol. XIV, pp. 290-291, July, 1903.

Sulaimaniya, Iraq:

Mountain Tribes of Iran and Iraq. By Harold Lamb. Vol. LXXXIX, pp. 385-408, 15 ills., 1 two-page map, Mar., 1946.

Sulphur Mine in Nevada. Vol. XV, p. 498, Dec., 1904.

Sultan, (Lt. Col.) Dan I.:

Army Engineer Explores Nicaragua: Mapping a Route for a New Canal Through the Largest of Central American Republics. By Lieut. Col. Dan I. Sultan. Vol LXI, pp. 593-627, 39 ills., 1 two-thirds-page map, May, 1932.

Sulu Archipelago, Philippine Islands:

"As the Tuan Had Said." By George M. Hanson. Vol. LXIV, pp. 631-644, 19 ills., Nov., 1933.

Sumatra:

Among the Hill Tribes of Sumatra. By W. Robert Moore. Vol. LVII, pp. 187-227, 31 ills. in black and white, 25 ills. in color, 1 half-page map, Feb., 1930.

Around the World for Animals. By William M. and Lucille Q. Mann. Vol. LXXIII, pp. 665-714, 33 ills. in black and white, 23 ills. in color, 1 page map, June, 1938.

By Motor Through the East Coast and Batak Highlands of Sumatra. By Melvin A. Hall. Vol. XXXVII, pp. 68-102, 27 ills., Jan., 1920.

The Face of the Netherlands Indies. 20 ills. from photographs by Maynard Owen Williams and others. Vol. LXXXIX, pp. 261-276, Feb., 1946.

Netherlands Indies: Patchwork of Peoples. 23 ills. in color from natural-color photographs by Maynard Owen Williams. Vol. LXXIII, pp. 681-712, June, 1938.

Sumatra, a Ribbon of Color on the Equator. 25 ills. in color from autochromes by W. Robert Moore. Vol. LVII, pp. 194-219, Feb., 1930.

Sumerians (People):

New Light on Ancient Ur: Excavations at the Site of the City of Abraham Reveal Geographical Evidence of the Biblical Story of the Flood. By M. E. L. Mallowan. Vol. LVII, pp. 95-130, 44 ills., 1 three-quarters-page map, Jan., 1930.

Summer Holidays on the Bosporus. By Maynard Owen Williams. Vol. LVI, pp. 487-508, 13 ills. in black and white, 11 ills. in color, 1 half-page map, Oct., 1929.

Summer Meeting of the American Forestry Association. Vol. XIII, pp. 352-358, Sept., 1902.

Summering in an English Cottage: Quiet and Loveliness Invite Contemplation in the Extra "Room," the Garden of the Thatched House. By Helen Churchill Candee. Vol. LXVI, pp. 429-456, 32 ills., Apr., 1935.

Summering in Styria, Austria's Rural Playground. 14 ills. in color from natural-color photographs by Hans Hildenbrand. Vol. LXII, pp. 430-439, Oct., 1932.

Sun. *See* Astronomy; Solar Radiation.

Sun-Compass, Bumstead:

First Flight to the North Pole. By Lieut. Comdr. Richard Evelyn Byrd. Vol. L, pp. 357-376, 14 ills., Sept., 1926.

Sun-Painted Scenes in the Near East. 32 ills. in color from autochromes lumière by Gervais Courtellement. Vol. XLVII, pp. 541-556, Nov., 1925.

Sun Shines Bright in Kentucky. 21 ills. in color from natural-color photographs by B. Anthony Stewart, Volkmar Wentzel, and Ray Scott. Vol. LXXXII, pp. 65-88, July, 1942.

Sun Shines on San Diego (California). 9 ills. in color from natural-color photographs by B. Anthony Stewart. Vol. LXXXI, pp. 57-64, Jan., 1942.

Sunda Islands, Greater. *See* Borneo; Celebes; Java; Sumatra.

Sunda Islands, Lesser. *See* Bali; Timor.

Sunday in Mezőkövesd (Hungary). By Margery Rae. Vol. LXVII, pp. 489-504, 22 ills., Apr., 1935.

Sungmas (Oracles):

Demon-Possessed Tibetans and Their Incredible Feats. 12 ills. in color from natural-color photographs. Vol. LXVIII, pp. 479-486, Oct., 1935.

Sungmas, the Living Oracles of the Tibetan Church. By Joseph F. Rock. Vol. LXVIII, pp. 475-486, 1 ill. in black and white, 12 ills. in color, Oct., 1935.

Sunny Corners in a Friendly Isle (Isle of Man). 12 ills. in color from natural-color photographs by B. Anthony Stewart. Vol. LXXI, pp. 601-608, May, 1937.

Sunny Corners of Kangaroo Land (Australia). 12 ills. in color from natural-color photographs by W. Robert Moore. Vol. LXX, pp. 713-720, Dec., 1936.

Sunny Siberia. 26 ills. in color from natural-color photographs by Owen Lattimore. Vol. LXXXVI, pp. 649-672, Dec., 1944.

Sunny South Africa. 9 ills. in color from natural-color photographs by W. Robert Moore. Vol. LXXXII, pp. 749-756, Dec., 1942.

Sunrise and Sunset from Mount Sinai. By Sartell Prentice, Jr. Vol. XXIII, pp. 1242-1282, 34 ills., 1 page map, Dec., 1912.

Sunset Hues in the Pacific Northwest (Washington). 13 ills. in color from natural-color photographs by Clifton Adams and Asahel Curtis. Vol. LXIII, pp. 154-163, Feb., 1933.

Sunset in the East (Japan). By Blair A. Walliser. Vol. LXXXIX, pp. 797-812, 17 ills., June, 1946.

Sunshine in Turkey. By Howard S. Bliss. Vol. XX, pp. 66-76, 1 ill., Jan., 1909.

Sunshine Land of Fruits, Flowers, Movies, and Sport (California). 41 ills. in color from natural-color photographs by Clifton Adams and Fred Payne Clatworthy. Vol. LXVI, pp. 545-592, Nov., 1934.

Sunshine over Oklahoma. 19 ills. in color from natural-color photographs by B. Anthony Stewart. Vol. LXXIX, pp. 277-308, Mar., 1941.

Sunshine Over the Chilean Lakes. 10 ills. in color from natural-color photographs by W. Robert Moore and John Swope. Vol. LXXX, pp. 97-104, July, 1941.

Superior, Lake:

Wild Life of Lake Superior, Past and Present: The Habits of Deer, Moose, Wolves, Beavers, Muskrats, Trout, and Feathered Wood-Folk Studies with Camera and Flashlight. By George Shiras, 3d. Vol. XL, pp. 113-204, 77 ills., supplement, 1 half-page map, Aug., 1921.

Winter Sky Roads to Isle Royal. By Ben East. Vol. LX, pp. 759-774, 18 ills., 1 half-page map, Dec., 1931.

Supplements. *See* National Geographic Society: Map Supplements; Pictorial Enlargements and Panoramas; *and* Index to Maps, p. 594.

Supply:

Oil for Victory Piped under the Sea. 9 ills. from photographs. Vol. LXXXVIII, pp. 721-726, Dec., 1945.

War, Patriotism, and the Food Supply. By Frederick V. Coville. Vol. XXXI, pp. 254-256, Mar., 1917.

Winning the War of Supply. By F. Barrows Colton. Vol. LXXXVIII, pp. 705-736, 23 ills., Dec., 1945.

See also Lend-Lease; U. S. Army Quartermaster Corps; Water Supply.

Supposed Birthplace of Civilizations. Vol. XVI, pp. 499-504, 6 ills., Nov., 1905.

Surf-Board Riding:

Surf-Boarders Capture California. 8 ills. from photographs by J. H. Ball. Vol. LXXXVI, pp. 355-362, Sept., 1944.

Waves and Thrills at Waikiki (Honolulu). 8 ills. in duotone by Thomas Edward Blake. Vol. LXVII, pp. 597-604, May, 1935.

Surf-Boarders Capture California. 8 ills. from photographs by J. H. Ball. Vol. LXXXVI, pp. 355-362, Sept., 1944.

Surinam:

Color Glows in the Guianas, French and Dutch. By Nicol Smith. Vol. LXXXIII, pp. 459-480, 8 ills. in black and white, 13 ills. in color, 1 two-thirds-page map, Apr., 1943.

Picturesque Paramaribo. By Harriet Chalmers Adams. Vol. XVIII, pp. 365-373, 7 ills., June, 1907.

Surinam Subjects of Queen Wilhelmina. 13 ills. in color from natural-color photographs by Philip Hanson Hiss. Vol. LXXXIII, pp. 465-472, Apr., 1943.

Survey of the Grand Canyon. Vol. XIV, pp. 162-163, Apr., 1903.

Surveying, Hydrographic. *See* Hydrography.

Surveying the Grand Canyon of the Colorado: An Account of the 1923 Boating Expedition of the United States Geological Survey. By Lewis R. Freeman. Vol. XLV, pp. 471-548, 62 ills., 1 three-quarters-page map, May, 1924.

Surveying the 141st Meridian (Boundary Line Between Canada and Alaska). By Thomas Riggs, Jr. Vol. XXIII, pp. 685-713, 46 ills., 1 page map, July, 1912.

Surveying the Philippine Islands. By George H. Putnam. Vol. XIV, pp. 437-441, 4 ills., Dec., 1903.

Surveying Through Khoresm: A Journey Into Parts of Asiatic Russia Which Have Been Closed to Western Travelers Since the World War. By Lyman D. Wilbur. Vol. LXI, pp. 753-780, 31 ills., 1 two-thirds-page map, June, 1932.

Survival at Sea:
They Survived at Sea. By Lt. Comdr. Samuel F. Harby. Vol. LXXXVII, pp. 617-640, 22 ills., May, 1945.

Susa (Shush), Iran:
Excavations of M. de Morgan at Susa. Vol. XII, p. 315, Aug., 1901.

Sussex (County), England:
Penn Country in Sussex: Home of Pennsylvania's Founder Abounds in Quaker History and Memories of Adventurous Smugglers. By Col. T. P. Etherton. Vol. LXVIII, pp. 59-90, 32 ills., 1 page map, July, 1935.

Susu (Tribespeople):
Dusky Tribesmen of French West Africa. 26 ills. in color from natural-color photographs by Enzo de Chetelat. Vol. LXXIX, pp. 639-662, May, 1941.

Suter, H. M.:
Forest Fires in the Adirondacks in 1903. By H. M. Suter. Vol. XV, p. 224, May, 1904.

Sutherland, Mason:
Aboard a Blimp Hunting U-boats: A Day above the Atlantic Reveals Navy Talk and Navy Ways, Creeping Convoys, and Torpedoed Wrecks. By Mason Sutherland. Vol. LXXXIV, pp. 79-96, 18 ills., July, 1943.
Bornholm—Denmark in a Nutshell. By Mason Sutherland. Vol. LXXXVII, pp. 239-256, 20 ills., 1 half-page map, Feb., 1945.
Navy Artist Paints the Aleutians. By Mason Sutherland. Paintings by Lt. William F. Draper. Vol. LXXXIV, pp. 157-176, 4 ills. in black and white, 16 ills. in color, Aug., 1943.

Sutton Courtenay (Manor), England:
Vacation in a Fifteenth Century English Manor House. By George Alden Sanford. Vol. LIII, pp. 629-636, 8 ills., May, 1928.

Sutton Hoo Burial Ship:
Ancestor of the British Navy: England's Oldest Known War Vessel Is Unearthed, Laden with Remarkable Treasures of an Anglo-Saxon Ruler. By C. W. Phillips. Vol. LXXIX, pp. 247-268, 22 ills. in black and white, 4 drawings, Feb., 1941.

Suwannee (River), Georgia:
Okefinokee Wilderness: Exploring the Mystery Land of the Suwannee River Reveals Natural Wonders and Fascinating Folklore. By Francis Harper. Vol. LXV, pp. 597-624, 35 ills., 1 two-thirds-page map, May, 1934.

Svalbard. *See* Spitsbergen.

Svans (People):
Roaming Russia's Caucasus: Rugged Mountains and Hardy Fighters Guard the Soviet Union's Caucasian Treasury of Manganese and Oil. By Rolf Singer. Vol. LXXXII, pp. 91-121, 33 ills., July, 1942.

Sven Hedin in Tibet. Vol. XIII, pp. 96-97, Mar., 1902.

Sven Hedin's Explorations in Central Asia. Vol. XII, pp. 393-395, Nov., 1901.

Sverdrup's Work in the Arctics. Vol. XIII, pp. 460-461, 1 page map, Dec., 1902.

Swallows:
Some Songsters and Flyers of Wide Repute. 42 portraits in color from paintings by Maj. Allan Brooks. Vol. LXIX, pp. 529-544, Apr., 1936.
Thrushes, Thrashers, and Swallows: Robins and Bluebirds are Familiar Members of a Famous Musical Family Which Includes the Hermit Thrush and European Nightingale. By T. Gilbert Pearson. Paintings by Maj. Allan Brooks. Vol. LXIX, pp. 523-546, 6 ills. in black and white, 42 paintings from life, Apr., 1936.

Swamp Drainage. *See* Reclamation of Land.

Swans:
Far-Flying Wild Fowl and Their Foes. By Maj. Allan Brooks. Vol. LXVI, pp. 487-528, 6 ills. in black and white, 3 portraits in color, Oct., 1934.
Fowls of Forest and Stream Tamed by Man. By Morley A. Jull. Vol. LVII, pp. 327-371, 27 ills. in black and white, 16 ills. in color, Mar., 1930.
Wild Geese, Ducks, and Swans. 3 portraits in color from paintings by Maj. Allan Brooks. Vol. LXVI, pp. 493-524, Oct., 1934.

Swayne, H. G. C.:
Rock of Aden: The Volcanic Mountain Fortress, on the Sea Route from Suez to India, Assumes New Importance. By H. G. C. Swayne. Vol. LXVIII, pp. 723-742, 24 ills., 1 half-page map, Dec., 1935.

Sweden:
Color and Customs of Sweden's Château Country. 13 ills. in color from natural-color photographs by Gustav Heurlin. Vol. LXVI, pp. 33-40, July, 1934.
Comparison of Norway and Sweden. Vol. XVI, pp. 429-431, Sept., 1905.
Country-House Life in Sweden: In Castle and Cottage the Landed Gentry Gallantly Keep the Old Traditions. By Amelie Posse-Brázdová. Vol. LXVI, pp. 1-64, 51 ills. in black and white, 13 ills. in color, 1 page map, July, 1934.
Flying Around the Baltic. By Douglas Chandler. Vol. LXXIII, pp. 767-806, 31 ills. in black and white, 13 ills. in duotone, 1 half-page map, June, 1938.
In Beautiful Delecarlia. By Lillian Gore. Vol. XX, pp. 464-477, 13 ills., May, 1909.

Sweden—*Continued*

King Herring: An Account of the World's Most Valuable Fish, the Industries It Supports, and the Part It Has Played in History. By Hugh M. Smith. Vol. XX, pp. 701-735, 21 ills., Aug., 1909.

Life's Flavor on a Swedish Farm: From the Rocky Hills of Småland Thousands of Sturdy Citizens Have Emigrated to the United States. By Willis Lindquist. Vol. LXXVI, pp. 393-414, 23 ills., 1 quarter-page map, Sept., 1939.

Nomads of Arctic Lapland: Mysterious Little People of a Land of the Midnight Sun Live Off the Country Above the Arctic Circle. By Clyde Fisher. Vol. LXXVI, pp. 641-676, 28 ills. in black and white, 12 ills. in color, 1 page map, Nov., 1939.

Rural Sweden Through American Eyes: A Visitor in Peacetime Finds Warmth, Welcome, and Strange Folkways On a Century-old Farm. By Elizabeth W. Nilson. Vol. LXXVII, pp. 795-822, 8 ills. in black and white, 22 ills. in color, June, 1940.

Sweden, Land of White Birch and White Coal. By Alma Luise Olson. Vol. LIV, pp. 441-484, 51 ills. in black and white, 29 ills. in color, Oct., 1928.

Types and Costumes of Old Sweden. 30 ills. in color from autochromes lumière by Gustav Heurlin, G. W. Cronquist, Wilhelm Tobien, and Charles Martin. Vol. LIV, pp. 424-441, Oct., 1928.

Under Swedish Roofs and Skies. 22 ills. in color from natural-color photographs by Volkmar Wentzel. Vol. LXXVII, pp. 799-822, June, 1940.

See also Stockholm.

Swifts (Birds):

Humming Birds, Swifts and Goatsuckers. 5 ills. in color from paintings by Maj. Allan Brooks. Vol. LXII, pp. 75-88, July, 1932.

Seeking the Smallest Feathered Creatures: Humming Birds, Peculiar to the New World, Are Found from Canada and Alaska to the Strait of Magellan. Swifts and Goatsuckers, Their Nearest Relatives. By Alexander Wetmore. Paintings by Maj. Allan Brooks. Vol. LXII, pp. 65-89, 2 ills. in black and white, 5 ills. in color, July, 1932.

Swingle, Charles F.:

Across Madagascar by Boat, Auto, Railroad, and Filanzana. By Charles F. Swingle. Vol. LVI, pp. 179-211, 42 ills., 1 half-page and 1 three-quarters-page maps, Aug., 1929.

Awarded Jane M. Smith Life Membership. Vol. XXXVII, p. 342, Apr., 1920.

Swiss Cherish Their Ancient Liberties. 21 ills. from photographs. Vol. LXXIX, pp. 481-496, Apr., 1941.

Switzerland:

Amid the Snows of Switzerland. 16 ills. in duotone by Albert Steiner. Vol. XLI, pp. 277-292, Mar., 1922.

Switzerland—*Continued*

Ascent of Mont Blanc. By Walter Woodburn Hyde. Vol. XXIV, pp. 861-942, 69 ills., Aug., 1913.

Citizen Army of Switzerland. Vol. XXVIII, pp. 502-510, 7 ills., Nov., 1915.

Flights from Arctic to Equator: Conquering the Alps, the Ice Peaks of Spitsbergen, of Persia, and Africa's Mountains of the Moon. By Walter Mittelholzer. Vol. LXI, pp. 445-498, 53 ills., 1 three-quarters-page map, Apr., 1932.

In Valais. By Louise Murray. Vol. XXI, pp. 249-256, 6 ills., Mar., 1910.

Italy, France, Switzerland. Vol. XXVIII, pp. 439-454, 16 ills. in color, Nov., 1915.

Lake Geneva: Cradle of Conferences. By F. Barrows Colton. Vol. LXXII, pp. 727-742, 12 ills., 1 third-page map, Dec., 1937.

Landslides and Rock Avalanches. By Guy Elliott Mitchell. Vol. XXI, pp. 277-287, 6 ills., Apr., 1910.

Majesty of the Matterhorn. Vol. XXIII, supplement, May, 1912.

Manless Alpine Climbing: The First Woman to Scale the Grépon, the Matterhorn, and Other Famous Peaks Without Masculine Support Relates Her Adventures. By Miriam O'Brien Underhill. Vol. LXVI, pp. 131-170, 30 ills. in black and white, 12 ills. in color, Aug., 1934.

Races of Europe. By Edwin A. Grosvenor. Vol. XXXIV, pp. 441-534, 62 ills., 2 page maps, special map supplement, Dec., 1918.

Republics—The Ladder to Liberty. By David Jayne Hill. Vol. XXXI, pp. 240-254, 5 ills., 2 page maps, Mar., 1917.

Scenes in Switzerland. Vol. XXI, pp. 257-268, 13 ills., Mar., 1910.

Skiing in Switzerland's Realm of Winter Sports. 10 ills. in duotone from photographs by Jean Gaberell, E. Gyger, and A. Klopfenstein. Vol. LXIII, pp. 344-353, Mar., 1933.

Snowy Peaks and Old Costumes of Switzerland. 12 ills. in color from natural-color photographs by Hans Hildenbrand. Vol. LXVI, pp. 147-154, Aug., 1934.

Swiss Cherish Their Ancient Liberties. 21 ills. from photographs. Vol. LXXIX, pp. 481-496, Apr., 1941.

Woman's Climbs in the High Alps. By Dora Keen. Vol. XXII, pp. 642-675, 26 ills., July, 1911.

See also Geneva; Gruyères.

Swope, John:

Sunshine Over the Chilean Lakes. 10 ills. in color from natural-color photographs by W. Robert Moore and John Swope. Vol. LXXX, pp. 97-104, July, 1941.

Swordfish:

Fighting Giants of the Humboldt. By David D. Duncan. Vol. LXXIX, pp. 373-400, 28 ills., 1 half-page map, Mar., 1941.

Sydney, Australia :

Capital Cities of Australia. By W. Robert Moore. Vol. LXVIII, pp. 667-722, 32 ills. in black and white, 24 ills. in color, 1 two-page map, Dec., 1935.

Lonely Australia : The Unique Continent. By Herbert E. Gregory. Vol. XXX, pp. 473-568, 68 ills., 1 two-page and 4 half-page maps, Dec., 1916.

Sydney Faces the War Front Down Under. By Howell Walker. Vol. LXXXIII, pp. 359-374, 8 ills. in black and white, 10 ills. in color, Mar., 1943.

Sykes, Ella C. :

Talk About Persia and Its Women. By Ella C. Sykes. Vol. XXI, pp. 847-866, 22 ills., Oct., 1910.

Sykes, Robert B., Jr. :

Uncle Sam's Icebox Outposts. 19 ills. in color from natural-color photographs by John E. Schneider and Robert B. Sykes, Jr. Vol. XC, pp. 473-496, Oct., 1946.

Sylvester, A. H. :

Is Our Noblest Volcano Awakening to New Life : A Description of the Glaciers and Evidences of Volcanic Activity of Mount Hood. By A. H. Sylvester. Vol. XIX, pp. 515-525, 5 ills., 1 page map, July, 1908.

Symbol of Service to Mankind (American National Red Cross). By Stockton Axon. Vol. XXXIII, pp. 375-390, 11 ills., Apr., 1918.

Syracuse, Sicily. *See* Siracusa.

Syria :

Antioch the Glorious. By William H. Hall. Vol. XXXVIII, pp. 81-103, 20 ills., 1 half-page map, Aug., 1920.

Bombs over Bible Lands. By Frederick Simpich and W. Robert Moore. Vol. LXXX, pp. 141-180, 34 ills., 1 two-page map, Aug., 1941.

Change Comes to Bible Lands. By Frederick Simpich. Vol. LXXIV, pp. 695-750, 40 ills. in black and white, 25 ills. in color, special map supplement, Dec., 1938.

Damascus, the Pearl of the Desert. By Archibald Forder. Vol. XXII, pp. 62-82, 19 ills., 1 three-quarters-page map, Jan., 1911.

Damascus and Mecca Railway. Vol. XII, p. 408, Nov., 1901.

From Jerusalem to Aleppo. By John D. Whiting. Vol. XXIV, pp. 71-113, 30 ills., 1 half-page map, Jan., 1913.

Impressions of Asiatic Turkey. By Stephen van Rensselaer Trowbridge. Vol. XXVI, pp. 598-609, 6 ills., Dec., 1914.

In the Land of Moses and Abraham. 25 ills. in color from natural-color photographs by W. Robert Moore. Vol. LXXIV, pp. 711-742, Dec., 1938.

New Alphabet of the Ancients Is Unearthed : An Inconspicuous Mound in Northern Syria Yields Archeological Treasures of Far-Reaching Significance. By F. A. Schaeffer. Vol. LVIII, pp. 477-516, 47 ills., 1 quarter-page map, Oct., 1930.

Syria—*Continued*

One Thousand Miles of Railway Built for Pilgrims and Not for Dividends. By Col. F. R. Maunsell. Vol. XX, pp. 156-172, 13 ills., 1 three-quarters-page map, Feb., 1909.

Secrets from Syrian Hills : Explorations Reveal World's Earliest Known Alphabet, Deciphered from Schoolboy Slates and Dictionaries of 3,000 Years Ago. By Claude F. A. Schaeffer. Vol. LXIV, pp. 97-126, 40 ills., 1 third-page map, July, 1933.

Skirting the Shores of Sunrise : Seeking and Finding "The Levant" in a Journey by Steamer, Motor-Car, and Train from Constantinople to Port Said. By Melville Chater. Vol. L, pp. 649-728, 60 ills. in black and white, 34 ills. in color, 1 two-thirds-page map, Dec., 1926.

Syria : The Land Link of History's Chain. By Maynard Owen Williams. Vol. XXXVI, pp. 437-462, 20 ills., 1 quarter-page map, Nov., 1919.

Syria and Lebanon Taste Freedom. By Maynard Owen Williams. With 21 ills. in color from natural-color photographs by the author. Vol. XC, pp. 729-763, 16 ills. in black and white, Dec., 1946.

See also Deir ez Zor.

Szechwan (Province), China :

China Fights Erosion with U. S. Aid. By Walter C. Lowdermilk. Vol. LXXXVII, pp. 641-680, 10 ills. in black and white, 26 ills. in color, June, 1945.

Eden of the Flowery Republic. By Joseph Beech. Vol. XXXVIII, pp. 355-390, 18 ills. in black and white, 16 ills. in color, Nov., 1920.

Populous and Beautiful Szechuan : A Visit to the Restless Province of China in which the Present Revolution Began. By Rollin T. Chamberlin. Vol. XII, pp. 1094-1119, 26 ills., 1 half-page map, Dec., 1911.

Salt for China's Daily Rice. 11 ills. from photographs. Vol. LXXXVI, pp. 329-336, Sept., 1944.

T

Taal Volcano and Its Recent Destructive Eruption (Philippine Islands). By Dean C. Worcester. Vol. XXIII, pp. 313-368, 40 ills., 4 half-page maps, 1 diagram, Apr., 1912.

Tabasco (State), Mexico :

Wildlife of Tabasco and Veracruz. By Walter A. Weber. With 19 ills. in color from paintings by the author. Vol. LXXXVII, pp. 187-216, 7 ills. in black and white, 1 two-thirds-page map, Feb., 1945.

See also La Venta.

Tableaux in an English Lilliput (Bekonscot). 15 ills. in color from natural-color photographs by B. Anthony Stewart. Vol. LXXI, pp. 653-660, May, 1937.

Tacoma, Washington :

Our Pacific Northwest. By N. H. Darton. Vol. XX, pp. 645-663, 12 ills., 2 half-page maps, July, 1909.

Taft, William Howard:

Annual Dinner of the National Geographic Society (Speech by William Howard Taft). Vol. XVII, pp. 22-37, Jan., 1906.

Arbitration Treaties. By William Howard Taft. Vol. XXII, pp. 1165-1172, Dec., 1911.

Election of William Howard Taft as Member of the Board of Managers of The Society. Vol. XXXIII, p. 371, Apr., 1918.

Great Britain's Bread Upon the Waters: Canada and Her Other Daughters. By William Howard Taft. Vol. XXIX, pp. 217-272, 56 ills., Mar., 1916.

Health and Morale of America's Citizen Army: Personal Observations of Conditions in Our Soldier Cities by a Former Commander-in-Chief of the United States Army and Navy. By William Howard Taft. Vol. XXXIII, pp. 219-245, 22 ills., Mar., 1918.

In Honor of the Army and Aviation (Address upon Election as Honorary Member of The Society). Vol. XXII, pp. 267-284, 1 ill., Mar., 1911.

Islands of Bermuda: A British Colony with a Unique Record in Popular Government. By William Howard Taft. Vol. XLI, pp. 1-26, 15 ills., 1 three-quarters-page map, Jan., 1922.

League of Nations, What It Means and Why It Must Be. By William Howard Taft. Vol. XXXV, pp. 43-66, 15 ills., Jan., 1919.

Lincoln Memorial (Washington, D. C.). By William Howard Taft. Vol. XLIII, pp. 597-602, 5 ills., June, 1923.

Philippines. By William Howard Taft. Vol. XVI, pp. 361-375, 3 ills., special map supplement, Aug., 1905.

Poisoned World. By William Howard Taft. Vol. XXXI, pp. 459-467, 7 ills., May, 1917.

Progressive World Struggle of the Jews for Civil Equality. By William Howard Taft. Vol. XXXVI, pp. 1-23, 14 ills., July, 1919.

Race for the South Pole (Presentation of Hubbard Gold Medal to Sir Ernest H. Shackleton by President Taft). Vol. XXI, pp. 185-186, Mar., 1910.

Some Impressions of 150,000 Miles of Travel. By William Howard Taft. Vol. LVII, pp. 523-598, 80 ills., May, 1930.

Some Recent Instances of National Altruism: The Efforts of the United States to Aid the Peoples of Cuba, Porto Rico, and the Philippines. By William Howard Taft. Vol. XVIII, pp. 429-438, July, 1907.

Ten Years in the Philippines. By William Howard Taft. Vol. XIX, pp. 141-148, Feb., 1908.

Washington (D.C.): Its Beginning, Its Growth, and Its Future. By William Howard Taft. Vol. XXVII, pp. 221-292, 33 ills. in black and white, 32 ills. in color, panorama, 1 page map, 1 diagram in colors, Mar., 1915.

TAG. See Transport Air Group.

Tagus (River), Spain-Portugal. See Tejo.

Tahiti (Island), Society Islands:

Diary of a Voyage from San Francisco to Tahiti and Return, 1901. By S. P. Langley. Vol. XII, pp. 413-429, 10 ills., 1 page and 1 half-page maps, Dec., 1901.

Dream Ship: The Story of a Voyage of Adventure More Than Half Around the World in a 47-Foot Lifeboat. By Ralph Stock. Vol. XXXIX, pp. 1-52, 43 ills., 1 page map, Jan., 1921.

Notes on Tahiti. By Harrison W. Smith. Vol. XXII, pp. 947-963, 17 ills., Oct., 1911.

Tahiti: A Playground of Nature. By Paul Gooding. Vol. XXXVIII, pp. 301-326, 16 ills., 1 half-page map, Oct., 1920.

Tahltan Indians:

Life on a Yukon Trail. By Alfred Pearce Dennis. Vol. X, pp. 377-391, 8 ills., 1 page map, Oct., 1899.

Tai Pusam (Hindu Festival):

Fire-Walking Hindus of Singapore. By L. Elizabeth Lewis. Vol. LIX, pp. 513-522, 12 ills., Apr., 1931.

Tai Shan, Sacred Mountain of the East (China). By Mary Augusta Mullikin. Vol. LXXXVII, pp. 699-719, 18 ills., 1 page map, June, 1945.

Taian, China:

Tai Shan, Sacred Mountain of the East. By Mary Augusta Mullikin. Vol. LXXXVII, pp. 699-719, 18 ills., 1 page map, June, 1945.

Taihoku, Formosa:

Formosa the Beautiful. By Alice Ballantine Kirjassoff. Vol. XXXVII, pp. 246-292, 60 ills., 1 half-page map, Mar., 1920.

I Lived on Formosa. By Joseph W. Ballantine. Vol. LXXXVII, pp. 1-24, 19 ills., 1 page and 1 half-page maps, Jan., 1945.

Tailed People of Nigeria. Vol. XXIII, pp. 1239-1242, 3 ills., Dec., 1912.

Tairen, Manchuria. See Dairen.

Taiwan (Island). See Formosa.

Taj Mahal (Mausoleum), India:

Through the Heart of Hindustan: A Teeming Highway Extending for Fifteen Hundred Miles, from the Khyber Pass to Calcutta. By Maynard Owen Williams. Vol. XL, pp. 433-467, 29 ills., Nov., 1921.

Take-off for Japan. 22 ills. in color from U. S. Navy official photographs. Vol. LXXXVIII, pp. 193-208, Aug., 1945.

Talbot, P. A.:

Notes on the Ekoi (Nigeria). By P. A. Talbot. Vol. XXIII, pp. 32-38, 8 ills., Jan., 1912.

Tale (Block Talc):

India's Treasures Helped the Allies. By John Fischer. Vol. LXXXIX, pp. 501-522, 18 ills., Apr., 1946.

Tale of Three Cities (Prague, Vienna, Budapest). By Thomas R. Henry. Vol. LXXXVIII, pp. 641-669, 23 ills., Dec., 1945.

Tales of the British Air Service. By Maj. William A. Bishop. Vol. XXXIII, pp. 27-37, 12 ills., Jan., 1918.

Talk About Persia and Its Women. By Ella C. Sykes. Vol. XXI, pp. 847-866, 22 ills., Oct., 1910.

Tallest Tree That Grows (Eucalyptus). By Edgerton K. Young. Vol. XX, pp. 664-667, 5 ills., July, 1909.

Tallinn, Estonian Soviet Socialist Republic:

Estonia: At Russia's Baltic Gate: War Often Has Ravaged This Little Nation Whose Identity Was Long Submerged in the Vast Sea of Russian Peoples. By Baroness Irina Ungern-Sternberg. Vol. LXXVI, pp. 803-834, 33 ills., 1 half-page map, Dec., 1939.

Flying Around the Baltic. By Douglas Chandler. Vol. LXXIII, pp. 767-806, 31 ills. in black and white, 13 ills. in duotone, 1 half-page map, June, 1938.

Tambs, Erling:

Modern Saga of the Seas: The Narrative of a 17,000-Mile Cruise on a 40-Foot Sloop by the Author, His Wife, and a Baby, Born on the Voyage. By Erling Tambs. Vol. LX, pp. 645-688, 49 ills., 1 half-page map, Dec., 1931.

Taming "Flood Dragons" Along China's Hwang Ho (River). By Oliver J. Todd. Vol. LXXXI, pp. 205-234, 26 ills., 1 half-page map, Feb., 1942.

Taming the Outlaw Missouri River. By Frederick Simpich. Vol. LXXXVIII, pp. 569-598, 25 ills., 1 two-page map, Nov., 1945.

Taming the Wild Blueberry. By Frederick V. Coville. Vol. XXII, pp. 137-147, 5 ills., Feb., 1911.

Tampico, Mexico:

Naturalist's Journey Around Vera Cruz and Tampico. By Frank M. Chapman. Vol. XXV, pp. 532-562, 31 ills., May, 1914.

Tanager (Ship):

Bird Life Among Lava Rock and Coral Sand: The Chronicle of a Scientific Expedition to Little-Known Islands of Hawaii. By Alexander Wetmore. Vol. XLVIII, pp. 77-108, 36 ills., 1 half-page map, July, 1925.

Tanagers (Birds):

Bird Beauties of the Tanager and Finch Families. 55 portraits in color from paintings by Maj. Allan Brooks. Vol. LXVII, pp. 513-528, Apr., 1935.

Tanagers and Finches: Their Flashes of Color and Lilting Songs Gladden the Hearts of American Bird Lovers East and West. By Arthur A. Allen. Paintings by Maj. Allan Brooks. Vol. LXVII, pp. 505-532, 6 ills. in black and white, 55 portraits in color, Apr., 1935.

Tanahmerah, Netherlands New Guinea:

New Guinea's Mountain and Swampland Dwellers. By Col. Ray T. Elsmore. Vol. LXXXVIII, pp. 671-694, 15 ills. in black and white, 7 ills. in color, 1 half-page map, Dec., 1945.

Tanganyika Lake, Belgian Congo-Tanganyika:

Where Exploration Is Needed (Africa). Vol. XI, p. 163, Apr., 1900.

Tanganyika Territory:

Flashlights from the Jungle. Vol. XVIII, pp. 534-548, 11 ills., Aug., 1907.

Wings Over Nature's Zoo in Africa. 20 ills. in duotone from photographs by Reginald A. Bourlay. Vol. LXXVI, pp. 527-542, Oct., 1939.

Tangier, International Zone, Morocco:

Eastward from Gibraltar: Overland Route Across North Africa to Tunisia and Libia. By Cyrus French Wicker. Vol. LXXXIII, pp. 115-142, 28 ills., Jan., 1943.

Journey in Morocco: "The Land of the Moors." By Thomas Lindsey Blayney. Vol. XXII, pp. 750-776, 21 ills., Aug., 1911.

Morocco, the "Land of the Extreme West," and the Story of My Captivity. By Ion Perdicaris. Vol. XVII, pp. 117-157, 24 ills., Mar., 1906.

Two Great Moorish Religious Dances. By George Edmund Holt. Vol. XXII, pp. 776-785, 6 ills., Aug., 1911.

Tankers:

Ships That Won the Greatest Naval War. 26 ills. in color from U. S. Navy official photographs. Vol. LXXXIX, pp. 697-736, June, 1946.

Tannura, Ras at (Cape), Saudi Arabia:

Guest in Saudi Arabia. By Maynard Owen Williams. Vol. LXXXVIII, pp. 463-487, 24 ills., 1 two-thirds-page map, Oct., 1945.

Taoist Shrines:

Tai Shan, Sacred Mountain of the East. By Mary Augusta Mullikin. Vol. LXXXVII, pp. 699-719, 18 ills., 1 page map, June, 1945.

Tarascan Indians:

Mexican Land of Lakes and Lacquers (Pátzcuaro Region). 22 ills. from photographs by Helene Fischer and Luis Marquez. Vol. LXXI, pp. 633-648, May, 1937.

Paricutín, the Cornfield That Grew a Volcano (Mexico). By James A. Green. Vol. LXXXV, pp. 129-164, 16 ills. in black and white, 21 ills. in color, 1 third-page map, Feb., 1944.

Tarawa (Atoll), Gilbert Islands:

Gilbert Islands in the Wake of Battle. By W. Robert Moore. Vol. LXXXVII, pp. 129-162, 11 ills. in black and white, 19 ills. in color, 1 two-thirds-page map, Feb., 1945.

Round About Grim Tarawa. 19 ills. in color from natural-color photographs by W. Robert Moore. Vol. LXXXVII, pp. 137-160, Feb., 1945.

Tarheelia on Parade: Versatile and Vibrant, North Carolina in a Generation Has Climbed New Economic Heights. By Leonard C. Roy. Vol. LXXX, pp. 181-224, 24 ills. in black and white, 21 ills. in color, 1 map (two-page spread), Aug., 1941.

Tarr, Ralph S.:

National Geographic Society's Alaskan Expedition of 1909. By Ralph S. Tarr and Lawrence Martin. Vol. XXI, pp. 1-54, 42 ills., 12 maps, Jan., 1910.

Teaching of Geography. By Ralph S. Tarr. Vol. XIII, pp. 55-64, Feb., 1902.

Tartan Tints New Scotland (Nova Scotia). 21 ills. in color from natural-color photographs; 12 ills. by John Mills, Jr.; 7 ills. by W. R. MacAskill. Vol. LXXVII, pp. 591-622, May, 1940.

Tarxien (Temple), Malta:

Malta: The Halting Place of Nations: First Account of Remarkable Prehistoric Tombs and Temples Recently Unearthed on the Island. By William Arthur Griffiths. Vol. XXXVII, pp. 445-478, 35 ills., 1 third-page map, May, 1920.

Tashi-Cho-Jong (Monastery), Bhutan:

Castles in the Air—Experiences and Journeys in Unknown Bhutan. By John Claude White. Vol. XXV, pp. 365-455, 74 ills., 1 page map, Apr., 1914.

Tatars (People):

Young Russia: The Land of Unlimited Possibilities. By Gilbert H. Grosvenor. Vol. XXVI, pp. 421-520, 85 ills. in black and white, 17 ills. in color, Nov., 1914.

Tate, G. H. H.:

Through Brazil to the Summit of Mount Roraima. By G. H. H. Tate. Vol. LVIII, pp. 585-605, 24 ills., 1 half-page map, Nov., 1930.

Taurine World: Cattle and Their Place in the Human Scheme—Wild Types and Modern Breeds in Many Lands. By Alvin Howard Sanders. Vol. XLVIII, pp. 591-710, 76 ills. in black and white, 20 ills. in color, Dec., 1925.

Tautira, Tahiti, Society Islands:

Notes on Tahiti. By Harrison W. Smith. Vol. XXII, pp. 947-963, 17 ills., Oct., 1911.

Tauu Islands, Pacific Ocean:

American Pathfinders in the Pacific. By William H. Nicholas. Vol. LXXXIX, pp. 617-640, 17 ills., 1 two-page map, May, 1946.

Tayman, Nelson Grant:

Stilwell Road—Land Route to China. By Nelson Grant Tayman. Vol. LXXXVII, pp. 681-698, 18 ills., June, 1945.

Teaching of Geography. By Ralph S. Tarr. Vol. XIII, pp. 55-64, Feb., 1902.

Teaching of Physical Geography in Elementary Schools. By Richard E. Dodge. Vol. XI, pp. 470-475, Dec., 1900.

Teak (Trees):

Working Teak in the Burma Forests: The Sagacious Elephant Is Man's Ablest Ally in the Logging Industry of the Far East. By A. W. Smith. Vol. LVIII, pp. 239-256, 5 ills. in black and white, 15 ills. in color, Aug., 1930.

Technical Training Schools, U. S. Army Air Forces. *See* Army Air Forces Training Command.

Teddy (Ship):

Modern Saga of the Seas: The Narrative of a 17,000-Mile Cruise on a 40-Foot Sloop by the Author, His Wife, and a Baby, Born on the Voyage. By Erling Tambs. Vol. LX, pp. 645-688, 49 ills., 1 half-page map, Dec., 1931.

Tehran, Iran:

Iran in Wartime: Through Fabulous Persia, Hub of the Middle East, Americans, Britons, and Iranians Keep Sinews of War Moving to the Embattled Soviet Union. By John N. Greely. Vol. LXXXIV, pp. 129-156, 26 ills., 1 page map, Aug., 1943.

Modern Persia and Its Capital: And an Account of an Ascent of Mount Demavend, the Persian Olympus. By F. L. Bird. Vol. XXXIX, pp. 353-400, 47 ills., Apr., 1921.

Tehuantepec (Isthmus), Mexico:

In Honor of the Army and Aviation (Banquet). Vol. XXII, pp. 267-284, 1 ill., Mar., 1911.

Isthmus of Tehuantepec. By Herbert Corey. Vol. XLV, pp. 549-579, 25 ills., May, 1924.

Isthmus of Tehuantepec: The Bridge of the World's Commerce. By Helen Olsson-Seffer. Vol. XXI, pp. 991-1002, 6 ills., Dec., 1910.

Tehuelche Indians:

Indian Tribes of Southern Patagonia, Tierra del Fuego, and the Adjoining Islands. By J. B. Hatcher. Vol. XII, pp. 12-22, 4 ills., Jan., 1901.

Tejo (River), Portugal:

Lisbon, the City of the Friendly Bay. By Clifford Albion Tinker. Vol. XLII, pp. 504-552, 30 ills. in black and white, 16 ills. in color, 1 quarter-page map, Nov., 1922.

Tekes Valley, Sinkiang:

With the Nomads of Central Asia: A Summer's Sojourn in the Tekes Valley, Plateau Paradise of Mongol and Turkic Tribes. By Edward Murray. Vol. LXIX, pp. 1-57, 43 ills. in black and white, 26 ills. in color, 1 half-page map, Jan., 1936.

Tel Aviv, Palestine:

American Fighters Visit Bible Lands. By Maynard Owen Williams. With 23 ills. in color from natural-color photographs by the author. Vol. LXXXIX, pp. 311-340, 10 ills. in black and white, Mar., 1946.

Palestine Today. By Francis Chase, Jr. Vol. XC, pp. 501-516, 16 ills., Oct., 1946.

Telegraphy:

Building the Alaskan Telegraph System. By Capt. William Mitchell. Vol. XV, pp. 357-361, Sept., 1904.

Cape to Cairo Telegraph. Vol. XII, pp. 162-163, Apr., 1901.

Cape to Cairo Telegraph. Vol. XIII, pp. 76-77, Feb., 1902.

Telegraphy—*Continued*

Special Telegraphic Time Signal from the Naval Observatory. Vol. XV, pp. 411-415, Oct., 1904.

United States Government Telegraph and Cable Lines. Vol. XV, pp. 490-494, 3 page maps, Dec., 1904.

See also Cables.

Telephone:

Miracle of Talking by Telephone. By F. Barrows Colton. Vol. LXXII, pp. 395-433, 41 ills., Oct., 1937.

Prehistoric Telephone Days. By Alexander Graham Bell. Vol. XLI, pp. 223-241, 17 ills., Mar., 1922.

Voice Voyages by the National Geographic Society: A Tribute to the Geographical Achievements of the Telephone. Vol. XXIX, pp. 296-326, 15 ills., 1 chart, Mar., 1916.

World's Highest International Telephone Cable. Vol. LVIII, pp. 722-731, 8 ills., Dec., 1930.

Telescopes:

Exploring the Glories of the Firmament. By William Joseph Showalter. Vol. XXXVI. pp. 153-181, 17 ills., 3 charts, 1 diagram, Aug., 1919.

Television:

Your New World of Tomorrow. By F. Barrows Colton. Vol. LXXXVIII, pp. 385-410, 25 ills., Oct., 1945.

Tell el-Kheleifeh (Mound), Trans-Jordan:

On the Trail of King Solomon's Mines: The Bible, in Addition to Its Spiritual Values, Continues to Prove a Rich Geography and Guide to Exploration of the Holy Land. By Nelson Glueck. Vol. LXXXV, pp. 233-256, 20 ills., 1 page map, Feb., 1944.

Temple Mound Builders:

Indians of the Southeastern United States. By Matthew W. Stirling. Paintings by W. Langdon Kihn. Vol. LXXXIX, pp. 53-74, 8 ills. in black and white, 8 ills. in color, Jan., 1946.

Temples:

Chichen Itzá, an Ancient American Mecca: Recent Excavations in Yucatan Are Bringing to Light the Temples, Palaces, and Pyramids of America's Most Holy Native City. By Sylvanus Griswold Morley. Vol. XLVII, pp. 63-95, 34 ills., 1 half-page map, 1 diagram, Jan., 1925.

Excavations at Quirigua, Guatemala. By Sylvanus Griswold Morley. Vol. XXIV, pp. 339-361, 24 ills., 1 diagram, Mar., 1913.

Five Thousand Temples of Pagãn: Burma's Sacred City Is a Place of Enchantment in the Midst of Ruins. By William H. Roberts. Vol. LX, pp. 445-454, 9 ills., Oct., 1931.

"Glory That Was Greece." By Alexander Wilbourne Weddell. Vol. XLII, pp. 571-630, 51 ills., 1 three-quarters-page map, Dec., 1922.

Temples—*Continued*

Home of a Forgotten Race: Mysterious Chichen Itzá, in Yucatan, Mexico. By Edward H. Thompson. Vol. XXV, pp. 585-648, 59 ills., June, 1914.

Madura Temples. By J. S. Chandler. Vol. XIX, pp. 213-222, 4 ills., Mar., 1908.

Malta: The Halting Place of Nations: First Account of Remarkable Prehistoric Tombs and Temples Recently Unearthed on the Island. By William Arthur Griffiths. Vol. XXXVII, pp. 445-478, 35 ills., 1 third-page map, May, 1920.

Marble Dams of Rajputana. By Eleanor Maddock. Vol. XL, pp. 468-499, 13 ills. in black and white, 16 ills. in color, Nov., 1921.

Mysterious Temples of the Jungle: The Prehistoric ruins of Guatemala. By W. F. Sands. Vol. XXIV, pp. 324-338, 10 ills., Mar., 1913.

Peiping Panorama in Vivid Pigments. 16 ills. in color from camera paintings by H. C. and J. H. White, Deng Bao-ling, and Hwang Yao-tso. Vol. LXX, pp. 753-784, Dec., 1936.

Peiping's Happy New Year: Lunar Celebration Attracts Throngs to Temple Fairs, Motley Bazaars, and Age-old Festivities. By George Kin Leung. Vol. LXX, pp. 749-792, 31 ills. in black and white, 16 ills. in color, Dec., 1936.

Puto, the Enchanted Island. By Robert F. Fitch. Vol. LXXXIX, pp. 373-384, 11 ills., 1 third-page map, Mar., 1946.

Tai Shan, Sacred Mountain of the East (China). By Mary Augusta Mullikin. Vol. LXXXVII, pp. 699-719, 18 ills., 1 page map, June, 1945.

Temples and Ceremonies of Kaleidoscopic Bangkok. 12 ills. in color from natural-color photographs by Amos Burg, Gervais Courtellemont, and W. Robert Moore. Vol. LXV, pp. 547-554, May, 1934.

Temples of India. 54 ills. from photographs by W. M. Zumbro. Vol. XX, pp. 922-971, Nov., 1909.

See also Cave Temples.

Tempo and Color of a Great City (New York City). 42 ills. in color from natural-color photographs by Clifton Adams and Edwin L. Wisherd. Vol. LVIII, pp. 538-579, Nov., 1930.

Ten Thousand Smokes Now a National Monument: The President of the United States Sets Aside for the American People the Extraordinary Valley Discovered and Explored by the National Geographic Society. Vol. XXXV, pp. 359-366, 5 ills., Apr., 1919.

Ten Years in the Philippines. By William Howard Taft. Vol. XIX, pp. 141-148, Feb., 1908.

Ten Years of the Peary Arctic Club. By Herbert L. Bridgman. Vol. XIX, pp. 661-668, 3 ills., Sept., 1908.

Tennessee:

Highlights of the Volunteer State: Men and Industry in Tennessee Range from Pioneer Stages to Modern Machine Age. By Leonard Cornell Roy. Vol. LXXV, pp. 553-594, 20 ills. in black and white, 22 ills. in color, 1 map, May, 1939.

Home Folk Around Historic Cumberland Gap. By Leo A. Borah. Vol. LXXXIV, pp. 741-768, 25 ills., 1 quarter-page map, Dec., 1943.

Rambling Around the Roof of Eastern America (Great Smoky Mountains). By Leonard C. Roy. Vol. LXX, pp. 243-266, 25 ills., 1 page map, Aug., 1936.

Reelfoot—An Earthquake Lake. By Wilbur A. Nelson. Vol. XLV, pp. 95-114, 20 ills., Jan., 1924.

Tennessee Tableaux. 22 ills. in color from natural-color photographs; 19 ills. by J. Baylor Roberts. Vol. LXXV, pp. 569-592, May, 1939.

Tennessee (Battleship):

Victory's Portrait in the Marianas. By Lt. William Franklin Draper, USNR. With 17 ills. in color from paintings by the author. Vol. LXXXVIII, pp. 599-616, Nov., 1945.

Tēnos (Island), Aegean Sea:

Isles of Greece. By Lt. Richard Stillwell, USNR. Vol. LXXXV, pp. 593-622, 11 ills. in black and white, 20 ills. in color, 1 page map, May, 1944.

Ter Goes, Netherlands. *See* Goes.

Terceira (Island), Azores:

American Airmen in the Azores. 10 ills. in color from natural-color photographs. Vol. LXXXIX, pp. 177-184, Feb., 1946.

Termination Land (Antarctica). By Edwin Swift Balch. Vol. XV, pp. 220-221, May, 1904.

Terns (Birds):

Fairy Terns of the Atolls. By Lewis Wayne Walker. Vol. XC, pp. 807-814, 9 ills., Dec., 1946.

Pelican Profiles. By Lewis Wayne Walker. Vol. LXXXIV, pp. 589-598, 5 ills. in black and white, 8 ills. in color, Nov., 1943.
Contains information on the Gull-billed Tern of the Salton Sea Area, California.

Terra, Hellmut de:

On the World's Highest Plateaus: Through an Asiatic No Man's Land to the Desert of Ancient Cathay. By Hellmut de Terra. Vol. LIX, pp. 319-367, 39 ills. in black and white, 32 ills. in color, 1 two-thirds-page map, Mar., 1931.

Terrestrial Magnetism. *See* Geomagnetism.

Terriers:

Dogs in Toyland. 16 ills. in color from natural-color photographs by Willard R. Culver. Vol. LXXXV, pp. 473-480, Apr., 1944.

Terriers—*Continued*

Gallant Little Sportsmen of the Terrier Tribe. 33 portraits in color from paintings by Edward Herbert Miner. Vol. LXIX, pp. 253-268, Feb., 1936.

Man's Oldest Ally, the Dog: Since Cave-Dweller Days This Faithful Friend Has Shared the Work, Exploration, and Sport of Humankind. By Freeman Lloyd. Paintings by Edward Herbert Miner. Vol. LXIX, pp. 247-274, 13 ills. in black and white, 33 portraits in color, Feb., 1936.
Contains descriptions and illustrations of the following breeds: Airedale Terrier, Bedlington Terrier, Bull Terrier, Cairn Terrier, Dandie Dinmont Terrier, Irish Terrier, Kerry Blue Terrier, Lakeland Terrier, Manchester Terrier, Miniature Schnauzer, Scottish Terrier, Sealyham Terrier, Skye Terrier, Smooth Fox Terrier, Standard Schnauzer, Welsh Terrier, West Highland White Terrier, and Wire-haired Fox Terrier.

Toy Dogs, Pets of Kings and Commoners. By Freeman Lloyd. Vol. LXXXV, pp. 459-480, 8 ills. in black and white, 16 ills. in color, Apr., 1944.

Testing of Arctic Currents. Vol. XII, p. 404, Nov., 1901.

Testing the Currents of Lake Erie. By E. L. Moseley. Vol. XIV, pp. 41-42, Jan., 1903.

Tetrahedral Kites:

Aërial Locomotion: With a Few Notes of Progress in the Construction of an Aërodrome. By Alexander Graham Bell. Vol. XVIII, pp. 1-34, 36 ills., Jan., 1907.

The Tetrahedral Kite. Vol. XIV, p. 294, 1 ill., July, 1903.

The Tetrahedral Principle in Kite Structure. By Alexander Graham Bell. Vol. XIV, pp. 219-251, 79 ills., 15 diagrams, June, 1903.

Tetrahedral Tower:

Dr. Bell's Tetrahedral Tower. By Gilbert H. Grosvenor. Vol. XVIII, pp. 672-675, 7 ills., Oct., 1907.

Texan Teaches American History at Cambridge University. By J. Frank Dobie. Vol. LXXXIX, pp. 409-441, 9 ills. in black and white, 19 ills. in color, Apr., 1946.

Texas:

Along Our Side of the Mexican Border. By Frederick Simpich. Vol. XXXVIII, pp. 61-80, 9 ills., 1 quarter-page map, July, 1920.

Boundaries of Territorial Acquisitions. Vol. XII, pp. 373-377, 1 page chart, Oct., 1901.

Down the Rio Grande: Tracing this Strange, Turbulent Stream on Its Long Course from Colorado to the Gulf of Mexico. By Frederick Simpich. Vol. LXXVI, pp. 415-462, 28 ills. in black and white, 24 ills. in color, 6 maps, Oct., 1939.

Expedition into Texas of Fernando del Bosque, Standard-Bearer of the King, Don Carlos II, in the Year 1675. Translated from an Old, Unpublished Spanish Manuscript. By Betty B. Brewster. Vol. XIV, pp. 339-348, Sept., 1903.

Texas—*Continued*

Gulf Coast Towns Get into the Fight. 19 ills. in color from natural-color photographs; 17 ills. by J. Baylor Roberts. Vol. LXXXV, pp. 17-40, Jan., 1944.

How We Use the Gulf of Mexico. By Frederick Simpich. Vol. LXXXV, pp. 1-40, 20 ills. in black and white, 19 ills. in color, 1 two-page map (two-page spread), Jan., 1944.

Hurricanes on the Coast of Texas. By Maj. Gen. A. W. Greely. Vol. XI, pp. 442-445, Nov., 1900.

Lessons of Galveston. By W J McGee. Vol. XI, pp. 377-383, Oct., 1900.

Lost Boundary of Texas. By Marcus Baker. Vol. XII, pp. 430-432, Dec., 1901.

Oil Fields of Texas and California. Vol. XII, pp. 276-278, July, 1901.

Riatas and Romance on the Rio Grande. 24 ills. in color from natural-color photographs; 23 ills. by Luis Marden. Vol. LXXVI, pp. 431-462, Oct., 1939.

Rio Grande Cornucopia Under a Winter Sun. 24 ills. in color from natural-color photographs by B. Anthony Stewart. Vol. LXXV, pp. 65-96, Jan., 1939.

So Big Texas. By Frederick Simpich. Vol. LIII, pp. 637-693, 72 ills., 1 two-page map, June, 1928.

Texas, Our Largest State. By N. H. Darton. Vol. XXIV, pp. 1330-1360, 22 ills., 2 half-page maps, Dec., 1913.

Texas Delta of an American Nile: Orchards and Gardens Replace Thorny Jungle in the Southmost Tip of the Lone Star State. By McFall Kerbey. Vol. LXXV, pp. 51-96, 27 ills. in black and white, 24 ills. in color, 1 page map, Jan., 1939.

Wandering Islands in the Rio Grande. By Mrs. Albert S. Burleson. Vol. XXIV, pp. 381-386, 2 ills., 1 three-quarters-page map, Mar., 1913.

Yield of Texas. By Frederick Simpich. Vol. LXXXVII, pp. 163-184, 15 ills., 1 two-page map, Feb., 1945.

Textiles:

Chemists Make a New World: Creating Hitherto Unknown Raw Materials, Science Now Disrupts Old Trade Routes and Revamps the World Map of Industry. By Frederick Simpich. Vol. LXXVI, pp. 601-640, 22 ills. in black and white, 26 ills. in color, Nov., 1939.

From Nature's Hidden Building Blocks. 26 ills. in color from natural-color photographs by Willard R. Culver. Vol. LXXVI, pp. 609-640, Nov., 1939.

Thaelmann Collective Farm, U. S. S. R. *See* Ernst Thaelmann (Collective Farm).

Thailand. *See* Siam.

Thames (River), England:

Thames, England's Gateway to the World. 10 ills. in color from natural-color photographs by B. Anthony Stewart. Vol. LXXV, pp. 253-260, Feb., 1939.

Thames (River), England—*Continued*

Through the Heart of England in a Canadian Canoe. By R. J. Evans. Vol. XLI, pp. 473-497, 26 ills., 1 half-page map, May, 1922.

Time and Tide on the Thames. By Frederick Simpich. Vol. LXXV, pp. 239-272, 23 ills. in black and white, 10 ills. in color, 1 map, Feb., 1939.

Thaw, Lawrence Copley:

Africa on Parade. 14 ills. in color from natural-color photographs by Lawrence Thaw. Vol. LXXIV, pp. 343-350, Sept., 1938.

Along the Old Silk Routes: A Motor Caravan with Air-conditioned Trailer Retraces Ancient Roads from Paris across Europe and Half of Asia to Delhi. By Lawrence Copley Thaw and Margaret S. Thaw. Vol. LXXVIII, pp. 453-486, 33 ills., 1 map, Oct., 1940.

In the Realms of the Maharajas. By Lawrence Copley Thaw and Margaret S. Thaw. Vol. LXXVIII, pp. 727-780, 14 ills. in black and white, 40 ills. in color, 1 page map, Dec., 1940.

Princely India, Resplendent with Jewels and Gold. 40 ills. in color from natural-color photographs by Lawrence Copley Thaw. Vol. LXXVIII, pp. 733-780, Dec., 1940.

Trans-Africa Safari: A Motor Caravan Rolls Across Sahara and Jungle Through Realms of Dusky Potentates and the Land of Big-Lipped Women. By Lawrence Copley Thaw and Margaret Stout Thaw. Vol. LXXIV, pp. 327-364, 29 ills. in black and white, 14 ills. in color, 1 two-thirds-page map, Sept., 1938.

Thaw, Margaret S.:

Along the Old Silk Routes: A Motor Caravan with Air-conditioned Trailer Retraces Ancient Roads from Paris across Europe and Half of Asia to Delhi. By Lawrence Copley Thaw and Margaret S. Thaw. Vol. LXXVIII, pp. 453-486, 33 ills., 1 map, Oct., 1940.

In the Realms of the Maharajas. By Lawrence Copley Thaw and Margaret S. Thaw. Vol. LXXVIII, pp. 727-780, 14 ills. in black and white, 40 ills. in color, 1 page map, Dec., 1940.

Trans-Africa Safari: A Motor Caravan Rolls Across Sahara and Jungle Through Realms of Dusky Potentates and the Land of Big-Lipped Women. By Lawrence Copley Thaw and Margaret Stout Thaw. Vol. LXXIV, pp. 327-364, 29 ills. in black and white, 14 ills. in color, 1 two-thirds-page map, Sept., 1938.

Thebes, Egypt:

Reconstructing Egypt's History. By Wallace N. Stearns. Vol. XXIV, pp. 1021-1042, 21 ills., Sept., 1913.

Resurrection of Ancient Egypt. By James Baikie. Vol. XXIV, pp. 957-1020, 46 ills., 1 page map, Sept., 1913.

Their Monument Is in Our Hearts: Address by M. Viviani Before the Tomb of Washington, at Mount Vernon, April 29, 1917. Vol. XXXI, p. 367, Apr., 1917.

Theories of Volcanic Action. Vol. XIV, pp. 110-111, Mar., 1903.

Thēra (Island), Aegean Sea. *See* Santorin.

Thermopylae (Pass), Greece:

"Glory That Was Greece." By Alexander Wilbourne Weddell. Vol. XLII, pp. 571-630, 51 ills., 1 three-quarters-page map, Dec., 1922.

These Missourians. By Frederick Simpich. Vol. LXXXIX, pp. 277-310, 12 ills. in black and white, 22 ills. in color, 1 map (two-page spread), Mar., 1946.

Thessaly (Division), Greece:

With the Monks at Meteora : The Monasteries of Thessaly. By Elizabeth Perkins. Vol. XX, pp. 799-807, 5 ills., Sept., 1909.

They Survived at Sea. By Lt. Comdr. Samuel F. Harby. Vol. LXXXVII, pp. 617-640, 22 ills., May, 1945.

They Sustain the Wings (Ground Crews). By Frederick Simpich. Vol. LXXXIV, pp. 333-354, 19 ills., Sept., 1943.

38th Engineers, U. S. Army:

Ascension Island, an Engineering Victory. By Lt. Col. Frederick J. Clarke. Vol. LXXXV, pp. 623-640, 21 ills., May, 1944.

This Giant That Is New York. By Frederick Simpich. Vol. LVIII, pp. 517-583, 26 ills. in black and white, 8 ills. in gravure, 42 ills. in color, Nov., 1930.

This Is My Own : How the United States Seems to a Citizen Soldier Back from Three Years Overseas. By Frederick G. Vosburgh. Vol. LXXXIX, pp. 113-128, 14 ills., Jan., 1946.

This Was Austria. 18 ills. from photographs. Vol. LXXXVIII, pp. 71-86, July, 1945.

Thomason, (Maj.) John W., Jr.:

Approach to Peiping. By Maj. John W. Thomason, Jr. Vol. LXIX, pp. 275-308, 24 ills., 1 page map, Feb., 1936.

Thompson, Edward H.:

Henequen—The Yucatan Fiber. By Edward H. Thompson. Vol. XIV, pp. 150-158, 6 ills., Apr., 1903.

Home of a Forgotten Race : Mysterious Chichen Itzá, in Yucatan, Mexico. By Edward H. Thompson. Vol. XXV, pp. 585-648, 59 ills., June, 1914.

Thomson, J. P.:

Islands of the Pacific. By J. P. Thomson. Vol. XL, pp. 543-558, 15 ills., special map supplement, Dec., 1921.

Thoreau, Henry David:

Winter Rambles in Thoreau's Country. By Herbert W. Gleason. Vol. XXXVII, pp. 165-180, 15 ills., Feb., 1920.

Thorndike, Townsend W.:

Game and Fur-Bearing Animals and Their Influence on the Indians of the Northwest. By Townsend W. Thorndike. Vol. XV, p. 431, Oct., 1904.

Thousand Miles Along the Great Wall of China : The Mightiest Barrier Ever Built by Man Has Stood Guard Over the Land of Chin for Twenty Centuries. By Adam Warwick. Vol. XLIII, pp. 113-143, 27 ills., panorama, 1 page and 1 half-page maps, Feb., 1923.

Thrashers (Birds) :

Some Songsters and Flyers of Wide Repute. 42 portraits in color from paintings by Maj. Allan Brooks. Vol. LXIX, pp. 529-544, Apr., 1936.

Thrushes, Thrashers, and Swallows : Robins and Bluebirds are Familiar Members of a Famous Musical Family Which Includes the Hermit Thrush and European Nightingale. By T. Gilbert Pearson. Paintings by Maj. Allan Brooks. Vol. LXIX, pp. 523-546, 6 ills. in black and white, 42 paintings from life, Apr., 1936.

Three Drawings of the World War. 3 ills. from drawings by Lucien Jonas. Vol. XXXIII, pp. 355-357, Apr., 1918.

Three Old Ports on the Spanish Main. By G. M. L. Brown. Vol. XVII, pp. 622-638, 12 ills., Nov., 1906.

Three Sisters (Peaks), Oregon:

Scenes Among the High Cascades in Central Oregon. By Ira A. Williams. Vol. XXIII, pp. 578-592, 11 ills., June, 1912.

Three-Wheeling Through Africa : Two Adventurers Cross the So-Called Dark Continent North of Lake Chad on Motorcycles with Side Cars. By James C. Wilson. Vol. LXV, pp. 37-92, 64 ills., 1 two-page map, Jan., 1934.

Through Brazil to the Summit of Mount Roraima. By G. H. H. Tate. Vol. LVIII, pp. 585-605, 24 ills., 1 half-page map, Nov., 1930.

Through Franz Josef Land. Vol. X, p. 362, Sept., 1899.

Through Java in Pursuit of Color. By W. Robert Moore. Vol. LVI, pp. 333-362, 9 ills. in black and white, 29 ills. in color, 1 third-page map, Sept., 1929.

Through Paraguay and Southern Matto Grosso. By Sir Christopher H. Gibson. Vol. LXXXIV, pp. 459-488, 20 ills. in black and white, 11 ills. in color, 1 two-thirds-page map, Oct., 1943.

Through the Back Doors of Belgium : Artist and Author Paddle for Three Weeks Along 200 Miles of Low-Countries Canals in a Canadian Canoe. By Melville Chater. Vol. XLVII, pp. 499-540, 39 ills., 1 half-page map, May, 1925.

Through the Back Doors of France : A Seven Weeks' Voyage in a Canadian Canoe from St. Malo, Through Brittany and the Château Country, to Paris. By Melville Chater. Vol. XLIV, pp. 1-51, 55 ills., 1 half-page map, July, 1923.

Through the Deserts and Jungles of Africa by Motor: Caterpillar Cars Make 15,000-Mile Trip from Algeria to Madagascar in Nine Months. By Georges-Marie Haardt. Vol. XLIX, pp. 651-720, 95 ills., 1 two-thirds-page map, June, 1926.

Through the English Lake District Afoot and Awheel. By Ralph A. Graves. Vol. LV, pp. 577-603, 19 ills. in black and white, 15 ills. in color, 1 quarter-page map, May, 1929.

Through the Great River Trenches of Asia: National Geographic Society Explorer Follows the Yangtze, Mekong, and Salwin Through Mighty Gorges, Some of Whose Canyon Walls Tower to a Height of More Than Two Miles. By Joseph F. Rock. Vol. L, pp. 133-186, 47 ills., 1 half-page map, Aug., 1926.

Through the Heart of England in a Canadian Canoe. By R. J. Evans. Vol. XLI, pp. 473-497, 26 ills., 1 half-page map, May, 1922.

Through the Heart of Hindustan: A Teeming Highway Extending for Fifteen Hundred Miles, from the Khyber Pass to Calcutta. By Maynard Owen Williams. Vol. XL, pp. 433-467, 29 ills., Nov., 1921.

Thrushes (Birds):

Some Songsters and Flyers of Wide Repute. 42 portraits in color from paintings by Maj. Allan Brooks. Vol. LXIX, pp. 529-544, Apr., 1936.

Thrushes, Thrashers, and Swallows: Robins and Bluebirds are Familiar Members of a Famous Musical Family Which Includes the Hermit Thrush and European Nightingale. By T. Gilbert Pearson. Paintings by Maj. Allan Brooks. Vol. LXIX, pp. 523-546, 6 ills. in black and white, 42 paintings from life, Apr., 1936.

Thurber, (Lt.) H. R.:

Collarin' Cape Cod (Massachusetts): Experiences on Board a U. S. Navy Destroyer in a Wild Winter Storm. By Lieut. H. R. Thurber. Vol. XLVIII, pp. 427-472, 46 ills., Oct., 1925.

Tiahuanacu, Bolivia:

Heart of Aymará Land: A Visit to Tiahuanacu, Perhaps the Oldest City of the New World, Lost Beneath the Drifting Sand of Centuries in the Bolivian Highlands. By Stewart E. McMillin. Vol. LI, pp. 213-256, 23 ills. in black and white, 18 ills. in color, 1 half-page map, Feb., 1927.

Some Wonderful Sights in the Andean Highlands: The Oldest City in America. Sailing on the Lake of the Clouds: The Yosemite of Peru. By Harriet Chalmers Adams. Vol. XIX, pp. 597-618, 19 ills., 1 half-page map, Sept., 1908.

Tibet:

Across Tibet from India to China. By Lt. Col. Ilia Tolstoy. Vol. XC, pp. 169-222, 41 ills., 1 half-page map, Aug., 1946.

Crosby Expedition to Tibet. Vol. XV, pp. 228-231, 3 ills., May, 1904.

Tibet—Continued

Life Among the People of Eastern Tibet. By Dr. A. L. Shelton. Vol. XL, pp. 293-326, 35 ills., 1 half-page map, Sept., 1921.

Sky-high in Lama Land. 12 ills. from photographs by C. Suydam Cutting. Vol. XC, pp. 185-196, Aug., 1946.

Sven Hedin in Tibet. Vol. XIII, pp. 96-97, Mar., 1902.

The Tsangpo (Matsang). By James Mascarene Hubbard. Vol. XII, pp. 32-35, Jan., 1901.

See also Lhasa.

Tibetan Highland:

Climbing Mighty Minya Konka: Americans First Scaled Mountain That Now Is Landmark of China's New Skyway. By Richard L. Burdsall and Terris Moore. Vol. LXXXIII, pp. 625-650, 23 ills., 1 page map, May, 1943.

Tibetans:

Demon-Possessed Tibetans and Their Incredible Feats. 12 ills. in color from natural-color photographs. Vol. LXVIII, pp. 470-486, Oct., 1935.

Exploring a Grass Wonderland of Wild West China. By Ray G. Johnson. Vol. LXXXV, pp. 713-742, 24 ills., 1 half-page map, June, 1944.

Life Among the People of Eastern Tibet. By Dr. A. L. Shelton. Vol. XL, pp. 293-326, 35 ills., 1 half-page map, Sept., 1921.

Sungmas, the Living Oracles of the Tibetan Church. By Joseph F. Rock. Vol. LXVIII, pp. 475-486, 1 ill. in black and white, 12 ills. in color, Oct., 1935.

Tiburon (Island), Mexico:

Mexican Land of Canaan: Marvelous Riches of the Wonderful West Coast of Our Neighbor Republic. By Frederick Simpich. Vol. XXXVI, pp. 307-330, 16 ills., 1 page map, Oct., 1919.

Tides and Tidal Waves:

Charting a World at War. By William H. Nicholas. Vol. LXXXVI, pp. 617-640, 23 ills., 1 drawing, Nov., 1944.

Cotidal Lines for the World. By R. A. Harris. Vol. XVII, pp. 303-309, 2 page and 1 half-page maps, special map supplement, June, 1906.

Lessons of Galveston. By W J McGee. Vol. XI, pp. 377-383, Oct., 1900.

Our Guardians on the Deep. By William Joseph Showalter. Vol. XXV, pp. 655-677, 15 ills., 1 chart, June, 1914.

Some Personal Experiences with Earthquakes (Arica). By Rear Adm. L. G. Billings. Vol. XXVII, pp. 57-71, 7 ills., Jan., 1915.

Tides in the Bay of Fundy. Vol. XVI, pp. 71-76, 4 ills., Feb., 1905.

Tides of Chesapeake Bay. By E. D. Preston. Vol. X, pp. 391-392, Oct., 1899.

World's Most Cruel Earthquake (Messina). By Charles W. Wright. Vol. XX, pp. 373-396, 22 ills., 1 page and 1 three-quarters-page maps, Apr., 1909.

Tidewater Virginia, Where History Lives. By Albert W. Atwood. Vol. LXXXI, pp. 617-656, 18 ills. in black and white, 20 ills. in color, 1 page map, May, 1942.

Tierra del Fuego (Archipelago), South America :

Indian Tribes of Southern Patagonia, Tierra del Fuego, and the Adjoining Islands. By J. B. Hatcher. Vol. XII, pp. 12-22, 4 ills., Jan., 1901.

Inside Cape Horn. By Amos Burg. Vol. LXXII, pp. 743-783, 29 ills. in black and white, 10 ills. in color, 1 two-page map, Dec., 1937.

Land of the Horn, America's Tiptoe. 10 ills. in color from natural-color photographs by Amos Burg. Vol. LXXII, pp. 751-758, Dec., 1937.

Longitudinal Journey Through Chile. By Harriet Chalmers Adams. Vol. XLII, pp. 219-373, 60 ills., 1 half-page map, Sept., 1922.

Ties That Bind : Our Natural Sympathy with English Traditions, the French Republic, and the Russian Outburst for Liberty. By John Sharp Williams. Vol. XXXI, pp. 281-286, 4 ills., Mar., 1917.

Tiflis, Georgian Soviet Socialist Republic :

Land of the Stalking Death : A Journey Through Starving Armenia on an American Relief Train. By Melville Chater. Vol. XXXVI, pp. 393-420, 23 ills., Nov., 1919.

Tigara, Alaska :

Discovering Alaska's Oldest Arctic Town : A Scientist Finds Ivory-eyed Skeletons of a Mysterious People and Joins Modern Eskimos in the Dangerous Spring Whale Hunt. By Froelich G. Rainey. Vol. LXXXII, pp. 319-336, 15 ills., Sept., 1942.

Tiger-Hunting in India. By Brig. Gen. William Mitchell. Vol. XLVI, pp. 545-598, 46 ills., 1 quarter-page map, Nov., 1924.

Tigers:

King of Cats and His Court. By Victor H. Cahalane. Paintings by Walter A. Weber. Vol. LXXXIII, pp. 217-259, 9 ills. in black and white, 20 ills. in color, Feb., 1943.

Tiger-Hunting in India. By Brig. Gen. William Mitchell. Vol. XLVI, pp. 545-598, 46 ills., 1 quarter-page map, Nov., 1924.

Warfare of the Jungle Folk : Campaigning Against Tigers, Elephants, and Other Wild Animals in Northern Siam. By Merian C. Cooper. Photographs by Ernest B. Schoedsack. Vol. LIII, pp. 233-268, 33 ills., Feb., 1928.

Tigris (River), Iraq :

Cradle of Civilization : The Historic Lands Along The Euphrates and Tigris Rivers Where Briton Is Fighting Turk. By James Baikie. Vol. XXIX, pp. 127-162, 25 ills., Feb., 1916.

Where Adam and Eve Lived (Baghdad). By Frederick and Margaret Simpich. Vol. XXVI, pp. 546-588, 35 ills., Dec., 1914.

Timber. *See* Forests and Forestry.

Timberlines. Vol. XIV, pp. 80-81, Feb., 1903.

Timberlines. By Israel C. Russell. Vol. XV, pp. 47-49, Jan., 1904.

Timbuktu (Tombouctou), French Sudan :

Timbuktu, in the Sands of the Sahara. By Capt. Cecil D. Priest. Vol. XLV, pp. 73-85, 16 ills., Jan., 1924.

Timbuktu and Beyond : Desert City of Romantic Savor and Salt Emerges into World Life Again as Trading Post of France's Vast African Empire. By Laura C. Boulton. Vol. LXXIX, pp. 631-670, 18 ills. in black and white, 26 ills. in color, 1 map (two-page spread), May, 1941.

Time and Tide on the Thames (England). By Frederick Simpich. Vol. LXXV, pp. 239-272, 23 ills. in black and white, 10 ills. in color, 1 map, Feb., 1939.

"Time Will not Dim the Glory of Their Deeds" (World War Memorials). 11 ills. in color from natural-color photographs by W. Robert Moore. Vol. LXV, pp. 17-24, Jan., 1934.

Timeless Arans : The Workaday World Lies Beyond the Horizon of Three Rocky Islets Off the Irish Coast. By Robert Cushman Murphy. Vol. LIX, pp. 747-775, 35 ills., 1 quarter-page map, June, 1931.

Time's Footprints in Tunisian Sands. By Maynard Owen Williams. Vol. LXXI, pp. 345-386, 43 ills., 1 page and 1 half-page maps, Mar., 1937.

Timor a Key to the Indies. By Stuart St. Clair. Vol. LXXXIV, pp. 355-384, 33 ills., 1 third-page map, Sept., 1943.

Tin:

Bolivia—Tin Roof of the Andes. By Henry Albert Phillips. Vol. LXXXIII, pp. 309-332, 5 ills. in black and white, 20 ills. in color, Mar., 1943.

Tin, the Cinderella Metal. By Alicia O'Reardon Overbeck. Vol. LXXVIII, pp. 659-684, 24 ills., Nov., 1940.

Tinajas Altas (Water Basins). *See* Yuma Trail.

Tingmissartoq (Seaplane) :

Flying Around the North Atlantic. By Anne Morrow Lindbergh. Foreword by Charles A. Lindbergh. Vol. LXVI, pp. 259-337, 82 ills., 1 two-page and 1 two-thirds-page maps, Sept., 1934.

Tinian (Island), Marianas Islands :

Saipan and Tinian, Take-offs to Tokyo. 17 ills. in color from natural-color photographs ; 15 ills. by W. Robert Moore. Vol. LXXXVII, pp. 453-468, Apr., 1945.

South from Saipan. By W. Robert Moore. Vol. LXXXVII, pp. 441-474, 11 ills. in black and white, 17 ills. in color, 1 half-page map, Apr., 1945.

Springboards to Tokyo. By Willard Price. Vol. LXXXVI, pp. 385-407, 16 ills., Oct., 1944.

Tinker, Clifford Albion:

Lisbon, the City of the Friendly Bay. By Clifford Albion Tinker. Vol. XLII, pp. 504-552, 30 ills. in black and white, 16 ills. in color, 1 quarter-page map, Nov., 1922.

Tintagel, England :

Channel Ports—And Some Others. By Florence Craig Albrecht. Vol. XXVIII, pp. 1-55, 45 ills., July, 1915.

Tirnova, Bulgaria :

Tirnova, the City of Hanging Gardens. By Felix J. Koch. Vol. XVIII, pp. 632-640, 7 ills., Oct., 1907.

Tirol (Region). *See* Tyrol.

Tisdel, Edine Frances:

Guatemala, the Country of the Future. By Edine Frances Tisdel. Vol. XXI, pp. 596-624, 33 ills., 1 three-quarters-page map, July, 1910.

Titicaca (Lake), Bolivia-Peru :

Heart of Aymará Land : A Visit to Tiahuanacu, Perhaps the Oldest City of the New World, Lost Beneath the Drifting Sand of Centuries in the Bolivian Highlands. By Stewart E. McMillin. Vol. LI, pp. 213-256, 23 ills. in black and white, 18 ills. in color, 1 half-page map, Feb., 1927.

Some Wonderful Sights in the Andean Highlands : The Oldest City in America. Sailing on the Lake of the Clouds : The Yosemite of Peru. By Harriet Chalmers Adams. Vol. XIX, pp. 597-626, 19 ills., 1 half-page map, Sept., 1908.

Titmice (Birds) :

Winged Denizens of Woodland, Stream, and Marsh. By Alexander Wetmore. Paintings by Maj. Allan Brooks. Vol. LXV, pp. 577-596, 11 portraits in color, May, 1934.

Tittmann, O. H.:

Definite Location of Bouvet Island. By O. H. Tittmann. Vol. X, pp. 413-414, Oct., 1899.

Ketchikan. Vol. XVI, p. 508, 1 ill., Nov., 1905.

National Geographic Society (Speech by O. H. Tittmann). Vol. XXIII, pp. 273-298, 5 ills., Mar., 1912.

National Geographic Society (Election of O. H. Tittmann as President of the Society). Vol. XVII, p. 218, Feb., 1915.

Progress in Surveying the United States. By O. H. Tittmann. Vol. XVII, pp. 110-112, 1 ill., Feb., 1906.

United States Coast and Geodetic Survey. By O. H. Tittmann. Vol. XIV, pp. 1-9, Jan., 1903.

Tlapehuala, Mexico :

Down Mexico's Río Balsas. 9 ills. in color from natural-color photographs by John W. Webber, Kenneth Segerstrom, and Jack Breed. Vol. XC, pp. 257-264, Aug., 1946.

Tlingit (Indian Tribe) :

Indians of Our North Pacific Coast. By Matthew W. Stirling. Paintings by W. Langdon Kihn. Vol. LXXXVII, pp. 25-52, 3 ills. in black and white, 16 ills. in color, Jan., 1945.

Totem-pole Builders. 16 ills. in color from paintings by W. Langdon Kihn. Vol. LXXXVII, pp. 33-48, Jan., 1945.

To Bogotá and Back by Air : The Narrative of a 9,500-Mile Flight from Washington, Over Thirteen Latin-American Countries and Return, in the Single-Seater Airplane *Spirit of St. Louis.* By Col. Charles A. Lindbergh. Vol. LIII, pp. 529-601, 98 ills., 1 two-thirds-page map, May, 1928.

To-day on "The Yukon Trail of 1898." By Amos Burg. Vol. LVIII, pp. 85-126, 52 ills., 1 two-thirds-page map, July, 1930.

To Market in Guatemala. By Luis Marden. With 19 ills. in color from natural-color photographs by Giles Greville Healey and Charles S. Pineo. Vol. LXXXVIII, pp. 87-104, July, 1945.

To Seek the Unknown in the Arctic : United States Navy Fliers to Aid MacMillan Expedition Under the Auspices of the National Geographic Society in Exploring Vast Area. Vol. XLVII, pp. 673-675, 1 ill., 1 half-page map, June, 1925.

Toads:

Iridescent Beauty of Frogs and Toads. 14 ills. in color from paintings by Hashime Murayama. Vol. LXI, pp. 635-642, May, 1932.

Our Friend the Frog. By Doris M. Cochran. Vol. LXI, pp. 629-654, 16 ills. in black and white, 14 ills. in color, May, 1932.

Toba (Lake), Sumatra :

By Motor Through the East Coast and Batak Highlands of Sumatra. By Melvin A. Hall. Vol. XXXVII, pp. 68-102, 27 ills., Jan., 1920.

Tobacco Industry:

Cuba—The Sugar Mill of the Antilles. By William Joseph Showalter. Vol. XXXVIII, pp. 1-33, 24 ills., 1 page map, July, 1920.

Helping the Farmers. Vol. XV, pp. 82-85, 1 ill., Feb., 1905.

Tobien, Wilhelm:

Azores, Communications Hub of the Atlantic. 13 ills. in color from natural-color photographs by Wilhelm Tobien. Vol. LXVII, pp. 41-48, Jan., 1935.

Bulgaria : In the Shadow of Bulgarian Monasteries. 13 ills. in color from natural-color photographs by Wilhelm Tobien. Vol. LXII, pp. 202-211, Aug., 1932.

Bulgaria's Valley of Roses. 12 ills. in color from natural-color photographs by Wilhelm Tobien. Vol. LXII, pp. 186-195, Aug., 1932.

Canary Islands : Elysium for the Beauty-Seeking Traveler. 14 ills. in color from natural-color photographs by Wilhelm Tobien. Vol. LVII, pp. 630-639, May, 1930.

Canary Islands : In the Canary Islands, Where Streets Are Carpeted With Flowers. 13 ills. in color from natural-color photographs by Wilhelm Tobien. Vol. LVII, pp. 614-623, May, 1930.

Canary Islands : Scenes in the Fortunate Isles. 12 ills. in color from natural-color photographs by Wilhelm Tobien. Vol. LVII, pp. 598-607, May, 1930.

Tobien, Wilhelm—*Continued*

Frisian Islands, North : Demolishing Germany's North Sea Ramparts. 10 ills. in color from natural-color photographs by Wilhelm Tobien. Vol. XC, pp. 637-644, Nov., 1946.

Germany : Grimm's Fairyland in Northwestern Germany. 5 ills. in color from natural-color photographs by Wilhelm Tobien. Vol. LIX, pp. 640-649, May, 1931.

Germany : Life and Luster of Berlin. 24 ills. in color from natural-color photographs by Wilhelm Tobien and Hans Hildenbrand. Vol. LXXI, pp. 147-177, Feb., 1937.

Madeira : Mirrors of Madeira, Rock Garden of the Atlantic. 13 ills. in color from natural-color photographs by Wilhelm Tobien. Vol. LXVI, pp. 89-96, July, 1934.

Netherlands : Nooks and Bays Around the Zuider Zee. 11 ills. in color from natural-color photographs by Wilhelm Tobien. Vol. LXIV, pp. 301-308, Sept., 1933.

Netherlands : Tulip Time in the Netherlands. 9 ills. in color from natural-color photographs by Wilhelm Tobien. Vol. LXIV, pp. 325-332, Sept., 1933.

Romania : Palaces and Peasants in Rome's Old Colony. 14 ills. in color from natural-color photographs by Wilhelm Tobien. Vol. LXV, pp. 439-446, Apr., 1934.

Romania, Land of Color and Contrast. 15 ills. in color from natural-color photographs by Wilhelm Tobien. Vol. LXV, pp. 415-422, Apr., 1934.

Sweden : Types and Costumes of Old Sweden. 4 ills. in color from autochromes lumière by Wilhelm Tobien. Vol. LIV, pp. 424-441, Oct., 1928.

Today in the Feathered Serpent's City (Chichen Itzá). 25 ills. in color from natural-color photographs by Luis Marden. Vol. LXX, pp. 599-614, Nov., 1936.

Today in the Land of Penn and Franklin (Pennsylvania). 39 ills. in color from natural-color photographs by Edwin L. Wisherd. Vol. LXVIII, pp. 13-52, July, 1935.

Today on the China Coast. By John B. Powell. Vol. LXXXVII, pp. 217-238, 17 ills., 1 page map, Feb., 1945.

Today's Evidence of Grecian Glory. 22 ills. in color from natural-color photographs by B. Anthony Stewart. Vol. LXXVII, pp. 307-322, Mar., 1940.

Today's World Turns on Oil. By Frederick Simpich. Vol. LXXIX, pp. 703-748, 22 ills. in black and white, 2 drawings, 21 ills. in color, June, 1941.

Todd, Oliver J.:

Taming "Flood Dragons" Along China's Hwang Ho (River). By Oliver J. Todd. Vol. LXXXI, pp. 205-234, 26 ills., 1 half-page map, Feb., 1942.

Toilers of the Sky : Tenuous Clouds Perform the Mighty Task of Shaping the Earth and Sustaining Terrestrial Life. By McFall Kerbey. Vol. XLVIII, pp. 163-189, 33 ills., Aug., 1925.

Tokyo, Japan :

Behind the Mask of Modern Japan. By Willard Price. Vol. LXXXVIII, pp. 513-535, 14 ills., Nov., 1945.

Japan, Child of the World's Old Age : An Empire of Mountainous Islands, Whose Alert People Constantly Conquer Harsh Forces of Land, Sea, and Sky. By William Elliott Griffis. Vol. LXIII, pp. 257-301, 37 ills. in black and white, 12 ills. in color, Mar., 1933.

Life and Color Under the Rising Sun. 4 ills. in color from natural-color photographs by W. Robert Moore and Kiyoshi Sakamoto. Vol. LXIII, pp. 288-297, Mar., 1933.

Sakurajima, Japan's Greatest Volcanic Eruption : A Convulsion of Nature Whose Ravages Were Minimized by Scientific Knowledge, Compared with the Terrors and Destruction of the Recent Tokyo Earthquake. By Dr. Thomas Augustus Jaggar. Vol. XLV, pp. 441-470, 32 ills., 1 half-page map, Apr., 1924.

South from Saipan. By W. Robert Moore. Vol. LXXXVII, pp. 441-474, 11 ills. in black and white, 17 ills. in color, 1 half-page map, Apr., 1945.

　　Contains a two-page aerial photograph of Tokyo.

Sunset in the East. By Blair A. Walliser. Vol. LXXXIX, pp. 797-812, 17 ills., June, 1946.

Tokyo To-day. By William R. Castle, Jr. Vol. LXI, pp. 131-162, 33 ills., Feb., 1932.

Tolstoy, (Lt. Col.) Ilia:

Across Tibet from India to China. By Lt. Col. Ilia Tolstoy, AUS. Vol. XC, pp. 169-222, 41 ills., 1 half-page map, Aug., 1946.

Toltecs (Indians) :

Interesting Visit to the Ancient Pyramids of San Juan Teotihuacan. By A. C. Galloway. Vol. XXI, pp. 1041-1050, 8 ills., 1 page map, Dec., 1910.

Luster of Ancient Mexico. By William H. Prescott. Vol. XXX, pp. 1-32, 22 ills., July, 1916.

Tombouctou, French Sudan. *See* Timbuktu.

Tombs:

At the Tomb of Tutankhamen : An Account of the Opening of the Royal Egyptian Sepulcher Which Contained the Most Remarkable Funeral Treasures Unearthed in Historic Times. By Maynard Owen Williams. Vol. XLIII, pp. 461-508, 53 ills., 1 half-page map, May, 1923.

China's Treasures. By Frederick McCormick. Vol. XXIII, pp. 996-1040, 50 ills., Oct., 1912.

Malta : The Halting Place of Nations : First Account of Remarkable Prehistoric Tombs and Temples Recently Unearthed on the Island. By William Arthur Griffiths. Vol. XXXVII, pp. 445-478, 35 ills., 1 third-page map, May, 1920.

Monte Albán, Richest Archeological Find in America : A Tomb in Oaxaca, Mexico, Yields Treasures Which Reveal the Splendid Culture of the Mixtecs. By Dr. Alfonso Caso. Vol. LXII, pp. 487-512, 28 ills., Oct., 1932.

Tombs—_Continued_

Mukden, the Manchu Home, and Its Great Art Museum. By Eliza R. Scidmore. Vol. XXI, pp. 289-320, 30 ills., Apr., 1910.

Secrets from Syrian Hills: Explorations Reveal World's Earliest Known Alphabet, Deciphered from Schoolboy Slates and Dictionaries of 3,000 Years Ago. By Claude F. A. Schaeffer. Vol. LXIV, pp. 97-126, 40 ills., 1 third-page map, July, 1933.

See also Taj Mahal.

Tomsk, Siberia, U. S. S. R.:

Western Siberia and the Altai Mountains: With Some Speculations on the Future of Siberia. By James Bryce. Vol. XXXIX, pp. 469-507, 39 ills., May, 1921.

Tondorf, (Rev.) Francis A.:

How the Earth Telegraphed Its Tokyo Quake to Washington. By Rev. Francis A. Tondorf. Vol. XLIV, pp. 453-454, 1 ill., Oct., 1923.

Tonga Islands, Pacific Ocean:

Dream Ship: The Story of a Voyage of Adventure More Than Half Around the World in a 47-Foot Lifeboat. By Ralph Stock. Vol. XXXIX, pp. 1-52, 43 ills., 1 page map, Jan., 1921.

Falcon, the Pacific's Newest Island. By J. Edward Hoffmeister and Harry S. Ladd. Vol. LIV, pp. 757-766, 8 ills., 1 half-page map, Dec., 1928.

Living on a Volcano: An Unspoiled Patch of Polynesia Is Niuafoō, Nicknamed "Tin Can Island" by Stamp Collectors. By Thomas A. Jaggar. Vol. LXVIII, pp. 91-100, 17 ills., 1 half-page map, July, 1935.

Tongareva Island (Penrhyn), Pacific Ocean:

On the Bottom of a South Sea Pearl Lagoon. By Roy Waldo Miner. Vol. LXXIV, pp. 365-390, 17 ills. in black and white, 8 ills. in color, Sept., 1938.

Sailing the Seven Seas in the Interest of Science: Adventures Through 157,000 Miles of Storm and Calm, from Arctic to Antarctic and Around the World, in the Non-Magnetic Yacht _Carnegie._ By J. P. Ault. Vol. XLII, pp. 631-690, 47 ills., 1 chart, Dec., 1922.

Tongsa Jong (Fort), Bhutan:

Castles in the Air—Experiences and Journeys in Unknown Bhutan. By John Claude White. Vol. XXV, pp. 365-455, 74 ills., 1 page map, Apr., 1914.

Tonkin, French Indo-China:

Along the Old Mandarin Road of Indo-China. By W. Robert Moore. Vol. LX, pp. 157-199, 32 ills. in black and white, 28 ills. in color, 1 quarter-page map, Aug., 1931.

Toogood, Stanley:

Southampton—Gateway to London: The Port of Double Tides Where the "Mayflower" Moored is Rich in Sea History and Lore of Early England. By Stanley Toogood. Vol. LXXVII, pp. 91-114, 21 ills., 1 map, Jan., 1940.

Topographic Work of the United States Geological Survey in 1902. Vol. XIII, pp. 326-328, Aug., 1902.

Tops:

Primitive Gyroscope in Liberia. By G. N. Collins. Vol. XXI, pp. 531-535, 3 ills., June, 1910.

Toradja (Tribe):

Life and Death in Toradjaland (Celebes). 22 ills. from photographs; 11 ills. by Maynard Owen Williams; 8 ills. by Helene Fischer. Vol. LXXVIII, pp. 65-80, July, 1940.

Torbert, John B.:

Africa, the Largest Game Preserve in the World. By John B. Torbert. Vol. XI, pp. 445-448, 1 page map, Nov., 1900.

Torday, E.:

Among the Cannibals of Belgian Kongo (Taken from the Notes of E. Torday). Vol. XXI, pp. 968-971, 4 ills., Nov., 1910.

Curious and Characteristic Customs of Central African Tribes (Belgian Congo). By E. Torday. Vol. XXXVI, pp. 342-368, 35 ills., Oct., 1919.

Torii Gate, Japan. Vol. XXII, color plate, p. 982, Nov., 1911.

Torlanini, Enrico:

Speediest Boat. Vol. XXII, pp. 875-878, 2 ills., Sept., 1911.

Tornadoes:

Forecasting the Weather and Storms. By Willis L. Moore. Vol. XVI, pp. 255-305, 5 ills., 20 charts, June, 1905.

Tornow, Max L.:

Economic Condition of the Philippines. By Max L. Tornow. Vol. X, pp. 33-64, 10 ills., Feb., 1899.

Toronto, Canada:

Ontario, Next Door: Alert, Energetic, and Resourceful, Its British Pluck and Skill in Arts and Trades Gain for This Province a High Place Under the Union Jack. By Frederick Simpich. Vol. LXII, pp. 131-183, 54 ills., 1 three-quarters-page map, Aug., 1932.

See also Little Norway (Training Center).

Total Eclipse of the Sun, May 28, 1900. By Frank H. Bigelow. Vol. XI, pp. 33-34, Jan., 1900.

Totem-pole Builders (Indians). 16 ills. in color from paintings by W. Langdon Kihn. Vol. LXXXVII, pp. 33-48, Jan., 1945.

Totem Poles:

Indians of Our North Pacific Coast. By Matthew W. Stirling. Paintings by W. Langdon Kihn. Vol. LXXXVII, pp. 25-52, 3 ills. in black and white, 16 ills. in color, Jan., 1945.

Totem-pole Builders. 16 ills. in color from paintings by W. Langdon Kihn. Vol. LXXXVII, pp. 33-48, Jan., 1945.

Tour in the English Fenland. By Christopher Marlowe. Vol. LV, pp. 605-634, 26 ills. in black and white, 5 ills. in color, 1 half-page map, May, 1929.

Touring for Birds with Microphone and Color Cameras. By Arthur A. Allen. Vol. LXXXV, pp. 689-712, 3 ills. in black and white, 24 ills. in color, June, 1944.

Towers:

Dr. Bell's Tetrahedral Tower. By Gilbert H. Grosvenor. Vol. XVIII, pp. 672-675, 7 ills., Oct., 1907.

Parsees and the Towers of Silence at Bombay, India. By William Thomas Fee. Vol. XVI, pp. 529-554, 16 ills., Dec., 1905.

Singing Towers of Holland and Belgium. By William Gorham Rice. Vol. XLVII, pp. 357-376, 22 ills., Mar., 1925.

Towhees:

Sparrows, Towhees, and Longspurs. 43 paintings in color from life by Maj. Allan Brooks and Walter A. Weber. Vol. LXXV, pp. 361-375, Mar., 1939.

Sparrows, Towhees, and Longspurs : These Happy Little Singers Make Merry in Field, Forest, and Desert Throughout North America. By T. Gilbert Pearson. Vol. LXXV, pp. 353-376, 5 ills. in black and white, 43 ills. in color, Mar., 1939.

Town of Many Gables (Münster, Germany). By Florence Craig Albrecht. Vol. XXVII, pp. 107-140, 28 ills., Feb., 1915.

Townley-Fullam, C.:

Hungary : A Land of Shepherd Kings. By C. Townley-Fullam. Vol. XXVI, pp. 311-393, 92 ills., 1 page map, Oct., 1914.

Townsend, Charles Haskins:

Our Heritage of the Fresh Waters : Biographies of the Most Widely Distributed of the Important Food and Game Fishes of the United States. By Charles Haskins Townsend. Vol. XLIV, pp. 109-159, 25 ills. in black and white, 16 ills. in color, Aug., 1923.

Toy Dogs:

Dogs in Toyland. 16 ills. in color from natural-color photographs by Willard R. Culver. Vol. LXXXV, pp. 473-480, Apr., 1944.

Toy Dogs, Pets of Kings and Commoners. By Freeman Lloyd. Vol. LXXXV, pp. 459-480, 8 ills. in black and white, 16 ills. in color, Apr., 1944.

Toy Fishes:

Iridescent Denizens of the Miniature Aquarium. 8 ills. in color from paintings by Hashime Murayama. Vol. LIX, pp. 291-300, Mar., 1931.

Tropical Toy Fishes : More Than 600 Varieties of Aquarium Pygmies Afford a Fascinating Field of Zoölogical Study in the Home. By Ida Mellen. Vol. LIX, pp. 287-317, 20 ills. in black and white, 8 ills. in color, Mar., 1931.

Tozeur, Tunisia :

The Date Gardens of the Jerid. By Thomas H. Kearney. Vol. XXI, pp. 543-567, 20 ills., July, 1910.

Tozzi, (Gen.) P.:

Italy's Eagles of Combat and Defense : Heroic Achievements of Aviators Above the Adriatic, the Apennines, and the Alps. By Gen. P. Tozzi. Vol. XXXIII, pp. 38-47, 8 ills., Jan., 1918.

Tracking the Columbian Ground-Squirrel to Its Burrow : Loss of Millions to Crops and Danger of the Spread of Spotted Fever Necessitated Study of Peculiar Rodent of Western North America. By William T. Shaw. Vol. XLVII, pp. 587-596, 13 ills., May, 1925.

Tradition Lingers in Modern Japan. 11 ills. in color from natural-color photographs by W. Robert Moore. Vol. LXXIII, pp. 117-124, Jan., 1938.

Traditions and Glamour of Insignia. By Arthur E. Du Bois. Vol. LXXXIII, pp. 652-655, 3 ills., June, 1943.

Traffic on the Suez Canal. Vol. XII, p. 380, Oct., 1901.

Trailer Camps:

America on the Move. 26 illustrations from photographs by J. Baylor Roberts, B. Anthony Stewart, and others. Vol. XC, pp. 357-378, Sept., 1946.

Trailing History Down the Big Muddy : In the Homeward Wake of Lewis and Clark, a Folding Steel Skiff Bears Its Lone Pilot on a 2,000-Mile Cruise on the Yellowstone-Missouri. By Lewis R. Freeman. Vol. LIV, pp. 73-120, 51 ills., 1 half-page map, July, 1928.

Training Center (Little Norway), Toronto, Canada :

Norway, an Active Ally. By Wilhelm Morgenstierne. Vol. LXXXIII, pp. 333-357, 24 ills., 1 two-thirds-page map, Mar., 1943.

Training Schools:

Aviation Cadet : Pocket Carriers Fight the Submarines. 20 ills. in color from U. S. Navy official photographs. Vol. LXXXIV, pp. 521-544, Nov., 1943.

Blimp : Aboard a Blimp Hunting U-boats : A Day above the Atlantic Reveals Navy Talk and Navy Ways, Creeping Convoys, and Torpedoed Wrecks. By Mason Sutherland. Vol. LXXXIV, pp. 79-96, 18 ills., July, 1943.

U. S. Army Air Forces : They Sustain the Wings (Ground Crews). By Frederick Simpich. Vol. LXXXIV, pp. 333-354, 19 ills., Sept., 1943.

Training the New Armies of Liberty : Camp Lee, Virginia's Home for the National Army. By Granville Fortescue. Vol. XXXII, pp. 421-437, 8 ills., 1 page map in colors, Nov.-Dec., 1917.

Trains:

Trains of Today—and Tomorrow. By J. R. Hildebrand. Vol. LXX, pp. 535-589, 51 ills., Nov., 1936.

Your New World of Tomorrow. By F. Barrows Colton. Vol. LXXXVIII, pp. 385-410, 25 ills., Oct., 1945.

Tralee (Boat) :

Chesapeake Odyssey : An 18-foot Sailboat Follows the Course of Captain John Smith around This Spacious Bay of History, Commerce, Sea Food, and Nautical Lore. By John Maloney. Vol. LXXVI, pp. 357-392, 32 ills., 1 page map, Sept., 1939.

Tralles (Ancient City) :

Ruined Cities of Asia Minor. By Ernest L. Harris. Vol. XIX, pp. 741-760, 11 ills., Nov., 1908.

Trans-African Safari : A Motor Caravan Rolls Across Sahara and Jungle Through Realms of Dusky Potentates and the Land of Big-Lipped Women. By Lawrence Copley Thaw and Margaret Stout Thaw. Vol. LXXIV, pp. 327-364, 29 ills. in black and white, 14 ills. in color, 1 two-thirds-page map, Sept., 1938.

Transandine Railway, Argentina-Chile :

First Transandine Railroad from Buenos Aires to Valparaiso. By Harriet Chalmers Adams. Vol. XXI, pp. 397-417, 41 ills., 1 quarter-page map, May, 1910.

Trans-Asiatic Expedition:

Citroën Trans-Asiatic Expedition Reaches Kashmir : Scientific Party Led by Georges-Marie Haardt Successfully Crosses Syria, Iraq, Persia, and Afghanistan to Arrive at the Pamir. By Maynard Owen Williams. Vol. LX, pp. 387-443, 62 ills., 1 page map, Oct., 1931.

First Over the Roof of the World by Motor : The Trans-Asiatic Expedition Sets New Records for Wheeled Transport in Scaling Passes of the Himalayas. By Maynard Owen Williams. Vol. LXI, pp. 321-363, 45 ills., 2 half-page maps, Mar., 1932.

From the Mediterranean to the Yellow Sea by Motor : The Citroën-Haardt Expedition Successfully Completes Its Dramatic Journey. By Maynard Owen Williams. Vol. LXII, pp. 513-580, 45 ills. in black and white, 25 ills. in color, 2 half-page maps, Nov., 1932.

Trans-Asiatic Expedition Starts. By Georges-Marie Haardt. Vol. LIX, pp. 776-782, 6 ills., June, 1931.

Transcaucasia (Region), U. S. S. R. :

Armenia and the Armenians. By Hester Donaldson Jenkins. Vol. XXVIII, pp. 329-360, 27 ills., 1 half-page map, Oct., 1915.

British Take Baku. Vol. XXXIV, pp. 163-164, 1 ill., Aug., 1918.

Island in a Sea of History : The Highlands of Daghestan. By George Kennan. Vol. XXIV, pp. 1086-1140, 49 ills., 1 page map, Oct., 1913.

Transcaucasia (Region), U.S.S.R.—*Continued*

Land of the Stalking Death : A Journey Through Starving Armenia on an American Relief Train. By Melville Chater. Vol. XXXVI, pp. 393-420, 23 ills., Nov., 1919.

Old Post-Road from Tiflis to Erivan. By Esther Lancraft Hovey. Vol. XII, pp. 300-309, 9 ills., Aug., 1901.

Races of Europe. By Edwin A. Grosvenor. Vol. XXXIV, pp. 441-534, 62 ills., 2 page maps, special map supplement, Dec., 1918.

Roaming Russia's Caucasus : Rugged Mountains and Hardy Fighters Guard the Soviet Union's Caucasian Treasury of Manganese and Oil. By Rolf Singer. Vol. LXXXII, pp. 91-121, 33 ills., July, 1942.

Russia's Orphan Races : Picturesque Peoples Who Cluster on the Southeastern Borderland of the Vast Slav Dominions. By Maynard Owen Williams. Vol. XXXIV, pp. 245-278, 26 ills., 1 page map, Oct., 1918.

Transformation of Turkey : New Hats and New Alphabet are the Surface Symbols of the Swiftest National Changes in Modern Times. By Douglas Chandler. Vol. LXXV, pp. 1-50, 27 ills. in black and white, 23 ills. in color, 1 map, Jan., 1939.

Transformation of Washington (District of Columbia) : A Glance at the History and Along the Vista of the Future of the Nation's Capital. By Charles Moore. Vol. XLIII, pp. 569-595, 16 ills., 2 page maps, June, 1923.

Trans-Jordan:

Bedouin Life in Bible Lands : The Nomads of the "House of Hair" Offer Unstinted Hospitality to an American. By John D. Whiting. Vol. LXXI, pp. 59-83, 27 ills., 1 third-page map, Jan., 1937.

Geography of the Jordan. By Nelson Glueck. Vol. LXXXVI, pp. 719-744, 23 ills., 1 page map, Dec., 1944.

On the Trail of King Solomon's Mines : The Bible, in Addition to Its Spiritual Values, Continues to Prove a Rich Geography and Guide to Exploration of the Holy Land. By Nelson Glueck. Vol. LXXXV, pp. 233-256, 20 ills., 1 page map, Feb., 1944.

One Thousand Miles of Railway Built for Pilgrims and Not for Dividends (Damascus to Mecca). By Col. F. R. Maunsell. Vol. XX, pp. 156-172, 13 ills., 1 three-quarters-page map, Feb., 1909.

Visit to Three Arab Kingdoms : Transjordania, Iraq, and the Hedjaz Present Many Problems to European Powers. By Junius B. Wood. Vol. XLIII, pp. 535-568, 30 ills., 1 three-quarters-page map, May, 1923.

See also Petra.

Transport Air Group (TAG) :

Flying Our Wounded Veterans Home. By Catherine Bell Palmer. Vol. LXXXVIII, pp. 363-384, 17 ills., Sept., 1945.

Transportation:

America on the Move. 26 ills. from photographs by J. Baylor Roberts, B. Anthony Stewart, and others. Vol. XC, pp. 357-378, Sept., 1946.

American Transportation Vital to Victory. By Thornton Oakley. With 16 ills. in color from paintings by the author. Vol. LXXXIV, pp. 671-688, Dec., 1943.

Animals Were Allies, Too. 16 ills. from photographs. Vol. LXXXIX, pp. 75-88, Jan., 1946.

Bonds Between the Americas. By Frederick Simpich. Vol. LXXII, pp. 785-808, 22 ills., Dec., 1937.

Burma: Where India and China Meet: In the Massive Mountains of Southeast Asia, Swarming Road Builders Wage the "War of the Highways" for Free China and Her Allies. By John LeRoy Christian. Vol. LXXXIV, pp. 489-512, 18 ills., 1 page map, Oct., 1943.

Burma Road: China Opens Her Wild West: In the Mountain-girt Heart of a Continent a New China Has Been Created During the Years of War. By Owen Lattimore. Vol. LXXXII, pp. 337-367, 21 ills. in black and white, 11 ills. in color, 1 map (two-page spread), Sept., 1942.

Kunming, Southwestern Gateway to China. By Joseph E. Passantino. With 18 ills. in color from natural-color photographs by the author. Vol. XC, pp. 137-168, 12 ills. in black and white, Aug., 1946.

Landing Craft for Invasion. By Melville Bell Grosvenor. Vol. LXXXVI, pp.1-30, 26 ills., July, 1944.

Mother Volga Defends Her Own. By Maynard Owen Williams. Vol. LXXXII, pp. 793-811, 21 ills., Dec., 1942.

Queer Methods of Travel in Curious Corners of the World. By O. P. Austin. Vol. XVIII, pp. 687-715, 29 ills., Nov., 1907.

6,000 Miles over the Roads of Free China. By Josephine A. Brown. Vol. LXXXV, pp. 355-384, 30 ills., 1 two-thirds-page map, Mar., 1944.

Some Mexican Transportation Scenes. By Walter W. Bradley. Vol. XXI, pp. 985-991, 10 ills., Dec., 1910.

This Is My Own: How the United States Seems to a Citizen Soldier Back from Three Years Overseas. By Frederick G. Vosburgh. Vol. LXXXIX, pp. 113-128, 14 ills., Jan., 1946.

Transportation in England. Vol. XVI, p. 88, Feb., 1905.

Transportation Methods in Alaska. By Capt. George S. Gibbs. Vol. XVII, pp. 69-82, 19 ills., Feb., 1906.

U. S. Roads in War and Peace. By Frederick Simpich. Vol. LXXX, pp. 687-716, 27 ills., Dec., 1941.

Winning the War of Supply. By F. Barrows Colton. Vol. LXXXVIII, pp. 705-736, 23 ills., Dec., 1945.

Transportation—*Continued*

Your New World of Tomorrow. By F. Barrows Colton. Vol. LXXXVIII, pp. 385-410, 25 ills., Oct., 1945.

See also Air Carrier Contract Personnel; Air Transport Command; Boats; Highways and Roads; Railroads; Ships and Shipping; U. S. Army Transportation Corps.

Transporting a Navy Through the Jungles of Africa in War Time. By Frank J. Magee. Vol. XLII, pp. 331-362, 31 ills., Oct., 1922.

Trans-Siberian Railway, U. S. S. R. :

Land of Promise (Siberia). By Maj. Gen. A. W. Greely. Vol. XXIII, pp. 1078-1090, 7 ills., Nov., 1912.

Siberia. By Edwin A. Grosvenor. Vol. XII, pp. 317-324, Sept., 1901.

Western Siberia and the Altai Mountains: With Some Speculations on the Future of Siberia. By James Bryce. Vol. XXXIX, pp. 469-507, 39 ills., May, 1921.

Transvaal (Province), Union of South Africa :

British South Africa and the Transvaal. By F. F. Hilder. Vol. XI, pp. 81-96, 7 ills., Mar., 1900.

Cities That Gold and Diamonds Built : Transvaal Treasures Have Created Bustling Johannesburg and Fostered Pretoria, Administrative Capital of the South African Union. By W. Robert Moore. Vol. LXXXII, pp. 735-766, 20 ills. in black and white, 9 ills. in color, 1 two-thirds-page map, Dec., 1942.

Sunny South Africa. 9 ills. in color from natural-color photographs by W. Robert Moore. Vol. LXXXII, pp. 749-756, Dec., 1942.

Transvaal: The Treasure-House Province. By Melville Chater. Vol. LIX, pp. 479-512, 28 ills., Apr., 1931.

Transylvania (Division), Romania :

American Girl Cycles Across Romania : Two-wheel Pilgrim Pedals the Land of Castles and Gypsies, Where Roman Empire Traces Mingle With Remnants of Oriental Migration. By Dorothy Hosmer. Vol. LXXIV, pp. 557-588, 31 ills., 1 page map, Nov., 1938.

Roumania and Its Rubicon. By John Oliver La Gorce. Vol. XXX, pp. 185-202, 11 ills., Sept., 1916.

Transylvania and Its Seven Castles: A Motor Circuit Through Rumania's New Province of Racial Complexity and Architectural Charm. By J. Theodore Marriner. Vol. XLIX, pp. 319-352, 35 ills., 1 half-page map, Mar., 1926.

Trapdoor Spiders:

California Trapdoor Spider Performs Engineering Marvels. By Lee Passmore. Vol. LXIV, pp. 195-211, 23 ills., Aug., 1933.

Marvels of Metamorphosis : A Scientific "G-man" Pursues Rare Trapdoor Spider Parasites for Three Years With a Spade and a Candid Camera. By George Elwood Jenks. Vol. LXXIV, pp. 807-828, 39 ills., Dec., 1938.

Traveler's Notes on Java. By Henry G. Bryant. Vol. XXI, pp. 91-111, 17 ills., Feb., 1910.

Traveling in the Highlands of Ethiopia. By Leo B. Roberts. Vol. LXVIII, pp. 297-328, 37 ills., Sept., 1935.

Travels in Arabia and Along the Persian Gulf. By David G. Fairchild. Vol. XV, pp. 139-151, 20 ills., Apr., 1904.

Travels of George Washington: Dramatic Episodes in His Career as the First Geographer of the United States. By William Joseph Showalter. Vol. LXI, pp. 1-63, 50 ills., 5 maps, special map supplement, Jan., 1932.

Travels with a Donkey in Mexico: Three Adventurers Trudge from Oaxaca to Acapulco, 400 Miles, Through Back Country, Their Equipment Carried by Burros. By Bernard Bevan. Vol. LXVI, pp. 757-788, 36 ills., 1 page map, Dec., 1934.

Treasure Chest of Mercurial Mexico (Silver Mines in Guanajuato). By Frank H. Probert. Vol. XXX, pp. 55-68, 55 ills., July, 1916.

Treasure-House of the Gulf Stream: The Completion and Opening of the New Aquarium and Biological Laboratory at Miami, Florida. By John Oliver La Gorce. Vol. XXXIX, pp. 53-68, 5 ills. in black and white, 16 ills. in color, Jan., 1921.

Treasure Islands of Australasia: New Guinea, New Caledonia, and Fiji Trace across the South Pacific a Fertile Crescent Incredibly Rich in Minerals and Foods. By Douglas L. Oliver. Vol. LXXXI, pp. 691-722, 23 ills., 1 two-page map, June, 1942.

Treasure-trove of Old Mexican Jade (Cerro de las Mesas). 20 ills. in color from natural-color photographs by Richard H. Stewart. Vol. LXXX, pp. 293-316, Sept., 1941.

Treasures of the Pacific: Marine Fishes and Fisheries Yield Vast Wealth from Alaska to Baja California. By Leonard P. Schultz. Vol. LXXIV, pp. 463-498, 10 ills. in black and white, 31 portraits in color, Oct., 1938.

Treat, Ida:

Sailing Forbidden Coasts. By Ida Treat. Vol. LX, pp. 357-386, 31 ills., 1 quarter-page map, Sept., 1931.

Tree Rings:

Pueblo Bonito, the Ancient: The National Geographic Society's Third Expedition to the Southwest Seeks to Read in the Rings of Trees the Secret of the Age of Ruins. By Neil M. Judd. Vol. XLIV, pp. 99-108, 9 ills., 1 diagram, July 1923.

Secret of the Southwest Solved by Talkative Tree Rings: Horizons of American History Are Carried Back to A. D. 700 and a Calendar for 1,200 Years Established by National Geographic Society Expeditions. By Andrew Ellicott Douglass. Vol. LVI, pp. 737-770, 33 ills., 1 two-thirds-page map, Dec., 1929.

Trees:

American Berries of Hill, Dale, and Wayside. Vol. XXXV, pp. 168-184, 1 ill. in black and white, 28 ills. in color, Feb., 1919.

Among the Big Trees of California. By John R. White. Vol. LXVI, pp. 219-232, 14 ills., Aug., 1934.

California's Coastal Redwood Realm: Along a Belt of Tall Trees a Giant Bridge Speeds the Winning of Our Westernmost Frontier. By J. R. Hildebrand. Vol. LXXV, pp. 133-184, 31 ills. in black and white, 17 ills. in color, 1 page-and-a-half map, Feb., 1939.

Cork. Vol. XIX, pp. 690-693, 3 ills., Oct., 1908.

Fight at the Timber-Line. By John Oliver La Gorce. Vol. XLII, pp. 165-196, 32 ills., Aug., 1922.

Formosa the Beautiful (Camphor). By Alice Ballantine Kirjassoff. Vol. XXXVII, pp. 246-292, 60 ills., 1 half-page map, Mar., 1920.

Golden Gate, and Redwood Evergreens. 17 ills. in color from natural-color photographs by B. Anthony Stewart. Vol. LXXV, pp. 149-160, Feb., 1939.

Hardy Catalpa. Vol. XIV, pp. 348-353, 4 ills., Sept., 1903.

Hunting the Chaulmoogra Tree. By Joseph F. Rock. Vol. XLI, pp. 243-276, 39 ills., 1 page map, Mar., 1922.

Introduction of the Mango. Vol. XIV, pp. 320-327, 5 ills., Aug., 1903.

Isle of Frankincense (Socotra, Arabian Sea). By Charles K. Moser. Vol. XXXIII, pp. 266-278, 11 ills., Mar., 1918.

Kingdom of Flowers: An Account of the Wealth of Trees and Shrubs of China and of What the Arnold Arboretum, with China's Help, Is Doing to Enrich America. By Ernest H. Wilson. Vol. XXII, pp. 1003-1035, 24 ills., Nov., 1911.

Lonely Australia: The Unique Continent. By Herbert E. Gregory. Vol. XXX, pp. 473-568, 68 ills., 1 two-page and 4 half-page maps, Dec., 1916.

National Geographic Society Completes Its Gifts of Big Trees. Vol. XL, pp. 85-86, July, 1921.

New World to Explore: In the Tree-Roof of the British Guiana Forest Flourishes Much Hitherto-Unknown Life. By Maj. R. W. G. Hingston. Vol. LXII, pp. 617-642, 35 ills., Nov., 1932.

Notes on the Eucalyptus Tree from the United States Forest Service. Vol. XX, pp. 668-673, 4 ills., July, 1909.

Oldest Living Thing ("General Sherman Tree"). Vol. XXIX, supplement, Apr., 1916.

Our Big Trees Saved. Vol. XXXI, pp. 1-11, 10 ills., Jan., 1917.

Our National Parks. By L. F. Schmeckebier. Vol. XXIII, pp. 531-579, 41 ills., 1 page map, June, 1912.

The Palms. Vol. XXII, supplement, Dec., 1911.

Redwood Forest of the Pacific Coast. By Henry Gannett. Vol. X, pp. 145-159, 6 ills., 1 page map, May, 1899.

Trees—*Continued*

Rubber Plantations in Mexico and Central America. Vol. XIV, pp. 409-414, 7 ills., Nov., 1903.

Saving the Redwoods. By Madison Grant. Vol. XXXVII, pp. 519-536, 10 ills., June, 1920.

Strange Sights in Far-Away Papua (Stinging Trees). By A. E. Pratt. Vol. XVIII, pp. 559-572, 7 ills., Sept., 1907.

Tallest Tree That Grows (Eucalyptus). By Edgerton R. Young. Vol. XX, pp. 664-667, 3 ills., July, 1909.

Wonderland of California. By Herman Whitaker. Vol. XXVIII, pp. 56-104, 45 ills., July, 1915.

See also Forests and Forestry.

Trekking South Africa with a Color Camera. 11 ills. in color from natural-color photographs by Melville Chater. Vol. LIX, pp. 412-421, Apr., 1931.

Tres Zapotes, Mexico :

Discovering the New World's Oldest Dated Work of Man : A Maya Monument Inscribed 291 B. C. is Unearthed Near a Huge Stone Head by a Geographic-Smithsonian Expedition in Mexico. By Matthew W. Stirling. Vol. LXXVI, pp. 183-218, 40 ills., 1 half-page map, Aug., 1939.

Great Stone Faces of the Mexican Jungle : Five Colossal Heads and Numerous Other Monuments of Vanished Americans Are Excavated by the Latest National Geographic-Smithsonian Expedition. By Matthew W. Stirling. Vol. LXXVIII, pp. 309-334, 26 ills., 1 map, Sept., 1940.

Tribute to America. By Herbert Henry Asquith. Vol. XXXI, pp. 294-296, 2 ills., Apr., 1917.

Tribute to American Topographers. Vol. XVI, p. 358, July, 1905.

Tricolor Rules the Rainbow in French Indo-China. 27 ills. in color from natural-color photographs by Maynard Owen Williams. Vol. LXVIII, pp. 495-518, Oct., 1935.

Trinidad (Island), West Indies :

Americans in the Caribbean. By Luis Marden. Vol. LXXXI, pp. 723-758, 16 ills. in black and white, 22 ills. in color, 1 half-page map, June, 1942.

Crossroads of the Caribbean. By Laurence Sanford Critchell. Vol. LXXII, pp. 319-344, 18 ills. in black and white, 14 ills. in color, 1 half-page map, Sept., 1937.

East Indians in the New World. By Harriet Chalmers Adams. Vol. XVIII, pp. 485-491, 6 ills., July, 1907.

Tropic Color in Trinidad. 14 ills. in color from natural-color photographs by Edwin L. Wisherd. Vol. LXXII, pp. 327-334, Sept., 1937.

War Echoes in the West Indies. 22 ills. in color from natural-color photographs by Luis Marden. Vol. LXXXI, pp. 731-754, June, 1942.

Trip Through Siberia. By Ebenezer J. Hill. Vol. XIII, pp. 37-54, 17 ills., 1 quarter-page map, Feb., 1902.

Tripoli, Lebanon :

From Jerusalem to Aleppo. By John D. Whiting. Vol. XXIV, pp. 71-113, 30 ills., 1 half-page map, Jan., 1913.

Tripoli, Libia :

Americans on the Barbary Coast. By Willard Price. Vol. LXXXIV, pp. 1-31, 13 ills. in black and white, 10 ills. in color, 1 map (two-page spread), July, 1943.

Tripoli : A Land of Little Promise. By Adolf L. Vischer. Vol. XXII, pp. 1035-1047, 6 ills., 1 half-page map, Nov., 1911.

Tripolitania (Region), North Africa :

Here and There in Northern Africa. By Frank Edward Johnson. Vol. XXV, pp. 1-32, 113 ills., Jan., 1914.

Mysteries of the Desert. By Hanns Vischer. Vol. XXII, pp. 1056-1059, Nov., 1911.

Tripoli : A Land of Little Promise. By Adolf L. Vischer. Vol. XXII, pp. 1035-1047, 6 ills., 1 half-page map, Nov., 1911.

Tripolitania, Where Rome Resumes Sway : The Ancient Trans-Mediterranean Empire, on the Fringe of the Libyan Desert, Becomes a Promising Modern Italian Colony. By Col. Gordon Casserly. Vol. XLVIII, pp. 131-161, 27 ills. in black and white, 9 ills. in color, 1 two-thirds-page map, Aug., 1925.

Tristan da Cunha, Isles of Contentment : On Lonely Sea Spots of Pirate Lore and Shipwrecks Seven Families Live Happily Far from War Rumors and World Changes. By W. Robert Foran. Vol. LXXIV, pp. 671-694, 23 ills., 1 half-page map, Nov., 1938.

Tri-State Medley (Virginia, Maryland, and Delaware). 10 ills. in color from natural-color photographs by Willard R. Culver. Vol. LXXIV, pp. 33-40, July, 1938.

Troglodytes and Christian "Troglodytes":

Cone-Dwellers of Asia Minor : A Primitive People Who Live in Nature-Made Apartment Houses, Fashioned by Volcanic Violence and Trickling Streams. By J. R. Sitlington Sterrett. Vol. XXXV, pp. 281-331, 52 ills., 1 half-page map, Apr., 1919.

Here and There in Northern Africa. By Frank Edward Johnson. Vol. XXV, pp. 1-132, 113 ills., Jan., 1914.

Mole Men : An Account of the Troglodytes of Southern Tunisia. By Frank Edward Johnson. Vol. XXII, pp. 787-846, 60 ills., Sept., 1911.

Multicolored Cones of Cappadocia. 20 ills. in color from natural-color photographs by Eric Matson. Vol. LXXVI, pp. 769-800, Dec., 1939.

Peculiar Caves of Asia Minor. By Elizabeth H. Brewer. Vol. XXII, pp. 870-875, 5 ills., Sept., 1911.

Troglodytes and Christian "Troglodytes"—
Continued

Star and Crescent on Parade (Turkey). 29 ills. in color from natural-color photographs by Maynard Owen Williams. Vol. LXXXVII, pp. 585-616, May, 1945.

Turkish Republic Comes of Age. By Maynard Owen Williams. Vol. LXXXVII, pp. 581-616, 4 ills. in black and white, 29 ills. in color, 1 map (two-page spread), May, 1945.

Where Early Christians Lived in Cones of Rock: A Journey to Cappadocia in Turkey Where Strange Volcanic Pinnacles Are Honeycombed with Hermit Cells and Monasteries. By John D. Whiting. Vol. LXXVI, pp. 763-802, 20 ills. in black and white, 20 ills. in color, 1 half-page map, Dec., 1939.

Trondheim, Norway:

White War in Norway. By Thomas R. Henry. Vol. LXXXVIII, pp. 617-640, 23 ills., 1 three-quarters-page map, Nov., 1945.

Troop Carrier Command, U. S. Army Air Forces:

Flying Our Wounded Veterans Home. By Catherine Bell Palmer. Vol. LXXXVIII, pp. 363-384, 17 ills., Sept., 1945.

Tropic-Birds:

Birds of the High Seas: Albatrosses and Petrels; Gannets, Man-o'-war-birds, and Tropic-birds. By Robert Cushman Murphy. Vol. LXXIV, pp. 226-251, 7 ills. in black and white, 36 portraits in color, Aug., 1938.

Tropic Color in Trinidad. 14 ills. in color from natural-color photographs by Edwin L. Wisherd. Vol. LXXII, pp. 327-334, Sept., 1937.

Tropical Fish Immigrants Reveal New Nature Wonders. By Walter H. Chute. Vol. LXV, pp. 93-110, 8 ills. in black and white, 16 ills. in color, Jan., 1934.

Tropical Toy Fishes: More Than 600 Varieties of Aquarium Pygmies Afford a Fascinating Field of Zoölogical Study in the Home. By Ida Mellen. Vol. LIX, pp. 287-317, 20 ills. in black and white, 8 ills. in color, Mar., 1931.

Trouts (Fishes):

Fishing in Pacific Coast Streams. By Leonard P. Schultz. Vol. LXXV, pp. 185-212, 10 ills. in black and white, 54 portraits in color, Feb., 1939.

Fresh-Water Denizens of the Far West. 54 portraits in color from paintings by Hashime Murayama. Vol. LXXV, pp. 193-204, Feb., 1939.

Golden Trout. Vol. XVII, p. 424, July, 1906.

Wild Life of Lake Superior, Past and Present: The Habits of Deer, Moose, Wolves, Beavers, Muskrats, Trout, and Feathered Wood-Folk Studied with Camera and Flashlight. By George Shiras, 3d. Vol. XL, pp. 113-204, 77 ills., supplement, 1 half-page map, Aug., 1921.

Trowbridge, Stephen van Rensselaer:

Impressions of Asiatic Turkey. By Stephen van Rensselaer Trowbridge. Vol. XXVI, pp. 598-609, 6 ills., Dec., 1914.

Troy (Ancient City):

Homer's Troy Today. By Jacob E. Conner. Vol. XXVII, pp. 520-532, 11 ills., 1 half-page map, May, 1915.

Notes on Troy. Vol. XXVII, pp. 531-532, 1 half-page map, Apr., 1915.

Trujillo, Ciudad, Dominican Republic:

Land Columbus Loved. By Oliver P. Newman. Vol. LXXXV, pp. 197-224, 15 ills. in black and white, 11 ills. in color, 1 two-thirds-page map, Feb., 1944.

Truk Islands, Caroline Islands:

Hidden Key to the Pacific: Piercing the Web of Secrecy Which Long Has Veiled Japanese Bases in the Mandated Islands. By Willard Price. Vol. LXXXI, pp. 759-785, 28 ills., 1 map (two-page spread), June, 1942.

Yap and Other Pacific Islands Under Japanese Mandate. By Junius B. Wood. Vol. XL, pp. 591-627, 34 ills., 1 two-thirds-page map, Dec., 1921.

Trulli (Dwellings): Italy:

Stone Beehive Homes of Italian Peasants. 4 ills. in color from autochromes by Luigi Pellerano. Vol. LVII, pp. 234-243, Feb., 1930.

Stone Beehive Homes of the Italian Heel: In Trulli-Land the Native Builds His Dwelling and Makes His Field Arable in the Same Operation. By Paul Wilstach. Vol. LVII, pp. 229-260, 25 ills. in black and white, 12 ills. in color, 1 quarter-page map, Feb., 1930.

Truman, Harry S.:

Map rack presented to. Vol. LXXXIX, p. 290. Mar., 1946.

President Truman presents Hubbard Medal to Gen. H. H. Arnold, Nov. 16, 1945. Vol. LXXXIX, ill. 141, Feb., 1946.

Truth About the Congo. Vol. XVIII, pp. 807-813, 6 ills., Dec., 1907.

Tsangpo (Brahmaputra River). By James Mascarene Hubbard. Vol. XII, pp. 32-35, Jan., 1901.

Tsankawi, New Mexico:

Prehistoric Ruin of Tsankawi. By George L. Beam. Vol. XX, pp. 807-822, 12 ills., Sept., 1909.

Tschiffely, A. F.:

Buenos Aires to Washington by Horse: A Solitary Journey of Two and a Half Years, Through Eleven American Republics, Covers 9,600 Miles of Mountain and Plain, Desert and Jungle. By A. F. Tschiffely. Vol. LV, pp. 135-196, 75 ills., 1 page map, Feb., 1929.

Tsimshian (Indian Tribe):

Indians of Our North Pacific Coast. By Matthew W. Stirling. Paintings by W. Langdon Kihn. Vol. LXXXVII, pp. 25-52, 3 ills. in black and white, 16 ills. in color, Jan., 1945.

Tsinghai (Province), China :

Across Tibet from India to China. By Lt. Col. Ilia Tolstoy, AUS. Vol. XC, pp. 169-222, 41 ills., 1 half-page map, Aug., 1946.

China Fights Erosion with U. S. Aid. By Walter C. Lowdermilk. Vol. LXXXVII, pp. 641-680, 10 ills. in black and white, 26 ills. in color, June, 1945.

Tsingning, China :

"Where the Mountains Walked" : An Account of the Recent Earthquake in Kansu Province, China, Which Destroyed 100,000 Lives. By Upton Close and Elsie McCormick. Vol. XLI, pp. 445-464, 23 ills., 1 three-quarters-page map, May, 1922.

Tsung-Li-Yamen (Foreign Office, China). By Eliza R. Scidmore. Vol. XI, pp. 291-292, 1 diagram, 1 two-thirds-page map, July, 1900.

Tuamotu (Archipelago), Pacific Ocean :

Romance of Science in Polynesia : An Account of Five Years of Cruising Among the South Sea Islands. By Robert Cushman Murphy. Vol. LXVIII, pp. 355-426, 66 ills. in black and white, 16 ills. in color, 3 half-page maps, Oct., 1925.

Tuaregs (Tribespeople) :

Africa on Parade. 14 ills. in color from natural-color photographs by Lawrence Thaw. Vol. LXXIV, pp. 343-350, Sept., 1938.

Mysteries of the Desert (Sahara). By Hanns Vischer. Vol. XXII, pp. 1056-1059, Nov., 1911.

Trans-Africa Safari : A Motor Caravan Rolls Across Sahara and Jungle Through Realms of Dusky Potentates and the Land of Big-Lipped Women. By Lawrence Copley Thaw and Margaret Stout Thaw. Vol. LXXIV, pp. 327-364, 29 ills. in black and white, 14 ills. in color, 1 two-thirds-page map, Sept., 1938.

Tuatara (Reptile) :

Tuatara : "Living Fossils" Walk on Well-Nigh Inaccessible Rocky Islands off the Coast of New Zealand. By Frieda Cobb Blanchard. Vol. LXVII, pp. 649-662, 14 ills., 1 half-page map, May, 1935.

Tugeri (Tribespeople) :

Strange Sights in Far-Away Papua. By A. E. Pratt. Vol. XVIII, pp. 559-572, 7 ills., Sept., 1907.

Tulasne, (Maj.) Joseph:

America's Part in the Allies' Mastery of the Air. By Maj. Joseph Tulasne. Vol. XXXIII, pp. 1-5, 2 ills., Jan., 1918.

Tules (Indians). *See* San Blas Indians.

Tulips:

Some Odd Pages from the Annals of the Tulip : A "Made" Flower of Unknown Origin Took Medieval Europe by Storm and Caused a Financial Panic in the Netherlands. By Leo A. Borah. Vol. LXIV, pp. 321-343, 13 ills. in black and white, 10 ills. in color, Sept., 1933.

Tulips—*Continued*

Tulip Time in the Netherlands. 10 ills. in color from natural-color photographs by Wilhelm Tobien and A. Buyssens. Vol. LXIV, pp. 325-332, Sept., 1933.

Tulsa, Oklahoma :

So Oklahoma Grew Up. By Frederick Simpich. Vol. LXXIX, pp. 269-314, 30 ills. in black and white, 19 ills. in color, 1 page map, Mar., 1941.

Tumen (River), China-Korea :

Exploring Unknown Corners of the "Hermit Kingdom." By Roy Chapman Andrews. Vol. XXXVI, pp. 24-48, 30 ills., 1 page map, July, 1919.

Tuna Harvest of the Sea : A Little-known Epic of the Ocean Is the Story of Southern California's Far-ranging Tuna Fleet. By John Degelman. Vol. LXXVIII, pp. 393-408, 17 ills., Sept., 1940.

Tunis, Tunisia :

Eastward from Gibraltar : Overland Route Across North Africa to Tunisia and Libia. By Cyrus French Wicker. Vol. LXXXIII, pp. 115-142, 28 ills., Jan., 1943.

Tunis of Today. By Frank Edward Johnson. Vol. XXII, pp. 723-749, 24 ills., Aug., 1911.

Tunisia:

Americans on the Barbary Coast. By Willard Price. Vol. LXXXIV, pp. 1-31, 13 ills. in black and white, 10 ills. in color, 1 map (two-page spread), July, 1943.

Ancient Carthage in the Light of Modern Excavation. By Count Byron Khun de Prorok. Vol. XLV, pp. 391-423, 27 ills. in black and white, 16 ills. in color, 1 half-page map, Apr., 1924.

Country of the Ant Men. By Thomas H. Kearney. Vol. XXII, pp. 367-382, 11 ills., 1 half-page map, Apr., 1911.

Date Gardens of the Jerid. By Thomas H. Kearney. Vol. XXI, pp. 543-567, 20 ills., July, 1910.

Eastward from Gibraltar : Overland Route Across North Africa to Tunisia and Libia. By Cyrus French Wicker. Vol. LXXXIII, pp. 115-142, 28 ills., Jan., 1943.

From Africa to the Alps. 8 ills. in color from U. S. Army Air Forces official photographs. Vol. LXXXIX, pp. 161-168, Feb., 1946.

Greek Bronzes of Tunisia. By Frank Edward Johnson. Vol. XXIII, pp. 89-103, 11 ills., Jan., 1912.

Here and There in Northern Africa. By Frank Edward Johnson. Vol. XXV, pp. 1-132, 113 ills., Jan., 1914.

In Civilized French Africa. By James F. J. Archibald. Vol. XX, pp. 302-311, 14 ills., Mar., 1909.

Mole Men : An Account of the Troglodytes of Southern Tunisia. By Frank Edward Johnson. Vol. XXII, pp. 787-846, 60 ills., Sept., 1911.

Tunisia—*Continued*

Sacred City of the Sands (Kairouan). By Frank Edward Johnson. Vol. XXII, pp. 1061-1093, 25 ills., 1 half-page map, Dec., 1911.

Time's Footprints in Tunisian Sands. By Maynard Owen Williams. Vol. LXXI, pp. 345-386, 43 ills., 1 page and 1 half-page maps, Mar., 1907.

Tunis of Today. By Frank Edward Johnson. Vol. XXII, pp. 723-749, 24 ills., Aug., 1911.

Where Sea and Desert Meet. 16 ills. in color from autochromes by Gervais Courtellemont. Vol. XLV, pp. 415-423, Apr., 1924.

Turbulent Spain. By Ruth Q. McBride. Vol. LXX, pp. 397-427, 25 ills., 1 two-page map, Oct., 1936.

Turkestan. *See* Sinkiang ; Soviet Central Asia.

Turkey:

Alert Anatolia. 13 ills. from photographs. Vol. LXXXV, pp. 481-492, Apr., 1944.

American Alma Maters in the Near East. By Maynard Owen Williams. Vol. LXXXVIII, pp. 237-256, 16 ills., Aug., 1945.

Ancient Capital (Boghaz Keui). By Isabel F. Dodd. Vol. XXI, pp. 111-124, 11 ills., Feb., 1910.

Archeology, the Mirror of the Ages : Our Debt to the Humble Delvers in the Ruins at Carchemish and at Ur. By C. Leonard Woolley. Vol. LIV, pp. 207-226, 19 ills., Aug., 1928.

Armenia and the Armenians. By Hester Donaldson Jenkins. Vol. XXVIII, pp. 329-360, 27 ills., 1 half-page map, Oct., 1915.

Asia Minor in the Time of the Seven Wise Men. By Mary Mills Patrick. Vol. XXXVII, pp. 47-67, 19 ills., Jan., 1920.

Beside the Bosporus, Divider of Continents. 11 ills. in color from natural-color photographs by Maynard Owen Williams. Vol. LVI, pp. 492-501, Oct., 1929.

Buried Cities of Asia Minor. By Ernest Lloyd Harris. Vol. XX, pp. 1-18, 10 ills., Jan., 1909.

Changing Map in the Balkans. By Frederick Moore. Vol. XXIV, pp. 199-226, 27 ills., 1 page map, Feb., 1913.

Cone-Dwellers of Asia Minor : A Primitive People Who Live in Nature-Made Apartment Houses, Fashioned by Volcanic Violence and Trickling Streams. By J. R. Sitlington Sterrett. Vol. XXXV, pp. 281-331, 52 ills., 1 half-page map, Apr., 1919.

Crossing Asia Minor, the Country of the New Turkish Republic. By Maj. Robert Whitney Imbrie. Vol. XLVI, pp. 445-472, 31 ills., 1 quarter-page map, Oct., 1924.

East of Constantinople : Glimpses of Village Life in Anatolia, the Battleground of East and West, Where the Turks Reorganized Their Forces After the World War. By Melville Chater. Vol. XLIII, pp. 509-534, 27 ills., 1 three-quarters-page map, May, 1923.

Emancipation of Mohammedan Women. By Mary Mills Patrick. Vol. XX, pp. 42-66, 19 ills., Jan., 1909.

Turkey—*Continued*

Flags of Austria-Hungary, Bulgaria, Germany, and Turkey. By Byron McCandless and Gilbert Grosvenor. Vol. XXXII, pp. 386-388, 38 ills. in color, Oct., 1917.

Fringe of Verdure Around Asia Minor. By Ellsworth Huntington. Vol. XXI, pp. 761-775, 15 ills., Sept., 1910.

From England to India by Automobile : An 8,527-Mile Trip Through Ten Countries, from London to Quetta, Requires Five and a Half Months. By Maj. F. A. C. Forbes-Leith. Vol. XLVIII, pp. 191-223, 33 ills., 1 third-page map, Aug., 1925.

Gates to the Black Sea : The Dardanelles, the Bosphorus, and the Sea of Marmora. By Harry Griswold Dwight. Vol. XXVII, pp. 435-459, 27 ills., May, 1915.

German Route to India. By Gilbert H. Grosvenor. Vol. XI, pp. 202-204, 1 page map, May, 1900.

"Grass Never Grows Where the Turkish Hoof Has Trod." By Edwin Pears. Vol. XXIII, pp. 1132-1148, 19 ills., Nov., 1912.

Historic Islands and Shores of the Ægean Sea. By Ernest Lloyd Harris. Vol. XXVIII, pp. 231-262, 29 ills., 1 half-page map., Sept., 1915.

Homer's Troy Today. By Jacob E. Conner. Vol. XXVII, pp. 520-532, 11 ills., 1 half-page map, May, 1915.

Impressions of Asiatic Turkey. By Stephen van Rensselaer Trowbridge. Vol. XXVI, pp. 598-609, 6 ills., Dec., 1914.

Kizilbash Clans of Kurdistan. By Melville Chater. Vol. LIV, pp. 485-504, 22 ills., Oct., 1928.

Land of the Stalking Death : A Journey Through Starving Armenia on an American Relief Train. By Melville Chater. Vol. XXXVI, pp. 393-420, 23 ills., Nov., 1919.

Looking in on the Everyday Life of New Turkey. 12 ills. in color from natural-color photographs by Herman H. Kreider, Maynard Owen Williams, and Gervais Courtellemont. Vol. LXI, pp. 501-508, Apr., 1932.

Lost Wealth of the Kings of Midas. By Ellsworth Huntington. Vol. XXI, pp. 831-846, 15 ills., Oct., 1910.

Most Historic Lands on Earth. Vol. XXVI, pp. 614-615, 1 page map, Dec., 1914.

Mountaineers of the Euphrates. By Ellsworth Huntington. Vol. XX, pp. 142-156, 13 ills., Feb., 1909.

Multicolored Cones of Cappadocia. 20 ills. in color from natural-color photographs by Eric Matson. Vol. LXXVI, pp. 769-800, Dec., 1939.

New Map of Europe : Showing the Boundaries Established by the Peace Conference at Paris and by Subsequent Decisions of the Supreme Council of the Allied and Associated Powers. By Ralph A. Graves. Text accompanying special map supplement in colors. Vol. XXXIX, pp. 157-177, 18 ills., Feb., 1921.

Notes on Troy. Vol. XXVII, pp. 531-532, 1 half-page map, Apr., 1915.

Turkey—*Continued*

Old Pattern and New in Turkey. 23 ills. in color from natural-color photographs by Bernard F. Rogers, Jr. Vol. LXXV, pp. 17-48, Jan., 1939.

On the Turks' Russian Frontier : Everyday Life in the Fastnesses between the Black Sea and Ararat, Borderland of Oil and Minerals that Hitler Covets. By Edward Stevenson Murray. Vol. LXXX, pp. 367-392, 21 ills., 1 half-page map, Sept., 1941.

Peculiar Caves of Asia Minor. By Elizabeth H. Brewer. Vol. XXII, pp. 870-875, 5 ills., Sept., 1911.

Races of Europe. By Edwin A. Grosvenor. Vol. XXXIV, pp. 441-534, 62 ills., 2 page maps, special map supplement, Dec., 1918.

Road of the Crusaders : A Historian Follows the Steps of Richard the Lion Heart and Other Knights of the Cross over the "Via Dei." By Harold Lamb. Vol. LXIV, pp. 645-693, 46 ills. in black and white, 13 ills. in color, 1 page map, Dec., 1933.

Ruined Cities of Asia Minor. By Ernest Lloyd Harris. Vol. XIX, pp. 741-760, 11 ills., Nov., 1908.

Scenes in Asia Minor. Vol. XX, pp. 174-193, 34 ills., 1 three-quarters-page map, Feb., 1909.

Seeing 3,000 Years of History in Four Hours : A Panorama of Ancient, Medieval, and Modern Events Against a Background of Mythology Unfolds During an Airplane Journey from Constantinople to Athens. By Maynard Owen Williams. Vol. LIV, pp. 719-739, 24 ills., 1 two-thirds page map, Dec., 1928.

Sketch of the Geographical History of Asia Minor. By Sir William Ramsay. Vol. XLII, pp. 553-570, 12 ills., Nov., 1922.

Skirting the Shores of Sunrise : Seeking and Finding "The Levant" in a Journey by Steamer, Motor-Car, and Train from Constantinople to Port Said. By Melville Chater. Vol. L, pp. 649-728, 60 ills. in black and white, 34 ills. in color, 1 two-thirds-page map, Dec., 1926.

Some Ruined Cities of Asia Minor. By Ernest Lloyd Harris. Vol. XIX, pp. 833-858, 19 ills., Dec., 1908.

Star and Crescent on Parade. 29 ills. in color from natural-color photographs by Maynard Owen Williams. Vol. LXXXVII, pp. 585-616, May, 1945.

Summer Holidays on the Bosporus. By Maynard Owen Williams. Vol. LVI, pp. 487-508, 13 ills. in black and white, 11 ills. in color, 1 half-page map, Oct., 1929.

Sunshine in Turkey. By Howard S. Bliss. Vol. XX, pp. 66-76, 1 ill., Jan., 1909.

Transformation of Turkey : New Hats and New Alphabet are the Surface Symbols of the Swiftest National Changes in Modern Times. By Douglas Chandler. Vol. LXXV, pp. 1-50, 27 ills. in black and white, 23 ills. in color, 1 map, Jan., 1939.

Turkey—*Continued*

Turkey, Where Earthquakes Followed Timur's Trail. 15 ills. from photographs by Maynard Owen Williams. Vol. LXXVII, pp. 395-406, Mar., 1940.

Turkey Goes to School. By Maynard Owen Williams. Vol. LV, pp. 95-108, 17 ills., Jan., 1929.

Turkish Republic Comes of Age. By Maynard Owen Williams. Vol. LXXXVII, pp. 581-616, 4 ills. in black and white, 29 ills. in color, 1 map (two-page spread), May, 1945.

Two Possible Solutions for the Eastern Problem. By James Bryce. Vol. XXIII, pp. 1149-1157, 5 ills., 1 page map, Nov., 1912.

Under the Heel of the Turk : A Land with a Glorious Past, a Present of Abused Opportunities, and a Future of Golden Possibilities. By William H. Hall. Vol. XXXIV, pp. 50-69, 14 ills., July, 1918.

Where Early Christians Lived in Cones of Rock : A Journey to Cappadocia in Turkey Where Strange Volcanic Pinnacles Are Honeycombed With Hermit Cells and Monasteries. By John D. Whiting. Vol. LXXVI, pp. 763-802, 20 ills. in black and white, 20 ills. in color, 1 half-page map, Dec., 1939.

Young Turk. By Rear Adm. Colby M. Chester. Vol. XXIII, pp. 42-89, 39 ills., Jan., 1912.

See also İstanbul ; Van.

Turkeys:

Domestic Fowls of Field, Park, and Farmyard. 4 ills. in color from paintings by Hashime Murayama. Vol. LVII, pp. 328-361, Mar., 1930.

Fowls of Forest and Stream Tamed by Man. By Morley A. Jull. Vol. LVII, pp. 327-371. 27 ills. in black and white, 16 ills. in color, Mar., 1930.

Turkic Tribes:

With the Nomads of Central Asia : A Summer's Sojourn in the Tekes Valley, Plateau Paradise of Mongol and Turkic Tribes. By Edward Murray. Vol. LXIX, pp. 1-57, 43 ills. in black and white, 26 ills. in color, 1 half-page map, Jan., 1936.

See also Tatars ; Turkomans.

Turkish Republic Comes of Age. By Maynard Owen Williams. Vol. LXXXVII, pp. 581-616, 4 ills. in black and white, 29 ills. in color, 1 map (two-page spread), May, 1945.

Turkistan. *See* Sinkiang ; Soviet Central Asia.

Turkmen Soviet Socialist Republic:

Afghan Borderland. By Ellsworth Huntington. Part I : The Russian Frontier. Vol. XX, pp. 788-799, 14 ills., Sept., 1909.

Life in the Great Desert of Central Asia. By Ellsworth Huntington. Vol. XX, pp. 749-760, 12 ills., Aug., 1909.

Turkomans (Tribespeople) :

Life in the Great Desert of Central Asia. By Ellsworth Huntington. Vol. XX, pp. 749-760, 12 ills., Aug., 1909.

Turkomans—*Continued*

Russia's Orphan Races : Picturesque Peoples Who Cluster on the Southeastern Borderland of the Vast Slav Dominions. By Maynard Owen Williams. Vol. XXXIV, pp. 245-278, 26 ills., 1 page map, Oct., 1918.

Turner, Daniel S.:

Voyage of the *Morrissey*. 10 ills. in color from natural-color photographs by Daniel S. Turner and Sherman A. Wengerd. Vol. LXXXIX, pp. 609-616, May, 1946.

Turning Back Time in the South Seas (Fatu-Hiva Island). By Thor Heyerdahl. Vol. LXXIX, pp. 109-136, 33 ills., 2 maps, Jan., 1941.

Turocz, Sz. Márton, Czechoslovakia :

Czechoslovakia, the Keyland to Central Europe. By Maynard Owen Williams. Vol. XXXIX, pp. 111-156, 45 ills., 1 quarter-page map, Feb., 1921.

Turtles:

Capturing Giant Turtles in the Caribbean. By David D. Duncan. Vol. LXXXIV, pp. 177-190, 13 ills., 1 quarter-page map, Aug., 1943.

Certain Citizens of the Warm Sea. By Louis L. Mowbray. Vol. XLI, pp. 27-62, 18 ills. in black and white, 16 ills. in color, Jan., 1922.

Cultivation of Marine and Fresh Water Animals in Japan. By K. Mitsukuri. Vol. XVII, pp. 524-531, 5 ills., Sept., 1906.

Notes on the Remarkable Habits of Certain Turtles and Lizards. By H. A. Largelamb. Vol. XVIII, pp. 413-419, 12 ills., June, 1907.

Reptiles of All Lands. By Raymond L. Ditmars. Vol. XXII, pp. 601-633, 32 ills., July, 1911.

Turtling:

Capturing Giant Turtles in the Caribbean. By David D. Duncan. Vol. LXXXIV, pp. 177-190, 13 ills., 1 quarter-page map, Aug., 1943.

Tuscany (Department), Italy :

Holidays Among the Hill Towns of Umbria and Tuscany. By Paul Wilstach. Vol. LIII, pp. 401-442, 40 ills., 1 page map, Apr., 1928.

Inexhaustible Italy. By Arthur Stanley Riggs. Vol. XXX, pp. 273-368, 76 ills., 1 page map, Oct., 1916.

Italy, From Roman Ruins to Radio : History of Ancient Bridge Building and Road Making Repeats Itself in Modern Public Works and Engineering Projects. By John Patric. Vol. LXXVII, pp. 347-394, 27 ills. in black and white, 9 ills. in color, Mar., 1940.

Tutankhamen (Pharaoh) :

At the Tomb of Tutankhamen : An Account of the Opening of the Royal Egyptian Sepulcher Which Contained the Most Remarkable Funeral Treasures Unearthed in Historic Times. By Maynard Owen Williams. Vol. XLIII, pp. 461-508, 53 ills., 1 half-page map, May, 1923.

Tutuila (Island), Samoa :

America's South Sea Soldiers. By Lorena MacIntyre Quinn. Vol. XXXVI, pp. 267-274, 8 ills., Sept., 1919.

Tweedsmuir, (Lady) Susan Charlotte. *See* Buchan, Susan Charlotte.

Tweedsmuir Park (British Columbia) : The Diary of a Pilgrimage. By The Lady Tweedsmuir of Elsfield. Vol. LXXIII, pp. 451-476, 22 ills., 1 half-page and 1 third-page maps, Apr., 1938.

Tweedy, Owen:

Unbeliever Joins the Hadj : On the Age-Old Pilgrimage to Mecca, Babies Are Born, Elders Die, and Families May Halt a Year to Earn Funds in Distant Lands. By Owen Tweedy. Vol. LXV, pp. 761-789, 30 ills., 1 page map, June, 1934.

Twenty-third Psalm:

Among the Bethlehem Shepherds : A Visit to the Valley Which David Probably Recalled When He Wrote the Twenty-third Psalm. By John D. Whiting. Vol. L, pp. 729-753, 19 ills., Dec., 1926.

Twin Stars of Chile : Valparaiso, the Gateway, and Santiago, the Capital—Key Cities with a Progressive Present and a Romantic Past. By William Joseph Showalter. Vol. LV, pp. 197-247, 35 ills. in black and white, 25 ills. in color, Feb., 1929.

Twitchell, K. S.:

Kano, Mud-made City. 10 ills. in color from natural-color photographs by George W. Scott and K. S. Twitchell, Vol. LXXXV, pp. 545-552, May, 1944.

Two Fighting Tribes of the Sudan. By Merian C. Cooper. Photographs by Ernest B. Schoedsack. Vol. LVI, pp. 465-486, 27 ills., 1 two-thirds-page map, Oct., 1929.

Two Great Moorish Religious Dances (Tangier, Morocco). By George Edmund Holt. Vol. XXII, pp. 776-785, 6 ills., Aug., 1911.

Two Great Undertakings (Work of U. S. Bureau of Reclamation and U. S. Forest Service). Vol. XVII, pp. 645-647, Nov., 1906.

Two Possible Solutions for the Eastern Problem. By James Bryce. Vol. XXIII, pp. 1149-1157, 5 ills., 1 page map, Nov., 1912.

Tyosen. *See* Korea.

Types and Customs of Old Sweden. 30 ills. in color from autochromes lumière by Gustav Heurlin, G. W. Cronquist, Wilhelm Tobien, and Charles Martin. Vol. LIV, pp. 424-441, Oct., 1928.

Typhoid Fever:

Economic Loss to the People of the United States Through Insects That Carry Disease. By L. O. Howard. Vol. XX, pp. 735-749, Aug., 1909.

Our Army Versus a Bacillus. By Alton G. Grinnell. Vol. XXIV, pp. 1146-1152, 5 ills., 1 diagram, Oct., 1913.

Redeeming the Tropics. By William Joseph Showalter. Vol. XXV, pp. 344-364, 13 ills., Mar., 1914.

Tyrol (Region), Austria-Italy:

Austro-Italian Mountain Frontiers. By Florence Craig Albrecht. Vol. XXVII, pp. 321-376, 60 ills., 1 page map, Apr., 1915.

Entering the Front Doors of Medieval Towns: The Adventures of an American Woman and Her Daughter in a Folding Boat on Eight Rivers of Germany and Austria. By Cornelia Stratton Parker. Vol. LXI, pp. 365-394, 23 ills., 1 two-thirds-page map, Mar., 1932.

Land of Contrast: Austria-Hungary. By D. W. and A. S. Iddings. Vol. XXIII, pp. 1188-1218, 34 ills., Dec., 1912.

Merry Maskers of Imst. 14 ills. from photographs by Francis C. Fuerst. Vol. LXX, pp. 201-208, Aug., 1936.

Over the Alps to Brenner Pass. 15 ills. from photographs, 1 two-page map. Vol. LXXXIV, pp. 701-714, Dec., 1943.

This Was Austria. 18 ills. from photographs. Vol. LXXXVIII, pp. 71-86, July, 1945.

Tyrol, the Happy Mountain Land. 11 ills. in color from natural-color photographs by Hans Hildenbrand. Vol. LXI, pp. 370-379, Mar., 1932.

Tzeliutsing, China:

Salt for China's Daily Rice. 11 ills. from photographs. Vol. LXXXVI, pp. 329-336, Sept., 1944.

Tzotzils (Indians). *See* Zotzils.

U

Uaxactun, Mexico:

Unearthing America's Ancient History: Investigation Suggests That the Maya May Have Designed the First Astronomical Observatory in the New World in Order to Cultivate Corn. By Sylvanus Griswold Morley. Vol. LX, pp. 99-126, 28 ills., July, 1931.

Udaipur (State), India:

Marble Dams of Rajputana. By Eleanor Maddock. Vol. XL, pp. 468-499, 13 ills. in black and white, 16 ills. in color, Nov., 1921.

Uganda:

Amid the Snow Peaks of the Equator: A Naturalist's Explorations Around Ruwenzori, with an Excursion to the Congo State, and an Account of the Terrible Scourge of Sleeping Sickness. By A. F. R. Wollaston. Vol. XX, pp. 256-277, 11 ills., Mar., 1909.

Elephant Hunting in Equatorial Africa with Rifle and Camera. By Carl E. Akeley. Vol. XXIII, pp. 779-810, 30 ills., Aug., 1912.

Great African Lake (Victoria). By Sir Henry M. Stanley. Vol. XIII, pp. 169-172, 1 half-page map, May, 1902.

Uganda, "Land of Something New": Equatorial African Area Reveals Snow-Crowned Peaks, Crater Lakes, Jungle-Story Beasts, Human Giants, and Forest Pygmies. By Jay Marston. Vol. LXXI, pp. 109-130, 22 ills., 1 two-thirds-page map, Jan., 1937.

Where Roosevelt Will Hunt. By Sir Harry Johnston. Vol. XX, pp. 207-256, 43 ills., special map supplement, Mar., 1909.

Uganda—*Continued*

Wild Man and Wild Beast in Africa. By Theodore Roosevelt. Vol. XXII, pp. 1-33, 41 ills., 1 page map, Jan., 1911.

Ukraine, Past and Present. By Nevin O. Winter. Vol. XXXIV, pp. 114-128, 14 ills., Aug., 1918.

Ukrainian Soviet Socialist Republic, U.S.S.R.:

Liberated Ukraine. By Eddy Gilmore. Vol. LXXXV, pp. 513-536, 22 ills., 1 page map, May, 1944.

Races of Europe. By Edwin A. Grosvenor. Vol. XXXIV, pp. 441-534, 62 ills., 2 page maps, special map supplement, Dec., 1918.

Society's New Map of Soviet Russia. Text accompanying special map supplement in colors. Vol. LXXXVI, pp. 716-718, Dec., 1944.

Ukraine, Past and Present. By Nevin O. Winter. Vol. XXXIV, pp. 114-128, 14 ills., Aug., 1918.

Ulithi (Island), Caroline Islands:

American Pathfinders in the Pacific. By William H. Nicholas. Vol. LXXXIX, pp. 617-640, 17 ills., 1 two-page map, May, 1946.

Ulm, (Lt.) Charles T. P.:

Our Conquest of the Pacific: The Narrative of the 7,400-Mile Flight from San Francisco to Brisbane in Three Ocean Hops. By Squadron-Leader Charles E. Kingsford-Smith and Flight-Lt. Charles T. P. Ulm. Vol. LIV, pp. 371-402, 27 ills., 1 two-thirds-page map, Oct., 1928.

Ulster (Northern Ireland). *See* Northern Ireland.

Ultimate Washington (Plan Laid Out by the Commission of 1901 for the National Capital). Vol. XXVII, colored panorama, Mar., 1915.

Umbrella Ants. *See* Atta Ants.

Umbria (Department), Italy:

Holidays Among the Hill Towns of Umbria and Tuscany. By Paul Wilstach. Vol. LIII, pp. 401-442, 40 ills., 1 page map, Apr., 1928.

Umnak (Island), Aleutian Islands:

Navy Artist Paints the Aleutians. By Mason Sutherland. Paintings by Lt. William F. Draper. Vol. LXXXIV, pp. 157-176, 4 ills. in black and white, 16 ills. in color, Aug., 1943.

Unalaska (Island), Aleutian Islands:

Shishaldin as a Field for Exploration. By Joseph Stanley-Brown. Vol. X, pp. 281-288, 3 ills., 1 quarter-page map, Aug., 1899.

Unbeliever Joins the Hadj: On the Age-Old Pilgrimage to Mecca, Babies Are Born, Elders Die, and Families May Halt a Year to Earn Funds in Distant Lands. By Owen Tweedy. Vol. LXV, pp. 761-789, 30 ills., 1 page map, June, 1934.

Uncle Sam's Icebox Outposts (Greenland). 19 ills. in color from natural-color photographs by John E. Schneider and Robert B. Sykes, Jr. Vol. XC, pp. 473-496, Oct., 1946.

Uncompahgre Valley, Colorado:

Home-Making by the Government: An Account of the Eleven Immense Irrigating Projects to be Opened in 1908. By C. J. Blanchard. Vol. XIX, pp. 250-287, 23 ills., Apr., 1908.

Spirit of the West: The Wonderful Agricultural Development Since the Dawn of Irrigation. By C. J. Blanchard. Vol. XXI, pp. 333-360, 15 ills., Apr., 1910.

Under Egypt's Golden Sun. 22 ills. in color from natural-color photographs by B. Anthony Stewart. Vol. LXXVII, pp. 451-466, Apr., 1940.

Under Radiant Italian Skies. 8 ills. in color from autochromes by Hans Hildenbrand. Vol. L, pp. 248-257, Aug., 1926.

Under Swedish Roofs and Skies. 22 ills. in color from natural-color photographs by Volkmar Wentzel. Vol. LXXVII, pp. 799-822, June, 1940.

Under the French Tricolor in Indo-China. 28 ills. in color from natural-color photographs by W. Robert Moore. Vol. LX, pp. 166-100, Aug., 1931.

Under the Heel of the Turk: A Land with a Glorious Past, a Present of Abused Opportunities, and a Future of Golden Possibilities. By William H. Hall. Vol. XXXIV, pp. 50-69, 14 ills., July, 1918.

Under the South African Union. By Melville Chater. Vol. LIX, pp. 391-512, 97 ills. in black and white, 38 ills. in color, 1 two-page map, Apr., 1931.
Contents. Cape of Good Hope. The Floral Province.—Orange Free State: The Prairie Province.—Natal: The Garden Province.—The Transvaal: The Treasure-House Province.

Underground:

White War in Norway. By Thomas R. Henry. Vol. LXXXVIII, pp. 617-640, 23 ills., 1 three-quarters-page map, Nov., 1945.

Underhill, Miriam O'Brien:

Manless Alpine Climbing: The First Woman to Scale the Grépon, the Matterhorn, and Other Famous Peaks Without Masculine Support Relates Her Adventures. By Miriam O'Brien Underhill. Vol. LXVI, pp. 131-170, 30 ills. in black and white, 12 ills. in color, Aug., 1934.

Undersea Gardens of the North Atlantic Coast. 8 ills. in color from paintings by Else Bostelmann. Vol. LXX, pp. 217-224, Aug., 1936.

Underwood, Eric:

British Commonwealth of Nations: "Organized Freedom" Around the World. By Eric Underwood. Vol. LXXXIII, pp. 485-524, 31 ills., Apr., 1943.

Preservation of England's Historic and Scenic Treasures. By Eric Underwood. Vol. LXXXVII, pp. 413-440, 24 ills., 1 two-page map, Apr., 1945.

Unearthing America's Ancient History: Investigation Suggests That the Maya May Have Designed the First Astronomical Observatory in the New World in Order to Cultivate Corn. By Sylvanus Griswold Morley. Vol. LX, pp. 99-126, 28 ills., July, 1931.

Unexplored Philippines from the Air: Map-making Over Jungle Lands Never Before Seen by White Men. By Lieut. George W. Goddard. Vol. LVIII, pp. 311-343, 38 ills., 1 quarter-page map, Sept., 1930.

Unfurling Old Glory on Canton Island. 11 ills. in color; 1 painting by Charles Bittinger and 10 natural-color photographs. Vol. LXXIII, pp. 753-760, June, 1938.

Ungern-Sternberg, (Baroness) Irina:

Estonia: At Russia's Baltic Gate: War Often Has Ravaged This Little Nation Whose Identity Was Long Submerged in the Vast Sea of Russian Peoples. By Baroness Irina Ungern-Sternberg. Vol. LXXVI, pp. 803-834, 33 ills., 1 half-page map, Dec., 1939.

Unimak (Island), Aleutian Islands:

Mountains on Unimak Island, Alaska. By Ferdinand Westdahl. Vol. XIV, pp. 90-99, 4 ills., 1 page and 1 half-page maps, Mar., 1903.

Union of South Africa:

British Commonwealth of Nations: "Organized Freedom" Around the World. By Eric Underwood. Vol. LXXXIII, pp. 485-524, 31 ills., Apr., 1945.

British South Africa and the Transvaal. By F. F. Hilder. Vol. XI, pp. 81-96, 7 ills., Mar., 1900.

Busy Corner—the Cape of Good Hope: Ships Bound for Faraway Battlegrounds Stream Past Capetown, "Tavern of the Seas," and Other Ports of Virile South Africa. By W. Robert Moore. Vol. LXXXII, pp. 197-223, 11 ills. in black and white, 11 ills. in color, 1 two-thirds-page map, Aug., 1942.

Cairo to Cape Town, Overland: An Adventurous Journey of 135 Days, Made by an American Man and His Wife, Through the Length of the African Continent. By Felix Shay. Vol. XLVII, pp. 123-260, 118 ills., 1 half-page map, Feb., 1925.

Cities That Gold and Diamonds Built: Transvaal Treasures Have Created Bustling Johannesburg and Fostered Pretoria, Administrative Capital of the South African Union. By W. Robert Moore. Vol. LXXXII, pp. 735-766, 20 ills. in black and white, 9 ills. in color, 1 two-thirds-page map, Dec., 1942.

Color of Africa's Southern Tip. 11 ills. in color from natural-color photographs by W. Robert Moore. Vol. LXXXII, pp. 213-220, Aug., 1942.

Diamond Mines of South Africa. By Gardiner F. Williams. Vol. XVII, pp. 344-356, 11 ills., June, 1906.

Faces and Flowers Below the Tropics. 14 ills. in color from natural-color photographs by Melville Chater. Vol. LIX, pp. 452-461, Apr., 1931.

Great Britain's Bread Upon the Waters: Canada and Her Other Daughters. By William Howard Taft. Vol. XXIX, pp. 217-272, 56 ills., Mar., 1916.

Union of South Africa—*Continued*

Influence of Geographical Conditions on Military Operations in South Africa. By Maj. W. A. Simpson. Vol. XI, pp. 186-192, 1 half-page map, May, 1900.

Natal : The Garden Colony. By Russell Hastings Millward. Vol. XX, pp. 278-291, 16 ills., Mar., 1909.

Scenes on High Veld and Low. 13 ills. in color from natural-color photographs by Melville Chater. Vol. LIX, pp. 492-501, Apr., 1931.

Sunny South Africa. 9 ills. in color from natural-color photographs by W. Robert Moore. Vol. LXXXII, pp. 749-756, Dec., 1942.

Trekking South Africa with a Color Camera. 11 ills. in color from natural-color photographs by Melville Chater. Vol. LIX, pp. 412-421, Apr., 1931.

Under the South African Union. By Melville Chater. Vol. LIX, pp. 391-512, 97 ills. in black and white, 38 ills. in color, 1 two-page map, Apr., 1931.

> Contents : Cape of Good Hope : The Floral Province.—Orange Free State : The Prairie Province.—Natal : The Garden Province.—The Transvaal : The Treasure-House Province.

Union of Soviet Socialist Republics :

Afghan Borderland. By Ellsworth Huntington. Part I : The Russian Frontier. Vol. XX, pp. 788-799, 14 ills., Sept., 1909.

Armenia and the Armenians. By Hester Donaldson Jenkins. Vol. XXVIII, pp. 329-360, 27 ills., 1 half-page map, Oct., 1915.

British Take Baku. Vol. XXXIV, pp. 163-164, 1 ill., Aug., 1918.

Evolution of Russian Government. By Edwin A. Grosvenor. Vol. XVI, pp. 309-332, 16 ills., July, 1905.

Far Eastern Republic. By Junius B. Wood. Vol. XLI, pp. 565-592, 29 ills., 1 three-quarters-page map, June, 1922.

Few Glimpses into Russia. By Lieut. Zinovi Pechkoff. Vol. XXXII, pp. 238-253, 10 ills., Sept., 1917.

First Airship Flight Around the World : Dr. Hugo Eckener Tells of an Epochal Geographic Achievement Upon the Occasion of the Bestowal of the National Geographic Society's Special Gold Medal. Vol. LVII, pp. 653-688, 37 ills., June, 1929.

Geographical Pivot of History (Steppes of Central Asia). By H. J. Mackinder. Vol. XV, pp. 331-335, Aug., 1904.

Glimpses of Siberia, the Russian "Wild East." By Cody Marsh. Vol. XXXVIII, pp. 512-536, 26 ills., Dec., 1920.

Glimpses of the Russian Empire. By William Wisner Chapin. Vol. XXIII, pp. 1043-1078, 51 ills. in color, 1 three-quarters-page map, Nov., 1912.

Growth of Russia. By Edwin A. Grosvenor. Vol. XI, pp. 169-185, 2 page and 3 half-page maps, May, 1900.

I Learn About the Russians. By Eddy Gilmore. Vol. LXXXIV, pp. 619-640, 21 ills., Nov., 1943.

Union of Soviet Socialist Republics—*Continued*

Island in the Sea of History : The Highlands of Daghestan. By George Kennan. Vol. XXIV, pp. 1086-1140, 49 ills., 1 page map, Oct., 1913.

Japan Faces Russia in Manchuria. By Willard Price. Vol. LXXXII, pp. 603-634, 30 ills., 1 page map, Nov., 1942.

Land of Lambskins : An Expedition to Bokhara, Russian Central Asia, to Study the Karakul Sheep Industry. By Robert K. Nabours. Vol. XXXVI, pp. 77-88, 15 ills., July, 1919.

Land of Promise (Siberia). By Maj. Gen. A. W. Greely. Vol. XXIII, pp. 1078-1090, 7 ills., Nov., 1912.

Land of the Stalking Death : A Journey Through Starving Armenia on an American Relief Train. By Melville Chater. Vol. XXXVI, pp. 393-420, 23 ills., Nov., 1919.

Lend-Lease and the Russian Victory. By Harvey Klemmer. Vol. LXXXVIII, pp. 499-512, 6 ills., Oct., 1945.

Life in the Great Desert of Central Asia. By Ellsworth Huntington. Vol. XX, pp. 749-760, 12 ills., Aug., 1909.

"Magnetic City" (Magnitogorsk), Core of Valiant Russia's Industrial Might. By John Scott. Vol. LXXXIII, pp. 525-556, 27 ills., 1 two-page map, May, 1943.

Mother Volga Defends Her Own. By Maynard Owen Williams. Vol. LXXXII, pp. 793-811, 21 ills., Dec., 1942.

Murman Coast : Arctic Gateway for American and Allied Expeditionary Forces in Northern European Russia. Vol. XXXV, pp. 331-348, 30 ills., 1 half-page map, Apr., 1919.

New Map of Europe : Showing the Boundaries Established by the Peace Conference at Paris and by Subsequent Decisions of the Supreme Council of the Allied and Associated Powers. By Ralph A. Graves. Text accompanying special map supplement in colors. Vol. XXXIX, pp. 157-177, 18 ills., Feb., 1921.

New Road to Asia. By Owen Lattimore. Vol. LXXXVI, pp. 641-676, 15 ills. in black and white, 26 ills. in color, Dec., 1944.

Observations on the Russo-Japanese War in Japan and Manchuria. By Louis Livingston Seaman. Vol. XVI, pp. 80-82, Feb., 1905.

Observing an Eclipse in Asiatic Russia. By Irvine C. Gardner. Vol. LXXI, pp. 179-197, 19 ills. in black and white, 1 ill. in color, Feb., 1937.

Old Post-Road from Tiflis to Erivan. By Esther Lancraft Hovey. Vol. XII, pp. 300-309, 9 ills., Aug., 1901.

Races of Europe. By Edwin A. Grosvenor. Vol. XXXIV, pp. 441-534, 62 ills., 2 page maps, special map supplement, Dec., 1918.

Rebirth of Religion in Russia : The Church Reorganized While Bolshevik Cannon Spread Destruction in the Nation's Holy of Holies. By Thomas Whittemore. Vol. XXXIV, pp. 378-401, 16 ills., Nov., 1918.

Revolution in Russia. By William Eleroy Curtis. Vol. XVIII, pp. 302-316, May, 1907.

Union of Soviet Socialist Republics—*Continued*

Roaming Russia's Caucasus : Rugged Mountains and Hardy Fighters Guard the Soviet Union's Caucasian Treasury of Manganese and Oil. By Rolf Singer. Vol. LXXXII, pp. 91-121, 33 ills., July, 1942.

Russia. By Charles Emory Smith. Vol. XVI, pp. 55-68, Feb., 1905.

Russia from Within : Her War of Yesterday, Today, and Tomorrow. By Stanley Washburn. Vol. XXXII, pp. 91-120, 30 ills., Aug., 1917.

Russia in Recent Literature. By Maj. Gen. A. W. Greely. Vol. XVI, pp. 564-568, Dec., 1905.

Russia of the Hour : Giant Battle Ground for Theories of Economy, Society, and Politics, as Observed by an Unbiased Correspondent. By Junius B. Wood. Vol. L, pp. 519-598, 81 ills., Nov., 1926.

Russian Situation and Its Significance to America. By Stanley Washburn. Vol. XXXI, pp. 371-382, 8 ills., Apr., 1917.

Russia's Democrats. By Montgomery Schuyler. Vol. XXXI, pp. 210-240, 25 ills., Mar., 1917.

Russia's Man of the Hour : Alexander Kerensky's First Speeches and Proclamations. Vol. XXXII, pp. 24-45, 17 ills., July, 1917.

Russia's Orphan Races : Picturesque Peoples Who Cluster on the Southeastern Borderland of the Vast Slav Dominions. By Maynard Owen Williams. Vol. XXXIV, pp. 245-278, 26 ills., 1 page map, Oct., 1918.

Russia's Wheat Surplus. Vol. XVII, pp. 580-583, Oct., 1906.

Siberia. By Edwin A. Grosvenor. Vol. XII, pp. 317-324, Sept., 1901.

Society's New Map of Soviet Russia. Text accompanying special map supplement in colors. Vol. LXXXVI, pp. 716-718, Dec., 1944.

Some Impressions of 150,000 Miles of Travel. By William Howard Taft. Vol. LVII, pp. 523-598, 80 ills., May, 1930.

Sunny Siberia. 26 ills. in color from natural-color photographs by Owen Lattimore. Vol. LXXXVI, pp. 649-672, Dec., 1944.

Supposed Birthplace of Civilizations. Vol. XVI, pp. 499-504, 6 ills., Nov., 1905.

Surveying Through Khoresm : A Journey Into Parts of Asiatic Russia Which Have Been Closed to Western Travelers Since the World War. By Lyman D. Wilbur. Vol. LXI, pp. 753-780, 31 ills., 1 two-thirds-page map, June, 1932.

Ties That Bind : Our Natural Sympathy with English Traditions, the French Republic, and the Russian Outburst for Liberty. By John Sharp Williams. Vol. XXXI, pp. 281-286, 4 ills., Mar., 1917.

Trip Through Siberia. By Ebenezer J. Hill. Vol. XIII, pp. 37-54, 17 ills., 1 quarter-page map, Feb., 1902.

Voyaging on the Volga Amid War and Revolution : War-Time Sketches on Russia's Great Waterway. By William T. Ellis. Vol. XXXIII, pp. 246-265, 16 ills., Mar., 1918.

Union of Soviet Socialist Republics—*Continued*

Western Siberia and the Altai Mountains : With Some Speculations on the Future of Siberia. By James Bryce. Vol. XXXIX, pp. 469-507, 39 ills., May, 1921.

Where Slav and Mongol Meet. Vol. XXXVI, pp. 421-436, 16 ills. in color, Nov., 1919.

With an Exile in Arctic Siberia : The Narrative of a Russian Who Was Compelled to Turn Polar Explorer for Two Years. By Vladimir M. Zenzinov. Vol. XLVI, pp. 695-718, 30 ills., 1 half-page map, Dec., 1924.

Young Russia : The Land of Unlimited Possibilities. By Gilbert H. Grosvenor. Vol. XXVI, pp. 421-520, 85 ills. in black and white, 17 ills. in color, Nov., 1914.

See also Crimean Autonomous Soviet Socialist Republic ; Ukrainian Soviet Socialist Republic.

Unique Gifts of Washington to the Nation. 11 ills. in color from natural-color photographs by Charles Martin, Edwin L. Wisherd, Jacob Gayer, and Clifton Adams. Vol. LV, pp. 472-481, Apr., 1929.

Unique Island of Mount Desert (Maine). By George B. Dorr, Ernest Howe Forbush, and M. L. Fernald. Vol. XXVI, pp. 75-89, 7 ills., July, 1914.

Unique Republic, Where Smuggling Is an Industry (Andorra). By Herbert Corey. Vol. XXXIII, pp. 279-299, 16 ills., 1 half-page map, Mar., 1918.

United States :

Aces Among Aces (Aviators). By Laurence La Tourette Driggs. Vol. XXXIII, pp. 568-580, 9 ills., June, 1918.

Aerial Color Photography Becomes a War Weapon. By H. H. Arnold. Vol. LXXVII, pp. 757-766, 8 ills. in color, June, 1940.

Along Our Side of the Mexican Border. By Frederick Simpich. Vol. XXXVIII, pp. 61-80, 9 ills., 1 quarter-page map, July, 1920.

America Fights on the Farms. 21 ills. in color from natural-color photographs. Vol. LXXXVI, pp. 33-48, July, 1944.

America in the Air : The Future of Airplane and Airship, Economically and as Factors in National Defense. By Brig. Gen. William Mitchell. Vol. XXXIX, pp. 339-352, 8 ills., 1 three-quarters-page map, Mar., 1921.

America on the Move. 26 ills. from photographs by J. Baylor Roberts, B. Anthony Stewart, and others. Vol. XC, pp. 357-378, Sept., 1946.

American Deserts. Vol. XV, pp. 152-163, 7 ills., 1 half-page map, Apr., 1904.

American Fable (Conservation of Resources). By Gifford Pinchot. Vol. XIX, pp. 345-350, May, 1908.

American Industries Geared for War. By Thornton Oakley. With 16 ills. in color from paintings by the author. Vol. LXXXII, pp. 716-734, 1 ill. in black and white, Dec., 1942.

American People Must Become Ship-Minded. By Edward N. Hurley. Vol. XXXIV, pp. 201-211, 7 ills., Sept., 1918.

United States—*Continued*

American Scene. 29 ills. from winning photographs to the Sixth Annual Newspaper National Snapshot Awards, with explanatory note. Vol. LXXIX, pp. 220-246, Feb., 1941.

American Transportation Vital to Victory. By Thornton Oakley. With 16 ills. in color from paintings by the author. Vol. LXXXIV, pp. 671-688, Dec., 1943.

Americana. 11 ills. from winning photographs in the Seventh Annual Newspaper National Snapshot Awards. Vol. LXXXI, pp. 657-666, May, 1942.

America's Amazing Railway Traffic. By William Joseph Showalter. Vol. XLIII, pp. 353-404, 46 ills., 1 third-page map, Apr., 1923.

America's Duty. By Newton D. Baker. Vol. XXXI, pp. 453-457, 4 ills., May, 1917.

America's Part in the Allies' Mastery of the Air. By Maj. Joseph Tulasne. Vol. XXXIII, pp. 1-5, 2 ills., Jan., 1918.

Animal Wealth of the United States. By Francis E. Warren. Vol. XVII, pp. 511-524, 6 ills., Sept., 1906.

Another Important Map. Text accompanying special map supplement in colors. Vol. XLIII, p. 336, Mar., 1923.

As 2,000 Ships Are Born. By Frederick Simpich. Vol. LXXXI, pp. 551-588, 34 ills., May, 1942.

Automobile Industry: An American Art That Has Revolutionized Methods in Manufacturing and Transformed Transportation. By William Joseph Showalter. Vol. XLIV, pp. 337-414, 76 ills., Oct., 1923.

Battle-Ground of Nature: The Atlantic Seaboard. By John Oliver La Gorce. Vol. XXXIII, pp. 511-546, 23 ills., 4 half-page maps, June, 1918.

Big Things of the West. By Charles F. Holder. Vol. XIV, pp. 279-282, 2 ills., July, 1903.

Billions of Barrels of Oil Locked Up in Rocks. By Guy Elliott Mitchell. Vol. XXXIII, pp. 195-205, 10 ills., Feb., 1918.

Boundaries of Territorial Acquisitions. Vol. XII, pp. 373-377, 1 page chart, Oct., 1901.

Building America's Air Army. By Hiram Bingham. Vol. XXXIII, pp. 48-86, 43 ills., Jan., 1918.

By Car and Steamer Around Our Inland Seas. By Maynard Owen Williams. Vol. LXV, pp. 451-491, 29 ills. in black and white, 8 ills. in duotone, 1 two-page map, Apr., 1934.

Calculations of Population in June, 1900. By Henry Farquhar. Vol. X, pp. 406-413, Oct., 1899.

Call of the West. By C. J. Blanchard. Vol. XX, pp. 403-437, 20 ills., 1 half-page map, May, 1909.

Canyons and Cacti of the American Southwest. 22 ills. in color from natural-color photographs by Edwin L. Wisherd, Jacob Gayer, and Charles Martin. Vol. XLVIII, pp. 275-290, Sept., 1925.

United States—*Continued*

Census of 1900. By Dr. F. H. Wines. Vol. XI, pp. 34-36, Jan., 1900.

Center of Population of the United States. Vol. XII, p. 241, June, 1901.

Central Great Plains. Vol. XVI, pp. 389-397, Aug., 1905.

Character of Our Immigration, Past and Present. By Z. F. McSweeny. Vol. XVI, pp. 1-15, 1 chart, Jan., 1905.

China and the United States. By Sir Chentung Liang-Cheng. Vol. XVI, pp. 554-557, Dec., 1905.

Coal, Prodigious Worker for Man. By Albert W. Atwood. Vol. LXXXV, pp. 569-592, 19 ills., 1 drawing, May, 1944.

Columbia (River) Turns on the Power. By Maynard Owen Williams. Vol. LXXIX, pp. 749-792, 25 ills. in black and white, 18 ills. in color, June, 1941.

Commerce of Mexico and the United States. By O. P. Austin. Vol. XIII, pp. 25-26, Jan., 1902.

Conservation League of America. By Henry Gannett. Vol. XIX, pp. 737-739, Oct., 1908.

Conservation of Our National Resources. Vol. XIX, p. 384, May, 1908.

Controlling Sand Dunes in the United States and Europe. By A. S. Hitchcock. Vol. XV, pp. 43-47, 4 ills., Jan., 1904.

Correct Display of the Stars and Stripes. By Byron McCandless and Gilbert Grosvenor. Vol. XXXII, pp. 404-413, 8 ills., Oct., 1917.

Cotton: Foremost Fiber of the World. By J. R. Hildebrand. Vol. LXXIX, pp. 137-192, 31 ills. in black and white, 34 ills. in color, Feb., 1941.

Dealings of the United States with the Nations of the World. Vol. XV, pp. 186-187, Apr., 1904.

Deep-Water Route from Chicago to the Gulf. Vol. XVIII, pp. 676-685, 3 ills., 1 page map, Oct., 1907.

Down the Rio Grande: Tracing this Strange, Turbulent Stream on Its Long Course from Colorado to the Gulf of Mexico. By Frederick Simpich. Vol. LXXVI, pp. 415-462, 28 ills. in black and white, 24 ills. in color, 6 maps, Oct., 1939.

Drowned Empire (Swamp Drainage). By Robert H. Chapman. Vol. XIX, pp. 190-199, 10 ills., Mar., 1908.

Economic Loss of the People of the United States Through Insects That Carry Disease. By L. O. Howard. Vol. XX, pp. 735-749, Aug., 1909.

Exploring the Atlantic Seaboard with a Color Camera. 18 ills. in color from autochromes by Charles Martin and Jacob Gayer. Vol. XLIX, pp. 532-549, May, 1926.

Exports of Manufactures. Vol. XVI, pp. 434-437, Sept., 1905.

Fantastic Plants of Our Western Deserts. 8 ills. by Frank M. Campbell. Vol. XLV, pp. 33-40, Jan., 1924.

United States—*Continued*

Farmers Keep Them Eating. By Frederick Simpich. Vol. LXXXIII, pp. 435-458, 22 ills., Apr., 1943.

Fearful Famines of the Past: History Will Repeat Itself Unless the American People Conserve Their Resources. By Ralph A. Graves. Vol. XXXII, pp. 68-90, 11 ills., July, 1917.

First Alaskan Air Expedition. By Capt. St. Clair Streett. Vol. XLI, pp. 499-552, 37 ills., 1 page map, May, 1922.

Fishes and Fisheries of Our North Atlantic Seaboard. By John Oliver La Gorce. Vol. XLIV, pp. 567-634, 35 ills. in black and white, 16 ills. in color, Dec., 1923.

Flags of Our Army, Navy, and Government Departments. By Byron McCandless and Gilbert Grosvenor. Vol. XXXII, pp. 305-322, 3 ills. in black and white, 300 ills. in color, Oct., 1917.

Flags of the World. By Gilbert Grosvenor and William J. Showalter. Vol. LXVI, pp. 339-396, 10 ills. in black and white, 808 ills. in color, Sept., 1934.

Flaming Cliffs of Monument Valley. By Lt. Jack Breed, USNR. With 9 ills. in color from natural-color photographs by the author and Warren T. Mithoff. Vol. LXXXVIII, pp. 452-461, Oct., 1945.

Flow Onward, Connecticut (River)! 24 ills. in color from natural-color photographs; 22 ills. by B. Anthony Stewart. Vol. LXXXIII, pp. 409-432, Apr., 1943.

Flying. By Gilbert Grosvenor. Vol. LXIII, pp 585-630, 33 ills in black and white, 17 ills. in duotone, May, 1933.

Foreign-Born of the United States. Vol. XXVI, pp. 265-271, 14 diagrams, Sept., 1914.

Foreign Commerce of the United States in 1903. Vol. XIV, pp. 359-360, Sept., 1903.

Forest Reserves of the United States. By Gifford Pinchot. Vol. XI, pp. 369-372, 1 three-quarters-page map, Sept., 1900.

Freighters of Fortune on Our Great Lakes. 8 ills. in duotone from photographs by Maynard Owen Williams. Vol. LXV, pp. 463-470, Apr., 1934.

From the War-Path to the Plow. By Franklin K. Lane. Vol. XXVII, pp. 72-87, 12 ills., Jan., 1915.

Gardens of the West. Vol. XVI, pp. 118-123, 7 ills., Mar., 1905.

Geographic Names in the United States and the Stories They Tell. By R. H. Whitbeck. Vol. XVI, pp. 100-104, Mar., 1905.

Geography of a Hurricane: A Doughnut-shaped Storm Turned Back Time in New England to Candlelight Days, but Revealed Anew Yankee Courage and Ingenuity. By F. Barrows Colton. Vol. LXXV, pp. 529-552, 20 ills., 1 page map, Apr., 1939.

Geography of Our Foreign Trade. By Frederick Simpich. Vol. XLI, pp. 89-108, 25 ills., Jan., 1922.

United States—*Continued*

Glass "Goes to Town." By J. R. Hildebrand. Vol. LXXXIII, pp. 1-48, 28 ills. in black and white, 22 ills. in color, Jan., 1943.

Glimpses East and West in America. Vol. XLV, pp. 531-546, 16 ills., May, 1924.

Crops Growing Industry in the United States. Vol. XIV, pp. 445-451, 5 ills., Dec., 1903.

Great Canals of the World. Vol. XVI, pp. 475-479, Oct., 1905.

Great Mississippi Flood of 1927: Since White Man's Discovery This Mighty River Has Served Him Well, Yet It Has Brought Widespread Devastation Along Its Lower Reaches. By Frederick Simpich. Vol. LII, pp. 243-289, 53 ills., 1 half-page map, Sept., 1927.

Gulf Coast Towns Get into the Fight. 19 ills. in color from natural-color photographs; 17 ills. by J. Baylor Roberts. Vol. LXXXV, pp. 17-40, Jan., 1944.

Highest Point in Each State. Vol. XX, pp. 539-541, 2 ills., June, 1909.

Home Folk around Historic Cumberland Gap. By Leo A. Borah. Vol. LXXXIV, pp. 741-768, 25 ills., 1 quarter-page map, Dec., 1943.

Home-Making by the Government: An Account of the Eleven Immense Irrigating Projects to be Opened in 1908. By C. J. Blanchard. Vol. XIX, pp. 250-287, 23 ills., Apr., 1908.

How Long Will the Coal Reserves of the United States Last? By Marius R. Campbell. Vol. XVIII, pp. 129-138, 5 diagrams, 1 half-page map, Feb., 1907.

How the United States Grew. By McFall Kerbey. Vol. LXIII, pp. 631-649, 17 ills., 1 page map, May, 1933.

How We Use the Gulf of Mexico. By Frederick Simpich. Vol. LXXXV, pp. 1-40. 20 ills. in black and white, 19 ills. in color, 1 two-page map, Jan., 1944.

Immigration to the Southern States. Vol. XVI, pp. 517-519, Nov., 1905.

Is Climatic Aridity Impending on the Pacific Slope? The Testimony of the Forest. By J. B. Leiberg. Vol. X, pp. 160-181, May, 1899.

Japan, America, and the Orient. By Eki Hioki. Vol. XVII, pp. 498-504, Sept., 1906.

Japan and the United States. Vol. XVI, pp. 432-434, 1 ill., Sept., 1905.

Land of a Million Smiles (Ozarks). By Frederick Simpich. Vol. LXXXIII, pp. 589-623, 14 ills. in black and white, 20 ills. in color, 1 two-thirds-page map, May, 1943.

Land of the Best. By Gilbert H. Grosvenor. Vol. XXIX, pp. 327-430, 71 ills. in black and white, 33 ills. in color, panorama, Apr., 1916.

Lend-Lease and the Russian Victory. By Harvey Klemmer. Vol. LXXXVIII, pp. 499-512, 6 ills., Oct., 1945.

Life on the Grand Banks: An Account of the Sailor-Fishermen Who Harvest the Shoal Waters of North America's Eastern Coasts. By Frederick William Wallace. Vol. XL, pp. 1-28, 29 ills., July, 1921.

United States—*Continued*

Limited Water Supply of the Arid Region. By Frederick H. Newell. Vol. XI, pp. 438-442, Nov., 1900.

Long River of New England: In War and Peace, from Mountain Wilderness to the Sea, Flows the Connecticut River, Through a Valley Abounding in History, Scenery, Inventive Genius, and Industry. By Albert W. Atwood. Vol. LXXXIII, pp. 401-434, 12 ills. in black and white, 24 ills. in color, 1 two-thirds-page map, Apr., 1943.

Magnetic Survey of the United States. By Dr. L. A. Bauer. Vol. XIII, pp. 92-95, 1 half-page map, Mar., 1902.

Maneuvers of Military Planes Disclose Majestic Aërial Views. 17 ills. in duotone from U. S. Army and Navy official photographs. Vol. LXIII, pp. 598-615, May, 1933.

Marvelous Prosperity of the South. Vol. XVIII, p. 685, Oct., 1905.

Men Against the Rivers (Mississippi and Ohio Rivers). By Frederick Simpich. Vol. LXXI, pp. 767-794, 22 ills., 1 page-and-a-half and 1 quarter-page maps, June, 1937.

Metal Sinews of Strength: This Is a War of Many Metals, for We Live in an Age of Alloys. By Frederick G. Vosburgh. Vol. LXXXI, pp. 457-491, 35 ills., Apr., 1942.

Mind's-Eye Map of America. By Franklin K. Lane. Vol. XXXVII, pp. 479-518, 25 ills. in black and white, 8 ills. in color, June, 1920.

Miracle of War Production: For Victory the United States Transforms Its Complex Industry into the Biggest Factory and Mightiest Arsenal the World Has Ever Known. By Albert W. Atwood. Paintings by Thornton Oakley. Vol. LXXXII, pp. 693-715, 17 ills. in black and white, 16 ills. in color, Dec., 1942.

National Geographic Society's Map of Northeastern United States. Text accompanying special map supplement in colors. Vol. LXXXVIII, pp. 361-362, Sept., 1945.

National Growth and National Character. By W J McGee. Vol. X, pp. 185-206, June, 1899.

Nation's Pride (Natural Resources). By Franklin K. Lane. Vol. XXVIII, pp. 589-606, 6 ills., Dec., 1915.

Nation's Undeveloped Resources. By Franklin K. Lane. Vol. XXV, pp. 183-225, 32 ills., Feb., 1914.

Native Oysters of the West Coast. By Robert E. C. Stearns. Vol. XIX, pp. 224-226, Mar., 1908.

Nature's Scenic Marvels of the West. 17 ills. in duotone. Vol. LXIV, pp. 16-33, July, 1933.

New Map Reveals the Progress and Wonders of Our Country. Text accompanying special map supplement in colors. Vol. LXIII, pp. 650-652, 1 ill., May, 1933.

New United States Map Shows Census Changes. Text accompanying special map supplement in colors. Vol. LXXVIII, pp. 821-824, 2 ills., Dec., 1940.

United States—*Continued*

Non-Stop Flight Across America. By Lieut. John A. Macready. Photographs by Lieut. Albert W. Stevens. Vol. XLVI, pp. 1-83, 68 ills., 1 page and 1 half-page maps, July, 1924.

Northeast of Boston. By Albert W. Atwood. Vol. LXXXVIII, pp. 257-292, 12 ills. in black and white, 17 ills. in color, special map supplement, Sept., 1945.

Notes on the Deserts of the United States and Mexico (Extracted from a Publication of Dr. Daniel T. MacDougal). Vol. XXI, pp. 691-714, 16 ills., Aug., 1910.

Oldest Free Assemblies: Address of Right Hon. Arthur J. Balfour, in the United States House of Representatives, May 5, 1917. Vol. XXI, pp. 368-371, Apr., 1917.

Origin of American State Names. By Frederick W. Lawrence. Vol. XXXVIII, pp. 104-143, 34 ills., Aug., 1920.

Original Territory of the United States. By David Jayne Hill. Vol. X, pp. 73-92, Mar., 1899.

Our Coal Lands. By Guy Elliott Mitchell. Vol. XXI, pp. 446-451, 5 ills., May, 1910.

Our First Alliance. By J. J. Jusserand. Vol. XXXI, pp. 518-548, 8 ills., June, 1917.

Our Foreign-Born Citizens. Vol. XXXI, pp. 95-130, 36 ills., 1 page map, 8 diagrams, Feb., 1917.

Our Immigration During 1904. Vol. XVI, pp. 15-27, 6 ills., 2 charts, Jan., 1905.

Our Immigration in 1905. Vol. XVI, pp. 434-435, Sept., 1905.

Our Industrial Victory. By Charles M. Schwab. Vol. XXXIV, pp. 212-229, 17 ills., Sept., 1918.

Our Map of the United States. Text accompanying special map supplement in colors. Vol. XLIII, p. 460, Apr., 1923.

Our National Parks. By L. F. Schmeckebier. Vol. XXIII, pp. 531-579, 41 ills., 1 page map, June, 1912.

Our Neglected Southern Coast. By Alfred Goldsborough Mayer. Vol. XIX, pp. 859-871, 10 ills., Dec., 1908.

Our New Possessions and the Interest They Are Exciting. By O. P. Austin. Vol. XI, pp. 32-33, Jan., 1900.

Our Present Population. Vol. XV, p. 232, May, 1904.

Our State Flowers: Floral Emblems Chosen by the Commonwealths. By Gilbert Grosvenor. Vol. XXXI, pp. 481-517, 30 ills. in color, June, 1917.

Pages from the Floral Life of America. Vol. XLVIII, pp. 44-75, 55 ills. in color, July, 1925.

Patriotic Pilgrimage to Eastern National Parks: History and Beauty Live Along Paved Roads, Once Indian Trails, Through Virginia, North Carolina, Tennessee, Kentucky, and West Virginia. By Leo A. Borah. Vol. LXV, pp. 663-702, 18 ills. in black and white, 28 ills. in color, 1 two-page map, June, 1934.

United States—*Continued*

Photographing the Marvels of the West in Colors. By Fred Payne Clatworthy. Vol. LIII, pp. 694-719, 30 ills. in color, June, 1928.

Pirate Rivers and Their Prizes: The Warfare of Waterways Has Sometimes Changed the Geography of Our Continents. By John Oliver La Gorce. Vol. L, pp. 87-132, 48 ills., 1 half-page map, July, 1926.

Place Names of the United States. Vol. XIII, pp. 403-405, Nov., 1902.

Population of the United States. By Henry Gannett. Vol. XXII, pp. 34-48, 9 diagrams, 3 half-page maps, Jan., 1911.

Postwar Portrait of the United States. Text accompanying special map supplement in colors. Vol. XC, pp. 135-136, July, 1946.

Proportion of Children in the United States. Vol. XVI, pp. 504-508, 2 charts, Nov., 1905.

Protecting the United States from Plant Pests. By Charles Lester Marlatt. Vol. XL, pp. 205-218, 16 ills., Aug., 1921.

Reclaiming the Swamp Lands of the United States. By Herbert M. Wilson. Vol. XVIII, pp. 292-301, 1 half-page map, 1 diagram, May, 1907.

Reclamation of the West. By F. H. Newell. Vol. XV, pp. 15-30, 6 ills., 7 half-page maps, Jan., 1904.

Republics—The Ladder to Liberty. By David Jayne Hill. Vol. XXXI, pp. 240-254, 5 ills., 2 page maps, Mar., 1917.

Revolution in Eating: Machine Food Age—Born of Roads, Research, and Refrigeration—Makes the United States the Best-fed Nation in History. By J. R. Hildebrand. Vol. LXXXI, pp. 273-324, 33 ills. in black and white, 25 ills. in color, Mar., 1942.

Riatas and Romance on the Rio Grande. 24 ills. in color from natural-color photographs; 23 ills. by Luis Marden. Vol. LXXVI, pp. 431-462, Oct., 1939.

Salton Sea and the Rainfall of the Southwest. By Alfred J. Henry. Vol. XVIII, pp. 244-248, Apr., 1907.

Santa Fe Trail, Path to Empire. By Frederick Simpich. Vol. LVI, pp. 213-252, 35 ills. in black and white, 12 ills. in color, 1 half-page map, Aug., 1929.

Scenery of North America. By James Bryce. Vol. XLI, pp. 339-389, 45 ills., Apr., 1922.

Seals of Our Nation, States, and Territories. By Elizabeth W. King. Paintings by Carlotta Gonzales Lahey, Irvin E. Alleman, and Theodora Price. Vol. XC, pp. 1-42, 14 ills. in black and white, 84 ills. in color, July, 1946. Contents: Seals of the States and District of Columbia; Seals of the Territories, Island Possessions, the Canal Zone, and the Philippine Commonwealth; Great Seal of the United States and Other Federal Seals; Seals of the President and of the Government Departments.

United States—*Continued*

Secret of the Southwest Solved by Talkative Tree Rings: Horizons of American History Are Carried Back to A. D. 700 and a Calendar for 1,200 Years Established by National Geographic Society Expeditions. By Andrew Ellicott Douglass. Vol. LVI, pp. 737-770, 33 ills., 1 two thirds page map, Dec., 1929.

Seeing America from the *Shenandoah*: An Account of the Record-Making 9,000-Mile Flight from the Atlantic to the Pacific Coast and Return in the Navy's American-built American-manned Airship. By Junis B. Wood. Vol. XLVII, pp. 1-47, 39 ills., 1 page map, 1 diagram, Jan., 1925.

Seeing America with Lindbergh: The Record of a Tour of More Than 20,000 Miles by Airplane Through Forty-eight States on Schedule Time. By Lieut. Donald E. Keyhoe. Vol. LIII, pp. 1-46, 46 ills., 1 page map, Jan., 1928.

Seeing Our Spanish Southwest. By Frederick Simpich. Vol. LXXVII, pp. 711-756, 25 ills. in black and white, 17 ills. in duotone, special map supplement, June, 1940.

Sex, Nativity, and Color of the People of the United States. Vol. XII, pp. 361-389, 17 charts, Nov., 1901.

Ships for the Seven Seas: The Story of America's Maritime Needs, Her Capabilities and Her Achievements. By Ralph A. Graves. Vol. XXXIV, pp. 165-200, 24 ills., Sept., 1918.

Shortening Time Across the Continent. By Henry Herbert McClure. Vol. XIII, pp. 319-321, Aug., 1902.

Society Maps Northwestern United States and Neighboring Canadian Provinces. Text accompanying special map supplement in colors. Vol. LXXIX, pp. 805-806, June, 1941.

Society's Map of the United States: New Map Reveals the Progress and Wonders of Our Country. Text accompanying special map supplement in colors. Vol. LXIII, pp. 650-652, 1 ill., May, 1933.

Some Early Geographers of the United States. By Rear Adm. Colby M. Chester. Vol. XV, pp. 392-404, Oct., 1904.

Some of Our Immigrants. Vol. XVIII, pp. 317-334, 21 ills., May, 1907.

Southwest: Its Splendid Natural Resources, Agricultural Wealth, and Scenic Beauty. By N. H. Darton. Vol. XXI, pp. 631-665, 21 ills., 1 page map, Aug., 1910.

Southwest Trails from Horse to Motor. Text accompanying special map supplement in colors. Vol. LXXVII, p. 767, June, 1940.

Spirit of the West: The Wonderful Agricultural Development Since the Dawn of Irrigation. By C. J. Blanchard. Vol. XXI, pp. 333-360, 15 ills., Apr., 1910.

Statistical Atlas of the United States. Vol. XV, pp. 50-52, 2 diagrams, Jan., 1904.

Statistics of Cities. Vol. XVI, p. 437, Sept., 1905.

United States—*Continued*

Storm of February 25-28, 1902. By Alfred J. Henry. Vol. XIII, pp. 110-112, 1 chart, Mar., 1902.

Taming the Outlaw Missouri River. By Frederick Simpich. Vol. LXXXVIII, pp. 569-598, 25 ills., 1 two-page map, Nov., 1945.

This Is My Own : How the United States Seems to a Citizen Soldier Back from Three Years Overseas. By Frederick G. Vosburgh. Vol. LXXXIX, pp. 113-128, 14 ills., Jan., 1946.

Trailing History Down the Big Muddy : In the Homeward Wake of Lewis and Clark, a Folding Steel Skiff Bears Its Lone Pilot on a 2,000-Mile Cruise on the Yellowstone-Missouri. By Lewis R. Freeman. Vol. LIV, pp. 73-120, 51 ills., 1 half-page-map, July, 1928.

Tribute to America. By Herbert Henry Asquith. Vol. XXXI, pp. 294-296, 2 ills., Apr., 1917.

United States : Her Industries. By O. P. Austin. Vol. XIV, pp. 301-320, 24 diagrams, Aug., 1903.

United States : Her Mineral Resources. By C. Kirchhoff. Vol. XIV, pp. 331-339, Sept., 1903.

United States : Its Soils and Their Products. By Harvey W. Wiley. Vol. XIV, pp. 263-279, 11 ills., July, 1903.

"United States—Land and Waters." By Cyrus C. Adams. Vol. XIV, pp. 170-185, 8 ills., 1 half-page map, May, 1903.

United States and the British Empire. By Leonard David Gammans. Vol. LXXXVII, pp. 562-564, May, 1945.

U. S. Roads in War and Peace. By Frederick Simpich. Vol. LXXX, pp. 687-716, 27 ills., Dec., 1941.

Urban Population of the United States. Vol. XII, pp. 345-346, Sept., 1901.

Warfare on Our Eastern Coast. By John Oliver La Gorce. Vol. XXVIII, pp. 195-230, 29 ills., 2 charts, Sept., 1915.

Wartime in the Pacific Northwest. By Frederick Simpich. Vol. LXXXII, pp. 421-464, 25 ills. in black and white, 23 ills. in color, 1 half-page map, Oct., 1942.

Wasteful Nation (Report of Conservation Commission). Vol. XX, pp. 203-206, Feb., 1909.

Western National Parks Invite America Out of Doors. 17 ills. in duotone from photographs by G. A. Grant, W. M. Rush, Merl La Voy, and J. S. Dixon. Vol. LXVI, pp. 65-80, July, 1934.

Western Views in the Land of the Best. 16 ills. in color from autochromes by Fred Payne Clatworthy. Vol. XLIII, pp. 405-420, Apr., 1923.

What Is It to be an American ? By Franklin K. Lane. Vol. XXXIII, pp. 348-354, 4 ills., 1 diagram, Apr., 1918.

What the Latin American Republics Think of the Pan-American Conferences. Vol. XVII, pp. 474-479, Aug., 1906.

When Our Country Is Fifty Years Older. By Raphael Zon. Vol. XX, pp. 573-580, 2 ills., 1 diagram, June, 1909.

United States—*Continued*

Where Fog and Sun Paint the Pacific (Pacific Northwest). 23 ills. in color from natural-color photographs by J. Baylor Roberts. Vol. LXXXII, pp. 437-460, Oct., 1942.

Where New England Meets the Sea. 17 ills. in color from natural-color photographs by B. Anthony Stewart. Vol. LXXXVIII, pp. 265-288, Sept., 1945.

Where the World Gets Its Oil : But Where Will Our Children Get It When American Wells Cease to Flow ? By George Otis Smith. Vol. XXXVII, pp. 181-202, 21 ills., 1 page and 2 half-page maps, Feb., 1920.

Winning the West. By C. J. Blanchard. Vol. XVII, pp. 82-99, 10 ills., 1 page map, Feb., 1906.

Work and Play in the Ozarks. 20 ills. in color from natural-color photographs by B. Anthony Stewart and J. Baylor Roberts. Vol. LXXXIII, pp. 597-620, May, 1943.

See also names of individual states *and* Washington, D. C.

U. S. Air Mail Service:

Flying. By Gilbert Grosvenor. Vol. LXIII, pp. 585-630, 33 ills. in black and white, 17 ills. in duotone, May, 1933.

Flying the World's Longest Air-Mail Route : From Montevideo, Uruguay, Over the Andes, Up the Pacific Coast, Across Central America and the Caribbean to Miami, Florida, in 67 Thrilling Flying Hours. By Junius B. Wood. Vol. LVII, pp. 261-325, 65 ills., 1 half-page map, Mar., 1930.

On the Trail of the Air Mail : A Narrative of the Experiences of the Flying Couriers Who Relay the Mail Across America at a Speed of More than 2,000 Miles a Day. By Lieut. J. Parker Van Zandt. Vol. XLIX, pp. 1-61, 67 ills., 1 two-thirds-page map, Jan., 1926.

U. S. Armed Forces:

At Ease in the South Seas. By Maj. Frederick Simpich, Jr. Vol. LXXXV, pp. 79-104, 32 ills., Jan., 1944.

Insignia and Decorations of the United States Armed Forces. By Gilbert Grosvenor. Vol. LXXXVII, pp. 185-186, Feb., 1945.

Insignia of the United States Armed Forces. By Gilbert Grosvenor. With 991 illustrations in color. Vol. LXXXIII, p. 651, June, 1943.

Navy Artist Paints the Aleutians. By Mason Sutherland. Paintings by Lt. William F. Draper. Vol. LXXXIV, pp. 157-176, 4 ills. in black and white, 16 ills. in color, Aug., 1943.

See also U. S. Army ; U. S. Coast Guard ; U. S. Marine Corps ; U. S. Navy ; *and* the various branches of service.

U. S. Army:

American Decorations and Insignia of Honor and Service. By Col. Robert E. Wyllie. Vol. XXXVI, pp. 502-526, 6 ills. in black and white, 119 ills. in color, Dec., 1919.

U. S. Army—*Continued*

Americans Help Liberated Europe Live Again. By Lt. Col. Frederick Simpich. Vol. LXXXVII, p. 747-768, 17 ills., June, 1945.

America's New Soldier Cities: The Geographical and Historical Environment of the National Army Cantonments and National Guard Camps. By William Joseph Showalter. Vol. XXXII, pp. 438-476, 18 ills., 1 page map in colors, Nov.-Dec., 1917.

Animals Were Allies, Too. 16 ills. from photographs. Vol. LXXXIX, pp. 75-88, Jan., 1946.

Around the Clock with Your Soldier Boy. By Frederick Simpich. Vol. LXXX, pp. 1-36, 42 ills., July, 1941.

Bringing the World to Our Foreign Language Soldiers: How a Military Training Camp Is Solving a Seemingly Unsurmountable Problem by Using The Geographic. By Christian Krysto. Vol. XXXIV, pp. 81-90, 4 ills., Aug., 1918.

Celebrating Christmas on the Meuse. By Capt. Clifton Lisle. Vol. XXXVI, pp. 527-537, 5 ills., Dec., 1919.

A City Learns to Smile Again (Nancy, France). By Maj. Frederick G. Vosburgh. Vol. LXXXVII, pp. 361-384, 23 ills., 1 two-thirds-page map, Mar., 1945.

Conserving the Nation's Man-Power: Disease Weakens Armies, Cripples Industry, Reduces Production. How the Government Is Sanitating the Civil Zones Around Cantonment Areas. A Nation-Wide Campaign for Health. By Rupert Blue. Vol. XXXII, pp. 254-278, 17 ills., Sept., 1917.

Cooties and Courage. By Herbert Corey. Vol. XXXIII, pp. 495-509, 10 ills., June, 1918.

Europe's Looted Art. By John Walker. Vol. LXXXIX, pp. 39-52, 11 ills., Jan., 1946.

Flags of Our Army, Navy, and Government Departments. By Byron McCandless and Gilbert Grosvenor. Vol. XXXII, pp. 305-322, 3 ills. in black and white, 300 ills. in color, Oct., 1917.

Health and Morale of America's Citizen Army: Personal Observations of Conditions in Our Soldier Cities by a Former Commander-in-Chief of the United States Army and Navy. By William Howard Taft. Vol. XXXIII, pp. 219-245, 22 ills., Mar., 1918.

Heroes' Return. By William H. Nicholas. Vol. LXXXVII, pp. 333-352, 19 ills., Mar., 1945.

In Honor of the Army and Aviation (Banquet). Vol. XXII, pp. 267-284, 1 ill., Mar., 1911.

Infantrymen—The Fighters of War. By Brig. Gen. W. H. Wilbur. Vol. LXXXVI, pp. 513-538, 22 ills., Nov., 1944.

Insignia of the Uniformed Forces of the United States. By Byron McCandless and Gilbert Grosvenor. Vol. XXXIII, pp. 413-419, 318 ills., Oct., 1917.

U. S. Army—*Continued*

Lend-Lease Is a Two-way Benefit: Innovation in Creative Statesmanship Pools Resources of United Nations, and Supplies American Forces Around the World. By Francis Flood. Vol. LXXXIII, pp. 745-761, 14 ills., June, 1943.

New Guinea's Mountain and Swampland Dwellers. By Col. Ray T. Elsmore. Vol. LXXXVIII, pp. 671-694, 15 ills. in black and white, 7 ills. in color, 1 half-page map, Dec., 1945.
    Contains references to the Army plane crash and illustrations of the survivors.

Our Army Versus a Bacillus. By Alton G. Grinnell. Vol. XXIV, pp. 1146-1152, 5 ills., 1 diagram, Oct., 1913.

Painting the Army on Maneuvers. By Arthur Beaumont. Text accompanying 16 colored illustrations from paintings by the author. Vol. LXXXVII, pp. 601-602, Nov., 1942.

Romance of Military Insignia: How the United States Government Recognizes Deeds of Heroism and Devotion to Duty. By Col. Robert E. Wyllie. Vol. XXXVI, pp. 463-501, 97 ills., Dec., 1919.

San Francisco: Gibraltar of the West Coast. By La Verne Bradley. Vol. LXXXIII, pp. 279-308, 28 ills., Mar., 1943.

Shopping Abroad for Our Armies in France. By Herbert Corey. Vol. XXXIII, pp. 206-218, 6 ills., Feb., 1918.

Training the New Armies of Liberty: Camp Lee, Virginia's Home for the National Army. By Granville Fortescue. Vol. XXXII, pp. 421-437, 8 ills., 1 page map in colors, Nov.-Dec., 1917.

United States Military Insignia. Vol. LXXXIII, pp. 656-693, 7 ills. in black and white, 12 drawings, 311 ills. in color, June, 1943.

Winning the War of Supply. By F. Barrows Colton. Vol. LXXXVIII, pp. 705-736, 23 ills., Dec., 1945.

Your Dog Joins Up. By Frederick Simpich. Vol. LXXXIII, pp. 93-113, 25 ills., Jan., 1943.

See also Women's Army Corps (WAC).

U. S. Army Air Forces:

Aerial Color Photography Becomes a War Weapon. By H. H. Arnold. Vol. LXXVII, pp. 757-766, 8 ills. in color, June, 1940.

Aerial Invasion of Burma. By Gen. H. H. Arnold. Vol. LXXXVI, pp. 129-148, 20 ills., Aug., 1944.

Air Power for Peace. By Gen. H. H. Arnold. Vol. LXXXIX, pp. 137-193, 35 ills. in black and white, 28 ills. in color, special map supplement, Feb., 1946.

Aircraft Insignia, Spirit of Youth. By Gerard Hubbard. Vol. LXXXIII, pp. 710-722, 3 ills. in black and white, 337 ills. in color, June, 1943.

American Bombers Attacking from Australia. By Howell Walker. Vol. LXXXIII, pp. 49-70, 19 ills., 1 map (two-page spread), Jan., 1943.

U. S. Army Air Forces—*Continued*

American Wings Soar Around the World : Epic Story of the Air Transport Command of the U. S. Army Is a Saga of Yankee Daring and Doing. By Donald H. Agnew and William A. Kinney. Vol. LXXXIV, pp. 57-78, 22 ills., July, 1943.

Americans Stand Guard in Greenland. By Andrew H. Brown. Vol. XC, pp. 457-500, 23 ills. in black and white, 19 ills. in color, 1 page map, Oct., 1946.

Cosmic Rays : Series of flights under auspices of National Geographic Society, U. S. Army Air Forces, and Bartol Research Foundation of the Franklin Institute. Vol. XC, p. 387 ; ill. 388, Sept., 1946.

8th Air Force in England. 10 ills. in color from U. S. Army Air Forces official photographs. Vol. LXXXVII, pp. 297-304, Mar., 1945.

Exploring the Stratosphere. By Capt. Albert W. Stevens. Vol. LXVI, pp. 397-434, 43 ills., 1 two-thirds-page chart, Oct., 1934.

First natural-color photograph taken in the stratosphere. 1 ill. in color by Maj. Albert W. Stevens. Vol. LXXI, p. 340, Mar., 1937.

Flying Our Wounded Veterans Home. By Catherine Bell Palmer. Vol. LXXXVIII, pp. 363-384, 17 ills., Sept., 1945.

Gliders—Silent Weapons of the Sky. By William H. Nicholas. Vol. LXXXVI, pp. 149-160, 8 ills., Aug., 1944.

Greens Grow for GI's on Soilless Ascension. By W. Robert Moore. Vol. LXXXVIII, pp. 219-230, 12 ills., Aug., 1945.

How Latin America Looks from the Air : U. S. Army Airplanes Hurdle the High Andes, Brave Brazil Jungles, and Follow Smoking Volcanoes to Map New Sky Paths Around South America. By Maj. Herbert A. Dargue. Vol. LII, pp. 451-502, 52 ills., 1 page map, Oct., 1927.

How We Fight with Photographs. By F. Barrows Colton. Vol. LXXXVI, pp. 257-280, 22 ills., Sept., 1944.

Maneuvers of Military Planes Disclose Majestic Aërial Views. 7 ills. in duotone from U. S. Army official photographs. Vol. LXIII, pp. 598-615, May, 1933.

Man's Farthest Aloft : Rising to 13.71 Miles, The National Geographic Society–U. S. Army Stratosphere Expedition Gathers Scientific Data at Record Altitude. By Capt. Albert W. Stevens. Action Photographs of the Balloon's Perfect Landing included. Vol. LXIX, pp. 59-94, 39 ills., 1 quarter-page map, Jan., 1936.

National Geographic Society-U. S. Army Air Corps Stratosphere Flight of 1935 in Balloon *Explorer II* (Contributed Technical Papers, Stratosphere Series No. 2). Vol. LXXI, p. 340, Mar., 1937; p. 802, June, 1937.

New Frontier in the Sky. By F. Barrows Colton. Vol. XC, pp. 379-408, 28 ills., 1 diagram, Sept., 1946.

U. S. Army Air Forces—*Continued*

Our Air Frontier in Alaska. By Major General H. H. Arnold. Vol. LXXVIII, pp. 487-504, 15 ills., 1 page map, Oct., 1940.

Photograph Showing the Division Between the Troposphere and Stratosphere and also the Actual Curvature of the Earth. Special supplement from aërial photograph by Capt. Albert W. Stevens. Vol. LXIX, supplement, May, 1936.

Photographing the Eclipse of 1932 from the Air : From Five Miles Above the Earth's Surface, the National Geographic Society–Army Air Corps Survey Obtains Successful Photographs of the Moon's Shadow. By Capt. Albert W. Stevens. Vol. LXII, pp. 581-596, 18 ills., Nov., 1932.

Return to Florence. By 1st Lt. Benjamin C. McCartney. Vol. LXXXVII, pp. 257-296, 18 ills. in black and white, 18 ills. in color, Mar., 1945.

They Sustain the Wings (Ground Crews). By Frederick Simpich. Vol. LXXXIV, pp. 333-354, 19 ills., Sept., 1943.

World's Largest Free Balloon to Explore Stratosphere. Vol. LXVI, pp. 107-110, 2 ills., July, 1934.

Your Society Sponsors an Expedition to Explore the Stratosphere. Vol. LXV, pp. 528-530, 1 ill., Apr., 1934.

See also Air Carrier Contract Personnel ; Civil Air Patrol ; Women's Airforce Service Pilots (WASPS).

U. S. Army Engineers :

Alaskan Highway an Engineering Epic : Mosquitoes, Mud, and Muskeg Minor Obstacles of 1,671-mile Race to Throw the Alcan Life Line Through Thick Forests and Uninhabited Wilderness. By Froelich Rainey. Vol. LXXXIII, pp. 143-168, 21 ills., 3 maps, Feb., 1943.

Army Engineer Explores Nicaragua : Mapping a Route for a New Canal Through the Largest of Central American Republics. By Lieut. Col. Dan I. Sultan. Vol. LXI, pp. 593-627, 39 ills., 1 two-thirds-page map, May, 1932.

Ascension Island, an Engineering Victory. By Lt. Col. Frederick J. Clarke. Vol. LXXXV, pp. 623-640, 21 ills., May, 1944.

Engineering : Men Against the Rivers (Mississippi and Ohio Rivers). By Frederick Simpich. Vol. LXXI, pp. 767-794, 22 ills., 1 page-and-a-half and 1 quarter-page maps, June, 1937.

Greens Grow for GI's on Soilless Ascension. By W. Robert Moore. Vol. LXXXVIII, pp. 219-230, 12 ills., Aug., 1945.

More Water for California's Great Central Valley. By Frederick Simpich. Vol. XC, pp. 645-664, 16 ills., 1 page map, Nov., 1946.

Stilwell Road—Land Route to China. By Nelson Grant Tayman. Vol. LXXXVII, pp. 681-698, 18 ills., June, 1945.

Taming the Outlaw Missouri River. By Frederick Simpich. Vol. LXXXVIII, pp. 569-598, 25 ills., 1 two-page map, Nov., 1945.

U. S. Army Map Service:

Making of Military Maps. By William H. Nicholas. Vol. LXXXIII, pp. 765-778, 17 ills., June, 1943.

U. S. Army Nurse Corps:

Flying Our Wounded Veterans Home. By Catherine Bell Palmer. Vol. LXXXVIII, pp. 363-384, 17 ills., Sept., 1945.

Heroes' Return. By William H. Nicholas. Vol. LXXXVII, pp. 333-352, 19 ills., Mar., 1945.

Women in Uniform. By La Verne Bradley. Vol. LXXXIV, pp. 445-458, 10 ills., Oct., 1943.

U. S. Army Quartermaster Corps:

Fit to Fight Anywhere (Equipment Tests). By Frederick Simpich. Vol. LXXXIV, pp. 233-256, 26 ills., Aug., 1943.

QM, the Fighting Storekeeper. By Frederick Simpich. Paintings by Arthur Beaumont. Vol. LXXXII, pp. 561-600, 22 ills. in black and white, 16 ills. in color, Nov., 1942.

U. S. Army Signal Corps:

U. S. Signal Corps. Vol. XIII, p. 407, Nov., 1902.

The U. S. Signal Corps. By Gilbert H. Grosvenor. Vol. XIV, pp. 467-468, Dec., 1903.

The U. S. Signal Corps in Porto Rico. Vol. XI, pp. 242-243, 1 page map, June, 1900.

Winged Words—New Weapon of War. By F. Barrows Colton. Vol. LXXXII, pp. 663-692, 29 ills., 2 two-thirds-page maps, Nov., 1942.

U. S. Army Transportation Corps:

Heroes' Return. By William H. Nicholas. Vol. LXXXVII, pp. 333-352, 19 ills., Mar., 1945.

U. S. Army Transportation Corps Vessels:

Heroes of Wartime Science and Mercy. By Elizabeth W. King. Vol. LXXXIV, pp. 715-740, 11 ills. in black and white, 334 ills. in color, Dec., 1943.

U. S. Board on Geographic Names. *See* U. S. Geographic Board.

U. S. Bureau of American Ethnology:

Work of the Bureau of American Ethnology. By W J McGee. Vol. XII, pp. 367-372, Oct., 1901.

U. S. Bureau of Biological Survey:

Bird Life Among Lava Rock and Coral Sand: The Chronicle of a Scientific Expedition to Little-Known Islands of Hawaii. By Alexander Wetmore. Vol. XLVIII, pp. 77-108, 36 ills., 1 half-page map, July, 1925.

Plague of Mice. Vol. XX, pp. 479-485, 7 ills., May, 1909.

The Policemen of the Air: An Account of the Biological Survey of the Department of Agriculture. By Henry Wetherbee Henshaw. Vol. XIX, pp. 79-118, 38 ills., Feb., 1908.

U. S. Bureau of Fisheries:

America's Surpassing Fisheries: Their Present Condition and Future Prospects, and How the Federal Government Fosters Them. By Hugh M. Smith. Vol. XXIX, pp. 546-583, 35 ills., June, 1916.

Bureau of Fisheries. By Barton Warren Evermann. Vol. XV, pp. 191-212, 11 ills., 3 diagrams, May, 1904.

Federal Fish Farming: or, Planting Fish by the Billion. By Hugh M. Smith. Vol. XXI, pp. 418-446, 22 ills., May, 1910.

Our Fish Immigrants. By Hugh M. Smith. Vol. XVIII, pp. 382-400, 3 ills., June, 1907.

Planting Fishes in the Ocean. By George M. Bowers. Vol. XVIII, pp. 715-723, 5 ills., Nov., 1907.

When the Father of Waters Goes on a Rampage: An Account of the Salvaging of Food-Fishes from the Overflowed Lands of the Mississippi River. By Hugh M. Smith. Vol. XXXVII, pp. 369-386, 18 ills., Apr., 1920.

U. S. Bureau of Insular Affairs:

The Work of the Bureau of Insular Affairs. By Col. Clarence R. Edwards. Vol. XV, pp. 239-255, 8 ills., June, 1904.

U. S. Bureau of Reclamation:

Call of the West. By C. J. Blanchard. Vol. XX, pp. 403-437, 20 ills., 1 half-page map, May, 1909.

Four Prominent Geographers. Vol. XVIII, pp. 425-428, 4 ills., June, 1907.

Home-Making by the Government: An Account of the Eleven Immense Irrigating Projects to be Opened in 1908. By C. J. Blanchard. Vol. XIX, pp. 250-287, 23 ills., Apr., 1908.

Millions for Moisture. By C. J. Blanchard. Vol. XVIII, pp. 217-243, 22 ills., Apr., 1907.

More Water for California's Great Central Valley. By Frederick Simpich. Vol. XC, pp. 645-664, 16 ills., 1 page map, Nov., 1946.

Reclamation of the West. By F. H. Newell. Vol. XV, pp. 15-30, 6 ills., 7 half-page maps, Jan., 1904.

Spirit of the West: The Wonderful Agricultural Development Since the Dawn of Irrigation. By C. J. Blanchard. Vol. XXI, pp. 332-360, 15 ills., Apr., 1910.

Two Great Undertakings. Vol. XVII, pp. 645-647, Nov., 1906.

Winning the West. By C. J. Blanchard. Vol. XVII, pp. 82-99, 10 ills., 1 page map, Feb., 1906.

U. S. Bureau of Standards:

Natural-color photograph of an eclipse. 1 ill. in color by Irvine C. Gardner. Vol. LXXI, p. 178, Feb., 1937.

Observing an Eclipse in Asiatic Russia. By Irvine C. Gardner. Vol. LXXI, pp. 179-197, 19 ills. in black and white, 1 ill. in color, Feb., 1937.

Wonderland of Science. Vol. XXVII, pp. 153-169, 15 ills., Feb., 1915.

U. S. Bureau of the Census:

Statistics of Cities. Vol. XVI, p. 437, Sept., 1905.

U. S. Coast and Geodetic Survey:

Charting a Coast-Line of 26,000 Miles (Alaska). Vol. XX, pp. 608-609, July, 1909.

Charting a World at War. By William H. Nicholas. Vol. LXXXVI, pp. 617-640, 23 ills., 1 drawing, Nov., 1944.

Coast and Geodetic Survey. By O. H. Tittmann. Vol. XIV, pp. 1-9, Jan., 1903.

Coast and Geodetic Survey: Its Present Work. By E. D. Preston. Vol. X, pp. 268-269, July, 1899.

Heroes of Wartime Science and Mercy. By Elizabeth W. King. Vol. LXXXIV, pp. 715-740, 11 ills. in black and white, 334 ills. in color, Dec., 1943.

Hidden Perils of the Deep. By G. R. Putnam. Vol. XX, pp. 822-837, 19 diagrams, 3 charts, Sept., 1909.

Magnetic Work of the Coast and Geodetic Survey. By Dr. L. A. Bauer. Vol. X, pp. 288-289, Aug., 1899.

Our Guardians on the Deep. By William Joseph Showalter. Vol. XXV, pp. 655-677, 15 ills., 1 chart, June, 1914.

Progress in Surveying the United States. By O. H. Tittmann. Vol. XVII, pp. 110-112, 1 ill., Feb., 1906.

Recent Contributions to Our Knowledge of the Earth's Shape and Size, by the United States Coast and Geodetic Survey. By C. A. Schott. Vol. XII, pp. 36-41, 1 ill., 1 chart, Jan., 1901.

San Francisco Earthquake of April 18, 1906, as Recorded by the Coast and Geodetic Survey Magnetic Observatories. Vol. XVII, pp. 298-300, May, 1906.

U. S. Coast Guard:

Coast Guard Patrol in Greenland. 9 ills. in color from natural-color photographs by Lieut. Thomas S. La Farge. Vol. LXXXIII, pp. 565-572, May, 1943.

Great Mississippi Flood of 1927: Since White Man's Discovery This Mighty River Has Served Him Well, Yet It Has Brought Widespread Devastation Along Its Lower Reaches. By Frederick Simpich. Vol. LII, pp. 243-289, 53 ills., 1 half-page map, Sept., 1927.

Life with Our Fighting Coast Guard. By F. Barrows Colton. Vol. LXXXIII, pp. 557-588, 22 ills. in black and white, 9 ills. in color, May, 1943.

Standing Iceberg Guard in the North Atlantic: International Patrol Safeguards the Lives of Thousands of Travelers and Protects Trans-atlantic Liners from a "Titanic" Fate. By Lieut. Comdr. F. A. Zeusler. Vol. L, pp. 1-28, 29 ills., 1 half-page map, July, 1926.

Uncle Sam's Icebox Outposts (Greenland). 19 ills. in color from natural-color photographs by John E. Schneider and Robert B. Sykes, Jr. Vol. XC, pp. 473-496, Oct., 1946.

U. S. Coast Guard—*Continued*

United States Navy, Marine Corps, and Coast Guard Insignia. Vol. LXXXIII, pp. 694-709, 5 ills. in black and white, 343 ills. in color, June, 1943.

Your Dog Joins Up. By Frederick Simpich. Vol. LXXXIII, pp. 93-113, 25 ills., Jan., 1943.

See also Women's Reserve of the U. S. Coast Guard Reserve (SPARS).

U. S. Commission of Fine Arts:

Washington, D. C. 32 ills. and 2 panoramas in color from illustrations from the Commission of Fine Arts. Vol. XXVII, pp. 222-276, Mar., 1915.

U. S. Defense Bases:

Alaska—Our Northwestern Outpost. 16 ills. in color from natural-color photographs by Ernest H. Gruening, Amos Burg, and Froelich Rainey. Vol. LXXXII, pp. 297-308, Sept., 1942.

Alaskan Highway an Engineering Epic: Mosquitoes, Mud, and Muskeg Minor Obstacles of 1,671-mile Race to Throw the Alcan Life Line Through Thick Forests and Uninhabited Wilderness. By Froelich Rainey. Vol. LXXXIII, pp. 143-168, 21 ills., 3 maps, Feb., 1943.

American Soldier in Reykjavík. By Corporal Luther M. Chovan. Vol. LXXXVIII, pp. 536-568, 6 ills. in black and white, 34 ills. in color, Nov., 1945.

Americans in the Caribbean. By Luis Marden. Vol. LXXXI, pp. 723-758, 16 ills. in black and white, 22 ills. in color, 1 half-page map, June, 1942.

Americans Stand Guard in Greenland. By Andrew H. Brown. Vol. XC, pp. 457-500, 23 ills. in black and white, 19 ills. in color, 1 page map, Oct., 1946.

America's New Crescent of Defense. 8 ills. from photographs, 1 page map. Vol. LXXVIII, pp. 621-628, Nov., 1940.

Ancient Iceland, New Pawn of War. 21 ills. from photographs, 1 page map. Vol. LXXX, pp. 75-90, July, 1941.

Ascension Island, an Engineering Victory. By Lt. Col. Frederick J. Clarke. 21 ills., May, 1944.

Bizarre Battleground—the Lonely Aleutians. By Lonnelle Davison. Vol. LXXXII, pp. 316-317, 1 ill., Sept., 1942.

Coast Guard Patrol in Greenland. 9 ills. in color from natural-color photographs by Lieut. Thomas S. La Farge. Vol. LXXXIII, pp. 565-572, May, 1943.

Desolate Greenland, Now an American Outpost. 17 ills. from photographs; 12 ills. by Willie Knutsen; 4 ills. by F. Vogel. Vol. LXXX, pp. 393-406, Sept., 1941.

Greenland—U. S. Base in the Arctic. 5 ills. in color from natural-color photographs by James K. Penfield. Vol. LXXXII, pp. 373-376, Sept., 1942.

Greenland Turns to America. By James K. Penfield. Vol. LXXXII, pp. 369-383, 7 ills. in black and white, 5 ills. in color, 1 two-page map, Sept., 1942.

U. S. Defense Bases—_Continued_

Greens Grow for GI's on Soilless Ascension. By W. Robert Moore. Vol. LXXXVIII, pp. 219-230, 12 ills., Aug., 1945.

Life on the Hawaii "Front": All-Out Defense and Belt Tightening of Pacific Outposts Foreshadow the Things to Come on Mainland. By Lieut. Frederick Simpich, Jr. Vol. LXXXII, pp. 541-560, 19 ills., 1 half-page map, Oct., 1942.

Navy Artist Paints the Aleutians. By Mason Sutherland. Paintings by Lt. William F. Draper. Vol. LXXXIV, pp. 157-176, 4 ills. in black and white, 16 ills. in color, Aug., 1943.

Newfoundland, North Atlantic Rampart: From the "First Base of American Defense" Planes Fly to Britain's Aid over Stout Fishing Schooners of the Grand Banks. By George Whiteley, Jr. Vol. LXXX, pp. 111-140, 26 ills., 1 two-thirds-page map, July, 1941.

Our Air Frontier in Alaska. By Major General H. H. Arnold. Vol. LXXVIII, pp. 487-504, 15 ills., 1 page map, Oct., 1940.

Servicing Arctic Airbases. By Robert A. Bartlett. Vol. LXXXIX, pp. 602-616, 3 ills. in black and white, 10 ills. in color, 1 half-page map, May, 1946.

Uncle Sam's Icebox Outposts (Greenland). 19 ills. in color from natural-color photographs by John E. Schneider and Robert B. Sykes, Jr. Vol. XC, pp. 473-496, Oct., 1946.

War Echoes in the West Indies. 22 ills. in color from natural-color photographs by Luis Marden. Vol. LXXXI, pp. 731-754, June, 1942.

West Indies Links in a Defense Chain. 21 ills. in color from natural-color photographs; 20 ills. by Edwin L. Wisherd. Vol. LXXXIX, pp. 9-32, Jan., 1941.

U. S. Department of Agriculture:

Discovery of Cancer in Plants. Vol. XXIV, pp. 53-70, 12 ills., Jan., 1913.

Hunter of Plants. By David Fairchild. Vol. XXXVI, pp. 57-77, 18 ills., July, 1919.

Hunting Useful Plants in the Caribbean. By David Fairchild. Vol. LXVI, pp. 705-737, 39 ills., Dec., 1934.

Modern Alchemist. By James Wilson. Vol. XVIII, pp. 778-795, 6 ills., Dec., 1907.

New Plant Immigrants. By David Fairchild. Vol. XXII, pp. 879-907, 34 ills., Oct., 1911.

Our Plant Immigrants. By David Fairchild. Vol. XVII, pp. 179-201, 29 ills., Apr., 1906.

Peacetime Plant Hunting About Peiping. By P. H. and J. H. Dorsett. Vol. LXXII, pp. 509-534, 21 ills., 1 two-thirds-page map, Oct., 1937.

Pests and Parasites. By Charles Lester Marlatt. Vol. XXII, pp. 321-346, 29 ills., 2 three-quarters-page maps, Apr., 1911.

Protecting the United States from Plant Pests. By Charles Lester Marlatt. Vol. XL, pp. 205-218, 16 ills., Aug., 1921.

What the United States Government Does to Promote Agriculture. Vol. XIV, pp. 35-39, Jan., 1903.

U. S. First Air Commando Force:

Aerial Invasion of Burma. By Gen. H. H. Arnold. Vol. LXXXVI, pp. 129-148, 20 ills., Aug., 1944.

U. S. Forest Service:

Government Assistance in Handling Forest Lands. Vol. XV, pp. 150-159, Nov., 1904.

Notes on the Eucalyptus Tree from the United States Forest Service. Vol. XX, pp. 668-673, 4 ills., July, 1909.

Notes on the Forest Service. Vol. XVIII, pp. 142-145, 3 ills., Feb., 1907.

Two Great Undertakings (Work of U. S. Bureau of Reclamation and U. S. Forest Service). Vol. XVII, pp. 645-647, Nov., 1906.

Value of the United States Forest Service. Vol. XX, pp. 29-41, 14 ills., Jan., 1909.

U. S. Geographic Board:

Decisions by U. S. Board on Geographic Names. Vol. XII, p. 87, Feb., 1901.

Decisions of the U. S. Board on Geographic Names. Vol. XI, pp. 478-480, Dec., 1900.

Decisions of the U. S. Board on Geographic Names. Vol. XIII, pp. 178-179, May, 1902.

Decisions of the U. S. Board on Geographic Names. Vol. XIII, p. 409, Nov., 1902.

Decisions of the U. S. Board on Geographic Names. Vol. XIV, pp. 82-83, Feb., 1903.

Decisions of the U. S. Board on Geographic Names. Vol. XIV, pp. 258-259, June, 1903.

Decisions of the U. S. Board on Geographic Names. Vol. XV, pp. 49-50, Jan., 1904,

Decisions of the U. S. Board on Geographic Names. Vol. XV, p. 501, Dec., 1904.

Decisions of the U. S. Board on Geographic Names. Vol. XVI, pp. 131-132, Mar., 1905.

Decisions of the U. S. Board on Geographic Names. Vol. XVI, pp. 358-359, July, 1905.

Geographic Names. Vol. XII, p. 125, Mar., 1901.

Geographic Names. Vol. XII, p. 242, June, 1901.

National Geographic Magazine and the U. S. Board on Geographic Names. Vol. X, pp. 517-519, Dec., 1899.

Recent Decisions of U. S. Board on Geographic Names. Vol. XIII, pp. 28-30, Jan., 1902.

U. S. Board on Geographic Names. Vol. XI, pp. 329-330, Aug., 1900.

U. S. Board on Geographic Names. Vol. XII, p. 316, Aug., 1901.

U. S. Board on Geographic Names. Vol. XVII, p. 177, Mar., 1906.

United States Board on Geographic Names and Its Foreign Critics. Vol. X, p. 16, Jan., 1899.

U. S. Board on Geographic Names Changed to U. S. Geographic Board by President Theodore Roosevelt. Vol. XVII, p. 588, Oct., 1906.

U. S. Geological Survey:

Central Great Plains. Vol. XVI, pp. 389-397, Aug., 1905.

U. S. Geological Survey—*Continued*

Down Idaho's River of No Return (Salmon River). By Philip J. Shenon and John C. Reed. Vol. LXX, pp. 95-136, 43 ills., 1 page and 1 two-thirds-page maps, July, 1936.

Fieldwork of the United States Geological Survey for the Season 1902. Vol. XIII, pp. 322-325, Aug., 1902.

Four Prominent Geographers. Vol. XVIII, pp. 425-428, 4 ills., June, 1907.

Geologic Folios in Schools. Vol. XVI, pp. 244-247, May, 1905.

Hydrographic Work of the U. S. Geological Survey. Vol. XI, pp. 324-325, 1 ill., Aug., 1900.

Map Showing the Location of the Principal River Stations Maintained in the United States by the U. S. Geological Survey. Vol. XVII, p. 357, 1 page map, June, 1906.

Maps Recently Published by the United States Geological Survey. Vol. XVI, pp. 423-427, Sept., 1905.

Survey of the Grand Canyon. Vol. XIV, pp. 162-163, Apr., 1903.

Surveying the Grand Canyon of the Colorado: An Account of the 1923 Boating Expedition of the United States Geological Survey. By Lewis R. Freeman. Vol. XLV, pp. 471-548, 62 ills., 1 three-quarters-page map, May, 1924.

Topographic Work of the United States Geological Survey. Vol. XIII, pp. 326-328, Aug., 1902.

Twenty-fifth Anniversary of the U. S. Geological Survey. Vol. XV, p. 234, May, 1904.

What the Geological Survey Has Done in Twenty-five Years. Vol. XV, pp. 365-366, Sept., 1904.

U. S. Government Agencies and Employees:

Our Nation's Capital on Parade. 16 ills. in color from natural-color photographs by B. Anthony Stewart, Walter M. Edwards, and others. Vol. LXXXIV, pp. 265-288, Sept., 1943.

Wartime Washington. By William H. Nicholas. Vol. LXXXIV, pp. 257-290, 12 ills. in black and white, 16 ills. in color, Sept., 1943.

U. S. Hydrographic Office:

Work of the United States Hydrographic Office. By Comdr. W. H. H. Southerland. Vol. XIV, pp. 61-75, Feb., 1903.

U. S. Marine Corps:

Aircraft Insignia, Spirit of Youth. By Gerard Hubbard. Vol. LXXXIII, pp. 710-722, 3 ills. in black and white, 337 ills. in color, June, 1943.

Animals Were Allies, Too. 16 ills. from photographs. Vol. LXXXIX, pp. 75-88, Jan., 1946.

Flying Our Wounded Veterans Home. By Catherine Bell Palmer. Vol. LXXXVIII, pp. 363-384, 17 ills., Sept., 1945.

Gilbert Islands in the Wake of Battle. By W. Robert Moore. Vol. LXXXVII, pp. 129-162, 11 ills. in black and white, 19 ills. in color, 1 two-thirds-page map, Feb., 1945.

U. S. Marine Corps—*Continued*

Jungle War: Bougainville and New Caledonia. 17 ills. in color from paintings by Lieut. William F. Draper. Vol. LXXXV, pp. 417-432, Apr., 1944.

Okinawa, Threshold to Japan. By Lt. David D. Duncan, USMC. With 22 ills. in color from natural-color photographs by the author and others. Vol. LXXXVIII, pp. 411-428, Oct., 1945.

Palms and Planes in the New Herbrides. By Maj. Robert D. Heinl, Jr. Vol. LXXXVI, pp. 229-256, 17 ills. in black and white, 12 ills. in color, 1 four-fifths-page map, Aug., 1944.

United States Navy, Marine Corps, and Coast Guard Insignia. Vol. LXXXIII, pp. 694-709, 5 ills. in black and white, 343 ills. in color, June, 1943.

Victory's Portrait in the Marianas. By Lt. William Franklin Draper, USNR. With 17 ills. in color from paintings by the author. Vol. LXXXVIII, pp. 599-616, Nov., 1945.

Your Navy as Peace Insurance. By Fleet Admiral Chester W. Nimitz. Vol. LXXXIX, pp. 681-736, 32 ills. in black and white, 26 ills. in color, June, 1946.

See also U. S. Marine Corps Women's Reserve.

U. S. Marine Corps Women's Reserve:

Decorations, Medals, Service Ribbons, Badges, and Women's Insignia. Vol. LXXXIV, pp. 414-444, 6 ills. in black and white, 376 ills. in color, Oct., 1943.

Women in Uniform. By La Verne Bradley. Vol. LXXXIV, pp. 445-458, 10 ills., Oct., 1943.

U. S. Maritime Service:

Heroes of Wartime Science and Mercy. By Elizabeth W. King. Vol. LXXXIV, pp. 715-740, 11 ills. in black and white, 334 ills. in color, Dec., 1943.

U. S. Military Academy:

West Point, Mother of Army Men. 10 ills. in color from natural-color photographs by Edwin L. Wisherd. Vol. LXIX, pp. 779-786, June, 1936.

West Point and the Gray-Clad Corps. By Lieut. Col. Herman Beukema. Vol. LXIX, pp. 777-788, 10 ills. in color, June, 1936.

United States Military Insignia. Vol. LXXXIII, pp. 656-693, 7 ills. in black and white, 12 drawings, 311 ills. in color, June, 1943.

U. S. Naval Academy:

Annapolis, Cradle of the Navy. By Lieut. Arthur A. Ageton. Vol. LXIX, pp. 789-800, 13 ills. in color, June, 1936.

June Week at Annapolis, Cradle of the Navy. 13 ills. in color from natural-color photographs. Vol. LXIX, pp. 791-798, June, 1936.

Old Line State Cyclorama. 22 ills. in color from natural-color photographs by W. Robert Moore, B. Anthony Stewart, and others. Vol. LXXIX, pp. 409-432, Apr., 1941.

U. S. Naval Air Station, Lakehurst, New Jersey :

Aboard a Blimp Hunting U-boats : A Day above the Atlantic Reveals Navy Talk and Navy Ways, Creeping Convoys, and Torpedoed Wrecks. By Mason Sutherland. Vol. LXXXIV, pp. 79-96, 18 ills., July, 1943.

U. S. Naval Observatory:

Chronometer and Time Service of the U. S. Naval Observatory and the Present Status of Standard Time. By Lieut. Comdr. Edward Everett Hayden. Vol. XV, pp. 430-431, Oct., 1904.

Special Telegraphic Time Signal from the Naval Observatory. Vol. XV, pp. 411-415, Oct., 1904.

U. S. Navy:

Aboard a Blimp Hunting U-boats : A Day above the Atlantic Reveals Navy Talk and Navy Ways, Creeping Convoys, and Torpedoed Wrecks. By Mason Sutherland. Vol. LXXXIV, pp. 79-96, 18 ills., July, 1943.

Across the Equator with the American Navy. By Herbert Corey. Vol. XXXIX, pp. 571-624, 53 ills., June, 1921.

Aircraft Insignia, Spirit of Youth. By Gerard Hubbard. Vol. LXXXIII, pp. 710-722, 3 ills. in black and white, 337 ills. in color, June, 1943.

American Decoration and Insignia of Honor and Service. By Col. Robert E. Wyllie. Vol. XXXVI, pp. 502-526, 6 ills. in black and white, 119 ills. in color, Dec., 1919.

Battleship *Missouri* Comes of Age. 11 ills. in color from U. S. Navy official photographs. Vol. LXXXVII, pp. 353-360, Mar., 1945.

Call to the colors. Vol. XXXI, pp. 345-361, 17 ills., Apr., 1917.

Collarin' Cape Cod (Massachusetts) : Experiences on Board a U. S. Navy Destroyer in a Wild Winter Storm. By Lieut. H. R. Thurber. Vol. XLVIII, pp. 427-472, 46 ills., Oct., 1925.

Cruise on an Escort Carrier. By Melville Bell Grosvenor. Vol. LXXXIV, pp. 513-546, 14 ills. in black and white, 20 ills. in color, Nov., 1943.

Eclipse Adventures on a Desert Isle (Canton). By Capt. J. F. Hellweg. Vol. LXXII, pp. 377-394, 14 ills., 1 two-thirds-page map, Sept., 1937.

Farewell to Bikini. By Carl Markwith. Vol. XC, pp. 97-116, 16 ills., July, 1946.

Flags of Our Army, Navy, and Government Departments. By Byron McCandless and Gilbert Grosvenor. Vol. XXXII, pp. 305-322, 3 ills. in black and white, 300 ills. in color, Oct., 1917.

Flying Over the Arctic. By Lieut. Comdr. Richard E. Byrd. Vol. XLVIII, pp. 519-532, 10 ills., Nov., 1925.

Gem of the Ocean : Our American Navy. By Josephus Daniels. Vol. XXXIII, pp. 313-335, 35 ills., Apr., 1918.

Honors to the American Navy (National Geographic Society Banquet). Vol. XX, pp. 77-95, Jan., 1909.

U. S. Navy—*Continued*

How We Fight with Photographs. By F. Barrows Colton. Vol. LXXXVI, pp. 257-280, 22 ills., Sept., 1944.

Insignia of the Uniformed Forces of the United States. By Byron McCandless and Gilbert Grosvenor. Vol. XXXII, pp. 412-419, 318 ills., Oct., 1917.

Jungle War : Bougainville and New Caledonia. 17 ills. in color from paintings by Lieut. William F. Draper. Vol. LXXXV, pp. 417-432, Apr., 1944.

Landing Craft for Invasion. By Melville Bell Grosvenor. Vol. LXXXVI, pp. 1-30, 26 ills., July, 1944.

Life in Our Fighting Fleet. By F. Barrows Colton. Vol. LXXIX, pp. 671-702, 30 ills., June, 1941.

MacMillan Arctic Expedition Returns : U. S. Navy Planes Make First Series of Overland Flights in the Arctic and National Geographic Society Staff Obtains Valuable Data and Specimens for Scientific Study. By Donald B. MacMillan. Vol. XLVIII, pp. 477-518, 42 ills., Nov., 1925.

Maneuvers of Military Planes Disclose Majestic Aërial Views. 10 ills. in duotone from U. S. Navy official photographs. Vol. LXIII, pp. 598-615, May, 1933.

Nature's Most Dramatic Spectacle (Eclipse). By S. A. Mitchell. Vol. LXXII, pp. 361-376, 16 ills., 1 half-page map, Sept., 1937.

Navy Artist Paints the Aleutians. By Mason Sutherland. Paintings by Lt. William F. Draper. Vol. LXXXIV, pp. 157-176, 4 ills. in black and white, 16 ills. in color, Aug., 1943.

Navy Wings over the Pacific. 12 ills. in color from U. S. Navy official photographs. Vol. LXXXVI, pp. 241-248, Aug., 1944.

New Queen of the Seas (Aircraft Carrier). By Melville Bell Grosvenor. Vol. LXXXII, pp. 1-30, 27 ills., 1 drawing, 1 two-page map, July, 1942.

North Sea Mine Barrage. By Capt. Reginald R. Belknap. Vol. XXXV, pp. 85-110, 23 ills., 1 diagram, 1 page map, Feb., 1919.

Painting History in the Pacific. 19 ills. in color from paintings by Lt. William F. Draper. Vol. LXXXVI, pp. 409-424, Oct., 1944.

Palms and Planes in the New Hebrides. By Maj. Robert D. Heinl, Jr. Vol. LXXXVI, pp. 229-256, 17 ills. in black and white, 12 ills. in color, 1 four-fifths-page map, Aug., 1944.

Pocket Carriers Fight the Submarines. 20 ills. in color from U. S. Navy official photographs. Vol. LXXXIV, pp. 521-544, Nov., 1943.

Removal of the North Sea Mine Barrage. By Lieut. Comdr. Noel Davis. Vol. XXXVII, pp. 103-133, 28 ills., 2 half-page maps, Feb., 1920.

Romance of Military Insignia : How the United States Government Recognizes Deeds of Heroism and Devotion to Duty. By Col. Robert E. Wyllie. Vol. XXXVI, pp. 463-501, 27 ills., Dec., 1919.

U. S. Navy—*Continued*

Saga of the Carrier *Princeton*. By Capt. William H. Buracker, USN. Vol. LXXXVIII, pp. 189-218, 8 ills. in black and white, 22 ills. in color, 1 map (two-page spread), Aug., 1945.

San Francisco : Gibraltar of the West Coast. By La Verne Bradley. Vol. LXXXIII, pp. 279-308, 28 ills., Mar., 1943.

Seeing America from the *Shenandoah*: An Account of the Record-Making 9,000-Mile Flight from the Atlantic to the Pacific Coast and Return in the Navy's American-built, American-manned Airship. By Junius B. Wood. Vol. XLVII, pp. 1-47, 39 ills., 1 page map, 1 diagram, Jan., 1925.

Ships of Our Navy. 8 ills. in color from paintings by Arthur Beaumont. Vol. LXXX, pp. 329-336, Sept., 1941.

Ships That Guard Our Ocean Ramparts. By F. Barrows Colton. Paintings by Arthur Beaumont. Vol. LXXX, pp. 328-337, 8 ills. in color, Sept., 1941.

Ships That Won the Greatest Naval War. 26 ills. in color from U. S. Navy official photographs. Vol. LXXXIX, pp. 697-736, June, 1946.

Take-off for Japan. 22 ills. in color from U. S. Navy official photographs. Vol. LXXXVIII, pp. 193-208, Aug., 1945.

They Survived at Sea. By Lt. Comdr. Samuel F. Harby. Vol. LXXXVII, pp. 617-640, 22 ills., May, 1945.

To Seek the Unknown in the Arctic : United States Navy Fliers to Aid MacMillan Expedition Under the Auspices of the National Geographic Society in Exploring Vast Area. Vol. XLVII, pp. 673-675, 1 ill., 1 half-page map, June, 1925.

Unfurling Old Glory on Canton Island. 11 ills. in color ; 1 painting by Charles Bittinger and 10 natural-color photographs. Vol. LXXIII, pp. 753-760, June, 1938.

United States Navy, Marine Corps, and Coast Guard Insignia. Vol. LXXXIII, pp. 694-709, 5 ills. in black and white, 343 ills. in color, June, 1943.

Victory's Portrait in the Marianas. By Lt. William Franklin Draper, USNR. With 17 ills. in color from paintings by the author. Vol. LXXXVIII, pp. 599-616, Nov., 1945.

Your Navy as Peace Insurance. By Fleet Admiral Chester W. Nimitz. Vol. LXXXIX, pp. 681-736, 32 ills. in black and white, 26 ills. in color, June, 1946.

See also Naval Air Transport Service ; U. S. Coast Guard ; U. S. Navy Nurse Corps ; Women's Reserve of the U. S. Naval Reserve (WAVES).

United States Navy, Marine Corps, and Coast Guard Insignia. Vol. LXXXIII, pp. 694-709, 5 ills. in black and white, 343 ills. in color, June, 1943.

U. S. Navy Nurse Corps:

Flying Our Wounded Veterans Home. By Catherine Bell Palmer. Vol. LXXXVIII, pp. 363-384, 17 ills., Sept., 1945.

U. S. Navy Nurse Corps—*Continued*

Women in Uniform. By La Verne Bradley. Vol. LXXXIV, pp. 445-458, 10 ills., Oct., 1943.

U. S. Public Health Service:

Heroes of Wartime Science and Mercy. By Elizabeth W. King. Vol. LXXXIV, pp. 715-740, 11 ills. in black and white, 334 ills. in color, Dec., 1943.

U. S. Roads in War and Peace. By Frederick Simpich. Vol. LXXX, pp. 687-716, 27 ills., Dec., 1941.

U. S. Shipping Board:

American People Must Become Ship-Minded. By Edward N. Hurley. Vol. XXXIV, pp. 201-211, 7 ills., Sept., 1918.

Ships for the Seven Seas : The Story of America's Maritime Needs, Her Capabilities and Her Achievements. By Ralph A. Graves. Vol. XXXIV, pp. 165-200, 24 ills., Sept., 1918.

U. S. Signal Corps. *See* U. S. Army Signal Corps.

U. S. War Agencies. *See* War Agencies.

U. S. Weather Bureau:

Forecasting the Weather and Storms. By Willis L. Moore. Vol. XVI, pp. 255-305, 5 ills., 20 charts, June, 1905.

International Cloud Work of the Weather Bureau. By Frank H. Bigelow. Vol. X, pp. 351-354, Sept., 1899.

Kite Work of the Weather Bureau. By H. C. Frankenfield. Vol. XI, pp. 55-62, Feb., 1900.

Loss of Life by Lightning. Vol. XIII, p. 115, Mar., 1902.

Loss of Property From Lightning. Vol. XII, p. 82, Feb., 1901.

Our Heralds of Storm and Flood. By Gilbert H. Grosvenor. Vol. XVIII, pp. 586-601, 15 ills., 1 chart, Sept., 1907.

Record of the Great Earthquake Written in Washington by the Seismograph of the United States Weather Bureau. By C. F. Marvin. Vol. XVII, pp. 296-298, May, 1906.

Scientific Work of Mount Weather Meteorological Research Observatory. By Frank H. Bigelow. Vol. XV, pp. 442-445, Nov., 1904.

United States Weather Bureau. Vol. XIII, pp. 71-72, Feb., 1902.

United States Weather Bureau. By James Wilson. Vol. XV, pp. 37-39, Jan., 1904.

United States Weather Bureau at the Paris Exposition. Vol. XII, pp. 81-82, Feb., 1901.

Weather Bureau. By Willis L. Moore. Vol. XII, pp. 363-369, Oct., 1901.

Weather Bureau and the Recent Floods. By H. C. Frankenfield. Vol. XIV, pp. 285-290, 2 ills., July, 1903.

Universities and Colleges:

American Alma Maters in the Near East. By Maynard Owen Williams. Vol. LXXXVIII, pp. 237-256, 16 ills., Aug., 1945.

Contains text references and illustrations of the following: American University at Cairo, American University of Beirut, Istanbul Woman's College, Robert College.

Flow Onward, Connecticut (River)! 24 ills. in color from natural-color photographs; 22 ills. by B. Anthony Stewart. Vol. LXXXIII, pp. 409-432, Apr., 1943.

Contains colored illustrations of the following: Amherst College, Dartmouth College, Smith College.

Geography in the University of Chicago. Vol. XIV, pp. 163-164, Apr., 1903.

Long River of New England: In War and Peace, from Mountain Wilderness to the Sea, Flows the Connecticut River, Through a Valley Abounding in History, Scenery, Inventive Genius and Industry. By Albert W. Atwood. Vol. LXXXIII, pp. 401-434, 12 ills. in black and white, 24 ills. in color, 1 two-thirds-page map, Apr., 1943.

Contains information on the following: Amherst College, Dartmouth College, Mount Holyoke College, Smith College, Wesleyan University, Yale University.

Oxford, Mother of Anglo-Saxon Learning. By E. John Long. Vol. LVI, pp. 563-596, 31 ills., Nov., 1929.

Sculptured Gates to English Learning (Cambridge University). 15 ills. in color from natural-color photographs by B. Anthony Stewart. Vol. LXXXIX, pp. 417-440, Apr., 1946.

A Texan Teaches American History at Cambridge University. By J. Frank Dobie. Vol. LXXXIX, pp. 409-441, 9 ills. in black and white, 19 ills. in color, Apr., 1946.

Where the Winding Cam Mirrors Cambridge Spires (England). 12 ills. in color from natural-color photographs by Bernard Wakeman and Walter M. Edwards. Vol. LXX, pp. 339-346, Sept., 1936.

Within the Halls of Cambridge (England). By Philip Broad. Vol. LXX, pp. 333-349, 7 ills. in black and white, 12 ills. in color, Sept., 1936.

See also Cornell University; Harvard University; Johns Hopkins University; Lingnan University.

Unknown Japan: A Portrait of the People Who Make Up One of the Two Most Fanatical Nations of the World. By Willard Price. Vol. LXXXII, pp. 225-252, 30 ills., Aug., 1942.

Unknown New Guinea: Circumnavigating the World in a Flying Boat, American Scientists Discover a Valley of 60,000 People Never Before Seen by White Men. By Richard Archbold. Vol. LXXIX, pp. 315-344, 28 ills., 1 two-thirds-page map, Mar., 1941.

Unspoiled Cyprus: The Traditional Island Birthplace of Venus Is One of the Least Sophisticated of Mediterranean Lands. By Maynard Owen Williams. Vol. LIV, pp. 1-55, 55 ills. in black and white, 10 ills. in color, 1 half-page map, July, 1928.

Untouchables:

India Mosaic. By Peter Muir and Frances Muir. Vol. LXXXIX, pp. 443-470, 5 ills. in black and white, 22 ills. in color, 1 half-page map, Apr., 1946.

Untoured Burma. By Charles H. Bartlett. Vol. XXIV, pp. 835-853, 17 ills., July, 1913.

Up and Down on Saba (Island). 12 ills. in color from natural-color photographs by Charles W. Herbert. Vol. LXXVIII, pp. 605-612, Nov., 1940.

Ur, Iraq:

Archeology, the Mirror of the Ages: Our Debt to the Humble Delvers in the Ruins at Carchemish and at Ur. By C. Leonard Woolley. Vol. LIV, pp. 207-226, 19 ills., Aug., 1928.

New Light on Ancient Ur: Excavations at the Site of the City of Abraham Reveal Geographical Evidence of the Biblical Story of the Flood. By M. E. L. Mallowan. Vol. LVII, pp. 95-130, 44 ills., 1 three-quarters-page map, Jan., 1930.

Urari (Poison):

Fishing and Hunting Tales from Brazil. By Dewey Austin Cobb. Vol. XX, pp. 917-920, Oct., 1909.

Urban Population of United States. Vol. XII, pp. 345-346, Sept., 1901.

Urga, Outer Mongolia:

The Lama's Motor-Car: A Trip Across the Gobi Desert by Motor-Car. By Ethan C. Le Munyon. Vol. XXIV, pp. 640-670, 34 ills., May, 1913.

Urgub, Turkey:

Peculiar Caves of Asia Minor. By Elizabeth H. Brewer. Vol. XXII, pp. 870-875, 5 ills., Sept., 1911.

USBR. *See* U. S. Bureau of Reclamation.

Useful Facts About the Countries of the World. Vol. XVIII, pp. 420-425, June, 1907.

Usher, Roland G.:

Oldest Nation of Europe: Geographical Factors in the Strength of Modern England. By Roland G. Usher. Vol. XXVI, pp. 393-414, 11 ills., Oct., 1914.

Utah:

Beyond the Clay Hills: An Account of the National Geographic Society's Reconnaissance of a Previously Unexplored Section in Utah. By Neil M. Judd. Vol. XLV, pp. 275-302, 28 ills., 1 half-page map, Mar., 1924.

Bursts of Color in Sculptured Utah. 22 ills. in color from natural-color photographs. Vol. LXIX, pp. 593-616, May, 1936.

Utah—*Continued*

Colossal Natural Bridges of Utah. Vol. XV, pp. 367-369, 2 ills., Sept., 1904.

Encircling Navajo Mountain with a Pack-Train: An Expedition to a Hitherto Untraversed Region of Our Southwest Discovers a New Route to Rainbow Natural Bridge. By Charles L. Bernheimer. Vol. XLIII, pp. 197-224, 33 ills., 1 half-page map, Feb., 1923.

Experiences in the Grand Canyon. By Ellsworth and Emery Kolb. Vol. XXVI, pp. 99-184, 70 ills., 1 page map, Aug., 1914.

Flaming Cliffs of Monument Valley. By Lt. Jack Breed, USNR. With 9 ills. in color from natural-color photographs by the author and Warren T. Mithoff. Vol. LXXXVIII, pp. 452-461, Oct., 1945.

Great Natural Bridges of Utah. Vol. XVIII, pp. 199-204, 3 ills., Mar., 1907.

Great Natural Bridges of Utah. By Byron Cummings. Vol. XXI, pp. 157-167, 7 ills., Feb., 1910.

Great Rainbow Natural Bridge of Southern Utah. By Joseph E. Pogue. Vol. XXII, pp. 1048-1056, 6 ills., Nov., 1911.

Utah, Carved by Winds and Waters: The Beehive State, Settled Only 89 Years Ago, Stands a Monument to the Courage of Its Founders. By Leo A. Borah. Vol. LXIX, pp. 577-623, 20 ills. in black and white, 22 ills. in color, 1 two-page map, May, 1936.

Why Great Salt Lake Has Fallen. By L. H. Murdoch. Vol. XIV, pp. 75-77, Feb., 1903.

Utrecht, Netherlands:

Holland Rises from War and Water. By Thomas R. Henry. Vol. LXXXIX, pp. 237-260, 18 ills., 1 seven-eighths-page map, Feb., 1946.

Uzbek Soviet Socialist Republic, U. S. S. R.:

Land of Lambskins: An Expedition to Bokhara, Russian Central Asia, to Study the Karakul Sheep Industry. By Robert K. Nabours. Vol. XXXVI, pp. 77-88, 15 ills., July, 1919.

New Road to Asia. By Owen Lattimore. Vol. LXXXVI, pp. 641-676, 15 ills. in black and white, 26 ills. in color, Dec., 1944.

Russia's Orphan Races: Picturesque Peoples Who Cluster on the Southeastern Borderland of the Vast Slav Dominions. By Maynard Owen Williams. Vol. XXXIV, pp. 245-278, 26 ills., 1 page map, Oct., 1918.

Where Slav and Mongol Meet. Vol. XXXVI, pp. 421-436, 16 ills. in color, Nov., 1919.

V

V-1 (Robot Bomb). *See* Robot Bombs.

V-2 (Rockets):

Air Power for Peace. By Gen. H. H. Arnold. Vol. LXXXIX, pp. 137-193, 35 ills. in black and white, 28 ills. in color, special map supplement, Feb., 1946.

New Frontier in the Sky. By F. Barrows Colton. Vol. XC, pp. 379-408, 28 ills., 1 diagram, Sept., 1946.

See also Rocket Bombs.

Vacation in a Fifteenth Century English Manor House. By George Alden Sanford. Vol. LIII, pp. 629-636, 8 ills., May, 1928.

Vacation in Holland. By George Alden Sanford. Vol. LVI, pp. 363-378, 6 ills. in black and white, 8 ills. in color, 1 two-thirds-page map. Sept., 1929.

Vagabonding in England: A Young American Works His Way Around the British Isles and Sees Sights from an Unusual Point of View. By John McWilliams. Vol. LXV, pp. 357-398, 39 ills., 1 three-quarters-page map, Mar., 1934.

Vai (Tribespeople):

Land of the Free in Africa. By Harry A. McBridge. Vol. XLII, pp. 411-430, 22 ills., Oct., 1922.

Vail, Theodore N.:

Voice Voyages by the National Geographic Society: A Tribute to the Geographical Achievements of the Telephone (Address by Theodore N. Vail). Vol. XXIX, pp. 296-326, 15 ills., 1 chart, Mar., 1916.

Valais (Canton), Switzerland:

In Valais. By Louise Murray. Vol. XXI, pp. 249-256, 6 ills., Mar., 1910.

Vâlcov, Romania:

Caviar Fishermen of Romania: From Vâlcov, "Little Venice" of the Danube Delta, Bearded Russian Exiles Go Down to the Sea. By Dorothy Hosmer. Vol. LXXVII, pp. 407-434, 29 ills., 1 third-page map, Mar., 1940.

Valdez, Alaska:

National Geographic Society's Alaskan Expedition of 1909. By Ralph S. Tarr and Lawrence Martin. Vol. XXI, pp. 1-54, 42 ills., 4 page and 7 half-page maps, Jan., 1910.

Valley of Ten Thousand Smokes, Alaska:

Awe-Inspiring Spectacle of the Valley of Ten Thousand Smokes, Discovered and Explored by National Geographic Society Expeditions. Vol. XXXIII, panorama, Feb., 1918.

Our Greatest National Monument: The National Geographic Society Completes Its Explorations in the Valley of Ten Thousand Smokes. By Robert F. Griggs. Vol. XL, pp. 219-292, 73 ills. in black and white, 16 ills. in color, 1 page and 1 three-quarters-page maps, Sept., 1921.

Ten Thousand Smokes Now a National Monument: The President of the United States Sets Aside for the American People the Extraordinary Valley Discovered and Explored by the National Geographic Society. Vol. XXXV, pp. 359-366, 5 ills., Apr., 1919.

Valley of Ten Thousand Smokes: An Account of the Discovery and Exploration of the Most Wonderful Volcanic Region in the World. By Robert F. Griggs. Vol. XXXIII, pp. 115-169, 46 ills., 1 half-page map, panorama, Feb., 1918.

Valley of Ten Thousand Smokes, Alaska—*Continued*

Valley of Ten Thousand Smokes: National Geographic Society Explorations in the Katmai District of Alaska. By Robert F. Griggs. Vol. XXXI, pp. 12-68, 51 ills., 1 half-page map, Jan., 1917.

Valparaiso, Chile:

Capital and Chief Seaport of Chile. By W. Robert Moore. Vol. LXXXVI, pp. 477-500, 15 ills. in black and white, 8 ills. in color, 1 third-page map, Oct., 1944.

From Panama to Patagonia. By Charles M. Pepper. Vol. XVII, pp. 449-452, 1 ill., Aug., 1906.

Longitudinal Journey Through Chile. By Harriet Chalmers Adams. Vol. XLII, pp. 219-273, 60 ills., 1 half-page map, Sept., 1922.

Twin Stars of Chile: Valparaiso, the Gateway, and Santiago, the Capital—Key Cities with a Progressive Present and a Romantic Past. By William Joseph Showalter. Vol. LV, pp. 197-247, 35 ills. in black and white, 25 ills. in color, Feb., 1929.

Value of Arctic Exploration. By Comdr. Robert E. Peary. Vol. XIV, pp. 429-436, Dec., 1903.

Value of the United States Forest Service. Vol. XX, pp. 29-41, 14 ills., Jan., 1909.

Van, Turkey:

Between Massacres in Van. By Maynard Owen Williams. Vol. XXXVI, pp. 181-184, 3 ills., Aug., 1919.

Vandercook, John W.:

Mandate of Cameroun: A Vast African Territory Ruled by Petty Sultan Under French Sway. By John W. Vandercook. Vol. LIX, pp. 225-260, 49 ills., 1 two-thirds-page map, Feb., 1931.

Vanderlip, F. A.:

World's Production of Gold (From an Address to the American Bankers' Convention by F. A. Vanderlip, October 11, 1905). Vol. XVI, pp. 571-572, Dec., 1905.

Van der Meulen, D.:

Into Burning Hadhramaut (Arabia): The Arab Land of Frankincense and Myrrh, Ever a Lodestone of Western Explorations. By D. Van der Meulen. Vol. LXII, pp. 387-429, 44 ills., 1 two-thirds-page map, Oct., 1932.

Van Ess, John:

Forty Years Among the Arabs. By John Van Ess. Vol. LXXII, pp. 385-420, 27 ills., 1 two-page map, Sept., 1942.

Vanishing People of the South Seas: The Tragic Fate of the Marquesan Cannibals, Noted for Their Warlike Courage and Physical Beauty. By John W. Church. Vol. XXXVI, pp. 275-306, 22 ills., 1 half-page map, Oct., 1919.

Van Loon, Henrik Willem:

Citizen Army of Holland. By Henrik Willem Van Loon. Vol. XXIX, pp. 609-622, 9 ills., June, 1916.

Van Zandt, (Lt.) J. Parker:

Looking Down on Europe: The Thrills and Advantages of Sight-Seeing by Airplane, as Demonstrated on a 6,500-Mile Tour Over Commercial Aviation Routes. By Lieut. J. Parker Van Zandt. Vol. XLVII, pp. 261-326, 67 ills., 1 half-page map, Mar., 1925.

Looking Down on Europe Again: Crisscrossing Air Tracks Reveal Nature's Scenic Masterpieces and Man's Swift-Changing Boundaries and Structures. By J. Parker Van Zandt. Vol. LXXV, pp. 791-822, 31 ills., 1 page map, June, 1939.

On the Trail of the Air Mail: A Narrative of the Experiences of the Flying Couriers Who Relay the Mail Across America at a Speed of More Than 2,000 Miles a Day. By Lieut. J. Parker Van Zandt. Vol. XLIX, pp. 1-61, 67 ills., 1 two-thirds-page map, Jan., 1926.

Variations in Lake Levels and Atmospheric Precipitation. By Alfred J. Henry. Vol. X, pp. 403-406, 1 diagram, Oct., 1899.

Vasco da Gama. *See* Gama, Vasco da.

Vasco da Gama at the Court of the Zamorin of Calicut. Reproduction in color of the painting by José Velloso Salgado, Sociedade de Geographia de Lisboa. Vol. LII, supplement, Nov., 1927.

Vast Timber Belts of Canada. Vol XVII, pp. 509-511, Sept., 1906.

Vatican City:

Smallest State in the World: Vatican City on Its 100 Acres Is a Complete Sovereignty Internationally Recognized. By W. Coleman Nevils. Vol. LXXV, pp. 377-412, 37 ills., 1 two-page map, Mar., 1939.

Vatican City: Treasure House of the Ages. 8 ills. from photographs. Vol. LXXV, pp. 393-400, Mar., 1939.

Vatopéthi (Monastery), Greece:

Hoary Monasteries of Mt. Athos. By H. G. Dwight. Vol. XXX, pp. 249-272, 24 ills., 1 half-page map, Sept., 1916.

Vegetables:

America Fights on the Farms. 21 ills. in color from natural-color photographs. Vol. LXXXVI, pp. 33-48, July, 1944.

Black Acres (Mucklands of New York): A Thrilling Sketch in the Vast Volume of Who's Who Among the Peoples That Make America. By Dorothea D. and Fred Everett. Vol. LXXX, pp. 631-652, 13 ills. in black and white, 12 ills. in color, Nov., 1941.

Farmers Keep Them Eating. By Frederick Simpich. Vol. LXXXIII, pp. 435-458, 22 ills., Apr., 1943.

Fruitful Shores of the Finger Lakes (New York). By Harrison Howell Walker. Vol. LXXIX, pp. 559-594, 15 ills. in black and white, 22 ills. in color, 1 two-thirds-page map, May, 1941.

Vegetables—*Continued*

Greens Grow for GI's on Soilless Ascension. By W. Robert Moore. Vol. LXXXVIII, pp. 219-230, 12 ills., Aug., 1945.

More Water for California's Great Central Valley. By Frederick Simpich. Vol. XC, pp. 645-664, 16 ills., 1 page map, Nov., 1946.

Rio Grande Cornucopia Under a Winter Sun. 24 ills. in color from natural-color photographs by B. Anthony Stewart. Vol. LXXV, pp. 65-96, Jan., 1936.

Texas Delta of an American Nile : Orchards and Gardens Replace Thorny Jungle in the Southmost Tip of the Lone Star State. By McFall Kerbey. Vol. LXXV, pp. 51-96, 27 ills. in black and white, 24 ills. in color, 1 page map, Jan., 1939.

Vegetables, Dried :

Forming New Fashions in Food : The Bearing of Taste on One of Our Great Food Economies, the Dried Vegetable, Which Is Developing Into a Big War Industry. By David Fairchild. Vol. XXXIII, pp. 356-368, 11 ills., Apr., 1918.

Reviving a Lost Art. Vol. XXXI, pp. 475-481, 9 ills., June, 1917.

Venezuela:

Anglo-Venezuelan Boundary Dispute. By Marcus Baker. Vol. XI, pp. 129-144, 2 ills., 1 page map, Apr., 1900.

Countries of the Caribbean. By William Joseph Showalter. Vol. XXIV, pp. 227-250, 23 ills., Feb., 1913.

I Kept House in a Jungle : The Spell of Primeval Tropics in Venezuela, Riotous With Strange Plants, Animals, and Snakes, Enthralls a Young American Woman. By Anne Rainey Langley. Vol. LXXV, pp. 97-132, 28 ills., 1 third-page map, Jan., 1939.

In Humboldt's Wake : Narrative of a National Geographic Society Expedition Up the Orinoco and Through the Strange Casiquiare Canal to Amazonian Waters. By Ernest G. Holt. Vol. LX, pp. 621-644, 27 ills., 1 two-thirds-page map, Nov., 1931.

Journey by Jungle Rivers to the Home of the Cock-of-the-Rock : Naturalists Enter the Amazon, Voyage Through the Heart of Tropical South America, and Emerge at the Mouth of the Orinoco. By Ernest G. Holt. Vol. LXIV, pp. 585-630, 49 ills., 1 two-thirds-page map, Nov., 1933.

Modern Venezuelan Vignettes. 9 ills. from photographs. Vol. LXXV, pp. 113-120, Jan., 1939.

Some Notes on Venezuela. Vol. XIV, pp. 17-21, 3 ills., 1 page map, Jan., 1903.

Three Old Ports on the Spanish Main. By G. M. L. Brown. Vol. XVII, pp. 622-638, 12 ills., Nov., 1906.

See also Caracas.

Venezuela's Capital—City of Contrasts. 19 ills. in color from natural-color photographs by Luis Marden. Vol. LXXVII, pp. 483-506, Apr., 1940.

Venice, Italy :

Frontier Cities of Italy. By Florence Craig Albrecht. Vol. XXVII, pp. 533-586, 45 ills., June, 1915.

Geography of Medicines : War's Effect upon the World's Sources of Supply. By John A. Foote. Vol. XXXII, pp. 213-238, 25 ills., Sept., 1917.

Northern Italy : Scenic Battleground. 18 ills. in color from natural-color photographs ; 13 ills. by B. Anthony Stewart and 3 ills. by Lt. Benjamin C. McCartney. Vol. LXXXVII, pp. 265-288, Mar., 1945.

Republics—The Ladder to Liberty. By David Jayne Hill. Vol. XXXI, pp. 240-254, 5 ills., 2 page maps, Mar., 1917.

Venice. By Karl Stieler. Vol. XXVII, pp. 587-630, 42 ills., 1 page and 1 quarter-page maps, June, 1915.

Venice : Home City of Marco Polo. 8 ills. from photographs. Vol. LIV, pp. 559-566, Nov., 1928.

Venice of Mexico (Aztec Lake Country). By Walter Hough. Vol. XXX, pp. 69-88, 18 ills., July, 1916.

Venizelos, Eleutherios:

Greece and Montenegro. By George Higgins Moses. Vol. XXIV, pp. 281-310, 24 ills., Mar., 1913.

Veracruz (State), Mexico :

Discovering the New World's Oldest Dated Work of Man : A Maya Monument Inscribed 291 B. C. is Unearthed Near a Huge Stone Head by a Geographic-Smithsonian Expedition in Mexico. By Matthew W. Stirling. Vol. LXXVI, pp. 183-218, 40 ills., 1 half-page map, Aug., 1939.

Expedition Unearths Buried Masterpieces of Carved Jade. By Matthew W. Stirling. Vol. LXXX, pp. 277-302, 14 ills. in black and white, 20 ills. in color, 1 two-thirds-page map, Sept., 1941.

Great Stone Faces of the Mexican Jungle : Five Colossal Heads and Numerous Other Monuments of Vanished Americans Are Excavated by the Latest National Geographic-Smithsonian Expedition. By Matthew W. Stirling. Vol. LXXVIII, pp. 309-334, 26 ills., 1 map, Sept., 1940.

Jungle Housekeeping for a Geographic Expedition. By Marion Stirling. Vol. LXXX, pp. 303-327, 15 ills., Sept., 1941.

Naturalist's Journey Around Vera Cruz and Tampico. By Frank M. Chapman. Vol. XXV, pp. 532-562, 31 ills., May, 1914.

Treasure-trove of Old Mexican Jade. 20 ills. in color from natural-color photographs by Richard H. Stewart. Vol. LXXX, pp. 293-316, Sept., 1941.

Wildlife of Tabasco and Vera Cruz. By Walter A. Weber. With 19 ills. in color from paintings by the author. Vol. LXXXVII, pp. 187-216, 7 ills. in black and white, 1 two-thirds-page map, Feb., 1945.

Vergil. *See* Virgil.

Verhoogen, (Dr.) Jean:

We Keep House on an Active Volcano: After Flying to Study a Spectacular Eruption in Belgian Congo, a Geologist Settles Down on a Newborn Craterless Vent for Eight Months' Study, By Dr. Jean Verhoogen, Vol. LXXVI, pp. 511-550, 28 ills., 1 two-thirds-page map, Oct., 1939.

Vermont:

Flow Onward Connecticut (River)! 24 ills. in color from natural-color photographs; 22 ills. by B. Anthony Stewart. Vol. LXXXIII, pp. 409-432, Apr., 1943.

Green Mountain State. By Herbert Corey. Vol. LI, pp. 333-369, 40 ills. in black and white, 6 ills. in color, 1 page map, Mar., 1927.

Long River of New England: In War and Peace, from Mountain Wilderness to the Sea, Flows the Connecticut River, Through a Valley Abounding in History, Scenery, Inventive Genius and Industry. By Albert W. Atwood. Vol. LXXXIII, pp. 401-434, 12 ills. in black and white, 24 ills. in color, 1 two-thirds-page map, Apr., 1943.

New England's Wonderland of Mountain, Lake, and Seascape. 5 ills. in color from natural-color photographs by Clifton Adams. Vol. LX, pp. 262-271, Sept., 1931.

Verner, Samuel P.:

Some Peculiar Features of Central African Geography. By Samuel P. Verner. Vol. XV, p. 448, Nov., 1904.

Verona, Italy:

Frontier Cities of Italy. By Florence Craig Albrecht. Vol. XXVII, pp. 533-586, 45 ills., June, 1915.

Versailles (Palace), France:

From the Trenches to Versailles. By Carol Corey. Vol. XXXII, pp. 535-550, 12 ills., Nov.-Dec., 1917.

Palace of Versailles, Its Park and the Trianons. By Franklin L. Fisher. Vol. XLVII, pp. 49-62, 4 ills. in black and white, 14 ills. in color, Jan., 1925.

Versailles the Magnificent. 14 ills. in color from autochromes lumière by Gervais Courtellemont. Vol. XLVII, pp. 53-60, Jan., 1925.

Vesuvius (Volcano), Italy:

Behind the Lines in Italy. By Corporal Macon Reed, Jr. Vol. LXXXVI, pp. 109-128, 20 ills., July, 1944.

Eruption of Mount Vesuvius, April 7-8, 1906. By Dr. Thomas Augustus Jaggar. Vol. XVII, pp. 318-325, 6 ills., June, 1906.

Mount Vesuvius. Vol. XVII, pp. 272-279, 7 ills., May, 1906.

Vialles, (Dr.) André:

Camargue, the Cowboy Country of Southern France. By Dr. André Vialles. Vol. XLII, pp. 1-34, 33 ills., 1 half-page-map, July, 1922.

Victoria, British Columbia:

Factors Which Modify the Climate of Victoria, British Columbia. By Arthur W. McCurdy. Vol. XVIII, pp. 345-348, 2 quarter-page maps, May, 1907.

Victoria Falls, Southern Rhodesia:

African Rainbow. 10 ills. in color from natural-color photographs by W. Robert Moore. Vol. LXXXVI, pp. 289-296, Sept., 1944.

Rhodesia, Hobby and Hope of Cecil Rhodes. By W. Robert Moore. Vol. LXXXVI, pp. 281-306, 13 ills. in black and white, 10 ills. in color, 1 half-page map, Sept., 1944.

Wonders of the Mosi-oa-Tunga: The Falls of the Zambesi. By Louis Livingston Seaman. Vol. XXII, pp. 561-571, 6 ills., June, 1911.

World's Great Waterfalls: Visits to Mighty Niagara, Wonderful Victoria, and Picturesque Iguazu. By Theodore W. Noyes. Vol. L, pp. 29-59, 29 ills., July, 1926.

Victoria Island (Wollaston Land), Canada:

Origin of Stefansson's Blond Eskimo. By Maj. Gen. A. W. Greely. Vol. XXIII, pp. 1224-1238, 10 ills., 1 page map, Dec., 1912.

Victoria Lake, Kenya-Tanganyika-Uganda:

Great African Lake. By Sir Henry M. Stanley. Vol. XIII, pp. 169-172, 1 half-page map, May, 1902.

Where Roosevelt Will Hunt. By Sir Henry Johnston. Vol. XX, pp. 207-256, 43 ills., special map supplement, Mar., 1909.

Victory's Portrait in the Marianas. By Lt. William Franklin Draper, USNR. With 17 ills. in color from paintings by the author. Vol. LXXXVIII, pp. 599-616, Nov., 1945.

Vicuñas:

Camels of the Clouds. By W. H. Hodge. Vol. LXXXIX, pp. 641-656, 15 ills., 1 half-page map, May, 1946.

Vienna, Austria:

Tale of Three Cities. By Thomas R. Henry. Vol. LXXXVIII, pp. 641-669, 23 ills., Dec., 1945.

Vienna—A Capital Without a Nation. By Solita Solano. Vol. XLIII, pp. 77-102, 27 ills., Jan., 1923.

Views and Hues of the Sunflower State (Kansas). 12 ills. in color from natural-color photographs by Richard H. Stewart. Vol. LXXII, pp. 151-158, Aug., 1937.

Views of Lhasa (Tibet). Vol. XVI, pp. 27-38, 11 ills., Jan., 1905.

Views of the Lincoln Memorial in Washington. Vol. XLII, pp. 197-204, 8 ills., Aug., 1922.

Vignettes of Guadalajara (Mexico). By Frederick Simpich. Vol. LXV, pp. 329-356, 20 ills. in black and white, 15 ills. in color, 1 third-page map, Mar., 1934.

Viking Life in the Storm-Cursed Faeroes. By Leo Hansen. Vol. LVIII, pp. 607-648, 49 ills., 1 half-page map, Nov., 1930.

Vila, Efate (Island), New Hebrides:

Palms and Planes in the New Hebrides. By Maj. Robert D. Heinl, Jr. Vol. LXXXVI, pp. 229-256, 17 ills. in black and white, 12 ills. in color, 1 four-fifths-page map, Aug., 1944.

Village Life in the Holy Land. By John D. Whiting. Vol. XXV, pp. 249-314, 27 ills. in black and white, 22 ills. in color, Mar., 1914.

Villari, Luigi:

Races and Religions of Macedonia. By Luigi Villari. Vol. XXIII, pp. 1118-1132, 14 ills., Nov., 1912.

Villiers, Alan J.:

Cape Horn Grain-Ship Race : The Gallant *Parma* Leads the Vanishing Fleet of Square-Riggers Through Raging Gales and Irksome Calms 16,000 Miles from Australia to England. By A. J. Villiers. Vol. LXIII, pp. 1-39, 38 ills., Jan., 1933.

North About (*Joseph Conrad*). By Alan J. Villiers. Vol. LXXI, pp. 221-250, 24 ills., Feb., 1937.

Rounding the Horn in a Windjammer (*Grace Harwar*). By A. J. Villiers. Vol. LIX, pp. 191-224, 36 ills., 1 two-thirds-page map, Feb., 1931.

Where the Sailing Ship Survives (Åland Islands). By A. J. Villiers. Vol. LXVII, pp. 101-128, 31 ills., 1 half-page map, Jan., 1935.

Vineyards. *See* Grape Culture.

Vinton, Kenneth W.:

Frog That Eats Bats and Snakes : In Captivity, This Big Jungle Amphibian Exhibits an Extraordinary Appetite. By Kenneth W. Vinton. Vol. LXXIII, pp. 657-664, 11 ills., May, 1938.

Vinton, S. R.:

China. 3 ills. in color from photographs by S. R. Vinton. Vol. XXXVIII, pp. 382-390, Nov., 1920.

Vireos:

Blackbirds and Orioles. By Arthur A. Allen. Paintings by Maj. Allan Brooks. Vol. LXVI, pp. 111-130, 7 portraits in color, July, 1934.

Virgil:

Perennial Geographer : After 2,000 Years Vergil Is Still the Most Widely Read of Latin Poets—First to Popularize the Geography of the Roman Empire. By W. Coleman Nevils. Vol. LVIII, pp. 439-465, 29 ills., Oct., 1930.

Virgin Islands, West Indies :

American Gibraltar : Notes on the Danish West Indies. Vol. XXX, pp. 89-96, 4 ills., 1 page map, July, 1916.

American Virgins : After Dark Days, These Adopted Daughters of the United States Are Finding a New Place in the Caribbean Sun. By DuBose Heyward and Daisy Reck. Vol. LXXVIII, pp. 273-308, 15 ills. in black and white, 23 ills. in color, 1 two-thirds-page map, Sept., 1940.

Danish West Indies. Vol. XIII, pp. 72-73, Feb., 1902.

Haunts of the Caribbean Corsairs : The West Indies a Geographic Background for the Most Adventurous Episodes in the History of the Western Hemisphere. By Nell Ray Clarke. Vol. XLI, pp. 147-187, 27 ills., Feb., 1922.

Virgin Islands, West Indies—*Continued*

Is Germany the Cause of Denmark's Refusal to Sell Her West Indian Possessions? Vol. XIV, p. 39, Jan., 1903.

Island Treasures of the Caribbean. 23 ills. in color from natural-color photographs by Edwin L. Wisherd and C. W. Herbert. Vol. LXXVIII, pp. 281-304, Sept., 1940.

Southward Ho ! in the "Alice." By Henry Howard. Vol. LXXIII, pp. 265-312, 38 ills. in black and white, 13 ills. in color, 2 maps, Mar., 1938.

Virginia:

Approaching Washington by Tidewater Potomac. By Paul Wilstach. Vol. LVII, pp. 372-392, 7 ills., Mar., 1930.

Chesapeake Odyssey : An 18-foot Sailboat Follows the Course of Captain John Smith around This Spacious Bay of History, Commerce, Sea Food, and Nautical Lore. By John Maloney. Vol. LXXVI, pp. 357-392, 32 ills., 1 page map, Sept., 1939.

Dismal Swamp in Legend and History . George Washington Owned Large Tracts in Region Which He Describes as a "Glorious Paradise." By John Francis Ariza. Vol. LXII, pp. 121-130, 11 ills., July, 1932.

Fame's Eternal Camping Ground : Beautiful Arlington, Burial Place of America's Illustrious Dead. By Enoch A. Chase. Vol. LIV, pp. 621-638, 19 ills., Nov., 1928.

Gardens and Shrines of Old Virginia. 20 ills. in color from natural-color photographs by B. Anthony Stewart and J. Baylor Roberts. Vol. LXXXI, pp. 623-646, May, 1942.

George Washington's Historic River (Potomac). 18 ills. in color from natural-color photographs by Willard R. Culver and Robert F. Sisson. Vol. LXXXVIII, pp. 41-64, July, 1945.

Home of the First Farmer of America (Mount Vernon). By Worth E. Shoults. Vol. LIII, pp. 603-628, 6 ills. in black and white, 26 ills. in color, May, 1928.

Jefferson's Little Mountain : Romance Enfolds Monticello, the Restored Home of the Author of the Declaration of Independence. By Paul Wilstach. Vol. LV, pp. 481-503, 12 ills. in black and white, 12 ills. in color, Apr., 1929.

Luray Caverns. Vol. XVII, pp. 358-362, 3 ills., June, 1906.

Monticello, One of America's Most Historic Shrines. 12 ills. in color from natural-color photographs by Edwin L. Wisherd, Charles Martin, and Jacob Gayer. Vol. LV, pp. 488-497, Apr., 1929.

National Geographic Society's Eclipse Expedition to Norfolk, Virginia. By Marcus Baker. Vol. XI, p. 320, Aug., 1900.

Patriotic Pilgrimage to Eastern National Parks : History and Beauty Live Along Paved Roads, Once Indian Trails, Through Virginia, North Carolina, Tennessee, Kentucky, and West Virginia. By Leo A. Borah. Vol. LXV, pp. 663-702, 18 ills. in black and white, 28 ills. in color, 1 two-page map, June, 1934.

Virginia—*Continued*

Potomac, River of Destiny. By Albert W. Atwood. Vol. LXXXVIII, pp. 33-70, 15 ills. in black and white, 18 ills. in color, 1 map (two-page spread), July, 1945.

Restoration of Colonial Williamsburg. By W. A. R. Goodwin. Vol. LXXI, pp. 402-443, 21 ills. in black and white, 25 ills. in color, Apr., 1937.

Roads from Washington. By John Patric. Vol. LXXIV, pp. 1-48, 27 ills. in black and white, 30 ills. in color, special map supplement, July, 1938.

Scenes and Shrines of the Cavalier Country. 13 ills. in color from natural-color photographs by Charles Martin, Edwin L. Wisherd, Jacob Gayer, and Clifton Adams. Vol. LV, pp. 424-433, Apr., 1929.

Scientific Work of Mount Weather Meteorological Observatory. By Frank H. Bigelow. Vol. XV, pp. 442-445, Nov., 1904.

Skeleton in Luray Cave. By H. C. Hovey. Vol. XVII, pp. 425-426, July, 1906.

Society's Map of Historic and Scenic Reaches of the Nation's Capital. Text accompanying special map supplement in colors. Vol. LXXIV, pp. 57-58, July, 1938.

Tidewater Virginia, Where History Lives. By Albert W. Atwood. Vol. LXXXI, pp. 617-656, 18 ills. in black and white, 20 ills. in color, 1 page map, May, 1942.

Training the New Armies of Liberty : Camp Lee, Virginia's Home for the National Army. By Granville Fortescue. Vol. XXXII, pp. 421-437, 8 ills., 1 page map in colors, Nov.-Dec., 1917.

Travels of George Washington : Dramatic Episodes in His Career as the First Geographer of the United States. By William Joseph Showalter. Vol. LXI, pp. 1-63, 50 ills., 5 maps, special map supplement, Jan., 1932.

Tri-State Medley. 10 ills. in color from natural-color photographs by Willard R. Culver. Vol. LXXIV, pp. 33-40, July, 1938.

Virginia—A Comonwealth That Has Come Back. By William Joseph Showalter. Vol. LV, pp. 403-472, 69 ills. in black and white, 13 ills. in color, 1 page map, Apr., 1929.

Virginia's Colonial Heritage (Williamsburg). 25 ills. in color from natural-color photographs. Vol. LXXI, pp. 417-440, Apr., 1937.

See also Arlington County ; Cumberland Gap (Region).

Vischer, Adolph L.:

Tripoli : A Land of Little Promise (Libia). By Adolph L. Vischer. Vol. XXII, pp. 1035-1047, 6 ills., 1 half-page map, Nov., 1911.

Vischer, Hanns:

Mysteries of the Desert (Sahara). By Hanns Vischer. Vol. XXII, pp. 1056-1059, Nov., 1911.

Visit to Carlsbad Cavern : Recent Explorations of a Limestone Cave in the Guadalupe Mountains of New Mexico Reveal a Natural Wonder of the First Magnitude. By Willis T. Lee. Vol. XLV, pp. 1-40, 42 ills., Jan., 1924.

Visit to Lonely Iceland. By Perley H. Noyes. Vol. XVIII, pp. 731-741, 12 ills., Nov., 1907.

Visit to the Brazilian Coffee Country. By Robert De C. Ward. Vol. XXII, pp. 908-931, 19 ills., 1 half-page map, Oct., 1911.

Visit to Three Arab Kingdoms : Transjordania, Iraq, and the Hedjaz Present Many Problems to European Powers. By Junius B. Wood. Vol. XLIII, pp. 535-568, 30 ills., 1 three-quarters-page map, May, 1923.

Visits to the Old Inns of England : Historic Homes of Hospitality for the Wayfarer Dot the Length and Breadth of the Kingdom. By Harold Donaldson Eberlein. Vol. LIX, pp. 261-285, 17 ills. in black and white, 15 ills. in color, Mar., 1931.

Visoki Dečani (Monastery), Yugoslavia :

Clock Turns Back in Yugoslavia : The Fortified Monastery of Mountain-girt Dečani Survives Its Six Hundredth Birthday. By Ethel Chamberlain Porter. Vol. LXXXV, pp. 493-512, 20 ills., 1 page map, Apr., 1944.

Viviani, M.:

Our Heritage of Liberty : An Address Before the United States Senate by M. Viviani, President of the French Commission to the United States. Vol. XXXI, pp. 365-367, 1 ill., Apr., 1917.

Their Monument Is in Our Hearts : Address by M. Viviani Before the Tomb of Washington, at Mount Vernon, April 29, 1917. Vol. XXXI, p. 367, Apr., 1917.

Vladivostok, U. S. S. R. :

Glimpses of Siberia, the Russian "Wild East." By Cody Marsh. Vol. XXXVIII, pp. 512-536, 26 ills., Dec., 1920.

Japan Faces Russia in Manchuria. By Willard Price. Vol. LXXXII, pp. 603-634, 30 ills., 1 page map, Nov., 1942.

Land of Promise (Siberia). By Maj. Gen. A. W. Greely. Vol. XXIII, pp. 1078-1090, 7 ills., Nov., 1912.

Siberia. By Edwin A. Grosvenor. Vol. XII, pp. 317-324, Sept., 1901.

Vogel, F.:

Desolate Greenland, Now an American Outpost. 17 ills. from photographs ; 12 ills. by Willie Knutsen ; 4 ills. by F. Vogel. Vol. LXXX, pp. 393-406, Sept., 1941.

Voice Voyages by the National Geographic Society : A Tribute to the Geographical Achievements of the Telephone. Vol. XXIX, pp. 296-326, 15 ills., 1 chart, Mar., 1916.

Volcanic Eruptions on Martinique and St. Vincent. By Israel C. Russell. Vol. XIII, pp. 415-436, 10 ills., Dec., 1902.

Volcanic Rocks of Martinique and St. Vincent: Collected by Robert T. Hill and Israel C. Russell. By J. S. Diller. Vol. XIII, pp. 285-296, July, 1902.

Volcano-Girded Salvador: A Prosperous Central American State with the Densest Rural Population in the Western World. By Harriet Chalmers Adams. Vol. XLI, pp. 189-200, 10 ills., Feb., 1922.

Volcano Islands, Pacific Ocean. *See* Kazan Retto.

Volcanoes:

Africa: We Keep House on an Active Volcano: After Flying to Study a Spectacular Eruption in Belgian Congo, a Geologist Settles Down on a Newborn Craterless Vent for Eight Months' Study. By Dr. Jean Verhoogen. Vol. LXXVI, pp. 511-550, 28 ills., 1 two-thirds-page map, Oct., 1939.

Alaska: Awe-Inspiring Spectacle of the Valley of Ten Thousand Smokes, Discovered and Explored by National Geographic Society Expeditions. Vol. XXXIII, panorama, Feb., 1918.

Alaska: Evidence of Recent Volcanic Action in Southeast Alaska. Vol. XVII, pp. 173-176, Mar., 1906.

Alaska: Mapping the Home of the Great Brown Bear: Adventures of the National Geographic Society's Pavlof Volcano Expedition to Alaska. By Dr. Thomas Augustus Jaggar. Vol. LV, pp. 109-134, 30 ills., 1 three-quarters-page map, Jan., 1929.

Alaska: Monarchs of Alaska. By R. H. Sargent. Vol. XX, pp. 610-623, 9 ills., July, 1909.

Alaska: Our Greatest National Monument: The National Geographic Society Completes Its Explorations in the Valley of Ten Thousand Smokes. By Robert F. Griggs. Vol. XL, pp. 219-292, 73 ills. in black and white, 16 ills. in color, 2 page and 1 three-quarters-page maps, Sept., 1921.

Alaska: Recent Eruption of Katmai Volcano in Alaska. By George C. Martin. Vol. XXIV, pp. 131-181, 45 ills., 1 page map, 1 diagram, Feb., 1913.

Alaska: Valley of Ten Thousand Smokes: An Account of the Discovery and Exploration of the Most Wonderful Volcanic Region in the World. By Robert F. Griggs. Vol. XXXIII, pp. 115-169, 46 ills., 1 half-page map, panorama, Feb., 1918.

Alaska: Valley of Ten Thousand Smokes: National Geographic Society Explorations in the Katmai District of Alaska. By Robert F. Griggs. Vol. XXXI, pp. 12-68, 51 ills., 1 half-page map, Jan., 1917.

Alaska: Volcanoes of Alaska (Eruption of Mt. Katmai in June, 1912). By Capt. K. W. Perry. Vol. XXIII, pp. 824-832, 11 ills., Aug., 1912.

Alaska: World Inside a Mountain: Aniakchak, the New Volcanic Wonderland of the Alaska Peninsula, Is Explored. By Bernard R. Hubbard. Vol. LX, pp. 319-345, 34 ills., 1 half-page map, Sept., 1931.

Volcanoes—*Continued*

Aleutians: Jack in the Box: An Account of the Strange Performances of the Most Wonderful Island in the World (Bogoslof Volcano). By Capt. F. M. Munger. Vol. XX, pp. 194-199, 8 ills., Feb., 1909.

Aleutians: Mountains on Unimak Island, Alaska. By Ferdinand Westdahl. Vol. XIV, pp. 90-99, 4 ills., 1 page and 1 half-page maps, Mar., 1903.

Aleutians: Riddle of the Aleutians: A Botanist Explores the Origin of Plants on Ever-misty Islands Now Enshrouded in the Fog of War. By Isobel Wylie Hutchison. Vol. LXXXII, pp. 769-792, 24 ills., Dec., 1942.

Aleutians: Shishaldin as a Field for Exploration. By Joseph Stanley-Brown. Vol. X, pp. 281-288, 3 ills., 1 quarter-page map, Aug., 1899.

Caribbean Regions: Suggested Field for Exploration. Vol. XIV, pp. 290-291, July, 1903.

Central America: Shattered Capitals of Central America. By Herbert J. Spinden. Vol. XXXVI, pp. 185-212, 32 ills., 1 page map, Sept., 1919.

Chile's Land of Fire and Water: Smoking Volcanoes and Ice-hooded Peaks Stand Sentinel Over Limpid Lakes in the Far Southern Andes. By W. Robert Moore. Vol. LXXX, pp. 91-110, 9 ills. in black and white, 10 ills. in color, 1 page map, July, 1941.

Costa Rica: Land of the Painted Oxcarts. By Luis Marden. With 31 ills. in color from natural-color photographs by the author. Vol. XC, pp. 409-456, 30 ills. in black and white, 1 half-page map, Oct., 1946.

Costa Rica—Vulcan's Smithy. By Henry Pittier. Vol. XXI, pp. 494-525, 30 ills., 2 half-page maps, June, 1910.

Do Volcanic Explosions Affect Our Climate? By C. G. Abbot. Vol. XXIV, pp. 181-198, 9 ills., 1 diagram, Feb., 1913.

Ecuador: Volcanoes of Ecuador, Guideposts in Crossing South America. By G. M. Dyott. Vol. LV, pp. 49-93, 42 ills. in black and white, 12 ills. in color, 1 half-page map, Jan., 1929.

El Salvador: Coffee Is King in El Salvador. By Luis Marden. With 27 ills. in color from natural-color photographs by the author and David Duncan. Vol. LXXXVI, pp. 575-616, 22 ills. in black and white, 1 half-page map, Nov., 1944.

Falcon, the Pacific's Newest Island. By J. Edward Hoffmeister and Harry S. Ladd. Vol. LIV, pp. 757-766, 8 ills., 1 half-page map, Dec., 1928.

Guatemala: Land of Volcanoes and Progress: Cradle of Ancient Mayan Civilization, Redolent With Its Later Spanish and Indian Ways, Now Reaping Prosperity from Bananas and Coffee. By Thomas F. Lee. Vol. L, pp. 599-648, 32 ills. in black and white, 20 ills. in color, 1 page map, Nov., 1926.

Volcanoes—*Continued*

Hawaii, Territory of : America's Strongest Outpost of Defense—The Volcanic and Floral Wonderland of the World. By Gilbert Grosvenor. Vol. XLV, pp. 115-238, 106 ills. in black and white, 21 ills. in color, 1 page, 4 half-page, and 1 quarter-page maps, 1 diagram, Feb., 1924.

Hawaii, Then and Now : Boyhood Recollections and Recent Observations by an American Whose Grandfather Came to the Islands 102 Years Ago. By William R. Castle. Vol. LXXIV, pp. 419-462, 30 ills. in black and white, 10 ills. in color, 1 page-and-a-half map, Oct., 1938.

Italy : Behind the Lines in Italy. By Corporal Macon Reed, Jr. Vol. LXXXVI, pp. 109-128, 20 ills., July, 1944.
    Contains text references and illustrations of the 1944 eruption of Vesuvius.

Italy : Eruption of Mount Vesuvius, April 7-8, 1906. By Dr. Thomas Augustus Jaggar. Vol. XVII, pp. 318-325, 6 ills., June, 1906.

Italy : Mount Vesuvius. Vol. XVII, pp. 272-279, 7 ills., May, 1906.

Japan : Face of Japan. By W. Robert Moore. Vol. LXXXVIII, pp. 753-768, 14 ills., special map supplement, Dec., 1945.

Japan : Geography of Japan : With Special Reference to Its Influence on the Character of the Japanese People. By Walter Weston. Vol. XL, pp. 45-84, 23 ills. in black and white, 16 ills. in color, July, 1921.

Japan : Sakurajima, Japan's Greatest Volcanic Eruption : A Convulsion of Nature Whose Ravages Were Minimized by Scientific Knowledge, Compared with the Terrors and Destruction of the Recent Tokyo Earthquake. By Dr. Thomas Augustus Jaggar. Vol. XLV, pp. 441-470, 32 ills., 1 half-page map, Apr., 1924.

Krakatau : Eruption of Krakatau. By Sir Robert Ball. Vol. XIII, pp. 200-204, June, 1902.

Mexico : Greatest Volcanoes of Mexico. By A. Melgareio. Vol. XXI, pp. 741-760, 22 ills., Sept., 1910.

Mexico : Paricutín, the Cornfield That Grew a Volcano. By James A. Green. Vol. LXXXV, pp. 129-164, 16 ills. in black and white, 21 ills. in color, 1 third-page map, Feb., 1944.

Nicaragua : Land of Lakes and Volcanoes. By Luis Marden. With 17 ills. in color from natural-color photographs by the author. Vol. LXXXVI, pp. 161-192, 11 ills. in black and white, 1 two-thirds-page map, Aug., 1944.

Niuafoö : Living on a Volcano : An Unspoiled Patch of Polynesia Is Niuafoö, Nicknamed "Tin Can Island" by Stamp Collectors. By Thomas A. Jaggar. Vol. LXVIII, pp. 91-106, 17 ills., 1 half-page map, July, 1935.

Philippine Islands : Taal Volcano and Its Recent Destructive Eruption. By Dean C. Worcester. Vol. XXIII, pp. 313-368, 40 ills., 4 half-page maps, 1 diagram, Apr., 1912.

Theories of Volcanic Action. Vol. XIV, pp. 110-111, Mar., 1903.

Volcanoes—*Continued*

Tonga Islands : Living on a Volcano : An Unspoiled Patch of Polynesia Is Niuafoö, Nicknamed "Tin Can Island" by Stamp Collectors. By Thomas A. Jaggar. Vol. LXVIII, pp. 91-106, 17 ills., 1 half-page map, July, 1935.

United States : Crater Lake and Yosemite Through the Ages. By Wallace W. Atwood, Jr. Paintings by Eugene Kingman. Vol. LXXI, pp. 327-343, 7 ills. in black and white, 13 ills. in color, Mar., 1937.

United States : Is Our Noblest Volcano Awakening to New Life : A Description of the Glaciers and Evidences of Volcanic Activity of Mount Hood. By A. H. Sylvester. Vol. XIX, pp. 515-525, 5 ills., 1 page map, July, 1908.

Volcanoes. By Gilbert H. Grosvenor. Vol. XIII, pp. 204-208, 1 page map, June, 1902.

West Indies : Chemical Discussion of Analyses of Volcanic Ejecta from Martinique and St. Vincent. By W. F. Hillebrand. Vol. XIII, pp. 296-299, July, 1902.

West Indies : Destruction of Pompeii as Interpreted by the Volcanic Eruptions of Martinique. By Angelo Heilprin. Vol. XV, p. 431, Oct., 1904.

West Indies : Eruptions of La Soufrière, St. Vincent, in May, 1902. By Edmund Otis Hovey. Vol. XIII, pp. 444-459, 4 ills., Dec., 1902.

West Indies : Magnetic Disturbance Caused by the Explosion of Mont Pelée. Vol. XIII, pp. 208-209, June, 1902.

West Indies : National Geographic Society Expedition in the West Indies. Vol. XIII, pp. 200-213, 2 half-page maps, June, 1902.

West Indies : New Cone of Mont Pelée (Martinique). Vol. XIV, pp. 422-423, 2 ills., Nov., 1903.

West Indies : Recent Volcanic Eruptions in the West Indies (Martinique and St. Vincent). By Israel C. Russell. Vol. XIII, pp. 267-285, 7 ills., July, 1902.

West Indies : Report by Robert T. Hill on the Volcanic Disturbances in the West Indies. Vol. XIII, pp. 223-267, 13 ills., 2 page and 1 half-page maps, July, 1902.

West Indies : Report of the Eruption of the Soufrière of St. Vincent, 1812 (From the *Evening News* of June 30, 1812). Vol. XIV, pp. 158-161, Apr., 1903.

West Indies : Reports of Vessels as to the Range of Volcanic Dust (Martinique and St. Vincent). By James Page. Vol. XIII, pp. 299-301, July, 1902.

West Indies : Shattered Obelisk of Mont Pelée (Martinique). By Angelo Heilprin. Vol. XVII, pp. 465-474, 5 ills., Aug., 1906.

West Indies : Volcanic Eruptions on Martinique and St. Vincent. By Israel C. Russell. Vol. XIII, pp. 415-436, 10 ills., Dec., 1902.

West Indies : Volcanic Rocks of Martinique and St. Vincent : Collected by Robert T. Hill and Israel C. Russell. By J. S. Diller. Vol. XIII, pp. 285-296, July, 1902.

Volendam, Netherlands :

Glimpses of Holland. By William Wisner Chapin. Vol. XXVII, pp. 1-29, 26 ills., Jan., 1915.

Volga (River), U. S. S. R. :

Mother Volga Defends Her Own. By Maynard Owen Williams. Vol. LXXXII, pp. 793-811, 21 ills., Dec., 1942.

Voyaging on the Volga Amid War and Revolution : War-Time Sketches on Russia's Great Waterway. By William T. Ellis. Vol. XXXIII, pp. 245-265, 16 ills., Mar., 1918.

Vosburgh, Frederick G.:

A City Learns to Smile Again (Nancy, France). By Maj. Frederick G. Vosburgh. Vol. LXXXVII, pp. 361-384, 23 ills., 1 two-thirds-page map, Mar., 1945.

Dogs of Duty and Devotion. By Frederick G. Vosburgh. Vol. LXXX, pp. 769-774, 3 ills., Dec., 1941.

Fabulous Yellowstone : Even Stranger Than the Tales of Early Trappers is the Truth About This Steaming Wonderland. By Frederick G. Vosburgh. Vol. LXXVII, pp. 769-794, 15 ills. in black and white, 9 ills. in color, 1 two-thirds-page map, June, 1940.

Henry Hudson, Magnificent Failure : Just 330 Years Ago He and His Mutinous Crew Found Manhattan Covered With "Goodly Oakes" and Fought Indians in New York Harbor. By Frederick G. Vosburgh. Vol. LXXV, pp. 461-490, 21 ills., Apr., 1939.

Men-Birds Soar on Boiling Air. By Frederick G. Vosburgh. Vol. LXXIV, pp. 123-140, 15 ills., July, 1938.

Metal Sinews of Strength : This Is a War of Many Metals, for We Live in an Age of Alloys. By Frederick G. Vosburgh. Vol. LXXXI, pp. 457-491, 35 ills., Apr., 1942.

New York State's Air-Conditioned Roof (Adirondacks). By Frederick G. Vosburgh. Vol. LXXIII, pp. 715-748, 23 ills. in black and white, 10 ills. in color, 1 three-quarters-page map, June, 1938.

Our Insect Fifth Column : Alien Enemies Take Steady Toll of Food, Trees, and Treasures by Boring from Within. By Frederick G. Vosburgh. Paintings by Hashime Murayama. Vol. LXXX, pp. 225-248, 14 ills. in black and white, 10 ills. in color, Aug., 1941.

This Is My Own : How the United States Seems to a Citizen Soldier Back from Three Years Overseas. By Frederick G. Vosburgh. Vol. LXXXIX, pp. 113-128, 14 ills., Jan., 1946.

Wonders of the New Washington : Efficient Modern Structures Rise in the Biggest Government Building Program Since the Capital City Was Founded in a Wilderness. By Frederick G. Vosburgh. Vol. LXVII, pp. 457-488, 20 ills. in black and white, 13 ills. in color, Apr., 1935.

Voyage of the *Morrissey.* 10 ills. in color from natural-color photographs by Daniel S. Turner and Sherman A. Wengerd. Vol. LXXXIX, pp. 609-616, May, 1946.

Voyages:

American Pathfinders in the Pacific. By William H. Nicholas. Vol. LXXXIX, pp. 617-640, 17 ills., 1 two-page map, May, 1946.

Around the World in the *Islander* (Ship) : A Narrative of the Adventures of a Solitary Voyager on His Four-Year Cruise in a Thirty-Four-Foot Sailing Craft. By Capt. Harry Pidgeon. Vol. LIII, pp. 141-205, 75 ills. 1 two-page map, Feb., 1928.

At Home on the Oceans : Whales and Sharks Make Exciting Neighbors for a Professor's Wife, Turned Able Seaman, On a Three-year Voyage Around the World. By Edith Bauer Strout. Vol. LXXVI, pp. 33-86, 54 ills., 1 map. July, 1939.

Bird Life Among Lava Rock and Coral Sand : The Chronicle of a Scientific Expedition to Little-Known Islands of Hawaii. By Alexander Wetmore. Vol. XLVIII, pp. 77-108, 36 ills., 1 half-page map, July, 1925.

By Felucca Down the Nile : Giant Dams Rule Egypt's Lifeline River, Yet Village Life Goes On As It Did in the Time of the Pharaohs. By Willard Price. Vol. LXXVII, pp. 435-476, 21 ills. in black and white, 22 ills. in color, 1 two-page map, Apr., 1940.

By Sail Across Europe. By Merlin Minshall. Vol. LXXI, pp. 533-567, 38 ills., 1 two-thirds-page map, May, 1937.

Cape Horn Grain-Ship Race : The Gallant *Parma* Leads the Vanishing Fleet of Square-Riggers Through Raging Gales and Irksome Calms 16,000 Miles, from Australia to England. By A. J. Villiers. Vol. LXIII, pp. 1-39, 38 ills., Jan., 1933.

Capturing Giant Turtles in the Caribbean. By David D. Duncan. Vol. LXXXIV, pp. 177-190, 13 ills., 1 quarter-page map, Aug., 1943.

Chesapeake Odyssey : An 18-foot Sailboat Follows the Course of Captain John Smith around This Spacious Bay of History, Commerce, Sea Food, and Nautical Lore. By John Maloney. Vol. LXXVI, pp. 357-392, 32 ills., 1 page map, Sept., 1939.

Columbus of the Pacific : Captain James Cook. Foremost British Navigator, Expanded the Great Sea to Correct Proportions and Won for Albion an Insular Empire by Peaceful Exploration and Scientific Study. By J. R. Hildebrand. Vol. LI, pp. 85-132, 45 ills., 1 page and 1 three-quarters-page maps, Jan., 1927.

Convoys to Victory. By Harvey Klemmer. Vol. LXXXIII, pp. 193-216, 24 ills., Feb., 1943.

Cruise Among Desert Islands (Baja California). By G. Dallas Hanna and A. W. Anthony. Vol. XLIV, pp. 71-99, 32 ills., 1 quarter-page map, July, 1923.

Cruise of the *Kinkajou:* Among Desert Islands of Mexico Voyagers Find Outdoor Laboratories for the Naturalist and Ideal Fishing Grounds for the Sportsman. By Alfred M. Bailey. Vol. LXXX, pp. 339-366, 13 ills. in black and white, 12 ills. in color, 1 page map, Sept., 1941.

Voyages—*Continued*

Cruising to Crete: Four French Girls Set Sail in a Breton Yawl for the Island of the Legendary Minotaur. By Marthe Oulié and Mariel Jean Brunhes. Vol. LV, pp. 249-272, 15 ills. in black and white, 14 ills. in color, 1 page map, Feb., 1929.

Danube, Highway of Races: From the Black Forest to the Black Sea, Europe's Most Important River Has Borne the Traffic of Centuries. By Melville Chater. Vol. LVI, pp. 643-697, 54 ills., Dec., 1929.

Deep-Sea Exploring Expedition of the Steamer *Albatross*. By Hugh M. Smith. Vol. X, pp. 291-296, 2 ills., 1 diagram, Aug., 1899.

Diary of a Voyage from San Francisco to Tahiti and Return, 1901. By S. P. Langley. Vol. XII, pp. 413-429, 10 ills., 1 page and 1 half-page maps, Dec., 1901.

Dream Ship: The Story of a Voyage of Adventure More Than Half Around the World in a 47-foot Lifeboat. By Ralph Stock. Vol. XXXIX, pp. 1-52, 43 ills., 1 page map, Jan., 1921.

Greatest Voyage in the Annals of the Sea. By J. R. Hildebrand. Vol. LXII. pp. 699-739, 35 ills., 2 half-page maps, Dec., 1932.

Greenland from 1898 to Now: "Captain Bob," Who Went North with Peary, Tells of 42 Years of Explorations in the Orphan Island of New Aerial and Naval Interest. By Robert A. Bartlett. Vol. LXXVIII, pp. 111-140, 25 ills., 1 two-page map, July, 1940.

Henry Hudson, Magnificent Failure: Just 330 Years Ago He and His Mutinous Crew Found Manhattan Covered With "Goodly Oakes" and Fought Indians in New York Harbor. By Frederick G. Vosburgh. Vol. LXXV, pp. 461-490, 21 ills., Apr., 1939.

Inside Cape Horn. By Amos Burg. Vol. LXXII, pp. 743-783, 29 ills. in black and white, 10 ills. in color, 1 two-page map, Dec., 1937.

Isles of Greece. By Lt. Richard Stillwell, USNR. Vol. LXXXV, pp. 593-622, 11 ills. in black and white, 20 ills. in color, 1 page map, May, 1944.

Journey by Jungle Rivers to the Home of the Cock-of-the-Rock: Naturalists Enter the Amazon, Voyage Through the Heart of Tropical South America, and Emerge at the Mouth of the Orinoco. By Ernest G. Holt. Vol. LXIV, pp. 585-630, 49 ills., 1 two-thirds-page map, Nov., 1933.

Modern Saga of the Seas: The Narrative of a 17,000-Mile Cruise on a 40-Foot Sloop by the Author, His Wife, and a Baby, Born on the Voyage. By Erling Tambs. Vol. LX, pp. 645-688, 49 ills., 1 half-page map, Dec., 1931.

North About. By Alan J. Villiers. Vol. LXXI, pp. 221-250, 24 ills., Feb., 1937.

Pathfinder of the East: Setting Sail to Find "Christians and Spices," Vasco da Gama Met Amazing Adventures, Founded an Empire, and Changed the History of Western Europe. By J. R. Hildebrand. Vol. LII, pp. 503-550, 43 ills., 1 two-thirds-page map, Nov., 1927.

Voyages—*Continued*

"Pilgrim" Sails the Seven Seas: A Schooner Yacht Out of Boston Drops in at Desert Isles and South Sea Edens in a Leisurely Two-Year Voyage. By Harold Peters. Vol. LXXII, pp. 223-262, 36 ills., Aug., 1937.

Rediscovering the Rhine: A Trip by Barge from the Sea to the Headwaters of Europe's Storied Stream. By Melville Chater. Vol. XLVIII, pp. 1-43, 44 ills., July, 1925.

Revealing Earth's Mightiest Ocean (Pacific). By Albert W. Atwood. Vol. LXXXIV, pp. 291-306, 10 ills., special map supplement, Sept., 1943.

Road to Bolivia. By William E. Curtis. Vol. XI, pp. 208-224, 7 ills., June, 1900.

Romance of Science in Polynesia: An Account of Five Years of Cruising Among the South Sea Islands. By Robert Cushman Murphy. Vol. XLVIII, pp. 355-426, 66 ills. in black and white, 16 ills. in color, 3 half-page maps, Oct., 1925.

Rounding the Horn in a Windjammer. By A. J. Villiers. Vol. LIX, pp. 191-224, 36 ills., 1 two-thirds-page map, Feb., 1931.

Sailing Forbidden Coasts (Africa). By Ida Treat. Vol. LX, pp. 357-386, 31 ills., 1 quarter-page map, Sept., 1931.

Sailing the Seven Seas in the Interest of Science: Adventures Through 157,000 Miles of Storm and Calm, from Arctic to Antarctic and Around the World, in the Non-Magnetic Yacht *Carnegie*. By J. P. Ault. Vol. XLII, pp. 631-690, 47 ills., 1 chart, Dec., 1922.

Seafarers of South Celebes. By G. E. P. Collins. Vol. LXXXVII, pp. 53-78, 25 ills., 1 two-thirds-page map, Jan., 1945.

Servicing Arctic Airbases. By Robert A. Bartlett. Vol. LXXXIX, pp. 602-616, 3 ills. in black and white, 10 ills. in color, 1 half-page map, May, 1946.

Sindbads of Science: Narrative of a Windjammer's Specimen-Collecting Voyage to the Sargasso Sea, to Senegambian Africa and Among Islands of High Adventure in the South Atlantic. By George Finlay Simmons. Vol. LII, pp. 1-75, 89 ills., 1 two-thirds-page map, July, 1927.

Skirting the Shores of Sunrise: Seeking and Finding "The Levant" in a Journey by Steamer, Motor-Car, and Train from Constantinople to Port Said. By Melville Chater. Vol. L, pp. 649-728, 60 ills. in black and white, 34 ills. in color, 1 two-thirds-page map, Dec., 1926.

Southward Ho! in the "Alice." By Henry Howard. Vol. LXXIII, pp. 265-312, 38 ills. in black and white, 13 ills. in color, 2 maps, Mar., 1938.

Storied Islands of the South Sea. 20 ills. in color from natural-color photographs by Irving Johnson, Malcolm Evans, and others. Vol. LXXXI, pp. 9-40, Jan., 1942.

Contains illustrations of Easter Island, Galápagos Islands, Pitcairn, Samoa, Santa Cruz, and Solomon Islands.

Voyages—*Continued*

Surveying the Grand Canyon of the Colorado : An Account of the 1923 Boating Expedition of the United States Geological Survey. By Lewis R. Freeman. Vol. XLV, pp. 471-548, 62 ills., 1 three-quarters-page map, May, 1924.

Voyage of the *Morrissey*. 10 ills. in color from natural-color photographs by Daniel S. Turner and Sherman A. Wengerd. Vol. LXXXIX, pp. 609-616, May, 1946.

Voyage to the Island Home of Robinson Crusoe (Juan Fernández). By Waldo L. Schmitt. Vol. LIV, pp. 353-370, 24 ills., Sept., 1928.

Voyaging on the Volga Amid War and Revolution : War-Time Sketches on Russia's Great Waterway. By William T. Ellis. Vol. XXXIII, pp. 245-265, 16 ills., Mar., 1918.

Westward Bound in the *Yankee*. By Irving and Electa Johnson. Vol. LXXXI, pp. 1-44, 25 ills. in black and white, 20 ills. in color, 1 three-quarters-page map, Jan., 1942.
    Contains information and illustrations of Easter Island, Galápagos Islands, Pitcairn, Samoa, Santa Cruz, and Solomon Islands.

See also Antarctic Regions ; Arctic Regions ; Canoes and Canoe Trips.

Voyaging on the Volga Amid War and Revolution : War-Time Sketches on Russia's Great Waterway. By William T. Ellis. Vol. XXXIII, pp. 245-265, 16 ills., Mar., 1918.

Vultures (Birds) :

Eagle, King of Birds, and His Kin. By Alexander Wetmore. Paintings by Maj. Allan Brooks. Vol. LXIV, pp. 43-95, 23 ills. in black and white, 28 ills. in color, July, 1933.

Eagles, Hawks, and Vultures. 28 ills. in color from paintings by Maj. Allan Brooks. Vol. LXIV, pp. 65-94, July, 1933.

W

WAC. *See* Women's Army Corps.

Wadsworth, Eliot:

Red Cross Spirit. By Eliot Wadsworth. Vol. XXXI, pp. 464-474, 8 ills., May, 1917.

Waikiki Beach, Honolulu :

Waves and Thrills at Waikiki. 8 ills. in duotone by Thomas Edward Blake. Vol. LXVII, pp. 597-604, May, 1935.

Waimangu and the Hot-Spring Country of New Zealand : The World's Greatest Geyser Is One of Many Natural Wonders in a Land of Inferno and Vernal Paradise. By Joseph C. Grew. Vol. XLVIII, pp. 109-130, 19 ills., 1 third-page map, Aug., 1925.

Wake (Island), Pacific Ocean :

Navy Wings over the Pacific. 12 ills. in color from U. S. Navy official photographs. Vol. LXXXVI, pp. 241-248, Aug., 1944.

Wakeman, Bernard:

Wayfaring Down the Winding Severn. 9 ills. in color from natural-color photographs by Bernard Wakeman. Vol. LXIII, pp. 433-440, Apr., 1933.

Where the Winding Cam Mirrors Cambridge (University) Spires. 12 ills. in color from natural-color photographs by Bernard Wakeman and Walter M. Edwards. Vol. LXX, pp. 339-346, Sept., 1936.

Wakeman, Frank:

Beauties of the Severn Valley. By Frank Wakeman. Vol. LXIII, pp. 417-452, 24 ills. in black and white, 15 ills. in color, 1 three-quarters-page map, Apr., 1933.

Wayfaring Down the Winding Severn. 6 ills. in color from natural-color photographs by Frank Wakeman. Vol. LXIII, pp. 433-440, Apr., 1933.

Walcheren Island, Netherlands :

Holland Rises from War and Water. By Thomas R. Henry. Vol. LXXXIX, pp. 237-260, 18 ills. in black and white, 1 seven-eighths-page map, Feb., 1946.

Mending Dikes in th Netherlands. 20 ills. from photographs by Lawrence Earl. Vol. XC, pp. 791-806, Dec., 1946.

Walcott, Charles D.:

Four Prominent Geographers. Vol. XVIII, pp. 425-428, 4 ills., June, 1907.

Geologist's Paradise (Canadian Rockies). By Charles D. Walcott. Vol. XXII, pp. 509-536, 28 ills., panorama, June, 1911.

Monarch of the Canadian Rockies (Mount Robson). Vol. XXIV, pp. 626-639, 13 ills., panorama, May, 1913.

Walcott, Frederic C.:

Devastated Poland. By Frederic C. Walcott. Vol. XXXI, pp. 445-452, 7 ills., May, 1917.

Forerunners of Famine. By Frederic C. Walcott. Vol. XXXIII, pp. 336-347, 4 ills., 1 half-page map, 4 diagrams, Apr., 1918.

Walcott, Stuart:

Life Story of an American Airman in France : Extracts from Letters of Stuart Walcott, Who, Between July and December, 1917, Learned to Fly in French Schools of Aviation, Won Fame at the Front, and Fell Near Saint Souplet. Vol. XXXIII, pp. 86-106, 9 ills., Jan., 1918.

Walde-Waldegg, Hermann von:

Stone Idols of the Andes Reveal a Vanished People : Remarkable Relics of One of the Oldest Aboriginal Cultures of America are Unearthed in Colombia's San Agustín Region. By Hermann von Walde-Waldegg. Vol. LXXVII, pp. 627-647, 22 ills., 1 map, May, 1940.

Waldseemüller Maps:

Famous Waldseemüller Map of 1507. Vol. XV, p. 50, Jan., 1904.

Two Famous Maps of America. Vol. XIII, p. 72, Feb., 1902.

Wales:

Races of Europe. By Edwin A. Grosvenor. Vol. XXXIV, pp. 441-534, 62 ills., 2 page maps, special map supplement, Dec., 1918.

Sheep Dog Trials in Llangollen : Trained Collies Perform Marvels of Herding in the Cambrian Stakes, Open to the World. By Sara Bloch. Vol. LXXVII, pp. 559-574, 17 ills., Apr., 1940.

Short Visit to Wales : Historic Associations and Scenic Beauties Contend for Interest in the Little Land Behind the Hills. By Ralph A. Graves. Vol. XLIV, pp. 635-675, 37 ills., 1 half-page map, Dec., 1923.

Wales in Wartime. By Isobel Wylie Hutchison. Vol. LXXXV, pp. 751-768, 16 ills., 1 page map, June, 1944.

See also Skokholm (Island).

Wales, Alaska :

Exploring Frozen Fragments of American History : On the Trail of Early Eskimo Colonists Who Made a 55-Mile Crossing from the Old World to the New. By Henry B. Collins, Jr. Vol. LXXV, pp. 633-656, 24 ills., 1 two-thirds-page map, May, 1939.

Walker, Harrison Howell:

Adirondack Idyls. 10 ills. in color from natural-color photographs by Harrison Howell Walker. Vol. LXXIII, pp. 729-736, June, 1938.

American Bombers Attacking from Australia. By Howell Walker. Vol. LXXXIII, pp. 49-70, 19 ills., 1 map (two-page spread), Jan., 1943.

Camera Pastels in French Canada. 25 ills. in color from natural-color photographs by Harrison Howell Walker. Vol. LXXV, pp. 601-624, May, 1939.

Facing War's Challenge "Down Under." 20 ills. in color from natural-color photographs by Howell Walker. Vol. LXXXI, pp. 425-456, Apr., 1942.

France Farms as War Rages : An American Explores the Rich Rural Region of the Historic Paris Basin. By Harrison Howell Walker. Vol. LXXVII, pp. 201-238, 16 ills. in black and white, 18 ills. in color, 1 map, Feb., 1940.

Fruitful Shores of the Finger Lakes. By Harrison Howell Walker. Vol. LXXIX, pp. 559-594, 15 ills. in black and white, 22 ills. in color, 1 two-thirds-page map, May, 1941.

Gentle Folk Settle Stern Saguenay : On French Canada's Frontier Homespun Colonists Keep the Customs of Old Norman Settlers. By Harrison Howell Walker. Vol. LXXV, pp. 595-632, 15 ills. in black and white, 25 ills. in color, 1 map, May, 1939.

Life in Dauntless Darwin : A National Geographic Staff Writer Gives a Vivid Description of the Australian Town That Guards the Continent's Northern Door. By Howell Walker. Vol. LXXXII, pp. 123-138, 17 ills., 1 sixth-page map, July, 1942.

Making of an Anzac. By Howell Walker. Vol. LXXXI, pp. 409-456, 31 ills. in black and white, 20 ills. in color, 1 two-page map, Apr., 1942.

Walker, Harrison Howell—*Continued*

Old Ireland, Mother of New Eire : By Whatever Name, 'Tis the Same Fair Land With the Grass Growing Green on the Hills of Her and the Peat Smoke Hanging Low. By Harrison Howell Walker. Vol. LXXVII, pp. 649-691, 19 ills. in black and white, 18 ills. in color, 1 page map, May, 1940.

Pennsylvania's Land of Plenty. 22 ills. in color from natural-color photographs by Harrison Howell Walker. Vol. LXXX, pp. 41-64, July, 1941.

Some French Pastorals. 18 ills. in color from natural-color photographs by Harrison Howell Walker. Vol. LXXVII, pp. 207-230, Feb., 1940.

Spring's Gay Bouquets Deck the Nation's Capital. 10 ills. in color from natural-color photographs by Harrison Howell Walker. Vol. LXXIV, pp. 17-24, July, 1938.

Sydney Faces the War Front Down Under. By Howell Walker. Vol. LXXXIII, pp. 359-374, 8 ills. in black and white, 10 ills. in color, Mar., 1943.

When Irish Skies Are Smiling. 18 ills. in color from natural-color photographs by Harrison Howell Walker. Vol. LXXVII, pp. 663-686, May, 1940.

Walker, J. Bernard:

Cathedrals of the Old and New World. By J. Bernard Walker. Vol. XLII, pp. 61-114, 50 ills., July, 1922.

Walker, John:

Europe's Looted Art. By John Walker. Vol. LXXXIX, pp. 39-52, 11 ills., Jan., 1946.

Walker, Lewis Wayne:

Fairy Terns of the Atolls. By Lewis Wayne Walker. Vol. XC, pp. 807-814, 9 ills., Dec., 1946.

Pelican Profiles. By Lewis Wayne Walker. Vol. LXXXIV, pp. 589-598, 5 ills. in black and white, 8 ills. in color, Nov., 1943.

Photoflashing Western Owls. By Lewis W. Walker. Vol. LXXXVII, pp. 475-486, 6 ills. in black and white, 7 ills. in color, Apr., 1945.

Walking Tour Across Iceland. By Isobel Wylie Hutchison. Vol. LIII, pp. 467-497, 36 ills., 1 half-page map, Apr., 1928.

Wall of China. *See* Great Wall of China.

Wallace, Frederick William:

Life on the Grand Banks : An Account of the Sailor-Fishermen Who Harvest the Shoal Waters of North America's Eastern Coasts. By Frederick William Wallace. Vol. XL, pp. 1-28, 29 ills., July, 1921.

Wallace, Henry A.:

People's Fight Against Slavery. By Hon. Henry A. Wallace. Reprint of address delivered at a dinner of the Free World Association, May 8, 1942. Vol. LXXXII, pp. 276-280, 1 ill., Aug., 1942.

Walliser, Blair A.:

Sunset in the East (Japan). By Blair A. Walliser. Vol. LXXXIX, pp. 797-812, 17 ills., June, 1946.

Walmsley, Leo:

Between the Heather and the North Sea : Bold English Headlands Once Sheltered Sea Robbers, Later Were Ports of Wooden Ships, Centers of the Jet and Alum Trades, To-day Are Havens of Adventurous Fishing Fleets. By Leo Walmsley. Vol. LXIII, pp. 197-232, 41 ills., Feb., 1933.

Walruses:

Hunting the Walrus. Vol. XXII, pp. 285-290, 10 ills., Mar., 1911.

Walter, Richard:

Wanderers Awheel in Malta : British Stronghold Has Been a Steppingstone of Conquest Since Phoenicians Cruised the Mediterranean and St. Paul Was Shipwrecked There. By Richard Walter. Vol. LXXVIII, pp. 253-272, 17 ills., 2 maps, Aug., 1940.

Walter Wellman's Expedition to the North Pole. Vol. XVII, pp. 205-207, 1 chart, Apr., 1906.

Wanderers Awheel in Malta : British Stronghold Has Been a Steppingstone of Conquest Since Phoenicians Cruised the Mediterranean and St. Paul Was Shipwrecked There. By Richard Walter. Vol. LXXVIII, pp. 253-272, 17 ills., 2 maps, Aug., 1940.

Wandering Islands in the Rio Grande. By Mrs. Albert S. Burleson. Vol. XXIV, pp. 381-386, 2 ills., 1 three-quarters-page map, Mar., 1913.

Wandering Through the Black Forest (Germany). 13 ills. in color from autochromes by Hans Hildenbrand. Vol. LIV, pp. 658-667, Dec., 1928.

Wang Ye Fu, China :

Road to Wang Ye Fu : An Account of the Work of the National Geographic Society's Central-China Expedition in the Mongol Kingdom of Ala Shan. By Frederick R. Wulsin. Vol. XLIX, pp. 197-234, 44 ills., 1 third-page map, Feb., 1926.

War, Patriotism, and the Food Supply. By Frederick V. Coville. Vol. XXXI, pp. 254-256, Mar., 1917.

War Agencies, Washington, D. C. :

Our Nation's Capital on Parade. 16 ills. in color from natural-color photographs by B. Anthony Stewart, Walter M. Edwards, and others. Vol. LXXXIV, pp. 265-288, Sept., 1943.

Wartime Washington. By William H. Nicholas. Vol. LXXXIV, pp. 257-290, 12 ills. in black and white, 16 ills. in color, Sept., 1943.

War and Ocean Geography. By Gilbert Grosvenor. Vol. XXXIV, pp. 230-242, 6 ills., 1 page map, Sept., 1918.

War Awakened New Caledonia : Swift Changes on the South Pacific Island of Mineral Wealth Defended by Free French and American Troops. By Enzo de Chetelat. Vol. LXXXII, pp. 31-55, 14 ills. in black and white, 12 ills. in color, 1 two-thirds-page map, July, 1942.

War Clouds Over Danzig and Poland's Port (Gdynia). 8 ills. from photographs. Vol. LXXVI, pp. 551-558, Oct., 1939.

War Dogs:

Animals Were Allies, Too. 16 ills. from photographs. Vol. LXXXIX, pp. 75-88, Jan., 1946.

Mankind's Best Friend : Companion of His Solitude, Advance Guard in the Hunt, and Ally of the Trenches. By Ernest Harold Baynes. Vol. XXXV, pp. 185-201, 11 ills., Mar., 1919.

Sagacity and Courage of Dogs : Instances of the Remarkable Intelligence and Unselfish Devotion of Man's Best Friend Among Dumb Animals. Vol. XXXV, pp. 253-275, 14 ills., Mar., 1919.

Your Dog Joins Up. By Frederick Simpich. Vol. LXXXIII, pp. 93-113, 25 ills., Jan., 1943.

War Echoes in the West Indies. 22 ills. in color from natural-color photographs by Luis Marden. Vol. LXXXI, pp. 731-754, June, 1942.

War Finds Its Way to Gilbert Islands : United States Forces Dislodge Japanese from Enchanted Atolls Which Loom Now as Stepping Stones along South Sea Route from Australia to Hawaii. By Sir Arthur Grimble. Vol. LXXXIII, pp. 71-92, 19 ills., 1 half-page map, Jan., 1943.

War Meets Peace in Egypt. By Grant Parr and G. E. Janssen. Vol. LXXXI, pp. 503-526, 25 ills., 1 page map, Apr., 1942.

Warblers (Birds) :

Birds of Timberline and Tundra. By Arthur A. Allen. With 24 ills. in color from natural-color photographs by the author. Vol. XC, pp. 313-339, 8 ills. in black and white, Sept., 1946.

Birds on the Home Front. By Arthur A. Allen. Vol. LXXXIV, pp. 32-56, 7 ills. in black and white, 30 ills. in color, July, 1943.

Friends of Our Forests. By Henry Wetherbee Henshaw. Vol. XXXI, pp. 297-321, 1 ill. in black and white, 32 ills. in color, Apr., 1917.

Ward, Robert De C.:

Our Immigration Laws from the Viewpoint of National Eugenics. By Robert De C. Ward. Vol. XXIII, pp. 38-41, Jan., 1912.

Visit to the Brazilian Coffee Country. By Robert De C. Ward. Vol. XXII, pp. 908-931, 19 ills., 1 half-page map, Oct., 1911.

Wards of the United States : Notes on What Our Country Is Doing for Santo Domingo, Nicaragua, and Haiti. Vol. XXX, pp. 143-177, 36 ills., Aug., 1916.

Warfare of the Jungle Folk : Campaigning Against Tigers, Elephants, and Other Wild Animals in Northern Siam. By Merian C. Cooper. Photographs by Ernest B. Schoedsack. Vol. LIII, pp. 233-268, 33 ills., Feb., 1928.

Warfare on Our Eastern Coast. By John Oliver La Gorce. Vol. XXVIII, pp. 195-230, 29 ills., 2 charts, Sept., 1915.

Warner, Arthur H.:

Country Where Going to America Is an Industry (Italy). By Arthur H. Warner. Vol. XX, pp. 1063-1102, 41 ills., Dec., 1909.

Warren, Francis E.:

Animal Wealth of the United States. By Francis E. Warren. Vol. XVII, pp. 511-524, 6 ills., Sept., 1906.

War's Wake in the Rhineland. By Thomas R. Henry. Vol. LXXXVIII, pp. 1-32, 29 ills., 1 third-page map, July, 1945.

Warsaw, Poland :

Partitioned Poland. By William Joseph Showalter. Vol. XXVII, pp. 88-106, 12 ills., Jan., 1915.

Wartime in the Pacific Northwest (United States and Canada). By Frederick Simpich. Vol. LXXXII, pp. 421-464, 25 ills. in black and white, 23 ills. in color, 1 half-page map, Oct., 1942.

Wartime Washington (D. C.). By William H. Nicholas. Vol. LXXIV, pp. 257-290, 12 ills. in black and white, 16 ills. in color, Sept., 1943.

Warwick, Adam:

Farmers Since the Days of Noah : China's Remarkable System of Agriculture Has Kept Alive the Densest Population in the World. By Adam Warwick. Vol. LI, pp. 469-500, 37 ills., Apr., 1927.

People of the Wilderness : The Mongols, Once the Terror of All Christendom, Now a Primitive, Harmless Nomad Race. By Adam Warwick. Vol. XXXIX, pp. 507-551, 59 ills., May, 1921.

Thousand Miles Along the Great Wall of China : The Mightiest Barrier Ever Built by Man Has Stood Guard Over the Land of Chin for Twenty Centuries. By Adam Warwick. Vol. XLIII, pp. 113-143, 27 ills., panorama, 1 page and 1 half-page maps, Feb., 1923.

Warwick, England :

How Warwick (Castle) Was Photographed in Color. By Maynard Owen Williams. Vol. LXX, pp. 83-93, 13 ills. in color, July, 1936.

Warwick Castle, Stage for Old England's Pageantry. 13 ills. in color from natural-color photographs by Maynard Owen Williams. Vol. LXX, pp. 85-92, July, 1936.

Washburn, Bradford:

Conquest of Mount Crillon (Alaska). By Bradford Washburn. Vol. LXVII, pp. 361-400, 40 ills., 1 half-page map, Mar., 1935.

Washburn, Bradford—*Continued*

Exploring Yukon's Glacial Stronghold. By Bradford Washburn. Vol. LXIX, pp. 715-747, 28 ills., 1 two-page map, June, 1936.

Over the Roof of Our Continent (Mount McKinley). By Bradford Washburn. Vol. LXXIV, pp. 78-98, 17 ills. in duatone, 1 half-page map, July, 1938.

Washburn, Stanley:

Russia from Within : Her War of Yesterday, Today, and Tomorrow. By Stanley Washburn. Vol. XXXII, pp. 91-120, 30 ills., Aug., 1917.

Russian Situation and Its Significance to America. By Stanley Washburn. Vol. XXXI, pp. 371-382, 8 ills., Apr., 1917.

Washington, George:

Dismal Swamp in Legend and History : George Washington Owned Large Tracts in Region Which He Described as a "Glorious Paradise." By John Francis Ariza. Vol. LXII, pp. 121-130, 11 ills., July, 1932.

Home of the First Farmer of America (Mount Vernon). By Worth E. Shoults. Vol. LIII, pp. 603-628, 6 ills. in black and white, 26 ills. in color, May, 1928.

Our First Alliance. By J. J. Jusserand. Vol. XXXI, pp. 518-548, 8 ills., June, 1917.

Their Monument Is in Our Hearts : Address by M. Viviani Before the Tomb of Washington, April 29, 1917. Vol. XXXI, p. 367, Apr., 1917.

Travels of George Washington : Dramatic Episodes in His Career as the First Geographer of the United States. By William Joseph Showalter. Vol. LXI, pp. 1-63, 50 ills., 5 maps, special map supplement, Jan., 1932.

Washington (State) :

Call of the West. By C. J. Blanchard. Vol. XX, pp. 403-437, 20 ills., 1 half-page map, May, 1909.

Columbia (River) Turns on the Power. By Maynard Owen Williams. Vol. LXXIX, pp. 749-792, 25 ills. in black and white, 18 ills. in color, June, 1941.

Forest Lookout. By Ella E. Clark. With 9 ills. in color from natural-color photographs by the author. Vol. XC, pp. 73-96, 8 ills. in black and white, July, 1946.

Great White Monarch of the Pacific Northwest (Mount Rainier). By A. H. Barnes. Vol. XXIII, pp. 593-626, 31 ills., 1 half-page map, June, 1912.

Home-Making by the Government : An Account of the Eleven Immense Irrigating Projects to be Opened in 1908. By C. J. Blanchard. Vol. XIX, pp. 250-287, 23 ills., Apr., 1908.

Our Pacific Northwest. By N. H. Darton. Vol. XX, pp. 645-663, 12 ills., 2 half-page maps, July, 1909.

Spirit of the West : The Wonderful Agricultural Development Since the Dawn of Irrigation. By C. J. Blanchard. Vol. XXI, pp. 333-360, 15 ills., Apr., 1910.

Washington (State)—*Continued*

Sunset Hues in the Pacific Northwest. 13 ills. in color from natural-color photographs by Clifton Adams and Asahel Curtis. Vol. LXIII, pp. 154-163, Feb., 1933.

Wartime in the Pacific Northwest. By Frederick Simpich. Vol. LXXXII, pp. 421-464, 25 ills. in black and white, 23 ills. in color, 1 half-page map, Oct., 1942.

Washington, the Evergreen State : The Amazing Commonwealth of the Pacific Northwest Which Has Emerged from the Wilderness in a Span of Fifty Years. By Leo A. Borah. Vol. LXIII, pp. 131-196, 50 ills. in black and white, 26 ills. in color, 1 two-page map, Feb., 1933.

Where Fog and Sun Paint the Pacific. 23 ills. in color from natural-color photographs by J. Baylor Roberts. Vol. LXXXII, pp. 437-460, Oct., 1942.

Where the Last of the West Was Won. 13 ills. in color from natural-color photographs by Clifton Adams and Asahel Curtis. Vol. LXIII, pp. 178-187, Feb., 1933.

Wonderland of Glaciers and Snow. By Milnor Roberts. Vol. XX, pp. 530-537, 8 ills., June, 1909.

Washington, D. C. :

Approaching Washington by Tidewater Potomac. By Paul Wilstach. Vol. LVII, pp. 372-392, 7 ills., Mar., 1930.

Capitol, Wonder Building of the World. By Gilbert Grosvenor. Vol. XLIII, pp. 603-638, 17 ills., June, 1923.

Color Camera's First Aërial Success. 5 ills. in color from natural-color photographs by Melville Bell Grosvenor. Vol. LVIII, pp. 344-353, Sept., 1930.

Culture Still Lights Our Wartime Capital. 9 ills. in color from natural-color photographs by B. Anthony Stewart. Vol. LXXXI, pp. 337-344, Mar., 1942.

George Washington's Historic River (Potomac). 18 ills. in color from natural-color photographs by Willard R. Culver and Robert F. Sisson. Vol. LXXXVIII, pp. 41-64, July, 1945.

How the Earth Telegraphed Its Tokyo Quake to Washington. By Rev. Francis A. Tondorf. Vol. XLIV, pp. 453-454, 1 ill., Oct., 1923.

Lincoln Memorial. By William Howard Taft. Vol. XLIII, pp. 597-602, 5 ills., June, 1923.

Mall. Vol. XXVII, colored panorama, Mar., 1915.

Nation's Capital. By James Bryce. Vol. XXIV, pp. 717-750, 26 ills., June, 1913.

Nation's Capital by Night. By Volkmar Wentzel. With 16 ills. in duotone from photographs by the author. Vol. LXXVII, pp. 514-530, Apr., 1940.

Old Masters in a New National Gallery. By Ruth Q. McBride. Vol. LXXVIII, pp. 1-50, 11 ills. in black and white, 32 color reproductions of masterpieces, July, 1940.

Original Boundary Stones of the District of Columbia. By Ernest A. Shuster, Jr. Vol. XX, pp. 356-359, 6 ills., 1 half-page map, Apr., 1909.

Washington, D. C.—*Continued*

Our Colorful City of Magnificent Distances. 49 ills. in color from natural-color photographs by Staff Photographers and Capt. A. W. Stevens. Vol. LX, pp. 530-611, Nov., 1931.

Our Nation's Capital on Parade. 16 ills. in color from natural-color photographs by B. Anthony Stewart, Walter M. Edwards, and others. Vol. LXXXIV, pp. 265-288, Sept., 1943.

Potomac, River of Destiny. By Albert W. Atwood. Vol. LXXXVIII, pp. 33-70, 15 ills. in black and white, 18 ills. in color, 1 map (two-page spread), July, 1945.

Secrets of Washington's Lure. 15 ills. in color from natural-color photographs by Staff Photographers. Vol. LVII, pp. 376-385, Mar., 1930.

Sources of Washington's Charm. By J. R. Hildebrand. Vol. XLIII, pp. 639-680, 46 ills., June, 1923.

Spring's Gay Bouquets Deck the Nation's Capital. 10 ills. in color from natural-color photographs by Harrison Howell Walker. Vol. LXXIV, pp. 17-24, July, 1938.

Springtime Wreathes a Garland for the Nation's Capital. 13 ills. in color from natural-color photographs. Vol. LXVII, pp. 473-480, Apr., 1935.

Transformation of Washington : A Glance at the History and Along the Vista of the Future of the Nation's Capital. By Charles Moore. Vol. XLIII, pp. 569-595, 16 ills., 2 page maps, June, 1923.

Ultimate Washington (Plan Laid Out by the Commission of 1901 for the National Capital). Vol. XXVII, colored panorama, Mar., 1915.

Unique Gifts of Washington to the Nation. 11 ills. in color from natural-color photographs by Charles Martin, Edwin L. Wisherd, Jacob Gayer, and Clifton Adams. Vol. LV, pp. 472-481, Apr., 1929.

Views of the Lincoln Memorial in Washington. Vol. XLII, pp. 197-204, 8 ills., Aug., 1922.

Wartime Washington. By William H. Nicholas. Vol. LXXXIV, pp. 257-290, 12 ills. in black and white, 16 ills. in color, Sept., 1943.

Washington : Its Beginning, Its Growth, and Its Future. By William Howard Taft. Vol. XXVII, pp. 221-292, 33 ills. in black and white, 32 ills. in color, panorama, 1 map, 1 diagram in color, Mar., 1915.

Washington—Storehouse of Knowledge. By Albert W. Atwood. Vol. LXXXI, pp. 325-359, 20 ills. in black and white, 9 ills. in color, Mar., 1942.

Washington, Home City and Show Place : To Residents and Visitors the Nation's Capital Presents Varied Sides as the City Steadily Grows in Beauty and Stature. By Leo A. Borah. Vol. LXXI, pp. 663-695, 11 ills. in black and white, 20 ills. in color, June, 1937.

Washington, the Pride of the Nation. 16 ills. in color from autochromes by Charles Martin. Vol. XLIII, pp. 617-632, June, 1923.

Washington, D. C.—*Continued*

Washington of Tradition Builds for the Future. 20 ills. in color from natural-color photographs. Vol. LXXI, pp. 671-694, June, 1937.

Washington Through the Years: On Rolling Wooded Hills and Colonial Tobacco Fields, Where George Washington Dreamed Our Nation's Great Capital His Gorgeous Vision Comes True. By Gilbert Grosvenor. Vol. LX, pp. 517-619, 67 ills. in black and white, 49 ills. in color, 1 page map, Nov., 1931.

Winter Lights and Shadows in the Nation's Capital. 21 ills. in duotone. Vol. LXVII, pp. 201-216, Feb., 1935.

Wonders of the New Washington: Efficient Modern Structures Rise in the Biggest Government Building Program Since the Capital City Was Founded in a Wilderness. By Frederick G. Vosburgh. Vol. LXVII, pp. 457-488, 20 ills. in black and white, 13 ills. in color, Apr., 1935.

See also Arlington National Cemetery; Great Falls of the Potomac; Mount Vernon.

Washington Academy of Sciences:

Harriman Alaska Expedition in Coöperation with the Washington Academy of Sciences. By Gilbert H. Grosvenor. Vol. X, pp. 225-227, June, 1899.

Washington Cathedral, Washington, D. C.:

Cathedrals of the Old and New World. By J. Bernard Walker. Vol. XLII, pp. 61-114, 50 ills., July, 1922.

WASPS. *See* Women's Airforce Service Pilots.

Wasps:

Farmers' Friends Among the Wasps and Hornets. 12 ills. in color from paintings by Hashime Murayama. Vol. LXXII, pp. 57-64, July, 1937.

Marvels of Metamorphosis: A Scientific "G-man" Pursues Rare Trapdoor Spider Parasites for Three Years With a Spade and a Candid Camera. By George Elwood Jenks. Vol. LXXIV, pp. 807-828, 39 ills., Dec., 1938.

Potent Personalities—Wasps and Hornets: Though Often Painfully Stung Mankind Profits Immeasurably from the Pest-Killing Activities of These Fiery Little Flyers. By Austin H. Clark. Vol. LXXII, pp. 47-72, 18 ills. in black and white, 12 ills. in color, July, 1937.

Wasteful Nation (Report of Conservation Commission). Vol. XX, pp. 203-206, Feb., 1909.

Water Supply:

Artesian Water Predictions. Vol. XXI, pp. 361-363, 1 ill., Apr., 1910.

Carrying Water Through a Desert: The Story of the Los Angeles Aqueduct. By Burt A. Heinly. Vol. XXI, pp. 568-596, 19 ills., 1 half-page map, July, 1910.

Central Great Plains. Vol. XVI, pp. 389-397, Aug., 1905.

Limited Water Supply of the Arid Region. By Frederick H. Newell. Vol. XI, pp. 438-442, Nov., 1900.

Water Supply—*Continued*

More Water for California's Great Central Valley. By Frederick Simpich. Vol. XC, pp. 645-664, 16 ills., 1 page map, Nov., 1946.

National Geographic Society's Memorial to American Troops: Fountain and Water Supply System Presented to Historic French Town of Cantigny, Where Our Overseas Soldiers Won Their First Victory in the World War. Vol. XLIV, pp. 675-678, 4 ills., Dec., 1923.

New York—The Metropolis of Mankind. By William Joseph Showalter. Vol. XXXIV, pp. 1-49, 29 ills., July, 1918.

Old Jewel in the Proper Setting: An Eye-Witness' Account of the Reconquest of the Holy Land by Twentieth Century Crusaders. By Charles W. Whitehair. Vol. XXXIV, pp. 325-344, 17 ills., Oct., 1918.

Water Supply for the Nicaragua Canal. By Arthur P. Davis. Vol. XI, pp. 363-365, Sept., 1900.

Wateree (Ship):

Some Personal Experiences with Earthquakes (Arica). By Rear Adm. L. G. Billings. Vol. XXVII, pp. 57-71, 7 ills., Jan., 1915.

Waterfalls:

African Rainbow. 10 ills. in color from natural-color photographs by W. Robert Moore. Vol. LXXXVI, pp. 289-296, Sept., 1944.

Falls of Iguazu. By Marie Robinson Wright. Vol. XVII, pp. 456-460, 4 ills., Aug., 1906.

Geography of Japan: With Special Reference to Its Influence on the Character of the Japanese People. By Walter Weston. Vol. XL, pp. 45-84, 23 ills. in black and white, 13 ills. in color, July, 1921.

Great Falls of the Potomac. By Gilbert Grosvenor. Vol. LIII, pp. 385-400, 19 ills., Mar., 1928.

Kaieteur and Roraima: The Great Falls and the Great Mountain of the Guianas. By Henry Edward Crampton. Vol. XXXVIII, pp. 227-244, 12 ills., 1 half-page map, Sept., 1920.

Niagara at the Battle Front. By William Joseph Showalter. Vol. XXXI, pp. 413-422, 6 ills., May, 1917.

Niagaras of Five Continents. Vol. XXXVIII, pp. 211-226, 16 ills., Sept., 1920.

Potomac, River of Destiny. By Albert W. Atwood. Vol. LXXXVIII, pp. 33-70, 15 ills. in black and white, 18 ills. in color, 1 map (two-page spread), July, 1945.

Rhodesia, Hobby and Hope of Cecil Rhodes. By W. Robert Moore. Vol. LXXXVI, pp. 281-306, 13 ills. in black and white, 10 ills. in color, 1 half-page map, Sept., 1944.

Wonders of the Mosi-oa-Tunga: The Falls of the Zambesi. By Louis Livingston Seaman. Vol. XXII, pp. 561-571, 6 ills., June, 1911.

World's Great Waterfalls: Visits to Mighty Niagara, Wonderful Victoria, and Picturesque Iguazu. By Theodore W. Noyes. Vol. L, pp. 29-59, 29 ills., July, 1926.

Waterfalls—_Continued_

World's Greatest Waterfall : The Kaieteur Fall, in British Guiana. By Leonard Kennedy. Vol. XXII, pp. 846-859, 6 ills., 1 page map, Sept., 1911.

Waterways. _See_ Canals ; Rivers.

Watson, Thomas :

Voice Voyages by the National Geographic Society : A Tribute to the Geographical Achievements of the Telephone (Address by Thomas Watson). Vol. XXIX, pp. 296-326, 15 ills., 1 chart, Mar., 1916.

Watts, Harvey Maitland :

Chinese Paradox. ·By Harvey Maitland Watts. Vol. XI, pp. 352-358, 2 ills., Sept., 1900.

Watts, W. A. :

Flame-Feathered Flamingos of Florida. By W. A. Watts. With 9 ills. in color from natural-color photographs by W. F. Gerecke. Vol. LXXIX, pp. 56-65, Jan., 1941.

Watussi (Tribespeople) :

Land of Giants and Pygmies (Ruanda). By Duke Adolphus Frederick of Mecklenburg. Vol. XXIII, pp. 367-388, 16 ills., 1 page map, Apr., 1912.

WAVES. _See_ Women's Reserve of the U. S. Naval Reserve.

Waves and Thrills at Waikiki (Honolulu). 8 ills. in duotone by Thomas Edward Blake. Vol. LXVII, pp. 597-604, May, 1935.

Wayfaring Down the Winding Severn. 15 ills. in color from natural-color photographs by Frank and Bernard Wakeman. Vol. LXIII, pp. 433-440, Apr., 1933.

Ways and Byways of an Island Paradise (Bali). 9 ills. from photographs. Vol. LXXV, pp. 345-352, Mar., 1939.

Wayside Scenes in Europe. 19 ills. in duotone. Vol. XXV, pp. 229-244, Feb., 1914.

Wayside Scenes in Europe. 16 ills. in duotone. Vol. XXVII, pp. 401-416, Apr., 1915.

Waziristan (Region), India :

South of Khyber Pass. By Maynard Owen Williams. Vol. LXXXIX, pp. 471-500, 31 ills., Apr., 1946.

We Escape from Madrid. By Gretchen Schwinn. Vol. LXXI, pp. 251-268, 15 ills., Feb., 1937.

We Keep House on an Active Volcano : After Flying to Study a Spectacular Eruption in Belgian Congo, a Geologist Settles Down on a Newborn Craterless Vent for Eight Months' Study. By Dr. Jean Verhoogen. Vol. LXXVI, pp. 511-550, 28 ills., 1 two-thirds-page map, Oct., 1939.

We Live Alone and Like It—On an Island (Skokholm). By R. M. Lockley. Vol. LXXIV, pp. 252-278, 27 ills., Aug., 1938.

Wealth of Nations. Vol. XIII, p. 145, Apr., 1902.

Weapon of Food. By Herbert Hoover. Vol. XXXII, pp. 197-212, 15 ills., Sept., 1917.

Weapons :

Air Power for Peace. By Gen. H. H. Arnold. Vol. LXXXIX, pp. 137-193, 35 ills. in black and white, 28 ills. in color, special map supplement, Feb., 1946.

Infantrymen—The Fighters of War. By Brig. Gen. W. H. Wilbur. Vol. LXXXVI, pp. 513-538, 22 ills., Nov., 1944.

Pirate-Fighters of the South China Sea. By Robert Cardwell. Vol. LXXXIX, pp. 787-796, 11 ills., June, 1946.

Weather. _See_ Meteorology.

Weather Fights and Works for Man. By F. Barrows Colton. Vol. LXXXIV, pp. 641-670, 22 ills. in black and white, 3 drawings, Dec., 1943.

Weather Proverbs. Vol. XV, p. 133, Mar., 1904.

Weather Stations :

Americans Stand Guard in Greenland. By Andrew H. Brown. Vol. XC, pp. 457-500, 23 ills. in black and white, 19 ills. in color, 1 page map, Oct., 1946.

New Frontier in the Sky. By F. Barrows Colton. Vol. XC, pp. 379-408, 28 ills., 1 diagram, Sept., 1946.

Servicing Arctic Airbases. By Robert A. Bartlett. Vol. LXXXIX, pp. 602-616, 3 ills. in black and white, 10 ills. in color, 1 half-page map, May, 1946.

Uncle Sam's Icebox Outposts. 19 ills. in color from natural-color photographs by John E. Schneider and Robert B. Sykes, Jr. Vol. XC, pp. 473-496, Oct., 1946.

Weaver Birds :

Bright-hued Pets of Cage and Aviary. 51 portraits in color from paintings by Maj. Allan Brooks. Vol. LXXIV, pp. 783-790, Dec., 1938.

Canaries and Other Cage-Bird Friends. By Alexander Wetmore. Vol. LXXIV, pp. 775-806, 19 ills. in black and white, 51 portraits in color, Dec., 1938.

Weavers of the World. 8 ills. in duotone. Vol. XXXVI, pp. 145-152, Aug., 1919.

Weaving :

Totem-pole Builders. 16 ills. in color from paintings from W. Langdon Kihn. Vol. LXXXVII, pp. 33-48, Jan., 1945.

Weavers of the World. 8 ills. in duotone. Vol. XXXVI, pp. 145-152, Aug., 1919.

Webber, John W. :

Down Mexico's Río Balsas. By John W. Webber. With 9 ills. in color from natural-color photographs by the author, Kenneth Segerstrom, and Jack Breed. Vol. XC, pp. 253-272, 5 ills. in black and white, 1 half-page map, Aug., 1946.

Weber, Walter A.:

Birds: Sparrows, Towhees, and Longspurs. 43 paintings in color from life by Maj. Allan Brooks and Walter A. Weber. Vol. LXXV, pp. 361-375, Mar., 1939.

Cats: King of Cats and His Court (Leopards, Lions, and Tigers). 20 ills. in color from paintings by Walter A. Weber. Vol. LXXXIII, pp. 223-254, Feb., 1943.

Deer: Antlered Majestics of Many Lands. 23 ills. in color from paintings by Walter A. Weber. Vol. LXXVI, pp. 479-510, Oct., 1939.

Dogs: Non-sporting Dogs. 8 ills. in color from paintings from life by Walter A. Weber. Vol. LXXXIV, pp. 577-584, Nov., 1943.

Dogs: Wild Dogs and Working Dogs. 9 ills. in color from paintings by Walter A. Weber. Vol. LXXXVI, pp. 369-376, Sept., 1944.

Wildlife of Tabasco and Veracruz (Mexico). By Walter A. Weber. With 19 ills. in color from paintings by the author. Vol. LXXXVII, pp. 187-216, 7 ills. in black and white, 1 two-thirds-page map, Feb., 1945.

Webster, (Comdr.) Harrie:

China and Her People: Some Reflections on Their Manners and Customs, Habits and Lives. By Comdr. Harrie Webster. Vol. XI, pp. 309-319, 3 ills., Aug., 1900.

Japan and China—Some Comparisons. By Comdr. Harrie Webster. Vol. XII, pp. 69-77, 2 ills., Feb., 1901.

Korea—The Hermit Nation. By Comdr. Harrie Webster. Vol. XI, pp. 145-155, 7 ills., Apr., 1900.

Samoa: Navigators Islands. By Comdr. Harrie Webster. Vol. X, pp. 207-217, 9 ills., June, 1899.

Weddell, Alexander Wilbourne:

"Glory That Was Greece." By Alexander Wilbourne Weddell. Vol. XLII, pp. 571-630, 51 ills., 1 three-quarters-page map, Dec., 1922.

Week-Ends with the Prairie Falcon: A Commuter Finds Recreation in Scaling Cliffs to Observe the Nest Life and Flying Habits of These Elusive Birds. By Frederick Hall Fowler. Vol. LXVII, pp. 611-626, 21 ills., May, 1935.

Weeks, John M.:

Honors to the American Navy (Address by John M. Weeks). Vol. XX, pp. 77-95, Jan., 1909.

Weights and Measures:

Our Heterogeneous System of Weights and Measures. By Alexander Graham Bell. Vol. XVII, pp. 158-169, Mar., 1906.

Wonderland of Science. Vol. XXVII, pp. 153-169, 15 ills., Feb., 1915.

Weisshorn (Peak), Switzerland:

Woman's Climbs in the High Alps. By Dora Keen. Vol. XXII, pp. 642-675, 26 ills., July, 1911.

Welcome to Wyoming. 19 ills. in color from natural-color photographs; 18 ills. by B. Anthony Stewart. Vol. LXXXVIII, pp. 161-184, Aug., 1945.

Welker, P. A.:

Surveys in the Philippines. By P. A. Welker. Vol. XXII, pp. 82-83, 1 page map, Jan., 1911.

Wellfleet, Massachusetts:

Cape Cod People and Places. By Wanda Burnett. Vol. LXXXIX, pp. 737-774, 17 ills. in black and white, 24 ills. in color, 1 half-page map, June, 1946.

Welliver, Judson C.:

What the War Has Done for Britain. By Judson C. Welliver. Vol. XXXIV, pp. 278-297, 13 ills., Oct., 1918.

Wellman, Walter:

Meteorological Observations of the Second Wellman Expedition. By Evelyn B. Baldwin. Vol. X, pp. 512-516, Dec., 1899.

No Man's Land—Spitzbergen. Vol. XVIII, pp. 455-458, July, 1907.

Polar Airship. By Walter Wellman. Vol. XVII, pp. 208-228, 4 diagrams, Apr., 1906.

Return of Wellman. By J. Howard Gore. Vol. X, pp. 348-351, 2 ills., Sept., 1899.

Walter Wellman's Expedition to the North Pole. Vol. XVII, pp. 205-207, 1 chart, Apr., 1906.

Wellman Polar Expedition. Vol. X, pp. 361-362, Sept., 1899.

Wellman Polar Expedition. Vol. X, pp. 481-505, 10 ills., 1 half-page map, 1 diagram, Dec., 1899.

Wellman Polar Expedition. Vol. XVII, p. 712, Dec., 1906.

Wellman Polar Expedition. By J. Howard Gore. Vol. X, pp. 267-268, July, 1899.

Wells, A. J.:

Seed Farms in California. By A. J. Wells. Vol. XXIII, pp. 515-530, 14 ills., May, 1912.

Wendle, Joseph:

Hunting the Grizzly in British Columbia. By Joseph Wendle. Vol. XVIII, pp. 612-615, 3 ills., Sept., 1907.

Wends of the Spreewald (Germany). By Frederick Simpich. Vol. XLIII, pp. 327-336, 12 ills., Mar., 1923.

Wentzel, Volkmar:

Kentucky: Sun Shines Bright in Kentucky. 21 ills. in color from natural-color photographs by B. Anthony Stewart, Volkmar Wentzel, and Ray Scott. Vol. LXXXII, pp. 65-88, July, 1942.

New York: Empire State Onions and Pageantry. 12 ills. in color from natural-color photographs by J. Baylor Roberts and Volkmar Wentzel. Vol. LXXX, pp. 641-648, Nov., 1941.

Sweden: Under Swedish Roofs and Skies. 22 ills. in color from natural-color photographs by Volkmar Wentzel. Vol. LXXVII, pp. 799-822, June, 1940.

Wentzel, Volkmar—*Continued*

Washington, D. C.: Nation's Capital by Night. By Volkmar Wentzel. With 16 illustrations in duotone from photographs by the author. Vol. LXXVII, pp. 514-530, Apr., 1940.

West Virginia: High Road and Low through the Mountain State. 21 ills. in color from natural-color photographs by B. Anthony Stewart and Volkmar Wentzel. Vol. LXXVIII, pp. 157-180, Aug., 1940.

West Indian Hurricane of August 7-14, 1899. By E. B. Garriott. Vol. X, pp. 343-348, 1 diagram, Sept., 1899.

West Indian Hurricane of September 1-12, 1900. By E. B. Garriott. Vol. XI, pp. 384-392, Oct., 1900.

West Indian Hurricane of September 10-11, 1898. By E. B. Garriott. Vol. X, pp. 17-20, Jan., 1899.

West Indies:

Americans in the Caribbean. By Luis Marden. Vol. LXXXI, pp. 723-758, 16 ills. in black and white, 22 ills. in color, 1 half-page map, June, 1942.

America's New Crescent of Defense. 8 ills. from photographs, 1 page map. Vol. LXXVIII, pp. 621-628, Nov., 1940.

British Commonwealth of Nations: "Organized Freedom" Around the World. By Eric Underwood. Vol. LXXXIII, pp. 485-524, 31 ills., Apr., 1943.

British West Indian Interlude. By Anne Rainey Langley. Vol. LXXIX, pp. 1-46, 23 ills. in black and white, 21 ills. in color, 2 page maps, Jan., 1941.

Countries of the Caribbean. By William Joseph Showalter. Vol. XXIV, pp. 227-250, 23 ills., Feb., 1913.

Haunts of the Caribbean Corsairs: The West Indies a Geographic Background for the Most Adventurous Episodes in the History of the Western Hemisphere. By Nell Ray Clarke. Vol. XLI, pp. 147-187, 27 ills., Feb., 1922.

Heart of a Hemisphere: Of Vital Importance is the Area Portrayed in The Society's New Map of Mexico, Central America, and the West Indies. Text accompanying special map supplement in colors. Vol. LXXVI, pp. 739-740, Dec., 1939.

How Latin America Looks from the Air: U. S. Army Airplanes Hurdle the High Andes, Brave Brazil Jungles, and Follow Smoking Volcanoes to Map New Sky Paths Around South America. By Maj. Hergert A. Dargue. Vol. LII, pp. 451-502, 52 ills., 1 page map, Oct., 1927.

Hunting Useful Plants in the Carribbean. By David Fairchild. Vol. LXVI, pp. 705-737, 39 ills., Dec., 1934.

Important New Guide for Shipping: Navassa Light, on a Barren Island in the West Indies, Is the First Signal for the Panama Canal. By George R. Putnam. Vol. XXXIV, pp. 401-406, 3 ills., 1 half-page map, Nov., 1918.

West Indies—*Continued*

On the Shores of the Caribbean. Vol. XLI, pp. 157-172, 16 ills., Feb., 1922.

Our Map of the Countries of the Caribbean. Text accompanying special map supplement in colors. Vol. XLI, pp. 221-222, Feb., 1922.

Report by Robert T. Hill on the Volcanic Disturbances in the West Indies. Vol. XIII, pp. 223-267, 13 ills., 2 page and 1 half-page maps, July, 1902.

Skypaths Through Latin America: Flying From Our Nation's Capital Southward Over Jungles, Remote Islands, and Great Cities on an Aërial Survey of the East Coast of South America. By Frederick Simpich. Vol. LIX, pp. 1-79, 77 ills., 1 page map, Jan., 1931.

Society's New Caribbean Map: Mexico, Central America, and the West Indies—Gateway of Discovery. Text accompanying special map supplement in colors. Vol. LXVI, pp. 738-740, 1 ill., Dec., 1934.

Southward Ho! in the "Alice." By Henry Howard. Vol. LXXIII, pp. 265-312, 38 ills. in black and white, 13 ills. in color, 2 maps, Mar., 1938.

To Bogotá and Back by Air: The Narrative of a 9,500-Mile Flight from Washington, Over Thirteen Latin-American Countries and Return, in the Single-Seater Airplane *Spirit of St. Louis.* By Col. Charles A. Lindbergh. Vol. LIII, pp. 529-601, 98 ills., 1 two-thirds-page map, May, 1928.

War Echoes in the West Indies. 22 ills. in color from natural-color photographs by Luis Marden. Vol. LXXXI, pp. 731-754, June, 1942.

West Indian Hurricane of August 7-14, 1899. By E. B. Garriott. Vol. X, pp. 343-348, 1 diagram, Sept., 1899.

West Indian Hurricane of September 1-12, 1900. By E. B. Garriott. Vol. XI, pp. 384-392, 4 charts, Oct., 1900.

West Indian Hurricane of September 10-11, 1898. By E. B. Garriott. Vol. X, pp. 17-20, Jan., 1899.

West Indies Links in a Defense Chain. 21 ills. in color from natural-color photographs; 20 ills. by Edwin L. Wisherd. Vol. LXXIX, pp. 9-32, Jan., 1941.

See also Aruba; Bahama Islands; Bonaire; Cayman Islands; Cuba; Curaçao; Dominican Republic; Guadeloupe; Haiti; Jamaica; Martinique; Puerto Rico; Saba; St. Vincent; Trinidad; Virgin Islands.

West Point, New York:

West Point, Mother of Army Men. 10 ills. in color from natural-color photographs by Edwin L. Wisherd. Vol. LXIX, pp. 779-786, June, 1936.

West Point and the Gray-Clad Corps. By Lieut. Col. Herman Beukema. Vol. LXIX, pp. 777-788, 10 ills. in color, June, 1936.

West Virginia:

George Washington's Historic River (Potomac). 18 ills. in color from natural-color photographs by Willard R. Culver and Robert F. Sisson. Vol. LXXXVIII, pp. 41-64, July, 1945.

West Virginia—*Continued*

High Road and Low through the Mountain State. 21 ills. in color from natural-color photographs by B. Anthony Stewart and Volkmar Wentzel. Vol. LXXVIII, pp. 157-180, Aug., 1940.

Potomac, River of Destiny. By Albert W. Atwood. Vol. LXXXVIII, pp. 33-70, 15 ills. in black and white, 18 ills. in color, 1 map (two-page spread), July, 1945.

Roads from Washington. By John Patric. Vol. LXXIV, pp. 1-48, 27 ills. in black and white, 30 ills. in color, special map supplement, July, 1938.

Travels of George Washington : Dramatic Episodes in His Career as the First Geographer of the United States. By William Joseph Showalter. Vol. LXI, pp. 1-63, 50 ills., 5 maps, special map supplement, Jan., 1932.

West Virginia : Treasure Chest of Industry. By Enrique C. Canova. Vol. LXXVIII, pp. 141-184, 19 ills. in black and white, 21 ills. in color, 1 two-page map, Aug., 1940.

Westdahl, Ferdinand:

Mountains on Unimak Island. By Ferdinand Westdahl. Vol. XIV, pp. 90-99, 4 ills., 1 page and 1 half-page maps, Mar., 1903.

Western Front Map Embraces Three Continents (Europe, Africa, Asia). Text accompanying special map supplement in colors. Vol. LXXXII, pp. 139-140, July, 1942.

Western Hemisphere:

Map of Discovery. Reproduction in color of the painting by N. C. Wyeth, National Geographic Society, Washington, D. C. Vol. LV, text, p. 93 ; supplement, Jan., 1929.

Western National Parks Invite America Out of Doors. 17 ills. in duotone from photographs by G. A. Grant, W. M. Rush, Merl La Voy, and J. S. Dixon. Vol. LXVI, pp. 65-80, July, 1934.

Western Progress in China. Vol. XII, pp. 434-436, Dec., 1901.

Western Siberia and the Altai Mountains : With Some Speculations on the Future of Siberia. By James Bryce. Vol. XXXIX, pp. 469-507, 39 ills., May, 1921.

Western Views in the Land of the Best. 16 ills. in color from autochromes by Fred Payne Clatworthy. Vol. XLIII, pp. 405-420, Apr., 1923.

Westminster, Palace of, London, England :

Democracy's Royal Palace. 19 ills. in color from natural-color photographs by B. Anthony Stewart. Vol. XC, pp. 233-248, Aug., 1946.

Yanks at Westminster. By Capt. Leonard David Gammans. Vol. XC, pp. 223-252, 6 ills. in black and white, 19 ills. in color, Aug., 1946.

Weston, Harold F.:

Persia. 11 ills. in color from photographs by Harold F. Weston. Vol. XXXIX, pp. 401-416, Apr., 1921.

Persian Caravan Sketches : The Land of the Lion and the Sun as Seen on a Summer Caravan Trip. By Harold F. Weston. Vol. XXXIX, pp. 417-468, 46 ills. in black and white, 16 ills. in color, 1 three-quarters-page map, Apr., 1921.

Weston, Walter:

Geography of Japan : With Special Reference to Its Influence on the Character of the Japanese People. By Walter Weston. Vol. XL, pp. 45-84, 23 ills. in black and white, 16 ills. in color, July, 1921.

Some Aspects of Rural Japan. By Walter Weston. Vol. XLII, pp. 275-301, 12 ills. in black and white, 16 ills. in color, Sept., 1922.

Westward Bound in the *Yankee*. By Irving and Electa Johnson. Vol. LXXXI, pp. 1-44, 25 ills. in black and white, 20 ills. in color, 1 three-quarters-page map, Jan., 1942.
    Contains information and illustrations of Easter Island, Galápagos Islands, Pitcairn, Samoa, Santa Cruz, and Solomon Islands.

Wetmore, Alexander:

Bird Life Among Lava Rock and Coral Sand : The Chronicle of a Scientific Expedition to Little-Known Islands of Hawaii. By Alexander Wetmore. Vol. XLVIII, pp. 77-108, 36 ills., 1 half-page map, July, 1925.

Birds of the Northern Seas. By Alexander Wetmore. Paintings by Maj. Allan Brooks. Vol. LXIX, pp. 95-122, 12 ills. in black and white, 34 portraits in color, Jan., 1936.

Canaries and Other Cage-Bird Friends. By Alexander Wetmore. Vol. LXXIV, pp. 775-806, 19 ills. in black and white, 51 portraits in color, Dec., 1938.

Eagle, King of Birds, and His Kin. By Alexander Wetmore. Paintings by Maj. Allan Brooks. Vol. LXIV, pp. 43-95, 23 ills. in black and white, 28 ills. in color, July, 1933.

Game Birds of Prairie, Forest, and Tundra. By Alexander Wetmore. Vol. LXX, pp. 461-500, 5 ills. in black and white, 60 portraits in color, Oct., 1936.

Parrots, Kingfishers, and Flycatchers ; Strange Trogons and Curious Cuckoos are Pictured with these Other Birds of Color, Dash, and Courage. By Alexander Wetmore. Paintings by Maj. Allan Brooks. Vol. LXIX, pp. 801-828, 9 ills. in black and white, 36 portraits in color, June, 1936.

Seeking the Smallest Feathered Creatures : Humming Birds, Peculiar to the New World, Are Found from Canada and Alaska to the Strait of Magellan. Swifts and Goatsuckers, Their Nearest Relatives. By Alexander Wetmore. Paintings by Maj. Allan Brooks. Vol. LXII, pp. 65-89, 9 ills. in black and white, 36 ills. in color, July, 1932.

Shadowy Birds of the Night (Owls). By Alexander Wetmore. Vol. LXVII, pp. 217-240, 5 ills. in black and white, 21 portraits in color, Feb., 1935.

Wetmore, Alexander—*Continued*

Winged Denizens of Woodland Stream, and Marsh (Birds). By Alexander Wetmore. Paintings by Maj. Allan Brooks. Vol. LXV, pp. 577-596, 37 portraits in color, May, 1934.

Whalers (Men) :

American Pathfinders in the Pacific. By William H. Nicholas. Vol. LXXXIX, pp. 617-640, 17 ills., 1 two-page map, May, 1946.

Whalers (Ships) :

American Pathfinders in the Pacific. By William H. Nicholas. Vol. LXXXIX, pp. 617-640, 17 ills., 1 two-page map, May, 1946.

Whales:

Discovering Alaska's Oldest Arctic Town : A Scientist Finds Ivory-eyed Skeletons of a Mysterious People and Joins Modern Eskimos in the Dangerous Spring Whale Hunt. By Froelich G. Rainey. Vol. LXXXII, pp. 319-336, 15 ills., Sept., 1942.

Production of Whalebone. Vol. XIX, pp. 883-885, 2 ills., Dec., 1908.

South Georgia, an Outpost of the Antarctic. By Robert Cushman Murphy. Vol. XLI, pp. 409-444, 41 ills., 2 half-page maps, Apr., 1922.

Whales, Giants of the Sea : Wonder Mammals, Biggest Creatures of All Time, Show Tender Affection for Young, But Can Maim or Swallow Human Hunters. By Remington Kellogg. Vol. LXXVII, pp. 35-90, 25 ills. in black and white, 31 ills. in color, Jan., 1940.

Whales, Porpoises, and Dolphins. 31 ills. in color from paintings by Else Bostelmann. Vol. LXXVII, pp. 41-80, Jan., 1940.

Whaling:

Discovering Alaska's Oldest Arctic Town : A Scientist Finds Ivory-eyed Skeletons of a Mysterious People and Joins Modern Eskimos in the Dangerous Spring Whale Hunt. By Froelich G. Rainey. Vol. LXXXII, pp. 319-336, 15 ills., Sept., 1942.

How Long a Whale May Carry a Harpoon. By William H. Dall. Vol. X, pp. 136-137, Apr., 1899.

Indians of Our North Pacific Coast. By Matthew W. Stirling. Paintings by W. Langdon Kihn. Vol. LXXXVII, pp. 25-52, 3 ills. in black and white, 16 ills. in color, Jan., 1945.

Shore-Whaling : A World Industry. By Roy Chapman Andrews. Vol. XXII, pp. 411-442, 34 ills., May, 1911.

South Georgia, an Outpost of the Antarctic. By Robert Cushman Murphy. Vol. XLI, pp. 409-444, 41 ills., 2 half-page maps, Apr., 1922.

Wharton, (Sir) W. J. L.:

Geography. By Sir W. J. L. Wharton. Vol. XVI, pp. 483-498, Nov., 1905.

What Great Britain Is Doing (War Preparations). By Sydney Brooks. Vol. XXXI, pp. 193-210, 7 ills., Mar., 1917.

What Has Been Accomplished by the United States Toward Building the Panama Canal. By Theodore P. Shonts. Vol. XVI, pp. 558-564, Dec., 1905.

What Is It to be an American ? By Franklin K. Lane. Vol. XXXIII, pp. 348-354, 4 ills., 1 diagram, Apr., 1918.

What Is the Saar ? By Frederick Simpich. Vol. LXVII, pp. 241-264, 5 ills. in black and white, 23 ills. in duotone, 1 half-page and 1 third-page maps, Feb., 1935.

What Luzon Means to Uncle Sam. By Frederick Simpich. Vol. LXXXVII, pp. 305-332, 25 ills., special map supplement, Mar., 1945.

What the Fighting Yanks See. By Wanda Burnett. Vol. LXXXVI, pp. 451-476, 27 ills., Oct., 1944.

What the Latin American Republics Think of the Pan-American Conferences. Vol. XVII, pp. 474-479, Aug., 1906.

What the United States Geological Survey Has Done in Twenty-five Years. Vol. XV, pp. 365-366, 2 ills., Sept., 1905.

What the United States Government Does to Promote Agriculture. Vol. XIV, pp. 35-39, Jan., 1903.

What the War Has Done for Britain. By Judson C. Welliver. Vol. XXXIV, pp. 278-297, 13 ills., Oct., 1918.

Wheat:

How the World Is Fed. By William Joseph Showalter. Vol. XXIX, pp. 1-110, 101 ills., Jan., 1916.

Russia's Wheat Surplus. Vol. XVII, pp. 580-583, Oct., 1906.

Wheeler, William Morton:

Notes About Ants and Their Resemblance to Man. By William Morton Wheeler. Vol. XXIII, pp. 731-766, 32 ills., 2 diagrams, Aug., 1912.

Wheeler National Monument, Colorado :

Wheeler National Monument. Vol. XX, pp. 837-840, 4 ills., Sept., 1909.

When a Drought Blights Africa : Hippos and Elephants Are Driven Insane by Suffering, in the Lorian Swamp, Kenya Colony. By Capt. A. T. Curle. Vol. LV, pp. 521-528, 9 ills., Apr., 1929.

When Czechoslovakia Puts a Falcon Feather in Its Cap. By Maynard Owen Williams. Vol. LXIII, pp. 40-49, 13 ills. in color, Jan., 1933.

When GI Joes Took London. By Maj. Frederick Simpich, Jr. Vol. LXXXVI, pp. 337-354, 18 ills., Sept., 1944.

When Golden Praha Entertains the Majestic Sokol Festival. 13 ills. in color from natural-color photographs by Hans Hildenbrand. Vol. LXIII, pp. 40-49, Jan., 1933.

When Irish Skies Are Smiling. 18 ills. in color from natural-color photographs by Harrison Howell Walker. Vol. LXXVII, pp. 663-686, May, 1940.

When Our Country Is Fifty Years Older. By Raphael Zon. Vol. XX, pp. 573-580, 2 ills., 1 diagram, June, 1909.

When Red Men Ruled Our Forests (Northeastern Indians). 24 ills. in color from paintings by W. Langdon Kihn. Vol. LXXII, pp. 551-590, Nov., 1937.

When the Father of Waters Goes on a Rampage: An Account of the Salvaging of Food-Fishes from the Overflowed Lands of the Mississippi River. By Hugh M. Smith. Vol. XXXVII, pp. 369-386, 18 ills., Apr., 1920.

When the Herring Fleet Comes to Great Yarmouth. By W. Robert Moore. Vol. LXVI, pp. 233-250, 19 ills., Aug., 1934.

Where Adam and Eve Lived (Baghdad). By Frederick and Margaret Simpich. Vol. XXVI, pp. 546-588, 35 ills., Dec., 1914.

Where Ancient Sea Kings Held Sway (Crete). 14 ills. in color from autochromes by Maynard Owen Williams. Vol. LV, pp. 254-263, Feb., 1929.

Where Bible Characters Live Again: Everyday Life in Oberammergau, World Famous for Its Passion Play, Reaches a Climax at Christmas. By Anton Lang, Jr. Vol. LXVIII, pp. 743-769, 19 ills. in black and white, 11 ills. in color, 1 third-page map, Dec., 1935.

Where Birds and Little Animals Find Haven (Eaton Canyon Bird and Game Sanctuary). By Agnes Akin Atkinson. Vol. LXX, pp. 232-241, 14 ills., Aug., 1936.

Where Bretons Wrest a Living from the Sea (Guérande Peninsula). 23 ills. from photographs by F. W. Goro. Vol. LXXI, pp. 751-766, June, 1937.

Where Early Christians Lived in Cones of Rock: A Journey to Cappadocia in Turkey Where Strange Volcanic Pinnacles Are Honeycombed With Hermit Cells and Monasteries. By John D. Whiting. Vol. LXXVI, pp. 763-802, 20 ills. in black and white, 20 ills. in color, 1 half-page map, Dec., 1939.

Where East Meets West: A Visit to Picturesque Dalmatia, Montenegro, and Bosnia. By Marian Cruger Coffin. Vol. XIX, pp. 309-344, 26 ills., 1 half-page map, May, 1908.

Where Exploration Is Needed (Africa). Vol. XI, p. 163, Apr., 1900.

Where Fog and Sun Paint the Pacific (Pacific Northwest). 23 ills. in color from natural-color photographs by J. Baylor Roberts. Vol. LXXXII, pp. 437-460, Oct., 1942.

Where Hot Pools Seethe and Geysers Spout (Yellowstone). 9 ills. in color from natural-color photographs by Edwin L. Wisherd. Vol. LXXVII, pp. 775-782, June, 1940.

Where Man's Garb Rivals the Quetzal (Guatemala). 13 ills. in color from natural-color photographs by Luis Marden. Vol. LXX, pp. 437-444, Oct., 1936.

Where Nature Runs Riot: On Australia's Great Barrier Reef Marine Animals Grow to Unusual Size, Develop Strange Weapons of Attack and Defense, and Acquire Brilliant Colors. By T. C. Roughley. Vol. LXXVII, pp. 823-850, 18 ills. in black and white, 15 ills. in color, 1 page map, June, 1940.

Where New England Meets the Sea. 17 ills. in color from natural-color photographs by B. Anthony Stewart. Vol. LXXXVIII, pp. 265-288, Sept., 1945.

Where Our Bananas Come From (Costa Rica). By Edwin R. Fraser. Vol. XXIII, pp. 713-730, 14 ills., July, 1912.

Where Our Moths and Butterflies Roam. Vol. LII, pp. 105-126, July, 1927.

"Where Rolls the Oregon." 28 ills. in color from natural-color photographs by Ray Atkeson. Vol. XC, pp. 689-728, Dec., 1946.

Where Roosevelt Will Hunt (Africa). By Sir Harry Johnston. Vol. XX, pp. 207-256, 43 ills., special map supplement, Mar., 1909.

Where Slav and Mongol Meet. Vol. XXXVI, pp. 421-436, 16 ills. in color, Nov., 1919.

Where Snow Peaks Temper the Tropics (Ecuador). 9 ills. in color from natural-color photographs by W. Robert Moore. Vol. LXXX, pp. 727-734, Dec., 1941.

Where Spring Paints a State with Wild Flowers (California). 18 ills. in color from natural-color photographs by B. Anthony Stewart. Vol. LXIX, pp. 365-380, Mar., 1936.

Where the Blue Begins on the Italian Coast. 12 ills. in color from natural-color photographs by Hans Hildenbrand. Vol. LXVII, pp. 81-88, Jan., 1935.

Where the Last of the West Was Won (Washington). 13 ills. in color from natural-color photographs by Clifton Adams and Asahel Curtis. Vol. LXIII, pp. 178-187, Feb., 1933.

"Where the Mountains Walked": An Account of the Recent Earthquake in Kansu Province, China, Which Destroyed 100,000 Lives. By Upton Close and Elsie McCormick. Vol. XLI, pp. 445-464, 23 ills., 1 three-quarters-page map, May, 1922.

Where the New South Challenges the Old (Alabama). 26 ills. in color from natural-color photographs by Edwin L. Wisherd. Vol. LX, pp. 716-749, Dec., 1931.

Where the Sailing Ship Survives (Åland Islands). By A. J. Villiers. Vol. LXVII, pp. 101-128, 31 ills., 1 half-page map, Jan., 1935.

Where the Sard Holds Sway. Vol. XLIX, pp. 464-474, 1 ill. in black and white, 9 ills. in color, Apr., 1926.

Where the Wind Does the Work (Cape Hatteras). By Collier Cobb. Vol. XVII, pp. 310-317, 9 ills., 1 page map, June, 1906.

Where the Winding Cam Mirrors Cambridge (University) Spires. 12 ills. in color from natural-color photographs by Bernard Wakeman and Walter M. Edwards. Vol. LXX, pp. 339-346, Sept., 1936.

Where the Winning of the West Began (Ohio). 13 ills. in color from natural-color photographs by Jacob Gayer. Vol. LXI, pp. 562-571, May, 1932.

Where the World Gets Its Oil: But Where Will Our Children Get It When American Wells Cease to Flow? By George Otis Smith. Vol. XXXVII, pp. 181-202, 21 ills., 1 page and 2 half-page maps, Feb., 1920.

Where Women Vote (Finland). By Baroness Alletta Korff. Vol. XXI, pp. 487-493, June, 1910.

Whirlpool of the Balkans. By George Higgins Moses. Vol. XXXIX, pp. 179-197, 15 ills., Feb., 1921.

Whitaker, Herman:

Wonderland of California. By Herman Whitaker. Vol. XXVIII, pp. 56-104, 45 ills., July, 1915.

Whitbeck, R. H.:

Geographic Names in the United States and the Stories They Tell. By R. H. Whitbeck. Vol. XVI, pp. 100-104, Mar., 1905.

Whitby, England:

Between the Heather and the North Sea: Bold English Headlands Once Sheltered Sea Robbers, Later Were Ports of Wooden Ships, Centers of the Jet and Alum Trades, To-day Are Havens of Adventurous Fishing Fleets. By Leo Walmsley. Vol. LXIII, pp. 197-232, 41 ills., Feb., 1933.

White, Abbie M.:

Recent Bequests by Members of the National Geographic Society. Vol. XLIX, p. 474, Apr., 1926.

White, Clifford:

Peaks and Trails in the Canadian Alps. 3 ills. in duotone from photographs by Clifford White. Vol. LXV, pp. 627-642, May, 1934.

White, H. C.:

China's Wonderland—Yen Tang Shan (Chekiang Province). 8 ills. in color from camera paintings by Herbert Clarence White, Deng Bao-ling, and Hwang Yao-tso. Vol. LXXII, pp. 687-694, Dec., 1937.

Peiping Panorama in Vivid Pigments. 16 ills. in color from camera paintings by H. C. and J. H. White, Deng Bao-ling, and Hwang Yao-tso. Vol. LXX, pp. 753-784, Dec., 1936.

White, J. H.:

Peiping Panorama in Vivid Pigments. 16 ills. in color from camera paintings by H. C. and J. H. White, Deng Bao-ling, and Hwang Yao-tso. Vol. LXX, pp. 753-784, Dec., 1936.

White, James:

Location of the Sir John Franklin Monument. By James White. Vol. XIX, p. 596, Aug., 1908.

White, John Claude:

Castles in the Air: Experiences and Journeys in Unknown Bhutan. By John Claude White. Vol. XXV, pp. 365-455, 74 ills., 1 page map, Apr., 1914.

Nepal: A Little-Known Kingdom. By John Claude White. Vol. XXXVIII, pp. 245-283, 32 ills., 1 half-page map, Oct., 1920.

World's Strangest Capital (Lhasa, Tibet). By John Claude White. Vol. XXIX, pp. 273-295, 19 ills., panorama, Mar., 1916.

White, John R.:

Among the Big Trees of California. By John R. White. Vol. LXVI, pp. 219-232, 14 ills., Aug., 1934.

White, (Dr.) William A.:

Geographical Distribution of Insanity in the United States. By William A. White. Vol. XIV, pp. 361-378, 6 charts, Oct., 1903.

White City of Algiers. By Lieut. Col. Gordon Casserly. Vol. LIII, pp. 206-232, 9 ills. in black and white, 32 ills. in color, Feb., 1928.

White Mountains, New Hampshire-Maine:

From Notch to Notch in the White Mountains: Soaring Heights of New Hampshire Attract Multitudes to America's Oldest Mountain Recreation Area. By Leonard Cornell Roy. Vol. LXXII, pp. 73-104, 30 ills., special map supplement, July, 1937.

White Pelicans:

Pelican Profiles. By Lewis Wayne Walker. Vol. LXXXIV, pp. 589-598, 5 ills. in black and white, 8 ills. in color, Nov., 1943.

White Population of the Chief British Colonies. Vol. XIV, p. 360, Sept., 1903.

White River, Yukon Territory:

Ice Cliffs on White River, Yukon Territory. By Martin W. Gorman. Vol. XI, pp. 113-117, Mar., 1900.

White Russian Soviet Socialist Republic, U. S. S. R.:

Society's New Map of Soviet Russia. Text accompanying special map supplement in colors. Vol. LXXXVI, pp. 716-718, Dec., 1944.

White Sands of Alamogordo (New Mexico): A Dry Ocean of Granular Gypsum Billows Under Desert Winds in a New National Playground. By Carl P. Russell. Vol. LXVIII, pp. 250-264, 12 ills., Aug., 1935.

White Sheep, Giant Moose, and Smaller Game of the Kenai Peninsula, Alaska. By George Shiras, 3d. Vol. XXIII, pp. 423-494, 59 ills., 1 page and 1 two-page maps, May, 1912.

White War in Norway. By Thomas R. Henry. Vol. LXXXVIII, pp. 617-640, 23 ills., 1 three-quarters-page map, Nov., 1945.

Whitehair, Charles W.:

Old Jewel in the Proper Setting : An Eyewitness' Account of the Reconquest of the Holy Land by Twentieth Century Crusaders. By Charles W. Whitehair. Vol. XXXIV, pp. 325-344, 17 ills., Oct., 1918.

Whiteley, George, Jr.:

Newfoundland, North Atlantic Rampart : From the "First Base of American Defense" Planes Fly to Britain's Aid over Stout Fishing Schooners of the Grand Banks. By George Whiteley, Jr. Vol. LXXX, pp. 111-140, 26 ills., 1 two-thirds-page map, July, 1941.

Whiting, John D.:

Among the Bethlehem Shepherds : A Visit to the Valley Which David Probably Recalled When He Wrote the Twenty-third Psalm. By John D. Whiting. Vol. L, pp. 729-753, 19 ills., Dec., 1926.

Bedouin Life in Bible Lands : The Nomads of the "Houses of Hair" Offer Unstinted Hospitality to an American. By John D. Whiting. Vol. LXXI, pp. 59-83, 27 ills., 1 third-page map, Jan., 1937.

Bethlehem and the Christmas Story. By John D. Whiting. Vol. LVI, pp. 699-735, 27 ills. in black and white, 14 ills. in color, Dec., 1929.

Canoeing Down the River Jordan : Voyagers in Rubber Boats Find the Bible Stream Little Tamed Today as It Plunges to the Dead Sea Over the Earth's Lowest River Bed. By John D. Whiting. Vol. LXXVIII, pp. 781-808, 19 ills., 1 page map, Dec., 1940.

From Jerusalem to Aleppo. By John D. Whiting. Vol. XXIV, pp. 71-113, 30 ills., 1 half-page map, Jan., 1913.

Jerusalem's Locust Plague : Being a Description of the Recent Locust Influx Into Palestine, and Comparing Same with the Ancient Locust Invasions as Narrated in the Old World's History Book, the Bible. By John D. Whiting. Vol. XXVIII, pp. 511-550, 25 ills., 1 page map, Dec., 1915.

Last Israelitish Blood Sacrifice : How the Vanishing Samaritans Celebrate the Passover on Sacred Mount Gerizim. By John D. Whiting. Vol. XXXVII, pp. 1-46, 40 ills., 1 half-page map, Jan., 1920.

Petra, Ancient Caravan Stronghold : Mysterious Temples and Tombs, Carved in Glowing Cliffs of Eroded Sandstone, Are Remnants of a City David Longed to Storm. By John D. Whiting. Vol. LXVII, pp. 129-165, 15 ills. in black and white, 21 ills. in color, 1 half-page and 1 quarter-page maps, Feb., 1935.

Village Life in the Holy Land. By John D. Whiting. Vol. XXV, pp. 249-314, 27 ills. in black and white, 22 ills. in color, Mar., 1914.

Whiting, John D.—*Continued*

Where Early Christians Lived in Cones of Rock : A Journey to Cappadocia in Turkey Where Strange Volcanic Pinnacles Are Honeycombed With Hermit Cells and Monasteries. By John D. Whiting. Vol. LXXVI, pp. 763-802, 20 ills. in black and white, 20 ills. in color, 1 half-page map, Dec., 1939.

Whittemore, Thomas:

Rebirth of Religion in Russia : The Church Reorganized While Bolshevik Cannon Spread Destruction in the Nation's Holy of Holies. By Thomas Whittemore. Vol. XXXIV, pp. 378-401, 16 ills., Nov., 1918.

Who Shall Inherit Long Life ? On the Existence of a Natural Process at Work Among Human Beings Tending to Improve the Vigor and Vitality of Succeeding Generations. By Alexander Graham Bell. Vol. XXXV, pp. 505-514, 13 ills., June, 1919.

Who Treads Our Trails ? A Camera Trapper Describes His Experiences on an Island in the Canal Zone, a Natural-History Laboratory in the American Tropics. By Frank M. Chapman. Vol. LII, pp. 331-345, 18 ills., 1 half-page map, Sept., 1927.

Who's Who Among the Butterflies. By Austin H. Clark. Vol. LXIX, pp. 679-692, 15 ills. in black and white, 9 ills. in color, May, 1936.

Who's Who in the Monkey World. 40 portraits in color from paintings by Elie Cheverlange. Vol. LXXIII, pp. 625-648, May, 1938.

Why Great Salt Lake Has Fallen. By L. H. Murdoch. Vol. XIV, pp. 75-77, Feb., 1903.

Why Nik-ko Is Beautiful. By J. H. De Forest. Vol. XIX, pp. 300-308, 8 ills., Apr., 1908.

Wicker, Cyrus French:

Eastward from Gibraltar : Overland Route Across North Africa to Tunisia and Libia. By Cyrus French Wicker. Vol. LXXXIII, pp. 115-142, 28 ills., Jan., 1943.

Wideawake Field, Ascension Island :

Ascension Island, an Engineering Victory. By Lt. Col. Frederick J. Clarke. Vol. LXXXV, pp. 623-640, 21 ills., May, 1944.

Wight, Isle of, England :

England's Island Garden of Rocks and Flowers. 14 ills. in color from natural-color photographs by W. Robert Moore. Vol. LXVII, pp. 17-24, Jan., 1935.

England's Sun Trap Isle of Wight. By J. R. Hildebrand. Vol. LXVII, pp. 1-33, 22 ills. in black and white, 14 ills. in color, 1 half-page map, Jan., 1935.

Wilbur, Curtis D.:

Commander Byrd Receives the Hubbard Gold Medal : The First Explorer to Reach the North Pole by Air Receives Coveted Honor at Brilliant National Geographic Society Reception (Address by Secretary Wilbur). Vol. L, pp. 377-388, 5 ills., 1 chart, Sept., 1926.

Wilbur, Lyman D.:

Surveying Through Khoresm : A Journey Into Parts of Asiatic Russia Which Have Been Closed to Western Travelers Since the World War. By Lyman D. Wilbur. Vol. LXI, pp. 753-780, 31 ills., 1 two-thirds-page map, June, 1932.

Wilbur, (Brig. Gen.) W. H.:

Infantrymen—The Fighters of War. By Brig. Gen. W. H. Wilbur. Vol. LXXXVI, pp. 513-538, 22 ills., Nov., 1944.

Wilcox, Walter D.:

Among the Mahogany Forests of Cuba. By Walter D. Wilcox. Vol. XIX, pp. 485-498, 6 ills., 1 page map, July, 1908.

Recent Exploration in the Canadian Rockies. By Walter D. Wilcox. Part I, Vol. XIII, pp. 151-168, 12 ills., 1 page map, May, 1902. Part II, Vol. XIII, pp. 185-200, 9 ills., June, 1902.

Sources of the Saskatchewan. By Walter D. Wilcox. Vol. X, pp. 113-134, 5 ills., 1 chart, Apr., 1899.

Wild Animals That Took Their Own Pictures by Day and by Night. By George Shiras, 3d. Vol. XXIV, pp. 763-834, 68 ills., 1 page map, July, 1913.

Wild Blueberry Tamed : The New Industry of the Pine Barrens of New Jersey. By Frederick V. Coville. Vol. XXIX, pp. 535-546, 10 ills., June, 1916.

Wild Cats:

King of Cats and His Court. By Victor H. Cahalane. Paintings by Walter A. Weber. Vol. LXXXIII, pp. 217-259, 9 ills. in black and white, 20 ills. in color, Feb., 1943.

Wild Dogs:

Other Working Dogs and the Wild Species. By Stanley P. Young. Paintings by Walter A. Weber. Vol. LXXXVI, pp. 363-384, 12 ills. in black and white, 9 ills. in color, Sept., 1944.

Wild Dogs and Working Dogs. 9 ills. in color from paintings by Walter A. Weber. Vol. LXXXVI, pp. 369-376, Sept., 1944.

Wild Ducks as Winter Guests in a City Park. By Joseph Dixon. Vol. XXXVI, pp. 331-342, 11 ills., Oct., 1919.

Wild Flowers. *See* Flowers.

Wild Flowers of the West (United States). By Edith S. Clements. Vol. LI, pp. 566-622, 206 ills. in color, May, 1927.

Wild Gardens of the Southern Appalachians. 13 ills. in color from natural-color photographs by Edwin L. Wisherd, Laurence V. Jolliffe, and Clifton Adams. Vol. LXV, pp. 679-686, June, 1934.

Wild Geese, Ducks, and Swans. 93 portraits in color from paintings by Maj. Allan Brooks. Vol. LXVI, pp. 493-524, Oct., 1934.

Wild Life of Lake Superior, Past and Present : The Habits of Deer, Moose, Wolves, Beavers, Muskrats, Trout, and Feathered Wood-Folk Studied with Camera and Flashlight. By George Shiras, 3d. Vol. XL, pp. 113-204, 77 ills., supplement, 1 half-page map, Aug., 1921.

Wild Life of the Atlantic and Gulf Coasts : A Field Naturalist's Photographic Record of Nearly Half a Century of Fruitful Exploration. By George Shiras, 3d. Vol. LXII, pp. 261-309, 62 ills., Sept., 1932.

Wild Man and Wild Beast in Africa. By Theodore Roosevelt. Vol. XXII, pp. 1-33, 41 ills., 1 page map, Jan., 1911.

Wildlife:

High Country of Colorado. By Alfred M. Bailey. With 23 ills. in color from natural-color photographs by the author, Robert J. Niedrach, and F. G. Brandenburg. Vol. XC, pp. 43-72, 9 ills. in black and white, July, 1946.

Wildlife of Tabasco and Veracruz (Mexico). By Walter A. Weber. With 19 ills. in color from paintings by the author. Vol. LXXXVII, pp. 187-216, 7 ills. in black and white, 1 two-thirds-page map, Feb., 1945.

Wiley, Harvey W.:

National Geographic Society (Speech by Harvey W. Wiley). Vol. XXIII, pp. 273-298, 5 ills., Mar., 1912.

United States : Its Soils and Their Products. By Harvey W. Wiley. Vol. XIV, pp. 263-279, 11 ills., July, 1903.

Wilkes, (Rear Adm.) Charles:

American Discoverers of the Antarctic Continent. By Maj. Gen. A. W. Greely. Vol. XXIII, pp. 298-312, 7 ills., 1 page map, Mar., 1912.

Gem of the Ocean : Our American Navy. By Josephus Daniels. Vol. XXXIII, pp. 313-335, 35 ills., Apr., 1918.

Memorial Monument to, erected by National Geographic Society. Vol. LIV, p. 633, Nov., 1928.

Revealing Earth's Mightiest Ocean (Pacific). By Albert W. Atwood. Vol. LXXXIV, pp. 291-306, 10 ills., special map supplement, Sept., 1943.

Some Early Geographers of the United States. By Rear Adm. Colby M. Chester. Vol. XV, pp. 392-404, Oct., 1904.

Termination Land (Antarctica). By Edwin Swift Balch. Vol. XV, pp. 220-221, May, 1904.

Wilkes' and D'Urville's Discoveries in Wilkes Land. By Rear Adm. John Elliott Pillsbury. Vol. XXI, pp. 171-173, Feb., 1910.

Wilkins, (Sir) Hubert:

Our Search for the Lost Aviators : An Arctic Area Larger Than Montana First Explored in Hunt for Missing Russians. By Sir Hubert Wilkins. Vol. LXXIV, pp. 141-172, 29 ills., 1 two-page map, Aug., 1938.

Wilkinson, Norman:

Cathedrals of England: An Artist's Pilgrimage to These Majestic Monuments of Man's Genius and Faith. By Norman Wilkinson. Vol. LXXVI, pp. 741-762, 3 ills. in black and white, 16 ills. in gravure from dry-point engravings by the author, Dec., 1939.

Ships of the Centuries. 16 ills. in gravure from etchings by Norman Wilkinson. Vol. LXXIII, pp. 65-80; text, p. 98, Jan., 1938.

Willemstad, Curaçao (Island):

Curaçao and Aruba, Oil Isles of the Caribbean. 10 ills. in color from natural-color photographs by Philip Hanson Hiss and Robert Yarnall Richie. Vol. LXXXIII, pp. 175-182, Feb., 1943.

Curaçao and Aruba on Guard. By W. Robert Moore. Vol. LXXXIII, pp. 169-192, 12 ills. in black and white, 10 ills. in color, 4 maps, Feb., 1943.

Willey, Day Allen:

Barrage of the Nile. By Day Allen Willey. Vol. XXI, pp. 175-184, 14 ills., Feb., 1910.

William I, The Conqueror:

Land of William the Conqueror (Normandy): Where Northmen Came to Build Castles and Cathedrals. By Inez Buffington Ryan. Vol. LXI, pp. 89-99, 13 ills. in color, Jan., 1932.

Williams, C. B.:

Butterfly Travelers: Some Varieties Migrate Thousands of Miles. By C. B. Williams. Vol. LXXI, pp. 568-585, 1 ill. in black and white, 8 ills. in color, May, 1937.

Williams, Gardiner F.:

Diamond Mines of South Africa. By Gardiner F. Williams. Vol. XVII, pp. 344-356, 11 ills., June, 1906.

Williams, Ira A.:

Scenes Among the High Cascades in Central Oregon. By Ira A. Williams. Vol. XXIII, pp. 578-592, 11 ills., June, 1912.

Williams, John Sharp:

Ties That Bind: Our Natural Sympathy with English Traditions, the French Republic, and the Russian Outburst for Liberty. By John Sharp Williams. Vol. XXXI, pp. 281-286, 4 ills., Mar., 1917.

Williams, Maynard Owen:

Adventures with a Camera in Many Lands. By Maynard Owen Williams. Vol. XL, pp. 87-112, 24 ills., July, 1921.

Afghanistan Makes Haste Slowly. By Maynard Owen Williams. Vol. LXIV, pp. 731-769, 33 ills. in black and white, 12 ills. in color, 1 two-thirds-page map, Dec., 1933.

Williams, Maynard Owen—*Continued*

Airplanes Come to the Isles of Spice: Once Magnet of World Explorers, the Moluccas Again Stand at Crossroads of History in the Netherlands Indies. By Maynard Owen Williams. Vol. LXXIX, pp. 535-558, 26 ills., 1 page map, May, 1941.

Along London's Coronation Route. By Maynard Owen Williams. Vol. LXXI, pp. 609-632, 22 ills., 1 half-page map, May, 1937.

American Alma Maters in the Near East. By Maynard Owen Williams. Vol. LXXXVIII, pp. 237-256, 16 ills., Aug., 1945.

American Fighters Visit Bible Lands. By Maynard Owen Williams. With 23 ills. in color from natural-color photographs by the author. Vol. LXXXIX, pp. 311-340, 10 ills. in black and white, Mar., 1946.

Amidst the Templed Hills of Greece. 13 ills. in color from natural-color photographs by Maynard Owen Williams. Vol. LVIII, pp. 664-673, Dec., 1930.

Ancient Temples and Modern Guns in Thailand. 10 ills. from photographs; 6 ills. by Maynard Owen Williams. Vol. LXXX, pp. 653-660, Nov., 1941.

At the Tomb of Tutankhamen: An Account of the Opening of the Royal Egyptian Sepulcher Which Contained the Most Remarkable Funeral Treasures Unearthed in Historic Times. By Maynard Owen Williams. Vol. XLIII, pp. 461-508, 53 ills., 1 half-page map, May, 1923.

Back to Afghanistan. By Maynard Owen Williams. Vol. XC, pp. 517-544, 27 ills., 1 page map, Oct., 1946.

Bahrein: Port of Pearls and Petroleum. By Maynard Owen Williams. Vol. LXXXIX, pp. 195-210, 6 ills. in black and white, 11 ills. in color, 1 half-page map, Feb., 1946.

Bali, Gem of the Netherlands Indies. 11 ills. in color from natural-color photographs; 10 ills. by Maynard Owen Williams. Vol. LXXV, pp. 329-336, Mar., 1939.

Bali and Points East: Crowded, Happy Isles of the Flores Sea Blend Rice Terraces, Dance Festivals, and Amazing Music in Their Pattern of Living. By Maynard Owen Williams. Vol. LXXV, pp. 313-352, 33 ills. in black and white, 11 ills. in color, 1 two-thirds-page map, Mar., 1939.

Behind New Delhi's News. 13 ills. in color from natural-color photographs by Maynard Owen Williams. Vol. LXXXII, pp. 477-484, Oct., 1942.

Beside the Bosporus, Divider of Continents. 11 ills. in color from natural-color photographs by Maynard Owen Williams. Vol. LVI, pp. 492-501, Oct., 1929.

Between Massacres in Van. By Maynard Owen Williams. Vol. XXXVI, pp. 181-184, 3 ills., Aug., 1919.

Bright Pages from an Asiatic Travel Log. 12 ills. in color from natural-color photographs by Maynard Owen Williams. Vol. LXII, pp. 544-553, Nov., 1932.

Williams, Maynard Owen—*Continued*

Buddhist Calm Survives Along China's Great Wall. 10 ills. in color; 3 ills. from natural-color photographs by Maynard Owen Williams. Vol. LXXIII, pp. 321-328, Mar., 1938.

Buenos Aires: Queen of the River of Silver. By Maynard Owen Williams. Vol. LXXVI, pp. 561-600, 22 ills. in black and white, 24 ills. in color, 1 half-page map, Nov., 1939.

Buenos Aires—Metropolis of the Pampas. 24 ills. in color from natural-color photographs by Luis Marden and Maynard Owen Williams. Vol. LXXVI, pp. 577-600, Nov., 1939.

Bulgaria, Farm Land Without a Farmhouse: A Nation of Villagers Faces the Challenge of Modern Machinery and Urban Life. By Maynard Owen Williams. Vol. LXII, pp. 185-218, 19 ills. in black and white, 27 ills. in color, 1 half-page map, Aug., 1932.

By Car and Steamer Around Our Inland Seas. By Maynard Owen Williams. Vol. LXV, pp. 451-491, 29 ills. in black and white, 8 ills. in duotone, 1 two-page map, Apr., 1934.

By Motor Trail Across French Indo-China. By Maynard Owen Williams. Vol. LXVIII, pp. 487-534, 31 ills. in black and white, 27 ills. in color, 1 page map, Oct., 1935.

Carnival Days on the Riviera. By Maynard Owen Williams. Vol. L, pp. 467-501, 21 ills., Oct., 1926.

Celebes: New Man's Land of the Indies. By Maynard Owen Williams. Vol. LXXVIII, pp. 51-82, 33 ills., 1 page map, July, 1940.

Citroën Trans-Asiatic Expedition Reaches Kashmir: Scientific Party Led by Georges-Marie Haardt Successfully Crosses Syria, Iraq, Persia, and Afghanistan to Arrive at the Pamir. By Maynard Owen Williams. Vol. LX, pp. 387-443, 62 ills., 1 page map, Oct., 1931.

Clans in Kilt and Plaidie Gather at Braemar (Scotland). 11 ills. in color from natural-color photographs by Maynard Owen Williams. Vol. LXVIII, pp. 153-160, Aug., 1935.

Classic Greece Merges Into 1941 News. 19 ills. from photographs; 15 ills. by B. Anthony Stewart; 3 ills. by Maynard Owen Williams. Vol. LXXIX, pp. 93-108, Jan., 1941.

Coasts of Corsica: Impressions of a Winter's Stay in the Island Birthplace of Napoleon. By Maynard Owen Williams. Vol. XLIV, pp. 221-312, 88 ills., special supplement, 1 page and 1 quarter-page maps, Sept., 1923.

Color Records from the Changing Life of the Holy City (Jerusalem). By Maynard Owen Williams. Vol. LII, pp. 682-707, 27 ills. in color, Dec., 1927.

Columbia (River) Turns on the Power. By Maynard Owen Williams. Vol. LXXIX, pp. 749-792, 25 ills. in black and white, 18 ills. in color, June, 1941.

Czechoslovakia, the Key-Land to Central Europe. By Maynard Owen Williams. Vol. XXXIX, pp. 111-156, 45 ills., 1 quarter-page map, Feb., 1921.

Descendants of Confucius (Industries in Shantung). By Maynard Owen Williams. Vol. XXXVI, pp. 253-265, 16 ills., Sept., 1919.

Williams, Maynard Owen—*Continued*

East of Suez to the Mount of the Decalogue: Following the Trail Over Which Moses Led the Israelites from the Slave-Pens of Egypt to Sinai. By Maynard Owen Williams. Vol. LII, pp. 709-743, 32 ills., 1 three-quarters-page map, Dec., 1927.

Empire of Romance—India. 16 ills. in color from photographs by Maynard Owen Williams and others. Vol. XL, pp. 481-496, Nov., 1921.

The Face of the Netherlands Indies. 20 ills. from photographs by Maynard Owen Williams and others. Vol. LXXXIX, pp. 261-276, Feb., 1946.

Festival Days on the Slopes of Mount Parnassus (Greece). 14 ills. in color from natural-color photographs by Maynard Owen Williams. Vol. LVIII, pp. 712-721, Dec., 1930.

First Natural-Color Photographs from the Arctic. 3 ills. in color from natural-color photographs by Maynard Owen Williams. Vol. XLIX, pp. 300-317, Mar., 1926.

First Over the Roof of the World by Motor: The Trans-Asiatic Expedition Sets New Records for Wheeled Transport in Scaling Passes of the Himalayas. By Maynard Owen Williams. Vol. LXI, pp. 321-363, 45 ills., 2 half-page maps, Mar., 1932.

France of Sunshine and Flowers. 16 ills. in color from autochromes lumière by Maynard Owen Williams. Vol. L, pp. 481-496, Oct., 1926.

Freighters of Fortune on Our Great Lakes. 8 ills. in duotone from photographs by Maynard Owen Williams. Vol. LXV, pp. 463-470, Apr., 1934.

From the Mediterranean to the Yellow Sea by Motor: The Citroën-Haardt Expedition Successfully Completes Its Dramatic Journey. By Maynard Owen Williams. Vol. LXII, pp. 513-580, 45 ills. in black and white, 25 ills. in color, 2 half-page maps, Nov., 1932.

Grand Duchy of Luxemburg: A Miniature Democratic State of Many Charms Against a Feudal Background. By Maynard Owen Williams. Vol. XLVI, pp. 501-528, 28 ills., 1 quarter-page map, Nov., 1924.

Great Britain on Parade. By Maynard Owen Williams. Vol. LXVIII, pp. 137-184, 40 ills. in black and white, 11 ills. in color, Aug., 1935.

Guest in Saudi Arabia. By Maynard Owen Williams. Vol. LXXXVIII, pp. 463-487, 24 ills., 1 two-thirds-page map, Oct., 1945.

How Warwick (Castle) Was Photographed in Color. By Maynard Owen Williams. Vol. LXX, pp. 83-93, 13 ills. in color, July, 1936.

Idaho Made the Desert Bloom. 20 ills. in color from natural-color photographs; 17 ills. by Maynard Owen Williams. Vol. LXXXV, pp. 657-688, June, 1944.

In the Birthplace of Christianity. 17 ills. in color from autochromes lumière by Maynard Owen Williams. Vol. L, pp. 696-721, Dec., 1926.

Williams, Maynard Owen—*Continued*

India at Work and Play. 22 ills. in color from natural-color photographs by Peter Upton Muir, Maynard Owen Williams, and Frances Muir. Vol. LXXXIX, pp. 449-464, Apr., 1946.

Informal Salute to the English Lakes. By Maynard Owen Williams. Vol. LXIX, pp. 511-521, 10 ills. in color, Apr., 1936.

Isles of Greece. 20 ills. in color from natural-color photographs by Maynard Owen Williams and B. Anthony Stewart. Vol. LXXXV, pp. 601-616, May, 1944.

Kingdom of Many Tribes (Afghanistan). 12 ills. in color from natural-color photographs by Maynard Owen Williams. Vol. LXIV, pp. 745-752, Dec., 1933.

Land of Genghis Khan in Its True Colors. 13 ills. in color from natural-color photographs by Maynard Owen Williams. Vol. LXII, pp. 568-577, Nov., 1932.

Latvia, Home of the Letts : One of the Baltic Republics Which Is Successfully Working Its Way to Stability. By Maynard Owen Williams. Vol. XLVI, pp. 401-443, 48 ills., 1 half-page map, Oct., 1924.

Life and Death in Toradjaland. 22 ills. from photographs ; 11 ills. by Maynard Owen Williams ; 8 ills. by Helene Fischer. Vol. LXXVIII, pp. 65-80, July, 1940.

Looking in on the Everyday Life of New Turkey. 4 ills. in color from natural-color photographs by Maynard Owen Williams. Vol. LXI, pp. 500-509, Apr., 1932.

Modern Odyssey in Classic Lands : Troy's Treasures, Athens' Parthenon, and Rome's First "Broad Way" Influence Today's Banks, Costumes, Jewelry, and Railroad Timetables. By Maynard Owen Williams. Vol. LXXVII, pp. 291-337, 27 ills. in black and white, 22 ills. in color, Mar., 1940.

Mother Volga Defends Her Own. By Maynard Owen Williams. Vol. LXXXII, pp. 793-811, 21 ills., Dec., 1942.

Netherlands Indies : Patchwork of Peoples. 23 ills. in color from natural-color photographs by Maynard Owen Williams. Vol. LXXIII, pp. 681-712, June, 1938.

New Delhi (India) Goes Full Time. By Maynard Owen Williams. Vol. LXXXII, pp. 465-494, 17 ills. in black and white, 13 ills. in color, 1 page map, Oct., 1942.

New Greece, the Centenarian, Forges Ahead. By Maynard Owen Williams. Vol. LVIII, pp. 649-721, 51 ills. in black and white, 40 ills. in color, 1 three-quarters-page map, Dec., 1930.

Oil Comes to Bahrein, Port of Pearls. 11 ills. in color from natural-color photographs by Maynard Owen Williams. Vol. LXXXIX, pp. 201-208, Feb., 1946.

Paris in Spring. By Maynard Owen Williams. Vol. LXX, pp. 501-534, 30 ills., Oct., 1936.

Paris Lives Again. By M. O. Williams. Vol. XC, pp. 767-790, 24 ills., Dec., 1946.

Williams, Maynard Owen *Continued*

Pilgrims Still Stop at Plymouth (England). By Maynard Owen Williams. Vol. LXXIV, pp. 59-77, 19 ills., July, 1938.

Poland of the Present. By Maynard Owen Williams. Vol. LXIII, pp. 319-344, 19 ills. in black and white, 11 ills. in color, Mar., 1933.

Round About Liechtenstein : A Tiny Principality Which the Visitor May Encompass in a Single View Affords Adventurous Climbs Among Steep Pastures and Quaint Villages. By Maynard Owen Williams. Vol. LII, pp. 611-634, 18 ills., 1 half-page map, Nov., 1927.

Russia's Orphan Races : Picturesque Peoples Who Cluster on the Southeastern Borderland of the Vast Slav Dominions. Vol. XXXIV. pp. 245-278, 26 ills., 1 page map, Oct., 1918.

Scenes Along the Byways of Hellas. 13 ills. in color from natural-color photographs by Maynard Owen Williams. Vol. LVIII, pp. 688-697, Dec., 1930.

Scillion : Isles of Wrecks and Golden Daffodils. 13 ills. in color from natural color photographs ; 3 ills. by Maynard Owen Williams. Vol. LXXIV, pp. 759-766, Dec., 1938.

Seeing 3,000 Years of History in Four Hours : A Panorama of Ancient, Medieval, and Modern Events Against a Background of Mythology Unfolds During an Airplane Journey from Constantinople to Athens. By Maynard Owen Williams. Vol. LIV, pp. 719-739, 24 ills., 1 two-thirds-page map, Dec., 1928.

Sicily Again in the Path of War. By Maynard Owen Williams. Vol. LXXXIV, pp. 307-320, 7 ills., 1 map (two-page spread), Sept., 1943.

Singapore : Far East Gibraltar in the Malay Jungle. 23 ills. from photographs ; 5 ills. by Maynard Owen Williams. Vol. LXXIII, pp. 599-614, May, 1938.

South of Khyber Pass (India). By Maynard Owen Williams. Vol. LXXXIX, pp. 471-500, 31 ills., Apr., 1946.

Star and Crescent on Parade (Turkey). 29 ills. in color from natural-color photographs by Maynard Owen Williams. Vol. LXXXVII, pp. 585-616, May, 1945.

Struggling Poland : A Journey in Search of the Picturesque Through the Most Populous of the New States of Europe. By Maynard Owen Williams. Vol. L, pp. 203-244, 48 ills., 1 two-thirds-page map, Aug., 1926.

Suez Canal : Short Cut to Empires. By Maynard Owen Williams. Vol. LXVII, pp. 611-632, 19 ills., 1 half-page map, Nov., 1935.

Summer Holidays on the Bosporus. By Maynard Owen Williams. Vol. LVI, pp. 487-508, 13 ills. in black and white, 11 ills. in color, 1 half-page map, Oct., 1929.

Syria : The Land Link of History's Chain. By Maynard Owen Williams. Vol. XXXVI, pp. 437-462, 20 ills., 1 quarter-page map, Nov., 1919.

Williams, Maynard Owen—*Continued*

Syria and Lebanon Taste Freedom. By Maynard Owen Williams. With 21 ills. in color from natural-color photographs by the author. Vol. XC, pp. 729-763, 16 ills. in black and white, Dec., 1946.

Through the Heart of Hindustan: A Teeming Highway Extending for Fifteen Hundred Miles, from the Khyber Pass to Calcutta. By Maynard Owen Williams. Vol. XL, pp. 433-467, 29 ills., Nov., 1921.

Time's Footprints in Tunisian Sands. By Maynard Owen Williams. Vol. LXXI, pp. 345-386, 43 ills., 1 page and 1 half-page maps. Mar., 1937.

Tricolor Rules the Rainbow in French Indo-China. 27 ills. in color from natural-color photographs by Maynard Owen Williams. Vol. LXVIII, pp. 495-518, Oct., 1935.

Turkey, Where Earthquakes Followed Timur's Trail. 15 ills. from photographs by Maynard Owen Williams. Vol. LXXVII, pp. 395-406, Mar., 1940.

Turkey Goes to School. By Maynard Owen Williams. Vol. LV, pp. 95-108, 17 ills., Jan., 1929.

Turkish Republic Comes of Age. By Maynard Owen Williams. Vol. LXXXVII, pp. 581-616, 4 ills. in black and white, 29 ills. in color, 1 map (two-page spread), May, 1945.

Unspoiled Cyprus: The Traditional Island Birthplace of Venus Is One of the Least Sophisticated of Mediterranean Lands. By Maynard Owen Williams. Vol. LIV, pp. 1-55, 55 ills. in black and white, 10 ills. in color, 1 half-page map, July, 1928.

Warwick Castle, Stage for Old England's Pageantry. 13 ills. in color from natural-color photographs by Maynard Owen Williams. Vol. LXX, pp. 85-92, July, 1936.

When Czechoslovakia Puts a Falcon Feather in Its Cap. By Maynard Owen Williams. Vol. LXIII, pp. 40-49, 13 ills. in color, Jan., 1933.

Where Ancient Sea Kings Held Sway (Crete). 14 ills. in color from autochromes by Maynard Owen Williams. Vol. LV, pp. 254-263, Feb., 1929.

Where Slav and Mongol Meet. 16 ills. in color from photographs by Maynard Owen Williams. Vol. XXXVI, pp. 421-436, Nov., 1919.

Wilno, Stepchild of the Polish Frontier. 13 ills. in duotone; 3 ills. by Maynard Owen Williams. Vol. LXXIII, pp. 777-784, June, 1938.

Williams, Talcott:

Link Relations of Southwestern Asia. By Talcott Williams. Part I, Vol. XII, pp. 249-265, 12 page and 1 half-page maps, July, 1901. Part II, Vol. XII, pp. 291-299, 1 half-page map, Aug., 1901.

Williamsburg, Virginia:

Genesis of the Williamsburg Restoration. By John D. Rockefeller, Jr. Vol. LXXI, p. 401, Apr., 1937.

Williamsburg, Virginia—*Continued*

Restoration of Colonial Williamsburg. By W. A. R. Goodwin. Vol. LXXI, pp. 402-443, 21 ills. in black and white, 25 ills. in color, Apr., 1937.

Virginia's Colonial Heritage. 25 ills. in color from natural-color photographs. Vol. LXXI, pp. 417-440, Apr., 1937.

Willis, Bailey:

Awakening of Argentina and Chile: Progress in the Lands That Lie Below Capricorn. By Bailey Willis. Vol. XXX, pp. 121-142, 14 ills., Aug., 1916.

International Millionth Map of the World. By Bailey Willis. Vol. XXI, pp. 125-132, 1 diagram, Feb., 1910.

Willoughby, (Hon.) William F.:

Proceedings of the National Geographic Society (Report of Lecture on Puerto Rico by Hon. William F. Willoughby). Vol. XIII, pp. 466-470, Dec., 1902.

Willow Run, Michigan: Bomber Plant:

Michigan Fights. By Harvey Klemmer. Vol. LXXXVI, pp. 677-715, 20 ills. in black and white, 19 ills. in color, 1 page-and-a-half map, Dec., 1944.

Wilno, Poland:

Wilno, Stepchild of the Polish Frontier. 13 ills. in duotone. Vol. LXXIII, pp. 777-784, June, 1938.

Wilson, Alan D.:

Hunting Bears on Horseback. By Alan D. Wilson. Vol. XIX, pp. 350-356, 4 ills., May, 1908.

Wilson, Ernest H.:

Kingdom of Flowers: An Account of the Wealth of Trees and Shrubs of China and of What the Arnold Arboretum, with China's Help, Is Doing to Enrich America. By Ernest H. Wilson. Vol. XXII, pp. 1003-1035, 24 ills., Nov., 1911.

Wilson, Eugene E.:

Anticosti Island, Nugget of the North. By Eugene E. Wilson. Vol. LXXXI, pp. 121-140, 19 ills., 1 two-thirds-page map, Jan., 1942.

Wilson, Herbert M.:

Reclaiming the Swamp Lands of the United States. By Herbert M. Wilson. Vol. XVIII, pp. 292-301, 2 ills., 1 half-page map, 1 diagram, May, 1907.

Wilson, J. A.:

Canada from the Air: Flights Aggregating 10,000 Miles Reveal the Marvelous Scenic Beauties and Amazing Natural Resources of the Dominion. By J. A. Wilson. Vol. L, pp. 389-466, 76 ills., 1 page map, Oct., 1926.

Gentlemen Adventurers of the Air: Many Regions of Canada's Vast Wilderness, Long Hidden Even from Fur Trappers, Are Now Revealed by Exploring Airmen. By J. A. Wilson. Vol. LVI, pp. 597-642, 55 ills., 1 page map, Nov., 1929.

Wilson, James:

Modern Alchemist (Work of the Department of Agriculture). By James Wilson. Vol. XVIII, pp. 778-795, 6 ills., Dec., 1907.

Protecting Our Forests from Fire. By James Wilson. Vol. XXII, pp. 98-106, 5 ills., Jan., 1911.

United States Weather Bureau. By James Wilson. Vol. XV, pp. 37-39, Jan., 1904.

Wilson, James C.:

Three-Wheeling Through Africa: Two Adventurers Cross the So-called Dark Continent North of Lake Chad on Motorcycles with Side Cars. By James C. Wilson. Vol. LXV, pp. 37-92, 64 ills., 1 two-page map, Jan., 1934.

Wilson, James H.:

Great Wall of China. By James H. Wilson. Vol. XI, pp. 372-374, 1 ill., Sept., 1900.

Wilson, (Gen.) John M.:

In Honor of the Army and Aviation (Speeches by Gen. John M. Wilson). Vol. XXII, pp. 267-284, 1 ill., Mar., 1911.

National Geographic Society's Notable Year (Announcement of the Death of Brig. Gen. John M. Wilson). Vol. XXXVII, pp. 338-345, 2 ills., Apr., 1920.

Wilson, Woodrow:

Do Your Bit for America: A Proclamation by President Wilson to the American People. Vol. XXXI, pp. 287-293, 2 ills., Apr., 1917.

Election of Woodrow Wilson as Honorary Member of The Society. Vol. XXXIII, p. 369, Apr., 1918.

Honors to Colonel Goethals: The Presentation by President Woodrow Wilson, of the National Geographic Society Special Gold Medal, and Addresses by Secretary of State Bryan, the French Ambassador, the German Ambassador, and Congressman James R. Mann. Vol. XXV, pp. 677-690, 6 ills., June, 1914.

Wilson, Mount, California:

Magic Mountain. By J. N. Patterson. Vol. XIX, pp. 457-468, 9 ills., July, 1908.

Wilstach, Paul:

Approaching Washington by Tidewater Potomac. By Paul Wilstach. Vol. LVII, pp. 372-392, 7 ills., Mar., 1930.

Holidays Among the Hill Towns of Umbria and Tuscany. By Paul Wilstach. Vol. LIII, pp. 401-442, 40 ills., 1 page map, Apr., 1928.

Jefferson's Little Mountain: Romance Enfolds Monticello, the Restored Home of the Author of the Declaration of Independence. By Paul Wilstach. Vol. LV, pp. 481-503, 12 ills. in black and white, 12 ills. in color, Apr., 1929.

Stone Beehive Homes of the Italian Heel: In Trulli-Land the Native Builds His Dwelling and Makes His Field Arable in the Same Operation. By Paul Wilstach. Vol. LVII, pp. 229-260, 25 ills. in black and white, 12 ills. in color, 1 quarter-page map, Feb., 1930.

Winchester, England:

Winchester, England's Early Capital. By Frederick Simpich. Vol. LXXIX, pp. 67-92, 25 ills., 1 third-page map, Jan., 1941.

Winchester (Ship):

Cannon on Florida Reefs Solve Mystery of Sunken Ship. By Charles M. Brookfield. Vol. LXXX, pp. 807-824, 20 ills., 1 map (on pen and ink drawing), Dec., 1941.

Windermere (Lake), British Columbia:

On the Trail of a Horse Thief. By Herbert W. Gleason. Vol. XXXV, pp. 349-358, 6 ills., Apr., 1919.

Windjammers:

Cape Horn Grain-Ship Race: The Gallant *Parma* Leads the Vanishing Fleet of Square-Riggers Through Raging Gales and Irksome Calms 16,000 Miles from Australia to England. By A. J. Villiers. Vol. LXIII, pp. 1-39, 38 ills., Jan., 1933.

Rounding the Horn in a Windjammer. By A. J. Villiers. Vol. LIX, pp. 191-224, 36 ills., 1 two-thirds-page map, Feb., 1931.

Sindbads of Science: Narrative of a Windjammer's Specimen-Collecting Voyage to the Sargasso Sea, to Senegambian Africa and Among Islands of High Adventure in the South Atlantic. By George Finlay Simmons. Vol. LII, pp. 1-75, 89 ills., 1 two-thirds-page map, July, 1927.

Winds:

Americans Stand Guard in Greenland. By Andrew H. Brown. Vol. XC, pp. 457-500, 23 ills. in black and white, 19 ills. in color, 1 page map, Oct., 1946.

Forecasting the Weather. By Alfred J. Henry. Vol. XV, pp. 285-292, 6 ills., 1 chart, July, 1904.

Polar Airship. By Walter Wellman. Vol. XVII, pp. 208-228, 4 diagrams, Apr., 1906.

Sailing Ship and the Panama Canal. By James Page. Vol. XV, pp. 167-176, 2 charts, Apr., 1904.

Weather Fights and Works for Man. By F. Barrows Colton. Vol. LXXXIV, pp. 641-670, 22 ills. in black and white, 3 drawings, Dec., 1943.

Where the Wind Does the Work (Cape Hatteras). By Collier Cobb. Vol. XVII, pp. 310-317, 9 ills., 1 page map, June, 1906.

Windward Islands, West Indies:

British West Indian Interlude. By Anne Rainey Langley. Vol. LXXIX, pp. 1-46, 23 ills. in black and white, 21 ills. in color, 2 page maps, Jan., 1941.

See also St. Lucia; St. Vincent.

Wines, (Dr.) F. H.:

Census of 1900 (United States). By Dr. F. H. Wines. Vol. XI, pp. 34-36, Jan., 1900.

Wingate, (Maj. Gen.) Orde C.:

Aerial Invasion of Burma. By Gen. H. H. Arnold. Vol. LXXXVI, pp. 129-148, 20 ills., Aug., 1944.

Winged Denizens of Woodland, Stream, and Marsh (Birds). By Alexander Wetmore. Paintings by Maj. Allan Brooks. Vol. LXV, pp. 577-596, 37 portraits in color, May, 1934.

Winged Jewels from Many Lands (Butterflies). 9 ills. in color; 3 paintings by Hashime Murayama and 6 natural-color photographs by Willard R. Culver. Vol. LXIX, pp. 673-688, May, 1936.

Winged Words—New Weapon of War (Radio). By F. Barrows Colton. Vol. LXXXII, pp. 663-692, 29 ills., 2 two-thirds-page maps, Nov., 1942.

Wings Over Nature's Zoo in Africa. 20 ills. in duotone from photographs by Reginald A. Bourlay. Vol. LXXVI, pp. 527-542, Oct., 1939.

Wings Over the Bounding Main (Ocean Birds). 36 portraits in color from paintings by Maj. Allan Brooks. Vol. LXXIV, pp. 237-251, Aug., 1938.

Winning the War of Supply. By F. Barrows Colton. Vol. LXXXVIII, pp. 705-736, 23 ills., Dec., 1945.

Winning the West. By C. J. Blanchard. Vol. XVII, pp. 82-99, 10 ills., 1 page map, Feb., 1906.

Winter, Nevin O.:

Ukraine, Past and Present. By Nevin O. Winter. Vol. XXXIV, pp. 114-128, 14 ills., Aug., 1918.

Winter Expedition in Southwestern Mexico. By E. W. Nelson. Vol. XV, pp. 341-356, 14 ills., Sept., 1904.

Winter Lights and Shadows in the Nation's Capital. 21 ills. in duotone. Vol. LXVII, pp. 201-216, Feb., 1935.

Winter Rambles in Thoreau's Country. By Herbert W. Gleason. Vol. XXXVII, pp. 165-180, 15 ills., Feb., 1920.

Winter Scenes. 16 ills. from photographs. Vol. XXXVII, pp. 135-150, Feb., 1920.

Winter Sky Roads to Isle Royal (Michigan). By Ben East. Vol. LX, pp. 759-774, 18 ills., 1 half-page map, Dec., 1931.

Wiscasset, Maine:

The Worm Turns. By Samuel Sandrof. Vol. LXXXIX, pp. 775-786, 14 ills., June, 1946.

Wisconsin:

Life's Color in Wisconsin. 27 ills. in color from natural-color photographs: 23 ills. by B. Anthony Stewart. Vol. LXXII, pp. 17-40, July, 1937.

On Goes Wisconsin: Strength and Vigor Mark This Midwestern State, With Its Woods and Lakes and Its Blend of Sturdy Nationalities. By Glanville Smith. Vol. LXXII, pp. 1-46, 25 ills. in black and white, 27 ills. in color, 1 two-page map, July, 1937.

Wisherd, Edwin L.:

Alabama: Where the New South Challenges the Old. 26 ills. in color from natural-color photographs by Edwin L. Wisherd. Vol. LX, pp. 716-749, Dec., 1931.

Connecticut: Old and New Blend in Yankeeland. 25 ills. in color from natural-color photographs; 4 ills. by Edwin L. Wisherd. Vol. LXXIV, pp. 295-326, Sept., 1938.

Fish: Rainbow Denizens of the Aquarium. 16 ills. in color from natural-color photographs by Edwin L. Wisherd. Vol. LXV, pp. 97-104, Jan., 1934.

Indians: Friendly Crows in Festive Panoply. 13 ills. in color from natural-color photographs by Edwin L. Wisherd. Vol. LII, pp. 314-323, Sept., 1927.

Insect Rivals of the Rainbow. 21 ills. in color from natural-color photographs by Edwin L. Wisherd. Vol. LVI, pp. 28-85, July, 1929.

Kentucky: Modern Scenes in the Land of Lincoln's Birth. 15 ills. in color from natural-color photographs by Edwin L. Wisherd. Vol. LXV, pp. 695-702, June, 1934.

Louisiana: Color Camera Records of New Orleans. 15 ills. in color from natural-color photographs by Edwin L. Wisherd. Vol. LVII, pp. 458-467, Apr., 1930.

Louisiana: Flecks of Color in the Fertile Fields of Louisiana. 14 ills. in color from natural-color photographs by Edwin L. Wisherd. Vol. LVII, pp. 418-427, Apr., 1930.

Minnesota: State of Sky-Blue Water and Verdure. 11 ills. in color from natural-color photographs by Clifton Adams and Edwin L. Wisherd. Vol. LXVII, pp. 289-296, Mar., 1935.

Monticello, One of America's Most Historic Shrines. 8 ills. in color from natural-color photographs by Edwin L. Wisherd. Vol. LV, pp. 488-497, Apr., 1929.

New Jersey: Beaches and Bathers of the Jersey Shore. 11 ills. in color from natural-color photographs by Edwin L. Wisherd. Vol. LXIII, pp. 534-543, May, 1933.

New Jersey: Farms and Workshops of "The Garden State." 13 ills. in color from natural-color photographs by Edwin L. Wisherd. Vol. LXIII, pp. 558-567, May, 1933.

New York (City): Tempo and Color of a Great City. 42 ills. in color from natural-color photographs by Clifton Adams and Edwin L. Wisherd. Vol. LVIII, pp. 538-579, Nov., 1930.

New York (State): Color Highlights of the Empire State. 4 ills. in color from natural-color photographs by Edwin L. Wisherd. Vol. LXIV, pp. 569-576, Nov., 1933.

Pennsylvania: Today in the Land of Penn and Franklin. 39 ills. in color from natural-color photographs by Edwin L. Wisherd. Vol. LXVIII, pp. 13-52, July, 1935.

Philadelphia: Colorful Corners of the City of Homes. 13 ills. in color from natural-color photographs by Clifton Adams and Edwin L. Wisherd. Vol. LXII, pp. 674-683, Dec., 1932.

Wisherd, Edwin L.—*Continued*

Puerto Rico Polychromes. 23 ills. in color from natural-color photographs by Edwin L. Wisherd. Vol. LXXVI, pp. 713-736, Dec., 1939.

United States: Canyons and Cacti of the American Southwest. 7 ills. in color from natural-color photographs by Edwin L. Wisherd. Vol. XLVIII, pp. 275-290, Sept., 1925.

United States: Wild Gardens of the Southern Appalachians. 10 ills. in color from natural-color photographs by Edwin L. Wisherd. Vol. LXV, pp. 679-686, June, 1934.

Virgin Islands: Island Treasures of the Caribbean. 23 ills. in color from natural-color photographs by Edwin L. Wisherd and C. W. Herbert. Vol. LXXVIII, pp. 281-304, Sept., 1940.

Virginia: Scenes and Shrines of the Cavalier Country. 2 ills. in color from natural-color photographs by Edwin L. Wisherd. Vol. LV, pp. 424-433, Apr., 1929.

Virginia's Colonial Heritage (Williamsburg). 25 ills. in color from natural-color photographs; 12 ills. by Edwin L. Wisherd. Vol. LXXI, pp. 417-440, Apr., 1937.

Washington, D. C.: Springtime Wreathes a Garland for the Nation's Capital. 13 ills. in color from natural-color photographs; 3 ills. by Edwin L. Wisherd. Vol. LXVII, pp. 473-480, Apr., 1935.

Washington, D. C.: Unique Gifts of Washington to the Nation. 2 ills. in color from natural-color photographs by Edwin L. Wisherd. Vol. LV, pp. 172-181, Apr., 1929.

Washington, D. C.: Winter Lights and Shadows in the Nation's Capital. 21 ills. in duotone; 9 ills. by Edwin L. Wisherd. Vol. LXVII, pp. 201-216, Feb., 1935.

West Indies: Colorful Paths in Martinique and Guadeloupe. 13 ills. in color from natural-color photographs by Edwin L. Wisherd. Vol. LXXIII, pp. 281-288, Mar., 1938.

West Indies: Tropic Color in Trinidad. 14 ills. in color from natural-color photographs by Edwin L. Wisherd. Vol. LXXII, pp. 327-334, Sept., 1937.

West Indies Links in a Defense Chain. 21 ills. in color from natural-color photographs; 20 ills. by Edwin L. Wisherd. Vol. LXXIX, pp. 9-32, Jan., 1941.

West Point, Mother of Army Men. 10 ills. in color from natural-color photographs by Edwin L. Wisherd. Vol. LXIX, pp. 779-786, June, 1936.

Wyoming: Where Hot Pools Seethe and Geysers Spout (Yellowstone). 9 ills. in color from natural-color photographs by Edwin L. Wisherd. Vol. LXXVII, pp. 775-782, June, 1940.

With an Exile in Arctic Siberia: The Narrative of a Russian Who Was Compelled to Turn Polar Explorer for Two Years. By Vladimir M. Zenzinov. Vol. XLVI, pp. 695-718, 30 ills., 1 half-page map, Dec., 1924.

With the Devil Dancers of China and Tibet. 43 ills. in color from natural-color photographs by Joseph F. Rock. Vol. LX, pp. 18-59, July, 1931.

With the Italians in Eritrea: Torrid Colony Between the Red Sea and Ethiopia, 2,600 Miles by Sea from Rome, Is Mobilization Place of Fascist Troops and Planes. By Harald P. Lechenperg. Vol. LXVIII, pp. 265-295, 34 ills., 1 two-page map, Sept., 1935.

With the Monks at Meteora: The Monasteries of Thessaly. By Elizabeth Perkins. Vol. XX, pp. 799-807, 5 ills., Sept., 1909.

With the Nomads of Central Asia: A Summer's Sojourn in the Tekes Valley, Plateau Paradise of Mongol and Turkic Tribes. By Edward Murray. Vol. LXIX, pp. 1-57, 43 ills. in black and white, 26 ills. in color, 1 half-page map. Jan., 1936.

With Wild Animals in the Rockies. By Lucie and Wendell Chapman. Vol. LXVIII, pp. 231-249, 26 ills. in duotone, Aug., 1935.

Within the Halls of Cambridge (University). By Philip Broad. Vol. LXX, pp. 333-349, 7 ills. in black and white, 12 ills. in color, Sept., 1936.

Witwatersrand (Region), Transvaal:

Under the South African Union. By Melville Chater. Vol. LIX, pp. 391-512, 97 ills. in black and white, 38 ills. in color, 1 two-page map, Apr., 1931.

Wokas, a Primitive Indian Food. Vol. XV, pp. 182-185, 5 ills., Apr., 1904.

Wollaston, A. F. R.:

Amid the Snow Peaks of the Equator: A Naturalist's Explorations Around Ruwenzori, with an Excursion to the Congo State, and an Account of the Terrible Scourge of Sleeping Sickness. By A. F. R. Wollaston. Vol. XX, pp. 256-277, 11 ills., Mar., 1909.

Wolves:

Other Working Dogs and the Wild Species. By Stanley P. Young. Paintings by Walter A. Weber. Vol. LXXXVI, pp. 363-384, 12 ills. in black and white, 9 ills. in color, Sept., 1944.

Wild Life of Lake Superior, Past and Present: The Habits of Deer, Moose, Wolves, Beavers, Muskrats, Trout, and Feathered Wood-Folk Studied with Camera and Flashlight. By George Shiras, 3d. Vol. XL, pp. 113-204, 77 ills., supplement, 1 half-page map, Aug., 1921.

Wolves. Vol. XVIII, pp. 145-147, 2 ills., Feb., 1907.

Woman's Climbs in the High Alps. By Dora Keen. Vol. XXII, pp. 642-675, 26 ills., July, 1911.

Woman's Experiences among Stone Age Solomon Islanders: Primitive Life Remains Unchanged in Tropical Jungleland Where United States Forces Now Are Fighting. By Eleanor Schirmer Oliver. Vol. LXXXII, pp. 813-836, 26 ills., 1 half-page map, Dec., 1942.

Woman's Winter on Spitsbergen. By Martha Phillips Gilson. Vol. LIV, pp. 227-246, 20 ills., 1 three-quarters-page map, Aug., 1928.

Women and Children of the East. Vol. XVIII, pp. 248-271, 28 ills., Apr., 1907.

Women at Work. By La Verne Bradley. Vol. LXXXVI, pp. 193-220, 23 ills., Aug., 1944.

Women in Uniform. By La Verne Bradley. Vol. LXXXIV, pp. 445-458, 10 ills., Oct., 1943.

Women of All Nations. Vol. XXII, pp. 49-61, 12 ills., Jan., 1911.

Women's Airforce Service Pilots (WASPS) :

Women in Uniform. By La Verne Bradley. Vol. LXXXIV, pp. 445-458, 10 ills., Oct., 1943.

Women's Army Corps (WAC) :

Decorations, Medals, Service Ribbons, Badges, and Women's Insignia. Vol. LXXXIV, pp. 414-444, 6 ills. in black and white, 376 ills. in color, Oct., 1943.

Paris Freed. By Maj. Frederick Simpich, Jr. Vol. LXXXVII, pp. 385-412, 14 ills. in black and white, 12 ills. in color, Apr., 1945.

Seeing Paris on a 48-Hour Pass. 12 ills. in color from natural-color photographs. Vol. LXXXVII, pp. 401-412, Apr., 1945.

Women in Uniform. By La Verne Bradley. Vol. LXXXIV, pp. 445-458, 10 ills., Oct., 1943.

Women's Insignia:

Decorations, Medals, Service Ribbons, Badges, and Women's Insignia. Vol. LXXXIV, pp. 414-444, 6 ills. in black and white, 376 ills. in color, Oct., 1943.

Women's Reserve of the U. S. Coast Guard Reserve (SPARS) :

Decorations, Medals, Service Ribbons, Badges, and Women's Insignia. Vol. LXXXIV, pp. 414-444, 6 ills. in black and white, 376 ills. in color, Oct., 1943.

Women in Uniform. By La Verne Bradley. Vol. LXXXIV, pp. 445-458, 10 ills., Oct., 1943.

Women's Reserve of the U. S. Naval Reserve (WAVES) :

Decorations, Medals, Service Ribbons, Badges, and Women's Insignia. Vol. LXXXIV, pp. 414-444, 6 ills. in black and white, 376 ills. in color, Oct., 1943.

Women in Uniform. By La Verne Bradley. Vol. LXXXIV, pp. 445-458, 10 ills., Oct., 1943.

Women's Work in Japan. By Mary A. Nourse. Vol. LXXIII, pp. 99-132, 32 ills. in black and white, 11 ills. in color, Jan., 1938.

Wonder Island of the Amazon Delta (Marajó Island) : On Marajó Cowboys Ride Oxen, Tree-dwelling Animals Throng Dense Forests While Strange Fishes and Birds Help Make a Zoologist's Paradise. By Hugh B. Cott. Vol. LXXIV, pp. 635-670, 30 ills. in black and white, 12 ills. in color, 1 half-page map, Nov., 1938.

Wonderer Under Sea. By William Beebe. Vol. LXII, pp. 741-758, 13 ills. in black and white, 8 ills. in color, Dec., 1932.

Wonderful Canals of China. By George E. Anderson. Vol. XVI, pp. 68-69, Feb., 1905.

Wonderful Canals of China. By F. H. King. Vol. XXIII, pp. 931-958, 35 ills., 5 half-page maps, Oct., 1912.

Wonderful Strides of Africa. Vol. XVII, pp. 176-177, Mar., 1906.

Wonderland of California. By Herman Whitaker. Vol. XXVIII, pp. 56-104, 45 ills., July, 1915.

Wonderland of Glaciers and Snow (Mount Rainier National Park). By Milnor Roberts. Vol. XX, pp. 530-537, 8 ills., June, 1909.

Wonderland of Science. Vol. XXVII, pp. 153-169, 15 ills., Feb., 1915.

Wonders of the Mosi-oa-Tunga : The Falls of the Zambesi. By Louis Livingston Seaman. Vol. XXII, pp. 561-571, 6 ills., June, 1911.

Wonders of the New Washington : Efficient Modern Structures Rise in the Biggest Government Building Program Since the Capital City Was Founded in a Wilderness. By Frederick G. Vosburgh. Vol. LXVII, pp. 457-488, 20 ills. in black and white, 13 ills. in color, Apr., 1935.

Wong, Kinchue:

Changing Canton (China). 20 ills. from photographs by Siukee Mack, Alfred T. Palmer, and Kinchue Wong. Vol. LXXII, pp. 711-726, 20 ills., Dec., 1937.

Wood, Arnold:

Leach's Petrel : His Nursery on Little Duck Island. By Arnold Wood. Vol. XX, pp. 360-365, 7 ills., Apr., 1909.

Wood, Edward Frederick Lindley. *See* Halifax, Lord.

Wood, H. P.:

Hawaii for Homes. By H. P. Wood. Vol. XIX, pp. 298-299, Apr., 1908.

Wood, Junius B.:

Far Eastern Republic (U. S. S. R.). By Junius B. Wood. Vol. XLI, pp. 565-592, 29 ills., 1 three-quarters-page map, June, 1922.

Flying the World's Longest Air-Mail Route : From Montevideo, Uruguay, Over the Andes, Up the Pacific Coast, Across Central America and the Caribbean to Miami, Florida, in 67 Thrilling Flying Hours. By Junius B. Wood. Vol. LVII, pp. 261-325, 65 ills., 1 half-page map, Mar., 1930.

Wood, Junius B.—*Continued*

Illinois, Crossroads of the Continent. By Junius B. Wood. Vol. LIX, pp. 523-594, 51 ills. in black and white, 27 ills. in color, special map supplement, May, 1931.

Russia of the Hour: Giant Battleground for Theories of Economy, Society, and Politics, as Observed by an Unbiased Correspondent. By Junius B. Wood. Vol. L, pp. 519-598, 81 ills., Nov., 1926.

St. Malo (France), Ancient City of Corsairs: An Old Brittany Seaport Whose Past Bristles with Cannons and Cutlasses. By Junius B. Wood. Vol. LVI, pp. 131-177, 28 ills. in black and white, 29 ills. in color, 1 two-thirds-page map, Aug., 1929.

Seeing America from the *Shenandoah:* An Account of the Record-Making 9,000-Mile Flight from the Atlantic to the Pacific Coast and Return in the Navy's American-built, American-manned Airship. By Junius B. Wood. Vol. XLVII, pp. 1-47, 39 ills., 1 page map, 1 diagram, Jan., 1925.

Visit to Three Arab Kingdoms: Transjordania, Iraq, and the Hedjaz Present Many Problems to European Powers. By Junius B. Wood. Vol. XLIII, pp. 535-568, 30 ills., 1 three-quarters-page map, May, 1923.

Yap and Other Pacific Islands Under Japanese Mandate. By Junius B. Wood. Vol. XL, pp. 591-627, 34 ills., 1 two-page map, Dec., 1921.

Wood, (Maj. Gen.) Leonard:

In Honor of the Army and Aviation (Speech by Maj. Gen. Leonard Wood.) Vol. XXII, pp. 267-284, 1 ill., Mar., 1911.

Wood, R. W.:

Remarkable Photograph of Lilienthal's Gliding Machine. By R. W. Wood. Vol. XIX, p. 596, 1 ill., Aug., 1908.

Woodpeckers (Birds):

North American Woodpeckers. 25 ills. in color from paintings by Maj. Allan Brooks. Vol. LXIII, pp. 465-478, Apr., 1933.

Woodpeckers, Friends of Our Forests. By T. Gilbert Pearson. Paintings by Maj. Allan Brooks. Vol. LXIII, pp. 453-479, 12 ills. in black and white, 25 ills. in color, Apr., 1933.

Woods and Gardens of Portugal. By Martin Hume. Vol. XXI, pp. 883-894, 8 ills., Oct., 1910.

Woodworth, Francis:

California Says It with Wild Flowers. By Francis Woodworth. With 9 ills. in color fom natural-color photographs by B. Anthony Stewart. Vol. LXXXI, pp. 492-501, Apr., 1942.

Cologne, Key City of the Rhineland. By Francis Woodworth. Vol. LXIX, pp. 829-848, 18 ills., 1 half-page map, June, 1936.

Wool:

Beyond Australia's Cities. By W. Robert Moore. Vol. LXX, pp. 709-747, 27 ills. in black and white, 12 ills. in color, Dec., 1936.

Wool—*Continued*

Indispensable Sheep. Vol. LIII, pp. 512-528, 20 ills., Apr., 1928.

Woolf, Bella Sidney:

Fishing for Pearls in the Indian Ocean. By Bella Sidney Woolf. Vol. XLIX, pp. 161-183, 24 ills., Feb., 1926.

Woolley, C. Leonard:

Archeology, the Mirror of the Ages: Our Debt to the Humble Delvers in the Ruins at Carchemish and at Ur. By C. Leonard Woolley. Vol. LIV, pp. 207-226, 19 ills., Aug., 1928.

Worcester, Dean C.:

Field Sports Among the Wild Men of Northern Luzon. By Dean C. Worcester. Vol. XXII, pp. 215-267, 17 ills., 1 half-page map, Mar., 1911.

Head-Hunters of Northern Luzon. By Dean C. Worcester. Vol. XXIII, pp. 833-930, 102 ills., 1 page map, Sept., 1912.

Non-Christian Peoples of the Philippine Islands. By Dean C. Worcester. Vol. XXIV, pp. 1157-1256, 41 ills. in black and white, 48 ills. in color, Nov., 1913.

Philippines. 48 ills. in color from photographs by Dean C. Worcester and Charles Martin. Vol. XXIV, pp. 1161-1192, Nov., 1913.

Taal Volcano and Its Recent Destructive Eruption (Philippine Islands). By Dean C. Worcester. Vol. XXIII, pp. 313-368, 40 ills., 4 half-page maps, 1 diagram, Apr., 1912.

Work and Play in the Ozarks. 20 ills. in color from natural-color photographs by B. Anthony Stewart and J. Baylor Roberts. Vol. LXXXIII, pp. 597-620, May, 1943.

Work and War in the World of Ants. 18 ills. in color from paintings by Hashime Murayama. Vol. LXVI, pp. 179-186, Aug., 1934.

Work in the Far South. Vol. XIV, p. 109, 1 half-page chart, Mar., 1903.

Work in the Pacific Ocean of the Magnetic Survey Yacht *Galilee.* By Dr. L. A. Bauer. Vol. XVIII, pp. 601-611, 15 ills., Sept., 1907.

Work of the Bureau of American Ethnology. By W J McGee. Vol. XII, pp. 369-372, Oct., 1901.

Work of the Bureau of Insular Affairs. By Col. Clarence R. Edwards. Vol. XV, pp. 239-255, 8 ills., June, 1904.

Work of the United States Hydrographic Office. By Comdr. W. H. H. Southerland. Vol. XIV, pp. 61-75, Feb., 1903.

Work on the Isthmus. Vol. XVII, pp. 586-587, Oct., 1906.

Working Dogs:

Dogs of Duty and Devotion. By Frederick G. Vosburgh. Vol. LXXX, pp. 769-774, 3 ills., Dec., 1941.

Working Dogs—*Continued*

Other Working Dogs and the Wild Species. By Stanley P. Young. Paintings by Walter A. Weber. Vol. LXXXVI, pp. 363-384, 12 ills. in black and white, 9 ills. in color, Sept., 1944.

Wild Dogs and Working Dogs. 9 ills. in color from paintings by Walter A. Weber. Vol. LXXXVI, pp. 360 376, Sept., 1044.

Working Dogs of the World. By Freeman Lloyd. Paintings by Edward Herbert Miner. Vol. LXXX, pp. 776-806,, 12 ills. in black and white, 20 ills. in color, Dec., 1941.

Working Teak in the Burma Forests : The Sagacious Elephant Is Man's Ablest Ally in the Logging Industry of the Far East. By A. W. Smith. Vol. LVIII, pp. 239-256, 5 ills. in black and white, 15 ills. in color, Aug., 1930.

World Inside a Mountain : Aniakchak, the New Volcanic Wonderland of the Alaskan Peninsula, Is Explored. By Bernard R. Hubbard. Vol. LX, pp. 319-345, 34 ills., 1 half-page map, Sept., 1931.

World Map Articles:

Map of the Northern and Southern Hemispheres. Text accompanying special map supplement in colors. Vol. LXXXIII, pp. 481-483, Apr., 1943.

National Geographic Society's New Map of the World. Text accompanying special map supplement in colors. Vol. LXVIII, pp. 796-798, Dec., 1935.

New World Map Gives Backdrop for Headlines. Text accompanying special map supplement in colors. Vol. LXXX, pp. 741-742, 1 ill., Dec., 1941.

Society's New Map of the World. Text accompanying special map supplement in colors. Vol. XLII, p. 690, Dec., 1922.

Story of the Map. Text accompanying special map supplement in colors. Vol. LXII, pp. 759-774, 11 ills., Dec., 1932.

World That Rims the Narrowing Atlantic : Latest Ten-color Map Supplement Shows Four Continents and New Transatlantic Air Routes Which Make This Ocean Only One Day Wide. By James M. Darley. Text accompanying special map supplement in colors. Vol. LXXVI, pp. 139-142, 1 ill., July, 1939.

World War I:

Aces Among Aces. By Laurence La Tourette Driggs. Vol. XXXIII, pp. 568-580, 9 ills., June, 1918.

Aces of the Air. By Capt. Jacques De Sieyes. Vol. XXXIII, pp. 5-9, 2 ills., Jan., 1918.

America's Duty. By Newton D. Baker. Vol. XXXI, pp. 453-457, 4 ills., May, 1917.

America's Part in the Allies' Mastery of the Air. By Maj. Joseph Tulasne. Vol. XXXIII, pp. 1-5, 2 ills., Jan., 1918.

Appeal to Members of the National Geographic Society (Food Conservation). Vol. XXXIII, pp. 347-348, 2 ills., Apr., 1918.

World War I—*Continued*

Armistice Day and the American Battle Fields. By J. J. Jusserand. Vol. LVI, pp. 509-554, 32 ills. in black and white, 23 ills. in color, Nov., 1929.

Belgium : The Innocent Bystander. By William Joseph Showalter. Vol. XXVI, pp. 223-264, 36 ills., Sept., 1914.

Belgium's Plight. By John H. Gade. Vol. XXXI, pp. 433-439, 3 ills., May, 1917.

Bind the Wounds of France. By Herbert C. Hoover. Vol. XXXI, pp. 439-444, 5 ills., May, 1917.

British Take Baku. Vol. XXXIV, pp. 163-164, 1 ill., Aug., 1918.

Burden France Has Borne. By Granville Fortescue. Vol. XXXI, pp. 322-344, 19 ills., Apr., 1917.

Celebrating Christmas on the Meuse. By Capt. Clifton Lisle. Vol. XXXVI, pp. 527-537, 5 ills., Dec., 1919.

Conserving the Nation's Man Power : Disease Weakens Armies, Cripples Industry, Reduces Production. How the Government Is Sanitating the Civil Zones Around Cantonment Areas. A Nation-Wide Campaign for Health. By Rupert Blue. Vol. XXXII, pp. 254-278, 17 ills., Sept., 1917.

Cooties and Courage. By Herbert Corey. Vol. XXXIII, pp. 495-509, 10 ills., June, 1918.

Day with Our Boys in the Geographic Wards. By Carol Corey. Vol. XXXIV, pp. 69-80, 8 ills., July, 1918.

Devastated Poland. By Frederic C. Walcott. Vol. XXXI, pp. 445-452, 7 ills., May, 1917.

Do Your Bit for America : A Proclamation by President Wilson to the American People. By Woodrow Wilson. Vol. XXXI, pp. 287-293, 2 ills., Apr., 1917.

Flying in France. By Capt. André de Berroeta. Vol. XXXIII, pp. 9-26, 12 ills., Jan., 1918.

Food Armies of Liberty. By Herbert Hoover. Vol. XXXII, pp. 187-196, 6 ills., Sept., 1917.

Food for Our Allies in 1919. By Herbert Hoover. Vol. XXXIV, pp. 242-244, Sept., 1918.

Forerunners of Famine. By Frederic C. Walcott. Vol. XXXIII, pp. 336-347, 4 ills., 4 diagrams, 1 half-page map, Apr., 1918.

From the Trenches to Versailles. By Carol Corey. Vol. XXXII, pp. 535-550, 12 ills., Nov.-Dec., 1917.

Germany's Air Program. Vol. XXXIII, p. 114, Jan., 1918.

Germany's Dream of World Domination. Vol. XXXIII, pp. 559-567, 3 ills., June, 1918.

Healer of Humanity's Wounds. Vol. XXXIV, pp. 308-324, 16 ills., Oct., 1918.

Health and Morale of America's Citizen Army. By William Howard Taft. Vol. XXXIII, pp. 219-245, 22 ills., Mar., 1918.

World War I—*Continued*

Helping to Solve Our Allies' Food Problem : America Calls for a Million Young Soldiers of the Commissary to Volunteer for Service in 1918. By Ralph A. Graves. Vol. XXXIII, pp. 170-194, 23 ills., Feb., 1918.

Hospital Heroes Convict the Cootie. Vol. XXXIII, p 510, June, 1918

How Canada Went to the Front. By T. B. Macaulay. Vol. XXXIV, pp. 297-307, 6 ills., Oct., 1918.

Immediate Necessity for Military Highways. By A. G. Batchelder. Vol. XXXII, pp. 477-499, 22 ills., Nov.-Dec., 1917.

In French Lorraine : That Part of France Where the First American Soldiers Have Fallen. By Harriet Chalmers Adams. Vol. XXXII, pp. 499-518, 16 ills., Nov.-Dec., 1917.

Italy's Eagles of Combat and Defense : Heroic Achievements of Aviators Above the Adriatic, the Apennines, and the Alps. By Gen. P. Tozzi. Vol. XXXIII, pp. 38-47, 8 ills., Jan., 1918.

Letters from the Italian Front. By Marchesa Louise de Rosales to Ethel Mather Bagg. Vol. XXXI, pp. 46-67, 22 ills., July, 1917.

Life Story of an American Airman in France : Extracts from the Letters of Stuart Walcott, Who, Between July and December, 1917, Learned to Fly in French Schools of Aviation, Won Fame at the Front, and Fell Near Saint Souplet. Vol. XXXIII, pp. 86-106, 9 ills., Jan., 1918.

National Geographic Society in War Time. By Maj. Gen. A. W. Greely. Vol. XXXIII, pp. 369-375, 5 ills., Apr., 1918.

National Geographic Society's Memorial to American Troops : Fountain and Water Supply System Presented to Historic French Town of Cantigny, Where Our Overseas Soldiers Won Their First Victory in the World War. Vol. XLIV, pp. 675-678, 4 ills., Dec., 1923.

National Geographic War Zone Map. Text accompanying special map supplement. Vol. XXXIII, p. 494, May, 1918.

Needs Abroad. By Ian Malcolm. Vol. XXXI, pp. 427-433, 5 ills., May, 1917.

New Map of Europe : Showing the Boundaries Established by the Peace Conference at Paris and by Subsequent Decisions of the Supreme Council of the Allied and Associated Powers. By Ralph A. Graves. Text accompanying special map supplement in colors. Vol. XXXIX, pp. 157-177, 18 ills., Feb., 1921.

North Sea Mine Barrage. By Capt. Reginald R. Belknap. Vol. XXXV, pp. 85-110, 23 ills., 1 page map, 1 diagram, Feb., 1919.

Old Jewel in the Proper Setting : An Eyewitness' Account of the Reconquest of the Holy Land by Twentieth Century Crusaders. By Charles W. Whitehair. Vol. XXXIV, pp. 325-344, 14 ills., Oct., 1918.

On the Monastir Road. By Herbert Corey. Vol. XXXI, pp. 383-412, 31 ills., May, 1917.

Our Armies of Mercy (American National Red Cross). By Henry P. Davison. Vol. XXXI, pp. 423-427, 3 ills., May, 1917.

World War I—*Continued*

Our National War Memorials in Europe. By Gen. John J. Pershing. Vol. LXV, pp. 1-36, 24 ills. in black and white, 11 ills. in color, 1 half-page map, Jan., 1934.

Our Second Alliance. By J. J. Jusserand. Vol. XXXI, pp. 565-566, 1 ill., June, 1917.

Outspeaking of a Great Democracy. The Proceedings of the Chamber of Deputies of France on Friday, April 6, 1917, As Reported in the "Journal Officiel de La République Française." Vol. XXXI, pp. 362-365, 1 ill., Apr., 1917.

Plain Tales from the Trenches : As Told Over the Tea Table in Blighty—A Soldier's "Home" in Paris. By Carol Corey. Vol. XXXIII, pp. 300-312, 7 ills., Mar., 1918.

Poisoned World. By William Howard Taft. Vol. XXXI, pp. 459-467, 7 ills., May, 1917.

Practical Patriotism (National Geographic Society's War Work). Vol. XXXII, pp. 279-280, Sept., 1917.

Price of Liberty, Equality, Fraternity. Vol. XXXIV, p. 377, Nov., 1918.

Prussianism. By Robert Lansing. Vol. XXXIII, pp. 546-557, 5 ills., June, 1918.

Removal of the North Sea Mine Barrage. By Lieut. Comdr. Noel Davis. Vol. XXXV, pp. 103-133, 28 ills., 2 half-page maps, Feb., 1920.

Russia from Within : Her War of Yesterday, Today, and Tomorrow. By Stanley Washburn. Vol. XXXII, pp. 91-120, 30 ills., Aug., 1917.

Russian Situation and Its Significance to America. By Stanley Washburn. Vol. XXXI, pp. 371-382, 8 ills., Apr., 1917.

Russia's Man of the Hour : Alexander Kerensky's First Speeches and Proclamations. Vol. XXXII, pp. 24-45, 17 ills., July, 1917.

Shopping Abroad for Our Armies in France. By Herbert Corey. Vol. XXXIII, pp. 206-218, 6 ills., Feb., 1918.

Spirit of The Geographic. Vol. XXXIV, pp. 434-440, 4 ills., Nov., 1918.

Stand by the Soldier. By Gen. John J. Pershing. Vol. XXXI, pp. 457-459, 1 ill., May, 1917.

Tales of the British Air Service. By Maj. William A. Bishop. Vol. XXXIII, pp. 27-37, 12 ills., Jan., 1918.

Three Drawings of the World War. 3 ills. from drawings by Lucien Jonas. Vol. XXXIII, pp. 355-357, Apr., 1918.

Ties That Bind : Our Natural Sympathy with English Traditions, the French Republic, and the Russian Outburst for Liberty. By John Sharp Williams. Vol. XXXI, pp. 281-286, 4 ills., Mar., 1917.

"Time Will Not Dim the Glory of Their Deeds." 11 ills. in color from natural-color photographs by W. Robert Moore. Vol. LXV, pp. 17-24, Jan., 1934.

Transporting a Navy Through the Jungles of Africa in War Time. By Frank J. Magee. Vol. XLII, pp. 331-362, 31 ills., Oct., 1922.

World War I—*Continued*

Tribute to America. By Herbert Henry Asquith. Vol. XXXI, pp. 294-296, 2 ills., Apr., 1917.

War, Patriotism, and the Food Supply. By Frederick V. Coville. Vol. XXXI, pp. 254-256, Mar., 1917.

Weapon of Food. By Herbert Hoover. Vol. XXXII, pp. 197-212, 15 ills., Sept., 1917.

What Great Britain Is Doing. By Sydney Brooks. Vol. XXXI, pp. 193-210, 7 ills., Mar., 1917.

What the War Has Done for Britain. By Judson C. Welliver. Vol. XXXIV, pp. 278-297, 13 ills., Oct., 1918.

World War II:

Aboard a Blimp Hunting U-Boats: A Day above the Atlantic Reveals Navy Talk and Navy Ways, Creeping Convoys, and Torpedoed Wrecks. By Mason Sutherland. Vol. LXXXIV, pp. 79-96, 18 ills., July, 1943.

Aerial Invasion of Burma. By Gen. H. H. Arnold. Vol. LXXXVI, pp. 129-148, 20 ills., Aug., 1944.

America Fights on the Farms. 21 ills. in color from natural-color photographs. Vol. LXXXVI, pp. 33-48, July, 1944.

American Bombers Attacking from Australia. By Howell Walker. Vol. LXXXIII, pp. 49-70, 19 ills., 1 map (two-page spread), Jan., 1943.

American Industries Geared for War. By Thornton Oakley. With 16 ills. in color from paintings by the author. Vol. LXXXII, pp. 716-734, 1 ill. in black and white, Dec., 1942.

American Soldier in Reykjavík. By Corporal Luther M. Chovan. Vol. LXXXVIII, pp. 536-568, 6 ills. in black and white, 34 ills. in color, Nov., 1945.

American Transportation Vital to Victory. By Thornton Oakley. With 16 ills. in color from paintings by the author. Vol. LXXXIV, pp. 671-688, Dec., 1943.

American Wings Soar Around the World: Epic Story of the Air Transport Command of the U. S. Army Is a Saga of Yankee Daring and Doing. By Donald H. Agnew and William A. Kinney. Vol. LXXXIV, pp. 57-78, 22 ills., July, 1943.

Americans Help Liberated Europe Live Again. By Lt. Col. Frederick Simpich, Jr. Vol. LXXXVII, pp. 747-768, 17 ills., June, 1945.

Americans on the Barbary Coast. By Willard Price. Vol. LXXXIV, pp. 1-31, 13 ills. in black and white, 10 ills. in color, 1 map (two-page spread), July, 1943.

Ancient Iceland, New Pawn of War. 21 ills. from photographs, 1 page map. Vol. LXXX, pp. 75-90, July, 1941.

Animals Were Allies, Too. 16 ills. from photographs. Vol. LXXXIX, pp. 75-88, Jan., 1946.

As 2,000 Ships Are Born. By Frederick Simpich. Vol. LXXXI, pp. 551-588, 34 ills., May, 1942.

World War II—*Continued*

At Ease in the South Seas. By Maj. Frederick Simpich, Jr., Vol. LXXXV, pp. 79-104, 32 ills., Jan., 1944.

Battleship *Missouri* Comes of Age. 11 ills. in color from U. S. Navy official photographs. Vol. LXXXVII, pp. 353-360, Mar., 1945.

Behind the Lines in Italy. By Corporal Macon Reed, Jr. Vol. LXXXVI, pp. 109-128, 20 ills., July, 1944.

"Blood, Toil, Tears, and Sweat": An American Tells the Story of Britain's War Effort, Summed up in Prime Minister Churchill's Unflinching Words. By Harvey Klemmer. Vol. LXXXII, pp. 141-166, 19 ills., Aug., 1942.

Britain Fights in the Fields. By Francis A. Flood. Vol. LXXXVI, pp. 31-65, 17 ills. in black and white, 21 ills. in color, July, 1944.

Canada's War Effort: A Canadian Pictures the Swift and Sweeping Transformation from a Peaceful Dominion to a Nation Geared for War. By Bruce Hutchison. Vol. LXXX, pp. 553-590, 40 ills., Nov., 1941.

China Opens Her Wild West: In the Mountain-girt Heart of a Continent a New China Has Been Created During the Years of War. By Owen Lattimore. Vol. LXXXII, pp. 337-367, 21 ills. in black and white, 11 ills. in color, 1 map (two-page spread), Sept., 1942.

A City Learns to Smile Again (Nancy, France). By Maj. Frederick G. Vosburgh. Vol. LXXXVII, pp. 361-384, 23 ills., 1 two-thirds-page map, Mar., 1945.

A City That Refused to Die (Plymouth, England). By Harvey Klemmer. Vol. LXXXIX, pp. 211-236, 13 ills. in black and white, 9 ills. in color, 1 half-page map, Feb., 1946.

Convoys to Victory. By Harvey Klemmer. Vol. LXXXIII, pp. 193-216, 24 ills., Feb., 1943.

Crimea Reborn. By Eddy Gilmore. Vol. LXXXVII, pp. 487-512, 23 ills., 1 half-page map, Apr., 1945.

Cruise on an Escort Carrier. By Melville Bell Grosvenor. Vol. LXXXIV, pp. 513-546, 14 ills. in black and white, 20 ills. in color, Nov., 1943.

Demolishing Germany's North Sea Ramparts (Helgoland). By Stuart E. Jones. Vol. XC, pp. 635-644, 1 ill. in black and white, 10 ills. in color, Nov., 1946.

8th Air Force in England. 10 ills. in color from U. S. Army Air Forces photographs. Vol. LXXXVII, pp. 297-304, Mar., 1945.

Europe's Looted Art. By John Walker. Vol. LXXXIX, pp. 39-52, 11 ills., Jan., 1946.

Everyday Life in Wartime England. By Harvey Klemmer. Vol. LXXIX, pp. 497-534, 48 ills., Apr., 1941.

Facing War's Challenge "Down Under" (Australia and New Zealand). 20 ills. in color from natural-color photographs by Howell Walker. Vol. LXXXI, pp. 425-456, Apr., 1942.

World War II—*Continued*

Fiji Patrol on Bougainville. By David D. Duncan. Vol. LXXXVII, pp. 87-104, 9 ills. in black and white, 11 ills. in color, Jan., 1945.

Flying Our Wounded Veterans Home. By Catherine Bell Palmer. Vol. LXXXVIII, pp. 363-384, 17 ills., Sept., 1945.

French West Africa in Wartime. By Paul M. Atkins. Vol. LXXXI, pp. 371-408, 37 ills., 2 maps, Mar., 1942.

From Africa to the Alps. 8 ills. in color from U. S. Army Air Forces photographs. Vol. LXXXIX, pp. 161-168, Feb., 1946.

Front-line Town of Britain's Siege (Dover). By Harvey Klemmer. Vol. LXXXV, pp. 105-128, 21 ills., Jan., 1944.

Gilbert Islands in the Wake of Battle. By W. Robert Moore. Vol. LXXXVII, pp. 129-162, 11 ills. in black and white, 19 ills. in color, 1 two-thirds-page map, Feb., 1945.

Gliders—Silent Weapons of the Sky. By William H. Nicholas. Vol. LXXXVI, pp. 149-160, 8 ills., Aug., 1944.

Greens Grow for GI's on Soilless Ascension. By W. Robert Moore. Vol. LXXXVIII, pp. 219-230, 12 ills., Aug., 1945.

Gulf Coast Towns Get into the Fight. 19 ills. in color from natural-color photographs; 17 ills. by J. Baylor Roberts. Vol. LXXXV, pp. 17-40, Jan., 1944.

Healing Arts in Global War : As Weapons Grow Deadlier. Scientific Medicine Pits Its Ever-rising Skill Against Them. By Albert W. Atwood. Vol. LXXXIV, pp. 599-618, 17 ills., Nov., 1943.

Heroes of Wartime Science and Mercy. By Elizabeth W. King. Vol. LXXXIV, pp. 715-740, 11 ills. in black and white, 334 ills. in color, Dec., 1943.

Heroes' Return. By William H. Nicholas. Vol. LXXXVII, pp. 333-352, 19 ills., Mar., 1945.

Holland Rises from War and Water. By Thomas R. Henry. Vol. LXXXIX, pp. 237-260, 18 ills., 1 seven-eighths-page map, Feb., 1946.

How We Fight with Photographs. By F. Barrows Colton. Vol. LXXXVI, pp. 257-280, 22 ills., Sept., 1944.

How We Use the Gulf of Mexico. By Frederick Simpich. Vol. LXXXV, pp. 1-40, 20 ills. in black and white, 19 ills. in color, 1 map (two-page spread), Jan., 1944.

India's Treasures Helped the Allies. By John Fischer. Vol. LXXXIX, pp. 501-522, 18 ills., Apr., 1946.

Infantrymen—The Fighters of War. By Brig. Gen. W. H. Wilbur. Vol. LXXXVI, pp. 513-538, 22 ills., Nov., 1944.

Japan Faces Russia in Manchuria. By Willard Price. Vol. LXXXII, pp. 603-634, 30 ills., 1 page map, Nov., 1942.

Jungle War : Bougainville and New Caledonia. 17 ills. in color from paintings by Lieut. William F. Draper. Vol. LXXXV, pp. 417-432, Apr., 1944.

World War II—*Continued*

Landing Craft for Invasion. By Melville Bell Grosvenor. Vol. LXXXVI, pp. 1-30, 26 ills., July, 1944.

Lend-Lease and the Russian Victory. By Harvey Klemmer. Vol. LXXXVIII, pp. 499-512, 6 ills., Oct., 1945.

Lend Lease Is a Two-way Benefit : Innovation in Creative Statesmanship Pools Resources of United Nations, and Supplies American Forces Around the World. By Francis Flood. Vol. LXXXIII, pp. 745-761, 14 ills., June, 1943.

Liberated Ukraine. By Eddy Gilmore. Vol. LXXXV, pp. 513-536, 22 ills., 1 page map, May, 1944.

Life Grows Grim in Singapore. By H. Gordon Minnigerode. Vol. LXXX, pp. 661-686, 17 ills. in black and white, 9 ills. in color, 1 half-page map, Nov., 1941.

Life in Dauntless Darwin : A National Geographic Staff Writer Gives a Vivid Description of the Australian Town That Guards the Continent's Northern Door. By Howell Walker. Vol. LXXXII, pp. 123-138, 17 ills., 1 sixth-page map, July, 1942.

Life on the Hawaii "Front" : All-out Defense and Belt Tightening of Pacific Outpost Foreshadow the Things to Come on Mainland. By Lieut. Frederick Simpich, Jr. Vol. LXXXII, pp. 541-560, 19 ills., 1 half-page map, Oct., 1942.

Lisbon—Gateway to Warring Europe. By Harvey Klemmer. Vol. LXXX, pp. 259-276, 18 ills., Aug., 1941.

London Wins the Battle. By Marquis W. Childs. Vol. LXXXVIII, pp. 129-152, 21 ills., Aug., 1945.

Making of an Anzac. By Howell Walker. Vol. LXXXI, pp. 409-456, 31 ills. in black and white, 20 ills. in color, 1 two-page map, Apr., 1942.

Malta Invicta. By Bartimeus (A Captain in the Royal Navy). Vol. LXXXIII, pp. 375-400, 27 ills., 1 half-page map, Mar., 1943.

Mediterranean Checkerboard. By Frederick Simpich. Vol. LXXXI, pp. 527-550, 20 ills., 1 map (two-page spread), Apr., 1942.

Metal Sinews of Strength : This Is a War of Many Metals, for We Live in an Age of Alloys. By Frederick G. Vosburgh. Vol. LXXXI, pp. 457-491, 35 ills., Apr., 1942.

Michigan Fights. By Harvey Klemmer. Vol. LXXXVI, pp. 677-715, 20 ills. in black and white, 19 ills. in color, 1 page-and-a-half map, Dec., 1944.

Mindanao, on the Road to Tokyo. By Frederick Simpich. Vol. LXXXVI, pp. 539-574, 26 ills. in black and white, 12 ills. in color, 1 two-page map, Nov., 1944.

Miracle of War Production : For Victory the United States Transforms Its Complex Industry into the Biggest Factory and Mightiest Arsenal the World Has Ever Known. By Albert W. Atwood. Paintings by Thornton Oakley. Vol. LXXXII, pp. 693-715, 17 ills. in black and white, 16 ills. in color, Dec., 1942.

World War II—*Continued*

Navy Artist Paints the Aleutians. By Mason Sutherland. Paintings by Lt. William F. Draper. Vol. LXXXIV, pp. 157-176, 4 ills. in black and white, 16 ills. in color, Aug., 1943.

Navy Wings over the Pacific. 12 ills. in color from U. S. Navy official photographs. Vol. LXXXVI, pp. 241-248, Aug., 1944.

New Map of Europe and the Near East. Text accompanying special map supplement in colors. Vol. LXXXIII, pp. 762-763, 1 ill., June, 1943.

New Queen of the Seas (Aircraft Carrier). By Melville Bell Grosvenor. Vol. LXXXII, pp. 1-30, 27 ills., 1 drawing, 1 two-page map, July, 1942.

Newfoundland, North Atlantic Rampart: From the "First Base of American Defense" Planes Fly to Britain's Aid over Stout Fishing Schooners of the Grand Banks. By George Whiteley, Jr. Vol. LXXX, pp. 111-140, 26 ills., 1 two-thirds-page map, July, 1941.

Normandy's Made-in-England Harbors. Vol. LXXXVII, pp. 565-580, 16 ills., 1 quarter-page map, May, 1945.

Norway, an Active Ally. By William Morgenstierne. Vol. LXXXIII, pp. 333-357, 24 ills., 1 two-thirds-page map, Mar., 1943.

Oil for Victory Piped under the Sea. 9 ills. from photographs. Vol. LXXXVIII, pp. 721-726, Dec., 1945.

Okinawa, Threshold to Japan. By Lt. David D. Duncan, USMC. With 22 ills. in color from natural-color photographs by the author and others. Vol. LXXXVIII, pp. 411-428, Oct., 1945.

Our Global Strong Arm. 10 ills. in color from U. S. Army Air Forces official photographs. Vol. LXXXIX, pp. 145-152, Feb., 1946.

Painting History in the Pacific. 19 ills. in color from paintings by Lt. William F. Draper. Vol. LXXXVI, pp. 409-424, Oct., 1944.

Palms and Planes in the New Hebrides. By Maj. Robert D. Heinl, Jr. Vol. LXXXVI, pp. 229-256, 17 ills. in black and white, 12 ills. in color, 1 four-fifths-page map, Aug., 1944.

Paris Delivered. 10 ills. from photographs. Vol. LXXXVII, pp. 79-86, Jan., 1945.

Paris Freed. By Maj. Frederick Simpich, Jr. Vol. LXXXVII, pp. 385-412, 14 ills. in black and white, 12 ills. in color, Apr., 1945.

Paris Lives Again. By M. O. Williams. Vol. XC, pp. 767-790, 24 ills., Dec., 1946.

People's Fight Against Slavery. By Hon. Henry A. Wallace. Reprint of address delivered at a dinner of the Free World Association, May 8, 1942. Vol. LXXXII, pp. 276-280, 1 ill., Aug., 1942.

Pocket Carriers Fight the Submarines. 20 ills. in color from U. S. Navy official photographs. Vol. LXXXIV, pp. 521-544, Nov., 1943.

QM, the Fighting Storekeeper. By Frederick Simpich. Paintings by Arthur Beaumont. Vol. LXXXII, pp. 561-600, 22 ills. in black and white, 16 ills. in color, Nov., 1942.

World War II—*Continued*

Red Cross Girl Overseas. By Margaret Cotter. Vol. LXXXVI, pp. 745-768, 22 ills., Dec., 1944.

Rehearsal at Dieppe (France). By W. Robert Moore. Vol. LXXXII, pp. 495-502, 6 ills., Oct., 1942.

Return to Florence (Italy). By 1st Lt. Benjamin C. McCartney. Vol. LXXXVII, pp. 257-296, 18 ills. in black and white, 18 ills. in color, Mar., 1945.

Round About Grim Tarawa. 19 ills. in color from natural-color photographs by W. Robert Moore. Vol. LXXXVII, pp. 137-160, Feb., 1945.

Rural Britain Carries On. By Harvey Klemmer. Vol. LXXX, pp. 527-552, 27 ills., Oct., 1941.

Saga of the Carrier *Princeton*. By Capt. William H. Buracker, USN. Vol. LXXXVIII, pp. 189-218, 8 ills. in black and white, 22 ills. in color, 1 map (two-page spread), Aug., 1945.

Saipan and Tinian, Take-offs to Tokyo. 17 ills. in color from natural-color photographs; 15 ills. by W. Robert Moore. Vol. LXXXVII, pp. 453-468, Apr., 1945.

San Diego Can't Believe It. By Frederick Simpich. Vol. LXXXI, pp. 45-80, 26 ills. in black and white, 9 ills. in color, Jan., 1942.

San Francisco: Gibraltar of the West Coast. By La Verne Bradley. Vol. LXXXIII, pp. 279-308, 28 ills., Mar., 1943.

Scotland in Wartime. By Isobel Wylie Hutchison. Vol. LXXXIII, pp. 723-743, 19 ills., June, 1943.

Seeing Paris on a 48-Hour Pass. 12 ills. in color from U. S. Army official photographs. Vol. LXXXVII, pp. 401-412, Apr., 1945.

Ships That Won the Greatest Naval War. 26 ills. in color from U. S. Navy official photographs. Vol. LXXXIX, pp. 697-736, June, 1946.

South from Saipan. By W. Robert Moore. Vol. LXXXVII, pp. 441-474, 11 ills. in black and white, 17 ills. in color, 1 half-page map, Apr., 1945.

Springboards to Tokyo. By Willard Price. Vol. LXXXVI, pp. 385-407, 16 ills., Oct., 1944.

Sydney Faces the War Front Down Under. By Howell Walker. Vol. LXXXIII, pp. 359-374, 8 ills. in black and white, 10 ills. in color, Mar., 1943.

Take-off for Japan. 22 ills. in color from U. S. Navy official photographs. Vol. LXXXVIII, pp. 193-208, Aug., 1945.

A Tale of Three Cities (Prague, Vienna, Budapest). By Thomas R. Henry. Vol. LXXXVIII, pp. 641-669, 23 ills., Dec., 1945.

They Sustain the Wings (Ground Crews). By Frederick Simpich. Vol. LXXXIV, pp. 333-354, 19 ills., Sept., 1943.

This Is My Own: How the United States Seems to a Citizen Soldier Back from Three Years Overseas. By Frederick G. Vosburgh. Vol. LXXXIX, pp. 113-128, 14 ills., Jan., 1946.

World War II—*Continued*

Today on the China Coast. By John B. Powell. Vol. LXXXVII, pp. 217-238, 17 ills., 1 page map, Feb., 1945.

Victory's Portrait in the Marianas. By Lt. William Franklin Draper, USNR. With 17 ills. in color from paintings by the author. Vol. LXXXVIII, pp. 599-616, Nov., 1945.

War Meets Peace in Egypt. By Grant Parr and G. E. Janssen. Vol. LXXXI, pp. 503-526, 25 ills., 1 page map, Apr., 1942.

War's Wake in the Rhineland. By Thomas R. Henry. Vol. LXXXVIII, pp. 1-32, 29 ills., 1 third-page map, July, 1945.

Wartime in the Pacific Northwest (United States and Canada). By Frederick Simpich. Vol. LXXXII, pp. 421-464, 25 ills. in black and white, 23 ills. in color, 1 half-page map, Oct., 1942.

What Luzon Means to Uncle Sam. By Frederick Simpich. Vol. LXXXVII, pp. 305-332, 25 ills., special map supplement, Mar., 1945.

What the Fighting Yanks See. By Wanda Burnett. Vol. LXXXVI, pp. 451-476, 27 ills., Oct., 1944.

When GI Joes Took London. By Maj. Frederick Simpich, Jr., Vol. LXXXVI, pp. 337-354, 18 ills., Sept., 1944.

White War in Norway. By Thomas R. Henry. Vol. LXXXVIII, pp. 617-640, 23 ills., 1 three-quarters-page map, Nov., 1945.

Winning the War of Supply. By F. Barrows Colton. Vol. LXXXVIII, pp. 705-736, 23 ills., Dec., 1945.

Women at Work. By La Verne Bradley. Vol. LXXXVI, pp. 193-220, 23 ills., Aug., 1944.

Women in Uniform. By La Verne Bradley. Vol. LXXXIV, pp. 445-458, 10 ills., Oct., 1943.

Yank Meets Native. By Wanda Burnett. Vol. LXXXVIII, pp. 105-128, 24 ills., July, 1945.

Yanks in Northern Ireland. 15 ills. from photographs. Vol. LXXXIV, pp. 191-204, Aug., 1943.

Your Navy as Peace Insurance. By Fleet Admiral Chester W. Nimitz. Vol. LXXXIX, pp. 681-736, 32 ills. in black and white, 26 ills. in color, June, 1946.

Your Society Aids War Effort. Vol. LXXXIII, pp. 277-278, 1 ill., Feb., 1943.

See also articles of the war years (1939-1945) under the following headings: Alaska; Aleutian Islands; Algeria; Baja California; Belgium; Borneo; Brazil; China; Fiji Islands; Gilbert Islands; Greenland; Insignia; Iran; Japan; Java; Madagascar; Manipur (State), India; Map Articles; Marseille; Micronesia; Morocco; Netherlands; New Caledonia; New Guinea; Philippine Islands; Ryukyu Retto; Sicily; Solomon Islands; Timor; Tunisia; Union of Soviet Socialist Republics; U. S. Army; U. S. Army Air Forces; U. S. Army Engineers; U. S. Army Map Service; U. S. Army Quartermaster Corps; U. S. Army

World War II *Continued*

Signal Corps; U. S. Coast Guard; U. S. Defense Bases; U. S. Marine Corps; U. S. Navy; War Agencies; West Indies.

World's Ancient Porcelain Center (Kingtehchen, China). By Frank B. Lenz. Vol. XXXVIII, pp. 391-406, 11 ills., Nov., 1920.

World's Debt to France. Vol. XXVIII, pp. 491-501, 7 ills., Nov., 1915.

World's Great Waterfalls: Visits to Mighty Niagara, Wonderful Victoria, and Picturesque Iguazu. By Theodore W. Noyes. Vol. L, pp. 29-59, 29 ills., July, 1926.

World's Greatest Overland Explorer: How Marco Polo Penetrated Farthest Asia, "Discovered" Many Lands Unknown to Europe, and Added Numerous Minerals, Animals, Birds, and Plants to Man's Knowledge. By J. R. Hildebrand. Vol. LIV, pp. 505-568, 53 ills., 1 two-page map, Nov., 1928.

World's Greatest Waterfall; The Kaieteur Fall, in British Guiana. By Leonard Kennedy. Vol. XXII, pp. 846-859, 6 ills., 1 page map, Sept., 1911.

World's Highest Altitudes and First Ascents. By Charles E. Fay. Vol. XX, pp. 493-530, 25 ills., June, 1909.

World's Highest International Telephone Cable. Vol. LVIII, pp. 722-731, 8 ills., Dec., 1930.

World's Largest Free Balloon to Explore Stratosphere. Vol. LXVI, pp. 107-110, 2 ills., July, 1934.

World's Most Cruel Earthquake (Messina, Sicily). By Charles W. Wright. Vol. XX, pp. 373-396, 22 ills., 1 page and 1 three-quarters-page maps, Apr., 1909.

World's Production of Gold (From an Address to the American Bankers' Convention, by F. A. Vanderlip, October 11, 1905). Vol. XVI, pp. 571-572, Dec., 1905.

World's Strangest Capital (Lhasa, Tibet). By John Claude White. Vol. XXIX, pp. 273-295, 19 ills., panorama, Mar., 1916.

World's Words. By William H. Nicholas. Vol. LXXXIV, pp. 689-700, 8 ills., 1 two-page map, Dec., 1943.

Worm Turns. By Samuel Sandrof. Vol. LXXXIX, pp. 775-786, 14 ills., June, 1946.

Worms, Marine:

The Worm Turns. By Samuel Sandrof. Vol. LXXXIX, pp. 775-786, 14 ills., June, 1946.

Wounded, Evacuation of. *See* Air Evacuation of Wounded.

Wrangell Mountains, Alaska:

Wrangell Mountains. By Walter C. Mendenhall. Vol. XIV, pp. 395-407, 3 ills., panorama, Nov., 1903.

Wrangell Mountains, Alaska—*Continued*

Wrangell Mountains. Panorama taken by W. C. Mendenhall from the ridge east of the Dadina River. Vol. XIV, supplement, Nov., 1903.

Wrens:

Fairy Wrens of Australia : The Little Long-tailed "Blue Birds of Happiness" Rank High Among the Island Continent's Remarkable Birds. By Neville W. Cayley. With 8 ills. in color from paintings by the author. Vol. LXXXVIII, pp. 488-498, 1 ill. in black and white, Oct., 1945.

Pastel Wrens from "Down Under." 8 ills. in color from paintings by N. W. Cayley. Vol. LXXXVIII, pp. 489-496, Oct., 1945.

Winged Denizens of Woodland, Stream, and Marsh. By Alexander Wetmore. Paintings by Maj. Allan Brooks. Vol. LXV, pp. 577-596, 10 portraits in color, May, 1934.

Wright, Charles W.:

World's Most Cruel Earthquake (Messina, Sicily). By Charles W. Wright. Vol. XX, pp. 373-396, 22 ills., 1 page and 1 three-quarters-page maps, Apr., 1909.

Wright, Helen Dunstan:

Little-Known Sardinia. By Helen Dunstan Wright. Vol. XXX, pp. 97-120, 23 ills., 1 page map, Aug., 1916.

Wright, Marie Robinson:

Falls of Iguazu. By Marie Robinson Wright. Vol. XVII, pp. 456-460, 4 ills., Aug., 1906.

Wright, Orville and Wilbur:

Air Conquest: From the Early Days of Giant Kites and Birdlike Gliders, the National Geographic Society Has Aided and Encouraged the Growth of Aviation. Vol. LII, pp. 233-242, 13 ills., Aug., 1927.

In Honor of the Army and Aviation (Speech by Wilbur Wright). Vol. XXII, pp. 267-284, 1 ill., Mar., 1911.

Wright Field, Ohio :

New Frontier in the Sky. By F. Barrows Colton. Vol. XC, pp. 379-408, 28 ills., 1 diagram, Sept., 1946.

Wulsin, Frederick R.:

Road to Wang Ye Fu : An Account of the Work of the National Geographic Society's Central-China Expedition in the Mongol Kingdom of Ala Shan. By Frederick R. Wulsin. Vol. XLIX, pp. 197-234, 44 ills., 1 third-page map, Feb., 1926.

Württemberg (Region), Germany :

Corner of Old Württemberg. By B. H. Buxton. Vol. XXII, pp. 931-947, 17 ills., 1 half-page map, Oct., 1911.

Wyeth, N. C.:

Caravels of Columbus. Reproduction in color of the painting by N. C. Wyeth, National Geographic Society, Washington, D. C. Vol. LIV, text, p. 55 ; supplement, July, 1928.

Wyeth, N. C.—*Continued*

Commander Byrd at the North Pole. Reproduction in color of the painting by N. C. Wyeth, National Geographic Society, Washington, D. C. Vol. LIII, supplement, May, 1928.

The Discoverer. Reproduction in color of the painting by N. C. Wyeth, National Geographic Society, Washington, D. C. Vol. LIII, text, p. 347 ; supplement, Mar., 1928.

Map of Discovery (Eastern Hemisphere). Reproduction in color of the painting by N. C. Wyeth, National Geographic Society, Washington, D. C. Vol. LIV, text, p. 568 ; supplement, Nov., 1928.

Map of Discovery (Western Hemisphere). Reproduction in color of the painting by N. C. Wyeth, National Geographic Society, Washington, D. C. Vol. LV, text, p. 93 ; supplement, Jan., 1929.

Wyllie, (Col.) Robert E.:

American Decorations and Insignia of Honor and Service. By Col. Robert E. Wyllie. Vol. XXXVI, pp. 502-526, 6 ills. in black and white, 119 ills. in color, Dec., 1919.

Romance of Military Insignia : How the United States Government Recognizes Deeds of Heroism and Devotion to Duty. By Col. Robert E. Wyllie. Vol. XXXVI, pp. 463-501, 27 ills., Dec., 1919.

Wyoming:

Bighorn Mountains. By N. H. Darton. Vol. XVIII, pp. 355-364, 7 ills., 1 page map, June, 1907.

Call of the West. By C. J. Blanchard. Vol. XX, pp. 403-437, 20 ills., 1 half-page map, May, 1909.

"Compleat Angler" Fishes for Fossils. By Imogene Powell. Vol. LXVI, pp. 251-258, 7 ills., Aug., 1934.

Fabulous Yellowstone : Even Stranger Than the Tales of Early Trappers is the Truth About This Steaming Wonderland. By Frederick G. Vosburgh. Vol. LXXVII, pp. 769-794, 15 ills. in black and white, 9 ills. in color, 1 two-thirds-page map, June, 1940.

Grass Makes Wyoming Fat. By Frederick Simpich. Vol. LXXXVIII, pp. 153-188, 13 ills. in black and white, 19 ills. in color, 1 two-page map, Aug., 1945.

Hunting Bears on Horseback. By Alan D. Wilson. Vol. XIX, pp. 350-356, 4 ills., May, 1908.

Land of the Best. By Gilbert H. Grosvenor. Vol. XXIX, pp. 327-430, 71 ills. in black and white, 33 ills. in color, panorama, Apr., 1916.

Our National Parks. By L. F. Schmeckebier. Vol. XXIII, pp. 531-579, 41 ills., 1 page map, June, 1912.

Wyoming—Continued

Welcome to Wyoming. 19 ills. in color from natural-color photographs ; 18 ills. by B. Anthony Stewart. Vol. LXXXVIII, pp. 161-184, Aug., 1945.

Where Hot Pools Seethe and Geysers Spout (Yellowstone). 9 ills. in color from natural-color photographs by Edwin L. Wisherd. Vol. LXXVII, pp. 775-782, June, 1940.

Wild Animals That Took Their Own Pictures by Day and by Night. By George Shiras 3d. Vol. XXIV, pp. 763-834, 68 ills., 1 page map, July, 1913.

Wyoming Fossil Fields Expedition of July, 1899. By Wilbur C. Knight. Vol. XI, pp. 449-465, 8 ills., Dec., 1900.

X

Xochimilco (Lake), Mexico:

Venice of Mexico (Aztec Lake Country). By Walter Hough. Vol. XXX, pp. 69-88, 18 ills., July, 1916.

Y

Yachts:

Most Curious Craft Afloat : The Compass in Navigation and the Work of the Non-Magnetic Yacht Carnegie. By Dr. L. A. Bauer. Vol. XXI, pp. 223-245, 31 ills., Mar., 1910.

Sailing the Seven Seas in the Interest of Science : Adventures Through 157,000 Miles of Storm and Calm, from Arctic to Antarctic and Around the World, in the Non-Magnetic Yacht Carnegie. By J. P. Ault. Vol. XLII, pp. 613-690, 47 ills., 1 chart, Dec., 1922.

See also Physalia; Pilgrim.

Yahgans (Indians) :

Indian Tribes of Southern Patagonia, Tierra del Fuego, and the Adjoining Islands. By J. B. Hatcher. Vol. XII, pp. 12-22, 4 ills., Jan., 1901.

Inside Cape Horn. By Amos Burg. Vol. LXXII, pp. 743-783, 29 ills. in black and white, 10 ills. in color, 1 two-page map, Dec., 1937.

Yakutat Bay, Alaska :

National Geographic Society's Alaskan Expedition of 1909. By Ralph S. Tarr and Lawrence Martin. Vol. XXI, pp. 1-54, 42 ills., 4 page and 7 half-page maps, Jan., 1910.

Yakuts (People) :

New Road to Asia. By Owen Lattimore. Vol. LXXXVI, pp. 641-676, 15 ills. in black and white, 26 ills. in color, Dec., 1944.

Yalu (River), Korea-Manchuria :

Exploring Unknown Corners of the "Hermit Kingdom." By Roy Chapman Andrews. Vol. XXXVI, pp. 24-48, 30 ills., 1 page map, July, 1919.

Yambos (Tribespeople) :

Across Widest Africa. By A. Henry Savage Landor. Vol. XIX, pp. 694-737, 38 ills., 1 half-page map, Oct., 1908.

Yangtze (River), China :

Eden of the Flowery Republic. By Joseph Beech. Vol. XXXVIII, pp. 355-390, 18 ills. in black and white, 16 ills. in color, Nov., 1920.

Mrs. Bishop's "The Yangtze Valley and Beyond." By Eliza R. Scidmore. Vol. XI, pp. 366-368, Sept., 1900.

Through the Great River Trenches of Asia : National Geographic Society Explorer Follows the Yangtze, Mekong, and Salwin Through Mighty Gorges, Some of Whose Canyon Walls Tower to a Height of More than Two Miles. By Joseph F. Rock. Vol. L, pp. 133-186, 47 ills., 1 half-page map, Aug., 1926.

Yank Meets Native. By Wanda Burnett. Vol. LXXXVIII, pp. 105-128, 24 ills., July, 1945.

Yankee (Schooner) :

Storied Islands of the South Sea. 20 ills. in color from natural-color photographs by Irving Johnson, Malcolm Evans, and others. Vol. LXXXI, pp. 9-40, Jan., 1942.

Westward Bound in the Yankee. By Irving and Electa Johnson. Vol. LXXXI, pp. 1-44, 25 ills. in black and white, 20 ills. in color, 1 three-quarters-page map, Jan., 1942.

Yankovsky, George M.:

Jap Rule in the Hermit Nation (Korea). By Willard Price. Vol. LXXXVIII, pp. 429-451, 19 ills., 1 page map, Oct., 1945.

Yanks at Westminster. By Capt. Leonard David Gammans. Vol. XC, pp. 223-252, 6 ills. in black and white, 19 ills. in color, Aug., 1946.

Yanks in Northern Ireland. 15 ills. from photographs. Vol. LXXXIV, pp. 191-204, Aug., 1943.

Yap (Island), Caroline Islands :

Hidden Key to the Pacific : Piercing the Web of Secrecy Which Long Has Veiled Japanese Bases in the Mandated Islands. By Willard Price. Vol. LXXXI, pp. 759-785, 28 ills., 1 map (two-page spread), June, 1942.

Mysterious Micronesia : Yap, Map, and Other Islands Under Japanese Mandate are Museums of Primitive Man. By Willard Price. Vol. LXIX, pp. 481-510, 37 ills., 1 half-page map, Apr., 1936.

Yap and Other Pacific Islands Under Japanese Mandate. By Junius B. Wood. Vol. XL, pp. 591-627, 34 ills., 1 two-thirds-page map, Dec., 1921.

Yap Meets the Yanks. By David D. Duncan, USMC. With 11 ills. in color from natural-color photographs by the author. Vol. LXXXIX, pp. 364-372, Mar., 1946.

Yapanese (People) :

Yap Meets the Yanks. By David D. Duncan, USMC. With 11 ills. in color from natural-color photographs by the author. Vol. LXXXIX, pp. 364-372, Mar., 1946.

Yaqui Indians:

Adventuring Down the West Coast of Mexico. By Herbert Corey. Vol. XLII, pp. 449-503, 44 ills., 1 half-page map, Nov., 1922.

Mexican Land of Canaan: Marvelous Riches of the Wonderful West Coast of Our Neighbor Republic. By Frederick Simpich. Vol. XXXVI, pp. 307-330, 16 ills., 1 page map, Oct., 1919.

Yarmouth, England:

When the Herring Fleet Comes to Great Yarmouth. By W. Robert Moore. Vol. LXVI, pp. 233-250, 19 ills., Aug., 1934.

Yarmouth Port, Massachusetts:

Cape Cod People and Places. By Wanda Burnett. Vol. LXXXIX, pp. 737-774, 17 ills. in black and white, 24 ills. in color, 1 half-page map, June, 1946.

Yawl (Boat):

Cruising to Crete: Four French Girls Set Sail in a Breton Yawl for the Island of the Legendary Minotaur. By Marthe Oulié and Mariel Jean-Brunhes. Vol. LV, pp. 249-272, 15 ills. in black and white, 14 ills. in color, 1 page map, Feb., 1929.

Yellow Fever:

Economic Loss to the People of the United States Through Insects That Carry Disease. By L. O. Howard. Vol. XX, pp. 735-749, Aug., 1909.

Map-Changing Medicine. By William Joseph Showalter. Vol. XLII, pp. 303-330, 26 ills., Sept., 1922.

Yellow River, China. *See* Hwang Ho.

Yellowstone National Park, Wyoming:

Fabulous Yellowstone: Even Stranger Than the Tales of Early Trappers is the Truth About This Steaming Wonderland. By Frederick G. Vosburgh. Vol. LXXVII, pp. 769-794, 15 ills. in black and white, 9 ills. in color, 1 two-thirds-page map, June, 1940.

Land of the Best. By Gilbert H. Grosvenor. Vol. XXIX, pp. 327-430, 71 ills. in black and white, 33 ills. in color, panorama, Apr., 1916.

Our National Parks. By L. F. Schmeckebier. Vol. XXIII, pp. 531-579, 41 ills., 1 page map, June, 1912.

Where Hot Pools Seethe and Geysers Spout. 9 ills. in color from natural-color photographs by Edwin L. Wisherd. Vol. LXXVII, pp. 775-782, June, 1940.

Wild Animals That Took Their Own Pictures by Day and by Night. By George Shiras, 3d. Vol. XXIV, pp. 763-834, 68 ills., 1 page map, July, 1913.

Yellowstone River, Montana-Wyoming:

Trailing History Down the Big Muddy: In the Homeward Wake of Lewis and Clark, a Folding Steel Skiff Bears Its Lone Pilot on a 2,000-Mile Cruise on the Yellowstone-Missouri. By Lewis R. Freeman. Vol. LIV, pp. 73-120, 51 ills., 1 half-page map, July, 1928.

Yemen (Kingdom), Arabia:

"Flower of Paradise": The Part Which Khat Plays in the Life of the Yemen Arab. By Charles Moser. Vol. XXXII, pp. 173-186, 10 ills., 1 page map, Aug., 1917.

Yen Tang Shan:

China's Wonderland—Yen Tang Shan (Chekiang Province). 8 ills. in color from camera paintings by Herbert Clarence White, Deng Baoling, and Hwang Yao-tso. Vol. LXXII, pp. 687-694, Dec., 1937.

Yezdikhast, Iran:

Persian Caravan Sketches: The Land of the Lion and the Sun as Seen on a Summer Caravan Trip. By Harold F. Weston. Vol. XXXIX, pp. 417-468, 46 ills. in black and white, 16 ills. in color, 1 three-quarters-page map, Apr., 1921.

Yezidis (Tribespeople):

Mountain Tribes of Iran and Iraq. By Harold Lamb. Vol. LXXXIX, pp. 385-408, 15 ills., 1 two-page map, Mar., 1946.

Yield of Texas. By Frederick Simpich. Vol. LXXXVII, pp. 163-184, 15 ills., 1 two-page map, Feb., 1945.

Yorkshire, England:

Between the Heather and the North Sea: Bold English Headlands Once Sheltered Sea Robbers, Later Were Ports of Wooden Ships, Centers of the Jet and Alum Trades, To-day Are Havens of Adventurous Fishing Fleets. By Leo Walmsley. Vol. LXIII, pp. 197-232, 41 ills., Feb., 1933.

Yorktown (Aircraft Carrier):

Victory's Portrait in the Marianas. By Lt. William Franklin Draper, USNR. With 17 ills. in color from paintings by the author. Vol. LXXXVIII, pp. 599-616, Nov., 1945.

Yosemite National Park, California:

Crater Lake and Yosemite Through the Ages. By Wallace W. Atwood, Jr. Paintings by Eugene Kingman. Vol. LXXI, pp. 327-343, 7 ills. in black and white, 13 ills. in color, Mar., 1937.

Land of the Best. By Gilbert H. Grosvenor. Vol. XXIX, pp. 327-430, 71 ills. in black and white, 33 ills. in color, panorama, Apr., 1916.

Our National Parks. By L. F. Schmeckebier. Vol. XXIII, pp. 531-579, 41 ills., 1 page map, June, 1912.

Wonderland of California. By Herman Whitaker. Vol. XXVIII, pp. 56-104, 45 ills., July, 1915.

Young, Edgerton R.:

Tallest Tree That Grows (Eucalyptus). By Edgerton R. Young. Vol. XX, pp. 664-667, 3 ills., July, 1909.

Young, Stanley P.:

Other Working Dogs and the Wild Species. By Stanley P. Young. Paintings by Walter A. Weber. Vol. LXXXVI, pp. 363-384, 12 ills. in black and white, 9 ills. in color, Sept., 1944.

Young Japan. By Eliza R. Scidmore. Vol. XXVI. pp. 36-38, 54-64, 11 ills. in color, July, 1914.

Young Russia : The Land of Unlimited Possibilities. By Gilbert H. Grosvenor. Vol. XXVI. pp. 421-520, 85 ills. in black and white, 17 ills. in color, Nov., 1914.

Young Turk. By Rear Adm. Colby M. Chester. Vol. XXIII, pp. 42-89, 39 ills., Jan., 1912.

Youngblood, F. J.:

Little Journey in Honduras. By F. J. Youngblood. Vol. XXX, pp. 177-184, 6 ills., Aug., 1916.

Your Dog Joins Up. By Frederick Simpich. Vol. LXXXIII, pp. 93-113, 25 ills., Jan., 1943.

Your Navy as Peace Insurance. By Fleet Admiral Chester W. Nimitz. Vol. LXXXIX, pp. 681-736, 32 ills. in black and white, 26 ills. in color, June, 1946.

Your New World of Tomorrow. By F. Barrows Colton. Vol. LXXXVIII, pp. 385-410, 25 ills., Oct., 1945.

Your Society (National Geographic Society) Aids War Effort. Vol. LXXXIII, pp. 277-278, 1 ill., Feb., 1943.

Your Society Sponsors an Expedition to Explore the Stratosphere. Vol. LXV, pp. 528-530, 1 ill., Apr., 1934.

Youth Explores Its World (Boy Scouts). By Frederick Simpich. Vol. LXV, pp. 643-662, 21 ills., May, 1934.

Yucatán (State), Mexico :

Chichen Itzá, an Ancient American Mecca : Recent Excavations in Yucatan Are Bringing to Light the Temples, Palaces, and Pyramids of America's Most Holy Native City. By Sylvanus Griswold Morley. Vol. XLVII, pp. 63-95, 34 ills., 1 half-page map, 1 diagram, Jan., 1925.

Henequen—The Yucatan Fiber. By E. H. Thompson. Vol. XIV, pp. 150-158, 6 ills., Apr., 1903.

Home of a Forgotten Race : Mysterious Chichen Itzá, in Yucatan, Mexico. By Edward H. Thompson. Vol. XXV, pp. 585-648, 59 ills., June, 1914.

Life and Death in Ancient Maya Land. 10 ills. in color from paintings by H. M. Herget. Vol. LXX, pp. 623-630, Nov., 1936.

Today in the Feathered Serpent's City (Chichen Itzá). 25 ills. in color from natural-color photographs by Luis Marden. Vol. LXX, pp. 599-614, Nov., 1936.

Yucatán, Home of the Gifted Mayas : Two Thousand Years of History Reach Back to Early American Temple Builders, Corn Cultivators, and Pioneers in Mathematics. By Sylvanus Griswold Morley. Vol. LXX, pp. 591-644, 28 ills. in black and white, 35 ills. in color, 1 two-thirds-page map, Nov., 1936.

Yucay Valley, Peru :

Some Wonderful Sights in the Andean Highlands : The Oldest City in America. Sailing on the Lake of the Clouds : The Yosemite of Peru. By Harriet Chalmers Adams. Vol. XIX, pp. 597-618, 19 ills., 1 half-page map, Sept., 1908.

Yugoslavia :

Changing Map in the Balkans. By Frederick Moore. Vol. XXIV, pp. 199-226, 27 ills., 1 page map, Feb., 1913.

Clock Turns Back in Yugoslavia : The Fortified Monastery of Mountain-girt Dečani Survives Its Six Hundredth Birthday. By Ethel Chamberlain Porter. Vol. LXXXV, pp. 493-512, 20 ills., 1 page map, Apr., 1944.

Color Brightens Rustic Life in Jugoslavia. 25 ills. in color from natural-color photographs by Hans Hildenbrand and Wilhelm Tobien. Vol. LVIII, pp. 272-305, Sept., 1930.

Dalmatian Days : Coasting Along Debatable Shores Where Latin and Slav Meet. By Melville Chater. Vol. LIII, pp. 47-90, 26 ills. in black and white, 17 ills. in color, 1 two-thirds-page map, Jan., 1928.

Danube, Highway of Races : From the Black Forest to the Black Sea, Europe's Most Important River Has Borne the Traffic of Centuries. By Melville Chater. Vol. LVI, pp. 643-697, 54 ills., Dec., 1929.

East of the Adriatic : Notes on Dalmatia, Montenegro, Bosnia, and Herzegovina. By Kenneth McKenzie. Vol. XXIII, pp. 1159-1187, 37 ills., 1 page map, Dec., 1912.

Echoes from Yugoslavia. 16 ills. from photographs. Vol. LXXIX, pp. 793-804, June, 1941.

From England to India by Automobile : An 8,527-Mile Trip Through Ten Countries, from London to Quetta, Requires Five and a Half Months. By Maj. F. A. C. Forbes-Leith. Vol. XLVIII, pp. 191-223, 33 ills., 1 third-page map, Aug., 1925.

Great Turk and His Lost Provinces. By William E. Curtis. Vol. XIV, pp. 45-61, 7 ills., Feb., 1903.

Greece and Montenegro. By George Higgins Moses. Vol. XXIV, pp. 281-310, 24 ills., Mar., 1913.

In Quaint, Curious Croatia. By Felix J. Koch. Vol. XIX, pp. 809-832, 37 ills., Dec., 1908.

Jugoslavia—Ten Years After. By Melville Chater. Vol. LVIII, pp. 257-309, 44 ills. in black and white, 25 ills. in color, 1 three-quarters-page map, Sept., 1930.

Kaleidoscopic Land of Europe's Youngest King : Yugoslavia Holds a Mosaic of Slavs and the City Where Pistol Shots Touched Off the World War. By Douglas Chandler. Vol. LXXV, pp. 691-738, 18 ills. in black and white, 34 ills. in color, 2 maps, June, 1939.

Kingdom of Servia. By William Joseph Showalter. Vol. XXVII, pp. 417-432, 12 ills., 1 page map, Apr., 1915.

Land of Contrast : Austria-Hungary. By D. W. and A. S. Iddings. Vol. XXIII, pp. 1188-1218, 34 ills., Dec., 1912.

Yugoslavia—*Continued*

Medieval Glory Haunts the Eastern Adriatic. 17 ills. in color from autochromes by Hans Hildenbrand. Vol. LIII, pp. 64-81, Jan., 1928.

New Map of Europe: Showing the Boundaries Established by the Peace Conference at Paris and by Subsequent Decisions of the Supreme Council of the Allied and Associated Powers. By Ralph A. Graves. Text accompanying special map supplement in colors. Vol. XXXIX, pp. 157-177, 18 ills., Feb., 1921.

Races of Europe. By Edwin A. Grosvenor. Vol. XXXIV, pp. 441-534, 62 ills., 2 page maps, special map supplement, Dec., 1918.

Servia and Montenegro. Vol. XIX, pp. 774-789, 24 ills., Nov., 1908.

Where East Meets West: A Visit to Picturesque Dalmatia, Montenegro, and Bosnia. By Marian Cruger Coffin. Vol. XIX, pp. 309-344, 26 ills., 1 half-page map, May, 1908.

Whirlpool of the Balkans. By George Higgins Moses. Vol. X, pp. 179-197, 15 ills., Feb., 1921.

Yugoslavia: Where Oriental Hues Splash Europe. 34 ills. in color from natural-color photographs by Konstantin J. Kostich and Rudolf Balogh. Vol. LXXV, pp. 699-738, June, 1939.

Yukon River, Alaska-Canada:

"Breaking Up" of the Yukon. By Capt. George S. Gibbs. Vol. XVII, pp. 268-272, 3 ills., May, 1906.

To-day on "The Yukon Trail of 1898." By Amos Burg. Vol. LVIII, pp. 85-126, 52 ills., 1 two-thirds-page map, July, 1930.

Yukon Territory, Canada:

Alaskan Highway an Engineering Epic: Mosquitoes, Mud, and Muskeg Minor Obstacles of 1,671-mile Race to Throw the Alcan Life Line Through Thick Forests and Uninhabited Wilderness. By Froelich Rainey. Vol. LXXXIII, pp. 143-168, 21 ills., 3 maps, Feb., 1943.

Exploring Yukon's Glacial Stronghold. By Bradford Washburn. Vol. LXIX, pp. 715-747, 28 ills., 1 two-page map, June, 1936.

Family Afoot in Yukon Wilds: Two Young Children and Their Parents Live Off the Country in the Northwest Canada Wilderness Now To Be Traversed by the Alaska Highway. By William Hamilton Albee, with Ruth Albee. Vol. LXXXI, pp. 589-616, 18 ills. in black and white, 14 ills. in color, May, 1942.

Ice Cliffs on White River, Yukon Territory. By Martin W. Gorman. Vol. XI, pp. 113-117, Mar., 1900.

Ice Cliffs on White River, Yukon Territory. By C. Willard Hayes and Alfred H. Brooks. Vol. XI, pp. 199-201, May, 1900.

Life on a Yukon Trail. By Alfred Pearce Dennis. Vol. X, pp. 377-391, 8 ills., 1 page map, Oct., 1899.

Life on a Yukon Trail. By Alfred Pearce Dennis. Vol. X, pp. 457-466, 7 ills., Nov., 1899.

To-day on "The Yukon Trail of 1898." By Amos Burg. Vol. LVIII, pp. 85-126, 52 ills., 1 two-thirds-page map, July, 1930.

Yuma Trail, Arizona-Mexico:

Old Yuma Trail. By W J McGee. Part I, Vol. XII, pp. 103-107, Mar., 1901. Part II, Vol. XII, pp. 129-143, 7 ills., 1 page map, Apr., 1901.

Contents: Tinajas Altas (Water Basins).

Yun Kang Caves, China:

Buddhist Calm Survives Along China's Great Wall. 10 ills. in color; 4 paintings by Mary Augusta Mullikin and Anna M. Hotchkiss and 6 natural-color photographs. Vol. LXXIII, pp. 321-328, Mar., 1938.

China's Great Wall of Sculpture: Man-hewn Caves and Countless Images Form a Colossal Art Wonder of Early Buddhism. By Mary Augusta Mullikin. Vol. LXXIII, pp. 313-348, 23 ills. in black and white, 10 ills. in color, 1 third-page map, Mar., 1938.

Yünnan (Province), China:

Banishing the Devil of Disease Among the Nashi: Weird Ceremonies Performed by an Aboriginal Tribe in the Heart of Yünnan Province, China. By Joseph F. Rock. Vol. XLVI, pp. 473-499, 26 ills., 1 half-page map, Nov., 1924.

Burma Road, Back Door to China: Like the Great Wall of Ancient Times, This Mighty Mountain Highway Has Been Built by Myriad Chinese to Help Defend Their Homeland. By Frank Outram and G. E. Fane. Vol. LXXVIII, pp. 629-658, 26 ills., 1 two-thirds-page map, Nov., 1940.

China Opens Her Wild West: In the Mountain-girt Heart of a Continent a New China Has Been Created During the Years of War. By Owen Lattimore. Vol. LXXXII, pp. 337-367, 21 ills. in black and white, 11 ills. in color, 1 map (two-page spread), Sept., 1942.

Kunming, Southwestern Gateway to China. By Joseph E. Passantino. With 18 ills. in color from natural-color photographs by the author. Vol. XC, pp. 137-168, 12 ills. in black and white, Aug., 1946.

Land of the Crossbow. By George Forrest. Vol. XXI, pp. 132-156, 15 ills., 1 page map, Feb., 1910.

National Geographic Society's Yünnan Province Expedition. By Gilbert Grosvenor. Vol. XLVII, pp. 493-498, 5 ills., Apr., 1925.

South of the Clouds—Yünnan. 11 ills. in color from natural-color photographs by Owen Lattimore and Frank Outram. Vol. LXXXII, pp. 349-356, Sept., 1942.

Stilwell Road—Land Route to China. By Nelson Grant Tayman. Vol. LXXXVII, pp. 681-698, 18 ills., June, 1945.

Sungmas, the Living Oracles of the Tibetan Church. By Joseph F. Rock. Vol. LXVIII, pp. 475-486, 1 ill. in black and white, 12 ills. in color, Oct., 1935.

Through the Great River Trenches of Asia: National Geographic Society Explorer Follows the Yangtze, Mekong, and Salwin Through Mighty Gorges, Some of Whose Canyon Walls Tower to a Height of More Than Two Miles. By Joseph F. Rock. Vol. L, pp. 133-186, 47 ills., 1 half-page map, Aug., 1926.

Yushu, China. *See* Jyekundo.

Z

Zaandam, Netherlands:

Glimpses of Holland. By William Wisner Chapin. Vol. XXVII, pp. 1-29, 26 ills., Jan., 1915.

Zacatecas (State), Mexico:

Mexican Hacienda. By J. E. Kirkwood. Vol. XXV, pp. 563-584, 18 ills., May, 1914.

Zambesi (River), Africa:

Impressions and Scenes of Mozambique. By O. W. Barrett. Vol. XXI, pp. 807-830, 31 ills., Oct., 1910.

Wonders of the Mosi-oa-Tunga : The Falls of the Zambesi. By Louis Livingston Seaman. Vol. XXII, pp. 561-571, 6 ills., June, 1911.

Zanzibar (Island), Africa:

Zanzibar. By Mrs. Harris R. Childs. Vol. XXIII, pp. 810-824, 11 ills., Aug., 1912.

Zapotec Indians:

Among the Zapotecs of Mexico : A Visit to the Indians of Oaxaca, Home State of the Republic's Great Liberator, Juárez, and Its Most Famous Ruler, Diaz. By Herbert Corey. Vol. LI, pp. 501-553, 59 ills., 1 two-thirds-page map, May, 1927.

Hewers of Stone (Mitla, Mexico). By Jeremiah Zimmerman. Vol. XXI, pp. 1002-1020, 11 ills., Dec., 1910.

Isthmus of Tehuantepec : The Bridge of the World's Commerce. By Helen Olsson-Seffer. Vol. XXI, pp. 991-1002, 6 ills., Dec., 1910.

Monte Albán, Richest Archeological Find in America : A Tomb in Oaxaca, Mexico, Yields Treasures Which Reveal the Splendid Culture of the Mixtecs. By Dr. Alfonso Caso. Vol. LXII, pp. 487-512, 28 ills., Oct., 1932.

Zara, Italy:

East of the Adriatic : Notes on Dalmatia, Montenegro, Bosnia, and Herzegovina. By Kenneth McKenzie. Vol. XXIII, pp. 1159-1187, 37 ills., 1 page map, Dec., 1912.

Zeeland (Province), Netherlands:

City of Jacqueline (Goes, Netherlands). By Florence Craig Albrecht. Vol. XXVII, pp. 29-56, 31 ills., Jan., 1915.

See also Walcheren Island.

Zenzinov, Vladimir M.:

With an Exile in Arctic Siberia : The Narrative of a Russian Who Was Compelled to Turn Polar Explorer for Two Years. By Vladimir M. Zenzinov. Vol. XLVI, pp. 695-718, 30 ills., 1 half-page map, Dec., 1924.

Zeusler, (Lt. Comdr.) F. A.:

Standing Iceberg Guard in the North Atlantic : International Patrol Safeguards the Lives of Thousands of Travelers and Protects Transatlantic Liners from a "Titanic" Fate. By Lieut. Comdr. F. A. Zeusler. Vol. L, pp. 1-28, 29 ills., 1 half-page map, July, 1926.

Ziegler, William:

Baldwin-Zeigler Arctic Expedition. Vol. XIII, pp. 358-359, Sept., 1902.

Biography of William Ziegler. Vol. XVI, pp. 355-357, 1 ill., July, 1905.

Fighting the Polar Ice. Vol. XVIII, pp. 72-78, 7 ills. Jan., 1907.

Mr. Ziegler and the National Geographic Society. Vol. XIV, pp. 251-254, June, 1903.

Ziegler Polar Expedition. Vol. XIV, pp. 414-417, 5 ills., Nov., 1903.

Ziegler Polar Expedition. Vol. XV, pp. 427-428, Oct., 1904.

Ziegler Polar Expedition. Vol. XVI, pp. 439-440, Sept., 1905.

Zigzagging Across Sicily. By Melville Chater. Vol. XLVI, pp. 303-352, 44 ills., 1 half-page map, Sept., 1924.

Zimbabwe (Ruins), Southern Rhodesia:

Rhodesia, Hobby and Hope of Cecil Rhodes. By W. Robert Moore. Vol. LXXXVI, pp. 281-306, 13 ills. in black and white, 10 ills, in color, 1 half-page map, Sept., 1944.

Zimmerman, Jeremiah:

Hewers of Stone (Mitla, Mexico). By Jeremiah Zimmerman. Vol. XXI, pp. 1002-1020, 11 ills., Dec., 1910.

Zion National Park, Utah:

Bursts of Color in Sculptured Utah. 22 ills. in color from natural-color photographs. Vol. LXIX, pp. 593-616, May, 1936.

Photographing the Marvels of the West in Colors. By Fred Payne Clatworthy. Vol. LIII, pp. 694-719, 30 ills. in color, June, 1928.

Zon, Raphael:

When Our Country Is Fifty Years Older. By Raphael Zon. Vol. XX, pp. 573-580, 2 ills., 1 diagram, June, 1909.

Zoques (Indians):

Finding Jewels of Jade in a Mexican Swamp. By Matthew W. and Marion Stirling. Vol. LXXXII, pp. 635-661, 15 ills. in black and white, 12 ills. in color, 1 two-thirds-page map, Nov., 1942.

Isthmus of Tehuantepec : The Bridge of the World's Commerce. By Helen Olsson-Seffer. Vol. XXI, pp. 991-1002, 6 ills., Dec., 1910.

Zoroastrianism:

Parsees and the Towers of Silence at Bombay, India. By William Thomas Fee. Vol. XVI, pp. 529-554, 16 ills., Dec., 1905.

Zotzils (Indians):

Finding Jewels of Jade in a Mexican Swamp. By Matthew W. and Marion Stirling. Vol. LXXXII, pp. 635-661, 15 ills. in black and white, 12 ills. in color, 1 two-thirds-page map, Nov., 1942.

Zuider Zee, Netherlands:

Glimpses of Holland. By William Wisner Chapin. Vol. XXVII, pp. 1-29, 26 ills., Jan., 1915.

Zuider Zee, Netherlands—*Continued*

New Country Awaits Discovery: The Draining of the Zuider Zee Makes Room for the Excess Population of the Netherlands. By J. C. M. Kruisinga. Vol. LXIV, pp. 293-320, 20 ills. in black and white, 13 ills. in color, 1 three-quarters and 1 half-page maps, Sept., 1933.

Nooks and Bays Around the Zuider Zee. 13 ills. in color from natural-color photographs by Wilhelm Tobien, Gervais Courtellemont, and Franklin Price Knott. Vol. LXIV, pp. 301-308, Sept., 1933.

Zululand, Natal:

Under the South African Union. By Melville Chater. Vol. LIX, pp. 391-512, 97 ills. in black and white, 38 ills. in color, 1 two-page map, Apr., 1931.

Zulus (Tribespeople):

Natal: The Garden Colony. By Russell Hastings Millward. Vol. XX, pp. 278-291, 16 ills., Mar., 1909.

Zumbro, W. M.:

Religious Penances and Punishments Self-Inflicted by the Holy Men of India. By W. M. Zumbro. Vol. XXIV, pp. 1257-1314, 69 ills., Dec., 1913.

Zumbro, W. M.—*Continued*

Temples of India. 54 ills. from photographs by W. M. Zumbro. Vol. XX, pp. 922-971, Nov., 1909.

Zuñi Indians:

Everyday Life in Pueblo Bonito: As Disclosed by the National Geographic Society's Archeologic Explorations in the Chaco Canyon National Monument, New Mexico. By Neil M. Judd. Vol. XLVIII, pp. 227-262, 37 ills., 1 two-thirds-page map, Sept., 1925.

Indian Tribes of Pueblo Land. By Matthew W. Stirling. Vol. LXXVIII, pp. 549-596, 16 ills. in black and white, 25 ills. in color, Nov., 1940.

Red Men of the Southwest. 25 ills. in color from paintings by W. Langdon Kihn. Vol. LXXVIII, pp. 557-596, Nov., 1940.

Zwemer, S. M.:

Mecca the Mystic: A New Kingdom Within Arabia. By S. M. Zwemer. Vol. XXXII, pp. 157-172, 13 ills., Aug., 1917.

Notes on Oman. By S. M. Zwemer. Vol. XXII, pp. 89-98, 8 ills., 1 half-page map, Jan., 1911.

VOLUME II AND SUPPLEMENTS

Volume II of this Cumulative Index, covering issues beginning January, 1947, will be periodically revised and expanded to include issues of additional years. To keep Volume II currently up to date, a Cumulative Supplement will be made available at nominal cost about February 1 of each year until a new complete edition of Volume II is published. An envelope pocket for the Supplement is provided at the back of Volume II.

MAPS

Large Maps, issued as Special Map Supplements to The NATIONAL GEOGRAPHIC MAGAZINE for wall and desk use, are indicated by *italics*.

Abyssinia. *See* Ethiopia.

Aden Peninsula, Arabia:

Map showing Position of Aden and Little Aden Peninsulas. Vol. LXVIII, p. 726, 1 half-page, Dec., 1935.

Adirondack State Park, New York:

Adirondack State Park. Vol. LXXIII, p. 720, 1 three-quarters-page, June, 1938.

Aegean Regions:

Aegean Regions, and an Inset of the Bosphorus. Vol. LVI, p. 489, 1 half-page, Oct., 1929.

Aegean Regions, showing the Isles of Greece and the Italian Islands of the Aegean. Vol. LXXXV, p. 596, 1 page, May, 1944.

Asia Minor, the Dardanelles, and the Islands of the Aegean Sea. Vol. XLII, p. 554, 1 half-page, Nov., 1922.

Asia Minor and the Holy Land. Vol. XXXVII, p. 46, 1 half-page, Jan., 1920.

Classical Lands of the Mediterranean. Vol. LXXVII, special supplement in colors, 35¼ x 26 inches, Mar., 1940.

Crete and Greece. Vol. LV, p. 250, 1 half-page, Feb., 1929.

Gates to the Black Sea. Vol. XXVII, p. 532, 1 half-page, May, 1915.

Greece, and Inset showing Expansion of Greece. Vol. LVIII, p. 652, 1 two-thirds-page, Dec., 1930.

Greece, Asia Minor, and Mediterranean Regions, showing Route of the *Bonita.* Vol. LV, p. 250, 1 half-page, Feb., 1929.

Greece, Bulgaria, Turkey. Vol. XXX, p. 271, 1 half-page, Sept., 1916.

Greece and the Aegean, showing Sites of Antiquity and the Necklace of Hellenic Cities that Adorned the Coast of Asia Minor. Vol. LXXXV, pp. 280-281, 1 two-page, Mar., 1944.

Italian Islands of the Aegean. Vol. LXXIX, p. 451, 1 two-thirds-page, Apr., 1941.

"Shores of Sunrise" (The Levant). Vol. L, p. 652, 1 two-thirds-page, Dec., 1926.

Shores of the Aegean, Which Have Provided the Geographic Panorama for Much of the History of Civilization. Vol. LIV, p. 725, 1 two-thirds-page, Dec., 1928.

Afghanistan:

Afghanistan, Buffer Between Russia and India. Vol. XC, p. 521, 1 page, Oct., 1946.

Afghanistan and Adjacent Regions. Vol. XLIV, p. 742, 1 two-thirds-page, Dec., 1933.

Afghanistan and Its Border Lands. Vol. XXXIX, p. 90, 1 three-quarters-page, Jan., 1921.

Africa:

Africa (Prepared from Latest Geographical Data by Gilbert H. Grosvenor, Editor). Vol. XX, special supplement in colors, 15½ x 20 inches, Mar., 1909.

Africa. Vol. XLII, special supplement in colors, 27 x 30 inches, Oct., 1922.

Africa, as Described by Ptolemy in the Second Century. By Mattiolo: Venice, 1548. Vol. XXII, p. 390, 1 page, Apr., 1911.

Africa, showing Darfur. Vol. XLV, p. 46, 1 three-quarters-page, Jan., 1924.

Africa, showing Possessions of Each European Power. Vol. XXII, p. 393, 1 page, Apr., 1911.

Africa, showing Territory Within Which the Convention of May 19, 1900, Places Restrictions on the Killing of Wild Animals. Vol. XI, p. 447, 1 page, Nov., 1900.

Africa, showing the Homes of the Fighting Tribes of the Sudan. Vol. LVI, p. 466, 1 two-thirds-page, Oct., 1929.

Africa, with Da Gamma's Discoveries, 1498, by Mattiolo, 1548. Vol. XXII, p. 391, 1 page, Apr., 1911.

Africa, with Inset showing Airways and Relief. Vol. LXVII, special supplement in colors, 29 x 31½ inches, June, 1935.

Africa, with Insets of the Cape Verde Islands, Relief Map, and a Table of Airline Distances in Statute Miles. Vol. LXXXIII, special supplement in colors, 29¼ x 31½ inches, Feb., 1943.

Atlantic Ocean, showing West Coast of Africa. Vol. LXXVI, special supplement in colors, 31 x 25 inches, July, 1939.

Atlantic Ocean, showing West Coast of Africa, with a Table of Airline Distances in Statute Miles. Vol. LXXX, special supplement in colors, 31¼ x 25 inches, Sept., 1941.

Countries Bordering the Mediterranean Sea. Vol. XXIII, special supplement in colors, 10 x 18 inches, Jan., 1912.

Europe and Northern Africa, showing Extent of Roman Empire, with Table of Historical Facts. Vol. XC, pp. 552-553, 1 two-page, Nov., 1946.

French West Africa, with Pictographs, showing Route followed by Mrs. Boulton. Vol. LXXIX, pp. 636-637, two-page spread, May, 1941.

Geographic Relation of France and Her African Colonies. Vol. XI, p. 233, 1 page, June, 1900.

Gulf of Guinea Region, with Enlargement of São Tomé, the Chocolate Island. Vol. LXXXIX, p. 659, 1 third-page, May, 1946.

Africa—*Continued*

Indian Ocean, including Australia, New Zealand and Malaysia, showing East Coast of Africa and Suez Canal. Vol. LXXIX, special supplement in colors, 25½ x 32¾ inches, Mar., 1941.

Madagascar in Its Relation to Africa and Compared with the Eastern United States. Vol. LVI, p. 183, 1 half-page, Aug., 1929.

Map of the Seat of War in Africa, Prepared in the War Department, Adjutant General's Office, Military Information Division, with an Inset of South Africa. Vol. X, special supplement, 33 x 45 inches, Dec., 1899.

Mediterranean Coast of Libia and Egypt. Vol. LXXVIII, p. 810, Dec., 1940.

North Africa. Vol. XXII, p. 751, 1 page, Aug., 1911.

North Africa, showing Countries Bordering on the Mediterranean and Bombing Ranges from Bizerte, Tunisia. Vol. LXXXIV, pp. 8-9, two-page spread, July, 1943.

North-Central Africa, showing Route of Flood-Wilson Expedition. Vol. LXV, pp. 40-41, 2 half-pages, Jan., 1934.

Northwest Africa, showing Mileage Between Dakar, French West Africa, and Important Points in the Eastern and Western Hemispheres. Vol. LXXXI, p. 374, 1 three-quarters-page, Mar., 1942.

Railways in South Africa. Vol. XI, p. 188, 1 half-page, May, 1900.

Roosevelt's Route and Hunting Trips in Africa (British East Africa). Vol. XXII, p. 2, 1 page, Jan., 1911.

Route of Felix Shay from Cairo to Capetown. Vol. XLVII, p. 128, 1 half-page, Feb., 1925.

Route of Hassanein Bey Through the Libian Desert. Vol. XLVI, p. 236, 1 half-page, Sept., 1924.

Route of the Citroën African Expedition. Vol. XLIX, p. 652, 1 two-thirds-page, June, 1926.

Route of the Thaw Expedition from Algiers to Nairobi. Vol. LXXIV, p. 330, 1 two-thirds-page, Sept., 1938.

South-West Africa, showing Mt. Brukkaros and Neighboring Region. Vol. LVII, p. 489, 1 third-page, Apr., 1930.

South-West Africa in the Vicinity of the New Observatory (National Geographic Society's Solar Radiation Station). Vol. L, p. 504, 1 quarter-page, Oct., 1926.

Sudan. Vol. XVII, p. 245, 1 quarter-page, May, 1906.

Sudan, French West Africa, and British East Africa. Vol. XIX, p. 736, 1 half-page, Oct., 1908.

Theater of War in Europe, Africa, and Western Asia, with Table of Airline Distances in Statute Miles. Vol. LXXXII, special supplement in colors, 26½ x 31 inches, July, 1942.

Africa—*Continued*

Uganda Railway. Vol. XIII, p. 170, 1 half-page, May, 1902.

Western Africa, showing Strategic Position of Dakar. Vol. LXXXI, p. 377, 1 quarter-page, Mar., 1942.

Western Rift Valley and Surrounding Country, with Inset of the Virunga Mountains, Belgian Congo. Vol. LXXVI, p. 515, 1 two-thirds-page, Oct., 1939.

See also Egypt; Suez Canal; Union of South Africa.

Air Routes:

Airway Routes of the United States. Vol. LXIII, p. 634, 1 page, May, 1933.

Atlantic Ocean, showing Air Routes to Norway, Britain, and Portugal from Newfoundland, Greenland, and Iceland. Vol. LXXX, p. 77, 1 page, July, 1941.

Canada, showing the Route Flown by the Author, (J. A. Wilson) in His Air Survey of the Dominion. Vol. L, pp. 392-393, Oct., 1926.

Flying Around the North Atlantic: Route of the Lindberghs in the *Tingmissartoq*. Vol. LXVI, pp. 266-267, 2 half-pages, Sept., 1934.

Four Years of Aerial Trail Blazing in Ancient China (Routes Flown by Capt. Hans Koester). Vol. LXXIII, p. 574, 1 two-thirds-page, May, 1938.

How Commander Byrd Plots a New Transatlantic Route Along Which Future Flyers May Cross on Schedule. Vol. LII, p. 348, 1 half-page, Sept., 1927.

How the *Southern Cross* (Airplane) Blazed an Aërial Trail Across the Pacific. Vol. LIV, p. 373, 1 two-thirds-page, Oct., 1928.

Northern Hemisphere, showing Proposed Routes of Aircraft Over the Arctic Zone. Vol. XLII, p. 206, 1 page, Aug., 1922.

Pinedo's 60,000-Mile Air Cruise in the *Santa María* (Seaplane) to Six Continents. Vol. LIV, pp. 248-249, 1 two-page, Sept., 1928.

Route Flown by the Days. Vol. LXI, p. 656, 1 half-page, June, 1932.

Route Flown by the National Geographic Aërial Survey Party from Washington to Buenos Aires. Vol. LIX, p. 4, 1 page, Jan., 1931.

Route Followed by Air Mail Planes from Montevideo to Miami. Vol. LVII, p. 264, 1 half-page, Mar., 1930.

Route Followed by Lindbergh in His Flight Over 13 Latin-American Countries. Vol. LIII, p. 532, 1 two-thirds-page, May, 1928.

Route Followed by Sir Ross Smith from London to Australia. Vol. XXXIX, p. 230, 1 page, Mar., 1921.

Route Followed by U. S. Army Aviators on the First Alaskan Air Expedition from New York to Nome. Vol. XLI, pp. 500-501, May, 1922.

Route of the *Norge* (Airship) from Rome to Alaska—A Flight of 8,500 Miles Across the Top of the World. Vol. LII, p. 188, 1 page, Aug., 1927.

Air Routes—*Continued*

Route of the Trail-Blazing Flight of U. S. Army Airplanes Through 20 Countries of Latin America. Vol. LII, p. 452, 1 page, Oct., 1927.

Route of Transandean Mail and Passenger Planes. Vol. LIX, p. 596, 1 third-page, May, 1931.

Routes Flown by Sir Alan J. Cobham Over Europe, Asia, Australia, and Africa. Vol. LIII, p. 350, 1 three-quarters-page, Mar., 1928.

Southern Greenland: Route of the Lindberghs. Vol. LXVI, p. 262, 1 two-thirds-page, Sept., 1934.

Territory Covered in Flights of Walter Mittelholzer. Vol. LXI, p. 466, 1 three-quarters-page, Apr., 1932.

United States, showing Route followed by Lindbergh in the *Spirit of St. Louis* and Its Companion Plane. Vol. LIII, p. 5, 1 page, Jan., 1928.

United States Air Mail Routes in Operation and Proposed. Vol. XLIX, p. 5, 1 two-thirds-page, Jan., 1926.

Alabama:

Alabama. Vol. LX, p. 706, 1 page, Dec., 1931.

Åland (Islands), Finland:

Åland Islands. Vol. LXVII, p. 105, 1 half-page, Jan., 1935.

Alaska:

Alaska. Vol. XV, special supplement in colors, 36 x 42 inches, May, 1904.

Alaska. Vol. XX, p. 674, 1 page, July, 1909.

Alaska. Vol. XXV, special supplement in colors, 15¼ x 20 inches, Feb., 1914.

Alaska—Springboard for Attack on Japan and Key to Continental Defense. Vol. LXXXII, pp. 286-287, 1 two-page, Sept., 1942.

Alaska, showing Alcan Highway. Vol. LXXXIII, pp. 150-151, 1 two-page, Feb., 1943.

Alaska, showing Distribution of Timber. Vol. XVIII, p. 172, 1 page, Mar., 1907.

Alaska, showing Mineral Deposits so far as Known. Vol. XVI, p. 512, 1 page, Nov., 1905.

Alaska, showing Navigable Waters and Railroads. Vol. XVIII, p. 164, 1 page, Mar., 1907.

Alaska, showing Railway Routes and Known Occurrences of Economically Important Minerals. Vol. XVIII, p. 181, 1 page, Mar., 1907.

Alaska, showing so far as Known, the Distribution of Metamorphic Rocks and the Localities Where Gold Has Been Mined. Vol. XVIII, p. 168, 1 page, Mar., 1907.

Alaska, showing the Distribution of the Coal-Bearing Rocks so far as Known. Vol. XVIII, p. 170, 1 page, Mar., 1907.

Alaska, showing the Sections That Have Been Mapped and Surveyed. Vol. XXIII, p. 424, 1 page, May, 1912.

Alaska, showing the Unexplored Areas in 1905. Vol. XVII, p. 112, 1 third-page, Feb., 1906.

Alaska—*Continued*

Alaska and Adjoining Yukon Territory. Vol. LVIII, p. 89, 1 two-thirds-page, July, 1930.

Alaska Boundary in Portland Canal. Vol. XV, p. 5, 1 half-page, Jan., 1904.

Alaska-Canada Boundary Line. Vol. XXIII, p. 693, 1 page, July, 1912.

Alaska Telegraph and Cable Lines. Vol. XV, p. 491, 1 page, Dec., 1904.

Alaskan Boundary Decision. Vol. XV, special supplement, 12 x 12½ inches, Jan., 1904.

Alaskan Boundary Lines Claimed by the United States and Canada. Vol. XIV, p. 90, 1 page, Mar., 1903.

Base of the Alaska Peninsula: Showing the Major Features of the Katmai District and the Adjoining Country. Vol. XL, p. 222, 1 page, Sept., 1921.

British Map, 1832. Vol. X, p. 438, 1 page, Nov., 1899.

Canadian Map of 1831. Vol. X, p. 441, 1 page, Nov., 1899.

Canadian Map of 1857. Vol. X, p. 442, 1 page, Nov., 1899.

Chart Shewing Part of the Coast of N. W. America (Vancouver's Chart, No. I). Vol. X, special supplement, 15½ x 18 inches, Nov., 1899.

Chart Shewing Part of the Coast of N. W. America (Vancouver's Chart, No. II). Vol. X, special supplement, 15½ x 18 inches, Nov., 1899.

Coastal Region, Mapped by the International Boundary Commission in 1906-1908, and Adjoining Yukon and British Columbia, Surveyed by Bradford Washburn in 1935. Vol. LXIX, pp. 720-721, 1 two-page, June, 1936.

Columbia Glacier, Prince William Sound. Vol. XXI, p. 9, 1 page, Jan., 1910.

Copper-Bearing Areas of Alaska, so far as Known. Vol. XVIII, p. 169, 1 half-page, Mar., 1907.

Copper River and Northwestern Railway. Vol. XXI, p. 25, 1 page, Jan., 1910.

Fairweather Peninsula with Inset showing Location of Mount Crillon. Vol. LXVII, p. 363, 1 half-page, Mar., 1935.

French Map, 1844. Vol. X, p. 445, 1 page, Nov., 1899.

Geographic Provinces of Northwestern North America. Vol. XVIII, p. 176, 1 page, Mar., 1907.

Glaciers of Prince William Sound and Copper River. Vol. XXII, p. 540, 1 page, June, 1911.

Golofin Bay and Cape Nome Gold Fields. Vol. XI, p. 16, 1 page, Jan., 1900.

Government Reindeer Stations in Alaska. Vol. XIV, p. 131, 1 half-page, Apr., 1903.

Hidden Glacier in 1899, 1905, 1906, and 1909. Vol. XXI, p. 45, 1 page, Jan., 1910.

Hudson's Bay Company Map, 1857. Vol. X, p. 425, 1 page, Nov., 1899.

Katmai Volcano and Vicinity. Vol. XXXI, p. 23, 1 half-page, Jan., 1917.

Alaska—*Continued*

Kenai Peninsula, showing the Best Portion of the Sheep Country and Location of Seward and Resurrection Bay. Vol. XXIII, pp. 428-429, 2 pages, May, 1912.

Lake Clark and Vicinity. Vol. XV, p. 330, 1 half-page, Aug., 1904.

Location of Aniakchak Crater and Topographical Detail. Vol. LX, p. 322, 1 half-page, Sept., 1931.

Location of Mount McKinley. Vol. XII, p. 312, 1 three-quarters-page, Aug., 1901.

Lower Copper River, Controller Bay Region. Vol. XIII, p. 24, 1 page, Jan., 1910.

Lower Hubbard Glacier. Vol. XXI, p. 5, 1 half-page, Jan., 1910.

Malaspina Glacier. Vol. XXI, p. 9, 1 half-page, Jan., 1910.

Malaspina Glacier, showing Atrevida, Lucia and Marvine Lobes. Vol. XXI, p. 34, 1 half-page, Jan., 1910.

Model of the Valley of Ten Thousand Smokes and Vicinity. Vol. XL, p. 227, 1 three-quarters-page, Sept., 1921.

Mt. McKinley Region, Alaska. Vol. XIV, p. 32, 1 page, Jan., 1903.

Muir Inlet and Front of Muir Glacier, showing Positions of the Ice Front in 1890 and in May, 1903. Vol. XIV, p. 444, 1 quarter-page, Dec., 1903.

Nunatak Glacier in 1895, 1899, and 1909. Vol. XXI, p. 44, 1 page, Jan., 1910.

Pacific Coast of the Gulf of Alaska. Vol. XXI, p. 3, 1 quarter-page, Jan., 1910.

Port Wells, Prince William Sound, in 1899. Vol. XXII, p. 550, 1 half-page, June, 1911.

Port Wells in 1910, showing the Extraordinary Retreat of Barry and Surprise Glaciers. Vol. XXII, p. 550, 1 half-page, June, 1911.

Probable Summer Migration Route of Alaska Geese. Vol. LIII, p. 116, 1 third-page, Jan., 1928.

Proposed Mount McKinley National Park from Surveys by the United States Geological Survey. Vol. XXXI, p. 71, 1 half-page, Jan., 1917.

Provinces of Northwestern America. Vol. XVIII, p. 176, 1 page, Mar., 1907.

Recession of the Glaciers of Glacier Bay. Vol. XIX, p. 77, 1 three-quarters-page, Jan., 1908.

Region Affected by the Katmai Eruption, showing the Ash Fall at Varying Distances. Vol. XXIV, p. 132, 1 page, Feb., 1913.

Route Followed by Bradford Washburn up Mount Crillon in the Fairweather Range. Vol. LXVII, p. 385, 1 half-page, Mar., 1935.

Route Followed by the *Nakwasina* from Washington State to Alaska, by Way of the Inside Passage. Vol. LXIV, p. 6, 1 page, July, 1933.

Route of Harriman Alaska Expedition. Vol. X, p. 506, 1 page, Dec., 1899.

Russian Imperial Map, 1827. Vol. X, p. 437, 1 page, Nov., 1899.

Alaska—*Continued*

Scottish Geographical Map, 1898. Vol. X, p. 448, 1 page, Nov., 1899.

Seward Peninsula. Vol. LXXV, p. 638, 1 two-thirds-page, May, 1939.

Soundings in Port Wells, Prince William Sound. Vol. XXII, p. 559, 1 half-page, June, 1911.

Southeastern Alaska. Vol. LXXIV, p. 79, 1 half-page, July, 1938.

Southeastern Alaska, 1824. Vol. X, p. 428, 1 page, Nov., 1899.

Southeastern Alaska, showing Boundary Lines of American and British Claims. Vol. X, p. 454, 1 page, Nov., 1899.

Southeastern Alaska and Klondike Region. Vol. X, p. 376, 1 page, Oct., 1899.

State Department Map, 1867. Vol. X, p. 446, 1 page, Nov., 1899.

Territory Mapped by the Pavlof Expedition of 1928, and an Inset showing the Location of the Peninsula. Vol. LV, p. 112, 1 three-quarters-page, Jan., 1929.

Topographic Reconnaissance Map from Controller Bay to Prince William Sound. Vol. XVIII, p. 178, 1 page, Mar., 1907.

Unexplored Areas of Alaska. Vol. XIII, p. 132, 1 three-quarters-page, Apr., 1902.

United States Army and Navy Air Bases in Alaska. Vol. LXXVIII, p. 490, 1 page, Oct., 1940.

Upper Part of Port Wells, Prince William Sound, Alaska. Vol. X, p. 511, 1 page, Dec., 1899.

Valdez Glacier Highway. Vol. XXI, p. 11, 1 page, Jan., 1910.

Valley of Ten Thousand Smokes. Vol. XXXIII, p. 155, 1 half-page, Feb., 1918.

Variegated and Haenke Glaciers. Vol. XXI, p. 35, 1 third-page, Jan., 1910.

Volcanic Axes and Structure Lines in Eastern Asia and Alaska and Why Japan Is Subject to Frequent Destructive Earthquakes. Vol. XLIV, p. 446, 1 page, Oct., 1923.

See also Aleutian Islands.

Alaska Military Highway:

Alaska, showing Alcan Highway. Vol. LXXXIII, pp. 150-151, 1 two-page, Feb., 1943.

Western Canada, showing Alcan Highway. Vol. LXXXIII, p. 148, 1 half-page, Feb., 1943.

Albania:

Albania. Vol. LIX, p. 133, 1 half-page, Feb., 1931.

Albania and Its Border Countries of the Balkan Peninsula. Vol. XXXIV, p. 95, 1 half-page, Aug., 1918.

Alberta (Province), Canada:

Map of Northwestern United States and Neighboring Canadian Provinces. Vol. LXXIX, special supplement in colors, 24½ x 36 inches, June, 1941.

Sources of the Saskatchewan. Vol. X, p. 115, 1 page, Apr., 1899.

"Alcan" Highway. *See* Alaska Military Highway.

Aleutian Islands, Alaska :

Alaska—Springboard for Attack on Japan and Key to Continental Defense. Vol. LXXXII, pp. 286-287, 1 two-page, Sept., 1942.

Detailed Map of the Aleutian Islands. Vol. LXXXIII, pp. 152-153, two-page spread, Feb., 1943.

North America, with Inset of Aleutian Islands. Vol. LXXXI, special supplement in colors, 26½ x 33 inches, May, 1942.

See also Attu ; Bogoslof ; Kiska ; Unimak.

Algeria:

Souf Country. Vol. XXII, p. 377, 1 half-page, Apr., 1911.

Alps:

Bavarian Alps, Germany. Vol. LXVIII, p. 746, 1 third-page, Dec., 1935.

Amami Gunto (Islands), Ryukyu Retto, Japan :

Southeast Asia and Pacific Islands from the Indies and the Philippines to the Solomons, with inset of Nansei Islands, Amami to Okinawa. Vol. LXXXVI, special supplement in colors, 41 x 26½ inches, Oct., 1944.

Anatolia:

Asia Minor. Vol. XLVI, p. 450, 1 quarter-page, Oct., 1924.

Crusader Trails and Castles. Vol. LXIV, p. 654, 1 page, Dec., 1933.

Sketch Map of the Near East, showing Egypt, Anatolia, and the Arab Kingdoms of Hedjaz, Transjordania, and Iraq. Vol. XLIII, p. 534, 1 three-quarters-page, May, 1923.

Turkey, Greece, and Aegean Sea, with Inset showing Dardanelles. Vol. XLII, p. 554, 1 half-page, Nov., 1922.

See also Asia Minor ; Turkey.

Andorra:

Andorra. Vol. LXIV, p. 495, 1 third-page, Oct., 1933.

Anglo-Egyptian Sudan:

Eastern Anglo-Egyptian Sudan, Egypt, Ethiopia, Western Arabia, and Adjacent Countries. Vol. LXV, p. 765, 1 page, June, 1934.

Antarctic Regions:

Antarctic Regions, showing Explorations of the American Discoverers of the Continent, Palmer and Wilkes. Vol. XXIII, p. 308, 1 page, Mar., 1912.

Antarctic Regions, with Inset Maps showing Antarctic Archipelago, King Edward VII Land, and Part of Marie Byrd Land, and Byrd's South Pole Flight. Vol. LXII, special supplement in colors, 19½ x 26½ inches. Oct., 1932.

Antarctica, showing Course Followed by Lincoln Ellsworth in the *Polar Star* from Cape Eielson to Little America. Vol. LXX, p. 4, 1 page, July, 1936.

Antarctica, showing Routes of Lincoln Ellsworth's Flights, 1935 and 1939. Vol. LXXVI, p. 132, 1 page, July, 1939.

Antarctic Regions—*Continued*

Island of South Georgia, Outpost of the Antarctic. Vol. XLI, p. 412, 1 half-page, Apr., 1922.

Location of Byrd Antarctic Expedition Activities, with Details of Antarctic Continent and Little America. Vol. LVIII, p. 132, 1 page, Aug., 1930.

Map of the Continent, showing Airplane, Dog, and Tractor Party Trails Made by Byrd Antarctic Expedition. Inset of Alexandra and Rockefeller Mountains. Vol. LXVIII, pp. 450-451, 2 pages, Oct., 1935.

Northern and Southern Hemispheres, with Insets of Time Zones, World Terrain, and Tables of Airline Distances in Four Hemispheres. Vol. LXXXIII, special supplement in colors, 41 x 22 inches, Apr., 1943.

Route of Amundsen to South Pole. Vol. XXIII, p. 207, 1 page, Feb., 1912.

Routes Followed by Ships and Planes of Byrd Antarctic Expedition in the South Pacific. Vol. LXVIII, p. 405, 1 page, Oct., 1935.

South Polar Regions. Vol. XVIII, p. 114, 1 half-page, Feb., 1907.

South Polar Regions. Vol. XX, p. 399, 1 half-page, Apr., 1909.

South Polar Regions. Vol. XX, p. 1007, 1 half-page, Nov., 1909.

South Polar Regions. Vol. XXI, p. 168, 1 page, Feb., 1910.

South Polar Regions. Vol. XXII, p. 406, 1 page, Apr., 1911.

South Polar Regions—Showing Routes of the Proposed Antarctic Expeditions. Vol. X, special supplement, 8 x 8 inches, Aug., 1899.

Work in the Far South. Vol. XIV, p. 109, 1 two-thirds-page, Mar., 1903.

World, with Insets showing Arctic and Antarctic Regions, Natural Vegetation and Ocean Currents, and Density of Population and Prevailing Winds. Vol. LXII, special supplement in colors, 26 x 38½ inches, Dec., 1932.

World Map, with Insets of Arctic and Antarctic Regions, Territories Occupied by Belligerents in First and Second World Wars, and Table of Geographical Equivalents and Abbreviations. Vol. LXXXIV, special supplement in colors, 41 x 26½ inches, Dec., 1943.

Anticosti Island, Canada :

Southeastern Canada, with Enlargement of Anticosti Island. Vol. LXXXI, p. 122, 1 two-thirds-page, Jan., 1942.

Antilles, Greater. *See* Cuba ; Dominican Republic ; Haiti ; Jamaica ; Puerto Rico.

Antilles, Lesser. *See* Aruba ; Bonaire ; Curaçao ; Leeward Islands ; Tobago ; Trinidad ; Windward Islands.

Arabia:

Arabia. Vol. XX, p. 1117, 1 page, Dec., 1909.

Arabia—*Continued*

Arabia. Vol. XXXII, p. 181, 1 page, Aug., 1917.

Arabia, showing the Geographical Relation of the New Kingdom of Hejaz to Syria, Mesopotamia, and Armenia. Vol. XXXVI, p. 374, 1 page, Nov., 1919.

Arabia, Turkey, and Egypt. Vol. XXII, p. 63, 1 two-thirds-page, Jan., 1911.

Arabia, with Inset of Hadhramaut Province. Vol. LXII, p. 389, 1 two-thirds-page, Oct., 1932.

Near East, showing Egypt, Anatolia, and the Arab Kingdoms of Hedjaz, Transjordania, and Iraq. Vol. XLIII, p. 534, 1 three-quarters-page, May, 1923.

Western Arabia, Adjacent Countries, and Northeastern Africa. Vol. LXV, p. 765, 1 page, June, 1934.

See also Aden Peninsula ; Oman ; Saudi Arabia.

Aran Islands, Eire :

Aran Islands, with Inset Map of Ireland. **Vol.** LIX, p. 752, 1 quarter-page, June, 1931.

Arctic Regions:

Amundsen's Route (Northwest Passage). **Vol.** XVII, p. 39, 1 page, Jan., 1906.

Arctic Regions. Vol. XLVIII, special supplement in colors, 19¼ x 18 inches, Nov., 1925.

Arctic Regions, showing Capt. Bob Bartlett's World, as seen from 10,000 Miles in Space. Vol. LXXXIX, p. 604, 1 half-page, May, 1946.

Arctic Regions, showing Outline of Indicated North Polar Land. Vol. XV, p. 256, 1 page, June, 1904.

Arctic Regions, showing the Known Route of the Lost Soviet Aviators and the Network of Sir Hubert Wilkins' Search Flights. Vol. LXXIV, pp. 144-145, 1 two-page, Aug., 1938.

Canada, Alaska, Greenland, showing Distribution of Blond Eskimo. Vol. XXIII, p. 1224, 1 page, Dec., 1912.

Captain O. Sverdrup's Explorations, 1898-1902. Vol. XIII, p. 460, 1 page, Dec., 1902.

Field of Activity of the MacMillan Arctic Expedition Under the Auspices of the National Geographic Society. Vol. XLVII, p. 674, 1 half-page, June, 1925.

Franz Josef Land Archipelago, showing Explorations by the Wellman Expedition. Vol. X, p. 502, 1 page, Dec., 1899.

Global Map of Arctic Regions, showing Greenland, Important for Weather Stations and Air Bases. Vol. XC, p. 459, 1 page, Oct., 1946.

Greenland, Aerial Stepping Stone to Europe. Vol. LXXXII, pp. 370-371, 1 two-page, Sept., 1942.

Greenland, as seen from the North Pole. Vol. LXXVIII, pp. 118-119, 1 two-page, July, 1940.

Lapland. Vol. LXXVI, p. 645, 1 page, Nov., 1939.

Arctic Regions—*Continued*

North Polar Regions. Vol. XVIII, special supplement in colors, 17½ x 17½ inches, July, 1907.

North Polar Regions. Vol. XX, p. 916, 1 page, Oct., 1909.

Northern and Southern Hemispheres, with Insets of Time Zones, World Terrain, and Tables of Airline Distances in Four Hemispheres. Vol. LXXXIII, special supplement in colors, 41 x 22 inches, Apr., 1943.

Northern Hemisphere, showing Proposed Routes of Aircraft Over the Arctic Zone. Vol. XLII, p. 206, 1 page, Aug., 1922.

Northern Hemisphere, with Tables showing Airline Distances in the Pacific, the Atlantic, the Arctic, and the Americas. Vol. LXXXIX, special supplement in colors, 21¾ x 24 inches, Feb., 1946.

Peary's Sledge Routes and Surveys. Vol. XIV, p. 28, 1 page, Jan., 1903.

Record of Rear Admiral Peary's 20 Years of Polar Exploration, Finally Crowned with Success, April 6, 1909. Vol. XXXVII, p. 297, 1 page, Apr., 1920.

Route of the *Frithjof,* 1898. Vol. X, p. 483, 1 third-page, Dec., 1899.

Route of the *Norge* (Airship) from Rome to Alaska : A Flight of 8,500 Miles Across the Top of the World. Vol. LII, p. 188, 1 page, Aug., 1927.

World, with Insets showing Arctic and Antarctic Regions, Natural Vegetation and Ocean Currents, and Density of Population and Prevailing Winds. Vol. LXII, special supplement in colors, 26 x 38½ inches, Dec., 1932.

World Map, with Insets of Arctic and Antarctic Region, Territories Occupied by Belligerents in First and Second World Wars, and Table of Geographical Equivalents and Abbreviations. Vol. LXXXIV, special supplement in colors, 41 x 26½ inches, Dec., 1943.

Argentina:

Buenos Aires Region. Vol. LXXVI, p. 565, 1 half-page, Nov., 1939.

Route of Transandean Mail and Passenger Planes. Vol. LIX, p. 596, 1 third-page, May, 1931.

Arizona:

Arizona. Vol. LV, p. 8, 1 two-thirds-page, Jan., 1929.

Arizona and New Mexico, showing Location of Indian Ruins. Vol. LVI, p. 743, 1 two-thirds-page, Dec., 1929.

Grand Canyon, from Wyoming to Mexico. Vol. XXVI, p. 152, 1 page, Aug., 1914.

Grand Canyon of the Colorado River : 1923 Expedition of the U. S. Geological Survey. Vol. XLV, p. 474, 1 three-quarters-page, May, 1924.

Arizona—*Continued*

Old Yuma Trail Region. Vol. XII, p. 132, 1 page, Apr., 1901.

Route to Rainbow Natural Bridge. Vol. XLIII, p. 198, 1 half-page, Feb., 1923.

Southwestern United States. Vol. XXI, p. 632, 1 page, Aug., 1910.

Southwestern United States. Vol. LXXVII, special supplement in colors, 35 x 26 inches, June, 1940.

Arkansas:

Arkansas. Vol. XC, pp. 280-281, two-page spread, Sept., 1946.

Ozark Plateau, showing Missouri and Arkansas with Bordering States. Vol. LXXXIII, p. 593, 1 two-thirds-page, May, 1943.

Armenia:

Ancient Armenia, and the Country Where the Armenians Now Live. Vol. XXVIII, p. 359, 1 half-page, Oct., 1915.

See also Turkey.

Aruba (Island), West Indies:

Caribbean Regions, with Enlargements of Aruba, Bonaire, and Curaçao. Vol. LXXXIII, p. 172, 1 page, Feb., 1943.

Asia:

Arabia, Turkey, Persia, Egypt. Vol. XXIV, p. 72, 1 two-thirds-page, Jan., 1913.

Arid Regions and Closed Basins of Asia. Vol. XII, p. 254, 1 quarter-page, July, 1901.

Asia, from "Theatrum Orbis Terrarum," Sixteenth Century. Vol. LXIV, p. 771, 1 half-page, Dec., 1933.

Asia, showing Route Flown by the Days. Vol. LXI, p. 656, 1 half-page, June, 1932.

Asia and Adjacent Areas, with Table of Airline Distances in Statute Miles. Vol. LXXXII, special supplement in colors, 40 x 26½ inches, Dec., 1942.

Asia and Adjacent Regions. Vol. LXIV, special supplement in colors, 30¾ x 38 inches, Dec., 1933.

Asia and Adjoining Europe with a Portion of Africa. Vol. XXXIX, special supplement in colors, 28 x 36 inches, May, 1921.

Central Asia. Vol. LXIX, p. 7, 1 half-page, Jan., 1936.

Central Asia, showing the Route of the Morden-Clark Asiatic Expedition. Vol. LII, p. 374, 1 page, Oct., 1927.

Central Asia and the Route Followed by Mr. and Mrs. Owen Lattimore from Peiping to India. Vol. LV, p. 664, 1 two-thirds-page, June, 1929.

China-India War Route, with Enlargement showing Minya Konka and the Route Followed by the Sikang Expedition. Vol. LXXXIII, p. 628, 1 page, May, 1943.

Eastern Hemisphere, showing Interrelation of the Races. Vol. XII, p. 264, 1 page, July, 1901.

Asia—*Continued*

Europe and the Near East. Vol. LVI, special supplement in colors, 34¼ x 39¼ inches, Dec., 1929.

Far East. Vol. XI, p. 290, 1 three-quarters-page, July, 1900.

India, from "Geographia Universalis," 1552. Vol. LXII, p. 765, 1 half-page, Dec., 1932.

Indian Ocean, including Australia, New Zealand and Malaysia, with Insets of Singapore and Canton-Hong-Kong Area. Vol. LXXIX, special supplement in colors, 25½ x 32¾ inches, Mar., 1941.

Japan and Adjacent Regions of Asia and the Pacific Ocean, with Insets of Industrial Centers of Japan and the Marshall Islands. Vol. LXXXV, special supplement in colors, 26½ x 34½ inches, Apr., 1944.

Marco Polo's Travels Through Asia. Vol. LIV, pp. 508-509, 1 two-page, Nov., 1928.

Mongolia, Manchuria, Chosen, East Turkestan, Tibet, Northern India. Vol. XXIII, special supplement in colors, 17 x 23 inches, Oct., 1912.

Near East, showing Egypt, Anatolia, and the Arab Kingdoms of Hedjaz, Transjordania, and Iraq. Vol. XLIII, p. 534, 1 three-quarters-page, May, 1923.

Northern Europe and Asia, showing Advance of Russia in Asia. Vol. XVI, p. 404, 1 third-page, Sept., 1905.

Philippine Islands as the Geographical Center of the Far East. Vol. XI, special supplement, 7½ x 10¾ inches, Jan., 1900.

Physical Map of Asia, Illustrating the Obstacles to Land Transportation Which Rendered Early Commerce Between Occident and Orient Extremely Difficult. Vol. XVI, p. 400, 1 page, Sept., 1905.

Ptolemy's Map. Vol. LXII, p. 765, 1 half-page, Dec., 1932.

Relief Map of Eurasia. Vol. XII, p. 251, 1 half-page, July, 1901.

Route Followed by Sir Ross Smith, in First Aëroplane Voyage from London to Australia. Vol. XXXIX, p. 230, 1 page, Mar., 1921.

Route Followed by the Citroën-Haardt Trans-Asiatic Expedition. Vol. LXII, p. 522, 2 half-page, Nov., 1932.

Route Followed by the Citroën-Haardt Trans-Asiatic Expedition from Beyrouth to Peiping. Vol. LXI, p. 324, 1 half-page, Mar., 1932.

Route of the Citroën Trans-Asiatic Expedition in Asia. Vol. LX, p. 388, 2 half-page, Oct., 1931.

Southeast Asia and Pacific Islands from the Indies and the Philippines to the Solomons, with 22 Inset Maps of Important Cities and Islands. Vol. LXXXVI, special supplement in colors, 41 x 26½ inches, Oct., 1944.

Asia—*Continued*

Telegraph Lines of China, 1904. Vol. XVI, p. 409, 1 half-page, Sept., 1905.

Thaw Trans-Asia Expedition Following the Old Silk Routes. Vol. LXXVIII, pp. 456-457, Oct., 1940,

Theater of War in Europe, Africa, and Western Asia, with Table of Airline Distances in Statute Miles. Vol. LXXXII, special supplement in colors, 26½ x 31 inches, July, 1942.

Trade Routes from the East to Egypt. Vol. XII, p. 293, 1 half-page, Aug., 1901.

Turkey, Persia, Afghanistan, and Southern Russia. Vol. XXXIV, p. 277, 1 page, Oct., 1918.

Union of Soviet Socialist Republics, with International Boundaries according to Russian Treaties and Claims as of October 1, 1944. Boundaries of January 1, 1938, are shown in red. Vol. LXXXVI, special supplement in colors, 40 x 25 inches, Dec., 1944.

Volcanic Axes and Structure Lines in Eastern Asia and Alaska and Why Japan Is Subject to Frequent Destructive Earthquakes. Vol. XLIV, p. 446, 1 page, Oct., 1923.

See also names of individual countries.

Asia Minor:

Greece and the Aegean, showing Sites of Antiquity and the Necklace of Hellenic Cities that Adorned the Coast of Asia Minor. Vol. LXXXV, pp. 280-281, 1 two-page, Mar., 1944.

Railways Constructed in Asia Minor and Persia. Vol. XI, p. 202, 1 page, May, 1900.

See also Anatolia ; Turkey.

Atafu (Island), Tokelau Islands :

Pacific Ocean and the Bay of Bengal, with Inset of Atafu. Vol. LXXXIV, special supplement in colors, 36½ x 26½ inches, Sept., 1943.

Athens, Greece :

Classical Lands of the Mediterranean, with Inset of Ancient Athens. Vol. LXXVII, special supplement in colors, 35¼ x 26 inches, Mar., 1940.

Atlantic Ocean:

Atlantic Ocean, showing Mileage of Air Routes to Norway, Britain, and Portugal from Newfoundland, Greenland, and Iceland. Vol. LXXX, p. 77, 1 page, July, 1941.

Atlantic Ocean, with Inset of Isthmus of Panama. Vol. LXXVI, special supplement in colors, 25 x 31 inches, July, 1939.

Atlantic Ocean, with Inset of Isthmus of Panama and a Table of Airline Distances in Statute Miles. Vol. LXXX, special supplement in colors, 31¼ x 25 inches, Sept., 1941.

General Direction of the Gulf Stream and Other Currents in the North Atlantic Ocean. Vol. XXIII, p. 772, 1 half-page, Aug., 1912.

Atlantic Ocean—*Continued*

How Commander Byrd Plots a New Transatlantic Route Along Which Future Flyers May Cross on Schedule. Vol. LII, p. 348, 1 half-page, Sept., 1927.

Iceberg Danger Zone in the North Atlantic. Vol. L, p. 4, 1 half-page, July, 1926.

Military Outposts Leased from Britain Put New Teeth in Uncle Sam's Defenses. Vol. LXXVIII, p. 621, 1 page, Nov., 1940.

Pilot Chart of the North Atlantic Ocean for February, 1903. Vol. XIV, special supplement, 32 x 21¾ inches, Feb., 1903.

Route of the *Alice* (Yacht). Vol. LXXIII, p. 268, 1 half-page, Mar., 1938.

Route of the *Blossom* (Ship). Vol. LII, p. 5, 1 three-quarters-page, July, 1927.

Route of the Lindberghs in the *Tingmissartoq.* Vol. LXVI, pp. 266-267, 2 half-page, Sept., 1934.

Route of the *Yankee,* from Gloucester, Massachusetts, through the Panama Canal to Pitcairn Island. Vol. LXXXI, p. 4, 1 two-thirds-page, Jan., 1942.

South Atlantic Ocean, showing Location of Tristan da Cunha. Vol. LXXIV, p. 674, 1 half-page, Nov., 1938.

Western Atlantic Ocean and Caribbean Sea, showing Location of New United States Defense Bases. Vol. LXXVIII, p. 621, 1 page, Nov., 1940.

World Globe, showing Submarine Mountain Ranges and Deeps of Atlantic Ocean. Vol. LXXXVII, p. 112, 1 two-thirds-page, Jan., 1945.

Attu (Island), Aleutian Islands :

Pacific Ocean and the Bay of Bengal, with Inset of Attu. Vol. LXXXIV, special supplement in colors, 36½ x 26½ inches, Sept., 1943.

Austral Islands, Pacific Ocean :

Marquesas, Tuamotu, and Austral Islands. Vol. XLVIII, p. 366, 1 half-page, Oct., 1925.

See also Vavitao.

Australia:

Australia. Vol. XXX, pp. 480-481, 1 two-page, Dec., 1916.

Australia, with Enlargement of Central Primordial Lands Inhabited by Aborigines. Vol. LXXXIX, p. 91, 1 half-page, Jan., 1946.

Australia, with Inset of Tasmania. Vol. LXVIII, pp. 672-673, 2 pages, Dec., 1935.

Australia and Neighboring Islands. Vol. LXXXII, p. 124, 1 sixth-page, July, 1942.

Australia Superposed on Outline of North America of Same Scale, in Correct Latitude. Vol. XXX, p. 477, 1 two-thirds-page, Dec., 1916.

Australia Superposed on Outline of the United States, to Show Relative Sizes. Vol. XXX, p. 476, 1 half-page, Dec., 1916.

Distribution of the Population of Australia. Vol. XXX, p. 512, 1 half-page, Dec., 1916.

Australia *Continued*

East Coast of Australia, showing Great Barrier Reef. Vol. LVIII, p. 359, 1 half-page, Sept., 1930.

Great Barrier Reef, with Inset of Australia. Vol. LXXVII, p. 827, 1 page, June, 1940.

Indian Ocean, including Australia, New Zealand and Malaysia. Vol. LXXXIX, special supplement in colors, 25½ x 32¾ inches, Mar., 1941.

Isolation of Australia. Vol. XXX, p. 475, 1 half-page, Dec., 1916.

New Guinea, New Caledonia, and Fiji Command the Shortest Supply Routes from America to Australia, with Table of Airline Distances. Vol. LXXXI, pp. 698-699, 1 two-page, June, 1942.

Northwest Coast of Australia. Vol. XLV, p. 332, 1 half-page, Mar., 1924.

Pacific Islands, showing Limit of Long-range Bombing from Northern Australia, with Table of Airline Distances in Statute Miles. Vol. LXXXIII, pp. 56-57, 1 two-page, Jan., 1943.

Pacific War Area, showing Australia, New Zealand, Netherlands Indies, and Surrounding Islands. Vol. LXXXI, pp. 416-417, 1 two-page, Apr., 1942.

Philippine Islands as the Geographical Center of the Far East. Vol. XI, special supplement, 7½ x 10¾ inches, Jan., 1900.

Physical Map of Australia. Vol. XXX, p. 489, 1 half-page, Dec., 1916.

Railroad Map of Australia. Vol. XXX, p. 550, 1 eighth-page, Dec., 1916.

Rainfall in Australia. Vol. XXX, p. 488, 1 half-page, Dec., 1916.

Austria:

Austria, showing Rivers Paddled by Cornelia Stratton Parker. Vol. LXI, p. 368, 1 two-thirds-page, Mar., 1932.

Austria-Hungary. Vol. XXIII, p. 1284, 1 page, Dec., 1912.

Austria-Hungary. Vol. XXVI, p. 392, 1 page, Oct., 1914.

Austro-Italo Alpine Region, with Surrounding Territory. Vol. XXVII, p. 374, 1 page, Apr., 1915.

Frontier Cities of Italy and Austria-Hungary. Vol. XXVII, p. 628, 1 page, June, 1915.

Salzkammergut (District). Vol. LXXI, p. 446, 1 third-page, Apr., 1937.

Azores (Islands), Atlantic Ocean:

Azores, with Inset of Atlantic Ocean. Vol. LXVII, p. 36, 1 half-page, Jan., 1935.

Three Groups of the Azores and the Routes of the Successful American Aviators in Their Transatlantic Flight; also the Route Chosen by the Ill-Fated Hawker-Grieve Expedition. Vol. XXXV, p. 515, 1 page, June, 1919.

Baffin Island, Canada :

Arctic Regions, showing Capt. Bob Bartlett's World, as Seen from 10,000 Miles in Space. Vol. LXXXIX, p. 604, 1 half-page, May, 1946.

Bahama Islands, West Indies :

Bahama Islands, with Inset of New Providence Island. Vol. LXIX, p. 223, 1 half-page, Feb., 1936.

Cuba and Bahama Islands. Vol. LXIV, p. 348, 1 page, Sept., 1933.

Bahrein Island, Persian Gulf :

Bahrein, with Inset of Middle East. Vol. LXXXIX, p. 199, 1 half-page, Feb., 1946.

Baily Group, Pacific Ocean. *See* Haha Jima Retto.

Baja California (Lower California), Mexico :

Baja California, with Inset showing Relationship to California, Mexico, and States of the Southwest. Vol. LXXXII, p. 258, 1 page, Aug., 1942.

Cruise of the *Kinkajou* to Desert Islands of Mexico. Vol. LXXX, p. 340, 1 page, Sept., 1941.

Desert Islands of Lower California. Vol. XLIV, p. 73, 1 quarter-page, July, 1923.

Lower California, showing Route of E. W. Nelson. Vol. XXII, p. 446, 1 page, May, 1911.

Mexico and the Peninsula of Lower California. Vol. XXXVI, p. 310, 1 page, Oct., 1919.

Baker (Island), Pacific Ocean :

Pacific Ocean and the Bay of Bengal, with Inset of Baker Island. Vol. LXXXIV, special supplement in colors, 36½ x 26½ inches, Sept., 1943.

Balearic Islands, Spain :

Balearic Islands. Vol. LIV, p. 179, 1 quarter-page, Aug., 1928.

Majorca, Balearic Islands. Vol. XLV, p. 431, 1 quarter-page, Apr., 1924.

Bali (Island), Netherlands Indies :

Bali. Vol. LXXV, p. 316, 1 third-page, Mar., 1939.

Balkan Peninsula:

Balkan States. Vol. XXIV, p. 224, 1 page, Feb., 1913.

Balkan States and Central Europe. Vol. XXVI, special supplement in colors, 17 x 22½ inches, Aug., 1914.

Bulgaria, Servia, Albania, Montenegro, and Turkey in Europe. Vol. XXII, p. 421, 1 page, Apr., 1915.

Bulgaria, Servia, and Turkey in Europe. Vol. XXIII, p. 1152, 1 page, Nov., 1912.

Southeastern Europe, showing the Balkan States and European Turkey. Vol. XIX, p. 799, 1 page, Nov., 1908.

See also names of individual countries.

Balsas, Río, Mexico:

Río Balsas Region. Vol. XC, p. 254, 1 half-page, Aug., 1946.

Baltic Regions:

Baltic Region, with Inset of Bornholm (Island). Vol. LXXXVII, p. 240, 1 half-page, Feb., 1945.

Estonia, with Inset of the Baltic Region. Vol. LXXVI, p. 805, 1 half-page, Dec., 1939.

Southeast Baltic Coast. Vol. LXXIII, p. 770, 1 half-page, June, 1938.

Barro Colorado Island, Panama Canal Zone:

Barro Colorado, the Largest Island in the Canal Zone. Vol. LII, p. 332, 1 half-page, Sept., 1927.

Bavaria (Region), Germany:

Map showing Location of Oberammergau. Vol. LXVIII, p. 746, 1 third-page, Dec., 1935.

Beechey Group, Pacific Ocean. *See* Chichi Jima Retto.

Belgian Congo:

Ruanda, "The Land of Giants and Pygmies." Vol. XXIII, p. 388, 1 page, Apr., 1912.

Western Rift Valley and Surrounding Country, with Inset of the Virunga Mountains. Vol. LXXVI, p. 515, 1 two-thirds-page, Oct., 1939.

Belgium:

Route of the *Nageoma* (Canoe). Vol. XLVII, p. 507, 1 half-page, May, 1925.

Western Theatre of War, with Inset of France and Belgium. Vol. XXXIII, special supplement, 26 x 31 inches, May, 1918.

Bengal, Bay of:

Pacific Ocean and the Bay of Bengal, with Inset Maps of Important Islands, and Table of Air-line Distances in Statute Miles. Vol. LXXXIV, special supplement in colors, 36½ x 26½ inches, Sept., 1943.

Bering Sea Region:

Bering Sea, showing Location of Pribilof Islands. Vol. XXII, p. 1141, 1 half-page, Dec., 1911.

Bering Sea Region. Vol. LXXV, p. 638, 1 two-thirds-page, May, 1939.

Bermuda (Islands), Atlantic Ocean:

Bermuda Islands. Vol. XLI, p. 2, 1 three-quarters-page, Jan., 1922.

Bermuda Islands, showing Location of Beebe Deep-Sea Dives. Vol. LXVI, p. 670, 1 third-page, Dec., 1934.

Location of Nonsuch Island and Deep-Sea Explorations off Bermuda. Vol. LIX, p. 656, 1 quarter-page, June, 1931.

Location of Nonsuch Island and Deep-Sea Explorations off Bermuda. Vol. LXI, p. 66, 1 half-page, Jan., 1932.

Bermuda (Islands), Atlantic Ocean—*Continued*

Mexico, Central America, and the West Indies, with Inset of the Bermuda Islands. Vol. LXVI, special supplement in colors, 23 x 40 inches, Dec., 1934.

Mexico, Central America, and the West Indies, with Inset of the Bermuda Islands. Vol. LXXVI, special supplement in colors, 24 x 41 inches, Dec., 1939.

Military Outposts Leased from Britain Put New Teeth in Uncle Sam's Defenses. Vol. LXXVIII, p. 621, 1 page, Nov., 1940.

Bhutan:

Bhutan, showing Journeys by John Claude White. Vol. XXV, p. 453, 1 page, Apr., 1914.

Bible Lands:

Bible Lands, showing Palestine, Trans-Jordan, and Egypt. Vol. LXXXV, p. 236, 1 page, Feb., 1944.

Bible Lands, showing Palestine, Trans-Jordan, and Syria. Vol. LXXXVI, p. 722, 1 page, Dec., 1944.

Bible Lands and the Cradle of Western Civilization, with Insets showing Jerusalem, the Holy Land, Economic Development, Route of the Exodus, St. Paul's Travels, Crusades, and Empire of Alexander the Great. Vol. LXXIV, special supplement in colors, 25 x 35 inches, Dec., 1938.

Bible Lands and the Cradle of Western Civilization, with Insets showing the Holy Land Today, Holy Land in Biblical Times, Jerusalem, Traditional Route of the Exodus, St. Paul's Travels and the Seven Churches, and the Crusades. Vol. XC, special supplement in colors, 32 x 22 inches, Dec., 1946.

Jordan River from Galilee to Dead Sea. Vol. LXXVIII, p. 784, 1 page, Dec., 1940.

World Trouble Spot, the Oil-Rich Middle East. Vol. LXXXIX, pp. 396-397, 1 two-page, Mar., 1946.

World's Deepest Land Depression Separates Palestine from Trans-Jordan. Vol. LXXI, p. 72, 1 third-page, Jan., 1937.

Bird Migration Routes:

Bird Migration Routes from South America to North America Converge Funnel-like in Central America. Inset of Veracruz and Tabasco, Mexico, showing La Venta Region, a Natural Bird Observatory. Vol. LXXXVII, p. 188, 1 two-thirds-page, Feb., 1945.

Breeding Ground, Winter Home, and Curious Migration Routes of the White-Winged Scoter. Vol. XXIV, p. 365, 1 half-page, Mar., 1913.

Breeding Ground and Winter Home of the Ross Goose. Vol. XXIV, p. 367, 1 half-page, Mar., 1913.

Breeding Grounds of Wild Ducks and Geese. Vol. XXIV, p. 362, 1 half-page, Mar., 1913.

Connecticut Warbler Chooses a Different Route to Return to Its Winter Home Than It Used When Leaving in Spring. Vol. XXII, p. 353, 1 three-quarters-page, Apr., 1911.

Bird Migration Routes—*Continued*

Evolution of the Present Migration Route of the Golden Plover. Vol. XXII, p. 357, 1 three-quarters-page, Apr., 1911.

How the Golden Plover Is Able to Navigate to the Hawaiian Islands in the Mid-Pacific. Vol. XXII, p. 359, 1 three-quarters-page, Apr., 1911.

Location of 46 out of the 56 National Bird Reservations. Vol. XXIV, p. 369, 1 half-page, Mar., 1913.

Longest Single Flight Made by any Bird—2,500 Miles Across the Ocean from Nova Scotia to South America. Vol. XXII, p. 354, 1 page, Apr., 1911.

Migration Route of the Black-Poll Warblers That Nest in Alaska. Vol. XXII, p. 348, 1 page, Apr., 1911.

Migration Route of the Bobolink is Changing. Vol. XXII, p. 365, 1 three-quarters-page, Apr., 1911.

Migration Route of the Cliff Swallows That Nest In Nova Scotia. Vol. XXII, p. 349, 1 half-page, Apr., 1911.

Principal Routes Used by Birds in Their Migrations Between North and South America. Vol. XXII, p. 347, 1 half-page, Apr., 1911.

Principal Winter Resorts of the Wild Ducks and Geese. Vol. XXIV, p. 368, 1 half-page, Mar., 1913.

Probable Summer Migration Route of Alaska Geese. Vol. LIII, p. 116, 1 third-page, Jan., 1928.

Robin Moves Much More Quickly on the Pacific Than on the Atlantic. Vol. XXII, p. 362, 1 page, Apr., 1911.

Scarlet Tanager. Vol. XXII, p. 363, 1 three-quarters-page, Apr., 1911.

Summer and Winter Homes of the Bird That Hates Darkness. Vol. XXII, p. 360, 1 page, Apr., 1911.

Two of the Principal Migration Routes of the Palm Warbler. Vol. XXII, p. 352, 1 three-quarters-page, Apr., 1911.

Ward-McIlhenny and the Louisiana Refuges for Game Birds. Vol. XXIV, p. 373, 1 three-quarters-page, Mar., 1913.

Bismarck Archipelago, Pacific Ocean. *See* New Britain ; New Ireland.

Bogoslof (Volcanic Island), Aleutian Islands :

Bogoslof Island in September, 1908. Vol. XX, p. 194, 1 quarter-page, Feb., 1909.

Bolabola (Island), Society Islands :

Topography of Two Coral-Ringed Volcanic Isles : Bolabola of the Society Group and Vavitao of the Austral Group. Vol. XLVIII, p. 369, 1 three-quarters-page, Oct., 1925.

Bolivia:

Lake Titicaca Region. Vol. LI, p. 214, 1 half-page, Feb., 1927.

Western Bolivia. Vol. LXVI, p. 649, 1 half-page, Nov., 1934.

Bonaire (Island), West Indies :

Caribbean Regions, with Enlargements of Aruba, Bonaire, and Curaçao. Vol. LXXXIII, p. 172, 1 page, Feb., 1943.

Bonin Islands, Pacific Ocean. *See* Ogasawara Shoto.

Borneo:

Borneo and Java. Vol. LXXXVIII, p. 297, 1 page, Sept., 1945.

Sarawak (State), Borneo. Vol. XXXV, p. 161, 1 half-page, Feb., 1919.

Bornholm (Island), Denmark :

Baltic Region, with Inset of Bornholm. Vol. LXXXVII, p. 240, 1 half-page, Feb., 1945.

Bosporus (Strait) :

Aegean Regions. Vol. LVI, p. 489, 1 half-page, Oct., 1929.

Bougainville (Island), Solomon Islands :

Solomon Islands, with Inset Maps showing Guadalcanal-Tulagi Area and Bougainville Area. Vol. LXXXII, p. 815, 1 half-page, Dec., 1942.

Brazil:

Basin of the Amazon, the World's Greatest River. Vol. XLIX, p. 354, 1 page, Apr., 1926.

Brazil. Vol. LXXXV, pp. 44-45, 1 two-page, Jan., 1944.

Brazil, showing State Boundaries. Vol. LVIII, p. 738, 1 page, Dec., 1930.

Brazil, Venezuela, and British Guiana, showing Mt. Roraima. Vol. LVIII, p. 588, 1 half-page, Nov., 1930.

Marajó Island. Vol. LXXIV, p. 638, 1 half-page, Nov., 1938.

North-Central South America, showing Brazil-Venezuela Boundary. Vol. LXIV, p. 589, 1 two-thirds-page, Nov., 1933.

Rio de Janeiro, Its Famous Bay and Surrounding Hills. Vol. XXXVIII, p. 173, 1 half-page, Sept., 1920.

Southern Matto Grosso (State) and Paraguay, with Inset showing River System. Vol. LXXXIV, p. 461, 1 two-thirds-page, Oct., 1943.

See also São Paulo (State).

British Columbia (Province), Canada :

Coastline of British Columbia. Vol. LXIV, p. 6, 1 page, July, 1933.

Columbia Ice Field Photographic Expedition. Vol. XLVII, p. 382, 1 half-page, Apr., 1925.

Kananaskis Lakes. Vol. XIII, p. 167, 1 page, May, 1902.

Map of Northwestern United States and Neighboring Canadian Provinces. Vol. LXXIX, special supplement in colors, 24½ x 36 inches, June, 1941.

Pacific Coast Defense Area. Vol. LXXXII, p. 425, 1 half-page, Oct., 1942.

Tweedsmuir Park. Vol. LXXIII, p. 454, 1 half-page, Apr., 1938.

British Columbia (Province), Canada—*Continued*

Unexplored Territory of British Columbia. Vol. LXXIII, p. 452, 1 third-page, Apr., 1938.

Victoria, British Columbia. Vol. XVIII, p. 347, 1 quarter-page, May, 1907.

Yukon-British Columbia, Area Surveyed by Bradford Washburn in 1935, and Adjoining Alaska, Mapped by the International Boundary Commission in 1906-1908. Vol. LXIX, pp. 720-721, 1 two-page, June, 1936.

British East Africa:

Roosevelt's Route and Hunting Trips in Africa. Vol. XXII, p. 2, 1 page, Jan., 1911.

British Guiana:

Boundaries Claimed by Great Britain and Venezuela and Awarded by the Paris Tribunal, 1899. Vol. XI, p. 129, 1 page, Apr., 1900.

British Guiana. Vol. XXII, p. 847, 1 page, Sept., 1911.

Guianas, with an Inset showing the Territory Traversed by the "Kaieteur and Roraima" Expedition. Vol. XXXVIII, p. 229, 1 page, Sept., 1920.

Roraima and Contiguous Territory. Vol. LVIII, p. 588, 1 half-page, Nov., 1930.

British Isles:

British Harbors. Vol. XXXI, p. 85, 1 page, Jan., 1917.

British Isles and North Sea, showing Fishing Banks and War Zone. Vol. XXVII, p. 149, 1 half-page, Feb., 1915.

Isle of Man, with Inset of the British Isles. Vol. LXXI, p. 588, 1 third-page, May, 1937.

Modern Pilgrim's Map of the British Isles. Vol. LXXI, special supplement in colors, 29 x 35 inches, June, 1937.

Scilly Isles, with Inset of the British Isles. Vol. LXXIV, p. 757, 1 half-page, Dec., 1938.

See also Channel Islands ; England ; Scotland ; Wales ; Wight, Isle of.

Brittany (Region), France :

Northwest France, including Normandy and Brittany. Vol. LXXXIV, pp. 218-219, 1 two-page, Aug., 1943.

Brown (Island), Marshall Islands. *See* Eniwetok.

Bulgaria:

Bulgaria. Vol. LXII, p. 197, 1 half-page, Aug., 1932.

Bulgaria, Serbia, and Macedonia. Vol. XXIII, p. 1152, 1 page, Nov., 1912.

Bulgaria and Serbia. Vol. XXVII, p. 421, 1 page Apr., 1915.

Burma:

Burma, Home of the Chaulmoogra Oil Tree. Vol. XLI, p. 242, 1 page, Mar., 1922.

Burma and Eastern India, showing Manipur, Scene of Battle for Upper Burma. Vol. LXXXV, p. 750, 1 page, June, 1944.

Burma—*Continued*

Burma to China as the Crow Flies. Vol. LXXXIV, p. 492, 1 page, Oct., 1943.

India and Burma, with Insets of Bombay and Calcutta Areas. Verso of Map : Political Subdivisions and The Political Geography of India. Vol. LXXXIX, special supplement in colors, 30 x 25 inches, Apr., 1946.

Southwestern China and Burma, showing Route of the Burma Road. Vol. LXXVIII, p. 631, 1 two-thirds-page, Nov., 1940.

California:

Central Valley. Vol. XC, p. 648, 1 page, Nov., 1946.

Colorado Desert Region. Vol. XI, p. 339, 1 page, Sept., 1900.

Geographical Distribution of Redwood on the Pacific Coast. Vol. X, p. 146, 1 page, May, 1899.

Great New Lake Rising in Salton Sink. Vol. XVIII, p. 36, 1 page, Jan., 1907.

Los Angeles Aqueduct. Vol. XXI, p. 595, 1 half-page, July, 1910.

Northern California, with Inset of San Francisco Bay and Vicinity. Vol. LXIX, pp. 312-313, 1 two-page, Mar., 1936.

Northern Coast, showing Route of Redwood Highway. Vol. LXXV, pp. 138-139, 1 page-and-a-half, Feb., 1939.

Relief Map of the Lower Colorado River, showing Irrigable Lands. Vol. XVII, p. 94, 1 page, Feb., 1906.

San Francisco Bay and Vicinity. Vol. XVII, p. 281, 1 page, May, 1906.

San Francisco Peninsula (Showing Principal Fault Lines). Vol. XVII, p. 287, 1 page, May, 1906.

Southern California. Vol. LXVI, pp. 534-535, 1 two-page, Nov., 1934.

Southwestern United States. Vol. LXXVII, special supplement in colors, 35 x 26 inches, June, 1940.

United States of America, with Inset Maps of San Francisco and Los Angeles. Vol. XLIII, special supplement in colors, 36¼ x 26½ inches, Apr., 1923.

Yosemite National Park. Vol. LXIX, p. 344, 1 third-page, Mar., 1936.

Cameroons:

Cameroun. Vol. LIX, p. 228, 1 two-thirds-page, Feb., 1931.

Canada:

Alaska-Canada Boundary Line. Vol. XXIII, p. 693, 1 page, July, 1912.

British Map, 1832. Vol. X, p. 438, 1 page, Nov., 1899.

Canada. Vol. LVI, p. 600, 1 page, Nov., 1929.

Canada, showing the Route Flown by the Author (J. A. Wilson) in His Air Survey of the Dominion. Vol. L, pp. 392-393, Oct., 1926.

Canada—*Continued*

Canada, with Insets showing Natural Regions, Precipitation and Temperature, Main Natural Resources, Routes of Explorers and Time Zones. Vol. LXIX, special supplement in colors, 27 x 40 inches, June, 1936.

Canada and Alaska, Map of the Hudson's Bay Company, 1857. Vol. X, p. 425, 1 page, Nov., 1899.

Canadian Map of 1831. Vol. X, p. 441, 1 page, Nov., 1899.

Canadian Map of 1857. Vol. X, p. 442, 1 page, Nov., 1899.

Chart Shewing Part of the Coast of N. W. America (Vancouver's Chart, No. I). Vol. X, special supplement, 15½ x 18 inches, Nov., 1899.

Chart Shewing Part of the Coast of N. W. America (Vancouver's Chart, No. II). Vol. X, special supplement, 15½ x 18 inches, Nov., 1899.

Columbia Ice Field Photographic Expedition. Vol. XLVII, p. 382, 1 half-page, Apr., 1925.

French Map, 1811. Vol. X, p. 115, 1 page, Nov., 1899.

Hudson's Bay Company Map, 1857. Vol. X, p. 424, 1 page, Nov., 1899.

Mackenzie River and Basin, with an Inset showing Amos Burg's Route from McPherson, Northwest Territories, to Fort Yukon, Alaska. Vol. LX, p. 132, 1 page, Aug., 1931.

Map of Northwestern United States and Neighboring Canadian Provinces. Vol. LXXIX, special supplement in colors, 24½ x 36 inches, June, 1941.

New Brunswick Faces Strategic Newfoundland Across the Gulf of St. Lawrence. Vol. LXXIX, p. 597, 1 page, May, 1941.

North America. Vol. XLV, special supplement in colors, 27 x 37 inches, May, 1924.

North America, with Inset of the Aleutian Islands. Vol. LXXXI, special supplement in colors, 26½ x 33 inches, May, 1942.

Provinces of Northwestern North America. Vol. XVIII, p. 176, 1 page, Mar., 1907.

Route and Landing Fields of the First Air Expedition from New York to Alaska, Completed in 53 Hours and 30 Minutes Flying Time. Vol. XLI, pp. 500-501, 1 page, May, 1922.

Route of New Trans-Canadian Railway. Vol. XIV, p. 214, 1 third-page, May, 1903.

Scottish Geographical Magazine Map, 1898. Vol. X, p. 448, 1 page, Nov., 1899.

Southeastern Alaska, showing Boundary Lines of American and British Claims. Vol. X, p. 454, 1 page, Nov., 1899.

Southeastern Canada, with Enlargement of Anticosti Island. Vol. LXXXI, p. 122, 1 two-thirds-page, Jan., 1942.

Southeastern Canada, with Inset of Gaspé Peninsula. Vol. LXVIII, p. 210, 1 two-thirds-page, Aug., 1935.

Unexplored Territory, British Columbia–Yukon. Vol. LXXIII, p. 452, 1 third-page, Apr., 1938.

Canada—*Continued*

United States and Adjoining Portions of Canada and Mexico. Vol. LXIII, special supplement in colors, 26 x 40 inches, May, 1933.

Western Canada, showing Alcan Highway. Vol. LXXXIII, p. 148, 1 half-page, Feb., 1943.

Yukon–British Columbia, Area Surveyed by Bradford Washburn in 1935, and Adjoining Alaska, Mapped by the International Boundary Commission in 1906-1908. Vol. LXIX, pp. 720-721, 1 two-page, June, 1936.

See also Alberta ; British Columbia ; Nova Scotia ; Ontario ; Quebec ; Yukon Territory.

Canal Zone. *See* Panama.

Canary Islands, Atlantic Ocean :

Canary Islands and an Inset showing Their Location in Relation to Africa and Spain. Vol. LVII, p. 612, 1 third-page, May, 1930.

Canton Island, Phoenix Islands :

Pacific Ocean and the Bay of Bengal, with Inset of Canton Island. Vol. LXXXIV, special supplement in colors, 36½ x 26½ inches, Sept., 1943.

South Pacific, showing Date Line and Canton Island, Site of 1937 Eclipse Expedition. Vol. LXXII, p. 380, 1 two-thirds-page, Sept., 1937.

Cape Breton Island, Nova Scotia :

Cape Breton Island Vol. XXXVIII, p. 35, 1 three-quarters-page, July, 1920.

Cape Cod, Massachusetts. *See* Cod, Cape.

Cape Verde Islands, Atlantic Ocean :

Africa, with Insets of the Cape Verde Islands, Relief Map, and a Table of Airline Distances in Statute Miles. Vol. LXXXIII, special supplement in colors, 29¼ x 31½ inches, Feb., 1943.

Cappadocia :

Location of Mt. Argæus and of the Troglodytes. Vol. XXXV, p. 315, 1 half-page, Apr., 1919.

Turkey and the Near East, with Inset of Cappadocia. Vol. LXXVI, p. 767, 1 half-page, Dec., 1939.

Caribbean Regions :

American Bases in the Lesser Antilles Protect the Panama Canal. Vol. LXXXI, p. 729, 1 half-page, June, 1942.

Caribbean Regions, showing Airline Distances in Statute Miles, with Enlargements of Aruba, Bonaire, and Curaçao. Vol. LXXXIII, p. 172, 1 page, Feb., 1943.

Central America and Neighboring Islands, showing Turtling Areas. Vol. LXXXIV, p. 181, 1 quarter-page, Aug., 1943.

Caribbean Regions—*Continued*

Countries of the Caribbean, Including Mexico, Central America, the West Indies and the Panama Canal, with Detailed Insets of the Panama Canal and the Canal Zone, Porto Rico and the Virgin Islands, and Guantanamo Bay, Cuba. Vol. XLI, special supplement in colors, 25 x 44 inches, Feb., 1922.

Geographical Relation of Venezuela to the Isthmian Canal Routes, to the West Indies and Florida. Vol. XIV, p. 18, 1 page, Jan., 1903.

Map of Central America, Cuba, Porto Rico and the Islands of the Caribbean Sea, with Inset of the Panama Canal and Canal Zone. Vol. XXIV, special supplement in colors, 12½ x 19 inches, Feb., 1913.

Mexico, Central America, and the West Indies. Vol. LXVI, special supplement in colors, 23 x 40 inches, Dec., 1934.

Mexico, Central America, and the West Indies. Vol. LXXVI, special supplement in colors, 24 x 41 inches, Dec., 1939.

Military Outposts Leased from Britain Put New Teeth in Uncle Sam's Defenses. Vol. LXXVIII, p. 621, 1 page, Nov., 1940.

Route Followed by Lindbergh in His Flight Over 13 Latin-American Countries. Vol. LIII, p. 532, 1 two-thirds-page, May, 1928.

Western Atlantic Ocean and Caribbean Sea, showing Location of New United States Defense Bases. Vol. LXXVIII, p. 621, 1 page, Nov., 1940.

See also West Indies *and* names of individual countries and islands.

Caroline Island, Line Islands :

Pacific Ocean and the Bay of Bengal, with Inset of Caroline Island. Vol. LXXXIV, special supplement in colors, 36½ x 26½ inches, Sept., 1943.

Caroline Islands, Pacific Ocean :

Strategic Isles of the Pacific : Chichi Jima, Eniwetok, Guam, Hachijo, Haha Jima, Jaluit, Kwajalein, Kusaie, Marcus, Palau, Paramushiro, Ponape, Rota, Saipan, Tinian, Truk, Wake, Yap. Vol. LXXXV, pp. 392-393, 17 island maps (two pages), Apr., 1944.

The Taking of Saipan Opens the Gate in Japan's Wall of Island Defenses. Vol. LXXXVII, p. 447, 1 half-page, Apr., 1945.

Truk, Ruk, Hogolu Islands, of the Caroline Group, showing Encircling Coral Reef. Vol. XL, p. 648, Dec., 1921.

See also Palau Islands ; Ponape ; Truk Islands ; Yap.

Celebes (Island), Netherlands Indies :

Celebes. Vol. LXXVIII, p. 56, 1 page, July, 1940.

South Celebes. Vol. LXXXVII, p. 58, 1 two-thirds-page, Jan., 1945.

Central America :

Atlantic Ocean, with Inset of Isthmus of Panama. Vol. LXXVI, special supplement in colors, 25 x 31 inches, July, 1939.

Central America—*Continued*

Bird Migration Routes from South America to North America Converge Funnel-like in Central America. Inset of Veracruz and Tabasco, Mexico, showing La Venta Region, a Natural Bird Observatory. Vol. LXXXVII, p. 188, 1 two-thirds-page, Feb., 1945.

Central America. Vol. XVIII, p. 273, 1 half-page, Apr., 1907.

Central America, showing the Principal Volcanoes Whose Eruptions Have for Centuries Levied a Heavy Toll on Life and Property. Vol. XXXVI, p. 194, 1 page, Sept., 1919.

Central America, with Special Reference to Nicaragua. Vol. XX, p. 1104, 1 page, Dec., 1909.

Central America and Neighboring Islands, showing Turtling Areas. Vol. LXXXIV, p. 181, 1 quarter-page, Aug., 1943.

Central America and Southern Mexico. Vol. XLVII, p. 64, 1 half-page, Jan., 1925.

Countries of the Caribbean, Including Mexico, Central America, the West Indies and the Panama Canal, with Detailed Insets of the Panama Canal and the Canal Zone, Porto Rico and the Virgin Islands, and Guantanamo Bay, Cuba. Vol. XLI, special supplement in colors, 25 x 44 inches, Feb., 1922.

Map of Central America, Cuba, Porto Rico, and the Islands of the Caribbean Sea, with Inset of the Panama Canal and Canal Zone. Vol. XXIV, special supplement in colors, 12½ x 19 inches, Feb., 1913.

Mexico, Central America, and the West Indies. Vol. LXVI, special supplement in colors, 23 x 40 inches, Dec., 1934.

Mexico, Central America, and the West Indies. Vol. LXXVI, special supplement in colors, 24 x 41 inches, Dec., 1939.

Route Followed by Lindbergh in His Flight Over 13 Latin-American Countries. Vol. LIII, p. 532, 1 two-thirds-page, May, 1928.

Route of A. F. Tschiffely on His Horseback Journey from Buenos Aires to Washington. Vol. LV, p. 140, 1 page, Feb., 1929.

Route of the Trail-Blazing Flight of U. S. Army Airplanes Through 20 Countries of Latin-America. Vol. LII, p. 452, 1 page, Oct., 1927.

See also Costa Rica ; El Salvador ; Guatemala ; Nicaragua ; Panama.

Ceylon (Island), Indian Ocean :

Ceylon, with Location Map. Vol. XC, p. 666, 1 two-thirds-page, Nov., 1946.

Outline of Ceylon. Vol. XXIII, p. 193, 1 quarter-page, Feb., 1912.

Chaco (Region), South America :

Paraguay, showing Part of Chaco Area. Vol. LXIII, p. 387, 1 third-page, Apr., 1933.

Channel Islands :

Channel Islands. Vol. LXII, p. 104, 1 half-page, July, 1932.

Channel Islands—*Continued*

Channel Islands, showing Their Geographical Relation to France and England. Vol. XXXVIII, p. 151, 1 quarter-page, Aug., 1920.

Charleston, South Carolina :

Streets and Historic Sights of Charleston. Vol. LXXV, p. 279, 1 page, Mar., 1939.

Chesapeake Bay Region:

Chesapeake Bay Region, showing Route of the *Tralee.* Vol. LXXVI, p. 361, 1 page, Sept., 1939.

Chichi Jima Retto, Ogasawara Shoto, Pacific Ocean :

Pacific Ocean and the Bay of Bengal, with Inset of Chichi Jima. Vol. LXXXIV, special supplement in colors, 36½ x 26½ inches, Sept., 1943.

Southeast Asia and Pacific Islands from the Indies and the Philippines to the Solomons, with Inset of Chichi Jima Retto. Vol. LXXXVI, special supplement in colors, 41 x 26½ inches, Oct., 1944.

Strategic Isles of the Pacific. Vol. LXXXV, pp. 392-393, 17 island maps (two pages), Apr., 1944.

Chile:

Central Chile, showing Valparaíso-Santiago Region. Vol. LXXXVI, p. 481, 1 third-page, Oct., 1944.

Chile. Vol. XLII, p. 223, 1 half-page, Sept., 1922.

Lake District. Vol. LXXX, p. 94, 1 page, July, 1941.

Route of A. F. Tschiffely on His Horseback Journey from Buenos Aires to Washington. Vol. LV, p. 140, 1 page, Feb., 1929.

Route of Transandean Mail and Passenger Planes. Vol. LIX, p. 596, 1 quarter-page, May, 1931.

China:

Aerial Routes Blazed by Capt. Hans Koester, in Four Years. Vol. LXXIII, p. 574, 1 two-thirds-page, May, 1938.

Canals in 718 Square Miles of Chekiang Province. Vol. XXIII, p. 932, 1 half-page, Oct., 1912.

Chekiang and Kiangsu Provinces (Showing Canals). Vol. XXIII, p. 933, 1 half-page, Oct., 1912.

China. Vol. LI, p. 625, 1 three-quarters-page, June, 1927.

China. Vol. LXXXVII, special supplement in colors, 37 x 26½ inches, June, 1945.

China, showing Areas of Japanese Penetration. Vol. LXXXV, p. 359, 1 two-thirds-page, Mar., 1944.

China *Continued*

China, showing Location of Choni in Kansu Province. Vol. LIV, p. 576, 1 half-page, Nov., 1928.

China, showing Szechwan. Vol. XXII, p. 1097, 1 half-page, Dec., 1911.

China and Its Territories. Vol. XXIII, special supplement in colors, 17 x 23 inches, Oct., 1912.

China Coast, showing Extent of Japanese Penetration. Vol. LXXXVII, p. 223, 1 page, Feb., 1945.

China-India War Route, with Enlargement showing Minya Konka and the Route Followed by the Sikang Expedition. Vol. LXXXIII, p. 628, 1 page, May, 1943.

China-Tibetan Border, showing Route of Joseph F. Rock to the Amnyi Machen Mountains. Vol. LVII, pp. 138-139, 1 two-page, Feb., 1930.

Chinese Empire and Japan : Showing the Provinces, Treaty Ports, Railways, etc., and the Present Condition of the Russian Railway Through Manchuria to Port Arthur. Vol. XI, insert, two-page, Aug., 1900.

Country from Ta-ku to Pekin. Vol. XI, p. 292, 1 three-quarters-page, July, 1900.

Eastern China. Vol. LXIX, p. 278, 1 page, Feb., 1936.

Eastern China, with Inset of Hong Kong. Vol. LXVI, p. 603, 1 page, Nov., 1934.

Eastern Part of Hunan as Delineated by William B. Parsons. Vol. XI, p. 394, 1 half-page, Oct., 1900.

Foreign Concessions in North China. Vol. XV, p. 469, 1 page, Dec., 1904.

Foreign Concessions in South China. Vol. XV, p. 470, 1 page, Dec., 1904.

Grand Canal Stretches 1,000 Miles Southward from Peiping. Vol. LXXI, p. 488, 1 two-thirds-page, Apr., 1937.

Hong Kong Island. Vol. LXXVII, p. 534, 1 half-page, Apr., 1940.

Indian Ocean, including Australia, New Zealand and Malaysia, with Inset of the Canton-Hong Kong Area. Vol. LXXIX, special supplement in colors, 25½ x 32¾ inches, Mar., 1941.

Joseph F. Rock's Route from Tungchwan to Choni. Vol. XLVIII, p. 334, 1 quarter-page, Sept., 1925.

Kwangsi, One of China's Least-Known Provinces. Vol. LXXII, p. 674, 1 half-page, Dec., 1937.

Land of the Nashi, in Yünnan Province, China. Vol. XLVI, p. 478, 1 half-page, Nov., 1924.

Northeast China. Vol. LXXII, p. 489, 1 two-thirds-page, Oct., 1937.

Northeast China, showing Canals. Vol. XXIII, p. 934, 1 half-page, Oct., 1912.

Northeast China, showing Strategic Position of Peiping and Tientsin. Vol. LXXII, p. 512, 1 two-thirds-page, Oct., 1937.

Northeastern China. Vol. XI, p. 336, special supplement, 18½ x 35½ inches, Sept., 1900.

China—*Continued*

Northeastern China, showing Location of Yun Kang Caves. Vol. LXXIII, p. 315, 1 third-page, Mar., 1938.

Northern China, showing Route of Hwang Ho (Yellow River) Across the Great Plain. Vol. LXXXI, p. 207, 1 half-page, Feb., 1942.

Northern China, showing the Meanderings of the Great Wall. Vol. XLIII, p. 116, 1 page, Feb., 1923.

Photograph of Model Relief Map showing China's Supply Roads and the Territories Now Occupied by Japan. Vol. LXXXII, pp. 344-345, two-page spread, Sept., 1942.

Portion of the Route of the National Geographic Society's Central-China Expedition. Vol. XLIX, p. 199, 1 third-page, Feb., 1926.

Railways Constructed and Proposed in China. Vol. XVI, p. 408, 1 half-page, Sept., 1905.

Route of Joseph F. Rock from Muli to the Konkaling Peaks. Vol. LX, p. 7, 1 three-quarters-page, July, 1931.

Shanghai, China, and Adjacent Regions. Vol. XXIII, p. 958, 1 half-page, Oct., 1912.

Shanghai's Geographic Position Makes It the Major Seaport of the Yangtze Valley. Vol. LXXII, p. 491, 1 third-page, Oct., 1937.

Shantung. Vol. XXXVI, p. 235, 1 two-thirds-page, Sept., 1919.

Sikang's Mountain Grasslands, Route Followed by Ray G. Johnson and Party. Vol. LXXXV, p. 718, 1 half-page, June, 1944.

Southeast China, showing Pearl River Delta. Vol. LXXVII, p. 534, 1 quarter-page, Apr., 1940.

Southwestern China, showing Hainan Island. Vol. LXXIV, p. 394, 1 two-thirds-page, Sept., 1938.

Southwestern China and Burma, showing Route of the Burma Road. Vol. LXXVIII, p. 631, 1 two-thirds-page, Nov., 1940.

Szechwan, Yünnan, and Sikang Provinces. Vol. LVIII, p. 388, 1 two-thirds-page, Oct., 1930.

Telegraph Lines of China in 1904. Vol. XVI, p. 409, 1 half-page, Sept., 1905.

Tibet, showing Adjacent Areas of India and China. Vol. XC, p. 172, 1 half-page, Aug., 1946.

Upper Salwin. Vol. XXI, p. 147, 1 page, Feb., 1910.

See also Kansu ; Manchuria ; Mongolia ; Puto Shan (Island) ; Sikang ; Sinkiang ; Tai Shan (Mountain) ; Tibet ; Yünnan.

Chishima Retto (Kuril Islands), Japan :

Japan and Adjacent Regions of Asia and the Pacific Ocean, with Insets of Industrial Centers of Japan and the Marshall Islands. Vol. LXXXV, special supplement in colors, 26½ x 34½ inches, Apr., 1944.

See also Paramushiro Jima.

Christmas Island, Line Islands :

Pacific Ocean and the Bay of Bengal, with Inset of Christmas Island. Vol. LXXXIV, special supplement in colors, 36½ x 26½ inches, Sept., 1943.

Classical Lands :

Classical Lands of the Mediterranean. Vol. LXXVII, special supplement in colors, 35¼ x 26 inches, Mar., 1940.

Europe and Northern Africa, showing Extent of Roman Empire, with Table of Historical Facts. Vol. XC, pp. 552-553, 1 two-page, Nov., 1946.

Extent of the Empire, at the Death of Augustus (A.D. 14). Vol. LXXIV, p. 538, 1 half-page, Oct., 1938.

Greece and the Aegean, showing Sites of Antiquity and the Necklace of Hellenic Cities that Adorned the Coast of Asia Minor. Vol. LXXXV, pp. 280-281, 1 two-page, Mar., 1944.

Rome-Naples Area, showing Main Arteries and Important Sites of Antiquity. Vol. XC, p. 569, 1 half-page, Nov., 1946.

See also Greece.

Cod, Cape, Massachusetts :

Cape Cod. Vol. LXXXIX, p. 741, 1 half-page, June, 1946.

Coffin Group, Pacific Ocean. *See* Haha Jima Retto.

Colombia :

Northwestern Colombia. Vol. LXXVII, p. 629, 1 quarter-page, May, 1940.

Republic of Colombia. Vol. XLIX, p. 132, 1 third-page, Feb., 1926.

Western Colombia. Vol. LXXVIII, p. 509, 1 third-page, Oct., 1940.

Colorado :

Colorado. Vol. LXII, p. 6, 1 page, July, 1932.

Course of the Rio Grande (River) from Its Source in Colorado through Northern New Mexico. Vol. LXXVI, p. 419, 1 third-page, Oct., 1939.

Southwestern United States. Vol. LXXVII, special supplement in colors, 35 x 26 inches, June, 1940.

Connecticut :

Connecticut. Vol. LXXIV, pp. 282-283, 1 two-page, Sept., 1938.

Northeastern United States. Vol. LXXXVIII, special supplement in colors, 41 x 26½ inches, Sept., 1945.

Reaches of New York City. Vol. LXXV, special supplement in colors, 26½ x 29 inches, Apr., 1939.

Connecticut (River), United States :

Route of the Connecticut River through New England. Vol. LXXXIII, p. 405, 1 two-thirds-page, Apr., 1943.

Coral Sea Area:

Coral Sea Area, showing the Solomons and New Hebrides, with an Inset of Efate. Vol. LXXXVI, p. 233, 1 four-fifths-page, Aug., 1944.

Corsica (Island), Mediterranean Sea:

Geographical Relation of Corsica to the Mother Country, France. Vol. XLIV, p. 223, 1 quarter-page, Sept., 1923.

Island of Corsica. Vol. XLIV, p. 224, 1 page, Sept., 1923.

Costa Rica:

Boundary Between Nicaragua and Costa Rica. Vol. XII, p. 27, 1 half-page, Jan., 1901.

Costa Rica, with Location Map of the Caribbean. Vol. XC, p. 412, 1 half-page, Oct., 1946.

Part of Costa Rica Which Was Overwhelmed by the Earthquake of May 4, 1910. Vol. XXI, p. 516, 1 half-page, June, 1910.

Crete (Island), Greece:

Eastern Mediterranean, with an Enlargement of Crete. Vol. LXXXIV, p. 550, 1 page, Nov., 1943.

Island of Crete, and Map showing Route of the *Bonita* (Breton Yawl) on Its Mediterranean Voyage. Vol. LV, p. 250, 1 page, Feb., 1929.

Crimean Autonomous Soviet Socialist Republic, R. S. F. S. R.:

Crimea. Vol. LXXXVII, p. 496, 1 half-page, Apr., 1945.

Cuba:

Countries of the Caribbean, Including Mexico, Central America, the West Indies and the Panama Canal, with Detailed Insets of the Panama Canal and the Canal Zone, Porto Rico and the Virgin Islands, and Guantanamo Bay, Cuba. Vol. XLI, special supplement in colors, 25 x 44 inches, Feb., 1922.

Cuba. Vol. XVII, special supplement in colors, 12 x 24 inches, Oct., 1906.

Cuba and Bahama Islands. Vol. LXIV, p. 348, 1 page, Sept., 1933.

Cuba and the Neighboring Bahama Islands. Vol. XXXVIII, p. 4, 1 page, July, 1920.

Gulf of Mexico, showing Cuba and Gulf Coast Areas. Vol. LXXXV, pp. 8-9, 1 two-page, Jan., 1944.

Map of Central America, Cuba, Porto Rico, and the Islands of the Caribbean Sea, with Inset of the Panama Canal and Canal Zone. Vol. XXIV, special supplement in colors, 12½ x 19 inches, Feb., 1913.

Mexico, Central America, and the West Indies, with Inset of Cuba. Vol. LXVI, special supplement in colors, 23 x 40 inches, Dec., 1934.

Mexico, Central America, and the West Indies, with Inset of Cuba. Vol. LXXVI, special supplement in colors, 24 x 41 inches, Dec., 1939.

Railways of Cuba. Vol. XIV, p. 113, 1 half-page, Mar., 1903.

Cumberland Gap (Region), United States:

Cumberland Gap, First High Gateway to the West. Vol. LXXXIV, p. 745, 1 quarter-page, Dec., 1943.

Curaçao (Island), West Indies:

Caribbean Regions, with Enlargements of Aruba, Bonaire, and Curaçao. Vol. LXXXIII, p. 172, 1 page, Feb., 1943.

Cyclades (Islands), Greece:

Aegean Regions, showing the Isles of Greece and the Italian Islands of the Aegean. Vol. LXXXV, p. 596, 1 page, May, 1944.

Cyprus (Island), Mediterranean Sea:

Island of Cyprus and an Inset showing its Location Near the Eastern Limits of the Mediterranean. Vol. LIV, p. 4, 1 half-page, July, 1928.

Czechoslovakia:

Czechoslovakia. Vol. LXXIV, pp. 176-177, Aug., 1938.

Czechoslovakia, Whose Place Names Present Serious Problems for the Student. Vol. XXXIX, p. 156, 1 quarter-page, Feb., 1921.

Daghestan Autonomous Soviet Socialist Republic, R. S. F. S. R.:

Caucasus, showing the Highlands of Daghestan. Vol. XXIV, p. 1086, 1 page, Oct., 1913.

Danger Islands, Pacific Ocean:

Pacific Ocean and the Bay of Bengal, with Inset of Danger Islands. Vol. LXXXIV, special supplement in colors, 36½ x 26½ inches, Sept., 1943.

Dardanelles:

Asia Minor, the Dardanelles, and the Islands of the Aegean Sea. Vol. XLII, p. 554, 1 half-page, Nov., 1922.

Davao, Mindanao, Philippine Islands:

Southeast Asia and Pacific Islands from the Indies and the Philippines to the Solomons, with Inset of Davao Area. Vol. LXXXVI, special supplement in colors, 41 x 26½ inches, Oct., 1944.

Delaware:

Delaware. Vol. LXVIII, p. 371, 1 page, Sept., 1935.

Historic and Scenic Reaches of the Nation's Capital. Vol. LXXIV, special supplement in colors, 26½ x 31¼ inches, July, 1938.

Maryland, Delaware, and District of Columbia. Vol. LI, special supplement in colors, 12 x 18 inches, Feb., 1927.

Northeastern United States. Vol. LXXXVIII, special supplement in colors, 41 x 26½ inches, Sept., 1945.

Delhi, India:

Delhi, showing Eight Sites of the City, including New Delhi. Vol. LXXXII, p. 469, 1 page, Oct., 1942.

Denmark:

Denmark. Vol. XLII, p. 124, 1 three-quarters-page, Aug., 1922.

Denmark. Vol. LXXVII, p. 3, 1 three-quarters-page, Jan., 1940.

See also Bornholm (Island).

District of Columbia. *See* Washington, D. C.

Dodecanese Islands, Aegean Sea:

Aegean Regions, showing Sites of Antiquity, with a boundary line between the Greek and Italian Islands of the Aegean. Vol. LXXXV, pp. 280-281, 1 two-page, Mar., 1944.

Aegean Regions, showing the Isles of Greece and the Italian Islands of the Aegean. Vol. LXXXV, p. 596, 1 page, May, 1944.

Italian Islands of the Aegean. Vol. LXXIX, p. 451, 1 two-thirds-page, Apr., 1941.

Dominican Republic:

Haiti and Santo Domingo. Vol. XIX, p. 215, 1 quarter-page, Mar., 1908.

Island of Haiti, showing Its Two Republics. Vol. XXXVIII, p. 489, 1 half-page, Dec., 1920.

West Indies from Cuba to Puerto Rico, with an Enlargement of Haiti and the Dominican Republic. Vol. LXXXV, p. 200, 1 two-thirds-page, Feb., 1944.

Dutch East Indies. *See* Netherlands East Indies.

East Prussia:

East Prussia, Danzig, and the Polish Corridor. Vol. LXXIII, p. 770, 1 half-page, June, 1938.

Easter Island, Pacific Ocean:

Easter Island. Vol. XL, p. 630, 1 page, Dec., 1921.

Eastern Hemisphere:

Map of Discovery. Reproduction in color of the painting by N. C. Wyeth, National Geographic Society, Washington, D. C. Vol. LIV, text, p. 568; supplement, Nov., 1928.

Map of the World (in Eastern and Western Hemispheres), with Insets showing Land and Water Hemispheres, Density of Population, Time Zones, and World Mapping. Vol. LXXX, special supplement in colors, 41 x 22 inches, Dec., 1941.

Routes Flown by Sir Alan J. Cobham Over Europe, Asia, Australia, and Africa. Vol. LIII, p. 350, 1 three-quarters-page, Mar., 1928.

Eastern Theater of War Map. *See* World War II: *Theater of War in the Pacific Ocean.*

Eclipses:

Map of Pacific Ocean, showing Position of Total Eclipse (1937) Every 15 Minutes. Vol. LXXII, p. 364, 1 half-page, Sept., 1937.

Ecuador:

Ecuador. Vol. LXV, p. 136, 1 half-page, Feb., 1934.

Ecuador—*Continued*

The Oriente, Where Fever Fighters Combed the Jungle for Quinine. Vol. LXXXIX, p. 349, 1 half-page, Mar., 1946.

Volcanic Peaks of Ecuador, and Inset of Northern South America. Vol. LV, p. 52, 1 half-page, Jan., 1929.

Efate (Island), New Hebrides:

Coral Sea Area, showing the Solomons and New Hebrides, with an Inset of Efate. Vol. LXXXVI, p. 233, 1 four-fifths-page, Aug., 1944.

Egypt:

Bible Lands, showing Palestine, Trans-Jordan, and Egypt. Vol. LXXXV, p. 236, 1 page, Feb., 1944.

Bible Lands and the Cradle of Western Civilization, with Insets showing Jerusalem, the Holy Land, Economic Development, Route of the Exodus, St. Paul's Travels, Crusades, and Empire of Alexander the Great. Vol. LXXIV, special supplement in colors, 25 x 35 inches, Dec., 1938.

Bible Lands and the Cradle of Western Civilization, with Insets showing the Holy Land To-day, Holy Land in Biblical Times, Jerusalem, Traditional Route of the Exodus, St. Paul's Travels and the Seven Churches, and the Crusades. Vol. XC, special supplement in colors, 32 x 22 inches, Dec., 1946.

Mediterranean Coast of Libia and Egypt. Vol. LXXVIII, p. 810, Dec., 1940.

Narrow Ribbon of Fertile Land Which Runs the Length of Egypt. Vol. XLIX, p. 272, 1 half-page, Mar., 1926.

Nile and Surrounding Territory from Aswân to the Mediterranean Sea, with Pictographs. Vol. LXXVII, pp. 438-439, 1 two-page, Apr., 1940.

Nile from Its Mouth to the First Cataract. Vol. XXIV, p. 972, 1 page, Sept., 1913.

Nile Valley, World's Greatest Mine of History. Vol. LXXX, p. 426, 1 two-thirds-page, Oct., 1941.

Route of Hassanein Bey Through the Libian Desert. Vol. XLVI, p. 236, 1 half-page, Sept., 1924.

Route of the Exodus. Vol. XX, p. 1013, 1 page, Dec., 1909.

Sinai and the Route of the Exodus. Vol. XXIII, p. 1282, 1 page, Dec., 1912.

Sinai Peninsula, showing in General the Route of the Children of Israel in Their Flight from Egypt to the Promised Land. Vol. LII, p. 713, 1 three-quarters-page, Dec., 1927.

Suez Canal District. Vol. LXVIII, p. 612, 1 half-page, Nov., 1935.

Suez-Red Sea Region. Vol. LXXXI, p. 507, 1 page, Apr., 1942.

Temples and Tombs of Ancient Egypt at Thebes. Vol. XLIII, p. 467, 1 half-page, May, 1923.

Egypt—*Continued*

Territory Observed in the Authors' (Brig. Gen. P. R. C. Groves and Maj. J. R. McCrindle) Flight Over Egypt, Sinai, and Palestine. Vol. L, p. 315, 1 half-page, Sept., 1926.

Eire:

Ireland, Mother of New Eire. Vol. LXXVII, p. 653, 1 page, May, 1940.

Ellesmere (Island), Arctic Region:

Arctic Regions, with Inset of Ellesmere Island. Vol. XLVIII, special supplement in colors, 19¼ x 18 inches, Nov., 1925.

Ellice Islands, Pacific Ocean. *See* Funafuti; Nukufetau; Nukulaelae.

El Salvador:

El Salvador. Vol. LXXXVI, p. 580, 1 half-page, Nov., 1944.

Enderbury Island, Phoenix Islands:

Pacific Ocean and the Bay of Bengal, with Inset of Enderbury Island. Vol. LXXXIV, special supplement in colors, 36½ x 26½ inches, Sept., 1943.

England:

Canoeists' Trip Through the Heart of England. Vol. XLI, p. 475, 1 half-page, May, 1922.

Central England, showing the Canals Connecting London and Liverpool. Vol. LXXVIII, p. 191, 1 two-thirds-page, Aug., 1940.

Cornwall. Vol. XLVI, p. 657, 1 half-page, Dec., 1924.

Devon and Cornwall, and Inset Sketch Map of the British Isles, showing Location of the Lake and Fen Districts and Devon. Vol. LV, p. 532, 1 two-thirds-page, May, 1929.

Fen District. Vol. LV, p. 609, 1 half-page, May, 1929.

Isle of Wight. Vol. LXVII, p. 6, 1 half-page, Jan., 1935.

Lake District. Vol. LV, p. 581, 1 quarter-page, May, 1929.

London, showing Route of Coronation Procession. Vol. LXXI, p. 611, 1 half-page, May, 1937.

Modern Pilgrim's Map of the British Isles. Vol. LXXI, special supplement in colors, 29 x 35 inches, June, 1937.

Northern England. Vol. LXV, p. 359, 1 three-quarters-page, Mar., 1934.

Scenic and Historic Properties of the National Trust. Vol. LXXXVII, pp. 420-421, 1 two-page, Apr., 1945.

Severn River Valley. Vol. LXIII, p. 421, 1 three-quarters-page, Apr., 1933.

Southampton Region. Vol. LXXVII, p. 92, Jan., 1940.

Southeastern England, showing Harassed Channel Coast. Vol. LXXIX, p. 70, 1 third-page, Jan., 1941.

England—*Continued*

Southern England, showing Historic Sites and Cities Along the Thames. Vol. LXXV, pp. 244-245, 2 half-pages, Feb., 1939.

Southwestern England, with Enlargement of Plymouth Area. Vol. LXXXIX, p. 215, 1 half-page, Feb., 1946.

Sussex County. Vol. LXVIII, p. 63, 1 page, July, 1935.

See also Channel Islands.

Eniwetok (Atoll), Marshall Islands:

Pacific Ocean and the Bay of Bengal, with Inset of Eniwetok. Vol. LXXXIV, special supplement in colors, 36½ x 26½ inches, Sept., 1943.

Southeast Asia and Pacific Islands from the Indies and the Philippines to the Solomons, with Inset of Eniwetok. Vol. LXXXVI, special supplement in colors, 41 x 26½ inches, Oct., 1944.

Strategic Isles of the Pacific. Vol. LXXXV, pp. 392-393, 17 island maps (two pages), Apr., 1944.

Eritrea:

Ethiopia, Eritrea, and Adjacent Territory. Vol. LXVIII, pp. 270-271, 2 pages, Sept., 1935.

Eskimos:

Distribution of Blond Eskimos. Vol. XXIII, p. 1224, 1 page, Dec., 1912.

Estonia:

Estonia, with Inset of the Baltic Region. Vol. LXXVI, p. 805, 1 half-page, Dec., 1939.

Ethiopia:

Eritrea, Ethiopia, and Surrounding Territory. Vol. LXVIII, p. 270-271, 2 pages, Sept., 1935.

Ethiopia. Vol. LIV, p. 123, 1 two-thirds-page, Aug., 1928.

Ethiopia, showing Mountainous Regions. Vol. LIX, p. 702, 1 two-thirds-page, June, 1931.

Route of Harry V. Harlan. Vol. XLVII, p. 618, 1 half-page, June, 1925.

Europe:

Asia and Adjacent Areas, with Table of Airline Distances in Statute Miles. Vol. LXXXII, special supplement in colors, 40 x 26½ inches, Dec., 1942.

Atlantic Ocean. Vol. LXXVI, special supplement in colors, 25 x 31 inches, July, 1939.

Atlantic Ocean, with Inset of Isthmus of Panama and a Table of Airline Distances in Statute Miles. Vol. LXXX, special supplement in colors, 31¼ x 25 inches, Sept., 1941.

Automobile Route from England to India. Vol. XLVIII, p. 193, 1 third-page, Aug., 1925.

Balkan States and Central Europe. Vol. XXVI, special supplement in colors, 17 x 22½ inches, Aug., 1914.

Europe—*Continued*

Boundary Lines of European Nations as Drawn by the Gaunt Hand of Hunger. Vol. XXXIII, p. 338, 1 half-page, Apr., 1918.

Central Europe and the Mediterranean. Vol. LXXVI, special map supplement in colors, 36½ x 26½ inches, Oct., 1939.

Countries Bordering the Mediterranean Sea. Vol. XXIII, special supplement in colors, 10 x 18 inches, Jan., 1912.

Europe, Asia, Africa, Australia, showing Relation of the Races. Vol. XII, p. 264, 1 page, July, 1901.

Europe, Showing Countries as Established by the Peace Conference at Paris. Vol. XXXIX, special supplement in colors, 30 x 33 inches, Feb., 1921.

Europe, showing Route Flown by the Days. Vol. LXI, p. 656, 1 half-page, June, 1932.

Europe, showing Routes of J. Parker Van Zandt's Flights. Vol. LXXV, p. 794, 1 page, June, 1939.

Europe, showing Territory Covered in Flights of Walter Mittelholzer. Vol. LXI, p. 466, 1 three-quarters-page, Apr., 1932.

Europe, showing the Great Sheet of Ice That Covered the British Isles, Scandinavia, Germany, and Half of Russia During the Second Glacial Age. Vol. XXIX, p. 115, 1 half-page, Feb., 1916.

Europe and Adjoining Portions of Africa and Asia. Vol. XXVIII, special supplement in colors, 28 x 32 inches, July, 1915.

Europe and Northern Africa, showing Extent of Roman Empire, with Table of Historical Facts. Vol. XC, pp. 552-553, 1 two-page, Nov., 1946.

Europe and the Mediterranean. Vol. LXXIII, special supplement in colors, 34 x 39 inches, Apr., 1938.

Europe and the Near East. Vol. LVI, special supplement in colors, 34¼ x 39¼ inches, Dec., 1929.

Europe and the Near East, as of April 1, 1940. Vol. LXXVII, special supplement in colors, 39 x 34 inches, May, 1940.

Europe and the Near East, with Inset Map of the Middle East, and a Table of Distances between Principal Ports via Shortest Navigable Routes. Vol. LXXXIII, special supplement in colors, 39 x 34 inches, June, 1943.

Europe at a Period When the British Isles and Scandinavian Peninsula Were a Part of the Mainland. Vol. XXIX, p. 113, 1 half-page, Feb., 1916.

Europe—*Continued*

Germany and Its Approaches, with International Boundaries as of September 1, 1939, the day Germany Invaded Poland and Boundaries as of January 1, 1938, before Germany seized Austria and Czechoslovakia. Vol. LXXXVI, special supplement in colors, 33½ x 26½ inches, July, 1944.

Map of Central Europe, showing Strategic Position of the Saar Basin. Vol. LXVII, p. 243, 1 half-page, Feb., 1935.

Map of the New Balkan States and Central Europe. Vol. XXVI, special supplement in colors, 17 x 22½ inches, Aug., 1914.

Map showing Territorial Changes in Area Around Poland. Vol. LXXV, p. 744, 1 two-thirds-page, June, 1939.

Physical Map of Europe. Vol. XXXIV, p. 506, 1 page, Dec., 1918.

Races of Europe and Adjoining Portions of Asia and Africa. Vol. XXXIV, special supplement in colors, 19¾ x 31 inches, Dec., 1918.

Relative Density of Railroads in Europe. Vol. XVI, p. 521, 1 half-page, Dec., 1905.

Relief Map of Europe. Vol. XII, p. 255, 1 third-page, July, 1901.

Roman Empire (A. D. 14). Vol. LXXIV, p. 538, 1 half-page, Oct., 1938.

Route Followed by Lieut. J. Parker Van Zandt in His 6,500-Mile Airplane Tour of Europe. Vol. XLVII, p. 275, 1 half-page, Mar., 1925.

Route Followed by Merlin Minshall on His Voyage in the *Hawke.* Vol. LXXI, pp. 536-537, May, 1937.

Route Followed by Sir Ross Smith, in First Aëroplane Voyage from London to Australia. Vol. XXXIX, p. 230, 1 page, Mar., 1921.

Route of the Lindberghs in the *Tingmissartoq.* Vol. LXVI, pp. 266-267, 2 half-page, Sept., 1934.

Southeast Baltic Coast. Vol. LXXIII, p. 770, 1 half-page, June, 1938.

Southeastern Europe, showing the Balkan States and European Turkey. Vol. XIX, p. 799, 1 page, Nov., 1908.

Theater of War in Europe, Africa, and Western Asia, with Table of Airline Distances in Statute Miles. Vol. LXXXII, special supplement in colors, 26½ x 31 inches, July, 1942.

Western Europe During the Third Inter-Glacial Age. Vol. XXIX, p. 118, 1 page, Feb., 1916.

Western Theatre of War, with Inset of France and Belgium. Vol. XXXIII, special supplement in colors, 26 x 31 inches, May, 1918.

See also names of individual countries.

Faeroe Islands, North Atlantic Ocean:

Faeroe Islands. Vol. LVIII, p. 610, 1 half-page, Nov., 1930.

Fakaofo (Atoll), Tokelau Islands :

Pacific Ocean and the Bay of Bengal, with Inset of Fakaofo. Vol. LXXXIV, special supplement in colors, 36½ x 26½ inches, Sept., 1943.

Falcon Island, Pacific Ocean :

New Zealand in the Samoa Group, with an Enlargement of Falcon Island. Vol. LIV, p. 760, 1 two-thirds-page, Dec., 1928.

Fanning Island, Line Islands :

Pacific Ocean and the Bay of Bengal, with Inset of Fanning Island. Vol. LXXXIV, special supplement in colors, 36½ x 26½ inches, Sept., 1943.

Far East:

Far East, showing the Strategic Position of Formosa. Vol. LXXXVII, p. 6, 1 half-page, Jan., 1945.

Far East, with Enlargement of Java. Vol. LXXXI, p. 91, 1 two-thirds-page, Jan., 1942.

Far East, with Inset of the Moluccas. Vol. LXXIX, p. 538, 1 page, May, 1941.

Indian Ocean, including Australia, New Zealand and Malaysia. Vol. LXXIX, special supplement in colors, 25½ x 32¾ inches, Mar., 1941.

Japan and Adjacent Regions of Asia and the Pacific Ocean, with Insets of Industrial Centers of Japan and the Marshall Islands. Vol. LXXXV, special supplement in colors, 26½ x 34½ inches, Apr., 1944.

Malay States, Thailand, and French Indo-China, with Inset of Singapore. Vol. LXXX, p. 662, 1 half-page, Nov., 1941.

Philippine Islands as the Geographical Center of the Far East. Vol. XI, special supplement, 7½ x 10¾ inches, Jan., 1900.

Singapore, Manila, and Hong Kong Form a Tripod of American and British Influence in the Far East. Vol. LXXVII, p. 534, 1 quarter-page, Apr., 1940.

Fatu-Hiva (Island), Marquesas Islands :

Marquesas Islands, showing Fatu-Hiva. Vol. LXXIX, p. 112, 1 quarter-page, Jan., 1941.

Federated Malay States:

Strategic Geographic Position of Singapore, with an Inset of the Malay Peninsula. Vol. XLIX, p. 238, 1 half-page, Mar., 1926.

Fiji Islands, Pacific Ocean :

Pacific Ocean and the Bay of Bengal, with Inset of Fiji. Vol. LXXXIV, special supplement in colors, 36½ x 26½ inches, Sept., 1943.

Finger Lakes Region, New York :

Central New York, showing Finger Lakes Region. Vol. LXXIX, p. 561, 1 two-thirds-page, May, 1941.

Finland:

Finland. Vol. LXXIV, p. 502, 1 page, Oct., 1938.

Finland and Lapland, showing Murman Railway. Vol. XXXV, p. 332, 1 two-thirds-page, Apr., 1919.

Norway, showing the Petsamo Region of Finland, Ceded to the U. S. S. R. Vol. LXXXVIII, p. 620, 1 three-quarters-page, Nov., 1945.

See also Åland (Islands).

Flint Island, Line Islands :

Pacific Ocean and the Bay of Bengal, with Inset of Flint Island. Vol. LXXXIV, special supplement in colors, 36½ x 26½ inches, Sept., 1943.

Florida:

Florida, with Insets of the following Areas : Miami-Palm Beach, Pensacola, Jacksonville-St. Augustine, St. Petersburg-Sarasota-Tampa. Vol. LVII, special supplement in colors, 12½ x 13¼ inches, Jan., 1930.

Gulf of Mexico, showing Florida and Coastal Areas of United States and Mexico. Vol. LXXXV, pp. 8-9, 1 two-page, Jan., 1944.

South Florida. Vol. XVII, p. 6, 1 half-page, Jan., 1906.

Southern Florida. Vol. LXXVII, p. 118, 1 page, Jan., 1940.

Florida (Island), Solomon Islands :

Islands of the South Pacific, with Insets of Florida Island and Ontong Java. Vol. LXV, p. 268, 1 half-page, Mar., 1934.

Florida Keys:

Florida Keys, showing Location of Wreck of H. M. S. *Winchester.* Vol. LXXX, p. 811, 1 two-thirds-page, Dec., 1941.

Formosa (Island), China Sea :

Far East, showing the Strategic Position of Formosa. Vol. LXXXVII, p. 6, 1 half-page, Jan., 1945.

Formosa. Vol. LXXXVII, p. 7, 1 page, Jan., 1945.

Formosa, showing Its Geographical Relations to Japan, China, and the Philippines. Vol. XXXVII, p. 262, 1 half-page, Mar., 1920.

Japan and Korea, with Insets of Kuril Islands, Pescadores, Karafuto, Ryukyu Islands, Okinawa, Formosa, Tokyo Area, and a Location Map of Japan in the Western Pacific. Vol. LXXXVIII, special supplement in colors, 37 x 26½ inches, Dec., 1945.

France:

British Mulberry and Omaha Beach, Artificial Harbors, off the Normandy Coast. Vol. LXXXVII, p. 565, 1 quarter-page, May, 1945.

France, showing the Route of the *Nageoma* (Canoe). Vol. LII, p. 133, 1 half-page, Aug., 1927.

France—*Continued*

Geographical Relation of Corsica to the Mother Country, France. Vol. XLIV, p. 223, 1 quarter-page, Aug., 1923.

La Camargue, the Island "Wild West" of Southern France. Vol. XLII, p. 4, 1 half-page, July, 1922.

Location of the Montespan Cavern in the Foothills of the Pyrenees. Vol. XLVI, p. 126, 1 half-page, Aug., 1924.

Metz, Nancy, and Epinal Regions. Vol. LXXXVII, p. 367, 1 two-thirds-page, Mar., 1945.

Normandy. Vol. LXIX, p. 629, 1 two-thirds-page, May, 1936.

Northwest France, including Normandy and Brittany. Vol. LXXXIV, pp. 218-219, 1 two-page, Aug., 1943.

Northwestern France, Belgium and Luxembourg, showing Cemeteries and Monuments to American Soldiers. Vol. LXV, p. 9, 1 half-page, Jan., 1934.

Paris Basin, with Inset of Northern France. Vol. LXXVII, p. 202, 1 half-page, Feb., 1940.

Provinces of France. Vol. XXVIII, p. 471, 1 half-page, Nov., 1915.

Route of the *Nageoma* (Canoe) Through the Back Doors of France. Vol. XLIV, p. 3, 1 half-page, July, 1923.

Southeastern France, showing Mediterranean Coast. Vol. LXXXVI, p. 428, 1 three-quarters-page, Oct., 1944.

Western Peninsula of France and an Inset of St. Malo and Its Environs. Vol. LVI, p. 138, 1 two-thirds-page, Aug., 1929.

Western Theatre of War, with Inset of France and Belgium. Vol. XXXIII, special supplement, 26 x 31 inches, May, 1918.

See also Corsica (Island.)

Franz Josef Land, Arctic Region:

Arctic Regions, with Inset of Franz Josef Land. Vol. XLVIII, special supplement in colors, 19½ x 18 inches, Nov., 1925.

Franz Josef Land Archipelago, showing the New Lands Discovered and Explored by the Wellman Expedition. Vol. X, p. 502, 1 half-page, Dec., 1899.

French Guiana:

Surinam and French Guiana, with Insets showing the Location and Comparable Sizes of the Guianas. Vol. LXXXIII, p. 462, 1 two-thirds-page, Apr., 1943.

French Guinea:

French Guinea. Vol. LXVII, p. 699, 1 half-page, June, 1935.

French Indo-China:

French Indo-China. Vol. LX, p. 159, 1 quarter-page, Aug., 1931.

French Indo-China. Vol. LXVIII, p. 491, 1 page, Oct., 1935.

French Indo-China, showing the Location of the Ruins at Angkor, Cambodia. Vol. XXIII, p. 210, 1 page, Mar., 1912.

French Indo-China—*Continued*

Location of Angkor, the Capital of the Vast Empire Ruled by the Khmers. Vol. LIV, p. 304, 1 third-page, Sept., 1928.

Ruins of Angkor, Cambodia. Vol. XXIII, p. 225, 1 three-quarters-page, Mar., 1912.

French Somaliland:

French Somaliland. Vol. LX, p. 364, 1 quarter-page, Sept., 1931.

French West Africa:

French West Africa, with Pictographs, showing Route Followed by Mrs. Boulton. Vol. LXXIX, pp. 636-637, two-page spread, May, 1941.

Northwest Africa, showing Mileage Between Dakar, French West Africa, and Important Points in the Eastern and Western Hemispheres. Vol. LXXXI, p. 374, 1 three-quarters-page, Mar., 1942.

Funafuti (Island), Ellice Islands:

Pacific Ocean and the Bay of Bengal, with Inset of Funafuti. Vol. LXXXIV, special supplement in colors, 36½ x 26½ inches, Sept., 1943.

Galápagos Islands, Pacific Ocean:

South America, with Inset Maps of Airways and Relief, Chief Natural Resources, Precipitation and Temperature, and the Galápagos Islands. Vol. LXXII, special supplement in colors, 26¾ x 37½ inches, Dec., 1937.

South America, with Insets of the Galápagos Islands, Chief Natural Resources, Precipitation and Temperature, Airways and Relief, and a Table of Airline Distances and Flying Times in Hours. Vol. LXXXII, special supplement in colors, 26½ x 37¼ inches, Oct., 1942.

Garda (Lake), Italy:

Lake of Garda Region. War Zone on Austro-Italian Frontier Indicated. Vol. LXVIII, p. 334, 1 third-page, Sept., 1935.

Gardner Island, Phoenix Islands:

Pacific Ocean and the Bay of Bengal, with Inset of Gardner Island. Vol. LXXXIV, special supplement in colors, 36½ x 26½ inches, Sept., 1943.

Gaspé Peninsula, Canada:

Gaspé Peninsula, with Detailed Inset. Vol. LXVIII, p. 210, 1 two-thirds-page, Aug., 1935.

Geneva, Lake, Switzerland-France:

Lake Geneva Region. Vol. LXXII, p. 728, 1 third-page, Dec., 1937.

Georgia:

North Carolina, South Carolina, Georgia and Eastern Tennessee, with Inset Map of Atlanta. Vol. L, special supplement in colors, 14¾ x 19 inches, Sept., 1926.

Georgia—*Continued*

Okefinokee Swamp, Georgia. Vol. LXV, p. 603, 1 two-thirds-page, May, 1934.

Sea Islands, Georgia. Vol. LXV, p. 239, 1 two-thirds-page, Feb., 1934.

Germany:

Germany and Its Approaches, with International Boundaries as of September 1, 1939, the day Germany invaded Poland and Boundaries as of January 1, 1938, before Germany seized Austria and Czechoslovakia. Vol. LXXXVI, special supplement in colors, 33½ x 26½ inches, July, 1944.

Map of Bavarian Alps, showing Location of Oberammergau. Vol. LXVIII, p. 746, 1 third-page, Dec., 1935.

Map showing Strategic Position of the Saar Basin. Vol. LXVII, p. 243, 1 half-page, Feb., 1935.

New Germany as Limited by the Peace Treaty. Vol. XXXV, p. 546, 1 page, June, 1919.

Old and New Württemberg. Vol. XXII, p. 933, 1 half-page, Oct., 1911.

Rhineland. Vol. LXXXVIII, p. 4, 1 third-page, July, 1945.

Rhineland, showing Former Demilitarized Zone. Vol. LXIX, p. 832, 1 two-thirds-page, June, 1936.

Rivers Paddled by Cornelia Stratton Parker. Vol. LXI, p. 368, 1 two-thirds-page, Mar., 1932.

Ruhr Basin. Vol. XLI, p. 554, 1 third-page, May, 1922.

Saar Basin. Vol. LXVII, p. 242, 1 half-page, Feb., 1935.

States Forming Germany in November, 1918. Vol. XXXIV, p. 510, 1 page, Dec., 1918.

Western Theatre of War, with Inset of France and Belgium. Vol. XXXIII, special supplement, 26 x 31 inches, May, 1918.

Gilbert Islands, Pacific Ocean:

Gilbert Islands, with Insets of Tarawa and Makin. Vol. LXXXVII, p. 135, 1 two-thirds-page, Feb., 1945.

Pacific Islands, with Inset of Gilbert Islands. Vol. LXXXIII, p. 74, 1 half-page, Jan., 1943.

See also Makin; Tarawa.

Glaciers:

Atrevida, Lucia, and Marvine Lobe of Malaspina Glacier. Vol. XXI, p. 34, 1 half-page, Jan., 1910.

Bulb Glaciers of Lower Copper River (Copper River and Northwestern Railway Passing Between Childs and Miles Glaciers and Over the Stagnant Ice of Baird Glacier). Vol. XXI, p. 25, 1 half-page, Jan., 1910.

Columbia Glacier, Prince William Sound, with City of Washington Drawn to the Same Scale for Purposes of Comparison. Vol. XXI, p. 10, 1 page, Jan., 1910.

Glaciers—*Continued*

Comparing Sizes of Copper River Glaciers with Glaciers in the Rocky Mountains, Selkirks, and Cascades of the United States and Canada. Vol. XXII, p. 543, 1 half-page, June, 1911.

Fronts of Johns Hopkins, Grand Pacific, and Muir Glaciers, 1894 and 1907. Vol. XIX, p. 11, 1 page, Jan., 1908.

Hidden Glacier in 1899, 1905, 1906, and 1909. Vol. XXI, p. 45, 1 page, Jan., 1910.

Hubbard Glacier (Lower Portion), with Three Glaciers of the Swiss Alps Superimposed Upon It. Vol. XXI, p. 5, 1 half-page, Jan., 1910.

Location of the Glaciers of Prince William Sound. Vol. XXII, p. 540, 1 page, June, 1911.

Lower Copper River and Controller Bay Regions. Vol. XXI, p. 24, 1 half-page, Jan., 1910.

Malaspina Glacier (Largest in the World Outside of the Polar Regions). Vol. XXI, p. 9, 1 half-page, Jan., 1910.

Malaspina Glacier, Mount Saint Elias and Yakutat Bay. Vol. XXI, p. 4, 1 page, Jan., 1910.

Nunatak Glacier in 1895, 1899, and 1909. Vol. XXI, p. 44, 1 page, Jan., 1910.

Pacific Coast of the Gulf of Alaska. Vol. XXI, p. 3, 1 quarter-page, Jan., 1910.

Port Wells, Prince William Sound, Alaska, in 1899. Vol. XXII, p. 550, 1 half-page, June, 1911.

Valdez Glacier Highway. Vol. XXI, p. 11, 1 page, Jan., 1910.

Variegated and Haenke Glaciers. Vol. XXI, p. 35, 1 half-page, Jan., 1910.

Gobi (Desert), Outer Mongolia-China:

Mongolia, showing the Gobi. Vol. LXIII, p. 656, 1 half-page, June, 1933.

Gozo (Island), Mediterranean Sea:

Malta, Gozo, Comino and Filfla. Vol. LXXXIII, p. 378, 1 half-page, Mar., 1943.

Grand Canyon, Arizona:

Grand Canyon from Green River, Wyoming, to Mouth of Colorado, in Mexico. Vol. XXVI, p. 153, 1 page, Aug., 1914.

Grand Canyon of the Colorado River: 1923 Expedition of the U. S. Geological Survey. Vol. XLV, p. 474, 1 three-quarters-page, May, 1924.

Grand Union Canal, England:

Grand Union Canal, and Adjoining Canals. Vol. LXXVIII, p. 191, 1 two-thirds-page, Aug., 1940.

Grand Valley, Netherlands New Guinea:

New Guinea, with Inset showing Grand Valley and the Balim River. Vol. LXXXVIII, p. 674, 1 half-page, Dec., 1945.

Great Barrier Reef, Australia:

East Coast of Australia, showing Great Barrier Reef. Vol. LVIII, p. 359, 1 half-page, Sept., 1930.

Great Barrier Reef. Vol. LXXVII, p. 827, 1 page, June, 1940.

Great Britain. *See* England; Scotland; Wales.

Great Lakes:

Great Lakes Region. Vol. LXV, pp. 454-455, 1 two-page, Apr., 1934.

Lake Superior, showing Northern Michigan and Wisconsin, Eastern Minnesota, and Western Ontario. Vol. XL, p. 114, 1 half-page, Aug., 1921.

Lake Superior Region, showing Location of Isle Royal. Vol. LX, p. 760, 1 half-page, Dec., 1931.

Marquette's Map of Great Lakes Region. Vol. LXII, p. 768, 1 half-page, Dec., 1932.

Northeastern United States. Vol. LXXXVIII, special supplement in colors, 41 x 26½ inches, Sept., 1945.

Ontario, showing Great Lakes. Vol. LXII, p. 139, 1 three-quarters-page, Aug., 1932.

Great Smoky Mountains National Park:

Great Smoky Mountains National Park, with Inset showing Main Roads Across the Park. Vol. LXX, p. 246, 1 page, Aug., 1936.

Greater Antilles, West Indies. *See* Cuba; Dominican Republic; Haiti; Jamaica; Puerto Rico.

Greater Sunda Islands. *See* Borneo; Celebes; Java; Sumatra.

Greece:

Bulgaria, Serbia, and Macedonia. Vol. XXIII, p. 1152, 1 page, Nov., 1912.

Classical Lands of the Mediterranean. Vol. LXXVII, special supplement in colors, 35¼ x 26 inches, Mar., 1940.

Greece, with Inset showing Territorial Expansion. Vol. LVIII, p. 652, 1 three-quarters-page, Dec., 1930.

Greece and the Aegean, showing Sites of Antiquity and the Necklace of Hellenic Cities that Adorned the Coast of Asia Minor. Vol. LXXXV, pp. 280-281, 1 two-page, Mar., 1944.

Saloniki and Adjacent Countries. Vol. XXX, p. 271, 1 page, Sept., 1916.

Southern Greece—Attic Plain and the Peloponnesus. Vol. XLII, p. 574, 1 three-quarters-page, Dec., 1922.

See also Crete (Island).

Greenland:

Arctic Regions, showing Capt. Bob Bartlett's World, as seen from 10,000 Miles in Space. Vol. LXXXIX, p. 604, 1 half-page, May, 1946.

Atlantic Ocean, showing Air Routes to Norway and Britain, via Newfoundland, Greenland, and Iceland. Vol. LXXX, p. 77, 1 page, July, 1941.

Global Map of Arctic Regions, showing Greenland, Important for Weather Stations and Air Bases. Vol. XC, p. 459, 1 page, Oct., 1946.

Greenland—an Aerial Stepping Stone to Europe. Vol. LXXXII, pp. 370-371, 1 two-page, Sept., 1942.

Greenland—*Continued*

Greenland, as seen from the North Pole. Vol. LXXVIII, pp. 118-119, 1 two-page, July, 1940.

Southern Greenland. Vol. LXVI, p. 262, 1 two-thirds-page, Sept., 1934.

Guadalcanal (Island), Solomon Islands:

Solomon Island, with Inset Maps showing Guadalcanal-Tulagi Area and Bougainville Area. Vol. LXXXII, p. 815, 1 half-page, Dec., 1942.

Guam (Island), Marianas Islands:

Indian Ocean, including Australia, New Zealand and Malaysia, with Inset of Guam. Vol. LXXIX, special supplement in colors, 25½ x 32¾ inches, Mar., 1941.

Pacific Islands, with Inset of Guam. Vol. LXXIV, p. 102, 1 third-page, July, 1938.

Pacific Ocean and the Bay of Bengal, with Inset of Guam. Vol. LXXXIV, special supplement in colors, 36½ x 26½ inches, Sept., 1943.

Southeast Asia and Pacific Islands from the Indies and the Philippines to the Solomons, with Inset of Guam. Vol. LXXXVI, special supplement in colors, 41 x 26½ inches, Oct., 1944.

Strategic Isles of the Pacific. Vol. LXXXV, pp. 392-393, 17 island maps (two pages), Apr., 1944.

Guatemala:

Guatemala. Vol. XXI, p. 613, 1 half-page, July, 1910.

Guatemala. Vol. L, p. 604, 1 page, Nov., 1926.

Highlands of Guatemala, with Inset showing Whole of Republic. Vol. LXX, p. 432, 1 page, Oct., 1936.

Guerrero (State), Mexico:

Río Balsas Region. Vol. XC, p. 254, 1 half-page, Aug., 1946.

Gulf Coast, United States:

Gulf of Mexico, showing Coastal Areas of United States and Mexico, and the Gulf Intracoastal Waterway. Vol. LXXXV, pp. 8-9, 1 two-page, Jan., 1944.

Southeastern Louisiana, showing Terrebonne Parish, with Inset of Gulf Coast. Vol. LXXXVI, p. 509, 1 two-thirds-page, Oct., 1944.

Gulf Stream:

Direction of the Gulf Stream and Other Currents in the North Atlantic Ocean. Vol. XXIII, p. 772, 1 half-page, Aug., 1912.

Hachijo Shima (Island), Pacific Ocean:

Strategic Isles of the Pacific. Vol. LXXXV, pp. 392-393, 17 island maps (two pages), Apr., 1944.

Hadhramaut:

Map of Arabia, with Inset of Hadhramaut Province. Vol. LXII, p. 389, 1 two-thirds-page, Oct., 1932.

Haha Jima Retto, Ogasawara Shoto, Pacific Ocean:

Southeast Asia and Pacific Islands from the Indies and the Philippines to the Solomons, with Inset of Haha Jima Retto. Vol. LXXXVI, special supplement in colors, 41 x 26½ inches, Oct., 1944.

Strategic Isles of the Pacific. Vol. LXXXV, pp. 392-393, 17 island maps (two pages), Apr., 1944.

Hainan (Island), China:

Southeastern China, showing Hainan Island. Vol. LXXIV, p. 394, 1 two-thirds-page, Sept., 1938.

Haiti:

Haiti. Vol. LXXXVI, p. 312, 1 half-page, Sept., 1944.

Haiti, with Inset showing Caribbean Region. Vol. LXVI, p. 439, 1 quarter-page, Oct., 1934.

Haiti and Santo Domingo. Vol. XIX, p. 215, 1 quarter-page, Mar., 1908.

Island of Haiti, showing Its Two Republics. Vol. XXXVIII, p. 489, 1 half-page, Dec., 1920.

West Indies from Cuba to Puerto Rico, with an Enlargement of Haiti and the Dominican Republic. Vol. LXXXV, p. 200, 1 two-thirds-page, Feb., 1944.

Harbors, Artificial, Normandy Coast, France:

British Mulberry and Omaha Beach, Artificial Harbors, off the Normandy Coast. Vol. LXXXVII, p. 565, 1 quarter-page, May, 1945.

Hawaii, Territory of:

Hawaiian Islands. Vol. XLV, p. 123, 1 page, Feb., 1924.

Hawaiian Islands. Vol. XLVIII, p. 79, 1 half-page, July, 1925.

Hawaiian Islands, with Inset of Pearl Harbor and Vicinity. Vol. LXXXII, p. 545, 1 half-page, Oct., 1942.

Hawaiian Islands, with Inset showing Route of Clipper Ships Across the Pacific Ocean. Vol. LXXIV, pp. 424-425, 1 page-and-a-half, Oct., 1938.

Island of Hawaii, showing the Four Volcanoes, Mauna Kea, Hualalai, Mauna Loa, and Kilauea, Which Have Created the Island. Vol. XLV, p. 183, 1 three-quarters-page, Feb., 1924.

Pacific Ocean and the Bay of Bengal, with Inset of Hawaiian Islands. Vol. LXXXIV, special supplement in colors, 36½ x 26½ inches, Sept., 1943.

Relief Map of the Island of Maui. Vol. XLV, p. 145, 1 quarter-page, Feb., 1924.

Relief Map of the Island of Oahu. Vol. XLV, p. 134, 1 half-page, Feb., 1924.

Hemisphere Maps:

Map of the World (in Eastern and Western Hemispheres), with Insets showing Land and Water Hemispheres, Density of Population, Time Zones, and World Mapping. Vol. LXXX, special supplement in colors, 41 x 22 inches, Dec., 1941.

Northern and Southern Hemisphere, with Insets of Time Zones, World Terrain, and Tables of Airline Distances in Four Hemispheres. Vol. LXXXIII, special supplement in colors, 41 x 22 inches, Apr., 1943.

Northern Hemisphere, showing Parallels of Latitude, 10 to 60, to be Used with Sky Charts. Vol. LXXXIV, pp. 98-99, two-page spread, July, 1943.

Northern Hemisphere, with Tables showing Airline Distances in the Pacific, the Atlantic, the Arctic, and the Americas. Vol. LXXXIX, special supplement in colors, 21¾ x 24 inches, Feb., 1946.

Hispaniola (Island), West Indies. *See* Dominican Republic; Haiti.

Holland. *See* Netherlands.

Hong Kong, China:

Hong Kong Island. Vol. LXXVII, p. 534, 1 half-page, Apr., 1940.

Indian Ocean, including Australia, New Zealand and Malaysia, with Inset of Hong Kong. Vol. LXXIX, special supplement in colors, 25½ x 32¾ inches, Mar., 1941.

Southeast Asia and Pacific Islands from the Indies and the Philippines to the Solomons, with Inset of Hong Kong Area. Vol. LXXXVI, special supplement in colors, 41 x 26½ inches, Oct., 1944.

Honolulu, Hawaii:

Pacific Ocean and the Bay of Bengal, with Inset of Honolulu and Pearl Harbor Areas. Vol. LXXXIV, special supplement in colors, 36½ x 26½ inches, Sept., 1943.

Howland (Island), Pacific Ocean:

Pacific Ocean and the Bay of Bengal, with Inset of Howland Island. Vol. LXXXIV, special supplement in colors, 36½ x 26½ inches, Sept., 1943.

Hull Island, Phoenix Islands:

Pacific Ocean and the Bay of Bengal, with Inset of Hull Island. Vol. LXXXIV, special supplement in colors, 36½ x 26½ inches, Sept., 1943.

Humboldt Current, Pacific Ocean:

Pacific Coast of South America, showing Location of Humboldt Current. Vol. LXXIX, p. 376, 1 half-page, Mar., 1941.

Hungary:

Austria-Hungary. Vol. XXIII, p. 1284, 1 page, Dec., 1912.

Austria-Hungary. Vol. XXVI, p. 392, 1 page, Oct., 1914.

Hungary—*Continued*

Frontier Cities of Italy and Austria-Hungary. Vol. XXVII, p. 628, 1 page, June, 1915.

Hungary. Vol. LXI, p. 707, 1 half-page, June, 1932.

Hungary. Vol. LXXIII, p. 7, 1 half-page, Jan., 1938.

Iceland:

Atlantic Ocean, showing Air Routes to Norway and Britain, via Newfoundland, Greenland, and Iceland. Vol. LXXX, p. 77, 1 page, July, 1941.

Isobel Wylie Hutchison's Route from Reykjavík to Akureyri (inset) and Iceland's Location in the North Atlantic. Vol. LIII, p. 470, 1 half-page, Apr., 1928.

Idaho:

Central Idaho, showing Extent of Batholith (Granite Mass). Vol. LXX, p. 105, 1 two-thirds-page, July, 1936.

"Craters of the Moon" (Volcanic Lava Beds). Vol. XLV, p. 306, 1 three-quarters-page, Mar., 1924.

Idaho. Vol. LXXXV, p. 644, 1 page, June, 1944.

Map of Northwestern United States and Neighboring Canadian Provinces. Vol. LXXIX, special supplement in colors, 24½ x 36 inches, June, 1941.

Salmon River District. Vol. LXX, p. 100, 1 page, July, 1936.

Illinois:

Illinois, with Inset of Chicago. Vol. LIX, special supplement in colors, 12½ x 19 inches, May, 1931.

Main Features of the Chicago Plan. Vol. XXXV, p. 40, 1 page, Jan., 1919.

United States of America, with Inset of Chicago. Vol. XLIII, special supplement in colors, 26½ x 36¼ inches, Apr., 1923.

India:

Burma, Home of the Chaulmoogra Oil Tree. Vol. XLI, p. 242, 1 page, Mar., 1922.

Burma and Eastern India, showing Manipur, Scene of Battle of Upper Burma. Vol. LXXXV, p. 750, 1 page, June, 1944.

Geographical Relation of Nepal to India, Burma, Kashmir, and Tibet. Vol. XXXVIII, p. 249, 1 half-page, Oct., 1920.

India. Vol. LXXXI, p. 238, 1 sixth-page, Feb., 1942.

India, superimposed on a Map of America. Vol. LXXXIX, p. 470, 1 half-page, Apr., 1946.

India, with Inset showing Route of Thaw Expedition from Paris to India. Vol. LXXVIII, p. 729, 1 page, Dec., 1940.

India—*Continued*

India and Adjacent Countries, with Inset showing Areas Covered by British India and the Indian States. Vol. LXXXIV, pp. 392-393, 1 two-page, Oct., 1943.

India and Burma, with Insets of Bombay and Calcutta Areas. Verso of map: Political Subdivisions and The Political Geography of India. Vol. LXXXIX, special supplement in colors, 30 x 25 inches, Apr., 1946.

Mongolia, Manchuria, Chosen, East Turkestan, Tibet, Northern India. Vol. XXIII, special supplement in colors, 17 x 23 inches, Oct., 1912.

Network of Railroads Covering India. Vol. XVI, p. 407, 1 three-quarters-page, Sept., 1905.

Ptolemy's Map of India, Ancient Scythia, and China. Vol. LXII, p. 765, 1 half-page, Dec., 1932.

Tibet, showing Adjacent Areas of India and China. Vol. XC, p. 172, 1 half-page, Aug., 1946.

Two of the Areas in Which Brig. Gen. William Mitchell Hunted Tigers. Vol. XLVI, p. 550, 1 quarter-page, Nov., 1924.

See also Delhi ; New Delhi.

Indian Ocean:

Indian Ocean, including Australia, New Zealand and Malaysia. Vol. LXXIX, special supplement in colors, 25½ x 32¾ inches, Mar., 1941.

Indian Ocean, showing Importance of Madagascar in the Control of Vital Sea Lanes. Vol. LXXXI, p. 803, 1 half-page, June, 1942.

Indiana:

Indiana, showing Population Center of the U. S. (1930 Census). Vol. LXX, pp. 272-273, 1 two-page, Sept., 1936.

Northeastern United States. Vol. LXXXVIII, special supplement in colors, 41 x 26½ inches, Sept., 1945.

Indo-China. *See* French Indo-China.

Indonesia. *See* Netherlands East Indies.

Intracoastal Waterway, United States :

North Carolina, with Intracoastal Waterway marked. Vol. LXXX, pp. 184-185, two-page spread, Aug., 1941.

See also Gulf Coast, *for* Gulf Intracoastal Waterway.

Iowa:

Iowa—The Hawkeye State. Vol. LXXVI, pp. 146-147, 1 two-page, Aug., 1939.

Iran (Persia) :

Iran, showing Route of Trans-Iranian Railway. Vol. LXXVI, p. 329, 1 two-thirds-page, Sept., 1939.

Iran and Adjacent Regions, showing Highways, Railways, and Oil Pipe Lines. Vol. LXXXIV, p. 132, 1 page, Aug., 1943.

Persepolis and Adjacent Regions. Vol. LXIV, p. 383, 1 half-page, Oct., 1933.

Persia. Vol. XIX, p. 384, 1 quarter-page, May, 1908.

Persia. Vol. XXXIX, p. 418, 1 three-quarters-page, Apr., 1921.

Railways Constructed in Asia Minor and Persia. Vol. XI, p. 202, 1 page, May, 1900.

Iran (Persia)—*Continued*

World Trouble Spot, the Oil-Rich Middle East. Vol. LXXXIX, pp. 396-397, 1 two-page, Mar., 1946.

Iraq:

Bible Lands and the Cradle of Western Civilization, with Insets showing Jerusalem, the Holy Land, Economic Development, Route of the Exodus, St. Paul's Travels, Crusades, and Empire of Alexander the Great. Vol. LXXIV, special supplement in colors, 25 x 35 inches, Dec., 1938.

Bible Lands and the Cradle of Western Civilization, with Insets showing the Holy Land Today, Holy Land in Biblical Times, Jerusalem, Traditional Route of the Exodus, St. Paul's Travels and the Seven Churches, and the Crusades. Vol. XC, special supplement in colors, 32 x 22 inches, Dec., 1946.

Europe and the Near East. Vol. LVI, special supplement in colors, 34¼ x 39¼ inches, Dec., 1929.

Location of Ancient Ruins in Modern Iraq. Vol. LVII, p. 101, 1 three-quarters-page, Jan., 1930.

Near East, showing Naval Bases, Airports, Highways, Railways, Oil Pipe Lines, and Oil Pumping Stations. Vol. LXXX, pp. 144-145, 1 two-page, Aug., 1941.

Near East, showing Turkey, Iraq, and Adjacent Regions, with Naval Bases, Airports, Highways, Railways, and Oil Pipe Lines. Vol. LXXXII, pp. 388-389, 1 two-page, Sept., 1942.

Railways Constructed in Asia Minor and Persia. Vol. XI, p. 202, 1 page, May, 1900.

World Trouble Spot, the Oil-Rich Middle East. Vol. LXXXIX, pp. 396-397, 1 two-page, Mar., 1946.

Ireland:

Aran Islands, with Inset of Ireland. Vol. LIX, p. 752, 1 quarter-page, June, 1931.

Ireland. Vol. LI, p. 262, 1 page, Mar., 1927.

Ireland. Vol. LXXVII, p. 653, 1 page, May, 1940.

Northern Ireland. Vol. LXVIII, p. 574, 1 two-thirds-page, Nov., 1935.

Israel. *See* Palestine.

Italian Islands of the Aegean. *See* Dodecanese Islands.

Italy:

Austro-Italo Alpine Region, with Surrounding Territory. Vol. XXVII, p. 374, 1 page, Apr., 1915.

Central and Northern Italy. Vol. LXXXIV, pp. 708-709, 1 two-page, Dec., 1943.

Central Italy. Vol. LXX, p. 353, 1 two-thirds-page, Sept., 1936.

Central Italy, showing Route Followed by Horace (Roman poet) from Rome to Brindisi. Vol. LXVIII, p. 774, 1 page, Dec., 1935.

Italy—*Continued*

Classical Lands of the Mediterranean. Vol. LXXVII, special supplement in colors, 35¼ x 26 inches, Mar., 1940.

Frontier Cities of Italy and Austria-Hungary. Vol. XXVII, p. 628, 1 page, June, 1915.

Italy. Vol. XXX, p. 360, 1 page, Oct., 1916.

Italy, with a Detail of the Umbrian and Tuscan Hill Towns. Vol. LIII, p. 404, 1 page, Apr., 1928.

Italy, with a Detail of Trulli-Land. Vol. LVII, p. 233, 1 quarter-page, Feb., 1930.

Lake of Garda District. War Zone on Austro-Italian Frontier Indicated. Vol. LXVIII, p. 334, 1 third-page, Sept., 1935.

Northern Italy. Vol. LXVIII, p. 332, 1 page, Sept., 1935.

Pontine Marshes, with Inset of Italy. Vol. LXVI, p. 202, 1 two-thirds-page, Aug., 1934.

Position of Venice on a Group of Mud Banks. Vol. XXVII, p. 630, 1 quarter-page, June, 1915.

Relation of Sardinia to the Mainland of Italy. Vol. XLIII, p. 5, 1 quarter-page, Jan., 1923.

Riviera Region. Vol. LXVII, p. 69, 1 half-page, Jan., 1935.

Rome-Naples Area, showing Main Arteries and Important Sites of Antiquity. Vol. XC, p. 569, 1 half-page, Nov., 1946.

Site of Carthage : Also the Pontine Marshes. Vol. XLV, p. 394, 1 half-page, Apr., 1924.

See also Sardinia (Island) ; Sicily (Island).

Iwo Jima (Sulphur Island), Pacific Ocean :

Southeast Asia and Pacific Islands from the Indies and the Philippines to the Solomons, with Inset of Iwo Jima. Vol. LXXXVI, special supplement in colors, 41 x 26½ inches, Oct., 1944.

Izu Shichito (Islands), Pacific Ocean. *See* Hachijo Shima.

Jaluit (Island), Marshall Islands :

Pacific Ocean and the Bay of Bengal, with Inset of Jaluit. Vol. LXXXIV, special supplement in colors, 36½ x 26½ inches, Sept., 1943.

Strategic Isles of the Pacific. Vol. LXXXV, pp. 392-393, 17 island maps (two pages), Apr., 1944.

Jamaica (Island), West Indies :

Jamaica, the Key to the Caribbean. Vol. LI, p. 4, 1 page, Jan., 1927.

Mexico, Central America, and the West Indies, with Inset of Jamaica. Vol. LXVI, special supplement in colors, 23 x 40 inches, Dec., 1934.

Mexico, Central America, and the West Indies, with Inset of Jamaica. Vol. LXXVI, special supplement in colors, 24 x 41 inches, Dec., 1939.

Japan:

Chinese Empire and Japan : Showing the Provinces, Treaty Ports, Railways, etc., and the Present Condition of the Russian Railway Through Manchuria to Port Arthur. Vol. XI, insert, two-page, Aug., 1900.

Development of the Commerce of Japan Between 1874 and 1904 Resulting from the Construction of Railways. Vol. XVI, p. 406, 1 page, Sept., 1905.

Formosa (Taiwan), showing Its Geographical Relation to Japan, China, and the Philippines. Vol. XXXVII, p. 262, 1 half-page, Mar., 1920.

Japan. Vol. LXIX, p. 444, 1 three-quarters-page, Apr., 1936.

Japan and Adjacent Regions of Asia and the Pacific Ocean, with Insets of Industrial Centers of Japan and the Marshall Islands. Vol. LXXXV, special supplement in colors, 26½ x 34½ inches, Apr., 1944.

Japan and Korea, with Insets of Kuril Islands, Pescadores, Karafuto, Ryukyu Islands, Okinawa, Formosa, Tokyo Area, and a Location Map of Japan in the Western Pacific. Vol. LXXXVIII, special supplement in colors, 37 x 26½ inches, Dec., 1945.

Sakurajima, showing the Lava Flows of Japan's Greatest Volcanic Eruption. Vol. XLV, p. 449, 1 half-page, Apr., 1924.

See also Iwo Jima ; Ogasawara Shoto ; Okinawa Gunto ; Paramushiro Jima ; Ryukyu Retto ; *and* the following mandates and occupied territories : Caroline Islands ; Formosa ; Korea ; Manchuria (Manchukuo) ; Marianas Islands ; Marshall Islands ; Palau Islands.

Jarvis (Island), Line Islands :

Pacific Ocean and the Bay of Bengal, with Inset of Jarvis Island. Vol. LXXXIV, special supplement in colors, 36½ x 26½ inches, Sept., 1943.

Java:

Borneo and Java. Vol. LXXXVIII, p. 297, 1 page, Sept., 1945.

Dutch East Indies. Vol. LVI, p. 347, 1 third-page, Sept., 1929.

Far East, with Enlargement of Java. Vol. LXXXI, p. 91, 1 two-thirds-page, Jan., 1942.

Jerusalem, Holy Land :

Bible Lands and the Cradle of Western Civilization, with Insets showing Jerusalem, the Holy Land, Economic Development, Route of the Exodus, St. Paul's Travels, Crusades, and Empire of Alexander the Great. Vol. LXXIV, special supplement in colors, 25 x 35 inches, Dec., 1938.

Jerusalem, Holy Land—*Continued*

Bible Lands and the Cradle of Western Civilization, with Insets showing the Holy Land Today, Holy Land in Biblical Times, Jerusalem, Traditional Route of the Exodus, St. Paul's Travels and the Seven Churches, and the Crusades. Vol. XC, special supplement in colors, 32 x 22 inches, Dec., 1946.

Jordan. *See* Trans-Jordan.

Jugoslavia. *See* Yugoslavia.

Kansas:

Kansas, showing Geographic Center of the United States. Vol. LXXII, pp. 138-139, 1 two-page, Aug., 1937.

Kansu (Province), China :

China, showing Location of Choni in Kansu Province. Vol. LIV, p. 576, 1 half-page, Nov., 1928.

Quake-Stricken Area in Kansu Province, China. Vol. XLI, p. 448, 1 three-quarters-page, May, 1922.

Karafuto (Island), Japan :

Japan and Korea, with Insets of Kuril Islands, Pescadores, Karafuto, Ryukyu Islands, Okinawa, Formosa, Tokyo Area, and a Location Map of Japan in the Western Pacific. Vol. LXXXVIII, special supplement in colors, 37 x 26½ inches, Dec., 1945.

Kazan Retto (Volcano Islands), Pacific Ocean. *See* Iwo Jima.

Kentucky:

Kentucky. Vol. LXXXII, pp. 62-63, two-page spread, July, 1942.

Southeastern Kentucky, showing Cumberland Gap Region. Vol. LXXXIV, p. 745, 1 quarter-page, Dec., 1943.

Virginia, North Carolina, Kentucky, and Tennessee. Vol. LXV, pp. 666-667, 1 two-page, June, 1934.

Kenya Colony, Africa :

Route of Uganda Railway. Vol. XIII, p. 170, 1 half-page, May, 1902.

Territory Covered in Flights of Walter Mittelholzer. Vol. LXI, p. 466, 1 three-quarters-page, Apr., 1932.

Kiska (Island), Aleutian Islands :

Pacific Ocean and the Bay of Bengal, with Inset of Kiska. Vol. LXXXIV, special supplement in colors, 36½ x 26½ inches, Sept., 1943.

Korea:

Chosen and Adjacent Islands. Vol. LXIV, p. 424, 1 two-thirds-page, Oct., 1933.

Japan and Korea, with Insets of Kuril Islands, Pescadores, Karafuto, Ryukyu Islands, Okinawa, Formosa, Tokyo Area, and a Location Map of Japan in the Western Pacific. Vol. LXXXVIII, special supplement in colors, 37 x 26½ inches, Dec., 1945.

Korea—*Continued*

Korea. Vol. LXXXVIII, p. 433, 1 page, Oct., 1945.

Korea : The Region Traversed by Mr. Andrew's Expedition Extends Along the Upper Courses of the Tumen and the Yalu Rivers. Vol. XXXVI, p. 24, 1 page, July, 1919.

Monastic Establishments in the Diamond Mountains. Vol. XLVI, p. 355, 1 quarter-page, Oct., 1924.

Mongolia, Manchuria, Chosen, East Turkestan, Tibet, Northern India. Vol. XXIII, special supplement in colors, 17 x 23 inches, Oct., 1912.

War Map of Manchuria and Korea. Vol. XV, special supplement, 36 x 42 inches, Mar., 1904.

Kuril Islands, Japan :

Japan and Korea, with Insets of Kuril Islands, Pescadores, Karafuto, Ryukyu Islands, Okinawa, Formosa, Tokyo Area, and a Location Map of Japan in the Western Pacific. Vol. LXXXVIII, special supplement in colors, 37 x 26½ inches, Dec., 1945.

See also Chishima Retto.

Kusaie (Island), Caroline Islands :

Strategic Isles of the Pacific. Vol. LXXXV, pp. 392-393, 17 island maps (two pages), Apr., 1944.

Kwajalein (Atoll), Marshall Islands :

Pacific Ocean and the Bay of Bengal, with Inset of Kwajalein. Vol. LXXXIV, special supplement in colors, 36½ x 26½ inches, Sept., 1943.

Strategic Isles of the Pacific. Vol. LXXXV, pp. 392-393, 17 island maps (two pages), Apr., 1944.

Kwangsi (Province), China :

Kwangsi, One of China's Least-Known Provinces. Vol. LXXII, p. 674, 1 half-page, Dec., 1937.

Languages:

World, showing Distribution of Languages and Areas Occupied by U. S. Soldiers with Dates of Their Arrival. Vol. LXXXIV, pp. 696-697, 1 two-page, Dec., 1943.

Lapland:

Northern Portions of Norway, Sweden, Finland, and the Kola Peninsula of the U. S. S. R. Vol. LXXVI, p. 645, 1 page, Nov., 1939.

Latakia:

Bible Lands and the Cradle of Western Civilization, with Insets showing Jerusalem, the Holy Land, Economic Development, Route of the Exodus, St. Paul's Travels, Crusades, and Empire of Alexander the Great. Vol. LXXIV, special supplement in colors, 25 x 35 inches, Dec., 1938.

Latakia—*Continued*

Crusader Castles. Vol. LIX, p. 371, 1 third-page, Mar., 1931.

Crusader Trails and Castles. Vol. LXIV, p. 654, 1 page, Dec., 1933.

Eastern Shores of the Mediterranean. Vol. XXXVIII, p. 89, 1 quarter-page, Aug., 1920.

Latakia. Vol. LVIII, p. 485, 1 quarter-page, Oct., 1930.

Latakia and Lebanon. Vol. LXIV, p. 103, 1 third-page, July, 1933.

Latin America:

Miami-Montevideo Air-Mail Route. Vol. LVII, p. 264, 1 half-page, Mar., 1930.

Route Followed by Lindbergh in His Flight Over 13 Latin American Countries. Vol. LIII, p. 532, 1 two-thirds-page, May, 1928.

Route of A. F. Tschiffely on His Horseback Journey from Buenos Aires to Washington. Vol. LV, p. 140, 1 page, Feb., 1929.

Route of the Trail-Blazing Flight of U. S. Army Airplanes Through 20 Countries of Latin America. Vol. LII, p. 452, 1 page, Oct., 1927.

South America, Central America, and West Indies. Vol. LIX, p. 4, 1 page, Jan., 1931.

See also names of individual countries and islands.

Latvia:

Baltic Republic of Latvia. Vol. XLVI, p. 405, 1 half-page, Oct., 1924.

Lebanon:

Bible Lands and the Cradle of Western Civilization, with Insets showing Jerusalem, the Holy Land, Economic Development, Route of the Exodus, St. Paul's Travels, Crusades, and Empire of Alexander the Great. Vol. LXXIV, special supplement in colors, 25 x 35 inches, Dec., 1938.

Bible Lands and the Cradle of Western Civilization, with Insets showing the Holy Land Today, Holy Land in Biblical Times, Jerusalem, Traditional Route of the Exodus, St. Paul's Travels and the Seven Churches, and the Crusades. Vol. XC, special supplement in colors, 32 x 22 inches, Dec., 1946.

Crusader Castles. Vol. LIX, p. 371, 1 third-page, Mar., 1931.

Crusader Trails and Castles. Vol. LXIV, p. 654, 1 page, Dec., 1933.

Eastern Shores of the Mediterranean. Vol. XXXVIII, p. 89, 1 quarter-page, Aug., 1920.

Lebanon. Vol. LVIII, p. 485, 1 quarter-page, Oct., 1930.

Lebanon and Latakia. Vol. LXIV, p. 103, 1 third-page, July, 1933.

Leeward Islands, West Indies:

Hispaniola, Puerto Rico, and the Leeward Group of Islands. Vol. LXXIII, pp. 274-275, two-page spread, Mar., 1938.

Leeward and Windward Islands. Vol. LXXIX, p. 5, 1 page, Jan., 1941.

See also Saba.

Lesser Antilles, West Indies. *See* Aruba; Bonaire; Curaçao; Leeward Islands; Tobago; Trinidad; Windward Islands.

Lesser Sunda Islands:

Lesser Sunda Islands. Vol. LXXV, p. 316, 1 third-page, Mar., 1939.

See also Timor.

Levant States:

Asia Minor and the Levant. Vol. L, p. 652, 1 two-thirds-page, Dec., 1926.

Bible Lands and the Cradle of Western Civilization. Vol. LXXIV, special supplement in colors, 25 x 35 inches, Dec., 1938.

Crusader Castles. Vol. LIX, p. 371, 1 third-page, Mar., 1931.

Crusader Trails and Castles. Vol. LXIV, p. 654, 1 page, Dec., 1933.

Eastern Shores of the Mediterranean. Vol. XXXVIII, p. 89, 1 quarter-page, Aug., 1920.

Latakia and Lebanon. Vol. LVIII, p. 485, 1 quarter-page, Oct., 1930.

Latakia and Lebanon. Vol. LXIV, p. 103, 1 third-page, July, 1933.

Syria. Vol. XXXVI, p. 441, 1 quarter-page, Nov., 1919.

Libia:

Italian Libia. Vol. XLVIII, p. 138, 1 two-thirds-page, Aug., 1925.

Italian Libia and Environs. Vol. LVII, p. 690, 1 two-thirds-page, June, 1930.

Mediterranean Coast of Libia and Egypt. Vol. LXXVIII, p. 810, Dec., 1940.

Route of Hassanein Bey Through the Libian Desert. Vol. XLVI, p. 236, 1 half-page, Sept., 1924.

Liechtenstein:

Liechtenstein. Vol. LII, p. 612, 1 half-page, Nov., 1927.

Line Islands, Pacific Ocean. *See* Caroline Island; Christmas Island; Fanning Island; Flint Island; Jarvis; Malden Island; Palmyra; Starbuck Island; Vostok Island.

Lingayen Gulf, Philippine Islands:

Philippines, with Insets of Manila, Lingayen Gulf, and a Location Map of the Philippines. Vol. LXXXVII, special supplement in colors, 17½ x 26 inches, Mar., 1945.

Lord Howe (Island), New South Wales:

Lord Howe Island (Inset). Vol. LXVIII, p. 118, 1 two-thirds-page, July, 1935.

Lorraine (Region), France:

Metz, Nancy, and Epinal Regions. Vol. LXXXVII, p. 367, 1 two-thirds-page, Mar., 1945.

Louisiana:

Bird Refuges of Louisiana. Vol. XXIV, p. 373, 1 two-thirds-page, Mar., 1913.

Gulf of Mexico, showing Coastal Areas of United States and Mexico. Vol. LXXXV, pp. 8-9, 1 two-page, Jan., 1944.

Louisiana, with Inset of New Orleans. Vol. LVII, special supplement in colors, 13 x 13¼ inches, Apr., 1930.

Mississippi Delta Formations. Vol. XXXIII, p. 533, 1 half-page, June, 1918.

Southeastern Louisiana, showing Terrebonne Parish, with Inset of Gulf Coast. Vol. LXXXVI, p. 509, 1 two-thirds-page, Oct., 1944.

United States of America, with Inset of New Orleans. Vol. XLIII, special supplement in colors, 26½ x 36¼ inches, Apr., 1923.

Lower California. *See* Baja California.

Luxembourg (Grand Duchy):

Luxembourg. Vol. XLVI, p. 506, 1 quarter-page, Nov., 1924.

Madagascar:

Africa, with Insets of the Cape Verde Islands, Relief Map, and a Table of Airline Distances in Statute Miles. Vol. LXXXIII, special supplement in colors, 29¼ x 31½ inches, Feb., 1943.

Madagascar. Vol. LXXXI, p. 803, 1 half-page, June, 1942.

Map of Madagascar, Superimposed on the Eastern Seaboard of North America. Vol. LXXXI, p. 802, 1 quarter-page, June, 1942.

Route Followed by Charles F. Swingle in Madagascar. Vol. LVI, p. 184, 1 three-quarters-page, Aug., 1929.

Madeira (Island), Atlantic Ocean:

Madeira and Porto Santo Islands. Vol. LXVI, p. 85, 1 half-page, July, 1934.

Maine:

Maine. Vol. LXVII, pp. 538-539, 2 pages, May, 1935.

Northeastern United States. Vol. LXXXVIII, special supplement in colors, 41 x 26½ inches, Sept., 1945.

Makin (Atoll), Gilbert Islands:

Gilbert Islands, with Insets of Tarawa and Makin. Vol. LXXXVII, p. 135, 1 two-thirds-page, Feb., 1945.

Pacific Ocean and the Bay of Bengal, with Inset of Makin. Vol. LXXXIV, special supplement in colors, 36½ x 26½ inches, Sept., 1943.

Malay Archipelago:

Far East, with Inset of the Moluccas. Vol. LXXIX, p. 538, 1 page, May, 1941.

Indian Ocean, including Australia, New Zealand and Malaysia. Vol. LXXIX, special supplement in colors, 25½ x 32¾ inches, Mar., 1941.

Southeast Asia and Pacific Islands from the Indies and the Philippines to the Solomons, with 22 Inset Maps of Important Cities and Islands. Vol. LXXXVI, special supplement in colors, 41 x 26½ inches, Oct., 1944.

See also Borneo; Celebes; Java; Netherlands East Indies; New Guinea; Philippine Islands; Sumatra; Timor.

Malay Peninsula:

Indian Ocean, including Australia, New Zealand and Malaysia. Vol. LXXIX, special supplement in colors, 25½ x 32¾ inches, Mar., 1941.

Malay States, Thailand, and French Indo-China, with Inset of Singapore. Vol. LXXX, p. 662, 1 half-page, Nov., 1941.

Southeast Asia and Pacific Islands from the Indies and the Philippines to the Solomons, with 22 Inset Maps of Important Cities and Islands. Vol. LXXXVI, special supplement in colors, 41 x 26½ inches, Oct., 1944.

Strategic Geographic Position of Singapore, with an Inset of the Malay Peninsula. Vol. XLIX, p. 238, 1 half-page, Mar., 1926.

Malden Island, Line Islands:

Pacific Ocean and the Bay of Bengal, with Inset of Malden Island. Vol. LXXXIV, special supplement in colors, 36½ x 26½ inches, Sept., 1943.

Malta (Island), Mediterranean Sea:

Malta, a Tiny Island Which Has Played a Great Role in World History. Vol. XXXVII, p. 449, 1 third-page, May, 1920.

Malta, Gozo, and Comino. Vol. LXVIII, p. 650, 1 half-page, Nov., 1935.

Malta, Gozo, Comino, and Filfla. Vol. LXXXIII, p. 378, 1 half-page, Mar., 1943.

Maltese Islands. Vol. LXXVIII, p. 257, 1 half-page, Aug., 1940.

Man, Isle of, England:

Isle of Man, with Inset of the British Isles. Vol. LXXI, p. 588, 1 third-page, May, 1937.

Manchukuo. *See* Manchuria.

Manchuria:

Manchuria. Vol. LVI, p. 384, 1 two-thirds-page, Oct., 1929.

Manchuria: Japan Brews Another War with Russia. Vol. LXXXII, p. 607, 1 page, Nov., 1942.

Manchuria—*Continued*

Manchuria, with Inset Map showing Where Railway Interests of Japan, Russia, and China Clash. Vol. LXI, p. 106, 1 three-quarters-page, Jan., 1932.

Military Operations in the Far East. Vol. XV, p. 129, 1 half-page, Mar., 1904.

Mongolia, Manchuria, Chosen, East Turkestan, Tibet, Northern India. Vol. XXIII, special supplement in colors, 17 x 23 inches, Oct., 1912.

Seat of War in Manchuria (Beginning Just North of Mukden, and Covering the Country North to Harbin and East to Vladivostok). Vol. XVI, special supplement in colors, 18 x 44 inches, June, 1905.

War Map of Manchuria and Korea. Vol. XV, special supplement, 36 x 42 inches, Mar., 1904.

Manihiki (Island), Pacific Ocean:

Pacific Ocean and the Bay of Bengal, with Inset of Manihiki. Vol. LXXXIV, special supplement in colors, 36½ x 26½ inches, Sept., 1943.

Manila, Luzon, Philippine Islands:

Philippines, with Insets of Manila, Lingayen Gulf, and a Location Map of the Philippines. Vol. LXXXVII, special supplement in colors, 17½ x 26 inches, Mar., 1945.

Southeast Asia and Pacific Islands from the Indies and the Philippines to the Solomons, with Inset of Manila Area. Vol. LXXXVI, special supplement in colors, 41 x 26½ inches, Oct., 1944.

Marajó Island, Brazil:

Marajó Island. Vol. LXXIV, p. 638, 1 half-page, Nov., 1938.

Marcus (Minami Tori Shima, Island), Pacific Ocean:

Pacific Ocean and the Bay of Bengal, with Inset of Marcus Island. Vol. LXXXIV, special supplement in colors, 36½ x 26½ inches, Sept., 1943.

Southeast Asia and Pacific Islands from the Indies and the Philippines to the Solomons, with Inset of Marcus. Vol. LXXXVI, special supplement in colors, 41 x 26½ inches, Oct., 1944.

Strategic Isles of the Pacific. Vol. LXXXV, pp. 392-393, 17 island maps (two pages), Apr., 1944.

Marianas Islands, Pacific Ocean:

Strategic Isles of the Pacific: Chichi Jima, Eniwetok, Guam, Hachijo, Haha Jima, Jaluit, Kwajalein, Kusaie, Marcus, Palau, Paramushiro, Ponape, Rota, Saipan, Tinian, Truk, Wake, Yap. Vol. LXXXV, pp. 392-393, 17 island maps (two pages), Apr., 1944.

Marianas Islands, Pacific Ocean—*Continued*

The Taking of Saipan Opens the Gate in Japan's Wall of Island Defenses. Vol. LXXXVII, p. 447, 1 half-page, Apr., 1945.

See also Guam ; Pagan ; Rota ; Saipan ; Tinian.

Marquesas Islands, Pacific Ocean :

Marquesas, Tuamotu, and Austral Islands. Vol. XLVIII, p. 366, 1 half-page, Oct., 1925.

Marquesas Islands. Vol. LXXIX, p. 112, 1 quarter-page, Jan., 1941.

Marshall Islands, Pacific Ocean :

Marshall Islands, with Inset of Pacific Islands. Vol. LXXXVIII, p. 329, 1 half-page, Sept., 1945.

Strategic Isles of the Pacific : Chichi Jima, Eniwetok, Guam, Hachijo, Haha Jima, Jaluit, Kwajalein, Kusaie, Marcus, Palau, Paramushiro, Ponape, Rota, Saipan, Tinian, Truk, Wake, Yap. Vol. LXXXV, pp. 392-393, 17 island maps (two pages), Apr., 1944.

See also Eniwetok ; Jaluit ; Kwajalein ; Wotje.

Martinique (Island), West Indies :

Martinique. Vol. XIII, p. 231, 1 quarter-page, June, 1902.

Martinique, showing Mountainous Character of the Island. Vol. XIII, p. 211, 1 half-page, June, 1902.

Sketch Map of Martinique. Vol. XIII, p. 231, 1 quarter-page, July, 1902.

Zones of Devastation in Martinique. Vol. XIII, p. 260, 1 half-page, July, 1902.

Maryland:

George Washington's Travels in Maryland and West Virginia. Vol. LXI, pp. 36, 1 third-page, Jan., 1932.

Historic and Scenic Reaches of the Nation's Capital. Vol. LXXIV, special supplement in colors, 26½ x 31¼ inches, July, 1938.

Maryland. Vol. LXXIX, pp. 404-405, two-page spread, Apr., 1941.

Maryland, Delaware, and District of Columbia, with Inset of Baltimore. Vol. LI, special supplement in colors, 12 x 18 inches, Feb., 1927.

Potomac River Windings in Maryland, Virginia, and West Virginia. Vol. LXXXVIII, pp. 36-37, two-page spread, July, 1945.

Tidewater Maryland, showing Route of the *Tralee.* Vol. LXXVI, p. 361, 1 page, Sept., 1939.

United States of America, with Inset of Baltimore. Vol. XLIII, special supplement in colors, 26½ x 36¼ inches, Apr., 1923.

Massachusetts:

Cape Cod. Vol. LXXXIX, p. 741, 1 half-page, June, 1946.

Cape Cod Canal. Vol. XXVI, p. 186, 1 half-page, Aug., 1914.

Massachusetts—*Continued*

Lynn Harbor : Where the Land Has Scored Signal Victories Over the Sea. Vol. XXXIII, p. 534, 1 half-page, June, 1918.

Northeastern United States. Vol. LXXVIII, special supplement in colors, 41 x 26½ inches, Sept., 1945.

Reaches of New York City. Vol. LXXV, special supplement in colors, 26½ x 29 inches, Apr., 1939.

Six Maps showing Changes in Shore of Nantucket Island, Massachusetts, from 1890 to 1908. Vol. XX, p. 831, 1 page, Sept., 1909.

Travels of George Washington, with Inset of Boston. Vol. LXI, special supplement in colors, 20 x 29 inches, Jan., 1932.

United States of America, with Inset of Boston. Vol. XLIII, special supplement in colors, 26½ x 36¼ inches, Apr., 1923.

Matto Grosso (State), Brazil :

Southern Matto Grosso and Paraguay, with Inset showing River System. Vol. LXXXIV, p. 461, 1 two-thirds-page, Oct., 1943.

Mediterranean Regions:

Central Europe and the Mediterranean. Vol. LXXVI, special supplement in colors, 36½ x 26½ inches, Oct., 1939.

Classical Lands of the Mediterranean. Vol. LXXVII, special supplement in colors, 35¼ x 26 inches, Mar., 1940.

Cotidal Lines for the Mediterranean Sea. Vol. XVII, p. 306, 1 page, June, 1906.

Countries Bordering the Mediterranean Sea. Vol. XXIII, special supplement in colors, 9 x 18 inches, Jan., 1912.

Eastern Mediterranean, showing Location of Italian Islands of the Aegean. Vol. LXXIX, p. 451, 1 two-thirds-page, Apr., 1941.

Eastern Mediterranean, with an Enlargement of Crete. Vol. LXXXIV, p. 550, 1 page, Nov., 1943.

Europe and Northern Africa, showing Extent of Roman Empire. Vol. XC, pp. 552-553, 1 two-page, Nov., 1946.

Europe and the Mediterranean. Vol. LXXIII, special supplement in colors, 34 x 39 inches, Apr., 1938.

Island of Crete, and Map showing Route of the *Bonita* (Breton Yawl) on Its Mediterranean Voyage. Vol. LV, p. 250, 1 page, Feb., 1929.

Map showing Central Position of Maltese Islands. Vol. LXVIII, p. 651, 1 third-page, Nov., 1935.

Mediterranean, showing Strategic Position of Malta. Vol. LXXVIII, p. 257, 1 third-page, Aug., 1940.

Mediterranean Regions. Vol. XXII, pp. 1047, 1089, 2 half-pages, Nov., 1911.

Mediterranean Regions. Vol. LXXXI, pp. 530-531, two-page spread, Apr., 1942.

Mediterranean Regions—*Continued*

Mediterranean Regions, showing Bombing Ranges from Bizerte, Tunisia. Vol. LXXXIV, pp. 8-9, two-page spread, July, 1943.

Mediterranean Regions, with Inset Map of Sicily. Vol. LXXXIV, pp. 312-313, two-page spread, Sept., 1943.

Southeastern France, showing Mediterranean Coast. Vol. LXXXVI, p. 428, 1 three-quarters-page, Oct., 1944.

Tunisia, Africa's Northernmost Tip, Nearly Divides the Mediterranean into Two Great Lakes. Vol. LXXI, p. 349, 1 half-page, Mar., 1937.

See also names of individual countries and islands.

Melanesia:

New Guinea, New Caledonia, and Fiji Command the Shortest Supply Routes from America to Australia, with Table of Airline Distances. Vol. LXXXI, pp. 698-699, 1 two-page, June, 1942.

Pacific Ocean and the Bay of Bengal, with Inset Maps of Important Islands, and Table of Airline Distances in Statute Miles. Vol. LXXXIV, special supplement in colors, 36½ x 26½ inches, Sept., 1943.

Sovereignty and Mandate Boundary Lines in 1921 of the Islands of the Pacific. Vol. XL, special supplement in colors, Dec., 1921.

See also Fiji Islands ; New Caledonia ; New Guinea ; New Hebrides ; Solomon Islands.

Mexico:

Archeological Sites in Veracruz and Tabasco Explored by National Geographic Society-Smithsonian Expedition of 1940. Vol. LXXVIII, p. 313, 1 third-page, Sept., 1940.

Area Drained by the Great Canal. Vol. XIII, p. 7, 1 page, Jan., 1902.

Baja California, with Inset showing Relationship to Mexico, California, and States of the Southwest. Vol. LXXXII, p. 258, 1 page, Aug., 1942.

Bird Migration Routes from South America to North America Converge Funnel-like in Central America. Inset of Veracruz and Tabasco, Mexico, showing La Venta Region, a Natural Bird Observatory. Vol. LXXXVII, p. 188, 1 two-thirds-page, Feb., 1945.

Central America and Southern Mexico. Vol. XLVII, p. 64, 1 half-page, Jan., 1925.

Central Mexico. Vol. LXVI, p. 760, 1 page, Dec., 1934.

Central Mexico, showing Belt of Volcanoes. Vol. LXXXV, p. 131, 1 third-page, Feb., 1944.

Changes in the Estuary of the Colorado River. Vol. XIX, p. 54, 1 page, Jan., 1908.

Colorado Desert Region. Vol. XI, p. 339, 1 page, Sept., 1900.

Mexico—*Continued*

Countries of the Caribbean, Including Mexico, Central America, the West Indies and the Panama Canal, with Detailed Insets of the Panama Canal and the Canal Zone, Porto Rico and the Virgin Islands, and Guantanamo Bay, Cuba. Vol. XLI, special supplement in colors, 29 x 44 inches, Feb., 1922.

Country of the Old Yuma Trail. Vol. XII, p. 132, 1 page, Apr., 1901.

Course of the Rio Grande (River). Vol. LXXVI, 4 maps, pp. 427, 428, 440, 453, Oct., 1939.

Cruise of the *Kinkajou* to Desert Islands of Mexico. Vol. LXXX, p. 340, 1 page, Sept., 1941.

Desert Islands of Lower California. Vol. XLIV, p. 73, 1 quarter-page, July, 1923.

Gulf of Mexico, showing Coastal Areas of United States and Mexico. Vol. LXXXV, pp. 8-9, 1 two-page, Jan., 1944.

Jalisco and Central Mexico. Vol. LXV, p. 331, 1 third-page, Mar., 1934.

Location of Cuicuilco and the Pedregal Lava Flow Which Has Preserved the Ancient Mound. Vol. XLIV, p. 207, 1 quarter-page, Aug., 1923.

Lower California, showing Route of E. W. Nelson. Vol. XXII, p. 446, 1 page, May, 1911.

Mexico. Vol. XXI, p. 1050, 1 page, Dec., 1910.

Mexico. Vol. XXII, special supplement in colors, 17 x 24½ inches, May, 1911.

Mexico. Vol. XXV, special supplement in colors. 17 x 24½ inches, May, 1914.

Mexico. Vol. XXX, special supplement in colors, 20 x 29 inches, July, 1916.

Mexico, Central America, and the West Indies. Vol. LXVI, special supplement in colors, 23 x 40 inches, Dec., 1934.

Mexico, Central America, and the West Indies. Vol. LXXVI, special supplement in colors, 24 x 41 inches, Dec., 1939.

Mexico, showing the Route of the Old Spanish Road. Vol. XLIII, p. 230, 1 half-page, Mar., 1923.

Mexico and the Peninsula of Lower California. Vol. XXXVI, p. 310, 1 page, Oct., 1919.

New Center of Maya Culture Discovered in Vera Cruz by National Geographic Society-Smithsonian Institution Expedition. Vol. LXXVI, p. 184, 1 half-page, Aug., 1939.

Railways of Mexico. Vol. XIII, p. 1, 1 page, Jan., 1902.

Río Balsas Region. Vol. XC, p. 254, 1 half-page, Aug., 1946.

Route of Cortés from Veracruz to Mexico City. Vol. LXXVIII, pp. 338-339, 2 half-pages, Sept., 1940.

Southern Mexico, showing the Route of Collins and Doyle. Vol. XXII, p. 317, 1 quarter-page, Mar., 1911.

State of Oaxaca. Vol. LI, p. 504, 1 two-thirds-page, May, 1927.

Mexico—*Continued*

United States and Adjoining Portions of Canada and Mexico. Vol. LXIII, special supplement in colors, 26 x 40 inches, May, 1933.

United States-Mexico Boundary. Vol. XXXVIII, p. 75, 1 quarter-page, July, 1929.

Veracruz, Tabasco, Oaxaca, and Chiapas, showing Archeological Sites Explored by National Geographic Society-Smithsonian Institution Expeditions. Vol. LXXX, p. 283, 1 two-thirds-page, Sept., 1941.

Veracruz, Tabasco, Oaxaca, and Chiapas, showing Archeological Sites Explored by National Geographic Society-Smithsonian Institution Expeditions. Vol. LXXXII, p. 642, 1 two-thirds-page, Nov., 1942.

Veracruz, Tabasco, Oaxaca, and Chiapas, showing Archeological Sites Explored by National Geographic Society-Smithsonian Institution Expeditions. Vol. LXXXIV, p. 325, 1 two-thirds-page, Sept., 1943.

Wanderings of the Rio Grande and of the Old Boundary. Vol. XXIV, p. 384, 1 three-quarters-page, Mar., 1913.

West Coast of Mexico. Vol. XLII, p. 452, 1 half-page, Nov., 1922.

Yucatán, Campeche, and Quintana Roo. Vol. LXX, p. 595, 1 two-thirds-page, Nov., 1936.

Mexico, Gulf of (Region). *See* Gulf Coast.

Michigan:

Isle Royale. Vol. LX, p. 760, 1 half-page, Dec., 1931.

Michigan. Vol. LXXXVI, pp. 680-681, 1 page-and-a-half, Dec., 1944.

Michigan's Lower Peninsula and the Eastern Half of the Upper Peninsula. Vol. LIII, p. 275, 1 page, Mar., 1928.

Northeastern United States. Vol. LXXXVIII, special supplement in colors, 41 x 26½ inches, Sept., 1945.

United States of America, with Inset of Detroit. Vol. XLIII, special supplement in colors, 26½ x 36¼ inches, Apr., 1923.

Western Half of Michigan's Upper Peninsula. Vol. LIII, p. 274, 1 three-quarters-page, Mar., 1928.

Michoacán (State), Mexico:

Río Balsas Region. Vol. XC, p. 254, 1 half-page, Aug., 1946.

Micronesia:

Japanese Micronesia, with Insets of Yap, Ponape, and Palau Islands. Vol. LXIX, p. 483, 1 half-page, Apr., 1936.

Pacific Islands, showing Japanese Mandate, with Insets of Palau, Ponape, and Truk Islands. Vol. LXXXI, pp. 764-765, two-page spread, June, 1942.

Micronesia—*Continued*

Pacific Islands, showing Micronesia and Surrounding Islands, with a Table of Airline Distances. Vol. LXXXI, pp. 698-699, 1 two-page, June, 1942.

Pacific Ocean, with Inset Maps of Important Islands and Groups. Vol. LXX, special supplement in colors, 31 x 38 inches, Dec., 1936.

Pacific Ocean and the Bay of Bengal, with Inset Maps of Important Islands, and Table of Airline Distances in Statute Miles. Vol. LXXXIV, special supplement in colors, 36½ x 26½ inches, Sept., 1943.

South Pacific Archipelagoes, Including the Marquesas Group: Note the Location of Yap Among the Caroline Islands. Vol. XXXVI, p. 281, 1 half-page, Oct., 1919.

Sovereignty and Mandate Boundary Lines in 1921 of the Islands of the Pacific. Vol. XL, special supplement in colors, 19 x 25 inches, Dec., 1921.

See also Caroline Islands; Gilbert Islands; Guam; Marianas Islands; Marshall Islands; Palau Islands; Truk Islands.

Mid-Atlantic Ridge, Atlantic Ocean:

World Globe, showing Submarine Mountain Ranges and Deeps of Atlantic Ocean. Vol. LXXXVII, p. 112, 1 two-thirds-page, Jan., 1945.

Middle East:

Bahrein, with Inset of Middle East. Vol. LXXXIX, p. 199, 1 half-page, Feb., 1946.

Europe and the Near East, with Inset Map of the Middle East, and a Table of Distances between Principal Ports via Shortest Navigable Routes. Vol. LXXXIII, special supplement in colors, 39 x 34 inches, June, 1943.

Europe and the Near East, with Inset of the Middle East, as of April 1, 1940. Vol. LXXVII, special supplement in colors, 39 x 34 inches, May, 1940.

World Trouble Spot, the Oil-rich Middle East. Vol. LXXXIX, pp. 396-397, 1 two-page, Mar., 1946.

Middleton Island, Alaska:

Sketch Map showing the Location of Middleton Island. Vol. XLIV, p. 315, 1 eighth-page, Sept., 1923.

Midway Islands, Pacific Ocean:

Pacific Ocean and the Bay of Bengal, with Inset of Midway Islands. Vol. LXXXIV, special supplement in colors, 36½ x 26½ inches, Sept., 1943.

Migration Routes. *See* Bird Migration Routes.

Minami Tori Shima (Island), Pacific Ocean. *See* Marcus.

Mindanao (Island), Philippine Islands:

Mindanao and the Sulu Archipelago. Vol. LXXXVI, pp. 542-543, 1 two-page, Nov., 1944.

Minnesota:

Minnesota. Vol. LXVII, pp. 278-279, 2 pages, Mar., 1935.

Miquelon (Island), Atlantic Ocean:

St. Pierre and Miquelon. Vol. LXXX, p. 746, **1** fifth-page, Dec., 1941.

Mississippi:

Mississippi. Vol. LXXII, pp. 268-269, **1** two-page, Sept., 1937.

Mississippi (River), United States:

Changes in the Mississippi Delta in Less Than a Century. Vol. LXXI, p. 772, 1 quarter-page, June, 1937.

Growth of Land at Cubits Gap, Mississippi Delta, From 1852 to 1905. Vol. XX, p. 833, 1 page, Sept., 1909.

How Distant Tributaries Help Make Lower Mississippi Floods. Vol. LII, p. 245, 1 half-page, Sept., 1927.

Mississippi Delta, showing Formations. Vol. XXXIII, p. 533, 1 two-thirds-page, June, 1918.

Mississippi River. Vol. LXXII, pp. 268-269, 1 two-page, Sept., 1937.

Ohio and Mississippi River Basins. Vol. LXXI, pp. 770-771, 1 page-and-a-half, June, 1937.

Missouri:

Missouri. Vol. LXXXIX, pp. 280-281, two-page spread, Mar., 1946.

Ozark Plateau, showing Missouri and Arkansas with Portions of Bordering States. Vol. LXXXIII, p. 593, 1 two-thirds-page, May, 1943.

United States of America, with Inset of St. Louis. Vol. XLIII, special supplement in colors, 26½ x 36¼ inches, Apr., 1923.

Missouri (River), United States:

Route of Lewis R. Freeman's 2,000-Mile Voyage Down the Yellowstone-Missouri. Vol. LIV, p. 77, 1 half-page, July, 1928.

Missouri River Basin:

Missouri River Basin, showing Dams, Completed and Projected, and Wildlife Sanctuaries. Vol. LXXXVIII, pp. 576-577, 1 two-page, Nov., 1945.

Moll's Atlas:

Map of the World as Depicted by Map-Makers Before Captain Cook's First Voyage to "The Great South Sea." Vol. LI, p. 84, 1 page, Jan., 1927.

Moluccas (Islands), Netherlands Indies:

Far East, with Inset of the Moluccas. **Vol.** LXXIX, p. 538, 1 page, May, 1941.

Mongolia:

Divisions of Inner and Outer Mongolia. Vol. LXIII, p. 656, 1 half-page, June, 1933.

Mongolia, Manchuria, Chosen, East Turkestan, Tibet, Northern India. Vol. XXIII, special supplement in colors, 17 x 23 inches, Oct., **1912.**

Mongolia—*Continued*

Route of the National Geographic Society's Central-China Expedition. Vol. XLIX, p. 199, **1** third-page, Feb., 1926.

Montana:

Map of Northwestern United States and Neighboring Canadian Provinces. Vol. LXXIX, special supplement in colors, 24½ x 36 inches, June, 1941.

Morocco:

French and Spanish Morocco. Vol. XLVII, p. 331, 1 half-page, Mar., 1925.

Morocco. Vol. LXI, p. 266, 1 two-thirds-page, Mar., 1932.

Mulberry (Artificial Harbor), Normandy Coast, France:

British Mulberry and Omaha Beach, Artificial Harbors, off the Normandy Coast. Vol. LXXXVII, p. 565, 1 quarter-page, May, 1945.

Nansei Islands, Japan. *See* Ryukyu Retto.

Nantucket (Island), Massachusetts:

Nantucket, with Inset showing Mainland. Vol. LXXXV, p. 435, 1 half-page, Apr., 1944.

Nauru (Island), Pacific Ocean:

Pacific Ocean and the Bay of Bengal, with Inset of Nauru. Vol. LXXXIV, special supplement in colors, 36½ x 26½ inches, Sept., 1943.

Near East:

Europe and the Near East. Vol. LVI, special supplement in colors, 34¼ x 39¼ inches, Dec., 1929.

Europe and the Near East, as of April 1, 1940. Vol. LXXVII, special supplement in colors, 39 x 34 inches, May, 1940.

Europe and the Near East, with Inset Map of the Middle East, and a Table of Distances between Principal Ports via Shortest Navigable Routes. Vol. LXXXIII, special supplement in colors, 39 x 34 inches, June, 1943.

Near East, showing Naval Bases, Airports, Highways, Railways, Oil Pipe Lines, and Oil Pumping Stations. Vol. LXXX, pp. 144-145, 1 two-page, Aug., 1941.

Near East, showing Turkey, Iraq, and Adjacent Regions, with Naval Bases, Airports, Highways, Railways, and Oil Pipe Lines. Vol. LXXXII, pp. 388-389, 1 two-page, Sept., 1942.

Nebraska:

Nebraska. Vol. LXXXVII, pp. 516-517, two-page spread, May, 1945.

Nepal:

Geographical Relations of Nepal to India, Burma, Kashmir, and Tibet. Vol. XXXVIII, p. 249, 1 half-page, Oct., 1920.

Nepal, with Inset Map showing Location of Katmandu (Capital). Vol. LXVII, p. 323, 1 half-page, Mar., 1935.

Netherlands:

Flood Chart : Condition of Holland Without Dikes During Mean High Tide and Highest Stage of Rivers. Vol. XII, p. 233, 1 page, June, 1901.

Holland. Vol. XLIII, p. 286, 1 third-page, Mar., 1923.

Location and Extent of Zuider Zee Reclamation Project. Vol. LXIV, p. 295, 1 three-quarters-page, Sept., 1933.

Netherlands. Vol. LVI, p. 364, 1 two-thirds-page, Sept., 1929.

Netherlands, showing Area Below Sea Level. Vol. LXXXIX, p. 240, 1 seven-eighths-page, Feb., 1946.

Netherlands, with Inset showing Neighboring Countries. Vol. LXXVII, p. 261, 1 two-thirds-page, Feb., 1940.

Netherlands during the Sixth Century. Vol. XII, p. 219, 1 quarter-page, June, 1901.

Netherlands of Today and the State of Ohio Compared. Vol. XII, p. 220, 1 quarter-page, June, 1901.

Successive Enlargements of Haarlem Lake. Vol. XII, p. 223, 1 two-thirds-page, June, 1901.

Three Diagrams (Westvoorne, Goeree and Overflakkee) show the Enlargement of One Small Mud Flat to Ten Times Its Original Size. Vol. XII, p. 226, 1 page, June, 1901.

Zeeland About the Year 1200. Vol. XII, p. 225, 1 two-thirds-page, June, 1901.

Zuider Zee Reclamation Project. Vol. LXIV, p. 297, 1 half-page, Sept., 1933.

Netherlands East Indies:

East Indies. Vol. XIX, p. 471, 1 half-page, July, 1908.

Far East, with Enlargement of Java. Vol. LXXXI, p. 91, 1 two-thirds-page, Jan., 1942.

Far East, with Inset of the Moluccas. Vol. LXXIX, p. 538, 1 page, May, 1941.

Indian Ocean, including Australia, New Zealand and Malaysia. Vol. LXXIX, special supplement in colors, 25½ x 32¾ inches, Mar., 1941.

Netherlands Indies, with Inset of Malay States and Northern Sumatra. Vol. LXXIII, p. 668, 1 page, June, 1938.

Pacific War Area, showing Australia, New Zealand, Netherlands Indies, and Surrounding Islands. Vol. LXXXI, pp. 416-417, 1 two-page, Apr., 1942.

Philippine Islands as the Geographical Center of the Far East. Vol. XI, special supplement, 7½ x 10¾ inches, Jan., 1900.

Route of Magellan's Voyage. Vol. LXII, pp. 700-701, 2 half-pages, Dec., 1932.

Southeast Asia and Pacific Islands from the Indies and the Philippines to the Solomons, with 22 Inset Maps of Important Cities and Islands, and a Table of the Netherlands Indies' Administrative Areas and their Capital Cities. Vol. LXXXVI, special supplement in colors, 41 x 26½ inches, Oct., 1944.

Netherlands East Indies—*Continued*

See also Bali ; Borneo ; Celebes ; Java ; Lesser Sunda Islands ; New Guinea ; Nias (Island) ; Sumatra ; Timor.

Netherlands West Indies. *See* Aruba ; Bonaire ; Curaçao ; Saba.

Nevada:

Death Valley Region, Nevada. Vol. XVIII, p. 486, 1 page, Sept., 1906.

Southwestern United States. Vol. LXXVII, special supplement in colors, 35 x 26 inches, June, 1940.

New Britain (Island), Bismarck Archipelago :

Pacific Ocean and the Bay of Bengal, with Inset of New Britain and New Ireland. Vol. LXXXIV, special supplement in colors, 36½ x 26½ inches, Sept., 1943.

New Brunswick (Province), Canada :

New Brunswick Faces Strategic Newfoundland Across the Gulf of St. Lawrence. Vol. LXXIX, p. 597, 1 page, May, 1941.

New Caledonia (Island), Pacific Ocean :

Pacific Islands, with Inset of New Caledonia and the Loyalty Islands. Vol. LXXXII, p. 43, 1 two-thirds-page, July, 1942.

New Delhi, India :

New Delhi, showing the Seven Previous Sites of the City. Vol. LXXXII, p. 469, 1 page, Oct., 1942.

New England, United States :

Map showing Direction of Hurricane Air Currents and Path of Storm Center. Vol. LXXV, p. 534, 1 page, Apr., 1939.

Northeastern United States, with Inset of Southeastern New England. Vol. LXXXVIII, special supplement in colors, 41 x 26½ inches, Sept., 1945.

Route of the Connecticut River. Vol. LXXXIII, p. 405, 1 two-thirds-page, Apr., 1943.

See also Cod, Cape ; Connecticut ; Maine ; Massachusetts ; New Hampshire ; Rhode Island ; Vermont.

New Guinea:

Archbold Expedition Explores Interior of Netherlands New Guinea. Vol. LXXIX, p. 318, 1 two-thirds-page, Mar., 1941.

New Guinea, New Caledonia, and Fiji Command the Shortest Supply Routes from America to Australia, with Table of Airline Distances. Vol. LXXXI, pp. 698-699, 1 two-page, June, 1942.

New Guinea, with Inset showing Grand Valley and the Balim River. Vol. LXXXVIII, p. 674, 1 half-page, Dec., 1945.

New Guinea and an Inset Sketch Map of the Fly River Basin. Vol. LVI, p. 255, 1 three-quarters-page, Sept., 1929.

New Guinea or Papua. Vol. XIX, p. 471, 1 half-page, July, 1908,

New Hampshire:

New Hampshire. Vol. LX, p. 260, 1 page, Sept., 1931.

Northeastern United States. Vol. LXXXVIII, special supplement in colors, 41 x 26½ inches, Sept., 1945.

White Mountains of New Hampshire. Vol. LXXII, special supplement in colors, 17 x 20 inches, July, 1937.

New Hebrides (Islands), Pacific Ocean:

Coral Sea Area, showing the Solomons and New Hebrides, with an Inset of Efate. Vol. LXXXVI, p. 233, 1 four-fifths-page, Aug., 1944.

New Ireland (Island), Bismarck Archipelago:

Pacific Ocean and the Bay of Bengal, with Inset of New Britain and New Ireland. Vol. LXXXIV, special supplement in colors, 36½ x 26½ inches, Sept., 1943.

New Jersey:

Northeast Section of New Jersey. Vol. LXIII, p. 529, 1 two-thirds-page, May, 1933.

Northeastern United States. Vol. LXXXVIII, special supplement in colors, 41 x 26½ inches, Sept., 1945.

Reaches of New York City, with Inset of Southern New Jersey. Vol. LXXV, special supplement in colors, 26½ x 29 inches, Apr., 1939.

State of New Jersey. Vol. LXIII, p. 521, 1 page, May, 1933.

New Mexico:

Arizona and New Mexico, showing Location of Indian Ruins. Vol. LVI, p. 743, 1 two-thirds-page, Dec., 1929.

Carlsbad Caverns, with Diagrammatic Cross-Sections. Vol. XLVIII, p. 302, 1 three-quarters-page, Sept., 1925.

Course of the Rio Grande (River) from Its Source in Colorado Through Northern New Mexico, with Inset of the Entire River. Vol. LXXVI, p. 419, 1 third-page, Oct., 1939.

Course of the Rio Grande (River) from Northern New Mexico to El Paso, Texas. Vol. LXXVI, p. 424, 1 half-page, Oct., 1939.

Map of New Mexico, with Pictographs. Vol. LXXIII, pp. 532-533, 1 two-page, May, 1938.

New Mexico and Eastern Arizona. Vol. XLVIII, p. 232, 1 two-thirds-page, Sept., 1925.

Southwestern United States. Vol. LXXVII, special supplement in colors, 35 x 26 inches, June, 1940.

Texas, New Mexico, and Oklahoma. Vol. LIII, pp. 642-643, 1 two-page, June, 1928.

New South Wales (State), Australia. *See* Lord Howe (Island).

New York (City):

Chart of New York Harbor Made in 1737. Vol. XX, p. 825, 1 half-page, Sept., 1909.

New York (City)—*Continued*

Greater New York . . . Metropolis of Mankind. Special supplement from aërial photograph by Capt. Albert W. Stevens. Vol. LXIV, Nov., 1933.

Reaches of New York City. Vol. LXXV, special supplement in colors, 26½ x 29 inches, Apr., 1939.

Travels of George Washington, with Inset of New York and the Lower Hudson. Vol. LXI, special supplement in colors, 20 x 29 inches, Jan., 1932.

United States of America, with Inset of Greater New York. Vol. XLIII, special supplement in colors, 26½ x 36¼ inches, Apr., 1923.

New York (State):

Adirondack State Park. Vol. LXXIII, p. 720, 1 three-quarters-page, June, 1938.

Central New York, showing Finger Lakes Region. Vol. LXXIX, p. 561, 1 two-thirds-page, May, 1941.

Chart of New York Harbor Made in 1737. Vol. XX, p. 825, 1 half-page, Sept., 1909.

Front-Line Trenches of the Rivers of New York. Vol. L, p. 92, 1 half-page, July, 1926.

Greater New York . . . Metropolis of Mankind. Special supplement from aërial photograph by Capt. Albert W. Stevens. Vol. LXIV, Nov., 1933.

Mosaic Map of Rochester, N. Y., a City of 300,000 Inhabitants, Made from an Elevation of 10,000 Feet in a Single Flight. Vol. XXXIX, p. 344, 1 three-quarters-page, Mar., 1921.

Northeastern United States. Vol. LXXXVIII, special supplement in colors, 41 x 26½ inches, Sept., 1945.

One of Our Soldier Cities: Map of Camp Upton, Yaphank, Long Island, New York. Vol. XXXII, p. 437, 1 page in colors, Nov.-Dec., 1917.

Reaches of New York City. Vol. LXXV, special supplement in colors, 26½ x 29 inches, Apr., 1939.

Route of the New Erie Canal. Vol. XVI, p. 569, 1 page, Dec., 1905.

State of New York. Vol. LXIV, pp. 520-521, 1 two-page, Nov., 1933.

Two Maps showing Movement of Rockaway Beach and Inlet from 1835 to 1908. Vol. XXVIII, p. 206, 1 page, Sept., 1915.

Travels of George Washington, with Inset of New York and the Lower Hudson. Vol. LXI, special supplement in colors, 20 x 29 inches, Jan., 1932.

United States of America, with Insets of Greater New York and Buffalo. Vol. XLIII, special supplement in colors, 26½ x 36¼ inches, Apr., 1923.

New Zealand:

Indian Ocean, including Australia, New Zealand and Malaysia. Vol. LXXIX, special supplement in colors, 25½ x 32¾ inches, Mar., 1941.

New Zealand—*Continued*

New Zealand, with Insets of Hot Springs and Mountainous Regions. Vol. LXIX, pp. 170-171, 1 two-page, Feb., 1936.

Pacific War Area, showing Australia, New Zealand, Netherlands Indies, and Surrounding Islands. Vol. LXXXI, pp. 416-417, 1 two-page, Apr., 1942.

Rotorua Hot Springs Region of New Zealand. Vol. XLVIII, p. 113, 1 half-page, Aug., 1925.

South Island and Stephen Island. Vol. LXVII, p. 651, 1 half-page, May, 1935.

Newfoundland:

Military Outposts Leased from Britain Put New Teeth in Uncle Sam's Defenses. Vol. LXXVIII, p. 621, 1 page, Nov., 1940.

New Brunswick Faces Strategic Newfoundland Across the Gulf of St. Lawrence. Vol. LXXIX, p. 597, 1 page, May, 1941.

Newfoundland, showing British and American Defense Bases. Vol. LXXX, p. 113, 1 two-thirds-page, July, 1941.

Starting Point for Aviators Flying Planes to Britain, Norway, and Portugal. Vol. LXXX, p. 77, 1 page, July, 1941.

Nias (Island), Netherlands Indies:

Nias Island. Vol. LX, p. 205, 1 quarter-page, Aug., 1931.

Nicaragua:

Basins of the Rio Grande and Rio Las Lajas. Vol. X, p. 242, 1 page, July, 1899.

Boundary Between Nicaragua and Costa Rica. Vol. XII, p. 27, 1 half-page, Jan., 1901.

Lake Nicaragua. Vol. X, p. 239, 1 page, July, 1899.

Map of the Region Adjacent to the Nicaragua Canal Route. By C. Willard Hayes. Vol. X, special supplement, 7½ x 10½ inches, July, 1899.

Nicaragua. Vol. LXI, p. 594, 1 two-thirds-page, May, 1932.

Nicaragua. Vol. LXXXVI, p. 165, 1 two-thirds-page, Aug., 1944.

Route of Nicaragua Canal as Proposed by Isthmian Canal Commission. Vol. XII, p. 29, 1 page, Jan., 1901.

Nigeria:

Nigeria, with Inset showing Position in Africa. Vol. LXXXV, p. 540, 1 half-page, May, 1944.

Nile (River), Egypt:

Narrow Ribbon of Fertile Land Which Runs the Length of Egypt. Vol. XLIX, p. 272, 1 half-page, Mar., 1926.

Nile from Aswân, Egypt, to the Mediterranean Sea, with Pictographs. Vol. LXXVII, pp. 438-439, 1 two-page, Apr., 1940.

Nile from Its Mouth to the First Cataract. Vol. XXIV, p. 972, 1 page, Sept., 1913.

Niuafoō (Island), Tonga Islands:

Niuafoō (Inset). Vol. LXVIII, p. 95, 1 two-thirds-page, July, 1935.

Nonsuch Island, Bermuda :

Nonsuch Island. Vol. LXI, p. 66, 1 half-page, Jan., 1932.

Normandy (Region), France:

British Mulberry and Omaha Beach, Artificial Harbors, off the Normandy Coast. Vol. LXXXVII, p. 565, 1 quarter-page, May, 1945.

Normandy. Vol. LXIX, p. 629, 1 two-thirds-page, May, 1936.

Northwest France, including Normandy and Brittany. Vol. LXXXIV, pp. 218-219, 1 two-page, Aug., 1943.

North America:

Atlantic Ocean. Vol. LXXVI, special supplement in colors, 25 x 31 inches, July, 1939.

Atlantic Ocean, with Inset of Isthmus of Panama and a Table of Airline Distances in Statute Miles. Vol. LXXX, special supplement in colors, 31¼ x 25 inches, Sept., 1941.

Bird Migration Routes from South America to North America Converge Funnel-like in Central America. Inset of Veracruz and Tabasco, Mexico, showing La Venta Region, a Natural Bird Observatory. Vol. LXXXVII, p. 188, 1 two-thirds-page, Feb., 1945.

North America. Vol. XLV, special supplement in colors, 27 x 37 inches, May, 1924.

North America, with Inset of the Aleutian Islands. Vol. LXXXI, special supplement in colors, 26½ x 33 inches, May, 1942.

North America at the Time of Maximum Extent of the Ice. Vol. XXI, p. 526, 1 three-quarters-page, June, 1910.

Track of West Indian Hurricane, 1900. Vol. XI, p. 385, 1 page, Oct., 1900.

Track of West Indian Hurricane, 1900. Vol. XI, p. 390, 1 page, Oct., 1900.

United States, Canada, and Alaska, showing Route of the First Air Expedition to Alaska. Vol. XLI, pp. 500-501, 2 half-pages, May, 1922.

See also names of individual countries.

North Carolina:

Great Smoky Mountains National Park, with Inset showing Main Roads Across the Park. Vol. LXX, p. 246, 1 page, Aug., 1936.

North Carolina. Vol. XLIX, p. 512, 1 third-page, May, 1926.

North Carolina. Vol. LXXX, pp. 184-185, two-page spread, Aug., 1941.

North Carolina, South Carolina, Georgia, and Eastern Tennessee, with Inset of Charlotte. Vol. L, special supplement in colors, 14¾ x 19 inches, Sept., 1926.

Northeastern Coast and Islands of North Carolina. Vol. LXIV, p. 701, 1 two-thirds-page, Dec., 1933.

Sand Reefs Along the North Carolina Coast. Vol. XVII, p. 311, 1 page, June, 1906.

North Carolina—*Continued*

Virginia, North Carolina, Kentucky, and Tennessee. Vol. LXV, pp. 666-667, 1 two-page, June, 1934.

North Sea:

Denmark, with Inset of the North Sea. Vol. LXXVII, p. 3, 1 three-quarters-page, Jan., 1940.

Fishing Banks of the North Sea and the "War Zone" About the British Isles. Vol. XXVII, p. 149, 1 half-page, Feb., 1915.

Location of the Mine Barrage Laid by the American and British Mining Squadrons. Vol. XXXV, p. 86, 1 page, Feb., 1919.

Location of the Mine Fields. Vol. XXXVII, p. 104, 1 half-page. Feb., 1920.

Mine Groups. Vol. XXXVII, p. 105, 1 half-page, Feb., 1920.

Northern Hemisphere:

Average Lines Along Which the Centers of Storms Move in January and July in the Northern Hemisphere. Vol. XVI, p. 290, 1 page, June, 1915.

Diagram showing Arrangement of Sheets for the International Map on the Scale of 1: 1,000,000. Vol. XXI, p. 131, 1 two-thirds-page, Feb., 1910.

Lines of January Storms in the Northern Hemisphere. Vol. XVI, p. 291, 1 page, June, 1905.

Lines of July Storms in the Northern Hemisphere. Vol. XVI, p. 290, 1 page, June, 1905.

Northern and Southern Hemispheres, with Insets of Time Zones, World Terrain, and Tables of Airline Distances in Four Hemispheres. Vol. LXXXIII, special supplement in colors, 41 x 22 inches, Apr., 1943.

Northern Hemisphere, showing Parallels of Latitude, 10 to 60, to be Used with Sky Charts. Vol. LXXXIV, pp. 98-99, two-page spread, July, 1943.

Northern Hemisphere, with Tables showing Airline Distances in the Pacific, the Atlantic, the Arctic, and the Americas. Vol. LXXXIX, special supplement in colors, 21¾ x 24 inches, Feb., 1946.

Northern Ireland:

Ulster. Vol. LXVIII, p. 574, 1 two-thirds-page, Nov., 1935.

Northern Rhodesia:

Northern and Southern Rhodesia. Vol. LXXXVI, p. 284, 1 half-page, Sept., 1944.

Northwest Territories, Canada:

Mackenzie River and Basin. Vol. LX, p. 132, 1 page, Aug., 1931.

Norway:

Norway. Vol. LXXV, p. 496, 1 two-thirds-page, Apr., 1939.

Norway. Vol. LXXXIII, p. 336, 1 two-thirds-page, Mar., 1943.

Norway—*Continued*

Norway, showing the Petsamo Region of Finland, Ceded to the U. S. S. R. Vol. LXXXVIII, p. 620, 1 three-quarters-page, Nov., 1945.

Southern Norway. Vol. LXVII, p. 631, 1 half-page, May, 1935.

Nova Scotia (Province), Canada:

Cape Breton Island. Vol. XXXVIII, p. 35, 1 three-quarters-page, July, 1920.

Nova Scotia. Vol. LXXVII, pp. 580-581, 1 two-page, May, 1940.

Nukufetau (Island), Ellice Islands:

Pacific Ocean and the Bay of Bengal, with Inset of Nukufetau. Vol. LXXXIV, special supplement in colors, 36½ x 26½ inches, Sept., 1943.

Nukulaelae (Island), Ellice Islands:

Pacific Ocean and the Bay of Bengal, with Inset of Nukulaelae. Vol. LXXXIV, special supplement in colors, 36½ x 26½ inches, Sept., 1943.

Nukunono Island, Tokelau Islands:

Pacific Ocean and the Bay of Bengal, with Inset of Nukunono Island. Vol. LXXXIV, special supplement in colors, 36½ x 26½ inches, Sept., 1943.

Ocean (Island), Pacific Ocean:

Pacific Ocean and the Bay of Bengal, with Inset of Ocean Island. Vol. LXXXIV, special supplement in colors, 36½ x 26½ inches, Sept., 1943.

Oceania. *See* Pacific Islands.

Ogasawara Shoto (Bonin Islands), Pacific Ocean:

Strategic Isles of the Pacific: Chichi Jima, Eniwetok, Guam, Hachijo, Haha Jima, Jaluit, Kwajalein, Kusaie, Marcus, Palau, Paramushiro, Ponape, Rota, Saipan, Tinian, Truk, Wake, Yap. Vol. LXXXV, pp. 392-393, 17 island maps (two pages), Apr., 1944.

See also Chichi Jima Retto; Haha Jima Retto.

Ohio:

Northeastern United States. Vol. LXXXVIII, special supplement in colors, 41 x 26½ inches, Sept., 1945.

Ohio. Vol. LXI, p. 529, 1 three-quarters-page, May, 1932.

Sandusky and Vicinity. Vol. XIII, p. 401, 1 page, Nov., 1902.

United States of America, with Inset of Cleveland. Vol. XLIII, special supplement in colors, 26½ x 36¼ inches, Apr., 1923.

Ohio (River), United States:

Ohio and Mississippi River Basins. Vol. LXXI, pp. 770-771, 1 page-and-a-half, June, 1937.

Okinawa Gunto (Islands), Ryukyu Retto, Japan:

Detailed Map of Okinawa, which Offers a Fine Base for the United States Navy. Vol. LXXXVII, p. 548, 1 half-page, May, 1945.

Japan and Korea, with Insets of Kuril Islands, Pescadores, Karafuto, Ryukyu Islands, Okinawa, Formosa, Tokyo Area, and a Location Map of Japan in the Western Pacific. Vol. LXXXVIII, special supplement in colors, 37 x 26½ inches, Dec., 1945.

Southeast Asia and Pacific Islands from the Indies and the Philippines to the Solomons, with Inset of Nansei Islands, Amami to Okinawa. Vol. LXXXVI, special supplement in colors, 41 x 26½ inches, Oct., 1944.

Oklahoma:

Oklahoma. Vol. LXXIX, p. 289, 1 page, Mar., 1941.

Texas, New Mexico, and Oklahoma. Vol. LIII, pp. 642-643, 1 two-page, June, 1928.

Omaha Beach (Artificial Harbor), Normandy Coast, France:

British Mulberry and Omaha Beach, Artificial Harbors, off the Normandy Coast. Vol. LXXXVII, p. 565, 1 quarter-page, May, 1945.

Oman (Sultanate), Arabia:

Oman. Vol. XXII, p. 89, 1 quarter-page, Jan., 1911.

Ontario (Province), Canada:

Northeastern United States. Vol. LXXXVIII, special supplement in colors, 41 x 26½ inches, Sept., 1945.

Ontario. Vol. LXII, p. 139, 1 three-quarters-page, Aug., 1932.

Ontong Java (Islands), Solomon Islands:

Islands of the South Pacific, with Insets of Florida Island and Ontong Java. Vol. LXV, p. 268, 1 half-page, Mar., 1934.

Oregon:

Map of Northwestern United States and Neighboring Canadian Provinces. Vol. LXXIX, special supplement in colors, 24½ x 36 inches, June, 1941.

Oregon. Vol. XXIII, p. 626, 1 half-page, June, 1912.

Oregon. Vol. LXV, pp. 176-177, 1 two-page, Feb., 1934.

Oregon. Vol. XC, pp. 686-687, 1 two-page, Dec., 1946.

Rainfall Map of Washington and Oregon. Vol. XX, p. 647, 1 two-thirds-page, July, 1909.

Relief Map of Mount Hood. Vol. XIX, p. 519, 1 page, July, 1908.

United States of America, with Inset of Portland. Vol. XLIII, special supplement in colors, 26½ x 36¼ inches, Apr., 1923.

Washington and Oregon. Vol. XX, p. 646, 1 three-quarters-page, July, 1909.

Ozarks (Plateau), United States:

Ozark Plateau, showing Missouri and Arkansas with Portions of Bordering States. Vol. LXXXIII, p. 593, 1 two-thirds-page, May, 1943.

Pacific Islands:

Coral Sea Area, showing the Solomons and New Hebrides, with an Inset of Efate. Vol. LXXXVI, p. 233, 1 four-fifths-page, Aug., 1944.

Cruises of the *Princeton,* from the Time of Commissioning at Philadelphia to Her Loss in the Philippine Sea. Vol. LXXXVIII, pp. 210-211, two-page spread, Aug., 1945.

Hawaiian Islands, with Inset showing Route of Clipper Ships Across the Pacific Ocean. Vol. LXXIV, pp. 424-425, 1 page-and-a-half, Oct., 1938.

Islands of the South Pacific, with Insets of Florida Island and Ontong Java. Vol. LXV, p. 268, 1 half-page, Mar., 1934.

Japan and Adjacent Regions of Asia and the Pacific Ocean, with Insets of Industrial Centers of Japan and the Marshall Islands. Vol. LXXXV, special supplement in colors, 26½ x 34½ inches, Apr., 1944.

Japanese Micronesia, with Insets of Palau, Ponape, and Truk Islands. Vol. LXXXI, pp. 764-765, two-page spread, June, 1942.

Japanese Micronesia, with Insets of Yap, Ponape, and Palau Islands. Vol. LXIX, p. 483, 1 half-page, Apr., 1936.

Map of Pacific Islands, showing Route of Flying Clippers. Vol. LXXIV, p. 102, 1 third-page, July, 1938.

Marquesas, Tuamotu, and Austral Islands. Vol. XLVIII, p. 366, 1 half-page, Oct., 1925.

New Guinea, New Caledonia, and Fiji Command the Shortest Supply Routes from America to Australia, with Table of Airline Distances. Vol. LXXXI, pp. 698-699, 1 two-page, June, 1942.

New Zealand to the New Hebrides, with an Enlargement of Lord Howe Island. Vol. LXVIII, p. 118, 1 two-thirds-page, July, 1935.

New Zealand to the Samoa Group, with an Enlargement of Falcon Island. Vol. LIV, p. 760, 1 half-page, Dec., 1928.

Pacific Islands. Vol. XIX, p. 547, 1 three-quarters-page, Aug., 1908.

Pacific Islands: Aircraft Carrier Men's Vision of the Battle for the Pacific. Vol. LXXXII. pp. 8-9, two-page spread, July, 1942.

Pacific Islands, showing Date Line and Canton Island, Site of 1937 Eclipse Expedition. Vol. LXXII, p. 380, 1 two-thirds-page, Sept., 1937.

Pacific Islands, showing Limit of Long-range Bombing from Northern Australia, with Table of Airline Distances in Statute Miles. Vol. LXXXIII, pp. 56-57, 1 two-page, Jan., 1943.

Pacific Islands, showing Location of Marquesas Islands. Vol. LXXIX, p. 112, 1 twelfth-page, Jan., 1941.

Pacific Islands—*Continued*

Pacific Islands, with History of Discovery and an Inset showing Proposed American Bases. Vol. LXXXIX, pp. 624-625, 1 two-page, May, 1946.

Pacific Islands, with Inset of Gilbert Islands. Vol. LXXXIII, p. 74, 1 half-page, Jan., 1943.

Pacific Islands, with Inset of New Caledonia and the Loyalty Islands. Vol. LXXXII, p. 43, 1 two-thirds-page, July, 1942.

Pacific Ocean, with Inset Maps of Important Islands and Groups. Vol. LXX, special supplement in colors, 31 x 38 inches, Dec., 1936; revised in 1942.

Pacific Ocean and the Bay of Bengal, with Inset Maps of Important Islands, and Table of Airline Distances in Statute Miles. Vol. LXXXIV, special supplement in colors, 36½ x 26½ inches, Sept., 1943.

Pacific War Area, showing Australia, New Zealand, Netherlands Indies, and Surrounding Islands. Vol. LXXXI, pp. 416-417, 1 two-page, Apr., 1942.

Polynesian Archipelago. Vol. XLVIII, p. 358, 1 half-page, Oct., 1925.

Position of Tahiti in Mid-Pacific. Vol. XII, facing p. 413, 1 page, Dec., 1901.

South Pacific, showing Date Line and Canton Island, Site of 1937 Eclipse Expedition. Vol. LXXII, p. 380, 1 two-thirds-page, Sept., 1937.

South Pacific, with Inset of Niuafoō Island. Vol. LXVIII, p. 95, 1 two-thirds-page, July, 1935.

South Pacific Archipelagoes. Vol. XXXVI, p. 281, 1 half-page, Oct., 1919.

Southeast Asia and Pacific Islands from the Indies and the Philippines to the Solomons, with 22 Inset Maps of Important Cities and Islands. Vol. LXXXVI, special supplement in colors, 41 x 26½ inches, Oct., 1944.

Sovereignty and Mandate Boundary Lines in 1921 of the Islands of the Pacific. Vol. XL, special supplement in colors, 19 x 25 inches, Dec., 1921.

Strategic Isles of the Pacific: Chichi Jima, Eniwetok, Guam, Hachijo, Haha Jima, Jaluit, Kwajalein, Kusaie, Marcus, Palau, Paramushiro, Ponape, Rota, Saipan, Tinian, Truk, Wake, Yap. Vol. LXXXV, pp. 392-393, 17 island maps (two pages), Apr., 1944.

The Taking of Saipan Opens the Gate in Japan's Wall of Island Defenses. Vol. LXXXVII, p. 447, 1 half-page, Apr., 1945.

Theater of War in the Pacific Ocean, with Table of Airline Distances in Statute Miles. Vol. LXXXI, special supplement in colors, 20½ x 26½ inches, Feb., 1942.

Topography of Two Coral-Ringed Volcanic Isles: Bolabola, of the Society Group, and Vavitao, of the Austral Group. Vol. XLVIII, p. 369, 1 three-quarters-page, Oct., 1925.

Pacific Islands—*Continued*

See also Aleutian Islands; Caroline Islands; Fiji Islands; Gilbert Islands; Guam; Hawaii; Marianas Islands; Marquesas Islands; Marshall Islands; New Caledonia; New Guinea; New Hebrides; Philippine Islands; Ryukyu Retto; Society Islands; Solomon Islands; Tahiti; Truk Islands.

Pacific Northwest, United States:

Map of Northwestern United States and Neighboring Canadian Provinces. Vol. LXXIX, special supplement in colors, 24½ x 36 inches, June, 1941.

Pacific Northwest Defense Area. Vol. LXXXII, p. 425, 1 half-page, Oct., 1942.

See also Oregon; Washington.

Pacific Ocean:

Air and Water Currents of the Pacific. Vol. XVI, p. 420, 1 half-page, Sept., 1905.

Charts of 1869 and 1903, of the Pacific Ocean West of the Hawaiian Islands, to Illustrate the Removal of Doubtful Dangers. Vol. XX, p. 836, 1 page, Sept., 1909.

Crossroads of the Pacific Showing Trade Routes and Distances. Vol. XIX, p. 296, 1 half-page, Apr., 1908.

Doubtful Islands Region. Vol. XV, p. 479, 1 page, Dec., 1904.

Hawaiian Islands, with Inset showing Route of Clipper Ships Across the Pacific Ocean. Vol. LXXIV, pp. 424-425, 1 page-and-a-half, Oct., 1938.

How the *Southern Cross* (Airplane) Blazed an Aërial Trail Across the Pacific. Vol. LIV, p. 373, 1 two-thirds-page, Oct., 1928.

Humboldt Current. Vol. LXXIX, p. 376, 1 half-page, Mar., 1941.

Location of Hawaiian Islands. Vol. XLV, p. 116, 1 half-page, Feb., 1924.

Manila as a Distributing Point for Commerce. Vol. XIII, p. 314, 1 page, Aug., 1902.

Map showing Position of Total Eclipse (1937) Every 15 Minutes. Vol. LXXII, p. 364, 1 half-page, Sept., 1937.

Migration Routes of Hawaiian Islanders from Asia. Vol. XLV, p. 127, 1 half-page, Feb., 1924.

Migration Routes of the Golden Plover. Vol. XXII, p. 359, 1 two-thirds-page, Apr., 1911.

National Frontage and Way Stations on the Pacific. Vol. XIII, p. 308, 1 half-page, Aug., 1902.

"Pacific Is, and Will Remain, an American Ocean." Vol. XIII, p. 318, 1 half-page, Aug., 1902.

Pacific Ocean, with Inset Maps of Important Islands and Groups. Vol. LXX, special supplement in colors, 31 x 38 inches, Dec., 1936; revised in 1942.

Pacific Ocean—*Continued*

Pacific Ocean and the Bay of Bengal, with Inset Maps of Important Islands, and Table of Airline Distances in Statute Miles. Vol. LXXXIV, special supplement in colors, 36½ x 26½ inches, Sept., 1943.

Polynesian Archipelagoes. Vol. XLVIII, p. 358, 1 half-page, Oct., 1925.

Position of Reported Islands in Doubtful Region. Vol. XV, p. 481, 1 page, Dec., 1904.

Position of Reported Islands in the Doubtful Region, and the Sailing Tracks of Vessels Sent to Seek Them. Vol. XVIII, p. 207, 1 page, Mar., 1907.

Position of Tahiti in the Mid-Pacific. Vol. XXXVIII, p. 303, 1 half-page, Oct., 1920.

Principal Productions of the Countries Fronting on the Pacific. Vol. XIII, p. 305, 1 half-page, Aug., 1902.

Proposed Routes for Pacific Cables. Vol. XIII, p. 312, 1 three-quarters-page, Aug., 1902.

Relative Position of Doubtful Islands Region, the Hawaiian Islands, and the American Coast. Vol. XVIII, p. 206, 1 page, Mar., 1907.

Route Followed by Capt. Harry Pidgeon. Vol. LIII, p. 144, 1 two-page, Feb., 1928.

Route Followed by Capt. James Cook. Vol. LI, p. 87, 1 half-page, Jan., 1927.

Route of Flying Clippers. Vol. LXXIV, p. 102, 1 third-page, July, 1938.

Route of the *Yankee*, from Gloucester, Massachusetts, through the Panama Canal, to the Galápagos Islands, Easter Island, and Pitcairn. Vol. LXXXI, p. 4, 1 two-thirds-page, Jan., 1942.

Routes Followed by Ships and Planes of Byrd Antarctic Expedition in the South Pacific. Vol. LXVIII, p. 405, 1 page, Oct., 1935.

Shortest Route between Nantucket and Honolulu, via Cape Horn, is 15,600 Miles (Inset). Vol. LXXXIX, p. 625, May, 1946.

Sixteenth-Century Map of the Pacific. Vol. LXII, p. 763, 1 three-quarters-page, Dec., 1932.

Theater of War in the Pacific Ocean, with Table of Airline Distances in Statute Miles. Vol. LXXXI, special supplement in colors, 20½ x 26½ inches, Feb., 1942.

Transportation Routes of the Pacific. Vol. XIII, p. 310, 1 half-page, Aug., 1902.

Pagan (Island), Marianas Islands:

Southeast Asia and Pacific Islands from the Indies and the Philippines to the Solomons, with Inset of Pagan. Vol. LXXXVI, special supplement in colors, 41 x 26½ inches, Oct., 1944.

Pago Pago, Samoa:

Pacific Ocean and the Bay of Bengal, with Inset of Pago Pago Area. Vol. LXXXIV, special supplement in colors, 36½ x 26½ inches, Sept., 1943.

Palau Islands, Caroline Islands:

Japanese Micronesia, with Insets of Palau, Ponape, and Truk Islands. Vol. LXXXI, pp. 764-765, two-page spread, June, 1942.

Japanese Micronesia, with Insets of Yap, Ponape, and Palau Islands. Vol. LXIX, p. 483, 1 half-page, Apr., 1936.

Pacific Ocean and the Bay of Bengal, with Inset of Palau Islands. Vol. LXXXIV, special supplement in colors, 36½ x 26½ inches, Sept., 1943.

Southeast Asia and Pacific Islands from the Indies and the Philippines to the Solomons, with Inset of Palau Islands. Vol. LXXXVI, special supplement in colors, 41 x 26½ inches, Oct., 1944.

Strategic Isles of the Pacific. Vol. LXXXV, pp. 392-393, 17 island maps (two pages), Apr., 1944.

The Taking of Saipan Opens the Gate in Japan's Wall of Island Defenses. Vol. LXXXVII, p. 447, 1 half-page, Apr., 1945.

Palestine:

Bible Lands, showing Palestine, Trans-Jordan, and Egypt. Vol. LXXXV, p. 236, 1 page, Feb., 1944.

Bible Lands, showing Palestine, Trans-Jordan, and Syria. Vol. LXXXVI, p. 722, 1 page, Dec., 1944.

Bible Lands and the Cradle of Western Civilization, with Insets showing Jerusalem, the Holy Land, Economic Development, Route of the Exodus, St. Paul's Travels, Crusades, and Empire of Alexander the Great. Vol. LXXIV, special supplement in colors, 25 x 35 inches, Dec., 1938.

Bible Lands and the Cradle of Western Civilization, with Insets showing the Holy Land Today, Holy Land in Biblical Times, Jerusalem, Traditional Route of the Exodus, St. Paul's Travels and the Seven Churches, and the Crusades. Vol. XC, special supplement in colors, 32 x 22 inches, Dec., 1946.

Crusader Castles. Vol. LIX, p. 371, 1 third-page, Mar., 1931.

Crusader Trails and Castles. Vol. LXIV, p. 654, 1 page, Dec., 1933.

Eastern Shores of the Mediterranean. Vol. XXXVIII, p. 89, 1 quarter-page, Aug., 1920.

Jordan River from Galilee to Dead Sea. Vol. LXXVIII, p. 784, 1 page, Dec., 1940.

Mount Sinai and the Route of the Exodus. Vol. XXIII, p. 1282, 1 page, Dec., 1912.

Palestine, Syria, Iraq, Trans-Jordan, and Saudi Arabia. Vol. LXV, p. 496, 2 quarter-pages, Apr., 1934.

Palestine, Trans-Jordan, and Adjacent Territory. Vol. LXVII, p. 133, 1 quarter-page, Feb., 1935.

Philippine Islands (Republic of the Philippines)
—*Continued*

Relief Map of the Philippine Islands, showing Telegraph and Cable Lines. Vol. XV, p. 492, 1 page, Dec., 1904.

Southeast Asia and Pacific Islands from the Indies and the Philippines to the Solomons, with 22 Inset Maps of Important Cities and Islands. Vol. LXXXVI, special supplement in colors, 41 x 26½ inches, Oct., 1944.

Theater of Military Operations in Luzon, 1899. Vol. X, special supplement, 23½ x 38 inches, June, 1899.

Phoenix Islands, Pacific Ocean. *See* Canton Island; Enderbury Island; Gardner Island; Hull Island; Sydney Island.

Plymouth Area, England:

Southwestern England, with Enlargement of Plymouth Area. Vol. LXXXIX, p. 215, 1 half-page, Feb., 1946.

Poland:

Poland. Vol. L, p. 213, 1 two-thirds-page, Aug., 1926.

Poland. Vol. LXXV, p. 744, 1 two-thirds-page, June, 1939.

Southern Poland, showing Bicycle Route of Dorothy Hosmer. Vol. LXXV, p. 743, 1 third-page, June, 1939.

Polar Regions. *See* Antarctic Regions; Arctic Regions.

Polynesia:

Archipelago of Polynesia. Vol. XLVIII, p. 358, 1 half-page, Oct., 1925.

Marquesas, Tuamotu, and Austral Islands. Vol. XLVIII, p. 366, 1 half-page, Oct., 1925.

Migration Routes of Hawaiian Islanders from Asia. Vol. XLV, p. 127, 1 half-page, Feb., 1924.

New Zealand to the Samoa Group, with an Enlargement of Falcon Island. Vol. LIV, p. 760, 1 half-page, Dec., 1928.

Pacific Ocean, with Inset Maps of Important Islands and Groups. Vol. LXX, special supplement in colors, 31 x 38 inches, Dec., 1936; revised in 1942.

Pacific Ocean and the Bay of Bengal, with Inset Maps of Important Islands, and Table of Airline Distances in Statute Miles. Vol. LXXXIV, special supplement in colors, 36½ x 26½ inches, Sept., 1943.

Position of Tahiti in the Mid-Pacific. Vol. XXXVIII, p. 303, 1 half-page, Oct., 1920.

Route Followed by Capt. Harry Pidgeon in His Circumnavigation of the Globe. Vol. LIII, p. 144, 1 two-page, Feb., 1928.

Routes of Captain Cook's Three Voyages Through the Great South Sea. Vol. LI, p. 87, 1 three-quarters-page, Jan., 1927.

South Pacific, showing Date Line and Canton Island, Site of 1937 Eclipse Expedition. Vol. LXXII, p. 380, 1 two-thirds-page, Sept., 1937.

Polynesia—*Continued*

South Pacific, with Inset of Niuafoō Island. Vol. LXVIII, p. 95, 1 two-thirds-page, July, 1935.

South Pacific Archipelagoes, including the Marquesas Group: Note the Location of Yap Among the Caroline Islands. Vol. XXXVI, p. 281, 1 half-page, Oct., 1919.

Sovereignty and Mandate Boundary Lines in 1921 of the Islands of the Pacific. Vol. XL, special supplement in colors, 19 x 25 inches, Dec., 1921.

Topography of Two Coral-Ringed Volcanic Isles: Bolabola, of the Society Group, and Vavitao, of the Austral Group. Vol. XLVIII, p. 369, 1 three-quarters-page, Oct., 1925.

See also Hawaii; Marquesas Islands; Society Islands; Tahiti.

Ponape (Island), Caroline Islands:

Japanese Micronesia, with Insets of Palau, Ponape, and Truk Islands. Vol. LXXXI, pp. 764-765, two-page spread, June, 1942.

Japanese Micronesia, with Insets of Yap, Ponape, and Palau Islands. Vol. LXIX, p. 483, 1 half-page, Apr., 1936.

Pacific Ocean and the Bay of Bengal, with Inset of Ponape. Vol. LXXXIV, special supplement in colors, 36½ x 26½ inches, Sept., 1943.

Southeast Asia and Pacific Islands from the Indies and the Philippines to the Solomons, with Inset of Ponape. Vol. LXXXVI, special supplement in colors, 41 x 26½ inches, Oct., 1944.

Strategic Isles of the Pacific. Vol. LXXXV, pp. 392-393, 17 island maps (two pages), Apr., 1944.

Population:

Density of Population of the United States: The Number of Inhabitants Per Square Mile. Vol. XXII, p. 41, 1 half-page, Jan., 1911.

Foreign Stock in the Population of the United States—By Foreign Stock Is Meant Foreign-Born and Children of a Foreign-Born Father or Mother. Vol. XXXI, p. 96, 1 page, Feb., 1917.

Proportion of the Urban to Total Population in the United States. Vol. XXII, p. 43, 1 half-page, Jan., 1911.

United States, with Insets showing Army Corps Areas and Population of the States (1940). Vol. LXXVIII, special supplement in colors, 41 x 26½ inches, Dec., 1940.

Porto Rico. *See* Puerto Rico.

Portugal:

Lisbon and the Friendly Bay. Vol. XLII, p. 510, 1 quarter-page, Nov., 1922.

Portugal. Vol. LII, p. 568, 1 two-thirds-page, Nov., 1927.

Portugal. Vol. LXXIII, p. 134, 1 half-page, Feb., 1938.

See also Azores (Islands).

Potomac (River), United States:

Potomac River Windings in Maryland, Virginia, and West Virginia. Vol. LXXXVIII, pp. 36-37, two-page spread, July, 1945.

Pratas (Island), South China Sea:

Southeast Asia and Pacific Islands from the Indies and the Philippines to the Solomons, with Inset of Pratas. Vol. LXXXVI, special supplement in colors, 41 x 26½ inches, Oct., 1944.

Princeton (Aircraft Carrier):

Cruises of the *Princeton,* from the Time of Commissioning at Philadelphia to Her Loss in the Philippine Sea. Vol. LXXXVIII, pp. 210-211, two-page spread, Aug., 1945.

Puerto Rico:

Countries of the Caribbean, Including Mexico, Central America, the West Indies and the Panama Canal, with Detailed Insets of the Panama Canal and the Canal Zone, Porto Rico and the Virgin Islands, and Guantanamo Bay, Cuba. Vol. XLI, special supplement in colors, 25 x 44 inches, Feb., 1922.

Main Highway System of the Island. Vol. XLVI, p. 602, 1 half-page, Dec., 1924.

Map of Central America, Cuba, Porto Rico and the Islands of the Caribbean Sea, with Inset of the Panama Canal and Canal Zone. Vol. XXIV, special supplement in colors, 12½ x 19 inches, Feb., 1913.

Mexico, Central America, and the West Indies, with Inset of Puerto Rico. Vol. LXVI, special supplement in colors, 23 x 40 inches, Dec., 1934.

Mexico, Central America, and the West Indies, with Inset of Puerto Rico and the Virgin Islands. Vol. LXXVI, special supplement in colors, 24 x 41 inches, Dec., 1939.

Military Telegraph Lines in Porto Rico Operated by the Signal Corps, United States Army, Military Posts, Ports of Entry, and Area Compared with That of the State of Connecticut. Vol. XI, p. 242, 1 page, June, 1900.

Relief Map of Porto Rico, showing Telegraph Lines. Vol. XV, p. 493, 1 page, Dec., 1904.

Puto Shan (Island), East China Sea:

Puto Shan, with Enlargement showing Location of Island Off the China Coast. Vol. LXXXIX, p. 375, 1 third-page, Mar., 1946.

Quebec (Province), Canada:

Saguenay Region, with Inset of the St. Lawrence. Vol. LXXV, pp. 598-599, two-page spread, May, 1939.

St. Lawrence-Saguenay Region, with Inset showing Whole of Province. Vol. LXVII, p. 170, 1 page, Feb., 1935.

Races of Europe:

Races of Europe and Adjoining Portions of Asia and Africa. Vol. XXXIV, special supplement in colors, 19¾ x 31 inches, Dec., 1918.

Radio:

Paths of Short-wave Radio Beams from New York City Follow Great Circle Routes over Surface of the Earth. Vol. LXXXII, p. 679, 1 two-thirds-page, Nov., 1942.

Paths of Short-wave Radio Beams from San Francisco Follow Great Circle Routes over Surface of the Earth. Vol. LXXXII, p. 687, 1 two-thirds-page, Nov., 1942.

Raiatea (Island), Society Islands:

Relief Map of Raiatea and Tahaa Islands. Vol. LXV, p. 716, 1 third-page, June, 1934.

Rakahanga (Island), Pacific Ocean:

Pacific Ocean and the Bay of Bengal, with Inset of Rakahanga. Vol. LXXXIV, special supplement in colors, 36½ x 26½ inches, Sept., 1943.

Red Sea Region:

Pearl-Fishing Islands and Inset of Arabia. Vol. LXXII, p. 600, 1 two-thirds-page, Nov., 1937.

Suez-Red Sea Region. Vol. LXXXI, p. 507, 1 page, Apr., 1942.

Rhineland (Region), Germany:

Rhineland. Vol. LXXXVIII, p. 4, 1 third-page, July, 1945.

Rhineland, showing Former Demilitarized Zone. Vol. LXIX, p. 832, 1 two-thirds-page, June, 1936.

Rhode Island:

Northeastern United States. Vol. LXXXVIII, special supplement in colors, 41 x 26½ inches, Sept., 1945.

Rhodesia. *See* Northern Rhodesia; Southern Rhodesia.

Rio Grande (River), United States-Mexico:

Course of the Rio Grande from Its Source in Western Colorado to the Gulf of Mexico. Series of six maps. Vol. LXXVI, pp. 419, 424, 427, 428, 440, 453, Oct., 1939.

Rio Grande Delta, Texas:

Rio Grande Delta. Vol. LXXV, p. 54, 1 page, Jan., 1939.

Rivers:

Front-Line Trenches of the Rivers of New York. Vol. L, p. 92, 1 half-page, July, 1926.

Rivers in Germany and Austria Paddled by Cornelia Stratton Parker. Vol. LXI, p. 368, 1 two-thirds-page, Mar., 1932.

Where the Great River Trenches of Asia Run Parallel. Vol. L, p. 134, 1 half-page, Aug., 1926.

See also names of the following rivers: Balsas; Connecticut; Mississippi; Missouri; Nile; Ohio; Potomac; Rio Grande; Thames; Yellowstone; Yukon; *and* Saguenay River Region; St. Lawrence River Region.

Riviera (Region), France-Italy:

Riviera, with Inset Map showing Location of Monaco. Vol. LXVII, p. 69, 1 half-page, Jan., 1935.

Roman Empire:

Classical Lands of the Mediterranean, with Inset of the Roman Empire at the Time of Trajan. Vol. LXXVII, special supplement in colors, 35¼ x 26 inches, Mar., 1940.

Europe and Northern Africa, showing Extent of Roman Empire, with Table of Historical Facts. Vol. XC, pp. 552-553, 1 two-page, Nov., 1946.

Extent of the Empire, at the Death of Augustus (A. D. 14). Vol. LXXIV, p. 538, 1 half-page, Oct., 1938.

Rome-Naples Area, showing Main Arteries and Important Sites of Antiquity. Vol. XC, p. 569, 1 half-page, Nov., 1946.

Romania (Rumania):

Eastern Romania. Vol. LXXVII, p. 411, 1 third-page, Mar., 1940.

Romania. Vol. XLIX, p. 323, 1 half-page, Mar., 1926.

Romania. Vol. LXV, p. 401, 1 half-page, Apr., 1934.

Romania. Vol. LXXIV, p. 562, 1 page, Nov., 1938.

Rome (Ancient City):

Classical Lands of the Mediterranean, with Inset of Ancient Rome. Vol. LXXVII, special supplement in colors, 35¼ x 26 inches, Mar., 1940.

Rota (Island), Marianas Islands:

Southeast Asia and Pacific Islands from the Indies and the Philippines to the Solomons, with Inset of Rota. Vol. LXXXVI, special supplement in colors, 41 x 26½ inches, Oct., 1944.

Strategic Isles of the Pacific. Vol. LXXXV, pp. 392-393, 17 island maps (two pages), Apr., 1944.

Ruanda (District), Belgian Congo:

Ruanda, "The Land of Giants and Pygmies." Vol. XXIII, p. 388, 1 page, Apr., 1912.

Russia. *See* Union of Soviet Socialist Republics.

Russian Soviet Federated Socialist Republic. *See* Crimean Autonomous Soviet Socialist Republic; Daghestan Autonomous Soviet Socialist Republic.

Russian Turkistan. *See* Soviet Central Asia.

Ryukyu Retto (Nansei Islands), Japan:

Japan and Adjacent Regions of Asia and the Pacific Ocean, with Insets of Industrial Centers of Japan and the Marshall Islands. Vol. LXXXV, special supplement in colors, 26½ x 34½ inches, Apr., 1944.

Japan and Korea, with Insets of Kuril Islands, Pescadores, Karafuto, Ryukyu Islands, Okinawa, Formosa, Tokyo Area, and a Location Map of Japan in the Western Pacific. Vol. LXXXVIII, special supplement in colors, 37 x 26½ inches, Dec., 1945.

Ryukyu Retto (Nansei Islands), Japan *Continued*

Ryukyus, with Inset showing Location of the Islands in relation to Japan, Formosa, Philippines, and the China Coast. Vol. LXXXVII, p. 545, 1 two-thirds-page, May, 1945.

Southeast Asia and Pacific Islands from the Indies and the Philippines to the Solomons, with Inset of Nansei Islands, Amami to Okinawa. Vol. LXXXVI, special supplement in colors, 41 x 26½ inches, Oct., 1944.

See also Okinawa Gunto.

Saar Basin, Germany:

Saar Basin. Vol. LXVII, p. 242, 1 half-page, Feb., 1935.

Strategic Position of the Saar. Vol. LXVII, p. 243, 1 half-page, Feb., 1935.

Saba (Island), Leeward Islands:

Military Outposts Leased from Britain Put New Teeth in Uncle Sam's Defenses, with Inset of Saba. Vol. LXXVIII, p. 621, 1 page, Nov., 1940.

Saguenay River Region, Quebec, Canada:

Region of the Saguenay River, Quebec. Vol. LXXV, pp. 598-599, two-page spread, May, 1939.

St. Lawrence-Saguenay Region, with Inset showing Quebec Province. Vol. LXVII, p. 170, 1 page, Feb., 1935.

St. Lawrence River Region, Canada-United States:

Saguenay Region, with Inset of the St. Lawrence. Vol. LXXV, pp. 598-599, two-page spread, May, 1939.

St. Lawrence-Saguenay Region, with Inset showing Quebec Province. Vol. LXVII, p. 170, 1 page, Feb., 1935.

St. Pierre and **Miquelon** (Islands), Atlantic Ocean:

St. Pierre and Miquelon. Vol. LXXX, p. 746, 1 fifth-page, Dec., 1941.

St. Thomas (Island), Virgin Islands:

Mexico, Central America, and the West Indies, with Inset of Saint Thomas. Vol. LXXVI, special supplement in colors, 24 x 41 inches, Dec., 1939.

St. Vincent (Island), West Indies:

Zones of Devastation in St. Vincent. Vol. XIII, p. 282, 1 quarter-page, July, 1902.

Saipan (Island), Marianas Islands:

Southeast Asia and Pacific Islands from the Indies and the Philippines to the Solomons, with Inset of Saipan and Tinian Islands. Vol. LXXXVI, special supplement in colors, 41 x 26½ inches, Oct., 1944.

Strategic Isles of the Pacific. Vol. LXXXV, pp. 392-393, 17 island maps (two pages), Apr., 1944.

Salmon River District, Idaho:

Map of Salmon River District. Vol. LXX, p. 100, 1 page, July, 1936.

Salzkammergut (Region), Austria:

Salzkammergut. Vol. LXXI, p. 446, 1 third-page, Apr., 1937.

Samoa (Islands), Pacific Ocean:

Pacific Ocean and the Bay of Bengal, with Inset of Tutuila. Vol. LXXXIV, special supplement in colors, 36½ x 26½ inches, Sept., 1943.

Santo Domingo. *See* Dominican Republic.

São Paulo (State), Brazil:

Area Between Santos and São Paulo. Vol. LXXV, p. 660, 1 two-thirds-page, May, 1939.

São Paulo Coffee District of Brazil. Vol. XXII, p. 909, 1 half-page, Oct., 1911.

São Tomé (Island), Gulf of Guinea:

São Tomé, the Chocolate Island, with Location Map. Vol. LXXXIX, p. 659, 1 third-page, May, 1946.

Sardinia (Island), Mediterranean Sea:

Island of Sardinia. Vol. XLIII, p. 4, 1 three-quarters-page, Jan., 1923.

Relation of Sardinia to the Mainland of Italy. Vol. XLIII, p. 5, 1 quarter-page, Jan., 1923.

Sardinia and Her Relative Position to Adjacent Mediterranean Countries. Vol. XXX, p. 102, 1 page, Aug., 1916.

Saskatchewan (Province), Canada:

Map of Northwestern United States and Neighboring Canadian Provinces. Vol. LXXIX, special supplement in colors, 24½ x 36 inches, June, 1941.

Saudi Arabia:

Saudi Arabia, with Insets of Medina to Mecca Area and Ras at Tannura to Dhahran Area. Vol. LXXXVIII, p. 469, 1 two-thirds-page, Oct., 1945.

Western Arabia, Adjacent Countries, and Northeastern Africa. Vol. LXV, p. 765, 1 page, June, 1934.

Scilly Isles, England:

Scilly Isles, with Inset of the British Isles. Vol. LXXIV, p. 757, 1 half-page, Dec., 1938.

Scotland:

Scotland. Vol. LXXXIX, pp. 552-553, 1 two-page, May, 1946.

Southeastern Scotland. Vol. LXIX, p. 551, 1 two-thirds-page, Apr., 1936.

Serbia:

Bulgaria, Servia, and Macedonia. Vol. XXIII, p. 1152, 1 page, Nov., 1912.

Bulgaria and Serbia. Vol. XXVII, p. 421, 1 page, Apr., 1915.

Shanghai, China:

Southeast Asia and Pacific Islands from the Indies and the Philippines to the Solomons, with Inset of Shanghai Area. Vol. LXXXVI, special supplement in colors, 41 x 26½ inches, Oct., 1944.

Shantung (Province), China:

Shantung, China's Holy Land. Vol. XXXVI, p. 235, 1 half-page, Sept., 1919.

Siam:

Siam, French Indo-China, and Federated Malay States. Vol. LXV, p. 533, 1 two-thirds-page, May, 1934.

Siberia:

Far Eastern Republic. Vol. XLI, p. 567, 1 three-quarters-page, June, 1922.

Great Siberian Railway. Vol. XV, p. 129, 1 half-page, Mar., 1904.

Great Trans-Siberian Railway, showing Its Principal Connections. Vol. XXIII, p. 1076, 1 three-quarters-page, Nov., 1912.

Route of Trans-Siberian Railway. Vol. XII, p. 438, 1 quarter-page, Dec., 1901.

Seat of War in Manchuria (Beginning Just North of Mukden, and Covering the Country North to Harbin and East to Vladivostok). Vol. XVI, special supplement in colors, 18 x 44 inches, June, 1905.

Siberian Railway. Vol. XIII, p. 38, 1 quarter-page, Feb., 1902.

Where Vladimir M. Zenzinov Was Exiled in Arctic Siberia. Vol. XLVI, p. 699, 1 half-page, Dec., 1924.

Sicily (Island), Mediterranean Sea:

Classical Lands of the Mediterranean. Vol. LXXVII, special supplement in colors, 35¼ x 26 inches, Mar., 1940.

Geology in the Vicinity of Messina. Vol. XX, p. 394, 1 page, Apr., 1909.

Mediterranean Regions, with Inset Map of Sicily. Vol. LXXXIV, pp. 312-313, two-page spread, Sept., 1943.

Messina: Showing Principal Buildings, the City Wall, and Sickle-Shaped Harbor. Vol. XX, p. 375, 1 sixth-page, Apr., 1909.

Sicily. Vol. XLVI, p. 306, 1 half-page, Sept., 1924.

Sicily and South Italy. Vol. XX, p. 118, 1 three-quarters-page, Jan., 1909.

Sikang (Province), China:

China-India War Route, with Enlargement showing Minya Konka and the Route Followed by the Sikang Expedition. Vol. LXXXIII, p. 628, 1 page, May, 1943.

China-Tibetan Border, showing Route of Joseph F. Rock to the Amnyi Machen Mountains. Vol. LVII, pp. 138-139, 1 two-page, Feb., 1930.

Sikang, Yünnan, and Szechwan Provinces of China. Vol. LX, p. 7, 1 two-thirds-page, July, 1931.

Sikang (Province), China—*Continued*

Sikang's Mountain Grasslands, Route Followed by Ray G. Johnson and Party. Vol. LXXXV, p. 718, 1 half-page, June, 1944.

Szechwan, Yünnan, and Sikang Provinces. Vol. LVIII, p. 388, 1 two-thirds-page, Oct., 1930.

Singapore, Straits Settlements :

Indian Ocean, including Australia, New Zealand and Malaysia, with Inset of Singapore. Vol. LXXIX, special supplement in colors, 25½ x 32¾ inches, Mar., 1941.

Malay States, Thailand, and French Indo-China, with Inset of Singapore. Vol. LXXX, p. 662, 1 half-page, Nov., 1941.

Map of Equatorial Regions of the World, showing Importance of Singapore's Location. Vol. LXXVIII, p. 86, 1 quarter-page, July, 1940.

Southeast Asia and Pacific Islands from the Indies and the Philippines to the Solomons, with Inset of Singapore Area. Vol. LXXXVI, special supplement in colors, 41 x 26½ inches, Oct., 1944.

Strategic Geographic Position of Singapore, with an Inset of the Malay Peninsula. Vol. XLIX, p. 238, 1 half-page, Mar., 1926.

Sinkiang (Chinese Turkistan) :

Eastern Turkistan. Vol. XIV, p. 13, 1 quarter-page, Jan., 1903.

Khotan Valley. Vol. XIV, p. 12, 1 half-page, Jan., 1903.

Mongolia, Manchuria, Chosen, East Turkistan, Tibet, Northern India. Vol. XXIII, special supplement in colors, 17 x 23 inches, Oct., 1912.

Route of the Morden-Clark Asiatic Expedition. Vol. LII, p. 374, 1 page, Oct., 1927.

Sinkiang and Adjacent Countries. Vol. LIX, p. 323, 1 third-page, Mar., 1931.

Western Sinkiang. Vol. LXIX, p. 7, 1 half-page, Jan., 1936.

Smoky Mountains, North Carolina-Tennessee. *See* Great Smoky Mountains National Park.

Society Islands, Pacific Ocean :

Relief Map of Raiatea and Tahaa Islands. Vol. LXV, p. 716, 1 third-page, June, 1934.

See also Bolabola ; Tahiti.

Soerabaja, Java :

Southeast Asia and Pacific Islands from the Indies and the Philippines to the Solomons, with Inset of Soerabaja Area. Vol. LXXXVI, special supplement in colors, 41 x 26½ inches, Oct., 1944.

Solar Radiation Station, National Geographic Society :

South-West Africa in the Vicinity of the New Observatory. Vol. L, p. 504, 1 quarter-page, Oct., 1926.

Solomon Islands, Pacific Ocean :

Coral Sea Area, showing the Solomons and New Hebrides, with an Inset of Efate. Vol. LXXXVI, p. 233, 1 four-fifths-page, Aug., 1944.

Pacific Ocean and the Bay of Bengal, with Inset of Solomon Islands. Vol. LXXXIV, special supplement in colors, 36½ x 26½ inches, Sept., 1943.

Solomon Islands, with Inset Maps showing Guadalcanal-Tulagi Area and Bougainville Area. Vol. LXXXII, p. 815, 1 half-page, Dec., 1942.

Somaliland. *See* French Somaliland.

South Africa. *See* Union of South Africa.

South America:

Amazon Valley. Vol. XLIX, p. 354, 1 page, Apr., 1926.

Atlantic Ocean. Vol. LXXVI, special supplement in colors, 31 x 25 inches, July, 1939.

Atlantic Ocean, with Inset of Isthmus of Panama and a Table of Airline Distances in Statute Miles. Vol. LXXX, special supplement in colors, 31¼ x 25 inches, Sept., 1941.

Map of the Guianas, with an Inset showing the Territory Traversed by the "Kaieteur and Roraima" Expedition. Vol. XXXVIII, p. 229, 1 half-page, Sept., 1920.

Mexico, Central America, the West Indies, and Northern South America. Vol. LXVI, special supplement in colors, 23 x 40 inches, Dec., 1934.

Miami-Montevideo Air-Mail Route. Vol. LVII, p. 264, 1 half-page, Mar., 1930.

North-Central South America, showing Brazil-Venezuela Boundary. Vol. LXIV, p. 589, 1 two-thirds-page, Nov., 1933.

Pacific Coast of South America, showing Location of Humboldt Current. Vol. LXXIX, p. 376, 1 half-page, Mar., 1941.

Peru and Bolivia. Vol. XIX, p. 606, 1 half-page, Sept., 1908.

Railroad from Buenos Aires to Santiago, 888 Miles Long. Vol. XXI, p. 401, 1 quarter-page, May, 1910.

Route of A. F. Tschiffely on His Horseback Journey from Buenos Aires to Washington. Vol. LV, p. 140, 1 page, Feb., 1929.

Route of the National Geographic Society's Aërial Survey Flight from Washington to Buenos Aires. Vol. LIX, p. 4, 1 page, Jan., 1931.

Route of the Trail-Blazing Flight of U. S. Army Airplanes Through 20 Countries of Latin America. Vol. LII, p. 452, 1 page, Oct., 1927.

Route of Transandean Mail and Passenger Planes. Vol. LIX, p. 596, 1 third-page, May, 1931.

South America. Vol. XVII, special supplement in colors, 8 x 11 inches, Aug., 1906.

South America—*Continued*

South America. Vol. XL, special supplement in colors, 26 x 36 inches, Oct., 1921.

South America, with Inset Maps of Airways and Relief, Chief Natural Resources, Precipitation and Temperature, and the Galápagos Islands. Vol. LXXII, special supplement in colors, 26¾ x 37½ inches, Dec., 1937.

South America, with Insets of the Galápagos Islands, Chief Natural Resources, Precipitation and Temperature, Airways and Relief, and a Table of Airline Distances and Flying Times in Hours. Vol. LXXXII, special supplement in colors, 26½ x 37¼ inches, Oct., 1942.

Tierra del Fuego, with Inset of South America. Vol. LXXII, pp. 746-747, 1 two-page, Dec., 1937.

See also Argentina ; Bolivia ; Brazil ; British Guiana ; Chile ; Colombia ; Ecuador ; French Guiana ; Paraguay ; Peru ; Surinam ; Venezuela.

South Carolina:

North Carolina, South Carolina, Georgia, and Eastern Tennessee. Vol. L, special supplement in colors, 14¾ x 19 inches, Sept., 1926.

South Dakota:

Route Followed by Stratosphere Balloon, *Explorer II.* Vol. LXIX, p. 63, 1 quarter-page, Jan., 1936.

South Georgia (Island), Scotia Sea :

Author's Sketch Map of the Bleak and Lonely Bay of Isles. Vol. XLI, p. 412, 1 half-page Apr., 1922.

Island of South Georgia, Outpost of the Antarctic. Vol. XLI, p. 412, 1 half-page, Apr., 1922.

South Pole. *See* Antarctic Regions.

South Sea Islands. *See* Melanesia ; Micronesia ; Polynesia.

South-West Africa:

Map of the Seat of War in Africa, Prepared in the War Department, Adjutant General's Office, Military Information Division, with an Inset of South Africa. Vol. X, special supplement, 33 x 45 inches, Dec., 1899.

South-West Africa. Vol. LVII, p. 489, 1 sixth-page, Apr., 1930.

South-West Africa in the Vicinity of the New Observatory (National Geographic Society's Solar Radiation Station). Vol. L, p. 504, 1 quarter-page, Oct., 1926.

Southern Hemisphere:

Northern and Southern Hemispheres, with Insets of Time Zones, World Terrain, and Tables of Airline Distances in Four Hemispheres. Vol. LXXXIII, special supplement in colors, 41 x 22 inches, Apr., 1943.

Southern Rhodesia:

Northern and Southern Rhodesia. Vol. LXXXVI, p. 284, 1 half-page, Sept., 1944.

Soviet Central Asia:

Khoresm, U. S. S. R. : With Inset Map showing Relative Location of Khoresm. Vol. LXI, p. 754, 1 two-thirds-page, June, 1932.

Spain:

Location of the Montespan Cavern in the Foothills of the Pyrenees. Vol. XLVI, p. 126, 1 half-page, Aug., 1924.

Mountainous Regions of Spain. Vol. LIX, p. 124, 1 two-thirds-page, Jan., 1931.

Spain. Vol. XXI, p. 188, 1 half-page, Mar., 1910.

Spain. Vol. LV, p. 314, 1 two-thirds-page, Mar., 1929.

Spain. Vol. LXIX, p. 409, 1 half-page, Mar., 1936.

Spain, showing Location of Andorran Republic on the French Border. Vol. XXXIII, p. 281, 1 half-page, Mar., 1918.

Spain, with Inset Map of Madrid and Vicinity. Vol. LXX, pp. 402-403, 1 two-page, Oct., 1936.

Spain and the Basque Provinces. Vol. XLI, p. 66, 1 three-quarters-page, Jan., 1922.

See also Balearic Islands.

Spitsbergen (Archipelago), Arctic Region :

Arctic Regions, with Inset of Spitsbergen. Vol. XLVIII, special supplement in colors, 19¼ x 18 inches, Nov., 1925.

Spitsbergen and an Inset showing Its Location in the North Atlantic. Vol. LIV, p. 228, 1 three-quarters-page, Aug., 1928.

Sporades, Southern (Islands). *See* Dodecanese Islands.

Starbuck Island, Line Islands :

Pacific Ocean and the Bay of Bengal, with Inset of Starbuck Island. Vol. LXXXIV, special supplement in colors, 36½ x 26½ inches, Sept., 1943.

Stephen (Island), New Zealand :

Map showing Location of Stephen Island. Vol. LXVII, p. 651, 1 half-page, May, 1935.

Straits Settlements, Malay Peninsula. *See* Singapore.

Suez Canal, Egypt :

Indian Ocean, including Australia, New Zealand and Malaysia, with Inset of the Suez Canal. Vol. LXXIX, special supplement in colors, 25½ x 32¾ inches, Mar., 1941.

Suez-Red Sea Region. Vol. LXXXI, p. 507, 1 page, Apr., 1942.

Suez Canal. Vol. LXVIII, p. 612, 1 half-page, Nov., 1935.

Sulphur Island, Pacific Ocean. *See* Iwo Jima.

Sulu Archipelago, Philippine Islands :

Mindanao and the Sulu Archipelago. Vol. LXXXVI, pp. 542-543, 1 two-page, Nov., 1944.

Sumatra:

Netherlands Indies, with Inset of Malay States and Northern Sumatra. Vol. LXXIII, p. 668, 1 page, June, 1938.

Sumatra. Vol. LX, p. 205, 1 quarter-page, Aug., 1931.

Sumatra and an Inset of the Dutch East Indies. Vol. LVII, p. 189, 1 half-page, Feb., 1930.

Sunda Islands, Greater. *See* Borneo ; Celebes ; Java ; Sumatra.

Sunda Islands, Lesser. *See* Lesser Sunda Islands ; Timor.

Surinam:

Surinam and French Guiana, with Insets showing the Location and Comparable Sizes of the Guianas. Vol. LXXXIII, p. 462, 1 two-thirds-page, Apr., 1943.

Suvorov (Island), Pacific Ocean :

Pacific Ocean and the Bay of Bengal, with Inset of Suvorov. Vol. LXXXIV, special supplement in colors, 36½ x 26½ inches, Sept., 1943.

Sussex (County), England :

Scenic and Historic Properties of the National Trust. Vol. LXXXVII, pp. 420-421, 1 two-page, Apr., 1945.

Southeastern England, showing Harassed Channel Coast. Vol. LXXIX, p. 70, 1 third-page, Jan., 1941.

Sussex County. Vol. LXVIII, p. 63, 1 page, July, 1935.

Svalbard. *See* Spitsbergen.

Swains (Island), Pacific Ocean :

Pacific Ocean and the Bay of Bengal, with Inset of Swains Island. Vol. LXXXIV, special supplement in colors, 36½ x 26½ inches, Sept., 1943.

Sweden:

Southern Sweden. Vol. LXVI, p. 5, 1 page, July, 1934.

Southern Sweden, with Inset of Småland. Vol. LXXVI, p. 396, 1 quarter-page, Nov., 1939.

Switzerland:

Lake Geneva Region. Vol. LXXII, p. 728, 1 third-page, Dec., 1937.

Sydney Island, Phoenix Islands :

Pacific Ocean and the Bay of Bengal, with Inset of Sydney Island. Vol. LXXXIV, special supplement in colors, 36½ x 26½ inches, Sept., 1943.

Syria:

Asia Minor and the Levant. Vol. L, p. 652, 1 two-thirds-page, Dec., 1926.

Bible Lands and the Cradle of Western Civilization, with Insets showing Jerusalem, the Holy Land, Economic Development, Route of the Exodus, St. Paul's Travels, Crusades, and Empire of Alexander the Great. Vol. LXXIV, special supplement in colors, 25 x 35 inches, Dec., 1938.

Bible Lands and the Cradle of Western Civilization, with Insets showing the Holy Land Today, Holy Land in Biblical Times, Jerusalem, Traditional Route of the Exodus, St. Paul's Travels and the Seven Churches, and the Crusades. Vol. XC, special supplement in colors, 32 x 22 inches, Dec., 1946.

Crusader Castles. Vol. LIX, p. 371, 1 third-page, Mar., 1931.

Crusader Trails and Castles. Vol. LXIV, p. 654, 1 page, Dec., 1933.

Eastern Shores of the Mediterranean. Vol. XXXVIII, p. 89, 1 quarter-page, Aug., 1920.

Latakia and Lebanon. Vol. LVIII, p. 485, 1 quarter-page, Oct., 1930.

Latakia and Lebanon. Vol. LXIV, p. 103, 1 third-page, July, 1933.

Syria. Vol. XXXVI, p. 441, 1 quarter-page, Nov., 1919.

Szechwan (Province), China :

China. Vol. XXII, p. 1097, 1 two-thirds-page, Dec., 1911.

Szechwan Province, China. Vol. LVIII, p. 388, 1 three-quarters-page, Oct., 1930.

Tabasco (State), Mexico :

Bird Migration Routes from South America to North America Converge Funnel-like in Central America. Inset of Veracruz and Tabasco, Mexico, showing La Venta Region, a Natural Bird Observatory. Vol. LXXXVII, p. 188, 1 two-thirds-page, Feb., 1945.

Tahaa (Island), Society Islands :

Relief Map of Raiatea and Tahaa Islands. Vol. LXV, p. 716, 1 third-page, June, 1934.

Tahiti (Island), Society Islands :

Position of Tahiti in the Mid-Pacific. Vol. XXXVIII, p. 303, 1 half-page, Oct., 1920.

Profile Map of Tahiti, showing the Eroded Volcanic Core, the Lagoon, Fringing Reef, and Barrier Reef. Vol. XLVIII, p. 362, 1 page, Oct., 1925.

Tahiti, showing the Many Rivers That Flow from the High Mountains in the Interior. Vol. XII, p. 418, Dec., 1901.

Tai Shan (Mountain), China :

Pen and Ink Drawing of Tai Shan, with Pictographs. Vol. LXXXVII, p. 700, 1 page, June, 1945.

Taiwan (Island). *See* Formosa.

Tarawa (Atoll), Gilbert Islands:

Gilbert Islands, with Insets of Tarawa and Makin. Vol. LXXXVII, p. 135, 1 two-thirds-page, Feb., 1945.

Pacific Ocean and the Bay of Bengal, with Inset of Tarawa. Vol. LXXXIV, special supplement in colors, 36½ x 26½ inches, Sept., 1943.

Tasmania (Island), Australia:

Australia, with Inset of Tasmania. Vol. LXVIII, pp. 672-673, 2 pages, Dec., 1935.

Tennessee:

Great Smoky Mountains National Park, with Inset showing Main Roads Across the Park. Vol. LXX, p. 246, 1 page, Aug., 1936.

North Carolina, South Carolina, Georgia, and Eastern Tennessee. Vol. L, special supplement in colors, 14¾ x 19 inches, Sept., 1926.

Northeastern Tennessee, showing Cumberland Gap Region. Vol. LXXXIV, p. 745, 1 quarter-page, Dec., 1943.

Tennessee. Vol. LXXV, pp. 556-557, 2 half pages, May, 1939.

Virginia, North Carolina, Kentucky, and Tennessee. Vol. LXV, pp. 666-667, 1 two-page, June, 1934.

Texas:

Course of the Rio Grande (River) from Candelaria to Eagle Pass. Vol. LXXVI, p. 428, 1 quarter-page, Oct., 1939.

Course of the Rio Grande (River) from Eagle Pass to Rio Grande. Vol. LXXVI, p. 440, 1 quarter-page, Oct., 1939.

Course of the Rio Grande (River) from El Paso to Presidio. Vol. LXXVI, p. 427, 1 third-page, Oct., 1939.

Course of the Rio Grande (River) from Rio Grande to the Gulf of Mexico. Vol. LXXVI, p. 453, 1 quarter-page, Oct., 1939.

Galveston Hurricane, 1900. Vol. XVI, p. 278, 1 page, June, 1905.

Gulf of Mexico, showing Coastal Areas of United States and Mexico. Vol. LXXXV, pp. 8-9, 1 two-page, Jan., 1944.

Rio Grande Delta. Vol. LXXV, p. 54, 1 page, Jan., 1939.

Texas. Vol. XXIV, p. 1353, 1 half-page, Dec., 1913.

Texas. Vol. LXXXVII, pp. 168-169, 1 two-page, Feb., 1945.

Texas, New Mexico, and Oklahoma. Vol. LIII, pp. 642-643, 1 two-page, June, 1928.

Texas, showing Annual Rainfall and Mean Annual Temperature Zones. Vol. XXIV, p. 1355, 1 three-quarters-page, Dec., 1913.

Two Maps showing the Effect of Improvements at the Entrance to Galveston, Texas, from the Charts of 1867 and 1909. Vol. XX, p. 826, 1 page, Sept., 1909.

Thailand. *See* Siam.

Thames (River), England:

Thames River from Oxford to the North Sea. Vol. LXXV, pp. 244-245, 2 half-pages, Feb., 1939.

Theater of War Maps. *See* World War I *and* World War II.

Tibet:

Mongolia, Manchuria, Chosen, East Turkestan, Tibet, Northern India. Vol. XXIII, special supplement in colors, 17 x 23 inches, Oct., 1912.

Tibet, showing Adjacent Areas of India and China. Vol. XC, p. 172, 1 half-page, Aug., 1946.

Tibet and Border Countries. Vol. XL, p. 296, 1 half-page, Sept., 1921.

Tibetan Highland:

China-India War Route, with Enlargement showing Minya Konka and the Route Followed by the Sikang Expedition. Vol. LXXXIII, p. 628, 1 page, May, 1943.

Tides:

Cotidal Lines for the Gulf of Saint Lawrence. Vol. XVII, p. 308, 1 page, June, 1906.

Cotidal Lines for the Mediterranean Sea. Vol. XVII, p. 306, 1 page, June, 1906.

Cotidal Lines for the World; or, Lines of Simultaneous High Water at Each Hour and Half Hour of Greenwich Lunar Time. Vol. XVII, special supplement, 8 x 14 inches, June, 1906.

Systems of Semi-Diurnal Tide. Vol. XVII, p. 305, 1 half-page, June, 1906.

Tierra del Fuego (Archipelago), South America:

Tierra del Fuego, with Inset of South America. Vol. LXXII, pp. 746-747, 1 two-page, Dec., 1937.

Timor (Island), Netherlands Indies:

Pacific Ocean and the Bay of Bengal, with Inset of Timor. Vol. LXXXIV, special supplement in colors, 36½ x 26½ inches, Sept., 1943.

Timor. Vol. LXXXIV, p. 359, 1 third-page, Sept., 1943.

Tinian (Island), Marianas Islands:

Southeast Asia and Pacific Islands from the Indies and the Philippines to the Solomons, with Inset of Saipan and Tinian Islands. Vol. LXXXVI, special supplement in colors, 41 x 26½ inches, Oct., 1944.

Strategic Isles of the Pacific. Vol. LXXXV, pp. 392-393, 17 island maps (two pages), Apr., 1944.

Tobago (Island), West Indies:

Trinidad and Tobago Islands, with Inset of West Indies. Vol. LXXII, p. 321, 1 half-page, Sept., 1937.

Tokelau Islands, Pacific Ocean. *See* Atafu; Fakaofo; Nukunono.

Tokyo Area, Japan:

Japan and Korea, with Insets of Kuril Islands, Pescadores, Karafuto, Ryukyu Islands, Okinawa, Formosa, Tokyo Area and a Location Map of Japan in the Western Pacific. Vol. LXXXVIII, special supplement in colors, 37 x 26½ inches, Dec., 1945.

Tonga Islands, Pacific Ocean:

Tonga Islands, with Inset of Niuafoō Island. Vol. LXVIII, p. 95, 1 two-thirds-page, July, 1935.

Tongareva (Island), Pacific Ocean:

Pacific Ocean and the Bay of Bengal, with Inset of Tongareva. Vol. LXXXIV, special supplement in colors, 36½ x 26½ inches, Sept., 1943.

Trans-Jordan:

Bible Lands, showing Palestine, Trans-Jordan, and Egypt. Vol. LXXXV, p. 236, 1 page, Feb., 1944.

Bible Lands, showing Palestine, Trans-Jordan, and Syria. Vol. LXXXVI, p. 722, 1 page, Dec., 1944.

Bible Lands and the Cradle of Western Civilization, with Insets showing Jerusalem, the Holy Land, Economic Development, Route of the Exodus, St. Paul's Travels, Crusades, and Empire of Alexander the Great. Vol. LXXIV, special supplement in colors, 25 x 35 inches, Dec., 1938.

Bible Lands and the Cradle of Western Civilization, with Insets showing the Holy Land Today, Holy Land in Biblical Times, Jerusalem, Traditional Route of the Exodus, St. Paul's Travels and the Seven Churches, and the Crusades. Vol. XC, special supplement in colors, 32 x 22 inches, Dec., 1946.

Near East, showing Egypt, Anatolia, and the Arab Kingdoms of Hedjaz, Transjordania, and Iraq. Vol. XLIII, p. 534, 1 three-quarters-page, May, 1923.

Trans-Jordan, Palestine, and Adjacent Territory. Vol. LXVII, p. 133, 1 quarter-page, Feb., 1935.

World's Deepest Land Depression Separates Palestine from Trans-Jordan. Vol. LXXI, p. 72, 1 third-page, Jan., 1937.

Trinidad (Island), West Indies:

Trinidad and Tobago Islands, with Inset of West Indies. Vol. LXXII, p. 321, 1 half-page, Sept., 1937.

Tristan da Cunha (Islands), Atlantic Ocean:

South Atlantic Ocean, with Inset of Tristan da Cunha. Vol. LXXIV, p. 674, 1 half-page, Nov., 1938.

Truk Islands, Caroline Islands:

Japanese Micronesia, with Insets of Palau, Ponape, and Truk Islands. Vol. LXXXI, pp. 764-765, two-page spread, June, 1942.

Truk Islands, Caroline Islands—*Continued*

Pacific Ocean and the Bay of Bengal, with Inset of Truk Islands. Vol. LXXXIV, special supplement in colors, 36½ x 26½ inches, Sept., 1943.

Southeast Asia and Pacific Islands from the Indies and the Philippines to the Solomons with Inset of Truk Islands. Vol. LXXXVI, special supplement in colors, 41 x 26½ inches, Oct., 1944.

Strategic Isles of the Pacific. Vol. LXXXV, pp. 392-393, 17 island maps (two pages), Apr., 1944.

Truk, Ruk, and Hogolu Islands, of the Caroline Group, showing Encircling Coral Reef. Vol. XL, p. 648, Dec., 1921.

Truk Islands. Vol. LXV, p. 707, 1 two-thirds-page, June, 1934.

Tuamotu (Archipelago), Pacific Ocean:

Marquesas, Tuamotu, and Austral Islands. Vol. XLVIII, p. 366, 1 half-page, Oct., 1925.

Tulagi Area, Solomon Islands:

Solomon Islands, with Inset Maps showing Guadalcanal-Tulagi Area and Bougainville Area. Vol. LXXXII, p. 815, 1 half-page, Dec., 1942.

Tunisia:

Tunisia, Africa's Northernmost Tip, Nearly Divides the Mediterranean into Two Great Lakes. Vol. LXXI, p. 349, 1 half-page, Mar., 1937.

Tunisia, with Inset of Tunis. Vol. LXXI, p. 350, 1 page, Mar., 1937.

Location of Kairouan. Vol. XXII, p. 1089, 1 half-page, Dec., 1911.

Site of Carthage: Also the Pontine Marshes. Vol. XLV, p. 394, 1 half-page, Apr., 1924.

Turkey:

Aegean Regions. **Vol. LVI,** p. 489, **1** half-page, Oct., 1929.

Ancient Armenia, and the Country Where the Armenians Now Live. Vol. XXVIII, p. 359, 1 half-page, Oct., 1915.

Asia Minor. Vol. XLVI, p. 450, 1 quarter-page, Oct., 1924.

Asia Minor, showing Turkey. Vol. L, p. 652, 1 two-thirds-page, Dec., 1926.

Bible Lands and the Cradle of Western Civilization, with Insets showing Jerusalem, the Holy Land, Economic Development, Route of the Exodus, St. Paul's Travels, Crusades, and Empire of Alexander the Great. Vol. LXXIV, special supplement in colors, 25 x 35 inches, Dec., 1938.

Turkey—*Continued*

Bible Lands and the Cradle of Western Civilization, with Insets showing the Holy Land Today, Holy Land in Biblical Times, Jerusalem, Traditional Route of the Exodus, St. Paul's Travels and the Seven Churches, and the Crusades. Vol. XC, special supplement in colors, 32 x 22 inches, Dec., 1946.

Classical Lands of the Mediterranean. Vol. LXXVII, special supplement in colors, 35¼ x 26 inches, Mar., 1940.

Constantinople. Vol. XLI, p. 650, 1 three-quarters-page, June, 1922.

Crusader Trails and Castles. Vol. LXIV, p. 654, 1 page, Dec., 1933.

Eastern Turkey. Vol. LXXX, p. 370, 1 half-page, Sept., 1941.

Europe and the Near East. Vol. LVI, special supplement in colors, 34¼ x 39¼ inches, Dec., 1929.

Gates to the Black Sea. Vol. XXVII, p. 532, 1 half-page, May, 1915.

Gates to the Black Sea. Vol. XXVIII, p. 232, 1 half-page, Sept., 1915.

Location of Mt. Argæus and of the Troglodytes. Vol. XXXV, p. 315, 1 half-page, Apr., 1919.

Near East, showing Naval Bases, Airports, Highways, Railways, Oil Pipe Lines, and Oil Pumping Stations. Vol. LXXX, pp. 144-145, 1 two-page, Aug., 1941.

Near East, showing Turkey, Iraq, and Adjacent Regions, with Naval Bases, Airports, Highways, Railways, and Oil Pipe Lines. Vol. LXXXII, pp. 388-389, 1 two-page, Sept., 1942.

Railways Constructed in Asia Minor and Persia. Vol. XI, p. 202, 1 page, May, 1900.

"Shores of Sunrise" (The Levant). Vol. L, p. 652, 1 two-thirds-page, Dec., 1926.

Turkey. Vol. LXXV, pp. 8-9, Jan., 1939.

Turkey. Vol. LXXXVII, pp. 594-595, two-page spread, May, 1945.

Turkey, Arabia, Persia, and Egypt. Vol. XX, p. 173, 1 two-thirds-page, Feb., 1909.

Turkey, Arabia, Persia, and Egypt. Vol. XXII, p. 63, 1 two-thirds-page, Jan., 1911.

Turkey, Greece, and Aegean Sea, with Inset showing Dardanelles. Vol. XLII, p. 554, 1 half-page, Nov., 1922.

Turkey and the Near East, with Inset of Cappadocia. Vol. LXXVI, p. 767, 1 half-page, Dec., 1939.

Turkey in Asia. Vol. XXVI, p. 614, 1 page, Dec., 1914.

World Trouble Spot, the Oil-rich Middle East, Vol. LXXXIX, pp. 396-397, 1 two-page, Mar., 1946.

World's Most Historic Lands. Vol. XXIX, p. 216, 1 page, Feb., 1916.

See also Anatolia; Asia Minor.

Turkistan. *See* Sinkiang; Soviet Central Asia.

Tutuila (Island), Samoa:

Pacific Ocean and the Bay of Bengal, with Inset of Tutuila. Vol. LXXXIV, special supplement in colors, 36½ x 26½ inches, Sept., 1943.

Tweedsmuir Park, British Columbia:

Tweedsmuir Park. Vol. LXXIII, p. 454, 1 half-page, Apr., 1938.

Uganda:

Uganda Borders the Largest Fresh-Water Lake in the Old World and Contains the Source of the Nile. Vol. LXXI, p. 113, 1 two-thirds-page, Jan., 1937.

Ukrainian Soviet Socialist Republic, U.S.S.R.:

Western U. S. S. R., showing Extent of German Invasion. Vol. LXXXV, p. 516, 1 page, May, 1944.

Ulster (Northern Ireland):

Northern Ireland. Vol. LXVIII, p. 574, 1 two-thirds-page, Nov., 1935.

Unimak (Island), Aleutian Islands:

Unimak Island. Vol. XIV, p. 92, 1 half-page, Mar., 1903.

Union Group, Pacific Ocean. *See* Tokelau Islands.

Union of South Africa:

Map of the Seat of War in Africa, Prepared in the War Department, Adjutant General's Office, Military Information Division, with an Inset of South Africa. Vol. X, special supplement, 32 x 45 inches, Dec., 1899.

Union of South Africa, with Inset Maps of Africa and Cape of Good Hope. Vol. LIX, pp. 400-401, 1 two-page, Apr., 1931.

Union of South Africa, with Inset Maps of Africa and Cape of Good Hope. Vol. LXXXII, p. 203, 1 two-thirds-page, Aug., 1942.

Union of South Africa, with Inset showing Witwatersrand (Region). Vol. LXXXII, p. 739, 1 two-thirds-page, Dec., 1942.

Union of Soviet Socialist Republics:

Amu Darya Valley, with Inset Map showing the Location of Khoresm. Vol. LXI, p. 754, 1 two-thirds-page, June, 1932.

Caucasus, showing the Highlands of Daghestan. Vol. XXIV, p. 1086, 1 page, Oct., 1913.

Diagram showing Successive Advances of Russia Toward India. Vol. XI, p. 183, 1 half-page, May, 1900.

Ethnographic Russia in 1900. Vol. XI, p. 172, 1 half-page, May, 1900.

Growth of Russia in Europe from 1303 to 1645. Vol. XI, p. 175, 1 three-quarters-page, May, 1900.

Growth of Russia in Europe from 1645 to 1900. Vol. XI, p. 178, 1 three-quarters-page, May, 1900.

Murman Coast and the Territory Through Which Runs the New Murman Railway. Vol. XXXV, p. 332, 1 half-page, Apr., 1919.

Union of Soviet Socialist Republics—*Continued*

Russian Empire in Its Geographic Relation to Europe and Asia. Vol. XI, p. 185, 1 page, May, 1900.

Trans-Siberian Railway, showing Its Principal Connections. Vol. XXIII, p. 1076, 1 three-quarters-page, Nov., 1912.

Union of Soviet Socialist Republics, with International Boundaries according to Russian Treaties and Claims as of October 1, 1944. Boundaries of January 1, 1938, are shown in red. Vol. LXXXVI, special supplement in colors, 40 x 25 inches, Dec., 1944.

Union of Soviet Socialist Republics, with Outline Map of the United States Superimposed, to Show the Northern Latitude of Russian-Siberian Industry. Vol. LXXXIII, pp. 532-533, 1 two-page, May, 1943.

Western U. S. S. R., showing Extent of German Invasion. Vol. LXXXV, p. 516, 1 page, May, 1944.

Where Russia's Orphan Races Reside. Vol. XXXIV, p. 277, 1 page, Oct., 1918.

See also Crimean Autonomous Soviet Socialist Republic ; Siberia.

United Nations Area:

The United States of America, with Insets of United Nations Area and East of Maine. Vol. XC, special supplement in colors, 26½ x 41 inches, July, 1946.

United States:

Airway Routes of the United States. Vol. LXIII, p. 634, 1 page, May, 1933.

Approximate Location and Extent of Open Range in the United States. Vol. XV, p. 21, 1 three-quarters-page, Jan., 1904.

Arid, Semi-Arid and Humid Regions of the United States. Vol. XV, p. 16, 1 half-page, Jan., 1904.

Arizona, New Mexico, and Northern Mexico. Vol. XXXVIII, p. 75, 1 third-page, July, 1920.

Arizona, New Mexico, Utah, and Colorado, showing Sites of Ruins. Vol. LVI, p. 743, 1 third-page, Dec., 1929.

Boundaries of Territorial Acquisitions of the United States. Vol. XII, p. 375, 1 page, Oct., 1901.

Clark's Survey of the Boundary of Texas. Vol. XII, p. 431, 1 sixth-page, Dec., 1901.

Coal Areas of the United States. Vol. XVIII, p. 135, 1 half-page, Feb., 1907.

Cold Wave, January 7, 1886, 7 A. M. Vol. XVI, p. 271, 1 page, June, 1905.

Cold Wave, January 8, 1886, 7 A. M. Vol. XVI, p. 272, 1 page, June, 1905.

Cold Wave, January 9, 1886, 7 A. M. Vol. XVI, p. 273, 1 page, June, 1905.

Cold Wave, January 10, 1886, 7 A. M. Vol. XVI, p. 274, 1 page, June, 1905.

United States—*Continued*

Course of the Rio Grande (River) from Its Source in Colorado to the Gulf of Mexico. Series of six maps. Vol. LXXVI, pp. 419, 424, 427, 428, 440, 453, Oct., 1939.

Cumberland Gap, First High Gateway to the West. Vol. LXXXIV, p. 745, 1 quarter-page, Dec., 1943.

Distribution of the Chestnut-Bark Disease. Vol. XXII, p. 345, 1 three-quarters-page, Apr., 1911.

Foreign Stock in the Population of the United States—By Foreign Stock Is Meant Foreign-Born and Children of a Foreign-Born Father or Mother. Vol. XXXI, p. 96, 1 page, Feb., 1917.

Forest Reserves of the United States. Vol. XI, p. 370, 1 page, Sept., 1900.

Forests and Woodlands of the West. Vol. XV, p. 19, 1 three-quarters-page, Jan., 1904.

Geological Survey River Stations : Map showing the Location of the Principal River Stations Maintained in the United States by the United States Geological Survey. Vol. XVII, p. 357, 1 page, June, 1906.

Government Reclamation Projects. Vol. XX, p. 437, 1 three-quarters-page, May, 1909.

Grand Canyon from Green River, Wyoming, to Mouth of Colorado, in Mexico. Vol. XXVI, p. 153, 1 page, Aug., 1914.

Grand Canyon of the Colorado River : 1923 Expedition of the U. S. Geological Survey. Vol. XLV, p. 474, 1 three-quarters-page, May, 1924.

Great Lakes Region. Vol. LXV, pp. 454-455, 1 two-page, Apr., 1934.

Gulf of Mexico, showing Coastal Areas of United States and Mexico. Vol. LXXXV, pp. 8-9, 1 two-page, Jan., 1944.

Historic and Scenic Reaches of the Nation's Capital. Vol. LXXIV, special supplement in colors, 26½ x 31¼ inches, July, 1938.

How Distant Tributaries Help Make Lower Mississippi Floods. Vol. LII, p. 245, 1 half-page, Sept., 1927.

Irrigated and Irrigable Lands. Vol. XV, p. 20, 1 three-quarters-page, Jan., 1904.

Lake Superior, showing Northern Michigan and Wisconsin, Eastern Minnesota, and Western Ontario. Vol. XL, p. 114, 1 half-page, Aug., 1921.

Lights That Mark the Approaches to the Great Harbors of Boston, New York, and Philadelphia. Vol. XXIV, p. 6, 1 three-quarters-page, Jan., 1913.

Location of and Annual Precipitation at Certain Stations in the Arid Region of Western America. Vol. XV, p. 162, 1 half-page, Apr., 1904.

Location of Cities Having a Population of 50,000 or More, Census 1890. Vol. XIV, p. 367, 1 half-page, Oct., 1903.

Location of Fisheries. Vol. XVI, p. 522, 1 page, Nov., 1905.

United States—*Continued*

Location of 46 Out of the 56 National Bird Reservations. Vol. XXIV, p. 369, 1 half-page, Mar., 1913.

Location of Some of the Important Finds of Dinosaurian Remains and Areas Where Deposits were Laid Down During the Time That These Animals Lived. Vol. XXXV, p. 425, 1 page, May, 1919.

Location of the Principal River Stations Maintained in the United States by the United States Geological Survey. Vol. XVII, p. 357, 1 page, June, 1906.

Map of Northwestern United States and Neighboring Canadian Provinces. Vol. LXXIX, special supplement in colors, 24½ x 36 inches, June, 1941.

Map showing Direction of Hurricane Air Currents and Path of Storm Center in New England. Vol. LXXV, p. 534, 1 page, Apr., 1939.

Mean Annual Rainfall in the United States. Vol. XV, p. 16, 1 half-page, Jan., 1904.

Mexico, Central America, the West Indies, and Southern United States. Vol. LXVI, special supplement in colors, 23 x 40 inches, Dec., 1934.

Missouri River Basin, showing Dams, Completed and Projected, and Wildlife Sanctuaries. Vol. LXXXVIII, pp. 576-577, 1 two-page, Nov., 1945.

National Monuments and National Parks. Vol. XXIII, p. 538, 1 page, June, 1912.

National Parks of the United States. Vol. XI, p. 370, 1 page, Sept., 1900.

Normal Storm Tracks for May. Vol. XVI, p. 281, 1 page, June, 1905.

North Carolina, South Carolina, Georgia and Eastern Tennessee, with Insets of Charleston, Charlotte, and Atlanta. Vol. L, special supplement in colors, 15¼ x 18¾ inches, Sept., 1926.

Northeastern United States, with Inset of Southeastern New England. Vol. LXXXVIII, special supplement in colors, 41 x 26½ inches, Sept., 1945.

Number of Children under 5 Years of Age to 1,000 Females 15 to 49 Years of Age: 1890. Vol. XVI, p. 506, 1 page, Nov., 1905.

Number of Children under 5 Years of Age to 1,000 Females 15 to 49 Years of Age: 1900. Vol. XVI, p. 507, 1 page, Nov., 1905.

Number of Colored Population for Each Colored Insane, Census 1880. Vol, XIV, p. 376, 1 half-page, Oct., 1903.

Number Population for Each Insane Person, Census 1880. Vol. XIV, p. 363, 1 half-page, Oct. 1903.

Ohio and Mississippi River Basins. Vol. LXXI, pp. 770-771, 1 page-and-a-half, June, 1937.

Ozark Plateau, showing Missouri and Arkansas with Portions of Bordering States. Vol. LXXXIII, p. 593, 1 two-thirds-page, May, 1943.

United States—*Continued*

Pipe-Line System Which Forms a Network Beneath the Surface of the Eastern Half of the United States. Vol. XXXVII, p. 183, 1 half-page, Feb., 1920.

Population of the United States: The Number of Inhabitants Per Square Mile. Vol. XXII, p. 41, 1 quarter-page, Jan., 1911.

Primary Triangulation in the United States About 10,000 Linear Miles by the Coast and Geodetic Survey and about 2,000 Miles by the Lake Survey. Vol. XXV, p. 664, 1 page, June, 1914.

Production of Petroleum in the United States in 1918, and the Outlines of the Petroleum Areas. Vol. XXXVII, p. 187, 1 half-page, Feb., 1920.

Proportion of Urban to Total Population. Vol. XXII, p. 43, 1 half-page, Jan., 1911.

Rate of Growth Throughout the United States (In Population): 1900-1910. Vol. XXII, p. 35, 1 half-page, Jan., 1911.

Ratio of Total Insane per 100,000 Population, Census 1880. Vol. XIV, p. 362, 1 half-page, Oct., 1903.

Ratio of Total Insane per 100,000 Population, Census 1890. Vol. XIV, p. 368, 1 half-page, Oct., 1903.

Reaches of New York City. Vol. LXXV, special supplement in colors, 26½ x 29 inches, Apr., 1939.

Relative Density of Railroads in the United States. Vol. XVI, p. 521, 1 half-page, Dec., 1905.

Route Followed by Lindbergh in the *Spirit of St. Louis,* and Its Companion Plane. Vol. LIII, p. 5, 1 page, Jan., 1928.

Route of Lewis R. Freeman's 2,000-Mile Voyage Down the Yellowstone-Missouri. Vol. LIV, p. 77, 1 half-page, July, 1928.

Route of Santa Fe Trail. Vol. LVI, p. 216, 1 half-page, Aug., 1929.

Route of the Connecticut River through New England. Vol. LXXXIII, p. 405, 1 two-thirds-page, Apr., 1943.

Routes Followed by Lieut. John A. Macready and Lieut. Oakley G. Kelly in Their Transcontinental, Non-stop Flights, and of Lieut. Macready and Lieut. A. W. Stevens on Their Later Photographic Flights. Vol. XLVI, p. 6, 1 page, July, 1924.

Sections Mapped by the U. S. Geological Survey. Vol. XII, p. 122, 1 half-page, Mar., 1901.

Southwestern United States. Vol. XXI, p. 632, 1 page, Aug., 1910.

Southwestern United States. Vol. LXXVII, special supplement in colors, 35 x 26 inches, June, 1940.

Storm Tracks for August. Vol. XVI, p. 279, 1 page, June, 1905.

Storm Tracks for February. Vol. XVI, p. 280, 1 page, June, 1905.

United States—*Continued*

Swamp Areas in the United States. Vol. XVIII, p. 298, 1 half-page, May, 1907.

Territories from Which Each National Army Cantonment Camp Received Its Troops: Also Showing the Location of Cantonments, Regular Army Organization Camps, National Guard Mobilization Camps, and Aviation Camps. Vol. XXXII, p. 438, 1 page in colors, Nov.-Dec., 1917.

Texas, New Mexico, and Oklahoma. Vol. LIII, pp. 642-643, 2 page maps, June, 1928.

Tornado at Louisville, Kentucky, Mar. 27, 1890. Weather Map 8 P. M. of That Date. Vol. XVI, p. 282, 1 page, June, 1905.

Tornadoes of 1889—A Year of Small Frequency. Vol. XVI, p. 283, 1 page, June, 1905.

Tornadoes of 1893—A Year of Great Frequency. Vol. XVI, p. 284, 1 page, June, 1905.

Transcontinental Routes of the *Shenandoah* on Its Record-Making Voyage. Vol. XLVII, p. 5, 1 page, Jan., 1925.

Travels of George Washington, with Insets of New York and the Lower Hudson, Tidewater Virginia, Philadelphia, Boston, and Mount Vernon. Vol. LXI, special supplement in colors, 20 x 29 inches, Jan., 1932.

United States, showing Territory Acquired by Texas Annexation and Mexican Cessions. Vol. XXII, p. 474, 1 half-page, May, 1911.

United States, showing Waterways That Probably Could be Made Navigable for Commerce. Vol. XVIII, p. 676, 1 page, Oct., 1907.

United States, with Insets showing Army Corps Areas and Population of the States (1940). Vol. LXXVIII, special supplement in colors, 41 x 26½ inches, Dec., 1940.

United States Air Mail Routes in Operation and Proposed. Vol. XLIX, p. 5, 1 two-thirds-page, Jan., 1926.

United States and Adjoining Portions of Canada and Mexico. Vol. LXIII, special supplement in colors, 26 x 40 inches, May, 1933.

United States Interior Navigation. Vol. XIV, p. 183, 1 half-page, May, 1903.

United States of America, with Insets of Important Cities. Vol. XLIII, special supplement in colors, 26½ x 36¼ inches, Apr., 1923.

The United States of America, with Insets of United Nations Area and East of Maine. Vol. XC, special supplement in colors, 26½ x 41 inches, July, 1946.

Vacant Public Lands. Vol. XV, p. 18, 1 three-quarters-page, Jan., 1904.

Virginia, North Carolina, Kentucky, and Tennessee. Vol. LXV, pp. 666-667, 1 two-page, June, 1934.

United States—*Continued*

Voice Voyages Made by the National Geographic Society from Washington to Pittsburgh, Chicago, Omaha, Denver, Salt Lake City, San Francisco, Portland, Seattle, El Paso, Ottawa, Jacksonville, and Intermediate Points. Vol. XXIX, p. 296, 1 half-page, Mar., 1916.

Wanderings of the Rio Grande and of the Old Boundary. Vol. XXIV, p. 384, 1 three-quarters-page, Mar., 1913.

Weather Map, 8 A. M., February 28, 1902. Vol. XIII, p. 111, 1 page, Mar., 1902.

Weather Maps showing the Conditions Under Which the Transcontinental Non-Stop Flight Was Made (May, 1923). Vol. XLVI, p. 4, 1 half-page, July, 1924.

West Indian Hurricane, August 27, 1893, 8 A. M. Vol. XVI, p. 275, 1 page, June, 1905.

West Indian Hurricane, August 28, 1893, 8 A. M. Vol. XVI, p. 276, 1 page, June, 1905.

West Indian Hurricane, August 29, 1893, 8 A. M. Vol. XVI, p. 277, 1 page, June, 1905.

White Insane Only: Census 1880. Vol. XIV, p. 375, 1 half-page, Oct., 1903.

Winter Storm, December 15, 1893, 8 A. M. Vol. XVI, p. 268, 1 page, June, 1905.

Winter Storm, Dec. 15, 1893, 8 P. M. Vol. XVI, p. 269, 1 page, June, 1905.

Winter Storm, December 16, 1893, 8 A. M. Vol. XVI, p. 270, 1 page, June, 1905.

See also Washington D. C. *and* names of individual states.

U. S. Defense Bases:

Alaska—Springboard for Attack on Japan and Key to Continental Defense. Vol. LXXXII, pp. 286-287, 1 two-page, Sept., 1942.

Alaska, showing Alcan Highway. Vol. LXXXIII, pp. 150-151, 1 two-page, Feb., 1943.

American Bases in the Lesser Antilles Protect the Panama Canal. Vol. LXXXI, p. 729, 1 half-page, June, 1942.

American Military Bases near the Arctic Circle. Vol. LXXXIX, p. 604, 1 half-page, May, 1946.

The American Virgins Guard a Main Route from Europe to the Panama Canal. Vol. LXXVIII, p. 277, 1 two-thirds-page, Sept., 1940.

Arctic Regions, as seen from 10,000 Miles in Space, the World of Capt. Bob Bartlett, Who Supplied American Military Bases near the Arctic Circle for Four Summers. Vol. LXXXIX, p. 604, 1 half-page, May, 1946.

Atlantic Ocean, showing Air Routes to Norway and Britain, via Newfoundland, Greenland, and Iceland. Vol. LXXX, p. 77, 1 page, July, 1941.

Detailed Map of the Aleutian Islands—Battleground of the Northern Pacific. Vol. LXXXIII, pp. 152-153, two-page spread, Feb., 1943.

Global Map of Arctic Regions showing Greenland, Important for Weather Stations and Air Bases. Vol. XC, p. 459, 1 page, Oct., 1946.

U. S. Defense Bases—*Continued*

Greenland—an Aerial Stepping Stone to Europe. Vol. LXXXII, pp. 370-371, 1 two-page, Sept., 1942.

Greenland, as seen from the North Pole, with Emphasis upon its Strategic Importance to North America. Vol. LXXVIII, pp. 118-119, 1 two-page, July, 1940.

Leeward and Windward Islands—Like a Curving Shield the West Indies Guard the Panama Canal. Vol. LXXIX, p. 5, 1 page, Jan., 1941.

Like a Curving Shield the West Indies Guard the Panama Canal. Vol. LXXIX, p. 5, 1 page, Jan., 1941.

Military Outposts Leased from Britain Put New Teeth in Uncle Sam's Defenses. Vol. LXXVIII, p. 621, 1 page, Nov., 1940.

New Brunswick Faces Strategic Newfoundland Across the Gulf of St. Lawrence. Vol. LXXIX, p. 597, 1 page, May, 1941.

Newfoundland—Starting Point for Aviators Flying Planes to Britain, Norway, and Portugal. Vol. LXXX, p. 77, 1 page, July, 1941.

Newfoundland, showing British and American Defense Bases. Vol. LXXX, p. 113, 1 two-thirds-page, July, 1941.

Pacific Islands, with History of Discovery and an Inset showing Proposed American Bases. Vol. LXXXIX, pp. 624-625, 1 two-page, May, 1946.

Pacific Northwest Defense Area. Vol. LXXXII, p. 425, 1 half-page, Oct., 1942.

United States Army and Navy Air Bases in Alaska. Vol. LXXVIII, p. 490, 1 page, Oct., 1940.

Western Hemisphere, showing U. S. Defense Bases. Vol. LXXIX, p. 41, 1 page, Jan., 1941.

Utah:

Newly Discovered Route to Rainbow Natural Bridge. Vol. XLIII, p. 198, 1 half-page, Feb., 1923.

Route of the National Geographic Society's San Juan Expedition. Vol. XLV, p. 278, 1 half-page, Mar., 1924.

Southwestern United States. Vol. LXXVII, special supplement in colors, 35 x 26 inches, June, 1940.

Utah, with Insets of Bryce and Zion Canyons. Vol. LXIX, pp. 580-581, 1 two-page, May, 1936.

Vatican City:

Vatican City. Vol. LXXV, pp. 382-383, 1 two-page, Mar., 1939.

Vavitao (Island), Austral Islands:

Topography of Two Coral-Ringed Volcanic Isles: Bolabola, of the Society Group, and Vavitao, of the Austral Group. Vol. XLVIII, p. 369, 1 three-quarters-page, Oct., 1925.

Venezuela:

Boundaries as Claimed by Great Britain and Venezuela and as Awarded by the Paris Tribunal, 1899. Vol. XI, p. 129, 1 page, Apr., 1900.

North-Central South America, showing Brazil-Venezuela Boundary. Vol. LXIV, p. 589, 1 two-thirds-page, Nov., 1933.

Northeastern Venezuela. Vol. LXXV, p. 100, 1 third-page, Jan., 1939.

Venezuela. Vol. LX, p. 622, 1 third-page, Nov., 1931.

Veracruz (State), Mexico:

Archeological Sites in Veracruz and Tabasco Explored by National Geographic Society-Smithsonian Expedition of 1940. Vol. LXXVIII, p. 313, 1 third-page, Sept., 1940.

Bird Migration Routes from South America to North America Converge Funnel-like in Central America. Inset of Veracruz and Tabasco, Mexico, showing La Venta Region, a Natural Bird Observatory. Vol. LXXXVII, p. 188, 1 two-thirds-page, Feb., 1945.

New Center of Maya Culture Discovered by National Geographic Society-Smithsonian Institution Expedition. Vol. LXXVI, p. 184, 1 half-page, Aug., 1939.

Vermont:

Northeastern United States. Vol. LXXXVIII, special supplement in colors, 41 x 26½ inches, Sept., 1945.

Vermont. Vol. LI, p. 340, 1 page, Mar., 1927.

Virgin Islands, West Indies:

Countries of the Caribbean, Including Mexico, Central America, the West Indies and the Panama Canal, with Detailed Insets of the Panama Canal and the Canal Zone, Porto Rico and the Virgin Islands, and Guantanamo Bay, Cuba. Vol. XLI, special supplement in colors, 25 x 44 inches, Feb., 1922.

Greater and Lesser Antilles with Inset of the Virgin Islands. Vol. LXXVIII, p. 277, 1 two-thirds-page, Sept., 1940.

Mexico, Central America, and the West Indies, with Inset of Puerto Rico and the Virgin Islands. Vol. LXXVI, special supplement in colors, 24 x 41 inches, Dec., 1939.

Mexico, Central America, and the West Indies, with Inset of the Virgin Islands. Vol. LXVI, special supplement in colors, 23 x 40 inches, Dec., 1934.

Relative Position of Danish West Indies. Vol. XXX, p. 93, 1 page, July, 1916.

Virginia:

Assateague Island, Virginia, showing Land Defenses Built Since 1849. Vol. XXXIII, p. 534, 1 half-page, June, 1918.

Chain of Forts Recommended by George Washington. Vol. LXI, p. 40, 1 two-thirds-page, Jan., 1932.

Virginia—*Continued*

Cumberland Gap Region. Vol. LXXXIV, p. 745, 1 quarter-page, Dec., 1943.

Historic and Scenic Reaches of the Nation's Capital. Vol. LXXIV, special supplement in colors, 26½ x 31¼ inches, July, 1938.

Potomac River Windings in Maryland, Virginia, and West Virginia. Vol. LXXXVIII, pp. 36-37, two-page spread, July, 1945.

Tidewater Virginia. Vol. LXXXI, p. 621, 1 page, May, 1942.

Tidewater Virginia, with Inset of Hampton Roads. Vol. LXXVI, p. 361, 1 page, Sept., 1939.

Travels of George Washington, with Insets of Mount Vernon and Tidewater Virginia. Vol. LXI, special supplement in colors, 20 x 29 inches, Jan., 1932.

Virginia. Vol. LV, p. 405, 1 page, Apr., 1929.

Virginia, by Capt. John Smith. Vol. LXII, p. 700, 1 half-page, Dec., 1932.

Virginia, North Carolina, Kentucky, and Tennessee. Vol. LXV, pp. 666-667, 1 two-page, June, 1934.

Virginia and Florida, from an Amsterdam Atlas of the World Published in 1638. Vol. XLV, p. 242, 1 page, Mar., 1924.

Virunga Mountains, Belgian Congo:

Western Rift Valley and Surrounding Country, with Inset of the Virunga Mountains. Vol. LXXVI, p. 515, 1 two-thirds-page, Oct., 1939.

Volcano Islands (Kazan Retto), Pacific Ocean. *See* Iwo Jima.

Vostok Island, Line Islands:

Pacific Ocean and the Bay of Bengal, with Inset of Vostok Island. Vol. LXXXIV, special supplement in colors, 36½ x 26½ inches, Sept., 1943.

Wake (Island), Pacific Ocean:

Pacific Ocean and the Bay of Bengal, with Inset of Wake Island. Vol. LXXXIV, special supplement in colors, 36½ x 26½ inches, Sept., 1943.

Strategic Isles of the Pacific. Vol. LXXXV, pp. 392-393, 17 island maps (two pages), Apr., 1944.

Wales:

Severn River Valley. Vol. LXIII, p. 421, 1 three-quarters-page, Apr., 1933.

Wales. Vol. XLIV, p. 639, 1 half-page, Dec., 1923.

Wales. Vol. LXXXV, p. 754, 1 page, June, 1944.

War Maps. *See* World War I; World War II; *and* names of individual countries and islands.

Washington, George:

Location of Washington's Chain of Forts. Vol. LXI, p. 40, 1 two-thirds-page, Jan., 1932.

Route Followed by Washington on His Trip to Fort Le Boeuf. Vol. LXI, p. 10, 1 page, Jan., 1932.

Travels of George Washington, with Insets of New York and the Lower Hudson, Tidewater Virginia, Philadelphia, Boston, and Mount Vernon. Vol. LXI, special supplement in colors, 20 x 29 inches, Jan., 1932.

Washington's Travels in Southwestern Pennsylvania. Vol. LXI, p. 12, 1 two-thirds-page, Jan., 1932.

Washington's Travels in the Maryland-West Virginia Sector. Vol. LXI, p. 36, 1 half-page, Jan., 1932.

Washington (State):

Location of Mount Rainier. Vol. XXIII, p. 626, 1 half-page, June, 1912.

Map of Northwestern United States and Neighboring Canadian Provinces. Vol. LXXIX, special supplement in colors, 24½ x 36 inches, June, 1941.

Pacific Northwest Defense Area. Vol. LXXXII, p. 425, 1 half-page, Oct., 1942.

Rainfall Map of Washington and Oregon. Vol. XX, p. 647, 1 two-thirds-page, July, 1909.

State of Washington. Vol. LXIII, pp. 136-137, 1 two-page, Feb., 1933.

United States of America, with Inset of Seattle. Vol. XLIII, special supplement in colors, 26½ x 36¼ inches, Apr., 1923.

Washington and Oregon. Vol. XX, p. 646, 1 three-quarters-page, July, 1909.

Washington, D. C.:

Central Part of Washington, D. C., 1904. Vol. XV, p. 375, 1 page, Sept., 1904.

Historic and Scenic Reaches of the Nation's Capital. Vol. LXXIV, special supplement in colors, 26½ x 31¼ inches, July, 1938.

Location of Government Buildings and New Developments. Vol. LX, p. 521, 1 page, Nov., 1931.

Mall, Washington, D. C. Vol. XXVII, special supplement in colors, Mar., 1915.

Mall and the Principal Public Buildings. Vol. XLIII, p. 576, 1 page, June, 1923.

Maryland, Delaware, and District of Columbia, with Inset of Washington, D. C., and Vicinity. Vol. LI, special supplement in colors, 12 x 18 inches, Feb., 1927.

Nation's Capital: 1915 (Showing Location of Public Buildings, Monuments, and Existing and Proposed Public Grounds). Vol. XXVII, p. 245, 1 two-thirds-page, Mar., 1915.

Original Boundary Stones of the District of Columbia. Vol. XX, p. 357, 1 three-quarters-page, Apr., 1909.

Washington, D. C.—*Continued*

The Ultimate Washington (Plan Laid Out by the Commission of 1901 for the National Capital). Vol. XXVII, special supplement in colors, Mar., 1915.

United States of America, with Inset of Washington, D. C. Vol. XLIII, special supplement in colors, 26½ x 36¼ inches, Apr., 1923.

Washington. Vol. XLIII, p. 574, 1 page, June, 1923.

West Indies:

American Bases in the Lesser Antilles Protect the Panama Canal. Vol. LXXXI, p. 729, 1 half-page, June, 1942.

Atlantic Ocean, with Inset of Isthmus of Panama. Vol. LXXVI, special supplement in colors, 31 x 25 inches, July, 1939.

Caribbean Regions, showing Airline Distances in Statute Miles, with Enlargements of Aruba, Bonaire and Curaçao. Vol. LXXXIII, p. 172, 1 page, Feb., 1943.

Central America, Cuba, Porto Rico and the Islands of the Caribbean Sea, with Relief Elevation Sketch of the Canal. Vol. XXIV, special supplement in colors, 12½ x 19 inches, Feb., 1913.

Countries of the Caribbean, Including Mexico, Central America, the West Indies, and the Panama Canal, with Detailed Insets of the Panama Canal and the Canal Zone, Porto Rico and the Virgin Islands, and Guantanamo Bay, Cuba. Vol. XLI, special supplement in colors, 25 x 44 inches, Feb., 1922.

Geographical Relation of Venezuela to the Isthmian Canal Routes, to the West Indies and Florida. Vol. XIV, p. 18, 1 page, Jan., 1903.

Greater and Lesser Antilles, with Inset of the Virgin Islands. Vol. LXXVIII, p. 277, 1 two-thirds-page, Sept., 1940.

Hispaniola, Puerto Rico, and the Leeward Group of Islands. Vol. LXXIII, pp. 274-275, Mar., 1938.

Leeward and Windward Islands. Vol. LXXIX, p. 5, 1 page, Jan., 1941.

Mexico, Central America, and the West Indies. Vol. LXVI, special supplement in colors, 23 x 40 inches, Dec., 1934.

Mexico, Central America, and the West Indies. Vol. LXXVI, special supplement in colors, 24 x 41 inches, Dec., 1939.

Military Outposts Leased from Britain Put New Teeth in Uncle Sam's Defenses. Vol. LXXVIII, p. 621, 1 page, Nov., 1940.

Trinidad and Tobago Islands, with Inset of West Indies. Vol. LXXII, p. 321, 1 half-page, Sept., 1937.

Volcanic Islands of the West Indies. Vol. XIII, p. 213, 1 page, June, 1902.

West Indian Hurricane of August 7-14, 1899. Vol. X, p. 345, 1 page, Sept., 1899.

West Indies from Cuba to Puerto Rico, with an Enlargement of Haiti and the Dominican Republic. Vol. LXXXV, p. 200, 1 two-thirds-page, Feb., 1944.

West Indies—*Continued*

See also Bahama Islands ; Cuba ; Dominican Republic ; Haiti ; Jamaica ; Martinique ; Puerto Rico ; St. Vincent ; Virgin Islands ; Windward Islands.

West Virginia:

Chain of Forts Recommended by George Washington. Vol. LXI, p. 40, 1 two-thirds-page, Jan., 1932.

Historic and Scenic Reaches of the Nation's Capital. Vol. LXXIV, special supplement in colors, 26½ x 31¼ inches, July, 1938.

Potomac River Windings in Maryland, Virginia, and West Virginia. Vol. LXXXVIII, pp. 36-37, two-page spread, July, 1945.

West Virginia. Vol. LXXVIII, pp. 144-145, 1 two-page, Aug., 1940.

Western Hemisphere:

Map of Discovery. Reproduction in color of the painting by N. C. Wyeth, National Geographic Society, Washington, D. C. Vol. LV, text, p. 93 ; supplement, Jan., 1929.

Map of the World (in Eastern and Western Hemispheres), with Insets showing Land and Water Hemispheres, Density of Population, Time Zones, and World Mapping. Vol. LXXX, special supplement in colors, 41 x 22 inches, Dec., 1941.

Western Hemisphere, showing U. S. Defense Bases. Vol. LXXIX, p. 41, 1 page, Jan., 1941.

Western Theater of War Maps. *See* World War I *and* World War II : *Theater of War in Europe, Africa, and Western Asia.*

White Mountains, New Hampshire-Maine :

White Mountains of New Hampshire. Vol. LXXII, special supplement in colors, 17 x 20 inches, July, 1937.

Wight, Isle of, England :

Isle of Wight. Vol. LXVII, p. 6, 1 half-page, Jan., 1935.

Windward Islands, West Indies :

Direction of the Currents in the Passages of the Windward Islands. Vol. XXIII, p. 775, 1 page, Aug., 1912.

Leeward and Windward Islands. Vol. LXXIX, p. 5, 1 page, Jan., 1941.

Political Map of Windward Islands. Vol. XIII, p. 227, 1 half-page, July, 1902.

Wisconsin:

Wisconsin. Vol. LXXII, pp. 6-7, 1 two-page, July, 1937.

Witwatersrand (Region), Transvaal :

Union of South Africa, with Inset showing Witwatersrand. Vol. LXXXII, p. 739, 1 two-thirds-page, Dec., 1942.

World:

Active and Recently Extinct Volcanoes. Vol. XIII, p. 205, 1 page, June, 1902.

Black Shadow Which the Dream of Pan-Germanism Casts Over the World. Vol. XXXIII, p. 558, 1 page, June, 1918.

Chart of the World on Mercator's Projection Vol. XVI, special supplement in colors, 25 x 45 inches, Feb., 1905.

Coast Surveys of the World. Vol. XVI, pp. 64-65, 1 two-page, Feb., 1905.

Cotidal Lines for the World ; or, Lines of Simultaneous High Water at Each Hour and Half Hour of Greenwich Lunar Time. Vol. XVII, special supplement, 8 x 14 inches, June, 1906.

Distribution of Atlantic and Pacific Coast Types. Vol. XII, p. 256, 1 half-page, July, 1901.

Distribution of Rainfall on Earth's Surface. Vol. XII, p. 258, 1 page, July, 1901.

Distribution of Republics and Democracy in 1917. Vol. XXXI, p. 243, 1 page, Mar., 1917.

Distribution of Republics in 1776, the Year of Our Declaration of Independence. Vol. XXXI, p. 242, 1 page, Mar., 1917.

Extent of the Bubonic Plague Area. Vol. XI, p. 248, 1 quarter-page, June, 1900.

Known and Possible Oil Resources of the World. Vol. XXXVII, p. 200, 1 page, Feb., 1920.

Map of the World (in Eastern and Western Hemispheres), with Insets showing Land and Water Hemispheres, Density of Population, Time Zones, and World Mapping. Vol. LXXX, special supplement in colors, 41 x 22 inches, Dec., 1941.

Northern and Southern Hemispheres, with Insets of Time Zone, World Terrain, and Tables of Airline Distances in Four Hemispheres. Vol. LXXXIII, special supplement in colors, 41 x 22 inches, Apr., 1943.

Paths of Short-wave Radio Beams from New York City Follow Great Circle Routes over Surface of the Earth. Vol. LXXXII, p. 679, 1 two-thirds-page, Nov., 1942.

Paths of Short-wave Radio Beams from San Francisco Follow Great Circle Routes over Surface of the Earth. Vol. LXXXII, p. 678, 1 two-thirds-page, Nov., 1942.

Pinedo's 60,000-Mile Air Cruise in the *Santa María.* Vol. LIV, pp. 248-249, 1 two-page, Sept., 1928.

Principal Arcs of the Meridian, the Parallel and Oblique Arcs. Vol. XII, p. 39, 1 page, Jan., 1901.

Principal Ocean Currents. Vol. XXIII, p. 768, 1 page, Aug., 1912.

Principal Ocean Currents. Vol. XXXIV, p. 234, 1 page, Sept., 1918.

Route of the Dream Ship. Vol. XXXIX, p. 4, 1 page, Jan., 1921.

World—*Continued*

Route of the *Grace Harwar's* Voyage from Australia to the British Isles. Vol. LIX, p. 192, 1 two-thirds-page, Feb., 1931.

Route of the *Igdrasil* on Its 38,000-Mile Cruise. Vol. LXXVI, pp. 38-39, July, 1939.

Routes Flown by Sir Alan J. Cobham. Vol. LIII, p. 350, 1 three-quarters-page, Mar., 1928.

Routes Traversed by the *Carnegie* During Three Voyages, Covering 157,000 Miles. Vol. XLII, p. 634, 1 half-page, Dec., 1922.

Second Oldest Map of the World : By Berlinghieri, before Columbus. Vol. XXII, p. 388, 1 page, Apr., 1911.

Systems of Semi-Diurnal Tide. Vol. XVII, p. 305, 1 half-page, June, 1906.

World. Vol. XLII, special supplement in colors, 27½ x 40 inches, Dec., 1922.

World (in Eastern and Western Hemispheres), with Insets showing Land and Water Hemispheres, and Time Zones. Vol. LXVIII, special supplement in colors, 23 x 44 inches, Dec., 1935.

World, showing Distribution of Languages and Areas Occupied by U. S. Soldiers with Dates of Their Arrival. Vol. LXXXIV, pp. 696-697, 1 two-page, Dec., 1943.

World, with Insets showing Arctic and Antarctic Regions, Natural Vegetation and Ocean Currents, and Density of Population and Prevailing Winds. Vol. LXII, special supplement in colors, 26 x 38½ inches, Dec., 1932.

World as Depicted by Map-Makers before Captain Cook's First Voyage to "The Great South Sea." Vol. LI, p. 84, 1 page, Jan., 1927.

World as Depicted by Waldseemüller in 1507. Vol. LXII, p. 770, 1 page, Dec., 1932.

World at the End of the XVIII Century, showing Explored and Unexplored Territory. Vol. XII, p. 151, 1 half-page, Apr., 1901.

World at the End of the XIX Century, showing Explored and Unexplored Territory. Vol. XII, p. 151, 1 half-page, Apr., 1901.

World Chart : By Mattiolo, 1548. Vol. XXII, p. 389, 1 page, Apr., 1911.

World Globe, showing Submarine Mountain Ranges and Deeps of Atlantic Ocean. Vol. LXXXVII, p. 112, 1 two-thirds-page, Jan., 1945.

World Map, with Insets of Arctic and Antarctic Regions, Territories Occupied by Belligerents in First and Second World Wars, and Table of Geographical Equivalents and Abbreviations. Vol. LXXXIV, special supplement in colors, 41 x 26½ inches, Dec., 1943.

World War I:

Austro-Italo Alpine Region, with Surrounding Territory. Vol. XXVII, p. 374, 1 page, Apr., 1915.

World War I—*Continued*

Black Shadow Which the Dream of Pan-German-ism Casts Over the World. Vol. XXXIII, p. 558, 1 page, June, 1918.

Boundary Lines of European Nations as Drawn by the Gaunt Hand of Hunger. Vol. XXXIII, p. 338, 1 half-page, Apr., 1918.

British Isles and North Sea, showing Fishing Banks and War Zone. Vol. XXVII, p. 149, 1 half-page, Feb., 1915.

Bulgaria and Serbia. Vol. XXVII, p. 421, 1 page, Apr., 1915.

Europe and Adjoining Portions of Africa and Asia. Vol. XXVIII, special supplement in colors, 28 x 32 inches, July, 1915.

Frontier Cities of Italy and Austria-Hungary. Vol. XXVII, p. 628, 1 page, June, 1915.

Lake of Garda Region. War Zone on Austro-Italian Frontier Indicated. Vol. LXVIII, p. 334, 1 third-page, Sept., 1935.

Map of the New Balkan States and Central Europe. Vol. XXVI, special supplement in colors, 17 x 22½ inches, Aug., 1914.

New Germany as Limited by the Peace Treaty. Vol. XXXV, p. 546, 1 page, June, 1919.

One of Our Soldier Cities : Map of Camp Upton, Yaphank, Long Island, New York. Vol. XXXII, p. 437, 1 page in colors, Nov.-Dec., 1917.

States Forming Germany in November 1918. Vol. XXXIV, p. 510, 1 page, Dec., 1918.

Territories from Which Each National Army Cantonment Camp Received Its Troops : Also Showing the Location of Cantonments, Regular Army Organization Camps, National Guard Mobilization Camps, and Aviation Camps. Vol. XXXII, p. 438, 1 page in colors, Nov.-Dec., 1917.

Western Theatre of War, with Inset of France and Belgium. Vol. XXXIII, special supplement, 26 x 31 inches, May, 1918.

World Map, with Insets of Arctic and Antarctic Regions, Territories Occupied by Belligerents in First and Second World Wars, and Table of Geographical Equivalents and Abbreviations. Vol. LXXXIV, special supplement in colors, 41 x 26½ inches, Dec., 1943.

World War II:

Africa, with Insets of the Cape Verde Islands, Relief Map, and a Table of Airline Distances in Statute Miles. Vol. LXXXIII, special supplement in colors, 29¼ x 31½ inches, Feb., 1943.

Asia and Adjacent Areas, with Table of Airline Distances in Statute Miles. Vol. LXXXII, special supplement in colors, 40 x 26½ inches, Dec., 1942.

World War II—*Continued*

Atlantic Ocean, with Inset of Isthmus of Panama and a Table of Airline Distances in Statute Miles. Vol. LXXX, special supplement in colors, 31¼ x 25 inches, Sept., 1941.

British Mulberry and Omaha Beach, Artificial Harbors, off the Normandy Coast. Vol. LXXXVII, p. 565, 1 quarter-page, May, 1945.

China. Vol. LXXXVII, special supplement in colors, 37 x 26½ inches, June, 1945.

Europe and the Near East, as of April 1, 1940. Vol. LXXVII, special supplement in colors, 39 x 34 inches, May, 1940.

Europe and the Near East, with Inset Map of the Middle East, and a Table of Distances between Principal Ports via Shortest Navigable Routes. Vol. LXXXIII, special supplement in colors, 39 x 34 inches, June, 1943.

Germany and Its Approaches, with International Boundaries as of September 1, 1939, the day Germany invaded Poland, and Boundaries as of January 1, 1938, before Germany seized Austria and Czechoslovakia. Vol. LXXXVI, special supplement in colors, 33½ x 26½ inches, July, 1944.

Indian Ocean, including Australia, New Zealand, and Malaysia. Vol. LXXIX, special supplement in colors, 25½ x 32¾ inches, Mar., 1941.

Japan and Adjacent Regions of Asia and the Pacific Ocean, with Insets of Industrial Centers of Japan and the Marshall Islands. Vol. LXXXV, special supplement in colors, 26½ x 34½ inches, Apr., 1944.

Japan and Korea, with Insets of Kuril Islands, Pescadores, Karafuto, Ryukyu Islands, Okinawa, Formosa, Tokyo Area, and a Location Map of Japan in the Western Pacific. Vol. LXXXVIII, special supplement in colors, 37 x 26½ inches, Dec., 1945.

Pacific Ocean and the Bay of Bengal, with Inset Maps of Important Islands, and Table of Airline Distances in Statute Miles. Vol. LXXXIV, special supplement in colors, 36½ x 26½ inches, Sept., 1943.

Philippines, with Insets of Manila, Lingayen Gulf, and a Location Map of the Philippines. Vol. LXXXVII, special supplement in colors, 17½ x 26 inches, Mar., 1945.

Southeast Asia and Pacific Islands from the Indies and the Philippines to the Solomons, with 22 Inset Maps of Important Cities and Islands. Vol. LXXXVI, special supplement in colors, 41 x 26½ inches, Oct., 1944.

Theater of War in Europe, Africa, and Western Asia, with Table of Airline Distances in Statute Miles. Vol. LXXXII, special supplement in colors, 26½ x 31 inches, July, 1942.

Theater of War in the Pacific Ocean, with Table of Airline Distances in Statute Miles. Vol. LXXXI, special supplement in colors, 20½ x 26½ inches, Feb., 1942.

World War II—*Continued*

Union of Soviet Socialist Republics, with International Boundaries according to Russian Treaties and Claims as of October 1, 1944. Boundaries of January 1, 1938, are shown in red. Vol. LXXXVI, special supplement in colors, 40 x 25 inches, Dec., 1944.

World, showing Distribution of Languages and Areas Occupied by U. S. Soldiers with Dates of Their Arrival. Vol. LXXXIV, pp. 696-697, 1 two-page, Dec., 1943.

World Map, with Insets of Arctic and Antarctic Regions, Territories Occupied by Belligerents in First and Second World Wars, and Table of Geographical Equivalents and Abbreviations. Vol. LXXXIV, special supplement in colors, 41 x 26½ inches, Dec., 1943.

See also Mediterranean Regions; Pacific Islands; U. S. Defense Bases; *and* names of individual countries and islands for the war years, 1939-1945.

Wotje (Island), Marshall Islands:

Pacific Ocean and the Bay of Bengal, with Inset of Wotje. Vol. LXXXIV, special supplement in colors, 36½ x 26½ inches, Sept., 1943.

Wyoming:

Map of Northwestern United States and Neighboring Canadian Provinces. Vol. LXXIX, special supplement in colors, 24½ x 36 inches, June, 1941.

South End Yellowstone Lake, Valley of the Upper Yellowstone River and Adjacent Country. Vol. XXIV, p. 818, 1 page, July, 1913.

Topographic Map of the Cloud Peak Region, Summit of Bighorn Mountains, Wyoming. Vol. XVIII, p. 357, 1 page, June, 1907.

Wyoming. Vol. LXXXVIII, pp. 156-157, 1 two-page, Aug., 1945.

Yellowstone National Park. Vol. LXXVII, p. 771, 1 two-thirds-page, June, 1940.

Yap (Island), Caroline Islands:

Japanese Micronesia, with Insets of Yap, Ponape, and Palau Islands. Vol. LXIX, p. 483, 1 half-page, Apr., 1936.

Pacific Ocean and the Bay of Bengal, with Inset of Yap. Vol. LXXXIV, special supplement in colors, 36½ x 26½ inches, Sept., 1943.

Southeast Asia and Pacific Islands from the Indies and the Philippines to the Solomons, with Inset of Yap. Vol. LXXXVI, special supplement in colors, 41 x 26½ inches, Oct., 1944.

Strategic Isles of the Pacific. Vol. LXXXV, pp. 392-393, 17 island maps (two pages), Apr., 1944.

Yellowstone (River), Montana-Wyoming:

Map showing Route of Lewis R. Freeman's 2,000-Mile Voyage Down the Yellowstone-Missouri. Vol. LIV, p. 77, 1 half-page, July, 1928.

Yellowstone National Park, Wyoming:

Yellowstone National Park. Vol. LXXVII, p. 771, 1 two-thirds-page, June, 1940.

Yosemite Valley, California:

Yosemite National Park. Vol. LXIX, p. 344, 1 third-page, Mar., 1936.

Yucatán (Peninsula), Mexico-Central America:

Yucatán Peninsula. Vol. LXX, p. 595, 1 two-thirds-page, Nov., 1936.

Yugoslavia:

Bulgaria, Serbia, and Macedonia. Vol. XXIII, p. 1152, 1 page, Nov., 1912.

Bulgaria and Serbia. Vol. XXVII, p. 421, 1 page, Apr., 1915.

Dalmatian Coast. Vol. LIII, p. 50, 1 two-thirds-page, Jan., 1928.

Julian Alps, showing Frontiers of Yugoslavia, Germany, and Italy. Vol. LXXV, p. 605, 1 third-page, June, 1939.

Yugoslavia. Vol. XIX, p. 313, 1 half-page, May, 1908.

Yugoslavia. Vol. LVIII, p. 264, 1 three-quarters-page, Sept., 1930.

Yugoslavia, showing Bordering Countries. Vol. LXXV, p. 694, 1 two-thirds-page, June, 1939.

Yugoslavia and Adjoining Countries, showing International Boundaries as of Sept. 1, 1939, the day Germany invaded Poland. Vol. LXXXV, p. 498, 1 page, Apr., 1944.

Yukon River, Alaska-Canada:

Alaska and Adjoining Yukon Territory. Vol. LVIII, p. 89, 1 two-thirds-page, July, 1930.

Yukon Territory, Canada:

Alaska and Adjoining Yukon Territory. Vol. LVIII, p. 89, 1 two-thirds-page, July, 1930.

Yukon-British Columbia, Area Surveyed by Bradford Washburn in 1935, and Adjoining Alaska, Mapped by the International Boundary Commission in 1906-1908. Vol. LXIX, pp. 720-721, 1 two-page, June, 1936.

Yünnan (Province), China:

Land of the Nashi, in Yünnan Province, China. Vol. XLVI, p. 478, 1 half-page, Nov., 1924.

Territory, Where a National Geographic Society Expedition Was at Work For Two Years. Vol. XLVII, p. 450, 1 half-page, Apr., 1925.

Upper Salwin. Vol. XXI, p. 147, 1 page, Feb., 1910.

Yünnan Province, showing the Yangtze, Mekong, and Salwin Rivers. Vol. L, p. 134, 1 half-page, Aug., 1926.